THE ACADEMIC WHO'S WHO
1975-1976

The Academic Who's Who

1975–1976

UNIVERSITY TEACHERS IN THE BRITISH ISLES
IN THE ARTS, EDUCATION AND SOCIAL SCIENCES

Second Edition

GALE RESEARCH COMPANY
BOOK TOWER · DETROIT, MICHIGAN 48226

FIRST PUBLISHED BY A. AND C. BLACK LTD
4, 5 AND 6 SOHO SQUARE LONDON W1V 6AD

FIRST EDITION 1973
SECOND EDITION 1975

© 1973, 1975 BY A. AND C. BLACK LTD

ISBN 0-8103-2020-7

PUBLISHED IN THE UNITED STATES BY
GALE RESEARCH CO., BOOK TOWER,
DETROIT, MICHIGAN 48226

Printed in Great Britain by
Butler & Tanner Ltd, Frome and London

PREFACE

In preparing the second edition of this biennial work, the publishers have borne in mind the many helpful suggestions made to them by users of the first edition. In particular the coverage has been greatly increased, over 2000 entries having been added to bring the total number of entries to nearly 7000. These are confined, as in the first edition, to senior teachers in Universities in the British Isles in the fields of the arts, education and the social sciences. All these teachers – of the rank of senior lecturer or above, or who have taught for five years as a lecturer or assistant lecturer – should have received forms of invitation; invitations were also sent to those holding senior non-teaching University appointments.

Some omissions are inevitable in a work of this nature, and the publishers will be grateful for notification of any such omissions, which will be rectified in the third edition. Every care is taken to ensure accuracy, but neither the publisher nor the printer can accept liability for any loss through misprint or other cause. Inclusion in the book is not a matter for payment or of obligation to purchase the volume.

ABBREVIATIONS USED IN THIS BOOK

Some of the designatory letters in this list are used merely for economy of
space and do not necessarily imply any professional or other qualification

A

AA: Anti-Aircraft; Automobile Association; Architectural Association; Augustinians of the Assumption

AAA: Amateur Athletic Association

AA&QMG: Assistant Adjutant and Quartermaster-General

AAAS: American Association for Advancement of Science

AACCA: Associate of the Association of Certified and Corporate Accountants

AAF: Auxiliary Air Force (now RAuxAF)

AAG: Assistant Adjutant-General

AAI: Associate of Chartered Auctioneers' and Estate Agents' Institute

AAMC: Australian Army Medical Corps

A&AEE: Aeroplane and Armament Experimental Establishment

AASA: Associate of Australian Society of Accountants

AAUQ: Associate in Accountancy, University of Queensland

AB: Bachelor of Arts (US); able-bodied seaman

ABA: Amateur Boxing Association

ABC: Australian Broadcasting Commission

ABCA: Army Bureau of Current Affairs

ABCFM: American Board of Commissioners for Foreign Missions

Abp: Archbishop

ABPsS: Associate, British Psychological Society

ABSM: Associate, Birmingham and Midland Institute School of Music

ABTAPL: Association of British Theological and Philosophical Libraries

AC: *Ante Christum* (before Christ)

ACA: Associate of the Institute of Chartered Accountants

Acad.: Academy

ACAS: Assistant Chief of the Air Staff

ACCA: Association of Certified and Corporate Accountants

ACCM: Advisory Council for the Church's Ministry (formerly CACTM)

ACCS: Associate of Corporation of Secretaries (formerly of Certified Secretaries)

ACDS: Assistant Chief of Defence Staff

ACF: Army Cadet Force

ACG: Assistant Chaplain-General

ACGI: Associate of City and Guilds of London Institute

ACII: Associate of the Chartered Insurance Institute

ACIS: Associate of the Chartered Institute of Secretaries

ACLS: American Council of Learned Societies

ACOS: Assistant Chief of Staff

ACS: Additional Curates Society

ACSEA: Allied Command SE Asia

ACSM: Associate of the Camborne School of Mines

ACT: Australian Capital Territory; Australian College of Theology; Associate of the College of Technology

ACMA: Associate of the Institute of Cost and Management Accountants

AD: *Anno Domini*

ADB: Asian Development Bank

ADC: Aide-de-camp

ADCM: Archbishop of Canterbury's Diploma in Church Music

AD Corps: Army Dental Corps

Ad eund.: *Ad eundem gradum* (admitted to the same degree); and *see under* a e g

ADFW: Assistant Director of Fortifications and Works

ADGB: Air Defence of Great Britain

ADGMS: Assistant Director-General of Medical Services

ADH: Assistant Director of Hygiene

Adjt: Adjutant

ADJAG: Assistant Deputy Judge Advocate General

Adm.: Admiral

ADMS: Assistant Director of Medica lServices

ADOS: Assistant Director of Ordnance Services

ADPR: Assistant Director of Public Relations

ADS&T: Assistant Director of Supplies and Transport

Adv.: Advisory; Advocate

ADVS: Assistant Director of Veterinary Services

ADWE&M: Assistant Director of Works, Electrical and Mechanical

AEA: Atomic Energy Authority; Air Efficiency Award

AEAF: Allied Expeditionary Air Force

AEC: Agricultural Executive Council; Army Educational Corps (now RAEC)

AEF: Amalgamated Union of Engineering and Foundry Workers; American Expeditionary Forces

a e g: *ad eundem gradum* (to the same degree—of the admission of a graduate of one university to the same degree at another without examination)

AEGIS: Aid for the Elderly in Government Institutions

AEI: Associated Electrical Industries

AEM: Air Efficiency Medal

AER: Army Emergency Reserve

AERE: Atomic Energy Research Establishment (Harwell)

Æt., Ætat.: *Ætatis* (aged)

AEU: Amalgamated Engineering Union

AFA: Amateur Football Alliance

AFAIAA: Associate Fellow of American Institute of Aeronautics and Astronautics (and *see under* AFIAS)

AFC: Air Force Cross; Association Football Club

AFCAI: Associate Fellow of the Canadian Aeronautical Institute

AFD: Doctor of Fine Arts (US)

AFHQ: Allied Force Headquarters

AFIA: Associate of Federal Institute of Accountants (Australia)

AFIAS: (now *see under* AFAIAA) (formerly) Associate Fellow Institute of Aeronautical Sciences (US)

AFICD: Associate Fellow Institute of Civil Defence

AFM: Air Force Medal

AFRAeS: Associate Fellow Royal Aeronautical Society

AFV: Armoured Fighting Vehicles

AG: Attorney-General

AGH: Australian General Hospital

AGI: Artistes Graphiques Internationales; Associate of the Institute of Certificated Grocers

AGSM: Associate of Guildhall School of Music

AHQ: Army Headquarters

AH-WC: Associate of Heriot-Watt College, Edinburgh

AIA: Associate of the Institute of Actuaries; American Institute of Architects

AIAL: Associate Member of the International Institute of Arts and Letters

AIArb: Associate, Institute of Arbitrators

AIAS: Associate Surveyor Member, Incorporated Association of Architects and Surveyors

AIB: Associate of the Institute of Bankers

AIBD: Associate of the Institute of British Decorators

AIBP: Associate of the Institute of British Photographers

AIC: Agricultural Improvement Council; also formerly Associate of the Institute of Chemistry (see ARIC)

AICA: Associate Member Commonwealth Institute of Accountants; Association Internationale des Critiques d'Art

AICE: Associate, Institution of Civil Engineers

AICTA: Associate of the Imperial College of Tropical Agriculture

AIEE: Associate of the Institution of Electrical Engineers

AIF: Australian Imperial Forces

AIG: Adjutant-Inspector-General

AIIA: Associate Insurance Institute of America

AIL: Associate of the Institute of Linguists

AILA: Associate of the Institute of Landscape Architects

AILocoE: Associate of Institution of Locomotive Engineers

AIM: Associate, Institution of Metallurgists

AIME: American Institute of Mechanical Engineers

AIMarE: Associate of the Institute of Marine Engineers

AInstP: Associate of Institute of Physics

AInstPI: Associate of the Institute of Patentees (Incorporated)

AIOB: Associate of the Institute of Building

AIS: Associate of Institute of Statisticians; now see MIS

AISA: Associate of the Incorporated Secretaries' Association

AIWSP: Associate Member of Institute of Work Study Practitioners

AJAG: Assistant Judge Advocate General

AKC: Associate of King's College (London)

ALA: Associate of the Library Association

Ala: Alabama (US)

ALAS: Associate of Chartered Land Agents' Society

ALCD: Associate of London College of Divinity

ALCM: Associate of London College of Music

ALFSEA: Allied Land Forces South-East Asia

ALI: Argyll Light Infantry

ALLC: Association for Literary and Linguistic Computing

ALS: Associate of the Linnaean Society

Alta: Alberta

AM: Albert Medal; Master of Arts (US); Alpes Maritimes

AMA: Associate of the Museums Association; Australian Medical Association

Amb.: Ambulance

AMBritIRE: (now see under AMIERE) (formerly) Associate Member of British Institution of Radio Engineers

AMC: Association of Municipal Corporations

AMet: Associate of Metallurgy (Sheffield University)

AMF: Australian Military Forces

AMGOT: Allied Military Government of Occupied Territory

AMIAgrE: Associate Member of Institution of Agricultural Engineers

AMICE: Associate Member of Institution of Civil Engineers (formerly lower rank of corporate membership of Instn, now see under MICE; change dated July 1968)

AMIChemE: Associate Member of Institution of Chemical Engineers

AMIEA: Associate Member of Institute of Engineers, Australia

AMIED: Associate Member of Institution of Engineering Designers

AMIEE: Associate Member of Institution of Electrical Engineers (formerly lower rank of corporate membership of Instn, now see under MIEE; change dated Dec. 1966)

AMIE(Ind): Associate Member, Institution of Engineers, India

AMIERE: Associate Member of Institution of Electronic and Radio Engineers (and see under AMBritIRE)

AMIMechE: Associate Member of Institution of Mechanical Engineers (formerly lower rank of corporate membership of Instn, now see under MIMechE, change dated April 1968)

AMIMinE: Associate Member of Institution of Mining Engineers

AMIMM: Associate Member of Institution of Mining and Metallurgy

AMInstBE: Associate Member of Institution of British Engineers

AMInstCE: Associate Member of Institution of Civil Engineers (changed 1946 to AMICE)

AmInstEE: American Institute of Electrical Engineers

AMInstR: Associate Member of Institute of Refrigeration

AMInstT: Associate Member of the Institute of Transport

AMIStructE: Associate Member of the Institution of Structural Engineers

AMP: Advanced Management Program

AMRINA: Associate Member of Royal Institution of Naval Architects

AMS: Assistant Military Secretary; Army Medical Service

AMTPI: Associate Member of Town Planning Institute

ANA: Associate National Academician (America)

Anat.: Anatomy; Anatomical

ANECInst: Associate of NE Coast Institution of Engineers and Shipbuilders

Anon.: Anonymously

ANU: Australian National University

ANZAAS: Australian and New Zealand Association for the Advancement of Science

AO: Air Officer

AOA: Air Officer in charge of Administration

AOC: Air Officer Commanding

AOC-in-C: Air Officer Commanding-in-Chief

AOD: Army Ordnance Department

AOER: Army Officers Emergency Reserve

APA: American Psychiatric Association

APD: Army Pay Department

APS: Aborigines Protection Society

APsSI: Associate, Psychological Society of Ireland

APSW: Association of Psychiatric Social Workers

APTC: Army Physical Training Corps

AQMG: Assistant Quartermaster-General

AR: Associated Rediffusion (Television)

ARA: Associate of the Royal Academy

ARACI: Associate, Royal Australian Chemical Institute

ARAD: Associate of the Royal Academy of Dancing

ARAeS: Associate of the Royal Aeronautical Society

ARAM: Associate of the Royal Academy of Music

ARAS: Associate of the Royal Astronomical Society

ARBA: Associate of the Royal Society of British Artists

ARBC: Associate Royal British Colonial Society of Artists

ARBS: Associate Royal Society of British Sculptors

ARC: Architects' Registration Council; Agricultural Research Council; Aeronautical Research Council

ARCA: Associate Royal College of Art; Associate Royal Canadian Academy

ARCamA: Associate Royal Cambrian Academy (formerly ARCA)

ARCE: Academical Rank of Civil Engineers

Archt: Architect

ARCM: Associate Royal College of Music

ARCO: Associate Royal College of Organists

ARCO(CHM): Associate Royal College of Organists with Diploma in Choir Training

ARCS: Associate Royal College of Science

ARCST: Associate Royal College of Science and Technology (Glasgow)

ARCVS: Associate of Royal College of Veterinary Surgeons

ARE: Associate of Royal Society of Painter-Etchers and Engravers; Arab Republic of Egypt

ARIAS: Associate, Royal Incorporation of Architects in Scotland

ARIBA: Associate of the Royal Institute of British Architects

ARIC: Associate of the Royal Institute of Chemistry

ARICS: Professional Associate of the Royal Institution of Chartered Surveyors

Ark: Arkansas (US)

ARLT: Association for the Reform of Latin Teaching

ARMS: Associate of the Royal Society of Miniature Painters

ARP: Air Raid Precautions

ARPS: Associate of the Royal Photographic Society

ARRC: Associate of the Royal Red Cross

ARSA: Associate Royal Scottish Academy

ARSM: Associate Royal School of Mines

ARTC: Associate Royal Technical College (Glasgow) (name changed) *see* *under* ARCST

ARVIA: Associate Royal Victoria Institute of Architects

ARWA: Associate Royal West of England Academy

ARWS: Associate Royal Society of Painters in Water-Colours

AS: Anglo-Saxon

ASA: Associate Member, Society of Actuaries

ASAA: Associate of the Society of Incorporated Accountants and Auditors

ASAM: Associate of the Society of Art Masters

AScW: Association of Scientific Workers

ASE: Amalgamated Society of Engineers

ASIA(Ed): Associate, Society of Industrial Artists (Education)

ASLEF: Associated Society of Locomotive Engineers and Firemen

ASLIB: Association of Special Libraries and Information Bureaux

ASO: Air Staff Officer

ASSET: Association of Supervisory Staffs, Executives and Technicians

AssocISI: Associate of Iron and Steel Institute

AssocMCT: Associateship of Manchester College of Technology

AssocMIAeE: Associate Member Institution of Aeronautical Engineers

AssocRINA: Associate of the Royal Institution of Naval Architects

AssocSc: Associate in Science

Asst: Assistant

ASTMS: Association of Scientific, Technical and Managerial Staffs

Astr.: Astronomy

ASW: Association of Scientific Workers

ATA: Air Transport Auxiliary

ATAE: Association of Tutors in Adult Educationl

ATC: Air Training Corps

ATCDE: Association of Teachers in Colleges and Departments of Education

ATCL: Associate of Trinity College of Music, London

ATD: Art Teacher's Diploma

ATI: Associate of Textile Institute

ATII: Associate Member of the Institute of Taxation

ATS: Auxiliary Territorial Service

ATV: Associated TeleVision

AUEW: Amalgamated Union of Engineering Workers

AUS: Army of the United States

AVD: Army Veterinary Department

AVLA: Audio Visual Language Association

AVR: Army Volunteer Reserve

B

b: born; brother

BA: Bachelor of Arts

BAAL: British Association for Applied Linguistics

BAAS: British Association for the Advancement of Science

B&FBS: British and Foreign Bible Society

BAFO: British Air Forces of Occupation

BAI: Bachelor of Engineering (*Baccalarius in Arte Ingeniaria*)

BALPA: British Air Line Pilot's Association

BAO: Bachelor of Art of Obstetrics

BAOR: British Army of the Rhine (formerly *on the* Rhine)

BAOS: British Association of Oral Surgeons

BARC: British Automobile Racing Club

Bart or **Bt:** Baronet

BAS: Bachelor in Agricultural Science

BASc: Bachelor of Applied Science

BASW: British Association of Social Workers

Batt.: Battery

BB&CIRly: Bombay, Baroda and Central India Railway

BBC: British Broadcasting Corporation

BC: Before Christ; British Columbia

BCE (Melb): Bachelor of Civil Engineering (Melbourne Univ.)

BCh or **BChir:** Bachelor of Surgery

BCL: Bachelor of Civil Law

BCMS: Bible Churchmen's Missionary Society

BCOF: British Commonwealth Occupation Force

BCom: Bachelor of Commerce

BComSc: Bachelor of Commercial Science

BCS: Bengal Civil Service

BCURA: British Coal Utilization Research Association

BD: Bachelor of Divinity

Bd: Board

BDA: British Dental Association

Bde: Brigade

BDS: Bachelor of Dental Surgery

BDSc: Bachelor of Dental Science

BE: Bachelor of Engineering; British Element

BEA: British East Africa; British European Airways; British Epilepsy Association

BEAMA: British Electrical and Allied Manufacturers' Association

BEc: Bachelor of Economics (Australian)

BEd: Bachelor of Education

Beds: Bedfordshire

BEE: Bachelor of Electrical Engineering

BEF: British Expeditionary Force

BEM: British Empire Medal

BEngE: Bachelor of Electrical Engineering (Canada)

Berks: Berkshire

BFI: British Film Institute

BFPO: British Forces Post Office

BGS: Brigadier General Staff

BHS: British Horse Society

BIF: British Industries Fair

BIM: British Institute of Management

BIS: Bank for International Settlements

BISF: British Iron and Steel Federation

BISFA: British Industrial and Scientific Film Association

BISRA: British Iron and Steel Research Association

BJ: Bachelor of Journalism

BJSM: British Joint Services Mission

BL: Bachelor of Law

BLA: British Liberation Army

BLE: Brotherhood of Locomotive Engineers

BLESMA: British Limbless Ex-Servicemen's Association

BLitt: Bachelor of Letters

BM: British Museum; Bachelor of Medicine

BMA: British Medical Association

BMH: British Military Hospital

BMJ: British Medical Journal

Bn: Battalion

BNAF: British North Africa Force

BNC: Brasenose College

BNEC: British National Export Council

BNOC: British National Opera Company

BOAC: British Overseas Airways Corporation

BomCS: Bombay Civil Service

BomSC: Bombay Staff Corps

BoT: Board of Trade

Bot.: Botany; Botanical

Bp: Bishop

BPharm: Bachelor of Pharmacy

BR: British Rail

Br: Branch

BRA: Brigadier Royal Artillery

BRCS: British Red Cross Society

Brig.: Brigadier

BritIRE: (now *see under* IERE) (formerly) British Institution of Radio Engineers

BRS: British Road Services

BS: Bachelor of Surgery; Bachelor of Science

BSA: Bachelor of Scientific Agriculture; Birmingham Small Arms

BSAA: British South American Airways

BSAP: British South Africa Police

BSC: British Steel Corporation; Bengal Staff Corps

BSc: Bachelor of Science

BSc (Dent): Bachelor of Science in Dentistry

BSE: Bachelor of Science in Engineering (US)

BSF: British Salonica Force

BSI: British Standards Institution

BSJA: British Show Jumping Association

BSocSc: Bachelor of Social Science

BT: Bachelor of Teaching

Bt: Baronet; Brevet

BTA: British Tourist Authority (*formerly* British Travel Association)

BTC: British Transport Commission

BTh: Bachelor of Theology

BUAS: British Universities Association of Slavists

Bucks: Buckinghamshire

BVM: Blessed Virgin Mary

BWI: British West Indies (now WI; West Indies)

BWM: British War Medal

C

(C): Conservative; 100

c: Child; cousin

CA: Central America; County Alderman; Chartered Accountant (Scotland, and Canada)

CACTM: Central Advisory Council of Training for the Ministry (now *see* ACCM)

CALE: Canadian Army Liaison Executive

Cambs: Cambridgeshire

CAMC: Canadian Army Medical Corps

CAMW: Central Association for Mental Welfare

Cantab: Of Cambridge University

CAS: Chief of the Air Staff

CASI: Canadian Aeronautics and Space Institute

Cav.: Cavalry

CB: Companion of the Bath

CBE: Commander Order of the British Empire

CBI: Confederation of British Industry (and *see under* FBI)

CBSA: Clay Bird Shooting Association

CC: Companion of the Order of Canada; City Council; County Council; Cricket Club; Cycling Club; County Court

CCC: Corpus Christi College; Central Criminal Court; County Cricket Club

CCF: Combined Cadet Force

CCG: Control Commission Germany

CCPR: Central Council of Physical Recreation

CCRA: Commander Corps Royal Artillery

CCS: Casualty Clearing Station; Ceylon Civil Service

CD: Canadian Forces Decoration; Commander of the Order of Distinction (Jamaica)

CDEE: Chemical Defence Experimental Establishment

Cdre: Commodore

CDS: Chief of the Defence Staff

CE: Civil Engineer

CEF: Canadian Expeditionary Force

CEGB: Central Electricity Generating Board

CEI: Council of Engineering Institutions

CEIR: Corporation for Economic and Industrial Research

CEMA: Council for the Encouragement of Music and the Arts

CEMS: Church of England Men's Society

CEng: Chartered Engineer

Cento: Central Treaty Organisation

CERN: Conseil (now Organisation) Européenne pour la Recherche Nucléaire

CETS: Church of England Temperance Society

CF: Chaplain to the Forces

CFA: Canadian Field Artillery

CFE: Central Fighter Establishment

CFR: Commander of Federal Republic of Nigeria

CFS: Central Flying School

CGIA: City and Guilds of London Insignia Award

CGLI: City and Guilds of London Institute

CGM: Conspicuous Gallantry Medal

CGS: Chief of the General Staff

CH: Companion of Honour

Chanc.: Chancellor; Chancery

Chap.: Chaplain

ChapStJ: Chaplain of Order of St John of Jerusalem (now ChStJ)

ChB: Bachelor of Surgery

Ch. Ch.: Christ Church

Ch. Coll.: Christ's College

(CHM): See under ARCO(CHM), FRCO(CHM)

ChM: Master of Surgery

Chm.: Chairman

ChStJ: Chaplain of Order of St John of Jerusalem

CI: Imperial Order of the Crown of India; Channel Islands

CIAD: Central Institute of Art and Design

CIAgrE: Companion, Institution of Agricultural Engineers

CIAL: Corresponding Member of the International Institute of Arts and Letters

CID: Criminal Investigation Department

CIE: Companion of the Order of the Indian Empire

CIGRE: Conférence Internationale des Grands Réseaux Electriques

CIGS: (formerly) Chief of the Imperial General Staff (now CGS)

CIMarE: Companion of the Institute of Marine Engineers

CIMechE: Companion of the Institution of Mechanical Engineers

C-in-C: Commander-in-Chief

CIPFA: Chartered Institute of Public Finance and Accountancy (formerly IMTA)

CIPM: Companion, Institute of Personnel Management (formerly FIPM)

CIR: Commission on Industrial Relations

CIV: City Imperial Volunteers

CJ: Chief Justice

CJM: Congregation of Jesus and Mary (Eudist Fathers)

CL: Commander of Order of Leopold

c.l.: *cum laude*

Cl.: Class

CLA: Country Landowners' Association

CLit: Companion of Literature (Royal Society of Literature Award)

CM: Medal of Courage (Canada); Congregation of the Mission (Vincentians); Master in Surgery; Certificated Master; Canadian Militia

CMA: Canadian Medical Association

CMAC: Catholic Marriage Advisory Council

CMB: Central Midwives' Board

CMF: Commonwealth Military Forces; Central Mediterranean Force

CMG: Companion of St Michael and St George

CMO: Chief Medical Officer

CMS: Church Missionary Society

CNAA: Council for National Academic Awards

CNR: Canadian National Railways

CNRS: Centre National du Recherche Scientifique

CO: Commanding Officer; Commonwealth Office (from Aug. 1966) (*see also* FCO); Colonial Office (before Aug. 1966); Conscientious Objector

Co.: County; Company

C of E: Church of England

C of S: Chief of Staff

CoID: Council of Industrial Design

Co.L or Coal.L Coalition Liberal

Col: Colonel

Coll.: College; Collegiate

Colo: Colorado (US)

Col. Sergt: Colour-Sergeant

Com: Communist

Comd: Command

Comdg: Commanding

Comdr: Commander

Comdt: Commandant

COMEC: Council of the Military Education Committees of the Universities of the UK

Commn: Commission

Commnd: Commissioned

ComplEE: Companion of the Institution of Electrical Engineers

ComplERE: Companion of the Institution of Electronic and Radio Engineers

CompTI: Companion of the Textile Institute

Comr: Commissioner

Comy-Gen.: Commissary-General

CON: Cross of Order of the Niger

Conn: Connecticut (US)

Const.: Constitutional

COPA: Comité des Organisations Professionels Agricoles de la CEE

COPEC: Conference of Politics, Economics and Christianity

Corp.: Corporation; Corporal

Corr. Mem. or **Fell.**: Corresponding Member or Fellow

COS: Chief of Staff; Charity Organization Society

COSA: Colliery Officials and Staffs Association

COSSAC: Chief of Staff to Supreme Allied Commander

COTC: Canadian Officers' Training Corps

Co.U or **Coal.U**: Coalition Unionist

CP: Central Provinces; Cape Province

CPA: Commonwealth Parliamentary Association; Chartered Patent Agent; also (formerly) Certified Public Accountant (Canada) (now merged with CA)

CPAS: Church Pastoral Aid Society

CPC: Conservative Political Centre

CPM: Colonial Police Medal

CPR: Canadian Pacific Railway

CPRE: Council for the Protection of Rural England

CPSU: Communist Party of the Soviet Union

CPU: Commonwealth Press Union

CR: Community of the Resurrection

cr: created or creation

CRA: Commander, Royal Artillery

CRASC: Commander, Royal Army Service Corps

CRE: Commander, Royal Engineers

Cres.: Crescent

CRO: Commonwealth Relations Office (before Aug. 1966; now *see* CO)

CS: Clerk to the Signet; Civil Service

CSB: Bachelor of Christian Science

CSC: Conspicuous Service Cross

CSI: Companion of the Order of the Star of India

CSIR: Commonwealth Council for Scientific and Industrial Research (re-named: Commonwealth Scientific and Industrial Research Organization; *see* below)

CSIRO: Commonwealth Scientific and Industrial Research Organization (and *see* above)

CSO: Chief Scientific Officer; Chief Signal Officer

CSP: Chartered Society of Physiotherapists; Civil Service of Pakistan

CSSp: Holy Ghost Father

CSSR: Congregation of the Most Holy Redeemer (Redemptorist Order)

CStJ: Commander of the Order of St John of Jerusalem

CTA: Chaplain Territorial Army

CTB: College of Teachers of the Blind

CTC: Cyclists' Touring Club

CTR (Harwell): Controlled Thermonuclear Research

CU: Cambridge University

CUAC: Cambridge University Athletic Club

CUAFC: Cambridge University Association Football Club

CUBC: Cambridge University Boat Club

CUCC: Cambridge University Cricket Club

CUF: Common University Fund

CUHC: Cambridge University Hockey Club

CUP: Cambridge University Press

CURUFC: Cambridge University Rugby Union Football Club

CVO: Commander of the Royal Victorian Order

CWS: Co-operative Wholesale Society

D

D: Duke

d: Died; daughter

DA: Diploma in Anaesthesia; Diploma in Art

DAA&QMG: Deputy Assistant Adjutant and Quartermaster-General

DAAG: Deputy Assistant Adjutant-General

DA&QMG: Deputy Adjutant and Quartermaster General

DACG: Deputy Assistant Chaplain-General

DAD: Deputy Assistant Director

DADMS: Deputy Assistant Director of Medical Services

DADOS: Deputy Assistant Director of Ordnance Services

DADQ: Deputy Assistant Director of Quartering

DADST: Deputy Assistant Director of Supplies and Transport

DAG: Deputy Adjutant-General

DAMS: Deputy Assistant Military Secretary

DAQMG: Deputy Assistant Quartermaster-General

DASc: Doctor in Agricultural Sciences

DATA: Draughtsmen's and Allied Technicians' Association

DBA: Doctor of Business Administration

DBE: Dame Commander Order of the British Empire

DC: District of Columbia (US)

DCAe: Diploma of College of Aeronautics

DCAS: Deputy Chief of the Air Staff

DCG: Deputy Chaplain-General

DCGS: Deputy Chief of the General Staff

DCh: Doctor of Surgery

DCH: Diploma in Child Health

DCIGS: (formerly) Deputy Chief of the Imperial General Staff (now DCGS)

DCL: Doctor of Civil Law

DCLI: Duke of Cornwall's Light Infantry

DCM: Distinguished Conduct Medal

DCMG: Dame Commander of St Michael and St George

DCnL: Doctor of Canon Law

DCS: Deputy Chief of Staff; Doctor of Commercial Sciences

DCSO: Deputy Chief Scientific Officer

DCT: Doctor of Christian Theology

DCVO: Dame Commander of Royal Victorian Order

DD: Doctor of Divinity

DDL: Deputy Director of Labour

DDME: Deputy Director of Mechanical Engineering

DDMI: Deputy Director of Military Intelligence

DDMS: Deputy Director of Medical Services

DDMT: Deputy Director of Military Training

DDNI: Deputy Director of Naval Intelligence

DDO: Diploma in Dental Orthopaedics

DDPR: Deputy Director of Public Relations

DDPS: Deputy Director of Personal Services

DDRA: Deputy Director Royal Artillery

DDS: Doctor of Dental Surgery; Director of Dental Services

DDSc: Doctor of Dental Sciences

DDSD: Deputy Director Staff Duties

DDST: Deputy Director of Supplies and Transport

DDWE&M: Deputy Director of Works, Electrical and Mechanical

DE: Doctor of Engineering

DEA: Department of Economic Affairs

Decd: Deceased

DEconSc: Doctor of Economic Science

DEd: Doctor of Education

Del: Delaware (US)

Deleg.: Delegate

DEng: Doctor of Engineering

DenM: Docteur en Médicine

DEOVR: Duke of Edinburgh's Own Volunteer Rifles

DEP: Department of Employment and Productivity

Dep.: Deputy

DèsL: Docteur ès lettres

DesRCA: Designer of the Royal College of Art

DèsS: Docteur ès sciences

DFA: Doctor of Fine Arts

DFC: Distinguished Flying Cross

DFM: Distinguished Flying Medal (Canada)

DG: Dragoon Guards

DGAMS: Director-General Army Medical Services

DGMS: Director-General of Medical Services

DGMT: Director-General of Military Training

DGMW: Director-General of Military Works

DGNPS: Director-General of Naval Personal Services

DGP: Director-General of Personnel

DGS: Diploma in Graduate Studies

DGStJ: (formerly) Dame of Grace, Order of St John of Jerusalem (now DStJ)

DHL: Doctor of Humane Letters; Doctor of Hebrew Literature

DHQ: District Headquarters

DIAS: Dublin Institute of Advanced Sciences

DIC: Diploma of the Imperial College

DIG: Deputy Inspector-General

DIH: Diploma in Industrial Health

Dio.: Diocese

DipCD: Diploma in Civic Design

DipEd: Diploma in Education

DipPA: Diploma of Practitioners in Advertising

DipTP: Diploma in Town Planning

DipTPT: Diploma in Theory and Practice of Teaching

DisTP: Distinction Town Planning

Div.: Division; divorced

DJAG: Deputy Judge Advocate General

DJStJ: formerly Dame of Justice of St John of Jerusalem (now DStJ)

DJur: Doctor Juris

DL: Deputy Lieutenant

DLC: Diploma Loughborough College

DLES: Doctor of Letters in Economic Studies

DLI: Durham Light Infantry

DLitt or DLit: Doctor of Literature; Doctor of Letters

DLO: Diploma in Laryngology and Otology

DM: Doctor of Medicine

DMD: Doctor of Medical Dentistry (Australia)

DME: Director of Mechanical Engineering

DMI: Director of Military Intelligence

DMJ: Diploma in Medical Jurisprudence

DMR: Diploma in Medical Radiology

DMRD: Diploma in Medical Radiological Diagnosis

DMRE: Diploma in Medical Radiology and Electrology

DMRT: Diploma in Medical Radio-Therapy

DMS: Director of Medical Services

DMus: Doctor of Music

DMT: Director of Military Training

DNB: Dictionary of National Biography

DNE: Director of Naval Equipment

DNI: Director of Naval Intelligence

DO: Diploma in Ophthalmology

DObstRCOG: Diploma Royal College of Obstetricians and Gynaecologists

DOC: District Officer Commanding

DocEng: Doctor of Engineering

DoE: Department of the Environment

DOL: Doctor of Oriental Learning

Dom.: *Dominus*

DOMS: Diploma in Ophthalmic Medicine and Surgery

DOR: Director of Operational Requirements

DOS: Director of Ordnance Services

Dow.: Dowager

DPA: Diploma in Public Administration; Discharged Prisoners' Aid

DPEc: Doctor of Political Economy

DPed: Doctor of Pedagogy

DPH: Diploma in Public Health

DPh or DPhil: Doctor of Philosophy

DPM: Diploma in Psychological Medicine

DPR: Director of Public Relations

DPS: Director of Postal Services; also (formerly) Director of Personal Services

DQMG: Deputy Quartermaster-General

Dr: Doctor

DRAC: Director Royal Armoured Corps

DrIng: Doctor of Engineering (Germany)

DrŒcPol: Doctor Œconomiæ Politicæ

DS: Directing Staff

DSAO: Diplomatic Service Administration Office

DSC: Distinguished Service Cross

DSc: Doctor of Science

DScA: Docteur en sciences agricoles

DSD: Director Staff Duties

DSIR: Department of Scientific and Industrial Research (now *see under* SRC)

DSM: Distinguished Service Medal

DSO: Companion of the Distinguished Service Order

DSP: Director of Selection of Personnel; Docteur en sciences politiques (Montreal)

d.s.p.: *decessit sine prole* (died without issue)

DSS: Doctor of Sacred Scripture

DSSc: Doctor of Social Science (USA)

DST: Director of Supplies and Transport

DStJ: Dame of Grace, Order of St John of Jerusalem; Dame of Justice, Order of St John of Jerusalem; and *see* GCStJ

DTD: Dekoratie voor Trouwe Dienst (Decoration for Devoted Service)

DTech: Doctor of Technology

DTH: Diploma in Tropical Hygiene

DTheol: Doctor of Theology

DThPT: Diploma in Theory and Practice of Teaching (Durham University)

DTI: Department of Trade and Industry

DTM&H: Diploma in Tropical Medicine and Hygiene

DUniv: Doctor of the University

DUP: Docteur de l'Université de Paris

DVH: Diploma in Veterinary Hygiene

DVM: Doctor of Veterinary Medicine

DVSM: Diploma in Veterinary State Medicine

E

E: East; Earl
e: eldest
EAHY: European Architectural Heritage Year
EAP: East Africa Protectorate
Ebor: (*Eboracensis*) of York
EBU: European Broadcasting Union
EC: East Central (postal district); Emergency Commission
ECA: Economic Co-operation Administration
ECAFE: Economic Commission for Asia and the Far East
ECE: Economic Commission for Europe
ECGD: Export Credits Guarantee Department
ECSC: European Coal and Steel Community
ECU: English Church Union
ED: Efficiency Decoration; Doctor of Engineering (US)
EdB: Bachelor of Education
EDC: Economic Development Committee
EdD: Doctor of Education
Edin.: Edinburgh
Edn: Edition
Educ.: Educated
Educn: Education
EEC: European Economic Community
EEF: Egyptian Expeditionary Force
EETS: Early English Text Society
EFTA: European Free Trade Association
e.h.: *ehrenhalber*; *see under* h.c.
EI: East Indian; East Indies
EICS: East India Company's Service
E-in-C: Engineer-in-Chief
EMS: Emergency Medical Service
Ency.Brit.: Encyclopaedia Britannica
Eng.: England
Engr: Engineer
ENSA: Entertainments National Service Association
ENT: Ear, Nose and Throat
er: elder
ER: Eastern Region (BR)
ERC: Electronics Research Council
ERD: Emergency Reserve Decoration (Army)
ESRO: European Space Research Organization
E-SU: English-Speaking Union
Euratom: European Atomic Energy Commission
Ext.: Extinct

F

FA: Football Association
FAA: Fellow of the Australian Academy of Science; also (formerly) Fleet Air Arm
FAAAS: Fellow of the American Association for the Advancement of Science
FACC: Fellow of the American College of Cardiology
FACCA: Fellow of the Association of Certified and Corporate Accountants
FACCP: Fellow of American College of Chest Physicians
FACD: Fellow of American College of Dentistry
FACE: Fellow of the Australian College of Education
FACI: (Changed to) FRACI

FACP: Fellow of American College of Physicians
FACR: Fellow of American College of Radiology
FACS: Fellow of American College of Surgeons
FAGS: Fellow American Geographical Society
FAHA: Fellow, Australian Academy of the Humanities
FAI: Fellow of Chartered Auctioneers' and Estate Agents' Institute
FAIA: Fellow of American Institute of Architects
FAIAA: Fellow of American Institute of Aeronautics and Astronautics (and *see under* FIAS)
FAIAS: Fellow of Australian Institute of Agricultural Science
FAIM: Fellow of the Australian Institute of Management
FAIP: Fellow of Australian Institute of Physics
FAMS: Fellow of the Ancient Monuments Society
FAmSCE: Fellow of the American Society of Civil Engineers
FANY: First Aid Nursing Yeomanry
FAO: Food and Agriculture Organization
FAPHA: Fellow American Public Health Association
FAPI: Fellow of the Australian Planning Institute
FARELF: Far East Land Forces
FAS: Fellow of the Antiquarian Society
FASA: Fellow of Australian Society of Accountants
F.ASCE: Fellow of American Society of Civil Engineers
FBA: Fellow of the British Academy
FBCS: Fellow of the British Computer Society
FBHI: Fellow of the British Horological Institute
FBI: Federation of British Industries (*see under* CBI, in which now merged)
FBIM: Fellow of the British Institute of Management (formerly FIIA; Fellow of the Institute of Industrial Administration)
FBOA: Fellow of British Optical Association
FBOU: Fellow British Ornithologists' Union
FBPsS: Fellow of British Psychological Society
FBritIRE: (formerly) Fellow of British Institution of Radio Engineers
FBS: Fellow Building Societies Institute
FBSI: Fellow of Boot and Shoe Institution
FBSM: Fellow of the Birmingham School of Music
FCA: Fellow of the Institute of Chartered Accountants
FCASI: (formerly FCAI) Fellow of the Canadian Aeronautics and Space Institute
FCCS: Fellow of Corporation of Secretaries (formerly of Certified Secretaries)
FCGI: Fellow of City and Guilds of London Institute
FCGP: Fellow of the College of General Practitioners (now *see* FRCGP)
FCH: Fellow of Coopers Hill College
FChS: Fellow of the Society of Chiropodists
FCI: Fellow of the Institute of Commerce
FCIC: Fellow Chemical Institute of Canada (formerly Canadian Institute of Chemistry)
FCII: Fellow of the Chartered Insurance Institute
FCIPA: (formerly used for) Fellow of the Chartered Institute of Patent Agents (now *see* CPA)
FCIS: Fellow of the Chartered Institute of Secretaries
FCIT: Fellow of Chartered Institute of Transport
FCMA: Fellow of the Institute of Cost and Management Accountants

FCO: Foreign and Commonwealth Office (departments merged Oct. 1968)

FCP: Fellow College of Preceptors

FCPath: Fellow of the College of Pathologists (now *see* FRCPath)

FCP(SoAf) Fellow of the College of Physicians, South Africa

FCPSO (SoAf): (and *see* FCP(SoAf) and FCS (SoAf) Fellow of the College of Physicians and Surgeons and Obstetricians, South Africa

FCRA: Fellow of the College of Radiologists of Australia

FCS or **FChemSoc:** Fellow of the Chemical Society

FCSP: Fellow of the Chartered Society of Physiotherapy

FCS(SoAf): Fellow of the College of Surgeons, South Africa

FCST: Fellow of the College of Speech Therapists

FCT: Federal Capital Territory (now ACT)

FCTB: Fellow of the College of Teachers of the Blind

FCU: Fighter Control Unit

FDS: Fellow in Dental Surgery

FDSRCS: Fellow in Dental Surgery, Royal College of Surgeons of England

FDSRCSE: Fellow in Dental Surgery, Royal College of Surgeons of Edinburgh

FEAF: Far East Air Force

FEIS: Fellow of the Educational Institute of Scotland

FES: Fellow of the Entomological Society; Fellow of the Ethnological Society

FF: Field Force

FFA: Fellow of Faculty of Actuaries (in Scotland)

FFARACS: Fellow of Faculty of Anaesthetists Royal Australian College of Surgeons

FFARCS: Fellow of Faculty of Anaesthetists, Royal College of Surgeons of England

FFARCSI: Fellow of Faculty of Anaesthetists Royal College of Surgeons in Ireland

FFAS: Fellow of Faculty of Architects and Surveyors, London

FFDRCSI: Fellow of Faculty of Dentistry, Royal College of Surgeons in Ireland

FFF: Free French Forces

FFHom: Fellow of Faculty of Homœopathy

FFI: French Forces of the Interior; Finance For Industry

FFR: Fellow of Faculty of Radiologists

FGA: Fellow of Gemmological Association

FGI: Fellow of the Institute of Certificated Grocers

FGS: Fellow of Geological Society

FGSM: Fellow of Guildhall School of Music

FHA: Fellow of the Institute of Health Service Administrators (formerly Hospital Administrators)

FHAS: Fellow of Highland and Agricultural Society of Scotland

FH-WC: Fellow of Heriot-Watt College (now University), Edinburgh

FIA: Fellow of Institute of Actuaries

FIAAS: Fellow of the Institute of Australian Agricultural Science

FIAA&S: Fellow of the Incorporated Association of Architects and Surveyors

FIAgrE: Fellow of the Institution of Agricultural Engineers

FIAI: Fellow of the Institute of Industrial and Commercial Accountants

FIAL: Fellow of the International Institute of Arts and Letters

FIArb: Fellow of Institute of Arbitrators

FIAS: (now *see under* FAIAA) (formerly) Fellow Institute of Aeronautical Sciences (US)

FIAWS: Fellow, International Academy of Wood Sciences

FIB: Fellow of Institute of Bankers

FIBD: Fellow of the Institute of British Decorators

FIBiol: Fellow of Institute of Biology

FIBP: Fellow of the Institute of British Photographers

FIC: *See* FRIC

FICA: Fellow of the Commonwealth Institute of Accountancy; Fellow of the Institute of Chartered Accountants in England and Wales (but *see* FCA)

FICD: Fellow of the Institute of Civil Defence; Fellow of the Indian College of Dentists

FICE: Fellow of the Institution of Civil Engineers (*see also* MICE)

FICeram: Fellow of the Institute of Ceramics

FIChemE: Fellow of Institution of Chemical Engineers

FICI: Fellow of the Institute of Chemistry of Ireland; Fellow of the International Colonial Institute

FICS: Fellow of Institute of Chartered Shipbrokers; Fellow of the International College of Surgeons

FIE: Fellow of Institute of Engineers

FIEE: Fellow of the Institution of Electrical Engineers (*see also* MIEE)

FIEEE: Fellow of Institute of Electrical and Electronics Engineers (NY)

FIEI: Fellow of the Institution of Engineering Inspection

FIERE: Fellow of Institution of Electronic and Radio Engineers

FIES: Fellow of Illuminating Engineering Society; now *see* FIllumES

FIFST: Fellow of Institute of Food Science and Technology

FIGasE: Fellow of Institution of Gas Engineers

FIGCM: Fellow Incorporated Guild of Church Musicians

FIHsg: (formerly) Fellow of Institute of Housing (now *see under* FIHM)

FIHE: Fellow of Institute of Health Education

FIHM: Fellow of Institute of Housing Managers

FIHVE: Fellow of Institution of Heating & Ventilating Engineers

FIIA: Fellow of Institute of Industrial Administration (now FBIM); Fellow of the British Institute of Management)

FIInst: Fellow of the Imperial Institute

FIL: Fellow of the Institute of Linguists

FILA: Fellow of the Institute of Landscape Architects

FILLM: Fédération Internationale des Langues et Littératures Modernes

FIllumES: Fellow of Illuminating Engineering Society

FIM: Fellow of the Institution of Metallurgists

FIMA: Fellow of the Institute of Mathematics and its Applications

FIMarE: Fellow, Institute of Marine Engineers

FIMechE: Fellow of the Institution of Mechanical Engineers (*see also* MIMechE)

FIMI: Fellow of the Institute of the Motor Industry (formerly FIMT; Fellow Institute of Motor Trade)

FIMinE: Fellow of the Institution of Mining Engineers

FIMIT: Fellow of the Institute of Music Instrument Technology

FIMTA: Fellow of the Institute of Municipal Treasurers and Accountants; now *see* IPFA

FIMunE: Fellow of Institution of Municipal Engineers

FIN: Fellow of the Institute of Navigation

FInstBiol: Fellow of Institute of Biology (now *see* FIBiol)

FInstD: Fellow of Institute of Directors

FInstF: Fellow of Institute of Fuel

FInstM: Fellow of the Institute of Meat; Fellow of the Institute of Marketing

FInstMet: Fellow of Institute of Metals

FInstMSM: Fellow of the Institute of Marketing and Sales Management (formerly FSMA)

FInstP: Fellow of Institute of Physics

FInstPet: Fellow of the Institute of Petroleum

FInstPI: Fellow of the Institute Patentees (Incorporated)

FInstPS: Fellow of Institute of Purchasing and Supply

FInstW: Fellow of the Institute of Welding

FIOB: Fellow of Institute of Building

FIPA: Fellow of the Institute of Practitioners in Advertising

FIPHE: Fellow of the Institution of Public Health Engineers

FIPM: Fellow of the Institute of Personnel Management; now *see* CIPM

FIPR: Fellow of Institute of Public Relations

FIProdE: Fellow, Institution of Production Engineers

FIRA(Ind): Fellow of Institute of Railway Auditors and Accountants (India)

FIRE(Aust): (now *see under* FIREE(Aust)); (formerly) Fellow of the Institution of Radio Engineers (Australia)

FIREE(Aust): Fellow of the Institution of Radio and Electronics Engineers (Australia) (and *see under* FIRE(Aust))

FIRI: Fellow of the Institution of the Rubber Industry

FIRTE: Fellow, Institute of Road Transport Engineers

FIS: Fellow of the Institute of Statisticians (formerly Assoc. of Incorporated Statisticians)

FISA: Fellow of the Incorporated Secretaries' Association

FISE: Fellow of Institution of Sanitary Engineers

FIST: Fellow of the Institute of Science Technology

FIStructE: Fellow of Institution of Structural Engineers

FIW: Fellow of the Welding Institute

FIWE: Fellow of the Institute of Water Engineers

FIWM: Fellow of the Institution of Works Managers

FIWSc: Fellow of the Institute of Wood Science

FJI: Fellow of Institute of Journalists

FKC: Fellow of King's College (London)

FLA: Fellow of Library Association

Fla: Florida (US)

FLAS: Fellow of the Chartered Land Agents' Society

FLCM: Fellow of the London College of Music

FLHS: Fellow of the London Historical Society

FLS: Fellow of the Linnaean Society

Flt: Flight

FM: Field-Marshal

FMA: Fellow of the Museums Association

FMS: Federated Malay States

FMSA: Fellow of the Mineralogical Society of America

FNA: Fellow of Indian National Science Academy

FNECInst: Fellow, North East Coast Institution of Engineers and Shipbuilders

FNI: Fellow of National Institute of Sciences in India (now see FNA)

FNZIA: Fellow of the New Zealand Institute of Architects

FNZIAS: Fellow of the New Zealand Institute of Agricultural Science

FNZIC: Fellow of the New Zealand Institute of Chemistry

FNZIE: Fellow of the New Zealand Institution of Engineers

FO: Foreign Office (*see also* FCO); Field Officer; Flying Officer

FOIC: Flag Officer in charge

FPhS: Fellow of the Philosophical Society of England

FPhysS: Fellow of the Physical Society

FPS: Fellow of the Pharmaceutical Society

FRACI: Fellow of the Royal Australian Chemical Institute (formerly FACI)

FRACP: Fellow of the Royal Australasian College of Physicians

FRACS: Fellow of the Royal Australasian College of Surgeons

FRAD: Fellow of the Royal Academy of Dancing

FRAeS: Fellow of the Royal Aeronautical Society

FRAgSs: Fellow of the Royal Agricultural Societies (*ie* of England, Scotland and Wales)

FRAHS: Fellow of Royal Australian Historical Society

FRAI: Fellow of the Royal Anthropological Institute

FRAIA: Fellow of the Royal Australian Institute of Architects

FRAIC: Fellow of the Royal Architectural Institute of Canada

FRAM: Fellow of the Royal Academy of Music

FRAS: Fellow of the Royal Astronomical Society; Fellow of the Royal Asiatic Society

FRASB: Fellow of Royal Asiatic Society of Bengal

FRASE: Fellow of the Royal Agricultural Society of England

FRBS: Fellow of Royal Society of British Sculptors; Fellow of the Royal Botanic Society

FRCGP: Fellow of the Royal College of General Practitioners

FRCM: Fellow of the Royal College of Music

FRCO: Fellow of the Royal College of Organists

FRCO(CHM): Fellow of the Royal College of Organists with Diploma in Choir Training

FRCOG: Fellow of the Royal College of Obstetricians and Gynaecologists

FRCP: Fellow of the Royal College of Physicians London

FRCPath: Fellow of the Royal College of Pathologists

FRCP(C) Fellow of the Royal College of Physicians of Canada

FRCPE and FRCPEd: Fellow of the Royal College of Physicians of Edinburgh

FRCPGlas: Fellow of the Royal College (formerly Faculty) of Physicians and Surgeons, Glasgow (and *see under* FRFPSG)

FRCPI: Fellow of the Royal College of Physicians in Ireland

FRCPS(Hon): Hon. Fellow of Royal College Physicians and Surgeons (Glasgow)

FRCPsych: Fellow of the Royal College of Psychiatrists

FRCS: Fellow of the Royal College of Surgeons of England

FRCSE and **FRCSEd:** Fellow of the Royal College of Surgeons of Edinburgh

FRCSGlas: Fellow of the Royal College of Surgeons of Glasgow

FRCSI: Fellow of the Royal College of Surgeons in Ireland

FRCSoc: Fellow of the Royal Commonwealth Society

FRCUS: Fellow of the Royal College of University Surgeons (Denmark)

FRCVS: Fellow of the Royal College of Veterinary Surgeons

FREconS: Fellow of Royal Economic Society

FREI: Fellow of the Real Estate Institute (Australia)

FRES: Fellow of Royal Entomological Society of London

FRFPSG: (formerly) Fellow of Royal Faculty of Physicians and Surgeons, Glasgow (now Royal College of Physicians and Surgeons, Glasgow) (and *see under* FRCPGlas)

FRGS: Fellow of the Royal Geographical Society

FRHistS: Fellow of Royal Historical Society

FRHS: Fellow of the Royal Horticultural Society

FRIAS: Fellow of the Royal Incorporation of Architects of Scotland

FRIBA: Fellow of the Royal Institute of British Architects

FRIC: (formerly FIC) Fellow of Royal Institute of Chemistry

FRICS: Fellow of the Royal Institution of Chartered Surveyors

FRIH: Fellow of Royal Institute of Horticulture (NZ)

FRINA: Fellow of Royal Institute of Naval Architects

FRIPHH: Fellow of the Royal Institute of Public Health and Hygiene

FRMCM: Fellow of Royal Manchester College of Music

FRMedSoc: Fellow of Royal Medical Society

FRMetS: Fellow of the Royal Meteorological Society

FRMS: Fellow of the Royal Microscopical Society

FRNS: Fellow of Royal Numismatic Society

FRPS: Fellow of the Royal Photographic Society

FRPSL: Fellow of the Royal Philatelic Society, London

FRS: Fellow of the Royal Society

FRSA: Fellow of Royal Society of Arts

FRSAI: Fellow of the Royal Society of Antiquaries of Ireland

FRSanI: Fellow of Royal Sanitary Institute (*see* FRSH)

FRSC: Fellow of the Royal Society of Canada

FRSCM: Fellow of the Royal School of Church Music

FRSE: Fellow of the Royal Society of Edinburgh

FRSGS: Fellow of the Royal Scottish Geographical Society

FRSH: Fellow of the Royal Society for the Promotion of Health (formerly FRSanI)

FRSL: Fellow of the Royal Society of Literature

FRSM or **FRSocMed:** Fellow of Royal Society of Medicine

FRSNZ: Fellow of Royal Society of New Zealand

FRSSAf: Fellow of Royal Society of South Africa

FRST: Fellow of the Royal Society of Teachers

FRSTM&H: Fellow of Royal Society of Tropical Medicine and Hygiene

FRTPI: Fellow, Royal Town Planning Institute

FRVIA: Fellow Royal Victorian Institute of Architects

FRZSScot: Fellow of the Royal Zoological Society of Scotland

fs: Graduate of Royal Air Force Staff College

FSA: Fellow of the Society of Antiquaries

FSAA: Fellow of the Society of Incorporated Accountants and Auditors

FSAM: Fellow of the Society of Art Masters

FSArc: Fellow of Society of Architects (merged with the RIBA 1952)

FSAScot: Fellow of the Society of Antiquaries of Scotland

FSASM: Fellow of the South Australian School of Mines

fsc: Foreign Staff College

FSDC: Fellow of Society of Dyers and Colourists

FSE: Fellow of Society of Engineers

FSG: Fellow of the Society of Genealogists

FSGT: Fellow of Society of Glass Technology

FSI: Fellow of Royal Institution of Chartered Surveyors (changed Aug. 1947 to FRICS)

FSIA: Fellow of Society of Industrial Artists and Designers

FSLAET: Fellow, Society of Licensed Aircraft Engineers and Technologists

FSMA: Fellow of Incorporated Sales Managers' Association; *see* FInstMSM, FIM

FSMC: Freeman of the Spectacle-Makers' Company

FSS: Fellow of the Royal Statistical Society

FTCD: Fellow of Trinity College, Dublin

FTCL: Fellow of Trinity College of Music London

FTI: Fellow of the Textile Institute

FTII: Fellow of the Institute of Taxation

FTS: Flying Training School

FUMIST: Fellow of University of Manchester Institute of Science and Technology

FWA: Fellow of the World Academy of Arts and Sciences

FZS: Fellow of the Zoological Society

FZSScot: (Changed to) FRZSScot

G

Ga: Georgia (US)

GAPAN: Guild of Air Pilots and Air Navigators

GATT: General Agreement on Tariffs and Trade

GB: Great Britain

GBA: Governing Bodies Association

GBE: Knight or Dame Grand Cross Order of the British Empire

GC: George Cross

GCB: Knight Grand Cross of the Bath

GCH: Knight Grand Cross of Hanover

GCIE: Knight Grand Commander of the Indian Empire

GCMG: Knight or Dame Grand Cross of St Michael and St George

GCON: Grand Cross, Order of the Niger

GCSI: Knight Grand Commander of the Star of India

GCStJ: Bailiff or Dame Grand Cross of the Order of St John of Jerusalem

GCVO: Knight or Dame Grand Cross of Royal Victorian Order

GDC: General Dental Council

Gdns: Gardens
Gen.: General
Ges.: Gesellschaft
GFS: Girls' Friendly Society
g g s: great grandson
GHQ: General Headquarters
Gib.: Gibraltar
GIMechE: Graduate Institution of Mechanical Engineers
GL: Grand Lodge
GLC: Greater London Council
Glos: Gloucestershire
GM: George Medal; Grand Medal (Ghana)
GMC: General Medical Council; Guild of Memorial Craftsmen
GMIE: Grand Master of Indian Empire
GMSI: Grand Master of Star of India
GOC: General Officer Commanding
GOC-in-C: General Officer Commanding-in-Chief
GOE: General Ordination Examination
Gov.: Governor
Govt: Government
GP: General Practitioner; Grand Prix
GPDST: Girls' Public Day School Trust
GPO: General Post Office
GQG: Grand Quartier Général (French GHQ)
Gr.: Greek
Gram. Sch.: Grammar School
GRSM: Graduate of the Royal Schools of Music
GS: General Staff
g s: Grandson
GSM: General Service Medal; Guildhall School of Music
GSO: General Staff Officer
GTS: General Theological Seminary (New York)
GUI: Golfing Union of Ireland
GWR: Great Western Railway

HH: His (or Her) Highness; His Holiness
HHD: Doctor of Humanities (US)
HIH: His (or Her) Imperial Highness
HIM: His (or Her) Imperial Majesty
HJ: Hilal-e-Jurat (Pakistan)
HLI: Highland Light Infantry
HM: His (or Her) Majesty, or Majesty's
HMAS: His (or Her) Majesty's Australian Ship
HMC: Headmasters' Conference; Hospital Management Committee
HMHS: His (or Her) Majesty's Hospital Ship
HMI: His (or Her) Majesty's Inspector
HMOCS: His (or Her) Majesty's Overseas Civil Service
HMS: His (or Her) Majesty's Ship
HMSO: His (or Her) Majesty's Stationery Office
Hon.: Honourable; Honorary
HP: House Physician
HPk: Hilal-e-Pakistan
HQ: Headquarters
(HR): Home Rule
HRCA: Honorary Royal Cambrian Academician
HRH: His (or Her) Royal Highness
HRHA: Honorary Member of Royal Hibernian Academy
HRI: Honorary Member of Royal Institute of Painters in Water Colours
HROI: Honorary Member of Royal Institute of Oil Painters
HRSA: Honorary Member of Royal Scottish Academy
HRSW: Honorary Member of Royal Scottish Water Colour Society
HS: House Surgeon
HSH: His (or Her) Serene Highness
Hum.: Humanity, Humanities (Latin)
Hunts: Huntingdonshire
Hy: Heavy

H

HA: Historical Association
HAA: Heavy Anti-Aircraft
HAC: Honourable Artillery Company
Hants: Hampshire
HARCVS: Honorary Associate of the Royal College of Veterinary Surgeons
Harv.: Harvard
HBM: His (or Her) Britannic Majesty (Majesty's)
hc: *honoris causa*
HCF: Hon. Chaplain to the Forces
HCIMA: Hotel, Catering and Institutional Management Association
HDA: Hawkesbury Diploma in Agriculture (Australian)
HDD: Higher Dental Diploma
HE: His Excellency; His Eminence
HEH: His Exalted Highness
HEIC: Honourable East India Company
HEICS: Honourable East India Company's Service
Heir-pres.: Heir-presumptive
Herts: Hertfordshire
HFARA: Honorary Foreign Associate of the Royal Academy
HFRA: Honorary Foreign Member of the Royal Academy
HG: Home Guard

I

I: Island
Ia: Iowa (US)
IA: Indian Army
IAF: Indian Air Force; Indian Auxiliary Force
IAHM: Incorporated Association of Headmasters
IAMC: Indian Army Medical Corps
IAMTACT: Institute of Advanced Machine Tool and Control Technology
IAOC: Indian Army Ordnance Control
IAPS: Incorporated Association of Preparatory Schools
IARO: Indian Army Reserve of Officers
IAS: Indian Administrative Service
IASS: International Association for Scandinavian Studies
IATA: International Air Transport Association
Ib. or Ibid.: *Ibidem* (in the same place)
IBA: Independent Broadcasting Authority; International Bar Association
IBG: Institute of British Geographers
IBRD: International Bank for Reconstruction and Development (World Bank)
i/c: In charge
ICA: Institute of Contemporary Arts
ICAA: Invalid Children's Aid Association

ICAO: International Civil Aviation Organization
ICE: Institution of Civil Engineers
Icel.: Icelandic
ICFC: Industrial and Commercial Finance Corporation
ICFTU: International Confederation of Free Trade Unions
IChemE: Institution of Chemical Engineers
ICI: Imperial Chemical Industries
ICMA: Institution of Cost and Management Accountants
ICOM: International Council of Museums
ICOMOS: International Council of Monuments and Sites
ICRC: International Committee of the Red Cross
ICS: Indian Civil Service
ICSS: International Committee for the Sociology of Sport
ICSU: International Council of Scientific Unions
ICT: International Computers and Tabulators Ltd
Id: Idaho (US)
IDA: International Development Association
idc: Completed a Course at, or served for a year on the Staff of, the Imperial Defence College
IEE: Institution of Electrical Engineers
IEEE: Institute of Electrical and Electronics Engineers (NY)
IERE: Institution of Electronic and Radio Engineers (and see under BritIRE)
IES: Indian Educational Service; Institution of Engineers and Shipbuilders in Scotland
IFLA: International Federation of Library Associations
IFS: Irish Free State; Indian Forest Service
IG: Instructor in Gunnery
IGasE: Institution of Gas Engineers
IGU: International Geographical Union; International Gas Union
IHA: Institute of Health Service Administrators
IIS: International Institute of Sociology
IISS: International Institute of Strategic Studies
ILEC: Inner London Education Committee
Ill: Illinois (US)
ILO: International Labour Office
ILP: Independent Labour Party
IMA: International Music Association
IMEA: Incorporated Municipal Electrical Association
IMechE: Institution of Mechanical Engineers
IMF: International Monetary Fund
IMinE: Institution of Mining Engineers
IMMTS: Indian Mercantile Marine Training Ship
Imp.: Imperial
IMS: Indian Medical Service
IMTA: Institute of Municipal Treasurers and Accountants; now see CIPFA
IMunE: Institution of Municipal Engineers
IN: Indian Navy
Inc.: Incorporated
Incog.: *Incognito* (in secret)
Ind.: Independent; Indiana (US)
Insp.: Inspector
Inst.: Institute
Instn: Institution
InstnMM: Institution of Mining and Metallurgy
InstT: Institute of Transport
IODE: Imperial Order of the Daughters of the Empire
I of M: Isle of Man

IOGT: International Order of Good Templars
IOM: Isle of Man; Indian Order of Merit
IOOF: Independent Order of Oddfellows
IOP: Institute of Painters in Oil Colours
IoW: Isle of Wight
IPCS: Institution of Professional Civil Servants
IPFA: Member, Chartered Institute of Public Finance and Accountancy
IPI: International Press Institute
IPM: Institute of Personnel Management
IPPS: Institute of Physics and The Physical Society
IPS: Indian Police Service; Indian Political Service
IPU: Inter-Parliamentary Union
IRA: Irish Republican Army
IRC: Industrial Reorganization Corporation
IREE(Aust): Institution of Radio and Electronics Engineers (Australia)
IRO: International Refugee Organization
Is: Island(s)
IS: International Society of Sculptors, Painters and Gravers
ISC: Imperial Service College, Haileybury; Indian Staff Corps
ISE: Indian Service of Engineers
ISI: International Statistical Institute
ISIS: Independent Schools Information Service
ISM: Incorporated Society of Musicians
ISMRC: Inter-Services Metallurgical Research Council
ISO: Imperial Service Order
IStructE: Institution of Structural Engineers
IT: Indian Territory (US)
ITA: Independent Television Authority; now see IBA
Ital. or It.: Italian
ITO: International Trade Organization
IUA: International Union of Architects
IUC: Inter-University Council for Higher Education Overseas
IUCN: International Union for the Conservation of Nature and Natural Resources
IUCW: International Union for Child Welfare
IUP: Association of Independent Unionist Peers
IVS: International Voluntary Service
IW: Isle of Wight
IWGC: Imperial War Graves Commission
IY: Imperial Yeomanry
IZ: I Zingari

J

A: Judge Advocate
JACT: Joint Association of Classical Teachers
JAG: Judge Advocate General
Jas: James
JCB: *Juris Canonici Bachelor* (Bachelor of Canon Law)
JCS: Journal of the Chemical Society
JCD: *Juris Canonici Doctor* (Doctor of Canon Law)
JD: Doctor of Jurisprudence
JDipMA: Joint Diploma in Management Accounting Services
JInstE: Junior Institution of Engineers
jls: Journals
JMN: *Johan Mangku Negara* (Malaysian Honour)

Joh. or Jno.: John
JP: Justice of the Peace
Jr: Junior
jsc: Qualified at a Junior Staff Course, or the equivalent, 1942–46
JSLS: Joint Services Liaison Staff
jssc: Joint Services Staff Course
jt, jtly: joint, jointly
JUD: *Juris Utriusque Doctor*, Doctor of Both Laws (Canon and Civil)
Jun.: Junior
Jun. Opt.: Junior Optime
JWS or jws: Joint Warfare Staff

K

Kans: Kansas (US)
KAR: King's African Rifles
KBE: Knight Commander Order of the British Empire
KC: King's Counsel
KCB: Knight Commander of the Bath
KCC: Commander of Order of Crown, Belgium and Congo Free State
KCH: King's College Hospital; Knight Commander of Hanover
KCIE: Knight Commander of the Indian Empire
KCL: King's College, London
KCMG: Knight Commander of St Michael and St George
KCSG: Knight Commander of St Gregory
KCSI: Knight Commander of the Star of India
KCSS: Knight Commander of St Silvester
KCVO: Knight Commander of the Royal Victorian Order
KDG: King's Dragoon Guards
KEH: King Edward's Horse
KG: Knight of the Order of the Garter
KGStJ: formerly Knight of Grace, Order of St John of Jerusalem (now KStJ)
KH: Knight of Hanover
KHC: Hon. Chaplain to the King
KHDS: Hon. Dental Surgeon to the King
KHNS: Hon. Nursing Sister to the King
KHP: Hon. Physician to the King
KHS: Hon. Surgeon to the King; Knight of the Holy Sepulchre
K-i-H: Kaisar-i-Hind
KJStJ: formerly Knight of Justice, Order of St John of Jerusalem (now KStJ)
KORR: King's Own Royal Regiment
KOSB: King's Own Scottish Borderers
KOYLI: King's Own Yorkshire Light Infantry
KP: Knight of the Order of St Patrick
KPM: King's Police Medal
KRRC: King's Royal Rifle Corps
KS: King's Scholar
KSG: Knight of St. Gregory
KSLI: King's Shropshire Light Infantry
KSLJ: Knight of St Lazarus of Jerusalem
KSS: Knight of St Silvester
KStJ: Knight of Order of St John of Jerusalem; and *see* GCStJ
KT: Knight of the Order of the Thistle
Kt or Knt: Knight
Ky: Kentucky (US)

L

(L): Liberal
LA: Los Angeles; Literate in Arts; Liverpool Academy
La: Louisiana (US)
(Lab): Labour
LAC: London Athletic Club
Lancs: Lancashire
LCC: London County Council (now *see under* GLC)
LCh: Licentiate in Surgery
LCJ: Lord Chief Justice
LCL: Licentiate of Canon Law
L.Corp. or Lance-Corp.; Lance-Corporal
LCP: Licentiate of the College of Preceptors
LDiv: Licentiate in Divinity
LDS: Licentiate in Dental Surgery
LDV: Local Defence Volunteers
LEA: Local Education Authority
LEPRA: British Leprosy Relief Association
LesL: Licencié ès lettres
LH: Light Horse
LHD: (*Literarum Humaniorum Doctor*) Doctor of Literature
LI: Light Infantry; Long Island
LicMed: Licentiate in Medicine
Lieut: Lieutenant
Lincs: Lincolnshire
Lit.: Literature; Literary
LitD: Doctor of Literature; Doctor of Letters
Lit. Hum.: *Literae Humaniores* (Classics)
LittD: Doctor of Literature; Doctor of Letters
LJ: Lord Justice
LLA: Lady Literate in Arts
LLB: Bachelor of Laws
LLCM: Licentiate London College of Music
LLD: Doctor of Laws
LLL: Licentiate in Laws
LLM: Master of Laws
LM: Licentiate in Midwifery
LMBC: Lady Margaret Boat Club
LMCC: Licentiate of Medical Council of Canada
LMR: London Midland Region (BR)
LMS: London, Midland and Scottish Railway (*see* BR); London Missionary Society
LMSSA: Licentiate in Medicine and Surgery, Society of Apothecaries
LMTPI: Legal Member of the Town Planning Institute
(LNat): Liberal National
LNER: London and North Eastern Railway (*see* BR)
L of C: Lines of Communication
LPTB: London Passenger Transport Board
LRAD: Licentiate of the Royal Academy of Dancing
LRAM: Licentiate of the Royal Academy of Music
LRCP: Licentiate of the Royal College of Physicians, London
LRCPE: Licentiate of the Royal College of Physicians, Edinburgh
LRCS: Licentiate of the Royal College of Surgeons of England
LRCSE: Licentiate of the Royal College of Surgeons, Edinburgh

LRFPS(G): formerly Licentiate of the Royal Faculty of Physicians and Surgeons, Glasgow (now Royal College of Physicians and Surgeons, Glasgow)

LRIBA: Licentiate, Royal Institute of British Architects

LSA: Licentiate of the Society of Apothecaries

LSE: London School of Economics

Lt: Light (*e.g.* Light Infantry)

Lt or Lieut: Lieutenant

LT Licentiate in Teaching

LTB: London Transport Board

LTCL: Licentiate of Trinity College of Music London

Lt-Col: Lieutenant-Colonel

LTE: London Transport Executive

Lt-Gen.: Lieutenant-General

LTh: Licentiate in Theology

(LU): Liberal Unionist

LUOTC: London University Officers' Training Corps

LXX: Septuagint

M

M: Marquess; Member; Monsieur

m: married

MA: Master of Arts

MAAF: Mediterranean Allied Air Forces

MACE: Member of the Australian College of Education

MACI: Member of the American Concrete Institute

MACS: Member of the American Chemical Society

MAEE: Marine Aircraft Experimental Establishment

MAFF: Ministry of Agriculture, Fisheries and Food

Mag.: Magnetism; Magazine

MAI: Master of Engineering (*Magister in Arte Ingeniaria*

MAIAA: Member of American Institute of Aeronautics and Astronautics (and *see under* MIAS)

MAICE: Member of American Institute of Consulting Engineers

MAIChE: Member of the American Institute of Chemical Engineers

Maj.-Gen.: Major-General

Man: Manitoba (Canada)

MAO: Master of Obstetric Art

MAOU: Member American Ornithologists' Union

MAP: Ministry of Aircraft Production

MArch: Master of Architecture

Marq.: Marquess

MASAE: Member American Society of Agriculture Engineering

M.ASCE: Member American Society of Civil Engineers

MASME: Member American Society of Mechanical Engineers

Mass: Massachusetts (US)

Math.: Mathematics; Mathematical

MB: Bachelor of Medicine

MBA: Master of Business Administration

MBASW: Member, British Association of Social Workers

MBE: Member of the Order of the British Empire

MBIM: Member of the British Institute of Management (formerly MIIA: Member of the Institute of Industrial Administration)

MBOU: Member British Ornithologists' Union

MBritIRE: (now *see under* MIERE) (formerly) Member of British Institution of Radio Engineers

MC: Military Cross

MCC: Marylebone Cricket Club

MCD: Master of Civic Design

MCE(Melb): Master of Civil Engineering (Melbourne University)

MChemA: Master in Chemical Analysis

MChOrth: Master in Orthopædic Surgery

MCL: Master in Civil Law

MCMES: Member of Civil and Mechanical Engineers' Society

MCom: Master of Commerce

MConsE: Member of Association of Consulting Engineers

MCP: Member of Colonial Parliament; Master of City Planning (US)

MCPA: Member of the College of Pathologists of Australia

MCPath: Member of College of Patholologists

MCPS: Member College of Physicians and Surgeons

MCS: Madras Civil Service; Malayan Civil Service

MD: Doctor of Medicine; Military District

Md: Maryland (US)

MDS: Master of Dental Surgery

Me: Maine (US)

ME: Mining Engineer; Middle East

MEAF: Middle East Air Force

MEC: Member of Executive Council

MEc: Master of Economics

MECAS: Middle East Centre for Arab Studies

Mech.: Mechanics; Mechanical

Med.: Medical

MEd: Master of Education

MEF: Middle East Force

MEIC: Member Engineering Institute of Canada

MELF: Middle East Land Forces

MEng: Master of Engineering

MetR: Metropolitan Railway

MEXE: Military Engineering Experimental Establishment

MFGB: Miners' Federation of Great Britain

MFH: Master of Foxhounds

MGA: Maj.-Gen. i/c Administration

MGC: Machine Gun Corps

MGCE: Maestro en Gestion Cuantitiva de Empresa

MGGS: Major-General, General Staff

MGI: Member of the Institute of Certificated Grocers

Mgr: Monsignor

MHA: Member of House of Assembly

MHR: Member of House of Representatives

MHRA: Modern Humanities Research Association

MHRF: Mental Health Research Fund

MI: Military Intelligence

MIAeE: Member Institute of Aeronautical Engineers

MIAgrE: Member of Institution of Agricultural Engineers

MIAS: (now *see under* MAIAA) (formerly) Member Institute of Aeronautical Science (US)

MIBF: Member Institute of British Foundrymen

MIBritishE: Member Institute of British Engineers

MICE: Member of Institution of Civil Engineers (formerly the higher rank of corporate membership of the Institution, now the lower rank; *see also* FICE; change dated July 1968)

MICEI: Member of Institution of Civil Engineers of Ireland

Mich: Michigan (US)

MIChemE: Member of the Institution of Chemical Engineers

MIEAust: Member Institution of Engineers, Australia

MIEE: Member of Institution' of Electrical Engineers (formerly the higher rank of corporate membership of the Institution, now the lower rank; *see also* FIEE; change dated Dec. 1966

MIEEE: Member of Institute of Electrical and Electronics Engineers (NY)

MIEI: Member of Institution of Engineering Inspection

MIE(Ind): Member of Institution of Engineers, India

MIERE: Member of Institution of Electronic and Radio Engineers (and *see under* MBritIRE)

MIES: Member Institution of Engineers and Shipbuilders, Scotland

MIEx: Member Institute of Export

MIGasE: Member, Institution of Gas Engineers

MIH: Member Institute of Hygiene

MIHVE: Member Institution of Heating and Ventilating Engineers

MIIA: Member of the Institute of Industrial Administration (now *see under* MBIM)

Mil.: Military

MILocoE: Member of Institution of Locomotive Engineers

MIMarE: Member of the Institute of Marine Engineers

MIMechE: Member of Institution of Mechanical Engineers (formerly the higher rank of corporate membership of the Institution, now the lower rank; *see also* FIMechE; change dated April 1968)

MIMI: Member of Institute of Motor Industry

MIMinE: Member of the Institution of Mining Engineers

MIMM: Member Institution of Mining and Metallurgy

MIMunE: Member Institution of Municipal Engineers

Min.: Ministry

MIN: Member of the Institute of Navigation

Minn: Minnesota (US)

MInstCE: Member of Institution of Civil Engineers (changed Feb. 1940 to MICE)

MInstF: Member of Institute of Fuel

MInstGasE: Member Institution of Gas Engineers

MInstHE: Member of the Institution of Highway Engineers

MInstM: Member of Institute of Marketing

MInstME: Member of Institution of Mining Engineers

MInstMet: Member of the Institute of Metals

MInstPet: Member of the Institute of Petroleum

MInstPI: Member of the Institute of Patentees (Inc.)

MInstR: Member of the Institute of Refrigeration

MInstRA: Member of the Institute of Registered Architects

MInstT: Member of the Institute of Transport

MInstW: Member Institute of Welding

MINucE: Member of Institution of Nuclear Engineers

MIOB: Member of the Institute of Building

MIPA: Member of the Institute of Practitioners in Advertising

MIPlantE: Member of the Institution of Plant Engineers

MIPM: Member of the Institute of Personnel Management

MIPR: Member of the Institute of Public Relations

MIProdE: (formerly MIPE) Member of the Institution of Production Engineers

MIRE: (now *see under* MIERE) (formerly) Member of the Institution of Radio Engineers

MIREE(Aust): Member of the Institution of Radio and Electronics Engineers (Australia)

MIRTE: Member of Institute of Road Transport Engineers

MIS: Member, Institute of Statisticians

MIS(India): Member of the Institution of Surveyors of India

MISI: Member of Iron and Steel Institute

Miss: Mississippi (US)

MIStructE: Member of the Institution Structural Engineers

MIT: Massachusetts Institute of Technology

MITA: Member, Industrial Transport Association

MIWE: Member of the Institution of Water Engineers

MIWPC: Member, Institute of Water Pollution Control

MIWSP: Member, Institute of Work Study Practitioners

MJI: Member of Institute of Journalists

MJIE: Member of the Junior Institute of Engineers

MJS: Member of the Japan Society

ML: Licentiate in Medicine; Master of Laws

MLA: Member of Legislative Assembly; Modern Language Association

MLC: Member of Legislative Council

MLitt: Master of Letters

Mlle: *Mademoiselle* (Miss)

MLO: Military Liaison Officer

MM: Military Medal

MME: Master of Mining Engineering

Mme: Madame

MMechE: Master of Mechanical Engineering

MMet: Master of Metallurgy

MMGI: Member of the Mining, Geological and Metallurgical Institute of India

MMSA: Master of Midwifery, Society of Apothecaries

MN: Merchant Navy

MNAS: Member of the National Academy of Sciences (US)

MO: Medical Officer

Mo: Missouri (US)

MoD: Ministry of Defence

Mods: Moderations (Oxford)

MOH: Medical Officer(s) of Health

MOI: Ministry of Information

Mon: Monmouthshire

Mont: Montana (US); Montgomeryshire

MOP: Ministry of Power

Most Rev.: Most Reverend

MoT: Ministry of Transport
MP: Member of Parliament
MPBW: Ministry of Public Building and Works
MPP: Member Provincial Parliament
MPS: Member of Pharmaceutical Society
MR: Master of the Rolls; Municipal Reform
MRAIC: Member Royal Architectural Institute of Canada
MRAS: Member of Royal Asiatic Society
MRC: Medical Research Council
MRCOG: Member of Royal College of Obstetricians and Gynaecologists
MRCP: Member of the Royal College of Physicians, London
MRCPA: Member of Royal College of Pathologists of Australia
MRCPE: Member of the Royal College of Physicians, Edinburgh
MRCPGlas: Member of the Royal College (formerly Faculty) of Physicians and Surgeons, Glasgow
MRCS: Member Royal College of Surgeons of England
MRCSE: Member of the Royal College of Surgeons, Edinburgh
MRCVS: Member of the Royal College of Veterinary Surgeons
MREmpS: Member of the Royal Empire Society
MRI: Member Royal Institution
MRIA: Member Royal Irish Academy
MRIAI: Member of the Royal Institute of the Architects of Ireland
MRICS: Member of the Royal Institution of Chartered Surveyors
MRINA: Member of Royal Institution of Naval Architects
MRSanI: Member of Royal Sanitary Institute (see MRSH)
MRSH: Member of the Royal Society for the Promotion of Health (formerly MRSanI)
MRST: Member of Royal Society of Teachers
MRTPI: Member of Royal Town Planning Institute
MRUSI: Member of the Royal United Service Institution
MS: Master of Surgery; Master of Science (US)
MS, MSS: Manuscript, Manuscripts
MSA: Master of Science, Agriculture (US); Mineralogical Society of America
MSAE: Member of the Society of Automotive Engineers (US)
MSAICE: Member of South African Institution of Civil Engineers
MSAInstMM: Member of South African Institute of Mining and Metallurgy
MS&R: Merchant Shipbuilding and Repairs
MSAutE: Member of the Society of Automobile Engineers
MSC: Madras Staff Corps
MSc: Master of Science
MScD: Master of Dental Science
MSE: Master of Science in Chemical Engineering (US)
MSH: Master of Stag Hounds
MSIA: Member Society of Industrial Artists
MSINZ: Member Surveyors' Institute New Zealand
MSIT: Member Society of Instrument Technology
MSM: Meritorious Service Medal; Madras Sappers and Miners
MSocSc: Master of Social Sciences

MSR: Member Society of Radiographers
Mt: Mountain
MT: Mechanical Transport
MTAI: Member of Institute of Travel Agents
MTCA: Ministry of Transport and Civil Aviation
MTh: Master of Theology
MTPI: Member of Town Planning Institute
MusB: Bachelor of Music
MusD: Doctor of Music
MusM: Master of Music
MV: Merchant Vessel, Motor Vessel (naval)
MVO: Member of the Royal Victorian Order
Mx: Middlesex

N

(N): Nationalist; Navigating Duties
N: North
n: Nephew
NA: National Academician (America)
NAACP: National Association for the Advancement of Colored People
NAAFI: Navy, Army and Air Force Institutes
NABC: National Association of Boys' Clubs
NALGO (Nalgo): National and Local Government Officers' Association
NAMH: National Association for Mental Health
NAPT: National Association for the Prevention of Tuberculosis
NASA: National Aeronautics and Space Administration (US)
NATCS: National Air Traffic Control Services
NATO: North Atlantic Treaty Organisation
Nat.Sci.: Natural Sciences
NB: New Brunswick
NBA: North British Academy
NBC: National Book Council (now National Book League); National Broadcasting Company (of America)
NBL: National Book League (formerly National Book Council)
NBPI: National Board for Prices and Incomes
NC: North Carolina (US)
NCA: National Certificate of Agriculture
NCB: National Coal Board
NCLC: National Council of Labour Colleges
NCU: National Cyclists' Union
NDA: National Diploma in Agriculture
NDak: North Dakota (US)
ndc: National Defence College (Canada)
NDD: National Diploma in Dairying; National Diploma in Design
NDH: National Diploma in Horticulture
NE: North-east
NEAC: New English Art Club
NEAF: Near East Air Force
Neb: Nebraska (US)
NECCTA: National Educational Closed Circuit Television Association
NECInst: North-East Coast Institution of Engineers and Shipbuilders
NEDC: National Economic Development Council; North East Development Council
NEDO: National Economic Development Office
NEL: National Engineering Laboratory
NERC: Natural Environment Research Council

Nev: Nevada (US)
New M: New Mexico (US)
NFER: National Foundation for Educational Research
NFS: National Fire Service
NFU: National Farmers' Union
NFWI: National Federation of Women's Institutes
NH: New Hampshire (US)
NI: Northern Ireland; Native Infantry
NIAB: National Institute of Agricultural Botany
NID: Naval Intelligence Division; National Institute for the Deaf; Northern Ireland District
NIH: National Institutes of Health (US)
NILP: Northern Ireland Labour Party
NJ: New Jersey (US)
NL: National Liberal
NLF: National Liberal Federation
Northants: Northamptonshire
Notts: Nottinghamshire
NP: Notary Public
NPFA: National Playing Fields Association
NPk: Nishan-e-Pakistan
NPL: National Physical Laboratory
NRA: National Rifle Association; National Recovery Administration
NRD: National Registered Designer
NRDC: National Research Development Corporation
NRR: Northern Rhodesia Regiment
NS: Nova Scotia: New Style in the Calendar (in Great Britain since 1752); National Society
ns: Graduate of Royal Naval Staff College, Greenwich
NSA: National Skating Association
NSPCC: National Society for Prevention of Cruelty to Children
N/SSF: Novice, Society of St Francis
NSW: New South Wales
NT: New Testament; Northern Territory of South Australia
NTDA: National Trade Development Association
NUGMW: National Union of General and Municipal Workers
NUI: National University of Ireland
NUM: National Union of Mineworkers
NUPE: National Union of Public Employees
NUR: National Union of Railwaymen
NUT: National Union of Teachers
NUTG: National Union of Townswomen's Guilds
NUTN: National Union of Trained Nurses
NW: North-west
NWFP: North-West Frontier Province
NWP: North-Western Provinces
NWT: North-Western Territories
NY: New York—City or State
NYC: New York City
NZ: New Zealand
NZEF: New Zealand Expeditionary Force
NZIA: New Zealand Institute of Architects

O

O: Ohio (US)
o: only
OA: Officier d'Académie

xxiv

OAS: On Active Service
O & E: Operations and Engineering (US)
O & O: Oriental and Occidental (Steamship Co.)
ob: died
OBE: Officer Order of the British Empire
OBI: Order of British India
oc: only child
OC and **o/c:** Officer Commanding
OCF: Officiating Chaplain to the Forces
OCTU: Officer Cadet Training Unit
ODA: Overseas Development Administration
ODI: Overseas Development Institute
ODM: Ministry of Overseas Development
OECD: Organization for Economic Co-operation and Development (formerly OEEC)
OEEC: Organization for European Economic Co-operation; *see* OECD
OFM: Order of Friars Minor
OFS: Orange Free State
OHMS: On His (or Her) Majesty's Service
OJ: Order of Jamaica
OL: Officer of the Order of Leopold
OM: Order of Merit
OMI: Oblate of Mary Immaculate
Ont: Ontario
OON: Officer of the Order of Niger
OP: *Ordinis Praedicatorum*—of the Order of Preachers (Dominican Ecclesiastical Title); Observation Post
ORC: Orange River Colony
Ore: Oregon (US)
ORS: Operational Research Society
ORSL: Order of the Republic of Sierra Leone
os: only son]
OSA: Ontario Society of Artists
OSB: Order of St Benedict
OSFC: Franciscan (Capuchin) Order
OSNC: Orient Steam Navigation Co.
OSRD: Office of Scientific Research and Development
OStJ: Officer of Order of St John of Jerusalem
OT: Old Testament
OTC: Officer's Training Corps
OU: Oxford University
OUAC: Oxford University Athletic Club
OUAFC: Oxford University Association Football Club
OUBC: Oxford University Boat Club
OUCC: Oxford University Cricket Club
OUDS: Oxford University Dramatic Society
OUP: Oxford University Press
OURC: Oxford Universisy Rifle Club
OURFC: Oxford University Rugby Football Club
Oxon: Oxfordshire; of Oxford

P

PA: Pakistan Army; Personal Assistant
Pa: Pennsylvania (US)
pac: Passed the final examination of the Advanced Class, The Military College of Science
PASI: Professional Associate Chartered Surveyors' Institution (changed August 1947 to ARICS)
PC: Privy Councillor; Police Constable; Perpetual Curate; Peace Commissioner (Ireland)
pc: *per centum* (by the hundred)

PCMO: Principal Colonial Medical Officer
PdD: Doctor of Pedagogy (US)
PEI: Prince Edward Island
PEN: (Name of Club: Poets, Playwrights, Editors, Essayists, Novelists)
PEng: Registered Professional Engineer (Canada)
PEP: Political and Economic Planning
PEST: Pressure for Economic and Social Toryism
PF: Procurator-Fiscal
pfc: Graduate of RAF Flying College
PGCE: Post Graduate Certificate of Education
PH: Presidential Medal of Honour (Botswana)
PhB: Bachelor of Philosophy
PhC: Pharmaceutical Chemist
PhD: Doctor of Philosophy
Phil.: Philology, Philological; Philosophy, Philosophical
PhM: Master of Philosophy (USA)
Phys.: Physical
PIB: Prices and Incomes Board (*see* NBPI)
PICAO: Provisional International Civil Aviation Organizations
pinx: (He) painted it
Pl: Place; Plural
PLA: Port of London Authority
Plen.: Plenipotentiary
PMG: Postmaster-General
PMN: *Panglima Mangku Negara* (Malaysian Honour)
PMO: Principal Medical Officer
PMRAFNS: Princess Mary's Royal Air Force Nursing Service
PMS: President Miniature Society
PNBS: *Panglima Negara Bintang Sarawak*
PNEU: Parents' National Educational Union
P&O: Peninsular and Oriental Steamship Co.
P&OSNCo.: Peninsular and Oriental Steam-Navigation Co.
PO: Post Office
Pop.: Population
POW: Prisoner of War; Prince of Wales's
PP: Parish Priest; Past President
Pp: Pages
PPCLI: Princess Patricia's Canadian Light Infantry
PPE: Philosophy, Politics and Economics (Oxford Univ.)
PPIStructE: Past President of the Institution of Structural Engineers
PPRA: Past President of the Royal Academy
PPRBA: Past President of the Royal Society of British Artists
PPRE: Past President of the Royal Society of Painter-Etchers and Engravers
PPS: Parliamentary Private Secretary
PPSIA: Past President of the Society of Industrial Artists
PPTPI: Past President Town Planning Institute
PQ: Province of Quebec
PRA: President of the Royal Academy
PRCS: President of the Royal College of Surgeons
PRE: President of the Royal Society of Painter-Etchers and Engravers
Preb.: Prebendary
PrEng.: Professional Engineer
Pres.: President
PRHA: President of the Royal Hibernian Academy
PRI: President of the Royal Institute of Painters in Water Colours

PRIA: President of the Royal Irish Academy
Prin.: Principal
PRO: Public Relations Officer; Public Records Office
Proc.: Proctor; Proceedings
Prof.: Professor
PROI: President of the Royal Institute of Oil Painters
Pro tem: *Pro tempore* (for the time being)
Prov.: Provost; Provincial
Prox.: *Proximo* (next)
Prox. acc.: *Proxime accessit* (next in order of merit to the winner, or a very close second)
PRS: President of the Royal Society; Performing Right Society Ltd
PRSA: President of the Royal Scottish Academy
PRSE: President of the Royal Society of Edinburgh
PRSH: President of the Royal Society for the Promotion of Health
PRSW: President of the Royal Scottish Water Colour Society
PRUAA: President of the Royal Ulster Academy of Arts
PRWS: President of the Royal Society of Painters in Water Colours
PS: Pastel Society
ps: passed School of Instruction (of Officers)
PSA: Property Services Agency
psa: Graduate of RAF Staff College
psc: Graduate of Staff College (†indicated Graduate of Senior Wing Staff College)
PSIA: President of the Society of Industrial Artists
PSM: *Panglima Setia Mahkota*
psm: Certificate of Royal Military School of Music
PSMA: President of Society of Marine Artists
PSNC: Pacific Steam Navigation Co.
Pte: Private (soldier)
Pty: Proprietary
PWD: Publc Works Department
PWO: Prince of Wales's Own

Q

Q: Queen
QAIMNS: Queen Alexandra's Imperial Military Nursing Service
QALAS: Qualified Associate Chartered Land Agents' Society
QARANC: Queen Alexandra's Royal Army Nursing Corps
QARNNS: Queen Alexandra's Royal Naval Nursing Service
QC: Queen's Counsel
QFSM: Queen's Fire Service Medal for Distinguished Service
QGM: Queen's Gallantry Medal
QHC: Queen's Honorary Chaplain
QHDS: Queen's Honorary Dental Surgeon
QHNS: Queen's Honorary Nursing Sister
QHP: Queen's Honorary Physician
QHS: Queen's Honorary Surgeon
Qld: Queensland
QMAAC: Queen Mary's Army Auxiliary Corps
QMC: Queen Mary College (London)
QMG: Quartermaster-General
Q(ops) Quartering (operations)

QPM: Queen's Police Medal

Qr: Quarter

QRV: Qualified Valuer, Real Estate Institute of New South Wales

QS: Quarter Sessions

qs: RAF graduates of the Military or Naval Staff College (symbol omitted if subsequently qualified psa)

QUB: Queen's University, Belfast

qv: *quod vide* (which see)

R

(R): Reserve

RA: Royal Academician; Royal Artillery

RAAF: Royal Australian Air Force

RAAMC: Royal Australian Army Medical Corps

RAC: Royal Automobile Club; Royal Agricultural College; Royal Armoured Corps

RACGP: Royal Australian College of General Practitioners

RAChD: Royal Army Chaplains' Dept

RACP: Royal Australasian College of Physicians

RACS: Royal Australasian College of Surgeons

RADA: Royal Academy of Dramatic Art

RAE: Royal Australian Engineers; Royal Aircraft Establishment

RAEC: Royal Army Educational Corps

RAeS: Royal Aeronautical Society

RAF: Royal Air Force

RAFO: Reserve of Air Force Officers (now Royal Air Force Reserve of Officers)

RAFRO: Royal Air Force Reserve of Officers

RAFVR: Royal Air Force Volunteer Reserve

RAIA: Royal Australian Institute of Architects

RAIC: Royal Architectural Institute of Canada

RAM: (Member of) Royal Academy of Music

RAMC: Royal Army Medical Corps

RAN: Royal Australian Navy

R&D: Research and Development

RANVR: Royal Australian Naval Volunteer Reserve

RAOC: Royal Army Ordnance Corps

RAPC: Royal Army Pay Corps

RARO: Regular Army Reserve of Officers

RAS: Royal Astronomical or Asiatic Society

RASC: (formerly) Royal Army Service Corps (now *see under* RCT)

RASE: Royal Agricultural Society of England

RAuxAF: Royal Auxiliary Air Force

RAVC: Royal Army Veterinary Corps

RB: Rifle Brigade

RBA: Member Royal Society of British Artists

RBC: Royal British Colonial Society of Artists

RBK&C: Royal Borough of Kensington and Chelsea

RBS: Royal Society of British Sculptors

RBSA: Royal Birmingham Soc. of Artists

RC: Roman Catholic

RCA: Member Royal Canadian Academy; Royal College of Art

RCAC: Royal Canadian Armoured Corps

RCAF: Royal Canadian Air Force

RCamA: Member Royal Cambrian Academy (formerly RCA)

RCAS: Royal Central Asian Society

RCDS: Royal College of Defence Studies

RCGP: Royal College of General Practitioners

RCHA: Royal Canadian Horse Artillery

RCHM: Royal Commission on Historical Monuments

RCM: Royal College of Music

RCN: Royal Canadian Navy

RCNC: Royal Corps of Naval Constructors

RCNR: Royal Canadian Naval Reserve

RCNVR: Royal Canadian Naval Volunteer Reserve

RCO: Royal College of Organists

RCOG: Royal College of Obstetricians and Gynaecologists

RCP: Royal College of Physicians, London

RCPath: Royal College of Pathologists

RCPE and RCPEd: Royal College of Physicians of Edinburgh

RCPGlas: Royal College of Physicians and Surgeons, Glasgow

RCS: Royal College of Surgeons of England; Royal Corps of Signals; Royal College of Science

RCSE and RCSEd: Royal College of Surgeons of Edinburgh

RCSI: Royal College of Surgeons in Ireland

RCT: Royal Corps of Transport

RCVS: Royal College of Veterinary Surgeons

RD: Rural Dean; Royal Navy Reserve Decoration

Rd: Road

RDA: Royal Defence Academy

RDC: Rural District Council

RDF: Royal Dublin Fusiliers

RDI: Royal Designer for Industry (Royal Society of Arts)

RDS: Royal Dublin Society

RE: Royal Engineers; Fellow of Royal Society of Painter-Etchers and Engravers

Rear-Adm.: Rear Admiral

REconS: Royal Economic Society

Rect.: Rector

Reg. Prof.: Regius Professor

Regt: Regiment

REME: Royal Electrical and Mechanical Engineers

RERO: Royal Engineers Reserve of Officers

RES: Royal Empire Society (now Royal Commonwealth Society)

Res.: Resigned; Reserve; Resident; Research

Rev.: Reverend; Review

RFA: Royal Field Artillery

RFC: Royal Flying Corps (now RAF); Rugby Football Club

RFPGS(G): *see under* FRFPSG (formerly)

RFU: Rugby Football Union

RGA: Royal Garrison Artillery

RGS: Royal Geographical Society

RHA: Royal Hibernian Academy; Regional Health Authority; Royal Horse Artillery

RHB: Regional Hospitals Board

RHG: Royal Horse Guards

RHistS: Royal Historical Society

RHR: Royal Highland Regiment

RHS: Royal Horticultural Society; Royal Humane Society

RI: Member Royal Institute of Painters in Water Colours; Rhode Island

RIA: Royal Irish Academy

RIAM: Royal Irish Academy of Music

RIAS: Royal Incorporation of Architects in Scotland

RIASC: Royal Indian Army Service Corps

RIBA: Royal Institute of British Architects

RIBI: Rotary International in Great Britain and Ireland

RIC: Royal Irish Constabulary; Royal Institute of Chemistry

RICS: Royal Institution of Chartered Surveyors

RIE: Royal Indian Engineering (College)

RIF: Royal Irish Fusiliers

RIIA: Royal Institute of International Affairs

RIM: Royal Indian Marine

RIN: Royal Indian Navy

RINA: Royal Institution of Naval Architects

RIPH&H: Royal Institute of Public Health and Hygiene

RM: Royal Marines; Resident Magistrate

RMA: Royal Marine Artillery; Royal Military Academy Sandhurst (now incorporating Royal Military Academy, Woolwich)

RMC: Royal Military College Sandhurst (now Royal Military Academy)

RMCS: Royal Military College of Science

RMedSoc: Royal Medical Society, Edinburgh

RMetS: Royal Meteorological Society

RMFVR: Royal Marine Forces Volunteer Reserve

RMLI: Royal Marine Light Infantry

RMO: Resident Medical Officer(s)

RMPA: Royal Medico-Psychological Association

RMS: Royal Microscopical Society; Royal Mail Steamer; Royal Society of Miniature Painters

RN: Royal Navy; Royal Naval

RNAS: Royal Naval Air Services

RNAY: Royal Naval Air Yard

RNC: Royal Naval College

RNEC: Royal Naval Engineering College

RNIB: Royal National Institute for the Blind

RNLI: Royal National Life-boat Institution

RNR: Royal Naval Reserve

RNS: Royal Numismatic Society

RNT: Registered Nurse Tutor

RNVR: Royal Naval Volunteer Reserve

RNVSR: Royal Naval Volunteer Supplementary Reserve

RNZN: Royal New Zealand Navy

RNZNVR: Royal New Zealand Naval Volunteer Reserve

ROC: Royal Observer Corps

ROF: Royal Ordnance Factories

R of O: Reserve of Officers

ROI: Royal Institute of Oil Painters

RoSPA: Royal Society for the Prevention of Accidents

(Rot.): Rotunda Hospital, Dublin (after degree)

Roy.: Royal

RP: Member Royal Society of Portrait Painters

RPC: Royal Pioneer Corps

RPMS: Royal Postgraduate Medical School (formerly PGMS)

RPS: Royal Photographic Society

RRC: Royal Red Cross

RRE: Royal Radar Establishment (formerly TRE)

RRS: Royal Research Ship

RSA: Royal Scottish Academician; Royal Society of Arts

RSAI: Royal Society of Antiquaries of Ireland

RSanI: *See* RSH

RSC: Royal Society of Canada

RSCM: Royal School of Church Music

RSCN: Registered Sick Children's Nurse

RSE: Royal Society of Edinburgh

RSF: Royal Scots Fusiliers

RSFSR: Russian Socialist Federated Soviet Republic

RSGS: Royal Scottish Geographical Society

RSH: Royal Society for the Promotion of Health (formerly Royal Sanitary Institute)

RSL: Royal Society of Literature

RSM: Royal Society of Medicine; Royal School of Mines

RSMA: (formerly SMA) Royal Society of Marine Artists

RSO: Rural Sub-Office; Railway Sub-Office; Resident Surgical Officer

RSPB: Royal Society for Protection of Birds

RSPCA: Royal Society for Prevention of Cruelty to Animals

RSSAILA: Returned Sailors, Soldiers and Airmen's Imperial League of Australia

RSSPCC: Royal Scottish Society for Prevention of Cruelty to Children

RSW: Member Royal Scottish Water Colour Society

Rt Hon.: Right Honourable

RTO: Railway Transport Officer

RTPI: Royal Town Planning Institute

RTR: Royal Tank Regiment

Rt Rev.: Right Reverend

RTS: Religious Tract Society; Royal Toxophilite Society

RU: Rugby Union

RUI: Royal University of Ireland

RUKBA: Royal United Kingdom Benevolent Institution

RUSI: Royal United Services Institute for Defence Studies (formerly Royal United Service Institution)

RWA (RWEA): Member of Royal West of England Academy

RWAFF: Royal West African Frontier Force

RWF: Royal Welch Fusiliers

RWS: Member Royal Society of Painters in Water Colours

RYA: Royal Yachting Association

RYS: Royal Yacht Squadron

RZS: Royal Zoological Society

S

(S): (in Navy) Paymaster

S: Succeeded; South; Saint

s: Son

SA: South Australia; South Africa; Société Anonyme

SAAF: South African Air Force

SACSEA: Supreme Allied Command, SE Asia

SADG: Société des Architectes Diplômés par le Gouvernement

Salop: Shropshire

SAMC: South African Medical Corps

Sarum: Salisbury

SAS: Special Air Service

SASO: Senior Air Staff Officer

SB: Bachelor of Science (US)

SBAC: Society of British Aircraft Constructors

SBStJ: Serving Brother, Order of St John of Jerusalem

SC: Senior Counsel (Eire); South Carolina (US)

sc: Student at the Staff College

SCAO: Senior Civil Affairs Officer
SCAPA: Society for Checking the Abuses of Public Advertising
ScD: Doctor of Science
SCF: Senior Chaplain to the Forces
Sch.: School
SCL: Student in Civil Law
SCM: State Certified Midwife; Student Christian Movement
SCONUL: Standing Conference of National and University Libraries
Sculpt.: Sculptor
SDak: South Dakota (US)
SDB: Salesian of Don Bosco
SDF: Sudan Defence Force; Social Democratic Federation
SE: South-east
SEAC: South-East Asia Command
SEALF: South-East Asia Land Forces
SEATO: South-East Asia Treaty Organization
Sec.: Secretary
SEN: State Enrolled Nurse
SESO: Senior Equipment Staff Officer
SG: Solicitor-General
SGA: Member Society of Graphic Art
Sgt: Sergeant
SHAEF: Supreme Headquarters, Allied Expeditionary Force
SHAPE: Supreme Headquarters, Allied Powers, Europe
SIB: Shipbuilding Industry Board
SinDrs: Doctor of Chinese
SITA: Société Internationale de Télécommunications Aéronautiques
SITPRO: Simplification of International Trade Procedures
SJ: Society of Jesus (Jesuits)
SJAB: St John Ambulance Brigade
SJD: Doctor of Juristic Science
SL: Serjeant-at-Law
SLA: Special Libraries Association
SLAS: Society for Latin-American Studies
SM: Medal of Service (Canada); Master of Science; Officer qualified for Submarine Duties
SMA: Society of Marine Artists (now *see under* RSMA)
SME: School of Military Engineering
SMIEEE: Senior Member of Institution of Electrical and Electronic Engineering (US)
SMIRE: Senior Member Institution of Radio Engineers (New York)
SMMT: Society of Motor Manufacturers and Traders Ltd
SMO: Senior Medical Officer; Sovereign Military Order
SNCF: Société Nationale des Chemins de Fer Français
SNP: Scottish National Party
SNTS: Society for New Testament Studies
SO: Staff Officer
SOAS: School of Oriental and African Studies
Soc.: Society
SODEPAX: Committee on Society, Development and Peace
SOE: Special Operations Executive
s.p. *sine prole* (without issue)
SP: Self-Propelled (Anti-Tank Regiment)
SPAB: Society for the Protection of Ancient Buildings

SPCK: Society for Promoting Christian Knowledge
SPD: Salisbury Plain District
SPG: Society for the Propagation of the Gospel (now USPG)
SPk: Sitara-e-Pakistan
SPRC: Society for Prevention and Relief of Cancer
sprl: *société de personnes à responsabilité limitée*
SPTL: Society of Public Teachers of Law
Sq.: Square
SR: Special Reserve; Southern Railway (*see* BR); Southern Region (BR)
SRC: Science Research Council (formerly DSIR)
SRHE: Society for Research into Higher Education
SRN: State Registered Nurse
SRO: Supplementary Reserve of Officers
SRP: State Registered Physiotherapist
SS: Saints; Straits Settlements; Steamship
SSA: Society of Scottish Arists
SS&AFA: Soldiers', Sailors', and Airmen's Families Association
SSC: Solicitor before Supreme Court (Scotland); Sculptors Society of Canada
SSEES: School of Slavonic and East European Studies
SSJE: Society of St John the Evangelist
SSM: Society of the Sacred Mission
SSO: Senior Supply Officer
SSRC: Social Science Research Council
SSStJ: Serving Sister, Order of St John of Jerusalem
St: Street; Saint
STB: *Sacrae Theologiae Bachelor* (Bachelor of Sacred Theology)
STC: Senior Training Corps
STD: *Sacrae Theologiae Doctor* (Doctor of Sacred Theology)
STh: Scholar in Theology
Stip.: Stipend; Stipendiary
STL: *Sacrae Theologiae Lector* (Reader or a Professor of Sacred Theology)
STM: *Sacrae Theologiae Magister*
STP: *Sacrae Theologiae Professor* (Professor of Divinity, old form of DD)
STRIVE: Society for Preservation of Rural Industries and Village Enterprises
STSO: Senior Technical Staff Officer
Supp. Res.: Supplementary Reserve (of Officers)
Supt: Superintendent
Surg.: Surgeon
Surv.: Surviving
SW: South-west
Syd.: Sydney

T

T: Telephone; Territorial
TA: Telegraphic Address; Territorial Army
TAA: Territorial Army Association
TAF: Tactical Air Force
T&AFA: Territorial and Auxiliary Forces Association
TANS: Territorial Army Nursing Service
TANU: Tanganyika African National Union

TARO: Territorial Army Reserve of Officers

T&AVR: Territorial and Army Volunteer Reserve

TA&VRA: Territorial Auxiliary and Volunteer Reserve Association

TC: Order of the Trinity Cross (Trinidad and Tobago)

TCD: Trinity College, Dublin (University of Dublin, Trinity College)

TCF: Temporary Chaplain to the Forces

TD: Territorial Efficiency Decoration; Efficiency Decoration (T&AVR) (since April 1967); (Teachta Dala) Member of the Dail, Eire

Temp.: Temperature; Temporary

Tenn: Tennessee (US)

TeolD: Doctor of Theology

Tex: Texas (US)

TF: Territorial Forces

TFR: Territorial Force Reserve

TGO: Timber Growers' Organisation

TGWU: Transport and General Workers' Union

ThL: Theological Licentiate

TIMS: The Institute of Management Sciences

TP: Transvaal Province

TPI: Town Planning Institute; now see RTPI

Trans.: Translation, Translated

Transf.: Transferred

TRC: Thames Rowing Club

TRE: (now see under RRE) (formerly) Telecommunications Research Establishment

TRH: Their Royal Highnesses

Trin.: Trinity

tsc.: passed a Territorial Army Course in Staff Duties

TSD: Tertiary of St Dominick

TTG: Teaching Qualification, Irish Language and Literature

TUC: Trades Union Congress

TV: Television

TYC: Thames Yacht Club

U

(U): Unionist

u: Uncle

UAR: United Arab Republic

UC: University College

UCET: Universities Council for Education of Teachers

UCH: University College Hospital (London)

UCL: University College, London

UCLA: University of California at Los Angeles

UCNW: University College of North Wales

UCW: University College of Wales

UDC: Urban District Council

UDF: Union Defence Force

UEA: University of East Anglia

UF: United Free Church

UGC: University Grants Committee

UJD: Utriusque Juris Doctor, Doctor of both Laws (Doctor of Canon and Civil Law)

UK: United Kingdom

UKAC: United Kingdom Automation Council

UKAEA: United Kingdom Atomic Energy Authority

UN: United Nations

UNA: United Nations Association

UNCIO: United Nations Conference on International Organisation

UNCSAT: United Nations Conference on the Application of Science and Technology

UNCTAD (Unctad): United Nations Commission for Trade and Development

UNDP: United Nations Development Programme

UNESCO (Unesco): United Nations Educational, Scientific and Cultural Organisation

UNICEF (Unicef): United Nations Children's Fund (formerly United Nations International Children's Emergency Fund)

Univ.: University

UNRRA: United Nations Relief and Rehabilitation Administration

UNRWA: United Nations Relief Works Agency

UNSCOB: United Nations Special Commission on the Balkans

UP: United Provinces; Uttar Pradesh; United Presbyterian

US: United States

USA: United States of America

USAAF: United States Army Air Forces

USAF: United States Air Force

USAR: United States Army Reserve

USDAW: Union of Shop Distributive and Allied Workers

USMA: United States Military Academy

USN: United States Navy

USNR: United States Naval Reserve

USPG: United Society for the Propagation of the Gospel (formerly SPG)

USS: United States Ship

USSR: Union of Soviet Socialist Republics

UTC: University Training Corps

(UU): Ulster Unionist

(UUUC): United Ulster Unionist Coalition

V

V: Five (Roman numerals); Version; Vicar; Viscount; Vice

v: Versus (against)

v or vid: Vide (see)

V&A: Victoria and Albert

Va: Virginia (US)

VAD: Voluntary Aid Detachment

VC: Victoria Cross

VCAS: Vice-Chief of the Air Staff

VD: Royal Naval Volunteer Reserve Officers' Decoration (now VRD); Volunteer Officers' Decoration; Victorian Decoration

VDC: Volunteer Defence Corps

Ven.: Venerable (of an Archdeacon)

Very Rev.: Very Reverend (of a Dean)

Vet.: Veterinary

VG: Vicar-General

VHS: Hon. Surgeon to Viceroy of India

Vice-Adm.: Vice-Admiral

Visc.: Viscount

VM: Victory Medal

VMH: Victoria Medal of Honour (Royal Horticultural Society)

Vol.: Volume; Volunteers

VP: Vice-President

VQMG: Vice-Quartermaster-General

VR: Victoria Regina (Queen Victoria)

VRD: Royal Naval Volunteer Reserve Officers' Decoration
VSO: Voluntary Service Overseas
Vt: Vermont (US)

W

W.: West
WA: Western Australia
WAAF: Women's Auxiliary Air Force (now WRAF)
Wash: Washington State (US)
W/Cdr: Wing Commander
WEA: Workers' Educational Association; Royal West of England Academy
WEU: Western European Union
WFTU: World Federation of Trade Unions
WHO: World Health Organization
WhSch: Whitworth Scholar
WI: West Indies (formerly BWI: British West Indies)
Wilts: Wiltshire
Wis: Wisconsin (US)
WJEC: Welsh Joint Education Committee
WLA: Women's Land Army
WLF: Women's Liberal Federation
Wm: William
WO: War Office
Worcs: Worcestershire
WOSB: War Office Selection Board

WR: West Riding; Western Region (BR)
WRAC: Women's Royal Army Corps
WRAF: Women's Royal Air Force (formerly WAAF)
WRNS: Women's Royal Naval Service
WRVS: Women's Royal Voluntary Service (previously WVS)
WS: Writer to the Signet
WSPU: Women's Social and Politica lUnion
WVa: West Virginia (US)
WVS: Women's Voluntary Services (*now see* WRVS)
Wyo: Wyoming (US)

X

X: Ten (Roman numerals)

Y

y: youngest
Yeo: Yeomanry
YHA: Youth Hostels Association
YMCA: Young Men's Christian Association
Yorks: Yorkshire
yr: younger
yrs: years
YWCA: Young Women's Christian Association

A

Abbott, George Clifford; Lecturer in Economics, Department of International Economic Studies, University of Glasgow, since 1966; *b* 1930; *m* 1956; two *s* two *d*. BA London 1955, MA Yale 1959 (Hons). Jnr Res. Fellow, Univ. of West Indies, 1960–63; Asst Lecturer, Univ. of Glasgow, 1963–66. *Publications: contrib.* Co-Existence, Econ. Hist. Rev., Canadian Jl of Hist., Government and Opposition, Int. Social and Econ. Studies, Jl of Political Econ. *Address:* Dept of International Economic Studies, Univ. of Glasgow, Glasgow G12 8QQ.

Abbott, Gerald William, BA; Lecturer, Department of Education, University of Manchester, since 1965; *b* 1935; *m* 1959; one *s* two *d*. BA London 1958 (English), PGCE London 1959; Mem., Linguistics Assoc. of GB, Mem., Internat. Assoc. of Teachers of English as a Foreign Lang. Lectr, Manchester Univ., 1965– ; seconded to Makerere Univ., 1971–73, to UNESCO, 1973–74. Army Commn, 1954; British Council Educn Officer, Jordan, 1964–65. *Publications:* Towards Better Reading and Writing (3 vols), Bangkok, 1961–62; Practical Reading, 1962; Down the Big River, 1964; Conditionals, 1969; Relative Clauses, 1970. *Address:* Dept of Education, Univ. of Manchester, Manchester M13 9PL.

Abel-Smith, Prof. Brian; Professor of Social Administration, London School of Economics and Political Science, since 1967; *b* 1926. BA Cambridge 1951 (2nd cl. Economics), MA and PhD Cambridge 1955. Asst Lectr in Social Science, LSE, 1955–57; Lectr in Social Science, LSE, 1957–61; Assoc. Prof., Yale Law School, Yale Univ., 1961; Reader in Social Administration, Univ. of London, 1961–67. Sen. Adv., Sec. of State for Soc. Serv., 1968–70. *Publications:* (with R. M. Titmuss) The Cost of the National Health Service in England and Wales, 1956; (with R. M. Titmuss) A History of the Nursing Profession, 1960; Social Policy and Population Growth in Mauritius, 1961; Paying for Health Services, 1963; The Hospitals 1800–1948, 1964; (with R. M. Titmuss et al.) The Health Services of Tanganyika, 1964; (with K. Gales) British Doctors at Home and Abroad, 1964; (with P. Townsend) The Poor and the Poorest, 1965; (with R. B. Stevens) Lawyers and the Courts, 1967; An International Study of Health Expenditure, 1967; (with R. B. Stevens) In Search of Justice, 1968; (with H. Rose) Doctors, Patients and Pathology, 1972; (with M. Zander and R. Brooke) Legal Problems and the Citizen, 1973; (with others) Accounting for Health, 1973; *contrib.* Med. Care. *Address:* London School of Economics, Houghton Street, WC2A 2AE.

Abercrombie, Prof. David; Professor of Phonetics, Department of Linguistics, Edinburgh University, since 1964; *b* 1909; *m* 1944. BA Hons Leeds 1930 (English). Asst Lectr in English, LSE, 1934–38; Dir of Studies, Inst. of English Studies, Athens, 1938–40; Lectr, Cairo Univ., 1940–45; LSE, 1945–47; Lectr in Phonetics, Leeds Univ., 1947–48; Edinburgh Univ., 1948–50; Sen. Lectr, 1951–57; Reader, 1957–63. *Publications:* Isaac Pitman: a pioneer in the scientific study of language, 1937; Problems and Principles in Language Study, 1956, 2nd edn 1963, Japanese trans., 1969; English Phonetic Texts, 1964; Studies in Phonetics and Linguistics, 1965; Elements of General Phonetics, 1967; *contrib.* English Language Teaching, Lingua, Trans Philol. Soc., Orbis, Linguistics, Brit. Jl of Disorders of Communication. *Address:* Dept of Linguistics, The Univ., Edinburgh EH8 9YL.

Aberg, Frederick Alan, BA; Lecturer, Department of Adult Education and Extra-Mural Studies, University of Leeds, since 1962; *m*; one *s* one *d*. BA Wales (Geog. and Anthropology Hons (2/I)). Sec., Moated Sites Res. Gp; Sec. Regional Gp 4, Council for British Archaeology; Mem., Council, Yorkshire Archaeol Soc. *Address:* Dept of Adult Education and Extra-Mural Studies, The University, Leeds LS2 9JT.

Abrams, Dr Hilton John; Lecturer in Chemical Engineering, University of Manchester Institute of Science and Technology, since 1960; *b* 1923; *m* 1956; one *s* two *d*. BSc Wales 1945; DipChemEng London 1948, BSc (Econ) London 1954; PhD Manchester 1971; MIMechE 1960, MACostE 1970, FIChemE 1971. Mem., Soc. Chem. Ind., REconS, R. Coll. Adv. Tech., Salford, 1958. *Publications: contrib.* Chem. Engineer (London), Jl of Bus Finance. *Address:* Univ. of Manchester Institute of Science and Technology, PO Box 88, Sackville Street, Manchester M60 1QD.

Abrams, Prof. Philip; Professor of Sociology, Department of Sociology and Social Administration, University of Durham, since 1970; *b* 1933; *m* 1956; one *s* and one *d*. BA Cantab 1955 (1st cl.), MA Cantab 1958, PhD Cantab 1962; BSA, PSA. Bye-Fellow, Peterhouse, Cambridge, 1958; Asst Lectr, London School of Economics, 1961; Asst Lectr, Cambridge, and Fellow and Tutor of Peterhouse, 1962; Lectr, Cambridge, 1965; Vis. Asst Prof., Univ. of Chicago, 1966. Sec., Social and Economic Archive Cttee, 1964–66; Mem. Editorial Board, Past and Present, 1958– . *Publications:* John Locke: Two Tracts on Government, 1967; The Origins of British Sociology, 1968; *contrib.* Brit. Jl of Sociology, Past and Present, Social Science Information. *Address:* 44 Old Elvet, Durham.

Abramsky, Chimen; Reader, Department of Hebrew and Jewish Studies, University College, London, since 1969; Senior Associate Fellow St Antony's College, Oxford, since 1972; *b* 1917; *m*; one *s* one *d*. BA Jerusalem (double first, with distinction), MA Oxon. Part-time Lectr, Dept of Hebrew and Jewish Studies, University Coll., London, 1966; Sen. Res. Fellow, St Antony's Coll., Oxford, 1967. *Publications:* (with H. Collins) Karl Marx and the English Labour Movement, 1965; Marx and the General Council of the IWMA, Paris 1968; The Birobidjan Project, in, Jews in the Soviet Union, 1970 (trans. French, Hebrew and Russian); Lenin and the Jews, Jerusalem, 1973 (Hebrew); many articles on Jewish art, Marx, modern Jewish history; *contrib.* Bull. Soc. Lab. Hist.; Jl Jew. Bibliog., Sov. Jew. Affairs, TLS.

Address: Univ. College, Dept of Hebrew and Jewish Studies, Gower Street, WC1E 6BT.

Ackrill, Prof. John Lloyd; Professor of the History of Philosophy, Oxford University, since 1966; *b* 1921; *m* 1953; one *s* three *d*. MA Oxon 1948 (1st cl. Literae Humaniores). Asst Lectr, Glasgow Univ., 1948–49; Univ. Lectr, Oxford, 1951–52; Fellow and Tutor, Brasenose Coll., Oxford, 1953–66; Mem., Inst. for Adv. Study, Princeton, 1950–51, 1961–62; Fellow, Council of Humanities and Vis. Prof., Princeton Univ., 1955, 1964. *Publications*: trans. and ed, Aristotle: Categories and De Interpretatione, 1963; Aristotle's Ethics, 1973; *contrib*. classical and philosophical jls. *Address*: Brasenose College, Oxford.

Ackroyd, Rev. Prof. Peter Runham, MA, PhD, DD, HonDD; Samuel Davidson Professor of Old Testament Studies, University of London, King's College, since 1961; *b* 1917; *m* 1940; two *s* three *d*. BD London 1940; MA Cambridge 1942; MTh London 1942; PhD Cambridge 1945; DD London 1970, HonDD St Andrews 1970; ordained Priest 1958. Pres., Soc. for Old Testament Studies, 1972. Mem., Palestine Exploration Fund. Lectr, Theology Dept, Univ. of Leeds, 1948–52; Univ. Lectr, Cambridge, 1952–61; Hulsean Lectr, Cambridge, 1960–62. Fellow King's Coll. London, 1969; Jt Ed., Cambridge Bible Commentary, SCM, OTL and SBT series. Examining chaplain to Bishop of Salisbury; Ed. Palestine Exploration Qly. *Publications*: The People of the Old Testament, 1959, Hindu version 1971; Continuity, 1962; The Old Testament Tradition, 1963; trans. Würthwein: Text of the Old Testament, 1957; trans. Eissfeldt: The Old Testament: an introduction, 1965; (ed jtly) Words and Meanings, 1968; Exile and Restoration, 1968; Mini-Commentary series, 7 (Chron.–Macc.) 1970; The Age of the Chronicler (Australian/New Zealand Theological Review) 1970; Israel under Babylon and Persia, 1970; 1 Samuel, Cambridge Bible Commentary, 1971; Isaiah in Interpreters Bible, 1971; 1, 2 Chron., Ezra, Nehemiah Torch Commentary, 1973; *contrib*. SOTS Book List, Svensk exegetisk årsbok, Vetus Testamentum, Annual of Swedish Theological Institute, The Expository Times, JTS, etc. *Address*: King's College, Strand, WC2R 2LS.

Adams, Rev. Arthur White, DD; Dean of Divinity, Fellow and Lecturer of Magdalen College, Oxford, since 1949; *b* 1912; *m* 1940; 1964; one *s* three *d*. BA Sheffield (1st cl. Eng. Lang. and Lit.) 1935, MA Sheffield 1936; MA Oxford 1949, BD Oxon 1950, DD Oxon 1967. Lectr in Theology, Oxford, 1950; Grinfield Lectr on the Septuagint, 1953–59. *Publications*: (with H. F. D. Sparks) Novum Testamentum . . . Latine Secundum edit. S. Hieronymi tom. III, 1954; (with F. C. Kenyon) Our Bible and The Ancient Manuscripts, 4th edn 1957; Der Text der griechischen Bibel, 2nd edn 1961; The Text of the Greek Bible, 4th edn 1974; The Bible in England, 1961. *Address*: Magdalen College, Oxford.

Adams, Prof. David Keith, MA, AM, MA, DPhil; Professor of American Studies, University of Keele, since 1972; *b* 1931; *m* 1961; three *s*. BA Cantab 1954 (1st cl. History), AM Yale 1955, MA Oxon 1957, MA Cantab 1960, DPhil Oxon 1962. Asst Lectr, Univ. Coll. N. Staffs, 1957–60; Lectr, 1960–65 (Univ. of Keele, 1962–); Sen. Lectr, 1965–72; Head of Dept of American Studies, 1965– . Mem., Exec. Cttee, Brit. Assoc. Amer. Studies, 1964– ; Dir, David Bruce Centre for Amer. Studies, Univ. of Keele, 1969– . *Publications*: America in the 20th Century, 1967; (jtly) An Atlas of North American Affairs, 1969; *contrib*. Chambers's Encyclopaedia World Survey; *contrib*. Bull. Brit. Assoc. Amer. Studies, Austral. Jl Pol. and Hist. *Address*: Dept of American Studies, Univ. of Keele, Keele, Staffs ST5 5BG.

Adams, David Stanley, LLB, BCL; Senior Part-time Lecturer, Law Faculty, University of Birmingham, since 1948; *b* 1922; *m* 1942; two *d*. LLB Birmingham 1941, BCL Oxon 1948; Solicitor 1949. Tutor, Univ. Coll., Oxford, 1948–49. Mem., Birmingham City Council, 1963–66; Mem., Council of Birmingham Law Soc., 1963– . *Address*: Law Faculty, Univ. of Birmingham, Edgbaston, Birmingham B15 2TT.

Adams, David William; Lecturer, School of Humanities and Social Sciences, University of Bath, since 1961; *b* 1929; *m* 1963: three *s* one *d*. BA Cambridge 1952, MA 1954. *Address*: School of Humanities and Social Sciences, Univ. of Bath, Claverton Down, Bath BA2 7AY.

Adams, Dr Ian Hugh; Lecturer in Geography, University of Edinburgh, since 1967; *b* 1937; *m* 1965; one *s* one *d*. MA Edinburgh 1964 (1st cl. Geography), PhD Edinburgh 1967; FSAScot, RSGS. Demonstrator, Edinburgh, 1965–67. Editor, Scottish Record Office 1964– ; Research Dir., Agrarian Landscape Research Gp, IBG. *Publications*: Descriptive List of plans in the Scottish Record Office, vol. 1, 1966, vol. 2, 1967, vol. 3, 1974; The Mapping of a Scottish Estate, 1971; Directory of former Scottish Commonties. 1971; *contrib*. Revue de l'Institut de Sociologie de Bruxelles; Jl Soc. Archivists; Scottish Geographical Magazine; Stair Society. *Address*: Dept of Geography, High School Yards, Edinburgh.

Adams, John Edward; Lecturer, Faculty of Law, University of Bristol, since 1957; *b* 1931; *m* 1956; two *s* four *d*. LLB Bristol 1954; Solicitor, admitted 1956. Mem., Law Soc. Land Law Cttee, 1969– ; Council Mem., Brit. Acad. Forensic Sciences, 1971– ; Mem., Law Soc. Advocacy Training Cttee, 1969– ; Bristol Educn Cttee, 1969–72; Bristol City Council, 1971–74; Avon County Council, 1973– . *Publications*: (with others) Modern Conveyancing Precedents, 1964; *contrib*. Conveyancer and Property Lawyer, Criminal Law Review, Law Soc. Gazette. *Address*: Faculty of Law, Univ. of Bristol, Wills Memorial Building, Queens Road, Bristol BS8 1RJ.

Adamson, Dr Donald; Senior Lecturer in French, Goldsmiths' College, London, since 1970; *b* 1939; *m* 1966; two *s*. BA Oxon 1959

(2nd cl. Modern Languages), BLitt Oxon 1962, MA Oxon 1963, DPhil Oxon 1971. Lectr, Goldsmiths' Coll., 1969. *Publications*: The Genesis of *Le Cousin Pons*, 1966; trans. Balzac: The Black Sheep, 1970; Ursule Mirouët, 1975; *contrib*. MLR, Symposium, etc. *Address*: Univ. of London Goldsmiths' College, New Cross, SE14 6NW.

Adamson, Graham Thomas, BSc; Senior Lecturer in Physical Education, University of Leeds, since 1946; *b* 1914. BSc London 1935; Dip. in Phys. Educn Carnegie Coll. of Physical Educn. *Publications*: (with R. E. Morgan) Circuit Training, 1955, 2nd edn 1961, Japanese edn 1961; *contrib*. Biomechanics, Brit. Assoc. for the Advancement of Science, Brit. Jl of Psychiatry, Ergonomics, Brit. Jl of Sports Medicine, Jl of American Coll. of Sports Medicine, Jl of Physiology, Proc. of Royal Soc. of London. *Address*: Physical Education Dept, The Univ., Leeds LS2 9JT.

Adamson, Mrs Robin; Lecturer, Department of French, University of Dundee, since 1968; *b* 1938; *m* 1967; one *d*. BA Queensland 1959, DipEd 1960, BPhil St Andrews 1973, Cert. of Phonetics and Gen. Linguistics, Sorbonne 1964. Tutor, Univ. of Western Australia, 1965–66; Sen. Tutor, 1967. *Address*: Dept of French, The Univ., Dundee DD1 4HN.

Adamson, Vera, MA BA, DipEd; Senior Tutor in English and Adviser to Overseas Students in the University of Birmingham; BA London 1931 (Hons English), MA Birmingham 1970, DipEd London 1932; Mem., Philolog. Soc.; Linguistics Assoc.; Brit. Assoc. of Applied Linguistics. Brit. Council Officer in London and Overseas, 1946–62; Pres., Ridge Hall of Residence, Birmingham Univ., 1962–65; Chm. Midland Region Advisory Council of the Brit. Broadcast. Assoc. 1971– ; Mem., Gen. Adv. Council, Brit. Broadcast. Assoc., 1971– ; Mem. Council, 1971–73, Ct of Governors, 1973– , Senate 1973– , Birmingham Univ. *Publication*: (with M. J. B. Lowe), General Engineering Texts, 1971. *Address*: Dept of English Language and Literature, Univ. of Birmingham, PO Box 363, Birmingham B15 2TT.

Addinall, Nigel Anthony, PhD; Lecturer in French, Department of Romance Studies, University College of Swansea, since 1968; *b* 1941; *m* 1966. BA Reading 1964, LèsL Bordeaux 1966, PhD Reading 1972. Lecteur, Univ. of Bordeaux, 1964–66; Res. Asst, Reading Univ., 1966–68. *Publications*: *contrib*. Ecrits de Paris. *Address*: Dept of Romance Studies, Univ. College of Swansea, Singleton Park, Swansea SA2 8PP.

Addison, Dr Paul; Lecturer, Department of History, University of Edinburgh, since 1967; *b* 1943. BA Oxon 1967, DPhil 1971. Lectr, Pembroke Coll., Oxford, 1966–67. *Publications*: Lloyd George and Compromise Peace, in, Lloyd George: Twelve Essays, ed A. J. P. Taylor, 1971; By-Elections of the Second World War, in, British By-Elections, ed C. Cook and J. Ramsden, 1973. *Address*: Dept of History, Univ. of Edinburgh, 50 George Square, Edinburgh EH8 9JY.

Adkins, Prof. Arthur William Hope, MA, DPhil; Professor of Classics, University of Reading, since 1966; *b* 1929; *m* 1961; one *s* one *d*. BA Oxon 1952, MA Oxon 1955, DPhil Oxon 1957. Asst in Humanity, Glasgow Univ. 1954–56; Lectr in Greek, Bedford Coll., London, 1956–61; Fellow, Exeter Coll., Oxford, 1961–65; Sen. Vis. Fellow, Soc. for the Humanities, Cornell Univ., 1969–70. *Publications*: Merit and Responsibility: a study in Greek values, 1960, Italian edn 1964; From the Many to the One: a study of personality and views of human nature in the context of Ancient Greek society, values and beliefs, 1970; Moral Values and Political Behaviour in Ancient Greece, 1972; *contrib*. Antichthon, CQ, JHS, Philosophy. *Address*: Dept of Classics, Univ. of Reading, Whiteknights, Reading, Berks RG6 2AH.

Adler, Catherine Elizabeth Marie; Staff Tutor in History and International Affairs, Department for External Studies, University of Oxford, since 1958; *b* 1912; *m* 1939, 1958. MA Oxon 1934 (Modern History), St Hugh's Coll., DipEd London 1935 (distinction). Staff Tutor, Univ. of Hull, 1946–58; Lectr, Management Courses, France, W Germany and England, 1966– ; Dean, Oxford Univ. Language Summer Sch., 1964– . Member: Mature State Scholarship Cttee, 1960–64; International Cttee, Townswomen's Guild, 1971– . Gold Medal, German Democratic Repub., 1973. *Publications*: *contrib*. Educational Jls in W and E Germany. *Address*: Rewley House, Wellington Square, Oxford.

Adrian, Lucy; Fellow, Lecturer and Director of Studies in Geography, Newnham College, Cambridge, since 1968; *b* 1935; *m* 1967. BA Cantab 1957, MA Cantab 1961, MA Wisconsin 1958, PhD Cantab 1966; FRGS. Asst Lectr, Univ. Coll. Wales, Aberystwyth, 1963–65; Lectr, 1965–67; Lectr, Univ. of Wisconsin, 1966. *Address*: Newnham College, Cambridge.

Adshead, David; Lecturer, Centre for Russian and East European Studies, University of Birmingham, since 1970; *b* 1940; *m* 1963. BA Birmingham 1967 (Hons Russian), Cert. in Educn Birmingham 1968; Mem. BNASEES. Res. Associate, Birmingham, 1968–70. *Publications*: (jtly) Birmingham University Language Laboratory Course in Russian for Social Scientists. *Address*: Centre for Russian and East European Studies, Univ. of Birmingham, Birmingham B15 2TT.

Ager, Prof. Dennis Ernest, BA, PhD; Professor of Modern Languages and Head of Department of Modern Languages, University of Aston in Birmingham, since 1971; *b* 1934; *m* 1958; one *s* one *d*. BA Lond 1955, P-GCE London 1958; PhD Salford 1972; Hon FIL, Mem., MLA, AVLA, BAAL, French Studies, MHRA, ALLC. Lectr in French Studies, Salford, 1964–71. Editor, Audio-Visual Lang. Jl, 1970– . *Publications*: Styles and Registers in Contemporary French, 1970; *contrib*. AVLJ. *Address*: Dept of Modern Languages, Univ. of Aston, Birmingham B4 7ET.

Agnew, Kenneth Malcolm; Senior Research Fellow, Department of Design Research, Royal College of Art, since 1971; *b* 1933; *m* 1970. Cert. in Architecture Lond. 1959, DipDes RCA 1962, MDes RCA 1969 (with distinction); MSIAD 1967, FRSA 1970; Res. Fellow RCA 1967–71. Mem., Advisory Cttee for Fire Res. Station. Silver Medallist of RCA 1962. *Publications* (as rapporteur): The Education of Industrial Designers: Seminar, 1964; The Education of Industrial Designers: Third Seminar, 1967; The Relevance of Industrial Design: Seminar, 1974; frequent contribs to Jls. *Address*: Dept of Design Research, RCA, SW7 2EU.

Aguirre, José Maria, PhD; Reader in Spanish, University of Wales, University College, Cardiff, since 1966; *b* 1924; *m* 1965; one *s* one *d*. Licenciado en Derecho (LIB) Zaragoza 1953, PhD Cantab 1960. Lector in Spanish, Cambridge, 1956–59; Lector in Spanish, Aberdeen, 1959–60; Asst Lectr, Univ. College, Cardiff, 1960–61; Lectr, 1961–66; Vis. Prof., Univ. of California, Los Angeles, 1968–69. Founder and Dir, Almenara, Zaragoza, 1951–52; Ansi, Zaragoza, 1952–53; La Niña, Huelva, 1954. *Publications*: Antologia de la poesia española contemporánea, 1961, 3rd edn 1971; Calisto y Melibea, amantes cortesanos, 1962; José de Valdivielso y la poesia religiosa tradicional, 1965; trans. T. S. Eliot: La tierra baldia (The Waste Land), 1965; Hernando del Castillo, Cancionero general (1511), Anthology, 1971; Antologia de la poesia española contemporánea, II, 1972; Antonio Machado, poeta simbolista, 1973; *contrib*. BHS, HR, Rev. Fil. Hisp., RF, Rev. Occidente, Est. Fil. (Chile), Universidad (Zaragoza). *Address*: Dept of Hispanic Studies, Univ. College, Cardiff, Cardiff CF1 1XL.

Ainger, William Dawson, TD, MA; Visiting Lecturer, Law Faculty, Southampton University, since 1969; *b* 1935; *m* 1964; one *s* one *d*. MA Oxford 1962; Barrister-at-law (of Lincoln's Inn) 1961. Lectr in Law, Southampton Univ., 1961–69. *Publications*: (with J. S. Barclay) Freshwater Fisheries in Rivers and The Impact of the Water Resources Act, 1963, 1964. *Address*: The Law Faculty, Southampton Univ., Highfield, Southampton SO9 5NH.

Airth, Alan Don; Senior Lecturer in Quantitative Economics, University of Lancaster, since 1966; *b* 1923; *m* 1949. BA Durham 1951; FSS. Lecturer: Durham, 1952; Newcastle; Dean, Faculty Econ. Studies, Durham, 1963–65; Dept of Employment: Dep. Chm., Wages Councils; Arbitrator, Industrial Relations Section. *Publications*: (with D. J. Newell) The Demand for Hospital Beds, 1962. *Address*: Lonsdale College, Bailrigg, Lancaster.

Aitcheson, Leslie William Drysdale; Lecturer in Private Law, University of Glasgow, since 1967; *b* 1927; *m* 1959; one *s* two *d*. MA, BL, LLB Glasgow 1951; Solicitor in Scotland and Notary Public; Comr for Oaths in England 1963, Advocate of Scottish Bar 1969. Chm., Nat. Insce, Local Appeal Tribunals, Glasgow Central etc., 1970; Reporter, Public Local Planning Enquiries, 1973; Assessor, Glasgow Police Courts, 1972. *Publications*: *contrib*. Jl Law Soc. Scotland, Scots Law Times. *Address*: Dept of Private Law, Univ. of Glasgow, Glasgow G12 8QQ.

Aitchison, Jean Margaret, MA, AM; Lecturer in Linguistics, Department of Language Studies, University of London (London School of Economics), since 1965; *b* 1938. BA Cantab (1st cl. Classics) 1960, AM Radcliffe Coll. USA 1961, MA Cantab 1962. Asst Lectr in Greek, Bedford Coll., Univ. of London, 1961–65. *Publications*: Teach Yourself General Linguistics, 1972; *contrib*. Brit. Jl of Disorders of Communication, Glotta. *Address*: Dept of Language Studies, London School of Economics (Univ. of London), Houghton Street, Aldwych WC2 2AE.

Aitken, Adam Jack; Senior Lecturer (part-time) in English Language, University of Edinburgh, since 1971; Editor, A Dictionary of the Older Scottish Tongue, since 1956 (Assistant Editor, 1948–56); *b* 1921; *m* 1952; three *s* one *d*. MA Hons Edinburgh 1947. Asst Lectr in Eng. Lang., Univ. of Edinburgh, 1947–48; Res. Fellow, Univs of Glasgow, Aberdeen and Edinburgh, 1948–53; Lectr, Univs of Glasgow and Edinburgh, 1953–65; Hon. Sen. Lectr, Univ. of Edinburgh, 1965–71. Member: Exec. Council, Scottish Nat. Dictionary Assoc., 1959– ; Council, Scottish Text Soc., 1962– ; Chm., Lang. Cttee, Assoc. for Scottish Lit. Studies, 1971– ; Consultative Mem., Editl Cttee, Dictionary of Early Modern English Pronunciation, 1972– . *Publications*: ed (with others), A Dictionary of the Older Scottish Tongue, vol. III (H–L), 1964; ed (with others), Edinburgh Studies in English and Scots, 1971; ed, A Dictionary of the Older Scottish Tongue, vol. IV (M–N), 1972; ed (with others), The Computer and Literary Studies, 1973; ed, Lowland Scots, 1973; contributions in: Chambers's Encyclopaedia; DNB; The Computer in Literary and Linguistic Research, ed R. A. Wisbey, 1971; Lexicography and Dialect Geography, ed H. Scholler and J. Reidy, 1973; Lexicography in English, ed R. I. McDavid, Jr, et al., 1973; Tavola Rotonda sui Grandi Lessici Storici, 1973; *contrib*. Sc. Hist. Rev., Scottish Lit. News, Soc. Studies, TLS. *Address*: Dept of English Language, Univ. of Edinburgh, Edinburgh EH8 9YL.

Aitken, Dr William Russell, MA, PhD, FLA; Senior Lecturer, Department of Librarianship, University of Strathclyde, since 1967; *b* 1913; *m* 1939; one *d*. MA Edinburgh 1935, PhD Edinburgh 1956; FLA 1948. Lectr, Dept of Librarianship, Strathclyde, 1964–67; Vis. Prof., Univ. of W Ontario, 1972. Co. Libr. Clackmannan, 1946–49; Perth and Kinross, 1949–58; Ayr County, 1958–62; Lectr, Scott. Sch. Librarianship, Scott. Coll. Commerce, 1962–64; Pres., Scott. Libr. Assoc., 1965; Ed., Libr. Rev., 1964– . *Publications*: ed, Soutar: Poems in Scots and English, 1961; A History of the Public Library Movement in Scotland to 1955, 1972; *contrib*. Bibliotheck, Libr. Assoc. Rec., Libr. Rev., Studies Scott. Lit. *Address*: Dept of Librarianship, Univ. of

Strathclyde, Livingstone Tower, Glasgow G1 1XH.

Akamatsu, Tsutomu; Lecturer, Department of Phonetics, University of Leeds, since 1966; *b* 1932; *m* 1964. BA Tokyo 1956, Postgrad. Dip. in Phonetics London 1960. Lectr, Aoyama Gakuin Univ., Tokyo, 1960–64. *Publications*: contrib. Bull. of the Phonetic Soc. of Japan, La Linguistique, Linguistische Berichte, Study of Sounds (Phonetic Soc. of Japan). *Address*: Dept of Phonetics, Univ. of Leeds, Leeds LS2 9JT.

Akehurst, Dr Michael Barton, MA, LLB, Docteur de l'Université, Barrister-at-Law; Senior Lecturer in Law, Keele University, since 1971; *b* 1940. BA Cantab 1961 (1st cl. Law), LLB Cantab (1st cl.) 1962, MA Cantab 1965, Docteur de l'Université Paris 1964, Diplômé of the Hague Academy of International Law 1965; Barrister-at-Law (Inner Temple) 1963. Asst Lectr in Law, Manchester, 1966–69; Lectr in Law, Keele, 1970–71; Vis. Lectr, Otago, 1972. Legal Officer, UNRWA, Beirut, 1967. *Publications*: The Law Governing Employment in International Organizations, 1967; A Modern Introduction to International Law, 1970, 2nd edn 1971, Spanish edn, 1973; contrib. International Disputes: the legal aspects, 1971; An Introduction to the Law of the European Economic Community, ed Wortley, 1972; *contrib.* Annuaire of the Assoc. of Attenders and Alumni of the Hague Academy of International Law, Brit. Year Book of International Law, International Rev. of Administrative Sciences, Jl de droit international, Modern Law Rev., New Law Jl, NZ Univs Law Rev., Otago Law Rev. *Address*: Law Dept, Keele Univ., Keele, Staffs ST5 5BG.

Alberich, José Maria, PhD; Reader in Modern Spanish Literature, Spanish Department, University of Exeter, since 1967; *b* 1929; *m* 1958; two *d.* Licenciado en Filosofía y Letras (Romance Philology) Madrid 1955, Doctor en Filosofía y Letras Madrid 1958; Mem., Assoc. Brit. Hispanists. Lectr, Southampton Univ., 1955–57; Lectr, Bristol Univ., 1957–58; Temp. Lectr, Oxford Univ., 1958–60; Lectr, Exeter Univ., 1960–67. Acting Head, Dept of Spanish, Exeter Univ., 1966–67. *Publications*: Los Ingleses y otros Temas de Pío Baroja, 1966; *contrib.* Arbor, BHS, Cuadernos de Literatura, HR, Papeles de Son Armadans, Revista de Occidente. *Address*: Dept of Spanish, Univ. of Exeter, Exeter, Devon EX4 4QJ.

Albrow, Martin C.; Senior Lecturer, Department of Sociology, University College, Cardiff, since 1967; *b* 1937; *m* 1962; three *s.* BA Cantab 1958. Tutorial Asst, Univ. of Leicester, 1961–62; Asst Lectr, Univ. of Leicester, 1962–63; Lectr, Univ. of Reading, 1963–67. *Publications*: Bureaucracy, 1970; *contrib.* Brit. Jl Sociol., Jew. Jl Sociol., Univs Qly. *Address*: Dept of Sociology, Univ. College, Cardiff CF1 1XL.

Alcock, John; Academic Secretary, London School of Economics, University of London, since 1967; *b* 1918; *m* 1941; two *d.* BA Manchester 1939. Registrar, LSE, 1958–67.

Address: LSE, Houghton Street, WC2A 2AE.

Alder, Dr Garry John, BA, PhD; Warden, Childs Hall and Lecturer, Department of History, University of Reading, since 1966; *b* 1932; *m* 1963; two *s* one *d.* BA Bristol 1953 (1st cl.), PhD Bristol 1959. Lectr, Univ. of Glasgow, 1958–60. Asst Hd, Educn Serv., Esso Petrol. Co., 1960–63; Hd Educn Serv., Esso Petrol. Co., 1963–66. *Publications*: British India's Northern Frontier, 1961; The Making of a Frontier, 1974; *contrib.* Jl Royal Cent. Asian Soc., Hist. Jl, Jl Asian Hist., Afghanistan Jl, ME Studies, Jl of Imperial and Commonwealth Hist. *Address*: Childs Hall, Upper Redlands Road, Reading RG1 5JW.

Alderman, Dr Geoffrey; Lecturer, Department of History, Royal Holloway College, University of London, since 1972; *b* 1944; *m* 1973. BA Oxon 1965 (Hons), MA, DPhil Oxon 1969; FRHistS 1971; Mem., Jewish Historical Soc. of England, Mem. numerous other historical societies. Res. Asst, Dept of History, University Coll., London, 1968–69; Temp. Lectr, Dept of Politics, University Coll. of Swansea, 1969–70; Postdoctoral Res. Fellow, Dept of History, Univ. of Reading, 1970–72. *Publications*: The History of Hackney Downs School, 1972; The Railway Interest, 1973; *contrib.* Hist. Jl, Marit. Hist., Transp. Hist., Jl Transp. Hist., Welsh Hist. Rev. *Address*: Dept of History, Royal Holloway College, Egham, Surrey TW20 0EX.

Alderman, Dr Robin Keith, BSc(Econ), PhD; Lecturer in Politics, University of York, since 1964; *b* 1938; *m* 1960. BSc(Econ) London 1961, PhD London 1971. Hon. Sec., Pol. Studies Assoc., 1969–70; Mem., Exec. Cttee, Pol. Studies Assoc., 1970– . *Publications*: co-author, The Tactics of Resignation, 1967; co-author, Management Training Survey, 1967; *contrib.* Parl. Aff., Parliamentarian, Pol. Studies. *Address*: Dept of Politics, Univ. of York, Heslington, York YO1 5DD.

Alexander, Alan; Lecturer, Department of Politics, University of Reading, since 1971; *b* 1943; *m* 1964; one *s* one *d.* MA Glasgow 1965. Lakehead Univ., Ontario, Canada: Lectr, 1966–69; Asst Prof., 1969–71. *Publications*: contrib. Brit. Jl of Polit. Sci., Parly Affairs, Public Admin. *Address*: Dept of Politics, The Univ., Whiteknights, Reading RG6 2AA.

Alexander, Flora; Lecturer, Department of English, University of Aberdeen, since 1965; *b* 1939; *m* 1970; one *d.* MA Aberdeen 1961, BLitt Oxon 1968. Asst Lectr, Dept of English Language, Univ. of Liverpool, 1963, *Address*: Dept of English, Univ. of Aberdeen, Aberdeen AB9 1AS.

Alexander, Ian Welsh, MA, DLitt, FIAL; Professor of French, Department of French and Romance Studies, University College of North Wales, Bangor, since 1951; *b* 1911; *m* 1935. MA Edinburgh 1932 (1st cl. Mod. Langs), DLitt Edinburgh 1949; FIAL, Officier des Palmes Académiques. Carnegie Research Scholar 1932–34, Carnegie Research Fellow

5

1936–37; Asst, 1934–36, Asst Lectr, 1937–38, Lectr, 1938–46, Univ. of Edinburgh; Lectr and Head of Dept. UC Dundee (St Andrews Univ.), 1946–51; Dean of Faculty of Arts, UC of N Wales, Bangor, 1958–60; G.T. Clapton Meml Lectr, Leeds Univ., 1967. Pres., Brit. Soc. for Phenomenology, 1967–72, Vice-Pres., 1972– . Mem. Adv. Cttee, The Human Context, 1970– ; Mem., Soc. for French Studies, Assoc. Internat. des Etudes Françaises, Royal Inst. of Philosophy. *Publications*: Bergson: philosopher of reflection, 1957; Benjamin Constant: Adolphe, 1973; (with others) Studies in Romance Philology and French Literature, 1953; Studies in Modern French Literature, 1961; Actes du Premier Colloque de la Société Britannique de Philosophie de Langue Française, 1962; Studi in onore di Carlo Pellegrini, 1963; Currents of Thought in French Literature, 1965; Penguin Companion to Literature Vol. 2 (European), 1969, 2nd edn 1972; Linguistic Analysis and Phenomenology, 1972; Mouvements premiers, 1972; *contrib.* Cambridge Jl, Forum for Mod. Lang. Stud., French Stud., Horizon, Jl of the Brit. Soc. for Phenomenology, Livres de France, MLR, Philos. Qly, Philosophy, Philos. Bks, Rev. de Métaphysique et de Morale, Rev. Philosophique, TLS. *Address*: Dept of French and Romance Studies, Univ. College of North Wales, Bangor, Caerns LL57 2DG.

Alexander, Rev. James Neil Stewart, MA, BD, STM; Senior Lecturer in New Testament Language and Literature, Faculty of Divinity, University of Glasgow, since 1967; *b* 1921; *m* 1949; two *d*. MA Glasgow 1942 (War Hons Classics), BD (Dist. in New Testament) Glasgow 1948, STM (magna cum laude) Union Seminary New York 1949; Minister of Church of Scotland, 1949; LRAM (Pianoforte), 1940; Mem., Soc. for New Testament Studies. Asst, Biblical Criticism, Aberdeen Univ., 1955–58; Lectr, Biblical Criticism, Aberdeen Univ., 1958–64; Lectr, New Testament Lang. and Lit., Glasgow Univ., 1964–67. Parish Minister, St Paul's, Cambuslang, Glasgow, 1949–55; Mem., Church of Scotland Panel on Doctrine, 1968–72; Mem., Church Hymnary Revision Cttee, 1963–72. *Publications*: The Epistles of John, 1962, pbk 1969; The Way of the Lord and The Way of the World, 1965; 1 and 2 Corinthians (IBRA), 1967; Life After Easter, 1968; contrib. The New Testament in Historical and Contemporary Perspective (Essays in memory G. H. C. Macgregor), 1965; *contrib.* Interpretation (Richmond, Virginia), 1958, The Preacher's Quarterly, 1967. *Address*: New Testament Dept, Univ. of Glasgow, 4 Southpark Terrace, Glasgow.

Alexander, Dr John Amyas, FSA; Senior Lecturer in Archaeology, Department of Extra Mural Studies, University of London, since 1964; *b* 1922; *m* 1948; two *s* two *d*. BA Cantab 1948, Academic Postgrad. Dip. (Archaeology) London 1953, PhD Cantab 1958; FSA. Vis. Res. Fellow, Jugoslavia, 1956; Tutor in Archaeology, Bd of Extra Mural Studies, Cambridge, 1957–64; Vis. Sen. Lectr, Univ. of Ghana, 1967; Vis. Sen. Lectr, Ibadan, Nigeria, 1973; Spec. Lectr, Inst. of Archaeology, London, 1971. Indian

Army, 1941–45; Sudan Educn Serv., 1948–51; Mem., Council Prehist. Soc., 1960–69; Council, Trust for Brit. Archaeol., 1970– ; Exec. Cttee, Council for Brit. Archaeol., 1971– ; Cllr Chesterton RDC, 1967–69. *Publications*: The Directing of Archaeological Excavations, 1969; Jugoslavia before the Romans, 1972; contrib. Symposia: The Domestication of Plants and Animals, 1969; Problems of Settlement and Urbanisation, 1971; Science and Archaeology Thames, 1969; *contrib.* Amer. Jl Archaeol., Antiquity, Proc. Prehist. Soc., Proc. Cong. Pre and Proto Hist. *Address*: Dept of Extra Mural Studies, 7 Ridgmount Street, WC1E 7AD.

Alexander, Dr John Huston; Lecturer in English, University of Aberdeen, since 1968; *b* 1941; *m* 1970; two *d*. BLitt 1963, MA 1966, DPhil 1969, Oxford. Sessional Lectr in English, Univ. of Saskatchewan, 1966–67; Asst Lectr in English, Univ. of Aberdeen, 1968–71. *Address*: Dept of English, Univ. of Aberdeen, Aberdeen AB9 2UB.

Alexander, Dr Jonathan James Graham; Reader, History of Art Department, Manchester University, since 1973; *b* 1935. BA Oxon 1960, MA Oxon, DPhil Oxon 1968. Lectr, Hist. of Art, Manchester Univ., 1971. Asst, Dept of Western MSS, Bodleian Library, Oxford, 1963–71. *Publications*: (with O. Pächt) Illuminated Manuscripts in the Bodleian Library, Vol. I 1966, Vol. II 1970, Vol. III 1973; (with A. C. de la Mare) The Italian Manuscripts in the Library of Major J. R. Abbey, 1969; Norman Illumination at Mont St Michel, 1970; The Master of Mary of Burgundy: A Book of Hours, 1970; *contrib.* Burlington Mag., Scriptorium, Arte Veneta, Antiquaries Jl. *Address*: History of Art Dept, Univ. of Manchester, Oxford Road, Manchester M13 9PL.

Alexander, Prof. Kenneth John Wilson; Professor of Economics, University of Strathclyde, since 1961; Dean of Scottish Business School, since 1973; *b* 1922; *m* 1949; one *s* four *d*. BSc(Econ) London 1949. Res. Asst, Univ. of Leeds, 1949–51; Lectr, Univ. of Sheffield, 1951–57; Lectr, Univ. of Aberdeen, 1957–61. Econ. Consultant to Sec. of State, Scotland, 1967– ; Mem., Bd Scott. Transport Gp, 1968– . *Publications*: The Economist in Business, 1967; Fairfields – A Study of Industrial Change, 1970; *contrib.* Bull. Econ. Res., Oxford Econ. Papers, Qly Jl Econ., Scott. Jl Pol. Econ., Sociol. Rev. *Address*: Dept of Economics, Univ. of Strathclyde, Glasgow G1 1XW.

Alexander, Michael Joseph; Lecturer, Department of English Studies, University of Stirling, since 1969; *b* 1941; *m* 1973. BA 1962, MA Oxon, Dip. in Italian Perugia 1963. Fellow, Princeton Grad. Coll., 1965–66; Lectr in English: Univ. of Calif, Santa Barbara, 1966–67; Sch. of English and American Studies, Univ. of E Anglia, 1968–69. Editor at: William Collins Ltd, Publishers, 1963–65; André Deutsch, Publishers, 1967–68. *Publications*: The Earliest English Poems, 1966; Beowulf, 1973; *contrib.* Agenda, Listener. *Address*: Dept of English Studies, Univ. of Stirling, Stirling FK9 4LA.

Alexander, Prof. Peter; Professor of Philosophy, University of Bristol, since 1971; *b* 1917; *m* 1943; one *s*. BSc London 1940 (Chemistry), BA London 1947 (Philosophy); Mem., Mind Assoc., Aristotelian Soc., Brit. Soc. for the Philosophy of Science. Asst Lectr, Leeds Univ., 1949, Lectr, 1951; Lectr Bristol Univ., 1957, Reader, 1960; Vis. Prof. Univ. of Pennsylvania, 1959; Univ. of Maryland, 1965; Univ. of Cincinnati, 1971. Treasurer, Mind Assoc., 1963–70; Mem., Cttees of Aristotelian Soc., 1961–64; and Brit. Soc. for Philosophy of Science, 1969. *Publications*: Sensationalism and Scientific Explanation, 1963; A Preface to the Logic of Science, 1963, Japanese edn 1969; An Introduction to Logic, 1969, Japanese edn forthcoming; *contrib*. BJPS, Mind, Philosophy, Phil. Rev., Proc. Arist. Soc., Ratio, Synthèse, The Technologist, TES. *Address*: Dept of Philosophy, The Univ., Wills Memorial Building, Bristol BS8 1RJ.

Alexiou, Dr Margaret Beatrice, MA, PhD; Lecturer in Byzantine and Modern Greek, University of Birmingham, since 1964; *b* 1939; *m* 1961; two *s*. BA Cantab 1961 (1st cl. Classics), MA Cantab 1964, PhD Cantab 1967. *Publications*: The Ritual Lament in Greek Tradition, 1974; *contrib*. Studi Med. *Address*: Dept of Greek, Univ. of Birmingham, Birmingham B15 2TT.

Alford, Dr Bernard William Ernest, BSc(Econ), PhD; Senior Lecturer in Economic History, Department of Economic and Social History, University of Bristol, since 1973; *b* 1937; *m*; two *s* one *d*. BSc(Econ) London, PhD London. Asst Lectr in Economic Hist., LSE, 1961–62; Asst Lectr, 1962–64, Lectr, 1964–73, Univ. of Bristol. *Publications*: (with T. C. Barker) A History of the Carpenters Company, 1968; Depression and Recovery? British Economic Growth 1918–1939, 1972; W.D. & H.O. Wills and the UK Tobacco Industry, 1786–1965, 1973; *contrib*. Business Hist., Econ. Hist. Rev., Expl. Entrepren. Hist. *Address*: Dept of Economic and Social History, Univ. of Bristol, Bristol BS8 1UL.

Alford, Roger Francis Gower; Cassel Reader in Economics, London School of Economics, since 1965; *b* 1926; *m* 1960; two *s* one *d*. BSc(Econ) LSE, 1952. Asst Lectr, LSE, 1952–56, Lectr, 1956–64, Sen. Lectr, 1964–65. Seconded, Bank of England, 1960–62. *Publications*: contrib. Sayers *Festschrift*; Robbins *Festschrift*; Monetary Confs, Hove 1969, Sheffield 1970; *contrib*. Economica, Lond. and Camb. Econ. Bull., Banker, Bankers Mag. *Address*: London School of Economics, Houghton Street, WC2A 2AE.

Allan, Charles M.; Senior Lecturer in Economics, University of Strathclyde, since 1972; *b* 1939; *m* 1961; two *s* two *d*. MA Aberdeen 1962; Mem., Royal Econ. Soc., Mem., Scottish Econ. Soc., Mem., Econ. Hist. Soc. Asst, Dept of Econ. Hist., Univ. of Glasgow, 1962–63; Asst, Dept of Econs, Univ. of Dundee, 1963–65; Lectr in Econs, Univ. of Strathclyde, 1965–71. *Publications*: The Theory of Taxation, 1971; *contrib*. Econ. Hist. Rev., Oxford Econ. Papers, Scottish Jl Pol. Econ-

omy. *Address*: McCance Building, Richmond Street, Glasgow G1 1XG.

Allchin, Dr Bridget; Fellow, since 1968 and Tutor, since 1969, Wolfson College, University of Cambridge; *b* 1927; *m* 1951; one *s* one *d*. BA Capetown 1949, PhD London 1956, MA Cambridge 1968; FRAI, FRGS; Mem.: Prehistoric Soc.; S African Archaeol Soc.; Indian Archaeol Soc. P. and E. Gibbs Travelling Fellow, Newnham College, Cambridge, 1970–71. *Publications*: The Stone Tipped Arrow, 1966; (with F. R. Allchin) The Birth of Indian Civilization, 1968; The Prehistory of the Indian Desert (forthcoming); *contrib*. Ancient India, Bull. Inst. Arch., Jl Royal Anthrop. Inst., Jl Geog. Soc., Man, S Asian Arch., World Arch. *Address*: Wolfson College, Cambridge.

Allchin, Dr Frank Raymond, FSA; Fellow of Churchill College, since 1963, and Reader in Indian Studies, since 1972, University of Cambridge; *b* 1923; *m* 1951; one *s* one *d*. BA London 1950 (1st cl. Hindi); MA Cantab 1959; PhD London 1954; FRAS, FSA. Lectr, London, 1954–59; Univ. Lectr, Cambridge, 1959–72. Mem. Adv. Council, V & A Museum, 1966–72; Consultant, UNESCO, 1969; Sen. Consultant, UNDP, 1970. *Publications*: Piklihal Excavations, 1960; Utnur Excavations, 1961; Neolithic Cattle Keepers of South India, 1963; The Kavitāvālī of Tulsī Dās, 1964; The Petition to Rām, 1966; (with B. Allchin) The Birth of Indian Civilization, 1968; *contrib*. Man, Bull. SOAS, Jl Econ. Soc., Hist. Orient, Antiquity, Jl R. Asiatic Soc. *Address*: Faculty of Oriental Studies, Sidgwick Avenue, Cambridge.

Allcock, John Bartlett; Lecturer, School of Social Sciences, University of Bradford, since 1968; *b* 1942; *m* 1963; two *s*. BA Leicester 1963 (Upper 2; Sociology); MA Carleton (Ottowa) 1967; Mem., Brit. Sociolog. Assoc. Tutorial Asst, Leicester, 1964; Asst Lectr, Bradford, 1966. *Publications*: *contrib*. Int. Dialog Zeitschrift, Sociological Rev., Sociology. *Address*: School of Social Sciences, Univ. of Bradford, Bradford, Yorks BD7 1DP.

Alldridge, James Charles; Lecturer, Department of German, Keele University, since 1967; *b* 1910. MA Oxon 1937. *Publications*: ed, Aichinger: Selected Short Stories, 1966; ed, German Narrative Prose, vol. III, 1968; Ilse Aichinger: a monograph, 1969; ed, Böll: 'Im Tal der donnernden Hufe, 1970; trans., Aichinger, The Young Lieutenant, 1967; Artmann – The Seriousness of Nonsense, in, Essays in Memory of Oswald Wolff, 1970; BBC Script, Modern German Poetry, 1972. *Address*: Dept of German, Univ. of Keele, Staffs ST5 5BG.

Allen, Christopher Hancorn; Lecturer, Department of Politics, Edinburgh University, since 1972; *b* 1942; *m* 1970; one *d*. BA (Hons) Oxford 1965, MA (Hons) 1968; Commonwealth Res. Fellow, Fourah Bay Coll., Univ. of Sierra Leone, 1966–67; Res. Fellow, Nuffield Coll., Oxford, 1968–70; Lectr in History, Ahmadu Bello Univ., Nigeria, 1970–71. *Publications*: ed (jtly) African Perspectives, 1970; *contrib*. African

Affairs. *Address*: Centre of African Studies, 40 George Square, Edinburgh EH8 9LL.

Allen, Prof. Harry Cranbrook, MC, MA; Professor of American Studies, School of English and American Studies, University of East Anglia, since 1971, and Dean since 1973; *b* 1917; *m* 1947; one *s* two *d*. BA Oxon 1938 (1st cl. Modern History); FRHistS; Cttee Mem., Brit. Assoc. for American Studies. Fellow Lincoln Coll., Oxford, 1946–55; Fellow of the Commonwealth Fund of New York, 1946; Commonwealth Fund Prof. of American History, University College London, 1955–71; Director, London Univ. Inst. of United States Studies, 1966–71; Vis. Prof., Univ. of Minnesota, 1949; Senior Research Fellow, Australian National Univ., 1953–54; Vis. Scholar, Univ. of California, Berkeley, 1953; Schouler Lectr, The Johns Hopkins Univ., 1956; American Studies Fellow, Commonwealth Fund of New York, 1957, at Univ. of Virginia; Vis. Prof., Univ. of Southern California, 1959; Vis. Member, Inst. for Advanced Study, Princeton, N.J., 1959; Vis. Prof., Univ. of Rochester, 1963, 1964; Vis. Prof., Univ. of Michigan, Ann Arbor, 1966; Vis. Prof., Univ. of Queensland, 1970; Vis. Prof., ANU, 1973. Mem., Dartmouth Royal Naval College Review Cttee, 1958; Mem., Naval Educ. Advisory Cttee, 1960–66; Mem., Academic Planning Board, Univ. of Essex, 1962. *Publications*: Great Britain and the United States, 1955, 1969; Bush and Backwoods, 1959; The Anglo-American Relationship since 1783, 1960; The Anglo-American Predicament, 1960; The United States of America, 1964 (Under the title, A Concise History of the USA, 1968); ed jtly. British Essays in American History, 1957, 1969. *Address*: School of English and American Studies, Univ. of East Anglia, Norwich NOR 88C.

Allen, Dr John Patrick Brierley; Lecturer, Department of Linguistics, University of Edinburgh, since 1967; *b* 1936; *m* 1965; two *s*. MA Oxon 1959 (Modern History); MA Indiana 1965 (Gen. Linguistics); PhD Essex 1967 (Applied Linguistics); Teaching Dip. London 1960 (English as a Foreign Lang.); Dip. Leeds 1964. (English as a Second Lang.). *Publications*: ed with Paul van Buren, Chomsky: selected readings, 1971; ed with S. P. Corder: Readings for Applied Linguistics, 1973; Techniques in Applied Linguistics, 1974; Papers in Applied Linguistics, 1974; (with H. G. Widdowson) English in Physical Science, 1974; *contrib*. Internat. Rev. of Applied Linguistics in Lang. Teaching. *Address*: Dept of Linguistics, Adam Ferguson Building, George Square, Edinburgh.

Allen, Kevin John, BA; Lecturer in Applied Economics, Department of Social and Economic Research, University of Glasgow, since 1966; *b* 1941; *m* 1969; one *s* one *d*. BA Nottingham 1963. Asst Lectr, Dept of Social and Economic Research, Univ. of Glasgow, 1964–66. Part time economic consultant to EFTA; Working Parties on Regional Development, 1966–71. *Publications*: (with Tormod Hermansen) published study papers in Regional Policy in EFTA: An Examination of the Growth Centre Idea, 1968; (with G. L. Reid) Nationalised Industries, 1970; (with M. C. MacLennan) Regional Problems and Policies in Italy and France, 1971; consultant and part author, Industrial Mobility, 1971. *Address*: Dept of Social and Economic Research, Adam Smith Building, University of Glasgow, Glasgow G12 8RT.

Allen, Louis; Senior Lecturer, Department of French, University of Durham, since 1959; *b* 1922; *m* 1949; four *s* one *d*. BA Manchester 1947, MA 1949; Member: Assoc. Int. des Etudes françaises; Assoc. Int. d'Etudes des Civilisations Méditerranéennes; Japan Soc. of London; Royal Asiatic Soc. Kemsley Travelling Fellow, Univ. of Manchester, 1947–48; Lectr in French, Univ. of Durham, 1948–59; Chief Examiner in French, Durham Univ. Schools Ex. Bd. Chm., Academic Bd Electors; Sometime Mem., Univ. Council, Senate, Academic Bd, Fac. of Arts, Buildings Cttee, Arts Finance Cttee; Chm., BBC NE Regional Adv. Council, 1970– ; Former Mem. North Regional Council and Radio Durham Council. Mem. BBC General Adv. Council. Mem. Literature Panel, Northern Arts Assoc. *Publications*: ed, Beaumarchais: Le Barbier de Séville, 1950; ed, Beaumarchais: Le Mariage de Figaro, 1950; (with Hidé Ishiguro) trans. Yuji Aida, Prisoner of the British, 1966; trans. Regis Debray: The Frontier, 1969; Japan: the Years of Triumph, 1971, Fr. and Spanish edns; Sittang: the Last Battle, 1972, Japanese edn; The End of the War in Asia (forthcoming); ed, Newman and the abbé Jager: a controversy on the Rule of Faith, (forthcoming); *contrib*. Bib. Hum. et Renaissance, French Studs, Mod. Lang. Review, Forum, Durham Univ. Jl, Mil. Hist., N & Q, Rev. Litt. Comp., Rev. d'Hist. Litt. de la France, Downside Rev., etc. *Address*: Univ. of Durham, Oldshire Hall, Durham DH1 3HP.

Allen, Dr Michael L.; Senior Lecturer in English, Queen's University, Belfast, since 1971; *b* 1935; *m* 1959; one *s* one *d*. BA Leeds 1958, MA Leeds 1960; PhD Birmingham 1965; Mem., BAAS. Res. Fellow, Univ. of Birmingham, 1960-63; ACLS Fellow, Yale, 1963–64; Lectr in English, Belfast, 1964–67, 1968–70; Vis. Lectr, Smith Coll., Mass, 1967–68. *Publications*: Poe and the British Magazine Tradition, 1969; *contrib*. The Black American Writer, ed C. W. E. Bigsby, 1969; Contemporary Irish Writing, ed D. Dunn, 1973; Penguin Companion to Literature; Mod. Lang. Rev., Jl Eng. Studies, Studi Americani, Jl of American Studies, Honest Ulsterman. *Address*: Dept of English, Queen's Univ., Belfast BT7 1NN.

Allen, Peter, BA; Lecturer, French Department, University of Edinburgh, since 1968; *b* 1942. BA Manchester 1963 (1st cl. French). Lecteur, Univ. of Geneva, 1963–64; Lectr, Ecole d'Interprètes, Geneva, 1963–64; Lectr, Univ. of Manchester, 1964–65; Lecteur, Univ. of Strasbourg, 1965–68. *Publications*: *contrib*. Bull. Jeunes Romanistes. *Address*: Dept of French, Univ. of Edinburgh, Edinburgh EH8 9YL.

Allen, William John; Director, Teaching Media Centre, University of Southampton, since 1971; *b* 1930. BA Bristol 1951 (2nd cl.

Geography), Cert. in Educn Bristol 1952. Mem., Royal Television Soc. Lectr in Educ. (Geography method and audio-visual techniques), 1966–71. Mem., School Broadcasting Council's Programme Cttee 3, 1970– ; Mem., Bd of Univ. Inst. of Educn; Mem., Bd of Univ. Faculty of Educn. *Publications*: (Films produced and directed): Gibraltar: Gateway to the Mediterranean, 1966; Malta: Mediterranean in Miniature, 1968; (with Dr M. J. Clark) Against the Sea: A Case Study of Coast Erosion, 1969; (with Mr W. B. Seacroft) Steig ein Nach Oberstdorf, 1970; (with Dr M. J. Clark) Rivers at Work: An Introduction to Channel Processes, 1971; Val D'Herens: an Alpine valley in Change, 1972. *Address*: Teaching Media Centre, Univ. of Southampton, SO9 5NH.

Allen, Prof. William Sidney, MA, PhD, FBA; Professor of Comparative Philology, University of Cambridge, since 1955; *b* 1918; *m* 1955. BA Cantab 1940 (Classics), MA Cantab 1946, PhD Cantab 1949; FBA 1971; Mem., Philological Soc. (Pres. 1965–67). Lectr (Phonetics; Comparative Linguistics) School of Oriental and African Studies, Univ. of London, 1948–55; Fellow Trinity Coll., Cambridge 1955– ; Vis. Prof., Univ. of Texas 1961, Washington 1962. Royal Tank Regt and General Staff (Int.), 1939–45; Governor (Council of Almoners), Christ's Hosp., 1968– . *Publications*: Phonetics in Ancient India, 1953; Sandhi, 1962; Vox Latina, 1965; Vox Graeca, 1968; Accent and Rhythm, 1973; *contrib.* Acta Linguistica, Archivum Linguisticum, Bull. Sch. Oriental and African St., Jl of Linguistics, Language, Lingua, Trans. Philological Soc., Word. *Address*: Faculty Rooms, Laundress Lane, Cambridge.

Allgrove, Joan, MA; Keeper of Textiles, Whitworth Art Gallery and Lecturer in the History of Art, University of Manchester, since 1961; *b* 1928; *m* 1956 (marr. diss. 1963). BA Reading 1952 (1st cl. Fine Art), MA Reading 1954 (History of Art); Mem., Museums Assoc., Mem., Egypt Exploration Soc., 1969. Lectr in Fine Art, Reading Univ., 1954–56; (married and living in Australia 1956–60). Tutor at Owens Park Student village, Manchester, 1964, Vice Chm. of Tutors, 1966–69; Mem., BEd Cttees, Manchester Univ., 1967, *Publications*: Brief Guide to the Whitworth Gallery, 1968; Exhibition catalogues: Textiles SIA, 1962; Age of Shakespeare, 1964; British Sources of Art Nouveau, 1969; in preparation: major catalogue of the Gallery's Coptic Textiles collection. *Address*: Whitworth Art Gallery, Whitworth Park, Manchester M15 6ER.

Allmand, Dr Christopher Thomas, MA, DPhil.; Senior Lecturer in Mediaeval History, University of Liverpool, since 1973 (Lecturer, 1967–73); *b* 1936; *m* 1964; three *d*. BA Oxon 1958, MA Oxon 1963, DPhil Oxon 1963; FRHistS. Asst Lectr, Univ. Coll. of N Wales, Bangor, 1963–65; Lectr, 1965–67. Mem., Council Historical Assoc., 1971–74. *Publications*: Henry V (Historical Assoc. booklet), 1968; (ed) Society at War: the experience of England and France during the Hundred Years' War, 1973; contrib. The Hundred Years' War, ed K. A. Fowler, 1971; contrib. Camden Miscellany, 1972; *contrib.* Bibl. Ecole des Chartes, BIHR, Econ. Hist. Rev., Speculum. *Address*: School of History, PO Box 147, Liverpool L69 3BX.

Allott, Anna Joan; Lecturer in Burmese, School of Oriental and African Studies, London, since 1953; *b* 1930; *m* 1952; two *s* one *d*. BA London (Russian Lang. and Lit.) 1951. *Publications*: ed (with others) Burmese–English Dictionary (in progress) pts iv–v, 1963–69. *Address*: School of Oriental and African Studies, Malet Street, WC1E 7HP.

Allott, Prof. Antony Nicolas; Professor of African Law, Department of Law, University of London, since 1964; *b* 1924; *m* 1952; two *s* two *d*. BA Oxon (Hons Jurisprudence) 1948, MA Oxon 1952, PhD London 1954; Mem., African Studies Assoc., Soc. of Public Teachers of Law, etc. Lectr in African Law, School of Oriental and African Studies, Univ. of London, 1948–60, Reader 1960–64; Head of Dept of Law, SOAS 1970– . Pres., African Studies Assoc. of the UK, 1969–70; Dir, Restatement of African Law Project, 1959– ; Vice-Pres., International African Law Assoc., 1967– . JP. *Publications*: Essays in African Law, 1960; ed Judicial and Legal Systems in Africa, 1962, 2nd edn 1970; New Essays in African Law, 1970; *contrib.* articles in numerous periodicals. *Address*: School of Oriental and African Studies, Malet St, WC1E 7HP.

Allott, Prof. Miriam; Andrew Cecil Bradley Professor of Modern English Literature, University of Liverpool, since 1974; *b* 1920; *m* 1952. BA Liverpool 1940, MA Liverpool 1948, PhD 1949. Liverpool University: William Noble Fellowship in English Literature, 1946–48; Asst Lectr and Lectr, 1948–58; Sen. Lectr, 1958–70; Reader, 1970–74. *Publications*: (with Kenneth Allott), The Art of Graham Greene, 1951; (with Kenneth Allott), The Pelican Book of English Prose, vol. V; Victorian Prose 183 1956; Novelists on–08, the Novel, 1959, paperback edns England and America, 1966; Elizabeth Gaskell, 1958, rev. 1970; The Complete Poems of John Keats, 1920, paperback edn 1972; Wuthering Heights: A Casebook, 1970; The Brontës: The Critical Heritage, 1973; Charlotte Brontë: Jane Eyre and Villette: A Casebook, 1973; *contrib.* Essays in Crit., Mod. Lang. Rev., JEGP, Rev. Eng. Stud., Vict. Stud. *Address*: English Dept, The Univ., Liverpool L69 3BX.

Allott, Dr Terence John Dobson, MA, BLitt, DPhil; Lecturer, Department of French, Westfield College, University of London, since 1962; *b* 1934. BA Oxon 1955, MA Oxon 1957; BLitt Oxon 1960; DPhil Oxon 1968; FRSA. Asst Univ. St Andrews, 1959–62. Mem., Council, Westfield Coll., 1970–73. *Publications*: *contrib.* BHR, Forum Mod. Lang. Studies, Library. *Address*: Dept of French, Westfield College, Kidderpore Avenue, NW3 7ST.

Allport, Dr Denison Alan; Lecturer in Psychology, Reading University, since 1969; *b* 1937; *m* 1965; one *s* one *d*. BA Oxon 1961

(1st cl. Psychology and Philosophy), MA Oxon 1966, PhD Cambridge 1966. Asst Lectr, Aberdeen Univ., 1965–66; Lectr, 1966–69. *Publications*: contrib. Brit. Jl Psychol., Percept. Psychophysics, Qly Jl Exper. Psychol. *Address*: Dept of Psychology, Univ. of Reading, Whiteknights, Reading RG6 2AL.

Allsop, Bruce; *see* Allsopp, H. B.

Allsopp (Harold) Bruce; Reader in the History of Architecture, School of Architecture, University of Newcastle upon Tyne, since 1973 (Senior Lecturer, 1969–73); *b* 1912; *m* 1936; two *s*. BArch Liverpool 1933 (1st cl.), DipCD Liverpool 1935; FRIBA, FSA, MRTPI. Lectr in Architecture, Univ. of Durham, 1946–55; Sen. Lectr, 1955–63; Sen. Lectr in Architecture, Univ. of Newcastle upon Tyne, 1963–69; Dir., Architectural Studies, 1965–69. Chm., Soc. Arch. Hist. GB, 1959–65; Chm., Oriel Press Ltd, 1962– ; Master, Art Workers Guild, 1970; Chm., Indep. Publishers Guild, 1971–72. *Publications*: Art and the Nature of Architecture, 1952; Decoration and Furniture, Vol. 1 1952, Vol. 2, 1953; A General History of Architecture, 1955, 2nd edn 1965; Style in the Visual Arts, 1957, pbk edn 1970; Possessed, 1959; The Future of the Arts, 1959, German edn 1960; A History of Renaissance Architecture, 1959; The Naked Flame, 1962; Architecture, 1964; To Kill a King, 1965, Portuguese edn 1967; A History of Classical Architecture, 1965; Historic Architecture of Newcastle upon Tyne, 1967, 2nd edn 1968; Civilization, the Next Stage, 1969, pbk edn 1971; The Romanesque Achievement, 1970; The Study of Architectural History, 1970; ed, Modern Architecture of Northern England, 1970; The Professional Artist in a Changing Society, 1970; Ecological Morality, 1972; The Garden Earth, 1972, pbk edn 1972; Towards a Humane Architecture, 1973; Return of the Pagan, 1974; (with U. Clark) Oriel Guides: Architecture of France, 1963; Architecture of Italy, 1964; Architecture of England, 1964; Photography for Tourists, 1966; (with U. Clark and H. W. Booton), The Great Tradition of Western Architecture 1966; contrib. numerous articles on French Architecture to Encyclop. Amer.; *contrib*. RIBA Jl, Jl Royal Soc. Arts. *Address*: School of Architecture, The Univ., Newcastle upon Tyne NE1 7RU.

Almansi, Prof. Guido; Professor of Italian, University College, Dublin, since 1972; *b* 1931; marr. diss.; one *d*. BA Hons London 1964 (1st cl.); MA Kent 1969. Glasgow University: Assistant, 1962–64; Lectr, 1964–66; University of Kent: Lectr, 1966–69; Sen. Lectr, 1969–71. Vis. Assoc. Prof., Univ. of BC, 1969–70; Vis. Prof., Carleton Univ., Ottawa, 1973. *Publications*: L'Estetica Dell' Osceno, 1974; *contrib*. Studi sul Boccaccio, Giornale Storico Della Letteratura Italiana, Paragone, Strumenti Critici, Studi Novecenteschi, Studi Secenteschi, TLS. *Address*: Dept of Italian, Univ. College, Dublin 4, Eire.

Alston, Robin Carfrae, PhD; Lecturer in English, Leeds University, since 1964; *b* 1933; *m* 1957; two *s* one *d*. BA British Columbia 1954; MA Oxon; MA Toronto; PhD London. Mem., Council, Bibliographical Soc., London; Founder, Chm, and principal editor, Scolar Press Ltd. *Publications*: An Introduction to Old English, 1961; An Introduction to Old English, 1966; A Catalogue of Books relating to the English Language (1500–1800) in Swedish Libraries, 1965; English Language and Medieval English Literature: a Select Reading-List for Students, 1966; A Bibliography of the English Language from the Invention of Printing to the Year 1800, 20 vols (in progress), 1965– ; Alexander Gil's Logonomia Anglica (1619): a translation into Modern English, 1973; (with B. Danielsson) The Works of William Bullokar (in progress), 1966– ; 'English Studies': Cambridge Bibliography of English Literature, vol. III, rev. edn, 1970; English Linguistics 1500–1800: a Collection of Texts in Facsimile, 365 vols, 1967–73; *contrib*. Eng. Studies, Leeds Studies in Eng., Studia Neophilologica, Trans. Bibliograph. Soc., etc. *Address*: School of English, Leeds Univ., Leeds LS2 9JT.

Altham, Dr James Edward John; Assistant Lecturer in Philosophy, University of Cambridge, since 1972; *b* 1941; *m* 1965; one *s*. BA Cantab 1963, MA 1967, PhD Cantab 1969; Mem., Aristotelian Soc. Gonville and Caius College: Res. Fellow, 1965; Official Fellow, 1968; Tutor, 1968–73; Registrary, 1972– . *Publication*: The Logic of Plurality, 1971. *Address*: Gonville and Caius College, Cambridge.

Amann, Ronald; Lecturer in Soviet Politics and Science Policy, Centre for Russian and East European Studies, University of Birmingham, since 1969; *b* 1943; *m* 1965; two *s*. BSocSc (Moral and Political Philosophy) Birmingham 1964, MSocSc Birmingham 1967; Mem., Nat. Assoc. for Soviet and East European Studies (NASEES). Consultant OECD and Hon. Res. Assoc., Univ. of Birmingham, 1965–68; Asst Lectr, Univ. of Birmingham, 1968–69. External examiner, Univ. of Sussex. *Publications*: Science Policy in the USSR, English and French edns, 1969, Japanese edn 1970, German edn 1971; *contrib*. La Recherche, Affari Esteri, Minerva, New Scientist, Scientific American. *Address*: Centre for Russian and East European Studies, Univ. of Birmingham, PO Box 363, Edgbaston, Birmingham B15 2TT.

Ambler, Rodney William; Lecturer in History, Department of Adult Education, University of Hull, since 1970. Admin. Asst, Dept of Adult Educn, Univ. of Hull, 1966–70. *Address*: Dept of Adult Education, Univ. of Hull, 195 Cottingham Road, Hull HU5 2EQ.

Ambrose, Dr Peter John; Lecturer, School of Cultural and Community Studies, University of Sussex, since 1967; *b* 1933; *m* 1964; one *s* one *d*. BA London, MA McGill, DPhil Sussex; AKC. Asst Lectr, Univ. of Sussex, 1965–67. *Publications*: Analytical Human Geography, 1969; The Quiet Revolution, 1974; *contrib*. Canadian Geographer, Tijdschrift voor Economische en Sociale Geografie, Town Planning Rev., Trans Inst. British Geographers. *Address*: Arts Building, Univ. of Sussex, Brighton, Sussex BN1 9RH.

Amey, Ronald Leslie; Director of Post-experience Studies, University of Aston Management Centre, since 1972; *b* 1929; *m* 1948; two *s* one *d*. BA (Hons Econ.) Sheffield 1960; CEng MIMechE Sheffield 1963. Lectr in Work Study, Coll. of Advanced Technology, Birmingham, 1960–65; Sen. Lectr in Technical Aspects of Management, Univ. of Aston, 1965–72. *Address:* Univ. of Aston Management Centre, Maple House, 158 Corporation Street, Birmingham B46 6TE.

Ancot, Jean-Pierre, FAMG; Lecturer in Econometrics, University of Bristol, since 1973; *b* 1941; *m* 1967; one *s*. Maître en Sciences Economiques et Sociales, Namur, 1967; Member: Econometric Soc., Amer. Statistical Assoc.; Research Asst, Univ. of Bristol, 1967–68; Assistant Lecturer: Univ. of Bristol, 1968–70; Namur, Belgium, 1970–71; Bristol, 1971–73. *Address:* Univ. of Bristol, Senate House, Bristol BS8 7TH.

Anderman, Gunilla Margareta; Lecturer in Linguistics and Swedish Language, Department of Linguistics and Regional Studies, University of Surrey, since 1966; *b* 1938; *m* 1963. Fil Mag Stockholm 1961, Academic Post-grad. Dip. in General Linguistics London 1969. Chief examiner, Swedish, Inst. of Linguists, 1969– . *Publications:* trans., (with S. D. Anderman), The Changing Roles of Men and Women, ed Dahlström, 1967; *contrib.* Year's Work in Mod. Lang. Studies (Swedish Lang. Sect.), Eng. Lang. Teaching. *Address:* Dept of Linguistic and Regional Studies, Univ. of Surrey, Guildford, Surrey GU2 5XH.

Anderman, Steven D.; Senior Lecturer in Law, University of Warwick, since 1973; *b* 1934; *m* 1963. BA (Econ) New York 1957; LLB Yale 1960; MSc London 1966. Res. Fellow, Stockholm, 1960–61; Lectr, Univ. of Maryland, 1961–66; Staff Tutor in Industrial Relations, Univ. of Oxford, 1966–68; Lectr in Law, Univ. of Warwick, 1968–73. Part-time Advr, NBPI, 1968; Part-time Advr, Dept of Employment, 1969–70. Advisory Editor, Industrial Relations Law Report, 1972. *Publications:* Trade Unions and Technological Change, 1967; Voluntary Dismissals, 1972; Procedure and the Industrial Relations Act, Unfair Dismissals and the Law, 1973. *Address:* Sch. of Law, Univ. of Warwick, Coventry CV4 7AL.

Anderson, Alexander; University Librarian, Heriot-Watt University, since 1967; *b* 1924; *m* 1947; one *s* one *d*. MA Edinburgh 1945, MA Southampton 1962; FLA 1952. Sen. Asst Librarian, aftw. Sub- Librarian, Southampton Univ. 1953–65; Deputy Librarian, Exeter Univ., 1966–67; Chm., Library Assoc. Univ. Coll. and Research Section, 1971–72; Mem., Executive of Assoc. of Univ. Teachers, 1971– ; Vice-Pres., 1973– . *Publications:* The Old Libraries of Fife, 1953; Catalogue of the Perkins Agricultural Library, Southampton, 1961; *contrib.* British academic libraries, 1973. *Address:* Heriot-Watt Univ. Library, Edinburgh EH1 1HX.

Anderson, Prof. George Wishart, MA, DD, TeolD, FBA; Professor of Hebrew and Old Testament Studies, University of Edinburgh, since 1968; *b* 1913; *m* 1959; one *s* one *d*. MA St Andrews 1935 (1st cl. Classics); BA Cantab 1937 (1st cl. Theology), MA Cantab 1946; Hon DD St Andrews 1959, Hon TeolD Lund 1971. Lectr, St Andrews, 1956–58; Prof. of Old Testament Studies, Durham, 1958–62; Prof. of Old Testament Literature and Theology, Edinburgh, 1962–68. Society for Old Testament Study: Editor, Book List, 1957–66; Pres., 1963; Hon. Sec. (Foreign), 1964– ; Sec., Internat. Organization for Study of OT, 1953–71, Pres., 1971–74. *Publications:* A Critical Introduction to the Old Testament, 1959; The History and Religion of Israel, 1966; trans. S. Mowinckel: He That Cometh, 1963; A. S. Kapelrud: The Ras Shamra Discoveries and the Old Testament, 1944; *contrib.* Etudes Théol. Rélig., Expos. Times, Jl Biblical Lit., Theol Studies. *Address:* New College, The Mound, Edinburgh EH1 2LX.

Anderson, Dr Graham; Lecturer in Classics, University of Kent, since 1973; *b* 1945; *m* 1969. MA Glasgow 1966 (1st cl. Classics), MPhil National Univ. of Ireland (distinction, Medieval Studies) 1972, DPhil Oxford 1974; ARCO 1968. Asst, UC Dublin, 1968–70; Asst Lectr, 1970–73. *Address:* Keynes College, Univ. of Kent at Canterbury, Canterbury, Kent CT2 7NZ.

Anderson, Rev. Prof. Hugh, MA, BD, PhD, DD; Professor of New Testament Language, Literature and Theology, University of Edinburgh, since 1966; *b* 1920; *m* 1945; one *s* one *d*. MA Glasgow 1941 and 1949 (2nd cl. Classics and 1st cl. Semitics), BD Glasgow 1945 (1st cl. New Testament), PhD Glasgow 1951, DD Glasgow (hon. causa) 1971. Lectr in Hebrew, Glasgow, 1946–51; A. B. Bruce Lectr, Glasgow, 1951–54; Prof. of Biblical Criticism, Duke Univ., North Carolina, 1957–66; Haskell Lectr, Oberlin College, Ohio, 1971. Minister of Trinity Church of Scotland, Glasgow, 1951–57; Convener of Cttee on Post-grad. Studies in Theology, Edinburgh, 1969– . *Publications:* Jesus and Christian Origins, 1964; Jesus, 1968; The Intertestamental Period, in, The Bible and History, ed W. Barclay; *contrib.* Expository Times, Interpretation, Scottish Jl of Theology. *Address:* Faculty of Divinity, Univ. of Edinburgh, New College, The Mound, Edinburgh EH1 2LX.

Anderson, James Ian; Lecturer in Management Operations, Loughborough University of Technology, since 1966; *b* 1914; *m* 1940; four *s*. Diploma in Management Studies 1954; MSc Loughborough 1971; MBIM 1962; Fellow, Inst. of Work Study Practitioners 1966. Sen. Lectr, Loughborough Coll. of Advanced Technology, 1956–66. *Publications:* *contrib.* Jl of Industrial Relations, Jl of Industrial Engineering (USA), Management Services. *Address:* Dept of Management Studies, Loughborough Univ. of Technology, Loughborough, Leics LE11 3TU.

Anderson, Prof. James Norman Dalrymple, OBE, LLD, FBA, QC; Professor of Oriental Laws, since 1953, and Director of the Institute of Advanced Legal Studies,

University of London, since 1959; *b* 1908; *m* 1933; two *d*. (one *s* decd). BA Cantab 1930 (1st cl. Pts I and II Law Tripos, Distinction in Pt I), LLB Cantab 1931 (1st cl.), MA Cantab 1934, LLD Cantab 1955; Hon. DD St Andrews 1974; FBA 1970. Called to the Bar (Gray's Inn) 1965. Superv., Clare Coll., Cambridge, 1930–31; Lectr, Sch. of Orient. Studies, Univ. of London, 1947–51, Reader, 1951–53; Hd, Dept of Law, SOAS, 1953–71; Dean, Fac. of Law, London Univ. 1964–68; Vis. Prof., Princeton and NY Univ., 1958; Vis. Prof., Harvard Univ. Law Sch., 1966. Pres., Soc. Public Teachers of Law, 1968–69; Chm., Hamlyn Trust; Mem., Colonial Office. Native Law Adv. Panel; Vice-Pres., Internat, Afr. Law Assoc., etc. Chm., House Laity, Gen. Synod C of E, 1970– . *Publications*: Islamic Law in Africa, 1954; Islamic Law in The Modern World, 1959; Into the World (the need and limits of Christian involvement), 1968; Christianity: The Witness of History, 1969; Christianity and Comparative Religion, 1970; Morality, Law and Grace, 1972; A Lawyer among the Theologians, 1973; ed, The World's Religions, 1950; ed, Changing Law in Developing Countries, 1963; ed, Family Law in Asia and Africa, 1968; *contrib*. Musl. Wld, Intern. Comp. Law Qly, Amer. Jl Comp. Law, Mod. Law Rev., Jl Royal Asian Soc., Jl Afr. Law, etc. *Address*: Institute of Advanced Legal Studies, 25 Russell Square, WC1B 5DR.

Anderson, Dr John Julian; Lecturer in English, Univ. of Manchester, since 1968; *b* 1938; *m* 1967; one *d*. BA (NZ) 1959, MA (NZ) 1960 (2nd cl. English); PhD Adelaide 1965. Tutor, Univ. of Adelaide, 1960-63; Lectr, Univ. of Sydney, 1964-67. *Publications*: ed, Patience, 1969; ed, The Canterbury Tales: a casebook, 1974; *contrib*. Modern Philology, Shakespeare Survey. *Address*: Dept of English, Univ. of Manchester, Manchester M13 9PL.

Anderson, Prof. Malcolm; Professor of Politics, University of Warwick, since 1973 (Senior Lecturer, 1965–73); *b* 1934; *m* 1957; two *s* one *d*. BA Oxford 1957, MA Oxford 1961, DPhil Oxford 1961. Asst Lectr in Govt, Univ. of Manchester, 1960-63; Lectr in Govt, Manchester, 1963–64; Rockefeller Res. Fellow, Inst. National des Politiques, Sciences, Paris, 1964–65; Vis. Prof., Univ. of Brit. Columbia, 1969. *Publications*: (jtly) The Right in France 1890-1919, 1962; Government in France: an Introduction to the Executive Power, 1970; Conservative Politics in France, 1972; *contrib*. Political Studies. *Address*: Dept of Politics, Univ. of Warwick, Coventry CV4 7AL.

Anderson, Dr Matthew Smith, MA, PhD, FRHistS; Professor of International History, Department of International History, London School of Economics, University of London, since 1972; *b* 1922; *m* 1954; two *d*. MA Edinburgh (1st cl. Hist.) 1947, PhD Edinburgh 1952. Asst in Hist., Edin., 1947–49; Asst Lectr in Political Hist., LSE, 1949–53; Lectr in International Hist., LSE, 1953–61, Reader 1961–72. *Publications*: Britain's Discovery of Russia, 1553–1815, 1958; Europe in the Eighteenth Century, 1961 (French edn

1968, Spanish edn 1964, Italian edn 1972); Eighteenth-Century Europe, 1966 (Spanish edn 1968); The Eastern Question, 1774–1923, 1966 (Hebrew edn 1972); The Great Powers and the Near East, 1774–1923, 1970; The Ascendancy of Europe, 1815–1914, 1972; *contrib*. American Slavic and East European Review; EHR; Bull. Inst. of Hist. Res.; Mariner's Mirror; Slavonic and East European Rev. *Address*: Dept of International History, London School of Economics, Houghton Street, Aldwych, WC2A 2AE.

Anderson, Michael John; Lecturer in Drama, University of Bristol, since 1966; *b* 1937; *m* 1973. BA Bristol 1961. Asst Lectr, in Drama, Bristol Univ., 1964–66. *Publications*: ed, Classical Drama and its influence, 1965; A Handbook of Contemporary Drama (with Jacques Guicharnaud and others), 1971, 2nd edn 1972; *contrib*. Greece and Rome. *Address*: Drama Dept, 29 Park Row, Bristol BS1 5LT.

Anderson, Olive; Reader in History, University of London, since 1969; *b* 1926; *m* 1954; two *d*. BA Oxon 1947 (1st cl. Mod. Hist.), BLitt Oxon 1949, MA Oxon 1951; FRHistS. Asst Lectr in History, Westfield Coll., Univ. of London, 1949–56, Lectr, 1958–69. *Publications*: A Liberal State at War, 1967; *contrib*. Bull. Inst. Hist. Res., Economica, Economic Hist. R., Engl. Hist. R., Hist. Jl, Jl Ecclesiastical Hist., Jl Mod. Hist., Law QR, Past and Present, Political Sci. Q., Public Adm., Victorian Stud., etc. *Address*: Westfield College, Univ. of London, Hampstead, NW3 7ST.

Anderson, Dr Robert David; Lecturer in History, University of Edinburgh, since 1969; *b* 1942. MA Oxon 1963, DPhil Oxon 1967. Univ. of Glasgow, 1967–69. *Publications*: *contrib*. Hist. of Educn, Past and Present. *Address*: Dept of History, William Robertson Building, George Square, Edinburgh.

Andison, Allan Charles; Director, The Language Centre, University of Newcastle upon Tyne, since 1969; *b* 1920; *m* 1948; one *d*. MA Oxon 1947, DipEd Oxon 1948. Lectr in Educn, 1959, Sen. Lectr in Educn, 1969, Univ. of Newcastle upon Tyne. *Address*: The Language Centre, Claremont Bridge, The Univ., Newcastle upon Tyne NE1 7RU.

Andreski, Prof. Stanislav Leonard; Professor of Sociology, University of Reading, since 1964; *b* 1919; *m* 1941; two *s* four *d*. BSc (Econ) London 1943 (1st cl.), MSc (Econ) London 1947, PhD London 1953; Mem., Brit. Soc. for Philosophy of Science; Mem., Cruising Assoc. Lectr in Sociology, Rhodes Univ., 1947–53; Sen. Res. Fellow in Anthropology, Manchester Univ., 1954–56; Lectr in Econs, Acton Tech. Coll., 1956–57; Lectr in Management Studies, Brunel Coll. of Tech., 1957–60; Prof. of Sociology, School of Soc. Sciences, Santiago, 1960–61; Sen. Res. Fellow, Nigerian Inst. of Social and Econ. Res., Ibadan, 1962–64; Vis. Prof. of Soc. and Anthropology, City Coll., City Univ. of NY, 1968–69. *Publications*: Military Organization and Society, 1954, 2nd edn 1968; (with Jan Ostaszewski and others) Class Structure and

Social Development, 1964; Elements of Comparative Sociology, 1964, American edn, as The Uses of Comparative Sociology, 1965, Spanish edn 1973; Parasitism and Subversion: The Case of Latin America, 1966, Spanish edn 1968; The African Predicament: A Study in Pathology of Modernisation, 1968; Social Sciences as Sorcery, 1972, Spanish edn 1973; The Prospects of a Revolution in America, 1973; *contrib*. American Soc. Rev., Brit. Jl Soc., Japanese Jl Soc., Jewish Jl Soc., Kultura, Science Jl, Social Forces, etc. *Address*: Dept of Sociology, Univ. of Reading, Whiteknights, Reading RG6 2AH.

Andrew, Dr Christopher Maurice; Director of Studies in History, Corpus Christi College, Cambridge, since 1968, and Lecturer in History, Cambridge University, since 1972; *b* 1941; *m* 1962; one *s* two *d*. BA Cantab 1962 (1st cl. History), MA Cantab 1965, PhD Cantab 1965. Res. Fellow, Gonville and Caius Coll., Cambridge, 1965–67; Asst Lectr, Cambridge Univ., 1967–72; Fellow, Corpus Christi Coll., 1967– ; Tutor, Corpus Christi Coll., 1969– ; Sec., Faculty Bd of History. *Publications*: Théophile Delcassé and the Making of the Entente Cordiale, 1968; The First World War: Causes and Consequences, 1970; contrib. Troubled Neighbours: Franco-British Relations in the Twentieth Century, ed N. Waites, 1971; *contrib*. Hist. Jl, Jl Contemp. Hist. *Address*: Corpus Christi College, Cambridge.

Andrewes, Prof. Antony, MBE, FBA; Wykeham Professor of Ancient History, University of Oxford, since 1953; *b* 1910; *m* 1938; two *d*. BA Oxon 1933 (1st cl. Lit. Hum.), MA Oxon 1936; FBA 1957; Pres. Hellenic Soc. 1962–64. Fellow Pembroke Coll., Oxford, 1933; Fellow New Coll., Oxford, 1946. *Publications*: (with R. Meiggs) Sources for Greek History, 478–431 BC, 1951; The Greek Tyrants, 1956; The Greeks, in History of Human Society, 1967, pbk edn, as Greek Society, 1971; (with K. J. Dover) vol. iv of A. W. Gomme's Historical Commentary to Thucydides, 1970; *contrib*. JHS, CQ, Phoenix, Historia, BSA, Hermes. *Address*: New College, Oxford.

Andrews, Dr Dennis Philip; Senior Research Fellow, Department of Communication, University of Keele, since 1969; *b* 1932. BA Cantab 1955 (Mech. Sciences Tripos), BSc London 1960 (Special Psychology), PhD London 1965. Res. Fellow, Univ. of Keele, 1960–69; Vis. Res. Fellow, Univ. of Calif., Berkeley, 1965–66. *Publications*: *contrib*. Jl Optical Soc. of America, Qly Jl Experim. Psych., Vision Res. *Address*: Dept of Communication, Univ. of Keele, Keele ST5 5BG.

Andrews, Prof. John A.; Professor of Law, University College of Wales, Aberystwyth, since 1967, and Head of Department; *b* 1935; *m* 1960; two *d*. BA Oxon 1956, BCL Oxon 1957, MA Oxon 1960; Barrister-at-Law, Gray's Inn, 1960. Asst Lectr, Manchester Univ., 1957–58; Lectr, Birmingham Univ., 1958–67. Member, Court of Governors; UCW, Aberystwyth; Univ. of Wales. *Publications*: ed, Welsh Studies in Public Law; *contrib*. Law Qly Rev., Mod. Law Rev., Conveyance and Property Lawyer,

British Tax Rev., Criminal Law Rev. etc. *Address*: Univ. Coll. of Wales, Aberystwyth SY23 2AX.

Andrews, Dr John Harwood; Lecturer in Geography, Trinity College, Dublin, since 1957. BA Cantab 1947, MA Cantab 1951; PhD London 1954; MA Dublin 1970, MLitt Dublin 1970; Mem., Inst. of Brit. Geographers, 1954. Asst Lectr, TCD, 1954, Tutor, 1962, Fellow, 1969. Pres., Geographical Soc. of Ireland, 1963–66; Sec., Irish National Cttee for Geography, 1963–73; Sec., Editorial Board of Atlas of Ireland, 1971–73. *Publications*: Ireland in maps, 1961; The Ordnance Survey in Nineteenth-Century Ireland, (forthcoming); *contrib*. Geography, Geographical Jl, Geographical Rev.; Imago Mundi, Irish Geography, etc. *Address*: Dept of Geography, Trinity College, Dublin 2.

Andrews, Dr Kenneth Raymond; Reader, Department of History, University of Hull, since 1964; *b* 1921; *m* 1969. BA London 1948 (1st cl. Hons History), PhD London 1951; FRHistS 1970. Mem. Council, Hakluyt Soc., 1958–62, 1966–70. *Publications*: English Privateering Voyages to the West Indies 1588–1595, 1959; Elizabethan Privateering, 1964, 2nd edn 1966; Drake's Voyages, 1967; The Last Voyage of Drake and Hawkins, 1972; *contrib*. Amer. Hist. Rev., EHR, History, Mar. Mirr., Wm and Mary Qly. *Address*: The Univ., Hull HU6 7RX.

Andrews, Lyman; Lecturer in American Literature, University of Leicester, since 1965; *b* 1938. BA Brandeis 1960 (Hons, Comparative Lit.); Mem., PEN; Mem., London Poetry Secretariat. Temp. Asst Lectr in English, Univ. of Wales, Swansea, 1964–65. Sunday Times Poetry Critic, 1968– . *Publications*: Ash Flowers, 1958; Fugitive Visions, 1962; The Death of Mayakovsky and Other Poems, 1969; Kaleidoscope, 1973. *Address*: Dept of English, The Univ. of Leicester, Leicester LE1 7RH.

Andrews, Richard Antony, MA; Senior Lecturer in Italian, University of Kent, since 1972; *b* 1939; *m* 1965. BA Oxon 1962 (Hons Modern Lang., Italian and French), MA Oxon 1967. Asst Lectr in Italian, Swansea, 1963, Lectr, 1963–72. *Publications*: ed, Antonio da Tempo, Summa Artis Rithmici Vulgaris Dictaminis (1332) (in preparation); *contrib*. Italian Studies, Studi e Problemi di Critica Testuale. *Address*: Univ. of Kent at Canterbury, Canterbury, Kent CT2 7NZ.

Andreyev, Dr Nikolay; Reader in Russian Studies, Cambridge University; *b* 1908; *m* 1954; two *s* one *d*. PhD Charles Univ., Prague 1933; MA Cantab 1951; Fellow, Inst. for Study of USSR, Munich, 1954–72; Fellow, Russian Historical Soc., Prague, 1934–45. T. G. Masaryk Res. Fellowship, 1933–38, Kondakov Inst. for Byzantine and Early Russian Studies, Prague; Lectr in Russian, Russian Free Univ., Prague, 1935–44; Fellow, 1933–45, and Actg Dir, Kondakov Inst., Prague, 1939–45; Lector in Russian, Cambridge Univ., 1948–51; Asst. Univ. Lectr, Cambridge, 1951–56, Univ. Lectr, 1956–73; Mem., Magdalene Coll., Cambridge,

1955– ; Official Fellow, Clare Hall, 1969– ; Vis. Lectr, London Univ., 1965–66. *Publications*: Studies in Muscovy, 1970; 13 Introductions to Everyman Library Series of Russian classics; *contrib.* Annales de l'Institut Kondakov, Slavonic and East European Rev., Slavic Rev., Revue des Etudes Slaves, Slavia, Jahrbücher für Geschichte Osteuropas, Trudy Otdela drevne-russkoy literatury (Acad. of Sciences of USSR), Novy Zhurnal (NY), Encyclopaedia Britannica, etc. *Address*: Dept of Slavonic Studies, Univ. of Cambridge, Cambridge.

Andrzejewski, Dr Bogumil Witalis; Reader in Cushitic Languages, School of Oriental and African Studies, University of London, since 1965; *b* 1922; *m* 1946. BA Oxon 1947 (English Lang. and Lit.), MA Oxon 1952, PhD London 1962 (Cushitic Lang.). Lectr in Cushitic Langs, SOAS, Univ. of London, 1952–64. Linguistic Res. Officer, Somaliland Protectorate, 1950–51; Lang. Superv. in Somali Service, BBC (part time), 1958–67; Asst Editor, Afr. Lang. Stud., 1963–65. *Publications*: (with M. H. I. Galaal) Hikmad Soomaali, 1956; The Declensions of Somali Nouns, 1964; (with I. M. Lewis) Somali Poetry – an introduction, 1964; *contrib.* Africa, Afr. Lang. Rev., Afr. Lang. Stud., Bull. SOAS, Jl Afr. Lang., Jl Folklore Inst. Indiana Univ., The Somaliland Jl. *Address*: School of Oriental and African Studies, Univ. of London, WC1E 7HP.

Angel, Rev. Gervais Thomas David, MA; Recognised Teacher in Theology, Department of Theology, Bristol University, since 1966; Dean of Studies, Trinity College; *b* 1936; *m* 1962; four *s* one *d*. BA Oxon 1959 (2nd cl. Classical Mods, 2nd cl. Litterae Humaniores, 2nd cl. Theology), MA Oxon 1962; Grad. Cert. in Educn London 1972; Mem., Eccles. Hist. Soc. of GB. Public examiner in NT Greek, Adv. Council to Church's Ministry, 1972– . Mem., Council, Trinity Coll., Bristol, 1972– . *Address*: Trinity College, Stoke Hill, Bristol BS9 1JP.

Angell, Alan Edward; Lecturer in Latin American Politics, Oxford University, and Fellow, St Antony's College, Oxford, since 1970; *b* 1939; *m* 1961; two *s*. BSc (Econ) London 1960. Member: Political Studies Assoc.; Soc. for Latin American Studies. Lectr, Univ. of Keele, 1961–66. Sen. Res. Fellow, St Antony's Coll., Oxford, and Royal Inst. of Internat. Affairs, 1966–70. *Publications*: Politics and the Labour Movement in Chile, 1972; *contrib.* Government and Opposition, Political Qly, Political Studies, Sociological Review Monographs, St Antony's Papers. *Address*: St Antony's College, Oxford.

Angell, Worcester Randolph; Lecturer in Physics and the History of Science and Technology, Heriot-Watt University, since 1961; *b* 1927; *m* 1956; three *s* one *d*. BS Tufts Univ. 1950 (Physics); Mem., Brit. Soc. Hist. Sci. Res. Asst, Harvard Coll. Observatory, 1950–53; Royal Coll. of Sci. and Technol., Glasgow, 1958–61. Trav. Fellowship, Goldsmiths' Co., 1972–73. Cnsltnt, Sci. Field; Ed., Clarendon Press, Oxford Univ., 1969–72.

Publications: Var. signed articles, in, Encyclopaedic Dictionary of Physics, 1960. *Address*: Physics Dept, Heriot-Watt Univ., Edinburgh EH1 1HX.

Anglo, Margaret Mary; *see* McGowan, M. M.

Anglo, Dr Sydney, PhD, FSA; Senior Lecturer in the History of Ideas, Department of History, University College of Swansea, since 1969; *b* 1934; *m* 1964. BA London 1955 (Hons History), PhD London 1959; FSA, FRHistS. Fellow, Reading Univ., 1958–61; Lectr, Univ. Coll., Swansea, 1961–69; Sen. Fellow, Warb. Inst., 1971–72. Sec., Soc. for Renaiss. Studies, 1967–70. *Publications*: The Great Tournament Roll of Westminster, 1968; Machiavelli: a Dissection, 1969; Spectacle Pageantry and Early Tudor Policy, 1969; *contrib.* Bull. J. Rylands Libr., Guildhall Misc., Jl Soc. Archiv., Jl Warb. and Court. Insts, Fêtes de la Renaiss. *Address*: Dept. of History, Univ. College of Swansea, Singleton Park, Swansea SA2 8PP.

Annan, The Lord; Noël Gilroy Annan, OBE; Provost of University College London, since 1966; *b* 1916; *m* 1950; two *d*. Hon. DLitt York, Ontario, DUniv Essex; FRHistS. Fellow of King's Coll., Cambridge, 1944–56, 1966; Asst Tutor, 1947; Lectr in Politics, Cambridge Univ., 1948–66; Provost of King's Coll., Cambridge, 1956–66; Romanes Lectr, Oxford, 1965; Fellow, Berkeley Coll., Yale, 1963; Hon. Fellow, UCL, 1968. Chm., Departmental Cttee on Teaching of Russian in Schools, 1960; Chm., Academic Planning Bd, Univ. of Essex, 1962; Mem., Academic Adv. Cttee, Brunel Coll., 1964; Mem., Academic Planning Bd., Univ. of E Anglia, 1960; Mem., Public Schools Commn, 1966–70. Sen. Fellow, Eton Coll., 1956–66; Governor, Stowe Sch., 1945–66; Governor, Queen Mary Coll., London, 1956–60; Trustee, Churchill Coll., 1958; Trustee, British Museum, 1963; Mem., Arts Cttee, Gulbenkian Foundn, 1957–64; Chm., Educn Cttee, Gulbenkian Foundn, 1971. Le Bas Prize, 1958; Diamond Jubilee Medal, Inst. of Linguists, 1971. *Publications*: Leslie Stephen: his thought and character in relation to his time, 1951 (James Tait Black prize, 1951); The Curious Strength of Positivism in English Political Thought, 1959; Roxburgh of Stowe, 1965; The Intellectual Aristocracy, in, Studies in Social History, 1956; Kipling's Place in the History of Ideas, in, Kipling's Mind and Art, 1964. *Address*: Univ. College London, Gower Street, WC1E 6BT.

Annan, Brian; *see* Annan, W. R. B.

Annan, William Robin Brian, MA; Lecturer, Department of Phonetics, University of Leeds, since 1963; *b* 1936; *m* 1967; one *d*. MA Edinburgh 1959; Mem., Philological Soc.; Mem., African Studies Assoc., U.K.; Mem., Brain Research Assoc.; Mem., Linguistics Assoc., UK; Mem., IPA. Asst Lectr, UC Ibadan, 1960–62; Lectr in Linguistics and African Languages, Univ. of Ibadan, 1962–63. Warden of Hall of Residence, 1964–71; Mem., Advisory Cttee for Speech Therapy, Leeds Polytechnic, 1971– . *Publications*:

contrib. various articles. *Address*: Dept of Phonetics, Univ. of Leeds, Leeds LS2 9JT.

Annett, Prof. John, MA, DPhil, ABsS; Professor of Psychology, University of Warwick, since 1974; *b* 1930; *m* 1955; one *s* one *d*. BA Oxon 1953 (2nd cl. PPP), MA Oxon 1957, DPhil Oxon 1959; ABPsS. Res. Worker, Oxford Univ., 1955–60; Vis. Scientist, US Naval Training Devices Center, 1960; Sen. Res. Worker, Sheffield Univ., 1960–63; Lectr, Univ. of Aberdeen, 1963–65; Sen. Lectr, Univ. of Hull, 1965–68, Reader, 1968–72; Prof. of Psychology, Open Univ., 1972–74. Mem., SSRC Educ. Res. Bd, 1970–74; Central Training Council, Res. Cttee, 1968– ; Chem. Indust. Training Bd, Res. Cttee, 1970– ; Council, Brit. Psychol. Soc., 1969–72; Chm., Training Sect., Ergonom. Res. Soc., 1968–72; Editor, Progr. Learning and Educn Technol., 1965–69; Co-Editor, Brit. Jl Psychol., 1970–73. *Publications*: Feedback and Human Behaviour, 1969; *contrib.* Acta Psychol., Ergonom., Jl Ment. Sci., Occupa. Psychol., Qly Jl Exper. Psychol. *Address*: Dept of Psychology, Univ. of Warwick, Coventry CV4 7AL.

Anscombe, Gertrude Elizabeth Margaret, FBA; Professor of Philosophy, University of Cambridge, since 1970; Fellow, New Hall, Cambridge, since 1970; *b* 1919; *m* 1941; three *s* four *d*. 2nd cl. Hon. Mods 1939, 1st cl. Greats 1941, Oxford; FBA 1967. Research studentships, Oxford and Cambridge, 1941–44; Somerville Coll., Oxford; Research fellowships, 1946–64; Fellow, 1964–70; Hon. Fellow, 1970– . *Publications*: Intention, 1957; An Introduction to Wittgenstein's Tractatus, 1959; (with Peter Geach) Three Philosophers, 1961; translator and co-editor of posthumous works of Ludwig Wittgenstein. *Address*: New Hall, Cambridge.

Anstey, Prof. Roger T.; Professor of Modern History, University of Kent, since 1968; *b* 1927; *m* 1954; one *s* two *d*. BA Cantab 1950, MA Cantab 1952, PhD London 1957; Mem., Hist. Assoc., African Studies Assoc., Royal African Soc. Lectr, Univ. of Ibadan, Nigeria, 1952–57; Lectr, Univ. of Durham, 1958–66; Vis. Prof., Univ. of Brit. Columbia, 1966–67; Reader, Univ. of Durham, 1967–68. Mem., Senate Exec. Cttee, Univ. of Kent; Governor of Kent Coll., Canterbury, and Kent Coll., Pembury. *Publications*: Britain and the Congo in the Nineteenth Century, 1962; King Leopold's Legacy: The Congo under Belgian Rule, 1966; The Atlantic Slave Trade and British Abolition, 1975; *contrib.* African Hist. Studies, Econ. Hist. Rev., EHR. *Address*: Eliot College, Univ. of Kent at Canterbury, Canterbury, Kent CT2 7NZ.

Anthony, Dr William Shaen; Lecturer in Education, School of Education, University of Leicester, since 1966; *b* 1932. BA Oxford 1955, MA Oxford 1958, DPhil Oxford 1958; ABPsS. Temp. Lectr in Psychol., Durham Univ., 1958–59; Lectr in Psychol., Auckland Univ., 1960–65; Lectr in Educn, Hull Univ., 1965–66. *Publications*: *contrib.* Br. Jl Educ. Psychol., Br. Jl Psychol., Jl Educ. Psychol. *Address*: School of Education, 21 University Road, Leicester LE1 7RF.

Antonovics, Dr Atis Valdis; Lecturer, Department of History, University of Bristol, since 1966; *b* 1941; *m* 1965; two *s*. BA Oxford 1963, DPhil Oxford 1971. *Publications*: *contrib.* Papers Brit. Sch. at Rome, Eur. Studies Rev. *Address*: Dept of History, Univ. of Bristol, Bristol BS8 1TH.

Anwar, Khaidir; Lecturer in Indonesian, SE Asia Department, School of Oriental and African Studies, University of London, since 1973; *b* 1932; *m* 1957; three *d*. BA Padjadjaran Univ., FKIP, Bandung, 1958, MA, TC Columbia Univ., NY, 1960, Dip. in Applied Linguistics, Edinburgh Univ. 1964. Lectr in Language and Linguistics, IKIP Bandung, 1961, Sen. Lectr, 1968– . IKIP Presidium, 1966; Mem. Cttee for Comprehensive Schs in Indonesia, 1972–73. *Publications*: (co-translator), Islam Djalan Mutlak (Islam the Straight Path), Djakarta 1962; Some Problems of Islamic Education (in Indonesian), IKIP Bandung, 1970; History of Islamic Movements in Indonesia (in Indonesian), FKSS, IKIP Bandung, 1972. *Address*: School of Oriental and African Studies, Malet Street, London WC1E 7HP.

Aplin, Kenneth Ernest; Lecturer, Building Economics and Measurement, Department of Building, University of Aston, since 1965; *b* 1930; *m* 1957. one *s*. BSc Aston 1968; AIAS, AIArb. *Address*: Dept of Building, Univ. of Aston in Birmingham, Gosta Green, Birmingham B4 7ET.

Appleton, Dr James Henry, MA MSc, PhD; Reader in Geography, University of Hull, since 1965; *b* 1919; *m* 1943; three *s*. BA Oxon 1943, MA Oxon 1945, BSc Dunelm 1950, MSc Dunelm 1956, PhD Hull 1964; FRGS. Asst Lectr, Univ. Coll., Hull, 1950–52; Lectr, 1952–54; Lectr, Hull Univ., 1954–64; Sen. Lectr, 1964–65; Vis. Lectr, UNE Armidale, 1961. *Publications*: The Geography of Communications in Great Britain, 1962; A Morphological Approach to the Geography of Transport, 1965; Disused Railways in the Countryside of England and Wales, 1970; *contrib.* Geography, Scot. Geog. Mag., Trans. Inst. Brit. Geog., Transports. *Address*: Dept of Geography, Univ. of Hull, Hull HU6 7RX.

Apter, Dr Michael John; Senior Lecturer, Department of Psychology, University College Cardiff, since 1973 (Lecturer, 1967–73); *b* 1939; *m* 1964. BSc Bristol 1960; PhD Bristol 1964; ABPS. Jun. Fellow, Bristol, 1962–63. Hd of Res. and Validation Dept, Teaching Programmes Ltd, 1964–67. *Publications*: Cybernetics and Development, 1966, pbk edn 1969, Russian edn 1970; An Introduction to Psychology, 1967; The New Technology of Education, 1968, Yugoslav edn 1971, Italian edn 1972; The Computer Simulation of Behaviour, 1970, US edn 1971, Japanese edn 1972, Polish edn 1973, Brazilian edn 1973; ed jtly, The Computer in Psychology, 1973; *contrib.* Jl Theoret. Biol., Leonardo, Monogr. Social Rev., Progr. Learn. *Address*: Dept of Psychology, Univ College Cardiff, Cathays Park, Cardiff CF1 1XL.

Ap-Thomas, Dafydd Rhys, MA, BD; Senior Lecturer in Hebrew and Biblical Studies,

University of Wales at Bangor, since 1964; *b* 1912; *m* 1940; one *s* one *d*. BA (Hebrew) Wales 1934, BA (Theol.) Oxon 1937, MA Oxon 1942, BD London 1943. Asst Lectr, Bangor, 1938; Lectr, 1941; Vis. Prof., Univ. of Toronto, 1965. Dean of Divinity, 1961–64; Mem., Council, Brit. Sch. of Archaeol. in Jerus., 1964–71; Hon. Sec., Soc. for OT Study, 1961–72, Pres., 1974. *Publications*: Primer of OT Text Criticism, 1947, 2nd edn 1964, US edn 1965; trans. O. Eissfeldt: 'Prophetic Literature' and W. Baumgartner: 'Wisdom Literature', in, OT and Modern Study, ed H. H. Rowley, 1951, 2nd edn 1968; trans. S. Mowinckel: The Psalms in Israel's Worship, 1962; trans. M. Noth: The Laws in the Pentateuch and Other Essays, 1966; 'Jerusalem', in, Archaeol and OT Study, ed D. W. Thomas, 1967; 'Two Notes on Isaiah', in, Essays in honour of G. W. Thatcher, ed E. C. B. MacLaurin, 1967; 'All the King's Horses', in, Proclamation and Presence, ed Durham and Porter, 1970; 'Archaeology', 'Geography', 'History', in, Understanding the OT, ed O. J. Lace, 1972; 'Phoenicia', in, Peoples of OT Times, ed D. J. Wiseman, 1973; ed, Efrydiau Beiblaidd Bangor, 1973; *contrib*. Expos. T., JBL, JNES, JSS, PEQ, SJTh, VT. *Address*: Univ. Coll. of North Wales, Bangor LL57 2DG.

Aquilecchia, Prof. Giovanni; Professor of Italian, University of London, since 1970; *b* 1923; *m* 1951 (div. 1973); two *s* one *d*. DottLett Rome 1946, Dip. Perfezionamento in Filologia Moderna, Rome 1948; MA Manchester 1965. Asst in Italian, Univ. of Rome, 1946–49; Boursier du Gouvernement Français at Collège de France, Univ. of Paris, 1949–50; British Council Scholar, Warburg Inst., Univ. of London, 1950–51; Asst, Dept of Italian Studies, Univ. of Manchester, 1951–53; Asst Lectr in Italian, UCL, 1953–55, Lectr, 1955–59; Libero Docente di Letteratura Italiana, Univ. of Rome, 1958– ; Reader in Italian, UCL, 1959–61; Prof. of Italian Lang. and Lit., Univ. of Manchester, 1961–70. Corr. Fellow, Arcadia, 1961. *Publications*: Giordano Bruno, 1971; critical editions of Giordano Bruno: La Cena de le Ceneri, 1955; Due Dialoghi sconosciuti, 1957; Dialoghi Italiani, 1958; Praelectiones geometricae e Ars deformationum, 1964; De la causa, principio et uno, 1973; Pietro Aretino: Sei Giornate, 1969; ed jtly, Essays on Italian Language and Literature, 1971; *contrib*. Atti dell'Accad. dei Lincei, Atti e Memorie dell'Arcadia, Bull. dell'Accad. della Crusca, Bull. John Rylands Library, Cultura Neolatina, Dizionario biografica degli italiani, Enciclopedia Dantesca, Encyclopaedia Britannica, Engl. Miscellany, Giornale storico della letteratura italiana, Lettere italiane, Studi Secenteschi, Studi Tassiani, etc. *Address*: Dept of Italian, Bedford Coll., Regent's Park, NW1 4NS.

'Arafat, Prof. Walid Najib, BA, PhD; Professor of Arabic and Islamic Studies, and Director, Institute of Arabic and Islamic Studies, University of Lancaster, since 1972; *b* 1921; *m* 1951; two *s*. Coll. Dipl. and Teachers Cert. Arab Coll., Jerusalem, 1941; BA London 1947 (Gen. Engl., Latin, Arabic), BA London 1949 (Hons Engl.), BA London 1950

(Arabic), PhD London 1953 (Arabic); FRAS. Lectr in Arabic, SOAS, 1951–61, Reader, 1961–72. *Publications*: Dīwān of Ḥassān Ibn Thābit (G. M. Series No. XXV), 1971: *contrib*. Bull. SOAS, EI, IQ, JRAS, JRAS Bengal, JSS, BJHS; In Arabic: al-Aqlām, Hunā London. *Address*: Institute of Arabic and Islamic Studies, Univ. of Lancaster, Bailrigg, Lancaster LA1 4YW.

Archer, Margaret; Senior Lecturer in Medieval History, School of History, University of Birmingham, since 1965. BA Liverpool (1st cl. Hist.) 1933, Cambridge Cert. of Educn 1934, BLitt Oxon 1936, MA Liverpool 1936. Lectr in Hist. and the Teaching of Hist., Educn Dept, Birmingham Univ., 1939; Lectr in Med. Hist., Birmingham Univ., 1947. *Publications*: ed, The Register of Bishop Philip Repingdon, 1405–19 (Lincoln Record Society), vols I and II, 1963 (other volumes in preparation); *contrib*. Univ. of Birmingham Hist. Jl. *Address*: School of History, Univ. of Birmingham, B15 2TT.

Archer, Dr Margaret Scotford; Lecturer in Sociology, Department of Sociology, University of Reading, since 1966; *b* 1943. BSc(Soc) London 1964, PhD London 1967. *Publications*: ed (with S. Giner), Contemporary Europe: Class, Status and Power, 1971; (with M. Vaughan), Social Conflict and Educational Change in England and France 1789–1848, 1971; ed, Students, University and Society; a comparative Sociological Review, 1972; trans. Sullerot: Women and Society, 1970; *contrib*. Brit. Jl Sociology, European Jl Sociology, State Sociale, Yearbook of Sociology of Religion in Britain. *Address*: Univ. of Reading, Whiteknights, Reading RG6 2AH.

Ardener, Edwin William; University Lecturer in Social Anthropology, University of Oxford, since 1963 and Fellow of St John's College Oxford, since 1969; *b* 1927. BA London 1948 (Anthropology), MA Oxon 1963; FRAI; Mem., Assoc. of Social Anthropologists (ASA). Research Fellow, WAISER/NISER (Univ. of Ibadan), 1952–62; Field Research, Nigeria and Cameroon; Oppenheimer Studentship, Oxford, 1961–62. Mem., Cttee ASA, 1966–70; Council RAI, 1968–73. *Publications*: Coastal Bantu of the Cameroons, 1956; Divorce and Fertility, 1962; ed, Social Anthropology and Language, 1971; (with S. Ardener and W. A. Warmington) Plantation and Village in the Cameroons, 1960; contrib. Social Change in Modern Africa, ed A. Southall, 1961; Witchcraft Accusations and Confessions, ed M. Douglas, 1970; History and Social Anthropology, ed I. Lewis, 1968; Malinowski Meml Lecture, 1971; The Interpretation of Ritual, ed J. S. La Fontaine, 1972; Specimens of Dialects by John Clarke, 1972; Problems of Population, ed H. B. Parry, 1974; *contrib*. Man, Africa, Brit. Jl Sociology. *Address*: Institute of Social Anthropology, 51 Banbury Road, Oxford; St John's College, Oxford.

Argyle, John Michael, MA, FBPsS; Reader in Social Psychology, Department of Experimental Psychology, Oxford University, since 1969; Fellow of Wolfson College, since 1965; *b* 1925; *m* 1949; one *s* three *d*. BA Cantab

1950 (1st cl. Experimental Psychology), MA Cantab 1951, Oxon 1952; Fellow of the Brit. Psychol. Soc., 1965; Chm., Social Psychol. Sect., Brit. Psychol. Soc., 1964–67, 1972–74; Mem., European Assoc. for Experimental Social Psych. Lectr in Social Psych., Oxford, 1952; Fellow at the Center for Advanced Studies in the Behavioural Sciences, Stanford, 1958–59; Acting Sen. Tutor, Wolfson Coll., 1972; Vis. Lectr or Prof. at univs in USA, Canada, Israel, Belgium and Africa. Social Psych. Editor of the Brit. Jl of Soc. and Clinical Psych., 1961–67; Editor, Penguin Books Science of Behaviour Monographs, Soc. Psych. Section. Chm., Soc. Psych. Section of the BPS 1964–67; Mem., Psych. Cttee of SSRC 1968–72. *Publications*: The Scientific Study of Social Behaviour, 1957; Religious Behaviour, 1958; Psychology and Social Problems, 1964; The Psychology of Interpersonal Behaviour, 1967, 1972; Social Interaction, 1969; The Social Psychology of Work, 1972; Social Encounters, 1973; *contrib*. Brit. Jl Psych., Brit. Jl Soc. and Clin. Psych., Human Relations, Sociometry, Eur. Jl of Experimental Soc. Psych., and other jls. *Address*: Dept of Experimental Psychology, South Parks Road, Oxford OX1 3PS.

Arkieson, George Kay Walker, DFC, MA, LLB; Registrar and Secretary, The University of Aston in Birmingham, since 1973; *b* 1923; *m* 1958; one *s* one *d*. MA Edinburgh 1947, LLB 1949; Admitted Solicitor in Scotland, 1949; Dip. in Administrative Law and Practice 1950. Asst Registrar, Fourah Bay Coll., Univ. Coll. of Sierra Leone, 1959–62; Academic Registrar, Coll. of Advanced Tech., Birmingham, 1962–66; Academic Registrar, The Univ. of Aston in Birmingham, 1966–73. *Address*: Univ. of Aston in Birmingham, Gosta Green, Birmingham B4 7ET.

Armitage, Prof. Arthur Llewellyn; Vice-Chancellor, University of Manchester, since 1970; *b* 1916; *m* 1940; two *d*. MA Cambridge 1936, LLB Cambridge 1937; LLD (Hon) Manchester 1970; called to the Bar, Inner Temple 1940, Pres., Soc, of Public Teachers of Law, 1967, Hon. Bencher 1969. Fellow and Dir. of Studies in Law, Queens' Coll., Cambridge, 1945–58; Lectr in Law, Univ. of Cambridge, 1947–70; Pres., Queens' Coll., Cambridge, 1958–70; Vice-Chancellor, Univ. of Cambridge, 1965–67; Prof. of Common Law, Univ. of Manchester, 1970– . Mem. and Chm., Wages Councils, 1955–70; Mem., Chm's Panel, Indust. Ct, 1961– ; Mem., UGC, 1967–70; Chm. of Brit. Cttee of Award, Harkness Fellowships, 1969– ; Chm., Adv., Cttee on Supply and Trng of Teachers, 1973– . *Publications*: (with J. W. C. Turner) Case Book on Criminal Law, edns 1952, 1958, 1964; (jtly), Clerk and Lindsell on Torts, edns 1954, 1961, 1969; *contrib*. Cambridge Law. *Address*: Univ. of Manchester, Oxford Road, Manchester M13 9PL.

Armstrong, Annette Elizabeth; Vice-Principal and Tutor in Modern Languages, Somerville College, Oxford, University Lecturer in French Literature, since 1950; *b* 1917; *m* 1953. BA Oxford 1940 (1st cl. Hons Mod. Langs), MA 1943, DPhil 1949; Member: The Bibliographical Soc., the Soc. for French Studies, Modern Humanities Res. Assoc., Soc. for Renaissance Studies etc. *Publications*: Robert Estienne, Royal Printer: an historical study of the elder Stephanus, 1954; Ronsard and the Age of Gold, 1968; *contrib*. Bibliothèque d'Humanisme et Renassance, Proceedings of the Huguenot Society of London, etc. *Address*: Somerville College, Oxford, OX2 6HD.

Armstrong, Dr Eric George Abbott; Senior Lecturer in Industrial Relations, Manchester Business School, University of Manchester, since 1967; *b* 1923; *m* 1948; two *d*. BA Birmingham 1950, MCom Birmingham 1962; PhD Birmingham 1966; Mem., British Univs Industrial Relations Assoc. Lectr in Industrial Relations, Univ. of Aston in Birmingham, 1966; Dean, Faculty of Business Admin., Univ. of Manchester, 1973– . *Publications*: Industrial Relations – an introduction, 1969; Straitjacket or Framework? – the implications for management of the Industrial Relations Act, 1973; *contrib*. Brit. Jl Indust. Rels, Bus. Horizs, Calif. Man. Rev., Indust. Rels, Manchester Sch., Scot. Jl Polit. Econ. *Address*: Manchester Business School, Booth Street West, Manchester M15 6PB.

Armstrong, Isobel M.; Lecturer, Department of English, University of Leicester, since 1971; *b* 1937; *m* 1961; one *s* one *d*. BA Leicester 1959 (1st cl. Hons), PhD Leicester 1963. Lectr in English, University Coll., London, 1963–70. *Publications*: Arthur Hugh Clough (British Council Pamphlet), 1962; The Major Victorian Poets: Reconsiderations, 1969; ed with introduction, Victorian Scrutinies: Reviews of Poetry, 1830–70, 1972; Browning, in, Writers and their Background series (forthcoming). *Address:* Dept of English, The Univ., University Road, Leicester LE1 7RH.

Armstrong, Terence Edward, PhD; Assistant Director of Research, Scott Polar Research Institute, University of Cambridge, since 1956; *b* 1920; *m* 1943; two *s* two *d*. BA Cantab 1941, MA Cantab 1947, PhD Cantab 1951; Hon LLD McGill 1963. Res. Fellow, Scott Polar Res. Inst., 1947–56; Fellow, Clare Hall, 1964– , Tutor, 1967– ; US Nat. Sci. Foundn Sen. Foreign Scientist Fellowship, Univ. of Alaska, 1970. Hon. Sec., Hakluyt Soc., 1965– . *Publications*: The Northern Sea Route, 1952; The Russians in the Arctic, 1958, 2nd edn, 1960; Sea Ice North of the USSR, 1958; Russian Settlement in the North, 1965; (jtly) Illustrated Glossary of Snow and Ice, 1966; *contrib*. Geog. Jl, Jl Glaciol., Inter-Nord, Polar Record. *Address*: Scott Polar Research Institute, Cambridge CB2 1ER.

Armstrong, Dr Walter Alan, BA, PhD, FRHistS; Senior Lecturer in Economic and Social History, University of Kent at Canterbury, since 1971; *b* 1936; *m* 1962; one *s* one *d*. BA Birmingham 1960 (Medieval and Modern History), PhD Birmingham 1967. Asst Lectr, later Lectr in Economic and Social History, Nottingham Univ., 1962–68; Lectr in History, Univ. of Warwick, 1968–69; Lectr in Economic and Social History, Univ. of Kent at

Canterbury, 1969-71. *Publications*: Stability and Change in an English County Town: a Social Study of York, 1801-51, 1974; contrib. Introduction to English Historical Demography, ed E. A. Wrigley, 1966; The Study of Urban History, ed H. J. Dyos, 1968; The Study of Nineteenth Century Society, ed E. A. Wrigley, 1972; Household and Family in Past Time, ed P. Laslett, 1972; British Censuses of the Nineteenth Century, ed R. Lawton, 1974; *contrib*. Annales de démographie historique, Econ. Hist. Rev. *Address*: Eliot College, Univ. of Kent at Canterbury, Canterbury, Kent CT2 7NZ.

Armstrong, Prof. William Arthur, MA, PhD; Professor of English, Birkbeck College, University of London, since 1974; *b* 1915; *m* 1951; one *s* one *d*. BA Sheffield 1938 (1st cl. English), DipEd Sheffield 1939, MA Sheffield 1940, PhD Yale 1943. Lectr, UCW, Aberystwyth, 1945; Lectr, KCL, 1948; Reader, KCL, 1961; Prof. Univ. of Hull, 1965; Prof. of English, Westfield Coll., 1967-74. Hon. Treas., English Assoc., 1959-62; Chm., Standing Conf. of Drama Assocs (Nat. Council for Social Service), 1965-68; Mem. of DES, Postgrad. Studentships Cttee, 1970- . *Publications*: The Elizabethan Private Theatres: facts and problems, 1958; Marlowe's Tamburlaine: the image and the stage, 1966; Sean O'Casey, 1967; Shakespeare's Typology: miracle and morality motifs in 'Macbeth', 1970; ed, Classic Irish Drama, 1964; ed, Elizabethan History Plays, 1965; assoc. ed, The Diary of Samuel Pepys, vols i-iii, 1970, vols. iv, v, 1971, vols vi, vii, 1972; Shakespeare's Histories: an anthology of modern criticism, 1972; *contrib*. English, English Studies, Modern Drama, Rev. of English Studies, Shakespeare Qly, Shakespeare Survey, Theatre Notebook, Teoria e Critica. *Address*: Birkbeck Coll., Malet Street, WC1E 7HX.

Armytage, Prof. Walter Harry Green; Professor of Education, Department of Education, University of Sheffield, since 1954; *b* 1915; *m* 1958; one *s*. 1st cl. History Tripos Cambridge 1937, Cert. in Educn Cambridge 1938. Lectr, Sheffield Univ., 1946-52; Senr Lectr, Sheffield Univ., 1952-54; Pro-Vice-Chancellor, Sheffield Univ., 1964-68; Vis. Lectr, Univ. of Michigan, 1955, 1959, 1961, 1963; Ballard Matthews Lectr, Univ. Coll. of N. Wales, 1963; Thomas. Hawksley Lectr, IMechE, 1969; Silvanus P. Thompson Lectr, IEE, 1972. Academic Planning Board, New Univ. of Ulster, 1964-68; Academic Advisory Board, New Univ. of Ulster, 1964-71. *Publications*: A. J. Mundella, 1951; Thomas Hughes, 1952; Civic Universities, 1955; Sir Richard Gregory, 1957; Heavens Below, 1962; Four Hundred Years of English Education, 1964; A Social History of Engineering, 1961, 3rd edn 1970; The Rise of the Technocrats, 1965; The American Influence on English Education, 1967; The French Influence on English Education, 1967; Yesterday's Tomorrows, 1967; The German Influence on English Education, 1969; The Russian Influence on English Education, 1969. *Address*: Dept of Education, Univ. of Sheffield, Sheffield S10 2TN.

Arnett, Dr Roger R.; Lecturer, Department of Geography, Hull University, since 1971; *b* 1943; *m* 1966; two *s*. BA Leeds 1965, MA Queensland, Australia 1968, PhD Hull 1972; Mem., Inst. of British Geographers; Tutor, Hull Univ., 1968-71. *Publications*: *contrib*. Australian Geog. Studies, Trans Inst. British Geographers, Révue de Géomorphologie Dynamique. *Address*: Dept of Geography, The Univ., Hull HN6 7RX.

Arnold, Dr Benjamin C. B.; Lecturer, Department of History, University of Reading, since 1974; *b* 1943. MA Oxon 1965 (Mod. History), DPhil Oxon 1973. Lectr, Univ. of Edinburgh, 1968-74. *Address*: Dept of History, Univ. of Reading, Whiteknights, Reading, Berks RG6 2AH.

Arnold, Prof. Denis Midgley, MA, BMus, Hon. RAM, ARCM; Heather Professor of Music, University of Oxford, from April 1975; *b* 1926; *m* 1951; two *s*. MA Sheffield 1950; Hon. RAM 1971; Mem., RMA, Internat. Musicological Soc., Gesellschaft für Musikforschung, Società Italiana di Musicologia. Lectr in Music, Queen's Univ., Belfast, 1951-60, Reader in Music, 1960-64; Sen. Lectr in Music, Univ. of Hull, 1964-68; Prof. of Music, Univ. of Nottingham, 1969-75. *Publications*: G. Gabrieli, Opera Omnia, 1957-73; Marenzio, 1965; Claudio Monteverdi 1963; Monteverdi Madrigals, 1967; Monteverdi Companion, 1968; Beethoven Companion, 1971; *contrib*. Acta Musicologica; Galpin Soc. Jl; Musica Disciplina; Music and Letters; Musical Qly; Proc. Royal Musical Assoc. *Address*: (to April 1975) Dept of Music, Lenton Grove, Beeston Lane, Nottingham NG7 2QN; (from April 1975) Faculty of Music, University of Oxford, Oxford OX1 3BD.

Arnold, John André; Lecturer in Accounting, Department of Accounting and Business Finance, University of Manchester, since 1971; *b* 1944. MSc London 1969 (Accounting and Finance); ACA 1967, ATII 1967. Teaching Fellow, London Sch. of Econs and Political Sci., 1967-69; Lectr in Accounting, Univ. of Kent, 1969-71. *Publications*: Pricing and Output Decisions, 1973; *contrib*. Account. and Bus. Res., Canad. Chart. Account. *Address*: Dept of Accounting and Business Finance, Univ. of Manchester, Manchester M13 9PL.

Arnott, Prof. David Whitehorn, MA, PhD; Professor of West African Languages, School of Oriental and African Studies, University of London, since 1966; *b* 1915; *m* 1942; two *d*. BA Cantab (1937 (Classics), MA Cantab 1944, PhD London 1960; Mem., Philol Soc. of GB, Afr. Studies Assoc. of UK. Lectr in West African Studies, SOAS, London Univ., 1951-60, Reader, 1961-66; Vis. Sen. Lectr, Ibadan Univ., 1962; Vis. Prof. UCLA, 1963; Vis. Prof., Abdullahi Bayero Coll (Ahmadu Bello Univ.), Kano, 1970, 1971, 1972. Colonial Admin. Service, N Nigeria, 1939-51; Mem., Council, Afr. Studies Assoc. of UK, 1968-71. *Publications*: The Nominal and Verbal Systems of Fula, 1970; *contrib*. Bull. SOAS, Africa, Afr. Lang. Studies, Jl W. Afr. Lang., Afr. und Übersee. *Address*: Dept of

Africa, School of Oriental and African Studies, Univ. of London, WC1E 7HP.

Arnott, Prof. James Fullarton, TD, MA, BLitt; Head of Department of Drama, University of Glasgow, since 1966, Professor since 1973; *b* 1914; *m* 1945; one *s*. MA Glasgow 1935 (1st cl. English Lang. and Lit.), BLitt Oxon 1938; Asst Lectr, Hull, 1938; asst Lectr, Glasgow, 1939–44; Lectr, 1944–62; Sen. Lectr, 1962–71; Reader 1971; Vis, Prof., Coll. of Wooster, Ohio, 1959–60; Rockefeller Fellow, 1950; Fellow, Folger Shakespeare Library, 1964; Editor, Theatre Research/Recherches Théâtrales, 1964– . Governor, Royal Scottish Acad. of Music and Drama, 1964– ; Dir, Citizens' Theatre, Glasgow, 1970– ; Dir, Scottish Theatre Ballet, 1970– ; Mem., Scottish Arts Council, 1972– . Major Productions: Love's Labour's Lost, 1964; The Man of Mode, 1966; The Way of the World, 1968; A Satire of the Three Estates, 1969; The Forrigan Reel, 1970; The Two Gentlemen of Verona, 1972. *Publications*: (with J. W. Robinson) English Theatrical Literature 1559–1900: a bibliography, 1970; Shakespeare and the Marvellous, in Le Merveilleux et les Arts du Spectacle, 1963; Nineteenth Century Drama in the New Cambridge Bibliography of English Literature, 1969; *contrib.* Theatre Notebook. *Address*: Dept of Drama, Univ. of Glasgow, Glasgow G12 8RZ.

Arnott, Prof. William Geoffrey, MA, PhD; Professor of Greek Language and Literature, University of Leeds, since 1968; *b* 1930; *m* 1955; three *d*. BA Cantab 1952 (1st cl. Classics), MA Cantab 1956, PhD Cantab 1960. Asst Lectr in Greek, Bedford Coll. Univ. of London, 1955–59; Asst Lectr in Classics, Univ. of Hull, 1960–61; Lectr in Classics, Univ. of Newcastle upon Tyne, 1961–66 (1961–63 King's Coll. in the Univ. of Durham); Sen. Lectr in Classics, Univ. of Newcastle upon Tyne, 1966–67; Mem., Inst. for Advanced Study, Princeton, 1973. Schoolmaster, Bristol Grammar School, 1952–53; Asst Dir of Examinations, Civil Service Commn, 1959–60; Mem. Council, Soc. for Promotion of Hellenic Studies, 1965–68; Council, Joint Assoc. of Classical Teachers, 1971– ; Council, Classical Assoc., 1971– ; Classical Jls Board, 1970– . *Publications*: Trans. Menander: Dyskolos, or The Man who did not like People, 1960; *contrib.* Arethusa, Bull. of the Inst. of Classical Studies, Classical Qly, Classical Rev., Classica et Mediaevalia, Greece and Rome, Gnomon, etc.; Encyclopaedia Britannica, Oxford Classical Dictionary, 2nd edn, 1970. *Address*: Dept of Greek, Univ. of Leeds, Leeds LS2 9JT.

Arnould, Prof. Emile Jules François; Professor, Department of French, University of Dublin, since 1945; *b* 1898. LèsL 1932, BA London 1933, MA London 1935 (Distinction), PhD London 1937, DLit London 1944, DèsL Paris 1947; Fellow, TCD; MRIA; Sòci dou Felibrige – Lauréat de l'Institut. Asst in French, Edinburgh, 1932–34; Asst, Manchester, 1934–37; Lectr and Head of Dept, Goldsmiths' Coll., London, seconded to Exeter, 1940; Prof. of French, Exeter, 1943–45. *Publications*: Le Manuel des Péchés, étude de littérature anglo-normande, 1940; The Livre des Seintes Medicines of Henry duke of Lancaster, 1940; Etude sur le Livre des Saintes Médecines, 1948; The Melos Amoris of Richard Rolle of Hampole, 1957; La Genèse du Barbier de Séville, 1965; ed, Le Mariage de Figaro, 1952; ed, Le Barbier de Séville, 1963; *contrib.* Medium Aevum, Romania, French Studies, MLR, Rev. d'Histoire Littéraire de la France. *Address*: Trinity College, Dublin 2.

Arthur, Christopher John; Lecturer in Philosophy, University of Sussex, since 1965; *b* 1940. BA Nottingham 1963, Postgrad. study Oxford 1963–65. Co-founder, and Mem., Ed. Bd Radical Philosophy. *Publications*: ed, Marx and Engels: The German Ideology, Part I, 1970; *contrib.* Hist. and Theory, Radical Philosophy. *Address*: School of Social Sciences, Arts Building, Univ. of Sussex, Falmer, Brighton BN1 9QN.

Artis, Prof. Michael John, BA; Professor of Applied Economics, University College of Swansea, since 1972; *b* 1938; *m* 1961; two *d*. BA Oxon 1959 (PPE). Asst Res. Officer, Oxford Univ. Inst. of Economics and Statistics, 1959–63; Jun. Lectr, Magdalen Coll., Oxford, 1963; Lectr in Economics, Adelaide Univ., 1964–66; Lectr and Sen. Lectr, Flinders Univ. of SA, 1966–67; Sen. Res. Officer, Nat. Inst. Economic and Social Res., London, 1967–72. *Publications*: Foundations of British Monetary Policy, 1964; Contrib. to Readings in Australian Monetary and Fiscal Policy, 1971; Contrib. to The Current Inflation, 1971; Contrib. to Labour's Economic Record, 1972; *contrib.* Bull, Oxford Univ. Inst. of Econs and Stats, Nat. Inst. Economic Rev. *Address*: Dept of Economics, Univ. College of Swansea, Singleton Park, Swansea SA2 8PP.

Asaad, Prof. Fikry N. M.; *see* Morcos-Asaad.

Ashby, The Lord; Eric Ashby, Kt; DSc, MA, DIC, FRS; Master of Clare College, Cambridge, since 1959; Fellow of Clare College, 1958; Chancellor, Queen's University, Belfast, since 1970; *b* 1904; *m* 1931; two *s*. Hon. LLD, St Andrews, Aberdeen, Belfast, Rand, London, Wales, Columbia, Chicago, Windsor, W. Australia, Hon. ScD Dublin, Hon. DSc, NUI, Nigeria, Southampton, Hon. DLitt W. Ontario, Sydney, Hon. DPhil Tech. Univ. Berlin, Hon. DCL East Anglia, Hon. DHL Yale; FRS 1963. Commonwealth Fund Fellow, 1929–31; Lectr, Imperial Coll. of Science, 1931–35; Reader in Botany, Bristol Univ., 1935–37; Prof. of Botany, Univ. of Sydney, 1938–46; Harrison Prof. of Botany, Univ. of Manchester, 1946–50; Pres. and Vice-Chancellor, Queen's Univ., Belfast, 1950–59; Vice-Chancellor, Cambridge Univ., 1967–69; Vis. Lectr, USA, 1964, 1970. Chm. Aust. Nat. Research Council, 1940–42; Chm. Professorial Bd, Univ. of Sydney, 1942–44; Trustee, Aust. Museum, 1942–46; Counsellor, Aust. Legation, Moscow, 1945–46; Mem., Adv. Council on Scientific Policy, 1950–53; Mem., Nuffield Prov. Hosps Trust, 1951–59; Mem., Adv.

19

Coun. on Scientific and Industrial Res., 1954–60. Chm. of DSIR Grants Cttees, 1955–60, and Past Chm. many other Cttees on Educn; Chm. Cttee of Award of Commonwealth Fund, 1963–68 (Mem. 1956–61); Mem., UGC, 1959–67; Mem., Commonwealth Scholarship Commn, 1960–63; Mem., Council of Royal Soc., 1964–65; Mem., Gov. Body, SOAS, 1965–70; Chm. Royal Commn on Environmental Pollution, 1970– ; Chm., working party on pollution control for UN Conf. on Environment, Stockholm, 1972; Vice-Chm., Assoc. of Univs of Brit. Commonwealth, 1959–61; Pres., Brit. Assoc. for the Advancement of Science, 1963; Trustee, CIBA Foundn, 1966– ; Trustee, Brit. Museum, 1969– ; Fellow, Imperial Coll. of Science; Fellow, Birkbeck Coll.; Fellow, Davenport Coll., Yale; Hon. Fellow, Royal Inst. of Chemistry; Hon. Foreign Mem. Amer. Acad. of Arts and Sciences. Order of Andres Bello, 1st cl. (Venezuela). *Publications*: trans., Environment and Plant Development, 1931; German-English Botanical Terminology, 1938; Challenge to Education, 1946; Scientist in Russia, 1947, trans. German; Technology and the Academics, 1958, trans. Spanish and Japanese; Community of Universities, 1963; African Universities and Western Tradition, 1964, trans. French 1964; (with M. Anderson) Universities: British, Indian, African, 1966, trans. Spanish; Masters and Scholars, 1970; (with M. Anderson) The Rise of the Student Estate, 1970; Any Student, any Study, 1971; (with M. Anderson) Portrait of Haldane, 1974. *Address*: Clare College, Cambridge.

Ashmore, Owen; Associate Director, Department of Extra Mural Studies, University of Manchester, since 1969; *b* 1920; *m* 1948; three *s* one *d*. MA Cambridge 1946, Dip. Educn Cambridge 1947; FSA 1972. Resident Staff Tutor, Extra Mural Dept, Manchester Univ., 1950–62; Dep. Dir, Extra Mural Dept, Manchester Univ., 1962–69. *Publications*: The Development of Power in Britain, 1967; The Industrial Archaeology of Lancashire, 1969; *contrib*. Trans. Hist. Soc. of Lancashire and Cheshire, Trans Lancashire and Chesire Antiquarian Soc. *Address*: Extra Mural Dept, Univ. of Manchester, Manchester M13 9PL.

Ashton, Brynmor Davies; Senior Lecturer and Secretary, Faculty of Education, University College, Cardiff, since 1971; *b* 1916 *m* 1941; one *s* one *d*. BA Wales (Cardiff) 1937 (1st cl.); Member: Chartered Inst. of Secs, 1949, Classical Assoc., Hon. Soc. Cymmrodorion, JACT. Lectr, Univ. of Wales (Cardiff), 1959–71. *Address*: Faculty of Education, Univ. College, Senghennydd Road, Cardiff.

Ashton, Prof. Robert; Professor of English History, University of East Anglia, since 1963; Dean of School of English Studies, 1964–67; *b* 1924; *m* 1966; two *d*. BA London 1949, PhD London 1953; FRHistS 1960. Asst Lectr, Economic History, Univ. of Nottingham, 1952–54; Lectr, 1954–61; Sen. Lectr, 1961–63; Vis. Assoc. Prof., History, Univ. of California, Berkeley, 1962–63; Vis. Fellow, All Souls Coll., Oxford, 1973–74. *Publications*: The Crown and the Money

Market 1603–40; James I by his contemporaries, 1969; 'Charles I and the City', in, Essays in The Economic and Social History of Tudor and Stuart England, ed F. J. Fisher, 1961; The Civil War and the Class Struggle', in, The Civil War and After, ed R. H. Parry, 1969; *contrib*. Econ. Hist. Rev., Past and Present. *Address*: School of English and American Studies, Univ. of East Anglia, Norwich NOR 88C.

Ashwell, Dr Ian Yorke; Lecturer in Geography, Department of Economics and Geography, University of Salford, since 1973; *b* 1923. DipMechE Loughborough Coll. 1944, BA 1950 (2nd cl. Hons), MA 1956 (Geog.), PhD 1964, PGCE 1951, Bristol; FRGS, FRMetS, Mem., corresp. American and Canadian Socs. Asst Prof., Univ. of Alberta, Calgary, Canada, 1962–65, Associate Prof., 1965–69, Prof. of Geography, 1969–70; Sen. Lectr in Geography, City of London Polytech., 1971–73. Actg Head, Geography Dept, Univ. of Calgary, 1967, Head, 1967–69. *Publications*: *contrib*. Annals Assoc. Am. Geogrs, Atmosphere, Can. Geogr, Geogr. Annlr, Geogr. Jl, Jl Glac., Jökull. *Address*: Dept of Economics and Geography, Univ. of Salford, Salford M5 4WT.

Ashworth, Anthony Eugene; Lecturer, Department of Sociology, University College Cardiff, University of Wales, since 1965; *b* 1935; *m* 1965; two *d*. Bsc Economics. Flying Officer, RAF, 1960–64. *Publications*: *contrib*. Brit. Jl of Sociology. *Address*: Dept of Sociology, Univ. College Cardiff, Cardiff CF1 1XL.

Ashworth, Prof. William; Professor of Economic and Social History, University of Bristol, since 1958; *b* 1920. BSc(Econ.) London 1946, PhD London 1950; FRHistS; Mem., Econ. Hist. Soc., Hist. Assoc. Asst Lectr in Econ. Hist., LSE, 1948–49; Lectr, 1949–55; Reader, 1955–58. Cabinet Off. (Hist. Sect.), 1947–48; Dean, Fac. of Soc. Sci., Univ. of Bristol, 1968–70; Mem., Council, Econ. Hist. Soc., 1958– ; Southmead Gp Gen. Hosp. Mt Cttee, 1967–74. *Publications*: A Short History of the International Economy, 1952, rev. edn 1962; Contracts and Finance (History of the Second World War: UK Civil Series), 1953; The Genesis of Modern British Town Planning, 1954; An Economic History of England 1870–1939, 1960; contrib. London: aspects of change, ed by Centre for Urban Studies, 1964; Victoria History of the County of Essex, vol. v, 1966; The Study of Economic History, ed, N. B. Harte, 1971; *contrib*. Economica, Econ. Hist. Rev., Yorkshire Bulletin of Econ. and Soc. Research. *Address*: University of Bristol, Dept of Economic and Social History, 67 Woodland Road, Bristol BS8 1UL.

Asmal, Abdul Kader; Lecturer in Law, University of Dublin, Trinity College, since 1966; *b* 1934; *m* 1961; two *s*. Natal Teachers' Dip. 1954; BA S Africa 1957, LLB London 1962, LLM London 1965, MA Dublin 1966; Barrister-at-Law (Lincoln's Inn, 1963); Mem., Europ. Inst. Soc. Security, Brit. Inst. Int. and Comp. Law. Jun. Lectr in Law.

TCD. 1963–66; Tutor, 1967. Hon. Sec., Irish Soc. Lab. Law Soc. Legis., 1968–70; Mem., Council, Irish Fed. Univ. Teachers, 1970– ; Mem., Bd TCD, 1970–74. Irish Editor, Industrial Law Jl, 1972– . *Publications*: Consumer Councils in Public Enterprise, 1972; Irish Labour Law (forthcoming); *contrib*. Admin, Int. Comp. Law Qly, Leargas – Public Aff. Jl. *Address*: 38 Trinity College, Dublin 2.

Aspinwall, Bernard; Lecturer in Modern History, Glasgow University, since 1965; *b* 1938; *m* 1971; one *d*. BA Manchester 1960 (Hons History), MA Manchester 1962. English Speaking Union Fellowship, Indiana Univ., 1961–62; Instructor in History, Eastern Kentucky Univ., 1962–63; Res. in Arts, Manchester, 1963–65; Vis. Lectr, Univ. of Notre Dame, 1973. Warden of Kelvin Lodge, Glasgow Univ., 1968–70; Warden of Dalrymple Hall, Glasgow Univ., 1970–72. *Publications*: *contrib*. Colloque: Les Catholiques libéraux au XIXe siècle, Grenoble, 1973, 1974; Revue d'Histoire de l'Eglise de France, Downside Rev., Month, Rev. of Politics. *Address*: Modern History Dept, Glasgow Univ., Glasgow G12 8QQ.

Astin, Prof. Alan Edgar, MA, MRIA; Professor of Ancient History, The Queen's University of Belfast, since 1967; *b* 1930; *m* 1955; two *s*. BA Oxon 1954 (1st cl. Lit. Hum.), MA Oxon 1957. Asst Lectr, The Queen's Univ. of Belfast, 1954–57; Lectr, 1957–67; Mem., Inst. Adv. Study, Princeton, NJ, 1964–65; Vis. Prof., Yale Univ., 1966. Dean, Fac. of Arts, The Queen's Univ. of Belfast, 1971–74. *Publications*: The Lex Annalis before Sulla, 1958; Scipio Aemilianus, 1967; *contrib*. Class. Philol., Class. Qly, Historia, Latomus. *Address*: Dept of Ancient History, The Queen's Univ. of Belfast, Belfast BT71 NN.

Aston, Prof. Peter, DPhil, GBSM, FTCL, ARCM; Professor of Music, University of East Anglia, since 1974; *b* 1938; *m* 1960; one *s*. ARCM 1959, GBSM 1960, FTCL 1960, DPhil York 1970. Lectr in Music, York Univ., 1964–72, Sen. Lectr, 1972–74. *Publications*: (jtly) Sound and Silence, 1970, German edn 1972; Music and Musicians at York Minster, 1972; miscellaneous choral works, church and chamber music; ed, Anthems and Sacred Songs by George Jeffreys; *contrib*. Mus. in Ed., Mus. Times, Proc. Royal Mus. Assoc. *Address*: Dept. of Music, Univ. of East Anglia, Norwich NOR 88C.

Aston, Trevor Henry; Director of Research and General Editor of the History of the University of Oxford, since 1968, Keeper of the Archives of the University of Oxford since 1969, Senior Research Fellow since 1968, and Librarian since 1956, of Corpus Christi College, Oxford; *b* 1925; *m* 1954. MA Oxon 1950; FRHistS 1958, FSA 1966. Junior Research Fellow in Medieval History, Corpus Christi Coll., Oxford, 1950–52; Fellow and Tutor in Medieval History, Corpus Christi Coll., and Univ. Lectr, 1952–68. Editor, Past and Present, 1960– ; Mem. Council of the Royal Hist. Soc., 1971. *Publications*: *contrib*. Trans Royal Hist. Soc., Past

and Present. *Address*: Corpus Christi Coll., Oxford.

Atherton, Judith; Lecturer in Management Science, Management Centre, University of Bradford, since 1968; *b* 1936; *m* 1959; two *d*. BSc Leeds 1958 (Hons Mathematics); Fellow, Royal Statistical Soc. Statistician: Monsanto Chemicals Ltd, 1958–60; Nairn-Williamson Ltd, 1960–63; Vis. Lectr in Management Studies, Univ. of Bradford, 1966–68. *Publication*: (co-author) Mathematics for Management Science, 1972. *Address*: Univ. of Bradford Management Centre, Emm Lane, Bradford BD9 4JL.

Atkinson, Prof. Anthony Barnes; Professor of Economics, University of Essex, since 1971; *b* 1944; *m* 1965. BA Cambridge 1966 (1st cl. Econ). Fellow, St John's Coll., Cambridge, 1967–71; Univ. Asst Lectr, Cambridge, 1968–71. Mem., Econs Bd, CNAA. *Publications*: Poverty in Britain and the Reform of Social Security, 1969; Unequal shares: wealth in Britain, 1972; *contrib*. Rev. of Econ. Studies, Econ. Jl. Qly Jl of Econs, Oxford Econ. Papers, Jl of Econ. Theory. *Address*: Dept of Economics, Univ. of Essex, Wivenhoe Park, Colchester, Essex C04 3SQ.

Atkinson, Dr Bruce Wilson, PhD; Lecturer in Geography, Queen Mary College, University of London, since 1964; *b* 1941. BSc London 1962, PhD London 1967; FRGS, FRMetS, Professional Mem., American Meteorological Soc. Editor, Weather (RmetS). *Publications*: The Weather Business, 1968, French edn 1970, German edn 1971; *contrib*. Trans Inst. of Brit. Geographers, Jl of Applied Meteorology, Qly Jl of Royal Meteorological Soc. *Address*: Dept of Geography, Queen Mary Coll., Mile End Road, E1 4NS.

Atkinson, Dorothy M., MA; Senior Lecturer in Portuguese, Department of Spanish, University of Birmingham, since 1964; *b* 1923. BA Sheffield 1944 (1st cl. French and Spanish DipEd Manchester 1944, MA Sheffield 1948. Asst Lectr, Birmingham Univ., 1946–49; Lectr, Birmingham, 1949–64. *Publications*: ed, Selections of Nineteenth Century Portuguese Prose, 1965; ed, Teach Yourself Portuguese, 1969; *contrib*. Estudios Dedicados a Menéndez Pidal, Mod. Lang. Rev., Occidente, Revista de Portugal, Série A. *Address*: Dept of Spanish, Univ. of Birmingham, Birmingham B15 2TT.

Atkinson, Prof. James, MA, MLitt, DrTheol; Professor of Biblical Studies, University of Sheffield, since 1967; *b* 1914; *m* 1939; one *s* one *d*. BA Durham 1936 (Classics and Theology), MA Durham 1939, MLitt Durham 1951, DrTheol Münster, Germany 1955. Fellow, Sheffield Univ., 1951–54; Lectr, Hull Univ., 1956–66; Vis. Prof., Chicago, USA, 1966–67. Canon Theologian, Leicester, 1954–71; Canon Theologian, Sheffield, 1971; Mem., Roman Catholic/Anglican Commn, 1967; Lutheran/Anglican Commn, 1969. *Publications*: Luther's Early Theological Works, 1962; Luther's Works, Vol. 44, 1966; Paternoster History, Vol. 4: Reformation, 1966; Rome and Reformation,

1966; Martin Luther and the Birth of Protestantism, 1968; The Trial of Luther, 1971; *contrib.* The Churchman, Theology, Jl Eccles. Hist., Jl Theolog. Studies, Scott. Jl Theology. *Address*: Dept of Biblical Studies, Sheffield Univ., Sheffield S10 2TN.

Atkinson, Joseph Rayner, LLB; Lecturer, Department of Law, Leeds University, since 1964; *b* 1925; *m* 1952. LLB 1964 (2nd cl. Hons). Solicitor of the Supreme Court of Judicature, 1950. Pres., Yorkshire Rent Assessment Panel (Dept of the Environment), 1965–72. *Publications*: Reviews, etc., of minor importance. *Address*: Faculty of Law, Leeds Univ., Leeds LS2 9JT.

Atkinson, Prof. Richard John Copland; Professor of Archaeology, University College, Cardiff, since 1958; *b* 1920; *m* 1942; three *s*. BA Oxon 1942 (War Degree, PPE), MA Oxon 1947; FSA. Asst Keeper, Ashmolean Museum, Oxford, 1944–49; Lectr, Edinburgh Univ., 1949–58; Dep. Principal, Univ. Coll., Cardiff, 1970– . Mem., Ancient Monuments Bd, Wales, 1959– ; Royal Commn on Ancient Monuments, Wales, 1963– ; Royal Commn on Historical Monuments, England, 1968– ; UGC, 1973– ; Vice-Pres. Prehistoric Soc., 1963–67; Council for Brit. Archaeology, 1970–73 (Hon. Sec., 1964–70). *Publications*: Field Archaeology, 1946, 2nd edn 1953; Stonehenge, 1956, 2nd edn 1960; *contrib.* Antiquity, Archaeologia, Archaeological Jl, Proc. Soc. Ant. Scot. *Address*: Dept of Archaeology, Univ. Coll., PO Box 78, Cardiff CF1 1XL.

Atkinson, Prof. Ronald Field; Professor of Philosophy, University of York, since 1967; *b* 1928; *m* 1951; one *s* two *d*. BA Oxon 1951 (1st cl. PPE), BPhil Oxon 1953. Asst Lectr, Univ. Coll., North Staffs (later Univ. Keele), 1953, Lectr, 1956, Sen. Lectr, 1962, Reader, 1966. Dep. Vice-Chancellor, Univ. of York, 1969– . *Publications*: Sexual Morality, 1965; Conduct: An Introduction to Moral Philosophy, 1970; *contrib.* Analysis, Mind, Philosophy, Philosophical Qtly, Philosophical Rev. *Address*: Dept of Philosophy, The Univ., Heslington, York YO1 5DD.

Attfield, Dr Robin; Lecturer in the Department of Philosophy, University College, Cardiff, since 1968; *b* 1941; *m* 1966; one *s* one *d*. BA Oxon 1964 (1st cl. Hons Lit. Hum.), 1966 (1st cl. Hons Theol.), MA Oxon 1967; PhD Wales 1972. Vis. Lectr in Philosophy, Dept of Religious Studies and Philosophy, Univ. of Ife, Nigeria, 1972–73. *Publications: contrib.* Analysis, Educn for Develt, Inquiry, Internat. Jl for Philos. of Religion, Jl of Critical Analysis, Noûs, Philosophy, Religious Studies, Second Order, Afr. Jl of Philosophy, Sophia. *Address*: Dept of Philosophy, Univ. Coll., Cardiff CF1 1XL.

Attwooll, Elspeth Mary-Ann, LLB, MA; Lecturer, Department of Jurisprudence, University of Glasgow, since 1969; *b* 1943. LLB St Andrews 1964, MA St Andrews 1966 (Hons Politics and Philosophy). Asst Lectr, Glasgow, 1966–69. Official, Labour Standards Br., ILO, 1968–69. *Address*: Dept of Jurisprudence, Univ. of Glasgow, Glasgow G12 8QQ.

Austin, Dr Alan Keith; Lecturer, Department of Pure Mathematics, University of Sheffield, since 1966; *b* 1937; *m* 1965; one *s* one *d*. Hon. BSc Manchester 1959 (1st cl. Maths), MSc Manchester 1960, PhD Manchester 1964; Mem., Maths Assoc. Asst Lectr, Sheffield Univ., 1964–66. *Publications: contrib.* Math. Gaz., Math. Teaching, Mind, Pacific Jl Math., Proc. Amer. Math. Soc., Publ. Math. Debrecen, Qly Jl Math. *Address*: Dept of Pure Mathematics, Univ. of Sheffield, Sheffield S10 2TN.

Austin, Dr Colin François Lloyd; Lecturer in Classics, University of Cambridge, since 1973; *b* 1941; *m* 1967; one *s* one *d*. MA Oxford and Cambridge 1965, DPhil Oxford 1965. Res. Fellow, Trinity Hall, Cambridge, 1965–69; Asst Lectr in Classics, Univ. of Cambridge, 1969–73. Treas., Cambridge Philological Soc., 1971– ; Member: Oxford Philological Soc., 1963– ; Hellenic Soc., 1972– . *Publications*: Nova Fragmenta Euripidea, in, Papyris Reperta, 1968; Papyrus Bodmer XXV – XXVI: Ménandre, La Samienne, Le Bouclier, 1969; Menandri Aspis et Samia, I, 1969, II, 1970; Comicorum Graecorum Fragmenta in Papyris Reperta, 1973; Mélanges Claire Préaux, 1975; *contrib.* Class. Rev., Dioniso, Gnomon, Maia, Oxyrhynchus Papyri, Proc. Camb. Phil. Soc., Recherches de Papyrologie, Zeitschrift für Papyrologie und Epigraphik. *Address*: Trinity Hall, Cambridge.

Austin, Prof. Lloyd James, FBA; Drapers Professor of French, University of Cambridge, since 1967; *b* 1915; *m* 1939; three *s* one *d*. BA Melbourne 1936 (1st cl. Hons French Lang. and Lit.), MA Melbourne 1947, Dr Univ. Paris 1940, MA Cantab 1955, MA Manchester 1956; FBA 1968; Dr hc Paris-Sorbonne 1973; Mem., Soc. for French Studies; Pres., Assoc. Internationale des Etudes Françaises, 1969–72. Lectr, Melbourne Univ., 1940–42, 1945–47; Lectr, St Andrews Univ., 1947–51; Fellow, Jesus Coll., Cambridge, 1955 and 1961– ; Prof., Mod. French Lit., Manchester Univ., 1956–61; Lectr, Cambridge Univ. 1961–66; Reader, 1966–67; Herbert F. Johnson Vis. Prof. Wisconsin Univ., 1962–63; General Ed., French Studies, 1967– . *Publications*: Paul Bourget, 1940; ed, Paul Valéry: Le Cimetière marin, 1954; L'Univers poétique de Baudelaire, 1956; (with H. Mondor) Les Gossips de Mallarmé, 1962; ed, (with H. Mondor) Correspondance de S. Mallarmé, vol. II, 1965, III, 1969, IV, 1973; ed, Baudelaire: L'Art romantique, 1968; *contrib.* AUMLA, AJFS, Bull. John Rylands Libr., FMLS, FS, MF, ML, MLR, RHLF, RLC, RR. RSH, etc. *Address*: Dept of French, Faculty of Modern and Medieval Languages, Sidgwick Avenue, Cambridge CB3 9DA.

Austin, Dr Michel Mervyn; Lecturer in Ancient History, Department of Ancient History, University of St Andrews, since 1968; *b* 1943. MA Cambridge 1965, PhD Cambridge 1968; Mem.: Soc. for Promotion of Hellenic Studies (Mem. Council, 1973–);

Société pour l'Encouragement des Etudes Grecques (Paris). *Publications*: Greece and Egypt in the Archaic Age, 1970; (with P. Vidal-Naquet) Economies et Sociétés en Grèce Ancienne, Paris, 1972, 2nd edn 1973. *Address*: Dept of Ancient History, St Salvator's College, The Univ., St Andrews, Fife.

Austin, Ralph William Julius, BA, PhD; Lecturer in Arabic, University of Durham, since 1963; *b* 1938; *m* 1963; one *s* one *d*. BA London 1960 (1st cl. Arabic), PhD London 1965. Research Asst, Univ. of California, Los Angeles, 1962. *Publications*: Sufis of Andalusia, 1971. *Address*: School of Oriental Studies, Univ. of Durham, Durham DH1 3HP.

Austwick, Prof. Kenneth, MSc, PhD, JP; Pro-Vice-Chancellor 1972–75, Professor and Head of School of Education, University of Bath, since 1966; *b* 1927; *m* 1956; one *s* one *d*. BSc Hons Sheffield 1948 (Mathematics), DipEd Sheffield 1949, MSc Sheffield 1951, PhD Sheffield 1963; FSS, FRSA, JP. Lectr, later Sen. Lectr in Educn, Sheffield Univ., 1959–65; Dep. Dir, Inst. of Educn, Reading Univ., 1965–66. Chm., Home Office Programmed Learning Cttee, 1967–72; Mem., Bath Educn Cttee, 1971; Home Office Jt Trng Cttee of Fire Brigades Council, 1972– . *Publications*: Logarithms, 1962; Equations and Graphs, 1963; (jtly) Objective Tests in A-Level Mathematics, 1973; ed, Teaching Machines and Programming, 1964; ed (jtly), Aspects of Educational Technology, vol. VI, 1972; several programmed texts in Mathematics, 1963–65; chapters in: Mechanisation in the Classroom, 1963; New Approaches to Mathematics Teaching, 1963; Educational Administration and the Social Sciences, 1968; Instructional Technology in Higher Education, 1969; *contrib.* BJEP, Jl of Programmed Learning, Universities Qly, Visual Educn. *Address*: Univ. of Bath School of Educn, Northgate House, Upper Borough Walls, Bath BA1 5AL.

Auty, Phyllis; Reader in South Slav History, School of Slavonic and East European Studies, University of London, since 1970; *b* 1910; *m* 1946; two *s*. BA Oxon 1931 (Hons History), BLitt Oxon 1935, MA Oxon 1950. Lectr, Oxford Univ. Tutorial Cttee, 1938–40; Lectr in History of Danubian Lands, School of Slavonic Studies, Univ. of London, 1947–70; Vis. Prof., Simon Fraser Univ., Canada, 1965–66; Vis. Prof., Stanford Univ., USA, 1969. *Publications*: Yugoslavia and Bulgaria, in, Central and South Eastern Europe, ed Betts, 1950; Yugoslavia, 1965; Tito's International Relations, in, Contemporary Yugoslavia, ed Vucinich, 1969; Yugoslavia since 1945, in, A Short History of Yugoslavia, ed Clissold, 1966; Tito: a biography, 1970; Yugoslavia in the Cold War, 1973; ed, British Policy to Resistance in Yugoslavia and Greece in the Second World War, 1974; *contrib.* Economist, Encycl. Brit., Eng. Hist. Rev., Slavic Rev., Slavonic Rev., Serbian Academy Istoriski Casopis, etc. *Address*: School of Slavonic and East European Studies, Univ. of London, WC1.

Auty, Prof. Robert, MA, DrPhil; Professor of Comparative Slavonic Philology, Oxford University, and Fellow of Brasenose College, Oxford, since 1965; *b* 1914; *m* 1944; one *s* one *d*. BA Cambridge 1935 (1st cl. Pts I and II Mod. Langs), Dr phil Münster 1937, MA Cambridge 1939, MA Oxford 1965; Josef Dobrovský Gold Medal, Czechoslovak Acad. of Sciences, 1968, Hon. Mem., Slovak Assoc. of Linguists (Bratislava), 1971, Mem., Philological Soc., Linguistic Soc. of America, Société de Linguistique de Paris, Societas Uralo-Altaica. Faculty Asst Lectr, Cambridge, 1937–45; Univ. Lectr, Cambridge, 1945–62; Fellow, Selwyn Coll., Cambridge, 1950–62; Prof., London Univ., 1962–65; Vis. Prof., UCLA, 1968; de Carle Lectr, Otago Univ., 1975. Pres., Brit. Univ. Assoc. of Slavists, 1964–67; Pres., Assoc. Int. des Langues et Littératures Slaves, 1966–72; Chm., Modern Humanities Res. Assoc., 1968–73; Vice-Pres., Internat. Cttee of Slavists, 1965– ; Vice-Pres., Internat. Fed. of Mod. Langs and Lits, 1966–72. *Publications*: Old Church Slavonic Texts and Glossary, 1960, 3rd edn 1968; *contrib.* Annali Istituto Universitario Orientale Sezione slava, Makedonski jazik, Mod. Lang. Rev., Oxford Slavonic Papers, Filologija, Revue des Etudes slaves, Slavonic and East European Rev., Studia z filologii polskiej i słowiańskiej, Slavia, Studia slavica, etc. *Address*: Brasenose Coll., Oxford OX1 4AJ.

Avery, Michael; Lecturer in Archaeology, Queen's University, Belfast, since 1967; *b* 1940; *m* 1970. BA Oxford 1963. Randall-MacIver student in Archaeology, The Queen's Coll., Oxford, 1965. *Publications*: various contribs to jls. *Address*: Dept of Archaeology, Queen's Univ., Belfast BT7 1NN.

Avery, Peter William; University Lecturer in Persian, Faculty of Oriental Studies, Cambridge University, since 1957, and Fellow of King's College, Cambridge, since 1965; *b* 1923. BA London 1949 (Hons Persian), MA Cambridge 1958; Mem., Royal Asiatic Soc., Royal Cent. Asian Soc., Chatham Hse; Cambridge Univ. Council of the Senate, 1969–74. Vis. Scholar, Univ. of Michigan, Ann Arbor, 1962; Vis. Prof., Harvard Univ., 1965; Vis. Prof., Univ. of Chicago, 1968. *Publications*: trans., (with J. Heath-Stubbs) Hafiz: Thirty Poems, 1952; Modern Iran, 1965, 2nd edn 1967; (with Paper and Jazairery) Advanced Persian Reader, 1965; (with J. Heath-Stubbs) The Rubā'īyāt of Omar Khayyām), 1974; Medieval Iran, 1975; The Culture of Tamburlaine's Sons, 1975; Persian History, in Encyclopaedia Britannica; *contrib.* Muslim World, Royal Cent. Asian Soc. Jl, Speculum: Jl Medieval Studies, Jl World Today. *Address*: King's Coll., Cambridge.

Avison, Neville Howard; Senior Lecturer in Criminology, Department of Criminology, University of Edinburgh, since 1970; Acting Head of Department, 1972–73; *b* 1934; *m* 1959; one *s* two *d*. BA (Mod.) TCD 1960 (Legal Science), MA TCD 1963. Res. Asst, Inst. of Criminology, Cambridge, 1961; Res. Officer, 1961; Sen. Res. Officer, 1962; Lectr, Univ. of Edinburgh, 1965–70. *Publications*: (with N. C. Savill and V. L. Worthington,

23

Sen. author F. H. McClintock) Crimes of Violence, 1963; (with F. H. McClintock) Crime in England and Wales, 1968; *contrib.* Juridical Rev., New Society. *Address*: Dept of Criminology, Univ. of Edinburgh, Old College, South Bridge, Edinburgh EH8 9YL.

Ayer, Sir Alfred (Jules); Wykeham Professor of Logic in the University of Oxford, since 1959; Fellow of New College, Oxford; *b* 1910; *m* 1932, 1960; two *s* one *d*. BA Oxon 1932 (1st cl. Lit. Hum.), MA Oxon 1936, Doc. hc Univ. of Brussels 1962; DUniv E. Anglia 1972. Hon Mem., Amer. Acad. of Arts and Sciences 1963; Pres., Aristotelian Soc., Modern Languages Assoc., 1966–67, Brit. Humanist Assoc., 1865–70. Lectr in Philosophy at Christ Church, 1932–35; Res. Student, 1935–44; Fellow of Wadham Coll., Oxford, 1944–46; Dean, 1945–46; Grote Prof. of the Philosophy of Mind and Logic, Univ. Coll., London, 1946–59; Hon. Fellow of Wadham Coll., 1957– . Served in Welsh Guards, Military Intell., 1940–45; Attaché to HM Embassy, Paris, 1945; Mem., Central Adv. Council for Educn, 1963–66. *Publications*: Language, Truth and Logic, 1936; The Foundations of Empirical Knowledge, 1940; Philosophical Essays, 1954; The Problem of Knowledge, 1956; The Concept of a Person and Other Essays, 1963; The Origins of Pragmatism, 1968; Metaphysics and Common Sense, 1969; Russell and Moore, the analytical heritage, 1971; Probability and Evidence, 1972; Russell, 1972; The Central Questions of Philosophy, 1973; *contrib.* Mind, Procs Aristot. Soc, Jl of Philosophy, Synthèse, Revue internationale de Philosophie, etc. *Address*: New College, Oxford.

Ayers, Dr Michael Richard; Fellow of Wadham College, Oxford, since 1965, Lecturer in Philosophy in University of Oxford, since 1966; *b* 1935; *m* 1962; one *s* one *d*. BA Cantab 1958, MA Cantab, PhD Cantab 1962. Fellow, St John's Coll., Cambridge, 1962–65; Vis. Lectr, Univ. of Calif., Berkeley, 1964; Vis. Prof., Univ. of Oregon, Eugene, 1970. *Publications*: Refutation of Determinism, 1968; *contrib.* American Phil. Qly, Mind, Phil. Qly. *Address*: Wadham College, Oxford.

Aylmer, Gerald Edward; Professor of History, University of York, since 1963; *b* 1926; *m* 1955; one *s* one *d*. MA Oxon 1951, BA Oxon 1950, DPhil Oxon 1955; FRHistS (Vice-Pres.), Mem., EconHistSoc, Past and Present Soc., etc. Junior Res. Fellow, Balliol Coll., Oxford, 1951–54; Asst Lectr, Manchester, 1954–57; Lectr, Manchester, 1957–62. Mem., Edit. Bd, History of Parliament. *Publications*: The King's Servants, 1961; The Struggle for the Constitution, 1963; (ed) The Interregnum, 1972; The State's Servants, 1973; *contrib.* Bull. Inst. of Hist. Res., Econ. Hist. Rev., EHR., Hist., Trans Royal Hist. Soc., Past and Present. *Address*: History Dept, Univ. of York, Heslington, York YO1 5DD.

Ayres, Reginald B.; *see* Barrett-Ayres.

24

B

Babiak, Harvey; Senior Lecturer in Accounting, London Graduate School of Business Studies, since 1972; *b* 1932; *m* 1959. BSc (Econs) London 1954, MBA Western Ontario 1962; FCA 1957; Mem., Canadian Inst. of Chartered Accountants, 1958. Univ. of BC, 1958–61; Univ. of Malaya (visiting), 1962–63; Univ. of Singapore (visiting), 1963–64; Univ. of Chicago, 1967–72; Univ. of the Witwatersrand (visiting), 1973. *Publications*: *contrib.* Jl Amer. Statist. Assoc., Kajian Ekonomi Malaysia. *Address*: London Graduate School of Business Studies, Regent's Park, NW1 4SA.

Babington Smith, Bernard, OBE; Senior Lecturer in Experimental Psychology, Oxford University, since 1953; *b* 1905; *m* 1940; two *s* one *d*. BA Cantab 1928 (2nd cl. Moral Sciences), MA Cantab 1932. Asst Lectr, St Andrews Univ., 1932; Lectr, Oxford Univ., 1946–53; Fellow, Pembroke Coll., Oxford, 1970. RAFVR (S and AD), 1940–45. Statistician, Min. Agriculture and Fisheries, 1945–46; Chief Examiner, Annual Schs Examn, Oxford City, 1949–51; Annual Selection Exam at 11 +, Wilts, 1954–59. *Publications*: Laboratory Experience in Psychology, 1965; Purpose and Choice, in, Sociology Theology and Conflict, ed Whiteley and Martin, 1969; *contrib.* Biometrika, Brit. Jl Psychol. *Address*: Dept Experimental Psychology, South Parks Road, Oxford.

Babister, Elizabeth A., MA; Lecturer in French, Department of Modern Languages, University of Strathclyde, Glasgow, since 1964; *b* 1923; *m* 1953. MA Glasgow 1944 (1st cl. French and German). Asst Lectr, French Dept, Univ. of Glasgow, 1950–54, 1956–57; Lectr, Dept of Modern Languages, Scottish Coll. of Commerce, Glasgow, 1961–64. *Address*: Dept of Modern Languages, Univ. of Strathclyde, Glasgow G1 1XW.

Bacarisse, Salvador, MA; Lecturer in Spanish and Portuguese Literature, University of St Andrews, since 1964; *b* 1923; *m* 1970; one *s* one *d*. BA London 1961 (1st cl. Hons Spanish); MA London 1963. Lectr, Bristol Univ., 1960–64. Asst Editor, Forum, 1970. *Publications*: *contrib.* Bull. Hispanic Studies, Forum. *Address*: Dept of Spanish, St Andrews Univ., St Andrews, Fife KY16 9AJ.

Bacharach, Michael Owen Leslie; Lecturer in Economics, Oxford University, since 1971, and Tutor in Economics, Christ Church, Oxford, since 1969; *b* 1936; *m* 1959; one *d*. BA Cambridge 1958 (1st cl. Economics), PhD Cambridge 1965; Board Mem., Econ. Study Soc. 1967, Mem., Econometric Soc., 1970. Junior Res. Officer, Dept Applied Econ., Cambridge, 1959; Res. Officer, 1964; Res. Fellow, Nuffield Coll., Oxford, 1965; Fellow, Balliol Coll., 1967; Student, Christ Church, 1970. *Publications*: (with J. M. Bates) Input–Output Relations 1954–66, 1963; ed (with E. Malinvaud), Activity Analysis in the Theory of Growth and Planning, 1967; Biproportional Matrices and Input–Output

Change, 1970; *contrib.* Internat. Econ. Rev., Management Science. *Address*: Christ Church, Oxford.

Backhouse, John Kenneth; Tutor, Department of Educational Studies, University of Oxford, since 1960; *b* 1927; *m* 1956; one *s* three *d*. BA Cantab 1948 (Mathematics), MA 1952; FIMA. Mem., Mathematical Assoc. Teaching Cttee, 1958–70; Mem., Sibford School Cttee, 1966–73. *Publications*: (with S. P. T. Houldsworth) Pure Mathematics – A First Course, 1957, SI edn 1972; (with S. P. T. Houldsworth and B. E. D. Cooper) Pure Mathematics – A Second Course, 1963, SI edn 1971; Statistics – An Introduction to Tests of Significance, 1967; (with D. L. Nuttall and A. S. Willmott) Comparability of Standards between Subjects, 1974; *contrib.* British Examinations: Techniques of Analysis (NFER), 1972. *Address*: Dept of Educational Studies, 15 Norham Gardens, Oxford OX2 6PY.

Bacon, Robert William; Tutorial Fellow in Economics, Lincoln College, and Faculty Lecturer in Econometrics, University of Oxford, since 1967; *b* 1942; *m* 1970. BA Bristol 1961, MA Oxford 1968. Mem. Bd, Soc. for Economic Analysis, 1970; Asst Gen. Editor, Oxford Economic Papers, 1973. *Publications*: The Cowley Shopping Centre, 1969; *contrib.* Bull. Oxf. Inst. Econs and Stats, Econ. Jl, Urban Stud. *Address*: Lincoln College, Oxford.

Badawi, Dr Mohamed Mustafa; Fellow of St Antony's College, Oxford, since 1967; *b* 1925; *m* 1954; one *s* three *d*. BA Alexandria 1946 (1st cl. English); BA London 1950, PhD London 1954, MA Oxon 1964. Asst Lectr, Alexandria Univ., 1947; Res. Fellow, 1948–54; Lectr, 1954–60; Asst Prof., 1960–64; Univ. Lectr, Oxford, 1964– ; Lectr, Brasenose Coll., Oxford, 1965– . Co-Editor, Jl of Arabic Lit., 1970– . *Publications*: An Anthology of Modern Arabic Verse, 1970; Coleridge, Critic of Shakespeare, 1973; trans. Haqqi: The Saint's Lamp, 1973; various books and articles in Arabic; *contrib.* Bull. Fac. of Arts, Alex. Univ., Cairo Studies in Eng., E in C, Jl of Arabic Lit., JWH, Med. Aev., Oxford Mag., Sh.Q., W.I. *Address*: St Antony's College, Oxford.

Baddeley, Dr Alan David; Director, Medical Research Council Applied Psychology Unit, Cambridge, since 1974; *b* 1934; *m* 1964; three *s*. BA London 1956 (Hons Psychology), MA Princeton 1957, PhD Cambridge 1962; Member: BPsS, EPS, Underwater Assoc. Lectr in Psychology, Univ. of Sussex, 1967–69; Reader in Experimental Psychology, 1969–72; Prof. of Psychology, Univ. of Stirling, 1972–74. *Publications*: *contrib.* Qly Jl of Experimental Psychology, Psychological Bull., Brit. Jl of Psychology, Neuropsychologia, Ergonomics, etc. *Address*: MRC Applied Psychology Unit, 15 Chaucer Road, Cambridge.

Badley, Prof. F. Stephen; Professor of Public Service Studies and Head of Public Services Studies Division, Institute of Continuing Education, New University of Ulster, since 1972; *b* 1924; *m* 1950; two *s* one *d*. BA (Admin) Manchester 1957 (distinction), Teachers' Cert. Manchester 1959 (with distinction). Staff Tutor in Public Admin, Manchester Univ., 1968; Acting Warden, Holly Royde Coll., 1969–70. *Address*: Institute of Continuing Education, New Univ. of Ulster, Londonderry, Northern Ireland BT52 1SA.

Baelz, Rev. Prof. Peter Richard, MA; Canon of Christ Church and Regius Professor of Moral and Pastoral Theology, University of Oxford, since 1972; BA Cantab 1944, MA Cantab 1948, BD Cantab 1971; Deacon 1947; Priest 1950. Dean, Jesus Coll., Cambridge, 1960–72; Lectr in Divinity, Univ. of Cambridge, 1966–72; Select Preacher, 1963; Hulsean Lectr, 1964–66. Asst Curate, Bournville, 1947–50, Sherborne, 1950–52; Asst Chaplain, Ripon Hall, Oxford, 1952–54; Rector, Wishaw, 1954–56; Vicar, Bournville, 1956–60; Licentiate to Officiate, Dio. Ely, 1961–72. Examining Chaplain to Bishop of Birmingham, 1962– ; Bishop of St Edmundsbury and Ipswich, 1967– . *Publications*: Christian Theology and Metaphysics, 1968; Prayer and Providence, 1968. *Address*: Christ Church, Oxford.

Bagley, Christopher; Reader, Department of Sociology, University of Surrey, since 1972; *b* 1937; *m* 1964; two *s*. Dip. Soc. Admin and Cert. Ed. Exeter 1962, 1964; MA Essex 1967 (Sociology). Res. Asst, Inst. of Neurology, London, 1964; Res. Officer, Univ. of Esex, 1967; Res. Fellow, Univ. of Sussex, 1969. *Publications*: Social Structure and Prejudice, 1970; Social Psychology of the Child with Epilepsy, 1971; The Dutch Plural Society, 1973; *contrib.* BMJ, Sociology, Brit. Jl Psychiat., Race, Brit. Jl Soc. Work, Soc. Sci. Med., Jl Soc. Psychol., Internal. Jl Psychol. *Address*: Dept of Sociology, Univ. of Surrey, Guildford, Surrey GU2 5XH.

Bagley, Frank Ronald Charles; Lecturer in Persian Studies, School of Oriental Studies, University of Durham, since 1958; *b* 1915; *m* 1947; one *s*. BA Oxford (Hons) 1937, MA Oxford 1953. Mem., Brit. Inst. Persian Studies, London and Tehran, Royal Central Asian Soc., Royal Inst. of Internat. Affairs, Middle East Inst., Washington. Asst Prof., McGill Univ., Inst. of Islamic Studies, 1953–58. Brit. Consular (later Foreign) Service, 1938–52. *Publications*: Ed and trans. Ghazali: Book of Counsel for Kings, 1964, 2nd edn 1971; trans. of The Muslim World: Part I, by B. Spuler, The Age of the Caliphs, 1960, 2nd edn 1969; Part II, by B. Spuler, The Mongol Period, 1960, 2nd edn 1969; Part III, by various contributors including self, The Last Great Muslim Empires, 1969; *contrib.* Der Islam, Durham Univ. Jl, Islamic Studies (Rawalpindi), Internat. Jl, Jl Internat. Affairs. *Address*: Univ. of Durham, School of Oriental Studies, Elvet Hill, Durham.

Bagley, John Joseph; Reader in History, Institute of Extension Studies, University of Liverpool, since 1967; *b* 1908; *m* 1935; one *s* one *d*. BA 1930 (Hons History), MA 1934,

25

DipEd 1931, Liverpool; FRHistS 1959– . Univ. of Liverpool: Staff Tutor in History, 1951; Sen. Lectr in History, 1960. Hon. Editor: Trans of the Historic Society of Lancs and Cheshire, 1949–69; A History of Cheshire, 12 vols. *Publications*: Margaret of Anjou, Queen of England, 1948; History of Lancashire, 1956, 5th edn 1970; Life in Mediaeval England, 1960, 5th edn 1970; Historical Interpretation I, 1965, 2nd edn 1971, Amer. edn 1973; Historical Interpretation 2, 1971, Amer. edn 1973; Documentary History of England, vol. I, 1966; Lancashire, 1972; Lancashire Diarists, 1974. *Address*: Institute of Extension Studies, 1 Abercromby Square, Liverpool L69 3BX.

Baier, Dr (Francis) Clair (W.); Reader in German, University of Hull, since 1971; *b* 1912; *m* 1937; one *s* two *d*. BA Liverpool 1933, DrPhil Tübingen 1937; Member: Mod. Humanities Res. Assoc., English Goethe Soc., Conf. of Univ. Teachers of German, Mod. Lang. Assoc. Assist Lectr, Univ. Sheffield, 1935–37; Asst Lectr, subseq. Lectr, Univ. Birmingham, 1938–45; Head, German Dept, UC, later Univ. Hull, 1946–70, Dean of Arts, 1957–60. Chevalier, Order of Pole Star, Sweden, 1963; Cross of Merit, Fed. Republic of Germany, 1971. *Publications*: Der Bauer in der Dichtung des Strichers, 1937; Deutschland und die Deutschen, 1952, 3rd edn 1965; Selections from Hans Carossa, 1960; *contrib*. German Life and Letters, Mod. Lang. Review. *Address*: Dept of German, Univ. of Hull, Hull HU6 7RX.

Bailey, Adrian Frank; Lecturer in American History, Department of History, Leicester University, since 1968; *b* 1944. BA Manchester 1966 (Politics and Modern History), MA 1967 (American History), PhD 1970; *Address*: Dept of History, Univ. of Leicester, Leicester LE1 7RH.

Bailey, Dr Ninette; Senior Lecturer, French Department, Birkbeck College, University of London, since 1971; *b* 1915; *m* 1940; two *s* one *d*. LèsL Dijon 1934–37 (Philosophy), Diplômée d'Etudes Supérieures Dijon 1938, BA London 1945 (1st cl. French), PhD London 1952; Lectr, Birkbeck Coll., 1956–71. Univ. Examiner to Coll. of Educn, 1965–69; Chm., Bd of Examiners, Gen. and Subsid. Exams in French, 1970– . *Publications*: Marcel Proust (forthcoming); *contrib*. Bull. des amis de M. Proust, French Studies, Mod. Lang. Rev. *Address*: Birkbeck College, Malet Street, WC1E 7HX.

Bailey, Richard Nigel; Lecturer in English Language and Medieval Literature, School of English, University of Newcastle, since 1967; *b* 1936; *m* 1960; one *s* one *d*. BA Dunelm 1967, MA Dunelm 1969. Lectr in English, Univ. Coll. of North Wales, 1960–67. *Address*: School of English, Univ. of Newcastle upon Tyne, Newcastle upon Tyne NE1 7RU.

Bain, Prof. Andrew David, MA, PhD; Esmée Fairbairn Professor of the Economics of Finance and Investment, University of Stirling, since 1970; *b* 1936; *m* 1960; three *s*.

BA Cambridge 1958, MA Cambridge 1962, PhD Cambridge 1963. Univ. Asst Lectr/ Lectr in Economics, Cambridge Univ., 1961–66; Prof. of Economics, Stirling Univ., 1967–70; Director, Inst. of Finance and Investment, Stirling Univ., 1970– . Head of National Economy Division of Bank of England, 1966–67. *Publications*: The Growth of Television Ownership in the United Kingdom, 1964; The Control of the Money Supply, 1970; *contrib*. Internat. Econ. Rev., Jl of Royal Stat. Soc., Econ. Jl, Jl of Econ. Studies, Manchester School, Scottish Jl of Political Econ. *Address*: Institute of Finance and Investment, Univ. of Stirling, Stirling FK9 4LA.

Bain, George Sayers; Deputy Director, SSRC Industrial Relations Research Unit, University of Warwick, since 1970; *b* 1939; *m* 1962; one *s* one *d*. BA (Hons) Manitoba 1961, MA Manitoba 1964, DPhil Oxon 1968. Mem., Brit. Univ. Indust. Relations Assoc., Canadian Econ. Assoc., Canadian Indust. Relations Res. Inst., Canadian Political Science Assoc., Canadian Sociol. and Anthropol. Assoc., Indust. Law Soc., Indust. Relations Res. Assoc., Internat. Indust. Relations Assoc., Soc. of Indust. Tutors, Soc. for Study of Labour Hist. Lectr, Univ. of Manitoba, 1962–63; Res. Fellow, Nuffield Coll., Oxford, 1966–69; Frank Thomas Prof. of Indust. Relations, Univ. of Manchester Inst. of Science and Tech., 1969–70. Mem., Soc. Science Working Party, TUC, 1970– ; Sec., Brit. Univ. Indust. Relations Assoc., 1971– . *Publications*: Trade Union Growth and Recognition: With Special Reference to White-Collar Unions in Private Industry, 1967; The Growth of White-Collar Unionism, 1970; (with others) The Reform of Collective Bargaining at Plant and Company Level, 1971; (with others) Social Stratification and Trade Unionism, 1973; *contrib*. Brit. Jl of Indust. Relations, Bull. Soc. for Study of Labour Hist., Indust. Relations Jl. Relations Industrielles. *Address*: Industrial Relations Research Unit, Univ. of Warwick, Coventry CV4 7AL.

Bain, Sheila Margaret; Research Assistant, Department of Geography, University of Aberdeen, since 1967; *b* 1929. MA Hons Edinburgh 1952 (Geography), DipEd St Andrews 1954, MEd Hons Aberdeen 1964 (Educn and Psychol.). Asst, Dept of Mental Health, Aberdeen, 1962–67; Research Fellow, 1964–67. *Publications*: In Community Psychiatry (North-East Region of Scotland), 1964: three chapters in Royal Grampian Country: A Report for the Scottish Tourist Board, 1969; The History and Production of Scotch Whisky in North-East Scotland: Geographical Essays, ed by C. Clapperton, 1971; The Geographical variation in psychiatric disorders in North-East Region of Scotland, in, Internat. Jl Med. Geog. Budapest, Hungary, 1971. *Address*: Dept of Geography, Univ. of Aberdeen, Aberdeen AB9 1AS.

Bainbridge, Dr Lisanne; Lecturer in Department of Psychology, University of Reading, since 1966. MA, MS, PhD. *Address*: Dept of Psychology, Univ. of

26

Reading, Whiteknights, Reading, Berks RG6 2AH.

Bainbridge, Margaret Nora; Lecturer in Turkish, School of Oriental and African Studies, University of London, since 1966; *b* 1924. MA Edinburgh 1945 (2nd cl. Geography), BA London 1965 (1st cl. Turkish); Teacher's Cert., Cambridge 1946; ARCM 1955. Mem., Folklore Soc., Philol. Soc.; Fellow, British Soc. for Middle Eastern Studies. *Address*: School of Oriental and African Studies, Univ. of London, WC1E 7HP.

Baird, Dr Alexander John, MA; Lecturer in Education, University of London Institute of Education, since 1965; *b* 1925; *m* 1954; two *d*. BA Cantab 1947, MA Cantab 1953, PhD London 1970; DipEd Liverpool 1953, Dip. in Applied Linguistics, Edinburgh 1963. Vis. Lectr in English Lang. and Lit., Univ. of Hiroshima, Japan, 1959–62. *Publications*: *novels*: The Mickey-Hunters, 1957; The Unique Sensation. 1959; *poetry*: Poems by Alexander Baird, 1963 (Poetry Book Society Summer Choice 1963); *contrib.* ELT. *Address*: Language Teaching Division, Univ. of London Institute of Education, Malet Street WC1E 7HS.

Baker, Alan George, MSc(Econ), MEd, ACIS; Senior Lecturer, School of Management, Bath University, since 1962; *b* 1929; *m* 1955; three *s* one *d*. BSc(Econ) London 1953, MSc(Econ) London 1960, MEd Durham 1965; ACIS. Lectr, Bath Univ., 1962–64; Dir of Studies, 1965–70. *Address*: School of Management, Univ. of Bath, Rockwell House, Kingsweston Road, Bristol.

Baker, Alan Reginald Harold, MA, PhD; Lecturer in Geography, University of Cambridge, since 1966; *b* 1938; *m* 1960; two *s*. BA London 1960 (1st cl. Geography), PhD London 1963, MA Cambridge 1966. Asst Lectr, Univ. Coll., London, 1963; Lectr, 1964–66; Fellow, Emmanuel Coll., Cambridge, 1970. Co-editor, Studies in Hist. Geog., 1970– . *Publications*: (with J. D. Hamshere and J. Langton) Geographical Interpretations of Historical Sources, 1970; Progress in Historical Geography, 1972; (with R. A. Butlin) Studies of Field Systems in the British Isles; ed (with J. B. Harley) Man Made the Land: essays in English historical geography, 1973; *contrib.* Agric. Hist. Rev., Canad. Geog., Econ. Hist. Rev., Geog., Professional Geog., Trans. Inst. Brit. Geogrs. *Address*: Dept of Geography, Univ. of Cambridge, Cambridge; Emmanuel Coll., Cambridge.

Baker, Derek; *see* Baker, L. G. D.

Baker, Felicity Ruth; Lecturer in French Language and Literature, University College London, since 1969; *b* 1940. BA Sydney 1962 (Hons); Mem.: British Soc. for 18th Century Studies; Soc. for French Studies. Teaching Fellow in French, Sydney Univ., 1962; Lectr, Dept of Romance Languages, Univ. of Pa, 1967–69. *Publications*: *contrib.* Annales de la Société J. J. Rousseau. *Address*: Dept of French Language

and Literature, Univ. College, Gower Street, WC1E 6BT.

Baker, Dr Gordon Park; Fellow of St John's College, and Lecturer in Philosophy, University of Oxford, since 1967; *b* 1938; *m* 1964; two *s*. AB Harvard 1960 (Mathematics), BA Oxon 1963 (Lit. Hum.), MA Oxon 1967, DPhil Oxon 1970. Asst Lectr in Philosophy, Univ. of Kent a+ Canterbury, 1966–67. *Publications*: *contrib.* Amer. Philosophical Qly, Ratio. *Address*: St John's College, Oxford.

Baker, (Leonard Graham) Derek, MA, BLitt, FRHistS; Lecturer in History, University of Edinburgh, since 1966; *b* 1931; *m* 1970. BA Oxford 1955 (1st cl. Hons), MA Oxford 1959, BLitt Oxford 1967; FRHistS (1971). Editor, Eccles. Hist. Soc., 1970; Sec., Brit. Sub-Commission, Commission Internationale d'Histoire Ecclésiastique Comparée. Mem., Oriel Coll. Development Cttee, 1971; Treas., Carter Foundation, 1971. *Publications*: Portraits and Documents I (871–1216), 1966, II (1216–1485), 1967; ed, Miscellanea Historiae Ecclesiasticae III, 1970; ed. Peter Abelard, 1970; ed, Studies in Church History VII, 1971, VIII, 1971, IX, 1972, X, 1973, XI, 1974; *contrib.* Ampleforth Jl, Analecta Cisterciensia, Hist., Northern Hist. *Address*: The Dept of History, William Robertson Building, George Square, Edinburgh 8.

Baker, Lionel Joseph Valentine; Lecturer in Psychology, Trinity College, Dublin, since 1969; *b* 1933; two *s*. BSc(Special) London 1964 (2nd cl. Psychol.), MA Dublin 1971. Mem., Council, Psychol. Soc. Ireland. Jun. Lectr, TCD, 1966–69; Asst Prof., Colorado Coll., USA, Spring 1972. Ed., Irish Jl Psychol. *Publications*: The Behaviour of Man and Animals, 1971; *contrib.* Papers in Psychol., Irish Jl Psychol. *Address*: Dept of Psychology, Trinity College, Dublin 2, Ireland.

Baker, Prof. Michael John; Professor and Head of Department of Marketing, Strathclyde University, since 1971; *b* 1935; *m* 1959; one *s* two *d*. BA Durham 1958, BSc(Econ) London 1962, CertITP Harvard 1968, DBA Harvard 1971, DipM Inst. of Marketing 1965; FInstM. Res. Associate, Harvard Univ., 1968–71. Richard Thomas & Baldwins (Sales) Ltd, 1958–64. Mem., Scottish Business Educn Council, 1973– . *Publications*: Marketing: an introductory text, 1971, 2nd edn 1974; ed, The Functions of Industry (forthcoming); Marketing New Industrial Products (forthcoming); *contrib.* Jl Advertising Res. *Address*: Strathclyde Univ., George Street, Glasgow G1 1XW.

Baker, Dr Peter Randall; Lecturer in Geography (Development Studies), University of East Anglia, since 1970; *b* 1944; *m* 1968. BSc Wales 1965; PhD E Africa 1968. Lecturer: Makerere UC, 1968–70; Overseas Develt Gp, UEA, 1970–73. Regional Planner, Western Region Plan, Saudi Arabia, 1971–72; Eastern Region Planning Team, Saudi Arabia, 1974; UN Reg. Planning Advr,

Saudi Arabia; FAO Expert Panel on Rangelands in Semi-Arid Areas; Project Manager, Eastern Regional Plan, Saudi Arabia, 1974–75. *Publications*: Western Regional Plan, Saudi Arabia; *contrib.* various j!s. *Address*: School of Development Studies, University Village, Norwich NOR 88C.

Baker, Prof. Samuel John Kenneth; Hon. Lecturer in Geography, University of Leicester, since 1968; *b* 1907. BA Liverpool 1927, MA Liverpool 1931; Hon. LittD Liverpool 1972; FRGS; Member: Inst. Brit. Geogrs; Geog. Assoc.; Afr. Studies Assoc. UK; Internat. Afr. Inst.; Uganda Geog. Assoc. (Pres., 1962); Uganda Soc. (Pres., 1966–67). Lecturer in Geography: Univ. of Liverpool, 1930–46; Makerere Coll., 1946–48; Makerere UC: Prof. of Geog., 1949–67; Prof. Emeritus, 1967; Vice-Principal, 1965–67; Advr (Academic Admin), 1967–68. Mem., Uganda Town and Country Planning Board, 1966–68. *Publications*: *contrib.* Oliver and Mathew, History of East Africa, vol. I, 1963; *contrib.* Africa, Bibliog. Internat. Géog., Encycl. Brit., Trans Inst. Brit. Geogrs, Uganda Jl, etc. *Address*: Dept of Geography, Univ. of Leicester, Leicester LE1 7RH.

Baker-Smith, Malcolm Philip Dominic; Director of Studies in English, Fitzwilliam College, Cambridge University, since 1968; University Assistant Lecturer in English, since 1972; *b* 1937; *m* 1961; two *s* one *d*. BA Cantab 1960, MA Cantab 1964, PhD Cantab 1969. Mem., Soc. Renaiss. Studies, Renaiss. Soc. Amer. Instructor, Univ. of Saskatchewan, 1961–64; Res. Fellow, Queens' Coll., Cambridge, 1966–68. Steward, Fitzwilliam Coll., 1971. *Publications*: Webster and Religion, in, John Webster, ed B. Morris, 1970; John Donne's Critique of True Religion, in, John Donne – Critical Approaches, ed A. J. Smith, 1972; *contrib.* Engl. Misc. *Address*: Fitzwilliam College, Cambridge CB3 0DG.

Balashov, Vladimir, PhD, FInstP; Lecturer in Russian, Modern Languages Centre, University of Bradford, since 1965; *b* 1918; *m* 1955; two *d*. Dip Moscow 1941 (1st cl. Phys Chem.), MScAcadSci USSR 1946, PhD Leeds 1956; Fellow, Inst. Physics 1958, Fellow, RMS. Mem., NASEES. Sen. Res. Fellow, Acad. Sci. USSR, 1945–48; Lectr, Moscow Univ., 1946–47; Res. Asst, Leeds Univ., 1950–57. Rep., Acad. Sci. USSR in E. Germany, 1948–49; Ch. Physicist, N Rhodesian Govt, 1957–64. *Publications*: trans., N. V. Belov: A Class-room Method for the Derivation of the 230 Space Groups, 1957; trans., V. L. Ginzburg: The Origin of Cosmic Radiation, 1958; *contrib.* Acta Cryst., Nature, Proc. Royal Soc. B. *Address*: Modern Languages Centre, Univ. of Bradford, Bradford BD7 1DP.

Balchin, Prof. William George Victor, MA, PhD, FRGS, FRMetS; Professor and Head of Department of Geography, University College of Swansea, since 1954; *b* 1916; *m* 1939; one *s* two *d*. BA Cambridge 1937 (1st cl. Part I Geog. Tripos), MA Cambridge 1941, PhD London 1951; FRGS, FRMS, Mem. of Inst. of Brit. Geographers. Demonstrator in Geography, Cambridge, 1937–39;

28

Lectr in Geography, King's Coll., London, 1945–54; Vice-Principal, Univ. Coll., Swansea, 1964–66 and 1970–73. Mem., Council of Roy. Geog. Soc., 1962–65; Trustee, Geog. Assoc., 1954– ; Pres., Geog. Assoc., 1971; Pres., Section E Brit. Assoc., 1972; Mem., Nature Conservancy Cttee for Wales, 1959–68; Roy. Soc. Brit. Nat. Cttee for Geog., 1964–70. *Publications*: ed, Geography and Man, 1947, 1955; Climate and Weather Exercises, 1949; Practical and Experimental Geography, 1952; Cornwall, The Making of the English Landscape, 1954; Cornwall, Landscape through Maps, 1967; ed, Geography for the Intending Student, 1970; ed, Swansea and Its Region, 1971; *contrib.* over 100 research and other contribs to Geog. Jl (RGS), Geog. (Geog. Assoc.), Proc. Geologists Assoc., Jl of Ecology, Nature, Times Educnl Supp., New Scientist, Geog. Magazine, Weather and Quart. Jl Royal Met. Soc., Water and Water Eng., Jl of Inst. of Water Eng., etc. *Address*: Univ. College of Swansea, Singleton Park, Swansea SA2 8PP.

Baldamus, Prof. Wilhelm, DrRerPol, DSocSc; Professor of Sociology, and Head of Department, University of Birmingham, since 1970; *b* 1908; *m* 1932; one *d*. Diplom Volkswirt, Frankfurt, 1930, DrRerPol, Frankfurt, 1932, DSocSc, Birmingham, 1963. Lectr in Sociology, Birmingham, 1961; Vis. Prof. at Soziologische Seminar, Technische Hochschule, Hannover, 1963–65; Reader in Economic Sociology, Birmingham, 1967. *Publications*: Der gerechte Lohn, 1960; Efficiency and Effort, 1961; *contrib.* Archiv für Rechts– und Socialphilosophie, Brit. Jl of Sociol., Jl of Industrial Econs, Economic Jl, Nature. *Address*: Dept of Sociology, Faculty of Commerce and Social Science, Univ. of Birmingham, P.O. Box 363, Birmingham B15 2TT.

Baldwin, Dr John Richard; Lecturer, Department of Phonetics and Linguistics, University College London, since 1965; *b* 1935; *m* 1961; two *s*. BA Nottingham 1957 (Russian), MA London 1966 (General Linguistics), PhD 1972. *Publications*: *contrib.* Jl of the International Phonetics Assoc., Zeitschrift für Phonetik. *Address*: Dept of Phonetics and Linguistics, Univ. College, London, Gower Street, WC1E 6BT.

Ball, Christopher John Elinger, MA; Fellow and Tutor in English Language at Lincoln College, Oxford, since 1964, and CUF Lecturer of the University of Oxford, since 1965; *b* 1935; *m* 1958; three *s* three *d*. BA Oxon 1959 (1st cl. English Language and Literature, course I), Dip. in Comparative Philology Oxon 1962, MA Oxon 1963; Mem., Philological Soc.; Linguistics Assoc. of Great Britain. Lectr in English Language, Merton Coll., Oxford, 1960–61; Lectr in Comparative Linguistics, Sch. of Oriental and African Studies, London Univ., 1961–64; Sen. Tutor and Tutor for Admissions, Lincoln Coll., 1971–72; Bursar, Lincoln Coll., 1972– . Sec., Linguistics Assoc. of Great Britain, 1964–67; Proproctor, Univ. of Oxford, 1967–68; Mem., English Studies Bd, CNAA, 1967– ; Pres., Oxford AUT, 1968–70; Publications Sec., Philological

Soc., 1969– . *Publications*: Questions of Old English Lexicography, in, Computers and Old English Concordance, ed A. Cameron et al., 1970; The English Vocabulary, in, The English Language, ed W. Bolton, 1972; (with A. Cameron) Some Specimen Entries for the Dictionary of Old English, in, A Plan for the Dictionary of Old English, ed R. Frank et al., 1973; *contrib*. Anglia, Arch. Ling., Engl. Studies, RES, TPS. *Address*: Lincoln College, Oxford.

Ball, Prof. Robert James, MA Oxon, PhD Pennsylvania; Principal, London Graduate School of Business Studies, since 1972; *b* 1933; *m* 1954; one *s* three *d*. Res. Officer, Oxford Univ. Inst. of Studies, 1957–58; IBM Fellow, Univ. of Pennsylvania, 1958–60; Lectr, Manchester Univ., 1960, Sen. Lectr, 1963–65; Dep. Principal, London Business Sch., 1969–72. Mem., Page Cttee on Nat. Savings, 1971; Mem., Econs Cttee, SSRC, 1971; Mem., Cttee on Social Forecasting, SSRC, 1972. *Publications*: An Econometric Model of the U.K., 1961; Inflation and the Theory of Money, 1964; ed, Inflation, 1969; ed, The International Linkage of National Economic Models, 1973; *contrib*. Economic Jl, Jl of Political Economy, Rev. of Economic Studies, Oxford Univ. Bull. of Stats, Rev. of Econs and Stats, Metroeconomica, Oxford Economic Papers, Economica, Internat. Economic Rev., Kyklos, Economic Record, Applied Statistics, Manchester Sch. *Address*: London Graduate School of Business Studies, Sussex Place, Regent's Park, NW1 4SA.

Ballhatchet, Prof. Kenneth Arthur, M.A., PhD; Professor of the History of South Asia in the University of London, since 1965; *b* 1922; *m* 1948; three *s* one *d*. MA Cantab (1st cl. Hist. Trip. Pt I, 1942, 1st cl. Hist. Trip. Pt II, 1947), PhD London 1954; FRHistS. Lectr, Sch. of Orient. and Afr. Studies, London Univ., 1948–59; Vis. Lectr., Ceylon Univ., 1948–49; Reader, London Univ., 1959–63; Reader, Oxford Univ., 1963–65; Faculty Fellow, St Antony's Coll., Oxford 1964–65; Assoc. Fellow, St. Antony's Coll., 1966– . Mem., Advisers' Panel, Commonwealth Schol. Commn, 1960– ; Mem., Council, Royal Asiatic Soc., 1968–72; Corresp. Mem., Indian Hist. Mss Commn. *Publications*: Social Policy and Social Change in Western India, 1817–1830, 1957; chapters in New Cambridge Modern History, vols. viii and ix, 1965; *contrib*. Bull. SOAS, Hist. Jl. *Address*: School of Oriental and African Studies, Univ. of London, WC1E 7HP.

Balme, David Mowbray, CMG, DSO, DFC, MA; Professor of Classics, Queen Mary College, London University, since 1964; *b* 1912; *m* 1936; four *s* one *d*. Res. student, Clare Coll., Cambridge, and Univ. of Halle, Germany, 1934–36; Lectr, Reading Univ., 1936–37; Res. Fellow, Clare Coll., 1937–40; Fellow of Jesus Coll., 1940; Tutor of Jesus Coll., 1945–47; Sen. Tutor, 1947–48; Univ. Lectr in Classics, 1947–48; Principal, Univ. Coll. of Ghana, 1948–57; Reader in Classics, Queen Mary Coll., London, 1957–64. *Publications*: Aristotle's De Partibus Animalium I and De Generatione Animalium I, 1972; *contrib*. articles in classica 'journals

on Greek Philosophy. *Address*: Queen Mary College, Mile End Road, E1 4NS.

Bamber, James Henry; Lecturer in Educational Psychology, Department of Education, Queen's University of Belfast, since 1968; *b* 1935; *m* 1961; one *s* one *d*. MA Glasgow 1959, DipEd Glasgow 1960, MEd Glasgow 1965; ABPS 1969, APSI 1972, FRSM; Mem. Brit. Soc. for Projective Psychol. and Personality Study. Mem.: Adv. Panel, NI Dyslexia Assoc., 1970– ; Bd of Governors, Rupert Stanley Coll., Belfast, 1973– . *Publications*: *contrib*. Brit. Jl Project. Psychol., Genet. Psychol. Monog., Irish Jl Psychol., Jl Genet. Psychol. *Address*: Dept of Education, Queen's Univ., Belfast BT7 1NN.

Bamborough, John Bernard; Principal of Linacre College, Oxford, since 1962; Pro-Vice-Chancellor, Oxford University, since 1966; *b* 1921; *m* 1947; one *s* one *d*. 1st cl. English Lang. and Lit. Oxford 1941, MA Oxford 1946. Junior Lectr, New Coll., Oxford, 1946; Fellow and Tutor, Wadham Coll., Oxford, 1947–62 (Dean, 1947–54; Domestic Bursar, 1954–56; Sen. Tutor, 1957–61); Univ. Lectr in English, 1951–62. Mem., Hebdomadal Council, Oxford; Editor, Review of English Studies, 1964– . Hon. Fellow, New Coll., Oxford, 1967. *Publications*: The Little World of Man, 1952; Ben Jonson, 1959; ed, Pope's Life of Ward, 1961; Jonson's Volpone, 1963; The Alchemist, 1967; Ben Jonson, 1970. *Address*: Linacre College, Oxford.

Bambrough, John Renford; University Lecturer in Philosophy, University of Cambridge, since 1966; *b* 1926; *m* 1952; one *s* three *d*. BA Cambridge 1948 (1st cl. in Pts I and II Classical Tripos), MA Cambridge 1952. Fellow, St John's Coll. Cambridge, 1950– ; Tutor, 1952–63; Dean, 1964– ; Dir of Studies in Philosophy, 1959– ; Supervisor in Classics and Philosophy, 1950–62; Coll. Lectr in Philosophy, 1962– ; Univ. Asst. Lectr in Classics, 1957–62; Stanton Lectr, 1962–65; Univ. Lectr in Classics, 1962–66; Mahlon Powell Lectr, Indiana Univ., 1962; H. B. Acton Lectr, Royal Inst. Philos., 1973; Vis. Prof., Cornell, 1962–63, Univ. Calif., Berkeley, 1967, Oregon, 1967. Univ. of Cambridge: Mem., Fac. Bd of Philosophy, 1953– (Chm., 1972–74); Fac. Bd of Classics, 1963–66; Council of Senate, 1964–70; Gen. Bd of Facs, 1965–66; Council, St John's Coll., 1957–61, 1970–71 (Sec. 1959–61); Council, New Hall, Cambridge, 1959–72; Mem., Mngt Cttee, Camb. Rev., 1951– , Chm. 1971– ; Steward, Cambridge Union Soc., 1955–61; Trustee, Cambridge Union Soc., 1963– ; Gov., Sedbergh Sch., 1961– ; Mem., Council and Exec. Cttee, Royal Inst. Philos., 1965–72; Editor: Camb. Rev., 1951–52; Philosophy (Jl Royal Inst. Philos.), 1972– . *Publications*: ed, The Philosophy of Aristotle, 1963; ed, New Essays on Plato and Aristotle, 1965; ed, Plato, Popper and Politics, 1967; Reason, Truth and God, 1969; Nature and Human Nature, 1973; Conflict and the Scope of Reason, 1974; ed, Wisdom; twelve essays, 1974; contrib. Philosophy,

29

Politics and Society, 1956; Religion and Humanism, 1964; New Cambridge Modern History, Vol. XII, 2nd edn 1968; Situationism and the New Morality, 1970; Understanding Wittgenstein, 1974; *contrib.* Amer. Jl Jurisp., Analysis, Phil., Phil. Qly, PAS, PASS. *Address:* St John's College, Cambridge.

Bance, Dr A. F.; Lecturer, Department of German, University of St Andrews, since 1967; *b* 1939; *m* 1964; one *d.* BA London 1961, PhD Cambridge 1968. Lektor, Univ. of Graz, Austria, 1964–65; Lectr, Univ. of Strathclyde, 1965–67; (leave of absence) Univ. of Cologne, 1972–73. *Publications:* ed with introd., notes and commentary, Joseph Roth: Die Kapuzinergruft, 1972; *contrib.* Seminar, FMLS, MLR. *Address:* Dept of German, Buchanan Building, Univ. of St Andrews, Fife.

Banham, Martin John; Fellow in Drama and Director of the Workshop Theatre, University of Leeds, since 1966; *b* 1932; *m* 1957; two *s* one *d.* BA Leeds 1955, MA Leeds 1962. Lectr, Univ. Coll., Ibadan, 1956; Sen. Lectr, Univ. of Ibadan, 1964; Vis. Lectr and Guest Dir of Theatre, Lake Erie Coll., USA, 1962–63. Mem., Council Yorkshire Arts Assoc., 1970– . *Publications:* Osborne, 1969; Mosquito (play), 1972; (ed) Drama in Education: the annual survey, 1972; *contrib.* Universities Qly, Rev. of Eng. Lit., Jl of Commonwealth Literature, New Theatre Magazine, Speech and Drama Books Abroad, Stratford Seminar Papers, Theatre Qly. *Address:* School of English, Univ. of Leeds, Leeds LS2 9JT.

Banham, Prof. (Peter) Reyner, BA, PhD; Professor of History of Architecture, School of Environmental Studies, University College, London, since 1969; *b* 1922; *m* 1946; one *s* one *d.* BA (Hist. of Art) London 1952, PhD London 1958. Sen. Lectr, Univ. Coll. London, 1964; Reader in Architecture, 1967; External Examiner in Humanities, Open University, 1970. Internat. Council of Societies of Industrial Design: Chm., Working Party on Doctrine and Definitions, 1964–68; Internat. Design Conf. in Aspen, Colorado: Adviser to the Bd, 1968– . *Publications:* Theory and Design in the First Machine Age, 1960; Guide to Modern Architecture, 1962; The New Brutalism, 1966; Architecture of the Well-Tempered Environment, 1969; Los Angeles, 1971; *contrib.* Arch. Rev., etc. *Address:* School of Environmental Studies, Univ. College, Gower Street, WC1E 6BT.

Banham, Prof. Reyner; *see* Banham, P. R.

Banks, Gerald Vincent, BA, PhD; Lecturer in French, Birmingham University, since 1964; *b* 1938; *m* 1961; two *s* one *d.* BA (Hons French) London 1960, PhD London 1966. *Publications:* ed, Giraudoux: Siegfried, 1967; ed, Camus: L'Etranger (forthcoming); *contrib.* reviews in Modern Languages Jl. *Address:* Dept of French, Birmingham Univ., PO Box 363, Birmingham B15 2TT.

Banks, Prof. J. A., MA; Professor of Socio-
30

logy, University of Leicester, since 1970; *b* 1920; *m* 1944. BA London 1950 (1st cl. Sociology), MA London 1952. Mem., Brit. Sociological Assoc. since 1951. Asst. Lectr in Sociology, Univ. Coll., Leicester, 1952–54; Sen. Res. Worker, Dept of Social Science, Univ. of Liverpool, 1954–59; Res. Lectr, 1959–60; Sen. Res. Lectr, 1960–70. *Publications:* Prosperity and Parenthood, 1954; (with W. M. Scott et al.) Technical Change and Industrial Relations, 1956; Industrial Participation, 1963; (with O. Banks) Feminism and Family Planning in Victorian England, 1964; ed, Studies in British Society, 1968; Marxist Sociology in Action, 1970; The Sociology of Social Movements, 1972; *contrib.* Brit. Med. Jl, Brit. Jl of Sociology, Daedalus, Population Studies, Sociological Rev., Sociologische Gids, Victorian Studies. *Address:* Dept of Sociology, Univ. of Leicester, Leicester LE1 7RH.

Banks, Michael Henry; Lecturer, Department of International Relations, London School of Economics, since 1961; *b* 1936. BScEcon London 1957 (1st cl. Hons International Relations), MA Lehigh (Pennsylvania) 1959 (International Relations). Sen. Res. Fellow, Centre for the Analysis of Conflict, Univ. Coll., London, 1967–69. Council Mem., Conflict Res. Soc., 1970– ; Consultant on Peace Res., UNESCO, 1969–71; Exec. Cttee Mem., Internat. Peace Res. Assoc., 1969–71; Editorial Bd Mem., Internat. Studies Qly, 1971–74. *Publications: contrib.* Clare Market Rev., Internat. Affairs, Internat. Studies Qly, Political Studies, Proc. IPRA, World Survey. *Address:* International Relations Dept, London School of Economics, Houghton Street, Aldwych, WC2A 2AE.

Banks, Prof. Olive, BA, PhD; Professor of Sociology, University of Leicester, since 1973 (Reader, 1970–73); *b* 1923; *m* 1944. BA London 1950 (2/I Sociology), PhD London 1953. Res. Asst, Liverpool, 1954; Sen. Res. Asst, Liverpool, 1956; Res. Lectr, Liverpool, 1959; Sen. Res. Lectr, Liverpool, 1969. *Publications:* Parity and Prestige in English Secondary Education, 1955; The Attitude of Steelworkers to Technical Change, 1960; (with J. A. Banks) Feminism and Family Planning, 1964; (with E. Mumford) The Computer and the Clerk, 1966; The Sociology of Education 1968, 2nd edn 1971; (with D. Finlayson) Success and Failure in the Secondary School, 1973; *contrib.* Brit. Jl of Educnl Studies, Brit. Jl of Sociology, Internat. Review of Educn, Occupational Psychology, Population Studies. *Address:* Dept of Sociology, Univ. of Leicester, Leicester LE1 7RH.

Bannerman, Dr John Walter MacDonald, MA, PhD; Lecturer, Scottish History, University of Edinburgh, since 1964; *b* 1932; *m* 1959; two *s* two *d.* MA Glasgow 1956 (Celtic Languages), BA Cambridge 1958 (Anglo-Saxon Tripos), PhD Cambridge 1964; FSAScot. *Publications:* Studies in the History of Dalriada; *contrib.* Celtica, Scott. Gael. Studies. *Address:* William Robertson Memorial Building, Univ. of Edinburgh, Edinburgh.

Bantock, Prof. Geoffrey Herman, MA; Professor of Education, School of Education, University of Leicester, since 1964; *b* 1914; *m* 1950. BA Cantab 1937, MA Cantab 1942. Lectr in Education, Univ. of Leicester, 1950; Reader in Education, Univ. of Leicester, 1954. Vis. Prof., Monash Univ., 1971. Mem., Exec., UCET, 1970– ; Trustee, Uppingham School, 1971– . *Publications*: Freedom and Authority in Education, 1952, 2nd edn 1965, pbk 1970; L. H. Myers: A Critical Study, 1956; Education in an Industrial Society, 1963; Education and Values, 1965; Education, Culture and the Emotions, 1967; Culture, Industrialisation and Education, 1968; trans. Spanish, 1972; T. S. Eliot and Education, 1970; *contrib.* Brit. Jl of Educ Studies, Cambridge Jl, Scrutiny, Melbourne Studies in Education, etc. *Address*: School of Education, Univ. of Leicester, 21 University Road, Leicester.

Banton, , Prof. Michael Parker, JP, PhD, DSc; Professor of Sociology, University of Bristol, since 1965; *b* 1926; *m* 1952; two *s* two *d*. BScEcon London 1950, PhD Edinburgh 1954, DSc Edinburgh 1964. Pres., Sect. N Brit. Assoc. Adv. Sci., 1970–1; FRAI; Mem., Brit. Social. Assoc.; Mem., Assoc. Soc. Anthrop.; Asst in Social Anthropology, Univ. of Edinburgh, 1953–55; Lectr, 1955–62; Reader, 1962–65; Vis. Prof. of Political Science, MIT, 1962–63; Malinowski Memorial Lectr, LSE, 1964; Munro Lectr, Univ. of Edinburgh, 1966; Vis Prof. of Sociology, Wayne State Univ., Detroit, 1971. Editor, Sociology: Jl Brit. Sociol. Assoc., 1966–69; Gen. Editor, Assoc. Soc. Anthrop. Monog., 1964–70; Dir, SSRC Res. Unit on Ethnic Relations, 1970; Mem., Home Sec's Adv. Cttee on Race Relations Res. *Publications*: The Coloured Quarter, 1955; West African City, 1957; White and Coloured, 1959; The Policeman in the Community, 1964; Roles, 1965; Race Relations, 1967; Racial Minorities, 1972; Police–Community Relations, 1973. *Address*: Dept of Sociology, Univ. of Bristol, 12 Woodland Road, Bristol BS8 1UB.

Barber, Rev. Charles Clyde; Senior Lecturer in German, Department of German, University of Aberdeen, since 1946; *b* 1905. BA Oxford 1926 (German), MA Oxford 1930, DPhil Giessen 1932, BD Oxford 1972. Lector in English: Heidelberg, 1926–27; Giessen, 1928–30; Lectr in German, Bristol Univ., 1930–41; Clerk in Holy Orders, 1932– . *Publications*: Vorgeschichtliche Betonung der germanischen Substantiva und Adjektiva, 1932; Old High German Reader, 1951; The Oldest Known Antiphoner of the Western Church (Codex Compendiensis), 1972; Codex Albensis (Transcription and Liturgical Introduction), 1972. *Address*: Dept of German, Univ. of Aberdeen, Aberdeen AB9 1AS.

Barber, Dr Charles Laurence; Reader in English Language and Literature, School of English, University of Leeds, since 1969; *b* 1915; *m* 1943; two *s* two *d*. BA Cambridge 1937 (1st cl. English), Teacher's Dip. London 1938, MA Cambridge 1941, Filosofie Licentiat Gothenburg 1956, Filosofie Doktor Gothenburg 1957. Lectr, Univ. of Gothenburg, 1947–56; Asst. Lectr, Queen's Univ. of Belfast, 1956–58; Lectr, Univ. of Leeds, 1959–62; Sen. Lectr, Univ. of Leeds, 1962–69. *Publications*: The Idea of Honour in the English Drama 1591–1700, 1957; The Story of Language, 1964; Linguistic Change in Present-Day English, 1964; ed, Shakespeare: Hamlet, 1964; ed, Thomas Middleton: A Trick to Catch the Old One, 1968; ed, Thomas Middleton: Women Beware Women, 1969; ed, Thomas Middleton: A Chaste Maid in Cheapside, 1969; *contrib.* ELT, E. Studies, REL. *Address*: School of English, The Univ., Leeds LS2 9JT.

Barber, Giles Gaudard; Librarian, Taylor Institution, Oxford, since 1970; Part-time Lecturer in Continental Bibliography, since 1969; Fellow of Linacre College, Oxford, since 1963; *b* 1930; *m* 1958; 1970; one *s* one *d*. BA Oxon 1954 (2nd cl. Hons Mod. Langs), MA 1958, BLitt Oxon 1963 (Mod. History); Gordon Duff prize in Bibliography (Oxford) 1962. Council Member: Oxford Bibliographical Soc.; Bibliographical Soc. Staff, Bodleian Library, 1954–70. *Publications*: French Letter-press Printing, 1969; ed, Bookmaking in Diderot's Encyclopedie, 1973; *contrib.* Library, Book Collector, Modern Language Review, Bodleian Library Record, Studies on Voltaire and the 18th Century. *Address*: Taylor Institution, St Giles, Oxford.

Barber, Dr James Peden; Reader, Department of Government, The Open University, since 1969; *b* 1931; *m* 1955; three *s* one *d*. BA Cantab 1952, MA Cantab 1962, PhD Cantab 1969. Univ. of New South Wales, 1962–65; Univ. of Exeter, 1965–69 (two years Secondment Univ. Coll. of Rhodesia and Nyasaland). Overseas Civil Service, Uganda, 1956–62; Dep. Dean Social Science, Univ. Coll. of Rhodesia, 1966–67; Pro-Vice Chancellor, Open Univ., 1971–73. *Publications*: Rhodesia: The Road to Rebellion, 1967; Imperial Frontier, 19̈68; South Africa's Foreign Policy, 1973; European Community, 1973; *contrib.* Jl of African Hist., Jl of Commonwealth Political Studies, Jl of Mod. African Studies. *Address*: The Open Univ., Walton Hall, Milton Keynes MK7 6AA.

Barber, Dr Malcolm Charles, BA, PhD; Lecturer in History, University of Reading, since 1966; *b* 1943; *m* 1968; one *s* one *d*. BA Nottingham 1964 (1st cl. History), PhD Nottingham 1968. *Publications: contrib.* Studia Monastica, Nottingham Mediæval Studies. *Address*: Dept of History, Whiteknights Park, Univ. of Reading, Berks RG6 2AH.

Barber, Prof. William Henry, MA, DPhil; Professor of French, University of London (Birkbeck College), since 1968; *b* 1918; *m* 1948. BA Oxon 1940, MA Oxon 1946, DPhil Oxon 1950; Hon. life mem., Mod. Hum. Res. Assoc. Asst. Lectr and Lectr, Univ. Coll., N Wales, 1948–55; Reader in French, London Univ. (Birkbeck Coll.), 1955–68; Editor, Year's Wk in Mod. Lang. Studies, 1959–62. Military service, 1940–46; Pres., Soc. for French Studies, 1964–66; Vice-Pres., 1966–67, Cttee Mem., 1962–64 and 1967– ; Mem., Brit. Soc. for 18th

Cent. Studies, 1971– ; Council, Whitelands Coll. of Educn, 1969–73. *Publications*: Leibniz in, France from Arnauld to Voltaire, 1955; Voltaire: Candide, 1960; ed, Racine, Britannicus, 1967; jt ed., The Age of Enlightenment, 1967; trans. Jolivet: Introduction to Kierkegaard, 1950; *contrib.* French Studies, MLR, Rev. de Litt. Comparée, Studies on Voltaire and the 18th Cent. *Address*: Dept of French, Birkbeck College, Malet Street, WC1E 7HX.

Barbour, Prof. Kenneth Michael; Professor of Geography, New University of Ulster, since 1973; *b* 1921; *m* 1946; four *d*. BA Oxon 1947, MA Oxon 1947, BLitt Oxon 1953, DPhil Oxon 1972. Lecturer in Geography: UC, Khartoum, 1948; UCL, 1956; Prof. of Geography, Univ. of Ibadan, Nigeria, 1962. *Publications*: The Republic of Sudan, 1961; Essays on African Population, 1961; Planning for Nigeria, 1972; The Growth, Location and Structure of Industry in Egypt, 1972; *contrib.* Geog. Rev., Jl of Mod. African Studies, ME Studies, Nigerian Geographical Jl, Trans Inst. British Geographers. *Address*: New Univ. of Ulster, Coleraine, Co. Londonderry, N Ireland BT52 1SA.

Barbour, Prof. Robert Stewart; Professor of New Testament Exegesis, Department of New Testament Exegesis, University of Aberdeen, since 1971; *b* 1921; *m* 1950; three *s* one *d*. MA Oxon 1947, DipEd Edinburgh 1948, BD St Andrews 1952, STM Yale 1953. Lectr in NT Language, Literature and Theology, Univ. of Edinburgh, 1955–59, Sen. Lectr, 1959–71. Sec., Studiorum Novi Testamenti Societas, 1970– ; Sec., Church of Scotland Special Cttee on Anglican-Presbyterian Relations, 1961–66; Mem., Council, Trinity Coll., Glenalmond, 1963– . *Publications*: The Scottish Horse, 1939–45, 1949; Traditio-Historical Criticism of the Gospels, 1972; What is the Church for?, 1973; *contrib.* New Testament Studies, Scottish Jl of Theology. *Address*: King's College, Old Aberdeen AB9 2UB.

Barbrook, Dr Alexander Thomas; Senior Lecturer in Politics and Government, University of Kent at Canterbury, since 1970, Lecturer, 1967–70; *b* 1927; *m* 1955; one *s* one *d*. BA Wales 1953 (2nd cl. History), DipEd Wales 1954, PhD Loughborough 1969. Asst. Lectr, Nottingham Univ., 1954–56; Lectr in Politics, Loughborough Univ., 1961–67; Sen. Res. Fellow, Massachusetts Inst. Tech., 1964. Warden, York Educnl Settlement, 1956; Monmouthshire Educn Cttee, 1960. *Publications*: The Civic Administration of York, in York, 1959 (British Association), 1959; God Save The Commonwealth; An Electoral History of Massachusetts, 1972; Patterns of Behavioural Politics, 1974; *contrib.* Urb. Aff. Qly, book rev. in Pol. Studies, etc. *Address*: Rutherford College, The Univ., Canterbury, Kent CT2 7NZ.

Barbu, Prof. Zevedei, DPhil, PhD; Professor of Sociology, University of Sussex, since 1968; *b* 1919; *m* 1946. DPhil, Cluj (Romania) 1942; PhD Glasgow 1954; Mem., British Sociological Assoc. Asst Lectr in Social Psychol., 1940–43; Lectr in Sociology

of Culture, 1943–51, Univ. of Cliy (Romania); Lectr in Social Psychology, 1951–60, Sen. Lectr in Sociology, 1960–63, Univ. of Glasgow; Sen. Lectr in Sociology, Univ. of Sussex, 1963–68; Professorial Fellow, Univ. of Sussex, 1966; Vis. Prof. of Sociology, Univ. of Nairobi, 1969–70. Under-Sec. of State, Nationalities, Bucarest, 1944–45; Dir, Cultural Relations with Abroad, Min. of Foreign Affairs, Bucarest, 1946; Mem., Romanian Delegn to Peace Conf., Paris, 1946; First Counsellor, Romanian Legation, London, 1946–49. *Publications*: Le Développement de la Pensée Dialectique, 1947; Democracy and Dictatorship, 1956; Problems of Historical Psychology, 1960 (Japanese edn 1968); Society, Culture and Personality, 1971 (Dutch edn 1972); *contrib.* European Jl of Sociology. *Address*: School of Social Science, Univ. of Sussex, Brighton, Sussex BN1 9RH.

Barclay, John Bruce, MA, PhD; Deputy Director, Department of Educational Studies, University of Edinburgh, since 1953; *b* 1909; *m* 1950; one *d*. MA Edinburgh 1931, PhD Edinburgh 1960; Scott. Teachers' Cert. 1932. Lectr, 1953, Sen. Lectr, 1962, Univ. of Edinburgh. Vice Chm. Scott. Cent. Film Libr., 1936– ; Council Mem., Scott. Educnl Film Assoc., 1933–69. Jt Editor, Scottish Jl of Adult Educn, 1973. *Publications*: Junior Cinema Clubs, 1951; Sound Films in the Primary School, 1955; Children's Film Tastes, 1956; Schools Television – the first six months in Scotland, 1958; Television in the Scottish Classroom, 1958; Viewing Tastes of Adolescents, 1961; Edinburgh from Earliest Times to Present, 1965; When Work is Done (Diamond Jub. Bk of Edin. Univ. Extra-Mural Assoc.), 1971; *contrib.* Scott. Adult Educn, Scott. Educn Jl, Lo Spettacolo. *Address*: Dept of Educational Studies, Univ. of Edinburgh, 11 Buccleuch Place, Edinburgh EH8 9JT.

Barden, Dr Garrett; Lecturer in Philosophy, University College Cork, since 1974; *b* 1939; *m* 1968; one *s* one *d*. BA NUI 1962; LicPh Heythrop 1965; Dip. Soc. Anthrop. Oxon 1966; BLitt Oxon 1967; PhD NUI 1973; Mem., Irish Philos. Soc.; FRAI. Lecturer in Philosophy: St John's Univ., NY, 1967–68; Inst. of Theol. and Philos., Dublin, 1970–72; Asst Lectr, Univ. Coll., Cork, 1972–74. Member: Council, Irish Fedn of Univ. Teachers, 1973– ; Nat. Cttee for Philos., RIA, 1972– . *Publications*: (with P. S. McShane) Towards Self-Meaning, 1969; translations: Lacroix: The Meaning of Modern Atheism, 1965; Ladrière: Language and Belief, 1973; ed, Gadamer: Truth and Method (forthcoming); *contrib.* Concilium, Human Context, Irish Theol. Qly, Philos. Studies, Studies. *Address*: Dept of Philosophy Univ. College, Cork, Ireland.

Bareham, Terence; Lecturer, Department of English Studies, New University of Ulster, since 1968; *b* 1937; *m* 1959; three *s*. BA Oxon 1962, MA Oxon 1967; Lectr, Univ. Coll. of Rhodesia, 1963–67; Univ. of York, 1967–68. *Publications*: *contrib.* Durham Univ. Jl, On the Novel: A Festschrift for Walter Allen, Orbis Litterarum, Studies in the Novel. *Address*: Dept of English Studies, New Univ. of Ulster, Coleraine, Co. Londonderry, Northern Ireland BT52 1SA.

Barelli, Dr Emma Spina; Lecturer in History of Art, University of Leeds, since 1969; *b* 1920; *m* 1954, Dott. in Scienze Pol. Milan 1944, Dott. in Lett. Pavia 1947. Lectr, Catholic Univ., Milan, 1954–67; Vis. Lectr, Newcastle Univ., 1968. Revisore dell' Indice dei disegni, Biblioteca Ambrosiana, 1959–65; Consulente al Gabinetto dei Restauri (Grafica), Museo Poldi Pezzoli, 1959–66. *Publications*: Disegni di Maestri Lombardi del Primo Seicento, 1959; La Decorazione Pittorica in Madonna di Campagna, 1961; L'Arazzo in Europa, 1963; Ascanio Condivi: Vita di Michelangelo Buonarroti, 1964; Francisco di Holanda, Dialoghi con Michelangelo, 1964; G. B. Moroni, 1966; Teorici e Scrittori d'Arte tra Manierismo e Barocco, 1966; *contrib*. Arte Lombarda, Vita e Pensiero, Studi in Onore di Mons C. Castiglioni, 1957, Studi Ist, stor, dell'Arte, Univ. Cat., 1966, Italian Studies, Storia dell'Arte. *Address*: Dept of Fine Art, Univ. of Leeds, Leeds LS2 9JT.

Barfield, Lawrence Harry, MA, PhD, FSA; Senior Lecturer, Department of Ancient History and Archaeology, University of Birmingham, since 1972, Lecturer 1966–72; *b* 1935; *m* 1969. BA Cantab 1958, MA Cantab 1961, PhD Cantab 1969; FSA 1971, Mem., Prehist. Soc.; Mem., Swiss Archaeological Soc.; Mem., Ist. Ital. di Preistoria e Protostoria. Asst, Institut für Vor- und Frühgeschichte, Bonn, 1961–62. Staff of Landesmuseum, Bonn, 1963; Council for Brit. Archaeology Gp 8 Secretary 1971. *Publications*: Northern Italy before Rome, 1971; *contrib*. Bonner Jahrbuch, Origini, Bullettino di Palentologia Italiana; Memorie del Museo di Verona; Rivista di Scienze Preistoriche. *Address*: Dept of Ancient History and Archaeology, Univ. of Birmingham, Birmingham B15 2TT.

Barford, Philip Trevelyan; Senior Lecturer in Music, Institute of Extension Studies, University of Liverpool, since 1969; *b* 1925; *m* 1950; two *s*. BMus Leeds 1949, MA Leeds 1950 (Philosophy); Mem., Royal Musical Assoc. Univ. of Liverpool, 1950– ; Vis. Associate Prof., Univ. of Calif. (Davis), 1967–68. *Publications*: The Keyboard Music of C. P. E. Bach, 1965; Gustav Mahler: Symphonies and Songs, 1970; Anton Bruckner: The Symphonies (forthcoming); contrib. The Beethoven Companion, 1971; *contrib*. Month. Mus. Record, Mus. Rev., Mus. and Letters, Musica. *Address*: Institute of Extension Studies, Univ. of Liverpool, PO Box 147, Liverpool L69 3BX.

Barič, Prof. Lorraine Florence, PhD; Professor of Sociology, Department of Sociology, Government and Administration, University of Salford, since 1970; *b* 1928; *m* 1st 1952, 2nd 1963; one *s* one *d*. BA Sydney 1950 (1st cl. Hons, Univ. Medal), Acad. Postgrad. Dipl. in Anthropology, London, LSE (Distinction), PhD London 1966; FRAI, Mem., Assoc. of Soc. Anthropol., Brit. Social. Assoc. (Sociology

Teachers' Sect.). Res. Asst, LSE, 1956; Asst Lectr, LSE, 1957; Lectr, LSE, 1961; Lectr, Manchester Univ., 1964; Lectr, Salford Univ. (RCAT), 1965; Sen. Lectr, Salford Univ., 1966. Res. Economist, Res. Service, Sydney, 1949–52; Chief Asst Planning Officer (Sociology), Liverpool Planning Dept, 1963. *Publications*: Contrib. (ed R. Firth and B. Yamey) Capital, Saving and Credit in Peasant Societies, 1964; (ed R. Firth) Themes in Economic Anthroplogy, 1967; (ed M. Freedman) Social Organization, 1967; *contrib*. Archives européennes de Sociologie, Brit. Jl Sociol., Current Anthróplogy. *Address*: Dept of Sociology, Government and Administration, Univ. of Salford, Salford M5 4WT.

Barker, Clive; Lecturer in Theatre Practice, Department of Drama and Theatre Arts, University of Birmingham, since 1966; *b* 1931; *m* 1964; two *s*. Entered Univ. in 1966 after career in professional theatre. Mem., Birmingham Arts Assoc. 1966– ; Course Dir Nat. Youth Theatre, 1966– ; Trustee, Interaction, 1967– ; Mem., Unesco Seminar on Theatre and Community, 1967; Assoc. Dir, Ambiance and Almost Free Theatre, 1970– . *Publications*: Woche für Woche, 1971; contrib. Nineteenth Century British Theatre, 1971; contrib., Drama: an outline for the intending student, 1971; *contrib*. Theatre Qly, Views, Jahrbuch-Deutschen Shakespeare-Gesellschaft, Zeitschfrift für Anglistik und Amerikanistik. *Address*: Dept of Drama and Theatre Arts, The Univ., Birmingham B15 2TT.

Barker, John Reginald; University Librarian, The Library, University of Dundee, since 1961; *b* 1924; *m* 1955; one *s* one *d*. MA Cantab 1948, Dip. in Librarianship, UCL, 1949; FLA 1950. Asst Librarian, Univ. of Liverpool, 1949–50; Sub-Librarian, Univ. of Bristol, 1950–61. *Publications*: contrib. Bibliotheck, Rev. Eng. Stud., Trans Bibliog. Soc. *Address*: University Library, Dundee DD1 4HN.

Barker, Philip Arthur, MA, FSA; Senior Lecturer in Post-Roman Archaeology, Department of Extra-Mural Studies, University of Birmingham, since 1972, Lecturer 1965–72; *b* 1920; *m* 1942; three *s*. MA Leicester 1965; FSA 1963. Editor, Worcs. Archaeological Soc. Trans., 1967–73; Mem., Council Royal Archaeological Inst., 1968–71; Res. Cttee, Royal Archaeological Inst., 1970– ; Exec. Cttee, Council for Brit. Archaeology, 1970–73; Chm., Avon-Severn Valleys Res. Project, 1969–73; Hon. Sec., Rescue, a Trust for Brit. Archaeology, 1970–73, Vice-Chm., 1973– . *Publications*: contrib. Medieval Archaeology, Trans Shropshire Archaeological Soc., Trans Worcs Archaeological Soc., World Archaeology. *Address*: Dept of Extra-Mural Studies, Univ. of Birmingham, Birmingham B15 2TT.

Barker, Dr Rodney Steven; Lecturer in Government, Department of Government, London School of Economics, since 1971; *b* 1942. BA Cantab 1963, MA Cantab 1968, PhD London 1968. Lectr in Politics, UC Swansea, 1967–71. *Publications*: ed and contrib., Studies in Opposition, 1971; Education

33

and Politics 1900-1951: a study of the Labour Party, 1972. *Address*: London School of Economics, Houghton Street, Aldwych, WC2A 2AE.

Barker, Terence Snarr, MA; Senior Research Officer, Department of Applied Economics, University of Cambridge, since 1972 (Research Officer, 1969-72); *b* 1941; *m* 1964; one *s*. MA (Hons) Edinburgh 1965, MA Cantab 1966, PhD Cantab 1973. Junior Res. Officer, Univ. of Cambridge, 1965; Fellow, Downing Coll. Cambridge, 1966. *Publications*: Exploring 1972, Vol. 9, in, A Programme for Growth (with J. R. C. Lecomber), 1970; The Determinants of Britain's Visible Imports 1949-1966, Vol. 10 in A Programme for Growth, 1970; *contrib*. Bull. Oxford Univ. Inst. of Econ. and Stats, Econ. Jl. Rev. of Econ. Studies. *Address*: Dept of Applied Economics, Univ. of Cambridge, Sidgwick Avenue, Cambridge.

Barker, Prof. Theodore Cardwell; Professor of Economic and Social History, University of Kent at Canterbury, since 1964; *b* 1923; *m* 1955. MA Oxon 1949; PhD Manchester 1951; FRHistS; Member: Economic Hist. Soc. (Sec. 1960-   ); British Nat. Cttee of Internat. Historical Congress, (Treasurer, 1973). Res. Fellow, Univ. of Aberdeen, 1952-53; Lectr in Economic History LSE, 1953-64. Dep. Dean, Faculty of Soc. Sci., Univ. of Kent, 1966-69. Member: Economics Cttee, CNAA, 1968-   ; Council, RHistS, 1967-70, 1973-   ; Nat. Cttee, Victoria County History, 1969- . *Publications*: (with J. R. Harris) A Merseyside Town in the Industrial Revolution, 1954; A History of the Girdlers' Company, 1957; (with others) Business History, 1960, 2nd edn 1970; Pilkington Brothers and the Glass Industry, 1960; (with R. M. Robbins) A History of London Transport, vol. I, 1963, vol. II, 1974; ed (with others) Our Changing Fare: two hundred years of British food habits, 1966; (with B. W. E. Alford) History of the Carpenters' Company, 1968; chapter on economic and social history, in, The Twentieth Century Mind, ed C. B. Cox and A. E. Dyson, vol. 1, 1972; (with John Hatcher) A History of Pewter, 1974; *contrib*. Econ. Hist. Rev., Jl of Econ. Hist., Hist., Business Hist., Jl of Transport Hist., Transport Hist., ecc. *Address*: Keynes College, Univ. of Kent, Canterbury.

Barley, Prof. Maurice Willmore, MA, FSA, FRHistS; Professor of Archaeology, Department of Classical and Archaeological Studies, University of Nottingham, since 1971; *b* 1909; *m* 1934; two *s* one *d*. BA Reading (2nd cl. Hist.), MA Nottingham 1952; FSA 1940, FRHistS 1965. Asst Lectr Univ. Coll., Hull, 1935-40; Tutor, Adult Educn Dept, Nottingham. 1946-62; Sen. Lectr and Reader, Classics Dept, Nottingham, 1962-71. Min. of Information and Labour, 1940-45, Sec., 1954-64, Pres., 1964-67, Council for Brit. Archaeology; Vice-Pres., Soc. of Antiquaries, 1965-68; Royal Commn Hist. Monuments, 1966- . *Publications*: Parochial Documents of the East Riding, 1939; Lincolnshire and the Fens, 1952; Documents relating to Newark on Trent,

1955; The English Farmhouse and Cottage, 1961; The House and Home, 1963, 1971; Guide to British Topographical Collections, 1974; *contrib*. Antiquaries Jl, Trans Thoroton Soc. *Address*: Dept of Classical and Archaeological Studies, The Univ., Nottingham NG7 6RD.

Barling, Thomas James, MA; Senior Lecturer in Education, University of Exeter, since 1968; *b* 1912; *m* 1940; two *s* two *d*. BA Birmingham 1933 (1st cl. French), MA Birmingham 1948; DipEd Birmingham 1934. Lectr in Educn, Univ. of Exeter, 1949-68. Chm, SW Br. Modern Language Assoc., 1958- . *Publications*: The Letter to the Philippians, 1958; Programming for the Language Laboratory (chapter on French), 1968; The Letter to the Colossians, 1973; *contrib*. Fre. St., St. Volt. and 18th Cent. *Address*: Univ. of Exeter, Thornlea, New North Road, Exeter EX4 4JZ.

Barlow, Derrick, BLitt, M.A; Fellow and Tutor in German, Jesus College, Oxford, since 1961; University Lecturer in German, Oxford, since 1948; *b* 1921; *m* 1953; one *s*. BA Oxford 1948, MA Oxford 1948, BLitt Oxford 1953. Lectr, Jesus Coll., Oxford, 1948; Lectr, Exeter Coll., Oxford, 1948. *Publications*: T. Fontane: Die Poggenpuhls, 1957; F. Hebbel: Selected Essays, 1962; C. Zuckmayer: Three Stories, 1963; C. Zuckmayer: Die Fastnachbeichte, 1966; C. Sternheim: Bürger Schippel, 1969; *contrib*. GLL, MLR. *Address*: Jesus College, Oxford.

Barlow, Prof. Frank, MA, DPhil, FBA, FRSL; Professor of History and Head of the Department of History, University of Exeter, since 1953; *b* 1911; *m* 1936; two s. BA Oxon 1933 (1st cl. Hist.), BLitt Oxon 1934, MA, DPhil Oxon 1937; FBA, FRHistS. FRSL. Fereday Fellow, St John's Coll. Oxford, 1935-38; Asst Lectr, Univ. Coll., London, 1936-40; Lectr, Univ. of Exeter, 1946-49; Reader, 1949, Dean of Arts, Univ. of Exeter, 1955-59; Dep. Vice-Chancellor, Univ. of Exeter, 1961-63; Mem., Council, Royal Hist. Soc., 1958-62. *Publications*: The Letters of Arnulf of Lisieux, 1939; Durham Annals and Documents of the Thirteenth Century, 1945; Durham Jurisdictional Peculiars, 1950; The Feudal Kingdom of England, 1955, 3rd edn 1972; The Life of King Edward the Confessor, 1962; The English Church, 1000-1066, 1963, 2nd edn 1966; William I and the Norman Conquest, 1965; Edward the Confessor, 1970; *contrib*. EHR, Jl Eccles. Hist., Speculum. *Address*: Univ. of Exeter, Dept of History, Queen's Building, The Queen's Drive, Exeter EX4 4QH.

Barlow, Dr Shirley A., MA; Lecturer in Classical Studies, University of Kent, since 1965; *b* 1934. BA London 1955 (Hons Classics), BA Cantab 1957 (Hons Classics), Certificate in Education, Cantab 1958, MA Cantab 1960, PhD London 1963. Teaching Fellow, Univ. of Michigan, 1959; Instructor, then Asst Prof, Univ. of Michigan, 1962-65. *Publications*: The Imagery of Euripides, 1971; *contrib*. book reviews to Jl of Hellenic Studies and Classical Rev. *Address*: Eliot College, The Univ., Canterbury, Kent CT2 7NZ.

Barna, Prof. Tibor, CBE; Professor of Economics, University of Sussex, since 1962; *b* 1919. Lectr, LSE, 1944; Official Fellow, Nuffield Coll., Oxford, 1947. Sen. posts in UN Econ. Commn for Europe, 1949; Asst Dir, Nat. Inst. of Econ. and Soc. Res., London, 1955. Mem., Monopolies Commn, since 1963. *Publications*: Redistribution of Income through Public Finance in 1937, 1945; Investment and Growth Policies in British Industrial Firms, 1962; *contrib.* Jl Royal Stat. Soc. *Address*: Univ. of Sussex, Falmer, Brighton BN1 9QQ.

Barnard, John Michael, MA, BLitt; Lecturer in English Literature, University of Leeds, since 1965; *b* 1936; *m* 1961; one *s* two *d*. BA Oxon 1959 (Eng. Lang. and Lit.), MA Oxon 1964, BLitt Oxon 1964. Res. Asst, Yale Univ., 1961–64; Vis. Lectr., Univ. of California at Santa Barbara, 1964–65; Post-Doctoral Fellow, Clark Memorial Library, Los Angeles, 1965. *Publications*: contrib. Sphere History of English Literature, 1970; New Cambridge Bibliography of English Literature, 1970; ed, Congreve: The Way of the World, 1972; ed, Pope: The Critical Heritage, 1973; ed, John Keats: The Complete Poems, 1973; *contrib.*Philolog. Qly, Bull. NY Pub. Lit., Pubs of the Bibliog. Soc. of America, Augustan Repr. Soc. *Address*: School of English, Univ. of Leeds, Leeds LS2 9JT.

Barnes, Anthony John Lane; Lecturer in Political Science, Government Department, London School of Economics (University of London), since 1965; *b* 1937; *m* 1965; one *s* one *d*. BA Cambridge 1960–61 (1st cl. Hons with distinction in Parts I and II of the Historical Tripos), MA Cantab; Council Mem., Navy Records Soc. Drosier Res. Fellowship in Hist., Gonville and Caius Coll., Cambridge, 1961–64; Asst Lectr in Polit. Science, London School of Econs, 1964–65. Conservative Parliamentary Candidate for Walsall North. 1964, 1966 and 1970 General Elections: Alderman, Greenwich Borough Council, 1968– . *Publications*: Teaching and Research in Contemporary British History, in, Contemporary History in Europe, ed D. C. Watt, 1969; (with R. K. Middlemas) Baldwin: A Biography, 1969; Consultant Historian to the Thames Television Series 'The Day Before Yesterday' and to the book of the same name by Alan Thompson, 1971, *Address*: London School of Economics, Houghton Street, WC2.

Barnes, Douglas Reginald; Senior Lecturer in Education, Institute of Education, University of Leeds, since 1972 (Lecturer, 1966–72); *b* 1927; *m* 1954; one *s* one *d*. BA Cantab 1948 (English), MA Cantab. Mem., Dartmouth Internat. Seminar on Teaching English, 1966; Chm, Nat. Assoc. for Teaching English, 1967–69; Dir, Schools Council Project 'Children as Readers', 1968–70. *Publications*: Drama in the English Classroom, 1968; (with H. Rosen and J. N. Britton) Language, the Learner and the School, 1969, 2nd edn 1971; Language in the Classroom, 1973; *contrib.* Use of English, English in Educn, Jl of Curric. Studies, Educnl Rev.

Address: Institute of Education, The Univ., Leeds LS2 9JT.

Barnes, Prof. John Arundel, DSC; Professor of Sociology, University of Cambridge, and Fellow of Churchill College, since 1969; *b* 1918; *m* 1942; three *s* one *d*. Fellow, St John's Coll., Cambridge, 1950–53; Simon Res. Fellow, Manchester Univ., 1951–53; Reader in Anthropology, London Univ., 1954–56; Prof. of Anthropology, Sydney Univ., 1956–58; Prof. of Anthropology, Inst. of Advanced Studies, ANU, Canberra, 1958–69; Overseas Fellow, Churchill Coll., Cambridge, 1965–66. *Publications*: Marriage in a Changing Society, 1951; Politics in a Changing Society, 1954; Inquest on the Murngin, 1967; Sociology in Cambridge, 1970; Three Styles in the Study of Kinship, 1971; Social Networks, 1972. *Address*: Churchill College, Cambridge CB3 0DS.

Barnes, Jonathan; Fellow and Tutor in Philosophy, Oriel College, Oxford, and Lecturer in Philosophy, University of Oxford, since 1968; *b* 1942; *m* 1964; two *d*. BA Oxon 1965, MA Oxon 1968; Member: Aristotelian Soc.; Mind Assoc.; Soc. for Promotion of Hellenic Studies. Lecturer in Philosophy: Univ. of Chicago, 1966–67; Exeter Coll., Oxford, 1967–68; Vis. Fellow, Inst. for Advanced Study, Princeton, 1972; Vis. Prof. of Classical Humanities, Univ. of Mass, 1973. *Publications*: The Ontological Argument, 1972; *contrib.* Archiv Gesch. Philos., Class. Qly, Philos. Qly, Phronesis, Proc. Aristot. Soc. *Address*: Oriel College, Oxford.

Barnett, Francis Joseph, MA; Fellow of Trinity College, Oxford, since 1952; *b* 1923; *m* 1950; three *d*. BA NZ 1944, MA NZ (1st cl. Greek) 1945. (1st cl. Latin) 1946, BA Oxon 1950 (1st cl. Mod. Langs), MA Oxon 1954. Asst Lectr Classics, Otago, 1947; Lectr Mod. Langs. Univ. Coll., Oxford, 1951. Trans. and Minute Writer, United Nations, 1951– ; Ed. adviser, Cassell's New Fr. Dict., 1966– . *Publications*: ed, Tallemant des Réaux: Portraits and Anecdotes, 1965; contrib. Studies presented to A. Ewert, 1961; contrib. and ed, The History and Structure of French, presd T. B. W. Reid, 1972; contrib. Cassell's Encyc. of Literature, 1973; *contrib.* French Studies, Trans. Philol. Soc., etc. *Address*: Trinity College, Oxford.

Barnicot, Prof. Nigel Ashworth; Professor of Physical Anthropology, Anthropology Department, University College, London, since 1960; *b* 1914. BSc UCL 1936 (1st cl. Hons Zool.), PhD 1950; Member: Royal Anthropolog. Inst.; Amer. Assoc. of Physical Anthropologists; Soc. for Study of Human Biology; Genet. Soc., Primate Soc. *Publications*: (co-author with Harrison, Weiner, Tanner and Barnicot) Human Biology, 1964; numerous papers on genetical and biochemical characteristics of human and non-human Primate populations; *contrib.* Annals Human Genetics, Human Biol., Folia Primat. *Address*: Dept of Anthropology, Univ. College London, Gower Street, WC1E 6BT.

Barnsley, David Graham; Professor of Law, University of Leicester, since 1973; *b* 1936; *m* 1960; two *d*. LLB Manchester 1956, LLM Manchester 1960; Solicitor of the Supreme Court, 1960. Univ. of Manchester: Asst Lectr, 1960–63;'Lectr, 1963–66; Sen. Lectr, Univ. of Leicester, 1966–73. *Publications:* Conveyancing Law and Practice, 1973; *contrib.* Convey. and Prop. Lawyer, Sol. Jl. *Address:* Faculty of Law, Univ. of Leicester, Leicester LE1 7RH.

Barnwell, Prof. Henry Thomas, MA, D de l'U; Marshall Professor of French Language and Literature, University of Glasgow, since 1971; *b* 1920; *m* 1951; one *s* one *d*. BA Birmingham 1941 (War Degree Regulations), BA Birmingham 1947 (1st cl. French), MA Birmingham 1949, Docteur de l'Université de Montpellier 1953 (mention très honorable); Mem. de l'Académie Racinienne. Lecteur d'Anglais, Montpellier, 1947; Asst Lectr in French, Sheffield, 1950; Lectr, Edinburgh, 1952; Reader, 1964; Prof., Belfast, 1965. *Publications:* Les idées morales et critiques de Saint-Evremond, 1957; ed, and trans, Selected Letters of Mme de Sévigné, 1960; ed, Corneille: Writings on the Theatre, 1965; The Tragic in French Tragedy, 1966; ed, Corneille: Pompée, 1971; ed, Pascal: Pensées, 1973; *contrib.* Dizionario critico della letteratura francese, 1972; Austln Jl for Fr. Studies, Forum for Mod. Lang. Studies, Fr. Studies, Jeunesse de Racine, MLR, Proc. Huguenot Soc. of London, Studi Francesi, Studies in Philology, XVIIe Siècle. *Address:* Dept of French, The Univ., Glasgow G12 8QL.

Baron, Prof. George, BA, MEd, PhD; Professor, and Head of Department of Educational Administration, University of London Institute of Education, since 1966; *b* 1911; *m* 1940; one *s* one *d*. BA Leeds 1933 (II Hons), DipEd Leeds 1934, MEd Leeds 1937, PhD London 1952. Mem., Royal Inst. Public Admin., Exec. Cttee Mem., Brit., Educnl Admin Soc., Vice-Pres., Commonwealth Council for Educnl Admin. Univ. of London Inst. of Educn: Lectr and Sen. Lectr, 1946–66; Reader, 1966–71; Vis. Prof., Univs of Alberta, 1961, 1963, Ontario Inst. for Studies in Educn, 1970, Univ. of British Columbia, 1972; Sen. Fulbright, Res. Fellowship, Univ. of Minnesota, 1954. Mem. Ed. Bd, Jl of Educnl Admin, 1967– ; London Educnl Rev., 1971– . *Publications:* A Bibliographical Guide to the English Educational System, 1952, 3rd edn 1965; Society, Schools and Progress in England, 1965; ed, Educational Administration: International Perspectives (with Dan Cooper and William G. Walker), 1969; ed, Educational Administration and the Social Sciences (with William Taylor), 1969; *contrib.* Brit. Jl of Educnl Studies. *Address:* Univ. of London Institute of Education, Malet Street, WC1E 7HS.

Barr, Prof. James, MA, BD, DD, FBA; Professor of Semitic Languages and Literatures, University of Manchester, since 1965; *b* 1924; *m* 1950; two *s* one *d*. MA Edinburgh 1948 (1st cl. Classics), BD Edinburgh 1951 (Distinction in Old Testament);

Hon DD Knox College, Toronto, 1964, MA Manchester 1969, Hon. DD Dubuque Univ., Iowa, 1974; FBA 1969, FRAS 1969, Pres., Soc. for Old Testament Study, 1973, Mem. Philological Soc. Prof., New Testament Presbyterian Coll., Montreal, 1953–55; Prof. of Old Testament, Edinburgh Univ., 1955–61; Prof. of Old Testament, Princeton Theological Seminary, 1961–65; Currie Lectr, Austin, Texas, 1964; Cadbury Lectr, Birmingham, 1969; Croall Lectr, Edinburgh, 1970; Vis. Prof., Hebrew Univ., Jerusalem, 1973. Editor, Jl of Semitic Studies, 1965– . *Publications:* The Semantics of Biblical Language, 1961, German edn 1965, Italian edn 1968, French edn 1971; Biblical Words for Time, 1962, 2nd edn 1969; Old and New in Interpretation, 1966, German edn 1967; Comparative Philology and the Text of the Old Testament, 1968; The Bible in the Modern World, 1973; trans. Ehrlich: Concise History of Israel, 1963; contrib. Peake's Commentary on the Bible, Hastings' Dictionary of the Bible, Encyclopaedia Judaica, etc.; *contrib.* Jl of Semitic Studies, Vetus Testamentum, Scot. Jl of Theol., Interpn, Bull. J. Rylands Lib., Svensk Exegetisk Årsbok, New Blackfriars, Biblica, Ecumenical Rev., Revue de théologie et de philosophie, Oudtestamentische Studiën, Jl Theol Studies. *Address:* Dept of Near Eastern Studies, Manchester Univ., Manchester M13 9PL.

Barr, Dr William; Senior Lecturer in Latin, University of Liverpool, since 1972, Lecturer 1953–72; *b* 1922. BA London (1st cl.) 1950, PhD London 1952. Asst Dir of Combined Hons., Univ. of Liverpool, 1969– . *Publications: contrib.* Athenaeum, Class. Rev., JRS, Latomus, Mnemosyne, Rh. Mus.; Encyclop. Brit., Oxford Class. Dict., 2nd edn. *Address:* School of Classics, Univ. of Liverpool, PO Box 147, Liverpool L69 3BX.

Barr, William Greig; Rector, Exeter College, Oxford, since 1972; *b* 1917; *m* 1954; two *s*. BA Oxon 1939 (1st cl. Hons Mod. Hist.). Fellow, Exeter Coll., Oxford, 1945–72; Sub-Rector, Exeter Coll., Oxford, 1947–54; Estates Bursar, Exeter Coll., Oxford, 1954–55; Sen. Tutor, Exeter Coll., Oxford, 1960–66; Lectr in Modern History, Univ. of Oxford, 1949–72, Jun. Proctor, Univ. of Oxford, 1951–52; Vis. Prof. of Mod. Hist., Univ. of S Carolina, 1968. Chm., Council, Brighton Coll., 1967– ; Governor, Plymouth Coll.; Governor, Sedbergh Sch; Trustee, Uppingham Sch. *Address:* Exeter College, Oxford.

Barratt Brown, Michael; Senior Lecturer, Department of Extramural Studies, Sheffield University, since 1964; *b* 1918; *m* 1947; three *s* one *d*. MA Oxon 1940; FRSS, Mem. Royal Econ. Soc., Industrial Relations Assoc., Industrial Tutors Soc., etc. Lectr, Shefield Univ., 1959–61; Vis. Prof., Centre for Advanced Studies, Univ. of Aligarh, India, 1972. Chm. Soc. of Industrial Tutors, 1968– . *Publications:* After Imperialism, 1963, 2nd edn 1970; What Economics is About, 1970; Essays on Imperialism, 1972; The Economics of Imperialism, 1974; *contrib.* Oxford Univ. Inst. of Econ. and Stats Bull., Yorkshire Bull. of Econ. and Soc.

Res., Econ. Studies. *Address*: 85 Wilkinson Street, Sheffield S10 2GS.

Barrell, Dr John Charles; University Lecturer in English, University of Cambridge and Fellow of King's College Cambridge, since 1972; College Lecturer in English at Newnham College, Cambridge, since 1972; *b* 1943; *m* 1965; two *s*. BA Cantab 1964, MA Cantab 1971; PhD Essex 1971. Asst Lectr in Literature, Univ. of Essex, 1968–69; Lectr, 1969–72. *Publications*: The Idea of Landscape and the Sense of Place, 1972; ed, and intro. S. T. Coleridge: On the Constitution of the Church and State, 1972; (with John Bull) The Penguin Book of Pastoral Verse, 1974. *Address*: King's College, Cambridge.

Barrère, Prof. Jean-Bertrand; Professor of French Literature, University of Cambridge, since 1954; Fellow of St John's College, Cambridge; *b* 1914; *m* 1941; three *s* three *d*. AdèsL 1938, DèsL Sorbonne 1949, MA Cantab 1954; Ancien élève, Ecole Normale Supérieure, 1935–38. Asst. Sorbonne, 1942–46; Lectr, French Inst., London, 1946–49; Prof., Univ of Lyons, 1949–54; Prof., Univ. Ibrahim, Cairo, 1950–52; Vis. Prof. UCLA, 1964; Vis. Fellow, Univ. of Brit. Columbia, 1966. *Publications*: La Fantaisie de Victor Hugo, 1949–60, 2nd edn 1972; Hugo, 1952, 8th edn 1971, trans. in Polish, 1969; Romain Rolland, 1955, 6th edn 1970, trans. in Portuguese, 1965; Le Regard d'Orphée, 1956; Critique de chambre, 1964; Un carnet des 'Misérables', 1965; La cure d'amaigrissement du roman, 1964; Victor Hugo à l'œuvre, 1966, 2nd edn 1970; Victor Hugo devant Dieu, 1965; Romain Rolland, l'âme et l'art. 1966; l'Idée de Goût, 1972; contrib. British Encyclopaedia; The art of criticism, ed, P. Nurse, 1969; Positions et Propositions sur le roman contemporain, 1970; Painting and Literature in XIX C France, 1972, *etc.*; *contrib.* Fr. Studies, Rev. Hist. Litt., Rev. Litt. Comp., Rev. Sci. Hum. *Address*: St. John's College, Cambridge.

Barrett, Rev. Prof. Charles Kingsley; Professor of Divinity, Department of Theology, University of Durham, since 1958; *b* 1917; *m* 1944; one *s* one *d*. BA Cantab 1938 (2nd cl. Mathematical Tripos Pt I; 1st cl. Theological Tripos Pts I and II), MA Cantab 1942, BD Cantab 1948, DD Cantab 1956; Hon. DD Hull 1970, Hon. DD Aberdeen 1972; FBA, Mem. SNTS (Pres., 1973), SOTS. Lectr in Theology, Durham Univ., 1945–54; Sen. Lectr in Theology, Durham Univ., 1954–58. *Publications*: The Holy Spirit and the Gospel Tradition, 1947, 2nd edn 1966; The Gospel according to St John, 1955; The New Testament Background: Selected Documents, 1956, German edn 1959; The Epistle to the Romans, 1957; Luke the Historian in Recent Study, 1961; From First Adam to Last, 1962; The Pastoral Epistles, 1963; Jesus and the Gospel Tradition, 1967; The First Epistle to the Corinthians, 1968; The Signs of an Apostle, 1970; Das Johannes evangelium und das Judentum, 1970; New Testament Essays, 1972; The Second Epistle to the Corinthians, 1973; *contrib.* Bull. J. Rylands Libr., Expos.

Times, Jl Theol. Studies, New Test Studies, Scott. Jl Theol., Svensk Exegetisk Årsbok, Zeits. Systemat. Theol. *Address*: Dept. of Theology, The Univ., Durham.

Barrett, Charles Richard; Lecturer, Department of Econometrics and Social Statistics, University of Birmingham, since 1966; *b* 1938. BSc Cape Town 1958 (1st cl. Math.), MSc Cape Town 1960 (with dist. Math.), BA Oxon 1963 (2nd cl. PPE). Res. Asst, Birmingham, 1964. *Publications*: contrib. Econ., Rev. of Econ. and Stat. *Address*: Faculty of Commerce and Social Science, Univ. of Birmingham, Birmingham B15 2TT.

Barrett, Dr Eric C., MSc, PhD, FRGS, FRMetS; Lecturer in Geography, University of Bristol, since 1965; *b* 1939; *m* 1967; two *c*. BSc Sheffield 1961 (1st cl. Geography), MSc Sheffield 1962, PhD Bristol 1969; FRGS, FRMetS, MIBG. Temp. Asst Lectr, Sheffield Univ., 1962–63; Asst Lectr, Leicester Univ., 1963–64; Vis. Lectr, Univ. New England, NSW, 1969. Sec., Brit. Climatol. Discussion Gp, 1971–72, Mem. Cttee 1972– . *Publications*: Viewing Weather from Space, 1967; (with J. O. Bailey) Weather and Climate, 1971; Geography from Space, 1972; Climatology from Satellites, 1974; ed (with L. F. Curtis), Environmental Remote Sensing: applications and achievements, 1974; *contrib.* Geog. Jl, Mon. Wea. Rev. (US Dept Commerce), Sci. Jl, Trans and Papers Inst. Brit. Geogrs, Weather. *Address*: Dept of Geography, The Univ., Bristol, BS8 1SS.

Barrett, Dr John D.; College Lecturer in English, University College Dublin, since 1971; *b* 1937; *m* 1968; one *s* two *d*. BA UCD 1960, MA UCD 1961, PhD UCD 1966. Assitant Professor: Midwestern Univ., Texas, 1965; Univ. of Texas, Austin, 1966; Asst Lectr, UCD, 1969. *Address* Dept of English, Univ. College, Dublin 4.

Barrett, William Spencer, FBA; Fellow of Keble College, Oxford, since 1952, Sub-Warden since 1968, and Tutor in Classics, since 1939; Reader in Greek Literature, University of Oxford, since 1966; *b* 1914; *m* 1939; one *s* one *d*. BA Oxon (Christ Church) 1937 (1st cl. Classical Hon. Mods, 1st cl. Lit. Hum.), MA Oxon 1939; FBA 1965. Lectr, Christ Church, Oxford, 1938–39; Lectr, Keble Coll., 1939–52; Librarian, 1946–66; Univ. Lectr in Greek Lit., 1947–66. *Publications*: (ed) Euripides: Hippolytos, 1964; *contrib.* CQ, Gnomon, Hermes. *Address*: Keble College, Oxford.

Barrett-Ayres, Reginald; Reader in Music, University of Aberdeen, since 1971; *b* 1920; *m* 1964; one *s* two *d*. BMus Edinburgh, 1942. Lectr in Music, Aberdeen Univ., 1951–71; Head of Dept of Music, Aberdeen Univ., 1956– . *Publications*: Singing for Fun, 1959; ed, New Songs for the Church, 1969; Communion Service, Series III, 1972; Joseph Haydn and the String Quartet, 1973; Study Score, and Performing Edition of Haydn Quartets, Vol. I, 1974; *contrib.* Musical Times, Times Educnl Suppl.

Address: Univ. Dept of Music, Powis Gate, Aberdeen.

Barrie, J. Edward, LLM, Barrister at Law; Senior Lecturer, The Law School, University of Strathclyde, since 1964; *b* 1923; *m* 1947; one *s*. LLB London 1956, LLM London 1966; ACIS 1950, Barrister at Law 1961. Vice-Dean, School of Business and Administration, Univ. of Strathclyde, 1969–71, Dean, 1972– . Town Clerk, Borough of Richmond, Yorkshire, 1955–57; Clerk to the Gainsborough UDC, 1957–60. *Address*: The Law School, Univ. of Strathclyde, Stenhouse Building, Cathedral Street, Glasgow.

Barringer, John Christopher; Resident Tutor in Norfolk, Board of Extra-Mural Studies. Cambridge, since 1966; *b* 1931; *m* 1958; one *s* one *d*. MA St John's Coll., Cambridge (BA Geography, Part I 1952 (Cl. II. Div. I), Part II 1953 (Cl. II. Div. I)), Post-Grad. Cert. in Educn, Cambridge, 1954; FRGS; Mem.: Inst. British Geographers; Regional Studies Assoc.; Town and Country Planning Assoc.; Geographical Assoc. Sen. Geography Master, Lancaster Royal Grammar Sch., 1954–65. Mem.: Council, Norfolk Res. Cttee, 1970– . *Publications*: *contrib.* East Anglian Studies, ed Munby, 1968; Lakeland Landscape, 1970; Yorkshire Dales: A social and economic geography (forthcoming). *Address*: Board of Extra-Mural Studies, Stuart House, Mill Lane, Cambridge CB2 1RY.

Barron, Dr Caroline Mary, MA, PhD; Lecturer in History, Bedford College, University of London, since 1968; *b* 1939; *m* 1962; two *d*. BA Oxon 1962 (2nd cl. History), MA Oxon 1965, PhD London 1970; FRHistS. Tutorial Res. Student, Bedford Coll., 1964–65; Tutorial Res. Fellow, Bedford Coll., 1965–67; Asst Lectr, Bedford Coll., 1967–68. *Publications*: ed (with F. R. H. Du Boulay) The Reign of Richard II, 1971; The Medieval Guildhall of London, 1974; *contrib.* Bull. of the Inst. of Hist. Res., Jl Royal Soc. Archiv. *Address*: Bedford College, Regent's Park, NW1 4NS.

Barron, Charles Aitken; Principal Lecturer and Head of Department of Drama, Aberdeen College of Education; part-time Lecturer, Aberdeen University, since 1970; *b* 1936; *m* 1961; one *s*. MA Aberdeen 1958 (1st cl. Hons English Lang. and Lit.; Cert. in Secondary Teaching, Aberdeen Coll. of Educn, 1959. Lectr, Jordanhill Coll. of Educn, English Dept, 1966–70. *Address*: Dept of Dramatic Art, Univ. of Aberdeen, Aberdeen College of Education, Hilton Place, Aberdeen AB9 1FA.

Barron, Prof. John Penrose, MA, DPhil, FSA; Professor of Greek Language and Literature, University of London (King's College), since 1971; Head of Department of Classics, King's College, since 1972; *b* 1934; *m* 1962; two *d*. BA Oxon 1957 (1st cl. Classical Hon. Mods), MA Oxon 1960, DPhil Oxon 1961; FSA 1967. Asst Lectr in Latin, Bedford Coll., 1959–61, Lectr, 1961–64; Lectr in Archaeology, Univ. Coll., London, 1964–67; Reader in Archaeology and Numismatics,

London Univ., 1967–71; Mem., Inst. for Advanced Study, Princeton, 1973–74. Mem. Council, Royal Numis. Soc., 1962–64, 1967–1970; Council, Soc. for Prom. Hellenic Studies, 1964–67, Trustee 1971– ; Managing Cttee, Brit. Sch. at Athens, 1971–73; Hon. Treas., St Martins in the Fields Youth Centre, 1972– . *Publications*: Greek Sculpture, 1965; The Silver Coins of Samos, 1966; *contrib.* Bull. Inst. Class. Studies, Class. Qly, Jl Hellenic Studies. *Address*: Dept of Classics, King's College, Strand, WC2R 2LS.

Barron, Michael John Burdett; Lecturer in Department of Economics, University of Southampton, since 1972; *b* 1945; *m* 1966; one *d*. BSc Southampton 1965. Univ. of Reading, 1965–72. *Publications*: *contrib.* Accountancy, Accounting and Business Res., Bus. Ratios, Jl Bus. Finance. *Address*: Dept of Economics, Univ. of Southampton, Southampton SO9 5NH.

Barron, Dr William Raymond Johnston; Senior Lecturer in English Language and Medieval Literature, Department of English, University of Manchester, since 1973 (Lecturer, 1957–73); *b* 1926. MA St Andrews 1948, BPhil St Andrews 1952, PhD St Andrews 1959. Asst in English, Aberdeen Univ., 1952–57; Asst Sec., Brit. Branch, Int. Arthurian Soc., 1966–69; Editor, Brit. Section, BBIAS, 1967–68; Vis. Prof., Pahlavi Univ., Iran, 1968–70. *Publications*: British Bibliography, BBIAS, 1966, 1967; ed jtly, Studies in Medieval Literature and Languages in Memory of Frederick Whitehead, 1973; ed and trans., Sir Gawain and the Green Knight, 1973; *contrib.* Chambers's Encyclopaedia, Medium Aevum, Romania. *Address*: Dept of English, The Univ. Manchester, M13 9PL.

Barrow, Prof. Geoffrey Wallis Steuart, MA, BLitt, DLitt, FRHistS; Professor of Medieval History, University of Newcastle upon Tyne, since 1961; *b* 1924; *m* 1951; one *s* one *d*. MA St Andrews 1944 (1st cl. Mod. and Med. Hist. 1948). BLitt Oxon 1950, DLitt St Andrews 1971; FRHistS, FSA Scot., Mem. Scot. Hist. Soc. Lectr, Univ. Coll., London, 1950–61; Dean of Faculty of Arts, Univ. of Newcastle upon Tyne, 1969–72. Mem., Council Royal Hist. Soc., 1963; Jt Lit. Dir, Royal Hist. Soc., 1964–74; Chm., Council Scot. Hist. Soc., 1964–68, Pres., 1972– ; Mem., Brit. Nat. Cttee, Internat. Congress of Hist. Sciences, 1968–72. *Publications*: Feudal Britain, 1956, 2nd (pbk) edn 1971; Acts of Malcolm IV King of Scots 1153–65, 1960; Robert Bruce and the Community of the Realm of Scotland, 1965; Acts of William I King of Scots 1165–1214, 1971; Kingdom of the Scots, 1973; *contrib.* Bull. Inst. Hist. Res., Jl of Ecclesiastical Hist., Juridical Rev., Northern Hist., Scot. Hist. Rev., Scot. Studies. *Address*: Dept of History, Univ. of Newcastle, Newcastle upon Tyne NE1 7RU.

Barry, Brian Michael; Fellow of Nuffield College, Oxford, since 1972; *b* 1936; *m* 1960; one *s*. BA Oxon 1958, MA, DPhil Oxon 1964. Res. Fellow and Asst Lectr, Dept of Philosophy, Birmingham, 1960–61; Vis. Fellow,

Harvard, 1961–62; Asst Lectr, Dept of Moral and Political Philosophy, Keele, 1962–63; Lectr, Dept of Politics, Southampton, 1963–1965; Fellow, UC Oxford, 1965–66; Fellow of Nuffield Coll., Oxford, 1966–69 (Sen. Tutor, 1968–69); Prof. of Govt, 1969–72; Dean, Sch. of Social Studies, 1970–72, Essex; Vis. Prof., Pittsburgh Univ., 1967. Editor, Brit. Jl of Political Science, 1971–72. *Publications*: Political Argument, 1965; Sociologists, Economists and Democracy, 1970; The Liberal Theory of Justice, 1973; *contrib.* Nomos, Philosophy, Proc. Aristotelian Soc., Analysis, Poltical Theory, Philosophy and Public Affairs, Brit. Jl of Political Science, Sociology. *Address*: Nuffield College, Oxford.

Barry, Michael Vincent; Lecturer, Department of English. The Queen's University of Belfast, since 1968; *b* 1935; *m* 1962; three *s* one *d*. BA Leeds 1958, MA Leeds 1960. Asst, Editor, Survey of English Dialects, Leeds, 1964–68. *Publications*: ed (with Prof. H. Orton), Survey of English Dialects, The Basic Material, The West Midland Counties, Vol. 2, Parts 1–3, 1969–71; *contrib.* Folk Life, Leeds Studies in English, Trans Yorks Dialect Soc., Trans Lakeland Dialect Soc., Ulster Folk Life. *Address*: The Queen's Univ. of Belfast, Belfast BT7 1NN.

Barston, Ronald Peter; Lecturer, Department of Politics, University of Lancaster, since 1968; *b* 1944; *m* 1969. BScEcon Wales 1967 (Aberystwyth), MScEcon Wales 1969 (Aberystwyth); Member: David Davies Inst., 1969– , Nobel Symposium 17, Oslo, 1970– , European Consortium for Pol Res. (Strasbourg), 1974– . Visiting Lectr, Univ. of Iceland, 1973. *Publications*: The Other Powers: Studies in the Foreign Politics of Small States, 1973; *contrib.* Internat. Affairs, Internat. Relations. *Address*: Dept of Politics, Fylde College, Univ. of Lancaster, Lancaster LA1 4YF.

Bartholomew, Prof. David John; Professor of Statistics, London School of Economics, since 1973; *b* 1931; *m* 1955; two *d*. BSc London 1953, PhD London 1955; FSS, Mem., Int. Stat. Inst., Inst. Math. Stats, Manpower Soc. Lectr in Stats, Univ. of Keele 1957–60; Lectr in Stats, Univ. Coll. of Wales, Aberystwyth, 1960–64; Vis. Lectr, Harvard Univ., 1964–65; Sen. Lectr, UCW, Aberystwyth, 1965–67; Prof. of Statistics, Sch. of Math. Studies, Univ. of Kent, 1967–72. Council Mem., Inst. of Manpower Studies, 1969– . Manpower Soc., 1969– , Royal Stat. Soc., 1970– . *Publications*: Stochastic Models for Social Processes, 1967, German edn 1970, 2nd edn 1973; (with E. E. Bassett) Let's Look at the Figures: The Quantitative Approach to Human Affairs, 1971; Jt Editor, two vols of papers on manpower topics, 1971; (with R. E. Barlow and others) Statistical Inference Under Order Restrictions, 1972; *contrib.* Jl Roy. Stat. Soc., Biometrika, Technometrics. *Address*: London School of Economics, WC2A 2AE.

Bartlett, Alan Gordon; Academic Registrar, University of Exeter (formerly University College of the South-West), since 1951;

b 1912; *m* 1939; one *s*. BA Cambridge 1936, (1st cl. Hons Pt I and Pt II, Classical Tripos); Mem., Lute Soc. Asst Registrar, Univ. of Reading, 1936–49; Asst Registrar and Sec. to Faculties, Univ. of Nottingham, 1949–51. *Address*: Northcote House, Univ. of Exeter, Exeter, Devon.

Bartlett, Dr Christopher John, BA, PhD, FRHistS; Reader in International History, Department of Modern History, University of Dundee, since 1968; *b* 1931; *m* 1958; two *s*. BA London (External) (1st cl. Hons Hist.), PhD London 1956; FRHistS. Res. Asst, Univ. Coll. London, 1956–57; Asst Lectr, Univ. of Edinburgh, 1957–59; Lectr, Univ. Coll. of the West Indies, 1959–62; Lectr, Queen's Coll., Dundee, Univ. of St. Andrews, 1962–68. *Publications*: Great Britain and Sea Power, 1815–53, 1963; Castlereagh, 1966; ed, Britain Preeminent, 1969; (with E. V. Goveia) Chapters in Caribbean History vol. ii, 1970; The Long Retreat: a short history of British Defence Policy, 1945–70, 1971; The Rise and Fall of the Pax Americana, 1975; *contrib.* EHR, Hispanic American, Hist. Rev., Jl Ecclesiast. Hist. *Address*: Dept of Modern History, The Univ., Dundee DD1 4HN.

Bartlett, Rev. John Raymond; Lecturer, Divinity School, Trinity College, Dublin, since 1969; *b* 1937; *m* 1965; three *d*. BA Oxon 1959 (2nd cl. Classics Hon. Mods, 2nd cl. Theology), MA Oxon 1962, BLitt Oxon 1962, MA (ad eundem gradum) TCD 1970. Jun. Lectr, TCD, 1966–69. *Publications*: Commentary on 1 and 2 Maccabees, 1973; *contrib.* A Source Book of the Bible for Teachers, ed J. S. Bowden and R. Walton, 1970; Peoples of Old Testament Times, ed D. J. Wiseman, 1973; *contrib.* Jl Theological Studies, Palestine Exploration Qly, Vetus Testamentum. *Address*: Divinity School, East Chapel, Trinity College, Dublin 2.

Barton, Anne, PhD; Fellow and Tutor in English Literature, New College, Oxford, since 1974; *b* 1933; *m* 1957; 1968. BA Bryn Mawr Coll. 1954; MA(statutory) Cambridge 1960, PhD Cambridge 1960. Lectr in History of Art, Ithaca Coll., New York, 1958; Research Fellow, Girton Coll., Cambridge, 1960–62; Univ. Asst Lectr, Cambridge, 1962–64; Official Fellow and Dir of Studies in English, Girton Coll., 1962; Univ. Lectr, Cambridge, 1964–72; Hildred Carlile Prof. of English Literature, Bedford Coll., Univ. of London, 1972–74. *Publications*: Shakespeare and the Idea of the Play, 1962; *contrib.* Shakespeare Survey, Stratford on Avon Studies, British Academy (Chatterton Lectures), Shakespeare Qly. *Address*: New College, Oxford.

Barton, Ian Maxwell; Senior Lecturer in Classics, Saint David's University College, Lampeter, since 1972; *b* 1926; *m* 1953; two *s* two *d*. BA Cantab 1951, MA Cantab 1955; Dip. Class. Archaeol. 1952. Asst Lectr, UCNS, Keele, 1952–55; Lectr, Univ. of Ghana, 1956–62; Fellow and Tutor of Legon Hall, Univ. of Ghana, 1956–61; Vice-Master, Legon Hall, Univ. of Ghana, 1961–62; Lectr, Saint David's UC, Lampeter, 1962–72; Acting Head, Dept of Classics, Saint David's

Coll., 1966–68. Vis. Prof., UC of Cape Coast, Ghana, 1970–71. Dean of Faculty of Arts, St David's UC, Lampeter, 1973–75. *Publications*: Africa in the Roman Empire, 1972; *contrib*. Greece and Rome, Museum Africum, Trivium. *Address*: Dept of Classics, Saint David's Univ. Coll., Lampeter, Dyfed SA48 7ED.

Bass, James Martin, BA, FCA; Lecturer in Accounting in the Department of Economics, University of Newcastle upon Tyne, since 1963; *b* 1939; *m* 1963; one *s* one *d*. BA(Econ) Dunelm 1960; ACA 1963, FCA 1973. Thornton Baker & Co., 1960–63. *Address*: Dept of Economics, Univ. of Newcastle upon Tyne, Newcastle upon Tyne NE1 7RU.

Bassett, Dr Edward Eryl; Lecturer in Statistics, University of Kent at Canterbury, since 1970; *b* 1966; one *s* one *d*. BA Oxon 1962, MSc Wales 1963, PhD Wales 1969; FSS. Asst Lectr in Statistics, Univ. Coll. of Wales, Aberystwyth, 1965–66; Lectr in Statistics, Imperial Coll., London, 1966–1970. *Publications*: (with D. J. Bartholomew) Let's Look at the Figures, 1971; *contrib*. Brit. Jl Psychol. *Address*: Cornwallis Building, The Univ. of Kent at Canterbury, Canterbury CT2 7NZ.

Bastable, Rev. Dr James D.; College Lecturer, Department of Logic and Psychology, University College Dublin, since 1968; *b* 1916. BA NUI 1937, MA NUI 1938, PhD NUI 1944. Prof. of Metaphysics, St Patrick's Coll., Maynooth, 1944; Dean Faculty of Philos., Maynooth, 1956–68. Member: Internat. Newman Conf., 1952–74; Gen. Bd of Studies, NUI, 1954–68. Pres., Philosophical Soc., Maynooth, 1949–68. Founding Editor, Philosophical Studies, 1951– . *Publications*: *contrib*. Irish Theol Qly, Irish Ecclesiastical Record. *Address*: Dept of Logic and Psychology, Univ. College, Belfield, Dublin 4.

Bastable, Dr Patrick Kevin, MA, PhD, MPsychSc; Lecturer, Department of Logic and Psychology, University College, Dublin, since 1960; *b* 1918. BA NUI 1938 (1st cl. Philos.), MA NUI 1939, PhD NUI 1946, MPsychSc. NUI 1966; Mem., BPS, MPSI, Mem., ASL. St Patrick's Coll., Maynooth, 1947–49; St Columban's Coll. and Major Seminary, Milton, Mass., 1953–59. Rector of St Columban's Coll., Dublin, 1959–72. *Publications*: Desire for God; Does Man Aspire Naturally to the Beatific Vision? An Analysis of this Question and of its History, 1947; *contrib*. Philosoph. Studies (asst rev. editor). *Address*: Dept of Logic and Psychology, Univ. College, Dublin 4.

Bastin, Dr John Sturgus; Reader in the Modern History of Southeast Asia, School of Oriental and African Studies, University of London, since 1965; *b* 1927; *m* 1966; two *s* two *d*. BA Melbourne 1949, MA Melbourne 1951, DLitt Leiden 1954, PhD Oxon 1956. Lectr, Queensland Univ., 1956–57; Fellow in Pacific Hist., Australian Nat. Univ., 1957–59; Prof. of Hist., Univ. of Malaya, 1959–63; Dean, Faculty of Arts, Univ. of Malaya, 1959–62; Mem., Univ. of Malaya Council, 1959–61; Lectr, School of Oriental and African Studies, Univ. of London, 1963–65. Mem., Council Muslim Coll., Malaya, 1959–61; Mem., Council and Vice Pres., Malayan Branch Royal Asiatic Soc., 1960–62; Mem., Malayan Govt Univ. Constitutional Cttee, 1961. *Publications*: Raffles' Ideas on Land Rent System in Java, 1954; Raffles in Java and Sumatra, 1957; ed, The Journal of Thomas Otho Travers 1813–19, 1960; Essays on Malayan and Indonesian History, 1961; The British in West Sumatra 1685–1825, 1964; A History of Modern Southeast Asia, 1968; *contrib*. Bijd TLV, Jl Malay. Branch Roy. Asiatic Soc., Jl Bibliog. Natural Hist., Bull. SOAS. *Address*: Dept of History, Univ. of London, School of Oriental and African Studies, Malet Street, WC1E 7HP.

Bastow, John David; Lecturer in Philosophy, University of Dundee, since 1964; *b* 1938; *m* 1962; three *d*. BA Oxon 1961 (PPP), MA Oxon 1967, BPhil Oxon 1963 (Philosophy). Asst, Univ. of Dundee, 1963. *Publications*: *contrib*. Philos. Books, Phil. Qly, Religious Studies. *Address*: Dept of Philosophy, The Univ., Dundee DD1 4HN.

Batchelor, Dr Ronald Ernest; Senior Lecturer, Department of French, University of Nottingham, since 1974; *b* 1934; *m* 1962; one *s* one *d*. BA 1956, DipEd 1957, MA 1960, Southampton, PhD Nottingham 1965. Lectr, Nottingham, 1962–74. *Publications*: Unamuno Novelist: a European perspective, 1972; *contrib*. MLR, FMLS, JES, ESR, Neophilologus, Essays in French Lit., Studi Francesi, NFS. *Address*: French Dept, Univ. of Nottingham, Nottingham NG7 2RD.

Bate, Selwyn Harold; Senior Lecturer (part-time), Faculty of Law, University of Birmingham, since 1949; *b* 1917; *m* 1948; three *d*. LLB Birmingham 1938, LLM Birmingham 1964; Solicitor of Supreme Court, 1940. Part-time Lectr in Law, Univ. of Birmingham, 1945–49. *Publications*: *contrib*. Atkin's Encyc. of Court Forms, Encyc. of Forms and Precedents. *Address*: Faculty of Law, Univ. of Birmingham, PO Box 363, Birmingham B15 2TT.

Bately, Janet Margaret, (Mrs L. J. Summers); Reader in English, Birkbeck College, University of London, since 1970; *b* 1932; *m* 1964; one *s*. BA Oxon 1954 (1st cl. English), MA Oxon 1958, Dip. in Comparative Philology Oxon 1956 (with distinction). Asst Lectr, Birkbeck Coll., Univ. of London, 1955–58; Lectr, 1958–69. *Publications*: contrib. England before the Conquest, Studies in Primary Sources presented to Dorothy Whitelock (ed, Peter Clemoes and Kathleen Hughes), 1971; *contrib*. Anglo-Saxon England, Anglia, Archaeologia, Classica et Mediaevalia, English Studies, Mediaeval Archaeol., Medium Aevum, Notes and Queries, Rev. of English Studies, Scriptorium, Studies in Philol. *Address*: Birkbeck College, Malet Street, WC1E 7HX.

Bates, James Arthur, BA, PhD; Professor of Business Economics, Queen's University, Belfast, since 1965; *b* 1926; *m* 1949; one *d*. BA Nottingham 1951, PhD Nottingham

1955. Asst Lectr, Univ. of Nottingham, 1953–55; Res. Off., Oxford Univ. (Inst. of Statistics), 1955–59; Lectr, Univ. of Glasgow, 1959–61; Lectr, Univ. of Bristol, 1961–65. Mem., numerous business and public cttees in N Ireland. *Publications*: (with J. R. Parkinson) Business Economics, 1962, 2nd edn 1969; The Financing of Small Business, 1963, 2nd edn 1970; (with M. Bell) The Management of Northern Ireland Industry, 1970; *contrib*. Banker, Bankers Mag., Brit Jl Finance, Jl Indust. Econ., Brit. Jl Indust. Relat., Sociol. Rev., Jl Mngmnt Studies, Jl Royal Stat. Soc. *Address*: Dept of Business Studies, Queen's Univ., Belfast BT7 1NN.

Bates, John Maynard, BA; Senior Lecturer in Economics, University of Nottingham, since 1972, Lecturer, 1962–72; *b* 1933; *m* 1959; two *s* one *d*. BA(Econ) Nottingham 1958 (2nd cl.); FSS, 1962. Junior Res. Officer, Dept of Applied Econ., Cambridge, 1958–62. *Publications*: *contrib*. Scot. Jl of Pol Econ., Operational Res. Qly. *Address*: Dept of Economics, Univ. of Nottingham, Nottingham NG7 2RD.

Bath, Michael Edwin; Lecturer, Department of English Studies, University of Strathclyde, since 1973; *b* 1942; *m* 1968; two *s*. BA Oxford 1965, MA Keele 1967. Univ. of Strathclyde, 1968. *Publications*: *contrib*. Essays Crit., Libr. Rev., Hardy Yearbook. *Address*: Dept of English Studies, Univ. of Strathclyde, Richmond Street, Glasgow.

Batho, Gordon Richard, MA, FRHistS; Senior Lecturer, Division of Education, University of Sheffield, since 1966; *b* 1929; *m* 1959; two *s*. BA (Hons) London 1950, PGCE London 1951, MA London 1953; FRHistS 1957. Asst Lectr, Dept of Educn, Sheffield, 1956–58, Lectr, 1958–66; Vis. Lectr, McMaster Univ., 1963, UBC 1963, 1964 and 1966, Carleton Univ. 1964, Univ. of Michigan, 1969. Mem., Council, Hist, Assoc., 1970– ; Exec. Cttee, Thomas Harriot Seminar, 1969– . *Publications*: The Household Papers of Henry Percy, 1962; chapter on 'Sources' in W. H. Burston and C. W. Green, Handbook for History Teachers, 1962; chapter on 'Syon House' in VCH Middlesex, vol. III, 1962; chapter on Crown and Lay Landownership 1500–1640 in Agrarian History of England, vol. IV, 1966; Calendar of the Talbot Papers, 1972, etc.; *contrib*. Archaeologia Aeliana, Brit. Jl of Educnl Studies, Derbys. Arch. Jl, Library, Econ. Hist. Rev., Hist. Jl, Scott. Hist. Rev., Sussex Arch. Coll., Trans Anc. Mon. Soc., Trans London and Mx Arch. Soc. *Address*: Division of Education, Univ. of Sheffield, Sheffield S10 2TN.

Bathurst, Maurice Edward, CMG, CBE, QC; Hon. Visiting Professor in International Law, King's College, London, since 1967; *b* 1913; *m* 1941; 1968; one *s*. LLB London 1937 (1st cl. Hons), LLM Columbia 1941, PhD Cantab 1949, LLD London 1966, Hon. DCL Sacred Heart NB 1946. Solicitor of Supreme Court, 1938–56; called to Bar, Gray's Inn, 1957; Master of the Bench, 1970. Mem. *ad eundem*, Inner Temple; Mem.:

Gen. Council of the Bar, 1970–71; Senate of Inns of Court, 1971–73; Senate of Inns of Court and the Bar, 1974– ; Council of Legal Educn, 1971–73. Legal Adviser, British Information Services, 1941–43, Legal Adviser, British Embassy, Washington, 1943–46; Legal Mem., UK Delegn to UN, 1946–48; UK Representative, Legal Advisory Cttee, Atomic Energy Commn, 1946–48; British Dep. Legal Adviser, Legal Adviser, and Judge, in Germany, 1949–57; British Judge, Arbitral Commn on Property, Rights and Interests in Germany, 1968–69. Mem. many UK Delegns to internat. organizations and confs, incl. UNRRA, UN General Assembly, FAO, WHO, Paris Conf. on WEU. Vice-Pres., UN League of Lawyers; Vice-Chm. Coun., Brit. Inst. of Internat. and Comparative Law. Mem., Panel of Arbitrators, Internat. Centre for Settlement of Investment Disputes; a Pres., Arbitration Tribunals, Internat. Telecom. Satellite Orgn; Mem., UK Cttee, UNICEF. Mem., Court of Assts, Haberdashers' Co. (Fourth Warden, 1973–74); Mem., Editorial Cttee, British Yearbook of Internat. Law; Chm., Governors, Haberdashers' Aske's Hatcham Schs; Pres., Brit. Insurance Law Assoc. Hon. Fellow, KCL. Freeman, City of London, City of Bathurst, NB. *Publications*: (with J. L. Simpson) Germany and the North Atlantic Community: a Legal Survey, 1956; *contrib*. Europe and the Law, 1968; ed jtly, Legal Problems of an Enlarged European Community, 1972; articles in legal jls, etc., British and American. *Address*: King's College, Strand, WC2R 2LS.

Batley, Edward Malcolm, BA. MLitt; Principal Lecturer and Head of German Department, Goldsmiths' College, University of London, since 1970; *b* 1935; *m* 1961; two *s* one *d*. BA Dunelm 1957 (Hons. German), DipEd Durham 1958, MLitt Durham 1965. Lectr in German, Goldsmiths' Coll., 1964–68; Univ. Examnr for German in BEd degree, 1968– . Mem., Assoc. of Teachers of German; Mem., Internationale Vereinigung der Germanisten; Mem., English Goethe Soc.; Mem., Conference of University Teachers of German. Mem., Council and Exec., MLA; Editor, Modern Languages 1970– . *Publications*: A Preface to The Magic Flute, 1969; *contrib*. Eighteenth Century Studies, German Life and Letters, Maske und Kothurn, Music and Letters, The Germanic Rev., The Music Rev., Pubs of the English Goethe Soc., Amer. Lessing Yearbook. *Address*: Dept of German, Univ., of London Goldsmiths' College, New Cross, SE14 6NW.

Battersby, Prof. Graham, BA; Professor of Law, University of Sheffield, since 1971; *b* 1937; *m* 1965; two *d*. BA Oxon 1960; Barrister 1964 (Lincoln's Inn). Asst Lectr, 1960–62, Lectr, 1962–68, Sen. Lectr, 1968–71, Sheffield Univ.; Dean of Faculty of Law, 1969–72; Vis. Associate Prof., Univ. of Manitoba, 1967–68. *Publications*: (with G. A. Lightman) Cases and Statutes on Real Property, 1965; Williams on Title, 4th edn 1974; *contrib*. Conv., Man. LJ, MLR, Sol. Qly, Sol. Jl. *Address*: Faculty of Law, The Univ., Sheffield S10 2TN.

Bauer, Prof. Peter Thomas, MA; Professor of Economics, London School of Economics, University of London, since 1960; *b* 1915. MA Cambridge 1942. Reader in Agricultural Economics, Univ. of London, 1947–48; Univ. Lectr in Economics, Cambridge Univ. 1948–56; Smuts Reader in Commonwealth Studies, Cambridge Univ., 1956–60; Fellow, Gonville and Caius Coll., Cambridge, 1946–60, 1968– ; Woodward Lecturer, Yale Univ., 1965. *Publications*: The Rubber Industry, 1948; West African Trade, 1954; (with B. S. Yamey) The Economics of Under-developed Countries, 1957; Economic Analysis and Policy in Under-developed Countries, 1958; Indian Economic Policy and Development, 1961; (with B. S. Yamey) Markets, Market Control and Marketing Reform, 1968; Dissent on Development: Studies and Debates in Development Economics, 1972; *contrib.* Economica, Econ. Jl, Jl Royal Stat. Soc., etc. *Address*: Dept of Economics, London School of Economics, Houghton Street, WC2A 2AE.

Bauman, Prof. Zygmunt, BA, MA, PhD; Professor of Sociology and Head of Department of Social Studies, University of Leeds, since 1971; *b* 1925; *m* 1948; three *d*. BA Warsaw 1950, MA Warsaw 1954, PhD Warsaw 1956, habilitation Warsaw 1960. Asst, 1953, Lectr, 1954, Asst Prof., 1960, Chair of Gen. Soc., 1964, Univ. of Warsaw; Prof. of Sociology, Univ. of Tel-Aviv, 1968. Mem., Polish, Israeli and Brit. Sociological Assocs. Chief Editor, Sociological Studies, Warsaw, 1960–68. *Publications*: (in Polish; Czech, Slovak, Serbo-Croat, Hungarian, Hebrew, Italian, French, English translations) Class-Movement Elite, 1960; Outline of Sociology, 1962; Images of the Human World, 1964; Culture and Society, 1966; Culture as Praxis, 1973; *contrib.* Annals of Am. Ac. of Science, Europen Jl of Sociology, Polish Sociological Bull., Social Res., Social Science Information, Sociological Studies, Sociol Rev., Brit. Jl of Sociol. *Address*: Dept of Social Studies, Univ. of Leeds, Leeds LS2 9JT.

Baumann, Dr Walter, Dr.phil; Senior Lecturer in Modern Languages (German), New University of Ulster, since 1973 (Lecturer, 1966–73), attached to Magee University College, Londonderry, 1966–72; *b* 1935; *m* 1961; one *s*. Dr.phil Zurich 1964; Zurich Grammar School Teacher's Dip., 1964. Lectr, Univ. Coll., Univ. of Toronto, 1964–66. *Publications*: The Rose in the Steel Dust: An Examination of the Cantos of Ezra Pound, 1967, American edn 1970; *contrib.* Colloquia Germanica, JEGP, MLQ, Seminar. *Address*: School of Humanities, New Univ. of Ulster, Coleraine, N Ireland.

Bawcutt, Nigel William, MA; Senior Lecturer in English Literature, University of Liverpool, since 1968; *b* 1930; *m* 1962; one *s*. BA Liverpool 1952 (1st cl. English Literature), DipEd Liverpool 1953, MA Liverpool 1955. William Noble Fellow, Liverpool, 1955; Asst Lectr, Liverpool, 1956–58; Lectr, Liverpool, 1958–68. *Publications*: ed, Middleton and Rowley: The Changeling, 1958, 2nd edn 1961; ed, Shorter Poems and Transla-

tions of Sir Richard Fanshawe, 1964; ed, John Ford: 'Tis Pity She's a Whore, 1966; *contrib.* ELR, Engl, Miscellany, MLR, Renaissance Drama. *Address*: Dept of English Literature, Univ. of Liverpool, Liverpool L69 3BX.

Bawden, Lisbeth-Anne Howard; Lecturer, Slade Film Department, University College London, since 1965; *b* 1931; *m* 1955 (marr. diss.); one *s* one *d*. St Hugh's Coll., Oxford, BA 1953 (Modern History), MA Oxon 1969. *Address*: Slade Film Dept, Univ. College London, Gower Street, WC1E 6BT.

Baxandall, Michael David Kighley; Reader in the History of the Classical Tradition, Warburg Institute, University of London, since 1973; *b* 1933; *m* 1963; one *s* one *d*. BA Cantab 1954, MA Cantab 1957. Junior Fellow. Warburg Inst., 1959–61; Asst Keeper, Dept of Architecture and Sculpture, Victoria and Albert Museum, 1961–65; Lectr in Renaissance Studies, Warburg Inst., 1965–73. *Publications*: Giotto and the Orators, 1971; Painting and Experience in 15th-century Italy, 1972; *contrib.* Jl of the Warburg and Courtauld Insts, Münchner Jahrbuch der bildenden Kunst. *Address*: Warburg Institute, Woburn Square, WC1H 0AB.

Baxter, Colin Robert; Lecturer in Law, University of Hull, since 1970; *b* 1943; *m* 1972. LLB Leeds 1965. Qualified as Solicitor, 1968. Asst Lectr, Hull, 1967. *Publications*: *contrib.* Camb. Law Jl. *Address*: Dept of Law, Univ. of Hull, Hull HU6 7RX.

Baxter, John Lamont; Lecturer, Division of Economic Studies, University of Sheffield, since 1968; *b* 1934; *m* 1963; one *s* one *d*. MA Glasgow 1954. *Publications*: *contrib.* Bull. Oxford Univ. Inst. of Econs and Stats, Scot. Jl Pol. Econ. *Address*: Div. of Economic Studies, The Univ., Sheffield S10 2TN.

Bayley, Prof. John; Warton Professor of English, University of Oxford, since 1973; *b* 1925; *m* 1956. BA Oxon 1950. Fellow of New Coll., Oxford, 1955; Professorial Fellow, St Catherine's Coll., Oxon, 1973. *Publications*: The Romantic Survival, 1956, 2nd edn 1968; The Character of Loves, 1959, 2nd edn 1968; Tolstoy and the Novel, 1964; Pushkin: A Comparative Commentary, 1969. *Address*: St Catherine's College, Oxford.

Bayley, Rev. Dr Michael John; Lecturer in Social Administration, Department of Sociological Studies, University of Sheffield, since 1973; *b* 1936; *m* 1963; two *s* two *d*. BA Cantab 1960 (Theol Tripos), Dip. in Social Studies Sheffield 1967, PhD 1972; Ind. Res. Worker, Sheffield, 1967–73. Asst Curate Gipton parish church, Leeds, 1962–66. *Publications*: Mental Handicap and Community Care, 1973; *contrib.* British Jl of Social Work, New Society. *Address*: Dept of Sociological Studies, Univ. of Sheffield, Shefield S10 2TN.

Bayley, Peter Charles; Master of Collingwood College, Durham, since 1971; *b* 1921; *m* 1951; one *s* two *d*. BA Oxon (1st cl.

English Language and Literature), MA Oxon 1947. Jun. Res. Fellow, Univ. Coll., Oxford, 1947–49; Fellow and Praelector in English, 1949–72; Univ. Lectr in English, Oxford, 1953–72; Vis. Lectr, Yale Univ. and Fellow, Jonathan Edwards Coll., 1970. Jun. Proctor, Oxford, 1957–58; Camerarius, Keeper of Coll. Bdgs, Dom. Bursar, Sen. Tutor, Tutor for Admiss., Univ. Coll., at various times 1949–72, Libr., 1966–72; Sen. examiner, awarder and Deleg. for Oxf. Local Exams, 1952–72; Sen. Mem., OUDS; Curator, Oxf. Univ. Theatre; Oxf. Univ. Corres., *The Times*, 1960–63. *Publications*: ed, Spenser: The Faerie Queene, Book II, 1965, Book I, 1966; Edmund Spenser, Prince of Poets, 1971; ed, Loves and Deaths: novelists' tales of the 19th century, 1972; *contrib*. Crit. Qly, Ess. Crit., Listener, RES, TLS, etc. *Address*: Collingwood College, Durham.

Bazell, Prof. Charles Ernest; Professor of General Linguistics, University of London, since 1957; *b* 1909. BA Oxon 1931 (1st cl. English), MA Oxon 1936. Fellow, Magdalen Coll., Oxford, 1934–42; Prof., Istanbul Univ., 1942–57. *Publications*: Linguistic Form, 1953; *contrib*. Archiv. Linguist., Trans Phil. Soc., Word. *Address*: School of Oriental and African Studies, Univ. of London, WC1E 7HP.

Bazire, Joyce; Senior Lecturer in English Language, University of Liverpool, since 1966; *b* 1923. BA Leeds 1944 (1st cl. English), MA Leeds 1949, DipEd Leeds 1945. Temp. Asst Lectr, Univ. of Hull, 1944–46; Asst Lectr in English, Univ. of Liverpool, 1946–49, Lectr 1949–66. Warden of Rankin Hall of Residence for Women Students, 1959–72. *Publications*: ed, The Metrical Life of St Robert of Knaresborough, 1953; (with Eric Colledge) The Chastising of God's Children, 1957; *contrib*. English and Germanic Studies, English Studies, Leeds Studies in English, MLR, YWES (Chaucer Chapter, 1953– , with David Mills 1966–). *Address*: Dept of English Language, The Univ. PO Box 147, Liverpool L69 3BX.

Beacham, Arthur, OBE, MA, PhD, LLD; Professor of Applied Economics, University of Liverpool, since 1966; *b* 1913; *m* 1938; one *s* one *d*. BA Wales 1935 (1st cl. Economics), MA Liverpool 1937, PhD Belfast 1941, Hon. LLD Otago 1969. Lectr in Economics, Queen's Univ., Belfast, 1938–45; Sen. Lectr in Economics, Univ. Coll., Wales, 1945–47; Prof. of Industrial Relations, Univ. Coll., Cardiff, 1947–51; Prof. of Economics, Univ. Coll. of Wales. 1951–63; Vice-Chancellor, Univ. of Otago, 1963–66. Mem., Council Royal Econ. Soc., 1970– ; North-West Econ. Planning Council, 1967– ; Chm., Post Office Arbitration Tribunal, 1972– . *Publications*: Economics of Industrial Organisation, 1947, 5th edn (with N. Cunningham) 1970; Industries in Welsh Country Towns, 1950; *contrib*. Econ. Jl, Qly Jl of Econs, Oxford Econ. Papers, etc. *Address*: Dept of Economics, Univ. of Liverpool, Liverpool L69 3BX.

Beales, Joan; Principal Tutor in Social Work, Department of Sociology, Bedford College, London University, since 1965; *b* 1920; *m* 1941; two *s*. Social Studies Dip. London 1941, Dip. Personnel Management London 1941, Mental Health Dip. London 1945. Mem., Assoc. Psychiatric Social Workers, subseq. Brit. Assoc. of Social Workers. *Address*: Sociology Dept, Bedford College, Regent's Park, NW1 4NS.

Bealey, Prof. Frank William; Professor of Politics, University of Aberdeen, since 1964; *b* 1922; *m* 1960; one *s* two *d*. BScEcon 1948 (1st cl. Government). Res. Asst, Passfield Trust, 1950–51; Extra-Mural Lectr (Burnley Area), Manchester Univ., 1951–52; Lectr, Univ. of Keele, 1952–64. *Publications*: (with Henry Pelling) Labour and Politics, 1958; (with J. Blondel and W. P. McCann) Constituency Politics, 1965; The Social and Political Thought of the British Labour Party, 1970; *contrib*. Manchester School, Brit. Jl of Sociology, Parly Aff., Mod. Hist., Mouvement Sociale, Western Pol. Qly. *Address*: Dept of Politics, Univ. of Aberdeen, Aberdeen AB9 1AS.

Bean, Ronald; Lecturer in Economics, University of Liverpool, since 1961; Senior Tutor, Faculty of Social and Environmental Studies, since 1971; *b* 1938; *m* 1962; two *s* one *d*. BCom, Liverpool 1959 (1st cl. Hons), Dip. in Industrial Sociology, Liverpool, 1960, MA McMaster Univ. (Canada) 1961 (Polit. Economy). Teaching Fellow in Political Economy, McMaster Univ., 1960–61; seconded to NBPI as an Industrial Relations Adviser, 1967. Sec., Merseyside Industrial Relations Soc. 1969–73; Joint Sec., Liverpool Economic and Statistical Soc., 1969–72. *Publications*: contrib.: Liverpool and Merseyside: Essays in the Economic and Social History of a Port, ed J. R. Harris, 1968; J. Saville and J. Bellamy, Dictionary of Labour Biography, 1972; Building the Union: Essays on the Growth of the Labour Movement, Merseyside, 1756–1967, ed H. R. Hikins, 1973; *contrib*. Brit. Jl Indust. Relns, Internat. Rev. Soc. Hist., Indust. Relns, Relations Industrielles, Lab. Hist., Pol Qly, Transp. Hist. *Address*: Dept of Economics, The Univ., Liverpool L69 3BX.

Beard, Geoffrey; Director, Visual Arts Centre, University of Lancaster, since 1972; *b* 1929; *m* 1948; one *d*. MA Leeds 1969 (History); ALA 1961. Manchester Poly., 1966–71; Sen. Res. Fellow, Dumbarton Oaks, Harvard Univ., 1968–69. Mem., Council, and Editor, *Furniture Hist. Jl*, 1964– ; Mem., Adv. panel, Central Council Care of Churches, 1969– ; Mem., Art History Panel, Nat. Council Diplomas in Art and Design. *Publications*: English Abbeys, 1948; XIXth Century Cameo Glass, 1956; Georgian Craftsmen and their Work, 1966; Modern Glass, 1968; Modern Ceramics, 1969; *contrib*. Apollo, Burl. Mag., Connoisseur. *Address*: Visual Arts Centre, Univ. of Lancaster, Bailrigg, Lancaster LA1 4YW.

Beard, Prof. Ruth M., PhD; Professor, Post-graduate School of Studies in Research in Education, Bradford University, since 1973; *b* 1919. BSc Hons London 1941 (1st cl. Advanced Subjects Maths), MSc London

1945 (Maths), MA London 1949 (Educn), PhD 1957; Post-grad. CertEd 1942. Univ. of Birmingham Sch. of Educn, 1959–65; i/c Univ. Teaching Methods Unit, Univ. of London Inst. of Educn, 1965–73. Member: Soc. for Res. into Higher Educn Governing Council, 1968– ; Assoc. for Study of Medical Educn, 1970–73, UGC Educnl Dev. Sub-Cttee, 1973– . *Publications*: An Outline of Piaget's Developmental Psychology, 1968; Research into Teaching Methods in Higher Education, 1968, 3rd edn (with D. A. Bligh) 1971; (with F. Healey and P. Holloway) Objectives in Higher Education, 1969, 2nd edn 1973; Teaching and Learning in Higher Education, 1970, 2nd edn 1972; *contrib*. Brit. Jl Educational Psychol., Brit. Jl Medical Educn. *Address*: Univ. of Bradford, Bradford BD7 1DP.

Beardsmore, Richard W.; Lecturer, Department of Philosophy, University College of North Wales, since 1968; *b* 1944; *m* 1965; one *d*. BA 1965, MA 1968, UCSW and Mon. Asst Lectr in Philosophy, St. David's Coll., Lampeter, 1967, Lectr., UCNW, 1968. *Publications*: Moral Reasoning, 1969; Art and Morality, 1971; *contrib*. Philosophy and the Arts, ed, G. N. A. Vesey, 1973; *contrib*. Analysis, Brit. Jl of Aesthetics, *Address*: Dept of Philosophy, Univ. Coll. of North Wales, Bangor LL57 2DG.

Bearne, Colin Gerald; Lecturer in Russian, School of European Studies, University of Sussex, since 1965; *b* 1939; *m* 1968; one *s*. one *d*. BA Hons Birmingham 1962 (German and Russian), MA Birmingham 1964 (Russian Lit.); Member: AUT; Assoc. of Teachers of Russian, Academic Sec., Sch. of European Studies, Univ. of Sussex, 1967–70. *Publications*: ed, Mikhail Sholokhov: Tales from the Don, 1967; ed, Modern Russian Short Stories, vols I and II, 1968 and 1969; ed, Vortex: Soviet Science Fiction, 1969; Sholokhov, 1970; trans. F. Maisch: Incest, 1971; trans. Giese/Gebhard: Female Sexuality; trans, Baranov. *Address*: Arts Building, Univ. of Sussex, Falmer, Brighton BN1 9QN.

Beasley, Nigel Alan, BA, PhD; Lecturer in Psychology, University of Keele, since 1966; *b* 1942; *m* 1965; one *s*. BA Nottingham 1964 (Hons Psychology), PhD Nottingham 1967. *Publications*: *contrib*. Canad. Jl Psychol., Jl Ment. Subnorm. *Address*: Dept of Psychology, Univ. of Keele, Keele, Staffs ST5 5BG.

Beasley, Prof. William Gerald, PhD, FBA; Professor of the History of the Far East, School of Oriental and African Studies, University of London, since 1954; *b* 1919, *m* 1955; one *s*. BA London 1940, PhD London 1950; FBA 1967. Lectr in the Hist. of the Far East, SOAS, London, 1947–54. Chm., Anglo-Japanese Mixed Cultural Commn, 1964–68; Mem., Hong Kong UGC, 1965–68. *Publications*: Great Britain and the Opening of Japan, 1951; Select Documents on Japanese Foreign Policy 1853–1868, 1955; The Modern History of Japan, 1963; The Meiji Restoration, 1972; *contrib*. Bull., School of Oriental and African Studies, Jl of Asian Studies. *Address*: School of Oriental

and African Studies, Malet Street, WC1E 7HP.

Beattie, Alan James; Senior Lecturer in Political Science, London School of Economics, since 1970; *b* 1938; *m* 1962; one *s*. BSc(Econ) London 1959 (1st cl. Political Science). Asst. Lectr in Political Sci., LSE, 1962–66, Lectr 1966–70. *Publications*: English Party Politics (2 vols), 1660–1970, 1970; *contrib*. Gov. and Opposition, Pol. Qly, Cultura e Politica, etc. *Address*: Dept of Government, London School of Economics, Aldwych, WC2A 2AE.

Beattie, Prof. Arthur James, FRSE; Professor of Greek at Edinburgh University since 1951; Dean of the Faculty of Arts, 1963–65; *b* 1914. 1st cl. Hons Classics Aberdeen 1935, 1st cl. Classical Tripos Cambridge, Part I 1936, Part II 1938; FRSE 1957. Wilson Travelling Fellowship, Aberdeen, 1938–40; Fellow and College Lectr, Sidney Sussex Coll., 1946–51; Faculty Asst Lectr and Univ. Lectr in Classics, Cambridge, 1946–51, Chm. Governors, Morrison's Acad., Crieff, 1962– . *Publications*: *contrib*. articles in classical jls. *Address*: Univ. of Edinburgh, Old College, South Bridge, Edinburgh EH8 9YL.

Beaumont, Adrian, DMus, ARCM; Lecturer, Department of Music, University of Bristol, since 1961; *b* 1937; *m* 1963. BA Wales 1958, DipEd 1959, MMus Wales 1961, DMus Wales 1973, ARCM (Oboe Performer) 1960. Musical Dir, Bristol Opera School, 1964–67; Founder-Conductor, Bristol Bach Choir, 1967– . *Publications*: Preliminary Exercises for the Oboe, 1971; *Compositions*: Songs for Little Children (Set 1), 1970; Sonata for Brass Quintet, 1973; Two Welsh Folk Songs, 1973; Anthem: The Spacious Firmament, 1974; Songs of all Seasons, 1974. *Address*: Dept of Music, Univ. of Bristol, Bristol BS8 1TH.

Beaumont, Dr Peter; Lecturer, Department of Geography, University of Durham, since 1965; *b* 1940; *m* 1963; two *s*. BA Durham 1962 (1st cl. Hons), PhD Durham 1968. Harkness Fellow of Commonwealth Fund of New York, 1969–71; NATO Fellow, 1972–73. *Publications*: *contrib*. Palaeogeography, Palaeoclimatology, Palaeoecology, New Phytologist, Jl Soil and Water Conservation, Trans Inst. Brit. Geographers, Geography, Bull. Internat. Assoc. Sci. Hydrology Proc. Yorks Geolog. Soc., Sedimentology, Bull. Geolog. Soc. of America, World Crops, Econ. Botany, Ground Water Geog. Jl, Water Well Jl, Weather. *Address*: Dept of Geography, Univ. of Durham, Durham DHA 3HP.

Beaver, Harold Lothar, MA; Reader in American Literature, University of Warwick; *b* 1929; *m* 1957; one *s* one *d*. BA Oxon 1951 (Mods and Greats), MA Harvard 1953 (Comparative Literature). Teaching Fellow and Resdt Tutor, Harvard, 1953–55; Lectr in Sch. of English, Leeds Univ., 1966; Sen. Lectr in Sch. of Literary Studies, Warwick, 1968. Editor with OUP, 1955–62. Fellow of Amer. Council of Learned Socs, Amherst Coll., 1973–74. *Publications*: American Critical Essays (Twentieth Century), 1959; ed, Mark Twain: Life on the Mississippi, 1962; The Confessions of Jotham Simiyu (a novel), 1965; Pardoner's Tale (a novel), 1966; ed, Melville: Billy Budd, Sailor and Other Stories, 1967, 2nd edn 1970; ed, Melville: Moby-Dick, 1972; contrib. The American Imagination, 1960; Essays and Studies, 1962; Penguin Companion to American Literature, 1972; contrib. Times Lit. Suppl. *Address*: Dept of English and Comparative Studies, Univ. of Warwick, Coventry CV4 7AL.

Bechhofer, Frank; Reader, Department of Sociology, University of Edinburgh, since 1971; *b* 1935; *m* 1960; one *s* one *d*. BA Cambridge 1959, MA 1962. Junior Research Officer, Dept of Applied Economics, Cambridge, 1962–65; Lectr, Univ. of Edinburgh, 1965–71. Brit. Sociological Assoc., Exec. Cttee, 1968–72. *Publications*: The Affluent Worker: Industrial Attitudes and Behaviour, 1968; The Affluent Worker: Political Attitudes and Behaviour, 1968; The Affluent Worker in the Class Structure, 1969 (all with J. H. Goldthorpe, D. Lockwood and J. Platt); ed, Population Growth and the Brain Drain, 1969; *contrib.* EJS, Scott. Jl of Pol Econ., Sociology. *Address*: Dept of Sociology, Univ. of Edinburgh, Adan Ferguson Building, George Square, Edinburgh.

Beckerman, Prof. Wilfred; Professor of Political Economy, Head of Department of Political Economy, University College London, University of London, since 1969; *b* 1925; *m* 1952; one *s* two *d*. BA Cantab 1948, MA Cantab 1951, PhD Cantab 1952. Lectr in Economics, Univ. of Nottingham, 1950–52; Dir Res. Project, Nat. Inst. Econ. Soc. Res., 1962–63; Fellow, Balliol Coll., Oxford, 1964–69. OEEC and OECD, 1952–61; Econ. Consultant, Dept of Econ. Aff., 1964–65; Econ. Adv., Bd of Trade, 1967–69; Mem., Royal Commn on Environmental Pollution, 1970–73. *Publications*: The British Economy in 1975 (with associates), 1965; Introduction to National Income Analysis, 1968; ed, The Labour Government's Economic Record: 1964–70, 1972; In Defence of Economic Growth, 1974; *contrib.* Econ. Jl, Economica, Econometrica, Rev. Econ. Stats, Rev. Econ. Studies, etc. *Address*: Dept of Political Economy, Univ. College London, Gower Street, WC1E 6BT.

Beckford, Dr James Arthur, BA, PhD; Lecturer in Sociology, Department of Sociology, University of Durham, since 1973; *b* 1942; *m* 1965; two *d*. BA Reading 1965 (1st cl. Hons), PhD Reading 1972. Lectr in Sociology, Reading, 1966–73. *Publications*: Jehovah's Witnesses in Britain (forthcoming); *contrib.* A Sociological Yearbook of Religion in Britain, Current Sociology. *Address*: Dept of Sociology, Univ. of Durham, 44 Old Elvet, Durham.

Beckingham, Prof. Charles Fraser; Professor of Islamic Studies, University of London, since 1965; *b* 1914; *m* 1946, 1970; one *d*. BA Cantab 1935, MA Cantab 1939. Lectr in Islamic History, Manchester Univ., 1951–55, Sen. Lectr, 1955–58, Prof. of Islamic Studies, 1958–65. Dept of Printed Books, British Museum, 1936–46. Seconded for service with military and naval Intelligence, 1942–46; Foreign Office, 1946–51. Mem. Council, RCAS, 1969–73, Vice-Pres., 1973– . Mem. Council, Hakluyt Soc., 1958–62, 1964–69, Pres., 1969–72, Vice-Pres., 1972– ; Treas., Royal Asiatic Soc., 1964–67, Pres., 1967–70; Jt Editor, 1961, Editor, 1965, Jl of Semitic Studies. *Publications*: contribs to Admiralty Handbook of Western Arabia, 1946; (with G. W. B. Huntingford) Some Records of Ethiopia, 1954; (with G. W. B. Huntingford) A True Relation of the Prester John of the Indies, 1961; Bruce's Travels (ed and selected), 1964; The Achievements of Prester John, 1966; (ed) Islam, in Religion in the Middle East, ed A. J. Arberry, 1969; *contrib.* Asian Affairs, Bull. SOAS, Jl RAS, Jl Semetic Studies. *Address*: School of Oriental and African Studies, Malet Street, WC1E 7HP.

Beckingsale, Bernard Winslow; Senior Lecturer, Department of History, University of Newcastle upon Tyne, since 1963; *b* 1917; *m* 1945; one *s*. one *d*. BA Cantab 1939, MA Cantab 1942; FRHistS; Mem., Historical Assoc. Coll. Lectr, Jesus Coll., Cambridge, 1946; Lectr, Univ. of Durham, 1948. *Publications*: Elizabeth I, 1963; Burghley: Tudor Statesman, 1967; *contrib.* Northern Hist. *Address*: Dept of History, Univ. of Newcastle upon Tyne, Newcastle upon Tyne NE1 7RU.

Beckinsale, Dr Robert Percy; Senior Lecturer, Geography Department, University of Oxford, since 1951; *b* 1908; *m* 1937; one *s* two *d*. BA London 1928 (History), BA London 1929 (Geography), MA London 1935 (Geography), DipEd Reading 1930, MA Oxon 1949, DPhil Oxon 1949; FRMetS, Mem., Soc. Authors. Saltley Coll., Birmingham, 1935–40; Lectr, Univ. of Oxford, 1944–51; Fulbright Vis. Prof., Chicago Univ., 1962–63; Fellow, Univ. Coll., Oxford, 1965. Argentine–Chile Boundary Dispute Commn, 1966–67; Sen. Res. Off., NID5, 1940–44. *Publications*: Companion into Gloucestershire, 1939, 6th edn 1974; Companion into Berkshire, 1951, 2nd edn 1972; The Trowbridge Woollen Industry, 1951; Land, Air and Ocean, 1943, 4th edn 1966; co-author, ed jtly, The History of the Study of Landforms, vol. 1, 1964; Urbanisation and its Problems, 1968, 2nd edn 1970; co-author, Life and Work of W. M. Davis, 1973; Southern Europe, 1973; *contrib.* Amer. Dict. Scientific Biog., Chambers's Encyclop., Encyclop. Amer., Encyclop. Britannica, Encyclop. Earth Sci., Geog. Jl. *Address*: University College, Oxford.

Beckley, Richard James; Lecturer in German Language and Literature, King's College, London, since 1962; *b* 1927. BA(Hons) London 1958 (1st cl. German), MA London 1960. Asst Lectr, King's Coll., London, 1960–62. Asst Editor, German Life and Letters, 1966– . *Publications*: Essay on Carl Sternheim in German Men of Letters, vol. II, 1963; Essay on Ernst Toller in German Men of Letters, vol. III, 1964; Es geht weiter: An Intermediate German Grammar, 1966; trans. and ed, J. H.

Negenman's A New Atlas of the Bible, 1969; contrib. German Life and Letters. Address: German Dept. King's College, Strand, WC2R 2LS.

Beddard, Dr Ralph; Lecturer in Law, Faculty of Law, University of Southampton, since 1967; b 1939. LLB Sheffield 1962. PhD Sheffield 1966. Temp. Lectr in Law, Univ. of Keele, 1966–67. Address: Faculty of Law, Univ. of Southampton, Southampton SO9 5NH.

Beddard, Dr Robert Anthony; Fellow, Tutor and Lecturer in Modern History, Oriel College, Oxford, since 1967; b 1939' BA London 1961 (1st cl.), MA Cantab 1965, MA, DPhil Oxon 1967; FRHistS. Lectr in Modern History, Univ. of Oxford, 1968. Publications: contrib. Oxford Dictionary of the Christian Church (forthcoming); contrib. Hist. Jl, Bull. Inst. Hist. Res., Guildhall Misc., Bodleian Qly, Wilts Archaeol. Mag., Sussex Archaeol. Collections, Notes and Queries, Jl Eccles. Hist., Archæologia Cantiana. Address: Oriel College, Oxford.

Bedford, Errol; Senior Lecturer in Philosophy, University of Edinburgh, since 1960; b 1921; m 1944; one s. BA London 1941. Asst, Univ. of Edinburgh, 1946–47, Lectr, 1947–60; Vis. Prof., Univ. of Maryland, 1966, 1971. Publications: contrib. Jl Philos., Mod. Lang. Rev., Proc. Aristot. Soc., Proc. 3rd Internat. Cong. Aesthetics, Proc. 11th and 12th Internat. Cong. Philosophy. Address: Dept of Philosophy, Univ. of Edinburgh.

Bedford, Dr Ronald David, MA, PhD; Lecturer in English, University of Exeter, since 1966; b 1940; m 1966; two s. BA Cantab 1962, MA Cantab 1965, PhD Cantab 1970. Address: Dept of English, Univ. of Exeter, Exeter, Devon.

Bednarowski, Dr Wladyslaw; Reader in Logic and Metaphysics, University of Aberdeen; b 1905. Dr of philos. Cracow 1933. Jun. Asst, Sen. Asst, Univ. of Lwow, 1934–39; Asst, Univ. of Aberdeen, 1946. Publications: only articles; contrib. Proc. Aristot. Soc., Aristot, Soc. Supp., Przeglad Filozoficzny, Szkice Filozoficzne. Address: Dept of Logic, Univ. of Aberdeen, King's College, Old Aberdeen, Scotland.

Beeby, Barry Michael; Staff Tutor in Archaeol., Department of Adult Education, University of Nottingham since 1967; b 1936; m 1964 (marr. diss.); 1972; one d. BA Hons Oxford 1960 (English Lang. and Lit.), MA 1964, Acad. Post-grad. Dip. London 1966 (Prehist. Archaeol.); Mem., Prehist. Soc. Address: Univ. of Nottingham, Dept of Adult Education, 14–22 Shakespeare Street, Nottingham NG1 4FJ.

Beechey, Dr Gwilym Edward, MA, MusB, PhD, FRCO; Lecturer in Music, University of Hull, since 1969; b 1938; m 1962; one s two d. BA, MusB Cantab 1959, MA Cantab 1963, PhD Cantab 1965; FRCO 1957. Asst Lectr in Music, Univ. of Glasgow, 1965–68. Publications: ed, Ten Eighteenth-Century Voluntaries (Bennett, Hine, Walond) –

Recent Researches in the Baroque Era, vol. VI, 1969; (with Thurston Dart) Eight Keyboard Sonatas, T. Arne, fascimile edn 1969; Shakespeare Ode – T. Linley, Jun. Musica Britannica XXX, 1970; Two Suites for Harpsichord, T. Chilcot, Penn State Music Series vol. 22, 1970; contrib. Consort, Music and Letters, Musical Qly, Music Rev., Musical Times, Rev. Belge de Musicologie, Organ. Address: Dept of Music, The Univ., Hull HU6 7RX, Yorkshire.

Beedell, Christopher John, BSc; Senior Lecturer in Residential Social Work, Department of Social Administration and Social Work, University of Bristol, since 1970; b 1924; m 1952; one s three d. BSc Special Psychology London 1947 (1st cl. Hons); Mem., British Psychological Soc., Assoc Teachers in Social Work Educn. Res. Fellow, Bristol, 1956; Lectr in Educn, 1960–70. Publications: Residential Life with Children, 1970, Italian edn 1972; contrib. Annual Rev. Res. Child Care Assoc., Brit. Jl Psychiatric Work, Jl Ment. Sci. Address: 6 Berkeley Square, Bristol BS8 1HQ.

Beer, Gillian Patricia Kempster; Fellow of Girton College and University Lecturer in English, Cambridge University, since 1966; b 1935; m 1962; three s. MA Oxon 1959, BLitt Oxon 1960. Asst Lectr, Bedford Coll., Univ. of London. 1959–62; Pt-time Lectr, Liverpool Univ., 1962–64; Univ. Asst Lectr, Cambridge, 1966–71. Publications: Meredith: A Change of Masks, 1970; The Romance, 1970; contrib. Mod. Lang. Rev., 19th Cent. Fiction, Rev. Engl. Studies, Vic. Studies. Address: Girton College, Cambridge.

Beer, Dr John Bernard; University Lecturer, Faculty of English, University of Cambridge, since 1964; b 1926; m 1962; three s. BA Cantab 1950 (1st cl. English I, 1950, 1st cl. Psychology II, 1952), MA Cantab 1955, PhD Cantab 1957. Fellow (Title A), St John's Coll., Cambridge, 1955–58; Asst Lectr, Manchester Univ., 1958–60; Lectr, 1960–64. Publications: Coleridge the Visionary, 1959, 2nd edn 1970; The Achievement of E. M. Forster, 1962; ed, Coleridge's Poems, 1963, new edn 1973; Milton, Lost and Regained (British Academy Chatterton Lecture), 1964; Blake's Humanism, 1968; Blake's Visionary Universe, 1969; ed and contrib., Coleridge's Variety, 1974; contrib. The English Moralists, ed Davies and Watson, 1964; English Poetry: Select Bibliographical Guides, ed A. E. Dyson, 1971; S. T. Coleridge, ed R. L. Brett, 1971; William Blake, ed M. D. Paley and M. Phillips, 1973; contrib. Camb. Rev., Crit. Qly, Notes and Queries, Times Lit. Supp., and numerous reviews. Address: Peterhouse, Cambridge.

Beesley, Prof. Michael Edwin; Professor of Economics, London Graduate School of Business Studies, since 1965; b 1924; m 1947; three s. two d. BCom Birmingham 1945 (Div. I), PhD Birmingham 1951. Univ. of Birmingham: Res. Associate, 1949; Lectr in Commerce, 1951–61; LSE: Rees Jeffreys Res. Fellow in Econs of Transport, 1961–64; Reader in Econs, 1964–65. Vis. Associate Prof. of Industry, Warton Sch., Univ. of

Pennsylvania, 1959-60; Vis. Prof. and Commonwealth Fellow, Univ. of BC, 1968; Vis. Prof., Harvard Business Sch. and Kennedy Sch., 1974. Mem., Management Studies Bd, CNAA; Management Studies Commn, SSRC. Consultant Chief Economic Advr, DoE, 1968- . *Publications*: Urban Transport: studies in economic policy, 1973; ed and contrib., Productivity and Amenity (forthcoming); ed and contrib., Britain: the new EEC opportunity, (forthcoming); The Machine Tool Industry, in, Symposium on the Structure of British Industry, 1958; (with R. T. Hamilton) New Enterprise Projects (forthcoming); *contrib*. Applied Econs, Bankers' Mag., Jl Birmingham Chamber of Commerce, Econ. Jl, Economica, Environment and Planning, Jl Industrial Econs, Netherlands Inst. of Transport Jl, New Scientist, Bull. Oxford Univ. Inst. Stats, Public Admin, Jl Royal Stat. Soc., Town Planning Rev., Traffic Engineering and Control, Urban Studies. *Address:* London Graduate School of Business Studies, Sussex Place, Regent's Park, NW1 4SA.

Beeson, Marxen; Lecturer in Criminology, Department of Adult Education and Extra Mural Studies, University of Leeds, since 1967; *b* 1931; *m* 1954; two *s* one *d*. BSc London 1953 ((Special) Psychology), Postgrad. Cert. Ed. London 1954; ABPsS 1963; Mem., British Soc. of Criminology. Sen. Res. Officer, LSE, 1961-64; Sen. Res. Fellow, Univ. of Durham, 1964-67. *Publications*: (with W. A. Belson), An Exploratory Study: Admitting Thefts, 1968; *contrib*. British Book News, Prison Service Jl. *Address:* 17 Lyddon Terrace, Leeds LS2 9IA.

Beeston, Prof. Alfred Felix L., DPhil, FBA; Laudian Professor of Arabic, University of Oxford, since 1955; *b* 1911. BA Oxon 1933 (1st cl. Oriental Studies), MA Oxon 1936, DPhil Oxon 1937; FBA, FRAsiaticS. Asst, Dept Oriental Books, Bodleian Libr., Oxford, 1935; Keeper of Oriental Books, 1945. *Publications*: Descriptive Grammar of Epigraphic South Arabian, 1962; The Arabic Language today, 1970. *Address:* St John's College, Oxford OX1 3JP.

Beet, Ernest Harold; Lecturer in Social Studies, Department of Adult Education, University of Keele, since 1962; *b* 1921; *m* 1947; three *d*. BA 1949 (Politics, Econs, IIi), MA (by thesis) 1954. Staff Tutor, Delegacy for Extra-Mural Studies, Univ. of Oxford, 1949-62. Staffs County Council: Mem., 1961- ; past Chm., Finance Cttee; Chm., Libraries, Records and Museums Cttee; Member: Health Exec. Council; Family Practitioners Cttee. *Publications*: *contrib*. Public Admin. *Address:* Univ. of Keele Dept of Adult Education, Keele, Staffs ST5 5BG.

Begbie, Dr George Hugh; Senior Lecturer, Department of Physiology, University Medical School, Edinburgh, since 1972; *b* 1920; *m* 1951; two *s*. MA Edinburgh 1941, PhD Edinburgh 1945, MB, ChB Edinburgh 1954; Mem., Brain Res. Assoc., Physiol. Soc. (London), Ergonomics Res. Soc., Brit. Biophysical Soc., Soc. of Authors. Vis. Prof.,

Fuh Tan Univ., Shanghai, 1946; Mem., MRC Applied Psychol. Unit, Cambridge, 1954-56; Lectr, Edinburgh Medical School, 1956-61; various visiting professorships in Canada and USA. Elected Mem., Senatus Academicus of Edinburgh Univ., 1970- ; Mem., Medical Faculty Cttees on Ageing, Behavioural Science Teaching; Dir of Studies, 1972- ; Mem., Court-Senate Cttee on Structure and Constitution of Univ. Editor, Qly Jl Experim. Phys., 1962-67 (now on Council and Board). WHO Consultant on Med. Educn, Indonesia, 1973. *Publications*: Seeing and the Eye, 1969; *contrib*. Jl of Phys., Qly Jl of Experimental Phys., Proc. Royal Soc., A, Nature, Qly Jl of Experimental Psych., Jl of Theor. Biol., Ergonomics, Physiotherapy, Ciba Foundation Symposium. *Address:* Dept of Physiology, Univ. Medical School, Teviot Place, Edinburgh.

Behrend, Prof. Hilde; Professor of Industrial Relations, Department of Business Studies, University of Edinburgh, since 1973; *b* 1917. BScEcon London 1944, PhD Birmingham 1951; Mem., Brit. Univs Industrial Relations Assoc., Mem., Scottish Econ. Soc. Asst Lectr and Res. Fellow, Commerce and Social Science, Univ. Birmingham, 1949-54; Lectr, Dept of Commerce, Univ. Edinburgh, 1954-64; Sen. Lectr, 1964-72; Reader, Dept of Business Studies, Univ. Edinburgh, 1972-73. *Publications*: Absence under Full Employment, 1951; (jtly) A National Survey of Attitudes to Inflation and Incomes Policy, 1966; (jtly), Incomes Policy and the Individual, 1967; (jtly) Views on Pay Increases, Fringe Benefits and Low Pay, 1970; (jtly) Views on Income Differentials and the Economic Situation, 1970; Public acceptability and a workable incomes policy, in, An Incomes Policy for Britain, 1972; Incomes Policy, Equity and Pay Increase Differentials, 1973; *contrib*. Brit. Jl Industrial Relations, Brit. Jl Sociology, Industrial and Labour Relations Rev., Industrial Relations Jl, Internat. Labour Rev., Jl Industrial Econs, Manchester Sch. Econ. and Social Studies, Nature, Occupational Psych., Scottish Jl Polit. Econ. *Address:* William Robertson Building, George Square, Edinburgh EH8 9LE.

Beishon, Prof. Ronald John; Professor of Systems, Open University, since 1971; *b* 1930; *m* 1954; two *s* two *d*. BSc London 1961 (Psychology), Grad. Dip. Birmingham 1954 (Metallurgy), DPhil Oxford 1966 (Psychology); ABPsS, AIM, MWeldI; Sen. Res. Asst, Oxford, 1961-64; Lectr in Psychology, Bristol, 1964-68; Reader in Behavioural Sciences, Sussex, 1968-71. Member: Council of Ergonomics Res. Soc. 1965-71; Scientific Advisory Cttee TUC, 1968-71. *Publications*: ed (with G. Peters) Systems Behaviour, 1972; *contrib*. Ergonomics, Internat. Studies of Management and Organisation. *Address:* Open Univ., Walton Hall, Milton Keynes. MK7 6AA.

Beith, Alan James, MP; Lecturer in Politics, Department of Politics, University of Newcastle upon Tyne, since 1966; MP (L) Berwick-upon-Tweed, since 1973; *b* 1943; *m* 1965. BA Oxon (PPE) 1964, BLitt, MA

Oxon 1969. Hon. Sec., Public Admin Cttee of Jt Univ. Council 1969. Hon. Sec., Public Admin Cttee of Jt Univ. Council for Social and Public Admin, 1970–73; Mem., Hexham Rural District Council, 1968– ; NE Transport Users' Consultative Cttee, 1970–74; Tynedale District Council, 1973– ; NE Regional Adv. Council of BBC, 1971– ; Chm., NE Gp of RIPA, 1970–72. *Publications*: *contrib*. New Soc., Local Govt Chronicle, Parliamentary Affairs, Public Admin Bull., Policy and Politics. *Address*: Dept of Politics, The Univ., Newcastle upon Tyne NE1 7RU.

Belfield, Eversley Michael Gallimore; Senior Lecturer, Extra-Mural Department, Southampton University, since 1966; *b* 1918; *m* 1950; three *s* two *d*. MA Oxon 1946. Mem., Council, Hist. Assoc., 1970– . *Publications*: (with Gen. Parham) Unarmed into Battle, 1956; Annals of the Addington Family, 1959; (with Gen. Essame) Battle for Normandy, 1965, French trans. 1967; Battle of Oudenarde, 1972; The Boer War, 1974. *Address*: Extra-Mural Dept, Univ. of Southampton, Highfield, Southampton SO9 5NH.

Belflower, Dr Robert; Lecturer in American Literature, Department of American Studies, University of Manchester, since 1970; *b* 1936. AB LaGrange 1958, AM Emory 1961, PhD Duke 1967, DPhil Oxon 1971; Mem., Brit. Assoc. Amer. Studies, Soc. Study Southern Lit. Grad. Tutor in English, Duke Univ., 1960–64; Instructor, Univ. of N Carolina at Chapel Hill, 1965–66. Fellow, Salzburg Seminar in Amer. Studies, 1973. *Address*: Dept of American Studies, The Univ., Manchester M13 9PL.

Bell, Colin Roy; Senior Lecturer, and Chairman, Department of Sociology, University of Essex, since 1971; *b* 1942; *m* 1964; one *s* one *d*. BA Keele 1964 (1st cl. in History and Geography), MScEcon Wales 1966; Mem., Brit. Sociological Assoc., Convenor of Family and Kinship Group. Res. Asst Univ. Coll., Swansea, 1965; Res. Fellow, Univ. Coll. Swansea, 1966–68; Lectr, Univ. of Essex 1968–71. Consultant to the Roskill Commn on the siting of the Third London Airport, 1969–70. *Publications*: Middle Class Families, 1969; The Disruption of Community Life, 1970; Community Studies, 1972; The Sociology of the Local Community, 1972; Persistence and Change: a second study of Banbury (forthcoming); *contrib*. Human Relations, Sociology, Sociol Rev., Sociologia Ruralis. *Address*: Dept of Sociology, Univ. of Essex, Colchester, Essex CO4 35Q.

Bell, Prof. Coral Mary; Professor of International Relations, University of Sussex, since 1972; *b* 1923. BA Sydney 1945, MSc Econ London 1954, PhD 1962; Mem., RIIA, Councillor, International Inst. of Strategic Studies. Lectr, Univ. of Manchester, 1956–61; Sen. Lectr, Univ. of Sydney, 1961–65; Reader, LSE, 1965–72. Member: Arms Control Advisory Panel, 1965– ; Political Science Cttee, SSRC, 1973– . *Publications*: Survey of International Affairs, 1956; Negotiation from Strength: a Study in the Politics of Power, 1961; Europe Without Britain, 1963; The Debatable Alliance, 1965;

The Conventions of Crisis, 1971. *Address*: Univ. of Sussex, Sussex House, Falmer, Brighton BN1 9RH.

Bell, Dr James Alan Morrison; Senior Lecturer, School of Architecture, University of Manchester, since 1971; *b* 1925; *m* 1956; one *s* one *d*. BArch (Hons) Liverpool 1950, MCD Liverpool 1951, PhD Manchester 1963; ARIBA, MRTPI. Lectr, Univ. of Manchester, 1954–71. Vice-Pres., Illum. Eng. Soc., 1973–74. *Publications*: Lighting section, in, Architectural Press: Specification 69, 1969 (and annual revisions); *contrib*. Trans Illum. Eng. Soc. *Address*: School of Architecture, Univ. of Manchester, Manchester M13 9PL.

Bell, Prof. Kathleen; Professor of Social Studies, Department of Social Studies, University of Newcastle upon Tyne, since 1971; *b* 1920; *m* 1945; one *s* one *d*. BA Manchester 1942; Mem., Exec. Cttee, Soc. Admin Assoc., 1968. Lectr, Dept of Extra Mural Studies, Univ. of Newcastle upon Tyne, 1963; Lectr in Social Studies, 1964–67; Sen. Tutor, 1967–69; Sen. Lectr, 1969–71. Mem.: Council on Tribunals, 1963– ; Davies Cttee on Hosp. Complaints Procedure, 1971–73; Ed. Bd, Jl Soc. Policy, 1971– ; Mem., N. Tyneside AHA, 1974– . *Publications*: Tribunals in the Social Services, 1969, American edn 1969; *contrib*. Pub. Admin, Soc. and Econ. Admin. *Address*: Dept of Social Studies, Univ. of Newcastle upon Tyne, Newcastle upon Tyne NE1 7RU.

Bell, Dr Peter Robinson; Senior Lecturer in Philosophy, School of Social Studies, University of East Anglia, since 1970; *b* 1936; *m* 1960; two *d*. BA Cantab 1960, MA Cantab 1963, PhD Cantab 1968. Res. Fellow, Sidney Sussex Coll., Cambridge, 1962–64; Lectr in Philosophy, East Anglia, 1964–70. *Address*: School of Social Studies, Univ. of East Anglia, Norwich, Norfolk NOR 88C.

Bell, Philip Michael Hett, BA, BLitt, FRHistS; Senior Lecturer, Department of Modern History, University of Liverpool, since 1970; *b* 1930; *m* 1955; one *s* one *d*. BA Oxon 1953 (1st cl. Modern History), BLitt Oxon 1957; FRHistS. Asst, Univ. of Aberdeen, 1954; Lectr, Univ. of Liverpool, 1957. *Publications*: Disestablishment in Ireland and Wales, 1969; *contrib*. Revue d'Histoire de la Deuxième Guerre Mondiale. *Address*: Dept of Modern History, Univ. of Liverpool, Liverpool L69 3BX.

Bell, Prof. Quentin (Claudian Stephen); Professor of the History and Theory of Art, Sussex University, since 1967; *b* 1910; *m* 1952; one *s* two *d*. MA Dunelm 1957. Lectr in Art Educn, King's Coll., Newcastle, 1952; Sen. Lectr, 1956; Prof. of Fine Art, Univ. of Leeds, 1962–67 (Head of Dept of Fine Art, 1959); Slade Prof. of Fine Art, Oxford Univ., 1965–66. Regular contributor to Listener, 1951– ; painter, sculptor, potter, author, art critic. *Publications*: On Human Finery, 1947; (with Helmut Gernsheim) Those Impossible English, 1951; Roger Montané, 1961; The Schools of Design, 1963; Ruskin, 1963;

48

Victorian Artists, 1967; Bloomsbury, 1968; Virginia Woolf, a biography, 2 vols, 1972; *contrib.* Burlington Magazine, Jl of Warburg and Courtauld Insts, History Today, Durham Res. Rev. *Address*: Univ. of Sussex, Falmer, Brighton BN1 9QN.

Bell, Robert Elliott; Lecturer, Faculty of Educational Studies, Open University, since 1971; *b* 1930. BA Cambridge 1953, MA 1957, DipEd TCD 1956, MEd Edinburgh 1965. Edinburgh Univ.: Res. Officer, Godfrey Thomson Unit for Educnl Res., 1965; Lectr Dept of Educn, 1966. Mem., Gen. Teaching Council for Scotland, 1968–71; Editor, Scottish Educational Studies, 1970– . *Publications*: (ed with G. Fowler and K. Little) Education in Great Britain and Ireland, 1973; (ed with A. J. Youngson) Present and Future in Higher Education, 1973; (with N. Grant) A Mythology of British Education, 1974. *Address*: Open Univ., Milton Keynes MK7 6AA.

Bellamy, Dr Joyce Margaret; Senior Research Officer, Department of Economic and Social History, University of Hull, since 1971; *b* 1921. BCom London 1941; PhD Hull 1966. Res. Asst, 1948; Sen. Res. Asst, 1966; Sen. Research Officer, 1971. Mem. Exec. Cttee, Business Archives Council, 1967–70, 1971– . *Publications*: British Markets for Flour and Wheatfeed, 1957; Trade and Shipping of Nineteenth-Century Hull, 1971; ed (with John Saville), Dictionary of Labour Biography, vol. 1, 1972, vol. 2 1974; *contrib.* Business Hist., Jl of Industrial Econs, Yorks Bull. of Economic and Social Res. *Address*: Dept of Economic and Social History, The Univ., Hull HU6 7RX.

Bellamy, Ronald; Senior Lecturer, School of Economic Studies, University of Leeds, since 1963; *b* 1917; *m* 1953; two *d.* BA Oxon 1945 (1st cl. PPE), MA Oxon 1947. Res. Off., Oxford Univ. Inst. Stats, 1945–46; Lectr in Economics, Christ Church, Oxford, 1946–48; Lectr in Economics, Leeds Univ., 1948–63; Sen. Res. Worker, Inst. Econs, USSR Acad. Sci., 1960–61; Sen. Lectr, Univ. of Ghana (Legon), 1963–66 (both on leave); Dean, Fac. Econ. Soc. Studies, 1970–72. *Publications*: The Pattern of Retail Distribution, 1946; Private and Social Cost in Retail Distribution, in, Explorations in Retailing, ed. Hollander, 1959; *contrib.* Bull. Oxf. Inst. Stats, Sci. and Soc. *Address*: School of Economic Studies, Univ. of Leeds, Leeds LS2 9JT.

Bellany, Dr Ian; Senior Lecturer, Department of Politics, University of Lancaster, since 1974; *b* 1941; *m* 1965; one *s* one *d.* BA Oxon 1962, MA 1966, DPhil 1966; Res. Fellow in International Relations, Australian Nat. Univ., 1968–70; Lectr in Politics, Univ. of Lancaster, 1970–74. *Publications*: Australia in the Nuclear Age, 1972; *contrib.* India Qly, Jl of Conflict Resolution, Jl Royal United Services Institute, Nature. *Address*: Dept of Politics, Univ. of Lancaster, University House, Bailrigg, Lancaster LA1 4YW.

Bellringer, Dr Alan Wayland, MA, Ph.D; Lecturer in English, University College of

North Wales, since 1963; *b* 1932; *m* 1965; two *s.* MA Glasgow 1954 (1st cl. English), PhD Aberdeen 1968. Asst in English, Univ. of Aberdeen, 1960–63. *Publications: contrib.* Critical Qly, Essays in Criticism, Jl of Amer. Studies, REL. *Address*: Dept of English, Univ. College of North Wales, Bangor LL57 2DG.

Beloff, Dr Halla, BSc, PhD; Lecturer, Department of Psychology, University of Edinburgh, since 1963; *b* 1930; *m* 1952; one *s* one *d.* BSc London 1952 (1st cl. Psychology), PhD Queen's Belfast 1956; FBPS. Res. Asst, Lab. for Personality Assess. and Gp Behavior, Univ. of Illinois, 1952–53; Res. Asst, Dept of Psychology, Queen's Univ. Belfast, 1953–62. Soc. Editor, Brit. Jl Soc. Clin. Psychol., 1971– . *Publications: contrib.* Genetic Psychol. Monog., Jl Abn. Soc. Psychol., Brit. Jl Soc. Clin. Psychol., Internat. Jl Psychol. *Address*: Dept of Psychology, Univ. of Edinburgh, 60 The Pleasance, Edinburgh EH8 9TJ.

Beloff, Dr John, PhD; Senior Lecturer, Department of Psychology, University of Edinburgh, since 1963; *b* 1920; *m* 1952; one *s* one *d.* Archit. Assoc. Dip 1946, BA (Hons) London 1952, PhD Belfast 1956; FBPsS. Lectr, Queen's Univ., Belfast, 1953–62; Vis. Prof., Cornell Univ., 1966. Mem., Council, Soc. Psychic. Res., 1963– ; Pres., Parapsychol. Assoc., 1972. *Publications*: The Existence of Mind, 1962; Psychological Sciences, 1973; *contrib.* Jl Amer. Soc. Psychic. Res., Jl Parapsychol., Jl Soc. Psychic. Res. *Address*: Dept of Psychology, Univ. of Edinburgh, 60 The Pleasance, Edinburgh EH8 9TJ.

Beloff, Prof. Max, BLitt, MA, FBA; Principal, University College at Buckingham, since 1974; *b* 1913; *m* 1938; two *s.* BA Oxon 1938 (1st cl. Hons Modern History), MA Oxon, BLitt 1937; Hon LLD Pittsburgh; FRHistS. Jun. Res. Fellow, Corpus Christi Coll., Oxford, 1937; Asst Lectr in History, Manchester Univ., 1939–46; Nuffield Reader in Comparative Study of Instns, Oxford Univ., 1946–56; Gladstone Prof. of Govt and Public Admin, 1957–74; Fellow of Nuffield Coll., 1947–57; Fellow of All Souls, 1957–74. Governor: St Paul's Schs; Haifa Univ., Trustee and Ex-Librarian, Oxford Union Soc. *Publications*: Public Order and Popular Disturbances, 1660–1714, 1938; The Foreign Policy of Soviet Russia, vol. 1, 1947, vol. 2, 1949; Thomas Jefferson and American Democracy, 1948; Soviet Policy in the Far East, 1944–51, 1953; The Age of Absolutism, 1660–1815, 1954; Foreign Policy and the Democratic Process, 1955; Europe and the Europeans, 1957; The Great Powers, 1959; The American Federal Government, 1959, 2nd edn 1970; New Dimensions in Foreign Policy, 1961; The United States and the Unity of Europe, 1963; The Balance of Power, 1967; The Future of British Foreign Policy, 1969; Imperial Sunset, vol. 1, 1969; The Intellectual in Politics, 1970; ed, The Federalist, 1948; ed, Mankind and his Story, 1948: ed, The Debate on the American Revolution, 1949; ed, On the Track of Tyranny, 1959; ed, L'Europe du XIXe et

XXe siècle, 1960–67; *contrib*. English, French, Italian and American Jls. *Address*: All Souls College, Oxford.

Benjamin, Bernard; Professor of Actuarial Science, Department of Social Sciences and Humanities, City University, since 1973; *b* 1910; *m* 1937; two *d*. BSc London 1933, PhD 1954; FIA 1941 (President, 1966–68), FSS (President, 1970). Vis. Prof. Applied Statistics, Graduate Business Centre, City Univ., 1970–73. Chief Statistician, General Register Office, 1954–63; Dir of Statistics, Min. of Health, 1963–66; Dir of Research and Intelligence, GLC, 1966–70; Dir of Statistical Studies, Civil Service Coll., 1970–73. *Publications*: Social and Economic Factors Affecting Mortality, 1965; Health and Vital Statistics, 1968; Demographic Analysis, 1969; Census, Procedures and Utilisation, 1969; (with H. W. Haycocks) Analysis of Mortality and other Actuarial Statistics, 1970; *contrib*. Brit. Med. Jl, Jl Inst. Act., Op. Res. Qly, Lancet, Population Studies, Jl Royal Stat. Soc., Jl Social Policy. *Address*: City Univ., St John Street, London EC1V 4PB.

Benn, Dr Thomas Vincent; Part-time Lecturer, University of Leeds, since 1968; *b* 1903; *m* 1935; one *s* one *d*. BA Leeds 1923 (Hons English–French), PhD Leeds 1925. Lectr, Clermont-Ferrand, 1925; Asst Lectr, Leeds, 1926–33; Lectr, 1933–52, Sen. Lectr, 1952–68. Mod. Lang. Assoc., Mem., Council, and Sec., Yorks Branch, 1927–35; Asst Sec., Yorks. Reg. Cttee for Educn in the Forces, 1940–46; Sub-Dean, Fac. of Arts, Leeds Univ., 1950–55. *Publications*: Learning to Speak Hindustani, 1943; *contrib*. Jl de Philologie, Rev. de litt. comparée, Rev. d'hist. litt. de la France, Mod. Lang., Jl Documents, Year's Wk in Mod. Lang. Studies. *Address*: Dept of French, Univ. of Leeds, Leeds LS2 9JT.

Bennathan, Prof. Esra; Professor of Political Economy, Department of Economics, University of Bristol, since 1969; *b* 1923; *m* 1949; two *s*. MCom Birmingham 1952; MA Cantab 1964. Lectr, Birmingham Univ., 1954–63; Fellow, Jesus Coll., Cambridge and Sen. Res. Officer, Dept of Applied Economics, Cambridge Univ., 1963–67. Chief, Economic Analysis and Survey Br., UN ECAFE, 1967–69. *Publications*: (with A. A. Walters) Economics of Ocean Freight Rates, 1969; chaps in UN Economic Survey of Asia and Far East, 1963, 1967, 1968, 1969; *contrib*. Jl Business History, Oxford Econ. Papers, Round Table Jl Maritime Law and Commerce. *Address*: Dept of Economics, University of Bristol, 40 Berkeley Square, Bristol 8.

Bennett, Alan John; Lecturer in Economics, Department of Industrial Administration, University of Aston, since 1966; *b* 1929; *m* 1961; one *s* one *d*. BCom Birmingham 1950, MCom Birmingham 1953; Rees Jefferies Student in Economics of Transport, LSE, 1952, Res. Asst, Faculty of Commerce, Univ. of Birmingham, 1954–55. Co. Sec. and Commercial Manager, J. H. Lavender & Co. Ltd (Aluminium Founders), 1955–66; Dir, Delta Diecastings Ltd, 1970– ; The Yarningale Co. Ltd, 1965– . *Publications*:

contrib. Brit. Foundryman, Jl Ind. Econs, Metal Bull., Financial Times. *Address*: Dept of Industrial Administration, Maple House, Corporation Street, Birmingham 4.

Bennett, Rev. Gareth Vaughan, MA, DPhil, FSA; Fellow, Dean of Divinity, and Lecturer in Modern History, New College, Oxford, since 1959; *b* 1929. BA Cantab 1951 (1st cl. with Distinction, Historical Tripos), PhD Cantab 1954, MA Cantab 1955; MA, DPhil Oxon (by incorporation) 1959; FSA, FRHistS. Lectr in History, King's Coll., London, 1954–59; Examiner, Hon. Sch. of Theology, Oxford, 1966–68; Examiner, Hon. Sch. of Modern History, Oxford, 1971. Ordained Deacon, 1956; Priest, 1957; Canon and Prebendary of Exceit, Chichester Cath., 1961; Gov. Harpur Trust, Bedford; Librarian, New Coll., 1964– , Sub-Warden, 1969–70. Junior Proctor, Oxford Univ., 1973–74. *Publications*: White Kennett (1660–1728) Bishop of Peterborough, 1957; ed and contrib. Essays in Modern English Church History in Memory of Norman Sykes, 1966; contrib. Studies in Church History, III, 1966, VII, 1971; Britain after the Glorious Revolution, 1969; Patristic Tradition in Anglican and Lutheran Thought, 1972; *contrib*. EHR, Mod. Churchman. *Address*: New College, Oxford.

Bennett, Prof. Jack Arthur Walter, MA, DPhil, FBA; Professor of Medieval and Renaissance English, University of Cambridge, since 1964; *b* 1911; *m* 1951; two *s*. MA New Zealand 1933, MA DPhil Oxford 1938, MA Cambridge 1964. Res. Fellow, The Queen's Coll., Oxford, 1938–46; Tutorial Fellow, Magdalen Coll., Oxford, 1947–64; Prof. Fellow, Magdalene Coll., Cambridge, 1964. Mem., Council, Early English Text Society, 1954– ; Exec. Cttee Soc. for the Study of Medieval Languages and Literature, 1952– ; Editor, Medium Ævum, 1954– . *Publications*: Devotional Pieces in Verse and Prose, 1948; (with H. R. Trevor Roper) The Poems of Richard Corbett, 1955; The Parlement of Foules, 1957 (1970); Chaucer's Book of Fame, 1968; (with G. V. Smithers) Early Middle English Verse and Prose, 1966 (1968); Selections from John Gower, 1968; Piers Plowman, 1972; *contrib*. Medium Ævum, Rev. of Eng. Studies, TLS. *Address*: Magdalene College, Cambridge.

Bennett, Dr John Herbert Buteux; Senior Lecturer, French Department, University of Glasgow, since 1972; *b* 1924; *m* 1956; one *s*. BA Hons London 1948, PhD London 1955. Lectr in French, Univ. of Glasgow, Jan. 1968–72. Asst French Master, Audenshaw Grammar Sch. for Boys, 1955–60; Sen. Mod. Langs Master, Quintin Sch., St John's Wood, 1960–67. *Publications*: contrib. FS, RBPH. *Address*: French Dept, Univ. of Glasgow, Glasgow G12 8QQ.

Bennett, Mary Letitia Somerville, MA; Principal, St. Hilda's College, Oxford, since 1965; *b* 1913; *m* 1955. 2nd cl. Mods, 1st cl. Lit. Hum. Oxford. Jt Broadcasting Cttee 1940–41; Transcription Service of BBC,

1941–45; Colonial Office, 1945–56. Hon. Sec., Society for the Promotion of Roman Studies, 1960– . *Address*: St Hilda's College, Oxford.

Bennett, Ralph Francis; Lecturer in History, Cambridge University, since 1947; Fellow of Magdalene College, since 1938; *b* 1911; *m* 1939; two *s*. BA 1932, MA 1936, Cambridge; FRHistS. Sen. Proctor, 1963–64; Member: Gen. Bd of Faculties, 1970– ; Financial Bd, 1973– . *Publications*: The Early Dominicans, 1937, 2nd edn 1971; trans. and introd., G. Tellenbach: Church, State and Christian Society, 1940 (repr. many times); ed jtly, Guillelmi de Ockham: Opera Politica, vols I, II and III, 1940–1963; trans. and introd., K. Hampe: Germany under the Salian and Hohenstaufen Emperors, 1973; First Class Answers in History, 1974. *Address*: Magdalene College, Cambridge.

Bennett, William Arthur, MA; Assistant Director of Research in Applied Linguistics, Department of Linguistics, University of Cambridge, since 1965; *b* 1930; *m* 1954; one *s* one *d*. BA Cantab 1954 (Modern Languages), Cert. in Educn, Cambridge 1957, MA Cantab 1959, Academic Dip. in Educn London 1960; Mem., Linguistics Assoc.; Philological Soc.; Brit. Assoc. for Applied Linguistics. Chm., Audio-Visual Language Assoc., 1965–66; Sec., Brit., Assoc. for Applied Linguistics, 1971– . *Publications*: Aspects of Language and Language Teaching, 1967; Applied Linguistics and Language Learning, 1974; *contrib*. Avla Jl, Bull. Péd. IUT, Camb. Rev., Rev. Phon. Appl., Univ. Qly, Vis. Educn. *Address*: Dept of Linguistics, Univ. of Cambridge, Sidgwick Avenue, Cambridge.

Bentley, Dr Arnold, BA PhD; Reader, School of Education, University of Reading, since 1973; *b* 1913; *m* 1954; one *s* two *d*. BA Reading 1935, DipEd 1936, PhD Reading 1963, ARCM 1940, LRAM 1946. Schoolmaster and RAF (Education Officer) to 1948; Lectr in Music, Weymouth Training Coll., 1948–49; Lectr in Music Educn, Univ. of Reading, 1949, Sen. Lectr, 1964; Vis. Prof., Univs of Michigan and Oregon (1966), Royal Coll. of Music, Stockholm (1967); Vis. Lectr, Univs of W Australia, Adelaide, Sydney, Melbourne, Canterbury (Christchurch) and Auckland, 1971. First Chm., Int. Soc. for Music Educn Res. Commn, 1968–72; First Chm., Soc. for Research in Psychology of Music and Music Educn. Editor, Music Educn Res. Papers; Dir, Schs Council Res. and Dev. Project on Music Educn of Young Children, 1970–76; Governor of schools, and Berkshire Coll. of Educn. *Publications*: Songs to Sing and Play: a basis of music reading, 1964 (also in Spanish); Aural Foundations of Music Reading, 1966 (also in Spanish); Musical Ability in Children and its Measurement, 1966; Measures of Musical Abilities, 1966 (both above also in German, Japanese and Spanish); Monotones: a comparison with normal singers in terms of incidence and musical abilities, 1968; *contrib*. Jl of Res. in Music Educn, Bull. of Council for Res. in Music Educn, Univ. of Brit. Columbia Jl of Educn, Comp. Educn Rev., Australian Jl of Music Educn.

Address: School of Education (Music Section), The Univ., London Road, Reading, Berks RG1 5AQ.

Beresford, Prof. Maurice Warwick, MA; Professor of Economic History, School of Economic Studies, The University of Leeds, since 1959; *b* 1920. BA Cambridge 1941 (1st cl. Historical Tripos), MA Cambridge 1946. Lectr in Economic History, Univ. of Leeds, 1948–57; Reader, 1957–59; Dean, 1955–57; Chm., Fac. Bds, 1968–70; Chm., Sch. Econ. Studies, 1965–68, 1971–72. Mem., Econ. and Soc. Hist. Cttee, SSRC, 1971– . Mem., Consumer Council, 1965–71; Hearing Aid Council, 1968–71; Yorkshire Dales National Park Cttee, 1964–72; Council, Econ. Hist. Soc., 1952– . Chm., No 1 Parole Cttee, Leeds Prison, 1970– ; co-opted Mem., Leeds Probation Cttee, 1972– . *Publications*: The Leeds Chambers of Commerce, 1951; The Lost Villages of England, 1954; History on the Ground, 1957; (with J. K. S. St Joseph) Medieval England: an Aerial Survey, 1958; Time and Place, 1962; New Towns of the Middle Ages, 1967; ed, (with G. R. J. Jones) Leeds and Its Region, 1967; (with J. G. Hurst) Deserted Medieval Villages, 1971; (with H. R. R. Finberg) English Medieval Boroughs, 1973; *contrib*. Agric. Hist. Rev., Econ. Hist. Rev., Medieval Archaeol., Yorks Archaeol. Jl. *Address*: The Univ., Leeds LS2 9JT.

Beresford, Michael; Senior Lecturer, Department of Russian Studies, University of Manchester, since 1968; *b* 1926; *m* 1957. BA Manchester 1949 (1st cl. Modern Languages, French and German), Graduate Cert. in Educn 1954. Asst Lectr, Manchester Univ., 1956–58; Lectr, Manchester Univ., 1958–68. *Publications*: Complete Russian Course for Scientists, 1965; ed, The Death of Ivan Ilyich, 1966. *Address*: Dept of Russian Studies, Univ. of Manchester, Manchester M13 9PL.

Beresford, Ronald, MA, DipEd; Lecturer in Phonetics, Sub-Department of Speech, Department of Education, University of Newcastle upon Tyne, since 1964; *b* 1925; *m* 1953; two *d*. MA Edinburgh 1951, DipEd Edinburgh 1952; Mem., Acoustical Soc. of America. Asst. Lectr, Univ. of Edinburgh, 1963–64. *Publications*: Some Comparative Descriptions of Children's Language in Applications of Linguistics: selected papers of the 2nd Int. Congress of Appl. Linguistics, Cambridge, 1969, ed by G. E. Perren and J. L. M. Trim, 1971; Deviant Language Acquisition: the Phonological Aspect in, The Child with Delayed Speech, ed by M. Rutter and J. A. M. Martin, 1972; The Acquisition of Speech: Some Phonological Aspects of Deviant Acquisition in Language, Cognitive Deficits and Retardation, ed N. O'Connor (forthcoming); *contrib*. Coll. of Speech Therapists Nat. Congress Report, 1966; Brit. Jl of Disorders of Communication, Jl NZ Coll. of Speech Therapeutists. *Address*: 46 Leazes Terrace, Newcastle upon Tyne NE1 4LZ.

Berghahn, Dr Volker R.; Reader, School of European Studies, University of East Anglia, since 1971; *b* 1938; *m* 1969; one *s*.

MA North Carolina 1961; PhD London 1964; Habilitation, Mannheim 1971. Mannheim Univ., 1966–69; Lectr, UEA, 1969–71. *Publications*: Der Stahlhelm BdF 1918–1935, 1966; Der Tirpitz-Plan, 1971; Rüstung und Machtpolitik, 1973; Germany and the Approach of War in 1914, 1973; *contrib.* Historische Zeitschrift, Revue d'Histoire de la Deuxième Guerre Mondiale, Vierteljahrshefte für Zeitgeschichte. *Address*: Sch. of European Studies, Univ. of East Anglia, Norwich NOR 88C.

Bergonzi, Prof. Bernard; Professor of English. University of Warwick, since 1971; *b* 1929; *m* 1960; one *s* two *d*. BA Oxon 1957, MA Oxon 1962, BLitt 1961. Asst Lectr, Univ. of Manchester, 1959–62, Lectr, 1962–66; Vis. Lectr, Brandeis Univ. 1964–65; Sen. Lectr, Univ. of Warwick, 1966–71. *Publications*: The Early H. G. Wells, 1961; Heroes' Twilight, 1965; ed, Innovations, 1968; ed, Four Quartets: A Casebook, 1969; ed, The Twentieth Century, 1970; The Situation of the Novel, 1970; T. S. Eliot, 1972; The Turn of a Century, 1973; *contrib.* Critical Qly, Encounter, Essays in Criticism, Hudson Rev., Jl of Contemp. Hist., Rev. of Engl. Studies. *Address*: Dept. of English, Univ. of Warwick, Coventry CV4 7AL.

Bergstrom, Prof. Albert Rex; Professor of Economics, University of Essex, since 1971; *b* 1925; *m* 1960; one *s*. MCom NZ 1948, PhD Cantab 1955. Asst Lectr, Massey Coll., 1948–49; Asst Lectr, Lectr, Sen. Lectr, Associate Prof., Univ. of Auckland, 1950–61; Reader, LSE, 1962–64; Prof., Univ. of Auckland, 1964–71. *Publications*: Construction and Use of Economics Models, 1967; *contrib.* Econometrica, Economica, Rev. of Economic Studies. *Address*: Dept of Economics, Univ. of Essex, Colchester CO4 3SQ.

Berki, Dr Robert N.; Lecturer, Department of Politics, University of Hull, since 1967; *b* 1936; *m* 1962; two *s* one *d*. BSc Econ., London 1964, PhD Cantab, 1967; Mem., Political Studies Assoc. *Publications*: ed (jtly), The Morality of Politics, 1972; ed (jtly), Knowledge and Belief in Politics, 1973; *contrib.* Ethics, Jl History of Ideas, Jl Politics, Philosophy, Political Studies, World Politics. *Address*: Dept of Politics, Univ. of Hull, Hull HU6 7RX.

Berlin, Sir Isaiah, OM, CBE, MA, FBA; President of Wolfson College, Oxford, since 1966; Chichele Professor of Social and Political Theory, 1957–67; Fellow of All Souls, 1932–38 and 1950–66; *b* 1909; *m* 1956. Hon. DLitt, Hull 1965, Glasgow 1967, Brandeis 1967; Hon. LittD, E Anglia 1967, Cambridge 1970, Liverpool 1972, Tel Aviv 1972; Hon. LLD, Columbia 1968, Jerusalem 1971. FBA 1957. Lectr in Philosophy, New Coll., 1932: Fellow of New Coll., 1938–50; Vis. Prof., USA, 1949, 1951, 1952, 1953, 1955, 1962, 1965, 1966– ; Northcliffe Lectr, UCL, 1953. Vice-Pres., British Academy, 1959–61; Pres., Aristotelian Soc., 1963–64. Mem., Cttee of Award, Commonwealth (Harkness) Fellowships, 1960–64; Mem., Academic Adv. Cttee, Univ. of Sussex, 1963–66; Mem., Cttee of Award, Kennedy Scholarships, 1969; Foreign Mem., Amer. Acad. of Arts and Sciences; For. Mem., Amer. Acad. Inst. of Arts and Letters; Governor, Univ. of Jerusalem; Mem., Bd of Dirs, Royal Opera House, Covent Garden, 1954–65. Hon. Fellow, Corpus Christi Coll., Oxford. *Publications*: Karl Marx, 1939, 1963; trans. of First Love by I. S. Turgenev, 1950; The Hedgehog and the Fox, 1953; Historical Inevitability, 1954; The Age of Enlightenment, 1956; Moses Hess, 1958; Two Concepts of Liberty, 1959; Mr Churchill in 1940, 1946; Four Essays on Liberty, 1969; *contrib.* Mind, Proc. Arist. Soc., Proc. British Acad., Encounter, etc. *Address*: Wolfson College, Oxford.

Berman, Dr David; Lecturer in Philosophy, Trinity College, Dublin, since 1968; *b* 1942; *m* 1971. BA New Sch. for Social Res.; MA Denver; PhD TCD. *Publications*: *contrib.* Hermathena, Jl of Hist. of Ideas, Mind. *Address*: Dept of Philosophy, Trinity College, Dublin 2, Eire.

Bermejo-Marcos, Dr Manuel, MA, PhD; Senior Lecturer in Spanish and Portuguese, University of Leeds, since 1972, Lecturer 1960–72; *b* 1928; *m* 1958; one *s* two *d*. BA Salamanca 1954 (Lic. Fil. y Letras), MA Salamanca 1955 (Filologia Románica), PhD Salamanca 1960; Mem., Assoc. Hispan., Mem., Assoc Latin Amer. Studies. Prof. Aux., Univ. de Salamanca, 1955–57; Lector, Univ. of Leeds, 1957–58; Asst Lectr, Univ. of Leeds, 1958–60. *Publications*: Don Juan Valera, critico literario, 1968; ed, Collins Spanish-English, English-Spanish Dictionary, 1971; Valle-Inclán: Introducción á su obra, 1971. *Address*: Spanish Dept, The Univ., Leeds LS2 9JT.

Bernal, Martin Gardiner; Fellow, King's College, Cambridge, since 1965; *b* 1937; *m* 1960; two *s* one *d*. BA Cantab 1961 (1st cl. Chinese), MA Cantab 1965, PhD Cantab 1966. Asst Tutor, King's Coll., 1967–70. Cttee of Management of the Contemporary China Inst., 1968– . *Publications*: Min Sheng Tsa-chih, 1967; *contrib.* Modern Asian Studies. *Address*: King's College, Cambridge.

Bernard, Joan Constance, MA, BD; Principal, Trevelyan College, University of Durham, and Honorary Lecturer in Theology, since 1966; *b* 1918. BA Oxon 1940 (Lit.Hum.); MA Oxon 1943; BD London 1961. Part-time Lectr in Theology, KCL, 1962–65; Warden, Canterbury Hall, Univ. of London, 1963–65. Staff Officer, ATS, HQ Anti-Aircraft Commd, 1942–44, Air Defence Div., Supreme HQ Allied Expeditionary Force, 1944–45; Dep. Admin. Officer, HQ NCB, 1946–50, Scientific Secretariat, 1946–48, Establishments Dept, 1948–50; Asst Sec. for Educn, Music and Drama, HQ Nat. Fedn of Women's Insts, 1950–57; Sec., later Chm., London Choral Soc., 1948–58. *Address*: Trevelyan College, Elvet Hill Road Durham DH1 3LN.

Bernbaum, Gerald; Senior Lecturer, School of Education, University of Leicester, since 1970; *b* 1936; *m* 1959; two *s*. BSc (Econ.)

52

1957. Postgraduate Cert. of Educn 1958. Lectr in Educn, Univ. of Leicester, 1964–70. Chm., BBC Radio Leicester, Educnl Advisory Panel, 1970– ; Res. Consultant, Organisation for Econ. Co-operation and Development, 1970– . *Publications*: Social Change and the Schools 1918–44, 1967; Case Studies of Educational Innovation, vol. III, 1972; contrib. Handbook for History Teachers, 1962, 2nd edn 1972; Sociology, History and Education, 1971; Education and its Disciplines, 1972. *contrib*. Educn for Teaching, Educn and Social Science, Educnl Rev., Paedagogica Europaea, Univ. Qly, Sociological Rev. *Address*: School of Education, University Road, Leicester.

Berrington, Prof. Hugh Bayard; Professor of Politics, University of Newcastle upon Tyne, since 1970; *b* 1928; *m* 1965; one *s* two *d*. BSc London (Econ.) (External), 1954; Mem., Political Studies Assoc., Royal Inst. of Public Admin, Politics Soc. Asst Lectr, Univ. Coll. of North Staffs (Keele), 1956–59, Lectr, 1959–65; Reader, Univ. of Newcastle upon Tyne, 1965–70. Sec./Treasurer, Political Studies Assoc., 1958–61, Treasurer, 1961–64. *Publications*: (with S. E. Finer and D. J. Bartholomew) Backbench Opinion in the House of Commons 1955–59, 1961; How Nations are Governed, 1964; Backbench Opinion in the House of Commons 1945–55, 1973. *contrib*. Parl. Aff., Jl Royal Stat. Soc., Int. Social Science Jl. *Address*: Politics Dept, The Univ., Newcastle upon Tyne NE1 7RU.

Berry, Dr David, MA, PhD; Lecturer, Department of French, University of Leeds, since 1966 *b* 1942. BA Hons Exeter 1964 (French), MA Exeter 1966, PhD Leeds 1972. *Publications*: *contrib*. Revue d'Histoire Littéraire de la France, Austr. Jl of French Studies. *Address*: Dept of French, Univ. of Leeds, Leeds LS2 9JT.

Berry, David Ronald; Lecturer, Department of Sociology, University College, Cardiff, since 1969; *b* 1942. BA Social Science Liverpool 1964, MA Liverpool 1967. Asst Lectr, Univ. of Strathclyde, 1966–68, Lectr, 1968–69. *Publications*: The Sociology of Grass Roots Politics, 1971; Central Themes in Sociological Theory, 1974; *contrib*. Political Studies. *Address*: Univ. College, Cardiff CF1 1XL.

Berry, Prof. Francis; Professor of English Langage and Literature, University of London at Royal Holloway College, since 1970; *b* 1915; *m* 1st 1947, 2nd 1970; one *s* one *d*. BA London 1947 (1st cl. English), MA Exeter 1961; FRSL. Asst Lectr, Sheffield Univ., 1947–59, Lectr, 1949–59; Sen. Lectr, 1959–63, Reader, 1963–67; Prof., 1967–70; Vis. Lectr, Carleton Coll., Minnesota, 1951; Vis. Lectr, Univ. Coll. of West Indies, 1957. *Publications*: Gospel of Fire, 1933; Snake in the Moon, 1936; The Iron Christ, 1938; Fall of a Tower, 1942; Murdock and Other Poems, 1947; The Galloping Centaur, 1952, 2nd edn 1970; Herbert Read, 1953, 2nd edn 1961; ed, An Anthology of Medieval Poems, 1954; Poets' Grammar: time, tense and mood

in poetry, 1958; Morant Bay and other poems, 1961; Poetry and the Physical Voice, 1962; The Shakespeare Inset, 1965, 2nd edn 1971; Ghosts of Greenland, 1967; John Masefield: the Narrative Poet, 1968; Thoughts on Poetic Time, 1972; *contrib*. Life and Letters, Erasmus, Orpheus, Essays in Criticism. *Address*: Dept of English, Royal Holloway College, Egham Hill, Egham, Surrey TW20 0EX,

Berry, Juliet Hilda; Tutor and Lecturer in Social Administration, Department of Sociological Studies, University of Sheffield, since 1968; *b* 1928. BSc Reading 1949 (Agric.), CertEd and Rural Domestic Econ., Worcester Trng Coll. 1952, Testamur Social Studies Bristol, 1959, Cert. Applied Social Studies, 1960; Member: BASW; Assoc. of Teachers in Social Work Educn; Nat. Children's Bureau. Farm Instructress, Greenacres Approved Sch., 1952–58; Field Worker/Administrator, Somerset Co. Children's Dept, 1960–68. *Publications*: Social Work with Children, 1972; Daily Experience: a study of residential care for children and staff (forthcoming); *contrib*. Brit. Jl Social Work, Case Conf., Child Adoption. *Address*: Dept of Sociological Studies, Univ. of Sheffield, Sheffield S10 2TN.

Berthoud, Jacques Alexandre, BA; Lecturer, English Department, University of Southampton, since 1967; *b* 1935; *m* 1958; one *s* two *d*. BA Witwatersrand 1955 (English French), BA Hons Witwatersrand 1958 (Comparative Literature). Junior Lectr, Univ. of Natal, 1958–60; Lectr, Univ. of South Africa, 1960–61; Lectr, Univ. of Natal, 1961–67. Chief Examiner, Matriculation English, Province of Natal, 1965–67. *Publications*: (with Dr C. van Heyningen) Uys Krige, 1967; (with C. O. Gardner) The Sole Function, 1970. *Address*: English Dept, The Univ., Southampton SO9 5NH.

Bertram, (Cicely) Kate, MA, PhD, JP; President, Lucy Cavendish College, Cambridge, since 1970 (Tutor, 1965–70); *b* 1912; *m* 1939; four *s*. MA PhD Cantab 1940; FLS. Jarrow Research Studentship, Girton Coll., Cambridge, 1937–40. Mem., Colonial Office Nutrition Survey, in Nyasaland, 1939; Adviser on Freshwater Fisheries to Govt of Palestine, 1940–43. Mem. Council, New Hall, Cambridge, 1954–66; Associate of Newnham Coll.; JP Co. Cambridge, and Isle of Ely, 1959. *Publications*: 2 Crown Agents' Reports on African Fisheries, 1939 and 1942; papers on African Fish, in zoological jls; papers and articles on Sirenia (with G. C. L. Bertram). *Address*: Lucy Cavendish College, Cambridge.

Bertram, Dr George Colin Lawder; Fellow (under Title E), St John's College, Cambridge, since 1972; *b* 1911; *m* 1939; four *s*. BA Cantab 1932, MA Cantab 1937, PhD Cantab 1939; FRGS (Hon. Sec), FZS, FIBiol. Dir, Scott Polar Res. Inst., 1945–56; Fellow and Tutor, St John's Coll., Cambridge, 1945–72, Senior Tutor, 1965–72. Chief Fisheries Office, Palestine, 1940–44; Fisheries Adviser, Middle East Supply Centre, 1944–45. *Publications*: Arctic and

Antarctic: The Technique of Polar Travel, 1939; Arctic and Antarctic: A Prospect of the Polar Regions, 1957; Adams Brood, 1959; In Search of Mermaids: The Manatees of Guiana, 1963; *contrib*. Biol., Jl Linn. Soc. Geogrl Jl, Proc. Zool. Soc. Lond. *Address*: St John's College, Cambridge.

Bescoby, John Henry; Lecturer in Industrial Relations, Faculty of Applied Science, University of Newcastle upon Tyne, since 1970; *b* 1922. DipSoc Studies Leicester 1951, BA Nottingham 1954 (Hons Sociology), MA Econ Manchester 1958; Mem., Manchester Stat. Soc., 1958; Brit. Univ. Indust. Relat. Assoc., 1961. Res. Asst, Manchester Univ., 1955–60; Staff Tutor, Indust. Studies, Dept Adult Educn, Newcastle upon Tyne, 1961–68; Asst Prof., Indust. Relat. Dept, Newark Coll. Engineering, NJ, 1968–69; Staff Tutor, Dept Adult Educn and temp. Lectr in Dept Naval Arch. and Shipbldg, Newcastle upon Tyne, 1969–70; Single Arbitrator, apptd by Sec. of State for Employmt, 1970; Mem., Indust. Tribunals, 1971. *Publications*: *contrib*. Brit. Jl Indust. Relat., Bull. Oxford Univ. Inst. Stats, Manchester Sch. Econ. Soc. Studies. *Address*: Dept of Naval Architecture and Shipbuilding, Univ. of Newcastle upon Tyne, Newcastle upon Tyne NE1 7RU.

Bessell, Dr James Edward; Lecturer, Department of Agriculture and Horticulture, University of Nottingham, teaching Statistics, Econometrics and Development Economics especially rural, since 1963; *b* 1923; *m* 1944; two *s* one *d*. PhD Nottingham 1970; FIS, 1956, FSS, AES, IAAE, FIMA. Mem., Economet. Soc. Mem., Council, Inst. Stat., 1960–62; Asst Editor, then Editor, Statistican, 1959–62; Examiner, Inst. Stat. in Agrig. Stat., 1960–68; Mem., Bd Gov., Brooksby Agric. Coll., Leicestershire, 1970–71. *Publications*: The Agricultural Labour Situation; projected labour requirements and employment, 1972; *contrib*. Jl Agric. Econ., Inc. Stat., Statistican, Jl Develt Studies. *Address*: School of Agriculture, Univ. of Nottingham, Sutton Bonington, Loughborough, Leicestershire LE12 5RD.

Best, Dr Albert Edward; Senior Lecturer in the History of Science, Department of History, University of Edinburgh, since 1970; *b* 1911; *m* 1947. BSc Manchester 1932, MA Manchester 1940, PhD London 1948, BLitt Oxon 1957. Assoc. Prof., Temple Univ., Philadelphia, 1963; Lectr, Dept of Educn, Univ. of Edinburgh, 1966; Lectr, Dept of History, Univ. of Edinburgh, 1968–70. *Publications: contrib*. Annals of Science, Medical Hist., Philosophy. *Address*: Dept of History, Univ. of Edinburgh, Edinburgh EH8 9JY.

Best, Prof. Ernest, MA, BD, PhD; Professor of Divinity and Biblical Criticism, University of Glasgow, since 1974; *b* 1917; *m* 1949; two *d*. BA Belfast 1938 (2nd cl. Mathematics), MA Belfast 1939, BD Belfast 1942, PhD Belfast 1948; Mem., SNTS, 1954. Temp. Lectr, Presbyt. Coll., Belfast and Queen's Univ., Belfast, 1953–54; Guest Prof., Austin Prebyt. Theol Seminary, 1955–57; Lectr in

Bib. Lit. and Theol., St Andrews, 1963–71; Sen. Lectr, 1971–74; Asst Minister, First Bangor Presbyt. Ch., Ireland, 1943–49; Minister, Caledon and Minterburn Presbyt. Chs, Ireland, 1949–63; Ed., Biblical Theol., 1962– . *Publications*: One Body in Christ, 1955; The Temptation and the Passion: the Markan Soteriology, 1966; The Letter of Paul to the Romans, 1967; 1 Peter: Commentary, 1971; 1 and 2 Thessalonians, 1972; *contrib*. Nov. Test., New Test Studies, Jl Theol Studies, Scott. Jl Theol., Interpret., Expos. Times. *Address*: St Mary's College, St Andrews, Fife.

Best, Prof. Geoffrey Francis Andrew; Professor of History, School of European Studies, University of Sussex, since 1974; *b* 1928; *m* 1955; two *s* one *d*. BA Cantab 1951 (1st cl. History), PhD Cantab 1956; Hist. Assoc., Internat. Inst. of Strategic Studies. Fellow, Trinity Hall, Cambridge, 1954–61; Joseph Hodges Choate Fellow, Harvard Univ., 1954–55; Asst Lectr, Cambridge, 1956–61; Lectr, Univ. of Edinburgh, 1961–66; Sir Richard Lodge Prof. of History, Edinburgh, 1966–73; Vis. Prof., Univ. of Chicago, 1964; Vis. Fellow, All Souls Coll., Oxford, 1969–70; Lees Knowles Lectr, Cambridge, 1970. Editor, Cambridge Rev., 1953–54; Brit. Editor, Victorian Studies, 1958–68. *Publications*: Temporal Pillars: Queen Anne's Bounty, The Ecclesiastical Commissioners, and the Church of England, 1700–1948, 1964; Shaftesbury, 1964; Bishop Westcott and the Miners, 1968; History, Politics, and Universities, 1969; Mid-Victorian Britain, 1971; ed, Church's Oxford Movement, 1971; *contrib*. EHR, Hist., Jl Theol. S., Theology, TRHS, Victn Studies, *Address*: Sch. of European Studies. Univ. of Sussex, Falmer, Brighton BN1 9QN.

Best, Dr Robin Hewitson, BSc, MSc, PhD; Reader in Land Use and Environmental Studies, Countryside Planning Unit, Wye College (University of London), since 1972; *b* 1926; *m* 1954; one *s* one *d*. BSc Dunelm 1952, MSc London 1957, PhD London 1963; Mem., Inst of Brit. Geogrs, Geog. Assoc., Town and Country Planning Assoc. Res. Asst, Wye Coll., 1954; Lectr, 1956–69; Sen. Tutor, 1969–71. Army Intelligence Corps, 1944–48; Land-Data Cttee, Min. of Land and Natural Resources, 1965–66; Vis. Mem., Land-Use Statistics Cttee, Resources for the Future, Washington DC, 1963; Mem., Terrestrial Life Sciences Cttee, NERC, 1972– ; Governor, Wye Coll., 1972– ; Governor, Queen Elizabeth Sch., Faversham, 1970– . *Publications*: (with J. T. Ward) The Garden Controversy, 1956; The Major Land Uses of Great Britain, 1959; (with J. T. Coppock) The Changing Use of Land in Britain, 1962; Land for New Towns, 1964; (with A. Rogers) The Urban Countryside, 1973. *contrib*. Geog. Jl, Jl Town Planning Inst., Town Planning Rev., Trans Inst. Brit. Geog., Urban Studies. *Address*: Countryside Planning Unit, Wye College, Ashford, Kent TN25 5AH.

Bethell, Denis; Statutory Lecturer in Medieval History, University College Dublin, since 1972; *b* 1934. BA Oxford 1957, BLitt Oxford 1962; FRHistS 1972. Asst Lectr, Univ. of Reading, 1962; College Lectr, UCD, 1966. *Publications*: trans. Renouard: The Avignon Papacy, 1305–1403, 1970; *contrib*. Analecta Bollandiana, English Hist. Rev., Jl Ecclesiastical Hist., Scottish Hist. Rev., Historical Studies. *Address*: Dept of Medieval History, Univ. Coll. Dublin, Belfield, Dublin 4.

Bethell, Dr Leslie; Reader in Hispanic American and Brazilian History, Department of History, University College London, since 1974; *b* 1937; *m* 1961; two *s*. BA London 1958 (1st cl. History), PhD London 1963; FRHistS. Asst Lectr and Lectr, Bristol Univ., 1961–66. Lectr in Hispanic American and Brazilian History, Dept of History, Univ. Coll. London, 1966–74. *Publications*: The Abolition of the Brazilian Slave Trade, 1970; *contrib*. EHR, Jl of African Hist., Jl of Latin Amer. Studies. *Address*: Dept of History, Univ. College London, Gower Street, WC1E 6BT.

Betjemann, Dr Alan Geoffrey; Director of Production, Media Services Unit, University of Lancaster, since 1971; *b* 1935; *m* 1963; one *s* one *d*. BSc London 1955 (2nd cl. Physics), PhD London 1959; Mem., Inst. Physics, 1961, Royal TV Soc., 1970. Res. Assoc., Univ. of Lancaster, 1964–68; Educnl TV Off., 1968–70; Dep. Dir, AV Aids, Univ. of Lancaster, 1970. *Publications*: *contrib*. Proc. Phys. Soc., Phys. Letters. *Address*: Media Services Unit, Univ. of Lancaster, Lancaster. LA1 4YW.

Bettenson, Ernest Marsden; Registrar, University of Newcastle upon Tyne, since 1963; *b* 1911; *m* 1946. BA Cantab 1932, MA, 1936, Cambridge Cert Ed 1934. Asst Registrar, Federal Univ. of Durham, 1947–52; Registrar, 1952–61; Registrar and Sec. King's College, Newcastle and Sec., federal Univ. Court and Senate, 1961–63. Governor, St Chad's Coll., Durham, 1954– ; Hon. Treas., 1954–63; Co-opted mem. (Univ.), Sunderland Education Cttee, 1954– . *Publication*: The University of Newcastle upon Tyne: An Historical Introduction, 1971. *Address*: Univ. of Newcastle upon Tyne, Newcastle upon Tyne NE1 7RU.

Betteridge, Dr Harold Thomas; Senior Lecturer, Department of German, University of Glasgow, since 1952; *b* 1910; *m* 1936; one *s* two *d*. BA Hons Birmingham 1931, MA 1933, PhD London 1937, Teaching Dip. Birmingham 1935; Member: Modern Humanities Res. Assoc; English Goethe Soc. Asst Lectr, LSE, 1935–39; Lectr, Glasgow Univ., 1946–52. *Publications*: Science German Course (grammatical intro.), 1952; ed. Albrecht von Haller, Die Alpen, 1959; Rapid German Course, 1960; ed Cassell's German and English Dictionary, 1957, 12th edn 1970; Klopstocks Briefe. Prolegomena zu einer Gesamtausgabe, 1963; *contrib*. Euph., GLL, JEGP, ML, MLR, OL, PEGS, PMLA, UQ. *Address*: Univ. of Glasgow, Glasgow G12 8QQ.

Bettinson, Christopher David, BA, PhD; Senior Lecturer in French Language and Literature, University College, Cardiff, since 1974; *b* 1943; *m* 1963; three *s*. BA Reading 1965 (1st cl. French), PhD Reading 1972. Asst Lectr, Glasgow Univ., 1966–69; Lectr, 1969–74. *Publications*: Gidc: Les Caves du Vatican (Studies in French Literature No. 20), 1972; *contrib*. French Rev., Modern Languages, etc. *Address*: Univ. College, PO Box 78, Cardiff CF1 1XL.

Betts, Christopher John; Lecturer in French Studies, University of Warwick, since 1965. MA Oxon, DPhil Oxon. *Address*: Dept of French Studies, Univ. of Warwick, Coventry CV4 7AL.

Betts, John Hamilton, BA; Lecturer in Classics, University of Bristol, since 1966; *b* 1940. BA London 1961 (1st cl. Classics). Lectr in Classics, Univ. of Auckland, NZ, 1962–66. *Publications*: Corpus der minoischen und mykenischen Siegel, Band X: Swiss Collections (forthcoming); *contrib*. AJA, BSA, JHS, Kadmos, Antike Kunst. *Address*: Dept of Classics, Univ. of Bristol, Bristol BS8 1RJ.

Bevan, Cecil Wilfrid Luscombe, CBE; Principal, University College, Cardiff, since 1966; Vice-Chancellor, University of Wales, since 1973; *b* 1920; *m* 1944; four *s*. BSc Wales 1940, PhD London 1949, DSc London 1971; FRIC 1957. Univ. of Exeter, 1949–53; Prof. and Hd of Dept of Chemistry, Univ. of Ibadan, 1953–66, Vice-Principal and Dep. Vice-Chancellor, 1960–64. Mem. Council, Univ. of Cape Coast, Ghana. Fellow, UCL, 1969. *Publications*: *contrib*. papers, mainly in Jl Chem. Soc., 1951– . *Address*: University College, Cathays Park, Cardiff CF1 3NS.

Bevan, Prof. Hugh Keith, LLM; Professor of Law, University of Hull, since 1969; *b* 1922; *m* 1950; one *s* one *d*. LLB Wales 1949 (1st cl.), LLM Wales 1966; Barrister-at-Law, Middle Temple. Asst Lectr, Univ. of Hull, 1950–51, Lectr, Univ. of Hull, 1951–61; Sen. Lectr, Univ. of Hull, 1961–69. Mem., Cttee, Soc. of Public Teachers of Law; Mem., UK Nat. Cttee of Comparative Law. *Publications*: (with P. R. H. Webb) A Source Book of Family Law, 1964; Law Relating to Children, 1973; *contrib*. Law Qly Review. *Address*: Dept of Law, Univ. of Hull, Hull HU6 7RX.

Bevan, John Michael; Senior Lecturer, Economic and Social Statistics, University of Kent at Canterbury, since 1969; *b* 1939; *m* 1963. BA Oxford 1961 (Mathematics), MA Oxford 1965, Dip. Stats Oxford 1963; Mem., Inst. Statisticians 1970; Mem., Royal Stat. Soc., Operational Res. Soc., Biometrics Soc., Brit. Social. Assoc. Res. Off., Dept of Biomathematics (formerly Unit of Biometry), Oxford, 1963–67; Lectr, Economic and Social Statistics, Univ. of Kent, 1967–69; Dep. Dir, Health Services Res. Unit, Univ. of Kent, 1971– . Mem., Exec. Cttee, Kent Postgrad.

Medical Centre, Canterbury, 1970- . *Publications*: (with G. J. Draper) Appointment Systems in General Practice, 1967; Introduction to Statistics, 1968. *Address*: Cornwallis Building, The Univ., Canterbury, Kent.

Bevan, Dr Jonquil; Lecturer and Director of Studies, Department of English Literature, University of Edinburgh, since 1967; *b* 1941. MA Oxon 1968, DPhil Oxon 1969. *Address*: Dept of English Literature, Univ. of Edinburgh, David Hume Tower, George Square, Edinburgh.

Bevington, Dorothy Mary; Lecturer, Department of Sociology, Leicester University, since 1961; *b* 1930. BA Nottingham 1951 (1st cl. Social Administration); Mem., Brit. Assoc. Soc. Works, Soc. Admin. Assoc. Bor. Welf. Dept, Chesterfield, 1951–53; City Welf. Dept, Leicester, 154–61; Mem., E. Midlands Old People's Welf. Cttee, 1961–71; Bd Assess, Women's Council Min. in the Ch., 1968–72. *Address*: Dept of Sociology, Univ. of Leicester.

Beynon, Victor Howel; Director, Agricultural Economics Unit, since 1974, Senior Lecturer, Department of Economics, University of Exeter, since 1965; *b* 1916; *m* 1946; one *s* one *d*. BScEcon Aberystwyth 1944 (1st cl. Hons); Mem., Agricultural Economics Soc. Agricultural Economist, Aberystwyth, 1944–46; Bristol, 1946–49; Sen. Agricultural Economist, Bristol, 1949–65. *Publications*: *contrib*. Westminster Bank Rev., Veterinary Record. *Address*: Dept of Economics, Univ. of Exeter, Exeter EX4 4QJ.

Biard, Dr Jean Dominique; Senior Lecturer, Department of French, University of Exeter, since 1957 ; *b* 1928; *m* 1951; three *s*. BA Hons external, London 1955, PhD 1965. *Publications*: BA Examination Papers for Translation, French edn 1961; The Style of La Fontaine's Fables, 1966, French trans 1970; Edition of: L. C. Discret 'Alizon', 1972; Edition of: Quinault 'La Comédie sans Comédie', 1974; *contrib*. French Studies, Studi Francesi. *Address*: Dept of French, Queen's Building, Univ. of Exeter, Exeter EX4 4QJ.

Bicat, Andre, OBE; Tutor, Department of Print Making, Royal College of Art; *b* 1909; *m* 1944; two *s* one *d*. Mem., London Group. *Address*: Royal College of Art, Kensington Gore, SW7 3EU.

Bickmore, David Pelham; Director, Experimental Cartography Unit, Royal College of Art, since 1967; *b* 1917; *m* 1939 and 1971; two *s* two *d*. BA Oxon 1938, MA Oxon 1946. Clarendon Press, Oxford, 1946–67. *Publications*: Oxford Atlas, 1951; Atlas of Britain, 1963; contribs to professional Jls. *Address*: Royal College of Art, 6A Cromwell Place, SW7.

Biddiss, Dr Michael Denis; Lecturer in Modern European History, Department of History, University of Leicester, since 1973; *b* 1942; *m* 1967; two *d*. BA Cantab 1964 (Double 1st cl. History), MA, PhD Cantab 1968; Assoc. Mem., Centre Universitaire des Hautes Etudes Européennes, Strasbourg, 1965–66; Fellow 1966–73, Tutor 1969–73, Dir of Studies in Soc. and Pol. Sci., 1969–71; Dir of Studies in History, 1970–73, Downing Coll.; Asst Lectr in Faculty of History, Univ. of Cambridge, 1968–73; Vis. Prof., Dept of History, Univ. of Victoria, BC, 1973. Mem., Inst. of Race Relat., 1965. *Publications*: Father of Racist Ideology: the social and political thought of Count Gobineau, 1970; ed, Gobineau: Selected Political Writings, 1970, pbk edn 1971, Spanish edn 1973; (with Dr F. F. Cartwright) Disease and History, 1972; chapter in Justice First, ed L. F. Donnelly 1969; *contrib*. Alta, Etudes Gobiniennes, Hist. Jl, Hist. Today, Horizon, Race, Wiener Libr. Bull. *Address*: Dept of History, Univ. of Leicester, Leicester LE1 7RH.

Biddlecombe, Mrs G.; *see* McGuinness, R.

Bide, Rev. Peter William; Chaplain and Tutor in Theology, Lady Margaret Hall, Oxford; *b* 1912; *m* 1941; two *s* four *d*. BA Hons, 1939 (2nd cl. Eng. Lang. and Lit.), MA 1945. Librarian, Theol. Faculty Library, 1970- . *Address*: Lady Margaret Hall, Oxford.

Bieler, Prof. Ludwig, DrPhil, MRIA; Professor of Palaeography and Late Latin, University College, Dublin, since 1960; *b* 1906; *m* 1939; one *s* one *d*. DrPhil Vienna 1929, Dip. Wissenschaftlicher Bibliotheksdienst Vienna 1935, Hon LittD TCD 1970, Hon. DrPhil Munich 1972; Mem., Royal Irish Academy 1947; Corresp. Fellow: Mediaeval Academy of America 1963, Österr. Academy d. Wissenschaften 1964, Brit. Academy 1971. Instructor in Greek, Vienna, 1932, Priv. Doz. Classics, Vienna, 1936; Vis. Lectr, Nat. Univ. Ireland, 1940; Asst Prof. Classics, Notre Dame, USA, 1946; Asst Lectr Classics, Univ. Coll. Dublin, 1948; Lectr, Palaeography, 1951; Vis. Prof., Pontifical Institute Mediaeval Studies, Toronto, 1969. Asst Keeper of MSS, Nat. Libr. Vienna, 1935–38; Archivist, Nat. Libr. of Ireland, 1946–47; Vis. Mem., Inst. for Advanced Study, Princeton, USA, 1954–55. *Publications*: Theîos Anér, 1935–36 (reprint 1967); The Life and Legend of St. Patrick, 1949; Libri Epistolarum S Patricii, 1952; ed, Boethius: Philosophiae Consolatio, 1957; Irland Wegbereiter des Mittelalters, 1961, English edn 1963; Geschichte der römischen. Literatur, 1961, 3rd edn 1972, Greek edn 1965, English edn 1966, Spanish edn 1968; The Irish Penitentials, 1963; St Patrick and the Coming of Christianity (History of Irish Catholicism 1, 1), 1967; Four Latin Lives of St Patrick, 1971; ed E. A. Lowe, Palaeographical Papers 1907–65, 1972; *contrib*. AJP, Anzeiger Österr. Akademie d. Wissensch., Celtica, Irish Hist. Studies, Proc. RIA, Scriptorium, Studies (Dublin), Texte u. Untersuchungen, Traditio, Wiener Studien. *Address*: Univ. College, Belfield, Arts Building, Dublin 4, Ireland.

Biggart, John; Lecturer in History, Schoo of European Studies, University of East Anglia, since 1966; *b* 1941; *m* 1963; one *s* one *d*. MA Glasgow 1964, BLitt Glasgow 1969; Mem., Royal Inst. Internat. Aff., Nat. Assoc. Sov. and E Eur. Studies, Univ. Assoc. for Contemp. Eur. Studies. Asst Lectr, Univ. of E. Anglia, 1966–69. *Publications:* trans., (with I. Nove) M. Lewin: Russian Peasants and Soviet Power, 1968; *contrib.* Sov. Studies, E European Qly. *Address:* School of European Studies, Univ. of East Anglia, Norwich NOR 88C.

Bigsby, Dr Christopher William Edgar; Lecturer in American Literature, School of English and American Studies, University of East Anglia, since 1969; *b* 1941; *m* 1965; one *s* two *d*. BA Sheffield 1962 (English), MA Sheffield 1964; PhD Nottingham 1966; Mem., British Assoc. American Studies. Lectr, University College of Wales, Aberystwyth, 1966–69. Ed., Newsletter of European Assoc. for American Studies. *Publications:* Confrontation and Commitment: a study of contemporary American drama, 1959–66, 1967; Albee, 1969; ed, Three Negro Plays, 1969; The Black American Writer, 1969; Dada and Surrealism, 1972; *contrib.* American Literary Realism, Negro Literary Forum, Contemporary Literature, Jl American Studies, Kansas Qly, Modern Drama, Twentieth Century Literature. *Address:* School of English and American Studies, Univ. of East Anglia, Norwich NOR 88C.

Bindoff, Stanley Thomas, MA; Professor of History, Queen Mary College, University of London, since 1951; *b* 1908; *m* 1936; one *s* one *d*. BA London (Upper 2nd cl. History), MA London (with mark of distinction) 1933; Alexander Medallist, RHistS, 1935. FRHistS 1946 (Vice-Pres., 1967); Fellow, UCL 1958; Mem., Utrecht Hist. Soc., 1947; Royal Dutch Soc. Lit., 1950. Successively Asst Lectr, Lectr, and Reader in History, UCL, 1935–51; Vis. Prof. in History: Columbia, Univ., NY, 1960; Claremont Grad. Sch. Calif, 1963; Wellesley Coll., Mass, 1968; Harvard Univ., 1968; Cornell Vis. Prof., Swarthmore Coll., Pa, 1973. Senate, Univ. of London, 1966–70. Neale Lectr, Univ. Coll. Lond., 1973. *Publications:* (with E. F. Malcolm Smith and C. K. Webster) British Diplomatic Representatives, 1789–1852, 1934; The Scheldt Question to 1839, 1945; Ket's Rebellion (Hist. Assoc. Pamphlet), 1949, 2nd edn 1968; Tudor England, 1950, 12th edn 1972; (with J. Hurstfield and C. H. Williams) Elizabethan Government and Society, 1961; The Fame of Sir Thomas Gresham (Neale Lecture) 1973; *contrib.* EHR, Econ. Hist. Rev., History. *Address:* Queen Mary College, Univ. of London, Mile End Road, E14 N5.

Binfield, Dr John Clyde Goodfellow; Lecturer, Department of Medieval and Modern History, University of Sheffield, since 1967; *b* 1940; *m* 1969; two *d*. BA Cantab 1961 (1st cl. History), MA Cantab 1965, PhD Cantab 1966. Asst Lectr, Sheffield Univ., 1964-67. Mem., Brit. Council of Churches, 1969- ; Sheffield Amenities Council, 1970- ; Congregational and United Reformed Church Chaplain, Sheffield Univ. 1966- . *Publications:* George Williams and the YMCA, 1973; *contrib.* EHR, Hist., Trans Congregational Hist. Soc. *Address:* Dept of Modern History, The Arts Tower, The Univ., Western Bank, Sheffield S10 2JN.

Binns, Alan Lawrie; Senior Lecturer in English Language, English Department, Hull University, since 1960; *b* 1925; *m* 1947; 1970; three *s*. BA Manchester 1944 (Hons English). Lectr, Hull, 1946- ; Vis. Lectr, Univ. of Leningrad, 1969. Dep. Warden, Camp Hall, 1947–54; Admissions Off., Arts, 1954–57; Pres., AUT, 1965. *Publications:* The Viking Century in East Yorkshire, 1963; East Yorkshire in the Sagas, 1966; trans., Arbman: The Vikings, 1961; Stenberger: Sweden, 1964; Kivikoski: Finland, 1967; *contrib.* Acta Archaeol. Scand., Bergens Museums Årbog, Engl. Germ. Studies, J. Rylands Libr. Bull., Saga Bk. *Address:* Dept of English, The Univ., Hull HU6 7RX.

Binns, Dr James Wallace; Lecturer, Department of Latin, University of Birmingham, since 1965; *b* 1940. BA Birmingham 1964 (1st cl. Latin), MA Birmingham 1965, PhD Birmingham 1969. War Office, 1958–61. *Publications:* ed, Ovid, 1973; *contrib.* Humanistics Lovaniensia, Studies in the Renaissance, Sixteenth Century Jl. *Address:* Dept of Latin, Univ. of Birmingham, PO Box 363, Birmingham B15 2TT.

Binyon, Timothy John; University Lecturer in Russian, University of Oxford, since 1965; *b* 1936. BA Oxon 1959 (1st cl. Mod. Langs), MA Oxon 1963, DPhil Oxon 1969. Lectr in Russian, Leeds Univ., 1962; Sen. Research Fellow, Wadham Coll., Oxford, 1968- . *Publications:* A Soviet Verse Reader, 1964. *Address:* Wadham College, Oxford.

Biran, Dr Leonard Arie; Lecturer in Medical Education, University of Dundee, since 1972; *b* 1937; *m* 1965; one *s* one *d*. BSc Birmingham 1958 (Chemistry); DPhil Oxon 1962 (Biochemistry). University of Birmingham: Res. Fellow in Biochem., 1963; Res. Fellow in Educn, 1964–68; Lectr in Educn (Psychology), 1968–70; Associate Prof., Internat. Centre for Advanced Technical and Vocational Training (ILO), Turin, 1970–72. Dir, Nat. Centre for Programmed Learning, 1968–70. *Publications: contrib.* Biochem. Jl, Brit. Jl of Med. Educn, Jl of Chromatography, Assoc. Programmed Learning and Educnl Technol. YB. *Address:* Dept of Medical Education, Univ. of Dundee, Dundee DD1 4HN.

Birch, Prof. Anthony Harold, PhD; Professor of Political Science, University of Exeter, since 1970; *b* 1924; *m* 1953; one *s* one *d*. BSc(Econ) London 1945 (1st cl. Hons), PhD London 1951. Asst Lectr in Govt, 1947–51, Lectr, 1951–58, Sen. Lectr in Govt, 1958-61, Univ. of Manchester; Prof. of Political Studies, Univ. of Hull, 1961–70. Commonwealth Fund Fellow, USA, 1951–52; Vis. Prof., Tufts Univ., 1968. Asst Principal, Board of Trade, 1945–47; Consultant to Govt of Western Region of Nigeria, 1956-58.

Publications: Federalism, Finance and Social Legislation, 1955; Small-Town Politics, 1959; Representative and Responsible Government, 1964; The British System of Government, 1967; Representation, 1971; *contrib*. articles in various jls. *Address*: Univ. of Exeter, Exeter EX4 4QJ.

Birch, Brian Charles; Lecturer in Literature and Drama, Adult Education Department, University of Hull, since 1973 (Staff Tutor, 1964–73); three *s* one *d*. BA Oxford 1961 (Hons. Eng. Lang. and Lit.), MA Oxon 1965. Governor, Grimsby Coll. of Technology, 1970– ; Chm., Friends of Whitgift Regional Film Theatre, 1973– . Author and director, film, Happening, 1973. *Publications*: ed, Lincolnshire Writers 1967–69; ed, Not for Ambition or Bread (poetry anthology), 1973; contrib. Lines and Levels, 1972; Lincolnshire Writers, 1970–73; *contrib*. The Library. *Address*: Dept of Adult Education, Univ. of Hull, 207 Cottingham Road, Hull, Yorkshire.

Birch, Dr Brian Peter; Lecturer in Geography, Southampton University, since 1964; *b* 1935; *m* 1961; three *s*. BA Durham 1959 (1st cl. Geography), MA Indiana 1962, PhD Durham 1966. Lectr, Univ. of Northern Iowa, 1961; Asst Lectr, Southampton, 1962–64; Vis. Assoc. Prof., Miami Univ., Ohio, 1970, San Diego State Univ., Calif., 1973. Mem., Governing Body Coll. of Sarum St Michael, Salisbury, 1971– . *Publications*: *contrib*. Southampton Res. Series, Tijdschift voor Econ. en Soc. Geografie, Annals Assoc. Am. Geogs. *Address*: Dept of Geography, Southampton Univ., Southampton SO9 5NH.

Birch, Prof. J. William; Professor of Geography, University of Leeds, since 1967; *b* 1925; *m* 1950; one *s* ond *d*. BA Reading 1949 (1st cl. Geography), PhD Reading 1957; Mem., Inst. Br. Geogrs. (Vice-Pres., 1974), Canadian Assoc. Geogrs, American Assoc. Geogrs, FRGS. Lectr, Bristol Univ., 1950–60; Prof., Grad. School Geog., Clark Univ., Worcester, Mass, 1960–63; Prof. and Chm. of Dept of Geog., Univ. of Toronto, 1963–67; Prof. and Head, Dept of Geog., Univ. Leeds, 1967– . Sec., Section E. Brit. Assoc., 1956–60; Mem., Council Inst. Br. Geog., 1958–60; Ed., Econ. Geog., 1962–63; Mem., Advisory Cttee on Geog. Res., Dept of Energy, Mines and Resources, Ottawa, 1965–67; Mem., Geog. Cttee of SSRC, 1968– , Vice-Chm., 1972– . *Publications*: The Isle of Man: a study in economic geography, 1964; *contrib*. Trans Inst. Br. Geogrs, Econ. Geog., Geog. Jl, Environmental Management. *Address*: Dept of Geography, Univ. of Leeds, Leeds LS2 9JT.

Birch, Julian, BSocSc; Lecturer in Soviet Politics, University of Sheffield, since 1968; *b* 1945. BSocSc Birmingham 1966 (Russian Studies); Mem., Nat. Assoc. Soviet and E European Studies. Temp. Lectr in Russian, Univ. of Aston in Birmingham, 1966–67. *Publications*: The Ukrainian Nationalist Movement in the USSR; Political Opposition in One Party States; *contrib*. Government and Opposition, Soviet Studies, Ukrainian Rev. *Address*: Dept of Political Theory and Institutions, Univ. of Sheffield, Sheffield S10 2TN.

Bird, Prof. James Harold, PhD; Professor of Geography, University of Southampton, since 1967; *b* 1923; *m* 1955. BA London 1951 (Hons Geog.), PhD London 1953; FRGS, MCIT. Asst Lectr, Univ. Coll., Southampton, 1953–54; King's Coll., Univ. of London, 1954–57; Lectr, KCL, 1957–62; Vis. Lectr, Univ. of New England, NSW, 1963; Reader, UCL, 1964–67. Mem., Council, RGS, 1968–71; Inst. of British Geographers, 1969–73; Brit. Nat. Cttee for Geography (Royal Soc.). *Publications*: The Geography of the Port of London, 1957; The Major Seaports of the United Kingdom, 1963; Seaport Gateways of Australia, 1968; Seaports and Seaport Terminals, 1971; Economic Geography, Geographical Jl, Geography. *Address*: Dept of Geography, Univ. of Southampton, Southampton SO9 5NH.

Bird, Prof. Peter Ashby, BScEcon, FCA; Professor of Accounting, University of Kent at Canterbury, since 1970; *b* 1934; *m* 1959; two *s*. BScEcon, London 1956; Chartered Accountant, 1961. Lectr, London School of Economics, 1963–66; Vis. Assoc. Prof., Univ. of Minnesota, 1965; Sen. Lectr, Univ. of Kent at Canterbury, 1966–70. Chm., Assoc. of Univ. Teachers of Accounting, 1969–71; Mem., Canterbury Diocesan Bd of Finance, 1972– . Mem., Advisory Bd of Accountancy Educn, 1970– . *Publications*: Economic Charges for Water, in, Essays in the Theory and Practice of Pricing, 1967; A Casebook on Auditing Procedures, together with A Manual of Possible Solutions, 1969, 2nd edn 1971; The Interpretation of Published Accounts, 1971; Accountability, 1972; Standard Accounting Practice, in, Debits, Credits, Finance and Profits, 1974; *contrib*. Accounting and Business Res., Brit. Tax Rev., Jl of Accounting Res. *Address*: Rutherford College, The Univ., Canterbury, Kent CT2 7NZ.

Birdsall, Dr James Neville, MA, PhD; Reader in New Testament Studies and Textual Criticism, Department of Theology, University of Birmingham, since 1971; *b* 1928; *m* 1951; two *s* two *d*. BA Cantab 1950, Jeremie Hellenistic Prize, Cambridge 1951, MA Cantab 1953, PhD Nottingham 1959; Mem., Studiorum Novi Testamenti Societas, 1957. Asst Lectr, Leeds Univ., 1956, Lectr in Biblical Studies, 1959; Lectr in Theology, Birmingham Univ., 1961; Vis. Assoc. Prof. of Caucasian Languages, Univ. of California, Los Angeles, 1965–66; Sen. Lectr in Theology, Birmingham Univ., 1967. Exec. Ed., Internat. Greek New Testament Project, 1969– . *Publications*: The Bodmer Papyrus of the Gospel of John, 1960; ed, (with R. W. Thomson) Biblical and Patristic Studies in memory of R. P. Casey, 1963; Cambridge History of the Bible, vol. I (ed. P. R. Ackroyd, C. R. Evans), chapter 11 The New Testament Text, 1970; *contrib*. Evangel. Qly, JTS, Le Muséon, NTS, Novum Testamentum, Oriens Christianus. *Address*: Dept of Theology, Univ. of Birmingham, Birmingham B15 2TF.

Birley, Prof. Anthony Richard, MA, DPhil, FSA; Professor of History, University of Manchester, since 1974; *b* 1937; *m* 1963; one *s* one *d*. BA Oxon 1960 (1st cl. Litt. Hum.), MA 1963, DPhil 1966, Oxon; FSA 1969. Mem., Council, Soc. for Promotion of Roman Studies, Faculty of Archaeology, Hist. and Letters, Brit. School at Rome. Craven Fellow, Oxford, 1960–62; Res. Fellow, Birmingham, 1963–65; Temp. Asst Lectr (Latin), Leeds, 1965–66; Lectr in Ancient History, Leeds, 1966–73, Reader in History 1973–74. Vis. Lectr, Duke Univ., 1968–69. *Publications*: Hadrian's Wall, 1963; Life in Roman Britain, 1964; Marcus Aurelius, 1966; trans. Mark Aurel: Kaiser and Philosoph, 1968; ed, Universal Rome, 1967; (with A. Sorrell) Imperial Rome, 1970; Septimius Severus: the African Emperor, 1971; trans. Alföldy: Noricum (forthcoming); *contrib.* Bonner Jahrbücher, Chiron, Epigraphische Studein, Historia., etc. *Address*: School of History, Univ. of Manchester, Manchester M13 9PL.

Bishop, Ian Benjamin; Lecturer in English, University of Bristol, since 1956; *b* 1927; *m* 1968; two *d*. BLitt, MA Oxon 1954. Asst Lectr, Bristol Univ., 1953–56. *Publications*: Pearl in its Setting, 1968; *contrib.* Encycl. Britannica, M. Aev., RES. *Address*: Dept of English, Univ. of Bristol, 40 Berkeley Square, Bristol BS8 1HY.

Bishop, Dr Thomas Gordon; Lecturer, Department of Education, Durham University, since 1965; *b* 1915; *m* 1939; five *s*. BA 1936, BSc (Econ.) London 1949, PhD Leeds 1958, CertEd Cambridge 1937. Lectr in Adult Educn (Services' Educn), Dept of Extra-Mural Studies, Leeds Univ., 1950–65. Vice-Chm., Nat. Exec., Approved Schs Managers' Assoc., 1968–74. *Address*: Dept of Education, 48 Old Elvet, Durham.

Bissett-Johnson, Alastair; Senior Lecturer in Law, Department of Law, Leicester University, since 1972; *b* 1941; *m* 1967. LLB Nottingham 1962, LLM Michigan 1963; Barrister, Inner Temple, 1969; Barrister and Solicitor, Vic., 1969. Asst Lectr, Sheffield Univ., 1963; Lectr, Bristol Univ., 1964; Sen. Lectr, Monash Univ., Melbourne, 1969. *Publications*: Family Law in Australia (with H. A. Finlay), 1972; *contrib.* Aust. Law Jl, Canad. Bar Rev., ICLQ. *Address*: Faculty of Law, The Univ., Leicester LE1 7RH.

Bivar, Dr Adrian David Hugh; Lecturer in Iranian and Central Asian Archaeology, Department of the Near and Middle East, School of Oriental and African Studies, University of London, since 1960; *b* 1926; *m* 1954. BA Oxon 1948 (1st cl. Shortened Lit. Hum.), MA Oxon 1952, DPhil Oxon 1956; FRNS, FRAS, Res. Lectr, Christ Church, Oxford, 1952–57. Curator, Nigerian Antiqu. Service, 1957–60; Mem., Council, Royal Numism. Soc., 1954–56, 1960–61, 1964–65; Council, Royal Asiatic Soc., 1968– , Dir, Royal Asiatic Soc., 1971– . *Publications*: Catalogue of the Western Asiatic Seals in the British Museum: Stamp Seals II, The Sassanian Dynasty, 1969; *contrib.* Memorial Vols; W. B. Henning, V. Minorsky; *contrib.* Bull. SOAS, JNSI, JRAS, Num Chron..

Address: School of Oriental and African Studies, Univ. of London, WC1E 7HP.

Bivon, Dr Roy; Lecturer, School of European Studies, University of East Anglia, since 1969; *b* 1944; *m* 1971; one *d*. BA Liverpool 1965 (Russian); PhD Essex 1969 (Linguistics of Russian); Member: Assoc. of Teachers of Russian; British Univs Assoc. of Slavists; Linguistics Assoc. Res. Asst, Essex, 1968. *Publications*: Element Order, 1971; *contrib.* Jl of Russian Studies. *Address*: School of European Studies, Univ. of East Anglia, Norwich NOR 88C.

Black, Christopher Freeman, MA, BLitt; Lecturer, Department of History, Glasgow University, since 1969; *b* 1941; *m* 1965. BA Oxon 1963, BLitt Oxon 1967, MA Oxon 1967. Asst Lectr, Glasgow Univ., 1965–69. *Publications*: *contrib.* Annali della Fondazione Italiana per la Storia Amministrativa, EHR, Dictionary of World History (1973). *Address*: Dept of History, The Univ., Glasgow G12 8QQ.

Black, David William, RD, BA, MLitt; Lecturer, Department of Classics, Queen Mary College, University of London, since 1964; *b* 1935; *m* 1964; one *s* one *d*. BA Durham 1956 (1st cl. Latin and Greek), MLitt Cambridge 1964. Asst. Lectr in Classics, QMC, 1961–64. Mem., Central Religious Advisory Cttee (BBC and ITA), 1968–72. *Publications*: *contrib.* Proc. Virg. Soc. *Address*: Dept of Classics, Queen Mary College, E1 4NS.

Black, Prof. John; Professor of Economic Theory, Department of Economics, University of Exeter, since 1967; *b* 1931; *m* 1960; one *s* one *d*. BA Oxon 1952, MA Oxon 1956. Fellow, Magdalen Coll., Oxford, 1956–57; Fellow and Tutor, Merton Coll., Oxford, 1957–66, Lectr in Econs, Oxford, 1957–66; Vis. Prof., Univ. of Illinois, 1963–64. Asst Ed., Rev. of Econ. Studies, 1958–63 and 1965–71. Asst Ed., Econ. Jl, 1971– . *Publications*: (with J. F. Bradley) Essential Mathematics for Economists, 1973; *contrib.* Econ. Jl, Economica, Rev. of Econ. Studies, Oxford Econ. Papers. *Address*: Dept of Economics, Univ. of Exeter, Exeter EX4 4PU.

Black, John Nicholson, MA, DPhil, DSc, FRSE; Principal, Bedford College, London University, since 1971; *b* 1922; *m* 1952; 1967; three *s* one *d*. BA Hons 1949 (1st cl. Agriculture), MA 1952, DPhil 1952, Oxford; DSc Adelaide 1965; FRSE 1965. Oxford Univ., 1946–49; ARC Studentship, 1949–52; Lectr, Sen. Lectr, Reader, Univ. of Adelaide (Waite Agricl Res. Inst.), 1952–63; André Mayer Fellowship (FAO), 1958; Prof. of Forestry and Natural Resources, Univ. of Edinburgh, 1963–71. Mem. Nat. Environment Res. Council, 1968– . *Publications*: The Dominion of Man, 1970; *contrib.* many papers on ecological subjects in scientific jls. *Address*: Bedford College, Regent's Park, NW1 4NS.

Black, Very Rev. Principal Matthew, DD, FBA; Principal of St Mary's College and Professor of Biblical Criticism in the University of

59

St Andrews, since 1954; b 1908; m 1938; one s
one d. MA Glasgow 1st cl. Hons (Classics)
1930, MA 2nd cl. Hons (Mental Philosophy)
1931, BD with distinction in Old Testament
1934, DLitt 1944, PhD Bonn 1937, Hon.
DTheol Münster 1960, Hon. DD Glasgow
1954, Hon. DD Cambridge 1965, Hon. DD
Queen's, Ontario 1967. Mem., Soc. for Old
Testament Study (Pres., 1968); Pres.,
Studiorum Novi Testamenti Societas;
Corr. Mem., Göttingen Akademie der Wissenschaften, 1957; Hon. Member: American
Soc. of Biblical Exegesis, 1958; American
Bible Society, 1966; FBA 1955. Asst to
Prof. of Hebrew, Univ. of Glasgow, 1935–37;
Asst Lectr in Semitic Languages and Litera-
tures, Univ. of Manchester, 1937–39; Lectr
in Hebrew and Biblical Criticism, Univ. of
Aberdeen, 1939–42; Lectr in New Testament
Language and Literature, Univ. of Leeds,
1947–52; Prof. of Biblical Criticism and Bibli-
cal Antiquities, Univ. of Edinburgh, 1952–
54; Morse Lectr and de Hoyt Lectr, Union
Theological Seminary, NY, 1963; Thomas
Burns Lectr, Univ. of Otago, 1967; Croall
Lectr, 1972; Chm., Advisory Cttee of Peshitta
Project of the Univ. of Leiden, 1968– .
Burkitt Medal for Biblical Studies, 1962.
Publications: Rituale Melchitarum, 1938; An
Aramaic Approach to the Gospels and Acts,
3rd edn 1967; A Christian Palestinian Syriac
Horologion, Texts and Studies, Contribu-
tions to Patristic Literature, New Series, vol.
I, 1954; The Scrolls and Christian Origins,
1961; General and New Testament Editor,
Peake's Commentary on the Bible, 1962;
Bible Societies' edn of the Greek New Testament, 1966; ed jtly, In Memoriam Paul
Kahle, 1968; ed, The Scrolls and Christianity,
1968; (with A. M. Denis) Apocalypsis Heno-
chi Graeca Fragmenta Pseudepigraphorum,
1970; Commentary on Romans, 1973;
Organizing Editor, The History of the
Jewish People in the Age of Jesus Christ,
by Emil Schürer (new translation and
revision, vol. I 1973; vol. II 1974; Editor,
New Testament Studies, 1954– ; Forthcoming: Edition of 4Q Enoch, in collaboration
with J. T. Milik; contrib. Language, Culture
and Religion: In Honor of Eugene A. Nida
(ed M.Black and W. A. Smalley),1974. *Address*:
St Mary's College, Univ. of St Andrews, St
Andrews, KY16 9JT.

Black, Prof. Robert Denis Collison, MA,
BComm, PhD; FBA; Professor of Economics
and Head of Department of Economics,
Queen's University Belfast, since 1962;
b 1922; m 1953; one s one d. BA TCD 1941
(1st cl. Econs and Pol. Sci.), BComm TCD
1941, PhD TCD 1943, MA TCD 1945; Dep.
Prof. of Pol Econ., TCD, 1943–45; Asst
Lectr, QUB, 1945, Lectr, QUB, 1946–58,
Sen. Lectr, 1958–61, Reader, 1961; Rocke-
feller Post-Doct. Fellow, Princeton Univ.,
1950–51; Vis. Prof. of Econs, Yale Univ.,
1964–65. Dean. Fac. of Econs and Social
Sciences, QUB, 1967–70; Pro-Vice-Chan-
cellor, QUB, 1971– . Member: Council,
Royal Econ. Soc., 1963– ; Council, Econ.
Soc. Res. Inst., Dublin, 1962– ; Hon. Sec.,
Stat. Soc. of Ireland, 1955– . *Publications*:
Centenary History of the Statistical and
Social Inquiry Society of Ireland, 1947;
Economic Thought and the Irish Question,

1960; Catalogue of Pamphlets on Economic
Subjects, 1750–1900, 1969, ed, W. S. Jevons:
The Theory of Political Economy, 1970; ed,
Economic Writings of Mountifort Longfield,
1971; Readings in the Development of
Economic Analysis, 1971; ed, Papers and
Correspondence of W. S. Jevons, vol. I, 1972,
vol. II, 1973, vol. III, 1974, vol. IV, 1975;
contrib. Economica, Econ. Jl, Hermathena,
Manchester Sch., Oxford Econ. Papers.
Address: Dept of Economics, Queen's Univ.,
Belfast BT7 1NN.

Blackburn, Dr Simon Walter; Fellow and
Lecturer in Philosophy, Pembroke College,
Oxford, since 1969; b 1944; m 1968; one d.
BA Hons Cambridge 1965, PhD 1970. Res.
Fellow, Churchill Coll., Cambridge, 1967–69.
Publications: Reason and Prediction, 1973;
contrib. Mind, Amer. Philosophical Qly, etc.
Address: Pembroke Coll., Oxford.

Blackhall, James Cameron; Senior Lec-
turer, Town and Country Planning, Univer-
sity of Newcastle upon Tyne since 1966;
b 1932; m 1959; two s. BA (Hons) Dunelm
1956 (Town and Country Planning), Dip.
Landscape Design, Dunelm 1957; MRTPI
1960, Assoc. Inst. Landscape Architects 1961.
Course Dir, BA (Hons) T & CP, 1969– ;
Dir of Res. SSRC 'Public Participation in
Planning', June 1971. *Publications*: *contrib*.
Danish Planning Jl, Traffic Eng., Jl Royal
Town Planning Inst. *Address*: The Univ.,
Newcastle upon Tyne NE1 7RU.

Blackie, Prof. James Campbell, MA, BD,
STM; Professor of Christian Ethics and
Practical Theology, University of Edinburgh,
since 1965; b 1921; m 1950; three s one d.
MA Edinburgh 1948, BD Edinburgh 1951,
STM (Union Theological Seminary, New
York) 1952. Lectr in Biblical Studies, Univ.
of Aberdeen, Chaplain to the Univ. Of
Edinburgh, 1956–64; Lectr, Edinburgh
Univ., 1964–65. Captain, RHA, 1942–46;
Vice-Chm., Edinburgh Council Soc. Service,
1967– ; Vice-Chm., Scottish Council Soc.
Service; Mem., George Heriot's Trust,
1967– . *Publications*: First Year at Univer-
sity, 1964; *contrib*. Contact (ed. 1960–66);
The Case of the Dying: a companion to
medical studies. *Address*: Dept of Christian
Ethics and Practical Theology, New College,
The Mound, Edinburgh.

Blacking, Prof. John Anthony Randoll,
PhD, DLitt; Professor and Head of Depart-
ment of Social Anthropology, The Queen's
University of Belfast, since 1970; b 1928; m
1955; one s two d. BA Cantab 1953 (Hons
Social Anthropology), MA Cantab 1957;
PhD Rand 1965; DLitt 1972; FRAI. Lectr
in Social Anthropology and African Govt,
Univ. of the Witwatersrand, 1959–65; Prof.
and Hd of Dept and Chm. of African Studies
Prog., 1966–69; Vis. Prof. in African Studies
Prog., Makerere Univ., 1965; Prof. of
Anthropology, Western Michigan Univ.,
1970–72; John Danz Lectr, Univ. of Wash-
ington, 1971. *Publications*: Black Background:
a study of Venda childhood, 1964; Venda
Children's Songs: a study in ethnomusico-
logical analysis, 1967; Process and Product in
Human Society, 1969; How Musical is Man?

1973; Man and Fellow man, 1974; *Records*: Music from Petauke, vol. I 1963, vol. II 1965; *contrib*. African Music, African Studies, Ethnomusicology, Man, Studies in Ethnomusicology, Yearbooks of Internat. Folk Music Council, Essays on Music and History in Africa. *Address*: Dept of Social Anthropology, The Queen's Univ. of Belfast, Belfast BT7 1NN.

Blackman, David John, MA, FSA; Lecturer, Department of Classics, University of Bristol, since 1967; *b* 1938; *m* 1962; three *d*. BA Cantab 1962 (1st cl. Classics), MA Cantab 1965; FSA 1972. Jun. Fellow, Bristol Univ., 1964–65; Asst Lectr, 1965–67; Commonwealth Fund Fellow and Jun. Fellow, Center for Hellenic Studies, Washington, DC, 1968–69; Adv. Ed., Int. Jl Naut. Archaeol., 1971–. Mem.: Council (formerly Cttee) Naut. Archaeol., 1964– ; Council, Soc. Prom. Hellenic Studies, 1971–74; Managing Cttee, British Sch. at Athens, 1974–. *Publications*: ed, Marine Archaeology, 1973; *contrib*. Arch. Anzeiger; Ann. Brit. Sch. at Athens, GRBS, JHS, Arch., Rep., Trans. Amer. Phil. Assoc. *Address*: Dept of Classics, Univ. of Bristol, Bristol BS8 1TH.

Blacksell, Dr Andrew Mark; Lecturer, Department of Geography, Exeter University, since 1970; *b* 1942; *m* 1965; one *d*. BA (Hons) Oxford 1964, DPhil Oxford 1967; Mem., Inst. of British Geogr., FRGS. Asst Lectr in Geography, Exeter Univ., 1967–70; Vis. Asst Prof., Southern Illinois Univ., 1968–69; Vis. Asst Prof., Colombia Univ., NY, 1970. *Publications*: Recent changes in the morphology of West German townscapes, in, Urbanization and its Problems, ed R. Beckinsale and J. Houston, 1968; Recreation and Land Use – a study in the Dartmoor National Park, in, Exeter Essays in Geography, ed, K. Gregory and W. Ravenhill, 1971. *Address*: Dept of Geography, Queen's Building, Queen's Drive, Exeter EX4 4AF.

Blackstone, Dr Tessa Ann Vosper; Lecturer in Social Administration, London School of Economics, since 1969, and Fellow, Centre for Studies in Social Policy, since 1972; *b* 1942; *m* 1965; one *s* one *d*. BSc(Soc) London (LSE) 1964, PhD London (LSE) 1969. Asst Lectr in Social Admin LSE, 1966–69. Mem.: Educational Adv. Council, IBA, 1973– ; City Poverty Cttee, 1973– . *Publications*: (co-author) Students in Conflict, 1970; A Fair Start, 1971; (co-author) The Academic Labour Market, 1974; *contrib*. BJS, Comp. Educn, Comp. Educn Rev., Higher Educn, Jewish Jl Sociol., Social and Econ. Admin, Trends Educn, etc. *Address*: London School of Economics, Houghton Street, WC2A 2AE.

Bladon, Richard Anthony Warren; Lecturer, Department of Linguistics, University College of North Wales, Bangor, since 1969; *b* 1943; *m* 1966. BA Cantab (Modern and Medieval Languages) 1965, MA Cantab 1968, MPhil Reading 1969. Lectr, Rijksuniversiteit Gent (Belgium), 1965. *Publications*: *contrib*. Engl. Studs, Trans Philol. Soc. *Address*: Dept of Linguistics, Univ. College of N Wales, Bangor LL57 2DG.

Blaess, Madeleine Marie Félicie; Senior Lecturer, French Department, University of Sheffield, since 1973 (Lecturer, 1951–73); *b* 1918. BA Leeds 1939 (1st cl. French Hons), LèsL Paris (Sorbonne) 1944; Arthurian Soc., Rencesvals Soc., Soc. for French Studies. Lectrice in the English Dept, Univ. of Paris, 1941; Asst Lectr, Sheffield Univ., 1948. Centre de Documentation de la Bibliothèque nationale, 1941–44; Lectr for Min. of Information. 1945–46; Part-time Lectr, Brit. Inst., Paris, 1947–48; Full-time tutor, Brit. Correspondence Course for the LèsL, 1947–48. *Publications*: (with M. Bigot) trans. Ogrizek: France, Paris and the provinces, 1944; *contrib*. Currents of Thought in French Literature: essays in memory of G. T. Clapton, 1965; Studies in Fr. Lit. presented to H. W. Lawton, 1968; *contrib*. Arthurian Bull., Romania. *Address*: French Dept, The Univ., Sheffield S10 2TN.

Blaikie, Dr Piers Macleod; Lecturer, School of Development Studies, University of East Anglia, since 1972; *b* 1942; *m* 1968; one *d*. BA Cantab 1965, MA Cantab 1966, PhD Cantab 1971; FRGS 1970. Lectr, Univ. of Reading, 1967–72. *Publications*: The Family Planning Programme of India: a Locational Approach, 1974; *contrib*. Trans Inst. of British Geographers, Geografiska Annaler Series B, Population Studies. *Address*: Overseas Development Group, University Village, Univ. of East Anglia, Norwich NOR 88C.

Blake, The Lord; Robert Norman William Blake, FBA; Provost of the Queen's College, Oxford University, since 1968; *b* 1916; *m* 1953; three *d*. BA Oxon 1938 (1st cl. PPE), MA Oxon 1946, Hon DLitt Glasgow 1972; FBA, FRHistS. Lectr, Christ Church, Oxford, 1946–47; Student of Christ Church, Oxford, 1947–68; Ford Lectr, Oxford, 1967–68. Mem., Oxford City Council, 1957–64; JP Oxford City, 1964; Life peer created 1971; Chm., Governors of Trent Coll.; Governor of Bradfield Coll., King Edward VI Sch., Norwich, Malvern Coll., and St Edward's Sch., Oxford. *Publications*: ed, The Private Papers of Douglas Haig, 1952; The Unknown Prime Minister, the Life and Times of Andrew Bonar Law, 1955; Disraeli, 1966; The Conservative Party from Peel to Churchill, 1970. *Address*: The Provost's Lodgings, The Queen's College, Oxford OX1 4AW.

Blake, Prof. Christopher; Professor of Economics, University of Dundee, since 1968; *b* 1926; *m* 1951; two *s* two *d*. MA St Andrews 1950, PhD St Andrews 1965. Instructor, Princeton Univ., 1952–53; Asst, Edinburgh Univ., 1953–55; Lectr, St Andrews Univ., 1960–65; Sen. Lectr, St Andrews Univ., 1965–67; Sen. Lectr, Dundee Univ., 1967–68. Organisation and Methods Officer, Stewarts and Lloyds Ltd, 1955–60; Chm., Council, St Leonard's School, 1972– ; Dean of Faculty of Social Sciences and Letters, Univ. of Dundee, 1968–72; Director, Scottish Academic Press, 1969– ; Dep. Chm. or Independent Mem.,

61

of several wages councils. *Publications*: *contrib*. Mind, Phil Qly, Scot. Jl of Pol. Econ. *Address*: Dept of Economics, The Univ., Dundee DD1 4HN.

Blake, David Leonard, MA; Senior Lecturer in Music, University of York, since 1971; *b* 1936; *m* 1960; two *s* one *d*. BA Cantab 1960, MA Cantab 1963. Lectr in Music, Univ. of York. 1964. *Publications*: It's a Small War: musical for schools, 1963; Variations for Piano, 1964; On Christmas Day, 1965; Three Songs of Ben Jonson, 1966; The Almanack, 1968; Lumina, 1969; Metamorphoses, Scenes, The Bones of Chuang Tzu, 1974. *Address*: Dept of Music, Univ. of York, Heslington, York YO1 5DD.

Blake, Dr Gerald Henry, MA, PhD; Senior Lecturer in Geography, University of Durham, since 1973 (Lecturer, 1964–73); *b* 1936; *m* 1965; one *s* two *d*. BA Oxon 1960, MA Oxon 1964, PhD Southampton 1964; Mem., Inst. Brit. Georg. Governor, Richmond School, Yorks, 1969– . *Publications*: Misurata: a market town in Tripolitania, 1967; *contrib*. Contemp. Rev., Geog., Kulturgeografi, Tijdschrift voor Econ. en Soc. Geografie, Univ. Southampton Res. Ser. in Geog., Asian Affairs, ME Internat., Geog. Mag., Méditerranée, Fin. Times. *Address*: Dept of Geography, Science Laboratories, Univ. of Durham, Durham DH1 3LE.

Blake, Prof. John William, CBE; Professor of History, New University of Ulster, since Jan. 1972; *b* 1911; *m* 1938; two *s* one *d*. BA Hons London (Hist.), MA London 1938; Hon. DLitt Keele 1971, Hon. DLitt. Univ. of Botswana, Lesotho and Swaziland 1971. Asst Lectr, Lectr, Senior Lectr, QUB, 1934–50; Prof., Univ. of Keele, 1950–64; Vice-Chancellor, Univ. of Botswana, Lesotho and Swaziland, 1964–71. *Publications*: European Beginnings in West Africa, 1937; Europeans in West Africa, 2 vols, 1942; Official War History of Northern Ireland, 1956; *contrib*. historical jls. *Address*: Dept of History, New Univ. of Ulster, Coleraine, Co. Londonderry, Northern Ireland BT52 1SA.

Blake, Prof. Norman Francis, MA, BLitt; Professor of English Language, University of Sheffield, since 1973; *b* 1934; *m* 1965. BA Oxon 1956, BLitt Oxon 1959, MA Oxon 1960. Asst Lectr, Liverpool, 1959–61; Lectr, 1961–68; Sen. Lectr, 1968–73; Vis. Prof., Univ. Coll. Toronto, 1963–64. *Publications*: The History of the Jomsvikings, 1962; The Phoenix, 1964; Caxton and his World, 1969; Caxton's History of Reynard the Fox, 1970; Middle English Religious Prose, 1972; Selections from William Caxton, 1973; Caxton's Own Prose, 1974; *contrib*. Anglia, Archiv, Book Collector, Bull. J. Rylands Lib., Chaucer Rev., Essays and Studies, Gutenberg Jahrbuch, Leeds Stud. in Eng., Neophilologus, Neuphilologische Mitteilungen, Mod. Phil., Proc. Suffolk Inst. of Arch., Stud. in Phil., Traditio. *Address*: Dept of English Language, Univ. of Sheffield, Sheffield S10 2TN.

Blakemore, Harold, BA, PhD; Secretary, Institute of Latin American Studies, University of London, since 1965; *b* 1930; *m* 1955; one *s* one *d*. BA London 1951 (1st cl. Hons History), PhD London 1955; FRHistS 1965, Chilean Acad. of Hist. 1970. Asst to Director, Extramural Dept, Sheffield, 1955; Staff Tutor in History, Sheffield, 1957; Educn Officer, School of Oriental and African Studies, London, 1960; Co-ed. Jl of Latin American Studies, 1969– . *Publications*: Latin America, 1966, 4th edn 1972, Dutch edn 1966, Norwegian edn 1966; (with C. T. Smith), co-ed., Latin America: Geographical Perspectives, 1971; British Nitrates and Chilean Politics, 1886-1896, 1974; *contrib*. Aportes, Boletin de la Academie Chilena de la Historia, Hist. Today, Hispanic American Hist. Rev., Latin American Res. Rev., Pacific Hist. Rev., Ybk of World Affairs. *Address*: Institute of Latin American Studies, 31 Tavistock Square, WC1H 9HA.

Blamires, Dr David Malcolm; Reader in German, Manchester University, since 1973; *b* 1936. BA Cambridge 1957, MA PhD Cambridge 1963. Asst Lectr in German, Manchester, 1960-63; Lectr, 1963–69; Sen. Lectr, 1969–73. Mem., Cttee, Brit. Branch of the Internat. Arthurian Soc., 1969– . *Publications*: Characterization and Individuality in Wolfram's 'Parzival', 1966; David Jones: Artist and Writer, 1971; A History of Quakerism in Liversedge and Scholes, 1973; trans. German tales in Medieval Comic Tales, ed Derek Brewer, 1973, *contrib*. Agenda, Mod. Lang. Rev. *Address*: Dept of German, The Univ., Manchester M13 9PL.

Blanchard, Dr Ian Stewart William, BSc (Econ), PhD; Lecturer, Department of Economic History, University of Edinburgh, since 1965; *b* 1942; *m* 1963. BSc (Econ) LSE 1963, PhD LSE 1967. *Publications*: The Duchy of Lancaster Estates in Derbyshire, 1485–1540, 1967; *contrib*. AHR, Econ. Hist. Rev., Northern Hist., Business Hist. *Address*: Dept of Economic History, Univ. of Edinburgh.

Bland, Beresford Maurice; University Librarian, University of Southampton, since 1961; *b* 1914; *m* 1945; one *s* one *d*. BCom Birmingham 1936, MCom Birmingham 1960; Mem., Library Assoc., 1936– (Mem., 1963– , Pres., 1968, SW Br.). University of Birmingham: Asst Librarian, 1936-40; 1946-50; Dep. Librarian, 1950-61. Mem., SCONUL, 1967– (Hon. Treasurer, 1968-73). *Address*: The Univ., Southampton SO9 5NH.

Bland, Dr David Edward; Lecturer in Economic History, University of Sheffield, since 1966; *b* 1940. BA Dunelm 1962, MLitt Dunelm 1968, PhD Sheffield 1968; ACommA 1970. Douglas Knoop Fellow in Econ. Hist., Sheffield, 1964; Sub-Dean of Social Sciences, 1970– . *Publications*: (with K. W. Watkins) Can Britain Survive?, 1971. *Address*: The Univ., Sheffield S10 2TN.

Bland, Desmond Sparling, MA; Deputy Director, Institute of Extension Studies, University of Liverpool, since 1970; *b* 1916; *m* 1944; one *s* one *d*. BA Cambridge 1938 (Eng.), MA Cambridge 1942, Teacher's Dip. Cambridge 1939. Staff Tutor, Dept of Extra-

Mural Studies, King's Coll., Newcastle upon Tyne, 1946–58; Asst Dir, Dept of Extra-Mural Studies, Univ. of Liverpool, 1958–69. *Publications*: Chapbooks and Garlands, 1956; Early Records of Furnival's Inn, 1957; A Bibliography of the Inns of Court and Chancery, 1966; ed, Gesta Grayorum, 1968; *contrib.* Eng. Studies, Notes and Queries, Rev. English Studies, Shakespeare Survey. *Address*: Inst. of Extension Studies, Univ. of Liverpool, Liverpool L69 3BX.

Blanning, Dr Timothy Charles William; Assistant Lecturer in History, University of Cambridge, since 1972, and Fellow and Tutor, Sidney Sussex College, Cambridge, since 1968; *b* 1942. BA Cambridge 1963, MA 1967, PhD 1967; Res. Fellow, Sidney Sussex Coll. Cambridge, 1965; Tutor for Admissions, 1968–73. *Publications*: Joseph II and Enlightened Despotism, 1970; Reform and Revolution in Mainz, 1743–1803, 1974. *Address*: Sidney Sussex College, Cambridge.

Blaug, Prof. Mark, PhD; Professor of the Economics of Education, University of London Institute of Education, since 1967; *b* 1927; *m* 1969; two *s*. BA Queens Coll., New York City 1950, MA Columbia Univ., New York City 1952, PhD 1955; Mem., Royal Econ. Soc. Asst Prof. of Economics, Yale Univ., 1954–63; Reader, Univ. of London Inst. of Educn, 1965–67. Mem., SSRC Economics Bd, CNAA Economics Bd. *Publications*: Ricardian Economics, 1958; Economic Theory in Retrospect, 1962, 2nd edn 1968; (with R. Layard and M. Woodhall) Causes of Graduate Unemployment in India, 1969; Introduction to the Economics of Education, 1970; *contrib.* Jl Political Econ., Qly Jl Econ., Economica, Manchester School Econ. Jl, Jl of Human Resources. *Address*: 56 Gordon Square, WC1.

Blench, Dr John Wheatley; Senior Lecturer, Department of English, University of Durham, since 1970; *b* 1926. BA Cantab 1949 (English Tripos pt 1, cl. 2, div. 1 (1949); pt 2, cl. 1 (1950)), MA Cantab 1954, PhD Cantab 1956, Hart Prize for Original Composition, St John's Coll., Cambridge, 1950 Asst Lectr, Edinburgh Univ., 1953–55; Lectr, Aberdeen Univ., 1956–65; Lectr, Durham Univ., 1965–70. Acting Editor, Durham Univ. Jl, 1971–72. *Publications*: Preaching in England in the late Fifteenth and Sixteenth Centuries, 1964; *contrib.* Cambridge Jl, Durham Univ. Jl, RES. *Address*: Dept of English, Univ. of Durham, Elvet Riverside, New Elvet, Durham DH1 3JT.

Bligh, Donald Arthur; Lecturer, University Teaching Methods Unit, London, since 1970; *b* 1936; *m* 1968; one *d.* Teacher's Cert. Leeds 1958, BA Hons Leeds 1961 (Geography), BA Jt Hons London, 1967 (Psychology and Philosophy); Lectr, London Inst. of Educn 1967–70. *Publications*: (with Ruth M. Beard) Research into Teaching Methods in Higher Education, 1967, 3rd edn 1971; Teaching Students in Groups, 1971; What's the Use of Lectures?, 1971, 3rd edn 1972; ed, Background Papers, for New Lecturers Introductory Course, 1973. *Address*: UTMU, 55 Gordon Square, WC1H 0NT.

Blight, Dr Barry James Norman; Lecturer, Department of Statistics, Birkbeck College, University of London, since 1967; *b* 1939; *m* 1965; one *d.* MA Cambridge 1961 (Mathematics), Postgraduate Diploma in Math. Stats Cambridge 1962, MPhil London 1967, PhD London 1971; FSS 1962. Lectr, Bath, 1964–67. *Publications*: *contrib.* American Statistician, Biometrika, Jl Royal Stat. Soc., Technometrics. *Address*: Dept of Statistics, Birkbeck College, Malet Street, WC1E 7HX.

Blinkhorn, Dr Richard Martin, BA, AM, DPhil; Lecturer in History, University of Lancaster, since 1968; *b* 1941; *m* 1967. BA Oxon 1963 (1st cl. History), AM Stanford 1964, DPhil Oxon 1970. Asst Lectr, Univ. of Lancaster, 1966–68. *Publications*: *contrib.* Euro. Studies Rev., Hist. Jl, Jl Contemp. History, Iberian Studies. *Address*: Dept of History, Univ. of Lancaster, Lancaster LA1 4YW.

Bliss, Prof. Alan Joseph, MA, BLitt, MRIA; Professor of Old and Middle English, University College, Dublin, since 1974; *b* 1921; *m* 1949; four *s* three *d.* BA London 1940, BLitt Oxon 1948, MA Oxon 1948; MRIA 1965. Lectr, Wadham Coll., Oxford, 1948; Lectr, Oriel and Brasenose Colls, Oxford, 1949–53; Prof. of English, Royal Univ. of Malta, 1953–57; Prof. of English Language, Istanbul, 1957–59; Lectr, Univ. Coll., Dublin, 1961–66; Assoc. Prof., 1966–74. *Publications*: Sir Orfeo, 1954, 2nd edn 1966; The Metre of Beowulf, 1958, 2nd edn 1962; Sir Launfal, 1960; An Introduction to Old English Metre, 1962; A Dictionary of Foreign Words and Phrases, 1966; (with T. P. Dunning) The Wanderer, 1969; *contrib.* Anglia, Archivum Linguisticum, Litera, Medium Ævum, Notes and Queries, PRIA, RES, Speculum. *Address*: Dept of English, Univ. College, Belfield, Dublin 4.

Bliss, Prof. Christopher John: Professor of Economics, University of Essex, since 1971; *b* 1940; *m* 1964; one *s* one *d.* BA Cantab 1962, PhD Cantab 1966. Part-time Research Officer, Dept of Applied Econ., 1964–65; Asst Lectr, 1965–68; Lectr, 1968–71, Cambridge. *Publications*: *contrib.* Econ. Jl, Rev. of Econ. Studies. *Address*: Univ. of Essex, Wivenhoe Park, Colchester CO4 3SQ.

Bliss, Prudence, BA, ATD; Lecturer in History of Art, Fine Art Department, University of Newcastle upon Tyne, since 1965; *b* 1932. BA Hons London 1955 (2/I History of Art); NDD 1960, ATD, 1961. *Address*: Dept of Fine Art, Univ. of Newcastle upon Tyne, Newcastle upon Tyne NE1 7RU.

Blit, Lucjan; Lecturer, Government Department, LSE, and History Department, SSEES (London), since 1968; *b* 1908; *m* 1948; one *s* two *d.* MA Warsaw 1932; Mem.; Pol. Sci., Assoc.; Royal Inst. of Internat. Affairs; Inst. of History, London. Heyter Fellow, SSEES, 1965; Fellow, Centre for Internat. Studies, LSE, 1967. *Publications*: Gomułka's Poland, 1959; The Eastern

Pretender, 1965; Anti-Jewish Campaign in People's Poland, 1968; The Origins of Polish Socialism, 1971; *contrib.* Slavonic and E Europ. Rev. *Address*: LSE, Houghton Street, WC2A 2AE.

Bloch, Jean Helen; Lecturer, Department of French, Bedford College, London, since 1968; *b* 1940; *m* 1963; one *s* one *d*. BA London 1961 (1st cl. Hons French), MA 1964; Temp. Asst Lectr, Bedford Coll., 1966–67; Asst Lectr, 1967–68. *Publications: contrib.* French Studies, Paedagogica Historica. *Address*: Bedford College, Regent's Park, London NW1 4NS.

Blois, Keith John; Senior Lecturer, Department of Management Studies, Loughborough University of Technology, since 1973 (Lecturer, 1966–73); Post-Graduate Course Tutor, since 1973; *b* 1939; *m* 1967; two *s*. BA Bristol 1960 (Economics with Statistics); Mem., Soc. Business Econ. Assoc., Ind. Marketing Res. Assoc. *Publications:* (with D. W. Cowell) Short Cases in Marketing Management, 1973; *contrib.* Jl of Ind. Econ., Qly Jl of Econs. *Address*: Dept of Management Studies Loughborough Univ. of Technology, Loughborough LE11 3TU.

Blondel, Prof. Jean Fernand Pierre; Professor of Government, University of Essex, since 1964; *b* 1929; *m* 1954; two *d*. Diplôme Institut d'Etudes Politiques Paris 1953, L en Droit Paris 1954, Dipl Et. Supres de Droit Paris 1955, BLitt Oxon 1955. Asst Lectr, Univ. of Keele, 1958–61; Lectr, Univ. of Keele, 1961–63; Vis. ACLS Fellow, Yale Univ., 1963–64; Vis. Prof., Carleton Univ., Ottawa, 1969–70; Vis. Prof., Institut d'Et. Pol., Paris, 1967– . Mem., Political Science Cttee, Social Science Res. Council, 1965–69; Mem., Nat. Cttee Foreign Area Fellowship Program, 1970– ; Exec. Dir, European Consortium for Political Res., 1970– . *Publications*: As condiçoes da vida politica in Paraiba, 1960; Voters Parties and Leaders, 1963, 3rd edn 1970, French edn 1964, German edn 1964; (with F. Ridley) Public Administration in France, 1964, 2nd edn 1968; (with F. Bealey and P. McCann) Constituency Politics, 1964; The Government of France, 4th edn 1973; A Reader in Comparative Government, 1968; An Introduction to Comparative Government, 1969; (with V. Herman) A Workbook in Comparative Government, 1972; Comparing Political Systems, 1972; Comparative Legislatures, 1973; *contrib.* Canadian Jl of Polit. Science, Government and Opposition, Parl. Aff., Polit. Studies, Public Admin, Revue française de science politique, Revue française de sociologie. *Address*: Dept of Government, Univ. of Essex, Wivenhoe Park, Colchester CO4 3SQ.

Bloomfield, Barry Cambray; Librarian, School of Oriental and African Studies, University of London, since 1971; *b* 1931; *m* 1958. University Coll. of SW, 1949–52 (BA); University Coll., London, 1954–55 (Dipl. in Librarianship); Birkbeck College, London, 1956–60 (MA); FLA 1959; Mem.: Library Assoc.; Bibliographical Soc.; Printing Historical Soc. Asst Librarian, British

Library of Political and Econ. Sci., LSE, 1961–63; Deputy Librarian, Sch. of Oriental and African Studies, 1963–71. *Publications*: W. H. Auden: a bibliography, 1964. 2nd edn 1972; ed, The Autobiography of Sir James Kay Shuttleworth, 1964; Theses on Asia, 1877–1964, 1967; ed, The acquisition and provision of foreign books by national and university libraries in the United Kingdom, 1972; *contrib.* Brit. Jl Educnl Stud., Library. *Address*: School of Oriental and African Studies, Malet Street, WC1E 7HP.

Bloor, David Charles, MA, PhD; Lecturer in Science Studies, Science Studies Unit, University of Edinburgh, since 1967; *b* 1942; *m* 1965; one *s*. BA Keele 1964 (Mathematics and Philosophy), BA Cambridge 1966 (Psychology), MA Cambridge 1972, PhD Edinburgh 1972. Asst Lectr, Univ. of Strathclyde, 1966–67. *Publications: contrib.* Australasian Jl of Philosophy, Brit. Jl for the Philosophy of Science, Perception and Psychophysics, Science Studies. *Address*: Science Studies Unit, 34 Buccleuch Place, Edinburgh.

Blumenthal, Dr Henry J.; Lecturer in Greek, University of Liverpool, since 1967; *b* 1936; *m* 1966; one *s* one *d*. BA Cantab 1960, PhD Cantab 1964. Lectr in Classics, Mount Allison Univ., 1963–65; Asst Lectr in Greek, Univ. of Liverpool, 1965–67. *Publications*: Plotinus' Psychology, 1971; *contrib.* Arch. Gesch. Phil., Hermes, Int. Philos. Qly, Philologus, Phronesis. *Address*: Dept of Greek, Univ. of Liverpool, Liverpool L69 3BX.

Blunden, Dr John Russell; Senior Lecturer in Geography, The Open University, since 1970; on secondment, Environmental Research Unit, Imperial College, University of London, since 1973; *b* 1934; *m* 1966; one *s* one *d*. BA Social Studies Exon 1958, PhD Exon 1965; FRGS, Mem., Inst. of Brit. Geog. Lectr in Geography and Fellow, Centre for Educ. Technology, Univ. of Sussex, 1966–69. *Publications*: (jtly) Studies in Adult Education, 1969; (jtly) Understanding Society, 1970; Spatial Aspects of Society, 1971; (jtly) Exeter Essays in Geography, 1971; (jtly) New Trends in Geography, 1972; Britain's Extractive Industries and Land Use Planning, 1972; Mineral Resources of Britain, 1974; *contrib.* Adult Educn, Geog., Home Studies, Jl of Film and Television Arts, NECCTA Jl, Times Ed. Supp., Trans Inst. Quarrying, US Bureau of Mines Symposium, William and Mary Qly. *Address*: Faculty of Social Science, The Open Univ., Walton Hall, Milton Keynes MK7 6AA; Imperial Coll. of Science and Technology, SW7 2AZ.

Blunt, Dr Michael Edward; Senior Lecturer in Politics, Department of Sociology, Government and Administration, University of Salford, since 1971; *b* 1932; *m* 1963; one *s* two *d*. BSc (Econ.) London 1953, PhD London 1957. Lectr: Univ. of Ife, Nigeria 1962–64; Univ of Salford (previously Royal Coll. of Advanced Technology, Salford), 1965–71. *Publications: contrib.* African Affairs.

Parliamentary Affairs. *Address*: Dept of Sociology, Government and Administration, Univ. of Salford, Salford M5 4WT.

Blyth, Prof. William Alan Lansdell; Sydney Jones Professor of Education, School of Education, University of Liverpool, since 1964; *b* 1921; *m* 1948; one *s*. BA (Hons) Cambridge 1943 (Historical Tripos Part I; Geographical Tripos Pt I), Cert. in Educn Cambridge 1944, MA Cambridge 1947, MEd Nottingham 1951, PhD Manchester 1961. Lectr in Educn, Keele, 1951–53; Lectr, and Sen. Lectr, in Educn, Manchester, 1954–64. Univ. Mem., Lancashire Educn Cttee, 1964–67; Univ. Mem., Liverpool Educn Cttee, 1970– ; Dir, Schools Council Project on History, Geography and Social Science 8–13, 1971–74. *Publications*: English Primary Education: a Sociological Description, 1965; contrib. Field Studies for Schools, ed M. S. Dilke, 1965; Linking Home and School, ed Craft, Raynor and Cohen, 1967; Development in Learning, vol. 3, Contents of Education, ed Lunzer and Morris, 1969; The Curriculum: Research, Innovation and Change, ed Taylor and Walton, 1973; *contrib*. Brit. Jl Educnl Studies, Educn 3–13, Educn Rev., Jl Curric. Studies, Sociological Rev. *Address*: School of Education, Univ. of Liverpool, PO Box 147, Liverpool L69 3BX.

Boa, Elizabeth; Lecturer, German Department, Nottingham University, since 1965; *b* 1939. MA Glasgow 1961. Lektorin, Univ. Des Saarlandes, Saarbrücken, 1964–65. *Publications*: The Rococo Verserzählung, in, Periods in German Literature, vol. II, ed J. H. Ritchie, 1969; (with J. H. Reid) Critical Strategies: German fiction in the twentieth century, 1972; six entries in A Dictionary of Modern Critical Terms, ed Roger Fowler, 1973; *contrib*. GLL, MLR. *Address*: German Dept, The Univ., Nottingham NG7 2RD.

Boag, Hugh Alexander; Senior Lecturer, Department of Modern Languages, University of Strathclyde, since 1972, Lecturer 1964–72; *b* 1930; *m* 1956; one *s* one *d*. MA Glasgow 1953 (1st cl. French and German), DipEd Glasgow 1954, MLitt Glasgow 1971. *Address*: Dept of Modern Languages, Univ. of Strathclyde (Livingstone Tower), Richmond Street, Glasgow.

Boakes, Dr Robert Alan; Lecturer in Experimental Psychology, Laboratory of Experimental Psychology, University of Sussex, since 1967; *b* 1939; *m* 1967; two *s* one *d*. BA Cantab 1962, PhD Harvard 1966; Mem., EPS, 1969. Asst Lectr, Sussex, 1966–67; Vis. Lectr, Harvard, 1968; Vis. Lectr, Princeton, 1971–72. *Publications*: ed (with M. S. Halliday), Inhibition and Learning, 1972; *contrib*. Jl Experimental Analysis Behavior, Qly Jl Experimental Psychology. *Address*: Lab. of Experimental Psychology, Univ. of Sussex, Brighton BN1 9RH.

Boal, Dr Frederick Wilgar, MA, MS, PhD; Senior Lecturer, Department of Geography, Queen's University, Belfast, since 1972 (Lecturer, 1963–72); *b* 1934; *m* 1961; two *s* one *d*. BA Belfast 1956, MA Belfast 1958, MS Michigan 1960, PhD Michigan 1963.

Mem.: Inst. Brit. Geogs, Regional Sci. Assoc., Assoc. Amer. Geogs. Asst Prof., Univ. of Calgary, 1961–63. Mem.: Ulster Countryside Cttee, 1967–68; Lagan Valley Country Pk Co-ord. Cttee, 1969– . *Publications*: contrib. Canad. Geog., Econ. Geog., Econ. Soc. Rev., Geog. Jl, Irish Geog., Traffic Qly. *Address*: Dept of Geography, Queen's Univ., Belfast BT7 1NN.

Board, Dr Christopher; Senior Lecturer in Geography, Geography Department, London School of Economics, since 1969; *b* 1932. BA London 1955 (Hons), MA Cantab 1959, PhD Rhodes 1961; Mem.: RGS; Inst. of Brit. Geographers; Geographical Assoc.; Brit. Cartographic Assoc.; S Afr. Geographical Soc. Rhodes University: Asst Res. Officer, 1955; Res. Officer, 1957; Tutor, University Coll., Swansea, 1958; Univ. Demonstrator, Cambridge, 1959; Lectr, LSE, 1963. Mem., Cartography sub-Cttee, Brit. Nat. Cttee for Geography. *Publications*: The Border Region: natural environment and land use in the Eastern Cape Province (ed E. D. Mountain and J. V. L. Rennie), 1962; *contrib*. Annals, Assoc. Amer. Geog., Internat. Yearbook Cartog., Reg. Stud., S Afr. Geograph. Jl, S Afr. Jl Econs, S Afr. Jl Sci. *Address*: London School of Economics, Houghton Street, WC2A 2AE.

Boardman, John, FBA; Reader in Classical Archaeology, University of Oxford, since 1959 and Fellow of Merton College, Oxford, 1963 (Sub-Warden, 1971–73); *b* 1927; *m* 1952; one *s* one *d*. MA Cambridge 1952; FBA 1969, FSA, Fellow of German Archaeological Inst., Corresponding Fellow of Bavarian Academy of Sciences. Asst Dir., Brit. School at Athens, 1952–55; Asst Keeper, Ashmolean Museum, Oxford, 1955–59; Ed., Jl Hellenic Studies, 1958–65; Vis. Prof., Columbia Univ., NY, 1965. Mem.: Managing Cttees of Hellenic Soc., Brit. School at Athens, Soc. for Promotion of Libyan Studies. *Publications*: The Cretan Collection in Oxford, 1961; The Date of the Knossos Tablets, 1963; Island Gems, 1963; Greek Art, 1964, rev. edn 1973; The Greeks Overseas, 1964, rev. edn 1974; Excavations at Tocra 1963–65, 1966; Greek Emporio, 1967; Pre-Classical Style and Civilisation, 1967; Engraved Gems, 1968; Archaic Greek Gems, 1968; Greek Gems and Finger Rings, 1970; (with D. Kurtz) Greek Burial Customs, 1971; Athenian Black Figure Vases, 1974; *contrib*. Jl Hellenic Studies, Ann. Brit. School at Athens, Revue Archéologique. *Address*: Ashmolean Museum, Oxford.

Bocock, Robert James; Lecturer in Sociology, Brunel University, since 1966; *b* 1940; *m* 1964. BA Leeds 1962; PGCE Inst. Educn London 1963; PhD Brunel 1973; Mem., BSA. *Publications*: Ritual in Industrial Society, 1974; *contrib*. Brit. Jl of Sociology, Social Compass. *Address*: Dept of Sociology, Brunel Univ., Uxbridge, Mddx UB8 3TH.

Boddy, David; Lecturer in Business Economics, Department of Management Studies, University of Glasgow, since 1965; *b* 1940;

m 1967; one *s* one *d*. BSc (Econ) London (University College) 1961. Asst in Dept of Social and Economic Research, 1963–65. Additional Mem., Industrial Tribunals, 1971– . *Publications*: Labour Problems of Technological Change, 1970; Labour Markets under Different Employment Conditions, 1971; *contrib*. Scott. Jl Political Econ. *Address*: Adam Smith Building, Univ. of Glasgow, Glasgow.

Boddy, Dr John; Lecturer in Psychology, Department of Psychology, University of Manchester, since 1968; *b* 1941; *m* 1964. BA Reading 1964 (2/I Psychology), PhD Manchester 1970 (Science); Graduate Mem., BPsS. Res. Asst, Univ. of Aston in Birmingham, 1964–65; Asst Lectr, Manchester Univ., 1965–68. Asst Sec., Manchester AUT, 1966–68. *Publications*: *contrib*. Electroenceph. clin. Neurophysiol., Psychol. Reports, Qly Jl Exp. Psychol. *Address*: Dept of Psychology, Univ. of Manchester, Oxford Road, Manchester M13 9PL.

Boden, Dr Margaret Ann, MA, PhD; Reader in Philosophy and Psychology, School of Social Sciences, University of Sussex, since 1973 (Lecturer, 1965–73); *b* 1936; *m* 1967; one *s* one *d*. BA Cantab 1958 (1st cl. Natural Sciences for Medicine), Pt II Moral Sciences Tripos (1st cl.) Cantab 1959 (History of Modern Philosophy), MA Cantab 1962, AM Harvard 1964 (Social Psychology), PhD Harvard 1969 (Social Psychology). Asst Lectr in Philosophy, Univ. of Birmingham, 1959–62; Lectr in Philosophy, Univ. of Birmingham, 1962–65; Harkness Fellow, Harvard Grad. Sch., 1962–64. Sec., Analysis Cttee, 1964–71; Mem., 1971– ; Sec., Brit. Soc. Philos. Sci., 1967–68; Cttee Mem., 1966–68. *Publications*: Purposive Explanation in Psychology, 1972; *contrib*. Jl Personal., Philos. Qly, Philos., Philos. Sci., Proc. Aristot. Soc., Ratio, Brit. Jl Philos. Sci. *Address*: School of Social Sciences, Univ. of Sussex, Falmer, Brighton BN1 9RH.

Boer, George de; *see* de Boer.

Boffey, Dr Thomas Brian; Lecturer, Department of Computational and Statistical Science, University of Liverpool, since 1969; *b* 1939; *m* 1965; two *s* one *d*. BSc Liverpool 1960 (Maths), MSc Liverpool 1962 (Pure Maths), PhD London 1967 (Applied Maths); MBCS 1972, Mem., OR Soc. Lectr, Malawi Univ., 1967–69. Sec./Treas., AISB, 1973– . *Address*: Dept of Computational and Statistical Science, Univ. of Liverpool, Brownlow Hill, Liverpool.

Bogdanow, Dr Fanni; Reader, Department of French, Manchester University, since 1974; *b* 1927. BA Hons Manchester 1948 (French), MA 1953, PhD 1957, DipEd 1949; Leverhulme Res. Fellow, Liverpool Univ., 1956–57; Asst Lectr, Manchester Univ., 1957–60; Lectr, 1960–74. *Publications*: The Romance of the Grail, 1966; La Folie Lancelot, 1965; *contrib*. Univ. of Texas Studies in English, Bull. Internat. Arthurian Soc., French Studies, Medium Ævum, Romania, Romance Philology, Nottingham Medieval Studies, Zeitschrift für Romanische Philologie. *Ad-*

dress: French Dept, Manchester Univ., Oxford Road, Manchester M13 9PL.

Bolgar, Robert Ralph, MA, PhD; Fellow and Director of Studies in Modern Languages, King's College, Cambridge, since 1956; Reader in the History of the Classical Tradition, University of Cambridge, since 1973; *b* 1913; *m* 1940; one *s* two *d*. BA Cantab 1936, MA Cantab 1938, PhD Cantab 1939. Fellow, King's Coll., Cambridge, 1939–54; Research Fellow, Univ. of Durham Inst. of Educn, 1954–56. *Publications*: The Classical Heritage and its Beneficiaries 1954; ed, Classical Influences on European Cultures, 1970; part-author: Cambridge Modern History, vol. 6, 1965; Governing Elites, ed R. Wilkinson, 1967; Humanism in France, ed A. Levi, 1970; The Changing Curriculum (History of Education Society), 1971; Cambridge Bibliography of English Literature, vol. I, ed G. Watson (Writings in Latin; Literary Relations with the Continent), 1974; *contrib*. Cambridge Jl, Didaskalos, Durham Res. Rev., Forum Mod. Lang. Studies, French Studies, Theology, 20th Century Studies, Year Book of Educn (1956). *Address*: King's College, Cambridge.

Bolger, Anthony William, MA; Lecturer in Educational Psychology, Institute of Education, University of Keele, since 1968; *b* 1927; *m* 1953; two *s* one *d*. Teachers' Cert. London 1944, BA Tasmania 1960, MA Tasmania 1965; Associate, British Psychological Soc. Asst Prof. of Education, Memorial Univ. of Newfoundland, 1963. Educnl Psychologist, Cornwall, CC, 1964–68. *Publications*: Child Study and Guidance, 1974; *contrib*. Forum in Educn, New Era, Brit. Jl Guid. and Counselling, Therapeutic Educn. *Address*: Institute of Education, Univ. of Keele, Staffs ST5 5BG.

Bolsover, George Henry, CBE, MA PhD; Director of School of Slavonic and East European Studies, University of London, since 1947; *b* 1910; *m* 1939; one *d*. BA Liverpool 1931 (1st cl. History), MA Liverpool 1933; PhD London 1933; FRHistS. Resident Tutor in Adult Educn, Univ. of Birmingham, 1937–38; Asst Lectr in History, Univ. of Manchester, 1938–43. Attaché and First Sec., British Embassy, Moscow, 1943–47. Mem., Cttee of Governors, LSE, 1955– . Treasury Cttee for Studentships in Foreign Languages and Cultures, 1948–58; UGC Sub-Cttee on Oriental, African, Slavonic and E European Studies, 1961–71; Adv. Cttee on Educn of Poles in Great Britain, 1948–67; Min. of Educn Cttee on Teaching of Russian, 1960–62; Inst. of Historical Research Cttee, 1948– ; Treasurer, British Nat. Historical Cttee, 1966–72; Chm., Council for Extra-Mural Studies, Univ. of London, 1968– . *Publications*: contrib. Essays presented to Sir Lewis Namier, 1956; Trans RHistS, 1957; *contrib*. EHR, Int. Affairs, Jl Modern History, Slavonic and East European Rev. *Address*: School of Slavonic and East European Studies, Univ. of London, Malet Street, WC1E 7HU.

Bolster, Richard Henry; Lecturer, Department of French, Bristol University, since

1967; b 1937; m 1973. BA TCD 1960 (1st cl. Modern Languages and Literature); Doctorate in French Literature Paris 1966. Asst Lectr, Bristol, 1965–67; Sen. Lectr in French, Ahmadu Bello Univ., Kano, 1974–75. *Publications*: Stendhal, Balzac et le féminisme romantique, 1970; *contrib.* Fr. Studies, Hermathena, Stendhal Club. *Address*: The Univ., Bristol BS8 1TH.

Bolt, Dr Christine Anne; Senior Lecturer in History, University of Kent at Canterbury, since 1973; b 1940; m 1962. BA London 1961, PhD London 1966; Mem., Brit. Assoc. Amer. Studies, Amer. Hist. Assoc. Asst Lectr, Univ. of Kent, 1966–67, Lectr, 1967–73; Vis. apptmts, American univs: Hobart and William Smith Colls, NY, 1968; Wayne State Univ., Detroit, 1969–70; Univ. of Maine, Orono, 1970; Univ. of North. Illinois, 1970–71. *Publications*: The Anti-Slavery Movement and Reconstruction, 1969; Victorian Attitudes to Race, 1971, 1974. A History of the United States, 1974. *Address*: Eliot College, Univ. of Kent, Canterbury, Kent CT2 7NZ.

Bond, Brian James; Lecturer in War Studies, Department of War Studies, King's College, London, since 1966; b 1936; m 1962. BA Oxon 1959, MA London 1962; Mem., Council, RUSI, Mem., IISS. Tutor in History, Exeter Univ., 1961–62; Lectr in Modern History, Liverpool, 1962–66; Vis. Prof. of Military History and Strategy, Univ. of W Ontario, 1972–73. Moderator in History, Royal Naval Coll., Dartmouth, 1969– . *Publications*: ed, Victorian Military Campaigns, 1967– ; The Victorian Army and the Staff College 1854–1914, 1972; ed, Chief of Staff: the diaries of Lt-Gen. Sir Henry Pownall, vol. 1: 1933–1940, 1972, Vol. 2: 1940–1944, 1973; *contrib.* New Cambridge Modern History, vol. XII; Hist. Today, Military Affairs, Royal United Service Inst. Jl, Victorian Studies. *Address*: Dept of War Studies, King's College, Strand, WC2R 2LS.

Bond, Godfrey William, MA; Fellow since 1950, and Senior Tutor since 1963, Pembroke College, Oxford; Lecturer in Classics, since 1950; b 1925; m 1959; one s two d. BA Dublin 1949 (1st cl. Classics), MA Oxon 1951; Mem., Cttee Egypt. Exploration Soc. Mem., Inst. for Advanced Study, Princeton, 1969; Oxford Univ. Sen. Proctor, 1964; General Board, 1970. *Publications*: ed, Euripides: Hypsipyle, 1963; *contrib.* Cl. Rev., Gnomon, Hermathena. *Address*: Pembroke College, Oxford.

Bonner, Stanley Frederick; Reader in Latin, University of Liverpool, since 1973; b 1912; m 1937. BA Cantab 1933 (1st cl. Classics), MA 1937; Cromer Prize (British Acad.) 1936, Hon. Sec., Classical Assoc. (Liverpool Branch), 1935–40, 1947– , Mem., Central Council, 1950–53. Asst Lectr in Latin, Univ. of Liverpool, 1933–36, Lectr, 1936–40; Lectr in Latin and Greek, 1945–49; Sen. Lectr in Classics, 1949–73; External Examiner, Univ. of Sheffield, 1956–59. Staff Officer, Royal Army Educnl Corps, 1941–45; Hon. Major, 1945. *Publications*: The Literary Treatises of Dionysius of Halicarn-

ssaus, 1939; Roman Declamation in the late Republic and early Empire, 1949; Roman Oratory, in, Fifty Years of Classical Scholarship, 1954; *contrib.* American Jl of Philol., Classical Rev. *Address*: School of Classics, Univ. of Liverpool, 12 Abercromby Square, Liverpool.

Bonwick, Colin Charles, MA, PhD; Lecturer in US History, Department of American Studies, University of Keele, since 1964; b 1935; m 1965; two s. BA Oxford 1959 (History), MA Oxford 1962, PhD Maryland 1969. *Address*: Dept of American Studies, The Univ., Keele, Staffs ST5 5BG.

Booth, Dr David A.; Senior Lecturer, Department of Psychology, University of Birmingham, since 1973; b 1938; m 1966; two s. BA Oxon 1958, MA Oxon 1963, BSc Oxon 1960, BA London 1962, PhD London 1964; Member: Exptl Psychol. Soc.; Biochem. Soc.; European Brain and Behaviour Soc.; European Chemoreception Res. Organisation. Res. Faculty, Yale Univ., 1964–66; Asst Prof., Rockefeller Univ., 1966; Res. Fellow, Univ. of Sussex, 1966–72; Lectr, Univ. of Birmingham, 1972–73. *Publications*: *contrib.* Biochim. Biophys. Acta, Brit. Jl Nutr., Brit. Jl Psychiat., Jl Chem. Soc., Jl Comp. Physiol. Psychol., Jl Neurochem., Jl Pharmacol. exptl Ther., Nature, Physiol. Behav., Qly Jl Exptl Psychol., Science. *Address*: Dept of Psychology, Elms Road, PO Box 363, Birmingham B15 2TT.

Booth, James; Lecturer, Department of English, University of Hull, since 1968; b 1945. BA Oxon 1966, BLitt Oxon 1971. *Address*: Dept of English, The Univ., Cottingham Road, Hull HU6 7RX.

Booth, Marjorie Brenda; Fellow and Tutor in Old French, St Anne's College, Oxford; m 1961; one s. BLitt Oxon 1953, MA Oxon 1954; Mem., Philological Soc. CUF Lectr, 1956. *Publications*: articles for encyclopaedia; working on Study of Old Provençal literature. *Address*: St Anne's College, Oxford.

Booth, Dr Thomas Geoffrey, BPharm, PhD, FPS, FIPharmM; Senior Lecturer, Pharmacy Practice Research Unit, University of Bradford, School of Studies in Pharmacy, since 1970; b 1927; m 1954, BPharm London 1951, PhD Bradford 1969; FPS 1951, FIPharmM 1964. Lectr, Univ. of Bradford, 1964. Chm., Inst. Pharmacy Management, 1971–73; Chm., Educn Cttee, Inst. Pharmacy Management, 1964– ; Examiner, Pharmaceutical Soc. of Gt Brit., 1960–71, Portsmouth Poly. (external), 1966– ; Mem., Senate, Univ. of Bradford, 1971– . *Publications*: *contrib.* Jl Pharm. Pharmacol., Pharm. Jl, Jl Hosp. Pharm., South African Pharm. Jl, Jl Occ. Therapy, Chem and Druggist, Retail Chem., Inquiry. *Address*: Pharmacy Practice Research Unit, School of Studies in Pharmacy, Univ. of Bradford, Bradford BD7 1DP.

Booth, Vera Southgate, MA, BCom; Senior Lecturer in Curriculum Studies, School of Education, University of Manchester, since

1972; *m* 1961. BCom Birmingham 1953 (Social Studies), Dip. Psych. Child. Birmingham 1954, MA Birmingham 1958 (Ed); Mem.: Brit. Psychol. Soc., NATE, UK Reading Assoc., Internat. Reading Assoc. Lectr in Curriculum Development, Manchester, 1960-72. Pres., UKRA, 1971-72; Mem., various Exec. Sub-Cttees of Internat. Reading Assoc. Mem., Govt's Cttee of Inquiry into Reading and the Use of English (Bullock Cttee), 1971-73. Ed. Consultant, Education Three to Thirteen, 1971- . *Publications*: Southgate Gp Reading Tests, One-Word Selection Test, 1959; Sounds and Words, Teachers' Book, 1959; Southgate Gp Reading Tests, Two-Sentence Completion Test, 1962; (with F. W. Warburton) i.t.a.: An Independent Evaluation, 1969; (with G. R. Roberts) Reading – Which Approach?, 1970; i.t.a.: What Is The Evidence?, 1970; Beginning Reading, 1972; ed, Literacy at all Levels, 1972; and 60 children's reading books, 1959-72; *contrib.* Brit. Jl Educnl Psychol., Educnl Res., Educnl Rev., Reading Res. Qly, Trends in Educn, Educn 3-13, Reading Teachers, Reading. *Address*: School of Education, Univ. of Manchester, Manchester M13 9PL.

Boothroyd, Hylton; Reader in Operational Research, School of Industrial and Business Studies, University of Warwick, since 1966; *b* 1934; *m* 1959; one *s* two *d*. BSc London 1955 (Mathematics); Mem., Operational Research Soc.; Operational Research, NCB, 1956-66. *Publications*: *contrib.* OR Quarterly. *Address*: School of Industrial and Business Studies, Univ. of Warwick, Coventry CV4 7AL.

Borger, Robert; Senior Lecturer, Psychology Department, Brunel University, since 1967; *b* 1927; *m* 1957; three *s* one *d*. BSc Wales 1947 (Mathematics), MA Oxon 1954 (Psychology and Philosophy); Member: BPsS; Experimental Psychology Soc.; Brit. Soc. for the Philosophy of Science; Artificial Intelligence and Simulation of Behaviour Group. Univ. of Manchester, 1954-58; Brunel Univ., 1958- . *Publications*: (with A. E. M. Seaborne) The Psychology of Learning, 1st edn 1966, 6th Reprint 1973; (with Frank Cioffi) Explanation in the Behavioural Sciences, 1974; *contrib.* Qly jl of Experimental Psychology. *Address*: Dept of Psychology, Brunel Univ., Uxbridge, Middlesex.

Borkowski, Jerzy Andrzej, LLB; Lecturer in Law, University of Bristol, since 1968; *b* 1943; *m* 1967 (marr. diss. 1972); *m* 1973. LLB London 1965 (1st cl. Hons); Barrister, Gray's Inn. Asst Lectr, Univ. of Bristol, 1965-68. *Publications*: *contrib.* Mod. Law Rev., Law Qly Rev. *Address*: Faculty of Law, Univ. of Bristol, Bristol BS8 1TH.

Borland, Dr Harold Howie; Reader in Scandinavian Studies, University of Hull, since 1971; *b* 1911; *m* 1960. BA Cantab 1933, MA Cantab 1946, PhD Cantab 1954. Lector in English, Heidelberg, 1936-39; Coll. Lectr in German, St Catharine's Coll., Cambridge, 1948-51; Dir of Studies in German, St Catharine's Coll., Cambridge,

1952-53; Asst Lectr in Scandinavian Studies, Manchester, 1955-59; Lectr in Swedish, Hull, 1960-66; Sen. Lectr in Swedish, Hull, 1966-71; in charge of Scandinavian Studies, Hull, 1970- . *Publications*: Nietzsche's Influence on Swedish Literature, 1956; Swedish for Students, 1970; *contrib.* Mod. Drama, Scandinavian Studies. *Address*: Dept of Scandinavian Studies, The Univ., Hull HU6 7RX.

Borland, Winifred Margaret Dodd; Senior Lecturer in Spanish, University of Hull, since 1970; *b* 1921; *m* 1960. BA Cantab 1943 (1st cl. Mod. and Med. Langs), MA Cantab 1949. Asst Lectr, Leeds Univ., 1946-48; Asst Lectr, Manchester Univ., 1949-52; Lectr, Manchester Univ., 1952-60; Lectr, Hull Univ., 1963-70. Mem., Cttee, Assoc. of Brit. Hispanists, 1956-59. *Publications*: as Margaret Wilson: ed, Tirso de Molina: Antona Garcia, 1957; Spanish Drama of the Golden Age, 1969; *contrib.* BHS, HR, MLR. *Address*: Dept of Hispanic Studies, The Univ. Hull HU6 7RX.

Borras, Prof. Frank Marshall; Professor of Russian Studies, University of Leeds, since 1966; *b* 1918; *m* 1947; one *d*. BA Oxon 1947, MA Oxon 1960. Lectr, Glasgow Univ., 1951-56; Univ. of Leeds: Lectr, 1956-59; Sen. Lectr, 1959-66. *Publications*: Russian Syntax, 1959, 2nd edn 1971; Russian Prose Composition, 1962; Maxim Gorky the Writer, 1967. *Address*: Dept of Russian Studies, Univ. of Leeds, Leeds LS2 9JT.

Borrie, Prof. Gordon Johnson, LLM; Professor of English Law and Director of the Institute of Judicial Administration, University of Birmingham, since 1969; *b* 1931; *m* 1960. LLB Manchester 1950 (Hons), LLM Manchester 1952; Barrister and Harmsworth Schol. (Middle Temple) 1952, Mem., Soc. of Public Teachers of Law. Sen. Lectr in Law, Univ. of Birmingham 1965-68. Sen. Treasurer, National Union of Students, 1955-58; Mem., Law Commn Adv. Panel and Contract Law, 1966- ; Governor, Birmingham Coll. of Commerce, 1966-70; Mem., Parole Bd for England and Wales, 1971- ; CNAA Legal Studies Bd, 1971- ; Consumer Protection Adv. Cttee, 1974- . *Publications*: Stevens and Borrie's Mercantile Law, 16th edn 1973; Commercial Law, 1962, 3rd edn 1970; (with A. L. Diamond) The Consumer, Society and the Law, 1964, 3rd edn 1973, Japanese edn 1972; Public Law, 1967, 2nd edn 1970; (with N. V. Lowe) Contempt of Court, 1973; *contrib.* Mod. Law Rev., New Law Jl, New Society. *Address*: Institute of Judicial Administration, Univ. of Birmingham, Birmingham B15 2TT.

Borthwick, Dr Edward Kerr; Reader in Greek, University of Edinburgh, since 1970; *b* 1925; *m* 1954; two *s* one *d*. MA Aberdeen 1946 (1st cl. Classics), BA Cantab 1948, MA, PhD Cantab 1951. Lectr in Classics, Leeds, 1951-55; Lectr in Greek, Edinburgh, 1955-70. *Publications*: *contrib.* Class. Rev., Class. Qly, Hermes, Jl Hellenic Studies, Mnemosyne, Class, Philol., etc. *Address*: Dept of Greek, David Hume Tower, George Square, Edinburgh.

Boss, Peter, MA; Senior Lecturer, School of Social Work, University of Leicester, since 1967; *b* 1925; *m* 1951; two *s* two *d*. Dip. Soc. Studies London 1951, Dip. Public Admin Bristol 1953, MA Liverpool 1965; Mem., Brit. Assoc. Social Workers, Social Admin Assoc. Social Science Dept, Liverpool Univ., 1961–67. Social Work, Children's Dept, Bristol, 1954–57; Children's Dept, Cheshire, 1957–61. *Publications:* Social Policy and the Young Delinquent, 1967; Exploration into Child Care, 1971; *contrib.* Child Care, Case Conf. *Address:* 107 Princes Road, Leicester LE1 7LA.

Bossanyi, Jo, BA, MIBiol; Senior Tutor in Biological Sciences, (teaching also Environmental Science), Department of Extra-Mural Studies, University of Southampton, since 1966; *b* 1924; *m* 1950; two *s* one *d*. BA Oxon 1946 (2nd cl. Zoology); Mem., Inst. Biol., Scient. Fellow, Zoological Soc., London; Mem. Mar. Biol. Assoc. UK, Brit. Ecol. Soc. Zoologist, Dove Marine Lab., Cullercoats (Dept of Zoology, Univ. of Newcastle upon Tyne), 1948–57. *Publications:* contrib. Jl Anim. Ecol., Jl Mar. Biol. Assoc. UK, Rep. Dove Mar. Lab., 3rd Ser. *Address:* Dept of Extra-Mural Studies, The Univ., Southampton SO9 5NH.

Bostock, David; Fellow and Tutor in Philosophy, Merton College, Oxford, since 1968; University Lecturer (CUF) in Philosophy, Oxford University, since 1969; *b* 1936; *m* 1961; one *s* one *d*. BA Oxon 1961 (Lit. Hum.), BPhil Oxon 1963 (Philosophy), MA Oxon 1968. Temp. Lectr in Philosophy, Leicester Univ., 1963–64; Lectr in Philosophy, ANU, Canberra, 1964–67; Loeb Fellow in Classical Philosophy, Harvard Univ, Boston, Mass, 1967–68. *Publication:* Logic and Arithmetic – Natural Numbers, 1974. *Address:* Merton College, Oxford.

Boston, Dr John Shipway, DPhil, MA, BLitt; Lecturer, University of Hull, since 1967; *b* 1930; *m* 1954; two *s* one *d*. MA Cambridge 1956, BLitt Oxon 1958, DPhil Oxon 1965; FRAI, Mem. ASA. Res. Fellow, Univ. of Ibadan, 1960–66; Lectr, Univ. of Ibadan, 1966–67. Ethnographer, Fed. Govt of Nigeria, 1955–60. *Publications:* The Igala Kingdom, 1968; Ikenga figures among the NW Ibo and the Igala (forthcoming); *contrib.* Africa, Jl African Hist., Man. *Address:* Sociology Dept, Univ. of Hull, Hull HU6 7RX.

Boswell, Jane Elizabeth; see de Sausmarez, J. E.

Boswell, Jonathan Stewart; Senior Lecturer in Managerial Economics, The City University, since 1971; *b* 1932; three *d*. BA Oxon, PPE; Mem., Soc. of Business Economists. Varied industrial experience, 1955–69; Sen. Res. Fellow TCU, 1969–71; Mem., Court of the Univ., 1973– . *Publications:* The Rise and Decline of Small Firms, 1973; various articles. *Address:* City Univ., Lionel Denny House, 23 Goswell Road, EC1.

Bosworth, Prof. Clifford Edmund, MA, PhD; Professor of Arabic Studies, Department of Near Eastern Studies, University of Manchester, since 1967; *b* 1928; *m* 1957; three *d*. BA Oxon 1952 (1st cl. Modern History), MA Oxon 1957, MA Edinburgh 1956 (1st cl. Oriental Languages), PhD Edinburgh 1961, Hon. MA Manchester 1971; FRAS. Lectr in Arabic. St Andrews Univ., 1956; Vis. Assoc. Prof., Toronto Univ., 1965–66; Vis. Prof., Univ. of California at Los Angeles, 1969. Co-ed., Iran, Jl of the British Inst. of Persian Studies, 1967– ; Co-ed., Jl of Semitic Studies, 1968– . *Publications:* The Ghaznavids, 1963; The Islamic Dynasties, 1968, Russian trans. 1971, Persian trans. 1971; Sistan under the Arabs, 1968; The book of curious and entertaining information, 1969; *contrib.* Der Islam, Muslim World, Central Asiatic Jl, Arabica, Bull. SOAS, Jl RAS, Oriens, Isis, Islamic Qly, Iran, Jl Semitic Studies, Jl Econ. and Social Hist. Orient, Internat. Jl ME Studies. *Address:* Dept of Near Eastern Studies, Univ. of Manchester, Manchester M13 9PL.

Bosworth, Stuart Ralph; Registrar, University of Salford, since 1970; *b* 1936; *m* 1961; one *d*. BA Oxford 1960; Admin. Asst, Univ. of Manchester, 1960–65; Sen. Admin. Asst, 1965–66; Dep. Registrar (Academic) Univ. of Salford (formerly Royal Coll. of Advanced Technology, Salford), 1966–70. *Address:* Univ. of Salford, Salford, Lancashire M5 4WT.

Botting, Joseph Henry Alfred, BA, MSc (Econ), AKC; Lecturer in Social Administration, University College of Swansea, since 1964; *b* 1914; *m* 1957; one *s* one *d*. AKC King's Coll., London 1941 (1st cl. Hons), BA South Africa 1962, MSc(Econ) Wales 1970. Sen. Social Welfare Off., Zambia, 1954–60; African Personnel Manager (Welfare), Zambia, 1960–61; Asst Dir of Studies, Social Training Centre, Tanzania, 1961–63; Adv. on Social Welfare, Govt of Lesotho, 1966; Consultant on Social Welfare Admin, Cyprus, 1970. *Publications:* Rwanda, Land of a Thousand Hills (occasional paper); *contrib.* Community Develt Jl; Internat. Social Work. *Address:* Social Administration Division, Univ. College of Swansea, Swansea SA2 8PP.

Bottomley, John Anthony; Professor, Department of Economics, University of Bradford, since 1966; *b* 1927; *m*; two *s* one *d*. BA British Columbia 1951 (Hons Economics), MA Virginia 1955, PhD Virginia 1961. Lectr in Economics, Univ. of Virginia, 1955–56; Univ. of Maryland European Program, 1956–61; Univ. of Singapore, 1961–63; Adviser, Govt of Ecuador, 1963–64, Lebanon, 1964–66; various part-time consultancies, 1967–73; Chm., Bradford Univ. Press; Ed., Bull. of Econ. Res. *Publications:* Factor Pricing and Growth in Underdeveloped Rural Area, 1971; (with J. E. Dunworth et al.) Studies in Institutional Management in Higher Education: Costs and Potential Economies, 1972; *contrib.* numerous (over 50) jls. *Address:* School of Social Sciences, Univ. of Bradford, Bradford BD7 1DP.

Bottomore, Prof. Thomas; Professor of Sociology, School of Social Sciences,

University of Sussex, since 1968; b 1920; m 1953; one s two d. BSc(Econ) London 1943, MSc(Econ) London 1949; Mem., Brit. Sociol. Assoc. (Pres., 1969–71), American Sociol. Assoc., Mind Assoc. Fellow of the Rockefeller Foundation, Univ. of Paris, 1951–52; Lectr and Reader in Sociology, London School of Economics, 1952–64; Prof. and Head, Dept of Political Science, Sociology and Anthropology, Simon Fraser Univ., Vancouver, 1965–68. Mem., Sociol. Cttee, Soc. Science Res. Council, 1971–72. *Publications*: (with Maximilien Rubel) Karl Marx: Selected Writings in Sociology and Social Philosophy, 1956; Sociology: A Guide to Problems and Literature, 1962, 2nd edn 1972; Karl Marx: Early Writings, 1963; Elites and Society, 1964; Classes in Modern Society, 1965; Critics of Society, 1967, 2nd edn 1969; Karl Marx, 1973; Sociology as Social Criticism, 1974; *contrib*. Brit. Jl of Sociol., Cahiers Internationaux de Sociologie, European Jl of Sociol., Encyclop. Britann., Internat. Encyclop. of the Social Sciences. *Address*: Univ. of Sussex, Brighton BN1 9QN.

Bottoms, Anthony Edward; Senior Lecturer in Criminology, Faculty of Law, University of Sheffield, since 1972, Lecturer 1968–72; b 1939; m 1962; one s two d. MA Oxford 1965, DipCrim Cambridge 1962. Res. Off., Inst. Criminology, Univ. of Cambridge, 1964–68. Probation Off., 1962–64. *Publications*: (with F. H. McClintock) Criminals Coming of Age, 1973; *contrib*. Crim. Law Rev. *Address*: Dept of Law, The Univ., Sheffield S10 2TN.

Boulton, Denise Bryers; Part-time Tutor in Italian, University of East Anglia, since 1970; b 1942; m 1964; one d. BA Hons Birmingham 1964 (Russian and Italian). University of East Anglia: Tutor of Russian, 1968; Part-time Tutor, 1969. Member: Standing Adv. Cttee on Italian; Associated Examining Bd, 1967– . *Address*: Language Centre, Univ. of East Anglia, Norwich NOR 88C.

Boulton, Dr Geoffrey Stewart; Lecturer, School of Environmental Science, University of East Anglia, since 1968; b 1940; m 1964; one d. BSc Birmingham 1961, PhD Birmingham 1968; FGS 1960. Keele, 1964–65; Birmingham, 1965–68. *Publications*: contrib. Till a Symposium, ed Goldthwait; *contrib*. Jl Geol Soc., Jl Glaciology. *Address*: School of Environmental Science, Univ. of East Anglia, Norwich NOR 88C.

Boulton, Prof. James Thompson, PhD; Professor of English Literature, University of Nottingham, since 1964; b 1924; m 1949; one s one d. BA Dunelm 1948 (1st cl. English), DipEd Dunelm 1949, BLitt Oxon 1952, PhD Nottingham 1960; FRSL, FRHistS. Asst Lectr, Nottingham Univ., 1951–53, Lectr, 1953–62, Sen. Lectr, 1962–63, Reader, 1963–64; John Cranford Adams Prof., Hofstra Univ., NY, 1967; Dean, Fac. of Arts, Nottingham Univ., 1970–73. Editor, Renaiss. and Mod. Studies, 1969– ; Gen. Editor, The Letters of D. H. Lawrence, 1973– . Pilot in RAF, 1943–46; Ed. Adv., Studies in

Burke and his Time, 1960– ; Mem., Exec. Cttee, Anglo-Amer. Associates, 1968– . *Publications*: ed, Burke: Philosophical Enquiry into . . . the Sublime and Beautiful, 1958, 2nd edn 1968, American pbk edn 1968; ed. C. F. G. Masterman: The Condition of England, 1960; The Language of Politics in the Age of Wilkes and Burke, 1963; ed, Dryden: Of Dramatick Poesie etc., 1964, 2nd edn 1971; ed, Defoe, 1965; ed (with J. Kinsley), English Satiric Poetry, 1966; ed, Lawrence in Love, 1968, 2nd edn 1969, Japanese edn 1972; ed, Samuel Johnson – The Critical Heritage, 1971; ed (with S. T. Bindoff), Research in Progress in English and Historical Studies, 1971; ed, Defoe, Memoirs of a Cavalier, 1972; *contrib*. DUJ, English, EIC, Mod. Drama, Renaiss. and Mod. Studies, Studies in Burke and his Time, etc. *Address*: School of English Studies, Univ. of Nottingham, Nottingham NG7 2RD.

Boulton, Dr John Victor, BA, PhD; Lecturer in Bengali and Oriya, India Department, School of Oriental and African Studies, London University, since 1962; b 1934; m 1960; two s. BA London 1956 (1st cl. Hons Bengali), PhD London 1967 (Oriya Literature). Asst Lectr, 1959–62. *Publications*: Two articles in 'Storia della Letteratura d'Oriente', 1969. *Address*: School of Oriental and African Studies, Univ. of London, WC1E 7HP.

Bourke, Dr John; Registrar, National University of Ireland, since 1972; b 1909; m 1946; four s two d. BComm UC Dublin 1930, MComm UC Dublin 1933, PhD UC Dublin 1962, LLD *de jure officii* 1974. NUI: Admin. Officer, 1932; Accountant, 1950; Asst Registrar, 1969; Mem. of Univ. Senate, 1972. Member: Irish Statistical and Social Enquiry Soc.; Economic and Soc. Res. Inst., Ireland. *Address*: 49 Merrion Square, Dublin 2.

Bourn, Prof. Alan Michael, BSc(Econ), FCA; Professor of Business Studies, University of Liverpool, since 1972; b 1934; m 1960; two s. BSc(Econ) London 1955; FCA 1969; MBIM. Lectr, Univ. of Liverpool, 1963–67; Sen. Lectr, UMIST, 1967–69; Prof., Univ. of Canterbury, NZ, 1969. *Publications*: ed, Studies in Accounting for Management Decision, 1969; *contrib*. Accountancy, Jl Accounting Res., Business Hist. *Address*: Dept of Business Studies, Univ. of Liverpool, Liverpool L69 3BX.

Bourne, Dr Kenneth, BA, PhD; Reader in International History, University of London, since 1969; b 1930; m 1955; one s one d. BA London and Exeter 1951 (1st cl. History), PhD London 1955. Res. Fellow, Inst. Hist. Res., London, 1955–56; Res. Fellow, Reading Univ., 1956; Lectr, LSE, 1957–69; Fulbright Fellow and Sen. Res. Fellow, Brit. Assoc. Amer. Studies, 1961–62; Vis. Lectr, Univ. of California, Davis, 1966–67; Scaife Vis. Disting. Lectr, Kenyon Coll., 1971. *Publications*: Britain and the Balance of Power in North America, 1815–1908, 1967 (Albert B. Corey Prize); (with D. C. Watt) Studies in International History, 1967; The Foreign Policy of Victorian England, 1970; *contrib*. Slav. and E Europ. Rev., Jl Mod. Hist., EHR. *Address*: Dept of International History, London School of Economics, Houghton Street, WC2A 2AE.

Bowcott, Ernest; Lecturer in Education, Department of Education, University of Durham, since 1961; *b* 1929; *m* 1956; one *d*. BA Durham 1952 (Hons Class. and Gen. Lit.), DipEd Durham 1953, MA Durham 1960, MEd Durham 1969. Founder Mem., Philosophy of Educn Soc. of GB; Member: British Soc. of Aesthetics; Soc. for Research in Psychology of Music and Music Educn. Friends Ambulance Unit (Nursing Orderly, Thornbury Hospital, Bristol), 1953–54. Asst Classics Master, Colfe's Grammar Sch., London, 1954; Head of Latin Dept, Barking Abbey Sch., Essex 1960. *Address*: Univ. of Durham Dept of Educn., 48 Old Elvet, Durham.

Bowen, David James, MA; Senior Lecturer, Department of Welsh Language and Literature, University College of Wales, Aberystwyth, since 1963; *b* 1925. BA Wales 1949 (1st cl. in Welsh), MA Wales 1952. Asst Lectr, Aberystwyth, 1953–56; Lectr, Aberystwyth, 1956–63. *Publications*: Barddoniaeth yr Uchelwyr, 1957; Gruffudd Hisaethog a'i Oes, 1958; *contrib*. Llên Cymru, Trans Hon. Soc. of Cymmrodorion. *Address*: Univ. College of Wales, Aberystwyth SY23 2AX.

Bowen, Dr David Quentin, BSc, PhD; Senior Lecturer in Geography, University College of Wales, since 1967; *b* 1938; *m* 1965; two *s*. BSc London 1960, PhD London 1965; FGS. Sen. Fellow, Univ. of Wales, 1965; Lectr, Univ. of Strathclyde, 1966. Treas., Quaternary Res. Assoc., 1969–72; Mem., Royal Soc. Brit. Nat. Cttee for Geology, INQUA sub-cttee, 1969–74. *Publications*: The Glaciations of Wales, 1970; A Concise Physical Geography, 1972; *contrib*. Jl Geol. Soc., Proc. Geol. Assoc., Nature, Trans Cardiff Nat. Soc. *Address*: Dept of Geography, Univ. College of Wales, Aberystwyth SY23 2AX.

Bowen-Jones, Howard; Professor, Department of Geography, since 1963, and Director, Middle East Centre, University of Durham, since 1968; *b* 1921; *m* 1952; one *s* one *d*. BA Cambridge 1941, MA Cambridge 1944; FRGS. Mem., Inst. Brit. Geogrs, Commonwealth Hum. Ecol. Council, Royal Commonwealth Soc. Lectr in Geography, Durham, 1947–58; Sen. Lectr, 1958–63; Vis. Prof., Univ. of Kuwait, 1963. Mem., Gov. Bd, Commonwealth Hum. Ecol. Council. *Publications*: Spain, 1956, 3rd edn 1968; Malta: Background to Development, 1961; Atlas of Durham City, 1960, 4th edn 1970; contrib. Iran (Cambridge History of Iran, vol. I), 1968. *Address*: Dept of Geography, Science Laboratories, Univ. of Durham, Durham.

Bowett, Dr Derek William, MA, LLB, PhD; President, Queens' College, Cambridge, since 1970; *b* 1927; *m* 1953; two *s* one *d*. MA, LLB Cantab 1951, PhD Manchester 1956; Barrister-at-law, Middle Temple 1953. Asst Lectr, Faculty of Law, Manchester Univ., 1951–54; Lectr, 1954–60; Lectr,

Faculty of Law, Cambridge Univ., 1960– ; Fellow, Queens' Coll., Cambridge, 1960–70. Legal Officer, United Nations, 1957–59; Mem., General Council of UNRWA, 1966–68. Mem., Royal Commn on Environmental Pollution, 1973– . *Publications*: Self-defence in International Law, 1958; Law of International Institutions, 1964, 2nd edn 1971; United Nations Forces, 1964; Law of the Sea, 1968; Search for Peace, 1972; *contrib*. Brit. Yearbook of Internat. Law, American Jl of Internat. Law, Internat. and Comparative Law Qly, Virginia Law Jl. *Address*: Queens' College, Cambridge CB3 9ET.

Bowie, Ewen Lyall; E. P. Warren Praelector in Classics, Corpus Christi College, Oxford, since 1965, and CUF Lecturer in Classics, Oxford University, since 1968; *b* 1940; *m* 1966. BA Oxon 1962 (1st cl. Lit. Hum.), MA Oxon 1965. Woodhouse Res. Fellow, St John's Coll., Oxford, 1963–65. Dean, Corpus Christi Coll., 1968–73; Ed., Oxford Mag., 1969–70. *Publications*: *contrib*. Jl Roman Studies, Past and Pres., Zeits. Papyrol. Epigraf. *Address*: Corpus Christi College, Oxford.

Bowker, Prof. John Westerdale; Professor, Department of Religious Studies, University of Lancaster, since 1974; *b* 1935; *m* 1963; one *s*. BA Oxon 1958. Stephenson Res. Fellow, Sheffield, 1961; Fellow, Corpus Christi Coll., Cambridge, 1962–74; Univ. Asst Lectr, Cambridge, 1965, Lectr, 1969; Wilde Lectr, Oxford, 1972–75. Mem.: Durham Commn on Religious Educn, 1970; Commn on Marriage, 1971; Commn on Prisons and Prisoners, 1973. *Publications*: Targums and Rabbinic Literature, 1969; Problems of Suffering in Religions of the World, 1970; Uncle Bolpenny Tries Things Out, 1973; Jesus and the Pharisees, 1973; The Sense of God: Sociological, Anthropological and Psychological Approaches to the Origin of the Sense of God, 1973; *contrib*. Making Moral Decisions, 1969; *contrib*. Humanitas, Jl Sem. Stud., Jl Theol. Stud., New Test. Stud., Relig. Stud., Stud. Evang., Vet. Test. *Address*: Univ. of Lancaster, Bailrigg, Lancaster LA1 4YW.

Bowker, Margaret, MA, BLitt; Lecturer in History and Fellow of Girton College, Cambridge University, since 1963 *b* 1936; *m* 1963; one *s*. BA Oxon 1958 (1st cl. History), MA, BLitt Oxon 1962; FRHistS 1968; Bryce Res. Student, Oxon, 1959, Alexander Prize 1970. Res. Fellow, Girton Coll., Cambridge, 1960; Dir of Studies, 1965. Sec., Faculty Bd of Hist., Cambridge Univ., 1967–69. *Publications*: ed, An Episcopal Court Book 1514–20; The Secular Clergy in the Diocese of Lincoln 1495–1520; *contrib*. ed D. Baker, Studies in Church History, 1972; ed D. A. Bullough and R. L. Storey, Study of Medieval Records; *contrib*. Jl. of Eccles. Hist. *Address*: Faculty of History, West Road, Cambridge.

Bowley, Prof. Marian E. A.; Professor of Political Economy, University of London, since 1965; *b* 1911. BSc(Econ) London 1931, PhD London 1936; Mem., Royal Econ. Soc. Temp. Asst Lectr, Univ. Coll. of Aberystwyth, 1932–33; Temp. Asst. Lectr, Univ. of

Birmingham, 1934–35; Asst Lectr and Lectr, Sch. of Econ., Dundee, 1938–46; (leave of absence, wartime civil service, Economist in various Govt Depts, 1940–46); Lectr, 1946–50, Reader 1950–65, Univ. Coll. London. *Publications*: Nassau Senior and Classical Economics, 1937 (repr. 1967); Housing and the State 1919–1944, 1945; Innovations in Building Materials – An Economic Study, 1960; The British Building Industry, 1965; Studies in the History of Economic Theory before 1870, 1973; *contrib.* Economica, Internat. Labour Rev., Manchester Sch., Political Qly, Rev. of Econ. Studies, Royal Stat. Soc. Jl. *Address*: Dept of Political Economy, Univ. College, Gower Street, WC1E 6BT.

Bowman, Bernard Clifford; Senior Lecturer, Department of Jurisprudence, University of Dundee, since 1967; *b* 1908; *m* 1936; two *s* one *d*. MA St Andrews 1928, LLB Edinburgh 1931; Solicitor 1932, Notary Public 1948. St Andrews Univ., Lectr in Jurisprudence, 1939–46; Scots Law, 1946–49, Law, 1949–50, Jurisprudence, 1950–65; Sen. Lectr in Jurisprudence, 1965–67; Adv. of Studies to Law Students, 1949–69; Dean of Fac. of Law, 1969. Hon. Sheriff of Perth and Angus at Dundee. *Address*: Faculty of Law, The Univ. of Dundee, Dundee DD1 4HN.

Bowman, Derek Edward; Lecturer, Department of German, University of Edinburgh, since 1965; *b* 1931; *m* 1958; two *d*. BA Liverpool 1953 (1st cl. German), MA Liverpool 1963, Cert. of Educn Cambridge 1956. Asst Lectr, Edinburgh Univ., 1964. *Publications*: trans. U. Bräker: The Life-Story and Real Adventures of the Poor Man of Toggenburg, 1970; Life into Autobiography: A Study of Goethe's Dichtung und Wahrheit, 1971; ed, Jetzt geht's los, 1974; *contrib.* Downside Rev., Forum for Mod. Lang., German Life and Letters, Proc. English Goethe Soc., Schweizer Monatshefte. *Address*: Dept of German, Univ. of Edinburgh, George Square, Edinburgh.

Bowmer, Pamela Maud, (Mrs Collard); Lecturer, Social Work Courses, Sociology Department, University of Keele, since 1972; *b* 1923; *m* 1971. Social Science Testamur Bristol 1953, Cert. of Psychiatric Social Work Manchester 1955; AAPSW. Lectr, Adult Educn Dept, Keele, 1966–72. *Address*: Univ. of Keele, Keele, Staffs ST5 5BG.

Bowyer, Tony Harold; Librarian of Queen Mary College, University of London, since 1971; *b* 1924; *m* 1952; one *s* one *d*. BSc(Econ) LSE 1949, Dip. in Librarianship UCL 1952; FLA 1954; Mem., Bibliographical Soc. Asst Librarian, British Library of Political and Econ. Sci., 1952–60; Sen. Asst Librarian, Univ. of London Library, 1960–62; Dep. Librarian, Univ. of Birmingham, 1962–71. Hon. Treas., Standing Conf. of Nat. and Univ. Libraries, 1973– . *Publications*: A Bibliographical Examination of the Earliest Editions of The Letters of Junius, 1957; *contrib.* J. Doc., Library. *Address*: Queen Mary College, Mile End Road, E1 4NS.

Box, Steven; Senior Lecturer, Department of Sociology, University of Kent, since 1971;

b 1937; *m* 1972; one *s*. BSc(Econ) London 1961 (Hons), PhD London 1967. Lectr, Sociology, Univ. of Kent, 1967–71. *Publications*: (with Stephen Cotgrove) Science, Industry and Society, 1970; Deviance, Reality and Society, 1971; *contrib.* Brit. Jl Sociol., Sociological Rev., and Sociology. *Address*: Rutherford College, Univ. of Kent, Canterbury, Kent.

Boyce, David George, BA, PhD, FRHistS; Lecturer, Department of Political Theory and Government, University College Swansea, since 1971; *b* 1942; *m* 1969. BA QUB 1965, PhD QUB 1969; Mem., Soc. of Archivists 1970; FRHistS, 1973. Asst Grade I, Dept of Western Manuscripts, Bodleian Library, Oxford, 1968–71. *Publications*: Englishmen and Irish Troubles, 1972; *contrib.* Irish Hist. Studies, Hist. Jl. *Address*: Dept of Political Theory and Government, Univ. College of Swansea, Swansea SA2 8PP.

Boyce, Prof. Mary, MA, PhD; Professor of Iranian Studies, University of London, since 1963; *b* 1920. BA Cantab Pt 1 1941 (1st cl. English), Pt 2 1943 (1st cl. with distinction, Archaeology), MA 1945, PhD 1952; FRAS. Asst Lectr in Anglo-Saxon Literature and Archaeology, Royal Holloway Coll., Univ. of London, 1944–46; Gough Studentship, Newnham Coll., Cambridge, 1946–47; Lectr, Iranian Studies, Sch. of Oriental and African Studies, London, 1947–58, Reader, 1958–63. Sec. and Treas., Corpus Inscriptionum Iranicarum, 1955–70; Mem. Council, RAS, 1956–60; 1965–68; Ed. Bd, Asia Major, 1962– . Burton Memorial Medal, 1972. *Publications*: The Manichaean Hymn-Cycles in Parthian, 1954; A Catalogue of the Iranian Manuscripts in Manichean Script in the German Turfan Collection, 1960; The Letter of Tansar, 1968; *contrib.* Acta Orient., Asia Major, Bull. SOAS, JAOS, JRAS, Persica, Saeculum. *Address*: School of Oriental and African Studies, Univ. of London, WC1E 7HP.

Boyd, Prof. Maurice James, MA, MRIA; Professor of Latin, The Queen's University of Belfast, since 1939; *b* 1911; *m* 1936; two *s* one *d*. BA QUB 1931 (1st cl. Classics), BA Oxon 1933 (2nd cl. Lit. Hum.), MA Oxon; MRIA. Sometime Dean of Faculties of Arts and of Theology, Dep. Chm. General Bd of Studies, Univ. Adviser on Schools, 1962–72; Mem. Univ. Senate (Governing Body), Chm. Convocation, 1956–65. Chm., NI GCE Bd, Dep. Chm., NI Sch's Examinations Council; sometime Chm., NI Library Adv. Council; sometime Chm., Ulster Soc. for Promoting the Educn of the Deaf and Dumb and the Blind. *Publications*: *contrib.* Classical Philology, Classical Qly, Classical Rev., Papers of Brit. Sch. at Rome. *Address*: Queen's University, Belfast BT7 1NN.

Boydell, Prof. Brian Patrick, BA, MusD, FTCD, LRIAM; Professor of Music, University of Dublin (Trinity College), since 1962; *b* 1917; *m* 1944; three *s*. BA Cantab 1938 (1st cl. Nat. Science Tripos), BA ad eundem Dublin 1939, MusB Dublin 1941, MusD Dublin 1959; FTCD 1972; LRIAM (Singing). Founder and Mem., Council, Music Assoc. of Ireland, 1948– ; Mem.,

Irish Arts Council; Conductor, Dublin Orchestral Players, 1942–52 (now President); Founder and Dir, Dowland Consort, 1958–69; Vice-Pres., Assoc. for Promotion of Music in Educn (Ireland); guest conductor, Radio Telefis Eirann Symph. Orch., CBC Symph. Orch. (Toronto). *Publications*: Article Ireland–Music, in, Cyclopedia Americana, 1969; Article, Dublin (et alia), in, Grove: Dictionary of Music and Musicians, 6th edn (forthcoming); The Irish Music Trade up to 1850 (forthcoming); *Musical Compositions include*: 3 String Quartets, Violin Concerto, Cantata: Mors et Vita, symphonic works, chamber music and songs. *Address*: No 5, Trinity College, Dublin 2.

Boyle of Handsworth, The Rt. Hon. Lord; Edward Charles Gurney Boyle, PC; Vice-Chancellor of Leeds University, since 1970; *b* 1923. Hon. LLD Leeds and Southampton 1965, Bath 1968, Sussex 1972, Hon. DSc Aston in Birmingham 1966. Pro-Chancellor, Sussex Univ., 1965–70; Richard Feetham Memorial Lectr on Academic Freedom, Univ. of Witwatersrand, 1965; Earl Grey Lectr Newcastle, 1966; Sidney Ball Meml Lectr, Oxford, 1967; Eleanor Rathbone Meml Lectr on Race Relations and Educn, Univ. of Liverpool, 1970; Boutwood Lectr, Corpus Christi, Cambridge, 1971; Gregynog Lectr, UCW, 1972. MP (C) Handsworth Div. of Birmingham, 1950–70; Parly Private Sec. to Under-Sec. for Air, 1951–52, and to Parly Sec. to Min. of Defence, 1952–53; Parly Sec., Min. of Supply, 1954–55; Economic Sec. to the Treasury, 1955–56; Parly Sec., Min. of Educn, 1957–59; Financial Sec. to the Treasury, 1959–62; Min. of Educn, 1962–64; Min. of State, DES, 1964. Dir, Penguin Books Ltd, 1966– ; Chm., Top Salaries Rev. Body, 1971– . Chm., Youth Service Develt Council, 1962–64; Pres., Incorporated Soc. of Preparatory Schls, 1970–72; Mem., Fulton Cttee on Civil Service, 1966–68; Mem., IBRD Commn on Internat. Develt, 1968–69; Trustee of Brit. Museum, Glyndebourne Arts Trust, Acton Soc. Trust; Pilgrim Trust; a Governor of Ditchley Foundn, and of Brit. Inst. of Recorded Sound. *Publications*: contrib. The Politics of Education, ed M. Kogan. *Address*: The Vice-Chancellor's Lodge, Grosvenor Road, Leeds LS6 2DZ.

Boyle, Anthony John; Reader in Laws, Faculty of Law, Queen Mary College, London, since 1970; *b* 1934; *m* 1965. LLB London 1956 (2/I), LLM 1958, SJD Harvard 1967, Study Fellowship Harvard Law School 1960–61; Mem., Grays Inn (called to Bar 1958), Selden Soc., Soc. of Public Teachers of Law. Lectr, Durham Univ., 1961–63; Lectr, Birmingham Univ., 1963–65; Lectr, King's Coll., London, 1965–70. Mem., Cttees of Management of the Inst. of US Studies and of the Inst. of Adv. Legal Studies (London Univ.); Mem., Gov. Body of Queen Mary Coll. *Publications*: ed, Gore Browne on Companies, 42nd edn 1972; *contrib*. Internat. and Compar. Law Qly, Jl of Business Law, Mod. Law Rev. *Address*: Law Faculty, Queen Mary College, Mile End Road, E1 4NS.

Boyle, Christopher Kevin, LLB, DipCrim, BL; Lecturer in Law, Queen's University Belfast, since 1969; *b* 1943. LLB QUB 1965 (Hons), DipCrim Cantab 1966; Barrister-at-Law (Grays Inn, Northern Ireland Bar). Asst Lectr, Queen's Univ. of Belfast, 1966–68; Temp. Lectr, 1968. Res. Fellow, Yale Law Sch., 1972–73. *Publications*: Police in Ireland since 1800 (forthcoming); *contrib*. NILQ. *Address*: Dept of Civil Law, Faculty of Law, The Queen's Univ., Belfast BT7 1NN.

Boyle, Prof. John Andrew, PhD; Professor, Department of Persian Studies, University of Manchester, since 1966; *b* 1916; *m* 1945; three *d*. BA Birmingham 1936 (1st cl. Hons German), PhD London 1947, Hon. MA Manchester 1970; Mem., RAS. Exchange Fellowship, Berlin Univ., 1936–39. Sen. Lectr, Manchester Univ., 1950–59, Reader, 1959–66; Vis. Prof., Univ. of California, 1959–60. FO, 1941–50; Mem., Council, Brit. Inst. Persian Studies, 1964– ; Ed. Bd, Cambridge Hist. of Iran, 1966– ; Adv. Bd, Tehran Jl Iran-Shenasi, 1969; Gibb Meml Trust, 1970; Soc. of Authors; Council, Brit. Soc. for ME Studies, 1973– ; Cttee, Folklore Soc., 1973– ; Chm., Anglo-Mongolian Soc., 1970– ; Hon. Fellow, Körösi Csoma Társaság, 1973. Order and Decoration of Sepass, Ist cl. (Persia), 1958; Certificate of Merit of Turkish Govt, on 50th anniversary of Republic, for outstanding contribution to study and promotion of Turkish Culture. *Publications*: A Practical Dictionary of the Persian Language, 1949; Modern Persian Grammar, 1966; ed and contrib. Cambridge History of Iran, vol. V, 1968; trans. Juvaini: History of the World-Conqueror, 1958; Rashid al-Din, The Successors of Genghis Khan, 1971; *contrib*. AO, CAJ, Folklore, HJAS, Islamic Studies, JRAS, JSS. *Address*: Dept of Persian Studies, Univ. of Manchester, Manchester M13 9PL.

Boyle, Dr Peter G.; Lecturer, Department of American Studies, University of Nottingham, since 1967; *b* 1941. MA Hons Glasgow 1963 (History), PhD California (Los Angeles) 1970. Visiting Professor: Cornell Univ., 1971; Beloit Coll., 1973. *Publications*: *contrib*. Jl of Amer. Studies, Univ. Vision. *Address*: Dept of American Studies, Univ. of Nottingham, Nottingham NG7 2RD.

Boyle, Timothy, BA, MPhil; Senior Lecturer in Modern History, Goldsmiths' College, University of London, since 1971; *b* 1936; *m* 1961; two *s*. BA London 1960 (Hist.), CertEd. Cambridge 1961, MPhil London 1969. Lectr in Modern Hist., Goldsmiths' Coll., Univ. of London, 1965–71. *Publications*: *contrib*. Bull. Inst. Hist. Res. *Address*: Dept of History, Goldsmiths' College, Lewisham Way, New Cross, SE14 6NW.

Boynton, Lindsay Oliver John; Reader, Department of History and History of Art, Westfield College, London, since 1972 (Lecturer, 1966–72); *b* 1934. MA Oxon 1959, DPhil Oxon 1962; FRHistS 1968, FSA 1967. Asst. Lectr, Leeds Univ., 1958–61; Lectr, Leeds Univ., 1961–66. Mem., Council of Furniture Hist. Soc., 1964– , Council of

Walpole Soc., 1971– . *Publications*: The Elizabethan Militia, 1967; *contrib.* Burling. Mag., EHR, Furniture Hist. *Address*: Westfield College, Kidderpore Avenue, Hampstead, NW3 7ST.

Bradbrook, Dr Frank W., MA, PhD; Senior Lecturer, Department of English, University of Wales (Bangor), since 1966; *b* 1917; *m* 1956. BA Cantab 1939 (Double 1st in English), Cert. competent knowledge in French Cantab 1940, MA Cantab 1946, PhD Wales 1964; Mem., Mod. Humanities Res. Assoc., Brit. Assoc. for American Studies, English-Speaking Union, Jane Austen Soc., Brit. Soc. for 18th-Century Studies. Asst Lectr in Eng., Univ. Coll. of North Wales, Bangor, 1947–51; Lectr, 1951–66. *Publications*: Essays in The Pelican Guide to English Literature, vols. 3, 4, and 7, 1956, 1957, and 1961; Jane Austen: Emma, 1961, Amer. edn 1962; Jane Austen and her Predecessors, 1966; ed, Jane Austen: Pride and Prejudice, 1970; *contrib.* Cambridge Jl, N&Q, Univ. Qly, Books Abroad, MLR, Eng. Lang. Notes. *Address*: Dept of English, Univ. College of North Wales, Bangor LL57 2DG.

Bradbrook, Prof. Muriel Clara; Professor of English Literature, University of Cambridge, since 1965; *b* 1909. BA Cantab 1930, MA, PhD Cantab 1933, LittD Cantab 1955, Hon. LittD Liverpool 1964, Sussex 1972, London 1973, Hon. LLD Smith Coll. USA 1965; FRSL 1947, FRSA 1968, Foreign Mem., Norwegian Acad. Arts and Sciences, 1966. Fellow of Girton 1932–35 and 1936–68; Lectr in English, Univ. of Cambridge, 1945–62; Reader, 1962–65. Chm. English Fac., Cambridge, 1965–66; Trustee, Shakespeare's Birthplace, 1967– ; Mem., various Univ. Cttees in Cambridge; Vice-Mistress, Girton Coll., 1962–66, Mistress, Girton Coll., 1968– . *Publications*: Elizabethan Stage Conditions, 1932; Themes and Conventions of Elizabethan Tragedy, 1934; The School of Night, 1936, US edn 1965; (with M. G. Lloyd Thomas) Andrew Marvell, 1940; Joseph Conrad, 1941, US edn 1965; Ibsen the Norwegian, 1946; T. S. Eliot, 1950; Shakespeare and Elizabethan Poetry, 1951; The Queen's Garland, 1953; The Growth and Structure of Elizabethan Comedy, 1955; Sir Thomas Malory, 1957; Tbe Rise of the Common Player, 1962; English Dramatic Form, 1965; That Infidel Place, 1969; Shakespeare the Craftsman, 1969; Literature in Action, 1972; Malcolm Lowry, 1974; *contrib.* Ibsen-årbok, MLR, Rev. of Engl. Studies, Shakesp. Surv., Shakesp. Qly, Stratford upon Avon Studies, etc. *Address*: Girton College, Cambridge CB3 0JG.

Bradbury, Prof. Malcolm Stanley, PhD; Professor of American Studies, School of English and American Studies, University of East Anglia, since 1970; *b* 1932; *m* 1959; two *s*. BA London 1953 (1st cl. Hons), MA London 1955, PhD Manchester 1962. Staff Tutor in Lit. and Drama, Univ. of Hull, 1959–61; Lectr in English, Univ. of Birmingham, 1961–65; Lectr, Sen. Lectr and Reader in English and American Lit., Univ. of East Anglia, 1965–70; Vis. Fellow, All Souls, Oxford, 1969; Guest Prof., Univ. of

Zürich, 1972. *Publications*: Eating People Is Wrong (novel), 1959; Evelyn Waugh, 1962; ed, E. M. Forster: A Collection of Critical Essays, 1965; Stepping Westward (novel), 1965; ed, Mark Twain: Pudd'nhead Wilson, 1969; What Is a Novel?, 1969; E. M. Forster: A Passage to India: a casebook, 1970; ed (with David Palmer), Metaphysical Poetry, 1970; ed (with David Palmer), Contemporary Criticism, 1971; The Social Context of Modern English Literature, 1971; ed (with Eric Mottram and Jean Franco), Penguin Companion to Literature, vol. iii: American, 1971; ed (with David Palmer), The American Novel and the 1920s, 1971; ed (with David Palmer), Shakespearean Comedy, 1972; ed (with David Palmer), Victorian Poetry, 1972; ed (with David Palmer), Medieval Drama, 1973; Possibilities: essays on the state of the novel, 1973; *contrib.* Critical Qly, Jl of American Studies, Perspectives in Hist. *Address*: School of English and American Studies, Univ. of East Anglia, Norwich NOR 88C.

Bradby, David Henry, MA, CertEd, PhD; Lectr in French, University of Kent at Canterbury, since 1971; *b* 1942; *m* 1965; one *s* one *d*. BA Oxon 1965 (1st cl. French), MA Oxon 1968, CertEd. Bristol 1966, PhD Glasgow 1972. Lectr, Strathclyde Univ., 1966–67; Lectr, Glasgow Univ., 1967–71. *Publications*: Adamov, 1974; ed, Sartre: Kean, 1973; *contrib.* Philosoph. Jl, La Nouvelle Critique. *Address*: Darwin College, The Univ., Canterbury, Kent.

Braddock, David Wilson; Resident Tutor in East Dorset and Bournemouth, Department of Extra-Mural Studies, University of Southampton, since 1970; *b* 1929; *m* 1953; one *s*. BA Birmingham 1950 (1st cl. Hons Geog.). Univ. of Southampton: Tutor to HM Forces, 1957–67; Resident Tutor, W Hants, 1967–70. Co-opted Mem., New Dorset Educn Cttee, 1973– . *Publication*: The Campaigns in Egypt and Libya 1940–42, 1964. *Address*: Univ. of Southampton, Southampton SO9 5NH.

Brading, Dr D. A.; University Lecturer in Latin American Studies, Department of History, University of Cambridge, since 1973; *b* 1936; *m* 1966; one *s*. BA Cantab 1960, MA Cantab 1965, PhD London 1965. Asst Prof. of History, Univ. of Calif., Berkeley, 1965–71; Associate Prof. of History, Yale Univ., 1971–73. *Publications*: Miners and Merchants in Bourbon Mexico 1763–1810, 1971; Los Origenes del Nacionalismo Mexicano, 1973; *contrib.* HAHR, Hist. Mex., Jls. *Address*: History Faculty Building, West Road, Cambridge.

Bradley, Prof. Anthony Wilfred; Professor of Constitutional Law, University of Edinburgh, since 1968; *b* 1934; *m* 1959; one *s* three *d*. BA Cantab (Law) 1957, LLB Cantab 1958, MA Cantab 1960; Solicitor of the Supreme Court (England and Wales) 1960, Clifford's Inn Prizeman 1960. Univ. Asst Lectr, 1960–64; Univ. Lectr, Cambridge Univ., 1964–68; Fellow, Trinity Hall, Cambridge, 1960–68; Vis. Reader, Univ. Coll., Dar es Salaam, 1966–67. *Publications*:

ed (jtly), Constitutional Law by E. C. S. Wade and G. G. Phillips, 7th edn 1965 and 8th edn 1970; *contrib.* Cambridge Law Jl, East African Law Jl, Ann, Survey of Commonwealth Law. *Address*: Faculty of Law, Univ. of Edinburgh, Old College, Edinburgh EH8 9YL.

Bradley, Dennis Rennard, MA; Senior Lecturer in Greek and Latin and Classical Philology, University of Manchester, since 1970; *b* 1923; *m* 1956; two *s* one *d*. BA Dunelm 1948, MA Dunelm 1948. Asst Lectr, Queen's Univ., Belfast, 1950–53; Asst Lectr, Manchester Univ., 1953–56, Lectr, 1956–69. Dir., Gen. Studies, Fac. of Arts, 1967– . *Publications: contrib.* Class. et Mediaev., Eranos, Latomus, Med. Stud., Riv. cult. class. and med. *Address*: Faculty of Arts, Univ. of Manchester, Manchester M13 9PL.

Bradley, Howard William; Lecturer and Tutor for In-Service Training, School of Education, University of Nottingham, since 1967; *b* 1938; *m* 1963; one *s* and *d*. BA Cambridge 1962, Cert. in Educn Cambridge 1963, MA Cambridge 1967. Mem., Universities' Council for Edn of Teachers, 1968– ; Hon. Sec., Assoc. of Inst. and Sch. of Educn In-Service Tutors, 1972– . *Publications*: An Enquiry into In-Service Training, 1972; (with J. G. Goulding) Handling Mixed Ability Groups in the Secondary School, 1973; In-Service Education after the White Paper, 1974; Technology Projects for Schools, 1974. *Address*: School of Education, University Park, Nottingham NG7 2RD.

Bradley, John; Lecturer, School of Education, University of Leicester, since 1964; *b* 1913; *m* 1944; three *d*. Dip. Psych. Oxford 1946, MEd Leicester 1962; ABPsS. Sen. Educl Psych., Leicestershire County Council, 1947–64. Mem., Parole Board, 1970; JP 1972. *Publications: contrib.* Nature. *Address*: School of Education, University Road, Leicester LE1 7RH.

Bradley, Dr John Francis Nejez; Lecturer in Government, Department of Government, Manchester University, since 1962; *b* 1930; *m* 1954; two *s* two *d*. BA Hons Cambridge 1955, MA, MLitt Cambridge 1958, Docteur de l'Université de Paris 1962. Res. Fellow, Fitzwilliam House, Cambridge, 1955–58; CNRS Fellow, Paris Univ., 1958–60; Lectr in Liberal Studies, Salford Univ., 1960–62. *Publications*: La Légion tchécoslovaque en Russie, 1964; Allied Intervention in Russia, 1968; Czechoslovakia: A Short History, 1971; *contrib.* Revue historique, Revue d'Histoire Moderne et Contemporaine, EHR, Slavonic Rev., Slavic Rev., Soviet Studies, Revue des Etudes Slaves. *Address*: Dept of Government, Manchester Univ., Manchester M13 9PL.

Bradley, Prof. John Lewis, BA, MA, PhD; Professor of English, University of Durham, since 1969 (currently Head of Department); *b* 1917; *m* 1943; one *d*. BA Yale 1940, MA Harvard 1946, PhD Yale 1950. Wellesley Coll., 1948–51; Clark Univ., 1952–54; Mount Holyoke Coll., 1954–63; Ohio State Univ.,

1963–65; Univ. of S. Carolina (Grad. Sch. of English), 1965–69. *Publications*: An Introduction to Ruskin, 1971; ed, Ruskin's Letters from Venice, 1955; ed, The Letters of John Ruskin to Lord and Lady Mount-Temple, 1964; ed, Selections from Mayhew's London Labour and the London Poor, 1965; *contrib.* Burlington Mag., Mod. Lang. Rev., Vict. Studies, N & Q, Jl Eng. Germ. Philol., Mod. Lang. Qly, Studies in English Literature, TLS, Victorian Newsletter. *Address*: Dept of English, Univ. of Durham, Durham DH1 3HP.

Bradshaw, Arnold Theodore von Salis, MA; Vice-Master and Senior Tutor of Van Mildert College and Part-time Lecturer in Classics, University of Durham, since 1965; *b* 1928; *m* 1953; two *s* two *d*. BA Dublin 1951 (1st cl. Classics), MA Dublin. Lectr, Univ. Coll., Ibadan, Nigeria, 1951–59; Univ. Coll., Sierra Leone, 1962–65. Teacher, Cambridge-shire High Sch. for Boys, 1960–62. *Publications: contrib.* Class. Qly, Philologus, Rhein. Museum, Sierra Leone Lang. Rev. *Address*: Van Mildert College, Durham.

Bradshaw, Dr John; Senior Lecturer in the Psychology of Language, Communication Science and Linguistics, University of Aston in Birmingham, since 1968; *b* 1924; *m* 1954; two *s* one *d*. BSc Lond. 1945 (Elec. Eng), MSc Lond. 1949 (Psychol.), MA Oxon 1956 (Theology), DPhil Oxon 1954; Grad. Mem., Brit. Psychol. Soc. Lectr, Univ. of Aston, 1965–68. Principal, Malua Theol. Coll., W Samoa, 1955–64. *Publications*: Chief trans., The Bible in Samoan, 1969. *Address*: Communication Science and Linguistics, Room 732, Univ. of Aston in Birmingham, Birmingham B4 7ET.

Bradshaw, Jonathan Richard; Research Fellow, Department of Social Administration and Social Work, University of York, since 1970; *b* 1944; *m* 1967; one *s*. BSoc Studies Dublin (1st cl. Hons), MA Dublin (Philosophy), MPhil York (Social Admin). Fellow, Dept of Social Admin, Univ. of York, 1968–69. York City Councillor. Mem., Nat. Exec., World Poverty Action Group. *Publications: contrib.* Political Qly, Brit. Jl of Social Work, Ybk of Social Policy, Applied Social Studies, Brit. Hosp. Jl and Social Service Rev. Jl of Social and Econ. Admin, New Society. *Address*: Dept of Social Administration and Social Work, Univ. of York, Heslington, York YO1 5DD.

Brady, Dr James C.; College Lecturer, Faculty of Law, University College, Dublin, since 1969; *b* 1940; *m* 1965; one *s* two *d*. BCL, LLB NUI 1963; PhD QUB 1970. University of Hull: Asst Lectr, 1966–68; Lectr, 1968–69. *Publications*: Religion and the Law of Charities in Ireland (forthcoming); *contrib.* Irish Jurist (New Series), Northern Ireland Legal Qly. *Address*: Faculty of Law, Univ. Coll., Belfield, Dublin 4.

Brady, Dr Philip Valentine, MA, PhD; Senior Lecturer, German Department, Birkbeck College London, since 1972 (Lecturer, 1960–72); *b* 1932; *m* 1961; one *s*. BA Cantab 1954 (1st cl. Mod. Langs). MA Cantab 1957,

PhD London 1966. *Publications*: *contrib.* FMLS, GLL, MLR, NGS, ZDA. *Address*: Birkbeck College, Malet Street, WC1E 7HX.

Bragg, Richard John; Lecturer, Department of Law, University of Hull, since 1970; *b* 1945; *m* 1972. LLB (Hons) Hull 1966, LLM Hull 1969; Mem., SPTL. Asst Lectr in Law, Univ. of Hull, 1968-70. *Publications*: *contrib*. Conv. *Address*: Dept of Law, Univ. of Hull, Hull HU6 7RX.

Bragg, Stephen Lawrence, MA, SM; Vice-Chancellor, Brunel University, since 1971; *b* 1923; *m* 1951; three *s*. BA Cantab 1945, MA Cantab 1949, SM MIT 1949, Hon. DEng Sheffield 1969. Rolls-Royce Ltd, 1944-48; Commonwealth Fund Fellow, 1948-49; Wm Jessop Ltd, Steelmakers, 1949-51; Rolls-Royce Ltd, 1951-71; Chief Scientist, 1960-63, Chief Research Engr, 1964-68; Dir, Aero Div., 1969-71; Mem., UGC, 1966-71; Mem., Aeronautical Res. Coun., 1970-73; Chm., Adv. Cttee on Falsework, 1973- . Mem. Ct, ASC Henley, 1972- . *Publications*: Rocket Engines, 1962; articles on Jet Engines, Research Management, University/Industry Collaboration, etc. *Address*: Brunel Univ., Kingston Lane, Uxbridge, Mddx UB8 3TH.

Braidwood, Prof. John, MA; Professor of English, The Queen's University of Belfast, since 1969; *b* 1918; *m* 1945; two *s*. MA Glasgow 1940 (1st cl. English Lang., Lit.). Geo. A. Clark Post-Grad. Schol. Asst. Lectr and Clark Schol., Glasgow, 1946-48; Lectr, 1948-49; Lectr, QUB, 1949-59; Sen. Lectr, 1959-69; Dean elect, Faculty of Arts. Governor, Belfast High Sch., 1970- ; Vice-Chm. Bd of Governors, 1973- . Served War, 1940-46, Maj., SEAC (despatches 1943). *Publications*: Ulster and Elizabethan English, 1965; The Ulster Dialect Lexicon, 1969; *contrib*. Ulster Folklife, RES, MLN. *Address*: Dept of English, The Queen's Univ. of Belfast, Belfast BT7 1NN.

Brake, Michael David; Lecturer in Sociology of Deviance, Department of Applied Social Studies, Bradford University, since 1972; *b* 1936; *m* 1960; one *d*. BA Hons Leeds 1967 (Sociology and Psychology), MSc LSE 1968. Part-time Lectr, Univ. of London Inst. of Educn, 1968-71; Lectr, Univ. of Bradford, 1971-72. Mem., Nat. Deviancy Symposium, 1968. *Publications*: *contrib*. Drugs and Society, Brit. Jl Crim.; Youth and Society (USA). *Address*: Dept of Applied Social Studies, The Univ., Bradford BD7 1DP.

Branch, Dr Michael Arthur; Lecturer in Finnish Language and Literature, Department of East European Language and Literature, School of Slavonic and East European Studies, University of London, since 1972; *b* 1940; *m* 1963; three *d*. BA (Hons) London 1963 (Hungarian Lang. and Lit.), PhD London 1967 (Finno-Ugrian Philology); Member: Finno-Ugrian Soc., Soc. for Hist. of Learning, Kotikieli Soc., Finnish Literature Soc., Kalevala Soc. (all of Helsinki), Porthan Soc. (Turku). Lectr in Hungarian and Finno-Ugrian Studies, Sch. of Slavonic and E European Studies, Univ. of London, 1967-72. Mem., Council, Anglo-Finnish Soc., 1969- . *Publications*: A. J. Sjögren: Studies of the North, 1973; A Student's Vocabulary of Finnish, 1974; A. J. Sjögren: Letters from the North, 1975; *contrib*. Virittäjä, Studia Fennica, Terra, Jl de la Société Finnoougrienne, Historiallinen Aikakauskirja, Kalevalaseuran vuoskirja (all of Helsinki). *Address*: Sch. of Slavonic and East European Studies, Univ. of London, WC1E 7HU.

Brand, Prof. Charles Peter; Professor of Italian, University of Edinburgh, since 1966; *b* 1923; *m* 1948; one *s* three *d*. BA Mod. Langs Cantab 1948 (1st cl. Hons), PhD Cantab 1951. Asst Lectr, Edinburgh Univ., 1952; Asst Lectr, subseq. Lectr, Cambridge Univ., 1952-66. General Editor, Modern Language Review, 1971- . *Publications*: Italy and the English Romantics, 1957; (jtly) Italian Studies presented to E. R. Vincent, 1962; Torquato Tasso, 1965; *contrib*. learned jls. *Address*: David Hume Tower, George Square, Edinburgh EH8 9YL.

Brandis, Walter; Research Officer, Sociological Research Unit, University of London Institute of Education, since 1966; *b* 1937. BSc(Soc) Regent Street Polytechnic 1961. Res. Asst, Psychology Dept, LSE, 1961-65. *Publications*: (with D. Henderson) Social Class, Language, and Communication, 1970, German trans. 1973; (with B. Bernstein) Selection and Control: a Study of Teacher's Ratings in the Infant School, 1974. *Address*: Sociological Res. Unit, Univ. of London Inst. of Education, Malet Street, WC1E 7HS.

Branigan, Dr Keith, BA, PhD, FSA; Lecturer in Archaeology, Department of Classics, University of Bristol, since 1966; *b* 1940; *m* 1965; one *s* one *d*. BA Birmingham 1963 (1st cl., Archaeol. and Anc. Hist.), PhD Birmingham 1966; FSA 1970. Res. Fellow, Univ. of Birmingham, 1965-66. Mem., Areas Museum Council, 1966; Chm., Bristol Archaeol. Res. Grp, 1970-72. *Publications*: Copper and Bronzeworking in Early Bronze Age, Crete, 1968; The Foundations of Palatial Crete, 1970; The Tombs of Mesara, 1970; Latimer, 1971; Town and Country, 1973; Aegean Metalwork of the Early and Middle Bronze Ages, 1974; Reconstructing the Past (forthcoming); ed, The Civitates of Roman Britain (series, first vols published Spring 1973); *contrib*. Amer. Jl of Archaeol.; Archaeol. Jl, Britannia, Ann. of Brit. Sch. at Athens, Kadmos, Studi Micenei ed Egeo-Anatolici, Wilts Archaeol. Mag. *Address*: Dept of Classics, Univ. of Bristol, Bristol BS8 1TH.

Branscombe, Peter John; Senior Lecturer in German, University of St Andrews, since 1970; *b* 1929; *m* 1967; two *s* one *d*. BA Oxon 1953, MA Oxon 1957; MHRA. Asst Lectr, St Andrews Univ., 1959; Lectr, 1960-70. Gov., Royal Scott. Acad. Music and Drama, 1967- ; Judge, Schlegel-Tieck Prize, 1971- . *Publications*: Heine (Penguin Poets), 1968; trans. Deutsch: Mozart and his world in contemporary pictures, 1961; co-trans.,

76

Deutsch: Mozart: a documentary biography, 1965, 2nd edn 1966; *contrib.* MT, Proc. RMA. *Address*: Dept of German, The Univ., St Andrews, Fife KY16 9AJ.

Branthwaite, William Guy; Assistant Director, Institute of Education, University of Newcastle upon Tyne, since 1972; *b* 1926; *m* 1952; two *s* one *d*. BSc Dunelm 1951, MSc Newcastle 1973; PGC-E London 1952, FRGS. Staff Tutor, Inst. of Educn: Durham, 1962–66; Newcastle upon Tyne, 1966–72; Lectr, Sch. of Educn, Newcastle upon Tyne, 1972. Governor, Jarrow Multilateral Schs, 1971– ; Mem. Delegacy , Newcastle Univ., 1972– . *Publications*: Teaching General Knowledge Subjects, 1962; *contrib.* Jl Insts Educn of Univs of Durham and Newcastle. *Address*: Sch. of Education, Univ. of Newcastle upon Tyne, Newcastle upon Tyne NE1 7RU.

Brasington, Ronald William Page; Lecturer, Department of Linguistic Science, University of Reading, since 1966; *b* 1936; *m* 1960; three *s* one *d*. BA Oxon 1959, MA Oxon 1961. Coll. Lectr, New Coll., Oxford, 1960; New Coll. and St Catherine's, Oxford, 1961; Asst Lecturer, UCNW, Bangor, 1962–64; Brit. Council, Argentina, 1965. *Publications*: *contrib.* Jl Ling., Lingua, Arch. Ling. *Address*: Dept of Linguistic Science, Univ. of Reading, Whiteknights, Reading, Berks RG6 2AH.

Bratchell, Dr Dennis Frank, BA, PhD; Head of Department of English and Liberal Studies, University of Wales Institute of Science and Technology, since 1960; *b* 1920; *m* 1955; two *s*. BA Birmingham 1953 (1st cl. English), PhD Birmingham 1955, Cert. in Educ. Bristol 1949; Mem., Mod. Hum. Res. Assoc., English Assoc., Nat. Assoc. for Teaching of English. Lectr, Univ. of Iowa, 1955; Vis. Lectr, Univ. of Birmingham, 1957–60. *Publications*: (with Morrell Heald) The Aims and Organization of Liberal Studies, 1966; The Aims and Organization of Further Education, 1968; *contrib.* English, English in Educn, Vocational Aspect, Jl of Tech. Writing and Communication. *Address*: Dept of English, Univ. of Wales Institute of Science and Technology, 57 Park Place, Cardiff CF1 3AT.

Braun, Thomas Felix Rudolf Gerhard; Fellow and Tutor in Ancient History, Merton College, Oxford, since 1963; *b* 1935. BA Oxon 1959 (1st cl. Hon. Mods, 1st cl. Lit. Hum.), Craven Fellow, A. M. P. Read Scholar, Merton Sen. Scholar 1959, MA Oxon 1962. Asst Lectr, Leicester Univ., 1962–63. Dean of Graduates, Merton College, 1966–72. *Address*: Merton College, Oxford.

Bray, Roger William; Lecturer, Department of Music, University of Manchester, since 1970; *b* 1944; *m* 1967; one *s* one *d*. BA Oxford 1965 (Hons), MA, DPhil Oxford 1970. Asst Prof., Univ. of Victoria, BC, Canada, 1968–70. *Publications*: Revision of edns of church music by Byrd and Weelkes, 1973, etc; *contrib.* Mus. Disc., Mus. and Letters, Proc. Royal Mus. Assoc., RMA Res.

Chron. *Address*: University Music Dept, Denmark Road, Manchester M15 6FY.

Bray, Dr Warwick Michael; Senior Lecturer in Latin American Archaeology, Institute of Archaeology and Institute of Latin American Studies, London University, since 1973 (Lecturer, 1966–73); *b* 1936; *m* 1960; three *d*. BA Cambridge 1957, MA Cambridge 1961, PhD Cambridge 1962; FSA 1965, Mem., Prehist. Soc., Royal Anthropol. Inst. Lecturer in European Prehistory, Univ. of Sheffield, 1963–66. *Publications*: Everyday Life of the Aztecs, 1968; (with David Trump) A Dictioanry of Archaeology, 1970; *contrib.* Antiquity, Nawpa Pacha, Revista Colombiana de Antropologia, Rivista di Scienze Preistoriche, Proc. Prehist. Soc. *Address*: London Univ. Institute of Archaeology, 31–34 Gordon Square, WC1H 0PY.

Brealey, Prof. Richard A.; Barclaytrust Professor of Finance, London Business School, since 1973; *b* 1936; *m* 1967; two *s*. MA Hons Oxon 1959; Sen. Res. Officer, London Business School, 1968–73. *Publications*: Introduction to Rule and Return from Common Stocks, 1969; Security Prices in a Competitive Market, 1971; (with J. H. Lorie) Modern Developments in Investment Management, 1972; (with C. Pyle) Bibliography of Finance and Investment, 1973. *Address*: London Business School, Sussex Place, Regents Park, London.

Breatnach, Prof. R. A.; Professor of Irish Language and Literature, University College, Cork, since 1946; *b* 1911; *m* 1941; three *s* two *d*. BA NUI 1937, MA NUI 1939; MRIA, 1951. Asst, Dept of Early and Mediaeval Irish, UCD, 1945–46. Dean, Faculty of Celtic Studies, 1970– ; Member: Governing Body, UCC, 1959–71; Senate, NUI, 1964– . *Publications*: *contrib.* Celtica, Érin, Éigse, Studia Hibernica, Studies. *Address*: Univ. College, Cork.

Bredin, Dr Hugh T., MA, PhD; Lecturer in Scholastic Philosophy, Queen's University, Belfast, since 1969; *b* 1939; *m* 1968; two *s* one *d*. BA NUI 1959, MA Belfast 1965, PhD Belfast 1967. Asst Lectr, Belfast, 1966–69. *Publications*: *contrib.* Res. Studies, Il Verri, Eire–Ireland. *Address*: Dept of Scholastic Philosophy, Queen's Univ., Belfast BT7 1NN.

Bredsdorff, Dr Elias Lunn, MA, DrPhil; Reader in Scandinavian Studies, University of Cambridge, since 1960; *b* 1912; *m* 1954; one *s* one *d*. Cand. Mag. Copenhagen 1938, MA Cantab 1949, DrPhil Copenhagen 1964; Corresp. Mem., Swedish Royal Soc. of Lit., Hist. and Antiquities, Stockholm. Queen Alexandra Lectr in Danish, Univ. Coll. London, 1946–49; Lectr in Danish, Cambridge Univ., 1949–60; Fellow of Peterhouse, 1963– . Editor, Scandinavica, 1962– . Hans Christian Andersen Prize, 1973. *Publications*: D. H. Lawrence, 1937; John Steinbeck, 1943; A Bibliography of Danish Literature in English Translation, 1950; (with B. Mortensen and R. G. Popperwell) An Introduction to Scandinavian Literature,

1951, 2nd edn 1971; H. C. Andersen og England, 1954; Hans Andersen and Charles Dickens, 1956; Danish: An Elementary Grammar and Reader, 1956, 3rd edn 1965; Sir Edmund Gosse's Correspondence with Scandinavian Writers, 1960; Bag Ibsens maske, 1962; Goldschmidt's Corsaren, 1962; Henrik Pontoppidan og Georg Brandes I–II, 1964; Kommer det os ved?, 1971; Literatura i obcestvo v Skandinavii, 1971; Den store nordiske krig om seksualmoralen, 1974; *contrib.* Orbis Litterarum, Edda, Scandinavica, Scandinavian Studies. *Address:* Dept of Scandinavian Studies, Univ. of Cambridge, Sidgwick Avenue, Cambridge.

Brenikov, Prof. Paul, MA, DipCD, FRTPI; Professor of Town and Country Planning, University of Newcastle upon Tyne, since 1964; *b* 1921; *m* 1942; two *s* one *d*. BA Liverpool 1948 (Hons Geog.), Dip CD Liverpool 1950, MA Liverpool 1956; FRTPI; Mem.: Inst. Brit. Geogrs, Town and Country Planning Assoc. Lectr, Univ. of Liverpool, 1955–64. Sen. Planning Off., Lancs CC, 1950–55; Planning Consultant, 1957– ; UN Planning Consultant, 1961–64; Mem.: Council, RTPI, 1970– ; Civic Trust for NE, 1970– ; Vice-Chm., RTPI Internal Affairs Cttee, 1973– . *Publications:* contrib. Land Use in an Urban Environment, 1961; The Dublin Regional Plan, Pt I, 1966, Pt II, 1967; Liverpool Essays in Geography, 1967; Construction Industry Handbook, 1971; *contrib.* Archit. Jl, Jl RTPI, Planning Outlook, Town Planning Rev., Urb. Studies. *Address:* Dept of Town and Country Planning, The Univ., Newcastle upon Tyne NE1 7RU.

Brennan, Dr Elizabeth M.; Lecturer in English, Westfield College, University of London, since 1965; *b* 1931. BA Queen's University Belfast 1952 (1st cl. Hons English Lit.), MA by thesis 1955, PhD London 1958. Asst Lectr in English, Univ. Coll. of N Wales, Bangor, 1959–62; Lectr, 1962–65. *Publications:* ed, John Webster: The Duchess of Malfi, 1964, NY 1965; ed, John Webster: The White Devil, 1966, NY 1968. *Address:* Dept of English, Westfield College, Kidderpore Avenue, NW3 7ST.

Brennan, John Desmond, MA; Lecturer in English, University College, Cork, since 1965; *b* 1919; *m* 1961; one *s* one *d*. BA NUI 1947, MA NUI 1948, HDipEd NUI 1951. *Publication:* The Dialect of Thomas Hardy, in, Thomas Hardy Year Book, 1974. *Address:* Dept of English, Univ. College, Cork, Ireland.

Brenner, Nathaniel; Special Lecturer in Drama, Drama Department, University of Bristol, since 1963; *b* 1915; *m* 1943; two *d*. Hon. MA Bristol 1971. Principal: Bristol Old Vic Theatre School 1963– ; Associate Dir, Bristol Old Vic Company. *Address:* Drama Dept, Univ. of Bristol, Bristol BS8 1TH.

Brett, Edwin Allan; Lecturer in Political Science, Sussex University, 1967–72 and since 1974; *b* 1936; *m* 1961; one *s* two *d*. BA (Hons) Witwatersrand 1959, PhD London 1966.

78

Lectr in Politics, Witwatersrand Univ., 1960–61; Lectr in Political Science, Univ. of E Africa, Makerere, 1964–67, 1972–74. *Publications:* African Attitudes, 1963; Colonialism and Underdevelopment in East Africa, 1972; *contrib.* Cah. d'Et. Afr., Race, Race Relat. Jl, Soc. Sci. Inf. *Address:* School of Social Sciences, Univ. of Sussex, Brighton BN1 9QN.

Brett, Prof. Raymond Laurence; G. F. Grant Professor of English, University of Hull, since 1952; *b* 1917; *m* 1947; two *s*. BA (Hons) Bristol 1937 (1st cl. English and Philosophy), BLitt Oxon 1940. Admiralty (Special Reserve RNVR), 1940–46. Lectr in English, Univ. of Bristol, 1946–52; Dean, Faculty of Arts, Univ. of Hull, 1960–62; Vis. Prof. of Rochester, USA, 1958–59. *Publications:* The Third Earl of Shaftesbury: a study in 18th century literary theory, 1951; Coleridge's Theory of Imagination (English Essays), 1949; George Crabbe, 1956; Reason and Imagination, 1961; (with A. R. Jones) a critical edn of Lyrical Ballads by Wordsworth and Coleridge, 1963; Thomas Hobbes (The English Mind), 1964; An Introduction to English Studies, 1965; Fancy and Imagination, 1969; ed, Poems of Faith and Doubt, 1965; ed, S. T. Coleridge, 1971; *contrib.* The Times, Telegraph, Time and Tide, Essays and Studies, Rev. of English Studies, MLR, Philosophy, English, S. Atlantic Qly, etc. *Address:* Univ. of Hull, Hull HU6 7RX.

Bretten, George Rex; Lecturer in Law, Department of Law, London School of Economics, since 1970; *b* 1942; *m* 1965; one *d*. BA 1964, LLB 1965, MA 1968, Cantab; Barrister, Lincoln's Inn, 1965. Lectr in Law, Univ. of Nottingham, 1964–68; Vis. Lectr in Law, Univ. of Auckland, NZ, 1967; Asst Dir, Inst. of Law Res. and Reform, Univ. of Alberta, Canada, 1968–70. *Publications:* contrib. Studies in Canadian Business Law, 1971; *contrib.* Brit. Tax Rev., Convey. and Prop. Lawyer, Internat. and Compar. Law Qly, Jl Bus. Law. *Address:* London School of Economics, Houghton Street, WC2A 2AE.

Brewer, Anthony Alan; Lecturer in Economics, University of Bristol, since 1967; *b* 1942; *m* 1967; two *s*. BA Cambridge 1964, MA Cambridge 1968. Asst Lectr, Leeds, 1966–67. *Address:* Economics Dept, Univ. of Bristol, Bristol BS8 1TH.

Brewer, Dr Derek Stanley; Lecturer in English and Fellow of Emmanuel College, Cambridge, since 1965; *b* 1923; *m* 1951; three *s* two *d*. BA Oxon 1947 (2nd cl. English), MA Oxon 1948, PhD Birmingham 1956, MA Cantab 1965, Matthew Arnold Prize Essay Oxford 1948, Seatonian Prize Poem Cambridge 1969, 1972. Lectr, Birmingham Univ., 1949–56; Prof., Internat. Christian Univ., Japan, 1956–58; Lectr and Sen. Lectr, Birmingham, 1958–64. Brit. Acad. Sir Israel Gollancz Meml Lectr, 1974. Founder and Man. Dir, D. S. Brewer Ltd (for pubn of medieval and renaissance lit. texts and studies). Infantry Off., 1942–45; Capt. and Adjt, 1st Bn Royal Fusiliers, 1944–45; Mem.,

Governing Body, Birmingham Coll. of Arts, 1962–64; Studentship Selection Cttee, Dept of Educn and Science, 1971–74. *Publications*: Chaucer, 1953, 3rd (Supplemented) edn 1973; Proteus: Studies in English Literature, 1958; ed, Chaucer: The Parlement of Foulys, 1960; Chaucer in his Time, 1963; ed, and contrib. Chaucer and Chaucerians, 1966; ed, Malory: The Morte D'Arthur, Pts Seven and Eight, 1968; ed. Chaucer: Facsimile of 16th Century Editions, 1969; ed, Chaucer: Troilus and Criseyde (abridged), 1969; ed, Chaucer: the critical heritage (forthcoming); contrib. Essays on Malory (ed J. A. W. Bennett), 1963; Patterns of Love and Courtesy (ed J. A. W. Lawlor), 1966; Companion to Chaucer Studies (ed B. Rowland), 1968; Chaucer's Mind and Art (ed A. C. Cawley), 1969; Sphere History of English Literature, vol. i (ed W. F. Bolton), 1970; Arthurian Studies (ed D. D. R. Owen), 1971; *contrib.* Anglia, EC, Engl, and Germ. St., Engl. Phil. St., Forum, Japanese learned jls. MÆ, MLR, MLN, NATE Bull., REL, RES, Speculum. *Address*: Emmanuel College, Cambridge.

Brick, Samuel Keith P.; *see* Panter-Brick.

Bridge, Dr Francis Roy; Lecturer, Department of International History, University of Leeds, since 1972; *b* 1939; *m* 1972; one *s*. BA London 1961, PhD London 1966, AKC 1961; FRHistS 1969. Asst Lectr, Internat. History Dept, LSE, 1964–67; Lectr, 1967–72. *Publications*: The Habsburg Monarchy 1804–1918: A critical bibliography, 1967; Great Britain and Austria-Hungary 1906–14: A diplomatic history, 1972; From Sadowa to Sarajevo: The foreign policy of Austria-Hungary 1866–1914, 1972; *contrib.* Slavonic and E European Rev., Middle Eastern Studies. *Address*: Dept of International History, Univ. of Leeds, Leeds LS2 9JT.

Bridge, Ian Cressy; Professor of Shipbuilding and Naval Architecture, University of Strathclyde, since 1970; *b* 1913; *m* 1940; two *d*. BSc Glasgow 1935 (1st cl. Hons Naval Arch.); FRINA; Lectr, Royal Tech. Coll., 1946–55; Sen. Lectr, 1955–65; Reader, Univ. of Strathclyde, 1965–70. Head of Dept, 1946– . *Publications*: *contrib.* Trans IESS, Trans RINA. *Address*: Univ. of Strathclyde, Richmond Street, Glasgow G1 1XH.

Bridge, John Neville, BA, AM; Lecturer in the Economics of the Middle East, University of Durham, since 1969; *b* 1942; *m* 1966; one *s* one *d*. BA Dunelm 1964 (Geography), AM Indiana 1966 (Economics). Lecturer in Economics, Durham, 1966–69. Internat. Editor, Jl of Modern ME Studies. *Publications*: *contrib.* Bank. Mag., Internat. Curr. Rev., Papers of David Horowitz Inst., Kuwait Econ. Soc. Bull., Seminar for Arabian Aff. *Address*: Dept of Economics, Univ. of Durham, 23–26 Old Elvet, Durham DH1 3HY.

Bridge, John William, LLB, LLM, PhD; Professor of Law, University of Exeter, since 1974; *b* 1937; *m* 1962; one *d*. LLB Bristol 1959. LLM Bristol 1962, PhD Bristol 1973;

Mem., Soc. of Public Teachers of Law, Justice, Univ. Assoc. for Contemp. European Studies. Asst Lectr, Univ. of Exeter, 1961–64; Lectr, 1964–71, Sen. Lectr, 1971–74. Governor, Wadham Sch., Crewkerne, Somerset. *Publications*: (with D. Lasok) Introduction to the Law and Institutions of the European Communities, 1973; (ed jtly) Fundamental Rights, 1973; *contrib.* Internat. and Comp. Law Qly, Law Qly Rev., Mod. Law Rev., Neb. Law Rev., Pub. Law, UMKC Law Rev., Jurid. Rev. *Address*: Faculty of Law, Univ. of Exeter, Rennes Drive, Exeter EX4 3LZ.

Bridge, Paul Anthony; Senior Lecturer, Design and Technology, University of London, Goldsmiths' College, since 1966; *b* 1925; *m* 1957; two *d*. Nat. Dip. Design Rotherham College of Art. Lectr, Leeds Coll. of Educn, 1965–66. Hd, Students Hall of Res. *Publications*: Designs in Metal, 1964; Designs in Wood, 1968. *Address*: Univ. of London, Goldsmiths' College, SE14 6NW.

Bridges, Edwin Michael; Senior Lecturer, Department of Geography, University College of Swansea, since 1972, Lecturer, 1961–72; *b* 1931; *m* 1957; 1969; one *s* two *d*. BSc (Hons) Sheffield 1954, DipEd 1955, MSc Sheffield 1958; PhD Wales 1971; Mem.: Internat. Soc. Soil Science, Brit Soc. Soil Science, Inst. Brit. Geogr., Geog. Assoc. Demonstrator in Geography, Sheffield Univ., 1955–56; Vis. Sen. Lectr, Dept of Geography, Univ. of New England, Armidale, NSW, 1966. Surveyor with Soil Survey of England and Wales, 1956–61; Regional Off., East Midlands, 1958–61; Mem., Council Brit. Soc. Soil Science, 1964–67. *Publications*: The Soils and Land Use of the District North of Derby, 1966; World Soils, 1970; ed, Soil Heterogeneity and Podzolization, 1971; *contrib.* Agriculture, Trans Internat. Soc. Soil Science, Jl of Soil Science, Trans Inst. Brit. Geogrs, Geog., Scot. Geog. Mag. *Address*: Dept of Geography, Univ. College of Swansea, Singleton Park, Swansea SA2 8PP.

Bridges, Dr Roy Charles, BA, PhD; Senior Lecturer in History, Department of History, University of Aberdeen, since 1970; *b* 1932; *m* 1960; two *s* two *d*. BA Keele 1957 (1st cl. History and Geography), DipEd 1957, PhD London 1963 (African History); Mem.: Afr. Studies Assoc. UK, Royal Geog. Soc., Hist. Assoc. Asst Lectr, Makerere Univ., Uganda, 1960–62, Lectr, 1962–64; Lectr, Univ. of Aberdeen, 1964–70; Vis. Asst Prof., Indiana Univ., USA, 1967. Adv. of Studies, Fac. of Arts, Univ. of Aberdeen, 1970– ; Mem.: Council, Afr. Studies Assoc. UK, 1970–73; Sec., Aberdeen Univ. Afr. Studies Gp, 1966– . *Publications*: Biog. Introd., 2nd edn J. L. Krapf: Travels, 1968; co-ed., Nations and Empires, 1969; Speke, in, Africa and Its Explorers, ed Rotberg, 1971; Livingstone and Africa (forthcoming); *contrib.* Afr. Hist. Studies, Geog. Jl, Ugan. Jl. *Address*: Dept of History, King's College, Aberdeen AB9 2UB.

Bridgwater, Dr Anthony Victor; Lecturer in Chemical Engineering, University of

Aston in Birmingham (also teaching Economics), since 1965; *b* 1942; *m* 1968. BSc (Tech.) Manchester 1963, MSc Aston 1967, PhD Aston 1971; CEng, MIChemE. *Publications*: contrib. Technological Forecasting, ed R. V. Arnfield, 1970; *contrib*. Chem. Engr, Powder Met. *Address*: Dept of Chemical Engineering, Univ. of Aston, Birmingham B4 7ET.

Brierley, Dr Harry, MA, DipEd, PhD, ABPsS; Consultant Psychologist, Newcastle University Hospital Group and Hon. Clinical Tutor, University of Newcastle Medical School, since 1966; *b* 1927; *m* 1951; one *d*. BA Cambridge 1951 (Exp. Psychol.), CertEd Cantab 1952, DipEd Cantab 1959, MA Liverpool 1960, PhD Leeds 1970; ABPsS. Clin. Services Sub-Cttee, Clin. Div., Brit. Psychol. Soc.; Cttee, NE Branch, Clin. Div., Brit. Psychol. Soc. *Publications*: *contrib*. Jl Neurol. Neurosurg, and Psychiatry, Brit. Jl Soc. Clin. Psychol., Brit. Jl Psychiatry, Brit. Jl Psychol. (General), Psychol. Med., Brit. Jl Criminol., Brit. Jl Educ. Psychol. *Address*: The General Hospital, Newcastle upon Tyne.

Briggs, Dr Anthony David, MA, PhD; Lecturer, Russian Studies, University of Bristol, since 1968; *b* 1938; *m* 1962; two *d*. BA Cantab 1961 (2nd cl.), MA Cantab 1965, PhD London 1968. Lectr in Russian, Queen's Univ., Kingston, Ontario, 1963–65. *Publications*: *contrib*. Forum (Univ. of St Andrews), Slavonic and East European Rev., Slavic Rev., Russian Lit. (Ardis), Oxf. Slavonic Papers, NZ Slavonic Jl. *Address*: Dept of Russian Studies, Univ. of Bristol, Bristol BS8 1TH.

Briggs, Prof. Asa, MA, BSc (Econ); Professor of History; Vice-Chancellor, University of Sussex, since 1967; *b* 1921; *m* 1955; two *s* two *d*. 1st cl. History Tripos Pts I and II Cambridge 1941, BSc (Econ) London 1941 (1st cl.); Hon DLitt East Anglia 1966, Hon DSc Florida Presbyterian 1966, Hon LLD York Canada 1968. Gerstenberg studentship in Economics, London, 1941; Fellow of Worcester Coll., Oxford, 1944–55; Reader in Recent Social and Economic History, Oxford, 1950–55; Mem., Inst. for Advanced Study, Princeton, USA, 1953–54; Faculty Fellow of Nuffield Coll., 1953–55; Prof. of Modern History, Leeds Univ., 1955–61; Dean, Sch. of Social Studies, Sussex Univ., 1961–65; Pro Vice-Chancellor, 1961–67; Visiting Prof., Australian National Univ., 1960, Chicago Univ., 1966 and 1972. Dep. Pres., WEA, 1954–58, Pres., 1958–67; Mem., UGC, 1959–67; Trustee, Glyndebourne Arts Trust, 1966– ; Chm., Standing Conf. for Study of Local History, 1969– ; Trustee, Internat. Broadcasting Inst., 1968– ; Governor, British Film Inst., 1970– ; Mem., Court of Governors, Admin. Staff Coll., 1971– ; Mem., Amer. Acad. of Arts and Sciences, 1970– . Hon. Fellow, Sidney Sussex Coll., Cambridge, 1968; Hon. Fellow, Worcester Coll., Oxford, 1969. *Publications*: (with D. Thomson and E. Meyer) Patterns of Peace-making, 1945; History of Birmingham (1865–1938), 1952; Victorian People, 1954; Friends of the People, 1956; The Age of Improvement, 1959; ed, Chartist Studies,

1959; ed (with John Saville), Essays in Labour History, vol. i, 1960, vol. ii, 1971; ed, They Saw it Happen, 1897–1940, 1961; A Study of the Work of Seebohm Rowntree, 1871–1954, 1961; History of Broadcasting in the United Kingdom, vol. i; The Birth of Broadcasting, 1961; vol. ii, The Golden Age of Wireless, 1965; vol. iii, The War of Words, 1970; Victorian Cities, 1963; William Cobbett, 1967; How They Lived, 1700–1815, 1969; ed, The Nineteenth Century, 1970. *Address*: Univ. of Sussex, Falmer, Brighton BN1 9RH.

Briggs, John Henry York, MA; Lecturer, Department of History, University of Keele, since 1964; *b* 1938; *m* 1965; three *s*. BA Cantab 1961, MA Cantab; Mem., Eccles. Hist. Soc. Holland Rose Prize, Christ's Coll., Cambridge, 1961; Univ. Postgrad. Schol., Univ. of Exeter, 1961–63; Sir Arthur Reed Grad. Schol., Univ. of Exeter, 1963–64. Pilot Officer, RAF, 1956–58; Pres., N Staffs Branch of Hist. Assoc., 1970– (Sec., 1965–70); Mem., Council, Baptist Union of GB, 1970– ; Cttee, Baptist Hist. Soc., 1971– ; Cttee, Univ. Teachers' Gp, 1968– . *Publications*: *contrib*. Baptist Qly, Faith and Thought. *Address*: Dept of History, Univ. of Keele, Staffs ST5 5BG.

Brightwell, Peter; Lecturer in Modern History, Durham University, since 1968; *b* 1938; *m* 1970. BA Cantab 1961 (1st cl. History), MA Cantab 1967, PhD Cantab 1967. Fellow, Emmanuel Coll., Cambridge, 1965. *Address*: History Dept, 43 North Bailey, Durham.

Brindle, Prof. Reginald Smith, DMus; Professor of Music, University of Surrey, since 1970; *b* 1917; *m* 1947; one *s* three *d*. BMus Wales 1949, Dip. Accademia S. Cecilia Rome 1952, DMus Wales 1959. Lectr, 1957–62, Sen. Lectr, 1962–63, Reader, 1963–67, Prof., 1967–70, UC N Wales. *Publications*: Serial Composition, 1966; Contemporary Percussion, 1971; ed, New Sounds for Woodwind, by Bruno Bartolozzi, 1967; contrib. Encyclopaedia Britannica, Enc. dello Spettacolo (Rome), Enc. de la Musique Religeuse, Paris; *contrib*. Musical Qly, Musical Times. *Address*: Music Dept, Univ. of Surrey, Guildford, Surrey GU2 5XH.

Briscoe, Dr John, MA, DPhil; Senior Lecturer in Greek and Latin, University of Manchester, since 1974; *b* 1938; *m* 1966; one *s* one *d*. BA Oxon 1960 (1st cl. Classical Mods, 1st cl. Lit. Hum.), MA Oxon 1963, DPhil Oxon 1965. Jun. Res. Fellow, Corpus Christi Coll., Oxford, 1962–67; Lectr, Corpus Christi Coll., Oxford, 1967–68; Lectr, Gk and Latin, Univ. of Manchester, 1968–74. Mem., Oxford City Council, 1962–68; Vice-Chm., Planning Cttee, 1964–66; Dep. Leader, Labour Group, 1967–68. *Publications*: Commentary on Livy, xxxi–xxxiii, 1973; Chapter in Livy, 1971; Studies in Ancient Society, 1974; *contrib*. Historia, JRS, Latomus, Past and Present, Classical Rev. *Address*: Departments of Greek and Latin, Univ. of Manchester, Manchester M13 9PL.

Briscoe, Lynden Margaret, MA; Lecturer, Department of Economics, University of Manchester, since 1969; *b* 1935; *m* 1966; one *s* one *d.* BA Oxon 1957 (PPE); Mem., Royal Econ. Soc., Res. Asst, Lady Hall, on comparative study of the distinctive trades, 1957–59; Res. Asst, Agricultural Econ. Res. Inst., Oxford, 1959–61; helped Colin Clark with book entitled British Trade in the Common Market, 1961–62; Deptl Demonstrator, Agricultural Econ. Res. Inst., Oxford, 1962–68. *Publications:* (some as L. M. Moore) Textile and Clothing Industries of the United Kingdom, 1971; contrib. The World Situation and Outlook for Cotton, in, Agricultural Producers and their Markets, ed T. K. Warley, 1967; *contrib.* Bull. Oxford Univ. Inst. of Stats, Farm Econ., Malayan Econ. Rev., Westminster Bank Rev. *Address:* Faculty of Economic and Social Studies, Dover Street, Manchester.

Briston, Prof. Richard Jeremy, BSc (Econ), ACA; Professor of Accountancy, University of Strathclyde, since 1972; *b* 1938; *m* 1964; one *d.* BSc(Econ) LSE 1958; ACA 1961. Lectr in Accounting, Univ. of Hull, 1963–69; Sen. Lectr in Finance, Bradford Management Centre, Univ. of Bradford, 1969–72. Dir of Res. and Mem., Council of Brit. Accounting and Finance Assoc.; Mem., Ed. Bd, Jl of Business Finance. *Publications:* The Stock Exchange and Investment Analysis, 1970, 2nd edn 1972; *contrib.* Econ. Jl, Jl of Business Finance, Jl of Business Policy, Accounting and Business Res. *Address:* Dept of Accounting and Finance, Univ. of Strathclyde, Glasgow G1 1XW.

Bristow, John Anthony; Associate Professor of Economics, Trinity College, University of Dublin, since 1972; *b* 1938; *m* 1962; two *s* one *d.* BA(Econ) Manchester 1961, MA Dublin 1970; Mem., Royal Econ. Soc., American Econ. Assoc. Asst Lectr and Lectr in Economics, QUB, 1963–66; Lectr, TCD, 1967–72. Economist, NI Govt, 1961–63; Jt Ed., Econ. and Soc. Rev., 1970– . *Publications:* (with A. A. Tait) Economic Policy in Ireland, 1968; (with C. F. Fell) Bord na Mona – a Cost-Benefit Study, 1971; (with A. A. Tait) Ireland – Some Problems of a Developing Economy, 1972; *contrib.* Econ. Jl. *Address:* 6 Trinity College, Dublin 2.

Britton, Prof. Denis King, MA, BSc(Econ), FRAgSs; Professor of Agricultural Economics, Wye College, University of London, since 1970; *b* 1920; *m* 1942; one *s* two *d.* BSc(Econ) London 1940, MA(Oxon) (by decree) 1948; FRAgS, FSA, Pres.-Elect, Internat. Assoc. of Agricultural Economists, Mem., Agricultural Econ. Soc. Lectr, Agricultural Econ. Res. Inst., Oxford, 1947–52; Prof. of Agricultural Econ., Nottingham, 1961–70; Dean of Faculty of Agric. and Hortic., 1967–70. Economist, UN Food and Agriculture Organisation, Geneva, 1952–59; Gen. Manager, Marketing and Econ. Res., Massey-Ferguson (UK) Ltd, 1959–61; Mem.: Econ. Develop. Cttee for Agriculture 1967– 73, Home-Grown Cereals Authority 1969– , Working Party on Management and Conservation of Natural Resources (Dept of the Environment), 1971–72, Adv. Council for

Agriculture and Horticulture in England and Wales, 1973– , Jt Cons. Org. for Research and Develt in Agriculture and Food: Arable Crops and Forage Bd, 1973– . Econ. Editor, World Atlas of Agriculture, 1961– . *Publications:* Cereals in the United Kingdom: Production, Marketing and Utilisation, 1969; *contrib.* Jl Agric. Econ., Jl Roy. Stat. Soc., Jl Farmers' Club. *Address:* School of Rural Economics and Related Studies, Wye College (Univ. of London), Ashford, Kent TN25 5AH.

Britton, Geoffrey Clifford, MA, PhD; Senior Lecturer in English, Bedford College, University of London, since 1965; *b* 1924; *m* 1950; one *s* three *d.* BA Birmingham 1948, MA Birmingham 1950, PhD Birmingham 1957. Asst Lectr, Bedford Coll., Univ. of London, 1950–53; Lectr, 1953–65. *Publications: contrib.* Anglia, EGS, EPS, Neophiloiogus, NM, N & Q, YWES. *Address:* Dept of English, Bedford College (Univ. of London), Regent's Park, NW1 4NS.

Britton, Prof. James Nimmo, MA; Goldsmiths' Professor of Education, University of London, since 1970; *b* 1908; *m* 1938; two *d.* BA (Hons) London 1929 (Engl.), Teachers' Dip. London 1930, MA London 1952 (with Distinction); Campbell Clarke Schol. 1926, John Oliver Hobbs Memorial Schol. 1928, Sen. Lectr in Educn, Univ. of London Inst. of Educn, 1954–66; Reader, 1966–70. Educn Ed., John Murray (publishers), 1938–53; Mem.: SSEC Engl. Lang. Examng Cttee, 1961–63; Schools' Council Engl. Cttee, 1965– 70; Dir, Schools' Council Writing Research Project, 1966–71; Chm., Nat. Assoc. for Teaching of Engl., 1971–73. *Publications:* (with Douglas Barnes and Harold Rosen) Language, the Learner and the School, 1969, rev. edn 1971; Language and Learning, 1970, American edn 1971, Dutch, German, Italian edns 1972; *contrib.* Brit. Jl Psychol., Educnl Rev., Engl. in Educn, Jl of Curriculum Studies. *Address:* Goldsmiths' College, Lewisham Way, New Cross, SE14 6NW.

Britton, Prof. Karl William; Professor of Philosophy, University of Newcastle upon Tyne, since 1951; *b* 1909; *m* 1936; one *s* two *d.* MA Cantab 1934 (1st cl.) MA Harvard 1934; Pres., Mind Assoc., 1963 (Sec. 1949–62). Lectr in Philosophy: UC, Aberystwyth, 1934–37; UC, Swansea, 1937–50. Dean, Fac. of Arts, Durham, 1961–63; Public Orator, Durham, 1959–62; Dean, Fac. of Arts, Newcastle, 1966–69. *Publications:* Communication, 1939, 1970; John Stuart Mill, 1953, 1969; Philosophy and the Meaning of Life, 1969; *contrib.* Proc. Aristotelian Soc., Mind, Philosophy, Philos. Rev. *Address:* The Univ., Newcastle upon Tyne NE1 7RU.

Broadbent, Prof. John Barclay, MA, PhD; Professor of English Literature, School of English and American Studies, University of East Anglia, since 1968; *b* 1926; *m* 1949; three *s* one *d.* MA Edinburgh 1952 (1st cl. English Lit. and Lang.), PhD Cantab 1955. Res. Fellow, St Catharine's Coll., Cambridge, 1955; Fellow, King's Coll., Cambridge, 1957; Sen. Tutor, 1963–68; Lectr in English, Cambridge 1955–68; Vis. Prof., Univ of Chicago, 1955; British Council Lectr, India, 1967, 1970. *Publications:* Some graver subject: an essay on 'Paradise Lost', 1960; ed, Smart: A Song to David, 1960; Milton: 'Comus' and 'Samson', 1961; Poetic love, 1964; ed, Paradise Lost I–II, 1972; 'Paradise Lost': introduction, 1972. *Address:* School of English and American Studies, Univ. of East Anglia, Univ. Plain, Norwich NOR 88C.

Broadhurst, Anne, BSc, DipPsychol., PhD, FBPsS; Lecturer, Department of Psychology, University of Birmingham, since 1971; *b* 1930; *m* 1956; one *s* one *d.* BSc London 1951 (1st cl. Psychol.), DipPsychol. London 1953, PhD London 1956; Mem.: Brit. Psychol. Soc., 1952, ABPsS 1955, FBPsS 1973. Div. Clin. Psychol., 1956. Asst Lectr, Inst. Psychiatry, London, 1954; Lectr in Clinical Psychol., Univ. of Birmingham, 1963–71. *Publications:* Abnormal sexual behaviour – female, in, Handbook of Abnormal Psychology, 2nd edn, ed, H. J. Eysenck, 1972; *contrib.* Brit. Jl Psychiatry, Brit. Jl Psychol., Jl Experim. Res. in Personality, Jl Ment. Sci., Acta Psychologia, Brit. Jl Social and Clinical Psychol. *Address:* Dept of Psychology, Univ. of Birmingham, Birmingham B15 2TT.

Broadhurst, Prof. Peter Lovell, DSc, FBPsS, FIBiol; Professor of Psychology, Head of Department of Psychology, University of Birmingham, since 1965; *b* 1924; *m* 1956; one *s* one *d.* BA London 1950, MA Stanford, California 1951, PhD London 1956, DSc London 1970; FBPsS, FIBiol For. Affiliate, Amer. Psychol. Assoc., Mem.: Assoc. Study of Animal Behaviour, Experim. Psychol. Soc., Genet. Soc. (all of GB); Corresp. Mem., Pavlov. Soc. (USA). Res. Psychol., 1951–56; Lectr, 1956–59; Sen. Lectr in Psychol., 1960–63, Inst. Psychiatry, Univ. of London; Sen. Lectr in Psychol., Univ. of Birmingham, 1963–65. Dir, Animal Lab., Inst. Psychiatry, Univ. of London, 1955–63; Fellow, Center Adv. Stud. Behav. Sci., Calif, 1961–62; Chm., Biol. Gp, Fac. of Sci. and Eng., Univ. of Birmingham, 1971–73; Fellow, Neth. Inst. Adv. Stud., 1973–74. *Publications:* The Science of Animal Behaviour, 1963; (with Charlotte Banks) Stephanos: Studies in Psychology presented to Cyril Burt, 1965; *contrib.* Acta Psychol., Activas Nervosa Superior, Amer. Psychol., Animal Behav., Ann. NY Acad. Sci., Behav. Genet., Behav. Res. Therap., Brain Res., Brit. Jl Psychol., Canad. Jl Psychol., Condit. Reflex, Folia Primatolog., Genetika, Heredity. Jl Comp. Physiol. Psychol., Jl Experim. Psychol., Jl Endocrin., Jl Genet. Psychol., Jl Psychosom. Res., Nature (London), Proc. Royal Soc. (B), Psychol. Bull., Psychol. Rep., Qly Jl Studies in Alcohol, and numerous edited books and encyclopaedias. *Address:* Univ. of Birmingham, PO Box 363, Birmingham B15 2TT.

Broady, Prof. Maurice, BA; Professor of Social Administration, University College of Swansea, since 1970; *b* 1926; *m* 1953; three *d.* BA Liverpool 1952 (1st cl. Social Science); Mem., Brit. Social. Assoc., Regional Studies Assoc. Jun. Res. Worker, Liverpool, 1953–56; Sen. Res. Worker, Glasgow, 1956–59; Lectr,

1959–65, Sen. Lectr, 1965–70, Southampton; Andrew Mellon Fellow, Pittsburgh, 1966. Chm., Salzburg Congress on Urban Planning, 1968–70; Mem., Publications Cttee, Nat. Council of Soc. Sci., 1967– ; Consult. Sociol., Tayside Study, 1968–70. *Publications:* (with Vereker and others) Urban Redevelopment and Social Change, 1961; Planning for People, 1969; ed, Marginal Regions: essays on social planning, 1973; *contrib.* Architect. Assoc. Qly, Koelner Zeitschrift für Soziologie, Town Planning Rev., Urban Affairs Qly. Univ. Qly. *Address:* Dept of Social Administration, Univ. College, Singleton Park, Swansea SA2 8PP.

Brock, David Le Marchant; Lectr in Architecture, Department of Architecture, University of Liverpool, since 1964; *b* 1923; *m* 1947; four *d.* BArch Liverpool (Hons), Dip. Civic Design Liverpool; ARIBA 1950. *Address:* Dept of Architecture, Univ. of Liverpool, Liverpool L69 3BX.

Brock, Michael George, MA, FRHistS; Vice-President and Bursar, Wolfson College, Oxford University, since 1967; *b* 1920; *m* 1949; three *s.* BA Oxon 1943, MA Oxon 1948 (1st cl. History); FRHistS 1965. Jun. Res. Fellow, Corpus Christi Coll., Oxford, 1948–50; Fellow and Tutor, 1950–66; Lectr (CUF), Oxford Univ., 1951–70; Jun. Proctor, 1956–57; Mem., Hebdomodal Council, 1965– ; Vis. Prof., Univ. of South Carolina, 1959–60. Mem., Oxford City Educn Cttee, 1957–61; Oxford Univ. correspondent, The Guardian, 1960–65; Pres., Oxford Assoc., AUT, 1964–66; Mem., Council, Eastbourne Coll., 1964–71. *Publications:* The Great Reform Act, 1973; *contrib.* British Prime Ministers, 1953, Wellingtonian Studies, 1959, Britain and the Netherlands, 1960. *Address:* Wolfson College Office, 47 Banbury Road, Oxford OX2 6NN.

Brock, Dr Sebastian Paul; University Lecturer in Aramaic and Syriac, University of Oxford, since 1974; *b* 1938; *m* 1966. BA Cantab 1962, MACantab 1965, MA and DPhil Oxon 1966. Asst Lectr, 1964–66, Lectr, 1966–67, Dept of Theology, Univ. of Birmingham; Lectr, Hebrew and Aramaic, Univ. of Cambridge, 1967–74. *Publications:* Pseudepigrapha Veteris Testamenti Graece II; Testamentum Iobi, 1967; The Syriac Version of the Pseudo-Nonnos Mythological Scholia, 1971; (with C. T. Fritsch and S. Jellicoe) A Classified Bibliography of the Septuagint, 1973, *contrib.* JSS, JST, Le Muséon, Oriens Christianus, Orientalia Christiana Periodica, Parole de l'Orient, Revue des études arméniennes. *Address:* Wolfson College, Oxford.

Brock, Dr William Hodson; Reader in History of Science, and Director, Victorian Studies Centre, University of Leicester, since 1974; *b* 1936; *m* 1960; two *s* one *d.* BSc London 1959, MSc Leicester 1961, PhD Leicester 1967; FCS, Mem., Brit. Soc. Hist. Science, Mem., Soc. Study Hist. Alchemy and Early Chemistry. Tutorial Asst, Leicester, 1960–62, Lectr in History of Science, 1962–74. Hon. Ed., Ambix, 1968– . Mem.: Council Brit. Soc. Hist. Science, 1968–72, Council

Soc. Study Alchemy and Early Chemistry, 1967– , Brit. Nat. Comm. Hist. of Science, Medicine, Technology (Roy. Soc.), 1971– . *Publications*: ed. Atomic Debates, 1967; ed, Science Case Histories, 1971; Henry Armstrong and the Teaching of Science, 1973; *contrib*. Med. Hist., Ambix, Isis, Notes and records Roy. Soc., Ann. Sci. *Address*: Dept of History of Science, Univ. of Leicester, Leicester LE1 7RH.

Brock, Prof. William Ranulf; Professor of Modern History, Department of History, Glasgow University, since 1967; *b* 1916; *m* 1950; one *s* one *d*. BA Cambridge 1937, PhD Cambridge 1946, MA Cambridge 1948; FRHistS.; Mem.: Hist. Assoc., Econ. Hist. Soc., Amer. Hist. Assoc., Org. of Amer. Hist., Brit. Assoc. Amer. Studies, Camb. Hist. Soc. Fellow, Selwyn Coll., Cambridge, 1947 (now Life Fellow); Univ. Lectr, 1949–67; Sec. Fac. Bd of Hist., 1961–64; Sec., Higher Degree Cttee, 1961–67; Vis. Prof., Univ. of Michigan, 1968; Vis. Prof., Univ. of Washington, 1970. *Publications*: Lord Liverpool and Liberal Toryism, 1941; Britain and the Dominions, 1950; The Character of American History, 1960, 2nd edn 1965; An American Crisis, 1963, American edn 1968; The Evolution of American Democracy, 1970; Conflict and Transformation, 1973; Sources of History: US 1790–1890, 1974; Chapters in, New Cambridge Modern History, vol. VII and vol. XI, 1957, 1962; *contrib*. Jl Amer. Studies, Hist. *Address*: Dept of History, Univ. of Glasgow, Glasgow G12 8QQ.

Brockbank, Prof. John Philip, MA, PhD; Professor of English Literature, University of York, since 1963; *b* 1922; *m* 1946; one *s*. BA Cantab 1949, MA Cantab 1953, PhD Cantab 1953; Charles Oldham Shakespeare Schol. 1950. Prof. of English, Univ. of Saarbrücken, 1953–54; Asst Lectr, Cambridge, 1954–58; Lectr, Jesus Coll., 1954–58; Lectr, Reading Univ., 1958–63. Mem.: UGC Arts Sub-Cttee, 1967– ; Council of Nat. Academic Awards, 1969– . *Publications*: Marlowe, Dr. Faustus, 1962; ed., Selected Poems of Pope, 1964; ed, Ben Jonson, Volpone, 1968; general ed, with B. Morris, New Mermaid Playwright; contrib. Early Shakespeare, 1961, later Shakespeare, 1966, ed Brown and Harris; Approaches to Paradise Lost, ed Patrides, 1968; Sphere History of English Literature, ed Ricks, 1971; *contrib*. Essays and Studies, Shakespeare Survey. *Address*: Dept of English, Univ. of York, York YO1 5DD.

Brockington, Dr John Leonard; Lecturer, Sanskrit Department, University of Edinburgh, since 1965; *b* 1940; *m* 1966; one *s* one *d*. BA Hons Oxford 1963 (Sanskrit), MA 1966, DPhil 1968; *Publications*: *contrib*. JAOS, JOIB, JRAS. *Address*: Sanskrit Dept, 7 Buccleuch Place, Edinburgh EH8 9LW.

Brocklehurst, Dr John Brian, MA, DMus, LRAM, ARCM; Senior Lecturer in Education (Music), University of Birmingham, since 1972, Lecturer in Music Education, 1959–72; BA Nottingham 1952, MA Sheffield 1957, DMus Sheffield 1959; LRAM, ARCM 1950. *Publications*: Music in Schools, 1962;

Pentatonic Song Book, 1968; Response to Music, 1971; *contrib*. Mus. and Lett., Educnl Rev. *Address*: School of Education, Univ. of Birmingham, PO Box 363, Edgbaston, Birmingham B15 2TT.

Bromhead, Prof. Peter Alexander; Professor of Politics, University of Bristol, since 1964; *b* 1919; *m* 1946; two *d*. BA Oxon 1941 (PPE), MA Oxon 1947, DPhil Oxon 1950. Lectr, Durham Univ., 1947–58; Sen. Lectr, 1958–62; Reader 1962; Vis. Prof., Univ. of Florida, 1959–60; Prof. of Politics, Univ. Coll. Swansea, 1963–64; Dean of Social Sciences, Bristol Univ., 1970–72. Mem., UGC Social Studies Sub-Cttee, 1968–73. *Publications*: Private Members' Bills, 1956; The House of Lords and Contemporary Politics, 1958; Life in Modern Britain, 1962, 3rd edn 1971; Life in Modern America, 1970; The Great White Elephant of Maplin Sands: the neglect of comprehensive transport planning in government decision-making, 1973; *contrib*. Church Qly Rev., Durham Univ. Jl, New Society, Parliamentary Affairs, Political Qly, Political Studies, Eur. Community. *Address*: Dept of Politics, Univ. of Bristol, 40 Berkeley Square, Bristol BS8 1HY.

Bromley, Mrs Jean; *see* Robertson, J.

Bromley, Prof. John Selwyn; Professor of Modern History, University of Southampton, since 1960; *b* 1913; *m* 1939. BA Oxford 1935 (1st cl. Hons), MA Oxford 1943; FRHistS. Lectr, Liverpool Univ., 1937–47; Lectr and subsequently Fellow, Keble Coll., Oxford, 1947–59; Vis. Res. Fellow, Merton College, 1971; Dean of Faculty of Arts, Southampton, 1965–68, Public Orator, 1973– . Admin. Asst, HM Treasury, 1941–45; Mem.: Councils of R. Hist. Soc., Hist. Assoc., Navy Records Soc., Hakluyt Soc., Soc. for Nautical Res., Brit. Nat. Cttee of Internat. Congress for Hist. Sciences, 1970– . *Publications*: John Balthorpe's The Straights Voyage, 1959; ed (with R. Hatton), William III and Louis XIV, 1968; The New Cambridge Modern History, vol. VI (The Rise of Great Britain and Russia), 1970; ed (with E. H. Kossmann), Britain and the Netherlands (4 vols), 1960–72; *contrib*. EHR, Revue d'histoire économique et sociale. *Address*: Dept of History, Univ. of Southampton, Highfield, Southampton, Hants SO9 5NH.

Bromley, Prof. Peter Mann; Professor of Law, University of Manchester, since 1965; *b* 1922; *m* 1963. BA Oxon 1947 (1st cl. Jurisprudence), MA Oxon 1948; Barrister Middle Temple 1951. Asst Lectr, Manchester Univ., 1947–50; Lectr, 1950–61; Sen. Lectr, 1961–65. Mem., Adv. Cttee on Legal Educn. *Publications*: Family Law, 1957, 4th edn 1971. *Address*: Faculty of Law, Univ. of Manchester, Manchester M13 9PL.

Bromwich, John I'anson, TD, MA; University Lecturer in English, University of Cambridge, since 1955; *b* 1915; *m* 1939; one *s*. BA Cantab 1937 (1st cl. Archaeology and Anthropology), MA Cantab 1941; FRNS, FRGS. Fellow, St John's Coll., Cambridge, 1949; Univ. Asst Lectr, Cambridge Univ., 1949–55; Fellow, Univ. Coll., Cambridge,

1965, Wolfson Coll., 1973. Univ. Candidate, Regular Army, 1935; Overseas Service (Middlesex Regt, Manchester Regt, British Military Mission to Greece) in Albania, Bulgaria, Egypt, Greece, Italy, Lebanon, Northern Ireland, Palestine, Syria and Trans-Jordan; Sec., 1952, Ed., 1954 Camb. Antiqu. Soc. *Publications*: Who was the Translator of the Paris Psalter?, 1950; ed, The Paris Psalter, 1958; (co-author) The Fenland in Roman Times, 1970; (co-author). A Semasiological Dictionary of the English Language (description of a computerized archive started in 1937), in, The Computer and Literary Studies, ed A. J. Aitkin et al., 1973; *contrib*. Camb. Bibliog. Soc., Numism. Chron. *Address*: Wolfson College, Cambridge.

Bromwich, Michael; Professor, Department of Business Administration and Accountancy, University of Wales Institute of Science and Technology, since 1971; *b* 1941; *m* 1972. BSc Econ London; ACMA 1962, ABIM 1972. Lectr, LSE, 1965–71. Dir, Graduate Management Centre, UWIST, 1970– . *Publications*: *contrib*. Accounting and Business Res., Jl Business Finance. *Address*: UWIST, King Edward VII Avenue, Cardiff CF1 3NU.

Bromwich, Dr Rachel, LittD; Reader in Celtic Languages and Literature, Department of Anglo-Saxon, Norse, and Celtic, University of Cambridge, since 1973; *b* 1915; *m* 1939; one *s*. BA Cambridge 1938 (English (Anglo-Saxon, Norse and Celtic)), LittD Cambridge 1971; Mem.: Internat. Arthurian Soc.; Soc. for Study of Medieval Languages and Literature; Hon. Soc. of Cymmrodorion; Irish Texts Soc. Univ. Lectr, Cambridge, 1945; O'Donnell Lectr: Univ. of Wales, 1962; Univ. of Oxford, 1967; Rhys Fellowship in Celtic Studies, Univ. of Oxford, 1974–75. Mem.: Council, Irish Texts Soc.; Cttee, British Branch of Internat. Arthurian Soc.; Exec. Cttee, Soc. for Study of Mediaeval Languages and Literature, 1967–69. *Publications*: Trioedd Ynys Prydein: The Welsh Triads, 1961; Tradition and Innovation in the Poetry of Dafydd ap Gwilym, 1967; Matthew Arnold and Celtic Literature: A Retrospect, 1967; Trioedd Ynys Prydain, in, Welsh Literature and Scholarship, 1969; ed, The Beginnings of Welsh Poetry (Studies by Sir Ifor Williams), 1972; ed, Armes Prydein: The Prophecy of Britain, 1972; *contrib*. Trans Hon. Soc. Cymmrod., Etudes Celt., Bull. Bd Celtic Stud., Med. Aev. *Address*: Wolfson College, Cambridge.

Brook, Prof. George Leslie, MA, PhD; Professor of English Language, since 1946, and of Medieval English Literature, University of Manchester, since 1950; *b* 1910; *m* 1948. BA Leeds 1931 (1st cl. English), PhD 1935, MA Manchester 1949. Asst Lectr, 1932–37; Lectr, 1937–46; Vis. Prof., UCLA, 1951. *Publications*: English Sound Changes, 1935; ed, The Harley Lyrics, 1948, 4th edn 1968; An Introduction to Old English, 1955; A History of the English Language, 1958; ed (with R. F. Leslie), La 3 amon: Brut, 1963; English Dialects, 1963; The Modern University, 1965; The Language of Dickens, 1970; Varieties of English, 1973; *contrib*. Leeds

Studies in English. *Address*: Dept of English Language and Literature, The Univ., Manchester M13 9PL.

Brook, Dr Leslie Charles, PhD; Lecturer in French, University of Birmingham, since 1962; *b* 1933; *m* 1959; four *s* two *d*. BA Bristol 1954 (1st cl. French), CertEd. Bristol 1959, PhD Bristol 1969; Mem., Internat. Arthurian Soc. and Soc. Rencesvals. Lecteur, Univ. Bordeaux, 1959–61; Res. Asst, Univ. Coll. London, 1961–62. *Publications*: ed, J. de Meun: Letters of Abelard and Héloïse (forthcoming); *contrib*. Actes et Mém. Soc. Rencesvals. *Address*: Dept of French, Univ. of Birmingham, PO Box 363, Birmingham B15 2TT.

Brooke, Prof. Christopher Nugent Lawrence, FBA; Professor of History, Westfield College, University of London, since 1967; *b* 1927; *m* 1951; three *s*. BA Cantab 1948 (1st cl. Hist. Tripos), MA Cantab 1952; FBA 1970. Fellow of Gonville and Caius Coll., 1949–56; Lectr in History, 1953–56; Praelector Rhetoricus, 1955–56; Asst Lectr in History, Cambridge, 1953–54; Univ. Lectr, 1954–56; Prof. of Mediaeval History, Univ. of Liverpool, 1956–67. *Publications*: From Alfred to Henry III 871–1272, 1961; The Saxon and Norman Kings, 1963; Europe in the Central Middle Ages, 1964; (with A. Morey) Gilbert Foliot and his Letters, 1965; (with A. Morey) The Letters and Charters of Gilbert Foliot: Bishop of London (1163–87), 1967; The Twelfth Century Renaissance, 1969–70; Structure of Medieval Society, 1971; (with D. Knowles and V. London) The Heads of Religious Houses, England and Wales, 940–1216, 1972; *contrib*. Bull. Inst. Hist. Res., Cambridge Hist. Jl, EHR, Jl Soc. Archivists, Traditio, Trans RHistS. *Address*: Dept of History, Westfield College, Kidderpore Avenue, NW3 7ST.

Brooke, Dr John Hedley; Lecturer in History of Science, Lancaster University, since 1969; *b* 1944; *m* 1972. BA Hons Cantab 1965, MA Cantab, PhD Cantab 1969, Cert. in Hist. and Philos. of Science, with Distinction, Cambridge, 1965; Member: Soc. for Study of Alchemy and Early Chemistry; British Soc. for Hist. of Science. Research Fellow, Fitzwilliam Coll., Cambridge, 1967–68; Tutorial Fellow, Univ. of Sussex, 1968–69. *Publications*: Open Univ. Correspondence Texts for AMST 283, Science and Belief from Copernicus to Darwin: Newton and the Mechanistic Universe; Natural Theology in Britain from Boyle to Paley; Precursors of Darwin?; Darwin (all 1974); *contrib*. Ambix, Brit. Jl for Hist. of Science, Historical Studies in Physical Scis, Studies in Hist. and Philos. of Science. *Address*: Dept of History, Univ. of Lancaster, LA1 4YW.

Brooke, Dr Michael Zachary, MA, PhD; Senior Lecturer in Management Sciences, University of Manchester Institute of Science and Technology, since 1973 (Lecturer, 1966–73); *b* 1921; *m* 1953; two *s* one *d*. BA Cambridge 1943 (1st cl. History), MA Cambridge 1945, MA Manchester 1964, PhD Manchester 1969; Mem.: Brit. Sociological Assoc., Internat. Inst. of Sociology, European Foundation for Management Develt. Director of the Internat. Business Unit at UMIST; Man. Director of FOBAS Ltd (Foreign Business Advisory Service). *Publications*: Le Play: Engineer and Social Scientist, 1970; (with H. L. Remmers) The Strategy of Multinational Enterprise, 1970; The Multinational Enterprise in Europe, 1972; *contrib*. Christ und Welt, Financial Times, Management Decision, Sociological Abstract, Sociologia Internationalis. *Address*: PO Box No 88, Sackville Street, Manchester.

Brooke, Prof. Nicholas Stanton, MA; Professor of English Literature, School of English and American Studies, University of East Anglia, since 1964; *b* 1924; *m* 1949; two *s* two *d*. BA Cantab 1948 (1st cl. English), MA Cantab 1950. Asst Coll. Lectr, Jesus Coll., Cambridge, 1948; Lectr, Durham Colls, Univ. of Durham, 1949–62; Sen. Lectr, 1962–63 (Librarian, Hatfield Coll., 1953–60); Sen. Lectr, Univ. of E Anglia, 1963–64; Vis. Prof., Univ. of Washington, 1969; Vis. Prof., Hollins Coll., Virginia, 1970; Wm Evans Vis. Prof., Univ. of Otago, 1970. Dean, Sch. of English and American Studies, Univ. of E Anglia, 1970–73. *Publications*: Shakespeare: King Lear, 1963, repr. 1964, 1967, 1969, 1971, 1973; George Chapman: Bussy D'Ambois, 1964; Shakespeare's Early Tragedies, 1968, repr. 1973; Shakespeare: Richard II, a casebook, 1973; contribs to: Shakespeare: The Tragedies, ed Clifford Leech, 1964; Shakespeare, 1564–1964; ed, Edward A. Bloom, 1964; *contrib*. Cambridge Jl, Critical Qly, Durham Univ. Jl, Shakespeare Survey, Stratford-upon-Avon Studies, Essays and Studies. *Address*: School of English and American Studies, Univ. of East Anglia, Univ. Plain, Norwich, NOR 88C.

Brooker, William Dixon; Tutor-Organiser, Department of Adult Education and Extra-Mural Studies, University of Aberdeen, since 1966; *b* 1931; *m* 1959; one *s* one *d*. BSc Aberdeen 1953 (Geography), 1958 (Hons). *Address*: Dept of Adult Education, King's College, Univ. of Aberdeen, Aberdeen.

Brookner, Dr Anita; Lecturer, History of Art, Courtauld Institute, London University, since 1964; *b* 1928. BA King's College, London 1949 (1st cl.), PhD Courtauld Institute 1952. Vis. Lectr, Reading Univ., 1959–64; Slade Prof., Cambridge, 1967–68. *Publications*: Watteau, 1967; The Genius of the Future, 1971; Greuze: The rise and fall of an eighteenth century phenomenon, 1972; *contrib*. Burlington Mag., Apollo, Encounter, New Statesman. *Address*: Courtauld Institute of Art, 20 Portman Square, W1H 0BE.

Brooks, Dr Douglas; Lecturer, English Department, Manchester University, since 1970; *b* 1942. BA Oxon 1965, PhD Liverpool 1967. Lectr, Sch. of English, Univ. of Leeds, 1967–70. *Publications*: ed, Henry Fielding: Joseph Andrews, and, Shamela, 1970; Number and Pattern in the Eighteenth-Century Novel, 1973; *contrib*. EC, Med. Æv., MLR, MP. *Address*: English Dept, Univ. of Manchester, Manchester M13 9PL.

Brooks, Edwin, MA, PhD, FRGS; Senior Lecturer, Department of Geography, Liverpool, since 1972; *b* 1929; *m* 1956; four *s* one *d*. BA Cambridge 1952, MA 1956, PhD 1958; FRGS. Lectr, Dept of Geography, Liverpool, 1954–66, 1970–72. MP, 1966–70; Mem., Cttee of Public Accounts, 1966–70. *Publications*: This Crowded Kingdom, 1973; Tribes of the Amazon Basin in Brazil 1972, 1973; *contrib*. Jl Biol. Soc. Science, Jl Repr. Fest. *Address*: Dept of Geography, PO Box 147, Liverpool L69 3BX.

Brooks, Prof. James Leslie, MA; Professor of Spanish, University of Durham, since 1963; Principal, St Cuthbert's Society; *b* 1919; *m* 1947; one *s* two *d*. BA Dublin 1942 (1st cl. Mod., Mod. Lang.), BA Dublin 1943 (2nd cl. Mod., Celtic Lang.), MA Dublin 1967. Asst, Queen's Univ., Belfast, 1946; Asst Lectr, Manchester Univ., 1947–49; Asst Lectr and Lectr, Sheffield Univ., 1949–58; Reader, Durham Univ., 1958–63. *Publications*: *contrib*. BHS, Est . . . R. Menéndez Pidal, RFE. *Address*: Dept of Spanish, Univ. of Durham, Elvet Riverside, Durham.

Brooks, Dr Kenneth Robert; Senior Lecturer, Department of English, University of Southampton, since 1947; *b* 1914; *m* 1944, (*d* 1967), 1971; two *s*. BA 1937 (1st cl. Hons Eng.), MA, DPhil 1942, Oxon; Mem., Philol Soc., 1936–   (Mem. Council, 1955–62). Actg Head, Dept of English, Univ. of Southampton, 1951–52, 1958–59 (part), and 1968–69. *Publications*: ed, Andreas and Fates of the Apostles, 1961; *contrib*. English and Germanic Studies (now English Philol Studies), Mod. Lang. Rev., Med. Æv., etc. *Address*: Dept of English, The Univ., Southampton SO9 5NH.

Brooks, Dr Nicholas Peter, DPhil, FRHistS, FSAScot; Lecturer in Mediaeval History, Department of Mediaeval History, University of St Andrews, since 1964; *b* 1941; *m* 1967; one *s* one *d*. BA Oxon 1962, MA Oxon 1969, DPhil Oxon 1969; FRHistS, FSAScot. *Publications*: *contrib*. Mediaeval Archaeology, Anglo-Saxon England. *Address*: Dept of Mediaeval History, St Salvator's College, St Andrews, Fife KY16 9AJ.

Brooks, Dr Peter Newman; Lecturer in Divinity (Modern Church History), University of Cambridge, since 1970; *b* 1931; *m* 1956; one *d*. BA Cantab 1954 (Historical Tripos), MA Cantab 1958, PhD Cantab 1960. Lectr and Sen. Lectr, Univ. Kent at Canterbury, 1965–70; Fellow Downing Coll., Cambridge, 1970, Dean of Coll., 1971, Dir of Studies in History, 1973–   . *Publications*: Thomas Cranmer's Doctrine of the Eucharist, 1965; Gen. Ed., The Evolution of Western Society, 1969–   . *Address*: Downing College, Cambridge.

Broome, Prof. Jack Howard; Professor, Department of French, Keele University, since 1968; *b* 1920; *m* 1941; one *s* one *d*. BA London 1947 (1st cl. French), PhD London 1949, DU Paris 1953, Res. Fellowship, Univ. of Nottingham, 1949–51; Asst Lectr, Univ. of Keele, 1951–53; Lectr, 1953–63; Sen. Lectr, 1963–66; Reader, 1966–68. Pres., Lancs

85

Chesh. Brch, Mod. Lang. Assoc., 1969–70. *Publications*: Rousseau: a study of his thought, 1963; Pascal, 1965; Corneille: a student's guide, 1971; *contrib*. Fr. Studies, Mod. Lang. Rev., Rev. Litt. Comp., Studies Volt. and 18th Cent., YW Mod. Lang. Studies. *Address*: Dept of French, Univ. of Keele, Keele, Staffs ST5 5BG.

Brothers, Anthony James, MA, BPhil; Lecturer, Department of Classics, St David's University College, Lampeter, since 1966; *b* 1938. BA Oxon 1962, BPhil Oxon 1964, MA Oxon 1965. Asst Lectr in Classics, Lampeter, 1964–66. Mem., Univ. Wales Court, 1971–74; Mem., Senate, St David's Univ. Coll., 1971–74. *Publications*: *contrib*. Class. Qly, Greece Rome, Trivium. *Address*: Dept of Classics, St David's Univ. College, Lampeter, Dyfed SA48 7ED.

Brotherston, Dr J. Gordon; Reader, University of Essex Department of Literature, since 1973; *b* 1939; *m* 1962; four *d*. BA Leeds 1961 (1st cl.), PhD Cambridge 1965. Asst. Lectr, King's Coll., London, 1964–65; Lectr, Univ. of Essex, 1965–68, Sen. Lectr, 1968–73; Vis. Assoc. Prof., Univ. of Iowa, 1968–69; Humboldt Fellowship, 1970–71. Ed., Latin American Series, Pergamon Press, 1965– . *Publications*: ed, J. E. Rodó: Ariel, 1967; Manuel Machado: A Revaluation, 1968; (with E. Dorn) Our Word (anthology of Latin American poetry), 1968; Spanish American Modernista Poets: A Critical Anthology, 1968; Seven Stories from Spanish America, 1968; César Vallejo: Selected Poems, 1974; Confines of Solitude: the new novel in Latin America, 1974; trans. Arenas: Hallucinations, 1971; *contrib*. Amer. Lit., Arcadia, Arion, Books Abroad, Bull. of Hisp. Studies, Comp. Lit. Studies, Estudios de Cultura Náhuatl, Romance Notes, Style, Times Lit. Supp., Twentieth-Century Lit. *Address*: Dept of Literature, Univ. of Essex, Colchester CO4 3SQ.

Brothwell, John Frederick, BA(Econ); Senior Lecturer in Economics, University of Leeds, since 1969; *b* 1924; *m* 1949. BA(Econ), Nottingham (1st cl. Hons). Res. Asst, Leeds Univ., 1951; Asst Lectr, Leeds Univ., 1952–54; Lectr, Leeds Univ., 1954–69; Vis. Lectr, Clark Univ., Mass, 1958. *Publications*: (with G. F. Rainnie and E. M. Sigsworth) The Woollen and Worsted Industry, An Economic Analysis, 1965; *contrib*. Bull. Econ. Res., Yorks Bull. Econ. and Soc. Res. *Address*: School of Economic Studies, Univ. of Leeds, Leeds LS2 9JT.

Brough, Prof. John, MA, DLitt, FBA; Professor of Sanskrit, University of Cambridge, since 1967; Fellow of St John's College; *b* 1917; *m* 1939; one *d*. 1st cl. Hons Classics Edinburgh 1939, 1st cl. Classical Tripos, Pt II Cambridge 1940, 1st cl. Oriental Langs Tripos, Pts I and II Cambridge 1941 and 1942, DLitt Edinburgh 1945; Fellow, St John's Coll., Cambridge, 1945–48; Lectr in Sanskrit, SOAS, Univ. of London, 1946–48; Prof. of Sanskrit, Univ. of London, 1948–67. Asst Keeper, Dept of Oriental Printed Books and MSS, BM, 1944–46. *Publications*: Selections from Classical Sanskrit Literature,

1951; The Early Brahmanical System of Gotra and Pravara, 1953; The Gāndhārī Dharmapada, 1962; Poems from the Sanskrit, 1968; *contrib*. Chambers's Encyclopaedia, Encyclopaedia Britannica, specialist jls. *Address*: St John's College, Cambridge.

Brough, Ronald; Lecturer in Economics with special reference to Accounting, Economics Department, University College of Swansea (University of Wales), since 1966; *b* 1918; *m* 1941; two *s* one *d*. BCom London 1946; ACCA, ACIS. *Address*: Dept of Economics, Univ. College of Swansea, Singleton Park, Swansea SA2 8PP.

Broughton, Geoffrey; Lecturer in Education (English as a Foreign Language), London University, Institute of Education, since 1962; *b* 1927; *m* 1950; one *s* two *d*. BA London 1948 (2nd cl. English), Postgrad. CertEd. London 1953, ACP 1953, MPhil London 1968, PhD London 1973; FRSA. *Publications*: ed, Bandoola, 1959; ed, Climbing Everest, 1960; ed, The Splendid Tasks, 1961; ed, Pattern Readers, 1965–66; An Advanced Technical Reader, 1965; English is Fun, 1966; Success with English, 1968–70; *contrib*. English by Radio and Television, English Lang. Teaching. *Address*: Univ. of London, Institute of Education, Malet Street, WC1E 7HS.

Broughton Harris, James; *see* Harris, J.B.

Brown, Alan, MA, Med, DLC; Lecturer in Physical Education, University of Newcastle upon Tyne, since 1960; *b* 1933; *m* 1961; one *s* one *d*. Dip. Loughborough Coll. (Hons) 1956, MA Newcastle 1970 (Service Degree), MEd Newcastle 1973. FA Staff Coach, MCC Adv. Coach. Consultant in PE to Percy Hedley Sch. for Spastics, 1963–72; Mem., NE Standing Coun. for Sport and Recreation, 1968–72. *Publications*: *contrib*. Brit. Jl Phys. Educn, Special Educn Jl. *Address*: Physical Education Centre, Univ. of Newcastle upon Tyne, Newcastle upon Tyne NE1 7RU.

Brown, Alan Brock; Member of Faculty of Law, Oxford University and Supernumerary Fellow, Worcester College, Oxford, since 1971; *b* 1911; *m* 1940; four *s*. BA Oxon 1934, BCL Oxon 1935, MA Oxon 1938; Barrister at Law, Inner Temple 1935– ; admitted to bar of NSW 1936; Mem., Soc. of Public Teachers of Law. Official Fellow, Worcester Coll., Oxford, 1938–71, Sen. Tutor, 1961–66, Vice-Provost, 1967–71; CUF Lectr, Oxford Univ., 1947–71; Examiner, Honour Sch. of Jurisprudence, 1949, 1951, 1952. Sen. Proctor, Oxford Univ., 1950–51. Mem. Hebdomadal Council, Oxford Univ., 1951–65; Sen. Mem., Oxford Univ. Law Soc., 1945–65; Sen. Mem., Oxford Univ. Athletic Club, 1945–54; Domestic Bursar, Worcester Coll., Oxford, 1947–58; Estates Bursar, Worcester Coll., Oxford, 1957–66. Pres., Oxford Consumers Group, 1961– . *Address*: Worcester College, Oxford.

Brown, Albert James; Lecturer, Department of Marketing, University of Strathclyde, since 1964; b 1925; m 1945; one s four d. BCom Edinburgh 1957, Teacher Training Edinburgh 1958; AMBIM 1969, AMMRS 1973. *Publications*: *contrib*. Scientific Bus., Statist, Int. Jl of Physical Distn. *Address*: Dept of Marketing, Univ. of Strathclyde, Glasgow G1 1XW.

Brown, Dr Alexander William; Senior Lecturer, Department of French, and Adviser of Studies, University of Aberdeen, since 1967; b 1921; m 1956; one s two d. MA Edinburgh 1950 (1st cl. French), PhD Edinburgh 1960. Asst in French, 1953–56. Lectr, Univ. of West Indies, 1956–57; Lectr, Univ. of Aberdeen, 1957–67. *Publications*: Victor Jacquemont et l'Inde anglaise, in Jacquemont, 1959; *contrib*. Forum for Modern Language Studies. *Address*: French Dept., Univ. of Aberdeen, AB9 1AS.

Brown, Prof. Alfred Lawson, Professor, Department of History, University of Glasgow, since 1972; b 1927; m 1963; one s. MA Glasgow 1948 (1st cl. History), DPhil Oxon 1955; FRHistS. Lectr, Glasgow Univ., 1951–63, Sen. Lectr, 1963–72. RAF 1948–49. *Publications*: (with S. B. Chrimes) Select Documents of English Constitutional History, 1961; The Early History of the Clerkship of the Council, 1969; *contrib*. Bull. Inst. Hist. Res., EHR, Trans Royal Hist. Soc. *Address*: Dept of History, Univ. of Glasgow, Glasgow G12 8QQ.

Brown, Anthony David F.; see Fitton-Brown.

Brown, Anthony Ernest; Staff Tutor in Archaeology, Department of Adult Education, University of Leicester, since 1969. Styring Scholar, The Queen's Coll., Oxford; BA 1960, MA 1964. Organising Tutor for Leicestershire, Dept of Adult Education, Univ. of Leicester, 1964–65; Organising Tutor for Northamptonshire, 1965–69. *Publications*: ed, The Growth of Leicester, 1970; *contrib*. Archaeol Jl, Trans London and Mddx Archaeol Soc., Trans Woolhope Club, Trans Radnorshire Soc., Northants Archaeology. *Address*: Dept) of Adult Education, Univ. of Leicester, Leicester LE1 7RH.

Brown, Archibald Haworth, Fellow of St Antony's College, Oxford, and Lecturer in Soviet Institutions in the University of Oxford since 1971; b 1938; m 1963; one s one d. BSc (Econ) London 1962 (1st cl.), MA Oxford 1972. Lectr in Pol., Glasgow Univ., 1964–71; Brit. Council Exch. Studshp, Moscow Univ., 1967–68. Mem., Nat. Cttee, Soviet and E Europ. Studies, 1969–71, 1973– ; Edit. Bd, CUP Soviet and E Europ. Monogrs; Nat. Adv. Bd, Soviet Studies. *Publications*: Soviet Politics and Political Science, 1974; (with G. Wightman) The Communist Party of Czechoslovakia, 1975; ed (with M. C. Kaser) The Soviet Union since the Fall of Krushchev, 1975; Prime Ministerial Power, in, European Politics, ed M. Dogan and R. Rose, 1971; Political Change in Czechoslovakia, in, Political Opposition in One-Party States, ed L. Schapiro, 1972; Adam Smith's First Russian

Followers, in, Adam Smith: Bicentenary Essays, ed T. Wilson, 1974; *contrib*. Govt and Opposit., Oxford Slavonic Papers, Public Law, Soviet Studies, Pravník (Prague), Vestnik Moskovskogo Universiteta – Istoriya (Moscow). *Address*: St Antony's College, Oxford OX2 6JF.

Brown, Prof. Arthur Joseph, MA, DPhil, FBA; Professor of Economics, University of Leeds, since 1947; b 1914; m 1938; two s. BA 1936 (1st cl. PPE), MA 1939, DPhil 1939, Oxon; Mem., Royal Econ. Soc., Royal Stat. Soc., RIIA, Brit. Assoc. Fellow, All Souls Coll., Oxford, 1937; Lectr, Hertford Coll., Oxford, 1937; Vis. Prof., Columbia Univ., 1950; Vis. Prof., Australian National Univ., 1963. Foreign Res. and Press Service, 1940–43; Foreign Office Res. Dept, 1943–45; Econ. Adviser, Cabinet Office, 1945–47; Mem., Council, Royal Econ. Soc., 1950–68; UGC, 1969; Pres., Sect. 'F', Brit. Assoc., 1958; Cttee on Intermediate Areas, 1967. *Publications*: Applied Economics: Aspects of the World Economy in Peace and War, 1948; The Great Inflation 1939–51, 1955; Introduction to the World Economy, 1959; Framework of Regional Economics in the UK, 1972; *contrib*. EJ, Oxf EP, Econ. Record, Scott. JPE, Rev. Inc. and Wealth, Yorks Bull. *Address*: School of Economic Studies, Univ. of Leeds, Leeds LS2 9JT.

Brown, Prof. Charles Victor, BA, PhD; Professor of Economics, University of Stirling, since 1970; b 1935; m 1959; two s. BA Haverford 1957, PhD London 1964. Lectr, Univ. of Ibadan, 1959–64; Lectr and Sen. Lectr, Univ. of Glasgow, 1964–70. *Publications*: Government and Banking in Western Nigeria, 1964; The Nigerian Banking System, 1966; ed, Economic Principles Applied, 1970; *contrib*. Bankers' Mag., Nigerian Jl of Econ., Scott. Jl of Pol. Econ. *Address*: Dept of Economics, Univ. of Stirling, Stirling FK9 4LA.

Brown, Rev. Dr Colin, Lecturer, Trinity College, since 1972, and Teacher in Theology, University of Bristol, since 1961; b 1932; m 1958; one s two d. BA Liverpool 1953, BD London 1958, MA Nottingham 1961, PhD Bristol 1970. Tutor, Tyndale Hall, Bristol, 1961; Vice-Principal 1967; Dean of Studies 1969–71. Mem., C of E Working Party on Specialised Ministries, 1971. *Publications*: Karl Barth and the Christian Message, 1967; Philosophy and the Christian Faith, 1969, 2nd edn 1971; Contrib. Creative Minds in Contemporary Theology, 1966, 2nd edn 1969; We Believe in God, 1968; Ministry in the Seventies, 1970; *contrib*. Churchman, Faith and Thought. *Address*: Trinity College, Bristol 9.

Brown, Dr David Clifford; Senior Lecturer in Music, University of Southampton, since 1970; b 1929; m 1953; two d. BA Sheffield 1950 (General Hons). BMus Sheffield 1951, DipEd Sheffield 1952, MA Sheffield 1960, PhD Southampton 1971; LTCL (Piano performer), 1948. Lectr in Music, Southampton Univ., 1962–70. Music Librarian, London Univ. 1959–62. *Publications*: Ed jtly. The Anthems of Thomas Weelkes, 1966; Thomas

Weelkes: a biographical and critical study, 1969; Mikhail Glinka: a biographical and critical study, 1974; John Wilbye, 1974; *contrib.* Music and Letters, Monthly Musical Record, Music Rev., Musical Times, Survey, etc. *Address*: Dept of Music, The Univ., Southampton SO9 5NH.

Brown, David John, BSc(Econ), FCA; Lecturer, Division of Economic Studies, University of Sheffield since 1963; *b* 1935; *m* 1963; one *s* one *d.* BSc(Econ) London 1956; FCA. *Publications*: *contrib.* Accountancy. *Address*: Division of Economic Studies, The Univ., Sheffield S10 2TN.

Brown, Dorothy Betty B.; *see* Byers Brown.

Brown, Prof. Edward Duncan, PhD, BL; Professor in the Department of Law, University of Wales Institute of Science and Technology, since 1974; *b* 1934; *m* 1958; one *s* two *d.* BL Edinburgh 1957, LLM London 1964 (Distinction), PhD London 1970; Solicitor (Scotland) 1957. Asst Lectr, Univ. Coll. London, 1961–63; Lectr, 1963–68; Sen. Lectr, 1968–71; Reader, 1971–74. Fellow, Woodrow Wilson Internat. Center for Scholars, Washington DC, 1970–71. Sec., London Inst. World Affairs, 1962. *Publications*: Arms Control in Hydrospace, 1971; The Legal Regime of Hydrospace, 1971; *contrib.* Australian Year Book of Internat. Law; Current Legal Problems; Common Market Law Rev., Indian Jl of Internat. Law, Natural Resources Jl, Year Book of World Affairs. *Address*: Dept of Law, Univ. of Wales Inst. of Science and Technology, Cardiff CF1 3NU.

Brown, Dr Edward Keith; University Lecturer in Linguistics, University of Edinburgh, since 1965; *b* 1935; *m* 1959; three *d.* BA Cambridge 1959, PhD Edinburgh 1971. Lectr, Univ. Coll. of Cape Coast, Ghana, 1962–64. *Address*: Adam Ferguson Building, George Square, Edinburgh.

Brown, Prof. Eric Herbert, MSc, PhD; Professor of Geography, since 1966, Dean of Students since 1972, University College London; *b* 1922; *m* 1945; two *d.* BSc London 1947 (1st cl. Geography), MSc Wales 1949 PhD London 1955; FRGS. Asst Lectr, UCW, Aberystwyth, 1947–49; Lectr, Reader, UCL, 1950–66; Vis. Lectr, Indiana Univ., USA, 1953–54; Vis. Prof., Monash Univ., Melbourne, 1971. RAF 1941–45; Geog. Adviser, Govt of Argentina, 1965–68; Chm., Brit. Geomorphological Res. Group, 1971– . *Publications*: The Relief and Drainage of Wales, 1961; (with W. R. Mead) The USA and Canada, 1962; *contrib.* Geog. Jl, Phil. Trans Roy. Soc., Proc. Geol. Assoc., Trans Inst. Brit. Geog. *Address*: Dept of Geography, Univ. College, Gower Street, WC1E 6BT.

Brown, Geoffrey; Senior Lecturer in Occupational Psychology, University of Aston, since 1970; *b* 1923; *m* 1963; one *s* one *d.* BSc Nottingham 1951 (2/I Psychology), MSc London 1961, PhD Aston 1968; ABPsS. Lectr, Univ. of Aston, 1965–70. *Address*: Applied Psychology Dept, Univ. of Aston, Birmingham B4 7ET.

Brown, Geoffrey Radley; Tutor in Philosophy, Department for External Studies, University of Oxford, since 1956; *b* 1930; *m* 1957. BA Oxon 1952, MA Oxon 1956. *Address*: Dept for External Studies, Univ. of Oxford, Oxford.

Brown, Dr Gillian, MA, PhD; Lecturer, Department of Linguistics, University of Edinburgh, since 1965; *b* 1937; *m* 1959; three *d.* BA Cantab 1959, MA Cantab 1964, PhD Edinburgh 1971. Lectr, Univ. of Cape Coast, Ghana, 1962–64. *Publications*: Phonological Rules and Dialect Variation: a study of the phonology of Lumasaaba, 1972; *contrib.* Jl African Lang., Jl Linguistics, Lingua. *Address*: Dept of Linguistics, Univ. of Edinburgh, Edinburgh EH8 9YL.

Brown, Prof. Godfrey Norman, MA, D.Phil; Professor of Education, and Director of Institute of Education, University of Keele, since 1967; *b* 1926; *m* 1960; three *s.* BA Oxon 1950, MA Oxon 1952, DPhil Oxon 1954. Lectr, UC of Ghana, 1958–61; Sen. Lectr, Univ. of Ibadan, 1961–62, Associate Prof., 1962–63, Prof., 1963–66. Social Affairs Officer, UN HQ, 1953–54; Sen. History Master, Barking Abbey Sch., 1954–57; Editor, West African Jl of Educn, 1962–66. Mem., Exec. Cttee, Univ. Council for Educn of Teachers, 1971– , Treas., 1973– ; Mem., Nat. Council for the Supply and Training of Teachers for Overseas, 1967–73; ODA Adv. Cttee on Teacher Trng, 1973– ; Staffs Educn. Cttee, 1968– ; Mem., Governing Bodies, Madeley and Radbrook Colls of Educn. *Publications*: An Active History of Ghana, 2 vols, 1961–64; Stories from the South of Nigeria, 1966; (with S. J. Eggleston) Towards an Education for the 21st Century, 1970; All African Readers, 1970; jt ed and contrib., Africa in the Nineteenth and Twentieth Centuries, 1966; ed, Towards a Learning Community, 1971; ed jtly and contrib., Harmony and Conflict in Education in Tropical Africa; *contrib.* Educn Forum (USA), Illiteracy Work (Iran), Intellect (USA), Internat. Relations, Jl Mod. African Studies, West African Jl of Educn. *Address*: Univ. of Keele Institute of Education, Keele, Staffs ST5 5BG.

Brown, Helen Wingate; Senior Assistant Keeper, Heberden Coin Room, Ashmolean Museum, University of Oxford, since 1967 (Assistant Keeper, 1958); occasional Lecturer in Oriental Numismatics; Fellow, St Cross College; *b* 1934; *m* 1970; one *s.* BA Oxon in Oriental Studies 1957 (Arabic with Persian), MA Oxon 1962; FRNS, FRAS. *Publications*: *contrib.* Numismatic Chronicle. *Address*: Ashmolean Museum, Oxford.

Brown, Iain; *see* Brown, R. I. F.

Brown, Prof. James Alan Calvert, MA; Professor of Applied Economics, Oxford University, and Fellow of Merton College, since 1970; *b* 1922. BA Cantab 1946, MA Cantab 1951, MA Oxon 1970. Res. Off., Dept of Applied Econs, Cambridge Univ., 1952–65; Fellow of Queen's Coll., 1961–65; Prof. of Econometrics, Bristol Univ. 1965–70.

MAFF, 1947–52; Mem., SW Electricity Bd, 1966–72. *Publications*: Monographs: (with J. Aitchison) Lognormal Distribution, 1957; (with R. Stone) Computable Model of Economic Growth; Exploring 1970; *contrib.* econ. and statistical lit. *Address*: Merton College, Oxford.

Brown, James Clifford, MA, MusB, FRCO; Senior Lecturer and University Organist, Music Department, Leeds University, since 1972 (Lecturer, 1948–72); *b* 1923. BA Cantab 1946 (2nd cl. English), MA Cantab 1949, MusB Cantab; FRCO (Read Prize). Mem., Internat. Organ Comp. Jury, Aosta, Italy, 1969. *Publications*: Andante sospirando for organ, 1954; Scherzo for organ, 1973. *Address*: Music Dept, Univ. of Leeds, Leeds LS2 9JT.

Brown, James Maclean; Lecturer in Philosophy, New University of Ulster, since 1968; *b* 1941; *m* 1972. BA Hons Manchester 1964 (Philosophy), MA Manchester 1970; MSc London 1973. Asst Lectr in Philosophy, Magee UC, Londonderry, 1966–68. *Publications: contrib.* Ratio. *Address*: Dept of Philosophy, New Univ. of Ulster, Coleraine, N Ireland BT52 1SA.

Brown, Dr James Murray, Hon. FTCL, LRAM; Senior Lecturer in Music, University of Durham, since 1973 (Lecturer, 1964–73); *b* 1913; *m* 1951; one *s* one *d*. BMus Dunelm, DMus Dunelm; Hon. FTCL, LRAM. *Address*: Dept of Music, Palace Green, Durham.

Brown, Jennifer Mary, MA; Lecturer, Department of Scottish History, University of Glasgow, since 1970; *b* 1942; *m* 1963; one *s*. MA Glasgow 1963 (1st cl. History); Asst Lectr, Glasgow Univ., 1966–70. *Publications: contrib.*, James VI and I, ed A. G. R. Smith, 1973; The Scottish Nation, ed G. Menzies, 1972. *Address*: Dept of Scottish History, The Univ., Glasgow G12 8QQ.

Brown, Dr John; Lecturer in History, Edinburgh University, since 1965; *b* 1937; *m* 1969; one *s*. MA Edinburgh 1960 (1st cl. History); PhD London 1964. Asst Lectr, Edinburgh Univ., 1962–65. *Publications: contrib.* Bull. Inst. History Res., Econ. History Rev., Scott. History Rev. *Address*: Dept of History, Univ. of Edinburgh, Edinburgh EH8 9YL.

Brown, Prof. John Russell; Professor of English, Sussex University, since 1971; *b* 1923; *m* 1961; one *s* two *d*. MA Oxon 1954, PhD, BLitt Oxon 1952. Fellow Shakespeare Inst., Stratford-upon-Avon, 1951–55; Lectr and Sen. Lectr, Dept of English, Birmingham Univ., 1955–63; Hd of Dept of Drama and Theatre Arts, Univ. of Birmingham, 1964–71; Reynolds Lectr, Colorado Univ., 1957; Vis. Prof., Grad. Sch., NY Univ., 1959; Mellon Prof. of Drama, Carnegie Inst., Pittsburgh, 1964; Vis. Prof., Zürich Univ., 1969–70; Univ. Lectr in Drama, Univ. of Toronto, 1970. Associate Dir, Nat. Theatre, London, 1973– . Gen. Editor: Stratford-upon-Avon Studies, 1960–67; Stratford-upon-Avon Library, 1964– . *Publications*: Shakespeare and his Comedies, 1957; Shakespeare: the tragedy of Macbeth, 1963; Shakespeare's Plays in Performance, 1966; Effective Theatre, 1969; Shakespeare's The Tempest, 1969; Shakespeare's Dramatic Style, 1971; Theatre Language, 1972; Free Shakespeare, 1974; ed, The Merchant of Venice, 1955; ed, The White Devil, 1960; ed, The Duchess of Malfi, 1965; ed, Henry V, 1965; *contrib.* Shakespeare Survey, Critical Qly, Tulane Drama Rev., Studies in Bibliography. *Address*: Univ. of Sussex, Falmer, Brighton BN1 9QQ.

Brown, Dr Judith Margaret; Lecturer, Department of History, University of Manchester, since 1971; *b* 1944. BA Cambridge 1965 (Hons History), MA Cambridge 1968 (Hons History), PhD Cambridge 1968 (History); FRHistS. Girton Coll., Cambridge: Res. Fellow, 1968–70; Official Fellow, 1970–71; Dir of Studies in History, 1969–71. *Publication*: Gandhi's Rise to Power: Indian Politics, 1915–1922, 1972. *Address*: Dept of History, Univ. of Manchester, Manchester M13 9PL.

Brown, Kenneth, MA, ABPsS; Lecturer in Psychology, Department of Psychology, The Queen's University of Belfast, since 1968; *b* 1941; *m* 1964. MA Aberdeen 1964 (1st cl. Psychology); ABPsS. Tutorial Student, Aberdeen, 1964; Asst Lectr, Aberdeen, 1965–67; Lectr, Aberdeen, 1968. NI Rep, Gen. Council, Brit. Psychol. Soc., 1972– . *Publications: contrib.* Anim. Behav., Develop. Psychobiol., Nature, Psychol. Sci., Psychopharmacol., IRCS (Med. Sci). *Address*: Dept of Psychology, The Queen's Univ. of Belfast, Belfast BT7 1NN.

Brown, Dr Kenneth Lewis; Lecturer in Social Anthropology, University of Manchester, since 1972; *b* 1936; *m* 1958; two *s* one *d*. BA MA PhD UCLA 1969 (Islamic Studies); Fellow, Cttee for the Comparative Study of New Nations, Univ. of Chicago, 1967–68; Res. Assoc. Dept of History and Center for Middle Eastern Studies, 1968–71; Sen. Simon Fellow, Univ. of Manchester, 1971–72. *Publications*: Profile of a Nineteenth Century Moroccan Scholar, in Sufis, Saints and Scholars, ed N. Keddie, 1972; The Impact of the Dahir Berbère in Sale, in, Arabs and Berbers: From Tribe to Nation in North Africa, ed E. Gellner and C. Micaud, 1973; *contrib.* Bull. of the Middle East Studies Assoc., Bull. Econ. et Soc. du Maroc; Hespéris-Tamuda. *Address*: Dept of Social Anthropology, Univ. of Manchester, Manchester M13 9PL.

Brown, Prof. L. Neville; Professor of Comparative Law and Dean, Faculty of Law, University of Birmingham, since 1966; *b* 1923; *m* 1957; three *s* one *d*. MA, LLB Cambridge 1949, Docteur en Droit, Lyon 1953; Solicitor, 1951. Rotary Foundation Fellow, Lyon Univ., 1951–52; Lectr in Law, Sheffield Univ., 1952–55; Lectr, 1955–57, Sen. Lectr, 1957–64, Reader, 1964–66, Birmingham Univ. Sen. Res. Fellow, Univ. of Michigan, 1960; Vis. Prof., Univ. of Tulane, 1968. Dir of Legal Studies, Birmingham Univ., 1968–73; Dean of Faculty of

Law, 1970– ; Chm., UK Nat. Cttee of Comparative Law, 1971– ; Treas., Soc. of Public Teachers of Law, 1971– . *Publications*: ed (with F. H. Lawson and A. E. Anton), Amos and Walton: Introduction to French Law, 2nd edn 1963, 3rd edn 1967; (with J. F. Garner), French Administrative Law 1967, 2nd edn 1973; *contrib*. Mod. Law Rev., Internat. and Comparative Law Qly, American Jl of Comparative Law, Tulane Law Rev., Toronto Law Jl; Ottawa Law Rev., Jl of Family Law; Annuaire de Législation Française et Etrangère. *Address*: Faculty of Law, Univ. of Birmingham, PO Box 363, Birmingham B15 2TT.

Brown, Maurice Joseph; Senior Lecturer, Department of Environmental Studies, University College London, since 1964; *b* 1916; *m* 1949. Dip. in Architecture, Edinburgh Coll. of Art, 1938, Dip. in Town Planning, Edinburgh Coll of. Art, 1939; ARIBA 1939, FRTPI 1962 (Associate MRTPI 1947). Asst Planning Officer, Dept of Health for Scotland, 1946–48; Asst Chief Architect (Planning), E Kilbride New Town Develt Corp., 1948–51; Polytechnic, Regent Street, London, 1952–63, Sen. Lectr i/c Town Planning, 1954–63. Member: RTPI Educn Cttee, 1959–66; RTPI Council, 1965–66; CNAA Town Planning Bd, 1966–71. *Publications*: contrib. Urban and Regional Ground Transportation, ed James J. Murray, 1973; *contrib*. High Speed Ground Transport. Jl, Jl RTPI. *Address*: School of Environmental Studies, Univ. College London, Gower Street, WC1E 6BT.

Brown, Michael; *see* Brown, Peter M.

Brown, Michael B.; *see* Barratt Brown.

Brown, Michael George, MA, BSc (Oxon), FRIC; Director, Postgraduate Certificate in Education, University of Sussex, since 1971; *b* 1927; *m* 1950; two *s* two *d*. BA Oxon 1949 (1st cl. Chem.), MA Oxon 1952, BSc Oxon 1952; Fellow, Royal Inst. of Chem., ASE, Mem., Chem. Soc., Lectr, Dept of Educn, Nottingham Univ., 1960–64; Dir, Arts/Science Programme, Univ. of Sussex, 1964– ; Lectr in Chemistry and Educn, 1965–69; Reader in Chemistry and Educn, 1969– . Mem., Council, Moira House School. *Publications*: Practical Inorganic and Organic Problems, 1961; Practical Chemistry, 1963; Critical Readings in Chemistry, 1965; Carbon Chemistry, 1965; *contrib*. Jl Chem. Soc., Trans Far. Soc., Jl Chem. Phys., Sch. Science Rev. *Address*: School of Molecular Sciences (or Education Building), Univ. of Sussex, Falmer, Brighton.

Brown, Neville George; Senior Lecturer, Department of Politics, University of Birmingham, since 1971. Academic Consultant at National Defence College, Latimer, since 1972; *b* 1932. BSc (Econ) London 1954 (2nd cl. Econs and Geography), BA Oxon 1957 (2nd cl. Mod. History), MA Oxon 1962; Fellow Royal Met. Soc., 1959; Trench Gascoigne Prize 1960. Lectr in Politics, Univ. of Birmingham, 1965–71. Lieut, Meteorol. Br. Fleet Air Arm, 1957–60; Lectr in Mod. Subjects, RMA, Sandhurst, 1960–62; Res. Assoc., Inst. Strategic Studies, 1962–64;

Defence Corresp., New Statesman, 1965–69; Defence Corresp., New Scientist, 1968–70. *Publications*: Strategic Mobility, 1963; Nuclear War: The Impending Strategic Deadlock, 1965; Arms Without Empire, 1967; (with D. C. Watt and F. Spencer) A History of the World in the Twentieth Century, 1967, American edn 1968, pbk edn 1970; British Arms and Strategy: 1970–80, 1969; European Security: 1972–80, 1972; *contrib*. Internat. Aff., Jl Royal United Service Inst., New Middle East, Monde Diplomatique, Military Rev., World Today. *Address*: Dept of Politics, The Univ. of Birmingham, PO Box 363, Birmingham B15 2TT.

Brown, Dr Peter; Lecturer in Education, School of Education, University of Nottingham, since 1965; *b* 1934; *m* 1959; two *d*. BSc Birmingham 1954, PhD Birmingham 1957; ARIC 1960. Res. Assoc. in Chemistry, Univ. of Virginia, 1957–58. Chief Examiner, A Level Chemistry Assoc. Exam. Board, 1969– . *Publications*: (with P. J. Hitchman and G. D. Yeoman) CSE: An Experiment in the Oral Examining of Chemistry, 1971; (with B. Hudson) Handbook of Objective Testing in Chemistry, 1972; *contrib*. Jl of Organic Chem., Tetrahedron. *Address*: School of Education, Univ. Park, Nottingham NG7 2RD.

Brown, Peter George McCarthy, MA; Fellow and Tutor in Classics, Trinity College, Oxford, since 1968; *b* 1945; *m* 1968. MA Oxon 1970. CUF Lectr in Greek and Latin Langs and Lit., Oxford, 1971. *Address*: Trinity College, Oxford OX1 3BH.

Brown, (Peter) Michael; Lecturer, Department of Humanity, University of Glasgow, since 1960; *b* 1934; *m* 1961; one *s* one *d*. MA Oxon 1956. Asst Lectr, Univ. of Glasgow, 1958–60. Advr of Studies, Glasgow Univ., 1971– . *Address*: Dept of Humanity, The Univ., Glasgow G12 8QQ.

Brown, Philip David Comely; Assistant Keeper, Department of Antiquities, Ashmolean Museum, Oxford, since 1966; *b* 1939; *m* 1971; one *s*. BA Cantab 1963, MA 1967; FSA. Dir, Excavations, Cirencester Excavation Cttee, 1965–67. *Publications*: contrib. Britannia. *Address*: Ashmolean Museum, Oxford.

Brown, Dr R. Allen, MA, DPhil, FSA, FRHistS; Reader in History, University of London, King's College, since 1964; *b* 1924; *m* 1952; one *s* one *d*. BA Oxon 1948, MA Oxon 1949, DPhil Oxon 1954; FSA, FRHistS. Bryce Res. Student, Oxford, 1949–50; Adv. Res. Student in Arts, Manchester, 1950–51; Asst Keeper, Public Record Off., 1951–59; Lectr, King's Coll., London, 1959–64. Editor, Public Record Off., 1959– ; Mem., Council, Pipe Roll Soc., Suffolk Records Soc. *Publications*: Castles, 1954, 2nd edn 1957; English Medieval Castles, 1954; ed, Sibton Abbey Charters (Pipe Roll Soc., NS XXXVI), 1962; ed, Memoranda Roll 10 John (Pipe Roll Soc., NS XXXI), 1955; English Castles, 1962; (with H. M. Colvin and A. J. Taylor) The

History of the King's Works, vols 1 and 2, The Middle Ages, 1962; ed, Pipe Roll 17 John (Pipe Roll Soc., NS XXXVII), 1964; The Normans and the Norman Conquest, 1969; The Origins of Modern Europe, 1972; The Origins of English Feudalism, 1973; *contrib.* Antiqu. Jl, Archaeol. Jl, EHR, Trans Royal Hist. Soc., etc. *Address*: Dept of History, King's College, Strand, WC2R 2LS.

Brown, Raymond; Lecturer, Department of Economic and Social History, University of Hull, since 1967; *b* 1926; one *s*. BScEcon London 1951, Dip. in Education Hull 1952, MScEcon Hull 1966. *Publications*: Waterfront Organisation in Hull 1870–1900, 1972. *Address*: Dept of Economic and Social History, Univ. of Hull, Hull HU6 7RX.

Brown, Prof. Reginald Francis, PhD; (First) Cowdray Professor of Spanish Language and Literature, University of Leeds, since 1953; *b* 1910; *m* 1939; one *s* one *d*. BA Liverpool 1932 (1st cl. Hons Spanish), PhD Liverpool 1939; Univ. Fellowship, Liverpool 1934. On staff of Spanish depts in Univs of Liverpool, Columbia and New York, NYC, and Dartmouth Coll., NH, USA, 1937–43; Hd of Dept of Spanish, Univ. of Leeds, 1945–53; Vis. Prof. of Spanish, Princeton Univ., 1958–59. Pres., Mod. Language Assoc., 1970. Diamond Jubilee Gold Medal, Inst. of Linguists, 1972. *Publications*: Bibliografia de la Novela Española, 1700–1850 (Madrid), 1953; Spanish–English, English–Spanish Pocket Dictionary, 1954, 2nd edn 1956; *contrib.* Spain, A Companion to Spanish Studies, ed E. Allison Peers, 5th edn revised and enlarged, 1956; D. F. Sarmiento, Facundo, ed Boston, 1960; *contrib.* Bull. Hispanic Studies, Hispania, Hispanic Rev., Mod. Languages, Year's Work in Mod. Language Studies. *Address*: Univ. of Leeds, Leeds LS2 9JT.

Brown, Richard Kemp; Senior Lecturer in Sociology, Department of Sociology and Social Administration, University of Durham, since 1970; *b* 1933; *m* 1961; three *s* one *d*. BA Cantab 1956, Cert. in Personnel Management LSE 1958. Sen. Res. Off., Univ. of Leicester, 1959–60; Asst Lectr in Sociology, 1960–62, Lectr in Sociology, 1962–66; Lectr in Sociology, Univ. of Durham, 1966–70; Dean, Faculty of Social Sciences, Durham, 1972–74. Mem., Exec. Cttee, Brit. Sociological Assoc., 1968–72. *Publications*: (jtly) The Sociology of Industry, 1967, 2nd edn 1972; ed, Knowledge, Education and Cultural Change, 1972; *contrib.* Man and Organization, 1973; *contrib.* Brit. Jl Industrial Relations, Sociological Rev., Sociology. *Address*: Dept of Sociology and Social Administration, Univ. of Durham, 44 Old Elvet, Durham.

Brown, (Robert) Iain (Froude); Lecturer, Department of Psychology, Glasgow University, since 1968. MA Hons, MEd Hons; ABPsS. Hon. Consultant Psychologist, Gambler's Anonymous; Trustee, Gambler's Anonymous Ltd (GB). *Publications*: *contrib.* Annals NY Acad. of Sciences, Scandanavian Jl of Rehabilitation Medicine, Perceptnal and Motor Skills. *Address*: Dept of Psychology, Univ. of Glasgow, Glasgow G12 8RT.

Brown, Dr Ronald Gordon Sclater; Senior Lecturer in Social Administration, University of Hull, since 1967; *b* 1929; *m* 1952; two *s*. MA St Andrews 1951, PhD Hull 1972. Tutor, then Lectr, in Social Administration, Univ. of Manchester, 1958–62; Lectr in Social Administration, Univ. of Hull, 1965–67. Min. of Health and Local Govt, NI, 1953–58; Scott. Home and Health Dept, 1962–65. *Publications*: The Administrative Process in Britain, 1970, 2nd edn 1971; The Changing National Health Service, 1973; (with R. W. H. Stones) The Male Nurse, 1973; The Management of Welfare, 1974; *contrib.* Public Administration, Yorks Bull. Social and Econ. Res., PAC Bull., Soc. and Econ. Admin, Int. Jl Nursing Studies, Jl RCGP, New Society, Nursing Times. *Address*: Dept of Social Administration, The Univ., Hull HU6 7RX.

Brown, Sally; Part-time Tutor, Department of Russian and Slavonic Studies, University of Sheffield, since 1970; *b* 1941; *m* 1968; one *s*. BA Leeds 1963 (Russian and German). Asst Lectr in Russian, Univ. of Sheffield, 1966–69; Lectr, 1969–70. *Address*: Dept of Russian and Slavonic Studies, Univ. of Sheffield, Sheffield S10 2TN.

Brown, Prof. Thomas Julian, MA, FSA; Professor of Palaeography, King's College, University of London, since 1961; *b* 1923; *m* 1959; two *d*. BA Oxon 1948 (2nd cl. Classical Hon. Moderations, 1942, 2nd cl. Lit. Hum., 1948), MA Oxon 1961; FSA 1956. Mem., Inst. for Advanced Study, Princeton, NJ, 1966–67. Asst Keeper, Dept of Manuscripts, BM, 1950–60. *Publications*: (with R. L. S. Bruce-Mitford and others) Codex Lindisfarnensis, 1956–60; The Stonyhurst Gospel, 1969; (with F. Wormald and others) The Durham Ritual, 1969; *contrib.* Anglo-Saxon England; Book Collector; Trans Cambridge Bibliographical Soc. *Address*: Dept of Palaeography, King's College, Strand, WC2 2LS.

Browne, Joan Dillon, CBE, JP, MA; Principal, Coventry College of Education, since 1948; Associate Professor, University of Warwick, since 1973; *b* 1912. BA Oxon 1933 (Modern History), MA 1947; Postgraduate Dip. Teaching 1934; Margaret Pollock Postgraduate scholarship from Somerville Coll. to Univ. of Bordeaux, 1934–35. Chm., ATCDE, 1960–61; Member: Schools Council and Steering Cttee Bd, 1967– ; NCET., 1968– ; Academic Cttee, Univ. of Warwick, 1973– . *Publications*: The Development of Educational Technology in Colleges of Education (NCET Occasional Paper 3), 1971; *contrib.* Colston Papers, 1969; The Curriculum: The Training of Teachers – a factual survey, ed Hewett, 1971; *contrib.* Education for Teaching, Educational Rev. *Address*: Univ. of Warwick, Coventry CV4 7AL.

Browning, Dr David George, University Lecturer in the Geography of Latin America, St Cross College, Oxford, since 1968; *b* 1938; *m* 1961; two *s* one *d*. BA Reading

1961, MA DPhil Oxon 1968. |*Publication*:
El Salvador: Landscape and Society, 1971.
Address: St Cross College, Oxford.

Browning, Prof. Robert; Professor of
Classics, University of London, since 1965;
b 1914; *m* 1946; two *d*. MA Glasgow 1935
(1st cl. Classics), BA Oxon 1939 (1st cl. Lit.
Hum.). Lectr, UCL, 1947–55; Reader, 1955;
Vis. Scholar, Dumbarton Oaks Center for
Byzantine Studies, 1973–74. Jt Editor, Jl of
Hellenic Studies, 1964; Mem., Classical Jls
Bd, 1965, Sec., 1970; Mem., Editorial Bd,
Past and Present, 1965; Mem., Internation-
aler Beirat, Philologus, 1971; Mem., Brit.
Nat. Cttee for Byzantine Studies, 1964.
Publications: Medieval and Modern Greek,
1969; Justinian and Theodora, 1971; *contrib*.
Balkan Studies, Byzantion, Class. Qly, Class.
Rev., Das Altertum, Jl Hell. Stud., Jl Rom.
Stud., Philologus, Revue des Etudes Byzan-
tines, Revue des Etudes Grecques, Vizanti-
jskij Vremennik. *Address*: Birkbeck College,
Malet Street, WC1E 7HX.

Brownlie, Dr Ian; Fellow and Tutor in Law,
Wadham College, Oxford, Lecturer in the
University of Oxford, since 1963; *b* 1932;
m 1957; one *s* two *d*. BA Oxon 1953, MA
Oxon 1959, DPhil Oxon 1961; Barrister of
Gray's Inn, 1958. Asst Lectr, Leeds Univ.,
1956–57; Lectr, Nottingham Univ., 1957–63;
Vis. Prof. Univ. of East Africa, 1968–69;
Vis. Prof., Univ. of Ghana, 1971. Jt Editor,
Brit. Year Book of Internat. Law. *Publica-
tions*: International Law and the Use of
Force by States, 1963; Principles of Public
International Law, 1966, 2nd edn 1973; ed,
Basic Documents in International Law,
1967, 2nd edn 1972; The Law Relating to
Public Order, 1968; ed, Basic Documents on
Human Rights, 1971; Basic Documents on
African Affairs, 1971. *Address*: Wadham
College, Oxford.

Brownsword, Roger; Lecturer in Law,
University of Sheffield, since 1968; *b* 1946;
m 1971. LLB London 1968. *Address*: Fac. of
Law, Univ. of Sheffield, Sheffield S10 2TN.

Bruce, Dr David James, MA, PhD;
University Lecturer in Psychology in the
Department of Education, University of
Cambridge, since 1961; *b* 1928; *m* 1952; one *s*
one *d*. BA Reading 1952 (1st cl. Psychology),
PhD Reading 1960, MA Cantab 1961; Mem.,
BPsS, EPS, ASAB, BRA. Asst Lectr,
Reading, 1952–55; Lectr, 1955–61; Fellow,
Corpus Christi Coll., Cambridge, 1962– ;
Tutor for Admissions, 1964–66; Bursar for
Leckhampton, 1968–71. Mem., Bd of Govs,
King Edward VI Sch., Norwich, 1965– ;
Mem., Bd of Govs, King Edward VI Sch.,
Bury St Edmunds, 1967– ; Mem., Council,
Univ. Coll. Sch., Hampstead, 1968– .
Publications: Psychology for Education, 1973;
contrib. Rev. Int. de Film., Lang. and Speech,
Brit. Jl Educnl Psychol., Acta Psychol.,
Paedagog. Europ., Nature. *Address*: Dept of
Education, 17 Brookside, Cambridge.

Bruce, Donald James; Lecturer in English
Literature, Department of English, Westfield
College, University of London, since 1968;
b 1930; *m* 1957; 1971; one *s* one *d*. BA

London 1953 (Hobbes Meml Schol.), MA
London 1959, Postgrad. Cert. in Educn 1954;
Mem., RSPCA. Recognised Lectr, Univ. of
London Inst. of Educn. 1961–68. Taught
English in Sweden, 1955–57; Schoolmaster,
1957–61. *Publications*: Radical Doctor
Smollett, 1964, American edn 1965; Topics
of Restoration Comedy, 1974; *contrib*.
Contemp. Rev. *Address*: Westfield College,
Hampstead, NW3 7ST.

Bruce, Prof. Frederick Fyvie, MA, DD,
FBA; Rylands Professor of Biblical Criticism
and Exegesis, University of Manchester,
since 1959; *b* 1910; *m* 1936; one *s* one *d*. MA
Aberdeen 1932, BA Cantab 1934, MA Cantab
1945, DD Aberdeen 1957, MA Manchester
1963; Mem., Soc. for OT Study (Pres., 1965),
Mem., Soc. for NT Studies (Pres., 1975).
Asst in Greek, Univ. of Edinburgh, 1935–38;
Lectr in Greek, Univ. of Leeds, 1938–47;
Head of Dept of Biblical Hist. and Lit., Univ.
of Sheffield, 1947–59 (Prof., 1955–59). Dean
of the Fac. of Theol., Univ. of Manchester,
1963–64. *Publications*: The Books and the
Parchments, 1950; The Acts of the Apostles,
1951; Second Thoughts on the Dead Sea
Scrolls, 1956; The Spreading Flame, 1957;
Biblical Exegesis in the Qumran Texts, 1960;
The English Bible, 1961; Paul and his
Converts, 1962; Israel and the Nations, 1963;
Expanded Paraphrase of the Epistles of Paul,
1965; New Testament History, 1969; This
is That, 1969; Tradition Old and New, 1970,
etc.; *contrib*. Bull. J. Rylands Lib., Erasmus,
Expository Times, Interpretation; Jl of
Semitic Studies, Jl of Theol. Studies, Mod.
Churchman, Scott. Jl of Theol. *Address*:
Faculty of Theology, Univ. of Manchester,
Manchester M13 9PL.

Bruce, Ian Macrae; Senior Lecturer in
Music, since 1956, and Assistant Director of
Studies, since 1969, University College,
Cardiff; *b* 1913. MA Edinburgh 1935,
MusBac 1938; Asst Lectr, University Coll.,
Cardiff, 1946–48; Lectr, 1948–56. *Publica-
tions*: *contrib*. Haydn Year-Book, Music
Rev., Soundings. *Address*: Dept of Music,
UC, Cardiff, Cathays Park, Cardiff CF1
3NS.

Bruce, Robert Richard Fernie, DFC,
MusBac; Lecturer in Music, University
College Cardiff, since 1947; *b* 1915; *m* 1941;
two *s* one *d*. MusBac Edinburgh 1938. *Address*:
Music Dept, Univ. College, Cardiff CF1
1XL.

Bruford, Alan James, PhD; Archivist
(Lecturer), School of Scottish Studies,
University of Edinburgh, since 1965; *b* 1937;
m 1969; one *d*. BA Cantab 1960 (2nd cl.
History and Anglo-Saxon), PhD Edinburgh
1965. Editor, Tocher, 1971– . *Publications*:
Gaelic Folk-Tales and Mediaeval Romances,
1969; ed (with D. A. MacDonald), Scottish
Traditional Tales, 1974; (with A. Munro),
The Fiddle in the Highlands, 1974; *contrib*.
Béaloideas, Éigse, Scott. Studies. *Address*:
School of Scottish Studies, 27 George
Square, Edinburgh EH8 9LD.

Brüggemann, Prof. Diethelm, Dr phil;
Professor of German, University College

Dublin, since 1968; *b* 1934. Staatsexamen Marburg 1961, Dr phil Marburg 1967. Assistent, Universität Bonn, 1961; Assistent, Technische Hochschule, Aachen, 1966. *Publications*: Vom Herzen direkt in die Feder: Die Deutschen in ihren Briefstellern, 1968; Die sächsische Komödie: Studien zum Sprachstil, 1970; *contrib.* Deutsche Vierteljahrsschrift für Literaturwissenschaft und Giestesgeschichte, Merkur, Neue Rundschau, Zeitschrift für deutsche Philologie. *Address*: Dept of German, Univ. College, Dublin 4.

Brumfitt, Prof. John Henry; Professor of French, University of St Andrews, since 1969; *b* 1921; *m* 1963; two *d*. MA Oxon 1947, DPhil Oxon 1953. Lectr, UC Oxford, 1948–51; Lectr, St Andrews Univ., 1951, Sen. Lectr, 1959. Mem., Adv. Cttee on new edn of Complete Works of Voltaire, 1968– ; Mem., Editorial Bd, FMLS, 1970– . *Publications*: Voltaire Historian, 1948, 2nd edn, 1971; Editions of: Voltaire's L'Ingénu, 1960; Selected Historical Works of Voltaire, 1963; Voltaire's La Philosophie de l'histoire, 1963, 2nd edn, 1969; Anatole France's Les Dieux ont soif, 1964; Voltaire's Candide, 1968; The French Enlightenment, 1972; *contrib.* Studies on Voltaire and the 18th century, French Studies, FMLS. *Address*: Dept of French, The Univ., St Andrews, Fife KY16 9AJ.

Brunner, Elizabeth; Reader in Economics, University of Lancaster, since 1971; Senior Research Associate, Case Western Reserve University, USA; *b* 1920. BA Oxon 1942, MA Oxon 1947. Mem., Res. Staff, Nuffield Coll., Oxford, 1945–67; Sen. Res. Fellow, Univ. of Lancaster, 1967–68; Sen. Lectr, Univ. of Lancaster, 1968–71; Asst Ed., Jl of Indust. Econ., 1952–71, Gen. Ed., 1971– . *Publications*: Holiday Making and the Holiday Trades, 1945; (with P. W. S. Andrews) Capital Development in Steel, 1951; (with P. W. S. Andrews) The Life of Lord Nuffield, 1955; (with P. W. S. Andrews) The Eagle Ironworks, 1965; *contrib.* Economia Internazionale, Jl of Indust. Econ., Oxford Econ. Papers, Omega. *Address*: Dept of Economics, Univ. of Lancaster, Bailrigg, Lancaster LA1 4YW.

Brunsden, Dr Denys; Lecturer, Department of Geography, University of London, since 1963; *b* 1936; *m* 1961; one *s* one *d*. BSc London 1959 (special), PhD London 1964; FRGS, Mem., Inst. Brit. Geogs; Mem., Geog. Assoc.; Mem., Brit. Geomorph. Res. Gp; Mem., Quaternary Res. Assoc. Tutorial Student, King's Coll., London, 1959–60; Asst Lectr, King's Coll., 1960–63. Hon. Conf. Org., Geog. Assoc., 1969–74; Tech. Ed., Brit. Geomorph. Res. Gp, 1968– . *Publications*: Papers on Dartmoor topics, and on Landslide topics; Dartmoor: The British Landscape through maps; *contrib.* Trans Inst. Brit. Geogrs. Geog., Jl Geol., Qly Jl Engrg Geol. *Address*: Dept of Geography, Univ. of London, King's College, Strand, WC2 RLS.

Brunskill, Dr Ronald William, MA, PhD, ARIBA; Senior Lecturer in Architecture, University of Manchester, since 1973

(Lecturer, 1960–73); *b* 1929; *m* 1960; two *d*. BA Manchester 1951 (1st cl. Architecture), MA Manchester 1952, PhD Manchester 1963; ARIBA 1951. Studio Asst, Univ. of Manchester, 1951–53; Vis. Fellow, Massachussets Inst. of Tech., 1956–57; Vis. Asst Prof., Univ. of Florida, 1969–70. Chie Architect, Williams Deacon's Bank, 1957–60; Partner in Carter, Brunskill and Associates, Chartered Architects, 1966–69, now Consultant. *Publications*: Illustrated Handbook of Vernacular Architecture, 1971; Vernacular Architecture of the Lake Counties, 1974; *contrib.* Trans Ancient Monuments Soc., Trans Cumberland and Westmorland Antiqu. and Archaeol. Soc., Jl of Folk Life Inst. (Indiana), Jl of Royal Archaeol. Inst. *Address*: School of Architecture, Univ. of Manchester, Manchester M13 9PL.

Brunt, Prof. Peter Astbury; Camden Professor of Ancient History, University of Oxford, since 1970; *b* 1917. BA Oxon 1939 (1st cl. Hon. Moderations in Classics, 1st cl. Lit. Hum.), MA 1946; FBA 1969. Lectr in Ancient History, St Andrews, 1947–51; Fellow, Tutor and Lectr in Anc. Hist., Oriel Coll., Oxford, 1951–67, Hon. Fellow, 1973; Sen. Bursar and Fellow of Gonville and Caius Coll., Cambridge, 1968–70. Asst Principal, later Principal (Temp.), Min. of Shipping, later War Transport, 1940–45; Dean of Oriel Coll., 1959–64; Ed., Oxford Mag., 1963–64; Gen. Bd of Fac., Oxford Univ., 1963–67; Chm., Cttee on Ashmolean Museum, 1967; Delegate Clarendon Press, 1970– . *Publications*: (with J. M. Moore) Res Gestae Div Augusti; Italian Manpower 225 BC–AD 14, 1971; Social Conflicts in Roman Republic, 1971; also contrib. Ancient Society and Institutions Studies presented to Victor Ehrenberg, 1966; R. Seager, Crisis of Roman Republic, 1969; *contrib.* AJP, CR, CQ, Gnomon, Historia, JHS, JRS, Latomus, PBSR, Past and Present, Phoenix, Proc. of Camb. Phil. Soc., RÉG. *Address*: Brasenose College, Oxford.

Brunyate, Margaret I.; Senior Lecturer, French Department, Goldsmiths' College, London, since 1968; *b* 1938; *m* 1968. BA London 1960 (2/I French), MA London 1963. Asst Lectr, Univ. of Glasgow, 1964–66; Lectr, 1966–68. Recognised Teacher, Univ. of London, and Univ. Examiner, 1970– . *Publications*: Renaissance themes in some works of Sympholien Champier, in, Cinq Etudes lyonnaises, 1966. *Address*: Dept of French, Goldsmiths' College, Lewisham Way, SE14 6NW.

Bryan, Margaret A.; Lecturer in Swahili, Department of Africa, School of Oriental and African Studies, University of London, since 1964; *b* 1909. BA Cantab 1930, MA Cantab, Dipl. SOS, 1934; Mem., Afr. Studies Assoc. UK. Colonial Service Course (later Overseas Services Course), Cambridge, 1950–60; Part-time Lectr, SOAS London, 1961–63; Vis. Lectr, UCLA, 1963–64. *Publications*: trans., in Swahili, Safari ya Msafiri (Pilgrim's Progress), c. 1941; The Distribution of the Semitic and Cushitic Languages of Africa, 1947; (with A. N. Tucker) The Distribution of the Nilotic and Nilo-Hamitic Languages of

Africa, 1948; trans., from French, Chitlangou, Son of a Chief, 1950; (with D. Westermann) Languages of West Africa, 1952, 2nd edn 1970; (with A. N. Tucker) The non-Bantu Languages of North-eastern Africa, 1956; comp., The Bantu Languages of Africa, 1959; trans. from French to Swahili, Agano la Kale na Kanisa la Kristo la leo (The Old Testament and the Christian Church of today), 1959; (with A. N. Tucker) Linguistic Analyses, 1965; *contrib.* Africa, Afri. Lang. Studies, Jl of Afri. Langs. *Address*: School of Oriental and African Studies, Univ. of London, WC1E 7HP.

Bryant, Christopher G. A., MA, PhD; Lecturer in Sociology, University of Southampton, since 1968; *b* 1944; *m* 1967; two *d.* BA Leicester 1965 (1st cl. Sociology), MA Leicester 1966, PhD Southampton 1974; Mem., Brit. Sociol Assoc. Tutorial Asst, Leicester Univ., 1965–66; Asst Lectr, Southampton Univ., 1966–68. *Publications*: *contrib.* Brit. Jl of Sociol., Soc. Res. *Address*: Dept of Sociology and Social Administration, Univ. of Southampton, Southampton SO9 5NH.

Bryant, Christopher John, BA, BPhil; Lecturer in Moral Philosophy, University of St Andrews, since 1966; *b* 1940; *m* 1964; one *s.* BA Oxon 1962, BPhil Oxon 1964. Asst Lectr, Univ. of St Andrews, 1964; Hon. Treas., Philosoph. Qly, 1968–72, Asst Ed., 1972– . *Address*: Dept of Moral Philosophy, Univ. of St Andrews, St Andrews, Fife KY16 9AL.

Bryant, Margaret Elizabeth; Senior Lecturer in Teaching of History and History of Education, University of London, Institute of Education, since 1972 (Lecturer, 1956–72); *b* 1916. BA Cantab 1937, MA Cantab 1943; CertEd, Cambridge 1938. Teaching posts and Edit. work, Brit. Council and Royal Inst. Internat. Aff., 1944–48; Educn Off., Essex Rec. Off. and Geffrye Mus., 1948–51. *Publications*: The Museum and the School, 1961; World Outlook, 1900–1965, 1968; Private Education, 16th to 20th Centuries, in, Victoria County History of Middlesex, vol. I, 1969; articles in Handbook for History Teachers, ed Burston and Green, 1972; Topographical Resources, in, Local Studies and the History of Education (History of Educn Soc.), 1972; *contrib.* Didask., Paedagog. Studien, Teaching Hist., TES. *Address*: Univ. of London Institute of Education, Malet Street, WC1E 7HS.

Bryden, Dr John Marshall; Lecturer, Overseas Development Group, University of East Anglia, since 1967; *b* 1941; *m* 1967; one *s* one *d.* BSc (Hons) Glasgow 1965 (Ag. Econs and Pol Econ.), PhD East Anglia 1973; Member: Agricultural Econs Soc., Scottish Econ. Soc., Royal Highland and Agricultural Soc., Royal Scottish Forestry Soc., British Deer Soc. Econ. Asst, Min. of Overseas Development, 1966–67; Econ. Development Adviser, E Caribbean, 1968–70; Head of Land Development Division, Highlands and Islands Development Bd, 1972– . Mem., West Indies Cttee. *Publications*: Tourism and Development: A Case Study of the Common-

wealth Caribbean, 1973; *contrib.* JAE, SES. *Address*: Overseas Development Gp, Univ. of East Anglia, Norwich NOR 88C.

Bryer, Dr Anthony Applemore Mornington; Senior Lecturer in Medieval History since 1973 (Lecturer, 1965–73); Acting Director of Byzantine Studies since 1970, Department of Medieval History, University of Birmingham; *b* 1937; *m* 1961; three *d.* BA Oxford 1961 (Mod. History), MA Oxford 1967, DPhil Oxford 1967. Res. Fellow, Athens Univ., 1961; Res. Fellow, Univ. of Birmingham, 1964; Vis. Fellow, Center for Byzantine Studies, Dumbarton Oaks, Harvard Univ., 1970. *Publications*: Byzantium and the Ancient East, 1970; contrib. The Making of the Modern World, ed D. W. Johnson, 1971; Byzantium: an Introduction, ed P. D. Whitting, 1971; The Greeks of Trebizond in the Pontos, 1974; (with D. Winfield) Monuments and Topography of the Empire of Trebizond, 1974; (with N. Panayotakis) The Acts of Vazelon, 1974; *contrib.* Antiquity, Apollo, Ararat, Archeion Pontou, Balkan Studies, Bedi Kartlisa, Byzantinische Zeitschrift, Byzantino-slavica, Hist. Today, Kypriakai Spoudai, Neo-Hellenika, Univ. of Birmingham Hist. Jl, etc. *Address*: School of History, Univ. of Birmingham, PO Box 363, Birmingham B15 2TT.

Bubb, Alfred Charles, BA, FLA; Librarian, University of Salford, since 1967; *b* 1923; *m* 1950; two *d.* BA London; FLA 1957. *Address*: Library, Univ. of Salford, Salford M5 4WT.

Buchan, Hon. Alastair Francis, CBE, MA; Montague Burton Professor of International Relations, University of Oxford, since 1972; *b* 1918; *m* 1942; two *s* one *d.* MA Oxon; Jun. Fellow, Univ. of Virginia, 1939. Asst Ed, The Economist, 1948–51; Washington Corres., The Observer, 1951–55; Diplomatic and Defence Corres., The Observer, 1955–58; Dir, Inst. for Strategic Studies, 1958–69; Comdt, Royal Coll. of Defence Studies (formerly IDC), 1970–71. Reith Lectr, 1973. *Publications*: The Spare Chancellor: the life of Walter Bagehot, 1959; NATO in the 1960's, 1960, rev. edn 1963; The United States, 1963; (jtly) Arms and Stability in Europe, 1963; War in Modern Society, 1966; ed, China and the Peace of Asia, 1965; ed, A World of Nuclear Powers?, 1966; ed, Europe's Futures, Europe's Choices, 1969; Power and Equilibrium in the 70's, 1973; ed, Problems of Modern Strategy, 1970; *contrib.* Foreign Affairs, etc. *Address*: Balliol College, Oxford.

Buchan, Dr David Duncan; Senior Lecturer, Department of English Studies, University of Stirling, since 1971; *b* 1939; *m* 1965; one *s* one *d.* MA Aberdeen 1960, PhD Aberdeen 1965. Fellow, Univ. of Aberdeen, 1960; Instructor, Univ. of Victoria, 1961–65; Asst Prof., Univ. of Massachusetts, 1965–68; Lectr, Univ. of Stirling, 1968–71. Mem., Univ. Cttee on Scott. Lit., 1969– ; Treas., Assoc. for Scott. Lit. Studies, 1971–73. *Publications*: The Ballad and the Folk, 1972 (Chicago Folklore Prize 1973, Blackwell Prize 1973); A Scottish Ballad Book, 1973; *contrib.* Ariel, Jl Folklore Inst., Malahat Rev.,

South. Folklore Qly. *Address*: Dept of English Studies, Univ. of Stirling, Stirling FK9 4LA.

Buchan, Ogilvie Milne Clarke, MA, BA; Staff Tutor in Philosophy, Department of Extra-Mural Studies, University of Durham, since 1964; *b* 1925; *m* 1967. MA Aberdeen 1951 (1st cl. Philosophy-English); BA Oxon 1954 (1st cl. PPE); Mem., Mind Assoc. Staff Tutor in Philosophy, Univ. of Oxford Delegacy for Extra-Mural Studies, 1955-57; Asst Dir, Examinations, Civil Service Commn, 1957-60; Lectr in Political Thought, Univ. of W Indies, 1960-64. *Address*: Dept of Extra-Mural Studies, Univ. of Durham, 32 Old Elvet, Durham.

Buchanan, Ian Loraine; Senior Lecturer, Economics, University of Dundee, since 1969; *b* 1930; *m* 1957; two *d*. BA Durham 1957 (Economic Studies); AIB 1952. Lectr in Econ., Queen's Coll., Univ. of St Andrews, 1962-69. Econ. Adv., Min. of Housing and Local Govt, 1968; Consultant to Tayside Study, 1969; Consultant for the Moray Firth Study, 1967. *Address*: Dept of Economics, Univ. of Dundee, Perth Road, Dundee.

Buchanan, Dr Robert Angus, MA, PhD; Senior Lecturer in the History of Technology, School of Humanities and Social Sciences, University of Bath, since 1965; *b* 1930; *m* 1955; two *s*. BA Cambridge 1953, MA Cambridge 1957, PhD Cambridge 1957. Asst Lectr, Bristol Coll. Sci. Technol. (later Univ. Bath), 1960; Lectr, 1961-65. Mem., Council; Mem., Newcomen Soc.; Mem., Brit. Soc. Hist. Sci.; Mem. (Royal Soc. nomin.), Brit. Nat. Cttee Hist. Sci. Technol. and Med. *Publications*: Technology and Social Progress, 1965; (with N. Cossons) Industrial Archaeology of the British Region, 1969; Industrial Archaeology in Britain, 1972; *contrib*. Trans Newcomen Soc., Trans Bristol and Gloucs. Archaeol. Soc., Antiqu. *Address*: School of Humanities and Social Sciences, Univ. of Bath, Bath, Somerset.

Buchanan, Dr Robert Thomson; Lecturer, Economics Department, University of Strathclyde, since 1968; *b* 1923; *m* 1959; one *d*. MA Aberdeen 1951, PhD Edinburgh 1958. Lectr, Dept of Economics, Univ. of Bristol, 1961-68. *Publications*: *contrib*. Brit. Jl Indust. Relat. *Address*: Dept of Economics, Univ. of Strathclyde, Glasgow.

Buchanan, Dr Ronald Hull, BA, PhD; Senior Lecturer, Department of Geography, Queen's University, Belfast, since 1968; *b* 1931; *m* 1958; one *s* one *d*. BA QUB 1953 (2nd cl. Geography), PhD QUB 1958; F. Amer. Geog. Soc.; Mem., Inst. Brit. Geogs; Mem., Geog. Assoc. Res. Asst, Queen's Univ., Belfast, 1953-55; Asst Lectr, 1955-58; Asst Prof., Montana State Univ., 1958-59; Lectr, Queen's Univ., Belfast, 1959-67; Assoc. Prof., Univ. of Washington, and Vis. Res. Fellow, Cornell Univ., 1967-68. Mem., Ulster Countryside Cttee, 1965-   . *Publications*: (with E. Jones and D. McCourt) Man and his Habitat, 1971; *contrib*. Econ. Geog., Folk Life, Ulster Folklife. *Address*: Dept of Geography, Queen's Univ., Belfast BT7 1NN.

Buchdahl, Gerd; Reader in History and Philosophy of Science, University of Cambridge, since 1958, Head of Dept of History and Philosophy of Science since 1972; *b* 1914; *m* 1947; three *s*. HND in Building Eng., 1936, BA Melbourne 1945 (1st cl. Philosophy), MA Melbourne 1953 (1st cl.), MA Cantab 1958; Licentiate, Inst. of Builders 1936. Lectr, Melbourne Univ., 1947-49; Sen. Lectr, 1949-57; Lectr, Oxford, 1954-55; Lectr, Cambridge, 1958-66; Vis. Prof., Stanford Univ., 1965; Univ. W Ontario, 1966-67; Univ. of Texas at Austin, 1969, 1971. Jt Ed., Studies Hist. Philos. Sci., 1966-   . *Publications*: The Image of Newton and Locke in the Age of Reason, 1961; Metaphysics and the Philosophy of Science, The Classical Origins: Descartes to Kant, 1969; Science and Metaphysics, in, The Nature of Metaphysics, ed. D. Pears, 1957; The Natural Philosophy, in, The Making of Modern Science, ed. A. R. Hall, 1960; Descartes' Anticipation of a Logic of Scientific Discovery, in, Scientific Change, ed. A. C. Crombie, 1963; Semantic Sources of the Concept of Law, in, Boston Studies in the Philosophy of Science, vol. 3, ed R. S. Cohen et al., 1968; The Kantian 'Dynamic of Reason', with Special Reference to the Place of Causality in Kant's System, in, Kant Studies Today, ed C. W. Beck, 1969; Gravity and Intelligibility: Newton to Kant, in, The Methodological Heritage of Newton, ed R. Buttes et al., 1970; History of Science and Criteria of Choice, in, Minnesota Studies in the Philosophy of Science, vol. 5, ed R. H. Stuewer; The Conception of Lawlikeness in Kant's Philosophy of Science, in, Proc. 3rd Int. Kant. Congress, ed L. W. Beck, 1972; The Methodology of Mathias Schleiden, in, The Foundations of Scientific Method: the nineteenth century, ed R. N. Giere and R. S. Westfall, 1972; Methodological Aspects of Kepler's Theory of Refraction, in, Internationalés Kepler-Symposium Weil der Stadt 1971, ed Krafft, Meyer and Sticker, 1972; Explanation and Gravity, in, Changing Perspectives in the History of Science, ed Teich and Young, 1972; *contrib*. Proc. Aristot. Soc., Aust. Jl Philos., Brit. Jl Hist. Sci., Brit. Jl Philos. Sci., Contemp. Phys, Hist. Sci., Isis, Mind, Monist, New Educn Rev., Philos. Phen. Res., Ratio, Synthese, Stud. Hist. Phil. Sci., Kant-Studien. *Address*: Dept of History and Philosophy of Science, Free School Lane, Cambridge.

Buck, Christopher Hearn; Lecturer in Product Design in University of Aston Management Centre (formerly in Department of Industrial Administration), since 1960; *b* 1912; *m* 1936. BSc Birmingham 1933; MInstP 1941, MIGasE 1950. Scient. Off., Royal Airc. Estab., 1940-45; various technical positions, Radiation Ltd, 1936-40 and 1945-60. *Publications*: Problems of Product Design and Development, 1963; (with D. M. Butler) Economic Product Design, 1970. *Address*: The Univ. of Aston in Birmingham, Gosta Green, Birmingham B4 7ET.

Buck, Timothy; Lecturer, German Department, University of Edinburgh, since 1966; *b* 1940; *m*; one *s* two *d*. BA Southampton 1963 (Hons), MA Southampton 1966. Lektor in

95

English, Göttingen, W Germany, 1963–65. *Publications*: German into English I, 1967, 3rd edn 1972; German into English II, 1972; trans., European Anecdotes and Jests, ed Ranke, 1972; Penguin German Dictionary (German–English) (forthcoming); *contrib.* Euphor., Forum Mod. Lang. Stud., Germ. Life and Letters, Mod. Lang. Rev., Oxf. Germ. Stud., Times, Die Zeit. *Address*: German Dept, Edinburgh Univ., Edinburgh EH8 9YL.

Budge, Dr Ian; Reader in Government, University of Essex, since 1971; *b* 1936; *m* 1964; one *s* one *d*. MA Edinburgh 1959 (1st cl. Hist.), AM Yale 1961, PhD Yale 1966. Temp. Asst, Univ. of Edinburgh, 1962–64; Asst, Univ. of Strathclyde, 1963–64, Lectr, 1964–66; Lectr, Univ. of Essex, 1966–68, Sen. Lectr, 1968–71; Vis. Lectr, Univ. of Wisconsin, 1969–70. Dir, Essex Summer Schools in Soc. Sci. Data-Analysis, 1968–72. *Publications*: (with D. W. Urwin) Scottish Political Behaviour, 1966; Agreement and the Stability of Democracy, 1970; (with J. A. Brand and others) Political Stratification and Democracy, 1972; (with C. O'Leary) Belfast: The Approach to Crisis, 1972; *contrib.* Pol Studies, Midwest Jl of Pol Science, Brit. Jl of Pol Science, Eur. Jl of Pol Science. *Address*: Dept of Government, Univ. of Essex, Colchester CO4 3SQ.

Bujic, Bojan; Lecturer in Music, Department of Music, University of Reading, since 1969; *b* 1937. BA Univ. of Sarajevo 1961 (Eng. Lang. and Lit.), BA Acad. of Music, Univ. of Sarajevo 1963 (Musicology), DPhil Oxford Univ. (Lincoln Coll.) 1967 (Music); Member: Royal Musical Assoc.; Brit Soc. of Aesthetics. Lectr in History of Music, Acad. of Music, Univ. of Sarajevo, Yugoslavia, 1967–68; Sen. Vis. Fellow, Soc. for the Humanities, Cornell Univ., Ithaca, NY, 1971. *Publications*: *contrib.* Grove's Dict. of Music, Arti musices (Univ. of Zagreb), IRMAS, MA. *Address*: Dept of Music, Univ. of Reading, 35 Upper Redlands Road, Reading.

Bulloch, Anthony William, MA, PhD; Fellow since 1967 and Dean-in-College, since 1968, King's College, Cambridge; *b* 1942; *m* 1967. BA Cantab 1964 (Classics), MA Cantab 1968, PhD Cantab 1972. Financial Tutor, King's Coll., Cambridge, 1970–72. *Publications*: CRAC Classics Degree Course Guide, 1972–73, 1974–75; The Fifth Hymn of Callimachus, 1975; contrib., Cambridge History of Classical Literature (forthcoming); The Legacy of Greece (forthcoming); *contrib.* Bull. Corr. Hell., Class. Qly, Hermes, Proc. Camb. Phil. Soc. *Address*: King's College, Cambridge CB2 1ST.

Bullock, Sir Alan (Louis Charles); Vice-Chancellor of Oxford University, 1969–73, and Master of St Catherine's College, Oxford University, since 1960; *b* 1914; *m* 1940; three *s* one *d*. BA Oxford 1936 (1st cl. Literae Humaniores), BA Oxford 1938 (1st cl. Modern History), MA 1940, DLitt 1969; FBA 1967; For. Mem., Amer. Acad. of Arts and Scis, 1972. Fellow, Tutor and Dean, New Coll., Oxford, 1945–52; Censor, St Catherine's Soc., Oxford, 1952–60. Chm.

Trustees, Tate Gallery; Trustee and Fellow, Aspen Inst. for Humanities. Chairman: Res. Cttee, RIIA; Nat. Adv. Council Training and Supply of Teachers, 1963–65; Schools Council, 1966–69; Cttee on Literary and Teaching of English, 1972– ; Mem., Arts Council, 1961–64; Mem., SSRC, 1966; Mem., Adv. Council on Public Records, 1965– ; Mem., British Library Organising Cttee, 1972–73; Mem., Cttee of Vice-Chancellors and Principals, 1969–73. *Publications*: Hitler: A Study in Tyranny, 1952, rev. edn 1964; The Liberal Tradition, 1956; Life and Times of Ernest Bevin, vol 1, 1960, vol. 2, 1967; ed, The Twentieth Century, 1971; (jt ed.) Oxford History of Modern Europe. *Address*: Master's Lodgings, St Catherine's College, Oxford.

Bullock, Alan Oswald, MA; Lecturer in Italian, University of Leeds, since 1964; *b* 1938; *m* 1961. BA Oxon 1960, MA Oxon 1964. Jun. Fellow, Bristol Univ., 1960–62; Asst, King's Coll., Aberdeen, 1962–64. Oral Examiner GCE, Oxford and Cambridge Schools Exam. Bd, 1962, 1967, 1971, 1973; Asst Oral Examiner GCE, London Univ., 1962, 1965– ; Sen. Examiner GCE, Oxford Local Exam., 1965– ; Oral Examiner GCE, JMB, 1966–69; Chm., Examiners, O level Italian, JMB, 1966– ; Mem., Subject Cttee, Mod. Foreign Lang., JMB, 1966– ; Oral Examiner, Army Cert. of Educn 1st cl., 1967; Examiner in Gen. Studies Italian, JMB, 1969– ; Sen. Oral Examiner, O level Italian, JMB, 1970– . *Publications*: contrib. G. Ragazzini, Dizionario Inglese–Italiano/Italiano–Inglese, 1967; *contrib.* Ital. Studies, Italica, Studi e Problemi di Critica Testuale. *Address*: Dept of Italian, The Univ., Leeds LS2 9JT.

Bullough, Prof. Donald Auberon; Professor of Medieval History, University of St Andrews, since 1973; *b* 1928; *m* 1963; two *d*. BA Oxford 1950, MA 1952; FRHistS 1958, FSA 1968, FSAScot; Fereday (Res.) Fellow, St John's Coll. Oxford, 1952–55; Lectr in Medieval Hist. Univ. of Edinburgh, 1955–66; Vis. Prof., Southern Methodist Univ., Dallas, Texas, 1965–66; Prof. of Medieval Hist., Univ. of Nottingham, 1966–73. Member: Faculty of History, Archaeology and Letters of British School at Rome, 1962–66, 1968–72, 1974– ; Council of Royal Hist. Soc., 1968–72; Council of Henry Bradshaw Soc., 1959– ; Director, Elek Books, 1968– . *Publications*: The Age of Charlemagne, 1965, 2nd edn 1974; Fr. Germ. and It. eds; (ed jtly) The Study of Medieval Records: Essays in Honour of Kathleen Major, 1971; *contrib.* Deutsches Archiv, English Hist. Rev., Le Moyen Age, Papers of the British School at Rome, Past and Present, Settimane di Studi del Centro Italiano di Studi sull'Alto Medioevo. *Address*: Dept of Medieval History, Univ. of St Andrews, South Street, St Andrews KY16 9AJ.

Bulmer, Martin; Lecturer in Sociology, Department of Sociology and Social Administration, University of Durham, since 1970; *b* 1943; *m* 1966. BSc London 1967 (Sociology). Mem., Brit. Soc. Assoc.; Mem., Amer. Soc. Assoc. Jun. Res. Fellow in Sociology, Rowntree Research Unit, Univ. of Durham, 1968–70. *Publications*: ed, Working Class Images of Society, 1974; *contrib*. Brit. Jl of Sociology, Durham Univ. Jl, Industrial Relations Jl, Sociology. *Address*: Univ. of Durham, Old Shire Hall, Durham DH1 3HP.

Burchell, Robert Arthur; Lecturer in American History and Institutions, University of Manchester, since 1968; *b* 1941. BA Oxon 1963, MA Oxon 1968, BLitt Oxon 1970. Asst Lectr in American History and Institutions, Univ. of Manchester, 1965–68. *Publications*: Westward Expansion, 1974; *contrib*. California Historical Soc. Qly, Jl of American Studies, S California Qly. *Address*: Dept of American History and Institutions, Univ. of Manchester, Oxford Road, Manchester M13 9PL.

Burchfield, Robert William; Fellow and Tutor in English Language, St Peter's College, Oxford, since 1963; Editor, A Supplement to the Oxford English Dictionary, since 1957; Chief Editor, The Oxford English Dictionaries, since 1971; *b* 1923; *m* 1949; one *s* two *d*. MA Victoria Univ. Coll., Wellington, NZ, 1948, BA Oxon 1951, MA Oxon 1955. Jun. Lectr in English, Victoria Univ. Coll., Wellington, 1948–49; Jun. Lectr in English Lang., Magdalen Coll., Oxford, 1952–53; Lectr in English Lang.: Christ Church, Oxford, 1953–57; St Peter's Coll., Oxford, 1955–63. Hon. Sec., Early English Text Soc., 1955–68 (Mem. Council, 1968–); Editor, Notes and Queries, 1959–62. *Publications*: (with E. M. Burchfield) The Land and People of New Zealand, 1953; (with C. T. Onions and G. W. S. Friedrichsen) The Oxford Dictionary of English Etymology, 1966; A Supplement of Australia and New Zealand Words, in the Pocket Oxford Dictionary, 5th edn, 1969; A Supplement to the Oxford English Dictionary, vol. I (A–G), 1972; *contrib*. Med. Æv., Notes and Quer., Rising Generation (Tokyo), Times Lit. Suppl., Trans Philolog. Soc. *Address*: St Peter's College, Oxford.

Burchnall, Herbert Henry; Registrar, University of Liverpool, since 1962; *b* 1919; *m* 1946; two *s*. BA Oxon 1947, MA Oxon 1951; Admin. Asst, NUJMB, 1948–50; Asst Sec., 1950–51; Asst Registrar, Liverpool Univ., 1951–56; Academic Sec., 1956–61; Dep. Registrar, 1961–62; Chm., Northwestern Univs O&M Unit Management Cttee, 1970– ; Mem., Liverpool Area Health Authority (Teaching), 1973– . *Address*: Univ. of Liverpool, PO Box 147, Liverpool L69 3BX.

Burges, (Norman) Alan, MSc, PhD, FInstBiol; Vice-Chancellor, New University of Ulster, Coleraine, Northern Ireland, since 1966; *b* 1911; *m* 1940; three *d*. BSc Hons Sydney 1931, MSc Sydney 1932, PhD Cambridge 1937; Hon. LLD Belfast, 1973. Res. Fellow, Emmanuel Coll., 1938; Prof. of Botany, Sydney Univ., 1947–52; Dean of Faculty of Science and Fellow of Senate, 1949–52; Holbrook Gaskell Prof. of Botany, Univ. of Liverpool, 1952–66, Acting Vice-Chancellor, 1964–65, Pro Vice-Chancellor, 1965–66. Chm., NI Adv. Council for

Educn, 1966– . Pres., Brit. Ecological Soc., 1958, 1959; Pres., Brit. Mycological Soc., 1962; Mem., Cttee, Nature Conservancy, England, 1959–66; Jt Ed., Flora Europaea Project, 1956– . *Publications*: Micro-organisms in the Soil, 1958; (with F. Raw) Soil Biology, 1967; *contrib*. to scientific jls on plant disease and fungi. *Address*: Vice-Chancellor's Lodge, Mountsandel Road, Coleraine, Northern Ireland.

Burgess, Colin Brian, BA; Staff Tutor in Archaeology, Department of Adult Education, University of Newcastle upon Tyne, since 1966; *b* 1938; *m* 1965; two *s*. BA Wales 1960 (Hons Archaeology); FSAScot, Mem.: Prehist. Soc., Royal Archaeol. Inst., Cambrian Archaeol. Assoc. Sir James Knott Fellow, Dept of Classics and Anc. Hist., Univ. of Newcastle upon Tyne, 1963–65. Archaeologist, Reading Museum, 1965–66; Mem., Council, Prehist. Soc., 1966–68; Mem., various Cttees, Council for Brit. Archaeol. *Publications*: Bronze Age Metalwork in Northern England, 1968; ed (with F. Lynch), Prehistoric Man in Wales and The West: essays in honour of Lily F. Chitty, 1972; *contrib*. Antiqu. Jl, Archaeol. Jl, Current Archaeol. *Address*: Dept of Adult Education, The Univ., Newcastle Upon Tyne NE1 7RU.

Burgess, Dr Glyn Sheridan; Lecturer, Department of French, University of Liverpool, since 1971; *b* 1943; *m* 1967; one *s* one *d*. BA Hons Oxon 1965 (Mod. Lang.), MA McMaster 1966, MA Oxon 1970, DUP 1968. Lectr, later Asst Prof., Queen's Univ., Kingston, Ontario, 1966–70; Asst Prof., Univ. of S Carolina, 1970–71. *Publications*: Contribution à l'étude du vocabulaire précourtois, 1970; *contrib*. Mod. Lang. Rev., Romance Notes, Symposium, Zeitschrift für romanische Philologie. *Address*: Dept of French, Univ. of Liverpool, PO Box 147, Liverpool L69 3BX.

Burgess, Malcolm Archer Sheridan, MA, PhD; University Lecturer in Salvonic Studies, Department of Slavonic Studies, Faculty of Modern and Medieval Languages, University of Cambridge, since 1967; *b* 1926. BA Cambridge 1948, MA Cambridge 1952, PhD Cambridge 1953 (1st cl. Hons Mod. and Med. Lang. Tripos: Spanish, Russian, Czechoslovak). Graham Robertson Res. Fellow, Downing Coll., Cambridge, 1953–57; Conducted courses of Russian for Scientists (Pressland Fund), Cambridge, 1960; Open Lectr on Hist. of Russian Art and Archit., Fac. of Fine Arts, Cambridge Univ., Lent Term, 1957; Lectr in Russian Lang. and Lit., Sch. of Slavonic and E European Studies, Univ. of London, 1957–62; Freelance Lectr on Slavonic and East European Art and Archit. Hon. Sec., Cambridge Univ. Slav. Soc.; Hon. Sec., Cambridge Univ. Mod. Lang. Soc.; Mem., Gov. Body, Downing Coll., Cambridge, 1953–56; Mem., Cttee, Cambridge Univ. Footlights Club, 1950–56; Designer, BBC TV, 1958. *Publications*: The First Empire Style in Furniture, in, Antiques International, ed P. Wilson, 1966; Peter the Great and the New Capital, 1700–1762, The Zenith of Imperial

Russia, 1762–1855, in, Art Treasures in Russia: Monuments, Masterpieces, Commissions and Collections, 1970; chaps VIIc, VIIIa, VIIIb (18th Century Literature, History of the Theatre to 1917), in, Cambridge Companion to Russian Studies (forthcoming); entries on Russian Drama and Theatre, in Oxford Companion to the Theatre, 4th edn (forthcoming); contrib. The Slavonic and East European Review, in, Modern Humanities Research Association, vol. II; Discovering Antiques, Issues 54, 56. *Address*: Dept of Slavonic Studies, Faculty of Modern and Medieval Languages, 2 Sidgwick Avenue, Cambridge.

Burkart, Arthur John; Senior Lecturer, Department of Hotel, Catering and Tourism Management, University of Surrey, since 1970; *m* 1st 1947, 2nd 1962; two *d*. MA Oxon 1947; FSS. Hon. Res. Fellow, Dept Econs, Univ. Lancaster, 1968–69. Advertising Man., British European Airways, 1957–63; Man. Dir, Illustrated Newspapers Ltd, 1963–65; Dir, Cunard Line Ltd, 1966–67; Dir, HTS Management Consultants Ltd, 1969–72. *Publications*: (with Prof. S. Medlik), Tourism, 1974; *contrib*. Jl Industrial Econs, Tourist Review (Switz.). *Address*: Dept of Hotel and Catering and Tourism Management, Univ. of Surrey, Guildford, Surrey GU2 5XH.

Burke, Dr Gerald Louis, MC; Head of Town Planning Section, Department of Land Management and Development, University of Reading, since 1970; *b* 1914; *m* 1949; one *s* one *d*. BSc (Est. Man.) London 1946, MSc Est. Man.) London 1951, PhD (Econ.) London 1962; ARICS 1947, MRTPI 1948. Lectr, Coll. of Estate Management, London, 1946–51; Head of Sch. of Survey, Royal Tech. Coll., Nairobi, 1956–58; Head of Town Planning Dept, Coll. of Estate Management, 1958–70. Town Planning Surveyor, Govt of Kenya, 1952–56. Educn Policy and other Educn Cttees, RICS, 1959–73 (incl. Wells and Eve Cttees). *Publications*: The Making of Dutch Towns, 1956; Greenheart Metropolis, 1966; Towns in the Making, 1971; Townscapes (forthcoming); *contrib*. Chartered Surveyor, The Planner, Nutrition Soc., Inst. of Biol. *Address*: Dept of Land Management and Development, Univ. of Reading, Whiteknights, Reading RG6 2AH.

Burke, Dr Thomas Edmund; Lecturer, Department of Philosophy, University of Reading, since 1964; *b* 1930; *m* 1956; two *s* one *d*. BA TCD 1952 (1st cl. Hons Phil.), PhD TCD 1955. Lectr, St David's Coll., Lampeter, 1958–64. Asst Principal, Brit. Admin. Civil Service, 1954–58. *Publications*: *contrib*. Hermathena, Inquiry, Mind. *Address*: Dept of Philosophy, Univ. of Reading, Reading, Berks RG6 2AH.

Burke, Ulick Peter; Lecturer in History, School of European Studies, University of Sussex, since 1962; *b* 1937. BA Oxon 1960 (1st cl. History), MA Oxon 1964; FRHistS. Herodotus Fellow, Institute for Advanced Study, Princeton, 1967; Leverhulme Fellowship, 1972. *Publications*: ed, The Renaissance, 1964; ed/trans., Sarpi, 1967; The

Renaissance Sense of the Past, 1969; Culture and Society in Renaissance Italy, 1972; Venice and Amsterdam, 1974; *contrib*. European Jl of Sociology, Hist. and Theory, Jl of World Hist. *Address*: Arts Building, Univ. of Sussex, Falmer, Brighton, Sussex BN1 9QN.

Burkett, Anthony John; Senior Lecturer in Politics, Department of European Studies, Loughborough University of Technology, since 1971; *b* 1933. BA Nottingham 1958 (2nd cl. Politics), MA Nottingham 1961; Mem., AUT; Mem., Pol Studies Assoc. Lectr, Loughorough Coll. Technol., 1961–66; Lectr, Loughborough Univ. Technol., 1966–71; Vis. Lectr, Univ. of Nancy. Warden, Forest Court Hall, 1964–72; Chm. Wardens' Cttee, 1970–72; Mem., Senate, 1969– ; Mem., Univ. Council, 1970–72; Chm., AUT, 1968–69. *Publications*: Parties and Elections in West Germany, 1974; *contrib*. Loughborough Jl Soc. Sci., Pol Studies, Social. Comment. *Address*: Dept of European Studies, Loughborough Univ. of Technology, Loughborough LE11 3TU.

Burnett, Prof. George Murray; Principal and Vice-Chancellor of Heriot-Watt University, since 1974; *b* 1921; *m* 1946; one *s* three *d*. BSc Aberdeen 1943, PhD Aberdeen 1947; DSc Birmingham 1954; FRIC 1956; FRSE 1956. Lectr, Univ. of Birmingham, 1948–54; Prof., Univ. of Aberdeen, 1955–74. *Publications*: Mechanism of Polymer Reaction, 1954; Transfer and Storage of Energy by Molecules, 1970; *contrib*. Trans Faraday Soc., Proc. Royal Soc., Jl Chem. Soc. *Address*: Heriot-Watt Univ., Chambers Street, Edinburgh EH1 1HX.

Burnett, James T. M., MA; Head of German Studies, Department of Modern Languages, University of Strathclyde, since 1968; *b* 1922; *m* 1947; two *d*. MA Glasgow 1950 (2nd cl. German and Russian); Teacher Training, General Cert. Lectr, 1963–71; Sen. Lectr in charge of German, 1971– . *Address*: Dept of Modern Languages, Univ. of Strathclyde, George Street, Glasgow G1 1XW.

Burnett, Prof. John, MA, LLB, PhD; Professor of Social History, Department of Government Studies, Brunel University, since 1972; *b* 1925; *m* 1951; one *s*. BA Cantab 1946, MA Cantab 1950, LLB Cantab 1951, PhD London 1958. Head of Dept of General Studies, Brunel CAT, 1962–66. Convener of Undergrad. Studies, School of Social Services, 1966–71; Reading in Econ. and Soc. Hist., 1966–72. *Publications*: Plenty and Want: A Social History of English Diet, 1966, 2nd edn 1968; A History of the Cost of Living, 1969; The Challenge of the Nineteenth Century, 1970; Useful Toil, 1974; *contrib*. Bull. Inst. Hist. Res., Business Hist., Hist. Today, etc. *Address*: School of Social Sciences, Brunel Univ., Uxbridge, Mddx UB8 3TH.

Burnett, Prof. John Harrison; Sibthorpian Professor of Rural Economy, Oxford, since 1970; *b* 1922; *m* 1945; two *s*. BA ,MA Oxon 1947, DPhil Oxon 1953; FRSE 1957. Fellow (by exam.), Magdalen Coll., 1949–53; Univ. Lectr and Demonstrator, Oxford, 1949–53; Lectr, Liverpool Univ., 1954–55; Prof. of Botany, Univ. of St Andrews, 1955–60; Prof. of Botany, King's Coll., Newcastle, Univ. of Durham, 1961–63, Univ. of Newcastle, 1963–68; Dean, Faculty of Science, St Andrews, 1958–60, Newcastle, 1966–68; Public Orator, Newcastle, 1966–68; Regius Prof. of Botany, Univ. of Glasgow, 1968–70. Chm., Scottish Horticultural Res. Inst., 1959– ; Mem., Nature Conservancy (Scottish Cttee), 1961–66; Mem., Academic Adv. Council, Univs of St Andrews and Dundee, 1964–66; Trustee, The New Phytologist, 1962– . *Publications*: Fundamentals of Mycology, 1968, 2nd edn 1972; Introduction to the Genetics of Fungi, 1972; ed and contrib. The Vegetation of Scotland, 1964; *contrib*. scientific jls. *Address*: St John's College, Oxford.

Burnett, Margaret Evelyn; Senior Lecturer in Social Work, Social Administration Department, University of Birmingham, since 1971; *b* 1933. BSc (Soc.) LSE 1955, Dip. Applied Social Studies LSE 1956. Lectr in Social Work, Univ. of Birmingham, 1963–71. Mem.: Professional Practices Cttee, Inst. of Med. Social Workers, 1965–70; Professional Practices and Devt Cttee Brit. Assoc. of Social Workers, 1973– ; Editorial Bd, Brit. Jl of Social Work. *Publications*: *contrib*. Med. Soc. Work, Social Work. *Address*: Social Administration Dept, Univ. of Birmingham, PO Box 363, Birmingham B15 2TT.

Burney, Charles Allan, MA, FSA; Lecturer in Near Eastern Archaeology in Departments of History and Archaeology, University of Manchester, since 1958; *b* 1930; *m* 1960; one *s* one *d*. BA Cantab 1952 (1st cl. History Pt I, 2nd cl. Archaeology and Anthropology Pt II), MA Cantab 1959; FSA 1964; Mem.: Council, Mgt and Exec. Cttee, Brit. Inst. Archaeol at Ankara; Brit. Inst. Persian Studies. *Publications*: (with D. M. Lang) The Peoples of the Hills: Ancient Ararat and Caucasus, 1971; *contrib*. Anatolian Studies, Iran. *Address*: Dept of Archaeology, Univ. of Manchester, Manchester M13 9PL.

Burns, Adelaide, BA; Lecturer, Department of Spanish, University of Birmingham, since 1971; *b* 1910; *m* 1933; three *s*. BA Liverpool (1st cl. Spanish). Asst Lectr, Birmingham Univ., 1931; Part-time Lectr, Birmingham, 1950–71. O Level Oral Examiner, JMB, 1969, 1970, 1971, 1972, 1973. *Publications*: España, ayer y hoy, 1965; Doce Cuentistas españoles de la posguerra, 1968; Cervantes: dos novelas ejemplares, 1971; *contrib*. MLR. *Address*: Dept of Spanish, Univ. of Birmingham, PO Box 363, Birmingham B15 2TT.

Burns, Dr Campbell Blain, MA, LLB, PhD; Senior Lecturer, The Law School, University of Strathclyde, since 1971; *b* 1936; *m* 1971. MA Glasgow 1959, LLB Glasgow 1962, PhD Strathclyde 1970. Mem., Law Soc. of Scotland, 1962. Lectr, Univ. of Strathclyde, 1964–71. *Publications*: The Commercial Law of Scotland, 1967, 2nd edn 1972; *contrib*. Accts. Mag., Jl LSS, SLT. *Address*: The Law School, Stenhouse Building, Univ. of Strathclyde, 173 Cathedral Street, Glasgow C4.

Burns, Prof. James Henderson; Professor of the History of Political Thought, University College London, since 1966, and Head of Department of History since 1970; *b* 1921; *m* 1947; two *s*. MA Edinburgh and Oxford, PhD Aberdeen; FRHistS 1962. Lectr in Polit. Theory, Univ. of Aberdeen, 1947–60; Hd of Dept of Politics, 1952–60; Reader in the History of Political Thought, Univ. Coll. London, 1961–66. Gen. Editor, The Collected Works of Jeremy Bentham, 1961– ; Hon. Sec., Royal Historical Soc., 1965–70; Sec., Bentham Cttee, 1966– . Sub-Ed., Home News Dept, BBC, 1944–45. *Publications*: (with D. Sutherland Graeme) Scottish University, 1944; Scottish Churchmen and the Council of Basle, 1962; (with S. Rose) contrib. to: D. E. Butler, The British General Election of 1951, 1952; Essays on the Scottish Reformation, ed D. McRoberts, 1962; Mill: a collection of critical essays, ed J. B. Schneewind, 1968; ed (with H. L. A. Hart), Jeremy Bentham, An Introduction in the Principles of Morals and Legislation, 1970; *contrib*. Scott. Hist. Rev., Innes Rev., Political Studies, Hist., Trans of RHistS, etc. *Address*: Univ. College London, Gower Street, WC1E 6BT.

Burns, Prof. Tom, BA; Professor of Sociology, University of Edinburgh, since 1964; *b* 1913; *m* 1944; one *s* four *d*. BA Bristol 1933; Mem.: Brit. Sociol. Soc., Amer. Sociol Assoc. Lectr, Univ. of Edinburgh, 1949–51; Sen. Lectr, 1951–59; Reader, 1959–64; Vis. Prof.: Univ. of Brit. Columbia, 1962; Univ. of Washington, 1966; Columbia Univ., 1966; Harvard Univ., 1973–74; Sen. Vis. Schol., Univ. of Cambridge, 1969–70. Mem.: Subcttee on Social Studies, UGC, 1967–70; Social Science Res. Council (Chm. Sociology Cttee, 1968–70); Human Sciences Cttee, DSIR, 1959–64; Sociology Cttee, SSRC, 1965–70. *Publications*: Local Government and Central Control, 1954; (with A. K. Cairncross) Local Development in Scotland, 1955; (with G. M. Stalker) The Management of Innovation, 1961, 3rd edn, 1972; ed, Industrial Man, 1969; (with E. Burns) ed, Sociology of Literature and Drama, 1972; *contrib*. Admin. Sci. Qly, Amer. Jl Sociology, Amer. Sociol. Rev., Brit. Jl Sociology, Human Relat., Europ. Jl Sociology, Sociologie du Travail. *Address*: Dept of Sociology, Univ. of Edinburgh, Adam Ferguson Building, George Square, Edinburgh EH8 9LL.

Burrough, Thomas Hedley Bruce; Special Lecturer, Department of Architecture, University of Bristol, since 1965; *b* 1910; *m* 1941; two *s*. ARIBA 1935, FRIBA 1947, Royal West of England Academician 1950. Mem.: Arts Lectures Cttee, Bristol Univ., 1955; Council Care Churches, 1965– ; Council Places Worship, Gen. Synod of C of E, 1972– ; Exec. Cttee, Soc. Architectural Historians GB, 1969– ; Council, Bristol and Gloucs. Archaeol. Soc., 1955– , Pres., 1970–72. Council for Training Architects in Conservn, 1960– ; Pres., Bristol and Somerset Soc. Architects, 1961–63; Council RIBA, 1963. *Publications*: An Approach to Planning, 1953; (jtly) South German Baroque, 1956; (jtly) Making the Building Fit the Liturgy, 1962; Bristol Buildings, 1971. *Address*: Dept of

Architecture, Univ. of Bristol, Bristol BS8 1TH.

Burroughs, Prof. George Edward Richard, BSc, PhD; Professor of Education, University of Birmingham, since 1965; *b* 1915; *m* 1950. BSc London 1937, PhD Birmingham 1950. ABPsS. Res. Fellow, Birmingham, 1948–50; Lectr, Birmingham, 1950–60; Sen. Lectr, Birmingham, 1960–65. UNESCO Mission to Ceylon and Siam, 1955–56; UNESCO Mission to Pakistan, 1958–59; UNESCO mission to Venezuela, 1963–66. *Publications*: The Vocabulary of Young Children, 1957; Design and Analysis in Educational Research, 1971; *contrib*. Brit. Jl of Educnl Psych. *Address*: School of Education, Univ. of Birmingham, PO Box 363, Birmingham B15 2TT.

Burrow, John Anthony, MA; Fellow and Tutor in English, Jesus College, Oxford, and University Lecturer in English, since 1960; *b* 1932; *m* 1956; three *s*. BA Oxon 1953 (1st cl. English), MA Oxon 1957. Asst Lectr, King's Coll., London, 1955–57; Lectr at Christ Church and BNC, Oxford, 1957–60. *Publications*: A Reading of Sir Gawain and the Green Knight, 1965; Geoffrey Chaucer (Penguin Critical Anthologies), 1969; Ricardian Poetry, 1971; Sir Gawain and the Green Knight (Penguin Poets), 1972; *contrib*. Essays in Criticism, Notes and Queries, Rev. of English Studies. *Address*: Jesus College, Oxford.

Burrow, Dr John Wyon; Reader in History, University of Sussex, since 1969; *b* 1935; *m* 1958; one *s* one *d*. BA Cantab 1957 (Hist.). MA Cantab 1960, PhD Cantab 1961; FRHistS 1971. Research Fellow, Christ's Coll., Cambridge, 1959–62; Fellow, Downing Coll., Cambridge, 1962–65; Lectr in Hist., UEA, 1965–69. *Publications*: Evolution and Society, 1966; *contrib*. Victorian Studies. *Address*: Arts Building, Univ. of Sussex, Falmer, Brighton BN1 9QN.

Burrows, Donald Ivan; Staff Tutor in Music and Senior Lecturer, Faculty of Arts, The Open University, since 1970; *b* 1930; *m* 1954; one *s* one *d*. ARCM 1951, FRCO 1953; Mem., Incorp. Soc. of Musicians, 1960. Univ. of Manchester Extra-Mural Bd, 1960–63; Part-time Tutor in Music, Oxford Univ. Delegacy for Extra-Mural Studies, 1964–70. Examiner: Birmingham Univ. Sch. of Educn, 1974– ; Birmingham Sch. of Music, 1974. *Publications*: Music entries, in, Blond Educational Encyclopaedia, 1970. *Address*: Faculty of Arts, The Open Univ., Milton Keynes MK6 7AA.

Burrows, Dr Paul; Senior Lecturer in Economics, University of York, since 1974 (Lecturer, 1965–74); *b* 1940; *m* 1963; two *d*. BSc(Econ) London 1962, DPhil York 1967. Res. Fellow, Inst. Social. Econ. Res., Univ. of York, 1963–65. *Publications*: (with M. Hauser) The Economics of Unemployment Insurance, 1969; (with T. Hitiris) Macroeconomic Theory: A Mathematical Introduction; *contrib*. App. Econ., Bull. Econ. Res., Jl Business Policy, Oxford Econ. Papers, Scott. Jl Pol Economy. *Address*: Dept of Economics, Univ. of York, Heslington, York YO1 5DD.

Burston, Wyndham Hedley; Professor of Education since 1972, Head of History Department since 1958, University of London Institute of Education; *b* 1915. BA Bristol 1936 (1st cl. Philosophy and Economics), MA(Ed) Bristol 1947. Lectr in Educn, Durham Univ., 1946–48; Lectr in Educn, London Univ. Inst. of Educn, 1948–58; Sen. Lectr, 1958–64, Reader, 1964–72. Sometime Mem., Council, Hist. Assoc., sometime Chm., Teaching Hist. Cttee; Chm., Higher Educn Cttee. *Publications*: Principles of History Teaching, 1963, 2nd edn 1972; James Mill on Philosophy of Education, 1973; ed, Studies in the Nature and Teaching of History, 1967, Italian edn 1971; ed jtly, Handbook for History Teachers, 1962, 2nd edn 1972; ed, James Mill on Education, 1969; *contrib*. Hist., Camb. Jl. *Address*: Univ. of London Institute of Education, Malet Street, WC1E 7HS.

Burt, Roger, BSc(Econ), PhD; Lecturer in Economic History, Department of Economic History, University of Exeter, since 1966; *b* 1942; *m* 1965. BSc(Econ) 1964 (2nd cl. Econ. Hist.). PhD LSE 1970. *Publications*: ed, Cornish Mining, 1969; ed, Industry and Society in the South West, 1970; intro., Cornish Mining, 1972; *contrib*. Econ. Hist. Rev., Business Hist. *Address*: Dept of Economic History, Streatham Court, Univ. of Exeter.

Burton, Ivor Flower; Senior Lecturer, Department of Sociology, Bedford College, University of London, since 1965; *b* 1923; *m* 1944; one *s* two *d*. BA Belfast (1st cl. Hons in Hist.) 1949; PhD London 1960. Asst Lectr in Hist., Bedford Coll., 1950, Lectr, 1953, Sen. Lectr, 1964. JP 1967. *Publications*: The Captain General: the career of John Churchill, 1st Duke of Marlborough 1702–1711, 1968; *contrib*. Bull. of Inst. of Hist. Res., EHR, Encyclopaedia Britannica, Hist. Jl, Parliamentary Affairs. *Address*: Bedford College, Regent's Park, NW1 4NS.

Burton, J. W., BA, PhD, DSc; Reader in International Relations, University College London, since 1963; *b* 1915. BA Sydney 1937 (First Hons), PhD London 1942; DSc London 1970. Tutor in Econs and Psychol., Wesley Coll., Univ. of Sydney, 1936–37; Dir of an independent res. organisation 'Policy Research', 1951–60; Res. Fellow and Rockefeller Grantee, Australian Nat. Univ., 1960–63. *Publications*: The Alternative, 1954; Peace Theory, 1962; International Relations: A General Theory, 1965; (ed and contrib.) Nonalignment, 1966; Systems, States, Diplomacy and Rules, 1968; Conflict and Communication, 1969; World Society, 1972; ed., vol. XVII, No 3, UNESCO International Social Science Journal; contrib. The World in 1984, vol. 2, 1964; The Natural History of Aggression, 1964; Conflict in Society, 1966; *contrib*. Australian Outlook, Disarmament and Arms Control, Conflict Resolution, etc. *Address*: Univ. Coll. London, 4–8 Endsleigh Gardens, WC1H 0EG.

Burton, Joseph Cyril George, MA; Senior Lecturer in Adult Education, Department of Extra-Mural Studies, University of Bristol, since 1966; b 1910; m 1934; one s one d. BA Cambridge 1931 (2nd cl. Moral Science), MA Cambridge 1938. Manchester Coll., Oxford, and St Catherine's Coll., Oxford, 1931–34; Minister of Religion, 1934–47; Graduate Mem., Brit. Psychol Soc. Lectr, Lund Univ., Sweden, Vacation Courses, 1951– ; Lectr in Adult Educn, Univ. of Bristol, 1947–66. Sec., Bristol Anglo-Scandinavian Soc., 1956–60; Mem., Council, Folk House, Bristol, 1956– . *Publications*: Life and Conditions in Britain, 1956, 8th edn 1968; Contemporary Britain, 1971, 2nd edn 1974; *contrib.* Hibbert Jl. *Address*: Dept of Extra-Mural Studies, Univ. of Bristol, Bristol BS8 1TH.

Burton, Michael; Tutor to BA in Architecture Degree, Department of Architecture, University of Bristol, since 1973; b 1928. BArch Liverpool 1955; Hoffman Wood Scholar 1949, British Council Scholar 1951; ARIBA 1956. Univ. of Bristol: Lectr, 1964; Tutor to BArch Degree, 1965; Sen. Lectr, 1969. Mem.: Wilts CC, 1970 (Chm., Further Educn sub-Cttee, 1973; Chm., Town Planning sub-Cttee, 1974); Bristol Avon River Authority, 1971; Governor: Chippenham Boys' Sch., 1970; Chippenham Sch., 1971; Vice-Chm., Chippenham Tech. Coll., 1972. *Address*: Dept of Architecture, Univ. of Bristol, Bristol BS1 5RA.

Burton, Reginald William Boteler; Fellow and Tutor in Classics, Oriel College, Oxford, since 1932; b 1908; m 1937; three d. BA Oxon 1931, MA Oxon 1933. Lectr in Classics, Oriel Coll., Oxford, 1931. *Publication*: Pindar's Pythian Odes, 1962. *Address*: Oriel College, Oxford.

Burton-Page, John Garrard, MA, FSA; Reader in the Art and Archaeology of South Asia, at the School of Oriental and African Studies, University of London, since 1971; b 1921; m 1945; three s. BA Oxon 1950, MA Oxon 1953; FSA 1965, FRAS (Dir, 1968–71, Vice-Pres., 1971–), 1948. Lectr in Nepali, SOAS, 1950, in Nepali and Hindi, 1952, in Hindi, 1958; Reader in Hindi, 1967–71; Vis. Prof., Deccan Coll., Univ. of Poona, 1958–59; Vis. Prof., Univ. of Toronto, 1966; Mem., Cttee of Management, Inst. of Archaeology, 1969– . War service with 1st KG V's O. Gurkha Rifles; Staff Capt. 115 Brigade, 1943–44; seconded to Kalibahadur Regt, Nepalese Army, 1945; Hon. Capt., RARO, 1947– . Ed. Sec., Encyclopaedia of Islam, 1960–63; Mem., Governing Council, Brit. Inst. of Persian Studies, 1968–72; Pres., Islamic Art Circle, 1972– . *Publications*: Mediaeval India: a cultural history, from the coming of the Muslims to the eighteenth century, 1972; (with Joanna M. Strub) History of Indian Civilization from Archaeological Sources, 1974; ed and revised T. W. Clark: Introduction to Nepali, 2nd edn 1972; some 70 articles in Encyclopaedia of Islam; *contrib.* Bull. SOAS, Indian Linguistics, JRAS. *Address*: School of Oriental and African Studies, Univ. of London, Malet Street, WC1E 7HP.

Bury, John Patrick Tuer, MA; Fellow of Corpus Christi College, Cambridge, since 1933 , University Lecturer in History, Cambridge, since 1937, Warden of Leckhampton, Corpus Christi College, since 1969; b 1908; m 1944; one s one d. BA Cambridge 1930 (1st cl. History), MA 1933; FRHistS, Membre Associé de l'Académie du Second Empire (France) 1970. Dean, Corpus Christi Coll., 1935–39; Libr., 1937–55, Pres., 1960–65; Steward of Estates, 1966–69. Principal, Ministry of Supply, 1939–44; Foreign Office Res. Dept, 1944–45; Mem., Council, Royal Hist. Soc., 1967–69; Governor, Royal Grammar Sch., Colchester, 1971– . Ed., (Cambridge) Hist. Jl, 1953–60. *Publications*: Gambetta and the National Defence, 1936; France 1814–1940, 1949, 4th edn 1969; The College of Corpus Christi and the Blessed Virgin Mary – A History from 1822 to 1952, 1952; ed (with J. C. Barry), An Englishman in Paris, 1953; ed (with Rohan Butler), Documents on British Foreign Policy 1919–1939, first series, vols. X–XV, 1960–67; ed, vol. X New Cambridge Modern History, 1960; Napoleon III and the Second Empire, 1964; ed, Romilly: Cambridge Diary 1832–42, 1967; Gambetta and the Making of the Third Republic, 1973; *contrib.* EHR, (Cambridge) Hist. Jl, French Hist. Studies, Revue Historique. *Address*: Corpus Christi College, Cambridge.

Busst, Dr Alan James Lawrence; Reader in French, University College of North Wales, Bangor, since 1973; b 1935; m 1958; two s two d. BA Reading 1957 (1st cl. French), PhD Reading 1961. Asst Lectr, Univ. Coll. of Wales, Bangor, 1961–63, Lectr, 1963–69, Sen. Lectr 1969–72. *Publications*: The Image of the Androgyne in the Nineteenth Century: Romantic Mythologies, 1967; ed, Ballanche: La Vision d'Hébal, 1969; *contrib.* AJFS, Fr. Studies, ML, MLR, RLMC, Romantisme, TLS. *Address*: Dept of French, Univ. College of North Wales, Bangor LL57 2DG.

Butcher, Prof. Harold John, BA, PhD; Professor of Educational Psychology, University of Sussex, since 1970; b 1920; m 1948; two s one d. BA Cantab 1941, DipEd Manchester 1956, PhD Manchester 1959; FBPsS. Lectr in Educn, Manchester 1956–63; Lectr in Psychol., Edinburgh, 1963–67; Prof., Higher Educn, Manchester, 1967–70., Council, Soc. Res. Higher Educn, 1968–72; Mem., Cttee, BPsS Educn Sect., 1968–72; Ed., Res. in Educn. *Publications*: Human Intelligence, 1968; Educational Research in Britain, 1968; (with R. B. Cattell) Prediction of Achievement and Creativity, 1968; (with J. Freeman, T. Christie) Creativity, 1968; (with H. B. Pont) Educational Research in Britain 2, 1970; (with D. Lomax) Readings in Human Intelligence, 1972; (with E. Rudd) Contemporary Problems in Higher Education, 1972; *contrib.* Brit. Jl Educnl Psychol., Brit. Jl Psychol., Brit. Jl Soc. Clinic. Psychol., Res. in Educn. *Address*: Univ. of Sussex, Arts Building, Falmer, Brighton BN1 9RH.

Butler of Saffron Walden, The Rt. Hon. Lord; Richard Austen Butler, KG, PC, CH, MA; Master of Trinity College, Cambridge; b 1902; m 1926; 1959; three s one d. Double 1st cl. Cambridge; Mod. Lang. Tripos French Section 1924, Historical Tripos

Part II 1925, First Div. 1st cl. Hon. LLD, Cambridge 1952, Nottingham 1953, Bristol 1954, Sheffield 1955, St Andrews 1956, Glasgow 1959, Reading 1959; Hon. DCL Oxon 1952, Durham 1968, Calgary 1968, Liverpool 1968, Witwatersrand 1969; Hon. LittD Leeds 1972. Pres., Cambridge Union Soc., 1924; Fellow, Corpus Christi Coll., Cambridge, 1925–29. MP (C) Saffron Walden, 1929–65; Under-Secretary of State, India Office, 1932–37; Parly Sec., Min. of Labour, 1937–38; Under-Sec. of State for Foreign Affairs, 1938–41; Minister of Educn, 1941–45; Minister of Labour, June–July 1945; Chancellor of the Exchequer, 1951–55; Lord Privy Seal, 1955–59; Leader of the House of Commons, 1955–61; Home Secretary, 1957–62; First Sec. of State, 1962–63; Minister in Charge of Central African Office, 1962–63; Secretary of State for Foreign Affairs, 1963–64. Rector of Glasgow Univ., 1956–59; High Steward, Cambridge Univ., 1958–66; High Steward, City of Cambridge, 1963– ; Chancellor of Sheffield Univ., 1960– ; Chancellor of Univ. of Essex, 1962– . Azad Meml Lecture, Delhi, 1970. Chm, Conservative Party Org., 1959–61; Chm., Conservative Res. Dept, 1945–64; Chm., Conservative Adv. Cttee on Policy, 1950–64; Chm., Coun. of Nat. Union of Conservative Assocs, 1945–56, Pres., 1956– ; Pres., Nat. Assoc. of Mental Health, 1946– ; Pres., Royal Soc. of Literature, 1951– . Hon. Fellow, Pembroke Coll., Cambridge, 1952; Hon. Fellow, Corpus Christi Coll., Cambridge, 1952; Hon. Fellow, St Anthony's Coll., Oxford, 1957. Freedom of Saffron Walden, 1954. *Publication*: The Art of the Possible, 1971. *Address*: The Master's Lodge, Trinity College, Cambridge.

Butler, Christopher; Official Student and Tutor in English Literature, Christ Church, and Lecturer in English Literature, University of Oxford, since 1970; *b* 1940; *m* 1966; two *d*. MA Oxon. Sen. Hulme Res. Scholar, Brasenose Coll., 1962–64; Res. Lectr, Christ Church,1964–70. Jun. Censor, Christ Church, 1972– . *Publications*: Number Symbolism, 1969; (with Alastair Fowler) Topics in Criticism, 1971. *Address*: Christ Church. Oxford.

Butler, David Edgeworth; Fellow of Nuffield College, Oxford, since 1951; *b* 1924; *m* 1962; three *s*. BA Oxon 1947, MA 1949, DPhil 1951. Vis. Appointments, Univ. of Illinois, 1960; Univ. of Michigan, 1965; Australian Nat. Univ., 1967, 1972. Personal Asst to HM Ambassador, Washington, 1955–56. *Publications*: The Electoral System in Britain, 1953, 2nd edn 1963; The British General Election of 1951, 1952, of 1955, 1955, (with R. Rose) of 1959, 1960, (with A. S. King) of 1964, 1965, (with A. S. King) of 1966, 1966, (with Pinto-Duschinsky) of 1970, 1971; The Study of Political Behaviour, 1958; ed, Elections Abroad, 1959; (with J. Freeman) British Political Facts, 1960, 4th edn 1974; (with D. Stokes) Political Change in Britain, 1969; The Canberra Model, 1973. *Address*: Nuffield College, Oxford.

Butler, John Richard, MA; Senior Research Fellow and Lecturer in Social Administration, University of Kent, since 1972 (Senior

Research Associate, 1969–72); *b* 1942; *m* 1963; one *s*. BA Nottingham 1963, MA Nottingham 1965; Res. Fellow, Manchester Univ., 1965–69. Mem., SE Metropolitan Mental Health Review Tribunal, 1973– . Governor, Kent Coll., Canterbury, 1971– . *Publications*: Who goes Home, 1970; Family Doctors and Public Policy, 1973; *contrib.* Brit. Jl of Sociol., Polit. Qly, Sch. Sci. Rev., Social and Econ. Admin, Sociol Rev. *Address*: Health Services Research Unit, Univ. of Kent, Canterbury, Kent CT2 7NZ.

Butler, Lawrence Arnold Stanley, PhD, FSA; Lecturer in Medieval Archaeology, University of Leeds, since 1965; *b* 1934; *m* 1958; two *d*. BA Cantab 1955, MA Cantab 1961, DipEd Oxon 1958, PhD Nottingham 1962; FSA. Investigating staff, Royal Commn on Ancient Monuments (Wales), 1959–65; Mem.: Council, Soc. for Medieval Archaeol., 1969–72; Council and Editor, Soc. for Post-Medieval Archaeol., 1967–72; Chm., Council for Brit. Archaeol. (Yorks Gp), 1969–72. *Publications*: chapters, in, Leeds and its Regions, 1967; Deserted Medieval Villages, 1971; Glamorgan County History, 1971; *contrib.* Archaeological Jl, Brit. Archaeological Assoc., Archaeologia Cambrensis, Hist. Soc. Church in Wales Jl. *Address*: Dept of Archaeology, The Univ., Leeds LS2 9JT.

Butler, Dr Lionel Harry; Principal, Royal Holloway College, University of London, since 1973; *b* 1923; *m* 1949; one *d*. BA Oxon 1945 (1st cl. History), MA Oxon 1949, DPhil Oxon 1951; Libr., Venerable Order of St John, Clerkenwell, London. Fellow of All Souls Coll., Oxford, 1946–56; Prof. of Mediaeval History, St Andrews, 1955–73; Vice-Principal, Univ. of St Andrews, 1971–73; Leverhulme Lectr, Royal Univ. of Malta, 1962; Vis. Prof., Univ. of Pennsylvania, 1964; Mem. Cttee of Management, London Univ. Centre of Internat. and Area Studies, 1973. Historical Dir, Council of Europe Exhibition on The Order of St John, Malta, 1970. Governor, Strode's Sch., Egham, 1973. *Publications*: trans. (with R. J. Adam) Robert Fawtier: Les Capétiens et la France, 1960; The Order of St John at Rhodes, 1306–1523 (forthcoming); *contrib.* Jl Eccles. Hist., Proc. Brit. Acad. *Address*: Royal Holloway Coll., Egham, Surrey TW20 0EX.

Butler, Rohan D'Olier, CMG; Fellow of All Souls, Oxford, since 1938, a Senior Research Fellow, since 1956; Historical Adviser to the Secretary of State for Foreign and Commonwealth Affairs, since 1968; *b* 1917; *m* 1956. BA Oxford 1938 (1st cl. Hons History), MA Oxford 1942; FRHistS. Leverhulme Res. Fellow, 1955–57; Sub-Warden, All Souls, 1961–63. On management of Inst. of Historical Res., Univ. of London, 1967– ; Mem. Court, Univ. of Essex, 1971– ; Governor of Felsted Sch., 1959– . *Publications*: The Roots of National Socialism, 1941 (Spanish trans. 1943); (ed) Documents on British Foreign Policy 1919–1939, 1st series, vols i–ix, 2nd series, vol. ix, 1947– . *Address*: All Souls College, Oxford.

Butler, Ronald Joseph; Professor of Philosophy, Humanities Faculty, University of

Kent at Canterbury, since 1971; *b* 1929. BA NZ 1951, MA NZ 1954. Fellow, Knox Coll., Dunedin, NZ, 1954–55; Teaching Fellow, Univ. of Otago, NZ, 1954–55; Part-time Instructor, Cornell Univ., 1955–56; Instructor, Princeton Univ., 1956–59; Asst Prof., Oberlin Coll., Ohio, 1959–60; Asst Prof., 1960–64, Assoc. Prof., Univ. of Toronto, 1964–67; Vis. Prof., 1967–68. Prof., 1968–71, Univ. of Waterloo. *Publications*: ed, Analytical Philosophy, first series 1962, 2nd edn 1966, second series 1965; *contrib*. Archiv. für Geschichte der Philosophie, Australasian Jl of Philosophy, Mind, Philosoph. Rev., Jl Symbolic Logic, Proc. Aristotelian Soc. *Address*: Eliot College, The Univ., Canterbury, Kent.

Butrym, Zofia Teresa, AIMSW; Senior Lecturer in Social Work, The London School of Economics, since 1958; *b* 1927. Cert. in Social Science and Administration, LSE, 1949; AIMSW 1950, Mem., Brit. Assoc. of Social Workers. Lectr. in Social Casework, LSE, 1958–70. Chm., Educn Cttee, Inst. of Medical Social Workers, 1961–69; Council Member: IMSW, 1961–69; Brit. Assoc. of Social Workers, 1970–71; Jt Univ. Council in Public and Social Admin. Social Work Educn Cttee, 1970– . *Publications*: Social Work in Medical Care, 1967; Medical Social Work in Action, 1968; *contrib*. Medical Social Work, Service Social dans le Monde. *Address*: Social Work Courses, The London School of Economics, Houghton Street, WC2A 2AE.

Butt, A. J.; *see* Butt Colson, A. J.

Butt, Dr John, BA, PhD; Senior Lecturer in Economic History, University of Strathclyde, since 1968; *b* 1929; *m* 1959; three *d*. BA London 1950 (1st cl. History), PhD Glasgow 1964; Mem., Council, Econ. History Soc. Lectr, Royal Coll. of Science and Technology, 1959–64. Editor, Indust. Archaeol., 1969; Sec., Scott. Soc. for Indust. Archaeol., 1968–72. *Publications*: The Industrial Archaeology of Scotland, 1967; Industrial History: Scotland, 1968; ed, The Industries of Scotland, their rise and progress, 1969; ed, Robert Owen, Prince of Cotton Spinners, 1971; ed, Life of Robert Owen by himself, 1971; *contrib*. Ayrshire Archaeol. Soc. Coll., Econ. Hist. Rev., Expl. Entreps. Hist., IA, Econ. Studies, Scott. Hist. Rev., Scott. Jl Pol Econ., Trans Hist. *Address*: McCance Building, Univ. of Strathclyde, Glasgow C1.

Butt Colson, Dr Audrey Joan; Lecturer in Ethnology, Department of Ethnology and Prehistory, University of Oxford, since 1955; *b* 1926; *m* 1968. BA London Ext. 1947 (2nd cl. History), Dip. in Anthropology Oxon 1949 (Distinction), BLitt Oxon 1950, DPhil Oxon 1954; FRGS, FRAI, Assoc. Soc. Anthropol. Fellow, St Hugh's Coll., Oxford, 1966– ; Vis. Schol., Inst. Venezolan de Investigaciones Cientificas (IVIC), Caracas, 1968. Res. Off., London Communications HQ, Foreign Off., 1948; Mem.: Council, RAI, 1962–65; Council, RGS 1966–69. *Publications*: (as A. J. Butt): The Nilotes of the Sudan and Uganda, 1952; (with P. T. W. Baxter) The Azande and Related Peoples, 1953; (with S. Wavell, ed., and N. Epton) Trances, 1966;

(as A. J. Butt Colson): contrib., Human Ecology in the Tropics, ed J. P. Garlick, 1970; The Ongoing Evolution of Latin American Populations, ed. F. Salzano, 1971; *contrib*. Antropológica, Folk, Jl Royal Anthrop. Inst., L'Homme, Man, Nieuwe West-Indische Gids, Proc. Int. Cong. Amer., Rev. Museu Paulista, Timehri, JRACS Brit. Guiana. *Address*: St Hugh's College, Oxford.

Butter, Prof. Peter Herbert, MA; Regius Professor of English Language and Literature, University of Glasgow, since 1965; *b* 1921; *m* 1958; one *s* two *d*. MA Oxon 1948 (1st cl. English). Asst, Edinburgh Univ., 1948–51, Lectr, 1951–58; Prof., Queen's Univ., Belfast, 1958–65. Sec., Treas., Internat. Assoc. of Univ. Prof. of English, 1962–71; Mem., Council, Trinity Coll., Glenalmond 1965– . *Publications*: Shelley's Idols of the Cave, 1954; Francis Thompson, 1961; Edwin Muir, 1962; Edwin Muir: Man and Poet, 1966; ed, Shelley: Alastor, Prometheus Unbound, Adonais, 1970; ed, Selected Letters of Edwin Muir, 1974; *contrib*. MLR, Rev. of English Lit., Rev. of English Studies. *Address*: Dept of English, Univ. of Glasgow, Glasgow G12 8QQ.

Butterfield, Peter, MA; College Lecturer, Department of History, University College Dublin (National University of Ireland), since 1968; *b* 1931; *m* 1959; two *s* three *d*. BA Cantab 1953, MA Cantab 1957. Admin Asst, Univ. of Cambridge, 1956–59; Asst Registrar, UC of Rhodesia and Nyasaland, 1960–63; Admin. Asst, Univ. of Birmingham, 1964; Asst Lectr in History, UC Dublin, 1964–68. *Address*: Dept of History, Univ. College Dublin, Belfield, Dublin 4, Ireland.

Butterfield, William John Hughes, OBE, DM, FRCP; Vice-Chancellor, University of Nottingham, since 1971; *b* 1920; *m* 1946; 1950; three *s* one *d*. FRSA, Member, Scientific Staff, Medical Res. Council, 1946–58; Prof. of Experimental Medicine, Guy's Hosp., 1958–63; Prof. of Medicine, Guy's Hosp. Medical Sch., and Additional Physician, Guy's Hosp., 1963–71. Examiner in Medicine, Oxford Univ., 1960–66, Cambridge Univ., 1967– ; Pfizer Vis. Prof., NZ and Australia, 1965; Vis. Prof., Yale, 1966; Olivier-Sharpey Lectr, 1967; Rock Carling Fellow, 1968; Banting Lectr, 1970; Oslin Lectr, 1971; Joslin Clinic Vis. Physician, 1973. Chairman: Woolwich/Erith New Town Medical Liaison Cttee, 1965–70; SE Met. Reg. Hosp. Board's Clinical Res. Cttee; Scientific Advisory Panel, Army Personnel Res. Cttee; Council for the Educn and Training of Health Visitors, 1971– ; Member: UGC Medical Sub-Cttee, 1966–71; Council, Brit. Diabetic Assoc., 1963–74 (Chm., 1967–74); MRC Cttee on Gen. Epidemiology, 1965–73; MRC Clinical Res. Grants Bd, 1969–71; Anglo-Soviet Consultative Cttee; Minister of Health's Long Term Study Gp; DHSS Cttee on Medical Aspects of Food Policy, 1964– ; Cambridge Univ. Clinical Sch. Planning Cttee, 1969– ; Med. Cttee British Council, 1970– ; Blackfriars Settlement, 1970– ; Trustees Cttee, Globe Playhouse, 1970–73; Exec. Cttee, Inter-Univ. Council, 1972– ; Trent RHA, 1973– ;

DHSS Chief Scientist Panel, 1973– ; Consultant, WHO Expert Cttee on Diabetes, 1964– ; Vice-Pres., European Assoc. for the Study of Diabetes, 1968–71. Mem., Editorial Bd, Diabetalogia, 1964–69; Mem., Editorial Bd, Jl Chronic Diseases, 1968– . Hon. Fellow, NY Acad. Science, 1962; Patron, Richmond Soc., 1968–71. *Publications*: (jtly) On Burns, 1953; Tolbutamide after 10 years, 1967; Priorities in Medicine, 1968; Health Behaviour in an Urban Community, 1971; *contrib*. various contribs to medical jls. *Address*: Univ. of Nottingham, Univ. Park, Nottingham NG7 2RD.

Butterworth, John; Lecturer in Industrial Economics, Department of Industrial Economics, University of Birmingham, since 1966; *b* 1937; *m* 1962; one *s* one *d*. BSocSci Birmingham 1963 (Russian Studies). Asst Lectr, Dept of Econs, Birmingham, 1964–65. *Address*: Dept of Industrial Economics and Business Studies, Univ. of Birmingham, PO Box 363, Birmingham B15 2TT.

Butterworth, John Blackstock, MA, DL, JP; Vice-Chancellor, University of Warwick, since 1963; *b* 1918; *m* 1948; one *s* two *d*. MA Oxford 1946. Fellow, New Coll., Oxford, 1946–63, Dean, 1952–56, Bursar and Fellow, 1956–63, Sub-Warden, 1957–58; Junior Proctor, 1950–51; Faculty Fellow of Nuffield Coll., 1953–58; Member of Hebdomadal Council, Oxford Univ., 1953–63. Managing Trustee, Nuffield Foundn, 1964– . Chm., Inter-Univ. Council for Higher Educn Overseas, 1968– . Called to Bar, Lincoln's Inn, 1947. DL Warwickshire, 1967; JP City of Oxford, 1962, Coventry, 1963– . Mem., Royal Commn on the Working of the Tribunals of Inquiry (Act), 1921, 1966; Mem., Intergovernmental Cttee on Law of Contempt in relation to Tribunals of Inquiry, 1968; Chm., Inquiry into Work and Pay of Probation Officers and Social Workers, 1971. Governor, Royal Shakespeare Theatre, 1964– ; Trustee, Shakespeare Birthplace Trust, 1966. *Address*: The Univ. of Warwick, Coventry CV4 7AL.

Button, Dr Leslie; Senior Lecturer in Education, University College of Swansea, since 1970; *b* 1916; *m* 1940; two *s* one *d*. BSc(Econ) London 1939, PhD London 1953. Lectr, Univ. Coll., Swansea, 1961–70. *Publications*: Youth Service, 1955; Leadership Training, 1965; Friendship Patterns of Older Adolescents, 1965; Some Experiments in Informal Group Work, 1967; Training for Youth Work in Colleges of Education, 1969; The Harbour Gate Group, 1970; The Seniors, 1970; Discovery and Experience, 1971; Developmental Group Work, 1974. *Address*: Dept of Education, Univ. College of Swansea, Hendrefoilan, Sketty, Swansea.

Buttress, Donald R., MA, DipArch, ARIBA, FSA; Lecturer in Architecture, University of Manchester, since 1964; *b* 1932; *m* 1956; two *s* two *d*. DipArch Manchester 1956, MA Manchester 1965; ARIBA 1958, FSA 1971. Vis. Prof., Univ. of Florida, 1967–68. Mem.: Manchester Corp. Hist. Bldgs Cttee, 1970–72; Chester Dioc. Adv. Cttee Care of Chs, 1970– . *Publications*: Manchester Buildings, 1967; contrib. Banister Fletcher: History of

Architecture, 18th edn 1972; National Trust Guide Book: Gawthorpe, 1972: *contrib*. Church in Wales, Historical Soc. Jl, Victorian Soc. Trans. *Address*: Dept of Architecture, Univ. of Manchester, Manchester M13 9PL.

Buxton, Edward John Mawby; Reader in English Literature, Oxford, since 1972; Fellow of New College, Oxford, since 1949; *b* 1912; *m* 1939. MA Oxon 1938 (Lit. Hum.); FSA. Lectr, New Coll., Oxford, 1946; Univ. Lectr, 1967–72; Vis. Fellow, Centre for Adv. Studies, Wesleyan Univ., Middletown, Conn, 1966; Warton Lectr, Brit. Acad., 1970; Chm., Council, Malone Soc., Mem. Cttee, Wiltshire Record Soc., 1969– . *Publications*: ed, Poems of Michael Drayton, 1953; Sir Philip Sidney and The English Renaissance, 1954, 2nd edn 1964; ed, Poems of Charles Cotton, 1958; Elizabethan Taste, 1963; A Tradition of Poetry, 1967; Byron and Shelley, 1968; Gen. Editor, Oxford Paperback English Texts since inception, 1968– ; Gen. Editor, Oxford History of English Literature, 1973– ; *contrib*. Apollo, Bodleian Libr. Record, English Literary Renaissance, MLR, Rev. of English Studies, TLS, The Library, etc. *Address*: New College, Oxford.

Buxton, Neil Keith; Senior Lecturer in Economic History, Department of Economics, Heriot-Watt University, since 1972, Lecturer, 1969–72); *b* 1940; *m* 1962; two *s* one *d*. MA (Economics) Aberdeen 1962. Asst Lectr, Aberdeen Univ., 1962–64; Lectr, Univ. of Hull, 1964–69; Vis. Lectr in Econ. History, Sydney Univ., 1973. *Publications*: (with T. L. Johnston and D. Mair) Structure and Growth of the Scottish Economy, 1971; *contrib*. Econ. Hist. Rev., Jl Royal Statistical Soc., Scott. Jl Polit. Econ., Business Hist. *Address*: Dept of Economics, Heriot-Watt Univ., Edinburgh EH1 1HX.

Buxton, Richard Joseph, BCL, MA; Lecturer in Law (part-time), Oxford University; *b* 1938. BA Oxon 1961 (1st cl. Jurisprudence), BCL Oxon 1962 (1st cl.), Vinerian Scholar 1962; Barrister-at-Law. Lectr, Christ Church, Oxford, 1962–63; Fellow of Exeter Coll., Oxford, 1964–73, Sub-Rector, 1966–71. Mem., Oxford City Council, 1966–69. *Publications*: Local Government, 1970, 2nd edn 1973; *contrib*. Law Qly Rev., Ann. Surv. of Commonwealth Law, Modern Law Rev., Criminal Law Rev., Jl of Planning and Environmental Law, Amer. Jl of Comp. Law. *Address*: Gray's Inn Chambers, WC1R 5JA.

Byard, Herbert; Lecturer in Music, University of Bristol, since 1948; *b* 1912; *m* 1932. MA Bristol 1952. Chief Examiner in Music, Bristol Sch. Exam. Bd, 1948–53; SUJB, 1953–56; Moderator in Music, Univ. of London Univ. Entrance and Sch. Exam. Council, 1962–73; Schools Council Music A Level Sub-Cttee, 1965–73. *Publications*: The Bristol Madrigal Society, 1968; *contrib*. Music and Letters, Musical Qly, Musical Times, Organ, Musical Opinion. *Address*: Dept of Music, Univ. of Bristol, Royal Fort House, Bristol BS8 1UJ.

Byers Brown, Dorothy Betty; Lecturer in Speech Pathology and Therapy, Department

104

of Audiology and Education of the Deaf, Faculty of Education, University of Manchester, since 1968; *b* 1927; *m* 1964 (marr. diss. 1970). LCST 1947, MCST 1958. Clinical Supervisor, Dept of Communicative Disorders, Univ. of Wisconsin, USA, 1963–68. Dir, Speech Therapy Dept, Central School of Speech and Drama, London, 1960–63; Mem., Council, Coll. of Speech Therapists, 1968–71. Editor, Brit. Jl Discord. Communic. *Publications*: Speak for yourself, 1971; *contrib*. Applications of Linguistics: Selected Papers, 1971; Handicapped Children: their potential and fulfilment, 1971. *Address*: Dept of Audiology and Deaf Education, Manchester Univ., Manchester M13 9PL.

Byres, Terence James; Lecturer in Economics, Department of Economic and Political Studies, School of Oriental and African Studies, University of London, since 1964; *b* 1936; *m* 1960; one *s* one *d*. MA Aberdeen 1958 (1st cl. Economic Science), BLitt Glasgow 1962. Res. Fellow in Economics, Sch. of Oriental and African Studies, Univ. of London, 1962–64. *Publications*: ed, Foreign Resources and Economic Development, 1972. *Address*: Dept of Economic and Political Studies, School of Oriental and African Studies, Univ. of London, Malet Street, WC1E 7HP.

Byrn, Richard Francis MacDermot; Lecturer in German, University of Leeds, since 1964; *b* 1940; *m* 1968; two *s*. BA(Mod) TCD 1963 (Modern Languages), MA TCD 1967. Mem., Ripon Dioc. Ecumen. Commn, 1969– . *Address*: Dept of German, The Univ., Leeds LS2 9JT.

Byrne, Andrew William Arthur, DMus, FRAM; Lecturer in Music, University of Reading, since 1965; *b* 1925; *m* 1955; three *d*. BMus London 1952, DMus London 1959, LRAM 1950, ARAM 1958, FRAM 1962; Mem.: Inc. Soc. Musicians, Composers Guild. Prof. of Composition and Harmony, RAM, 1954–66; Examiner Theoretical and Practical Exams, Ass. Bd Royal Schs Music, 1960– ; Mem., Music Panel, Southern Univs Jt Bd for Sch. Examinations, 1966–71; Mem., Catholic Liturgical Cttee, 1964–66; Mem., Council for Nat. Acad. Awards, 1967–70. *Publications*: Two Pieces for Clarinet and Piano, 1959; Suite for Clarinet and Piano, 1961; Four Pieces for Oboe and Piano, 1964; 'Introduction, Blues and Finale' for 3 equal-pitch instruments, 1967; Three Bagatelles for Flute and Piano, 1968. *Address*: Dept of Music, Univ. of Reading, 35 Upper Redlands Road, Reading.

Byrne, Francis John, MA; Professor of Early (including Medieval) Irish History, University College Dublin, since 1964; *b* 1934. BA NUI 1956 (1st cl. Early Irish History, Latin and Old Irish), MA NUI 1959 (1st cl.). Lectr in Celtic Philology, Uppsala 1959–60; Asst in Early Irish History, UCD, 1962–64. Mem.: Irish Mss Commn, 1964– ; Chm., Depts of History, UCD, 1970–73; Asst Sec., Irish Cttee Hist. Sci., 1971; jt ed., Royal Irish Acad.: New History of Ireland, 1969– . *Publications*: Irish Kings and High Kings, 1973; ed (with F. X. Martin), The Scholar Revolutionary: Eoin MacNeill 1867–

1945, 1973; *contrib*. Ériu, Irish Eccles. Rec., Irish Hist. Studies, Proc. Royal Irish Acad., Studia Hibern. *Address*: Dept of History, Univ. College, Belfield, Dublin 4.

Byrne Hill, Graham, MA; Senior Lecturer in Education, Goldsmiths' College, University of London, since 1971; *b* 1936; *m* 1966; one *s* one *d*. BA Oxon 1960 (History), MA Oxon 1964, DipEd Oxon 1964, AcDip London 1968. Lectr, Goldsmiths' Coll., 1969–71. *Publications*: *contrib*. Occ. Psy. *Address*: Education Dept, Goldsmiths' College, Univ. of London, SE14 6NW.

Byth, Dr William; Lecturer in Psychology, Queen's University of Belfast, since 1971; *b* 1940; *m* 1963; two *d*. MA Hons Aberdeen 1962 (1st cl. Psychol.), PhD Aberdeen 1969; ABPsS (Hon. Sec., NI Br., 1972–); APsSI (Mem. Council, 1973–74); For. Affiliate, Amer. Psychol. Assoc. University of Aberdeen: Asst Lectr, 1965; Lectr, 1966. *Publications*: *contrib*. Brit. Jl Psychol., Psychonomic Sci., Jl Cross-Cultural Psychol. *Address*: Dept of Psychology, The Queen's Univ. of Belfast, Belfast BT7 1NN.

Bythell, Dr Duncan; Lecturer in Economic History, University of Durham, since 1965; *b* 1940. BA Oxon 1962, MA Oxon 1966, DPhil Oxon 1968; FRHistS. *Publications*: The Handloom Weavers, 1969; *contrib*. Econ. Hist. Rev. *Address*: Dept of Economic History, The Univ., Durham DH1 3HP.

Bywater, Rev. Vincent; Tutor in Geography, Campion Hall, Oxford, 1963, Departmental Lecturer, School of Geography, University of Oxford, since 1965; *b* 1914. BA Oxon 1940 (1st cl. Geography), MA Oxon 1945; FRGS (Life Fellow) 1946. Coll. Libr., Campion Hall, Oxford, 1971– . *Address*: Campion Hall, Oxford OX1 1QS.

C

Cachia, Dr Pierre Jacques Elie, BA, PhD; Reader in Arabic, Department of Arabic and Islamic Studies, University of Edinburgh, since 1969; *b* 1921; *m* 1953; one *s* two *d*. BA American Univ. at Cairo 1942 (with distinction), PhD Edinburgh 1951. Lectr, American Univ. at Cairo, 1946–48; Asst Lectr, Edinburgh Univ., 1949–50, Lectr, 1950–64, Sen. Lectr, 1964–69; Vis. Prof., Columbia Univ., 1969–70. Jt Editor, Jl Arabic Lit., 1970– . *Publications*: Ṭāhā Husayn: his Place in the Egyptian Literary Renaissance, 1956; ed, Kitāb al-Burhān by Eutychius of Alexandria, 1960–61; sections on literature in W. M. Watt's History of Islamic Spain, 1965, Spanish edn 1970; The Monitor: a dictionary of Arabic Grammatical Terms, 1973; *contrib*. Ethnomusicology, Jl Amer. Oriental Soc., Jl Arabic Lit., Internat. Jl ME Studies, Jl Maltese Studies, Jl Semitic Studies, Univ. of Toronto Qly. *Address*: Dept of Arabic and Islamic Studies, Univ. of Edinburgh, Edinburgh EH8 9YL.

Cadoux, Dr Theodore John, MA, DPhil; Senior Lecturer and Head of Department of

Ancient History, University of Edinburgh, since 1959; *b* 1916; *m* 1950. BA Oxon 1939 (Lit. Hum.), MA Oxon 1946, DPhil Oxon 1951; Mem.: Classical Assoc., Classical Assoc., of Scotland, Soc. for Prom. Hellenic Studies, Soc. for Prom. Roman Studies. Asst Lectr, 1947, then Lectr in Greek, Univ. Coll., Cardiff, 1947–52; Lectr and Head of Dept of Ancient History, Univ. of Edinburgh, 1952–59. Sec. Gen. Council of Univ. of Edinburgh, 1962–65. *Publications*: trans. H. Volkmann: Cleopatra, 1958; articles in Oxford Classical Dictionary, 2nd edn 1970; *contrib*. Jl Hellenic Studies, Jl Roman Studies. *Address*: Dept of Ancient History, David Hume Tower, Edinburgh 8.

Cain, Maureen Elizabeth; Lecturer, Department of Sociology, Brunel University, since 1969; *b* 1938; *one s*. BA London 1959 (Hons Sociology), PhD 1969; Mem., Brit. Sociol Assoc. Res. Asst, LSE, 1960–61; Res. Off., Manchester, 1964–65; Res. Fellow, Brunel, 1968–69. *Publications*: Society and the Policeman's Role, 1973; *contrib*. Brit. Jl Criminol., Brit. Jl Sociol., Anglo-Amer. Law Rev. *Address*: Dept of Sociology, Brunel Univ., Kingston Lane, Uxbridge, Mddx UB8 3TH.

Caird, Rev. George Bradford, MA, DPhil, DD, FBA; Principal of Mansfield College, Oxford, since 1970, Reader in Biblical Studies, Oxford University, since 1969; *b* 1917; *m* 1945; three *s* one *d*. MA Cantab; DPhil, DD Oxon; Hon. DD St Stephen's Coll. Edmonton 1959, Hon. DD Diocesan Coll. Montreal 1959, Hon. DD Aberdeen 1966. Prof. of OT Lang. and Lit., St Stephen's Coll., Edmonton, Alberta, 1946–50; Prof. of NT Lang. and Lit., McGill Univ., Montreal, 1950–59; Principal, United Theological Coll., Montreal, 1955–59; Sen. Tutor, Mansfield Coll., Oxford, 1959–70. Grinfield Lectr on the Septuagint, Oxford Univ., 1961–65. Minister of Highgate Congregational Church, London, 1943–46. *Publications*: The Truth of the Gospel, 1950; The Apostolic Age, 1955; Principalities and Powers, 1956; The Gospel according to St Luke, 1963; The Revelation of St John the Divine, 1966; Our Dialogue with Rome, 1967; contribs to Interpreter's Dictionary of the Bible; *contrib*. Jl of Theological Studies; New Testament Studies; Expository Times. *Address*: Principal's Lodgings, Mansfield College, Oxford.

Caird, Dr James Brown; Senior Lecturer in Geography, University of Glasgow, since 1967; *b* 1928; *m* 1954; one *s* three *d*. MA Edinburgh 1950 (1st cl. Geography), D de l'Univ. Rennes 1951. Asst, Glasgow, 1955–57; Lectr, 1958–64; seconded Reader and Actg Hd of Dept of Geography, Univ. of Ife, Nigeria, 1964–66; Lectr, Glasgow, 1966–67. *Publications*: *contrib*. Scott. Geog. Mag., Soc. Rev. *Address*: Dept of Geography, Univ. of Glasgow, Glasgow G12 8QQ.

Cairncross, Sir Alexander Kirkland, KCMG, FBA; Master of St Peter's College, Oxford, since 1969; Chancellor, University of Glasgow, since 1972; *b* 1911; *m* 1943; three *s* two *d*. MA Glasgow 1933 (1st cl. Economic Science), PhD Cantab 1936, Hon

LLD, DLitt, LittD, DSc; FBA 1961; Pres., Royal Econ. Soc , 1968–70; Pres., Section F, Brit. Assoc., 1969; Pres., Brit. Assoc., 1970–71; Pres., Scott. Econ. Soc., 1969–72. Lectr, Univ. of Glasgow, 1935; Prof. of Applied Economics, 1951–61; Wicksell Lectr, Stockholm, 1960. Ed., Scott. Jl Pol Econ., 1954–61. Dir, Econ. Develop. Inst., Washington DC, 1955–56; Econ. Adv. to HM Govt, 1961–64; Head of Govt Econ. Service, 1964–69; Chm., Local Develop. Cttee, 1951–52; Mem.: Crofting Commn, 1951–54, Phillips Cttee, 1953–54, Anthrax Cttee, 1957–59, Radcliffe Cttee, 1957–59; Mem., Council of Management, Nat. Inst. of Econ. and Soc. Res., PEP; Court of Governors, LSE. *Publications*: Introduction to Economics, 1944, 5th edn 1973; Home and Foreign Investment 1870–1913, 1953; Monetary Policy in a Mixed Economy, 1960; Economic Development and the Atlantic Provinces, 1961; Factors in Economic Development, 1962; Essays in Economic Management, 1971; Control of Long-term International Capital Movements, 1973; ed, The Scottish Economy, 1954, The Managed Economy, 1970; Britain's Econ. Prospects Reconsidered, 1971; *contrib*. Econ. Hist. Rev., Econ. Jl, Kyklos, Weltwirtsch. Archiv., etc. *Address*: St Peter's College, Oxford.

Cairns, Dr Christopher Shannon, MA PhD; Lecturer in Italian, University College of Wales, Aberystwyth, since 1974; *b* 1940; *m*; one *s*. BA Leeds 1964 (2/1 Hons, Italian), MA Toronto 1965, PhD Reading, 1971. Teaching Asst in Italian, Toronto Univ., 1964; Teaching Fellow, Toronto, 1965–66; Lectr in Italian, Southampton, 1967–73. *Publications*: An Introduction to Italian Literature, 1974; Domenico Bollani, bishop of Brescia: devotion to Church and State in the Republic of Venice in the 16th Century, 1975; *contrib*. Ren. News, BIHR, Comm. Aten. Brescia, Studi Veneziani. *Address*: Dept of Romance Languages, Univ. Coll. of Wales, Aberystwyth SY23 2AX.

Cairns, Francis; Professor of Latin, Liverpool University, since 1979; *b* 1939; *m* 1969. MA Glasgow 1961, BA Oxon 1963, MA Oxon 1968. Asst Lectr, Edinburgh Univ., 1963–65, Lectr in Humanity (Latin), 1966–73. *Publications*: Generic Composition in Greek and Roman Poetry, 1972; *contrib*. AJPh, CQ, CR, Eranos, Hermes, Mnemosyne, Mus. Phil. Lond., RhM, Symb. Oslo. *Address*: Dept of Latin, School of Classics, Liverpool Univ., Abercromby Square, PO Box 147, Liverpool L69 3BX.

Cairns, Dr Mary Bell, LLM, PhD; Lecturer in Public Law, University of Keele, since 1953; *b* 1914. LLB Bristol 1937, LLM Bristol 1947, PhD London 1950; Barrister Middle Temple 1938, Mem., West. Circuit 1939. Asst Lectr, Dept of Political Institutions, Univ. Coll. of N Staffs, 1952–53. Mem., Bristol City Council, 1941–44; Min. of Food (Enforcement and Rationing and Catering Brchs), 1944–46; Wynn Parry Dept, Cttee on Conditions and Pay in Prison Services, 1957–58; Gen. Cttee, Soc. of Public Teachers of Law, 1959–65. *Publications*: The Law of Tort in Local Government, 1954, 2nd edn 1969; *contrib*. Indust. Law Rev., JALT, Law and

Contemp. Prob., Solic. Jl. *Address*: Dept of Law, Univ. of Keele, Keele, Staffs ST5 5BG.

Calderwood, Matthew Thomas; Lecturer in Psychology, Institute of Extension Studies, University of Liverpool, since 1966; *b* 1938. BA Hons Liverpool 1961. Demonstrator in Psychol., Univ. of Liverpool, 1961–64; Asst Lectr in Psychol., Univ. of Sussex, 1964–65, Lectr, 1965–66. *Address*: The Royal Instn, Colquitt Street, Liverpool.

Caldin, Prof. Edward Francis, MA, DPhil, DSc; Professor of Physical Chemistry, University of Kent at Canterbury (also teaches History and Philosophy of Science), since 1966; *b* 1914; *m* 1944; two *s*. BA Oxon 1937 (1st cl. Chemistry), MA Oxon 1950, DPhil Oxon 1950, DSc Oxon 1973; FChemSoc.; Mem., Brit. Soc. Hist. Sci.; Brit. Soc. Philos. Sci. Jun. Res. Fellow, Queen's Coll., Oxford, 1939–45; Lectr, Univ. of Leeds, 1945–54, Sen. Lectr, 1954–64, Reader, 1964–65; Reader, Univ. of Kent, 1965–66. *Publications*: The Power and Limits of Science, 1949; Introduction to Chemical Thermodynamics, 1958; The Structure of Chemistry, 1961; Fast Reactions in Solution, 1964; Russian trans., 1966; *contrib.* Chem. Rev., Jl Chem. Soc., Nature, Proc. Phys. Soc., Proc. Royal Soc. A, Trans Faraday Soc., etc. *Address*: Univ. Chemical Laboratory, Canterbury, Kent CT2 7NZ.

Caldwell, Dr James Alexander Malcolm, MA, PhD; Lecturer in the Economic History of East and South East Asia, School of Oriental and African Studies, University of London, since 1960; *b* 1931; *m* 1954; two *s* two *d*. MA Edinburgh 1953 (1st cl. Economics), PhD Nottingham 1956. Tutor in Politics, Nottingham, 1953–56; Res. Fellow, SOAS, 1958–61; Vis. Lectr, Univ. of Malaya, 1964–65. Editor, Jl Contemp. Asia. *Publications*: Indonesia, 1968, Dutch edn 1970; The Chainless Mind, 1968; Cambodia in the South East Asian War, 1973. *Address*: School of Oriental and African Studies, Malet Street, WC1E 7HP.

Caldwell, Dr John Anthony; Lecturer in Music, Oxford, since 1966, Research Fellow in Music, Keble College, since 1967; *b* 1938; *m* 1967; one *s* one *d*. BA Oxon 1960 (1st cl. Music), BMus Oxon 1961, MA Oxon 1964, DPhil Oxon 1965; FRCO 1957; Mem., Royal Mus. Assoc., Inc. Soc. Musicians, RCO, Soc. Renaiss. Studies. Lectr, Bristol, 1963–66. Organist: St Giles Ch., Oxford, 1966–68; Sts Philip and James Ch., Oxford, 1968– . *Publications*: English Keyboard Music before the Nineteenth Century, 1973; Medieval Music (forthcoming); *contrib.* Musica Disciplina, Mus. Times, Mus. and Lett., Organ Ybk. *Address*: Keble College, Oxford.

Caldwell, John Bernard, BEng, PhD CEng, FRINA, MIStructE; Professor and Head of Department of Naval Architecture and Shipbuilding, University of Newcastle upon Tyne, since 1966; *b* 1926; *m* 1955; two *s*. BEng Liverpool 1947, PhD Bristol 1953; CEng 1968, FRINA 1965, MIStructE 1965; Mem., NE Coast Instn of Engineers and Shipbuilders. Res, Fellow, Civil Engrg

Dept, Bristol Univ., 1953–55; Asst Prof. of Mechanical Engrg, Royal Naval Coll., Greenwich, 1960–66; Vis. Prof., Mass Inst. of Technology, 1962–63; Mem.: Council, RINA, 1966; Council, NECIES, 1966; Standing Cttee, ISSC, 1967; Ship and Marine Technology Requirements Bd, 1972; Aeronautical and Mech. Enrg Cttee, SRC, 1971. *Publications*: *contrib.* Die Ingen., Europ. Shipbuild, Trans Japan Soc. Naval Archs, Trans Roy. Aero. Soc., Trans Roy. Inst. Nav. Archs., Trans NE Coast Instn, Proc. Roy. Soc., Qly Jl Mechs App. Maths. *Address*: Dept of Naval Architecture and Shipbuilding, Univ. of Newcastle upon Tyne, Newcastle NE1 7RU.

Cali, Dr Pietro, DottLett, MA; Senior Lecturer in Italian, Head of Department, University College, Cork, since 1968; *b* 1927; *m* 1957; three *s*. Laurea in Lettere, Milan 1950, MA Cork 1967. Asst Lectr, Univ. Coll. Dublin, 1955–56; Special Asst Lectr, Univ. Coll. Cork, 1956–67. Pres., Dante Alighieri Soc., Cork, 1969– ; Consular Agent for Italy in Cork, 1970– . *Publications*: Allegory and Vision in Dante and Langland, 1971. *Address*: Dept of Italian, Univ. College, Cork, Ireland.

Callan, Prof. Norman Rainer; Professor of English Literature and Language in the University of London, Head of English Department, Queen Mary College, since 1964; *b* 1909; *m* 1934; one *s* one *d*. MA Cantab 1938 (Classics), BA London 1945 (English), (George Smith Student 1945). Lectr, Queen Mary Coll., 1945–54, Reader, 1954–64. *Publications*: Poetry in Practice, 1938, 2nd edn 1952; The Poems of Christopher Smart, 2 vols; (with Prof. Maynard Mack) Pope's Iliad and Odyssey, 1965; *contrib.* RES, IEGP, TLS, NQ. *Address*: Queen Mary College, Mile End Road, E1 4NS.

Callander, Margaret M.; Senior Lecturer, Department of French, University of Birmingham, since 1972 (Lecturer, 1956–72); *b* 1929. BA Manchester 1950, MA Manchester 1952, PhD Manchester 1962. Asst Lectr, Birmingham, 1956. *Publications*: The Poetry of Pierre Jean Jouve, 1965. *Address*: Dept of French, Univ. of Birmingham, PO Box 363, Birmingham B15 2TT.

Calvert, Prof. Harry, LLM; Professor of Law, University of Newcastle upon Tyne, since 1970; Dean of the Faculty of Law, since 1972; *b* 1932; *m* 1956; three *d*. LLB Leeds 1955 (Hons cl. II [i]), LLM Leeds 1959. Lectr, Univ. of Tasmania, 1956–59; Lectr, Univ. of Singapore, 1959; Lectr, Univ. of Wales, 1960–63; Lectr, QUB, 1963–65, Sen. Lectr, 1965–68, Reader, 1968–70. Mem., Senate, Newcastle Univ., 1971– ; Gen. Cttee, Soc. of Public Teachers of Law, 1971– ; Ed., Northern Ireland Legal Qly, 1965–70. *Publications*: The British Commonwealth: the development of its laws and constitutions; (ed. L. A. Sheridan) Malaya, Singapore and the Borneo Territories, 1961; Constitutional Law in Northern Ireland, 1968; *contrib.* various. *Address*: Dept of Law, Univ. of Newcastle upon Tyne, Newcastle upon Tyne NE1 7RU.

107

Calvert, John Stanley, TD, BA; Senior Lecturer in Physical Education, University of Newcastle upon Tyne, since 1969; *b* 1929; *m* 1952; two *s*. BA Birmingham 1950, Grad. Cert. Educn Birmingham 1951. Pt-time Acad. Warden, Havelock Hall, Univ. of Newcastle upon Tyne. Dep. Chm., Northern Sports Council; Vice-Chm., Northumberland Playing Fields Assoc. *Publications*: (with R. Morgan and C. Sayer) Physical Education and Sport in the Soviet Union, 1961. *Address*: Physical Education Centre, Univ. of Newcastle upon Tyne, Newcastle upon Tyne NE1 7RU.

Calvert, Mrs M. A. T.; *see* Hodge, M. A. T.

Calvert, Dr Peter Anthony Richard; Senior Lecturer in Politics, University of Southampton, since 1971; *b* 1936; *m* 1962; one *s* one *d*. BA Cantab 1960, AM Michigan 1961, MA and PhD Cantab 1964; FRHistS. Teaching Fellow, Univ. of Michigan, Ann Arbor, 1960-61; Lectr, Univ. of Southampton, 1964-71; Vis. Lectr, Univ. of California, Santa Barbara, 1966; Res. Fellow, Chas Warren Center for Studies in Amer. Hist., Harvard Univ., 1969-70. Mem., Cambridge City Council, 1962-64; Gov., Cambs Coll. Arts and Technol., 1962-64; Mem., Cttee, Soc. Lat. Amer. Studies, 1970-71. *Publications*: The Mexican Revolution, 1910-14: the diplomacy of Anglo-American conflict, 1968; Latin America: internal conflict and international peace, 1969, Hebrew edn 1973; Revolution (Key Concepts in Political Science), 1970, Swedish edn 1971; A Study of Revolution, 1970; Mexico (Nations of the Modern World), 1973; The Mexicans: how they live and work, 1974; *contrib*. Ann. Regist., Internat. Aff., Jl Lat. Amer. Studies, Pol Studies, etc. *Address*: Dept of Politics, Univ. of Southampton, Highfield, Southampton SO9 5NH.

Cameron, Prof. Alan Douglas Edward; Professor of Latin at King's College, University of London, since 1972; *b* 1938; *m* 1962; one *s* one *d*. BA Oxon 1961 (1st cl. Lit. Hum.), MA Oxon 1963. Craven Schol., 1958; De Paravicini Schol., 1960; Chancellor's Prize for Latin Prose, 1960, N. H. Baynes Prize, 1967; John Conington Prize, 1968. Asst Lectr in Humanity, Glasgow Univ., 1961-63; Lectr, Glasgow, 1963-64; Lectr, Bedford Coll., London, 1964-71, Reader, 1971-72; Vis. Prof., Columbia Univ., 1967-68. *Publications*: Claudian: Poetry and Propaganda at the Court of Honorius, 1970; Porphyrius the Charioteer, 1973; Circus Factions, 1975; contrib. Cambridge Prosopography of the Later Roman Empire, 1971; *contrib*. Athenaeum, Bull. Inst. Class. Studies, Class. Qly, Class. Rev., Greek Rom. and Byz. Studies, Hermes, Historia, Jl Hell. Studies, Jl Rom. Studies, Philologus, Proc. Camb. Philol. Soc. *Address*: Dept of Latin, Univ. of London, King's College, Strand, WC2R 2LS.

Cameron, Dr Averil M., MA, PhD; Reader in Ancient History, King's College London, since 1970; *b* 1940; *m* 1962; one *s* one *d*. BA Oxon 1962 (1st cl. Lit. Hum.), MA Oxon 1964, PhD London 1966; Mem., Council, Hellenic Soc., 1970. Asst Lectr, KCL, 1965-68; Lectr, KCL, 1968-70; Vis. Prof., Columbia Univ., 1967-68. *Publications*: Procopius (The Great Histories), 1967; Agathias, 1970; Corippus, De laudibus Iustini II, 1974; *contrib*. Byz. Zeit., Class. Qly, Dumbarton Oaks Papers, Historia, Jl Hell. Studies, Jl Rom. Studies, etc. *Address*: Dept of Classics, King's College London, Strand, WC2R 2LS.

Cameron, Duncan Inglis, JP, BL, CA; Secretary of Heriot-Watt University, since 1965; *b* 1927; *m* 1955; two *s* one *d*. BL Glasgow 1950; CA 1951, Mem., Soc. Investment Analysts; Mem., Scottish Econ. Soc.; Asst Accountant, Univ. Edinburgh, 1952-65. JP County of City of Edinburgh; Governor, Keil Sch., Dumbarton, 1966- ; Trustee, RSGS, 1972- ; Mem., Scottish Univs Council on Entrance, 1968- ; Mem., Management Cttee, Scottish Univs Organisation and Methods Unit, 1967- . *Address*: Heriot-Watt Univ., Chambers Street, Edinburgh EH1 1HX.

Cameron, Prof. Gordon Campbell, BA; Titular Professor in Applied Economics (Urban Studies), Department of Social and Economic Research, University of Glasgow, since 1971; *b* 1937; *m* 1962; one *s* one *d*. BA Durham 1960 (Hons Politics and Economics). Res. Asst, Univ. of Durham, 1960-62; Asst Lectr, Univ. of Glasgow, 1962-63; Lectr, Univ. of Glasgow, 1963-68; Assoc. Prof., Univ. of Pittsburgh, 1966; Vis. Schol., Resources for the Future, Washington DC, 1967; Sen. Lectr, Univ. of Glasgow, 1968-71; Vis. Prof., Univ. of California, Berkeley, 1974. Ed., Urban Studies Jl, 1968-73. Project Sec., Scottish War-on-Want, 1968-70. *Publications*: Regional Economic Development – The Federal Role, 1970; ed (wtih L. Wingo), Cities, Regions and Public Policy, 1973; *contrib*. Scott. Jl Pol Econ. Regional Studies, Urban Studies, New Society. *Address*: Adam Smith Building, Univ. of Glasgow.

Cameron, J. R.; Senior Lecturer, Department of Philosophy, University of Dundee, since 1973 (Lecturer, 1963-73); *b* 1936; *m* 1959; one *s* two *d*. MA St Andrews 1958 (1st cl. Maths), BPhil St Andrews 1961 (Philosophy). Asst, Queen's Coll., Dundee, 1962-63. *Publications*: *contrib*. Philos. Qly, Philos. *Address*: Dept of Philosophy, The Univ., Dundee DD1 4HN.

Cameron, Rev. Prof. James Kerr; Professor of Ecclesiastical History, University of St Andrews, since 1970; *b* 1924; *m* 1956; one *s*. MA St Andrews 1946, BD St Andrews 1949 (dist. Eccl. Hist.), PhD Hartford USA 1953 (Summa cum laude). Lectr, Aberdeen Univ., 1955-56; Lectr, St Andrews Univ., 1956-68; Sen. Lectr, St Andrews Univ., 1968-70. *Publications*: Letters of John Johnston and Robert Howie, 1963; Bibliographie de la Reforme 1450-1648; ed, The First Book of Discipline, 1972; contrib. to M. Spinka, Advocates of Reform, 1953; Studies on Voltaire and the eighteenth century, vol. 58, 1967; *contrib*. Aberdeen Univ. Rev., SHR. *Address*: Dept of Ecclesiastical History, St Mary's College, St Andrews, Fife KY16 9AJ.

Cameron, John; Lecturer, Department of Education in Developing Countries, University of London Institute of Education, since 1964; b 1914; m 1940; one s two d. BA Leeds 1939 (Hons Classics), Graduate Cert. Educn London 1947. Educn and Sen. Educn Off., Tanganyika, 1947-60; Asst Chief Educn Off., Tanganyika, 1960-64; Specialist in Educn Planning, UNESCO, Malta, July 1968-Dec. 1969, July-Sept. 1970. *Publications*: The Development of Education in East Africa, 1970; (with W. A. Dodd) Society, Schools and Progress in Tanzania, 1970; (with D. Carver and M. Wallace) Collins English Learners Dictionary, 1974; *contrib*. African Abst., Comp. Educn Rev., Teacher Educn in New Countries. *Address*: Univ. of London Institute of Education, Malet Street, WC1E 7HS.

Cameron, Dr Keith Colwyn, BA, LèsL, Doct. d'Univ.; Lecturer in French, University of Exeter, since 1966; b 1939; m 1962; three d. BA Exeter 1961, Cert. Educn Cambridge 1962, LèsL Rennes 1964, Doct. d'Univ. Rennes 1964. Lecteur, Rennes, 1962-64; Asst Lectr, Aberdeen, 1964-66. Gen. Editor, Textes littéraires, 1970- . Dir, Exeter Tapes, 1972. *Publications*: Montaigne et l'Humour, 1966; co-ed, Bèze: Abraham Sacrifiant, 1967; ed, Rivaudeau: Aman, 1969; ed, Chantelouve: La Tragédie de feu Gaspard de Colligny . . ., 1971; *contrib*. Bibliothèque d'Humanisme et Renaissance, L'Esprit Créateur, Renaissance Qly. *Address*: Dept of French and Italian, Queen's Building, The Univ., Exeter EX4 4QH.

Cameron, Prof. Kenneth; Professor of English Language, School of English Studies, Nottingham University, since 1963; b 1922; m 1947; one s one d. BA Leeds 1947 (Hons), PhD Sheffield 1951; FRHistS, Sir Israel Gollancz Meml Prize, Brit. Acad., 1969. Asst Lectr, Univ. of Sheffield, 1947-50; Lectr, Univ. of Nottingham, 1950-59; Sen. Lectr, 1959-62; Reader, 1962-63. Hon. Dir, English Place-Name Soc., 1966- ; Mem., Council, Viking Soc., 1966-69, 1971- , Pres., 1972- . *Publications*: The Place-Names of Derbyshire, 1959; English Place-Names, 1961, pbk 1969; Scandinavian Settlement in the Territory of the Five Boroughs: The Place-Name Evidence, 1965; *contrib*. Festschriften to Bruce Dickins and Dorothy Whitelock; *contrib*. Engl. Place-Name Soc. Jl, Med. Scand., Nottm Med. Studies. *Address*: School of English Studies, The Univ., Nottingham NG7 2RD.

Cameron, William Donald Bruce; Lecturer, Department of Accountancy, University of Glasgow, since 1959; b 1931; m 1955; two s. Chartered Accountant. *Address*: Dept of Accountancy, Glasgow Univ., Southpark Avenue, Glasgow.

Cameron Wilson, John; *see* Wilson, J. C.

Camp, Jeffery Bruce; Lecturer (part-time) in Fine Art, Slade School of Fine Art, University College, London, since 1961; b 1923; m 1963. DA Edinburgh. *Address*: Slade School of Fine Art, University Coll. London, WC1E 6BT.

Campbell, Prof. Alexander Elmslie, MA, PhD; Professor of American History, University of Birmingham, since 1972; b 1929; m 1956; one s one d. BA Cantab 1952 (1st cl. History), MA Cantab 1956, PhD Cantab 1956, MA Oxon 1959; FRHistS. Fellow, King's Coll., Cambridge, 1955-59; Fellow and Tutor, Keble Coll., Oxford, 1960-72; CUF Lectr, Oxford Univ., 1960-72; Vis. Prof., Hobart Coll., USA, 1970. *Publications*: Great Britain and the United States 1895-1903, 1960; America Comes of Age, 1971, French and Spanish edns 1971; ed, Expansion and Imperialism, 1970; ed, The USA in World Affairs, 1974; *contrib*. New Cambridge Modern History; *contrib*. Hist. Jl, Jl Southern Hist. *Address*: School of History, Univ. of Birmingham, PO Box 363, Birmingham B15 2TT.

Campbell, Prof. Archibald Duncan, CBE, MA; Professor of Applied Economics, University of Dundee, 1967-74; Chief Executive, Sidlaw Industries, since 1974; b 1919; m 1950; one s two d. MA Glasgow 1940 (1st cl. Economic Science). Lectr, Glasgow Univ., 1945-52, Sen. Lectr, 1952-55; Prof., St Andrews Univ., 1955-67. Economic Consultant to Sec. of State for Scotland, 1962- ; Mem., Scottish Gas Bd, 1966-72; British Gas Corp., 1973- ; Dir, Sidlaw Indust., 1969- ; Chm., Commn on Sugar Indust. (St Kitts), 1965; Mem.: Fleck Cttee on Fishing Indust., 1959-60; Boundary Commn for Scotland, 1961- ; Hunter Cttee on Salmon and Trout Fisheries, 1962-65; EDC for Building, 1967-73; Rochdale Cttee on Shipping, 1967-70; Dept of Environment, Planning and Transport Res. Adv. Cttee, 1972- ; Chm., EDCs for Building and Civil Engrg, 1973- ; Chm. of various arbitration bodies and courts, etc., of inquiry in labour matters. Mem., Council, Royal Econ. Soc., 1971- . *Publications*: Tayside, 1970; *contrib*. Econ. Jl, Scottish Jl Pol Economy.

Campbell, Dr Colin Barnsley, PhD; Lecturer in Sociology, Department of Sociology, University of York, since 1965; b 1940; m 1962; one s one d. BSc(Econ) London 1961 (2nd cl. external), PhD London (external) 1968. Asst Lectr, Birmingham Coll. of Comm., 1961-64; Asst Lectr, Univ. of York, 1964-65. *Publications*: Toward a Sociology of Irreligion, 1971; *contrib*. Soc. Ybk Relig. Brit., Soc. Rev. *Address*: Dept of Sociology, Univ. of York, Heslington, York YO1 5DD.

Campbell, David M. A., MA; Lecturer in Moral Philosophy, University of Glasgow, since 1968; b 1939. MA Aberdeen 1962 (Hons Mental Philosophy). Asst Lectr, Glasgow Univ., 1965-68. *Address*: Dept of Moral Philosophy, Univ. of Glasgow, Glasgow G12 8QQ.

Campbell, Dr Ian; Lecturer in English Literature, University of Edinburgh, since 1967; b 1942. MA Aberdeen 1964, PhD Edinburgh 1970; FSAScot 1970; Council Mem., Assoc. of Scottish Literary Studies, 1968- ; Mem., Univs Cttee on Scottish Literature, 1968- ; Vice-Pres., Carlyle Soc. *Publications*: mem. editorial team,

Letters of Thomas and Jane Welsh Carlyle (Duke-Edinburgh edn), 4 vols 1970, 3 vols, 1974, continuing; Carlyle, 1974; ed, Carlyle: Reminiscences, 1972; ed, Carlyle: Selected Essays, 1973; ed (jtly) MacLellan: Jamie the Saxt, 1971; *contrib*. Bibliotheck, Criticism, English Lang. Notes, Liturgical Rev., Scottish Literary News, Scottish Tradition, Studies in Scottish Lit., Guelph Univ. Colloq. *Address*: Dept of English, David Hume Tower, George Square, Edinburgh EH8 9JX.

Campbell, Prof. Ian McIntyre, MA; Professor of Humanity, University of Edinburgh, since 1959; Dean of Faculty of Arts, since 1971; *b* 1915; *m* 1945; two *s* one *d*. MA Glasgow 1936, MA Oxon 1946. Lectr in Humanity and Comparative Philology, Glasgow Univ., 1947–54; Prof. of Latin, UC of S Wales and Mon., 1954–59. Jt Editor, Archivum Linguisticum, 1949– . *Publications*: *contrib*. learned jls. *Address*: Univ. of Edinburgh, David Hume Tower, George Square, Edinburgh EH8 9JX.

Campbell, James; Fellow of Worcester College, since 1957, and Lecturer in Modern History, University of Oxford, since 1958; *b* 1935. BA Oxon 1955, MA; FSA 1972. Junior Res. Fellow, Merton College, 1956–58. Dean of Worcester Coll.; Senior Proctor of the Univ., 1973–74. *Publications*: *contrib*. Ampleforth Jl, Latin Historians, Studies in the Late Middle Ages. *Address*: Worcester College, Oxford.

Campbell, James Joseph, JP, HDipEd, MA; Director of the Institute of Education, The Queen's University of Belfast, since 1969; *b* 1910; *m* 1934; five *s* one *d*. BA QUB 1930 (1st cl. Classics), MA QUB 1934; HDipEd (with distinction) 1948. Mem., Univ. Senate, QUB, 1959–69; Chm., Convocation, QUB, 1971– . Govt Cttees: Youth Welfare, 1942; Legal Aid, 1958; Registered Clubs .1960: Public Libraries .1966; NI Adv. Council of Educn; Child Welfare Council; Educn and Trng of Teachers; Cameron Royal Commn on Disturbances in Northern Ireland, 1969; Ed., Irish Bookman, 1946–48; numerous dramatised documentaries for BBC. *Publications*: Primary and Secondary Education in Ulster since 1800, 1957; Television in Ireland, 1961; 'Between The Wars' in Belfast: origin and growth of an industrial city, 1967; ed, Cicero: Pro lege Manilia and Pro Archia, 1948; Legends of Ireland, 1955, Italian edn 1971; anthologised in: Die Jungfrau and her Teufel, 1964; The Irish Reader, 1963. *Address*: Institute of Education, The Queen's Univ. of Belfast, Belfast BT7 1NN.

Campbell, Prof. Peter Walker; Professor of Politics, University of Reading, since 1964; *b* 1926. BA Oxon 1947 (2nd cl. PPE), MA Oxon 1951. Mem., Pol Studies Assoc. UK, etc. Asst Lectr in Government, Univ. of Manchester, 1949–51; Lectr in Government, 1951–60; Prof. of Political Economy, Univ. of Reading, 1960–64. Dean, Fac. of Lett. and Soc. Sci., Reading, 1966–69; Chm., Grad. Sch. Contemp. Europ. Studies, Reading, 1971–73; Ed., Pol Studies, 1963–69. *Publications*: (with W. Theiner) Encyclopaedia of World Politics, 1950; (with B. Chapman) Constitution of the Fifth Republic: Translation and Commentary, 1958; French Electoral Systems and Elections, 1958, 2nd edn 1965; *contrib*. Parl. Aff., Pol Sci., Pol Studies, Public Admin. *Address*: Dept of Politics, The Univ., Reading RG6 2AA.

Campbell, Robin Neil, BSc; Lecturer in Psychology, University of Stirling, since 1969; *b* 1942; *m* 1966; one *d*. BSc Edinburgh 1964 (2nd cl. Math. Sci.), BSc Edinburgh 1966 (1st cl. Psychology); Mem., Lingu. Assoc. Res. Asst, Edinburgh, 1966–69. *Publications*: Chapters in, New Horizons in Linguistics, ed J. Lyons, 1970; Advances in Psycholinguistics, ed D. Arcais and Lovell, 1971; *contrib*. Jl Lingu. *Address*: Dept of Psychology, Univ. of Stirling, Stirling FK9 4LA.

Campbell, Scott; Lecturer in Art Education, Department of Fine Art, University of Newcastle upon Tyne, since 1961; *b* 1924; *m* 1953; one *s* two *d*. BA Durham 1952 (Hons Fine Art), MA Durham 1954. Admin. Asst, Dept of Fine Art, 1956–61. Asst Reg. Dir (NE), Arts Council of GB, 1953–55. *Address*: Dept of Fine Art, Univ. of Newcastle upon Tyne, Newcastle upon Tyne NE1 7RU.

Campbell, Prof. Thomas Douglas, PhD; Professor of Philosophy, University of Stirling, since 1973; *b* 1938; *m* 1967; one *s* one *d*. MA Glasgow 1962 (1st cl. Philosophy), BA Oxon 1964 (1st cl. Theology), PhD Glasgow 1969. Asst Lectr in Political Philosophy, Univ. of Glasgow, 1964–65; Lectr, 1965–70; Lectr, Dept of Moral Philosophy, Glasgow, 1970–73. *Publications*: Adam Smith's Science of Morals, 1971; *contrib*. Philosoph. Qly, Il Pensiero Politico, Analysis, Brit. Jl Pol Science. *Address*: Dept of Philosophy, Univ. of Stirling, Stirling FK9 4LA.

Campos, Dr Christophe, LèsL, DES, PhD; Lecturer in European Studies, University of Sussex, since 1964; *b* 1938. LèsL Paris 1958, DES Paris 1960, PhD Cambridge 1963. Lector in French, Gonville and Caius Coll., Cambridge, 1959–63; Lectr in French, Univ. of Maryland (European Division), 1963–64; Lectr in English, Univ. of Oslo, 1970–71. *Publications*: The View of France, 1965; trans. Sauvy: General Theory of Population, 1968; trans. Laslett: Un Monde que nous avons perdu, 1969; *contrib*. Nordisk Forum, Revue de l'AUPELF, Times Lit. Supp., Univ. Qly, Theatre Qly. *Address*: School of European Studies, Univ. of Sussex, Brighton BN1 9QN.

Camps, William Anthony; Master of Pembroke College, Cambridge, since 1970; *b* 1910; *m* 1953. Fellow, Pembroke College, 1933; Univ. Lectr in Classics, 1939; Temp. Civil Servant, 1940–45; Asst Tutor, Pembroke Coll., 1945, Sen. Tutor, 1947–62; Tutor for Advanced Students, 1963–70, Pres., 1964–70. Mem., Inst. for Advanced Study, Princeton, 1956–57; Vis. Assoc. Prof., UC Toronto, 1966; Vis. Prof., Univ. of N Carolina at Chapel Hill, 1969. *Publications*: edns of Propertius I, 1961, IV, 1965, III, 1966, II, 1967; An Introduction to Virgil's Aeneid,

1969; notes and reviews in classical periodicals. *Address*: Pembroke College, Cambridge.

Cann, Dr Johnson Robin; Reader, School of Environmental Sciences, University of East Anglia. *Address*: Sch. of Environmental Sciences, Univ. of East Anglia, Norwich NOR 88C.

Cannell, Robert Leslie; Pro-Vice Chancellor and Director, Centre for Extension Studies, University of Technology, Loughborough, since 1966; *b* 1920; *m* 1945; two *s*. BEng (Hons), Liverpool 1941, MEng Liverpool 1951; FIEE 1951. Electrical Engr Officer, RAF, 1942–46; English Electric Co. Ltd, Bradford, 1946–49; Lectr in Electrical Engrg, Univ. of Bristol, 1949–52; Sen. Educn Officer, English Electric Group, 1952–57; Vice Principal, Loughborough Coll. of Technology, 1957-66. *Publication*: Co-operative Education in Engineering in USA, 1960. *Address*: Centre for Extension Studies, Univ. of Technology, Loughborough LE11 3TU.

Cantor, Prof. Leonard Martin, MA; Schofield Professor of Education and Head of the Education Department, Loughborough University of Technology, since 1969; *b* 1927; *m* 1961; two *s*. BA Hons London 1951, Postgrad. CertEd London 1952, MA(Ed) London 1960. Lectr, Univ. of Keele, 1958–67; Sen. Lectr, 1967–69; Vis. Lectr, Reed Coll., Portland, Oregon, 1964–65; Vis. Lectr, Univ. of Michigan, 1967, 1969. *Publications*: Water and Man: A Geography of Hydroelectricity and Irrigation, 1963; A World Geography of Irrigation, 1967, 2nd edn 1970; (with I. F. Roberts) Further Education in England and Wales, 1969, 2nd edn 1972; *contrib*. Geog. Jl, Geog., Jl of Geog. *Address*: Dept of Education, Loughborough Univ. of Technology, Loughborough LE11 3TU.

Capp, Dr Bernard Stuart; Lecturer in History, University of Warwick, since 1968; *b* 1943; *m* 1966; one *s* one *d*. BA Oxon 1965, MA 1970, DPhil 1970; FRHistS 1972. Bryce res. studentship, Oxford, 1966–67. *Publications*: Extreme Millenarianism, in, Puritans, the Millennium and the Future of Israel, ed P. Toon, 1970; The Fifth Monarchy Men, 1972; *contrib*. Past and Present. *Address*: Dept of History, Univ. of Warwick, Coventry CV4 7AL.

Caracciolo, Peter L., BA; Lecturer in English Literature, University of London, since 1967; *b* 1933; *m* 1962; two *d*. BA London 1962 (2nd cl. English). Asst Lectr, Royal Holloway Coll. 1965–67. *Publications*: *contrib*. BC, Encounter, ES, NCF. *Address*: Dept of English, Royal Holloway College, Egham, Surrey TW20 0EX.

Caracciolo-Trejo, Dr Enrique E.; Senior Lecturer, Department of Literature, University of Essex, since 1974 (Lecturer, 1967–74); *b* 1932; *m* 1952; one *s*. LicDoc Univ. of Córdoba, Argentina 1955 and 1962. Col. Monserrat, Univ. of Córdoba 1958–62; Fac. Filosofía y Letras, Univ. of Córdoba, 1962–63; Univ. of Bristol, 1963–64. *Publications*: trans. William Blake: Poemas y Profeofas (in Spanish), 1957; Los Poetas metasfisicos ingleses del Siglo XVII, 1962;

Hawthorne, Melville y el Pasado Puritano, 1963; ed, Penguin Book of Latin American Verse, 1971; V. Huidobro y la Vanguardia, 1972; Visiones de William Blake, 1974; (jtly) Baroque Poetry: an anthology in 5 languages with English Prose translations (forthcoming); *contrib*. Pepeles de Son Armadans, L'Herne, Amaru, Rev. UNAM. *Address*: Dept of Literature, Univ. of Essex, Colchester, Essex CO4 3SQ.

Carbery, Dr Thomas Francis; Senior Lecturer in Government – Business Relations, University of Strathclyde, since 1964; *b* 1925; *m* 1954; one *s* two *d*. BScEcon London 1956, MScEcon London 1962, PhD London 1966, Dip. Public Admin Glasgow 1956; Mem., RIPA; Former Nat. Chm., Soc. for Coop. Studies; Sec., Scott. Branch of Public and Coop. Enterprise. Sen. Lectr in Govt and Economics, Scott. Coll. of Commerce, Glasgow, 1961–64. Mem., IBA, 1970– , Mem., Senate (Univ. of Strathclyde), 1964–71, 1973– ; Mem., Court (Univ. of Strathclyde), 1968–71. *Publications*: Consumer in Politics, 1969; Decision-making by Scottish Local Authorities on the Fluoridation of Water, 1972. *Address*: Dept of Economics, Univ. of Strathclyde, Glasgow G1 1XW.

Carby-Hall, Joseph Roger, RD; Lecturer in Law, University of Hull, since 1970; *b* 1933; *m* 1962; one *d*. MA Aberdeen 1958, LLB Aberdeen 1961; Advocate 1962; Mem., Industrial Law Soc.; Mem., SPTL. Research, Univ. Bristol, 1968–70. Asst Legal Adviser, David Brown Industries, 1961–65. *Publications*: Principles of Industrial Law, 1969; Studies in Labour Law, 1974; Cases in Labour Law, 1974; *contrib*. Industrial Soc., LQR, MLR, Sol. Jl. *Address*: Dept of Law, University of Hull, Hull HU6 7RX.

Cardell, Dr Brian Southwell, MD, FRCPath; Reader in Morbid Anatomy, King's College Hospital Medical School, University of London, since 1956; *b* 1920; *m* 1946; two *s*. MBBS London 1942, MD London 1950; FRCPath, FRSM. Mem., Assoc. Clin. Pathols, ASME, Int. Acad, Path, Path. Soc. GB and Ireland. Lectr, London Univ., 1949–55. Vice-Dean, King's Coll. Hosp. Med. Sch., 1963–66; Postgrad. Sub-Dean, 1969– . *Publications*: *contrib*. Brit. Jl Ophthal., Brit. Med. Jl, Jl Obst-Gyn. Brit. Commonwealth, Jl Pathol., etc. *Address*: Dept of Pathology, King's College Hospital Medical School, SE5.

Cardinal, Dr Roger Thomas; Lecturer in French, University of Kent, since 1968; *b* 1940; *m* 1965; one *s*. BA Cantab 1962 (1st cl. Mod. Langs), MA Cantab 1966, PhD Cantab 1966. Asst Prof., Univ. of Manitoba, 1965–67; Lectr, Univ. of Warwick, 1967–68. *Publications*: (jtly) Surrealism: permanent revelation, 1970; Outsider Art, 1972; German Romantics, 1974. *Address*: Keynes College, Univ. of Kent, Canterbury, Kent.

Cardwell, Prof. Donald Stephen Lowell; Professor of History of Science and Technology, University of Manchester Institute of Science and Technology and Manchester University, since 1974; *b* 1919; *m* 1953; one *s*

111

one d. BSc London 1940 (1st cl. Physics), PhD London 1949. Lectr, Dept of Philosophy, Leeds Univ., 1960–63; Reader in Hist. of Science and Technology, UMIST, 1963–73. Indust. Res., 1949–51; Nuffield Res. Schol., 1951–54; Res. Off., Sci. Indust. Cttee (Brit. Assoc.), 1955–57; Jt Hon. Sec., Manch. Lit. and Phil. Soc., Ed., Memoirs, 1971– . *Publications*: The Organisation of Science in England, 1957, 2nd edn 1972; Steam Power in the Eighteenth Century, 1963; ed, John Dalton and the Progress of Science, 1968; From Watt to Clausius: the Rise of Thermodynamics in the Early Industrial Age, 1971 (Dexter Prize, Soc. for Hist. of Technology, US); Technology, Science and History, 1972 (US, as Turning Points in Western Technology); *contrib*. Brit. Jl Hist. Sci. Technol. Cult. *Address*: Univ. of Manchester Institute of Science and Technology, Manchester.

Cardwell, Richard Andrew, BA; Lecturer in Spanish, University of Nottingham, since 1967; *b* 1938; *m* 1961. BA Southampton 1960 (1st cl. English and Spanish), Cert. Ed. Southampton 1961. Mem., Assoc. of Hispanists of GB, Soc. for Lat. Amer. Studies, Anglo-Catalan Soc. Asst Lectr, UCW Aberystwyth, 1964; Lectr in charge Spanish, Aberystwyth, 1965–67. Chief Examiner (Spanish Oral), Univ. of London GCE; Examiner (Oral) Camb. and Oxf. Bds. *Publications*: V. Blasco Ibáñez's La barraca, 1972; ed, R. Gil's La caja de música, 1972; contrib. Pérez Galdós' Doña Perfecta, ed Cardona, 1974; *contrib*. MLR, BHS, IB, ReMS, AG, Studies in Romanticism, Revista de Letras. *Address*: Dept of Spanish, Univ. of Nottingham, Nottingham NG7 2RD.

Care, Elaine, MA BLitt; Lecturer , German Department, Reading University, since 1966; *b* 1940. BA Oxon 1963, MA Oxon 1970, BLitt Oxon 1970. Asst Lectr, Reading Univ., 1964 (pt-time), 1965 (full time). *Address*: German Dept, Reading Univ., Berks RG6 2AH.

Carey, Dr John, MA, DPhil; Lecturer in English Literature and Fellow, St John's College, Oxford, since 1964; *b* 1934; *m* 1960. BA Oxon 1957 (1st cl. English Lang. and Lit.), MA Oxon 1960, DPhil Oxon 1960. Harmsworth Sen. Schol., Merton Coll., Oxford, 1957; Lectr, Christ Church, Oxford, 1958; Andrew Bradley Res. Fellow, Balliol Coll., Oxford, 1959; Fellow, Keble Coll., Oxford, 1960. *Publications*: Milton, 1969; ed (with Alastair Fowler), The Poems of John Milton, 1969; ed, James Hogg: The Confessions of a Justified Sinner, 1969; ed, Andrew Marvell, in, Penguin Critical Anthologies, 1969; Sixteenth and Seventeenth Century Prose, in, Sphere History of Literature, vol. 2, ed Christopher Ricks, 1970; The Violent Effigy: a study of Dickens' Imagination, 1973; trans., John Milton: Christian Doctrine, 1973; D. H. Lawrence's Doctrine, in, D. H. Lawrence: novelist, poet, prophet, ed Stephen Spender, 1973; *contrib*. RES, MLR. *Address*: 38 St John Street, Oxford.

Carey Jones, Norman Stewart; Director in Development Administration, Department of Social Studies, Leeds University, since 1965; *b* 1911; *m* 1946; two *s*. BA Oxford 1933, MA Oxford 1965; FRGS 1934, FRCommonwealth Soc. 1938. Mem., Pol Studies Assoc. UK, 1965; Afr. Studies Assoc. UK, 1965. Colonial Audit Service, 1935–54; Colonial Admin. Service, 1954–65. *Publications*: The Pattern of a Dependent Economy, 1952; The Anatomy of Uhuru, 1966; *contrib*. Afr. Qly, E Afr. Econ. Rev., Geog. Jl, Jl Admin. Overseas. *Address*: Dept of Politics, The Univ., Leeds LS2 9JT.

Carey Taylor, Alan; *see* Taylor, A. C.

Cargill Thompson, Dr William David James; Lecturer in Ecclesiastical History, Department of Ecclesiastical History, University of London King's College, since 1969; *b* 1930; *m* 1966; two *s*. BA Cambridge 1954 (1st cl. Historical Tripos Pts I and II), MA Cambridge 1959, PhD Cambridge 1960; FRHistS. Fellow, King's Coll., Cambridge, 1956–65; Lectr in History, Univ. of Sussex, 1965–69; Vis. Lectr, Univ. Coll. of Rhodesia and Nyasaland, 1962; Commonwealth Fund Fellowship, Harvard and Huntington Library, 1957–58; Alexander von Humboldt Fellowship, Göttingen, 1964–65. Governor of Harrow Sch., 1962– . *Publications*: contrib. Essays in Modern English Church History in Memory of Norman Sykes, ed G. V. Bennett and J. D. Walsh, 1966; Political Ideas, ed David Thomson, 1966, pbk edn 1969; Studies in Richard Hooker, ed W. Speed Hill, 1972; *contrib*. Harvard Theological Rev., Jl of Eccles. Hist., Jl of Theological Studies, Studies in Church Hist., Trans of Cambridge Bibliographical Soc. *Address*: Dept of Ecclesiastical History, Univ. of London King's College, Strand, WC2R 2LS.

Carl, George Edmund; Lecturer in History, University of Bristol, since 1969; *b* 1937. BSc Southwest Missouri State Coll. 1960 (magna cum laude), MA Univ. of Calif. at Berkeley 1962, PhD Tulane Univ. 1968. Instr of History, Fla State Univ., 1965–66; Asst Prof. of History, Ga State Univ., 1966–68; Lectr in History, Univ. of the WI (Barbados), 1968–69. *Publications*: contrib. Boletin Historico (Venezuela). *Address*: Dept of History, Univ. of Bristol, Bristol BS8 1TH.

Carlebach, Dr Julius; Reader in Sociology, University of Sussex, since 1974; *b* 1922; *m*; two *s*. MLitt Cantab, DPhil Sussex, DipSoc London, Dip CrimCantab; Lectr in Education, Bristol, 1966–68; Lectr in Sociology, Sussex, 1968–74. Sub-Dean, School of African and Asian Studies; Chm., Graduate Division-Sociology. *Publications*: The Jews of Nairobi, 1962; Juvenile Prostitutes in Nairobi, 1962; The Future of Youth Aliyah, 1968; Caring for Children in Trouble, 1970; Karl Marx and the Radical Critique of Judaism (forthcoming); Promiscuous Puritans: Difficult Adolescent Girls in Residential Care (forthcoming). *Address*: Arts Bldgs, Univ. of Sussex, Falmer, Brighton BN1 9RH.

Carmichael, Dr William Fleming; Senior Lecturer, Department of Architecture, Heriot-Watt University, since 1967; *b* 1923; *m* 1953; three *d*. PhD Heriot-Watt 1973; MICE 1953,

MIMunE 1948. *Address*: Dept of Architecture, Heriot-Watt Univ., Edinburgh.

Carnall, Geoffrey Douglas; Reader, Department of English Literature, University of Edinburgh, since 1969; *b* 1927; *m* 1962; one *s* two *d*. BA Oxford, 1948 (1st cl. English Lang. and Lit.), MA 1952, BLitt 1953. Lectr in English, The Queen's Univ. of Belfast, 1952–60; Lectr in English Lit., Univ. of Edinburgh, 1960–65; Sen. Lectr, 1965–69. *Publications*: Robert Southey and his Age; 1960; Robert Southey, 1964, 2nd edn 1971; *contrib*. Rev. of Engl. Studies, Victorian Studies. *Address*: Dept of English Literature, Univ. of Edinburgh, Edinburgh EH8 9YL.

Carnochan, Prof. Jack; Professor of Phonetics, Department of Phonetics and Linguistics, School of Oriental and African Studies, University of London, since 1972, Reader 1964–72; *b* 1918; *m* 1941; four *s* one *d*. BA London 1939 (2/1 French), DipEd Cambridge 1943; Chm., Linguistics Assoc. of GB, 1968–71; Mem., Council, Philolog. Soc. Special Lectr in Phonetics, SOAS, 1943–45; Lectr in Phonetics, SOAS, 1945–56; Sen. Lectr, 1956–64. *Publications*: (with B. Iwuchuku) An Igbo Revision Course, 1963; *contrib*. African Lang. Studies, Bull. SOAS, Jl of African Lang., Trans Philolog. Soc. *Address*: School of Oriental and African Studies, Univ. of London, WC1E 7HP.

Carr, Prof. (Albert) Raymond (Maillard); Warden of St Antony's College, Oxford, since 1968 (Sub-Warden, 1966–68), Fellow since 1964; *b* 1919; *m* 1950; three *s* one *d*. Gladstone Research Exhnr, Christ Church, 1941; Fellow of All Souls' Coll., 1946–53; Fellow of New Coll., 1953–64; Prof. of History of Latin America, Oxford, 1967–68. Dir, Latin American Centre, 1964–68; Chm., Soc. for Latin American Studies, 1966–68; Mem., Nat Theatre Bd, 1968– . Corresp. Mem., Royal Academy of History, Madrid. *Publications*: Spain 1808–1939, 1966; Latin America (St Antony's Papers), 1969; ed, The Republic and the Civil War in Spain, 1971; The Spanish Civil War, 1971; articles on Swedish, Spanish, and Latin American history. *Address*: St Antony's College, Oxford.

Carr, Antony David; Lecturer in Welsh History, University College of North Wales, Bangor, since 1964; *b* 1938; *m* 1962; one *s* one *d*. BA Wales 1959, MA Wales 1963, DAA Wales 1960. *Publications*: *contrib*. Bull. Bd Celtic Studies, History, Welsh History Review. *Address*: Dept of Welsh History, Univ. College of North Wales, Bangor LL57 2DG.

Carr, Dr John Laurence, BA, LèsL, PhD, DipEd; Senior Lecturer, Department of French, Glasgow University, since 1946; *b* 1916; *m* 1944; one *s* one *d*. BA Leeds 1938, DipEd Leeds, 1939, LèsL Paris and Lille 1944, PhD Glasgow 1954. Officier des Palmes Académiques. Lectr, Glasgow, 1946–65; Mem., Glasgow Corp. Cttee for Educl TV, 1966–67. *Publications*: Le Collège des Ecossais à Paris, 1963; ed, Voltaire: Le Philosophe ignorant, 1965; Life in France

under Louis XIV, 1966, pbk edn 1970; France, 1969; Robespierre, 1972; *contrib*. French Studies, Hist. Today, Jl Warburg Inst. *Address*: Dept of French, Glasgow Univ., Glasgow G12 8QQ.

Carr, Michael George; Lecturer in German Language, Language Centre, University of East Anglia, since 1968; *b* 1942; *m* 1971; one *s*. BA Hons Bangor 1965 (cl. I German). Lektor, Univ. Tübingen, 1965–67; Asst Lectr, Sch. of European Studies, UEA, 1967. Asst Dean of Students, 1970–73, Sen. Asst Dean of Students, 1973– , UEA. *Address*: Language Centre, University Plain, Norwich NOR 88C.

Carr, Dr William, BA, PhD, FRHistS, JP; Reader in Modern History, University of Sheffield, since 1970; *b* 1921; *m* 1950; one *d*. BA Birmingham 1948 (1st cl. History), DipEd Birmingham 1949, PhD Sheffield 1955; FRHistS 1970. Asst Lectr in History, Sheffield Univ., 1949–52; Lectr, 1952–63; Sen. Lectr, 1963–70; Chm., Sheffield Univ. Panel on Instruction in Lecturing Techniques, 1969– . Mem., National Health Exec., Sheffield, 1966–71, Sheffield Educ. Cttee, 1968– , Bd of Visitors, Wakefield Prison, 1967– ; JP, City of Sheffield, 1969. *Publications*: Schleswig–Holstein 1815–1848, a Study in National Conflict, 1963; A History of Germany 1815–1945, 1969; Arms, autarky and aggression: Nazi foreign policy 1933–39, 1972. *Address*: Dept of Modern History, Univ. of Sheffield S10 2TN.

Carroll, Dr David Roger, MA, PhD; Reader in English Literature, University of Lancaster, since 1972; *b* 1932; *m* 1956; two *d*. BA Dunelm 1953, MA London 1957, PhD Dunelm 1962. Lectr, UC Sierra Leone, 1957–63; UC Toronto: Lectr, 1963–64; Asst Prof., 1964–67; Assoc. Prof., 1967–70; Prof., 1970–72; Lectr, Univ. Lancaster, 1972–73. *Publications*: Chinua Achebe, 1970; George Eliot: The Critical Heritage, 1971; *contrib*. EC, ELT, MLR, MP, RES, VS. *Address*: Dept of English, Univ. of Lancaster, Bailrigg, Lancaster LA1 4YW.

Carroll, Dr Robert Peter; Lecturer, Department of Hebrew and Semitic Languages; University of Glasgow, since 1970; *b* 1941, *m* 1968; one *s* one *d*. BA Dublin 1962 (1st cl.), MA Dublin 1967, PhD Edinburgh 1967; Mem., Soc. for Old Testament Study. Asst Lectr, Glasgow, 1968–70. *Publications*: *contrib*. Trans Glasgow Univ. Oriental Soc., Vetus Testamentum. *Address*: Dept of Hebrew and Semitic Languages, 3 Southpark Terrace, Glasgow.

Carsaniga, Dr Giovanni; Reader in Italian, School of European Studies, University of Sussex, since 1971; *b* 1934; *m* 1959. DottLett Pisa 1956, DipScNormSup Pisa 1956. Asst Lectr, Birmingham Univ., 1959–61; Lectr, 1961–66; Lectr, Sussex Univ., 1966–71. Chm., ATI, 1971–72. *Publications*: (with A. L. Lepschy) Incontri in Italia, 1968; Geschichte der Italienischen Literatur, 1970; *contrib*. Belfagor, Comp. Lit., Ital. Studies. *Address*: Arts Building, Univ. of Sussex, Falmer, Brighton BN1 9QN.

Carsberg, Prof. Bryan Victor, MSc(Econ), FCA; Professor of Accounting, University of Manchester, since 1969; *b* 1939; *m* 1960; two *d*. MSc(Econ) London 1967; FCA 1960, MRI. Chartered Accountancy practice, Amersham, Bucks, 1962–64; Lectr in Accounting, LSE, 1964–68; Vis. Lectr, Grad. Sch. of Business, Univ. of Chicago, 1968–69. Mem., Res. Cttee, and Mem., Cttee on Develt Policy, Inst. of Chartered Accountants. *Publications:* An Introduction to Mathematical Programming for Accountants, 1969; (ed with H. C. Edey), Modern Financial Management, 1969; (with others), An Introduction to Economics for Engineers, 1969; *contrib.* Jl Accounting Res. *Address:* Dept of Accounting and Business Finance, Faculty of Economic and Social Studies, Univ. of Manchester, Manchester M13 9PL.

Carstairs, Andrew McLaren, MA, BPhil; Senior Lecturer in Economic History, Department of Modern History, University of Dundee, since 1965; *b* 1914; *m* 1949; two *s* one *d*. MA St Andrews 1937 (1st cl. Modern History and Political Economy), BPhil St Andrews. Lectr in Political Economy, Univ. of St Andrews, 1948–51; Lectr in Economic History, 1951–59; Sen. Lectr, 1959–65. Sen. Ad. of Studies, Fac. Soc. Sci. and Lett., 1969–71; Sub-Dean, 1970–71; Hon. Vice-Pres., Scott. Univs Sports Bd, 1967– . *Publications: contrib.* Scott. Jl Pol Econ., Scott. Hist. Rev. *Address:* The Univ., Dundee, DD1 4HN.

Carstairs, Dr George Morrison; Vice-Chancellor, University of York, since 1974; *b* 1916; *m* 1950; two *s* one *d*. MA Edinburgh 1938, MB, ChB Edinburgh 1941, DPM London 1948, MRCP Edinburgh 1947, MD Edinburgh 1959, FRCP Edinburgh 1959. Recognised Teacher, Inst. Psychiatry, London Univ., 1957; Prof. of Psychiatry, Univ. of Edinburgh, 1961–73, teaching: General Psychiatry, Social Psychiatry, Behavioural Science, Culture and Personality. Mem., Royal Commn Medical Educn, 1956–68; Pres., World Fedn Mental Health, 1967–71. *Publications:* The Twice-Born: a Study of a Community of High-caste Hindus, 1957; This Island Now: the 1962 Reith Lectures, 1963; *contrib.* Amer. Jl Psychiatry, Brit. Jl Psychiatry, Brit. Jl Prev. Soc. Med., Brit. Jl Med. Psychol., Nature. *Address:* Vice-Chancellor's House, University of York, York YO1 5DD.

Carsten, Prof. Francis Ludwig, DPhil, DLitt, FBA; Masaryk Professor of Central European History, University of London, since 1961; *b* 1911; *m* 1945; two *s* one *d*. State examination Berlin 1933, DPhil Oxon 1942, DLitt Oxon 1961; FBA. Lectr in Modern History, Westfield Coll., Univ. of London, 1947–60; Reader in Modern History, Univ. of London, 1960–61; Ed. Slav. and E European Rev., 1966– . Mem., Council, Inst. Hist. Res., Univ. of London, 1970– , Council, Institut für Europäische Geschichte, Mainz, 1970– . *Publications:* The Origins of Prussia, 1954, 2nd edn 1968, German edn 1968; Princes and Parliaments in Germany from the Fifteenth to the Eighteenth Century, 1959; ed, The New Cambridge Modern

History, vol. V (1648–1688), 1961; Reichswehr und Politik 1918–1933, 1964, English edn 1966; The Rise of Fascism, 1967, 2nd edn 1970, German edn 1968, Italian edn 1970, Japanese edn 1970, Spanish edn 1971; Revolution in Central Europe 1918–1919, 1972, German edn 1973; *contrib.* EHR, Hist., Slav. and E European Rev., Survey. *Address:* School of Slavonic and East European Studies, Univ. of London, WC1E 7HU.

Carter, Alice Clare, MA; Senior Lecturer, Department of Economic History, London School of Economics, since 1971; *b* 1909; *m* 1935; three *s* one *d*. BA London 1930 (1st cl. History), MA London 1934, Teaching Diploma 1931; FRHistS, EconHistS. Teaching Asst, Bedford Coll., 1934, Westfield Coll., 1935, LSE, 1946, Asst Lectr, 1950, Lectr, 1954, LSE; Fellow, Netherlands Inst. for Adv. Study, 1973–74. *Publications:* The English Reformed Church in Amsterdam in the Seventeenth Century, 1965; The English Public Debt in the Eighteenth Century, 1968; The Dutch Republic in Europe in the Seven Years War, 1971; Neutrality or Commitment? Dutch foreign policy, 1667–1795 (forthcoming); contrib. England and the Netherlands in Europe and Asia, ed Bromley and Kossmann; Studies in Diplomatic History, ed Hatton and Anderson; The Low Countries: handbook for history teachers, 2nd edn; *contrib.* BIHR, CHJ, Economica, Econ. Hist. Rev., ICLQ, Proc. Hug. Soc. L., SCH, TvG, Acta Historiae Neerlandicae, Actes du XIIe Congrès Internat., Comité Internat. des Sciences Historiques. *Address:* Dept of Economic History, London School of Economics, Aldwych, WC2A 2AE.

Carter, Charles Frederick, FBA; Vice-Chancellor, University of Lancaster, since 1963; *b* 1919; *m* 1944; one *s* two *d*. Hon. DEconSc NUI, FBA 1970. Lectr in Statistics, Univ. of Cambridge, 1945–51; Fellow of Emmanuel Coll., 1947–51 (Hon. Fellow, 1965–); Prof. of Applied Economics, The Queen's Univ., Belfast, 1952–59; Stanley Jevons Prof. of Political Economy and Cobden Lectr, Univ. of Manchester, 1959–63. Chm., Schools' Broadcasting Coun., 1964–71; Chm., NW Economic Planning Coun., 1965–68; Sec.-Gen., Royal Econ. Soc., 1971– ; Chm., Centre for Studies in Social Policy, 1972– ; Mem., Coun. for Scientific and Industrial Res., 1959–63; Mem., Commn on Higher Educn, Republic of Ireland, 1960–67; Mem., Heyworth Cttee on Social Studies, 1963; Mem., Adv. Coun. on Technology, 1964–66. Vice-Pres., WEA; Dir, Friends' Provident and Century Life Office. Jt Editor: Jl of Indus. Econs, 1955–61; Econ. Jl, 1961–70. Hon. Mem., Royal Irish Academy; Trustee, Joseph Rowntree Meml Trust, 1966; Trustee, Sir Halley Stewart Trust, 1969. *Publications:* The Science of Wealth, 1960; (with W. B. Reddaway and J. R. N. Stone) The Measurement of Production Movements, 1948; (with G. L. S. Shackle and others) Uncertainty and Business Decisions, 1954; (with A. D. Roy) British Economic Statistics, 1954; (with B. R. Williams) Industry and Technical Progress, 1957; Investment in Innovation, 1958; Science in Industry, 1959; (with D. P. Barritt) The Northern Ireland Problem, 1962, 2nd

114

edn 1972; Wealth, 1968; (with G. Brosan and others) Patterns and Policies in Higher Education, 1971; On Having a Sense of All Conditions, 1971; (with J. L. Ford et al.) Uncertainty and Expectation in Economics, 1972; *contrib.* articles in Econ. Jl, etc. *Address*: Univ. House, Bailrigg, Lancaster LA1 4YW.

Carter, Francis William; Joint Hayter Lecturer in the Geography of Eastern Europe, University College London and School of Slavonic and East European Studies, since 1967; *b* 1938. BA Hons Sheffield 1960, DipEd Cambridge 1961, MA LSE 1967. Mem., Inst. of Brit. Geographers, FRGS, FRAS. Res. Asst, Geog. Dept, LSE, 1963–65; Lectr, Kings Coll., London, 1965–67. Treas. Assoc. of Univ. Teachers (UCL) Br.), 1970–72. *Publications*: Dubrovnik (Ragusa): a classic city-state, 1972; *contrib.* Econ. Hist. Rev. Geografiska Annaler, Tijd. E. S. Geog., L'information géographique, East European Qly, Slavonic and E European Rev., Geography, Revue géog. de l'est, Annales de géographie, etc. *Address*: Dept of Geography, Univ. College, Gower Street, WC1E 6BT.

Carter, Prof. Harold; Gregynog Professor of Human Geography, Department of Geography, University College of Wales, since 1969; *b* 1925; *m* 1952. BA Wales 1949, MA Wales 1951. Lectr, 1949, Sen. Lectr, 1966, Dept of Geography, UCW Aberystwyth; Dean, Faculty of Arts, 1965–67. *Publications*: The Towns of Wales: A study in urban geography, 1965; The Study of Urban Geography, 1972; ed jtly, Geography at Aberystwyth, 1969; ed (with W. K. D. Davies), Urban Essays: studies in the geography of Wales, 1970; *contrib.* Trans Inst. of British Geographers, Economic Geography. *Address*: Dept of Geography, Univ. College of Wales, Llandinam Building, Penglais, Aberystwyth, Cards, Wales.

Carter, Jean, BA, BLitt; Senior Lecturer, Geography Department, University of Manchester, since 1969; *b* 1921. BA Hons Manchester 1942 (1st cl. Geog.), BLitt Oxon 1950. Res. Asst, AERI, Oxford Univ., 1950–51; Asst Lectr, 1951–54, Lectr, 1954–69, Geog. Dept, Univ. of Manchester; Lecturer: Univ. of Ibadan, Nigeria, 1954–55; Univ. of Singapore, 1956–57. Cartographer, Hydrographic Dept, Admiralty, 1942–47. *Publications*: *contrib.* Jl Tropical Geog., IBG Trans. *Address*: Dept of Geography, Univ. of Manchester, Manchester M13 9PL.

Carter, Dr Jennifer J.; Senior Lecturer in History, University of Aberdeen, since 1970; *b* 1933. BA London 1954 (Hons History), PhD London 1958. Tutorial Res. Fellow, Bedford Coll., London, 1957–58; Lectr, Makerere Coll., Univ. of E Africa, 1958–62; Lectr, Univ. of Aberdeen, 1963–70. Warden of Johnston Hall, Univ. of Aberdeen, 1968– ; Mem., Aberdeen Univ. Court, 1969–73, Broadcasting Council for Scotland, 1972– . *Publications*: contrib. Britain After the Glorious Revolution, ed G. Homes, 1969; *contrib.* EHR. *Address*: Johnston Hall, College Bounds, Old Aberdeen AB9 2TT.

Carter, Dr (Joan) Hazel, MA, PhD; Reader in Bantu Languages, Department of Africa, School of Oriental and African Studies, University of London, since 1971; *b* 1928; *m* 1953; one *s* one *d*. BA Oxon 1950, MA Oxon 1954, PhD London 1971; Mem., African Studies Assoc. of UK, Linguistics Assoc. of GB, Philolog. Soc. Lectr, SOAS, Univ. of London, 1954–57 and 1961–71. *Publications*: ed, H. W. Chitepo: Soko Risina Musoro, 1958; Notes on the Tonal System of Northern Rhodesian Plateau Tonga, 1962; Syntax and Tone in Kongo, 1973; *contrib.* African Lang. Studies, Jl African Lang., Jl Folklore Inst., Bull. SOAS. *Address*: Dept of Africa, School of Oriental and African Studies, Univ. of London, WC1E 7HP.

Carter, Prof. Michael P., BA, PhD; Professor of Sociology, since 1970, and Head of the Department of Sociology, since 1972, King's College, University of Aberdeen; *b* 1929; *m* 1953; one *s* two *d*. BA Nottingham 1952 (Hons Econ. and Sociology), PhD Edinburgh 1969; Mem., British Sociological Assoc.; Mem., Assoc. Social Anthropologists. Res. Asst, Nottingham Univ., 1952–54; Res. Associate, Birmingham Univ., 1957–58; Sen. Res. Worker, Sheffield Univ., 1958–63; Lectr in Social Anthropology, Edinburgh Univ., 1963–70; Prof. of Sociology, Univ. of Sierra Leone (Fourah Bay Coll.), 1968–70. *Publications*: (with Pearl Jephcott) The Social Background of Delinquency, 1954; Home, School and Work, 1962; Education, Employment and Leisure, 1963; Into Work, 1966, repr. 1969, 1971; *contrib.* Sociological Rev. *Address*: Dept of Sociology, King's College, Univ. of Aberdeen.

Carter, Peter Basil; Fellow of Wadham College, Oxford, since 1949; *b* 1921; *m* 1960 (widower). BA Oxon 1941 (1st cl. Juris.), MA 1946, BCL Oxon 1949 (1st cl.), Vinerian Scholar; Barrister at Law (Middle Temple, 1947). Wadham Coll.: Dean, 1954–56; Sec. to Gov. Body, 1961–65; Sen. Bursar, 1965– ; Chm., Bd of Fac. of Law, Oxforc Univ., 1967–69; Vis. Prof., Univ. of Melbourne, 1953; New York Univ., 1961 and 1969; Osgoode Hall Law Sch., 1971 and 1973; Canada Commonwealth Vis. Fellow, 1970; Jt Editor, Int. and Comp Law Qly, 1951– ; JP, 1959– . *Publications*: (with Z. Cowen) Essays on the Law of Evidence, 1956; *contrib.* Ann. Survey of Commonwealth Law, Law Qly Rev., Int. and Comp. Law Qly, Brit. Ybk of Internat. Law. *Address*: Wadham College, Oxford.

Carter, Dr Robert Lewis; Senior Lecturer, Department of Industrial Economics, University of Nottingham, since 1973; *b* 1932; *m* 1954; one *s* two *d*. BSc(Econ) London 1961, DPhil Sussex 1968; FCII. Brighton Coll. of Technology (now Brighton Polytechnic), 1963–69; Lectr, Univ. of Nottingham, 1969. Asst Insurance Manager, The Dunlop Co. Ltd, 1957–63. *Publications*: Essays in the theory and practice of pricing, 1967; Economics and Insurance, 1972; Handbook of Insurance, 1973; *contrib.* Jl Chart. Ins. Inst., Jl Risk and Ins. *Address*: Dept of Industrial Economics, Univ. of Nottingham, Nottingham NG7 2RD.

115

Carter, Thomas Albert; Director, Language Centre, since 1968, and Senior Lecturer, Southampton University, since 1970; *b* 1925; *m* 1952; two *s* one *d*. BA Hons Cantab 1950 (Modern and Medieval Langs), MA Cantab 1953; Lectr, Southampton Univ., 1968–70; Asst Chief Examiner, Internat. Baccalaureate Office, Geneva, 1969– ; Nat. Chm., Audio-Visual Lang. Assoc. of GB, 1971–73; Conference Officer, Jt Council of Lang. Assocs, 1970–73. *Publications:* Notes on French, 1954; Le Français Moderne Books 1–4, 1955–59; Modern Languages Teachers Guide, 1968, 3rd edn 1971; *contrib.* Bull. of the Internat. Baccalaureate, AVLA Jl. *Address:* Language Centre, Univ. of Southampton, Southampton SO9 5NH.

Casey, John; Senior Lecturer in Legal Studies, Heriot-Watt University, Edinburgh, since 1963; *b* 1929. MA, LLB Edinburgh 1952; FIArb 1967; Dip. Comp. Law, London, 1967; Solicitor, 1953. Mem., Senate, 1964–70. Mem., Univ. Examnrs Bd, Inst. Chartered Accountants of Scotland, 1967– ; Ext. Examnr in Commercial Law, Dundee Univ., 1972. *Publications:* Sale of Goods, Hire Purchase and Trade Descriptions, 1970; *contrib.* Scots Law Times. *Address:* Heriot-Watt Univ., Grassmarket, Edinburgh EH1 1HX.

Casey, Prof. Timothy Joseph; Professor of German, University College, Galway, since 1967; *b* 1927; *m* 1955; two *s* two *d*. BA NUI 1947, MA NUI 1949, Drphil Bonn 1953; Qualified Solicitor, 1950, Mem., Mod. Hum. Res. Assoc. Lektor, Frankfurt Univ., 1953–55; Junr Lectr, TCD, 1955–59; Lectr, QUB, 1959–66; Reader, 1966–67. Chm., Nat. Cttee for Mod. Lang. Studies, 1973– . *Publications:* Manshape That Shone: An Interpretation of Trakl, 1964; *contrib.* Expressionismus als Literatur (ed W. Rothe), 1969; *contrib.* Deuts. Viert. Jahrs., Lit. Geistes., Germ. Life Lett., Hermathena, Mod. Lang. Rev. *Address:* Dept of German, Univ. College, Galway.

Cashdan, Asher; Senior Lecturer in Educational Studies, The Open University, since 1970; *b* 1931; *m* 1956; one *s* one *d*. BA Oxford 1954, MA 1958, DipEd 1957, BEd 1958, MEd 1968, QUB; FBPsS 1970. Pinsent-Darwin Student in Mental Pathology, Cambridge Univ., 1960-62; Lectr in Educn of Handicapped Children, Manchester Univ., 1962–70. Pres., UKRA (UK Reading Assoc.), 1974–75. *Publications:* ed, Personality Growth and Learning, 1971; ed, Language and Learning, 1972; *contrib.* BJEP, Br. Jl Med. Psychol., Ed. Res. *Address:* The Open Univ., Walton Hall, Milton Keynes MK7 6AA.

Cassirer, Dr Eva, PhD, FRAS; Senior Lecturer in Logic and Metaphysics, St Andrews University, since 1969 (Lecturer since 1965); *b* 1920. BSc UCLA 1950, BA UCLA 1952, PhD London 1957; FRAS 1953; Mem., Brit. Soc. Philos. Sci., Arist. Soc., Internat. Soc. for Study of Time. Res. Fellow, Birmingham Univ., 1955–57; Lectr in Philosophy, Free Univ., Berlin, 1957–65; Vis. Prof. of Philosophy, Technical Univ. Berlin, 1974. Mem., Cttee, Brit. Soc. Phil.

Sci., 1969–72. *Publications:* trans., B. Russell: My Philosophical Development (into German: Der Monat), 1959; *contrib.* Procs Arist. Soc., Brit. Jl Phil. Science, Philos. Qly, Studium Generale. *Address:* Dept of Logic and Metaphysics, The Univ., St Andrews, Fife KY16 9AJ.

Castein, Hanne Clara, Dr phil; Lecturer in German, German Department, Goldsmiths' College, University of London, since 1969; *b* 1941. Dr phil Univ. of Freiburg/Breisgau 1967. *Publications:* Die anglo-irische Strassenballade, 1971 (Munich); *contrib.* Year's Work in English Studies. *Address:* Univ. of London, Goldsmiths' College, Lewisham Way, New Cross, SE14 6NW.

Castell, John Henry Fellows; Senior Lecturer, Psychology Department, University College of Swansea, since 1970; *b* 1929; *m* 1954; one *s* two *d*. BA London 1952 (2nd cl. Psychol.), Dip Psych London 1953; ABPsS. Mem., BPsS Divns, Clinical and Educl and Child Psych., 1959– . Lectr, Univ. Coll. Swansea, 1964–70. Psychologist, HM Prison Commn, 1953–57, Sen. Psychologist, 1957–58; Sen. Psychologist, Little Plumstead Hosp., 1958–62, Princ. Psychologist, 1962–64. Mem., Council, BPsS, 1967–70; Sec., BPsS Welsh Branch, 1966–70; Chm., Welsh Branch, BPsS Clin. Divn, 1973– ; Mem., Glantawe Hosp. Mgmt Cttee, 1969– ; Examiner, DHSS Training Council for Teachers of Mentally Handicapped, 1968– . *Publications: contrib.* Brit. Jl Psychiatry, Lancet. *Address:* Psychology Dept, Univ. College, Singleton Park, Swansea SA2 8PP.

Castles, Francis Geoffrey; Lecturer in Political Science, The Open University, since 1970; *b* 1943; *m* 1963; one *s* two *d*. BA Leeds 1964 (Sociol.). Asst Lectr in Politics, Univ. of York, 1965–67; Lectr in Pol Sci., ANU, 1968–70. *Publications:* Pressure Groups and Political Culture, 1967; Politics and Social Insight, 1971; co-ed, Decisions, Organizations and Society, 1971; *contrib.* Pol Studies, Survey, Politics, Australian and NZ Jl of Social., Govt and Opposition. *Address:* The Open Univ., Walton Hall, Milton Keynes MK7 6AA.

Caston, Geoffrey Kemp; Registrar, and Fellow of Merton College, University of Oxford, since 1972; *b* 1926; *m* 1956; two *s* one *d*. MA Cambridge and Oxford 1950, MPA Harvard 1951; Colonial Office, 1951–58; UK Mission to UN, NY, 1958–61; Dept of Techn. Co-op., 1961–64; Asst Sec., Dept of Educn and Sci., 1964–66; Jt Sec., Schs Council, 1966–70; Under Sec., UGC, 1970–72. Chairman: SE Survey Assoc. for Advancement of State Educn, 1962–64; UK Delegn to Commonwealth Educn Conf., Ottawa, 1964; Steering Gp, OECD Workshops on Educl Innovation, Cambridge, 1969, W Germany, 1970, Illinois, 1971; Ford Foundn Anglo-Amer. Primary Educn Project, 1968–70; Library Adv. Council (England), 1973– ; Educn Res. Bd, SSRC, 1973– ; Governor Centre for Educnl Develt Overseas, 1969–70 *Publications: contribs* to educnl jls. *Address:* Clarendon Building, Broad Street, Oxford.

Catani, Remo Damiano; Lecturer in Italian, University College, Cardiff, since 1966; *b* 1938; *m* 1970. MA Glasgow 1961 (1st cl. French and Italian). Res. Fellow, Scuola Normale Superiore, Pisa, 1961–62; Lectr, Bristol Univ., 1964–66. Chief Examiner in Italian, Welsh Jt Educn Cttee, 1971– . *Address*: Dept of Italian, Univ. College, Cardiff CF1 1XL.

Catephores, George; Lecturer in Economics, Department of Political Economy, University College, London, since 1969; *b* 1935; *m* 1964; one *s*. Degree in Law Athens 1958, MSc(Econ) London 1966. Res. Asst, Univ. Coll. London, Dept of Pol Econ., 1966–69. *Publications: contrib.* Oxford Econ. Papers. *Address*: Dept of Political Economy, Univ Coll. London, Gower Street WC1E 6BT

Cato, Brian Hudson; Special Lecturer, Department of Town and Country Planning, University of Newcastle upon Tyne, since 1956; *b* 1928; *m* 1963; one *s*. MA Oxon 1953, LLB London 1952; Barrister of Gray's Inn, 1952. Examiner in Law to Inst. of Landscape Arch., 1960– ; Chm., Mental Health Rev. Trib., Newcastle upon Tyne Reg. Hosp. Bd, 1967. *Address*: Dept of Town and Country Planning, Univ. of Newcastle upon Tyne, Newcastle upon Tyne NE1 7RU.

Caudle, Peter Robert K.; *see* Kaim-Caudle.

Cavanagh, Dr Bernard Michael; John Buchanan Lecturer in Modern Languages (Esperanto), University of Liverpool, since 1972; *b* 1899; *m* 1928; one *s* three *d*. BA Hons Oxon 1922, MA Oxon 1926, DSc London 1928; Sometime Fellow: Chemical Soc., Inst. of Chemistry, 1951 Exhibition Sen. Res. Fellow, 1928. Univ. Demonstrator, Balliol, Oxford, 1923–24; Asst Lectr, Manchester, 1924–28; Sen. Lectr, Melbourne, 1928–34; Res. Fellow, Manchester, 1934–39; Dir of Res., Physical Chemistry, Porton, 1939–46; Principal Scientist, Waltham Abbey, 1946–72. *Publications*: A First Foreign Language for All Mankind, 1971; *contrib.* Jl Chm. Soc., Jl Physiological Chem., Nature, Trans Royal Soc. *Address*: Mod. Languages Bdg, Room 403, Univ. of Liverpool, PO Box 147, Liverpool L69 3BX.

Cave, Dr Terence Christopher, MA PhD; Fellow in French Language and Literature, St John's College, Oxford, since 1972; *b* 1938; *m* 1965; one *s* one *d*. BA Cambridge 1960 (1st cl. Modern and Medieval Languages), MA Cambridge 1964, PhD Cambridge 1966. Asst, Univ. of St Andrews, 1962–63; Lectr, Univ. of St Andrews, 1963–65; Lectr, Univ. of Warwick, 1965–70, Sen. Lectr, 1970–72; Vis. Asst Prof., Cornell Univ., 1967–68; Vis. Fellow, All Souls Coll., Oxford, 1971. *Publications*: Devotional Poetry in France c. 1570–1613, 1969; Metamorphoses spirituelles, 1972; Ronsard the Poet, 1973; *contrib.* French Studies, Forum for Mod. Lang. Studies, Gazette des Beaux-Arts, L'Esprit Créateur, Yale French Studies, etc. *Address*: St John's College, Oxford OX1 3JP.

Caven, Brian McMurrough; Lecturer in Department of Classics, Birkbeck College,

University of London, since 1954; *b* 1921; *m* 1954; four *s* one *d*. BA Cambridge 1947, MA Cambridge 1952. Fellow of King's Coll., Cambridge, 1950–54; Tutor to Faculty of Arts, Birkbeck Coll., 1967– . *Address*: Birkbeck College, Malet Street, WC1E 7HX.

Cavenagh, Prof. Winifred Elizabeth; Professor of Social Administration and Criminology, Faculty of Commerce and Social Science, University of Birmingham, since 1972. BSc(Econ) London 1927, PhD Birmingham 1959, Barrister-at-Law (Gray's Inn) 1964; Nat. Chm., Assoc. Social Workers, 1955–57. Lectr and Sen. Lectr in Social Admin, Birmingham, 1946–72; Vis. Prof. Criminology, Ghana, 1971. JP, Birmingham, 1949– ; Co-opted individual Mem., Birmingham Educn Cttee, 1946–66; Mem.: Lord Chancellor's Standing Adv. Council on Mgts Training, 1965– ; Standing Adv. Cttee on Legal Aid and Advice, 1960–71; Home Off. Probation Adv. Cttee, 1958–67; Independent Mem., five Wages Councils; Assessor, Race Relations Act, 1968; Mem., W Midlands Econ. Planning Council, 1967–71; Mem. Industrial Tribunal, 1973– . *Publications*: Four Decades of Students in Social Work, 1952; The Child and the Court, 1959, 2nd edn as The Child, The Law and the Juvenile Court, 1967; *contrib.* Brit. Jl Criminology, Jl Royal Inst. Public Admin, JoP, etc. *Address*: Faculty of Commerce and Social Science, Univ. of Birmingham, PO Box 363, Birmingham B15 2TT.

Cawkwell, George Law; Fellow, since 1949, and Praelector in Ancient History, University College, Oxford; *b* 1919; *m* 1945; two *s* one *d*. MA New Zealand 1941, BA Oxon 1949, MA Oxon 1953; Mem.: Soc. for Promotion of Hellenic Studies, Soc. for Promotion of Roman Studies, Classical Assoc. Robert Bates Vis. Fellow, Jonathan Edwards Coll., Yale, 1969; William Evans Vis. Prof., Univ. of Otago, NZ, 1971. Mem., Council, Univ. Classical Depts, 1969–71. *Publications: contrib.* Classical Qly, Historia, Jl of Hellenic Studies, Revue des Etudes Grecques. *Address*: University College, Oxford.

Cawley, Prof. Arthur Clare, MA, PhD; Professor of English Language and Medieval English Literature, School of English, University of Leeds, since 1965; *b* 1913; *m* 1939; one *s*. BA London 1934, MA London 1938, PhD London 1953; Mem.: Philological Soc., English Assoc., Mod. Lang. Assoc. of America. Quain Student in English, Univ. Coll., London, 1935–38; Prof., Univ. of Iasi, Rumania, 1939–40; Lectr, Univ. of Cairo, 1941–43; Lectr, Univ. of Iceland, 1945–46; Lectr, Univ. of Sheffield, 1946–47; Lectr and Sen. Lectr, Univ. of Leeds, 1947–59; Darnell Prof. of English, Univ. of Queensland, 1959–65; Distinguished Vis. Prof., Ohio State Univ., 1969–70; Co-editor, Leeds Studies in English, Nos 8 and 9, 1952, Vols 1–5, New Series, 1967–72; Gen. Editor: Leeds Texts and Monographs, Nos 1 (Vols 1, 3–4), 2–4, New Series, 1966–72; Medieval Drama Facsimiles, 1. *Publications*: Everyman and Medieval Miracle Plays, 1965; The Wakefield Pageants in the Towneley Cycle, 1958; Chaucer: The Canterbury Tales, 1958;

George Meriton: A Yorkshire Dialogue, 1959; Everyman, 1961; Pearl and Sir Gawain and the Green Knight, 1962; Chaucer's Mind and Art, 1968; *contrib.* English and Germanic Studies, English Studies, Leeds Studies in English, London Mediaeval Studies, Meanjin, Mod. Lang. Notes, Mod. Lang. Rev., Procs of Leeds Phil. and Lit. Soc., Rev. of English Lit., Rev. of English Studies, Speculum, Trans Yorkshire Dialect Soc. *Address*: English School, Univ. of Leeds, Leeds LS2 9JT.

Cawthra, David Michael; Senior Lecturer in Music, University of Exeter, since 1970; *b* 1933; *m* 1955; one *s* two *d*. BA Oxon 1956 (2nd cl. Music), MA Oxon 1960; LRAM, ARCM, ARCO. Mem., Inc. Soc. Musicians, RCO. Staff Tutor and Lectr in Music, Univ. of Exeter, 1965–67; Lectr, 1967–70. Conductor, Plymouth Symphony Orchestra, 1968– . *Address*: Dept of Music, The Univ., Exeter EX4 4QJ.

Ceadel, Eric Bertrand; University Librarian, University of Cambridge, since 1967; *b* 1921; *m* 1946; three *s*. BA Cantab 1941 (1st cl. Classical Tripos Pts I and II), MA Cantab 1945; Univ. Lectr in Japanese, Cambridge Univ., 1947–67; Fellow, Corpus Christi Coll., Cambridge, 1962– ; Sen. Tutor, 1962–66; Vis. Prof. of Japanese, Univ. of Michigan, 1960, 1961. Mem., Brit. Libr. Organising Cttee, 1971– . *Publications*: Literatures of the East, 1953; Classified Catalogue of Modern Japanese Books in Cambridge University Library, 1962; *contrib.* Asia Major, Bull. SOAS, Class. Qly, Monumenta Nipponica. *Address*: Cambridge Univ. Library, West Road, Cambridge.

Cecil, Robert, CMG; Reader, Department of German, University of Reading, since 1968; *b* 1913; *m* 1938; one *s* two *d*. BA Cambridge 1935, MA Cambridge 1961; Mem.: Royal Inst. of Internat. Affairs; Univ. Assoc. of Contemporary European Studies. Dep. Chm., Graduate Sch. of Contemporary European Studies, 1970–73. Chm., Inst. for Cultural Res., 1971– ; Vice-Chm., European Schs Day, 1968– ; Treasurer, GB–E Europe Centre, 1968– . *Publications*: Levant and other Poems, 1940; Time and other Poems, 1955; Life in Edwardian England, 1969; Myth of the Master Race, 1972, Italian edn 1973; *contrib.* Amer. Herit., Hist. Today, Internat. Affs. *Address*: German Dept, Univ. of Reading, Reading, Berks. RG6 2AH.

Cerny, Philip George; Lecturer in Politics, University of York, since 1970; *b* 1946; *m* 1969; two *s*. BA Kenyon Coll. 1967; Certificat d'Etudes Politiques Paris 1966. Res. Asst in Govt, Univ. of Manchester, 1967–70. *Publications: contrib.* Brit. Jl of Political Sci., Govt and Opposition, Rev. of Politics. *Address*: Dept of Politics, Univ. of York, Heslington, York YO1 5DD.

Chadwick, Dr Anthony Samuel; Staff Tutor in Philosophy, Department for External Studies, University of Oxford, since 1957; *b* 1915; *m* 1942; one *s* one *d*. BD 1942, BA 1947 London, (1st cl. Hons Philos.), MA

118

1949, PhD 1952, Columbia. Asst Prof., Princeton Univ., 1951–55. *Address*: Dept for External Studies, Rewley House, Wellington Square, Oxford.

Chadwick, Prof. Charles; Professor of French, University of Aberdeen, since 1968; *b* 1924; *m* 1950. BA Liverpool 1946 (1st cl. French), MA Liverpool 1949, DU Paris 1954. Asst Lectr, Liverpool Univ., 1951–54; Lectr, Liverpool Univ., 1954–62; Sen. Lectr, Liverpool Univ., 1962–66; Reader, Manchester Univ., 1966–68. *Publications*: Etudes sur Rimbaud, 1959; Mallarmé, sa pensée dans sa poésie, 1960; Symbolism, 1971; Verlaine, 1973; ed, Sagesse, 1973; *contrib.* Fr. Studies, MLN, MLR, RHLF, RScH, etc. *Address*: Dept of French, The Univ., Aberdeen AB9 1AS.

Chadwick, Prof. George Fletcher, PhD; Professor of Town and Country Planning, University of Newcastle upon Tyne, since 1970; *b* 1923; *m* 1948; one *s* one *d*. BSc Tech Manchester 1943, DipTP Manchester 1946, MA Manchester 1950, PhD Manchester 1959, FRTPI 1943, FILA 1953. Lectr, Univ. of Manchester, 1955–62; Sen. Lectr, 1962–67; Dir of Planning Res., 1967–70; Vis. Lectr and Tutor, Inst. Adv. Architectural Studies, York, 1956–62. Various Local Planning Authorities, 1943–51; Hemel Hempstead New Town, 1951–55; TPI Exam. Bd, 1967–70; UN Technical Assistance Expert, 1970. *Publications*: The Works of Sir Joseph Paxton, 1961; The Park and The Town, 1966; A Systems View of Planning, 1971; *contrib.* TPI Jl, Planning Outlook. *Address*: Dept of Town and Country Planning, The Univ., Newcastle upon Tyne NE1 7RU.

Chadwick, Very Rev. Dr Henry, DD, MusB, FBA; Dean of Christ Church, Oxford, since 1969; *b* 1920; *m* 1945; three *d*. BA, MusB 1941, MA Cantab 1945, DD 1957, Hon. DD Glasgow 1957, Uppsala 1967, Yale 1970; FBA 1960, Mem., American Acad. of Arts and Sciences, 1970. Fellow, Queen's Coll., Cambridge, 1946–58 (Hon. Fellow, 1958); Regius Prof. of Divinity, Oxford Univ., 1959–69; Gifford Lectr, St Andrews, 1962–64; Forwood Lectr, Liverpool Univ., 1961; Birkbeck Lectr, Cambridge 1965; Ed., Jl Theological Studies, 1954– ; Hon. Fellow, Magdalene Coll., Cambridge, 1962. Delegate, OUP, 1960– ; Curator, Bodleian Library; Spalding Trustee. *Publications*: Origen contra Celsum, 1953, 2nd edn 1965; Alexandrian Christianity, 1954; Lessing's Theological Writings, 1956; The Sentences of Sextus, 1959; Early Christian Thought and the Classical Tradition, 1966; The Early Church, 1967; Die Kirche in der antiken Welt, 1972; *contrib.* Harvard Theol Rev., Jl Theol Studies; Reallexikon für Antike und Christentum. *Address*: The Deanery, Christ Church, Oxford.

Chadwick, Dr John, FBA; Reader in Greek Language, Faculty of Classics, University of Cambridge, since 1966; *b* 1920; *m* 1947; one *s*. BA Cantab 1946, MA Cantab 1949, Hon. Dr Athens 1958, Hon. Dr Brussels 1968, Hon. LittD TCD 1971; FBA 1967. Asst Lectr, Cambridge Univ., 1952–54; Lectr, 1954–66;

P. M. Laurence Reader in Classics, 1969– ; Collins Fellow, Downing Coll., Cambridge, 1960– . Mem.: Adv. Revision Bd, Swedenborg Soc., 1945– . *Publications*: (with W. N. Mann) trans., Hippocrates: The Medical Works, 1950; (with M. Ventris) Documents in Mycenaean Greek, 1956; The Decipherment of Linear B, 1958, 2nd edn 1970 (trans. in German, Italian, Swedish, Dutch, Danish, Japanese, Greek, Polish, Spanish and French); ed (with L. R. Palmer) jt ed., Proceedings of the Cambridge Colloquium on Mycenaean Studies, 1966; ed jtly, The Knossos Tablets, 2nd edn 1959, 3rd edn 1964, 4th edn 1971; *contrib*. Annual Brit. Sch. Athens, Camb. Ancient Hist. vol. II, Glotta, Jl Hellenic Studies, Minos. *Address*: Downing College, Cambridge CB2 1DQ.

Chadwick, Prof. William Owen, DD, FBA; Regius Professor of Modern History, University of Cambridge, since 1968; Master of Selwyn College, Cambridge, since 1956; *b* 1916; *m* 1949; two *s* two *d*. BA Camb 1939, MA Camb 1942, BD Camb 1951, DD Camb 1955, Hon. DD St Andrews 1960, Oxford 1973, Hon. DLitt Kent 1970; FBA 1962, FRHistS. Fellow, Trinity Hall, Cambridge, 1947–56; Hulsean Lectr, 1949–50; Birkbeck Lectr in Ecclesiastical History, 1956; Dixie Prof. of Ecclesiastical History, 1958–68. Vice-Chancellor, Cambridge Univ., 1969–71. *Publications*: John Cassian, 1950, 2nd edn 1968; The Founding of Cuddesdon, 1954; From Bossuet to Newman, 1957; Western Asceticism, 1958; The Mind of the Oxford Movement, 1960; Victorian Miniature, 1960; The Reformation, 1964, 6th edn 1973; The Victorian Church, vol. 1, 1966, 3rd edn 1971, vol. 2, 1969, 2nd edn 1972; *contrib*. Jl Eccles Hist., Jl Theol. Studies. *Address*: Faculty of History, West Road, Cambridge.

Chaffin, Dr Christopher Ellis; Lecturer in Classical and Medieval Studies, University of Sussex, since 1967; *b* 1937; *m* 1968. BA Cantab 1960 (1st cl. History), MA Cantab 1964, DPhil Oxon 1970. Asst Lectr, Univ. of Sussex, 1965–67. *Publications*: Church and Society in North Italy in the Age of Alaric (forthcoming); *contrib*. Rivista di Letteratura Italiana, Studia Patristica. *Address*: School of European Studies, Arts Building, Univ. of Sussex, Falmer, Brighton BN1 9RH.

Chalk, Derrick W.; *see* Wilbie-Chalk.

Chalklin, Christopher William; Lecturer in Economic History, University of Reading, since 1965; *b* 1933; *m* 1959; one *s* two *d*. BA New Zealand 1953, BA Oxon 1955, BLitt Oxon 1960. Sen. Fellow, Univ. of Wales, 1963–65. *Publications*: Seventeenth-Century Kent, 1965. *Address*: Dept of History, Univ. of Reading, Whiteknights, Reading, Berks RG6 2AH.

Challis, Dr Christopher Edgar, BA, PhD; Lecturer, School of History, University of Leeds, since 1967; *b* 1939; *m* 1967. BA Bristol 1961, PhD Bristol 1968; FRHistS. Asst Lectr, Leeds Univ., 1964–67. *Publications*: ed (with C. J. Black), Henry VIII to his Ambassadors at the Diet of Ratisbon, 1968; *contrib*. Econ. Hist. Rev. ,Eng. Hist. Rev., Brit. Numis. Jl.

Address: School of History, The Univ., Leeds LS2 9JT.

Chalmers, Walter Reid, MA; Senior Lecturer in Classics, since 1972, and Warden of Sherwood Hall, University of Nottingham, since 1964; *b* 1922; *m* 1948; one *s* two *d*. MA Edinburgh 1947 (1st cl. Classics). Asst Lectr in Classics, Univ. of Nottingham, 1948; Lectr, 1949–72. *Publications*: Chapter in, Roman Drama, ed, Dudley and Dorey, 1965; *contrib*. Class. Qly, Class. Rev., Phronesis, Rhein. Mus. *Address*: Dept of Classics, Univ. of Nottingham, Nottingham NG7 2RD.

Chaloner, Dr William Henry; Reader in Modern Economic History, Department of History, University of Manchester, since 1962; *b* 1914; *m* 1949; three *s*. BA Manchester 1936 (Hons History), MA Manchester 1937, PhD Manchester 1939, Vice-Pres., Newcomen Soc. for Study of Hist. of Engineering and Technology. Asst Lectr, 1945; Lectr, 1946–49; Sen. Lectr, 1949–62. Hon. Ed., Trans Lancashire and Cheshire Antiq. Soc. *Publications*: Social and Economic Development of Crewe, 1780–1923, 1951; Vulcan Boiler: one hundred years of engineering and insurance, 1959; National Boiler, 1864–1964, 1964; (with A. E. Musson) Industry and Technology, 1963; *contrib*. J. Rylands Libr. Bull. *Address*: Dept of History, Arts Building, Univ. of Manchester, Manchester M13 9PL.

Chamberlain, James Patrick; College Lecturer, Department of Psychology, University College Dublin, since 1971; *b* 1934; *m* 1967; one *s* two *d*. BA UCD 1959, Higher DipEd UCD 1960, BSocSc UCD 1963, DipPsych UCD 1966, MPsychSc UCD 1970; Mem.: BPsS, 1967; Psychol. Soc. Ireland, 1970. Tutor, 1966; Asst Lectr, 1967–71. *Address*: Room D 415, Dept of Psychology, Univ. College, Dublin 4.

Chamberlain, Dr Muriel Evelyn, MA, DPhil; Senior Lecturer in History, University College of Swansea, University of Wales, since 1972 (Lecturer 1958–72); *b* 1932. BA Oxon 1954 (1st cl. History), MA Oxon 1958, DPhil Oxon 1961. Temp. Asst Lectr, Royal Holloway Coll., London, 1955, 1957–58. Chief examiner, A Level History, WJEC. *Publications*: The New Imperialism, 1970; Britain and India, 1974; The Scramble for Africa, 1974; *contrib*. Morgannwg, Welsh Hist. Rev., Eng. Hist. Rev., Jl Brit. Studies, Glamorgan Historian. *Address*: Dept of History, Univ. College of Swansea, Singleton Park, Swansea SA2 8PP.

Chambers, David Sanderson; Lecturer in Renaissance Studies, Warburg Institute, University of London, since 1969; *b* 1934; *m* 1973. BA Oxon 1956, DPhil Oxon 1962. Lectr in Mediaeval History, Univ. of St Andrews, 1963–69. *Publications*: Cardinal Bainbridge in the Court of Rome, 1965; Materials for West African History in Italian Archives (with J. R. Gray), 1965; Vatican Office Registers 1534–1549, 1966; The Imperial Age of Venice, 1970; Patrons and Artists in The Italian Renaissance, 1970; *contrib*. Bull. Inst. Hist. Res., Stud. Med. and

119

Renaiss. Hist. *Address*: The Warburg Institute, Woburn Square, WC1H 0AB.

Chambers, Prof. William Walker, MBE, PhD, MA, LèsL; William Jacks Professor of German, since 1954, Vice-Principal since 1972, University of Glasgow; *b* 1913; *m* 1947; one *s* one *d*. MA Glasgow 1937 (1st cl. French and German and 1st cl. Germanic Language), PhD Munich 1939, LèsL Paris 1940; FEIS, FAncMonSoc, FRHS. Asst Lectr and Lectr in German, Leeds, 1946–50; Prof., Mod. Languages, Univ. Coll. of N Staffs, 1950–54. Pres., AUT, 1962–63; Dean, Faculty of Arts (Glasgow), 1961–64; Mem., Univ. Court, 1967–71; Vice-Chm, Governors, Jordanhill Trg Coll., 1962–66; Mem.: Commonwealth Scholarship Commn, 1961–64; Standing Cttee on Student Gts, 1955–58. *Publications*: ed, Paul Ernst: Selected Short Stories, 1953; ed, Paul Ernst: Erdachlte Gespräche, 1958; ed, F. de la Motte Fouqué: Undine, 1956; (with J. Wilkie), A Short History of German Language, 1970; *contrib.* MLR, German Life and Letters. *Address*: Dept of German, Univ. of Glasgow, Glasgow G12 8QQ.

Champernowne, Prof. David Gawen, MA, FBA; Professor of Economics and Statistics, Cambridge University, since 1970; Fellow of Trinity College, Cambridge, since 1959; *b* 1912; *m* 1948; two *s*. BA Cantab 1934, MA Cantab 1938; FBA 1970. Asst Lectr, LSE, 1936–38; Fellow, King's Coll., Cambridge, 1937–48; Univ. Lectr in Statistics, Cambridge, 1938–40; Dir, Oxford Univ. Inst. of Statistics, 1945–48; Fellow, Nuffield Coll., Oxford, 1945–59; Prof. of Statistics, Oxford Univ., 1948–59; Reader in Economics, Cambridge Univ., 1959–70. Asst in Prime Minister's statistical dept, 1940–41; Asst Dir of Programmes, Min. of Aircraft Production, 1941–45. Editor, Econ. Jl, 1971– . *Publications*: Uncertainty and Estimation in Economics (3 vols), 1969; The Distribution of Income between Persons, 1973. *Address*: Trinity College, Cambridge.

Chandaman, Prof. Cecil Douglas, PhD; Professor of History, St David's University College, Lampeter, since 1962; *b* 1916; *m* 1944; two *d*. BA London 1939 (1st cl. History), PhD London 1954; FRHistS. Derby Student, London, 1939–40; Asst Lectr, Glasgow Univ., 1947–48; Lectr, 1948–60; Sen. Lectr, 1960–62. Pres., W Wales Br. of Historical Assoc., 1967–69. *Publications*: The English Public Revenue 1660–88, 1975; *contrib.* British Government and Administration, ed Hearder and Loyn, 1974. *Address*: Dept of History, St David's Univ. College, Univ. of Wales, Lampeter, Dyfed SA48 7ED.

Chandler, Edmund Richard; Academic Registrar (Administration), Brunel University, since 1966; *b* 1923; *m* 1953; one *d*. BA London 1946 (English), MA 1954. *Publication*: Pater on Style, Anglistica Series, 1958. *Address*: Brunel Univ., Uxbridge, Mddx UB8 3TH.

Chandler, Frank Walter; Deputy Director, Department of Extra Mural Studies, University of Manchester, since 1963; *b* 1909; *m* 1937, 1971; two *s* one *d*. BA London 1934, MA London 1936. Staff-Tutor Librarian, Extra Mural Dept, Manchester Univ., 1947–63. *Address*: Univ. of Manchester, Manchester M13 9PL.

Chandler, Prof. Tony John, MSc, PhD; Professor of Geography, Department of Geography, University of Manchester, since 1973; *b* 1928; *m* 1954; one *s* one *d*. BSc London 1949 (1st cl. Geography and Mathematics), AKC London 1949, DipEd London 1950, MSc London 1956, PhD London 1964; FRGS, FRMetS. Lectr, Birbeck Coll., London, 1952–56; Lectr, Univ. Coll., London, 1956–65; Reader, 1965–69; Prof. of Geography, 1969–73. Mem., Ed. Bd, Weather, 1958–61; Mem., Council, Roy. Met. Soc., 1961–64; Rapporteur on Urban Climates, World Met. Org., 1965–69; Consultant, AWRE, 1965–69; Sec. Roy. Met. Soc., 1969– ; Mem., Roy. Soc. Cttee on Human Biomet. In Urban Env., 1972– . Mem., Royal Commn on Environmental Pollution, 1973– . *Publications*: The Climate of London, 1965; The Air Around Us, 1968; Modern Meteorology and Climatology, 1972; *contrib.* Geogl Jl, Geog., Weather, Meteorol Mag., Bull. Amer. Meteorol Soc. *Address*: School of Geography, Univ. of Manchester, Manchester M13 9PL.

Chang, Dr Hsin-Chang; University Lecturer in Chinese Studies, Faculty of Oriental Studies, Cambridge University, since 1959; Fellow of Wolfson College, Cambridge, since 1972; *b* 1923; *m* 1944; one *s* one *d*. BA Univ. of Shanghai 1942, PhD Univ. of Edinburgh 1949, MA Univ. of Cambridge 1960. Lectr in English, Provisional Univ. of Nanking, 1945–46; Lector in Chinese, Univ. of Cambridge, 1953–55; Lectr in English, Univ. of Malaya, Singapore and Kuala Lumpur, 1956–59; Vis. Prof. of Comparative Literature, National Univ. of Taiwan, 1967. *Publications*: Allegory and Courtesy in Spenser: A Chinese View, 1955; Chinese Literature: Popular Fiction and Drama, 1973; *contrib.* Asia Major. *Address*: Faculty of Oriental Studies, Sidgwick Avenue, Cambridge.

Channon, Derek F.; Senior Research Fellow, Manchester Business School, University of Manchester, since 1970; *b* 1939; *m* 1963; one *d*. BSc London 1960, Dip. BA Manchester 1967, DBA Harvard 1970. Ford Foundn European Doctoral Fellow, Harvard Business School, 1968–70, and concurrently Lectr in Marketing, Manchester Bus. Sch., Univ. of Manchester. Dir, Evode Holdings Ltd, 1974– ; Mem. Council, Case Clearing House of GB and Ireland, 1972– . *Publications*: The Strategy and Structure of British Enterprise, 1973; *contrib.* Jl of Bus. Policy, Direction et Gestion, Ind. Mkting Management. *Address*: Manchester Bus. Sch., Booth Street West, Manchester.

Chaplin, Peggy Elaine; Lecturer in French, University of Keele, since 1970; *b* 1943. BA Exeter 1965, MA Exeter 1968. Tutor in French, Exeter Univ., 1967–68 and 1969–70; Professeur étranger, Faculté de Brest, 1968–

69. *Publications*: ed, Pierre Du Ryer: Themistocle, 1972. *Address*: Dept of French, Univ. of Keele, Keele, Staffs ST5 5BG.

Chaplin, Robin A., MA; Senior Lecturer in Midland History, Extramural Department, University of Birmingham, since 1973; *b* 1931; *m* 1955; three *s* one *d*. BA Oxon 1953, MA Oxon 1957. Staff Tutor for S Warwicks, 1962-73. Chm. of Exec. Standing Conf. for Local History, 1971-72, 1972-73, 1973-74. Review editor: Midland History Jl; Local Historian. *Publications*: *contrib*. Warwickshire History, Local Historian, Trans Birmingham Archaeol Soc. *Address*: Extramural Dept, Univ. of Birmingham, Birmingham B15 2TT.

Chaplin, Stephen; painter; Senior Lecturer in Art History, University of Leeds, since 1973 (Lecturer, 1961-73); *b* 1934; *m* 1961; one *s* one *d*. Dipl. in Fine Art London 1955 (Slade Diploma), BA London 1958 (Hons). Asst Librarian, Courtauld Inst. of Art (Univ. of London), 1958-59; Admin. Asst, Chelsea Sch. of Art, 1959-61; Head of Art History and Complementary Studies Section, Leeds Coll. of Art, 1961-66. *Publications*: *contrib*. Apollo. *Address*: Dept of Fine Art, The Univ., Leeds LS2 9JT.

Chapman, Prof. Brian; Professor of Government, University of Manchester, since 1961; *b* 1923; *m* 1972. MA Oxon 1947, DPhil Oxon 1951, MA(Econ) Manchester. Nuffield Student, 1948-49; Res. Assoc. Lectr, Sen. Lectr, Univ. of Manchester; Vis. Prof at several European Univs, 1949-59; Foundation Prof. of Government and Dir, Public Admin programme, Univ. of West Indies, 1960-61; Dean, Faculty of Econ. and Social Studies, Univ. of Manchester, 1967-70; Vis. Prof., Queen's Univ., Kingston, Ont, 1972. Jt Editor, Minerva Series; Mem., Council, Manch. Business Sch.; Mem., Court Cranfield Inst. Technology; Mem. Court, Univ. of Manchester. *Publications*: French Local Government, 1953; The Prefects and Provincial France, 1954; (jtly) The Life and Times of Baron Haussmann, 1956; The Profession of Government, 1959; British Government Observed, 1963; The Police State, 1970; *contrib*. various contribs learned jls. *Address*: Dept of Government, Univ. of Manchester, Manchester M13 9PL.

Chapman, David; Lecturer, Department of French, University of Stirling, since 1968; *b* 1939; *m* 1968; one *d*. BA Keele 1963. Asst Lectr, Magee Univ. Coll., 1966. *Publications*: (with R. Sibley) French Civilization: a select bibliography, 1971. *Address*: Dept of French, Univ. of Stirling, Stirling FK9 4LA.

Chapman, Elizabeth Kate; Lecturer and Tutor to Advanced Course for Teachers of Visually Handicapped, University of Birmingham School of Education, since 1969; *b* 1925. BA Leeds 1947 (Hons English), DipEd Leeds 1948, Diploma of Coll. of Teachers of the Blind, 1961 (Arthur Pearson Award); Member: CTB; NAEPS. Member: Exec., CTB; Examination Bd, CTB; Liaison Cttee, CTB and NAEPS; Examination Bd for Overseas Training, CTB; Examiner, Royal Coll. of Preceptors; Editor, The Teacher (Jl of CTB). *Publications*: Modern Trends (reprint from Modern Ophthalmology, vols 3 and 4), 2nd edn 1972; Partially-Sighted Children (a survey of their needs and existing provisions), NAEPS 1972; 24 selected articles, CTB, 1970. *Address*: Univ. of Birmingham School of Education, PO Box 363, Birmingham B15 2TT.

Chapman, Graham Peter, MA, PhD; Lecturer, Department of Geography, Cambridge University, since 1974; Fellow, Downing College, Cambridge, since 1973; *b* 1944; *m* 1970; one *s* one *d*. BA Cambridge 1965 (1st cl. Hons), PhD Cambridge 1970; Mem., Inst. of British Geographers. Dept of Geog., Edinburgh, 1968-69; Asst Lectr, Cambridge, 1969-74. *Address*: Dept of Geography, Downing Place, Cambridge.

Chapman, John Walter Mann, MA, DPhil; Lecturer in International Relations, School of African and Asian Studies, University of Sussex, since 1968; *b* 1939; *m* 1964; one *s* one *d*. MA St Andrews 1961, DPhil Oxford 1967; Assoc. Mem., Royal Inst. of Internat. Affairs and Internat. Inst. for Strategic Studies. Jun. Res. Fellow, St. Antony's Coll., Oxford, 1966-67; Sub-Dean, Sch. of African and Asian Studies, Univ. of Sussex, 1970-73. Assoc. Fellow, Inst. for Develt Studies, 1972- ; Vis. Fellow, Seishin Joshi Univ., Tokyo, 1974. *Address*: Arts Building, Univ. of Sussex, Falmer, Brighton, Sussex BN1 9RH.

Chapman, Nigel Vance; Tutor, School of Industrial Design, Royal College of Art, since 1968; *b* 1927; *m* 1960; two *d*. BArch McGill 1951, DesRCA 1954; MSIA 1970. Mem., Design Cttee, Plastics Inst., 1970- ; Mem. Adv. Panel on Art and Design, Hatfield Polytechnic. *Publications*: Heating, 1966, rev. edn 1971. *Address*: Sch. of Industrial Design, Royal College of Art, Kensington Gore, SW7 2EU.

Chapman, Raymond, MA; Senior Lecturer in English, London School of Economics, University of London, since 1968; *b* 1924; *m* 1964; one *s* one *d*. BA Oxon 1945, MA Oxon 1959, MA London 1947; Asst Lectr, London Sch. of Econs, 1948-51, Lectr, 1951-68, Warden of Passfield Hall, 1950-61. Mem., Council of Religious Drama Soc., 1956-62; Mem., Governing Body, Battersea Grammar Sch., 1956-65; Governing Body, Mayfield Sch., 1965-71. *Publications*: A Short Way to Better English, 1956; ed, Religious Drama, 1959; The Ruined Tower, 1961; The Loneliness of Man, 1963; The Victorian Debate, 1968; Faith and Revolt, 1970; Linguistics and Literature, 1973; *contrib*. Church Qly Rev., Mod. Language Rev., Notes and Queries, Theology, Rev. of Eng. Studies. *Address*: Language Studies Dept, London School of Economics, WCA2 2AE.

Chapman, Dr Richard A., BA, MA, PhD, AMBIM; Reader in Politics, University of Durham, since 1971; *b* 1937. BA Leicester 1961, MA Carleton 1962; PhD Leicester 1966; AMBIM 1966; Member: Royal Inst. of Public Administration, Political Studies

Assoc. of UK, British Inst. of Management. Asst in Political Science, Carleton Univ., 1961–62; Asst Lectr in Politics, Leicester Univ., 1962–63; Leverhulme Lectr in Public Administration, Liverpool Univ., 1963–68; Senior Lectr in Local Govt and Administration, Birmingham Univ., 1968–71. Civil Servant, 1953–61. *Publications*: Decision Making, 1968; The Higher Civil Service in Britain, 1970; ed with A. Dunsire, Style in Administration, 1971; ed and contrib., The Role of Commissions in Policy Making, 1973; Teaching Public Administration, 1973; *contrib*. Administration, Public Administration, Rev. Politics. *Address*: Dept of Politics, Univ. of Durham, 23–26 Old Elvet, Durham DH1 3HY.

Chapman, Dr Stanley David; Pasold Reader in Textile History, Department of Economic and Social History, University of Nottingham, since 1973 (Lecturer, 1968–73); *b* 1935; *m* 1960; two *s*. BSc Econ, Hons II, London 1956, Graduate Cert. in Educn Manchester 1957, MA Econ. History Nottingham 1960, PhD London 1966. Lectr in Mod. Econ. and Social History, Univ. of Aston in Birmingham, 1966–68. *Publications*: The Early Factory Masters, 1967; (with J. D. Chambers) The Beginnings of Industrial Britain, 1970; ed, The History of Working Class Housing: a Symposium, 1971; The Cotton Industry in the Industrial Revolution, 1972; Jesse Boot of Boots The Chemists, 1973; *contrib*. Business Hist., Econ. Hist. Rev., Midland Hist., Trans Thoroton Soc., Textile Hist. *Address*: Dept of Economic and Social History, Univ. of Nottingham, Nottingham NG7 2RD.

Chapple, Prof. John Alfred Victor, MA; Professor of English, University of Hull, since 1971; *b* 1928; *m* 1955; four *s* one *d*. BA London 1953, MA London 1955. Asst, UCL, 1953–55; Res. Asst. Yale Univ., 1955–58; Asst, Aberdeen Univ., 1958–59; Asst Lectr, Manchester Univ., 1959–61; Lectr, Manchester Univ., 1961–67; Sen. Lectr, Manchester Univ., 1967–71. *Publications*: Documentary and Imaginative Literature 1880–1920, 1970; ed jtly, The Letters of Mrs Gaskell, 1966, American edn 1967; *contrib*. Q. Bull. (John Rylands Libr.), etc. *Address*: Dept of English, Univ. of Hull, Hull HU6 7RX.

Charlton, Prof. Donald Geoffrey; Professor of French, and Chairman, Department of French Studies, University of Warwick, since 1964; *b* 1925; *m* 1952; one *s* two *d*. BA Cambridge 1948 (1st cl. Mod. Languages), MA Cambridge 1953, PhD London 1955. Mem., Soc. French Studies. Assoc. Prof. of French. Lectr and Sen. Lectr, Univ. of Hull, 1949–64; Vis. Prof., Univ. of Toronto, 1961–62; Vis. Prof., Univ. of California, Berkeley, 1966. Mem., Advisory Editorial Bd, European Studies Rev. *Publications*: Positivist Thought in France during the Second Empire, 1852–1870, 1959; Secular Religions in France, 1815–1870, 1963, 2nd edn 1970; ed, Companion to French Studies, 1972; ed, Balzac and the Nineteenth Century, 1972; *contrib*. French Studies, Forum for Mod. Language Studies, Univ. Toronto Qly. *Ad-*

122

dress: Dept of French Studies, Univ. of Warwick, Coventry CV4 7AL.

Charlton, Prof. John Maxwell Town, MA, FSA; Professor of Classics, Department of Classics, University of Keele, since 1953; *b* 1917; *m* 1942; one *s* one *d*. BA Manchester 1939 (1st cl. Classics), MA Manchester 1940, BA Cantab 1947 (1st cl. Classical Tripos); FSA. Lectr, Reading Univ., 1947–50; Reader, Univ. Coll. of N Staffs, 1950–53. Military service 1939–46, commissioned RA. *Publications*: *contrib*. classical jls and local archaeol. jls. *Address*: Dept of Classics, Univ. of Keele, Keele, Staffs ST5 5BG.

Charlton, Prof. Kenneth, MA, MEd; Professor of the History of Education and Head of the Department of Education, King's College, London, since 1972; *b* 1925; *m* 1953; one *s* one *d*. MA Glasgow 1949, MEd Glasgow 1953; Teacher's Cert., 1950. Lectr in Educn, UC of N Staffs, 1954–64; Sen. Lectr, Univ. of Keele, 1964–66; Prof. of Hist. and Philosophy of Educn, Univ. of Birmingham, 1966–72. *Publications*: Recent Historical Fiction for Children, 1960, 2nd edn 1969; Education in Renaissance England, 1965; *contrib*. Educnl Rev., Brit Jl Educnl Psych., Year Bk of Educn, Jl Hist. of Ideas, Brit. Jl Educnl Studies, Int. Rev. of Educn, Trans Hist. Soc. Lancs and Cheshire, Irish Hist. Studies, Northern Hist. *Address*: Faculty of Education, University of London, King's College, The Strand, WC2R 2LS.

Charlton, William Edward Walmesley; Lecturer in Philosophy, University of Newcastle upon Tyne, since 1968; *b* 1935; *m* 1959; four *s* one *d*. BA Oxon 1959, MA Oxon 1963, BPhil Oxon 1963. Asst in Humanity, Glasgow, 1959–61; Jun. Lectr in Philosophy, Trinity Coll., Dublin, 1963–66, Lectr, 1966–68. *Publications*: (with A. Reynolds) Arthur Machen, a biography, 1963; Aristotle's Physics, Bks I and II, 1970; Aesthetics, an Introduction, 1970. *Address*: Dept of Philosophy, Univ. of Newcastle upon Tyne, Newcastle upon Tyne NE1 7RU.

Charsley, Simon Robert; Lecturer in Sociology, University of Glasgow, since 1968; *b* 1939; *m* 1968. BA Cantab 1962, MA Cantab 1965, MA(Econ) Manchester 1965, PhD Manchester 1969. Asst Res. Fellow, Univ. of E Africa, Makerere, 1965; SSRC Fellow, Manchester, 1967. *Publications*: The Princes of Nyakyusa, 1969; *contrib*. E African Geog. Rev., Uganda Jl, Africa. *Address*: Dept of Sociology, Univ. of Glasgow, Glasgow G12 8RT.

Charvet, John Christopher Raymond; Lecturer in Government, London School of Economics, since 1965; *b* 1938; *m* 1963; one *s*. BA Cantab 1960, BPhil Oxon 1963, MA Cantab 1963. *Publications*: *contrib*. Jl Polit. Studies, Mind. *Address*: London School of Economics, Houghton Street, Aldwych, WC2A 2AE.

Chaudhuri, Dr Kirti N., BA, PhD; Reader in Economic History of Asia, Department of History, School of Oriental and African Studies, University of London, since 1974 (Lecturer, 1963–74); *b* 1934; *m* 1961; one *s*. BA London 1959 (1st cl. History), PhD London 1961; FREconS, Mem., Econ. Hist. Soc. Res. Fellow, SOAS, Univ. of London, 1961–63. *Publications*: The English East India Company: the study of an Early Joint-Stock Company 1600–1640, 1965; The Economic Development of India under the East India Company 1814–1858, 1971; *contrib.* Econ. Hist. Rev., Mariner's Mirror, Jl of Mod. Asian Studies, Indian Econ. and Social Hist. Rev. *Address*: Dept of Hist., Sch. of Oriental and African Studies, Univ. of London, WC1E 7HP.

Chazan, Maurice, MA, FBPsS; Reader in Education, Department of Education, University College of Swansea, since 1971; *b* 1922; *m* 1945; two *d*. BA Wales 1943 (1st cl. Latin), MA Birmingham 1951, BA London 1956, DipEd Wales 1944; Training as educational psychologist, 1949–50, FBPsS. Lectr in Educational Psychology, Univ. Coll. of Swansea, 1960–64; Sen. Lectr, 1964–71. Mem.: Welsh Jt Educn Cttee, 1968–71; NFER Bd of Management, 1970–71. *Publications*: ed, Reading Readiness, 1970; ed (with G. Downes), Compensatory Education and the New Media, 1971; (with Alice Laing and Susan Jackson) Just Before School, 1971; ed, Aspects of Primary Education, 1972; ed, Compensatory Education, 1973; ed, Education in the Early Years, 1973; (jtly) The Practice of Educational Psychology (forthcoming); *contrib.* Brit. Jl Educnl Psych., Educnl Res., Jl Child Psych. Psychiat., Amer. Jl Ment. Defic., Rem. Educn, Comm. Dev. Jl. *Address*: Hendrefoilan, Swansea SA2 7NB.

Checkland, Prof. Sydney George, MA, MCom, PhD; Professor of Economic History, University of Glasgow, since 1957; *b* 1916; *m* 1942; two *s* three *d*. BCom Birmingham 1941 (1st cl.), MCom Birmingham 1947, PhD Liverpool 1952; Assoc., Canadian Bankers Assoc., 1937. Lectr, then Sen. Lectr in Econ. Science, Univ. of Liverpool, 1946–53; Lectr in Hist., Cambridge, 1953–57; Mem., Inst. for Adv. Study, Princeton, 1958, 1964; Senate Assessor, Univ. Court, Glasgow, 1971–73; Chm., Jt Council (staff–students), 1971–72. Mem.: E Kilbride Develop. Corp., 1965–69; Scott. Rec. Adv. Council, 1966– ; Council, Econ. Hist. Soc., 1957– ; Econ. Hist Cttee, SSRC, 1968–71; Chm., Nat. Register Archives (Scotland), 1971– ; Bd Management, Urban Studies; Vice-Chm., Business Archives Council (Scotland). *Publications*: The Rise of Industrial Society in England 1815–1885, 1964; The Mines of Tharsis; Roman, French and British Enterprise in Spain, 1967; The Gladstones, a family biography, 1764–1851, 1971; *contrib.* Econ. Hist. Rev., Scott. Jl Polit. Economy. *Address*: 5, The Univ., Glasgow G12 8QQ.

Chedzoy, Olaf Barrington, BSc, FSS, FBCS; Lecturer in Mathematics, University of Bath, since 1965; *b* 1929; *m* 1952; one *s* one *d*. BSc Bristol 1950; FSS 1965, FBCS 1959. Lectr in Mathematics (special interest in teaching Statistics and Mathematics to Social Scientists), Bristol Coll. of Science and Technology, subseq. Univ. of Bath, 1965– . *Publications*: An Introduction to Elliott 803 Autocode, 1963–66; (with S. E. Ford) Pro-

gramming by Case Studies, an Algol Primer, 1970; *contrib.* Technology and Society. *Address*: School of Mathematics, Univ. of Bath, Bath BA2 7AY.

Cheetham, Juliet; Lecturer in Applied Social Studies, Department of Social and Administrative Studies, Oxford University, since 1968; *b* 1939; *m* 1965; one *s* one *d*. MA St Andrews 1959 (English and History), Dip. in Social and Admin. Studies Oxford 1960; Mem., Brit. Assoc. Social Workers. Tutor in Applied Social Studies, Oxford Univ., 1965–68. Probation Off., 1961–65. Mem., Hunt Cttee on Immigration and Youth Service, 1966–67; Youth Service Develop. Council, 1968–70; Lane Cttee of Enquiry into Working of Abortion Act, 1971– . *Publications*: Social Work with Immigrants, 1972; *contrib.* Brit. Jl of Social Work, Race. *Address*: 28 Little Clarendon Street, Oxford.

Cheney, John Colin, BA; Lecturer in Physical Education, Birmingham University, since 1966; *b* 1934; *m* 1959; two *d*. BA Bristol 1955 (1st cl. Hons English and Philosophy); Dip. Loughborough Coll. of Educn 1958 (1st cl. Hons Physical Educn); Teaching Cert. 1958, Nottingham Univ. *Address*: Dept of Physical Education, Univ. of Birmingham, Birmingham B15 2TT.

Cheng, Prof. Bin, LLD, Lic.-en-Dr; Professor of Air and Space Law in the University of London, since 1967, and Dean, Faculty of Laws, University College, London, 1971–73; *b* 1921; *m* 1950; one *s* one *d*. Lic.-en-Dr Geneva 1944, PhD London 1950, LLD London 1966; Corresp. Mem., Inst. Aeronaut. Interplan. Law, Buenos Aires, Inst. Air Space Law, Nat. Univ. of Cordoba, Argentina, Brazilian Soc. Aeronaut. Space Law, Venezuelan Soc. Aeronaut. Space Law. Asst Lectr, UCL, 1950–53, Lectr, 1953–62; Reader in Internat Law, Univ. of London, 1962–67. Vice-Dean, Fac. of Laws, Univ. Coll., London, 1969–71; Chm., Air Law Cttee, Internat. Law Assoc., 1965– ; Hon. Sec., Brit. Br., Internat. Law Assoc., 1960-67; Mem., Council, 1956– , and Bd of Studies, 1954– , London Inst. World Aff. *Publications*: General Principles of Law as applied by International Courts and Tribunals, 1953; The Law of International Air Transport, 1962; *contrib.* Aeronaut. Jl, Curr. Legal Prob., Indian Jl Internat. Law, Internat. Comp. Law Qly, Internat. Law Assoc. Rep., Jl Droit Internat. (Clunet), Jl Air Law Comm., Jl Royal Aeronaut. Soc., Law Soc. Gaz., Solicitor, Trans Grotius Soc., World Aff., YBk Air Space Law, YBk World Aff. *Address*: Faculty of Laws, Univ. College London, 4–8 Endsleigh Gardens, WC1H 0EG

Cheng, Dr Te-k'un, BA, MA, PhD; Reader in Chinese Archaeology, University of Cambridge, since 1966; *b* 1907; *m* 1934; three *s*. BA Yenching 1930, MA Yenching 1931, PhD Harvard 1941; Academician, China Acad., 1966. Res. Fellow, Harvard-Yenching Inst., Peking, 1931–33, Harvard, 1938–41; Asst Prof., Amoy Univ., 1933–36; Prof. of Chinese History, West China Union Univ., 1941–47; Lectr, Univ. of Cambridge, 1951–66; Fellow, Wolfson Coll., Cambridge,

123

1966– ; Vis. Prof., Princeton Univ., 1961, Univ. of Malaya, 1962–63; 1966–67, Nanyang Univ., Singapore, 1968. Dir, Univ. Museum, Chengtu, 1941–47; Dir, Inst. of Comp. Cultures, Chengtu, 1945–46; Adv., Provincial Govt, Szechwan, 1944–46; Counsellor, Generalissimo's Headquarter, Chengtu, 1944–46; Ed., Jl Amoy Univ., 1934–36, Jl West China Border Res. Soc., 1944–47. *Publications*: A brief History of Chinese Mortuary Objects, 1942; Index to Shui-ching-chu, 1934; A History of Ancient Szechwan, 1946; Archaeological Studies in Szechwan, 1957; Archaeology in China, I. Prehistoric China, 1959; Supplement, 1966; II. Shang China, 1960; III. Chou China 1963; Archaeology in Sarawak, 1969; Jade Flowers and Floral Patterns in Chinese Decorative Art, 1969; T'ang Ceramic Wares of Ch'ang-sha, 1970; The Inconstancy of Character Structure in Chinese Writing, 1971; The Study of Ceramic Wares in South-east Asia, 1972; *contrib*. Amoy Univ. Jl, Antiquity, Artibus Asiae, Asia Major, China Qly, Harvard Jl of Asiatic Studies, Museum of Far Eastern Antiqu. Bull., Oriental Art, Oriental Ceramic Soc., Trans Royal Asiatic Soc., NCB Jl, W China Border Res. Soc. Jl, Yenching Jl Chinese Studies. *Address*: Faculty of Oriental Studies, Sidgewick Avenue, Cambridge.

Cherns, Prof. Albert Bernard, MA, FBPsS; Professor of Social Sciences, and Head of Department of Social Sciences, Loughborough University, since 1966; *b* 1921; *m* 1946; one *s* one *d*. MA Cambridge 1949; FBPsS 1960. Nuffield Unit on Res. into Problems of Ageing, Univ. of Cambridge, 1947–48; Dept of Scientific Adviser, Air Min., Chief Res. Off., Trg Comd, RAF, 1949–59; Head of Human Sciences Section, DSIR; Head of Human Sciences Div., SRC; Sec., Govt. Cttee on Soc. Studies (Heyworth Cttee); Scientific Sec., SSRC, 1959–66. Mem., Council, Tavistock Inst., Brit. Assoc.; Governor, Ashorne Hill Coll.; Actg Chm., Internat. Council for Quality of Working Life. *Publications*: Organization for Change, in, Manpower Research, ed N. A. B. Wilson, 1969; Social Sciences and Policy (Sociological Review Monograph No 16), 1970; Applied Sociology, in, Sociology: An Outline for the Intending Student, ed G. D. Mitchell, 1970; (with Clark and others) Structures and Aggregates: Two Complementary Paradigms, in, Manpower and Management Sciences, ed Bartholomew and Smith, 1971; ed (with Wilson and Mitchell) Social Science Research and Industry, 1971; ed (with Sinclair and Jenkins) Social Science and Government: Policies and Problems, 1972; (with Clark and Jenkins) Action Research and the Development of the Social Sciences, in, Symposium on Action Research, ed A. W. Clark, 1972/3; Social Sciences in Six Countries, 1973; (with L. E. Davis) The Quality of Working Life, 2 vols, 1974; *contrib*. Bull. Brit. Psych. Soc., Hum. Relat., Internat. Soc. Sci. Jl, Occup. Psychol., Personnel Rev., Social Sci. Inf., Sociol. Rev. *Address*: Dept of Social Sciences, Univ. of Loughborough, Loughborough LE11 3TU.

Cherry, Gordon E.; Senior Lecturer and Deputy Director, Centre for Urban and Regional Studies, University of Birmingham, since 1968; *b* 1931; *m* 1957; one *s* two *d*. BA London 1953 (Geog.); FRTPI, FRICS. Univ. of Birmingham, 1968– ; Asst Dean (Clerical and Technical Services), Faculty of Commerce and Social Science, 1973– . Vice-Chm., Regional Studies Assoc., 1970–71; Mem. Council, Royal Town Planning Inst., 1971– ; Chm., Sociological Surveys Study Group, Sports Council, 1972– . *Publications*: Town Planning in its Social Context, 1970, 2nd edn 1973; (with T. L. Burton) Social Research Techniques for Planners, 1971; Urban Change and Planning, 1972; The Evolution of British Town Planning, 1974; ed, Urban Planning, 1974. *Address*: Selly Wick House, Selly Wick Road, Birmingham B29 7JF.

Chester, Sir (Daniel) Norman, CBE, MA; Warden of Nuffield College, Oxford, since 1954; *b* 1907; *m* 1936. BA Manchester 1930, MA 1933, MA Oxon 1946; Hon. LittD Manchester 1968. Rockefeller Fellow, 1935–36, Lectr in Public Administration, 1936–45; Manchester Univ. Mem. of Economic Section, War Cabinet Secretariat, 1940–45; Official Fellow of Nuffield College, 1945–54. Editor, Jl of Public Admin, 1943–66; Mem., Oxford CC, 1952– ; Chm., Oxford Centre for Management Studies; Chm., Police Promotion Examinations Bd, 1969; Chm., Cttee on Association Football, 1966–68; Vice-Pres. (ex-Chm.), Royal Inst. of Public Admin; Past Pres., Internat. Political Science Assoc. Corresp. Mem., Acad. des Sciences Morales et Politiques, Institut de France, 1967. *Publications*: Public Control of Road Passenger Transport, 1936; Central and Local Government: Financial and Administrative Relations, 1951; The Nationalised Industries, 1951; ed, Lessons of the British War Economy, 1951; ed, The Organization of British Central Government, 1914–56; (with Nona Bowring) Questions in Parliament 1962; *contrib*. articles in learned jls. *Address*: Nuffield College, Oxford.

Chester, Robert Louis Charles; Senior Lecturer in Sociology, Department of Social Administration, University of Hull, since 1973; *b* 1929; *m* 1960; one *s* one *d*. Cert. in Social Studies Southampton 1957 (with Distinction); BSc (Econ) Southampton 1959 (1st cl.). Asst Lectr in Sociology, Univ. of Hull, 1959–61, Lectr, 1961–73. Warden, Needler Hall, 1964– ; Mem., Bd of Visitors, Hull Prison, 1968–73; Mem. Council, Eugenics Soc., 1970– . *Publications*: Towards a Satisfactory Way of Academic Life, 1968; contrib. Anarchy and Culture, ed D. Martin, 1969; *contrib*. Brit. Jl Sociol., Sociol., Jl Biosoc. Sci., Soc. and Econ. Admin, Brit. Jl Soc. Work, Postgrad. Med. Jl, Med. Gynaecol. and Sociol., Brit. Jl Prev. Soc. Med., Jl Marr. Fam., Bull. Eugen. Soc., Jl Psychosom. Res. *Address*: Dept of Social Adminstration, The Univ., Hull, Yorks HU6 7RX.

Chester, Prof. Theodore Edward, CBE; Professor of Social Administration, University of Manchester, since 1955; *b* 1908; *m* 1940; one *s*. Dr jur Vienna 1930; MA Manchester 1958; Dip. in Commerce Vienna

1929. Various Deptl Ctees of Dept Health and Dept of Educn and Science, 1956– . *Publications*: Hospitals and the State, 1956; Graduate Education for Hospital Administration in the USA, 1969; The British National Health Service, 1969; The Swedish Health Services System, 1971; *contrib*. Acta Hospitalia, Amer. Hosp. Admin, Austrian Hosp. *Address*: Dept of Social Administration, Univ. of Manchester, Manchester M13 9PL.

Chesterman, Michael Rainsford; Senior Lecturer in Law, University of Warwick, since 1973; *b* 1940; *m* 1970; one *s*. BA (Hons) Sydney 1961, LLB Sydney 1965, LLM London 1966. Solicitor, NSW, 1965; called to Bar, Lincoln's Inn, 1969. Asst Lectr in Law, KCL, 1966, Lectr, 1967–71, 1972–73; Vis. Sen. Lectr in Law, Univ. of Nairobi, 1971–72. *Publications*: Conflict of Laws, 1969; Specialist Editor, Gore-Browne on Companies, 42nd edn, 1972; *contrib*. Internat. and Comparative Law Qly, MLR. *Address*: Sch. of Law, Univ. of Warwick, Coventry CV4 7AL.

Chesterman, Sir Ross, PhD; Warden of Goldsmiths' College, University of London, since 1953; *b* 1909; *m* 1938. BSc London 1930 (1st cl. Hon Chemistry), MSc London 1932, PhD London 1937, DIC London 1931. Chief Inspector of Schs, Worcestershire, 1948–53; Vice-Master, Coll. of Craft Educn, 1960; Chm., Adv. Cttee on Teacher Training, ODA, 1971. *Publications*: Chapters in numerous pubns; *contrib*. Jl Chem. Soc., Nature, London Inst. Educn Bull., etc. *Address*: Goldsmiths' College, New Cross, SE14 6NW.

Chew, Dr Geoffrey Alexander; Lecturer, Department of Music, University of Aberdeen, since 1972; *b* 1940; *m* 1967; one *s*. BMus London 1961, MusB Cambridge 1964, PhD Manchester 1968, MA Cambridge 1970; ARCM 1959, FRCO 1964, Mem., Royal Music Assoc. Lectr in Music, Univ. of the Witwatersrand, 1967–70; Res. Asst, Univ. of Aberdeen, 1970–72. *Publications*: *contrib*. Haydn-Studien, Music and Letters. *Address*: Dept of Music, Univ. of Aberdeen, Aberdeen AB9 1AS.

Cheyne, Rev. Prof. Alexander C.; Professor, Ecclesiastical History Department, University of Edinburgh, since 1964; *b* 1924. MA Edinburgh 1946 (1st cl. Hons in History); BLitt Oxford 1954; BD Edinburgh 1956. Asst Lectr in History, Glasgow, 1950–51, Lectr, 1951–53; Lectr in Ecclesiastical History, Edinburgh, 1958–64. *Publications*: introduction to Tulloch: Movements of Religious Thought (repr.); *contrib*. New Coll. Bull., Rec. Scott. Ch. Hist. Soc., Scott. Jl Theol., Theol. Today. *Address*: New College, Mount Place, Edinburgh.

Cheyne, Dr George James Gordon; Senior Lecturer in Spanish and Latin American Studies, University of Newcastle upon Tyne, since 1970; *b* 1916; *m*; one *s* one *d*. BA London 1959; PhD Newcastle upon Tyne 1968; Consejero correspondiente de la Institución Fernando el Católico (CSIC), Zaragoza, 1964; Mem., Anglo-Catalan Soc. Soc. for Latin American Studies. Chm., North East Dyslexia Assoc. Part-time Lectr, KCL, 1960–61; Lectr, King's Coll., Newcastle, now Univ. of Newcastle upon Tyne, 1961–70. *Publications*: Joaquin Costa, el gran desconocido. Esbozo biográfico, 1972; A Bibliographical Study of the Writings of Joaquin Costa (1846–1911), 1972; *contrib*. Bull. Hispanic Studies, Bull. Hispanique, Anales galdosianos, Vida Nova. *Address*: Dept of Spanish and Latin American Studies, The Univ., Newcastle upon Tyne NE1 7RU.

Child, Dr Dennis; Senior Lecturer in Psychology of Education, Postgraduate School of Studies in Research in Education, University of Bradford, since 1973; *b* 1932; *m* 1954; one *s* one *d*. Teachers' Certif. in Educn St John's Coll. 1957, BSc London 1962 (2nd cl. hons), MEd Leeds 1968 (with dist.), PhD Bradford 1973; ABPsS 1971. Lectr in Psychology of Educn, Bradford Univ. 1967–73; Vis. Research Prof., Univ. of Illinois, 1972. University Representative: Committee A of UCET; Nat. Council for Adult Educn. *Publications*: jtly, Initiating Research in Colleges of Education, 1968; The Essentials of Factor Analysis, 1970; Psychology and the Teacher, 1973; with R. B. Cattell, Motivation and Dynamic Structure, 1974; *contrib*. British Jl Educn. Psychol., Bulletin (BPS), Brit. Jl Soc. Clin. Psychol., Durham Research Rev., Educn in Chemistry, Educational Research, Education, Educn for Teaching, Educational Review, Internat. Jl of Educ. Sci., Research in Educn, Soc. Rev., Univ. Qly Educn. *Address*: School of Education, Univ. of Bradford, Bradford BD7 1DP.

Child, Douglas; Lecturer, Department of Architecture, University of Sheffield, since 1968; *b* 1929; *m* 1952; four *s* three *d*. MA Sheffield 1974. FRICS 1954. *Publication*: Geometric Economics (forthcoming). *Address*: Dept of Architecture, Arts Tower, Sheffield S10 2TN.

Childs, Christopher Edward Nicholas; University Librarian, Brunel University, since 1967; *b* 1929; *m* 1955; two *s* one *d*. BA Oxon 1952. Asst Keeper, Dept of Printed Books, British Museum. *Address*: Brunel Univ., Kingston Lane, Uxbridge, Mddx UB8 3TH.

Childs, Dr David Haslam, BSc(Econ), PhD; Senior Lecturer in Politics, University of Nottingham, since 1971; *b* 1933; *m* 1964; two *s*. BSc(Econ) London 1956, PhD London 1962. Tech. Coll., 1965–66; Lectr, Nottingham Univ., 1966–71. TV Documentaries, 1961–64. *Publications*: From Schumacher to Brandt: The Story of German Socialism 1945–65, 1966; East Germany, 1969; Germany since 1918, 1971; Marx and the Marxists: An Outline History of Practice and Theory, 1973; *contrib*. Contemp. Rev., Internat. Aff., Pol Studies, Times Ed. Supp., Geog., Ger. Life and Letters, Guardian, World Today. *Address*: Dept of Politics, The Univ., University Park, Nottingham NG7 2RD.

Chilton, Dr Cecil William, MA, PhD; Reader in Classics, University of Hull, since

1971; *b* 1914; *m* 1942; one *s* one *d*. BA Cantab 1936 (1st cl. Class. Trip. Pts I & II), MA Cantab 1946, PhD Hull 1963; FRNS. Asst. Lectr, Univ. Coll., Hull, 1947–49, Lectr, 1949–54; Lectr, Hull Univ., 1954–62, Sen. Lectr, 1962–71; Special Lectr, Univ. Coll., Toronto, 1963–64. Mem., Council, Hellenic Soc., 1970–73. *Publications*: Diogenis Oenoandensis Fragmenta, 1967; Diogenes of Oenoanda: a Translation and Commentary, 1971; trans. Festugière: Epicurus and His Gods, 1955; Malraux: Saturn – An Essay on Goya, 1957; Wildenstein: The Paintings of Fragonard, 1960; *contrib.* Jl of Rom. Studies, Phronesis, Amer. Jl of Philol. *Address*: Dept of Classics, The Univ., Hull HU6 7RX.

Chilver, Dr Amos Henry; Vice-Chancellor, Cranfield Institute of Technology, since 1970; *b* 1926; *m* 1959; three *s* two *d*. BSc Bristol 1947, PhD Bristol 1951, MA Cantab 1955, DSc Bristol 1962. MICE 1964, MIStructE 1964, Associate Fellow, RAeS 1966. Asst Lectr, Bristol Univ., 1950–52, Lectr, 1952–54; Demonstrator, Cambridge Univ., 1954–56, Lectr, 1956–58; Fellow, Corpus Christi Coll., Cambridge, 1958–61; Prof. of Civil Engineering, UCL, 1961–69; Dir, Centre for Environmental Studies, 1967–69. Director: De La Rue Ltd; English China Clays Ltd; SKF (UK) Ltd. Member: SRC, 1970– ; ARC, 1972– ; Planning and Transport Res. Adv. Council, 1972– ; CNAA, 1973– . *Publications*: (with J. Case) Strength of Materials, 1959, 2nd edn 1971; (with R. J. Ashby) Problems in Engineering Structures, 1958, 2nd edn 1965; ed, Thin-walled Structures, 1967; *contrib.* Jls of Engrg Instns, Jl of Mechanics and Physics of Solids, Philosophical Trans, Royal Soc. *Address*: Cranfield Inst. of Technology, Cranfield, Bedford MK43 0AL.

Chilver, Elizabeth Millicent, (Mrs R. C. Chilver); Principal of Lady Margaret Hall, Oxford, since 1971; *b* 1914; *m* 1937. Dir, Univ. of Oxford Inst. of Commonwealth Studies. 1957–61; Sen. Res. Fellow, Univ. of London Inst. of Commonwealth Studies, 1961–64; Principal, Bedford Coll., Univ. of London, 1964–71. Journalist, 1937–39; temp. Civil Servant, 1939–45; Daily News Ltd, 1945–47; temp. Principal and Sec., Colonial Social Science Res. Coun. and Colonial Economic Res. Cttee, Colonial Office, 1948–57; Mem., Royal Commn on Medical Educn, 1965–68. Trustee, Brit. Museum, 1970– . Médaille de la reconnaissance française, 1945. *Publications*: articles on African historical and political subjects. *Address*: Lady Margaret Hall, Oxford.

Chilver, Prof. Guy Edward Farquhar; Professor of Classical Studies, University of Kent at Canterbury, since 1964; *b* 1910; *m* 1945, 1973. MA Oxon 1935, DPhil Oxon 1936; Vice-Pres., Soc. for Prom. Rom. Studies. Fellow and Praelector in Ancient History, Queen's Coll., Oxford, 1935–64; Univ. Lectr in Ancient History, 1946–64; Sen. Tutor, Queen's Coll., Oxford, 1948–64; Mem., Hebdomadal Council, Oxford Univ., 1949–64; Dean of Humanities, Univ. of Kent at Canterbury, 1964–74; Dep. Vice-Chancellor, 1966–72; Mem., Kent Educ.

Cttee, 1967–71. *Publications*: Cisalpine Gaul, 1941; trans. and ed, Unesco: History of Mankind, vol. II, 1965; *contrib.* Jl of Rom. Studies, Historia, Classical Rev. *Address*: Eliot College, Univ. of Kent, Canterbury CT1 3PA.

Chisholm, Prof. John Stephen Roy; Professor of Applied Mathematics, University of Kent at Canterbury, since 1965; *b* 1926; *m* 1953; one *s* two *d*. BA Cantab 1948, MA Cantab 1952, PhD Cantab 1952; MRIA 1963; Fellow, Physical Soc. Nuffield Res. Fellow, Glasgow, 1951–54; Lectr in Applied Maths, Cardiff, 1954–60; Sen. Lectr in Applied Maths, Cardiff, 1960–62; Prof of Natural Philosophy, TCD, 1962–65; Distinguished Vis. Prof. of Physics, Texas A. and M. Univ., 1965–66. Res. Assoc., CERN, Geneva, 1962–63. *Publications*: (with A. M. de Borde) An Introduction to Statistical Mechanics, 1956; (with Rosa Morris) Mathematical Methods, 1963; *contrib.* Jl Computational Physics, Jl Mathematical Physics, Nuclear Physics, Nuovo Cimento, Philosophical Mag., Physical Rev., Proc. Cambridge Philosophical Soc., Proc. Roy. Soc. *Address*: Mathematical Institute, The Univ., Canterbury, Kent CT2 7NZ.

Chisholm, Prof. Michael Donald Inglis; Professor of Economic and Social Geography, Department of Geography, University of Bristol, since 1972; *b* 1931; *m* 1959; one *s* two *d*. BA Cambridge 1954, MA Cambridge 1957; Mem., Inst. Brit. Geogrs, Royal Geogr. Soc., Reg. Sci. Assoc., Reg. Studies Assoc., Royal Econ. Soc. Deptl Demonstr, Agric. Econ. Inst., 1954–59; Asst Lectr, then Lectr in Geography, Bedford Coll., Univ. of London, 1960–64. Vis. Sen. Lectr in Geography, Univ. of Ibadan, Nigeria, 1964–65; Lectr in Geography, Univ. of Bristol, 1965–67, then Reader in Economic Geography, 1967–72. Mem. SSRC (Chm. Human Geography Cttee), 1967–72; Local Govt Boundary Commn for England, 1971– . Editor, Hutchinson University Library Geography Section, 1973. *Publications*: Rural Settlement and Land Use: an Essay in Location, 1962, 2nd edn 1968, Japanese edn 1971; Geography and Economics, 1966, 2nd edn 1970, Spanish edn 1969, Japanese edn 1969; Research in Human Geography, 1971; ed (with G. Manners), Spatial Policy Problems of the British Economy, 1971; ed (with A. E. Frey and P. Haggett), Regional Forecasting, 1971; ed, Resources for Britain's Future, 1972; (with P. O'Sullivan) Freight Flows and Spatial Aspects of the British Economy, 1973; (with J. Oeppen) The Changing Pattern of Employment: regional specialisation and industrial localisation in Britain, 1973; ed (with B. Rodgers), Studies in Human Geography, 1973; *contrib.* App. Stat., Geogr Jl, Geography, Oxford Econ. Papers, Progr. in Geography, Urban Studies. *Address*: Dept of Geography, The Univ. of Bristol, Bristol BS8 1TH.

Chitnis, Dr A. C.; Lecturer in History, University of Stirling, since 1968; *b* 1942; *m* 1970; one *s*. BA Hons. Birmingham 1963, MA Kansas 1965, PhD Edinburgh 1968; Mem., Hist. Assoc. Vis. Lectr, Univ. of

California, Santa Barbara and Washington State Univ., Pullman, USA, 1973. *Publications*: *contrib.* Annals of Sci., Enlightenment Essays, Med. Hist. *Address*: Dept of History, The Univ., Stirling FK9 4LA.

Chitnis, Bernice Anne; Lecturer, Department of French, University of Stirling, since 1972; *b* 1942; *m* 1970; one *s*. BA London 1965. Lectr, Univ. of Edinburgh, 1967–72. *Address*: Dept of French, Univ. of Stirling, Stirling FK9 4LA.

Chivite, Manuel F.; *see* Ferrer-Chivite.

Chloros, Prof. Alexander George; Professor of Comparative Law, University of London, King's College, since 1966; *b* 1926; *m* 1965; two *d*. BA Oxon 1951, MA Oxon 1955, LLD London 1972. Mem., Soc. Pub. Teach. of Law, 1951– , UK Cttee on Comp. Law; UK delegate, Coun. of Europe, Sub-Cttee on Fundamental Legal Concepts. Asst. Lectr in Law, Univ. Coll. of Wales, Aberystwyth, 1951–54, Lectr, 1954–59; Lectr in Laws, King's Coll., London, 1959–63; Reader in Comparative Law, King's Coll. 1963–66; Dean, Fac. of Laws, King's Coll., London, 1971– ; Inst. of Comp. Law, Belgrade, 1963–64. Adviser to Seychelles Govt for recodification and reform of Code Napoléon, 1973. *Publications*: Chapter 2, in, Graveson: Law and Society, 1967; Yugoslav Civil Law, 1970; ed, Bibliographical Guide to the Law of the UK, 2nd edn 1972; *contrib.* Acta juridica, Arch. de Philos. de Droit, Internat. and Comp. Law Qly, Mod. Law Rev., Rev. Internationale de Droit Comparé, etc. *Address*: Faculty of Laws, King's College, Strand, WC2R 2LS.

Chown, Dr Sheila Margaret; Reader, Department of Psychology, Bedford College, University of London, since 1973 (Lecturer, 1961–73); *b* 1931; *m* 1954. BScSpec London 1953 (1st Cl.), PhD Liverpool 1957; FBPsS 1969. MRC Unit on occup. aspects of ageing, 1956–60; Mem., Coun., Brit. Psychol Soc., 1963–72; Treas., Brit. Psychol Soc, 1965–67, Sec., 1967–70, Dep. Pres., 1970–72. *Publications*: (with A. Heron) Ageing and the Semi-skilled, 1961; (with A. Heron) Age and Function, 1967; ed, Human Ageing: Selected Readings, 1972; *contrib.* Ann. Rev. Psychol., Brit. Jl Educnl Psychol., Jl Abnorm. Soc. Psychol., Jl Gerontol., Occupat. Psychol, Psychol. Bull. *Address*: Bedford College, Regent's Park, NW1 4NS.

Christian, Harold; Lecturer, Department of Sociology, University of Keele, since 1970; *b* 1938; *m* 1968. BA Leicester 1965, MA Leicester 1967; Cert. of Nat. Council for Training Journalists, 1959; Mem., Brit. Sociol Assoc., BSA, Teachers Section. Tutorial Asst, Leicester Univ., 1965–66, Asst Lectr, 1966–68; Res., LSE, Part-time Lectr, London Univ. Extra-Mural Dept, 1968–70. *Address*: Dept of Sociology, Keele Univ., Keele, Staffs ST55BG.

Christian, Prof. Reginald Frank; Professor of Russian, St Andrews University, since 1966; *b* 1924; *m* 1952; one *s* one *d*. BA Oxon 1949 (1st cl. Russian), MA Oxon1950; Mem., Brit. Univs Assoc. of Slavists (Pres., 1967–70). Lectr, Liverpool Univ., 1950–55; Sen. Lectr, Birmingham Univ., 1956–63; Prof., Birmingham Univ., 1963–66; Vis. Prof., McGill Univ., 1961–62; Exchange Lectr, Moscow, 1964–65. RAF 1943–46 (Aircrew), Commd, 1944; Foreign Office 1949–50 (Brit. Emb., Moscow); Pres., BUAS, 1967–70; Mem., Internat. Cttee Slavists, 1970– ; Mem., Univ. Court of St Andrews, 1970–73. *Publications*: Korolenko's Siberia, 1954; (with F. M. Borras) Russian Syntax, 1959, 2nd edn 1971; Tolstoy's War and Peace: a study, 1962; (with F. M. Borras) Russian Prose Composition, 1964, 2nd edn 1974; Tolstoy: a critical introduction, 1969; *contrib.* Forum, Mod. Lang. Studies, Mod. Lang. Rev., Slavonic and E European Jl, Slav. and E European Rev., Survey, Times Lit. Supp. *Address*: Dept of Russian, Univ. of St Andrews, St Andrews, Fife KY16 9AJ.

Christie, Prof. Ian Ralph, MA; Professor of Modern British History, University College London, since 1966; *b* 1919. BA and MA Oxon 1948; FRHistS. Asst Lectr, Univ. Coll., London, 1948–51, Lectr 1951–60, Reader, 1960–66. Jt Lit. Dir, Royal Hist. Soc., 1964–70. *Publications*: The End of North's Ministry, 1780–1782, 1958; Wilkes, Wyvill and Reform, 1962; Crisis of Empire: Great Britain and the American Colonies, 1754–1783, 1966; Myth and Reality in late eighteenth-century British Politics, 1970; ed, Essays in Modern History selected from the Transactions of the Royal Historical Society, 1968; The Correspondence of Jeremy Bentham, vol. 3, January 1781 to October 1788, 1970; *contrib.* EHR, Hist. Jl, 1HR Bull., Hist. Today, Jl of Brit. Studies. *Address*: Dept of History, Univ. College London, Gower Street, WC1E 6BT.

Christodoulou, Anastasios; University Secretary, The Open University, since 1969; *b* 1932; *m* 1955; two *s* two *d*. BA Oxon 1955, MA Oxon 1960. Asst Registrar, Univ. Leeds, 1963–65, Dep. Sec. 1965–68. *Address*: Open Univ., Walton Hall, Milton Keynes MK7 6AA.

Christophersen, Dr Paul Hans; Reader in English, New University of Ulster, since 1969; *b* 1911; *m* 1950; one *s*. MA Copenhagen 1937, Dr Phil Copenhagen 1939, PhD Cantab 1943; MPhilSoc., Mem., Norwegian Acad. Sciences, Oslo, Mem., Linguistic Assoc. of GB, Mem., Brit. Assoc. for Applied Linguisitics. Fellow Commoner, Corpus Christi Coll., Cambridge, 1968. Prof. of Eng. Lang. and Lit., Copenhagen, 1946–48; Prof. of Eng., Ibadan, Nigeria, 1948–54; Prof. of Eng. Phil., Oslo, 1954–68; Vis. Prof., Emory Univ., Atlanta, 1965–66. Res. Asst, RIIA, Chatham House, 1944–46; Danish Rep., UNESCO Preparatory Commn, 1945–46. *Publications*: The Articles, 1939, Japanese edn 1958; Bilingualism, 1949; The Ballad of Sir Aldingar, 1952; An English Phonetics Course, 1956; Some Thoughts on the Study of English as a Foreign Language, 1957; (with O. Jespersen) A Modern English Grammar, vol. VI, 1942; (with A. O. Sandved) An Advanced English Grammar, 1969; Second-Language Learning, 1973; *contrib.* Engl.

Studies, Engl. Lang. Teaching, Trans Phil Soc. *Address*: Dept of English, New Univ. of Ulster, Coleraine, Co. Londonderry BT52 1SA.

Christopherson, Sir Derman (Guy), OBE, FRS, DPhil, MICE, FIMechE; Vice-Chancellor and Warden of Durham University, since 1960; *b* 1915; *m* 1940; three *s* one *d*. DPhil Oxon 1941; Hon. DCL Kent 1966, Hon. DCL Newcastle 1971, Hon. DSc Aston 1967, Hon. DSc Sierra Leone 1970, Hon. LLD Leeds 1969, Hon. LLD Royal Univ. of Malta 1969; FRS 1960. Lectr, Cambridge Univ. Engineering Dept, 1946; Prof. of Mechanical Engrg, Leeds Univ., 1949–55; Prof. of Applied Science, Imperial Coll. of Science and Technology. 1955–60; Fellow of Magdalene Coll., Cambridge, 1945, Bursar, 1947; Scientific Officer, Res. and Experiments Dept, Min. of Home Security, 1941–45; Mem., Nat. Advisory Coun. for Trng and Supply of Teachers, 1961; Chm., Cttee of Vice-Chancellors and Principals, 1967–70; Mem., Science Research Coun., 1965–70; Mem., CNAA (Chm. Educn Cttee), 1964– ; Chm., Central Council for Educn and Trng in Social Work, 1971– . Hon. Fellow, Imperial Coll. of Science and Technology, 1966; Hon. Fellow, Magdalene Coll., Cambridge, 1969; Clayton Prize, Instn of Mechanical Engrs, 1963. *Publications*: The Engineer in the University, 1967; The University at Work, 1973; *contrib.* various papers in Proc. Royal Soc., Proc. IMechE, Jl of Appl. Mechs, etc. *Address*: Durham Univ., Old Shire Hall, Old Elvet, Durham DH1 3HP.

Chroston, Dr Peter Neil; Lecturer, School of Environmental Sciences, University of East Anglia, since 1968; *b* 1943; *m* 1971. BSc Wales 1965, PhD Wales 1970; FGS. *Publications*: *contrib.* Norges geol. undersökelse, Notsk geol. tidsskr, Nature. *Address*: Sch. of Environmental Sciences, Univ. of East Anglia, Norwich NOR 88C.

Chubb, Prof. Frederick Basil, MA, DPhil; Professor of Political Science, University of Dublin, Trinity College, since 1962; *b* 1921; *m* 1946. BA Oxon, MA Oxon 1946, DPhil Oxon 1950; MRIA. Lectr in Pol Sci., TCD, 1948–52; Fellow, TCD, 1952–62. Bursar, TCD, 1957– ; Chm., Nat. Employer-Labour Conf., 1970– ; Chm., Comhairle na nOspidéal, 1972. *Publications*: The Control of Public Expenditure, 1952; The Government: an Introduction to the Cabinet System in Ireland, 1961; The Constitution of Ireland, Dublin, 1963, 3rd edn 1970; ed, A Source Book of Irish Government, 1964; ed (with P. Lynch), Economic Development and Planning, 1969; The Government and Politics of Ireland, 1970; *contrib.* Admin, Parly Affairs, Pol Studies, Studies. *Address*: Dept of Political Science, Trinity College, Dublin 2, Ireland.

Chuilleanáin, Eiléan N.; *see* Ní Chuilleanáin.

Church, Clive Hilborne; Joint Lecturer in French History, Departments of French and History, University of Lancaster, since 1965;

b 1939; *m* 1965; two *d*. BA Exeter 1960 (1st cl. Hons History), PhD London 1963 (History). Junior Lectr in Modern History, TCD, 1963–65. Mem., CNAA Hist. Studies and Combined Studies (Humanities) Bds, 1973– ; Sec., Lancaster AUT, 1973– . Mem., Editorial Bd, European Studies Rev., 1970– . *Publications*: *contrib.* French Government and Society, ed J. F. Bosher, 1973; *contrib.* European Studies Rev., French Hist. Studies, Irish Hist. Studies, Past and Present, Rassegna Storica del Risorgimento Italiano. *Address*: Dept of History, Furness College, Bailrigg, Lancaster.

Church, Prof. Ronald James H.; *see* Harrison-Church.

Church, Prof. Roy Anthony, BA, PhD, FRHistS; Professor of Economic History, University of East Anglia, since 1972; *b* 1935; *m* 1959; three *s*. BA Nottingham 1957, PhD Nottingham 1961; FRHistS; Mem., Council, Economic History Soc. Asst Prof., Purdue Univ., US, 1960–61; Asst Prof., Univ. of Washington, US, 1961–62; Asst Prof., UBC, Canada, 1962–63; Lectr, Univ. of Birmingham, 1963–72. Mem., SSRC Economic History Cttee. *Publications*: Economic and Social Change in a Midland Town, 1815–1900: Victorian Nottingham; Kenricks in Hardware: Family Business 1791–1966, 1969; Gravener Henson and The Making of the English Working Class, in, G. Mingay and E. L. Jones: Land, Labour and Population in the Industrial Revolution, 1967; *contrib.* Econ. Hist. Rev., Jl Econ. Hist., Bus. Hist., Hist., Yorks Bull. *Address*: School of Social Studies, University Plain, Univ. of East Anglia, Norwich NOR 88C.

Cigman, Gloria; Lecturer in English, University of Warwick, since 1968; *b* 1928; *m* 1949 (marr. diss. 1958); two *d*. BA London 1965, BLitt Oxon 1968. *Publications*: ed, Chaucer: Wife of Bath's and Clerk's Tales, 1974; *contrib.* 2 sections in New Cambridge Bibliography of English Literature, vol. I, 1974; *contrib.* Essays and Studies. *Address*: Univ. of Warwick, Coventry CV4 7AL.

Cigno, Prof. Alessandro; Professor of Economic Theory, University of Birmingham since 1974; *b* 1940; *m* 1962; one *s* one *d*. Laurea(Econ) Catania 1962, Dip(Econ) Naples 1964, PhD (Math. Econ.) Birmingham 1972. Assistente, Istituto Universitario Di Architettura, Venice, 1965–67; Lectr, 1967–73, Sen. Lectr, 1973–74, Dept of Math. Econs, Birmingham. Mem., Istituto di Ricerche Economiche e Sociali, Ente Nazionale Tre Venezie, 1964–67. *Publications*: *contrib.* Produzione e mercato del Latte nel Veneto, 1967; Input–Output in the United Kingdom, 1970; ed and contrib. Economic Thought of the 20th Century, 1972; contrib. Simulating Economic Development: the recursive programming approach, 1974; *contrib.* Giornale Degli Economisti, Reg. Studies, Rev. of Econ. Studies. *Address*: Univ. of Birmingham, PO Box 363, Birmingham B15 2TT.

Clague-Smith, Sydney Herbert, BA; Lecturer in Education, Tutor to Advanced

Course for Commonwealth Educationists, School of Education, Birmingham University, since 1963; b 1911; m 1936; one s one d. BA Birmingham 1934 (1st cl. History), Postgrad. CertEd. Cambridge 1935, CertProf in Divinity Cambridge 1936. *Address*: School of Education, Birmingham Univ., PO Box 363, Birmingham B15 2TT.

Clanchy, Dr Michael Thomas; Lecturer in Medieval History, University of Glasgow, since 1966; b 1936; m 1963; one s one d. BA Oxon 1959, DipEd Oxon 1962; PhD Reading 1966; FRHistS, 1966. Asst, Glasgow Univ., 1964–66. *Publications*: Civil Pleas of the Wiltshire Eyre 1249, 1971; The Roll and Writ File of the Berkshire Eyre of 1248, 1972; *contrib*. EHR, Hist., Trans Royal Hist. Soc. *Address*: Dept of History, The Univ., Glasgow G12 8QQ.

Clapham, Dr Christopher; Senior Lecturer in Politics, University of Lancaster, since 1974; b 1941. MA Oxon, DPhil Oxon 1966. Lectr, Haile Sellassie I Univ., 1966; Inst. of African Studies, Cambridge, 1967; Res. Fellow in Govt, Manchester, 1968; Lectr in Govt, UWI, Jamaica, 1970; Lectr in Politics, Lancaster, 1971–74. *Publications*: Haile-Selassie's Government, 1969; *contrib*. African Affairs, Jl of Mod. African Studies. *Address*: Dept of Politics, Univ. of Lancaster, Lancaster LA1 4YF.

Clapham, Dr John; Reader, Department of Music, University of Edinburgh, since 1969; b 1908; m 1939, 1966; two s two d. DMus London 1947; FRAM; Member: RMA; Soc. of Aut.; AUT; ISM; Internat. Musicological Soc. Lectr, UC Wales, Aberystwyth, 1945–62; Sen. Lectr, Univ. of Edinburgh, 1962–69; *Publications*: Antonín Dvořák: musician and craftsman, 1966; Smetana (Master Musicians series), 1972; *contrib*. Hudební věda; Music and Letters; Music Rev; The Musical Qly, Musica (Cassel), Proc. of RMA, Musikforschung. *Address*: Dept of Music, Alison House, Nicolson Square, Edinburgh EH8 9BH.

Clapp, Brian William; Senior Lecturer, Department of Economic History, University of Exeter, since 1966; b 1927; m 1959; one s three d. BA London 1947. Res. Asst, Manchester Univ., 1950–54; Lectr, Univ. of Exeter, 1954–66. *Publications*: (with Arthur Redford) Manchester Merchants and Foreign Trade 1858–1939, 1956; John Owens, Manchester Merchant, 1965. *Address*: Dept of Economic History, Univ. of Exeter, Exeter EX4 4QJ.

Clapperton, Dr Chalmers Moyes; Senior Lecturer, Department of Geography, University of Aberdeen, since 1972 (Lecturer, 1963–72); b 1938; m 1962; two s. MA Edinburgh 1961 (Hons Geog.), PhD Edinburgh 1967. Asst Lectr, Aberdeen, 1962–63. *Publications*: *contrib*. Scott. Geog. Mag., Jl Glaciol., Trans Inst Brit. Geogrs, Geog. Ann., Geog. Mag., Brit. Antarc. Surv. Bull., Brit. Antarc. Surv. Scientific Rpt, Procs Yorks Geol. Soc. *Address*: Dept of Geography, Univ. of Aberdeen, Old Aberdeen, Scotland.

Claridge, Dr Gordon; Reader in Clinical Psychology, Department of Psychological Medicine, Glasgow University, since 1972 (Lecturer, 1964–72); b 1932; m 1969; one s one d. BA London 1953, PhD London 1956; DSc Glasgow 1971; FBPsS. Part-time Lectr, Univ. of Bristol, 1961–64. *Publications*: Personality and Arousal, 1967; Drugs and Human Behaviour, 1970; (with S. Canter and W. I. Hume) Personality Differences and Biological Variations: a study of twins, 1973; *contrib*. Behav. Res. Therapy, Brit. Jl Psychiatry, Brit. Jl Psychol., Brit. Jl Social and Clin. Psychol., Jl Psychiatric Res., Jl Biol Psychol., Brit. Jl of Anaesthesia. *Address*: Univ. of Glasgow, Dept of Psychological Medicine, Southern General Hospital, Glasgow SW1.

Clark, Dr David Stuart Thorburn; Lecturer, Department of History, University College, Swansea, since 1967; b 1942; m 1965; one s two d. BA Wales 1964 (1st cl. History), PhD Cantab 1971. *Publications*: Introduction to Facsimile Edition of James I *Daemonologie* (1597) (forthcoming); *contrib*. History and Theory. *Address*: History Dept, Univ. College of Swansea, Singleton Park, Swansea, SA2 8PP.

Clark, Dr Francis; Reader in Religious Studies, Faculty of Arts, The Open University, since 1971; b 1919; m 1968; two d. PhL Heythrop Coll., 1950, STL Heythrop Coll., 1955, DD (*Summa cum Laude*), Pontifical Gregorian Univ., Rome, 1958; Associate Prof. of Theology, Pontifical Gregorian Univ., Rome, 1963–68; Vis. Prof. of Theology, Fordham Univ., NY, USA, 1969–70; Sen. Lectr in History of Religion, Open Univ., 1970–71. Captain and Adjt, 8th Bn, The Royal Fusiliers, 1943. Hon. Sec., London Society for Study of Religion; Mem., Ecclesiastical History Soc. *Publications*: Anglican Orders and Defect of Intention, 1956; Eucharistic Sacrifice and the Reformation, 1960, 2nd edn 1967; A New Theology of the Real Presence?, 1967; Origins of the Reformation, 1972; Luther and Lutheranism, 1972; Calvin and Other Reformers, 1972; The Catholic Reformation, 1972; The Rise of Christianity, 1973; *contrib*. Gregor., Clergy Rev., Irish Theol Qly, Heythrop Jl, Unitas. *Address*: Faculty of Arts, The Open Univ., Walton Hall, Milton Keynes MK7 6AA.

Clark, Prof. John G., BA, DUP; Professor of French and Head of Department of Modern Languages, University of Strathclyde, since 1973; b 1924; m 1969. BA Wales 1947 (1st cl. French), DUP 1952, Lauréat de L'Académie Française, 1955; Fellow, University of Wales; Mem.: Soc. for French Studies; Assoc. of Univ. Professors of French, 1964– . University Coll., Cardiff, 1951–52; Lectr in French, Univ. of Edinburgh, 1952–64, Prof. of French, Magee University Coll., Londonderry, 1964–68; Prof. of Modern Languages, New Univ. of Ulster, 1968–73. Vice-Pres., Magee University Coll., Londonderry, 1966–67. *Publications*: La Pensée de Ferdinand Brunetière, Paris 1954; Articles in: Encyc. Britannica; Penguin Companion to European Literature; *contrib*. French Studies, Mod. Lang. Rev. *Address*: Modern Languages

129

Dept, Univ. of Strathclyde, Glasgow G1 1XW.

Clark, Prof. John Grahame Douglas, CBE, ScD, Hon. DLitt, PhD, FBA; Master of Peterhouse, Cambridge, since 1973; *b* 1907; *m* 1936; two *s* one *d*. BA Cambridge 1930, MA Cambridge 1933, PhD Cambridge 1933, ScD Cambridge 1953; Hon. DLitt Sheffield 1971; FSA, 1932; FBA, 1951; Hon. Editor (and Pres., 1958–62), Prehist. Soc., 1935–70. Fac. Asst Lectr, 1935–46, Univ. Lectr, 1946–52, Cambridge Univ.; Disney Prof. of Archaeology and Head of Dept of Archaeology, Cambridge, 1952–74; Vis. Lectr and Prof. at Harvard, Otago, Uppsala and California (Berkeley). Mem., Anc. Monuments Bd for England, 1954– ; former Comr for Hist. Monuments (England), 1957–69. *Publications:* The Mesolithic Age in Britain, 1933; The Mesolithic Settlement of Northern Europe, 1936; Archaeology and Society, 1939, 1947, 1957; Prehistoric England, 1940; From Savagery to Civilization, 1946; Prehistoric Europe: the Economic Basis, 1952; Excavations at Star Carr, 1954, 1972; World Prehistory, 1961, 1962, 1965; (with Stuart Piggot) Prehistoric Societies, 1965; The Stone Age Hunters, 1967; World Prehistory, a New Outline, 1969, 1971; Aspects of Prehistory, 1970, 1974; The Older Stone Age Settlement of Scandinavia, 1974; *contrib.* Antiqu. Jl, Antiqu., Econ. Hist. Rev., Procs Prehist. Soc., etc. *Address:* Peterhouse, Cambridge.

Clark, Dr John Howard; Senior Lecturer, Department of Psychology, University of Manchester, since 1967; *b* 1929; *m* 1964; one *s* one *d*. BA Cantab 1952, MB Cantab 1956, MA Cantab 1957; MA Oxon 1966; LRCP, MRCS 1955; DPM 1961. House Physician, Dept of Psychol Medicine, Guy's Hosp., London, 1957–58; MRC Clin. Res. Fellow, Burden Neurol Inst., and Dept of Psychol., Bristol Univ., 1962–65; Temp. Mem., Scientific Staff, MRC Psycholinguistics Res. Unit, Inst. of Exptl Psychol., Oxford, 1965–66. *Publications:* A Map of Inner Space (forthcoming); *contrib.* Proc. Internat. Fedn for Inform., Process. Congr. *Address:* Dept of Psychology, The Univ., Manchester M13 9PL.

Clark, Michael, MA; Lecturer in Philosophy, University of Nottingham, since 1968; *b* 1940; *m*; one *s*. BA Oxon 1962 (1st cl. PPP), MA Oxon 1966. Asst Lectr in Logic and Moral Philosophy, Aberdeen Univ., 1963–64; Lectr in Logic, 1964–68. Vis. Assoc. Prof., Univ. of New Orleands, 1974–75. *Publications: contrib.* Analysis, Analysis Suppl., Jl Phil., Mind, Philos. Qly, Philos., Procs Aristot. Soc., Procs Aristot. Soc. Suppl. Vol., Royal Inst. Philos. Lectures. *Address:* Dept of Philosophy, Univ. of Nottingham, University Park, Nottingham NG7 2RD.

Clark, Michael Jeremy, BA, PhD; Lecturer, Department of Geography, University of Southampton, since 1967; *b* 1940; *m* 1966; one *s* one *d*. BA Southampton 1962 (1st cl. Geography), PhD Southampton 1965; Mem., Inst. of Brit. Geographers, Brit.

Cartographic Soc., Geographical Assoc., Geologists Assoc. Asst Lectr, Southampton, 1965–67. Mem., Exec. Cttee, Brit. Univ. Film Coun., 1971– . *Publications:* ed, Visual Media in Geography and Geology, 1971; *contrib.* Geography, Jl Glaciology, Procs Geologists Assoc., Univ. Vision. *Address:* Dept of Geography, The Univ., Southampton SO9 5NH.

Clark, Peter Anthony, BA, MIWP, GMIPM; Lecturer in Sociology and Co-Director Centre for the Utilization of Social Science Research, Department of Social Sciences, Loughborough University of Technology, since 1966; Fellow, Netherlands Institute for Advanced Studies in the Social Sciences, Wassenaar, 1972–73; *b* 1938; *m* 1962; one *s* one *d*. BA Leicester 1960; Grad. Mem., Inst. Personnel Management, 1961, Inst. Work Study Practitioners, 1968; Internat. Fellow, Inter-Univ. Seminar: Armed Services and Society, 1971. Lectr in Sociology, Loughborough Univ. of Tech., 1966; Co-Dir, Centre for the Utilization of the Social Sciences, 1970. *Publications:* Organizational Design: theory and practice, 1972; Action Research and Organizational Change, 1972; *contrib.* Sociol. Rev. *Address:* Centre for the Utilization of Social Sciences, Social Sciences Dept, Univ. of Technology, Loughborough LE11 3TU.

Clark, Dr Roger John Bevir; Lecturer in French, University of Kent at Canterbury, since 1966; *b* 1940; *m* 1964; one *s*. BA Oxon 1961 (1st cl. Mod. Langs), Certificat de Hautes Etudes Européennes, Collège d'Europe, Bruges 1962, MA Oxon 1962, PhD Harvard 1966; Mem., Soc. for French Studies Teaching Fellow, Harvard Univ., 1964–66. *Publications:* ed Mérimée: Chronique du règne de Charles IX, 1969; ed Dumas fils: La Dame aux camélias, 1972; *contrib.* L'Année balzacienne, Cahiers naturalistes, French Studies, Revue d'histoire littéraire de la France. *Address:* Eliot College, Univ. of Kent at Canterbury, Canterbury, Kent.

Clarke, Dr Aidan; Lecturer in Modern History, University of Dublin, since 1965; *b* 1933; *m* 1962; one *s* one *d*. BA Dublin 1955 (1st cl. History and Political Science), MA, PhD Dublin 1959. Lectr, Magee Univ. Coll., Derry, 1959; Fellow, TCD, 1970, Sen. Tutor, 1971–73. Mem. Council, Irish Fedn of Univ. Teachers, 1969–73; Chm., TCD Acad. Staff Assoc., 1970–73; Pres., Dublin Hist. Assoc., 1973–74. *Publications:* The Old English in Ireland, 1625–42, 1966; The Graces, 1625–41, 1968; *contrib.* Past Pres., Irish Hist. Studies, Studia Hibern. *Address:* Dept of History, Trinity College, Dublin 2.

Clarke, Prof. Alan Douglas Benson; Professor and Head of Department of Psychology, University of Hull, since 1962; *b* 1922; *m* 1950; two *s*. BA Reading 1948 (1st cl. Hons), PhD London 1950; Fellow, British Psychological Soc., 1966. Senior Psychologist, Manor Hospital, Epsom, 1951–57; Consultant Psychologist, 1957–62; Dean of Science, Univ. of Hull, 1966–68; Pro-Vice-Chancellor, 1968–71. Member: Trng Council for Teachers of the Mentally Handicapped, 1964– (Chm.,

1969–); SSRC Psychology Cttee, 1968–73. MRC Clinical Research Bd 2, 1971– ; Standing Mental Health Adv. Cttee, 1972– ; Personal Social Services Council, 1973– ; Central Council for Educn and Trng in Social Work, 1973– . Editor, British Jl of Psychology, 1973– . *Publications*: Mental Deficiency: the Changing Outlook, 1958, 3rd edn 1974; Mental Retardation and Behavioural Research, 1973; Recent Advances in the Study of Subnormality, 1966, 3rd edn 1974; *contrib*. Brit. Jl Psychiat., Brit. Jl Psychol., Brit. Med. Bull., Developm. Med. Child Neurol., Jl Child Psychol. Psychiat., Lancet. *Address*: Dept of Psychology, The Univ., Hull HU6 7RX.

Clarke, Dr Anthony Hedley; Lecturer, Department of Spanish, University of Birmingham, since 1969; *b* 1939; *m* 1962; two *s*. BA Birmingham 1960 (1st cl. Spanish), PhD Birmingham 1963. Univ. of Auckland, NZ, 1964–66; Univ. of Aberdeen, 1966–69. *Publications*: ed (with S. Clarke), R. Sánchez Ferlosio: Industrias y andanzas de Alfanhuí, 1969; Pereda, paisajista: el sentimiento de la naturaleza en la novela española del siglo XIX, 1969; ed jtly and contrib., Spanish Studies in Honour of Joseph Manson, 1972; Manual de bibliografía perediana, 1974; Hardy in Translation: Short-title bibliography (forthcoming); *contrib*. various Hispanic jls. *Address*: Dept of Spanish, The Univ., P.O. Box 363, Edgbaston, Birmingham B15 2TT.

Clarke, Brian Glyn, BA, DPhil, DipTP; Lecturer, Environmental Sciences, University of East Anglia, since 1969; *b* 1942; *m*. 1965; two *s*. BA Manchester 1964 (2nd cl. Geog), Dip TP Manchester 1966, DPhil Sussex 1972. Fellow, Univ. of Sussex, 1966–68; Tutorial Fellow, Univ. of Sussex, 1968–69. *Publications*: Crawley Expansion Study, 1969; Urban Renewal (Course Units): Open University Urban Development Course, 1973; *contrib*. Jl Royal Town Planning Inst., Urban Studies. *Address*: School of Environmental Sciences. Univ. of East Anglia, Norwich NOR 88C.

Clarke, Colin Campbell; Reader in English Literature, University of East Anglia, since 1968; *b* 1919; *m* 1958; one *s* three *d*. BA Oxon 1948 (1st cl. English), MA Oxon 1957. Lectr, Univ. of New England, NSW, 1958–63; Lectr, 1963–66, Sen. Lectr, 1967–68, Univ. of East Anglia; Vis. Prof., Univ. of Wisconsin, 1968. *Publications*: Romantic Paradox: an essay on the poetry of Wordsworth, 1962; River of Dissolution: D. H. Lawrence and English Romanticism, 1969; ed, The Rainbow and Women in Love: a casebook, 1969; *contrib*. Durham Univ. Jl; Modern Lang. Qly; English Studies. *Address*: School of English and American Studies, Univ. of East Anglia, Norwich NOR 88C.

Clarke, Dr Colin Graham, DPhil; Lecturer, Department of Geography and Centre for Latin-American Studies, University of Liverpool, since 1966; *b* 1938; *m* 1962; one *s* one *d*. BA Oxon 1960, MA Oxon 1967, DPhil Oxon 1967. Leverhulme Fellow, Liverpool, 1964; Vis. Prof., Univ. of Toronto, 1967.

Publications: *contrib*. Canadian Geogr. Geogral Rev., Geog., Trans Inst. Brit. Geogrs. *Address*: Dept of Geography, Univ. of Liverpool, Liverpool L69 3BX.

Clarke, Dr David Robert; Lecturer, French Department, King's College, University of London, since 1964; *b* 1935. BA 1958, MA 1959, PhD 1964, Cantab. Asst Lectr, KCL, 1961–64. *Publications*: *contrib*. Forum for Mod. Lang. Studies. *Address*: French Dept, King's Coll., Univ. of London, Strand, WC2R 2LS.

Clarke, Derek Ashdown; Librarian, British Library of Political and Economic Science, London School of Economics, University of London, since 1966; *b* 1921; *m* 1964. MA Oxon 1947 (Lit. Hum.) (Open Class. Scholar Oriel Coll., 1939), Dip. Librarianship London 1950; ALA 1950, Mem., Bibliog. Soc. Asst Keeper, Dept of Printed Books, BM, 1947–53; Dep. Librarian, Univ. of Leeds, 1953–55; Librarian: Univ. Coll. of Rhodesia, and Nyasaland, 1955–61; Univ. of Liverpool, 1961–66. Fulbright Fellowship, USA, 1950–51. Mem., Internat. Cttee for Social Sci. Documentation, 1967– ; Chm., Subsec. of Social Sci. Libraries, Internat. Fedn of Library Assocs, 1970– . *Publications*: The College Library and the Community, 1961; Acquisition of Publications from the Third World, 1974; *contrib*. Chambers's Encyclopaedia; *contrib*. Aslib Proc., Getenberg-Jahrbuch, Jl of Documentation, Library, Papers of Bibliog. Soc. of Amer., SA Libraries, Studies in Bibliog. *Address*: British Library of Political and Economic Science, Houghton Street, WC2A 2AE.

Clarke, Geoffrey Mallin, MA, DipStat; Reader in Mathematics and Statistics, University of Sussex, since 1973 (Lecturer, 1966–73); *b* 1928; *m* 1960; one *s* one *d*. BA Oxon 1950 (Hons Mathematics), MA Oxon 1954, DipStat Oxon 1953; FSS. Statistician, Long Ashton Res. Stn, and Lectr in Statistics, Univ. of Bristol, 1953–66. *Publications*: Statistics and Experimental Design, 1969; *contrib*. App. Stats (Jl Royal Stat. Soc. C), Biometrics. *Address*: School of Mathematical and Physical Sciences, Univ. of Sussex, Falmer, Brighton BN1 9QH.

Clarke, Howard Brian; Assistant Lecturer in Medieval History, University College, Dublin, since 1971; *b* 1940; *m* 1972; one *d*. BA Birmingham 1962. Asst in Med. History, University Coll., Dublin, 1968–71. *Publications*: trans. Duby: The Early Growth of the European Economy, 1974; *contrib*. Midland History, Worcs Archaeological Soc. Trans. *Address*: Dept of Medieval History, Univ. College, Dublin 4.

Clarke, Prof. John Innes, MA, PhD; Professor of Geography, University of Durham, since 1968; *b* 1929; *m*, 1955; three *d*. MA Aberdeen 1950 (1st cl. Geography), PhD Aberdeen 1956; FRGS, Mem., Inst. Brit. Geogrs, Geog. Assoc. Asst Lectr, Aberdeen Univ., 1954–55; Lectr, Durham Univ., 1955–63; Prof., Univ. Coll. of Sierra Leone, 1963–65; Reader, Durham Univ., 1965–68; Vis. Prof., Univ. Wisconsin, 1967.

131

Mem., SSRC Geog. Cttee, 1971– . *Publications*: ed, Field Studies in Libya, 1960; Iranian City of Shirza, 1963; Africa and the Islands, 1964, 3rd edn 1972; Population Geography, 1965, 2nd edn 1972; ed, Sierra Leone in Maps, 1966, 2nd edn 1969; (with B. D. Clark) Kermanshah: An Iranian Provincial City, 1969; Population Geography and the Developing Countries, 1971; (with W. B. Fisher) ed, Populations of the Middle East and North Africa, 1972; *contrib*. Econ. Geog., Geog., Die Erde, Afrika Spectrum, Trans Inst. Brit. Geogrs. *Address*: Dept of Geography, Univ. of Durham, Durham.

Clarke, Dr Malcolm Alistair; Assistant Lecturer, Faculty of Law, University of Cambridge, since 1970; Fellow, St John's College Cambridge, since 1970; *b* 1943; *m* 1968; one *s*. LLB 1965, MA 1968, PhD 1973, Cantab. SPTL, LAG. Asst, Institut de Droit Comparé, Paris, 1965–66; Res. Fellow, Fitzwilliam Coll., Cambridge, 1966–68; Asst Lectr (Special Post), Cambridge, seconded to Univ. of Singapore, 1968–70. *Address*: St John's College, Cambridge CB2 1TP.

Clarke, P. R. F.; Senior Lecturer in Clinical Psychology, Department of Psychiatry, University of Sheffield, since 1970; *b* 1928; *m* 1956; one *s*. BA Oxon 1954 (PPP), MA Oxon 1957; PGDip. in Psychology (Abnormal) London 1955; Associate, British Psychological Soc., 1957 (Mem., Div. of Clinical Psychology; Mem., Council 1965–68). Lectr, Univ. of Sheffield, 1960–70. Clinical Psychologist: Barrow Hosp., 1955–56; Nat. Hosp., Queen Square, 1956–58; Sen. Psychologist, United Birmingham Hosp., 1959–60. *Publications*: *contrib*. Brit. Jl Anaesth., Brit. Jl Psychol., Lancet, Nature, Psychol. Reps. *Address*: Whiteley Wood Clinic, Woofindin Road, Sheffield S10 3TL.

Clarke, Dr Peter Frederick; Lecturer, Department of History, University College London, since 1966; *b* 1942; *m* 1969. MA, PhD Cantab 1967, FRHistS. Vis. Lectr, Harvard Univ., 1974. Review Editor of History, 1967–73. *Publications*: Lancashire and the New Liberalism, 1971; (ed.) L. T. Hobhouse, Democracy and Reaction, 1972; ed, J. A. Hobson, The Crisis of Liberalism, 1974; *contrib*. Eng. Hist. Rev., Hist. Jl, History, Trans Roy. Hist. Soc. *Address*: Dept of History, Univ. College London, Gower Street, WC1E 6BT.

Clarke, Peter John; Fellow and Tutor in Law, Jesus College, Oxford, since 1971; *b* 1945; *m* 1968; one *s* one *d*. BA Hons 1967, BCL Hons 1968, MA 1971, Oxon: Barrister, Lincoln's Inn, 1970. Asst Lectr in Law, Nottingham Univ., 1968–69, Lectr, 1969–71. *Address*: Jesus Coll., Oxford OX1 3DW.

Clarke, Roger Alfred; Lecturer, Department of Political Economy and Institute of Soviet and East European Studies, Glasgow University, since 1965; *b* 1940; *m* 1970. MA Glasgow 1962 (Hons Russian and German), Cert. of Proficiency in Political Economy Glasgow 1964; Mem., NASEES. Mem., Ed. Bd, Soviet Studies, 1968– . *Publications*: A Concise Statistical Compendium of the USSR, 1972; *contrib*. Soviet Studies. *Address*: Adam Smith Building, Univ. of Glasgow, Glasgow G12 8RT.

Clarkson, Elizabeth Margaret Ross, MA, AIMSW; Tutor to the Applied Social Studies Course and Lecturer in Social Casework, University College of Swansea, since 1964; *b* 1917. MA Glasgow 1940, DipSocSci. Glasgow 1941; Associate Mem., Inst. Med. Soc. Workers, 1942. Lectr, Sch. of Soc. Work, Univ. of Toronto, 1947–48, Field Work Supervr, 1948–55; Pt-time Lectr, Med. Sch., Univ. of Toronto, 1952–55; Vis. Prof. of Social Work, Univ. of Rajshahi, Bangladesh, 1973–74. Mem., Soc. Work Educn Cttee, Jt Univ. Council, 1968– ; Training Officer, Brit. Assoc. Soc. Workers, SW Wales Br., 1971– . *Publications*: *contrib*. Almoner, Case Conf., Internat. Soc. Work. *Address*: Dept of Social Administration, Univ. College of Swansea, Singleton Park, Swansea SA2 8PP.

Clarkson, Prof. Geoffrey P. E., BSc, MSc, MBA, PhD; Professor of Business Finance (National Westminster Bank), Manchester Business School, University of Manchester, since 1969; *b* 1934; *m* 1960; two *d*. BSc 1958, MSc 1959, PhD 1961 Carnegie-Mellon Univ., Pittsburgh; MBA Manchester 1970; Mem., Amer. Econ. Assoc., Amer. Psychol. Assoc., Econometric Soc., Philos. of Science Assoc. Asst Prof., Massachusetts Inst. of Tech., 1961–65, Associate Prof., 1965–67; Ford Foundation Fellow, 1965–66; Vis. Prof., London School of Economics, 1966–67; Prof. of Management Science, Univ. of Manchester, 1967–69. Consultant to and dir several companies. *Publications*: Portfolio Selection: A Simulation of Trust Investment, 1962; The Theory of Consumer Demand: A Critical Appraisal, 1963; Managerial Economics, 1968; Managing Money and Finance, 1969, 2nd edn 1971; *contrib*. Amer. Econ. Rev., Behav. Science, Jl Finance, Indust. Management Rev. *Address*: Manchester Business School, Univ. of Manchester, Booth Street West, Manchester M15 6PB.

Clarkson, Dr Leslie Albert, BA, PhD; Senior Lecturer in Economic and Social History, Queen's University, Belfast, since 1970; *b* 1933; *m* 1954; two *s* three *d*. BA Nottingham 1954, PhD Nottingham 1960; Mem., Econ. Hist. Soc. Sen. Tutor in Economic History, Melbourne Univ., 1958, Lectr, 1959–61; Lectr in Economics, Univ. of W Australia, 1962–65; Lectr in Economic and Social History, Queen's Univ., Belfast, 1965–70. *Publications*: The Pre-Industrial Economy in England, 1500–1750, 1971; *contrib*. Agric. Hist. Rev., Australian Econ. Hist. Rev. (formerly Business Arch. and Hist.), Bull. Inst. Hist. Res., Econ. Hist. Rev. *Address*: Dept of Economic and Social History, The Queen's Univ., Belfast BT7 1NN, Northern Ireland.

Clay, Christopher George Anthony; Lecturer in Economic History, Department of Economic and Social History, University of Bristol, since 1967; *b* 1940; *m* 1973. BA Cambridge 1961, MA Cambridge 1964, PhD Cambridge 1966. Asst Lectr in Economic

History: Aberdeen Univ., 1964–65; Univ. of Bristol, 1966. Asst Principal, HM Civil Service (Navy Dept), 1966. *Publications*: *contrib*. EcHR, Rec. Hist. *Address*: Department of Economic and Social History, Univ. of Bristol, 67 Woodland Road, Bristol.

Clayton, Dr Eric Sesford, BSc, PhD; Reader in Agricultural Economics of Developing Countries, Agrarian Development Unit, School of Rural Economics, Wye College, University of London, since 1966; *b* 1919; *m* 1954; two *s*. BSc (Econ.) London 1949, PhD London 1960; Mem., RES, AES. Res. Off., Univ. of Cambridge, 1949–54; Lectr, Wye Coll., Univ. of London, 1957–66. *Publications*: Agrarian Development in Peasant Agriculture, 1964; Economics of the Poultry Industry, 1967; *contrib*. Econ. Develt and Cult. Change, Jl of Agric. Econ., Internat. Lab. Rev. *Address*: Wye College, Univ. of London, nr Ashford, Kent.

Clayton, Prof. Frederick William; Professor of Classics, since 1948, and Public Orator, since 1965, University of Exeter; *b* 1913; *m* 1948; two *s* two *d*. BA Cantab 1934, MA Cantab 1938; Fellow, King's Coll., Cambridge, 1937. *Publications*: The Cloven Pine, 1942; *contrib*. various jls. *Address*: Univ. of Exeter, Exeter EX4 4GJ.

Clayton, Prof. Keith Martin, MSc, PhD; Professor of Environmental Sciences, University of East Anglia, since 1967; *b* 1928; *m* 1951; three *s* one *d*. BSc Sheffield 1949, MSc Sheffield 1951; PhD London 1958. Demonstrator, Univ. of Nottingham, 1949–51; Asst Lectr, 1953–54, Reader, 1964–67, LSE. Dean, Sch. of Environmental Scis, UEA, 1967–71, Pro-Vice-Chancellor, 1971–73; Mem., NERC, 1971– . *Publications*: Geo. Abstracts (founded as Geomorphological Abstracts, 1960). *Address*: Univ. of East Anglia, Norwich NOR 88C.

Cleary, Alan; Lecturer in Psychology, Department of Psychology, University of Newcastle upon Tyne, since 1966; *b* 1934; *m* 1958; two *s*. BSc London 1962; MIERE. *Publications*: Aspects of Educational Technology V, ed D. Packham, A. Cleary, T. Mayes, 1971; *contrib*. Jl Applied Behaviour Analysis, Programmed Learning and Educational Technology, Psychonomic Science. *Address*: Univ. of Newcastle upon Tyne, Dept of Psychology, Newcastle upon Tyne NE1 7RU.

Cleaver, Air Vice-Marshal Peter Charles, CB; OBE; Secretary, Cranfield Institute of Technology, since 1973; *b* 1919; *m* 1948; two *s*. DCAe Cranfield 1952, converted to MSc 1972; CEng, FRAeS. RAF 1939–72, retired. Bursar, Cranfield Inst. of Technology, 1972–73. *Publication*: The Strength of Tubes under Uniform External Pressure, ARC paper, 1956. *Address*: Cranfield Institute of Technology, Cranfield, Bedford MK43 0AL.

Clegg, Arthur Duckering; Senior Lecturer in Economics and History of Science, Social Science and Humanities, The City University, London, since 1966; *b* 1914; *m* 1940; 1967; one *s* one *d*. BSc(Econ) (2/I), 1936.

Mem., British History of Science Soc., Newcomen Soc. *Address*: The City Univ., St John Street, EC1V 4PB.

Clegg, Prof. Hugh Armstrong; Professor of Industrial Relations, University of Warwick, since 1967; *b* 1920; *m* 1941; two *s* two *d*. BA Oxon 1939, MA Oxon 1948. Official Fellow, Nuffield Coll., Oxford, 1949–66; Emeritus Fellow, 1966– ; Dir, Industrial Relations Research Unit, SSRC, 1970–74; Chm., CS Arbitration Tribunal, 1968–71; Mem.: Royal Commn on Trade Unions and Employers' Assoc., 1965–68; Cttee of Inquiry into Port Transport Industry, 1964–65; Ct of Inquiry into Seamen's Dispute, 1966–67; Ct of Inquiry into Local Authorities Manual Workers' Pay Dispute, 1970. *Publications*: Labour Relations in London Transport, 1950; Industrial Democracy and Nationalisation, 1951; (with T. E. Chester) The Future of Nationalisation, 1953; General Union, 1954; (with T. E. Chester) Wage Policy in the Health Service, 1957; (with R. Adams) The Employers' Challenge, 1957; A New Approach to Industrial Democracy, 1960; (with A. J. Killick and R. Adams) Trade Union Officers, 1961; General Union in a Changing Society, 1964; (with A. Fox and A. F. Thompson) A History of British Trade Unions, vol. I, 1964; The System of Industrial Relations in Great Britain, 1970; How to run an Incomes Policy and Why we made such a Mess of the Last One, 1971. *Address*: School of Industrial and Business Studies, Univ. of Warwick, Coventry, Warwickshire CV4 7AL.

Clegg, Joan Elisabeth, MA; Senior Lecturer in Social Administration, Department of Social Science and Humanities, The City University, London, since 1959; *b* 1927; *m* 1967. BA Cantab 1947, MA Cantab 1951; Mem.: Soc. Admin. Assoc., Brit. Assoc. of Soc. Workers. Asst Lectr, Bedford Coll., London, 1956–58; Temp. Lectr, Univ. of Leicester, 1958–59. Mem., Brit. Council Churches, Soc. Responsibility Dept, 1961– , Nat. Council Soc. Service, Publication Adv. Gp, 1968– . *Publications*: Dictionary of Social Services, 1972. *Address*: The City Univ., St John Street, EC1V 4PB.

Clement, Dr Mary, MA, PhD; Lecturer in Education, University College of Wales, Aberystwyth, since 1954; *b* 1916. BA Wales 1937 (Hons Welsh), MA Wales 1939, PhD Wales 1952; Sometime Fellow, Univ. of Wales. *Publications*: Correspondence and Minutes of the SPCK relating to Wales 1699–1740, 1952; The SPCK and Wales, 1954; Records and Correspondence of the SPG, 1701–1750, 1973; (jtly) Essays on Education (in Welsh–Ysgrifau ar Addysg), 1966; *contrib*. Hist. Mag. Protest. Episc. Ch., USA, Trans Hon. Soc. Cymmrodorion, London, and many provincial Hist. Jls. *Address*: Education Dept, Univ. College of Wales, Aberystwyth SY23 2AX.

Clement, Robert David; Lecturer and Co-editor, Linguistic Survey of Scotland, University of Edinburgh, since 1971; *b* 1943; *m* 1967; two *d*. BA Cantab 1965 (Modern and Mediaeval Langs), MA 1969, Dip. of General

Linguistics Edinburgh 1966; Mem., Linguistics Assoc. of GB; Lektor für englische Sprache, Univ. of Freiburg, 1966–69; Asst Lectr, Univ. of East Anglia, 1969–71. *Address*: Linguistic Survey of Scotland, 27 George Square, Edinburgh.

Clementi, Dr D. R.; Reader in History, London University, Queen Mary College, since 1963; *b* 1914. BA Oxon 1939, DPhil Oxon 1950; FRHistS; Mem., Int. Commn Hist. of Rep. Parly Instns. Asst Dir and Libr., Brit. Sch. in Rome, 1945–47; Susette-Taylor Trav. Fellow, Lady Margaret Hall, Oxford, 1948–50; Asst Lectr, then Lectr, Manchester Univ., 1951–55; Lectr, Queen Mary Coll., London Univ., 1955–63. War Off., 1941; Foreign Off, 1941–45. *Publications*: contributions, inc. Calendar of the diplomas of the Hohenstaufen emperor Henry VI concerning the kingdom of Sicily, Quelten und Forschungen aus italienischen Archiven und Bibliotheken 35, 1955; Alexandri Telesini, 'Ystoria serenissimi Rogerii prime regis Sicilie' Lib. IV, 6–10, Bullettino dell' Istituto Storico Italiano per il Medio Evo e Archivio Muratoriano 77, 1965; The Relations between the Papacy, the Western Roman Empire and the emergent Kingdom of Sicily and South Italy, 1050–1156, Bullettino dell' Istituto Storico Italiano . . . 80, 1968; also to Archiv. Storico Pugl., Bull. J. Rylands Libr., EHP, Papers Brit. Sch. Rome, Studies Int. Commn Hist. Rep. Parl. Inst. *Address*: Dept of History, Queen Mary College, Mile End Road, E1 4NS.

Clements, Dr Ronald Ernest, BD; Lecturer in Old Testament, University of Cambridge, since 1967; *b* 1929; *m* 1955; two *d*. BD London 1954 (2nd cl.); BA Cantab 1956 (1st cl.), MA 1960; PhD Sheffield 1961; BD Cantab 1969. Asst Lectr, Univ. of Edinburgh, 1960–64, Lectr, 1964–67; Fellow, Fitzwilliam Coll., Cambridge, 1968– . *Publications*: God and Temple, 1965; Prophecy and Covenant, 1965; God's Chosen People, 1968; Abraham and David, 1968; The Conscience of the Nation, 1968; Exodus (New Cambridge Comm.), 1972; *contrib*. Vetus Testamentum, Jl Semit. Studies. *Address*: Fitzwilliam College, Cambridge CB3 0DG.

Clemoes, Prof. Peter Alan Martin, PhD, FRHistS; Elrington and Bosworth Professor of Anglo-Saxon, Department of Anglo-Saxon, Norse, and Celtic, University of Cambridge, since 1969; *b* 1920; *m* 1956; two *s*. BA London 1950 (1st cl. English); PhD Cantab 1956; FRHistS. Res. Fellow, Reading Univ., 1954–55, Lectr in English, 1955–61; Lectr in Anglo-Saxon, Cambridge Univ., 1961–69; Official Fellow, Emmanuel Coll., Cambridge, 1962–69; Asst Libr., 1963–69; Coll. Lectr in English, 1963–69; Dir of Studies in English, 1963–65; Tutor, 1966–68; Professorial Fellow, Emmanuel Coll., Cambridge, 1969– ; Gen. Ed., Early English MSS in Facsimile, 1963– ; Mem., Council, Early English Text Soc., 1971– ; Ch. Ed., Anglo-Saxon England, 1972– . *Publications*: ed, The Anglo-Saxons: Studies . . . presented to Bruce Dickins, 1959; ed jtly, Ælfric's First Series of Catholic Homilies: BM Royal

7 C, xii (facsimile), 1966; ed jtly, England Before the Conquest. Studies . . . presented to Dorothy Whitelock, 1971; ed jtly, The Old English Illustrated Hexateuch (facsimile), 1974; *contrib*. Anglia. *Address*: Emmanuel College, Cambridge.

Clines, David John Alfred, BA, MA; Senior Lecturer in Biblical Studies, University of Sheffield, since 1973 (Lecturer, 1967–73); *b* 1938; *m* 1963; one *s* one *d*. BA Sydney 1960 (1st cl. Greek and Latin); BA Cantab 1963 (Oriental Studies), MA Cantab 1966. Asst Lectr in Biblical History and Literature, Univ. of Sheffield, 1964–67. *Publications*: contrib., A New Testament Commentary, ed G. C. D. Howley, 1969; *contrib*. Tynd. Bull., Vet. Test., Austr. Jl of Bibl. Archaeol., Jl of Bibl. Lit., Jl of Northwest Semitic Langs, Catholic Bibl. Qly. *Address*: Dept of Biblical Studies, The University of Sheffield, Sheffield S10 2TN.

Clissmann, Anne; Lecturer in English, Trinity College, Dublin, since 1971; *b* 1945; *m* 1969. BA Sussex 1967; MLitt TCD 1971. Jun. Lecturer, TCD, 1968. Member: Faculty of Arts (Letters) Exec. Cttee, TCD, 1971–72 1972–73. *Publications*: The Story-Teller's Book-Web: a critical introduction to the work of Flann O'Brien, 1974; *contrib*. Jl Irish Lit. *Address*: English Dept, 40 Trinity College, Dublin 2.

Clive, Dr Eric McCredie; Senior Lecturer, Department of Scots Law, University of Edinburgh, since 1969; *b* 1938; *m* 1962; one *s* three *d*. MA Edinburgh 1958, LlB Edinburgh 1960 (dist.), LlM Michigan 1962, SJD Virginia 1967; Solicitor (Scotland) 1961. Lectr, Dept of Scots Law, Edinburgh, 1962–69. Senatus Academicus, Edinburgh, 1968–72; Univ. Court, Edinburgh, 1971–72; Assoc. Dean, Faculty of Law, Edinburgh, 1970–72. *Publications*: (with G. A. Watt) Scots Law for Journalists, 1965, 2nd edn 1969; (with J. G. Wilson) Husband and Wife, 1974; *contrib*. Jur. Rev., SLT, JLSS. *Address*: Faculty of Law, Old College, South Bridge, Edinburgh EH8 9YL.

Clogg, Richard Ralph Mowbray; Lecturer in Modern Greek History, School of Slavonic and East European Studies and King's College, University of London, since 1969; *b* 1939; *m* 1962; one *s* one *d*. MA Edinburgh 1963. Lectr in Mod. Hist., Univ. of Edinburgh, 1968–69. *Publications*: ed (with George Yannopoulos) Greece under Military Rule, 1972; ed, The Struggle for Greek Independence, 1973; ed (with P. Anty), British Policy towards Wartime Resistance in Yugoslavia and Greece, 1974; trans. Inside the Colonels' Greece, 1972; *contrib*. Ann. Register, Anzeiger der phil.-hist. Klasse der Österreichischen Akademie der Wissenschaften, E Chs Rev., Eranistis, Greek Orthodox Theol Rev., Jl of Ecclesiastical Hist., ME Studies, Mikrasiatika Khronika, Revue des Etudes sud-est européennes, Univ. of Birmingham Hist. Jl, etc. *Address*: King's College, Strand, WC2R 2LS.

Clough, Dr Cecil Holdsworth; Senior Lecturer in Medieval History, University of

Liverpool, since 1970; b 1930; m 1970; one s. BA Oxon 1954 (2nd cl. History), MA Oxon 1958, DPhil Oxon 1962; FRHistS; Cavaliere nell'Ordine al Merito della Repubblica Italiana, 1970. Guggenheim Fellow. Norman Fellow in the Humanities, Columbia Univ., NY, 1959–61; Lectr in Modern History, Univ. of Toronto, 1961–63; Tatti Fellow, Harvard Univ., 1963–64; Res. Fellow, Dept of Italian, Birmingham Univ., 1964–67; Lectr in Medieval History, Univ. of Liverpool, 1967–70; Leverhulme Faculty Fellowship in European Studies, 1973–74. Commnd RAF 1949–51. *Publications*: Pietro Bembo's Library, 1965, 2nd edn 1971; Machiavelli Researches, 1967; *contrib.* Annali dell' Istituto Universitario Orientale di Napoli, Apollo, Arch. Veneto, Atti e Mem., Dep. St Patria per le Province di Romagna, Bod. Libr. Rec., Bull. JRL, Commentari dell' Ateneo di Brescia, EHR, Ital. Studies, Italica, Jl Warburg and Courtauld Insts, La Bibliofilia, Librarium, Manuscripta, MLN, RN, Medievalia et Humanistics, Studia Oliveriana, Studies in the Renaissance, Studi urbinati, Studi Veneziani. *Address*: School of History, Univ. of Liverpool, Liverpool L69 3BX.

Clowes, Prof. Max; Professor of Artificial Intelligence, School of Social Sciences, University of Sussex, since 1974; b 1934; m 1957; one s three d. BSc Reading 1955 (Special Hons Physics), PhD Reading 1959 (Physics). Senior Research Fellow, Experimental Psychology, Univ. Sussex, 1969–74. *Publications*: *contrib.* Artificial Intelligence, Information and Control, Optica Acta. *Address*: Arts Building, Univ. of Sussex, Falmer, Brighton BN1 9QN.

Cluysenaar, Anne Alice Andrée; Lecturer, Department of English Language and Literature, University of Birmingham, since 1973; b 1936. BA Dublin (1st cl. French and English Lit.), Dip. General Linguistics Edinburgh 1963. Lectr, Manchester Univ., 1957–58; Lectr, TCD, 1961–62; Lectr, King's Coll., Aberdeen, 1963–65, Lectr, Lancaster Univ., 1965–72, Sen. Lectr, Huddersfield Polytechnic, 1972–73. Poetry critic, Strand, 1970– . *Publications*: A Fan of Shadows, 1967; Nodes, 1970; contrib., British Poetry since 1960, 1972; A Dictionary of Modern Critical Terms, 1973; Aspects of Literary Stylistics, 1974; *contrib.* Strand, TLS, Lang. and Style, Poetry Nation. *Address*: Dept of English Language and Literature, Univ. of Birmingham, PO Box 363, Birmingham B15 2TT.

Clyde Barber, Charles; see Barber.

Coates, Bryan Ellis; Senior Lecturer, Department of Geography, University of Sheffield, since 1969; b 1933; m 1960; two s one d. BA Hons Leeds 1955 (Geog.) MA 1960; Mem., Inst. Brit. Geogrs. Temp. Asst Lectr, Univ. of Leeds, 1957–58; Jun. Res. Fellow, Asst Lectr, Lectr, 1958–69, Univ. of Sheffield. *Publications*: Regional Variations in Britain: Selected Studies in Economic and Social Geography, 1971; Census Atlas of South Yorkshire: computer and laser graphic mapping of 35 selected population characteristics in over 2700 enumeration districts, 1974; *contrib.* Geog. Trans Inst. Brit. Geogr. *Address*: Dept of Geography, Univ. of Sheffield, Sheffield S10 2TN.

Coates, John David; Lecturer, Adult Education Department, University of Hull, since 1970; b 1943; m 1969. BA Cantab 1965, Dip. English Studies Cantab 1966, MA Cantab 1969. *Address*: Adult Education Dept, Univ. of Hull, Hull HU6 7RX.

Coates, Dr John Gordon, DSO; Dean of Students and Lecturer in Finno-Ugrian Studies, School of European Studies, University of East Anglia, since 1968; b 1918; m 1946; two s. BA Cantab 1940 (Mod. and Med. Langs), MA Cantab 1945, Cert. of Competent Knowledge (Russian) Cantab 1950, PhD Cantab 1969; Mem., Finno-Ugrian Soc. (SUS), 1965. Asst Prof., Univ. of Idaho, 1962–63; Res. Fellow. Clare Hall, Cambridge, 1965–68. HM Diplomatic Serv., 1946–62; Secretariat, Royal Soc., 1964–65. *Address*: School of European Studies, Univ. of East Anglia, Norwich NOR 88C.

Coates, Kenneth; Senior Tutor, Department of Adult Education, University of Nottingham, since 1972; b 1930; m; three s three d. BA Nottingham 1959 (1st cl. Hons Sociology). Dir, Bertrand Russell Peace Foundation since 1966. Dept of Adult Educn, Univ. of Nottingham: Asst Tutor, 1960; Tutor, 1961. *Publications*: The Crisis of British Socialism, 1971; Essays in Industrial Democracy, 1971; ed, Essays on Socialist Humanism, 1972; with A. J. Topham: Industrial Democracy in Great Britain, 1968; The New Unionism, 1972; The Trade Union Register, Nos 1, 2, 3, 1969, 1970, 1973; with R. L. Silburn: Poverty, Deprivation and Morale, 1967; Poverty, The Forgotten Englishmen, 1970; The Partial View (forthcoming), etc., *contrib.* articles and occasional papers. *Address*: Dept of Adult Education, 14–22 Shakespeare Street, Nottingham.

Coats, Prof. A. W., (Bob); Professor and Head of Department of Economic and Social History, University of Nottingham, since 1964; Fellow, Netherlands Institute for Advanced Study in Humanities and Social Sciences, 1972–73; b 1924; m 1945; two s one d. BA(Intermediate) London External 1947, BSc(Econ) London 1948, MSc(Econ) London 1950; PhD Johns Hopkins 1953; Phi Beta Kappa (Graduate) 1953, Mem., Royal Econ. Soc., Econ. Hist. Soc. (Brit. and USA), Amer. Econ. Assoc. Grad. Asst in Economics, Univ. of Pittsburgh, 1950–51; Jun. Asst in Economics, Johns Hopkins, 1951–52; Gustav Bissing Fellowship, Johns Hopkins, 1952–53; Asst Lectr in Economic and Social History, Univ. of Nottingham, 1953–54, Lectr, 1954–62; Rockefeller Foundn Fellowship, US, 1958–59; Vis. Associate Prof. of Economics, Univ. of Virginia, 1962–63; Reader in Economic and Social History, Univ. of York, 1963–64; Vis. Prof., Stanford Univ., Fall Quarter, 1967; Vis. Lectr or Prof., Summer courses, Columbia Univ. 1962, Univ. of Wisconsin, 1963, 1967, Editor and Co-editor, Hist. Econ. Thought Newsletter, 1969– ; Mem., Ed. Bd, Hist.

Polit. Econ., 1970. *Publications*: ed (with R. M. Robertson), Essays in American Economic History, 1969; ed, The Classical Economists and Economic Policy, 1971; *contrib*. Amer. Econ. Rev., Brit. Jl Sociol., Econ. Hist. Rev., Econ. Jl, Economica, Hist. Polit. Econ., Jl Amer. Studies, Jl Econ. Lit., Jl Law and Econ., Kyklos, Qly Jl Econ., Renaiss. and Mod. Studies, Scand. Econ. Hist. Rev., Yorks Bull. Econ. and Soc. Res. *Address*: Dept of Economic and Social History, Univ. of Nottingham, University Park, Nottingham NG7 2RD

Cobb, Prof. Richard Charles, MA, FBA; Professor of Modern History, University of Oxford, since 19,73; *b* 1917; *m* 1963; three *s* one *d*. BA Oxon 1938, MA Oxon 1945; Lectr in History, University Coll., Aberystwyth, 1955–61; Sen. Simon Res. Fellow, Manchester, 1960; Lectr, Leeds, 1962; Fellow and Tutor in Modern History, Balliol, 1962–72; Reader in French Revolutionary History, Oxford, ₁969–72. Fellow of Worcester Coll., Oxford, 1973– . Vis. Prof. in the History of Paris, Collège de France, 1971. Chevalier des Palmes Académiques, 1956. *Publications*: L'armée révolutionnaire à Lyon, 1952; Les armées révolutionnaires du Midi, 1955; Les armées révolutionnaires, vol. 1, 1961, vol. 2, 1963; Terreur et Subsistances, 1965; A Second Identity: essays on France and French History, 1969; The Police and the People: French Popular Protest 1789–1820, 1970; Reactions to the French Revolution, 1972. *Address*: Worcester College, Oxford.

Cobb, Stephen Rhodes; Lecturer, Department of Psychology, Glasgow University, since 1971; *b* 1939; *m* 1961; four *s*. MSc UMIST, 1966; FBOA 1965; Associate, UMIST, 1967. Demonstration, Univ. of Manchester, 1965; Sen. Lectr, Glasgow Coll. of Science and Technol., 1967. *Publications*: *contrib*. Brit. Jl. Physiol. Opt., Clin. Genet., Jl Biosoc. Sci., Ophthalmic Optician, Vis. Res. *Address*: Dept of Psychology, Adam Smith Building, Univ. of Glasgow, Glasgow G12 8RT.

Cobban, Dr Alan Balfour, MA, PhD, FRHistS; Lecturer in Medieval History, University of Liverpool, since 1966; *b* 1939. MA Aberdeen 1961; MA Cambridge 1965, PhD Cambridge 1965; FRHistS. Fellow, Trinity Coll., Cambridge, 1963. *Publications*: The King's Hall within the University of Cambridge in the later Middle Ages, 1969; *contrib*. Bull. J. Rylands Libr., Past and Present, Studies in Ch. Hist. *Address*: School of History, Univ. of Liverpool, 8 Abercromby Square, PO Box 147, Liverpool L69 3BX.

Cochran, Dr Alastair Jack. Senior Research Fellow, Interdisciplinary Higher Degrees Scheme, Aston University, since 1970; *b* 1929; *m* 1955; three *s* one *d*. BSc Edinburgh 1952 (1st cl. Physics), PhD Edinburgh. Assist Lectr, Physics Dept, Edinburgh Univ., 1953–55; Sen. Lectr, Physics Dept. Royal Military Coll. of Science, 1956–60; Sen. Scientific Officer, UKAEA, 1960–63; Dir., Golf Soc. of Great Britain Scientific Programme, 1963–68.

Publications: The Search for the Perfect Swing, 1968; *contrib*. Proc. Phys. Soc. *Address*: Interdisciplinary Higher Degrees Scheme, Univ. of Aston in Birmingham, Gosta Green, Birmingham B4 7ET.

Cockcroft, Dr Robert; Lecturer, School of English Studies, University of Nottingham, since 1973; *b* 1939; *m* 1968; two *d*. BA Cantab 1961, MA Cantab 1965, PhD London 1967, CertEd 1962. Asst Lectr, Univ. of Nottingham, 1965–69; Lectr B, 1969–73; Lectr A, 1973. *Publications*: *contrib*. Ren. and Mod. Studies. *Address*: Sch. of English, Univ. of Nottingham, University Park, Nottingham NG7 2RD.

Cockerham, Harry; Lecturer, French Department, Royal Holloway College, University of London, since 1967, *b* 1937; *m* 1962; one *d*. BA Hons 1959 (French), Grad Cert Ed 1960, MA 1962, Manchester. Lecteur d'anglais, Université de Strasbourg, 1962–65; Asst Lectr in French, Univ. of Aberdeen, 1965–67. *Publications*: ed, Théophile Gautier: Poésies (1830), 1973; *contrib*. Bull. des jeunes Romanistes, Strasbourg, Gazette des Beaux Arts, Travaux de Linguistique et de Littérature de l'Université de Strasbourg, Univ. Vision, Yale Fr. Studies. *Address*: French Dept, Royal Holloway College, Egham Hill, Egham TW20 0EX.

Cockerton, Rev. John Clifford Penn; Principal, St John's College, Durham University, since 1970; *b* 1927. BA Liverpool 1948 (Hons Geog.), DipEd Liverpool 1949; BA Oxon 1954 (Hons Theol.), MA Oxon 1958. *Address*: St John's College, Durham DH1 3RJ.

Cocking, Prof. John Martin, MA; Professor of French Language and Literature, University of London, King's College, since 1952; *b* 1914; *m* 1941; one *s*. BA London 1935 (1st cl. French), MA London 1939; Diplôme d'études universitaires Sorbonne 1937; Teacher's Dip. London 1936, Certificat de l'Association Phonétique Internationale 1934; Fellow of King's Coll., 1965; Mem., Assoc. Internat. des Etudes Françaises, Mod. Humanities Res. Assoc., Soc. for French Studies, Assoc. Profs of French. Asst Lectr, Univ. of London, King's College, 1939–46, Lectr, 1946–52; Vis. Prof., Univ. of Ghana, 1960, Univ. of W Australia, 1965, Univ. of Wisconsin at Madison, 1971; George A. Miller Lectr at Urbana, Ill., 1971. Asst to Dir, Brit. Inst. in Paris, 1937–39. Officier de l'Ordre national du mérite, 1973. *Publications*: Proust, 1956; ed jtly, Order and Adventure in Post-Romantic French Poetry, 1973; contrib. French 19th-century Painting and Literature, ed Finke, 1972; *contrib*. AUMLA, South. Rev., Mod. Lang. Rev., Fr. Studies, Essays in Fr. Lit. (Univ. of W Australia), Australian Jl of Fr. Studies, Bull. Proust, Romanic Rev., Forum for Mod. Lang. Studies. *Address*: Dept of French, King's College, Strand, WC2R 2LS.

Cockshut, Anthony Oliver John; G. M. Young Lecturer in 19th Century English Literature, Oxford, since 1965, and Fellow,

Hertford College, since 1966; *b* 1927; *m* 1952; one *d*. BA Oxford 1948 (1st cl.), MA 1952. Res. Fellow, Balliol Coll., Oxford, 1950–54. Asst Master, Manchester Grammar Sch., 1954–64. *Publications*: Anthony Trollope, 1955; Anglican Attitudes, 1959; The Imagination of Charles Dickens, 1961; The Unbelievers, 1964; The Achievement of Walter Scott, 1969; Truth to Life, 1974. *Address*: Hertford College, Oxford.

Coddington, Dr Alan; Lecturer in Economics, Department of Economics, Queen Mary College, University of London, since 1967; *b* 1941. BSc Leeds 1963, DPhil York 1966. Sir Ellis Hunter Meml Fellow, Univ. of York, 1965; Asst Lectr in Economics, Queen Mary Coll., 1966–67. *Publications*: Theories of the Bargaining Process, 1967; *contrib*. Canad. Jl Econ. *Address*: Queen Mary College, Mile End Road, E1 4NS.

Coe, Prof. Richard Nelson; Professor of French Studies, University of Warwick, since 1972; *b* 1923. Dip. Slav. Stud. London 1943, MA Oxon 1949, PhD Leeds 1954; FAHA 1969. Asst Lectr, Leeds Univ., 1950–53; Lectr, 1953–62; Sen. Lectr, Queensland, 1962–64; Reader, Melbourne, 1964–66; Reader, Warwick, 1966–69; Personal Prof., Melbourne, 1969–72. Chm., Faculty Board (Arts), Univ. of Warwick, 1973– ; Mem., Editorial Board, Australian Journal of French Studies, 1964– . *Publications*: trans. Stendhal: Life of Rossini, 1956, 2nd edn 1970; trans. Stendhal: Rome, Naples and Florence in 1826, 1959; Ionesco, 1961, 2nd edn 1969; Beckett, 1964, 2nd edn 1969; Stendhal and the Art of Memory, in, Currents of Thought in French Literature, 1965; Eugène Ionesco: the Meaning of Un-Meaning, in, Aspects of Drama and the Theatre, 1965; The Vision of Jean Genet, 1968, German, Italian and Japanese edns; ed, The Theater of Jean Genet: A Casebook, 1970; trans. Stendhal: Lives of Haydn, Mozart and Metastasio, 1972; *contrib*. Stendhal Club, Brit. Jl Educnl Studies, French Studies, Rev. Proc. Leeds Philosophical and Literary Soc., Time and Tide, Australian Jl of French Studies, Cambridge Rev., Revue d'histoire littéraire de la France. *Address*: Dept of French Studies, Univ. of Warwick, Coventry CV4 7AL.

Coffey, Dr Michael; Senior Lecturer in Latin and Greek, University College London, since 1967; *b* 1926; *m* 1962; two *d*. BA Manchester 1947 (1st cl. Classics); BA Cantab 1949 (1st cl. Classical Tripos pt II), MA Cantab 1953, PhD Cantab 1954. Asst Lectr, Univ. Coll., London, 1951–54, Lectr, 1954–67. Treas., 3rd Internat. Cong. Class. Studies, 1959. *Publications*: Appendix on Roman Tragedy, in, Fifty Years (and Twelve) of Classical Scholarship, 1968; new introd. to Juvenal Satires, ed J. D. Duff, 1970; *contrib*. Amer. Jl Philol., Bull. Inst. Class. Studies, Lustrum. *Address*: Depts of Latin and Greek, Univ. College London, Gower Street, WC1E 6BT.

Coggins, Richard James; Lecturer in Old Testament Studies, University of London, since 1962; *b* 1929; *m* 1964; one *s* one *d*. BA Oxon 1950 (Mod. Hist.), Dip. Theol.

Oxon 1953, MA Oxon 1954. *Publications*: Samaritans and Jews, 1974; *contrib*. Annual of Swedish Theol Inst., Church Qly Rev., Jl Theol Studies. *Address*: King's College, Strand, WC2R 2LS.

Cogman, Dr Peter William Mauger; Lecturer, Department of French, University of Southampton, since 1968; *b* 1941; *m* 1970; BA 1963, MA 1967, PhD 1969, Cantab. *Address*: The Univ. Highfield, Southampton SO9 5NH.

Cohen, Gerald Allen; BA, BPhil; Lecturer in Philosophy, University College London, since 1964; *b* 1941; *m* 1965; one *s* one *d*. BA McGill 1961 (1st cl. Philosophy and Politics); BPhil Oxon 1963. Asst Lectr, UCL, 1963–64; Vis. Asst Prof. of Politics, McGill Univ., Autumn Term, 1965. *Publications*: *contrib*. Ethics, Jl of Hist. of Ideas, Praxis, Proc. Aristotelian Soc., Supplementary Vol., Philos. and Public Aff. *Address*: Dept of Philosophy, Univ. College London, Gower Street, WC1E 6BT.

Cohen, Prof. John, MA, PhD, FBPsS; Professor of Psychology, University of Manchester, since 1952; *b* 1911; *m* 1st 1939; one *s* one *d*; 2nd 1955; three *s*. BA London 1933, MA London 1936, PhD London 1940; Hon. MA Manchester 1954; FBPsS, Fellow, World Acad. of Arts and Sciences, Leeds, 1948–49; Jerusalem, 1949–51; London, 1951–52. Offices of War Cabinet, 1941–46; Cabinet Office, 1946–47; short periods of secondment to Home Office and Air Ministry; Mem., Working Parties: Human Factors in Industry, 1945; Scientific Manpower, 1945; Recruitment and Training of Nurses, 1945–47; Consultant to Unesco, 1949, 1950, 1963, 1966. *Publications*: Human Nature, War and Society, 1946; (with C. E. M. Hansel) Risk and Gambling, 1956, French edn 1958, German edn 1958, Japanese edn 1966; Humanistic Psychology, 1958, German edn 1960, Japanese edn 1968, Italian edn 1964; Chance, Skill and Luck, 1960, French edn 1963, Dutch edn 1965, Italian edn 1964; Behaviour in Uncertainty, 1964, Japanese edn 1968; Human Robots in Myth and Science, 1966, French edn 1968, German edn 1968, Spanish edn 1968; A New Introduction to Psychology, 1966, Danish edn 1968, Spanish edn 1968; Psychological Time in Health and Disease, 1967, Japanese edn 1968; (with B. Preston) Causes and Prevention of Road Accidents, 1968; (with I. P. Christensen) Information and Choice, 1970; Elements of Child Psychology for Student Teachers, 1970; Homo Psychologicus, 1971, French edn 1971, Japanese edn 1972; Psychological Probability, 1972; Everyman's Psychology, 1973; *contrib*. Acta Psychol., Annee Psychol., Brit. Jl Psychol., BM Jl, Bull. de Psychol., Nature, Operat. Res. Qly, Scientia, Scientific Amer., etc. *Address*: Dept of Psychology, The Univ. of Manchester, Oxford Road, Manchester M13 9PL.

Cohen, Laurence Jonathan, FBA; Fellow and Praelector in Philosophy, The Queen's College, Oxford, since 1957; *b* 1923; *m* 1953; three *s* one *d*. BA Oxon 1947 (1st cl. Classical Honour Mods, 1941; 1st cl.

Lit. Hum., 1947), MA Oxon 1947. Asst in Logic and Metaphysics, Edinburgh Univ., 1947–50; Lectr in Philosophy, Univ. Coll., Dundee, in Univ. of St Andrews, 1950–57; Vis. Lectr, Hebrew Univ. of Jerusalem, 1952; Commonwealth Fund Fellow, Princeton and Harvard Univs, 1952–53; Vis. Prof., Columbia Univ., 1967–68; Vis. Prof., Yale Univ., 1972–73. Naval Intelligence, UK and SEAC, 1942–45. Hebdomadal Council, Oxford Univ., 1966–67; Chm., Bd of Psychology Faculty, Oxford Univ., 1971–72. Gen. Editor, Clarendon Library of Logic and Philosophy. *Publications*: The Principles of World Citizenship, 1954; The Diversity of Meaning, 1962, 2nd edn 1966; The Implications of Induction, 1970; *contrib*. Brit. Jl Phil. of Science, Analysis, Amer. Phil. Qly, Jl Symbolic Logic, Logique et Analyse, Mind, Phil. Qly, Phil. Rev., Phil. Studies, Philosophy, Proc. Aristotelian Soc., Revue Internationale de Philosophie, Ratio, Synthese. *Address*: The Queen's College, Oxford.

Cohen, Prof. Percy Saul; Professor of Sociology, University of London, since 1971; *b* 1928; *m* 1956; three *d*. BCom Witwatersrand 1947; BSc. (Econ) London 1951, PhD London 1961; FRAI, Mem., Assoc. Social Anthropol., Brit. Sociol. Assoc. Lectr, Univ of Leicester, 1960–64; Lectr, Univ. of London, 1965–67, Reader, 1967; Dean, Undergrad. Studies, London Sch. of Economics, 1967–71; Fellow, Center for Advanced Studies in Behavioural Sciences, Stanford Univ., 1972–73. *Publications*: Modern Social Theory, 1968, Spanish, Italian, Dutch and German edns 1971–72; *contrib*. Brit. Jl Sociol., Man, Sociol. *Address*: Dept of Sociology, London School of Economics, Houghton Street, WC2A 2AE.

Cohen, Ronald Alban, LDS, FFD, RCSI; Part-time Senior Research Fellow in Dental History, Department in Oral Pathology, Dental School, University of Birmingham, since 1970; *b* 1907; *m* 1934; one *s* two *d*. LDS Birmingham 1930, RCS Ireland 1964; FSA; Mem., Brit. Dent. Assoc.; Hon. Mem., Société Française de l'Histoire de l'Art Dentaire; Hon. Mem., Amer. Acad. Hist. of Dentistry; Mem., Amer. Assoc. Hist. of Medicine; Mem., Fédération Dentaire Int.; Chm., Warwicks and Solihull Exec. Council, 1958– . *Publications*: *contrib*. Brit. Dent. Jl, etc. *Address*: Dept of Oral Pathology, Dental School, St Mary's Row, Birmingham.

Cohn, Ernst Joseph; Visiting Professor of European Laws, and Fellow, King's College, London, since 1967; *b* 1904; *m* 1972 (3rd *m*); one *s*. Dr jur Breslau 1927, PhD London 1949, LLD London 1965, Hon Dr jur Cologne 1959. Barrister, Lincoln's Inn, 1937. Lectr, Univ. of Frankfurt Main, 1929–32; Prof. of Law, Univ. of Breslau, 1932–33; Hon. Prof. Univ. of Frankfurt, 1958– . Pres. North Western Reform Synagogue, London, 1973– ; Mem., Academic Cttee, Leo Baeck Coll., 1968– . *Publications*: Manual of German Law, vol. 1 1950, 2nd edn 1968, vol. 2 1952, 2nd edn 1972; (with R. H. and D. Graveson) The Uniform Laws on International Sales Act, 1967; several books in

German; *contrib*. British Yearbook of Internat. Law, Internat. and Compar. Law Qly, Modern Law Review, Zeitschrift für Zivilprozessrecht. *Address*: King's College, Univ. of London, Strand, WC2 R2LS.

Cohn, Dr Henry Jacob, MA, DPhil, FRHistS; Senior Lecturer, Department of History, University of Warwick, since 1971; *b* 1936; *m* 1960; one *d*. BA Oxon 1957 (1st cl. History), MA Oxon 1962, DPhil Oxon 1963; FRHistS. Asst, Glasgow, 1960–61; Asst Lectr, Leicester, 1961–63, Lectr, 1963–66; Lectr, Warwick, 1967–71. Mem., Acad. Adv. Cttee World Jewish Congress, 1969– . *Publications*: The Government of the Rhine Palatinate in the Fifteenth Century, 1965; Government in Reformation Europe, 1971; *contrib*. Europ. Studies Rev., Jewish Social Studies. *Address*: Dept of History, Univ. of Warwick, Coventry CV4 7AL.

Colclough, Dr Nevill Thomas; Lecturer in Sociology, University of Kent, since 1966; *b* 1938; *m* 1966. BA Oxon 1961 (1st cl. History); PhD London 1969; Mem., ASA. *Address*: Darwin College, The Univ., Canterbury.

Coldstream, John Nicolas; Reader in Greek, Bedford College, University of London, since 1966; *b* 1927; *m* 1970. BA Cantab 1951 (Classical Tripos, cl. I), MA Cantab 1956; FSA 1964. Temp. Asst Keeper, Greek and Roman Antiquities, British Museum 1956–57. Lectr, Bedford Coll. 1960. Mem. Man. Cttee, British Sch. at Athens, 1966– . *Publications*: Greek Geometric Pottery, 1968; Kythera: Excavations and Studies, 1972; Knossos: The Sanctuary of Demeter, 1973; *contrib*. Annual Brit. Sch. at Athens, Bull. Inst. Class. Stud., Gnomon, Jl Hellenic Stud. *Address*: Bedford College, Regent's Park, NW1 4NS.

Coldstream, Prof. Sir William, CBE, DLitt; Slade Professor, Department of Fine Art, University College London, 1949–75; *b* 1908; *m* 1931; 1961; one *s* four *d*. Slade School of Fine Art, Univ. Coll., London, 1926–29. Fellow, Univ. Coll. Trustee, Nat. Gall., 1948–55, 1956–63; Trustee, Tate Gall., 1949–55, 1956–63; Chm., Art Panel, Arts Council, 1953–62; Dir, Royal Opera House, Covent Garden, 1957–62; Chm., Nat. Adv. Council on Art Educn, 1958–71; Vice-Chm., Arts Council of GB, 1962–69; Chm., Brit. Film Inst., 1964–70. Work in permanent exhibitions: Tate Gall., Nat. Gall. of Canada, Nat. Mus. of Wales, Ashmol. Mus., Imp. War. Mus., Arts Council, Brit. Council, Bristol Art Gall., etc. *Address*: Slade School of Fine Art, Univ. College London, Gower Street, WC1E 6BT.

Cole, Dr John Peter; Reader, Geography Department, University of Nottingham, since 1969; *b* 1928; *m* 1952; two *s*. BA Nottingham 1950, MA Nottingham 1952, PhD Nottingham 1962; Mem., Inst. Brit. Geogrs. Demonstrator, Nottingham Univ., 1951–52; Lectr, Reading Univ., 1955–56; Lectr, Nottingham Univ., 1956–69; Vis. Prof., Univ. of Washington, 1966. *Publications*: Geography of World Affairs, 1959, various edns since; (with F. C.

German) Geography of the USSR, 1961, 2nd edn 1970; Italy, 1964; Latin America, 1965; (with C. A. M. King) Quantitative Geography, 1968; (with N. J. Benyon) New Ways in Geography, 1969; *contrib.* Geog. Jl, Geog. Rivista Geografica Italiana, Bull. della Societa Geografica, Italiana, Tijdschrift voor Economische en Sociale Geografie. *Address*: Geography Dept, Univ. of Nottingham, Nottingham NG7 2RD.

Cole, Prof. Monica M.; Professor of Geography, Bedford College, University of London, since 1964; *b* 1922. BSc London, PhD London; Lectr in Geography: Univ. of Capetown, 1947; Univ of Witwatersrand, 1948–51; Univ. of Keele, 1951–64; Associate Prof., Univ. of Idaho summer sch., 1952; Vis. Lectr, Univs of Queensland, Melbourne, and Adelaide, 1960; Mem., Brit. delegn Internat. Geographical Congress in: Washington, 1952; Rio de Janeiro, 1956; London, 1964; New Delhi, 1968. Res., vegetation/soils/geomorphology: S Africa, 1948–51; Brazil, 1956, 1965; Central and E Africa, 1959; Australia, 1960, 1962, 1963, 1965, 1966, 1967, 1968, 1971, 1972; Venezuela, 1964; Southern Africa, 1967, 1968. *Publications*: The Transvaal Lowveld, 1956; South Africa, 1961, 1966; *contrib.* Geog. Jl, Geography, Trans Inst. Brit. Geographers, S African Geog. Jl, Trans Instn Mining and Metallurgy, Proc. Royal Soc. *Address*: Bedford College, Inner Circle, Regent's Park, NW1 4NS.

Cole, Prof. William Alan, MA, PhD; Professor of Economic History, University College of Swansea, since 1966; *b* 1926; *m* 1970; one step-*s* one step-*d*. BA Cantab 1950 (Double 1st History), MA Cantab 1952, PhD Cantab 1955. Jun. Res. Off., Dept of Applied Econs, Cambridge, 1955–57, Res. Off., 1957–59; Lectr, Bristol Univ., 1959–65; Sen. Lectr, 1965–66. Nat. Service: Coal mining, 1944–45, RAF, 1946–48. *Publications*: (with P. Deane) British Economic Growth, 1688–1959, 1962, 2nd edn 1967; *contrib.* Crisis in Europe, 1560–1660, ed T. Aston, 1965; (with P. Deane) Cambridge Economic History of Europe, vol. VI, ed H. J. Habakkuk and M. Postan, 1965; The Study of Economic History, ed N. B. Harte, 1971; *contrib.* Cam. Jl, Econ. Hist. Rev., Explorations in Econ. Hist., Jl Friends' Historical Soc., Past and Present. *Address*: Dept of Economic History, Univ. College of Swansea, Singleton Park, Swansea SA2 8PP.

Coleman, Dr Bruce Ivor, MA, PhD, FRHistS; Lecturer, Department of History, Exeter University, since 1969; *b* 1940. BA Cantab 1961 (1st cl. Hons), MA 1966, PhD 1968; FRHistS 1973. Fellow, Trinity Hall, Cambridge, 1966–69. *Publication*: The Idea of the City in Nineteenth-century Britain, 1973. *Address*: Dept of History, The Univ. Exeter EX4 4QJ.

Coleman, Prof. Donald Cuthbert, FBA; Professor of Economic History, University of Cambridge, since 1971; *b* 1920; *m* 1954. BSc(Econ) London 1949 (1st cl. Economic History), PhD London 1951; MA Cambridge 1971; FRHistS. Lectr in Industrial Hist.,

London Sch. of Econs, 1951–58, Reader in Econ. Hist., 1958–69, Prof. of Econ. Hist., 1969–71; Vis. Prof. of Econs, Yale Univ., 1957–58; Fellow, Pembroke Coll., Cambridge, 1971. English Editor, Scandinavian Econ. Hist. Rev., 1952–61; Editor, Econ. Hist. Rev., 1967–73; Mem., Council, Econ. Hist. Soc., 1959– . *Publications*: The British Paper Industry, 1495–1860, 1958; Sir John Banks: Baronet and Businessman, 1963; Courtaulds: an Economic and Social History, 1969; Revisions in Mercantilism, 1969; *contrib.* Econ. Hist. Rev., Economica, Hist., Scandinavian Econ. Hist. Rev. *Address*: Pembroke College, Cambridge.

Coleman, Dr Dorothy Gabe, MA, PhD; Lecturer in French, University of Cambridge, since 1966; *b* 1935; *m* 1958; one *s*. BA Cantab 1956 (starred 1st cl. Mod. and Med. Langs), MA Cantab 1960; PhD Glasgow 1961; Mem., Fr. Studies. Asst Lectr, Glasgow, 1957–60; Fellow, New Hall, 1960; Asst Lectr, Cambridge, 1961–66. *Publications*: Rabelais: a critical study in prose fiction, 1971; *contrib.* French Studies, Studi francesi, Mod. Lang. Rev., Kentucky Romance Qly. *Address*: New Hall, Cambridge.

Coleman, Olive, MA; Lecturer in Economic History, London School of Economics, University of London, since 1964; *b* 1928. BA Hons London 1949, MA London 1957. Res. Officer, LSE, 1959–64. *Publications*: The Brokage Book of Southampton 1443–44, vol. 1, 1960, vol. II, 1961; (with E. M. Carus-Wilson) England's Export Trade 1275–1547, 1963; *contrib.* Econ. Hist. Rev. *Address*: London School of Economics, Houghton Street, Aldwych, WC2A 2AE.

Coleman, Rev. Canon Peter Everard, LLB, AKC; Special Lecturer, Department of Theology, University of Bristol, since 1971; *b* 1928; *m* 1960; two *s* two *d*. LLB and AKC London 1953, Cambridge Ordination Course 1955; Blackstone Schol., Middle Temple, 1950, Bar Finals, 1953; called to Bar, Middle Temple, 1966. Chaplain and Lectr, King's Coll., Univ. of London, 1960–66; Recognised Teacher in Theology, Univ. of Bristol, 1967–71. Chaplain, Univ. of Bristol, 1966–71; Canon Residentiary, Bristol Cath. and Dir, Ordination Training, Diocese of Bristol, 1971– ; Mem., Archbps Advisers on Radio and TV, 1963–67; C of E Bd Social Responsibility – Cttees on Illegitimacy, 1963, Natural Law, 1965, Homosexuality, 1968. *Publications*: Experiments in Prayer, 1961; A Christian Approach to Television, 1968; chapter in. Is Gay Good? – Ethics, Theology and Homosexuality, 1971. *Address*: Dept of Theology, Univ. of Bristol, Bristol BS8 1TH.

Coleman, Robert George Gilbert, MA; Fellow of Emmanuel College and Lecturer in Classics, Cambridge University, since 1960; *b* 1929; *m* 1958; one *s*. MA Victoria Univ., Wellington 1951 (1st cl. Latin), BA Cantab 1954 (1st cl. Classical Tripos part II). Prendergast Studentship, Burney Prize, Cambridge 1954–55; Lectr, King's Coll., Aberdeen, 1955–60. Mem., Council, Philological Soc., 1966–72. *Publications*: chapter on Pastoral, in, Greek and Latin Literature, ed J. Higginbotham, 1969; *contrib.* Amer. Jl Philology, Classical Qly, Didaskalos, Greece and Rome, Lingua, Proc. Cambridge Philological Soc. Trans Philological Soc., etc. *Address*: Emmanuel College, Cambridge.

Coles, Colin Roy; Assistant Director, Teaching Media Centre, University of Southampton since 1971; *b* 1940; *m* 1965; two *s*. BSc Leicester 1962 (Gen. Science), BSc Leicester 1964 (Psychology); Grad. Mem. British Psychological Soc. Mem. Assoc. for the Study of Medical Information. Lectr in Psychology, City Univ., 1965–67; Lectr in Educn Tech., Loughborough Coll. of Educn, 1967–69; Head of Dept of Educn Tech., Coll. of St Mark and St John, 1969–71. Membership Sec., NECCTA. *Publications*: Has produced film: (with A. D. B. Chant) Varicose Veins: the logical treatment, 1973; *contrib.* New Educn, Creative Drama, Screen Educn, NECCTA Bull. *Address*: Teaching Media Centre, South Academic Block, Southampton General Hospital, Southampton

Coles, John Morton, MA, PhD, FSA; University Lecturer, Department of Archaeology, Cambridge University, since 1965; *b* 1930; *m* 1958; two *s* two *d*. BA Toronto 1952; PhD Edinburgh 1959; FSA. Carnegie Scholar, 1959; Univ. Asst Lectr, Cambridge, 1960–65; Fellow, Fitzwilliam Coll. Hon. Editor, Proc. Prehist. Soc., 1970– . *Publications*: (with E. S. Higgs) The Archaeology of Early Man, 1969; Field Archaeology in Britain, 1972; Archaeology by Experiment, 1973; *contrib.* Antiqu. Jl, Antiquity, Proc. Prehist. Soc., Proc. Soc. Ant. Scot. *Address*: Dept of Archaeology, Downing Street, Cambridge.

Collard, Christopher, MA, MLitt, Senior Lecturer in Classical Studies, University of Kent at Canterbury, since 1972 (Lecturer, 1965–72); Master of Rutherford College, since 1974; *b* 1934; *m* 1966. MA Cantab 1961, MLitt Cantab 1963. Asst Lectr and Lectr, Liverpool Univ., 1959–65. Mem. Council, Classical Assoc., 1970– ; Jt Hon. Sec., 1972– ; Mem. Council, Hellenic Soc., 1973– . *Publications*: Supplement, Allen-Italie Concordance to Euripides, 1971; ed, Euripides: Supplices (forthcoming); *contrib.* BICS, Class. Qly, Jl Hellenic Studies, Latomus, RIFC, etc. *Address*: Rutherford College, The Univ., Canterbury, Kent.

Collard, Pamela Maud; *see* Bowmer, P. M.

Collcutt, Prof. Roger Hugh; Professor of Operational Research, Manchester Business School, University of Manchester, since 1971; *b* 1923; *m* 1951; four *d*. BSc Hons London 1943 (Engineering), Dip. Mun. and Civil Eng. London 1943; Fellow Operational Research 1974. Member: Operational Res. Soc., British Computer Soc., The Metals Soc., Operational Res. Soc. of America. Scientific Advisers Dept, Air Ministry, 1943–55; Head Operational Res. Dept BISRA, 1955–66; Dir Management Sciences, Arthur D. Little Ltd, London, 1966–71. *Publications*: Operational Research the first 20 years, 1965; *contrib.* Jl of Iron and Steel Institute, Operational Res. Qly. *Address*: Manchester Business

School, Booth Street West, Manchester M15 6PB.

Colledge, Dr Malcolm Andrew Richard, MA, PhD; Lecturer in Classics, Westfield College, University of London, since 1967; *b* 1939; *m* 1962; one *s*. BA Cambridge 1961 (1st cl. Classics), MA Cambridge 1964, PhD Cambridge 1965. Asst Lectr, Univ. Coll. Swansea, 1964–66; Asst Lectr, Westfield Coll., Univ. of London, 1966. Mem., Council, Soc. for Promotion of Hellenic Studies, 1971– , Cttee of Management, Inst. Classical Studies, London, 1971– . *Publications*: The Parthians, 1967; The Art of Palmyra, 1975; Parthian Art, 1975. *Address*: Dept of Classics, Westfield College, Univ. of London, Kidderpore Avenue, NW3 7ST.

Collier, Leslie William, MA; Lecturer in English Language, University of Glasgow, since 1966; *b* 1939. BA Oxon 1961 (English), Dip. Comparative Philology Oxon 1963, MA Oxon 1965. Asst, Glasgow Univ., 1963–66. *Address*: Dept of English Language, The Univ., Glasgow G12 8QQ.

Collier, Simon Daniel White, MA, PhD; Senior Lecturer in History, University of Essex, since 1971; *b* 1938. BA Cantab 1961, MA Cantab 1965, PhD Cantab 1965. Asst Lectr, Univ. of Essex, 1965, Lectr, 1966–71; Dir, Univ. of Essex Latin Amer. Centre, 1968–70; Dean, Sch. of Comparative Studies, 1971– . *Publications*: Ideas and Politics of Chilean Independence 1808–1833, 1967. *Address*: School of Comparative Studies, Univ. of Essex, Colchester CO4 3SQ.

Collins, David Norman; Lecturer, Department of Russian Studies, University of Leeds, since 1968; *b* 1944; *m* 1967; one *s*. BA Leeds 1966 (1st cl. Hons); Member: SCONUL/SEEG, Nat. Assoc. for Soviet and East European Studies, British Univ. Assoc. of Slavists. Slavonic Subject Specialist, Brotherton Library, Leeds Univ., 1966–67. *Publications*: *contrib.* Cambridge Hist. Jl, Soviet Studies. *Address*: Dept of Russian Studies, Univ. of Leeds, Leeds LS2 9JT.

Collins, Dennis Ferguson, MA, LLB, SSC; Lecturer in Private Law (Scots Law), University of Dundee, since 1960; *b* 1930; *m* 1961; one *s* one *d*. MA St Andrews 1952, LLB St Andrews 1956; Solicitor, 1957; Notary Public, 1962; SSC, 1971. *Address*: Faculty of Law, Univ. of Dundee, Dundee DD1 4HN.

Collins, Michael Patrick; Senior Lecturer in Town Planning, School of Environmental Studies, University College London, since 1964; *b* 1933; *m* 1968; two *d*. BA Nottingham 1954 (Geography), Dip. Town Planning London 1960 (Distinction); FRTPI. Asst Gp Planning Off., Town Planning Div., Architects Dept, LCC, 1956–64. *Publications*: contrib. Study of Urban Complexes within the Southern Half of the Greater London Region (Royal Commission Cmnd 1164, vol. 5), 1960; Frontiers in Geographical Teaching, 1965; co-author, Urban Motorways in London, 1969; *contrib.* Geographical Essays in Honour of Professor K. C. Edwards, 1970. *Address*: School of Environmental Studies,

Flaxman House, 16 Flaxman Terrace, WC1H 9AT.

Collins, Prof. Philip Arthur William; Professor of English, University of Leicester, since 1964; *b* 1923; *m* 1965; two *s* one *d*. BA Cantab 1947 (1st cl. English), MA Cantab 1948. Staff Tutor in Adult Educn, Leicester 1947; Warden, Vaughan Coll., Leicester, 1954; Sen. Lectr in English, Leicester, 1962–64; Vis. Prof., Univ. of California, Berkeley, 1967, Columbia, 1969. Sec., Leicester Theatre Trust Ltd, 1963– ; Mem., Drama Panel, Arts Council of GB, 1970– *Publications*: James Boswell, 1956; Dickens and Crime, 1962, 2nd edn 1964; Dickens and Education, 1963, 2nd edn 1964; The Impress of the Moving Age, 1965; Thomas Cooper the Chartist, 1969; A Dickens Bibliography, 1970; Dickens's Bleak House, 1970; Reading Aloud: a Victorian Métier, 1972; ed, English Christmas, 1956; ed, Dickens, the Critical Heritage, 1971; ed, A Christmas Carol: the Author's Prompt-Copy, 1971; *contrib*. Dickensian, Essays and Studies, Notes and Queries, Rev. of English Studies. *Address*: The Univ., Leicester LE1 7RH.

Collins, Wilkie Gordon; Reader, Department of Civil Engineering, University of Aston in Birmingham, since 1971; *b* 1924; *m* 1950; two *d*. BSc London 1956, PhD Leeds 1967; Teacher's Cert. London 1950. Lectr, London Coll. of Estate Management, 1957–60; Lectr, Univ. of Leeds, 1960–71. Mem., Nat. Cttee Photogrammetry, 1971– . *Publications*: A study, with the aid of aerial photographs, of the land utilisation of the Parish of St Catherine, Jamaica (special report for Govt of Jamaica), 1966; *contrib*. Royal Town Planning Inst., etc. *Address*: Dept of Civil Engineering, Univ. of Aston in Birmingham, Gosta Green, Birmingham B4 7ET.

Collis, Prof. Arthur Thomas, BSc(Econ); Professor of Social Administration, University of Birmingham, since 1969; *b* 1916; *m* 1948; two *s* two *d*. BSc(Econ) London 1950 (2/1 Sociology), Dip. in Social Studies London (Extra-mural) 1946; ACII 1939. Lectr, Birmingham Univ., 1956–64, Sen. Lectr, 1964–69, Dean, Faculty of Comm. and Social Science, 1969–72. Dep. Children's Officer, Glamorgan CC, 1950–56; Governor, Nat. Inst. Social Work Training, 1965–71; Chm., then Vice-Pres., Assoc. Social Workers, 1963–70; Mem.: Mental Health Rev. Tribunal (Birmingham), 1960–67; Birmingham Settlement Management Cttee. *Publications*: (with V. E. Poole) These Our Children, 1950; *contrib*. Brit. Jl Delinquency, Case Conf., Chambers' Encyclopaedia World Survey, Internat. Social Work. *Address*: The Univ. of Birmingham, PO Box 363, Birmingham B15 2TT.

Collison, Prof. Peter, BCom, PhD, MA; Professor of Social Studies, University of Newcastle upon Tyne, since 1965; *b* 1925; *m* 1953; one *s* two *d*. BCom Birmingham 1950 (1st cl. Econs, Politics and Sociology), PhD Birmingham 1953; MA Oxford 1955. Tutor in Sociology, Oxford Univ., 1955–60, Lectr in Sociology, 1960–65; Rockefeller Foundation

Fellow. n Social Sciences, 1958–59. *Publications*: The Cutterlowe Walls, 1963; *contrib*. Amer. Jl Sociology, Brit. Jl Sociology, Sociology, Sociological Rev., etc. *Address*: Dept of Social Studies, The Univ., Newcastle upon Tyne 1.

Colman, Andrew Michael, MA; Lecturer in Psychology, Leicester University, since 1970; *b* 1944; *m* 1968. BA Cape Town 1964, BA Hons Cape Town 1965 (1st cl. Psychology), MA Cape Town 1968. Grad. Asst, Cape Town Univ., 1966, Jun. Lectr, 1967–68; Lectr, Rhodes Univ., 1969–70. *Publications*: *contrib*. Jl Soc. Psychol., Percept. Motor Skills, Psychologia Africana. *Address*: Dept of Psychology, Leicester Univ., Leicester LE1 7RH.

Colson, A. J. B.; *see* Butt Colson.

Coltham, Dr Jeanette Barbara, MA, PhD; Senior Lecturer in Education, University of Manchester, since 1966; *b* 1915; *m* 1947. BA Oxon 1947 (Hons. History), MA Oxon 1952; PhD Manchester 1960; Bd of Educn Teacher's Cert., 1936. Lectr, Manchester, 1947–66. Mem., Steering Cttee A, Schs Council, 1969–73. *Publications*: Beginning of Writing, 1953; (with W. H. Wright) Life Then; Norman Times; Series of six books, 1966–68; *contrib*. Educn for Teaching, Sch. Rev. *Address*: Dept of Education, The Univ., Manchester M13 9PL.

Coltham, Dr Stephen William; Senior Lecturer in History, Department of Adult Education, Keele University, since 1968; *b* 1914; *m* 1947, BA Oxford 1941 (Hons History), MA Oxford 1945, DPhil Oxford 1956. Extra-mural Staff Tutor, Oxford, 1941–62; Staff Tutor (Lectr), Dept of Adult Educn, Keele, 1962–68. *Publications*: The Bee-Hive Newspaper: Its Origin and Early Struggles, in, Essays in Labour History (ed A. Briggs and J. Saville), 1960; *contrib*. Internat. Rev. Soc. Hist., Victorian Studies. *Address*: Dept. of Adult Education, Univ. of Keele, Keele, Staffs ST5 5BG.

Coltheart, Dr Max; Reader in Psychology, University of Reading, since 1972; *b* 1939; *m* 1961, 1970; two *s*. BA Sydney 1961, MA 1962, PhD 1968; Member: Psychonomic Soc. 1971– ; Experimental Psychology Soc., 1973– . Lectr, Univ. of Sydney, 1965–66; Lectr, Monash Univ., 1967–68; Sen. Lectr, 1969; Asst Prof., Univ. Waterloo, 1969–71; Assoc. Prof. 1971–72. *Publications*: Readings in Cognitive Psychology, 1972; *contrib*. Cognitive Psychology, Nature, Jl Auditory Research, Perception and Psychophysics, Memory and Cognition, Amer. Jl of Psychology, Qly Jl of Experimental Psychology. *Address*: Dept of Psychology, Univ. of Reading, Whiteknights, Reading RG6 2AH.

Colvin, Howard Montagu, CBE, MA, FBA; Fellow, since 1948 and Librarian since 1950, St John's College, Oxford; Reader in Architectural History, Oxford University, since 1965; *b* 1919; *m* 1943; two *s*. BA London; MA Oxon 1948; Hon. FRIBA. Asst Lectr, Dept of History, UCL, 1946–48. Member: Royal Fine Art

Commn, 1962–72; Royal Commn on Historical Monuments, 1963– ; Historic Buildings Council for England, 1970– . *Publications*: The White Canons in England, 1951; A Biographical Dictionary of English Architects 1660–1840, 1954 (Sir Banister Fletcher Prize, 1957); (with R. A. Brown and A. J. Taylor) The History of the King's Works (vols 1 and 2), 1963; A History of Deddington, 1963; (with M. Craig) Catalogue of Architectural Drawings in the Library of Elton Hall, 1964; ed (with J. Harris), The Country Seat, 1970; Building Accounts of King Henry III, 1971; *contrib.* Archaeological Jl, Architectural Rev., etc. *Address*: St John's College, Oxford.

Combe, Dr Thomas George Sugden; Lecturer, French Department, University of Cambridge, since 1938; Fellow of Pembroke College, Cambridge, since 1949; *b* 1911; *m* 1939; one *s* three *d*. MA Edinburgh 1933 (Hons), Doctorat d'Université Bordeaux 1937, MA Cambridge 1938. Asst Lectr, Glasgow, 1937–38; War service, 1940–Jan. 1946. *Publications*: Sainte-Beuve poète et les poètes anglais, 1937; ed (with P. Rickard), The French Language (Studies presented to Lewis Charles Harmer), 1970; *contrib.* French Stud., Mod. Langs Rev. *Address:* Pembroke College, Cambridge.

Common, Robert, BSc, PhD; Reader in Geography, Queen's University, Belfast, since 1966; *b* 1922; *m* 1948; two *s* one *d*. BSc Dunelm 1949 (1st cl. Hons), PhD Edinburgh 1953; Asst Lectr, Edinburgh Univ., 1949–53; Lectr, Glasgow Univ., 1953–57; Assoc. Prof., Univ. of Alberta, 1957–60; Lectr, Sen. Lectr, Belfast, 1960–66. *Publications*: ed, N Ireland from the Air, 1964; ed, Laboratory Manual in Physical Geography, 1959. *Address*: Dept of Geography, Queen's Univ., Belfast BT7 1NN.

Connell, Rev. Prof. Desmond; Professor of General Metaphysics, University College, Dublin, since 1972; *b* 1926. BA National Univ. of Ireland 1946, MA National Univ. of Ireland 1947, BD St Patrick's Coll., Maynooth, PhD Louvain. Asst, Dept of Metaphysics, Univ. Coll., Dublin, 1953–57, Asst Lectr, 1957–61, Coll. Lectr, 1961–72. *Publications*: The Vision in God: Malebranche's Scholastic Sources, 1967; *contrib.* Irish Theological Qly, Rev. philosophique de Louvain. *Address*: Room D508, Arts Block, Univ. College, Belfield, Dublin 4.

Connell, Dr Geoffrey William; Senior Lecturer, Department of Hispanic Studies, University of Glasgow, since 1970; *b* 1928; *m* 1959; one *s* one *d*. BA Hons Manchester 1952 (Mod. Langs), MA Manchester 1954 (Spanish); PhD Nottingham 1964 (Spanish). Teaching-Fellow, Univ. of Texas, 1953–54; Asst, Univ. of Manchester, 1954–56; Asst Lectr, Univ. of Nottingham, 1956–58, Lectr, 1958–67; Lectr, Univ. of Glasgow, 1967–70. *Publications*: Rafael Alberti: Concerning the Angels, complete verse trans. and introduction, 1967; *contrib.* Bulletin of Hispanic Studies, Hispanic Review, New Directions, Renaissance and Modern Studies. *Address*: Dept of Hispanic Studies, The Univ., Glasgow G12 8QQ.

Connolly, John Augustine, MAgrSc, MS, PhD; Lecturer in the Department of Applied Agricultural Economics, University College, Dublin, since 1972; *b* 1938; *m* 1965; four *s*. BAgrSc National Univ. of Ireland 1961, MAgrSc National Univ. of Ireland 1968; MS(Econ) Michigan State Univ. 1970; Kellogg Fellow, Michigan State Univ., 1968–70. College Lectr, Dept of Farm Management, Univ. Coll. Dublin, 1965–72. *Publications*: *contrib.* Jl Agric. and Fish., Ireland. *Address*: Dept of Applied Agricultural Economics, Univ. Coll. Dublin, Glasnevin, Dublin 9, Ireland.

Connolly, Prof. Kevin J.; Professor of Psychology, Sheffield University, since 1972; *b* 1937; *m* 1963; three *d*. BSc Hull 1961 (2/1 Psychology); PhD London 1969; ABPsS; Mem., Assoc. Study Animal Behaviour, Royal Inst. Philosophy, Genetical Soc., Soc. Res. Child Develop. Asst Lectr, Birkbeck Coll., London, 1963–64, Lectr, 1964–65; Lectr, Sheffield Univ., 1965–69, Sen. Lectr, 1969–72. *Publications*: Capital Punishment, 1963; ed, Mechanisms of Motor Skill Development, 1970; ed (with J. S. Bruner), The Growth of Competence, 1974; *contrib.* Animal Behaviour, Brit. Jl Psychol., Child Develop., Develop. Med. Child Neurol., Evolution, Nature, Science, Jl Ins. Physiol., Experientia. *Address*: Dept of Psychology, Univ. of Sheffield, Sheffield S10 2TN.

Constable, Prof. Charles John; Professor of Operations Management, School of Management, Cranfield Institute of Technology, since 1971; *b* 1936; *m* 1960; three *s* one *d*. BA Cantab 1957, MA 1965, BSc ARSM London 1959, DBA Harvard 1971; MBIM. Lectr, Durham Univ., 1964–68; Asst Dir, Bus. Sch., Durham Univ., 1968–71. Consultant to: BSC, 1969–70; Lesney Products Ltd, 1969– ; General Motors Overseas Corp. 1973; Joseph Lucas Industries Ltd, 1973. Chm., Case Clearing House, GB and Ireland. *Publications*: (with D. A. Smith) Group Assessment Programmes, 1966; *contrib.* Internat. Jl of Prodn Res., Management Today. *Address*: Sch. of Management, Cranfield Inst. of Technology, Cranfield, Bedford MK43 0AL.

Conway, Freda, BSc, MA (Com); Senior Lecturer in Social and Economic Statistics, Department of Sociology, Government and Administration, University of Salford, since 1967; *b* 1911. BSc London 1932 (2nd cl. Maths); MA (Com) Manchester 1948; Mem., RSS, Econ. Soc., Mathematical Assoc. Lectr, Leicester, 1948–64; Lectr, Salford, 1965–67. Mem., Council, Manchester Statistical Soc., 1968– . *Publications*: Descriptive Statistics, 1963; Sampling: an introduction for social scientists, 1967; *contrib.* Applied Statistics (now JRSS, Series C), Manchester Sch. *Address*: Dept of Sociology, Government and Administration Univ. of Salford, Salford M5 4WT.

Cook, Dr Adrian E.; Lecturer, History Department, University of Reading, since 1971; *b* 1940. BA Cambridge 1961 (double 1st cl. Hons), MA, PhD Cambridge 1965;

Mem.: Amer. Historical Assoc.; Organization of Amer. Historians; Southern HA; Rockefeller Grant Fellow, BAAS, Johns Hopkins Univ., 1962–63. Lectr in History, Univ. of Reading, 1966–68; ACLS Fellow: Columbia Univ., 1968–69; Univ. of Va, 1969–70; Postdoctoral Fellow, Inst. for Res. in Humanities, Univ. of Wisconsin, Madison, 1970–71. *Publications*: The Armies of the Streets: The New York City Draft Riots of 1863, 1974; The Settlement of the Alabama Claims: The United States and Great Britain, 1865–1872 (forthcoming); *contrib*. Aust. Jl Polit. and Hist., Maryland Hist. Mag. *Address*: Dept of History, Univ. of Reading, Reading RG6 2AA.

Cook, David Allen; Director of Studies, School of Architecture and Building Tech-, nology, University of Bath, since 1973. BSc Bristol 1955, DIC Imperial Coll. London 1962, MSc Bath 1973; MICE 1959, MIStructE 1958. Lectr Sch. of Arch. and Bldg Technology, Bath, 1966. *Publications*: A practical method for field control of Embankment loading, in, British Geotechnical Society Conference on Field Instrumentation in Geotechnical Engineering, 1973; *contrib*. Quart. Jl Engrg Geol. *Address*: School of Architecture and Building Technology, Univ. of Bath, Claverton Down, Bath BA2 7AY.

Cook, Frederick George, MA, BA, AMBIM; Research Lecturer, Department of Sociology, University of Liverpool, since 1968; *b* 1927; *m* 1951; two *s*. BA Liverpool 1965 (2nd cl Social Science), MA Liverpool 1972; Dip. Management Studies, 1958; AMBIM 1967. Res. Worker, Univ. of Liverpool, 1965–67, Lectr, 1967–68. *Address*: Dept of Sociology, Univ. of Liverpool, Liverpool L69 3BX.

Cook, Prof. John Manuel, FSA, FBA; Professor of Ancient History and Classical Archaeology, Bristol University, since 1958; *b* 1910; *m* 1939; two *s*. BA Cantab 1934, MA Cantab 1947; FSA. Asst in Humanity and Lectr in Classical Archaeology, Edinburgh Univ., 1936–45; Dir, Brit. Sch. of Archaeol at Athens, 1946–54; Reader, 1954–58, Dean, Faculty of Arts, 1966–68, Pro-Vice-Chancellor, 1972– , Bristol Univ.; C E Norton Lectr of the Archaeological Inst. of America, 1961–62; Vis. Prof., Yale Univ., 1965; Gray Meml Lectr, Cambridge. 1969. *Publications*: The Greeks in Ionia and the East, 1962; The Troad, 1973; (with W. H. Plommer) The Sanctuary of Hemithea at Kastabos, 1966; chapters in Cambridge Ancient History and Cambridge History of Iran; *contrib*. classical, archaeological, and historical jls. *Address*: Univ. of Bristol, Bristol BS8 1TH.

Cook, Michael Allan; Lecturer in Economic History with special reference to the Middle East, History Department, School of Oriental and African Studies, University of London, since 1966; *b* 1940; *m* 1966; two *s*. BA Cambridge 1963 (1st classes in Part I History and Part II Oriental Studies). *Publications*: ed, Studies in the Economic History of the Middle East, 1970; Population Pressure in Rural Anatolia, 1450–1600, 1972. *Address*: School of Oriental and African Studies, Univ. of London, Malet Street, WC1E 7HU.

Cook, Michael Garnet; University Archivist, Archives and Medieval History Departments, University of Liverpool, since 1968; *b* 1931, *m* 1955; three *s* two *d*. BA 1954, MA 1968, Oxon. (Mod. Hist.), postgrad. course in archives, Bodleian Lib., 1955; Soc. of Archivists (Mem. Council), Mem., Brit. Records Assoc., Bus. Archives Council (Mem. Exec.). City Archivist, Newcastle upon Tyne, 1958–63; Dir of Nat. Archives, Tanzania, 1964–66; UNESCO Cons. in Archives Sci., 1973. *Publications*: The Diocese of Exeter in 1821, 2 vols, 1958, 1960; A New Manual of Archives Administration, 1974; *contrib*. Archives, Jl of Soc. of Archivists. *Address*: Univ. Archives, PO Box 147, Liverpool L69 3BX.

Cook, P. Lesley; Reader in Industrial Economics, School of Social Sciences, University of Sussex, since 1963. *b* 1922. BA Cantab 1947, MA Cantab 1948, PhD Cantab 1951. Lectr, Univ. of Exeter, 1951–53; Research Officer, Dept of Applied Econs, 1953–63; Newnham Coll., Cambridge: Fellow and Tutor, 1956–63; Sen. Tutor, 1959–63. Mem., Bd of Governors Cambridge United Hosps, 1961–63; Sen. Economic Advr, Min. of Power, 1967–69; Part-time Mem., SE Gas Bd, 1971–73. *Publications*: (with R. L. Cohen) Effects of Mergers, 1958; Railway Workshops: The problems of contraction, 1964; *contrib*. Economic Jl. *Address*: Univ. of Sussex, Falmer, Brighton BN1 9RH.

Cook, Prof. Robert Manuel; Laurence Professor of Classical Archaeology, Cambridge University, since 1962; *b* 1909; *m* 1938. BA Cambridge 1931. Asst Lectr in Classics, Manchester Univ., 1934–38, Lectr, 1938–45; Laurence Reader in Classical Archaeol., Cambridge Univ., 1945–62. Min. of Works, 1941–45. *Publications*: Corpus Vasorum Antiquorum, British Museum, fasc. 8, 1954; Greek Painted Pottery, 1960, 2nd edn 1972; The Greeks till Alexander, 1961; (with Kathleen Cook) Southern Greece, 1968; Greek Art, 1972; *contrib*. Annual Brit. Sch. Athens, Jl Hellenic Studies, etc. *Address*: Museum of Classical Archaeology, Little St Mary's Lane, Cambridge.

Cook, Prof. Stephen L., BSc; Professor of Operational Research, The University of Aston in Birmingham, since 1966; *b* 1919; *m* 1954; two *d*. BSc London 1940 (1st cl. Hons Electrical Engineering); Mem., ORS; Mem., BIM; Mem., ATM; Mem., BSSRS; Mem., TIMS (UK Chapter). Vis. Prof. of Operations Res., Case Inst. of Technology, Cleveland, Ohio, 1963–64. Exp. Officer, Admiralty, 1940–46; Nelson Res. Labs, English Electric Co., 1946–48; Dep. Hd, Field Investigation Gp, NCB, 1949–56; Manager, OR Dept, Richard Thomas & Baldwins, 1956–65. ORS Council Mem., 1959–62, 1971–73; Chm., ORS External and Future Affairs Cttee, 1973–75; Chm., SWORDS, 1962–63; Chm., MORS, 1969–71; ORS Educn Cttee, 1960–63, 1966–69; Chm., OR and Social Organisation Gp, 1965–68; ORS Public Affairs Cttee, 1967–69. *Publications*: chapters in: Operations Research for Management, 1956; Progress in

143

Operations Research, vol. II, 1964; Operational Research and the Social Sciences, 1966; Economics and Technical Change, 1969; *contrib.* Management Educn and Develop., Management Science, OR Qly, Trans Inst. Mining Engineers, Omega. *Address*: University of Aston Management Centre, Maple House, 158 Corporation Street, Birmingham B4 6TE.

Coombes, Prof. David Leslie, MA, BLitt; Professor of European Studies, Loughborough University of Technology, since 1971; *b* 1940; *m* 1962; one *s* two *d*. BA Oxon 1962 (PPE), MA Oxon 1967, BLitt Oxon 1964. Asst Lectr in Polit. Studies, Univ. of Hull, 1964–66; Lectr in Polit., Univ. of Reading, 1966–71. Res. Associate, Polit. and Econ. Planning, 1966– . *Publications*: The Member of Parliament and the Administration, 1966; Towards a European Civil Service, 1968; Politics and Bureaucracy in the European Community, 1970; State Enterprise: Business or Politics? 1971; The Power of The Purse in the European Community, 1972; *contrib.* Diritto Pubblico, Parliamentary Affairs, Public Law, Spettatore Internazionale. *Address*: Dept of European Studies, Univ. of Technology, Loughborough LE11 3TU.

Cooper, Cary Lynn, BS, MBA, PhD; Senior Lecturer in Psychology, University of Manchester Institute of Science and Technology, since 1973; *b* 1940; *m* 1968; one *s* one *d*. BS UCLA 1962, MBA UCLA 1964; PhD Leeds 1968; MBPsS, Internat. Assoc. of Humanistic Psychol., Amer. Acad. of Management. Res. Asst. Univ. of Leeds, 1964–66; Fellow, Sussex Univ., 1966–67; Lectr in Social Psychology, Dept of Psychology, Southampton, 1967–73. Mem., Exec. Cttee, Gp Relations Training Assoc., 1972–74. *Publications*: T-Groups: A Survey of Research, 1971; Group Training for Individual and Organizational Development, 1973; Theories of Group Processes, 1975; *contrib.* Admin. Sci. Qly, Brit. Jl Soc. Clin. Psychol., Hum. Relat., Interpers. Develt, Jl Mgt. Studies, Psychol. Reports, Small Gp. Behaviour. *Address*: Dept of Management Sciences, Univ. of Manchester Institute of Science and Technology, Sackville Street, Manchester M60 1QD.

Cooper, James Anthony; Lecturer, Division of Languages, Brunel University, since 1966; *b* 1939; *m* 1965; two *s*. MA Edinburgh 1962, Teacher's Cert. Moray House Coll. of Educn 1963. *Address*: Brunel Univ., Kingston Lane, Uxbridge, Middx UB8 3TH.

Cooper, Morley Bruce; Senior Lecturer in History, School of European Studies, University of East Anglia, since 1969; *b* 1932; *m* 1965; one *s* one *d*. BA California 1959. Lectr, UEA, 1964–69. *Publications*: *contrib.* Hist. Jl. *Address*: Sch. of European Studies, University Plain, Norwich.

Cooper, Margery Gascoigne, MEd, NFF; Lecturer in Education, University of Durham, since 1965; *b* 1916; *m* 1943. National Froebel Cert A Newcastle upon Tyne 1942 (1st cl.), MEd Leicester 1962. *Publications*: *contrib.* Educnl Res., NFF Bull., Trends in Educn.

Address: Institute of Education, Univ. of Durham, Durham DH1 3HP.

Cooper, Michael Hymie, BA, MRSH; Reader in Social Economics, University of Exeter, since 1971; *b* 1938; *m* 1972; one *d*. BA Leicester 1961; MRSH. Asst Lectr, Keele Univ., 1963–64; Asst Lectr, Exeter Univ., 1964–66, Lectr, 1966–71; Vis Prof., Stanford Univ., 1968–69; Editor, Soc. and Econ. Admin, 1966–73, Occ. Papers in Soc. and Econ. Admin, 1966– . Mem., NEDO Sub-Gp on Pharmaceuticals Marketing and Forecasting, 1970–71; European Consumer's Cttee on Civil Aviation (Zurich Cttee), 1970– . *Publications*: Prices and Profits in the Pharmaceutical Industry, 1966; The Price of Blood – An Economic Study of the Charitable and Commercial Principle, 1968; The Price of Air Travel, 1971; Economics of Health, 1972; International Price Comparison, 1973; The Pharmaceutical Industry in the UK, 1973; Social Policy, 1974; *contrib.* Sociological Studies in British Penal Services, 1965; Innovation and the Balance of Payments – The Experience of the Pharmaceutical Industry, 1967; Health Services Financing, 1970; Economics of Medical Care, 1972; Management and the Social Services, 1972; Economics of Health and Medical Care, 1974; The Economics of Charity, 1974; *contrib.* Brit. Med. Jl, Jl Royal Coll. Gp, Jl RSH, Jl Trans Econ. and Pol., Lancet, Med. Care, OEP, Soc. Rev. Mono., Soc. Sci. and Med., Soc. and Econ. Admin. *Address*: Economics Dept, Univ. of Exeter, Streatham Court, Rennes Drive, Exeter EX4 4PU.

Cooper, Neil Louis; Reader in Philosophy, Department of Philosophy, University of Dundee, since 1969; *b* 1930; *m* 1956; one *s* one *d*. BA London 1949 (2nd cl. Classics), BA Oxon 1953 (Classical Hon. Mods Oxon 1951 (1st cl.), Classical Greats Oxon 1953 (1st cl.)), BPhil Oxon 1955, MA Oxon 1956. Lectr in Philosophy, Queen's Coll., Dundee, 1956–67; Sen. Lectr in Philosophy, Univ. of Dundee, 1967–69. Dean of Students, Fac. of Social Science and Letters, Univ. of Dundee, 1972. *Publications*: *contrib.* The Definition of Morality, ed Wallace and Walker; Weakness of Will, ed G. W. Mortimore; *contrib.* Analysis, Brit. Jl Philos. Sci. Mind, Monist, Philos. Qly, Philos., Supp. Proc. Aristot. Soc. *Address*: Dept of Philosophy, The Univ., Dundee DD1 4HN.

Cooper, Theodora Constance; Fellow and Tutor in Economics, St Hugh's College, Oxford, University Lecturer (CUF), University of Oxford, since 1963; *b* 1934. BA Cantab 1956 (2nd cl. Economics), MA Cantab 1960. Res. Asst in Economics, Univ. of Manchester, 1960; Lectr in Economics, St Hugh's Coll., Oxford, 1960–63. Econ. Consultant, Cabinet Off., 1965–69; Fiscal Adv., Brit. Virgin Is, 1970. *Address*: St Hugh's College, Oxford.

Cope, Rev. Dr Gilbert, MSc, DipTheol; Deputy Director, Institute for the Study of Worship and Religious Architecture, University of Birmingham, since 1962; *b* 1910; *m* 1939; two *s*. BSc Birmingham 1931 (2nd cl. Biochemistry), MSc 1932; DipTheol Oxon

1934; PhD Birmingham 1960 (Theol.). Lectr, Dept of Extramural Studies, Birmingham Univ., 1947–64, Sen. Lectr, 1964–65. Proctor in Convocation and Mem., General Synod – Univs' Rep. (Province of Canterbury), 1970– ; Mem., Council for Places of Worship; Chm., New Churches Cttee, 1972; Univ. Rep., Bd of Govs, Warwick Schs Stratford-on-Avon Gr. Sch. for Girls, 1971– . Associate Editor, Kunst und Kirche. *Publications*: Symbolism in the Bible and the Church, 1959; Ecclesiology: Then and Now, 1963; Theology for Adults, 1963; ed, Making the Building Serve the Liturgy, 1962; Christianity and the Visual Arts, 1964; Cathedral and Mission, 1969; Dying, Death and Disposal, 1970; Problem Churches, 1972; *contrib*. An Experimental Liturgy, 1958; The Modern Architectural Setting of the Liturgy, 1963; Crisis for Baptism, 1965; School Worship, 1965; Church Architecture and Social Responsibility, 1968; For Church Builders, 1969; A Dictionary of Liturgy and Worship, 1972; University Studies for Adults, 1972. *Address*: Dept of Theology, Univ. of Birmingham, PO Box 363, Birmingham B15 2TT.

Cope, John Michael, BCom, ATII; Senior Lecturer in Accounting and Finance, University of Lancaster, since 1973 (Lecturer, 1970–73); *b* 1929; *m* 1952; one *s* one *d*. BCom Birmingham 1951; ATII 1963. Lectr, Sheffield Univ., 1966–70. *Publications*: Business Taxation, 1972; *contrib*. Brit. Tax Rev., Accountant, Jl Busin. Fin. *Address*: Dept of Accounting and Finance, Univ. of Lancaster, Bailrigg, Lancaster LA1 4YW.

Copley, Antony Robert Hanchett; Lecturer, History Department, Kent University, since 1967; *b* 1937. BA Oxford 1960, BPhil Oxford 1962, MA Oxford 1963. Lectr, Univ. Coll. of Wales, Bangor, 1963–67. *Publications*: C.R., A Historian's Tribute, Rajaji 93, 1971; *contrib*. Indo-British Rev., 20th Century Studies. *Address*: Rutherford College, The Univ., Canterbury.

Copley, James, MA; Lecturer, Overseas Educational Studies Group, Institute of Education, University of Leeds, since 1964; *b* 1916; *m* 1943; two *s*. BA Leeds 1938 (1st cl. English Language and Literature), MA Leeds 1940 (with Distinction), DipEd Leeds 1939; Mem., Brontë Soc., York. Dialect Soc. Lectr in English, Univ. of Malaya, 1951–56; Head of English Dept, Fourah Bay Univ. Coll., Sierra Leone, 1957–61; Lectr in Communication, Dept of Adult Educn, Univ. of Leeds, 1962–64. Team Leader, Teaching Eng. Overseas Courses, Leeds Inst. of Educn, 1969– . *Publications*: Seven English Songs and Carols of the Fifteenth Century, 1940; Shift of Meaning, 1961; Three Centuries, 1962; *contrib*. Durham Univ. Jl, Eng. Studies, Mod. Lang. Notes, Notes and Queries, Times Educnl Supp., Univs Rev., Univ. of Leeds Rev., Brontë Soc. Trans; articles on hist. of English theatres; dramatic documentaries for school, college, university. *Address*: Overseas Educational Studies Group, Institute of Education, Univ. of Leeds, Leeds LS2 9JT.

Coppock, John Terence, MA, PhD; Ogilvie Professor of Geography, University of Edinburgh, since 1965; *b* 1921; *m* 1953; one' *s* one *d*. BA Cantab 1949 (1st cl. pts I and II Geographical Tripos), MA Cantab 1954; PhD London 1960; FRGS. Asst Lectr, Univ. Coll., London, 1950–52, Lectr, 1952–63; Vis. Sen. Lectr, Univ. of Ibadan, 1963–64; Reader, Univ. Coll., London, 1964–65; Commonwealth Prestige Fellow, NZ, 1971; Vis. Prof., Univ of Waterloo, 1972. Mem., Council, Inst. of Brit. Geogrs, 1966– , Vice-Pres., 1971–73, Pres., 1973– ; Mem., England Cttee, Nature Conservancy, 1965–71; Land-use Grants Cttee, NERC, 1967– ; Sec. of State's Cttee on Educn and the Countryside, 1968– ; Brit. Nat. Cttee on Geography, 1973– ; Specialist Adviser, Select Cttee on Scottish Affairs, 1971–72. *Publications*: (with R. H. Best) The Changing Use of Land in Britain, 1962; ed (with H. C. Prince), Greater London, 1964; An Agricultural Atlas of England and Wales, 1964; An Agricultural Geography of Great Britain, 1971; *contrib*. Agric. Hist. Rev., Trans Inst. Brit. Geogrs. *Address*: Dept of Geography, Univ. of Edinburgh, High School Yards, Edinburgh EH1 1NR.

Corbet, Dr Sarah Alexandra; Lecturer in Zoology, Westfield College, University of London, since 1968; *b* 1940. BA Cantab 1962 (1st cl. Zoology), MA Cantab 1966, PhD Cantab 1966. Asst Lectr, Westfield Coll., 1965–68. *Address*: Westfield College, Hampstead, NW3 7ST.

Corbet, John David, BA; Lecturer in French, University of Keele, since 1969; *b* 1940. BA London 1963 (1st cl. French). Asst Lectr, Univ. of Keele, 1966–69. *Address*: French Dept, Univ. of Keele, Staffs ST5 5BG.

Corbett, Prof. John Patrick, MA; Professor of Philosophy, University of Bradford, since 1972; *b* 1916; *m* 1940; 1968; two *s* two *d*. MA Oxon 1945. Fellow, Balliol Coll., Oxford, 1945–61; Prof. of Philosophy, Sussex Univ., 1961–72; Jowett Lectr in Philosophy; Council of Europe Fellow, 1957; Vis. Lectr, Yale Univ., 1958; NATO Fellow, 1960; Vis. Prof., Univ. of Toronto, 1968. *Publications*: Europe and the Social Order, 1959; Ideologies, 1965. *Address*: Univ. of Bradford, Bradford BD7 1DP.

Corbett, Prof. Peter Edgar; Yates Professor of Classical Art and Archaeology in the University of London (University College), since 1961; *b* 1920. MA Oxon 1945. Thomas Whitcombe Greene Scholar, and Macmillan Student, Brit. Sch. at Athens, 1947–49; Lectr in Classics, Univ. of Calif, Los Angeles, 1956. Asst Keeper, Dept of Greek and Roman Antiquities, BM, 1949–61; *Publications*: The Sculpture of the Parthenon, 1959; *contrib*. Jl of Hellenic Studies, Hesperia, Annual of Brit. Sch. at Athens, BM Qly, Bull. Inst. of Classical Studies. *Address*: Univ. College, Gower Street, WC1E 6BT.

Corbin, Peter Francis; Lecturer, Department of English, University of Exeter, since 1966; *b* 1940; *m* 1964. BA Hons Birmingham

1963 (English), PhD 1966. Admissions Tutor, Univ. of Exeter, 1970–74. *Publications*: *contrib.* English Studies. *Address*: Queen's Building, Univ. of Exeter, Exeter EX4 4QJ.

Corcoran, Dr John Xavier Wellington Patrick, MA, PhD, FSA; Senior Lecturer in Archaeology, Department of Archaeology, Glasgow University, since 1970; *b* 1926; *m* 1959; two *d*. BA Manchester 1951 (Hons History), MA Manchester 1952 (Prehistory), PhD Manchester 1956; FSA 1958, FSAScot 1950. Staff Tutor, Dept of Extra-Mural Studies, London, 1957–61; Lectr in Archaeology, Glasgow, 1961–70. Editor, Proc. Soc. Antiq. Scot, 1970–72. *Publications*: The Young Field Archaeologist's Guide, 1966; (with T. G. E. Powell and others) Megalithic Enquiries in the West of Britain, 1969; Antiquities of the Scottish Countryside; Introduction to Prehistoric Archaeology (forthcoming); *contrib.* Antiq. Jl, Proc, Prehist. Soc., Proc. Soc., Antiq. Scot., Jl Royal Soc. Antiq. Ireland. *Address*: Dept of Archaeology, The Univ., Glasgow G12 8QQ.

Corden, Dr Warner Max; Nuffield Reader in International Economics and Fellow of Nuffield College, Oxford University, since 1967; *b* 1927; *m* 1957; one *d*. BComm Melbourne 1949, MComm Melbourne 1953, PhD London 1956, MA Oxon 1967. Lectr, Melbourne Univ., 1958–61; Prof. Fellow, Australian National Univ., 1962–67; Vis. Prof., Univ. of California, 1965, Univ. of Minnesota, 1971, Princeton Univ., 1973. *Publications*: The Theory of Protection, 1971; Trade Policy and Economic Welfare, 1974; *contrib.* Amer. Econ. Rev., Econ. Jl, Econ. Rec., Economica, Jl Polit. Econ., Oxford Econ. Papers. *Address*: Nuffield College, Oxford.

Corfield, Penelope Jane, MA; Lecturer, Department of History, Bedford College, University of London, since 1969; *b* 1944. BA Oxon 1965, MA 1970. Temp. Asst Lectr, Birmingham Univ., 1968–69. *Publications*: *contrib.*: Crisis and Order in English Towns, ed P. Clark and P. Slack, 1972; The Origins of the English Revolution, ed C. S. R. Russell, 1973. *Address*: Dept of History, Bedford Coll. Regent's Park, NW1 4NS.

Corina, Dr John Gordon, MA, DPhil; Fellow and Tutor in Economics, St Peter's College, Oxford, since 1965; Visiting Professor in Management Sciences, Manchester University, 1974; *b* 1931; *m*; two *s*. DipEconPolSci. Oxon 1954 (Distinc.), BA Oxon 1956 (1st cl. PPE), MA Oxon 1960, DPhil Oxon 1961, DSc Harvard 1965; Smithson medallist, 1971. Fellow, Nuffield Coll., Oxford, 1960–63; Lectr, St Peter's Coll., Oxford, 1960–63; Lectr, Sussex Univ., 1963–65; Harvard Univ., DAS, 1964; Vis. Prof., Buenos Aires Univ., 1965; Tutor, Oxford Business Sch., 1961–68; Vis. Prof., California Univ., 1966; Vis. Lectr, USSR Acad. of Sciences, 1967. Presidential Off., Chief Econ. Adv. (labour): Argentina, Brazil, Uruguay, 1964–67; Sen. Govt Consultant (prices and incomes policy): UK, USA, ILO, EEC, OECD, Canada, 1965–72; Presidential

Adviser, Zambia, 1973–75; Cons. Adviser, Tanzania, 1974; Mem., overseas arbitrn tribunals, 1972–74. *Publications*: Politica de Salarios, 1965; Incomes Policy, 1966; Systems of Wage and Salary Payment for High Productivity, 1970; Incomes Policy – An International Survey, 1969; ed, Self-Government in Industry, 1970; The Performance of Prices and Incomes Policy in the UK, 1970; Labour Market Economics, 1972; Theorie et Pratique de la Politique des Revenus, 1972; *contrib.* Econ. Jl, Economica, Brit. Jl Indust. Rel. *Address*: St Peter's College, Oxford.

Corker, Dr David Tom; Lecturer in American Literature, Department of English and American Studies, University of East Anglia, since 1968; *b* 1944; *m* 1969; two *s*. BA Birmingham 1965, PhD East Anglia 1973. *Address*: Univ. of East Anglia, University Plain, Norwich NOR 88C.

Corlett, Prof. Esmond Nigel; Professor of Industrial Ergonomics, Department of Engineering Production, University of Birmingham, since 1971; *b* 1922; *m* 1956; three *d*.BSc(Eng) London 1948 (external); MEng Sheffield 1957; PhD Birmingham 1960; FIProdE, FIMechE, Mem., Ergonomics Res. Soc., Brit. Psychol Soc., Human Factors Soc. (USA). Res. Fellow, Univ. of Birmingham, 1957–60, Lectr, 1960–63, Sen. Lectr, 1963–71; Vis. Prof., Purdue Univ., 1965, Univ. of Massachusetts, 1969–70. Associate Editor, Int. Jl Prodn Res., 1960– ; Mem.: Council, Inst. Prodn Engs, 1964, 1970– , Ergonomics Res. Soc., 1963–67; Chm., Ergonomics Res. Soc., 1972– . *Publications*: *contrib.* Ergonomics; Human Factors; Int. Jl Prodn Res., Occupl Psychol. *Address*: Dept of Engineering Production, Univ. of Birmingham, PO Box 363, Birmingham B15 2TT.

Corley, Thomas Anthony Buchanan; Senior Lecturer in Economics, University of Reading, since 1968; *b* 1923; *m* 1953 (wife died 1965); three *s* one *d*. BA Oxon 1949 (2nd cl. History), MA Oxon 1949; Mem., Royal Econ. Soc. Dept of Applied Economics, Cambridge Univ., 1956–58; Asst Lectr, Queen's Univ. of Belfast, 1958–60, Lectr, 1960–63; Lectr, Reading Univ., 1963–68. RN (Temp. Lieut, RNVR), 1942–46; Min. of Nat. Ins. (Temp. Asst Principal), 1949–50; Bank of England, 1950–56 (Dir, Issue Dept, Central Bank of Iraq, 1953–55). *Publications*: Democratic Despot: A Life of Napoleon III, 1961, US edn 1961, Spanish edn 1963, German edn 1970; contrib. Ouvrard, Speculator of Genius, 1962; Domestic Electrical Appliances, 1966; Quaker Enterprise in Biscuits: Huntley and Palmers of Reading 1822–1972, 1972; *contrib.* Bank. Mag., Jl Indust. Econ., Moorgate and Wall St. *Address*: Univ of Reading, Faculty of Letters, Whiteknights, Reading RG6 2AA.

Cormack, Prof. James Maxwell Ross; Regius Professor of Greek, University of Aberdeen, since 1965; *b* 1909; *m* 1968; one *s*. MA Aberdeen 1932 (1st cl. Classics), BA Cantab 1935 (1st cl. Pts I and II Class. Tripos), MA Cantab; FRNS. Lectr, Classics,

Univ. Reading, 1937–46, Prof., 1946–65; Dean, Fac. Letters, Reading, 1948–54, Dep. Vice-Chancellor, 1954–64. *Publications*: The Inscribed Monuments of Aphrodisias, 1955; ed, Monumenta Asiae Minoris Antiqua VIII, 1962; *contrib*. Amer. Jl Arch., Ann. Brit. Sch. Athens, Archiv f. Papyrusforschung, Bull. Inst. Cl. Studies Univ. London, Harvard Theol. Rev., Hesperia, Jl Hellenic Studies, Jl Roman Studies, Klio, Proc. Brit. Acad. *Address*: Dept of Greek, King's College, Old Aberdeen AB9 2UB.

Cormack, Prof. Richard M., FRSE; Professor of Statistics, University of St Andrews, since 1972; *b* 1935; *m* 1960; one *s* one *d*. BA Cantab 1955 (Major Scholar, King's Coll. Cambridge 1952), BSc London 1954, MA Cantab 1962, Dip.MathStat 1956, PhD Aberdeen 1961; Mem. Biometric Soc., FSS. FRSE. Asst in Stats, 1956–58, Lectr in Stats, 1958–66, Univ. of Aberdeen; Vis. Asst Prof., Univ. of Washington, 1964–65; Sen. Lectr, Univ. of Edinburgh, 1966–72. Sec., Biometric Soc. (Brit. Region), 1970– . *Publications*: The Statistical Argument, 1971; *contrib*. Biometrics, Biometrika, Jl RSS, Oceanogr., Mar. Biol., Ann. Rev. *Address*: Dept of Statistics, Univ. of St Andrews, Mathematical Inst., St Andrews, Fife KY16 9SS.

Cornford, Prof. James Peters; Professor of Politics, University of Edinburgh, since 1968; *b* 1935; *m* 1960; one *s* three *d*. BA Cantab 1958 (1st cl. History), MA Cantab 1961; Mem., Political Studies Assoc. Fellow, Trinity Coll., Cambridge, 1960; Harkness Fellow of the Commonwealth Fund, Univs of California (Berkeley) and Chicago, 1961–62; Lectr Dept of Politics, Univ. of Edinburgh, 1964–68. Mem., SSRC: Political Science Cttee, 1968–72; Economic and Social History Cttee, 1970–72. *Publications*: contrib. Cleavages, Ideologies and Party Systems, ed Allardt and Littunen, 1964; Ideas and Institutions of Victorian Britain, ed Robson, 1967; Government and Nationalism in Scotland, ed Wolfe, 1969; International Guide to Electoral Statistics, ed Rokkan and Meyriat, 1969; Mass Politics, ed Allardt and Rokkan, 1970; Philosophy, Politics and Society, ed Laslett, Runciman and Skinner, 1972; *contrib*. Victorian Studies. *Address*: William Robertson Building, George Square, Edinburgh EH8 9JY.

Cornish, Prof. William R., LLB, BCL; Professor of English Law, London School of Economics, since 1970; *b* 1937; *m* 1964; one *s* two *d*. LLB Adelaide 1960, BCL Oxon 1962; Barrister, Asst Lectr and Lectr, LSE, 1962–68; Reader in Law, Queen Mary Coll., 1969–70. *Publications*: The Jury 1968, 2nd edn 1970; ed jtly Sutton and Shannon on Contracts, 7th edn 1970; *contrib*. Mod. Law Rev., Jl of Busin. Law, Ann. Surv. Commonwealth Law. *Address*: Dept of Law, London School of Economics, Houghton Street, WC2A 2AE.

Corry, Prof. Bernard Alexander; Professor, Department of Economics, University of London (Queen Mary College), since 1968; *b* 1930; *m* 1956; one *s* two *d*. BSc(Econ)

London 1951, PhD(Econ) London 1958; Mem., Amer. Econ. Assoc., Assoc. Univ. Teachers Econ. Lectr, Univ. of Durham, 1956–58; Asst Lectr, Univ. of London (LSE), 1958–61, Lectr, 1961–66, Reader, 1966–68; Vis. Prof., Univ. of California, Berkeley, 1965–66. Chm., Public Admin Bd, CNAA 1971; Mem., Econ. Bd, CNAA, 1968– ; Res. Gp, SE Planning Council; Sec., Assoc. Univ. Teachers, 1964– . *Publications*: Money, Saving and Investment, 1963; *contrib*. Amer. Econ. Rev., Economica, Econ. Jl, Jl Appl. Econ. *Address*: Dept of Economics, Queen Mary College, Mile End Road, E1 4NS.

Cosgrove, Brian D.; College Lecturer, Department of English, University College, Dublin, since 1971; *b* 1941; *m* 1970; two *d*. BA Hons Belfast 1962, BLitt Oxford 1966. Asst Lectr: Dept of English, Aberdeen Univ., 1965–67; University Coll., Dublin, 1967–71; Asst Prof., Univ. of Windsor, Ontario, 1971–72 (leave of absence). *Address*: Dept of English, Univ. Coll., Belfield, Dublin 4.

Cosgrove, Isobel Mary, MA, MLitt, BA; Demonstrator in Geography, University of Oxford, since 1968; *b* 1943; *m* 1970. BA(SS) Exon 1964; MLitt Newcastle 1970; MA Oxon 1970. Coll. of Wm and Mary, Virginia, USA, Exchange Scholarship, 1964–65; Demonstrator in Geography, Univ. of Newcastle upon Tyne, 1966–68. *Publications*: The Geography of Recreation and Leisure, 1972. *Address*: School of Geography, Mansfield Road, Oxford.

Cossar, Clive Douglas McIntosh, MA, BA, PhD; Lecturer in German, University of Leeds, since 1964; *b* 1939. MA Glasgow 1960 (Ordinary); BA Leeds 1963 (1st cl. German), PhD Leeds 1970. Lektor Englisches Seminar, Univ. of Erlangen-Nürnberg, 1963–64. *Address*: Dept of German, The Univ., Leeds LS2 9JT.

Costa, Charles Desmond Nuttall; Senior Lecturer, School of Hellenic and Roman Studies, Birmingham University, since 1973; *b* 1932; *m* 1960; one *s* one *d*. BA Oxon 1958, BPhil Oxon 1960, MA Oxon 1961. Lectr, Dept of Latin, Birmingham Univ., 1959–73; Mem., Fac. of Art, 1968–71. *Publications*: Langenscheidt, Universal Dictionary (Latin-English), 1966; ed, Horace, 1973; Seneca, Medea, 1973; *contrib*. Greece and Rome. *Address*: School of Hellenic and Roman Studies, The Univ., PO Box 363, Birmingham B15 2TT.

Costello, Thomas Michael; Lecturer in Literature, Institute of Extension Studies, University of Liverpool, since 1967; *b* 1935; *m* 1963; two *s*. BA Hons Leeds 1967 English (Lit.). *Address*: Inst. of Extension Studies, Univ. of Liverpool, PO Box 147, Liverpool L69 3BX.

Cotgrove, Prof. Stephen, BSc(Econ), PhD; Professor of Sociology, University of Bath, since 1966; *b* 1920; *m* 1946; two *s* two *d*. BSc(Econ) London 1947 (Sociology), PhD London 1956; Brit. Sociological Assoc.,

1950. Mem., Council for National Academic Awards (Business Studies 1965–71, Sociological Studies, 1966– , Management Studies Bds 1969–72); Mem., Schools Council (Soc. Science Cttee), 1967–72; SRC: Total Technology Panel. *Publications*: Technical Education and Social Change, 1958; The Science of Society, 1967, 2nd edn 1972; (with Dr Box) Science, Industry and Society, 1970; (with J. Dunham and C. Vamplew) The Nylon Spinners, 1971; *contrib*. Brit. Jl of Sociology, Sociology, Sociol Rev. *Address*: School of Humanities and Social Sciences, Univ. of Bath, Claverton Down, Bath BA2 7AY.

Cotran, Dr Eugene; Lecturer in African Law, School of Oriental and African Studies. University of London, since 1962; *b* 1938; *m* 1963; three *s*. LLB Leeds 1958; Dip. in International Law Cantab 1959; LLM Leeds 1961; LLD London 1971; Barrister-at-Law (Lincoln's Inn 1959); Mem., Kenya Bar, Gambia Bar, Sierra Leone Bar. Res. Off., Sch. of Oriental and African Studies, Univ. of London, 1959–62; Customary Law Comr, Govt of Kenya, 1961–63; Lectr in African Law, UCLA, 1967. Mem. and Sec., Kenya Commns on Marriage, Divorce and Succession, 1967–68; Hon. Treas., Internat. African Law Assoc., 1964–66; Sec., Bd of Studies in Laws, Univ. of London, 1968–71; Gen. Editor, (with N. Rubin) Annual Survey of African Law, 1967– . *Publications*: Restatement of African Law, Kenya: Vol. I – The Law of Marriage and Divorce, 1968; Vol. II – The Law of Succession, 1969; (with N. Rubin) Readings in African Law, 1970; Report on Customary Criminal Offences in Kenya, 1963; (with other Commissioners) Report of Commission on the Law of Marriage and Divorce in Kenya, 1968; (with other Commissioners) Report of Commission on the Law of Succession in Kenya, 1968; *contrib*. JAL, ICLQ, EALJ. *Address*: School of Oriental and African Studies, Univ. of London, WC1E 7HP.

Cotter, Charles Henry; Senior Lecturer, Department of Maritime Studies, University of Wales Institute of Science and Technology, since 1965; *b* 1919; *m* 1941; four *s*. BSc (Special) London 1960 (Geography 2nd cl.); MSc Wales 1968; Extra Master Mariner 1948, FRINav, FRMetSoc, MSNR MBHistSci. Sen. Lectr, Dept of Maritime Studies UWIST (formerly Welsh CAT), 1965. Mem., Council of Royal Inst. Nav., 1968–72; Chm., Royal Inst. Nav. (Bristol Channel Branch), 1969–74. *Publications*: The Elements of Navigation, 1953, French edn (Quebec) 1964; The Principles and Practice of Radio Direction Finding, 1961; The Master and His Ship, 1962; The Apprentice and His Ship, 1963; The Complete Coastal Navigator, 1964; The Physical Geography of the Oceans, 1965; The Astronomical and Mathematical Foundations of Geography, 1966; A History of Nautical Astronomy, 1968; The Complete Nautical Astronomer, 1969; The Atlantic Ocean, 1974; *contrib*. Jl Royal Inst. Nav. *Address*: Dept of Maritime Studies, UWIST, Cathays Park, Cardiff CF1 3NU.

Cottle, Dr Arthur Basil; Senior Lecturer in English, University of Bristol, since 1962; *b* 1917. BA Wales 1937 (1st cl. Latin, 1938 1st cl. English and 2nd cl. Greek), MA Wales 1947; PhD Bristol 1958, DipEd Cardiff 1939. Asst Lectr in English, Univ. of Bristol, 1946–48. Lectr, 1948–62. *Publications*: (with J. W. Sherborne) The Life of a University, 1951, 2nd edn 1959; St Mary Redcliffe Church Guide, 1957; ed (with L. C. Knights), Metaphor and Symbol, 1960; Thomas Chatterton, 1963; The Penguin Dictionary of Surnames, 1967, 2nd edn 1969; The Triumph of English 1350–1400, 1969; *contrib*. Jl of English and Germanic Philology, Rev. of English Studies, Essays in Criticism. *Address*: Dept of English, Univ. of Bristol, Bristol BS8 1TH.

Cottrell, Sir Alan Howard, FRS; Master of Jesus College, Cambridge, since Apr. 1974; *b* 1919; *m* 1944; one *s*. BSc Birmingham 1939, PhD Birmingham 1944; MA Cantab 1958; Hon DSc: Columbia 1965; Newcastle 1967; Liverpool 1969; Manchester 1970; Warwick 1971; Sussex 1972; Bath 1973; FRS 1955; Fellow, Royal Swedish Acad. of Scis, 1955. University of Birmingham: Lectr in Metallurgy, 1943; Prof. of Physical Metallurgy, 1949–55; Goldsmiths' Prof. of Metallurgy, Univ. of Cambridge, 1958–65. Dep. Head of Metallurgy Div., AERE, Harwell, 1955–58; Dep. Chief Scientific Advr (Studies), Mod, 1965–67; Chief Advr (Studies), (MoD), 1967; Dep. Chief Scientific Advr to Govt, 1968–71, Chief Scientific Advr, 1971–74. Part-time Mem., UKAEA, 1962–65; Member: Adv. Council of Scientific Policy, 1963–64; Central Adv. Council for Science and Technol, 1967. For. Hon. Mem., Amer. Acad. of Arts and Scis, 1960; For. Assoc., Nat. Acad. of Scis, USA, 1972; Hon. Mem., Soc. for Metals, 1972. *Publications*: Theoretical Structural Metallurgy, 1948, 2nd edn 1955; Dislocations and Plastic Flow in Crystals, 1953; Theory of Crystal Dislocations, 1964; Mechanical Properties of Matter, 1964; Introduction to Metallurgy, 1967; *contrib*. various scientific jls. *Address*: Master's Lodge, Jesus College, Cambridge.

Coughlan, John Anthony; Senior Lecturer in Social Administration and Policy, Department of Social Studies, Trinity College, Dublin, since 1973 (Lecturer, 1964–73); *b* 1936. BA NUI 1956, MA NUI 1958, DipSoc. Studies London 1960; MA Dublin 1964; Mem., Inst. Public Admin, Econ. Soc. Res. Inst., Dublin, Stat. Soc. Enquiry Soc. Ireland, Irish Hist. Soc., Fabian Soc. Jun. Lectr, TCD, 1961–64. *Publications*: (with G. J. Bourke) Dublin General Hospital and Geriatric Study, 1967; (with G. J. Bourke and J. McGilvray) Dublin Hospital Paediatric Study, 1969; pamphlets inc.: The Northern Crisis, Which Way Forward?, 1969; Ireland and the Common Market, The Alternatives to Membership, 1972; *contrib*. Admin., Soc. Studies, Christ. Rex. *Address*: Dept of Social Studies, Trinity College, Dublin 2, Ireland.

Coull, Dr James Reid; Senior Lecturer, Department of Geography, Aberdeen University, since 1971; *b* 1935. MA Aberdeen

1957, PhD Aberdeen 1962. Asst Lectr, Univ, of Aberdeen, 1959, Lectr, 1961. *Publications*: The Fisheries of Europe: an Economic Geography, 1972; *contrib*. Scottish Geogr. Mag., Scottish Studies. *Address*: Dept of Geography, Univ. of Aberdeen, Aberdeen AB9 1AS.

Coulson, Dr Michael; Lecturer in Sanskrit and Head of Department, University of Edinburgh, since 1963; *b* 1936. BA Oxon 1959 (1st cl. Sanskrit), MA Oxon 1963, DPhil Oxon 1966. *Publications*: Teach Yourself Sanskrit: An Introduction to the Classical Language (forthcoming); Three Sanskrit Plays in Translation (forthcoming). *Address*: Dept of Sanskrit, Univ. of Edinburgh, Edinburgh EH8 9YL.

Coulson, Prof. Noel James, MA; Professor of Oriental Laws, University of London, since 1967; *b* 1928; *m* 1951; two *d*. BA Oxon 1950 (1st cl. Classical Hon. Mod. and Oriental Languages), MA Oxon 1961; Barrister of Gray's Inn, 1961. Lectr, SOAS, Univ. of London, 1954–64; Reader in Islamic Law, 1964–67; Vis. Prof. of Comparative Law, Law Schs, UCLA, 1961–62, Chicago, 1968, Pennsylvania, 1970. Dean, Fac. of Law, Ahmadu Bello Univ., Nigeria. 1965–66. *Publications*: A History of Islamic Law, 1964; Conflicts and Tensions in Islamic Jurisprudence, 1969; Succession in the Muslim Family, 1971; *contrib*. Encyclopaedia Britannica; *contrib*. Studia Islam., Int. Comp. Law Qly. *Address*: Dept of Law, School of Oriental and African Studies, Univ. of London, WC1E 7HP.

Coulson, Sidney John, BEM, BA, DPhil; Research Fellow in Theology, University of Bristol, since 1968; *b* 1919; *m* 1939; one *s* two *d*. BA Bristol 1949; DPhil Oxon 1968. Warden, Downside Centre for Religious Studies, 1964– . Central Religious Adv. Council, BBC, 1961–67; Catholic Theol Commn for England and Wales, 1968– ; Consultant-Observer, Brit. Council of Churches, 1965–70. *Publications*: ed, The Saints, 1958, French edn 1960; ed (with introduction, J. H. Newman), On Consulting the Faithful in matters of Doctrine, 1961; ed, Theology and the University, 1964; (with A. M. Allchin) Newman: a Portrait Restored, 1965; ed (with A. M. Allchin), Oxford Symposium, The Rediscovery of Newman, 1967; Newman and the Common Tradition, 1970; *contrib*. to published Downside Symposia (1956– , 9 vols, in progress); *contrib*. Downside Rev., JTS. *Address*: Dept of Theology, Royal Fort House, Tyndall Avenue, Bristol BS8 1UJ.

Coulton, Dr John James; Lecturer in Classical Archaeology, University of Edinburgh, since 1969; *b* 1940; *m* 1969. BA Cantab 1961, MA and PhD Cantab 1965. Lectr in Classics, Australian National Univ., Canberra, 1964–68; Asst Lectr in Classics, Univ. of Manchester, 1969. *Publications*: *contrib*. BSA. *Address*: Dept of Classical Archaeology, 19 George Square, Edinburgh EH8 9JZ.

Coupe, Prof. William Arthur; Professor of

German, University of Southampton, since 1971; *b* 1929; *m* 1959; three *s*. MA Cantab 1959, PhD Cantab 1959. Asst in German, Aberdeen, 1956–58; Lectr in German, Exeter, 1958–63; Lectr in German, Reading, 1963–67, Reader, 1967–71. *Publications*: ed, C. F. Meyer: Der Heilige, 1965; The German Illustrated Broadsheet in the 17th Century, 1966–67; A Sixteenth-Century German Reader, 1972; *contrib*. The Continental Renaissance, ed A. J. Krailsheimer, 1971; Penguin Companion to European Literature; Oxford Companion to the Theatre; *contrib*. Comp. Studies in Soc. and Hist., German Life and Letters, Jl Warb. and Courtd Inst., Mod. Lang. Rev. *Address*: Dept of German, Univ. of Southampton, Southampton SO9 5NH.

Couper, Prof. Alastair Dougal, MA, PhD; Professor of Maritime Studies, UWIST, since 1969; *b* 1931; *m* 1958; two *s* two *d*. Hon. MA Aberdeen, DipEd Aberdeen 1963, PhD Canberra 1966; Master Mariner 1957, MRIN 1969, MNI 1973. Lectr, Australian National Univ., 1963–65; Univ. of Durham, 1966–69. Editor, Jl of Maritime Studies and Management. *Publications*: Geography of Sea Transport, 1972; *contrib*. The Pacific in Transition, ed H. C. Brookfield, 1973. *contrib*. Built Environment, Jl Polynesian Soc., Jl Royal Inst. of Navigation, New Zealand Geographer, Pacific Viewpoint, Tijchshrift Voor Economische en Sociale Geographic. *Address*: UWIST, King Edward VII Avenue, Cardiff CF1 3NU.

Course, Dr Edwin Alfred, BSc(Econ), PhD, FCIT; Senior Tutor, Department of Extra-Mural Studies, University of Southampton, since 1968; *b* 1922; *m* 1945; 1971; one *s* one *d*. BSc(Econ) LSE 1954, PhD LSE 1957; FCIT. Resident Tutor, Univ. of Southampton, 1956–68. Mem., Council, Inst. Trspt, 1967; Recorder, Section X, Brit. Assoc., 1972– ; Indust. Archaeol. Cttee, Council for Brit. Archaeol., 1971– ; Council, Hants Field Club, 1965– . *Publications*: London Railways, 1963; Portsmouth Railways, 1971; Railways of Southern England, vol. I, 1973, vol. 2, 1974; *contrib*. Brit. Assoc. Handbk, Encyclop. Brit., Geog., Jl Rly and Canal Hist. Soc. *Address*: Dept of Extra-Mural Studies, The Univ., Southampton SO9 5NH.

Court, Dr John Mason; Lecturer in Biblical Studies, Board of Studies in Theology, Faculty of Humanities University of Kent, since May 1969; *b* 1943; *m* 1969. BA Hons Durham 1964 (Theol.), PhD Durham 1973; Mem., SNTS. Asst Lectr in Biblical Studies, Univ. of Kent, 1968–69. Chm., Bd of Studies in Theol., Univ. of Kent, 1973– . *Publications*: *contrib*. Jl Theol. Studies. *Address*: Keynes Coll., Univ. of Kent, Canterbury, Kent.

Courtney, Dr Cecil Patrick; University Lecturer in French, and Fellow since 1962, Director of Studies in Modern Languages since 1964, Librarian since 1972, Christ's College, Cambridge; *b* 1930; *m* 1959; two *s*. BA QUB 1951, DPhil Oxon 1960, PhD Cantab 1962; Member: Modern Humanities Res. Assoc., 1965; Assoc. internationale des

Etudes françaises, 1961. Res. Fellow, Univ. of Birmingham, 1958; Asst Lectr, Univ. of Sheffield, 1959–61; Lectr, Univ. of Sheffield, 1961–62; Vis. Prof. of French, Univ. of W Ontario, 1968–69; Vis. Res. Fellow, Univ. of Utrecht, 1974. Mem. Faculty Bd, Faculty of Mod. and Med. Langs, 1968– . *Publications*: Montesquieu and Burke, 1963; *contrib.* Revue d'Histoire littéraire de la France, Revue de Littérature comparée, Neophilologus. *Address*: Christ's College, Cambridge.

Courtney, Edward, MA; Reader in Classics, King's College, University of London, since 1970; *b* 1932; *m* 1962; two *s*. BA Dublin 1954 (1st cl. Classics), BA Oxford 1955 (by incorporation), MA Oxford 1957; Mem., Classical Assoc., Soc. for Promotion of Roman Studies. Res. Lectr, Christ Church, Oxford, 1955–59; Lectr in Classics, King's Coll., Univ. of London, 1959–70. Warden of King's Coll. Hall, 1961–62; Sec., Bd of Studies in Classics, Univ. of London, 1970–72. *Publications*: C. Valerius Flaccus, Argonautica, edidit E. Courtney, 1970; *contrib.* Bull. Inst. Classical Studies, Classical Rev., Mnemosyne, Philologus, Phoenix, Scriptorium. *Address*: Dept of Classics, King's College, Strand, WC2R 2LS.

Cousins, Dr Russell Frederick; Lecturer in French, University of Birmingham, since 1973; *b* 1943; *m* 1969. BA Hons Birmingham 1965 (French), PhD 1973; Arts Faculty Res. Fellowship, Univ. of Birmingham, 1968–70; Temporary Lectr, Dept of French, 1970–73. *Address*: Dept of French, Univ. of Birmingham, Edgbaston, Birmingham B15 2TT.

Coutts, Prof. John Archibald; Professor of Jurisprudence, University of Bristol, since 1950; Pro-Vice-Chancellor, since 1971; *b* 1909; *m* 1940; two *s*. BA Cantab 1931 (1st cl. Law Tripos), LLB Cantab 1933, MA Cantab 1934, MA Dublin 1937; Barrister, Gray's Inn, 1933. Lectr, Univs of Hull, London (King's College), Belfast and Dublin; Fellow, Trinity Coll., Dublin, 1944; Prof. of Law, Univ. of Dublin, 1944; Vis. Prof., Osgoode Hall Law Sch., Toronto, 1962–63, Univ. of Toronto, 1970–71. Mem., SW Reg. Hosp. Bd, 1953–1965; Pres., Bristol Rent Assess. Panel, 1965– . *Publications*: ed, The Accused, 1966; *contrib.* Mod. Law Rev., Law Qly Rev., etc. *Address*: Faculty of Law, Wills Memorial Building, Queen's Road, Bristol.

Coveney, Prof. James, BA, Dr de l'Univ. de Strasbourg; Professor of Modern Languages, and Head of School of Modern Languages, University of Bath, since 1969; Joint Director, Centre for European Industrial Studies, University of Bath, since 1969; *b* 1920; *m* 1955; two *s*. BA Reading 1950 (1st cl. French), Docteur de L'Université de Strasbourg, 1953. French Govt Res. Scholar, Univ. of Strasbourg, 1950–51, Lecteur d'anglais, Univ. of Strasbourg, 1951–53; Lectr in French, Univ. of Hull, 1953–58; Sen. Lectr, Head of Modern Languages, Univ. of Bath, 1964–68. Asst Dir of Exams (Mod. Langs), Civil Service Commn, 1958–59; UN Secretariat, NY, 1959–61, NATO Secretariat, 1961–64; Mem., Assoc. Internat. des Traducteurs de Conférence, 1967– ;

Comité Internat. Permanent des Directeurs des Instituts Universitaires de Traducteurs et Interprètes, 1971– ; Nat. Council for Modern Langs, 1972– ; French-British Mixed Commn, 1973– ; Jt Sec., Assoc. Univ. Profs of French, 1973– . *Publications*: La légende de l'empereur Constant, 1955; International Organization Documents for Translation from Freud, 1972; (jtly) Glossary of French and English Management Terms, 1972; (jtly) Le français pour l'ingénieur, 1974; *contrib.* Babel, Bull. Péd. IUT, Die Unterrichts praxis, Eur. Community, FT, Industrial Trng Internat., Jl de l'Audiovisuel, Saisons d'Alsace, Technol, and Soc., THES. *Address*: School of Modern Languages, Univ. of Bath, Bath BA2 7AY.

Coveney, Peter James, MA; Lecturer in History Department, and Warden of Lincoln Hall, University of Nottingham, since 1962; *b* 1924; *m* 1959; one *d.* BA Cantab 1945 (1st cl. History), MA Cantab 1948. Vice-Warden, Hulme Hall, Univ. of Manchester, 1949–52; Warden, Needler Hall, Univ. of Hull, 1952–62; Lectr in History, Univ. of Hull, 1958–62. *Publications*: Poor Monkey, the Child in English Literature, 1957; The Image of Childhood, 1967; ed, The Adventures of Huckleberry Finn, 1966; ed, G. Eliot: Felix Holt, 1972; *contrib.* EHR. *Address*: Dept of History, Univ. of Nottingham, Nottingham NG7 2RD.

Cowan, Prof. Charles Donald, MA, PhD; Professor of South East Asian History, University of London, since 1961; *b* 1923; *m* 1945; 1962; two *d.* BA Cambridge 1947, MA Cambridge 1949; PhD London. Lectr, Raffles Coll., Singapore, 1947–48; Lectr, Univ. of Malaya, 1948–50; Lectr, School of Oriental and African Studies, 1950–60; Vis. Prof., Cornell Univ., 1960–61. Pt-time Mem., FCO Jt Research Dept, 1964–66; Mem., Sec. of State for Educn's Postgraduate Awards Cttee, 1967–71. *Publications*: Nineteenth Century Malaya: the origins of British Political Control, 1961, 2nd edn 1962, Malay edn 1970; ed, The Economic Development of Southeast Asia: studies in economic history and political economy, 1964; ed, The Economic Development of China and Japan: studies in economic history and political economy, 1964; *contrib.* Jl Royal Asiatic Soc., Malayan Branch, New Camb. Mod. Hist., Jl SE Asian Hist., etc. *Address*: Dept of History, School of Oriental and African Studies, Univ. of London, Malet Street, WC1E 7HP.

Cowan, David, (Dawud); Senior Lecturer in Arabic, School of Oriental and African Studies, University of London, since 1965; *b* 1915; *m* 1945; one *s* one *d.* BA London 1937 (1st cl. Arabic), MA London 1940; FRAS. Lectr in Arabic, SOAS, 1945–65. Dir of Studies, MECAS, Shimlan, Lebanon, 1959–60, 1964–65. *Publications*: An Introduction to Modern Literary Arabic, 1958; *contrib.* several works on Arabic Literature. *Address*: School of Oriental and African Studies, Univ. of London, WC1E 7HP.

Cowan, Edward James; Lecturer, Department of Scottish History, University of Edinburgh, since 1967; *b* 1944; *m* 1963; one *s* two d. MA Edinburgh 1967. Pres., Scottish Soc. for Northern Studies, 1971–73; Editor, Trans E Lothian Antiqu. and Field Naturalists Soc. *Publications*: Montrose (forthcoming); Montrose and Argyll, in The Scottish Nation, ed G. Menzies, 1972; *contrib*. Studia Islandica. *Address*: William Robertson Building, 50 George Square, Edinburgh.

Cowan, John; Lecturer in German, University of Oxford, since 1954, and Fellow of New College, since 1959; *b* 1926; *m* 1961; one *s* one *d*. MA Cantab 1953. *Address*: New Coll., Oxford.

Cowan, Ian Borthwick, MA, PhD; Senior Lecturer in Scottish History, University of Glasgow, since 1970; *b* 1932; *m* 1954; three *d*. MA Edinburgh (2nd cl. History), PhD Edinburgh 1961; FRHistS. Asst Lectr, Edinburgh Univ., 1956–59; Lectr, Glasgow Univ., 1962–70. Treas., Scott. Hist. Soc., 1965– ; Pres., Scott. Church Hist. Soc., 1971–74; Mem.: Council, Hist. Assoc., 1971– ; Adv. Cttee on Papal Registers, Irish MSS Comm., 1971– . *Publications*: Blast and Counterblast, 1960; The Parishes of Medieval Scotland, 1967; ed (with A. I. Dunlop), Scottish Supplications to Rome, 1428–32; The Enigma of Mary Stuart, 1971; *contrib*. Innes Rev., Rec. Scott. Church Hist. Soc., Scott. Hist. Rev. *Address*: Dept of Scottish History, Univ. of Glasgow, Glasgow G12 8QQ.

Cowan, Prof. Peter David, DipArch, PhD, ARIBA; Professor of Planning Studies, University College London, since 1970; *b* 1929; *m* 1954; one *s*. DipArch (Hons) Northern Polytechnic 1951, PhD London 1969; ARIBA, FRStatSoc. Res. Asst, Univ. Coll., London, 1960–63, Lectr, 1963–67, Reader, 1967–70. Mem., Res. Adv. Gp, Min. of Hous. and Loc. Govt, 1965. *Publications*: The Office: a Facet of Urban Growth, 1969; ed, Developing Patterns of Urbanization, 1970; *contrib*. Regl Studies, Lond. Papers Regl Science, Environ. and Plan., RIBA Jl, Brit. Jl Social and Prev. Med., Med. Hist., etc. *Address*: Joint Unit for Planning Research, 171–174 Tottenham Court Road, W1P OBS.

Cowan, Prof. Ralph; Professor of Architecture, Heriot-Watt University, since 1968; *b* 1917; *m* 1940; two *s*. DipArch Edinburgh Coll. of Art 1939. DipTP, Edinburgh Coll. of Art 1944; FRIAS, ARIBA, MRTPI. Edinburgh Univ. 1950–55; Vis. Lect, Cornell Univ. 1961. Mem., RIBA Schs Cttee, 1956–72, RIBA Bd of Educn, 1964–69, ARCUK Bd of Educn, 1956– ; Faculty, Brit. Sch. at Rome, 1960– . *Address*: Dept of Architecture, Heriot-Watt Univ., Edinburgh EH1 1HX.

Coward, David Allen; Lecturer in French Language and Literature, University of Leeds, since 1966; *b* 1938; *m* 1962; two *s*. BA London 1960 (1st cl. French). Asst Lectr, Univ. of Leeds, 1963–66. *Publications*: *contrib*. Studies on Voltaire and the 18th Cent., 18th Cent. Studies. *Address*: Dept of French, The Univ., Leeds LS2 9JT.

Cowdrey, Rev. Herbert Edward John; Fellow and Tutor in Modern History, St Edmund Hall, Oxford, since 1956; *b* 1926; *m* 1959; one *s* two *d*. BA Oxon 1949 (1st cl. Modern History, 2nd cl. Theology); FRHistS. Mem., Council, Henry Bradshaw Soc., 1969– . *Publications*: The Cluniacs and the Gregorian Reform, 1970; The Epistolae vagantes of Pope Gregory VII, 1972; *contrib*. EHR, Hist., Jl Eccles. Hist., Jl Theol. Stud., Past and Present, Trans Royal Hist. Soc., Studi Gregoriani, Studia Patristica. *Address*: St Edmund Hall, Oxford OX1 4AR.

Cowie, Anthony Paul; Lecturer in Modern English Language, University of Leeds, since 1966; *b* 1931; *m* 1956; two *s* one *d*. BA Oxon 1955 (Modern Languages), MA Oxon 1965, DipEd London 1956, DipALing Edinburgh 1964. Temp. Lectr in Contemporary English, Univ. of Leeds, 1964–66. *Publications*: Associate Editor, The Oxford Advanced Learner's Dictionary of Current English, 3rd edn, 1974; ed (with R. Mackin), A Dictionary of Idioms and Collections in English (forthcoming). *Address*: The School of English, Univ. of Leeds, Leeds LS2 9JT.

Cowie, Evelyn E.; Lecturer, Faculty of Education, King's College London, since 1965; *b* 1924; *m* 1949; one *s*. BA London 1945 (History), Teaching Dip. London 1946, MA London 1948. *Publications*: Living Through History, 9 vols, 1964; Examining the Evidence, 1973. *Address*: King's Coll., Strand, WC2R 2LS.

Cowie, George Robert; Secretary, the Queen's University of Belfast, since 1948; *b* 1910; *m* 1942; two *s* one *d*. MA Hons 1933 (English), LLB 1935 (with Distinction) Aberdeen, Solicitor in Scotland 1936. Jun. Asst to Sec. of Univ. of Aberdeen, 1938–39, Sen. Asst Sec., 1945–47. War Service 1939–45, Major, RA and Special Ops (Mediterranean). Mem., Govt (NI) Electoral Adv. Cttee, 1972; Mem., Bd of Governors, Methodist Coll., Belfast 1972. *Publications*: *contrib*. occasional articles in TES. *Address*: The Queen's Univ. of Belfast, Belfast BT7 1NN.

Cowie, Prof. Gordon Strachan; Professor of Public Law, University of Glasgow, since 1973 (Senior Lecturer, 1967–73); *b* 1933; *m* 1961; three *s* one *d*. MA Aberdeen 1955, LLB Aberdeen 1958; Advocate 1962. Lecturer in International and Comparative Law, St Andrews, 1960–67. Consultant, Scott. Br., Inst. of Trading Standards Admin, 1969– . *Address*: Dept of Public Law, Univ. of Glasgow, Glasgow G12 8QQ.

Cowling, Prof. Keith; Professor of Economics, University of Warwick, since 1969; *b* 1936; *m* 1962; one *s* two *d*. BSc London 1958; PhD Illinois 1961. Manchester University: Asst Lectr, 1961; Lectr, 1962; Sen. Lectr, 1965; Sen. Lectr, Univ. of Warwick, 1966. Dir, Centre for Industrial, Economic and Business Res., 1972–73. *Publications*: (with D. Metcalf and A. J. Rayner) Resource Structure of Agriculture, 1970; ed, Market Structure and Corporate

Behaviour, 1972; *contrib.* Economica, Economic Jl, Jl of Polit. Econ., Manchester Sch., Ox. Bull. of Econs, Rev. of Econs and Stats, etc. *Address*: Dept of Economics, Univ. of Warwick, Coventry CV4 7AL.

Cowling, Maurice John, MA; Fellow and Director of Studies in History, Peterhouse, Cambridge, since 1963; University Lecturer in History; *b* 1926. BA Cantab 1949 (1st cl. Historical Tripos pts I and II), MA Cantab 1951. Fellow, Jesus Coll., Cambridge, 1951–53 and 1961–63; Res. Fellow, Univ. of Reading, 1953–54. Times Leader-writer, 1955–56; Mem., Cambs CC, 1966–70; Parliamentary candidate, Bassetlaw (C), 1959; Lit. Editor, Spectator, 1970–71. *Publications*: The Nature and Limits of Political Science, 1963; Mill and Liberalism, 1963; Disraeli, Gladstone and Revolution, 1967; The Impact of Labour, 1971. *Address*: Peterhouse, Cambridge.

Cox, Prof. Charles Brian; Professor of English, Manchester University, since 1966; *b* 1928; *m* 1954; one *s* two *d*. MA Cantab 1956, MLitt Cantab 1958; MA Manchester 1970. Asst Lectr, Univ. of Hull, 1954, Lectr, 1957, Sen. Lectr, 1962; Vis. Associate Prof., Univ. of California, Berkeley, 1964–65. Co-Editor, The Critical Quarterly. *Publications*: The Free Spirit, 1963; ed, Dylan Thomas: twentieth century views, 1966; (with A. E. Dyson) Modern Poetry, 1963; The Practical Criticism of Poetry, 1965; Poems of this Century, 1968; The Black Papers on Education, 1971; The Twentieth Century Mind, 3 vols., 1972–73; *contrib.* Crit. Qly, Crit. Survey, Bull. John Rylands Library. *Address*: Dept of English, The Univ., Manchester M13 9PL.

Cox, Charles James; Lecturer in Management Sciences, University of Manchester Institute of Science and Technology, since 1966; *b* 1932; *m* 1961; one *s* one *d*. BA Bristol 1954 (Hons Psychology and Philosophy). Grad. Mem., Brit. Psychol. Soc. UK Rep., Europ. Res. Gp on Mngmt. *Address*: Dept of Management Sciences, Univ. of Manchester Institute of Science and Technology, PO Box 88, Sackville Street, Manchester M60 1QD.

Cox, Cyril Edwin; Senior Lecturer in Education, Head of the Religious Education Department, University of London Institute of Education, since 1967; *b* 1916; *m* 1940; two *s* one *d*. BD London 1939 (1st cl.), MTh London 1945, AKC 1939 (1st cl.). Lectr in Theology, St David's Coll., Lampeter, 1946–49; Lectr in Education, Univ. of Birmingham, 1962–67; Vis. Prof., Memorial Univ. of Newfoundland, 1970–71. Mem. Governing Body, Bordesley Coll. of Educn, Birmingham, 1964–67, Queen Mary's Schs, Walsall, 1964–67, Channing Sch., Highgate, 1972– ; Mem., Council, Selly Oak Coll., 1965–67; Mem., Schs Council RE Main Cttee, 1967–72; Chm., Nat. Council of Religious Educn in England and Wales, 1973– ; Chm., Adv. Cttee Lancaster Univ. Curriculum Develt Project in Primary Sch. RE. *Publications*: Changing Aims in Religious Education, 1966; Sixth Form Religion, 1967; contrib. Let's Teach Them Right, ed Macy,

1969; Studies in Adolescence, ed Grunder, 1969; Adolescent Development, ed Gold and Douvain, 1969; Educational Research in Britain 2, ed Butcher and Pont, 1970; Religious Education and Integrated Studies, ed Birnie, 1972; A Reader in Religious and Moral Education, ed E. Lord and C. Bailey, 1973; *contrib.* Asp. of Educn, Brit. Jl Soc. Clin. Psychol., Educnl Rev., Jl Soc. Psychol., Relig. in Educn, Relig. Educn. *Address*: Univ. of London Institute of Education, Malet Street, WC1E 7HS.

Cox, Jeremy William R.; see Roxbee Cox.

Cox, Dr Reginald Gordon, MA, PhD; Reader, English Department, University of Manchester, since 1970; *b* 1914; *m* 1949. BA Cantab 1935 (1st cl. English Tripos pts I and II), MA Cantab 1939, PhD Cantab 1940. Res. Fellow, Downing Coll., Cambridge, 1937–40; Asst Lectr, Univ. Coll. of Wales, Aberystwyth, 1946–47; Lectr, Manchester Univ., 1947–70. Pubns Sec., Manch. Lit. Philos. Soc., 1963–71. *Publications*: contrib. Pelican Guide to English Literature, ed B. Ford: Literary Survey and Chap. on Donne, vol. 3, 1956; Chap. on periodicals, vol. 6, 1958; Chap. on Auden, vol. 7, 1961; prefatory essays on Richard III, Henry V, and The Winter's Tale, in, Shakespeare: Oeuvres Complètes, ed Evans and Leyris, 1954–61; ed, Thomas Hardy: the Critical Heritage, 1970; *contrib.* Scrutiny, Times Lit. Supp. *Address*: Dept of English, The Univ., Manchester M13 9PL.

Cox, William Harvey; Lecturer, Department of Political Theory and Institutions, Liverpool University, since 1966; *b* 1939; *m* 1966; three *d*. *Address*: Dept of Political Theory and Institutions, Univ. of Liverpool, PO Box 417, Liverpool L69 3BX.

Coxon, Dr Anthony Peter Macmillan, BA, PhD; Lecturer in Sociology, University of Edinburgh, since 1969; *b* 1938; *m* 1967; two *s* three *d*. BA Leeds 1961 (2nd cl. Sociology and Philosophy), PhD Leeds 1965 (Sociology); FSS, Mem., Brit. Sociol Assoc. Lectr, Dept of Sociology, Univ. of Leeds, 1964–68; Vis. Lectr, Dept of Political Science, Massachusetts Inst. of Tech., 1968–69. Mem., SSRC Sociol. Cttee, 1967–68, 1970– ; SSRC Cttee on Computing and Social Science, 1971– ; Mem. Exec. Cttee, Brit. Sociol. Assoc.; Convener and Editor, Newsletter of BSA Maths and Computing Gp, 1969–73; Mem., of Edit. Bd, Sociol., 1969–72. Quality and Quanity, 1970– . *Publications*: contrib. Sociol., Int. Jl Math. Educn in Sci. and Tech. *Address*: Dept of Sociology, Univ. of Edinburgh, Adam Ferguson Building, George Square, Edinburgh EH8 9LL.

Coy, Dr P. E. B.; Senior Lecturer in Sociology, University of Stirling, since 1971; at La Trobe University, 1974–75; *b* 1922; *m* 1959; two *s* two *d*. BA Durham 1961, DipAnth 1963, BLitt Oxford 1966, DPhil 1966. Monash, Australia, 1967–71. *Publications*: contrib. Jl of Interamer. Studies, Jl of Latin Amer. Studies, Man. *Address*: (until 1976) Sch. of Social Sciences, La Trobe

Univ., Victoria 3083, Australia; Dept of Sociology, Univ. of Stirling, Stirling FK9 4LA.

Crabtree, Dr Keith; Lecturer in Geography, University of Bristol, since 1966; *b* 1939; *m* 1966; two *s*. BSc Bristol 1961 (1st cl. Geography), PhD Bristol 1966; Mem., Inst. Brit. Geogrs, Freshwater Biol. Assoc., Geog. Assoc. Asst Lectr in Geography, Univ. of Bristol, 1963–66. *Publications*: contrib. New Phytol., Sci. Progress, Mitt. Internat. Verein. Limnol. *Address*: Dept of Geography, Univ. of Bristol, Bristol BS8 1SS.

Craft, Maurice, BScEcon, PhD; Senior Lecturer in Education, Institute of Education, University of Exeter, since 1967; *b* 1932; *m* 1957; two *d*. BScEcon London 1953, HDipEd Dublin 1956; AcadDipEd London 1959, PhD Liverpool 1972. Principal Lectr and Hd of Dept of Sociology, Edge Hill Coll. of Educn, Ormskirk, Lancs, 1960–67; Sub-Dean, Fac. of Educn, Exeter Univ., 1969–73; Prof. of Educn, and Chm., Centre for Urban Educn, La Trobe Univ., Melbourne (on secondment), 1973–75. Consultant, Devon Educn Cttee, 1970–72. Jt Editor (with Prof. J. B. Mays), Longman's Aspects of Modern Sociology library, 1965– . Chm., Nat. Interprofessional Working Party, 1972–74; Chm., Sociology Section, ATCDE, 1967–69, Mem., Nat. Exec. Cttee, 1968–69. *Publications*: Urban Education: a Dublin case study, 1973; ed (jtly), Linking Home and School, 1967, 2nd edn 1972; ed (jtly), Guidance and Counselling in British Schools, 1969, 2nd edn 1974; ed, Family, Class and Education, 1970; contrib. numerous books; *contrib.* Admin, Educn for Teaching, Higher Educn Jl, Internat. Rev. Educn, New Soc., Social and Econ. Admin Studies. *Address*: Sch. of Education, Univ. of Exeter, Gandy Street, Exeter EX4 3QL.

Cragg, Rt. Rev. (Albert) Kenneth, DPhil; Reader in Religious Studies, University of Sussex, since 1973; *b* 1913; *m* 1940; three *s*. BA Oxon 1934, MA 1937, DPhil 1950; Hon. DD Huron College, Ontario; Asst Prof. of Philos., Amer. Univ. of Beirut, 1942–47; Prof. of Arabic and Islamics, Hartford Seminary, Connecticut, USA, 1951–56; Warden, St Augustine's Coll., Canterbury, 1960–67; Canon, St George's Cathedral, Jerusalem, 1956–60; Hon. Canon, Canterbury Cathedral, 1960– ; Bye-Fellow, Gonville and Caius Coll., Cambridge, 1969–74; Asst Bishop in Jerusalem, 1970–74; Asst Bishop, Diocese of Chichester, 1974– . *Publications*: The Call of the Minaret, 1956, 2nd edn 1964; Sandals at the Mosque, 1959; The Dome and the Rock, 1964; The Privilege of Man, 1968; Christianity in World Perspective, 1968; The House of Islam, 1969, 2nd edn 1974; Alive to God, 1970; The Event of the Qur'an, 1970; The Mind of the Qur'an, 1973; trans from Arabic: City of Wrong, 1959; Theology of Unity, 1964; *contrib.* Jl of World History; Muslim World; Middle East Jl. *Address*: Arts Building, Univ. of Sussex, Falmer, Brighton BN1 9QN.

Cragg, Dr Richard Henry, BSc, PhD; Lecturer in Chemistry, University of Kent at Canterbury (also teaching history of chemistry), since 1966; *b* 1938; *m* 1963; one *s*. BSc Manchester 1961 (Hons Chemistry), PhD Manchester 1964. Mem., Chem. Soc. Lord Adams Fellow, Univ. of Newcastle upon Tyne, 1964–66. *Publications*: contrib. Jl Chem. Soc., Organomet. Chem. Rev., Qly Rep. Sulph. Chem., Royal Inst. Chem. Rev. *Address*: The Chemical Laboratory, Univ. of Kent at Canterbury.

Craig, Barbara Denise, MA; Principal of Somerville College, Oxford, since 1967; *b* 1915; *m* 1942. MA Oxon. Craven Fellow, 1938; Goldsmiths' Sen. Student, 1938. Asst to Prof. of Greek, Aberdeen Univ., 1940–42; Woolley Fellow in Archaeology, Somerville Coll., 1954–56. Temp. Asst Principal, Mins of Supply and Labour, 1939–40; Temp. Principal, Min. of Production, 1943–45. Unofficial work as wife of British Council officer in Brazil, Iraq, Spain, Pakistan, 1946–65; from 1956, archaeological work on finds from British excavations at Mycenae. *Address*: Somerville College, Oxford.

Craig, Dr David Main; Senior Lecturer, Lancaster University, since 1964; *b* 1932; *m* 1957; three *s* one *d*. MA Aberdeen 1954 (1st cl. English), PhD Cambridge 1958. Lectr in English, Univ. of Ceylon, 1959–61. Organising Tutor, WEA, N Yorks, 1961–64; Sen. Lectr, Dept of English, Lancaster Univ., 1964–72; Dean, Cartmel Coll., Univ. of Lancaster, 1966–68; Mem., Senate, Univ. of Lancaster, 1964–68. *Publications*: Scottish Literature and the Scottish People, 1680–1830, 1961; The Reel Foundations, 1973; ed, Alan Sillitoe: Saturday Night and Sunday Morning, 1968; ed, Moderna Prosa und Lyrik der Britischen Inseln, 1968; ed, Dickens: Hard Times, 1970, 4th edn 1972; ed, Hugh MacDiarmid: Selected Poems, 1970; *contrib.* Crit. Qly, Ess. in Crit., Mosaic (Winnipeg), Zeitschrift für Anglistik und Amerikanistik (Berlin). *Address*: Lonsdale College, Bailrigg, Lancaster.

Craig, James; Lecturer, Department of Economics, University of Strathclyde, since 1968; *b* 1936; *m* 1959; two *s*. MA Hons Glasgow 1957 (Econs and Pol.), Teachers Special Cert. (Ch. 5) Jordan Hill Coll. 1959. *Address*: Stenhouse Bldg, Univ. of Strathclyde, Glasgow G1 1XW.

Craig, John Alexander, BSc, MICE, AMInstHE, MRTPI; Lecturer, Department of Town and Country Planning, Heriot-Watt University/Edinburgh College of Art, since 1966; *b* 1932; *m* 1956; one *s* two *d*. BSc Glasgow 1954 (civ. eng.); DipTP Edinburgh College of Art 1966; MICE 1963, AMInstHE 1964, MRTPI. Private practice as Chartered Civil Engineer, 1968– . Mem., consultant team which prepared study 'Recreation Planning for the Clyde', 1970; Mem., consultant team on Central Area Study of Tranent, East Lothian. *Address*: Heriot-Watt University/Edinburgh College of Art, 39 Palmerston Place, Edinburgh EH12 5AU.

Craig, Robert Stewart; Lecturer in Economic History, Department of History, University College London, since 1966, b 1924; m 1948; one s one d. BSc(Econ) LSE 1966; FRHistS. Mem., Soc. for Nautical Res. Council Mem., Econ. Hist. Soc. Mem., Ship's Cttee, Maritime Trust, 1970– . Editor, Maritime History. *Publications*: (with R. C. Jarvis) Liverpool Registry of Merchant Ships, 1967; contributor to: The Autobiography of William Stout of Lancaster, 1665–1752, ed, J. D. Marshall, 1967; Aspects of Capital Investment in Great Britain, 1750–1850, ed J. P. P. Higgins and S. Pollard, 1971; *contrib*. Archives, Bus. Archives, Exeter Papers in Econ. Hist., Mariner's Mirror, Nat. Lib. of Wales Jl, Trans Hist. Soc. of Lancs and Ches. *Address*: Dept of History, Univ. Coll. London, Gower Street, WC1E 6BT.

Craik, Elizabeth Mary, MA, MLitt; Lecturer in Greek, University of St Andrews, since 1965; b 1939; m 1964; one s one d. MA St Andrews 1960 (1st cl. Classics), MLitt Cantab 1965. Res. Fellow, Birmingham Univ., 1963–64; Temp. Asst in Latin, St Andrews Univ., 1964–65. *Publications*: *contrib*. Class. Qly, Maia, Parola del Passato. *Address*: Dept of Greek, St Salvator's College, St Andrews.

Craik, Prof. Thomas Wallace, MA, PhD; Professor of English, University of Dundee, since 1973; b 1927; m 1955; one s. BA Cantab 1948 (1st cl. English), MA Cantab 1952, PhD Cantab 1952. Asst Lectr, Leicester Univ., 1953–55, Lectr, 1955–65; Vis. Lectr, Queens Coll., NY, 1958–59; Lectr, Aberdeen Univ., 1965–67, Sen. Lectr 1967–73. *Publications*: The Tudor Interlude, 1958, 3rd edn 1967; The Comic Tales of Chaucer, 1964, 4th edn 1967; *contrib*. Eng. Studies, MLR, Renaiss. Drama, RES, Scrutiny, Stratford-upon-Avon Studies. *Address*: Dept of English, The Univ., Dundee DD1 4HN.

Craik, Dr Wendy Ann, BA, PhD; Lecturer in English, University of Aberdeen, since 1965; b 1934; m 1955; one s. BA London 1955 (2nd cl. English), PhD Leicester 1963. *Publications*: Elizabeth Gaskell and the Provincial Novel, 1974; ed, Jane Austen: The Six Novels, 1965, pbk edn 1968; ed, The Brontë Novels, 1968, pbk edn 1970; Jane Austen in her Time, 1969. *Address*: Dept of English, Taylor Building, King's College, Old Aberdeen AB9 2UB.

Crane, Prof. Francis Roger; Professor of Law, and Dean, Faculty of Law, Queen Mary College, since 1965; b 1910; m 1938; two s one d. LLB London 1933; Solicitor, 1934 (Clifford's Inn Prize). Lectr in Law, KCL, and private practice, 1935–38; Lectr in Law, Univ. of Manchester, 1938–46; Prof. of Law, Univ. of Nottingham, 1946–52; Prof. of English Law, KCL, 1952–65; Vis. Prof., Tulane Univ., 1960; Univ. of Khartoum, 1963; Univ. of Canterbury, NZ, 1964; Univ. of Melbourne, 1972; Monash Univ., 1972. *Publications*: (jtly) A Century of Family Law, 1957; *contrib*. legal periodicals. *Address*: Queen Mary College, Mile End Road, E14 NS.

Crampton, Dr Richard John; Lecturer, Faculty of Humanities (History), University

of Kent at Canterbury, since 1967; b 1940; m 1965; two s. BA Dublin 1964; PhD London 1971. *Publications*: *contrib*. History, Slavonic and East European Rev. *Address*: Rutherford Coll., The Univ., Canterbury, Kent.

Cranfield, Rev. Charles Ernest Burland, MA; Reader in Theology, University of Durham, since 1966; b 1915; m 1953; two d. BA Cambridge 1936 (1st cl. pts I and II Classical Tripos, 1st cl. pt I Theological Tripos 1938), MA Cambridge 1940. Lectr in Theology, Univ. of Durham, 1950–62. Sen. Lectr, 1962–66. Jt gen. Editor, Internat. Crit. Comm., new series, 1966– . *Publications*: The First Epistle of Peter, 1950; The Gospel according to St Mark (Cambridge Greek Testament Commentary), 1959; 1 and 2 Peter and Jude, 1960; A Ransom for Many, 1963; The Service of God, 1965; A Commentary on Romans 12–13, 1965; Commentary on the Epistle to the Romans (forthcoming); *contrib*. ET, Interpret,. NTS, SJT, Theol. Today. *Address*: Dept of Theology, Univ. of Durham, Durham DH1 3HP.

Cranmer, Prof. Philip, MA, BMus, Hon. RAM, FRCO; Professor of Music, University of Manchester, since 1970; b 1918; m 1939; one s three d. BA, BMus Oxon 1939, FRCO 1946, MA Oxon 1948; Hon. RAM 1967. Lectr, Birmingham Univ., 1950–54; Hamilton Harty Prof., The Queen's Univ., Belfast, 1954–70. Pres., Incorp. Soc. of Musicians, 1971. *Publications*: The Technique of Accompaniment, 1970; songs, part-songs, pieces for organ, etc. *Address*: Dept of Music, The Univ., Manchester M13 9PL.

Cranston, Prof. Maurice (William); Professor of Political Science, London School of Economics, since 1969; b 1920; m 1958; two s. BA Oxon 1948 (PPE), MA Oxon, BLitt 1951 (Lit. Hum).; FRSL; Hon. Foreign Mem., American Academy of Arts and Sciences. Lectr (Part-time) in Social Philosophy, London Univ., 1950–59; Lectr in Political Science, 1959–64; Reader in Political Science, LSE, 1964–69; Vis. Prof., Harvard Univ., 1965–66; Dartmouth College, USA, 1969–70; UBC, Vancouver, 1973. *Publications*: Freedom, 1953, 3rd edn 1967; John Locke, 1957, 2nd edn 1961; Jean-Paul Sartre, 1962, 2nd edn 1965; ed, Western Political Philosophers, 1964, 2nd edn 1969; Political Dialogues, 1969; ed, The New Left, 1970; trans. Rousseau: The Social Contract, 1968, 3rd edn 1971; The Theatre of Politics, 1972. *Address*: London School of Economics, WC2A 2AE.

Craster, Mary D., FSA; Assistant Curator, Museum of Archaeology and Ethnology, University of Cambridge, since 1957; b 1928. BA Oxon 1951 (Litt. Hum.), DipAnth Oxon 1952, MA Oxon 1955; FSA 1962. *Publications*: *contrib*. Proc. Cambs Antiqu. Soc. *Address*: Museum of Archaeology and Ethnology, Downing Street, Cambridge.

Craven, Stanley; Lecturer in charge of German Studies, Department of Modern Languages, University of Aston, since 1971; b 1930; m 1960; two d. BA Cantab 1953,

CertEd Cantab 1954, MA Cantab 1957. Member: Modern Langs Assoc., Modern Humanities Res. Assoc. University of Aston: Lectr i/c Mod. Langs., 1964–71. *Publications: contrib.* Mod. Langs. *Address:* Univ. of Aston in Birmingham, Birmingham B4 7ET.

Crawford, Dorothy Joan, MA, PhD; College Lecturer and Fellow in Classics, Girton College, Cambridge, since 1965; *b* 1939; *m* 1966. BA Cantab 1961 (Classical Tripos), CertEd Bristol 1962, MA Cantab 1964, PhD Cantab 1966; Mem., Classical Assoc., Hellenic Soc. Librarian, Classical Faculty, Cambridge, 1967– ; Dir of Studies, Classics, Clare Coll., 1973– . Mem., Governing Body, Rutland High Sch., 1970– ; Mem., Council, Hellenic Soc., 1970–73, Council, Cheltenham Ladies Coll., 1971– . *Publications:* Kerkeosiris: an Egyptian village in the Ptolemaic period, 1971; *contrib.* Chronique d'Egypte, Jl Eg. Arch., Jl Juristic Papyr. *Address:* Girton College, Cambridge CB3 0JG.

Crawford, Michael Hewson, MA; Fellow, Christ's College, Cambridge, since 1964, Lecturer in Classics, Cambridge, since 1972; *b* 1939; *m* 1966. BA Oxford 1961 (1st cl. Lit. Hum.), MA Oxford 1964; Mem., Soc. for Promotion of Roman Studies; Fellow, Royal Numismatic Soc. Asst. Lectr in Classics, Cambridge, 1969–72. Mem., Faculty of Archaeol., Hist. and Letters. Brit. Sch. at Rome, 1968–72, Council, Roman Soc., 1970–73, Royal Numismatic Soc., 1968–70. *Publications:* Roman Republican Coin Hoards, 1969; The Roman Republican Coinage, 1973; *contrib.* Jl Roman Studies, Papers Brit. Sch. at Rome, Annales, Eirene. *Address:* Christ's College, Cambridge.

Crawford, Thomas; Reader in English, University of Aberdeen, since 1973; *b* 1920; *m* 1946; one *s* one *d.* MA Edinburgh 1944 (Hist.), MA Auckland 1953 (Eng.). Hon. Sec., Assoc. for Scottish Literary Studies, 1971– ; Mem. Council, Scottish Text Soc., 1972. *Publications:* Burns: A Study of the Poems and Songs, 1960, 1965; Scott, 1965; Sir Walter Scott: Selected Poems, 1972; *contrib.* Scot. Studies, Studies in Scot. Lit. *Address:* Dept of English, Univ. of Aberdeen, Old Aberdeen, AB9 2UB.

Crease, David Plaistow, MA, DA, RIBA, MIStructE; Chief Architect (Design Unit), Institute of Advanced Architectural Studies, York University, since 1969; *b* 1928; *m* 1969; one *d.* MA Cantab 1953 (2nd cl. Architectural Studies), DA Edinburgh Coll. of Art 1953, Dip. Architecture; RIBA 1953, MIStructE 1956. Res. Fellow, York, 1964–68, Sen. Fellow, 1968–69. Various architectural appts, Edinburgh, Hong Kong, London and Brasilia, public and private practice, 1953–64. *Publications: contrib.* Archit. Rev., Geogr. Mag. *Address:* King's Manor, York YO1 2EP.

Creaser, Harry, BSc, ARIC; Director, Audio Visual Communications, University of York, since 1968; *b* 1923; *m* 1945; one *s* one *d.* BSc Leeds 1944 (2nd cl. Chemistry), ARIC London 1957; FCS. Part-time Lectr, Bristol Univ., 1956–57; Lectr in Educn, Makerere Univ., Uganda, 1957–61, Sen. Lectr, 1961–63, Dean, 1963–64; Sen. Lectr in Educn, Univ. of York, 1964–68. Mem., Assoc. for Science Educn; Edit. Bd, NECCTA; Vice-Chm, Northern Univs Working Party for Cooperation in Educnl Technology; Mem., UCET Film Bd. *Publications:* A Course in Junior Science, 1960; Beginning Science in Nigeria, Book 5, 1962, Beginning Science in Nigeria, Book 6, 1963; An Introduction to Physical Science, 1963; (with A. Beleson) Techniques and Apparatus for Science Teachers, 1964; Educational Technology in Higher Education, 1971; *contrib.* Visual Educn, Resources in Educn. *Address:* Audio Visual Communications, Univ. of York, Heslington, York YO1 5DD.

Creber, John William Patrick; Senior Lecturer, Department of Education, University of Exeter, since 1971; *b* 1930; *m* 1957; one *s* two *d.* BA Birmingham 1952 (Hons English); CertEd Exeter 1954. Lectr, Manchester Univ., 1964–67; Lectr, Exeter Univ., 1967–71. Mem., Council, Nat. Assoc. Teaching English, 1969–72; English Cttee, Schs Council, 1971– . *Publications:* Sense and Sensitivity, 1965; Lost for Words, 1972; *contrib.* English in Educn, Use of English. *Address:* Dept of Education, Univ. of Exeter, Exeter EX4 4QJ.

Cregeen, Eric Radcliffe, MA; Senior Lecturer, School of Scottish Studies, Edinburgh University, since 1969; *b* 1921; *m* 1958; two *d.* BA Cambridge 1947 (Hons History), MA Cambridge 1949; FSAScot. Lectr, Univ. of Glasgow, 1954–64; Lectr, Univ. of Edinburgh, 1966–69; Carnegie Fellowship, 1962–63; Nuffield Sociological Scholarship, Cambridge, 1964–65; SSRC award for research, 1973–76. *Publications:* Inhabitants of the Argyll Estate, 1779, 1963; Argyll Estate Instructions, 1771–1805, 1964; chapter, in, I. M. Lewis: History and Social Anthropology, 1968; chapter, in, Phillipson and Mitchison: Scotland in the Age of Improvement, 1970; *contrib.* Scott. Studies, Chambers's Encyclopaedia. *Address:* 27 George Square, Edinburgh.

Creighton, Herbert Colin; Lecturer in Sociology, University of Hull, since 1966; *b* 1940; *m* 1961; two *s* one *d.* BA Oxon 1963, Dip. Public and Social Admin, Oxford 1964; Mem., Brit. Sociological Assoc. *Address:* Dept of Sociology and Social Anthropology, Univ. of Hull, Hull HU6 7RX.

Creighton, T. R. M., MA; Senior Lecturer in English Literature, University of Edinburgh, since 1966; *b* 1915; *m* 1951; one *s* one *d.* BA Cantab 1935 (2nd cl. Modern Languages), 1937 (1st cl. English), MA 1939. Lectr in English, Univ. of Amsterdam, 1939–40; Lectr in English and Warden of St Patrick's Hall, Univ. of Reading, 1949–61 (seconded to Makerere University Coll. of E Africa 1955–57 as Sen. Lectr); Prof. of English Lang. and Lit., Fourah Bay Univ. Coll., Sierra Leone, 1961–64; Lectr in English for Overseas Students, Univ. of Leeds, 1964–66. Organised Lindsay Commn on German Univs, 1947–48; Mem., W African Exams

Council, 1961–64. Founder and editor, Bull. of African Lit., 1963–64. *Publication*: The Anatomy of Partnership, 1961; Thomas Hardy: a selection with introd. and notes, 1974. *Address*: Dept of English, Univ. of Edinburgh, Edinburgh EH8 9YL.

Cressey, Rev. Prof. Martin Hawley; Barbour Professor of Systematic Theology and Apologetics, Westminster and Cheshunt Colleges, Cambridge, and member of Faculty of Divinity, University of Cambridge, since 1973; *b* 1930; *m* 1958; one *s* three *d*. BA Oxon 1954 (1st cl. Lit Hum), MA Oxon 1956, BA Cantab 1958 (1st cl. Theol. Pt 3), MA Cantab 1958. Ordained 1959, Presbyt. C of E (now United Reformed Church). Mem., Soc. for Study of Theology; Mem., Internat. Assoc. for Mission Studies. Lectr, Dept of Theology, Univ. of Birmingham, 1968–73 (while on staff of Selly Oak Colls). Minister, St Columba's Church, Coventry, 1959–67. Sec., Jt Cttee for Cong./Pres. Union Conversations, 1963–72; Vice-Pres., Selly Oak Colls, 1972–73; Chm., Missionary and Ecumenical Work at Home Cttee, United Reformed Church, 1972– . *Publications*: *contrib.* Bull. Scottish Inst. Missionary Studies, Theology. *Address*: Westminster and Cheshunt Colleges, Madingley Road, Cambridge CB3 0AA.

Cresswell, Roy William; Senior Lecturer, Department of Town Planning, University of Wales Institute of Science and Technology, since 1971; *b* 1931. BA Manchester 1957 (Hons Town and Country Planning); FRTPI (AMTPI 1957, MTPI 1966). Lectr in Town Planning, Univ. Nottingham, 1964–71. Mem. Educn Bd, RTPI; Mem. Exec., S Wales Br., RTPI; Mem., Council, Town and Country Planning Summer Sch. (under auspices of RTPI). *Publications*: (jtly); Runcorn New Town Master Plan, 1967; *contrib.* Built Environment, Planner. *Address*: Dept of Town Planning, Univ. of Wales Institute of Science and Technology, Cardiff CF1 3NU.

Cretney, Stephen Michael; University Lecturer in English Law, Fellow and Tutor in Law, Exeter College, Oxford, since 1969; *b* 1936; *m* 1973. BA Oxon 1959, MA 1966. Solicitor, 1962. Lectr, Kenya School of Law, Nairobi, 1966–67; Lectr, Univ. of Southampton, 1968–69; Pro-Proctor, Oxford Univ., 1974–75. *Publications*: (with G. Dworkin) Theobald on Wills, 13th edn 1971; Principles of Family Law, 1974; *contrib.* Conveyancer, Law Quarterly Review, Modern Law Review. *Address*: Exeter College, Oxford OX1 3DP.

Crewe, Ivor Martin; Lecturer, Department of Government, Essex University, since 1971; *b* 1945; *m* 1968; one *s* one *d*. BA Oxon 1966 (PPE); MScEcons London 1968. Asst Lectr, Dept of Politics, Lancaster Univ., 1967–69; Jun. Res. Fellow, Nuffield Coll., Oxford, 1969–71. Mem. Bd, British Jl of Political Science. *Publications*: (with A. H. Halsey) Social Survey of the Civil Service, vol. 3 (1) of Fulton Report, 1969; ed, The British Political Sociology Yearbook, vol. I, 1974; (with C. Payne) Analysing the Census Data, in, The British General Election of 1970,

1971; *contrib.* Brit. Jl of Political Sci., European Jl of Political Res. *Address*: Univ. of Essex, Wivenhoe Park, Colchester, Essex CO4 3SQ.

Cribb, Timothy John Llanwarne, MA; Fellow and College Lecturer in English, Churchill College, Cambridge, since 1969; *b* 1939. BA Cantab 1960, MA Cantab 1970. Graduate Teaching Asst, Univ. of Minnesota, 1960–61; Asst Lectr, Univ. of Glasgow, 1965–67, Lectr, 1967–69. *Publications*: *contrib.* Trans Rumanian Poetry, Encounter. *Address*: Churchill College, Cambridge CB3 0DS.

Crick, Prof. Bernard, BSc(Econ), PhD; Professor of Politics, Birkbeck College, University of London, since 1971; *b* 1929; *m* 1953; two *s*. BSc(Econ), London, PhD London. Teaching Fellow, Harvard Univ., 1952–54; Asst Prof., McGill Univ., 1954–55; Vis. Fellow, Berkeley, 1955–56; Asst Lectr, later Lectr and Sen. Lectr, LSE, 1957–65; Prof. of Polit. Theory and Institutions, Sheffield Univ., 1965–71. Jt Sec., Study of Parliament Gp, 1964–68. Jt Editor, Polit. Qly, 1966– . Hon. Pres., Politics Assoc., 1970– . *Publications*: The American Science of Politics, 1958; In Defence of Politics, 1962, 2nd edn 1964 (trans. German, Japanese, Spanish, Italian); The Reform of Parliament, 1964, 2nd edn 1968; Political Theory and Practice, 1972; ed, Essays on Reform, 1967; ed (with W. A. Robson), Protest and Discontent, 1970; ed, Machiavelli: The Discourses, 1971. *Address*: Birkbeck College, Malet Street, WC1E 7HX.

Crick, Joyce Pumfrey; Lecturer in German, Department of German, University College London, since 1963; *b* 1929; *m* 1953; two *s*. BA London 1950, MA 1956, PGCE 1956; Lectr in English, Univ. of Erlangen, 1951–53; Res. Asst, German Dept, Univ. Coll. London, 1961–63. *Publications*: *contrib.* The Notebooks of Samuel Taylor Coleridge, vol. III, 1808–1819, ed K. Colwin, 1973. *contrib.* The Listener, Literature and Psychology, Poetry Notion. *Address*: Dept of German, Univ. College London, Gower Street, London WC1.

Criddle, Byron; Lecturer in Politics, University of Aberdeen, since 1968; *b* 1942; *m*; one *s*. BA (Hons) Keele 1964 (Politics–Hist.), MA Leicester 1967 (Dist.). *Publications*: Socialists and European Integration: – a study of the French Socialist Party, 1969; *contrib.* Parly Affairs, New Soc., World Today (RIIA). *Address*: Dept of Politics, Univ. of Aberdeen, Aberdeen AB9 1AS.

Cripwell, Kenneth Richard; Lecturer, Department of Education in Developing Countries, University of London Institute of Education, since 1967; *b* 1931; *m* 1965; two *d*. BA Cape Town 1952, MA Cape Town 1953, BEd Cape Town 1954, STD Cape Town 1956, MA(Ed) London 1970; Res. Fellow, Inst. of Adult Educn, Univ. Coll. of Rhodesia and Nyasaland, 1963–65. Consultant, Educnl TV, Union Minière du Haut Katanga, Republic of Zaire. *Publications*: Teaching Adults by Television, 1968; *contrib.* A-V Media, Educnl TV Internat., Teacher Educn in New Countries. *Address*: Institute of Education, Malet Street, WC1E 7HS.

Crisp, Olga; Reader in Russian Economic History, University of London, since 1971; *b* 1921; *m* 1950; one *s* one *d*. BA London (1st cl. Hons Russian Regional Studies), PhD London 1954. Asst Lectr, Sch. of Slavonic Studies, London, 1950–54, Lectr, 1954–68, Sen. Lectr, 1968. *Publications*: Banking and Industrialisation – Russia, 1860–1914, in, Banking in the Early Stages of Industrialization, ed R. Cameron, 1967; The Pattern of Russia's Industrialization up to 1914, in, L'industrialisation en Europe au xixe siècle, 1972; *contrib*. Business Hist., Econ. Hist. Rev., Slav. and E Europe Rev. *Address*: School of Slavonic Studies, Univ. of London, Senate House, WC1E 7HU.

Critchley, Dr John Stewart; Lecturer, Department of History, University of Exeter, since 1968; *b* 1942; *m* 1964; one *d*. BA Nottingham 1964 (1st cl. History), PhD Nottingham 1968. Asst Lectr, Univ. of Glasgow, 1966–68. *Publications*: *contrib*. EHR, Bull. Inst. Hist. Res. *Address*: Dept of History, Univ. of Exeter, Exeter EX4 4QH.

Croft, Dr Pauline; Lecturer in History, Royal Holloway College, University of London, since 1968; *b* 1943; *m* 1969. MA Oxon 1969, DPhil Oxon 1969. Warden, Founder's Hall, RHC Univ. of London, 1970– ; Chm., Bd of Examiners in History, London Univ. Inst. of Educn (CertEd), 1972–74. *Publications*: The Spanish Company, 1973; *contrib*. EHR. *Address*: Royal Holloway College, Egham Hill. Egham, Surrey TW20 0EX.

Crofts, Roger, BA, MLitt, CertEd; Research Officer, Department of Geography, University College London, since 1972; *b* 1944; *m* 1971. BA Liverpool 1965 (Geography), CertEd Leicester 1966, MLitt Aberdeen 1971; Mem., Inst. Brit. Geogrs. Res. Officer, Dept of Geography, Univ. of Aberdeen, 1966–72. *Address*: Dept of Geography, University Coll. London, Gower Street, WC1E 6BT.

Crombie, Dr Alistair Cameron; University Lecturer in History of Science, since 1953 and Fellow of Trinity College, Oxford, since 1969; *b* 1915; *m* 1943; three *s* one *d*. BSc Melbourne 1938, PhD Cantab 1942, MA Oxon 1954; FRHistS; Mem., Brit. Soc. Hist. Sci. (Pres., 1964–66), Int. Acad. Hist. Sci. (Pres., 1968–71), Int. Acad. Hist. Med. Lectr, UCL, 1946–53; Vis. Prof., Univ. of Washington, 1953–54; Princeton Univ., 1959–60; Guest Vis., Australian Univs, 1963. Editor: Brit. Jl Philos. Sci., 1949–54; Hist. Sci., 1961– ; Dir, Oxford Univ. Symp. Hist. Sci., 1961. *Publications*: Augustine to Galileo, 1952, 3rd edn 1970; Robert Grosseteste and the Origins of Experimental Science, 1953, 3rd edn 1971; Scientific Change, 1963; The Mechanistic Hypothesis and The Scientific Study of Vision, 1967; *contrib*. Annals of Sci., Brit. Jl Hist. Sci., EHR, Isis, Jl Animal Ecol., Jl Exper. Biol., Organon, Physis, Proc. Royal Soc. Lond., Rev. de Synthèse, TLS, Dict. Sci. Biogr., Encyc. Brit., New Camb. Mod. Hist., etc. *Address*: Trinity College, Oxford.

Crompton, James, MA, BLitt, FSA, FRHistS; Warden of Digby Hall and Lecturer in History, University of Leicester, since 1961; b 1919. BA Manchester 1941 (1st cl. History), BLitt Oxon, MA Oxon 1950; FSA, FRHistS. Asst Lectr, UCL, 1947–50; Faculty and Coll. Lectr, Univ. Coll. Oxford, 1950–54; Sen. Lectr, Rhodes Univ., Grahamstown, S Africa, 1954–61. Sec., Leicestershire Archaeological and Historical Soc., 1964– ; Lay Rep. Gen. Synod, 1971–; Governor, Trinity Hosp., Leicester, 1970– ; Mem., Historic Buildings Adv. Panel, 1964– . Editor, Trans Leicestershire Archaeological and Historical Soc., 1962–73. *Publications*: *contrib*. Jl of Ecclesiastical Hist., Hist., Trans Leicestershire Archaeological and Hist. Soc., Sobornost, Medium Aevum, Archives, Hist., Lexikon für Theologie und Kirche. *Address*: Digby Hall, Stoughton Drive South, Leicester LE2 2NB.

Cromwell, Valerie, (Mrs John Kingman); Lecturer in History, School of English and American Studies, University of Sussex, since 1964; *b* 1935; *m* 1964; one *s* one *d*. BA London 1957 (1st cl. History), MA Cantab 1961; FRHistS 1963, Mem., Internat. Commn for Hist. of Represent. and Parly Instns, 1962– . Asst Lectr in Hist., Bedford Coll., London, 1960–61; Fellow and Lectr in Hist., Newnham Coll., Cambridge, 1961–64. Mem., Senate, Univ. of Sussex. *Publications*: *contrib*. Bull. Inst. Hist. Res., Hist. Jl, Trans Royal Hist. Soc., Victorian Studies. *Address*: Arts Building, Univ. of Sussex, Brighton, Sussex BN1 9QN.

Crook, John Anthony, MA, FBA; Reader in Roman History and Law, University of Cambridge, and President of St John's College, since 1971; *b* 1921. BA Cantab 1947, MA 1949; FBA 1970. Univ. Asst Lectr in Classics, Reading Univ., 1948, Lectr, 1949–51; Research Fellow, St John's Coll., Cambridge, 1951, Teaching Fellow, 1953– , Tutor, 1956–64; Univ. Asst Lectr in Classics, Cambridge Univ., 1953, Lectr, 1955–71. *Publications*: Consilium Principis, 1955; Law and Life of Rome, 1967. *Address*: St John's College, Cambridge.

Crook, John Hurrell, BSc, PhD; Reader in Ethology, Department of Psychology, University of Bristol, since 1969; *b* 1930; *m* 1958; one *s* one *d*. BSc Southampton 1953 (Hons Zoology), PhD Cambridge 1958; Fellowship, Center for Adv. Studies in the Behavioural Sciences, Stanford, Calif, 1968–69; Fellow Zool Soc., London; Mem., Assoc. for Study Animal Behav.; Council member: (in various years) ASAB; Brit. Ornithol. Union; Founder and Council Mem., Primate Soc. of GB. Lectr in Psychology, Bristol Univ., 1962–68. *Publications*: ed, Social Behaviour in Birds and Mammals, 1970; Social Organisation and Visual Communication in Weaver Birds, 1964; Social Systems and Evolutionary Ecology (forthcoming); *contrib*. Animal Behav., Behav. Folia Primatologica, Ibis. *Address*: Psychology Dept, 8–10 Berkeley Square, Bristol Univ., Brstol 8.

Crook, Dr Joseph Mordaunt, MA, DPhil, FSA; Lecturer in History, Bedford College,

University of London, since 1965; *b* 1937; *m* 1964. BA Oxon 1958 (1st cl. Modern History), DPhil Oxon 1961, MA Oxon 1962; FSA 1972. Res. Fellow, Inst. of Hist. Res., 1961–62; Res. Fellow, Bedford Coll., London, 1962–63; Asst Lectr, Leicester Univ., 1963–65; Res. Fellow, Warburg Inst., 1970–71. Mem., Exec. Cttee, Soc. Architect. Historians of Great Britain, 1964– ; Exec. Cttee, Georgian Gp, 1970– ; Exec. Cttee, Victorian Soc., 1970– . Editor, Architect. Hist., 1967– . *Publications*: The Greek Revival, 1968; ed, Eastlake: A History of the Gothic Revival, 1970; Victorian Architecture: a Visual Anthology, 1971; The British Museum, 1972; The Greek Revival: Neo-Classical Attitudes in British Architecture, 1760–1870, 1972; ed, Emmett: Six Essays, 1972; ed, Kerr: The Gentleman's House, 1972; (jtly) History of the King's Works, vol. VI, 1782–1851, 1972; contrib. Concerning Architecture, 1967; The Country Seat, 1970; The Age of Neo-Classicism, 1973; The Reform Club, 1973; *contrib.* Architect. Hist., Architect. Rev., Country Life, Hist. Today, Jl Royal Soc. Arts, RIBA Jl. *Address*: Dept of History, Bedford College, Regent's Park, NW1 4NS.

Croome, David Robin; Lecturer in Economics, Queen Mary College, University of London, since 1968; *b* 1941; *m* 1969; one *d*. BA Durham 1961 (Politics and Econ.), MA Pennsylvania 1965 (Economics). Res. Asst, Univ. of Durham, 1961–62; Univ. Coll., London, 1962–64; Teaching Fellow., Univ. of Pennsylvania, 1964–66; Asst Lectr, LSE, 1966–67; Teaching Fellow, Univ. of Pennsylvania, 1966–67; Lectr, Queen Mary Coll., London, 1968–70; Lectr, Civil Service Coll., London, and Adv., HM Treasury, 1970–72 (on secondment). *Publications*: ed (with H. G. Johnson), Money in Britain 1959–69, 1970; *contrib.* Banker, Bankers Mag. *Address*: Dept of Economics, Queen Mary College, Mile End Road, E1 4NS.

Crosbie, Dr Alexander John; Senior Lecturer, Geography Department, University of Edinburgh, since 1966; *b* 1926; *m* 1965; one *s* three *d*. MA Aberdeen 1952, PhD Edinburgh 1965; FRGS. Lectr (pt-time), Edinburgh, 1964–65. Dir of Studies, 1967– ; Associate Dean, Fac. Soc. Sci., 1970– ; Mem., Scott. Univs Council on Entrance, 1971– , Standing Conf. on Univ. Entrance, 1972– . Mem., Soil and Land Use Survey Dept, Ghana, 1952–58. *Publications*: *contrib.* Geog. Jl. *Address*: Dept of Geography, Univ. of Edinburgh, High School Yards, Edinburgh.

Crosland, Margaret; Senior Lecturer in Spanish, University of Edinburgh, since 1963; *b* 1922. BA Cantab 1944 (1st cl. Modern and Medieval Languages), Cert. of Competent Knowledge, German, 1946, MA Cantab 1949. Lectr, Edinburgh Univ., 1947–63. *Publications*: *contrib.* Mod. Lang. Rev., Yrs Wk Mod. Lang. *Address*: Dept of Spanish, David Hume Tower, George Square, Edinburgh.

Crosland, Prof. Maurice P.; Professor of the History of Science and Director of the Unit for the History, Philosophy and Social Relations of Science, University of Kent at Canterbury, since 1974; *b* 1931; *m* 1957; three *s* one *d*. BSc London 1951, MSc London 1953, PhD London 1959; Vice-Pres., Brit. Soc. Hist. Sci., 1971–74; Corres. Mem., Internat. Acad. Hist. Sci., 1971. Lectr in Hist. and Philosophy of Science, Univ. of Leeds, 1963–69; Reader in Hist. of Science, 1969–74; Hon. Ed., Brit., Jl Hist. Sci., 1965–70; Vis. Prof., Univ. of California, Berkeley, 1967; Cornell Univ., 1967–68; Univ. of Pennsylvania, 1971. Mem., Brit. Nat. Cttee, Hist. Sci., 1970–76. *Publications*: Historical Studies in the Language of Chemistry, 1962; The Society of Arcueil: a view of French science at the time of Napoleon I, 1967; ed, Science in France in the Revolutionary Era described by Thomas Bugge, 1969; ed, The Science of Matter: a historical survey, 1971; *contrib.* Ann. Sci., Proc. Internat. Cong. Hist. Sci., Isis, Studies on Voltaire and the 18th Cent. *Address*: Unit for the History, Philosophy and Social Relations of Science, Univ. of Kent, Canterbury, Kent.

Cross, Prof. Sir (Alfred) Rupert (Neale), FBA; Vinerian Professor of English Law in the University of Oxford, since 1964; *b* 1912; *m* 1937. MA Oxon 1937, DCL Oxon 1958; Solicitor 1939; FBA 1967. Tutor, Law Soc., 1945–48; Fellow, Magdalen Coll., Oxford, 1948–64; Vis. Prof., Univ. of Sydney, 1968. *Publications*: Evidence, 3rd edn 1967; Precedent in English Law, 2nd edn 1968; (with P. Asterley Jones) Introduction to Criminal Law, 6th edn 1968; Cases in Criminal Law, 4th edn 1968; (with Nancy Wilkins) An Outline of the Law of Evidence, 3rd edn 1971; The English Sentencing System, 1971; Punishment, Prison and the Public (Hamlyn lectures), 1971; *contrib.* Law Qly Rev., Mod. Law Rev., Criminal Law Rev. *Address*: All Souls College, Oxford.

Cross, Dr Anthony Glenn; Reader in Russian, School of European Studies, University of East Anglia, since 1972; *b* 1936; *m* 1960; two *d*. BA Cantab 1960, AM Harvard 1961, MA Cantab 1964, PhD Cantab 1966; Member: Brit. Univs Assoc. of Slavists, Brit. Soc. for Eighteenth-Century Studies, Brit. Univs Study Gp on Eighteenth-Century Russia. Lectr in Russian, Univ. East Anglia, 1964–69, Sen. Lectr, 1969–72. Co-editor, Jl of European Studies, 1972– ; Editor, Newsletter of Study Group on Eighteenth-Century Russia, 1973– . *Publications*: N. M. Karamzin: A Study of his Literary Career (1783–1803), 1971; Russia under Western Eyes, 1971; *contrib.* Can.-Amer. Slavic Studies, European Studies Rev., Forum for Mod. Lang. Studies, Mod. Lang. Rev., Oxford Slavonic Papers, Slavic Rev., Slavonic and E European Rev. *Address*: School of European Studies, Univ. of East Anglia, Norwich NOR 88C.

Cross, Donald Thomas; Senior Lecturer, Department of Town and Country Planning, University of Manchester, since 1971; *b* 1926. MA Cantab 1950; MCD Liverpool 1953; MRTPI. Head of Research Group GLC Planning Dept, 1965–68; Vis. Fellow,

Clare Hall, Cambridge, 1968–69; Asst Chief Planner (Strategy), GLC Planning and Transportation Dept, 1969–70. Mem., SSRC Planning Cttee, 1968–72. *Address*: Dept of Town and Country Planning Univ. of Manchester, Oxford Road, Manchester M13 9PL.

Cross, Dr Gordon Raymond; Lecturer, since 1965, and Head of Department of Educational Psychology, since 1973. Faculty of Education, King's College, University of London; *b* 1926; *m* 1954; one *s* one *d*. BA Cantab 1949, MA Cantab 1954, PhD Cantab 1958 (Psychol.); Grad. Mem., Brit. Psychol. Soc. Supervisor of Studies, Pembroke Coll., Cambridge, 1953–56; Loughborough Univ., 1956–65. Dir, BJEP, 1959– ; Mem., ATCDE/BJEP and Plowden Working Parties. *Publications*: The Measurement of Human Abilities and their Cultivation, in, The Teacher and the Needs of Society in Evolution, ed E. J. King, 1970; Psychology of Learning, 1st edn 1974; *contrib.* BJEP, Jl of Educnl Studies. *Address*: King's College, Strand, WC2R 2LS.

Cross, Dr John Arthur; Reader in Politics, University College, Cardiff, since 1974; *b* 1927; *m* 1959; three *d*. BA Cantab 1948, MA Cantab 1952, BSc (Econ.) London 1956, PhD London 1965, DipEd Liverpool, 1950; Lectr in Politics, Univ. Coll., Cardiff, 1964–68. Dep. Dir of Studies, Ashridge Coll. for residential adult educn, 1950–54; Ref. Div., COI, 1954–61; Lectr in Public Admin, Welsh Coll. of Adv. Tech., 1962–64; Sen. Lectr, Politics, Univ. Coll., Cardiff, 1968–74. *Publications*: Whitehall and the Commonwealth, 1967; (with R. K. Alderman) The Tactics of Resignation, 1967; British Public Administration, 1970; Modern British Government, 1972; *contrib.* Jl Commonwealth Polit. Studies; Parly Aff., Public Admin, etc. *Address*: Dept of Politics, Univ. College, PO Box 78, Cardiff CF1 1XL.

Cross, Margaret Claire; Senior Lecturer in History, University of York, since 1970; *b* 1932. BA Cambridge 1955, MA Cambridge 1958, PhD Cambridge 1959; FRHistS. Res. Schol., Girton Coll., 1955–58; Internat. Fellow, Amer. Assoc. Univ. Women, 1961–62. Res. Fellow, Univ. of Reading, 1962–65; Lectr, Univ. of York, 1965–70. County Archiv., Cambridgeshire, 1958–61; Mem., Eccles. Hist. Soc. *Publications*: The Free Grammar School of Leicester, 1953; The Puritan Earl: The Life of Henry Hastings, Third Earl of Huntingdon, 1536–1595, 1966; The Royal Supremacy in the Elizabethan Church, 1969; ed, The Letters of Sir Francis Hastings, 1574–1609, 1969; contrib. The Interregnum: the quest for settlement 1646–1660, ed G. E. Aylmer, 1972; *contrib.* Bull. Inst. Hist. Res., Hist. Jl, Agric. Hist. Rev., Studies in Ch. Hist., Recus. Hist., Archaeol. Ael., Trans Leics Arch. and Hist. Soc., etc. *Address*: Dept of Hist., Univ. of York, Heslington, York YO1 5DD.

Cross, Prof. Robert Craigie, CBE; Regius Professor of Logic, University of Aberdeen, since 1953; *b* 1911; *m* 1943; two *d*. MA Glasgow 1932 (1st cl. Classics), BA Oxon 1936 (1st cl. Classical Mods 1934, 1st cl. Lit. Hum. 1936), MA Oxon. Asst, Dept of Logic, Univ. of Edinburgh, 1936–37; Lectr, Jesus Coll., Oxford, 1937–38; Fellow and Tutor in Phil., Jesus Coll., Oxford, 1938–53, Sen. Tutor, 1948–53. Mem., NE Reg. Hosp. Bd, 1958–65; UGC, 1965– ; Trustee, Scott. Hosp. Endowments Res. Trust, 1968– . *Publications*: (with A. D. Woozley) Plato's Republic: a Philosophical Commentary, 1964; *contrib.* Mind, Proc. Aristot. Soc. *Address*: Dept of Logic, King's College, Univ. of Aberdeen.

Cross, Thomas Alfred; Senior Lecturer, Department of Fine Art, University of Reading, since 1964; *b* 1931; *m* 1959; one *s*. Slade Dip. London 1956 (Fine Art), Nat. Dip. of Des. Manchester Regional Coll. of Art 1953. Abbey Scholarship, Brit. Sch. at Rome, 1956–57; French Govt Scholarships, 1957–58. Lectr in Fine Art, Reading Univ., 1953; Asst Dir, Welsh Arts Council, 1959–63; Vis. Prof., Ohio State Univ., Colombus, Ohio, USA, 1971. Mem., Art Adv. Panel, S Regional Council for Further Educn, 1969–73, Chm., 1973. Exhibitions in London and Provincial galls incl. Liverpool, Oxford, Reading Mus., Univ. of Sussex, Birmingham, Manchester, Whitechapel Gall., AIA Gall., etc. *Publication*: The Slade Tradition, 1971. *Address*: Dept of Fine Art, Univ. of Reading, London Road, Reading.

Crossland, Richard Walker, BSc, MEd; Senior Lecturer in Education, University of Manchester, since 1965; Dean of the Faculty of Education, since 1974 (Dean-Elect, 1973–74); *b* 1914; *m* 1939; 1969; one *d*, one *s* decd, one step-*s*. BSc Manchester 1936 (1st cl. Biology), MEd Manchester 1956, Teacher's Dip Manchester 1937; MIBiol 1950. Staff Tutor in Natural Science, Extra-Mural Dept, Birmingham Univ., 1946–48; Lectr in Educn, Univ. of Manchester, 1949–65. Sch. teacher, 1937–40; Nat. Serv., 1940–46; Governor, Glossop Sch., 1950– , Elizabeth Gaskell Coll. of Educn, 1965– ; Consult. Eval., Schools Council, 1966–71. *Publications*: O Level Tests in Biology, 1957; (with M. E. J. Shewell) Junior Science, 1962–64; (with M. E. J. Shewell) How Your Body Works, 1967; *contrib.* Adult Educn, Biol. and Hum. Aff., Sch. Sci. Rev. *Address*: Dept of Education, Univ. of Manchester, Manchester M13 9PL.

Crossland, Prof. Ronald Arthur; Professor of Greek, Department of Greek, University of Sheffield, since 1958; *b* 1920. BA Cambridge 1946 (1st cl. Classics), MA Yale 1947, MA Cambridge 1948; Mem., Class. Assoc., Hellenic Soc., Linguistics Assoc. (Chm., Hist. Linguistics Sect.), Philol. Soc., Prehist. Soc., Brit. Inst. Archaeol., Ankara, Brit. Inst. Persian Studies. Instructor in Classics, Yale, 1947–48; Lectr in Ancient Hist., Univ. of Durham (King's Coll., Newcastle), 1951–58; Harris Fellow, King's Coll., Cambridge, 1952–56; Dean, Fac. of Arts, Univ. of Sheffield, 1973– . *Publications*: Immigrants from the North, in, Cambridge Ancient History 3rd edn, vol. 1/2, chap. XXVII, 1967; The origin and development of languages, Language families of the world, in, Thought and Ideals, ed B. Pattison, 1968; (with Ann Birchall) Bronze Age Migrations in the Aegean, 1974; *contrib.* Arch. Ling., Past and Present, Studia Balcanica, Trans Philol. Soc. *Address*: Dept of Greek, The Univ., Sheffield S10 2TN.

Crossley, Prof. John Rodney; Montague Burton Professor of Industrial Relations, School of Economic Studies, University of Leeds, since 1968; *b* 1934; *m* 1961; two *s*. BSc(Econ) London 1957; FSS, FREconS, Mem., London Math. Soc. Asst Lectr in Econ. Statistics, Univ. Manchester, 1957–61; Asst Lectr and Lectr in Econs, LSE, 1961–68; Industrial Relations Adviser, Nat., Bd for Prices and Incomes, 1967–69; Mem., Briggs Cttee on Nursing, 1970–72; Brit. Mem., EEC Cttee on Employment Problems of Econ. and Monetary Union, 1972– . *Publications*: *contrib.* BJIR, Eca, SJPE, LCESB, ER, MS. *Address*: School of Economic Studies, Univ. of Leeds, Leeds LS2 9JT.

Crowe, Rev. Dr Michael Bertram, MA, BD, PhD; University (Statutory) Lecturer in Ethics and Politics, University College, Dublin, 1972; *b* 1923. BA NUI 1944 (1st cl. Mental and Moral Science), MA NUI 1945, BD Lateran Univ. Rome 1948, PhD Louvain 1955. Asst Lectr in Philosophy, Univ. Coll., Dublin, 1950–61; Coll. Lectr in Ethics and Politics, Univ. Coll., Dublin, 1961–72; Vis. Scholar, Harvard Univ. Sch. of Divinity, Fall Term, 1973–74; Vis. Prof., Boston Theological Inst. (St John's Seminary), Fall Term, 1973–74. *Publications*: Private Morals and Public Life, 1965, 2nd edn 1968; Human Rights, 1972; *contrib.* Irish Eccles. Rec., Irish Theol. Qly, Nat. Law Forum, Studies. *Address*: Dept of Ethics and Politics, Univ. College, Dublin 4.

Crowley, Rev. Prof. Theodore, OFM; Professor of Scholastic Philosophy, The Queen's University of Belfast, since 1969; *b* 1910. PhD Louvain 1939, Maître Agrégé en Philosophie Louvain 1949, Lic.enSc.Hist Louvain 1938. Lectr, QUB, 1951–54, Reader, 1954–68. Mem., Internat. St Bonaventure Cttee, 1970. *Publications*: trans., The University of Louvain during second world war, 1948; Roger Bacon: the problem of the soul in his philosophical commentaries, 1950; Transcendence (inaug. lec.), 1970; Studies in the Philosophy of St Bonaventure (forthcoming); trans., Hidden God: how do we know that God exists?, 1966; ed jtly, St Bonaventure Centenary Volume, 1972–74; *contrib.* Irish Philos. Studies, Bull. J. Rylands Lib., Etudes Franciscaines. *Address*: Dept of Scholastic Philosophy, The Queen's Univ. Belfast BT7 1NN.

Crowther-Hunt, The Lord; Norman Crowther Crowther-Hunt, MA, PhD; Minister of State, Department of Education and Science, since 1974; Constitutional Adviser to the Government; Fellow and Lecturer in Politics, Exeter College, Oxford University, since 1952; *b* 1920; *m* 1944; three *d*. BA Cantab (1st cl. History Tripos, 1946 and 1947), MA Cantab 1949, PhD Cantab 1951. Res Fellow, Sidney Sussex Coll., Cambridge,

1949–51; Commonwealth Fund Fellow, Princeton Univ., USA, 1951–52; Vis. Prof., Michigan State Univ., USA 1961. Mem., Cttee on the Civil Service (Fulton Cttee), and Leader, Mngmt Cnsltncy Gp, 1966–68; Mem., Commn. on the Constitution, 1969–73, and principal author of the Memorandum of Dissent. Mem., Council, Headington Sch., Oxford, 1966– . *Publications*: Two Early Political Associations, 1961; ed, Whitehall and Beyond, 1964; ed, Personality and Power, 1970; *contrib.* Occid., Oxford Slav. Studies. *Address*: Exeter College, Oxford.

Crozier, Dr Andrew Thomas Knights; Lecturer in English, School of English and American Studies, University of Sussex, since 1973; *b* 1943; *m* 1970. BA Cantab 1964, MA Cantab 1967; PhD Essex 1973. Dept of American Studies, Univ. of Keele, 1967–73. *Address*: Arts Building, Univ. of Sussex, Brighton BN1 9QN.

Cruickshank, James George; Senior Lecturer in Geography, Queen's University of Belfast, since 1972 (Lecturer, 1959–72); *b* 1935; *m* 1962; one *s* one *d*. BSc Aberdeen 1957. Scientific Officer, Macaulay Inst. for Soil Res., Aberdeen, 1957–59. *Publications*: Soil Geography, 1972; *contrib.* Arctic, Can. Geog., Geog., Ann., Irish Geog., Scott. Geogl Mag., Trans Inst. Brit. Geog. *Address*: Dept of Geography, Queen's Univ. of Belfast, Belfast BT7 1NN.

Cruickshank, Prof. John, MA, PhD, LittD; Professor of French, University of Sussex, since 1962; *b* 1924; *m* 1949; one *s*. BA Dublin 1948 (1st cl. French & German), MA Dublin 1950, PhD Dublin 1951, LittD Dublin 1971; Mem., Cttee, Mod. Hums Res. Assoc., Mngmt Cttee, Brit. Inst. In Paris. Lectr in French, Univ. of Southampton, 1949–60; Sen. Lectr in French, Univ. of Southampton, 1960–62. Mem., UGC, 1970– . *Publications*: Albert Camus and the Literature of Revolt, 1959, Turkish edn 1965; Critical Readings in the Modern French Novel, 1961, 2nd edn 1968; The Novelist as Philosopher: Essays in French Fiction 1935–1960, 1962, Spanish edn 1968; Montherlant, 1964; ed, Vigny: Servitude et grandeur militaires, 1966; Aspects of the Modern European Mind, 1969; French Literature and its Background (6 vols), 1968–70; Benjamin Constant, 1974; *contrib.* French Studies; Mod. Lang. Rev., Times Lit. Supp., etc. *Address*: Univ. of Sussex, Falmer, Brighton BN1 9QN.

Cruickshank, John McInnes; Senior Lecturer in Accountancy, University of Glasgow, since 1968; *b* 1932; *m* 1956; two *s* one *d*. BCom Edinburgh 1952; FCA (ACA 1955), FCMA (ACWA 1958), JDipMA. Industrial appts until 1968; Adviser of Studies, Glasgow Univ., 1968– . *Address*: Univ. of Glasgow, Glasgow G12 8QQ.

Cruickshank, Dr Marjorie Alice; Senior Lecturer in Education, University of Keele, since 1972; *b* 1920; *m* 1953; one *s* one *d*. BA Manchester 1941 (1st cl. History), MA London 1950 (Educn), PhD Leeds 1955 (Educn). Lectr in Educn, Univ. Leeds, 1950–62; Lectr in Educn, Univ. Keele.

1968–72. *Publications*: Church and State in English Education, 1870 to the Present Day, 1963; History of the Training of Teachers in Scotland, 1970; *contrib*. Brit. Jl Educnl Studies, History of Educn, Paedagogica Historica. *Address*: Education Dept, Univ. of Keele, Keele, Staffs ST5 5BG.

Cruise O'Brien, Dr Donal Brian; Lecturer, Department of Political and Economic Studies, School of Oriental and African Studies, University of London, since 1969; *b* 1941; *m*; one *d*. BA Cantab 1963 (History), MA California 1964 (Pol Sci.), PhD LSE 1969 (Sociol.). Res. Fellow, SOAS, Univ. of London, 1966–69. *Publications*: The Mourides of Senegal, 1971; *contrib*. Africa, Cahiers d'Etudes Africaines, Civilisations, Jl of African Hist., Jl of Develt Studies. *Address*: Sch. of Oriental and African Studies, Univ. of London, Malet Street, WC1E 7HP.

Crystal, Dr David; Reader, Department of Linguistic Science, University of Reading, since 1969; *b* 1941; *m* 1963; one *s* two *d*. BA London 1962 (1st cl. English), PhD London 1966; Mem., Lingu. Assoc. GB, Philol. Soc. Res. Asst, UCL, 1962–63; Asst Lectr, UCNW, Bangor, 1963–65; Lectr, Reading, 1965–69. Assoc. Ed., Jl Lingu., 1970–73; Ed., Lang. Res. in Prog., 1966–70; Ed., Jl Child Language, 1974– ; Sec., Lingui. Assoc. GB, 1967–70; Adv, Ed., Penguin Modern Linguistics. *Publications*: (with R. Quirk) Systems of Prosodic and Paralinguistic Features in English, 1964; Linguistics, Language and Religion, 1965; What is Linguistics?, 4th edn 1974; Prosodic Systems and Intonation in English, 1969; (with D. Davy) Investigating English Style, 1969; (with W. Bolton) The English Language, vol. 2, 1969; Linguistics, 1971; *contrib*. Jl Lingu., Jl Int. Phonet. Assoc., Praxis, Brit. Jl Disorders Commun. *Address*: Dept of Linguistic Science, Univ. of Reading, Whiteknights, Reading RG6 2AH.

Cuddy, Dr Michael Patrick; Lecturer, Department of Economics, University College Galway, since 1971; *b* 1942. BAgrSc UC Dublin 1965 (1st cl. Hons), MAgrSc 1966, PhD NC State Univ. 1972 (Economics and Statistics); Res. Asst, UC Dublin, 1965–66; NC State Univ. 1966–71; Teaching Asst, 1969–71. *Address*: Dept of Economics, Univ. Coll. Galway, Galway.

Cudworth, Charles L. E., MA; Curator, Pendlebury Library of Music, Cambridge, since 1958; *b* 1908; *m* 1938. MA Cambridge 1958; Mem., Royal Music Assoc., 1951, Internat. Assoc. Music Libr., 1951. Asst, Mus. of Class. Archaeol., Cambridge, 1931–37; Sub-Libr., Class. Fac. Libr., Cambridge, 1937–46; Pendlebury Libr., 1946–57; Sen. Mem., Gonville and Caius Coll., 1958; Fellow, Univ. Coll., Cambridge, 1965; Vis. Prof., Univ. of S Calif Los Angeles, 1968. *Publications*: jtly, Shakespeare and Music, 1964; Handel, 1972; *contrib*. Belg. Tijds. Muziek., Galpin Soc. Jl, Music Lett., Music. Times, Notes, Proc. Royal Music Assoc, Encyc. Brit., MGG, Grove. *Address*: Univ. Music School, Downing Place, Cambridge.

Cullen, Dr James Stanislaus Benedict; Tutor and Lecturer in Modern History, Greyfriars, Oxford University, since 1967; *b* 1930. BA NUI 1952 (1st cl. Hons), MA NUI 1953, MA Oxon 1968, DPhil Oxon 1964; ALCM 1946. Faculty Lectr, Oxford Univ., 1968– , also Head, History Dept, University Hall, Buckland. *Publications*: several articles in newspapers and jls. *Address*: Greyfriars, Oxford.

Cullen, Prof. Louis Michael; Associate Professor of Modern History, University of Dublin, Trinity College, since 1963; *b* 1932; *m* 1964; one *s* one *d*. BA NUI 1953, MA NUI 1956, PhD London 1959. Fellow, TCD, 1968– ; Dean of Arts (Humanities), 1973– . Jt Dir, Survey Business Rec. Irish MSS Commn, 1970– ; Hon. Sec., Econ. Soc. Hist. Soc. Ireland, 1970– . *Publications*: Anglo-Irish Trade, 1660–1800, 1968; Life in Ireland, 1968; An Economic History of Ireland since 1660, 1972; *contrib*. Past Pres., Trans Royal Hist. Soc., Proc. Royal Irish Acad., Irish Hist. Studies, Studia Hibern. *Address*: 40 Trinity College, Dublin 2.

Cullingford, Robin Albert; Lecturer in Geography, University of Exeter, since 1965; *b* 1940; *m* 1963; two *s*. MA Edinburgh 1962 (1st cl. Geography); PhD Edinburgh 1972; Mem., Inst. Brit. Geogrs, Royal Scott. Geogl Soc., Glaciol Soc. *Publications*: *contrib*. Scott. Geog. Mag., Trans Inst. Brit. Geogrs. *Address*: Dept of Geography, The Univ., Exeter, Devon EX4 4QH.

Culmsee, Bent, mag.art; Lecturer in Danish, Department of German and Scandinavian Studies, University of Newcastle upon Tyne, since 1967; *b* 1925; *m* 1967. mag.art. Copenhagen 1950 (comparative literature). Lectr, Strasbourg Univ. 1956–65. Progr. asst, BBC, 1951–52; Asst libr., Royal Lib., Copenhagen, 1952–55; Lit. ed., Danmarks Radio, 1965–67. *Publications*: trans. (into Danish for Danish State Radio), M. Mihura: Maribel, 1966; Georges Schéhadé: Histoire de Vasco, 1967; M. Duras: Des Journées entières dans les Arbres, 1968; Jean Cocteau: La Machine infernale, 1969; Natalia Ginzburg: L'Inserzione, 1970; G. Schéhadé: L'Emigré de Brisbane, 1971; Denis Diderot: Le Neveu de Rameau, 1972; *contrib*. Etudes Gobin., Scandinavica. *Address*: Dept of German and Scandinavian Studies, Claremont Bridge, Univ. of Newcastle upon Tyne, Newcastle upon Tyne NE1 7RU.

Culyer, Anthony John, BA; Assistant Director, Institute of Social and Economic Research, University of York, since 1971; *b* 1942; *m* 1966; one *s* one *d*. BA Exon 1965; Mem., AUTE, AEA. Royal Econ. Soc. Teaching Asst, UCLA, 1965; Lectr, Exeter Univ., 1966–69; Lectr, York Univ., 1969–71. Asst Ed., Soc. and Econ. Admin, 1966–71. *Publications*: The Economics of Social Policy, 1973; ed jtly, Benham's Economics, 1973; ed jtly, Health Economics, 1973; *contrib*. Bull. Econ. Res., Economica, Kyklos, Med. Care, Oxf. Econ. Papers, SJPE, Soc. Sci. and Med., Soc. Econ. and Admin, Soc. Trends, Public Fin. *Address*: Institute of

Social and Economic Research, Univ. of York, Heslington, York YO1 5OD.

Cummins, Dr James S.; Professor of Spanish, University College, London, since 1964. BA Hons London 1953 (Spanish), PhD London 1955, Diploma de estudios hispánicos, Madrid 1951; Mem. Council, Hakluyt Soc., MRHistS. Mem., Cañada Blanch Cttee, London University, 1968– . *Publications*: Travels and Controversies of Domingo de Navarrete, 2 vols, 1960; ed, Lope de Vega: Triunfo de la Fe en los reynos del Japón, 1965; ed, A. de Morga: Sucesos de las islas Filipinas, 1971; (with N. Cushner, SJ) The Discurso Parenético of Gómez de Pspinosa, 1974; *contrib.* Archivum Fratrum Praedicatorum, Monumenta Nipponica, Bull. Hispanic Studies, History Today. *Address*: Univ. Coll., Gower Street, WC1E 6BT.

Cumpston, Dr Ina Mary, MA, DPhil, FRHistS; Reader in Commonwealth History, Department of History, Birkbeck College, University of London, since 1965. BA Sydney 1939 (1st cl. History), MA Sydney 1940, DPhil Oxon 1950; FRHistS. Tutor, New England Univ. Coll. (Sydney Univ.), 1942–44, Lectr, 1944–47; Lectr, Royal Holloway Coll., London, 1955–57; Lectr, Birkbeck Coll., London, 1957–65. Narrator, Hist. Sect., Cabinet Off., 1950–55; Mem., Panel of Experts, IFUW, 1970– . *Publications*: Indians Overseas in British Territories 1834–1854, 1953; The Growth of the British Commonwealth 1880–1932, 1972; *contrib.* Austr. Jl Pol. Hist., Bull. Inst. Hist. Res., EHR, Hist. Studies A and NZ, Pacific Hist. Rev., Popul. Studies, Trans Royal Hist. Soc. *Address*: Dept of History, Birkbeck College, Univ. of London, Malet Street, WC1E 7HX.

Cunliffe, Prof. Barrington Windsor, MA, PhD, FSA; Professor of European Archaeology, Oxford University, and Fellow of Keble College, since 1972; *b* 1939. BA Cantab 1961 (1st cl. Archaeology and Anthropology), MA Cantab 1964, PhD Cantab 1966; FSA. Lectr in Archaeology, Univ. of Bristol, 1963–66; Prof. of Archaeology, Univ. of Southampton, 1966–72. Chm., Solent Local Radio Cttee; Mem., BBC South Adv. Cttee, and of misc. Archaeol. Cttees. *Publications*: Winchester Excavations, vol. 1, 1965; Richborough, vol. 5, 1968; Roman Baths, 1969; Excavations at Fishbourne, vols 1 and 2, 1971; Roman Bath Discovered, 1971; Fishbourne: a Roman Palace and its Garden, 1971; The Regni, 1972; *contrib.* Antiqu. Jl, Proc. Prehis. Soc., Jl Post-Mediev. Archaeol., Mediev. Archaeol. *Address*: Institute of Archaeology, 35 Beaumont Street, Oxford.

Cunliffe, Prof. Marcus Falkner, MA, BLitt; Professor of American Studies, University of Sussex, since 1965; *b* 1922; *m* 1949; 1971; one *s* two *d*. BA Oxon 1944, MA and BLitt Oxon 1947, MA Manchester 1964; FRHistS. Lectr and Sen. Lectr, Manchester Univ., 1949–60; Vis. Prof., Harvard Univ., 1959–60; Prof of American History, Manchester Univ., 1960–64; Vis. Prof., Grad. Center, City Univ. of NY, 1970, Univ. of Michigan, 1973; Sec. and Chm., Brit. Assoc. Amer.

Studies, 1958–63. *Publications*: The Literature of the United States, 1954, 3rd edn 1957; George Washington: Man and Monument, 1958; The Nation Takes Shape, 1789–1837, 1959; ed, Weems' Life of Washington, 1963; Soldiers and Civilians: The Martial Spirit in America 1775–1865, 1968; ed (with R. Winks), Pastmasters: Some Essays on American Historians, 1969; American Presidents and the Presidency, 1969; ed, The Times History of Our Times, 1971; *contrib.* Amer. Qly, Hist. *Address*: Arts Building, Univ. of Sussex, Brighton BNI 9QN.

Cunningham, Dr Anthony Christopher, BComm, MEconSc, PhD; Associate Professor of Business Administration, Department of Business Administration, University College, Dublin, since 1972; *b* 1935; *m* 1960; one *s* one *d*. BComm Univ. Coll. Cork 1955, MEconSc Univ. Coll. Cork 1959, PhD Cornell 1964; MMII, AMBIM. Grad. Asst, Cornell Univ., 1960; Lectr in Marketing, Univ. Coll. Dublin, 1964–72; Vis. Prof., Univ. of Arizona, 1966; Vis. Sen. Fellow, ITC, UNCTAD/GATT, Geneva, 1970; Vis. Lectr, Queen's Univ., Belfast, 1968–72. *Publications*: Introduction to Business Administration, 1974; *contrib.* Worldwide Marketing, 1974; *contrib.* Brit. Jl Market., Eur. Jl Market., Manag. Studies. *Address*: Dept of Business Administration, Univ. College, Dublin 4.

Cunningham, Dr Hugh St Clair; Lecturer in History, University of Kent at Canterbury, since 1969; *b* 1942; *m* 1969. BA Cantab 1963, MA Cantab 1967, DPhil Sussex 1969. Lectr, Fourah Bay Coll., Univ. Coll. of Sierra Leone, 1963–66. *Publications*: *contrib.* Vict. Studies. *Address*: Darwin College, The Univ., Canterbury, Kent.

Cunningham, Joseph Sandy; Reader in English, University of York, since 1967; *b* 1928; *m* 1953; three *s* one *d*. BA Hons Durham 1949 (cl. I English); BLitt Oxon 1952. Asst Lectr, Manchester, 1954–56; Lectr, Durham, 1956–63; Lectr, later Sen. Lectr, York, 1963–67. Vis. Prof., Toronto, 1966–67. Chm., Bd of Studies, York, 1969–71. *Publications*: ed, William Collins: Drafts and Fragments, 1956; Alexander Pope: The Rape of the Lock, 1961; ed, Pope: The Rape of the Lock, 1966; The Powers That Be, 1969; *contrib.* Delta, Essays and Studies, Use of English. *Address*: Dept of English, Univ. of York, YO1 5DD.

Cunningham, Malcolm Terence, BSc, CEng, FIMechE; Senior Lecturer in Management Sciences, University of Manchester Institute of Science and Technology, since 1971; *b* 1927; *m* 1955; one *s* one *d*. BSc Leeds 1950 (1st cl. Mech. Eng); CEng, FIMechE. Lectr, UMIST, 1964–71. Ch. Eng., Dewrance and Co., 1958; Eng Mgr Dewrance and Co., 1960; Mem., CNAA Bd for Business Studies, 1971. *Publications*: *contrib.* Jl Mngmt Studies, Brit. Jl Market., Europ. Jl Market. *Address*: Dept of Management Sciences, Univ. of Manchester Institute of Science and Technology, Manchester M60 1QD.

Cunningham, William; Lecturer in Economics, University of Warwick, since 1963; *b* 1939; *m* 1964; one *s* one *d*. MA Edinburgh 1963, PhD Newcastle 1964– (still continuing). *Publications*: McConnell and Kennedy, Cotton Spinners, 1790–1840, 1972; *contrib*. Econ. Jl. *Address*: Dept of Economics, Univ. of Warwick, Warwick CV4 7AL.

Cunnison, Prof. Ian, MA, DPhil; Professor of Social Anthropology, Department of Sociology and Social Anthropology, University of Hull, since 1966; *m* 1956; two *d*. BA Cantab 1947 (1st cl. Arch. and Anth.), DPhil Oxon 1952; Mem., Assoc. of Social Anth. Res. Offr., Rhodes-Livingstone Inst., 1948–51; Temp. Res. Asst., Manchester, 1951–52; Anth. on Sudan Govt. Grant, 1952–55; Simon Res. Fellow, Manchester Univ., 1955; Lectr, Manchester, 1955–59; Head Dept of Anth., Khartoum Univ., 1959–65, Prof., 1964–65; Dean, Faculty of Social Sci. and Law, Hull, 1969–71. Mem., SSRC Social Anth. Cttee, 1969–73; Mem., Area Studies Panel, 1970–72; Ed., Sudan Notes and Records, 1962–66, Assoc. Ed., 1966– . *Publications*: The Luapula Peoples of Northern Rhodesia, 1959; Baggara Arabs, 1966; trans. Mauss, The Gift, 1954; trans. Gamitto, King Kazembe, 1960; ed (with W. R. James), Essays in Sudan Ethnography, 1972; *contrib*. Africa, Amer. Anthrop., Jl African Hist., Rhodes-Liv. Jl, Sudan Jl Vet. Sci. and Animal Husb., Sudan Phil. Soc. Ann. Conf. Procs., Sudan Soc. *Address*: Dept of Sociology and Social Anthropology, Hull Univ., Hull HU6 7RX.

Cupitt, Rev. Don; University Lecturer, Faculty of Divinity, Cambridge, since 1973; *b* 1934; *m* 1963; one *s* two *d*. BA 1955, MA 1958, Cantab. Univ. Asst Lectr in Divinity, Cambridge, 1968–73; Stanton Lectr, 1968–71. Sen. Proctor, Univ. of Cambridge 1967–68; Dean of Emmanuel Coll., 1966– . *Publications*: Christ and the Hiddenness of God 1971; Crisis of Moral Authority, 1972; contributor to: Crisis for Confirmation, ed, Michael Perry, 1967; Christ, Faith and History, ed, S. W. Sykes and J. P. Clayton, 1972; *contrib*. Anglican Theol Rev., Jl Theol Studies, Theol. *Address*: Emmanuel Coll., Cambridge.

Curran, Sir Samuel (Crowe), FRS; Principal and Vice-Chancellor, University of Strathclyde, since 1964; *b* 1912; *m* 1940; three *s* one *d*. DSc Glasgow 1950, MA Glasgow, BSc, PhD Glasgow 1937, PhD Cantab 1941; Hon. LLD Glasgow 1968, Hon. LLD Aberdeen 1971; Hon. ScD Poly. Lodz; FRS 1953, FRSE 1947, Hon. FRCPS, 1964; DL Glasgow 1969; Hon. Fellow, St John's Coll. Cambridge, 1971. Manhattan Project (Min. of Supply), Univ. of California, 1944–45 (Invention of Scintillation Counter, 1944). Principal, Royal Coll. of Sci. and Tech., Glasgow, 1959–64; UKAEA, 1955–58; Chief Scientist, AWRE, Aldermaston, Berks, 1958–59; Chief Scientific Adviser to Sec. of State for Scotland, 1967– . Mem., Coun. for Scientific and Indus. Res., 1962–65; Mem., SRC, 1965–68; Mem., Adv. Coun. on Tech., 1965–70; Mem., Scottish Economic Planning Coun., 1965–68; Mem., Oil Develt Council for Scotland, 1973– ; Chm., Adv. Cttee on Med. Research, 1962– ; Chm., Adv. Bd on Relations with Univs, 1966–70, Mem., Coun., Royal Soc. of Edinburgh, 1961–64; Hon. Pres., Scottish–Polish Cultural Assoc., 1972. Comdr, St Olav (Norway), 1966; Offr of Polonia Restituta, 1970. *Publications*: (with J. D. Craggs) Counting Tubes, 1949; Luminescence and the Scintillation Counter, 1953; Alpha, Beta and Gamma Ray Spectroscopy, 1964; *contrib*. Proc. Royal Soc., London, Philosophical Mag., Physical Rev., Nature, etc. *Address*: Univ. of Strathclyde, Royal College, 204 George Street, Glasgow G1 1XW.

Currie, Harry MacLeod, MA, BA; JP; Senior Lecturer in Classics, Queen Mary College, University of London, since 1968; *b* 1930; *m* 1959; three *s*. MA Glasgow 1953, BA Cantab 1955. Asst Lectr in Greek, Bedford College, London Univ., 1955–57; Asst Lectr in Classics, King's Coll., London Univ., 1957–58; Lectr in Classics, Queen Mary Coll., 1959–68; Vis. Prof. of Classics, Univ. of Victoria, BC, 1974. Hon. Sec., Virgil Soc., 1964–70; Ed., its Annual Proceedings, 1962– . *Publications*: Chapter on Seneca as Philosopher, in, Silver Latin Literature II, 1972; The Individual and the State, 1973; *contrib*. Bull. of Inst. of Classical Studies (London), Hermes, Latomus, Mnemosyne, New Rambler, Theology, etc. *Address*: Dept of Classics, Queen Mary College, Univ. of London, Mile End Road, E1 4NS.

Curtis, Bernard Lionel; Lecturer (Philosophy of Education), MEd Course Tutor, School of Education, University of Birmingham, since 1968; *b* 1921; *m* 1948; one *s* one *d*. BA Bristol 1965 (Hons), MLitt Bristol 1968; Teaching Cert. Goldsmiths' Coll., London 1950. Appointments Officer (part-time), Bristol, 1966–68. *Publications*: *contrib*. Brit. Jl Aesth., Educ. Rev., Proc. Phil. Educ. Soc. *Address*: School of Education, Univ. of Birmingham, PO Box 363, Birmingham B15 2TT.

Curtis, Dr Renée Lilian, BA, PhD; Senior Lecturer, French Department, Westfield College, University of London, since 1969. BA London 1950 (Hons French), PhD London 1953, Dip. in French Phonetics London 1948. Res. Asst, Univ. Coll., London, 1953–54; Lectr in Medieval French Lit., Univ. of Durham, 1954–55; Univ. Coll. of Ghana, 1955–59; Westfield Coll., Univ. of London, 1960–69; Vis. Assoc. Prof., Univ. of California, 1966–67. *Publications*: Le Roman de Tristan en prose, vol. I, 1963; Tristan Studies, 1969; Le Roman de Tristan en prose, vol. 2 (forthcoming); *contrib*. Mod. Lang. Rev., Romania, Mél. Frapp. *Address*: Westfield College, Hampstead, NW3 7ST.

Custard, John Douglas G.; *see* Goss-Custard.

Cuthbert, Prof. Norman; Professor of Applied Economics, The Queen's University of Belfast, since 1969; *b* 1909; *m* 1943; one *d*. BA Belfast 1932, MA 1934, BComSc 1937;

Mem., REconS; Coun. of Stat, and Soc.; Inquiry Soc. of Ireland. Res. Lectr, 1946–48, Lectr, 1948–54, Sen. Lectr, 1954–65, Reader, Queen's Univ. of Belfast, 1965–69; Prof., Royal Univ. of Malta, 1966–68. Welfare Br., Belfast Civil Defence Auth., 1941–45; Consult, BOT, 1965; Mem., NI GCE 1969– ; NI Schools Examination Coun., 1970– ; Bd, Ulster Coll., 1969– ; Trade Statistics Consult. Cttee, 1971– . *Publications*: Ulster under Home Rule, 1956; Economic Survey of Northern Ireland, 1957; Enquiry into SET in Retail Trade in NI, 1971; *contrib.* Jl of Industrial Econ., Scottish Jl of Political Economy, Jl of Statistical and Soc. Inquiry Soc. of Ireland. *Address*: Dept of Economics, Queen's Univ. Belfast, Belfast BT7 1NN.

D

Dabbagh, Dr Hussein Muhammad Ali; Lecturer in Arabic, University of Durham, since 1959; *b* 1929; *m* 1961; one *s* one *d*. BA (Hons) London 1958 (Classical Arabic); PhD Dunelm 1968 (Modern Arabic Studies); Mem., UTA. Asst Lectr, Univ. of Durham, 1956–59; on secondment from Durham Univ. to: Dept of Islamic Studies, Univ. of Malaya, 1964–66; Dept of Islamic Studies, Ibadan Univ., 1970–71; Dept of English, Kuwait Univ., 1971–72. *Publications*: contrib. Four Shakespearian Sonnets, trans. Arabic, Aswat, 1961; Reith Lectures, trans. Arabic, 1962; *contrib.* Arabic literary periodicals. *Address*: School of Oriental Studies, Elvet Hill, Univ. of Durham, Durham City.

Dahrendorf, Prof. Ralf, PhD, DrPhil; Director, London School of Economics, University of London, since 1974; *b* 1929; *m* 1954; three *d.* DrPhil Hamburg 1952 (philosophy and class. philology), PhD LSE 1956 (Leverhulme Res. Schol., 1953–54, Hon. Fellow); Hon. DLitt Reading 1973, Hon. LLD Manchester 1973, Hon. DSc Ulster 1973. Lectr, Saarbrücken, 1957; Fellow, Center for Advanced Study, Palo Alto, 1957–58; Professor of Sociology: Hamburg, 1958–60; Tübingen, 1960–64; Konstanz, 1966–69 (Vice-Chm., Founding Cttee, 1964–66); Parly Sec. of State, Foreign Office, W Germany, 1969–70; Mem., EEC Commn, Brussels, 1970–74. Vis. Prof., Columbia, 1960; Sydney Bell Lectr, Oxford, 1965; Henry Failing Distinguished Lectr, Oregon, 1966. Learned Publication Award, Journal Fund, 1966. *Publications*: Marx in Perspektive, 1953; Industrie und Betriebssoziologie, 1956; Soziale Klassen und Klassenkonflikt, 1957; Homo sociologicus, 1959; Sozialstruktur des Betriebes, 1959; Gesellschaft und Freiheit, 1961; Über den Ursprung der Ungleichheit, 1961; Die angewandte Aufklärung, 1963; Arbeiterkinder an deutschen Universitäten, 1965; Bildung 1st Bürgerrecht, 1965; Gesellschaft und Demokratie in Deutschland, 1965; Markt und Plan, 1966; Conflict After Class, 1967; Essays in the Theory of Society, 1967; Pfade aus Utopia, 1967; Die Soziologie und der Soziologe, 1967; Für eine Erneuerung der Demokratie in der Bundesrepublik, 1968; Konflikt und Freiheit, 1972. *Address*: London Sch. of

Economics and Political Science, Houghton Street, Aldwych, WC2 2AE.

Daiches, Prof. David, LittD, FRSL; Professor of English, University of Sussex, since 1961; *b* 1912; *m* 1937; one *s* two *d.* MA Edinburgh 1934 (1st cl. English Lit. and Lang.), MA Oxon 1937, DPhil Oxon 1939, Hon. LittD Brown Univ. 1964; Docteur *hc* Sorbonne, 1973; FRSL, Hon. Mem., Mod. Lang. Assoc. Amer.; Fellow, Balliol Coll., Oxford, 1936–37; Asst Prof., Univ. of Chicago, 1939–43; Prof. of English, Cornell Univ., 1946–51; Univ. Lectr in English, Cambridge, 1951–61; Fellow, Jesus Coll., Cambridge, 1957–62; Dean, Sch. of Eng. and Amer. Studies, Univ. of Sussex, 1961–68; Ellison Lectr, Univ. of Cincinnati, 1960; Whidden Lectr, McMaster Univ., 1964; Ewing Lectr, Univ. of California, 1968; Carpenter Vis. Prof., Univ. of Minnesota, 1969; Vis. Fellow, Wesleyan Univ. Middletown, Conn, 1970. *Publications*: The Place of Meaning in Poetry, 1935; New Literary Values, 1936; Literature and Society, 1938; The Novel and the Modern World, 1939, 2nd edn 1960; Poetry and the Modern World, 1940; The King James Bible: A Study of its Sources and Development, 1941; Virginia Woolf, 1942; Robert Louis Stevenson, 1947; A Study of Literature, 1948; Robert Burns, 1950, 2nd edn 1966; Willa Cather: A Critical Introduction, 1951; Critical Approaches to Literature, 1956; Two Worlds: An Edinburgh Jewish Childhood, 1956; Literary Essays, 1956; John Milton, 1957; The Present Age, 1958; A Critical History of English Literature, 1960; George Eliot's Middlemarch, 1963; The Paradox of Scottish Culture, 1964; ed, The Idea of a New University, 1964; English Literature (Princeton Studies in Humanistic Scholarship), 1965; More Literary Essays, 1968; Some Late Victorian Attitudes, 1969; Scotch Whisky, 1969; Sir Walter Scott and His World, 1971; A Third World (autobiography), 1971; Robert Burns and His World, 1971; ed, The Penguin Companion to Literature: Britain and The Commonwealth, 1971; Charles Edward Stuart, 1973; R. L. Stevenson and his World, 1973. *Address*: Mantell Building, Univ. of Sussex, Falmer, Brighton.

Daintith, Prof. Terence C.; Professor of Public Law, University of Dundee, since 1972; *b* 1942; *m* 1965; one *s* one *d.* MA Oxon 1968; Barrister, Lincoln's Inn, 1966. Associate in Law, Univ. California at Berkeley, 1963–64; Lectr in Constitutional Law, Univ. Edinburgh, 1964–72; Vis. Lectr in Law, Coll. of Europe, Bruges, 1966–68; Hon. Lectr in European Econ. Law, Univ. Edinburgh, 1972–73. *Publications*: contrib. Amer. Jl Compar. Law, Internat. Compar. Law Qly., Jl Business Law, Public Law, Revue des Droits de L'Homme. *Address*: Faculty of Law, Bonar House, 17 Bell Street, Dundee DD1 1HP.

Dakyns, Janine Rosalind; Lecturer, School of European Studies, University of East Anglia, since 1969; *b* 1939. BA Oxon 1960, MA Oxon, DPhil Oxon 1969. Temp. Asst Lectr, French Dept, UCL, 1964–66; Asst Lectr, Glasgow Univ., 1967–69. *Publi-*

cations: The Middle Ages in French Literature, 1851–1900, 1973. *Address*: School of European Studies, University Plain, Univ. of East Anglia, Norwich NOR 88C.

Dalby, Dr David; Reader in West African Languages, School of Oriental and African Studies, University of London, since 1967; *b* 1933; *m* 1957; two *d*. BA London 1954 (Mod. Languages), PhD London 1961. Lectr, Univ. Coll. of Sierra Leone, 1961–62; Lectr, SOAS, Univ. of London, 1962–67; Hans Wolff Vis. Prof., Indiana Univ., 1969; Chm., Centre Afr. Studies, SOAS, 1971–. Dir, Internat. Afr. Inst.; Mem., Brit. Cttee for Furthering of Relations with French-speaking Africa; Mem., Coun., Afr. Studies Assoc. UK, 1971–73. Editor, Afr. Lang. Rev., 1961– . *Publications*: Lexicon of the Mediæval German Hunt, 1965; ed, Language and History in Africa, 1970; Black through White: Patterns of Communication in Africa and the New World, 1970; *contrib*. Afr. Lang. Studies, Jl Afr. Lang., Jl W Afr. Lang. *Address*: School of Oriental and African Studies, Univ. of London, Malet Street, WC1E 7HP.

Dale, Dr Anthony John; Lecturer, Philosophy Department, Hull University, since 1965; *b* 1940; *m* 1961; one *s*. BA Bristol 1961, MA Bristol 1963, PhD Keele 1969. *Address*: Dept of Philosophy, Hull Univ., Hull HU6 7RX.

Dale, John Rodney; Bursar, University of Bradford, since 1966; *b* 1914; *m* 1939; two *s*. BSc(Econ) London 1951, LLB London 1955, MA Liverpool 1959 (Industrial Sociology). Sec., Bradford Inst. Technol., 1962–66. *Publications*: The Clerical Function, 1959; The Clerk in Industry, 1960; Elementary Economics, 1970. *Address*: Univ. of Bradford, Bradford, Yorkshire BD7 1DP.

Dalgleish, Robert, MSc, BCom, FCIS; Senior Lecturer, Department of Business Organisation, Heriot-Watt University; *b* 1926; *m* 1956; two *s* one *d*. BCom London 1952 (2nd cl.), Travelling Schol, Univ. of Poitiers, MSc Strathclyde 1969; FCIS. Lectr, Heriot-Watt Coll., Edinburgh, 1955–66; Senr Lectr, Dept of Industrial Admin, 1966–69; Vis. Prof. of Business Policy and Admin. Theory, Univ. of Washington, Seattle, 1969–70; also Lectr in various colls and univs in UK. Worked in industry, 1943–44; Brit. Army, 1944–48; Mem., various cttees in past 10 yrs; Hon. Sec., Univ. of London Convocation (SE Scotland), 1958– . *Publications*: co-author, Power System Economics, 1969; CME, Jl Compy Secs, Jl Inst. CA Scot., Mgmt Educn and Dev., Scotl., Scott. Econ. Rev. *Address*: Dept of Business Organisation, Heriot-Watt Univ., Edinburgh EH1 1HX.

Dalton, Kenneth Godfrey; Senior Lecturer, Department of Education, Queen's University, Belfast; *b* 1920; *m* 1953; two *s* two *d*. BA Leeds 1949 (1st cl. Geography), MA Leeds 1957, DipEd Leeds 1950. Lectr, then Sen. Lectr, Fourah Bay Coll. (Univ. Coll. of Sierra Leone), 1954–62; Lectr, then Sen.

Lectr, Queen's Univ., Belfast, 1962– ; on secondment as Prof., Sch. of Educn, Univ. of Zambia, 1972–74. Dean, Fac. of Arts, Fourah Bay Coll., 1960–62; Ed., Bull. Sierra Leone Geog. Assoc., 1954–62. *Publications*: A Geography of Sierra Leone, 1965; *contrib*. Geog. Viewpt, Bull. Sierra Leone Geog. Assoc. *Address*: Dept of Education, Queen's Univ., Belfast BT7 1NN.

Dalton, Robert Henry Francis; Lecturer in Education, Tutor in Charge, Courses for Commonwealth Teachers and Educational Administrators, University of Birmingham, since 1960; *b* 1919; *m* 1951. BA London 1950 (Hons Classics), DipEd Dunelm 1951, MEd Birmingham 1968; Adv. Dip. Course in Chinese Lang., Univ. of Hong Kong, 1971. Sec., Inst. of Educn, Univ. Coll. of Ghana, 1957–60; Vis. Lectr, Univ. of Hong Kong, 1965. Gov., Westhill Coll. of Educn, 1969– ; Conv., Conf. for Inspectors of Schs in Far East. and Pacif. areas of Commonwealth, 1969– . *Publications*: trans. Einaudi: Greatness and Decline of Planned Economy in the Hellenistic World, 1950; Education on the Move – A Handbook for Teachers and Administrators in the British Tropical Commonwealth, 1968; *contrib*. Educnl Papers, Univ. Durham, Educnl Rev., Greece and Rome, Teacher Educn, W Afr. Jl Educn, World Ybk of Educn, Malaysian Jl of Educn. *Address*: School of Education, Univ. of Birmingham, Birmingham B15 2TT.

Daly, Miriam Annette, MA; Lecturer in Irish Economic and Social History, Queen's University of Belfast, since 1969; *b* 1928; *m* 1953; 1965; one *s* one *d*. BA NUI 1948 (1st cl. History and Economics), MA NUI 1950 (1st cl. Economic History); Higher DipEd. 1949. Asst, Univ. Coll., Dublin, 1950–53; Lectr, Univ. of Southampton, 1964–68. Sec., Edit. Bd, Irish Hist. Studies, 1969– . *Publications*: *contrib*. Christus Rex, Furrow, Philos. Studies. *Address*: Dept of Economic and Social History, Queen's Univ. of Belfast, BT7 1NN.

Danby, Prof. Miles William, AADipl, RIBA; Professor of Architecture and Director of Project Office, University of Newcastle upon Tyne, since 1970; *b* 1925; *m* 1948; two *d*. AADiploma, 1953; Mem., RIBA, 1955, Mem., Architectural Assoc. Lectr, Kumasi Univ. of Science and Technology, 1959–63; Sen Lectr, Kumasi Univ. of Science and Technology, 1963; Reader and Head of Dept, Kumasi Univ. of Science and Technology, 1964–65; Prof. and Head of Dept, Khartoum Univ., 1965–70. Private Practice, London 1953–59; Private Practice, Ghana and Sudan, 1959–70; Consultant to UNESCO. RAF 1943–47. *Publications*: Grammar of Architectural Design, 1963, Spanish edn 1970; chaps in: The Volta Resettlement Experience, 1970; Shelter in Africa, 1971; *contrib*. Architects' Jl, Build Internat., Planning Outlook, Edilizia Moderna (Milano). *Address*: School of Architecture, The Univ., Newcastle upon Tyne NE1 7RU.

Daniel, Prof. Glyn Edmund, LittD, FSA; Fellow of St John's College, Cambridge, since 1938, Disney Professor of Archaeology, Cambridge University, since 1974; *b* 1914; *m* 1946. BA Cambridge 1935 (1st cl. with distinction Arch. and Anthrop.), MA 1939, PhD Cambridge 1938, LittD Cambridge 1962; FSA 1942. Lectr in Archaeology, Cambridge Univ., 1946–74; Vis. Prof., Aarhus, 1968; Ferens Prof., Hull, 1969; MacCurdy Lectr, Harvard, 1971–72. Ed. Antiquity, 1958– ; Ancient Peoples and Places, 1958– ; Dir, Anglia TV; Dir, Camb. Arts Theatre Trust. *Publications*: The Three Ages, 1942; A Hundred Years of Archaeology, 1950; The Prehistoric Chamber Tombs of England and Wales, 1950; The Idea of Prehistory, 1961; The First Civilisations, 1968; *contrib.* Proc. Prehist. Soc., Antiqu. Jl, Antiqu. *Address*: St John's College, Cambridge.

Daniel, Sir Goronwy Hopkin, KCVO, CB, DPhil; Principal, Aberystwyth University College, since 1969; *b* 1914; *m* 1940; one *s* two *d*. DPhil Oxon. Fellow of Univ. of Wales; Meyricke Scholar, Jesus Coll. Oxford Inst. of Statistics, 1937–40; Lectr, Dept of Economics, Bristol Univ., 1940–41; Clerk, House of Commons, 1941–43; Min. of Town and Country Planning, 1943–47; Chief Statistician, Min. of Fuel and Power, 1947–55; Under-Sec., Coal Div., 1955–62, Gen. Div., 1962–64; Permanent Under-Sec. of State, Welsh Office, 1964–69. Chm., Brit. Nat. Conf. on Social Welfare, 1970; Pres., W Wales Assoc. for the Arts, 1971– ; Chm., Home-grown Timber Adv. Cttee, 1973– ; Mem., BBC Gen. Adv. Council, 1973– ; Mem., Welsh Language Council, 1973– . *Publications*: *contrib.* Papers in statistical, fuel and power, and other Jls. *Address*: University College of Wales Aberystwyth, Aberystwyth SY23 2AX.

Daniel, Peter, MCd, BArch, FRIAS, ARIBA, MRTPI, AILA; Lecturer (part-time), School of Architecture, Heriot-Watt University, since 1965; Lecturer (part-time), Department of Landscape Architecture, Edinburgh University, since 1972; *b* 1924; *m* 1951; one *s* two *d*. BArch(Hons) Liverpool 1952, MCd Liverpool 1953; FRIAS 1968, ARIBA 1954, MRTPI 1963, AILA 1955. *Publications*: *contrib.* Archit. Rev., Town Planning Rev. *Address*: School of Architecture, Heriot-Watt Univ., Lauriston Place, Edinburgh.

Daniels, Dr David John; Director of Advanced Studies, School of Education, University of Bath, since 1971; *b* 1934; *m* 1956; two *s*. BSc Nottingham 1955, PhD Nottingham 1958, Dip. Advanced Educational Studies Newcastle upon Tyne 1956; ARIC 1957, FRIC 1964; Mem.: Chem. Soc.; Assoc. for Science Educn. Lectr in Educn, Univ. of Bath, 1967–71; Vis. Lectr, South African Foundn for Educn, Science and Technology, 1973. *Publications*: (co-author) Practical Chemistry: an Integrated Course 1962, 2nd edn 1966; (co-author) Chemistry: a Unified Approach, 1967, 3rd edn forthcoming; *contrib.* Educn in Chem., Sch. Sci. Rev. *Address*: Univ. of Bath, Northgate House, Upper Borough Walls, Bath BA1 5AL.

Daniels, Dr Gordon; Lecturer in Modern Far Eastern History, with Special reference to Japan, Centre for Japanese Studies, University of Sheffield, since 1966; *b* 1937; *m* 1964. BSc(Econ) London 1959 (1st cl.), Dphil Oxon 1968. Asst Lectr in Mod. Far Eastern Hist., Univ. of Sheffield, 1963–66. *Publications*: *contrib.* Mod. Asian Studies. *Address*: Centre for Japanese Studies, The Univ., Sheffield S10 2TN.

Daniels, John Clifford; Head of Further Professional Training Division of School of Education, University of Nottingham, since 1969; *b* 1915; *m* 1940; 1962; two *s* one *d*. BSc Dun 1938, DipEd 1939, MEd Dun 1948, PhD Nottingham 1959; ABPS; Ex-Pres., UK Read. Assoc. Lectr, Univ. of Nottingham Inst. of Educn, 1949–60; Sen. Lectr, 1960–69. *Publications*: Figure Reasoning Test, 1949; Handbook of Test Construction, 1949; Royal Road Readers, 1954; Standard Reading Tests, 1955; Statistical Methods in Educational Research, 1956; Progress in Reading, 1956; *contrib.* Brit. Jl Educnl Psychol., Race, Culture and Intelligence, 1972. *Address*: School of Education, University Park, Nottingham NG7 2RD.

Darby, Adrian Marten George; Fellow, since 1963 and Bursar, since 1968 of Keble College, Oxford; CUF Lecturer in Economics, University of Oxford, since 1964; *b* 1937; *m* 1964; one *s* one *d*. BA Oxon 1961 (1st cl. PPE), MA Oxon 1965. Lectr, Christ Church, Oxford, 1962–63. *Address*: Keble College, Oxford.

Darby, Prof. Henry Clifford, OBE, LittD, FBA; Professor of Geography, University of Cambridge, since 1966; *b* 1909; *m* 1941; two *d*. BA Cantab 1928 (1st cl. Geography), PhD Cantab 1931, MA Cantab 1932, LittD Cantab 1960; Hon. LHD Chicago 1967, Hon. LittD Liverpool 1968, Hon. LittD Durham 1970; FBA. Lectr, Cambridge Univ., 1931–45; Fellow, King's Coll., Cambridge, 1932–45 and 1966– ; Prof., Liverpool Univ., 1945–49; Prof., Univ. Coll., London, 1949–66; Vis. Prof.: Chicago Univ., 1952; Harvard Univ., 1959, 1964–65; Washington (Seattle), 1963. Mem.: Nat. Parks Commn, 1958–63; Water Resources Bd, 1964–68; Royal Commn Hist. Monum., 1953– ; Chm., Brit. Nat. Cttee for Geography. *Publications*: ed, An Historical Geography of England before AD 1800, 1936; The Medieval Fenland, 1940; The Draining of the Fens, 1940, 2nd edn 1956; (with H. Fullard) The University Atlas, 1937, 14th edn 1972; ed, The Domesday Geography of England, 5 vols, 1952–67; (with H. Fullard) The New Cambridge Modern History Atlas, 1970; ed, A New Historical Geography of England, 1973; *contrib.* Econ. Hist. Rev., Geog. Jl, Geog. Rev. *Address*: Dept of Geography, Downing Place, Cambridge CB2 3EN.

Darke, Hubert Seymour Garland, MA, MLitt; University Lecturer in Persian, Faculty of Oriental Studies, University of Cambridge, since 1961; *b* 1919; *m* 1948; two *s* one *d*. MA Cambridge 1949, MLitt Cambridge 1957; Member: RAS; Brit. Inst. of

Persian Studies; Brit. Inst. of Afghan Studies. Editorial Sec., Cambridge Hist. of Iran, 1969– . *Publication*: The Book of Government or Rules for Kings (The 'Siyar al-Mutuk' of Nizām al-Mulk, trans. from Persian), 1960. *Address*: Downing College, Cambridge.

Darling, Vivienne Honor; Director of Practical Training and Lecturer in Social Work, Department of Social Studies, Trinity College Dublin, since 1973; *b* 1927. Dip. Social Studies 1947, MA Dublin 1965, Cert. Social Work Josephine Butler Coll. 1968; Member: Irish Assoc. of Social Workers, (Hon. Sec., 1972–74); British Assoc. of Social Workers. Asst. Dir of Practical Training, Trinity Coll., Dublin, 1951–68; Tutor of Practical Work, 1968–73. Vice-Warden, Trinity Hall, 1961–68; Asst Dean of Women, 1969–72. *Publications*: *contrib*. Social Studies. *Address*: Dept of Social Studies, 6 Trinity College, Dublin 2.

Darlow, George Stephen; Librarian, University of Kent at Canterbury, since 1963; *b* 1917. BA Cantab 1939, MA 1946; ALA 1950. Asst Librarian, Univ. Leeds, 1947–50 and 1951–54; Reference Asst, Univ. Pittsburgh, 1950–51; Sub-Librarian, Durham Colls, 1954–58, Dep. Librarian 1958–63; College Tutor, Hatfield Coll., Durham, 1956–63. *Publications*: A union list of periodicals in the learned libraries of Durham, 1962. *Address*: The Univ., Canterbury, Kent CT2 7NU.

Dasgupta, Dr Biplab Kumar; Fellow, Institute of Development Studies, University of Sussex, since 1972; *b* 1939; *m* 1963. BA Calcutta 1957, MA Calcutta 1960 (Economics), LLB Calcutta 1962, PhD London 1966 (Economics), MSc London 1970 (Computer Science); Mem., AUT. Lectr in Econs and Stats, Univ. of London SOAS, 1966–72. *Publications*: The Oil Industry of India – some economic aspects, 1971; *contrib*. Econ. and Pol. Wkly, Jl Develop. Studies, Asian Surv., Jl Commonwealth Pol. Studies, Jl South Asian Studies. *Address*: Institute of Development Studies, Univ. of Sussex, Falmer, Brighton.

Dauncey, Kenneth Douglas Masson; Lecturer, Department of Management Studies, Loughborough University of Technology, since 1965; *b* 1918; *m* 1941, 1967; one *s* two *d*. MA Cantab (examinations 1940: proceeded to degree after war). Lectr in Ancient Hist. and Archaeol., Birmingham Univ., 1947–1953. Head of Personnel Organization, Steel Co. of Wales, Port Talbot, 1953–60; Dir of Personnel, Elliot-Automation Gp, 1960–62; Cons., The Emerson Consultants, 1962–64. *Address*: Loughborough Univ. of Technology, Loughborough LE11 3TU.

Daveney, Prof. Thompson Faulkner; Professor of Adult Education and Director of Extra-Mural Studies, Department of Extra-Mural Studies, University of Exeter, since 1968; *b* 1922; *m* 1955; two *s* one *d*. BA London 1951 (1st cl. Hons Philos.); Mem.,

Royal Inst. Philosophy; Mem., Mind Assoc. Staff Tutor in Philos., QUB, 1954–60; Dir of Extra-Mural Studies, Univ. Durham, 1960–68. Mem. Council, Inst. Cornish Studies, 1972; Mem. Adult Educn Cttees, Devon and Cornwall. *Publications*: Education, A Moral Concept: Inaugural lecture, 1970; *contrib*. Analysis, Mind, Philos. Qly. *Address*: Dept of Extra-Mural Studies, Univ. of Exeter, Exeter EX4 4QJ.

Davenport, William Anthony; Lecturer in English Language and Literature, Royal Holloway College, University of London, since 1964; *b* 1935; *m* 1960; one *d*. BA London 1955 (1st cl. English), MA London 1958; Res. Asst, Univ. Coll., London, 1958; Asst Lectr, Univ. of Leeds, 1959–62; Lectr, 1962–64. *Publications*: Study of V. Woolf's To the Lighthouse, 1968; *contrib*. Year's Wk Engl. Studies. *Address*: Department of English, Royal Holloway College, Englefield Green, Surrey.

Davey, Alfred George; Senior Lecturer in Social Psychology, School of Social Sciences, University of Bradford, since 1969; *b* 1926; *m*, widower. BA London 1961 (Hons Psychology), Academic Dip Educn London 1955; Academic Post-grad. Dip. in Educnl Psychol. London 1962. Chm., Undergrad. Sch. of Social Science, 1972– . Educnl Psychol., Essex Educn Cttee, 1962–64. *Publications*: Journal of Moral Education, 1972; *contrib*. Brit. Jl Educnl Psychol., Brit. Jl Soc. Clin. Psychol., Educnl Res., Univ. Qly. *Address*: School of Social Science, Univ. of Bradford, Bradford BD7 1DP.

Davey, Brian Humphrey, BSc(Agric), MEcon; Lecturer in Agricultural Economics, University of Newcastle upon Tyne, since 1966; *b* 1937; *m* 1960; one *s* one *d*. BSc Leeds 1959 (Agriculture), MEcon North Carolina 1966. Agric. Economist, Min. of Agric. Fish. and Food, 1961–66; Admin. Off., Agric. Adjustment Unit, Univ. of Newcastle upon Tyne, 1970– ; Mem., Adv. Cttee on Agric. and Land Mgmt, Countryside in 1970, 1969–70. *Publications*: *contrib*. Jl Agric. Econ. *Address*: Dept of Agricultural Economics, The Univ., Newcastle upon Tyne NE1 7RU.

Davey, Christopher John, BA; Lecturer in Modern History, University of Dundee, since 1964; *b* 1938; *m* 1962; one *s* one *d*. BA London 1960; FSAScot. Temp. Asst Lectr, Univ. of Sheffield, 1962–63; Asst, Univ. of St Andrews, 1963–64. *Address*: Dept of History, The Univ., Dundee.

David, Dr Nicholas; Lecturer in Anthropology, University College London, since 1971; *b* 1937; *m* 1962; one *s* one *d*. BA Cantab 1960, MA Harvard 1962, PhD Harvard 1966. Member: Royal Anthropological Inst., Prehist. Soc., Current Anthropology Associate. Instructor University of Pennsylvania: 1965–66; Asst-Prof., 1966–67; Asst-Curator i/c African Section, Univ. Museum, 1967–71. Special Consultant to War on Want, 1973. *Publications*: (with H. L. Movius. Jr *et al*) The Analysis of Certain Major Classes of Upper Palaeolithic Tools, 1968; (with Hilke

167

Hennig) The Ethnography of Pottery: a Fulani case seen in archaeological perspective, 1972; *contrib.* Bull. de la Société Préhistorique Française, World Archaeology. *Address:* Univ. College London, Gower Street, WC1E 6BT.

Davidson, Dr Donald Allen; Lecturer in Geography, St David's University College, Lampeter, since 1971; *b* 1945; *m* 1969; two *d.* BSc Aberdeen 1967; PhD Sheffield 1972. University of Sheffield: Jun. Res. Fellow, 1967–70; Temp. Lectr, 1970–71. *Publications:* ed (with M. L. Shackley) Studies in Geoarchaeology (forthcoming); *contrib.* Archaeometry, Rev. de Géomorphol. Dynamique. *Address:* Dept. of Geography, St David's Univ. Coll., Lampeter, Dyfed SA48 7ED.

Davidson, Eric Dalgleish; Lecturer (part-time), Department of Architecture, University of Edinburgh, since 1966; *b* 1928; *m* 1956; two *s* two *d.* DA Edinburgh 1954; FRIBA 1968, FRIAS 1966. Asst Dir, Building Div., Scottish Health Service. *Publications: contrib.* Building Technology and Management. *Address:* 18 George Square, Edinburgh EH8 9LE.

Davidson, Jeremy H. C. S.; Lecturer, Department of Southeast Asia, SOAS, University of London, since 1971; *b* 1941; *m* 1962; one *s.* BA Hons ANU 1962 (Oriental Studies). Vacation Scholar, ANU, 1961–62; Res. Asst, 1963–65; Res. Fellow, SOAS, 1968–71. *Publications:* (with D. Leslie) Author Catalogues of Western Sinologists, 1966; Catalogues of Chinese Local Gazetteers, 1967. *Address:* Dept of Southeast Asia, SOAS, Malet Street, London, WC1E 7HP.

Davidson, John; Lecturer in History, University College of Wales, Aberystwyth, since 1964; *b* 1939; *m* 1960: two *s* one *d.* MA Hons Edinburgh 1960 (Hist.); PhD Wisconsin 1969. *Address:* History Dept, Univ. Coll. of Wales, Aberystwyth SY23 2AX.

Davidson, Prof. Robert, MA, BD; Professor of Old Testament Language and Literature, University of Glasgow, since 1972; *b* 1927; *m* 1952; four *s* three *d.* MA St Andrews 1949 (1st cl. Classics), BD St Andrews 1952 (Distinction in Old Testament Studies). Asst, Biblical Studies, Aberdeen, 1952–54; Lectr in Biblical Studies, Aberdeen, 1954–60; Lectr, Hebrew and Old Testament, St Andrews, 1960–67; Lectr, Hebrew and Old Testament Studies, Edinburgh, 1967–71, Sen. Lectr, 1971–72. *Publications:* The Bible Speaks, 1959, French edn 1960; The Old Testament, 1966; Biblical Criticism (vol. 3, Pelican Guide to Modern Theology), 1970; Genesis 1–11 (Cambridge Bible Commentary), 1973; *contrib.* Ann. Swed. Theol. Inst., Expos. Times, Scott. Jl Theol., Vet. Testam. *Address:* Dept of Old Testament, Univ. of Glasgow, Glasgow W2.

Davidson, Dr Robert Norman; Lecturer in Geography, University of Hull, since 1969; *b* 1940. MA Glasgow 1963, PhD Glasgow 1968. Res. Asst, Hull Univ., 1967–69. *Publications:* Social Area Analysis of Hull and Haltemprice, 1966; *contrib.* Trans

Bartlett Soc., Urban Studies. *Address:* Dept of Geography, Univ. of Hull, Hull HU6 7RX.

Davie, Prof. Cedric Thorpe, OBE, LLD; Professor of Music, since 1973 (Reader in Music, 1956–73), and Master of Music, St Andrews, since 1945; *b* 1913; *m* 1937; two *s.* ARCM 1934, FRAM 1952, Hon LLD Dundee 1969. Lectr in Music, St Andrews, 1948–56. Vice-Chm., Scott. Arts Council, 1971–73; Mem., Arts Council of GB, 1968–73. *Publications:* Musical Structure and Design, 1953, American edn 1966; (with G. C. McVicar) Oxford Book of Scottish Songs, 1968; various musical compositions. *Address:* Dept of Music, The Univ., St Andrews, Fife.

Davie, Prof. Ronald; Professor of Educational Psychology, Department of Education, University College, Cardiff, since 1974; *b* 1929; *m* 1957; one *s* one *d.* BA Hons Reading 1954 (Psychology), PGCE Manchester 1955, Dip. in the Educn of the Deaf 1955, Dip. in Educational Psychology Birmingham 1961, PhD London 1970; FBPsS; Assoc. Mem., Assoc. of Educational Psychologists, Member: Assoc. for Child Psychology and Psychiatry, Nat. Assoc. for Mental Health; Co-Director Nat. Child Development Study, 1967– ; Chairman: Assoc. for Child Psychology and Psychiatry, 1972–73 (Hon. Sec., 1965–70); Training and Educn Cttee, NAMH, 1970–73; Member: Finance and General Purposes Cttee, NAMH, 1970– ; Council of Management, NAMH, 1970– ; Training and Employment Cttee, Nat. Deaf Children's Soc., 1973– ; Hon. Treas., Developmental Psychology Section, BPsS, 1973– . *Publications:* (with M.L.K. Pringle and N. R. Butler) 11,000 Seven-Year-Olds, 1966; (with M. L. K. Pringle and L. H. Hancock) Directory of Voluntary Organisations Concerned with Children, 1969; (with E. Younghusband, D. Birchall and M. L. K. Pringle) Living with Handicap, 1970; (with N. Butler and H. Goldstein) From Birth to Seven, 1972; *contrib.* Brit. Jl of Educational Psychology, Community Health, Early Child Development and Care, Forward Trends, Froebel Jl, Jl of Mental Subnormality, London Educational Rev., Public Health, Special Educn, Statistical News; Trends in Educn. *Address:* Dept of Educn, Univ. Coll. Cardiff, PO Box 78, Cardiff CF1 1XL.

Davies; *see* Llewelyn-Davies.

Davies, Alan Digby; Lecturer, Department of Overseas Administration, University of Manchester, and Senior Lecturer, University of the South Pacific, Fiji, since 1973; *b* 1939; *m* 1961; one *s* two *d.* BA London 1960; MBCS, AMBIM. Lectr (part-time), Cambridge Univ., 1964–66; Lectr, Warwick Univ., 1971–73. Dir, Educational Systems Ltd, 1964–68; Management Consultant, Urwick, Orr & Partners, 1968–71. *Address:* Dept of Overseas Administration, Univ. of Manchester, Manchester M13 9PL.

Davies, Prof. Anna Elbina; Professor of Comparative Philology, and Fellow of Somerville College, Oxford University, since

1971; *b* 1937; *m* 1962. Laurea in lettere Univ. Rome 1959, Libera docenza Univ. Rome 1963, MA Oxford 1964. Asst in Filologia Classica, Univ. of Rome, 1959–61; Jun. Fellow, Center for Hellenic Studies, Washington DC, 1961–62; Univ. Lecturer in Classical Philology, Oxford Univ., 1964–71; Fellow, St Hilda's Coll., Oxford, 1966–71; Hon. Fellow, St Hilda's Coll., Oxford, 1972; Vis. Prof. in Linguistics, Univ. of Pennsylvania, 1971. *Publications* (as A. Morpurgo, or A. Morpurgo-Davies): Mycenaeae Graecitatis Lexicon, 1963; *contrib.* Class. Rev., Glotta, Kadmos, Parola Pass., Rend. Acc. Lincei, Trans Philol Soc. *Address*: Somerville College, Oxford OX2 6HD.

Davies, Benjamin T., MCSP, MSc, PhD; Senior Lecturer, Department of Engineering Production (teaching Ergonomics), Birmingham University, since 1972. Lecturer 1967–72; *b* 1926; *m* 1957; two *s* one *d*. MSc Loughborough 1962 (Ergonomics and Cybernetics), MSc Birmingham 1965 (Production Engineering), PhD Birmingham 1967. Res. Fellow, Birmingham, 1962–65; Sen. Res. Fellow, 1965–67; Vis. Assoc. Prof., Univ. of Massachusetts, 1969–70. Mem.: Educ. Sub-Cttee, Chrtd Soc. Physiother., 1959–61; ERS Soc., 1963; Hon. Mem., Sec., Ergonom. Res. Soc., 1970. *Publications*: *contrib.* Ergonom., Hum. Fact., Royal Soc. Jl. *Address*: Dept of Engineering Production, Univ. of Birmingham, PO Box 363, Birmingham B15 2TT.

Davies, Dr Bleddyn Pryce, MA, DPhil, DipPubSocAdmin; Director, Social Services Research Unit, University of Kent, since 1974; *b* 1936; *m* 1962; two *d*. BA Cantab 1959 (Economics Tripos), DipPubSocAdmin Oxon 1960; DPhil Oxon 1968. Asst Lectr, Univ. Coll., Aberystwyth, 1962–63; Lectr, Dept of Social Admin, LSE, 1963–74. Ed., Policy and Politics, 1971. *Publications*: Social Needs and Resources in Local Services, 1968; Variations in Services for the Aged, 1971; Variations in Children's Services, 1972; Planning Resources for Personal Social Services, 1972; Gambling, Work and Leisure, 1974; The Statistics of Personal Social Services and Voluntary Organisations, 1974; University Costs and Outputs, 1974; University Selectivity and Effectiveness: The School Meals Case, 1974; *contrib.* Jl Royal Stat. Soc., Public Admin, Soc. Econ. Admin, Sociol. Rev, Policy and Politics. *Address*: Social Services Res. Unit, Univ. of Kent, Canterbury, Kent CT2 7NZ.

Davies, Dr Brian Ewart; Lecturer in Geography, University College of Wales, Aberystwyth, since 1965; *b* 1937; *m* 1964; two *d*. BSc Hons Wales, Bangor 1959 (Biochemistry and Soil Science), PhD Wales, Bangor 1963 (Soil Science); ARIC 1963. Asst Lectr, Wye Coll., Univ. of Cincinnati, 1964–65. Vis. Prof., Univ. of Cincinnati, Ohio, USA, 1970–71. Mem., Univ. Wales Court, 1969–70. *Publications*: (with others) A Concise Physical Geography, 1972; *contrib.* Geoderma, Jl Agricl Sci., Jl Environmental Pollution, Oikos, Proc. Soil Sci. Soc. Amer. *Address*: Dept. of Geography, UCW Aberystwyth, Aberystwyth SY23 2AX.

Davies, Ven. Carlyle W.; *see* Witton-Davies.

Davies, Cecil William; Senior Staff Tutor, Department of Extra-Mural Studies, University of Manchester, since 1973 (Staff Tutor, 1953–73); *b* 1918; *m* 1942; one *s* two *d*. BA London 1939 (1st cl. English), TD London 1940; Mem., Engl. Assoc., Life Mem., Brontë Soc. Vice-Chm., Century Theatre Ltd; Mem., Cheshire Comm. Council. *Publications*: The Night is Far Spent (Play), 1958; Crown Royal (Play), 1958; Beloved of Zeus (Play), 1958; various unpublished plays produced or broadcast, 1951– ; Nonconformity, in, History of Macclesfield, ed C. S. Davies, 1961; *contrib.* Engl., Adult Educn, Essays in Crit., Studies in Adult Educn, Theatre Qly. *Address*: Dept of Extra-Mural Studies, Univ. of Manchester, Manchester M13 9PL.

Davies, Clifford Stephen Lloyd, MA; Fellow and Tutor in Modern History, Wadham College, Oxford, since 1963, and University Lecturer (CUF), since 1964; *b* 1936; *m* 1962; one *s* one *d*. BA Oxon 1959 (Modern History), MA Oxon 1963. Asst, Dept of Econ. Hist., Univ. of Glasgow, 1962–63. *Publications*: *contrib.* Annales (Economies, Societés, Civilisations), Econ. Hist. Rev., EHR, Hist., Past and Present. *Address*: Wadham College, Oxford.

Davies, Clive Robin Michael; University Research Lecturer in Sociology, University of Liverpool, since 1970; *b* 1931; *m* 1954; three *d*. LLB London 1955, MA Liverpool 1968; Barrister-at-Law, Gray's Inn, 1962. Lectr in Laws, Victoria Univ. of Wellington, 1964; Univ. Res. Worker, Liverpool, 1967–70. Publisher's Rep., 1954–59; Fabian Bookshop Manager, 1956–57; Ind. Rep., 1959–62; Law Lectr, 1962–64; Practising Barrister, 1964–69. Member: Howard League; Justice; Legal Action Gp; NCCL (Cobden Trust); Radical Alternatives to Prison; Preservation of Rights of Prisoners. *Publications*: General Principles of Law, 1964, 2nd edn 1972; *contrib.* Brit. Jl Criminol., Criminal Law Rev., Howard Jl, Justice of the Peace, Law Guardian, New Law Jl, New Soc., New Statesman, Police Rev., Solicitors' Jl, Times. *Address*: Sociology Dept, The Univ., Liverpool L69 3BX.

Davies, Rev. David Protheroe, MA, BD; Lecturer in Theology, Saint David's University College, Lampeter, since 1967; *b* 1939; *m* 1963; one *d*. BA Cantab 1962 (Classics and Theol.), MA Cantab 1966, BA Oxon 1962 (by incorp.), MA Oxon 1969, BD Oxon 1969; Deacon (Church in Wales) 1964, Priest 1965; Mem. SNTS, IOSCS. Sen. Treas., Students Union, SDUC, Lampeter, 1971– ; Member: Council, Senate, SDUC, Lampeter, 1971– ; Univ. of Wales Court, 1971– ; Univ. of Wales Extension Bd, 1971– ; Univ. of Wales Faculty of Educn, 1973– . *Publications*: Geirfa Marc, 1973; *contrib.* Diwinyddiaeth, Expository Times, Trivium, Yr Haul, Y Traethodydd. *Address*: Dept of Theology, Saint David's Univ. College, Lampeter, Dyfed SA48 7ED.

Davies, David William; Senior Industrial Fellow, Faculty of Business Administration, University of Manchester, since 1966; *b* 1925; *m* 1953; one *s* two *d*. BA Wales 1949 (2nd cl. English), DipEd Wales 1950 (1st cl.). Sen. Tutor, Univ. of Manchester, 1966–67, 1968; Vis. Internat. Fellow, Harvard Univ., 1967–68; Dir, Management Course, Manchester Business Sch., 1971– . Cllr and Mem., Educn Cttee, Knutsford UDC and Macclesfield DC, Cheshire. *Address:* Manchester Business School, Booth Street West, Manchester M15 6PB.

Davies, David Wynne, MA (Oxon); Lecturer in Development Economics, University of Leeds, since 1965; *b* 1931. BA Oxon 1959, MA Oxon 1966. Lectr, Univ. of Science and Technology, Kumasi, Ghana, 1960–62; Univ. Coll. of Cape Coast, Ghana, 1962–65. Princ. Plann. Economist and Act. Ch. Economist, Malawi Govt, 1968–69. *Address:* The School of Economic Studies, The Univ., Leeds LS2 9JT.

Davies, Eirian Catherine; Lecturer, Department of English, Bedford College, London University, since 1972; *b* 1940. BA Hons London 1962 (English); Teaching Asst, Univ. of Minnesota, 1962–63; Res. Asst, Univ. of London Inst. of Educn, 1963–64; Res. Asst, UCL, 1964–67; Lectr in Linguistics, UWIST, 1967–72; Warden, Bedford Coll. Hall of Residence, 1972–73. *Publications: contrib.* TPS. *Address:* Dept of English, Bedford College, Regent's Park, NW1 4NS.

Davies, Hon. Francis Ronald; Senior Lecturer, Faculty of Law, The University of Manchester, since 1971; *b* 1920; *m* 1942; two *s* one *d*. MA Oxford 1947, called to the Bar, Gray's Inn 1948. In practice at the Bar 1948–54, Solicitor's Off., Inland Rev., 1954–66; Lectr, Manchester, 1966–71. Sec. for Admissions, Fac. of Law, 1970–72. *Publications:* Contract, 1970; *contrib.* Brit. Tax Rev., Mod. Law Rev. *Address:* Faculty of Law, The Univ., Manchester M13 9PL.

Davies, Prof. Glyndwr, BA, MSc(Econ); Sir Julian Hodge Professor of Banking and Finance, University of Wales Institute of Science and Technology, since 1970; Head of Department of Applied Economics; *b* 1919; *m* 1947; three *s* one *d*. BA Wales Univ. Coll. Cardiff 1947, BSc London 1953 (Econ.), MSc London 1956 (Econ.); FIL 1956. Sen. Lectr in Applied Economics, Scottish Coll. of Commerce/Univ. of Strathclyde, 1959–67. First Sen. Econ. Adv. to Sec. of State for Wales, 1968–70. *Publications:* The Galloway Project: a Study of Tourism in South-West Scotland, 1968; National Giro: Modern Money Transfer, 1973; *contrib.* Banker, Banker's Mag., Econ., Jl Econ. Studies, Jl Indust. Econ., Oxford Econ. Papers, Reg. Studies Bull. *Address:* Univ. of Wales Institute of Science and Technology, Cathays Park, Cardiff CF1 3NU.

Davies, Prof. Gordon Leslie; Associate Professor of Geography, Trinity College, University of Dublin, since 1970; *b* 1932; *m*

1955; two *s*. BA Manchester 1953, MA Manchester 1954, MA Dublin 1957, PhD Dublin 1967. Asst Lectr, Univ. of Dublin, 1954–57; Lectr, 1957–70; Fellow, TCD, 1967; Vis. Prof., Univ. of Oregon, 1967–68; Vis. Lectr, West and Cent. Washington State Colls, 1968; Vis. Prof., Cent. Washington State Coll., 1973. Mem., Irish Nat. Cttee Hydrological Decade, 1965– ; Pres., Geog. Soc. Ireland, 1960–63; Corresp. Mem., Internat. Cttee Hist. Geol.; Editor, Irish Geography, 1968. *Publications:* The Earth in Decay: A History of British Geomorphology, 1969; *contrib.* Geog. Jl, Proc. Geol. Assoc., Irish Geog., Jl Hist. Ideas, Ann. Sci., Proc. Royal Irish Acad., Jl Glaciol. *Address:* Dept of Geography, Trinity College, Dublin 2, Ireland.

Davies, Dr Graham Michael; Lecturer, Department of Psychology, University of Aberdeen, since 1968; *b* 1943; *m* 1966; one *s* one *d*. BA Hull 1964 (Psychology), PhD Hull 1970; ABPsS. Asst in Psychol., Univ. of Aberdeen, 1967. *Publications: contrib.* Jl of Exptl Child Psychol., Jl of Special Educn, Qly Jl of Exptl Psychol., Brit. Jl of Psychol. *Address:* Dept of Psychology, Kings Coll., The Univ., Old Aberdeen.

Davies, Harold Neville, MA; Lecturer, Department of English, University of Birmingham, since 1970; *b* 1939; *m* 1963; two *s* one *d*. BA Liverpool 1962 (English Language and Literature), DipEd Reading 1963, MA Liverpool 1965. Leverhulme Fellow, Univ. of Liverpool, 1965–67; Fellow, Shakespeare Inst., Univ. of Birmingham, 1967–70; Admissions Tutor, Dept of English, Univ. of Birmingham, 1970– ; Vis. Sen. Lectr (førstelektor), Univ. of Oslo, 1972–74. *Publications:* Gen. Ed., The Second Series of Adaptations of Shakespeare's Plays, 1970–73; *contrib.* Cassell's Encyclopaedia of World Literature, ed. J. Buchanan Brown; English Drama: Select Bibliographical Guides, ed S. W. Wells; Webster's New World Companion to English and American Literature, ed A. Pollard; Engl. Lang. Notes, Jl Warb. and Court. Inst., Library, Music and Letters, Notes and Queries; Silent Poetry, ed. A. Fowler, 1970. *Address:* Dept of English Language and Literature, University of Birmingham, Edgbaston B15 2TT.

Davies, Harold Richard John; Senior Lecturer in Geography, University College of Swansea (University of Wales), since 1970; *b* 1931; *m* 1957; one *s* one *d*. BA Oxon 1954, PGCE London 1955, MA Oxon 1959, BLitt Oxon 1962; FRGS, Mem.: African Studies Assoc. of UK, Inst. Brit. Geog., Geog. Assoc. Lectr, Khartoum Univ., Sudan, 1955–60; Lectr, Univ. Coll., Swansea, 1960–70; Sen. Res. Fellow, Rural Econ. Res. Unit, Ahmadu Bello Univ., Nigeria, 1965–66 (on secondment). Mem.: SCUSA (Standing Cttee on Univ. Studies on Africa), 1970– ; Archbishop's Commn (Church in Wales), 1971– ; Council RISW (Royal Inst. of S. Wales), 1961– ; Chwdn, Pennard Parish, 1970– . *Publications:* Tropical Africa: Atlas for Rural Development, 1973; *contrib.* Econ. Geog., Geog. Jl, Geog., Sudan N and R, Tijdschrift voor Economische on Social

Geografie. *Address*: Dept of Geography, Univ. College, Swansea SA2 8PP.

Davies, Hilda Margaret; Senior Lecturer, Department of Probability and Statistics, University of Sheffield, since 1972; *b* 1914. BSc Special London 1935 (Hons Maths; Stats added in 1953 as supplementary subject; DipEd Bristol 1936, Cert. RSS 1957. Univ. of Sheffield: Res. Asst, 1953–59; Tutor, 1959–64; Lectr, 1964–72; Actg Head of Dept of Statistics, 1959–60 and 1963–65. *Publications*: Chap. in, The Teaching of Probability and Statistics, ed, Lennart Råde, 1970; *contrib*. Math. Gaz., JRSS Series A, JRSS Series B, Statistician. *Address*: Dept of Probability and Statistics, The Univ., Sheffield S3 7RH.

Davies, Ina Mary; Visiting Lecturer, Department of Theology, Southampton University, since 1965; *b* 1929; *m* 1956; three *s*. BA Cantab 1950, PhD Manchester 1956. Mem., Society for Study of Theology. *Address*: Univ. of Southampton, Highfield, Southampton SO9 5NH.

Davies, Ivor John, NDD, ATD; Lecturer on Sources of the Modern Movements, Department of Fine Art, University of Edinburgh, since 1963; *b* 1935. Nat. Dip. of Design Cardiff 1956, Art Teacher's Dip. Swansea 1957. Asst of Lausanne, Switzerland, 1959–61; Pt-time Lectr, Univ. of S Wales Extra-Mural Dept, 1961–63. *Publications*: *contrib*. Art and Artists, Studio Internat. *Address*: Dept of Fine Art, Univ. of Edinburgh, 19 George Square, Edinburgh.

Davies, Dr Ivor Norman Richard; Lecturer in History, School of Slavonic and East European Studies, University of London, since 1971; *b* 1939; *m* 1966; one *s*. BA Hons Oxon 1961 (Mod. Hist.), MA 1965, MA Sussex 1966 (Russian Studies), Doktor Nauk Humanistycznych Cracow 1973, DipEd Oxford 1962, Diplôme de Langue et Littérature françaises Grenoble 1958; FRHistS 1973. Lektor, Jagiellonian Univ., Cracow, 1966–68; Alistair Horne Res. Fellow, St Antony's Coll., Oxford, 1970–71; Sen. Associate Mem., St Antony's Coll., Oxford, 1971– . *Publications*: White Eagle, Red Star: the Polish–Soviet war, 1919–20, 1972; *contrib*. Jl Cont. Hist., SEE Rev., Hist. Jl, Sov. Stud., Mod. Lang. Rev., Eur. Stud. Rev., Survey, Dzieje Najnowsze (Warsaw), Studia Historyczne (Cracow), Sobótkca (Wrocław), Rev. d'Etudes Slaves (Paris). *Address*: Sch. of Slavonic and East European Studies, Senate House, WC1E 7HU.

Davies, Dr James Atterbury; Lecturer in English, University College, Swansea, since 1967; *b* 1939; *m* 1966; one *d*. BA Wales 1965 (1st cl. Hons), PhD Wales 1969. *Publications*: *contrib*. Dickensian, RES, Use of English. *Address*: Univ. College, Singleton Park, Swansea SA2 8PP.

Davies, Jeffrey Lyn; Lecturer in Archaeology, Department of History, University College, Aberystwyth, since 1967; *b* 1943; *m* 1968; one *s*. BA Cardiff 1964; FSA. *Publications*: *contrib*. Archaeologia Cambrensis. *Address*: Dept of History, 1 Laura Place, Aberystwyth SY23 2AU.

Davies, John, BA, PhD; Lecturer, Department of Welsh History, University College of Wales, Aberystwyth, since 1973; *b* 1938; *m* 1966; one *s* two *d*. BA Wales (Cardiff) 1959 (1st cl. History), PhD Wales (Swansea) 1969. Lectr, Univ. of Wales, Swansea, 1963–73. *Publications*: *contrib*. Morgannwg, Welsh Hist. Rev. *Address*: Dept of Welsh History, Univ. Coll., Aberystwyth SY23 2AX.

Davies, John Derek; Fellow in Law, St Catherine's College, and University Lecturer, University of Oxford, since 1954; *b* 1931; *m* 1961; two *s* one *d*. LLB Wales 1951 (1st cl.), BCL Oxford 1953 (1st cl.), MA Oxford 1954; Barrister-at-Law 1956. *Publications*: *contrib*. Law Rev., Conveyancer. *Address*: St Catherine's College, Oxford.

Davies, Prof. John Gordon; Edward Cadbury Professor, and Head of Department and Director of the Institute for the Study of Worship and Religious Architecture, Department of Theology, University of Birmingham, since 1960; *b* 1919; *m* 1945; one *s* two *d*. BA Oxon 1942, MA 1945, BD Oxon 1946, DD Oxon 1956, MA (Official) Birmingham 1952, HonDD St Andrews 1968; Mem.: Studiorum Novi Testamenti Societas, Soc. for Study of Theology. Asst Lectr in Theology, Univ. of Birmingham, 1948; Lectr, 1950; Sen. Lectr, 1957; Reader, 1959; Dean of Faculty of Arts, 1967–70. *Publications*: The Theology of William Blake, 1948, 1966; The Origin and Development of Early Christian Church Architecture, 1952, American edn 1953; Daily Life in the Early Church, 1952, American edn 1955, French edn 1956; The Spirit, the Church and the Sacrament, 1954, German edn 1958; Social Life of Early Christians, 1954; Members One of Another, 1958; He Ascended into Heaven (Bampton Lectures), 1958; The Making of the Church, 1960; The Architectural Setting of Baptism, 1962; Holy Week: A Short History, 1963; The Early Christian Church, 1965, Italian edn 1965, Portuguese edn 1967; A Select Liturgical Lexicon, 1965, Swedish edn 1968; Worship and Mission, 1966, Japanese edn 1968; Dialogue with the World, 1967, Spanish edn 1967; The Secular Use of Church Buildings, 1968; Every Day God, Encountering the Holy in World and Worship, 1973; ed, A Dictionary of Liturgy and Worship, 1972; *contrib*. Jl of Theological Studies, Vigiliae Christianae, etc. *Address*: Dept of Theology, Univ. of Birmingham, PO Box 363, Birmingham B15 2TT.

Davies, Rev. John Howard, MA, BD, FRCO; Senior Lecturer in Theology, University of Southampton, since 1974; *d* 1929; *m* 1956; four *s*. BA Cantab 1950 (Music Tripos pt 1), MA Cantab 1954 (Theologica Tripos pts 2 and 3), BD Nottingham 1962; FRCO 1952. Succentor, Derby Cath., 1955–58; Chaplain, Westcott House, Cambridge, 1958–63; Lectr in Theology, Univ. of Southampton, 1963–74. *Publications*, A Letter to Hebrews, 1967. *Address*: Dept of Theology and the Study of Religion, The Univ., Southampton SO9 5NH.

Davies, Dr John Kenyon, MA, DPhil; Fellow and Tutor in Ancient History, Oriel College, Oxford, since 1968; *b* 1937; *m* 1962. BA Oxford 1959 (1st cl. Lit. Hum), MA Oxford 1962, DPhil Oxford 1965; Mem., Class. Assoc., JACT, Soc. Hellenic Studies, Soc. Rom. Studies. Harmsworth Sen. Schol., Merton Coll., Oxford, 1960–61 and 1962–63; Jun. Fellow, Center for Hellenic Studies, Washington DC, 1961–62; Dyson Jun. Res. Fellow, Balliol Coll., Oxford, 1963–65; Lectr in Ancient History, Univ. of St Andrews, 1965–68. Editor, Jl of Hellenic Studies, 1972– . *Publications*: Athenian Propertied Families, 600-300 BC, 1971; *contrib*. Historia, Jl Hellenic Studies, Riv. Storica Italiana. *Address*: Oriel College, Oxford OX1 4EW.

Davies, John Vivian; Lecturer in English and Education, University of York, since 1967; *b* 1935; *m* 1959; one *s* one *d*. BA Hons Cantab 1957, MA Hons Cantab 1962, DipEd London 1959. Various teaching posts in Schools, including Head of English at Thomas Bennett School, Crawley, Sussex. *Publications*: ed, Lawrence on Hardy and Painting, 1973; *contrib*. Use of English. *Address*: Langwith College, Univ. of York, York.

Davies, Rev. Joseph Elfed; Lecturer in Education, and Course Director, Department of Education, University College, Cardiff, since 1963; *b* 1920; *m* 1946; one *d*. BA Hons Wales 1943 (Philos.), BD Wales 1948; MA Oxon 1946 (Theol.); PGCE London 1956; DipEd London 1961; Mem., Philos. of Educn Soc. GB and Ireland; Founder Chm., Cardiff and South Wales Philos. of Educn Soc. Vis. Fellow, Regent's Park Coll., Oxford, 1972. Mem., Syllabus Co-ordinating Commn, Revised Syll. of Religious Instruction for Schs of Wales. *Publications*: *contrib*. Hon. Soc. of Cymmrodorion, Jl Philos. Studies Univ. of Wales, West African Jl of Educn. *Address*: Faculty of Education, Univ. Coll., Cardiff.

Davies, Keith, MA, LLM; Senior Lecturer in the Department of Law Relating to the Land, University of Reading, since 1973 (Lecturer, 1969–73); *b* 1929; *m* 1960; five *s*. BA Oxon 1952 (2nd cl. History), MA Oxon 1956, LLB (2nd cl.) London 1957; LLM London 1964; of Gray's Inn Barrister-at-Law 1959. Lectr, Coll. of Estate Mgmt, 1961–66; Lectr, Univ. of Southampton, 1966–69. Admin. Off., LCC, 1952–61. *Publications*: ed, West: Law of Housing, 3rd edn 1974; Concise Law of Highways, 1969; Planning Law, in, Land Law – Cases and Materials, ed Maudsley and Burn, 2nd edn 1970; Law of Compulsory Purchase and Compensation, 1972; Planning Law, in, Modern Real Property, ed Cheshire, 11th edn 1972; *contrib*. Modern Law Review, Estates Gazette, Conveyancer, New Law Jl. *Address*: Univ. of Reading, Whiteknights, Reading RG6 2AH.

Davies, Dr Margaret C., Reader, Department of French Studies, Reading University, since 1970; *m*; one *s* one *d*. BA Oxon 1944, DipEd Oxon 1945, MA Oxon 1947, D de l'U

Paris 1948. Lectr, Univ. of Reading, 1962–63; Lectr, Westfield Coll., Univ. of London, 1963–64; Lectr, Univ. of Reading, 1964–70. *Publications*: Two Gold Rings (Novel), 1958; Colette (Writers and Critics Series), 1961; Apollinaire, 1964; *contrib*. Fr. Studies, Rev. Lett. Mod., Rev. Litt. Comp., Times Lit. Supp. *Address*: Dept of French Studies, Univ. of Reading, Whiteknights, Reading RG6 2AH.

Davies, Dr Maurice Robert Russell, PhD, LLM, DPA; Senior Lecturer in Law, University of Leeds, since 1963; *b* 1920; *m* 1945; one *s* one *d*. LLB Leeds 1940 (1st cl. Hons), LLM Leeds 1943, DPA London 1942, PhD Cambridge 1947; Solicitor of the Supreme Court 1941–49, Barrister 1950– , of the Middle Temple and North Eastern Circuit. Rouse Ball Sen. Res. Student, Trinity Coll., Cambridge, 1945–47; Dean of the Faculty of Law, Univ. of Leeds, 1956–58; Vis. Prof., Louisville Law School, Kentucky, 1964–65. *Publications*: The Law of Road Traffic, 1954, 5th edn 1973; Principles and Practice of Planning, Compulsory Purchase and Rating Law, 1956; The Law of Burial, Cremation and Exhumation, 1956, 3rd edn 1971; *contrib*. Law Jl, Law Times, Conveyancer, Industrial Law Rev., Brit. Jl Admin. Law. *Address*: Faculty of Law, Univ. of Leeds, Leeds LS2 9JT.

Davies, Morton Rees; Leverhulme Lecturer in Public Administration, Department of Political Theory and Institutions, Liverpool University, since 1968; *b* 1939; *m* 1963; one *s* three *d*. BA Wales 1961 (Modern History and Politics), DipEd Wales 1962; Lectr in Politics, Univ. of Liverpool, 1964–68. *Publications*: (with V. A. Lewis) Models of Political Systems, 1971; *contrib*. Internat. Rev. Hist. and Pol. Sci., Pol. Studies. *Address*: Dept of Political Theory and Institutions, Social Studies Building, The Univ., Liverpool.

Davies, Paul Crompton, MA, BLitt; Lecturer, English Department, University College of North Wales, since 1966; *b* 1939; *m* 1964; two *s*. BA Aberystwyth 1961 (1st cl. English), BLitt Oxon 1963, MA Wales 1965. Asst Lectr, Univ. Coll., N Wales, 1963–66. *Publications*: ed, Dekker: The Shoemaker's Holiday, 1969; ed, Watkyns: Flamma sine Fumo, 1969; *contrib*. Comp. Lit., Durh. Univ. Jl, Et. Angl., Trivium, Univ. of Toronto Qly. *Address*: English Dept, Univ. College of North Wales, Bangor LL57 2DG.

Davies, Dr Peter Michael Cunliffe; Lecturer in Zoology, Department of Zoology, University of Nottingham (also teaches philosophy of science), since 1967; *b* 1936; *m* 1962; three *d*. BA Dublin 1961 (1st cl. Zoology), PhD Dublin 1964; MIBiol. Asst Lectr, Nottingham Univ., 1964–67. *Publications*: contrib. The Nature of Human Sexuality, 1972; *contrib*. Comp. Biochem. Physiol., Month, Nature, Philos. Studies. *Address*: Dept of Zoology, The Univ. of Nottingham, Nottingham NG7 2RD.

Davies, Dr Peter Neville, MA, PhD; Lecturer, Department of Economic History,

University of Liverpool, since 1968; *b* 1927; *m* 1962; one *s*. BA Liverpool 1961 (Special Studies, Hons Economics), MA Liverpool 1963, PhD Liverpool 1967; Cert. Educn, St John's College, York, 1955; FRSA 1973. Tutor, Univ. of Liverpool, 1964–66, Asst Lectr, 1966–68, Asst Dir, Soc. Studies, 1970– . Hon. Mem., Council for Nautical Archaeology, 1973– . *Publications*: A Short History of the Ships of John Holt and Co. (Liverpool) Ltd, and the Guinea Gulf Line Ltd, 1965; A Brief History of the Elder Dempster Line and its Predecessors, 1967; The Trade Makers, 1973; The African Steam Ship Company, in, Liverpool and Merseyside, ed J. R. Harris, 1969; *contrib.* W Africa, Sea Breezes, Sea, Business Hist. *Address*: Dept of Economic History, Univ. of Liverpool, Liverpool L69 3BX.

Davies, Reginald Thorne, MA; Reader in English Literature, University of Liverpool, since 1967, and Warden of Gladstone Hall of Residence, since 1965, Warden of Roscoe and Gladstone Hall since 1972; *b* 1923. BA and MA Oxon 1948 (2nd cl. English Lang. and Lit.). Asst Lectr, then Lectr, then Sen. Lectr in Dept of Eng. Lit., Liverpool, 1948–67; Tutor in Derby Hall of Res., then Sen. Tutor, 1949–65; Sub-Dean, Fac. of Arts, 1960–63. Lt, RA, 1942–45; Mem., Council, St Aidan's Coll., 1967–70; Adult Cttee, C of E Bd of Educn, 1960–62; Hon. Sec., Adult Educn Council, Dio. of Liverpool, 1954–62. *Publications*: ed, G. Chaucer: Prologue to the Canterbury Tales, 1953; ed, Medieval English Lyrics, 1963; ed, Samuel Johnson: Selected Writings, 1965; ed, Sir Thomas Malory: King Arthur and his Knights, 1967; ed, The Corpus Christi Play of the English Middle Ages, 1972; *contrib.* Rev. Eng. Studies, Etudes Ang., Studies Philol., Ess Crit. *Address*: Roscoe and Gladstone Hall, Greenbank Lane, Liverpool L17 1AH.

Davies, Robert Rees; Lecturer, Department of History, University College, London, since 1963; *b* 1938; *m* 1966; one *s* one *d*. BA London 1959 (1st cl. History), DPhil Oxon 1965; FRHistS. Asst Lectr, Univ. Coll., Swansea, 1961–63. Asst Ed., Hist., 1963–67, Rev. Ed., 1967– . Mem., Council, Hon. Soc. Cymmrodorion. *Publications*: contrib. Glamorgan County History, vol. 3, 1971; The Age of Richard II, ed Barron and du Boulay; *contrib.* Econ. Hist. Rev., Hist. Trans Cymmrodorion Soc., Welsh Hist. Rev. *Address*: Dept of History, Univ. College, Gower Street, WC1E 6BT.

Davies, Prof. Robert William; Director and Professor of Soviet Economic Studies, Centre for Russian and East European Studies, University of Birmingham, since 1963; *b* 1925; *m* 1953; one *s* one *d*. BA London 1950, PhD Birmingham 1954. Asst, Univ. of Glasgow, 1955–56; Res. Fellow, Lectr, Sen. Lectr, Univ. of Birmingham, 1956–63. Mem., Nat. Cttee, Nat. Assoc. Sov. and E European Studies, 1965– . *Publications*: The Development of the Soviet Budgetary System, 1958; Science and the Soviet Economy, 1967; (with E. Zaleski and others) Science Policy in the USSR, 1969; (with E. H. Carr) Foundations of a Planned Economy, 1926–1929, vol. 1,

1969; *contrib.* Econ. of Planning, EHR, Sov. Studies. *Address*: Centre for Russian and East European Studies, Univ. of Birmingham, Birmingham B15 2TT.

Davies, Rosser Llewelyn; Lecturer in Geography, University of Newcastle upon Tyne, since 1969; *b* 1940; *m* 1965; one *s* one *d*. BA 1962, MA 1966, Leeds; MSc Northwestern 1966. Instructor, Univ. of Massachusetts, 1966–67; Lectr, Lanchester Poly., 1967–69. Treas., Regional Studies Assoc., N Br., 1969–72. *Publications*: The Nature of Cities, 1973; *contrib.* Urban Studies, Regional Studies, Trans Inst. of Br. Geogrs. *Address*: Dept of Geography, Univ. of Newcastle upon Tyne, Newcastle upon Tyne NE1 7RU.

Davis, Alan G.; Research Fellow in Sociology, Department of Sociology, King's College, Aberdeen, since 1971; *b* 1941. BA Econ Sheffield. Lectr in Sociology, Aberdeen Univ., 1966–71. *Address*: Dept of Sociology, Aberdeen Univ., Aberdeen AB9 1AS.

Davis, Prof. Derek Russell, MD; Professor of Mental Health, University of Bristol, since 1962; Dean of Medicine, University of Bristol; *b* 1914; *m* 1939; one *s* one *d*. BA Cantab 1935, MRCS London, LRCPEng 1938, MA 1939, MBBChir 1939, MRCP London 1939, MD 1946; FRCP 1963, FRCPsych 1971, FBPsS 1957, Mem., Exper. Psychol. Gp, 1948. Lectr, Psychopathology, Univ. of Cambridge, 1948–50; Reader in Clinical Psychology, 1950–57; Reader in Medical Psychology, 1957–62; Fellow, Clare Coll., Cambridge, 1960–62; Vis. Prof., Univ. of Virginia, 1958. Editor, Qly Jl Exper. Psychol., 1949–58. Pres., Fed. Assoc. Mental Health Workers; Mem., Bd Sci. Educn, BMA; Mem., Avon AHA. *Publications*: Pilot Error, 1948; Introduction to Psychopathology, 1957, 3rd edn 1972; (with G. Clark and Visc. Maugham) The Campden Wonder, 1959; *contrib.* Brit. Jl Med. Psychol., Qly Jl Exper. Psychol. *Address*: 41 St Michael's Hill, Bristol BS2 8DZ.

Davis, Prof. Edward William; Lloyds Bank Professor, Management Centre, University of Aston, since 1971; *b* 1940; *m* 1969. MA St Andrews 1965. University Coll. of Wales, Aberystwyth, 1966–69; Dept of Applied Economics, Univ. of Cambridge, 1969–71. *Publication*: (with E. T. Nevin) The London Clearing Banks, 1970. *Address*: Univ. of Aston Management Centre, Maple House, Corporation Street, Birmingham B4 6TE.

Davis, Harry Clayton; Lecturer, Italian Department, University of Birmingham, since 1966; *b* 1927. BA Cantab 1950, MA Cantab 1955, BA London 1965 (1st cl. Italian). *Address*: Dept of Italian, Univ. of Birmingham, Birmingham B15 2TT.

Davis, Dr John H. R.; Senior Lecturer, Faculty of Social Sciences, University of Kent, since 1973 (Lecturer, 1966–73); *b* 1938. BA Oxon 1961, PhD London 1969. Res. Asst, LSE, 1963–64. Mem., Cttee, Assoc. Soc. Anthropol., 1971– ; Mem., SSRC Social Anthropology Cttee, 1973– . *Publications*: Land and Family in Pisticci, 1972; *contrib.*

173

Brit. Jl Sociol., Comp. Studies Soc. Hist., Proc. RAI, Man. *Address*: Eliot College, The Univ., Canterbury.

Davis, Prof. Norman, MBE, FBA; Merton Professor of English Language and Literature, University of Oxford, since 1959; *b* 1913; *m* 1944. MA NZ 1934 (NZ Rhodes Scholar 1934), BA Oxon 1937, MA 1944, Dip. in Comp. Philol. 1937; FBA 1969. Lectr in English: Univ. of Kaunas, Lithuania, 1937–38; Univ. of Sofia, Bulgaria, 1938–39; Lectr in Eng. Lang., Queen Mary Coll., Univ. of London, 1946–47, Oriel and Brasenose Colls., Oxford, 1947–49; Oxford Univ. Lectr in Medieval Eng., 1948–49; Prof. of Eng. Lang., Glasgow Univ., 1949–59. Asst Press Attaché, Brit. Legation, Sofia, 1939–41; attached GHQ, MEF 1941–44, Major, MBE (mil.). Jt Editor, RES, 1954–63; Hon. Dir, EETS, 1957– . *Publications*: ed, Sweet: Anglo-Saxon Primer, 9th edn 1953; Paston Letters, 1958; Beowulf facsimile, 2nd edn 1959; The Paston Letters: A Selection in Modern Spelling, 1963; glossary, Early Middle English Verse and Prose (ed Bennett and Smithers), 1966, 2nd edn 1968; Sir Gawain and the Green Knight (ed Tolkien and Gordon), rev. edn 1967; Non-Cycle Plays and Fragments, 1970; Paston Letters and Papers of the Fifteenth Century, Pt I, 1971; William Tyndale's English of Controversy (Chambers Memorial Lecture), 1971; *contrib.* EAGS, Med. Æv., N and Q, PBA, RES. *Address*: Merton College, Oxford OX1 4JD.

Davis, Prof. Ralph Henry Carless; Professor of Medieval History, University of Birmingham, since 1970; *b* 1918; *m* 1949; two *s*. MA Oxon 1947. Lectr, UCL, 1948–56; Fellow and Tutor, Merton Coll., Oxford, 1956–70; Mem., Hebdomadal Council, Oxford Univ., 1967–69. Asst Master, Christ's Hosp., Horsham, 1947–48. Editor, History, 1968– . *Publications*: The Mosques of Cairo, 1944; A History of Medieval Europe, 1957; King Stephen, 1967; ed, The Kalendar of Abbot Samson of Bury St Edmunds, 1954; ed (with H. A. Cronne), Regesta Regum Anglo-Normannorum, vol. III, 1968, vol. IV, 1969; *contrib.* historical and archaeological jls. *Address*: Univ. of Birmingham, PO Box 363, Birmingham B15 2TT.

Davis, Prof. Roy, MA, DPhil; Professor of Psychology, University of Reading, since 1973; *b* 1930; *m* 1963; one *s*. BA Oxon 1953 (PPP), MA. Oxon 1955, DPhil Oxon 1958; Mem.: Experl Psychol. Soc., Assoc. Psychol. Soc., Brain Res. Assoc., Assoc. Psychol. Scientif. Lang. Franc. Jun. Lectr in Experl Psychol., Oxford, 1955–59; Vis. Fellow, Univ. of Michigan, 1959–60; Vis. Fellow, Sorbonne, 1960–61; Lectr, Univ. of Reading, 1961–66, Sen. Lectr, 1966–68, Reader, 1968–69; Prof. of Psychology, Univ. of Newcastle upon Tyne, 1969–73. Treas., Experl Psychol. Soc., 1962–69; Ed., Qly Jl Experl Psychol., 1972– . *Publications*: *contrib.* Acta Psychol., Brit. Jl Psychol., Jl Experl Psychol., Année Psychol., Nature, Qly Jl Experl Psychol. *Address*: Dept of Psychology, Univ. of Reading, Earley Gate, Whiteknights, Reading RG6 2AL.

Davis, Dr Terence Newman; Senior Lecturer, Department of Education, Stirling University, since 1970; *b* 1930; *m* 1962; one *s* one *d*. MA Edinburgh 1964, MEd Birmingham 1965, PhD Birmingham 1970; CertEd, Liverpool 1955, ABPsS 1966, FRStatSoc. 1966, Full Mem., Internat. Assoc. App. Psychol., 1965. Lectr, Univ. of Bristol, 1967–70, Act. Hd of Dept, 1971. *Publications*: *contrib.* Brit. Jl Educnl Psychol., Educnl Res., Progr. Learn. *Address*: Dept of Education, Univ. of Stirling, Stirling FK9 4LA.

Davison, Dr Nigel St John; Senior Lecturer, Department of Music, Bristol University, since 1971; *b* 1929; *m* 1965; two *s* one *d*. BA Cantab 1953 (1st cl. Music), BMus Cantab 1954 (Organ, Composition, Palaeography and Criticism), MA Cantab 1957, DMus Edinburgh 1961; FRCO 1954. Lectr, Bristol Univ., 1967–71. Dir of Music, Wellington Coll., Berks, 1963–67; Conductor, Bristol Opera Co., 1967– . *Publications*: ed, Mozart: Magnificat (from K.321), 1962; Mozart: Epistle Sonata (K.336), 1963; P. de la Rue: Vier Motetten (Das Chorwerk, 91), 1964; P. de la Rue: Magnificat Quinti Toni, 1965; P. de la Rue: Five Motets, 1966–67; Tye: Western Wind Mass, 1970; Palestrina: Assumpta est Maria, 1971; P. de la Rue: Missa L'Homme armé (Das Chorwerk 114), 1972; *contrib.* Music Qly, Music Rev., Organ. *Address*: Dept of Music, Univ of Bristol, Royal Fort House, Tyndall Avenue, Bristol BS8 1UJ

Davison, Prof. Peter H.; Professor of English, St David's University College, since 1973; *b* 1926; *m* 1949; three *s*. BA Hons, London External 1954, MA London 1957, PhD Sydney 1963. Lectr, Sydney Univ., 1960–64; Fellow, Shakespeare Inst., 1964–65; Lectr, Birmingham Univ., 1965–69; Sen. Lectr, 1969–73; Vis. Prof., Univ. of Western Ontario, 1969 and 1971. Asst Sec., Internat. Wool Secretariat, 1952–60; Mem., Council of Malone Soc. since 1969; Ed., ALTA. Univ. of Birmingham Review, 1966–70; Ed., The Library, Bibliographical Soc., 1971– ; Mem., Univ. of Birmingham Rev. Body, 1971–72. *Publications*: ed: The Fair Maid of the Exchange, 1963, Richard II, 1964, The Merchant of Venice, 1967, and 1 Henry IV, 1968; The Dutch Courtesan, 1968; Songs of the British Music Hall, 1971; Book Production and Distribution, Literature and Mass Society, Newspapers and Journals, in, New Cambridge Bibliography of English Literature, vol. IV, 1972; Theatrum Redivivum series, 1972; *contrib.* Aumla, EB, ELH, The Library, MLQ, SB. *Address*: Dept of English, St David's Univ. Coll., Lampeter, Dyfed SA48 7ED.

Davison, Roy Malcolm, MA; Lecturer, Department of Russian, University of Liverpool, since 1963; *b* 1937. BA Oxon 1958 (2nd cl. Russian), MA Oxon 1963, DipEd Durham 1959. *Publications*: The Use of the Genitive in Negative Constructions, 1967; *contrib.* Eur. Studies Rev., Slav. Rev. *Address*: Dept of Russian, PO Box 147, The Univ., Liverpool L69 3BX.

Dawe, Alan Martin; Reader in Sociology, School of Sociology, University of Warwick, since 1974; b 1933; m 1963; two s. BA Leeds 1962 (Sociology). Asst Lectr in Sociology, LSE, 1963–64; Lectr in Sociology, Univ. of Leeds, 1964–72, Univ. of York, 1972–74. *Publications*: The Relevance of Values, in, Max Weber and Modern Sociology, ed A. Sahay, 1971; The Two Sociologies, in, Sociological Perspectives, ed J. Tunstall and K. Thompson, 1971; The Two Sociologies (forthcoming); *contrib*. Brit. Jl Sociol., Sociol Rev. *Address*: Sch. of Sociology, Univ. of Warwick, Coventry CV4 7AL.

Dawe, Dr Roger David; Lecturer in Classics, University of Cambridge, since 1967; Fellow of Trinity College, since 1963; b 1934; m 1960; one s one d. BA 1957, MA 1960, PhD 1961, LittD 1974, Cantab. Fellow of Gonville and Caius Coll., Cambridge, 1957–63; Asst Lectr, Cambridge Univ., 1965–67. *Publications*: Investigation and Collation of MSS of Aeschylus, 1964; Repertory of Conjectures on Aeschylus, 1965; Studies on the Text of Sophocles, 2 vols, 1973; Teubner edn of Sophocles, vol. I, 1975; *contrib*. Class. Qly, Eranos, Proc. Camb. Philol. Soc., etc. *Address*: Trinity Coll., Cambridge.

Daws, Dr Peter Philip; Senior Lecturer in Education, Institute of Education, University of Keele, since 1972; b 1926; m 1953; two s three d. BA Nottingham 1953 (Hons Psychology), PhD Nottingham 1957; ABPsS 1957. Asst Lectr, Dept of Psychology, Univ. of Edinburgh, 1956–59; Lectr, Dept of Psychology, Univ. of Leeds, 1959–69; Gulbenkian Sen. Lectr in Educn, Inst. of Educn, Keele, 1969–72. *Publications*: A Good Start in Life, 1968; *contrib*. Brit. Med. Jl, Educnl Res., Careers Qly, Voc. Asp. Educn. *Address*: Institute of Education, Univ. of Keele, Keele, Staffs ST5 5BG.

Dawson, Dr Andrew H., BA, PhD; Lecturer in Geography, University of St Andrews, since 1966; b 1942; m 1965; one s two d. BA London 1963 (1st cl. Geography), PhD London 1967. *Publications*: *contrib*. Scott. Geog. Mag., Tijdschrift voor Econ. en Soc. Geog., Trans Inst. Brit. Geog. *Address*: Dept of Geography, Univ. of St Andrews, Fife KY16 9AJ.

Dawson, Dr Bernard Ernest; Lecturer in Education, King's College, University of London, since 1963; b 1924; m 1957. BSc 1950, Postgrad. CertEd 1951, PhD 1956, London; FRIC 1963 (ARIC 1956), Member: Chem. Soc., Assoc. for Sci. Educn, Mem., ASE Sci. and Educn Cttee 1961–67; Nuffield Sci. Teaching Project: Chemistry, 1963–66; Physical Sci., 1965–73. Mem, Editorial Bd, London Educnl Rev., 1972– . *Publications*: ed, An Approach to Natural Science, 1960, 4th edn 1966; ed, Science in the Introductory Phase, 1967; Practical Inorganic Chemistry, 1963, 2nd edn 1967; Energy in Chemistry: an approach to thermodynamics, 1971; Kinetics and Mechanisms of Reactions, 1973; ed, Nuffield Advanced Science – Physical Science: Source Book, 1974; ed, Revised Nuffield Chemistry: Teachers' Guide II, 1975; *contrib*. Jl Phys. Chem., Sch. Sci. Rev., Jl Chem. Educn, Educnl Chem. *Address*: Fac. of Education, King's College, Strand, WC2R 2LS.

Dawson, George Ferguson Dempster, Lecturer, Department of Government, London School of Economics, University of London, since 1972; b 1941. MA (Hons) St Andrews 1964; PhD Dundee 1969; Hon. Sec., Political Studies Assoc. of UK, 1968. Res. Asst, Univ. of St Andrews, 1965–66; Lectr, LSE, 1966–72; Vis. Prof., Univ. of Wisconsin, USA, 1969–70. *Publications*: Nordic Cooperation in the Social and Labour Field, 1965; *contrib*. Encyclo. Brit. (various articles in Financial Times, New Society etc.), Political Studies, Political Qly Rev., Article in Scandinavian Dictinary of Biography. *Address*: London School of Economics, Houghton Street, WC2A 2AE.

Dawson, Peter F.; Lecturer in Political Science and Public Administration, Department of Government, London School of Economics, University of London, since 1964; b 1934, m 1969; one s one d. BA Cambridge 1959, MA 1963; Mem., Royal Inst. of Public Admin, Political Studies Assoc. of the UK, African Studies Assoc. of UK. *Address*: London School of Economics, Houghton Street, WC2A 2AE.

Dawson, Raymond Stanley, MA; University Lecturer in Chinese, Oxford University, since 1961, Fellow of Wadham College, Oxford, since 1963; b 1923; m 1944; two s one d. BA Oxon 1947 (Literae Humaniores), 1950 (1st cl. Chinese), MA Oxon 1949. Spalding Lectr in Chinese Philos., Durham Univ., 1952–57; Spalding Lectr in Chinese Lang. and Civilization, Durham Univ., 1957–61. Keeper, Gulbenkian Mus. of Oriental Art and Archaeol., 1959–60. *Publications*: The Legacy of China, 1964, 2nd edn (pbk) 1971, Spanish edn 1967, Dutch edn 1973; The Chinese Chameleon, an analysis of European conceptions of Chinese civilization, 1967, Spanish edn 1970, Japanese edn 1972; An Introduction to Classical Chinese, 1968; Imperial China, 1972. *Address*: Oriental Institute, Pusey Lane, Oxford.

Dawson, Sam William; Lecturer, Department of English, University College of Swansea, since 1951; b 1928; m 1952; one s yne d. BA Manchester 1949 (1st cl.), MA Manchester 1951. *Publications*: Drama and the Dramatic, 1970; *contrib*. Ess. in Crit. *Address*: Dept of English, Univ. College of Swansea, Singleton Park, Swansea SA2 8PP.

Day, Prof. Alan Charles Lynn; Professor of Economics, London School of Economics, University of London, since 1964; b 1924; m 1962. BA Cantab 1948. Asst Econ. then Lectr, LSE, 1949–54; Reader in Economics, London Univ., 1956–64; Brit. Acad. Leverhulme Vis. Prof., Graduate Inst. for Internat. Studies, Geneva, 1971. Econ. Adv., HM Treasury, 1945–56; Part-time Econ. Adv. on Civil Aviation, BoT, later DTI, later Civil Aviation Authority, 1968– ; Mem., Council, Consumers' Assoc., 1963; Mem., Bd, British Airports Authority, 1965–68; Mem., SE Region Econ. Planning Council, 1966–69; Mem., Road Research Lab. Traffic Res. Cttee, 1966–70; Mem., Min. of Housing Preservation Policy Gp, 1966–69; Mem., Home Office Cttee on the London Taxicab Trade, 1967–70.

Publications: The Future of Sterling, 1954; Outline of Monetary Economics, 1956; The Economics of Money, 1959; (with S. T. Beza) Wealth and Income, 1960. *Address*: London School of Economics and Political Science, Houghton Street, Aldwych, WC2A 2AE.

Day, Colin Leslie; Lecturer in Economics, University of Stirling, since 1971; *b* 1944; *m* 1966; one *s* one *d*. BA Oxon 1966, MA Oxon 1972; Mem., Amer. Econ. Assoc. Res. Fellow, Univ. of Stirling, 1968–71. *Address*: Dept of Economics, Univ. of Stirling, Stirling.

Day, Douglas; Senior Lecturer, French Department, Bristol University, since 1974 (Lecturer, 1961–74); *b* 1930; *m* 1959; one *d*. BA London 1952 (French and Russian), MA London 1955. Lecteur, Toulouse Univ., 1953–55; Bristol University: Junior Fellow, 1957–59; Asst Lectr, 1959–61; Fac. Accommodation Officer, 1971–74. *Publications*: *contrib*. Jl Value Inquiry, Mod. Lang. Rev., Revue de Littérature Comparée. *Address*: French Dept, Univ. of Bristol, Bristol BS8 1TH.

Day, John; Senior Lecturer in Politics, University of Leicester, since 1970; *b* 1931; *m* 1958; two *s* one *d*. BA Cantab 1953 (1st cl. History). Asst Lectr, Edinburgh Univ., 1957–59; Asst Lectr, Leicester Univ., 1959–61; Lectr, Leicester Univ., 1961–70; Vis. Lectr, Univ. Coll. of Rhodesia and Nyasaland, 1964. *Publications*: International Nationalism, 1968; *contrib*. Jl Mod. Af. Studies, Jl Commonwealth Pol. Studies, Philosophy, Pol. Studies. *Address*: Dept of Politics, The Univ., Leicester LE1 7RH.

Day, Peter Russell, MPhil; Lecturer in Social Work, Department of Applied Social Science, Nottingham University, since 1973; *b* 1933; *m* 1957; two *d*. Cert. in Social Studies Nottingham 1956, Cert. in Mental Health LSE 1959, MPhil Nottingham 1970; Mem., Brit. Assoc. Soc. Workers, Psychiat. Soc. Worker, 1959–63; Gulbenkian Fellow, Nat. Inst. Soc. Work Train., 1963; Tutor in Soc. Work, High Wycombe Tech. Coll., 1963–66; Tutor in Child Care, Dept of Adult Educn, Nottingham Univ., 1966–73. *Publications*: Communication in Social Work, 1972; *contrib*. Probation, Soc. Work Today. *Address*: Dept of Applied Social Science, Univ. Park, Nottingham NG7 2RD.

Deakin, Brian Measures, Senior Research Officer, Department of Applied Economics, University of Cambridge, since 1964; Fellow and Director of Studies in Economics, Magdalene College, Cambridge, since 1967; *b* 1922; *m* 1954; one *s* one *d*. BA Hons Oxon 1949 (PPE), MA Oxon 1953, MA Cantab 1967. Founder and Associate Mem., of ASEPELT (Assoc. Scientifique Européenne pour la prévision économique à moyen et à long terme), Brussels (Vice-Pres., 1967–71). Sen. Proctor, Univ. of Cambridge, 1973–74. *Publications*: (with T. Seward) Productivity in Transport: a study of employment, capital output, productivity, and technical change, 1969; (with T. Seward) Shipping Conferences: a study of their

origins, development and economic practices, 1973; contrib. Programming for Europe's Collective Needs, ed J. H. P. Paelinck, 1971; *contrib*. London and Cambridge Econ. Bull. *Address*: Magdalene College, Cambridge CB3 0AG.

Deane, Phyllis Mary; Reader in Economic History, Faculty of Economics and Politics, University of Cambridge, since 1971; *b* 1918. MA Glasgow 1940 (1st cl. Economic Science), MA Cantab 1951; FRHistS. Lectr, Faculty of Econ., 1961–71; Fellow, Newnham Coll., 1961– ; Vis. Prof., Univ. of Pittsburgh, 1969. Res. Off., Nat. Inst. Econ. Soc. Res., 1941–48; Colonial Res. Fellow, 1945–47; Res. Off., Colonial Off., 1948–50; Res. Off., Dept of Applied Econ., 1950–60; Chm., Council, Internat. Assoc. Res. Income and Wealth, 1967–69; Rev. Ed., Econ. Jl, 1968– ; Mngng Ed., Econ. Jl, 1971– ; Mem., E Anglian Econ. Planning Council, 1969– . *Publications*: (with J. Huxley) The Future of the Colonies, 1945; The Measurement of Colonial National Income, 1948; Colonial Social Accounting, 1953; British Economic Growth 1688–1959 (with W. A. Cole), 1962, 3rd edn 1968; (with B. R. Mitchell) Abstract of British Historical Statistics, 1962, 2nd edn 1970; The First Industrial Revolution, 1965, 2nd edn 1969; The Industrial Revolution in England, (Fontana Economic History of Europe), 1969; *contrib*. Econ. Develop. Cult. Chge, Econ. Hist. Rev., Jl Econ. Hist., Jl Royal Stat. Soc., Rev. Income Wealth. *Address*: Faculty of Economics, Univ. of Cambridge, Sidgwick Avenue, Cambridge.

Deane, Dr Seamus Francis; Statutory Lecturer, Department of English and American Literature, University College, Dublin, since 1972; *b* 1940; *m* 1963; two *s* one *d*. BA QUB 1961 (1st cl. Hons), MA QUB 1963, PhD Cantab 1968. Coll. Lectr, Dept of English and American Studies, UC Dublin, 1968–72. Vis. Fulbright Lectr, Reed Coll., Oregon, USA, 1966–67; Vis. Fulbright Lectr, Univ. of California, Berkeley, 1967–68. Editor, Atlantis, 1969–74. *Publications*: Gradual Wars (poems), 1972; The French Enlightenment and Revolution in England, 1789–1832, 1975; ed, Sale Catalogue of Libraries of Eminent Persons: Politicians, 1974; ed, The Adventures of Hugh Trevor, by Thomas Holcroft, 1972; *contrib*. Atlantis, Encounter, Jl History of Ideas, Revue de Litterature Comparée, Studies in Burke and His Time, etc. *Address*: Arts Block, English Dept, Belfield, Univ. College, Dublin 4.

Dearden, Derek George, MA, ARIBA; Senior Lecturer in Architecture, University of Manchester, since 1972; *b* 1929; *m* 1955; one *s* one *d*. BA Manchester 1951 (1st cl. Architecture), MA Manchester 1954; ARIBA 1951. Lectr, Univ. of Manchester, 1956–72. Architect, priv. pract., 1951– . *Address*: Dept of Architecture, Univ. of Manchester, Manchester M13 9PL.

Dearden, Dr Robert Frederick; Reader in Philosophy of Education, University of London Institute of Education, since 1972, (Lecturer, 1964–72); *b* 1934; *m* 1958; three *d*.

BA London 1964 (1st cl. Philos.), Acad. Dip-Ed London 1965 (Dist.), Teacher's Cert. 1956; PhD London 1973; Mem., Aristot. Soc., Philos. Educn Soc. of GB. *Publications*: The Philosophy of Primary Education, 1968; ed (with R. S. Peters and P. H. Hirst), Education and the Development of Reason, 1972; *contrib*. Brit. Jl Educnl Studies, Proc. Philos. Educn Soc. *Address*: Univ. of London Institute of Education, Malet Street, WC1E 7HS.

Dearnaley, Edmund John; Senior Lecturer in Psychology, University of Manchester, since 1972; *b* 1933; *m* 1957; one *s* two *d*. BSc Manchester 1954, MSc Manchester 1956; FBPsS. Res. Asst in Psychol., Univ. of Manchester, 1954–58; Asst Lectr in Psychol., Univ. of Manchester, 1960–62; Lectr, 1962–72. Commnd, RAF, 1958–60 and served RAF Inst. Aviat. Med., Mem., Psychol. Sub-Cttee, Flying Personnel Res. Cttee, 1962– ; Bredbury and Romiley UDC, 1963–66, 1967–70; Council, Brit. Psychol. Soc., 1969–71; Ct Governors, Univ. of Manchester, 1970– ; Governor, Huddersfield Polytechnic, 1973– . *Publications*: *contrib*. Acta Psychol., Aerosp. Med., Brit. Jl Psychol., Brit. Jl Educnl Psychol., Brit. Med. Jl, Durham Res. Rev., Educnl Res., Jl Gen. Psychol., Occup. Psychol., Oper. Res. Qly, Psycho-pharmocol., Sociol Rev. *Address*: Dept of Psychology, Univ. of Manchester, Manchester M13 9PL.

Deas, Malcolm Douglas, MA; University Lecturer in the Politics and Government of Latin America, Oxford University, since 1965, Acting Professor and Director of Latin American Centre, St Antony's College, 1968–70, 1971–72; *b* 1941; *m* 1964; one *d*. BA Oxon 1962 (1st cl. History), MA Oxon 1965. Fellow, All Souls Coll., 1962–65; Fellow, St Antony's Coll., 1965. *Address*: St Antony's College, Oxford.

de Bhaldraithe, Prof. Tomas; Professor of Modern Irish Language and Literature, University College, Dublin, since 1960; *b* 1916; *m* 1943; six *s* three *d*. BA NUI 1937 (Mod. Lang.), MA 1939 (Mod. Irish), PhD 1942; DLitt 1955; Member: Royal Irish Academy, 1952, Bd of Celtic Studies, Dublin Inst. for Advanced Studies, 1961– , Place Names Commission. Lectr, Mod. Irish Lang. and Lit., UCD, 1952–60. *Publications*: The Irish of Cois Fhairrge: A Phonetic Study, 1945, 2nd edn 1966; Gaeilge Chois Fhairrge: An Deilbhíocht, 1953; Scothscéalta le Pádraic Ó Conaire, 1956; English–Irish Dictionary, 1959; Cín Lae Amhlaoibh, 1970; *contrib*. Béaloideas, Celtica, Éigse, Ériu, Galvia. *Address*: Univ. College, Belfield, Dublin 4.

de Boer, George; Reader in Geography, University of Hull, since 1967; *b* 1920; *m* 1952; one *s* one *d*. BA Cantab 1942, MA Cantab 1946. CertEd Cambridge 1947; Member: Inst. of British Geographers; Internat. Glaciol Soc. University of Hull: Asst Lectr, 1947; Lectr, 1949; Sen. Lectr, 1964. Member: Hull Univ. Senate, 1951–55, 1956–57, 1965–66; Hull Univ. Council, 1956–57. *Publications*: *contrib*. Geographical

Jl, Imago Mundi, Trans Inst. of Brit. Geographers; Post-Medieval Archaeol., Proc. Yorks Geol. Soc. *Address*: Dept of Geography, The Univ., Hull HU6 7RX.

Decreus, Dr Juliette C., MA, DUP, Officier de l'ordre national des Palmes Académiques; Officier de l'ordre de Léopold II de Belgique; Senior Lecturer, French Department, University of London, Queen Mary College, since 1967; *b* 1911; *m* 1931; one *s*. MA Leeds 1943, Docteur de l'Univ. de Paris 1948. Asst Lectr, Univ. of Leeds, 1940–47; Univ. of Glasgow, 1951–53; Lectr, Univ. of London, Queen Mary Coll., 1953–58; Vis. Prof., Univ. of Houston, Texas, 1958–59, and Summer Schs, 1963; Lectr, Queen Mary Coll., 1959–67; Full Prof., Univ. of Manitoba, Winnipeg, 1972–73. Vice-Pres., Assoc. Drs Lettres, Univ. de Paris, 1965; Mem., Soc. Gens de Lettres de France, 1950. *Publications*: Sainte-Beuve et la Critique des Auteurs Féminins, 1949; Poésie et Transcendance, 1957; Henry Bulwer et Hortense Allart, 1961; Le Prêtre dans l'Œuvre d'André Billy, 1964; trans., Rafael Laffón (from Spanish), 1967; *contrib*. Comp. Lit. Studies, Humanidades, and reviews, France and Belgium. *Address*: French Dept, Queen Mary College, Mile End Road, E1 4NS.

Deech, Ruth Lynn; Fellow and Tutor in Law, St Anne's College Oxford, and CUF Lecturer, since 1970; *b* 1943; *m* 1967. BA Oxon 1965, MA Brandeis 1966, MA Oxon 1969. Barrister, Inner Temple, 1967. Asst Prof. Faculty of Law, Univ. of Windsor, 1968–1970. Legal Asst, Law Commn, 1966–67. *Publications*: *contrib*. Can. Bar Rev., MLR, NLJ. *Address*: St Anne's College, Oxford.

Deer, Prof. William Alexander, MSc, PhD, FRS, FGS; Professor of Mineralogy and Petrology, Cambridge University, since 1961; Master of Trinity Hall, Cambridge, since 1966; Vice-Chancellor, Cambridge University, 1971–73; *b* 1910; *m* 1939; two *s* one *d*. MSc Manchester, PhD Cantab; FRS 1962. Graduate Res. Schol., 1932, Beyer Fellow 1933, Manchester Univ.; Strathcona Studentship, St John's Coll., Cambridge, 1934; 1851 Exhbn Sen. Studentship, 1938; Fellow, St John's Coll., Cambridge, 1939; Jun. Bursar, St John's Coll., 1946; Tutor, St John's Coll., 1949; Prof. of Geology, Manchester Univ., 1950–61; Fellow of St John's Coll., 1961–66, Hon. Fellow, 1969. Percival Lectr, Univ. of Manchester, 1953. Petrologist on Brit. E Greenland Expdn, 1935–36; Murchison Fund Geol. Soc. of London, 1945; Leader, NE Greenland Expdn, 1948; Bruce Medal, Royal Soc. of Edinburgh, 1948; Jt Leader, E Greenland Geol. Expdn, 1953; Leader, Brit. E Greenland Expdn, 1966. Trustee, Brit. Museum (Nat. Hist.), 1967. Pres., Mineralogical Soc., 1968–69; Pres., Geological Soc., 1970–72; Mem., NERC, 1968–71. *Publications*: *contrib*. Petrology and Mineralogy. *Address*: The Master's Lodge, Trinity Hall, Cambridge.

Dees, Norman; Director, Department of Extra-Mural and Adult Education, University of Glasgow, since 1961; *b* 1916; *m* 1940; two *d*.

177

BA Manchester 1937 (Hons History). Staff Tutor, Univ. Manchester, 1945–47; Univ. Newcastle: Staff Tutor, 1947–53; Sen. Staff Tutor, 1953–56; Dep. Dir of Extra-Mural Studies, 1959–61; seconded Foreign Office, as Adult Educn adviser, Berlin, 1956–58; Exec. Governor, Newbattle Abbey Adult Coll, 1961– ; Chm., Exec. Cttee, Scottish Inst. of Adult Educn, 1970– . *Publications*: ed, Approaches to Adult Teaching, 1965; You Live and Learn, 1965; Prospects Before Us, 1966; Teachers and Taught, 1966; *contrib*. Scottish Jl Adult Educn, Studies in Adult Educn. *Address*: 57/59 Oakfield Avenue, Glasgow G12 8LW.

de Grouchy, Philip John, MA; Lecturer and Resident Tutor (West Sussex), Department of Extra-Mural Studies, University of Southampton, since 1947; *b* 1921; *m* 1948; one *s* one *d*. BA and MA Oxon 1947 (War Degree, 1st cl. Pt 1 Hist. Shortened degree course). Gov., Worthing High Sch. for Boys, 1967– . *Publications*: Britain in Ferment, 1968; Classic to Computer: A Study of Art in Revolution, 1970. *Address*: Dept of Extra-Mural Studies, The Univ., Southampton SO9 5NH.

Deighton, Herbert Stanley; Lecturer in International Politics, Brunel University, since 1967; *b* 1910; *m* 1947; one *s* two *d*. BA Oxford 1933, BLitt Oxford 1935, MA Oxford 1937; FZS; John Hay Whitney Res. Fellow, 1951–52, Leverhulme Res. Fellow, 1953–55; Mem., IHR, RIIA (Chm. Middle East Gp, 1943–46), ISS, RUSIDS, Hist. Assoc. Fellow, Pembroke Coll., Oxford, 1937– , Supernumerary Fellow, 1953– ; Dean, Pembroke Coll., 1937–39, and 1946–51, Tutor in Modern History, 1937–53; Univ. Lectr in Modern History, Oxford, 1947–53; Vis. Prof., Cairo Univ., 1941–46; Prof., Univ. of New Mexico, 1951; Prof., Emory Univ., Georgia, 1952; Consult. in Polit. Science, Brunel Univ., 1966; Acad. Consult. and Lectr, Nat. Def. Coll., 1971– . Chm., Educn Cttee, Lib. Party, 1948–50; Chm., Machinery of Govt Cttee, Lib. Party, 1967–68. *Publications*: contrib. The Unservile State, ed G. Watson, 1957; The Radical Alternative, ed G. Watson, 1963; ed, P. M. Holt, Political and Social Change in Modern Egypt, 1968; The Future of Man, ed F. J. Ebling and G. W. Heath, 1972; *contrib*. EHR, Internat. Aff., Politique Etrangere, TLS. *Address*: School of Social Science, Brunel Univ., Kingston Lane, Hillingdon, Mddx UB8 3TH.

de la Cruz Fernandez, Dr Juan Manuel, PhD, DFil; Senior Lecturer, Language Centre, University of Essex, since 1973; *b* 1940; *m* 1967; one *s* two *d*. LicFil Madrid 1964 (Mod. Philology), PhD QUB 1969 (English) DFil Madrid 1974 (Mod. Philology); Member: Assoc. Hispanists of GB and Ire.; AEPE; Linguistics Assoc. of GB. Queen's Univ. Belfast: Lector in Spanish, 1965–70; Asst Lectr in Spanish, 1970–71; Lectr in Spanish, 1971–72; Lectr in Hispanic Studies, Glasgow Univ., 1972–73; *Publications*: Ortografiá e Historia Lingüística: Contrastes Significativos entre el Inglés y el Español (Annex to Filología Moderna) (forthcoming); *contrib*. EPhS, FMod, IF, Linguis-tics, Orbis, RSEL, Studia Anglica Posnanien-sia. *Address*: Language Centre, The Univ., Wivenhoe Park, Colchester, Essex CO4 3SQ.

Delano Smith, Catherine, MA, BLitt; Lecturer in Geography, University of Nottingham, since 1967. BA Oxon 1962, MA Oxon 1969, BLitt Oxon 1968; FRGS. Asst Lectr, Durham Univ., 1964–67. Chevalier of the Order of Merit of the Grand-Duchy of Luxembourg, 1971. *Publications*: Land Use in E Madeira, Neolithic and Mediaeval Tavoliere, Italy (forthcoming); papers in Conference proceedings: Colloquio sulla Preistoria e Protoistoria della Daunia, Foggia, 1973; Perm. European Conf. for Study of Rural Landscapes, Perugia, 1973; Sediments in Archaeology, Southampton, 1973; *contrib*. Geogl Mag., Man, Mediterranée, Trans of Inst. of Brit. Geogrs. *Address*: Dept of Geography, University Park, Nottingham NG7 2RD.

de Lavigne, Dr Richard Louis, PhD; Lecturer in Mediaeval History, University of St Andrews, since 1964; *b* 1940; *m* 1967; two *s*. BA London 1961 (1st cl. Hist.), PhD London 1971. *Publications*: *contrib*. Annales du Midi. *Address*: Dept of Mediaeval History, St Salvator's College, St Andrews, Fife.

Dell, Geoffrey Alan; Hon. Lecturer, Department of Education, University of Glasgow, since 1965; *b* 1928; *m* 1959; one *d*. MA Oxon 1951, MEd QUB 1954; ABPsS 1960, Mem. Brit. Psychol. Soc. (Mem. Council, 1970–). Sen. Psychologist, Belfast Educn Dept, 1956–65; Principal Psychologist, Glasgow Educn Dept, 1965–74. Mem., Scottish Central Cttee on Primary Educn, Assessment Sub-Cttee, 1972–74. *Publications*: *contrib*. Brit. Jl Educnl Psychol., Scottish Educnl Studies. *Address*: Dept of Education, Univ. of Glasgow, Glasgow G12 8QG.

de Madariaga, Isabel; *see* Madariaga.

de Mourgues, Dr Odette Marie Hélène Louise; Reader, Department of French, University of Cambridge, since 1969; *b* 1914. Licence en droit Grenoble 1934, Licence d'anglais et diplôme d'études littéraires classiques Aix-en-Provence 1938 (Fr. and Eng.), Diplôme d'études supérieures de droit Aix 1938, Agrégation d'anglais 1945, PhD 1950. DLitt 1968, Cantab. Assistant Lecturer: Univ. of Aix-en-Provence 1945–46; Univ. of Cambridge, 1950–52; Lectr, Univ. of Cambridge, 1952–69. *Publications*: Metaphysical, Baroque and Précieux Poetry, 1953; La Fontaine, Fables, 1960; O Muse, fuyante proie, essai sur la poésie de La Fontaine, 1962; An Anthology of French 17C Poetry, 1966, Racine or the Triumph of Relevance, 1967; Autonomie de Racine, 1967; chapters in: The French Renaissance and its Heritage, ed, D. R. Haggis, 1968; Molière, Stage and Study, ed W. D. Howarth and M. Thomas, 1973; Ronsard the Poet, ed, T. Cave, 1973; *contrib*. Fr. Studies, RHLF etc. *Address*: Girton Coll. Cambridge CB3 0JG.

Dempsey, Prof. Peter James Rory; Professor of Applied Psychology, University College, Cork, since 1964; *b* 1914. BA NUI

1936, LicTheol Rome 1941, LicScript Rome 1943, DrTheol Rome 1944, MA NUI 1946, PhD Montreal 1949; FBPsS, Fellow, Amer. Assoc. Adv. of Science, Fellow, Irish Psychol. Soc. Asst, Univ. Coll., Cork, 1951–53; Lectr, 1952–64. Mem.: Human Sciences Cttee, Dublin, 1965– ; Cttee on Mngmt Studies, 1968–70; Vice-Pres., Internat. Cath. Psychiatric Assoc., 1954–57; Ed., Manp. App. Psychol., 1967– . *Publications*: The Psychology of Sartre, 1950; Psychology for All, 1952; Freud, Psychoanalysis, Catholicism, 1956; Psychology and the Manager, 1973; *contrib*. Manp. App. Psychol. *Address*: Dept of Applied Psychology, Univ. College, Cork.

Dempster, Dr Michael Alan Howarth; Fellow and Tutor, Balliol College, University Lecturer in Industrial Mathematics, University of Oxford, since 1967; *b* 1938; *m* 1963; two *s* one *d*. BA Toronto 1961 (Maths), MS Carnegie 1963 (Maths), PhD Carnegie 1965 (Maths), MA Oxon 1966; Mem.: Amer. Math. Soc., Amer. Stat. Assoc., Econometric Soc., Econ. Study Soc., Inst. Math. Stat., **Inst.** Man. Science, Lond. Math. Soc., Public Choice Soc. IBM Res. Fellow, Oxford, 1965; Res. Fellow, Nuffield Coll., Oxford, 1966; Vis. Prof., Univ. of Toronto, 1970; Vis. Sen. Fellow, Manchester Business Sch., 1970, 1971. *Publications*: (with P. R. Adby) Introduction to Optimization Methods, 1974; Elements of Optimization, 1975; Linear Econometric Models (forthcoming); Co-ed., Chapman and Hall Mathematics Series; *contrib*. Amer. Polit. Sci. Rev., Can. Jl Math., Jl Math. Anal. Applns. *Address*: Balliol College, Oxford.

Denbigh, Prof. Kenneth George, MA, DSc, FRS; Principal of Queen Elizabeth College, University of London, since 1966; *b* 1911; *m* 1935; two *s*. MA Cantab, DSc Leeds; Hon. DèsSc Toulouse 1960, Hon. DUniv. Essex 1967; FRS 1965. Imperial Chemical Industries, 1934–38, 1945–48; Lectr, Southampton Univ., 1938–41; Ministry of Supply (Explosives), 1941–45; Lectr, Cambridge Univ., Chemical Engineering Dept, 1948–55; Prof. of Chem. Techn., Edinburgh, 1955–60; Prof. of Chem. Engng Sci., London Univ., 1960–61; Courtauld's Prof., Imperial Coll., 1961–66. *Publications*: The Thermodynamics of the Steady State, 1951; The Principles of Chemical Equilibrium, 1955; Science, Industry and Social Policy, 1963; Chemical Reactor Theory, 1965; *contrib*. various scientific papers. *Address*: Queen Elizabeth College, Campden Hill Road, W8 7AH.

Denison, Norman, MA, PhD; Director, Department of Language Studies, London School of Economics and Political Science, University of London, since 1964; *b* 1925; *m* 1950; one *s* one *d*. BA Cantab 1949 (Mod. and Med. Langs), MA Cantab 1952, PhD Cantab 1955; Mem., Corr., Soc. Finno-Ougr. de Helsinki. Lectr, Helsinki Univ., 1951–54; Asst Lectr, Aberystwyth, 1954–56; Lectr, 1956; Lectr, Glasgow, 1956–58, 1960–63; Prof., Univ. of Punjab, 1958–60; Lectr, Univ. Ist. Inst. For. Langs, Moscow, 1963–64. Gov., CILT, 1971– ; Mem.: Exec. Cttee, BAAL since its creation; Internat. Exec. Cttee,

AILA, 1969– , (Gen. Sec., 1969); Chm, Langs Bd, CNAA, 1971. *Publications*: The Partitive in Finnish, 1957; sections, in, Giornale Internazionali di Sociolinguistica, Rome, 1969; Social Anthropology and Language, 1971; *contrib*. on plurilingualism and sociolinguistics in various collecs and jls. *Address*: Dept of Language Studies, London School of Economics, Houghton Street, Aldwych, WC2A 2AE.

Denman, Prof. Donald Robert, MA, MSc, PhD, FRICS; Professor of Land Economy, Cambridge University, since 1968; *b* 1911; *m* 1941; two *s*. BSc London 1938, MSc London 1940, PhD London 1945, MA Cantab 1948; FRICS 1949, Vice-Pres., Conservation Soc. Univ. Lectr, Cambridge, 1948–68; Fellow, Pembroke Coll., Cambridge, 1962– . Advr on Development of Land Economy, Univ. of Kumasi, Ghana and Univ. of Nigeria, 1963– ; Fellow, Royal Swedish Acad. Forestry and Agric., 1971– . Dep. Exec. Off., Cumberland War Agric. Exec. Cttee, 1939–46; Land Mngmt Cttee, Agric. Improvement Council, 1953–60; Mem.: Church Assembly, 1957– ; Stand. Cttee, Istituto Dintto Agrar. Int. Comp., Florence, 1960– ; Cttee, CNAA, 1966–72; Adv., Min. of Co-operation and Rural Affairs, Iran, 1963– ; Gov., Canford Sch., –1972; Mem., Gov. Bd, Commonwealth Hum. Ecol. Council, 1970– ; Nat. Commn for UNESCO, 1972– . *Publications*: Tenant Right Valuation in History and Modern Practice, 1942; Tenant Right Valuation and Current Legislation, 1948; Estate Capital: The Contribution of Landownership to Agricultural Finance, 1957; Origins of Ownership: A Brief History of Landownership and Tenure, 1958, 2nd edn 1959; Bibliography of Rural Land Economy and Landownership 1900–1957, 1958; Farm Rents: A Comparison of Current and Past Farm Rents in England and Wales, 1959; Landownership and Resources, 1960; Contemporary Problems of Landownership, 1963; Land in the Market, 1964; Commons and Village Greens: A Study in Land Use, Conservation and Management Based on a National Survey of Commons in England and Wales 1961–1966, 1967; Land and People, 1967; The Case for Capitalism (Capitalism and Property), 1967; Rural Land Systems: A General Classification of Rural Land Systems in Relation to the Surveyor's Profession and Rural Land Reform, 1968; Land Use and the Constitution of Property, 1969; Land Use: An Introduction to Proprietary Land Use Analysis, 1972; The King's Vista, a land reform which has changed the face of Persia, 1973; *contrib*. Chart. Survey., Jl RTPI, Land Econs, RSA Jl, Twent. Cent. *Address*: Dept of Land Economy, 19 Silver Street, Cambridge CB3 9EP.

Denmark, Dr John Clifford; Honorary Lecturer, Department of Audiology and Education of the Deaf, Manchester University, since 1967; *b* 1924; *m* 1945; one *s* one *d*. MB, ChB Liverpool 1952, MRCS, LRCP 1952, DPM Manchester 1958, MRCPsych 1972. Dir, Dept of Psychiatry for the Deaf, Whittingham Hosp., Preston; Hon. Psychiatrist, Royal Nat. Inst. for Deaf; Mem., Lewis Cttee, HMSO, 1968. *Publications*: Psychiatry

179

for the Deaf, in, Current Psychiatric Therapies, vol. II 1971; ed Masserman, Grune and Stratton; *contrib*. Brit. Jl Dis. Communication, Brit. Jl Psych., Brit. Jl Sociol. Brit. Med. Jl, Hearing, J. Men. Sci., Jl Soc. Teachers of Deaf, Lancet, Proc. Roy. Soc. Med., Sound. *Address*: Dept of Audiology and Education of the Deaf, Manchester Univ., Manchester M13 9PL.

Dennison, Dr Peter John; Assistant Lecturer, Faculty of Music, University of Cambridge, since 1971, Fellow and Director of Music, Clare College, Cambridge, since 1971; *b* 1942. BMus Sydney 1964, BA Oxford 1966, MA and DPhil Oxford 1970, MA and PhD by incorporation Cambridge 1971; FRCO 1966, Mem. Royal Musical Assoc. Lectr in Music, Univ. of Glasgow, 1968–71. Conductor, Cambridge Philharmonic Soc., 1971– ; Mem., Cttee, Purcell Soc., 1972– . *Publications*: Pelham Humfrey: Complete Church Music (Musica Britannica vols 34 and 35), 1972; Purcell: Sacred Music, Part 2 (Purcell Society vol. 14), 1973. *Address*: Clare College, Cambridge.

Dennison, Stanley Raymond, CBE; Vice-Chancellor, University of Hull, since 1972; *b* 1912. MA Dunelm 1937, MA Cantab 1939. Lectr in Econs, Manchester Univ., 1935–39; Prof. of Econs, Univ. Coll. of Swansea, 1939–45; Lectr in Econs, Cambridge Univ., 1945–58; Fellow of Gonville and Caius Coll., 1945–58; Prof. of Econs, Queen's Univ. of Belfast, 1958–61; David Dale Prof. of Econs, Univ. of Newcastle upon Tyne, 1962–72; Pro-Vice-Chancellor, 1966–72. Chief Econ. Asst, War Cabinet Secretariat, 1940–46. Mem., UGC, 1964–68; Mem., NE Electricity Bd, 1965–72. Chm of Wages Councils; Mem., Cttee on Land Utilisation in Rural Areas, 1942; Mem., Cttee on Medical Services in the Armed Forces, 1955; Mem., Cttee on Air Pollution, 1954; Mem., Cttee on Marketing and Distribution of Fatstock and Carcase Meat, 1964; Mem., Rev. Body on Remuneration of Doctors and Dentists in the NHS, 1962–70. Chm. Govs, Royal Grammar Sch., Newcastle upon Tyne, 1969– . *Publications*: The Location of Industry and the Depressed Areas, 1939; (with Sir Dennis Robertson) The Control of Industry, 1960; various articles etc. on economic questions. *Address*: Univ. of Hull, Hull HU6 7RX.

Denny, Dr Neville Vivian Edward; Senior Lecturer, Drama Department, Bristol University, since 1969; *b* 1931; *m* 1956; three *s* two *d*. BA Hons Witwatersrand 1954, MA, Cape Town 1956, DipEd, PhD Bristol 1966. Lecturer in English: Univ. of Cape Town, 1955–60; Univ. of East Africa, 1960–65; Lectr. in Drama, Univ. of Bristol, 1965–69. *Publications*: Luther, 1971; Medieval Interludes, 1972; Medieval Drama, 1973; Cornish Miracle Cycle, 1974; *contrib*. New Theatre Mag., Medium Aevum, Rev. of English Studies. *Address*: Drama Dept, Univ. of Bristol, Bristol BS8 1TH.

Denton, Dr Jeffrey Howard; Lecturer in History, Department of History, University of Manchester, since 1965; *b* 1939; *m* 1964; two *d*. BA Hons Hull 1960, PhD Cantab 1966;

FRHistS. *Publications*: English Royal Free Chapels 1100–1300, 1970; *contrib*. Bull John Rylands Lib., Eng. Hist. Rev., Jl Eccl Hist. *Address*: Dept of History, Univ. of Manchester, Manchester M20 9PL.

Derrett, Prof. John Duncan Martin; Professor of Oriental Laws, University of London, since 1965; *b* 1922; *m* 1950; four *s* one *d*. BA Oxon 1945 (Classics and Hist.), MA Oxon 1947, PhD London 1949, DCL Oxon 1966, LLD London 1971; Barrister (Gray's Inn). Lectr in Hindu Law, Sch. of Oriental and African Studies, London, 1949–56; Reader in Oriental Laws, 1956–65; Vis. Prof., Univ. of Chicago, 1963; Ann Arbor, 1970. *Publications*: The Hoysaḷas, 1957; Hindu Law Past and Present, 1957; Introduction to Modern Hindu Law, 1963; ed, Studies in the Laws of Succession in Nigeria, 1965; Religion, Law and the State in India, 1968; ed, Introduction to Legal Systems, 1968; Law in the New Testament, 1970; Critique of Modern Hindu Law, 1970; Jesus's Audience, 1973; *contrib*. ICLQ, Zeits. vergl. Rechtsw., NTS, NT, ZNW, Man. *Address*: School of Oriental and African Studies, Univ. of London, Malet Street, WC1E 7HP.

Derrick, Thomas; Lecturer in Education, School of Education, University of Bradford, since 1967; *b* 1916; *m* 1942; one *s*. MEd Manchester 1961, Advanced DipEd 1957; ABPsS 1971. Res. Associate, School of Educn, Univ. of Manchester, 1964–67. *Publications*: *contrib*. Educational Res. *Address*: School of Education, Univ. of Bradford, Bradford BD7 1DP.

Derry, Dr John Wesley; Senior Lecturer Department of History, University of Newcastle upon Tyne, since 1973; *b* 1933. MA Cantab 1958, PhD Cantab 1961. Res. Fellow, Emmanuel Coll., Cambridge, 1959–61; Asst Lectr, LSE, 1961–63; Lectr, LSE, 1963–65; Fellow and Dir of Studies in History, Downing Coll., Cambridge, 1965–70; Lectr in History, Univ. of Newcastle upon Tyne, 1970–73. *Publications*: William Pitt, 1962; Reaction and Reform, 1963, 3rd edn 1970; The Regency Crisis and The Whigs 1788–9, 1963; Parliamentary Reform, 1966; The Radical Tradition, 1967; Political Parties, 1968; Cobbett's England, 1968; Charles James Fox, 1972; *contrib*. Reviews in Eng. Hist. Rev., Hist. Jl, History. *Address*: Dept of History, The Univ. Newcastle upon Tyne NE1 7RU.

Desai, Dr Meghnad; Lecturer, Department of Economics, London School of Economics, since 1973; *b* 1940; *m* 1970; two *d*. BA Bombay 1958, MA Bombay 1960, PhD Pennsylvania 1964; Mem.: Amer. Economic Assoc.; Indian Economic Assoc, Assoc. of Univ. Teachers in Econs; Econometric Soc. Dept of Agricultural Economies, Univ. of Calif., Berkeley, 1963–65. *Publications*: *contrib*. Economet., Econom., Internat. Econ. Rev., Jl Econ. Theory, Sankhya. *Address*: Dept of Economics, London School of Economics, Houghton Street WC2A 2AE.

de Ste Croix, Geoffrey Ernest Maurice; Fellow and Tutor in Ancient History, New

180

College, Oxford, and University Lecturer in Ancient History, since 1953; *b* 1910; *m* 1959; two *s*. BA London 1949 (1st cl. Hons History), MA Oxon 1953; FBA 1972. Asst Lectr in Ancient Economic History, LSE, 1950–53; Part-time Lectr in Ancient History, Birkbeck Coll., London, 1950–53; J. H. Gray Lectr in Classics, Cambridge, 1972–73. *Publications*: contrib.: Studies in the History of Accounting, 1956; The Crucible of Christianity, 1969; The Origins of the Peloponnesian War, 1972; Debits, Credits, Finance and Profits, 1973; Studies in Ancient Society, 1974; *contrib.* various learned jls. *Address*: New College, Oxford.

de Sausmarez, Jane Elizabeth; Lecturer (part-time), Printed Textiles, University of London, Goldsmiths' College, since 1961; *b* 1938; *m* 1963; one *d*. Dip. with Distinction, Central Sch. of Art and Design 1960; Reg. of Designers, Design Centre, Haymarket W1. Part-time Lectr, Hornsey Coll. of Art, 1960–61; Harrow Coll. of Art, 1961–63; Central Sch. of Art and Design, 1962–63. Col. Consult, Hull Stafford Ltd, 1960–62; Mem., Consultative Cttee, London Coll. of Fashion, 1971– . *Address*: School of Art, Univ. of London, Goldsmiths' College, Lewisham Way, SE14 6NW.

Desborough, Vincent Robin d'Arba, MA, FBA, FSA; Senior Research Fellow in Ancient History, New College, Oxford, since 1968; *b* 1914; *m* 1950; one *d*. BA Oxon 1936, BLitt Oxon 1940, MA Oxon 1949; FBA, FSA. Asst Lectr, then Lectr, then Sen. Lectr in Hist., Manchester Univ., 1948–67; Reader, 1967–68. Mem.: Brit. Council, 1946–47; Asst Dir, Brit. Sch. at Athens, 1947–48; Chm. Brit. Sch. at Athens, 1968–72; Mem., Hellenic and Roman Socs. *Publications*: Protogeometric Pottery, 1952; The Last Mycenaeans and their Successors, 1964; The Greek Dark Ages, 1972; *contrib.* Revised Cambridge Ancient Hist., 1962; *contrib.* Ann. Brit. Sch. Athens, Jl Hellenic Studies. *Address*: New College, Oxford.

De Silva, Dr M. W. Sugathapala; Reader, Department of Language, University of York, since 1968; *b* 1931; *m* 1959; one *s* two *d*. BA Ceylon 1954 (1st cl. Hons), MA London 1958 (Gen. Linguistics), PhD London 1965; Member: Linguistics Assoc. Gt Britain, Philol Soc. Gt Britain, Royal Asiatic Soc. Lectr in Sinhalese, Ceylon, 1958–64; (on secondment) Research Associate, Cornell Univ., 1961–62; Lectr in Language, York Univ., 1964–66, Sen. Lectr, 1966–68. Chm., Bd of Studies in Language, York, 1966–70; Secr, Univ. of Ceylon Linguistic Soc. and Editor of Soc.'s Jl, 1964. *Publications*: Spoken Sinhalese for the Beginner, 1963; A Graduated Hindi Course, 1965; Colloquial Sinhalese I and II, 1968; Colloquial Sinhalese Reader, 1971; Vedda Language of Ceylon, 1972; Papers in Linguistics (in Sinhalese), 1972; *contrib.* Internat. Jl Dravidian Linguistics, Jl Amer. Oriental Soc., Linguistics, Mod. Ceylon Studies, Trans Philol, Soc., Univ. Ceylon Rev., York Papers in Linguistics. *Address*: Dept of Language, Univ. of York, Heslington, York, YO1 5DD.

Dessaint, William Y.; Lecturer in Social Anthropology and Sociology, The New University of Ulster, since 1968; *b* 1930; *m* 1956; four *s*. BA Minnesota (1st cl. Anthropology), MA Cornell (Anthropology); Hon. Mem., Société des Études Confucéenes; Mem.: Assoc. Internationale des Sociologues, FRAI, Associate in Current Anthropology, etc. Res. Asst, SOAS, Univ. of London, 1961–63; Lectr, Univ. of Strathclyde, 1965–68. Res.: SOAS, LSE and Sorbonne; field-work in Japan, Yugoslavia, India, Thailand and Nepal. *Publications*: numerous articles. *Address*: The New Univ. of Ulster, Coleraine, Northern Ireland BT52 1SA.

Devine, David McDonald; Secretary and Registrar, University of St Andrews, since 1972; *b* 1920; *m* 1946; one *d*. MA Glasgow 1945, LLB London 1952. Univ. of St Andrews: Asst Sec., 1946; Dep. Sec, 1961. *Publications*: 11 crime novels, 1961–72. *Address*: Univ. of St Andrews, College Gate, St Andrews, Fife KY16 9AJ.

Devine, Dr T. M., BA, PhD; Lecturer, Dept of History, University of Strathclyde since 1969; *b* 1946; *m* 1970; two *d*. BA Hons 1968 (1st cl. Econ. Hist.), PhD 1972, Strathclyde. Asst Lectr, Strathclyde, 1968–69. *Publications*: contrib. Land and Industry, ed J. T. Ward and R. G. Wilson; *contrib.* Bus. Hist., Jl Econ. Hist., Scot. Hist. Rev., Transport Hist. *Address*: Dept of History, McCance Bldg, Univ. of Strathclyde, Glasgow G1 1XW.

Devletoglou, Prof. Nicos E., PhD; Lecturer in Economics, London School of Economics, since 1966; Professor of Economics, School of Law, University of Athens, since 1973; *b* 1936; *m* 1971. BA Mc Gill 1959 (1st cl. Hons Econ. and Pol Sci.), MA(Econ) Univ. of Calif, Berkeley, 1961; PhD London 1965; Grand Master of the Laws of Ecumenical Patriarchate, Constantinople, 1971. *Publications*: Montesquieu and the Wealth of Nations, 1965; (with J. Buchanan) Academia in Anarchy: an economic diagnosis, 1970; Consumer Behaviour, 1972; *contrib.* Economica, EJ, JPE, QJE, AER, Kyklos. *Address*: London School of Economics, Houghton Street, WC2A 2AE.

Dew, Prof. Ronald Beresford; Professor of Management Sciences, Department of Management Sciences, University of Manchester Institute of Science and Technology, since 1967; *b* 1919; *m* 1944; one *s* one *d*. LLB Manchester 1936, MA Cantab 1940; of the Middle Temple, Barrister at Law 1940; FCA 1945, Fellow, Inst. Works Mngrs, 1964, FBIM 1966, Council Mem.: Manchester Business Sch., 1966, Brit. Inst. Mngmt, 1971. Vis. Prof. of Indust. Admin, UMIST, 1961–63; Prof. of Indust. Admin, 1963–67. Asst Mngng Dir, P-E Consulting Gp, 1955–63; Co-Chm., Conf. of Univ. Mngmt Schs, 1971– . *Publication*: (with K. P. Gee) Management Control and Information, 1973. *Address*: Dept of Management Sciences, Univ. of Manchester Institute of Science and Technology, Sackville Street, Manchester M60 1QD.

Dewdney, John Christopher, MA; Reader in Geography, University of Durham, since

1971; b 1928; m 1956; three s. MA Edinburgh 1952; Mem., Inst. Brit. Geogrs, Geogl Assoc., Fellow, Royal Scott. Geogl Soc. Demonstr, Durham Univ., 1952–53; Lectr, Durham Univ., 1953–68; Prof., Univ. of Sierra Leone, 1965–67 (on secondment); Sen. Lectr, Durham Univ., 1968–71. *Publications*: (with W. B. Fisher and H. Bowen-Jones) Malta: Background for Development, 1961; A Geography of the USSR, 1965, 2nd edn 1971; Turkey, 1971; ed, Durham County and City with Teesside (Brit. Assoc. Survey), 1970; *contrib.* Trans Inst. Brit. Geogrs, Geog., Scott. Geog. Mag., Town Planning Rev. *Address*: Dept of Geography, Univ. of Durham, Durham DH1 3HP.

Dewhurst, Roland Frederick James; Senior Lecturer, Department of Industrial and Business Studies, University of Warwick, since 1969; b 1920; m 1951; two s one d. MA Oxon 1947; FCA 1971. Lectr, Sch. of Management, Cranfield 1968–69; Manager, MSc course, Univ. of Warwick, 1971–72. *Publications*: Mathematics for Accountants and Managers, 1968, 2nd edn 1974; Business Cost Benefit Analysis, 1972; *contrib.* Accountant. *Address*: School of Industrial and Business Studies, Univ. of Warwick, Coventry CV4 7AL.

Deyermond, Prof. Alan David; Professor of Spanish, Westfield College, University of London, since 1969; b 1932; m 1957; one d. BA Oxon 1953 (2nd cl. Mod. Langs), MA Oxon 1957, BLitt Oxon 1957. Asst Lectr, 1955–58, Lectr, 1958–66, Reader, 1966–69, Sen. Tutor, 1967–72, Dean of Faculty of Arts, 1972–74, Westfield Coll.; Vis. Prof., Univ. of Wisconsin, 1972. Pres., London Medieval Soc., 1970–74. Jt Editor: Critical Guides to Spanish Texts, 1969– ; Res. Bibliographies and Checklists, 1971– ; Mem., Editorial Cttee, Colección Támesis, 1963– ; Mem., Editorial Cttee, Romance Philology, 1971– . *Publications*: The Petrarchan Sources of La Celestina, 1961, 2nd edn 1974; Epic Poetry and the Clergy: studies on the Mocedades de Rodrigo, 1969; A Literary History of Spain, I: The Middle Ages, 1971, 2nd (Spanish) edn 1973; Apollonius of Tyre: two 15th-century Spanish prose romances, 1973; (with D. S. Brewer *et al.*) Medieval Comic Tales, 1973; ed, F. Lecoy: Recherches sur le Libro de Buen Amor, 2nd edn 1974; *contrib.* AEM, BHS, Filología, FMLS, Hispanófila, MLN, MLR, Neophilologus, PQ, RF, Romance Notes, Studies in Short Fiction. *Address*: Dept of Spanish, Westfield College, Hampstead, NW3 7ST.

Diamond, Prof. Aubrey Lionel, LLM; Law Commissioner; Visiting Professor of Law, Queen Mary College, University of London, since 1971; b 1923; m 1955; one s one d. LLB London 1950, LLM London 1956; Solicitor of the Supreme Court, 1951. Asst Lectr, 1957–59, Lectr, 1959–63, Reader, 1963–66, LSE, Univ. of London; Prof. of Law, Queen Mary Coll., 1966–71; Vis. Prof., Univ. of East Africa (at Faculty of Law, Univ. Coll., Dar-es-Salaam), 1966–67; Vis. Prof., Law Sch. of Stanford Univ., 1971. Mem., Consumer Council, 1963–66 and 1967–71; Mem., Cttee on Age of Majority (Latey Cttee),

1965–67. *Publications*: (with G. J. Borrie) The Consumer, Society and the Law, 1963, 3rd edn 1973; Introduction to Hire-Purchase Law, 1967, 2nd edn 1971; ed, Instalment Credit, 1970; co-ed., Sutton and Shannon on Contracts, 7th edn 1970; *contrib.* Int. and Comp. Law Qly, Mod. Law Rev. *Address*: Faculty of Laws, Queen Mary College, Mile End Road, E1 4NS.

Diamond, Derek R., MA, MSc; Reader in Regional Planning, London School of Economics, since 1968; b 1933; m 1957; one s one d. BA Oxon 1955 (Geography), MA 1957, MSc Northwestern Univ. (Illinois) 1957; FRGS Mem., Inst. Brit. Geogrs. Lectr in Geography, Glasgow, 1957–65; Lectr in Town and Regional Planning, Glasgow, 1965–68; Vis. Sen. Lectr, Hebrew Univ. of Jerusalem, 1967. Mngng Ed., Urban Studies, 1964–68; Mem., SSRC Planning Cttee, 1967–71; Ed., Town and Country Planning, 1972– ; Treas., Inst. Brit. Geogrs, 1972– . *Publications*: 3 chapters, in, Lothians Regional Survey and Plan, vol. 1, ed D. J. Robertson, 1966; 2 chapters, in, Grangemouth-Falkirk Regional Survey and Plan, vol. 1, ed D. J. Robertson, 1968; chapter in, New Towns: the British experience, ed H. Evans, 1972; *contrib.* Scott. Jl Polit. Econ., Adv. Sci., Town Ctry Planning, Built Environment. *Address*: London School of Economics, Houghton Street, Aldwych, WC2A 2AE.

Dias, Reginald Walter Michael; University Lecturer, Law Faculty, University of Cambridge, since 1951, Fellow of Magdalene College, University of Cambridge, since 1955; b 1921; m 1947; two d. BA Hons Cantab 1942, LLB Cantab 1943, MA Cantab 1945; Barrister at Law (Inner Temple) 1945. Sen. Lectr, Univ. Coll. of Wales, Aberystwyth, 1949–51. Visiting Lectr, Univ. of Uppsala and Stockholm, 1972. Mem.: Council of Senate, Cambridge, 1971; Gen. Bd of Faculties, Cambridge, 1971. *Publications*: Jurisprudence, 1957, 3rd edn 1970; A Bibliography of Jurisprudence, 1964, 2nd edn 1970; ed, Wise and Winfield: Outlines of Jurisprudence, 6th edn 1948; ed, Clerk and Lindsell: On Torts, 12th edn 1961, 13th edn 1969; *contrib.* Roman Law of Sale, ed D. Daube, 1959; Enc. Brit., 1965– ; Dictionary of the History of Ideas, 1973; *contrib.* Acta Juridica, Ann. of Nat. Law Study, Camb. Law Jl, Camb. Rev., Ceylon Law Students' Rev., Duquesne Law Rev., Jl Soc. Public Teachers of Law, Law Qly Rev., Mod. Law Rev., Rechtstheorie, Ritsumeikan Law Rev., Tulane Law Rev., Univ. Toronto Law Jl. *Address*: Magdalene College, Cambridge.

Dick, Cecilia Rachel; Lecturer in Modern History, University of Oxford, since 1957; b 1927; m 1951 (marr. diss.); one s two d. BA Oxon 1949, MA Oxon 1951. Lectr, Lady Margaret Hall, Oxford, 1951–57; Domestic Bursar, Wolfson College, Oxford, 1966– . *Address*: Wolfson College, Oxford.

Dicken, Rev. Dr Eric William Trueman, MA, DD; Warden of Lenton Hall and Senior Lecturer in Christian Theology, University of Nottingham, since 1965; b 1919; m 1940; one s two d. BA Oxon 1946 (Mod. Langs, 1st cl. Theology 1948), MA Oxon 1946, BD 1964, DD 1964; Ordained Deacon, Cuddesdon Coll. (C of E), 1949, Ordained Priest, 1950. Priest-in-Charge, St John's Church, Hucknall, Notts, 1949–54; Vicar of Caunton and Maplebeck, Notts, 1954–65. *Publications*: Living with God, 1957; The Crucible of Love, 1963; Not This Way, 1968; Loving on Principle, 1969; trans. G. von Rad: The Problem of the Hexateuch and other Essays, 1966; *contrib*. Ephemerides Carmeliticae, Revista de Espiritualidad. *Address*: The Warden's House, Lenton Hall, Univ. of Nottingham.

Dickens, Prof. Arthur Geoffrey, DLit, FBA; Director of the Institute of Historical Research, and Professor of History, University of London, since 1967; *m* 1936; two *s*. BA Oxon 1932 (1st cl. History), MA Oxon 1936, DLit London 1965; FBA, FSA, FRHistS. Fellow, Keble Coll., Oxford, 1933–49; Prof. of Hist., Univ. of Hull, 1949–62; Pro-Vice-Chancellor, Univ. of Hull, 1959–62; Prof. of Hist. and Hd of Dept of Hist. at King's Coll., Univ. of London, 1962–67; Hon. Fellow, Keble Coll., Oxford, 1971– . Pres., Eccles. Hist. Soc., 1966–68; Mem.: Adv. Council on Public Records, 1968– ; Adv. Council on Export of Works of Art, 1968– ; Chm. and Gen. Sec., Brit. Nat. Cttee of Hist. Sciences, 1967– ; Foreign Sec., Brit. Acad., 1969– ; Vice-Pres., Brit. Acad., 1970–71. *Publications*: Lübeck Diary, 1947; The Register of Butley Priory, 1951; The East Riding of Yorkshire, 1954; Lollards and Protestants, 1959; Thomas Cromwell, 1959; Tudor Treatises, 1960; Clifford Letters, 1962; The English Reformation, 1964, and 5 later edns; Reformation and Society in 16th Century Europe, 1966 and French, Dutch, Portuguese edns; Martin Luther and the Reformation, 1967; The Counter Reformation, 1968 (French, Dutch and Portuguese edns); Europe in the Age of Humanism and Reformation, 1972; The German Nation and Martin Luther, 1974; *contrib*. numerous contrib. to jls (about 50). *Address*: Institute of Historical Research, Univ. of London, Senate House, WC1E 7HU.

Dickenson, Aubrey Fiennes T.; *see* Trotman-Dickenson.

Dickins, David William; Lecturer, Psychology Department, University of Liverpool, since 1964; *b* 1936; *m*; two *s*. BSc London 1956 (Special Zoology), Post Grad. CertEd London 1957, BSc London 1961 (1st cl. Special Psychology); Mem.: Brain Res. Assoc., Assoc. Study Animal Behav. Res. Asst, Dept of Pharmacology, Univ. Coll., London, 1961–64. Study leave, Dept of Psychology, Univ. of W Australia, 1974–75. *Publications*: *contrib*. Brit. Jl Pharmacol., Bull. Brit. Psych. Soc. *Address*: Dept of Psychology, Univ. of Liverpool, PO Box 147, Liverpool L69 3BX.

Dickie, Dr James; Lecturer in Religious Studies, University of Lancaster, since 1969; *b* 1934. MA Glasgow 1959, LenL Barcelona 1966, PhD Granada 1967. Univ. Manchester, 1967–69. *Publications*: Dīwān Ibn Shuhaid al-Andalust, 1969, trans. Spanish, as El dīwān de Ibn Suhayd, 1974; The Grecian Urn: an archaeological approach, 1969, 2nd edn 1973; The Undead, 1971, 2nd edn 1973; *contrib*. And., BJRL, BSOAS, IQ, Iqbal Rev., IR, MEAH, Oriental Art (NS), Encyc. Brit. (new edn). *Address*: Dept of Religious Studies, Univ. of Lancaster, Bailrigg, Lancaster LA1 4YW.

Dickinson, Alaric Keith, BA; Lecturer in Education, University of London, since 1966; *b* 1940; *m* 1967; one *d*. BA Wales 1962 (1st cl. History). *Address*: Dept of History, Univ. of London Institute of Education, Malet Street, WC1E 7HS.

Dickinson, Gordon Cawood, MA, MRTPI; Lecturer, Department of Geography, University of Leeds, since 1956; *b* 1927; *m* 1953; two *s* one *d*. BA Cantab 1948, MA Cantab 1953, DipTP Leeds 1954; MRTPI. Asst Lectr, Dept of Geography, Leeds Univ., 1953–56. *Publications*: Statistical Mapping. The Presentation of Statistics, 1963, 2nd edn 1972; Maps and Air Photographs, 1969; *contrib*. Jl Transp. Hist., Town Planning Rev. *Address*: Dept of Geography, The Univ., Leeds LS2 9JT.

Dickinson, Dr Harry Thomas, BA, DipEd, MA, PhD; Reader in History, Edinburgh University, since 1973; *b* 1939; *m* 1961; one *s* one *d*. BA Durham 1960, DipEd Durham 1961, MA Durham 1963, PhD Newcastle 1968. Earl Grey Fellow, Newcastle Univ., 1964–66; Fulbright Scholar, 1973; Huntington Library Fellowship, 1973; Folger Shakespeare Library Sen. Fellowship, 1973. *Publications*: ed, The Correspondence of Sir James Clavering 1708–1740, 1967; Bolingbroke, 1970; Walpole and the Whig Supremacy, 1973; ed, Politics and Literature in the 18th Century, 1974; *contrib*. Bull. Inst. Hist. Res., EHR, Durham Univ. Jl, Hist. Today, Hunt. Libr. Qly, Jl Army Hist. Res., Jl Brit. Studies, Mariners' Mirror, etc. *Address*: History Dept, Edinburgh Univ., Edinburgh EH8 9YL.

Dickinson, Ian Scott; Lecturer, Law School, University of Strathclyde, since 1966; *b* 1935; *m* 1967; one *s* one *d*. MA 1955, LLB 1958, Glasgow; Solicitor; Mem. Law Soc. of Scotland, 1958– . Univ. Repr., Council of Scottish Univs Law Inst., 1970– . *Publications*: *contrib*. Juridical Rev., Scots Law Times. *Address*: Law Sch., Stenhouse Bldg, 173 Cathedral Street, Glasgow.

Dickinson, Dr John Philip; Lecturer, Department of Accounting and Finance, University of Lancaster, since 1971; *b* 1945; *m* 1968; one *d*. MSc Leeds 1968, MA Cantab 1971, PhD Leeds, 1972; FSS 1968, AFIMA 1972. Lectr in Management Studies, Assoc. Lectr in Operational Res., Univ. Leeds, 1968–71, Hon. Lectr in Management Studies, 1971– ; Vice-Chm., Dept of Accounting and Finance, Lancaster, 1971–73. *Publications*: ed and contrib., Risk and Uncertainty in Accounting and Finance, 1974; ed and contrib., Portfolio Analysis, 1974; *contrib*. The Accountant, Accounting and Business Res., Jl Accounting Res., Jl Business, Jl Financial and Quantitative Analysis, Metrika, Operational Res. Qly, Statistician.

Address: Univ. of Lancaster, Bailrigg, Lancaster LA1 4YW.

Dickinson, Prof. Peter; Professor of Music, University of Keele, since 1974; *b* 1934; *m* 1964; two *s*. MA Cantab 1959; LRAM 1953, ARCM 1953, FRCO 1955. Birmingham Univ., 1966–1974. *Publications*: Printed Music: The Judas Tree (musical drama), 1965; Fanfares and Elegies (organ and brass), 1967; Martin of Tours (cantata), 1966; The Dry Heart (chorus), 1967; Outcry (cantata), 1968; Two Motets: Mark, John, 1963; Three Statements (organ), 1964; Paraphrase I (organ), 1967; Paraphrase II (piano), 1967; and many other musical works ranging from orchestra to song cycles; *contrib*. Composer, Music Rev., Musical Times, Music and Musicians, Music in Educn. *Address*: Music Dept, Keele Univ., Keele, Staffs ST5 5BG.

Dicks, Anthony Richard, MA, LLB; Lecturer in Oriental Laws, Department of Law, School of Oriental and African Studies, University of London, since 1970; *b* 1936; *m* 1969. BA Cantab 1959, LLB Cantab 1960 (1st cl.), MA Cantab 1963; Barrister-at-Law (Inner Temple), 1961; admitted to the Bar of Hong Kong, 1965, and of Brunei, 1971; Mem., Brit. Inst. of Internat. and Comparative Law; Royal Inst. of Internat. Affairs; Amer. Soc. Internat. Law. Teaching Fellow, Univ. of Chicago Law Sch., 1960–61; Sub-Lector in Law, Trinity Coll., Cambridge, 1962–64; Fellow of Trinity Hall, Cambridge, and Univ. Asst Lectr, 1968–70. Res. Fellow in Chinese Law, Inst. of Current World Affairs and Brit. Inst. of Internat. and Comparative Law, 1962–68. Mem., Univs China Cttee, 1971. *Address*: Dept of Law, School of Oriental and African Studies, Univ. of London, WC1E 7HP.

Dicks, Dr David Reginald; Lecturer, Department of Greek, Bedford College, University of London, since 1964; *b* 1923; *m* 1951; two *d*. BA London 1947 (Hons Classics), PhD London 1953. Lectr in Classics, Univ. Coll. of the West Indies, 1954–61; Prof. of Classics, Univ. of Ghana, 1961–63; Dir, Inst. of Classical Studies, 1963–64 (part-time); Vis. Prof., Princeton Univ., 1966; Mem., Inst. for Adv. Study, Princeton, 1967. *Publications*: The Geographical Fragments of Hipparchus, 1960; Early Greek Astronomy to Aristotle, 1970; *contrib*. Classical Qly, Classical Rev., Hermes, Jl of Hellenic Studies, Jl of Brit. Astronomical Assoc. *Address*: Dept of Greek, Bedford College, Regent's Park, NW1 4NS.

Dicks, Thomas Richard Brian; Senior Lecturer, Department of Geography, University of Strathclyde, Glasgow, since 1972; *b* 1938. BSc Wales 1960, PhD Wales 1964; FSAScot, Mem., Inst. Brit. Geogrs. Jun. Res. Fellow, Sheffield, 1964–65; Lecturer, 1965–72. *Publications*: The Greeks, 1972; *contrib*. Tidjschrift Econ. Social Geog., Nat. Libr. Wales Jl, Town Planning Rev., Area, Geogl Mag. *Address*: Dept of Geography, Univ. of Strathclyde, Glasgow G1 1XW.

Dickson, Douglas Ernest Norman, MA,

MSc, PhD; Senior Lecturer in Marketing, University of Strathclyde, since 1972 (Lecturer, 1964–72); *b* 1933; *m* 1966; one *d*. MA Glasgow 1958, 1964 (2nd cl. Economics and Economic History), MSc Strathclyde 1968 (Marketing); Assoc. Inst. Bankers Scotl., Internat. Mktg Inst., Harvard Business Sch., 1966; Salzburg Sem. Fellow, 1966; Vis. Lectr in Mktg, BIM Summer Sch., Oxford Univ., 1971–72. Ch. Examiner, Scott. Council Comm. Admin. Prof. Educn, 1965–71; Vice-Dean, Sch. Business Admin, 1972, Mem. Bd, 1969–72, Chm., Academic Policy Cttee. Consultant, Scott. Decorator Fedn, 1968–72; Consultant, SELNEC Passenger Transport Exec. *Publications*: *contrib*. Director, Mngmt Pract., Mktg, Mktg Wld, Scott. Agric., Industrial Advtg and Mktg. *Address*: Dept of Marketing, Univ. of Strathclyde, Glasgow G1 1XW.

Dickson, Keith Andrew, MA; Lecturer in German, University of Exeter, since 1962; *b* 1934; *m* 1966. BA Oxon 1955 (1st cl. Mod. Lang.), MA Oxon 1960, DipEd Oxon 1956 (with Dist.). Lay Preacher, Methodist Conf., 1961. *Publications*: ed, Kleist: Amphitryon, 1967; Brecht: Lehrstücke, 1968; Ludwig: Zwischen Himmel und Erde, 1971; Brecht: Kalendesgeschichten, 1971; *contrib*. Forum Mod. Lang. Studies, Germ. Rev., Greece and Rome, Rev. Mod. Langs, Mod. Drama, Mod. Lang. Rev., New German Studies, Brecht Ybk. *Address*: Queen's Building, The Univ., Exeter EX4 4QJ.

Dietz, Brian, BA, PhD; Lecturer in Modern History, University of Glasgow, since 1961; *b* 1933. BA London 1954 (1st cl. History), PhD London 1958. *Publications*: The Port and Trade of early Elizabethan London: Documents (London Record Society), 1972. *Address*: Dept of Modern History, Univ. of Glasgow, Glasgow G12 8QQ.

Dietz, John Edward Michael, ARIBA, DipTP; Director of the Evening School of Architecture, University of Newcastle upon Tyne, since 1966; *b* 1929. Dip. TP, Dunelm 1954; ARIBA 1958. *Publications*: Buildings for Music: The Concert Hall (forthcoming). *Address*: School of Architecture, Univ. of Newcastle upon Tyne, Newcastle upon Tyne NE1 7RU.

Diffey, Dr Terence John, PhD; Lecturer in Philosophy, School of English and American Studies, University of Sussex, since 1965; *b* 1938; *m* 1962. BA Bristol 1960 (2nd cl. Philosophy and English Literature), PhD Bristol 1966; Mem., Mind Assoc., Brit. Soc. Aesth., Amer. Soc. Aesth. Tutorial Fellow, Univ. of Sussex, 1962–63; Asst Lectr, 1963–65. Sub-Dean, Sch. Engl. Amer. Studies, 1969–72. Mem., Exec. Cttee, Brit. Soc. Aesth.. 1970– . *Publications*: *contrib*. Brit. Jl Aesth. *Address*: Arts Building, Univ. of Sussex, Falmer, Brighton, Sussex BN1 9QN.

Di Fidio, Dr Ottavio; Junior Lecturer in Italian Literature, University College, Galway, since 1968; *b* 1930. Degree in Lingue e Letterature Straniere Rome 1958, Abilitazione Rome 1959, Idoneità Rome 1966. Asst Volont., Univ. of Rome, 1964; Asst in Italian Lang. and Lit., Univ. Coll., Galway, 1966–68.

Publications: trans. in Italian: A. C. Bradley: Shakespearean Tragedy, 1964; T. S. Eliot: Hamlet, 1965; T. S. Eliot: Shakespeare and the Stoicism of Seneca, 1965; W. Hazlitt: Cymbeline, 1965; *contrib*. Parallelo 38. *Address*: Dept of Romance Languages, Univ. College, Galway, Eire.

Digby, Simon Everard; Assistant Keeper, Department of Eastern Art, Ashmolean Museum, Oxford, and Research Fellow, Wolfson College, since 1969; *b* 1932. BA Hons 1954, MA 1960, Cantab, MA Oxon 1973; FRAS 1960. Hon. Librarian, RAS of GB and Ireland, 1970– . *Publications*: War-horse and Elephant in the Delhi Sultanate: a study of military supplies, 1973; *contrib*. Aarp, Bull. Amer. Acad. of Benares, Bull. Prince of Wales Mus. of W India, Bull. SOAS, Indian Econ. and Social Hist. Rev., Iran, Jl RAS. *Address*: Wolfson Coll., Oxford.

Diggle, Dr James, MA; Fellow and Director of Studies in Classics, Queen's College, Cambridge, since 1966, and University Assistant Lecturer in Classics, since 1970; *b* 1944. BA Cambridge 1965, MA and PhD Cambridge 1969. Libr., Queens' Coll., Cambridge, 1969– ; Prael., Queens' Coll., 1971–73; Ed., Proc. Camb. Philol. Soc., 1970– . *Publications*: ed (with F. R. D. Goodyear), Flavii Cresconii Corippi Iohannidos Libri VIII, 1970; The Phaethon of Euripides, 1970; ed (with F. R. D. Goodyear), The Classical Papers of A. E. Housman, 1972; *contrib*. Class. Qly, Class. Rev., Proc. Camb. Philol. Soc., Rheinisches Museum, Latomus, Bull. Inst. Class. Studies, London, Gk Rom. Byz. Studies. *Address*: Queens' College, Cambridge.

Dilke, Prof. Oswald Ashton Wentworth, MA, DLitt et Phil; Professor of Latin, University of Leeds, since 1967; *b* 1915; *m* 1949; one *s*. BA Cantab 1938 (1st cl. Classics), MA Cantab 1945, DLitt et Phil Univ. of S Africa 1963. Lectr, Univ. Coll., Hull, 1946–50; Lectr, then Sen. Lectr, Glasgow Univ., 1950–67; Prof. of Class., Rhodes Univ., 1961–62; Vis. Prof., Ohio State Univ., 1969; Sir D. Owen Evans Meml Lectr, Aberystwyth, 1974–75. Lieut and Capt., Intell. Corps, 1941–44. Mem., Council, Class. Assoc., 1955–58; Council, Hellenic Soc., 1955–58; Council, Glasgow Archaeol. Soc., 1958-60, 1963–67 (Hon. Treas., 1966-67); Pres., Grahamstown Reg., Class. Assoc. S Africa, 1961–62; Mem., Ed. Cttee, Acta Class., 1964– . *Publications*: (with E. Mercanti) La Scuola nel Mondo: 5 Inghilterra, 1949; ed, Statius: Achilleid, 1954; ed, Horace: Epistles I, 1954, 3rd edn 1966; Lucan VII, rev. edn of J. P. Postgate, 1960; The Roman Land Surveyors, 1971; trans., The Battle of Pharsalia (Lucan VII), 1971; The Ancient Romans: how they lived and worked, 1974; *contrib*. Acta Class., Ann. Brit. Sch. Athens, Class. Qly, Class. Rev., Geogl Jl, Geogl Mag., Gnomon, Greece and Rome, Imago Mundi, Latomus, New Knowl., Studies in Latin. *Address*: Dept of Latin, The Univ., Leeds LS2 9JT.

Dilks, Prof. David Neville; Professor of International History, University of Leeds,

since 1969; *b* 1938; *m* 1963. BA Oxon 1959. Asst Lectr in Internat. Hist., LSE, 1962–65, Lectr LSE, 1965–69. Res. Asst to Rt Hon. Earl of Avon, 1960–62, to Marshal of the RAF Lord Tedder 1963–65, to Rt Hon. Harold Macmillan, 1964–67. Chm., Commonwealth Youth Exchange Council, 1968– . *Publications*: Sir Winston Churchill, 1964; Curzon in India, vol. I, 1969, vol. II, 1970; ed, The Diaries of Sir Alexander Cadogan, 1971. *Address*: School of History, The Univ., Leeds LS2 9JT.

Dilman, Dr Ilham; Reader, Department of Philosophy, University College of Swansea, since 1973; *b* 1930; *m* 1960. BA Cantab 1953, PhD Cantab 1958. Asst Lectr, subseq. Lectr in Philos., UC Swansea, 1961-67; Vis. Asst Prof., Univ. Calif. Los Angeles, 1965; Associate Prof., Univ. of Calif., Santa Barbara, 1967–68; Vis. Associate Prof., Univ. Oregon, 1968; Lectr, subseq. Sen. Lectr, Univ. Hull, 1968–71; Lectr, UC Swansea, 1971–73. *Publications*: (with D. Z. Phillips) Sense and Delusion, 1971; Induction and Deduction, A Study in Wittgenstein, 1973; Paradoxes and Discoveries, in Wisdom, Twelve Essays, ed, Bambrough, 1974; Wittgenstein on the Soul, in, Understanding Wittgenstein, ed G. Vesey, 1974; *contrib*. Analysis, Aristotelian Soc. Proc. Arist. Soc. Suppl. Vol., Human World, Mind, Monist, Philosophy, Philosophical Books, Ratio, Religious Studies, Review of Metaphysics. *Address*: Dept of Philosophy, Univ. Coll. of Swansea, Singleton Park, Swansea SA2 8PP.

Dimbleby, Prof. Geoffrey William, BSc, MA, DPhil; Professor of Human Environment, Institute of Archaeology, University of London, since 1964; *b* 1917; *m* 1945; four *d*. BA Oxon 1939, BSc Oxon 1941, MA Oxon 1943, DPhil Oxon 1951; FRSA; Mem., Brit. Ecol. Soc., Brit. Soc. Soil Science, Prehist. Soc. (Sometime Council Mem., all three). Demonst. in Forestry, Oxford, 1945–47; Univ. Lectr in Forestry, Oxford, 1947–64. RAFVR, 1941–45; Mem., Council, Conserv. Soc., 1969–72. *Publications*: The Development of British Heathlands and their Soils, 1962; Plants and Archaeology, 1967; ed (with P. J. Ucko), The Domestication and Exploitation of Plants and Animals, 1969; ed (with P. J. Ucko and R. Tringham), Man, Settlement and Urbanism, 1972; *contrib*. Jl Soil Sci., Proc. Prehist. Soc. *Address*: Institute of Archaeology, 31-34 Gordon Square, WC1H 0PY.

Dimond, Dr Stuart John; Senior Lecturer in Psychology, University College Cardiff, since 1973 (Lecturer, 1966–73); *b* 1938; *m* 1968; one *d*. BSc Bristol 1960, MA TCD 1966, PhD Bristol 1963. Lectr, TCD, 1963–66. Mem., Council, ASAB, 1967–69; NATO Studies visit, USA and Canada, 1971; Royal Soc. visit to Czechoslovak Acad. of Science, 1973. *Publications*: Social Behaviour of Animals, 1970; The Double Brain, 1972; ed (with J. G. Beaumont), Hemisphere Functions of the Human Brain, 1973; *contrib*. Qly Jl Exper. Psychol. *Address*: Dept of Psychology, Univ. College Cardiff, Cardiff CF1 1XL.

Dingley, James; Senior Lecturer in Russian Studies, Department of German, University of Reading, since 1966; *b* 1942; *m* 1967. BA Cantab 1963, MA Cantab 1966. Editor, Jl of Byelorussian Studies. *Publications*: *contrib.* Jl Byelorussian Studies, *Address*: Dept of German, Univ. of Reading, Whiteknights, Reading, Berks RG6 2AH.

Dinour, David; Reader in Economics and Dean of the School of Social Sciences, New University of Ulster, since 1967; *b* 1915; *m* 1951; one *s* one *d*. DipEcon (with Hons) Tel Aviv 1940, DPA London 1947, DScSoc (with distinction) Hebrew Univ. Jerusalem 1958; Mem., Royal Econ Soc., Amer. Econ. Assoc. Sen. Asst Dir, Econ. Res. Dept, Govt of Israel, 1949–51; Dir Div. Econ. Stats, CBS Israel, 1941–58; UN expert, Ghana and Congo, 1958–62; Dir, UN Stat. Training Centre for Engl. spkg countries of W Africa, Univ. of Ghana, 1962–66. UNCTAD consultant, 1966–67. *Publications*: Four-Year Development Plan of Israel, 1951; Structure of Israel's Industry, 1956; Industrial Statistics in Israel, in, Industry Book, 1957–58; Budgetary Problems in Ghana, 1959; contrib. Fiscal and Monetary Policies in Relation to the Seven Year Development Plan of Ghana; *contrib.* Econ. Bull. Ghana, UNCTAD Studies. *Address*: Economics Dept, New Univ. of Ulster, Coleraine, Co. Londonderry, Northern Ireland BT52 1SA.

Dinwiddy, Dr John Rowland; Lecturer, History Department, Royal Holloway College, University of London, since 1969; *b* 1939; *m* 1962; two *d*. BA Oxford 1960, MA Oxford 1965, PhD London 1971. Asst Lectr, Makerere Univ. Coll., Univ. of E Africa, 1963–64, Lectr, 1964–67; Res. Fellow, Inst. Hist. Res. Univ. of London, 1967–68. *Publications*: Christopher Wyvill and Reform 1790–1820, 1971; *contrib.* Bull. Inst. Hist. Res., Hist. Jl, Hist., Nineteenth Cent. Fiction, Jl. Hist. of Ideas, Notes and Queries, Past and Present, Studies in Burke and His Time, Victorian Newsletter. *Address*: Royal Holloway College, Egham, Surrey TW20 0EX.

Diverres, Prof. Armel Hugh, Officier des Palmes Académiques; Carnegie Professor of French, University of Aberdeen, since 1958; *b* 1914; *m* 1945; one *s* two *d*. BA Wales 1936 (1st cl. French), MA Wales 1938, LèsL Rennes 1938, D de l'Univ. Paris 1950; Vice-Pres., Brit. Brch, Int. Arthurian Soc. Asst Lectr, Manchester Univ., 1946–49, Lectr, 1949–54; Sen. Lectr, Aberdeen Univ., 1954–57; Prof. d'Etudes Bourguignonnes, Louvain Univ., 1964. Royal Artil., 1940–42; Intell. Corps, 1942–46 (Capt.); Dean, Fac. of Arts, Aberdeen Univ., 1967–70; Mem., Brit. Council Cttee for Scotland, 1965– ; CNAA Langs Cttee, 1965– ; Gov., Aberdeen Coll. Educn, 1971– ; Mem., Court, Aberdeen Univ., 1971– . *Publications*: ed, Froissart: Voyage en Béarn, 1953; ed. La Chronique métrique attribuée à Geffroy de Paris, 1956; ed, Vigny: Chatterton, 1967; *contrib.* Forum Mod. Lang. Studies, Jl Nat. Lib. Wales, Nouv. Rev. Bret., Rev. Litt. Comp. *Address*: Dept of French, Taylor Building, King's College, Old Aberdeen.

Dix, Prof. Gerald Bennett; Professor of Planning, and Director, Institute of Planning Studies, University of Nottingham, since 1970; *b* 1926; *m* 1956; 1963; two *s* one *d*. BA (Arch.) Manchester 1950, DipTCP Manchester 1951 (Distinction); Master in Landscape Arch. Harvard 1954; ARIBA 1950, FRTPI (AMTPI 1957, MTPI 1959), FRSA 1972. Studio Asst in Arch., Manchester Univ., 1950–51; Asst Lectr in Town and Country Planning Manchester, 1951–53; Sen. Res. Fellow, Univ. of Science and Tech., Kumasi, Ghana, 1959–63; Lectr in Planning, Nottingham Univ., 1966–68, Sen. Lectr, 1968–70. Chief Architect Planner (with Sir Patrick Abercrombie), Addis Ababa, 1954–56; Actg Planning Adviser, Singapore, 1959; with UN Planning Mission, Ghana, 1962; Overseas Div. Building Res. Station, Min. of Overseas Develt, 1963–65; reported on planning in Ethiopia, Ghana, Cyprus etc. to Govts. Mem. Libr Bd RIBA, 1969– ; Reports on planning education to Makerere Univ., 1971, Ahmadu Bello Univ., 1972. Member: RIBA Library Bd, 1969–72; Professional Literature Cttee, 1966– ; Edit. Adv. Bd, Ekistics, 1974– . *Publications*: Planning reports; *contrib.* Ekistics, Jl of RIBA, Jl of RTPI, TP Rev. *Address*: Institute of Planning Studies, Univ. of Nottingham, Nottingham NG7 2RD.

Dixon, Keith Frederick, MA; Lecturer, Department of Sociology, University of York, since 1969; *b* 1932; *m* 1954; three *d*. BA London 1960, MA London 1964, Dip Ed Leeds 1962; Mem., Mind Assoc., Aristotelian Soc., Phil. of Educn Soc. of GB. Lectr, Strathclyde Univ., 1965–68. *Publications*: ed, Philosophy of Education and the Curriculum, 1972; Sociological Theory: Pretence and Possibility, 1972; *contrib.* Brit. Jl of Educnl Studies. *Address*: Dept of Sociology, Univ. of York, Heslington, York YO1 5DD.

Dixon, Dr N. F., MBE, FBPS; Reader in Psychology, Psychology Department, University College, London, since 1953; *b* 1922; *m*; two *s* three *d*. BA Reading 1953, PhD Reading 1955; DSc London 1972. *Publications*: Subliminal Perception: the Nature of a Controversy, 1971; *contrib.* Acta Psychol., Brit. Jl Psychol., Jl Abn. Social Psychol., Qly Jl Exper. Psychol. *Address*: Dept of Psychology, Univ. College, Gower Street, WC1E 6BT

Dixon, Prof. Victor Frederick, MA, PhD; Professor of Spanish, Trinity College Dublin, since 1974; *b* 1932; *m* 1963; one *s* one *d*. BA Cantab 1954 (1st cl. Mod. Lang.), MA Cantab 1960, PhD Cantab 1960. Asst, Univ. of St Andrews, 1957–58, Lectr, 1958–60; Lectr, 1960–73, Sen. Lectr, 1973–74, Univ. of Manchester. Vis. Associate Prof., Adelphi Univ., NY, 1964–65. *Publications*: ed, Lope de Vega; El sufrimiento premiado, 1967; *contrib.* BHS, FMLS, MLN, HR, Hispanófila. *Address*: Dept. of Spanish, Trinity College, Dublin.

Dobb, Dr Maurice Herbert; Emeritus Reader in Economics, University of Cambridge; Fellow of Trinity College, Cambridge, since 1948; *b* 1900; *m* 1932. MA Cantab 1926, PhD London 1925; Hon. DEconSc

Charles Univ. Prague 1964, Hon. DLitt Leicester 1972; FBA, FREconS; Vis. Lectr, Russian Econ. Studies, Sch. of Slavonic Studies, Univ. London, 1943–46; Vis. Prof. Delhi Sch. of Econs, Univ. of Delhi, 1951. *Publications*: Capitalist Enterprise and Social Progress, 1925; Russian Economic Development since the Revolution, 1928; Political Economy and Capitalism, 1937; Studies in the Development of Capitalism, 1946, 8th edn 1963; Development of Soviet Economy since 1917, 1948, 6th edn 1966; An Essay on Economic Growth and Planning, 1960, 3rd edn 1964; Welfare Economics and the Economics of Socialism, 1969; Theories of Value and Distribution since Adam Smith: Ideology and Economic Theory, 1973; *contrib*. Econ. Jl, Economica, Soviet Studies, etc. *Address*: Trinity College, Cambridge.

Dobbins, Dr Frank; Lecturer, Department of Music, Goldsmiths' College, University of London, since 1973; *b* 1943; *m* 1969. BA Oxon 1965, MA and DPhil Oxon 1971. Lectr, KCL, 1969–73. *Publications*: *contrib*. Early Music, Jl American Musicol Soc., Music and Letters, Proc. Royal Musical Assoc., Musical Times. *Address*: Goldsmiths' College, Univ. of London, Lewisham Way, New Cross, SE14 6NW.

Dobson, Dr Brian; Staff Tutor in Extra-Mural Studies (Archaeology), University of Durham, since 1960; *b* 1931; *m* 1958; two *s* three *d*. BA Dunelm 1952 (1st cl. Mod. Hist.), PhD Dunelm 1955 (Archaeology), FSA 1972. Res. Fellow, Birmingham Univ., 1957–59. *Publications*: ed (with M. G. Jarrett), Britain and Rome, 1966; ed, A. von Domaszewski: Die Rangordnung des römischen Heeres, 1967. *Address*: Extra-Mural Dept, 32 Old Elvet, Durham.

Dobson, Prof. Eric John, MA, DPhil, FBA; Professor of English Language, Oxford University, since 1964; *b* 1913; *m* 1940; two *s* one *d*. BA Sydney 1934 (1st cl. English), BA Oxon 1937 (1st cl. English), MA Oxon 1941, DPhil Oxon 1951. Tutor, Sydney Univ., 1934–35; Asst Lectr, then Lectr, Reading Univ., 1940–48; Lectr, St Edmund Hall and Jesus Coll., Oxford, 1948–54; Reader in Eng. Lang., Oxford Univ., 1954–64 (title of Prof., 1960–64); Professorial Fellow, Jesus Coll., Oxford, 1954– . Intell. Div., Naval Staff, 1942–45; Studentship Cttee, DES, 1969–72. *Publications*: English Pronunciation 1500–1700, 1957, 2nd edn 1968; The Phonetic Writings of Robert Robinson, 1957; The Affiliations of the Manuscripts of Ancrene Wisse, in, English and Medieval Studies presented to J. R. R. Tolkien, 1962; The English Text of the Ancrene Riwle (B.M. Cotton MS. Cleopatra C. vi), 1972; *contrib*. Med. Aev., Notes and Queries, Proc. Brit. Acad. (Gollancz Memorial Lecture, 1966), RES, Trans Hon. Soc. Cymmrodorion, Trans Phil. Soc. *Address*: Jesus College, Oxford.

Dobson, Dr Richard Barrie; Reader in History, University of York, since 1971 (Senior Lecturer, 1966–71); *b* 1931; *m* 1959; one *s* one *d*. BA Oxon 1954, MA Oxon 1958, DPhil Oxon 1961; FRHistS. Sen. Demy, Magdalen Coll., Oxford, 1956; Jun. Lectr,

Magdalen Coll., Oxford, 1957–58; Lectr in Med. Hist., St Andrews, 1958–64; Chm., York Hist. Dept, 1970–71. Mem., Brit. Film Inst., Reg. Film Theatres Cttees, 1968– ; York Archaeol. Cttee, 1972. *Publications*: Selby Abbey and Town, 1970; ed, The Peasants' Revolt of 1381, 1971; (with M. J. Angold) The World of the Middle Ages, 1971; Durham Priory, 1400–1450, 1973; The Jews of Medieval York, 1974; *contrib*. Econ. Hist. Rev., Scott. Hist. Rev., Yorkshire Archeol. Jl, Studies in Ch. Hist., Northern Hist. *Address*: Dept of History, Univ. of York, Heslington, York YO1 5DD.

Dockrill, Dr Michael Lawrence; Lecturer, Department of War Studies, King's College, University of London, since 1970; *b* 1936. BScEcon London 1961, MA Illinois 1963, PhD London 1969; Member: Internat. Inst. of Strategic Studies; RIIA. Lecturer: University Coll., Wales, Aberystwyth, 1966–67; Portsmouth Polytechnic, 1967–70. *Publications*: (with C. J. Lowe) The Mirage of Power: British Foreign Policy 1902–1922 (3 vols), 1972; *contrib*. Lloyd George, Twelve Essays, ed A. J. P. Taylor, 1971. *Address*: Dept of War Studies, Univ. of London, King's College, Strand, WC2R 2LS.

Dodd, Raymond Henry; Senior Lecturer, Department of Music, Aberdeen University, since 1970; *b* 1929; *m* 1962; one *s* one *d*. MA, B Mus Oxon; ARAM. Lectr, Aberdeen Univ., 1956–70; Vis. Associate Prof., Wilson Coll., Chambersburg, Pa, 1972–73. *Publications*: Prelude, Air and Scherzo for clarinet and piano, 1960; ed. Schott Viola Album, 1966. *Address*: Dept of Music, Powis Gate, College Bounds, Old Aberdeen.

Dodgson, John McNeal, MA; Lecturer, Department of English, University College London, since 1957; *b* 1928; *m* 1953; one *s* one *d*. BA London 1952 (2nd cl. English), MA London 1957, Dip in Archive Admin London 1954; Asst Lectr, English Dept, Univ. Coll., London, 1953–57. Founder Mem., Crabtree Foundation, 1954– , Orator, 1973; Hon. Dir, Engl. Name-Studies, Univ. Coll. London; Asst Hon. Sec., Engl. Place-Name Soc., 1953–61, Hon. Sec., 1967– ; Sometime Mem., Council, Viking Soc. for North. Res. and Soc. Mediev. Archaeol.; Ed. Cttee, Brit. Rec. Assoc., 1970–73; Council, BRA, 1972; Founder-Mem., Council for Name-Studies in GB and Ireland, 1958– ; Mem., Int. Cttee Onomastic Sciences, 1969– ; Hon. Sec., 9th Internat. Cong. Onomastic Sciences, London, 1966; Jt Hon. Sec., Hugh Smith Meml, 1970– ; Ed., Jl Engl. Place Name Soc., 1969– . *Publications*: co-comp., Proceedings of IX ICOS 1966; Place-Names of Cheshire pt 1 1970, pt 2 1970, pt 3 1971, pt 4 1972 (EPNS vols 44–47), pt 5 (EPNS vol 48) (forthcoming); *contrib*. Beitr. für Namen., Mediev. Archaeol., Saga-Bk Viking Soc., Museums Journal, The Library, Dinnsean-chas, Early English and Norse Studies, Anglo-Saxon England, etc. *Address*: Dept of English, Univ. College London, Gower Street, WC1E 6BT.

Dodsworth, James Martin, MA; Lecturer in English, Royal Holloway College,

University of London, since 1967; *b* 1935; *m* 1967; one *s*. BA Oxon 1956 (English), MA Oxon 1961. Asst Lectr, then Lectr, Birkbeck Coll., London, 1961–67; Vis. Lectr, Svvarthmore Coll., 1966. Mem., Edit. Bd Rev., 1965–71. *Publications*: The Survival of Poetry: A Contemporary Survey, 1970; *contrib*. Essays in Crit., Rev. *Address*: Dept of English, Royal Holloway College, Egham Hill, Egham, Surrey TW20 0EX.

Dodwell, Barbara, MA, FRHistS; Reader, Department of History, University of Reading, since 1962; *b* 1912. BA London 1934 (2nd cl. history), MA London 1936 (with mark of Distinction); FRHistS. Asst Lectr, Univ. Coll. of SW Exeter, 1941–45; Lectr, 1945–46; Lectr, Reading Univ., 1946–62. Mem., Council, Pipe Roll Soc., 1962– ; Jt Gen. Ed., Pipe Roll Soc., 1971– . *Publications*: Feet of Fines for the County of Norfolk, 1198–1202 (PRS NS 27), 1952; Feet of Fines for the County of Norfolk, 1201–1215, for the County of Suffolk, 1199–1214 (PRS NS 32), 1958; *contrib*. Econ. Hist. Rev., EHR, Norfolk Archeol., Trans Royal Hist. Soc. *Address*: Dept of History, Faculty of Letters, Univ. of Reading, Whiteknights, Reading RG6 2AH.

Dodwell, Prof. Charles Reginald, MA, PhD, LittD, FBA, FRHistS, FSA; Pilkington Professor of History of Art and Director of Whitworth Art Gallery, University of Manchester, since 1966; *b* 1922; *m* 1942; one *s* one *d*. BA Cantab 1947, MA Cantab 1949, PhD Cantab 1950, LittD Cantab 1972; FRHistS, FSA. Res. Fellow, Gonville and Caius Coll., Cambridge, 1950–53; Sen. Res. Fellow, Warburg Inst., 1950–53, Lambeth Libr., 1953–58; Fellow, Lectr and Libr., Trinity Coll., Cambridge, 1958–66; Vis. Sch., Princeton Inst. Advanced Studies, 1965–66. Syndic Cambridge Univ. Lib., 1964–66; Mem., Manchester City Cultural Cttee; ICOM (British Section); Feoffee of Chetham's Hosp. *Publications*: The Canterbury School of Illumination, 1954; Lambeth Palace, 1958; The Great Lambeth Bible, 1959; (jtly) The St Alban's Psalter, 1960; Theophilus; de diversis artibus, 1961; Reichenau Reconsidered, 1965; Painting in Europe: 800–1200, 1971; *contrib*. Burlington Mag., Cahiers de Civilisation Médiévale, Gazette des Beaux Arts, Settimane di Studi Sull'Alto Medioevo. *Address*: Univ. of Manchester, Manchester M13 9PL.

Doe, Prof. Paul Maurice, MA; Professor of Music, University of Exeter, since 1971; *b* 1931; *m* 1957; two *s* two *d*. BA Oxon 1952 (1st cl. Music), MA Oxon 1956. Asst, Aberdeen Univ., 1956–59; Lectr, Birmingham Univ., 1959–71. Mem., Brit. Acad. Cttee, Early Engl. Ch Mus., 1970– , Gen. Editor 1972– ; Exec. Cttee, Grove's Dict. of Mus. (6th edn), 1970– ; Gov., Dartington Coll. Arts, 1971– ; Dolmetsch Foundn, 1971– . *Publications*: ed, Early Tudor Magnificats, 1964; Tallis (Oxford Studies of Composers, 4), 1968; *contrib*. Mus. and Lett., Proc. Roy. Mus. Assoc. *Address*: Dept of Music, Univ. of Exeter, Exeter EX4 4PD.

Doherty, Francis Michael Joseph; Senior Lecturer, Department of English Language and Literature, University of Keele, since 1968; *b* 1932; *m* 1959; four *s* three *d*. BA Sheffield 1959 (1st cl. English), MA Manchester 1962. Temp. Lectr, UC North Staffs, 1961–62; Asst, UC Dublin, 1962–63; Lectr, Univ. of Keele, 1963–68. *Publications*: Byron, 1968; Samuel Beckett, 1971; *contrib*. Essays in Criticism, Philological Qly, Neophilologus. *Address*: Dept of English Language and Literature, Univ. of Keele, Staffs ST5 5BG.

Dolamore, Charles Edward James; Lecturer, Department of French Language and Literature, University of Leeds, since 1967; *b* 1942; *m* 1968. BA Wales 1965. *Publications*: *contrib*. Forum for Mod. Lang. Studies, Sud. *Address*: Dept of French, Univ. of Leeds, Leeds LS2 9JT.

Dolley, Michael, MRIA; Reader, Department of Modern History, Queen's University of Belfast, since 1969; *b* 1925; *m* 1950; two *s* four *d*. BA London 1947 (2nd cl. Anc. and Med. Hist.); MRIA, FSA, FRHistS; For. Corresp. Mem., Royal Swedish Acad. Lett., Hist. Antiqu. Lectr in Mediaeval Hist., Queen's Univ. of Belfast, 1963–69. Asst Keeper: Nat. Marit. Mus., 1948–51; Brit. Mus., 1951–63; Jt Ed., Sylloge of Coins of the Brit. Isles, 1959– ; Jt Ed., Brit. Numis. Jl, 1965– ; Mem., Sylloge Cttee, Brit. Acad., 1959– ; Council Mem., Royal Irish Acad., 1970– , Senior Vice-President, 1972, etc. *Publications*: ed, Anglo-Saxon Coins, 1961; Anglo-Saxon Pennies, 1964; Viking Coins of the Danelaw and of Dublin, 1965; The Hiberno-Norse Coins in the British Museum, 1966; The Norman Conquest and the English Coinage, 1966; (with K. F. Morrison) The Carolingian Coins in the British Museum, 1966; (with W. A. Seaby) Ango-Irish Coins in the Ulster Museum – John – Edward III, 1968; (with C. E. Blunt and others) Anglo-Saxon and Norman Coins in the Reading University Collection; Anglo-Norman Pennies in the Royal Coin Cabinet Stockholm, 1969; (with I. D. Brown), Coin Hoards of Great Britain and Ireland 1500–1967, 1971; Medieval Anglo-Irish Coins, 1972; (with C. E. Blunt and L. V. Grinsell) Ancient British Coins and Coins of the Bristol and Gloucestershire Mints in the Bristol and Gloucester Museums; Anglo-Norman Ireland, 1973, etc.; *contrib*. Antikv. Arkiv, Brit. Numis. Jl, Jl Roy. Soc. Antiqu. Ireland, Nord. Numis. Arssk., Num. Chron., Proc. Roy. Irish Acad., etc. *Address*: Dept of Modern History, The Queen's Univ., Belfast BT7 1NN.

Donald, Sydney Greig; Lecturer in German Language and Literature, University of Leeds, since 1967; *b* 1943 *m* 1965; three *d*. MA St Andrews 1965. Lektor, Englisches Seminar, Universität Erlangen–Nürnberg, 1965–67; Asst Lectr, Univ. Leeds, 1967–70. Warden, Bodington Hall, 1970– . *Address*: Dept of German, Univ. of Leeds, Leeds LS2 9JT.

Donaldson, Alexander, MA, LLB; Lecturer in International Private Law, University of Glasgow, since 1949; *b* 1911; *m* 1941; two *s*. MA Glasgow 1932, LLB Glasgow 1934. Solicitor. *Address*: Dept of International

Private Law, Faculty of Law, Univ. of Glasgow, Glasgow G12 8QQ.

Donaldson, Prof. Gordon, MA, PhD, DLitt; Professor of Scottish History and Palaeography, University of Edinburgh, since 1963; *b* 1913. MA Edinburgh 1935 (1st cl. Hist.), PhD London 1938, DLitt Edinburgh 1954; FRHistS, FSAScot. Lectr, Edinburgh Univ., 1947–55; Reader, 1955–63. Mem., Royal Commn Anct Monum. Scotland; Anct Monum. Bd Scotland; Jt Editor, Scottish Historical Review. *Publications*: St Andrews Formulare, 1942–44; Protocol Book of James Young, 1950; Accounts of Collectors of Thirds, 1950; Source Book of Scottish History, 1952–54, 2nd edn 1959; The Making of the Scottish Prayer Book, 1954; Court Book of Shetland, 1955; Register of the Privy Seal of Scotland, vols v–vii, 1957–66; Shetland Life under Earl Patrick, 1958; Scotland: Church and Nation, 1960, 2nd edn 1972; The Scottish Reformation, 1960; Scotland – James V to James VII, 1965; The Scots Overseas, 1966; Northwards by Sea, 1966; Scottish Kings, 1967; Memoirs of Sir James Melville, 1969; The First Trial of Mary, Queen of Scots, 1969; Scottish Historical Documents, 1970; *contrib.* EHR, Proc. Soc. Antiqu. Scotl., Scott. Hist. Rev., Trans Roy. Hist. Soc. *Address*: William Robertson Building, George Square, Edinburgh.

Donaldson, Prof. William Anderson; Professor of Operational Research, University of Strathclyde, since 1971; *b* 1927; *m* 1965; one *s* one *d*. MA Glasgow 1946 (Hons), BA Cantab 1950 (Hons), DipMatStat Cantab 1951; Fellow Brit. Computer Soc. 1968, FRStatSoc 1952. Mem., Operat. Res. Soc. Asst Lectr (Maths), Glasgow, 1946–48; Lectr (Maths), Glasgow, 1951–55; Sen. Lectr (OR), Strathclyde, 1962–69; Reader (OR), 1969–71. *Publications*: (jtly) Operational Research Techniques, vol. 1, 1969; *contrib.* Operat. Res. *Address*: Dept of Operational Research, Univ. of Strathclyde, Glasgow G1 1XW.

Donchin, Dr Georgette; Reader in Russian Literature, School of Slavonic and East European Studies, University of London, since 1970; *b* 1922; *m* 1950; one *s*. BA Hons London 1949, PhD London 1953. Asst Lectr, SSEES, London Univ., 1960–63; Lectr, 1963–70. Jt Editor, Slavonic and East European Review. *Publications*: The Influence of French Symbolism on Russian Poetry, 1958; *contrib.* Revue de Littérature Comparée, Slavonic and E European Rev. Year's Work in Mod. Lang. Studies. *Address*: School of Slavonic and East European Studies, Univ. of London, Senate House, WC1E 7HU.

Donelan, Michael Denis; Senior Lecturer in International Relations, London School of Economics and Political Science, since 1971; *b* 1932; *m* 1966; three *d*. BA Oxon 1955 (1st cl. Mod. Hist.), MA Oxon 1964. Lectr, LSE, 1964–71. *Publications*: The Ideas of American Foreign Policy, 1963; (with F. S. Northedge) International Disputes, The Political Aspects, 1971; (with M. J. Grieve) International Disputes, Case Histories, 1945–70, 1973; *contrib.* Internat. Aff., Internat. Relat. *Address*: International Relations Dept, London School of Economics and Political Science, Houghton Street, WC2A 2AE.

Donnachie, Ian; Staff Tutor in History, The Open University, since 1970; *b* 1944; *m* 1969. MA Hons Glasgow 1966, MLitt Strathclyde 1969; FSAScot. 1965. Res. Asst, Univ. of Strathclyde, 1967–68; Part-time WEA and Univ. Extra-Mural Lectr, 1966– . Mem., Open Univ. bds and cttees, 1970– ; (incl. Res. Bd, Cttee on Publishing Policy). Asst Editor, Industrial Archaeology, 1968– . *Publications*: Industrial History: Scotland, 1968; The Industrial Archaeology of Galloway, 1971; War and Economic Growth in Britain 1793–1815, 1973; Old Galloway: essays in social and economic history, 1974. Transport: roads and canals, 1974; corresp. units for Open Univ. courses on War and Society and Great Britain 1750–1950; *contrib.* Explorns in Econ. Hist., Proc. Soc. Antiquaries of Scot., Ind. Archaeol. Tspt Hist., Trans Dumfries and Galloway Soc., Jl Scot. Georgian Soc., etc. *Address*: The Open Univ., 60 Melville Street, Edinburgh EH3 7HF.

Donnison, Prof. David Vernon; Director, Centre for Environmental Studies, University of London, since 1969; *b* 1926; *m* 1950; two *s* two *d*. BA Oxon. Asst Lectr, then Lectr, Manchester Univ., 1950–53; Lectr, Toronto Univ., 1953–55; Reader, 1956–61, Prof. of Social Admin, 1961–69, LSE; Vis. Prof. of Environmental Studies UCL. Chm., Public Schs Commn, 1968–70. *Publications*: The Neglected Child and the Social Services, 1954; Welfare Services in a Canadian Community, 1958; Housing since the Rent Act, 1961; Social Policy and Administration, 1965; The Government of Housing, 1967. *Address*: Centre for Environmental Studies, 5 Cambridge Terrace, Regent's Park, NW1 4JL.

Donoughue, Dr Bernard; Senior Lecturer in Politics, London School of Economics, since 1968; Senior Policy Adviser to the Prime Minister, since 1974; *b* 1934; *m* 1959; two *s* two *d*. MA, DPhil 1962 Oxon; FRHistS 1973 Lectr, LSE, 1963–68. Mem., Ct of Governors, LSE, 1968– ; Mem., UK Nat. Sports Council, 1965–71. *Publications*: Trade Unions in a Changing Society, 1963; British Politics and the American Revolution, 1964; (with C. W. Jones) Herbert Morrison: Portrait of a Politician, 1973. *Address*: London Sch. of Economics, Houghton Street, WC2A 2AE.

Donoghue, Prof. Denis; Professor of Modern English and American Literature, Department of English, University College, Dublin, since 1965; *b* 1928; *m* 1951; three *s* five *d*. BA Univ. Coll. Dublin 1949, MA Univ. Coll. Dublin 1952, PhD Univ. Coll. Dublin 1957, MA Cantab 1965; Mem., Internat. Cttee, Assoc. Univ. Profs English. Asst Lectr, Univ. Coll., Dublin, 1954–57, Coll. Lectr, 1957–62; Vis. Scholar, Univ. of Pennsylvania, 1962–63; Coll. Lectr, Univ. Coll., Dublin, 1963–64; Univ. Lectr, Cambridge Univ., 1964–65; Fellow, King's Coll., Cambridge, 1964–65. Admin. Off., Dept of Finance, Irish Civil Service, 1951–54. *Publications*: The Third Voice, 1959; Connoisseurs of Chaos, 1965;

189

co-ed., An Honoured Guest, 1965; The Ordinary Universe, 1967; Emily Dickinson, 1968; Jonathan Swift, 1969; ed, Swift, 1970; Yeats, 1971; Thieves of Fire; *contrib.* Hudson Rev., Kenyon Rev., Nineteenth Cent. Fiction, Sewanee Rev., Times Lit. Supp. *Address*: Dept of English, Univ. College, Dublin 4.

Doody, Dr Margaret Anne; Lecturer, English Department, University College of Swansea, since 1969; *b* 1939. BA Dalhousie 1960, BA Oxon 1962 (1st cl. Hons English), DPhil Oxon 1968. Instructor in English, Univ. Victoria, BC, 1962–64, Asst Prof. 1968–69. *Publications*: A Natural Passion: a study of the novels of Samuel Richardson, 1974; *contrib.* Anglo-Welsh Review. *Address*: English Dept. Univ. College of Swansea, Singleton Park, Swansea SA2 8PP.

Doornkamp, Dr John Charles, MSc, PhD, FGS; Senior Lecturer, Department of Geography, University of Nottingham, since 1973 (Lecturer, 1966–73); *b* 1938; *m* 1964; two *d*. BSc Sheffield 1959, MSc Sheffield 1962, PhD Nottingham 1966; FGS 1970. Jun. Res. Fellow, Sheffield, 1961–62; Asst Lectr, Makerere Univ. Coll., Uganda, 1962–64; Asst. Lectr, Nottingham Univ., 1964–66. Mem., Ct of Govs, Univ. of Sheffield, 1968–' ; Hon. Sec., Brit. Geomorphol. Res. Gp, 1968–71. *Publications*: Geomorphology of the Mbarara Area, 1970; ed (with R. H. Osborne and F. A. Barnes), Geographical Essays in Honour of K. C. Edwards, 1970; (with C. A. M. King) Numerical Analysis in Geomorphology, 1971; (with D. Krinsley) Atlas of Quartz Sand Surface Textures, 1973; Plausible Reasoning in Geomorphology, 1972; ed (with J. A. Dawson), Evaluating the Human Environment: essays in Applied Geography, 1973; (with R. U. Cooke) Geomorphology in Resource Management: an introduction, 1974; ed (with D. Brunsden), The Unquiet Landscape, 1974; *contrib.* Geogl Jl, Trans Inst. Brit. Geogrs, Geog., Sedimentol., E Afr. Geogl Rev., Geografiska Annaler, Zeitschrift für Geomorphology. *Address*: Dept of Geography, The Univ., Nottingham NG7 2RD.

Dorsch, Prof. Theodor Siegfried, MA; Professor of English Literature, Univ. of Durham, since 1968; *b* 1911; *m* 1937; one *s* one *d*. BA Adelaide 1933 (1st cl. Classics), BA Oxon 1936 (1st cl. English Lang. and Lit.), MA Oxon, 1947. Lectr, Westfield Coll., Univ. of London, 1947–61; Sen. Lectr, 1961–67; Reader, 1967–68. Mem., Exec. Cttee, Engl. Assoc., 1955– ; Chm., Publications Cttee, 1961–68; Gov., Phillippa Fawcett Coll., 1964–68; Prested Hall Spastics Home, 1964–68; Van Mildert Coll., 1968–69; Trustee, Wordsworth-Rydal Mt Trust, 1970– , Chm., 1972– ; Mem., Council, Durham Univ., 1970– ; DES Studentship Selection Cttee, 1973– . *Publications*: ed, Shakespeare: Julius Caesar (Arden edn), 1955; co-ed., The Year's Work in English Studies, 1958–66, ed, 1966–68; trans., W. Clemen: English Tragedy before Shakespeare, 1961; Classical Literary Criticism: Aristotle, Horace, Longinus, 1965; ed, English Short Stories of Today, 3rd Series, 1965; ed, Byron: Don Juan, Cantos I–IV, 1967; ed, Essays and Studies, 1972;

Shakespeare, in New Cambridge Bibliography of English Lit.,1974; *contrib.* Ess. and Studies, Boston Univ. Studies in Engl., Archiv. *Address*: Dept of English, Univ. of Durham, Durham DH1 3HP.

Dosser, Prof. Douglas G. M.; Professor of Economic Theory, University of York, since 1965; *b* 1927; *m* 1954; three *d*. BSc(Econ) London 1954 (1st cl. Economics). Lectr in Economics, Sheffield, 1954; Lectr in Economics, Edinburgh, 1958; Vis. Prof., Seattle, Washington, 1960; Vis. Prof., Columbia Univ., 1962; Reader in Economics, York, 1963–65. Res. and consultancy appointments: EEC, OECD, Brookings Inst., Chatham House, PEP, OAS. *Publications*: National Income of Tanganyika, 1958; Economic Analysis of Tax Harmonisation, in, Fiscal Harmonisation in Common Markets, 1967; Non-Tariff Barriers to Atlantic Economic Integration, in, Studies in Trade Liberalisation, 1967; Taxes in the EEC and Britain: The Problem of Harmonisation, 1968; The Tax System of Liberia, 1971; A Theory of Integration for Developing Countries, 1971; Taxation in The Economics of Europe, 1971; *contrib.* Economica, Econ. Jl, Kyklos, Manchester Sch., Public Finance, Rev. Econs and Stats, Rev. Econ. Studies, Scot. Jl of Political Economy. *Address*: Dept of Economics, University of York, York YO1 5DD.

Dougherty, Dr Christopher Robert Sykes; Lecturer, Department of Economics, London School of Economics, since 1973; *b* 1943. BA Cantab 1965, MA Cantab 1969, MA Harvard 1968, PhD Harvard 1972. Junior Research Fellow, King's College, Cambridge, 1968. *Publications*: *contrib.* Econ. Jl, Jl Polit. Economy, Qly Jl Econs. *Address*: London School of Economics, Houghton Street, Aldwych, WC2A 2AE.

Douglas, Prof. Alan Edward; Professor of Latin, University of Birmingham, since 1974; *b* 1922; *m* 1945; one *s*. BA and MA Oxon 1947 (1st cl. Lit. Hum.); Mem., Class. Assoc., JACT, Hellenic Soc., Roman Soc. Asst Lectr, Univ. Coll., Southampton, 1947–49; Lectr, 1949–63, Sen. Lectr, 1963–73, Reader, 1973–74. *Publications*: M. Tulli Ciceronis Brutus, 1966; *contrib.* Amer. Jl Phil. Class. Qly, Class. Rev., Eranos, Greece and Rome, Latomus, Mnemos. *Address*: Dept of Latin, Univ. of Birmingham, Birmingham B15 2TT.

Douglas, Dr James William Bruce; Director, Medical Research Council Unit on Environmental Factors in Mental and Physical Illness, London School of Economics, University of London, since 1962; Hon. Lecturer, London School of Economics, since 1962; *b* 1914; *m* 1967; three *s* one *d*. BA Oxon 1935 (Nat. Science), BSc Oxon 1936, BM, BCh Oxon 1939; Mem., many learned socs. Sen. Lectr in Social Medicine, Univ. of Edinburgh, 1954, Reader in Social Medicine, 1958–62. Mem. many cttees. *Publications*: (jtly) Maternity in Great Britain, 1948; (jtly) Children Under Four, 1958; The Home and the School, 1964; (jtly) All Our Future, 1968; *contrib.* 70 papers in med., sociolog. and other learned jls. *Address*: 20 Hanway Place, W1P 0AJ.

190

Douglas, Prof. Mary; Professor of Social Anthropology, Anthropology Department, University College, London, since 1970; *b* 1921; *m* 1951; two *s* one *d*. MA Oxon 1945, BSc Oxon 1947, PhD Oxon 1951; FRAI. Univ. Lectr in Social Anthropology, Oxford, 1949–51; Lectr, London, 1951–63, Reader, 1963–70. *Publications*: The Lele of the Kasai, 1963; Purity and Danger, 1966; Natural Symbols, 1970; *contrib*. Jl Royal Anthrop. Inst., Afr., Man, New Soc., Daedalus, Brit. Jl Sociol., Jl Psychosom. Res. *Address*: Dept of Anthropology, Univ. College London, Gower Street, WC1E 6BT.

Douglas, Dr Roy Ian, BSc, PhD, AKC, Barrister-at-Law; Lecturer, School of Humanities and Social Sciences, University of Surrey, since 1967; *b* 1924; *m* 1955; three *s* one *d*. BSc London 1946 (2nd cl. Zoology), AKC 1946, PhD Edinburgh 1952; Barrister-at-Law 1956. Demonst. in Biology, St Thomas's Hosp. Med. Sch., 1946–48; Asst in Zoology, Univ. of Edinburgh, 1949–51. *Publications*: Law for Technologists, 1964; History of the Liberal Party 1895–1970, 1971; *contrib*. Bull. Inst. Hist. Res., EHR, Hist. Jl, Jl Mod. Hist. *Address*: Dept of Humanities and Social Sciences, Univ. of Surrey, Guildford, Surrey GU2 5XH.

Douglas Jones, Prof. Aldwyn, OBE, RWA, MA, FRIBA; Professor of Architecture, University of Bristol, since 1963; *b* 1910; *m* 1933; two *s*. DipArch Liverpool 1933 (distinction), MA Bristol 1963; FRIBA 1948. Vis. Prof., Cornell, 1961 and Ahmadu Bello, 1962; Staff Mem., Architectural Assoc. 1936–40; Head, Manchester Sch. of Architecture Coll. of Art, 1940–47; Head, Birmingham Sch. of Architecture, 1947–63. Past Chm., RIBA, Schs Cttee and Prizes Cttee; Past Vice-Chm., Bd of Arch. Educn; Past Member: RIBA Vis. Bd; Architects Registration Council Bd of Arch. Educn; RIBA Gold Medal and Bronze Medal Juries; Civic Trust Award Panels; SW Regional Council; Past Pres., Bristol and Somerset Soc. of Architects. *Publications*: ed, Colston Papers: Communication and Energy in Changing Urban Environments, 1968; *contrib*. Architect and Building News, Listener, RIBA Jl. *Address*: Dept of Architecture, Univ. of Bristol, 25 Great George Street, Bristol BS1 5RA.

Dovell, Prof. Peter; Professor of Urban Design, University of Manchester, since 1968; *b* 1923; *m* 1949; one *s* one *d*. BArch Liverpool 1946 (1st. cl. Hons), MCD Liverpool 1953, MA Manchester 1972; RIBA 1952, MRTPI 1954, AMTPIC 1956, MRAIC 1958. Sen. Lectr, Birmingham Sch. of Architecture, 1962–65; Head, Birmingham Sch. of Planning and Landscape, Univ. of Aston, 1965–68. W Australia State Govt, 1953–55. Head of Projects Div., City of Toronto Planning Bd, Ontario, 1955–57; Ontario Regional Architect and Planner, CMHC, 1957–62; Mem., Council and Educn Cttee RTPI, 1970–73. *Publications*: Cork: An Environmental Study, 1971; *contrib*. Plan for Metropolitan Region, Perth and Fremantle, 1955; Redevelopment study of Halifax, Nova Scotia, 1957; professional press. *Address*: Univ. of Manchester, Manchester M13 9PL.

Dover, Prof. Kenneth James, MA, FBA; Professor, Department of Greek, St Andrews University, since 1955; *b* 1920; *m* 1947; one *s* one *d*. BA and MA Oxford 1946 (1st cl. Lit. Hum.); FBA 1966. Fellow and Tutor, Balliol Coll., Oxford, 1948–55; Vis. Lectr, Harvard Univ., 1960; Sather Vis. Prof., Univ. of California, 1967; Co-editor, Class. Qly, 1962–68; Pres., Soc. Prom. Hellenic Studies, 1971–74. *Publications*: Greek Word Order, 1960, 2nd edn 1968; ed, Thucydides: Book VI, 1965; ed, Thucydides: Book VII, 1965; ed, Aristophanes: Clouds, 1968; Lysias and the Corpus Lysiacum; (with A. Andrewes and A. W. Gomme), Historical Commentary on Thucydides, vol. IV, 1970; ed, Theocritus: Select Poems, 1971; Aristophanic Comedy, 1972. *contrib*. Amer. Jl Philol., Class. Qly, Class. Rev., Gnomon, Jl Hellenic Studies, Maia, Quad. Urb. *Address*: Dept of Greek, Univ. of St Andrews, St Andrews, Fife KY16 9AJ.

Dowdeswell, Prof. Wilfrid Hogarth; Professor, School of Education, Bath University, since 1972; *b* 1914; *m* 1940; one *s* two *d*. BA Oxford 1937 (2nd class Hons Zoology), MA 1951; FIBiol, FRES; Mem. Genetical Soc. Sen. Lectr, Sch. of Educn, Bath Univ. 1969–72. Organiser: Nuffield O-Level Biology Project; (with Dr P. J. Kelly), Nuffield A-level Biology Proj.; Inter-Univ. Biology Teaching Proj. *Publications*: Introduction to Animal Ecology, 1952, 3rd edn 1967 (Sinhalese, Swed., Span. and Amer. edns); Practical Animal Ecology, 1959, 3rd edn 1967 (Swed. edn); The Mechanism of Evolution, 1955, 5th edn (Amer. and Jap. edns); *contrib*. Proc. Roy. Soc., Heredity, J. Exp. Biol., J. Biol. Ed., Jl Ecol. *Address*: School of Education, Bath Univ., Northgate House, Upper Borough Walls, Bath BA1 5AL.

Dower, Nigel; Lecturer in Logic and Moral Philosophy, University of Aberdeen, since 1969; *b* 1942; *m* 1972; one *s*. MA Hons Oxford 1964 (2nd cl. Literae Humaniores), MA Leeds 1967. Assistant Lecturer, Univ. of Aberdeen, 1967–69. *Publication*: *contrib*. APQ. *Address*: Depts of Logic and Moral Philosophy, King's College, Aberdeen.

Downer, Prof. Gordon Boyd, BA; Professor of Chinese Studies, University of Leeds, since 1970; *b* 1926; *m* 1948; one *s* one *d*. BA London 1950 (1st cl. Chinese). Asst Lectr in Cantonese, SOAS, London, 1950; Lectr in Cantonese, 1951–58; Lectr in Chinese, 1958–70. *Publications*: *contrib*. Bull. SOAS, Asia Maj. *Address*: Dept of Chinese Studies, Univ. of Leeds, Leeds LS2 9JT.

Downes, Dr (John) Kerry, FSA, Reader, Department of Fine Art, Reading University, since 1971; *b* 1930; *m* 1962. BA 1951, PhD 1960 London; FRSA. Librarian and Hon. Lectr in Fine Arts, Barber Inst. of Fine Arts, Univ. of Birmingham, 1958–66; Lectr in Fine Art, Univ. of Reading, 1966–71; Vis. Lectr, Yale Univ., 1968. *Publications*: Hawksmoor, 1959; English Baroque Architecture, 1966; Hawksmoor, 1969; Christopher Wren, 1971; Vanbrugh, 1974; *contrib*. Arch. Hist., Burlington Mag. *Address*: Dept of

Fine Art, Univ. of Reading, London Road, Reading RG1 5AQ.

Downey, Meriel Elaine; Principal Lecturer and Head of Secondary Education and BEd Courses, Education Department, University of London, Goldsmiths' College, since 1962; *b* 1931; *m* 1966. BA London 1952 (1st cl. German), BA London 1961 (1st cl. Psychology); Grad. Mem., BPS. *Address:* Goldsmiths' College, New Cross, SE14 6NW.

Downie, Prof. Robert Silcock; Professor of Moral Philosophy, Glasgow University, since 1969; *b* 1933; *m* 1958; three *d.* MA Glasgow 1955 (1st cl. Hons Philosophy and English Lit.); BPhil Oxon 1959. Lectr in Moral Philosophy, Glasgow Univ., 1959; Vis. Prof. of Philosophy, Syracuse Univ., NY, USA, 1963–64; Sen. Lectr in Moral Philosophy, Glasgow Univ., 1968–69; Ext. Examiner, Edinburgh, Belfast. Chm., CCETSW Cttee on Values in Social Work. Russian linguist, Intelligence Corps, 1955–57. *Publications:* Government Action and Morality, 1964; (jtly) Respect for Persons, 1969; Roles and Values, 1971; (jtly) Education and Personal Relationships, 1974; *contrib.* Mind, Philosophy, Analysis, Aristotelian Soc., Philosophical Quarterly. *Address:* 7 The Univ., Glasgow.

Downing, M. F.; Lecturer in Landscape Design, University of Newcastle upon Tyne, since 1965; *b* 1934; *m* 1963; one *s* one *d.* DipLandArch Reading 1957, Advanced Dip-LandArch Reading 1958; MSc Newcastle 1972 (Lands. Des.); Assoc. Inst. Landsc. Architects 1967. Planning Asst, Essex CC, 1958–60; Landsc. Asst, Basildon Develt Corp., 1960–62; Chief Landsc. Architect, Newcastle Corp., 1962–65. *Publications:* (with others), Landscape Reclamation, vol. I, 1971, vol. 2, 1972; *contrib.* Jl Inst. Landsc. Archts, Jl Parks and Rec., Planning Outlk, Qly Jl Forest., Spectrum (Brit. Sci. News), Landscape Architecture (USA). *Address:* Dept of Town and Country Planning, Univ. of Newcastle upon Tyne, Newcastle upon Tyne NE1 7RU.

Dowrick, Prof. Frank Ernest, MA, Barrister-at-Law; Professor of Law, since 1966, and Dean of Faculty of Law, University of Durham, 1970–72; Head of Department of Law, 1964–72; *b* 1921; *m* 1948; three *s.* BA Oxon 1947 (Jurisprudence), MA Oxon 1950; Barrister-at-Law 1950, Mem., Inner Temple. Lectr in Law, Belfast Univ., 1949–50; Lectr in Law, TCD, 1950–56, Sen. Lectr, 1956–62, Reader, 1962–63; Lectr in Law, Univ. of Durham, 1963–64, Reader, 1964–66. Mem., Exec. Cttee, Council for Soc. Serv., Co. Durham. *Publications:* Notes on the Irish Law of Contracts: supplement to Cheshire and Fifoot on Contracts, 1954; Justice According to the English Common Lawyer, 1961; *contrib.* Amer. Jl Jurisp., Law Qly Rev., Mod. Law Rev., Public Law. *Address:* Dept of Law, 50 North Bailey, Durham.

Dowse, R. E.; Reader in Politics, University of Exeter, since 1971; *b* 1933; *m* 1959; two *s.* BSc(Econ) LSE 1958, PhD London 1962. Asst Edinburgh Univ., 1958–59; Asst, Hull Univ., 1959–64; Lectr, Exeter Univ., 1964–

71. *Publications:* Left in the Centre, 1966; ed, Readings on British Politics and Government, 1968; Modernisation in Ghana and the USSR, 1970; Political Sociology, 1972; *contrib.* Brit. Jl Sociol., Parly Aff., Pol. Studies, Sociol., Wld Pol. *Address:* Dept of Politics, Univ. of Exeter, Exeter EX4 4QJ.

Dowsett, Prof. Charles James Frank, MA, PhD; Calouste Gulbenkian Professor of Armenian Studies, University of Oxford, and Fellow of Pembroke College, since 1965; *b* 1924; *m* 1949. BA Cantab 1949 (1st cl. Modern and Medieval Languages), MA, PhD Cantab 1954; Diplôme de'arménien, Ecoles des Langues Orientales Vivantes, Paris 1952; diplôme de géorgien, Institut Catholique de Paris 1953; MA, DPhil Oxon 1965 (by incorporation); Member Council, Royal Asiatic Soc., Philological Soc.; Mem., Folklore Soc. Lectr, SOAS, Univ. of London, 1954–65, Reader, 1965. *Publications:* The History of the Caucasian Albanians by Movsēs Dasxuranci, 1961; The Penitential of David of Ganjak, 1961; (with J. Carswell) Kütahya Armenian Tiles, vol. I, 1972; *contrib.* BSOAS, Revue des Etudes Arméniennes, Le Muséon. *Address:* Oriental Institute, Pusey Lane, Oxford; Pembroke College, Oxford.

Doyle, Dr Anthony Ian; Reader in Bibliography and Keeper of Rare Books, University Library, Durham, since 1972; *b* 1925. MA Cantab 1949, PhD Cantab 1953; FRHistSoc 1970. Durham Univ. Library: Sen. Asst, 1950; Asst Librarian, 1953; Keeper of Rare Books, 1959; Sen. Keeper, 1966; Reader in Bibliography, 1972. Lyell Reader in Bibliography, Oxford, 1967. Member of Council: Early English Text Soc.; Surtees Soc.; Sub-Cttee on Manuscripts of Standing Conf. of Nat. and Univ. Libraries. *Publications: contrib.* Book Collector, Bull. John Rylands Library, Dominican Studies, Durham Univ. Jl, Innes Rev., Medium Aevum, Modern Language Assoc. of America, Speculum, Trans Cambridge Bibliog. Soc., Trans Essex Arch. Soc. *Address:* Univ. Library, Palace Green, Durham.

Doyle, Prof. Peter; Professor of Marketing, University of Bradford, since 1974; *b* 1943; *m* 1973; BA Hons Manchester 1964 (Econ. 1st cl.), MA 1965, MS Carnegie-Mellon Univ. 1970, PhD 1971; Member: Market Res. Soc., Amer. Econ. Assoc. Head of Marketing Dept, Univ. of Bradford, 1973. *Publications:* Inflation, 1969; Analytical Marketing Management, 1974; Product Management, 1974; Advertising, 1974; *contrib.* Admap, Econ. Jl, European Jl of Mkting, Jl of the Market Res. Soc., Management Decision, Oxford Econ. Papers, Operational Res. Qly. *Address:* Univ. of Bradford, Management Centre, Emm Lane, Bradford, Yorks.

Doyle, Dr William, MA, DPhil; Lecturer, Department of History, University of York, since 1967; *b* 1942; *m* 1968. BA Oxon 1964, MA and DPhil Oxon 1968. Vis. Prof., Univ. of S. Carolina, 1969. *Publications:* The Parlement of Bordeaux and the End of the Old Régime (forthcoming); *contrib.* Annales du Midi, Fr. Hist. Studies, Past and Present.

192

Address: Dept of History, Univ. of York, Heslington, York YO1 5DD.

Drake, Prof. Charles D.; Professor of Law, University of Leeds, since 1972; *b* 1924; *m* 1956; one *s* one *d*. BA Cantab 1947 (Law), LLB Cantab 1948, MA Cantab 1950; Barrister-at-Law, Middle Temple 1950. Lectr, Durham Univ., 1964–69, Sen. Lectr, 1969–72. Mem., CNAA Business Studies Bd. *Publications*: Labour Law, 1969, 2nd edn 1973; Ch. 2, in, Government Enterprise, a Comparative Symposium on the Public Corporation, 1970; Law of Partnership, 1972; ed, Pt 2, Encyclopaedia of Labour Relations, Law, 1972; *contrib.* Indust. Law Jl (ed statutory section), Bull. Indust. Law Soc., Curr. Law Statutes, Jl Business Law, Law Qly Rev., Mod. Law Rev., Public Admin. *Address*: Faculty of Law, Univ. of Leeds, Leeds LS2 9JT.

Drake, Prof. Michael, MA, PhD; Professor in the Faculty of Social Sciences, Open University, since 1969; *b* 1935; *m* 1958; two *s*. BA Cantab 1956 (History), MA Cantab 1960, PhD Cantab 1964. Temp. Lectr, Queen's Univ., Belfast, 1960–61; Jun. Lectr, TCD, 1961–63; Lectr, Queen's Univ., Belfast, 1963–65; Amer. Council of Learned Socs. Fellow, Univ. of Wisconsin, Madison, 1965–66; Lectr, Univ. of Kent at Canterbury, 1966–68; Sen. Lectr, 1968–69; Dean, Open Univ. Fac. Social Science, 1969–71. *Publications*: Population and Society in Norway, 1735–1865, 1969; ed, Population in Industrialisation, 1969; ed, Applied Historical Studies: an introductory reader, 1973; *contrib.* Econ. Hist. Rev., Jl Interdisc. Hist., Popn Studies, Scand. Econ. Hist. Rev. *Address*: Faculty of Social Sciences, The Open Univ., Walton Hall, Milton Keynes MK7 6AA.

Draper, Col G. I. A. D., OBE; Reader in charge of Law Studies, School of European Studies, University of Sussex, since 1969; *b* 1914; *m* 1951. LLB London 1935, LLM London 1938; Solicitor 1936, Barrister 1947; awarded NATO Fellowship 1958. Lectr in Law, London, 1957–63; Reader in Public Internat. Law, London, 1964–67; Vis. Prof., Univ. of Cairo, 1964–65; Reader in Law Studies, Univ. of Sussex, 1967–69, Chm., Law Subject Gp, 1970–72; Lionel Cohen Lectr, Hebrew Univ. of Jerusalem, 1972; Titular Prof., Sanremo Inst. of Internat. Humanitarian Law, 1971– . *Publications*: Red Cross Conventions, 1958; Civilians and the NATO Status of Forces Agreement, 1966; Hague Receuil Lectures, 1968; *contrib.* Brit. Yr Bk Internat. Law, Internat. Comp. Law Qly, Military Law, Law of War Rev., Internat. Aff. *Address*: Arts Building, Univ. of Sussex, Falmer, Sussex.

Draper, John Michael; Lecturer in Literature and Drama, Adult Education Department, University of Hull, since 1966; *b* 1930; *m* 1955. BA Hull 1961 (1st cl. English). Staff Tutor, Glasgow Univ., 1964–66. *Address*: Adult Education Dept, Univ. of Hull, Hull, Yorkshire.

Draper, Dr Ronald Philip, BA, PhD; Professor of English, University of Aberdeen,

since 1973; *b* 1928; *m* 1950; three *d*. BA Nottingham 1950 (1st cl. English), PhD Nottingham 1953. Lectr, Adelaide Univ., 1955–57; Sen. Lectr in English, Univ. of Leicester, 1957–73. *Publications*: D. H. Lawrence, 1964; D. H. Lawrence, 1969; D. H. Lawrence: the Critical Heritage, 1970; *contrib.* Crit. Qly, English Studies, Essays in Crit., Etudes Anglaises, New Literary History, Revue des Langues Vivantes, TLS. *Address*: Dept of English, Univ. of Aberdeen, Aberdeen AB9 2UB.

Drechsler, Dr Frank S.; Head of Department of Business Studies, University of Dublin, Trinity College, since 1969; *b* 1923; *m* 1951; one *s* three *d*. BE UCD 1944 (Mech. and Elec.), ME UCD 1947; MA TCD 1969, PhD TCD 1969 (Business Studies); MASME 1951; CEng, FIEI 1969. Assoc. Prof., Univ. of Delaware, 1953; UCD, 1955; TCD, 1965. Company Dir, 1954. Governor, Sandford Park Sch., 1954. Chm., IIC. *Publications*: Information, Decisions, Control, 1968, 2nd edn 1972; Network Analysis, 1969, 2nd edn 1972; The Business Graduate and his Job, 1970; Simulation, 1970; *contrib.* Irish Engineers Jl, Management, Operational Res. Qly, Accountant, Internat. Planning. *Address*: Department of Business Studies, Trinity College, Dublin 2.

Drever, James; Principal and Vice-Chancellor, University of Dundee, since 1967; *b* 1910; *m* 1936; one *s* one *d*. MA Edinburgh 1932 (Hons Philosophy), MA Cambridge 1934 (Moral Science Tripos); FRSE. Asst, Dept of Philosophy, Edinburgh, 1934–38; Lectr in Philosophy and Psychology, King's Coll., Newcastle, 1938–41; Prof. of Psychology, Univ. of Edinburgh, 1944–66. Vis. Prof., Princeton Univ., 1954–55. Editor, Brit. Jl of Psychol., 1954–58; Pres., Brit. Psychol Soc., 1960–61; Pres., Internat. Union of Scientific Psychology, 1963–66. Mem., Cttee on Higher Educn, 1961–63; Mem., Social Science Research Coun., 1965–69; Chm., Advisory Coun. on Social Work, in Scotland, 1970– ; Mem., Scottish Oil Develt Council, 1973– ; Mem., Adv. Council for Civil Service Coll., 1973– . *Publications*: *contrib.* papers and reviews. *Address*: The Univ., Dundee DD1 4HN.

Drew, Dr David P.; Lecturer in Geography, Trinity College Dublin, since 1971; *b* 1943. BA Hons Nottingham 1964; PhD Bristol 1967; Member: British Care Res. Assoc.; British Geomorphol Res. Gp. Head of Geography Dept, 1968–69, Assoc. Prof. of Geography, 1968–71, Univ. Saskatchewan. Mem., Irish Cttee on Science in Archaeology. *Publications*: (with D. Smith) Limestones and Caves of the Mendip Hills, 1974; *contrib.* Bristol Univ. Speleological Soc. Trans, British Cave Res. Assoc. Trans, Trans Internat. Geog. Union, Groundwater, Irish Geog. *Address*: Dept. Geography, Trinity Coll. of Dublin 2, Eire.

Drew, Prof. George Charles; Professor of Psychology, University College, London, since 1958; *b* 1911; *m*; one *s* one *d*. BA Bristol 1933 (1st cl. Hons Philos and English Lit.), MA 1948 (Psychology), DipEd 1934;

FBPsS, FEPsS. Lectr-in-charge of Psychology, Univ. of Bristol, 1946–50; Reader, 1950–51; Prof., 1951–58. Dean of Science, UCL, 1973– ; Vis. Prof., Univ. of California, Berkeley, 1967–68; Member: Science Res. Council, 1965–67; Parl and Scientific Cttees, 1968– . *Publications*: *contrib.* Brit. Jl of Psychology, BM Jl, Proc. Royal Institution, Qly Jl of Experimental Psychology, etc. *Address*: Univ. College London, Gower Street, WC1E 6BT.

Drew, (Kenneth) Philip (Arthur); Reader in English, University of Glasgow, since 1971; *b* 1925; *m* 1953; one *s* two *d*. BA Oxon 1949, MA Oxon 1954. Asst, Univ. of Glasgow, 1950–52, Lectr, 1952–66, Sen. Lectr, 1966–71. *Publications*: ed, Robert Browning: A Collection of Critical Essays, 1966; The Poetry of Browning: A Critical Introduction, 1970; *contrib.* Ess. Crit., ELH, NCF, SEL, VP, VS. *Address*: Dept of English, Univ. of Glasgow, Glasgow G12 8QQ.

Drewery, Rev. Benjamin, MA; Bishop Fraser Senior Lecturer in Ecclesiastical History, University of Manchester, since 1971; *b* 1918; *m* 1949; four *d*. BA Oxon 1939, MA Oxon 1946, BA Cantab 1948 (1st cl. Hons Theology); Mem., Soc. for Eccles. Hist. Lectr, Univ. of Manchester 1965–71. Methodist Chaplain to Oxford University 1957–64; Mem. of the Faith and Order Cttee of the Methodist Church 1957–73, and of the General Purposes Cttee 1964–73. *Publications*: Origen and the Doctrine of Grace, 1960; Oxford Sermons, 1964; (with others) Luther and Erasmus: Free Will and Salvation, 1969; (with E. G. Rupp) Martin Luther, 1970, 2nd edn 1971; *contrib.* Church Qly, Jl of Eccles. Hist., Jl of Theological Studies; London Qly and Holborn Rev. *Address*: Faculty of Theology, Univ. of Manchester, Manchester M13 9PL.

Drewry, Gavin Richard; Lecturer in Government, Department of Sociology, Bedford College, University of London, since 1969; *b* 1944; *m* 1966. BSc Southampton 1966 (Social Sciences). Member: Royal Inst. Public Administration; Hansard Soc.; Political Studies Assoc.; Politics Assoc.; Study of Parliament GP; Bedford College: Research Asst, Legal Research Unit, 1966–67; Asst Research Officer, 1967–69. *Publications*: (jtly), Final Appeal: A Study of the House of Lords in its Judicial Capacity, 1972; (ed jtly), Law and Morality, 1974; *contrib.* Law Quarterly Review, Modern Law Review, New Law Jl, Parliamentary Affairs, Political Quarterly. *Address*: Dept of Sociology, Bedford College, Regent's Park, NW1 4NS.

Dronke, Ernest Peter Michael; Lecturer in Medieval Latin, University of Cambridge, since 1961, and Fellow, Clare Hall, since 1964; *b* 1934; *m* 1960; one *d*. MA New Zealand 1954 (1st cl. English), BA Oxon 1957 (1st cl. English), MA Oxon 1961, MA Cantab 1961. Fellow, Merton Coll., Oxford, 1958–61; Gastdozent, Univ. of Munich, 1960; Sen. Res. Fellow, Alexander von Humboldt Foundn, 1966; Prof., Session d'Eté, Centre d'études supérieures médiévales, Poitiers, 1969; Lectr, Eranos Tagung, 1972; Leverhulme Res.

Award, 1972; Vis. Prof., Universidad Autónoma de Barcelona, 1974. Hon. Pres., Internat. Soc. for Study of Courtly Lit., 1973– . *Publications*: Medieval Latin and the Rise of European Love-Lyric, 1965–66, 2nd edn 1968; The Medieval Lyric, 1968 (German trans. 1973, Spanish trans. 1974); Poetic Individuality in the Middle Ages, new departures in poetry 1000–1150, 1970; Fabula: explorations into the uses of myth in medieval Platonism, 1974; chapter in, Literature and Western Civilization, vol. II, ed D. Daiches and A. Thorlby, 1973; *contrib.* Anuario Estudios Mediev., Beitr. Gesch. Deutsch. Sprache Lit., Cah. Civilis. Médiév., Class. Mediaev., Med. Aev., Orb. Litt., Roman. Forsch., Studi Mediev., Enanos-Jbh, Mittellateinisches Jbh. *Address*: Clare Hall, Cambridge.

Drower, Margaret Stefana, (Mrs C. Hackforth-Jones), MBE, BA; Reader in Ancient History, University College London, University of London, since 1966; *b* 1911; *m* 1947; two *d*. BA London 1935 (1st cl. Egyptology);FRAS. Hon. Sec., Egypt Explor. Soc., 1957–71; Mem., Cttee EES, Soc. Libyan Studies. Asst Lectr, Univ. Coll., London, 1937–40, Lectr, 1940–58, Sen. Lectr, 1958–66. Robert Mond Exp., 1935–37 (Egypt Explor. Soc.); Min. of Inform., 1940–45. *Publications*: Egypt in Colour, 1964; Nubia: a Drowning Land, 1967; Fascicles 55, 63 and 64, in, Cambridge Ancient History, rev. edn 1968–69; Chapters, in, Cemeteries of Armant I (Mond and Myers), 1937; Legacy of Egypt, 1940; Temples of Armant, 1940; History of Technology I (Singer, etc.), 1954; rev. edn, vol. I, M. Rostovtzeff: Storia del Mondo Antico, 1965; trans., P. Montet: Everyday Life in Egypt, 1958; *contrib.* Encyclop. Britt., Chambers' Encyclop., Oxf. Class. Dict; *contrib.* Jl Egypt. Archaeol., Antiqu., Bull. Inst. Archaeol. *Address*: Dept of History, Univ. College London, Gower Street, WC1E 6BT.

Drucker, Dr H. M.; Lecturer in Politics, University of Edinburgh, since 1967; *b* 1942. BA Allegheny, PhD London. Dir of Studies, Edinburgh, 1968– , Convenor, Gen. Assembly of Staff, 1970–72; Mem., Constitution and Structure Cttee, 1972– ; Mem., Educnl Policy Cttee, 1972– ; Vice Convenor Travel and Res. Cttee, 1971– . *Publications*: The Political Context of Ideology, 1974; *contrib.* Philosophy, Political Studies. *Address*: Dept of Politics, Univ. of Edinburgh, Edinburgh EH8 9YL.

Drummond, Stuart Hamilton; Resident-Tutor in West and Central Hampshire, Department of Extra-Mural Studies, University of Southampton, since 1970; *b* 1927; *m* 1958; one *d*. BA Oxon 1951 (Hons), MA Oxon 1955; Mem., Royal Inst. of Internat. Affairs. Tutor to HM Forces, Dept of Extra-Mural Studies, Southampton Univ., 1963–70. *Publications*: (with Helga Drummond) History of the Mongols, 1972 (trans. Bertold Spuler: Geschichte der Mongolen); *contrib.* Army Qly. and Defence Rev., Asian Surv., Pol. Stud., Pub. Admin., World Today. *Address*: Dept of Extra-Mural Studies, The Univ., Southampton SO9 5NH.

Drury, (Janet) Linda; Assistant Keeper, Department of Palaeography and Diplomatic, University of Durham, since 1967; *b* 1941; *m* 1970. MA St Andrews 1963 (Hons). *Address:* Dept of Palaeography and Diplomatic, Univ. of Durham, South Road, Durham DH1 3LE.

Drus, Ethel; Lecturer, Department of History, University of Southampton, since 1967; *b* 1919. BA Cape Town 1938, MA Cape Town 1939, BEd Cape Town 1940; FRHistS. Jun. Lectr in History, Univ. of Cape Town, 1945–46; Res. Fellow, Inst. Hist. Res., London, 1948–49; Lectr in History, Birkbeck Coll., London, 1949–57; Res. Fellow, Australian Nat. Univ., 1958–59; Lectr in History, Univ. of Hull, 1960–67. *Publications: contrib.* Bull. Inst. Hist. Res., Camden Misc., EHR, Trans Royal Hist. Soc. *Address:* Dept of History, The Univ., Southampton SO9 5NH.

Dryden, Prof. Myles Muir, BSc(Econ), MBA, PhD; Professor of Management Studies, University of Glasgow, since 1972; *b* 1931; *m* 1970. BSc(Econ) London 1955, MBA Cornell 1957 (with distinction), PhD Cornell 1961. Fellowships, Cornell Univ., 1957–60; Asst Prof. of Industrial Management, Massachusetts Inst. Technol., 1961–63; Lectr, Edinburgh Univ., 1963–67, Reader in Economics, 1967–72. *Publications: contrib.* Econ. Jl, Engg Econ., Jl App. Econ., Jl Business, Jl Finance, Jl Indus. Eng., Scott. Jl Pol. Econ. *Address:* Dept of Management Studies, Glasgow Univ., Glasgow G12 8QQ.

Dryhurst, Dr James; Senior Lecturer, Department of French, University of Leeds, since 1971; *b* 1931; *m* 1960; one *s* three *d.* BA Liverpool 1953 (1st cl. French), PhD Liverpool 1964. Asst Lectr, Leeds, 1958–61; Lectr, 1961–71. *Publications: contrib.* Year's Work Mod. Lang., ZFSL, CAIEF, RHLF. *Address:* Dept of French, Univ. of Leeds, Leeds LS2 9JT.

Dubois, Elfrieda Theresia, MA, DPhil, Docteur ès lettres; Reader, Department of French Studies, University of Newcastle upon Tyne, since 1973 (Senior Lecturer, 1964–73); *b* 1916; *m* 1948; one *s.* BA Birmingham 1943 (1st cl. French), MA Birmingham 1945, DPhil Vienna 1954, DèsL Paris 1970. Asst Lectr, Sheffield, 1947–48; Lectr, Newcastle upon Tyne (Univ. of Durham), 1948–64; Mem., Edit. Bd, Erasmus. *Publications:* ed, Rapin: Réflexions sur la poétique, in, Studies in French Literature, 1949; Portrait of Léon Bloy, 1950; Essays presented to C. M. Girdlestone, 1960; Currents in French Thought, 1965; Claudel: a reappraisal, 1968; Rapin, l'homme et l'œuvre, 1972; ed, Rotrou: Saint Genest, 1972; *contrib.* XVIIe Siècle, Durham Univ. Jl, Fr. Studies, Jl Aesth., Mod. Lang. Rev. *Address:* Dept of French Studies, Univ. of Newcastle upon Tyne, Newcastle upon Tyne NE1 7RU.

Du Boulay, Prof. Francis Robin Houssemayne; Professor of Mediaeval History in the University of London, at Bedford College, since 1960; *b* 1920; *m* 1948; two *s* one *d.* MA Oxon 1947; FRHistS (Hon. Sec., 1961–65). Asst Lectr, Bedford Coll., 1947, Lectr, 1949–55; Reader in Mediaeval History, Univ. of London, 1955–60. *Publications:* A Hand List of Medieval Ecclesiastical Terms, 1952; The Register of Archbishop Bourgchier, 1953; Medieval Bexley, 1961; Documents Illustrative of Medieval Kentish Society, 1964; The Lordship of Canterbury, 1966; An Age of Ambition, 1970; *contrib.* various jls and symposia. *Address:* Bedford College, Inner Circle, Regent's Park, NW1 4NS.

Duchêne, Louis-François; Director, Centre for Contemporary European Studies, Sussex University, since 1974; *b* 1927; *m* 1952; one *d.* Journalist, 1949–52, 1956–58, 1963–67; Press attaché, Luxembourg, 1952–55; Director: Documentation Centre of Action Cttee for United States of Europe, Paris, 1958–63; International Institute for Strategic Studies, 1969–74. *Publications:* ed, The Endless Crisis, 1970; The Case of the Helmeted Airman, a study of W. H. Anden, 1972. *Address:* Univ. of Sussex, Sussex House, Falmer, Brighton BN1 9RH.

Duckham, Baron Frederick; Senior Lecturer in Economic History, Department of History, University of Strathclyde, since 1971; *b* 1959; *m* 1959; two *s* one *d.* BA Manchester 1954 (Hons Politics and Modern History), Grad. CertEd, Leeds 1955, MA Manchester 1956; FRHistS. Lectr, then Sen. Lectr, Doncaster Coll. of Educn, 1962–66; Pt-time Lectr, Sheffield Univ., 1964–66; Lectr, Strathclyde Univ., 1966–71. Ed., Transp. Hist., 1968–73. *Publications:* The Yorkshire Ouse: the history of a river navigation, 1967; The Transport Revolution 1750–1830, 1967; A History of the Scottish Coal Industry 1700–1815, 1970; Great Pit Disasters: Britain 1700 to the Present Day, 1973; The Inland Waterways of East Yorkshire, 1700–1900, 1973; new edns, var. classics of mining history, 1969– ; *contrib.* Business Hist., Business Hist. Rev., Hist., Indust. Archaeol., Jl Local Hist., North Hist., Scott. Hist. Rev., Transp. Hist., Jl Transp. Hist., etc. *Address:* Dept of Economic History, Univ. of Strathclyde, Glasgow G1 1XW.

Duckworth, David, MA; Lecturer in German and Dutch, German Department, University of Nottingham, since 1966; *b* 1941; *m* 1965. BA Manchester 1962 (Hons German), MA Manchester 1964 (Hons German). *Publications: contrib.* Zeits. Deut. Spr. *Address:* Dept of German, Univ. of Nottingham, Nottingham NG7 2RD.

Dudbridge, Dr Glen; Lecturer in Modern Chinese, University of Oxford, since 1965; *b* 1938; *m* 1965; one *s* one *d.* BA Cantab 1962 (1st cl. Chinese), MA Cantab, Oxon 1966, PhD Cantab 1967. Fellow, Magdalene Coll., Cambridge, 1965; Fellow, Wolfson Coll., Oxford, 1966; Vis. Assoc. Prof., Yale Univ., 1972–73. *Publications:* The Hsi-yu chi, 1970; *contrib.* Asia Maj. *Address:* Oriental Institute, Pusey Lane, Oxford.

Dudley Edwards, Robert; *see* Edwards, R. D.

Duff, R. Antony; Lecturer in Philosophy, University of Stirling, since 1970; *b* 1945. BA Hons Oxon 1967 (1st cl. Lit. Hum.). Vis. Lectr and Tutor in Philosophy, Univ. of Washington, Seattle, USA, 1968–69. *Address:* Dept of Philosophy, Univ. of Stirling, Stirling FK9 4LA.

Duggan, Dr Edward Patrick, MA, PhD, BSc, FRAS; Senior Research Fellow, Centre for Social Science Research, University of Keele, since 1971; *b* 1912; *m* 1938; one *s* one *d*. King's Coll. London 1931–34; BSc (Gen.) 1934; BSc London 1951 (Special Chemistry), MA London 1955 (Education), PhD London 1969 (Education); Acad. DipEd 1953; FRAS; Mem., Brit. Astron. Assoc. (Sec., 1965–70). Sen. Res. Fellow, Inst. Educn, Univ. of Keele, 1966–71; Tutor, Dip. Adv. Studies in Educn, Univ. of Keele, 1967–70. Adj., RA, HAA Reg., 1943–45; Asst Comm., Demob. Unit, 1945–46; Pres., Kent Fedn Hd Teacher Assocs, 1963; Vice-Chm., Sen. Common Room, Univ. of Keele, 1971–72; Chm., 1972–73. *Publications:* The Choice of Work Area of Teachers (Sociological Rev. Monog., 15), 1970; Concurrent and Postgraduate Courses at Keele, 1966–1970, 1971; Concurrent and Postgraduate Courses in Four Colleges of Education, 1968–1970, 1971; The Alsager Experiment, 1971; The Relationship between Parental Encouragement and School Performance, 1972; The Relationship between the Watson-Glaser Critical Appraisal Test and Examination Performance among Advanced Education Students, 1972; The Geographical Mobility of Two Cohorts of Teachers in Reading and Stoke-on-Trent, 1973; *contrib.* Brit. Astron. Assoc. Jl, Sociol. Rev. *Address:* Centre for Social Science Research, Univ. of Keele, Keele, Staffs ST5 5BE.

Dugmore, Rev. Prof. Clifford William, DD, FRHistS; Professor of Ecclesiastical History, King's College, University of London, since 1958; *b* 1909; *m* 1938; one *d*. BA Oxon 1932, MA (and James Mew Rabbinical Hebrew Scholar) Oxon 1935, BD 1940, DD 1957, BA Cambridge (by incorp.) 1933, MA 1936; Norrisian Prizeman 1940; Deacon 1935, Priest 1936, FRHistS; Life Mem., Soc. OT Studies, 1933; Founder Mem. SNTS, EHS (Pres., 1963–64); Chm., Brit. Sous-Commn, Commn Internat. d'Hist. Eccles., 1952–62. Bishop Frazer Sen. Lectr in Ecclesiastical History, Univ. of Manchester, 1946–58; Select Preacher, Univ. of Cambridge, 1956; Hulsean Lecturer, Univ. of Cambridge, 1958–60; Mem., Senate, Univ. of London, 1964–71; Proctor, Conv. of Canterbury (Gen. Synod), for Univ. of London, 1971– . Ed., Jl Eccles. Hist., 1950– . *Publications:* Eucharistic Doctrine in England from Hooker to Waterland, 1942; The Influence of the Synagogue upon the Divine Office, 1944, 2nd edn 1964; The Mass and the English Reformers, 1958; Ecclesiastical History No Soft Option, 1959; ed, The Interpretation of the Bible, 1944; 2nd edn 1946; ed, Studies in Church History I, 1964; *contrib.* Chambers's Encyclopaedia, 1950, 1960; Weltkirchenlexikon, 1960; Studia Patristica, IV, 1961; Neotestamentica et Patristica, 1962; The English Prayer Book, 1963; A Companion to the Bible, 2nd rev. edn, 1963; Studies in Church History II, 1965; Man and his Gods, 1971; A Dictionary of Liturgy and Worship, 1972; *contrib.* Jl Eccles. Hist., Jl Theol. Studies. *Address:* Univ. of London, King's College, Strand, WC2R 2LS.

Dukes, Dr Paul; Senior Lecturer in History, University of Aberdeen, since 1972 (Lecturer, 1964–72); *b* 1934; *m* 1966 (marr. diss. 1972). BA Cantab 1954 (Hons History), MA Washington 1956, PhD London 1964. Teaching Fellow, Univ. of Washington, 1954–56; Lectr, Univ. of Maryland, 1958–64. *Publications:* Catherine the Great and the Russian Nobility, 1967; co-ed, Nations and Empires, 1969; The Emergence of the Super-Powers, 1970; A History of Russia, 1974; *contrib.* Hist., Hist. Today, Russ. Rev., Slav. and E Europ. Rev. *Address:* History Dept, King's College, Old Aberdeen.

Dummett, Michael Anthony Eardley, FBA; Fellow, All Souls College, Oxford, since 1950; Reader in the Philosophy of Mathematics, University of Oxford, since 1962; *b* 1925; *m* 1951; three *s* two *d*. BA Oxon 1950 (1st cl. Hons PPE), MA Oxon 1954; FBA 1968. Asst Lectr in Philosophy, Birmingham Univ., 1950–51; Commonwealth Fund Fellow, Univ. of California, Berkeley, 1955–56; Vis. Lectr, Univ. of Ghana, 1958; Vis. Prof., Stanford Univ., several occasions, 1960–66; Vis. Prof., Univ. of Minnesota, 1968. Founder Mem., Oxford Cttee for Racial Integration, 1965 (Chm., Jan–May 1966); Mem., Exec. Cttee Campaign against Racial Discrimination, 1966–67; Mem., Legal Civil Affairs Panel, Nat. Cttee for Commonwealth Immigrants, 1966–68; Chm., Jt Council for Welfare of Immigrants, 1970 (Vice-Chm., 1967–69). *Publications:* entry on Frege, in Encyclopedia of Philosophy, ed P. Edwards, 1967; (with A. Dummett) chapter on Rôle of the Government, in Justice First, ed L. Donnelly, 1969; *contrib.* Proc. Aristotelian Soc., Philos. Rev., Econometrica, Jl Symbolic Logic, Zeitschrift für Mathematische Logik, Dublin Rev., New Blackfriars, Clergy Rev. *Address:* All Souls College, Oxford.

Dunbabin, John Paul Delacour; Fellow and Tutor in Politics and Modern History, St Edmund Hall, Oxford, since 1964; *b* 1938; *m* 1962; two *d*. BA Oxon 1959 (1st cl. History), MA 1962; FRHistS. Res. Lectr, Christ Church, Oxford, 1962–63; Lectr, St Edmund Hall, 1963–64. Min. of Transp., 1961–62. *Publications:* Rural Discontent in Nineteenth Century Britain, 1974; *contrib.* Agric. Hist. Rev., EHR, Hist. Jl, Past and Present. *Address:* St Edmund Hall, Oxford.

Dunbar, Nan Vance, MA; Fellow and Tutor in Classics, Somerville College, Oxford, since 1965; *b* 1928. MA Glasgow 1950 (1st cl. Classics), BA Cantab 1952 (1st cl. Classical Tripos), MA 1955, MA Oxon 1965 (by incorporation). Lectr in Greek, Edinburgh Univ., 1952–55; Res. Fellow, Girton Coll., Cambridge, 1955–57; Lectr in Latin, St Andrews Univ., 1957–65. *Publications:* contrib. Class. Rev. *Address:* Somerville College, Oxford.

Duncan, Dr Alistair Matheson; Reader in History and Philosophy of Science and Technology, Department of Social Sciences, Loughborough University of Technology, since 1967; *b* 1926; *m* 1953; two *s* one *d*. BA and MA Oxford 1951, DipEd Oxford 1952, BSc London 1957, MSc London 1961, PhD London 1971; Mem., Brit. Soc. Hist. Sci. Assoc. Lib. Educn. Sen. Lectr in Liberal Studies, Loughborough Univ. Technol., 1966–67. Public Orator, Loughborough Univ. Technol.; Chm., Assoc. Liberal Educn, 1972– ; Chm., Lit. Panel, E Midlands Arts Assoc., 1971– . *Publications*: The Scientific Revolution of the Seventeenth Century, 1969; ed, Bergman: Dissertation on Elective Attractions, 1970; trans. Copernicus: On the Revolutions (forthcoming); *contrib.* Ambix, Ann. Sci., Lib. Educn. *Address*: Dept of Social Sciences, Univ. of Technology, Loughborough LE11 3TU.

Duncan, Andrew Gordon Macaulay; Senior Lecturer, Department of Scots Law, Edinburgh University, since 1971; *b* 1914. MA Edinburgh 1935, LLB Edinburgh 1937 (with distinction); Solicitor 1939, Writer to the Signet 1941. Part-time Tutor, Univ. of Edinburgh, 1937–40; part-time Asst to Prof. of Conveyancing, 1941, 1946–49; Lectr in Conveyancing, 1962–71. Dir of Studies, Fac. of Law, 1966–74; Assoc. Dean, Fac. of Law, 1972–74. *Publications*: *contrib.* Conveyancing Rev., Jl Law Soc. Scotl., Scots Law Times. *Address*: Room 167, Old College, South Bridge, Edinburgh.

Duncan, Prof. Archibald Alexander McBeth; Professor of Scottish History and Literature, Glasgow University, since 1962; *b* 1926; *m* 1954; two *s* one *d*. Lectr in Hist., QUB, 1951–53; Lectr in Hist., Edinburgh Univ., 1953–61; Leverhulme Res. Fellow, 1961–62. Mem., Royal Commn on the Ancient and Historical Monuments of Scotl., 1969– . *Address*: Univ. of Glasgow, Glasgow G12 8QQ.

Duncan, Cyril John; Director, Department of Photography and Teaching Aids Laboratory, University of Newcastle upon Tyne, since 1947; *b* 1916; *m* 1940; one *s* two *d*. BA Cantab 1938 (Maths and Nat. Sc. Pt II Physics), MA Cantab 1950; FRPS 1945, FRMS 1948, FIOP 1964, FIRT 1963, AIMBI 1969. Dir, Computer Typesetting Res. Project, 1965–70. Kodak Ltd, 1938–40; RAE Farnborough, 1940–46; Mem., Council, BUFC; NCET; CNAA Photog. Bd. *Publications*: chapter in, Media and Methods, ed Unwin, 1969; Computer Composing, HMSO, 1970; trans., L. P. Clerc: Properties of Photographic Materials, 1950; trans., A. H. S. Craeybeckx: Gevaert Manual of Photography, 1958; *contrib.* Brit. Univs Film Jl, Penrose Ann., Photog. Jl, etc. *Address*: Dept of Photography and Teaching Aids Laboratory, Univ. of Newcastle upon Tyne, Newcastle upon Tyne NE1 7RU.

Duncan, Jennifer Ann; Lecturer in French and Director of Studies in Modern Languages, Newnham College, University of Cambridge, since 1970; *b* 1940. BA Oxon 1962 (1st cl. Mod. Langs), MA and BLitt Oxon 1966; Mem., Soc. French Studies. Tutor, Dept of French, Exeter Univ., 1965–66; Asst Lectr, 1966–69; Lectr, 1969–70. Full time trans., Shell Internat. Petroleum Co., London, 1962–63. *Publications*: ed, Correspondence of Paul Adam (forthcoming); Le symbolisme des romans de Paul Adam (forthcoming); *contrib.* Mod. Lang. Rev. *Address*: Newnham College, Cambridge.

Duncan-Jones, Katherine, (Mrs K. Wilson), BLitt, MA; Fellow and Tutor in English Literature, Somerville College, Oxford, since 1966; *b* 1941; *m* 1971; one *d*. BA Oxford 1962 (1st cl. English Language and Literature), BLitt 1964; Mary Ewart Res. Fellow, Somerville Coll., 1963–65; Fellow in English Literature, New Hall, Cambridge, 1965–66. *Publications*: ed (with J. A. van Dorsten), Miscellaneous Prose of Sir Philip Sidney, 1973; Sir Philip Sidney: Selected Poems, 1973; *contrib.* Eng. Studies, Mod. Lang. Rev., Rev. Engl. Studies. *Address*: Somerville College, Oxford.

Duncan-Jones, Dr Richard Phare; Fellow of Gonville and Caius College, Cambridge, since 1963; *b* 1937. BA 1959, MA 1963, PhD 1965, Cantab. *Publications*: The Economy of the Roman Empire: quantitative studies, 1974; *contrib.* Class. Phil., Epig. Stud., Historia, Latomus, Jl Rom. Stud., Papers Brit. Sch. Rome. *Address*: Caius College, Cambridge.

Duncanson, Dennis J., OBE, MA; Reader in Southeast Asian Studies, University of Kent at Canterbury, since 1969; *b* 1917; *m* 1939. BA London 1936 (French), MA London 1938 (French), BA London 1951 (Chinese). Fellow in Internat. Studies, LSE, 1967–69. Brit. Mil. Admin. of Eritrea, 1941–46; Malayan Civil Service (Chinese Dept), 1946–57; Govt of Hong Kong, 1957–61; Diplomatic Service, 1961–67 (Brit. Adv. Mission to Vietnam, 1961–65). *Publications*: Government and Revolution in Vietnam, 1968; The Rise of the Indochina Communist Party; *contrib.* Africa, Asian Affs, Internat. Affs, Mod. Asian Stud., World Today. *Address*: Keynes College, Univ. of Kent at Canterbury, Canterbury.

Dundas-Grant, Valerie Hermine, MA; Lecturer in Education, University of Keele, since 1965; BA Oxon 1945 (2nd cl. French and German), MA Oxon 1949, DipEd Oxford 1951 (Distinction). Hon. Treas., Comp. Educn Soc. in Europe (Brit. Sect.), 1966–69; Mem., Consult. Cttee, Schs Council Mod. Langs Project, 1970; Pres., NW Brch, Mod. Lang. Assoc., 1972–73; Gov., Maryhill Comp. Sch., Kidsgrove, 1972– . *Publications*: *contrib.* Times Educnl Supp. *Address*: Dept of Education, Univ. of Keele, Newcastle, Staffs ST5 5BG.

Dungworth, David; Lecturer in Modern Languages, Department of European Studies and Modern Languages, University of Manchester Institute of Science and Technology, since 1963; *b* 1934; *m* 1963. BA Oxon 1955, MA Oxon 1959, DipEd Sheffield 1959. Assistant, Trier/Kaiserslautern, 1971–72. *Publications*: Versuch es mit Humor, 1968,

2nd edn 1974; Erzählende Bilder, 1970, 2nd edn 1972; German Translation for Scientists, 1971; *contrib*. Programmed Learning, Umschau in Wissenschaft und Technik, Educnl Forum, Times Educnl Supplement. *Address*: Dept of European Studies and Modern Languages, UMIST, Manchester 1.

Dunham, Jack, BSc(Econ.), MEd, DCP, ABPsS; Lecturer in Psychology, School of Humanities and Social Sciences, Bath University, since 1966; *b* 1926; *m* 1954; two *s*. BSc(Econ.) London 1951, DipPsych of Childhood Birmingham 1956, MEd Manchester 1959; ABPsS 1966. Sen. Res. Fellow, Univ. of Bath, 1964–66. Student Counsellor, Univ. of Bath, 1971. *Publications*: (with S. F. Cotgrove and C. Vamplen) The Nylon Spinners, 1971; Personality and Career Choice, 1974; *contrib*. Brit. Jl Educnl Psychol., Educnl Res., Soc. Res. High Educn Monogs., Technol. *Address*: School of Humanities and Social Sciences, The Univ., Claverton Down, Bath, Somerset BA2 7AY.

Dunn, Alfred; Tutor, Printmaking Department, Royal College of Art, since 1969; *b* 1937; *m* 1960; one *s* one *d*. ARCA *Address*: Royal College of Art, Kensington Gore, SW7 2EU.

Dunn, Prof. Charles James, PhD; Professor of Japanese, School of Oriental and African Studies, University of London, since 1970; *b* 1915; *m* 1940; one *d*. BA London 1936 (1st cl. French), PhD London 1959; Lectr, SOAS, Univ. of London, 1947–68, Reader, 1968–70. *Publications*: Early Japanese Puppet Drama, 1960; Everyday Life in Traditional Japan, 1969; trans. (with B. Torigoe), The Actors' Analects, 1969. *Address*: School of Oriental and African Studies, Univ. of London, Malet Street, WC1E 7HP.

Dunn, John Montfort; Fellow of King's College, Cambridge, since 1966, and University Lecturer in Politics, since 1971; *b* 1940; *m* 1973. BA Cantab 1962 (Hist.); Member: Past and Present Soc.; Pol Studies Assoc. Fellow Jesus Coll., Cambridge, 1965–66; Dir of Studies in History, King's Coll. Cambridge, 1967–74; Vis. Lectr, Univ. of Pol Sci., Univ. of Ghana, Legon, 1968. *Publications*: The Political Thought of John Locke, 1969; Modern Revolutions, 1972; (with Dr A. F. Robertson) Dependence and Opportunity: political change in Ahafo, 1973; *contrib*. Hist. Jl, Philos., Pol Studies, Brit. Jl Pol. Science, Trans Hist. Soc. of Ghana. *Address*: King's Coll., Cambridge.

Dunn, Mary Emma; Director, Centre for Secretarial Studies, Strathclyde University, since 1970; *b* 1912. MA Glasgow 1955 (Hon. Economics and Political Science); ACIS. Sen. Lectr, Scott. Coll. of Comm., 1960; Hd of Dept, Secretarial Studies, Strathclyde Univ., 1964–66; Sen. Lectr, Dept of Comm., Strathclyde Univ., 1966–70. Co. Sec. and Dir in Indust., 1932–59; Economist, Secretariat, Enquiry into Scott. Econ. Mem.: Comm. and Clerical Training Cttee, Central Training Council, 1964–69; Chm., Sub-Cttee, CTC, on Training Needs of Grads in Industr., 1969; Mem., Food Proc. Industr. in Scotl.

Cttee, Scott. Council (Develt and Ind.), 1969–70; Consultant, Govt Australia on Degrees in Secret. Studies, 1971. *Publications*: *contrib*. Scott. Coll., var. indust. and comm. jls. *Address*: Centre for Secretarial Studies, Univ. of Strathclyde, Stenhouse Building, 143 Cathedral Street, Glasgow G4 0RQ.

Dunning, Eric Geoffrey, BSc(Econ), MA; Senior Lecturer, Department of Sociology, University of Leicester, since 1971; *b* 1936; *m* 1969. BSc(Econ) London 1959 (2 I), MA Leicester 1961 (Sociology); BSA. Asst Lectr, Leicester, 1962–63, Lectr, 1962–71; Vis. Lectr, Univ. of Warwick, 1966–69; Vis. Prof., Brooklyn Coll., 1964; Univ. of Minnesota, 1968; State Univ. of NY, Buffalo, 1970. *Publications*: The Sociology of Sport: A Selection of Readings, 1971; *contrib*. Jl Sociol., Kölner Zeits. Sociol. Sozialpsychol., Sociol. Rev., Race. *Address*: Dept of Sociology, Univ. of Leicester, Leicester LE1 7RH.

Dunning, Prof. John Harry, BSc(Econ), PhD; Professor of International Investment and Business Studies, since 1974, and Head of Department of Economics, since 1964, University of Reading; *b* 1927; *m* 1948; one *s*. BSc(Econ) London 1951 (1st cl.), PhD Southampton 1957; Res. Asst, Univ. Coll., London, 1951; Asst Lectr, Southampton Univ., 1952–54, Lectr, 1954–62, Sen. Lectr, 1962–64; Prof. of Economics, Univ. of Reading, 1964–74; Vis. Prof. of Econs, Univ. of W Ontario, 1968–69; Vis. Prof. of Econs, Univ. of California (Berkeley), 1969. Mem.: SE Econ. Planning Council, 1967–71; Chemicals Econ. Develop. Cttee, 1971– ; Council, Royal Econ. Soc., 1970– ; UN Gp of Eminent Persons to study the impact of the Multinational Enterprise on Econ. Develt, 1973–74; Partner, Econ. Adv. Gp, 1966– . *Publications*: American Investment in British Manufacturing Industry, 1958; (with C. J. Thomas) British Industry, 1961, 2nd edn 1963; Economic Planning and Town Expansion, 1963; Studies in International Investment, 1970; (with E. V. Morgan) An Economic Study of the City of London, 1971; ed, The Multinational Enterprise, 1971; ed, Readings in International Investment, 1972; ed, Economic Analysis and the Multinational Enterprise, 1974; *contrib*. various learned and professional jls. *Address*: Dept of Economics, Univ. of Reading, Reading.

Dunsire, Andrew; Senior Lecturer, Department of Politics, University of York, since 1964; *b* 1924; *m* 1951; two *s* one *d*. MA Edinburgh 1949 (Hons Hist.). Commonwealth Foundation Fellow, 1951; Asst Lectr, LSE, 1952; Lectr, Univ. of Exeter, 1953–57, 1959–64. Principal, Min. of Transp. and Civil Aviat., 1957–59; Mem., Public Admin. Bd, CNAA, 1971– . *Publications*: ed, The Making of an Administrator, 1956; (with R. K. Alderman) Management Training Survey, 1968; (with R. A. Chapman) Style in Administration, 1971; Administration, the Word and the Science, 1973; *contrib*. Admin. (Dublin), Public Law. *Address*: Dept of Politics, The Univ., Heslington, York YO1 5DD.

Dunstan, Prof. The Rev. Canon Gordon Reginald; F. D. Maurice Professor of Moral and Social Theology, University of London, at King's College, since 1967; *b* 1917; *m* 1949; two *s* one *d*. BA Leeds 1938 (1st cl. History), MA 1939 (with distinction); Hon. DD Exeter 1973; FSA 1957. Prideaux Lectr, Univ. of Exeter, 1968; Gresham's Prof. in Divinity, 1969–71; Moorhouse Lectr, Melbourne, 1973. Sec., C of E Council Soc. Work, 1955–63; Church Assembly Jt Bd Studies, 1963–66; Ed., Crucible, 1962–66; Theology, 1965– ; Dep. Priest in Ordinary to the Queen, 1959–64; Priest in Ordinary, 1964– ; Select Preacher, Univ. of Cambridge, 1960, Leeds, 1970; Canon Theologian of Leicester Cathedral, 1966– ; Mem., Council, Canterbury and York Soc., 1950– ; Vice-Pres., 1965–66, and Chm., Brit. Cttee Internat. Union Family Organizations, 1964–66; Mem. Council, Tavistock Inst. of Human Relations and of Inst. of Marital Studies, 1968– ; Royal Soc. of Medicine, Lay and Library Sect., 1971– ; etc. *Publications*: The Family is not Broken, 1962; A Digger Still, 1968; Not Yet the Epitaph, 1968; ed, The Sacred Ministry, 1970; transcr. and ed, The Register of Edmund Lacy Bishop of Exeter, 1420–1455 (5 vols), 1963–72; The Artifice of Ethics, 1974; contrib. Industry and Values, ed M. Ivens, 1970; Personality and Science, ed I. T. Ramsey and R. Porter, 1971; The Rules of the Game, ed T. Shavin, 1972; Law and Ethics of AID and Embryo Transfer, ed G. E. W. Wolstenholme and D. FitzSimons, 1973; *contrib.* Theol., Jl Eccles. Hist., Race Relat., Relig. Studies, Brit. Jl Educnl Studies, Concilium. *Address*: King's College, Strand, WC2R 2LS.

Durbin, Prof. James; Professor of Statistics, University of London (London School of Economics), since 1961; *b* 1923; *m* 1958; two *s* one *d*. BA Cantab 1947, MA Cantab 1949. Dept of Applied Econs, Cambridge, 1948–49; Asst Lectr, then Lectr in Statistics, LSE, 1950–53; Reader in Statistics, 1953–61. *Publications*: *contrib.* Biometrika, Jl Royal Statistical Soc., etc. *Address*: London School of Economics and Political Science, Houghton Street, Aldwych WC2A 2AE.

Durrant, Michael, BA, BPhil; Senior Lecturer in Philosophy, University College, Cardiff, since 1972 (Lecturer 1964–72); *b* 1934; *m* 1963; two *s*. BA Leeds 1958 (1st cl. Philosophy with History), BPhil Oxon 1963. Asst Lectr, Univ. Coll., Cardiff, 1962–64; Vis. Prof. of Philosophy, Univ. of Nebraska, 1965–66. *Publications*: Theology and Intelligibility, 1972; The Logic of 'God', 1972; *contrib.* Analysis, Mind, Nous, Relig. Studies, Sophia. *Address*: Dept of Philosophy, Univ. College, Cardiff.

Dutch, Ralph Douglas; Principal Lecturer in Educational Psychology at Aberdeen College of Education, since 1964, Recognised Lecturer in Psychology at Aberdeen University, since 1966; *b* 1929; *m* 1955; two *d*. MA Aberdeen 1951 (1st cl. English), MEd Aberdeen 1953 (1st cl. Education and Psychology); ABPsS. *Address*: Educational Psychology Dept, College of Education, Hilton Place, Aberdeen.

Duthie, Rev. Principal Charles Sim, MA

BD, Hon. DD; Principal of New College, University of London and Lecturer in Systematic Theology and Christian Ethics, since 1964; *b* 1911; *m* 1941; one *s* one *d*. MA 1932 (1st cl. Philosophy), BD 1935, Hon. DD Aberdeen 1952. Lectr, Post-grad. Sch. of Theology, Univ. of Edinburgh, 1946–64. Tutor and Lectr, Paton Coll., 1936–38; Min. of Religion, Bathgate, 1938–44; Chap., HM Forces, 1940–44; Principal, Scott. Cong. Coll., 1944–64. *Publications*: God in His World, 1955, American edn 1956; Outline of Christian Belief, 1967, 2nd edn 1970; chapter, in, Providence, 1969; *contrib.* Cong. Qly, Scott. Jl Theology. *Address*: New College, 527 Finchley Road, NW3 7BE.

Duthie, Dr George Douglas, MA, BD, BPhil, PhD; Senior Lecturer in Moral Philosophy, University of Aberdeen, since 1972 (Lecturer, 1954–72); *b* 1919. MA Oxon 1947 (1st cl. Greats), BPhil Oxon 1949, PhD Cantab 1956, BD London External 1965. Asst in Philosophy, Queen's Univ., Belfast, 1953–54. *Publications*: *contrib.* Philos. Qly, various articles and reviews, 1957– . *Address*: Dept of Moral Philosophy, King's College, Old Aberdeen AB9 2UB.

Duthie, Dr John Hume, MA; Senior Lecturer, Department of Education, University of Stirling, since 1968; *b* 1933; *m* 1958; one *s* one *d*. MA Edinburgh 1956 (1st cl. Psychol.), DipEd Durham 1957, PhD Edinburgh 1965; Mem., Brit. Psychol. Soc. Lectr, Dept of Educn, Univ. of Stirling, 1968–69. Res. Dir, Scottish Primary Sch. Survey, 1966–68. *Publications*: The Primary School Survey: a study of the teacher's day, 1970; *contrib.* Qly Jl Exp. Psychol. *Address*: Dept of Education, Univ. of Stirling, Stirling FK9 4LA.

Dworkin, Prof. Ronald; Professor of Jurisprudence, Oxford University, since 1968; *b* 1931; *m* 1958; one *s* one *d*. BA Harvard Coll. 1953, BA Oxford 1955 (Jurisprudence), JD Harvard Law Sch. 1957, MA Yale 1965, MA Oxford 1969. Assoc. Prof. of Law, Yale Law Sch., 1962; Prof. of Law, Yale Univ., 1965; Hohfeld Prof. of Jurisprudence, Yale Law Sch., 1968; Vis. Prof., Princeton Univ. and Stanford Univ. Master, Trumbull Coll., Yale Univ., 1966–69. *Publications*: *contrib.* Ethics, Jl Philos., NY Rev. Books, Univ. Chicago Law Rev., Univ. of Pennsyl. Law Rev., Yale Law Jl. *Address*: Univ. College, Oxford.

Dyer, Dr Alan David, PhD; Lecturer in History, University College of North Wales, since 1965; *b* 1941; *m* 1965. BA Birmingham 1963 (1st cl. History), PhD Birmingham 1966. *Publication*: City of Worcester in the Sixteenth Century, 1973. *Address*: Dept of History, Univ. College of North Wales, Bangor, Caernarvonshire.

Dyson, Anthony Edward; Senior Lecturer, School of English and American Studies, University of East Anglia, since 1962; *b* 1928. BA Cantab 1952 (1st cl. Pts I and II English Tripos), MA Cantab 1954, MLitt Cantab 1958. Univ. Coll. of North Wales, Bangor, 1955–62. Co-Editor, Crit. Qly, Gen. Ed.,

Macmillan Casebooks, Co-Gen. Ed., Rutledge's Birth of Modern Britain series; ed, vols for Macmillan and OUP. *Publications*: Modern Poetry (with C. B. Box), 1962; The Crazy Fabric: Essays in Irony, 1965; (with C. B. Box) The Practical Criticism of Poetry, 1965; The Inimitable Dickens, 1970; Between Two Worlds: Aspects of Literary Form, 1972; *contrib*. Crit. Qly, Ess. and Studies, Ess. Crit., Mod. Fiction Studies, Novel, Rev. Eng. Studies, etc. *Address*: School of English and American Studies, Univ. of East Anglia, Norwich NOR 88C.

Dyson, Dr Roger Franklin, BA, PhD; Lecturer in Industrial Relations, Department of Adult Education and Extra-mural Studies, University of Leeds, since 1966; *b* 1940; *m* 1964; one *s* one *d*. BA Keele 1962 (1st cl. History and Economics), PhD Leeds 1971. Asst Lectr, Extra-mural Dept, Leeds, 1963–66; Assoc. Lectr in Industrial Relations, Nuffield Health Services Studies Centre, 1971. *Address*: Dept of Adult Education and Extra-mural Studies, The Univ., Leeds LS2 9JT.

E

Eadie, John; Lecturer in English, University College of North Wales, since 1965; *b* 1938; *m* 1963; two *d*. MA Edinburgh 1959 (2nd cl. English), Dip. in Celtic Studies Oxon 1961. Asst Lectr, Dept of English, UCNW, 1962–65. *Publications*: *contrib*. Neophilol. *Address*: Dept of English, Univ. College of North Wales, Bangor LL57 2DG.

Eagleton, Dr Terence Francis; Fellow of Wadham College, Oxford, and University Lecturer in English, since 1969; *b* 1943; *m* 1966; one *s*. Trinity College, Cambridge; BA 1964 (1st cl.), PhD 1969, Cantab. Fellow of Jesus Coll., Cambridge, 1964–69. *Publications*: The New Left Church, 1966; Shakespeare and Society, 1966; Exiles and Emigrés, 1970; The Body as Language, 1970; *contrib*. Essays in Crit., Crit. Qly. *Address*: Wadham Coll., Oxford.

Earl, Dr Donald Charles; Reader in Roman Politics, Department of Latin, University of Leeds, since 1970; *b* 1931; *m* 1956; two *s* three *d*. BA Cantab 1953, MA, PhD Cantab 1958. Asst Lectr in Classics, Leeds Univ., 1955–58; Lectr, 1958–67; Sen. Lectr, 1967–70; Vis. Assoc. Prof., Northwestern Univ., USA, 1965; Vanier Lectr, Ottawa Univ., 1971. Mem., Council, Soc. Prom. Roman Studies, 1962–65, 1968–71; Gov., Trinity and All Saints' Coll. of Educn, Horsforth, Leeds, 1967– . *Publications*: The Political Thought of Sallust, 1961; Tiberius Gracchus: A Study in Politics, 1963; The Moral and Political Tradition of Rome, 1967; The Age of Augustus, 1968, German edn 1969, French edn 1970; *contrib*. Athenaeum (Pavia), Historia, Jl Rom. Studies, Latomus. *Address*: Dept of Latin, The Univ., Leeds LS2 9JT.

Earle, Dr Peter; Lecturer in Economic History, London School of Economics, since 1965; *b* 1937; *m* 1963; two *s*. BSc (Econ.) London 1960, PhD 1969. *Publications*: Corsairs of Malta and Barbary, 1970; Life and Times of Henry V, 1971; Life and Times of James II, 1972; Robert E. Lee, 1973; Essays in European Economic History, 1974; The World of Daniel Defoe (forthcoming); *contrib*. Econ. Hist. Rev. *Address*: London Sch. of Economics, Houghton Street, WC2A 2AE.

Earnshaw, Frank, ALA; University Librarian, University of Bradford, since 1967; *b* 1922; *m* 1947; one *d*. BA Hons Leeds 1948 (Mod. Lang.); ALA 1951. Actg Librarian, Univ. of Bradford, 1966–67. *Publications*: *contrib*. Librarian, Library Assoc. Record. *Address*: Univ. of Bradford, Bradford, BD7 1DP.

Easson, Dr Angus William; Lecturer in English, Royal Holloway College, University of London, since 1971; *b* 1940. BA Nottingham 1962, DPhil Oxford 1968. Univ. of Newcastle upon Tyne, 1965–1971. *Publications*: ed, Dickens: The Old Curiosity Shop, 1972; ed, Gaskell: North and South, 1973; Dickens: Hard Times (commentary), 1973; Contrib. Webster's New World Companion to English and American Literature, 1973; *contrib*. Dickens Studies Annual, Dickensian, James Joyce Qly, Jl of Warburg and Courtauld Insts, Mod. Lang. Rev., Victorian Newsletter. *Address*: Royal Holloway Coll., Egham Hill, Egham, Surrey TW20 0EX.

Easterby, Ronald Scott; Senior Tutor, Applied Psychology Department, University of Aston, since 1970; *b* 1931; *m* 1955; two *s* one *d*. BEE Melbourne 1954, MSc Ergonomics Loughborough 1965; MIEE, Chartered Electrical Engineer. Lectr, Univ. of Aston, 1965–69; Senior Lectr, 1969–70. Committee Member: BSI; ISO. *Publications*: (with W. T. Singleton and D. C. Whitfield) Human Operation in Complex Systems, 1967; *contrib*. Ergonomics, Human Factors. *Address*: College House, Gosta Green, Birmingham B4 7ET.

Easthope, Dr Gary; Lecturer in Sociology, School of Social Studies, University of East Anglia, since 1973; *b* 1945; *m* 1967; one *s*. BA Leeds 1966, MA Leeds 1967, PhD Exeter 1973. Res. Asst/Officer, Inst. of Educn, Exeter, 1968–71; Lectr in Educn, New Univ. of Ulster, 1971–73. School teacher, 1967–68. *Publication*: A History of Social Research Methods, 1973. *Address*: Univ. of East Anglia, Earlham Hall, Norwich NOR 88C.

Easton, Dr Malcolm Fyfe; Reader in History of Art, Department of History, University of Hull, since 1973; *b* 1910; *m* 1945; one *d*. MA Oxon 1947, PhD Leeds 1954. Lectr, History of Art, Univ. Hull, 1957–73. Hon. Curator, Art Collection, Univ. of Hull, 1963. *Publications*: The Last Recollections of Captain Gronow (100 illustrations), 1935; Artists and Writers in Paris, 1964; Aubrey and the Dying Lady: a Beardsley Riddle, 1972, revised edn 1973; (with Michael Holroyd) The Art of Augustus John, 1974; numerous critical catalogues;

contrib. Apollo, Burlington Mag., Connoisseur, Gazette des Beaux Arts, Jl Warburg and Courtauld Insts. *Address*: Univ. of Hull, Hull HU6 7RX.

Eastwood, Charles Cyril, BD, PhD, FRHistS; Lecturer in Religion and Philosophy, Department of Adult Education, Keele University, since 1965; *b* 1916; *m* 1944; one *s* one *d*. BD London 1944, PhD London 1957; FRHistS. *Publications*: The Priesthood of All Believers, 1960; Wanted on Voyage, 1960; The Royal Priesthood of the Faithful, 1963; Life and Thought in the Ancient World, 1964; What You Make It, 1967; *contrib.* Scott. Jl Theol., Lon. Qly Rev. *Address*: Univ. of Keele, Keele, Staffs ST5 5BG.

Eaton, John Herbert; Senior Lecturer, Dept of Theology, University of Birmingham, since 1969; *b* 1927. BA Cantab 1948 (French and German, Theology 1st cl.), MA Cantab 1951, Dip. in Oriental Languages Cantab 1953; Mem., Soc. OT Study, 1958– , (Cttee 1970–). Asst Lectr, Univ. of Birmingham, 1956–59; Lectr, 1959–69. Admiss. Tutor, Theology, 1967– . *Publications*: Obadiah, Nahum, Habakkuk and Zephaniah: Introduction and Commentary, 1961; Psalms: Introduction and Commentary, 1967, pbk edn 1970; *contrib.* Ann. Swed. Theol. Inst., Bible Trans., Jl Theol. Studies, Theol., Vet Testam., Zeits. Alttestam. Wissens. *Address*: Dept of Theology, The Univ., PO Box 363, Birmingham B15 2TT.

Eaton, John Richard; Director of Computing Services, London Business School, since 1973; *b* 1942; *m* 1965; one *s* one *d*. BA (Econ) Manchester 1963; Member: Econometric Soc.; TIMS. Res. Associate, Manchester Univ., 1963–65; Lectr in Economics and Statistics, London Business Sch., 1965–70, Co-ordinator, Computing Services, 1970–73. *Publications*: *contrib.* Economica, Econ. Jl, Jl Agric. Econs. *Address*: London Business School, Sussex Place, Regents Park, NW1 4SA.

Eatwell, Ronald Francis; Librarian, Surrey University, since 1966; *b* 1922; *m* 1949; one *d*. MA London 1974; FLA 1962. Asst Librarian, Greenwich Public Library, 1946–50; Librarian, Battersea Polytechnic, later Battersea Coll. of Technology, 1950–66. Mem., Surrey Univ. Council, 1966–71. *Address*: Univ. of Surrey, Guildford, Surrey GU2 5XH.

Echenique, Dr Marcial, MA, DrArch; University Lecturer in Architecture, since 1970, and Fellow, Churchill College, Cambridge since 1972; *b* 1943; *m* 1963; two *s* one *d*. DipArch Barcelona 1964, DrArch 1966, MA Cantab 1972. Asst Prof., Univ. of Barcelona, 1964–65; Res. Officer, Dept of Architecture, Univ. of Cambridge, 1967–70. Chm., Res. Centre for Land Use and Built Form Studies, Dept of Architecture, Univ. of Cambridge, 1973– . *Publications*: Chaps in, Urban Space and Structures, ed L. Martin and L. March, 1972; *contrib.* London Papers, Arch. Des., Arch. Res. and Teaching, Planificacion, Regnl

Studies. *Address*: Land Use and Built Form Studies, 16 Brooklands Avenue, Cambridge.

Edden, Dr Valerie Jane; Lecturer, Department of English, University of Birmingham, since 1969; *b* 1943; *m* 1965; two *d*. BA Birmingham 1963 (1st cl.), MA Birmingham 1964, PhD Birmingham 1971. Fellow Shakespeare Inst., Univ. of Birmingham, 1965–69. *Publications*: *contrib.* A Second Series of Adaptations of Shakespeare Plays, 1970–71; Horace, ed C. D. N. Costa, 1973. *Address*: Dept of English, Univ. of Birmingham, PO Box 363, Birmingham B15 2TT.

Eden, Michael John; Lecturer, Department of Geography, Bedford College, London University, since 1965; *b* 1936. BA Oxon 1961, MA Oxon 1964, MSc McGill 1964; FRGS. Asst Lectr, Bedford Coll., 1964–65; Vis. Res. Fellow, Univ. of Papua, New Guinea, 1968–69. *Publications*: The Savanna Ecosystem, Northern Rupununi, British Guiana, 1964; *contrib.* Geoderma, Geog. Annal., Geog. Jl, Jl Trop. Geog., Zeits. Geomorphol. *Address*: Dept of Geography, Bedford College, NW1 4NS.

Edey, Prof. Harold Cecil; Professor of Accounting, University of London (London School of Economics and Political Science), since 1962; *b* 1913; *m* 1944; one *s* one *d*. Chartered Accountant 1935, BCom. 1947, Hon. LLD 1972. Lectr in Accounting and Finance, LSE, 1949–55; Reader in Accounting, Univ. of London (LSE), 1955–62. Mem., UK Adv. Council on Educn for Mngmt, 1961–65; Mem., Acad. Planning Bd for London Grad. Sch. of Business Studies, and Gov., 1965–71. Chm., Arts and Social Studies Cttee, CNAA, 1965–71, and Mem. Council, 1965–73; Chm. Bd of Studies in Econs, Univ. of London, 1966–71; Pro-Dir, LSE, 1967–70. Mem. Council, Inst. of Chartered Accountants in England and Wales, 1969– . Commissioned RNVR, 1940–46. *Publications*: (with A. T. Peacock) National Income and Social Accounting, 1954; Business Budgets and Accounts, 1959, 3rd edn 1966; Introduction to Accounting 1963, 2nd edn 1964; (with B. S. Yamey and H. Thompson) Accounting in England and Scotland 1543–1800, 1963; ed (with B. V. Carsberg), Modern Financial Management, 1969; (Mem., Edit. Cttee) An Introduction to Engineering Economics, 1969; ed (with B. S. Yamey), Debits, Credits, Finance and Profits, 1974; *contrib.* Accounting Res., Accounting Rev., Bankers' Mag., Brit. Tax Rev., Brit. Transp. Rev., London and Cambridge Econ. Bull., Mod. Law Rev. *Address*: Houghton Street, Aldwych, WC2A 2AE.

Edge, Dr David Owen, FRAS; Director, Science Studies Unit, University of Edinburgh, since 1966; *b* 1932; *m* 1959; two *s* one *d*. BA Cantab 1955 (Hons Physics), MA Cantab 1959, PhD Cantab 1959; FRAS. Teaching: the role of technology in social history, the historical 'conflict' between scientific and religious thought, ethical problems of science and technology, the origins of 'the environmental crisis'. Producer, Sci. Unit, BBC, 1959–66. Sen. Fellow, Soc. for

201

the Humanities and Sen. Res. Associate of Program on Science, Techn. and Society, Cornell Univ., Feb.–July, 1973; Jt Editor, Science Studies Jl. *Publications*: ed, Experiment, 1964; ed (with J. N. Wolfe), Meaning and Control: essays in social aspects of science and technology, 1972; ed, several vols broadcast scripts for BBC Publications; contrib. Science and Religion: the reopening dialogue, ed G. Walters, 1970; *contrib*. Mem. RAS, MNRAS. *Address*: Science Studies Unit, Univ. of Edinburgh, 34 Buccleuch Place, Edinburgh EH8 9JT.

Edgington, Dorothy Margaret Doig; Lecturer, Department of Philosophy, Birkbeck College, University of London, since 1968; *b* 1941; *m* 1965; one *s* one *d*. BA Oxon 1964, MA, BPhil Oxon 1968. *Address*: Dept of Philosophy, Birkbeck College, Univ. of London, Malet Street, WC1E 7HX.

Edgley, Prof. Roy, BA, BPhil; Professor of Philosophy, University of Sussex, since 1970; *b* 1925; *m* 1960; two *d*. BA Manchester 1952 (1st cl. Philosophy), BPhil Oxon 1954; Mem.: Aristot. Soc., Mind Assoc. Asst Lectr, Bristol, 1954–57; Lectr, 1957–64; Vis. Lectr, Ghana, 1960; Sen. Lectr, Bristol, 1964–70; Vis. Prof., Reed Coll., Oregon, 1969. *Publications*: Reason in Theory and Practice, 1969; *contrib*. Mind, Proc. Aristot. Soc. *Address*: Arts Building, Univ. of Sussex, Falmer, Brighton BN1 9QN.

Edminson, Mary, BA, PhD; Lecturer, School of Education, University of Newcastle upon Tyne, since 1962; *b* 1920; *m* 1939; one *s*. BA Dunelm 1955, PhD Dunelm 1962; Mem., AUT, Nat. Assoc. Teaching Engl. *Publications*: (jtly), A Survey of the Teaching of English in Local Secondary Schools, 1964; (jtly) Attitudes to English Usage, 1970; *contrib*. Dickensian, 19th Cent. Fict. *Address*: School of Education, Univ. of Newcastle upon Tyne, Newcastle upon Tyne NE1 7RU.

Edmonds, Martin Hugh Anthony, BA, MA; Senior Lecturer, Department of Politics, University of Lancaster, since 1972; *b* 1939; *m* 1963; two *s* one *d*. BA Keele 1962 (Internat. Relations), MA (Hons) Manchester 1964. Asst Lectr, Univ. of Manchester, 1965–66; Lectr, Univ. of Lancaster, 1966–72. *Publications*: contrib.: Military Technical Revolution, ed J. Erickson; Dilemmas of Accountability in Modern Government, ed B. Smith and D. Hague; Civil Wars in the 20th Century, ed R. Highams; Nation at War, ed R. Higham and R. Mardar; *contrib*. Internat. Aff., Europ. Archiv., Public Admin., ATM Bull. *Address*: Dept of Politics, Univ. of Lancaster, Bailrigg, Lancaster LA1 4RW.

Edwards, Dr Anthony William Fairbank; Assistant Director of Research, Department of Medicine, University of Cambridge, and Fellow, Gonville and Caius College, since 1970; *b* 1935; *m* 1958; one *s* two *d*. MA, PhD 1961, ScD 1972, Cantab; FSS. Res. Associate, Univ. of Pavia, 1961–64; Actg Asst Prof., Stanford Univ., 1969–65; Sen. Lectr, Univ. of Aberdeen, 1965–68; Bye-Fellow, Gonville and Caius Coll., Cambridge,

1968–70; Vis. Prof., Univ. of Aarhus, 1973. *Publications*: Likelihood, 1972; *contrib*. 34 statistical, genetical and mathematical jls. *Address*: Gonville and Caius Coll., Cambridge.

Edwards, Christopher John Wilfred, MA; Lecturer in Geography, School of Biological and Environmental Studies, New University of Ulster, since 1967; *b* 1940; *m* 1966; one *d*. BA Liverpool 1962 (Hons Special Studies Geography), MA Liverpool 1964. Asst Lectr, Magee Univ. Coll., Londonderry, 1964–66; Lectr, New Univ. of Ulster, 1966– . *Publications*: *contrib*. Arctic. *Address*: School of Biological and Environmental Studies, New Univ. of Ulster, Coleraine BT52 1SA.

Edwards, Edward George, PhD, BSc, FRIC; Vice-Chancellor and Principal, University of Bradford, since 1966; Principal of Bradford Institute of Technology, 1957–66; *b* 1914; *m* 1940; two *s* two *d*. Lectr, Chemistry, Univ. of Nottingham, 1938–40; Head of Dept of Chemistry and Applied Chemistry, Royal Technical Coll., Salford, 1945–54; Principal, Coll. of Technol., Liverpool, 1954–57. Mem. Council, Univ. of Science and Technology, Kumasi, Ghana. Res. Chemist (ICI Ltd), 1940–45. *Publications*: various research papers in chemical jls; articles and papers on higher education, technological innovation, university planning. *Address*: Univ. of Bradford, Richmond Road, Bradford, Yorkshire BD7 1DP.

Edwards, Elizabeth Rosemary, BA, MA, PhD, DipEd; Lecturer, English Department, and Warden of St Andrew's Hall, University of Reading, since 1967; *b* 1922; *m* 1947; one *s* three *d*. BA Bristol 1943 (Hons English), DipEd Bristol 1944, MA London 1953, PhD London 1963. Writer and Researcher on Hist. of Parliament, Inst. Hist. Res., 1964–67. *Address*: St Andrew's Hall, Univ. of Reading, Reading, Berks.

Edwards, Dr Elwyn, BA, PhD; Reader in Ergonomics, Loughborough University of Technology, since 1963; *b* 1932; *m* 1958; one *s* one *d*. BA Liverpool 1957, PhD Bristol 1960; ABPsS, FRStatS. Mem.: Ergonom. Res. Soc., Biol. Engin. Soc., Human Factors Soc.; Freeman, Guild of Air Pilots and Navigs. Lectr, Loughborough Coll. Technol., 1960–63. Mem., Council, Ergonom. Res. Soc., 1964–66; Cttee on Publicns, Brit. Psychol. Soc., 1964–69; Ed., Ergonomics, 1970– . *Publications*: Information Transmission, 1964; Man and Computer in Process Control, 1973; *contrib*. Ergonom., Occup. Psychol., Percept. Mot. Skills. *Address*: Dept of Ergonomics and Cybernetics, Univ. of Technology, Loughborough LE11 3TU.

Edwards, Evan Watts, MA; Senior Lecturer, Department of History, University College, Cardiff, since 1964; *b* 1914; *m* 1949; two *d*. BA Wales 1935 (1st cl. History), MA Wales 1939. Lectr, Univ. Coll., Cardiff, 1949–64. *Publications*: *contrib*. EHR, Hist., Jl Mod. Hist. *Address*: Dept of History, Univ. College, Cathays Park, Cardiff CF1 1XL.

Edwards, Dr Glynn Patrick; Senior Lecturer in Humanity, University of Aberdeen, since 1972 (Lecturer, 1960–72); *b* 1933; *m* 1962; one *s* one *d*. BA Cantab 1956 (1st cl. Classical Tripos Pt II), MA Cantab 1959, PhD Cantab 1965; Mem., Philol. Soc. 1956. *Publications*: The Language of Hesiod in its Traditional Context, 1971; *contrib*. Glotta. *Address*: Dept of Humanity, King's College, Old Aberdeen.

Edwards, Dr Kathleen; Reader in Medieval History, University of Aberdeen, since 1966; *b* 1912. BA London 1935 (Hons History), MA London 1937, PhD Manchester 1940; FRHistS, FSA. Lectr in Medieval History, Univ. Coll. of Wales, Aberystwyth, 1946–47; Lecturer in Medieval History, Univ. of Aberdeen, 1947–53; Sen. Lectr, 1953–66. Asst Registrar, Nat. Reg. of Archives, 1945–46. *Publications*: The English Secular Cathedrals in the Middle Ages, 1949, 2nd edn 1968; ed (with others), The Registers of Roger Martival, Bishop of Salisbury 1315–30, vols I–IV, 1962–74; contrib. Victoria Cty Hist. of England, Wiltshire, vol. 3; *contrib*. Brit. Archaeol. Jl, Ch. Qly Rev., EHR, Oxonien., Trans Royal Hist. Soc. *Address*: History Dept, King's College, The Univ., Aberdeen.

Edwards, Dr Michael; Senior Lecturer, Department of Literature, University of Essex, since 1973; *b* 1938; *m* 1964; one *s* one *d*. BA Cantab 1960, MA Cantab 1964, PhD Cantab 1965. Asst Lectr in French, Univ. of Warwick, 1965, Lectr, 1966. *Publications*: La Thébaïde de Racine, 1965; La Tragédie racinienne, 1972; co-editor, Prospice; *contrib*. Adam, Agenda, Crit. Qly, Jeunesse de Racine (Paris), TLS. *Address*: Dept of Literature, Univ. of Essex, Wivenhoe Park, Colchester, Essex CO4 3SQ.

Edwards, Paul Geoffrey; Reader in English Literature, Edinburgh University, since 1973; *b* 1926; *m* 1954; two *d*. BA Dunelm 1952 (1st cl. Hons Eng. Lang. and Lit.), BA Cantab 1954 (1st cl. Arch. and Anthrop. Section B), MA Cantab 1958. Lectr in English, Fourah Bay Coll., UC Sierra Leone, 1957–63; Lectr in Eng. Lit., Univ. Edinburgh, 1963–68, Sen. Lectr, 1968–73; Vis. Prof., New York State Univ., 1971–72. Sen. Examr in Oral English, W African Exams Council, 1961; Adviser to Overseas Students, Edinburgh Univ., 1964–68. *Publications*: West African Narrative, 1963; Equiano's Travels, 1967, 2nd edn 1969; (with H. Palsson) Gautrek's Saga and other medieval tales, 1968; ed, The Letters of the late Ignatius Sancho, 1969; ed, Ottobah Cugoano's Thoughts and Sentiments on the Evil of Slavery, 1969; (with H. Palsson) The Book of Settlements, 1972; (with H. Palsson) Eyrbyggja Saga, 1973; *contrib*. Afr. Lit. Today, Durham Univ. Jl, English, Eng. Lang. Teaching, Eng. Studies, Essays in Crit., Jl Commonwealth Lit., Mosaic, Notes and Queries, Papers in Lang. and Lit., Phylon. *Address*: Dept of English Literature, David Hume Tower, Edinburgh Univ., Edinburgh EH8 9JX.

Edwards. Prof. Philip Walter, MA, PhD; King Alfred Professor of English Literature,

University of Liverpool, since 1974; *b* 1923; *m* 1952; three *s* one *d*. BA Birmingham 1942 (English), MA Birmingham 1946, PhD Birmingham 1960, MA Dublin 1963 (jure officii). Lectr in English, Birmingham Univ., 1946–58; Commonwealth Fund Fellow, Harvard Univ., 1954–55; Sen. Lectr, Birmingham Univ., 1958–60; Prof. of English Literature, Dublin Univ. (Trinity Coll.), 1960–66; Prof. of Literature, Essex Univ., 1966–74; Vis. Prof., Michigan Univ., 1964–65; Vis. Prof., Williams Coll., Massachusetts, 1960; Vis. Fellow, All Souls Coll., Oxford, 1970–71. *Publications*: Sir Walter Ralegh, 1953; ed, Kyd: The Spanish Tragedy, 1959; Thomas Kyd and Early Elizabethan Tragedy, 1966; Shakespeare and the Confines of Art, 1968; ed, Shakespeare: Pericles, 1974; ed (jtly), Massinger: Plays and Poems, 1974; *contrib*. Shakesp. Survey, Proc. Brit. Acad., Rev. Engl. Lit. *Address*: Dept of English, Univ. of Liverpool, Liverpool L69 3BX.

Edwards, Prof. Robert Dudley; Professor of Modern Irish History, University College, Dublin, since 1945; *b* 1909; *m* 1933; one *s* two *d*. MA National Univ. of Ireland 1921, PhD London 1933, DLitt National Univ. of Ireland 1938; FRHistS. MRIA. Chairman: Irish Cttee of Historical Sciences; Irish Society for Archives; Formerly editor, Irish Historical Studies. Former President, Irish Historical Soc.; Sec., Irish Catholic Historical Cttee; Mem., Irish Manuscripts Commission; Lectr in Modern Irish History, UC, Dublin, 1939–44. Chm., History Depts, Univ. Coll., Dublin. *Publications*: Church and State in Tudor Ireland, 1935, repr. 1972; The Great Famine, 1956; New History of Ireland, 1972; *contrib*. Irish Hist. Studies. *Address*: Dept of Modern Irish History, Arts/Commerce Block, Univ. College, Dublin, Belfield, Dublin 4.

Edwards, Prof. Sir Ronald Stanley, KBE; Professor of Economics with special reference to Industrial Organisation in the University of London, since 1949; *b* 1910; *m* 1936; two *d*. BCom, DSc (Econ.) London, Hon. LLD Edinburgh 1966, Hon. DSc Bath 1966, Hon. LLD Strathclyde 1973, Hon. DLitt Warwick 1973; Certified Accountant. Asst Lectr, later Lectr, in Business Admin with special reference to Accounting, LSE, 1935–40; Sir Ernest Cassel Reader in Commerce with special reference to Industrial Admin, Univ. of London, 1946–49. Mem., British Airways Bd, 1971– ; Finance Mem., and Gen. Sec., Birmingham War Factories Jt Cttee, Dep. Dir of Labour and Asst Sec., Min. of Aircraft Production, 1940–45; Dep. Chm., Electricity Council, 1957–61, Chm., 1962–68; Chm., Beecham Gp Ltd, 1968– ; Dir, ICI Ltd, 1969– . Mem.: Interdeptl Cttee on Further Educn and Training, 1944; Min. of Fuel and Power Cttee on Electricity Peak Load in relation to Non-Industrial Consumers, 1948; Adv. Council, Dept of Scientific and Industrial Res., 1949–54; Min. of Fuel and Power Cttee of Inquiry into the Organisation and Efficiency of the Electricity Supply Industry, 1954–55; UGC, 1955–64; NEDC, 1964–68; Indep. Chm., Brit. Clock and Watch Manufacturers' Assoc. (Watch

Section), 1946–59, Hon. Pres., 1959– ; Pres., Market Research Soc., 1965–69; Chm., Govt Cttee of Inquiry into Civil Air Transport Industry, 1967–69; Chm., Govt Adv. Cttee on Appointment of Advertising Agents, 1970– ; Governor: Admin. Staff Coll., Henley, 1962–70; London Grad. Sch. of Business Studies, 1964– ; LSE. *Publications*: Co-operative Industrial Research, 1950; Industrial Research in Switzerland, 1951; (with H. Townsend) Business Enterprise, 1958; (with H. Townsend) Studies in Business Organisation, 1961; (with H. Townsend) Business Growth, 1966; (with R. Roberts) Status, Productivity and Pay: a major experiment, 1971; contribs to: Studies in Accounting, ed Baxter; Studies in Costing, ed Solomons; *contrib.* learned jls on econ. industrial and accounting questions. *Address*: London School of Economics, Houghton Street, WC2A 2AE.

Edwards, Stephen Charles; Lecturer in Environmental Engineering, School of Architecture and Building Technology, University of Bath, since 1968; *b* 1940; *m* 1963; two *d*. MSc Bath 1971; CEng, MIHVE, MInstF, MInstR. Consultant to Hoare Lea & Partners, Consulting Engineers. *Publications*: Thermal Environmental Engineering (3 vols), 1972; *contrib.* Instn Heat. Vent. Engrs. *Address*: School of Architecture and Building Technology, Univ. of Bath, Claverton Down, Bath BA2 7AY.

Eekelaar, John Michael; Fellow and Lecturer, Pembroke College, Oxford, since 1965; *b* 1942. LLB London 1963, BCL Oxon 1965, MA Oxon 1965; of the Inner Temple, Barrister-at-Law. CUF Lectr Oxford Univ., 1966– . *Publications*: Family Security and Family Breakdown, 1971; contrib. Annual Survey of Commonwealth Law, 1967–73; Oxford Essays in Jurisprudence (2nd series), 1972; *contrib.* legal jls. *Address*: Pembroke College, Oxford.

Eels, Francis Robert, MA; Lecturer, Industrial Administration, University of Strathclyde, since 1961; *b* 1915. MA St Andrews 1952 (Econ. and Pol Sci.). Res. in Econ., Sheffield, 1953–57; Res. Off., Oxford Inst. of Stats, 1957–58; Prof. of Economics, Univ. of Alaska, and Assoc. Ed., Rev. of Econ. Conditions in Alaska, 1965–67. Res. Off., Bd of Trade, 1959–61. *Publications*: *contrib.* Account. Res., Bull. Oxf. Univ. Inst. Stats, Jl Ind. Econ., Rev. Econ. Conditions Alaska. *Address*: Business School, Univ. of Strathclyde, Glasgow G1 1XH.

Egan, William; Co-ordinator for Educational Technology, London Graduate School of Business Studies, University of London, since 1971; *b* 1934; *m* 1959; one *s* one *d*. BA Dunelm 1959, MA Leeds 1966; GMBPS 1966. Senior Research Offr, LBS, 1968. *Address*: London Graduate School of Business Studies, Sussex Place, Regent's Park, NW1 4SA.

Eggleston, James Frederick; Senior Lecturer in Education, School of Education, University of Leicester, since 1971; *b* 1927; *m* 1955; three *s* two *d*. BSc Durham 1952

(Special Hons Zoology), DipEd Durham 1953; MIBiol 1954–71, FIBiol 1971. Res. Fellow, Univ. of Leicester, 1964– ; Sen. Res. Fellow, 1965; Lectr in Educn, 1966–71. Dir, Schs Council Res. Project, Evaluation of Sci. Teaching Methods, 1970–73. *Publications*: A Critical Review of Assessment Procedures in Secondary School Science, 1965; Problems in Quantitative Biology, 1968; Studies in Assessment, 1970; Thinking Quantitatively, I, Mathematical Models, II, Statistics and Experimental Design, 1970; Disciplines of the Curriculum – Biology, 1970; *contrib.* Educnl Res. *Address*: School of Education, 21 University Road, Leicester.

Eggleston, Prof. Samuel John, BSc(Econ), MA; Professor of Education and Head of Education Department, University of Keele, since 1967; *b* 1926; *m* 1957; two *s* two *d*. Leverhulme Scholar, LSE 1954–57, BSc (Econ) London 1957, MA London 1965; Teacher's Cert. 1948; Mem., Brit. Sociological Assoc., Amer. Sociological Assoc. Lectr, Leicester Univ., 1963–66, Sen. Lectr, 1966–67. Mem., Council of Europe; Res. Cttee and Wkg Party on Post Secondary Educn; Schs Council Wkg Party on Whole Curriculum; H of C Wkg Party on Racial Prejudice in Educn; Stoke on Trent Educn Cttee; Governor, Alsager Coll. of Educn; Consultant, OECD. Editor, 'Studies in Design Education', 1969– ; Editor, 'Paedagogia Europaea' (European Ybk of Educn), 1970– ; Chm., Sociological Rev. Edit. Bd. *Publications*: Social Context of the School, 1967; ed, Research in the Sociology of Education, 1974; The Sociology of the Curriculum, 1974; ed, European Year Book of Education, vols V, VI, VII, VIII and IX, 1970–74; *contrib.* Brit. Jl of Sociology, Ed. Res., Sociology. *Address*: Dept of Education, Univ. of Keele, Keele, Staffordshire ST5 5BG.

Ehrenberg, Prof. A. S. C.; Professor of Marketing, London Graduate School of Business Studies, since 1970; *b* 1926; *m* 1949; two *s* one *d*. BSc Durham 1947; Member: RSS, Market Res. Soc., BPsS. Demonstrator, Univ. of Durham, 1947–48; Res. Asst, Cambridge, 1949–51; Lectr, London, 1951–55; Associate Prof., Warwick, 1968–70; Vis. Lectr, Columbia, 1968; Vis. Prof., Pittsburgh, 1970–71. *Publications*: Consumer Behaviour, 1971; Repeat Buying, 1972; Konsument Beteende, 1973; Data Reduction, 1974; *contrib.* Jl RSS, Applied Statist., Jl Market Res. Soc., Jl Marktg Res., Jl Adv. Res., Op. Res. Qly. *Address*: London Business School., Sussex Place, NW1 4SA.

Ehrlich, Prof. Cyril; Professor of Economic and Social History, Queen's University, Belfast, since 1974 (Reader, 1969–74); *b* 1925; *m* 1954; two *s* one *d*. BSc(Econ) London 1950, PhD London 1958; Mem., Econ. Hist. Soc. Afr. Studies Assoc. Lectr, Makerere Coll., E Africa, 1952–58, Sen. Lectr, 1958–61; Lectr, Belfast, 1961–66, Sen. Lectr, 1966–69. Mem., CouncilAfr. Studies Assoc., 1966–69. *Publications*: The Uganda Company, 1953; contrib. Oxford History of East Africa, vol. 11 1965, vol. III 1972; *contrib.* Jl Afr. Hist., Jl Develt Studies,

Jl Mod. Afr. Studies. *Address*: Dept of Economic and Social History, Queen's Univ., Belfast BT7 1NN.

Eisler, Prof. Frieda G.; *see* Goldman-Eisler.

Eisner, Otto Z., LLD, BA; Senior Lecturer in German, University of Bradford, since 1964; *b* 1911; *m* 1946; one *s* one *d*. LLD Prague 1935 (Dr jur utr), BA London 1949 (1st cl. German with Russian). Lektor, Univ. of Wales (Univ. Coll., Cardiff), until 1955; Asst Ed., Structure Reports, 1955–57; Lectr, Liverpool Coll. of Comm., 1957–64. Dep. Chm., Sch. Mod. Langs, Univ. of Bradford, 1966– ; var. Ext. Examinerships. *Publications*: trans., in German (with H. Schönhof), V. Nezval: Gedichte 1938; contrib. var. Prague papers, 1938; ed, 'Cechoslovàk' and 'Obzor' (two war-time publications); contrib. Stimmen aus Böhmen; Advanced German Conversation, 1965; contrib. 'The Teaching of Languages to Adults', 1965; 'Language and Education' (Lyndale House papers), 1965; *contrib.* Universum Prague. *Address*: School of Modern Languages, Bradford Univ., Bradford BD7 1DP.

Elcock, Dr Howard James; Lecturer, Department of Political Studies, The University of Hull, since 1966; *b* 1942. BA Oxon 1964 (2nd cl. PPE), BPhil Oxon 1966 (Politics), MA Oxon 1968, PhD Hull 1973; Mem., Public Admin. Cttee, Jt Univ. Council Soc. Public Admin., 1968– . *Publications*: Administrative Justice, 1969; Portrait of a Decision: The Council of Four and the Treaty of Versailles, 1972; *contrib.* Hist. Jl, Pol Studies, Public Admin. *Address*: Dept of Political Studies, Univ. of Hull, Hull HU6 7RX.

Elcombe, (Denis) Keith; Lecturer in Music, University of Manchester, since 1967; *b* 1941; *m* 1972. BA 1964, MusB 1965, Cantab; LRAM 1961, FRCO 1964. Univ. Organist and Conductor, Manchester Univ. Chorus. *Address*: Univ. of Manchester, Manchester M13 9PL.

Elder, Neil Colbert McAulay), MA, BLitt; Senior Lecturer, Department of Political Studies, University of Hull, since 1967; *b* 1925; *m* 1966; one *d*. BA Oxon 1949 (1st cl. PPE), MA Oxon 1950, BLitt Oxon 1954. Lectr, Brasenose and St John's Colls, Oxford, 1950–53; Lectr, Univ. and St John's Coll., Oxford, 1953–56; Lectr, Queen's Coll., Dundee, 1956–63; Sen. Lectr, 1963–67. *Publications*: Government in Sweden, 1970; *contrib.* Amer. Pol Sci. Rev., Party Aff., Pol Studies. *Address*: Dept of Political Studies, University of Hull, Hull HU6 7RX.

Eldridge, Dr Colin Clifford; Lecturer, History Department, Saint David's University College, since 1968; *b* 1942; *m* 1970. BA Nottingham 1963, PhD Nottingham 1966. Post-Doctoral Fellow, Edinburgh Univ., 1966–68. *Publications*: England's Mission: The Imperial Idea in the Age of Gladstone and Disraeli, 1868–80, 1973; Victorian Imperialism (forthcoming); *contrib.* Jl NZ Hist., Renaiss. Mod. Studies, Trivium, Vict.

Studies. *Address*: Saint David's Univ. College, Lampeter, Dyfed SA48 7ED.

Eldridge, Prof. John E. T.; Professor of Sociology, University of Glasgow, since 1972; *b* 1936; *m* 1960; one *s* two *d*. BSc (Econ) London 1957; MA Leicester 1959; Member: British Sociological Assoc.; British Univs Industrial Relations Assoc. Sen. Res. Asst, Univ. of Durham, 1961–63; Lectr, Sen. Lectr, Univ. of York, 1964–69; Prof. of Sociology, Univ. of Bradford, 1969–72. Mem., SSRC Management and Industrial Relations Cttee, 1969–74. *Publications*: Industrial Disputes, 1968, 2nd edn 1972; Max Weber: the interpretation of social reality, 1970, 2nd edn 1972; Sociology and Industrial Life, 1971, 2nd edn 1973; *contrib.* Brit. Jl of Sociol., Jl of Management Studies, Sociol Rev. *Address*: Dept of Sociology, Adam Smith Building, Univ. of Glasgow.

Elfenbein, Dr Josef Horblit; Senior Lecturer in Mathematics, University of London, Goldsmiths' College (also teaches the history of mathematics), since 1965; *b* 1927; *m* 1953; one *s* one *d*. BA California 1947 (Maths), MA, PhD Princeton 1950 (Oriental Philology, Sanskrit with Iranian), MPhil London 1969 (Mathematics); FRAS, LMS. Jun. Fellow, Princeton, 1949–50; Lectr in Maths, Univ. of Teheran, 1961–62. *Publications*: A Vocabulary of Marw Baluchi, 1963; The Baluchi Language (RAS monograph), 1966; *contrib.* Archiv Orient., Bull. SOAS. *Address*: Dept of Mathematics, Univ. of London, Goldsmiths' College, New Cross, SE14 6NW.

El-Kafrawy, Mohamed; Department of Near Eastern Studies, Manchester University, since 1962; *b* 1915; *m* 1957; three *d*. BA Cairo 1944, London 1949, PhD London 1951. Cairo Univ., 1952–62. *Publications*: Ganin; Abdellah b al-Muatayy; Al-Shian al Arabi; Topiph al Shir, 4 vols; Ostonat al-Zuhd. *Address*: Dept of Near Eastern Studies, Manchester Univ., Manchester M13 9PL.

Elkan, Prof. Walter, BSc(Econ), PhD; Professor of Economics and Chairman of Department of Economics, University of Durham, since 1966; *b* 1923; *m* 1946; one *s* two *d*. BSc(Econ) LSE 1950 (2nd cl.), PhD LSE 1956; Mem., Royal Econ. Soc. (Council 1971–); Pres., Afr. Studies Assoc. UK (Council 1971–). Res. Asst, LSE, 1952–53; Res. Fellow, E African Inst. Soc. Res., 1954–58; Lectr, Makerere Univ. Coll., 1958–60; Lectr, Univ. of Durham, 1960–66; Visiting Res. Prof., Univ. of Nairobi, 1972–73. *Publications*: An African Labour Force, 1956; Migrants and Proletarians, 1960; Economic Development of Uganda, 1961; Introduction to Development Economics, 1972; *contrib.* Amer. Econ. Rev., Africa, Rev. Econ. Studies, Jl Develop. Studies, Internat. Aff. *Address*: Univ. of Durham, Dept of Economics, 23/6 Old Elvet, Durham.

Elkins, Prof. Thomas Henry; Professor of Geography, University of Sussex, since 1963; *b* 1926; *m* 1953; one *s* one *d*. BA London 1950; FRGS, Mem., Inst. Brit. Geogrs, etc. Asst Lectr, LSE, 1950–55; Lectr, King's

Coll., London, 1955–63. Hon. Org. Sec., 20th Internat. Geog. Cong., 1964; Mem., Crawley Local Cttee, Commn for New Towns. *Publications*: Germany, 1960, 2nd edn 1968; The Urban Explosion, 1973; *contrib*. Geog. Jl, Geog., Trans Inst. Brit. Geogrs, etc. *Address*: Arts Building, Univ. of Sussex, Falmer, Brighton, Sussex BN1 9QN.

Elliott, Anne Hynde; Fellow and Tutor in English Literature, St Hilda's College, Oxford, and Lecturer, Faculty of English Language and Literature, Oxford University, since 1954; *b* 1920. BA Oxon 1943, MA 1948. Mary Somerville Res. Fellow, Somerville Coll., 1953–54. *Address*: St Hilda's College, Oxford.

Elliott, Charles, MA, DipEd; Senior Lecturer, Department of English, University College, Cardiff, since 1964; *b* 1919; *m* 1943; two *s* one *d*. DipEd Wales 1946, BA Wales 1949 (1st cl. English), MA Wales 1950. Asst Lectr, Univ. Coll., Cardiff, 1951–53; Lectr, Univ. Coll., Cardiff, 1953–64; Asst Examiner, English (A Level, WJEC), 1958–64; Ch. Examiner, 1965–67. *Publications*: ed, Robert Henryson: Poems, 1963; *contrib*. Jl EGP, Mediev. Studies, Notes and Queries. *Address*: Dept of English, Univ. College, Cathays Park, Cardiff CF1 1XL.

Elliott, Prof. Charles Kenneth, PhD; Professor of Human Resource Management, University of Loughborough, since 1974; *b* 1936; *m* 1961; two *d*. BA Hull 1961 (1st cl. Psychology), PhD Liverpool 1965. Lectr in Psychology, Univ. of Bradford, 1963–71, Sen. Lectr, 1971–74. Sci. Staff, Med. Res. Council, 1961–63. *Publications*: A Guide to the Documentation of Psychology, 1971; Research Methods in Marketing, 1974; *contrib*. Brit. Jl Educnl Psychol., Brit. Jl Indust. Relat., Bull. Brit. Psychol. Soc., Jl Market Res. Soc., Libr. Assoc. Rec., Occup. Psychol. *Address*: Loughborough Univ. of Technology, Loughborough LE11 3TU.

Elliott, Rev. Dr Charles Middleton; Senior Research Associate and Visiting Lecturer, Overseas Development Group, University of East Anglia, since 1972; *b* 1939; *m* 1964; three *s*. BA Oxon (2nd cl. Hons) 1960, DPhil 1962; Asst Lectr then Lectr in Pure Economics, Nottingham, 1963–65; Reader in Economics, Zambia, 1965–69; Sen. Res. Fellow, UN Res. Inst. of Social Development, Geneva (on secondment), 1964–65; Asst Sec. and Res. Dir, SODEPAX, 1969–72. *Publications*: (with R. Dayal) Social and Economic Factors in Agricultural Development, 1966; The Development Debate, 1971, Swedish, Italian, US edns, 1971, Philippines 1973; ed, Constraints on Zambia's Economic Development, 1971; (jtly) Some Determinants of Labour Productivity in Zambian Agriculture: An Econometric Analysis with Policy Suggestions (report to Govt of Zambia), 1971; Fair Chance for All: Money and Trade between Unequal Partners, 1973; *Articles in Symposia and Books*: The Cost of Economic Development, in, Economic Growth in World Perspective, ed D. L. Munby, 1965; The Role of Agriculture in Economic Development, and The Process of Economic Growth, in, Agricultural Producers and their Markets, ed T. K. Warley, 1966; The Ideology of Economic Growth – A Case Study; in, Land, Labour and Population: Essays in Honour of J. D. Chambers, ed Jones and Mingay, 1967; Zambian Humanism and Zambian Agriculture, in, After Mulungushi: The Economics of Zambian Humanism, ed Fortman, 1969; Towards a Generalised Model of African Agricultural Progress, in, Agrarian Change and Economic Development, ed Jones and Woolf, 1970; The Effect of Ill-Health on Farm Productivity in Zambia, in, Change in Agriculture, ed A. H. Bunting, 1970; Wachstum, Entwicklung – oder Unabhängigkeit?, in, Probleme des Sozioökonomischen Wandels in Dualistischen Wirtschaften – Das Beispiel Zambia, ed H. and U. Simonis, 1970; Political Economy of English Dissent, 1780–1840, in, The Industrial Revolution, ed R. M. Hartwell, 1970; Agricultural Organization in Africa, in, Survey of Developments in African Law, International Association of Legal Science, 1970; Income Distribution and Social Stratification, in, Measuring Development, ed N. Baster, 1972; *contrib*. Jl Development Studies, Econ. Hist. Rev., Jl Applied Econs, Philippine Econ. Rev. *Address*: Sch. of Development Studies, Univ. Village, Norwich NOR 88C.

Elliott, Dr James Keith; Lecturer in New Testament Studies, University of Leeds, since 1967; *b* 1943; *m* 1971. BA Wales 1964 (1st cl.), DPhil Oxon 1967; Mem. Studiorum Novi Testamenti Societas. Warden, Charles Morris Hall, Univ. Leeds, 1971– . *Publications*: The Greek Text of the Epistles to Timothy and Titus, 1968; *contrib*. Expos. Times, Jl of Theol Studies, Novum Test., Theology, Zeitschrift für die Neutestamentliche Wissenschaft. *Address*: Dept of Theology, Univ. of Leeds, Leeds LS2 9JT.

Elliott, Kenneth Walter, MA, DipCrim; Lecturer, Department of Adult Education and Extra-Mural Studies, University of Leeds, since 1972; *b* 1915; *m* 1946. BA Cambridge 1963 (Law), MA Cambridge 1967, Postgrad. Dip. in Criminology, Cambridge 1964. Res. Asst, Dept of Social Theory and Institutions, Durham, 1964–68; Res. Fellow, Dept of Sociology, Southampton, 1968–72. Adviser, in, Studies, Central Training Organisation, HM Prison Dept, House Office. *Address*: Dept of Adult Educn and Extra-Mural Studies, Univ. of Leeds, 10 Clarendon Place, Leeds LS2 9JT.

Elliott, Dr Norman Robson; Senior Lecturer in Geography, University of Edinburgh, since 1969; *b* 1925; *m* 1957; one *d*. BA Dunelm 1950, PhD Dunelm 1955. Asst Lectr, Edinburgh Univ., 1953–56; Lectr, 1956–69. *Publications*: *contrib*. Trans Inst. Brit. Geogrs, Tijdschr. Econ. Soc. Geogr. *Address*: Dept of Geography, Univ. of Edinburgh, Edinburgh EH8 9YL.

Elliott, Philip; Research Officer, Centre for Mass Communication Research, University of Leicester, since 1968; *b* 1943; *m* 1964; one *s* one *d*. BA Oxon 1964, MA(Econ) Manchester 1967 (Sociology); BSA. Res. Asst,

CMCR, Univ. of Leicester, 1966–68. *Publications*: (with J. D. Halloran and G. Murdoch) Demonstrations and Communication: A Case Study, 1970; (with J. D. Halloran) Television for Children and Young People, 1970; The Making of a Television Series: A Case Study in the Sociology of Culture, 1972; The Sociology of the Professions, 1972; *contrib*. Sociol. Rev. *Address*: Centre for Mass Communication Research, Univ. of Leicester, Leicester LE1 7LT.

Elliott, Prof. Raymond Kenneth, BA, MA; Head of the History and Philosophy of Education Division, School of Education, University of Birmingham, since 1973; *b* 1924; *m* 1952; one *s* two *d*. BA Oxon 1951 (2nd cl. English), MA Oxon, BA London 1961 (1st cl. Philosophy). Lectr in Philosophy, Birkbeck Coll., London, 1962–68; Lectr, then Sen. Lectr in Philosophy of Educn, Univ. of London Inst. of Educn, 1968–73. *Publications*: contrib. Phenomenology and Linguistic Analysis, ed W. Mays and S. C. Brown, 1972; RIP Lectures, vol. 6 1971–72; *contrib*. Analysis, Brit. Jl of Aesthetics, Kant-Studien, Proc. Aristot. Soc., Proc. Philos. of Educn Soc. GB. *Address*: School of Education, Univ. of Birmingham, Birmingham B15 2TT.

Ellis, Charles Matthew, MSc, FRIC; Head of the Chemistry Department, Goldsmiths' College, University of London, since 1965; *b* 1921; *m* 1945; one *s* two *d*. BSc London 1948 (1st cl. Chemistry), MSc London 1955; ARIC 1948, FRIC 1965. Lectr, Woolwich Poly., 1948–59; Sen. Lectr, Goldsmiths' Coll., 1959–65. Rep., Univ. of London Inst. Educn, Chemistry Teachers' Centre Cttee, Thames Poly., 1971. *Publications*: *contrib*. Analyst, Jl Chem. Educn, Sch. Sci. Rev. *Address*: Chemistry Dept, Goldsmiths' College. Lewisham Way, SE14 6NW.

Ellis, Dr Geoffrey James; Official Fellow and Tutor in Modern History, Hertford College, Oxford, since 1974; *b* 1940; *m* 1969; one *s*. BA Rhodes 1962 (1st cl. Hons), BA Oxon 1966 (1st cl.), MA DPhil Oxon 1972. Jun. Lectr, Dept of History, Rhodes Univ., 1963–64; Sen. McKinnon Scholar, Magdalen Coll., Oxford, 1966–67; Res. Lectr, Christ Church, Oxford, 1967–72; Lectr, Dept of Econ. History, Durham, 1972–74; Tutor, Collingwood Coll., Durham, 1973–74. *Address*: Hertford Coll., Oxford OX1 3BW.

Ellis, Rev. Ieuan Pryce; Lecturer in Theology, Department of Theology, University of Hull, since 1965. BA Cantab 1958 (Theological Tripos), MA 1962, BA Oxford 1960, BLitt 1962, BD London 1963; Lectr in Theology, Fourah Bay Coll., Sierra Leone, 1962–64. *Publications*: *contrib*. Jl Ecclesiastical History, New Blackfriars, NT Studies, Theol. *Address*: Dept of Theology, The Univ., Hull HU6 7RX.

Ellis, John Clive Alexander; Senior Lecturer, Education Department, University of London, Goldsmiths' College, since 1968; *b* 1928; *m* 1954; two *s* one *d*. BA Auckland

UC, NZ 1949, BA Cantab. 1952, DipEd Cambridge Inst. Educn 1953, AcDip in Educn London 1968. Lectr in Education and English, Univ. of London Inst. of Educn, 1965–68. *Publications*: contrib. Bull. Univ. of London Inst. of Educn, Comprehensive Educn, English in Educn, Ideas (Univ. of London Goldsmiths' Coll.), The World and the Sch. *Address*: Goldsmiths' College, New Cross, SE14 6NW.

Ellis, Dr Kenneth Leslie; Lecturer, History Department, Durham University, since 1949; *b* 1924; *m* 1969. MA Oxon 1949, DPhil Oxon 1954. *Publication*: The Post Office in the Eighteenth Century, 1958. *Address*: History Dept, 43 North Bailey, Durham.

Ellis, Margaret Anne; Warden of University Hall of Residence and Lecturer, Department of English, University of Hull, since 1968; *b* 1930. Dip. Sociology London 1962, BA London 1968 (1st cl. Hons English). Various admin. posts in Univ. London and other educnl bodies, 1948–68. *Address*: Cleminson Hall, Cottingham, E Yorks.

Ellis, Stanley, MA; Senior Lecturer in English Language and Medieval English Literature, School of English, University of Leeds, since 1973; *b* 1926; *m* 1953; two *s* one *d*. BA Leeds 1951, MA Leeds 1952. Res. Asst, Leeds Univ., 1952–58, Lectr, 1958–73. Hon. Ed. Sec., Yorks Dial. Soc., 1961– ; Chm., Council, Yorks Dial. Soc., 1970–73; Treas., and Jt Ed., Leeds Studies in English. *Publications*: ed, Studies in Honour of Harold Orton (Leeds Studies in English vol. II), 1968; contrib. Survey of English Dialects, ed H. Orton and E. Dieth; *contrib*. Trans Yorks Dial. Soc. *Address*: School of English, Univ. of Leeds, Leeds LS2 9JT.

Ellis, William Ronald Archer; Lecturer in Geography and Education, University of Sheffield, since 1965; *b* 1913; *m* 1940; two *d*. BA Liverpool 1935, DipEd, Liverpool 1936. Mem. Inst. British Geographers. Chm., Geography Cttee, Schools Council, 1964–71; Jt Hon. Sec., Geographical Assoc., 1967– . *Publications*: (with D. M. Ellis) Geography around us, 1963; *contrib*. Geography. *Address*: Institute of Education, Univ. of Sheffield, Sheffield S10 2TN.

Ellison, Dr Mary Louise; Lecturer, Department of American Studies, Keele University, since 1971; *b* 1939; *m* 1960 (marr. diss.); one *s* one *d*; *m* 1973. BA Hons, London 1960, PhD London 1968. Hist. Dept, Univ. of Reading, 1968–71. *Publications*: Support for Secession, 1972; The Black Experience, 1974; chapter in, Europe and the American Conflict. *Address*: Dept of American Studies, Univ. of Keele, Keele, Staffs ST5 5BG.

Ellmann, Prof. Richard; Goldsmiths' Professor of English Literature, and Fellow of New College, Oxford, since 1970; *b* 1918; *m* 1949; one *s* two *d*. BA Yale 1939, MA Yale 1941, BLitt TCD 1947, PhD Yale 1947, MA Oxon 1970; FRSL, Fellow, Amer. Acad. Arts Sci., Mem., Nat. Inst. Art: Lett.

Instructor, Harvard, 1942–43, 1947–48; Briggs-Copeland Asst Prof., Harvard, 1948–51; Prof., Northwestern Univ., 1951–63; F. B. Snyder Prof., Northwestern, 1963–68; Prof., Yale, 1968–70; Rockefeller Fellow, 1946–47; Guggenheim Fellow, 1950, 1957, 1970; Kenyon Rev. Fellow in Criticism, 1955–56; Fellow, Sch. of Letters, Indiana Univ., 1956, 1960, Sen. Fellow, 1966–72. National Book Award, 1960. *Publications*: Yeats: The Man and the Masks, 1948; trans., Selected Writings of Henri Michaux, 1951; The Identity of Yeats, 1954; James Joyce: a biography, 1959; Eminent Domain, 1967; Ulysses on the Liffey, 1972; Golden Codgers, 1973; edited: S. Joyce: My Brother's Keeper, 1958; (with others) Masters of British Literature, 1958; Arthur Symons: The Symbolist Movement in Literature, 1958; (with E. Mason) The Critical Writings of James Joyce, 1959; Edwardians and Late Victorians, 1959; (with C. Feidelson Jr) The Modern Tradition, 1965; Letters of James Joyce, vols II and III, 1966; James Joyce, Giacomo Joyce, 1968; The Artist as Critic, Critical Writings of Oscar Wilde, 1969; Oscar Wilde (Twentieth Century Views), 1970; The Norton Anthology of Modern English and American Poetry, 1973; James Joyce, Selected Letters, 1974. *Address*: New College, Oxford.

El-Mokadem, Dr Ahmed Mohamed, BA, PhD; Lecturer in Econometrics, Economics Department, University of Lancaster, since 1970; Senior Economic Adviser, Battelle Memorial Institute, USA; *b* 1941; *m* 1967; two *s*. BA Cairo 1961, PhD Manchester 1969. Asst Lectr, Cairo, 1961–68; Res. Fellow, Stirling, 1968–70. *Publications*: Econometric Models of Personal Saving: the UK 1948–1966, 1973; *contrib.* Manchester Sch. *Address*: Dept of Economics, Univ. of Lancaster, Bailrigg, Lancaster LA1 4YW; Battelle Memorial Institute, 505 King Avenue, Columbus, Ohio 43201, USA.

Else, Peter Kenneth; Senior Lecturer in Economics, University of Sheffield, since 1973; *b* 1937; *m* 1971. BSc(Econ.) London 1959, MCom Birmingham 1963; Mem., Royal Econ. Soc. Asst Res. Off. Univ. Coll. of Wales, 1961–63; Asst Lectr, Univ. of Sheffield, 1963–65, Lectr, 1965–73. *Publications*: Public Expenditure, Parliament and PPB (PEP Broadsheet 522), 1970; *contrib.* Jl Transp. Econ. Policy, Oxford Econ. Papers. *Address*: Division of Economic Studies, The Univ., Sheffield S10 2TN.

Elsworth, John David, MA, PhD; Senior Lecturer in Russian, School of European Studies, University of East Anglia, since 1971; *b* 1939; *m* 1968; two *s* one *d*. BA Cantab 1961 (Mod. and Med. Langs), MA Cantab 1965, PhD Cantab 1968. Asst Lectr, Univ. of East Anglia, 1964–67; Lectr, 1967–71. *Publications*: Andrey Bely, 1972. *Address*: School of European Studies, University Plain, Norwich NOR 88C.

Eltis, Walter Alfred, MA; Official Fellow and Lecturer in Economics, Exeter College, Oxford, since 1963; *b* 1933; *m* 1959; one *s* two *d*. BA Cantab 1956 (1st cl. Economics), MA Oxon 1960. Res. Fellow, Exeter Coll.,

Oxford, 1958–60; Lectr, Exeter Coll. and Keble Coll., 1960–63; Vis. Reader, Univ. of W Australia, 1970. Econ. Consultant, NEDO, 1963–66 and 1972; Mem., Council of Govs, Wycliffe Coll., 1971– . *Publications*: Economic Growth, 1966; Jt Ed, Induction Growth and Trade: Essays in Honour of Sir Roy Harrod, 1970; Growth and Distribution, 1973; *contrib.* Econ. Jl, Econ. Rec., Oxford Econ. Papers. *Address*: Exeter College, Oxford.

Elton, Prof. G. R., LittD, FBA; Professor of English Constitutional History, University of Cambridge, since 1967; *b* 1921; *m* 1952. BA London 1943 (1st cl. Hons), PhD London 1949, MA Cantab 1949, LittD Cantab 1960; FBA, FRHistS (Pres., RHistS 1973–). Asst, Glasgow, 1948–49; Asst Lectr, Cambridge, 1949–53; Lectr, Cambridge, 1953–63; Reader in Tudor Studies, Cambridge, 1963–67. Syndic, Cambridge Univ. Press, 1963– . *Publications*: The Tudor Revolution in Government, 1953; England under the Tudors, 1955; Star Chamber Stories, 1958; ed, New Cambridge Modern History II, 1958; The Tudor Constitution, 1960; Reformation Europe, 1963; ed, Renaissance and Reformation, 1963; The Practice of History, 1967; Sources of History: England 1200–1640, 1969; Political History: Principles and Practice, 1970; Policy and Police: the enforcement of the Reformation in the age of Thomas Cromwell, 1972; Reform and Renewal: Thomas Cromwell and the Commonweal, 1973; Studies in Tudor and Stuart Politics and Government (2 vols), 1974; *contrib.* Econ. Hist. Rev., EHR, Hist. Jl, Hist., JBS, etc. *Address*: Clare College, Cambridge.

Elton, Prof. Lewis Richard Benjamin, DSc; Head of Institute for Educational Technology since 1967, and Professor of Science Education since 1971, University of Surrey; *b* 1923; *m* 1950; three *s* one *d*. BA Cantab 1945, BSc London 1947 (1st cl. Mathematics), MA Cantab 1948, PhD London 1950, DSc London 1961, Cambridge Cert. Educn 1945; FInstP, FIMA, FRSA. Asst Lectr, then Lectr, King's Coll., London, 1950–57; Hd of Physics Dept, Battersea Coll. of Technol., 1958–66; Hd of Physics Dept, Univ. of Surrey, 1966–69, Prof. of Physics, 1964–71; Res. Assoc., Massachusetts Inst. Technol., 1955, Stanford Univ., 1956, Niels Bohr Inst., Copenhagen, 1962; Vis. Prof., Univ. of Washington, Seattle, 1965, Univ. Coll. London, 1970– , Univ. of Sydney, 1971. Mem.: Gov. Body, Battersea Coll. Technol., 1962–66; Council, Univ. of Surrey, 1966–67; Conv., Stand. Conf. Physics Profs, 1971– ; Mem., Gov. Council, Soc. Res. Higher Educn, 1971– . *Publications*: Introductory Nuclear Theory, 1959, Spanish edn 1964, 2nd edn 1965; Nuclear Sizes, 1961, Russian edn 1962; Concepts in Classical Mechanics, 1971; *contrib.*: Proceedings of the Conference on Direct Interactions and Nuclear Reaction Mechanisms, 1963; Employment Problems of Automation and Advanced Technology, 1966; Proceedings of the International Conference on Electromagnetic Sizes of Nuclei, 1967; Landolt Börnstein, 1967; High Energy Physics and Nuclear Structure, 1970; Aspects of

208

Educational Technology, 1970–71; Computer und Angestellte, 1971; *contrib.* Nucl. Phys, Phys Rev., Phys Bull., Phys Educn, Proc. Phys Soc., Times Educnl Supp., Univ. Qly, etc. *Address:* Institute for Educational Technology, Univ. of Surrey, Guildford, Surrey GU2 5XH.

Elvin, Dr J. Mark D., MA, PhD; Lecturer in Oriental Studies, University of Oxford, from Oct. 1973, and Fellow of St Antony's College; *b* 1938; *m* 1962 (separated); two *s*. BA Cantab 1959 (1st cl. with distinction, History), MA Cantab 1964, PhD Cantab 1968 (Oriental Studies). Harkness-Commonwealth Fellow, Harvard Univ., 1962–64; Asst Univ. Lectr, Univ. of Cambridge, 1964–67; Res. Fellow, Clare Hall, Cambridge, 1966–67; Lectr in Economic History, Univ. of Glasgow, 1968–73. *Publications:* trans., Hoshi: The Ming Grain Tribute System, 1969; Shiba: Commerce and Society in Sung China, 1970; The Pattern of the Chinese Past – A Social and Economic Interpretation, 1973; ed (with G. W. Skinner), The Chinese City Between Two Worlds (forthcoming); *contrib.* Mod. Asian Studies. *Address:* Dept of Economic History, Adam Smith Building, Univ. of Glasgow, Glasgow G12 8RT.

Elwell-Sutton, Laurence Paul; Reader in Persian, University of Edinburgh, since 1969; *b* 1912; *m* 1940; 1950; 1969; four *s* two *d*. BA London 1934 (1st cl. Arabic); Mem.: Royal Asiatic Soc., Royal Central Asian Soc., Iran Soc., Brit. Assoc. Orientalists. Lectr in Arabic, Sch. Oriental and African Studies, London Univ., 1939– 40; Lectr in Persian, Univ. of Edinburgh, 1952–60; Sen. Lectr, 1960–69. Anglo-Iranian Oil Co., Iran, 1935–38; Min. of Information, 1939; BBC Near Eastern Services, 1940–43, 1948–52; Brit. Embassy, Tehran, 1943–47; Chm., Brit. Assoc. of Orientalists, 1971–72. *Publications:* Colloquial Persian, 1941, 8th edn 1972; Modern Iran, 1941, 4th edn 1944; The Wonderful Seahorse and other Persian Tales, 1950; Guide to Iranian Area Study, 1952; Persian Proverbs, 1954; Persian Oil: A Study in Power Politics, 1955; Elementary Persian Grammar, 1963, 3rd edn 1972; trans., Rahnema: Payambar the Prophet, 1964–66, 2nd edn 1971; Ali Dashti: In Search of Omar Khayyam, 1971; *contrib.* Aryan Path, Delos, Iran, Middle East Jl, NY Rev. Bks, Oriens, Rahnema-e Ketab, Royal Central Asian Jl (Asian Aff.), Sokhan. *Address:* Dept of Persian, Univ. of Edinburgh, Edinburgh.

Ely, John W.; see Wilton-Ely.

Embleton, Dr Clifford, MA, PhD, FRCO; Reader in Geography, University of London, King's College, since 1969; *b* 1931; *m* 1956; three *s*. BA Cantab 1952, MA Cantab 1956, PhD Cantab 1956; FRCO 1949, FRGS, Mem., Inst Brit. Geogs, Glaciol. Soc., Geol. Assoc. Asst Lectr, Bedford Coll., London, 1954–56, Lectr, 1958–64; Sen. Lectr, King's Coll., London, 1964–69; Vis. Prof., North-western Univ., Illinois, 1965; Toronto Univ., 1972. Hon. Ed., Inst. Brit. Geogrs, 1966–73; Mem.: Internat. Geog. Union Comms on Present-day Processes and Geomorphol

Mapping; Bd of Studies, Geog., London Univ. *Publications:* (with A. B. Mountjoy) Africa: A Geographical Study, 1966, 3rd edn 1970; (with C. A. M. King) Glacial and Periglacial Geomorphology, 1968; Glaciers and Glacial Erosion, 1972; *contrib.* Trans Inst. Brit. Geogrs, Geog. Jl, Proc. Geol. Assoc. *Address:* Dept of Geography, King's College, Strand, WC2R 2LS.

Emeny, Roger; Lecturer, Department of Land Management and Development, University of Reading, since 1964; *b* 1931; *m* 1958; two *s*. ARICS 1956. Mem. Council, RICS, 1963–65. *Publications:* (film) How a House is Built, 1960 (National Film Archives); (jtly with M. Roberts) Lands Tribunal Index, 1968; (jtly with H. M. Wilks) Principles and Practice of Rating Valuation, 3rd edn 1972; *contrib.* Chartered Surveyor. *Address:* Dept of Land Management and Development, Faculty of Urban and Regional Studies, Univ. of Reading, Whiteknights, Reading, Berks RG6 2AH.

Emerson, Prof. Anthony Roy; Professor of Sociology, School of Social Studies, University of East Anglia, since 1964; *b* 1925; *m* 1952; one *d*. BA Nottingham 1952, PhD Edinburgh 1957; ABPsS 1955; Mem., Brit. Sociol. Assoc. Asst, Dept of Public Health and Sociol Medicine, Edinburgh, 1953–56; Lectr, Dept of Social Science, Nottingham Univ., 1956–64; Dean, Sch. of Soc. Studies, Univ. of E Anglia, 1968–71. Mem.: E Anglia Reg. Planning Council, 1965– ; Norwich Educn Cttee, 1965– ; E Anglia Reg. Hosp. Bd, 1969–73; E Anglian RHA, 1973– . Past Editor, Students Lib. of Sociology. *Publications: contrib.* Brit. Jl Indust. Soc. Med., Occup. Psychol. *Address:* School of Social Studies, Univ. of East Anglia, Norwich NOR 88C.

Emerton, Rev. John Adney, DD; Regius Professor of Hebrew, Cambridge University, since 1968, and Fellow of St John's College, since 1970; *b* 1928; *m* 1954; one *s* two *d*. BA Oxon 1950 (1st cl. Hons Theology; 1st cl. Hons Oriental Studies 1952); MA Oxon 1954, MA Cantab 1955 (by incorporation), BD Cantab 1960, DD 1973, Deacon 1952, Priest 1953. Asst Lectr in Theology, Birmingham Univ., 1952–53; Lectr in Hebrew and Aramaic, Durham Univ., 1953–55; Lectr in Divinity, Cambridge Univ., 1955–62; Reader in Semitic Philology, and Fellow, St Peter's Coll., Oxford, 1962–68; Vis. Prof. of Old Testament and Near Eastern Studies, Trinity Coll., Toronto Univ., 1960. Curate of Birmingham Cathedral, 1952–53; Select Preacher before Univ. of Cambridge, 1962, 1971. Sec., Internat. Organization for the Study of OT, 1971– . *Publications:* The Peshitta of the Wisdom of Solomon, 1959; The Old Testament in Syriac: Song of Songs, 1966; *contrib.* Jl of Semitic Studies, Jl of Theological Studies, Theology, Vetus Testamentum, Zeitschrift für die Alttestamentliche Wissenschaft. *Address:* St John's College, Cambridge CB2 1TP.

Emmans, Keith Allen; Lecturer, Language Teaching Centre, University of York, since 1967; *b* 1932; *m* 1957; one *s* one *d*. BA Hons

London 1957, PGCE 1958; Member: Modern Languages Assoc., Nat. Assoc. of Language Advisers (Hon. Sec.), Audio-Visual Language Assoc. Univ. of York, 1967. *Publications*: (jtly) Pilot Survey of National Manpower Requirements in Foreign Languages, 1974; *contrib*. TES. *Address*: King's Manor, Univ. of York, York YO1 2EP.

Emslie, Dr MacDonald; Reader in English Literature, University of Edinburgh, since 1966; *b* 1920; *m* 1947; one *s* one *d*. BA Cantab 1950, MA Cantab 1955, PhD Cantab 1957; Scholar and Collins prizeman, Pembroke Coll., Cambridge 1951; Mem.: Malone Soc., 1957, Bibliog. Soc. 1958, Royal Musical Assoc. 1960, Fellowship, Folger Shakespeare Libr., Washington, 1968. Asst Lectr, Univ. Coll., London, 1954–56, Lectr, 1956–65; Lectr, Univ. of Edinburgh, 1965–66. Insp., Min. Health, 1939; RAF, 1940–46; Min. Nat. Insurance, Staff Training Brch, 1947–48. *Publications*: Goldsmith: The Vicar of Wakefield, 1963, 3rd edn 1965; chapters, in, Die Musik in Geschichte und Gegenwart, 1963, W. B. Yeats, Centenary Essays, 1965, and The Explicator Cyclopedia, 1967–68; ed. music and lyrics, The Diary of Samuel Pepys, 1970– (in progress); *contrib*. Lib., Ess. Crit., Rev. Eng. Lit., Cambridge Jl, Mod. Lang. Rev., Mus. and Lett., Rev. Engl. Studies, Use of Engl., Mod. Engl., Engl. Lang. Teaching, Engl. Studies. *Address*: Dept of English Literature, Univ. of Edinburgh, George Square, Edinburgh EH8 9JX.

Enfield, Roy L. A.; Lecturer in Sociology, University of Warwick, since 1973; *b* 1934. BA Leeds 1963 (Special Studies in Philos.). Dept Philos., Lancaster, 1965–68; Dept Sociol., Essex, 1968–73. External Examiner: Univ. of Cambridge, 1972–73; Univ. of Kent, 1973– . *Address*: Dept of Sociology, Univ. of Warwick, Coventry CV4 7AL.

English, Vernon Baxter; Hon. Senior Lecturer, Manchester Business School, University of Manchester, since 1971; *b* 1922. MA Cantab 1946. Sen. Lectr, Manchester Business Sch., 1966, Dir of Studies, Sen. Exec. Courses, 1968–71. Chief Exec., Marketing Planning, Davy Internat. Ltd, 1971– . *Address*: Manchester Business School, Booth Street West, Manchester.

Enos, Dr John Lawrence; Fellow and Tutor in Economics, Magdalen College, Oxford, since 1966; *b* 1924; *m* 1959; one *s* three *d*. BSc MIT 1949, MA Case-Western Reserve 1956, PhD MIT 1958. Asst Prof., MIT, 1955; Vis. Assoc. Prof., Indian Inst. Mngmt, Calcutta, 1961; Vis. Prof., Middle East Tech. Univ., Ankara, 1962; Prof., Inst. de Economia, Univ. of Chile, 1963–65. Jun. Dean of Arts, Magdalen Coll., Oxford, 1969–71; Sen. Dean of Arts, 1971–73. *Publications*: Petroleum Progress and Profits; A History of Process Innovation, 1962; Modelling the Economic Development of a Poorly Endowed Region: The North-east of Thailand, 1970; (with K. B. Griffin) Planning Development, 1970; *contrib*. Econ. Develop. Cult. Chge. Explorat. Entrepren.

History, Jl Indust. Econ. *Address*: Magdalen College, Oxford.

Enright, Dr Brian James; University Librarian and Keeper of the Pybus Collection, University Library, Newcastle upon Tyne, since 1973; *b* 1929; *m* 1957; one *s* one *d*. BA Oxon 1949, MA Oxon 1953, DPhil Oxon 1957. Bodleian Library, Oxford, 1949–57; House of Commons Library, 1957–62; BBC TV Film Librarian, 1962–65; Univ. Librarian, City Univ., 1965–68; Univ. Librarian, Sussex Univ., 1968–72. Member: UGC Educnl Develt Cttee, 1973; Library Adv. Council for England, 1971–75; Council for Educn Technology, 1973. *Publications*: New Media and the Library in Education, 1972; *contrib*. Bodleian Library Record, Library, Library Assoc. Record, Oxoniensia. *Address*: Univ. Library, Newcastle upon Tyne NE1 7RU.

Entwistle, Prof. Noel James, BSc, PhD, ABPsS; Professor of Educational Research, Department of Educational Research, University of Lancaster, since 1971; *b* 1936; *m* 1964; one *d*. BA Sheffield 1960 (2nd cl. Physics), PhD Aberdeen 1967; ABPsS. Res. Asst, Aberdeen Univ., 1964, Res. Fellow, 1964–67; Lectr, Lancaster Univ., 1968–70, Sen. Lectr, 1970–71. Mem: Educnl Res. Bd, SSRC; Council, Eur. Assoc. for Res. and Develt in Higher Educn. *Publications*: (with J. D. Nisbet) The Age of Transfer to Secondary Education, 1966; (with J. D. Nisbet) The Transition to Secondary Education, 1969; (with J. D. Nisbet) Educational Research Methods, 1970; Educational Research in Action, 1972; The Nature of Educational Research, 1972; *contrib*. Brit. Jl Educnl Psychol., Univ. Qly, Scott. Educnl Studies. *Address*: Dept of Educational Research, Cartmel College, Univ. of Lancaster.

Eppel, Prof. Emanuel Montague; Professor of Education, Director of Centre for Continuing Education, University of Sussex, since 1968; *b* 1920; *m* 1949; one *s*. MA Glasgow 1941 (Hons Eng. Lit./Lang.), DipEd Glasgow 1948, MEd Glasgow 1949 (1st cl. Psych., Educn); Teacher's Cert. (Scotland) 1947, Mem.: Brit. Psychol. Soc., Brit. Sociol. Assoc., Assoc. Child Psychol. Staff Tutor, London Univ. Extra-mural Dept, 1950–64; Vis. Lectr, LSE (Applied Soc. Studies), 1954–64; Vis. Lectr, Nat. Inst. Soc. Work Training, 1956–64; Sen. Lectr, Educnl Psychol., Univ. of Sussex, 1964–67; Reader, Human Relats, 1967–68. Mem.: Cttee, Youth Studies Foundn, King's Coll., London, 1960–64; Council, BBC, Radio Brighton, 1967– ; Univs Council for Adult Educn, 1968– ; Cttee, Extra-mural Officers, 1968– ; DES Cttee for State Schols, Mature Students, 1968– ; Adv. Cttee, Higher and Further Educn, Open Univ., 1969– ; Hon. Consultant, Medical Educn, SE Reg. Hosp. Bd, 1969– ; Probation and After-Care Cttee, E Sussex, 1972– ; Educn Cttee, Nat. Assoc. Mental Health, 1969–72. *Publications*: (with M. Eppel) Adolescents and Morality, 1966; contrib. to Moral Education in a Changing Society, ed, W. R. Niblett, 1963, 2nd edn 1970; Youth in New Society, ed, T. Raison, 1966; Trends in the Services for Youth, ed, Leicester and Farndale, 1967; ed, Education for Cultural Pluralism, 1972; *contrib*. Brit. Jl Educnl Psychol., Brit. Jl Sociol. *Address*: Centre for Continuing Education, Univ. of Sussex, Falmer, Brighton BN1 9RH.

Epstein, Prof. Arnold Leonard; Professor of Social Anthropology, School of African and Asian Studies, University of Sussex, since 1972; *b* 1924; *m* 1957; two *d*. LLB QUB 1944, PhD Manchester 1955; Barrister-at-Law 1948. Res. Asst, Manchester Univ., 1951–52, 1954–55; Res. Fellow, Austral. Nat. Univ., 1958–61; Sen. Lectr, Soc. Anthrop., Manchester, 1961–65; Prof. Fellow, Austral. Nat. Univ., 1966–70, Prof. and Head of Dept, 1970–72. *Publications*: The Administration of Justice and the Urban African, 1953; Politics in an Urban African Community, 1958; Matupit: Land, Politics and Change among the Tolai, 1969; ed, The Craft of Social Anthropology, 1968; ed, Contention and Dispute: aspects of law and social control in Melanesia, 1974; *contrib*. Africa, Oceania, Rhodes-Livingstone Jl, etc. *Address*: Univ. of Sussex, Falmer, Brighton BN1 9RH.

Eraut, Dr Michael Ruare; Acting Director and Senior Fellow, Centre for Educational Technology, University of Sussex, since 1973 (Assistant Director, 1971–73); *b* 1940; *m* 1964; two *s*. BA Cantab 1962, PhD Cantab 1965 (Chemistry). Res. Schol., Off. of Instruct. Resources, Univ. of Illinois, Chicago, 1965–66; Lectr, Univ. of Colorado, 1966; Vis. Asst Prof., Univ. of Illinois, Chicago, 1966–67; Fellow in Educnl Technol., Univ. of Sussex, 1967. *Publications*: The Impact of Educational Technology on Curriculum Development: Implications for Colleges of Education, in, Curriculum Innovation in Practice in Relation to Colleges of Education, ed, M. R. Bar, 1969; The Design of Variable Input Learning Systems, in, Aspects of Educational Technology, vol. 2, ed, W. R. Dunn and C. Holroyd, 1969; (with A. G. Howson) Continuing Mathematics (NCET Working Paper No. 2), 1969; The Role of Evaluation, in, The Teacher as Manager, ed, G. Taylor, 1970; (with N. MacKenzie and H. C. Jones) Teaching and Learning: New Methods and Resources in Higher Education, 1970, French edn 1970, German edn 1973; (with G. Squires) An Annotated Select Bibliography of Educational Technology, 1971; Fundamentals of Arithmetic: A Programme for Self Instruction, 1970, Spanish edn 1972; Fundamentals of Elementary Algebra: A Programme for Self Instruction, 1970, Spanish edn 1972; Fundamentals of Intermediate Algebra: A Programme for Self Instruction, 1970, Spanish edn 1972; Strategies for the Evaluation of Curriculum Materials, in, Aspects of Educational Technology, vol. 6, ed, K. Austwick and N. D. C. Harris, 1972; In-Service Training for Innovation, 1973; *contrib*. AV Commnctn Rev., Brit. Jl Educnl Technol., Jl Chem. Soc., Tech. Educn. *Address*: Education Development Building, Univ. of Sussex, Brighton, Sussex.

Erickson, Charlotte, MA, PhD; Senior Lecturer in Economic History, London School of Economics, since 1965; *b* 1923; *m* 1952; two *s*. BA Augustana Coll. 1945, MA Cornell 1947, PhD Cornell 1951; FRHistS, Mem.: Amer. Hist. Assoc., Amer. Hist., Econ. Hist. Soc., Econ. Hist. Assoc. Instructor, Vassar Coll., 1951–52; Asst Lectr, 1955–59, Lectr, London Sch. of Econ., 1959–65. Sec., Brit. Assoc. Amer. Studies, 1966– . *Publications*: American Industry and the European Immigrant 1860–85, 1957; British Industrialists, Steel and Hosiery 1850–1950, 1959; Invisible Immigrants, 1972; *contrib*. Populat. Studies; Explorat. Entrepren. Hist. *Address*: London School of Economics, Houghton Street, Aldwych, WC2 2AE.

Erskine-Hill, Dr Howard Henry; University Lecturer in English, Fellow since 1969, Tutor since 1970, Jesus College, Cambridge; *b* 1936. BA Nottingham 1957 (1st cl.), PhD Nottingham 1960, MA Cantab 1970. Tutor in English, UCW Swansea, 1960, Asst Lectr 1961, Lectr 1962; Lectr, Univ. of Cambridge, 1969. Sec., English Faculty Bd, Cambridge, 1971–72. *Publications*: Pope: Horatian Satires and Epistles, 1964; contrib. Renaissance and Modern Essays, ed G. R. Hibbard, 1965; Pope: The Dunciad, 1972; contrib. Donne: Essays in Celebration, ed A. J. Smith, 1972; contrib. Alexander Pope, ed Peter Dixon, 1972; *contrib*. Jl Warburg and Courtauld Inst., Renaissance and Modern Studies, Rev. English Studies. *Address*: Jesus College, Cambridge.

Eshag, Eprime, MA, FCA; Economics Fellow, Wadham College, and Senior Research Officer, University of Oxford Institute of Economics and Statistics, since 1962; *b* 1918. BSc(Econ) London 1942, PhD Course Cambridge; Mem., Inst. Chartd Accountants, 1943. Econ. Affairs Off., Econ. Res. Div., UN Secretariat, NY, 1953–62; Consultant, UN, 1966, 1967, 1968, 1971. *Publications*: From Marshall to Keynes, 1962; Present System of Trade and Payments Versus Full Employment and Welfare State, 1966; *contrib*. Bull. Oxford Univ., Inst. Econ. Stats, Econ. Jl, UN Period. of Econ. Bulls. *Address*: Wadham College, Oxford.

Estall, Dr Robert Charles, BSc(Econ), PhD; Reader (formerly Lecturer) in the Economic Geography of North America, London School of Economics, since 1955; *b* 1924; *m* 1956; three *s* one *d*. BSc(Econ) London 1955 (1st cl.), PhD London 1964. Vis. Prof., Clark Univ., Worcester, Mass., 1958; Fellow, Amer. Council Learned Socs, 1962–63; Vis. Prof., Univ. of Pittsburgh, Pa, 1967. Chm., Admissions Cttee, LSE, 1972– . *Publications*: (with R. O. Buchanan) Industrial Activity and Economic Geography, 1961, Spanish edn 1970, Portuguese edn 1971, 3rd edn 1973, Japanese edn 1974; New England: A Study in Industrial Adjustment, 1966; A Modern Geography of the United States, 1972; *contrib*. Econ. Geog., Jl Amer. Studies, etc. *Address*: London School of Economics, Houghton Street, WC2A 2AE.

Etchells, Dorothea Ruth; Vice-Principal of Trevelyan College and part-time Lecturer in

English, University of Durham, since 1972, Senior Lecturer since 1973; *b* 1931. BA Liverpool 1951, DipEd Liverpool 1952, MA Liverpool 1954, BD London 1967. Resident Tutor of Trevelyan Coll. and part-time Lectr in English, Univ. of Durham, 1968. Mem. Gov. Body, St John's Coll., Univ. of Durham, 1973– ; Mem. Gov. Body, Neville's Cross Coll., Univ. of Durham, 1974– . *Publications*: Unafraid to Be, 1969; The Man with the Trumpet, 1970. *Address*: Trevelyan College, Univ. of Durham, Durham.

Ettinghausen, Dr Henry Michael; Lecturer, Department of Spanish, University of Southampton, since 1965; *b* 1940; *m* 1962; one *s*. BA Oxon 1961, MA Oxon 1969, DPhil Oxon 1969. Asst Lectr, Hull Univ., 1964–65. *Publications*: Francisco de Quevedo and the Neostoic Movement, 1972; *contrib*. BHS, BRAE, Mod. Lang. Rev. *Address*: Dept of Spanish, Univ. of Southampton, Southampton SO9 5NH.

Eunson, Ronald John; Lecturer in Education, School of Education, University of Newcastle upon Tyne, since 1967; *b* 1938; *m* 1968; one *s*. BA Hons Durham 1960 (German), MEd Aberdeen 1963, Teacher's Cert. (Sec. Educn) Scotland 1961; Member: Comparative Educn Soc. in Europe (Brit. Section); Mod. Lang. Assoc. *Address*: Sch. of Education, St Thomas Street, Newcastle upon Tyne NE1 7RU.

Evans, Adrian R.; *see* Rowe-Evans.

Evans, Prof. Anthony John; University Librarian, Loughborough University of Technology, since 1964, and Professor, Department of Library and Information Studies, since 1973; *b* 1930; *m* 1954; two *d*. BPharm (Hons) London 1954, PhD London 1961; FLA 1969. Sch. of Pharmacy, London Univ.: Asst Lectr, 1954–58; Librarian, 1958–63; Dean of Sch. of Educnl Studies, Loughborough Univ., 1973–76. Pres., Internat. Assoc. of Technological Univ. Libraries, 1970–72 and 1973–75. Chm., IFLA Working Gp on Res. and Develt in Librarianship and Documentation, 1971–73; Member: ASLIB Council, 1970– ; Cttee of Vice-Chancellors and Principals, Cttee on Univ. Libraries, 1972– . *Publications*: A Bibliography of the Tabletting of Medicinal Substances, 1963 (Supplement 1964); *contrib*. IATUL Proc., Jl Pharm. Pharmacol. *Address*: Univ. of Technology, Loughborough, Leics LE11 3TU.

Evans, Dr Colin H., MA, DèsL; Lecturer, Department of French, University College, Cardiff, since 1963; *b* 1937; *m* 1964; one *s*. BA Wales 1958 (1st cl. French), DipEd 1961, MA Wales 1961, DèsL Paris 1971. Fellow, Univ. of Wales, 1961–63. *Address*: French Dept, Univ. College, Cardiff CF1 1XL.

Evans, Dr Dafydd Howells; Reader in Romance Philology, French Department, Queen Mary College, University of London, since 1970; *b* 1919. BA Wales 1950, MA Wales 1952, DU Paris 1953. Asst Lectr, Queen Mary Coll., 1953–55, Lectr, 1955–70. Warden, Beaumont Hall, QMC, 1968– .

Publications: ed, Lanier, Histoire d'un Mot, 1967. *Address*: Dept of French, Queen Mary College, Mile End Road, E1 4NS.

Evans, Prof. Daniel Simon; Professor of Welsh, St David's University College, since 1974; *b* 1921; *m* 1949; one *s*. BA Wales 1943 (1st cl. Welsh), BD Wales 1947 (Greek and Hebrew), MA Wales 1948, BLitt Oxon 1952. Asst Lectr in Welsh, Swansea Univ. Coll., 1948–51, Lectr, 1951–56; Prof. of Welsh, Univ. Coll., Dublin, 1956–62; Lectr in Welsh, St David's Coll., Lampeter, 1962–66; Head of Dept, Celtic Studies, Liverpool 1966–74; External Examr in Welsh, Univ. of Wales, 1960–63, 1970– ; Hon. Lectr in Linguistics, Liverpool, 1969–73. Founder Ed., Trivium, Jl of St David's Coll., Lampter, 1966. *Publications*: Gramadeg Cymraeg Canol, 1951, 2nd edn 1960; Buched Dewi, 1959, 2nd edn 1965; A Grammar of Middle Welsh, 1964, 2nd edn 1970; ed, G. H. Doble: Lives of the Welsh Saints, 1971; *contrib*. Bull. Bd Celtic Studies, Etudes Celt., Llên Cymru, Studia Celt., Trivium, Rev. Eng. Studies, Y Traethodydd. *Address*: St David's Univ. Coll., Lampter, Dyfed SA48 7ED.

Evans, Dr David; Senior Lecturer, School of Education, Exeter University, since 1970; *b* 1925; *m* 1951; one *d*. BA Wales 1949 (Hons Economics), DipEd Wales 1950, MA (Ed) Birmingham 1956, DipEdPsych Birmingham 1957, PhD Exon 1973; ABPsS 1960. Temp. Lectr, Birmingham, 1963–64; Lectr, Exeter, 1964–70. In charge MEd (Psych.) Course, Training Educnl Psychologists, 1972– . *Publications*: *contrib*. App. Schs Jl, Brit. Jl Dis. Comm., Brit. Jl Ment. Sub., Bull. London Inst. Educn, Educnl Psychologist. *Address*: School of Education, University of Exeter, Exeter EX4 4QJ.

Evans, Prof. David Ellis, MA; Professor of Welsh Language and Literature, University College of Swansea, since 1974; *b* 1930; *m* 1957; two *d*. BA Wales 1952 (1st cl. Welsh, 1st cl. Latin, 1st cl. Greek), MA Wales 1954, DPhil Oxon 1962. Asst Lectr, Univ. Coll., Swansea, 1957–60, Lectr, 1960–68, Reader, 1968–74. Mem., Council for Name Studies of GB and Ireland, 1962– ; Bd Celtic Studies, 1968– . *Publications*: Gaulish Personal Names, 1967; contrib. The Anatomy of Wales, ed, R. B. Jones, 1972; *contrib*. Antiqu., Bull. Bd Celtic Studies, Etudes Celt., Studia Celt., Y Traethodydd, Zts. f. celtische Philologie. *Address*: Dept of Welsh, Univ. College of Swansea, Singleton Park, Swansea SA2 8PP.

Evans, David Lloyd; Lecturer, Department of Law Relating to Land, Faculty of Urban and Regional Studies, University of Reading, since 1969; *b* 1938; *m* 1972. BA Cantab 1961, LLB Cantab 1963, MA Cantab 1965; Mem.: Gray's Inn, SPTL. Faculté de droit et des sciences économiques, Univ. of Paris, 1963; Graduate Sch. of Contemporary European Studies, Reading, 1971– . Mem., Law Commn, 1965; Sec., Law Commn Working Party on Landlord and Tenant, 1965–68; Mem., Educn Cttee of Inst. of Rent Officers, 1971– ; Hon. Fellow, 1974. *Publications*: Law of Landlord and Tenant, 1974; *contrib*.

Annuaire de Legislation Française et Etrangère, Current Law, Estates Gazette, Jl of Planning and Environmental Law. *Address*: Faculty of Urban and Regional Studies, Univ. of Reading, Whiteknights, Reading RG6 2AH.

Evans, David Myfyr; Lecturer in Economics, Department of Applied Economics, University of Wales Institute of Science and Technology, since 1968; *b* 1917; *m* 1944; one *s* one *d*. CertEd Wales 1946, BA Wales 1948 (History and Economics), BA Hons 1949 (Economics and Political Science); Member: REconS; RIPA (Chm., South Wales Branch); Town and Country Planning Assoc. WCAT, Cardiff, 1959–68. Member: Cardiff City Council, 1964–74; S Glam CC, 1974– (Chm., Environment and Planning Cttee); Cardiff City DC, 1974– . Rhoose Airport Consortium Exec.; Assoc. of County Councils Planning Exec.; Governor: UC Cardiff; Univ. of Wales. *Publications*: *contrib.* Political Qly. *Address*: Applied Economics Dept, UWIST, Cathays Park, Cardiff CF1 3NS.

Evans, Donald Morgan; Lecturer, Department of Philosophy, University of Wales (Cardiff), since 1968. *b* 1939; *m* 1961; two *s*. BA Wales (1st cl.). Non-Professorial Staff Rep., Senate, 1973– . *Publications*: *contrib.* Philos. *Address*: Univ. College, Cathays Park, Cardiff CF1 1XL.

Evans, Dr Eric John; Lecturer in Modern British History, University of Lancaster, since 1971; *b* 1945; *m* 1968; one *s* one *d*. BA Oxon 1966 (1st cl. Hons. Mod. History), MA Oxon 1970, PhD Warwick 1970. Lectr, History, Stirling, 1969–70. Asst Ed., Studies in Social History, 1972– . *Publications*: Tillicoultry, A Centenary History 1871–1971, 1972; *contrib.* Agric. Hist. Rev., Jl Friends Hist. Soc., Trans Cumberland and Westmorland Antiq. and Arch. Soc. *Address*: Dept of History, Univ. of Lancaster, Bailrigg, Lancaster LA1 4YW.

Evans, Eric Wyn; Senior Lecturer, Department of Economics, University of Hull, since 1966; *b* 1932; *m* 1960; two *d*. BA(Hons) Wales 1952, MA Wales 1953, PhD Wales 1955. Asst Lectr, Univ. Coll., Jamaica, 1955–58; Hallsworth Fellow, Manchester, 1958–59; Lecturer, Hull, 1959–66. *Publications*: Mabon: A Study in Trade Union Leadership, 1959; The Miners of South Wales, 1961; (with K. Hartley) Employment and Unemployment in the Hull Region, 1964; *contrib.* Oxford Bull., Yorks Bull., and Bank Jls. *Address*: Dept of Economics, Univ. of Hull, Hull HU6 7RX.

Evans, Dr Gareth Lloyd; Senior Lecturer, Extramural Department, University of Birmingham, since 1966; *b* 1923; *m* 1949; two *s* one *d*. BA Wales 1944, DipEd Wales 1945, PhD Birmingham 1969. Mem., Critics' Circle GB. Birmingham University: Sen. Lectr, 1966; Dir, Graduate Summer Sch., Shakespeare and Elizabethan Drama, 1969– ; Distinguished Vis. Prof., Pennsylvania State Univ. 1973. Mem. Drama Panel, West Midlands Arts Assoc. *Publications*: J. B.

Priestley – The Dramatist, 1964; Shakespeare in the Limelight, 1968; Shakespeare I – 1564–1592, 1969; Shakespeare II – 1592–1598, 1969; Shakespeare III – 1598–1603, 1971; Shakespeare IV – 1603–1607, 1972; Shakespeare V – 1607–1616, 1973; *contrib.* Shak. Qly, Mod. Lang. Rev., Shak. Surv. Stratford-upon-Avon Stud., Stud. Latin Lit., Encounter. *Address*: Extra Mural Dept, Univ. of Birmingham, Edgbaston, Birmingham B15 2TT.

Evans, George Frederick; Lecturer in French, University College of Swansea, since 1966; *b* 1939; *m* 1964; one *s* one *d*. BA Wales 1961 (1st cl. French). Asst Lectr, Magee Univ. Coll., 1963–65; Asst Lectr, The Queen's Univ., Belfast, 1965–66. *Publications*: *contrib.* Yrs Wk Mod. Langs. *Address*: Dept of Romance Studies, Univ. Coll. of Swansea, Singleton Park, Swansea SA2 8PP.

Evans, Dr Howard, BA, D de l'U; Lecturer in French Language and Literature, University of Leeds, since 1966; *b* 1932; *m* 1958; one *s* two *d*. BA Bristol 1953 (1st cl. French), D de l'U Bordeaux 1958. Internat. Staff, NATO, 1958–66. *Publication*: L'Administration locale, 1973. *Address*: Dept of French, Univ. of Leeds, Leeds LS2 9JT.

Evans, Hywel Iorwerth; Principal, Cartrefle College of Education, Wrexham, since 1973; also directing and teaching MEd courses, University College of North Wales; *b* 1930; *m* 1956; two *s* three *d*. BA Oxon 1953 (2nd cl. Hons Theology, Jesus Coll.), MA Oxon 1959, DipEd UCNW 1954 (1st cl. Hons). Lectr in Educn, and Faculty Officer, Dept and Faculty of Educn, UCNW, 1962–72. Chm., Christian Educn Movement in Wales, 1971– . *Address*: Cartrefle College of Education, Wrexham LL13 9NL.

Evans, Ian S.; Lecturer, Geography Department, Durham University, since 1970; *b* 1943; *m* 1966. BA Cantab 1964, MS Yale 1966, MA Cantab 1967. Member: RGS, Inst. British Geographers, British Geomorphological Res. Gp, Int. Glaciol. Soc., Liverpool Geol. Soc., British Cartographic Soc. Research Fellow, Experimental Cartography Unit, Royal Coll. of Art, 1968–70. *Publications*: contrib. Water, Earth and Man, ed R. J. Chorley; contrib. Spatial Analysis in Geomorphology, ed R. J. Chorley; *contrib.* Area, Revue de Géomorphologie dynamique. *Address*: Dept of Geography, Science Laboratories, South Road, Durham.

Evans, Dr Iorwerth Gwyn; Senior Lecturer in Statistics, University College of Wales, Aberystwyth, since 1968; *b* 1929; *m* 1952; one *s*. BSc Wales 1949 (1st cl. Pure Mathematics), MSc Wales 1950, Dip. in Mathematical Statistics and Computational Analysis, Swansea 1950, PhD Wales 1965; FRStatSoc 1956. FInstStat 1971. Lectr in Pure Mathematics, Univ. Coll. of Wales, Swansea, 1960–68. *Publications*: *contrib.* Jl Royal Stat. Soc., Jl Amer. Stat. Assoc. *Address*: Dept of Statistics, Univ. College of Wales, Aberystwyth SY23 2AX.

Evans, Dr John David Gemmill; Fellow since 1964 Tutor, Praelector and Lecturer in Classics, Sidney Sussex College, Cambridge; b 1942. BA Cantab 1963, MA Cantab 1967, PhD Cantab 1970. Mem., Cambridge Philological Soc., 1963- . Vis. Assoc. Prof., Philosophy Dept, Duke Univ., 1972–73. Address: Sidney Sussex College, Cambridge CB2 3HU.

Evans, Prof. John Davies, FBA; Director, University of London Institute of Archaeology, and Professor of Archaeology, London University, since 1973; b 1925; m 1957. BA Cantab 1948, MA Cantab 1950, PhD Cantab 1956; FBA 1973. Fellow, Brit. Inst. of Archaeology at Ankara, 1951–52; Res. Fellow, Pembroke Coll., Cambridge, 1953–56; Prof. of Prehistoric Archaeology, London Univ., 1956–73. Publications: Malta (Ancient Peoples and Places Series), 1959; (with Dr A. C. Renfrew) Excavations at Saliagos, near Antiparos, 1968; The Prehistoric Antiquities of the Maltese Islands, 1971; contrib. archaeological jls. Address: Institute of Archaeology, Gordon Square, WC1H 0PY.

Evans, John Maxwell; Lecturer, Department of Law, London School of Economics, since 1967; b 1942; m 1966; two d. BA Oxon 1964, BCL Oxon 1965. Teaching Fellow, Univ. of Chicago, 1965–66; Lectr, Worcester Coll., Oxford, 1966–67. Mem., Ed. Cttee, Mod. Law Rev., 1971- . Publications: contrib. Mod. Law Rev. Address: Dept of Law, London School of Economics, Houghton Street, WC2A 2AE.

Evans, M., MA; Lecturer in Government, Department of Government, University of Manchester, since 1965; b 1936; m 1961; one s two d. BA(Hons) Manchester 1960, MA Manchester 1963. Lectr in Political Science, Makerere Univ. Coll., Uganda, 1961–62; Asst Lectr, Univ. of Manchester, 1963–65. Publications: Karl Marx, 1974; contrib. Jl Commonwealth Polit. Studies, Polit. Studies, Gov. Opposit. Address: Dept of Government, Univ. of Manchester, Manchester M13 9PL.

Evans, Prof. Maurice; Professor of English, Exeter University, since 1968; b 1914; m 1942; 1966; two s one d. BA (Hons) Cantab 1936, PhD Cantab 1940. Lectr, Goldsmiths' Coll., Univ. of London, 1946–52; Sen. Lectr, Makerere Coll., Univ. of East Africa, 1952–55; Lectr and Sen. Lectr, Univ. of Aberdeen, 1955–64; Prof. McGill Univ. Montreal, 1964–68. Publications: G. K. Chesterton, 1939; An Anthology of Contemporary Poetry, 1949; English Poetry in the VXIth Century, 1955; ed, Bussy D'Ambois (New Mermaid edn), 1965; English Poetry in the XVIth Century (a new vol., re-written), 1967; Spenser's Anatomy of Heroism: A Commentary on The Faerie Queen, 1970; contrib. Cambridge Jl, ELH, English Studies, Essays in Criticism, Renaissance Qly, Rev. of English Studies, Studies in Philology. Address: Dept of English, Univ. of Exeter, Exeter EX4 4QJ.

Evans, Rev. Owen Ellis, MA, BD; Lecturer in Biblical Studies, University College of North Wales, Bangor, since 1969; b 1920; m 1953; two s two d. BD London 1949 (1st cl.), MA Leeds 1951 (with distinction);

Minister, Methodist Ch. (ordained 1951). Duckworth Chair of NT Language and Literature, Hartley Victoria Methodist Coll., Manchester, 1953–69; Lectr (part-time) in NT, Univ. of Manchester, 1955–69. Publications: The Gospel According to St John, 1965; ed, V. Taylor: The Passion Narrative of St Luke, 1972; contrib. Expos. Times. Address: Dept of Biblical Studies, Univ. College of North Wales, Bangor LL57 2DG.

Evans, Dr Patricia; see Thompson, P.

Evans, Prof. Peter Angus, MA, DMus; Professor of Music, University of Southampton, since 1961; b 1929; m 1953. BA Dunelm 1950 (1st cl. Music), BMus, MA Dunelm 1953, DMus Dunelm 1958; FRCO 1952. Lectr, Durham Univ., 1953–61. Mem.: Music Bd, CNAA, 1968- , Chm., 1971- ; Council, Royal Musical Assoc., 1970–74; Chm., Music Panel, South. Arts Assoc., 1969- . Publications: contrib. Die Musik in Geschichte und Gegenwart, 1958–63; Michael Tippett, a Symposium, 1965; New Oxford History of Music, vol. X (forthcoming); contrib. Mus. and Lett., Mus. Times, Perspect. New Music, Tempo. Address: Dept of Music, Univ. of Southampton, Highfield, Southampton SO9 5NH.

Evans, Sir (Robert) Charles, MA, FRCS; Principal, University College of North Wales; Vice-Chancellor, University of Wales, 1965–67, and 1971–73; b 1918; m 1957; three s. BM, BCh Oxon 1943, MA Oxon 1947; Hon. DSc Wales 1956; FRCS 1949. Surgical Registrar, United Liverpool Hosps, and Liverpool Regional Hosps, 1947–57. Hunterian Prof., Royal Coll. of Surg. Eng., 1953. Dep. Leader, Mt Everest Expedition, 1953; Leader, Kangchenjunga Expedition, 1955; Pres., Alpine Club, 1967–70; Mem.: Council, RGS, 1960–61. Cullum Medal, American Geog. Soc., 1954; Livingstone Medal, Scott. Geog. Soc., 1955; Founder's Medal, Royal Geog. Soc., 1956. Publications: Eye on Everest, 1955; On Climbing, 1956; Kangchenjunga: The Untrodden Peak, 1956; articles in Alpine Jl, Geographical Jl, etc. Address: Univ. College of North Wales, Bangor LL57 2DG.

Eveling, Harry Stanley; Senior Lecturer, Department of Philosophy, University of Edinburgh, since 1960; b 1925; m 1950; two s two d. BA Dunelm 1950 (2nd cl. English Lang. and Lit), BA Dunelm 1953 (1st cl. Philosophy), BPhil Oxon 1955; Asst Lectr, Aberdeen Univ., 1956–58; Lectr, Univ. Coll. of Wales, 1958–60. Publications: Plays, vol. I 1969, vol. II 1970, vol. III 1971; contrib. Proc. Aristot. Soc. Address: Dept of Philosophy, Univ. of Edinburgh, Edinburgh EH8 9YL.

Everett, Barbara, (Mrs Emrys Jones); Senior Research Fellow, Somerville College Oxford, since 1971 and CUF Lecturer in English at The University of Oxford, since 1972; b 1932; m 1965; one d. BA Oxford 1954, MA 1958; MA Cantab 1960; Lectr, Univ. of Hull, 1955–60; Fellow of Newnham College, Cambridge and University Lectr, 1960–65; Lectr, Somerville College, Oxford,

1965-71. *Publications*: ed, Antony and Cleopatra, 1964; W. H. Auden, 1964; ed, All's Well That Ends Well, 1970; Donne: A London Poet, 1972; *contrib*. Critical Qly. *Address*: Somerville College, Oxford.

Everitt, Prof. Alan Milner, MA, PhD, FRHistS; Hatton Professor of English Local History and Head of Department of English Local History, University of Leicester, since 1968; *b* 1926. MA St Andrews 1951, PhD London 1957; FRHistS. Mem.: Stand. Conf. Local Hist., Econ. Hist. Soc., Histl Assoc., Brit. Agric. Hist. Soc., Urban Hist. Gp, etc. Res. Asst in Agrarian Hist., Univ. of Leicester, 1957–59; Res. Fellow in Urban Hist., 1960–65; Lectr in English Local Hist., 1965–68. Mem.: Exec. Cttee, Brit. Agric. Hist. Soc.; Stand. Conf. Local Hist.; Brit. Rec. Soc., Mem., Northants Rec. Cttee, etc. *Publications*: The County Committee of Kent in the Civil War, 1957; Suffolk and the Great Rebellion 1640–1660, 1960; The Community of Kent and the Great Rebellion 1640–60, 1966; 'Farm Labourers' and 'The Marketing of Agricultural Produce', in, The Agrarian History of England and Wales, IV, 1500–1640, ed J. Thirsk, 1967; Change in the Provinces: the Seventeenth Century, 1969; The Local Community and the Great Rebellion, 1969; New Avenues in English Local History, 1970; Ways and Means in Local History, 1971; The Pattern of Rural Dissent: the Nineteenth Century, 1972; Perspectives in English Local History, 1973; The Food Market of The English Town, in, Troisième Conférence Internationale d'Histoire Economique, 1965; The County Community, in, The English Revolution, ed E. W. Ives, 1968; Nonconformity in Country Parishes, in, Land, Church and People, ed J. Thirsk, 1970; *contrib*. Agric. Hist. Rev., Amat. Hist., Geneals Mag., Local Hist., Past and Present. *Address*: Dept of English Local History, The Univ., Leicester LE1 7RH.

Everitt, Rev. Mark; Chaplain and Fellow, Merton College, Oxford, since 1963; *b* 1934; *m* 1969; one *s* one *d*. BA Oxon 1958 (1st cl. Mod. Langs), MA Oxon 1962; Clerk in Holy Orders (ordained 1960, 1961). Tutor in Russian, Merton Coll., Oxford, 1963– ; Lectr in Russian, Lincoln and Jesus Colls, 1964– . *Address*: Merton College, Oxford.

Everton, Dr Ann R.; Lecturer, Faculty of Laws, University of Leicester, since 1973; *b* 1941; *m* 1964. LLB Birmingham 1961, LLM Birmingham 1963, PhD Birmingham 1965. Called to Bar, Lincoln's Inn, 1966. Lectr in Law, UCL, 1968–71. *Publications*: Law as a Liberal Study, 1969; What is Equity About?, 1970; Fire and the Law, 1972; *contrib*. Conv. Prop. Lawyer, Current Legal Problems, Law Teacher. *Address*: Faculty of Law, Univ. of Leicester, University Road, Leicester LE1 7RH.

Evetts, Julia; Lecturer in Sociology, University of Nottingham, since 1968; *b* 1944; *m* 1967; one *s*. one *d*. BA(Econ) Hons Sheffield 1966 (Sociology); Mem., Brit. Sociol. Assoc. Lectr, Derby Coll. of Technol., 1967–68. *Publications*: The Sociology of Educational Ideas, 1973; *contrib*. Brit. Jl

Sociol. *Address*: Dept of Sociology, Univ. of Nottingham, Nottingham NG7 2RD.

Evetts, Leonard Charles, MA, ARCA; Senior Lecturer, Department of Fine Art, University of Newcastle upon Tyne, since 1937; *b* 1909; *m* 1937. MA Dunelm 1941, ARCA London 1933. Vice-Chm., Exec. Cttee of Council for Places of Worship, 1972; Mem., Council Care of Chs, 1959–71. *Publications*: Roman Lettering, 1938; *contrib*. Archaeol. Ael., Burl. Mag. *Address*: Dept of Fine Art, Univ. of Newcastle upon Tyne, Newcastle upon Tyne NE1 7RU.

Evison, Vera I., FSA; Reader in the Archaeology of the Anglo-Saxon Period, University of London, since 1963; BA London 1947 (Hons English); FSA; Corresp. Mem., Deutsches Arch. Inst. Part-time Lectr, Birkbeck Coll., London, 1947–49; Asst Lectr 1949–52; Lectr, 1952–63. *Publications*: The Fifth-century Invasions South of the Thames, 1965; *contrib*. Antiqu. Jl, Archaeol., Archaeol. Cant., Archaeol. Jl, Beds. Archaeol Jl, Berichten v. Rijksdienst voor Oudheidkundig Bodemonderzoek, Jl Glass Studies. *Address*: Birkbeck College, Univ. of London, Malet Street, WC1E 7HX.

Ewbank, Dr Inga-Stina; Reader in English Literature, Bedford College, University of London, since 1972; *b* 1932; *m* 1959; one *s* two *d*. BA Carleton 1952. MA Sheffield 1954, Fil.kand Gothenburg 1954, PhD Liverpool 1973; Phi Beta Kappa 1952. William Noble Fellow, Liverpool Univ., 1955–57; Res. Fellow, Birmingham Univ., 1957–60; Vis. Lectr, Munich, 1959–60; Asst Lectr, then Lectr, Liverpool, 1960–70; Sen. Lectr, 1970–72. Vis. Assoc. Prof., Northwestern Univ., USA, 1966, Harvard, 1974. *Publications*: Their Proper Sphere, 1966; contrib. A Book of Masques, 1967; John Webster, 1970; A New Companion to Shakespeare Studies, 1971; Shakespearian Comedy, 1972; A Bibliographical Guide to English Drama, 1974; Penguin Anthologies: John Webster, 1969; Henrik Ibsen, 1970; Shakespeare's Later Comedies, 1971; Emily Brontë, 1973; *contrib*. Engl. Lang. Hist., Engl. Studies, Ess. and Studies, Ibsen Ybk, Mod. Lang. Rev., Renaiss. Drama, Rev. Engl. Studies, Rev. Engl. Lit., Shakespeare Survey. *Address*: Dept of English, Bedford College, Regent's Park, NW1 4NS.

Ewing, John Eric Hugh O.; *see* Orr-Ewing.

Ewing, William Thomas, MA, LLB, JP; Registrar, The New University of Ulster, since 1966; *b* 1921; *m* 1951; one *d*. 1st cl. Moderatorship (Classics), MA, LLB, Dublin; JP 1971. Mem., Northern Ireland Boundary Commission, 1973; Chm., Employment and Training Advisory Cttee for County Londonderry, 1973. *Address*: New Univ. of Ulster, Coleraine, County Londonderry BT52 1SA.

Exshaw, Eldon Young, MA, LLB, Lecturer in Law, School of Law, University of Dublin, since 1964; *b* 1930; *m* 1960; one *s* one *d*. MOD BA Dublin 1953 (1st cl. Legal Science), LLB Dublin 1953 (1st cl.), MA Dublin 1957, Barrister-at-Law; called to Bar King's Inns

1953 (1st cl.), Barrister-at-Law Gray's Inn 1958. Reid Prof. of Penal Legislation, Const. and Crim. Law and Evid., Dublin Univ. 1955–60; Lectr, Exeter Univ., 1960–64; Registrar, Law Sch., Dublin Univ., 1964–70; Tutor, Dublin Univ., 1965–70. Mem., Law Reform Adv. Cttee. *Publications: contrib.* Ann. Légis. Franç. Etrang., Crim. Law Rev., Irish Law Times, Irish Jurist. *Address:* School of Law, Trinity College, Dublin 2.

Eynon, John, DipArch, FRIBA; Senior Lecturer, The Welsh School of Architecture, University of Wales, since 1969; *b* 1923; *m* 1950. DipArch Wales 1950, ARIBA 1951, FRIBA 1968; Mem.: Hist. Bldgs Council for Wales, 1967– ; Eur. Arch. Heritage Cttee, Wales; Consultant, local authorities and govt agencies Hist. Bldgs and Conserv.; Governor, Cardiff Coll. of Art; Mem.: Exec. Cttee, Jl Archit., Wales, 1960–65; Concrete Soc.; Central Housing Trust; Cardiff 2000; Cambrian Archaeol. Assoc., 1968– ; Former Mem., Exec. Cttee and Gen. Council, SWIA. Ed., SWIA Jl, 1960–64; Cult. Educnl Exch. Prog., Rumania, Hungary and Bulgaria, 1968–73. *Publications: contrib.* SWIA Jl, Archit. Wales, Welsh Med. Gaz., Isms of Modern Art, misc. Archit./Build. pubns. *Address:* Welsh School of Architecture, Univ. of Wales Institute of Science and Technology, Cathays Park, Cardiff CF1 3NU.

Eyre, Dr S. Robert; Senior Lecturer in Geography, University of Leeds, since 1966; *b* 1922; *m* 1948; two *s.* BSc London 1949, PhD Sheffield 1953; FRMetSoc., 1954. Res. Demonst., Univ. of Sheffield, 1949–52; Asst Lectr, Univ. of Leeds, 1952–54, Lectr, 1954–66. Mem.: Council, Royal Met. Soc., 1965–68; Council, Brit. Assoc. Adv. Sci., 1966–72; Pres. Sec. E, Brit. Assoc., 1971. *Publications:* Vegetation and Soils, 1963, 2nd edn 1968; (with G. R. J. Jones) Geography as Human Ecology, 1966; World Vegetation Types, 1971; *contrib.* Adv. Sci., Agric. Hist. Rev., Trans Inst. Brit. Geogs. *Address:* Dept of Geography, Univ. of Leeds, Leeds LS2 9JT.

Eysenck, Prof. Hans J., PhD; Professor of Psychology, Institute of Psychiatry, University of London, since 1955; *b* 1916; *m* 1938; 1950; four *s* one *d.* BA London 1938, PhD London 1940, DSc London 1964; FBPsS, FAPA. Sen. Res. Psychologist, Mill Hill Emergency Hosp., 1942–46; Sen. Psychologist, Maudsley Hosp., 1946–47; Dir, Psychology Dept, Maudsley Hosp., 1947–48; Reader in Psychology, Univ. of London, Dir, Psychology Dept, Inst. of Psychiatry, Sen. Clinical Psychologist, Maudsley and Bethlem Royal Hosps, 1948–55; Vis. Prof., Univ. of Pennsylvania, 1949–50; Vis. Prof., Univ. of California, 1954. *Publications:* Dimensions of Personality, 1947; The Scientific Study of Personality, 1952; The Structure of Human Personality, 1952; Uses and Abuses of Psychology, 1953; The Psychology of Politics, 1954; Sense and Nonsense in Psychology, 1956; The Dynamics of Anxiety and Hysteria, 1957; (with G. Granger and J. C. Brengelmann) Perceptual Processes and Mental Illness, 1957; Manual of the Maudsley Personality Inventory, 1959; ed, Handbook

of Abnormal Psychology, 1960, 2nd edn 1972; ed, Experiments in Personality, 1960; ed, Behaviour Therapy and the Neuroses, 1960; Know Your Own IQ, 1962; ed, Experiments with Drugs, 1963; Manual for the Eysenck Personality Inventory, 1963; ed, Experiments in Motivation, 1964; ed, Experiments in Behaviour Therapy, 1964; Crime and Personality, 1964; Eysenck Personality Inventory, 1964; (with S. Rachman) Causes and Cures of Neurosis, 1965; Fact and Fiction in Psychology, 1965; Smoking, Health and Personality, 1965; Check Your Own IQ, 1966; The Biological Basis of Personality, 1967; Personality, Structure and Measurement, 1969; Readings in Extraversion/Introversion, 1971; Race, Intelligence and Education, 1971; Psychology is about People, 1972; Encyclopedia of Psychology, 1972; *contrib.* some 500 articles in Brit., Amer., German, Spanish and French jls of psychology. *Address:* Dept of Psychology, Institute of Psychiatry, De Crespigny Park, Denmark Hill, SE5.

Eysenck, Dr Michael William; Lecturer in Psychology, Birkbeck College, University of London, since 1965; *b* 1944. BA London 1965 (1st cl. Hons Psychology), PhD 1972; Mem., British Psychological Soc. *Publications: contrib.* Developmental Psychology, Jl of Personality, Jl of Verbal Learning and Verbal Behavior. *Address:* Birkbeck College, Malet Street, WC1E 7HP.

F

Fage, Prof. John Donnelly; Professor of African History and Director of Centre of West African Studies, University of Birmingham, since 1963; *b* 1921; *m* 1949; one *s* one *d.* BA Cambridge 1946, MA Cambridge 1948, PhD Cambridge 1950; FRHistS. Bye-Fellow, Magdalene Coll., Cambridge, 1947–49; Lectr, Univ. of Ghana, 1949–52, Sen. Lectr and Hd of Dept of Hist., 1952–55, Prof., 1955–59; Vis. Prof., Univ. of Wisconsin, 1957, Lectr, Sch. of Oriental and African Studies, Univ. of London, 1959–63; Vis. Prof., Smith Coll., 1962. RAF, 1941–45; Dep. Principal, Univ. Coll. of Ghana, 1957–59; Dep. Dean, Fac. of Arts, Birmingham, 1973– ; Hon. Sec., Afr. Studies Assoc. UK, 1963–66, Pres., 1968–69; Mem.: Exec. Council, Internat. Afr. Inst., 1965– ; Brit. Nat. Cttee, Internat. Hist. Cong., 1969– ; Internat. Sci. Cttee, Gen. Hist. of Afr., UNESCO, 1970– ; Bureau Internat. Congress Africanists, 1971–73; Ed., Jl African Hist., 1960–73. *Publications:* A History of West Africa, 1955, 4th edn 1969; An Atlas of African History, 1958; Ghana – a historical interpretation, 1959; (with R. Oliver) A Short History of Africa, 1962, 4th edn 1972 (also edns in German, Swedish, Italian, Catalan, Dutch, Japanese, Finnish and Arabic); ed, Africa Discovers Her Past, 1970; (jt ed), Papers on African Prehistory, 1970; *contrib.* Afr. Aff., Boston Univ. Papers Afr. Hist., Jl Afr. Hist., Trans Ghana Hist. Soc. *Address:* Centre of West African Studies, Univ. of Birmingham, PO Box 363, Birmingham B15 2TT.

Fagg, Bernard Evelyn ller, MBE; Curator, Pitt Rivers Museum and Department of Ethnology and Prehistory, University of Oxford, since 1963; Fellow of Linacre College, Oxford; *b* 1915; *m* 1942; one *s* two *d*. BA Cantab 1939, MA Cantab 1944; MA Oxon 1964; FSA, FMA. Mem. Council: Royal Anthropological Inst.; British Inst. in Eastern Africa; Mem. Adv. Cttee, Horniman Museum. *Publications*: ed, Proceedings of the Third West African Conference, 1957; *contrib*. Africa, Archaeometry, Jl Hist. Soc. of Nigeria, Jl West African Archaeology, Museum, Man. Proc. Prehistoric Soc., World Archaeology. *Address*: Pitt Rivers Museum, South Parks Road, Oxford OX1 3PP.

Fahy, Prof. Conor, MA, PhD; Professor of Italian, Birkbeck College, University of London, since 1970; *b* 1928; *m* 1955; four *s* three *d*. BA Cantab 1948 (2nd cl. Mod. and Med. Languages), MA Cantab 1951, PhD Manchester 1954; Mem.: Bibliog. Soc., Mod. Humanities Res. Assoc., Soc. Italian Studies. Asst, Edinburgh Univ., 1954–55; Asst Lectr, Univ. Coll., London, 1955–58, Lectr, 1958–67; Reader, Birkbeck Coll., 1967–70. *Publications*: *contrib*. Bibliofilia, Gle storico lett. Ital., Lett. Ital., Ital. Studies, Library. *Address*: Dept of Italian, Birkbeck College, Malet Street, WC1E 7HX.

Fairclough, Norman, MA; Lecturer in English, University of Lancaster, since 1966; *b* 1941. BA London 1963 (English), MA London 1965 (English). Temp. Asst Lectr, London 1965. *Address*: Dept of English, Univ. of Lancaster, Bailrigg, Lancaster LA1 4YW.

Fairest, Prof. Paul Brant; Professor of Law, University of Hull, since 1974; *b* 1940; *m* 1965; two *s* one *d*. BA 1961, LLB 1962, MA 1965, Cantab. Univ. of Cambridge: Asst Lectr in Land Economy, 1964–66; Asst Lectr in Law, 1966–69, Lectr 1969–74; Sen. Proctor, 1969–70; Sec., Fac. of Law, 1972–74; Fellow 1964–74, Tutor 1966–74, Selwyn Coll. *Publications*: *contrib*. Cambridge Law Jl. *Address*: The Univ., Hull HU6 7RX.

Fairhurst, Harry; Librarian, University of York, since 1962; *b* 1923; *m* 1948; two *s* one *d*. BA Cantab 1949, MA Cantab 1954. Asst Librarian, Univ. of Leeds, 1951–56; Dep. Librarian, UC of Rhodesia and Nyasaland, 1956–62. IUC 1967– . *Publications*: University of Ghana Library (planning report), 1970; The New Universities, in, Librarianship in Britain today, ed, W. L. Saunders, 1967; contrib. Encyclopaedia of Education; *contrib*. ASLIB Proc., Educn, Library Assoc. Rec., Library World. *Address*: J. B. Morrell Library, Univ. of York, Heslington, York YO1 5DD.

Fairlie, Prof. Alison Anna Bowie; Professorial Fellow, Girton College, since 1972; Professor of French, University of Cambridge, since 1972; *b* 1917. BA Oxon 1938 (1st cl. Mediaeval and Modern Languages), MA, DPhil Oxon 1943. Lectr in French, Girton Coll., Cambridge, 1944–67, Staff Fellow and Dir of Studies in Mod. Langs, 1946–67;

Univ. Lectr in French, Cambridge, 1948–67, Reader, 1967–72; Hon. Fellow, St Hugh's, Coll., Oxford, 1972– . Temp. Asst, FO, 1942–44. Vice-Pres., 1965–66 and 1968–69, Pres., 1966–68, Soc. for French Studies; Mem., Council of Assoc. Internationale des Etudes françaises, 1969– . *Publications*: Leconte de Lisle's Poems on the Barbarian Races, 1947; Baudelaire: Les Fleurs du Mal, 1960, repr. 1972 (American edn 1962); Flaubert: Madame Bovary, 1962, repr. 1970 (American edn 1963); *contrib*. Australian Jl of French Studies, Europe, Essays in French Literature, Forum for Mod. Lang. Studies, French Studies, Mod. Lang. Rev., Revue d'Histoire Littèraire de France, Rev. des Sciences Humaines, Times Lit. Supp.; presentation vols to: Gustave Rudler, P. Mansell Jones, Alan M. Boase, A. R. Chisholm, H. J. Hunt, C. A. Hackett; Actes du Congrès B. Constant de Lausanne, 1967; Actes du Colloque Baudelaire de Nice, 1967; Manchester Symp. on Fr. 19th Century Painting and Literature, 1969; Cahiers de l'Assoc. Internat. des Etudes Françaises, 1970. *Address*: Girton College, Cambridge.

Falck, Colin; Lecturer, Humanities Department, Chelsea College, University of London, since 1965; *b* 1934. BA Oxon 1957 (PPE), BA Oxon 1959 (Philos., Psychol. and Physiol.). Asst Lectr in Sociol., LSE, 1961–62, Asst Lectr in Liberal Studies, Chelsea Coll., London, 1963–65. *Publication*: Backwards into the Smoke, 1973. *Address*: Humanities Dept, Chelsea Coll., Manresa Road, SW3 6LX.

Falvey, Dr John Francis; Senior Lecturer in French, University of Southampton, since 1972; *b* 1928; *m* 1954; three *s* one *d*. BA Hons Nottingham 1952, PhD Nottingham 1956. *Address*: Dept of French, Univ. of Southampton, Highfield, Southampton SO9 5NH.

Farish, John, MA; Senior Lecturer in English Language, University of Glasgow, since 1969; *b* 1921; *m* 1946; two *s*. MA Glasgow 1948 (1st cl. Hons English Language and Literature). Asst Lectr in English Language, Univ. of Glasgow, 1948–49, Lectr in English Language, 1949–69. *Publications*: *contrib*. Engl. Studies. *Address*: Dept of English Language, The Univ., Glasgow G12 8QQ.

Farley-Hills, David Leslie; Senior Lecturer, English Department, Queen's University, Belfast, since 1973; *b* 1931; *m* 1962; two *s* two *d*. MA, BLitt, DPhil Oxon; Queen's Coll., Oxford, 1953–60; Royal Univ. of Malta, 1961–68; Queen's Univ. Belfast, 1968– . *Publications*: Gawain's Fault in Sir Gawain and the Green Knight, in, Critical Essays on Sir Gawain and the Green Knight, ed Howard and Zacher, 1968; Rochester: The Critical Heritage, 1972; The Benevolence of Laughter, Comic Poetry of the Commonwealth and Restoration (forthcoming); *contrib*. Rev. Eng. Stud., Essays in Crit. *Address*: Dept of English, Queen's Univ. Belfast BT7 1NN.

Farmer, Bertram Hughes, MA; Fellow of St John's College, Cambridge, since 1948;

Reader in South Asian Geography, since 1967, and Director of the Centre of South Asian Studies, University of Cambridge, since 1964; *b* 1916; *m* 1947; three *s* one *d*. BA Cantab 1937, MA Cantab 1941; FRGS; Mem., Inst. Brit. Geogrs (Ed., 1961–66, Vice-Pres., 1970–71, Pres., 1972). Lectr, Univ. Coll., Swansea, 1946–48; Tutor, 1958–61, and Pres., 1967–71, St John's Coll., Cambridge; Univ. Demons. in Geography, 1948–52; Lectr, Univ. of Cambridge, 1952–67. War Service (Royal Tank Regt, Royal Engineers) 1940–46; Mem.: Ceylon Land Commn, 1955–58; Council, Royal Geog. Soc., 1963–66, Brit. Nat. Cttee Geog., 1969–72; Chm., Gal Oya Project Evaluation Cttee, Ceylon, 1966–69; Mem., Gov. Body, SOAS, Univ. of London, 1970– . *Publications*: Pioneer Peasant Colonization in Ceylon, 1957; Ceylon: a Divided Nation, 1963, Sinhalese edn 1964; Agricultural Colonization in India since Independence; *contrib*. Geog. Jl, Geog. Rev., Jl Develop. Studies, Trans Inst. Brit. Geogrs. *Address*: St John's College, Cambridge.

Farmer, David Hugh; Lecturer in History, University of Reading, since 1967; *b* 1923; *m* 1965; two *s*. BLitt Oxford 1967; FSA 1962, FRHistS 1968. *Publications*: (with D. L. Douie) The Life of St Hugh of Lincoln, 2 vols, 1961–62; The Monk of Farne, 1962; The Rule of St Benedict, 1968; Studies in Latin Biography, 1967; Pre-Reformation English Spirituality, 1964; Tenth Century Studies, 1973; St Wilfrid at Hexham, 1974; *contrib*. Analecta Bollandiana, Analecta Monastica, Revue d'Histoire Ecclesiastique, Jl of Ecclesiastical Hist., TLS. *Address*: Dept of History, Fac. of Letters, Univ. of Reading, Reading RG6 2AA.

Farmer, Mary Elwood; Senior Lecturer in Sociology, University of Liverpool, since 1972; *b* 1918; *m* 1942; one *s* two *d*. BA Liverpool 1940 (1st cl. Social Science). Lectr in Sociology, Univ. of Liverpool, 1962–72. *Publications*: The Family, 1970, Dutch edn 1971; *contrib*. Sociol. Rev. *Address*: Dept of Sociology, Univ. of Liverpool, Liverpool L69 3BX.

Farnie, Douglas Antony; Senior Lecturer in Economic History, Department of History, University of Manchester, since 1972; BA Manchester 1951, MA Manchester 1953, PhD Natal 1969; Mem.: Hist. Assoc., Econ. Hist. Soc. Lectr in Hist., Univ. of Natal, Durban, 1954–60; Lectr in Econ. Hist., Univ. of Manchester, 1961–72. *Publications*: East and West of Suez: The Suez Canal in History, 1854–1956, 1969; *contrib*. Econ. Hist. Rev., Bull. J. Rylands Lib., S Afr. Jl Econ. *Address*: Dept of History, Univ. of Manchester, Manchester M13 9PL.

Farrand, Prof. Julian Thomas, LLB, LLD; Professor of Law, University of Manchester, since 1968; *b* 1935; *m* 1957; one *s* two *d*. LLB London 1957 (1st cl.), LLD London 1966; Hon. LLM Manchester 1972; Solicitor of Supreme Court 1960. Asst Lectr, King's Coll., London, 1960–62; Lectr, 1962–63; Lectr, Sheffield Univ., 1963–65; Reader, Queen Mary Coll., London, 1958–68. Dean, 218

Faculty of Law, Manchester Univ., 1970–72. Chm., Manchester Rent Tribunal, 1973– . *Publications*: Contract and Conveyance, 1969, 2nd edn 1973; ed (with J. G. Smith), Emmet on Title, 15th edn 1967, 16th edn 1974; ed, Wolstenholme and Cherry's Conveyancing Statutes, 13th edn 1972; *contrib*. Solicitors Jl, Convey. Property Lawyer. *Address*: Faculty of Law, The Univ., Manchester M13 9PL.

Farrell, Brian, MA; College Lecturer in Political Institutions, Department of Ethics and Politics, University College of Dublin, since 1966; *b* 1929; *m* 1955; four *s* three *d*. BA NUI 1953 (1st cl. History), MA NUI 1956. Asst Registrar and Sec., UCD, 1955–66; Dir, Extramural Studies, UCD, 1960–66. Mem.: Mktg Cttee, Fed. Irish Indust., 1960–64; Cath. Communic. Inst. of Ireland, 1970– . Editor, Studies in Irish Political Culture. *Publications*: Chairman or Chief? the role of Taoiseach in Irish Government, 1971; The Founding of Dáil Éireann: Parliament and Nation-Building, 1971; ed, The Irish Parliamentary Tradition, 1973; *contrib*. Admin., Irish Jurist, Econ. Soc. Rev. *Address*: Room G 3–02, Arts Block, Univ. College, Dublin 4, Ireland.

Farrell, Michael James; Fellow of Gonville and Caius College, Cambridge, since 1958; Reader in Economics, Cambridge University, since 1970; *b* 1926; *m* 1952; five *s*. BA Oxon 1949 (1st cl. PPE), MA Oxon 1953, MA Cantab 1953; Fellow, Econ. Soc. Asst Lectr, Cambridge Univ., 1953–56, Lectr, 1956–70; Vis. Prof., Yale Univ., 1962; Vis. Prof., Univ. of California, Berkeley, 1966–67; Ford Foundn Disting. Vis. Res. Prof., Carnegie-Mellon Univ., 1969. Jt Mngng Ed., Rev. Econ. Studies, 1965–68. *Publications*: ed, Readings in Welfare Economics, 1973; *contrib*. Economica, Econometrica, Econ. Jl, Jl Indust. Econ., Jl Politl Econ., Jl Royal Statistical Soc. (series A), Oxford Econ. Papers, Rev. Econ. Studies. *Address*: Gonville and Caius College, Cambridge.

Farrington, Brian; Director, Language Laboratory, University of Aberdeen, since 1973; *b* 1925; *m* 1953; 1968; two *s* two *d*. BA TCD 1947, MA Manchester 1966. Lectr in French, Manchester Univ., 1965–66; Lectr in French, Aberdeen Univ., 1966–72, Sen. Lectr, 1972. *Publications*: Emigrant of a Hundred Townlands (poems), 1969; Malachi Stilt Jack (Essay on W. B. Yeats), 1965; *contrib*. AV Lang. Jl, Mod. Langs. *Address*: Language Laboratory, King's College, Univ. of Aberdeen, Aberdeen AB9 2UB.

Farrington, Dr John H.; Lecturer in Geography, University of Aberdeen, since 1969; *b* 1945; *m* 1973. BSc Hons Hull 1966, PhD 1970 (Geog.); Member: Inst. Brit. Geogrs, Geog. Assoc. Post-Doctoral Fellow, Univ. of Canterbury, Christchurch, NZ, 1974. *Publications*: Morphological Studies of English Canals, 1972; *contrib*. Geog. Mag., Trspt Hist. *Address*: Dept of Geography, St Mary's, High Street, Old Aberdeen AB9 2UF.

Faulkes, Anthony Robin; Lecturer in English, University of Birmingham, since 1973; *b* 1937; *m* 1958; two *s*. BA Oxon 1960

(2nd cl. English), MA Oxon 1964, BLitt Oxon 1965. Asst Lectr, Birkbeck Coll., 1963–66, Lectr, 1966–73. *Publications*: Rauðúlfs þáttr: a study, 1966; Two Icelandic Stories: Hreidars þáttr, Orms þáttr, 1967; *contrib*. Ling. Island., Saga-Bk Viking Soc., North. Res. *Address*: Dept of English, Univ. of Birmingham, Birmingham B15 2TT.

Faulkner, Peter; Senior Lecturer in English, University of Exeter, since 1973; *b* 1933; *m* 1959; one *s* one *d*. BA (Cantab) 1956 (1st cl. Hons), MA Cantab 1961, MA Birmingham 1959. Lectr in English, Univ. Durham, 1963–71; Vis. Sen. Lectr in English, Fourah Bay Coll., 1965–66; Lectr in English, Exeter, 1971–73. *Publications*: William Morris and W. B. Yeats, 1961; W. B. Yeats and the Irish Eighteenth Century, 1966; ed, T. Holcroft: Anna St Ives, 1970, paperback edn 1973; ed, William Morris: The Critical Heritage, 1973; ed, William Morris: Early Romances in Prose and Verse, 1973; *contrib*. Durham Univ. Jl, Yearbook of English Studies. *Address*: Dept, of English, Queen's Building, Queen's Drive, Exeter EX4 4QH.

Fawthrop, Prof. Roger A., BA(Econ), PhD, FCMA; Esme Fairbairn Professor of Financial Management, University of Warwick, since 1972; Chairman, School of Industrial and Business Studies, since 1973; *b* 1923; *m* 1948. BA(Econ) Leeds 1948, PhD Loughborough 1969; ACWA (subseq. ACMA) 1949, FCWA (subseq. FCMA) 1965. Lectr, Univ. of Loughborough, 1965–69; Sen. Lectr, and Dir of Postgrad. Studies in Financial Control, Univ. of Lancaster, 1969. Cost Acntnt, Bradford Dyers Assoc., 1949–58; Sen. Mngmnt Acntnt, Tarmac Gp, 1958–61; Chief Acntnt, Air Products Ltd, 1961–65; Mem., various cttees, profess. bodies. *Publications*: *contrib*. Jl Acntng and Business Res., Jl Business Fin., Jl Business Policy, etc. *Address*: School of Industrial and Business Studies, Univ. of Warwick, Coventry CV4 7AL.

Fearon, Peter Shaun; Lecturer, Department of Economic History, Leicester University, since 1966; *b* 1942; *m* 1966; one *s*. BA(Econ) Liverpool 1964. *Publications*: ed (with D. H. Aldcroft), Economic Growth in Twentieth Century Britain, 1969; ed (with D. H. Aldcroft), British Economic Fluctuations 1790–1939, 1972; *contrib*. Bus Hist. Rev. *Address*: Dept of Economic History, Univ. of Leicester, Leicester LE1 7RH.

Fehérvári, Géza, BA, PhD; Lecturer in Islamic Art and Archaeology, School of Oriental and African Studies, University of London, since 1963; *m* 1958; one *s*. BA Budapest 1952 (Arabic), PhD London 1961 (Islamic Art and Arch.); FRAS, FSA. *Publications*: Islamic Pottery from the Collection of Sir Alan Barlow, 1973; Islamic Metalwork in the Keir Collection, 1975; *contrib*. Orient. Art, IRAN, Kunst Orients, Bull. SOAS. *Address*: School of Oriental and African Studies, Univ. of London, WC1E 7HP.

Feldman, David Jonathan Peretz; Lecturer, School of Development Studies, University of East Anglia, since 1970; *b* 1940; *m* 1966; two *d*. BSc(Econ) LSE 1963, MSc(Econ) LSE 1965. Asst Lectr, Dept of Agricultural Economics, Univ. of Manchester, 1965–67; Fellow, Inst. of Development Studies, Univ. of Sussex, and Res. Fellow, Economic Res. Bureau, Univ. of Dar es Salaam, 1968–70. *Publications*: The Economics of Ideology, in, Politics and Change in Developing Societies, ed C. Leys, 1970; *contrib*. E African Jl of Rural Develt, Etudes Congolaises. *Address*: Sch. of Development Studies, Univ. of East Anglia, Norwich NOR 88C.

Feldman, Dr Maurice Philip, BA, Dip-Psychol, PhD; Reader in Clinical Psychology, University of Birmingham, since 1972; *b* 1933; *m* 1959; two *d*. BA Manchester 1959 (Psychol.), DipPsychol London 1960 (Dist.), PhD London 1963; FBPsS. Lectr, Birmingham, 1966–68; Sen. Lectr, 1969–72; Visiting Prof., Univ. of Hawaii, 1972–73. Mem., Commn on Training, British Psychol. Soc., 1969–72. *Publications*: Psychology in the Industrial Environment, 1971; (with M. J. MacCulloch) Homosexual Behaviour: Therapy and Assessment, 1971; (with M. J. MacCulloch) Human Sexual Behaviour (forthcoming); Criminal Behaviour: a psychological analysis (forthcoming); *contrib*. Acta Psychiatrica Scandinavica, Behaviour Res. and Therapy, Behaviour Therapy, Brit Med Jl, Psychol. Bull. *Address*: Dept of Psychology, Univ. of Birmingham, PO Box 363, Birmingham B15 2TT.

Fell, Christine Elizabeth; Lecturer in the School of English Studies, University of Nottingham, since 1971; *b* 1938. BA London 1959 (1st cl. English), MA London 1961. Asst Lectr, Aberdeen Univ., 1963–65; Lectr, Leeds Univ., 1965–71. Mem., Council, Viking Soc. North. Res., 1964–65, 1969–70. *Publications*: Dunstanus Saga, 1963; Edward King and Martyr, 1971; trans., Egils saga, 1974; contrib. Proc. Int. Saga Conf., 1, 1971; *contrib*. Angl. Sax. Engl., Leeds Studies in Engl., Saga-Bk, Scandinav. *Address*: School of English Studies, The Univ., Nottingham NG7 2RD.

Feltham, John David; Fellow and Tutor in Law, Magdalen College, Oxford, since 1965; *b* 1932; *m* 1959; two *s*. BA Melbourne 1953, BA Oxon 1956, MA Oxon 1961. Sen. Lectr in Law, Univ. of Melbourne, 1960–65; Sen. Proctor, Oxford Univ., 1972–73. *Address*: Magdalen Coll. Oxford.

Fenlon, Dr Dermot Brian; Fellow and Tutor, Gonville and Caius College, Cambridge, since 1970, and University Lecturer in History since 1973; *b* 1941; BA NUI 1963, MA, PhD 1969, Cantab. FRHistS 1973. Res. Fellow, Gonville and Caius Coll., Cambridge, 1968–70; Univ. Asst Lectr in Hist., Cambridge, 1970–73. *Publications*: Heresy and Obedience in Tridentine Italy: Cardinal Pole and the Counter Reformation, 1972. *Address*: Gonville and Caius Coll., Cambridge.

Fennell, Graham; Lecturer in Sociology, School of Social Studies, University of East

Anglia, since 1968; *b* 1943; *m* 1973. BA Oxon 1964 (Modern History), DipSocSc Stockholm 1965, MSocSc 1966, MA Oxon 1968; Mem., BSA. *Address*: Sch. of Social Studies, Univ. of East Anglia, Norwich NOR 88C.

Fennell, Prof. John Lister Illingworth; Professor of Russian, University of Oxford, since 1967; *b* 1918; *m* 1948; one *s* one *d*. MA Cantab, PhD Cantab. Asst Lectr, Cambridge, 1947–52; Reader in Russian and Head of Dept of Slavonic Langs, Nottingham Univ., 1952–56; Lectr, Oxford Univ., 1956–67; Vis. Lectr, Harvard Univ., 1963–64; Fellow, Univ. Coll., Oxford, 1964–67; Fellow, New Coll., Oxford, 1967– ; Vis. Prof., Univ. of California, Berkeley, 1971. Jt Ed., Oxford Slavonic Papers, 1968– ; Russia Mediaevalis, 1973– . *Publications*: The Correspondence between Kurbsky and Ivan IV, 1955; Ivan the Great of Moscow, 1961; The Penguin Russian Course, 1961; The Penguin Pushkin, 1964; Kurbsky's History of Ivan IV, 1965; The Emergence of Moscow 1304–1359, 1968; A Russian Historical Reader, 1969; Nineteenth Century Russian Literature, 1973; Early Russian Literature, 1974; *contrib.* Jahrb. Gesch. Osteurop., Slav. Rev., Slav. E Europ. Jl, etc. *Address*: New College, Oxford.

Fenton, Rev. John Charles; Principal, St Chad's College, Durham University, and part-time Lecturer, Department of Theology, since 1965; *b* 1921, *m* 1963; three *s* three *d*. BA Oxon 1943, MA Oxon 1947, BD Oxon 1953; *Publications*: Preaching the Cross, 1958; The Passion according to John, 1961; The Gospel of St Matthew, 1963; The Gospel according to John, 1970; What was Jesus' Message, 1971. *Address*: St Chad's Coll., Durham.

Fenwick, Ian M.; Lecturer, Department of Geography, Reading University, since 1964; *b* 1937; *m* 1961; three *d*. BSc(Hons) Reading 1958, MSc Reading 1960; Mem., Inst. Brit. Geogrs, Brit. Soc. Soil Science. Asst Lectr, Univ. Coll., Londonderry, 1962–64; Vis. Prof., McMaster Univ., 1967–68. *Publications*: contribs. Proc. Third Afr. Reg. Conf. Soil Mech.; (with B. J. Knapp) Soils – Process and Response (forthcoming); *contrib.* Ont. Archaeol. *Address*: Dept of Geography, Univ. of Reading, Reading RG6 2AF.

Ferguson, Prof. John, MA, BD, FIAL; Dean and Director of Studies in Arts, The Open University, since 1969; *b* 1921; *m* 1950. MA Cantab 1947 (1st cl.), BD London 1944 (1st cl.); FIAL 1962; Mem., Brit. Assoc. Adv. Sci., Class. Assoc., Engl. Assoc., Hellenic Soc., Hist. Assoc., Roman Soc., Royal Inst. Philos. Lectr in Classics, King's Coll., Newcastle, 1948–53; Sen. Lectr in Classics, Queen Mary Coll., London, 1953–56; Prof. of Classics, Univ. Coll., Ibadan (subseq. Univ. of Ibadan), 1956–66; Ext. Examiner, Univ. of Ghana, 1964–66; Hill Vis. Prof., Univ. of Minnesota, 1966–68; Prof., 1968–69; Old Dominion Vis. Prof. in Humanities, Hampton Inst., Virginia, 1968–69 (leave of absence from Minnesota). Chm., Fellowship of Reconcil., 1953–56; Vice-Chm., 1969– ; Jt Ed., Reconcil. Qly, 1969– ; Chm., Brit.

Council Chs Educn Dept, 1971–74; Dir Community Aff., 1974– ; Mem., Exec. Cttee, UN Assoc., 1971– ; Pres., Orbilian Soc., 1972. *Publications*: ed, Studies in Christian Social Commitment, 1954; Pelagius, 1956; ed, Plato: Republic X, 1957; The United Nations and the World's Needs, 1957; Moral Values in the Ancient World, 1958; The Enthronement of Love, 4th edn 1959; Africa in Classical Antiquity, 1969; Socrates: A Source-Book, 1970; The Place of Suffering, 1972; The Politics of Love, 1972; A Companion to Greek Tragedy, 1972; The Heritage of Hellenism, 1972; Aristotle, 1972; Sermons of a Layman, 1972; ed, War and the Creative Arts, 1972; many Open University course units; *contrib.* Amer. Jl Philol., Class. Qly, Engl. Studies in Afr., Expos. Times, Greece and Rome, Mod. Drama, Phronesis, Proc. Afr. Class. Assocs, Relig. Studies. *Address*: The Open Univ., Walton Hall, Milton Keynes MK7 6AA.

Ferguson, William; Senior Lecturer in Scottish History, University of Edinburgh, since 1968; *b* 1924; *m* 1958; two *s* two *d*. MA Glasgow 1950 (Hons Hist.), BA Oxon 1952 (Hons Hist.), PhD Glasgow 1957. Asst, Dept of Hist., Glasgow Univ. 1952–54; Asst, Dept of Scottish Hist., Edinburgh, 1954–57, Lectr, 1957–68, Dir of Studies, 1965–68. *Publications*: Scotland: 1689 to Present, 1968; *contrib.* Scottish Hist. Rev. *Address*: Dept of Scottish History, William Robertson Building, Univ. of Edinburgh, George Square, Edinburgh EH8 9JY.

Fernandez, Juan Manuel de la Cruz; *see* de la Cruz Fernandez.

Ferns, Prof. Henry Stanley; Professor of Political Science, University of Birmingham, since 1961; *b* 1913; *m* 1940; three *s* one *d*. BA Manitoba 1935, MA Queen's Univ. (Kingston Canada) 1936, BA Cambridge 1938, MA Cambridge 1945, PhD Cambridge 1951. Asst Prof. of Hist., Univ. of Manitoba, 1945–49; Res. Fellow, Canadian Soc. Sci. Res. Council, 1949–50; Lectr in Mod. Hist. and Govt, Univ. of Birmingham, 1950–55; Sen. Lectr, 1955–60. *Publications*: (with B. Ostry) The Age of Mackenzie King, 1955; Britain and Argentina in the Nineteenth Century, 1960; Gran Britañ y Argentina en el Siglo XIX, 1967; Argentina, 1969; National Economic Histories: The Argentine Republic, 1516–1971, 1973; *contrib.* Canad. Hist. Rev., Economic Hist. Rev., Past Pres., Sociol. Rev., Pol. Qly. *Address*: Faculty of Commerce and Social Service, Univ. of Birmingham, PO Box 363, Birmingham B15 2TT.

Ferrer-Chivite, Dr Manuel, PhD; Lecturer in Spanish, University College, Dublin, since 1969; *b* 1929. Lic. en Filosofía y Letras Zaragoza 1960; PhD Wisconsin 1967. Asst Prof., Marquette Univ., 1967–69. *Publications*: Borges y la Nada, 1971; El laberinto mexicano de Juan Rulfo, 1972; *contrib.* Revista Camoniana. *Address*: Dept of Spanish, Univ. College, Dublin 4.

Ferries, George William, MA, ABPsS; Lecturer in Applied Psychology, Department of Applied Psychology, The University of Aston in Birmingham, since 1966; *b* 1929; *m* 1956; three *s* one *d*. MA Aberdeen 1951 (Philosophy and Psychology), BA London 1958 (Psychology); HNC in Production Engineering 1962; Mem., Div. of Occupational Psy; Mem., Ergonomics Res. Soc. Assoc. Teachers of Mgnt, Coll. Teachers of Blind. *Publications*: The first steps in training design, in, New Media and Methods in Industrial Training, ed J. Robinson and N. Barnes, 1967; *contrib*. Brit. Jl Ophthalmol., Mid. Indust. Comm. *Address*: Applied Psychology Dept, The Univ. of Aston in Birmingham, Birmingham B4 7ET.

Feuchtwanger, Edgar Joseph, MA, PhD; Reader in History, since 1973, Deputy Director, since 1966, Department of Extramural Studies, University of Southampton; *b* 1924; *m* 1962; one *s* two *d*. BA Cantab 1947, MA Cantab 1950, PhD Southampton 1958. Lectr, Southampton Univ., 1949–66, Sen. Lectr, 1966–73. *Publications*: Disraeli, Democracy and the Tory Party, 1968; Prussia: Myth and Reality, 1970, German edn 1972; ed, Upheaval and Continuity: a century of German history, 1973; Gladstone: a political biography, 1974; *contrib*. Bull. Inst. Hist. Res., Vict. Studies. *Address*: Dept of Extra-mural Studies, The Univ., Southampton SO9 5NH.

Field, Dr Christopher David Steadman; Lecturer in Music, University of St Andrews, since 1966; *b* 1938. BA Oxon 1962, MA Oxon 1965, DPhil Oxon 1971; ARCM 1960. Warden, Southgait Hall, St Andrews, 1971. *Publications*: editions of 17th and 19th century Chamber music; *contrib*. Mus. Lett. *Address*: Dept of Music, The Univ., St Andrews, Fife KY16 9AJ.

Field, Dr Frank; Senior Lecturer in History, University of Keele, since 1962; *b* 1936; *m* 1965; two *d*. BA Oxon 1960, DPhil Oxon 1965. *Publications*: The Last Days of Mankind: Karl Kraus and his Vienna, 1967; *contrib*. TLS, Wiener Library Bull. *Address*: Dept of History, Univ. of Keele, Keele, Staffs ST5 5BG.

Field, Peter John Christopher, BLitt, MA; Lecturer in English, University College of North Wales, Bangor, since 1964; *b* 1939. BA Oxon 1962 (1st cl. English), MA Oxon 1966, BLitt Oxon 1967. *Publications*: Romance and Chronicle, 1971; ed, Sir Thomas Malory: Le Morte Darthur: Parts Seven and Eight, 1974; *contrib*. Med. Aev., Speculum, Studies in Philol., Durham Univ. Jl, Studia Neophilologica, Neuphilologische Mitteilungen, Rev. Eng. Stud., Bull. Inst. Hist. Res. *Address*: English Department, Univ. College, Bangor LL57 2DG.

Fielden, Richard Derrick Spensley; Tutor-in-charge, Adult and Further Education Division, University of Nottingham, since 1969; *b* 1926; *m* 1960; one *s* three *d*. BA 1951 (Hons English), MA Manchester 1952. Univ. of Indonesia, Djakarta, 1953–60; Res. Tutor in Lincoln, Extra-mural Dept, Univ. of Nottingham, 1960–69. Hon. Sec., Stand. Conf. Univ. Teaching and Res. in Educn Adults (SCUTREA), 1970–71. *Publications*: (with L. A. Hill), Comprehension and

Precis Pieces for Overseas Students, 1957, 3rd edn 1970; English Language Teaching Games, 1974; *contrib*. Adult Educn. *Address*: School of Education, Univ. Park, Nottingham NG7 2RD.

Fieldhouse, David Kenneth, MA; Beit Lecturer in Commonwealth History, Oxford University, since 1958; *b* 1925; *m* 1952; one *s* two *d*. BA Oxon 1949 (1st cl. Hist.), MA Oxon 1950; FRHistS. Lectr, Univ. of Canterbury, NZ, 1953–58; Fellow, Australian Nat. Univ., 1965– ; Vis. Prof., Yale Univ., 1969–70. Sub-Lieut (A), RN, 1945–47; Dom. Bursar, Nuffield Coll., Oxford, 1966– . *Publications*: Two Centuries of Change, vol. II, 2nd edn 1964; The Colonial Empires, 1966, German edn 1965, Italian edn 1967; The Theory of Capitalist Imperialism, 1967; Economics and Empire 1830–1914, 1973; *contrib*. Econ. Hist. Rev., Hist. Studies A. and NZ, Jl Commonwealth Pol. Studies. *Address*: Nuffield College, Oxford.

Fielding, Prof. Kenneth J.; Saintsbury Professor of English Literature, Edinburgh University, since 1966; *b* 1924. BA, MA Oxon 1948, DPhil Oxon 1953. William Noble Fellow, Liverpool, 1951–53. *Publications*: Charles Dickens: A Survey, 1954; Charles Dickens, A Critical Introduction, 1965; The Speeches of Charles Dickens, 1960; asst ed., vol. 1, Pilgrim edn of Dickens' Letters, 1965; assoc. ed., Letters of Thomas and Jane Welsh Carlyle, vols 1–4, 1970; *contrib*. Dickensian, Rev. Eng. Studies, Dickens Studies. *Address*: Dept of English Literature, David Hume Tower, George Square, Edinburgh EH8 9JX.

Fields, Alan; Lecturer, School of Management, Cranfield Institute of Technology, since 1964. BSc Sheffield 1951; MInst GasE 1958, AMInstFuel 1958. *Publication*: Method Study, 1969. *Address*: Cranfield Institute of Technology, Cranfield, Bedford MK43 0AL.

Fifoot, Erik Richard Sidney, MC, MA, ALA; University Librarian, University of Edinburgh, since 1960; *b* 1925; *m* 1949; two *d*. BAOxon 1948 (2nd cl. Hons Jurisprudence), Dip. Librarianship London 1951, ALA 1952. Temp. Asst Librarian, Leeds Univ., 1950, Sub-Librarian, 1952; Dep. Librarian, Nottingham Univ., 1958. Hon. Sec., Sconul Cttee on Buildings, 1963– ; Mem. Commn on Buildings, Internat. Fedn of Library Assocs, 1972– . *Publications*: A Bibliography of Edith, Osbert and Sacheverell Sitwell, 1963, 2nd edn 1971; *contrib*. Canadian Library, Educn Libraries Bull., Encyc. Library and Information Science, Library Assoc. Record. *Address*: University Library, George Square, Edinburgh EH8 9LJ.

Finch, Prof. Ronald George, MA, PhD; Professor of German, University of Glasgow, since 1974; *b* 1925; *m* 1953; one *s* one *d*. BA Wales 1948 (1st cl. German), MA Wales 1950, PhD Belfast 1963. Asst UCW, Aberystwyth, 1948; Asst Lectr, 1949–51, Lectr, 1951–54; Lectr, The Queen's Univ. of Belfast, 1954–62, Sen. Lectr, 1962–68, Reader, 1968–70, Prof., 1970–73. Ch. Exam-

221

iner, N Ireland A-Level GCE, 1961–66; Ext. Examiner, Nat. Univ. of Ireland, 1969–71; Ext. Examiner (Swedish), Univ. of Hull, 1972; Ext. Examiner, New Univ. of Ulster, 1972–73. *Publications*: The Saga of the Volsungs, 1965; trans., Danish Introductions for English edn, Corpus Codicum Danicorum Medii Ævi, vols I–X 1960–68; *contrib*. Neuphil Mitt., Saga-Bk, GLL. *Address*: Dept of German, Univ. of Glasgow, Glasgow G12 8QQ.

Findlay, Dr John Malcolm; Lecturer, Department of Psychology, University of Durham, since 1968; *b* 1942; *m* 1967; two *d*. BA Hons Cantab 1963, (Nat. Scis), MA Cantab 1966, PhD Cantab 1967. Sen. Res. Asst, Univ. of Reading, 1967–68. *Publications*: *contrib*. Kybernetik, Nature, Optica Acta, Vision Res. *Address*: Dept of Psychology, Univ. of Durham, Durham DH1 3LE.

Finer, Prof. Samuel Edward; Professor of Government, Chairman, Department of Government, University of Manchester, since 1966; *b* 1915; *m* 1949; two *s* one *d*. BA Oxon 1937 (1st cl. Hons Mod. Greats), BA Oxon 1938 (1st cl. Hons Mod. Hist.), MA Oxon 1946; Hon. MA (Econ) Manchester, 1970. Mem.: Bd Exec. Cttee, IPSA Political Studies Assoc., Amer. Pol. Science Assoc. Lectr in Politics, 1946–49, Jun. Res. Fellow, Balliol Coll., Oxford, 1949–50; Prof., Political Inst., Keele Univ., 1950-66, Dep. Vice-Chancellor, 1962-64; Vis. Prof. and Faculty Mem., Inst. of Social Studies, The Hague, 1957– . Mem.: SSRC; Inst. for Jewish Affairs; Inst. Strategic Studies; Inst. for Study of Conflict, etc. *Publications*: A Primer of Public Administration, 1950; The Life and Times of Sir Edwin Chadwick, 1952; (with Sir John Maud) Local Government in England and Wales, 1953; (with D. J. Bartholomew and H. B. Berrington) Backbench Opinion in the House of Commons, 1955; Anonymous Empire: a study of the lobby in Britain, 1958, 2nd edn 1966; Private Enterprise and Political Power, 1958; Man on Horseback: the role of the military in politics, 1962; (ed, Macridis and Ward) Great Britain in Modern Political Systems: Europe, 3rd edn 1972; ed, Siéyès: What is the Third Estate?, 1963; Pareto: sociological writings, 1966; Comparative Government, 1970; The transmission of Benthamite ideas, in, Studies in the Growth of 19th Century Government, 1972; (ed, G. Parry) chapter, in, Participation, 1972; Introduction to Ferrero (forthcoming); *contrib*. Encyclopaedia Britannica, Sociological Rev., The Economist, New Society, Govt and Opposition, Encounter, etc. *Address*: Dept of Government, Univ. of Manchester, Manchester M13 9PL.

Finlayson, Douglas S.; Senior Lecturer in Educational Research, School of Education, University of Liverpool, since 1973 (Lecturer, 1970–73); *b* 1923; *m* 1952; one *s* two *d*. MA Edinburgh 1949, MEd Edinburgh 1950; ABPsS. Lectr in Educnl Psychology, Liverpool Univ., 1960–70. *Publications*: Success and Failure in the Secondary School (with Olive Banks), 1973; *contrib*. Brit. Jl Educn. Psychol., Brit. Jl Soc. Clin. Psychol., Educnl Res., Pedagog. Europ., Res. Educn. *Address*:

School of Education, Univ. of Liverpool, Abercromby Square, Liverpool.

Finlayson, Geoffrey Beauchamp Alistair Moubray, MA, BLitt, FRHistS; Lecturer in History, University of Glasgow, since 1962; *b* 1934; *m* 1968; two *d*. MA Glasgow 1957 (1st cl. Hist.), BLitt Oxon 1960; FRHistS 1968. Asst in Hist., Univ. of Glasgow, 1959–61; Temp. Lectr in Hist., Univ. of Glasgow, 1961–62; Visiting Prof., City Univ. of NY, 1972–73. *Publications*: England in the Eighteen-Thirties, decade of reform, 1969; Shaftesbury, in, Pressure from Without, 1974; *contrib*. Bull. Inst. Hist. Res., EHR, History. *Address*: Dept of History, Univ. of Glasgow, Glasgow G12 8QQ.

Finley, Dr Moses I., FBA; Professor of Ancient History, Cambridge University, since 1970; Fellow of Jesus College, since 1957; *b* 1912; *m* 1932. BA Syracuse 1927 (magna cum laude) (PhiBetaKappa), MA Columbia 1929, PhD Columbia 1950; Hon. LittD Leicester 1972; FBA 1971. Fellow in Hist., Columbia Univ., 1934–35; Fellow, Amer. Council of Learned Socs, 1948; Lectr, then Asst Prof. of History, Newark Colls of Rutgers Univ., 1948–52; Faculty Fellow, Fund for the Advancement of Educn, 1951– 52; Lectr in Classics, Cambridge Univ., 1955–64; Reader in Ancient Social and Economic History, Cambridge Univ., 1964–70. Librarian, Jesus Coll., 1960–64; Chm., Faculty Bd of Classics, Cambridge Univ., 1967–69; Chm., Social and Political Scis Ctee, Cambridge Univ., 1973–74. Sec., Cambridge Philol. Soc., 1959–65; Convener, Ancient Hist. sect., Int. Econ. Hist. Conf., Aix-en-Provence, 1962, Munich, 1965; Chm., sub-cttee on Ancient Hist., Jt Assoc. Classical Teachers, 1964–70; Pres., Classical Assoc., 1973–74; Sather Prof. of Classical Lit., Univ. of California, Berkeley, 1972; First Mason Welch Gross Lectr, Rutgers Univ., 1972; Jane Harrison Meml Lecture, Cambridge, 1972; ed., Views and Controversies in Classical Antiquity, 1960– ; Ancient Culture and Soc., 1969– . *Publications*: Studies in Land and Credit in Ancient Athens, 1952; The World of Odysseus, 1954; ed, The Greek Historians, 1958; ed, Slavery in Classical Antiquity, 1960; The Ancient Greeks, 1963; ed, Josephus, 1965; Aspects of Antiquity, 1968; Ancient Sicily, 1968; Early Greece: the Bronze and Archaic Ages, 1970; The Ancestral Constitution (Inaug. Lecture), 1971; ed, Thucydides, 1972; Knowledge for What? (Enc. Brit. lecture), 1972; Democracy Ancient and Modern, 1973; ed, Problèmes de la terre en Grèce ancienne, 1973; The Ancient Economy, 1973; ed, Studies in Ancient Society, 1973; articles and reviews in classical, historical and legal jls, and in literary weeklies and monthlies in Britain and US. *Address*: Jesus College, Cambridge CB5 8DL.

Finnegan, Dr Ruth Hilary, (Mrs D. J. Murray), MA, DPhil; Senior Lecturer in Comparative Social Institutions, Faculty of Social Sciences, The Open University, since 1972; *b* 1933; *m* 1963; three *d*. BA Oxon 1956 (1st cl. Literae Humaniores), MA Oxon 1958, Dipl in Anthropology Oxon 1959 (with distinction); BLitt Oxon 1960, DPhil Oxon

1963; Fellow, Royal Anthropol. Inst.; Mem., Brit. Sociol Assoc., Assoc. Soc. Anthropol., Afr. Studies Assoc., UK. Mem. Council, Soc. for Res. in Higher Educn. Lectr in Soc. Anthrop., Univ. Coll. of Rhodesia and Nyasaland, 1963–64; Lectr in Soc., Univ. of Ibadan, 1965–67, Sen. Lectr, 1967–69; Lectr in Sociology, Open Univ., 1969–72; Visiting Prof., American Univ. in Cairo, 1971. *Publications*: Survey of the Limba of Northern Sierra Leone, 1965; Limba Stories and Storytelling, 1967; Oral Literature in Africa, 1970 (part. trans. in Japanese 1971); ed (with R. Horton), Modes of Thought: Essays on Thinking in Western and non-Western Societies, 1973; *contrib.* Hist. and Theory, Jl Comp. Sociol., Man, Odu, Sociol. *Address*: Faculty of Social Sciences, The Open Univ., Walton, Milton Keynes MK7 6AA.

Finnie, James; Senior Lecturer in Financial Management, Department of Management Studies, Loughborough University of Technology, since 1971; *b* 1933; *m* 1957; two *s* one *d*. MA 1955, LLB 1958 Glasgow; CA (Scotland) 1960, Associate MBIM, Member: Brit. Accounting and Finance Assoc.; Assoc. Univ. Teachers of Accounting. Lectr in Accounting, Univ. of W Indies, Kingston, Jamaica, 1964–70. Manager, Purchase Price Analysis, Ford Motor Co. Ltd., 1962–64. Cons. Financial Controller to Universal Stores Ltd., Kingston, Jamaica, 1970–71. *Publications*: *contrib.* Accountancy, Accountant's Mag. *Address*: Dept of Management Studies, Univ. of Technology, Loughborough, Leics LE11 3TU.

Finnis, Dr John Mitchell; Rhodes Reader in the Laws of the British Commonwealth and the United States, University of Oxford, since 1972; Fellow and Praelector in Jurisprudence, University College, Oxford, since 1966; *b* 1940; *m* 1964; one *s* two *d*. LLB Adelaide 1961 (1st cl.), DPhil Oxon 1965; of Gray's Inn, Barrister-at-Law. Assoc., Law School, Univ. of California, Berkeley, 1965–66; Vis. Lectr, Univ. of Adelaide, 1971. *Publications*: Halsbury's Laws of England, 4th edn, 1974, title Commonwealth and Dependencies; chapters, in Annual Survey of Commonwealth Law, 1967–73; Khanbai, Katz and Pineau: Jowett Papers 1968–1969, 1970; Noonan: The Morality of Abortion, 1970; *contrib.* Adel. Law Rev., Anal., Arch. Phil. Droit, Heythrop Jl, Law Qly Rev., Natural Law Forum, Phil. and Pub. Aff., Univ. Pa Law Rev. *Address*: Univ. Coll., Oxford.

Firth, Rosemary, MA; Lecturer, Department of Health and Welfare, London Institute of Education, since 1966; *b* 1912; *m* 1936; one *s*. MA Edinburgh 1935 (1st cl. Econ), Dip., Social Science and Admin LSE 1961; Fellow, Eugenics Soc.: Mem., Assoc. Social Anthropols, Brit. Soc. Assoc., Teachers Sect. Mem., Training and Educn Cttee, Nat. Assoc. Mental Health, 1971– ; Educn Cttee, Royal Coll. Midwives, 1970– ; Intermed. Technol. Develt Gp, 1968–72. *Publications*: Housekeeping among Malay Peasants, 1943, rev. edn 1966; *contrib.* Int. Yr Bk Educn, 1968, Crossing Cultura Boundaries, 1972, Jl Biosol. Sci., Kajian Ekon. Malaysia, Jl Anthrop. Soc. Oxford, Contemp. Rev. *Address*: London Univ. Institute of Education, Malet Street, WC1E 7HS.

Fisher, Prof. Charles Alfred, MA, FRGS; Professor of Geography with reference to Asia, School of Oriental and African Studies, University of London, since 1964; *b* 1916; *m* 1945; one *s* one *d*. BA Cantab 1938 (1st cl. Hons Geog. Tripos), MA Cantab 1942, MA Oxon 1950; FRGS; Mem. Coun., RGS, 1965–68. Asst Lectr in Geography, UC of Leicester, 1946; Lectr in Geography, UC of Wales, Aberystwyth, 1946–49; Sen. Res. Officer, Inst. of Colonial Studies, Oxford, 1950–51; Lectr in Geography, Univ. (Coll.) of Leicester, 1951–58, Reader, 1958–59; Prof. and Hd of Dept of Geography, 1959–64, and Dir, Centre of Japanese Studies, 1962–64, Univ. of Sheffield; RGS Travelling Fellowship, 1947– ; Vis. Lectr in Geography and Vis. Fellow of Trumbull Coll., Yale Univ., 1952–54; Chm., Assoc. of Brit. Orientalists, 1962–63. Ed., Mod. Asian Studies, 1967–70. *Publications*: South-east Asia: a Social Economic and Political Geography, 1964, 2nd edn 1966; (jtly), Geographical Essays on British Tropical Lands, 1956; ed, Essays in Political Geography, 1968; *contrib.* Geog. Jl, Econ. Geog., Internat. Affairs, Mod. Asian Studies, Politique Etrangère, etc. *Address*: School of Oriental and African Studies, Univ. of London, Malet Street, WC1E 7HP.

Fisher, Prof. Frederick Jack, MA; Professor of Economic History, London School of Economics, University of London, since 1954; *b* 1908; *m* 1943; one *s* one *d*. MA London 1930; FRHistS; Mem., Econ. Hist. Soc. Asst Lectr in Economic Hist., 1935–47; Reader in Economic Hist., Univ. of London, 1947–54. *Publications*: ed, Essays in the Economic and Social History of Tudor and Stuart England, 1961; ed, Calendar of Mss of Lord Sackville of Knole, vol. II, 1966; *contrib.* Economica, Econ. Hist. Rev., Trans Royal Hist. Soc. *Address*: London School of Economics, Houghton Street, Aldwych, WC2A 2AE.

Fisher, Dr Gerald Haigh, BSc, MEd, PhD; Senior Lecturer in Psychology, University of Newcastle upon Tyne, since 1967; *b* 1926; *m* 1970; one *s*. BSc Hull 1959, (1st cl. Psychology), PhD Hull 1962, MEd Dunelm 1968; ABPsS, ERS. Sen. Res. Fellow in Psychology, Univ. of Durham, 1961–62; Lectr in charge of Psychology, King's Coll., Newcastle, 1962–66. Investigator, DSIR, Min. of Defence, SSRC and MRC Res. Contracts. *Publications*: The New Form Statistical Tables, 1965; The Fisher Statistical Slide Rule, 1966–68; The Frameworks for Perceptual Localization, 1968; *contrib.* Amer. Jl Psychol., Brit. Jl Psychol., Qly Jl Exper. Psychol., Vision Res. *Address*: Dept of Psychology, Univ. of Newcastle upon Tyne, Newcastle upon Tyne NE1 7RU.

Fisher, Dr Harold Edward Stephen, BSc; Lecturer in Economic History, University of Exeter, since 1960; *b* 1930; *m* 1961; one *d*. BSc(Econ) London 1955 (Economic Hist.), PhD London 1961 (Economic Hist.). Asst

223

Lectr in Economic History, Univ. of Exeter, 1957–60; Warden, Murray Hse, Univ. of Exeter, 1963– ; Sen. Warden, Duryard Halls, 1971– . Mem., Govt Body, Dillington Hse Coll., 1967– . *Publications*: ed, The South-West and the Sea, 1968; The Portugal Trade, 1971; ed, Ports and Shipping in the South-West, 1971; ed (with W. E. Minchinton), Transport and Shipowning in the West Country, 1973; *contrib*. Econ. Hist. Rev. *Address*: Dept of Economic History, Univ. of Exeter, Exeter, Devon.

Fisher, Dr Humphrey John; Reader in African History, School of Oriental and African Studies, University of London, since 1970; *b* 1933; *m* 1958; four *s*. BA Harvard 1955 (English Hist. and Lit., magna cum laude, PhiBetaKappa), DPhil Oxon 1959. Lectr in African Hist., SOAS. 1962–70; Adviser to students, SOAS, 1967–72. *Publications*: Ahmadiyyah: a study in contemporary Islam on the West African coast, 1963; co-author, Slavery and Muslim society in Africa, 1970, USA edn 1971, pbk edn 1972; co-trans. and ed., G. Nachtigal: Sahara and Sudan, vol. iv: Wadai and Darfur, 1971; *contrib*. St Ant. Papers, Muslim Wld, Jl Afr. Hist., Jl Mod. Afr. Studies. *Address*: School of Oriental and African Studies, Univ. of London, WC1E 7HP.

Fisher, James, MS, FCCA, MBIM; Senior Lecturer in Accountancy and Finance, Heriot-Watt University, since 1966; *b* 1936; *m* 1960; two *s*. MS Minnesota 1969 (Accounting, Finance); FCCA 1962, MBIM 1962; Fulbright Scholar, 1968, Churchill Fellow, 1972; Mem., Beta Alpha Psi, 1969, Beta Gamma Sigma, 1970. Vis. Assoc. Prof., Univ. of Toronto, 1971. Finance Sections, Local and Central Govt, 1958–62. *Publications*: *contrib*. Abacus, Acntncy, Acntnt. Mag., Cert. Acntnt. *Address*: Dept of Accountancy and Finance, Heriot-Watt Univ., Edinburgh EH1 2HT.

Fisher, Dr John Robert; Lecturer in Latin American History, Department of Modern History/Centre for Latin American Studies, Liverpool University, since 1967; *b* 1943; *m* 1966; three *s*. BA London 1964 (History), MPhil London 1967, PhD Liverpool 1973. Mem. Soc. for Latin American Studies. *Publications*: Arequipa 1796–1811: La Relación del Gobierno del Intendente Salamanca, 1968; Government and Society in Colonial Peru: The Intendant System, 1970; Latin America: From Conquest to Independence, 1971; *contrib*. Hispanic American Historical Review, Anuario de Estudios Americanos. *Address*: Dept of Modern History, Univ. of Liverpool, PO Box 147, Liverpool L69 3BX.

Fisher, Dr Malcolm Robertson; University Lecturer in Economics, Cambridge University, since 1957; *b* 1923; *m* 1957; one *s* one *d*. BA New Zealand 1946, MA New Zealand 1948 (1st cl.), Post Grad. Scholar in Arts, New Zealand 1950, PhD Cantab 1953; FREconSoc; Mem., Amer. Econ. Assoc., Economet. Soc., Council of Europe Fellow 1963. Jun. Lectr, Univ. of Auckland, 1947–49; Lectr, Univ. of Auckland, 1949–53; Res. Off., Oxford Univ. Inst. of Stats, 1953–54; Asst.

Lectr in Economics, 1954–57; Fellow, Downing Coll., Cambridge, 1958– ; Vis. Ford Foundn Prof., Univ. of Chicago, 1968; Vis. Prof. of Economics, UCLA, 1971, 1974. Bursar, Downing Coll., 1959–74; Dir of Studies, Economics, Downing Coll., 1955– ; Mem., Financial Bd, Cambridge, 1961–70. *Publications*: Macro-Economic Models: their nature, purposes and limitations, 1964; Wage Determination in an Integrating Europe, 1966; The Economic Analysis of Labour, 1971; Measurement of Labour Disputes and their Economic Effects, 1973; *contrib*. Econ. Jl, Economet., Oxf. Econ. Papers, Oxf. Univ. Inst. Stats Bull. *Address*: Downing College, Cambridge.

Fisher, Prof. William Bayne, Ddel'U; Principal, Graduate Society, since 1965, Professor of Geography, since 1956, and Head of Department of Geography, University of Durham, since 1954; *b* 1916. BA Manchester 1937 (1st cl. Geog.), DipEd Manchester 1938 (1st cl.), Ddel'U Paris 1943; FRGS, FRAI. Asst, Univ. of Manchester, 1946–47; Lectr, Univ. of Aberdeen, 1947–53. RAF, 1941–46; Dir, Centre Mid. East Islamic Studies, Univ. of Durham, 1963–66; Pres., Sect. E, Brit. Assoc., 1969; Mem., Gov. Council, Inst. Persian Studies, Soc. for Afghan Studies, 1972– ; N Reg. Hosp. Cttee, 1972– . *Publications*: The Middle East, 1951, 8 Eng. edns to 1971, and others; (with H. B. Jones) Spain, 1958, 2nd edn 1966; (with H. B. Jones and J. C. Dewdney) Malta, 1960; (with J. I. Clarke) Populations of the Middle East and North Africa, 1972; ed, Cambridge History of Iran, vol. I, 1968; *contrib*. Ann. Geog., Geog. Jl, Geog. Rev., Geog. *Address*: Science Laboratories, South Road, Durham.

Fishman, Prof. Leslie; Professor of Economics, University of Keele, since 1969; *b* 1921; *m* 1941; two *s* one *d*. BA California (Berkeley) 1941, PhD California (Berkeley) 1957; Mem., Royal Econ. Soc., Amer. Econ. Assoc., Economet. Soc. Teaching Asst, then Lectr, Univ. of California (Berkeley), 1941, 1946–47, 1948–50; Instructor, then Asst Prof., Idaho State Coll., 1955–57; Asst, Assoc., and Prof., Univ. of Colorado, 1957–67; Ford Fellowships, 1951–52, 1962–63; Sen. Lectr, Univ. of Warwick, 1967–69. Dir, Cost of living project, Colorado Welfare Bd, 1960–64; Dir, US Arms Control and Disarmament Study, Reemployment of Defense Workers, 1966–69; Asst Dir, Res., CIO, 1947–48. *Publications*: Reemployment Experiences of Defense Workers, 1968; Reemployment Experiences of Martin Co. Employees, 1966; contrib. Thorstein Veblen, 1958; Disarmament and the Economy, 1963; *contrib*. Jl Pol Econ., Rev. Econ. Stat., West. Econ. Rev., Bull. Atomic Sci. *Address*: Dept of Economics, Univ. of Keele, Keele, Staffs ST5 5BG.

Fishwick, Francis; Senior Lecturer in Economics, School of Management, Cranfield, since 1966, *b* 1936; *m* 1959; three *s*. BA Econ Manchester 1957, MAEcon Manchester (external thesis). CAT Birmingham (Univ. of Aston), 1962–66. Planning Officer, Lancs CC 1957–62. *Publications*: (with C. J.

Harling) Shiftwork in the Motor Industry, 1974); *contrib*. Credit, Inst. Transport Jl, NEDO. *Address*: Cranfield School of Management, Cranfield, Bedford MK43 0AL.

Fitch, Frank John, BSc, FGS, FRGS; Reader in Geology (also teaches in Archaeology), Birkbeck College, University of London, since 1971; *b* 1925; *m* 1950; two *s* two *d*. BSc London 1953; Engineering Cadetship Dip. 1945; FRGS, FGS. Mem.: Mineral. Soc., Geol. Assoc., Assoc. Teachers Geol., Glacial. Soc. Demonstrator in Petrology, Birkbeck Coll., 1951–53; Asst Lectr in Geology, 1953–56; Lectr in Geology, 1956–71; Dir, Geochronological Res. Lab., 1965– . Commissioned Corps of RE, 1945–48; Dir, FM Cnsltnts, Ltd, 1966– ; Mem., Volcanic Studies Gp Cttee; Geol. Soc. London, 1965–70; Volcano Res. Cttee, Royal Soc. Lond., 1971–73, Stratigraphy Cttee Geol. Soc. Lond., 1971– . *Publications*: contrib. The Phanerozoic Time-Scale, 1964; Pre-Cambrian and Palaeozoic Rocks of Wales, 1969; Time and Place in Orogany, 1969; Calibration of Hominoid Evolution, 1971; C. R. 6th Internat. Cong. Carboniferous Stratigraphy and Geology, 1970; *contrib*. Amer. Min., Amer. Jl Sci., Assoc. Internat. Hydro. Sci., Bull. Volc., Jl Geol. Soc. Lond., Geol. Jl, Nature, Norsk Geol. Tids., Norsk Polarinst. Arbok, Phil. Trans Royal Soc. Lond., Proc. Geol. Assoc. Lond., Proc. Royal Soc. Lond., Palaeogeog. Palaeoclim. Palaeoecology, Tectonophysics, Union Geodes. Geophys. Internat. *Address*: Geochronological Research Laboratory, Dept of Geology, Birkbeck College, 7–15 Gresse Street, W1P 1PA.

Fitton Brown, Prof. Anthony David; Professor of Classics, University of Leicester, since 1969; *b* 1925; *m* 1953; two *s* one *d*. BA Cantab 1948 (1st cl. Classics), MA Cantab 1951. Asst Lectr, UC of North Wales, Bangor, 1949–51, Lectr, 1951–63; Fellow, Corpus Christi Coll., Cambridge, 1963–69. Mem., Council Hellenic Soc., 1962–65. *Publications*: Greek Plays as First Productions, 1970; *contrib*. Classical Qly, Classical Rev., Jl of Hellenic Studies. *Address*: Dept of Classics, Univ. of Leicester, Leicester LE1 7RH.

Fitzgerald, Peter; Senior Lecturer in Fine Art, Department of Fine Art, University of Reading, since 1967; *b* 1929; *m* 1954; 1972; two *s* one *d*. NDD 1950, ATD London 1951, BA London 1961 (2/1 Hist. of Art). Lectr in Fine Art, Reading, 1965–67. Mem.: Hist. of Art Panel, NCDAD, 1962–72; Art Panel, S Reg. Council for FE, 1966–70; Art Panel, SUJB, 1966–71; Conf. for Higher Educn in Art and Design, 1970– ; Gov., W Surrey Coll. of Art, 1971– . *Publications*: Daumier (forthcoming); *contrib*. Burl. Mag. *Address*: Dept of Fine Art, The Univ., London Road, Reading RG1 5AQ.

FitzGibbon, Thomas Gerald; Assistant Demonstrator, Department of English, University College, Cork, since 1973; *b* 1946; *m*; two *d*. BA 1967, Higher Dip. in Educn 1970, MA 1972; Univ. Demonstrator, UC, Cork, 1968–73. *Address*: English Dept, Univ. Coll., Cork.

Fitzroy, Dr Peter Trevor, PhD; Senior Research Fellow, Manchester Business School, University of Manchester, since 1970; *b* 1936; *m* 1966; one *d*. BMechE Melbourne 1958, MSIE Purdue 1961, PhD Purdue 1966; TIMS. Asst Prof., Univ. of Waterloo, 1966–67; Asst Prof., Univ. of Pennsylvania, 1967–70. *Publications*: Experiments on the Value of Information in Simulated Marketing Environments, 1967. *Address*: Manchester Business School, Booth Street West, Manchester M15 6PB.

Fleeman, Dr J. D.; Fellow and Tutor in English Literature, Pembroke College, Oxford, since 1965; *b* 1932; *m* 1957. MA St Andrews 1956, DPhil Oxford 1965; Member: Bibliog. Soc., Bibliog. Soc. of Univ. of Virginia, Oxford Bibliog. Soc. Bibliog. Consultant, Harvard Univ. Library, 1962–64, Fellow in Bibliog., 1964–65. *Publications*: Samuel Johnson: The Complete English Poems, 1971; *contrib*. Library, Papers of Bibliog. Soc of Amer., Rev. of English Studies. *Address*: Pembroke Coll. Oxford.

Fleischmann, Prof. Aloys, MA, DMus, HonMusD, MRIA; Professor of Music, University College, Cork, since 1934; *b* 1910; *m* 1941; two *s* three *d*. BA NUI 1930, BMus NUI 1931, MA NUI 1932, DMus NUI 1963; Hon. MusD Dublin 1964; Mem., Royal Irish Acad., 1966. Mem.: Adv. Cttee Cult. Relat., Dept of Ext. Aff.; Irish Nat. Commn for UNESCO; Off. of Merit, German Fed. Repub.; Chm., Irish Nat. Cttee, RILM; Dir, Cork Internat. Choral Folk Dance Fest.; Conductor, Cork Symph. Orch.; Chm., Cork Orch. Soc. Wks publicly performed include 3 ballets, 4 song cycles, 4 wks for choir and orch., 1 for horn and orch., 1 overture, 1 piano quint., mass for female choir and organ, unaccompanied part songs. *Publications*: Music in Ireland, 1952; Suite for Piano, 1938; Three Songs for Tenor and Orchestra, 1945; Elizabeth McDermott Roe – Lament for String Orchestra, 1950; *contrib*. Grove: Dictionary of Music; Encyclop. Amer.; Encyclop. Musique, Edn Fasquelle; *contrib*. Proc. Royal Irish Acad., Jl Cork Histol. Archaeol. Soc. *Address*: Music Dept, University College, Cork.

Fleming, Andrew Maurice; Lecturer in Prehistory and Archaeology, Department of Ancient History, Sheffield University, since 1967; *b* 1943; *m* 1971; one *s*. BA Cantab 1965, MA Cantab 1968; Mem. Prehistoric Soc., Mem. Agric. History Soc. *Publications*: contrib. Proc. Prehistoric Soc, World Archaeology, Man, Agric. History Review, etc. *Address*: Dept of Ancient History, Univ. of Sheffield, Sheffield S10 2TN.

Fleming, Gerald, LèsL, FIL; Senior Lecturer in Applied Linguistics, University of Surrey, since 1973 (Lecturer, 1968–73); *b* 1921; *m* 1950; two *d*. LèsL Lille 1953, Teachers Dip. 1947; FIL. Res. Fellow, Univ. of Surrey, 1965–68; Exec., Educn Div., Soc. Authors. *Publications*: Wall Pictures for Guided Composition, 1957; Guided Composition, 1960, 2nd edn 1965; Les Carré, 1966; Avec les Carré, 1966, 2nd edn 1969; French Visual Grammar, 1969; Grammaire visuelle de français, 1970, 2nd edn 1971; chapter in, Advances in the Teaching of Modern Languages, 1964; chapter in, Neue Wege im Sprachunterricht, 1965; *contrib.* AV Instr., AVL Jl, Babel, Contact, DaF, Film User, IRAL, Praxis, Pens. Zing., Vis. Educn. *Address*: Univ. of Surrey, Guildford, Surrey GU2 5XH.

Fleming, Prof. John Miles, BComSc; Professor of Economics, University of Bristol, since 1969; *b* 1919; *m* 1945; one *s* one *d*. BComSc Belfast 1944 (1st cl. Economics and Philosophy). Lectr, Bristol Univ., 1946–62; Sen. Lectr, 1962–69; Vis. Lectr, Univ. of Pennsylvania, 1962–63, 1967. Econ. Advr, HM Treasury, 1952–54; Mem., Council, Royal Econ. Soc., 1970–75. *Publications*: Introduction to Economic Analysis, 1969; Monetary Theory, 1972; *contrib.* Economica, Econ. Jl. *Address*: Dept of Economics, Univ. of Bristol, 40 Berkeley Square, Bristol BS8 1HY.

Fleming, Dr John Robb, ThD, DD; Senior Lecturer in Divinity, University of St Andrews, since 1968; *b* 1910; *m* 1938; one *d*. MA 1932, BD Glasgow 1935 (distinction NT), ThD 1961 Union Theological Seminary NY; Hon. DD Glasgow 1971. Chm., Scott. Inst. Mission. Studies, 1971– ; Hon-Pres., Scott. Ch. Theo. Soc., 1971–72. Lectr in Theology, Trinity Theol. Coll., Singapore, 1952–68; Dean, SE Asia Grad. Sch. Theol., 1965–68. Exec. Dir, Assoc. Theol. Schs, SE Asia, 1957–68; Foundn Theol. Educn SE Asia, 1957–68; Ed, SE Asia Jl Theol., 1959–68; Mem., Ch. Scot. Ch. and Nation Cttee, 1969– ; Dept Int. Aff., Brit. Council Chs, 1969– . *Publications*: ed, One people – one mission, 1963; Structures for a Missionary Congregation, 1964, Chinese edn 1965; chapters in, The Prospects of Christianity Throughout the World, 1964; Tendenzen der Theologie im 20 Jahr Hundert, 1966; Christianity in SE Asia, 1968; *contrib.* Concise Dictionary of Christian Missions, 1970; ed, J. R. Mott Meml Lectures, 1961, 1964, 1967; *contrib.* SE Asia Jl Theol. *Address*: St Mary's College, The Univ. of St Andrews, St Andrews, Fife KY16 9AJ.

Flemming, John Stanton; Official Fellow in Economics, Nuffield College, Oxford, since 1965; *b* 1941; *m* 1963; three *s* one *d*. BA Oxon 1962 (1st cl. PPE), MA Oxon 1966. Lectr, 1963, and Fellow, 1964, Oriel Coll., Oxford; Harkness Fellow, 1968–69. Jt Invest. Bursar, Nuffield Coll., 1970– ; Assoc. Gen. Ed., Oxf. Econ. Papers, 1970–73; Mem., Edit. Cttee Rev. Econ. Studies, 1973– . *Publications*: *contrib.* Bull. Oxf. Univ. Inst. Econ. Stats, Econ. Jl, Oxf. Econ. Papers, Rev. Econ. Studies. *Address*: Nuffield College, Oxford.

Flemming, Wilfred, MA, MSc, FIMA; Lecturer in Education, School of Education, Leicester University, since 1950; *b* 1910; *m* 1938; two *s*. BSc Liverpool 1931 (1st cl. Hons Mathematics, 1st cl. Physics), MSc Liverpool 1935, MA Liverpool 1949, DipEd Liverpool 1932; FIMA 1966. Prof. of Educn, Univ. of Ghana (Hd of Dept Educn, and Dir of Inst. of Educn), 1962–65.

UNESCO Consultancies, 1963– ; Chm., ATCDE Maths Sect., 1957–62; Mem., various Math. Assoc. Cttees, 1953– ; Leicester Dioc. Bd Educn, 1960– ; Candidates Cttee, ACCM, 1973– . *Publications*: (with E. H. Copsey) Individual Mathematics, pt V, 1963; *contrib.* Educnl Rev., Math. Gaz., Teacher Educn; var. reports to Math. Assoc., ATCDE, Unesco. *Address*: Univ. of Leicester, School of Education, 21 University Road, Leicester.

Flenley, Dr John Roger; Lecturer in Geography, University of Hull, since 1967; *b* 1936; *m* 1959; three *d*. BA Cantab 1958, CertEd Cantab 1959, PhD ANU 1967; Mem. Brit. Ecological Soc.; Mem. Quaternary Res. Assoc. *Publications*: *contrib.* Jl Ecol., Pollen Spores. *Address*: Geography Dept, Univ. of Hull, Hull HU6 7RX.

Flesch, Michael Charles; Lecturer in Laws, Faculty of Law, University College London, since 1964; *b* 1940; *m* 1972. LLB London 1962; Barrister-at-law. Bigelow Teaching Fellow, Law Faculty, Univ. of Chicago, 1963–64. *Publications*: *contrib.* Brit. Tax Rev., Convey., Cur. Legal Problems. *Address*: Law Faculty, Univ. College, London, 4–8 Endsleigh Gardens, WC1H 0EG.

Fletcher, Anthony John; Lecturer in Medieval and Modern History, University of Sheffield, since 1967, *b* 1941; *m* 1967; two *s*. BA Hons Oxon 1962 (Mod. Hist.), DipEd Oxon 1964; Mem., Ecclesiastical Hist. Soc. *Publications*: Elizabethan Village, 1967; Tudor Rebellions, 1968, 2nd edn 1973; *contrib.* N Hist., Brit. Jl of Educnl Studies, Derby Archaeol Jl. *Address*: Dept of Medieval and Modern History, Univ. of Sheffield, Sheffield S10 2TN.

Fletcher, Dr Ian, PhD; Reader in English Literature, University of Reading, since 1966; *b* 1920; *m* 1965; two *d*. PhD Reading 1965. Asst Lectr, Univ. of Reading, 1956–58, Lectr, 1958–66; Vis. Prof.: Univ. of Maryland 1965–66; Univ. of New York State at Buffalo 1970 and 1972. Selector, Poetry Book Soc., 1962–63. *Publications*: Orisons (poems), 1947; ed, The Complete Poems of Lionel Johnson, 1953; The Lovers' Martyrdom (trans. from Italian), 1957; Walter Pater, 1959, 2nd rev. edn, 1972; *contrib.* W. B. Yeats: Image of a Poet, 1961, 2nd edn 1971; Motets (poems), 1962; *contrib.* An Honoured Guest; Yeats Centenary Essays, 1965; Beaumont and Fletcher, 1967; Romantic Mythologies, 1967; The Milesian Intrusion, 1968; Meredith Now, 1971; Swinburne, 1972; *contrib.* Times Literary Supplement, Victorian Studies, Southern Qly, Book Collector, Yeats Studies, etc. *Address*: Faculty of Letters, Univ. of Reading, Reading RG6 2AH.

Fletcher, Ian F.; Lecturer in Law, University College of Wales, Aberystwyth, since 1967, *b* 1944; *m* 1974. BA Cantab 1965, LLB Cantab 1966, MCL Tulane 1967, MA Cantab 1969; Barrister-at-law. Mem. Adv. Cttee on Legal Educn, 1972– ; Mem. Exec. Cttee, Soc. of Public Teachers of Law, 1974 (Chm. Young Members' Gp,

1972–73). *Publications*: (with D. G. Lewis) The Law of Bankruptcy, 1974; *contrib*. Cambridge Law Jl. *Address*: Dept of Law, UCW, Penglais, Aberystwyth SY23 3DB.

Fletcher, Dr John Malcolm; Lecturer in European History, Department of Modern Languages, University of Aston in Birmingham, since 1967; *b* 1934; *m* 1961; two *s*. Merton Coll., Oxford: BA 1956 (Hons), MA 1960, DPhil 1961. Res. Fellow, Freiburg, 1961–62. Mem., Cambridge Bibliographical Soc.; Pres., Black Country Soc.; Gen. Editor, Worcs Historical Soc. *Publications*: Mediaeval Statutes of University of Freiburg, 1967; Liber Taxatorum, 1969; *contrib*. Camb. Bibliog. Soc. Trans, Pedag. Historica. *Address*: Dept of Modern Languages, Univ. of Aston in Birmingham, Birmingham B4 7ET.

Fletcher, Prof. John Walter James, MA, DTC; Professor of Comparative Literature, School of European Studies, University of East Anglia, since 1969; *b* 1937; *m* 1961. BA Cantab 1959, MA Cantab 1964, Dip d'Et Sup Toulouse 1961, DTC Toulouse 1964; MHRA. Lector, Toulouse Univ., 1961–64; Lectr, Durham Univ., 1964–66; Lectr, Univ. of E Anglia, 1966–68; Reader, 1968–69; Vis. Prof., Odense and Salzburg Univs, 1971. Gov., Jex Sch., Norwich, 1970– . *Publications*: The Novels of Samuel Beckett, 1964, 2nd edn 1970; Samuel Beckett's Art, 1967, German edn 1969; New Directions in Literature, 1968; Critical Commentary on Flaubert's Trois Contes, 1968; (with R. Federman) Samuel Beckett, His Works and His Critics, 1970; (with J. Spurling) Beckett, A Study of His Plays, 1972; ed (with B. S. Fletcher), Samuel Beckett: Fin de partie, 1970; Samuel Beckett, Waiting for Godot, 1971; Forces in Modern French Drama, 1972; *contrib*. Ann. Fac. Lett. Toulouse, Bks Bkmen, Comp. Lit., Crit. Qly, Durham Univ. Jl, Esp. Créat, Fr. Rev., Mod. Drama, Mod. Lang. Rev., Nott. Fr. Studies, Spectator, Univ. Vision. *Address*: Univ. of East Anglia (EUR), University Plain, Norwich NOR 88C.

Fletcher, Robin Anthony, DSC, MA, DPhil; Lecturer in Medieval and Modern Greek, Oxford University, since 1949 and Fellow of Trinity College, since 1950; *b* 1922; *m* 1950; two *s*. BA Oxon 1949 (2nd cl. Mod. Lang.), MA Oxon 1953, DPhil Oxon 1955. Dom. Bursar, Trinity Coll., 1951– ; Mem., Hebdom. Council 1968– ; Sen. Proctor, 1966–67; Mem., Hart Cttee on Student Relations, 1968; Councils Radley Coll. and Cheltenham Coll.; Governing Bodies, Marlborough Coll., Sherborne Sch. *Publications*: *contrib*. various articles and reviews. *Address*: Trinity College, Oxford.

Flew, Prof. Antony Garrard Newton; Professor of Philosophy, University of Reading, since 1973; *b* 1923; *m* 1952; two *d*. MA Oxon 1949, DLitt Keele 1974, John Locke Scholarship in Mental Philosophy, Oxford, 1948. Lecturer: Christ Church, Oxford, 1949–50; King's Coll., Aberdeen, 1950–54; Professor: Keele, 1954–71; Calgary, 1972–73. Sometime Mem., DES Adv.

Cttee on Postgraduate Awards in Humanities; Vice-Pres., Rationalist Press Assoc. *Publications*: A New Approach to Psychical Research, 1953; Hume's Philosophy of Belief, 1961; God and Philosophy, 1966; Evolutionary Ethics, 1967; An Introduction to Western Philosophy, 1971; Crime or Disease?, 1973; Editor of various works, incl. Malthus: An Essay on the Principle of Population, 1971; *contrib*. Mind, Philos. Philos. Qly, Praxis, Question, Stud. Philos. and Educn. *Address*: Dept of Philosophy, Univ. of Reading, Whiteknights, Reading RG6 2AA.

Flinn, Prof. Michael Walter; Professor of Social History, Department of Economic History, University of Edinburgh, since 1967; *b* 1917; *m* 1943; two *s*. BA Manchester 1950, DipEd Manchester 1951, MA Manchester 1952, DLitt Edinburgh 1965. Res. Fellow, Aberdeen Univ., 1954–55; Lectr, Edinburgh Univ., 1959–64; Sen. Lectr, 1964–65; Reader, 1965–67. *Publications*: An Economic and Social History of Britain, 1961; Men of Iron, 1962; Readings in Economic and Social History, 1963; Edwin Chadwick's Report on the Sanitary Condition of the Labouring Population (1842), 1965; Origins of the Industrial Revolution, 1967; British Population Growth, 1700–1850, 1971; *contrib*. Ann. Sci., Business Hist., Econ. Hist. Rev., Jl Econ. Hist., Scott. Jl Pol. Econ. *Address*: Dept of Economic History, Univ. of Edinburgh, Edinburgh EH8 9YL.

Flint, Prof. David, TD, MA, BL, CA; Johnstone Smith Professor of Accountancy, University of Glasgow, since 1964; *b* 1919; *m* 1953; two *s* one *d*. MA Glasgow 1939, BL Glasgow 1942; CA 1949. Pt-time Asst, Univ. of Glasgow, 1950–56; Pt-time Lectr, 1956–60; Dean, Fac. of Law, 1971–73. Mem., Council and Exec. Cttee, Scott. Business Sch. Mem.: Council, Scott. Econ. Soc., 1962– ; Mgmnt Training Develop. Cttee, Central Training Council, 1966–70; Soc. Sci. Panel, SUCE, 1968–72; Mngmnt Indust. Relations Cttee, SSRC, 1970–72. Inst. Chartered Accnts of Scotland: Mem. Educn Cttee; Vice-Pres., 1973– . *Publications*: *contrib*. Acntnt, Acntnts. Mag., Acntng Business Res., Local Govt Fin. *Address*: Dept of Accountancy, Univ. of Glasgow, Glasgow G12 8LE.

Flint, Dr Jack M., MA, PhD; Senior Lecturer in charge of Spanish and Latin American Studies, University of Strathclyde, since 1964; *b* 1928; *m* 1954. BA Manchester 1950 (1st cl. Mod. Langs), MA Manchester 1962, PhD Strathclyde 1971. Past Chm., Hist. Soc. Scotl., 1960–64. *Publications*: *contrib*. Bull. Hisp. Studies, Iberoromania. *Address*: Livingstone Tower, Univ. of Strathclyde, Glasgow.

Flood, John Lewis, MA; Senior Lecturer in German, University of London, King's College, since 1972; *b* 1938; *m* 1973. BA Nottingham 1961 (1st cl. German), MA Nottingham 1963 (German). Lektor in English, Univ. of Erlangen-Nuremberg, 1963–64; Asst Lectr in German, Univ. of Nottingham, 1964–65; Asst Lectr in German, Univ. of London, King's Coll., 1965–67,

Lectr, 1967–72; **Mem.** Cttee of Mngmnt, Univ. of London Inst. of Germanic Studies, 1972– . Hon. Sec., London Mediev. Soc., 1969– ; Hon. Sec., Conf. Univ. Teachers of German, GB and Ireland, 1971– ; Mem. Coun., Viking Soc. for Northern Res., 1972– . *Publications*: *contrib.* Yrs Wk Mod. Lang. Studies. 1967–72; Libr., Mod. Lang. Rev., Nottingham Med. Studies, Zeitsch. Deutsch. Alter., Zeitsch. Deutsche Philol. *Address*: Dept of German, Univ. of London, King's College, Strand, WC2R 2LS.

Flood Page, Colin Michael; Lecturer, School of Education, Bradford University, since 1970; *b* 1940; three *s*. MA Cantab 1943, CertEd 1940; Member: Soc. for Res. into Higher Educn; Geologists' Assoc., Internat. Voluntary Service. Leverhulme Res. Fellow in Dental Educn, London Hosp. Med. Coll., London Univ., 1966–70; Hon. Adv. in Dental Educn, 1970– . Council Mem., Soc. for Res. into Higher Educn, 1969– (Chm., NE England Br., 1973– .) *Publications*: Technical Aids to Teaching in Higher Education, 1970; Student Evaluation of Teaching, 1974; *contrib.* Univ. Qly, Brit. Dental Jl. *Address*: Bradford Univ., Bradford BD7 1DP.

Flook, Alfred John Melsom; Senior Lecturer, Psychology Department, University of Dundee, since 1967; *b* 1918; *m* 1942; two *d*. BA London 1948; FBPsS, Mem., Conflict Res. Soc. Res. Fellow and Lectr, St Andrews Univ., 1951–62, Sen. Lectr, 1962–67; Vis. Scholar, Michigan Univ., 1965. Mem., Bd Mngmnt, Dundee North. Hosp., 1961–66. *Publications*: *contrib.* Jl Educnl Psychol., Simulation, Vocat. Asp. *Address*: Psychology Dept, The Univ., Dundee DD1 4HN.

Floud, Jean Esther, MA, BSc(Econ), Hon. LittD Leeds; Principal, Newnham College, Cambridge, since 1972; *b* 1915; *m* 1938; one *s* two *d*. BSc(Econ) London. Teacher of Sociology, Univ. of London, LSE, 1947–62; Official Fellow, Nuffield Coll., Oxford, 1963–72. Dir of Educn, City of Oxford, 1940–46. Mem., Franks Commn of Inquiry into the Univ. of Oxford, 1964–66; Mem., UGC, 1969– ; Mem., SSRC, 1970– . *Publications*: (with A. H. Halsey and F. M. Martin) Social Class and Educational Opportunity, 1956; *contrib.* sociological jls. *Address*: Newnham College, Cambridge.

Floud, Dr Roderick Castle; Lecturer in Economic History, Faculty of History, University of Cambridge, since 1973; *b* 1942; *m* 1964; two *d*. BA Oxford 1964 (2nd cl. Mod. History), DPhil Oxford 1970. Asst Lectr in Economic History: UCL, 1966–69; Univ. of Cambridge, 1969–73. Fellow and Tutor, Emmanuel College, Cambridge, 1969– . Member: Econ. and Social History Cttee, SSRC 1970– ; Council of Econ. History Soc., 1972– . *Publications*: An Introduction to Quantitative Methods for Historians, 1973; ed, Essays in Quantitative Economic History, 1974; *contrib.* Econ. Hist. Rev. *Address*: Emmanuel Coll., Cambridge.

Flower, Prof. John Francis; Professor of Accounting, Department of Economics,

University of Bristol, since 1969; *b* 1934; *m* 1961; two *s* one *d*. BSc(Econ) London 1958; FCA. Lecturer in Accounting, LSE, 1963–69. *Publications*: Computer Models for Accountants, 1973; *contrib.* Acntncy, Acntng Business Res., Jl Acntng Res. *Address*: Dept. of Economics, Univ. of Bristol, Bristol BS8 1HY.

Flowerdew, Anthony David John; Senior Lecturer in Economics, London School of Economics, since 1971; *b* 1935; *m* 1959; one *s* one *d*. BA 1957, MA 1960, Cantab, Cert. RSS 1958; Mem., Operational Res. Soc. Mem., NCB Field Investigation Gp, 1957–61; Operational Res. Dept, Richard Thomas and Baldwins Ltd, 1961–66; Sen. Planner, GLC, 1966–68; Dep. Dir of Res., Commn on Third London Airport, 1968–70. *Publications*: *contrib.* Architects Jl, Computor Jl, Jl of Ind. Engrg, Jl RSS, Operational Res. Qly, Regnl Studies, Statistician. *Address*: London Sch. of Economics, Houghton Street, Aldwych, WC2A 2AE.

Floyd, Dr Barry Neil; Lecturer, Department of Geography, University of Durham, since 1972; *b* 1925; *m* 1953; two *s* three *d*. BA Hons Cantab 1949, MA Cantab 1951, MA Minnesota 1951, PhD Syracuse 1959. Member: Inst. of Brit. Geogrs, Geog. Assoc., Assoc. of American Geogrs. Univ. of Nigeria, 1962–66, Actg Head, Geog. Dept, 1965–66; Head, Geog. Dept, Univ. of West Indies, Jamaica, 1966–72. *Publications*: Eastern Nigeria: a geographical review, 1969; *contrib.* Area, Econ. Geography, Geography, Geog. Rev., Jl of Geography, Professional Geographer. *Address:* Dept of Geography, Univ. of Durham, South Road, Durham DH1 3LE.

Foakes, Prof. Reginald Anthony, MA, PhD; Professor of English Literature, University of Kent, since 1964; *b* 1923; *m* 1951; two *s* two *d*. BA Birmingham 1948, MA Birmingham 1949, PhD Birmingham 1952. Fellow, Shakespeare Inst., 1951–54; Lectr, Durham Univ., 1954–63; Sen. Lectr, 1963–64; Commonwealth Fund Fellow, Yale Univ., 1955–56; Vis. Prof., Univ. of Toronto, 1960–62; Vis. Prof., Univ. of California, 1968–69. *Publications*: ed, King Henry VIII and Comedy of Errors (Arden Shakespeare), 1957 and 1962; The Romantic Assertion, 1958; ed (with R. T. Rickert), Henslowe's Diary, 1961; ed, The Revenger's Tragedy (Revels Plays), 1966; ed, Romantic Criticism 1800–1850, 1968; ed, Macbeth and Much Ado about Nothing, 1968; Shakespeare, the Dark Comedies to the Last Plays: From Satire to Celebration, 1971; ed, Coleridge on Shakespeare: The Text of the Lectures of 1811–12, 1971; *contrib.* Philol. Qly. Shakesp. Qly, Shakesp. Surv., Univ. Toronto Qly. *Address*: Eliot College, Univ. of Kent, Canterbury, Kent CT1 3PA.

Foldes, Lucien Paul; Reader in Economics, University of London, since 1961; *b* 1930. BCom 1950 (1st cl.), DipBusAd 1951, MSc(Econ) 1952; Mem.: Royal Econ. Soc., Economet. Soc., Inst. Math. Stats, Amer. Econ. Soc. Asst, LSE, 1951–52; Asst Lectr, 1954–55; Lectr, 1955–61; Rockefeller Trav.

Fellow, 1961–62. Mem.: Cttee Investig. (Agricult. Mktng); Econ. Consltnt, Gas Council. *Publications*: contrib. var. symposia; *contrib*. Economica, Rev. Econ. Studies. *Address*: London School of Economics, Houghton Street, Aldwych, WC2A 2AE.

Folley, Terence T.; Lecturer, Department of Spanish, National University of Ireland (Cork), since 1963; *b* 1931; *m* 1956; four *s* two *d*. BA Cork 1951 (1st cl. German and Spanish), MA Cork 1955 (Spanish), PhD NUI 1969 (Spanish). Teacher, 1956–63; Ch. Adv. Examiner in Spanish, Dept of Educn, Dublin, 1967– . *Publications*: A Dictionary of Spanish Idioms and Colloquialisms, 1965; Spanish Vocabulary, 1966; Contemporary Spanish Passages for Advanced Study, 1967; Parallel Passages in Spanish and English, 1968; Spanish Comprehension Passages, 1972; *contrib*. Arbor, Bull. Hisp. Studies, Vida Hispán. *Address*: Dept of Spanish, Univ. College, Cork, Ireland.

Foot, David Hugh Stevens; Lecturer, Department of Geography, University of Reading, since 1969; *b* 1939; *m* 1969; two *d*. BSc Aberystwyth 1962 (2nd cl. Econ.), DipStats Aberystwyth 1963; FRStatSoc. Res. Asst, Bristol Univ., 1963–65; Res. Fellow, Manchester Univ., 1965–67. *Publications*: contrib. Reg. Studies, Environ. Planning, Official Archit. Planning. *Address*: Dept of Geography, Univ. of Reading, Whiteknights, Reading RG6 2AH.

Foot, Dr Hugh Corrie, BA, PhD; Lecturer in Psychology, Department of Applied Psychology, University of Wales Institute of Science and Technology, since 1968; *b* 1941; *m* 1968. BA Durham 1962 (2nd cl. Psychology), PhD St Andrews 1967; ABPsS. Res. Fellow, Dundee, 1965–68. Hon. Sec. and Treas., Welsh Brch, Brit. Psychol. Soc. *Publications*: contrib. Brit. Jl Soc. Clin. Psychol., Ergonom., Percept. Mot. Skills. *Address*: Dept of Applied Psychology, Llwyn-y-Grant Road, Penylan, Cardiff.

Foot, Philippa Ruth; Senior Research Fellow, Somerville College, Oxford, since 1969, and Professor in Residence, UCLA, since 1972; *b* 1920; *m* 1945 (marr. diss. 1959). BA Oxon 1942 (1st cl. Philosophy, Politics and Economics), MA Oxon 1947. Lectr in Philosophy, 1946–50, Fellow and Tutor, 1950–69; Vice Principal, Somerville Coll., 1967–69; Univ. Lectr, Oxford, 1954–69; Vis. Associate Prof., Cornell Univ., 1960; Vis. Prof., MIT, 1962–63; Vis. Prof., Society for the Humanities, Cornell Univ., 1967; Vis. Prof., Univ. of California at Berkeley, 1970; Vis. Prof., UCLA, 1972. *Publications*: ed (with introduction), Theories of Ethics, 1967; Morality and Art, 1970; *contrib*. Aristot. Soc. Proc. and Supplementary Vols, Mind, Philosophy, Philosophical Rev. *Address*: Somerville College, Oxford.

Foote, Jeffrey Ian; Lecturer in Law, Queen's University, Belfast, since 1968; *b* 1944. LLB Belfast 1965, LLM Tulane 1966; Called to N Ireland Bar 1970. Asst Lectr, Queen's Univ., Belfast, 1965–68; Now practising at the Bar, teaching pt-time; Sec.,

Fac. of Law, Queen's Univ., 1968–69. *Publications*: contrib. Dublin Univ. Law Rev., North. Ireland Legal Qly. *Address*: Faculty of Law, Queen's Univ., Belfast BT7 1NN.

Foote, Prof. Peter Godfrey; Professor of Old Scandinavian and Director of Scandinavian Studies, University College London, since 1963; *b* 1924; *m* 1951; one *s* two *d*. BA London 1948, MA London 1951; fildr *hc* Uppsala 1972; Mem.: Viking Soc. (Jt Sec., 1956–), Royal Gustav Adolfs Acad., Uppsala, Sweden, 1967; Kungl. Humanistiska Vetenskapssamfundet, Uppsala, 1968; Visindafélag Íslands, 1969; Hon. Mem., Ísl Bókmenntafélag, 1965. Asst Lectr, Lectr and Reader in Old Scandinavian, UCL, 1950–63. Jt Editor: Saga-Book of Viking Soc.; Mediaeval Scandinavia; Mem., Editorial Bd, Scandinavica. Crabtree Orator, 1968; Commander, Icelandic Order of the Falcon, 1973. *Publications*: Gunnlaugs saga ormstungu, 1957; Pseudo-Turpin Chronicle in Iceland, 1959; Laing's Heimskringla, 1961; Lives of Saints: Icelandic manuscripts in facsimile IV, 1962; (with G. Johnston) The Saga of Gisli, 1963; (with D. M. Wilson) The Viking Achievement, 1970; *contrib*. Saga-Book, Arv, Studia Islandica, Islenzk Tunga. *Address*: Univ. College, Gower Street, WC1E 6BT.

Forbes, Dom (Cyril Louis) James, OSB, MA; Master of St Benet's Hall, since 1964; *b* 1913. BA Oxon 1937; MA Oxon 1964. Sen. Hist. Master, Ampleforth Coll., York, 1937–64. *Address*: St Benet's Hall, Oxford.

Forbes, Dr Eric Gray, BSc, PhD, MSc, PhD; Reader in History of Science, History Department, University of Edinburgh, since 1973; *b* 1933; *m* 1966; one *s* one *d*. BSc St Andrews 1954 (1st cl. Astronomy), PhD St Andrews 1961, MSc London 1965, PhD London 1972; FRAS. Coll. Educn Lectr, 1961–65; Lectr in History of Science, Univ. of Edinburgh, 1965–72, Sen. Lectr, 1972–73; Alexander von Humboldt Fellow, 1973–74. Assoc. Ed., Jl Hist. Astron., 1971– ; Consltng Mem., IAU Commn 41 (Hist. of Astron.), 1965– ; Full Mem., IAU, 1973– ; Mem., BSHS, 1966– ; Council Mem., 1966–71; Mem., Deutsche Gesellschaft für Geschichte der Medizin, Naturwissenschaft und Technik, 1973– ; Addtl Mem., Brit. Nat. Cttee for Hist. of Science, Medicine and Technology. Recognized Teacher, Univ. of London Inst. of Educn, 1963– ; Reg. Off., Brit. Council, 1961. *Publications*: The Euler–Mayer Correspondence (1751–55), 1971; Tobias Mayer's Opera Inedita, 1971; The Unpublished Writings of Tobias Mayer, 3 vols, 1972; The Birth of Scientific Navigation, 1974; *contrib*. Ann. Sci., Brit. Jl Hist. Sci., Jl Hist. Astron., Qly Jl Royal Astron. Soc., etc. *Address*: Dept of History, Univ. of Edinburgh, Edinburgh EH8 9YL.

Forbes, Sebastian; Lecturer, Department of Music, University of Surrey, since 1972; *b* 1941; *m* 1968; two *d*. BA Cantab 1963 (1st cl. Hons), MusB Cantab 1964, MA Cantab 1967, LRAM 1960, ARCO 1960, ARCM 1960; Mem. Royal Coll. of Organists, Mem. Composers Guild of GB. UC of N Wales,

Bangor, 1968–72. Producer, Music Div. (Sound), BBC, London, 1964–67; Organist, St Giles, Cripplegate, 1966–67; Organist, Trinity Coll, Cambridge, Jan.–Sept. 1968. *Publications*: Compositions published, or available from a publisher: Symphony in Two Movements; Essay for clarinet and orchestra; String Quartet No 1; String Quartet No 2 and 4 other chamber works, Organ Sonata and 4 other organ works; Crete Songs (baritone, viola, and piano); First Sequence of Carols, and other choral works; 14 educational pieces. *Address*: Music Dept, Univ. of Surrey, Guildford, Surrey GU2 5XH.

Ford, Prof. Alec George; Professor of Economics, University of Warwick, since 1970; *b* 1926; *m* 1954; two *s* one *d*. BA Oxon 1951 (1st cl. PPE), MA Oxon 1954, DPhil Oxon 1956. Lectr, Univ. of Leicester, 1953–63, Senior Lectr, 1963–65; Reader, Univ. of Warwick, 1965–70; Pro-Vice-Chancellor, 1971–72. *Publications*: The Gold Standard, 1880–1914; Britain and Argentina, 1962, Spanish edn 1965; jt ed, Planning and Growth in Rich and Poor Countries, 1966; Income, Spending and the Price Level, 1971; *contrib*. Econ. Hist. Rev., Jl Econ. Hist., Manch. Sch., Oxf. Econ. Papers, Yorks Bull. Econ. Soc. Res. *Address*: Dept of Economics, Univ. of Warwick, Coventry CV4 7AL.

Ford, Anthony Dudley, BMus; Lecturer in Music, University of Hull, since 1964; *b* 1935; *m* 1965. BMus Birmingham 1957. Asst Lectr in Music, Hull, 1963–64. Conductor, Hull Bach Choir, 1969– . *Publications*: Bononcini: Aeterna fac, 1970; Bononcini: Arias from the Vienna Operas, 1971; Purcell: Fantazias, 1973; *contrib*. Curr. Musicol., Music. Times, Encyc. Brit., MGG. *Address*: Dept of Music, Univ. of Hull, Hull HU6 7RX.

Ford, Prof. Boris, MA; Director, College and Further Professional Studies, School of Education, University of Bristol, since 1974; *b* 1917; *m* 1950; one *s* three *d*. BA Cantab 1939 (1st cl. English), MA Cantab 1942. Prof. Sheffield Univ., 1960–63; Prof., Sussex Univ., 1963–73; Vis. Prof., Ann Arbor Univ., 1969; Vis. Prof., Seattle Univ., 1971. Ch. Ed. and Dir, Bureau of Current Aff., 1951; Secretariat, UN, 1951–53; Sec., Wood Cttee on liberalising tech. educn, 1953–54; Ed., Jl Educn, 1954–58; Ed., Univ. Qly, 1954– ; Educ. Sec., Camb. Univ. Press, 1958; Hd, Sch. Brdcstng, Assoc. Rediffus., 1957–58; Chm., NATE, 1959. *Publications*: Discussion Method, 1949; Teachers' Handbook to Human Rights, 1950; Liberal Education in a Technical Age, 1955; Young Readers, Young Writers, 1960; Gen. Ed., Pelican Guide to English Literature, 1954–61; *contrib*. Encounter, New Statesm. Scrutiny. *Address*: School of Education, 35 Berkeley Square, Bristol BS8 1JA.

Ford, Prof. James Lorne; Professor of Economics, Division of Economic Studies, University of Sheffield, since 1973; *b* 1939; *m* 1962; three *d*. BA Liverpool 1960 (Econ), MA Liverpool 1962 (Econ), Asst Lectr, then Lectr, Manchester Univ., 1961–68; Rocke-

feller Foundn Fellow, Stanford, Yale and MSU, 1964–65; Sen. Lectr, New Univ. of Ulster, 1968–70; Vis. Prof., UCLA, 1969; Esmee Fairbairn Sen. Res. Fellow, Univ. of Sheffield, 1970–73. *Publications*: The Ohlin-Heckscher Theory of Trade, 1965; (with T. Stark) Long- and Short-term Interest Rates, 1967; ed (with C. F. Carter), Uncertainty and Expectations in Economics, 1972; (with J. C. Dodds) Expectations, Uncertainty and the Term Structure of Interest Rates, 1974; (with G. Clayton and others) Financial Model Building, 1975; *contrib*. Bull. Oxf. Inst. Econ. Stats, Cahiers, Ser. P, ISEA, Economia Int., Econ. Jl, Kyklos, Manch. Sch., Riv. Int. Sci. Econ. Comm. *Address*: Research Section, Division of Economic Studies, The Univ., Sheffield S10 2TN.

Ford, Dr William Frederick; Reader, Department of Ceramics, Glasses and Polymers, University of Sheffield, since 1972; *b* 1916; *m* 1948; one *d*. BSc London, PhD Sheffield; Founder Fellow, Inst. of Ceramics, 1955. Lectr, 1955–60, Sen. Lectr, 1960–72, Univ. of Sheffield. *Publications*: The Effect of Heat on Ceramics, 1967; *contrib*. Brit. Ceramic Soc. *Address*: Dept of Ceramics, Glasses and Polymers, Univ. of Sheffield, Sheffield S10 2TN.

Fordham, Paul Ellis, BA; Director of Extra-Mural Studies, University of Southampton, since 1971; *b* 1925; *m* 1950; two *s*. BA Leeds 1950 (Geography). Asst Lectr, Nottingham Univ. (Adult Educn), 1951–54, Lectr, 1954–61; Lectr, Makerere Univ. Coll., Uganda (Extra-Mural), 1961–62; Principal, Coll. Social Studies, Kikuyu, Kenya, 1962–66; Dir of Adult Studies, Univ. Coll., Nairobi, 1966–68. Mem., Kenya Educn Commn, 1964–66; Chm., Kenya Agricult. Wages Adv. Bd, 1964–66; Principal, Dept Educn and Science, 1968–71. *Publications*: The Geography of African Affairs, 1965, 3rd edn 1972; (with P. Kinyanjui) The Geography of Kenya, 1968; Rural Development in the Kenya Highlands, 1973; *contrib*. Adult Educn, Univ. Qly. *Address*: Dept of Extra-Mural Studies, The Univ., Southampton SO9 5NH.

Forge, Anthony, MA; Senior Lecturer in Social Anthropology, London School of Economics, University of London, since 1970; *b* 1929; *m* 1965; one *s* one *d*. BA, 1953, MA 1957, Cantab; FRAI, Mem., ASA. Asst Lectr, 1961–64; Lectr, LSE, 1964–70; Curl Lectr, RAI, 1965; Vis. Prof., Yale, 1969; Malinowski Meml Lectr, 1972. Managing Editor, LSE Monographs on Social Anthropology, 1964–72. *Publications*: ed, Primitive Art and Society, 1973; *contrib*. Man, Proc. RAI. *Address*: London School of Economics, Houghton Street, Aldwych, London WC2A 2AE.

Forrest, Prof. Derek W., MA, PhD; Professor of Psychology, Trinity College Dublin, since 1968; *b* 1926; *m* 1953; one *d*. BA Oxon 1951, MA Oxon 1955; PhD London 1956; FBPsS, Fellow Psychological Soc. of Ireland, Fellow TCD; Lectr, Bedford Coll., Univ. of London, 1952–62; Reader, Trinity College, Dublin, 1962–68. *Publications*: Francis

Galton: the life and work of a Victorian genius, 1974; *contrib.* Brit. Jl Psychol, Jl Exp. Psychol., Jl Pers. Soc. Psychol., Psychol. Monogr. *Address*: Dept of Psychology, Trinity College, Univ. of Dublin, Dublin 2, Ireland.

Forrest, William George Grieve; Fellow and Tutor in Ancient History, Wadham College, Oxford, since 1951; *b* 1925; *m* 1956; two *d*. BA Oxon 1951 (1st cl. Hon. Mods, 1st cl. Lit. Hum.), MA Oxon 1954. Univ. Lectr, Oxford, 1952– ; Vis. Prof., Univ. and Trinity Colls, Toronto, 1961–62; Vis. Prof., Yale, 1968; Dean, Wadham Coll., 1963–69; Sen. Tutor, Wadham Coll., 1971–72. *Publications*: ed and trans., Herodotus, 1963; Emergence of Greek Democracy, 1966, French, German, Italian edns 1966, Spanish edn 1967, Japanese edn 1970; A History of Sparta, 1968; *contrib.* Ann. Brit. Sch. Athens, Bull. Corr. Hell., Class. Qly, Class. Rev., Gk Rom. Byz. Studies, Historia, Klio, Phoenix. *Address*: Wadham College, Oxford.

Forrester, David Alexander Roxburgh; Lecturer, Department of Accountancy, Strathclyde University, since 1964; *b* 1928; *m* 1967; one *s* one *d*. MA St Andrews 1947, BA Oxon 1952, ACWA 1959. *Publications*: *contrib.* Acntnt, Acntnts Mag., Bull. Brit. Computer Soc., Acctg and Bus. Res. *Address*: Dept of Accountancy, Univ. of Strathclyde, Glasgow G1 1XW.

Forrester, Prof. Peter Garnett; Professor, and Director of School of Management, Cranfield Institute of Technology, since 1967, and Dean of Faculty of Management, since 1972; *b* 1917; *m* 1942; two *d*. BSc Manchester 1938 (2nd cl. Hons Metallurgy), MSc Manchester 1939; MInstMet. 1938, FIM 1949. Prof. of Industrial Management, Coll. of Aeronautics, Cranfield, 1966. Cranfield Sch. of Management: Mem. Council, 1970– ; Mem. Staffing Cttee, 1967– (Chm. 1968–71); Mem. Academic Cttee, 1967–70. *Publications*: *contrib.* Jl IMechE, Jl Inst. Met., Metallurgical Reviews, Proc. Royal Soc. *Address*: School of Management, Cranfield Institute of Technology, Bedford MK43 0AL.

Forster, Gordon Colin Fawcett, BA, FSA, FRHistS; Senior Lecturer in Modern History, University of Leeds, since 1965; *b* 1928; *m* 1956. BA Leeds 1949; FSA, FRHistS. Douglas Knoop Fellow, Sheffield Univ., 1952–55; Asst Lectr, Leeds Univ., 1955–58; Lectr, Leeds Univ., 1958–65. Ed., North. Hist., 1966– ; Mem.: Central Cttee, Victoria Co. Hist., 1967– ; Brit. Cttee, Atlas of Hist. Towns, 1971– ; Council, Hist, Assoc., 1970. *Publications*: York in 17th century, in, VCH: City of York, 1961; Hull in 16th and 17th centuries, in, VCH: City of Kingston upon Hull, 1969; Leeds 1207–1725, in, Leeds and its Region, 1967; Descriptive Catalogue, Records of Corporation of Scarborough, 1967; The English Local Community and Local Government 1603–1625, in, The Reign of James VI and I, 1973; The East Riding Justices of the Peace in the 17th Century, 1973; contrib. University Teaching in Transition, 1968; Scarborough 966–1966,

1966; County Government in Stuart Yorkshire, 1975. *Address*: School of History, Univ., Leeds LS2 9JT.

Forster, Prof. Leonard Wilson, MA, Drphil; Schröder Professor of German, University of Cambridge, since 1961; *b* 1913; *m* 1939; one *s* two *d*. BA Cantab 1934, MA Cantab 1937; Drphil Basel 1939; Goethe Medal in gold 1965; Mem.: Deutsche Akad. Sprache und Dichtung, Royal Netherlands Acad. Sciences Lett., Maatschappij der nederlandse letterkunde, Kon, Akad. nederlandse taal en letterkunde, Gent. English Lektor, Univ. of Leipzig, 1934–35; Univ. of Königsberg, 1935–36; Univ. of Basel, 1936–38; Fellow, Selwyn Coll., Cambridge, 1937, Univ. Asst Lectr, 1937–39, Lectr, 1945–48; Prof., Univ. Coll., London, 1950–61; Vis. Prof., Univ. of Toronto, 1958; McGill Univ., 1968; Univ. of Heidelberg, 1964; Univ. of Otago, 1968. Foreign Off., 1939–45; Pres., Internat. Verein. germanische Sprach– und Literatur., 1970–75. *Publications*: G. R. Weckherlin, 1944; Conrad Celtis, 1948; German Poetry 1944–48, 1948; Penguin Book of German Verse, 1957; Janus Gruter's English Years, 1967; Die Niederlande und die Anfänge der deutschen Barockliteratur, 1967; The Icy Fire, 1969; The Poet's Tongues, 1970; *contrib.* Euphorion, Germ. Life Lett., Mod. Lang. Rev. *Address*: Dept of German, Sidgwick Avenue, Cambridge.

Forster, Michael Desmond; Academic Registrar, since 1966, and Deputy Secretary, since 1964, University of Lancaster; *b* 1931; *m* 1954; one *s* one *d*. BSc (1st cl. Econ.) Queen's Univ. of Belfast, 1953, MA 1959; Personal Res. Asst to the Vice-Chancellor, Queen's Univ. of Belfast, 1953–55; Admin. Asst to the Vice-Chancellor, Secretary, and Clerk of Examinations, 1955–58; Sen. Admin. Asst, Assoc. of Commonwealth Univs, 1958–64. *Publications*: An Audit of Academic Performance, 1959. *Address*: Univ. House, Univ. of Lancaster, Lancaster LA1 4YW.

Forster, Peter Glover, MA(Econ); Lecturer, Department of Sociology and Social Anthropology, University of Hull, since 1969; *b* 1944; *m* 1968. BA(Econ) Hons Manchester 1965 (2nd cl. Sociology and Social Anthropology), MA(Econ) Manchester 1967; Mem., Brit. Sociol Assoc. Asst Lectr, Hull Univ., 1966–69. *Publications*: *contrib.* Kölner Zeits. Sozio. Sozialpsychol., Pens. Lingua. Operaz., Social. Rev., Brit. Jl Sociol. *Address*: Dept of Sociology and Social Anthropology, The Univ., Hull HU6 7RX.

Forsyth, James; Reader and Head of Russian Department, Aberdeen University, since 1964; *b* 1928; *m* 1951; one *d*. MA Edinburgh 1957 (1st cl. Russian). Asst Lectr, Keele, 1958–61; Lectr, Glasgow, 1961–64. *Publications*: (with K. Brooke) Russian through Reading, 1962; A Practical Guide to Russian Stress, 1963; A Grammar of Aspect, 1970: ed, Vinokur: The Russian Language, 1971; ed, var. Russian literary texts; *contrib.* Mod. Langs, SEER, Forum Mod. Lang. Studies. *Address*: Dept of Russian, Univ. of Aberdeen, King's College, Old Aberdeen.

Forsyth, John; Lecturer in Extra Mural Studies, Queen's University of Belfast, since 1966; *b* 1929; *m* 1957; two *d*. BSc Hons Aberdeen 1952 (Zool.); MIBiol. Lectr in Agric. Entomology, Univ. of Ghana, 1959–62. Entomologist, RHS, Wisley Gardens, Woking, Surrey, 1963–66. *Publications:* Agricultural Insects of Ghana: an annotated check list, 1966; ed jtly, Conservation in the Development of Northern Ireland, 1971. *Address:* Dept of Extra Mural Studies, Queen's Univ. of Belfast, Belfast BT7 1NN.

Fortune, Dr Nigel Cameron; Part-time Reader in Music, Birmingham University, since 1970; *b* 1924. BA Birmingham 1950, PhD Cambridge 1954. Lectr in Music, Birmingham Univ., 1959–70. Sec., Royal Musical Assoc., 1957–71; Vice-pres., 1971– ; Text Ed.; Mem.: Edit. Bd, and Vice-Chm., Exec. Cttee, Grove's Dictionary of Music and Musicians, 6th edn 1970– . *Publications:* Solo Song and Cantata, in, New Oxford History of Music, IV, 1968; (Jt Ed.), The Monteverdi Companion, 1968; The Beethoven Companion, 1971; ed, various music. wks, including Purcell Soc., vols 28–30, 32 (jtly), 2nd edns respectively 1968, 1965, 1970, 1968; J. Dowland: Ayres for four voices (jtly), 2nd edn 1963; assoc. Ed., New Oxford History of Music, V, 1974; (Jt Ed.), Italian Baroque Opera (forthcoming); *contrib.* Music Lett., Music. Qly. *Address:* Dept of Music, Barber Institute of Fine Arts, The Univ., P.O. Box 363, Birmingham B15 2TT.

Foskett, Douglas John; Librarian, Institute of Education, University of London, since 1957; Part-time Lecturer, School of Library, Archives, and Information Studies, University College, London, since 1958; *b.* 1918; *m* 1948; one *s* two *d*. BA London 1939, MA 1954; FLA 1949 (Vice-Pres., 1966–73), Private Libraries Assoc. (Past Pres.). Asst, Ilford Municipal Libraries, 1939–48 (War Service, 1940–46); Inf. Officer, Metal Box Co., Res. Dept, 1948–57. Mem., Advisory Cttee on Scientific and Technical Inf., DES, 1967–71; Mem. and Rapporteur, Internat. Adv. Cttee on Documentation, Libraries and Archives, UNESCO, 1968–73; Hon. Library Adv., Royal Nat. Inst. for Deaf, 1965– . *Publications:* Assistance to Readers in Lending Libraries, 1952; (with E. A. Baker), Bibliography of Food, 1958; Information Service in Libraries, 1958, 1967; Classification and Indexing in the Social Sciences, 1963; Science, Humanism and Libraries, 1964; How to Find Out: Educational Research, 1965; *contrib.* Internat. Social Sci. Jl, Jl of Documentation, Jl of Librarianship, Lib. Assoc. Record, Nature, TLS. *Address:* Inst. of Education Library, Univ. of London, Malet Street, WC1E 7HS.

Foster, Dr Brian, MA, Ddel'U; Senior Lecturer, French Department, University of Southampton, since 1964; *b* 1920; *m* 1st 1946, 2nd 1953; two *s* one *d*. BA Dunelm 1942 (uncl. wartime degree), BA Dunelm 1947 (1st cl. French), MA Dunelm 1947, Doctorat de l'Université de Paris (Mention très honorable) 1949; Mem., Anglo-Norman Text Soc. Asst Lectr, Southampton Univ., 1950–51; Lectr, 1951–64. Examiner in French,

Oxford and Cambridge Schls Exams Bd, 1951–71. *Publications:* The local port book of Southampton for 1435–56, 1963; The changing English language, 1968, pbk edn 1970; *contrib.* French Studies, Mod. Lang. Rev., Anglia, Notes Queries, Engl. Studies, Studia Neophilol. *Address:* Dept of French, Univ. of Southampton, Southampton SO9 5NH.

Foster, Prof. Idris Llewelyn, FSA; Jesus Professor of Celtic, University of Oxford, since 1947; *b* 1911. BA Wales 1932 (1st cl.), MA Wales 1935 (distinction), DipEd Wales 1933 (1st cl.). Fellow, Soc. Antiqu., 1954. Fellow, Univ. of Wales, 1935–36; Lectr in Welsh and Hd of Dept of Celtic, Univ. of Liverpool, 1936–47; O'Donnell Lectr, Univ. of Edinburgh, 1960, Univ. of Wales, 1972. Mem.: Royal Commn Anc. Monum. Wales and Monmouth., 1949– ; Stand. Commn Mus. Galleries, 1964– ; Treas., Nat. Libr. Wales, 1964– . *Publications:* The Book of the Anchorite (Sir John Rhys Memorial Lecture, 1949), in, Proc. Brit. Acad., XXXVI, 1950; ed (with Leslie Alcock), Culture and Environment, 1963; (with G. E. Daniel), Prehistoric and Early Wales, 1965. *Address:* Jesus College, Oxford.

Foster, Jonathan Charles Brian; Lecturer in Latin, University of Liverpool, since 1965; *b* 1938; *m* 1968. MA Aberdeen 1959 (1st cl. Classics), 1st cl. Classical Mods Oxford 1961, BPhil Oxford 1964; Mem., Inst. Class. Studies, 1971. Asst Lectr, Liverpool Univ., 1962–65. *Publications:* *contrib.* Class. Qly, Class. Rev., Mnemosyne, Proc. Virg. Soc., Rh. Mus. *Address:* Dept of Latin, Univ. of Liverpool, Liverpool L69 3BX.

Foulds, Peter Barrington; Lecturer in German Language and Literature, University of Birmingham, since 1964; *b* 1938. BA London 1960. Lektor, Univ. of Tübingen, 1960–62. *Address:* Dept of German, Univ. of Birmingham, P.O. Box 363, Birmingham B15 2TT.

Foulger, Dr Lawrence Ernest; Lecturer in German Language and Literature, University of Manchester, since 1964; *b* 1939; *m* 1965. BA Leeds 1962 (1st cl. German), PhD Leeds 1970. *Address:* Dept of German, Univ. of Manchester, Manchester M13 9PL.

Foulkes, David Llewhelin, BA, LLM, JP; Senior Lecturer, Department of Law, University of Wales Institute of Science and Technology, Cardiff, since 1967; *b* 1924; *m* 1955; one *s* two *d*. BA (Econ) Wales 1947, LLB London 1949, LLM London 1956; Barrister 1951. Lectr, UWIST (formerly Welsh Coll. Adv. Technol.), 1955–67; Vis. Lectr, Wharton Sch., Univ. of Pennsylvania, 1964–65. RN, 1943–46; Admin. Asst, Wales Gas Bd, 1949–52; Mem., S Glamorgan CC. *Publications:* Introduction to Administrative Law, 3rd edn 1972; Law for Managers, 2nd edn 1971; *contrib.* Mod. Law Rev. *Address:* Dept of Law, Univ. of Wales Institute of Science and Technology, Cardiff CF1 3NU.

Fowler, Prof. Alastair David Shaw, FBA; Regius Professor of Rhetoric and English

232

Literature, University of Edinburgh, since 1972; *b* 1930; *m* 1950; one *s* one *d*. MA Edinburgh 1952, MA 1955, DPhil 1957, Oxon. Jun. Res. Fellow, Queen's Coll., Oxford, 1955–59; Instr, Indiana Univ., 1957; Lectr, UC, Swansea, 1959–62; Fellow and Tutor in English Literature, Brasenose College, Oxford, 1962–71; Visiting Professor, Univ. of Virginia, 1969. Mem., Inst. for Advanced Study, Princeton, 1966. *Publications*: Spenser and the Numbers of Time, 1964; Triumphal Forms, 1970; Silent Poetry, 1970; trans. and ed, Richard Wills, De re poetica, 1958; ed, C. S. Lewis, Spenser's Images of Life, 1967; ed (with J. Carey), The Poems of John Milton, 1968; ed (with C. Butler), Topics in Criticism, 1971; *contrib*. revs and articles in jls. *Address*: Dept of English, David Hume Tower, George Square, Edinburgh EH8 9JX.

Fowler, Dr Frank Macpherson, MA, DPhil; Reader in German, Queen Mary College, University of London, since 1970; *b* 1935. MA Aberdeen 1957 (1st cl.), DPhil Oxon 1962. Asst Lectr, Aberdeen, 1960–62, Lectr, 1962–65; Lectr, Univ. of Kent at Canterbury, 1965–67; Lectr, King's Coll., London, 1967–70. Hon. Sec., Univ. Teachers German, 1967–71; Hon. Sec., Engl. Goethe Soc., 1972– . *Publications*: (with B. J. Kenworthy and M. Würzl) Manual of German Prose Composition, 1966; ed, Schiller: Poems, 1969; *contrib*. Hebbel-Jbh, Mod. Lang. Rev., Publ. Engl. Goethe Soc. *Address*: Dept of German, Queen Mary College, Mile End Road, E1 4NS.

Fowler, Prof. Kenneth Alan, BA, PhD, FRHistS; Professor of Medieval History, University of Edinburgh, since 1974; *b* 1933; *m* 1959; one *s* one *d*. BA Leeds 1955 (Hons History), PhD Leeds 1961; FRHistS 1970. Asst Lectr, Edinburgh, 1958–61, Lectr, 1961–70, Reader 1970–74. *Publications*: The Age of Plantagenet and Valois: the Struggle for Supremacy 1328–1498, 1967, French edn 1968; The King's Lieutenant: Henry of Grosmont, First Duke of Lancaster, 1310–1361, 1969; ed, The Hundred Years War, 1971; *contrib*. Cahiers Vernonnais, Study of War and Soc. (Open Univ.), Ann. Bull. Hist. Lit., etc. *Address*: Dept of History, Univ. of Edinburgh, Edinburgh EH8 9YL.

Fowler, Roger; Senior Lecturer, School of English and American Studies, University of East Anglia, since 1969; *b* 1938; *m* 1959; two *s*. BA Hons London 1959 (English), MA 1962; Mem., Linguistics Association of GB. Asst Lectr/Lectr, Hull Univ., 1960–64; Lectr, Univ. of East Anglia, 1964–69; Vis. Lectr, Dept of Speech, Univ. of California, Berkeley, 1966–67; Vis. Prof. of Comparative Literature, Brown Univ., 1972–73. *Publications*: Essays on Style and Language, 1966; Old English Prose and Verse, 1966; Introduction to Transformational Syntax, 1971; The Languages of Literature, 1971; Wulfstan's 'Canons of Edgar', 1972; A Dictionary of Modern Critical Terms, 1973; Understanding Language, 1974; Style and Structure in Literature, 1974; *contrib*. Anglia, Ardivum Linguisticum, Critical Survey, Dutch Qly Rev., Essays in Criticism, Jl of

English and Germanic Philology, Jl of Linguistics, Lingua, Linguistics, Medium Ævum, Studia Neophilologica, Word. *Address*: Sch. of English and American Studies, Univ. of East Anglia, Norwich NOR 88C.

Fowlie, Ian Marshall; Senior Lecturer in Department of Moral Philosophy, University of Aberdeen, since 1971; *b* 1931; *m* 1962; two *s* one *d*. MA St Andrews 1955 (1st cl. Classics), BA Cantab 1957 (1st cl. Moral Science Tripos). Lectr in Moral Philosophy, Aberdeen Univ., 1959–71. *Publications*: *contrib*. Encyclop. Brit. *Address*: Dept of Moral Philosophy, King's College, Aberdeen.

Fox, Alan; Lecturer in Sociology, Department of Social and Administrative Studies, University of Oxford, since 1963; *b* 1920; *m* 1950; two *s*. Dip. Econs and Politics, Oxford 1948, BA Oxford 1950 (PPE), BLitt 1952. Res. Fellow, Nuffield Coll. Oxford, 1957–1963. *Publications*: History of the National Union of Boot and Shoe Operatives, 1958; (with H.A. Clegg and A. F. Thompson) History of British Trade Unions 1889–1910, 1964; A Sociology of Work in Industry, 1971; Beyond Contract, 1974; Man Mismanagement, 1974; *contrib*. Brit. Jl Ind. Rel., Jl Man. Studies, Oxford Econ. Papers. *Address*: Dept of Social and Administrative Studies, 28 Little Clarendon Street, Oxford.

Fox, David John; BSc, MA; Lecturer, School of Geography, University of Manchester, since 1959; *b* 1931. BSc London 1952 1st cl. Geography), MA California 1958; FRGS. Mem., Inst. Brit. Geogrs. Res. Asst, McGill Univ., Canada, 1955–56; Teaching Asst, Univ. of California, Berkeley, 1956–58; Tutor, Fac. of Arts, Univ. of Manchester, 1966– ; Tutor and Vice Warden, Woolton Hall, Univ. of Manchester, 1960– . Vice-Chm., Latin-Amer. Cttee, Oxfam, 1970– . *Publications*: *contrib*. Geog. Rev., Jl Trop. Geog., Tijd. Econ. Soc. Geog., Trans Inst. Brit. Geogrs. *Address*: School of Geography, The Univ., Manchester M13 9PL.

Fox, John Henry Malcolm; Tutor in Adult Education, Extra-Mural Department, University of Southampton, since 1974; *b* 1936; *m* 1965; two *d*. BA Nottingham 1961 (Hons English). Univ. of Nottingham: Tutor i/c Services Educn Dept of Adult Educn, 1962–65; Resident Tutor for N Leics and Warden of Quest House, 1965–67; Tutor in English Studies, Adult Studies Centre, Univ. of Nairobi (secondment), 1967–69; Warden, Univ. of Nottingham Adult Educn Centre, 1969–73. *Publications*: (with Thomas Mulusa) What is Socialism?, 1972 (E African Literature Bureau); *contrib*. Adult Educn, Stud. Adult Educn. *Address*: Dept of Extra-Mural Studies, Univ. of Southampton, Highfield, Southampton S09 5NH.

Fox, Prof. John Howard, BA, Ddel'U; Professor of French, University of Exeter, since 1967; *b* 1925; *m* 1947; four *s*. BA London 1946 (1st cl. French), Ddel'U Paris 1948. Asst Lectr, Univ. Coll. of SW, 1948–50; Lectr, 1950–64; Reader in French, Univ. of Exeter, 1964–67. Mem., Edit. Bd, French Studies, 1970– . *Publications*: Robert de

233

Blois, son œuvre didactique et narrative, 1950; The Poetry of Villon, 1962; (with B. Saklatvala) Complete Poems of François Villon, 1968; (with R. Wood) A Concise History of the French Language, 1968; The Lyric Poetry of Charles d'Orléans, 1969; Charles d'Orléans, Choix de poésies éditées d'après le ms Royal 16 FII du British Museum, 1973; A History of Medieval French Literature, 1974; *contrib.* Fr. Studies, Mod. Lang. Rev., Romania. *Address:* Queen's Building, Univ. of Exeter, Exeter EX4 4QJ.

Fox, Dr Robert, MA, DPhil; Senior Lecturer in the History of Science, Department of History, University of Lancaster, since 1966; *b* 1938; *m* 1964; three *d.* BA Oxon 1961 (Physics), MA Oxon 1965, DPhil Oxon 1967. Clifford Norton Res. Fellow, Queen's Coll., Oxford, 1965–66. Ed. Brit. Jl Hist. Science, 1971– . Mem., Council Brit. Soc. Hist. Science, 1970– . *Publications:* The caloric theory of gases from Lavoisier to Regnault, 1971; *contrib.* Bol. Acad. Nac. Cienc. Repub. Argent., Brit. Jl Hist. Sci., Minerva, Notes Rec. Royal Soc. London; Proc. Amer. Philosl Soc., Technol. Cult., Hist. Studies Phys Scis. *Address:* Dept of History, Univ. of Lancaster, Bailrigg, Lancaster LA1 4YW.

Foxon, David Fairweather; Reader in Textual Criticism, University of Oxford, since 1968; *b* 1923; *m* 1947; one *d.* BA Oxon 1948 (1st cl. English), MA Oxon 1953. Prof. Queen's Univ., Kingston, Ont., 1965–68. Foreign Off., 1942–45; Min. Town and Country Planning, 1949–50; Dept Printed Books, Brit. Mus., 1950–65; Harkness Fellow, 1959–61; Guggenheim Fellow, 1967–68; Vice-Pres., Bibliog. Soc., 1970– . *Publications:* The Technique of Bibliography, 1955; T. J. Wise and the Pre-Restoration Drama, 1959; Libertine Literature in England, 1660–1745, 1964; ed, English Bibliographical Sources, 1964–66; English Verse, 1701–1750: a catalogue, 1974; *contrib.* Bk Coll., Libr., Times Lit. Supp. *Address:* Wadham College, Oxford.

Foyle, Dr Arthur Montague; Lecturer, School of Environmental Studies, University College, London, since 1948; *b* 1915; *m* 1948. BA (Arch) 1938, PhD 1959, London; RIBA 1939, AMTPI 1940, AMIStructE 1943. *Publication:* General Editor, Conference on Tropical Architecture, 1953, 1954. *Address:* Univ. Coll., London, Gower Street, WC1E 6BT.

Fraile, Dr Medardo; Lecturer in Spanish, Department of Modern Languages, University of Strathclyde, since 1968; *b* 1925; *m* 1971. Filosofía y Letras Madrid 1957, Doctorate Madrid 1968. Asst in Language, Southampton Univ., 1964–67; Asst Lectr, Strathclyde Univ., 1967–68. *Publications:* Cuentos con algún amor, 1954; A la luz cambian las cosas, 1959; Cuentos de Verdad, 1964; Descubridor de nada y otros cuentos, 1970; Con los días contados, 1972; Samuel Ros (1904–1945): Hacia una generación sin crítica, 1972; La penúltima Inglaterra, 1973; Literatura española contemporánea: Teatro y Poesía, 1974; *contrib.* Abside, Agora, Caravelle, Cuadernos Hispano-ameri-234

canos, Cuadernos de Literatura, Insula, Prohemio, Revista de Occidente, Texas Qly. *Address:* Dept of Modern Languages, Univ. of Strathclyde, Glasgow G1 1XW.

France, Dr John; Lecturer in Medieval History, University College, Swansea, since 1966; *b* 1941; *m* 1968. BA Nottingham 1963 (1st cl. History), PhD Nottingham 1967. *Publications: contrib.* Biblioth. Ecole Chartes, Bull. Inst. Hist. Res., Byzantion, EHR 1972. *Address:* Dept of History, Univ. College, Swansea SA2 8PP.

France, Philip Roland; Lecturer in Law, University of Bradford, since 1966; *b* 1933. BA Manchester 1954 (Hons Modern History with Economics and Politics), LLB Manchester 1956; Solicitor, Supreme Court, 1966. *Publications:* The Discipline of an Academic Community, 1969; *contrib.* Univ. Qly. *Address:* School of Social Sciences, Univ. of Bradford, Bradford BD7 1DP.

Francis, Dr Kenneth Henry, BA, PhD; Senior Lecturer in French, Royal Holloway College, University of London, since 1962; *b* 1924; *m* 1950; one *s.* BA London 1945 (1st cl. French) at Univ. Coll. Southampton, PhD London 1948. Asst Lectr, Sheffield Univ., 1949–52, Lectr, 1952-62. Dean, Fac. of Arts, Royal Holloway Coll., 1970–73; Chm., Bd Examiners in French, Univ. of London, 1968–73. Hon. Sec., Soc. for Fr. Studies, 1973– . *Publications:* France 1871–1914, in, M. Bruce: The Shaping of the Modern World, 1958; contrib. Studies in French Literature presented to H. W. Lawton, 1968; *contrib.* Bibl Hum. et Ren., Fr. Studies, Mod. Lang. Rev. *Address:* Dept of French, Royal Holloway College, Egham, Surrey TW20 0EX.

Francis, Richard Andrew, MA, BLitt; Lecturer, Department of French, Nottingham University, since 1968; *b* 1942; *m* 1970; one *d.* BA 1963, MA BLitt 1968, Oxon; Member: Soc. for French Studies; Brit. Soc. for Eighteenth-Century Studies. Asst Lectr. in French, Nottingham Univ., 1966–68. Brit Sec., Assoc. des Amis du Fonds Romain Rolland. *Publications: contrib.* French Studies; Nottingham French Studies, Year's Work in Mod. Lang. Studies. *Address:* Dept of French, Univ. of Nottingham, Nottingham NG7 2RD.

Frank, H. Eric; Senior Lecturer, School of Management, University of Bath, since 1964, and Director of Studies, Post Experience Courses; *b* 1921; *m* 1968. BSc(Econ) London 1946, Teacher's Dip London 1949, Teacher's Cert. 1949; Mem., Inst. Personnel Mngnt, Brit. Assoc. Comm. Indust. Educn, Amer. Soc. Trng Develop; Mem., Central Trng Council, Trng Staff Cttee. Editor, Indust. Trng Internat. *Publications:* Organization Structuring, 1971. *Address:* Univ. of Bath, School of Management, Rockwell, Kings Weston Road, Bristol BS11 0UY.

Frank, Peter John; Lecturer in Soviet Government and Politics, Department of Government, University of Essex, since 1968; *b* 1934; *m* 1960; two *s* one *d.* BA Leeds

1963 (2nd cl. Russian Language and Literature); Teaching Cert., Univ. of Leeds Inst. Educn, 1956. Asst Lectr, Leeds Univ., 1964–65, Lectr, 1965–68. Mem., Nat. Exec. Cttee, Nat. Assoc. Sov. E Europ. Studies, 1968– , Chm., 1973– ; Mem., Edit. Adv. Bd, Sov. Studies, 1970– , and NASEES Monog. Series, 1970–72. *Publications: contrib.* Listener, Lond. Mag., New Soc., Sov. Studies, Brit. Jl Polit. Sci. *Address:* Dept of Government, Univ. of Essex, Colchester, Essex CO4 3SQ.

Frankel, Prof. Joseph; Professor of Politics, University of Southampton, since 1962; *b* 1913; *m* 1944; one *d*. Master of Laws Lwow, Poland, 1935; LLM WA 1948, PhD(Econ) London 1950. Temp. Asst Lectr, UCL, 1950–51; Lectr and Sen. Lectr, Univ. of Aberdeen, 1951–62. Legal practice, Solicitor, in Poland, 1935–38; farming in Western Australia, 1938–47; *Publications:* The Making of Foreign Policy, 1962, 1967; International Relations, 1963, 1970; International Politics: conflict and harmony, 1969; National Interest, 1970; *contrib.* Internat. Affairs, Ybk World Aff., etc. *Address:* Univ. of Southampton, Highfield, Southampton SO9 5NH.

Frankenberg, Prof. Ronald, BA, MA(Econ), PhD; Professor of Sociology, and Head of Department of Sociology, University of Keele, since 1969; *b* 1929; *m* 1st 1953, 2nd 1964; three *d*. BA Cantab 1949–50 (2nd cl. Nat. Sc. Tripos Pt 1, Anthropology Tripos, Pt II), MA(Econ) Manchester 1952, PhD Manchester 1954. Res. Asst, Industrial Relations Dept, Univ. Coll., Cardiff, 1954–56; Res. Asst, Univ. of Manchester, 1956; Lectr, then Sen. Lectr and Reader in Sociology, Univ. of Manchester, 1960–68; Seconded Prof. of Sociology and Dean, Sch. of Humanities and Social Science, Univ. of Zambia, 1966–68. Educnl Off., S Wales area, Nat. Union Mnwkrs, 1957–60. *Publications:* Village on the Border, 1957; Communities in Britain, 1966; *contrib.* Afr. Social Res., Monogs Assoc. Social Anthropol. *Address:* Dept of Sociology, Univ. of Keele, Keele, Staffs ST5 5BG.

Frankis, Percy John; Senior Lecturer, Department of English Language, University of Newcastle upon Tyne, since 1972; *b* 1926; *m* 1957; two *s*. BA Oxon 1950 (English), MA Oxon 1955, BLitt Oxon 1955. Lektor in English, Univ. of Tübingen, 1951–54; Lectr in English, Univ. of Helsinki, 1955–59; Lectr in English, Univ. of Tübingen, 1959–62; Fellow, Shakespeare Inst., Univ. of Birmingham, 1962–64; Lectr in English, Univ. of Newcastle upon Tyne, 1964–72. *Publications: contrib.* Med. Æv., Neuphilol. Mitteil., Anglo-Saxon England. *Address:* School of English, The Univ., Newcastle upon Tyne NE1 7RU.

Frankish, Clive Robert, BA; Lecturer, Department of French, University of Manchester, since 1970; *b* 1942. BA London 1964 (Hons French); Mem., Soc. Fr. Studies. Tutorial Asst, Univ. of E Anglia, 1966–67; Asst Lectr, Univ. of Manchester, 1967–70. *Publications:* ed, Th. de Bèze: Abraham Sacrifiant, 1550, 1969; *contrib.* BHR. *Address:*

Dept of French, The Univ. of Manchester, Manchester M13 9PL.

Franklin, Dr Mark Newman; Lecturer, Department of Politics, University of Strathclyde, since 1969; *b* 1942; *m* 1967; one *s* one *d*. BA Oxon 1965, MA 1968, PhD Cornell 1970. Teaching Asst, Cornell Univ., 1964–67, Research Fellow, 1967–69. Member: Study of Parliament Gp, 1970; European Consortium for Pol Res., Computer Applications Gp, 1971 (Chm., 1973). *Publications:* DAEDAL: A Data Archiving, Editing, Describing and Analysing Language, 1973; *contrib.* Amer. Pol Sci. Rev., Brit. Jl Pol. Sci., Parliamentarian. *Address:* Univ. of Strathclyde, Glasgow G1 1XQ.

Franks, The Rt. Hon. Lord; Oliver Shewell Franks, PC, GCMG, KCB, CBE, FBA; Provost of Worcester College, Oxford, since 1962; Chancellor of East Anglia University, since 1965; *b* 1905; *m* 1931; two *d*. MA Oxford; Hon. DCL Oxford, and other Hon. Doctorates; FBA 1960. Fellow and Praelector in Philosophy, Queen's Coll., Oxford, 1927–37; Univ. Lectr in Philosophy, 1935–37; Vis. Prof., Univ. of Chicago, 1935; Prof. of Moral Philosophy, Univ. of Glasgow, 1937–45; Provost of Queen's Coll., Oxford, 1946–48. Temp. Civil Servant, Min. of Supply, 1939–46; Permanent Sec., Min. of Supply, 1945–46; Brit. Ambassador at Washington, 1948–52. Dir, Lloyds Bank Ltd (Chm., 1954–62); Dir, Schroders. Mem. of Rhodes Trust, 1957–73; Chm., Bd of Governors, United Oxford Hosps, 1958–64; Chm., Wellcome Trust, 1965– (Trustee 1963–65); Pres., Kennedy Meml Cttee, 1963; Pres., Commn of Inquiry into Oxford Univ., 1964–66; Pres., Cttee on Official Secrets Act, Section 2, 1971– . Mem. NEDC, 1962–64. Trustee, Pilgrim Trust, 1947– ; Trustee, Rockefeller Foundn, 1961–70. Hon. Fellow, Queen's Coll., Oxford, 1948; Hon. Fellow, St Catharine's Coll., Cambridge, 1966; Hon. Fellow, Wolfson Coll., Oxford, 1967; Vis. Fellow, Nuffield Coll., 1959. *Address:* The Provost's Lodgings, Worcester College, Oxford.

Fraser, Colin; Lecturer in Psychology, Department of Psychology, University of Bristol, since 1968; *b* 1937; *m* 1965; three *s*. MA (Hons) Aberdeen 1958, Asst Lectr, Exeter, 1963–64; Lectr, Birmingham, 1965–68; Vis. Res. Worker, Ecole Pratique, Paris, 1971. Sec., and Mem. Exec. Cttee, Europ. Assoc. Exper. Soc. Psychol., 1972– . *Publications: contrib.* Europ. Jl Social Psychol., Jl Verb. Learn. Verb. Behav., Monog. Soc. Res. Child Develop. *Address:* Dept of Psychology, Univ. of Bristol, Bristol BS8 1TH.

Fraser, George Sutherland, MA; Reader in Modern English Literature, University of Leicester, since 1964; *b* 1915; *m* 1946; one *s* two *d*. MA St Andrews 1937. Lectr in English, Leicester, 1958–63; Vis. Prof., Rochester Univ., NY, 1963–64. Freelance lit. journalist and broadcaster, London, 1946–50, 1951–58; Poetry advr and occasional leader writer, Times Lit. Supp., 1952–62; Cultl Advr, UK Liaison Missn, Japan,

1950–51; Mem.: Arts Council Poetry Panel, 1951–58; E Midlands Arts Assoc. Lit. Panel, 1971– ; Lectr, Yeats Ann. Summer Sch., Sligo, 1961, 1965, 1972. *Publications*: The Fatal Landscape and Other Poems, 1943; Home Town Elegy, 1964; The Traveller Has Regrets and Other Poems, 1948; Leaves without a Tree, 1956; ed, Conditions: Selected Recent Poetry, 1969; The Modern Writer and His World, 1951 (Japan), English edns 1963, 1964, 1970; W. B. Yeats, 1954, rev. edns 1965, 1969; Dylan Thomas, 1957, rev. edns 1964, 1972; Vision and Rhetoric, 1959; Ezra Pound, 1960 (trans. French and Spanish); Lawrence Durrell, 1968, new edn 1972; Metre, Rhyme and Free Verse, 1970 (trans. Japanese); Case-Book on Keats' Odes, 1971; *contrib*. Arion, Shenandoah, Crit. Qly, Rev. Lang. Viv. Cah. Herne. *Address*: The English Dept, Univ. of Leicester, Leicester LE1 7RH.

Fraser, Ian A., MA; Lecturer in Scottish Studies, University of Edinburgh, since 1965; *b* 1941; MA Edinburgh 1964; Sec., Council for Name Studies, GB and Ireland, 1969– ; Scott. Soc. North. Studies, 1970– . *Publications*: *contrib*. Med. Æv., Local Hist., Scott. Studies, ONOMA. *Address*: School of Scottish Studies, Univ. of Edinburgh, 27 George Square, Edinburgh EH8 9LD.

Fraser, John M.; *see* Munro Fraser.

Fraser, Peter Marshall, MC, MA, FBA; Reader in Hellenistic History, Oxford, since 1964, and Fellow of All Souls College, since 1953; *b* 1918; *m* 1st 1940, 2nd 1955; three *s* three *d*. MA Oxon 1946; FBA 1960. Lectr in Hellenistic History, Oxford, 1948–64. Dir, Brit. Sch. Archaeol. Athens, 1968–71; Jun. Proctor, Oxford Univ., 1960–61; Dom. Bursar, All Souls Coll., 1962–65. *Publications*: (with G. E. Bean) The Rhodian Peraea and Islands, 1954; (with T. Rönne) Boeotian and West Greek Tombstones, 1957; ed, Rostovtzeff: Social and Economic History of the Roman Empire, 2nd edn 1957; Samothrace, the Inscriptions (vol. ii, Excavations of Samothrace), 1960; Ptolemaic Alexandria, 1972; trans. (from Swedish), Roman Literary Portraits, 1958; ed, The Wares of Autolycus: selected literary essays of Alice Meynell, 1965; trans. (from Swedish), E. Kjellberg and G. Säflund: Greek and Roman Art, 1968; *contrib*. various articles in learned jls. *Address*: All Souls College, Oxford.

Fraser, Dr William Hamish; Lecturer, Department of History, University of Strathclyde, since 1966; *b* 1941; *m* 1965. MA Aberdeen 1963 (1st cl. History), DPhil Sussex 1968. Ed., Jl Scott, Lab. Hist. Soc., 1969– . *Publications*: Trade Unions and Society: the struggle for acceptance, 1974; *contrib*. Scott. Hist. Rev. *Address*: Dept of History, Univ. of Strathclyde, Glasgow G1 1XW.

Frazier, Robert Llewellyn; Lecturer in Modern History, University of Nottingham, since 1966; *b* 1922; *m* 1948. BA Ohio State 1943 (Chemistry), BA London 1965 (History); Phi Beta Kappa, 1942. *Address*: Dept of History, Univ. of Nottingham, Univ. Park, Nottingham NG7 2RD.

Frears, John Russell; Lecturer in Politics, Department of European Studies, Loughborough University, since 1968; *b* 1936; *m* 1962; three *d*. BA Cantab 1960, MA Cantab 1966, LèsL Nantes 1968. JP, County Councillor. *Publications*: *contrib*. Polit. Qly, Polit. Studies. *Address*: Dept of European Studies, The Univ., Loughborough LE11 3TU.

Frederiksen, Martin William; University Lecturer in Ancient History, Oxford University, and Fellow of Worcester College, since 1959; *b* 1930. BA Sydney 1952, BA Oxon 1954, MA Oxon 1959. Craven Fellow, Schol., Brit. Sch. Rome, 1954; Jun. Res. Fellow, Corpus Christi Coll., 1956–59. *Publications*: *contrib*. P. Wissowa: Real-Encyclop.; *contrib*. Dial. Archaeol., Jl Rom. Studies, Papers Brit. Sch. Rome, etc. *Address*: Worcester College, Oxford.

Freear, John; Senior Lecturer in Accounting, Faculty of Social Sciences, University of Kent at Canterbury, since 1973; *b* 1941; *m* 1966; two *d*. BA Hons Cantab 1963, MA 1967, MA Kent 1969; ACA 1967. University of Kent: P. D. Leake Teaching Fellow, 1967; Lectr in Accounting, 1969; Chm., Bd of Studies in Accounting, 1972–74; Sen. Tutor, Faculty of Social Scis, 1973– . Convenor, Accounting History Soc., 1972– . *Publications*: Financing Decisions in Business, 1973; *contrib*. Abacus. *Address*: Rutherford Coll., The Univ., Canterbury, Kent CT2 7NX.

Freeborn, Prof. Richard H., MA, DPhil; Professor of Russian Literature, School of Slavonic and East European Studies, University of London, since 1967; *b* 1926; *m*, 1954; one *s* three *d*. BA Oxon 1950 (1st cl. Russian), MA Oxon 1955, DPhil Oxon 1957; BUAS, ATR. Univ. Lectr, Hulme Lectr, Brasenose Coll., Oxford, 1954–64; Vis. Prof., UCLA, 1964–65; Sir William Mather Chair of Russian, Manchester Univ., 1965–67. Pres., Brit. Univ. Assoc. Slavists, 1970–72; Hon. Vice-Pres., Assoc. Teachers of Russian. *Publications*: Turgenev, A Study, 1960; Two Ways of Life, 1962; The Emigration of Sergey Ivanovich, 1963, American edn 1965; A Short History of Modern Russia, 1966; The Rise of the Russian Novel, 1973; trans., Turgenev: Sketches from a Hunter's Album, 1967, Home of the Gentry, 1970; Rudin, 1974; *contrib*. Slav. Rev., Times Lit. Supp., Enc. Brit. *Address*: School of Slavonic and East European Studies, Univ. of London, Malet Street, WC1 E 7HU.

Freedman, Prof. Maurice; Professor of Social Anthropology, Institute of Social Anthropology, Oxford University, since 1970; *b* 1920; *m* 1946. BA London 1942 (English), MA London 1948 (Anthropology), PhD London 1956 (Anthropology), MA Oxon 1970 (by Sp. Resolution); Mem.: Royal Anthropol. Inst., Assoc. Soc. Anthropol., Assoc. SE Asian Studies UK, Univ. Assoc. Soc. Relig., etc. Lectr in Anthropology, LSE, 1951–57; Reader, 1957–65; Prof., 1965–70; Vis. Assoc. Prof. of Anthropol., Yale Univ., 1960–61; Vis. Prof. of Anthropol., Cornell Univ., 1965. Pres., Royal Anthropol. Inst., 1967–69; Org. Sec. (later Chm.),

London–Cornell Project, 1962–69; Chm., Assoc. SE Asian Studies UK, 1971–74; Mem., SSRC, 1972–73; Mem. (academic), Ct of Governors, LSE, 1967–70, (lay) 1970– . *Publications*: ed, A Minority in Britain, 1955; Chinese Family and Marriage in Singapore, 1957, 2nd edn 1971; Lineage Organization in Southeastern China, 1958. 2nd edn 1965; Chinese Lineage and Society, 1966, 2nd edn 1971; ed, Social Organization, Essays presented to Raymond Firth, 1967; ed, Family and Kinship in Chinese Society, 1970; Social and Cultural Anthropology, 1974; *contrib*. Brit. Jl Sociol., Comp. Studies Soc. and Hist., Jl Asian Studies, Jl Royal Anthropol. Inst., Man, Pacif. Aff., etc. *Address*: All Souls College, Oxford OX1 4AL.

Freegard, Malcolm Leslie; Director, Audio-Visual Centre, University of East Anglia, since 1968; *b* 1922; *m* 1947; three *s* one *d*. BA Cantab 1947 (IIi English), MA 1949; Mem., Royal Television Soc., 1970. Asst Master (English), Gresham's Sch., Holt, 1948–52; Lecturer (English), St Luke's Coll. Exeter, 1952–55; Producer, BBC Television, 1955–68. Mem., Adv. Cttee, Norwich Sch. of Art, 1971; Mem., Film and Television Panel, Eastern Arts Assoc., 1973. Cambridge Soccer Blue, 1946–47, 1947–48. *Address*: Audio-Visual Centre, University Plain, Univ. of East Anglia, Norwich NOR 88C.

Freeman, Edward, MA, BLitt; Lecturer, Department of French, University of Bristol, since 1970; *b* 1939; *m* 1962; two *d*. BA Oxon 1963 (Mod. Langs), MA Oxon 1968, BLitt Oxon 1968. Asst Lectr, Westfield Coll., Univ. of London, 1965–66; Lectr, Univ. of Ibadan, Nigeria, 1966–69; Temp. Lectr, Univ. of Bristol, 1969–70. *Publications*: The Theatre of Albert Camus – a Critical Study, 1971; *contrib*. Forum Mod. Lang. Studies, Mod. Lang. Qly, Sympos. *Address*: Dept of French, Univ. of Bristol, Bristol BS8 1TH.

Freeman, John Charles, BA, LLM; JP; Lecturer in Laws, Faculty of Laws, King's College, University of London, since 1966; *b* 1932; LLB Tasmania 1956, BA Tasmania 1957, LLM London 1962; Barrister and solicitor, Tasmania, 1956, Aust. Capital Territory, 1972; Barrister Inner Temple, 1963. Mem., Inner London Juvenile Courts Panel, 1972– . Assoc. Brit. Psych. Soc., 1963; Founder Mem., Aust. Psych. Soc. Head, Dept of Legal and General Studies, E London Coll., 1965–66. Chm., Assoc. of Law Teachers, 1970–71; Mem., Commn Scientifique of Soc. Internat. de Criminologie; Hon. Treas., Brit. Soc. of Criminology; Mem. Educn Cttee, Inst. for Study and Treatment of Delinquency. *Publications*: *contrib*. Jl of the Assoc. of Law Teachers, BJ Crim. *Address*: Faculty of Laws, King's College London, Strand, WC2R 2LS.

Freeman, Michael David Alan, LLM; Lecturer in English Law, University College London, since 1969; *b* 1943; *m* 1967; one *s* one *d*. LLB London 1965, LLM London 1966; Barrister, Gray's Inn, 1969. Lectr, Univ. of Leeds, 1966–69. *Publications*: The Legal Structure, 1974; *contrib*. Current Legal Problems, Family Law, Mod. Law

Rev. *Address*: Univ. College London, Gower Street, WC1E 6BT.

Freeman, Dr Michael John, Lecturer in French, University of Leicester, since 1968; *b* 1942; *m* 1966. BA Hons Leeds 1964 (French), PhD Leeds 1971. Lectr, Univ. of Lisbon, Portugal, 1964–66. *Publications*: Œuvres de Guillaume Coquillart: critical edition, 1974; *contrib*. Bibliothèque d'Humanisme et Renaissance. *Address*: Dept of French, Univ. of Leicester, Leicester LE1 7RH.

Freeman, Prof. Thomas Walter; Professor of Geography, University of Manchester, since 1974; *b* 1908; *m* 1941; two *s* one *d*. BA Leeds 1930 (1st cl. Geography), DipEd Leeds 1931, MA Leeds 1932, MA Dublin 1938; FRGS; Mem., Inst. Brit. Geogs, Hon. Mem., Geog. Soc. Ireland, Mem., Authors' Soc. Asst in Geography, Edinburgh Univ., 1933–36; Lectr, Dublin Univ., 1936–44, Reader 1944–49; Reader in Geography, Manchester Univ., 1949–74; Vis. Prof., Univ. of Rhode Island, 1967; Ed., Irish Geog., 1945–50; Pres., Geog. Soc., Ireland, 1945–48. Geographer, Naval Intell. Div., 1941–44; Chm. of Govs, Altrincham Girls' Gr. Sch., 1957–68; Sec., Commn on Hist. of Geogl Thought, Internat. Geogl Union, 1969– ; Mem., Council, Hakluyt Soc., 1970. *Publications*: Ireland, a general and regional geography, 1950, 4th edn 1969, Russian edn 1950; Pre-Famine Ireland, 1957; Geography and Planning, 1958, 4th edn 1974; The Conurbations of Great Britain, 1959, 2nd edn 1966; A Hundred Years of Geography, 1961; revised 1965, 1971; (with H. B. Rodgers) Lancashire, Cheshire and the Isle of Man, 1966; The Geographer's Craft, 1967; Geography and Regional Administration, 1968; The Writing of Geography, 1971; *contrib*. Geog. Jl, Irish Geog. *Address*: Dept of Geography, Univ. of Manchester, Manchester M13 9PL.

French, Dr Richard Antony; Senior Lecturer, Dept of Geography, University College London and School of Slavonic and East European Studies, since 1972; *b* 1929; *m* 1956; two *s* two *d*. BA Liverpool 1950 (1st cl. Geography), MA London 1953, PhD London 1968; FRGS; Mem., Inst. Brit. Geogrs, NASEES. Lectr, Univ. Coll., London, 1956–63; Lectr, UCL and Sch. of Slavonic and E Europ. Studies, 1963–72; Vis. Prof., Univ. of Wisconsin, Milwaukee, 1971. *Publications*: The USSR and Eastern Europe, 1965; *contrib*. Agric. Hist. Rev., Econ. Geog., Geog. Jl, Jl Byeloruss. Studies, Trans Inst. Brit. Geogrs. *Address*: Dept of Geography, Univ. College London, Gower Street, WC1E 6BT.

French, Dr Roger Kenneth; Lecturer in History and Philosophy of Science, Department of History and Philosophy of Science, Aberdeen University, since 1968; *b* 1938; *m* 1966; one *s* two *d*. BA Oxon 1961 (Zoology), MA Oxon 1964, DPhil Oxon 1965; Res. Fellow in Hist. of Science, Leicester Univ., 1965–66; Lectr, 1967–68. *Publications*: Robert Whytt, the soul and medicine, 1969; A History of Anatomy (forthcoming); The Establishment of Medicine at a Scottish

237

University (forthcoming); *contrib.* Clio Med., Med. Hist. *Address:* Dept of History and Philosophy of Science, King's College, Old Aberdeen.

Frend, Prof. William Hugh Clifford, TD (Clasp), DD, FSA; Professor of Ecclesiastical History, Glasgow University, since 1969, and Dean of Divinity, 1972–74; *b* 1916; *m* 1951; one *s* one *d.* BA Oxon 1937 (1st cl. Hons Mod. Hist.), Craven Fellowship 1937–40, DPhil Oxon 1940, BD Cantab 1964, DD Oxon 1966; FSA 1952, FRHistS 1954. Res. Fellow, Nottingham Univ., 1951; SA Cook Bye-Fellow, 1952, Fellow, 1956–69, Dir Studies, Archaeol., 1961–69, Gonville and Caius Coll., Cambridge; Univ. Asst Lectr, 1953, Lectr in Divinity, 1958–69, Univ. of Cambridge; Birkbeck Lectr in Ecclesiastical Hist., 1967–68; Guest Prof., and Peter Ainslie Mem. Lectr, Rhodes Univ., 1964; Licensed Lay Reader, 1956. Mem., Edit. Bd, German Foreign Min. Documents, 1947–51; Editor, Mod. Churchman, 1963. *Publications:* The Donatist Church, 1952; Martyrdom and Persecution in the Early Church, 1965; The Early Church, 1965; The Rise of the Monophysite Movement, 1972; contrib. The Layman in Christian History, 1963; contrib. Religion in the Middle East, 1968; *contrib.* Jl Theol Studies, Jl Roman Studies, Jl Eccles. Hist., etc. *Address:* Univ. of Glasgow, Glasgow G12 8QQ.

Frendo, Dr Joseph David; Lecturer in Ancient Classics, University College, Cork, since 1969; *b* 1937; *m* 1966; two *d.* BA London 1963 (1st cl. Classics), PhD London 1968; Lectr in Classics, Royal Univ. of Malta, 1965–69. *Publications:* trans. Agathias: The Histories (Engl. trans. based on Greek text of Rudolf Keydell's edition of 1967) (forthcoming). *Address:* Dept of Ancient Classics, Univ. College, Cork, Eire.

Frere, Prof. Sheppard Sunderland, MA, FBA, FSA; Professor of the Archaeology of the Roman Empire, Institute of Archaeology, University of Oxford, since 1966; *b* 1916; *m* 1961; one *s* one *d.* BA Cantab 1938 (1st cl. Classics), MA Cantab 1944; FBA, FSA. Lectr in Archaeol., Manchester, 1954–55; Reader in the Archaeol. of the Roman Provinces, London, 1955–61; Prof., 1961–66. Mem.: Royal Commn Hist. Monum. (England), 1966; Mem., Anc. Monum. Bd (England), 1966; Ed., Britannia, 1970. *Publications:* Problems of the Iron Age in Southern Britain, 1961; Britannia: a history of Roman Britain, 1967; Verulamium Excavations, vol. i, 1972; *contrib.* Antiqu. Jl, Archaeol. Jl, Britannia. *Address:* All Souls College, Oxford.

Freyne, John, BSc(Econ); Director of General Studies, since 1965, and Chairman of School of Humanities and Social Sciences, Surrey University, since 1972; *b* 1922; *m* 1952; one *s* three *d.* BSc(Econ) London 1951; Lectr, Sen. Lectr, and Principal Lectr, Battersea Coll. of Technology, 1957–62; Head of Humanities and Social Sciences Dept, Surrey, 1962–72. Dep. Educn Off., IMechE, 1951–54; Educn and Personnel Off., GEC, 1954–57; Mem., Sch. Council

(Home Economics), 1971. *Address:* School of Humanities and Social Sciences, Surrey Univ., Guildford GU2 5XH.

Friel, Joseph; Assistant Lecturer, Private Law Department, Glasgow University, since 1956; *b* 1932; *m* 1954; two *s.* BL Glasgow 1952; Notary Public, FIArb. *Address:* Dept of Private Law, Glasgow Univ., Glasgow G12 8QQ.

Frood, Andrew McKie, MA; Senior Lecturer in Geography, University of Reading, since 1962; *b* 1912; *m* 1942; three *s* one *d.* BA Liverpool 1933 (1st cl. Geography), DipEd Liverpool 1934, MA Liverpool 1937; FRGS; Mem. Geog. Assoc., Mem. Inst. Brit. Geogrs. Teaching Schol., Birmingham Univ., 1935–37; Lectr, Cairo Univ., 1937–39; Lectr, Reading Univ., 1945–62. Army, 1940–45. Mem. Governors, Reading Sch., 1969–72. *Publications:* contrib. Liverpool Essays in Geography: a jubilee collection, 1967; *contrib.* Adv. Sci., Chambers's Encyc., Geog. *Address:* Dept of Geography, Univ. of Reading, Whiteknights, Reading, Berks RG6 2AH.

Frost, Dr David Leonard, MA, PhD; Fellow and Director of Studies in English, St John's College, Cambridge University, since 1966, and University Assistant Lecturer in English, University of Cambridge, since 1969; *b* 1939. BA Cantab 1961, MA Cantab 1965, PhD Cantab 1965. Asst Lectr in English, Univ. Coll., Cardiff, 1965–66. Mem., C of E Liturg. Commn, 1969– . *Publications:* The School of Shakespeare, 1968; Twenty Five Psalms from a Modern Liturgical Psalter, 1973; The Language of Series 3, 1973; *contrib.* Shakespeare Qly, Theol. *Address:* St John's College, Cambridge.

Frowen, Stephen Francis, BSc(Econ); Lecturer in Economics, Department of Economics, University of Surrey, since 1966; *b* 1923; *m* 1949; one *s* one *d.* BSc(Econ) Bonn 1948; Vis. Lectr, Birmingham Univ., 1962–63. Jt Ed., Surrey Papers in Econ., 1967– . Asst Ed., Bank. Mag., 1954–55, Ed., 1956–60; Econ. Adv., Indust. and Comm. Fin. Corp. Ltd, 1959–60; Res. Off., Nat. Inst. Econ. Soc. Res., 1960–62; Lectr, Thames Poly. (formerly Woolwich Poly.), 1962–63, Sen. Lectr, 1963–66; Ed., Woolwich Econ. Papers, 1963–67. *Publications:* trans., K. Wicksell: Value, Capital and Rent, 1954; W. A. Jöhr and H. W. Singer: The Role of the Economist as Official Adviser, 1955; co-ed., Enzyklopädisches Lexikon für das Geld-, Bank- und Börsenwesen, 1957; (with H. C. Hillmann) Economic Issues, 1957; trans., in German, L. von Mises: Die Wurzeln des Antikapitalismus, 1958; *contrib.* Kred. Kap, Zeits. Gesam. Kred. *Address:* Dept of Economics, Univ. of Surrey, Guildford, Surrey GU2 5XH.

Froy, Prof. Martin; Professor of Fine Art, University of Reading, since 1972; *b* 1926; DFA London 1951; Gregory Fellow in Painting, Univ. of Leeds, 1951–54; Leverhulme Res. Award: Six months study in Italy, 1963; Arts Council Sabbatical Award,

1965. Mem., National Council for Diplomas in Art and Design: Fine Art Panel 1962–71; Council 1969–71; Trustee, National Gallery, 1972– . One-man Exhibitions: Hanover Gallery, 1952, 1969; University of Leeds, 1952, 1953; Wakefield City Art Gallery, 1953; Belgrade Theatre, Coventry, 1958; Leicester Galleries, London, 1961; RWEA, Bristol, 1964; Arts Centre, University of Sussex, 1968; Park Square Gallery, Leeds, 1970; Arnolfini Gallery, Bristol, 1970. contrib. to other Exhibitions. Commissions: Artist Consultant for the Arts Council to the City Architect, Coventry, 1953–58; Mosaic decoration at the Belgrade Theatre, Coventry, 1957–58; Two mural panels in the Concert Hall, Morley College, London, 1958–59. Works in Public Collections: Tate Gallery; Museum of Modern Art, NY; Chicago Art Institute; Arts Council; Contemporary Art Society; RWEA; Leeds University; City Art Galleries of Carlisle, Leeds, Southampton and Wakefield. *Address*: Dept of Fine Art, Univ. of Reading, London Road, Reading RG1 5AQ.

Fry, Prof. Dennis Butler, PhD; Professor of Experimental Phonetics, University College London, since 1958; *b* 1907; *m* 1937; one *s* two *d*. BA London 1929, PhD London 1947; FRSA 1970, Fellow Acoust. Soc. Amer., 1966, Hon. Fellow, Coll. Speech Therapists, 1964. Asst Lectr, Univ. Coll., London, 1934–37; Lectr, 1937–48; Reader in Experimental Phonetics, 1948–58; Hd of Dept of Phonetics, UCL, 1949–71; Ed., Lang. Speech, 1958– . Pres., Perm. Internat. Council Phonetic Sciences, 1961– ; Gov., Brit. Inst. Recorded Sound, 1955–70, 1971– ; Sadler's Wells Foundn, 1967. *Publications*: (with D. Kostić) Serbo-Croat Phonetic Reader, 1939; (with E. Whetnall) The Deaf Child, 1964, rev. edn 1971; (with E. Whetnall) Learning to Hear, 1970; *contrib*. Jl Acoust. Soc. Amer., Jl Laryngol. Otol., Lancet, Lang. Speech. *Address*: Dept of Phonetics and Linguistics, Univ. College London, WC1E 6BT.

Fry, Dr Geoffrey Kingdon; Lecturer in Politics, University of Leeds, since 1966; *b* 1937; *m* 1969; one *d*. BScEcon London 1962 (II i), PhD London 1967; Mem., Public Admin Cttee, Jt Univs Council for Social and Public Admin. *Publications*: Statesmen in Disguise, 1969; *contrib*. Parly Affairs, Political Studies, Political Qly, Public Admin, Public Admin (Aust.), Public Law. *Address*: Dept of Politics, The Univ., Leeds LS2 9JT.

Fryer, Alan, BA; Lecturer in Italian Language and Literature, University of Leeds, since 1967; *b* 1942; *m* 1964; one *s* one *d*. BA Leeds 1964 (1st cl. Italian); Mem., Soc. Ital. Studies. Asst Lectr, Leeds Univ., 1964–67. Examr in Italian, Oxford Local Examns, 1964– , JMB 1971– . *Publications*: Degree Course Guide, Italian, 1971, rev. edn 1973; *contrib*. ABELL, Internat. Med. Bibliog., Italian Studies, Times Lit. Supp., THES, Yrs Wk Mod. Lang. Studies. *Address*: Dept of Italian, Univ. of Leeds, Leeds LS2 9JT.

Fryer, Prof. Walter Ronald; Professor of Modern History, University of Nottingham, since 1966; Dean of Arts Faculty since 1973; *b* 1917; *m* 1945; one *d*. BA Oxon 1938 (1st cl. History), BLitt 1940, MA 1942; FRHistS 1964. Asst Lectr, Univ. of Nottingham, 1947–49; Lectr, 1949–60; Sen. Lectr, 1960–66. *Publications*: Republic or Restoration in France 1794–97?, 1965; *contrib*. Renaiss. Mod. Studies, Studies Burke and His Times. *Address*: Dept of History, The Univ. of Nottingham, Nottingham NG7 2RD.

Fudge, Prof. Erik Charles, PhD; Professor of Linguistics, University of Hull, since 1974; *b* 1933; *m* 1959; one *s* two *d*. BA Cantab 1955, MA Cantab 1959; PhD Cantab 1968; Assoc. Dir, Lingu. Res. Project, Indiana Univ., 1964; Lectr, Univ. of Edinburgh, 1965–68; Lectr, Univ. of Cambridge, 1968–74. *Publications*: ed, Penguin Readings in Modern Linguistics: Phonology, 1973; *contrib*. Jl Lingu., Lingua, Scott., Jl Theol. *Address*: The Univ., Hull HU6 7RX.

Fulcher, David James; Lecturer in Sociology, University of Leicester, since 1969; *b* 1942; *m* 1965; one *s*. BA Contab 1964 (Hist.), MSc (Econ.) LSE 1966 (Sociol.). Univ. of Leicester: Tutorial Asst., 1966–67; Asst Lectr, 1967–69. *Publications*: *contrib*. Brit. Jl Ind. Relns, Sociol. *Address*: Sociology Dept, Univ. of Leicester, Leicester LE1 7RH.

Fulcher, Margaret Norah; Lecturer, Department of Town and Regional Planning, Sheffield University, since 1968. BA Cantab 1959, MA, DipTP Regent Street Polytech. 1964. Lectr, Univ. of Lancaster, 1965–68. *Address*: Dept Town and Regional Planning, Univ. of Sheffield. Sheffield S10 2TT.

Fuller, John Leopold; Fellow and Tutor in English Literature, and Senior Dean of Arts, Magdalen College, Oxford University, since 1966; *b* 1937; *m* 1960; three *d*. BA Oxon 1960, MA Oxon 1964, BLitt Oxon 1965; Vis. Lectr, State Univ. of NY, Buffalo, 1962–63; Asst Lectr, Manchester Univ., 1963–66. *Publications*: Fairground Music, 1961; The Tree that Walked, 1967; A Reader's Guide to W. H. Auden, 1970; Cannibals and Missionaries, 1972; The Sonnet, 1972; Penguin Modern Poets 22, 1973; Epistles to Several Persons, 1973; *contrib*. Rev. Engl. Studies, Times Lit. Supp. *Address*: Magdalen College, Oxford.

Fuller, Dr Raymond Guy Cyril; Lecturer, Department of Psychology, Trinity College Dublin, since 1972; *b* 1943; *m* 1966; two *s*. MA St Andrews 1965; PhD Dundee 1970; Mem., PsSI. TCD: Jun. Res. Lectr, 1968; Jun. Lectr, 1971. Mem. Council, Inst. of Psychol., 1971–74. *Publications*: *contrib*. Irish Jl Psychol., Psychol Reports. *Address*: Dept of Psychology, Trinity Coll., Dublin 2.

Fullerton, Brian, MA; Senior Lecturer, Department of Geography, University of Newcastle upon Tyne, since 1970; *b* 1928; *m* 1956; one *s* one *d*. BA London 1948 (1st cl. Geography), MA London 1951; FRGS. Asst in Geography, Glasgow Univ., 1951–54; Lectr in Geography, Newcastle Univ.,

1954–70; Vis. Prof., Alberta Univ., Edmonton, 1963. *Publications*: (with J. W. House) Tees-side at mid-century – an industrial and economic survey, 1960; (with A. F. Williams) Scandinavia, 1972; *contrib*. Trans Inst. Brit. Geogrs, Tijds. Econ. Soc. Geog. *Address*: Dept of Geography, Univ. of Newcastle, Newcastle upon Tyne NE1 7RU.

Funnell, Prof. Brian Michael; Professor, since 1968, Dean, 1971–74, School of Environmental Sciences, University of East Anglia; *b* 1933; *m* 1957; one *s* two *d*. MA Cantab 1955 (Geology), PhD Cantab 1961; Member: Geol Soc. London; Geologists' Assoc.; Palaeontol Assoc.; Instn of Environmental Sciences. Res. Fellow, Trinity Coll., Cambridge, 1959–63; Harkness Fellow, Scripps Inst. of Oceanography, Calif., 1961–62; Univ. Demonstrator, Dept Geol., Cambridge, 1963–66; Univ. Lectr, Dept Geol., Cambridge, 1966–68. *Publications*: ed (with others), The Micropalaeontology of Oceans, 1971; *contrib*. Deep-Sea Res., Geol Magazine, Marine Geol., Palaeontol., Qly Jl of Geol. *Address*: Sch. of Environmental Sciences, Univ. of East Anglia, Norwich NOR 88C.

Funnell, Dr Victor Cecil; Lecturer in Politics, University of Hull, since 1971; *b* 1926; *m* 1964; two *s*. MA Cantab 1952; PhD London 1968. Flinders Univ., Adelaide, Australia, 1966–70. BBC Chinese Section, 1962–64; FO Res. Dept, 1964–66. *Publications*: *contrib* China Qly, Problems of Communism, Austr. Outlook, Studies in Comp. Communism, Community Develt Jl, World Today, Annual of Power and Conflict, Current Scene. *Address*: Dept of Politics, Univ. of Hull, HU6 7RX.

Furbank, Philip Nicholas; Lecturer, Faculty of Arts, The Open University, since 1972; *b* 1920. MA Cantab 1947. Fellow, Emmanuel Coll., Cambridge, 1947–53; Fellow, King's Coll., Cambridge, 1970–72. *Publications*: Samuel Butler: 1835–1902, 1948; Italo Svevo: The Man and the Writer, 1966; Reflections on the Word 'Image', 1970; *contrib*. Essays in Criticism, Critical Qly, Kenyon Review, Encounter. *Address*: Faculty of Arts, The Open Univ., Walton Hall, Milton Keynes MK7 6AA.

Fürer-Haimendorf, Prof. Christoph von; Professor of Asian Anthropology, School of Oriental and African Studies, University of London, since 1951; Dean of SOAS since 1970; *b* 1909; *m* 1938; one *s*. DPhil Vienna 1931; Corresp. mem., Austrian Acad. Science, Vice-Pres., Royal Anthropol. Inst., Royal Geogr. Soc. Asst Lectr, Univ. of Vienna, 1932–35; Lectr, Univ. of Vienna, 1936–39; Prof., Osmania Univ., 1945–49; Reader, SOAS, Univ. of London, 1949–50; Vis. Prof., Colégio de México, 1964, 1966; Asst Polit. Off., Govt of India, 1944–45; Adv., Hyderabad State Govt, 1945–49. *Publications*: The Naked Nagas, 1939, 3rd edn 1962; The Chenchus, 1943; The Reddis of the Bison Hills, 1945; The Raj Gonds of Adilabad, 1948; Himalayan Barbary, 1955; The Apa Tanis and their Neighbours, 1962; The Sherpas of Nepal, 1964; ed, Caste and Kin in Nepal, India and Ceylon, 1966; Morals and Merit, 1967; The Konyak Nagas, 1969; *contrib*. Anthrops, Bull. SOAS, Indian Soc., Jl Royal Anthropol Inst., Jl Royal Asiatic Soc., Geog. Soc., Anthropos, Man in India. *Address*: School of Oriental and African Studies, Univ. of London, Malet Street, WC1E 7HP.

Furley, Dr Peter Anthony; Lecturer in Biogeography, University of Edinburgh, since 1962; *b* 1935; *m* 1963; one *s* two *d*. MA Oxon, DPhil Oxon. Mem. Inst. Brit. Geographers, Mem. Brit. Soc. for Soil Science. Tutor, Oxford, 1961–62. *Publications*: ed, British Honduras: Yucatan (monograph of sci. expedn), 1968; ed, Central America (monograph of sci. expedn), 1972; Geography of Belize, 1974; The Nature and Distribution of Soils, Plants and Animals (forthcoming); *contrib*. Geogr. Jl, Jl Biogeog., Jl Soil Sci., Jl Trop. Geogr, Scottish Geogr. Mag., Trans Brit. Geogrs, Zeitschrift für Geomorphologie. *Address*: Physical Geography Laboratory, High School Yards, Edinburgh.

Furlong, Prof. Edmund James Joseph, MA, FTCD; Professor of Moral Philosophy, Department of Philosophy, University of Dublin, since 1949; *b* 1913; *m* 1944; two *s* three *d*. BA Dublin 1935 (1st cl. Mathematics, 1st cl. Mental and Moral Science), Testimonium in Divinity 1937 (1st cl.), MA Dublin 1938; MRIA 1958. Mem., Irish Philos. Club (Southern Sec., 1948–73). Fellow, TCD, 1947– ; Tutor, 1947–55; Study-year, Oriel Coll., Oxford, 1937–38; Ext. Examiner in Philos., Wales, Sheffield, New Univ. of Ulster, Nat. Univ. of Ireland, Queen's Univ., Belfast, 1961–73. Operational Res., RAF HQ, FC, 1942–43, seconded Admirality, 1943; HQ, AEAF, 1944; Ed., Hermathena (a Dublin Univ. Rev., founded 1873), 1963– . *Publications*: A Study in Memory, 1951; Imagination, 1961; *contrib*. Austral. Jl Philos. Psychol., Encyclop. Philos., Hermathena, Mind, Philos. Qly, Philos., Proc. Aristot. Soc., Internat. Cong. Philos., Royal Irish Acad. *Address*: Dept of Philosophy, Trinity College, Dublin 2.

Furlong, John Daniel George; Lecturer (Statistician), Physical Education Department, University of Birmingham, since 1966; *b* 1928; *m* 1958; one *s* one *d*. BSc London 1965 (Maths and Physics); FSS 1966, MIS 1969. *Address*: Physical Education Department, The Univ. of Birmingham, Birmingham B15 2TT.

Furmston, Michael Philip, TD; Fellow and Tutor in Jurisprudence, Lincoln College, Oxford, since 1964, and University Lecturer (CUF) in Law, since 1965; also Lecturer in Common Law, Council of Legal Education, since 1965; *b* 1933; *m* 1964; four *d*. BA Oxon 1956 (1st cl. Jurisprudence), BCL Oxon 1957 (1st cl.), MA Oxon 1960, LLM Birmingham 1962; Of Gray's Inn, Barrister-at-Law (1st cl. Bar Exam 1960, Cert. of Hon.). Lectr in English Law, Univ. of Birmingham, 1957–62; Lectr in Law, Queen's Univ., Belfast, 1962–63. Asst Dean, Fac. of Law, Queen's Univ., Belfast, 1963; Sen. Dean and Pro Proctor,

Lincoln Coll., Oxford, 1967–68; Sen. Tutor and Tutor for Admissions, Lincoln Coll., Oxford, 1969– ; Sec., Sen. Tutors' Cttee, 1972– ; Dep. Chm. Mngmnt Cttee, Oxford Colleges Admissions Office, 1973– ; Mem., Central Council, UCCA, 1970– . *Publications*: Chapter on Commercial Law, in, Annual Survey of Commonwealth Law 1965–70, 1972; ed (with G. C. Cheshire and C. H. S. Fifoot), Cheshire and Fifoot: Law of Contract, 8th edn 1972; *contrib*. Mod. Law Rev., Univ. Toronto Law Jl. *Address*: Lincoln College, Oxford.

Furneaux, Prof. Walter Desmond Charles, BSc, FBPsS; Professor of Education and Director of Further Education Group, Department of Education, Brunel University, since 1966; *b* 1919; *m* 1945. BSc London 1947 (Hons Psychology); Dip. Psychol. Hypnos. 1960; FRSM 1963, FBPsS. Nuffield Res. Fellow, 1948–56, Sen. Res. Fellow, 1956–63, Inst. of Psychiatry, Univ. of London. Experl. Officer, Watson Electromedical, Wembley, 1944–48; Dir, Res. and Stat. Gp, ILEA, 1963–66; Mem., Socio-Educnl Res. Cttee, Univ. of Sussex, 1962–65; Chm., SRHE Working Party on Univ. Teaching Methods, 1966–72; Mem., Gov. Council, Soc. for Res. in Higher Educn, 1967–73; Consultant on Medical Educn, WHO, 1968– ; Mem. CNAA Educn Panel, 1973– ; Chm., Regional Adv. Cttee (Educn), London and Home Counties, 1973– . *Publications*: Nufferno tests of problem solving abilities, 1955; The Chosen Few: a study of selection, 1961; (jtly) New Junior Maudsley Personality Inventory, 1961; chapters in: Experimental Hypnosis, 1952; Handbook of Abnormal Psychology, 1960; The Nature of Hypnosis, 1961; Yearbook of Education, 1962; Chambers Encyclopaedia, 1962; Structure of World Hypnosis, 1963; *contrib*. Brit. Jl Educn. Psychol., Int. Jl Clinic and Exper. Hypnosis., Jl Exper. Psychol., Jl Gen. Psychol., Jl Personality, Proc. RSM, Sociological Rev., Univ. Qly. *Address*: Dept of Education, Brunel Univ., Kingston Lane, Uxbridge UB8 3TH.

Furness, Prof. Nicholas Arthur; Professor of German, University of Edinburgh, since 1969; *b* 1923; *m* 1951; one *s* three *d*. BA Durham 1950 (King's Coll., Newcastle upon Tyne), Drphil Innsbruck 1952. Temporary Lectr, King's Coll., Newcastle, 1952–53; Asst Lectr, Univ. of Manchester, 1953–54; Lectr, Univ. of Edinburgh, 1954–62; Sen. Lectr, 1962–69. *Address*: Dept of German, Univ. of Edinburgh, David Hume Tower, George Square, Edinburgh EH8 9JX.

Furness, Dr Raymond Stephen; Lecturer, Department of German, University of Manchester, since 1962; *b* 1933; *m* 1965; one *s* one *d*. BA Wales 1955 (Swansea), MA Wales 1960 (Swansea), PhD Manchester 1963. Asst. Lectr, UMIST, 1959–62. *Publications*: Expressionism, 1973; *contrib*. German Life and Letters Mod. Lang. Rev. *Address*: Dept of German, Univ. of Manchester, Oxford Road, Manchester M13 9PL

G

Gabas, J.-J.; Lecturer in French, University College, Cardiff, since 1965; *b* 1937. LèsL Paris 1960, DES Paris 1961; MA Wales 1973. *Address*: Dept of French, Univ. Coll., Cardiff CF1 1XL.

Gabbey, William Alan; Lecturer, Department of History and Philosophy of Science, Queen's University, Belfast, since 1968; *b* 1938. BSc Belfast 1960, PhD Belfast 1964; Mem., Brit. Soc. Hist. Science. Asst Lectr, Queen's Univ., Belfast, 1965–68. *Publications*: *contrib*. Studies Hist. Philos. Sci., Rev. d'Histoire des Sciences. *Address*: Dept of History and Philosophy of Science, Queen's Univ., Belfast BT7 1NN.

Gable, Dr Anthony Terence; Lecturer in French, Queen Mary College, London University, since 1971; *b* 1944. BA Cantab 1965 (1st cl. Mod. Langs), MA Cantab 1968, PhD Cantab 1971. Lectr, Sch. of European Studies, East Anglia, 1968–71. *Publications*: *contrib*. Jl European Studies, French Studies. *Address*: French Dept, Queen Mary College, Mile End Road, E1 4NS.

Gadney, Reg; Tutor, Department of General Studies, Royal College of Art, since 1969; *b* 1941; *m* 1966; one *s* one *d*. Josephine de Kármán Scholarship, MA Cantab 1969. Research Fellow and Instructor, Sch. of Architecture and Planning, MIT, 1966–67. Lion and Unicorn Press, RCA, 1972. Dep. Controller, Nat. Film Theatre, 1968–69. *Publications*: Drawn Blanc, 1970; Somewhere in England, 1971; Seduction of a Tall Man, 1972; Something Worth Fighting For, 1974; The Hours Before Dawn (forthcoming); *contrib*. Leonardo, London Mag. *Address*: Dept of Gen. Studies, Royal College of Art, Kensington Gore, SW7 2EU.

Gadoffre, Prof. Gilbert, DèsL, PhD; Professor of Modern French Literature, University of Manchester, since 1966; *b* 1911; *m* 1953. LèsL and DES Sorbonne 1933 (1st), PhD Manchester 1958, DèsL Sorbonne 1968. Mem.: Société européenne de la Culture; Soc. for French Studies. Asst Lectr in French, Manchester Univ., 1938–39; Lectr in History of French Thought, 1954–63; Prof. of French Literature, Univ. of California, Berkeley, 1964–66. Directeur de l'Information, French Zone of Austria, 1945–47; Directeur, Centre culturel international de Royaumont, 1947–54; Mem. Foundator, Round Table Confs, Institut collégial européen, 1950. *Publications*: Introduction historique au discours de la Méthode, 1941, 5th edn 1965; Style du XXe siècle, 1945; Ronsard, 1960, 12th edn 1972; Claudel et l'Univers chinois, 1968; critical edn of Claudel's *Connaissance de l'Est*, 1973; Du Bellay (forthcoming); *contrib*. Annales d'histoire économique et Sociale, Mercure de France, French Studies, Esprit, Revue d'histoire de la philosophie et de la civilisation. *Address*: Dept of French, The Univ., Manchester M13 9PL.

Gage, Dr John Stephen, BA, PhD; Lecturer in Art History, University of East Anglia, since 1969; *b* 1938. BA Oxon 1960 (3rd cl. Modern History), PhD London 1968 (Art History). Teaching Fellow, Univ. of E. Anglia, 1966–67, Asst Lectr, 1967–69; Vis. Lectr, Yale Univ., 1970–71. *Publications*: Life in Italy at the Time of the Medici, 1968; Colour in Turner, Poetry and Truth, 1969; Turner: Rain, Steam and Speed, 1972; *contrib*. Anglia, Apollo, Art Qly. Burl. Mag., Coloquio Artes, Enc. Universalis, Jl Eur. Studies, Jl Royal Soc. Arts, Jl Warb. Court. Inst. *Address*: School of Fine Arts and Music, Univ. of East Anglia, Norwich NOR 88C.

Gaines, Dr Fergus John; College Lecturer in Mathematics, University College, Dublin, since 1970; *b* 1939; *m* 1964; four *s* one *d*. BSc UCD 1960, MSc UCD 1961 (1st cl. Maths), PhD Caltech 1966; Mem., London Math. Soc. 1968. Asst, UCD, 1961–62; Teaching Asst, Caltech, 1962–66; Asst Lectr, UCD, 1966–70. Mem., Arts Fac., UCD, 1971– . *Publications*: *contrib*. Amer. Math. Mly, Duke Jl, Lin. Alg. App. *Address*: Mathematics Dept, Univ. College, Dublin 4.

Galbraith, Katherine J.; Lecturer, History of Art Department, Birkbeck College, University of London, since 1968; *b* 1937. BA Columbia 1960, MA London 1962; FSA. *Address*: History of Art Dept, Birkbeck College, Malet Street, WC1E 7HX.

Gale, Maurice Anthony; Senior Lecturer in Psychology in Department of Applied Psychology, UWIST, Cardiff, since 1973; *b* 1937; *m* 1961; one *s* one *d*. BA Exeter 1963 (Philosophy and Psychology), DipEd Swansea 1964; ABPsS. Res. Asst, Exeter, 1964–65, Lectr, 1965–71; Lectr, Swansea, 1971–73. Assoc. Ed., Jl Biol. Psychol, 1972– . *Publications*: *contrib*. Psychophysiol., Brit. Jl Psychol., Qly Jl Exptl Psychol., Jl Biol Psychol. *Address*: Dept of Applied Psychology, UWIST, Lewyn-y-Grant, Cardiff CF3 7UX.

Gallagher, Prof. John Andrew; *b* 1919. MA Cantab. Fellow of Trinity Coll., Cambridge, 1948–63 (Dean of Coll., 1960–63, Sen. Res. Fellow, 1971–72); Univ. Lectr in History, Cambridge, 1953–63; Beit Prof. of History of British Commonwealth, Oxford, and Fellow of Balliol Coll., 1963–70; Harmsworth Prof. of Imperial and Naval History, Univ. of Cambridge, 1971–72; Ford Lectr in English History, Oxford Univ., 1973–74; Rockefeller Foundn Fellow, 1957. *Publications*: (with R. E. Robinson) Africa and the Victorians, 1961; chaps in New Cambridge Modern History, vols VII and XI; *conbrib*. learned jls. *Address*: Trinity College, Cambridge.

Gallie, Roger Douglas; Lecturer in Philosophy, Department of Philosophy, University of Leicester, since 1969; *b* 1942; *m* 1972; one *d*. MA Aberdeen 1964 (Upper 2nd cl. Hons in Mental Philos.), MLitt Cantab 1971; Mem. Aristotelian Soc. Asst

Lectr in Philos., Leicester, 1966. *Publications*: *contrib*. Analysis, Mind. *Address*: Philosophy Dept, The Univ., Leicester LE1 7RH.

Gallie, Prof. Walter Bryce; Professor of Political Science, and Fellow of Peterhouse, Cambridge University, since 1967; *b* 1912; *m* 1940; one *s* one *d*. BA Oxon 1934 (1st cl. PPE), BLitt Oxon 1937, MA Oxon 1947. Asst Lectr in Philosophy, 1935–38, Lectr, 1938–48, Sen. Lectr, 1948–50, UC of Swansea; Prof. of Philosophy, UC of N Staffs, 1950–54; Prof. of Logic and Metaphysics, QUB, 1954–67; Vis. Prof., New York Univ., 1962–63; Lewis Fry Meml Lectr, Bristol Univ., 1964. Croix de Guerre, 1945. *Publications*: An English School, 1945; Peirce and Pragmatism, 1952; Free Will and Determinism Yet Again (Inaugural Lecture), 1957; A New University: A. D. Lindsay and the Keele Experiment, 1960; Philosophy and the Historical Understanding, 1964; *contrib*. Mind, Aristotelian Soc. Proc., Philosophy, French Studies. *Address*: Peterhouse, Cambridge.

Galloway, Rev. Prof. Allan Douglas, MA, BD, STM, PhD; Professor of Divinity, University of Glasgow, since 1968, and Principal of Trinity College, Glasgow, since 1972; *b* 1920; *m* 1948; two *s*. MA Glasgow 1942 (1st cl. Philosophy), BD Glasgow 1945 (Distinction), STM Union Theol. Sem. NY 1947, PhD Cantab 1948; Ordained minister, Ch of Scotland. Prof. of Religious Studies, Univ. Coll., Ibadan, Nigeria, 1954–60; Sen. Lectr in Principles of Religion, Univ. of Glasgow, 1960–64, Sen. Lectr in Divinity, 1964–66, Reader in Divinity, 1966–68. Ordained Asst minister, Port Glasgow, 1948–50; Minister of Auchterhouse, 1950–54. *Publications*: The Cosmic Christ, 1951; Basic Readings in Theology, 1964; Faith in a Changing Culture, 1966; Wolfhart Pannenberg, 1973; *contrib*. Expos. Times, Relig. Studies, Scott, Jl Theol. *Address*: Dept of Divinity, The Univ., Glasgow G12 8QQ.

Gamberini, Spartaco, DottLing; Reader in Italian, University College Cardiff, since 1972; *b* 1920; *m* 1955; two *s*. DottLing Genova 1950 (110 con lode). Asst Vol. in English, Genova, 1950–55; Lectr, Cardiff, 1965–68, Sen. Lectr, 1968–72. *Publications*: La poesia di T. S. Eliot, 1954; Poeti metafisici e cavalieri in Inghilterra, 1959; Orientaciones actuales de la literatura inglesa, 1961; Saggio su John Donne, 1967; Lo studio dell'italiano in Inghilterra nel '500 e nel '600, 1970; Il ragazzo guarda il mondo, gramm. trasf. della lingua italiana, 1971; *contrib*. Belfagor, Ital. Studies, Yrs Wk Mod. Lang. Studies. *Address*: Dept of Italian, Univ. College, Cardiff CF1 1XL.

Gambling, Prof. Trevor Ellison; Professor of Accounting, University of Birmingham, since 1969; *b* 1929; *m* 1960; two *d*. BCom Dunelm 1950, PhD Birmingham 1969; FCA 1964 (ACA 1953). Lectr, Birmingham, 1961–69; Vis. Associate Prof., Berkeley, California, 1966–67; Vis. Prof., Univ. of Illinois, Urbana-Champaign, 1972. *Publications*: A One-Year Accounting Course, 1969;

Modern Accounting: accounting as the Information System of Technological Change (forthcoming); Societal Accounting (forthcoming); *contrib.* Abacus, Accounting Rev., Jl of Accounting Res. *Address*: Dept. of Accounting, Faculty of Commercial and Social Science, Univ. of Birmingham, PO Box 363, Birmingham B15 2TT.

Gandy, Dr Robin Oliver; Reader in Mathematical Logic, University of Oxford, since 1969; *b* 1919. BA Cantab 1941, MA Cantab 1946, PhD Cantab 1952; Grad., Inst. Elec. Eng 1946. Mem.: Assoc. Symbol. Logic, Lond. Math. Soc. Asst Lectr in Applied Maths, Leicester, 1950–53, Lectr, 1950–56; Lectr in Applied Maths, Leeds, 1956–61; Sen. Lectr in Math. Logic, Manchester, 1961–63, Reader, 1963–67, Prof., 1967–69; Vis. Associate Prof., Stanford, 1966–67, UCLA, 1968; Fellow, Wolfson Coll., 1970. RA 1940–43, REME 1943–46 (Capt. 1945); Mem.: Council. Assoc. Symbol. Logic, 1967–70; Omega Gp, Heidelberg Univ., 1969– . *Publications*: ed (with C. E. M. Yates), Logic Colloquium, 1969, 1971; *contrib.* Bull. Pol. Acad. Sci., Jl Assoc. Symbol. Logic. *Address*: Mathematical Institute, St Giles, Oxford.

Ganz, Joan Safran, BA, MA, PhD; Lecturer, Social Science and Humanities, The City University, since 1967; *b* 1937; one *d.* BA Cornell 1961, MA Pennsylvania 1962, PhD Pennsylvania 1967. Fellow, Univ. of Pennsylvania, 1962–66; Instructor, Temple Univ., 1966–67. *Publications*: Rules: a systematic study, 1971; *contrib.* Brit. Jl Phil. Sci. *Address*: Dept. of Social Science and Humanities, The City Univ., St John Street, EC1V 4PB.

Ganz, Prof. Peter Felix, MA, PhD; Professor of German Language and Literature, University of Oxford, and Fellow of St Edmund Hall, since 1972; *b* 1920; *m* 1949; two *s* two *d.* MA London 1950, PhD London 1954, MA Oxon 1960. Asst Lectr, Royal Holloway Coll., Univ. of London, 1948–49; Lectr, Westfield Coll., Univ. of London, 1949–60; Reader in German, Oxford, 1960–72; Vis. Prof., Univ. of Erlangen-Nürnberg, 1964–65, 1971; Vis. Prof., Univ. of Munich, 1970. Fellow, Hertford Coll., Oxford, 1963–72. *Publications*: Der Einfluss des Englischen auf den deutschen Wortschatz 1740–1815, 1957; Geistliche Dichtung des 12 Jahrhunderts, 1960; Graf Rudolf, 1964; (with F. Norman and W. Schwarz) Dukus Horant, 1964; (with W. Schröder) Probleme mittelalterlicher Überlieferung und Textkritik, 1967; ed, Discontinuous Tradition: studies in German Literature in honour of Ernest Ludwig Stahl, 1970; co-ed, German Life and Letters; *contrib.* periodicals. *Address*: 74 High Street, Oxford.

Garbutt, Douglas; Senior Lecturer, School of Management, Cranfield Institute of Technology, since 1966; *b* 1922; *m* 1947, 1973; one *s* one *d.* London Univ. Teachers Cert. 1952 (Distinction), London Univ. Acad. DipEd 1965, MEd Leics 1970; ACIS 1947, ACMA 1956, FCMA 1974. Visiting Professor: Southern Illinois Univ., 1968–69; Georgia State Univ., 1971, 1973. Member: Educn Cttee, ICMA, 1967–69 (Chm., Editorial Bd, 1973– ; Mem., Res. Cttee); East Anglia Further Educn Adv. Bd Sub-Cttee on Management Studies. *Publications*: Carter's Advanced Accounts, 5th edn 1962, 7th edn (repr.) 1973; (with E. F. Castle) Principles of Accounts, 1963, 1972; Planning for Profits, 1967; Simple Guide to Capital Expenditure Decisions, 1967; Training Costs, 1969; *contrib.* Accountant, Accountancy, Accountants' Mag. Business Systems, Business Systems and Equipment, Chem. and Ind., Commercial Accountant, Cost Accountant, Indian Admin. and Management Rev., Ind. Trng Internat., Jl Bus. Educn (USA), Jl Bus. Finance, Jl Savings Bank Inst., Management Accounting, Management Educn and Develt, Management Today, Personnel Mag., Prodn Engineer, Soc. of Management Inf. Technol., Socio-econ. Planning Science, Vocational Aspect. *Address*: Cranfield School of Management, Cranfield, Bedford MK43 0AL.

Garcia, Angel Maria; Lecturer, Department of Spanish and Latin American Studies, University College, London, since 1967; *b* 1932; *m* 1964; two *d.* LicFil Madrid 1956 (1st cl. Hons), BD Heythrop Coll. (now of London Univ.) 1961 (1st cl. Hons), BA King's Coll., London 1966 (1st cl. Hons); FIL (by invitation), 1973. Mem.: Bd of Studies in Romance Languages and Literatures, London Univ., 1967; Bd of Examiners in Modern Iberian and Latin American Regional Studies, London Univ., 1967; Spanish Subject Sub-Cttee, 1967. *Publications*: El fondo conceptual en el proceso de conversión de Segismundo, in, Hacia Calderón (ed W. de Gruyter) (forthcoming). *Address*: Univ. College, Gower Street, WC1E 6BT.

Garcia-Lora, Joseph, MA; Senior Lecturer in Spanish-American Studies, Department of Spanish, University of Birmingham, since 1966; *b* 1920; *m* 1949; two *d.* BA Birmingham 1940 (English, History, Spanish), MA Birmingham 1946; Mem., Soc. Latin Amer. Studies. Lectr in Spanish, Univ. of Liverpool, 1946–48; Lectr in Spanish, Univ. of Birmingham, 1948–66. Vis. Prof., UCLA, USA, 1967–68; Ext. Examiner, Cambridge Univ. Spanish Tripos, 1950–52; Reviser of Spanish Texts, UNESCO Gen. Conf., New Delhi, 1956. *Publications*: Tierra Cantiva: A play in three acts, 1962; La deidad tras la Fabula: Ensoyos solore dos literaturas, 1965; La caja del repocijo: A play in three acts, in, La palabra y el hombre, 1966; contrib. F. R. Ramón: Historia del teatro español, siglo XX, 1971; *contrib.* Insula, Papeles Son Armadans, Bol. Inst. Esp., Palabra y Hombre. *Address*: Univ. of Birmingham, Spanish Dept, PO Box 363, Edgbaston, Birmingham B15 2TT.

Gard, Dr Andrew Roger, MA, PhD; Lecturer in English, Queen Mary College, University of London, since 1965; *b* 1936; *m* 1964; one *s* one *d.* BA Cantab 1959 (1st cl. English), MA Cantab 1963, PhD Cantab

1965. Asst Lectr, Queen Mary Coll., London, 1962–65; Dir of Studies in English, Corpus Christi Coll., Cambridge, 1969–70. *Publications*: Henry James: The Critical Heritage, 1968; (with S. Bolt) Teaching Fiction in Schools, 1970; *contrib*. Delta Ess Crit., Melbourne Crit. Rev. *Address*: Dept of English, Queen Mary College, Mile End Road, E1 4NS.

Garden, Dr Edward, DMus, FRCO; Senior Lecturer in Music, and Organist to the University of Glasgow, since 1966; *b* 1930; *m* 1961; one *s* one *d*. BMus London 1957, DMus Edinburgh 1969; LRAM 1952, ARCM 1953, FRCO 1956. Dir, Glasgow Univ. Chapel Choir (has recorded). *Publications*: Balakirev: a critical study of his life and music, 1967; Tchaikovsky, 1973; various short musical compositions, including carol, Fairer than the sun at morning, 1963; *contrib*. Music Lett., Proc. Royal Music. Assoc. *Address*: Dept of Music, Univ. of Glasgow, 14 University Gardens, Glasgow.

Gardiner, Patrick Lancaster; Fellow and Tutor in Philosophy, Magdalen College, Oxford University, since 1958; *b* 1922; *m* 1955; two *d*. BA Oxon (1st cl. History 1942, 1st cl. Philosophy, Politics and Economics 1947), MA Oxon 1949. Lectr, Wadham Coll., Oxford, 1949–52; Fellow, St Antony's Coll., Oxford, 1953–58; Vis. Prof., Columbia Univ., NY, 1955. *Publications*: The Nature of Historical Explanation, 1952, pbk edn 1967, Mexican edn 1961; Schopenhauer, 1963, 2nd edn 1971; ed, Theories of History, 1959, 8th repr. 1967, Portuguese edn 1969, 2nd Portuguese edn forthcoming; ed, Nineteenth Century Philosophy, 1969; *contrib*. Hist. Theory, Proc. Aristot. Soc., Proc. Brit. Acad., Philos. Qly, Philos., etc. *Address*: Magdalen College, Oxford.

Gardiner, Dr Sunray C.; Lecturer, Department of Russian Studies, University of Manchester, since 1965; *b* 1927. Special Hons Degree Leeds 1953 (German), Hons Degree London 1956 (1st cl. Russian), MA London 1958 (Russian), PhD London 1965 (Russian). Asst Lectr in Modern Languages, UMIST, 1962–65. *Publications*: German Loanwords in Russian, 1550–1690, 1965; *contrib*. Slav. E Europ. Rev., Wiener Slav. Jahrb., Zeits. Slav. Philol. *Address*: Dept of Russian Studies, The Univ., Manchester M13 9PL.

Gardner, Dame Helen (Louise), DBE, DLitt, FBA; Merton Professor of English Literature, Oxford University, and Fellow of Lady Margaret Hall, Oxford, since 1966; *b* 1908. BA Oxon 1929 (1st cl. English), MA Oxon 1935, DLitt Oxon 1963, Hon. DLitt Durham 1960, East Anglia 1967, Birmingham 1969, Harvard 1971; Hon. DLitt London 1968; Hon. LLD Aberdeen 1967; Hon. DHL Yale 1972; FBA, FRSL. Temp. Asst Lectr, Birmingham, 1930–31; Asst Lectr, Royal Holloway Coll., 1931–34; Lectr, Birmingham, 1934–41; Fellow and Tutor, St Hilda's Coll., Oxford, 1941–54; Vis. Prof., UCLA, 1954; Reader in Renaissance English Literature, Oxford, 1954–66. Dele-

gate, Oxford Univ. Press, 1958– ; Mem.: Robbins Cttee Higher Educn, 1961–63; Council Nat. Acad. Awards, 1964–67; Trustee, Nat. Portrait Gall., 1968– . *Publications*: The Art of T. S. Eliot, 1949; ed, The Divine Poems of John Donne, 1952, 4th corrected imp. 1966; The Metaphysical Poets, anthology, 1957, 3rd edn 1972; The Business of Criticism, 1959; ed, John Donne: Elegies and Songs and Sonnets, 1965; A Reading of Paradise Lost, 1965; Religion and Literature, 1970; The Faber Book of Relitious Verse, 1972; The New Oxford Book of English Verse, 1972. *Address*: Lady Margaret Hall, Oxford.

Gardner, Prof. Julian Richard; Professor of the History of Art, University of Warwick, since 1974; *b* 1940; *m* 1973. BA Oxon 1962 (Mod. Hist.), DipHist. Art 1964 (dist.), MA Oxon 1965, PhD London 1969. Lectr, Courtauld Inst. of Art, 1966–74. Mem. Faculty, British Sch. at Rome, 1973– . *Publications*: *contrib*. Burlington Mag., Papers of Brit. Sch. Rome, Zeitschrift für Kunstgeschichte. *Address*: Dept of Art History, Univ. of Warwick, Coventry, Warwicks CV4 7AL.

Gardner, William Russell Williamson, MA, PhD; Senior Lecturer, Department of German, University of Glasgow, since 1967; *b* 1924; *m* 1962; two *s*. MA Glasgow 1948 (1st cl. French and German), PhD Glasgow 1956. Asst, Univ. of Glasgow, 1950–52; pt-time teaching, Bedford Coll., Westfield Coll., London, 1952–54; Lectr, Univ. of Glasgow, 1954–67; Asst Adv. of Studies, 1964–69; Chm. Cttee, Scottish-German Soc., 1961–69. *Publications*: *contrib*. Yrs Wk Mod. Lang. Studies. *Address*: Dept of German, Univ. of Glasgow, Glasgow G12 8QQ.

Garforth, Francis William; Senior Lecturer, Department of Educational Studies, University of Hull, since 1966; *b* 1917; *m* 1946; three *s* one *d*. MA Cantab 1938 (Classics), BA London 1956 (Philosophy). Lectr in Educn, Univ. of Hull, 1949–66; *Publications*: Education and Social Purpose, 1962; ed, J. Locke: Some Thoughts concerning Education, 1964, 2nd edn 1969; ed, J. Locke: Of the Conduct of the Understanding, 1966; ed, J. Dewey: selected educational writings, 1966; ed, Bede: Historia Ecclesiastica, a selection, 1967; ed, Aspects of Education: Education for the Seventies, 1969; ed, J. S. Mill on Education, 1971; The Scope of Philosophy, 1971. *Address*: Dept of Educational Studies, 173 Cottingham Road, Hull HU5 2EH.

Garland, Dr Mary, BA, PhD; Senior Lecturer in German, University of Exeter, since 1950; *b* 1922; *m* 1949; two *d*. BA London 1950 (1st cl. German), PhD Exeter 1968. *Publications*: ed, Hebbel: Agnes Bernauer, 1953; Friedrich Hebbel, in, German Men of Letters, 1961; ed, BA Examination Papers for Translation, 1962; Kleist's Prinz Friedrich von Homburg, 1969; Hebbel's Prose Tragedies, 1973; (with H. B. Garland) The Oxford Companion to German

Literature (forthcoming). *Address*: Dept of German, Univ. of Exeter, Exeter EX4 4QJ.

Garlick, Dr Kenneth John; Keeper of Western Art, The Ashmolean Museum, Oxford University, since 1968; *b* 1916. BA Oxon 1938, MA 1943, granted graduate status, London 1946; PhD Birmingham 1961; FMA; FSA. Lectr, Barber Inst. of Fine Arts, Univ. of Birmingham, 1949–62; Sen. Lectr, 1962–68, Professorial Fellow, Balliol Coll., 1968– . *Publications*: Sir Thomas Lawrence, 1954; Catalogue Raisonné of the Paintings, Drawings and Pastels of Sir Thomas Lawrence (Walpole Soc., vol. XXXIX), 1964; *contrib.* Apollo, Burl. Mag. *Address*: The Ashmolean Museum, Oxford.

Garner, John Clifford; Director, Department of Fine Arts and Complementary Studies, University of Salford, since 1972; *b* 1915; *m* 1939; one *s* one *d*. BA Manchester 1935, DipEd 1936; ALAM 1965. (Mem., Drama Bd). Lectr, 1967–69, Sen. Lectr 1969–72, Dept of Fine Arts and Complementary Studies, Univ. of Salford. Mem. Council, NWAA. *Address*: Dept of Fine Arts and Complementary Studies, Univ. of Salford, Salford M5 4WT.

Garner, Prof. John Francis; Professor of Public Law, University of Nottingham, since 1964; *b* 1914; *m* 1939; one *s* one *d*. LLB London 1936 (1st cl.), LLM London 1938, LLD London 1965; Solicitor 1940; Mem., Selden Soc., Council, Justice. Pt-time Asst Lectr, Southampton Univ., 1958–60; Sen. Lectr, Birmingham Univ., 1960–64; Vis. Prof., Oklahoma, 1971. Dep. Town Clerk, Barnstaple, 1946–48; Dep. Clerk of Council, Bognor Regis, 1948–50; Town Clerk, Andover, 1950–60. *Publications*: Local Land Charges, 1949, 6th edn 1971; Law of Sewers and Drains, 1950, 4th edn 1969; Law of Public Cleansing, 1952, 2nd edn 1965; Civic Ceremonial, 1953, 2nd edn 1957; Law of Allotments, 1953, 2nd edn 1963; Road Charges, 1955, 4th edn 1974; Clean Air, Law and Practice, 1957, 3rd edn (with R. K. Crow) 1969; Administrative Law, 1963, 4th edn 1974; (with L. N. Brown) French Administrative Law, 1967, 2nd edn 1973; *contrib.* Convey. and Property Lawyer, Mod. Law Rev., Public Law, Toronto Law Jl. *Address*: Dept of Law, The Univ., Nottingham NG7 2RD.

Garnett, John C.; Senior Lecturer in Strategic Studies, University College of Wales, Aberystwyth, since 1970; *b* 1936; *m* 1961; one *s* one *d*. BSc(Econ) 1961 (1st cl.), MSc (Econ) 1962; Mem., Inst. Strategic Studies. Lectr, Dept. of Internat. Politics, Univ. Coll. of Wales, 1962–70. *Publications*: Theories of Peace and Security, 1930; *contrib.* Internat. Aff., Internat. Relat., Jl Royal United Services Inst. *Address*: Dept of International Politics, Univ. College of Wales, Aberystwyth SY23 2AX.

Garrety, Michael Joseph; Lecturer in English Studies, Division of Languages, Brunel University, since 1966; *b* 1927; *m* 1954; two *s* one *d*. BA Nottingham 1951 (English Studies). *Address:* Division of Languages, Brunel Univ., Uxbridge UB8 3TH.

Garside, Donald; Warden, Holly Royde College, University of Manchester, since 1948, and Senior Staff Tutor, Department of Extra-Mural Studies, Manchester, since 1965; *b* 1911; *m* 1939; one *s* one *d*. BA Manchester 1934 (Hons Geography), Univ. Teachers Dipl. Manchester 1935; Mem.: Geographical Assoc.; Nat. Inst. of Adult Educn; Nat. Trust; CPRE. Staff Tutor, Dept of Extra-Mural Studies, Univ. of Manchester, 1945. Mem.: Central Training Council in Child Care, Home Office, 1958–64; Council, Nat. Inst. of Adult Educn, 1960–66. *Publications*: *contrib.* Studies in Adult Educn. *Address*: Holly Royde College, 56-64 Palatine Road, Manchester M20 9JP.

Garside, Kenneth; Director of Central Library Services and Goldsmiths' Librarian, University of London, since 1974; *b* 1913; *m* 1951; one *s*. BA Leeds 1935, DipEd Leeds 1936, MA Leeds 1937. Asst Librarian, Univ. of Leeds, 1937–45; Dep. Librarian, University College London, 1945–58; Librarian, King's College London, 1958–74. War service, 1941–46; CO (Lt-Col), Univ. of London OTC, 1958–63; Chm., ABTAPL, 1961–66; Hon. Sec., COMEC, 1966– ; Sec., Univ. Librs Sub-Sect. IFLA, 1967–73; Univ of London Cttee on Libr. Resources, 1969–71; CNAA Librarianship Bd, 1971– . *Publications*: *contrib.* Jl Documentation, Libr. Assoc. Record, Libri, Zs f. Bibliothekswesen u. Bibliographie. *Address*: University of London Library, Senate House, Malet Street, WC1E 7HU.

Garside, Dr Roger Forbes, BSc, PhD, FBPsS; Senior Lecturer in Applied Psychology, University of Newcastle upon Tyne, since 1958; *b* 1917; *m* 1940; one *s* one *d*. BSc London 1938 (Special Psychology), PhD Newcastle 1969; FBPsS 1966. Admin. Staff, London Univ., 1938–39; Lectr in Applied Psychology, Newcastle upon Tyne, 1949–58; Warden, Garnett Hse, Newcastle upon Tyne, 1964. Army, 1939–46; Res. Psychol., Rowntree & Co. Ltd, York, 1946–49. *Publications*: *contrib.* Brit. Jl Psychiat., Brit. Med. Jl, Psychol. Med., Psychomet. *Address*: Dept of Psychological Medicine, Univ. of Newcastle upon Tyne, Newcastle upon Tyne NE1 4LP.

Garside, Dr William Redvers; Lecturer, Department of Economic and Social History, University of Birmingham, since 1972; *b* 1944; *m* 1971. BA Hons Leeds 1965 (Sp. Studies Econs), PhD Leeds 1969; Member: Econ. Hist. Soc. Soc. for Study of Labour Hist. Lectr in Econ. Hist., Univ. of Leicester, 1968–72. *Publication*: The Durham Miners 1919–1960, 1972. *Address*: Dept of Economic and Social History, Univ. of Birmingham, PO Box 363, Birmingham B15 2TT.

Garvie, Alexander Femister, MA; Senior Lecturer in Greek, University of Glasgow, since 1972; *b* 1934; *m* 1966; one *s* one *d*. MA Edinburgh 1955 (1st cl. Classics), BA Cantab 1959 (1st cl. Classical Tripos Pts I and II), MA Cantab 1964. Asst, Glasgow Univ., 1960–61, Lectr, 1961–72; Vis. Gillespie Prof., Coll. of Wooster, Ohio, 1967–68; Vis. Asst Prof., Ohio State Univ. 1968. Treas., Class. Assoc. Scotl., 1966–71; Mem., Council, Hellenic Soc., 1971–74. *Publications*: Aeschylus' Supplices: play and trilogy, 1969; *contrib.* Bull. Inst. Class. Studies, Class. Qly, Class. Rev. *Address*: Dept of Greek, The Univ., Glasgow G12 8QQ.

Garvin, Thomas, MA; Assistant Lecturer in Politics, University College Dublin, since 1967; *b* 1943; *m* 1969. BA UCD 1964 (1st cl. Politics), MA UCD 1966 (1st cl.). Tutor, UCD, 1964–66; Asst Lectr, UCD, 1967–69; Res. Asst/Teaching Asst, Univ. of Georgia, USA, 1969–70. Admin. Offr, Dept of Finance, Irish Republic, 1966–67. *Publications*: The Irish Senate, 1969; *contrib.* Econ. Soc. Rev. *Address*: Dept of Ethics and Politics, Univ. College, Dublin, Belfield, Dublin 4.

Gash, Prof. Norman, FRHistS, FBA, FRSL; Professor of History, St Salvator's College, St Andrews University, since 1955; *b* 1912; *m* 1935; two *d*. BA Oxon 1933 (1st cl. Mod. History), MA Oxon 1938, BLitt Oxon 1934; FRHistS, FBA, FRSL. Temp. Lectr, Edinburgh Univ., 1935–36; Asst Lectr, Univ. Coll., London, 1936–40; Lectr, St Salvator's Coll., St Andrew's, 1946–53; Prof. Mod. Hist., Leeds Univ., 1953–55; Vis. Prof., Johns Hopkins Univ., Baltimore, 1962; Ford Lectr, Oxford, 1964; Vice-Principal, St Andrews Univ., 1967–71. War service, 1940–46; Major GS (War Off.), 1945–46; Pres., St Andrews Br., Hist Assoc., 1955–70; Mem., Council, Royal Hist. Soc., 1961–64. *Publications*: Politics in the Age of Peel, 1953, American edn 1971; Mr Secretary Peel, 1961; Reaction and Reconstruction in English Politics 1832–52 (Ford Lectures), 1965; Age of Peel, 1968; Sir Robert Peel, 1972; *contrib.* EHR, Oxonien, Proc. Leeds Philos. Soc., Trans Royal Hist. Soc. *Address*: St Salvator's College, St Andrews Univ., St. Andrews, Fife.

Gaskell, Dr John Philip Wellesley; Fellow and Librarian, Trinity College, Cambridge, since 1967, Tutor since 1973; *b* 1926; *m* 1948; two *s* one *d*. BA Cambridge 1949 (2nd cl. English), MA Cambridge 1954, PhD Cambridge 1956. Fellow, King's Coll., Cambridge, 1953–61, Dean, 1954–56, Asst Tutor, 1956–58; Lectr in English and Keeper of Special Collections, Univ. of Glasgow, 1962–66. *Publications*: The First Editions of William Mason, 1951; John Baskerville, 1959; The Foulis Press, 1964; Morvern Transformed, 1968; A New Introduction to Bibliography, 1972; *contrib.* Libr., Studies Bibliog., Trans Camb. Bibliog. Soc. *Address*: Trinity College, Cambridge.

Gaskell, Ronald W.; Lecturer in English, University of Bristol, since 1962; *b* 1926; *m* 1964; one *s* one *d*. MA Glasgow 1948 (1st cl. English). Asst Lectr, Bristol Univ., 1959–60, 1961–62; Asst Lectr, Nottingham Univ., 1960–61; Lectr, City Coll., NY, 1965–66. *Publications*: Drama and Reality, 1972; *contrib.* Crit. Qly, Drama Surv., Ess. Crit.,

Mod. Drama. *Address*: Dept of English, Univ. of Bristol, Bristol BS8 1TH.

Gaskin, John Charles Addison; Lecturer in Philosophy, Trinity College Dublin, since 1966; *b* 1936; *m* 1972. BA Oxon 1961, MA Oxon 1963, BLitt Oxon 1965; MA Dublin 1967. Trinity College Dublin: Asst in Philosophy, 1963–65; Jun. Lectr in Philosophy, 1965–66; Asst Jun. Dean, 1969– . *Publications*: Hume's Philosophy of Religion (forthcoming); *contrib.* Hermath. Hibb. Jl, Philos., Relig. Studies, Ratio. *Address*: Trinity College, Dublin 2.

Gaskin, Prof. Maxwell, DFC; Jaffrey Professor and Head of Department of Political Economy, University of Aberdeen, since 1965; *b* 1921; *m* 1952; one *s* three *d*. BA 1949, MA 1955, Liverpool; FREconS, Mem. Scott. Econ. Soc. Asst Lectr, Liverpool Univ., 1950–51; Asst Lectr, Glasgow Univ., 1951–52, Lectr, 1952–61, Sen. Lectr, 1961–65; Vis. Sen. Lectr, Nairobi Univ. Coll., 1964–65. Mem.: Cttee of Inquiry, Bank Interest Rates, NI Govt, 1965–66; Cttee of Inquiry, Trawler Safety, 1968–69; Scottish Agric. Wages Bd, 1972– . Chm., Bd of Mngmnt, Foresterhill and Associated Hosps, 1971–74. *Publications*: The Scottish Banks, 1965; ed (and dir. survey), North East Scotland: A Survey of its Development Potential, 1969; *contrib.* E Afr. Econ. Rev., Econ. Hist. Rev., Oxf. Econ. Papers, Scott. Jl Pol. Econ. *Address*: Dept of Political Economy, Univ. of Aberdeen, Study Block, King's College, Aberdeen AB9 2UB.

Gathercole, Peter William, MA; Curator, University Museum of Archaeology and Ethnology, Cambridge, since 1970; *b* 1929; *m* 1951, 1972; three *s* one *d*. BA Cantab 1952 (History Tripos, Pt I, 2:1 Archaeol. and Anthrop. Tripos, Pt II, 2:1), MA Cantab 1964; Post-Grad. Dip. European Archaeology London 1954; Dip. Mus. Assoc., 1958; AMA; Hon. Mem., NZ Archaeological Assoc. Lectr, 1958–62; Sen. Lectr, 1962–68; Associate Prof., Otago Univ., 1968; Lectr, Oxford Univ., 1968–70; Supernumerary Fellow, Worcester Coll., Oxford, 1969–70. Trainee Asst, Birmingham Museum, 1954–56; Curator, Scunthorpe Museum, 1956–58; Keeper in Anthropology, Otago Museum, 1958–62; Sec., NZ Archaeological Assoc., 1960–62 (Vice-Pres., 1967–68); Mem., Council RAI, 1970– . *Publications*: (with M. A. Cotton) Excavations at Clausentum, Southampton, 1951–54, 1958; ed jtly, Comparatively Speaking (Papers by H. D. Skinner), 1974; *contrib.* Antiquity, Jl Polynes. Soc., NZ Archaeol. Assoc. Newsletter, Trans Birmingham Archaeol. Soc., Trans Leics Archaeol. and Hist. Soc., Trans Thoroton Soc., World Archaeology. *Address*: University Museum of Archaeology and Ethnology, Downing Street, Cambridge CB2 3DZ.

Gatrell, Dr Valentine Arthur Charles, Assistant Lecturer in British Social and Economic History, Faculty of History, University of Cambridge, since 1973; Fellow and College Lecturer, Gonville and Caius College, since 1971; *b* 1941; *m* 1970; one *s*. BA Hons Rhodes 1962 (1st cl.), BA 1964 (1st cl.), MA 1967, PhD 1971, Cantab. Res. Fellow, Gonville and Caius Coll., Cambridge, 1967; Sec., Colls' Jt Entrance Exam. (Gp I), 1973. *Publications*: Robert Owen: A New View of Society, 1970; (with T. B. Hadden) Nineteenth Century Criminal Statistics and their Interpretation, in, Nineteenth Century Society, ed E. A. Wrigley, 1972; Commercial Men and Lancashire Cotton: society and politics in Manchester, 1800–57 (forthcoming). *Address*: Gonville and Caius Coll., Cambridge.

Gatt-Rutter, John, BA; Lecturer in Italian, University of Hull, since 1964; *b* 1941; *m* 1971. BA Cantab 1962 (2nd cl. Mod. Langs – Italian and Russian), CCK Czech. Asst Lectr, Univ. Coll. of Wales (Aberystwyth), 1963–64. *Publications*: Literature and Politics: Italy since the War (forthcoming); Senilita and the Unsaid, in Essays on Italo Svevo, ed T. F. Staley, 1969; Non-commitment in Italo Svevo, in Jl Eur. Studies, 1973; contrib. Italian entries, in Cassell's Encyclopaedia of World Literature, 1973. *Address*: Dept of Italian, Univ. of Hull, Hull HU6 7RX.

Gauld, Alan Ogilvie; Lecturer, Department of Psychology, University of Nottingham, since 1962; *b* 1932; *m* 1966; two *s*. BA Cantab 1956, MA Cantab 1958, PhD Cantab 1962. King George VI Memorial Fellowship, Harvard Univ., 1956–57; Res. Fellow, Emmanuel Coll., Cambridge, 1958–62. Mem., Council, Soc. Psychical Res., 1961– . *Publications*: The Founders of Psychical Research, 1968; *contrib*. Amer. Psychol., Brit. Jl Philos. Sci., Brit. Jl Psychol., Proc. Soc. Psychical Res. *Address*: Dept of Psychology, Univ. of Nottingham, Nottingham NG7 2RD.

Gaunt, David Martin, MBE, MA; Senior Lecturer in Classics, University of Bristol, since 1970; *b* 1918; *m* 1945; one *d*. BA Cantab 1940, MA Cantab 1945. Classics Master: Fettes Coll., 1945–46; Clifton Coll., 1946–65; Lectr in Classics, Univ. of Bristol, 1965–70. Foreign Off., 1940–45; Mem., Council, Clifton Coll., 1970– ; Vice-Chm., Western Coll. Trust, 1970– . *Publications*: Selections from Quintilian, 1952; Epic Poetry, in Comparative Studies in Greek and Latin Literature, ed J. Higginbotham, 1969– ; Surge and Thunder, 1971; *contrib*. Class. Rev., Greece and Rome. *Address*: Dept of Classics, Wills Memorial Building, Queen's Road, Bristol BS8 1RJ.

Gavin, Dr Evelyn Edith; Senior Lecturer in Law, University of Strathclyde, since 1970; *m* 1963. MA Aberdeen 1953 (Hons Psychology), LLB St Andrews 1956 (distinction), PhD Strathclyde 1969. Lectr, Law Sch., Strathclyde, 1964–70; Adviser of Studies, Sch. of Business and Admin, Strathclyde Univ., 1969– . *Address*: Law School, Univ. of Strathclyde, Glasgow G1 1XW.

Geach, Gertrude Elizabeth Margaret; *see* Anscombe, G. E. M.

Geach, Prof. Peter Thomas, FBA; Professor of Logic, University of Leeds, since 1966; *b* 1916; *m* 1941; three *s* four *d*. BA

Oxon 1938, MA Oxon 1949, MA Cantab (by incorporation) 1971; FBA 1965. Univ. of Birmingham: Asst Lectr in Philosophy, 1951; Lectr, 1952–59; Sen. Lectr, 1959–61; Reader in Logic, 1961–66; Stanton Lectr in the Philosophy of Religion, Cambridge, 1971– . *Publications*: Mental Acts, 1957; Reference and Generality, 1962; (with G. E. M. Anscombe) Three Philosophers, 1961; God and the Soul, 1969; Logic Matters, 1972; *contrib*. Mind, Philos. Rev., Analysis, Ratio. *Address*: Dept of Philosophy, The Univ., Leeds LS2 9JT.

Gearin-Tosh, Michael; Official Fellow and Tutor of St Catherine's College and University Lecturer in English, University of Oxford, since 1971; *b* 1940. BA Oxon 1961, MA Oxon. Lectr, Magdalen Coll., Oxford, 1963; Ford Foundn Fellow, St Catherine's Coll., 1965. Sec. to Gov. Body, St Catherine's Coll., 1973. *Publications*: *contrib*. Studia Neophilologica, Essays in Criticism, Notes and Queries. *Address*: St Catherine's College, Oxford.

Geddes, James Clarke; Director of Adult Education and Extra-Mural Studies, University of St Andrews, since 1967; *b* 1922; *m* 1955; two *s* two *d*. MA Aberdeen 1958, MA Aberdeen 1960 (1st cl. Hons English–History DipEd Aberdeen 1961; Cert. Secondary Educn 1961; Member: Scottish Council for Adult Educn, 1969– ; Univs Council for Adult Educn, 1967– . Sec., Univ. St Andrews Consultative Cttee for Adult Educn, 1968– . *Address*: Dept of Adult Education and Extra-Mural Studies, Univ. of St Andrews, 3 St Mary's Place, St Andrews KY16 9UZ.

Gedye, Ione; Head of Conservation of Antiquities Department, Institute of Archaeology, University of London, since 1964 (i/c Conservation Department, since 1937); *b* 1907. BA University Coll., London, 1930 (Classical Archaeology); Fellow, Internat. Inst. for Conservation of Historic and Artistic Works, 1952. Sec. UK Gp, Internat. Inst. for Conservation, 1958. *Publication*: Conservation of Pottery and Glass, in, The Conservation of Cultural Property, 1968 (UNESCO). *Address*: Institute of Archaeology, Univ. of London, 31–34 Gordon Square, WC1H 0PY.

Gee, Dr Kenneth Philip; Senior Lecturer, Department of Accounting and Finance, University of Lancaster, since 1974; *b* 1946; *m* 1971; one *d*. BSc Bristol 1968 (Econs and Accounting), PhD Manchester 1971. Lectr in Management Sciences, UMIST, 1972–74. *Publications*:(with R. Beresford Dew) Management Control and Information, 1973; *contrib*. Acctng and Business Res., Jl Business Fin., Mngmt Acctng, Mngmt Decision, Mngmt Educn and Develt, Mngmt Internat. Rev. *Address*: Dept of Accounting and Finance, Furness College, Univ. of Lancaster, Bailrigg, Lancaster.

Gelling, Peter Stanley, MA, FSA; Reader in Ancient History and Archaeology, Birmingham University, since 1971; *b* 1925; *m* 1952. BA Cantab 1947, MA Cantab 1950, Dip. Classical Archaeology 1948, Dip. Aramaic pt I 1949; FSA. Lectr, Birmingham Univ., 1953–66, Sen. Lectr, 1966–71. *Publications*: (with H. E. Davidson) The Chariot of the Sun, 1969; Urartu (trans. of B. B. Piotrovskii: Iskusstvo Urartu), 1967; *contrib*. Mediev. Archaeol., Proc. Prehist. Soc. *Address*: Dept of Ancient History and Archaeology, The Univ., PO Box 363, Birmingham B15 2TT.

Gellner, Prof. Ernest André, FBA; Professor, Sociology Department, London School of Economics, since 1962; *b* 1925; *m* 1954; two *s* two *d*. MA Oxon 1947, PhD London 1961; Mem., Assoc. Social Anthropol., Brit. Sociol. Assoc. Asst, Edinburgh, 1947–49; various grades, LSE, 1949–62. Mem. Editorial on Advisory Bd: Europ. Jl of Sociol., Brit. Jl Sociol., Mid. East. Studies. *Publications*: Words and Things, 1959, 2nd edn 1968; Thought and Change, 1964, 2nd edn 1969; Saints of the Atlas, 1969; ed, Arabs and Berbers, 1973; Cause and Meaning in the Social Sciences, 1973; Contemporary Thought and Politics, 1974. *Address*: London School of Economics, Aldwych, WC2.

Gelston, Rev. Anthony; Lecturer in Theology, University of Durham, since 1962; *b* 1935; *m* 1969. BA Oxon 1957 (2nd cl. Mods. 1955, 1st cl. Hon. Sch. Th. 1957, 2nd cl. Hon Sch. Oriental Studies 1959), MA Oxon 1960; Ordination in C of E (Deacon 1960, Priest 1961); Mem., Soc. OT Study 1960. Hon. Chaplain, Bernard Gilpin Soc., Durham, 1966– . *Publications: contrib*. Sc. Jl Theol., Vetus Testam., Z AW, Oudestamentische Studien. *Address*: Dept of Theology, Abbey House, Palace Green, Durham.

Gennard, John; Lecturer in Industrial Relations, Department of Industrial Relations, London School of Economics and Political Science, since 1970; *b* 1944; *m* 1968; one *s*. BA (Econ) Sheffield 1966, MA (Econ) Manchester 1968. Res. Officer, LSE, 1968–70. *Publications*: Multinational Corporations and British Labour: a review of attitudes and responses, 1972; (with M. D. Steuer) Industrial Relations, Labour Disputes and Labour Utilization in Foreign-Owned Firms in the United Kingdom, in, The Multinational Enterprise, ed J. H. Dunning, 1970; (with B. C. Roberts and R. J. Loveridge) The Reluctant Militants, 1972; The Impact of Foreign-Owned Subsidiaries on Host Country Labour Relations: the case of the United Kingdom, in, Industrial Relations and the Multinational Corporation, ed R. J. Flannagan (forthcoming); *contrib*. Brit. Jl Ind. Relns, Scot. Jl Pol Econ., Ind. Relns Tutor. *Address*: Dept of Industrial Relations, London School of Economics, Houghton Street, Aldwych, WC2A 1AE.

George, Edward F., BLitt, MA; Senior Lecturer in German, University of Edinburgh, since 1968; *b* 1922; *m* 1955. BA/MA Oxon 1949 (2nd cl. German), BLitt Oxon 1954. Lektor, Univ. of Bonn., 1950–51; Lectr, Univ. of Edinburgh, 1951–68. *Publications: contrib*. Forum Mod. Lang. Studies. *Address*: Dept of German, David Hume Tower, George Square, Edinburgh.

George, Prof. Frederick William Arthur, BA, PhD, Chevalier des Palmes Académiques; Professor of French Language and Literature, St David's University College, University of Wales, since 1969; *b* 1920; *m* 1946; one *s* one *d*. BA London 1948 (1st cl. French), PhD London 1951. Tutor, UCL, 1949; Asst Lectr, UCW Aberystwyth, 1950–52; Lectr, UC Swansea, 1952–62, Sen. Lectr, 1962–69; Prof., Univ. of Nigeria, Nsukka, 1966–67. Sub-Dean of Arts, Swansea, 1968–69; Sec. and Vice-Pres., Swansea branch of MLA; Mem., Modern Language Panel of Welsh Jt Educn Cttee. *Publications*: (with R. C. Knight) Advice to Students of French, 1960, 2nd edn 1966; The French Language, in, The Year's Work in Modern Languages, 1958–62; Arts, in, The Penguin Dictionary of European Literature, 1969, *contrib*.YWML. *Address*: Dept of French, St David's Univ. College, Lampeter, Dyfed SA48 7ED.

George, Prof. Kenneth Desmond; Professor of Economics, University College, Cardiff, since 1973; *b* 1937; *m* 1959; two *s* one *d*. BA Wales 1957, MA Wales 1959, MA Cantab 1966. Univ. Lectr, Western Australia, 1959–63; Univ. Coll., N, Wales 1963–64; Res. Officer, Dept Applied Econs, Cambridge, 1964–66; Univ. Asst Lectr, 1966–68; Univ. Lectr, 1968–73. Editor, Jl of Industrial Economics. *Publications*: Productivity in Distribution, 1966; Productivity and Capital Expenditure in Retailing, 1968; Industrial Organisation: Competition, Growth and Structural Change in Britain, 1971, 2nd edn 1974; *contrib*. Australian Econ. Papers, Econ. Jl, Jl Industrial Econs, Oxford Bull., Oxford Econ. Papers, Rev. of Econs and Stats. *Address*: Dept of Economics, Univ. College, Cardiff CF1 1XL.

George, Dr Kenneth Edward Morris, MA, DUP; Lecturer, Department of Language Studies, London School of Economics, since 1966; *b* 1937; *m* 1964; two *s* one *d*. BA Cardiff 1959 (1st cl. French), MA Wales 1961, DU Paris 1965; formerly Fellow, Univ. of Wales; Mem.: Soc. Ling. Rom., Soc. French Studies. Asst Lectr, LSE, 1964–66. *Publications*: contrib. Matériaux pour l'histoire du vocabulaire français, Datations et documents lexicographiques, 2ème série 1, 2, 3 and 4, 1970–72; Les noms du tisserand français (forthcoming); *contrib*. Franç. Mod., Mod. Lang., Rev. Ling. Romane, Romania, Studia Neophilol. *Address*: Dept of Language Studies, London School of Economics, WC2A 2AE.

George, Patrick H.; Senior Lecturer, Slade School of Fine Art, University College, London, since 1967; *b* 1923; *m* 1955; four *d*. Andrew Grant Scholar, Edinburgh Coll. of Art; NDD Camberwell Sch. of Art. Hd of Dept., Ahmadu Bello Univ., Nigeria, 1959–60. Mem., NCDAD resigned 1971. *Address*: Slade School of Fine Art, Univ. College, Gower Street, WC1.

George, Reginald Edmund, BA; Lecturer in Education, and Secretary, Department and Faculty of Education, University College of Swansea, since 1962; *b* 1931; *m* 1955. BA 1953 (1st cl. Latin), BA 1955 (1st cl. Greek),

DipEducn 1954 (1st cl.). *Address*: Dept of Education, Univ. College of Swansea, Hendrefoilan, Swansea SA2 7NB.

George, Prof. Vic; Professor of Social Administration and Social Work, University of Kent, since 1973; *b* 1930; *m* 1956; one *s* one *d*. BA Nottingham 1956 (2nd cl. Social Administration), MA Nottingham 1960 (Social Administration), PhD Nottingham 1970. Sen. Res. Offr, LSE, 1963–64; Lectr in Applied Social Science, Univ. of Nottingham, 1964–72, Sen. Lectr, 1972–73. Admin. Offr, Cyprus Govt, 1957–60; Child Care Offr, LCC, 1960–63. *Publications*: Social Security: Beveridge and After, 1968; Foster Care: Theory and Practice, 1970; (with P. Wilding) Motherless Families, 1972; Social Security and Society, 1973; *contrib*. Soc. Wk, Race, Brit. Sociol. Rev. *Address*: Keynes College, The Univ. of Kent, Canterbury, Kent.

Georgiades, Dr Nicholas J.; Lecturer, Department of Occupational Psychology, Birkbeck College, University of London, since 1968; *b* 1940; *m* 1971; one *s*. BA Reading 1961 (Hons Psychology), MPhil London 1967, PhD London 1972; ABPsS 1968. Res. Officer, Reading Research Unit, Univ. of London, Inst. of Educn, 1962–67. Vis. Prof. Cornell, 1973. Member: Educn and Res. Adv. Team, Jt Bd Clinical and Nursing Studies, 1970– ; Council, British Psychol. Soc., 1970– . *Publications*: ITA in Remedial Reading Classes: an experiment, 1969. *Address*: Dept of Occupational Psychology, Birkbeck College, Malet Street, WC1E 7HX.

Gershevitch, Dr Ilya, FBA; Reader in Iranian Studies, University of Cambridge, since 1965; *b* 1914; *m* 1951; one *d*. DLitt Rome 1937, PhD London 1943, MA Cantab 1948; HonDPhil Berne 1971; FBA 1967, MRAS 1944, Mem., Philol. Soc. GB 1946, Mem., Soc. Asiatique Paris 1959. Lectr, Cambridge, 1948–65; Fellow, Jesus Coll., Cambridge, 1962; Vis. Prof., Columbia Univ., 1960, 1965; Exch. Vis., USSR, 1965; Ratanbai Katrak Lectr, Oxford, 1968. Dialect exploration, Bashakard (Persian Makran), 1956; Mem.: Council, Philol. Soc. GB, 1964–68; Council, Corpus Inscriptionum Iranicarum, 1966– ; Governing 1968– ; Council, Soc. for Afghan Studies, 1972– ; Council, Brit. Inst. Persian Studies; Mem., Editorial Board: Camb. Hist. of Iran, 1970– ; Persian Heritage Series, UNESCO, 1971– . *Publications*: A Grammar of Manichean Sogdian, 1954, 2nd edn 1961; The Avestan Hymn to Mithra, 1959, 2nd edn 1968; *contrib*. AM, BSOAS, CAJ, IF, JAOS, JNES, JRAS, JRCAS, TPS. *Address*: Jesus College, Cambridge.

Giardelli, Vincent Charles Arthur, MBE (1973); MA; Senior Tutor in Art, Department of Extra-Mural Studies, University College of Wales, Aberystwyth, since 1968; *b* 1911; *m* 1937; one *s* one *d*. BA Oxon 1933 (2nd cl. French, Italian, distinc. Colloqu. Fr.), DipEd 1934, MA 1937. Tutor, Extra-Mural Dept, Aberystwyth, 1960–68; Pres., Oxford Univ. Music. Club and Union, 1933; Mem., Art Cttee, Welsh Arts Council, 1965–

72; Chm., Assoc. Tutors Adult Educn, 1964–66, Vice-Chm., 1971–73; Chm., 56 Gp, Wales, 1958–73. *Publications*: Artists in Wales, 1971; *contrib*. Adult Educn, Anglo-Welsh Rev., Agenda, Barn. *Address*: Dept of Extra-Mural Studies, 9 Marine Terrace, Aberystwyth.

Gibb, Andrew; Lecturer, Department of Geography, University of Glasgow, since 1972; *b* 1943; *m* 1964; one *s*. MA Hons Glasgow 1968 (1st cl. Geog./Archaeol.); FSA Scot; Member: Prehistoric Soc. of GB; Royal Scottish Geographical Soc.; Inst. of British Geographers. Asst Lectr, Univ. of Glasgow, 1968–72. *Address*: Dept of Geography, The Univ., Glasgow G12 8QQ.

Gibb, Ian Pashley; Lecturer in Management Studies, School of Librarianship, Archive and Information Studies, University College London, since 1967; *b* 1926; *m* 1953; two *s*. BA London 1950, Acad. Postgrad. Dip. in Librarianship 1952; ALA 1954 (Mem. 1950), Mem., Bibliographical Soc. (Hon., Treas., 1961–67). Sen. Library Asst, Univ. of London Library, 1951–52; Asst Librarian, UCL, 1952–58; Dep. Librarian, Nat. Central Library, 1958–73; Dep. Dir, The British Library, Science Ref. Library, 1973– . *Publications*: contrib. to: The Libraries of London, ed R. Irwin and R. Staveley, 2nd edn 1961; Five Years' Work in Librarianship, 1956–1960, ed (for Library Assoc.) P. H. Sewell, 1963; Five Years' Work in Librarianship, 1961–1965, ed (for Library Assoc.) P. H. Sewell, 1968; *contrib*. Jl of Documentation, Library Assoc. Record. *Address*: Sch. of Librarianship, Archive and Information Studies, Univ. Coll. London, Gower Street, WC1E 6BT.

Gibbens, Prof. Trevor Charles Noel, MBE, MD, MRCP, FRCPsych; Professor of Forensic Psychiatry, London University, since 1967; *b* 1912; *m* 1950; two *s* one *d*. MA Cantab 1938, MB BChir 1939, MD 1947; DPM 1946, MRCP 1966, FRCPsych 1971. Sen. Lectr in Forensic Psychiatry, London Univ., 1951–64, Reader, 1964–67. Mem.: Streatfield Cttee, 1958–60; Adv. Council on Probation and Aftercare, 1958–71; Royal Commn on Penal Reform, 1964–66; Pres., Brit. Acad. Foren. Sci., 1967–68; Pres., Internat. Soc. Criminol., 1967–73. Mem. Parole Bd. *Publications*: Trends in Juvenile Delinquency, 1961; Shoplifting, 1962; Psychiatric Studies of Borstal Lads, 1963; Cultural Factors in Delinquency, 1966; *contrib*. Brit. Jl Criminol., Brit. Jl Psychiat. *Address*: Institute of Psychiatry, de Crespigny Park, SE5 8AF.

Gibbons, Brian Charles; Lecturer, Department of English and Related Literature, University of York, since 1965; *b* 1938; *m* 1966; one *s* one *d*. BA Cantab (1st cl.), MA Cantab 1964, PhD Cantab 1966. *Publications*: ed, Tourneur: The Revenger's Tragedy, 1967; Jacobean City Comedy, 1968; Marlowe's Tragedy of Dido, in, Marlowe, ed B. R. Morris, 1968; ed, Congreve: The Way of the World, 1971. *Address*: Dept of English and Related Literature, Univ. of York, Heslington, York YO1 5DD.

Gibbs, Graham Charles, MA; Reader in Modern History, Department of History, Birkbeck College, University of London, since 1972; *b* 1928; *m* 1961; three *d*. BA Liverpool 1950, MA 1953; FRHistS 1963, Mem., Nederlands Historisch Genootschap, 1968; For. Mem. Provincial Utrechts Genootschap van Kunsten an Weten-schappen, 1973. Birkbeck College: Asst Lectr, 1953–56; Lectr, 1956–72. *Publications*: contribs to collections of essays, festschrift, etc.; *contrib*. Bijdragen en Mededelingen Betreffende de Geschiedenis der Nederlan-den, Eng. Hist. Rev. *Address*: Birkbeck Coll., Univ. of London, Malet Street, WC1E 7HX.

Gibbs, Dr Jack, BLitt, MA, DPhil; Lec-turer, Department of Spanish, University of Birmingham, since 1947; *b* 1917. BA Oxon 1938, BLitt Oxon 1940, MA Oxon 1946, DPhil Oxon 1950; Mem.: Int. Arthurian Soc., Int. Assoc. Hispanists, Soc. Rencesvals. Ch. Examiner, Advanced Spanish, JMB, 1950– . *Publications*: La vida de fray Antonio de Guevara, 1960; ed (with A. Burns), Dos novelas ejemplares de Cervantes, 1971; The Spanish Civil War, 1973; *contrib*. MLR, Proc. Int. Assoc. Hispanists, Proc. Soc. Rencesvals, Yrs Wk Mod. Lang. Studies. *Address*: Dept of Spanish, The Univ. of Birmingham, PO Box 363, Birmingham B15 2TT.

Gibbs, Marion Elizabeth; Lecturer, Depart-ment of German, Royal Holloway College, University of London, since 1967; *b* 1940. BA London 1961 (1st cl.), MA London 1965; Mem., Mod. Humanities Res. Assoc. Asst Lectr, Royal Holloway Coll., 1964–67. *Publications*: Wîplîches Wîbes Reht: A Study of the Women Characters in the Works of Wolfram von Eschenbach, 1972; *contrib*. Germ. Life Lett., Mod. Lang. Rev. *Address*: Dept of German, Royal Holloway College, Egham Hill, Egham, Surrey TW20 0EX.

Gibbs, Prof. Norman Henry, MA, DPhil; Chichele Professor of the History of War, University of Oxford, since 1953; *b* 1910; *m* 1955. MA Oxon 1935, DPhil Oxon 1936. Asst Lectr, UCL, 1934–36; Fellow and Tutor in Modern History, Merton Coll., Oxford, 1936; Research Associate, Center for Internat. Studies, Princeton, 1965–66. Mem., Naval Educn Adv. Cttee; Mem., Internat. Council Inst. Strategic Studies, 1965– . *Publications*: ed, Keith, British Cabinet System, 2nd edn 1952; The Origins of the Committee of Imperial Defence, 1955; ed, The Soviet System and Democratic Society, 1967; contribs to: Cambridge Mod-ern History, new edn; L'Europe du XIXme et du XXme siècles, 1966. *Address*: All Souls College, Oxford.

Gibson, Rev. John Clark Love, MA, BD, DPhil; Reader in Hebrew, University of Edinburgh, since 1973; *b* 1930; *m* 1956; four *s* one *d*. MA Glasgow 1953 (1st cl. Hebrew and Arabic), BD Glasgow 1956 (Distinction, Old Testament), DPhil Oxon 1959; Mem., Assoc. Brit. Ling., Mem., Brit. OT Soc. Minister, New Machar, Aberdeenshire, 1959–62; Lectr in Hebrew, Univ. of Edin-burgh, 1962–73. *Publications*: Textbook of
250

Syrian Semitic Inscriptions, 1971– ; *contrib*. Archiv. Ling., Jl Ling., Jl Near East. Studies, Jl Semit. Studies, Mul. Wld, Scott. Jl Theol. *Address*: Dept of Hebrew, New College, Univ. of Edinburgh.

Gibson, Dr Margaret Templeton, MA, DPhil; Lecturer in Medieval History, University of Liverpool, since 1964; *b* 1938. MA St Andrews 1959, BA Oxon 1961, DPhil Oxon 1968; FRHistS. *Publications*: *contrib*. Jl Theol. Studies. *Address*: School of History, Univ. of Liverpool, Liverpool L69 3BX.

Gibson, Michael A. J.; Lecturer in Economics, University of Leicester, since 1968; *b* 1940; *m* 1962; two *s*. Dip. Pol Econ. and Soc. Studies Nottingham 1962 (external), BA Essex 1967 (Econs). *Publications*: (with M. J. Pullen), Retail Trade Patterns in the East Midlands 1961–1981, 1971; *contrib*. Agenda, Bull. Soc. Co-op. Studies, Co-op. Management and Marketing, Economics, Reg. Studies. *Address*: Dept of Economics, The Univ., Leicester LE1 7RH.

Gibson, Prof. Norman James, BSc(Econ), PhD; Professor of Economics, New Univer-sity of Ulster, since 1967; *b* 1931; *m* 1959; two *s* one *d*. BSc(Econ) Belfast 1953 (1st cl.), PhD Belfast 1959. Asst Lectr, QUB, 1956–59, Lectr, 1959–62; Lectr, Manchester Univ., 1962–66, Sen. Lectr, 1966–67; Vis. Assoc. Prof., Wisconsin Univ. Madison, 1967. Dean, Sch. Soc. Sci., NUI, 1968–71; Mem., Council, Econ. Social Res. Inst., Dublin, 1968– . *Publications*: Monetary, Credit and Fiscal Policies, in, The UK Economy, ed. D. J. Coppock and A. R. Prest, 1966, 5th edn 1974; ed (with H. G. Johnson et al), Readings in British Monetary Econ-omics, 1972; *contrib*. Manch. Sch., Econ. Soc. Studies. *Address*: School of Social Sciences, New Univ. of Ulster, Coleraine, Co. Londonderry BT52 1SA.

Gibson, O. Duncan M.; *see* Macrae-Gibson.

Gibson, Prof. Robert Donald Davidson, BA, PhD; Professor of French, University of Kent at Canterbury, since 1965; *b* 1927; *m* 1953; three *s*. BA London 1948 (1st cl. French), PhD Cantab 1953. Asst Lectr, St Andrews Univ., 1954–55; Lectr, Queen's Coll., Dundee, 1955–58; Lectr, Aberdeen Univ., 1958–61; Prof., Queen's Univ., Belfast, 1961–65. Dep. Master, Rutherford Coll., Univ. of Kent, 1966–71; Sub-Dean, Fac. Humanities, Univ. of Kent, 1967–73. *Publications*: The Quest of Alain Fournier, 1953; Roger Martin du Gard, 1961; Modern French Poets on Poetry, 1961; ed, Le Bestiaire Inattendu, 1961; La Mésentente Cordiale, 1963; ed, Brouart et le Désordre, 1964; ed, Provinciales, 1965; ed, Le Grand Meaulnes, 1968; contrib.: Colliers Encyclop.; Brit.; French Literature and its Background; Penguin Companion to Literature; *contrib*. Austral. Jl Fr. Studies. *Address*: Rutherford College, Univ. of Kent, Canterbury, Kent.

Gibson, Dr Wendy; Lecturer, French Department, Reading University, since 1968; *b* 1944. BA Hons Birmingham 1965 (French), PhD 1972. *Address*: French Dept,

Univ. of Reading, Whiteknights Park, Reading RG6 2AH.

Giedymin, Dr Jerzy; Reader and Chairman of Logic and Scientific Method Division, School of Mathematics and Physical Sciences, Sussex University, since 1966; *b* 1925. MPhil Poznan 1950, MSciEcon Poznan 1950, PhD Poznan 1952. Lectr in Economic Planning, Poznan Sch. of Economics, 1950–53; Lectr in Logic and Philosophy of Science, Poznan Univ., 1953–59, Docent and Hd of Dept of Logic, 1959–65. Prof. of Logic and Scientific Method, 1965–66. *Publications*: Methodological Issues in Historical Research, 1961; Questions, Assumptions, Decisions, 1964; (with J. Kmita) Lectures on Logic, Information Theory and Methodology of Science, 1966; *contrib.* Ann. Pol. Econ. Soc., Brit. Jl Philos. Sci., Studia Filozof., Studia Logica, etc. *Address*: Dept of Logic and Scientific Method, Univ. of Sussex, Physics B1, Falmer, Brighton.

Gifford, Prof. Charles Henry; Winterstoke Professor of English, University of Bristol, since 1967; *b* 1913; *m* 1938; one *s* one *d*. Classical Hon. Mods 1934, BA Oxon 1936 (English Language and Literature), MA Oxon 1946. Asst Lectr, Bristol Univ., 1946–49, Lectr, 1949–55, Sen. Lectr, 1955–63, Prof. of Modern English Literature, 1963–67. *Publications*: The Hero of his Time: A Theme in Russian Literature, 1950; (with C. Tomlinson) Castilian Ilexes: Versions from Antonio Machado, 1963; The Novel in Russia, 1964, American edn 1965; Comparative Literature, 1969; Leo Tolstoy: A Critical Anthology, 1971; *contrib.* Ess. Crit., OSP, Rev. Engl. Studies, SEER, Times Lit. Supp. *Address*: Dept of English, Univ. of Bristol, Alfred Marshall Building, 40 Berkeley Square, Bristol BS8 1HY.

Gifford, Douglas John, TD, BLitt, MA; Senior Lecturer in the Department of Spanish, since 1962, Director of the Centre for Latin American Linguistic Studies, since 1968, St Andrews University; *b* 1924; *m* 1947; three *s* one *d*. BA Oxford 1949 (Spanish and French), MA Oxford 1950, BLitt Oxford 1954. Pres., Assoc. Brit. Hisp., 1973–75. Lectr, St Andrews Univ., 1950–62; CO (Lt Col), St Andrews Univ. OTC (TA), 1960–67; Mem., Senate, St Andrews Univ., 1968–71. *Publications*: (with F. W. Hodcroft) Textos Lingüísticos del Medioevo Español, 1959, 2nd edn 1966; *contrib.* Bull. Hisp. Studies, Forum Mod. Lang. Studies. *Address*: Dept of Spanish, The Univ., St Andrews, Fife KY16 9AJ.

Giggs, Dr John Alistair; Lecturer in Geography, University of Nottingham, since 1963; *b* 1938; *m* 1964. BSc (Hons) UC Wales, Aberystwyth 1959, PhD 1967. Jun. Res. Fellow, Sheffield Univ., 1962–63. Cttee Mem., World Atlas of Agri. Cttee (Internat.), HQ, Centro di Geografia Agraria Universita, Verona, Italy. *Publications*: ed, World Atlas of Agriculture, vol. III, Americas, 1970, vol. II, Asia and Oceania, 1973; (with B. Waites and K. Wheeler) Patterns and Problems in World Agriculture, 1971; *contrib.* East Midland Geogr, Geographia Polonica, Trans Inst. of Brit. Geogrs. *Address*: Geography Dept, The Univ., Nottingham NG7 2RD.

Gilbert, Martin; Fellow of Merton College, Oxford, since 1962; *b* 1936; *m*; one *d*. BA Oxon 1960. Vis. Prof., Univ. of South Carolina, USA, 1965. Official Biographer of Sir Winston Churchill, 1968– . *Publications*: The Appeasers, 1963 (with Richard Gott) (trans. German, Polish, Rumanian); Britain and Germany Between the Wars, 1964; The European Powers, 1900–1945, 1965 (trans. Italian, Spanish); Plough My Own Furrow: The Life of Lord Allen of Hurtwood, 1965; Servant of India: A Study of Imperial Rule 1905–1910, 1966; The Roots of Appeasement, 1966; Recent History Atlas 1860–1960, 1966; Winston Churchill (Clarendon Biogs, for young people), 1966; British History Atlas, 1968; American History Atlas, 1968; Jewish History Atlas, 1969; First World War Atlas, 1970; Winston S. Churchill, vol. iii, 1914–1916, 1971, Companion volume (in two parts) 1973; Russian History Atlas, 1972; Sir Horace Rumbold: portrait of a diplomat, 1973; Churchill: a photographic portrait, 1974; The Arab–Israeli Conflict: its history in maps, 1974; Churchill and Zionism (pamphlet), 1974; Winston S. Churchill, vol. iv, 1917–1922, 1975, Companion volume (in three parts) 1975; Ed: A Century of Conflict: Essays Presented to A. J. P. Taylor, 1966; Churchill, 1967, and Lloyd George, 1968 (Spectrum Books); compiled Jackdaws: Winston Churchill, 1970; The Coming of War in 1939, 1973; *contrib.* historical articles and reviews to jls (incl. Purnell's History of the Twentieth Century). *Address*: Merton College, Oxford.

Giles, Anthony Kent; Senior Lecturer, Department of Agricultural Economics and Management, University of Reading, since 1968; *b* 1928; *m* 1954; one *s* three *d*. BSc (Econ) Belfast 1953. Mem., Agric. Econ. Soc., Mem., Farm Mngmt Assoc. Mem., Internat. Assoc. Agric. Econ. Asst Agricultural Economist, Univ. of Bristol, 1953–57; Agricultural Economist, 1957–60; Lectr in Agricultural Economics, Univ. of Reading, 1960–68. Rep. of Univ. on Cttees: Min. of Ag., Fish. and Food; Nat. Econ. Develop. Off.; City and Guilds London Inst.; Agric. Hortic. Indust. Training Bd; Farm Mngmt Assoc. *Publications*: University of Reading: Agricultural Economics 1923–73; var. publicns, Univs of Bristol and Reading on Farm Business Mngmt and Agric. Labour; *contrib.* Jl Agric. Econ. Soc. *Address*: Dept of Agricultural Economics and Management, Univ. of Reading, Building No 4, Earley Gate, Whiteknights, Reading RG6 2AH.

Giles, Brian Douglas; Lecturer, Department of Geography, University of Birmingham, since 1964; *b* 1932; *m* 1960; two *d*. BA Birmingham 1955 (2nd cl. Geography), MA Birmingham 1956 (Geography); FRMeteorSoc, Mem., Geog. Assoc. *Publications*: *contrib.* Bull. Brit. Antarc. Surv., Notos, Trans Worcs Archaeol. Soc., Weather. *Address*: Dept of Geography, University of Birmingham, PO Box 363, Birmingham B15 2TT.

251

Giles, Geoffrey; Lecturer in Education, University of Stirling, since 1968; *b* 1929; *m* 1958; two *s* one *d*. BSc Hons Glasgow 1951, MEd 1959. *Address*: Dept of Education, Univ. of Stirling, Stirling FK9 4LA.

Gill, Rev. Joseph; research, Campion Hall, Oxford, lecturing in Modern History Faculty, University of Oxford, since 1970; *b* 1901. BA London 1924, STL Heythrop 1933, BA Hons London 1938, PhD London 1950. Lectr in Med. Greek Lang. and Prof. of Byzantine Hist., Pont. Oriental Inst., Rome, 1938–39 and 1946–68, Rector of Pont. Oriental Inst., 1962–67; Lectr in Anglican Theology, Pont. Gregorian Univ., Rome, 1949–66. *Publications*: La Chiesa Anglicana, 1948; Acta Graeca Concilii Florentini, 1953; The Council of Florence, 1959; Eugenius IV, Pope of Christian Union, 1961; Personalities of the Council of Florence, 1964; Constance, Bâle-Florence, 1965; Georgii Scholarii orationes in Concilio Florentini habitae, 1966; chapters in various books; *contrib*. Orientalia Christiana Periodica, Unitas, Jl Eccles. Hist., Byzantinische Zeitschrift, Studi bizantini e neoellenici, Heythrop Jl. *Address*: Campion Hall, Oxford OX1 1QS.

Gill, Roma; Senior Lecturer in English Literature, University of Sheffield, since 1970; *b* 1934. BA Cantab 1957, MA Cantab 1960, BLitt Oxon 1963. Asst Lectr, Univ. of Sheffield, 1963–65, Lectr, 1965–70. *Publications*: edns of Marlowe: Dr Faustus, 1965; Marlowe: Edward II, 1967; Middleton: Women Beware Women, 1968; Marlowe: Plays, 1971; Festschrift for William Empson, 1974; *contrib*. Engl. Studies, Libr., Rev. Engl. Studies, Ess. Crit., Yrs Wk Engl. Studies. *Address*: Dept of English Literature, The Univ., Sheffield S10 2TN.

Gill, Stephen Charles; Fellow and Tutor in English Literature, Lincoln College, Oxford University, since 1970; *b* 1941; *m* 1963; one *s* one *d*. BA Oxon 1963, BPhil Oxon 1965, PhD Edinburgh 1968, MA Oxon 1969. Lectr in English Literature, Edinburgh Univ., 1965–68; Lectr, Exeter Coll., Oxford, 1968–70. *Publications*: ed, Mrs Gaskell: Mary Barton, 1970; ed, C. Dickens: Our Mutual Friend, 1971; ed, W. Wordsworth: The Prelude, 1970; *contrib*. Ess. Crit., Engl. Lit. Hist., Mod. Lang. Rev., NCF, SIR. *Address*: Lincoln College, Oxford.

Gillam, John Pearson, MA, FSA; Reader in Roman British History and Archaeology, University of Newcastle upon Tyne, since 1956; *b* 1917; *m* 1942; two *s*. BA Dunelm 1938 (2nd cl. History), MA Dunelm 1947; FSA. Lectr in Roman British History and Archaeology, Durham Univ., 1948–56. Service in Indian Army (Major), 1942–46; Mem., Council. Soc. Antiquaries London, 1965–66; Pres., Soc. Antiquaries, Newcastle upon Tyne, 1970– . *Publications*: Types of Roman Coarse Pottery Vessels in Northern Britain, 1957, 3rd edn 1970; *contrib*. Antiqu. Jl, Archaeol. Ael., Derbys Archaeol. Jl, Proc. Soc. Antiqu. Scotl., Trans Cumb. Westm. Archaeol. Antiqu. Soc., Trans Dumfries. Galloway Archaeol. Nat. Hist. Soc., Trans

Durham Northumb. Archit. Archaeol. Soc., Yorks Archaeol. Jl. *Address*: Dept of Archaeology, The Univ., Newcastle upon Tyne NE1 7RU.

Gillard, Dr David Ronald, BA, PhD; Senior Lecturer in History, University of Glasgow, since 1969; *b* 1929; *m* 1960; one *s* one *d*. BA London Ext. 1949 (1st cl. History), PhD London Ext. 1952. Asst Lectr, Glasgow Univ., 1957, Lectr, 1957–69. *Publications*: Industrial Revolution and the New Wealth, 1970; The Great Game: Russo-British Rivalry in Eurasia (forthcoming); *contrib*. EHR. *Address*: Dept of History, The Univ., Glasgow G12 8QQ.

Gillespie, Dr George Turland, MA, PhD; Senior Lecturer, Department of German, University College Cardiff (University of Wales), since 1968; *b* 1917; *m* 1947; one *s* one *d*. BA London 1946 (2nd cl.), MA London 1957, PhD London 1966. Lectr in German, Univ. Coll., Cardiff, 1959–68. Army (Capt.), 1939–46; Foreign Service (German Sect.), 1946–49; Teaching, 1949–59. *Publications*: A Catalogue of Persons Named in German Heroic Literature (700–1600) including named animals and objects and ethnic names, 1973; *contrib*. Germanistik, Germ. Life Letters, Jahrb. Coburg. Landesst. Med. Germ. Studies, Mod. Lang. Rev., Oxf. Germ. Studies, Trivium. *Address*: Dept of German, Univ. College, Cardiff CF1 3NR.

Gillett, Arthur Nicholas, MA, BSc, MEd; Lecturer, School of Education, University of Bristol, since 1965; *b* 1914; *m* 1938; three *s* three *d*. BA Oxon 1937 (3rd cl. Modern Greats), MA Oxon BSc(Econ) London 1942, MEd Birmingham 1952; Teachers Cert. Unesco Tech. Assist. *Address*: 35 Berkeley Square, Bristol.

Gillett, Edward; Senior Lecturer, Adult Education, University of Hull, since 1972; *b* 1915; *m* 1946; two *s* one *d*. BA London 1937 (1st cl. Hons); Mem. Soc. of Archivists. Staff Tutor in History, Univ. Hull, 1941–69; Dep. Dir, Dept of Adult Educn, and Sen. Lectr in Adult Educn, 1969–72. Asst Sec. (Forces Educn), UC Hull, 1941–45. *Publication*: A History of Grimsby, 1970. *Address*: Dept of Adult Education, Univ. of Hull, Hull HU6 7RX.

Gillham, Dr Mary Eleanor; Senior Lecturer, Extra-Mural Department, University College, Cardiff, since 1968; *b* 1921. BSc Wales 1948 (Agric.), BSc Wales 1949 (1st cl. Hons Plant Ecology), PhD Wales 1953 (Bird Island Ecology); MIBiol, MBOU. Botany Dept, Univ. Exeter, 1953–57; Univ. Massey, 1957–58; Univ. Melbourne, 1958–59; research, CSIRO, Austr.; UC Cardiff, 1962– . Member: Brit. Trust for Ornithology Council, 1967–70; Soc. for Protection Nature Reserves, 1966–70; Monmouth section, Nat. Park Cttee, 1970–73; Brecon Nat. Park Jt Cttee, 1973– . *Publications*: Instructions to Young Ornithologists, Sea-birds, 1963; A Naturalist in New Zealand, 1966; Sub-Antarctic Sanctuary, 1967; chapters in Everyman's Nature Reserve, Wildlife Anthology, Flora of a Changing Britain, etc;

contrib. Bull. Glamorgan Naturalists' Trust, Jl Ecology, Nature in Wales, N Western Naturalist, Proc. Roy. Soc. Tasmania, Proc. Roy. Soc. NZ, Proc. Societé Guernesiaise, Trans Cardiff Naturalists, Trans Roy. Soc. Qld, Trans Roy. Soc. Victoria, W Australian Naturalist, various other Australian jls, etc. *Address:* Extra-Mural Dept, 40 Park Place, Cardiff, Glam.

Gillingham, John Bennett; Lecturer, Department of Economic History, London School of Economics, since 1965; *b* 1940; *m* 1966; two *d.* BA Oxon 1962, BPhil Oxon 1965. Laming Travelling Fellow, The Queen's Coll., Oxford, 1963–65. *Publications:* The Kingdom of Germany in the High Middle Ages, 1971; Richard I, 1973; trans., Mayer: The Crusades, 1972. *Address:* Dept of Economic History, London School of Economics, Houghton Street, WC2A 2AE.

Gillmor, Dr Desmond Alfred; Lecturer in Geography, Trinity College, University of Dublin, since 1966; *b* 1938; *m* 1966; two *s.* BA Dublin 1961 (1st cl. Geography), MA Dublin 1966, PhD Dublin 1966. Jun. Lectr, Univ. of Dublin, 1963–66; Vis. Prof., Univ. of Waterloo, 1970–71; Vis. Prof., California State Univ. at Hayward, 1971. Pres., Geog. Soc. Ireland, 1972–76; Editor, Geogr. Viewpoint, 1972– . *Publications:* (with F. H. Aalen and P. W. Williams) West Wicklow, background for development, 1966; (with F. H. Aalen, E. A. Colhoun and A. A. Horner) County Kildare, a geographical background for planning, 1970; A Systematic Geography of Ireland, 1971; Resources, Economy, Society: a socio-economic geography, 1974; *contrib.* Irish Geog., Geogr. Viewpoint, Trans Inst. Brit. Geogrs, Econ. Geog., Geog., etc. *Address:* Dept of Geography, Trinity College, Dublin 2, Ireland.

Gimson, Prof. Alfred Charles, BA; Professor of Phonetics, University of London, since 1966; *b* 1917; *m* 1942; one *d.* BA London 1939 (1st cl. French); Hon. FCST 1957. Lectr, Univ. Coll., London, 1945–61, Reader, 1961–66, Head of Dept, 1971– . Sec., Internat. Phonet. Assoc., 1949– ; Mem., Adv. Cttee, Linguaphone Inst., 1967– ; Editor: Everyman English Pronouncing Dictionary, 1964– ; Maître Phonetique, 1949–70; Jl Internat. Phonet. Assoc., 1971– . *Publications:* Engleska Fonetska Citanka, 1957; Introduction to the Pronunciation of English, 1962, 2nd edn 1970; Supplement, The Use of English (R. Quirk), 1962, 2nd edn 1968; (with G. F. Arnold) English Pronunciation Practice, 1965; *contrib.* Acta linguistica, MPhon, Praxis, Zeits. Phon. *Address:* Dept of Phonetics and Linguistics, Univ. Coll. London, WC1E 6BT.

Giner, Dr Salvador, MA, PhD; Senior Lecturer in Sociology, University of Lancaster, since 1972; *b* 1934; *m* 1966; one *s* one *d.* MA Barcelona 1957 (Law), MA Chicago 1962 (1st cl. Sociology), PhD Chicago 1968 (Sociology); Mem., Brit. Sociol. Assoc. Asst Lectr, Barcelona, 1959–60; Vis. Prof., Puerto Rico, 1963–64; Lectr, Barcelona, 1964–65; Lectr in Sociology, Reading, 1965–72. *Publications:* Societat de masses, 1961; Historia del pensamiento social, 1967; Social Stratification in Spain, 1968; ed (with M. S. Archer), Contemporary Europe: Class, Status and Power, 1971; Sociedad masa: ideologia y conflicto social, 1971; L'estructura social de lallibertat, 1971; ed, La sociologie au XXe siècle, 1972; Sociology, 1972, Spanish edn 1969, French edn 1970. *Address:* Sociology Dept, Univ. of Lancaster, Bailrigg, Lancaster LA1 4YW.

Ginestier, Paul Louis; Reader in Modern French Literature, University of Hull, since 1965; *b* 1922; *m* 1944; two *s* one *d.* LèsL 1946, DES 1947, Dr Paris 1959. Hull Univ.: Asst Lectr, 1947–49; Lectr, 1949–59; Sen. Lectr, 1959–65. Editor, Series De la Langue à la Civilisation Française (Didier International) and Classiques Etrangers Bordas. Chevalier de la Légion d'Honneur 1974. *Publications:* Le Poète et la Machine, 1953, trans. English 1961; La Pensée anglo-saxonne depuis 1900, 1956; Les Meilleurs Poèmes anglais et américains d'aujourd'hui, 1958; Vers la France, 1959, 12th edn 1972; Le Théâtre Contemporain dans le Monde, 1960; Culture et Civilisation Françaises, 1962, 5th edn 1974; La pensée de Camus 1964, 3rd edn 1971; En France, 1966, 5th edn 1974; La Pensée de Bachelard, 1968, trans. Portuguese 1974; Jean Anouilh, 1969; Henry de Montherlant, 1973; Philosophes anglais et américains d'aujourd'hui, 1973; Valeurs du théâtre classique, 1974; edns of plays of Corneille, Racine, Molière; *contrib.* La Revue d'Esthétique. *Address:* Univ. of Hull, Hull HU6 7RX.

Giorgetti, Dr Giovanni Pietro; Lecturer in Italian, Birkbeck College, University of London, since 1955; *b* 1927; *m* 1959; two *d.* Dott Pisa 1950; Dip. Scuola Normale Superiore Pisa 1950; Univ. of Zürich, Philos. Fakultät, Scholarship, 1950–51. Lecteur d'Italien, Univ. of Dijon, 1951–54; Vis. Prof., Univ. of California, Riverside, 1970–71. Editorial Manager, Sansoni Publ., Florence, 1954–55. *Publications:* contrib. Use Your Italian, an Advanced Radio Course (ed E. Ferguson), 1962, 2nd edn 1966; Talking Italian, a Radio Course for Beginners (ed E. Ferguson), 1964; (with J. Norman) Italian Phrase Book, 1968; *contrib.* Encyclopaedia Britannica; *contrib.* Year's Work in Modern Language Studies, 1961–65. *Address:* Birkbeck College, Univ. of London, Malet Street, WC1E 7HX.

Gladdish, Kenneth Raymond; Senior Lecturer, Department of Politics, University of Reading, since 1967; *b* 1928; *m* 1953; two *s* one *d.* BA Hons Manchester 1951 (2nd cl. Pol and Mod. Hist.); Member: Pol Studies Assoc., 1964; African Studies Assoc., 1965. Lectr in Politics (part-time), Univ. of Reading, 1962–67. Univ. of Reading: Fac. Sec., 1962–65; Sub-Dean of Fac., 1965. *Publications: contrib.* Acta Politica, Jl of Contemp. Hist., Pol Studies. *Address:* Dept of Politics, Univ. of Reading, Whiteknights, Reading RG6 2AA.

Glass, Prof. David Victor, FRS, FBA; Martin White Professor of Sociology, University of London (London School of

253

Economics), since 1949; *b* 1911; *m* 1942; one *s* one *d*. BSc(Econ) London 1931; PhD London 1940; Hon. DSc Michigan 1967; Hon. DSocSci Edinburgh, 1973; FBA 1964, FRS 1971. For. Hon. Mem., Amer. Acad. of Arts and Sciences, 1971; For. Associate, Nat. Acad. of Sciences, USA, 1973. Reader in Demography, London Univ., 1946–49. Chm., Population Investigation Cttee; Hon Pres., Internat. Union for Scientific Study of Population; Fellow, Internat. Stat. Inst., Formerly UK Rep., UN Population Commn. *Publications*: The Town, 1935; The Struggle for Population, 1936; Population Policies and Movements in Europe, 1940; ed, Introduction to Malthus, 1953; ed, Social Mobility in Britain, 1954; (with E. Grebenik). The Trend and Pattern of Fertility in Britain, 1954; (with D. E. C. Eversley) Population in History, 1965; ed (with R. Revelle), Population and Social Change, 1972; Numbering the People, 1973; *contrib*. Populat. Studies, Proc. Royal Soc. Series B. *Address*: Dept of Sociology, London School of Economics, Aldwych, WC2A 2AE.

Glass, Stanley Thomas; Lecturer, Department of Politics, University of Keele, since 1964; *b* 1932; *m* 1958; two *s*. BA Hons Durham 1958; BLitt Oxon 1963; Mem., Political Studies Assoc. of UK. Assistant Lecturer: QUB, 1960–1963; Keele Univ., 1963. *Publication*: The Responsible Society, 1966. *Address*: Dept of Politics, Univ. of Keele, Keele, Staffs ST5 5BG.

Glasscock, Dr Robin Edgar; Senior Lecturer in Geography, Queen's University Belfast, since 1972 (Lecturer, 1960–72); *b* 1935; *m* 1966. BA London 1957, PhD London 1963; FRGS, Mem.: Econ. Hist. Soc., Inst. Brit. Geogrs, Amer. Geog. Soc. Assoc. Amer. Geogs, Soc. Mediev. Archaeol. Hon. Treasurer: Medieval Village Res. Gp; Ulster Archaeology. Soc.; Hon. Sec., Gp for Study of Irish Historic Settlement. *Publications*: ed (with J. C. Beckett), Belfast: the origin and growth of an industrial city, 1967; ed (with N. Stephens), Irish Geographical Studies in Honour of E. Estyn Evans, 1970; chapters, in, Northern Ireland from the Air, ed R. Common, 1965; Deserted Medieval Villages, ed J. G. Hurst and M. W. Beresford, 1971; A New Historical Geography of England, ed H. C. Darby, 1973; *contrib*. Trans Inst. Brit. Geogs. *Address*: Dept of Geography, Queen's Univ., Belfast BT7 1NN.

Glatter, Ronald; Lecturer in Educational Administration, Institute of Education, University of London, since 1968; *b* 1939; *m* 1966; one *d*. BA Hons 1962, MA 1965, Oxford, Advanced Dip. in Pub. Admin Manchester 1966; Hon Sec., Brit. Educnl Admin Soc., Mem. Royal Inst. of Public Admin. Res. Associate, Univ. of Manchester, 1965–68. *Publications*: (with E. G. Wedell) Study by Correspondence, 1971; Management Development for the Education Profession, 1972; *contrib*. Adult Educn, Comparative Educn, Proc. Ann. Conf. of Brit. Educnl Admin. Soc. *Address*: Univ. of London Inst. of Education, Malet Street, WC1E 7HS.

Glazebrook, Peter Rowland; Fellow of

Jesus College, and University Lecturer in Law, University of Cambridge, since 1967; *b* 1936; *m* 1963; two *s* one *d*. BA Oxon 1958, MA Oxon 1962, MA Cantab 1967. Lectr, Exeter and Trinity Coll., Oxford, 1958–63, Lectr, Univ. of Exeter, 1963–67; Warden, Crossmead Hall, Univ. of Exeter, 1965–67; Gresham Prof. in Law, City of London, 1970– ; Gen. Editor, Classical English Law Texts Series, 1971– . *Publications*: *contrib*. Amer. Jl Leg. Hist., Camb. Law J, Crim. Law Rev., Law Qly Rev., Mod. Law Rev. *Address*: Jesus College, Cambridge.

Gleasure, James William, MA, DipLing; Lecturer in Celtic, University of Glasgow, since 1969; *b* 1940; *m* 1968; two *d*. BA Dublin 1963 (Hons Celtic Languages), Diploma in Linguistics Wales 1965, MA Dublin 1966. Scholar, Dublin Inst. Adv. Studies, 1965–66; Asst, Glasgow Univ., 1966–69. *Publications*: *contrib*. Studia Celt. Ériu. *Address*: Dept of Celtic, The Univ., Glasgow G12 8RZ.

Gleave, John T.; Director of Special Courses, Department of Adult Education and Extramural Studies, Leeds University, since 1969; *b* 1917; *m* 1940; two *d*. MA, MEd, DThPT. Dir, Extramural Classes and Courses, Leeds Univ., 1962–69. *Publications*: Geography for Uganda Schools, 1958; Introducing Geography, 1960; Civics for East African Schools, 1962; Visual Geography of East Africa, 1966; Handbooks for Teachers, 1959; World Atlas for Uganda Schools, 1960; Uganda our Homeland, 1961; *contrib*. Geographical Jl, Overseas Educn. *Address*: Dept of Adult Education and Extramural Studies, Univ. of Leeds, Leeds LS2 9JT.

Gleave, Michael Barrie, MA; Senior Lecturer in Geography, University of Salford, since 1971; *b* 1936; *m* 1961; one *s* one *d*. BA Hull 1957, MA Hull 1960, DipEd Reading 1960; Mem.: Royal Geog. Soc., Inst. Brit. Geogs, Geog. Assoc. Asst Lectr, Univ. of Ibadan, 1963; Lectr, 1963–64; Temp. Lectr, Univ. of Glasgow, 1964–65; Lectr, Univ. of Salford, 1965–71; seconded as Prof. of Geography, Fourah Bay Coll., Univ. of Sierra Leone, 1972–74. Actg Editor, Nigerian Geog. Jl, 1963–64. *Publications*: (with H. P. White) An Economic Geography of West Africa, 1971; *contrib*. Afr., Geog. Rev., Trans Inst. Brit. Geogrs. *Address*: Dept of Economics and Geography, Univ. of Salford, Salford M5 4WT.

Glendinning, Prof. Oliver Nigel Valentine; Professor of Spanish, Queen Mary College, University of London, since 1974; *b* 1929; *m* 1958; four *s*. BA Hons Cantab 1953 (1st cl.), MA Cantab 1957; MA Oxon 1958; PhD Cantab 1959; MA Dublin 1970. Jebb Studentship, Univ. of Cambridge, 1954–56; Temp. Lectr, Oxford, 1956–57; Res. Fellow, Trinity Hall, Cambridge, 1957–58; Lectr, Oxford, 1958–62; Professor: Southampton, 1962–70; TCD, 1970–74. Hon. Treas., Internat. Assoc. of Hispanists, 1962–67. Mem., Latin Amer. Sub-Cttee, UGC, 1969–72, etc. Gen. ed., Year's Work in Mod. Lang. Studies, 1966–68. *Publications*: ed, works of José Cadalso: Noches lúgubres, 1961, Los eruditos a la violeta, 1967, (with

Lucien Dupuis) Cartas marruecas, 1966, 2nd edn 1971; Vida y obra de Cadalso, 1962; trans. Julio Caro Baroja: The World of the Witches, 1964; A Literary History of Spain: the 18th Century, 1972 (Spanish edn 1973); Goya: the artist and his critics (forthcoming); ed, Studies in Modern Spanish Literature and Art presented to Helen F. Grant, 1972; chapters in: Art Treasures in Spain, 1970; The Varied Pattern: studies in the Eighteenth Century, 1971; Studies in Modern Spanish Literature, 1972; Spain: a Companion to Spanish Studies, 1973; *contrib.* Burlington Mag., Bull. Hispanic Studies, Jl of Warburg and Courtauld Insts, Hispanic Rev., Papeles de Son Armadans, Rev. de Filología Española, Rev. de literatura, Rev. de Littérature Comparée, etc. *Address*: Dept of Spanish, Queen Mary College, Univ. of London, Mile End Road, E1 4NS.

Glossop, John Antony; Lecturer in Education, Institute of Education, Leeds, since 1968; *b* 1936; *m* 1969; one *s* one *d*. BA London 1957 (Sociology), Cert. and DipEd. Sheffield 1958, MA London 1966 (Sociology). *Address*: Institute of Education, Leeds LS2 9JT.

Glover, George Neil; Senior Lecturer in Law, University of Leeds, since 1969; *b* 1921; *m* 1959; three *d*. LLB Leeds 1941; Solicitor 1948. Pt-time Lectr Univ. of Leeds, 1957–66, Lectr, 1966–69. Dean, Fac. of Law, 1970–74. *Publications*: *contrib.* Brit. Tax Rev., Law Soc. Gaz. *Address*: Faculty of Law, The University, Leeds LS2 9JT.

Glover, Jonathan Cureton Burdick; Fellow and Tutor in Philosophy, New College Oxford, since 1968, University Lecturer in Philosophy, Oxford University, since 1967; *b* 1941; *m* 1966; one *s*. BA Oxon 1966, MA Oxon 1970, PBhil Oxon 1966. Lectr in Philosophy, Pembroke, Jesus and Keble Colls, Oxford, 1965–66; Lectr in Philosophy, Christ Church, Oxford, 1966–68. *Publications*: Responsibility, 1970. *Address*: New College, Oxford.

Glowacki-Prus, Xenia; Lecturer, Department of Russian Studies, University of Hull, since 1970; *b* 1942. BA London (1st cl. Russian); MPhil London 1973. Lectr, Univ. of Hull, 1965–68; Lectr, Univ. Coll. of Wales, Aberystwyth, 1969–70. *Publications*: trans. (with A. McMillin), K. Malevich: Essays on Art, 1968; PILL (Programmed Intensive Language Learning) Russian Course, for tuition at home or in Language Laboratories, 6 records, 6 booklets, 1973; trans. (with T. E. Little and T. Andersen), K. Malevich, 2 vols (forthcoming); *contrib.* NZ Slavic Rev. *Address*: Dept of Russian Studies, The Univ., Hull HU6 7RX.

Glucker, John; Lecturer in Classics, University of Exeter, since 1965; *b* 1933; *m* 1968; two *d*. BA Jerusalem 1958, MA Jerusalem 1960. Res. Student, Pembroke Coll., Oxford, 1961–63; Asst Lectr, Exeter Univ., 1963–65; Jun. Fellow, Center for Hellenic Studies, Washington DC, 1971–72; Vis. Sen. Lectr, Tel-Aviv Univ., 1973–74. *Publications*: *contrib.* Class. Rev., Class. et Med., Eranos, Bibliog. d'humanisme et Renaiss., Scientia. Hist., Mnemosyne, Iyyun, Rev. Augustin., Pegasus, Latomus, Byzantion. *Address*: Dept of Classics, Queen's Building, The Univ., Exeter EX4 4QJ.

Gluckman, Prof. H. Max, DHC, MA, DPhil, FBA; Research Professor in Social Anthropology, and holder of Special Fellowship of Nuffield Foundation, University of Manchester, since 1971; *b* 1911; *m* 1939; three *s*. BA Witwatersrand 1930, DPhil Oxon 1936, MA Oxon 1947, MA Manchester 1953, Doc. Hon. Causa Bruxeles 1965; FBA 1968, Hon. For. Mem., Amer. Acad. Arts Science, 1970, Fellow, Center for Adv. Study in Behav. Science, 1967, 1971– . Univ. Lectr in Social Anthropology, Oxford, 1947–49; Prof. of Social Anthropology, Univ. of Manchester, 1947–71. Mem., Human Sci. Cttee, Dept Science Indust. Res., 1958–63; Chm., Assoc. Social Anthropologists Commonwealth, 1962–66; Pres., Sociol. Sect., Brit. Assoc., 1961; Soc. Studies Sub-cttee, UGC, 1965–70; Soc. Anthropol. Cttee, SSRC, 1966–69. *Publications*: Analysis of a Social Situation in Modern Zululand, 1940, 2nd edn 1958; Economy of the Central Barotse Plain, 1941; Essays on Lozi Land and Royal Property, 1943; Malinowski's Theory of Social Change, 1945; The Judicial Process among the Barotse of N Rhodesia, 1955, 2nd edn 1967; Custom and Conflict in Africa, 1955; Order and Rebellion in Tribal Africa: Collected Essays with an Autobiographical Introduction, 1963; The Ideas in Barotse Jurisprudence, 1965; Politics, Law and Ritual in Tribal Society, 1965; ed (with E. Colson), Seven Tribes of British Central Africa, 1951; Essays on the Ritual of Social Relations, 1962; Closed Systems and Open Minds, 1965; The Allocation of Responsibility, 1972; *contrib.* Afr., Afr. Studies, Amer. Anthropologist Bantu Studies, Curr. Anthropol., Law Soc., Man, Past Pres., Rhodes-Livingst. Jl, Yale Law Jl. *Address*: Dept of Social Anthropology, The Univ., Dover Street, Manchester M13 9PL.

Gluxon, Daniel; Lecturer in Law, School of Management, Bath, since 1961; *b* 1920; *m* 1956. BA Oxon (Jurisprudence), MA Oxon; FIWSP 1944. Central Work Study Engineer, BICC, 1948–56. *Address*: School of Management, Bath Univ., Claverton, Bath BA2 7AY.

Glynn, Sean; Lecturer in Economic and Social History, Faculty of Social Sciences, University of Kent at Canterbury, since 1968; *b* 1940; *m* 1964; two *s*. BScEcon London 1963, MEcon WA 1965. Univ. Western Australia, 1964–66; ANU, 1966–68. *Publications*: Urbanisation in Australian History, 1970; *contrib.* Austr. Econ. Hist. Rev., Econ. Hist. Rev., Jl Politics and Hist., Univ. Studies in Hist. *Address*: Darwin College, Univ. of Kent, Canterbury, Kent.

Goddard, Dr John Burgess; Lecturer in Geography, London School of Economics and Political Science, since 1973; *b* 1943; *m* 1965; one *d*. BA London 1965 (Hons Geog.), PhD London 1973. Member: Inst. British Geographers; Regional Studies Assoc.

255

LSE, 1968– . *Publications*: Office Linkages and Location, 1973; *contrib*. London Studies in Regional Science, Progress in Planning, Regional Studies, Urban Studies, Trans Inst. Brit. Geographers. *Address*: London School of Economics, Houghton Street, Aldwych, WC2A 2AE.

Goddard, Keith Arthur; Lecturer in French, Queen's University of Belfast, since 1970; *b* 1941. BA 1963, MA 1966, Leeds; Member: Société de Linguistique Romane, Philol Soc., Assoc. of Hispanists. Asst Lectr, later Lectr in Med. French, QUB, 1965–70. *Publications*: *contrib*. Revue de Linguistique Romane, Proc. RIA, Babel. *Address*: Dept of French, Queen's Univ., Belfast BT7 1NN.

Goddard, Prof. Leonard; Professor of Logic and Metaphysics, University of St Andrews, since 1966; *b* 1925; *m* 1945; two *d*. MA St Andrews 1951, BPhil St Andrews 1955. Asst in Logic and Metaphysics, St Andrews, 1952–56; Lectr in Philosophy, Univ. of New England, NSW, 1956–61, Prof. of Philosophy, 1961–66. Dean, Fac. of Arts, New England, 1964–65; Dean, Fac. of Arts, St Andrews, 1971–73. *Publications*: (with F. R. Routley) The Logic of Significance and Context, vol. I; *contrib*. Analysis, Austral. Jl Philos., Mind, Notre Dame Jl Formal Logic. *Address*: Dept of Logic and Metaphysics, The Univ., St Andrews, Fife KY16 9AJ.

Godfrey, Edward Martin, PhD; Lecturer in Economics, Manchester University, since 1964; *b* 1937; *m* 1961; two *s* one *d*. BA Cantab 1961, MA Cantab 1965; PhD Manchester 1971. Lectr in Economics, UC Cape Coast, Ghana, 1963–64; Asst Lectr in Economics, 1964–66, Lectr in Economics, 1966–71, Univ. of Manchester; Vis. Res. Fellow, Inst. for Develt Studies, Univ. of Nairobi, 1971–73. *Publications*: *contrib*. Econ. Devlt and Cultural Change, Jl of Devlt Studies, Jl of Econ. Studies, Jl of Modern African Studies, Nigerian Jl of Economic and Social Studies. *Address*: Economics Dept, Manchester Univ., Manchester M13 9PL.

Godin, Prof. Henri Jean Gustave; Professor of French, and Romance Philology, Queen's University of Belfast, since 1972; *b* 1910; *m* 1937. BA London 1932, LèsL Lille 1933, MA QUB 1938, PhD QUB 1940. Officier d'Académie, 1956. Lecteur, UC Cardiff, 1934–36; Queen's Univ., Belfast: Sen. Asst, 1936–39; Jun. Lectr, 1939–43; Lectr, 1943–54; Sen. Lectr, 1954–67; Reader, 1967–72. Mem., Northern Ireland GCE Cttee, then Bd, 1964– . *Publications*: trans., Le Charroi de Nîmes, 1936; Les Ressources stylistiques du français contemporain, 1948, 2nd edn 1964; critical edn, Giraudoux: La Guerre de Troie n'aura pas lieu, 1958; critical edn, Genevoix: Rémi des Rauches, 1965; chapter on Giraudoux, in, Forces in Modern French Drama, 1972; Jules Janin and Balzac, in Balzac and the Ninteeenth Century, 1972; *contrib*. French Studies. *Address*: Dept of French, Queen's Univ. of Belfast, Belfast BT7 1NN.

Godley, Hon. Wynne Alexander Hugh
256

MA; Director, Department of Applied Economics, University of Cambridge, since 1970; *b* 1926; *m* 1955; one *d*. MA Oxon 1969. Professional oboist, 1950–56; Economic Section, HM Treasury, 1956–70 (Dep. Dir, 1967–70); Fellow, King's College, Cambridge, 1970– . *Publications*: *contrib*. Nat. Inst. Rev., Economic Jl, London and Cambridge Econ. Bull. *Address*: King's College, Cambridge.

Goehr, Prof. Alexander; West Riding Professor of Music, Leeds University, since 1971; *b* 1932; *m* 1954; three *d*. Hon. FRMCM; Hon. DMus Southampton 1973. Lectr, Morley Coll., 1955–57; Music Asst, BBC, 1960–67; Winston Churchill Trust Fellowship, 1968; Composer in residence, New England Conservatory, Boston, Mass, 1968–69; Associate Prof. of Music, Yale Univ., 1969–70. Composer. *Publications*: Fantasia Op. 4; Violin Concerto; Little Symphony; Pastorals; Romanza for cello; Symphony in one Movement, Opus 29, 1970; Concerto for Eleven, 1972; Piano Concerto; Chamber music; Konzertstück; Opera: Arden must die; Cantatas: Sutter's Gold; The Deluge; Triptych (Naboth's Vineyard; Shadowplay; Sonata about Jerusalem). *Address*: Music Dept, Univ. of Leeds, Leeds LS2 9JT.

Golant, W.; Lecturer, Department of History, University of Exeter, since 1964; *b* 1937. BA California 1958, MA California 1960 (History), BLitt Oxon 1967. Teaching Asst, UCLA, 1959–61. *Publications*: *contrib*. Hist. Jl, Pol. Qly. *Address*: Dept of History, Queen's Building, Univ. of Exeter, Exeter EX4 4QJ.

Goldman, Prof. Arnold (Melvyn), AB, MA, PhD; Professor of American Studies, University of Keele, since 1974; *b* 1936; *m* 1963; two *s*. AB Harvard 1957 (summa cum laude English Literature), MA Yale 1959, PhD Yale 1964. Asst Lectr, Manchester Univ., 1960–63, Lectr, 1963–65; Vis. Lectr, Smith Coll., 1965–66, 1969; Lectr, Sussex Univ., 1966–71, Reader 1971–74; Vis. Reader, State Univ. of NY at Buffalo, 1973. *Publications*: The Joyce Paradox, 1966; James Joyce, 1968; ed, Twentieth Century Interpretations of Absalom, Absalom!, 1971; ed (with J. S. Whitley), Charles Dickens's American Notes, 1972; *contrib*. Notes Queries, New Lit. Hist. *Address*: Univ. of Keele, Keele, Staffs ST5 5BG.

Goldman-Eisler, Prof. Frieda; Professor of Psycholinguistics, Department of Phonetics and Linguistics, University College, London, since 1970; *b* 1915; *m* 1950. DrPhil Vienna 1937, Qualifying examination, University College, London 1938; FBPsS, FRSocMed, Mem.,Experim. Psychol. Soc. Scientific Staff, MRC, Inst. Psychiatry, 1948–55; Hon. Res. Assoc. Univ. Coll., London, 1955–62; Lectr, 1962–70. *Publications*: Psycholinguistics: Experiments in Spontaneous Speech, 1968; *contrib*. Brit. Jl Psychol., Discov., Jl Comm., Jl Personal., Jl Psychosom. Res., Jl Verb Learn. Verb. Behav., Lang. and Speech. Nature, Neuropsychopharm., Neurol. Psychiat. Belgia, New Scientist, Qly Jl Exper. Psychol., Psychopharm. *Address*: Psycholinguistics Research Unit, Wolfson House, 4 Stephenson Way, NW1.

Goldsmith Dr Margaret Elizabeth, PhD; Lecturer in English (Part-time), University of Bristol, since 1953; *b* 1920; *m* 1944; two *s*. BA London 1942 (1st cl. English), PhD Bristol 1968. Asst Lectr, Edinburgh Univ., 1943–44; Asst Lectr, Bristol Univ., 1944–47; Lectr, 1947–53. *Publications*: The Mode and Meaning of Beowulf, 1970; *contrib*. Compar. Lit. Med. Aev., Neophilol., Notes Queries, Rev. Engl. Studies, Ess. Crit., Anglo-Saxon England. *Address*: Dept of English, Univ. of Bristol, Bristol BS8 1HY.

Goldsmith, Prof. Maurice Marks; Professor of Political Theory, Department of Politics, University of Exeter, since 1969; *b* 1933. AB Columbia 1954, PhD Columbia 1964. Instructor, Columbia Univ., 1960–67; Asst Prof., 1964–68; SSRC (USA) Fellow in Political Theory and Legal Philosophy, 1959–60. Lawrence H. Chamberlain Fellow, Columbia Univ., 1965; Guggenheim Fellow, 1967–68. *Publications*: Hobbes's Science of Politics, 1966; Allegiance (Inaugural Lecture), 1971; ed, Hobbes: Elements of Law, 1968; Hobbes: Behemoth, 1969; Mandeville: Origin of Honour, 1971; *contrib*. A Case of Identity, in, Politics and Experience, ed King and Parekh, 1968; *contrib*. Pol. Studies. *Address*: Dept of Politics, Univ. of Exeter, Exeter EX4 4QJ.

Goldthorpe, Dr John Ernest, MA, BSc (Econ), PhD; Senior Lecturer in Sociology, University of Leeds, since 1967; *b* 1921; *m* 1950; two *s* two *d*. BA Cantab 1942 (Nat. Science), MA Cantab 1946, BSc(Econ) London 1949, PhD London 1961. Lectr in Sociology, Makerere Univ. Coll., Uganda, 1951–60, Sen. Lectr, 1960–62; Lectr, Leeds Univ., 1962–67. *Publications*: Outlines of East African Society, 1958, 2nd edn 1962; An African Elite, 1965; An Introduction to Sociology, 1968; *contrib*. Sociol. Rev., Brit. Jl Sociol., ZAIRE. *Address*: Dept of Sociology, Univ. of Leeds, Leeds LS2 9JT.

Goldthorpe, John Harry; Official Fellow, Nuffield College, Oxford University, since 1969; *b* 1935; *m* 1963; one *s* one *d*. BA London 1956 (1st cl. History), MA Cantab 1960, MA Oxon 1969; Mem., Brit. Sociol. Assoc. Res. Fellow, Dept of Sociology, Univ. of Leicester, 1957–60; Fellow, King's Coll., Cambridge, 1960–69; Asst Lectr, Faculty of Economics, Cambridge, 1962–64; Lectr, 1964–69. Editor, Sociology, 1969–72; Mem.: Exec. Brit. Sociol. Assoc., 1969–72; Sociol. and Social Admin Cttee, Soc. Science Res. Council, 1965–68; Pres., Sect. N, Brit. Assoc., 1969. *Publications*: (with D. Lockwood et al.) The Affluent Worker: Industrial Attitudes and Behaviour, 1968; (with D. Lockwood et al) The Affluent Worker: Political Attitudes and Behaviour, 1968; (with D. Lockwood et al) The Affluent Worker in the Class Structure, 1969; (with K. Hope) The Social Grading of Occupations, 1974; *contrib*. Archiv. Europ. Sociol., Brit. Jl

Sociol., Sociol. Rev., Sociol. Travail, Sociol. *Address*: Nuffield College, Oxford.

Gombrich, Dr Richard Francis; University Lecturer in Sanskrit and Pali, Oxford University, since 1965; *b* 1937; *m* 1964; one *s* one *d*. BA Oxon 1961 (1st cl. Oriental Studies), AM Harvard 1963, MA Oxon 1964, DPhil Oxon 1969; FRAS; Mem., Univ. Assoc. for Sociol. of Religion. *Publications*: Precept and Practice: Traditional Buddhism in the Rural Highlands of Ceylon, 1971; *contrib*. Hist. Relig., Jl Asian Studies, Man, WZKSO. *Address*: The Oriental Institute, Pusey Lane, Oxford OX1 2LE.

Gomme, Dr Austin Harvey; Senior Lecturer, Department of English, University of Keele, since 1968; *b* 1930; *m* 1960; one *s* three *d*. BA Cambridge 1954, MA Cambridge 1958, PhD Cambridge 1963. Fellow in English, Caius Coll., Cambridge 1956–59; Lectr in English, Dept of Extra-Mural Studies, Univ. of Glasgow, 1959–62; Lectr in English, Univ. of Keele, 1963–68. Vis. Prof., Univs of Montana and Rhode Island, USA, 1962–63. JP 1970. Mem. Exec. Cttee and Registrar of Research, Soc. of Architectl Historians, GB, 1967– . *Publications*: Attitudes to Criticism, 1966; The Architecture of Glasgow, 1968; Dickens, 1971; ed, Coriolanus, 1969; ed, Jacobean Tragedies, 1969; ed, The Roaring Girl, 1974; *contrib*. Delta, Essays in Crit., Human World, MLR, Oxford Rev., TLS, Univs Qly. *Address*: Dept of English, Univ. of Keele, Keele, Staffs ST5 5BG.

Gömöri, George Thomas; Lecturer in Slavonic Studies, Department of Slavonic Studies, Cambridge University, since 1973; *b* 1934; *m* 1961; two *d*. BA London 1958, BLitt Oxon 1962, MA Cantab 1969. Lectr, Univ. of California, 1963–64; Res. Fellow, Harvard, 1964–65; Res. Associate, Univ. of Birmingham, 1965–67; Sen. Res. Associate, Birmingham, 1967–69; Asst Lectr, Cambridge, 1969–73. Mem. Editorial Bd, Books Abroad, 1968– . *Publications*: Polish and Hungarian Poetry 1945 to 1956, 1966; ed. (with C. Newman), New Writing of East Europe, 1968; contrib., The Cry of Home, ed H. E. Lewald, 1972; contrib. World Literature since 1945, ed Ivask and Wilpert, 1973; (ed jtly), Attila József: Selected Poems and Texts, 1973; (ed jtly), Laszlo Nagy: Love of the Scorching Wind, 1973; *contrib*. Books Abroad, California Slavic Studies, Mosaic, Slavonic and East European Review, Tri-Quarterly. *Address*: Dept of Slavonic Studies, Sidgwick Avenue, Cambridge.

Gooch, Anthony Leonard, MA; Lecturer in Spanish, in charge of subject within Language Studies Department, LSE, University of London, since 1964; Lecturer, UCL; *b* 1930; *m* 1959; one *s* one *d*. MA Edinburgh 1954 (1st cl. Spanish with French). Mem., Assoc. Hispanists. Asst Lectr, Edinburgh Univ., 1959–64; Vis. Lectr, Santander (Menéndez Pelayo Univ.), 1972. Chm., Assoc. Teachers of Span. and Portug., 1968–69. *Publications*: Diminutive, Augmentative and Pejorative Suffixes in Modern Spanish, 1967, 2nd edn 1970; Cassell's Spanish Dictionary, rev. edn (forthcoming); trans. in

257

Spanish and Linguistic Commentary (forthcoming); *contrib.* Actas del IV Cong. Asoc. Int. de Hispan. *Address*: Dept of Spanish, Language Studies, London School of Economics, Houghton Street, WC2A 2AE.

Gooch, John Henry, MA, CEng; Lecturer in Organisation Analysis, School of Social Sciences, Brunel University, since 1965; *b* 1929; *m* 1962; two *d.* BA Cantab 1953, MA Cantab 1956; MIMechE 1958, AMIMarE 1958. Man. Dir, J. H. Gooch & Co. Ltd, Consultants. *Address*: School of Social Sciences, Brunel Univ., Uxbridge UB8 3TH.

Goodall, Brian, BSc(Econ); Senior Lecturer, Department of Geography, University of Reading, since 1973 (Lecturer, 1967–73); *b* 1937; *m* 1961; three *s.* BSc(Econ) London 1958 (2nd cl.); Mem.: Inst. Brit. Geogrs, Reg. Studies Assoc. Lectr in Economics, Coll. of Estate Management, London, 1960–66; Vis. Lectr, Geografisk Inst. Aarhus Univ., Denmark, 1969–70. Rees Jeffreys Res. Fellow, DSIR Road Res. Lab., 1959–60. *Publications*: (jtly) Aspects of Land Economics, 1966; The Economics of Urban Areas, 1972; (jtly) The Recreational Potential of Forestry Commission Holdings, 1973; *contrib.* Forest Research, Jl Town Planning Inst., Reg. Studies, Landscape Res. News. *Address*: Dept of Geography, Univ. of Reading, Whiteknights, Reading RG6 2AF.

Goode, Prof. Royston Miles, OBE, LLB; Crowther Professor of Credit and Commercial Law, University of London (Queen Mary College), since 1973; *b* 1933; *m* 1964; one *d.* LLB London 1954; Solicitor 1955. Prof. of Law, QMC, 1971–73. Mem., Cttee on Consumer Credit, 1968–71; Chm., Examination Bd Finance Houses Assoc. Diploma Examination. *Publications*: Hire-Purchase Law and Practice, 1962, 2nd edn 1970; The Hire-Purchase Act, 1964, 1964; (with Prof. J. S. Ziegel) Hire-Purchase and Conditional Sale: a comparative survey of Commonwealth and American Law, 1965; *contrib.* Modern Law Rev., Law Guardian, New Law Jl, Solicitors Jl, Encyclopaedia of Forms and Precedents. *Address*: Faculty of Laws, Queen Mary College, Mile End Road, E1 4NS.

Gooderson, Richard Norman; Reader in English Law, University of Cambridge, since 1967; *b* 1915; *m* 1939; two *s* one *d.* BA Cantab 1937 (1st cl. with distinction Law), MA Cantab 1947; George Long Prize Roman Law 1936; George Long Prize Jurisprudence 1937; Bhaonagar Medal 1938; Barrister 1946 (Cert. of Honour), Inner Temple. Fellow, St Catharine's Coll., Cambridge, 1948; Tutor, 1951–65; Sen. Tutor, 1965–67; Pres., 1962–65, 1972– ; Asst Lectr, 1948–49; Lectr, 1949–67; Chm., Law Faculty, 1970–73. Dep. Chm., QS, 1970–72; Recorder, 1972; Chm., Rent Trib., 1960–72. *Publications*: *contrib.* Canad. Bar Rev., Camb. Law Jl, Law Qly Rev., Mod. Law Rev. *Addrews*: St Catharine's College, Cambridge.

Goodey, Brian; Lecturer in Urban Studies, since 1969, and Tutor to Graduate Students, Centre for Urban and Regional Studies, University of Birmingham, since 1972; *b*

1941; *m* 1967; one *d.* BA Nottingham 1961 (Geography), MA Indiana 1967 (Geography); FRGS; Mem.: Inst. Brit. Geogrs, Educn for Planning Assoc., Assoc. Amer. Geogrs. Assoc. Faculty, Indiana Univ., Gary, 1965–67; Asst Prof. in Geography, Univ. of N Dakota, 1967–69; Vis. Lectr, Univ. of Arizona, 1971. Adv., Sci. Gp on Environmtl Health Criteria for Urban Planning, WHO, Geneva, June 1971; Consultant: Man and the Biosphere Programme, UNESCO, 1973; WHO Seminar Health Aspects of Urban Develt, Stuttgart, Dec. 1973; SSRC Res. Grant, Perception Studies for Planning, 1972–74; Leverhulme Res. Grant (personal), New Communities in Arizona, 1972–73. Mem., Cttee, Educn for Planning Assoc., 1971–72. *Publications*: Readings in the Geography of North Dakota, 1968; Perception of the Environment, 1971; Where You're At, 1974; *contrib.* Geog. Jl, Jlism Qly, Official Archit. Planning, Town and Country Planning. *Address*: Centre for Urban and Regional Studies, Selly Wick House, Selly Wick Road, Birmingham B29 7JF.

Goodger, John Michael, ATD, MSc; Lecturer in Art and Design, Arts and Complementary Studies Section, University of Salford, since 1967; *b* 1933; *m* 1960; one *s.* NatDip. in Design 1954, Art Teacher's Dip. 1955; MSc Salford 1973; ALCM 1955. Lectr in Art, Royal Coll. of Advanced Technol., Salford, subseq. Univ. of Salford, 1961–67. Corporate Mem., Brit. Kinematograph Sound and Television Soc. *Films*: Almost but not quite, 1969; The Making of a Mayor, 1970; The Changing Face of Salford, part 1, 1970, part 2, 1971; Salford: the other side, 1972. *Address*: Arts and Complementary Studies, Univ. of Salford, Salford M5 4WT.

Gooding, Dr David Willoughby; Reader in Classics, Queen's University, Belfast, since 1968; *b* 1925. BA Cantab 1950 (1st cl. Classics), MA Cantab 1953, PhD Cantab 1954; Kaye Prizeman Cantab 1959. Asst in Palaeography, Durham Univ., 1954–56; Res. Fellow in Arts, 1956–59; Asst Lectr in Classics, Queen's Univ., Belfast, 1959–61, Lectr, 1961–68; Grinfield Lectr on the Septuagint, Oxford, 1967–68. *Publications*: The Account of the Tabernacle, 1959; ed, P. Walters: The Text of the Septuagint, 1972; Relics of Ancient Exegesis (forthcoming); *contrib.* Jl Sem. Studies, Jl Theol. Studies, Textus, Vet. Testamen., Zeits. Allgem. Wissen. *Address*: Greek Dept, Queen's Univ., Belfast BT7 1NN.

Goodings, Richard Francis; Senior Lecturer in Education, University of Durham, since 1965; *b* 1928; *m* 1965; one *s* two *d.* BA Oxon 1952 (Mod. History), Certif. in Educn London 1953, MA Oxon 1956, DipEd London 1956; FRSA; Member: Comparative Educn Soc. in Europe; Soc. for Research into Higher Educn; Phi Delta Kappa; Kappa Delta Pi. Univ. of London, 1961–65; Vis. Prof. in USA, 1965, 1967, 1969. Staffing Officer, South Essex Divisional Executive, 1958–61. Consultant in Comparative Educn to Internat. Project for Evaluation of Educnl Achievement, 1964–68. Asst Editor, Year Book of Education, 1961–65. *Publications*:

258

contrib. International Study of Achievement in Mathematics, 2 vols, ed Almquist and Wiksall, 1967; contrib. Ideals and Ideologies: Essays in Comparative Education, 1969; contrib. Internat. Rev. of Educn, Univ. of London Inst. of Educn Libraries Bull., Year Book of Educn, World Book Encyclopaedia. Address: Univ. of Durham, Dept of Education, 48 Old Elvet, Durham.

Goodlad, Dr John Sinclair Robertson, MA, PhD; Lecturer in Associated Studies, Department of Electrical Engineering, Imperial College, London, since 1962; b 1938; m 1968. BA Cantab 1959, MA Cantab 1963, PhD London 1969. Lectr, St Stephen's Coll., Delhi Univ., India, 1959; Vis. Lectr, MIT, USA, 1961. Publications: A Sociology of Popular Drama, 1971; Science for Non-Scientists, 1972. Address: Imperial College, SW7 2BT.

Goodman, Anthony Eric; Lecturer in Medieval History, History Department, University of Edinburgh, since 1965; b 1936; m 1964; one d. BA Oxon 1958 (1st cl. History), MA Oxon 1966, BLitt Oxon 1966; FRHistS 1972. Asst Lectr, Edinburgh Univ., 1961–65. Publications: The Loyal Conspiracy: The Lords Appellant under Richard II, 1971; contrib. Bull. Inst. Hist. Res., Welsh Hist. Rev. Address: Dept of History, Univ. of Edinburgh, George Square, Edinburgh.

Goodman, Dr David Charles, MA DPhil; Lecturer in History of Science, Faculty of Arts, Open University, since 1971; b 1939; m 1972. Oxford Univ.: Dipl. in History and Philosophy of Science 1962, MA 1964, DPhil 1965; Mem.: British Soc. for History of Science; Chemical Soc. Vis. Asst Prof. in History of Science, Johns Hopkins Univ., Baltimore, USA, 1966–67. Publications: ed (with C. A. Russell), Science and the Rise of Technology since 1800, 1973; Science and Religious Belief: a selection of primary sources 1600–1900 (forthcoming); contrib. Ambix, Episteme, Hist. Stud. Phys. Scis, Med. Hist. Address: The Open Univ. Walton, Milton Keynes MK7 6AA.

Goodman, Dr John Francis Bradshaw; Senior Lecturer in Industrial Relations, University of Manchester, since 1970; b 1940; m 1967; one s one d. BScEcon London 1961 (1st cl.), Dip. Personnel Management, London 1962, PhD Nottingham 1970. MIPM. Lectr in Industrial Econs, Univ. of Nottingham, 1964–69. Personnel Officer, Ford Motor Co. Ltd, 1962–64; Industrial Relations Adviser, Nat. Bd for Prices and Incomes, 1969–70. Publications: Shop Stewards in British Industry, 1969; Shop Stewards, 1973; contrib. Brit. Jl Industrial Relations, Internat. Labour Rev., Jl Industrial Relations, Personnel Management. Address: Univ. of Manchester, Oxford Road, Manchester M13 9PL.

Goodman, Prof. Michael Jack, MA, PhD; Professor of Law, University of Durham, since 1971, and Dean of Faculty of Law, 1972-74; b 1931; m 1958; two s one d. BA Oxon 1953, MA Oxon 1961, PhD Manchester 1967; Solicitor 1956. Lectr, Man-

chester Univ., 1964–66, Sen. Lectr, 1966–70. Publications: contrib. Mod. Law Rev., Conveyan. Address: Faculty of Law, Univ. of Durham, 50 North Bailey, Durham City.

Goodridge, Jonathan Francis; Senior Lecturer, Department of English, University of Lancaster, since 1965; b 1924; m 1949; two s two d. BA Oxon 1949 (Hons Eng. Lang. and Lit.), MA Oxon 1956. Formerly Princ. Lectr in English, St Mary's Coll. of Educn, Twickenham. Founder-Editor, Catholic Education Today, 1959–65. Publications: trans., Langland: Piers the Ploughman, 1959, rev. edn 1966; Emily Brontë's Wuthering Heights (Studies in Eng. Lit. Series), 1964. Address: Dept of English, Univ. of Lancaster, Bailrigg, Lancaster LA1 4YQ.

Goodwin, Prof. Geoffrey Lawrence; Montague Burton Professor of International Relations, University of London, since 1962; b 1916; m 1951; one s two d. BSc(Econ) London 1945. Asst Lectr, LSE, 1948–59. Reader, 1959–62. Regular Army Offr., 1936–43; Foreign Off., 1945–48; Comr for Chs on Internat. Affs, 1969– ; Principal, St Catherine's, Cumberland Lodge, Windsor Gt Park, 1971–72; Mem., Res. Cttee, Royal Inst. Internat. Aff., 1965– ; (Mem. Council, 1969–71). Publications: ed, University Teaching of International Relations, 1952; Britain and the United Nations, 1958; (with S. Strange) Research in International Organization, 1969; contrib. Internat. Organiz., Internat. Aff., Internat. Relat. Address: London School of Economics and Political Science, Aldwych, WC2A 2AE.

Goodwin, Richard Murphey; Reader in Economics, University of Cambridge, since 1969; b 1913; m 1937. AB Harvard 1934, BA Oxon 1936, BLitt Oxon 1937, PhD Harvard 1941; Mem., Economet. Soc., 1942– . Instructor, Harvard, 1941–46; Asst Prof., Harvard, 1946–51; Lectr, Cambridge, 1951–69. Fellow, Peterhouse, Cambridge, 1957. Publications: Elementary Economics, 1970; contrib. Economet., Econ. Jl, Rev. Econ. Stats. Address: Peterhouse, Cambridge.

Goody, Dr Esther; Lecturer in Social Anthropology, University of Cambridge, and Fellow of New Hall, since 1972; b 1932; m 1956; two d. BA Antioch 1954 (Sociology), PhD Cantab 1961 (Social Anthropology). Fellow and Lectr in Social Anthropology, New Hall, Cambridge, 1966– . Publications: Contexts of Kinship, 1973; essays, in, Marriage in Tribal Society, ed M. Forbes, 1962; Socialization: The Approach from Social Anthropology, ed P. Mayer, 1969; Witchcraft Confessions and Accusations, ed M. Douglas, 1970; The Interpretation of Ritual, ed J. S. La Fontaine, 1972; contrib. Man, Race. Address: New Hall, Cambridge.

Goody, Prof. John Rankine, ScD; William Wyse Professor of Social Anthropology, University of Cambridge, since 1973; Director of the African Studies Centre, and Fellow of St John's College, Cambridge University, since 1961; b 1919. BA Cambridge 1946, DipAnth Cambridge 1947, BLitt Oxon 1962, PhD Cambridge 1954,

ScD Cambridge 1969. Asst Lectr, Cambridge, 1954–59, Lectr, 1959–61; Smuts Reader in Commonwealth Studies, 1971–73. Mem., Council, Internat. Afr. Inst. *Publications*: The Social Organisation of the LoWiili, 1956; ed, The Developmental Cycle in Domestic Groups, 1958; Death, Property and the Ancestors, 1962; ed, Succession to High Office, 1966; (with J. A. Braimah) Salaga: the Struggle for Power, 1967; ed, Literacy in Traditional Societies, 1968; Comparative Studies in Kinship, 1969; Technology, Tradition and the State in Africa, 1971; The Myth of The Bagre, 1972; ed, The Character of Kinship, 1973; (with S. J. Tambiah) Bridewealth and Dowry, 1973; *contrib.* Afr., Jl Royal Anthropol. Inst., Brit. Jl Sociol., Comp. Studies Soc. and Hist., Econ. Hist. Rev., Amer. Jl Sociol., Europ. Jl Sociol., Jl Afr. Hist., Jl Mod. Afr. Studies, Sociol. *Address*: St John's College, Cambridge.

Goodyear, Prof. Francis Richard David, MA, PhD; Hildred Carlile Professor of Latin, University of London, since 1966; *b* 1936; *m* 1967; one *s*. BA Cantab 1957 (1st cl. Classics), MA and PhD Cantab 1961; Craven Schol. 1956, Chancellor's Medal 1957. Res. Fellow, St John's Coll., Cambridge, 1959–60; Official Fellow, Queens' Coll., Cambridge, 1960–66, Libr., Queens' Coll., Cambridge, 1960–64; Dean, Fac. of Arts, Bedford Coll., London, 1971. *Publications*: Incerti auctoris Aetna, 1965; (with others) Appendix Vergiliana, 1966; (with J. Diggle) Corippi Iohannidos Libri VIII, 1970; Tacitus, a survey, 1970; Tacitus, Annals 1–6, vol. 1, 1972; ed jtly, A. E. Housman: Classical Papers, 1972; *contrib.* Bull. Inst. Class. Studies. Class. Qly, Class. Rev., Gnomon, Jl Rom. Studies, Proc. Camb. Philo. Soc. *Address*: Dept of Latin, Bedford College, Regent's Park, NW1 4NS.

Goold, Prof. George Patrick; Professor of Latin, University College London, since 1973; *b* 1922. BA 1948, PhD 1954, London, AM Hons Harvard 1965; Member: Class. Assoc.; JACT; Hellenic Soc.; Roman Soc.; Class. Assoc. of Canada (Sec., 1959–61); Amer. Philol Assoc. (Servius Cttee, 1963–). Lectr in Classics, UC, Hull, 1948–55; Prof. of Classics, Univ. of Cape Town, 1955–57; Associate Prof. of Classics, Univ. of Manitoba, 1957–60; Prof. of Classics, Univ. of Toronto, 1960–65; Prof. of Greek and Latin, Harvard Univ. 1965–73 (Chm., of Dept, 1971–72). Editor: Harvard Studies in Class. Philol., 1966–71; Loeb Class. Library, 1974– . *Publications*: ed, Catulli Carmina, 1973; *contrib.* Phoenix, Trans of Amer. Philol Assoc., Harvard Studies in Class. Philol. *Address*: Dept of Latin, Univ. Coll. London, Gower Street, WC1E 6BT.

Gordon, Charles P.; Lecturer, Law Faculty, University of Exeter, since 1971; *b* 1942. BA Chicago 1963, JD Chicago 1967; Mem. Illinois Bar. Temp. Asst Lectr, 1967, Asst Lectr, 1970, Univ. of Exeter. *Publications*: Civil Rights, a More Civil Remedy or Litigation not Demonstration, in, Fundamental Rights, 1973; *contrib.* New Law Jl. *Address*: Law Faculty, Exeter Univ., Exeter, Devon.

Gordon, Prof. Donald James, MA, PhD; Professor of English, University of Reading, since 1949; *b* 1915. MA Edinburgh, PhD Cantab; FRHistS, Corresp. Mem., Accademia Olimpico of Vicenza, Italy. Lectr in English, Univ. of Liverpool, 1942–46; Lectr in English, Univ. of Reading, 1946–49. *Publications*: (with J. Robertson) A Calendar of Dramatic Records in the Books of the Livery Companies of London 1485–1640, 1955; Images of a Poet: W. B. Yeats, 1961; ed, Fritz Saxl: Memorial Essays, 1957; *contrib.* Papers on problems connected with Renaissance Imagery, and on connexions between lit. and visual arts in late 19th century. *Address*: Dept of English, Univ. of Reading, Whiteknights, Reading, Berkshire RG6 2AH.

Gordon, Dr George; Lecturer, Department of Geography, University of Strathclyde, since 1966; *b* 1939; *m* 1965; two *d*. MA Edinburgh 1962 (1st cl. Geography), PhD Edinburgh 1971. Demonstrator, Dept of Geog., Edinburgh Univ., 1964–65; Asst Lectr, Dept of Geog., Strathclyde Univ., 1965–66. Convenor, West of Scotland Geography 14–18 Working Party. Mem., Cttee Inst. Brit. Geogrs, Urban Geog. Study Gp, 1972– . *Publication*: Atlas of the West Region (Scotland). *Address*: Dept of Geography, Univ. of Strathclyde, Glasgow G1 1XW.

Gordon, Prof. Gerald Henry, MA, LLB, PhD, LLD, QC; Professor of Scots Law, Edinburgh University, since 1972; Dean of the Faculty of Law, Edinburgh University, 1970–73; *b* 1929; *m* 1957; one *s* two *d*. MA Glasgow 1950 (1st cl. Philosophy with English Literature), LLB Glasgow 1953 (with distinction), PhD Glasgow 1960; Advocate (Scottish Bar) 1953; QC (Scot.) 1972; Mem.: Soc. Public Teachers of Law, Assoc. Internat. Droit Penal. Sen. Lectr in Criminal Law and Criminology, Edinburgh, 1965–68, Reader, 1968–69, Prof., 1969–72; Procurator-Fiscal Depute, Edinburgh, 1960–65; Mem., Thomson Cttee (Inter-Deptl Cttee on Crim. Procedure), 1969– ; Temporary Sheriff, 1973– . *Publications*: The Criminal Law of Scotland, 1967; ed, Renton and Brown's Criminal Procedure, 4th edn 1972; *contrib.* Jl Crim. Law, Jl Law Soc. Scotland, Law Qly Rev., Scots Law Times. *Address*: Old College, South Bridge, Edinburgh EH8 9YL.

Gordon, John Christopher Benedict; Lecturer in German, Language Centre, University of East Anglia, since 1970; *b* 1945. BA Oxon 1967; Mem. Phil Soc., Mem. Linguistics Assoc., of Gt Britain. Lektor in English, Universität des Saarlandes, Germany, 1967–68. *Address*: Language Centre, Univ. of East Anglia, University Plain, Norwich NOR 88C.

Gordon, Michael Colin, MA, MSc; Lecturer in International Relations, Department of Sociology, Government and Administration, University of Salford, since 1967; *b* 1929; *m* 1952; one *s* one *d*. BA Oxon 1953, MA Oxon 1966, MSc Salford 1968; NATO res. Fellow, 1970–71. Mem., Internat. Inst.

Strategic Studies. Lectr, Royal Coll. of Adv. Technol., Salford, 1959–67. Indust. Engrg Dept, T. Hedley and Co., 1953–56; Personnel Dept, 1956–59. *Address*: Dept of Sociology, Government and Administration, The Univ. of Salford, Salford M5 4WT.

Gordon, Prof. William Morrison, Douglas Professor of Civil Law, University of Glasgow, since 1969; *b* 1933; *m* 1957; two *s* two *d*. MA Aberdeen 1953, LLB Aberdeen 1955, PhD Aberdeen 1963; Solicitor 1956. Asst in Jurisprudence, Aberdeen, 1957–59; Lectr in Civil Law, Glasgow, 1960–65, Sen. Lectr in Private Law, 1965–69. *Publications*: Studies in the Transfer of Property by Traditio, 1970; *contrib*. Juridical Rev., Revue int. droits antiquité. *Address*: Faculty of Law, The Univ., Glasgow G12 8QQ.

Gore, Dr Keith Oakleigh; Fellow and Tutor in French, Worcester College, Oxford University, since 1967; *b* 1930; *m* 1960; one *s* one *d*. BA Wales 1955, MA Wales 1957, DU Paris 1967, MA Oxon 1967. Res. Fellow, Univ. of Wales, 1958–60; Asst Lectr, Queen Mary Coll., Univ. of London, 1960–63, Lectr, 1963–67. *Publications*: L'Idée de progrès dans la pensée de Renan, 1970; Sartre: La Nausée and Les Mouches (Studies in French Literature, 17), 1970; *contrib*. Bks Abroad, Rev. Hist. Litt. de la France, Jl Brit. Soc. Phenom. *Address*: Worcester College, Oxford.

Goring, Dr (John) Jeremy; Senior Lecturer in History, Goldsmiths' College, London, since 1969; *b* 1930; *m* 1958; three *s* one *d*. BA Oxon 1952 (2nd cl. Hist.), PhD London 1955, MA Oxon 1956, Dip. Theol. London 1961. Lectr, Goldsmiths' Coll., 1967. Trustee, Dr Williams's Library, 1958–68. *Publications*: (co-author) The English Presbyterians, 1968; (co-editor) Northamptonshire Militia Papers, 1973; *contrib*. EHR, Hist. *Address*: Dept of History, Goldsmiths' College, Lewisham Way, SE14 6NW.

Gorman, Prof. William Moore; Professor of Economics, London School of Economics, since 1967; *b* 1923; *m* 1950. BA(Econ) TCD 1948, BA(Maths) TCD 1949, MA Dublin and Oxon 1962; Hon. DSocSc Birmingham 1973. Asst Lectr, Lectr, and Sen. Lectr in charge, Dept. of Econometrics and Social Stats, Univ. of Birmingham, 1949–62; Prof. of Econ., Oxford Univ. and Fellow of Nuffield Coll., 1962–67; Vis. Prof. at various American Univs. Chm., Economic Studies Soc., 1964–67; Mem. Council: Royal Statistical Soc., 1966–67; Royal Econ. Soc., 1971–73; Vice-Pres., 1970–71, Pres., 1972, Econometric Soc. *Publications*: *contrib*. Econometrica, Jl of Polit. Economy, Rev. of Econ. Studies, etc. *Address*: Dept of Economics, London School of Economics and Political Science, Aldwych, WC2A 2AE.

Gorner, Paul Anthony; Lecturer, Department of Moral Philosophy, Aberdeen University, since 1966; *b* 1940; *m* 1965; three *s* one *d*. BA Manchester 1963, PhD Aberdeen 1972. *Publications*: *contrib*. Jl Brit. Soc. Phenom. *Address*: Dept of Moral Philosophy, King's College, Aberdeen.

Gosden, Dr Peter Henry John Heather, MA, PhD; Reader in Educational Administration and History, University of Leeds, since 1971; *b* 1927; *m* 1964. BA Cambridge 1948, MA Cambridge 1952, PhD London 1959; FRHistS. Lectr, Leeds Univ., 1960–67, Sen. Lectr, 1967–71. Jt Editor, Jl Educnl Admin. Hist. *Publications*: The Friendly Societies in England, 1815–1875, 1961; The Development of Educational Administration in England and Wales, 1966; The Development of Educational Administration in England and Wales; A Bibliographical Guide, 1967; (with D. W. Sylvester) History for the Average Child, 1968; How they were taught: learning and teaching in England, 1800–1950, 1969; The Evolution of a Profession, 1972; Self-Help: Voluntary Associations in the 19th Century, 1973. *Address*: Dept of Education, The Univ., Leeds LS2 9JT.

Goss, Prof. Anthony, FRTPI, DipTP, ARIBA; Professor of Urban Design and Head of Department of Town Planning, University of Wales Institute of Science and Technology, since 1967; *b* 1922; *m* 1949; one *s* one *d*. Dip. in TP London 1958; ARIBA 1951, FRTPI (AMTPI 1959, MTPI 1968). Sen. Lectr, Birmingham Sch. of Architecture, 1959–62; Head of the Leeds Sch. of Town Planning, 1962–67. Mem., Yorkshire and Humberside Econ. Planning Council, 1965–68. *Publications*: British Industry and Town Planning, 1962; The Architect and Town Planning, 1965; Homes, Towns and Traffic, 1965, 2nd rev. edn 1968; *contrib*. RIBA Jl, Jl RTPI, Town Planning Rev. *Address*: Dept of Town Planning, Univ. of Wales Institute of Science and Technology, King Edward VII Avenue, Cardiff CF1 3NU.

Gossip, Dr Christopher James, MA, PhD; Lecturer in French, University of Aberdeen, since 1967; *b* 1941; *m* 1970. MA Edinburgh 1962 (1st cl. French), PhD Edinburgh 1971. Asst Lectr, Aberdeen Univ., 1964–67. *Publications*: ed, T. Corneille: Stilicon, 1973; *contrib*. Jeunesse de Racine, Cahiers Raciniens, Studi Francesi. *Address*: Dept of French, Univ. of Aberdeen, Taylor Building, Old Aberdeen AB9 2UB.

Gossling, William Frank, MA, MSA, PhD; Lecturer in Economics, School of Social Studies, University of East Anglia, since 1969; *b* 1932; *m* 1956. BA Cantab 1955, MA Cantab 1959, MSA Toronto 1962, PhD Illinois 1965; Mem.: Economet. Soc., Amer. Econ. Assoc., Amer. Agric. Econ. Assoc., Soc. of the Sigma Xi. Res. Asst, Univ. of Toronto, 1959–61; Res. Asst, Univ. of Illinois, 1962–65; Res. Associate, Univ. of Illinois, 1965–66; Res. Fellow, Univ. of Manchester, 1966–69. Consultant: USDA, 1966; CSO, 1968; Director: 1968 Manchester Conf. on Input-Output; 1971 Norwich Conf. on Input-Output and Throughput; Chm., Input-Output Res. Assoc. (formerly Gp), 1966– . *Publications*: Productivity Trends in a Sectoral Macro-Economic Model, 1972; ed, Input-Output in the United Kingdom, 1970; *contrib*. Jl Agric. Econ. Soc., Canad. Jl Agric. Econ., Jl Farm Econ., Rev. Econ. Studies, Manchester Sch. *Address*: School of

Social Studies, Univ. of East Anglia, University Plain, Norwich NOR 88C.

Gottmann, Prof. Jean; Professor of Geography, University of Oxford, and Fellow of Hertford College, Oxford, since 1968; *b* 1915; *m* 1957. Hon. LLD Wisconsin; Hon. DSc S Illinois 1969; FRGS; Hon. Member: Amer. Geog. Soc., 1960; Royal Netherlands Geog. Soc., 1963; Amer. Acad. of Arts and Sciences, 1972. Res. Asst Human Geog., Sorbonne, 1937–40; Mem., Inst. for Advanced Study, Princeton, NJ, several times, 1942–65; Lectr, then Associate Prof. in Geog., Johns Hopkins Univ., Baltimore, 1943–48; Dir of Studies and Research, UN Secretariat, NY, 1946–47; Chargé de Recherches, CNRS, Paris, 1948–51; Lectr, then Prof., Institut d'Etudes Politiques, Univ. of Paris, 1948–56; Res. Dir, Twentieth Century Fund, NY, 1956–61; Prof., Ecole des Hautes Etudes, Sorbonne, 1960– ; Governor, Univ. of Haifa; Pres., World Soc. for Ekistics, 1971–73. Charles Daly Medal of Amer. Geog. Soc., 1964; Prix Bonaparte-Wyse, 1962; Palmes Académiques, 1968. *Publications*: Relations commerciales de la France, 1942; L'Amérique, 1949, 3rd edn 1960; A Geography of Europe, 1950, 4th edn 1969; La politique des états et leur géographie, 1952; Virginia at Mid-Century, 1955; Megalopolis, 1961; Essais sur l'aménagement de l'espace habité, 1966; The Significance of Territory, 1973. *Address*: School of Geography, Mansfield Road, Oxford OX1 3TB.

Gottschalk, Dr Hans Benedict; Lecturer in Classics, University of Leeds, since 1959; *b* 1930. BA Cantab 1952, MA and PhD Cantab 1957. Master, Uppingham Sch., 1957. Asst Lectr in Classics, Leeds Univ., 1958–59. *Publications*: ed, Strator of Lampsacus: Some Texts (Proc. Leeds Philos. and Lit. Soc.), 1965; *contrib.* Class. Philol., Class. Qly, Class. Rev., Erasmus, Gnomon, Hermes, Jl Hellenic Studies, Philologus, Phronesis, Brit. Jl for Hist. of Sci., Archives Internat. d'Histoire des Sciences. *Address*: Dept of Latin, The Univ., Leeds LS2 9JT.

Gough, Ian Roger, MA; Lecturer in Social Administration, University of Manchester, since 1968; *b* 1942; *m* 1964; three *s.* BA Cantab 1964 (Economics), MA Cantab 1967. Res. Associate, Manchester Univ., 1964–66, Asst Lectr, 1966–68. *Publications*: *contrib.* Manchester Sch., Econ. Social Admin, New Left Rev., CSE Bull. *Address*: Dept of Social Administration, Univ. of Manchester, Manchester M13 9PL.

Gough, John Vaughan; Lecturer, English Language and Mediaeval Literature, Leicester University, since 1969; *b* 1943; *m* 1969. BA Oxon 1965, MA Oxon 1969, Dip. Compar. Philology 1968. Mem. Philological Soc. Asst Lectr, Leicester Univ., 1967–69. *Publications*: *contrib.* English Studies, Anglia., railway magazines. *Address*: Dept of English, Univ. of Leicester, Leicester LE1 7RH.

Gould, Prof. John Philip Algernon, MA; Henry Overton Wills Professor of Greek, University of Bristol, since 1974; *b* 1927; *m* 1953; two *s* two *d.* BA Cantab 1948 (1st cl. Classics), MA Cantab 1951, MA Oxon 1953. Res. Fellow, Jesus Coll., Cambridge, 1952–53; Student and Tutor, Christ Church, Oxford, 1953–68; Prof. of Classics, Univ. Coll. of Swansea, 1968–74; Editor, Class. Qly, 1968–74; Vis. Jun. Fellow, Center Hellenic Studies, Washington, DC, 1962–63. Mem., Council, Hellenic Soc., 1969–72. *Publications*: The Development of Plato's Ethics, 1955; ed (with D. M. Lewis), Sir A. Pickard-Cambridge: Dramatic Festivals of Athens, rev. edn 1968. *Address*: Dept of Classics, Univ. of Bristol, Bristol BS8 1RJ.

Gould, Prof. Samuel Julius, MA; Professor of Sociology, University of Nottingham, since 1964; *b* 1924; *m* 1954; two *s.* BA and MA Oxon 1949. Mem., Brit. Sociol. Assoc. Asst Lectr, Univ. Coll., Swansea, 1949–50; Lectr, LSE, 1950–57, Reader in Sociol Insts, 1957–64; Vis. Prof., Univ. of California, Berkeley, 1959; Cornell Univ., 1971. Mem.: UK Nat. Commn for UNESCO. 1965– ; E Mid. Reg. Econ. Planning Council, 1965– . *Publications*: ed (with W. L. Kolb), A Dictionary of the Social Sciences, 1964; (with S. Esl) Jewish Life in Modern Britain, 1964; ed, Penguin Survey of Social Science, 1964; Penguin Social Sciences Survey, 1968; *contrib.* Brit. Jl Sociol., Govt Opposit. *Address*: Dept of Sociology, Univ. of Nottingham, Nottingham NG7 2RD.

Goulder, Rev. Michael Douglas; Staff Tutor in Theology, Department of Extramural Studies, University of Birmingham, since 1966, Senior Lecturer since 1972; *b* 1927; *m* 1953; two *s* two *d.* BA Cantab. 1948, BA Oxford 1954, MA 1967. Mem., Studiorum Novi Testamenti Societas, 1967. *Publications*: Type and History in Acts, 1964; Midrash and Lection in Matthew, 1974; *contrib.* Jl Theol Studies. *Address*: Dept of Extramural Studies, Univ. of Birmingham, Birmingham B15 2TT.

Gourvish, Dr Terence Richard; Senior Lecturer in Economic History, University of East Anglia, since 1974; *b* 1943; *m* 1967. BA London 1964 (1st cl. Hons Med. and Mod. History, King's Coll.), PhD LSE 1964 (Econ. History); Mem., Econ. History Soc. Asst Lectr in Econ. History, Univ. of Glasgow, 1967–69; Lecturer: Univ. of Glasgow 1969–70; Univ. of East Anglia 1971–74. Executive: Nat. Council Inland Transport, 1971– ; Transport 2000, 1973– . *Publications*: Mark Huish and the London and North Western Railway, 1972; *contrib.* Business History, Business History Rev., Econ. History Rev., Jl Econ. History, Scottish Jl Pol Econ. *Address*: School of Social Studies, Univ. of East Anglia, Norwich NOR 88C.

Gowan, Prof. Ivor Lyn, MA; Professor of Political Science, University College of Wales, Aberystwyth, since 1965; *b* 1922; *m* 1947; one *s.* BA Wales 1942, BA Oxon 1945 (PPE), MA Oxon 1951. Scholar, Balliol Coll., Oxford, 1945–47; Student, Nuffield Coll., Oxford, 1947–49; Lectr, Nottingham Univ., 1949–60, Sen. Lectr, 1960–65. Temp. Asst Principal, Treasury, 1947; Vis. Public Admin. Expert, UN, Colombia, 1966; Mem., Welsh Council,

1968– ; Treas., Jt Univ. Council Social Studies, 1969– . *Publications*: The Reform of Local Government, 1955; The Role and Power of Political Parties, 1963; Government in Wales in the Twentieth Century, 1970; *contrib.* Loc. Govt Chron., Public Admin. *Address*: Dept of Political Science, Univ. College of Wales, Llandinam Building, Aberystwyth, Dyfed.

Gower, Laurence Cecil Bartlett, FBA; Vice-Chancellor, University of Southampton, since 1971; *b* 1913; *m* 1939; two *s* one *d*. LLB London 1933, LLM London 1934; Hon. LLD York Ont, Edinburgh, Dalhousie; FBA 1965. Sir Ernest Cassel Prof. of Commercial Law in Univ. of London, 1948–62, Vis. Prof., Law School of Harvard Univ., 1954–55; Prof. and Dean of Faculty of Law of Univ. of Lagos, 1962–65; Holmes Lectr, Harvard Univ., 1966. Fellow of Univ. Coll. London. Admitted solicitor, 1937; Adviser on Legal Educn in Africa to Brit. Inst. of Internat. and Comparative Law and Adviser to Nigerian Coun. of Legal Educn, 1962–65; Law Comr, 1965–71. Mem.: Jenkins Cttee on Company Law Amendment; Denning Cttee on Legal Educn for Students from Africa, 1960; Ormrod Cttee on Legal Educn, 1967–70. Trustee, Brit. Museum, 1968– . Hon. Fellow, LSE, 1970. *Publications*: Principles of Modern Company Law, 1954, 3rd edn 1969; Independent Africa: The Challenge to the Legal Profession, 1967; numerous articles in legal periodicals. *Address*: The Univ., Southampton SO9 5NH.

Gowing, Prof. Lawrence Burnett, CBE, MA; Professor of Fine Art, University of Leeds, since 1967; *b* 1918; three *d*. MA Dunelm 1952. Prof. of Fine Art, Univ. of Durham, and Principal, King Edward VII Sch. of Art, Newcastle upon Tyne, 1948–58; Principal, Chelsea Sch. of Art, 1958–65. Keeper of Brit. Collection, and Dep. Dir, Tate Gallery, 1965–67; Painter, exhibitions: 1942, 1946, 1948, 1955, 1965; works in collections of Contemp. Art Soc., Tate Gallery, National Gallery of Canada, National Gallery of South Australia, British Council, Arts Council, Ashmolean Museum and Galleries of Brighton, Bristol, Manchester, Middlesbrough, Newcastle, Nottingham, etc. Mem.: Arts Council, 1970–72, (Art Panel, 1953–58, 1959–65, 1969–70, Dep. Chm., 1970–72; Chm., Art Films Cttee, 1970–72); Trustee: Tate Gallery, 1953–60, and 1961–64; National Portrait Gallery, 1960– ; Mem., National Council for Diplomas in Art and Design, 1961–65; Chm., Adv. Cttee on Painting, Gulbenkian Foundn, 1958–64. *Publications*: Renoir, 1947; Vermeer, 1952, 2nd edn 1971; Cézanne (catalogues of exhibns), 1954, 1973; Constable, 1960; Vermeer, 1961; Goya, 1965; Turner: Imagination and Reality, 1966; Matisse (Museum of Modern Art, New York), 1966, London, 1968; Hogarth (Tate Gallery Exhbn), 1971; Exhibn catalogues; *contrib.* periodicals. *Address*: Univ. of Leeds, Leeds LS2 9JT.

Gowing, Prof. Margaret Mary, BSc(Econ); Professor of the History of Science, University of Oxford, since 1973; *b* 1921; *m* 1944; two *s*. BSc(Econ) London 1941; FRHistS. Bd of Trade, 1941–45; Hist. Sect., Cabinet Off., 1945–59; Historian and Archivist, UK Atomic Energy Auth., 1959–66; Reader in Contemp. Hist., Univ. of Kent at Canterbury, 1966–72; Mem., Cttee on Deptal Records (Grigg Cttee), 1952–54; Publicns Adv. Cttee, PRO; SSRC Cttee on Govt; Exec. Cttee, Assoc. Contemp. Hist.; Royal Soc./RCHM Cttee on Sci. and Tech. Records. *Publications*: (with Sir K. Hancock) British War Economy, 1949, 2nd edn 1953; (with E. L. Hargreaves) Civil Industry and Trade, 1952; Britain and Atomic Energy, 1964, French edn 1965; Independence and Deterrence: I, Policy Making; II, Policy Execution, 1974; *contrib.* various jls. *Address*: Linacre College, Oxford.

Gowland, Dr David Alexander; Lecturer in Modern History, University of Dundee, since 1968; *b* 1942. BA Hons Manchester 1963 (Hist), PhD 1966, PGCE London 1967; Member: Univ. Assoc. for Contemporary European Studies; Ecclesiastical Hist. Soc.; Wesley Hist. Soc. Asst Lectr in European History, Univ. of Dundee, 1967–68; Open Univ. Course Tutor, 1970. *Publications*: Common Market or Community?, 1973; *contrib.* Proc. Wesley Hist. Soc. *Address*: Dept of Modern History, Univ. of Dundee, Dundee DD1 4HN.

Goy, Dr Edward Dennis; University Lecturer, Department of Slavonic Studies, Cambridge, since 1958; *b* 1926. MA 1954, PhD 1955, Cantab. Asst Lectr, Cambridge, 1955–58. *Publications*: trans.: Miodrag Bulatović: The Red Cockerel, 1962; Radomir Konstantinović: Exitus, 1965; Miodrag Bulatović: Hero on a Donkey, 1966; *contrib.* Annali Istituto Universitario Napoli, Slavonic and E European Rev. *Address*: Dept of Slavonic Studies, Sidgwick Avenue, Cambridge.

Grabiner, Anthony Stephen, LLM; Lecturer in Law, Queen Mary College, University of London, since 1968; *b* 1945. LLB London 1966 (1st cl.), LLM London 1967 (Distinction); Barrister-at-Law, Lincolns Inn, 1968. Pt-time Teacher, LSE, 1966–67; Asst Lectr, Queen Mary Coll., 1967–68. *Publications*: ed jtly, Sutton and Shannon on Contracts, 8th edn 1970; *contrib.* Mod. Law Rev. *Address*: Faculty of Laws, Queen Mary College, Mile End Road, E1 4NS.

Gradon, Pamela Olive Elizabeth, PhD; University Lecturer in Medieval English, since 1963, and Fellow and Lecturer, St Hugh's College, Oxford University, since 1950; *b* 1915. BA Oxon 1937 (2nd cl. English), MA Oxon 1941, PhD London 1948, Dip. in Comparative Philology Oxon 1942. Asst Lectr, then Lectr, Bedford Coll., London, 1943–50. Ed. Sec. Early English Text Soc., 1970– . *Publications*: The Old English 'Elene', 1958, rev. American edn 1966; Form and Style in early English Literature, 1971; contrib. Essays presented J. R. R. Tolkien; *contrib.* Engl. Germanic Studies, Mod. Lang. Rev. *Address*: St Hugh's College, Oxford.

Graebner, Dr Eric Hans; Lecturer in Music, University of Southampton, since

1968; *b* 1943; *m* 1968; one *s*. BA Cantab 1964
(1st cl.), MA Cantab 1967, DPhil York 1968.
Vis. Fellow, Princeton, 1973. Mem. Editorial
Bd, New Berlioz Edn, 1966– . *Publications*:
New Berlioz Edition, vol. 4; *contrib*. Perspectives of New Music, Soundings, Musical
Times. *Address*: Music Dept, Univ. of
Southampton, Highfield, Southampton SO9
5NH.

Graham, Dr Alexander John; Senior
Lecturer in Ancient History, University of
Manchester, since 1970; *b* 1930; *m* 1963;
two *s*. BA Cantab 1952 (1st cl. Classics),
MA Cantab 1956, PhD Cantab 1957; Member: Soc. Promotion Hellenic Studies, Soc.
Promotion Roman Studies, Class. Assoc.,
Brit. Sch. Athens, Cambridge Philol. Assoc.
Asst Lectr in Classics, Bedford Coll.,
London, 1955–57; Asst Lectr in Ancient
History, Manchester, 1957–59; Lectr, 1959–
70. Mem.: Council, Hellenic Soc., 1959–62;
Cttee, Bootham and Mount Schs, York,
1961–69. *Publications*: Colony and Mother
City in Ancient Greece, 1964; *contrib*. Ann.
Brit. Sch. Athens, Historia, Jl Hellenic
Studies, Jl Roman Studies. *Address*: Dept of
History, Univ. of Manchester, Manchester
M13 9PL.

Graham, Prof. Angus Charles, MA, PhD;
Professor of Classical Chinese, School of
Oriental and African Studies, University of
London, since 1971; *b* 1919; *m* 1955 (marr.
diss. 1967); one *d*. BA Oxon 1940 (Theology),
MA Oxon, BA London 1949 (Chinese), PhD
London 1953. Lectr, SOAS, 1950–66, Reader,
1966–71; Vis. Fellow, Hongkong Univ.,
1954–55; Vis. Prof., Yale, 1965–67; Michigan,
1970; Sen. Fellow, Soc. of Humanities,
Cornell, 1972–73; Cnsltng Editor: Foundations of Language, 1965– ; Jl of Chinese
Philosophy, 1973– . *Publications*: Two
Chinese Philosophers: Ch'eng Ming-tao and
Ch'eng Yi-ch'uan, 1958; Problem of Value,
1961; The Book of Lieh-tzu, 1960; Poems
of the late T'ang, 1965; The Sun beneath the
Coral, 1969; *contrib*. Asia Major, Bull. SOAS,
Founds of Lang, Hist. Relig., Mind, Tsinghua Jl. *Address*: School of Oriental and
African Studies, Univ. of London, Malet
Street, WC1E 7HP.

Graham, Dr Desmond Francis; Lecturer,
School of English, University of Newcastle
upon Tyne, since 1971; *b* 1940; *m* 1961; one *s*
one *d*. BA Leeds 1961, PhD 1969. Tübingen
Univ., 1961–62; UC of Rhodesia and Nyasaland, 1962–63; UC of Sierra Leone, 1963–66;
Munich Univ., 1968–70; Mannheim Univ.,
1970–71. *Publications*: Introduction to Poetry,
1968; Keith Douglas 1920–44: a biography,
1974; *Address*: Sch. of English, The Univ.,
Newcastle upon Tyne NE1 7RU.

Graham, Douglas; Senior Lecturer in
Psychology, University of Durham, since
1960; *b* 1920; *m* 1944; one *s* two *d*. MA St
Andrews 1940, BScEcon London 1947,
EdB Glasgow 1948; ABPsS. Res. Asst
Educational Psychology, Univ. of Durham,
1948–51; Lectr in Psychology, 1951–60. Dean
of Faculty of Social Science, Univ. of Durham, 1970–72. *Publications*: Moral Learning
and Development, 1972; trans. L. Chertok:

Hypnosis, 1966; trans. L. Chertok et al:
Motherhood and Personality, 1970; trans.
Claudine Herzlich: Health and Illness, 1973.
Address: Dept of Psychology, Science
Laboratories, South Road, Durham.

Graham, Ian Ewen; Registrar and Secretary, University of Durham, since 1963; *b*
1924. MA Edinburgh 1950 (History). Asst
Registrar, Univ. of Durham, 1950–59; Sec.
of Durham Colls, 1959–63. Mil. Service,
1943–47, commnd Royal Scots; served in
Italy and Austria. Chm., Registrar's Conf.,
1967–68. *Publication*: The University of
Durham, in, Durham County and City with
Teesside, ed J. C. Dewdney, 1970. *Address*:
Univ. of Durham, Old Shire Hall, Durham
DH1 3HP.

Graham, Ilse, BA, PhD; Reader, Department of German, University of London, since
1965; *b* 1914; *m* 1951; one *s* one *d*. BA London
1939 (Hons German), PhD London 1951.
Asst Lectr, Queen Mary Coll., 1942–46; Asst
Lectr, Univ. Coll., London, 1946–49, Lectr,
1949–51; Res. and Lectrg, USA, 1951–53;
Part-time Lectr, King's Coll., London, 1954–
57, Lectr, 1957–65. *Publications*: Creative
Configurations: Lessing and Goethe, 1973;
Schiller, Talent and Integrity: a Study of his
Dramas, 1974; Schiller, A Master of the
Tragic Form: His Theory in His Practice,
1974, German edn 1974; *contrib*. Deutsche,
Beitr., Eup., Germ. Life Lett., Mod. Lang.
Notes, Mod. Lang. Qly, Mod. Lang. Rev.,
Pubs. Engl. Goethe Soc., Jb. Deuts. Schiller
Gesell. *Address*: Dept of German, King's
College, Univ. of London, Strand, WC2R
2LS.

Graham, Dr Norman Christopher; Senior
Tutor and Senior Lecturer, Department of
Education, University of Aston, since 1972;
b 1928; *m* 1962; one *s* two *d*. BA, DipEd
Durham 1952, BA London 1963 (Psychol.),
PhD Birmingham 1970 (Ed. Psychol.); Associate Brit. Psychol Soc. Univ. of Aston: Sen.
Res. Associate, 1965–68; Lectr, 1968–72.
Publications: The Language of Educationally
Subnormal Children (DES Res. Report 1,
Birmingham Univ.), 1970; contrib. Proc.
Biennial Conf., Assoc. for Special Educn,
1968; *contrib*. Educnl Rev., Jl of Learning
Disabilities, Language Cognitive Defects
and Retardation, Lang. and Speech. *Address*:
Dept of Education, Univ. of Aston, Birmingham B4 7ET.

Granger, Prof. Clive William John, BA,
PhD; Professor of Applied Statistics and
Econometrics, Mathematics Department,
University of Nottingham, since 1965; *b* 1934;
m 1960; one *s* one *d*. BA Nottingham 1955
(1st cl. Maths), PhD Nottingham 1959
(Statistics); FRStatSoc. Asst Lectr, Univ. of
Nottingham, 1956–59, Lectr, 1959–64,
Reader, 1964–65; Res. Fellow, Princeton
Univ., 1959–60; Vis. Associate Prof., Stanford Univ., 1963; Vis. Prof., Univ. of California, San Diego, 1969–70. *Publications*:
(with M. Hatanaka) Spectral Analysis of
Economic Time Series, 1964; (with O.
Morgenstern) Predictability of Stock Market
Prices, 1970; (with W. Labys) Speculation,
Hedging and Commodity Price Forecasts,

1970; *contrib.* Jl Amer. Stat. Assoc., Jl Amer. Mktg Soc., Appl. Stats, Jl Int. Inst. Stats, Econometrica, Jl Royal Stat. Soc., etc. *Address*: Dept of Mathematics, Univ. of Nottingham, Nottingham NG7 2RD.

Gransden, Antonia; Reader in Medieval History, University of Nottingham, since 1973 (Lecturer, 1965–73); *b* 1928; *m* 1956; two *d*. BA Oxon 1951 (1st cl. History), MA 1956, PhD London 1957; FRHistS. Asst Keeper, Dept of Mss, Brit. Museum. 1952–62. *Publications*: The Letter-Book of William of Hoo, Sacrist of Bury St Edmunds 1280–1294 (Suffolk Records Soc. v), 1963; The Customary of the Benedictine Abbey of Eynsham in Oxfordshire (Corpus Consuetudinum Monasticarum, ii), 1963; The Chronicle of Bury St Edmunds 1212–1301 (Nelson's Medieval Texts), 1964; The Customary of the Benedictine Abbey of Bury St Edmunds in Suffolk (Henry Bradshaw Soc. xcix), 1973; Historical Writing in Medieval England, *c* 500–1307, 1974; *contrib.* Bull. Inst. Hist. Res., EHR, Rev. Bénédic., Speculum, Mediaeval Studies. *Address*: Dept of History, Univ. of Nottingham, Nottingham NG7 2RD.

Gransden, Karl Watts; Reader, Department of English, University of Warwick, 1973 (Senior Lecturer, 1965–73); *b* 1925; *m* 1956; two *d*. BA Cambridge 1949 (1st cl. Parts I and II, Classical Tripos), MA 1957. *Publications*: E. M. Forster, 1961, rev. edn 1970; Tennyson's 'In Memoriam', 1964; Tudor Verse Satire, 1970; *contrib.* Arethusa, Ess. Crit. *Address*: Univ. of Warwick, Coventry CV4 7AL.

Grant, Prof. Colin King, MA, DPhil; Professor of Philosophy, University of Durham, since 1959; *b* 1924; *m* 1961; two *s*. BA Oxon 1944 (1st cl. PPE), MA Oxon 1950, DPhil Oxon 1950; Mem., Mind Assoc., Aristot. Soc. Pollard Student, Wadham Coll., 1944–46; Asst Lectr in Moral Philosophy, Univ. of Glasgow, 1946–49; Lectr, Univ. of Nottingham, 1949–59; Vis. Prof., Univ. of Maryland, 1964–65; Vis. Prof., Univ. of Bergen, 1968. Mem., Council, Royal Inst. Philos., 1972. *Publications*: *contrib.* Mind, Proc. Aristot. Soc., etc. *Address*: Dept of Philosophy, 50 Old Elvet, Durham.

Grant, Damian, MA; Lecturer in English Literature, University of Manchester, since 1969; *b* 1940; *m* 1964; one *s* one *d*. BA London 1962 (1st cl. English Lang. and Lit.), MA London 1966. Asst Lectr in English, Manchester Univ., 1966–69. *Publications*: Realism, 1970; ed, Tobias Smollett: The Adventures of Ferdinand Count Fathom, 1971; *contrib.* Crit. Qly, Poetry Nation. *Address*: Dept of English, Univ. of Manchester, Manchester M13 9PL.

Grant, Helen Frances, MA; University Lecturer in Spanish (retired), Spanish Department, Cambridge, 1946–71, and Fellow of Girton College, since 1955, and Life Fellow since 1971; Leverhulme Emeritus Fellowship, 1973–75; *b* 1903; *m* 1930. BA Oxford 1930 (Spanish and French), MA Cambridge 1946 (by incorporation); Mem.,

Mod. Hum. Res. Assoc., Assoc. Hispan. GB, Int. Assoc. Hispan., Royal Inst. Int. Aff. Asst Lectr, Spanish Dept, Univ. of Birmingham, 1934–39; Teaching, Somerville and St Hilda's College, Oxford, 1934–39; Supervis., Tutor, Lectr in Spanish, Girton Coll., 1955–58; Lectr in Spanish and Supernum. Fellow, 1958–64; Grad. Tutor, 1968–71. Foreign Res. and Press Service, Spanish specialist, 1939–41 (Royal Inst. Int. Aff. for Foreign Off.); BBC European Service, Spanish Intell. Off., 1941–43; Asst Progr. Orgnsr, BBC Spanish Service, 1943–45; Mem., Fac. Bd Mod. and Mediev. Langs, Cambridge Univ. for ten years. *Publications*: contrib. Studies in Honour of Joseph Manson, 1972; Studies in Spanish Literature of the Golden Age, 1973; ed, Mariano Jose de Larra, Artículos de crítica literaria (with R. Johnson), 1964, 2nd edn 1971; *contrib.* Atlante, Bull. Hispan. Studies, Insula, Int. Aff., Mod. Lang. Rev., La Torre, Yrs Wk Mod. Langs. *Address*: Girton College, Cambridge.

Grant, Dr John James, CBE, Hon. DCL; Director, Institute of Education, University of Durham, since 1963; *b* 1914; *m* 1945; two *s*. MA Glasgow 1937, EdB Glasgow 1948; Hon. DCL Durham 1960; Qualified Teacher, Scottish Regs, 1938. Lectr in Educn, Univ. of Durham, 1948–53; Vice-Principal, Fourah Bay Coll., Sierra Leone, 1953–55; Principal, 1955–60; Principal, St Cuthbert's Soc., Univ. of Durham, 1960–63. *Address*: Univ. of Durham Institute of Education, 48 Old Elvet, Durham.

Grant, Dr Nigel D. C., MA, MEd, PhD; Reader, Department of Educational Studies, Edinburgh University, since 1972; *b* 1932; *m* 1957; one *s* one *d*. MA Glasgow 1954 (2nd cl. English), MEd Glasgow 1959 (1st cl.), PhD Glasgow 1969; Teacher's Secondary Cert. (Scotland) 1955. Lectr, Dept of Educnl Studies, Edinburgh Univ., 1965–72. Vis. Prof., Univ. of Michigan and Kent State, Ohio, 1968; Bowling Green State Univ., Ohio, 1971; Univ. of Michigan, 1972; Cnsltnt, Open Univ., 1971. Mem., Cttee, Comp. Educn Soc. in Europe, 1971– ; (Mem. Cttee, Brit. Sect., 1969– , Vice-Chm. 1971–73, Chm. 1973–); Chm., Scott. Univs Council for Studies in Educn. *Publications*: Soviet Education, 1964, 4th edn 1972, German edn 1966, Italian and Dutch edns 1972; Society, Schools and Progress in Eastern Europe, 1969; (with J. Lowe and T. D. Williams) Education and Nation-Building in the Third World, 1971; (with R. E. Bell) A Mythology of British Education, 1974; *contrib.* Comp. Educn, Comp. Educn Rev., Internat. Rev. Educn, Irish Jl Educn, Paedagogik, Rev. Legislaz. Scolast. Comp., Scott. Educnl Studies. *Address*: Dept of Educational Studies, Univ. of Edinburgh, 10/11 Buccleuch Place, Edinburgh, Scotland.

Grant, Valerie Hermine D.; *see* Dundas-Grant.

Grassby, Richard Bruce; Fellow and Tutor in Modern History, Jesus College, Oxford University, since 1964; *b* 1935; *m* 1962. BA Oxon 1957 (1st cl. History), MA Oxon 1962; FRHistS. P. S. Allen Jun. Res. Fellow,

Corpus Christi Coll., Oxford, 1961–64. *Publications*: contrib. Econ. Hist. EHR, Past Pres. *Address*: Jesus College, Oxford.

Grassie, Dr Alexander Donald Campbell; Lecturer in Experimental Physics, School of Mathematical and Physical Sciences, University of Sussex (also teaches combined Education/Physics), since 1962; *b* 1935; *m* 1960; two *s* one *d*. MA Aberdeen 1957, BA Cambridge 1959, PhD Cambridge 1962; MInstP. Mem., Nuffield Foundn Science. Teaching Project Adv. Cttee for Physical Science, 1964–70; Governor, Thomas Bennet Sch., Crawley, 1971– . *Publications*: Physical Science – Nuffield Advanced Science, 1972; *contrib*. Physical Rev., Jl Phys., Jl Low Temp. Phys. *Address*: Physics Laboratory, Univ. of Sussex, Brighton BN1 9QH.

Gratwick, Adrian Stuart; Lecturer, Department of Humanity, University of St Andrews, since 1967; *b* 1943; *m* 1970. MA Cantab 1964, DPhil Oxon 1968; Member: Roman Soc., Jt Assoc. of Classical Teachers, Oxford Philological Soc. Asst Lectr, St Andrews, 1967–70, Lectr, 1970– ; Admissions Officer, Faculty of Arts, 1971– . *Publications*: contrib. Classical Qly, Classical Rev., Glotta, Hermes, JRS. *Address*: Dept of Humanity, St Salvator's College, Univ. of St Andrews, St Andrews, Fife.

Grauberg, Walter; Director, Language Centre, University of Nottingham, since 1966; *b* 1923; *m* 1965; two *d*. BA 1944, MA 1948, Cantab, LèsL Lille 1953. Lectr in Educn, Univ. of Nottingham, 1960–66. Chm., Brit. Assoc. for Applied Linguistics, 1973. *Publications*: The Role and Structure of University Language Centres in Europe, 1972; *contrib*. Mod. Langs. *Address*: Language Centre, Univ. of Nottingham, Nottingham NG7 2RD.

Graves, Arthur Montague, TD; Special Lecturer in Geography, University of Bristol, since 1948; Warden of Wills Hall, since 1973; *b* 1920; *m* 1944; one *s*. BSc Bristol 1947. Mem., IBC. Warden of Burwalls Hall, Univ. of Bristol, 1959–73. *Address*: Department of Geography, The Univ., Bristol BS8 1TH.

Graves, Dr Norman John, BSc(Econ), MA, PhD; Senior Lecturer and Head of the Department of Geography, University of London Institute of Education, since 1963; *b* 1925; *m* 1950; one *s* one *d*. BSc(Econ) London 1949 (Economics and Geography), Teacher's Dip. 1950, MA London (Distinction – Education) 1957, PhD London 1964; FRGS. Lectr, Dept of Education, Univ. of Liverpool, 1960–63. Mem., Exec. Cttee, Geogl Assoc., 1969–72; Chm., Commn Geog. in Educn, Internat. Geogl Union; Chm., Geog Cttee, Schs Council. *Publications*: (with R. C. Honeybone) North America and Asia, 1966; (with J. T. White) Geography of the British Isles, 1971; Geography in Secondary Education, 1971; New Movements in the Study and Teaching of Geography, 1972; *contrib*. Cah. Geog. Québec, Bull. Univ. London. Inst. Educn, Geogl Jl, New Era, Persoon Gemeens. Vocat. Asp. Educn.

Address: Univ. of London Institute of Education, Malet Street, WC1E 7HS.

Graveson, Prof. Ronald Harry, CBE, QC, LLD; Professor of Private International Law, University of London, King's College, since 1974 (Professor of Law, 1947–74); Dean of the Faculty of Laws in the University; *b* 1911; *m* 1937; one *s* two *d*. LLB Sheffield 1932, LLM Sheffield 1933, LLD Sheffield 1955, SJD Harvard 1936, PhD London 1941, LLD London 1951, LLD (hc) Ghent 1964, DrJur (hc) Freiburg 1969; Solicitor 1934, Barrister-at-Law (Gray's Inn) 1945, Bencher 1965; QC 1966; Vice-Pres., Soc. Public Teachers of Law, 1971–72, Pres., 1972–73. Asst Lectr in Law, King's Coll., London, 1938–40; Reader in English Law, Univ. Coll., London, 1946–47; Vis. Prof. of Law, Harvard Law Sch., 1958–59. Army Service, 1940–46; Cnsltnt Editor, Law Reports and Weekly Law Reports, 1971– ; Mem., Rev. Body on Doctors' and Dentists' Pay, 1971. *Publications*: The Conflict of Laws, 1948, 7th edn 1974; Cases on the Conflict of Laws, 1949; Status in The Common Law, 1953; (jtly) A Century of Family Law, 1957; The Comparative Evolution of Principles of the Conflict of Laws in England and the USA, 1960; Comparative Aspects of the General Principles of Private International Law, 1963; (jtly) Law: an outline for the intending Student, 1967; (jtly) The Uniform Laws on International Sales Act 1967, 1968; *contrib*. Brit. Ybk Int. Law, Int. Comp. Law Qly, Law Qly Rev., Rev. Crit. Droit Int. Privé. *Address*: King's College, Strand, WC2R 2LS.

Gray, Barbara Joyce, BA, PhD; JP; Staff Tutor in Social Study, Department of Extramural Studies, University of Birmingham, since 1964; *b* 1923; *m* 1949. BA Birmingham 1946 (2nd cl. Soc. and Pol. Science), DipSS 1945, PhD 1948 (Psychology). Tutor in Social Studies, Dept of Social Studies, Leicester Univ., 1948–52; Res. Asst, Fac. of Commerce and Social Studies, Univ. of Birmingham, 1952–54; Sen. Res. Associate, 1961–64. County Councillor, Warwicks, 1958–61; Magistrate, Warwicks, 1959– ; Chm., Juvenile Ct Panel, 1964–70; Mem., Latey Cttee on Age of Majority, 1965–67; Dep. Chm., Solihull Bench, 1971; Co-opted mem., Birmingham Accident Prevention Cttee, 1961– . *Publications*: (with J. P. Davison et al.) Productivity and Economic Incentives, 1958; Home Accidents among Older People: report of research carried out in the Birmingham Area, 1966; *contrib*. Case Conf., Ment. Hlth, Sociol Rev. *Address*: Dept of Extramural Studies, Univ. of Birmingham, PO Box 363, Birmingham B15 2TT.

Gray, Denis Everett, MBE, BA, PhD; JP; Senior Lecturer, Department of Extramural Studies, University of Birmingham, since 1967; *b* 1926; *m* 1949. BA Birmingham 1948 (2nd cl. Hist.); PhD Manchester 1961. WEA Tutor-Organiser, Staffs, 1954–57. Lectr, Dept of Extramural Studies, Univ. of Birmingham, 1957–67. Chm., Solihull Magistrates, 1971– ; Mem., Lord Chancellor's Nat. Adv. Council on Training of Magistrates. *Publications*: Spencer Perceval: the Evangelical Prime Minister, 1963. *Address*: Dept of Extramural Studies, Univ. of Birmingham, PO Box 363, Birmingham B15 2TT.

Gray, Douglas; Fellow of Pembroke College, Oxford, since 1961; *b* 1930; *m* 1959; one *s*. MA Wellington 1952, MA Oxon 1960. Asst Lectr, Victoria Univ. of Wellington, 1953–54; Lectr, Pembroke and Lincoln Colls, Oxford, 1956–61. *Publications*: ed, Spenser: The Faerie Queene, Book 1, 1969; Themes and Images in the Medieval English Religious Lyric, 1972; *contrib*. Archiv für das Studium der Neueren Sprachen, Neuphilologische Mitteilungen, Notes and Queries. *Address*: Pembroke College, Oxford.

Gray, Eric William, MBE, MA; University Lecturer in Ancient History, Oxford University, since 1948; *b* 1910; *m* 1943; two *s* two *d*. BA Adelaide 1932 (1st cl. Classics), Rhodes Scholar for South Australia 1932, BA Oxon 1935 (1st cl. Classical Mods and Lit. Hum.), MA Oxon 1938; Asst Lectr in Classics, Birmingham Univ., 1936–38; Lectr in Ancient Hist., Christ Church, Oxford, 1938–39, Official Student and Tutor, 1939– , Censor, 1947–50; Vis. Lectr, Univ. of W Australia, 1967, 1973; Mem., Council Soc. Prom. Roman Studies, 1947–50, 1958–61 and 1967–70; Mem., Faculty, Brit. Sch. Rome, 1963–65. *Publications*: ed, Greenidge and Clay: Sources for Roman History (133–70 BC), rev. edn 1960; *contrib*. Class. Rev. Erasmus, Gnomon, Jl Roman Studies, Zeits. Papyrol. Epigraphie. *Address*: Christ Church, Oxford.

Gray, Dr Jeffrey Alan, MA, PhD; Lecturer in Psychology, Department of Experimental Psychology, since 1964, and Fellow of University College, Oxford, since 1965; *b* 1934; *m* 1961; two *s*. BA Oxon 1959 (1st cl. Mod. Lang.), BA Oxon 1959 (2nd cl. Psychology and Philosophy), Dip. Psychol. London 1960 (Distinction), MA Oxon 1964, PhD London 1964. *Publications*: Pavlov's Typology, 1964; The Psychology of Fear and Stress, 1971; The Biological Bases of Individual Behaviour, 1972; *contrib*. Acta Biol. Expers., Acta Psychol., Adv. Sci., Anim. Behav., Behav. Res. Therapy, Brit. Jl Psychol., Canad. Jl Psychol., Electroenceph Clin. Neurophysiol., Jl Exper. Psychol., Nature, Neuropharm., Phil. Qly, Physiol. Behav., Psychol. Bull., Psychol. Rev., Psychopharm., Qly Jl Exper. Psychol., Sci., Vopr. Psikhol. *Address*: Dept of Experimental Psychology, Oxford.

Gray, Rev. Prof. John; Professor of Hebrew, University of Aberdeen, since 1961; *b* 1913; *m*. MA Edinburgh, BD Edinburgh, PhD Edinburgh; Mem., Soc. for Old Testament Study. Lectr in Semitic Langs and Lits, Manchester Univ., 1946–53; Lectr in Hebrew and Biblical Criticism, Univ. of Aberdeen, 1953–61. Colonial Chaplain and Chaplain to Palestine Police, 1939–41; Minister of the Church of Scotland, Kilmory, Isle of Arran, 1942–46. *Publications*: The Kr Text in the Literature of Ras Sharma, 1955, 2nd edn 1964; The Legacy of Canaan, 1957, 2nd edn 1965; Archaeology and the Old Testament World, 1962; The Canaanites, 1964; Kings I

and II: a commentary, 1964, new edn 1970; Joshua, Judges and Ruth, 1967; A History of Jerusalem, 1969; Near Eastern Mythology, 1969; *contrib*. various Biblical Dictionaries, meml vols and learned jls. *Address*: Univ. of Aberdeen, Aberdeen AB9 1AS.

Gray, Rev. John, MA, BD, DD; Senior Lecturer in Christian Ethics and Practical Theology, University of Edinburgh, since 1969; *b* 1911; *m* 1939. MA Glasgow 1934 (1st cl. English), BD Glasgow 1937 (with Distinction), Hon. DD Glasgow 1967; Minister, Ch of Scotland, 1939. Bruce Lectr, Univ. of Glasgow, 1949; Hon. Lectr, Univ. of Edinburgh, 1954–66; Lectr, Univ. of Edinburgh, 1966–69. Dir of Studies, Divinity; Mem., var. Cttees on Religious Educn, Scotland. *Publications*: An Experimental Syllabus for Secondary Schools, 1960; A Second Experimental Syllabus for Secondary Schools, 1967; What about the Children, 1970; *contrib*. Expos. Times, Scott. Jl Theol. *Address*: New College, The Mound, Edinburgh.

Gray, Prof. John Richard; Professor of African History, University of London, since 1972; *b* 1929; *m* 1957; one *s* one *d*. BA Cantab 1951 (2nd cl. Hist.), MA Cantab 1955, PhD London 1957. Lectr, Univ. of Khartoum, 1959–61; Res. Fellow, SOAS, London, 1961–63; Reader, 1963–72; Vis. Prof., UCLA, 1967; Editor, Jl of Afr. Hist., 1968–71. *Publications*: The Two Nations, aspects of the development of race relations in the Rhodesias and Nyasaland, 1960; A History of the Southern Sudan, 1839–1889, 1961; (with D. Chambers) Materials for West African History in Italian Archives, 1965; ed (with D. Birmingham), Pre-Colonial African Trade, 1970; *contrib*. Jl Afr. Hist., Jl Contemp. Hist. *Address*: School of Oriental and African Studies, Univ. of London, WC1E 7HP.

Gray, John William Reid; Lecturer in Private Law, University of Dundee (formerly St Andrews), since 1964, and Warden of Airlie Hall, since 1966; *b* 1926. MA Aberdeen 1949 (2nd cl. Moral Philosophy and English), LLB Aberdeen 1952; Scots Bar 1954. Resident, Magistrate, Uganda, 1954–62; Temp. Procurator Fiscal Depute, Glasgow, 1962–63; Mem., Senate, Dundee Univ., 1971– . *Publications*: *contrib*. Jurid. Rev. Scots Law Times, Modern Law Rev., Jl SPTL. *Address*: Dept of Private Law, Univ. of Dundee, Dundee DD1 4HN.

Gray, Dr Ronald Douglas; Lecturer, German Department, University of Cambridge, since 1957; *b* 1919; *m* 1942; one *s* one *d*. BA Cambridge 1946, PhD Cambridge 1949. Univ. Asst Lectr, Cambridge 1949–57; Fellow, Emmanuel Coll., 1958. *Publications*: Goethe the Alchemist, 1952; Kafka's Castle, 1956; Brecht, 1961; ed, Kafka: A Collection of Critical Essays, 1962; An Introduction to German Poetry, 1965; The German Tradition in Literature, 1871–1945, 1965; Poems of Goethe, 1966; Goethe: A Critical Introduction, 1968; Franz Kafka, 1973. *Address*: Emmanuel College, Cambridge.

Gray, Timothy Stuart, BA; Lecturer in Politics, University of Newcastle upon Tyne,

267

since 1963; *b* 1942; *m* 1964; two *s* one *d*. BA Dunelm 1963 (1st cl. Politics and Economics). Mem., Newburn UDC, 1967–70. *Address*: Dept of Politics, Univ. of Newcastle upon Tyne, NE1 7RU.

Grayson, Prof. Cecil; Serena Professor of Italian Studies, University of Oxford, since 1958; *b* 1920; *m* 1947; one *s* three *d*. BA Oxon 1947 (1st cl. Mod. Langs), MA Oxon 1948. Foreign mem., Accad. Nazionale dei Lincei, Accad. della Crusca, Accad. delle Scienze di Bologna, Accad. Letteraria dell'Arcadia. Univ. Lectr in Italian, Oxford, 1948–57; Fellow, Magdalen Coll., 1958– ; Vis. Fellow, Newberry Libr., Chicago, 1965; Vis. Prof., Yale, 1966; Vis. Prof., Berkeley, 1969, 1973; Vis. Prof., Perth, WA, 1973. *Publications*: Opuscoli inediti di L. B. Alberti, 1954; Vincenzo Calmeta, Prose e Lettere, 1959; L. B. Alberti: Opere volgari, I 1960, II 1966, III 1973; L. B. Alberti: La prima grammatica della lingua volgare, 1964; Cinque saggi su Dante, 1972; L. B. Alberti: On Painting and Sculpture, 1972; trans. Ridolfi: Lives of Savonarola, 1959, Machiavelli, 1963, Guicciardini, 1967; *contrib.* Rinasc. Lett. Ital., Giorn. St. Lett. Ital., Rass. Lett. Ital., Ital. Studies, Burl. Mag., Romance Philol., etc. *Address*: Magdalen College, Oxford.

Grayson, Thomas John, CEng; Lecturer, Centre for Russian and East European Studies and Department of Engineering Production, University of Birmingham, since 1968; *b* 1939; *m* 1964. HND Glamorgan Coll. Technol. 1962 (Mech. Eng.), DIC 1963, MSc Birmingham 1969; CEng, MIMechE, MIProdE. Leverhulme Res. Fellow, Birmingham, 1965. Tech. Asst, NCB, 1963–65; Mem., GT Div., Inst. Prod. Eng., 1969–71; BSI Tech. Cttees, 1969– . *Publications*: Tech. Editor, series of books translated from Russian including: S. P. Mitrofanov: The Scientific Principles of Group Technology, 1966; E. K. Ivanov: Organisation and Technology of Group Production, 1968; V. A. Petrov: Flowline Group Production Planning, 1968; and part coll. wks J. Peklenik: Advances in Manufacturing Systems – Research and Development, 1971; *contrib.* Aslib Proc., Internat. Jl Prod. Res. *Address*: Centre for Russian and East European Studies, Univ. of Birmingham, PO Box 363, Birmingham B15 2TT.

Grayston, Rev. Prof. Kenneth, MA; Professor of Theology, Department of Theology and Religious Studies, University of Bristol, since 1965; Dean of Faculty of Arts since 1972; *b* 1914. BA Oxon 1937 (Chemistry), MA Oxon 1953, BA Cantab 1941 (Theology), MA Cantab 1943; Mem., Soc. OT Studies, Special Lectr, Bristol Univ., 1950–65. Asst Head, Religious Broadcasting, BBC, 1944–49; Sec., Studiorum Novi Testamenti Soc., 1955–65; Mem., Jt Cttee, New English Bible. *Publications*: Galatians and Philippians, 1957; Philippians and Thessalonians, 1967; *contrib.* symposia and dictionaries; *contrib.* NT Studies, Theol., Expo. Times, London Qly Rev., Ecumen. Rev. Bible Trans. *Address*: Dept of Theology, Royal Fort House, Tyndall Avenue, Bristol BS8 1UJ.

Greaves, Prof. Harold Richard Goring; Professor of Political Science, London School of Economics and Political Science, since 1960. Teaching at LSE, 1931– ; Vis. Prof., Columbia Univ., NY, 1959–60. Sometime Mem., Acad. Council, and Dean of Fac., Univ. of London. Literary Editor, Political Qly; English Editor, Internat. Pol Sci. Abstracts. *Publications*: The League Committees and World Order, 1931; The Spanish Constitution, 1933; Raw Materials and International Control, 1936; Reactionary England and Other Essays, 1936; The British Constitution, 1938; Federal Union in Practice, 1940; The Civil Service in the Changing State, 1947; The Foundations of Political Theory, 1958, 2nd edn 1966; Democratic Participation and Public Enterprise, 1964; *contrib.* Pol Qly, Pol Sci. Qly, Mod. Law Rev., CS in Brit. and France. *Address*: London Sch. of Economics and Political Science, Houghton Street, Aldwych, WC2A 1AE.

Green, Dr Christopher Paul; Lecturer in Geography, Bedford College, London, since 1966; *b* 1938; *m* 1965; two *s* one *d*. BA Oxon 1962 (2nd cl. Geography), DPhil Oxon 1965. Mem., Inst. Brit. Geogrs. Tutorial Res. Fellow, Geography Dept, Bedford Coll., London, 1965–66. *Publications*: *contrib.* Trans Inst. Brit. Geogrs, Geografiska Annaler. *Address*: Dept of Geography, Bedford College, Regent's Park, NW1 4NS.

Green, Prof. Dennis Howard; Professor of Modern Languages, Department of German, University of Cambridge, since 1966; *b* 1922. BA Cantab 1947, DPhil Basle 1949. Univ. Lectr, St Andrews, 1949–50; Fellow, Trinity Coll., Cambridge, 1949; Univ. Lectr, Cambridge, 1950–66; Vis. Prof., Cornell, 1965, Auckland, 1966, Yale, 1969, Australian Nat. Univ., 1971. Hd of Dept of Other Languages, Cambridge, 1956– . *Publications*: The Carolingian Lord, 1965; The Millstätter Exodus, 1966· *contrib.* Med. Æv., Mod. Lang. Rev. *Address*: Trinity College, Cambridge.

Green, Prof. Edward Rodney Richey, DPhil; Director, Institute of Irish Studies, Queen's University of Belfast, since 1970; *b* 1920; *m* 1948; two *s* one *d*. BA Hons Dublin 1942, DPhil Oxford 1952; MRIA, 1973. Lectr in Hist., TCD, 1943–45; Univ. of Manchester: Lectr in Hist., 1954–63; Sen. Lectr, 1963–70. Member: Historic Monuments Council, N Ireland, 1949; Council for Brit. Archaeol., 1960; Historic Buildings Council, N Ireland, 1973. *Publications*: The Lagan Valley, 1800–50, 1949; The Industrial Archaeology of Co. Down, 1963; ed, Essays in Scotch–Irish History, 1969; *contrib.* Irish Hist. Studies, William and Mary Qly, Ulster Jl of Archaeol. *Address*: Queen's Univ. of Belfast, 42 University Road, Belfast BT7 1NJ.

Green, Prof. H(arold) A(lfred) John; Professor of Economic Theory, University of Kent at Canterbury, since 1973; *b* 1923; *m* 1950; one *s* one *d*. BA Oxon 1947, MA Oxon 1948, PhD MIT 1954 (Industrial Econs); Member: Royal Econ. Soc., Econometric Soc., Amer. Econ. Assoc. Lectr, Clark

Univ., 1948–50; Instructor, Brown Univ., 1952–54; Res. Asst, Univ. Manchester, 1954–55; Lectr, Univ. Keele, 1955–58; Asst Prof. Univ. Calif. Santa Barbara, 1958–59; Univ. Toronto, 1959–72 (Prof. of Econs, 1963–72); Simon Vis. Prof., Univ. Manchester, 1965–66; Vis. Prof., Univ. Essex, 1971–72. Dir of Grad. Studies, Dept Polit. Econ., Univ. Toronto, 1970–71; Cons. to Econs Cttee of SSRC, 1973–74. *Publications:* Aggregation in Economic Analysis, 1964; Consumer Theory, 1971; *contrib.* American Econ., Rev. Can. Jl Econs and Polit. Sci., Economica, Econ. Jl, Economie Appliquée, Metroeconomica, Oxford Econ. Papers, Rev. Econ. Studies. *Address:* Darwin College., Univ. of Kent, Canterbury, Kent.

Green, John Nigel; Lecturer, in Romance and General Linguistics, Department of Language, University of York since 1967; *b* 1946; *m* 1972. BA Cantab 1967 (1st cl. Mod. and Mediaeval Langs), MA Cantab 1971; DPhil York 1973. Res. Fellow, Dept of Language, Univ. of York, 1969. Editor, York Papers in Linguistics. *Publications:* ed, W. D. Elcock: The Romance Languages (forthcoming); *contrib.* Archivum Linguisticum, Lingua, Romance Philol, Year's Work in Mod. Lang. Studies. *Address:* Dept of Language, Univ. of York, Heslington, York YO1 5DD.

Green, Dr Malcolm Robert; Lecturer in Roman History, Department of Humanity, University of Glasgow, since 1967; *b* 1943; *m* 1971. BA Oxon 1966, MA Oxon 1969, DPhil Oxon 1974; Mem. Soc. for Promotion of Roman Studies. *Address:* Dept of Humanity, Univ. of Glasgow, Glasgow G12 8QQ.

Green, Dr Peter; Senior Lecturer in Urban and Regional Planning, University of Strathclyde, since 1967; *b* 1931; *m* 1956; four *s.* BA Leeds 1953, MA Leeds 1955, PhD Strathclyde 1970; Mem. Inst. of British Geographers. Royal Coll. of Science and Technology, Glasgow, 1961. *Publications:* introd., Patrick Geddes: Dunfermline Report, 1973; *contrib.* Jl Indian History, Professional Geographer, Scottish Geog. Mag., Sociologia Ruralis. *Address:* Univ. of Strathclyde, George Street, Glasgow G1 1XW.

Green, Peter Stuart, MA, fil.kand; Senior Lecturer, Language Teaching Centre, University of York, since 1970; *b* 1929; *m* 1957; one *s* one *d.* BA Cantab 1952, MA Cantab 1956, fil.kand Lund 1959. Teaching and Res. Asst, York, 1965–67, Lectr, 1967–70. Export Sales Rep., English Steel Corp., Sheffield, 1952–56; Schoolmaster, Calday Grange GS, W Kirby, 1959–65. *Publications:* Consonant–Vowel Transitions, 1959; (with K. J. H. Creese) German, A Structural Approach, Bk I 1966, Bk II 1967, Bk III 1968, Dutch edns 1968–70; ed (with E. W. Hawkins and others), chapter on Testing, in Report of Research into Effectiveness of Language Laboratory (forthcoming); *contrib.* Int. Rev. App. Ling. *Address:* Language Teaching Centre, Univ. of York, Heslington, York YO1 5DD.

Green, Roger Philip Hywel; Lecturer, Department of Humanity, University of St Andrews, since 1967; *b* 1943; *m* 1970; one *d.* BA 1965 (Lit. Hum.), BLitt 1968, Oxon; Mem.: Class. Assoc., 1972– ; Soc. Prom. Rom. Stud., 1974– . *Publications:* The Poetry of Paulinus of Nola, 1971; *contrib.* VC, Latomus. *Address:* Dept of Humanity, Univ. of St Andrews, St Andrews, Fife KY16 9AJ.

Green, Rev. Dr Vivian Hubert Howard; Fellow since 1951, Senior Tutor in History since 1974 (Tutor 1951–74), and Sub Rector of Lincoln College, Oxford, since 1969; *b* 1915. BA Cantab 1937 (1st cl. Hist. Tripos), MA 1941, BD, DD Cantab and Oxon 1957 (Trinity Hall, Cambridge Sch., 1934–37, Goldsmiths' Exhibner; Lightfoot Sch. in Eccl Hist., 1938, Thirlwall Prize and Medal, 1941); FRHistS. *Publications:* Bishop Reginald Pecock, 1945; From St Augustine to William Temple, 1948, repr., NY, 1971; The Hanoverians, 1714–1815, 1948; Renaissance and Reformation, 1952, 2nd edn 1964, pbk 1972; The Later Plantagenets, 1955, pbk 1973; Oxford Common Room, 1957; The Swiss Alps, 1961; The Young Mr Wesley 1961; Religion at Oxford and Cambridge c 1160–1960, 1964; John Wesley, 1964; Martin Luther and the Reformation, 1964; The Universities, 1969; Medieval Civilization in Western Europe, 1971; A Short History of Oxford University, 1974. *Address:* Lincoln Coll., Oxford.

Greenall, Ronald Leslie, BSc(Econ), MA; Warden of the University Centre, Northampton, Department of Adult Education, University of Leicester, since 1967; *b* 1937; *m* 1959; two *s.* BSc(Econ) London 1958 (2nd cl.), MA Leicester 1970. *Publications:* ed, The Parish Register of Long Buckby 1558–1689, 1971; The People of a Northamptonshire Village in 1851: A Census Study of Long Buckby, 1971. *Address:* The Univ. Centre, Barrack Road, Northampton.

Greenan, Thomas Anthony; Lecturer, Department of Russian, University of Liverpool, since 1963; *b* 1932; *m* 1959; two *s.* BA Oxon 1956, MA Oxon 1961. Asst Libr., Liverpool Univ., 1960–63. *Publications:* ed, Turgenev: Mesyats v derevne, 1971. *Address:* Dept of Russian, Modern Languages Building, The Univ., PO Box 147, Liverpool L69 3BX.

Greene, Anthony Hamilton Millard K.; *see* Kirk-Greene.

Greene, Dr Judith, PhD; Lecturer in Psychology, Birkbeck College, University of London, since 1966; *b* 1936; *m* 1957. BA Oxon 1957 (Mod. Hist.), MA Oxon 1964; BA London 1964 (Psychol.), PhD London 1968 (Psychol); Member: BPsS; Exptl Psychol. Soc. Lectr, Birkbeck Coll., 1966–71; Temp. Lectr, Keele Univ., 1971–72. Sec., Bd of Studies in Psychol., Univ. of London, 1973–. *Publications:* Psycholinguistics: Chomsky and Psychology, 1972; *contrib.* Brit. Jl Psychol., Qly Jl Exptl Psychol., Perception and Psychophysics. *Address:* Birkbeck Coll., Malet Street, WC1E 7HX.

Greenhalgh, Dr Charles Michael Barrington; Lecturer in History of Art Department, University of Leicester, since 1968; *b* 1943; *m* 1966; two *s* one *d*. BA Manchester 1965 (1st cl. Hons French), MA Manchester 1966, PhD Manchester 1968. *Publications: contrib.* Apollo, Architectural Rev., Hist. Today, Numismatic Chronicle, Gazette des Beaux-Arts, Nouvelles de l'Estampe. *Address:* Univ. of Leicester, University Road, Leicester LE1 7RH.

Greenleaf, Prof. William Howard; Professor of Political Theory and Government, University College, Swansea, since 1967; *b* 1927; *m* 1956; one *s* one *d*. BSc(Econ) London 1951 (1st cl.), PhD London 1954; FRHistS. Asst, Economics Res. Sect., Manchester, 1953–54; Asst Lectr, Dept of Government, Hull, 1954–56, Lectr, 1956–64, Sen. Lectr, 1964–66, Reader, 1966–67; Vis. Prof., Univ. of Texas, Austin, 1970, Bryn Mawr Coll., Pa, 1973–74. *Publications:* Order, Empiricism and Politics, 1964; Oakeshott's Philosophical Politics, 1966; *contrib.* EHR, Hist Jl, Jl Soc. Army Hist. Res., Pol. Studies, Public Law, Vict. Studies. *Address:* Dept of Political Theory and Government, Univ. College, Swansea SA2 8PP.

Greenwood, Edward Baker; Senior Lecturer in English, Faculty of Humanities, University of Kent, since 1971; *b* 1933; *m* 1958; two *s*. BA Oxon 1954 (2nd cl. English), BLitt Oxon 1956, MA Oxon 1958. Asst Lectr, Univ. of Canterbury, Christchurch, NZ, 1960–64; Lectr, Univ. of Glasgow, 1964–66; Lectr, Univ. of Kent, 1966–71; Vis. Associate Prof., Univ. of California, Santa Barbara, 1967–68. *Publications: contrib.* Encounter, Ess. Crit., Landfall, Neophilol., Twent. Cent. *Address:* Rutherford College, Univ. of Kent, Canterbury, Kent.

Greenwood, John Alfred, BA, BPhil; Lecturer in Economics, University of Sussex, since 1967; *b* 1944. BA Oxon 1965 (2nd cl. PPE), BPhil Oxon 1967 (Economics). Sub-Dean, Sch. of Social Sciences, 1971; Pt-time Econ. Adv., Dept of Employment, 1970–71. *Publications:* Some Problems in the Implementation of An Equal Pay Policy (Indust., Educnl and Res. Foundn Res. Paper 2), 1969; (with J. F. Pickering and D. Hunt) The Small Firm in the Hotel and Catering Industry, 1971; *contrib.* Brit. Jl Indust. Relat., Indust. Relat. Jl. *Address:* School of Social Sciences, Univ. of Sussex, Falmer, Brighton BN1 9QN.

Greenwood, Prof. Richard Harold, MA; Professor of Geography, University College, Swansea, since 1970; *b* 1914; *m* 1947; two *d*. BA Cantab 1936, MA Cantab 1940; Mem.: Inst. Brit. Geogrs, Inst. Austral. Geogrs, Gt Barrier Reef Cttee. Lectr, Univ. of Otago, NZ, 1947–50; Sen. Lectr, Univ. of Queensland, 1950–58, Prof. of Geography, 1958–70. Dean, Fac. of Arts, Univ. of Queensland, 1959–62; Pres., Royal Soc. Queensland, 1967; Hon. Sec., Queensland, ANZAAS, 1963–68; Mem., Social Science Res. Council, Australia, 1964–70. *Publications:* Introducing Geography, 1953; The Darling Downs, 1957; Queensland, city, coast and country, 1959;

The regions of Queensland, 1971; *contrib.* Austral. Geog., Austral. Jl Sci., Die Erde, Pacific Aff., Proc. Roy. Soc. Qland. *Address:* Dept of Geography, Univ. College, Singleton Park, Swansea SA2 8PP.

Greenwood-Wilson, Alan Greenwood; Staff Tutor in Philosophy, Department of Adult Education, University of Newcastle upon Tyne, since 1953; *b* 1920; *m* 1942; one *s* one *d*. BA Hons Manchester 1949 (2nd cl. Philosophy). *Address:* Dept of Adult Education, The Univ. Newcastle upon Tyne NE1 7RU.

Greer, Prof. David Clive, MA; Hamilton Harty Professor of Music, Queen's University of Belfast, since 1972; *b* 1937; *m* 1961; two *s* one *d*. BA Oxon 1960; MA Oxon 1964. Mem., Royal Music. Assoc., Inc. Soc. Music. Asst Lectr, Birmingham Univ., 1963–65, Lectr, 1965–72. *Publications:* ed, English Madrigal Verse, 1967; ed, English Lute Songs, 9 vols, 1967–71; *contrib.* Music Lett., Proc. Royal Music Assoc., Music. Times, Shakesp. Qly, Notes Queries, Lute Soc. Jl. *Address:* Dept of Music, The Queen's Univ., Belfast BT7 1NN.

Greer, Prof. Desmond Sproule; Professor of Law, Queen's University, Belfast, since 1973; *b* 1940; *m* 1964; one *s* one *d*. LLB Belfast 1962, BCL Oxon 1964. Tutor in Legal Method, Law Sch., Univ. of Pennsylvania, 1964; Lectr, 1966–72, Sen. Lectr 1972–73, QUB. *Publications: contrib.* Brit. Jl Criminol., Irish Jurist., N Ireland Legal Qly. *Address:* Faculty of Law, Queen's Univ., Belfast BT7 1NN.

Greer, Dr John Edmund; Lecturer in Education (Religious Education), Education Centre, New University of Ulster, since 1972; *b* 1932; *m* 1964; one *s* one *d*. BSc QUB 1953, BAgr QUB 1954 (1st cl. Hons), PhD QUB 1956, BD TCD 1965, MPhil Ulster 1972. Part-time Lectr in Educn, New Univ. Ulster, 1968–72. *Publications:* A Questioning Generation: A report on Sixth Form Religion in N Ireland, 1972; Teachers and Religious Education, 1973; *contrib.* Biblical Theology, Educnl Rev. Irish Jl Educn, Jl Curriculum Studies, New Divinity, Social Studies. *Address:* New Univ. of Ulster, Coleraine, N Ireland BT52 1SA.

Greer, John V.; Lecturer, since 1968, and Assistant Adviser of Studies since 1972, Town and Country Planning Department, Queen's University, Belfast; *b* 1942; *m* 1968; two *d*. Hon. BA QUB 1963 (Geog.); MRTPI 1967. Mem. Consultative Panel, Nat. Inst. of Phys. Planning and Construction Res., 1970. *Publications: contrib.* Jl Inst. Landscape Archs. *Address:* 2 Lennoxvale, Malone Road, Belfast, BT9 5BY, Northern Ireland.

Gregor, Prof. Ian Copeland Smith; Professor of Modern English Literature, University of Kent, since 1969; *b* 1926. BA Durham 1950, PhD Durham 1954. Asst Lecturer, King's Coll., London, 1956–58; Asst Lectr, then Lectr, Univ. of Edinburgh, 1958–65; Sen. Lectr, then Reader, Univ. of Kent, 1965–69. Mem., Council Nat. Acad.

Awards, 1971. *Publications*: (with B. Nicholas) The Moral and the Story, 1962; (with M. Kinkead-Weekes) William Golding: A Critical Study, 1967; ed, M. Arnold: Culture and Anarchy, A Critical Edition, 1971; ed, Brontës: Selected Essays, 1971; *contrib*. Engl. Lit. Hist., Ess. Crit., Hudson Rev., Sewanee Rev. *Address*: Rutherford College, The Univ. of Kent, Canterbury, Kent.

Gregory, Dr Andrew H.; Senior Lecturer, Department of Psychology, Manchester University, since 1974; *b* 1935; *m* 1961; two *s*. BA Cambridge 1959; PhD Hull 1963; Assoc. Mem. BPsS; Mem. EPS. Asst Lectr, Manchester, 1961–64; Lectr, 1964–74. *Publications*: Basic Statistics, 1970; *contrib*. Jl Exp. Psychol., Qly Jl Exp. Psychol. *Address*: Psychology Dept, Univ. of Manchester, Manchester M13 9PL.

Gregory, Prof. Geoffrey; Professor of Management Sciences, Department of Management Studies, Loughborough University of Technology, since 1973; *b* 1929; *m* 1958; three *d*. BA Cambridge 1952, MS Stanford 1955, MA Cambridge 1955, PhD Stanford 1956; FSS. Staff Tutor in Operational Research, Birmingham, 1958–59; Sen. Lectr, Univ. of Melbourne, 1959–65, Reader, 1965–68; Vis. Res. Fellow, Lancaster, 1966; Sen. Res. Fellow, Lancaster, 1968–72. Pres., Operat. Res. Soc. Victoria, Australia, 1965; Chm., Austral. Jt Council Operat. Res. Socs, 1965. *Address*: Dept of Management Studies, Univ. of Technology, Loughborough LE11 3TJ.

Gregory, Dr Kenneth John, BSc, PhD; Reader in Physical Geography, University of Exeter, since 1972; *b* 1938; *m* 1962; one *s* two *d*. BSc London 1959 (Special), PhD London 1962; FRGS. Lectr, Univ. of Exeter, 1962–72. *Publications*: Southwest England, 1969; ed, Exeter Essays in Geography, 1971; Drainage Basin Geomorphology, 1973; An Advanced Geography of the British Isles, 1974; Fluvial Processes in Instrumented Watersheds, 1974; *contrib*. Trans Inst. Brit. Geogrs, Zeits. Geomorphol., Jl Hydrol. *Address*: Dept of Geography, The Univ., Exeter EX4 4QH.

Gregory, Peter Gordon; Lecturer in Social Administration, University of Hull, since 1966; *b* 1940; *m* 1968; two *s*. BA Oxford 1961 (2nd cl. PPE), Grad. Dip. in Social Policy and Administration LSE 1962. Res. Asst, Dept of Social Studies, Durham, 1963; Asst Lectr, in Social Administration, Hull, 1963–66. *Publications*: Deafness and Public Responsibility, 1964; Polluted Homes. 1965; (with Michael Young) Lifeline Telephone Service for the Elderly, 1972; Telephones for the Elderly, 1973. *Address*: Univ. of Hull, Cottingham Road, Hull HU6 7RX.

Gregory, Dr Roy; Reader in Politics, Department of Politics, University of Reading, since 1973; *b* 1935. BA 1959, MA, DPhil 1962, Oxford; Member: Pol Studies Assoc. of UK; Royal Inst. of Public Admin.; Queen's Coll., Dundee, 1962–64; Univ. of Reading, 1964–73. Mem., Co. Borough of Reading Council, 1966–69. *Publications*: The Miners and British

Politics, 1906–1914, 1968; The Price of Amenity: five studies in conservation and government, 1971; *contrib*. Internat. Jl of Environmental Studies; New Soc., Pol Studies, Public Admin. *Address*: Dept of Politics, Univ. of Reading, Reading RG6 2AA.

Gregory, Prof. Stanley, MA, PhD; Professor of Geography, University of Sheffield, since 1968; *b* 1926; *m* 1950; two *d*. BA London 1950 (1st cl. Geography), MA Liverpool 1952, PhD Liverpool 1958; Hon. DGeog Ottawa 1972; FRMetS. Mem., Inst. Brit. Geogrs, Geog. Assoc. Asst Lectr, Liverpool Univ., 1950–53; Lectr, 1953–60, 1961–62; Lectr, Univ. of Sierra Leone, 1960–61; Sen. Lectr, Liverpool, 1962–66, Reader, 1966–68; Vis. Prof., Univ. of Ottawa, 1970. Jt Hon. Sec., Geog. Assoc., 1968–72; Inst. Brit. Geogrs: Mem. Council, 1963–65; Vice-Pres., 1973–74; Brit. Nat. Cttee, Geog., 1964–69; Council Environ. Educn, 1968–71; Jt Matric. Bd, 1969– ; Chm., Assoc. Brit. Climatol., 1973– . *Publications*: Statistical Methods and the Geographer, 1963, 3rd edn 1973, Polish trans. 1970, Rainfall over Sierra Leone, 1965; *contrib*. Erdkunde, Geog., Jl Town Planning Inst., Qly Jl Royal Met. Soc., Tijd. Econ. Soc. Geog., Trans Inst. Brit. Geogrs, Water and Water Eng., Weather. *Address*: Dept of Geography, The Univ., Sheffield S10 2TN.

Grenville, Prof. John Ashley Soames; Professor of Modern History, University of Birmingham, since 1969; *b* 1928; *m* 1960; three *s*. BA London, PhD London; FRHistS (Mem. Council, 1971–73). Postgrad. Scholar, Univ. of London, 1951–53; Asst Lectr, then Lectr, Univ. of Nottingham, 1953–64; Reader in Modern History, Nottingham, 1964–65; Prof. of International History, Univ. of Leeds, 1965–69; Commonwealth Fund Fellow, 1958–59; Postdoctoral Fellow, Univ. of Yale, 1960–63; Vis. Prof., Queens Coll., City Univ. of NY, 1964, etc. Consultant: American and European Bibliographical Centre, Oxford and California, 1960– ; Clio Press, 1960– ; Editor, Fontana History of War and Society, 1969– . *Publications*: Lord Salisbury and Foreign Policy, 1964, 2nd edn 1970; with J. G. Fuller, The Coming of the Europeans, 1962; with G. B. Young, Politics, Strategy and American Diplomacy: studies in Foreign Policy, 1873–1917, 1966, 2nd edn 1971; The Major International Treaties 1914–73: a history and guide with texts, 1974; *Documentary films*: The Munich Crisis, 1968; (with N. Pronay) The End of Illusions: from Munich to Dunkirk, 1970. *Address*: Univ. of Birmingham, PO Box 363, Birmingham B15 2TT.

Greve, Prof. John; Professor of Social Policy and Administration, Leeds University, since 1974; *b* 1927; one *s* one *d*. BSc(Econ) London. LSE, 1958–66; Norwegian Building Res. Inst., Oslo, 1964–65, 1966–67; Sen. Lectr, Southampton, 1967–69; Prof. of Social Admin, Southampton, 1969; seconded to Home Office, 1969–74. *Publications*: Housing Problem, 1961; London's Homeless, 1964; Private Landlords in England, 1965; The

Housing Problem, 1969; (with others) Comparative Social Administration, 1969; Housing, Planning and Change in Norway, 1970; Voluntary Housing in Scandinavia, 1971; Homelessness in London, 1971. *Address*: Univ. of Leeds, Leeds LS2 9JT.

Greve, Stella; Lecturer in Social Policy, Department of Extra-Mural Studies, University of Southampton, since 1970; *b* 1931; *m*; one *s* one *d*. BA Nottingham, 1953 (Soc. Admin). Lectr, LSE, 1964–66; Sen. Res. Associate, Birmingham Univ., 1968–70. Psychiatric social work and res. until 1964. *Publications*: (jtly), Homelessness in London, 1971. *Address*: Univ. of Southampton, Southampton SO9 5NH.

Grice, Prof. Geoffrey Russell, MA, PhD; Professor of Philosophy, University of East Anglia, since 1971; Dean of the School of Social Studies, since 1973; *b* 1926; *m* 1959; two *s* one *d*. BA Oxon 1947 (Hon. Sch. Nat. Sci./Physics), MA Oxon 1951; PhD Cantab 1965. Lectr, E Anglia Univ., 1965–68, Sen. Lectr, 1968–70, Reader, 1970–71. *Publications*: The Grounds of Moral Judgement, 1967; *contrib*. Proc. Aristot. Soc. *Address*: School of Social Studies, Univ. of East Anglia, University Plain, Norwich NOR 88C.

Grierson, Prof. Philip, LittD, FBA; Professor of Numismatics, Faculty of History, Cambridge University, since 1971; *b* 1910. BA Cambridge 1932, MA Cambridge 1936, LittD Cambridge 1971; Hon. LittD Ghent 1958; FBA, FSA, FRHistS. Fellow, Gonville and Caius Coll., Cambridge, 1935– , Libr., 1944–69, Pres., 1966– ; Univ. Lectr in History, 1945–59; Reader in Medieval Numismatics, 1959–71; Prof. of Numismatics and the History of Coinage, Univ. of Brussels, 1948– ; Advr in Byzantine Numismatics to Dumbarton Oaks Library and Collections, Harvard Univ., Washington, USA, 1955– ; Ford's Lectr in History, Univ. of Oxford, 1956–57. Lit. Dir, Royal Hist. Soc., 1945–55; Pres., Royal Numism. Soc., 1961–66. *Publications*: Les Annales de Saint-Pierre de Gand et de Saint-Amand, 1937; Sylloge of Coins of the British Isles: Fitzwilliam Museum, 1958; Bibliographie Numismatique 1966; (with A. R. Bellinger) Catalogue of the Byzantine Coins in the Dumbarton Oaks Collection and in the Whittemore Collection, vols 1–3, 1966–73; *contrib*. Brit. Numism. Jl, EHR, Econ. Hist Rev., Museum Notes, Numism. Chron., Rev. Ben. *Address*: Gonville and Caius College, Cambridge.

Griew, Prof. Edward James; Professor of Law, University of Leicester, since 1972; *b* 1930; *m* 1959; one *s* one *d*. LLB Cantab 1952, MA Cantab 1955; Barrister 1954. Asst Lectr in Laws, King's Coll., London, 1956–59; Sen. Lectr in Law, Univ. of Leicester, 1966–72. *Publications*: The Theft Act, 1968, 2nd edn 1974; *contrib*. Crim. LR, CLJ. *Address*: Dept of Law, Univ. of Leicester, University Road, Leicester LE1 7RH.

Griffin, James Patrick; Fellow and Tutor in Philosophy, Keble College, University of Oxford, since 1966; *b* 1933; *m* 1966; one *s* one *d*. BA Yale 1955 (Summa cum Laude),

MA Oxon 1962, DPhil Oxon 1960. Lectr, Christ Church, Oxford, 1960–66; Vis. Prof., Univ. of Wisconsin, 1971. *Publications*: Wittgenstein's Logical Atomism, 1964, American edn 1967. *Address*: Keble College, Oxford OX1 3PG.

Griffin, Keith Broadwell; Fellow and Tutor in Economics, Magdalen College, Oxford University, since 1965; *b* 1938; *m* 1956; two *d*. BA Williams Coll. 1960, BPhil Oxon 1962, MA Oxon 1965, DPhil Oxon 1966; Mem., Amer. Econ. Assoc., Royal Econ. Soc. Vis. Prof., Inst. Econ., Santiago, Chile, 1962, 1964. Advr, Algerian Govt, on agricultural planning, and acting chief, FAO Mission, Algiers, 1963–64; Sen. Economist, UN Res. Inst. Soc. Develt, 1971–72. *Publications*: Comercio Internacional y Politicas de Desarrollo Economico, 1967; Underdevelopment in Spanish America, 1969; Planning Development, 1970; ed, Financing Development in Latin America, 1971; ed, Growth and Inequality in Pakistan, 1972; The Political Economy of Agrarian Change, 1974; *contrib*. Bull. Oxf. Univ. Inst. Stats, Oxf. Econ. Papers. *Address*: Magdalen College, Oxford.

Griffin, Miriam Tamara; Tutorial Fellow in Ancient History, Somerville College, Oxford, since 1967; *b* 1935; *m* 1960; three *d*. BA Columbia 1956, AM Harvard 1957, BA Oxon 1960 (1st cl. Greats), MA Oxon 1963, DPhil Oxon 1969. Teaching Fellow, Harvard Univ., 1960–61; Fulford Res. Fellow, St Anne's Coll., Oxford, 1961–67. *Publications*: chapter, in, Seneca: Studies in Literature and its Influence (forthcoming); *contrib*. Class. Qly, Jl Roman Studies. *Address*: Somerville College, Oxford.

Griffith, Prof. John Aneurin Grey, LLB, LLM; Professor of Public Law, London School of Economics and Political Science, University of London, since 1970; *b* 1918; *m* 1941; two *s* one *d*. LLB London, LLM London. Lectr in Law, UCW, Aberystwyth, 1946–48; Lectr in Law and Reader, LSE, 1948–59, Prof. of English Law, 1959–70; Vis. Prof. of Law, Univ. of California, Berkeley, 1966. Barrister-at-Law. Mem., Marlow UDC, 1950–55, and Bucks CC, 1955–61; Chm., Council for Academic Freedom and Democracy, 1970– . Editor, Public Law, 1970– . *Publications*: (with H. Street) A Casebook of Administrative Law, 1964; Central Departments and Local Authorities, 1966; (with H. Street) Principles of Administrative Law, 4th edn 1967; *contrib*. English, Commonwealth, and American jls of law, public admin. and politics. *Address*: London School of Economics and Political Science, Houghton Street, Aldwych, WC2A 2AE.

Griffith, John Godfrey; Fellow and Tutor in Classics, Jesus College, Oxford, and University Lecturer in Classics, since 1938; Public Orator, since 1973; *b* 1913. MA Oxon 1939. Correspondent, Thracological Section, Bulgarian Acad. of Scis. *Publications*: *contrib*. Class. Qly, Class. Rev., Jl Theol. Studies, Hermes, Mus. Helvet., Jl Hell. Studies, Greece and Rome. *Address*: Jesus College, Oxford.

Griffith, Prof. Thomas Gwynfor; Professor of Italian Language and Literature, University of Manchester, since 1971; *b* 1926; *m* 1953; three *d*. MA, BLitt Oxon 1950, MA Dublin 1955. Asst Lectr and Lectr in Italian, Leeds Univ., 1948–52; Lectr in Charge of Dept of Italian, Dublin Univ., 1952–55; Reader in Charge and Fellow of Trinity Coll., Dublin, 1955–58; Univ. Lectr in Italian, Oxford Univ., 1958–65, and Fellow of St Cross Coll., Oxford, 1965; Prof. of Italian, Univ. of Hull, 1966–71. Chm., Soc. for Italian Studies and editor of Italian Studies, 1974– . *Publications:* Boccaccio: Detholion o'r Decameron, 1951; Bandello's Fiction: an Examination of the Novelle, 1955; (with J. O. Davies) Luigi Pirandello: Fel y tybiwch, y mae, 1958; Avventure linguistiche del Cinquecento, 1961; (with B. Migliorini) The Italian Language, 1966; Italian Writers and the Italian Language, 1967; ed (with P. R. J. Hainsworth), Petrarch: Selected Poems, 1971; *contrib.* Cambridge Italian Dictionary, vol. I, Italian–English 1962, Italian Studies, Trans Hon. Soc. Cymmrodorion, etc. *Address:* Dept of Italian Studies, Univ. of Manchester, Manchester M13 9PL.

Griffiths, Albert, MA; Senior Lecturer in Education, Institute of Education, University of Leeds, since 1968; *b* 1918; *m* 1945; two *s* three *d*. BA Leeds 1949, DipEd Leeds 1950, MA Leeds 1954. Lectr in Education, Inst. of Educn, Univ. of Leeds, 1963–68. *Publications:* Secondary School Reorganisation in England and Wales, 1971; Some Recent British Research on the Social Determinants of Education: an annotated bibliography, 1971. *Address:* Institute of Education, The Univ., Leeds LS2 9JT.

Griffiths, Prof. Allen Phillips; Professor of Philosophy, University of Warwick, since 1964; *b* 1927; *m* 1948; one *s* one *d*. BA Wales 1951 (1st cl. Philosophy), BPhil Oxon 1953. Asst Lectr, Univ. of Wales, 1955–57; Lectr, Birkbeck Coll., Univ. of London, 1957–64; Vis. Prof., Swarthmore Coll., Pa, 1963; Univ. of Wisconsin, 1964–65, 1969–70; Univ. of California, 1966–67; Pro-Vice-Chancellor, Univ. of Warwick, 1970–71, 1973– . *Publications:* ed, Knowledge and Belief, 1967; contrib. Encyclopaedia of Philosophy; *contrib.* Analysis, Mind, Philos. Qly, Proc. Aristot. Soc., Amer. Philos. Qly. *Address:* Univ. of Warwick, Coventry CV4 7AL.

Griffiths, Brian; Lecturer in Economics, London School of Economics and Political Science, since 1965; *b* 1941; *m* 1965; one *s* two *d*. BSc (Econ.) 1963, MSc (Econ.) 1965, London. Asst Lectr, LSE, 1965–68. *Publications:* Competition in Banking, 1970; Monetary and Fiscal Policy in Mexican Economic Development 1940–1969, 1972; *contrib.* Economica, Jl Money, Credit and Banking. *Address:* London Sch. of Economics, Houghton Street, Aldwych, WC2A 2AE.

Griffiths, Dr Bruce; Lecturer, Department of French and Romance Studies, University College of North Wales, Bangor, since 1966; *b* 1938. BA Oxon 1959, MA Oxon 1963, DipLing Wales 1963, DPhil Oxon 1968; Member Yr Academi Gymreig (Welsh Acad.).

Asst Lectr, QUB, 1963–66. *Publications:* trans., Bordeaux: Yr Argae, 1972; trans., Molière: Y Claf Diglefyd, 1972; trans., Camus: Y Dieithryn, 1973; *contrib.* Forum for Mod. Lang. Studies. *Address:* French Dept, Univ. College of North Wales, Bangor LL57 2DG.

Griffiths, Rev. David Robert, MA, BD, MTh; Lecturer in Biblical Studies, University College, Cardiff, since 1955; *b* 1915; *m* 1944; one *d*. BD London 1937, BA Oxon 1939 (2nd cl. Theology), MTh London 1942, MA Oxon 1943. Jt Editor, Diwinyddiaeth, 1954–68. *Publications:* contrib. Christian Baptism, 1959; The New Testament and the Roman State, 1970; *contrib.* Diwinyddiaeth, Expos. Times. *Address:* Dept of Semitic Languages and Religious Studies, Univ. College, Cardiff CF1 1XL.

Griffiths, Prof. Hubert Brian; Professor of Pure Mathematics, Department of Mathematics, University of Southampton (also teaching Mathematics/Education), since 1964; *b* 1927; *m* 1954; one *s* one *d*. BSc Manchester 1948, MSc Manchester 1949, PhD Manchester 1951; FIMA; Mem.: Lond. Math. Soc., Math. Assoc., Assoc. Teachers Math., CASE, Amnesty, etc. Asst, Aberdeen Univ., 1951–53; Lectr, Bristol Univ., 1953–60; Lectr, Birmingham Univ., 1960–62, Sen. Lectr, 1962–64; Mem., Inst. Adv. Study, Princeton, NJ, 1956–58; Vis. Mem., Courant Inst., NY Univ., 1963–64. Mem., SRC Math. Cttee, 1971– ; SSRC Stat. Cttee, 1971– . *Publications:* (with J. V. Armitage) SMP A-level Companion, 1970; (with P. J. Hilton) Classical Mathematics, 1971; *contrib.* Jl Lond. Math. Soc., Acta Math., Comm. Pure Appl. Math., Educnl Studies in Math., etc. *Address:* Dept of Mathematics, The Univ., Southampton SO9 5NH.

Griffiths, Prof. Hywel; Professor of Social Administration, New University of Ulster, since 1972; *b* 1933; *m* 1960; one *s* three *d*. BA Wales 1955. Lectr, Adult Educn, Univ. of Manchester, 1965–70. Dir., NI Community Relations Commn, 1970–72. *Publications:* (As member of the Calouste Gulbennien Study Gp on Community Work in Britain) Community Work and Social Change, 1969; Current Issues in Community Work, 1973; *contrib.* Community Development Jl. *Address:* New Univ. of Ulster, Coleraine, Co. Londonderry, NI BT52 1SA.

Griffiths, Dr Ieuan Lloyd; Reader in Geography, University of Sussex, since 1972; *b* 1934; *m* 1959; two *s* one *d*. BSc Econ London 1956, PhD London 1959; Mem. Inst. of British Geographers. Lecturer: Rhodes Univ., SA, 1959; Natal Univ., Durban, SA, 1960; Rhodes Univ., SA, 1960; Sussex Univ., 1964 *Publications:* contrib. Geography, Geographical Rev., Tijdschrift v. Econ. en Soc. Geografie. *Address:* Geography Lab., Univ. of Sussex, Falmer, Brighton BN1 9QN.

Griffiths, Dr James Howard Eagle, OBE; President, Magdalen College, Oxford, since 1968; *b* 1908. 1st cl. Natural Science (Physics) Oxford 1930, DPhil Oxford 1933, MA

273

Oxford 1934; Hon. DEd, Mindanao, Philippines, 1968. Fellow. Magadalen Coll., Oxford, 1934–68; Sen. Dean of Arts, Magdalen Coll., 1947–50, 1956–60, 1965–66, Vice-Pres., 1951–52; Univ. Demonstrator and Lectr in Physics, 1945–66; Reader in Physics, 1966–68; Vice-Chancellor, Univ. of Malaya, Kuala Lumpur, 1967–68. Mem.: Hebdomadal Council, Oxford, 1951–63, 1968– ; Hale Cttee on Univ. Teaching Methods. CV Boys Prize, Physical Soc., London, 1951. *Publications: contrib.* Proc. Royal Soc., Proc. Phys. Soc. London and other physics jls. *Address:* Magdalen College, Oxford.

Griffiths, Prof. John Gwyn; Professor of Classics, University of Wales, since 1973; *b* 1911; *m* 1939; two *s*. BA Wales 1932 (1st cl. Classics), MA Liverpool 1936, DPhil Oxon 1949, DLitt Oxon 1972; Mem. Cttee, Classical Assoc., 1963–64, Egypt Exploration Soc. 1966– ; Corresp. Mem., German Archaeological Inst., Berlin, 1966. Fellow, Univ. of Wales, 1937–39; Lectr and Sen. Lectr, Univ. Coll., Swansea, 1946–65, Reader, 1965–73; Lady Wallis Budge Res. Lectr, Univ. Coll., Oxford, 1957–58; Guest Prof. in Classics and Egyptology, Univ. of Cairo, 1965–66; Editor, Jl of Egyptian Archaeology, 1970– . *Publications:* The Conflict of Horus and Seth, 1960; The Origins of Osiris, 1966; Cerddi Cairo, 1969; Plutarch's De Iside et Osiride, 1970; chapters in, Religions en Egypte hellénistique et romaine, 1969; *contrib.* Jl of Egyptian Archaeology, The Classical Rev. *Address:* Dept of Classics, Univ. Coll., Swansea SA2 8PP.

Griffiths, Dr Ralph Alan, FRHistS; Senior Lecturer in History, University College, Swansea, since 1971; *b* 1937. BA Bristol 1959, PhD Bristol 1962; FRHistS. Res. Asst, Bd of Celtic Studies, Wales, 1961–64; Asst Lectr, Univ. Coll., Swansea, 1964–66; Lectr, 1966–71; Vis. Prof., Dalhousie Univ., 1967. Mem., Hist. Law Cttee, Bd Celtic Studies; Council, Glamorgan Hist. Soc.; Asst Editor, Welsh Hist. Rev., 1966– . *Publications:* Principality of Wales in Later Middle Ages, I, South Wales, 1972; contrib. Glamorgan County History, vol. III, ed T. B. Pugh, 1972; The Fifteenth Century, 1399–1509, ed S. B. Chrimes, C. D. Ross, R. A. Griffiths, 1972; British Government and Administration in Action, ed H. Hearder and H. R. Loyn, 1974; ed, Student's History of Wales Series; *contrib.* Bull. Bd Celtic Studies, Bull. J. Rylands Libr., Bull. Inst. Hist. Res., Ceredigion, Glamorgan Hist., Morgannwg, Trans Brist. Glos. Archaeol. Soc., Welsh Hist. Rev., Speculum, Nat. Libr. Wales Jl, Trans Cymmrodorion Soc., Hist. Engl.-spkng Peoples, Trans Carmarthenshire Antiquarian Soc. *Address:* Dept of History, Univ. College, Swansea SA2 8PP.

Griffiths, Prof. Richard Mathias, MA, PhD; Professor of French, University College, Cardiff, since 1974; *b* 1935; *m* 1971. BA Cantab 1957 (1st cl. French and German), MA Cantab 1961, PhD Cantab 1961. Res. Fellow, Selwyn Coll., Cambridge, 1960–61; Official Fellow, 1961–66; Dean, 1962–65; Tutor, 1965–66; Fellow, Brasenose Coll.,

Oxford, 1966–74. Editor, Camb. Rev., 1962–63; Gov., Lancing Coll., 1962– ; Fellow, Woodard Corp., 1963– ; Governor: Pangbourne Coll., 1968–74; Brightlands Sch., 1970–74; Man. of St Barnabas Aided Primary Sch., 1969–74; Mem., Oxford Educn Cttee, 1968–71 (Vice-Chm., 1970–71). *Publications:* trans., Huysmans: Parisian Sketches, 1961; The Reactionary Revolution, 1966, French edn 1971; The Dramatic Technique of Antoine de Montchrestien, 1970; Marshal Pétain, 1970, American edn 1972; ed, Claudel: a Reappraisal, 1968; *contrib.* Fr. Studies, Mod. Lang. Rev., Rev. Sci. Hum., Bull. Soc. Huysmans. *Address:* Dept of French, Univ. Coll., Cardiff, PO Box 78, Cardiff CF1 1XL.

Grigg, Dr David Brian, MA, PhD; Reader in Geography, University of Sheffield, since 1968; *b* 1934; *m* 1964; one *s* two *d*. BA Cambridge 1956, MA Cambridge 1961, PhD Cambridge 1961. Asst Lectr, Univ. of Sheffield, 1959–62, Lectr, 1962–66, Sen. Lectr, 1966–68. *Publications:* The Agricultural Revolution in South Lincolnshire, 1966; The Harsh Lands, 1970; *contrib.* Ann. Assoc. Amer. Geogrs, Econ. Geog., Trans Inst. Brit. Geogrs. *Address:* Dept of Geography, The Univ., Sheffield S10 2TN.

Grillo, Dr Ralph David; Lecturer in Social Anthropology, School of African and Asian Studies, University of Sussex, since 1970; *b* 1940; *m* 1968; one *s* two *d*. BA Cantab 1963, PhD Cantab 1968; Member: Assoc. Social Anthropologists; Royal Anthropol. Inst. Asst Lectr, QUB, 1967–70. *Publications:* African Railwaymen, 1973; Race, Class and Militancy, 1974. *Address:* Sch. of African and Asian Studies, Univ. of Sussex, Falmer, Brighton BN1 9QN.

Grimsley, Prof. Ronald, MA, DPhil, LèsL; Professor of French Language and Literature, University of Bristol, since 1964; *b* 1915; *m* 1956; one *s* two *d*. BA London 1937 (1st cl. French), MA Oxon 1948, DPhil Oxon 1948, LèsL Lille 1948. Lectr in French, UC, N Wales, 1948–56, Sen. Lectr, 1956–62, Reader, 1962–64. *Publications:* Existentialist Thought, 1955, 2nd edn 1960; Jean d'Alembert, 1963; Jean-Jacques Rousseau: a study in self-awareness, 1958, 2nd edn 1961; Søren Kierkegaard and French Literature, 1966; Rousseau and the Religious Quest, 1968; ed, Rousseau's Religious Writings, 1970; Maupertuis, Turgot and Main de Biran, Sur l'origine du langage, 1971; Philosophy of Rousseau, 1973; Kierkegaard: a biographical introduction, 1973; *contrib.* Fr. Studies, MLR, Mod. Lang. Qly, Philos. Studies in Romanticism, Comp. Lit., Comp. Lit. Studies, etc. *Address:* Dept of French, Wills Memorial Building, Queen's Road, Bristol.

Grisbrooke, William Jardine, MA, BD, FRHistS, Lecturer, The Queen's College, Birmingham; Recognised Lecturer in Theology, University of Birmingham, since 1972; *b* 1932; *m* 1955. BA Cantab 1954 (1st cl. History), MA Cantab 1958, BD Cantab 1964; FRHistS. Jun. Fellow, Fac. of Theology, Univ. of Edinburgh, 1959–62;

Res. Fellow, Inst. for Study of Worship and Religious Architecture, Univ. of Birmingham, 1967-72. Asst Editor, Studia Liturgica, 1968. *Publications*: Anglican Liturgies of the XVII and XVIII Centuries, 1958; Spiritual Counsels of Father John of Kronstadt, 1967; contrib. Dying, Death and Disposal, 1970; The Eucharist at Solihull, 1970; A Dictionary of Liturgy and Worship, 1972; *contrib.* Aylesford Rev., East Chs Qly, East. Chs Rev., Jl Eccles. Hist., Life Worsh., Liturgy, Res. Bull. ISWRA, St Vlads Theol. Qly, Studia Liturg., Theol. *Address*: The Queen's College, Somerset Road, Birmingham B15 2QH.

Grodecki, Prof. J. K., MA, JP; Professor of Law, University of Leicester, since 1965; Dean of the Faculty of Law and Pro-Vice-Chancellor since 1973; *b* 1923; *m* 1950; one *s* one *d*. Bachelier en Droit Grenoble 1943, BA Oxon 1948 (1st cl. Jurisprudence), MA Oxon 1953; Barrister-at-Law Lincoln's Inn, 1952. Asst Lectr, Birmingham Univ., 1949; Lectr, Bristol Univ., 1949-62, Sen. Lectr, 1962-65. Magistrate, Leicester City Bench, 1969- ; Mem., Legal Studies Bd CNAA. *Publications*: *contrib.* Brit. Ybk Int. Law, Grotius Soc. Trans, Int. Comp. Law Qly, Law Qly Rev., Mod. Law Rev. *Address*: Faculty of Law, Univ. of Leicester, Leicester LE1 7RH.

Groom, A. J. R., BSc(Econ), MA, DèsScPol; Lecturer in International Relations (Laws), University College London, since 1965; *b* 1938; *m* 1971. BSc(Econ) London 1959, MA Lehigh 1961, DèsScPol Genève 1971. Grad. Asst, Lehigh Univ., 1959-61; Fellow, Inst. Univ. de Hautes Etudes Internat., 1961-64; Cours Commerciaux, Genève, 1963-64; Asst, Inst. Univ. de Hautes Etudes Internat., 1964-65; Dotation Carnegie pour la paix internationale, programme of training young diplomats (various); Lectr, London Inst. of World Affairs, 1965-67; Vis. Prof. in Internat. Relations, Univ. of S California, 1969- ; Brigham Young Univ., 1970; Victoria Univ. of Wellington, 1970; Univ of Colorado, 1972; Cnsltnt, GATT, 1963, Centre for the Analysis of Conflict, 1967- ; Vis. Res. Cnsltnt, SIPRI (Stockholm Internat. Peace Res. Inst.), 1971. *Publications*: ed (with R. Boardman), The Management of Britain's External Relations, 1973; British Thinking about Nuclear Weapons, 1974; ed (with P. Taylor), Functionalism: theory and practice in International Relations, 1974; Towards a New Relevance for Peacekeeping, 1974; The Study of World Society: a London perspective, 1974; Conflict Research and the Middle East Conflict, 1974; *contrib.* Contemp. Rev., Etudes Internat., Internat. Aff., Peace Sci., Pol. Studies, Rev. Mil. Suisse, Sch. Monats., Wld Pol., Ybk Wld Aff., Medjunarodni Proleml, Round Table, Jl Common Market Studies; chapters in various symposia. *Address*: Univ. College London, Faculty of Laws, 4-8 Endsleigh Gardens, WC1H 0EG.

Gross, Herbert, MA; Chevalier des Palmes Académiques; Lecturer in Education and Modern Languages, University of Bristol, since 1963; *b* 1928; *m* 1953. BA Cantab 1950 (1st cl. German), MA Cantab 1954, Cert. of competent knowledge Cantab 1958 (Czech and Slovak), CertEd Cantab 1958 (Distinction), Cert. of competent knowledge Cantab 1961 (Russian); Mem., Mod. Lang. Assoc., A.V. Lang. Ass., Assoc. Teachers of Russian, ATCDE. Vis. Lectr, Univ. of Baroda, 1967; Laval, Quebec, 1969-72; Assessor, Univ. of Cambridge Dept of Educn, 1969-71. Hon. Treas., A.V. Lang. Assoc., 1964-66; Governor, Colston's Girls' Sch., 1969- ; Mem., Bristol Educn Soc., 1969- ; Co-dir, DES Inservice courses, 1968, 1969, 1971. *Publications*: (with B. Mason) Bonjour Line: Teacher's Book, 1967, 2nd edn 1971; (with A. Brimer) Bristol Achievement Tests: English Tests, 1968; contrib. Wide-span Reading Test, 1972; Student Unrest and the Uncertain Ethos in a Free Democracy (Inst. for Parly and Const. Studies, Delhi), 1972; *contrib.* Educn Psychol. Rev. (Baroda), Problem of Student Unrest (Baroda). *Address*: School of Education, Univ. of Bristol, 35 Berkeley Square, Bristol BS8 1JA.

Grossman, Justin; Senior Lecturer in Politics, University of Leeds, since 1972; *b* 1926; *m* 1948; two *s*. BA Chicago 1951. Asst Lectr, Leeds, 1960-62, Lectr, 1962-72. Hon. Sec., Pol. Studies Assoc. UK, 1962-66. *Publications*: Merit Employment, 1953; *contrib.* Pol. Studies, Pol. Qly. *Address*: Dept of Politics, The Univ., Leeds LS2 9JT.

Grove, Robert Benjamin; Senior Lecturer, School of Education, Nottingham University, since 1965; *b* 1911; *m* 1936; one *d*. BA Leeds 1932 (2nd cl. French), MA Leeds 1937, MA London 1949. Lectr, Nottingham Univ., 1949-65; Vis. Prof., State Univ. of Iowa, 1962-63. JP 1962- . *Address*: School of Education, Univ. of Nottingham, Nottingham NG7 2RD.

Groves, Dr Roger Edward Vane; Senior Lecturer in Finance and Accounting, Department of Accounting, University of Birmingham, since 1974; *b* 1939; *m* 1964; two *s* one *d*. BCom Birmingham 1960, MSc Purdue (USA) 1968, PhD Purdue 1970; FCA 1974 (ACA 1963); Treas., Assoc. of Teachers of Management, 1973. Univ. of Birmingham: Asst Lectr, 1964-65; Lectr, 1965-69 (on leave of absence, 1967-69); Lectr, Grad. Centre for Management Studies, 1970-72; Lectr, Univ. of Birmingham, 1972-74. Articled Clerk, Howard Smith Thompson, Chartered Accts, 1960-63; Sen. Audit Clerk, Price Waterhouse, 1963-64. *Publications*: (with J. M. Samuels and C. S. Goddard) Company Finance in Europe (forthcoming); *contrib.* Accountancy, Accounting Rev., Accounting and Bus. Res., Bankers Mag., Internat. Jl Physical Distrib. *Address*: Fac. of Commerce, Univ. of Birmingham, PO Box 363, Birmingham B15 2TT.

Gruffydd, Prof. Robert Geraint; Professor, Department of Welsh Language and Literature, University College of Wales, Aberystwyth, since 1970; *b* 1928; *m* 1953; two *s* one *d*. BA Wales 1948, DPhil Oxford 1953. Lectr in Welsh, UC of North Wales, Bangor, 1955-70.

Asst Editor, Geiriadur Prifysgol Cymru, 1953–55. *Publications*: articles on Welsh literary history in various jls. *Address*: Dept of Welsh Language and Literature, Univ. College of Wales, Aberystwyth SY23 2AX.

Gruner, Dr Rolf; Lecturer, Department of Philosophy, University of Sheffield, since 1972; *b* 1928; *m* 1956; one *s*. DrPhil Berlin 1956, PhD Durham 1967. Research Asst, Free Univ. Berlin, 1958–61; Lectr, Univ. of Khartoum, 1961–65; Res. Fellow, Univ. of Durham, 1965–68; Associate Prof., St Mary's Univ., Halifax, 1968–71. *Publications*: *contrib*. Amer. Philos. Qly, Archiv f. Philosophie, Aristot. Soc., Durham Univ. Jl, Hist. and Theory, Inquiry, Jl of Value Inquiry, Metaphilosophy, Methodos, Mind, Philos. Qly, Philosophy. *Address*: Dept of Philosophy, The Univ., Sheffield S10 2TN.

Guder, Dr Gotthard; Senior Lecturer in German, University of Glasgow, since 1946; *b* 1910. PhD Edinburgh 1943 (comb. English–German Lit.). *Publications*: Else Lasker-Schüler: Deutung ihrer Lyrik, 1967; *contrib*. German Life Lett., Mod. Langs, Orbis Litt. *Address*: German Dept, Univ. of Glasgow, Glasgow G12 8QQ.

Guest, Prof. Anthony Gordon, MA; Professor of English Law, King's College, University of London, since 1966; *b* 1930. BA Oxon 1954 (1st cl. Jurisprudence), MA Oxon 1957; Barrister-at-Law (Gray's Inn) 1955. Lectr, Univ. Coll., Oxford, 1954–55; Fellow and Praelector in Jurisprudence, 1955–65; Dean, 1963–64. Travelling Fellowship, S Africa, 1957; Mem., Lord Chancellor's Law Reform Cttee, 1963– ; Adv. Cttee on establishment of Law Faculty in Univ. of Hong Kong, 1965; Reader in Common Law, Council of Legal Educn (Inns of Court), 1967– ; UK Deleg., UN Commn on Internat. Trade Law, 1968– ; Mem., Bd, Athlone Press, 1968–73; Governor, Rugby Sch., 1968– . *Publications*: ed, Anson's Law of Contract, 21st to 23rd edns, 1959–1969; ed jtly, Chitty on Contracts, 22nd edn 1961, Gen. Editor, 23rd edn 1968; ed, Oxford Essays in Jurisprudence, 1961; The Law of Hire-Purchase, 1966; *contrib*. Conveyan., Canad. Bar Rev., Law Qly Rev., Mod. Law Rev. *Address*: King's College, Strand, WC2R 2LS.

Guest, George Howell, MA, MusB, FRCO, FRSCM; Fellow and Organist, St John's College, Cambridge University, since 1951, and Lecturer in Music since 1956; *b* 1924; *m* 1959; one *s* one *d*. BA Cantab 1949, MusB Cantab 1950; FRCO 1942. Dir of Studies in Music, St John's, Downing, and Queens' Colls, Cambridge. Special Commnr, Royal Sch. of Ch Music; Mem. Council, Royal Coll. Organists. *Publications*: *contrib*. Music. Times. *Address*: St John's College, Cambridge.

Guest, Tanis Margaret, PhD; Lecturer, Department of Dutch, Bedford College, University of London, since 1965; *b* 1936; *m* 1960; three *s*. BA London 1959 (1st cl. Dutch), PhD London 1971. Asst Lectr, Bedford Coll., London, 1961–65. *Publica-*

tions: Hadewijch and Minne, in, European Context, 1971. *Address*: Dept of Dutch, Bedford College, Regent's Park, NW1 4NS.

Gulland, Robert Rainsford M.; *see* Milner-Gulland.

Gulley, Prof. Norman, MA; Professor of Classics, St David's University College, Lampeter, since 1968; *b* 1920; *m* 1945; two *s* one *d*. MA Oxon 1946. Asst Lectr in Classics, Bristol Univ., 1946–49, Lectr, 1949–61, Sen. Lectr in Classics and Ancient Philosophy, 1961–64, Reader, 1964–68. *Publications*: Plato's Theory of Knowledge, 1962, repr. 1973; The Philosophy of Socrates, 1968; Aristotle on the Purposes of Literature, 1971; *contrib*. Am. Jl Philol., Class. Qly, Class. Rev., Jl Hell. Stud., Mnemosyne, Phil. Qly, Phoenix, Phronesis. *Address*: Dept of Classics, St David's Univ. College, Lampeter, Dyfed SA48 7ED.

Gulliford, Ronald; Senior Lecturer, School of Education, University of Birmingham, since 1966; *b* 1920; *m* 1950; two *s* two *d*. BA London 1944 (Hons Psych.), DipEdPsych Birmingham 1949; ABPS. Lectr, Remedial Education Centre, Univ. of Birmingham, 1951–53; Tutor, Diploma in Special Educn, 1954– ; Educnl Psychol., Bolton, 1949–51; Hon. Editor, Special Educn, 1966– ; Pres., Assoc. Special Educn, 1962–64; Mem., Sec. of State's Adv. Cttee on Handicapped Children, 1966–72; DES Cttee on Educn of Deaf, 1964–67; DES Cttee on Educn of Blind, 1969–72. *Publications*: (with A. E. Tansley) The Education of Slow Learning Children, 1960; Backwardness and Educational Failure, 1969; Special Educational Needs, 1971. *Address*: School of Education, Univ. of Birmingham, PO Box 363, Birmingham B15 2TT.

Gunn, Prof. Lewis Arthur; Professor of Administration, School of Business and Administration, University of Strathclyde, since 1972; *b* 1935; *m* 1960; two *d*. MA Aberdeen 1957 (Economics–Politics). Teaching Asst, Cornell Univ., 1957–59; Asst Lectr, then Lectr, Manchester, 1960–66; Lectr, Glasgow, 1966–68, Sen. Lectr, 1968–72; Tutor and Adviser on Public Admin, Civil Service Coll. (London), 1969–70; Cnsltnt, OECD Scientific Aff. Directorate (Paris), 1965–69. *Publications*: chapters in symposia on National Health Service and on Science Policy, 1971 and 1972; *contrib*. Minerva, Pol. Qly, Public Admin, Scottish Med. Jl, New Atlantis, Pol. Studies. *Address*: School of Business and Administration, Univ. of Strathclyde, Glasgow G1 1XW.

Gurney, Prof. Oliver Robert, DPhil, FBA; Professor of Assyriology, University of Oxford, since 1965; *b* 1911; *m* 1957. BA Oxon 1933 (2nd cl. Lit. Hum.), MA 1937, DPhil Oxon 1939; FBA. Shillito Reader in Assyriology, Oxford, 1945–65. Royal Artillery, 1939–45. *Publications*: The Hittites, 1952; (with J. Garstang) The Geography of the Hittite Empire, 1959; (with J. J. Finkelstein and P. Hulin) The Sultantepe Tablets, I 1957, II 1964; Ur Excavations, Texts, vol. VII (forthcoming); *contrib*. Anatol. Studies,

Ann. Archaeol. Anthropol., Iraq. *Address*: Oriental Institute, Pusey Lane, Oxford.

Gurr, Dr Andrew John; Senior Lecturer, School of English, University of Leeds, since 1973; *b* 1936; *m* 1961; three *s*. BA NZ 1957, MA Auckland 1958, PhD Cantab 1963. Univ. Wellington, 1959; Univ. Leeds, 1962– ; Univ. Nairobi (on secondment from Leeds), 1969–73. *Publications*: ed, The Knight of the Burning Pestle, 1968; ed, The Maid's Tragedy, 1969; ed, Philaster, 1969, 2nd edn 1973; The Shakespearean Stage, 1574–1642, 1970; ed, Black Aesthetics, 1973; ed, Writers in East Africa, 1974; *contrib*. Essays in Criticism, Jl Commonwealth Lit., Rev. Eng. Lit., Shakespeare Survey, Studies in Philology. *Address*: School of English, Univ. of Leeds, Leeds LS2 9JT.

Gutteridge, William Frank; Director of Complementary Studies, University of Aston in Birmingham, since 1971; *b* 1919; *m* 1944; three *d*. BA Oxon 1948 (2nd cl. Hist.), MA Oxon 1953, DipEd Oxon 1949. Lectr, RMA, Sandhurst, 1949–50, Sen. Lectr, 1950–63; Nuffield Foundn Home Civil Service Travelling Fellowship, Africa, 1960–61; Hd of Dept, Lanchester Coll. Technol., Coventry (later Lanchester Poly)., 1963–71. Mem., Council for Nat. Acad. Awards, Cttee for Arts and Soc. Studies and relevant subject bds, 1965– ; Chm., CNAA Comb. Studies (Humanities) Bd, 1971– ; Chm., CNAA Political Studies Panel, 1973– ; Sec., Brit. Pugwash Gp for Scientists in World Aff., 1966– . *Publications*: Armed Forces in New States, 1962; Military Institutions and Power in New States, 1965; The Military in African Politics, 1969; *contrib*. Afr. Aff., Europa-Archiv, Internat. Inst. Strat. Studies, Adelphi Papers, Parl. Aff., etc. *Address*: Complementary Studies, Univ. of Aston in Birmingham, Birmingham B4 7ET.

Guttsman, Wilhelm Leo; University Librarian, University of East Anglia, since 1962; *b* 1920; *m* 1942; one *d*. BSc Econ London 1946, MSc Econ 1952; Member: Brit. Sociological Assoc.; Soc. for the Study of Labour History. Asst Librarian (later Sub-Librarian, Acquisitions), Brit. Library of Political and Economic Science, LSE, 1948–62. *Publications*: The British Political Elite, 1963; ed, A Plea for Democracy, 1967; ed, The English Ruling Class, 1969; *contrib*. Brit. Jl Sociology, Internat. Rev. Social History, Jl of Documentation, Jl of Librarianship. *Address*: The Library, Univ. of East Anglia, University Plain, Norwich, NOR 88C.

Guyatt, Prof. Richard, CBE; Professor, School of Graphic Design, Royal College of Art, since 1948; *b* 1914; *m* 1948; one *d*. Hon. ARCA 1949, FSIA, FRSA. Pro-Rector, Royal Coll. of Art, 1974. Mem. Stamp Adv. Cttee, Bank of England Design Adv. Cttee. *Publications*: *contrib*. Architectural Rev., Jl RSA, Graphis Annual, Penrose Annual. *Address*: Royal College of Art, Exhibition Road SW7 2EU.

Gwilliam, Prof. Kenneth Mason; Professor, Institute for Transport Studies and School of Economic Studies, University of Leeds, since 1967; *b* 1937; *m* 1961; two *s*. BA Oxon 1960; MCIT. Lectr, Univ. Nottingham, 1961–65; Lectr, Univ. East Anglia, 1965–67. Mem. Civil Engrg and Transport Cttee, SRC, 1970– ; Assessor, Greater London Develt Plan Inquiry, 1970–72. *Publications*: Transport and Public Policy, 1964; The Economics of British Transport Policy in the Seventies, 1974; *contrib*. Applied Econs, Jl Transport Econs and Policy, Jl Transport Planning and Techn., Regional Studies, Yorks Bull. Econ. and Social Res. *Address*: Institute for Transport Studies, Univ. of Leeds, Leeds LS2 9JT.

Gwyn Griffiths, J.; *see* Griffiths, J. G.

Gwynne, Gruffudd Eilydd, MA, DU; Senior Lecturer in French Studies, University of Manchester, since 1971; *b* 1923; *m* 1952; two *s* one *d*. BA Wales 1947 (1st cl.), MA Wales 1949, DU Paris 1953. Asst Lectr, Manchester, 1951–54; Lectr, 1954–70. *Publications*: Madame de Staël et la Révolution Française, 1969; contrib. Modern Miscellany presented to Prof. E. Vinaver. *Address*: Dept of French, The Univ., Manchester M13 9PL.

Gwynne Jones, Prof. H.; *see* Jones, H. G.

Gybbon-Monypenny, Dr Gerald Burney, MA, PhD; Senior Lecturer, Department of Spanish and Portuguese Studies, University of Manchester, since 1965; *b* 1923. BA Cambridge 1949 (1st cl. Spanish, 2nd cl. French Pt I, 2nd cl. French and Spanish Pt II), MA Cambridge 1952, PhD Cambridge 1955. Asst Lectr, Univ. of Manchester, 1955–57, Lectr, 1957–65. *Publications*: Libro de Buen Amor: Studies, 1970; *contrib*. An. Estudios Mediev., Bull. Hisp. Studies, Rev. Filol. Espan. *Address*: Dept of Spanish and Portuguese Studies, The Univ., Manchester M13 9PL.

H

Haack, Robin John, MA, BPhil, DPhil; Lecturer in Philosophy, University of Warwick, since 1966; *b* 1940; *m* 1967. BA Melbourne 1963 (1st cl. Philosophy), MA Melbourne 1966 (1st cl. Philosophy), BPhil Oxon 1966 (Philosophy), DPhil Oxon 1971 (Philosophy); Mem., Brit. Soc. Philos. Science. Tutor in Philosophy, Univ. of Melbourne, 1963–64; Lectr in Philosophy, Univ. of W Australia, 1964–66; Tutor in Philosophy, Worcester Coll., Oxford, 1966. *Publications*: *contrib*. Austral. Jl Philos., Mind, Nous. *Address*: School of Philosophy, Univ. of Warwick, Coventry, Warwickshire.

Haas, Prof. William, MA; Mont Follick Professor of Comparative Philology, Department of General Linguistics, University of Manchester, since 1963; *b* 1912; *m* 1939; one *s* one *d*. BA Wales 1942, Dip. in Economics and Allied Subjects Wales 1942, MA Wales 1945. Lectr, UC Cardiff, 1945–54; Senior Lectr, Manchester Univ., 1954–63; Linguistic Soc. of America Prof., 1962; Vis. Prof., Harvard, 1970. Mem., Council Phil. Soc., 1961–66; Mem., Editorial Bd, Brit. Jl of

277

Linguistics, 1965– ; Mem., Commn Soc. Ling. Eur., 1968– ; Mem., Internat. Phonol. Assoc., 1968– . *Publications:* Phonographic Translation, 1969; contrib. Studies in Linguistic Analysis, 1957; In Memory of J. R. Firth, 1966; Phonologie der Gegenwart, ed Hamm, 1967; The Theory of Meaning, ed Parkinson, 1968; Alphabets for English, 1969; *contrib.* Archiv. Linguisticum, Arist. Soc. Proc., Brit. Jl of Disorders in Comm., German Life and Letters, Brit. Jl of Linguistics, Language, Philosophy, Jl of Speech and Hearing Disorders, Trans Phil Soc., Word. *Address:* Dept of General Linguistics, Univ. of Manchester, Manchester M13 9PL.

Habakkuk, Hrothgar John, FBA; Principal, Jesus College, Oxford University, since 1968; Vice-Chancellor, University of Oxford, since 1973; *b* 1915; *m* 1948; one *s* three *d*. BA Cambridge 1936 (1st cl. with distinction, Pt II History Tripos), MA Cambridge 1940, MA Oxford 1950; Hon DLitt Wales 1971; Hon. DLitt Cantab 1973; FBA, FRHistS, FREconS. Foreign Mem., Amer. Philos. Soc., Amer. Acad. Arts Science. Fellow, Pembroke Coll., Cambridge, 1938; Lectr in Faculty of Economics and Politics, Cambridge, 1946–50; Chichele Prof. of Econ. Hist., Oxford, and Fellow of All Souls, 1950–68; Vis. Prof., Harvard, 1954, Berkeley, 1962; Vice-Chancellor-Elect, Oxford, 1971. Mem., Grigg Cttee on Departmental Records, 1952–54; Adv. Council on Public Records, 1958–69; SSRC, 1967–71; Dainton Cttee on National Libraries, 1968–69; Brit. Library Organising Cttee, 1971–73; Vice-Pres., Royal Hist. Soc., 1969–72; Editor, Econ. Hist. Rev., 1950–60. *Publications:* American and British Technology in the nineteenth century, 1962; Population Growth and Economic Development since 1750, 1971; *contrib.* Econ. Hist. Rev., Jl Econ. Hist. *Address:* Jesus College, Oxford.

Haber, Dr L. F.; Reader in Economics, University of Surrey, since 1970; *b* 1921; *m* 1949. BScEcon London 1943, PhD London 1949. *Publications:* The Chemical Industry during the 19th Century, 1958; The Chemical Industry 1900–30, 1971; *contrib.* Endeavour, Jl Inst. of Fuel, Minerva. *Address:* Dept of Economics, Univ. of Surrey, Guildford, Surrey GU2 5XH.

Hackel, Very Rev. Dr Sergei; Lecturer in Russian Studies, School of European Studies, University of Sussex, since 1964; *b* 1931; *m* 1953; two *s* two *d*. BA Oxon 1952 (Hons), MA Oxon 1965, DPhil Sussex 1973. Mem., Internat. Dept Brit. Council of Chs, 1968– . *Publications:* One of Great Price: the life of Mother Maria Skobtsova, martyr of Ravensbrück, 1965, German trans. 1967; The Orthodox Church, 1971; The Poet and the Revolution: Aleksandr Blok's 'The Twelve', 1975; contrib. Art Treasures in Russia, 1971; trans.: A. Hackel: The Icon, 1954; V. Tendryakov: Ruts, 1968; *contrib.* Contem. Lit., East. Chs Rev., Mod. Lang. Rev. *Address:* Arts Building, Univ. of Sussex, Falmer, Brighton BN1 9QN.

Hacker, Dr Peter Michael Stephan; Fellow and Tutor in Philosophy, St John's

College, Oxford, since 1966; *b* 1939; *m* 1963; two *s* one *d*. BA Oxford 1963, MA 1966, DPhil 1966; Junior Res. Fellow, Balliol College, Oxford, 1965–66; Vis. Lectr, Makerere Univ. Uganda, 1968; Vis. Prof., Swarthmore College, USA, 1973; Vis. Prof., Univ. of Michigan, 1974. *Publications:* Insight and Illusion, Wittgenstein on Philosophy and the Metaphysics of Experience, 1972, *contrib.* Kantstudien, Amer. Philosophical Qly, Philosophy and Phenomenological Res., Idealistic Studies, Philosophical Qly, Rivista di filosofia. *Address:* St John's College, Oxford.

Hackett, Prof. Brian; Professor of Landscape Architecture, Department of Town and Country Planning, University of Newcastle upon Tyne, since 1967; *b* 1911; *m* 1942; one *s* two *d*. MA Durham 1949; ARIBA 1934. MTPI 1947, FILA 1954 (AILA 1945), Hon. Corresp. Mem., Amer. Soc. Landscape Archit., 1962. Lectr in Town and Country Planning, Univ. of Durham, 1947–48, Lectr in Landscape Architecture, 1948–49, Sen. Lectr, 1949–60; Prof. of Landscape Architecture, Univ. of Illinois, 1960–62; Personal Readership in Landscape Architecture, Univ. of Newcastle, 1962–67. Mem., Landscape Planning Commn, IUCN, 1949– . Pres., Inst. Landscape Archit., 1967; Mem., Archit. Planning Sub-Cttee, UGC, 1971; Mem., Water Space Amenity Commn. *Publications:* Man, Society and Environment, 1950; Landscape Planning, 1971; *contrib.* Archaeol. Ael., Biol. Conserv., Gartenant, Industr. Archit., Jl Inst. Landscape Archit., Jl Royal Scott. Forest., Landscape Archit., Planning Outlk, Qly Rev., Jl RTPI. *Address:* Univ. of Newcastle upon Tyne, Newcastle upon Tyne NE1 7RU.

Hackett, Sir John Winthrop, GCB, CBE, DSO and Bar, MC, BLitt, MA; Principal of King's College, London, 1968–July 1975; *b* 1910; *m* 1942; three *d*. MA Oxon 1945, BLitt Oxon 1945; Hon. LLD: QUB; Perth, WA 1963; Fellow KCL, 1968; Hon. Fellow St George's Coll., Univ. of WA, 1965; Hon. Fellow, New Coll., Oxford, 1972. Lees Knowles Lectr, Cambridge, 1961; Basil Henriques Meml Lectr, 1970; Harmon Meml Lectr, USAF Acad., 1970. DQMG, BAOR, 1952; Comdr 20th Armoured Bde, 1954; GOC 7th Armoured Div., 1956–58; Comdt Royal Mil. Coll. of Science, 1958–61; GOC-in-C, NI Command, 1961–63; Dep. Chief of Imperial Gen. Staff, 1963–64; Dep. Chief of Gen. Staff, MOD, 1964–66; Comdr-in-Chief, BAOR, and Comdr, Northern Army Gp, 1966–68; ADC (Gen.), 1967–68. Pres., UK Classical Assoc., 1971; Pres. UK English Assoc., 1974. *Address:* King's College, Strand, WC2R 2LS.

Hackforth-Jones, Mrs Margaret Stefana; see Drower, M. S.

Hackney, Jefrey; Fellow of St Edmund Hall, since 1964, and CUF Lecturer since 1965, Oxford University; Senior Tutor, St Edmund Hall; *b* 1941; *m* 1962; one *s* one *d*. BA Oxford 1962, BCL Oxford 1964, MA Oxford 1965; Vinerian Scholar 1964; Barrister (Middle Temple). Vis. Prof., York

Univ., Toronto, 1972. *Address*: St Edmund Hall, Oxford.

Haddakin, Lilian Faith, MA, PhD; Senior Lecturer in English, University College, London, since 1961; *b* 1914; *m* 1938. BA London 1936 (1st cl. English), MA London 1938; PhD London 1948. Asst, Univ. Coll., London, 1945–48, Asst Lectr, 1948–50, Lectr, 1950–61. *Publications*: The Poetry of Crabbe, 1955; Silas Marner, in, Critical Essays on George Eliot, ed B. Hardy, 1970; *contrib*. Mod. Lang. Rev., Yrs Wk Engl. Studies. *Address*: Dept of English, Univ. College London, Gower Street, WC1E 6BT.

Hadley, Prof. Roger Denham; Professor in Social Administration, University of Lancaster, since 1974; *b* 1931; *m* 1962; one *s* one *d*. BSc(Econ) London 1955; Dip. in Industrial Sociology Liverpool 1959; PhD London 1971. Lectr in Social Admin, LSE, 1966–74. Outside Dir, Scott Bader and Co., 1970– . *Publication*: (with T. Blackstone, K. Gales and W. Lewis) Students in Conflict, 1970; (with A. Webb and C. Farrell) Across the Generations, 1974. *Address*: Dept of Social Administration, Univ. of Lancaster, Bailrigg, Lancaster LA1 4YW.

Hadrill, John Michael W.; *see* Wallace-Hadrill.

Hagan, Thomas; Head of Language Centre, New University of Ulster, since 1968; *b* 1933; *m* 1958; one *s* one *d*. BA QUB 1957; BA London 1961. Lectr in French, Univ. of Surrey, 1966–68. *Address*: Language Centre, New Univ. of Ulster, Coleraine, Co. Londonderry BT52 1SA.

Hagenbuch, Prof. Walter, MA; Professor of Economics, University of Kent at Canterbury, since 1964; *b* 1916; *m* 1949; one *s* one *d*. BA Manchester 1938; MA Cantab 1949; FSS. Lectr in Economics, Univ. of Manchester, 1945–49; Lectr in Economics, Univ. of Cambridge, 1949–64; Fellow, Queens' Coll., Cambridge, 1951–64; Tutor, 1955–58; Sen. Tutor, 1958–63; Proctor, Univ. of Cambridge, 1955–58; Sen. Proctor, 1956–57; Dean, Fac. Social Sciences, Univ. of Kent, 1964–69. Chm., several Wages Councils. *Publications*: Social Economics, 1958; *contrib*. Econ. Jl. *Address*: Keynes College, The Univ., Canterbury, Kent.

Haggard, Prof. Mark Peregrine; Professor of Psychology, Queen's University, Belfast, since 1971; *b* 1942; *m* 1962; two *s*. MA Edinburgh 1963; PhD Cantab 1966. Vis. Fellow, Haskins Labs, NY, 1966; Fellow, Corpus Christi Coll., and Univ. Demonstrator, Cambridge, 1967–71. Mem., Exp. Psychol. Soc.; Acoust. Soc. Amer. Ed., Qly Jl Exper. Psychol. 1970. *Publications*: *contrib*. Jl Acoust. Soc. Amer, Qly Jl Exper. Psychol. *Address*: Dept of Psychology, The Queen's Univ. of Belfast, BT7 1NN.

Haggett, Prof. Peter; Professor of Urban and Regional Geography, University of Bristol, since 1966; *b* 1933; *m* 1956; two *s* two *d*. BA Cantab 1954 (1st cl. Geography); MA Cantab 1957, PhD Cantab 1970. Asst

Lectr, Univ. Coll., London, 1955–57 Demonstrator and Lectr, Cambridge Univ., 1957–66; Fellow, Fitzwilliam Coll., Cambridge, 1964–66. Mem., SW Reg. Econ. Planning Council, 1967–72; Council, Royal Geog. Soc., 1971–72. *Publications*: Locational Analysis in Human Geography, 1965, Russian trans. 1967; co-ed, Frontiers in Geographical Teaching, 1965; co-ed, Models in Geography 1967, Russian trans. 1967; (with R. J. Chorley) Network Analysis in Geography, 1969; co-ed, Regional Forecasting, 1971; Geography: A Modern Synthesis, 1972; *contrib*. Geog. Jl, Annals Amer. Assoc. Geogrs, Trans Inst. Brit. Geogrs; Papers Reg. Sci. Assoc., etc. *Address*: Dept of Geography, Univ. of Bristol, Bristol BS8 1TH.

Haggis, Dr Donald Ross, BA, PhD; Reader in Modern French Literature, Department of French and Italian, University of Exeter, since 1968; *b* 1913; *m* 1938; two *s*. BA London 1939 (1st cl. General), BA London 1941 (2nd cl. French), PhD London 1950. Lectr, Glasgow, 1948–62; Sen. Lectr, 1962–68. Mem., Exec. Cttee, Soc. Fr. Studies, 1965–67. *Publications*: Camus: La Peste (Studies in French Literature, 9), 1962; C-F. Ramuz, ouvrier du langage (Situation, No. 16), 1968; *contrib*. MLR, Fr. Studies, Forum for Mod. Lang. Studies. *Address*: Dept of French and Italian, Univ. of Exeter, Exeter EX4 4QJ.

Hague, Prof. Douglas Chalmers; Professor of Managerial Economics, Manchester Business School, Manchester University, since 1965; *b* 1926; *m* 1947; two *d*. MCom Birmingham 1948, MBA Manchester 1967. Asst Lectr in Political Econ., Univ. Coll., London, 1947–50, Lectr, 1950–57; Reader in Political Economy, Univ. of London, 1957; Newton Chambers Prof. of Applied Econs, Univ. of Sheffield, 1957–63; Vis. Prof., Duke Univ., USA, 1960–61; Prof. of Applied Econs, Univ. of Manchester, 1963–65. Pt-time mem., NW Gas Bd, 1966–73; Mem., Working Party of Mngmt Training in the Civil Service, 1965–67; Jt Chm, Conf, of Univ. Mngmt Schs, 1971–73. Mem. Price Commn, 1973– . *Publications*: (with A. W. Stonier) A Textbook of Economic Theory, 1953, 4th edn 1972; (with A. W. Stonier) The Essentials of Economics, 1955; The Economics of Manmade Fibres, 1957; ed, Pricing in Various Economies, 1965; Managerial Economics, 1970; ed, The Dilemma of Accountability in Modern Government: Independence Versus Control, 1971; Pricing in Business, 1971; ed (with M. E. Beesley), Britain in the Common Market: a new business opportunity, 1973; *contrib*. Econ. Jl, Rev. Econ. Studies. *Address*: Manchester Business School, Booth Street West, Manchester M15 6PB.

Hahn, Prof. Frank Horace; Professor of Economics, University of Cambridge, since 1972; *b* 1925; *m* 1946. BSc(Econ) London 1946, MA Cantab 1960, PhD London 1951. Asst Lectr, then Lectr and later Reader, Univ. of Birmingham, 1948–59; Vis. Prof., MIT, 1956; Univ. of California, Berkeley, 1959; Lectr, Cambridge, 1960–66; Fellow, Churchill Coll., Cambridge, 1960– ; Fellow, Center for Adv. Studies in Social Sciences,

279

1966–67; Prof. of Economics, LSE, 1967–72. Pres., Econometric Soc., 1968–69; Mngng Ed., Rev. Econ. Studies, 1962–67. *Publications*: (with K. J. Arrow) General Competitive Analysis, 1971; The Share of Wages in the National Income, 1972; *contrib*. Economica, Rev. Econ. Studies, Econ. Jl. *Address*: Churchill College, Cambridge.

Haimendorf, Christoph von F.; *see* Fürer-Haimendorf.

Haines, John Courtney; Senior Lecturer, School of Social Work, University of Leicester, since 1972; *b* 1935. BA Oxon 1958 (Hons Mod. Hist.), MA Oxon 1962, Certif. Social Sci. and Admin London 1959 (distinction), Certif. Applied Social Studies London 1960. Lectr in Applied Social Studies, Univ. of Nottingham, 1964–69. Regional Trng Officer, Probation and After-Care Service, Midland Region, 1969–71; Sen. Asst Dir of Social Services, Leics CC Social Services Dept, 1971–72. *Publications*: The Nature of Social Work, 1970, 2nd edn 1973; Norway: a New Look at Crime, 1971. *Address*: School of Social Work, 107 Princess Road, Leicester LE1 7LA.

Hair, Dr Paul Edward Hedley; Senior Lecturer, Department of Modern History, University of Liverpool, since 1968; *b* 1926; *m* 1959; one *s* one *d*. BA Cantab 1948 (2nd cl. History), MA Cantab 1950, DPhil Oxon 1955; FRHistS. Res. Fellow, W Afr. Inst. Social Econ. Res., 1951–54; Lectr, Teacher Training Dept, Fourah Bay Coll., Sierra Leone, 1955–58; Lectr, Univ. of Sierra Leone, 1961–63; Sen. Lectr in African History, Univ. of Khartoum, 1963–65; Lectr in African History, Univ. of Liverpool, 1965–68. Sec., Teaching Staff Assoc., Univ. of Sierra Leone, 1957–58, 1962–63; Acad. Staff Assoc., Univ. of Khartoum, 1964–65. *Publications*: A History of West Africa for Schools and Colleges, 1959; The Early Study of Nigerian Languages, 1967; Before the Bawdy Court, 1972; *contrib*. Afr. Lang. Rev., Afr. Lang. Studies, Econ. Hist. Rev., Irish Hist. Stud., Jl Afr. Hist., Jl Eccles. Hist., Pop. Studies, Trans Philos. Soc. *Address*: School of History, Univ. of Liverpool, 8 Abercromby Square, Liverpool.

Haire, The Very Rev. Principal James Loughridge Mitchell; Principal of the Presbyterian College, Belfast, since 1963, and Lecturer in Theology, Queen's University, Belfast, since 1944; *b* 1909; *m* 1945; two *s* three *d*. BA Oxon 1933 (2nd cl. Cl. Mods, 2nd cl. Lit. Hum.), MA 1936, BD London and Belfast 1936, MTh London 1945, Hon DD Edinburgh 1960. Prof. of Systematic Theology, Presbyterian Coll., Belfast, 1944– . Vice-Pres., Brit. Council of Chs, 1965–67. *Publications*: (with J. Thompson) Commentary on Shorter Catechism, 1969; trans. (with I. Henderson) Barth: Knowledge of God and Service of God, 1939; (with I. Henderson) W. Luthi: In the Time of Earthquake, 1940; Barth: Church Dogmatics, vol. 2, 1, 1956; On behalf of Chalcedon, in, Essays in Christology for Karl Barth, ed Parker, 1956; Diaconia in the Reformed Churches, in, Service in Christ, 1966;

contrib. Biblical Theol., Scott. Jl Theol. *Address*: Presbyterian College, Rugby Road, Belfast 7.

Haksar, Dr Vinit Narain, DPhil; Lecturer in Philosophy, University of Edinburgh, since 1969; *b* 1937; *m* 1966; two *s* one *d*. BA Delhi 1956 (Hons), BA 1959, MA 1963, DPhil 1968, Oxon. Asst, Dept of Moral Philosophy and Dept of Logic and Metaphysics, St Andrews Univ., 1962–64; Lectr in Moral Philosophy, 1964–69. Mem.: Bd of Studies in Philosophy, St Andrews Univ., 1964–69; Bd of Studies in Mental Philosophy, Edinburgh Univ., 1969– ; Council, Fac. of Arts, Edinburgh Univ., 1972– . *Publications*: contrib. Aristotle's Ethics, ed H. Shapiro and J. Walsh; *contrib*. Analysis, Brit. Jl Pol Sci., Gandhi Marg, Philos. Bks, Philos. Qly, Philos. Rev. Philos., Proc. Aristot. Soc. Suppl. Vol. *Address*: Dept of Philosophy, The Univ. of Edinburgh, Edinburgh EH8 9YL.

Haldane, Dr Joan A., BA; Lecturer in Classics, University College of North Wales, Bangor, since 1965; *b* 1935. BA Classics London 1958 (1st cl.), PhD London 1963; Assoc. King's Coll., 1957. Asst Lectr, Magee Univ. Coll., Londonderry, 1963–64; Asst Lectr, Univ. Coll. of N Wales, Bangor, 1964. *Publications*: contrib. Class. Qly, Greece and Rome, Jl Hellenic Studies, Philologus, Phoenix, Poetry Rev., English. *Address*: Univ. College of North Wales, Bangor LL57 2DG.

Hale, David John; Lecturer in Psychology, Queen's University, Belfast, since 1972; *b* 1944; *m* 1965; four *d*. BSc Manchester 1965 (1st cl. Psychology), MSc Manchester 1967 (Psychology); Mem., Brit. Psychol. Soc., Exper. Psychol. Soc.; Associate Psychol. Soc. of Ireland. Asst Lectr in Psychology, Manchester Univ., 1965–67; Res. Fellow in Applied Psychology, Aston Univ., 1967–71. *Publications*: contrib. Acta Psychol., Jl Exper. Psychol., Percept. Mot. Skills, Psychon. Sci., Qly Jl Exper. Psychol., Irish Jl Psychol. *Address*: Psychology Dept, Queen's Univ., Belfast BT7 1NN.

Hale, Prof. John Rigby, MA, FSA; Professor of Italian, University College London, since 1970; *b* 1923; *m* 1951 and 1965; two *s* two *d*. BA Oxon 1948 (1st cl. History), MA Oxon 1953; FSA, FRHistS. Fellow, Jesus Coll., Oxford, 1949; Prof. of History, Warwick Univ., 1964–70; Vis. Prof., Cornell Univ., 1959; Vis. Prof., Berkeley, 1969 and 1970. Trustee, Nat. Gallery; Chm., Brit. Renaissance Soc. *Publications*: England and the Italian Renaissance, 1954, rev. ed 1963; The Italian Journal of Samuel Rogers, 1956; Machiavelli and Renaissance Italy, 1961, rev. edn 1972; The Evolution of British Historiography, 1964; ed, Certain Discourses Military by Sir John Smythe, 1964; ed (with B. Smalley and R. Highfield), Europe in the Late Middle Ages, 1965; Renaissance Exploration, 1968; Renaissance Europe, 1971; ed, Renaissance Venice, 1973; *contrib*. Past and Present, English Miscellany, Italian Studies, Shakespeare Qly, Huntington Library Qly, Newberry Library Bull., Studi Veneziani, New Cambridge

Modern History, vols i, ii and iii; Fest-schriften for Hans Baron, W. K. Ferguson, J. H. Whitfield, etc. *Address*: Dept of Italian, Univ. College, Gower Street, WC1E 6BT.

Hale, Dr Victor William Douglas, PhD, FBCS; Senior Lecturer in Mathematics, University of York, since 1963; *b* 1922; *m* 1952; one *s* one *d*. BA Cantab 1943 (Wrangler, Mathematics), MA Cantab 1947, PhD Cantab 1951; FBCS. Lectr, Hull Univ., 1949–63; Vis. Prof., York Univ., Toronto, 1970; Vis., Australian Nat. Univ., Canberra, 1972. Mem., Council, BCS, 1968–72. *Address*: Dept of Mathematics, Univ. of York, York YO1 5DD.

Haley, Prof. Kenneth Harold Dobson; Professor of Modern History, University of Sheffield, since 1962; *b* 1920; *m* 1948; one *s* two *d*. BA Oxon 1946 (1st cl. History), MA Oxon 1946, BLitt Oxon 1951; FRHistS. Asst Lectr, Sheffield Univ., 1947–50, Lectr, 1950–60, Sen. Lectr, 1960–62. Mem., Council, Hist. Assoc., 1966– . *Publications*: William of Orange and the English Opposition, 1672–74, 1953; Charles II (Hist. Assoc. pamphlet), 1966; The First Earl of Shaftesbury, 1968; The Dutch in the Seventeenth Century, 1972; *contrib.* Bull. Inst. Hist. Res., EHR. *Address*: Dept of Medieval and Modern History, Univ. of Sheffield, Sheffield S10 2TN.

Halkhoree, Dr Premraj Radhe Krishna; Lecturer, Department of Spanish, Westfield College, University of London, since 1967; *b* 1941; *m* 1968. MA Edinburgh 1965, PhD Edinburgh 1969; ATCL 1962, LRAM 1963; Mem. Assoc. Univ. Teachers, Mem. Assoc. Hispanists. *Publications*: Calderón de la Barca: El alcalde de Zalamea, 1972; *contrib.* Bull. Comediantes, Forum Mod. Lang. Studies, Romance Notes, Romanistiches Jahrbuch. *Address*: Dept of Spanish, West-field College, Kidderpore Avenue, Hampstead, NW3 7ST.

Hall, Prof. Alfred Rupert; Professor of History of Science and Technology, Imperial College, University of London, since 1963; *b* 1920; *m* 1941; 1959; two *d*. BA Cantab 1941, MA Cantab 1944, PhD Cantab 1950; FRHistS, Mem., Internat. Hist. des Sci., Brit. Soc. Hist. Science Fellow, Christ's Coll., Cambridge, 1949–59; Asst Lectr, then Lectr, Cambridge Univ., 1950–59; Assoc. Res. Medical Hist., UCLA, 1959–60; Prof. of Philosophy, 1960–61; Prof. of History and Logic of Science, Indiana Univ., 1961–63. Pres., Brit. Soc. Hist. Sci., 1966–68. Ballistics in the 17th Century, 1952; The Scientific Revolution, 1954, 2nd edn 1962; From Galileo to Newton, 1963; The Cambridge Philosophical Society, a History, 1969; (with M. B. Hall) Unpublished Scientific Papers of Isaac Newton, 1962; Brief History of Science, 1964; Correspondence of Henry Oldenburg, 1965 (in progress); ed (with L. Tilling), Correspondence of Isaac Newton; co-ed, A History of Technology, 1953–58; *contrib.* Ann. Sci., Brit. Jl Hist. Sci., Isis, Notes Rec. Royal Soc. *Address*: Dept of History of Science and Technology, Imperial College, SW7 2 AZ.

Hall, Prof. Basil, MA, PhD, MA(Theol) FSA, FRHistS; Professor of Ecclesiastical History, University of Manchester, since 1968; *b* 1915; *m* 1948; one *d*. BA Dunelm 1936 (English Language and Literature), MA Dunelm 1940; BA Cantab 1939 (Theol Tripos, Part III, Ecclesiastical History), MA Cantab 1942, PhD Cantab 1970; MA Manchester 1972 (Theol); FSA, FRHistS. Fac. of Theol., Univ. of Wales, 1949 (Prof. of Ecclesiastical Hist., United Theol Coll., Aberystwyth); Lectr in Reformation Studies, Fac. of Theol., Univ. of Cambridge, 1956–68 (concurrently Prof., Church History, Westminster Coll., Cambridge, 1963–68); Fellow of Fitzwilliam Coll., Cambridge, 1963. *Publications*: Biblical Scholarship and Commentaries in the sixteenth century, in, Cambridge History of the Bible, vol. II, 1965; Diakonia in Martin Butzer, in, Service in Christ, ed McCord and Parker, 1966; Jonathan Swift the Churchman, in, Essays on Swift, ed B. Vickers, 1969; Erasmus, biblical scholar and reformer, in, Erasmus, ed J. Dorey, 1970; The Great Polyglot Bibles, limited edn (San Francisco), 1966; *contrib.* Jl Theol Studies, Jl Ecclesiastical Hist., Scottish Jl Theol. *Address*: Dept of Ecclesiastical History, Faculty of Theology, University of Manchester, Manchester M13 9PL.

Hall, Bernard; Lecturer, Department of Economics, University of Durham, since 1964; *b* 1938; *m* 1959; two *s*. MA Edinburgh 1961 (Hons Econ. Science), DipEd Edinburgh 1962; Asst, Dept of Polit. Economy, Univ. of Glasgow, 1962–64. *Address*: Dept of Economics, Univ. of Durham, 23–26 Old Elvet, Durham.

Hall, Clifford Gregory; Lecturer in Law, Department of Law, University College of Wales, Aberystwyth, since 1970; *b* 1945; *m* 1969. MA Cantab 1971, LLM Wales 1971. Asst Lectr, UCW Aberystwyth, 1967–70. *Publications*: ed, Cambrian Law Review, 1970, vol. 5 1974; *contrib.* Cambrian Law Rev., Internat. Aff., Internat. and Compar. Law Qly. *Address*: Dept of Law, Univ. College of Wales, Aberystwyth SY23 2AX.

Hall, Dr David Clement; Lecturer in Psychology at Leeds University, since 1967; *b* 1942; *m* 1965; three *s*. BSc Edinburgh 1964 (Psychol.), PhD Edinburgh 1969 (Psychol.); ABPsS; Mem., AUT. *Publications: contrib.* Brit. Jl Psychol. *Address*: Dept of Psychology, The Univ., Leeds LS2 9JT.

Hall, Edward Thomas; Director, Research Laboratory for Archaeology and History of Art, Oxford, since 1954; *b* 1924; *m* 1957; two *s*. BA Oxon 1948, MA Oxon 1953, DPhil Oxon 1953; FPhysS. Fellow, Worcester Coll., Oxford, 1969– . Mem. Hon. Scientific Cttee, Nat. Gallery, 1971; Trustee of British Museum, 1973. *Publications: contrib.* Archaeometry. *Address*: 6 Keble Road, Oxford.

Hall, George Derek Gordon; President, Corpus Christi College, Oxford, since 1969; *b* 1924; *m* 1952. MA Oxon 1949; FRHistS. Lectr in Law, UCW Aberystwyth, 1948–49; Fellow and Tutor in Law, Exeter Coll.,

Oxford, 1949–69. Member: Hebdomadal Council, Univ. of Oxford, 1963–73; Gen. Bd of Faculties, 1963–73 (Vice-Chm., 1967–69); Literary Adviser, Selden Soc. *Publications*: Glanvill, 1965; contrib. Essays Presented to Bertie Wilkinson, 1969; with E. de Haas, Early Registers of Writs 1970; *contrib.* Amer. Jl of Legal History, Bull. of John Rylands Library, Eng. Hist. Rev., Law Qly Rev., Tulane Law Rev. *Address*: Corpus Christi College, Oxford OX1 4JF.

Hall, Prof. George Garfield, MA, BSc, PhD, FIMA; Dean of Pure Science and Professor of Applied Mathematics, University of Nottingham (also concerned with Mathematics in Education), since 1962, and Professor of Chemistry, University of Kansas (2 months annually), since 1970; *b* 1925; *m* 1951; one *s* two *d*. BSc Belfast 1946 (1st cl. Mathematics; 1st cl. Math. Phys,) 1947 (1st cl. Physics), MA Cantab 1950, PhD Cantab 1951; FIMA 1964. Asst in Res., Cambridge, 1950–55; Fellow, St John's Coll., Cambridge, 1953–55; Lectr, Imperial Coll., London, 1955–62; Vis. Res., Uppsala, 1957–58; Vis. Prof., Univ. of Kansas, 1969. Mem.: Council, IMA, 1968–71; Derbyshire Educn Cttee, 1969– ; Editl Adv. Cttees, Internat. Jl Quantum Chem., Internat. Jl Math. Educn Science Technol., Comput. Phys. Communic., Chem. Phys. Lett.; mem., Comput. Consult. Council, 1971– . *Publications*: Matrices and Tensors, 1962; Applied Group Theory, 1967; *contrib.* Internat. Jl Quantum Chem., Proc. Royal Soc. *Address*: Mathematics Dept, Univ. of Nottingham, Nottingham NG7 2RD.

Hall, Hugh Gaston, BA, MA, PhD; Senior Lecturer in French, University of Warwick, since 1966; *b* 1931; *m* 1955; one *s* two *d*. BA Millsaps College 1952, Dip pour l'enseignement du français Toulouse 1953, BA Oxford 1955 (Mod. Langs), MA Oxford 1959, PhD Yale 1959; Mem., Mod. Hum. Res. Assoc., Soc. Fr. Studies, Soc. Renaiss. Studies, Soc. 18th-cent. Studies. Instructor, Yale Univ., 1958–60; Asst then Lectr, Univ. of Glasgow, 1960–64; Vis. Asst Prof., Univ. of California, Berkeley, 1963; Vis. Sen. Lectr, Monash Univ., Australia, 1965; Special Lectr, 1968; Vis. Prof., Queens Coll. and Grad. Center, City Univ., NY, 1970–72. *Publications*: Molière: Tartuffe, 1960, 4th edn 1970, American edn 1962; ed, D. de Saint-Sorlin: Les Visionnaires, 1964; ed, Molière: Le Bourgeois Gentilhomme, 1966, Les Femmes Savantes, 1974; trans. from Italian, F. Simone: The French Renaissance, 1970; D. de Saint-Sorlin: His Background and Reception in the 17th Century, 1971; *contrib.* Austral. Jl Fr. Studies, Ball State Univ. Forum, Diz. Crit. Lett. Franc., Fr. Studies, Kentucky Rom. Qly, Mod. Lang. Rev., Studi Franc., Yale Fr. Studies, Year's Work Mod. Lang. Studies. *Address*: Dept of French, Univ. of Warwick, Coventry CV4 7AL.

Hall, John Bernard, BPhil, MA; Lecturer in charge of Spanish, Department of Romance Studies, University College, Swansea, since 1966; *b* 1941; *m* 1964; one *s*. BA Oxon 1963, BPhil Oxon 1967, MA Oxon 1968.

Publications: contrib. Studies of the Spanish and Portuguese Ballad, ed N. D. Shergold, 1972; *contrib.* Anales Galdosianos, Forum Mod. Lang. Studies, Iberomania, Rev. Litt. Comp. *Address*: Dept of Romance Studies, Univ. College, Swansea SA2 8PP.

Hall, John Cecil; Lecturer in Moral Philosophy, University of St Andrews, since 1960; *b* 1930; *m* 1961; two *s* one *d*. MA Oxford 1956. Asst Principal, MAFF, 1955–58. *Publications*: Rousseau: an introduction to his political philosophy, 1973; *contrib.* Class. Qly, Philos. Qly, Proc. Aristotelian Soc. *Address*: Dept of Moral Philosophy, The Univ., St Andrews, Fife KY16 9AJ.

Hall, John Challice, MA, LLB; Lecturer in Law, Cambridge University, since 1960, and Fellow of St John's College, Cambridge, since 1955; *b* 1928. BA Cantab 1948 (1st cl. Law), MA Cantab 1952, LLB Cantab 1951; Solicitor 1953. Sen. Tutor, St John's Coll., Cambridge, 1972; JP 1970– . *Publications*: Sources of Family Law, 1966, Supplement, 1971; Jt ed, Clerk and Lindsell on Torts, 12th and 13th edns and supplements, 1961–72; *contrib.* Cambridge Law Jl, Jl Soc. Public Teachers Law. *Address*: St John's College, Cambridge CB2 1TP.

Hall, John Ruthven; Lecturer in Education, University of Newcastle upon Tyne, since 1966; *b* 1929; *m* 1955; one *s* two *d*. BA Cantab 1952 (Nat. Sciences), Cert. Educn Bristol 1953; Asst Master (Biology), Rugby Sch., 1953–59; King's Coll., Budo, Kampala, 1960–64, Sen. Science Master, 1963–64. Lectr in Educn, Makerere Univ. Coll., 1964–66. *Publications*: Senior Tropical Biology, 1970; Teach Yourself Biology, 1974. *Address*: Univ. Sch. of Education, St Thomas Street, Newcastle upon Tyne.

Hall, Prof. John Sexton, MA, LLB; Professor of Law at the University College at Buckingham, since 1974; *b* 1919; *m* 1952; one *s* one *d*. Law Tripos Cambridge 1946 (2nd cl.); Lincoln's Inn, Barrister 1946. Asst Lectr in Law, Univ. of Exeter, 1947–49, Lectr, 1949–63, Sen. Lectr, 1963–72, Reader, 1972–74; Vis. Prof., Univ. of Missouri, Kansas City, 1964. Mem., Univ. Senate, 1961–64; Univ. Council, 1963–64. *Publications*: Taxation Ed., Jl Business Law; ed, Tax section, Palmer: Company Law, 21st edn, 1968; *contrib.* Acntng Res., Brit. Tax Rev., Conveyan. Prop Law, Jl Business Law, JP Local Govt Rev., Law Qly Rev., New Law Jl, Solic. Jl, Univ. Miss. Kansas City Law Rev. *Address*: Univ. Coll. at Buckingham, Old Bank Building, 2 Bridge Street, Buckingham.

Hall, Joseph Roger C.; see Carby-Hall.

Hall, Dr Kathleen M.; Senior Lecturer, Department of French, University of Southampton, since 1969; *b* 1924. BA Oxon 1944, MA Oxon 1949, DPhil Oxon 1953; Chev. de l'ordre des palmes académiques, 1970. Mem., Soc. Fr. Studies, Soc. Renaiss. Studies. Asst Lectr, Queen's Univ., Belfast, 1953–55; Lectr, Univ. of Southampton,

1955–69. *Publications*: Pontus de Tyard and his Discours Philosophiques, 1963; ed (with K. Cameron and F. Higman), T. de Bèze: Abraham Sacrifiant, 1967; ed (with C. N. Smith), J. de La Taille: Dramatic Works, 1972; *contrib*. Fr. Studies, Esp. Créat., Mod. Lang. Rev. *Address*: Dept of French, The Univ., Southampton S09 5NH.

Hall, Laura Margaret, (Lady Hall); Fellow and Tutor in Economics, Somerville College, Oxford University, since 1948, and University Lecturer in Economics, Oxford, since 1955; *b* 1910; *m* 1932, divorced 1968; two *d*. BA Oxon 1932, MA Oxon 1938; Lectr, Lincoln Coll., Oxford, 1946–48; Vis. Prof., Economics Dept, MIT, 1961–62. Mem.: Treasury Purchase Tax (Valuation) Cttee, 1953; Co-op. Independent Commn (Gaitskell Commn), 1958; Interdeptal Cttee on Social and Econ. Res., Agric. and Food Statistics, 1958; Min. of Agric. Cttee on Remuneration of Milk Distributors, 1962; Commn of Inquiry into Advertising (Reith Commn), 1964; Mem., Econ. Develt Cttee for the Distributive Trades, 1964; Census of Distribution Adv. Cttee, 1970; Covent Garden Market Authority Adv. Panel, 1972; Monopolies Commn, 1973. *Publications*: Distributive Trading, An Economic Analysis, 1948; Distribution in Great Britain and North America, 1961; The Small Unit in Distributive Trades (Research Report no 8 for Bolton Cttee), 1971; *contrib*. The British Economy, ed Worswich and Ady, 1952; *contrib*. Amer. Econ. Rev., Econ. Jl, Economica, Jl Indust. Econ., London Cambridge Bull., OECD Product. Rev., Oxford Econ. Papers, Oxford Univ. Inst. Stat. Bull., Rev. Econ. Stat., Westmin. Bank Rev. *Address*: Somerville College, Oxford.

Hall, Marie Boas; Reader, Department of History of Science and Technology, Imperial College, London, since 1964; *b* 1919; *m* 1959. AB Radcliffe College 1940, MA Radcliffe College 1942, PhD Cornell 1949; FRSA. Mem.: Brit. Soc. Hist. Science, Newcomen Soc., Hist. Science Soc. Asst Prof., Univ. of Massachusetts, 1949–52; Brandeis Univ., 1952–57; UCLA, 1957–61; Prof., Indiana Univ., 1961–63; Sen. Lectr, Imperial Coll., 1963–64. Sec., Hist. Science Soc., 1952–58; Mem. Council, Brit. Soc. Hist. Science, 1970–73. *Publications*: Robert Boyle and 17th Century Chemistry, 1958; The Scientific Renaissance, 1962, pbk edn 1970; Robert Boyle on Natural Philosophy, 1965; Nature and Nature's Laws, 1970; ed, Hero: Pneumatics, 1971; (with A. R. Hall) Unpublished Scientific Papers of Isaac Newton, 1962; Brief History of Science, 1964; Correspondence of Henry Oldenburg, 1964– ; *contrib*. Brit. Jl Hist. Science, Isis, Osiris, Rev. Hist. des Science. *Address*: Dept of History of Science and Technology, Imperial College, SW7 2AZ.

Hall, Prof. Peter Geoffrey; Professor and Head of Department of Geography, University of Reading, since 1968; *b* 1932; *m* 1967. BA Cantab 1953, MA Cantab 1958, PhD Cantab 1959; Mem.: Royal Geog. Soc., Inst. Brit. Geogrs, Reg. Studies Assoc. Asst

Lectr, Birkbeck Coll., Univ. of London, 1957–60; Lectr, 1960–65; Reader in Geography with reference to Reg. Planning, LSE, 1966–68. Mem.: SE Reg. Econ. Planning Council, 1966; Nature Conserv., 1967–72; Planning and Transport. Res. Adv. Council, 1971–73; Exec. Cttee, Reg. Studies Assoc.; Hon. Ed., Reg. Studies, 1966; Chm., Fabian Soc. Exec., 1971–72. *Publications*: The Industries of London, 1962; London 2000, 1963; Labour's New Frontiers, 1964; ed, Land Values, 1965; The World Cities, 1966; Theory and Practice of Regional Planning, 1970; Containment of Urban England, 1973; Planning and Urban Growth, 1973; Urban and Regional Planning, 1974; *contrib*. Trans Inst. Brit. Geogrs, Geog. Jl, Reg. Studies. *Address*: Dept of Geography, Univ. of Reading, Whiteknights, Reading, Berkshire RG6 2AF.

Hall, Peter Reginald Frederick, CBE, MA; Director of the National Theatre, since 1973; Associate Professor of Drama, Warwick University, since 1968; *b* 1930; *m* 1st 1956, 2nd 1966; two *s* two *d*. MA (Hons) Cambridge 1953. Director, Royal Shakespeare Co., 1960–68. Mem., Pilkington Cttee on Future of Broadcasting; Arts Council, 1969–73. *Publications*: Many articles on the theatre in various jls. *Address*: National Theatre, Waterloo Road, SE1.

Hall, Roland; Reader in Philosophy, University of York, since 1967; *b* 1930; *m* 1954; three *d*. BA Oxon 1954 (1st cl. Lit. Hum.), BPhil Oxon 1956, MA Oxon 1960; Asst in Logic, Univ. of St Andrews, 1956–57; Lectr in Philosophy, Queen's Coll., Dundee, 1957–66; Sen. Lectr, 1966–67. Asst Ed., Philos. Qly, 1961–67. Editor, The Locke Newsletter, 1970– . *Publications*: A Hume Bibliography, 1971; *contrib*. Chambers's Encyclopaedia, 1966; Encyclopaedia of Philosophy, 1967; Oxford English Dictionary, 1972– ; *contrib*. Analysis, Class Qly, Mind, Notes Queries, Philos Qly, Philos. Rev., Philos., Proc. Aristot. Soc. *Address*: Dept of Philosophy, Univ. of York, Heslington, York YO1 5DD.

Hall, Rev. Stuart George, MA, BD; Senior Lecturer in Theology, University of Nottingham, since 1973 (Lecturer, 1962–73); *b* 1928; *m* 1953; two *s* two *d*. BA Oxon 1952 (2nd cl. Classical Hon. Moderations; 1st cl. Lit. Hum.; 2nd cl. Theology), MA 1955; BD Oxon 1973; ordained deacon, C of E, 1954, priest 1955. Gov., Nottingham High Sch., 1963– . *Publications*: chapters in, Studia Evangelica, ed K. Aland, etc., 1959; Four Anchors from the Stern, ed A. Richardson, 1963; Difficulties for Christian Belief, ed R. P. C. Hanson, 1966; Studia Patristica VIII, ed F. L. Cross, 1966; *contrib*. Jl Theol. Studies, Theol. *Address*: Dept of Theology, Univ. Park, Nottingham NG7 2RD.

Hall, Victor, ERD, MSc, FRIBA, MRIAI; Senior Lecturer, Department of Architecture, Queen's University of Belfast, since 1968; *b* 1921; *m* 1942; two *s*. MSc Belfast 1969; FRIBA 1955, MRIAI 1964. Archit. Tech. Off., ICI Ltd, 1956–59; Acting Hd, Dept of

Archit., Coll. of Art, Belfast, 1959–65. Lectr, Queen's Univ. of Belfast, 1965–68. HM Forces, 1941–46; AER, RE, 1950–64; Sen. Archit., Corby New Town, 1954, 1956. *Address*: Dept of Architecture, Queen's Univ. of Belfast, Belfast BT7 1NN.

Halladay, Eric; Vice-Master and Senior Tutor, Grey College, and part-time lecturer in History, University of Durham, since 1964; *b* 1930; *m* 1956; one *s* two *d*. BA Cantab 1953 (2nd cl. both pts History Tripos), MA Cantab 1956, DipEd Oxon 1954; Sen. History Master, Exeter Sch., 1954–60; Sen. Lectr in History, RMA, Sandhurst, 1960–64. *Publications*: (with D. D. Rooney) The Building of Modern Africa, 1966, 2nd edn 1967; *contrib.* Africa and Its Explorers, ed R. I. Rotberg, 1970; The Emergent Continent–Africa in the Nineteenth Century, 1972. *Address*: Grey College, Durham.

Hallett, Graham, PhD, MA; Lecturer, Department of Economics, University College, Cardiff, since 1967; *b* 1929; *m* 1972. BA Oxon 1952 (PPE), MA Oxon 1957, PhD Wales 1962; Lectr in Agric. Econs, Univ. Coll., Aberystwyth, 1954–63; Assoc. Prof., Univ. of Manitoba, 1961–62; Fellow, Alexander von Humboldt Foundn, 1963–65; Lectr in Land Econ., Cambridge Univ., 1965–67. *Publications*: The Economics of Agricultural Land Tenure, 1960; The Economics of Agricultural Policy, 1968; (with P. Randall) Maritime Industry and Port Development in South Wales, 1970; *contrib.* Jl Agric. Econ. *Address*: Dept of Economics, Univ. College, Cardiff CF1 1XL.

Hallett, Richard William, BA; Lecturer, Department of Russian, University of Aberdeen, since 1967; *b* 1939; *m* 1969; one *s*. BA Nottingham 1963 (2nd cl. Russian and English); Asst Lectr, Aberdeen Univ., 1965–67. *Publications*: Isaac Babel, 1972, NY edn 1973; *contrib.* Russian Rev., Slavonic E Europ. Rev. *Address*: Dept of Russian, Univ. of Aberdeen, Aberdeen AB9 1AS.

Halliday, Dr Anita Josephine; Lecturer, Sociology Department, Birmingham University, since 1968; *b* 1940. BA (Econ) Cantab 1962, MA (Econ) Cantab 1965, PhD Keele 1967; Mem., Brit. Sociol. Assoc. Asst Lectr, Birmingham Univ., 1965–68. *Address*: Sociology Dept, Univ. of Birmingham, PO Box 363, Birmingham B15 2TT.

Halliday, Prof. John Menzies, CBE, MA, LLD; Professor of Conveyancing, University of Glasgow, since 1955; *b* 1909; *m* 1940; three *s*. MA Glasgow 1931, LLB Glasgow 1932 (distinction), LLD Edinburgh 1971. Solicitor. Mem., Law Soc. of Scotland, 1950. Faulds Fellow, Glasgow, 1934–37. Mem., Scott. Law Commn, 1965– ; Soc. Studies Sub-Cttee, UGC, 1971– ; Assessor Dean, Guild Ct, Glasgow, 1963– . *Publications*: (with G. H. Brown) Outline of Estate Duty in Scotland, 1962, 3rd edn 1967; Conveyancing and Feudal Reform (Scotland) Act 1970, 1970; *contrib.* Jl Law Soc. Scotland, Jurid. Rev., Scots Law Times. *Address*: Dept of Conveyancing, Univ. of Glasgow, 63 Hillhead Street, Glasgow G12 8QQ.

Halliday, Dr Michael Sebastian, MA, PhD; Lecturer in Experimental Psychology, University of Sussex, since 1965; *b* 1937; *m* 1958; three *s* two *d*. BA Cantab 1961 (1st cl. Psychology), MA Cantab 1963, PhD Cantab 1965; Asst in Res., Univ. of Cambridge, 1964–65. *Publications*: (with R. A. Boakes) Inhibition and Learning, 1972; *contrib.* Qly Jl Exper. Psychol., Jl Exper. Anal Behav. *Address*: Laboratory of Experimental Psychology, Univ. of Sussex, Brighton.

Halls, Dr Wilfred Douglas; Tutor and Lecturer, Department of Educational Studies, University of Oxford, since 1959; *b* 1918; *m* 1950; three *s* one *d*. BA London 1940, BSc (Econ) London 1949, MA London 1953, DPhil Oxon 1956, MA Oxon 1966; Mem., Comp. Educn Soc. Europe. Res. Fellow, Bedford Coll., London, 1955–59; Vis. Prof., Univ. of Toronto, 1967–68; Co-Ed., Comp. Educn, 1964– ; Gen. Editor, Oxford Rev. of Educn, 1974. Pres., Brit. Sect., Comp. Educn Soc.; Gov., W London (ILEA) Coll. *Publications*: Maurice Maeterlinck, 1960; Society, Schools and Progress in France, 1965; International Equivalences in Access to Higher Education, 1971; Foreign Languages and Education in Western Europe, 1971; (with A. D. C. Peterson) The Education of Young People in Europe, 1973; trans., Capelle: Tomorrow's Education: the French Experience, 1967; trans., Hubert and Mauss: Sacrifice: its Nature and Function, 1964; trans., C. Fuhr (ed): Education in the German Federal Republic, 1970; *contrib.* Bild. Erzieh., Comp. Educn, Comp. Educn Rev., Econ., Hibb. Jl, Internat. Rev. Educn, etc. *Address*: Dept of Educational Studies, Oxford Univ., Oxford.

Halmos, Prof. Paul, Dr Jur, BA, PhD; Professor of Sociology, The Open University, since 1974; *b* 1911; *m* 1937; one *s*. Doctor Juris Budapest 1935, BA London 1945, PhD London 1950; Lectr, Univ. of Keele, 1956–60; Sen. Lectr, Univ. of Keele, 1960–65; Prof. of Sociology, Univ. Coll. Cardiff, 1965–74; Vis. Prof., Wayne State Univ., 1972. Ed., Sociol. Rev. Monogr., 1958– ; Ed., Sociol. Soc. Welfare Series, 1965– . *Publications*: Solitude and Privacy, 1952; Towards a Measure of Man, 1957; The Faith of the Counsellors, 1965, 2nd edn 1970; The Personal Service Society, 1970; *contrib.* Philos., Ethics, Brit. Jl Sociol. *Address*: The Open Univ., Walton Hall, Milton Keynes MK7 6AA.

Halsall, Dr Elizabeth, MA, PhD; Senior Lecturer, Department of Educational Studies, University of Hull, since 1973 (Lecturer, 1964–73); *b* 1916. BA Oxon 1938 (2nd cl. Mod. Lang.), MA Oxon 1952, PhD London 1963; Mem., Comp. Educn Soc. Europe, 1965– . Leon Fellow, London Univ., 1957–58; Mod. Lang. Assoc. Cttee on the Sixth Form, 1954–57; Dept Hd, St Gregory's Comprehensive Sch., Kirkby, 1959–64. Mem., Council, Mod. Lang. Assoc., 1952–55; Cttee, Yorks Reg. Bd for CSE Exams, 1965– . *Publications*: French for the CSE, 1967; French as a Second Language: Levels of Attainment in Three Countries, 1968; Becoming Comprehensive: Case Histories, 1970; The Comprehensive School: guidelines to the reorganization of secondary education, 1973; *contrib.* Internat. Rev. Educn, Mod. Lang., Trends Educn. *Address*: Dept of Educational Studies, Univ. of Hull, Hull HU6 7RX.

Halsey, Dr Albert Henry; Director, Department of Social and Administrative Studies, University of Oxford, since 1962; *b* 1923; *m* 1949; three *s* two *d*. BSc (Econ) London 1950, PhD London 1954, MA Oxon 1962; Mem., Brit. Sociol. Assoc. Res. Worker, Univ. of Liverpool, 1952–54; Lectr, Univ. of Birmingham, 1954–58; Sen. Lectr, 1958–62. Adv. to Sec. of State for Educn, 1966–68; Chm., CERI, OECD, Paris, 1968–70. Foreign Associate, Amer. Nat. Acad. of Educn, 1972– . *Publications*: Social Class and Educational Opportunity, 1957; Education, Economy and Society, 1961; Power in Cooperatives, 1965; Social Survey of the Civil Service, 1968; The British Academics, 1971; Trends in British Society since 1900, 1972. *Address*: Nuffield College, Oxford.

Halstead, Cyril Arthur, BSc; Lecturer in Geography, University of Glasgow, since 1947; *b* 1922; *m* 1944. BSc (General) London 1941, BSc (Special) London 1946 (1st cl. Geography); Asst in Geography, Glasgow, 1946–47. RAFVR, 1941–45; RAAF, 1949– . *Publications*: Climate of Glasgow Region, 1958; ed and trans., Borisov: Climates of USSR, 1965; ed, Jorré: Soviet Union, 3rd edn 1967. *Address*: Dept of Geography, Univ. of Glasgow, Glasgow G12 8QQ.

Hamblin, Anthony Crandell; Lecturer, School of Management, University of Bath, since 1967; *b* 1935; *m* 1966; two *d*. BA Oxon 1957 (2nd cl. Lit. Hum.), MA Oxon 1962; Cert. in Personnel Management, LSE 1958; Mem.: Brit. Sociol. Assoc., Assoc. Teachers Mngnt. Res. Asst, LSE, 1959–61; Jun. Res. Off., LSE, 1961–63; Res. Assoc., Univ. Coll. of S Wales, 1963; Sen. Res. Fellow, Univ. of Bath, 1964. *Publications*: The Supervisor and his Job, 1963; The Basis of Supervisory Training Policy, 1967; Evaluation and Control of Training, 1974; *contrib.* Indust. Training Internat., Internat. Jl Product. Res., Social. Travail. *Address*: Bath Univ. School of Management, Claverton Down, Bath BA2 2AY.

Hamer, Richard Frederick Sanger; Tutor in English Literature, Christ Church, Oxford University, since 1966; *b* 1935; *m* 1966; three *d*. BA Oxon 1960, MA Oxon 1963. Student, Christ Church, Oxford, 1966. *Publications*: A Choice of Anglo-Saxon Verse, 1970. *Address*: Christ Church, Oxford.

Hamilton, Bernard, BA, PhD, FRHistS; Senior Lecturer in History, University of Nottingham, since 1972 (Lecturer, 1962–72); *b* 1932; *m* 1963; two *d*. BA London 1953, PhD London, 1960; FRHistS. Tutorial Research Asst, Royal Holloway College London, 1958–60; Asst Lectr in History, Univ. of Nottingham, 1960–62. Asst Editor, Studia Monastica, 1962– . *Publications*: contrib. Le Millénaire du Mont-Athos: études et mélanges, 1963; *contrib.* Orientalia

Christiana Periodica, Studia Monastica, Studies in Medieval and Early Renaissance History, Eastern Churches Rev. *Address*: Dept of History, The Univ., Nottingham NG7 2RD.

Hamilton, Dr John Noel; Lecturer in Celtic, Queen's University Belfast, since 1966; *b* 1933; *m* 1971. BA Belfast 1962, MA Belfast 1964, PhD Belfast 1968. Editor of An tUltach, 1969–70. *Publications*: *contrib.* Folksongs of Britain; *contrib.* Dinnseanchas, Eigse, Zeits. Celtis, Philol. *Address*: Celtic Dept, Queen's Univ., Belfast BT7 1NN.

Hamilton, Dr Vernon; Senior Lecturer, Department of Psychology, Reading University, since 1963; *b* 1922; *m* 1944; two *d*. BA London 1953, PhD London 1956, DipPsych London 1956; FBPsS (Mem. Council, 1973–). LSE 1962–63; York Univ., Toronto, 1967–68. Principal Psychologist, Mental Health Service, 1958–63. *Publications*: *contrib.* Brit. Jl Psychiat., Brit. Jl Psychol., Jl Child Psychol. Psychiat., Nature, Percept. and Motor Skills, Qly Jl Expt Psychol. *Address*: Dept of Psychology, Whiteknights, Earley Gate, Reading, Berks RG6 2AH.

Hamilton, Walter, MA, FRSL; Master of Magdalene College, Cambridge, since 1967; *b* 1908; *m* 1951; three *s* one *d*. 1st cl. Classical Tripos Part I 1927, Part II 1929, Hon. DLitt Durham. Fellow of Trinity Coll., Cambridge, 1931–35; Asst Lectr, University of Manchester, 1931–32; Asst Master, Eton Coll., 1933–46, Master in Coll., 1937–46, Fellow, 1972– ; Fellow and Classical Lectr, Trinity Coll., 1946–50; Tutor, 1947–50; University Lectr in Classics, 1947–50; Head Master of Westminster Sch., 1950–57; Head Master of Rugby Sch., 1957–66. Editor, Classical Quarterly, 1946–47. Chm., Scholarship Cttee, Lord Kitchener Nat. Meml Fund, 1953–59, Chm., Exec. Cttee, 1967– ; Chm., Headmasters' Conference, 1955, 1956, 1965, 1966; Chm., Governing Body, Shrewsbury Sch., 1968– ; Chm., Governing Bodies Assoc., 1969– . Mem., Exec. Cttee, British Council, 1958–70; Mem., Council of Senate of Cambridge Univ., 1969– . *Publications*: A New Translation of Plato's Symposium (Penguin Classics), 1951; Plato's Gorgias (Penguin Classics), 1960; Plato's Phaedrus and Letters VII and VIII (Penguin Classics), 1974; *contrib.* Classical Qly, Classical Review, etc. *Address*: Magdalene College, Cambridge.

Hamlin, Ann Elizabeth, MA; Lecturer in Medieval Archaeology, Department of History, University of Exeter, since 1967; *b* 1940. MA Oxon 1965, Dipl. Prehistoric Archaeol. London 1964. Mem. Churches Cttee, Council for British Archaeology; Mem., Area Museums Council for South West. *Publications*: *contrib.* Oxoniensia, Proc. Devon Arch. Soc., Ulster Jl Archaeol. *Address*: Queen's Building, Queen's Drive, Exeter EX4 4QH.

Hamlyn, Prof. David Walter; Professor of Philosophy, Birkbeck College, University of London, since 1964; *b* 1924; 1949; one *s* one *d*. BA Oxon 1948 (1st cl. Lit. Hum. 1950 1st cl. Philosophy and Psychology), MA

285

Oxon 1949. Res. Fellow, Corpus Christi Coll., Oxford, 1950–53; Lectr, Jesus Coll., Oxford, 1953–54; Lectr, Birkbeck Coll., London, 1954–63; Reader, 1963–64; Ed., Mind, 1972– . Mem., Council, Royal Inst. Philos., 1968– , Executive, 1971– ; Gov., Birkbeck Coll., 1965–69; Heythop Coll. (Chm.), 1971– . *Publications*: The Psychology of Perception, 1957, rep. with additional material, 1969; Sensation and Perception, 1961; Aristotle's De Anima, Books II and III, 1968; The Theory of Knowledge, 1970 (USA), British edn. 1971; contrib. Critical History of Western Philosophy, 1964; Encyclopaedia of Philosophy, 1967; Concept of Education, 1967; Historical Roots of Contemporary Psychology, 1968; Explanation in the Behavioural Sciences, 1970; Cognitive Development and Epistemology, 1971; Education and the Development of Reason, 1972; Reason and Reality, 1972; Philosophy of Psychology, 1974; Person-Perception and Interpersonal Behaviour, 1974; *contrib*. Analysis, Class. Qly, Mind, Monist, Philos. Qly, Philos., Phronesis, Proc. Aristot. Soc. *Address*: Dept of Philosophy, Birkbeck College, Univ. of London, Malet Street, WC1E 7HY.

Hammersley, George F., BA, PhD; Senior Lecturer in History, University of Edinburgh, since 1970; *b* 1918; *m* 1951; one *s* two *d*. BA London 1950 (History), PhD London 1971; FRHistS; Mem., Hist. Assoc., Econ. Hist. Soc. Pt-time Lectr, Queen Mary Coll., London, 1953–54; Asst Lectr, Queen's Univ., Belfast, 1954–58; Lectr in Economic History, 1958–64; Lectr, Univ. of Edinburgh, 1964–70. *Publications*: trans. in: Essays in European Economic History, ed Crouzet etc, 1969; G. Adelmann: Structural Change in the Rhenish Linen and Cotton Trades; rev. in Mercantilism, ed D. C. Coleman, 1969; I. Bog: Mercantilism in Germany; J. Van Klaveren: Fiscalism, Mercantilism and Corruption; K. Borchardt: The Industrial Revolution in Germany, 1700–1914, 1972; *contrib*. Bull. Inst. Hist. Res., Hist., Business Hist., Econ. Hist. Rev. *Address*: Univ. of Edinburgh, Dept of History, William Robertson Building, Edinburgh EH8 9JY.

Hammerton, Prof. Max; Professor of Psychology, University of Newcastle upon Tyne, since 1973; *b* 1930; *m* 1958. BSc London 1954, BSc London 1958, PhD London 1963; Member: Exptl Psychol. Soc.; BPsS. Visiting Professor: UCLA, 1969; Meml Univ. of Newfoundland, 1973. Mem., Royal United Services Inst. for Defence Studies; Fellow, Brit. Interplanetary Soc. *Publications*: *contrib*. Brit. Jl Psychol., Ergonomics, Jl Appl. Psychol., Jl Exptl Psychol., Jl Roy. United Services Inst., Monthly Notices RAS, Nature, Qly Jl Exptl Psychol. *Address*: Dept of Psychology, Ridley Building, Claremont Place, Newcastle upon Tyne.

Hammond, Graham Edward Anthony; Lecturer, School of Education, University of Exeter, since 1966; *b* 1930; *m* 1957; two *s* one *d*. BA Hons Durham 1953. *Address*: Univ. of Exeter, Sch. of Education, Gandy Street, Exeter EX4 3LZ.

Hamnett, Dr Ian; Senior Lecturer, Department of Sociology, University of Bristol, since 1967; *b* 1929; *m* 1964. MA Oxon (examined 1951: MA 1957), LLB Edinburgh 1957, Dip. Social Anthropol. Edinburgh 1962, PhD Edinburgh 1970; Advocate 1957. Mem., Assoc. Social Anthropol., 1967. Lectr in Social Anthropology, Centre of African Studies, Univ. of Edinburgh, 1965–67. Hon. Treas., Assoc. Social Anthropol., 1971– ; Dep. Dean, Fac. Soc. Sci. Univ. of Bristol, 1971–73. *Publications*: *contrib*. Afr., Jl Afr. Law, Jurid. Rev., Man, Race, Rass. Ital. Sociol. *Address*: Univ. of Bristol, Dept of Sociology, 12 Woodland Road, Bristol BS8 1UQ.

Hampshire, Dr Peter, (Peter Nurse), MA, DLitt; Reader in French, University of Kent at Canterbury, since 1966; *b* 1926; *m* 1951; two *s* one *d*. BA Oxford 1950 (1st cl. Mod Lang.), MA Oxford 1953, DLitt Kent 1971, Chevalier des Palmes Académiques 1963. Lectr, then Sen. Lectr, Queen's Univ., Belfast, 1952–65; Vis. Prof. of French, Univ. of California, 1965–66, 1969. *Publications*: as P. Nurse, Le Cymbalum Mundi de B. des Périers, 1957, 2nd edn 1967; Molière: L'Ecole des Maris, 1959; Corneille: Horace, 1963; Jules Romains: Un Grand Honnête Homme, 1963; Molière: Le Malade Imaginaire, 1965; The Art of Criticism, 1969; Lafayette: La Princesse de Clèves, 1970; Classical Voices, 1971; *contrib*. Rev. Sci. Hum., Univ Toronto Qly, etc. *Address*: Eliot College, Univ. of Kent, Canterbury CT1 3PA.

Hampshire, Stuart Newton, FBA; Warden of Wadham College, Oxford University, since 1970; *b* 1914; *m* 1961. 1st cl. Lit. Hum. Oxford 1936; Hon. DLitt Glasgow; FBA 1960. Fellow of All Souls Coll., and Lectr in Philosophy, Oxford, 1936–40; Lectr in Philosophy, University Coll. London, 1947–50; Fellow of New Coll., Oxford, 1950–55; Domestic Bursar and Research Fellow, All Souls Coll., 1955–60; Grote Prof. of Philosophy of Mind and Logic, Univ. of London, 1960–63; Prof. of Philosophy, Princeton Univ., 1963–70. Fellow, Amer. Acad. of Arts and Sciences, 1968. Personal Asst to Minister of State, Foreign Office, 1945. Mem., Arts Council, 1972– . *Publications*: Spinoza, 1951; Thought and Action, 1959; Freedom of the Individual, 1965; Modern Writers and other essays, 1969; Freedom of Mind and other essays, 1971; articles in philosophical jls. *Address*: Wadham College, Oxford.

Hampson, Prof. Norman, MA, DUP; Professor of History, University of York, since 1974; *b* 1922; *m* 1948; two *d*. BA and MA Oxon 1947, Docteur d'Université Paris 1955; FRHistS. Res. Staff Tutor, Extra Mural Dept, Manchester, 1948–54; Lectr in French History and Institutions, Manchester, 1954–62; Sen. Lectr, 1962–67; Prof. of Modern History, Univ. of Newcastle, 1967–74. *Publications*: La Marine de l'An II, 1959; Social History of the French Revolution, 1963, Italian edn 1964, Danish edn 1968, Spanish edn 1969; The Enlightenment, 1968, Italian edn 1969, French edn 1972; The First European Revolution, 1969,

French edn 1970, Portuguese edn 1970; The Life and Opinions of Maximilien Robespierre, 1974; *contrib*. Hist. Jl, Bull. J. Rylands Lib., Rev. Hist. Econ. Soc. *Address*: History Dept, The Univ., Heslington, York YO1 5DD.

Hampton, Dr John, BA, LèsL; Senior Lecturer, Department of French, University of Leicester, since 1949; *b* 1920; *m* 1945; two *s* one *d*. BA Sheffield 1943, LèsL Paris 1947, D de l'U Paris 1954; Mem., Soc. Fr. Studies, Brit. Soc. 18th Century Studies. *Publications*: Nicholas Antoine Boulanger et la Science de son Temps, 1955; *contrib*. Fr. Studies, Rev. Litt. Comp., Studies Voltaire and 18th Cent. *Address*: Dept of French, Univ. of Leicester, Leicester LE1 7RH.

Hampton, Dr William Albert; Senior Lecturer in Extra-mural Studies, University of Sheffield, since 1970; *b* 1929; *m* 1951; one *s* one *d*. BSc(Econ) London 1963 (1st cl. Government), PhD Sheffield 1970. Asst Lectr, Sheffield, 1963–64; Lectr, 1964–70. Mem., Ed. Adv. Cttee, Politics and Policy. *Publications*: Democracy and Community, 1970; *contrib*. Local Govt Studies, Parl. Aff., Pol. Qly, Pol. Studies. *Address*: Dept of Extra-mural Studies, 85 Wilkinson Street, Sheffield S10 2GS.

Hand, Prof. Geoffrey Joseph, MA, DPhil, MRIA, Barrister; Professor of Legal and Constitutional History, University College, Dublin, since 1972; *b* 1931. BA NUI 1952 (1st cl. History), MA NUI 1954, DPhil Oxon 1960; Barrister-at-law (King's Inns, Dublin) 1961, FRHistS 1961, MRIA 1970. Asst Lectr in British History, Univ. of Edinburgh, 1960–61; Lectr in (Constitutional) History, Univ. of Southampton, 1961–65; Lectr in Legal and Constitutional History, Nat. Univ. of Ireland, 1965–72. Dean, Fac. of Law, Univ. Coll., Dublin, 1970– . Chm., Arts Council of Republic of Ireland, 1974– . *Publications*: English Law in Ireland, 1290–1324, 1967; Report of the Irish Boundary Commission, 1925, 1969; (with Lord Cross of Chelsea) Radcliffe and Cross's English Legal System, 5th edn 1971; *contrib*. Irish Hist. Studies, Irish Jurist, Report. Novum. *Address*: Faculty of Law, Univ. College, Dublin 4.

Handley, Prof. Eric Walter, MA, FBA; Professor of Greek, University College, London, since 1968, and Director, Institute of Classical Studies, University of London, since 1967; *b* 1926; *m* 1952. BA Cantab 1946, MA 1950; FBA 1969, FRSA 1971. Asst Lectr in Latin and Greek, Univ. Coll., London, 1946–49; Lectr, 1949–61; Reader, 1961–67; Prof. of Greek and Latin, 1967–68; Vis. Lectr on the Classics, Harvard, 1966; Vis. Mem., Inst. Adv. Study, Princeton, 1971. Mem., Council, Hellenic Soc., 1969–72; Sec., Council of Univ. Classical Depts, 1970–71. *Publications*: (with J. Rea) The Telephus of Euripides, 1957; The Dyskolos of Menander, 1965; *contrib*. Bull. Inst. Class. Studies. *Address*: Dept of Greek, Univ. College London, Gower Street, WC1E 6BT.

Handley, John Peter Henry; Lecturer,

School of Management, Cranfield Institute of Technology, since 1967; *b* 1928; *m* 1957; two *d*. BA Hons Leeds 1954, CertEd Coll. of St Peters, Saltley 1951. *Address*: Cranfield Inst. of Technology, Cranfield, Bedford MK43 0AL.

Hands, Rosalie Rachel; Lecturer in English, Lady Margaret Hall and University College, Oxford, since 1971; *b* 1937; *m* 1965; two *d*. BA Oxon 1959 (cl. II Hons, English Language and Literature), MA 1963, BLitt 1968. Sheffield University: Asst Lectr, 1962–64, Lectr, 1964–68. *Publications*: English Hawking and Hunting in the Boke of St Albans (Oxford English Monographs), 1974; *contrib*. Archiv., Med. Aev., Med. Stud., Notes and Quer., Rev. Eng. Stud. *Address*: Lady Margaret Hall, Oxford.

Handy, Prof. Charles Brian; Professor of Management Development, London Graduate School of Business Studies, since 1972; *b* 1932; *m* 1962; one *s* one *d*. BA Hons Oxon 1955 (1st cl. Lit. Hum.), MA Oxon 1965; MS MIT 1967; Mem., Assoc. of Teachers of Management. Internat. Faculty Fellow, MIT, 1966–67. London Graduate School of Business Studies: Dir, London–Sloan Fellowship Programme, 1967–71; Sen. Tutor in Organisational Behaviour, 1971–72. Chm., MSc Programme, London Business Sch. Bd of Trustees, European Foundn of Management Develt. *Publications*: Understanding Organisations, 1974; *contrib*. European Business, Jl Management Studies, Management Educn and Develt. *Address*: London Graduate Sch. of Business Studies, Sussex Place, Regent's Park, NW1 4SA.

Hankey, Dr A. Teresa, PhD; Lecturer in Classical and Medieval Studies, Sussex University, since 1967; *b* 1929. BA London 1951 (History), PhD London 1955 (History). Tutorial Fellow, Bedford Coll., London, 1955–56; Asst Lectr (History), 1956–60; Lectr, 1960–67; Sen. Res. Fellow, Warburg Inst. Univ. of London, 1966–67. Mem., Cttee, Soc. Renaiss. Studies, 1967–72. *Publications*: ed, Riccobaldo da Farrara, Compendium de historia Romana (forthcoming); *contrib*. Ital. Studies, Jl Warb. Court. Inst. Rinasc. *Address*: Arts Building, The Univ. of Sussex, Falmer, Brighton BN1 9QN.

Hanlon, Dr James Patrick, PhD; Lecturer, Department of Transportation and Environmental Planning, University of Birmingham, since 1970; *b* 1942. BSc Hull 1967 (Econ), MA Manchester 1968 (Econ), PhD Birmingham 1973. Res. Fellow, Univ. of Salford, 1968–70. *Address*: Dept of Transportation, Univ. of Birmingham, Edgbaston, Birmingham B15 2TT.

Hanna, Alexander John; Reader, Department History, Southampton University, since 1968; *b* 1923; *m* 1952; two *s*. BA Belfast 1945, PhD London 1948. Asst Lectr, Southampton, 1948–49; Lectr, 1949–61; Sen. Lectr, 1961–68; Vis. Assoc. Prof., Columbia, NY, 1961–62; Prof. of History, Univ. Coll., Nairobi (on secondment), 1963–65. *Publications*: The Beginnings of Nyasaland and

287

North-Eastern Rhodesia, 1956, 2nd edn 1969; The Story of the Rhodesias and Nyasaland, 1960, 2nd edn 1965; European Rule in Africa (Historical Association Pamphlet), 1961, 2nd edn 1965. *Address*: Dept of History, The Univ., Southampton SO9 5NH.

Hannah, Leslie, MA, DPhil; Lecturer, Department of Economics, University of Essex, since 1973; *b* 1947. BA Oxon 1968 (1st cl. Hons Mod. Hist.), MA Oxon 1972, DPhil Oxon 1972 (Econs). Nuffield Coll., Oxford, 1968-69; St John's Coll., Oxford, 1969-73. Trustee, Oxford Student Publications Ltd, 1970- ; Historical Adviser, Electricity Council, 1973- . *Publications*: The Rise of the Corporate Economy, 1974; *contrib*. Business History, Economic History Rev., Oxford Econ. Papers. *Address*: Dept of Economics, Univ. of Essex, Wivenhoe Park, Colchester CO4 3SQ.

Hannan, Prof. Damian F.; Professor of Social Theory and Institutions, University College, Cork, since 1971; *b* 1935; *m* 1965; three *d*. BAgrSc University Coll., Dublin 1959, MAgrSc 1961, MA Michigan State Univ. 1964, PhD 1967 (Sociology); Member: Amer. Sociological Assoc.; Sociological Assoc. of Ireland; British Sociological Assoc.; Rural Sociology Society; European Soc. for Rural Sociology. Res. Officer then Sen. Res. Officer, Economic and Social Res. Institute, Dublin, 1967-71. *Publications*: Rural Exodus, 1970; *contrib*. Econ. and Social Rev., Rural Sociology, Social Studies, Sociologia Ruralis. *Address*: Dept of Social Theory and Institutions, Univ. College, Cork.

Hannay, Dr David Rainsford; Lecturer, Department of Community Medicine, Glasgow University, since 1968; *b* 1939; *m* 1963; two *s*. MB, BChir Cantab 1964-65, MA Cantab 1966, DCH London 1968, MFCM 1972. Mem., BMA, 1964, Soc. Antiqu. (Scotland), 1970, Soc. Social Medicine 1971. Resident Staff, St George's Hosp., London, 1964-67; Asst. Lectr in Anatomy, Manchester Univ., 1967-68. Extl Examiner in Soc. Biol., Univ. of Guyana, 1970- . *Publications*: *contrib*. Lancet, Brit. Jl Med. Educn, Scot. Med. Jl. *Address*: Dept of Community Medicine, Univ. of Glasgow, Glasgow G12 8QQ.

Hanson, Rev. Prof. Anthony Tyrrell; Professor of Theology, University of Hull, since 1963; *b* 1916; *m* 1945; two *s*. 1st cl. Hons (Gold Medal) Lit. Hum. Dublin 1938, 1st cl. Hons Mental and Moral Science Dublin 1938, BD Dublin 1941, DD Dublin 1954. *Publications*: (with R. H. Preston) Revelation of St John the Divine, 1949, latest edn 1957; (with E. M. Hanson) The Book of Job, 1953, latest edn 1970; The Wrath of the Lamb, 1957; The Pioneer Ministry, 1961; The Church of the Servant, 1962; Jesus Christ in the Old Testament, 1965; Beyond Anglicanism, 1965; ed, Vindications, 1966; The Pastoral Letters, 1966; Studies in the Pastoral Epistles, 1968; ed, Moberly: Ministerial Priesthood, Teilhard Reassessed, 1970; Studies in Paul's Technique and Theology, 1974; *contrib*. Jl Theol. Studies,

NT Studies, Theol. *Address*: Dept of Theology, The Univ., Hull HU6 7RX.

Hanson, Dr Charles Goring; Lecturer in Economics, University of Newcastle upon Tyne, since 1963; *b* 1934; *m* 1963; one *s* three *d*. BA 1958, MA 1959, Cantab, PhD Newcastle upon Tyne 1972. *Publications*: Welfare before the Welfare State, in, The Long Debate on Poverty, 1973; Trade Unions: a century of privilege?, 1973; *contrib*. Jl of Management Studies, Westminster Bank Rev. *Address*: Univ. of Newcastle upon Tyne Newcastle upon Tyne NE1 7RU.

Hanson, Owen Jerrold; Senior Lecturer in Systems Analysis, Graduate Business Centre, The City University, since 1970; *b* 1934; *m* 1965; two *d*. BA Cantab 1957, MA 1961, MSc London 1970; AIM 1961. Sec., ISO Working Gp on PL/I. *Address*: Graduate Business Centre, 23 Goswell Road, EC1M 7BB.

Hanson, Dr Philip; Senior Lecturer, Centre for Russian and East European Studies, Birmingham University, since 1973 (Lecturer, 1968-73); *b* 1936; *m* 1960; two *s*. BA (Hons) Cambridge 1960 (Economics), PhD Birmingham, 1971. Mem. and former Cttee mem., Nat. Assoc. Soviet and E European Studies. Lectr, Univ. of Exeter, 1961-67; Vis. Lectr, Univ. of Michigan, 1967-68. Econ. Asst, HM Treasury, 1960-61; First Sec., Brit. Embassy, Moscow, and Res. Off., Foreign and Commonwealth Off., London, 1971-72 (on leave of absence); Mem., Cttee, NASEES; Ed. Bd, ABSEES (Soviet and E European Abstracts Series), 1969-71. *Publications*: The Consumer in the Soviet Economy, 1968; Advertising and Socialism, 1974; *contrib*. Sov. Studies. *Address*: Centre for Russian and East European Studies, Univ. of Birmingham, PO Box 363, Birmingham B15 2TT.

Hanson, Prof. Richard Patrick Crosland; Professor of Historical and Contemporary Theology, Faculty of Theology, University of Manchester, since 1973; *b* 1916; *m* 1950; two *s* two *d*. BA TCD 1938 (1st cl. Hons, Classics and 1st cl. Hons Ancient History) BD TCD 1941 (1st cl.), DD 1950 (thesis). Mem. RAI 1972. Lectr, subseq. Sen. Lectr, then Reader, Dept of Theology, Univ. of Nottingham, 1952-62; Lightfoot Prof. of Divinity, Univ. of Durham, 1962-64, and Canon Residentiary of Durham Cathedral; Prof. of Theology and Head of Dept of Theology, Univ. of Nottingham, 1964-70. Bishop of Clogher (Anglican), Ireland, 1970-73; Asst Bishop of Manchester (Honorary), 1973- . *Publications*: Origen's Doctrine of Tradition, 1954; Torch Commentary upon Second Epistle to the Corinthians, 1954; Tradition in the Early Church, 1962; contrib. Institutionalism and Church Unity, 1963; Selections from Justin Martyr's Dialogue with Trypho, a Jew, 1963; New Clarendon Commentary on Acts, 1967; ed, Difficulties for Christian Belief, 1967; St Patrick, his Origins and Career, 1968; ed (with M. Barley), Christianity in Britain 300-700, 1968; contrib. Preparatory Essays to The Lambeth Conference, 1968, reprinted as Lambeth Essays on Ministry, 1968; ed, The Pelican Guide to Modern Theology, 3 vols, 1969–70; contrib. Cambridge History of the Bible, vol. I, 1970; Groundwork for Unity, 1971; contrib. Epektasis: Mélanges Patristiques Offerts au Cardinal Jean Daniélou, 1972; The Attractiveness of God, 1973; *contrib.* JTS, JEH, Vig. Chris., New Test. Stud., Church Quarterly. *Address:* Fac. of Theology, Univ. of Manchester, Manchester M13 9PL.

Hanson, William P.; Lecturer in German, University of Exeter, since 1964; *b* 1938; *m* 1960; two *d.* BA Wales 1960, MA Wales 1962. Asst Lectr, Univ. of Manchester, 1962–64. *Publications:* ed, W. Raabe: Stopfkuchen, 1970; *contrib.* Germ. Life Lett., Mod. Lang. *Address:* Dept of German, Queen's Building, The Queen's Drive, Exeter.

Hanton, William Baxter, MA, DipPsych, CertEd; Lecturer in Educational Psychology, Education Department, University College of North Wales, since 1968; *b* 1936; *m* 1960; one *s* two *d.* MA Aberdeen 1958 (1st cl. Psychology), Acad. Postgrad. Dip. Psychol. London 1959 (Section D: Abnormal), CertEd Birmingham 1960. Asst Schoolmaster Birmingham LEA, 1960–62; Asst Educl Psychol., Staffs CC 1962–64; Lectr, Univ. Coll. of Wales, Aberystwyth, 1964–68. *Address:* Dept of Education, Univ. College of North Wales, Bangor LL57 2DG.

Harbinson, Dr Denis Noel, BMus, PhD; Lecturer in Music, University College, Cardiff, since 1967; *b* 1932; *m* 1962; one *s* one *d.* BMus Wales 1962 (1st cl.), PhD Wales 1965. Fellow, Univ. of Wales, 1964; Asst Lectr, Univ. Coll., Cardiff, 1965–67. *Publications:* Songs for Edna, 1963; Adagio and Rondo Sonata, Cl. and Pfte, 1963; *contrib.* Music. Discip., Music Lett. *Address:* Dept of Music, Univ. College, Cathays Park, Cardiff CF1 1XL.

Harbour, Gerald; Lecturer in Econometrics, Department of Economics, University College, Cardiff, since 1968; *b* 1944; *m* 1970; two *s.* BScEcon Wales 1966. *Address:* PO Box 96, Cardiff CF1 1XB.

Harbury, Prof. Colin Desmond Barnard, BCom, PhD; Professor of Economics, and Head of Department of Social Science and Humanities, The City University, since 1971; *b* 1922; *m* 1948; one *s* one *d.* BCom LSE 1950 (2nd cl.), PhD Wales 1959. Asst Lectr, then Lectr, Univ. Coll. of Wales, Aberystwyth, 1950–57; Lectr, then Sen. Lectr, Univ. of Birmingham, 1957–71; Vis. Prof., San Diego State Coll., California, 1962–63; Vis. Sen. Lectr, Monash Univ., Australia, 1968–69; Dir Econ. Studies, Civil Service Coll., London, 1969–71. *Publications:* Descriptive Economics, 1957, 4th edn 1972; The Industrial Efficiency of Rural Labour, 1958; Workbook in Introductory Economics, 1969, rev. edn 1974, Australian edn 1969; Introduction to Economic Behaviour, 1971; ed, Fontana Introduction to Modern Economics, 1969–72; *contrib.* Econ Jl, Jl Econ.

Educn, Jl Royal Stat. Soc., Oxf. Bull. Stats., Oxf. Econ. Papers, Qly Jl Econ. *Address:* Dept of Social Science and Humanities, The City Univ., St John Street, EC1V 4BP.

Hardie, Charles Jeremy Mawdesley; Fellow and Tutor in Economics, Keble College, Oxford, since 1968; *b* 1938; *m* 1962; two *s* two *d.* BA Oxford (2nd Classical Hon. Mods) 1960, (1st Lit. Hum.) 1962, MA Oxford (by purchase) 1967, BPhil Econs Oxford 1967; ACA 1966. Jun. Res. Fellow, Trinity Coll., Oxford, 1967–68; Res. Officer, Econs and Org. of Transport, Oxford, 1968–70; Fellow, Oxford Centre for Management Studies, 1970– . Dir, Nat. Provident Instn, 1972– ; Mem. Council, Advertising Standards Authority, 1972– . *Publication:* Regional Policy, in, The Labour Government's Economic Record, ed Beckerman. *Address:* Keble College, Oxford.

Harding, Alan; Lecturer in History, University of Edinburgh, since 1962; Associate Dean, Faculty of Arts, 1972; *b* 1932; *m* 1958; one *s* one *d.* BA Oxon 1955 (2nd cl. Mod. History), MA Oxon 1957, BLitt Oxon 1957; FRHistS, FSA Scot. Asst Lectr in History, Univ. of Edinburgh, 1961–62. *Publications:* A Social History of English Law, 1966; The Law Courts of Medieval England, 1973; The Shropshire Eyre Roll of 1256 (forthcoming); *contrib.* Jurid. Rev., Trans Royal Hist. Soc. *Address:* Dept of History, Univ. of Edinburgh, William Robertson Building, 50, George Square, Edinburgh EH8 9JY.

Harding, Donald Malcolm, BSc, PhD, FRMetSoc; Lecturer in Geography, University College of Swansea, since 1966; *b* 1941; *m* 1967. BSc 1963 (Hons Geography); PhD 1972; FRMetS 1967. *Publications: contrib.* Trans Inst. Brit. Geogrs, Nature. *Address:* Dept of Geography, Univ. College of Swansea, Singleton Park, Swansea SA2 8PP.

Harding, Dr Graham Frederick Anthony, BSc, PhD, ABPsS; Head of the Neuropsychology Unit, Reader in Neuropsychology, Applied Psychology Department, University of Aston (also teaches Educational Psychology), since 1969; *b* 1937; *m* 1961; two *d.* BSc London 1961 (2nd cl.), PhD Birmingham 1968; ABPsS 1964, Council Mem., EEG Soc. Res. Asst, Univ. of Aston, 1961–62; Res. Fellow, 1962–65; Sen. Res. Fellow, 1965–68; Hon. Neuropsychologist, United Birmingham Hosps, 1964– ; Sen. Res. Fellow in Electroencephalography, All Saints Hosp. Gp, Dudley Rd Hosp. Gp, E Birmingham Hosp. Gp, Birmingham. *Publications: contrib.* Brit. Jl Psychol., Electroencephal. clin. Neurophysiol. *Address:* Applied Psychology Dept, University of Aston, Birmingham B4 7ET.

Hardingham, Martin; Senior Tutor, School of Textiles, Royal College of Art, since 1968; *b* 1933; *m* (marr. diss.); three *d.* DesRCA 1960; MSIA 1969–70. *Publications: contrib.* Des. Mag., Crafts Mag., SIAD Mag. *Address:* Royal Coll. of Art, Kensington Gore, SW7 2EU.

Hardman, Christopher Barrie; Lecturer in English Language and Literature, University of Reading, since 1968, and Assistant Warden, Childs Hall, University of Reading, since 1972; *b* 1943; *m* 1970. BA Oxon 1964, MA Oxon 1968. BLitt Oxon 1969. Asst Lectr, UEA, Norwich, 1966–68. *Address*: Dept of English, Faculty of Letters and Social Sciences, Univ. of Reading, Whiteknights, Reading RG6 2AH.

Hardman, Dr John David; Lecturer, Department of History, Edinburgh University, since 1969; *b* 1944. BA Oxon 1966, MA Oxon 1973, DPhil Oxon 1973. Tutorial Asst, Reading Univ., 1967–69. *Publications*: ed, French Revolution Documents, vol. 2, 1792–95, 1973. *Address*: Dept of History, Univ. of Edinburgh, William Robertson Building, George Square, Edinburgh EH8 9JY.

Hardy, Prof. Barbara Gladys; Professor of English Literature, Birkbeck College, University of London, since 1970; *m*; two *d*. BA London 1947, MA London 1949. Mem., Staff, English Dept, Birkbeck Coll., London; Prof. English, Royal Holloway Coll., Univ. of London, 1965–70. Mem., Bd of Dirs, Athlone Press. *Publications*: the Novels of George Eliot, 1959; The Appropriate Form, 1964; ed, George Eliot: Daniel Deronda, 1967; Middlemarch: critical approaches to the novel, 1967; The Moral Art of Dickens, 1970; ed, Critical Essays on George Eliot, 1970; The Exposure of Luxury: Radical Themes in Thackeray, 1972; Narrative (essay), in Novel, Fall, 1968. *Address*: Birkbeck College, Malet Street, WC1E 7HX.

Hardy, Rev. Daniel Wayne; Lecturer in Modern Theological Thought, Department of Theology, University of Birmingham, since 1965; *b* 1930; *m* 1958; two *s* two *d*. BA Haverford 1952, BST Gen. Theol Seminary 1955, MST Gen. Theol Seminary 1963; Mem. Soc. for Study of Theology. Fellow and Tutor, General Theological Seminary, New York, 1959–61. Member: Bd of Faculty of Arts, 1968– ; Broader Educn Cttee, 1970– ; Bds of Studies and Examrs for BEd Degree 1969– ; Supervisor, Postgrad. Studies in Religion and Humanism, 1970– ; Exec. Cttee, Soc. for Study of Theology, 1970–73; Synod of Dio. of Birmingham, 1970– ; Governor, Blue Coat Sch., Birmingham, 1970– . *Publications*: *contrib.* Theology. *Address*: Dept of Theology, Univ. of Birmingham, Birmingham B15 2TT.

Hardy, Rev. Edward Rochie; Lecturer in Divinity, University of Cambridge, since 1969; Dean of Jesus College since 1972; *b* 1908; *m* 1939; one *s*. BA Columbia 1923, MA Columbia 1924, PhD Columbia 1931. Past Pres., Amer. Soc. of Church History; Mem. Amer. Hist. Soc.; Mem. Eccles. History Soc. Prof., Berkeley Divinity Sch., assoc. with Yale, 1944–69. Mem., Faith and Order Commn, World Council of Churches, 1961– ; Mem., Anglican–Orthodox Theological Commn, 1966– . *Publications*: The Large Estates of Byzantine Egypt, 1931; Christian Egypt, Church and People, 1952; ed, Christology of the later Fathers, 1954, Faithful Witnesses: Records of Early Christ-

ian Martyrs, 1959, repr. 1970; *contrib.* Dumbarton Oaks Papers. *Address*: Jesus College, Cambridge.

Hardy, Dr John Richard, MA, PhD; Lecturer in Geography, University of Reading, since 1961; *b* 1931; *m* 1959; two *s* one *d*. BA Cantab 1955, MA Cantab 1959, PhD Cantab 1962; Mem., Inst. Brit. Geogrs. Asst Lectr, Reading Univ., 1960–61; Vis. Asst Prof., Univ. of Toronto, 1966–67. Directorate of Military Survey, 1958–59. *Publications*: contrib. Penguin Science Survey, 1964; (with J. B. Whittow) Geology and Scenery in England and Wales, by A. E. Trueman, 1938, rev. edn 1972; *contrib.* Berks Archaeol. Jl, E. Mid. Geogr., Jl Geophys. Res., Jl Glaciol., Trans Inst. Brit. Geogrs. *Address*: Dept of Geography, The Univ., Reading RG6 2AF.

Hardy, Dr Peter, MA, PhD; Reader in the History of Islam in South Asia, University of London, since 1962; *b* 1922; *m* 1953; one *d*. BA Cantab 1944 (1st cl. Historical Tripos Pts I and II), MA Cantab 1947, PhD London 1953; FRAS. Lecturer, Sch. Orient. Afr. Studies, Univ. of London, 1948–62; Vis. Lecturer, Univ. of Chicago, 1961; Prof. of History, Univ. of the Panjab, Lahore, 1963–65 (on secondment). *Publications*: Islam in Medieval India, in, Sources of Indian Tradition, 1958; Historians of Medieval India, 1960, 2nd edn 1966; Partners in Freedom – and True Muslims, 1971; The Muslims of British India, 1972; *contrib.* Encyclopaedia of Islam, Jl Panjab Univ., Hist. Soc., Jl Ind. Hist. *Address*: Dept of History, School of Oriental and African Studies, University of London, Malet Street, WC1E 7HP.

Hare, Dr Arnold, MA; Senior Lecturer in Adult Education, Department of Extra-Mural Studies, University of Bristol, since 1969; *b* 1921; *m* 1944; three *s* one *d*. BA (Hons) London 1942, Teachers' Dip. London 1946 (with Distinction), MA Bristol 1954, PhD Bristol 1973; Mem., Soc. for Theatre Res., 1945– . Univ. of Bristol: Resident Tutor in Wiltshire, 1946–69; Sen. Tutor for Wiltshire, 1969– . Vice-Chm., Nat. Drama Conf., 1967– ; Mem., The Drama Bd, 1971– ; Governor: Urchfont Manor Coll., 1969– ; Warminster Sch., 1972– ; Mem., Wilts Co. Libraries and Museums Cttee, 1969– . *Publications*: (jtly), City of Salisbury, 1957; The Georgian Theatre in Wessex, 1958; The Man Who Never Laughed, 1963, NY 1963; contrib. George Frederick Cooke: the actor and the man, in, The Eighteenth Century English Stage, 1972; ed, Theatre Royal Bath – The Orchard Street Calendar (forthcoming); *contrib.* Enciclopedia dello Spettacolo (Rome), Theatre Notebook, Theatre Res., Recherches Theatrales, Wilts Archaeol Mag. *Address*: Dept of Extra-Mural Studies, 32 Tyndall's Park Road, Bristol BS8 1HR.

Hare, Prof. Richard Mervyn, FBA; White's Professor of Moral Philosophy, Oxford University, since 1966; *b* 1919; *m* 1947; one *s* three *d*. BA and MA Oxon 1947 (1st cl. Lit. Hum.); FBA; Mem., Aristot. Soc. (Pres., 1972–73). Fellow and Tutor in

Philosophy, Balliol Coll., Oxford, 1947–66; Wilde Lecturer in Natural Religion, Oxford, 1964–66; Fellow of Corpus Christi Coll., Oxford, 1966– ; Vis. Fellow or Prof., Princeton, 1957; Australian Nat. Univ., Canberra, 1966; Univ. of Michigan, 1968; Univ. of Delaware, 1974. Mem., C of E Cttees on medical ethical problems, 1964– ; Nat. Road Safety Adv. Council, 1966–68. *Publications*: Oxford's Traffic, 1948; The Language of Morals, 1952, 2nd edn 1961; Freedom and Reason, 1963; Practical Inferences (with bibliography), 1971; Essays on Philosophical Method, 1971; Essays on the Moral Concepts, 1972; Applications of Moral Philosophy, 1972; *contrib.* Analysis, Mind, Philos. Qly, Philos. Rev., Proc. Aristot. Soc., Proc. Brit. Acad., Rev. Internat. Philos. *Address*: Corpus Christi College, Oxford.

Hargreaves, David H.; Senior Lecturer, Department of Education Manchester University, since 1972. *b* 1939. BA Cantab 1960, MA 1964. Manchester Univ.: Res. Associate, Dept of Sociology, 1964–65; Lectr, Dept of Education, 1965–72. *Publications*: Social Relations in a Secondary School, 1967; Interpersonal Relations and Education, 1972. *Address*: Dept of Education. Manchester Univ., Manchester M13 9PL.

Hargreaves, Henry; Senior Lecturer in English Language, University of Aberdeen, since 1966; *b* 1922; *m* 1948; three *d*. BA Liverpool 1948 (1st cl. English), MA Liverpool 1952, DipEd Liverpool 1949. Asst Lectr, then Lectr, Sheffield Univ., 1950–57; Lectr, Aberdeen Univ., 1957–66; Asst Dean, Fac. of Arts, Aberdeen, 1969–72. *Publications*: *contrib.* Aberd. Univ. Rev., Bull. J. Rylands Libr., Engl. Lang. Teaching, Ess. Studies, Med. Ævv., Mod. Lang. Qly, Neuer Sprach., Studia Neophilol. *Address*: Dept of English, University of Aberdeen, Aberdeen AB9 2UB.

Hargreaves, Prof. John Desmond; Professor of History, University of Aberdeen, since 1962; Dean of the Faculty of Arts, 1973–76; *b* 1924; *m* 1950; one *s* two *d*. Lectr in History, Manchester Univ., 1948–52; Lectr in History, Fourah Bay Coll., Sierra Leone, 1952–54; Aberdeen Univ., 1954–62; Vis. Prof., Union Coll., Schenectady, NY, 1960–61; Vis. Prof., Univ. of Ibadan, 1970–71. Asst Principal, War Office, 1948; Mem., Kidd Cttee on Sheriff Court Records, 1966; Mem., Scottish Records Adv. Council; Pres., African Studies Assoc. (UK), 1972–73; Jt Editor, Oxford Studies in African Affairs. *Publications*: A Life of Sir Samuel Lewis, 1958; Prelude to the Partition of West Africa, 1963; West Africa: the former French States, 1967; France and West Africa, 1969; West Africa Partitioned, vol. I: The Loaded Pause, 1974; *contrib.* jls and collaborative vols. *Address*: Univ. of Aberdeen, Aberdeen AB9 2UB.

Harkins, James, BSc, NDA; Senior Lecturer in Agriculture, University of Edinburgh, since 1971; *b* 1926; *m* 1952; three *s* one *d*. BSc(Agric.) Edinburgh 1950; NDA 1951. Lectr, Edinburgh Univ., 1953–71. *Address*: Edinburgh School of Agriculture, West Mains Road, Edinburgh.

Harkness, Dr David William; Senior Lecturer in History, and Chairman, Board of Studies in History, University of Kent at Canterbury, since 1973; *b* 1937; *m* 1964; one *s* two *d*. BA Cantab 1961 (History), MA Cantab 1966, PhD Dublin 1967. Asst Lectr, Univ. of Kent at Canterbury, 1965, Lectr, 1966–73; Vis. Fellow in History, Univ. of Ibadan, 1971–72. Associate Editor, Jl of Imperial and Commonwealth Hist., 1972– . *Publications*: The Restless Dominion, 1969; The Post-War World, 1974; *contrib.* Jl of Commonwealth Political Studies. *Address*: Rutherford College, The Univ., Canterbury, Kent.

Harlen, Dr Wynne; Director, Schools Council Project, Reading University School of Education, from 1973; *b* 1937; *m* 1958; one *s* one *d*. BA Oxon 1958 (2nd cl. Natural Science), MA Oxon 1961, MA Bristol 1965 (Education), PhD Bristol 1973. Res. Fellow, Sch. of Educn, Bristol Univ., 1966–73. *Publications*: With Objectives in Mind (with L. F. Ennever), 1972; Evaluation and Science 5/13, 1974; chapter, in, Evaluation in Curriculum Development: 12 case studies, 1973; *contrib.* Educnl Res., Jl Curric. Studies, Educnl Develt Internat., TES. *Address*: Reading University School of Education, Reading, Berks.

Harley, Dr John Brian, BA, PhD; Montefiore Reader in Geography, University of Exeter, since 1972; *b* 1932; *m* 1956; one *s* three *d*. BA Birmingham 1955 (Geog.), PhD Birmingham 1960; DipEd Birmingham 1956; Mem., Inst. British Geographers, Mem., Econ. Hist. Soc., Mem., British Agricultural Hist., Mem., RGS, Mem., Hakluyt Soc., Mem., British Cartographic Soc. Asst Lectr and Lectr, Liverpool Univ., 1958–69; Lectr, Univ. of Exeter, 1970–72; Post-Doctoral Res. Fellow, Brown Univ., USA, Jan–June 1966; Nebenzahl Lectr, Newberry Library, Chicago Univ., 1974. Mem. Council, Inst. of British Geographers, 1972–75; Mem. Council, Hakluyt Soc., 1972– ; Dir, Imago Mundi, 1973– ; Geography Editor, David & Charles (Publishers), 1969– . *Publications*: Christopher Greenwood, County Map-Maker, 1962; (with C. W. Phillips) The Historian's Guide to Ordnance Survey Maps, 1964; Maps for the Local Historian, 1972; ed, Reprint of the First Edition of the One-Inch Ordnance Survey of England and Wales, 1969–71; Ordnance Survey Maps: a descriptive manual, 1974; Gen. Editor (with Alan R. H. Baker), Studies in Historical Geography Series, 1970– ; *contrib.* Cartographic Jl, Econ. Hist. Rev., Geogr. Jl, Geog. Mag., Imago Mundi, Jl RSA, The Local Historian, Trans Inst. British Geographers, Trans Lancs and Cheshire Historic Soc. *Address*: Dept of Geography, Queen's Building, The Queen's Drive, Exeter EX4 4QH.

Harlow, Christopher Geoffrey, MA, BLitt, FSA; Senior Lecturer in English, Westfield College, University of London, since 1969; *b* 1924; *m* 1950; one *s* three *d*. BA Oxon 1949, BLitt Oxon 1955, MA Oxon 1958. Asst in English Language, Glasgow Univ., 1950–53; Lectr, 1953–61; Lectr, Westfield Coll., London, 1961–68. Mem., Council, Viking

Soc., 1964–69, 1971– ; Pres., London Mediev. Soc., 1966–70; Mem., Exec. Cttee, Engl. Assoc., 1966– ; Chm., Publicns Subcttee, Engl. Assoc., 1968– ; Asst Ed. Yrs Wk Engl. Studies, 1966–68, Ed., 1969–73; Ch. Ed., Early Engl. MSS in Facsim., 1972– . *Publications*: ed (with M. Avery), A Guide to English Courses in the Universities, 1970; *contrib.* Notes and Queries, Proc. Suff. Inst. Archaeol., Rev. Engl. Studies, Shakesp. Qly, Studies Engl. Lit. *Address*: Dept of English, Westfield College (Univ. of London), Hampstead NW3 7ST.

Harper, Anthony John, BA, MA; Lecturer, Department of German, University of Edinburgh, since 1964; *b* 1938; *m* 1964; one *s* two *d*. BA Bristol 1959 (1st cl. German), CertEd Exeter 1961, MA Bristol 1963. Asst Lectr, Edinburgh, 1962–64. *Publications*: (with E. McInnes) German Today, 1967; *contrib.* Eichend. Jrb., Forum Mod. Lang. Studies, Germ. Life Lett., Maske Kothurn, Neophilol. *Address*: Dept of German, Univ. of Edinburgh, George Square, Edinburgh.

Harper, Prof. John Lander, MA, DPhil, FIBiol; Professor of Agricultural Botany and Head of the School of Plant Biology, University College of North Wales, Bangor (also teaches ecology and conservation), since 1960; *b* 1925; *m* 1953; one *s* two *d*. BA Oxford 1947, MA Oxford 1950, DPhil Oxford 1950; FInstBiol; Mem.: Brit. Ecol. Soc. (Pres., 1965–67), Assoc. Appl. Biol., Amer. Assoc. Adv. Sci., Amer. Soc. Nat., Amer. Soc. Agron., Soc. Exper. Biol. Dept demonstrator, Univ. of Oxford, 1951–54; Univ. demonstrator and Lectr, 1954–60. Mem., Pesticides Cttee, Min. Agric. Fish and Food, 1967– . *Publications*: ed, The Biology of Weeds; *contrib.* Jl Ecol., New Phytol., Adv. Ecol. System., Plant Soil. *Address*: School of Plant Biology, Univ. College of North Wales, Bangor LL57 2DG.

Harper, Dr J. W.; Senior Lecturer, Department of English and Related Literatures, University of York, since 1973; *b* 1932; *m* 1956; one *d*. BA Knox Coll. 1954; MA Standford 1956; PhD Princeton 1960. Asst Prof., Haverford Coll., 1959–62; Vis. Fellow, Reading Univ., 1962–63; Lectr, Univ. of York, 1963–73. *Publications*: ed, Middleton: A Game at Chess, 1966; ed, Marlowe: Tambarlaine, 1971; Eternity Our Due, in, Victorian Poetry, 1972. *Address*: Dept of English and Related Literatures, Univ. of York, York YO1 5DD.

Harpin, William Sydney; Lecturer, School of Education, University of Nottingham, since 1967; *b* 1930; *m* 1953. BA Hons Birmingham 1951 (Eng.), Acad. Dip. in Educn London 1960, MEd 1962, PGCE 1952 Birmingham. *Publications*: Social and Educational Influences on Children's Acquisition of Grammar (SSRC Res. Report), 1973; *contrib.* Brit. Jl Educnl Psych., Educnl Res., Educnl Rev., English in Ed. Spoken English. *Address*: Sch. of Education, The Univ., University Park, Nottingham NG7 2RD.

Harré, Rom; University Lecturer in Philosophy of Science, and Fellow of Linacre

College, Oxford, since 1960; *b* 1927; *m* 1948; one *d*. BSc Auckland 1948, MA Auckland 1953, BPhil Oxon 1956, MA Oxon 1960; Mem., British Soc. for Philosophy of Science, Associate Mem.. Amer. Psychological Assoc. Lectr, Univ. of Punjab, Lahore, 1954–56; Res. Fellow, Birmingham Univ., 1956–57; Lectr, Leicester Univ., 1957–60; Vis. Prof., Univ. of Wisconsin, 1965; Vis. Prof., Univ. of Nevada, 1968; Vis. Prof., Univ. of Buffalo, 1971. Sec., Brit. Soc. for Philosophy of Science, 1968–69; Jt Editor, Jl for the Theory of Social Behaviour, 1971– . *Publications*: Introduction to the Logic of the Sciences, 1960, 2nd edn 1966; Theories and Things, 1961; Matter and Method, 1964; The Anticipation of Nature, 1965; The Principles of Scientific Thinking, 1970, 2nd edn 1972; The Method of Science, 1970; The Philosophies of Science, 1972; (with P. F. Secord) The Explanation of Social Behaviour, 1972; (with E. H. Madden) Causal Powers, 1974; ed, Principles of Linguistic Philosophy, by F. Waismann, 1965; ed, How I See Philosophy, by F. Waismann, 1968; ed, Early Seventeenth Century Scientists, 1965; ed, The Sciences, 1967; ed, Some Nineteenth Century British Scientists, 1969; ed, Scientific Thought 1900–1960, 1969; *contrib.* Brit. Jl for the Philosophy of Science, Mind, Philosophical Qly, Philosophy. *Address*: Linacre College, Oxford.

Harries, Dr David; Senior Lecturer, Music Department, University College of Wales, Aberystwyth, since 1970; *b* 1933; *m* 1958; one *s* one *d*. BMus Wales 1954, DMus Wales 1964. Lectr in Music, Univ. Coll. of Wales, Aberystwyth, 1962–70. Ch. Examiner in Music, A Level, Welsh Jt Educn Cttee, 1972– . *Publications*: Violin Concerto, 1965; Carol: 'Christchild', 1968; A Little Cantata, 1968; Four Impromptus for Piano, 1970; Three Stanzas for Harp, 1972; *contrib.* Anglo-Welsh Rev., Music Educn. *Address*: Music Dept, Univ. College of Wales, Aberystwyth SY23 2AX.

Harrington, Richard Lester; Lecturer, Department of Economics, University of Manchester, since 1968; *b* 1942. BScEcon Wales 1967, MScEcon London 1968. *Publications*: *contrib.* Man. School, Nat. West Bank Review. *Address*: Dept of Economics, Univ. of Manchester, Manchester M13 9PL.

Harriott, Rosemary Margaret, BA, MA; Lecturer, Department of Classics, Reading University, since 1970; *b* 1928. BA London 1950 (General), BA London 1959 (Hons), MA London 1961. Jun. Fellow, Univ. of Bristol, 1961–64; Lectr, Univ. of London, 1964–70. Warden, Hall of Res., Reading, 1970. *Publications*: Poetry and Criticism before Plato, 1969. *Address*: Dept of Classics, The Univ., Whiteknights, Reading RG6 2AH.

Harris, Dr Alan, MA, PhD; Reader in Geography, University of Hull, since 1968; *b* 1928; *m* 1965. BA London External 1949 (1st cl. Geography), MA London External 1951, PhD Hull 1961; Mem., Inst. Brit. Geogrs. Asst Lectr, Univ. of Hull, 1954–56, Lectr, 1956–65, Sen. Lectr, 1965–68. Mem.,

Council, Cumb. Westm. Antiqu. Archaeol. Soc., 1967– ; Asst Editor, Trans Cumb. Westm. Antiqu. Archaeol. Soc., 1970. *Publications*: The Rural Landscape of the East Riding of Yorkshire 1700–1850, 1961; ed (with H. King), A Survey of the Manor of Settrington, 1962; Cumberland Iron: the story of Hodbarrow mine 1855–1968, 1970; *contrib*. Trans Hist. Soc. Lancs Cheshire, Trans Cumb. Westm. Antiqu. Archaeol. Soc., Yorks Archaeol. Jl, etc. *Address*: Dept of Geography, Univ. of Hull, Hull HU6 7RX.

Harris, Christopher Charles, BA; Senior Lecturer in Sociology, University College of Swansea, since 1971; *b* 1934; *m* 1961. BA Oxon 1958 (2nd cl. PPE), Dip. Public and Social Administration Oxon 1959; Mem., Brit. Sociol. Assoc. Jun. Res. Off., Dept of Soc. Admin, Swansea, 1959–62; Res. Fellow, 1963–64; Lectr in Sociology, Faculty of Econ. and Soc. Studies, Swansea, 1964–71. Mem., Adv. Council, Nat. Corp. for Care of Old People, 1968–70; Archbishop's Commn on Structure and Boundaries of Ch in Wales, 1971– ; Council of Chs for Wales, 1968–72. *Publications*: (with C. Rosser) The Family and Social Change, 1965; The Family, 1969; ed, Kinship in Urban Society, 1970; *contrib*. Sociol. Rev. *Address*: School of Social Studies, Univ. College of Swansea, Singleton Park, Swansea SA2 8PP.

Harris, David John; Senior Lecturer in Law, University of Nottingham, since 1973; *b* 1938; *m* 1964; two *s*. LLB 1959, LLM 1961, London. Asst Lectr, QUB 1962–63; Lectr, Univ. of Nottingham, 1963–73. *Publications*: Cases and Materials on International Law, 1973; *contrib*. Brit. Yearbook of Internat. Law; Internat. and Comparative Law Qly: *Address*: Dept of Law, Univ. of Nottingham, Nottingham NG7 2RD.

Harris, Dr David Russell, MA, BLitt, PhD; Reader, Department of Geography, University College, London, since 1973 (Lecturer, 1964–73); *b* 1930; *m* 1957; four *d*. BA Oxford 1953 (Hons Geography), BLitt Oxford 1955, MA Oxford 1957, PhD California 1963; FRGS; Mem.: Inst. Brit. Geogrs, Assoc. Amer. Geogrs, Fellow, Amer. Geog. Soc. Mem.: Amer. Assoc. Adv. Sci., Soc. Econ. Bot. Teaching Asst and Instructor, Univ. of California, Berkeley, 1956–58; Asst Lectr, Queen Mary Coll., Univ. of London, 1958–61; Lectr, Queen Mary Coll., 1961–64. Vis. Prof., Univ. of New Mexico, 1962–63; Univ. of Toronto, 1970; Vis. Res. Fellow, ANU, 1974. *Publications*: Plants, Animals, and Man in the Outer Leeward Islands, West Indies: An Ecological Study of Antigua, Barbuda, and Anguilla, 1965; ed (with B. W. Hodder), Africa in Transition, 1967; contrib. The Domestication and Exploitation of Plants and Animals, ed P. J. Ucko and G. W. Dimbleby, 1969; Trends in Geography, ed R. U. Cooke and J. H. Johnson, 1969; Man, Settlement and Urbanism, ed P. J. Ucko et al., 1972; The Explanation of Culture Change: Models in Prehistory, ed C. Renfrew, 1973; *contrib*. Amer. Sci., Ann. Assoc. Amer. Geogrs, Geog. Jl, Geog. Rev., Proc. Linn. Soc. Lond., Proc. Prehist. Soc., Trans Inst. Brit. Geogrs. *Address*: Dept of Geography,

Univ. College London, Gower Street, WC1E 6BT.

Harris, Dr Derek Raymond, MA, PhD; Lecturer in Spanish, University College, London, since 1966; *b* 1939; *m* 1962; two *s*. BA Nottingham 1960, MA Nottingham 1962, PhD Hull 1968. Asst Lectr in Spanish, Univ. Coll., London, 1964–66. *Publications*: The Poetry of Luis Cernuda, 1971; Luis Cernuda: Perfil del aire, 1971; Luis Cernuda: a study of the poetry, 1973; *contrib*. Bull. Hisp. Studies. *Address*: Dept of Spanish and Latin American Studies, Univ. College London, Gower Street, WC1E 6BT.

Harris, Donald Renshaw; Fellow and Tutor in Jurisprudence, Balliol College, Oxford University, since 1956, and Associate-Director, Centre for Socio-legal Studies, since 1972; *b* 1928; *m* 1951; one *s* two *d*. BA New Zealand 1949 (Classics), LLB New Zealand 1952, LLM New Zealand 1953 (1st cl.), BCL Oxon 1955 (1st cl.), MA Oxon 1956; Barrister New Zealand 1952, Inner Temple 1958. Lectr in Law, Worcester Coll., Oxford, 1956–59; Vis. Prof., Univ. of W Ontario, 1968–69. Sen. Tutor, Balliol Coll., 1962–67; Estates Bursar, 1967–72. *Publications*: asst ed., Chitty on Contracts, 22nd and 23rd edns, 1968; asst ed., Benjamin's Sale of Goods, 1974; *contrib*. chapter on Contract, in, Annual Survey of Commonwealth Law. *Address*: Balliol College, Oxford.

Harris, Geoffrey Thomas; Lecturer, Department of French, Dundee University, since 1969; *b* 1941; *m* 1965; one *s* one *d*. BA Manchester 1963 (Hons French Studies), MA Manchester 1967. Asst Lectr, Univ. of Manchester, 1968–69. *Publications*: L'Ethique comme fonction de l'esthétique: André Malraux, 1972 (Paris); *contrib*. Mod. Lang. Rev., Nottingham French Stud. *Address*: Dept. of French, Univ. of Dundee, Dundee DD1 4HN.

Harris, James Broughton; Lecturer in Architecture, University of Manchester, since 1964; *b* 1931; *m* 1961; two *d*. DipArch Manchester, 1954, MA Manchester 1967; Member: RIBA, Design Res. Soc. Lectr in Architecture, 1959; Vis. Prof., Coll. of Environmental Design, Univ. Calif., Berkeley, 1964. *Address*: Dept of Architecture, Univ. of Manchester, Manchester M13 9PL.

Harris, James William, MA, BCL, PhD; Fellow of Keble College and Lecturer in Law, Oxford University, since 1973; *b* 1940; *m* 1968. BA Oxford 1962, MA and BC Oxford 1966; Solicitor 1965. Lectr, Law Dept, LSE, 1966–73. *Publications*: *contrib*. Camb. Law Jl, Conveyan. and Prop. Law, Law Qly Rev., Mod. Law Rev. *Address*: Keble Coll., Oxford.

Harris, Dr John; Lecturer in Science Education, Chelsea College, University of London, since 1970; *b* 1932; *m* 1962; one *s* one *d*. MA 1957, PhD 1959, Cantab; MInstP. Res. Associate and Lectr in Physics, Harvard Univ., 1964–68; Vis. Fellow, Chelsea Coll., 1968–70. *Publications*: contrib. (Harvard) Project Physics, 1970; Nuffield Advanced Physics, 1971.

Address: Centre for Science Education, Chelsea Coll., Bridges Place, SW6 4HR.

Harris, John Wesley, MA; Lecturer in Drama and Mass Media, University of Hull, since 1968; *b* 1935; *m* 1960; two *s* one *d*. BA Cantab 1957, MA Cantab 1961. Lectr, Univ. of Queensland, 1961; Research Fellow, Univ. of Birmingham, 1966; Lectr, Univ. of Hull, 1968. Gen. Staff Intelligence (Security), GHQ, MELF 1958–61. *Address*: Dept of Drama, Univ. of Hull, Hull HU6 7RX.

Harris, Nigel Gareth Evan; Lecturer in Philosophy, University of Dundee, since 1969; *b* 1940; *m* 1965; one *s* two *d*. BSc Bristol 1961, BA Leeds 1965, BPhil Oxon 1967. Asst Lectr, Univ. of Dundee, 1967–69; Asst Editor, Philosophical Qly, 1970–72. *Publications*: *contrib*. Analysis, Ethics, Jl Aesthetics and Art Criticism, Brit. Jl of Pol Sci. *Address*: Dept of Philosophy, Univ. of Dundee, Dundee DD1 4HN.

Harris, Norman Duncan Campany; Director of Educational Services, School of Education, University of Bath, since November 1970; *b* 1933; *m* 1961; two *d*. BSc (Hons) 2 (ii) Nottingham 1955, MSc Nottingham 1961, PhD Bath 1973; Cert. in Educn, Cambridge 1956; APLET. Lectr in Education, 1967–70; Univ. of Bath: Senate, 1972– ; Court, 1972– ; Univ. of Nottingham, Court, 1973– ; Bath and Wells Diocesan Educn Cttee, 1971– ; Schools Council: Engrg Science Develt Unit Steering Cttee, 1970– . *Publications*: Mechanics, 1969, 2nd edn 1970; (with K. Austwick) Aspects of Educational Technology VI, 1972; (with K. Austwick and P. N. Richards) Objective Questions in Modern 'A' Level Mathematics, 1973; *contrib*. Higher Educn, Indust. Trng Internat., Programmed Learning and Educnl Technology. *Address*: Educational Services Unit, Univ. of Bath, Upper Borough Walls, Bath BA1 5AL.

Harris, Onslow Edward; Senior Lecturer, Land Management and Development Department, University of Reading, since 1969; *b* 1926; *m* 1949; one *s*. DipTP London 1957; MRTPI 1957. Head of Planning Dept, Stevenage Develt Corp., 1959–66; Sen. Res. Officer, Nat. Inst. of Economic and Social Res., 1966–69. *Address*: Land Management and Development Dept, University of Reading, Reading, Berks RG6 2AH.

Harris, Dr Rosemary Lois; Lecturer, Department of Anthropology, University College London, since 1969; *b* 1930. BA Queen's University Belfast 1951, MA London 1956, PhD London 1960; Mem. Assoc. Social Anthropologists, FRAI. Lecturer: Queen's Univ., Belfast, 1960–65; Univ. of Sussex, 1965–69. *Publications*: The Political Organization of the Mbembe of SE Nigeria, 1965; Prejudice and Tolerance in Ulster: A Study of Neighbours and Strangers in a Border Community, 1972; *contrib*. Africa, Man, Soc. Rev. *Address*: Dept of Anthropology, University Coll. Gower Street, WC1E 6BT.

Harris, Sylvia Clare; Lecturer, German Department, Birkbeck College, University of London, since 1963; *b* 1931. MA London 1954 (German); Mem.: Mod. Hum. Res. Assoc., Philol. Soc., Brit. Brch, Int. Arthurian Soc. Lectr, Univ. Coll. of Wales, Aberystwyth, 1956–63. *Publications*: *contrib*. Jl Engl. Germ. Philol., Med. Aev., Mod. Lang. Rev. *Address*: Birkbeck College, Malet Street, WC1E 7HX.

Harris, William Jack Augustus; Lecturer in Adult Education, University of Manchester, since 1962; *b* 1912; *m* 1949; two *s* one *d*. BA Cardiff 1935; MSc Econ London 1940; Mem., Assoc. of Tutors in Adult Educn. Res. Tutor i/c, UC of E Africa, 1953; Staff Tutor, Univ. London (Dept of Extra Mural Studies), 1957. CO Welfare Dept. London, 1949–50. UNESCO consultancy, Thailand, 1974. *Publications*: (with others) Study by Correspondence, 1971; Home Study Students, 1972; *contrib*. Adult Educn, Highway, Jl Royal Television Soc., Home Study Rev., Continuous Learning. *Address*: Dept. of Adult Education, The Univ., Manchester M13 9PL.

Harrison, Alan, MA, MSc; Reader in Agricultural Economics, University of Reading, since 1971; *b* 1926; *m* 1952; two *d*. MA St Andrews 1950 (French Ord. Degree), MA St Andrews 1952 (1st cl. Economics, 2nd cl. Philosophy), MSc Reading 1956; Mem.: Agric. Econ. Soc., Int. Assoc. Agric. Econ. Asst Lectr, Reading, 1953–56; Lectr, 1956– 71. *Publications*: *contrib*. Jl Agric. Econ., Farm Econ., Econ. Rur. *Address*: Dept of Agricultural Economics, Univ. of Reading, Building 4, Earley Gate, Reading.

Harrison, Anthony Edward; Lecturer in Economic and Social History, Department of Economics, University of York, since 1968; *b* 1942; *m* 1965; two *s*. BA Leeds (2nd cl. special Economics). Tutorial Asst, York, 1964–65; Asst Lectr, 1965–68. *Publications*: *contrib*. Econ. Hist. Rev. *Address*: Dept of Economics, Univ. of York, Heslington, York YO1 5DD.

Harrison, Barry Joseph Douglas; Lecturer in Local History, Department of Adult Education and Extra-Mural Studies, University of Leeds, since 1966; *b* 1935; *m* 1965 one *d*. BA (Hons) Oxford 1957, MA Oxford 1965; Mem. Vernacular Architecture Gp, Econ. History Soc., Brit. Agric. History Soc., Soc. for Med. Archaeology, Standing Conference, Local History Tutors. Tutor, History, Exeter Univ., 1960–61; Asst Lectr, Edinburgh Univ., 1961–62. Mem., Jt Tutorial Classes Cttee, 1971– . *Publication*: Teesside (Cities and Counties series), 1974. *Address*: Dept of Adult Educn and Extra-Mural Studies, Univ. of Leeds, Leeds LS2 9JT.

Harrison, Dr Bernard Joseph; Reader in Philosophy, University of Sussex, since 1971; *b* 1933; *m* 1956; one *s* two *d*. BSc Birmingham 1954, BA Birmingham 1956, MA Birmingham 1957, PhD Michigan 1961; Mem., Aristot. Soc. Lectr, Univ. of Toronto, 1960– 62; Asst Lectr, Univ. of Birmingham, 1962– 63; Lectr, Univ. of Sussex, 1963–71. *Publications*: Meaning and Structure, 1972; Form and Content, 1974; Philosophy of Language (forthcoming); contrib. Contemporary Studies in Aesthetics, ed Coleman, 1968; Violence, ed Shaffer, 1971; *contrib.* Inquiry, Mind, Proc. Aristot. Soc., Jl Philos. Lingu. *Address:* Arts Building, Univ. of Sussex, Falmer, Brighton BN1 9QN.

Harrison, Dr Brian Howard, MA, DPhil, FRHistS; Fellow and Tutor in Modern History and Politics, Corpus Christi College, Oxford University, since 1967; *b* 1937; *m* 1967. BA Oxon 1961 (1st cl. Modern History), MA Oxon 1966, DPhil Oxon 1966; FRHistS. Res. Student, St Antony's Coll., Oxford, 1961–64; Res. Fellow, Nuffield Coll., Oxford, 1964–67; Vis. Prof., Univ. of Michigan, Ann Arbor, 1970; Vis. Lectr, Harvard, 1973. *Publications:* (with G. Barlow) History at the Universities, 1966; (with B. Trinder) Drink and Sobriety in an Early Victorian Country Town, 1969; Drink and the Victorians, 1971; *contrib.* Hist. Jl, EHR, Past Pres., Local Hist., Internat. Rev. Soc. Hist., Hist., Vict. Studies. *Address:* Corpus Christi College, Oxford.

Harrison, Colin; Lecturer in Geography, Department of Economics and Geography, University of Salford, since 1967; *b* 1942. BSc Wales 1964, MSc Manchester 1967; Mem., Inst. Brit. Geogrs, Geol. Assoc. Demonstrator, Sch. of Geography, Manchester Univ., 1966–67. *Publication:* The Analysis of Geographical Data, 1970. *Address:* Dept of Economics and Geography, Univ. of Salford, Salford M5 4WT.

Harrison, Edward Lawrence; Senior Lecturer in Classics, University of Leeds, since 1965; *b* 1921; *m* 1951; two *s* one *d.* BA Manchester 1946 (cl. I Classics), DipEd Manchester 1947; BLitt Oxon 1951; Member: Classical Assoc; Virgil Soc. Asst Lectr, UCD, 1949–52; Lectr, Univ. of Leeds, 1952–65; Assoc. Prof., Queen's Univ., Ontario, 1961–62. *Publications: contrib.* Classical Philol., Classical Qly, Classical Rev., Eranos, Hermes, Phoenix, Rev. Archéologique, Virgil Soc. Proc. *Address:* Dept of Latin, Univ. of Leeds, Leeds LS2 9JT.

Harrison, Eric, ARCA, ATI, MSIA; Senior Lecturer in Textile Design and Colour, School of Textile Technology and Textile Design, University of Bradford, since 1966; *b* 1919; *m* 1956; one *s* one *d.* Mem., sub-cttee on TrainingTextile Designers; Yorks Council for Further Educn, 1963–64; Syllabus sub-Cttee, Appreciation of Colour and Design, City and Guilds of London Inst., 1963. *Address:* School of Textile Technology and Textile Design, Univ. of Bradford, Bradford, Yorkshire BD7 1DP.

Harrison, Dr Geoffrey Ainsworth, MA, BSc, DPhil; Reader in Physical Anthropology, University of Oxford, since 1963; *b* 1927; *m* 1946; one *d.* BA Cantab 1950, BSc London 1952, BA Oxon 1953, MA Oxon 1955, DPhil Oxon 1957; FRAI, FZS. Deptal Demonstrator, Oxford Univ., 1953–54; Lectr, Liverpool Univ., 1954–63; Vis. Prof., Univ. of Rio Grande do Sul, Brazil, 1964; Vis. Fellow, Australian Nat. Univ., Canberra, 1969. Sec.. Soc. Study Hum. Biol., 1962–68; Vice-Pres,

and Sec., Eugenics Soc., 1968–71; Pres., Royal Anthropol. Inst., 1969–71; Chairman: Royal Soc. Hum. Adaptability, IBP Sub-Cttee, 1970; Royal Soc. Study Gp, Human Biol. in Urban Environments, 1972. *Publications:* ed (with D. F. Roberts), Natural Selection in Human Populations, 1959; ed, Genetical Variations in Human Populations, 1961; (with J. S. Weiner et al.) Human Biology, 1964; ed, Teaching and Research in Human Biology, 1964; ed (with A. J. Boyce), The Structure of Human Populations, 1972; *contrib.* Ann. Hum. Genet., Hum. Biol., Genet., Jl Zool., Philos. Trans Roy. Soc., Proc. Roy. Soc., Proc. Zool. Soc. *Address:* Physical Anthropology Laboratory, Dept of Human Anatomy, South Parks Road, Oxford OX1 3QX.

Harrison, Dr Godfrey James, BSc, PhD; Lecturer in Psychology, University College Cardiff (also teaches Psychology of Language), since 1970; *b* 1938; *m* 1960; two *s* one *d.* BSc Exeter 1962 (2nd cl.), PhD Sheffield 1967; Mem.: Brit. Psychol. Soc., Brain Res. Assoc. Res. Asst, Sheffield Univ., 1964–67; Independent Res. Worker, Sheffield Univ., 1967–68; Lectr, Hull Univ., 1968–70. Mem., Schools Council Subject Cttee on Soc. Scis; co-holder of SSRC grant on Acquisition of Bilingual Speech by Infants, Chm., Sheffield Campaign Against Racial Discrim., 1967–68. *Publications:* contrib. The Computer in Psychology, 1973; *contrib.* Acta Psychol. *Address:* Dept of Psychology, Univ. College, PO Box 78, Cathays Park, Cardiff CF1 1XL.

Harrison, Prof. John Fletcher Clews; Professor of History, University of Sussex, since 1970; *b* 1921; *m* 1945; one *s* one *d.* BA Cantab 1942 (1st cl. Hons Law), MA Cantab 1946, PhD Leeds 1955; Schol. and Prizeman, Selwyn Coll., Goldsmiths' Open Exhibn in History. Lectr, 1947–58, Dep. Dir of Extra Mural Studies, Leeds Univ., 1958–61; Prof. of History, Univ. of Wisconsin, 1961–70. War service, 1941–45, Captain, Royal Leicestershire Regt and King's African Rifles. *Publications:* History of the Working Men's College 1854–1954, 1954; Learning and Living 1790–1960, 1961; ed, Society and Politics in England, 1780–1960, 1965; Robert Owen and the Owenites, 1969; The Early Victorians 1832–51, 1971; *contrib.* Victorian Studies, Jl of British Studies, Labor History. *Address:* School of English and American Studies, Univ. of Sussex, Falmer, Brighton, Sussex.

Harrison, Prof. Jonathan, MA; Professor of Philosophy, University of Nottingham, since 1964; *b* 1924; *m* 1949 (wife *d* 1969); three *s* one *d.* BA Oxon 1945 (1st cl. PPE), MA Oxon 1951; Mem.: Mind Assoc., Aristotelian Soc., Brit. Soc. Philos. Sciences. Lectr in Philosophy, Univ. of Durham, 1947–59; Lectr in Philosophy, Univ. of Edinburgh, 1959–62; Sen. Lectr, 1962–64; Vis. Prof. of Philosophy, Northwestern Univ., USA, 1967. Pres., Mind Assoc., 1971; Pres., Jt Session, Mind Assoc. and Aristotel. Soc., 1971; Mem., Council, Royal Inst. Philos. *Publications:* Our Knowledge of Right and Wrong; *contrib.* Analysis, Aristot. Soc. Proc., Aristot. Soc. Supp. Proc., Austral. Jl Philos, Mind, Philos., Philos. Qly.

Address: Dept of Philosophy, The Univ., Nottingham NG7 2RD.

Harrison, Linda Rosemary; Lecturer, Department of Modern Languages, University of Salford, since 1968; *b* 1945. BA Leeds 1966 (Hons French). *Address*: Dept of Modern Languages, Univ. of Salford, Salford M5 4WT.

Harrison, Prof. Martin, BA (Econ), DES, DPhil; Professor of Politics, University of Keele, since 1966; *b* 1930; *m* 1957; two *s* one *d*. BA (Econ) Manchester 1952 (1st cl.), Diplôme Supérieur de Recherches et d'Etudes Politiques (DES) Paris 1959, DPhil Oxford 1958; Mem., Pol. Studies Assoc. UK. Res. Fellow, Nuffield Coll., Oxford, 1957–62; Lectr, then Sen. Lectr, Manchester, 1963–66. Chm., Bd of Soc. Sciences, Univ. of Keele, 1971–74. *Publications*: Trade Unions and the Labour Party, 1960; (with P. Williams) De Gaulle's Republic, 1960; French Politics, 1969; (with P. Williams) Politics and Society in de Gaulle's Republic, 1970; *contrib*. Amer. Pol. Science Rev., Jl Pol., Parl. Aff., Pol., Studies, Rev. Franç. Science Pol. *Address*: Dept of Politics, Univ. of Keele, Keele, Staffordshire ST5 5BG.

Harrison, Dr Reginald James; Senior Lecturer in Politics, University of Lancaster, since 1968; *b* 1927; *m* 1954; two *s* one *d*. BA De Pauw 1952 (Economics), BSc (Econ) London (ext. at Univ. Coll. of SW) 1953, PhD Ohio State 1964; Mem.: Pol. Studies Assoc., Univ. Assoc. Contemp. Europ. Studies. Graduate Asst, Ohio State Univ., 1954–57; Lectr, Victoria Univ. of Wellington, NZ, 1957–59; Sen. Lectr, 1959–67; Lectr, Lancaster Univ., 1967. *Publications*: The New Zealand Parliament, 1964; Integration Theory, 1974; contrib. The Other Powers: studies in the foreign policies of small states, ed R. P. Barston, 1973; Functionalism: theory and practice in international relations, ed J. Groom and P. Taylor, 1974; *contrib*. Austral. Qly, Comment (NZ), Ind. Jl Pol Science, Landfall (NZ), Listener, Mngmt Jl, Pacific Viewpt, Pol Etrang., Pol Science, Pol Studies, Rev. Marché Commun, Univ. Focus, Jl of Common Market Studies. *Address*: Dept of Politics, Lancaster Univ., Lancaster LA1 4YW.

Harrison, Prof. Richard Martin, MA, FSA; Professor of Archaeology, University of Newcastle upon Tyne, since 1968; *b* 1935; *m* 1959; one *s* three *d*. BA Oxon 1958 (Lit. Hum.), MA Oxon 1961; Fellow, Brit. Inst. Archaeol., Ankara, 1959–60; Rivoira Schol., Brit. Sch. Rome, 1960; Lectr, Bryn Mawr Coll., 1961; Glanville Res. Student, Lincoln Coll., Oxford, 1962–63; Lectr, Univ. of Newcastle upon Tyne, 1964–68; Vis. Fellow, Dumbarton Oaks Centre for Byzantine Studies, 1969. Controller of Antiquities, Prov. Govt of Cyrenaica, 1960–61; Dir, Saraçhane excavs, Istanbul, 1964–69; Mem., Council, British Inst. Archaeol., Ankara; Council, Roman Soc., Fac. of Archaeol., Hist. and Lett., Brit. Sch., Rome. *Publications*: *contrib*. Anat. Studies, Archaeol. Ael., DO Papers, Fast. Archaeol., Jl Rom. Studies, Pap. Brit. Sch. Rome. *Address*: Dept of

Archaeology, The Univ., Newcastle upon Tyne NE1 7RU.

Harrison, Roger Davis; Senior Lecturer, Institute of Educational Technology, Open University, since 1970; *b* 1927; *m* 1960; one *s* one *d*. BSc Birmingham 1948 (1st cl. Hons. Math. Physics); MInstP 1954. Asst Lectr in Physics, UC of N Staffs (Univ. of Keele), 1951–55; Extension Lectr in Science, King's Coll. Newcastle (Univ. of Newcastle), 1955–63; Sen. Lectr in Physics, Rutherford Coll. Technol. (Newcastle Polytech.), 1963–69. *Publications*: Forces, 1969; Book of Data, Nuffield Advanced Science, 1972; *contrib*. Adult Educn, Aspects of Educnl. Technol. *Address*: Open Univ., Walton Hall, Milton Keynes MK7 6AA.

Harrison, Prof. Royden John, MA, DPhil; Professor of Social History, and Director of the Centre for the Study of Social History, University of Warwick, since 1970; *b* 1927; *m* 1954; two *d*. MA Oxon, DPhil Oxon 1955. Lectr (extra-mural), Sheffield Univ., 1955–64; Sen. Lectr, 1964–69; Vis. Prof. in Modern History, Madison, Wisconsin, 1964; Sen. Leverhulme Res. Fellow, 1966–68; Reader, Dept of Politics, Sheffield, 1969–70. Co-Founder and co-ed., Bull. Soc. Study Labour Hist., 1960– ; Mem. Edit. Bd, Political Qly. *Publications*: Before the Socialists, 1965; ed, The English Defence of the Commune, 1971; contrib. Essays in Labour History, ed A. Briggs and J. Saville, vol. 1 1960, vol. 2 1971; *contrib*. Econ. Jl, Internat. Rev. Soc. Hist., I Protag., Pol. Qly, Sci. Soc., Slav. E Europ. Jl, Wisconsin Vict. Studies. *Address*: Centre for the Study of Social History, Univ. of Warwick, Coventry CV4 7AL.

Harrison, Dr Thomas Ross; Lecturer in Philosophy, University of Bristol, since 1970; *b* 1943; *m* 1968. BA Cantab 1964 (1st cl. Hons Moral Scis), MA Cantab 1968, PhD 1969. Mem., Aristotelian Society. Fellow of St John's Coll. Cambridge, 1967. *Publications*: On What There Must Be, 1974; contrib. Friedrich Überwegs Grundriss der Geschichte der Philosophie (forthcoming); *contrib*. Analysis, Political Studies, Philosophical Qly. *Address*: Dept of Philosophy, The Univ., Bristol BS8 1RJ.

Harrison, Prof. Wilfrid; Professor of Politics, Warwick University, since 1964; *b* 1909; *m* 1943; two *d*. MA Glasgow 1931, BA Oxford 1933, MA Oxford; Mem.: Amer. Pol. Sci. Assoc., Pol. Studies Assoc. UK. Lectr, Queen's Coll, Oxford, 1935–39; Fellow, 1939–57; Prof. of Political Theory and Institutions, Univ. of Liverpool, 1957–64. Pro-Vice Chancellor, Univ. of Warwick, 1964–69; Dean, Queen's Coll., Oxford, 1939–40; Temp. Civil Servant, 1939–45; Mem., Exec., Pol. Studies Assoc., 1952–63; Ed., Pol. Studies, 1952–63; Gen. Ed., Blackwell Political Texts, 1955– ; Local Govt Exams Bd, 1960–68; Training Bd, 1968–73; Chm., Hist. and Pol. Science Bd, Council for Nat. Acad. Awards, 1971–73. *Publications*: The Government of Britain, 1948, 9th edn 1964; ed, Bentham: Fragment on Government and Principles of Morals and Legislation, 1948;

Conflict and Compromise: History of British Political Thought, 1593–1900, 1965; ed, Sources in British Political Thought, 1593–1900, 1965; *contrib.* Parl. Aff., Pol. Studies. *Address*: Dept of Politics, The Univ. of Warwick, Coventry CV4 7AL.

Harrison-Church, Prof. Ronald James, BSc(Econ), PhD; Professor of Geography, London School of Economics and Political Science, University of London, since 1964; *b* 1915; *m* 1944; one *s* one *d*. BSc(Econ) London 1936 (1st cl.), DipEd London 1939, PhD London 1943; FRGS. Mem., Geog. Assoc., Inst. Brit. Geogrs, Afr. Studies Assoc. UK, Royal Afr Soc. Asst Lectr, LSE, 1944–47; Lectr, 1947–58; Reader, 1958–64; Vis. Professor: Wisconsin Univ., 1956; Indiana Univ., 1965; Tel-Aviv and Haifa Univs, 1972–73. Mem., Council, Royal Afr. Soc., 1972– . *Publications*: as R. J. H. Church: Modern Colonization, 1951; West Africa, 1957, 7th edn 1973; Russian edn 1959; Environment and Policies in West Africa, 1963; Looking at France, 1970, French and American edns 1970, Spanish edn 1973; (jtly) Africa and the Islands, 1964, 3rd edn 1971; An Advanced Geography of Northern and Western Europe, 1967, 2nd edn 1973; *contrib.* Econ. Geog., Geog., Geog. Jl, Geog. Mag., Geog. Rev., Trans Inst. Brit. Geogrs, W Afr. *Address*: Dept of Geography, London School of Economics, WC2A 2AE.

Harrop, Jeffrey; Lecturer in Economics, University of Hull, since 1966; *b* 1943; *m* 1967; one *d*. BA Liverpool 1964 (Hons. Economics), MA Liverpool 1966. *Publications*: *contrib.* J. Econ. Studies, Text. Hist., Yorks Bull. *Address*: Dept of Economics, Univ. of Hull, Hull HU6 7RX.

Hart, Gillian Rosemary, MA, BPhil; Lecturer in Classics, University of Durham, since 1969; *b* 1934. BA Oxon 1958 (2nd cl. Lit. Hum.), MA Oxon 1961, Dip. in Comparative Philology (with distinction) Oxon 1960, BPhil 1967 (Oriental Studies – Hittite). Mem.: Class. Assoc., Philol. Soc., Linguistics Assoc., Royal Asiatic Soc. Lectr in Classics, Univ. Coll. of Wales, Aberystwyth, 1960–69. *Publications*: Proceedings of the Cambridge Colloquium on Mycenaean Studies, ed, J. Chadwick and L. R. Palmer, 1966; *contrib.* Bull. Inst. Class. Studies, Mnemosyne, Trans Philol. Soc., Kadmos. *Address*: Dept of Classics, 38 North Bailey, Durham.

Hart, Harold, BA(Com), FCA; Senior Lecturer in Accountancy, Department of Economics, University of Southampton, since 1965; *b* 1915; *m* 1950. BA(Com) Manchester 1935; ACA 1937. Lectr, Southampton Univ., 1958–65. Chm., Educn Sub-Cttee. South. Soc. Chtd Actnts, 1965–67; Mem.: Cttee, South. Soc. Chtd Acntnts, 1965–69; Central Council, FSSU, 1960– ; Jt Stand. Cttee on Degree Studies and Acntncy Profession. *Publications*: contrib. Overhead Costs, 1973; Trade Credit Control, 1974; *contrib.* Acntncy, Acntnt, Acntnts' Jl, Business Ratios, Sci. Business. *Address*: Dept of Economics, Univ. of Southampton, Southampton SO9 5NH.

Hart, Prof. Herbert Lionel Adolphus, FBA; Principal, Brasenose College, Oxford, since 1973; *b* 1907; *m* 1941; three *s* one *d*. BA Oxon 1929 (1st cl. Lit. Hum.), MA Oxon 1942; Hon Dr of Law Stockholm 1960; Hon. LLD: Glasgow, 1966; Chicago, 1966; Hon DLitt Kent, 1969; FBA 1962; Fellow, Accademia delle Scienze, Turin, 1964; For. Mem., Amer. Acad. Arts and Sciences, 1966; Hon. Master of the Bench, Middle Temple, 1963. Practised at the Chancery Bar, 1932–40. Fellow and Tutor in Philosophy, New Coll., Oxford, 1945; Univ. Lectr in Philosophy, 1948, Prof. of Jurisprudence, 1952–68, Oxford; Fellow, University Coll., Oxford, 1952–68, Res. Fellow, 1969–73; Sen. Res. Fellow, Nuffield Foundn, 1969–73; Vis. Professor: Harvard Univ., 1956–57; Univ. of California, LA, 1961–62; Commonwealth Prestige Fellow, Govt of NZ, 1971. Delegate of OUP, 1960– ; Chm., OU Enquiry into Relations with Junior Members, 1969 (Report 1970). Mem., Monopolies Commn, 1967–73. Pres., Aristotelian Soc., 1959–60. *Publications*: (with A. M. Honoré) Causation in the Law, 1959; The Concept of Law, 1961; Law, Liberty and Morality, 1963; The Morality of the Criminal Law, 1965; Punishment and Responsibility, 1968; ed. (with J. H. Burns), Jeremy Bentham: An Introduction to the Principles of Morals and Legislation, 1970; ed, Jeremy Bentham: Of Laws in General, 1970; *contrib.* Proc. Aristotelian Soc.; Yale Law Rev., Harvard Law Rev., Philos. Rev. *Address*: Brasenose College, Oxford.

Hart, Jenifer Margaret; Tutor in Modern History and Fellow of St Anne's College, since 1952, and University Lecturer, Oxford, since 1953; *b* 1914; *m* 1941; three *s* one *d*. BA Hons Oxon 1935 (Mod. Hist.), MA Oxon. Supervisor of Studies, Extra-Mural Dept, Oxford, 1947–49; Res. Fellow, Nuffield Coll., 1950–51. Civil Servant (Admin. grade), Home Office, 1936–47. *Publications*: The British Police, 1951; chapter, in Studies in the Growth of 19th century Government, ed G. Sutherland, 1972; *contrib.* EHR, Past and Pres. Public Admin. *Address*: St Anne's College, Oxford.

Hart, John, ATD; Head of Art Teachers' Certificate Course, University of London, Goldsmiths' College, since 1967; *b* 1921; *m* 1951; three *d*. NDD Liverpool Coll. of Art 1950 (Painting), ATD Liverpool Coll. of Art 1951. Mem.: Univ. of London, Goldsmiths' Delegacy; Univ. of London Bd of Studies in Fine Art. One Man Shows: Beaux Arts Gallery, London, 1953; Midland Group, Nottingham, 1954; New Shakespeare Gallery, Liverpool, 1959; Midland Group, Nottingham, 1960; Liverpool University, 1961; Hamilton Galleries, London, 1961; Majorie Parr Gallery, London, 1965; Bear Lane Gallery, Oxford, 1960; New Gallery, Belfast, 1964; Galleria Torbandena, Trieste, 1971. *Address*: Univ. of London, Goldsmiths' College, New Cross, SE14 6NW.

Harte, Negley Boyd, BSc(Econ), FRHistS; Lecturer in Economic History, University College London, since 1969; *b* 1943; *m* 1970; one *d*. Lectr in Social History, London Univ. Extra-Mural Dept, 1966–69; Res. Fellow in

History, Inst. Hist. Res., 1968–69; Supervisor in Economic History, St John's Coll., Cambridge, 1968–69. Non-professional representative, University Coll. Cttee, 1972– ; Man. Editor, London Jl, 1974– . *Publications*: ed, The Study of Economic History, 1971; ed (with K. G. Ponting), Textile History and Economic History, 1973; *contrib*. Econ. Hist. Rev., Textile Hist. *Address*: Dept of History, Univ. College London, Gower Street, WC1E 6BT.

Harting, Henry Maria Robert Egmont M.; *see* Mayr-Harting.

Hartley, John Roger; Director, Computer Based Learning Project, since 1971; Senior Lecturer, Department of Education, University of Leeds, since 1972; *b* 1933; *m* 1957; one *s* one *d*. BA Keele 1956, Advanced Dip. Educnl Studies, Manchester 1961, MA Keele 1965; MInstP. Res. Associate, Manchester Univ., 1963–67; Lectr, Leeds Univ., 1967–72. *Publications*: (with A. H. Gregory and D. G. Lewis) Basic Statistics, 1969 (Spanish and Hebrew edns); *contrib*. British Jl Educational Psychol., Internat. Jl Man-Machine Studies. *Address*: Computer Based Learning Project, Leeds Univ., Leeds LS2 9JT.

Hartley, Keith; Senior Lecturer, Department of Economics, University of York, since 1972; *b* 1940; *m*; one *s* one *d*. BScEcon Hull 1962; Lectr, Univ. of York, 1964–72; Vis. Assoc. Prof., Univ. of Illinois, USA, 1974. Chm., Departmental Bd in Economics, 1971–73. *Publications*: (with R. Cooper) Export Performance and Pressure of Demand, 1970; *contrib*. Bull. Econ. Res., Brit. Jl Industrial Relations, Jl. of Industrial Economics, Econ. Jl, Oxford Econ. Papers, Scottish Jl Political Econ. *Address*: Economics Dept, Univ. of York, Heslington, York YO1 5DD.

Hartley, Dr Owen Arthur; Lecturer in Politics, Department of Politics, University of Leeds, since 1968; *b* 1943; *m* 1968; one *s* one *d*. BA Oxon 1965, MA Oxon 1969, DPhil Oxon 1969. *Publications*: *contrib*. Local Govt Studies, Policy and Politics, Public Admin (London), Public Admin (Sydney). *Address*: Dept of Politics, Univ. of Leeds, Leeds LS2 9JT.

Hartley, Trevor Clayton, LLM; Lecturer, Law Department, London School of Economics, since 1973; *b* 1939; *m* 1961; two *s* one *d*. BA Cape Town 1959, LLB Cape Town 1961, LLM London 1964; Mem., SPTL. Asst Prof. of Law, Univ. of Western Ontario, Canada, 1964–68; Associate Prof., 1968–69. *Publications*: (with J. A. G. Griffith) Government and Law, 1974; *contrib*. Buffalo Law Rev., Internat. and Comparative Law Qly, Mod. Law Rev., Public Law. *Address*: London School of Economics, Houghton Street, Aldwych, WC2A 2AE.

Hartley, Walter Colin Farrar; Assistant Director of Post Experience Programmes Management Centre, University of Bradford, since 1968; *b* 1932; *m* 1953; two *s*. FCA (ACA 1953), FCMA (ACWA 1956), JDipMA 1963; Mem. Inst. Directors 1970. *Publications*: An Introduction to Business Accounting for Managers, 1965, 2nd edn 1970; *contrib*. Corporate Planning and the Role of the Management Accountant (ICMA pubn); *contrib*. Acctncy Age, Long Range Planning. *Address*: Univ. of Bradford Management Centre, Heaton Mount, Keighley Road, Bradford BD9 4JU.

Hartmann, Dr Reinhard Rudolf Karl; Director, Language Centre, University of Exeter, since 1974; *b* 1938; *m* 1965; one *s* one *d*. BSc Vienna Sch. of Econs 1960, Transl. Dip. Vienna 1960, MA S Illinois 1962, DComm Vienna Sch. of Econs 1965. Member: Brit. Assoc. Applied Linguistics; Linguistics Assoc. of GB, Societas Linguistica Europaea. Lectr in Mod. Langs, UMIST, 1964–68; Lectr in Applied Linguistics, Univ. of Nottingham, 1968–74. Mem., Editorial Adv. Panel, Lebende Sprachen, 1965– ; Co-editor, Nottingham Linguistic Circular, 1971–74; Vis. Ch. Examnr for German Orals, Jt Matric. Bd, Manchester, 1967–74. *Publications*: (with F. C. Stork) Dictionary of Language and Linguistics, 1972; German Linguistics, 1973; The Language of Linguistics, 1973; *contrib*. Beitr. Sprachk. Inf. verarbeitung, Deutsche Sprache, Folia Linguistica, Incorp. Linguist, Lang. Sciences, Lebende Sprachen, Linguistics, Ling. & Didaktik, Rev. of ITL, Unterrichtspraxis. *Address*: Language Centre, Univ. of Exeter, Exeter EX4 4QH.

Hartwell, Ronald Max, MA, DPhil; Reader in Recent Social and Economic History, University of Oxford, since 1956; *b* 1921; *m* 1945; four *d*. BA Sydney 1945 (1st cl. Econs), MA Sydney 1947 (1st cl. Econs), DPhil Oxon 1956, MA Oxon 1956. Teaching Fellow in Economics, Univ. of Sydney, 1946–48; Prof. of Economic History and Dean of the Faculty of Humanities and Social Sciences, Univ. of Technology, NSW, 1950–56. Fellow Librarian of Nuffield Coll., Oxford, 1958– ; Editor, The Economic History Review, 1957–72. *Publications*: The Economic Development of Van Diemens Land, 1820–1850, 1954; ed, The Causes of the Industrial Revolution, 1967; ed, The Industrial Revolution, 1970; The Industrial Revolution and Economic Growth, 1971; *contrib*. Econ. Hist. Rev., Jl Econ. Hist. *Address*: Nuffield College, Oxford.

Harvey, Dr Adrian Michael; Lecturer, Department of Geography, University of Liverpool, since 1965; *b* 1940; two *s* one *d*. BSc London 1962, PhD London 1967; Mem., Inst. Brit. Geogrs. *Publications*: *contrib*. Jl Hydrol., Water and Water Eng., Inst. Brit. Geogrs Sp. Publn 6. *Address*: Dept of Geography, Univ. of Liverpool, PO Box 147, Liverpool L69 3BX.

Harvey, Barbara Fitzgerald; Fellow and Tutor in Modern History, Somerville College, Oxford, since 1956; *b* 1928. BA Oxon 1949 (1st cl. Hons Modern History), MA Oxon 1953, BLitt Oxon 1953; FRHistS. Asst, Dept of Scottish History, Univ. of Edinburgh, 1951–52; Asst Lectr, Queen Mary Coll., London, 1952–54, Lectr, 1954–55; Tutor, Somerville Coll., Oxford, 1955–56. *Publications*: ed (with intro.) Walter de Wenlok, Abbot of Westminster, 1283–1307 (Camden, 4th series, ii), 1965; contrib. Victoria County History, Oxon, vi; contrib. Bull. Inst. Hist. Res., Econ. Hist. Rev., Trans Roy. Hist. Soc., Jl Eccles. Hist. Address: Somerville College, Oxford.

Harvey, Prof. Brian Wilberforce; Professor of Law, Birmingham University, from April 1973; b 1936; m 1962; two s two d. BA Cantab 1957, LLB Cantab 1959, MA Cantab 1961. Solicitor (England); Assoc. Inst. of Taxation. Lectr, Birmingham Univ., 1962–63; Sen. Lectr, Nigerian Law Sch., 1965–67; Lectr, 1967–70, Sen. Lectr, 1970–71, QUB. Mem., Working Party on NI Land Law, 1967–71; Statute Law Cttee of NI, 1971. Publications: The Nigerian Law of Wills, Probate and Succession, 1968; (jtly) Survey of Northern Ireland Land Law, 1971; Settlements of Land, 1973; chapter on Northern Ireland, in, Le régime matrimonial dans les législations contemporaines, 1972; contrib. Nigerian Law Jl, NI Legal Qly, Solicitors' Jl. Address: Faculty of Law, Univ. of Birmingham, Birmingham B15 2TT.

Harvey, Francis David; Lecturer in Classics, University of Exeter, since 1965; b 1937; m 1964; one s one d. BA Oxon 1960 (1st cl. Hon. Mods 1958, 2nd cl. Lit, Hum. 1960), MA Oxon 1963; Mem.: Class. Assoc., Soc. Prom. Hellenic Studies, Soc. Prom. Roman Studies, etc. Asst Lectr in Classics (Ancient History), Univ. of Exeter, 1962–65; Sec., Classical Assoc. (SW Br.), 1963–67, 1971– ; Fellow, Center for Hellenic Studies, Washington DC, 1967–68. Mem., Council, Soc. Prom. Hellenic Studies, 1970–73. Publications: trans. (with H. M. Harvey), Reinhardt: Sophokles (forthcoming); contrib. Class. et Med., Class. Philol., Cornish Archaeol., Historia, Jl Hellenic Studies, Mnemosyne, Pegasus, REG. Address: Dept of Classics, The Queen's Building, Univ. of Exeter, Exeter, Devon.

Harvey, Jack; Lecturer in Economics, University of Reading, since 1965; b 1917; m 1952; two s three d. BSc(Econ) London 1949, DipEd Oxford 1950. Publications: Elementary Economics, 1957, 3rd edn 1971; (with L. Bather) The British Constitution, 1963, 3rd edn 1972; Intermediate Economics, 1965, 2nd edn 1970; (with M. Harvey) Producing and Spending, 1966, 3rd edn 1969; Modern Economics, 1969; (with M. K. Johnson) Workbook for Modern Economics, 1969; How Britain is Governed, 1970; (with M. K. Johnson) Introduction to Macro-economics, 1971; Multiple Choice Questions for Intermediate Economics, 1972; (with M. K. Johnson) Workbook for Introduction to Modern Economics, 1973. Address: Economics Dept, Univ. of Reading, Reading RG6 2AH.

Harvey, Dr John Robert, MA, PhD; Fellow and Lecturer in English, Emmanuel College, Cambridge, since 1969; b 1942; m 1968; one d. BA Cantab 1964 (1st cl.), MA Cantab 1968, PhD Cantab 1969. Emmanuel College, Cambridge: Research Fellow, 1967, Director of Studies, English, 1970; Praelector, 1971. Trustee, Dickens Soc., 1972.

Publications: Victorian Novelists and their Illustrators, 1970. contrib. Cambridge Qly, Princeton Univ. Library Chronicle. Address: Emmanuel College, Cambridge.

Harvey, Dr Jonathan Dean; Senior Lecturer in Music, University of Southampton, since 1973 (Lecturer, 1965–73); b 1939; m 1960; one s one d. BA Cantab 1960, PhD Glasgow 1965; MA Cantab 1971, DMus Cantab 1972; Mem., Composers' Guild GB; Mem. Cttee, ISCM (Brit. Sect.); Mem. Exec. Cttee, SPNM. Asst Lectr, Southampton Univ., 1964–65; Harkness Fellow, Princeton Univ., 1969–70. Mem., South. Arts Music Panel. Publications: musical compositions; The Music of Stockhausen, 1974; contrib. Music Rev., Perspect. New Music. Address: Dept of Music, The Univ., Southampton SO9 5NH.

Harvey, Prof. Leonard Patrick; Cervantes Professor of Spanish, King's College, University of London, since 1973; b 1929; m 1954; two s. BA Oxon 1952 (1st cl. Mod. Langs, 2nd cl. Oriental Studies 1954), MA Oxon 1956, DPhil Oxon 1958. Univ. Lectr in Spanish, Oxford, 1957–58; Lectr, Southampton Univ., 1958–60; Lectr, Queen Mary Coll., London, 1960–63; Reader, 1963–67; Vis. Prof., Victoria BC, 1966; Prof. of Spanish, Queen Mary Coll., 1967–73; Dean, Fac. of Arts, QMC, 1970–73. Publications: contrib. Al-Andalus, Bull. Hisp. Studies, Jl Semit. Studies, Misc. Estudios Arab. Hebraic. Address: Dept of Spanish, King's Coll., Strand, WC2R 2LS.

Harvey, Margaret Mary, MA, DPhil; Part-time Lecturer in History and Resident Tutor, Department of History and St Aidan's College, Durham University, since 1964; BA Oxon 1958 (2nd cl. History), MA and DPhil Oxon 1964; FRHistS, Mem., Eccles. Hist. Soc. Asst Lectr, Royal Holloway Coll., 1960–64. Publications: contrib. Studies Ch. Hist., Ann. Hist. Concil. Address: St Aidan's College, Durham Univ.

Harvey, Dr Paul Dean Adshead; Senior Lecturer, Department of History, Southampton University, since 1970; b 1930; m 1968. BA Oxon 1953, MA, DPhil Oxon 1960; FSA, FRHistS. Asst Archivist, Warwicks County Rec. Off., 1954–57; Asst Keeper, Dept of Mss, Brit. Mus., 1957–66; Lectr, Southampton Univ., 1966–70. Jt Gen. Ed., Southampton Rec. Series, 1967– ; Gen. Ed., Portsmouth Rec. Series, 1969– ; Mem., Council, Brit. Rec. Assoc., 1963–66; Libr. Cttee, Soc. Antiqu., 1966–73. Publications: (with H. Thorpe) The Printed Maps of Warwickshire, 1576–1900, 1959; A Medieval Oxfordshire Village, 1965; articles on Banbury, in, Victoria History of Oxfordshire, vol. x, 1972; Manorial Records of Cuxham, 1974; contrib. Agric. Hist. Rev., Past and Present, Econ. Hist. Rev. Address: Dept of History, The Univ., Southampton SO9 5NH.

Harvey, Ruth Charlotte, MA, PhD; Fellow and Tutor in German, St Anne's College, Oxford, since 1971, and Lecturer, Faculty of Modern Languages, Oxford, since 1959; b 1918. BA Oxon 1938 (1st cl. Mod. Langs),

299

MA Oxon 1942, Dip. Comparative Philology (Dist.), Oxon 1940, PhD St Andrew's 1959. Asst Lectr, Westfield Coll., 1943–46; Lectr, St Andrews, 1950–58; Supernum. Fellow, and Lectr in German, St Anne's Coll., Oxford, 1959–71. Educn Br., Brit. Mil. Govt, Berlin, 1946–50; Mem., Gov. Body, Westminster Coll., Oxford, 1969– . *Publications*: Moriz von Craûn and the Chivalric World, 1961; ed, Der Ritter vom Turn (forthcoming); Prolegomena to an Edition of Der Ritter vom Turn, in, Probleme mittelalterlicher Überlieferung u. Textkritik, 1968; *contrib*. Germ. Life Lett., Med. Æv., PBB (Tüb.). *Address*: St Anne's College, Oxford OX2 6HS.

Harvey, Dr Sally Patricia Joyce; Lecturer in History, University of Leeds, since 1971; *b* 1941. BA Birmingham 1963, MA Cantab 1966, PhD Birmingham 1972; FRHistS. Fellow, Girton Coll., Cambridge, 1966–71; Sub-Warden, Charles Morris Hall, 1972– . *Publications*: *contrib*. Econ. Hist. Rev., Eng. Hist. Rev., Past and Present. *Address*: School of History, Univ. of Leeds, Leeds LS2 9JT.

Harvey, Dr Simon; Lecturer in French, Westfield College, University of London, since 1970; *b* 1941. BA Cantab 1963, PhD Cantab 1971. Teaching Fellow in French, Univ. of Michigan, 1963–64; Asst Lectr in French, Univ. of Manchester, 1967–70; Course Tutor in Arts, Open Univ., 1972–73. *Address*: Wolfson House, Westfield College, Kidderpore Avenue, NW3 7ST.

Haskell, Prof. Francis James Herbert, FBA; Professor of Art History, Oxford University, and Fellow of Trinity College, Oxford, since 1967; *b* 1928; *m* 1965. BA Cantab 1950, MA Cantab 1955; FBA 1971. Fellow, King's Coll., Cambridge, 1954–67; Librarian of Fine Arts Faculty, Cambridge Univ., 1962–67. Junior Library Clerk, House of Commons, 1953–54. *Publications*: Patrons and Painters: a study of the relations between Art and Society in the Age of the Baroque, 1963; Géricault (The Masters), 1966; *contrib*. Burlington Mag., Jl Warburg Inst., New Statesman, NY Rev. of Books, etc. *Address*: Trinity College, Oxford OX1 2HG.

Haskell, Dr Simon Hai; Tutor and Lecturer i/c DipEd Physically Handicapped Children Course, Department of Child Development and Educational Psychology, University of London Institute of Education, since 1970; *b* 1928; *m* 1956; one *s* two *d*. BA Calcutta 1950, BT Calcutta 1954 (1st cl.), Academic Diploma in Educn, London, 1957, MA London 1959, PhD London 1969; ABPsS; Member: Assoc. of Child Psychologists and Psychiatrists; Assoc. of Univ. Teachers. Trained as Educational Psychologist, Tavistock Clinic, 1959–60; Lecturer, Dept of Child Develt and Educnl Psychology, Univ. of London Inst. of Educn, 1965. Member: Univ. of London Central Academic Bd; Subcttee on courses for handicapped children; Adv. Cttee on courses relating to educn of handicapped children; Adv. Cttee on Special Educn, ILEA; Educn Commn, Internat. Soc. for Rehabilitation of Disabled; Chm, Bishops Stortford and District Soc. for Mentally Handicapped. *Publications*: Elective Mutism: The child who does not talk, in, Clinics in Developmental Medicine, 1963; Some speculations on effects of sensory deprivation upon cerebral palsied infants and adults, in, Learning Problems of the Cerebrally Palsied, 1964; Programmed instruction and the mentally retarded, in, The Application of Research to the Education and Training of the Severely Subnormal Child, ed H. C. Gunzburg, 1966; (co-author) The Psychological Assessment of Young Cerebral Palsied and Brain Damaged Children in Uganda, 1969; (co-author) Getting Ready to Read, 1971; (co-author) Training in Basic Cognitive Skills (28 workbooks), 1972; Arithmetical Disabilities in Cerebral Palsied Children, Illinois 1973; Why Special Education?, 1973; Training in Motor Skills (8 booklets), 1973; (co-author) Training in Basic Cognitive Skills: Training in Motor Skills (manual), 1973; (co-author) Look I'm Reading, in, New Reading Scheme, 1974; Handicapped children, in, Educational Research in Britain, vol. 3, ed H. J. Butcher and H. B. Pont; Programmed instruction for physically handicapped children: some educational and sociological implications, in, Advances in the Care of the Mentally Handicapped, ed H. C. Gunzburg; Report of Survey in Psychological and Educational Handicaps in Pupils Attending Eugeniahemmet; contrib.: Commun. II Congress. Pedosich., 1963; Internat. Copenhagen Congress on Sci. Study Mental Retard., 1964; Proc. 11th World Congress, ISRDk 1970; Proc. Preview 12th World Congr. Rehab. Internat., ISRD, 1972; Proc. 5th Internat. Seminar Special Educn, 1972; Proc. Conf. Mentally Handicapped, 1972; Proc. Conf., Dr Barnardo's, Liverpool; *contrib*. Jl Educnl Res., Brit. Orthopt. Jl, Jl Ment. Subnorm., Spec. Educn, Jl Spec. Educn, Irish Jl Educn, Develt Med. Child Neurol., Sygepae dagogen, Brit. Jl Ment. Subnorm., Teaching Atyp. Stud. Alberta, Slow Learn. Child, Percept. Motor Skills. *Address*: Univ. of London Institute of Education, Malet Street, WC1E 7HS.

Haslam, Richard B., BComm; Lecturer (Part-time), Public Administration Department, University College, Cork, since 1962; *b* 1925; *m* 1969; one *s* one *d*. BComm Cork 1951. Town Clerk, Youghal, 1954–58; City Acntnt, Cork Corpn, 1958–63; County Sec., Limerick CC, 1963–65; Asst County Mngr, Cork CC, 1966–70; County Mngr, Limerick CC, 1970– . *Address*: Public Administration Dept, Univ. College, Cork.

Hassall, Mark William Cory, MA, FSA; Lecturer, Archaeology of the Roman Provinces, Institute of Archaeology, London University, since 1968; *b* 1940. BA Oxon 1963 (Classics), MA Oxon 1967, Dip. in Archaeology London 1965 (Distinction); FSA. Asst Lectr, London Univ., 1966–68. *Publications*: The Romans, 1971. *Address*: Institute of Archaeology, 31–4 Gordon Square, WC1H 0PY.

Hassell Smith, A.; *see* Smith, A. H.

Hasson, Reuben Alex, LLM; Lecturer in Law, Queen Mary College, London, since

1971; *b* 1938. BA Cape Town 1958 (Dist. in Roman Law, Constitutional Law and African Law), LLB LSE 1962 (2nd cl.), LLM Yale 1968. Asst Lectr SOAS 1962–66; Res. Associate, Yale Law Sch., 1968–69; Teaching Fellow, Stanford Law Sch., 1969–70. *Publications*: (with Prof. S. A. de Smith and L. H. Leigh) chap., in, Annual Survey of Commonwealth Law, 1966; *contrib*. Mod. Law Rev., Public Law. *Address*: Fac. of Law, Queen Mary College, Mile End Road, E1 4NS.

Hatcher, Dr (Melvyn) John; Lecturer, History Department, University of Kent, since 1967; *b* 1942; *m* 1967. BSc(Econ) London 1964 (1st cl.), PhD London 1967. *Publications*: Rural Economy and Society in the Duchy of Cornwall, 1300–1500, 1970; English Tin Production and Trade to 1550, 1973; A History of British Pewter, 1974; *contrib*. Agric. Hist. Rev., Econ. Hist. Rev. *Address*: Eliot College, The Univ., Canterbury, Kent.

Hattaway, Dr Michael, MA, PhD; Lecturer in English, University of Kent at Canterbury, since 1966; *b* 1941; *m* 1965. BA New Zealand 1962, MA Wellington 1963 (1st cl. English), PhD Cantab 1967. Asst Lectr, Victoria Univ. of Wellington, 1963–66; Vis. Asst Prof., Univ. of Brit. Columbia, 1970–71. *Publications*: ed, Beaumont: The Knight of the Burning Pestle, 1969; *contrib*. Jl Hist. Ideas, Renaiss. Drama. *Address*: Eliot College, The Univ., Canterbury, Kent CT1 3PA.

Hatto, Prof. Arthur Thomas, MA; Head of the Department of German, Queen Mary College, University of London, since 1938; *b* 1910; *m* 1935; one *d*. BA London 1931, MA London 1934 (with Distinction); FRAI, FRAS, Fellow, King's Coll., London, 1971. Lektor für Englisch, Univ. of Berne, 1932–34; Asst Lectr in English, KCL, 1934–38; Pt-time Lectr in German, UCL, 1944–45; Reader in German Lang. and Lit., 1946–53; Prof. of German Lang. and Lit., 1953, Univ. of London; Lectured Tübingen, Heidelberg, Munich, Göttingen, 1961; Vienna, Graz, Salzburg, Innsbruck, 1971; Vis. Prof. of German, Auckland, 1965; Foundn Day Lectr, SOAS, 1970. Governor: SOAS, Univ. of London, 1960; Queen Mary Coll., Univ. of London, 1968–70; Chm., London Seminar on Epic; Cttee 'A' (Theol. and Arts) Central Res. Fund, Univ. of London, 1969. *Publications*: (with R. J. Taylor) The Songs of Neidhart von Reuental, 1958; Gottfried von Strassburg, Tristan (trans. entire for first time) with Tristan of Thomas (newly trans.) with an Introduction, 1960; The Nibelungenlied: a new trans., with introduction and notes, 1964; ed, Eos (an enquiry by 50 scholars into the theme of the alba in world literature), 1965; *contrib*. learned periodicals. *Address*: Queen Mary College, Mile End Road, E1 4NS.

Hatton, Peter Harry Sverre; Lecturer in History, Westfield College, London University, since 1967; *b* 1940; *m* 1964, divorced 1971. BA Cantab 1962 (1st cl. History), MA Cantab 1965, PhD Cantab 1972. Asst Lectr, Westfield Coll., London, 1965–67. *Publications*: *contrib*. Europ. Studies Rev.,

Hist., Jl Af. Hist., Past and Present, Eng. Hist. Rev., Jl Imperial and Commonwealth Hist. *Address*: History Dept, Westfield College, Univ. of London, Kidderpore Avenue, NW3 7ST.

Hatton, Prof. Ragnhild Marie; Professor of International History, University of London, since 1968; *b* 1913; *m* 1936; two *s*. Cand Mag Oslo 1936, PhD London 1947; FRHistS, Corresp. Mem. (Swedish), Kungl. Vitterhets, Hist. Antikv. Akad. Pt-time Tutor, Westfield Coll., London, 1948–49; Asst Lectr, LSE, 1949–50; Lectr, 1950–58; Reader, 1958–68; Mershon Prof., State Univ. of Ohio, Columbus (on leave of absence), 1964 (fall semester); Rose Morgan Prof., State Univ. of Kansas, Lawrence (on leave of absence), 1968 (fall semester). *Publications*: Diplomatic Relations (Anglo-Dutch) 1714–21, 1950; Captain James Jefferyes' Letters from the Swedish Army 1707–09, 1954; Charles XII of Sweden, 1968; War and Peace 1680–1720, 1969; Europe in the Age of Louis XIV, 1969, French edn 1970, Portuguese edn 1971; Louis XIV and his World, 1972; co-ed, William III and Louis XIV, 1968; Studies in Diplomatic History, 1970; ed, History of European Ideas, 1972; *contrib*. New Cambridge Modern History vols VI, 1970 and VII, 1957; Studies in International History, ed K. Bourne and D. C. Watt, 1967; Louis XIV and the Craft of Kingship, ed J. C. Rule, 1969; *contrib*. Bull. Inst., Europ. Studies Rev., Hist., Hist. Tids. (Sweden), Hist. Tids. (Norway), Jl Army Hist. Res., Scott. Geneal., etc. *Address*: Dept of International History, London School of Economics (Univ. of London), Houghton Street, WC2A 2AE.

Hatwell, John Michael, BA; Lecturer in Italian, University of Birmingham, since 1966; *b* 1928; *m* 1968; two *s*. BA London 1963; Mem., Soc. Ital. Studies. Asst Lectr, Univ. Coll., London, 1963–65; Lectr, Sheffield Univ., 1965–66. 'A' Level Examiner, Italian, JMB, 1968– ; Ed. Asst Ital. Studies, 1969– ; Gen. Ed. St George's Press and Hamish Hamilton ELT series. *Publications*: *contrib*. Yrs Wk Mod. Lang. Studies. *Address*: Dept of Italian, Univ. of Birmingham, PO Box 363, Birmingham B15 2TT.

Haughton, Prof. Joseph Pedlow, MA, MSc, MRIA; Professor of Geography, University of Dublin, since 1966; *b* 1920; *m* 1953; two *s* two *d*. BA Dublin 1941 (Moderatorship in Natural Sciences), MSc Dublin 1943; Mem. Council, Royal Irish Acad. Asst Lecturer, TCD, 1944–56; Reader, 1956–66; Prof. of Geography and Dean, Fac. of Arts, Univ. of Lagos, 1963–64; Fellow, TCD, 1967– . Past-Pres., Geog. Soc. Ireland; Mem., Irish Nat. Cttee for Geog.; Council Mem., Inst. Brit. Geog., 1956–57; Nat. Soc. Science Council, 1970– ; Mem., Exec., Irish Freedom from Hunger Council, 1968– ; Friends' World Cttee, 1970– . *Publications*: *contrib*. Geog. Rev., Econ. Geog., Irish Geog. *Address*: Dept of Geography, Trinity College, Univ. of Dublin, Dublin 2.

Havard-Williams, Prof. Peter; Professor of Library Studies and Head of Department

301

of Library and Information Studies, Loughborough University of Technology, since 1972; *m*; two *d*. BA Wales 1943, DipEd Oxon 1945, MA Wales 1949; ALA 1952, ANZLA 1958, FLAI 1970. Sub-Librarian, Univ. of Liverpool, 1951–56; Librarian and Keeper of Hocken Collection, Univ. of Otago, 1956–60; Dep. Librarian, Univ. of Leeds, 1960–61; Librarian, 1961–71, and Dir Sch. of Library and Information Studies, 1964–70, QUB. Dean and Prof. Library Sch., Univ. of Ottawa, 1971–72. Vice-Pres., Internat. Fedn of Library Assocs, 1970– ; Vice-Pres., Library Assoc., 1968–70, 1974– ; Member: Adv. Cttee on Public Library Service, Northern Ireland, 1964–65; CNAA Librarianship Bd, 1970– ; Consultant for several new university library buildings in UK and abroad, 1960– . *Publications*: *contrib.* Jl Lib., An Leabh., Libr, Unesco Bull. for Libs, NZ Libs. *Address*: Loughborough Univ. of Technology, Loughborough, Leics LE11 3TU.

Havinden, Michael Ashley, MA, BLitt; Lecturer in Economic History, University of Exeter, since 1965; *b* 1928; *m* 1954; one *d*. BA Cambridge 1950 (2nd cl. (i) History), MA Cambridge, 1959, BLitt Oxford 1961; Mem.: Econ. Hist. Soc., Agric. Hist. Soc. Farmer, 1950–57. Res. Asst, Reading Univ., 1960–63; Vis. Lectr, Sierra Leone Univ., 1966, 1969–70. Hist. Asst, Survey of London, 1964–65; Sec., Brit. Agric. Hist. Soc., 1966– ; Mem., Stand. Cttee on Univ. Studies of Africa, 1971–. *Publications*: ed, Household and Farm Inventories in Oxfordshire, 1550–1590, 1965; ed jtly, People in the Countryside, 1965; Estate Villages, 1966; ed jtly, Rural Change and Urban Growth 1500–1800, Essays in English Regional History in Honour of W.G. Hoskins, 1974; *contrib.* Agric. Hist. Rev., Econ. Hist. Rev. *Address*: Dept of Economic History, Univ. of Exeter, Exeter EX4 4QJ.

Hawcroft, Francis Wilson, BA, FMA; Keeper of the Whitworth Art Gallery, and Lecturer in Art History, University of Manchester, since 1959; *b* 1925. BA London 1951 (History of Art); FMA 1972. Dep. Curator, Norwich Castle Mus., 1951–59; Mem.: Norwich Triennial Festival Cttee, 1956–59; Art Panel, Arts Council, 1961–63, 1970–72; Exec. Cttee, Georgian Gp, 1964– ; Pres., NW Federn of Mus. and Gall., 1967–68; Council, Mus. Assoc., 1968–71; Dir, Northern Dance Theatre, 1969– . *Publications*: A Visual History of Modern Britain: The Arts, 1967; various exhibition catalogues including John Crome: Bicentenary (Arts Council), 1968; Water Colours by J. R. Cozens (Whitworth and V and A), 1971; *contrib.* Burl. Mag., Country Life, Connoisseur, Gaz. Beaux Arts, Old Water-Colour Soc., Museums Jl, Museum. *Address*: Whitworth Art Gallery, Univ. of Manchester, Manchester M15 6ER.

Hawkes, Dr Ron; Lecturer in Environmental Studies, University College London, since 1971; *b* 1943; *m*; one *d*. BSc 1963 (Psychol.), PhD 1969, (Environmental Des.), UCL. Hon. Res. Asst, UCL, 1964. Member: Nat. Illumination Cttee, 1973– ; Lighting Quality Panel, IES, 1972– ; Consultant: DES, 1967– ; DoE, 1970– . *Publications*: *contrib.* Acustica, Bldg, Educn, Jl Arch. Res. and

302

Teach., Jl Amer. Inst. Plann., Jl Traffic Engr. and Contr. *Address*: Sch. of Environmental Studies, University Coll. London, Gower Street, WC1E 6BT.

Hawkes, Dr Terence Frederick, MA, PhD; Senior Lecturer in English, University College, Cardiff, since 1967; *b* 1932; *m* 1961; two *s*. BA Wales 1955, MA Wales 1958, PhD Wales 1963. Instructor/Asst Prof., State Univ. of NY, Buffalo, 1957–59; Asst Lectr, Univ. Coll., Cardiff, 1959–60; Lectr, Univ. Coll., Aberystwyth, 1960–61; Lectr, Univ. Coll., Cardiff, 1961–67; Vis. Prof., State Univ. of NY, Buffalo, 1963; Univ. of Waterloo, Ontario, 1968, 1969; Rutgers Univ., NJ, 1971. *Publications*: ed, Coleridge's Writings on Shakespeare, 1959, British Edn 1969; (with E. L. Epstein) Linguistics and English Prosody, 1959; Shakespeare and the Reason, 1964; Metaphor, 1972; Shakespeare's Talking Animals, 1973; *contrib.* Lang. Style. Mod. Lang. Rev., Notes Queries, Rev. Engl. Lit., Rev. Engl. Studies, Shakesp. Qly, Shakesp. Surv., TLS, THES. *Address*: Dept of English, Univ. College, Cardiff CF1 1XL.

Hawkins, Christopher James; Lecturer, Department of Economics, University of Southampton, since 1965; *b* 1937. BA Bristol 1959. *Publications*: Capital Investment Appraisal, 1971; Theory of the Firm, 1973. *contrib.* AER, JIE. *Address*: Dept of Economics, Univ. of Southampton, Highfield, Southampton SO9 5NH.

Hawkins, David Cedric; Lecturer in International Politics, Department of Extra-Mural Studies, University of Southampton, since 1949; *b* 1921; *m* 1945; two *s* one *d*. BSc(Econ) London 1949. *Publications*: The Defence of Malaysia and Singapore, 1972; *contrib.* Asian Surv., Wld Surv., Wld Today. *Address*: Dept of Extra-Mural Studies, The Univ., Southampton SO9 5NH.

Hawkins, Prof. Eric William, CBE, MA, FIL; Professor of Education, and Director of Language Teaching Centre, University of York, since 1965; *b* 1915; *m* 1938; one *s* one *d*. BA Cantab 1936 (Spanish and French), MA Cantab 1946, CertEd Cantab 1937; Fellow Inst Linguists 1971. Gov., Centre Information Lang. Teaching, 1968– ; Mem.: Nat. Adv. Council England (Plowden Cttee), 1963–67; Nat. Cttee Commonwealth Immigrants, 1965–68; Chm., Mod. Lang. Cttee, Schs Council, 1968– . *Publications*: ed, Modern Languages in the Grammar School, 1961, rev. edn 1966; ed (with D. S. Mair), New Patterns in Sixth Form Modern Language Teaching, 1970; A Time For Growing – Handbook on Summer Projects for disadvantaged children, 1971; contrib. Post O Level Studies in Modern Languages, ed C. V. Russell, 1970. *Address*: Language Teaching Centre, The Univ., York YO1 5DD.

Hawkins, John David; Lecturer in Ancient Anatolian Languages, Near and Middle East Department, University of London, since 1967; *b* 1940. BA Oxon 1962 (Lit. Hum.), Dip. Archaeol. London 1964. Res. Fellow in Hittite, SOAS, 1964–67. *Publications*: (jtly) Hittite Hieroglyphs and Luwian: new evidence for the connection (Nachrichten der Göttinger Akad. der Wissenschaft, 1973); *contrib*. Revue Hittite et Asianique, Anatolian Studies, Reallexikon der Assyriologie. *Address*: Sch. of Oriental and African Studies, Univ. of London, Malet Street, WC1E 7HP.

Hawkins, Peter Gerald; Lecturer in French, University of Bristol, since 1968; *b* 1942; *m* 1966. BA London 1964 (1st cl. French), MA London 1967 (Distinction French). Ecole Normale Supérieure, Rue d'Ulm, Paris, 1964–65; Lecteur, Inst. Etudes Angl. et Nord-Amer., Paris, 1966–68. *Publications*: Vers et Prose, in, L'Année 1913: les formes esthétiques de l'œuvre d'art à la veille de la première guerre mondiale, ed L. Brion-Guerry, 1971. *Address*: Dept of French, Wills Memorial Building, Queen's Road, Bristol BS8 1RJ.

Hawkridge, Prof. David Graham; Professor of Applied Educational Sciences, and Director of Institute of Educational Technology, The Open University, since 1970; *b* 1933; *m* 1956; one *s* three *d*. BA 1952, MA 1953, BEd 1954, STC 1954, Cape Town, PhD London 1963; ABPsS. Lectr in Educn, Rhodesia and Nyasaland, 1961–67. Sen. Res. Scientist, Amer. Insts for Res., 1967–70. *Publications*: (with W. D. Michie) A Secondary Geography of Central Africa, 1965, 3rd edn 1968; (with P. L. Campeau and P. K. Trickett) Preparing Evaluation Reports of Educational Programs: a guide for authors, 1969; (with W. Schramm and H. H. Howe) An Everyman's University for Israel, 1972; *contrib*. Jl Assoc. Programmed Learning, Jl Med. Educ., Brit. Jl Med. Educ., Jl Ed. Tech., AV Comm. Rev., Educ. Broadcasting Internat. *Address*: The Open Univ., Milton Keynes MK7 6AA.

Hawthorn, Geoffrey Patrick; University Lecturer in Sociology, Social and Political Sciences Commitee, and Fellow of Churchill College, Cambridge, since 1970; *b* 1941; *m* 1969; one *s*. BA Oxon 1962. Lectr in Sociology, Essex Univ., 1964–70; Vis. Prof. of Sociology and Demography, Harvard Univ., 1973. *Publications*: The Sociology of Fertility, 1970; *contrib*. Demography, Human Relations, Jl Biosocial Science, Quaderni Storici, Science Studies, Sociology. *Address*: Churchill College, Cambridge CB3 0DS.

Hawthorne, Prof. Sir William (Rede), CBE, FRS, MA, ScD, FIMechE, FRAeS; Master of Churchill College, Cambridge, since 1968; Hopkinson and ICI Professor of Applied Thermodynamics, University of Cambridge, since 1951; Head of Department of Engineering, 1968–73; *b* 1913; *m* 1939; one *s* two *d*. FRS 1955. Mem., Council, Royal Soc., 1968–70; a Vice-Pres., Royal Soc., 1969–70. Assoc. Prof. of Mechanical Engineering, 1946; George Westinghouse Prof. of Mech. Engineering, 1948; Massachusetts Inst. of Technology; Jerome C. Hunsaker Prof. of Aeronautical Engng, MIT, 1955–56. Vis. Inst. Prof., MIT, 1962–63. Develop. Engr, Babcock and Wilcox Ltd, 1937–39; Scientific Off., RAE, 1940–44; Brit. Air Commn, Washington, 1944; Dep. Dir, Engine Research, Min. of Supply, 1945;

Dir, Dracone Develop. Ltd, 1958– . Foreign Associate, US Nat. Acad. of Sciences, 1965; Chm., Advisory Council on Scientific Res. and Technical Develop., 1966–71; Governor, Westminster Sch., 1956– . Medal of Freedom (US), 1947. *Publications*: Secondary Circulation in Fluid Flow, 1951; Some Aerodynamic Problems of Aircraft Engines, 1957; (ed) Aerodynamics of Turbines and Compressors, vol. x, High Speed Aerodynamics and Jet Propulsion, 1964; *contrib*. papers in mechanical and aeronautical jls. *Address*: The Master's Lodge, Churchill College, Cambridge.

Hay, Alan Malcolm; Lecturer, Department of Geography, University of Sheffield, since 1972; *b* 1942; *m* 1967; two *s* one *d*. MA Cantab 1966, PhD Cantab 1967. Assoc. Res. Fellow, Univ. Ibadan, 1965–66; Lectr, Univ. Leicester, 1967–71; Res. Assoc., Univ. Wisconsin, 1969–70; Vis. Prof., Univ. Washington, 1973. Mem., Editorial Bd, Jl Transport History. *Publications*: Interregional Trade and Money Flows in Nigeria 1964, 1970; Transport for the Space Economy, 1973; *contrib*. Econ. Geog., Geog. Analysis, Jl Transport Econs and Policy, Jl Transport History. *Address*: Dept of Geography, Univ. of Sheffield, Sheffield S10 2TN.

Hay, Andrew Leslie; Lecturer in Taxation Law, University of Aberdeen, since 1961; *b* 1905; *m* 1933; two *s* one *d*. MA Aberdeen 1925, LLB 1927; Lectr in Procedure and Evidence, Aberdeen Univ., 1945–64. *Address*: Law Dept, Taylor Building, Old Aberdeen, AB9 2UB.

Hay, Brigitte Elisabeth; Lecturer in German, Department of Language Studies, London School of Economics; *b* 1926; *m* 1969. BA London 1942 (Hons German), MA London 1944 (German). Recognised teacher, Univ. of London. *Publications*: var. edns, articles and reviews. *Address*: London School of Economics, Houghton Street, WC2A 2AE.

Hay, David; *see* Hay, J. D. L.

Hay, Prof. Denys, Hon. DLitt, FBA; Professor of Medieval History, University of Edinburgh, since 1954; *b* 1915; *m* 1937; one *s* two *d*. BA Oxon 1937 (1st cl. History), MA Oxon 1945; Hon. DLitt Newcastle 1970; FBA, FRHistS, FSA Scot. Sen. Demy, Magdalen Coll., Oxford, 1938; Temp Lectr, Glasgow Univ., 1938–39; Asst Lectr, Univ. Coll., Southampton, 1939–40; Lectr, Edinburgh Univ., 1945–54; Lit. Dir, RHistS, 1955–58; Ed., EHR, 1958–65; Italian Lectr, Brit. Acad., 1959; Wiles Lectr, Belfast, 1960; Vis. Prof., Cornell Univ., 1963; Sen. Fellow, Newberry Libr., Chicago, 1966; Birkbeck Lectr, Trinity Coll., Cambridge, 1971. Army 1940–42; Official historian, Cabinet Off., 1942–45; Pres., Hist. Assoc., 1967–70; Trustee, Nat. Libr. Scot., 1966– ; Vice-Principal, Edinburgh Univ., 1971–74. *Publications*: Anglica Historia of P. Vergil, 1950; P. Vergil, 1952; From Roman Empire to Renaissance Europe, 1953, reissued as The Medieval Centuries, 1964; ed, R. K. Hannay: Letters of James V, 1954; Europe, the Emergence of an Idea, 1957, 2nd edn 1968;

Italian Renaissance in its Historical Background, 1961, German edn 1962, Italian edn 1966; (with M. M. Postan and J. D. Scott) Design and Development of Weapons (History of Second World War), 1964; Europe in the XIV and XV Cents, 1966, French edn 1972; (with W. K. Smith) Aeneas Sylvius Piccolomini, De gestis concilii Basiliensis, 1967; contrib. Bull. Inst. Hist. Res., EHR, Scott. Hist. Rev. Address: History Dept, William Robertson Building, George Square, Edinburgh EH8 9JY.

Hay, Donald Andrew; Fellow and Tutor in Economics, Jesus College, Oxford, since 1970; b 1944; m 1967; one s one d. BA Cantab 1965, MA Cantab 1969, BPhil Oxon 1968 (Econs). Asst Res. Officer, Oxford Univ. Inst. of Econs and Statistics, 1968–69; Foreign Area Fellow of American Council of Learned Socs and Social Science, Research Council of America, in Brazil, 1969–70. Address: Jesus College, Oxford.

Hay, (John) David (Lumsden); Lecturer in Education, Nottingham University, since 1966; b 1935; m 1964; three s. BSc (Hons), Aberdeen 1958, MSc Nottingham 1961, DipEd Nottingham 1966; MIBiol. Vice-Chm., Catholic Renewal Movement, 1969–70. Publications: Human Populations, 1973 (TES Educational Information Book of the Year Award, 1973); contrib. Converg., New Blackfr., Newman, Christ. Renew. Address: School of Education, Nottingham Univ., Nottingham NG7 2RD.

Hay, Rev. Raymond; Tutor in Theology, St John's College, Durham University, since 1968; b 1938; m 1964; one s one d. BScEcon QUB 1960, BD TCD 1968, DipTh, Durham 1962. Address: St John's College, Durham DH1 3RJ.

Hayes, John; Lecturer in Management Studies, Department of Management Studies, University of Leeds, since 1967; b 1943; m 1965; one s one d. BSc (Econ) Hull 1965, PhD Leeds 1970; Mem.: Gp Relat. Training Assoc., Organisat. Develop. Ntwk. Res. Asst, Dept of Psychology, Univ. of Leeds, 1965–66; Asst Lectr, Dept of Management Studies, Univ. of Leeds, 1966–67. Dir of Studies, MA progr. in Organisat. Studies, Univ. of Leeds, 1969– . Publications: The Theory and Practice of Vocational Guidance, a collection of readings, 1968; Careers Guidance: the role of the school in vocational development, 1971; Occupational Perceptions and Occupational Information: An Analysis of the way in which work is perceived before and after employment, 1971; contrib. Educl Res., Guid. Counsel., Tech. Educn Abstracts, Interpers. Develop., Occupat. Psychol., Vocat. Asp. Educn. Address: Dept of Management Studies, Univ. of Leeds, Leeds LS2 9JT.

Hayes, Dr Paul Martin, MA, DPhil; Fellow and Tutor in Modern History and Politics, Keble College, University of Oxford, since 1965, and University Lecturer in International History, since 1973 (in International Relations, 1965–73); b 1942; m 1966. Dip. Dijon 1960, Dip. Marburg 1961, BA Oxon 1963 (1st cl. History), MA Oxon 1967, DPhil Oxon 1969. Dir of Studies in Internat. Relat., Foreign Service Course, Oxford, 1968– ; Jun. Dean, Keble Coll., 1966–71; Sen. Dean, 1971– . Publications: Quisling: The career and political ideas of Vidkun Quisling, 1887–1945, 1971; Fascism, 1973; contrib. EHR, Hist. Studies, Hist. Today, Jl Contemp. Hist., Rev. Hist. 2ème Guerre Mond. Address: Keble College, Oxford.

Hayes-McCoy, Prof. Gerard A., MA, PhD, DLitt, MRIA; Professor of History, University College, Galway, since 1958; b 1911; m 1941; two s three d. BA NUI 1931, BComm NUI 1931, MA NUI 1932, PhD Edinburgh 1934, DLitt NUI 1950; MRIA 1949. Travelling student, NUI, 1935–37; Asst, Nat. Mus. Ireland, 1939–53; Asst Keeper, 1953–58. Vice-Pres., Mil. Hist. Soc. Ireland, 1949– ; Cdr Order of Naval Merit, Argentina, 1957; Mem., Irish MSS Commn, 1960– . Publications: Scots Mercenary Forces in Ireland, 1937; ed, Historical Studies IV, 1963; Ulster and other Irish maps c. 1600, 1964; ed, The Irish at War, 1965; Sixteenth Century Irish Swords, 1966; M. W. Keogh, US Army (O'Donnell Lecture), 1967; Irish Battles, 1969; contrib. Irish Hist. Studies, Irish Sword, Jl Arms Armour Soc., Jl Royal Soc. Antiquaries Ireland, Studies. Address: Dept of History, Univ. College, Galway, Ireland.

Hayhurst, Dr George; Lecturer in Financial Control, University of Lancaster, since 1970; b 1939; m 1971. BSc Manchester 1961, MSc Loughborough 1966, PhD Loughborough 1971; AFIMA, AMBIM. Res. Fellow. In Management, Dept of Industrial Engineering and Management, Loughborough Univ. of Technol., 1966–68; Lectr in Management Science, 1968–70. Publications: contrib. IFAC; Jl Business Fin., Jl Business Policy, Opl. Res. Q., Product, Eng. Address: Dept of Financial Control, Univ. of Lancaster, Lancaster LA1 4YW.

Haynes, Dr Valerie Mildred; Lecturer, Geography Department, University of Strathclyde, since 1967; b 1941. Scholarship Girton Coll., Cambridge, 1960, BA Cantab 1963 (Hons), MA Cantab 1967, PhD Cantab 1972; Mem.: Royal Geographical Soc.; Glaciological Soc.; Inst. of British Geographers; Royal Scottish Geographical Soc.; Edinburgh Geological Soc.; Quaternary Res. Assoc. Tutor, Geography Dept, University Coll., Swansea, 1966–67. Publications: contrib. Geograf. Annal., Nature. Address: Dept of Geography, Livingstone Tower, Univ. of Strathclyde, Glasgow G1 1XH.

Hayter, Sir William Goodenough, KCMG; Warden of New College, Oxford, since 1958; b 1906; m 1938; one d. Entered HM Diplomatic Service, 1930; served Foreign Office, 1930; Vienna, 1931; Moscow, 1934; Foreign Office, 1937; China, 1938; Washington, 1941; Foreign Office, 1944 (Asst Under Sec. of State, 1948); HM Minister, Paris, 1949; Ambassador to USSR, 1953–57; Deputy Under-Sec. of State, Foreign Office, 1957–58. Fellow of Winchester Coll. Chm., UGC Cttee Oriental, Slavonic, East European and

African Studies, 1961; Mem., Standing Commn on Museums and Galleries, 1962–70; Pres., Anglo-Austrian Soc.; Trustee, British Museum, 1960–70. Grosses Goldenes Ehrenzeichen mit dem Stern für Verdienste (Austria), 1967. *Publications*: The Diplomacy of the Great Powers, 1961; The Kremlin and the Embassy, 1966; Russia and the World, 1970; William of Wykeham, Patron of the Arts, 1970. *Address*: The Warden's Lodgings, New College, Oxford.

Hayton, David John; Fellow, Jesus College, Cambridge, and Assistant Lecturer in Law, University of Cambridge, since 1973; *b* 1944; *m* 1973. LLB Newcastle 1966 (1st cl. Hons), MA Cantab 1973; Barrister 1968. Univ. of Sheffield: Asst Lectr, 1966–68; Lectr, 1968–69; Lectr, Queen Mary Coll., London, 1970–73. *Publications*: Registered Land, 1973; *contrib*. Conveyancer, Law Qly. Review. *Address*: Jesus College, Cambridge CB5 8BL

Hayward, Prof. Jack Ernest Shalom; Professor of Politics, University of Hull, since 1973; *b* 1931; *m* 1965; one *d*. BSc(Econ) London 1952, PhD London 1958. Asst Lectr and Lectr, Sheffield Univ., 1959–63; Lectr and Sen. Lectr in Politics, Keele, 1963–73; Sen. Res. Fellow, Nuffield Coll., Oxford, 1968–69. *Publications*: Private Interests and Public Policy: the experience of the French economic and social council, 1966; The One and Indivisible French Republic, 1973; *contrib*. Brit. Jl of Ind. Rels, Int. Rev. Soc. Hist., Parl. Aff., Pol. Studies, Rev. Française de Sociologie, Sociological Rev. *Address*: Dept of Political Studies, Univ. of Hull, Hull HU6 7RX.

Haywood, John Alfred; Reader in Arabic, School of Oriental Studies, University of Durham, since 1967; *b* 1913; *m* 1948. BA Sheffield 1935 (History), MA Sheffield 1936, DipEd Sheffield 1936, BMus Durham 1936; FRAsiatSoc, Mem., Asiat. Soc. Bangladesh, AUT. Sudan Civil Service, 1946–55; Lectr in Arabic, Durham, 1955–63; Sen. Lectr, 1963–67. Comd TA, 1938, Army (Major), Indian Army, Burma, etc., 1939–46. *Publications*: Arabic Lexicography, 1959, 2nd edn 1965; (with M. Nahmad) A Modern Arabic Grammar, 1962, 2nd edn 1965; Modern Arabic Literature, 1971; Helen of Kirkconnell (Pt-song), 1969; *contrib*. Encyclop. Brit., Encyclop. of Islam, Urdu Encyclop. of Islam; *contrib*. Acta Orient., Composer, Durham Univ. Jl, Jl Royal Asiat. Soc. *Address*: School of Oriental Studies, Elvet Hill, Durham.

Haywood, Stuart Collingwood; Lecturer, Department of Social Administration, University of Hull; si nce 1936; *m* 1959 two *s* two *d*. BA Hons Hull 1959, Postgrad. Dip. in Social Admin, Manchester 1961 (distinction) Inst. of Hospital Administrators, Prof. examinations, 1962. Asst Lectr, Dept of Social Admin., Univ. of Hull, 1965–66. Vis. Lectr, Chinese Univ. Hong Kong, 1971–72. School governor: gp of primary schs, 1969–71; two secondary schs, 1972– ; Mem., Beverley District Council. *Publications*: Managing the Health Service, 1974; *contrib*. various jls, particularly Hospital and Health

Service Management. *Address*: Dept of Social Administration, The Univ., Hull HU6 7RX.

Hazlewood, Arthur Dennis; Senior Research Officer, Institute of Economics and Statistics, Oxford, since 1956, and Fellow and Lecturer in Economics, Pembroke College, Oxford, since 1961; *b* 1921; *m* 1954; one *d*. BSc(Econ) London 1948 (1st cl., Gonner Prize), BPhil Oxon 1950, MA Oxon 1954. Tutor in Economics, Oxford Univ. Inst. of Commonwealth Studies, 1950–56; Pro-Proctor, Oxford Univ., 1964–65. Domestic Bursar, Pembroke Coll., Oxford, 1970– ; Dir, Common Market Secretariat, Off. of Pres., Nairobi, 1965–66; Mngng Ed., Jl Develop. Studies, 1967–70. *Publications*: The Economics of Under-developed Areas, 1954, 2nd edn 1959; (with P. D. Henderson) Nyasaland: the Economics of Federation, 1960; (with Klein, Ball and Vandome) An Econometric Model of the United Kingdom, 1961; The Economy of Africa, 1961; The Economics of Development, 1964; Rail and Road in East Africa, 1964; African Integration and Disintegration, 1967; *contrib*. E Afr. Econ. Rev., E Afr. Econ. Stat. Rev., Econ. Jl, Inst. Econ. Stats Bull., Rev. Econ. Studies, Soc. Econ. Studies. *Address*: Pembroke College, Oxford.

Headey, Dr Bruce W.; Lecturer, Department of Politics, Strathclyde University, since 1968; *b* 1943; *m* 1966; two *s*. BA Oxford 1965, MA Tulane 1967, MA Wisconsin 1968, PhD Strathclyde 1973. *Publications*: British Cabinet Ministers: the roles of politicians in executive office, 1974; *contrib*. Pol Studies, Jl Politics, Internat. Jl Admin. Scis. *Address*: Dept of Politics, Univ. of Strathclyde, Glasgow G1 1XW.

Headington, Christopher John Magenis; Tutor in Music, Department for External Studies, University of Oxford, since 1965; *b* 1930. LRAM 1950, ARAM 1954, ARCM 1953, BMus Dunelm 1965; Mem. Composers' Guild of Gt Britain, Mem. Incorp. Soc. of Musicians. Mem. Exec. Cttee, Composers' Guild of Gt Britain, 1958–61 and 1974– . *Publications*: The Orchestra and its Instruments, 1965; The Bodley Head History of Western Music, 1974; *contrib*. Chesterian, Music and Letters. *Address*: Dept for External Studies, Univ. of Oxford, Rewley House, Wellington Square, Oxford OX1 2JA.

Heafford, Philip Ernest, MA, BSc; Senior Tutor and Lecturer in Science, Oxford University Department of Educational Studies, since 1950; *b* 1906; *m* 1932; one *s*. BSc Leeds 1926 (Hons Physics), CertEd Ontario 1928, DipEd Oxford 1938, MA Oxford 1943; Brit. Beekeepers Master Craftsman 1938, Mem., Swiss Alpine Club 1946–50, Assoc. Sci. Educn 1946– . Lectr, Clarendon Lab., Oxford Univ., 1940–46; Demonstrator in charge 1st yr Physics, 1944–46; Off. in charge, Oxf. Schs Squadron, ATC, 1941–46; Hon. Treas., Oxf. Inst. Psychiat., 1964. *Publications*: Mathematics for Fun, 1955, 3rd edn 1966; Science for Fun, 1956, 2nd edn 1960, trans. Polish, Japanese, Singalese, etc.; A New Mathematics for Fun, 1966; Science on

305

the March, Units 7, 8, 9, 11 and 14, 1956–69; The Math Entertainer, 1959; Discovering Physics, 1964, 7th SI edn 1971; Physics Topics, 2 units, 1969–70, 2nd edn 1971, Dutch edn 1972; Techniques of Teaching, vol. 2, 1965. *Address*: Dept of Educational Studies, 15 Norham Gardens, Oxford OX2 6PY.

Heal, Dr Geoffrey Martin, BA, MA, PhD; Professor of Economics, University of Sussex, since 1973; *b* 1944; *m* 1967; one *d*. BA Cantab 1966 (1st cl. Economics), MA Cantab 1970, PhD Cantab 1970. Fellow, Christ's Coll., Cambridge, 1968–72; Asst Lectr, Cambridge, 1968–72; Vis., Yale, 1972. Managing Ed., Rev. of Economic Studies, 1971. *Publications*: The Theory of Economic Planning, 1973; (with G. A. Hughes and R. J. Tarling), Linear Algebra and Linear Economics, 1974; (with P. S. Dasgupta) Economic Theory and Exhaustible Resources, 1974; contrib. Essays in Modern Economics, ed M. Parkin, 1973; Economic Aspects of Natural Resource Depletion, ed D. W. Pearce, 1974; *contrib*. Oxford Econ. Papers, Rev. of Econ. Studies. *Address*: School of Social Studies, Sussex Univ., Falmer, Brighton BN1 9RH.

Heald, Dr David Ronald Lacey; Lecturer in German, University of Kent at Canterbury, since 1967; *b* 1940. BA London 1964; MA Johns Hopkins 1965; PhD London 1970. Lektor, Univ. Münster, 1966–67. *Publications*: *contrib*. German Life and Letters, Mod. Langs, New German Studies, Oxford German Studies, Univs Qly. *Address*: Darwin Coll., Univ. of Kent, Canterbury, Kent.

Heale, Dr Michael John; Lecturer in History, Department of History, University of Lancaster, since 1967; *b* 1941. BA Manchester 1962 (1st cl.), DPhil Oxon 1967; Member: Amer. Hist. Assoc., Brit. Assoc. for Amer. Studies, Amer. Studies Assoc. Asst Lectr in History, Univ. Lancaster, 1965–67; Vis. Asst Prof., State Univ. New York at Buffalo, 1969; Amer. Studies Fellow, from Amer. Council of Learned Socs, Rutgers Univ., 1972–73. *Publications*: *contrib*. European Studies Rev., Jl Amer. Studies, NY Hist. Soc. Qly, Societas, Western Hist. Qly. *Address*: Dept of History, Univ. of Lancaster, Lancaster LA1 4YW.

Healey, Prof. Frank George; Professor and Head of Department of Linguistic and Regional Studies, University of Surrey, since 1972; *b* 1923; *m* 1951; two *s* two *d*. BA Birmingham 1948 (1st cl. Hons), MA Birmingham 1949, PhD Birmingham 1954; Member: Assoc. of Univ. Profs of French, Soc. for French Studies, MLA. Lectr in French, Univ. Birmingham, 1949–60; Prof. of French, Magee UC, Londonderry, 1960–64. Leader, Univ. Educn Res. Project, Manchester Univ., 1964–67; Head Dept Mod. Langs, Portsmouth Polytechnic, 1967–72. Member: Cttee for Arts and Social Studies, CNAA, 1968–71; CNAA Langs Panel, 1968–71; CNAA Cttee for Res. and Higher Degrees, 1972– ; co-opted mem., Nat. Council for Mod. Langs, 1971– ; Contributing Editor for Mod. Langs,Times Higher Educn Supplement, 1971– . *Publications*: Rousseau et

Napoléon, 1957; The Literary Culture of Napoleon, 1959; Foreign Language Teaching in the Universities, 1967; *contrib*. French Studies, Revue de l'Institut Napoléon, Studies in Voltaire and the Eighteenth Century. *Address*: Univ. of Surrey, Guildford, Surrey GU2 5XH.

Healy, Prof. John Francis, MA, PhD, FRNS, FRSA; Professor of Classics, Royal Holloway College (University of London), since 1966; *b* 1926; *m* 1957; one *s*. BA Cantab 1950 (1st cl. Classics), MA Cantab 1952, PhD Cantab 1955; FRNS, FRSA. Asst Lectr, Manchester, 1953–56; Lectr, 1956–61; Reader in Greek, Bedford Coll., Univ. of London, 1961–66. Hon. Asst Keeper (Numismatic coll.), Manchester Mus., Univ. of Manchester, 1953– ; Chm., Fin. and Gen. Purposes Cttee, Inst. Class. Studies, London. *Publications*: (with A. Rowe) Cyrenaican Expeditions of the University of Manchester, 1955–57; *contrib*. Bull. J. Rylands Libr., Class. Rev., Gnomon, Jl Hellenic Studies, Jl Semit. Studies, Numism. Chron. *Address*: Dept of Classics, Royal Holloway College (Univ. of London), Egham Hill, Egham, Surrey TW20 0EX.

Heaney, Henry Joseph; Librarian, Queen's University, Belfast, since 1972; *b* 1935. BA 1957 (Mod. Hist.), MA 1970, QUB; FLA 1969 (ALA 1962). Queen's Univ., Belfast: Sen. Library Asst, 1957–59; Asst Librarian, 1959–63; Librarian, Magee Univ. Coll., Londonderry, 1963–69; Dep. Librarian, New Univ. of Ulster, Coleraine, 1967–69; Asst Sec., Standing Conf. of Nat. and Univ. Libraries, 1969–72. Mem., NI Min. of Educn Cttee on Public Library Service, 1966; Chm., NI Br., Library Assoc., 1965, 1973, 1974. Editor, IFLA Annual, 1971. *Publications*: *contrib*. Jl Documentation, An Leabharlann, Irish Lib., Lib. Assoc. Record, Lib. Hist. *Address*: Queen's Univ., Belfast BT7 1NN.

Hearder, Prof. Harry, PhD; Professor of Modern History, University College, Cardiff, since 1967; *b* 1924; *m* 1954; two *s* one *d*. BA London External 1951, PhD London 1954; FRHistS 1967, Mem., Hist. Assoc., Soc. Ital. Studies. Asst Lectr in Political History, LSE, 1954–57; Lectr in Internat. History, 1957–64; Vis. Lectr, Wellesley Coll., Mass., 1963; Sen. Lectr in Internat. History, LSE, 1964–67; Vis. Prof., Columbia Univ., 1966; Vis. Prof., Harvard Univ., 1970. *Publications*: ed (with D. P. Waley), A Short History of Italy, 1963, pbk edn 1966, Spanish trans. 1966; Europe in the Nineteenth Century, 1966, pbk edn 1970, French edn 1973; *contrib*. Atti Cong. Stor. Risorg., EHR, Rass. Stor. Risorg. *Address*: Dept of History, Univ. College, PO Box 78, Cardiff CF1 1XL.

Hearnshaw, Prof. Leslie Spencer; Professor of Psychology, University of Liverpool, since 1947; *b* 1907; *m* 1937; one *s* three *d*. BA Oxon 1930 (1st cl. Lit. Hum.), MA 1933, BA London 1932 (1st cl. Hons Psychology); FBPsS 1940 (Pres., 1955–56); Vice-Pres., Internat. Assoc. of Applied Psychology, 1964–74. Lectr, Victoria UC Wellington, NZ, 1938–47. Investigator, National Institute of Industrial Psychology, 1933–37; Dir, Industrial Psychology Division, DSIR (NZ); Hon. Dir, MRC Unit for Res. on Occupational Aspects of Ageing, 1963–70; Editor, Internat. Jl of Applied Psychology, 1964–74. *Publications*: (with R. Winterbourn) Human Welfare and Industrial Efficiency, 1945; A Short History of British Psychology, 1964; *contrib*. Brit. Jl Psychol., Occupational Psychology, etc. *Address*: Dept of Psychology, Eleanor Rathbone Building, Univ. of Liverpool, PO Box 147, Liverpool L69 3BX.

Heasman, Kathleen Joan, MA, PhD; Senior Lecturer in Social Studies, Queen Elizabeth College, London University, since 1948; *b* 1913; *m* 1941. MA Cantab 1935 (Economics), PhD London 1959 (Sociology); Mem., Brit. Sociol. Assoc. Lectr, Hong Kong Univ., 1936–46. Mem., Bd Govs, All Saints Coll., Tottenham; Ch Army Bd. *Publications*: Evangelicals in Action, 1962; Christians and Social Work, 1964; Army of the Church, 1967; An Introduction to Pastoral Counselling, 1969; The Study of Society, 1972; *contrib*. Community Develop. Jl, Hist. Jl. *Address*: The White Cottage, Leigh, near Tonbridge, Kent.

Heath, Michael John; Lecturer, Department of French, University College of North Wales, Bangor, since 1968; *b* 1944; *m* 1973. BA Exeter 1966, MA 1967. *Publications*: *contrib*. BHR. *Address*: Dept of French, Univ. Coll. of North Wales, Bangor LL57 2DG.

Heath, Peter, MA; Senior Lecturer in History, University of Hull, since 1971; *b* 1932; *m* 1964; one *d*. BA London 1954 (1st cl. History), MA London 1961 (History); Mem., Eccles. Hist. Soc. Selden Soc. Asst Lectr in History, Hull Univ., 1959–61; Lectr, 1961–71. *Publications*: Medieval Clerical Accounts, 1964; English Parish Clergy on the Eve of the Reformation, 1969; The Visitations of Bishop Geoffrey Blythe *c*. 1515–1525, 1973; The Origins of the English Reformation, 1974; John Colet (forthcoming); *contrib*. Bull. Inst. Hist. Res., Jl Eccles. Hist., North. Hist. Vict. County Hist. *Address*: Dept of History, University of Hull, Hull HU6 7RX.

Heathcote, Rev. Dr Arthur Weston; Principal Lecturer, and Head of Religious Studies, Redland College, Bristol, since 1967; *b* 1916; *m* 1948. BSc Birmingham 1937 (1st cl. Physics), BA Cantab 1940 (1st cl. Theol. Trip), BD London 1941, MTh London 1943, MA Cantab 1945, PhD London 1949, BSc London 1950, MSc London 1952; Life Fellow, Internat. Inst. Arts Lett. Lectr, Keele Univ., 1962–65; Sen. Lectr, 1965–67; Recogn. Lectr, Bristol Univ., 1967– . Methodist Min., 1938– . *Publications*: From the Death of Solomon to the Captivity of Judah, 1959; Israel to the Time of Solomon, 1960; From the Exile to Herod the Great, 1964; Introduction to the Letters of St Paul, 1963; trans., Jacob: Theology of the Old Testament, 1958; trans., Corswant: Dictionary of Life in Bible Times, 1960 trans., Héring: First Epistle of St Paul to the Corinthians, 1962; trans., Tournier: Guilt and Grace, 1962; trans., Héring: Second

Epistle of St Paul to the Corinthians, 1967; trans., Héring: Commentary on Epistle to the Hebrews, 1970; *contrib*. Brit. Jl Philos. Sci., Lond. Qly Holb. Rev. *Address*: Redland College, Redland Hill, Bristol BS6 6UZ.

Heathcote, Dorothy, MA, LRAM; Staff Tutor in Drama in Education, School of Education (formerly Institute of Education), University of Newcastle upon Tyne, since 1954; *b* 1926; *m* 1955; one *d*. MA Dunelm 1961; LRAM 1952. *Address*: School of Education, Univ. of Newcastle upon Tyne, Newcastle upon Tyne NE1 7RU.

Hedderwick, (Frederic) Karl; Lecturer in Economics and Industrial Studies, Department of Extramural Studies, University of Sheffield, since 1964; *b* 1937; *m* 1965; two *d*. Dip. Econs and Pol Sci. Oxon 1962, BA Hons Oxon 1964 (PPE); Member: Soc. of Ind. Tutors; Soc. for Study of Labour Hist. *Publications*: Statistics for Bargainers, 1974; *contrib*. Jl Soc. of Ind. Tutors. *Address*: Broomspring House, 85 Wilkinson Street, Sheffield S10 2GS.

Hedgecoe, Dr John; Reader in Photography, since 1970, and Head of Photography Department, since 1965, Royal College of Art; *b* 1937; *m* 1960; two *s* one *d*. Guildford Sch. of Art: Surrey Major Scholarship, Art Sch. Dipl. 1958; Doctor RCA 1972; Associate, Royal Photographic Soc., 1958. Associate Editor, Queen Magazine, 1967–71. *Publications*: Henry Moore, 1968; Photography Material and Methods, 1970, repr. 1973; Henry Moore, Energy and Space, 1973; The Thames (forthcoming); Photography, Aspects of (forthcoming); *contrib*. illustrated art and photographic jls throughout world. *Address*: Dept of Photography, Royal College of Art, Kensington Gore, SW7 2EU.

Hedges, Anthony John, MA, BMus, LRAM; Senior Lecturer in Music, University of Hull, since 1968; *b* 1931; *m* 1948; two *s* two *d*. BA Oxon 1953 (1st cl. Music), BMus Oxon 1955, MA Oxon 1957; LRAM 1950, Mem., Composers Guild GB. Teacher, Royal Scottish Acad. of Music, 1957–63; Lectr in Music, Univ. of Hull, 1963–68. Founder-Chm., Northern Br., Composers Guild, 1965; Mem., Exec. Cttee, Composers Guild, 1969; Chm., 1972–73; Mem., Council, Central Music Lib., 1970. *Publications*: Over 80 compositions, these include: Five Preludes, 1959; Comedy Overture, 1962; Overture 'October '62', 1962; Sinfonia Semplice, 1963; Gloria, 1965; Concertante Music, 1965; Four Pieces for Piano, 1966; Rondo Concertante, 1967; Four Miniature Dances, 1967; A Holiday Overture, 1968; Variations on a Theme of Rameau, 1969; Epithalamion, 1969; String Quartet, 1970; Four Diversions, 1971; To Music, 1973; Psalm 104, 1973; Piano Sonata, Symphony, 1974; *contrib*. Curr. Musicol., Music. Times, Guardian, Scotsman, Glasgow Her., Yorks Post. *Address*: Dept of Music, Univ. of Hull, Cottingham Road, Hull HU6 7RX.

Heesom, Alan John; Lecturer, Department of Modern History, University of Durham, since 1966; *b* 1941; *m* 1963; one *s* one *d*. BA

307

(Hons) Cantab 1963 (1st cl. Hist.), MA Cantab 1967. *Address*: Dept of History, 43 North Bailey, Durham.

Heesterman, A. R. G.; Senior Lecturer, Department of Econometrics and Social Statistics, University of Birmingham, since 1972 (Lecturer, 1965–72); *b* 1932; *m* 1958; one *s* one *d*. Drs. Pol. and Soc. Sci. Amsterdam 1959. Res. Off., Central Planning Bureau, Min. of Econ. Aff., Netherlands, 1961–65. *Publications*: Forecasting Models for National Economic Planning, 1970, 2nd edn 1972; paper in The Econometric Study of the UK, ed K. Hilton and D. Heathfield, 1970; Allocation Models and their Use in Economic Planning, 1971; Macroeconomic Market Regulation, 1974; *contrib.* Management Science, Numberische Mathematik, 12, Economics of Planning Stat. Neerlandica. *Address*: Econometrics Dept, Univ. of Birmingham, PO Box 363, Birmingham B15 2TT.

Heggie, Ian G.; Director, Transport Studies Unit, Oxford University, since 1973 (Senior Research Officer in the Economics and Organisation of Transport, Oxford University, 1968–72); *b* 1936; *m* 1962; one *s* one *d*. BSc Witwatersrand 1958 (Civil Engineering), BA Oxon 1964 (1st cl. PPE), MA Oxon 1968; CEng, MICE 1971. Design Eng. and Resid. Eng., 1959–62; Cnsltnt and Dep. Res. Dir, Economist Intelligence Unit, 1964–68; Sen. Res. Fellow, Nuffield Coll., Oxford, 1968– ; Vis. Associate Prof., Univ. of British Columbia, 1972–73. Cnsltnt (Economics), Freeman, Fox & Assoc., 1971– ; Mem., Transp. Planning and Operat. Panel, Sci. Res. Council, 1971. *Publications*: Transport Engineering Economics, 1972; ed jtly, Transport and the Urban Environment, 1974; ed jtly, The Management of Water Quality and the Environment, 1974; contrib. ICE Conf. on Engineering Problems Overseas, 1968; *contrib.* Proc. ICE, Jl Transpt Econ. Policy. *Address*: 4 George Street, Oxford OX1 2AE.

Heim, Dr Alice W.; MRC Scientific Staff, Department of Experimental Psychology (teaches Intelligence, Personality and Psychological Assessment), Cambridge University, since 1939; Fellow of Clare Hall, Cambridge, since 1972; *b* 1913; one *s* one *d*, both adopted. BA Cambridge 1934 (Psychology), MA Cambridge 1938 (Psychology), PhD Cambridge 1939 (Psychology); FBPsS 1956. Smith Mundt–Fulbright Fellowship, Stanford Univ., California, 1951–52; Lecturing and researching, Cambridge Univ., 1946– ; Dir of Studies, Psychology, Newnham Coll., Cambridge, 1960– ; Examiner for BPS Dip. in Clinical Psychol., 1971–73. Mem., Cttee, Educnl Sect., BPS, 1967–70; Pres., Camb. Psychol. Soc., 1968–70; Sec., Science Gp, Newnham Assoc., 1968–74; Ed. Adv., Occupat. Psychol., 1970–74; Pres., Camb. Science Lunch Club, 1970–73; SSRC Vis. Prof., Paris, 1972. *Publications*: The Appraisal of Intelligence, 1954; Intelligence and Personality, 1970; OUP Biology Reader on Psychological Testing, 1974; seven psychometric tests published by NFER, 1955–74; *contrib.* Brit. Jl Educnl Psychol., Brit. Jl Psychol., Occupat. Psychol., Percept. Mot.

Skills, Psychol. Rep., Qly Jl Exper. Psychol. *Address*: Psychological Laboratory, Downing Street, Cambridge.

Heinemann, Margot Claire, BA; Senior Lecturer in English, University of London, Goldsmiths' College, since 1967; *b* 1913; one *d*. BA Cantab 1934 (English Tripos Pt I, 1933, 1st cl. with disinction, Pt II, 1934, 1st cl.), Gladstone Scholar, 1934–35. Res. Worker, Labour Res. Dept, 1937–49; Lectr in English, Goldsmiths' Coll., Univ. of London, 1965. *Publications*: Britain's Coal, 1943; Wages Front, 1947; The Adventurers (novel), 1960; (with N. Branson) Britain in the Nineteen Thirties, 1971. *Address*: Goldsmiths' College, New Cross, SE14 6NW.

Hellen, Dr John Anthony; Lecturer in Geography, University of Newcastle upon Tyne, since 1964; *b* 1935; *m* 1959; three *s* two *d*. BA Oxon 1959, MA Oxon 1963, DPhil Bonn 1964; FRGS. Asst, Univ. of Bonn, 1963–64. *Publications*: Rural Economic Development in Zambia, 1890–1964, 1969; North Rhine–Westphalia, 1974; trans., Kanter: Libya, 1967; Fischer: Afghanistan, 1968; Kuls and Schaller: Ethiopia, 1972; *contrib.* Agric. Hist. Rev., Erdkunde, Internat. Aff. *Address*: Dept of Geography, Univ. of Newcastle upon Tyne, Newcastle upon Tyne NE1 7RU.

Helm, Paul, BA; Lecturer, Department of Philosophy, University of Liverpool, since 1964; *b* 1940; *m* 1962; three *s* one *d*. BA Oxon 1962 (2nd cl. PPE). Vis. Associate Prof., Univ. of Rhode Island, 1971–72. *Publications*: The Varieties of Belief, 1973; *contrib.* Analysis, Jl Hist. Philos., Mind, Philos. Qly, Philos., Rel. Studies. *Address*: Dept of Philosophy, Univ. of Liverpool, PO Box 147, Liverpool L69 3BX.

Hemming, Dr Timothy Dominic; Lecturer in French, University of Bristol, since 1963; *b* 1934; *m* 1957. BA Oxon 1955 (1st cl. Mod. Langs), MA Oxon 1960, DPhil Oxon 1963. Jun. Fellow in French, Bristol, 1960–63. Sec., Brit. Sect., Soc. Rencesvals. *Publications*: *contrib.* Med. Æv., Mod. Lang. Rev., Romania. *Address*: Dept of French, Univ. of Bristol, Bristol BS8 1TH.

Hemmings, Prof. Frederic William John; Professor of French Literature, Department of French, University of Leicester, since 1963; *b* 1920; *m* 1942, 1972; one *s* one *d*. BA Oxon 1941 (1st cl. French and German), MA, DPhil Oxon 1950. Asst Lectr, Univ. Coll., Leicester, 1948–50; Lectr, 1950–54; Reader, Univ. of Leicester, 1954–63; Vis. Prof., Yale Univ., 1966–67. *Publications*: The Russian Novel in France 1884–1914, 1950; Emile Zola, 1953, 2nd edn 1966; ed, Zola: Salons, 1959; Stendhal, a Study of his Novels, 1964; Balzac, an interpretation of La Comédie humaine, 1967; Culture and Society in France 1848–1898, 1971; The Age of Realism, 1974; *contrib.* Cah. Natural., Fr. Studies, PMLA, Rev. Hist. Lit. France, Rev. Sci. Hum., Romanic Rev. *Address*: Dept of French, The Univ., Leicester LE1 7RH.

Henderson, Arthur; Senior Lecturer in Management, Department of Business Administration and Accountancy, University of Wales Institute of Science and Technology, since 1963; *b* 1918; *m* 1947; one *s* one *d*. BA (Administration) Manchester 1939 BSc (Econ) London 1946; MBIM. Founder mem., Assoc. Teachers Mngmt, 1960; Mem., Exec. Cttee, 1963; Sec., 1965–73; Sec., Case Clearing House of GB and Ireland, 1974. *Publications*: ed, Policies for Management Education, 1966; *contrib*. Assoc. Teachers Mngmt Bull., Mngmt Educn Develop. *Address*: Univ. of Wales Institute of Science and Technology, Cathays Park, Cardiff CF1 3NU.

Henderson, Barbara M., MA, MLitt; Lecturer in German, Department of Modern Languages, University of Aston in Birmingham, since 1966; *b* 1936. MA Glasgow 1958 (1st cl. French, German), MLitt Glasgow 1966; Ch V Teaching Cert., Moray Hse, Edinburgh, 1963. *Address*: Dept of Modern Languages, Univ. of Aston in Birmingham, Gosta Green, Birmingham B4 7ET.

Henderson, Dr George David Smith; Lecturer and Head of Department, Department of History of Art, University of Cambridge, since 1974; Fellow, Downing College, Cambridge; *b* 1931; *m* 1957; one *s* one *d*. MA Aberdeen 1953, BA London 1956, MA, PhD Cantab 1960. Res. Fellow, Barber Inst. Fine Arts, Univ. Birmingham, 1959–60; Graham Robertson Res. Fellow, Downing Coll., Cambridge, 1960–63; Asst Lectr, History of Art Dept, Univ. Manchester, 1962–64, and Lectr, 1964–65; Lectr, Dept of Fine Art, Univ. Edinburgh, 1966–71, and Reader, 1971–73. *Publications*: Gothic, 1967, repr. 1972; Chartres, 1968; Early Medieval, 1972; *contrib*. Art Bull., Jl Brit. Archaeological Assoc., Jl Warburg and Courtauld Insts. *Address*: Univ. of Cambridge, Dept of History of Art, 1 Scroope Terrace, Cambridge CB2 1PX; Downing Coll., Cambridge CB2 1DQ.

Henderson, Prof. George Patrick, MA; Professor of Philosophy, University of Dundee, since 1967; Dean, Faculty of Social Sciences and Letters, since 1973; *b* 1915; *m* 1939. MA St Andrews 1936 (1st cl. Philosophy), BA Oxon 1938 (2nd cl. Lit. Hum.), MA Oxon 1943. Asst, St Andrews Univ., 1938–40; Lectr, 1945–53; Sen. Lectr, 1953–59; Prof. of Philosophy, Queen's Coll., Dundee, 1959–67; Ed., Philos. Qly, 1962–72. Army service, UK, Italy, Greece, 1940–46. *Publications*: The Revival of Greek Thought 1620–1830, 1970; *contrib*. Amer. Philos. Qly, Brit. Jl Aesthet., Dialogue, Mind, Philos., Philos. Qly, Proc. Aristot. Soc., Ratio. *Address*: Dept of Philosophy, Univ. of Dundee, Dundee DD1 4HN.

Henderson, Hamish McNaughton, MA, LLB; Senior Lecturer in Scots Law, Edinburgh, since 1972 (Lecturer, 1969–72); *b* 1926; *m* 1960; three *d*. BA Cantab 1949 (1st. cl. Classics Pt I, 2(i) Classics Pt II 1950), MA Cantab 1957, LLB Aberdeen 1957; Solicitor, Advocate in Aberdeen, 1960. Mem.: Soc. Public Teachers of Law, Royal Inst. Internat. Aff. Lectr in Constitutional Law, Edinburgh, 1958–69. Mem., Edinburgh Airport Cnsltve Cttee, 1971– . *Publications*: *contrib*. Jl Law

Soc. Scotl., Law Qly Rev., Scott. Law Times. *Address*: Dept of Scots Law, Old College, Edinburgh EH8 9YL.

Henderson, Harry John Radford, BSc, MA; Lecturer, Department of Geography, University College of Swansea, since 1962; *b* 1934; *m* 1965; one *s* two *d*. BSc Sheffield 1955, DipEd Sheffield 1956, MA Liverpool 1959; Mem., Inst. Brit. Geog., Geog. Assoc. Temp. Lectr, Rhodes Univ., S Africa, 1956–57; Leverhulme Fellow, Liverpool, 1957–59; Tutor, Univ. Coll. of Swansea, 1959–61; Asst Lectr, 1961–62; Vis. Lectr, Rhodes Univ., S Africa, 1963; Vis. Sen. Lectr, 1969–70. *Publications*: (with R. J. Harrison Church, etc.), Africa and the Islands, 1964, 3rd edn 1971; *contrib*. Trans Inst. Brit. Geog. *Address*: Dept of Geography, Univ. College, Swansea SA2 8PP.

Henderson, Dr James Lewis; Senior Lecturer in History and Industrial Affairs, London University Institute of Education, since 1963; *b* 1910; *m* 1946; two *s* three *d*. MA Oxon, 1932, MA 1952, PhD 1955, London; Chm., World Educn Fellowship; Jt Chm., Educn Adv. Cttee, Parly Gp for World Govt. Chairman: Pictorial Charts Educnl Trust; London Hist. Teacher's Assoc. *Publications*: Education for World Understanding, 1968; Dag Hammarskjold, 1968; Hiroshima, 1974; *contrib*. Teaching History. *Address*: Inst. of Education, Malet Street, WC1E 7HS.

Henderson, James Walker; Lecturer, Department of Geography, University of Glasgow, since 1966; *b* 1939; *m* 1968; two *s*. MA Edinburgh 1961; Asst, Glasgow Univ., 1965–66. *Address*: Dept of Geography, Univ. of Glasgow, Glasgow G12 8QQ.

Hendrie, Prof. Gerald Mills, MA, MusB, PhD, FRCO, ARCM; Professor of Music, The Open University, since 1971; *b* 1935; *m* 1962; two *s*. BA Cantab 1957, MusB Cantab 1958, PhD Cantab 1961, MA Cantab 1962; ARCM (triple Dip.) 1954, FRCO 1955; Mem., Royal Musical Assoc. Supervisor in Music, Cambridge Univ., 1958–63; Lectr in the Hist. of Music and Musical Palaeography, Manchester Univ., 1963–67; Chm., Dept of Music, Univ. of Victoria, BC, 1967–69; Reader in Music, Open Univ., 1969–71. *Publications*: The English Lute-Songs, first series vol. 17, John Coprario (transcribed and ed with T. Dart); Musica Britannica XX, Orlando Gibbons: Keyboard Music, 1962, 2nd edn 1967, two vols of off-prints 1968; The Keyboard Music of Orlando Gibbons (1583–1625) (RMA paper), 1962; (transcribed and ed) George Friederic Handel: The Chandos and related Anthems (forthcoming); Carol: As I Outrode this enderis night, 1964; Carol: Sweet was the Song the Virgin Sang, 1966; *contrib*. Die Musik in Geschichte und Gegenwart. *Address*: Faculty of Arts, The Open Univ., Walton Hall, Walton, Milton Keynes MK7 6AA.

Hendy, Michael Frank, MA; Lecturer in Numismatics and Curator of the Coin Collections, Department of Fine Arts, University of Birmingham, since 1972; *b* 1942. MA Oxon

309

1968, MA Cantab 1970; FSA, FRNS, FRHistS. Asst Curator, Fitzwilliam Museum, Univ. of Cambridge, 1967–72. *Publications*: Coinage and Money in the Byzantine Empire 1081–1261, 1969; *contrib*. Archaeom, Byzant. Zeitsch., Jl Roman Stud., Numis. Chron., Rev. Numis., Trans Roy. Hist. Soc., Univ. Birmingham Hist. Jl. *Address*: Barber Institute of Fine Arts, The Univ., Birmingham B15 2TT.

Henig, Ruth Beatrice; Lecturer in History, Lancaster University, since 1968; *b* 1943; *m* 1966; two *s*. BA Hons London 1965 (1st cl. History); ARIIA. *Publications*: ed, The League of Nations, 1973; *contrib*. Internat. Affairs. *Address*: Dept of History, Furness Coll., Lancaster Univ., Bailrigg, Lancaster.

Hennessy, Charles Alistair Michael, MA, DPhil; Professor of History, University of Warwick, since 1971; *b* 1926; *m* 1952; one *s*. BA Oxon 1951, MA Oxon 1952, DPhil Oxon 1959; Lectr, Univ. of Exeter, 1954–65; Sen. Lectr, Univ. of Warwick, 1965–66, Reader, 1966–71; Assoc. Fellow, St Antony's Coll., Oxford, 1965–70. *Publications*: The Federal Republic in Spain, 1962; chapters, in, Political Systems of Latin America, ed M. Needler, 2nd edn 1970; The Politics of Conformity in Latin America, ed C. Veliz, 1967; Latin America and the Caribbean: a handbook, ed C. Veliz, 1968; Populism: its nature and national characteristics, ed Ionescou and Gellner, 1969; The Twentieth Century, ed A. Bullock, 1971; *contrib*. Internat. Affairs, Jl of Latin American Studies, TLS, Jl Contemporary History. *Address*: Dept of History, Univ. of Warwick, Coventry CV4 7AL.

Hennings, Dr Klaus Hinrich; Volkswagen Lecturer in Economics, University of Reading, since 1971; *b* 1937. Diplom-Volkswirt Tübingen 1966; DPhil Oxford 1972; Qualification as accountant, 1960; Member: Royal Econ. Soc., Amer. Econ. Soc.; List-Gesellschaft. Part-time Res. Asst, Tübingen, 1964–66, Res. Asst, 1966; Res. Student (Michael Foster Meml Scholar and Michael Wills Scholar), Pembroke and Nuffield Colls, Oxford, 1966–71; Part-time Lectr, Univ. of Reading, 1970–71. *Publications*: *contrib*. Zeitschrift für die gesamte Staatswissenschaft, Kyklos, Econ. Jl. *Address*: Dept of Economics, Univ. of Reading, Whiteknights, Reading RG6 2AH.

Hennock, Dr Ernest Peter; Reader in History, School of Cultural and Community Studies, University of Sussex, since 1968; *b* 1926; *m* 1954; two *s* one *d*. BA Cantab 1950, MA 1955, PhD 1956; FRHistS 1973. Asst Lectr, Univ. of Keele History Dept, 1953–57; Political Institutions Dept, 1953–56; Lectr, History Dept, 1957–63; Univ. of Sussex, Lectr in History, 1963–65; Sen. Lectr, 1965–68; Vis. Fellow, All Souls Coll., Oxford, 1966–67. *Publications*: Fit and Proper Persons. Ideal and Reality in Nineteenth-Century Urban Government, 1973; *contrib*. Archiv f. Kommunalwissenschaften, Econ. Hist. Rev., Historical Jl, Victorian Studies. *Address*: Arts Building, Univ. of Sussex, Falmer, Brighton BN1 9QN.

Henriques, Prof. Louis Fernando, MA, DPhil; Professorial Fellow and Director of Centre for Multi-Racial Studies (formerly Research Unit for Study of Multi-Racial Societies), University of Sussex, since 1964; *b* 1916; *m* 1948; three *s*. MA Oxon 1948, DPhil Oxon 1948; Carnegie Res. Fellow, Oxford, 1946–47; Grad. Asst, Inst. of Social Anthropology, Univ. of Oxford, 1947–48; Lectr in Social Anthropology, Univ. of Leeds, 1948–64; Dean, Faculty of Econs and Social Studies, 1960–62, Wyndham Deedes Schol., 1963; Ford Prof. in Comp. Hist., MIT, 1971. Broadcaster, Overseas Services, BBC, 1939– . Dir, Sociological res. projects, sponsored by Nuffield Foundn, 1952–54; Coal Industry Social Welfare Organ., 1954–58; DSIR, 1955–56; Sociol. Mem., UN Tech. Assistance Admin. Rural Electrification Survey, Ghana, 1957; Mem., Council, Inst. of Race Relations, London, 1965– ; Mem., SE Econ. Planning Council, 1966–68. English Language Ed., Library of Sexual Behaviour, 1970; Gen. Ed., Library of Race Relations, Conway Maritime Press, 1971– . *Publications*: Family and Colour in Jamaica, 1953, rev. edn 1968; Jamaica, Land of Wood and Water, 1957; (with N. Dennis and C. Slaughter) Coal is Our Life, 1956, rev. edn 1969; Love in Action, 1959; Prostitution and Society, vol. I, 1962, vol. II, 1963, vol. III, 1967; contribs to: Handbook of Latin American Studies, 1966; Ciba Foundn Report on Immigration, 1966; Encyclop. Britannica, 1966; *contrib*. sociol. jls. *Address*: Univ. of Sussex, Falmer, Brighton BN1 9QQ.

Henriques, Dr Ursula R. Q., PhD, BLitt, MA; Senior Lecturer, Department of History, University College, Cardiff, since 1973 (Lecturer, 1963–73); *b* 1914. BA Oxon 1935 (1st cl. History), BLitt Oxon 1941, PhD Manchester 1959; Asst Lectr, Univ. Coll., Cardiff, 1961–63. Admin. Asst, Admiralty, London, 1940–45; Sen. Hist. Mistress, St Leonards Sch., St Andrews, 1947–53. *Publications*: Religious Toleration in England, 1780–1833, 1961; *contrib*. Hist., Past and Present, Scott. HR. *Address*: Dept of History, Univ. College, Cardiff CF1 1XL.

Henry, A. K.; Lecturer in English, University of Exeter, since 1971; *b* 1935. BA Oxon 1964 (Hons English), MA Oxon 1968, Nat. Dip. Design 1956, Art Teachers Dip. London 1957 (Distinction); Fulford Sen. Schol., St Hugh's Coll., Oxford, 1964; Asst Lectr in English, Queen Mary Coll., Univ. of London, 1965–68; Lectr in English, Homerton Coll. of Educn, Cambridge, 1968–71; Sen. Mem., Lucy Cavendish Coll., Cambridge, 1968–71. *Publications*: *contrib*. Engl. Studies, South. Rev. (Adelaide). *Address*: Dept of English, Queen's Building, Univ. of Exeter, Exeter EX4 4QH.

Henry, Dr Desmond Paul; Reader in Philosophy, University of Manchester, since 1969; *b* 1921; *m* 1945; three *d*. BA Leeds 1948 (1st cl. Philosophy), PhD Manchester 1962; Emsley Schol., Leeds Univ., 1946; Asst Lectr, Manchester Univ., 1948–51; Lectr, 1951–65; Sen. Lectr, 1965–69; Vis. Prof., Brown Univ., 1966; Vis. Prof., Univ. of Pennsylvania, 1970. *Publications*: The De

Grammatico of St Anselm, 1964; The Logic of St Anselm, 1967; Medieval Logic and Metaphysics, 1972; Commentary on De Grammatico, 1974; *contrib.* Archiv. Latin. Med. Æv., Dominic. Studies, Francisc. Studies, Jl Comput. Syst., Law Qly Rev., Log. Analyse, Mind, Notre Dame Jl, Formal Logic, Philos. Qly, Ratio, Sophia, Synth. *Address*: Dept of Philosophy, The Univ., Manchester M13 9PL.

Henry, Prof. Patrick Leo, DPhil, DLitt, MRIA; Professor of Old and Middle English, University College, Galway, since 1966; *b* 1918; *m* 1956; two *s* four *d*. BA National Univ. of Ireland 1940, MEconSc National Univ. of Ireland 1941, HDipEd National Univ. of Ireland 1943, DPhil Zurich 1952, DLitt National Univ. of Ireland 1970; Mem., Royal Irish Acad., 1969- . Asst ,Univ. Coll., Dublin, 1953–56; Asst Lectr in English, 1956–60; Lectr in Celtic, then Reader, Queen's Univ., Belfast, 1960–66. Mem., Royal Irish Acad. Cttee for Anglo-Irish Lang. and Lit., 1969- . *Publications*: An Anglo-Irish Dialect of North Roscommon, 1957; The Early English and Celtic Lyric, 1966; *contrib.* Lochlann, Zeits. Vergleich. Sprach., Zeits. Celt. Philol. *Address*: Univ. College, Galway, Ireland.

Henry, Peter; Senior Lecturer in Charge, Department of Russian Studies, Hull University, since 1965; *b* 1926; *m* 1951 (marr. diss. 1970); one *s* three *d*. BA Oxon 1950 (2nd cl. Hons Russian and German), MA 1954, DipEd Leeds 1951 (distinction in practical teaching); Lectr in Russian, Liverpool Univ., 1957–63; Lectr in Charge, Hull Univ., 1963–65. Cttee member: Assoc. of Teachers of Russian, 1958–64; Brit. Univs Assoc. of Slavists, 1969–72. *Publications*: Modern Russian Prose Composition, Book 1, 1963, 2nd edn 1964; Book 2, 1964, 2nd edn, 1969; Manual of Modern Russian Usage, 1963, 2nd edn 1971; ed, Pushkin: The Gypsies, 1962, 2nd edn 1968; Bunin: Selected Stories, 1964, 2nd edn 1968; Chekhov: The Seagull, 1964; Paustovsky: Stories, 1967; Anthology of Soviet Satire, vol. 1, 1972, vol. 2, 1974; trans stories by Sholokhov, Tendryakov, Paustovsky; *contrib.* Jl of Russian Studies, Modern Langs, Slavonic and East European Rev. *Address*: Dept of Russian Studies, Univ. of Hull, Hull HU6 7RX.

Henry, Zygmunt L.; *see* Layton-Henry.

Hepburn, Prof. Ronald William, MA, PhD; Professor of Philosophy, University of Edinburgh, since 1964; *b* 1927; *m* 1953; two *s* one *d*. MA Aberdeen 1951, PhD Aberdeen 1955; Mem.: Mind Assoc., Aristotelian Soc., Brit. Soc. of Aesthetics, Phil. of Educn Soc. of GB. Asst, Moral Philosophy, 1952–55; Lectr, 1955–60, Univ. of Aberdeen; Prof. of Philosophy, Univ. of Nottingham, 1960–64; Vis. Assoc. Prof., NY Univ., 1959–60; Stanton Lectr, Univ. of Cambridge, 1965–68. *Publications*: Christianity and Paradox, 1958, 2nd edn 1966; (jtly), Metaphysical Beliefs, 1957, 2nd edn 1970; chapters, in, Objections to Humanism, 1963; Collected Papers on Aesthetics, 1965; Christian Ethics and Con-temporary Philosophy, 1966; British Analytical Philosophy, 1966; Hobbes and Rousseau, 1972; Education and the Development of Reason, 1972; *contrib.* Encyclopaedia of Philosophy, ed Edwards, 1967; Brit. Jl of Aesthetics, Jl of the Hist. of Ideas, Mind, Philosophy, Philosophical Qly, Proc. Aristotelian Soc., Religious Studies. *Address*: Dept of Philosophy, Univ. of Edinburgh, Hume Tower, George Square, Edinburgh EH8 9JX.

Heppell, Muriel; Lecturer in Medieval History of Orthodox Eastern Europe, School of Slavonic and East European Studies, University of London, since 1968; *b* 1917. BA London (Westfield Coll.) 1939 (Cl. I), MA London 1951, PhD London 1954. Tutorial Res. Fellowship, Univ. of Nottingham, 1953–56; Lector in English Language: Univ. of Novi Scid, Yugoslavia, 1956–66; Univ. of Belgrade, Yugoslavia, 1966–68. *Publications*: (part author) Yugoslavia (Nations of the Modern World), 1961, 2nd edn 1966; *contrib.* Byzantinoslavica, Jl Eccles. Hist. *Address*: School of Slavonic and East European Studies, Malet Street, WC1E 7HU.

Hepple, Bob Alexander; Fellow of Clare College and Lecturer in Law, Cambridge University, since 1968; *b* 1934; *m* 1960; one *s* one *d*. BA Witwatersrand 1954, LLB Witwatersrand 1957 (cum laude), LLB Cambridge 1966 (1st cl.), MA Cambridge 1968; of Gray's Inn, Barrister, 1966, Advocate of Supreme Court of S Africa, 1961. Lectr, Witwatersrand Univ., 1959–62; Lectr, Nottingham Univ., 1966–68; Ed., Indust. Law Jl, 1969- ; Co-Ed., Encyclop. of Labour Relations Law, 1972- . Sec., Fac. Bd of Law, Cambridge, 1970–72; Mem., Gen. Cttee, Soc. Public Teachers of Law, 1970–72. *Publications*: (jtly) Union of South Africa: Development of its Law and Constitutions, 1960; Race, Jobs and the Law in Britain, 1968, 2nd edn 1970; (jtly) Public Employee Trade Unionism in UK: Legal Framework, 1971; (jtly) Individual Employment Law, 1971; (jtly) Prevention of Racial Discrimination in Britain, 1971; (jtly) Sourcebook on Tort, 1974; (jtly) Bibliography of Labour Law, 1974; *contrib.* Camb. Law Jl, Mod. Law Rev., New Community, Race, S Afr. Law Jl. *Address*: Clare College, Cambridge CB2 1TL.

Herbert, Barry; Lecturer in Fine Art, University of Leeds, since 1968; *b* 1937; *m* 1960; one *s* one *d*. CertEd Leeds 1961; Inter. Cert. SBI 1958. York City Savings Bank, 1954–58; Studio Demonstrator in Fine Art, Leeds, 1964–68; Warden, Bodington Hall, 1969–73. Sec., Print-makers from Yorkshire, 1969–73. One-man Exhibitions: Ilkley, 1965; Israel, 1968, 1969; Leeds, 1969, 1971, 1973; London (Serpentine Gallery), 1971; Switzerland (Grenchen), 1972; Sheffield, 1972; Bradford, 1974; Numerous Gp Exhibitions: In England, Canada, Switzerland, Israel and USA; 1st Brit. Internat. Print Biennale, 1968; Swiss Internat. Print Triennale, 1970 (commendation) 1973. *Address*: Dept of Fine Art, The Univ. of Leeds, Leeds LS2 9JT.

Herbert, Dr David Thomas, BA, PhD; Lecturer in Geography, University College,

Swansea, since 1965; *b* 1935; *m* 1967; one *s*. BA Wales 1959, DipEd Wales 1960, PhD Birmingham 1964; Demonstrator in Geography, Keele, 1962–64; Asst Lectr, Keele, 1964–65; Vis. Prof., Toronto, 1965; Manitoba, 1967; York (Ontario), 1969. Sub-Dean, Fac. Econ-Soc. Studies, Swansea, 1971; Secretary: Cttee, Inst. Brit. Geogr., Urban Study Gp; Census Res. Gp, 1970. *Publications*: Overspill in Winsford, 1965; Urban Geography: A Social Perspective, 1972; chapters, in, Applied Geography, 3, 1964; Urban Essays: Studies in the Geography of Wales, 1969; *contrib.* Geog., Jl Inst. Planner, Prof. Geog., Sociol. Rev., Town Country Planning, Tijds. Econ. Soc. Geog., Urban Studies IBG Trans, Acta Geog. Louvaniensia. *Address*: Dept of Geography, Univ. College, Singleton Park, Swansea SA2 8PP.

Herbert, Harry; Senior Lecturer in Environmental Health, Department of Building, University of Aston, since 1966; *b* 1916; *m* 1940; two *d.* MSc Aston 1969; Fellow Assoc. Public Health Insp., 1965, FRSoc. Health, 1965, FInst. Public Health Eng., 1968. Lectr, Coll. of Technol., Birmingham (subsequently Coll. of Adv. Technol., then became Univ. of Aston), 1948–66. Local Govt, 1935–48; Mem. Public Health Insp. Educn Bd, 1961– , Chm. 1973– ; Mem. Gen. Council, Assoc. Public Health Insp., 1967– . *Publications*: *contrib.* Environm. Health, Municipal Eng., Royal Soc. Health Jl. *Address*: Dept of Building, Univ. of Aston, Gosta Green, Birmingham B4 7ET.

Herbert, Jack; Staff Tutor in Literature, Board of Extra-Mural Studies, University of Cambridge, since 1965; *b* 1931; *m* 1960. BA Nottingham 1953 (Hons Eng.), MLitt Cambridge 1958. Lectr in English: Kyushu Univ., Fukuoka, Japan, 1958–61; Univ. of Munich, 1961–63. *Address*: Cambridge Univ. Bd of Extra-Mural Studies, Stuart House, Mill Lane, Cambridge CB2 1RY.

Herity, Michael, MA, PhD, FSA; Lecturer in Celtic Archaeology, University College, Dublin, since 1967; *b* 1929; *m* 1960; two *s* two *d.* BA NUI 1957, MA NUI 1960, PhD NUI 1966; FSA 1969. Asst, Univ. Coll., Dublin, 1961–67. Ed., Jl Royal Soc. Antiqu. Ireland. *Publications*: Irish Passage Graves, 1974; (with G. Eogan) Ireland in Prehistory, 1974; *contrib.* Antiqu. Jl, Jl Royal Soc. Antiqu. Ireland, Proc. Royal Irish Acad., Studia Hibern., Ulster Jl Archaeol. *Address*: Dept of Celtic Archaeology, Univ. College, Dublin 4.

Herman, Samuel J.; Senior Tutor in Glass, Glass Department, Royal College of Art, since 1966; *b* 1936; *m* 1963; one *s* one *d.* BA Western Washington State Coll. 1962, MS Univ. of Wisconsin 1964. *Exhibitions*: 1967: Primavera '69, London (contributor); 1968: PUB, Stockholm (contributor); Museum of Glass and Jewellery, Jablonec Roseliushaus, Böttcherstrasse, Bremen; Heal's, London; 1969: Fulham Gall., London; Compendium Gall., Birmingham; Crafts Centre of GB, London; Seibu, Tokyo; Gemeente Mus. voor Stad en Lande, Groningen; Mus. Boymans van Beuningen, Rotter-

dam; 1970: Design Centre, London; Röhsska Konstslöjdmuseet, Goteborg; Pace Gall., London; Galerie Lecuyer, Brussels; 1971: Archer Gall., London; Pilkington Mus., St Helens; Oxford Gall., V and A Mus. (one man show); Camden Arts Centre; Fine Arts Soc. *Address*: Glass Dept, Royal College of Art, Kensington Gore, SW7 2EU.

Herrington, Paul Raymond; Lecturer in Economics, University of Leicester, since 1967; *b* 1939; *m* 1967; one *s* one *d.* BA Nottingham 1961, MSc Southampton 1966; Lectr in Econs, Univ. of Lancaster, 1964–67. *Address*: Dept of Economics, Univ. of Leicester, Leicester LE1 7RH.

Herrity, Peter; Lecturer, Department of Slavonic Studies, University of Nottingham, since 1971; *b* 1936; *m* 1966; two *d.* BA London 1965 (1st cl. Hons Russian Lang. and Lit.); Member: Philological Soc.; British Univs Assoc. of Slavists; Modern Humanities Research Assoc.; Soc. for Slovene Studies (USA). Lectr in Russian, New Univ. of Ulster, 1968–71. *Publications*: *contrib.* Slavonic and E European Rev., Year's Work in Mod. Lang. Studies, Zbornik Meðunarodnog slavističkog centra, Belgrade. *Address*: Dept of Slavonic Studies, Univ. of Nottingham, University Park, Nottingham NG7 2RD.

Herrmann, Prof. Luke John; Professor of the History of Art, University of Leicester, since 1973; *b* 1932; *m* 1965; two *s.* MA Oxon 1957. Dept of Western Art, Ashmolean Museum, Oxford: Asst Keeper, 1958; Sen. Asst Keeper, 1966; Univ. of Leicester: Paul Mellon Foundn Lectr in History of British Art, 1967; Sen. Lectr i/c History of Art Dept, 1970; Head of Dept, 1972. Asst Editor, Illustrated London News, 1955–58. *Publications*: J. M. W. Turner, 1963; Ruskin and Turner, 1968; British Landscape Paintings of the 18th Century, 1973; *contrib.* Apollo, Burlington Mag., Connoisseur. *Address*: History of Art Dept, Univ. of Leicester, University Road, Leicester LE1 7RH.

Hersh, Alan Laurence; Lecturer in French, Division of Languages, Brunel University, since 1967; *b* 1934; *m* 1962; three *d.* BA London 1955, Certif. Educn London 1966, MA London 1971; FIL 1966. French Master, Crosfields Sch., Reading, 1956–57; Asst Lectr in Mod. Langs, Corby Techn Coll., 1958–60; Lectr in Mod. Langs, Hall Green Techn. Coll., 1960–67. *Address*: Brunel Univ., Kingston Lane, Uxbridge, Mddx UB8 3PH.

Hesketh, Peter; Lecturer, Building Department, University of Manchester Institute of Science and Technology, since 1965; *b* 1926; *m* 1953; two *d.* BA Cambridge 1950; Res. Officer, UMIST, 1963–65. Business Consultancy, 1965– . *Address*: Dept of Building, Univ. of Manchester Institute of Science and Technology, Manchester M60 1QD.

Heskin, Kenneth Joseph; Lecturer in Psychology, School of Biological and Environmental Studies, University of Ulster, since 1972; *b* 1945; *m* 1967; two *s* one *d.* BA QUB 1968; Member: Assoc. of Univ. Teachers;

BPsS (Mem. Cttee, NI Br., 1973–). Res. Asst, Univ. of Durham, 1968–72. *Publications*: *contrib.* Brit Jl Criminol., Brit. Jl Soc. Clin. Psychol. *Address*: Sch. of Biological and Environmental Studies, Univ. of Ulster, Coleraine, Co. Londonderry BT52 1SA.

Hess, Hans, OBE, MA; Reader in History and Theory of Art, University of Sussex, since 1969; *b* 1908; *m* 1944; one *d*. MA Leeds 1964 (History of Art); Lectr, History and Theory of Art, Univ. of Sussex, 1967–69. *Publications*: Lyonel Feininger, 1959; *contrib.* The Burlington Mag., Museums Jl, Brit. Jl of Aesthetics. *Address*: School of European Studies, Univ. of Sussex, Falmer, Brighton BN1 9QN.

Hesse, Dr Mary Brenda, FBA; Reader in Philosophy of Science, University of Cambridge, since 1968; *b* 1924. BSc London 1945 (1st cl. Mathematics), PhD London 1948, MSc London 1950, MA Cantab 1960; FBA 1971; Mem., Aristotelian Soc., Brit. Soc. Phil. Science; Brit. Soc. Hist. Sci. Asst Lectr, Royal Holloway Coll., 1947–51; Lectr, Leeds, 1951–55; Lectr, UCL, 1955–59; Lectr, Cambridge, 1960–68; Vis. Prof., Yale, 1962; Minnesota, 1966; Chicago, 1968. Pres. Brit. Soc. Phil. Science, 1970–72; Cttee mem., Phil. Science Div. of Internat. Union Hist. and Phil. Sci., 1971– ; Ed., Brit. Jl Phil. Sci., 1965–69. *Publications*: Science and the Human Imagination, 1954; Forces and Fields, 1961; Models and Analogies in Science, 1963; The Structure of Scientific Inference, 1974; *contrib.* Brit. Jl Phil. Sci., Ann. Sci., Isis, Proc. Aris. Soc. Rev., Metaphysics, Dialectica, Amer. Jl Phys, Phil. Qly, Jl Phil., Philosophy, Phil. Sci. *Address*: Whipple Museum, Free School Lane, Cambridge.

Hetherington, Dr Ralph Railton; Secretary-General, British Psychological Society, since 1973; Visiting Professor in Clinical Psychology, University of Liverpool, since 1973 (Director, Sub-Department of Clinical Psychology, 1971–73); *b* 1917; *m* 1945; two *s* two *d*. BSc London 1947 (1st cl. Psychology), PhD London 1954; FBPsS. Part-time Lectr, Liverpool Univ., 1960–64; Co-Ed., Brit. Jl Soc. Clin. Psychol., 1965–69. Registrar, Bd of Examiners, Brit. Psychol. Soc., 1970– . *Publications*: An Introduction to Psychology for Medical Students, 1964; *contrib.* Brit. Jl Anaes., Brit. Jl Med. Educn, Brit. Jl Med. Psychol., Jl Ment. Sci., Brit. Jl. Psychiat., Bull. Brit. Psychol. Soc. *Address*: 18/19 Albemarle Street, W1X 4DN.

Heughan, Hazel E.; Lecturer in Economics, University of Edinburgh, since 1949; *b* 1918. MA Edinburgh 1941 (1st cl. Economic Science). Min. of Labour and Nat. Service. 1941–48. *Publications*: Pit Closures at Shotts and the Migration of Miners, 1953; *contrib.* Turkish Econ. Rev. *Address*: Dept of Economics, Univ. of Edinburgh, EH8 9YL.

Heuston, Prof. Robert Francis Vere, DCL; Regius Professor of Laws, Trinity College, Dublin, since 1970; *b* 1923; *m* 1962; four step *c*. DCL Oxon 1970. Barrister, King's Inns, 1947, Gray's Inn, 1951. Fellow,

Pembroke Coll., Oxford, 1947–65 (Supernumerary Fellow, 1965–), Dean, 1951–57, Pro-Proctor, 1953; Prof. of Law, Univ. of Southampton, 1965–70; Vis. Prof., Univ. of Melbourne, 1956; Vis. Prof., Univ. of BC, 1960; Gresham Prof. in Law, 1964–70. Mem., Law Reform Cttee, 1968–70. *Publications*: Essays in Constitutional Law, 2nd edn 1964; Lives of the Lord Chancellors, 1964; ed, Salmond on Torts, 11th edn 1953, 16th edn 1973; *contrib.* learned periodicals. *Address*: Trinity College, Dublin 2.

Hewitt, Dr David Sword, MA, PhD; Lecturer in English, University of Aberdeen, since 1968; *b* 1942; *m* 1967; one *d*. MA Edinburgh 1964, PhD Aberdeen 1969; Asst Lectr, Aberdeen, 1964–68. *Publications*: *contrib.* AUJ, Scott. Literary News, TES. *Address*: Dept of English, Univ. of Aberdeen, Taylor Building, Old Aberdeen AB9 2UB.

Hewitt, Douglas John; Staff Tutor, Department for External Studies, Oxford, since 1956; Research Lecturer, Pembroke College, Oxford, since 1973; *b* 1920; *m* 1951 (widowed); *m* 1965; five *s* two *d*. BA Cantab 1941, MA Cantab 1945, MA Oxon 1972 (by incorporation). *Publications*: Conrad: A Reassessment, 1952, 2nd edn 1969; The Approach to Fiction: Good and Bad Readings of Novels, 1972; *contrib.* RES, Essays in Criticism. *Address*: Dept for External Studies, Rewley House, Wellington Square, Oxford.

Heywood, Dr Jean Schofield, BA, PhD, AIMSW, JP; Reader in Social Administration, University of Manchester, since 1973; *b* 1915. BA Manchester 1937 Hons Classics, Dipl. in Social Admin. Manchester 1938, PhD Leeds 1959 (Sociology); AIMSW 1939. Principal, Admiralty, 1939–46; Med. Social Worker, 1946–48; Children's Officer, Rochdale, 1948–54; Lectr, Leeds Univ., 1954–58; Manchester University: Lectr, 1958–68; Sen. Lectr, 1968–73. Member: Ed. Bd, Jl of Economic and Social Admin., 1972– ; Manchester Diocesan Bd of Social Responsibility, 1972– . *Publications*: Children in Care, 1959, 2nd edn 1964, 3rd edn forthcoming; An Introduction to Teaching Casework Skills, 1964; Casework and Pastoral Care, 1967; Financial Help in Social Work, 1971; *contrib.* Soc. Work Today, Brit. Jl Soc. Work. *Address*: Dept of Social Administration, The Univ., Dover Street, Manchester.

Heywood, John; Research Associate Professor of Education, Trinity College, Dublin, since 1973; *b* 1930; *m* 1960; three *s* two *d*. MLitt Lancaster 1969, FCP 1963 (LCP 1962), AMBIM, FRAS, FRSA, SMIEEE (NY). Leverhulme Sen. Res. Fellow in Higher Educn, 1964–67, Lectr in Higher Educn, 1967–70, Univ. of Lancaster; Lectr in Industrial Studies, Univ. of Liverpool, 1970–73. Mem. Council Brit. Ast. Assoc. 1956–64 (Dir, Radio Electronics Sect.); Coll. of Preceptors, 1963; Soc. for Res. into Higher Educn, 1964– (Treasurer); Mem., Lancashire Educn Cttee. *Publications*: Bibliography of British Technological Education and Training, 1971; *contrib.* Bull. Mech. Eng. Educn, Int. Jl Elec. Eng. Ed., Jl Jun. Inst. E., Memoirs, Brit. Ast. Ass., NFER

313

Occasional Publ., Nature, Proc. Royal Soc., Universities Qly. *Address*: School of Education, Trinity Coll., Dublin 2.

Heywood Thomas, Rev. John, DD; Reader in Divinity, University of Durham, since 1965; *b* 1926; *m* 1935; one *d*. BA Wales 1947 (Hons Philosophy), BD Wales 1950, STM Union Seminary, NY 1953, DD Wales 1965; Res. Fellow, Durham Univ., 1955–57; Asst Lectr, Manchester Univ., 1957–60; Lectr, 1960–65; Croall Lectr, Edinburgh, 1969; Montgomery Lectr for CEM, 1972–74. *Publications*: Subjectivity and Paradox, 1957; Paul Tillich: An Appraisal, 1963; Paul Tillich, 1965; *contrib*. Relig. Studies, Rev. Relig., Scott. Jl Theol. *Address*: Dept of Theology, 46 Saddler Street, Durham.

Hick, Rev. Prof. John Harwood, MA, PhD, DPhil; H. G. Wood Professor of Theology, University of Birmingham, since 1967; *b* 1922; *m* 1953; three *s* one *d*. MA Edinburgh 1948 (1st cl. Philosophy), DPhil Oxon 1950, PhD Cantab 1964 (by incorporation); Mem.: Mind Assoc., Royal Inst. Philos., Soc. Psychical Res., Soc. Study Theol., Ed. Bd Theol. Today, Relig. Studies, Encyclop. of Philos. Asst. Prof. of Philosophy, Cornell Univ., 1956–59; Stuart Prof. of Christian Philosophy, Princeton Theol. Seminary, 1959–64; Lectr in Divinity, Cambridge Univ., 1964–67; S.A. Cook Bye-Fellow, Gonville and Caius Coll., Cambridge, 1963–64; Guggenheim Fellow, 1963–64; Mead-Swing Lectr, Oberlin Coll., 1962; Mary Farnum Brown Lectr, Haverford Coll., 1964; Disting. Vis. Lectr, Univ. of Oregon, 1969; James W. Richard Lectr, Univ. of Virginia, 1969; Vis. Prof., Benares Hindu Univ., 1971; Brit. Acad. Overseas Vis. Fellow, Univ. of Ceylon, 1974; Arthur Stanley Eddington Lectr, Cambridge Univ., 1972. *Publications*: Faith and Knowledge, 1957, 2nd edn 1966; Philosophy of Religion, 1963, 2nd edn 1973, Spanish, Portuguese, Finnish and Japanese trans.; ed, Faith and the Philosophers, 1963; ed, Classical and Contemporary Readings in the Philosophy of Religion, 1963, 2nd edn 1970; ed, The Existence of God, 1963; Evil and the God of Love, 1966; ed, The Many-Faced Argument, 1967; Christianity at the Centre, 1968; Arguments for the Existence of God, 1971; Biology and the Soul, 1972; God and the Universe of Faiths, 1973; ed, Truth and Dialogue, 1974; *contrib*. Jl Theol. Studies, Relig. Studies, Jl Philos., Philos., Australian Jl Philos., Canadian Jl Philos., Scottish Jl Theol. *Address*: Dept of Theology, Univ. of Birmingham, PO Box 363, Birmingham B15 2TT.

Hickey, Dr Leo, MA, LLB, Lic en Fil y Let, Dr en Fil y Let, Barrister-at-Law; Lecturer in Spanish, Department of Modern Languages, University of Salford, since 1966; *b* 1934; *m* 1969; one *s* one *d*. BA NUI 1956, MA NUI 1958, LLB NUI 1958; Barrister-at-Law King's Inn 1957, Lic en Fil y Let Madrid 1966, Dr en Fil y Let Madrid 1966. *Publications*: Cinco horas con Miguel Delibes, 1968; *contrib*. Jl Aesthet. Art Crit., Rev. Occid. *Address*: Dept of Modern Languages, The Univ., Salford M5 4WT.

Hickling, Rev. Colin John Anderson; Lecturer in New Testament Studies, University of London, King's College, since 1968; *b* 1931. BA Cantab 1953 (Pt 1, 1st cl. English, with Distinction, Pt 2, 2nd cl. (i) French and Italian), Theological Tripos Sect. 2 (New Testament) 1955 (2nd cl. (i)), Carus Prize for Greek New Testament (half share) 1956, MA Cantab 1957. Mem., Soc. OT Study. Lectr and Tutor in Old Testament, Chichester Theol. Coll., 1961–65; Asst Lectr in New Testament Studies, Univ. of London, King's Coll., 1965–68. Dep. Priest in Ordinary to HM The Queen, 1971–74, Priest in Ordinary 1971– ; Subwarden, King's Coll. Hall, 1969–; Boyle Lectr, 1973– . *Publications*: contrib. Anglican Catholics Today, 1968; *contrib*. Ch Qly Rev., Faith Unity, Theol., Foi Vie – Cahiers Bibl. *Address*: Univ. of London, King's College, Strand, WC2R 2LS.

Hickman, Dr Aubrey Thomas; Senior Lecturer, Department of Education, University of Manchester, since 1968; *b* 1922; *m* 1950; two *s* one *d*. BA London 1947, BMus Durham 1952, PhD Manchester 1968; LRAM 1949. Lectr, Dept of Educn, Univ. of Manchester, 1959–68. Treasurer, SRPMME, 1972– . Mem., Univ. Senate, 1969–72. *Publications*: Electronic Apparatus for Music Research, 1968; *contrib*. Jl Acoust. Soc. America, Jl Res. Music Educn, Res. in Educn, Psychol. Mus., ISME Res. Bull. *Address*: Dept of Education, Univ. of Manchester, Manchester M13 9PL.

Hickson, Prof. David John, MScTech; Professor of Behavioural Studies, University of Bradford Management Centre, since 1970; *b* 1931; *m* 1954; one *s* one *d*. MScTech Manchester 1961; AICS 1954, Assoc. Inst. Personnel Mngmt 1958; Member: Brit. Sociol. Assoc.; Internat. Sociol. Assoc.; American Sociol Assoc. Res. Fellow, Univ. of Aston, 1960–63; Lectr in Indust. Sociol., 1963–70; Vis. Prof. of Organizational Behaviour, Univ. of Alberta, 1968–70. Asst to Sec., Bristol Stock Exch., 1957; Mem., Ed. Bd, Admin. Sci. Qly, 1969– . *Publications*: (jtly) Writers on Organizations, 1964, later edn 1971; *contrib*. Admin. Sci. Qly, Jl Mngmt Studies, Mens Maatsch, Occupat. Psychol., Sociol. *Address*: Organizational Analysis Research Unit, Univ. of Bradford Management Centre, Bradford BD9 4JL.

Hiddleston, Dr James Andrew, MA, PhD; Fellow in French, Exeter College, Oxford University, since 1966; *b* 1935; *m* 1971. MA Edinburgh 1957 (1st cl. French), PhD Edinburgh 1961, MA Oxon 1966. Lectr in French, Leeds Univ., 1960–66. *Publications*: L'univers de Jules Supervielle, 1965; Malraux: La Condition humaine, 1973; ed, Laforgue: Poems, 1974. *Address*: Exeter College, Oxford.

Higgins, Rev. Prof. Angus John Brockhurst; Professor of Theology, University of Wales, since 1970; *b* 1911; *m* 1939; one *d*. BA Wales 1934, MA 1937, BD Manchester 1939, PhD 1945, DD 1965; Mem.: Soc. for Old Testament Study, Studiorum Novi Testamenti Societas. Asst Lectr in Hebrew,

Manchester Univ., 1945–46; Lectr in New Testament, New Coll., London Univ., 1946–52; Lectr, Leeds Univ., 1953–61; Sen. Lectr, 1961–66; Reader, 1966–70; Vis. Prof., Trinity Coll., Univ. of Toronto, 1958–59. *Publications*: The Christian Significance of the Old Testament, 1949; The Reliability of the Gospels, 1952; The Lord's Supper in the New Testament, 1952, repr. 1972; ed, Cullmannn: The Early Church, 1956; ed, New Testament Essays: in memory of T. W. Manson, 1959; The Historicity of the Fourth Gospel, 1960; Jesus and the Son of Man, 1964; Menschensohn-Studien, 1965; The Tradition about Jesus, 1969; *contrib.* Jl of Theological Studies; New Testament Studies; Novum Testamentum; Scott. Jl of Theology; Vigiliae Christianae. *Address*: Dept of Theology, St David's Univ. College, Lampeter, Dyfed SA48 7ED.

Higgins, David Henry, MA; Lecturer in charge of Italian, University of Bristol, since 1966; *b* 1935; *m* 1961; two *s* two *d*. BA Cantab 1959, MA Cantab 1969. Lectr Auckland Univ., NZ, 1963–66. Assessor (MA) Wellington Univ., NZ, 1970– . *Publications*: *contrib.* FMLS, Dante Studies, MLR, YWMLS. *Address*: Sub-Dept of Italian, Univ. of Bristol, Bristol BS8 1TH.

Higgins, Prof. John Christopher, MA, MSc; Professor of Management and Information Sciences, Management Centre, University of Bradford, since 1970, Director since 1972; *b* 1932; *m* 1960; three *s*. MA Cantab 1957, MSc London 1959, BSc London 1964; C. Eng., MIEE, MInstP, Mem. of OR Soc., BIM. RAF, 1953–56; Scientific Civil Service, 1962–64; Consultancy and Business 1964–70 (Dir, IPC Newspapers Ltd, 1969–70). Chm., Publications Cttee, OR Soc., 1970–72. *Publications*: Problems in Applied Physics, 1962; Problems in Electronics, 1964; Introduction to Linear Programming, 1966; Operational Research, 1967; *contrib.* IEE Jl, Jl of Business Policy, Management Decision. *Address*: Univ. of Bradford, The Management Centre, Emm Lane, Bradford BD9 4JL.

Higgins, Patrick Farrel Phillips; Reader in Law, University of Wales, since 1972; *b* 1913; *m* 1947; one *d*. LLB London 1960, LLM Tasmania 1964; Solicitor (Hons) 1954; Member: Law Soc. 1954, Soc. of Public Teachers of Law 1957, Assoc. of Pakistani Papists 1968. Sen. Lectr in Law, Univ. Tasmania, 1960–68; Reader in Law, Monash Univ., 1968–71; Sen. Lectr, Univ. Wales Inst. of Science and Technology, 1971–72. Sen. Lectr, Law Soc. Sch. of Law, 1956–60; Chief Justice of Victoria's Law Reform (sub-cttee on age of majority), 1970. Regular Army 60th Rifles, 1934–49. *Publications*: Law of Partnership in Australia and New Zealand, 1963, 2nd edn 1971; ed (with J. G. Starke) Australian edn, Cheshire and Fifoot's Law of Contract, 1966, 3rd edn 1974; sections on Agency, Bailment, Guarantees, Insurance, Loan, Money Had and Received, Bankruptcy, Bills of Exchange, Currency and Personal Property, in, The Judgments of Sir Owen Dixon, 1973; *contrib.* Cambrian Law Rev., Malaya Law Rev., Modern Law Rev., Univ.

Tasmania Law Rev., Univ. W Australia Law Rev. *Address*: Dept of Law, Univ. of Wales Institute of Science and Technology, Cathays Park, Cardiff CF1 3NU.

Higgs, Eric S.; Assistant Director of Research, Department of Archaeology, Cambridge University, since 1966; *b* 1908; *m* 1964; one *s* three *d*. BCom London 1930, MA Cantab 1956; FZS; Mem. Brit. Ecological Soc., Mem. Prehistoric Soc. Asst in Research, Cambridge Univ., 1956–61, Sen. Asst 1961–66; Dir of Studies, Magdalene Coll. and Gonville and Caius Coll., Cambridge. *Publications*: Science in Archaeology, 1963; The Archaeology of Early Man, 1965; Papers in Economic Prehistory, 1972; Palaeoeconomy, 1973; *contrib.* Procs. Prehistoric Soc., Man, etc. *Address*: Dept of Archaeology, Downing Street, Cambridge.

Higgs, John Walter Yeoman; Fellow of Exeter College, Oxford University (Senior Research Fellow), and College Lecturer in Agriculture and Agricultural Development, since 1962; *b* 1923; *m* 1948; two *d*. BA Cantab 1943, MA Cantab 1947, BA Oxon 1946, MA Oxon 1950 (Incorporation); Sec., Brit. Agricultural Hist. Soc., 1952–64; Mem., Council, Museums Assoc., 1954–58. Res. Asst, Agricultural Economics Inst., Univ. of Oxford, 1946–48; Lectr, Fac. of Agriculture, Univ. of Reading, 1948–57; Lectr, Agricultural Devlt, Dept of Agriculture, Univ. of Oxford, 1957–65; Fellow and Bursar, Exeter College, Univ. of Oxford, 1962–68. Keeper, Museum of English Rural Life, Univ. of Reading, 1951–57; Warden, Whiteknight Park House, Univ. of Reading, 1952–57. Chief, Agricultural Educn, Extension and Rural Youth Service, FAO, UN, 1971– . *Publications*: The Land, 1964; (with R. K. Kerkham and J. R. Raeburn) Problems in the Modernization of Agriculture in Tropical African Colonies, 1950; ed, People in the Countryside, 1966. *Address*: Exeter College, Oxford.

Higgs, Malcolm Slade, AADip, PhD, ARIBA, ARIAS; Lecturer in Architecture, University of Edinburgh, since 1964; *b* 1935; *m* 1965; one *s* one *d*. AADip 1960; PhD, Edinburgh, 1972; ARIBA, ARIAS. Dir of Studies, Edinburgh Univ., 1968– . Mem., Univ. Senate, 1968–71. Amer. Council of Learned Socs Fellow, Columbia and Harvard Univs, 1972–73. *Publications*: *contrib.* Jl Soc. Archit. Hist. *Address*: 16–18 George Square, Edinburgh.

Higham, Norman; University Librarian, University of Bristol, since 1966; *b* 1924; *m* 1954; one *s* one *d*. BA Sheffield 1951 (1st cl. Hons Philos., Span., English), MA Leeds 1962; ALA 1955. Asst Librarian, Univ. of Sheffield, 1953–57; Univ. of Leeds, 1957–62; Leverhulme Res. Fellow, Dept of Philosophy, Univ. of Leeds, 1961; Librarian, Loughborough Coll. of Technol., 1962–63; Deputy Librarian, Univ. of Leeds, 1963–66. Chm. UCR Section, Library Assoc., 1974– ; Mem., Sconul Cttee 1972– . *Publications*: A Very Scientific Gentleman: The Major Achievements of Henry Clifton Sorby, 1963; Computer Needs for University Library

Operations, 1973; contrib. A Biographical Dictionary of Scientists, ed T. I. Williams, 1969; Encyclopaedia of World Biography, 1972; contrib. Program, Jl Documentation. Address: The Library, Univ. of Bristol, Bristol BS8 1RJ.

Higman, Prof. Francis Montgomery; Professor of French, Trinity College, Dublin, since 1970; b 1935; m 1960; one s two d. BA Oxon 1959 (French, German), MA Oxon 1964, BLitt Oxon 1964. Asst. Lectr, Bristol Univ., 1961–64, Lectr, 1964–69; Vis. Associate Prof., Univ. of Saskatchewan (Regina), 1969–70. Publications: The Style of John Calvin in his French polemical treatises, 1967; ed with K. Cameron and K. M. Hall, Th. de Bèze, Abraham Sacrifiant, 1967; ed, J. Calvin, Three French Treatises, 1970; Ronsard's Political and Polemical Poetry, in Ronsard the Poet, 1973; contrib. Bibliothèque d'Humanisme et Renaissance, Western Canadian Studies in Mod. Lang. Address: No. 35, Trinity College, Dublin 2, Ireland.

Hilbourne, Marion Phoebe, BA, MA; Lecturer, Department of Mental Health, University of Bristol, since 1969; b 1939; m 1971. BA Exeter 1960 (Hons Sociology), MA McGill 1962 (Sociology); Mem., Brit. Sociol. Assoc. Res. Asst, Univ. Coll., Cardiff, 1962–65; Lectr, Univ. Coll., Cardiff, 1965–66; Res. Assoc., Univ. of Bristol, 1966–69. Publications: contrib. Hum. Relat., Sociol., Jl Psychosom. Res., Sociol. Rev. Address: Dept of Mental Health, 41 St Michael's Hill, Bristol BS2 8DZ.

Hill, Alan Geoffrey, MA, BLitt; Senior Lecturer in English, University of Dundee, since 1968; b 1931; m 1960; three d. MA St Andrews (1st cl. Eng. Lang. and Lit.), BLitt Oxon 1957. Asst Lectr, then Lectr, Exeter Univ., 1958–62; Lectr, St Andrews Univ., 1962–68; Vis. Prof. of English, Saskatchewan Univ., 1973–74. Trustee, Dove Cottage, 1969– . Publications: ed (with Mary Moorman), The Letters of William and Dorothy Wordsworth: The Middle Years, Pt II, 1970; contrib. Crit. Qly, Essays in Crit., Forum Mod. Lang. Studies, Notes Queries, Rev. Engl. Studies, Scott. Jl Theol., Theol., Times Lit. Supp. Address: Dept of English, Univ. of Dundee, Dundee DD1 4HN.

Hill, Dr Brian Ernest; Lecturer in Agricultural Economics, Department of Economics, University of Nottingham, since 1970; b 1937; m 1960; two s one d. BSc Nottingham 1959, MSc London 1963, PhD Nottingham 1971; Mem., Agric Econs Soc. Asst Lectr in Agricl Econs, Univ. of Exeter, 1963–66; Lectr in Agricl Econs, Dept of Agricl Econs, Univ. of Nottingham, 1966–70. Res. Cons. to FAO (Rome), 1970–71. Publications: contrib. Jl Agricl Econs. Address: Dept of Economics, University Park, Nottingham NG7 2RD.

Hill, Dr Brian William, BA, PhD; Lecturer in English History, School of English and American Studies, University of East Anglia, since 1963; b 1932; m 1968; one s. BA London 1957 (1st cl. History), PhD Cantab 1962. Res. Asst, Burke Correspondence (Copeland edn),

1961–63. Publications: Edmund Burke on Government, Politics and Society; contrib. Econ. Hist. Rev., Hist. Jl, Hist., Eng. Hist. Rev. Address: School of English and American Studies, Univ. of East Anglia, Univ. Plain, Norwich NOR 88C.

Hill, Charles Peter, MA; Senior Lecturer, School of Education, University of Exeter; b 1914; m 1st 1938, 2nd 1971; one s. BA Oxon 1936 (Hons Mod. Hist.), DipEd Oxon 1937, MA Oxon 1940; Mem. Council Historical Assoc. Lectr, Univ. Exeter, 1960–66, Sen. Lectr, 1966–75. Publications: History of the United States, 1942, 2nd edn 1966; The History of Bristol Grammar School, 1951; Suggestions on the Teaching of History, 1953; British Social and Economic History since 1700, 1957, 3rd edn 1970; Who's Who in History: England, 1603–1714, 1965; Franklin Roosevelt, 1966. Address: School of Education, Univ. of Exeter, Exeter EX4 4QJ.

Hill, Christine Muriel, MA; Lecturer in French, University of Manchester, since 1958; b 1927. BA Oxon 1948 (Hons Mod. Lang. French), MA Manchester 1951, MA Oxon 1952, Dip. Ed. Oxon 1949. Asst Lectr in French, Univ. Coll., London, 1953–56; Asst Lectr in French, Manchester, 1956–58. Mem., Council, Univ. of Manchester, 1961–64 and 1972– ; elected non-professorial Mem., Senate, 1970–73, 1973–76; Mem., Stand. Cttee, Senate, 1971–73. Publications: ed (with M. Morrison), R. Garnier: Hippolyte and Marc Antoine (forthcoming); contrib. Fr. Studies. Address: Dept of French, Univ. of Manchester, Manchester M13 9PL.

Hill, Christopher Peter; Lecturer in Education, with Special Reference to the Teaching of English as a Foreign Language, Institute of Education, University of London, since 1965; b 1929; m 1954; three s. BA Dublin 1951 (Mod.-Mod. Lang/English and French), MA Dublin 1959. DipEd Belfast 1952, Cert. TESL California 1962. Dep. Leader, Survey of Language Use and Language Teaching in Tanzania, 1969–70; Dir, Univ. of London Dept of Extra-Mural Studies' Summer Sch. of English, 1974. Mem., Lingu. Assoc. Gt Brit., Internat. Assoc. Teachers Engl. as Foreign Langs. Publications: contrib. Engl. Lang. Teaching. Address: Dept of English as a Foreign Language, Division of Language Teaching, Univ. of London, Institute of Education, Malet Street, WC1E 7HS.

Hill, Christopher Richard; Lecturer in Politics, University of York, since 1966, and Director, Centre for Southern African Studies, since 1972; b 1935. BA Cantab 1956, MA Cantab 1960. Foreign Off., 1959–62; Asst Dir, Inst. Race Relat., London, 1962–65; Lectr in Govt, Univ. Coll. of Rhodesia, 1965–66. Publications: Bantustans; the Fragmentation of South Africa, 1964; ed, Rights and Wrongs: Some Essays on Human Rights, 1969. Address: Dept of Politics, Univ. of York, Heslington, York YO1 5DD.

Hill, Rev. Dr David, BA, BD, STM, PhD; Senior Lecturer, Department of Biblical Studies, University of Sheffield, since 1971; b 1935. BA Belfast 1956 (2nd cl. Classics),

BD St Andrews 1959, STM Union Theol. Sem., NY 1960, PhD St Andrews 1964; Mem., Studiorum NT Soc. 1965. Asst Lectr, Univ. of Sheffield, 1964–66; Lectr, 1966–71. *Publications*: Greek Words and Hebrew Meanings, 1967; The Gospel of Matthew, A Commentary, 1972; *contrib*. Expos. Times, Nov. Test., NT Studies. *Address*: Dept of Biblical Studies, The Univ., Sheffield S10 2TN.

Hill, Donald Edward; Lecturer, Department of Classics, University College, Cardiff, since 1969; *b* 1938; *m* 1967; two *s* one *d*. BA Cantab 1960; MA Washington 1963; MA Cantab 1964. Member: Amer. Philol Assoc.; Classical Assoc.; Classical Assoc. of Canada. Instructor, Washington Univ., 1961–63; Lecturer: Univ. of New Brunswick, 1963–64; Univ. of Western Ontario, 1964–67; Asst Prof., Univ. of Western Ontario. 1967–69. *Publications*: *contrib*. CQ, CR, Hermes, Phoenix, RhM. *Address*: Univ. Coll., Cardiff CF1 1XA.

Hill, Graham B.; *see* Byrne Hill.

Hill, Howard Henry E.; *see* Erskine-Hill.

Hill, Dr (John Edward) Christopher; Master of Balliol College, University of Oxford, since 1965; *b* 1912; *m* 2nd, 1956; one *s* two *d*. BA Oxon 1934, MA Oxon 1938, DLitt Oxon 1965; Hon DLitt Hull, Sheffield, E Anglia; FBA, FRHistS. Fellow, All Souls Coll. Oxford, 1934–38; Asst Lecturer in Modern History, Univ. Coll., Cardiff, 1936–38; Fellow and Tutor in Modern History, Balliol Coll., Oxford, 1938–65; Univ. Lectr in 16th and 17th c. History, Oxford 1958–65; Ford Lectr, Oxford, 1962. Pres., Past Pres. Soc., 1970– . *Publications*: The English Revolution, 1940; Lenin and The Russian Revolution, 1947; ed, (with E. Dell), The Good Old Cause, 1949; Economic Problems of the Church, 1956; Puritanism and Revolution, 1958; The Century of Revolution, 1961; Society and Puritanism in Pre-Revolutionary England, 1964; Intellectual Origins of the English Revolution, 1965; Reformation to Industrial Revolution, 1967; God's Englishman: Oliver Cromwell and the English Revolution, 1970; Antichrist in 17th century England, 1971; The World Turned Upside Down, 1972; ed, The Law of Freedom and Other Writings of Gerrard Winstanley, 1973; *contrib*. Brit. Jl Sociol., Econ. Hist. Rev., Engl. Hist. Rev., Essays Crit., Hist., Hist. Theory, Notes Rec. Royal Soc. Lond., Past Pres., Rev. Hist., Scrutiny, Soviet Studies, Texas Qly, Trans Royal Hist. Soc., Vop. Hist *Address*: Balliol College, Oxford.

Hill, John Kaye, MA; Lecturer in French, The Language Centre, University of Kent at Canterbury, since 1965; *b* 1931; *m* 1958; two *s*. BA Wales 1953 (Hons French), MA Wales 1964, Cert. Ed. Bristol 1956. *Publications*: (with R. Coulon etc) Le français à travers les sciences humaines (Univ. of Kent Lang. Centre audiolingual reading course in French), 1972. *Address*: The Language Centre, Univ. of Kent, Canterbury.

Hill, Lewis George, MA, BLitt; Lecturer in

South East Asian Social Anthropology, Department of South-East Asian Sociology, University of Hull, since 1969; *b* 1935; *m* 1962. BA Oxon 1959 (Geography), DipAnth Oxon 1960 (Social Anthropology), BLitt Oxon 1962 (Social Anthropology), MA Oxon 1963; FRAI, ASA. Lectr, Univ. of Khartoum, 1962–68. *Address*: Centre for SE Asian Studies, Univ. of Hull, Hull HU6 7RX.

Hill, Dr Michael; Lecturer, Department of Sociology, London School of Economics, since 1967; *b* 1943; *m* 1967; two *s*. BA London 1965 (1st cl. Hons Sociology), PhD London 1971; Hobhouse Meml Prize, LSE, 1965; Nuffield Coll. Studentship, 1967. *Publications*: A Sociological Yearbook of Religion in Britain, No 4, 1971, No 5, 1972, No 6, 1973, No 7 (forthcoming); A Sociology of Religion, 1973; The Religious Order, 1973; *contrib*. Soc. Compass, Expos. Times, New Soc., New Christian. *Address*: London School of Economics, Houghton Street, WC2A 2AE.

Hill, Dr Polly, (Mrs M. E. Humphreys); Smuts Reader, Department of Social Anthropology, Cambridge University, since 1973; Fellow of Clare Hall, Cambridge, since 1965; *b* 1914; *m* 1953; one *d*. BA Cantab 1936 (Econs), PhD Cantab 1967. Mem. Assoc. of Social Anthropologists, 1972– . Sen. Res. Fellow, Univ. of Ghana, 1954–65; Sen. Associate, Univ. of Michigan, 1965–69. SSRC grant for research in northern Nigeria, 1971–73. Civil Servant, 1940–51; journalist, W Africa, 1951–54. *Publications*: The Unemployment Services, 1940; The Gold Coast Cocoa Farmer, 1956; The Migrant Cocoa-Farmers of Southern Ghana, 1963, new edn 1970; Studies in Rural Capitalism in West Africa, 1970; Rural Hausa: A Village and a Setting, 1973; chapters in several books; *contrib*. Africa, Cahiers d'Etudes Africaines, Econ. Develop. and Cult. Change, Jl African Hist., Man. *Address*: Clare Hall, Cambridge CB3 9AL.

Hill, Prof. Rosalind Mary Theodosia; Professor of History, University of London, since 1971; *b* 1908. BA Oxon 1931 (1st cl. Hons History), MA Oxon 1936, BLitt Oxon 1937; FRHistS, FSA, FRSA. Asst Lecturer, University Coll., Leicester, 1932–37; Lectr, Westfield Coll., London, 1937–55; Reader, London, 1955–71. Gen. Ed., Canterbury and York Soc., 1961–69. Chm., 1969– ; Hon. Sec., Eccles. Hist. Soc., 1963–73, Pres., 1973–74; Dir, UFAW, 1962– ; Chm., Educnl Adv. Cttee, UFAW, 1962–73. *Publications*: ed, The Rolls and Register of Bishop Oliver Sutton, 1948; Both Small and Great Beasts, 1956; ed, Gesta Francorum, 1962; The Labourer in the Vineyard, 1969; ed, Register of Archbishop Melton (forthcoming); A Chaunterye for Soules, in, The Reign of Richard II, ed Du Boulay and Barron; *contrib*. Hist., Jl Eccles. Hist., Jl Hants Field Club and Archaeol. Soc. *Address*: Westfield College, Kidderpore Avenue, NW3 7ST.

Hill, Stanley Rowland; Senior Lecturer in Economics and Marketing, Aston Management Centre (formerly Department of Industrial Administration), University of

Aston in Birmingham, since 1969; *b* 1928; *m* 1952; two *d*. BSc London 1959 (Econ.); MISM 1966. Lectr, Univ. of Aston in Birmingham, 1962–69; Course Tutor, Executive Development Programme, 1964–71; Vis. Prof., Amos Tuck Sch., Dartmouth Coll., NH, 1966, 1969; Vis Prof., Colombia Univ., NY, 1966; Vis. Prof., Univ. of Michigan, Ann Arbor, 1966, 1971; Vis. Prof., Kent State Univ., Ohio, 1969, 1971; Vis. Prof., New York Univ., 1971; Vis. Prof., Michigan State Univ., E Lansing, 1971; Vis. Prof., Rutgers, Grad. Sch. Business, 1969, 1971; Vis. Prof., San Francisco State Coll., 1971; Vis. Prof., Drexel Univ., Philadelphia, 1971. Bd Mem., Distrib. Indust. Training Bd, 1968–   ; Chm., Res. Cttee, DITB, 1969–   ; Mem.: RTEC/DITB, Res. Cttee, 1969–70; Cttee on Equal Pay, 1970; Sen. Cnsltnt, UN, 1969–70; Mngmt Cnsltnt, Britain, USA, Sweden and W Germany, 1963–   ; Cnsltnt, US Bureau of Customs, 1971–73. Cnsltnt Editor, Retail and Distribution Management. Arthur H. Elliot Fellow, 1971. *Publications*: The Distributive System, 1964; contrib. An Economic Atlas, 1965; Industrial Relations, Law and Economics, 1969; contrib. Problems of Public Manufacturing Enterprises, 1971; *contrib*. Mktng, New Univ., Retail and Distribution Mngmt, Jl Retailing. *Address*: Aston Management Centre, Univ. of Aston in Birmingham, Gosta Green, Birmingham B4 7ET.

Hill, Dr Stephen Roderick; Lecturer, Sociology Department, London School of Economics, University of London, since 1974; *b* 1946; *m* 1969; one *s*. BA Oxon 1966 (Mod. Hist.), MSc London 1968 (Sociology), PhD London 1973 (Sociology); Mem.: Brit. Sociolog. Assoc.; Brit. Univs Ind. Relns Assoc. Asst Lectr in Sociology, Bedford Coll., London, 1968–69, Lectr 1969–70; Lectr, Ind. Relns, LSE, 1971–74. *Publications contrib*. Brit. Jl Industrial Relations, Brit. Jl Sociology. *Address*: Sociology Dept, London School of Economics, Houghton Street, WC2A 2AE.

Hill, Prof. Thomas Peter, MA; Professor of Economics, since 1967, Dean of School of Social Studies, 1971–73, Pro-Vice-Chancellor, 1973–76, University of East Anglia; *b* 1929; *m* 1961; three *s*. BA Oxon 1952, MA Oxon 1956; Research Officer, Inst. of Statistics, Oxford, 1952–61; Rockefeller Fellow, Yale Stanford, 1957–58; Lectr, Magdalen Coll., Oxford, 1958; Sen. Lectr, Univ. of East Anglia, 1964–67. Administrator, OECD, Paris, 1961–64; Consultant, Statistical Office of the European Communities, 1971–   . *Publications*: The Measurement of Real Product, 1971; A System of Integrated Price and Volume Measures, EEC, 1972; trans. EEC: European System of Integrated Economic Accounts, 1972; *contrib*. Econometrica, Econ. Jl, Rev. Income and Wealth, Bull. Oxford Inst. Econs and Stats. *Address*: School of Social Studies, Univ. of East Anglia, Norwich NOR 88C.

Hill, Trevor Howard H.; *see* Howard-Hill.

Hillebrandt, Dr Patricia M.; Senior Lecturer, School of Environmental Studies, University College, London, since 1967; *b* 1929;

318

m 1957; two *s*. BScEcon London 1952, PhD London 1958. Plant Protection Ltd, 1952–56; Economist, Richard Costain Ltd, 1957–62; Nat. Econ. Develt Office, 1962–67. *Publications*: Small Firms in the Construction Industry, 1971; Economic Theory and the Construction Industry, 1974; *contrib*. Agrarwirtschaft, Farm Economist, Jl Agric. Econs. *Address*: School of Environmental Studies, Univ. College London, Gower Street WC1E 6BT.

Hilliard, John Vincent; Lecturer in Economics, University of Leeds, since 1972; *b* 1946. Lectr in Economics, Univ. of Lancaster, 1969–71. *Address*: Dept of Economics, Univ. of Leeds, Leeds LS2 9JT.

Hilliard, Prof. Frederick Hadaway; Head of the Colleges of Education Division, University of Birmingham School of Education, since 1967; Chairman of the School of Education, 1970–73; *b* 1912; *m* 1937; one *s* one *d*. BD London 1938 (2nd cl. Hons). PhD London 1944, Postgrad. CertEd Cambridge 1947. Mem., Philos. Educn Soc. GB. Principal. Fourah Bay Coll., Univ. of Sierra Leone, 1947–50; Head of Univ. Dept in enlarged Coll., 1950–52; Sen. Lectr in Education, Univ. Coll. of Gold Coast, 1952–55; Sen. Lectr, Univ of London Inst. of Education, 1955–64; Reader, 1964–67. Chm., Universities Council for Educn of Teachers, 1973–   . Chm., Educnl Adv. Cttee ATV Corp. Mem., Adv. Cttee on Supply and Trng of Teachers; Educnl Adv. Council, Independent TV Authority. *Publications*: A Short History of Education in British West Africa, 1957; The Teacher and Religion, 1963; contrib. Christianity in Education (Hibbert Lectures 1965), 1966; ed. Teaching the Teachers, 1971; *contrib*. Brit. Jl Educnl Psychol., Brit. Jl Educnl Studies. Dur. Res. Rev., Educnl Rev. *Address*: School of Education, Univ. of Birmingham, PO Box 363, Birmingham B15 2TT.

Hilling, David, MSc, MCIT; Lecturer in Geography, Bedford College, University of London, since 1966; *b* 1935; *m* 1962; two *s*. BSc Wales 1957 (Hons Geog.). Postgrad. CertEd London 1958, MSc Wales 1961; FRGS, Mem., Inst. Brit. Geogrs, Geog. Assoc., Afr. Studies Assoc. UK. Jun. Res. Fellow, Sheffield, 1959–61; Lectr in Geography, Univ. of Ghana, 1961–66. Transp. cnsltnt, UN Econ. Commn, Africa, 1971–   . *Publications*: ed (with B. S. Hoyle) Seaports and Development in Tropical Africa, 1970; *contrib*. Geog. Jl. Geog. Mag., Geog. *Address*: Dept of Geography, Bedford College, Regent's Park, NW1 4NS.

Hills, D. L. F.; *see* Farley-Hills.

Hills, Peter John; Assistant Director of Research, Institute for Transport Studies, University of Leeds, since 1973; *b* 1938; *m* 1968; two *d*. BSc(Eng) London 1961, MSc Birmingham 1962; CEng 1969, MICE 1969, AMInstHE 1963, MCIT 1963. Lectr in Transport, Imperial Coll., London, 1963–72; Recognised Teacher, Univ. of London, 1965–72. Mem., Exec. Cttee, London Amenity and Transp. Assoc. (LATA), 1967–

71; Working Gp on Buchanan Report: Traffic in Towns, Min. of Transp., 1962–63; Assoc. Ed., UK, Transportation (qly jl). *Publications: contrib*. Buchanan (Report): Traffic in Towns, 1963; (jtly), Kaduna Plan, 1967; (jtly), Motorways in London, 1969. *Address*: Inst. for Transport Studies, Univ. of Leeds, Leeds LS2 9JT.

Hills, Dr Richard Leslie, MA, PhD, DIC; Director, North Western Museum of Science and Industry, and Honorary Senior Lecturer at Manchester University and UMIST, since 1969; *b* 1936. BA Cantab 1960 (History), MA 1963, CertEd 1962, DIC 1965, PhD UMIST 1968; Member: Newcomen Soc.; Historical Assoc.; Museums Assoc. Res. Asst UMIST, 1965–68; Mem. Council, Newcomen Soc., 1967– . *Publications*: Machines, Mills and Uncountable Costly Necessities, a short history of the drainage of the Fens, 1967; Power in the Industrial Revolution, 1970; Sir Richard Arkwright, 1973; *contrib*. Industrial Archaeology, Textile History, Museums Assoc. Jl, Newcomen Soc. Trans, Technology and Culture. *Address*: North Western Museum of Science and Industry, 97 Grosvenor Street, Manchester M1 7HF.

Hilton, Dr Ian; Senior Lecturer, Department of German, University College of North Wales, Bangor, since 1970; *b* 1935; *m* 1961; two *s*. BA Southampton 1956 (1st cl. German), PhD Southampton 1962. Res. Asst, Univ. of Southampton, 1958–60; Asst Lectr, Bangor Univ. Coll., 1960–62; Lectr, 1962–69; Assoc. Prof., Univ. of Calgary, 1969–70; Vis. Assoc. Prof., Univ. of Brit. Columbia, Vancouver, 1971. Rev. Ed., Mod. Langs, 1970– ; Sec., Assoc. Teachers German, GB and Ireland, 1971– . *Publications*: Peter Weiss: A Search for Affinities, 1970; contrib. Essays, German Men of Letters series: Gertrud von Le Fort, vol. II, 1963; Gottfried Benn, vol. III, 1964; Gerd Gaiser, vol. IV, 1966; Clemens Brentano, vol. V, 1969; Vernon Watkins as Translator, in, Vernon Watkins 1906–67, 1970. *Address*: Dept of German, Univ. College of North Wales, Bangor LL57 2DG.

Hilton, Prof. Kenneth; Professor of Financial Control, Department of Economics, University of Southampton, since 1970; *b* 1937; *m* 1963; three *d*. BA Liverpool 1960; ACIS. Asst Lectr, Reading Univ., 1961–62; Lectr, Southampton Univ., 1964–66; Sen. Res. Fellow, Southampton Univ., 1966–70. Nat. Econ. Develop. Office, 1962–64. *Publications*: Jt Ed., The Econometric Study of the United Kingdom, 1970; *contrib*. Appl. Econ., Bull. Oxf. Univ. Inst. Stats Econ., Jl Business Fin., etc. *Address*: Dept of Economics, Univ. of Southampton, Southampton SO9 5NH.

Hilton, Prof. Rodney Howard; Professor of Medieval Social History, University of Birmingham, since 1963; *b* 1916. BA Oxon, DPhil Oxon. Lectr and Reader in Medieval History, Univ. of Birmingham, 1946–63; Ford Lectr, Univ. of Oxford, 1973. *Publications*: The Economic Development of Some Leicestershire Estates in the 14th and 15th Centuries, 1947; (with H. Fagan) The English Rising of 1381, 1950; A Medieval Society, 1966; The Decline of Serfdom in Medieval England, 1969; Bondmen Made Free, 1973; ed, Ministers' Accounts of the Warwickshire Estates of the Duke of Clarence, 1952; ed, The Stoneleigh Leger Book, 1960; *contrib*. Past and Present, EHR, Econ. Hist. Rev. *Address*: School of History, Univ. of Birmingham, Birmingham B15 2TT.

Himmelweit, Prof. Hildegard Therese; Professor of Social Psychology, London School of Economics, since 1964; *m* 1940; one *d*. BA Cantab 1940 (1st cl Modern Languages), BA Cantab 1942 (1st cl. Moral Sciences Tripos: Part II Psychology), PhD London 1945; Fellow, British Psychol. Soc., 1952. Res. Fellow, Maudsley Hosp., 1943–45; Clinical Psychologist, Inst. of Psychiatry, Maudsley Hosp., 1945–48; Lectr, LSE, 1949–53, Reader, 1953–64. Mem., Editorial Board of British Jl of Social and Clinical Psychology, 1962– ; Mem. of Res. Bd, Inst. of Jewish Affairs, 1966– ; Chm., Academic Adv. Cttee, Open Univ., 1969– ; Mem., Educn. Cttee; Community Relations Commn, 1971– . *Publications*: (with A. N. Oppenheim, and P. Vince) Television and the Child, 1958; chapters, in: T. H. Pear, Psychological Factors of Peace and War; D. Glass, Social Mobility in Great Britain; Yearbook of Education, 1960; L. Arons, Television and Human Behaviour; P. Mussen, et al., Trends and Issues in Developmental Psychology; *contrib*. Jl European Soc. Psychol., Sociol. Rev. Mono., Universities' Qly, Brit. Psych. Soc. Bull., New Soc., Jl of Soc. Issues, Acta Psychol., Brit. Jl Psych., Brit. Jl Sociol., Brit. Jl Educl Psych., Eugen. Rev., Jl Pers. *Address*: London School of Economics, Houghton Street, WC2A 2AE.

Hinchliffe, Dr Arnold P.; Senior Lecturer in Literature, Department of English, University of Manchester, since 1970; *b* 1930. BA Manchester 1954, MA Manchester 1955, MA Yale 1956 (American Studies), PhD Manchester 1963. Asst Lectr, Manchester, 1956–59; Lectr, 1959–70. *Publications*: Harold Pinter, 1967; Private File (poems), 1967; ed (with C. B. Cox), Casebook on the Waste Land, 1968; The Absurd, 1969 (trans. into Japanese and Greek); Drama, in The Twentieth Century Mind, ed Cox and Dyson, 1972; British Theatre: 1950–70 (forthcoming); *contrib*. Mod. Drama, Speech Drama, Studi Amer., Texas Studies Lit. Lang., Twent. Cent., Crit. Qly. *Address*: Dept of English, Univ. of Manchester, Manchester M13 9PL.

Hinchliffe, Gerald; Senior Lecturer in Education, School of Education, University of Nottingham, since 1967; *b* 1922; *m* 1955; one *s* one *d*. BA Leeds 1943 (Hons English), MEd Leeds 1955, Dip Ed Leeds 1947. Lectr in Education, Nottingham Univ., 1955–67. Gov., Ockbrook Sch., Ashfield Sch., Eaton Hall Coll. of Educn. *Publications*: A History of King James's Grammar School in Almondbury, 1963; *contrib*. Educnl Rev., Forw. Trends, Jl Educn, Schoolmaster, Times Euducnl Supp., Use Engl., Vis. Educn. *Address*: School of Education, Univ. of Nottingham, Nottingham NG7 2RD.

Hinde, Prof. Robert Aubrey, MA, ScD, DPhil; Royal Society Research Professor, and Honorary Director, Medical Research Council Unit on the Development and Integration of Behaviour, since 1963; *b* 1923; *m* 1st 1950, 2nd 1971; two *s* three *d*. BA Cambridge 1948, BSc London 1948, DPhil Oxford 1950, ScD Cambridge 1958. Mem., various academic societies. Fellow, St John's Coll., Cambridge, 1951–54, 1958– ; Curator, then Sen. Asst in Res., Sub-Dept of Animal Behaviour, 1950–63. Pres., Assoc. Study Anim. Behav., 1969–71. *Publications*: Animal Behaviour, 1966, 2nd edn 1970; Biological Bases of Human Social Behaviour, 1974; jt ed., Advances in the Study of Behaviour, vol. I, 1965; II, 1969; III, 1970; ed, Bird Vocalizations, 1969; ed (with G. Horn), Short Term Changes in Neural Activity, 1970; ed, Non-verbal Communication, 1972; *contrib*. Anim. Behav., Jl Child Psychol. Psychiat., Sci. *Address*: Medical Research Council Unit on the Development and Integration of Behaviour, Madingley, Cambridge CB3 8AA.

Hindle, Dr Anthony, BA, Dip Psychol, PhD; Research Director, Unit for Operational Research in the Health Services, University of Lancaster, since 1971; *b* 1940; *m* 1962; two *s* one *d*. BA Liverpool 1961 (Hons Psychology and Statistics), Dip Psychol Liverpool 1962 (Industrial Psychology), PhD Nottingham 1966 (Control Systems). Mem., Operat. Res. Soc., 1967. Res. Fellow, Lougborough, 1962–65; Asst Lectr, Lancaster, 1965–66; Lectr, Lancaster, 1966–71; Vis. Res. Associate, Regenstrief Inst. of Health Care, Indiana Univ. Sch. of Medicine, 1974–75. Mem., Cttee of Health and Welfare Study Gp, Operat. Res. Soc., 1971– . *Publications*: A Simulation Approach to Surgical Scheduling, 1970; OR in the Health Services and A Practical Approach to Surgical Scheduling, in, Health Services Management, ed H. P. Ferrer, 1972; and jtly, Operations Research in Library and Information Services (forthcoming); *contrib*. Jl Document., Ergonom., Operat. Res. Qly. *Address*: Operational Research Dept, Cartmel College, Bailrigg, Lancaster.

Hindley, Dr Alan; Lecturer, Department of French, University of Hull, since 1968; *b* 1941; *m* 1965; one *s* one *d*. BA Hull 1962, PhD Hull 1965; Mem. Soc. for French Studies. Tutor, Dept of Romance Studies, UC Swansea, 1965–66; Asst Lectr, UC Swansea, 1966–68. *Publications: contrib*. Revue d'Histoire du Théâtre. *Address*: Dept of French, Univ. of Hull, Hull HU6 7RX.

Hindley, Prof. Colin Boothman, MB, ChB, BSc; Professor of Child Development since 1972, and Director, Centre for Study of Human Development, Institute of Education, London, since 1967; *b* 1923; *m* 1945; two *s*. MB, ChB Manchester 1946, BSc London 1949 (1st cl. Psychology); FBPsS, Mem., Assoc. Child Psychol. Psychiat. Res. Psychologist, Inst. of Educn, London Univ., 1949–66; Dir, Longitudinal Res., 1966– ; Recognized Teacher, Univ. of London, 1967–; Hd of Adolescent Development Dip. Course, 1968– . Psychol. Adv., Centre

Internat. Enfance Growth Studies, 1954– ; Ed. Jl Child Psychol. Psychiat., 1959–69; Chm., Assoc. Child Psychol. Psychiat., 1967–68; Mem., Council, Brit. Psychol. Soc., 1970–73; Cttee, Internat. Soc. Study Behav. Develop., 1969– . *Publications*: *contrib*. chapters in books; Brit. Jl Med. Psychol., Brit. Med. Jl, Develop. Med. Child Neurol., Enfance, Hum. Biol., Jl Child Psychol. Psychiat., Jl Genet. Psychol. *Address*: Dept of Child Development, Institute of Education, Univ. of London, Malet Street, WC1E 7HS.

Hindley, Reginald; Lecturer in Geography, University of Bradford, since 1965; *b* 1929; *m* 1954; two *s* two *d*. BA Leeds 1950 (1st cl. Geography), MA Leeds 1952 (with Distinction); FRGS, Mem., Inst. Brit. Geogrs, Geog. Assoc., Geog. Soc. Ireland, Royal Inst. Int. Aff. Asst Lectr, Univ. Coll. of S West, Exeter, 1954–55. *Address*: School of Social Sciences, Univ. of Bradford, Bradford BD7 1DP.

Hindmarch, Dr Ian, BSc. PhD, ABPsS; Lecturer in Cognitive Psychology, Department of Psychology, University of Leeds, since 1966; *b* 1944; *m* 1965; two *s* one *d*. BSc Leeds 1966 (Hons Psychology), PhD Leeds 1970; ABPsS, MICAA. Mem., Soc. Study Addiction. NATO Fellowship, 1967; IBS Res. Fellowship, 1968; Assoc. Prof., Univ. of Maryland, European Div., 1969– ; Hon. Sec. and Treas., Northn Br., Brit. Psychol. Soc., 1968–73; Mem., Adv. Cttee, Soc. and Psychol. Aspects of Drugs, 1968–70; Mem., UN Expert Cttee Social Aspects Drug Use, 1972. *Publications*: Eyes, Eye Spots and Pupil Dilation in Nonverbal Communication (European Monographs in Social Psychology No 3), 1972; Student Drug Surveys, 1972; *contrib*. Brit. Jl Addiction, Drugs Soc., Internat. Jl Addictions, Papers Psychol., Psychol. Belg., Bull. on Narcotics, Psychopharm., Synapse, Nature, Bull. Hist. Med. *Address*: Dept of Psychology, Univ. of Leeds, Leeds LS2 9JT.

Hindmarsh, Miss Irene, JP; Principal St Aidan's College, University of Durham, since 1970; *b* 1923. BA Lady Margaret Hall, Oxford 1945 (Hons French), MA Oxon 1949. *Address*: St Aidan's College, Durham.

Hinds, Alfred Edward, MA; Lecturer in Classics, Trinity College, University of Dublin, since 1965; *b* 1930; *m* 1955; one *s* one *d*. BA Dublin 1952 (1st cl. Classics, Gold Medal, Univ. Studentship in Classics), MA Dublin 1957. Asst Lectr, Queen Mary Coll., Univ. of London, 1953–55; Jun. Lectr, Trinity Coll., Dublin, 1955–65. Tutor, 1965–72. *Publications*: *contrib*. Class. Qly. *Address*: 40 Trinity College, Dublin 2. Ireland.

Hinds, Dr (George) Martin; University Lecturer in Arabic, University of Cambridge, since 1970; Fellow of Trinity Hall, Cambridge, since 1972; *b* 1941; *m* 1963; two *s*. BA London 1962, MA Cantab 1966, PhD London 1969. Asst Lectr in Arabic, Univ. of London, 1963–66; Univ. Asst Lectr in Arabic, Cambridge, 1965–70. Exec. Dir, Center for

Arabic Study Abroad (Univ. of California at Berkeley and American Univ. in Cairo), 1970–72. *Publications*: *contrib*. IJMES, JSS. *Address*: Trinity Hall, Cambridge CB2 1TJ.

Hine, Robert Charles; Lecturer, Department of Economics, University of Nottingham, since 1970; *b* 1944. BA Hons London 1965 (Geog.), MSc Nottingham 1967 (Agric. Econ.). Asst Lectr, Dept of Agric. Econs, Univ. of Nottingham, 1967–70. *Publications*: *contrib*. Jl of Agric. Econs. *Address*: Dept of Economics, University Park, Nottingham NG7 2RD.

Hiner, Owen Stanley, MA; Senior Lecturer in Economics, University of Hull, since 1964; *b* 1922. BA Cantab 1949, MA Cantab 1954. Lectr, Hull Univ., 1951–64; Vis. Prof., Rochester Univ., 1970. *Publications*: The Business Schools and Management Education in the United States, 1958; Business Administration, 1969. *Address*: Dept of Economics and Commerce, Univ. of Hull, Hull HU6 7RX.

Hines, Prof. Albert Gregorio; Professor of Economics, University of London, since 1972; *b* 1935; *m* 1962; two *s* one *d*. Cert. in Trade Union Studies LSE 1957, BSc(Econ) London 1961. Asst Lectr, Bristol Univ., 1962–64; Lectr, Univ. Coll. London, 1964–68; Prof., Durham Univ., 1968–72; Vis. Prof., MIT, 1971–72. *Publications*: The Reappraisal of Keynesian Economics, 1971; *contrib*. Amer. Econ. Rev., Econ. Jl, Rev. Econ. Stats., Rev. Econ. Studies. *Address*: Dept of Economics, Birkbeck College, Univ. of London, 7–15 Gresse Street, W1P 1PA.

Hinings, Christopher Robin; Senior Research Fellow, Institute of Local Government Studies, University of Birmingham, since 1973; *b* 1937; *m* 1959; three *d*. BA Leeds 1960 (1st cl. Hons Sociology); Mem. British Sociological Assoc. Res. Asst, Univ. of Aston, 1961–63; Lectr in Sociology, Univ. of Birmingham, 1963–71; Vis. Assoc. Prof., Univ. of Alberta, 1968–70; Sen. Lectr in Sociology, Univ. of Aston, 1971–73; Admissions Tutor in Social Science, Univ. of Birmingham, 1965–67; Actg Head, Org. Behaviour, Univ. of Aston, 1972–73. Mem. Adv. Bd, Inst. for Study of Worship and Religious Architecture, Univ. of Birmingham, 1964– ; Hon. Res. Fellow, Irish Inst. of Public Admin., 1973– . *Publications*: D. S. Pugh, D. J. Hickson and C. R. Hinings: Writers on Organization, 1964, 2nd edn, revised and enlarged, 1970; *contrib*. Admin. Science Qly, Sociology, Human Relations, Jl Acad. Management, Policy and Politics. *Address*: Institute of Local Government Studies, Univ. of Birmingham, Birmingham B15 2TT.

Hinnells, John Russell; Lecturer in Comparative Religion, Manchester University, since 1970; *b* 1941; *m* 1965; two *s*. BD London 1964; AKC, FRAS, Mem. Internat. Assoc. for History of Religions, Mem. Soc. for New Testament Studies, Mem. Soc. for Afghan Studies, Mem. Brit. Inst. of Persian Studies. Lectr, Newcastle upon Tyne Univ., 1967–70;

Actg Head of Dept, Manchester, 1971–73. Vice-Chm. of Shap Working Party on World Religions in Educn, 1971– ; Treas. and Mem. Council, Soc. for Mithraic Studies, 1971– ; Editorial Sec., Religion: Jl of Religion and Religions, 1971–72, Mem. Editorial Bd, 1971– ; Ed. (series) Makers of New Worlds, 1973– ; Convenor, 1st and 2nd Internat. Congress of Mithraic Studies, Manchester and Iran, 1971 and 1974. *Publications*: ed, Comparative Religion in Education, 1970; ed jtly, Hinduism, 1972 and 1973; ed jtly, Man and his Salvation, Studies in memory of S. G. F. Brandon, 1973; Persian Mythology, 1974; ed, Mithraic Studies, 1974; Zoroaster, 1975; *contrib*. Acta Iran., Jl K. R. Cama Or. Inst., Bombay, Numen, Religion, Religious Studies. *Address*: Dept of Comparative Religion, Univ. of Manchester, Manchester M13 9PL.

Hinsley, Prof. Francis Harry, OBE; Fellow of St John's College, since 1944, and Professor of the History of International Relations, University of Cambridge, since 1969; *b* 1918; *m* 1946; two *s* one *d*. BA Cantab 1944, MA Cantab 1946. Res. Fellow, St John's Coll., Cambridge, 1944–50; Lectr in Hist., Univ. of Cambridge, 1949–65; Tutor, St John's Coll., Cambridge, 1956–63; Reader, Hist. of Internat. Relats. Univ. of Cambridge, 1965–69; Chm., Faculty Bd of Hist., Cambridge, 1970–72; Lees-Knowles Lectr on Military Science, Trinity Coll., 1970–71. Editor, The Historical Jl, 1960–71. UK Rep., Provisional Acad. Cttee of European University Inst., 1973– . *Publications*: Command of the Sea, 1950; Hitler's Strategy, 1951; Power and the Pursuit of Peace, 1963; Sovereignty, 1966; Nationalism and the International System, 1972; (ed), New Cambridge Modern History, vol. XI, 1962. *Address*: St John's College, Cambridge.

Hinton, Prof. Denys, MSc, AADipl, FRIBA; Professor of Architecture, University of Aston in Birmingham, since 1966; *b* 1921; *m* 1971; one *d*. AADipl 1951, MSc Aston 1968; FRIBA. Mem., Council, RIBA, 1963–66; Vice-Chm., Bd Archit, Educn, 1966–70; Chm., ARCUK Bd Educn, 1971– . *Publications*: *contrib*. Archit. Jl, RIBA Jl. *Address*: Univ. of Aston in Birmingham, Gosta Green, Birmingham B4 7ET.

Hinton, John Michael; Fellow and Tutor in Philosophy, Worcester College, Oxford, since 1960; *b* 1923; *m* 1964. MA St Andrews 1948. Member: Mind Assoc.; Aristotelian Soc. Asst in Logic and Metaphysics, Edinburgh Univ., 1950–53; Lectr in Philosophy, Wellington Univ., 1953–58; Lectr in Philosophy, Worcester Coll., Oxford, 1958–60. *Publications*: Experiences, 1973; *contrib*. Inquiry, Mind, Philos. Quart., Philos. Rev., Philosophy. *Address*: Worcester College, Oxford.

Hinton Thomas, Richard; *see* Thomas, R. H.

Hirschmann, Henry David; Lecturer in Philosophy, University of Bristol, since 1967; *b* 1939; *m* 1965; one *d*. BA Bristol 1961. Asst Lectr in Philosophy, Univ. of Bristol, 1964–67. Vis. Lectr in Philosophy, Univ. of

Nevada, 1973–74. *Publications*: *contrib*. Proc. Arist. Soc., Proc. Arist. Soc. Supp. Vol. *Address*: Dept of Philosophy, The Univ., Bristol BS8 1RJ.

Hirst, Prof. Paul Heywood; Professor of Education, University of Cambridge, and Fellow of Wolfson College, Cambridge, since 1971; *b* 1927. BA Cantab 1948, MA Cantab 1952. CertEd Cantab 1952, DipEd London 1955, MA Oxon 1955 (by incorporation). Lectr and Tutor, Univ. of Oxford Dept of Educn, 1955–59; Lectr in Philosophy of Educn, Univ. of London Inst. of Educn, 1959–65; Prof. of Educn, KCL, 1965–71; Vis. Prof., Univ. of BC, 1964, 1967; Vis. Prof., Univ. of Malawi, 1969. Asst Master, William Hulme's Grammar Sch., Manchester, 1948–50; Maths Master, Eastbourne Coll. 1950–55; Governor, Cheshunt Sch.; Mem. Council, Gordonstoun Sch.; Vice-Chm., Philosophy of Educn Soc. of GB; Vice-Chm., UCET. *Publications*: (with R. S. Peters) The Logic of Education, 1970; ed (with R. F. Dearden and R. S. Peters), Education and Development of Reason, 1971; papers, in, Philosophical Analysis and Education, ed R. D. Archambault, 1965; The Study of Education, ed J. W. Tibble, 1965; The Concept of Education, ed R. S. Peters, 1966; Let's Teach Them Right, ed C. Macy, 1969; *contrib*. Brit. Jl Educnl Studies, Jl Educnl, Jl Curriculum Studies, Hibbert Jl, Proc. Philos. of Educn Soc. *Address*: Wolfson College, Cambridge.

Hirst, Prof. Rodney Julian; Professor of Logic, Glasgow University, since 1961; *b* 1920; *m* 1942; two *d*. MA Oxford 1948 (1st cl. Lit. Hum.). Lectr in Logic and Metaphysics, St Andrew's, 1948–49; Lectr in Logic, Glasgow, 1949–59; Sen. Lectr in Logic, Glasgow, 1959–61. Dean, Fac. of Arts, Glasgow, 1971–73. *Publications*: Problems of Perception, 1959; (jtly) Human Senses and Perception, 1964; ed, Perception and the External World, 1965; ed, Philosophy: an Outline for the Intending Student, 1968; *contrib*. Mind, Philos. Qly, Proc. Aristot. Soc. *Address*: Logic Dept, Glasgow Univ., Glasgow G12 8QQ.

Hitch, Peter John, BA; Lecturer in Social Psychology, School of Applied Social Studies, University of Bradford, since 1966; *b* 1932; *m* 1963; one *s* two *d*. BA London 1954 (Hons Sociology). Production trainee, Mullard, 1956–58; Asst Exec., Assoc. Newspapers, 1958–60; Sci. Off., Air Min., 1960–62; Govt Social Survey, 1962–63; Dept of General Studies, West Ham Coll. of Further Educn, 1963–64; Asst Lectr in Social Psychology, Rutherford Coll. of Techn., 1964–66. *Publications*: *contrib*. Appl. Social Studies. *Address*: School of Applied Social Studies, The Univ., Bradford BD7 1DP.

Hitchcock, Dr Richard; Lecturer in Spanish, University of Exeter, since 1966; *b* 1940. MA St Andrews 1964, PhD St Andrews 1971. *Publications*: contrib. Spain: Companion to Spanish Studies, 2nd edn, ed P. E. Russell, 1972; ed, Richard Ford: Letters to Gayangos, 1973; *contrib*. Anu. Estudios Mediev., Bull. Hisp. Studies, Estudios

Orientales, Mod. Lang. Notes. *Address*: Dept of Spanish, Univ. of Exeter, Exeter EX4 4QJ.

Hitiris, Dr Theodore, BA, DPhil; Lecturer in Economics, University of York, since 1969; *b* 1938; *m*; one *s*. BA(Econ) Athens 1961, DPhil York 1969 (Economics). Asst, Higher Sch. of Econ., Athens, 1963–64; Fellow, York, 1967–69. Min. of Econ. Co-ord., Greece, 1963; Center of Planning and Econ. Res., 1964. *Publications*: Trade Effects of Economic Association with the EEC, 1972; (with P. Burrows) Macroeconomic Theory: a mathematical introduction, 1974; *contrib*. Bull. Econ. Res., Jl Econ. Studies, Manchester Sch. *Address*: Alcuin College, Univ. of York, York YO1 5DD.

Hoare, Geoffrey, MA; Lecturer in Education, University of Exeter, since 1963; *b* 1928; *m* 1967; one *s* two *d*. BA Cantab 1949 (1st cl. English), Cert. Prof. Ed. 1951 (1st cl.), MA Cantab 1953. Dir, TV Studio. Univ. Fine Art Cttee, 1964–67. Editor, Jl of Education, 1957–58. *Publications*: Experiments in Education at Sevenoaks, 1964; *film*: Parents are Welcome, 1970. *Address*: Sch. of Education, Univ. of Exeter, Thornlea, New North Road, Exeter.

Hobbis, Peter Derwent, MA; Lecturer in Philosophy, School of Social Studies, University of East Anglia, since 1966; *b* 1939; *m* 1965; two *d*. BA Cantab 1962, MA Cantab 1967. *Address*: School of Social Studies, Univ. of East Anglia, Norwich NOR 88C.

Hobbs, Alan Charles, BA, BPhil; Lecturer in Philosophy, School of Social Studies, University of East Anglia, since 1966; *b* 1941; *m* 1963; two *s*. BA Keele 1963 (1st cl.), BPhil Oxon 1966. *Address*: School of Social Studies, Univ. of East Anglia, Norwich NOR 88C.

Hobday, Dr Thomas Lyrian, TD, DL; Senior Lecturer in Social Medicine and Clinical Epidemiology, University of Liverpool, since 1966; *b* 1920. MB ChB Liverpool 1951, MRCS England, LRCP London 1951, Dip. in Public Health Liverpool 1957, Dip. in Public Administration Liverpool 1957; Barrister-at-Law (Inner Temple) 1962; Dip. in Med. Jurisprudence, Soc. of Apothecaries, 1973. Mem., Brit. Acad. Forensic Sciences, 1962. Lectr in Public Health, Univ. of Liverpool, 1964–66. Col., RAMC (TA); Sen. Specialist in Army Health; Hon. Physician to HM The Queen, 1970; Min. of Health Smallpox Cnsltnt, Liverpool, Manchester and Welsh Reg. Hosp. Bds; WHO Travelling Fellow, India, 1960; Ciba Anglo-French Res. Bursar, 1955; JP, Liverpool, 1968; City Councillor and Chm., Environm. Health and Protection Cttee, City of Liverpool, 1969–70; Chm., Educn Cttee, City of Liverpool, 1970–71; Mem., Merseyside Metrop. Council, 1974. *Publications*: *contrib*. Brit. Med. Jl, Bull. Wld Health Org., Jl RAMC, Lancet, etc. *Address*: Univ. of Liverpool, Liverpool L69 3BX.

Hobsbaum, Dr Philip D.; Senior Lecturer, Department of English, University of Glasgow, since 1971; *b* 1932. BA Cantab 1955, LRAM 1956, LGSM 1957, MA Cantab 1961, PhD Sheffield 1968. Asst Lectr in English, QUB, 1962–63, Lectr 1963–66; Lectr in English, Glasgow Univ., 1966–71. *Publications*: (with E. Lucie-Smith) ed, A Group Anthology, 1963; The Place's Fault and Other Poems, 1964; In Retreat and Other Poems, 1966; Coming Out Fighting: Poems, 1969; ed, Ten Elizabethan Poets, 1969; A Theory of Communication, 1969; Women and Animals: Poems, 1972; A Reader's Guide to Charles Dickens, 1973; *contrib*. Brit. Jl Aesthetics, Brit. Jl for Amer. Studies, Encounter, Hudson Rev., Mod. Lang. Rev., etc. *Address*: Univ. of Glasgow, Glasgow G12 8QQ.

Hobsbawm, Prof. Eric John Ernest; Professor of Economic and Social History, Birkbeck College, University of London, since 1970; *b* 1917; *m* 1962; one *s* one *d*. BA Cantab 1939 (History), MA Cantab 1943, PhD Cantab 1951; Hon DPhil Stockholm 1969; Silas Marcus Macvane Prize of Harvard (distinguished achievement in mod. Europ. hist.) 1970, Foreign Hon. Mem., Amer. Acad. Arts and Sciences, 1971; Hon. Fellow, King's Coll., Cambridge, 1973. Lectr, Birkbeck Coll., 1947–59; Fellow, King's Coll., Cambridge, 1949–55; Reader, 1959–70; Vis. Prof., MIT, 1967. Mem., Ed. Bd, Past and Present, 1952– (Vice-Chm.); Council, Econ. Hist. Soc., 1951– ;Chm., Soc. Study Labour Hist., 1966–70. *Publications*: ed, Labour's Turning Point, 1948; Primitive Rebels, 1959 (US, German, French, Italian, Spanish, Portuguese edns); The Age of Revolution 1789–1848, 1962 (US, French, German, Italian, Spanish, Dutch, Japanese, Hebrew, Hungarian edns); Labouring Men, 1964 (US, Italian, Japanese edns); ed, K. Marx: Precapitalist Economic Formations, 1964 (US, Italian, Spanish, Japanese edns); Industry and Empire, 1968 (US, German, Italian edns); (with G. Rudé) Captain Swing, 1969 (US edn); Bandits, 1969 (US, Italian, German, French edns); *contrib*. Econ. Hist. Rev., Past and Pres., and var. symposia. *Address*: Dept of History, Birkbeck College, Malet Street, WC1E 7HX.

Hockey, Stanley Llewellin, MA; Senior Tutor, Higher Degrees Division, and Senior Lecturer in Education, University of Newcastle upon Tyne, since 1965; *b* 1911; *m* 1937; one *s*. BA Bristol 1932 (1st cl. Hons Geography), MA Bristol 1935, DipEd Bristol 1933. Lecturer in Education, Durham Univ., 1949–58; Prof. of Education, Univ. of Sierra Leone, 1964–65. Pres., Tyneside Geog. Assoc., 1966–71; Mem., Gateshead Educn Cttee, 1967–74. *Address*: School of Education, The Univ., Newcastle upon Tyne NE1 7RU.

Hockley, Graham Charles; Senior Lecturer, Department of Economics, University College, Cardiff, since 1972; *b* 1931; *m* 1963; one *s* one *d*. BA Nottingham (Hons Economics), MA Cantab 1962. Mem., Royal Econ. Soc. Jun. Res. Off., Dept of Applied Economics, Univ. of Cambridge, 1959–62; Lecturer, Dept of Industrial Economics, Univ. of Nottingham, 1963–64; Lectr, UC, Cardiff,

1964–72. *Publications*: contrib. J. Moyle: The Wealth of the Nation: the National Balance of the United Kingdom 1957–61, by J. Revell, 1967; Monetary Policy and Public Finance, 1970; *contrib*. Banker, Britann. Bk of Yr, Brit. Tax Rev., Local Govt Fin., Bldg Socs Gazette, Econ. Age. *Address*: Dept of Economics, Univ. College, PO Box 78, Cardiff CF1 1XL.

Hodd, Michael Robert Velleck; Lecturer, Economics and Politics Department, School of Oriental and African Studies, London University, since 1969; *b* 1941. MA 1963, MSc(Econ) 1965. La Trobe Univ., Melbourne, Australia, 1967–69. *Publications*: *contrib*. Economica. *Address*: Sch. of Oriental and African Studies, Malet Street, WC1E 7HP.

Hodder, Prof. Bramwell William, Professor of Geography, University of London, since 1970; *b* 1923; *m* 1947; three *s* two *d*. BA Oxon 1951 (Geography), MA Oxon 1955, BLitt Oxon 1956, PhD London 1964; FRGS. Lectr, Malaya Univ., Singapore, 1952–56; Lectr, Ibadan Univ., Nigeria, 1956–63; Lectr, Glasgow Univ., 1963–64; Lectr, London Univ., 1964–67; Reader, 1967–70. Chm., Commonwealth Geog. Bureau, 1968–72; Vice-Pres., Wld Expedit. Assoc. *Publications*: Man in Malaya, 1959; ed (with D. R. Harris), Africa in Transition, 1967; Economic Development in the Tropics, 1968, 2nd edn 1973; ed (with U. I. Ukwu), Markets in West Africa, 1969; *contrib*. Econ. Geog., Trans Inst. Brit. Geog. *Address*: Dept of Geography, School of Oriental and African Studies, Univ. of London, WC1E 7HP.

Hodder-Williams, Richard, MA; Lecturer in Politics, University of Bristol, since 1967; *b* 1943; *m* 1972. BA Oxon 1965, MA Oxon 1970. Jun. Fellow, Univ. Coll. of Rhodesia and Nyasaland, 1965–67. Mem., Stand. Cttee on Univ. Studies of Africa, 1972. Co-editor, Jl Southern African Studies, 1974; *contrib*. editor, Internat. Jl Politics, 1972. *Publications*: Public Opinion Polls and British Politics, 1970; *contrib*. Afr. Aff., Jl Commonwealth Pol. Studies, Jl Mod. Afr. Studies, Round Table, Rhodesian Hist., Africa Soc. Res. *Address*: Dept of Politics, 40 Berkeley Square, Bristol BS8 1HY.

Hoddinott, Prof. Alun, DMus; Professor of Music, University College of South Wales and Monmouthshire, since 1967; *b* 1929; *m* 1953; one *s*. DMus Wales; Hon. RAM. Lectr, Cardiff Coll. of Music and Drama, 1951–59; Lectr, UC of S Wales and Mon., 1959–65; Reader, Univ. of Wales, 1965–67. Mem., BBC Music Central Adv. Cttee, 1971– ; Mem., Welsh Arts Council, 1968–73; Artistic Dir, Cardiff Festival of 20th Century Music; Governor, Welsh Nat. Theatre, 1968– ; Walford Davies Prize, 1954; Arnold Bax Medal, 1957. *Publications*: *opera*: The Beacon of Falesa, 1974; *symphonies*: 1955, 1962, 1968, 1969, 1973; *concertos for*: clarinet, 1951; oboe, 1954; harp, 1958; viola, 1958; piano, 1940, 1960, 1967; violin, 1961; organ, 1967; horn, 1969; *sonatas for*: piano, 1959, 1962, 1965, 1966, 1968, 1972; harp, 1964; clarinet, 1967;

violin, 1969, 1970, 1971; cello, 1970; horn, 1971; *other compositions:* Nocturne, 1951; Welsh Dances, 1958, 2nd suite 1969, Investiture Dances 1969; 2nd Nocturne, 1959; Two Welsh Nursery Tunes, 1959; Sextet, 1960; Rebecca, 1962; Septet, 1962; Folk Song Suite, 1962; Sonatina, 1963; Variations, 1963; Medieval Songs, 1963; Divertimento, 1963; Danegeld, 1964; 4 Welsh Songs, 1964; Dives and Lazarus, 1965; String Quartet, 1965; Concerto Grosso, 1965; Variants, 1966; Night music, 1966; Suite for harp, 1967; Aubade, 1967; Roman Dream, 1968; Nocturnes and Cadenzas, 1968; Divertimenti for 8 instruments, 1968; Piano Quintet, 1972; Sinfonietta, no 2, 1969, no 3, 1970, no 4, 1971; Piano Trio, 1970; Fioriture, 1968; An Apple Tree and a Pig, 1968; Black Bart, 1968; The Tree of Life, 1971; song cycle, Ancestor Worship, 1972; and numerous other shorter works. *Address:* Univ. College, Cardiff, PO Box 78, Cardiff CF1 1XL.

Hodge, Barbara Joan; Lecturer in Education with Special Reference to the Teaching of Classics, Institute of Education, London University, since 1952; *b* 1917. BA Cantab 1938 (2nd cl. Classics), MA Cantab 1942, DipEd Reading 1939; LRAM 1944. Mem., AUT, Class. Assoc., Jt Assoc. Class. Teachers, Asst Ed., Didaskalos, 1963– . *Publications:* (with F. K. Smith) Poetry and Prose (The Roman World), 1956; (with F. K. Smith) Scenes from Euripides' Trojan Women, 1961; (with G. L. Lewis and J. A. Lauwerys) Cyprus School History Textbooks, 1966. *Address:* Univ. of London Institute of Education, Malet Street, WC1E 7HS.

Hodge, Margaret Ada Tomsett, (Mrs Calvert); Lecturer, Department of Accounting and Business Finance, University of Manchester, since 1957; *b* 1924; *m* 1953; four *s*. BA London 1949; Inst. of Chartered Accountants, 1952, Fellow, 1958; Fellow, Inst. of Taxation, 1964. Principal Accountant Univ. of Oxford, 1952–53; Accountant (with special duties), Univ. of Liverpool, 1953–55. Dep. Adviser to Women Students, Univ. of Manchester, 1966– ; Mem.: Tribunal, Dept of Health and Social Security, 1963–69; VAT Tribunal, 1973– . JP 1963– . *Publications:* contrib. Office Management Encyclopaedia, ed Standingford, 1965; *contrib.* Accountant, Accountancy. *Address:* Dept of Accounting and Business Finance, The Univ., Manchester M13 9PL.

Hodges, Henry Woolmington Mackenzie, FIIC; Senior Lecturer in Archaeological Technology, Institute of Archaeology, London University, since 1957; *b* 1920; *m* 1965; one *s* one *d*. Dip. in Archaeology, London 1953; FIIC. Lectr, Queen's Univ., Belfast, 1943–47. Treas., Internat. Inst. Cnsrvtn Hist. Artistic works. *Publications:* Artifacts, 1964; Technology in the Ancient World, 1970; Pottery: A Technical History, 1972; Technology in the Medieval World (forthcoming); *contrib.* Studies Cnsrvtn. *Address:* Institute of Archaeology, 31 Gordon Square, WC1H 0PY.

Hodgett, Gerald Augustus John, MA; Reader in History, University of London,

King's College, since 1961; *b* 1917. BA London 1937 (1st cl. History), MA London 1947; FRHistS, FSA. Lectr in History, King's Coll., 1947–61; Vis. Prof., Univ. of British Columbia, 1967. Mem., Council, Hist. Assoc., 1959– , Vice-Pres., 1972. *Publications:* ed, The State of the Ex-Religious and former Chantry Priests in the Diocese of Lincoln, 1959; ed, The Cartulary of Holy Trinity Aldgate, 1971; A Social and Economic History of Medieval Europe, 1972; ed, A Book of Medieval Recipes from a MS in Samuel Pepys's Library, 1972; Tudor Lincolnshire (forthcoming); contrib. Victoria County History, Wiltshire vol. 5; *contrib.* Jl Eccles. Hist., Lincs Archit. Archaeol. Soc., Reps and Papers. *Address:* King's College, Strand, WC2R 2LS.

Hodgkinson, John Francis Nicholas; Registrar, University of Keele, since 1953; *b* 1918; *m* 1947; three *s*. MA Oxon 1943. Asst Registrar, Univ. of Birmingham, 1948–53. *Address:* Univ. of Keele, Keele, Staffs ST5 5BG.

Hodgson, Dr Peter Edward; Lecturer in Nuclear Physics, University of Oxford, since 1967; *b* 1928; *m* 1958; three *s* one *d*. BSc London 1948 (1st cl. Physics), ARCS, PhD London 1951, MA Oxon 1960, DIC, DSc London 1964; FInstP. Lectr, Univ. of Reading, 1956–58; Sen. Res. Off., Nuclear Physics Lab., Oxford, 1958–67; Sen. Res. Fellow, Corpus Christi Coll., Oxford, 1962– . *Publications:* The Optical Model of Elastic Scattering, 1963; Nuclear Reactions and Nuclear Structure, 1971; *contrib.* Nature, Nuclear Phys., Phys. Lett., Phys. Rev. Lett., Phys. Rev., Proc. Phys. Soc. *Address:* Nuclear Physics Laboratory, Oxford.

Hogan, Brian; Professor of Law, University of Leeds, since 1967; *b* 1932; *m* 1957; one *s* one *d*. LLB Manchester 1956; Barrister at law, Gray's Inn 1959; Lectr, Univ. of Nottingham, 1956–67. *Publications:* (with J. C. Smith) Criminal Law, 1965, 3rd edn 1973; *contrib.* Crim. Law Rev. *Address:* Faculty of Law, Univ. of Leeds, Leeds LS2 9JT.

Hogarth, Cyril Edmund; Adult Education Tutor, Department of Adult Education, University of Nottingham, since 1948; *b* 1916; *m* 1960. BA 1938, DipEd 1939, MA 1957, Manchester. *Publications: contrib.* Bull. Internat. Affairs, Univ. of Nottingham, Derbys Archaeol. Jl. *Address:* Dept of Adult Education, Univ. of Nottingham, 14–22 Shakespeare Street, Nottingham NG1 4FJ.

Hogarth, Dr Paul; Visiting Lecturer, Department of Illustration, Royal College of Art, since 1964; *b* 1917; *m* 1960; one *s*. Dr RCA 1972; Fellow, Soc. of Ind. Artists and Designers. Vis. Prof., Philadelphia Coll. of Art, Philadelphia, Pa, USA, 1968–69. *Publications:* Artist as Reporter, 1967; Artists on Horseback, 1972; Arthur Boyd Houghton, 1975; *contrib.* Amer. West. Mod. Qly. *Address:* Dept of Illustration, Sch. of Graphic Design, Royal College of Art, Exhibition Road, SW7 2RL.

Hogg, Anne Patricia; Lecturer in Spanish, St Anne's College, Oxford University, since 1966; *b* 1939; *m* 1961; two *d*. BA Oxon 1960, MA Oxon 1964, PhD London 1967. *Address*: St Anne's College, Oxford.

Hogg, Gordon Welch; Lecturer, School of Education, University of Newcastle upon Tyne, since 1972; *b* 1930; *m* 1964; two *d*. BA Lordon, MEd Durham. Part-time Lectr, Dept of Educn, Univ. of Newcastle upon Tyne, 1968-72. *Publication*: (with J. C. Tyson), Popular Education, 1700-1870, 1970. *Address*: Sch. of Education, Univ. of Newcastle upon Tyne, St Thomas' Street, Newcastle upon Tyne NE1 7RU.

Hoggan, Dr David George; Senior Lecturer, Department of Romance Studies, University College of Wales, Aberystwyth, since 1974 (Lecturer, 1958-74); *b* 1927; *m* 1959; one *s* one *d*. MA St Andrews 1948 (1st cl. French and German), LésL Strasbourg 1952, Docteur de l'Université, Strasbourg, 1953. *Publications*: contrib. Medium Ævum, Romania. *Address*: Dept of Romance Studies, Univ. College of Wales, Aberystwyth SY23 2AX.

Holborow, Leslie Charles, MA, BPhil; Senior Lecturer in Philosophy, University of Dundee, since 1973 (Lecturer, 1965-73); *b* 1941; *m* 1965; one *s* two *d*. BA Auckland 1961, MA Auckland 1962 (1st cl. Philosophy), BPhil Oxon 1965. Mem., Aristot. Soc. Pt-time Lectr, Auckland Univ., 1962; Jun. Lectr, 1963; Asst Ed., Philos. Qly, 1967-72. Hon. Sec., Scott Philos. Club, 1966-70. *Publications*: contrib. Analysis, Austral. Jl Philos., Nous, Philosophy, Philos. Qly, Proc. Aristot. Soc., Proc. Royal Inst. Phil. *Address*: Dept of Philosophy, Univ. of Dundee, Dundee DD1 4HN.

Hold, Trevor, MA, BMus; Music Tutor, Department of Adult Education, University of Leicester, since 1970; *b* 1939; *m* 1962; two *d*. BMus Nottingham 1961 (1st cl.), MA Nottingham 1963. Asst Lectr, Univ. Coll. of Wales, Aberystwyth, 1963-65; Lectr, Liverpool Univ., 1965-70. *Publications*: (music) The Unreturning Spring, 1965; Fun with 12-Notes, 1966; Three Songs of the Countryside, 1970; (poetry) Time and the Bell, 1971; *contrib*. Composer. IBIS, Music Lett. *Address*: Univ. Centre, Barrack Road, Northampton.

Holdcroft, David; Senior Lecturer, Department of Philosophy, University of Warwick, since 1972 (Lecturer, 1966-72); *b* 1934; *m* 1959; one *s* two *d*. BA Cambridge 1958 (2nd cl. Pt II Moral Sciences Tripos). Asst Lectr, then Lectr, Univ. of Manchester, 1960-66. *Publications*: contrib. Mind, Philosophia, Philos., Philos. Qly, Ratio, Supp. Proc. Aristot. Soc. *Address*: Dept of Philosophy, Univ. of Warwick, Coventry CV4 7AL.

Holden, Barry Barfield, BA; Senior Lecturer, Politics Department, University of Reading, since 1971; *b* 1936; *m* 1963; one *s* one *d*. BA Keele 1959 (2nd cl. Political Institutions and Philosophy). Temp. Asst Lectr, Southampton Univ., 1962-63; Asst Lectr, Reading Univ., 1963-64; Lectr, 1964-71. GCE Awarder, Oxf. and Camb. Schs Exam. Bd, 1969-72. *Publication*: The Nature of Democracy (forthcoming). *Address*: Dept of Politics, Univ. of Reading, Whiteknights, Reading RG6 2AA.

Holden, Dr James Milnes; Reader in Business Law, Department of Accountancy and Business Law, University of Stirling, since 1973; *b* 1918; *m* 1951; one *s* one *d*. LLB 1947 (1st cl. Hons), PhD 1951, LLD 1971, London; AIB 1936; Barrister, 1948. Asst Lectr, LSE, 1949-51, Part-time Lectr, 1952-67; Sen. Lectr, Univ. of Stirling, 1972-73. Legal Advr, Inter-Bank Res. Orgn, 1969-72; Special Legal Advr, UN, 1969-71. *Publications*: ed, Payne's Carriage of Goods by Sea, 6th edn 1954; History of Negotiable Instruments in English Law, 1955; ed jtly, Chalmers' Marine Insurance Act, 1906, 5th edn 1956; Law and Practice of Banking, vol. 1, Banker and Customer, 2nd edn 1974, vol. 2, Securities for Bankers' Advances, 5th edn 1971; Jones and Holden's Studies in Practical Banking, 6th edn 1971; numerous contribs to jls. *Address*: Dept of Accountancy and Business Law, Univ. of Stirling, Stirling FK9 4LA.

Holderness, Bryan Alexander, MA, PhD; Lecturer in Economic History, University of East Anglia, since 1972; *b* 1941; *m* 1965; two *s* one *d*. BA Cambridge 1963 (1st cl. History Tripos). MA Cambridge 1970, PhD Nottingham 1968. Lectr in Dept of Economic History, Univ. of Sheffield, 1965-72. *Publications*: contrib. Aspects of Capital Investment in Great Britain 1750-1850, ed S. Pollard and J. P. P. Higgins, 1971; *contrib*. Agric. Hist. Rev.. Econ. Hist. Rev., Mid. Hist., Business Hist., Lincs Hist. and Archaeol., Yorks ASJ, Hunterian ASJ. *Address*: School of Social Sciences, Univ. of East Anglia, Norwich NOR 88C.

Holdsworth, Dr Christopher John; Reader in Medieval History, University College, London, since 1973; *b* 1931; *m* 1957; one *s*. BA Cantab 1953 (1st cl. Historical Tripos Pts I and II), MA Cantab 1955, PhD Cantab 1960; FRHistS. Asst Lectr, Univ. Coll., London, 1956-59; Lectr, 1959-67; Sen. Lectr, 1967-73; Vis. Fellow, Clare Hall, Cambridge, 1968; Tutor, Arts Students, Univ. Coll., London, 1968-73. *Publications*: Rufford Charters, vols I and II (Thoroton Soc. Rec. Series), 1972, 1974; vol. III (forthcoming); *contrib*. Citeaux, EHR, Jl Eccles. Hist., Hist., Trans Royal Hist. Soc. *Address*: Univ. College London, Gower Street, WC1E 6BT.

Holgate, Sidney, MA, PhD; Master of Grey College, University of Durham, since 1959; *b* 1918; *m* 1942. BA Dunelm 1940 (1st cl. Maths), DThPT Dunelm 1941, MA Dunelm 1943, PhD Dunelm 1945. Lectr in Mathematics, Univ. of Durham, 1942-46; Sec. of Durham Colls, 1946-59; Pro-Vice-Chancellor, Univ. of Durham, 1964-69. Mem., Standing Conf. on Univ. Entrance, 1965-69; Mem., Schs Council General Studies Cttee, 1967-70; Mem., Academic Adv. Cttee, Open Univ., 1969- ; Chm.,

BBC Radio Durham, 1968-72. *Publications*: *contrib*. Proc. of Camb. Phil. Soc., Proc. of Roy. Soc. London. *Address*: Grey College, Durham.

Holl, Peter; Lecturer in Econometrics, Department of Social Science and Humanities, City University, since 1968 (on leave to Worcester Polytechnic Institute, Massachusetts, USA, academic year 1974-75); *b* 1944; *m* 1967; one *d*. BScEcon London 1966, MAEcon Sussex 1967. *Address*: Dept of Social Science and Humanities, City Univ., St John Street, EC1V 4PB.

Holladay, Alfred James; Fellow and Tutor since 1949, and Tutor for Graduates since 1967, Trinity College, University of Oxford; University Lecturer in Ancient History, since 1950; *b* 1921; *m* 1950. BA Oxon 1943, MA Oxon 1946 (1st cl. Class. Hons Mods, 1941; 1st cl. Lit. Hum., 1947). Harmsworth Sen. Schol., Merton Coll., Oxford, 1947; Craven Fellow, 1947; Fellow, All Souls Coll., 1947. Dean, Trinity Coll., Oxford, 1950-59. *Address*: Trinity College, Oxford.

Holland, Prof. Roy Fraser; Professor of Philosophy, University of Leeds, since 1967; *b* 1923; *m* 1951; one *s* three *d*. MA Oxon 1948, BPhil Oxon 1950. Asst Lectr, then Lectr, Univ. Coll. of Swansea, 1950-59; Sen. Lectr, 1959-66; Vis. Prof., Rochester Univ., 1962; Reader, Leicester Univ., 1966-67. Ed., Studies in Philos. Psychol. *Publications*: *contrib*. Amer. Jl Philos., Austral. Jl Philos., Class. Qly, Human Wld, Mind, Philos. Qly, Philosophy, Proc. Aristot. Soc., Ratio. *Address*: Dept of Philosophy, Univ. of Leeds, Leeds LS2 9JT.

Holland, Prof. Walter Werner; Director, Department of Clinical Epidemiology and Social Medicine, St Thomas's Hospital Medical School (London University), since 1968; *b* 1929; *m* 1964; three *s*. BSc London 1951, MB, BS London 1954, MD London 1964, MRCP (without exam) 1971; FFCM 1972, FRCP 1973, FRSM, FSS., Mem., Soc. Schols, Johns Hopkins Univ., BMA, Soc. Soc. Med., Soc. Hum. Biol. Lectr, St Thomas's Hosp. Med. Sch., 1958-59; Sen. Lectr, 1962-64; Reader, 1965-68; Prof., 1968- ; Vis. Prof., Univ. of California, 1969; Vis. Prof., Monash Univ., 1973. Ed., Internat. Jl Epidemiol., 1971; Sec., MRC Cttee on General Epidemiology, 1967; Mem., Working Party on Collaboration; Mem., Independent Cttee on Smoking; Asst Sec., MRC Cttee on Research into Chronic Bronchitis. *Publications*: Data Handling in Epidemiology, 1970; contrib. Challenges for Change, 1971; *contrib*. BMJ, Lancet. Brit. Jl Prev. Soc. Med. *Address*: Dept of Clinical Epidemiology and Social Medicine, St Thomas's Hospital Medical School, SE1 7EH.

Hollenweger, Prof. Walter J., DTh; Professor of Mission, Department of Theology, University of Birmingham, since 1971; *b* 1927; *m* 1951. Swiss Immatriculation Ex. (Type A) 1955; Hebraicum Zürich 1956. Propedeuticum Zürich 1958; TheolEx Basel 1961; DTh Zürich 1966. Res. Asst for Social

Ethics and Church History, Zürich, 1961-64. Study Dir, Evangelical Acad., Zürich. 1964-65; Exec. Sec., World Council of Churches, Geneva, 1965-71. *Publications*: Handbuch der Pfingstbewegung, 10 vols, 1965-67; Enthusiastisches Christentum: die Pfingstbewegung in Geschichte und Gegenwart, 1969; The Pentecostals, 1972 (Spanish and French trans forthcoming); ed, Die Pfingstkirchen, 1971; ed, Kirche, Benzin und Bohnensuppe, 1971; Marxist and Kimbanguist Mission: a comparison, 1973; New Wine in Old Wineskins: Protestant and Catholic Neo-Pentecostals, 1973; Evangelisation gestern und heute, 1973; *contrib*. Areopag. Concept, Concilium, Ecumenical Rev., Ev. Theologie, Internat. Rev. of Mission, Reformatio, Studia Liturgica. *Address*: Dept of Theology, Univ. of Birmingham, Birmingham B15 2TT.

Hollindale, Peter, MA; Lecturer in English and Education, University of York, since 1965; *b* 1936; *m* 1967; two *s*. BA Cantab 1957 (1st cl. Parts I and II of the English Tripos), MA Cantab 1962; CertEd Bristol 1959 (Distinction). *Publications*: Shakespeare's King Henry IV Part Two: a critical commentary, 1971; Choosing Books for Children, 1974; ed, Shakespeare: As You Like It, 1974; *contrib*. Use of English. *Address*: Dept of English and Related Literature, Univ. of York, Heslington, York YO1 5DD.

Hollings, Laurence Alred; Lecturer in Philosophy, School of Social Sciences, University of Sussex, since 1967; BA Bristol 1964. *Address*: Arts Building, Univ. of Sussex, Falmer, Brighton BN1 9QN.

Hollingsworth, Barry, MA, PhD; Senior Lecturer, Department of Russian Studies, University of Manchester, since 1971; *b* 1935; *m* 1963; one *s* one *d*. BA Cantab 1958, MA Cantab 1961, PhD Cantab 1966. Asst Lectr in Russian Studies, Univ. of Manchester, 1959-62; Lectr in Russian Studies, Univ. of Manchester, 1962-71. *Publications*: *contrib*. Jl Mod. Hist., Oxf. Slav. Papers, Slav. E Europ. Rev., Sov. Studies. *Address*: Dept of Russian Studies, Univ. of Manchester, Manchester M13 9PL.

Hollingsworth, Dr Thomas Henry; Senior Lecturer in Demography, University of Glasgow, since 1972; *b* 1932. BA Cantab 1953, Dipl. Math. Stat. Cantab 1954, MA Cantab 1957, PhD London 1963; FSS. Asst in Res., Cambridge, 1954-57; Univ. of Glasgow: Res. Fellow, 1963-66; Lectr in Social Statistics, 1966-72; Vis. Fellow, ANU, Canberra, 1970; Vis. Prof., Cairo, 1971-72. Technical Officer, ICI Ltd, 1957-60; Sen. Adv., UN in Philippines, 1969-70; Consultant, UN in Egypt, 1972. *Publications*: The Demography of the British Peerage, 1964; Historical Demography, 1969; Migration, 1970; *contrib*. Annales de dém. hist., Daedalus, Eug. Rev., Jl Biosoc. Sci., Jl Roy. Statist. Soc. A. Pop. Studs. *Address*: Adam Smith Building, Univ. of Glasgow, Glasgow G12 8RT.

Hollingworth, Brian Charles, MA; Lecturer in the Department of Education, University of Leeds, since 1968; *b* 1935; *m* 1967; one *s* one *d*. BA Manchester 1956 (1st cl. English), MA Manchester 1959, CertEd Leeds 1957. Asst Master, Dursley Grammar Sch., 1958–59; Hd of English Dept, Methodist Coll., Kowloon, 1960–66; Temp. Lectr, Dept of Educn, Leeds, 1966–68. *Address*: Dept of Education, Univ. of Leeds, Leeds LS2 9JT.

Hollis, Adrian Swayne; Fellow of Keble College, University of Oxford, and Lecturer at University College, Oxford, since 1967; *b* 1940; *m* 1967; one *d*. BA Oxon 1962, MA 1964, BPhil Oxon 1964; FRNS. Asst Lectr, Dept of Humanity, Univ. of St Andrews, 1964–67. Gov., Churcher's Coll., Petersfield, 1971– . *Publications*: ed, Ovid: Metamorphoses bk 8, 1970; *contrib*. Ovid, ed J. W. Binns, 1973; Class. Rev. *Address*: Keble College, Oxford.

Hollis, Martin, MA; Senior Lecturer in Philosophy, School of Social Studies, University of East Anglia, since 1972; *b* 1938; *m* 1965; two *s*. BA Oxon 1961, MA Oxon 1965. Commonwealth Fellowship, Berkeley and Harvard, 1961–63; Lectr in Philosophy, New Coll., Oxford, 1964–65; Balliol Coll., Oxford, 1965–67; Univ. of E Anglia, 1967–72. Foreign Office, 1963–66; Sch. Gov., 1971– ; JP 1972– . *Publications*: (with E. J. Nell) Rational Economic Man, 1974; ed, The Light of Reason: Rationalist Philosophers of the Seventeenth Century, 1973; *contrib*. Analysis, Europ. Jl Sociol., Fndtns Lang., Mind, Philos., Proc. Aristot. Soc., Soc. Res. *Address*: School of Social Studies, Univ. of East Anglia, Norwich NOR 88C.

Hollis, Dr Patricia; Lecturer, School of English and American Studies, University of East Anglia, Norwich, since 1967; *b* 1941; *m* 1965; two *s* BA Hons Cantab 1962; DPhil, MA Oxon 1968; FRHistS 1971. *Publications*: Poor Man's Guardian, 1969; The Pauper Press, 1970; Class and Conflict in early 19th Century England, 1973; Pressure from Without, 1974; *contrib*. English Historical Rev, Victorian Studies, THES. *Address*: Univ of East Anglia, Earlham Hall, Norwich NOR 88C.

Holloway, Prof. John, MA, DPhil, DLitt, LittD, FRSL; Professor of Modern English, University of Cambridge, since 1972; *b* 1920; *m* 1946; one *s* one *d*. BA Oxon 1941 (1st cl. Mod. Greats), MA Oxon 1945, DPhil Oxon 1947, DLitt Aberdeen 1954, LittD Cambridge 1969; FRSL 1956, Mem., Soc. Authors 1965. Fellow, All Souls Coll., 1946–60; Lectr, Aberdeen, 1949–54; Lectr, Cambridge (and Fellow, Queens' Coll.), 1954–66, Reader in Modern English, 1966–72; Byron Prof., Athens (seconded), 1961–63; Vis. Prof., Chicago, 1965; Johns Hopkins, 1972. Sec., English Fac., 1955–57, 1969, Fac. Libr., 1964–66, Chm., 1969–71; Mem., Council, Brit. Council, 1964– ; Mem., Arts Council Poetry Panel, 1958–60. *Publications*: Language and Intelligence, 1951; The Victorian Sage, 1953; The Charted Mirror (essays), 1960; The Colours of Clarity (essays), 1964; The Story of the Night (Shakespearean tragedy), 1961; The Lion Hunt (on modern poetry), 1964; Blake's Lyric Poetry, 1968; Verse: The Minute, 1956; The Fugue, 1960; The Landfallers, 1962; Wood and Windfall, 1964; New Poems, 1970; *contrib*. Crit. Qly, Ess. Crit., Hudson Rev., Mod. Lang. Forum, Rev. Engl. Studies, etc. *Address*: Queens' College, Cambridge.

Holman, Michael John de Koby; Lecturer in Russian Studies, University of Leeds, since 1966; *b* 1940; *m* 1965. BA Oxon 1964 (Russian and German); Mem. Brit. Univs Assoc. of Slavists. *Address*: Dept of Russian Studies, Univ. of Leeds, Leeds LS2 9JT.

Holman, Dr Robert; Senior Lecturer, Department of Social Administration and Social Work, Glasgow University, since 1973; *b* 1936; *m* 1963; one *s* one *d*. BA London 1960, Certif. Social Admin London 1961, Dip. Applied Social Studies London 1962, PhD Birmingham 1971. Lectr in Social Work and Social Admin, Univ. of Birmingham, 1966–72. Child Care Officer, Herts CC, 1962–64; Lectr, Stevenage Coll. of Further Educn, 1964–66; Mem., Gulbenkian Working Gp on Community Work, 1970–73. *Publications*: Socially Deprived Families in Britain, 1970, 2nd edn 1973; Unsupported Mothers and the Care of Their Children, 1970; Trading in Children: A Study of Private Fostering, 1973; *contrib*. Univs Qly, Brit. Jl Social Work, Jl Social Policy, Policy and Politics. *Address*: Dept of Social Administration, 53 Southpark Avenue, Glasgow G12 8LF.

Holmes, Dr Brian, BSc, PhD, MInstP; Reader in Comparative Education, Institute of Education, University of London, since 1964; *b* 1920; *m* 1st 1945, 2nd 1971; two *s* one *d*. BSc London 1941 (2nd cl. physics), PhD London 1962; DipEd 1946; Assoc. Inst. Physics 1947; Pres., Comp. Educn Soc. in Europe (Brit. Sect.) 1970–71. Lectr, Univ. of Durham, 1951–53; Asst Ed., Univ. of London, Inst. of Educn, 1953–59; Lectr, 1959–63; Sen. Lectr, 1963–64; Vis. Prof., Chicago, Boston, Illinois, New York Univs. Sec., Treas., Comp. Educn Soc. in Europe, 1961–73, Pres., 1973– ; Vice Pres., Comp. Educn Soc. in USA. *Publications*: General Science Textbooks, 1947–48; 'American Criticism of American Education' (Ohio State Memorial Lectures), 1956; Problems in Education, 1965; ed, Educational Policy and the Mission Schools, 1967; (with T. Bristow) Comparative Education through the Literature, 1968; *contrib*. Brit. Jl Educnl Studies, Nat. Soc. Study Educn Ybk, Wld Ybk Educn. *Address*: Univ. of London, Institute of Education, Malet Street, WC1E 7HS.

Holmes, Colin, MA; Senior Lecturer in Economic History, University of Sheffield, since 1972; *b* 1938; *m* 1962. BA Nottingham 1960 (2nd cl. Econ. and Soc. Hist.), MA Nottingham 1964; CertEd 1962. Asst Lectr, Sheffield Univ., 1963–66, Lectr, 1966–72. *Publications*: ed (with S. Pollard), The Process of Industrialization, 1750–1870 (Documents of European Economic History vol. I), 1968; ed (with S. Pollard), Industrial

327

Power and National Rivalry, 1870–1914 (Documents of European Economic History vol. II), 1972; ed (with S. Pollard), The End of the Old Europe, 1914–1939 (Documents of European Economic History vol. III), 1973; (with B. J. Elliott) World Society in the Twentieth Century, 1973. *Address*: Dept of Economic History, Univ. of Sheffield, Sheffield S10 2TN.

Holmes, Prof. Geoffrey Shorter; Professor, Department of History, University of Lancaster, since 1973; *b* 1928; *m* 1955; one *s* one *d*. BA Oxon 1948, MA Oxon 1952, BLitt Oxon 1952; FRHistS, Mem., Assoc. Univ. Teachers. Univ. Glasgow: Asst in History, 1952–56; Lectr, 1956–66; Sen. Lectr, 1966–69; Reader in History, Univ. Lancaster, 1969–72. *Publications*: British Politics in the Age of Anne, 1967; (with W. A. Speck) The Divided Society, 1967; ed and contrib., Britain after the Glorious Revolution 1969; The Trial of Doctor Sacheverell, 1973; *contrib*. Bull. Inst. Hist. Res., English Hist. Rev. *Address*: Dept of History, Furness College, Univ. of Lancaster, Lancaster.

Holmes, Dr George Arthur, MA, PhD; Fellow and Tutor in Modern History, St Catherine's College, Oxford University, since 1962; *b* 1927; *m* 1953; one *s* two *d*. BA Cantab 1948 (1st cl. History), PhD Cantab 1952; FRHistS. Res. Fellow, St John's Coll., Cambridge, 1951–54; Tutor, St Catherine's Soc., Oxford, 1954–62; Asst Ed., Econ. Hist. Rev., 1961–67; Vice-Master, St Catherine's Coll., 1969–71. Mem., Council, Royal Hist. Soc., 1964–67. *Publications*: The Estates of the'Higher Nobility in Fourteenth-Century England, 1957; The Later Middle Ages, 1962; The Florentine Enlightenment, 1969; trans. Mazzarino: The End of the Ancient World, 1966; *contrib*. Econ. Hist. Rev., EHR. *Address*: St Catherine's College, Oxford.

Holmes, Terence Michael; Lecturer, Department of German, University College of Swansea, since 1966; *b* 1942; *m* 1964; one *s*. BA Southampton 1964, MPhil Southampton 1971. *Publications*: *contrib*. GLL, MLR. *Address*: Dept of German, Univ. Coll. of Swansea, Singleton Park, Swansea SA2 8PP.

Holmström, Dr Mark; Lecturer in Social Anthropology, School of Development Studies, University of East Anglia, since 1973; *b* 1934; *m* 1960; two *d*. BA Oxon 1958 (Mod. Langs), DipSocAnthrop. Oxon 1963, DPhil Oxon 1968 (Social Anthrop.), Mem. Assoc. Social Anthropologists. Lectr, Sch. of Social Studies, Univ. E Anglia, 1967–73. UN, New York, 1960–62; Sociologist, SE Johore Project, Malaysia, 1969–70 (with gp consultants to Govt of Malaysia, from Univ. E Anglia). *Publications*: *contrib*. Contributions to Indian Sociology (New Series), Jl Royal Asiatic Soc., Econ. and Political Weekly (Bombay). *Address*: School of Development Studies, Univ. of East Anglia, University Village, Norwich, NOR 88C.

Holt, Prof. James Clarke; Professor of History, University of Reading, since 1966; Dean of the Faculty of Letters and Social Sciences, since 1972; *b* 1922; *m* 1950; one *s*. BA Oxon 1947 (1st cl. History), MA Oxon 1947; DPhil Oxon 1952; FSA, FRHistS. Asst Lectr, Nottingham, 1949–51; Lectr, 1951–60; Sen. Lectr, 1960–62; Prof. of Medieval Hist., 1962–66. Mem., Council, Royal Hist. Soc., 1966–69; Council, Selden Soc., 1966– ; Council, Pipe Roll Soc., 1969– ; Jt Gen. Ed., Pipe Roll Soc., 1971– . *Publications*: The Northerners, 1961;Magna Carta, 1965, pbk rev. edn 1969; The Making of Magna Carta, 1966; ed, Magna Carta and the Idea of Liberty, 1972; ed, Praestita Roll 14–18 John, and other documents, in, Pipe Roll Society n.s. vol. 37, 1964; *contrib*. Econ. Hist. Rev., EHR, Past Pres., Trans Royal Hist. Soc. *Address*: Dept of History, Faculty of Letters, Univ. of Reading, Whiteknights, Reading RG6 2AH.

Holt, Prof. Peter Malcolm; Professor of Arab History, University of London, since 1964; *b* 1918; *m* 1953; one *s* one *d*. BA Oxon 1940, MA Oxon 1945, DLitt Oxon 1969. Lectr, Sch. of Oriental and African Studies, London, 1955–60; Reader, 1960–64. *Publications*: The Mahdist State in the Sudan 1881–1898, 1958, 2nd edn 1970; A Modern History of the Sudan, 1961, 2nd edn 1963; Egypt and the Fertile Crescent 1516–1922, 1966; Studies in the History of the Near East, 1973; ed, Political and Social Change in Modern Egypt, 1968; ed jtly, Historians of the Middle East, 1962; The Cambridge History of Islam, 1971; *contrib*. Archives, Bull. SOAS, Jl Afr. Hist., Sudan Notes Rec. *Address*: School of Oriental and African Studies, Malet Street, WC1E 7HP.

Holt, Prof. Stephen Campbell; Professor of European Studies, University of Bradford, since 1970; *b* 1935; *m* 1959; two *s* one *d*. BA Cantab 1959, MA Cantab 1963, PhD Manchester 1966. Asst Lectr in Politics, Sheffield Univ., 1963–66; Lectr, 1966–69; Vis. Prof., Colorado Univ., 1969–70. Mem., Bolton Co. Bor. Council, 1961–64. *Publications*: The Common Market: the conflict of theory and practice, 1967; Six European States: the countries of the European Community and their political systems, 1970, American edn 1970; *contrib*. Jl Common Mkt Studies, Pol. Qly. *Address*: School of European Studies, Univ. of Bradford, Bradford BD7 1DP.

Holtom, Christopher William Dupen; Senior Lecturer in Adult Education (in Social Work), University of Bristol, since 1970; *b* 1927; *m* 1952; one *s* five *d*. Cert. Social Studies LSE 1954 (Distinction), Cert. Appl. Social Studies LSE 1955; MBASW. Asst, Edinburgh Univ., 1958–61; Tutor in Social Casework, Bristol Univ., 1961–65; Tutor, in charge of Home Office courses, 1965–70. Hon. Sec., Scott. Br., Howard League, 1959–61; Mgr, Kingswood Approved Schs, 1962–70; Mem., Home Office Adv. Cttee on Juvenile Delinquency, 1963–64; Chm., Bristol Assoc. Care and Resettlement of Offenders, 1964– ; Bristol Probation and After-Care Cttee, 1964– ; Vice-Chm., NACRO Reg. Council, 1969– ; Mem., Local Review Cttee for Parole, Leyhill Prison, 1968– ; Sec. UCAES Social Work

Educn Sub-Cttee, 1970– ; Chm., Bristol New Careers Project, 1972– ; Bristol Victims Support Scheme, 1972– ; Governor, New Barnes Sch., Toddington, Glos, 1969– . *Publications*: contrib. Fieldwork Training for Social Work, 1971; *contrib.* Case Conf., Child in Care, Soc. Wk, Procs Assoc. for Psychiatric Study of Adolescents. *Address*: Social Work Courses, Dept of Extra-Mural Studies, 13 Woodland Road, Bristol BS8 1UG.

Honan, Park; Senior Lecturer, Department of English, University of Birmingham, since 1972 (Lecturer, 1968–72); *b* 1928; *m* 1952; one *s* two *d*. MA Chicago 1951, PhD London 1959; Mem., Mod. Lang. Assoc. Teaching Asst, Univ. of Illinois, 1953–54; Instructor, Connecticut Coll., 1959–62; Asst Prof., Brown Univ., 1963–66; Assoc. Prof., 1966–68. Fellow, John Simon Guggenheim Mem. Foundn, 1962–63; Mngng Editor, Novel: A Forum on Fiction, 1967–69, British Editor, 1970– . *Publications*: Browning's Characters, 1961, 3rd edn 1970; co-ed, Shelley, 1962; ed, Bulwer-Lytton: Falkland, 1967; co-ed, Complete Works of Browning: Variorum Edn, 1969– ; jtly, The Book, the Ring and the Poet: a Biography of Robert Browning. 1974; *contrib.* ES, MP, TSL, VNL, VP, VS, ELN. *Address*: Dept of English, Univ. of Birmingham, PO Box 363, Birmingham B15 2TT.

Honderich, Dr Ted; Reader in Philosophy, University College London, since 1972; *b* 1933; *m* 1965; one *s* one *d*. BA Toronto Hons 1959 (Phil. and English), PhD London 1968; Member: Mind Soc.; Aristotelian Soc. Lectr in Philosophy: Univ. of Sussex, 1962–64; UCL, 1965–72; Vis. Prof., Yale and Grad. Center of Univ. of NY, 1970–71. Gen. Editor, Internat. Lib. of Philosophy and Scientific Method. *Publications*: Punishment, the Supposed Justifications, 1969, 3rd edn 1971; ed, Essays on Freedom of Action, 1973; *contrib.* Inquiry, Mind, Philosophy and Public Affairs, Proc. Aristotelian Soc. *Address*: Dept of Philosophy, Univ. College London, Gower Street, WC1E 6BT.

Hones, Dr G. H.; Senior Lecturer in Education, School of Education, University of Bath, since 1973; *b* 1922; *m* 1951; one *s* one *d*. BSc London 1942, BSc (Hons) London 1947, DipEd Exeter 1948, MA Clark Univ. 1953, PhD Bath Univ. 1973; Mem., Geographical Association; Mem., Comparative Edcn Soc. in Europe. Lectr in Educn, Bath 1967. Jt Sec., Working Party, Internat. Geographical Union, for 22nd International Congress (Montreal). *Publications*: Motivation, in, New Movements in the Study and Teaching of Geography, ed N. J. Graves 1971; chapter in New Directions in the Teaching of Geography, ed R. Walford, 1972; *contrib.* Geography, Jl of Geography, Universities Qly. *Address*: School of Education, Univ. of Bath, Bath BA2 7AY.

Honigmann, Prof. Ernst A. J., MA, BLitt, DLitt; Joseph Cowen Professor of English Literature, Department of English Literature, University of Newcastle upon Tyne, since 1970; *b* 1927; *m* 1958; two *s* one *d*. MA Glasgow 1948, BLitt Oxon 1950, DLitt Glasgow 1966. Asst, Univ. of Glasgow, 1951; Fellow, Shakespeare Inst., Univ. of Birmingham, 1951–54; Lectr, Univ. of Glasgow, 1954–66; Sen. Lectr, 1966–67; Reader, 1967; Reader, Univ. of Newcastle upon Tyne, 1968–70; Vis. Lectr, Tufts Univ., USA, 1966–67; Vis. Prof., Univ. of Washington, Seattle, 1967. Sec., Glasgow Bibliog. Soc., 1963–66; Mem., Bd of New-, castle People's Theatre Arts Trust Ltd, 1970– ; Adv. Bd, Shakesp. Studies, 1970– . *Publications*: The Stability of Shakespeare's Text, 1965; ed, King John (New Arden Shakespeare), 1954; Milton's Sonnets, 1966; Richard III (New Penguin Shakespeare), 1968; Twelfth Night (Macmillan Shakespeare), 1972; contrib. P. Alexander: Introductions to Shakespeare, 1964; A Book of Masques in Honour of Allardyce Nicoll, 1967; *contrib.* Durham Univ. Jl, Forum Mod. Lang., Libr., Mod. Lang. Rev., New Saltire, Phil. Qly, Rev. Engl. Studies, Shakesp. Qly, Shakesp. Survey, Stratford Studies, Theatre Res., Times Lit. Supp., etc. *Address*: School of English, Univ. of Newcastle upon Tyne, Newcastle upon Tyne NE1 7RU.

Honoré, Prof. Antony Maurice, DCL, FBA; Regius Professor of Civil Law, University of Oxford, since 1971; *b* 1921; *m* 1948; one *s* one *d*. BA S Africa 1946, BA Oxon 1947 (1st cl. Jurisprudence), BCL Oxon 1948 (1st cl.); Lincoln's Inn, Barrister at Law, Advocate of the Supreme Court of S Africa. Asst Lectr, Nottingham Univ., 1948–49; Lectr, Queen's Coll., Oxford, 1948–49; Fellow, 1949–64; Fellow, New Coll., Oxford, 1964–70; Rhodes Reader in Roman–Dutch Law, 1958–70. Hon. Bencher, Lincoln's Inn, 1971; Assoc. Mem., Internat. Acad. Comp. Law, 1971. *Publications*: (with R. W. Lee) The South African Law of Obligations, 1952; The South African Law of Property etc, 1956; (with H. L. A. Hart) Causation in the Law, 1959; Gaius, 1962; The South African Law of Trusts, 1967; *contrib.* Z. Sav. Stif. *Address*: All Souls College, Oxford.

Hood, Dr Roger Grahame; University Reader in Criminology and Fellow of All Souls College, Oxford, since 1973; *b* 1936; *m* 1963; one *d*. BSc London 1957 (Sociology), PhD Cantab 1963; Mem., Brit. Soc Criminol., Brit. Sociol. Assoc. Jun. Res. Off., LSE, 1957–58; Res. Off., 1961–63; Lectr in Social Admin., Durham Univ., 1963–67; Res. Assoc., Columbia Law Sch., 1971; Fellow, Clare Hall, Cambridge, 1969–73; Asst Dir of Res., Inst. of Criminology, Univ. of Cambridge, 1967–73. *Publications*: Sentencing in Magistrates' Courts, 1962, pbk edn 1969; Borstal Re-Assessed, 1965; Homeless Borstal Boys, 1966; (with R. Sparks) Key Issues in Criminology, 1970; trans., Sentencing the Motoring Offender, 1972; *contrib.* Brit. Jl Criminol. *Address*: All Souls College, Oxford.

Hook, Dr Andrew Dunnett; Senior Lecturer in English, University of Aberdeen, since 1971; *b* 1932; *m* 1966; one *s* one *d*. MA Edinburgh 1954 (1st cl. Hons English),

PhD Princeton 1960; Vans Dunlop Scholar, Manchester Univ., 1956, Jane Eliza Prcctor Visiting Fellow, Princeton, 1957–58. Instructor in English, Duke Univ., 1959–60; Temp. Lectr in English, Magee UC, 1960; Vis. Lectr in Amer. Lit., TCD, 1960; Asst Lectr in English, Univ. of Edinburgh, 1961–63; Lectr in Amer. Lit. Univ. of Edinburgh, 1963–70. *Publications*: ed, Scott: Waverley, 1972; ed, John dos Passos: A Collection of Critical Essays, 1974; ed with Judith Hook, C. Brontë: Shirley, 1974; *contrib*. Nineteenth Century Fiction, Texas Studies in Lang. and Lit., *Address*: English Dept, Taylor Building King's College, Aberdeen.

Hook, Brian George; Lecturer in Chinese Studies, University of Leeds, since Apr. 1963; *b* 1935; *m* 1961. BA Hons London 1958 (Modern Chinese); FRAS 1973. Member Executive Council: Univs China Cttee 1972– ; Contemp. China Inst, 1973– . *Publications*: China, in Education within Industry, ed J. Lauwreys and D. Scanlon, 1969; contrib. (with others) China's 3000 Years, 1973. *Address*: Dept of Chinese Studies, Univ. of Leeds, Leeds LS2 9JT.

Hooker, Edna Margaret, MA; Lecturer in Latin, University of Birmingham, since 1959; *b* 1920; *m* 1942; two *s* one *d*. BA Hons London 1941 (1st cl. Classics), MA London 1947; Life Mem., Class. Assoc., Hellenic Soc., Roman Soc., Brit. Sch. Athens. Asst Lectr in Classics, Birmingham Univ., 1947–50; Lectr in Classics, 1950–59. Treas., Class. Assoc., 1957–63. *Publications*: contrib. Greece Rome, Jl Hellenic Studies, Numen, Proc. Class. Assoc. *Address*: Sch. of Hellenic and Roman Studies, Univ. of Birmingham, PO Box 363, Birmingham B15 2TT.

Hooker, Geoffrey Thomas William, MC, MA; Lecturer in Classics, University of Birmingham, since 1947; *b* 1917; *m* 1942; two *s* one *d*. BA London 1940 (1st cl. Classics), MA London 1947; Mem., Class. Assoc., Hellenic Soc., Roman Soc., Life Mem., Brit. Sch. Athens, Brit. Sch. Rome. Jt Ed., Greece and Rome, 1953–63; Sec., Sch. of Hellenic and Roman Studies, Birmingham Univ., 1971– . War service, 1940–45; Educnl Broadcasts Off., BAOR, 1945; Mem., Council, Hellenic Soc., 1956–59; Council, Roman Soc., 1956–59; Council, Class. Assoc., 1951–64, 1971–74. *Publications*: contrib. University Choice, ed, K. Boehm, 1966; Penguin Companion to Literature, vol. 4 (Classical and Byzantine), 1969; *contrib*. Jl Hellenic Studies, Proc. Class. Assoc. *Address*: School of Hellenic and Roman Studies, Univ. of Birmingham, PO Box 363, Birmingham B15 2TT.

Hooker, Dr Morna Dorothy; Lecturer in Theology, University of Oxford, and Fellow of Linacre College, since 1970; Lecturer in Theology, Keble College, since 1972; *b* 1931. BA Bristol 1953 (1st cl. Hons Theol.), MA Bristol 1956, PhD Manchester 1966, MA Oxford; Member: Soc. for OT Study; Studiorum Novi Testamenti Societas, Res. Fellow, Univ. of Durham, 1959–61; Lectr in NT Studies, KCL, 1961–70. *Publications*: Jesus and the Servant, 1959; The Son of Man in Mark, 1967; *contrib*. Jl of Theol Studies, NT Studies, Theol. *Address*: Linacre College, Oxford OX1 1SY.

Hooker, William Ian; Lecturer in Law, University of Nottingham since 1966; *b* 1940; *m* 1963; three *d*. LLB Cantua, Canterbury NZ 1963. *Address*: Univ. of Nottingham, Nottingham NG7 2QF.

Hooper, Dr Douglas Frederick; Senior Lecturer in Clinical Psychology, Department of Mental Health, University of Bristol, since 1969; *b* 1927; *m* 1950; two *s* one *d*. BA (Hons) Reading 1954, PhD Cambridge 1960; FBPsS, 1968. Res. Asst, Cambridge, 1955–57; Res. Project Officer, Tavistock Inst. of Human Relations, 1960–62; Res. Assoc., Harvard 1962–64; Res. Fellow, Bristol, 1964–65; Lectr in Clinical Psychology, 1965–69. Hon. Consultant Psychologist, United Bristol Hospitals, 1974– . *Publications*: Disordered Lives, 1st edn 1967, 2nd edn 1973; *contrib*. Jl Med. Psychol., Brit. Jl. Soc. Clin. Psychol., Human Organisation, Human Relations, Internat. Jl Social Psychiatry, Jl Psychosom. Res., Lancet, Med. Social Work, Soc. Sci. and Med. *Address*: Univ. of Bristol, Dept of Mental Health, 41 St Michael's Hill, Bristol BS2 8DZ.

Hope, Dr Keith; University Lecturer in Methods of Social Research, Department of Social and Administrative Studies, Oxford, since 1968; Fellow of Nuffield College, Oxford, since 1968; *b* 1936; *m* 1961; one *s*. BA Oxon 1958 (PPE), BA London 1961 (Psychology), PhD London 1963 (Clin. Psych.). Hon. Lectr, Dept of Psychology, Edinburgh Univ., 1965–67. *Publications*: Elementary Statistics: A Workbook, 1967, Spanish edn 1971; (with G. A. Foulds and T. M. Caine), Personality and Personal Illness Scales, 1967; Methods of Multivariate Analysis, 1969, Spanish edn 1972; ed, Oxford Studies in Social Mobility Working Papers vol. 1, The Analysis of Social Mobility: Methods and Approaches, 1972; (with J. H. Goldthorpe) The Social Grading of Occupations: a new approach and scale, 1974; *contrib*. Amer. Soc. Rev., Brit. Jl Psychiatry, Brit. Jl Psychology, Sociology. *Address*: Nuffield College, Oxford.

Hope, Robert Page, BSc (Econ); Lecturer in Management Studies, Management Centre, University of Bradford, since 1966; *b* 1940; *m* 1969; one *s*. BSc (Econ) Hull 1962 (2nd cl.). Dip. Operational Research Hull 1963; Mem., Operat. Res. Soc. *Address*: Management Centre, Emm Lane, Bradford, Yorkshire.

Hope, Prof. Thomas Edward, DSC, MA, PhD; Professor of French Language and Romance Philology, University of Leeds, since 1968; *b* 1923; *m* 1949; three *s*. BA Oxon 1947, MA Oxon 1948, PhD Glasgow 1968. Asst, Glasgow, 1948–53; Lectr, Newcastle, 1953–61; Sen. Lectr, Manchester, 1962–68. RNVR, 1942–45. *Publications*: Lexical Borrowing in the Romance Languages, 1971; *contrib*. Archiv. Lingu., Trans Philol. Soc.

Address: Dept of French, Univ. of Leeds, Leeds LS2 9JT.

Hopkins, (Glen) James; Lecturer in Philosophy, King's College London, since 1972; *b* 1941; *m* 1963; two *d*. AB Economics Harvard 1963, BA Cambridge 1965 (Philosophy); Lectr in Philosophy, Lincoln Coll., Oxford, 1967–68; Jun. Res. Fellow in Philosophy, King's Coll., Cambridge, 1968–72. Director of Studies in Philosophy, King's Coll., Cambridge, 1969–72; Tutor and Official Fellow, King's Coll., Cambridge, 1971–72. *Publications*: *contrib*. Philosophical Rev. *Address*: Dept of Philosophy, King's College, Strand, WC2R 2LS.

Hopkinson, (Henry) Thomas, CBE; Director, Centre for Journalism Studies, University College, Cardiff, since 1970; *b* 1905; *m* 1953; three *d*. BA Oxon 1927, MA Oxon 1930; CBE 1967. Sen. Fellow in Press Studies, Univ. Sussex, 1967–69; Vis. Prof. of Journalism, Univ. Minnesota, 1968–69. Editor, Picture Post, 1940–50; Editor-in-chief, Drum Magazine in Africa, 1958–61; Dir for Africa of Internat. Press Inst, i/c trng of African Journalists in Nairobi and Lagos, 1963–66. *Publications*: Short life of George Orwell (series Writers and their Work), 1953; In the Fiery Continent, 1962; South Africa, 1964; Picture Post, 1938–50; novels, collections of short stories, etc.; *contrib*. Journalism Today. *Address*: Centre for Journalism Studies, 34 Cathedral Road, Cardiff.

Hopkinson, Prof. Ralph Galbraith, CEng, FIEE, Hon.FRIBA; Professor of Environmental Design and Engineering, School of Environmental Studies, University College, London, since 1965; Dean, Faculty of Environmental Studies, University College, London, since 1972 (Vice-Dean, 1970–72); *b* 1913; *m* 1938; two *s*. BSc(Eng) London 1934 (2nd cl. Electrical Engineering), Dip. Faraday House (Elec. Eng. 1st cl. 1935), PhD 1940; CEng, FIEE, FIES, FRPS, FIHVE, Hon. FRIBA. Sen. Prin. Scientific Officer, DSIR Bldg Res. Station, to 1964; Vis. Res. Fellow, Cornell Univ., Ithaca, NY, 1958–66. Sec., Sci. and Tech. Cttee, and Council, Royal Photog. Soc., 1946–50; Mem., Council, Ergonom. Res. Soc., 1956–58; Council, Illum. Eng. Soc., 1957–60; Pres., Illum. Eng. Soc., 1965–66, Gold Medallist 1972; Chm., Royal Inst. Brit. Archit. Res. Cttee, 1969; Vice Chm., Nat. Illum. Cttee, 1967–71; Mem., Royal Soc. Study Gp on Human Biology in Urban Environment, 1972. *Publications*: Architectural Physics: Lighting, 1963; ed, Hospital Lighting, 1964; ed, Sunlight in Buildings, 1965; (with P. Petherbridge and J. Longmore) Daylighting, 1966; (with J. D. Kay) The Lighting of Buildings, 1969; Lighting and Seeing, 1969; (with J. B. Collins) The Ergonomics of Lighting, 1970; *contrib*. Brit. Jl Ophthal., Brit. Jl Psychol., Byggmasteren, Ergonom., Illum. Eng., Jl Inst. Elec. Eng., Jl Opt. Soc. Amer., Jl Royal Inst. Brit. Archit., Jl Royal Inst. Town Planning, Light. Res. Technol., Lux, Nature, Photog. Jl, Trans Illum. Eng. Soc. *Address*: School of Environmental

Studies, Univ. College London, Gower Street, WC1E 6BT.

Hopkinson, Thomas; *see* Hopkinson, H. T.

Hoppen, Dr Karl Theodore, MA, PhD; Lecturer in History, University of Hull, since 1966; *b* 1941; *m* 1970. BA University College Dublin 1961 (1st cl. History and Economics), MA University College Dublin 1963, PhD Cambridge 1967. *Publications*: The Common Scientist in the 17th Century: A Study of the Dublin Philosophical Society 1683–1708, 1970; *contrib*. Hist. Jl, Irish Hist Studies, Jl Eccles. Hist., Notes Rec. Royal Soc. London. *Address*: Dept of History, Univ. of Hull, Hull HU6 7RX.

Hopper, Earl, BA, MSc; Lecturer, Sociology Department, London School of Economics, since 1967; *b* 1940. BA Washington 1962, MSc Washington 1965. Mem.: Brit. Sociol. Assoc., Amer. Sociol. Assoc., Assoc. of Psychotherapists, Group-Analytic Soc. Asst Lectr, Univ. of Leicester, 1962–63; Asst Lectr, Univ. of Cambridge, 1963–67. Mem., Mngmt Cttee, London Centre Psychotherapy, 1972. *Publications*: ed, Readings in The Theory of Educational Systems, 1971; *contrib*. Brit. Jl Sociol., Sociol., Sociol. Rev. *Address*: Sociology Dept, London School of Economics, Houghton Street, WC2A 2AE.

Hopper, Prof. Robert John, BA, PhD, FSA; Professor of Ancient History, University of Sheffield, since 1955; *b* 1910; *m* 1939. BA Wales 1932 (1st cl. Classics), PhD Cantab 1935, Dip. Classical Arch. Cantab 1934; FSA, Lectr in Classics, Univ. Coll. of Wales, 1938–41, 1945–47; Sen. Lectr in Ancient History, Univ. of Sheffield, 1947–55. Trustee, Brit. Sch. Athens. *Publications*: The Glory that was Greece, 4th edn 1964; The Acropolis, 1971; *contrib*. Ann. Brit. Sch. Athens, Jl Hellenic Studies. *Address*: Dept of Ancient History, Arts Tower, The Univ., Sheffield S10 2TN.

Hopson, Dr Barrie; Director, Vocational Guidance Research Unit, Department of Psychology, University of Leeds, since 1969; *b* 1943; *m* 1967; one *s* one *d*. BA Hull 1964 (Psychology/Sociology), PhD Leeds 1969; ABPsS 1969. Res. Asst, Leeds, 1964–66; Lectr, 1966– . Ed., Brit. Jl of Guidance and Counselling. *Publications*: The Theory and Practice of Vocational Guidance: A Selection of Readings, 1968; Uses of Psychological Tests in Vocational and Educational Counselling, 1968; Careers Guidance, 1971; Exercises in Personal and Career Development, 1973; Twosome Plus: a guide to cohabitation, 1973; *contrib*. Careers Qly, Guid. Coun., New Soc. *Address*: Dept of Psychology, Univ. of Leeds, Leeds LS2 9JT.

Horbury, Rev. Dr William; Member of Faculty of Divinity, University of Cambridge, since 1969; *b* 1942; *m* 1966; one *d*. Oriel Coll. Oxford: BA 1964, MA 1967, Mew Rabbinical Hebrew Prize 1966; Clare Coll. Cambridge: BA 1966, MA (incorp.) 1968, Hebrew Prize 1966, PhD 1971; Mem., Studiorum Novi

Testamenti Societas, 1973. Fellow of Clare Coll., Cambridge, 1968–72. Vicar of Great Gransden and Rector of Little Gransden, 1972– ; Exam. Chaplain to Bishop of Peterborough, 1973. *Publications*: contributor to: The Trial of Jesus, ed E. Bammel, 1970; The Zealots and Jesus, ed E. Bammel and C. F. D. Moule (forthcoming); ed, Samuel Krauss: The Jewish–Christian Controversy (forthcoming); *contrib*. JTS, Theol., Trans Camb. Bibliog. Society. *Address*: Great Gransden Vicarage, Sandy, Beds.

Horden, John Robert Backhouse; Director, Institute of Bibliography and Textual Criticism, University of Leeds, since 1969; *m*; one *s*. MA Oxford, BLitt Oxford, Cambridge, Heidelberg, Sorbonne; Hon. DHL Indiana State Univ., 1974. Editor, Leeds Studies Bibliog. and Text. Crit., 1966– ; Disting. Vis. Prof., Univ. of Saskatoon, 1966; Editor: Ann. Bibliog. Engl. Lang. Liter., 1967– ; revision of Halkett and Laing: Dict. Anon. Pseudon. Engl. Lit., 1971– ; Cecil Oldman Mem. Lectr in Bibliography and Textual Criticism, Leeds, 1971; Vis. Fellow elect, Pennsylvania State Univ.; Consultancy, Humanities Research Center, Univ. of Texas at Austin, 1974. Mem., Cttee, MHRA, 1967– ; Cttee, Leeds Libr., 1968– ; Brotherton Collections Adv. Cttee, 1971– . *Publications*: Francis Quarles: a bibliography of his works to the year 1800, 1953; currently ed. series emblem bks: latest is J. Hall: Emblems with Elegant Figures, 1658, 1970; Index of English Literary Manuscript Sources (in preparation); *contrib*. Anglia, Encyclopaedia Britannica, New Cambridge Bibliography of English Literature, Times, Times Lit. Supp., Trans Camb. Bibliog. Soc. *Address*: The School of English, The Univ. of Leeds, Leeds LS2 9JT.

Horlock, Dr John Harold; Vice Chancellor of Salford University, since Apr. 1974; *b* 1928; *m* 1953; one *s* two *d*. BA Cantab 1949, MA Cantab 1954, PhD Cantab 1955; CEng; FIMechE; FRAeS; MASME. Univ. Demonstrator, Cambridge, 1952–56; Res. Fellow, St John's Coll., Cambridge, 1955–57; Asst Prof., MIT, 1956–57; Lectr, Cambridge, 1957–58; Harrison Prof. of Mech. Eng, Liverpool, 1958–66; Prof. of Engineering, Cambridge, and Fellow, St John's Coll., 1967–74; Vis. Prof., Penn State Univ., 1966–67. *Publications*: Axial Flow Compressors, 1958, 2nd edn 1973; Axial Flow Turbines, 1966, 2nd edn 1973; *contrib*. Proc. Royal Soc., Proc. IMechE, Proc. Amer. Soc. of Mech. Eng, RAeS. *Address*: Salford Univ., Salford M5 4WT.

Hornby, Prof. James Angus; Professor of Law, University of Bristol, since 1961; *b* 1922. BA Cantab 1944, LLB Cantab 1945, MA Cantab 1948; Barrister (Lincoln's Inn) 1947. Lectr, Manchester Univ., 1947–61. Dean of Law, Bristol, 1962–65, 1971–74. *Publications*: Introduction to Company Law, 1957, 4th edn 1973; *contrib*. Camb. Law Jl, Law Qly Rev., Mod. Law Rev. *Address*: Faculty of Law, Univ. of Bristol, Queens Road, Bristol BS8 1RJ.

Hornsby-Smith, Dr Michael Peter; Lecturer, Department of Sociology, Surrey University, since 1965; *b* 1932; *m* 1960; three *s* one *d*. BSc(Tech) Sheffield 1954, PhD Sheffield 1958 (Fuel Technology and Chemical Engineering), BSc(Soc) London 1968; Mem., Brit. Sociol. Assoc. Lectr in Fuels, Battersea Coll. of Technol. (now Univ. of Surrey), 1959–65. Mem., Catholic Educn Council for Engl. and Wales, 1970– . *Publications*: ed (with G. Dann), Towards the Whole Truth, 1974; *contrib*. Town Planning Rev., Vocat. Asp. Educn, Durham Res. Rev., Society and Leisure, Management Decision, etc. *Address*: Dept of Sociology, Univ. of Surrey, Guildford, GU2 5XH.

Hornsey, Geoffrey; Senior Lecturer in Public and Comparative Law, Queens University, Belfast, since 1964; *b* 1924; *m* 1955; two *s* one *d*. LLB Leeds 1946 (1st cl.), LLM Leeds 1950. Asst Lectr, Manchester Univ., 1946–47; Lectr, Leeds Univ., 1947–64. Asst Sec. Gen., Internat. Inst. Unification of Private Law, Rome, 1955–57. *Publications*: *contrib*. Internat. Law Qly, Jurid. Rev., Law Qly Rev., Mod. Law Rev., North Irel. Law Qly, Rev. Soc. *Address*: Faculty of Law, Queens Univ., Belfast BT7 1NN.

Horobin, Gordon William; Assistant Director, Medical Sociology Unit (Medical Research Council), University of Aberdeen (also part-time Lecturer in Sociology), since 1969; *b* 1926; *m* 1950; one *s* one *d*. BSc(Econ) London 1952 (1st cl.). Res. Asst, Hull, 1953–54; Asst Lectr, then Lectr, Hull, 1954–62; Sociologist, MRC, Aberdeen, 1963–69. Edit. Adv., Sociol., 1969– , Editor 1973–75. *Publications*: (with H. G. Birch et al.) Mental Subnormality in the Community, 1970; ed, Experience with Abortion: A Case Study of North-East Scotland, 1973; *contrib*. Brit. Jl Sociol., Jl Biosoc. Sci., Sociol. Rev., Sociol. *Address*: Centre for Social Studies, Westburn Road, Aberdeen AB9 2ZE.

Horsfall, Dr Ben; Senior Lecturer in Music, University of Manchester, since 1966; *b* 1908; *m* 1950; one *s* one *d*. MusB Durham 1935, MusD Manchester 1948; ARMCM 1929; Hon. FRMCM 1962. Lectr in Music, Manchester Univ., 1948–66. Sec. for Admissions, Dept of Music, Manchester, 1963– . *Address*: Dept of Music, Univ. of Manchester, Manchester M13 9PL.

Hoskin, Dr Michael Anthony, MA, PhD, FRAS; Lecturer in the History of Science, University of Cambridge, since 1959, and Fellow and Librarian of Churchill College, Cambridge, since 1969; *b* 1930; *m* 1956; four *s* one *d*. BA London 1951 (1st cl. Mathematics), MA London 1952 (Mathematics), PhD Cantab 1956 (Mathematics); FRAS. Mem., Internat. Astronom. Union, Corresp. Mem., Internat. Acad. Hist. Sci. Fellow, Jesus Coll., Cambridge, 1956–57; Lectr in History of Science, Leicester Univ., 1957–59; Fellow, Tutor and Vice-Master, St Edmund's Hse, Cambridge, 1965–69; Sandars Reader in Bibliography, Cambridge Univ., 1972–73.

Ed., Hist., Sci., 1961– ; Jl Hist. Astron., 1970– . *Publications*: William Herschel and the Construction of the Heavens, 1963; Thomas Wright's Second Thoughts, 1968; The Mind of the Scientist, 1971; ed, Thomas Wright, An Original Theory of the Universe, 1971; *contrib*. Brit. Jl Hist. Sci., Jl Hist. Astron., Jl London Math. Soc., Proc. London Math. Soc., Thomist. *Address*: Churchill College, Cambridge CB3 0DS.

Hosking, Geoffrey Alan, MA, PhD; Lecturer, Department of History, University of Essex, since 1972; *b* 1942; *m* 1970. BA Cambridge 1963 (1st cl. Modern Lang.), PhD Cambridge 1970. Asst Lectr, Dept of Govt, Univ. of Essex, 1966–68, Lectr, 1968–72; Vis. Lectr, Univ. of Wisconsin, 1971. *Publications*: The Russian Constitutional Experiment: Government and Duma, 1907–14, 1973; *contrib*. Slav. E Europ. Rev., Slavic Rev., Soviet Studies. *Address*: Dept of History, Univ. of Essex, Wivenhoe Park, Colchester CO4 3SQ.

Houghton, David Sidney Eude; Lecturer in Philosophy, School of Social Studies, University of East Anglia, since 1968; *b* 1942; *m* 1971. BA Oxford 1964, MA Oxford 1967, BPhil Oxford 1966. Asst Lectr, Univ. of E Anglia, 1966–68. *Address*: School of Social Studies, Univ. of East Anglia, Norwich NOR 88C.

Houghton, Rev. Ralph Edward Cunliffe; Fellow and Tutor, St Peter's College, University of Oxford, 1930–63, and Fellow Emeritus, since 1963 (still teaching); *b* 1896; *m* 1931; two *s* one *d*. BA Oxon 1921, MA Oxon 1923; Univ. Lectr in English Literature, Oxford, 1955–63. *Address*: St Peter's College, Oxford.

Houlden, Prof. Brian Thomas; Institute of Directors Professor of Business Studies, School of Industrial and Business Studies, University of Warwick, since 1966; *b* 1926; *m* 1951; two *s*. BSc London 1947 (1st cl.), ARSM 1947, PhD London 1949, Dip. Imperial Coll. London 1949; Mem., Operat. Res. Soc., Long Range Planning Soc. Res. Metallurgist, Brit. Non Ferrous Metals Res. Assoc., 1949–51; OR Scientist, NCB, 1951–60; Dir. Operat. Res., 1960–65. Mem., Min. of Transp. Cttee on Highway Maintenance, 1968–70; Min. of Technol. Cttee on Quality Assurance, 1968–70. *Publications*: Some Applications of Operational Research in the British Coal Industry, 1960; contrib. var. conf. proc.; ed, Some Techniques of Operational Research, 1962, Japanese and Czech edns; *contrib*. Coll. Guard., Iron Coal Trades Rev., Metallurgia, Mngmt Techniq., Mining Eng., Operat. Res. Qly, Purchas. Jl, Trans Inst. Mining Eng. *Address*: Univ. of Warwick, Coventry CV4 7AL.

Houlden, Rev. James Leslie, MA; Principal, Cuddesdon Theological College, since 1970; and Member of Faculty of Theology, Oxford University, since 1960; *b* 1929. BA Oxon 1952 (2nd cl. History, 1st cl.

Theology 1954), MA Oxon 1956. Chaplain and Fellow, Trinity Coll., Oxford, 1960–70; CUF Lectr, 1961–70. Mem., Archbps' Liturg. Commn, 1968– ; Archbps' Doctr. Commn, 1969– . *Publications*: Paul's Letters from Prison, 1970; ed, A Celebration of Faith, 1970; Ethics and the New Testament, 1973; The Johannine Epistles, 1973; contrib. Theology and Modern Education, ed Bright, 1965; Catholic Anglicans To-day, ed Wilkinson, 1968; Man Fallen and Free, ed Kemp, 1969; Thinking about the Eucharist, ed Ramsey, 1972; *contrib*. Ch Qly Rev. *Address*: Cuddesdon College, Oxford OX9 9EX.

House, Prof. John William, MA; Halford Mackinder Professor of Geography, University of Oxford, since 1974; Fellow of St Peter's College, Oxford; *b* 1919; *m* 1942; two *s* two *d*. BA Oxon 1940, MA Oxon 1946; FRGS. Mem., Inst. Brit. Geogrs, Geog. Assoc., Reg. Studies Assoc. Lectr, King's Coll., Univ. of Durham, 1946–58; Sen. Lectr, 1958–61; Leverhulme Fellow, 1957–58; Reader in Applied Geog., 1961–64; Prof. and Head of Dept of Geography, Newcastle upon Tyne, 1964–74; Fulbright Prof., Univ. of Nebraska, 1962–63; Vis. Prof., Univ. of S Illinois, 1970. Mem., North. Econ. Planning Council, 1966– ; North. Pennines Rural Develop. Bd, 1967–70; Council, Inst. Brit. Geogrs, 1961–62; Murchison Award, RGS, 1970; Mem., Conseil Internat. Econ. Reg., 1966– . *Publications*: Northumbrian Tweedside, 1956; Tees-side at Mid Century, 1960; Papers on Migration and Mobility in Northern England, 1965–68; Industrial Britain, the North East, 1969; *contrib*. Cronache Econ., Geog. Jl, Geog. Mag., Trans Papers Inst. Brit. Geogrs. *Address*: St Peter's College, Oxford.

Houston, Prof. George Frederick Barclay; Titular Professor of Political Economy, University of Glasgow, since 1970; *b* 1920; *m* 1950; one *s* two *d*. MA Edinburgh 1950 (1st cl. Econ. Science), BLitt Oxon 1954. Mem., Royal Econ. Soc., Econ. Hist. Soc., Agric. Hist. Soc., Agric. Econ. Soc., Amer. Agric. Econ. Soc. Lectr, Glasgow Univ., 1951–65; Sen. Lectr, 1965–70. Econ. Cnsltnt, FAO, 1962–64; Agric. Cnsltnt, Highlands and Islands Develop. Bd, 1967– . *Publications*: chapters, in, The Scottish Economy, ed A. K. Cairncross, 1954; The Control of Public Expenditure, ed A. T. Peacock and D. J. Robertson, 1963; Economic Change and Agriculture, ed J. Ashton and S. J. Rogers, 1967; ed, Third Statistical Account of Scotland, County of Dumfries, 1962; (jtly) The World Meat Economy, 1965; *contrib*. Agric. Hist. Rev., Farm Econ., Jl Agric. Econ., Jl Royal Stat. Soc., Scott. Jl Pol. Econ. *Address*: Dept of Political Economy, Univ. of Glasgow, Glasgow G12 8QQ.

Houston, Dr Joseph; Lecturer in Divinity, University of Glasgow, since 1970; *b* 1939. MA St Andrews 1961, BD Edinburgh 1964, DPhil Oxon 1972. Asst Lectr in Logic, Glasgow Univ., 1966–69; Lectr in Logic, 1969–70. *Publications*: contrib. Philos. Qly.

Address: Dept of Divinity, Southpark Terrace, Glasgow.

Houston, Louise Helen; Lecturer, Department of Public Law, Dundee University, since 1965; *b* 1926. MA Edinburgh 1947 (Hons), LLB Edinburgh 1953; Enrolled Solicitor, Law Soc. of Scotland 1954. Warden, Hall of Res., 1965- ; Pt-time Lectr, Sch. of Town and Regional Planning, Duncan of Jordanstone Coll. of Art, Dundee, 1966- . Mem., Supplem. Benefits Tribunal, Perth, Dundee and Angus, 1969- . *Address*: Faculty of Law, Bonar House, Bell Street, Dundee.

Hovell, Peter John; Assistant Director (Senior Lecturer), School of Business Studies, University of Liverpool, since 1970; *b* 1934; *m* 1957; two *s*. BA Cantab 1965 (Econs), MA Cantab 1968. Research Fellow in Exporting, Univ. of Salford, 1965-67; Lectr in Management Studies, Univ. of Salford, 1967-70. Export Marketing Manager, Pye Ltd, Cambridge, 1955-62; Export Adviser to Dept of Trade and Industry, 1970-72. *Publications*: The Management of Urban Passenger Transport: a market perspective, 1974; *contrib*. District Bank Rev., European Jl Marketing, Jl Management Studies. *Address*: School of Business Studies, Univ. of Liverpool, Liverpool L69 3BX.

Howard, Christopher Henry Durham, MA; Reader in History, King's College, London, since 1954; *b* 1913; *m* 1957; two *s* three *d*. BA Oxon 1935 (1st cl. PPE), MA Oxon 1944; FRHistS. Asst Lectr, 1938, Lectr, 1946, KCL. Seconded to British Council, 1940-45; Mem., Council, Historical Assoc., 1947-61. *Publications*: Sir John Yorke of Nidderdale, 1939; ed. A Political Memoir, by Joseph Chamberlain, 1953; Splendid Isolation, 1967; *contrib*. Bull. of Inst. of Historical Res., EHR, Historische Zeitschrift, Historical Jl, History, Irish Historical Studies. *Address*: King's College, Univ. of London, Strand, WC2R 2LS.

Howard, Constance Mildred, (Mrs C. M. Parker), ATD, ARCA; Senior Lecturer, Fine Art Department, Goldsmiths' College, University of London, since 1947; *b* 1910; *m* 1945; one *d*. Assoc. Royal Coll. of Art 1934, Art Teachers Dip. 1935; Mem., Soc. Designer Craftsmen, Craft Centre GB, World Craft Council. Ext. examiner, several Insts of Educn, 1961- . *Publications*: Design for Embroidery from Traditional English Sources, 1956; Inspiration for Embroidery, 1966, 5th edn 1971. *Address*: Fine Art Dept, Univ. of London, Goldsmiths' College, New Cross, SE14 6NW.

Howard, Michael Eliot, MC, FBA; Fellow of All Souls College, Oxford University, since 1968; *b* 1922. BA Oxford (Final Shortened Hons History Course, Pt I (1st cl.) 1942, Pt II (2nd cl.) 1946), MA 1948; FBA, FRHistS, FRSL. Asst Lectr in History, King's Coll., London, 1947-50; Lectr, 1950-53; Lectr in War Studies, 1953-61; Reader, 1961-63; Professor of War Studies, 1963-68. Dean, Fac. of Arts, Univ. of London, 1964-68; Vice-Chm., Inst. for Strategic Studies; Vice-

Chm., Royal Inst. Internat. Aff.; Chm., Army Educnl Adv. Bd, 1968-71. *Publications*: (with John Sparrow) The Coldstream Guards, 1951; Disengagement in Europe, 1958; ed, Soldiers and Governments, 1958; The Franco-Prussian War, 1961; ed, The Theory and Practice of War, 1965; The Mediterranean Strategy in the Second World War, 1967; Studies in War and Peace, 1970; Grand Strategy vol. IV (UK History of 2nd World War, Military Series), 1972; The Continental Commitment, 1972; *contrib*. Adelphi Papers (Inst. Strategic Studies), Internat. Aff., Jl RUSI. *Address*: All Souls College, Oxford.

Howarth, Janet; Fellow and Tutor in History, St Hilda's College, Oxford, since 1969; *b* 1943; *m* 1963. BA Oxon 1963, MA Oxon 1966; FRHistS. Fellow and Lectr, Girton Coll., Cambridge, 1965-69. *Publications*: *contrib*. Hist. Jl *Address*: St Hilda's College, Oxford.

Howarth, Richard Wagstaff, MA, Dip AgricEcon: Lecturer in Agricultural Economics, Department of Agriculture, University College of North Wales, since 1964; *b* 1940; *m* 1963; two *s*. MA St Andrews 1963 (2nd cl. Moral Philosophy and Political Economy), DipAgricEcon Oxon 1964. *Publications*: Market Pricing for Agriculture, in Essays in the Theory and Practice of Pricing, 1967; Agricultural Support in Western Europe (Res. Mono. 25, IEA), 1971; *contrib*. Pol. Studies, Westm. Bk Rev. *Address*: Dept of Agriculture, Univ. College of North Wales, Bangor LL57 2DG.

Howarth, Prof. William Driver; Professor of Classical French Literature, University of Bristol, since 1966; *b* 1922; *m* 1950; two *s* two *d*. BA Oxon 1947 (1st cl. Mod. Langs), MA Oxon 1948. Laming Travelling Fellow, Queen's Coll., Oxford, 1967-68; Fellow, Jesus Coll., Oxford, 1948-66; Senior Tutor, 1963-66. Gen. Ed., Clarendon French Series, 1962- . *Publications*: Life and Letters in France, vol. I: The Seventeenth Century, 1965; (with C. L. Walton) Explications: The Technique of French Literary Appreciation, 1971; Sublime and Grotesque: A Study of French Romantic Drama, 1975; ed, Molière: Don Juan, 1958; L'Ecole des femmes, 1963; ed, Anouilh: Pauvre Bitos, 1958; Le Bal des voleurs, 1960; Becket, 1962; ed (with J. M. Thomas), Molière: Stage and Study, essays in honour of W. G. Moore, 1973; *contrib*. Fr. Studies, Jl Europ. Studies, Mod. Lang. Rev., Trivium, Rev. Sciences humaines. *Address*: Dept of French, Univ. of Bristol, Bristol BS8 1TH.

Howatt, Anthony Philip Reid; Lecturer in Department of Linguistics, University of Edinburgh, since 1965; *b* 1938; *m* 1971. MA Edinburgh 1959, Dip. in Applied Linguistics Edinburgh 1963. *Publications*: (with H. G. Hoffmann) Einführung in das Technische Englisch, 1962, 5th edn 1971; (with H. G. Hoffman) Weltsprache Englisch für Anfänger, 1963, 5th edn 1970; (with J. Webb and M. Knight) A Modern Course in Business English, 1967, 2nd edn 1972; Programmed Learning and the Language Teacher, 1969;

Put It In Writing, 1970. *Address*: c/o 14 Buccleuch Place, Edinburgh.

Howe, Alan; Lecturer in French, University of Liverpool, since 1968; *b* 1942; *m* 1967; one *d*. BA Wales 1966. *Publications*: *contrib*. French Studies. *Address*: Dept of French, Univ. of Liverpool, PO Box 147, Liverpool L69 3BX.

Howe, Prof. G(eorge) Melvyn, MSc, PhD; Professor of Geography, University of Strathclyde, since 1967; *b* 1920; *m* 1947; three *d*. BSc Wales 1940, BSc Wales 1947 (1st cl. Geography), MSc Wales 1949, PhD Wales 1957; FRGS, FRSGS, FRMetSoc. Lectr in Geog., Univ. Coll. of Wales, Aberystwyth, 1948–61; Sen. Lectr in Geog., Aberystwyth, 1961–64; Reader in Geog., Univ. of Wales, 1964–67. *Publications*: Wales from the Air, 1957, 2nd edn 1966; (with P. Thomas) Welsh Landforms and Scenery, 1963; National Atlas of Disease Mortality in the United Kingdom, 1963, 2nd edn 1970; The Soviet Union, 1968; The USSR, 1972; ed, Atlas of Glasgow and the West Region of Scotland, 1972; Man, Environment and Disease, 1972; ed (with J. A. Loraine), Environmental Medicine, 1973; *contrib*. Geog. Jl, Jl Prev. Soc. Med., Lancet, Nature, Scott. Geog. Mag., Trans Inst. Brit. Geogrs. *Address*: Dept of Geography, Univ. of Strathclyde, Glasgow G1 1XH.

Howe, Dr Patricia Anne; Lecturer, Department of German, Bedford College, University of London, since 1969; *b* 1941; *m* 1967; one *s* one *d*. BA London 1964, PhD London 1971. Asst Lectr, Dept of German, Bedford Coll., 1966–69. *Address*: Bedford College, Regent's Park, NW1 4NS.

Howell, Dr Paul Philip, CMG, OBE, MA, DPhil; Director, Cambridge University Course on Development, Fellow of Wolfson College, Cambridge, and Director of Development Studies, since 1969; *b* 1917; *m* 1949; two *s* two *d*. MA Cantab, MA Oxon 1946, DPhil Oxon 1949. Sudan Political Service, 1938–54; Uganda Govt. 1955–61; Foreign Service and Min. of Overseas Develt, 1961–69. Mem. Govg Body, Inst. of Devlt Studies, Sussex, 1971– ; Mem. Council, Overseas Develt Inst. 1972– ; Mem. and Sec., Cambridge Univ. Overseas Studies Cttee, 1969– , etc. *Publications*: A Manual of Nuer Law, 1954, 2nd ed. 1971; *contrib*. Jl of RAI, Man, Africa, etc. *Address*: Wolfson College, Cambridge.

Howell, Peter Adrian; Lecturer, Department of Latin, Bedford College, University of London, since 1967; *b* 1941. BA Oxon 1963, BPhil and MA Oxon 1966. Asst Lectr, Dept of Latin, Bedford Coll., London, 1964–67. Mem., Cttee, Victorian Soc., 1968– . *Publications*: Victorian Churches, 1968; (with E. Beazley) Companion Guide to Wales (forthcoming); Martial: a Commentary on Book I (forthcoming). *Address*: Dept of Latin, Bedford College, Regent's Park, NW1 4NS.

Howells, Brian Elwyn, MA; Lecturer in Welsh History, University College of Wales, Aberystwyth, since 1968; *b* 1929; *m* 1954; one *s*. BA Wales 1953 (1st cl. History), MA Wales 1956; Mem., Agric. Hist. Soc. Res. in Welsh Hist., Univ. of Wales, 1954–56; Fellow, Univ. of Wales, 1956–58; Teacher Pembroke Grammar Sch., 1958–64; Lectr in Hist., St David's Univ. Coll., Lampeter, 1964–67. *Publications*: ed, A Calendar of Letters Relating to North Wales, 1967; Pembrokeshire Life, 1972; Elizabethan Pembrokeshire, 1974; *contrib*. Jl Nat. Libr. Wales, Pembs Hist., Local Historian, Land of Dyfed. *Address*: Dept of Welsh History, Univ. College of Wales, Aberystwyth SY23 2AX.

Howells, Kristijana Apolonia; Lecturer in German, St David's University College, Lampeter, since 1965; *b* 1930; *m* 1954; one *s*. Absolventorium, Zagreb 1953; Dipl. Philos., Zagreb 1956; BA Cantab 1958, MA Cantab 1961; Member: Goethe Soc.; Conf. of Univ. Teachers of German. *Publications*: Pembrokeshire Life, 1972; *contrib*. Nat. Lib. of Wales Jl. *Address*: Dept of German, St David's Univ. Coll., Lampeter, Dyfed SA48 7ED.

Howes, Graham Anthony Kingston; Staff Tutor in Social Sciences, Board of Extra-Mural Studies, University of Cambridge, since 1965, and Fellow, Tutor and Director of Studies in Social and Political Sciences, Trinity Hall, Cambridge, since 1968; *b* 1938; *m* 1970; one *d*. BA Cantab 1962, MA Cantab 1965. Vis. Lectr, Dept of Sociology, Univ. of Essex, 1966–73. Mem. Cttee, Victorian Soc., 1971– . *Publications*: Dr Arnold and Bishop Stanley, in, Studies in Church History II, ed G. J. Cuming, 1965; *contrib*. Amer. Hist. Rev., Jl Eccles. Hist., Sociology. *Address*: Trinity Hall, Cambridge.

Howie, Alan Crawford, BMus, PhD; Lecturer in Music, University of Manchester, since 1966; *b* 1942; *m* 1969. BMus Edinburgh 1964 (1st cl. Hons), PhD Manchester 1969; Mem., RMA. Tutor, Open Univ., 1971–73. *Publications*: various biog. articles, in, Musik in Geschichte und Gegenwart, 1969–71; trans., eight vols, Das Musikwerk series 1970–73; *contrib*. articles on Bruckner, in Encyclopaedia Britannica, Soundings. *Address*: Dept of Music, Univ. of Manchester, Denmark Road, Manchester M15 6FY.

Howie, Dr David Ian Dickson; Registrar, University of Dublin, Trinity College, since 1966; Associate Professor in Zoology, University of Dublin, Trinity College, since 1967; *b* 1928; *m* 1950; two *d*. BSc St Andrews 1950, PhD 1957, MA TCD 1957; MIBiol. Lectr, TCD, 1953–67. Dean of Grad. Studies, 1964–67; Member: ad hoc body, Higher Education Authority, 1968–72; Statutory body, 1972– ; Central Council, Federated Dublin Voluntary Hospitals, 1966– ; Chm., St James's Hospital Bd, 1972–73. *Publications*: *contrib*. Jl Marine Biological Assoc., General and Comparative Endocrinology. *Address*: Univ. of Dublin, Trinity College, Dublin 2.

Howie, James Gordon; Lecturer, Department of Greek, Edinburgh University, since 1966; b 1941; m 1969. MA Glasgow 1963 (1st cl. Classics), Hon. Mods. Classics Oxford 1965 (1st cl.). *Address:* Dept of Greek, The David Hume Tower, Edinburgh EH8 9JX.

Howitt, David Robert; Lecturer in Hispanic Studies, University of Hull, since 1965; b 1939; m 1967. BA Birmingham 1962. *Address:* Dept of Hispanic Studies, Univ. of Hull, Hull HU6 7RX.

Howson, Dr Albert Geoffrey; Senior Lecturer, Department of Mathematics, University of Southampton, since 1966; b 1931; m 1965; one d. BSc Manchester 1952 (1st cl. Maths), MSc Manchester 1954, PhD Manchester 1955; FIMA. Sen. Lectr, Royal Naval Coll., Greenwich, 1957–62; Lectr, Univ. of Southampton, 1962–66. Asst Dir, Centre for Curric. Renewal and Educnl Develop. Overseas, 1967–69; Trustee, Sch. Math. Project, 1967– ; Hon. Sec., Math. Assoc., 1969– . *Publications:* ed, Texts of the School Mathematics Project, 1964– ; trans, M. Jeger: Transformation Geometry, 1966; (with M. R. Eraut) Continuing Mathematics, 1969; ed, Children at School – Primary Education in Britain Today, 1969; ed, Developing a New Curriculum, 1970; ed, Mathematics Apparatus for Primary Schools, 1971; A Handbook of Terms used in Algebra and Analysis, 1972; ed, Developments in Mathematical Education, 1973; (with H. B. Griffiths) Mathematics: Society and Curricula, 1974; *contrib.* Jl London Math. Soc. *Address:* Dept of Mathematics, The Univ., Southampton SO9 5NH.

Hoy, Peter Charles, MA; Fellow and Modern Languages Tutor, Merton College, University of Oxford, and CUF Lecturer in the University of Oxford, since 1967; b 1934; m 1958; two d. BA Wales 1955 (1st cl. French), MA Wales 1958, MA Oxon 1967; Asst Lectr, Univ. of Leicester, 1960–64; Lectr, 1964–67. Ed., Calepins de bibliographie, Biblionotes and Biblio-thèque, 1969– . *Publications:* Silence at Midnight, 1967; Camus in English, 1968, 2nd French edn 1971; Bibliographie des études critiques consacreés à Albert Camus, 1969, 3rd edn 1972; Bibliographie des études critiques consacrées à Julien Green, 1969; Ponge in English, 1972; Julien Gracq, essai de bibliographie, 1973; *contrib.* Adam, Rev. Lett. Mod., Rev. Sci. Hum. *Address:* Merton College, Oxford OX1 4JD.

Hoyle, Dr Brian Stewart, MA PhD; Lecturer in Geography, University of Southampton, since 1970; b 1936; m 1960; two s one d. BA Nottingham 1957, MA Nottingham 1959, PhD London 1966; FRGS. Asst Lectr, Makerere Univ., 1960–62; Lectr, Makerere Univ., 1962–66; Ed., E Afr. Geog. Rev., 1963–66; Lectr, Univ. Coll. of Wales, Aberystwyth, 1966–69; Vis. Assoc. Prof., Columbia Univ., 1971. *Publications:* The Seaports of East Africa, 1967; ed, Seaports and Development in Tropical Africa, 1970; ed, Transport and Development, 1973; ed, Spatial Aspects of Development, 1974; *contrib.* E Afr. Geog. Rev., Geog., Geog.

Rev., Tijd. Econ. Soc. Geog., Trans Inst. Brit. Geogrs. *Address:* Dept of Geography, Univ. of Southampton, Southampton SO9 5NH.

Hoyle, Prof. Eric; Professor of Education, University of Bristol, since 1971; b 1931; m 1954; one s two d. BSc London 1958 (Sociology), Acad DipEd London 1960, MA London 1962 (Education); CertEd London 1953. Lectr in Educn, Univ. of Manchester, 1965–70; Sen. Lectr in Educn, 1970–71; Vis. Prof., Western Michigan Univ., 1967; Sir George Williams Univ., Montreal, 1970. Founding co-ed. (with H. J. Butcher), Res. Educn; Cnsltnt, Public Schs Commn (2nd Stage: Direct Grant Schs), 1969–70. *Publications:* The Role of the Teacher, 1968; *contrib.* Educational Administration and the Social Sciences, ed G. Baron and W. Taylor, 1969; Curriculum Organization and Design, ed J. Walton, 1971; The Curriculum: Context, Design and Development, ed R. Hooper, 1971; Interpreting Education: a Sociological Approach, ed L. W. Drabick, 1971; *contrib.* Educnl Res., Jl Curric. Studies, Jl Soc. Pol., Ped. Europ., Res. Educn, Soc. Rev., Soc. Sci. Inf. *Address:* Univ. of Bristol School of Education, Helen Wodehouse Building, 35 Berkeley Square, Bristol.

Hoyles, (Francis) John, MA, PhD; Lecturer in English Literature, University of Hull, since 1965; b 1936; m 1960; one s one d. BA Cantab 1960, MA Cantab 1965, PhD Hull 1969. Tutor, Open Univ., 1971– . *Publications:* Littérature Anglaise, 1965; The Waning of The Renaissance, 1971; The Edges of Augustanism, 1972; D. H. Lawrence and the Counter-revolution, 1973. *Address:* English Dept, Univ. of Hull, Hull HU6 7RX.

Hubbard, Margaret Eileen, MA; Fellow and Tutor in Classics, St Anne's College, Oxford University, since 1957; b 1924. BA Adelaide 1945 (1st cl. Latin and English), MA Adelaide 1948, BA Oxon 1953 (1st cl. Litt. Hum.), MA Oxon 1956; Hertford Schol. 1950, Craven Schol. 1950, Ireland Schol. 1951. Tutor, Univ. of Adelaide, 1946–48; Craven Fellow, 1953–55; Mary Somerville Res. Fellow, Somerville Coll., Oxford, 1955–57. Assessor, 1964–65; Vice-Principal, St Anne's Coll., 1967–70. *Publications:* Propertius, 1974; (with R. Nisbet) Commentary on Horace: Odes I, 1970; trans., Aristotle: Poetics and Rhetoric 3, in, D. M. Russell and M. Winterbottom: Ancient Literary Criticism, 1972. *Address:* St Anne's College, Oxford.

Huby, Pamela Margaret; Senior Lecturer, Department of Philosophy, University of Liverpool, since 1971; b 1922; m 1956; two s one d. BA Oxon 1944 (1st cl. Classical Hon. Moderations 1942, 1st cl. Lit. Hum. 1944), MA Oxon 1947. Asst Lectr in Classics, Reading Univ., 1944–45; Lectr in Philosophy, St Anne's Soc., Oxford, 1947–49; Asst Lectr in Philosophy, Liverpool Univ., 1949–52; Lectr, 1952–71. *Publications:* Greek Ethics, 1967; Plato and Modern Morality, 1972; chapter, in, Critical History of Western Philosophy, ed D. J. O'Connor, 1964;

336

contrib. Apeiron, Class. Rev., Class. Qly, Jl Clin. Pharm. Therap., Jl Soc. Psych. Res., Philos., Philos. Qly, Phronesis. *Address*: Dept of Philosophy, The Univ., PO Box 147, Liverpool L69 3BX

Hudson, Dr Anne Mary; Fellow and Tutor in English, and CUF lecturer, Lady Margaret Hall, Oxford University, since 1963; *b* 1938. BA Oxford 1960 (1st cl. English), MA and DPhil Oxford 1964; Lectr, Lady Margaret Hall, Oxford, 1961–63. Exec. Sec., Early Engl. Text Soc., 1969– . *Publications*: *contrib.* Bull. Inst. Hist. Res., Jl Theol. Studies, Med. Æv., Neophilol., Notes Queries, Rev. Engl. Studies. *Address*: Lady Margaret Hall, Oxford.

Hudson, Prof. Anthony Hugh; Professor of Law, University of Liverpool, since 1971; *b* 1928; *m* 1962; one *s* three *d*. BA Cantab 1949, MA Cantab 1953, LLB Cantab 1950, PhD Manchester 1966; Barrister-at-Law, Lincoln's Inn 1954. Asst Lectr, Hull Univ. Coll., 1951–54; Lectr, Hull Univ., 1954–57; Lectr, Birmingham Univ., 1957–62; Lectr, Manchester Univ., 1962–64; Sen. Lectr, Liverpool Univ., 1964–71; Dean, Fac. of Law, 1971– . *Publications*: *contrib.* Canadian Bar Rev., Conv., Law Qly Rev., Mod. Law Rev. *Address*: Faculty of Law, Univ. of Liverpool, Liverpool L69 3BX.

Hudson, Dr Frederick, DMus, FRCO; Reader in Music, University of Newcastle upon Tyne, since 1949; *b* 1913; *m* 1941; two *s*. BMus Durham 1941; DMus Durham 1950, ARCO 1935, FRCO 1939. Vis. Prof. of Music, Univ. of Cincinnati, Ohio, 1967–68; Vis. Lectr, Princeton Univ., 1967; Rutgers Univ., 1968; Univ. of Cincinnati, 1970; Guest Lectr, Princeton, Rutgers, Cincinnati, and N Texas State Univ., 1974. *Publications*: Neue Bach-Ausgabe, I/33, Trauungskantaten, 1957; Hallische Handel-Ausgabe, IV/11, Sechs Concerti Grossi Op. 3, 1959; IV/12, Acht Concerti, 1971; IV/16, Concerti a due cori, 1976; Urtext edns of J. Merbecke, W. Byrd, G. Gabrieli; Reconstructions of incomplete Bach Wedding Cantatas: BWV 120a, 1955; BWV 34a, 1972; *contrib.* Grove: Dictionary of Music, 6th edn; *contrib.* Amer. Chor. Rev., Curr. Musicol., Händel-Jrb., Music Lett., Music Rev., Musica, Music. Times, Musik Gesch. Gegen., Musikfors., Paper Maker. *Address*: Dept of Music, The Univ., Newcastle upon Tyne NE1 7RU.

Hudson, Prof. Liam; Professor of Educational Sciences, University of Edinburgh, since 1968; *b* 1933; *m* 1st 1955, 2nd 1965; three *s* one *d*. BA Oxon 1957, MA Oxon 1960, PhD Cantab 1961. Dir, Res. Unit on Intellectual Develop., 1964– ; Fellow, King's Coll., Cambridge, 1966–68. Chm., Thomson Res. Fund, 1968– ; Co-dir., Nuffield Foundn 'Anabas' Project, 1971– . *Publications*: Contrary Imaginations, 1966; Frames of Mind, 1968; ed, The Ecology of Human Intelligence, 1970; The Cult of the Fact, 1972; *contrib.* Nature. *Address*: Centre for Research in the Educational Sciences, Univ. of Edinburgh.

Hudson, Michael Anthony; Lecturer in Economics, University of Leeds, since 1966; *b* 1937; *m* 1961; one *s*. BEc Hons Sydney 1960; MA Hons Otago 1962. Univ. of NSW, 1961; Univ. of Otago, 1962; Univ. of Canterbury, 1963–65. *Publications*: *contrib.* Econ. Hist. Rev., Econ. Record, Jl of Finance. *Address*: Sch. of Economic Studies, Univ. of Leeds, Leeds LS2 9JT.

Hudson, Dr Richard Anthony; Lecturer, Department of Phonetics and Linguistics, University College, London, since 1970; *b* 1939; *m* 1970; one *d*. BA Cantab 1961, PhD London 1964. Mem., Linguistics Assoc. of Great Britain. Research Asst, UCL 1964–70. *Publications*: ed (with A. R. Meatham), Encyclopedia of Linguistics, Information and Control, 1969; English Complex Sentences: An introduction to Systemic Grammar, 1971; *contrib.* Foundns of Language, Jl Linguistics, Language, Lingua. *Address*: Dept of Phonetics and Linguistics, Univ. Coll. London, Gower Street, WC1E 6BT.

Hudson, Dr William Donald; Reader in Moral Philosophy, Philosophy Department, Exeter University, since 1969; *b* 1920; *m* 1944; one *s* two *d*. MA London 1954, BD London 1943, PhD London 1958. Lectr in Philosophy, Exeter, 1960–66; Sen. Lectr in Philosophy, 1966–69. Sub-Dean of Arts, Exeter Univ., 1969–73; Gen. Ed., New Studies in Ethics, New Studies in Philos. of Religion, New Studies in Practical Philos. *Publications*: Ludwig Wittgenstein, 1968; Ethical Intuitionism, 1967; The Is-Ought Question, 1969; Reason and Right, 1970; Modern Moral Philosophy, 1970; A Philosophical Approach to Religion, 1974; *contrib.* Analysis, Mind, Philos., Philos. Qly, Relig. Studies, Scott. Jl Theol., Theol. *Address*: Queen's Building, The Univ., Exeter EX4 4QH.

Hudson-Williams, Prof. Harri Llwyd, MA; Professor of Greek, Department of Classics, University of Newcastle upon Tyne, since 1952; *b* 1911; *m* 1946; two *d*. BA Wales 1931 (1st cl. Greek), BA Cambridge 1936 (1st cl. Parts I and II Classical Tripos), MA Cambridge 1940. Asst Lectr in Greek, Liverpool Univ., 1937–40; Lectr in Greek, 1945–50; Reader in Greek, King's Coll., Newcastle upon Tyne, 1950–52. Dean, Fac. of Arts, Newcastle Univ., 1963–66; Hd of Dept of Classics, 1970– . Mem., Council, Hellenic Soc., 1951–54, 1962–65; Council, Class. Assoc., 1969–72; Gov., Royal Grammar Sch., Newcastle upon Tyne, 1969– ; Barnard Castle Sch., 1959– . *Publications*: Ch. on Rhetoric, in, Fifty Years of Classical Scholarship, 1954, 2nd edn (entitled Fifty Years (and Twelve) of Classical Scholarship) 1968; *contrib.* Amer. Jl Philos., Class. Qly, Class. Rev., Greece Rome, Jl Hellenic Studies. *Address*: Dept of Classics, The Univ., Newcastle upon Tyne NE1 7RU.

Hughes, Anthony Dowdall, BCL, MA; Sub-Dean, Faculty of Laws, University of London, King's College, since 1968, and Senior Lecturer, King's College, since 1972; *b* 1933; *m* 1960; one *s* four *d*. BA Oxon 1955 (1st cl. Jurisprudence), BCL Oxon 1956 (1st

337

cl.), MA Oxon 1958; Barrister (Lincoln's Inn) 1965. Asst Lectr, King's Coll., London, 1959–60; Lectr, 1960–72; Vis. Assoc. Prof., Manitoba Law Sch., 1965–66. Chm., Bd of Examiners, LLB External, Univ. of London, 1968– . *Publications*: contrib. Jl Business Law, Law Qly Rev., Mod. Law Rev. *Address*: Faculty of Laws, Univ. of London, King's College, Strand, WC2R 2LS.

Hughes, Prof. Anthony George; Professor of Music, University College, Dublin since 1958; *b* 1928; *m* 1960; one *s* three *d*. BMus Dublin 1949, DMus 1955; Member: IMS, RMA. Travelling Studentship, NUI, 1952; Graduate, Akademie für Musik und d. kunst, 1953–54; Lectr, RIAM, 1948–58. Chm., RDS Music Cttee, 1963– ; Member: Council RDS, 1969– ; Irish Cultural Relations Cttee, 1964– ; President Dublin Grand Opera Soc., 1967– ; Trustee, National Library of Ireland, 1970– . Arnold Bax Medal, 1956. *Address*: Univ. College, Dublin, Belfield, Dublin 4.

Hughes, Anthony Owen, BSc, MSc, MPhil; Lecturer, Department of Community Health, University of Nottingham Medical School, since 1970; *b* 1944; *m* 1965; one *s* one *d*. BSc Nottingham 1964 (2nd cl. Maths/Econs), MSc Nottingham 1965 (Statistics), MPhil Nottingham 1972 (Economics). Tutorial Asst, Econs Dept, Nottingham, 1964–66, Lectr, 1966–68, Lectr, Mathematics Dept, 1968–70. *Publications*: contrib. Jl Royal Stat. Soc. *Address*: Dept of Community Health, The Medical School, Nottingham Univ., Nottingham NG7 2RD.

Hughes, Prof. Christopher John; Professor of Politics, University of Leicester, since 1962, Head of Department 1962–74; *b* 1918; *m* 1957. BA Oxon 1939, MA Oxon 1946, BPhil Oxon 1948, DLitt Oxon 1974; Mem., Royal Inst. Internat. Affairs, Mem., Political Studies Assoc., Mem., Swiss Political Studies Assoc., Mem., Swiss Historical Assoc. Student of Nuffield Coll., 1948; Lectr, Univ. of Glasgow, 1949–53; Lectr, Univ. of Leicester, 1957–62. Foreign Office, German Section (Cultural Relations), 1954–55. *Publications*: The Federal Constitution of Switzerland: text and commentary, 1954; The British Statute Book, 1957; The Parliament of Switzerland, 1962; Confederacies. Inaugural Lecture, 1963; Switzerland, 1974; contrib. Switzerland, in, European Political Parties, 1971; Leibholz Festschrift, 1966; de Salis Festschrift, 1972; *contrib.* Annuaire Suisse de Science politique, Jahrbuch des Öffentlichen Rechts, Internat. Affairs, Parly Affairs, Public Admin. *Address*: Univ. of Leicester, University Road, Leicester LE1 7RH.

Hughes, Dr Derek William; Lecturer, Department of English and Comparative Literary Studies, University of Warwick, since 1972; *b* 1944. BA Oxon 1967, MA 1970, PhD Liverpool 1972; Lectr, Brock University, Ontario, 1967–70; William Noble Fellow, Univ. of Liverpool, 1971–72. *Publications*: contrib. ELH, SEL, UTQ. *Address*: Dept of English, Univ. of Warwick, Coventry CV4 7AL.

Hughes, Edward William; Director of Adult Education, University of Newcastle upon Tyne, since 1964; *b* 1920; *m* 1969; two *s* one *d*. BA Oxon 1942, MA Oxon 1947, BLitt Oxon 1947, LLB London 1951; Student Nuffield Coll., Oxford, 1946–47; Lectr in Politics, King's Coll., Newcastle upon Tyne (Univ. of Durham) and Univ. of Newcastle upon Tyne, 1947–64; Vis. Lectr in Politics, Univ. of Michigan, 1956–57. Pres., Assoc. of Univ. Teachers, 1969–70. *Address*: Dept of Adult Education, The Univ., Newcastle upon Tyne.

Hughes Dr (James) Quentin, MC; Reader, School of Architecture, University of Liverpool, since 1968; *b* 1920; *m* 1948; two *d*. BArch Liverpool 1946 (Hons), Dipl. Civic Design Liverpool 1947, PhD Leeds 1952; ARIBA 1948, FRIBA 1957, FRSA 1972, FRHistS 1972. Sch. of Architecture, Liverpool University: Lect., 1955; Sen. Lectr and Sub Dean, 1960; Reader, 1968; (seconded to) Royal Univ. of Malta: Prof. 1968–72; Dean, 1968–72. Chairman: RIBA Professional Books Cttee, 1963–66; Chester Civic Trust, 1964–66; Victorian Soc., Liverpool, 1965–68; Bi-Centenary and Royal Visit, Royal Univ. of Malta, 1969; Governor, Liverpool Polytechnic, 1973– ; Mem. Senate: Univ. of Malta, 1968–72; Liverpool Univ., 1973–74. *Publications*: Building of Malta, 1956, 2nd edn 1968; Renaissance Architecture, 1962, 3rd edn 1965; Seaport, 1964, 2nd edn 1968; Fortress, 1966, German edn 1972; Liverpool, 1966; ed, Le fabbriche e i desegni di Andrea Palladio, 1968; Military Architecture (forthcoming); *contrib.* Architec. Assoc. Jl, Architect. Rev., Casabellag, Chambers's Encyc. *Address*: School of Architecture, Univ. of Liverpool, PO Box 147, Abercromby Square, Liverpool L69 3BX.

Hughes, James Thomas; Senior Lecturer, Department of Social and Economic Research, University of Glasgow, since 1973; *b* 1940; *m* 1964; one *s* two *d*. MA Glasgow 1962. University of Glasgow: Asst, Dept of Social and Economic Res., 1962–64; Lectr, Dept of Political Econ., 1964–69. Lectr, Dept of Social and Econ. Res., 1969–73. Vis. Res. Fellow, Washington Centre for Metropolitan Studies, 1967–68. Consultant, Govt of New Brunswick, Canada, 1968, 1969. *Publications*: Chapters in: Lothians Regional Survey and Plan, vol. 1, ed D. J. Robertson, 1966; Grangemouth–Falkirk Regional Survey and Plan, vol. 1, ed D. J. Robertson, 1968; Employment Projection and Urban Development, in, Urban and Regional Analysis, ed S. C. Orr and J. B. Cullingworth, 1969; (with J. Kozlowski) Threshold Analysis: a quantitative planning method, 1972; *contrib.* Jl of Develt Studies, Jl of RTPI, Urban Studies, Scottish Jl of Political Econ. *Address*: Dept of Social and Economic Research, Univ. of Glasgow, Adam Smith Building, Glasgow G61 8RT.

Hughes, John Anthony; Lecturer in Sociology, Department of Sociology, University of Lancaster, since 1970; *b* 1941. BSocSc (MPP) Birmingham 1963 (1st cl.). Univ Birmingham, 1964–65; Univ. Exeter, 1965–70.

Publications: (with R. E. Dowse) Political Sociology, 1972; Sociological Methods, 1975; *contrib*. Brit. Jl Sociology, Sociology. *Address*: Univ. of Lancaster, University House, Bailrigg, Lancaster LA1 4YW.

Hughes, Dr Kathleen; Lecturer in the Early History and Culture of the British Isles, Department of Anglo-Saxon, Norse and Celtic, University of Cambridge, since 1958: Fellow since 1955, and Director of Studies in History, since 1959, Newnham College, Cambridge; *b* 1926. BA London 1947 (History), PhD London 1951, LittD Cantab 1973; FRHistS, FSA. Asst Lectr in Hist., Royal Holloway Coll., Univ. of London, 1951–55; Asst Lectr in Hist., Univ. of Cambridge, 1957–58. O'Donnell Lectr, Univ. of Wales, 1969; Jarrow Lectr, 1970; Sir John Rhŷs Lectr in Brit. Acad., 1973. *Publications*: contrib. Studies in the Early British Church, ed N. K. Chadwick, 1958; The English Church and the Papacy, ed C. H. Lawrence, 1965; The Church in Early Irish Society, 1966; A. J. Otway-Ruthven: A History of Medieval Ireland, 1968; England Before the Conquest, ed Clemoes and Hughes, 1971; Early Christian Ireland: Introduction to the Sources, 1972; *contrib*. EHR, Irish Hist. Studies, Jl Eccles. Hist., Anal. Bolland., Studia Celt., Studies in Church Hist. *Address*: Newnham College, Cambridge.

Hughes, Dr Meredydd Glyn, MA, PhD; Senior Lecturer, Faculty of Education, University College, Cardiff, since 1974; *b* 1922; *m* 1953; one *s* one *d*. BA Cantab Senior Optime in Maths Tripos 1948, MA 1950, DipEd London 1949, PhD Wales 1972; Barrister, Lincoln's Inn, 1956. Member: Mathematical Assoc.; British Educational Administration Soc. (Council of Management). Lectr and Administrative Officer, Faculty of Education, Univ. Coll., Cardiff, 1965–74. Headmaster of Dynevor School, Swansea, 1957–65; Chairman, Council for Education in World Citizenship (Wales), 1963–74. Editor: Educn Admin Bulletin, Jl Brit. Educn Admin Soc., 1972– ; Admin Abstracts. *Publications*: Modernising School Mathematics, 1962; ed, Secondary School Administration: A Management Approach, 1st edn 1970, 2nd edn 1974; *contrib*. Educn for Develt, HMA Rev., Lond. Educn Qly, Mathematical Gazette, Trends in Educn, Y Gwyddonydd. *Address*: Faculty of Education, Univ. College, Cardiff, PO Box 78, Cardiff CF1 1XL.

Hughes, Patrick Michael, MA, MEd, ABPS; Senior Lecturer in Education, University of Reading, in charge of Guidance Unit, since 1972; *b* 1923. BA Belfast 1943, BEd Belfast 1952 (with Distinction), MA Belfast 1959, LRAM 1960; ABPS (Mem. Div. Educnl Child Psychol.). Lectr, Univ. Coll., Swansea, 1963–67; Lectr in Educnl Psychology, Reading, 1967–72. Mem. Exec. Cttee, Reading Area Youth Counsel. Service; Mem. Exec. Cttee, Standing Conf. for Advancement of Counselling. *Publications*: Guidance and Counselling in Schools: a response to change, 1971. *Address*: Univ. of Reading School of Education, Guidance

Unit, Old Red Building, London Road, Reading RG1 5AQ.

Hughes, Quentin; *see* Hughes, J. Q.

Hughes, Thomas Erasmus Vaughan; Senior Lecturer in Town Planning, University of Wales Institute of Science and Technology, since 1968; *b* 1927; *m* 1955; two *s* one *d*. BA Hons Liverpool 1951 (Geog. cl. 2), MCD Liverpool 1953; DipPA Liverpool 1959; Cert. Traffic Eng., Lanchester Polytechnic, 1963; FRTPI. Dir, Mid-Career Educn in Town Planning, 1973– ; Mem., Bd of Celtic Studies. External Examiner: Edinburgh Univ. 1969–72; RTPI, 1974– . *Publications*: contrib. Jl RTPI, Jl Architectural Res., Welsh Jl. *Address*: Univ. of Wales Institute of Science and Technology, Cardiff CF1 3NU.

Hughes, Prof. Thomas Jones; Professor of Geography, University College, Dublin, since 1960; *b* 1922; *m* 1952; two *s* three *d*. BA Wales 1948, MA Wales 1950. Lectr, Univ. Coll., Dublin, 1950–60. *Publications*: contrib. Irish Geog. *Address*: Dept of Geography, Univ. College, Dublin 4, Ireland.

Hulin, Peter; University Lecturer in Near Eastern Archaeology, University of Oxford, since 1957; Fellow of Wolfson College, Oxford, since 1965; *b* 1923; *m* 1954; one *s* three *d*. MA Oxon 1949. Mem., Brit. Sch. Archaeol. Iraq; Mem., Brit. Inst. Archaeol. Ankara; Mem., Brit. Inst. Persian Studies. Univ. Registry, Oxford, 1954–57. *Publications*: contrib. Anatol. Studies, Iraq, Jl Cuneif. Studies, etc. *Address*: Oriental Institute, Oxford.

Hull, Dr John Martin; Lecturer in Education (Theology), School of Education, University of Birmingham, since 1968; *b* 1935; *m* 1962; one *d*. BA Melbourne 1955, DipEd Melbourne 1956, BEd Melbourne 1958, MA Cantab 1965, PhD Birmingham 1969. Taught in secondary schs, Australia and Britain, 1957–59 and 1962–66; Lectr in Divinity, Westhill Coll. of Educn, Birmingham, 1966–68; Editor, Learning for Living, 1970– ; Nat. Vice-Chm., Christian Educn Movt, 1971– . *Publications*: Hellenistic Magic and the Synoptic Tradition, 1974; Sense and Nonsense about God, 1974; Education and Worship (forthcoming); *contrib*. Educn for Teaching, Educnl Rev., Jl Curriculum Studies, Scottish Jl Theology. *Address*: School of Education, Univ. of Birmingham, Birmingham B15 2TT.

Hulton, Angus Orpe; Senior Lecturer, Departments of Greek and Latin, University of Sheffield, since 1966; *b* 1920; *m* 1956; two *s* two *d*. MA Oxford 1948. Asst Lectr, Univ. of Sheffield, 1948–51, Lectr, 1951–66. *Publications*: contrib. Class. Philol., Class. Qly, Class. Rev., Greece and Rome, Latomus, Mnemosyne, Orpheus. *Address*: Dept of Classics, The Univ., Sheffield S10 2TN.

Hume, John Robert, BSc, ARCST; Lecturer, Department of History (formerly Department of Economic History), University of Strathclyde, since 1964; *b* 1939; *m* 1965;

339

two *s*. BSc Glasgow 1961; ARCST 1961; Mem., Econ. Hist. Soc., Newcomen Soc. Jt Sec., Scott. Econ. Hist. Conf., 1969– ; Jt Editor, Transp. Hist., 1968– ; Mem., Council for Brit. Archaeol., Res. Cttee on Indust. Archaeol. *Publications*: The Industrial Archaeology of Glasgow, 1974; *contrib.* Indust. Archaeol., Scott. Hist. Rev. *Address*: Dept of History, Univ. of Strathclyde, Glasgow G1 1XW.

Hume, Dr Wilfrid Ian, PhD, DCP; Lecturer in Clinical Psychology, Department of Psychiatry, University of Leeds, since 1970; *b* 1940; *m* 1968; one *s* one *d*. BSc Bristol 1963 (Hons Psychology), PhD Bristol 1970; DCP Glasgow 1966; ABPsS. Lectr, Univ. of Glasgow, 1966–70. *Address*: Dept of Psychiatry, Univ. of Leeds, 15 Hyde Terrace, Leeds LS2 9LT.

Humphreys, Prof. Arthur Raleigh; Professor of English, University of Leicester, since 1947; *b* 1911; *m* 1947. BA Cantab 1933, MA Cantab 1936; AM Harvard 1935 (Commonwealth Fund Fellow). Supervisor in English, Cambridge Univ., 1935–37; Lectr in English, Liverpool Univ., 1937–46; Brit. Council Lectr in English, Istanbul Univ., 1942–45. Fellow, Folger Shakespeare Libr. Washington, DC, 1960, 1961, 1964; Vis. Fellow, All Souls, Oxford, 1966. *Publications*: William Shenstone, 1937; The Augustan World, 1954; Steele, Addison and their Periodical Essays, 1959; Melville, 1962; Shakespeare, Richard II, 1967; Shakespeare, The Merchant of Venice, 1973; ed, Henry IV, Part I, 1960, Part II, 1966; ed, Tom Jones, 1962; ed, Amelia, 1963; ed, Jonathan Wild, 1964; ed, Melville's White-Jacket, 1966; ed, Henry V, 1968; ed, Henry VIII, 1971; ed, Joseph Andrews and Shamela, 1973; *contrib.* From Dryden to Johnson, ed B. Ford, 1957; Alexander Pope, ed P. Dixon, 1972; Shakespeare's Art, ed M. Crane, 1973; Shakespeare: Select Bibliographical Guides, ed S. Wells, 1973; *contrib.* learned jls. *Address*: Univ. of Leicester, University Road, Leicester LE1 7RH.

Humphreys, Dr Kenneth William; Librarian, University of Birmingham, since 1952; *b* 1916; *m* 1939; two *s*. BA Oxon 1938 (English), MA Oxon 1943, BLitt Oxon 1949, PhD Birmingham 1969; Hon LittD Dublin 1969; FLA 1969. Asst, Bodleian Libr., 1935–50; Dep., Brotherton Libr., Leeds, 1950–52. Hon. Lectr in Palaeography, Leeds, 1951–52; Birmingham, 1953– . Mem. Cttee, Sec. and Chm., SCONUL, 1953– ; Chm., Univ. Libr. Sub-Sect., IFLA, 1967– ; Sec., LIBER, 1971– ; Chm., Nat. Acad. and Med. Libraries Cttee, Lib. Assoc., 1972– ; Chm. Council, Lib. Assoc., 1973– ; Chm., Nat. Cttee on Regional Libr. Co-op., 1970– ; Libr. Adv. Panel, Brit. Council, 1971– . *Publications*: The book provisions of the Mediaeval Friars, 1964; The library of the Carmelites at Florence at the end of the fourteenth century, 1964; The library of the Franciscans of the Convent of St Anthony, Padua, at the beginning of the fifteenth century, 1967; Reports on the Libr. of the Indian Inst. of Technol., Delhi, Jewish Nat. and Univ. Libr., Israeli acad. libraries, Tel-Aviv Univ. Libr., Nat Libr. Ireland; *contrib.* Libr. Assoc. Rec. Libri, etc. *Address*: The Main Library, Univ. of Birmingham, PO Box 363, Birmingham B15 2TT.

Humphreys, Mrs M. E.; *see* Hill, Polly.

Humphrys, Dr Graham; Senior Lecturer in Geography, University College of Swansea, since 1973 (Lecturer, 1960–73); *b* 1934; *m* 1957; one *s*. BSc Bristol 1956 (1st cl. Geog.); MA McGill 1959; PhD Wales 1967. Res. Asst, McGill Sub-Arctic Res. Lab., 1956–57; Teaching Asst, McGill Univ., 1958–59; Asst Lectr, Edinburgh Univ., 1959–60; Vis. Prof., Univ. of Alberta, 1966–67, York Univ., Toronto, 1972. Resident Sen. Tutor, Nevadd Lewis Jones Hall of Residence, Univ. Coll., Swansea, 1962–68; Sub-Dean, Fac. of Econ. and Soc. Studies, Univ. Coll., Swansea, 1968–71; Mem., Council, Inst. Brit. Geogrs, 1969–72. *Publications*: Industrial South Wales, 1972; Power and the Industrial Structure, in The UK Space, ed J. W. House, 1974; *contrib.* Geog. Rev., Scott. Geog. Mag., Trans Inst. Brit. Geogrs. *Address*: Dept of Geography, Univ. College of Swansea, Swansea SA2 8PP.

Hunt; *see* Crowther-Hunt, The Lord.

Hunt, Arthur John, BA; Senior Lecturer, Department of Geography, University of Sheffield, since 1959; *b* 1915; *m* 1941; one *d*. BA London 1938; Cambridge Teacher's Cert. 1940. Mem., Inst. Brit. Geogs, Geog. Assoc., Reg. Studies Assoc. Univ. Asst, Edinburgh Univ., 1938–39; Asst Lectr, Sheffield Univ., 1947–49, Lectr, 1949–59. RE (Survey), 1941–46. *Publications*: ed, Population Maps of the British Isles, 1961; trans., Pinchemel: France, 1969; *contrib.* Trans Inst. Brit. Geogrs. *Address*: The Univ. of Sheffield, Sheffield S10 2TN.

Hunt, Charles Henry; Senior Lecturer, Computer Centre, University of Aston in Birmingham (also teaches social implications of computers), since 1971; *b* 1928; *m* 1957; one *s* one *d*. BA Oxon 1952, MA Oxon 1956; PhD Liverpool 1970; FSS, FIMA. Dept Hd, Pioneer Life Ass. Co. Ltd, 1954–55; Mngr, O and M, Tate and Lyle Ltd Liverpool, 1955–58; Lectr, A. T. and E. Co. Ltd (later the Plessey Co. Ltd), 1958–64; Computer Training Mngr, Plessey Telecomms Gp, 1964–66; Res. Fellow, Liverpool, 1966–70, Sen. Res. Fellow 1970–71, and Dir, Data Processing Res. Unit, 1968–71. *Publications*: *contrib.* Comput. Jl. *Address*: Computer Centre, Univ. of Aston in Birmingham, 15 Coleshill Street, Birmingham B4 7PA.

Hunt, Dr Edward H., BSc(Econ), PhD; Lecturer in Economic History, London School of Economics, University of London, since 1969; *b* 1939; *m* 1966. BSc(Econ) LSE 1964, PhD London 1971. Asst Lectr, Queen's Univ., Belfast, 1966–68, Lectr, 1969. Asst Editor, Econ. Hist. Rev., 1971– . *Publications*: Regional Wage Variations in Britain, 1850–1914, 1973; *contrib.* Econ. Hist. Rev., Hist. *Address*: London School of Economics, Houghton Street, WC2A 2AE.

Hunt, Gregory Max Kneale; Lecturer in Philosophy, University of Warwick, since 1970; *b* 1942; *m* 1964; one *d*. BSc Melbourne 1963, MA Melbourne 1972; Dip. Applied Physics, Royal Melbourne Inst. of Tech. 1960. Temp. Lectr, Univ. of Melbourne, 1967. *Publications: contrib.* Brit. Jl Phil Sci. *Address*: Dept of Philosophy, Univ. of Warwicks, Coventry CV4 7AL.

Hunt, Kenneth Edward; Director, Institute of Agricultural Economics, University of Oxford, since 1969; *b* 1916; *m* 1941; one *s* two *d*. BA Cantab 1938, Dip. Agric. Science Cantab 1939, MA Cantab 1942; MA Oxon 1947. Mem., Brit. Agricultural Economics Soc.; Mem., Nutrition Soc.; Mem., Animal Production Soc.; Internat. Assoc. of Agricultural Economists (Vice-Pres.). Res. Asst, Dept of Agriculture, Cambridge, 1939–47; Lectr, Agricultural Economics Inst., Oxford, 1947–69. *Publications*: The State of British Agriculture, 1953–66; Colonial Agricultural Statistics, 1952, 1957; Agricultural Statistics for Developing Countries, 1969. *Address*: Institute of Agricultural Economics, Dartington House, Little Clarendon Street, Oxford OX1 2HP.

Hunt, Martin Robert; Tutor, Department of Ceramics, Royal College of Art, since 1968; *b* 1942; *m* 1963; one *s* one *d*. Nat. Dip. in Des. 1963, Des (RCA) 1966. Vis. Lectr, RCA, 1966. Indep. Mem., Design Council (formerly Council of Ind. Design); Design Index Cttee. Partner, (design firm) Queensberry and Hunt, 1966– . *Publications*: Selling Modern Pottery and Glass, 1972; *Address*: Royal Coll. of Art, Sch. of Ceramics, Kensington Gore, SW7 2EU.

Hunt, Prof. Norman Charles, BCom, PhD; Professor of Business Studies, University of Edinburgh, since 1953; *b* 1918; *m* 1942; two *s*. BCom London 1943 (1st cl. Economics), PhD Edinburgh 1948, FBIM. Lectr, Univ. of Edinburgh, 1946–52; Dean of Social Sciences, 1961–64. Mem., Home Off. Cttee on Fire Service, 1968–70; UGC, 1969– ; Chm., Mngmt Develt Cttee, Council for Tech. Educn and Training in Overseas Countries, 1971– . *Publications*: Methods of Wage Payment in British Industry, 1951; University Education for Business in the United States, 1954; ed. Modern Thinking on Management, 1966; (with H. A. Nicholls) The Economy of Edinburgh: present and future prospects, 1968; ed (with W. D. Reekie), Management in the Social and Safety Services, 1974. *Address*: Dept of Business Studies, William Robertson Building, 50 George Square, Edinburgh EH8 9JY.

Hunt, Peter Leonard; Lecturer in English, University of Wales Institute of Science and Technology, since 1968; *b* 1945. BA Aberystwyth 1966, MA Wales 1969. *Address*: Dept of English, Univ. of Wales Institute of Science and Technology, Cardiff CF1 3NU.

Hunter, Geoffrey Basil Bailey; Reader, Department of Logic and Metaphysics, University of St Andrews, since 1972; *b* 1925; *m* 1951; three *d*. BA Oxon 1950, MA Oxon 1953. Lectr, Queen's Univ., Kingston, Ont.,

1950–52; Asst Lectr, Leeds Univ., 1952–54, Lectr, 1954–65; Vis. Associate Prof., Univ. of N Carolina, Chapel Hill, 1964; Lectr, Univ. of St Andrews, 1965–66, Sen. Lectr, 1966–72. *Publications*: Metalogic, 1971, rev. American edn 1973; contrib. Hume, American edn 1966, British edn 1968; The Is–Ought Question, 1969; *contrib.* Mind, Philos. Qly, Philos. Studies, Philos., Texas Studies Lit. Lang. *Address*: Dept of Logic and Metaphysics, The Univ., St Andrews, Fife KY16 9AJ.

Hunter, Prof. Ian Melville Logan; Professor of Psychology, University of Keele, since 1962; *b* 1927. BSc (Hons) Edinburgh 1950 (Psychology, 1st cl.), DPhil Oxon 1953; FBPsS. Lectr in Psychology, Edinburgh Univ., 1953–62. Pres., Section J, Brit. Assoc. for the Advancement of Science, 1972–73. *Publications*: Memory, 1957, rev. edn, 1964; *contrib.* Brit. Jl of Psychology, Qly Jl of Experimental Psychology. *Address*: Psychology Dept, Keele Univ., Keele ST5 5BG.

Hunter, Prof. Laurence Colvin; Professor of Applied Economics, University of Glasgow, since 1970; *b* 1934; *m* 1958; three *s* one *d*. MA Glasgow; DPhil Oxon. Asst, Manchester Univ., 1958–59; Post-Doctoral Fellow, Univ. of Chicago, 1961–62; Lectr, 1962–67, Sen. Lectr, 1967–69, Titular Prof., 1969–70, Univ. of Glasgow. Editor, Scottish Jl of Political Economy. *Publications*: (with G. L. Reid) Urban Worker Mobility, 1968; (with D. J. Robertson) Economics of Wages and Labour, 1969; (with G. L. Reid and D. Boddy) Labour Problems of Technological Change, 1970; (with A. W. J. Thomson) The Nationalized Transport Industries, 1972; (with R. B. McKersie) Pay, Productivity and Collective Bargaining, 1973; *contrib.* econ. jls. *Address*: Univ. of Glasgow, Glasgow G12 8RT.

Hunter, Robert Brockie, MBE, FRCP; Vice-Chancellor and Principal, University of Birmingham, since 1968; *b* 1915; *m* 1940; three *s* one *d*. MB ChB Edinburgh 1938; Hon. LLD Dundee 1969; FRCPE 1950; FACP 1963; FRSEd 1964; FInstBiol 1968. Asst Dir, Edinburgh Post-Grad. Bd for Medicine, 1947; Lectr in Therapeutics, Univ. of Edinburgh, 1947; Commonwealth Fellow in Medicine, 1948; Lectr in Clinical Medicine, Univ. of St Andrews, 1948; Prof. of Materia Medica, Pharmacology and Therapeutics, 1948–67, Dean, Faculty of Medicine, 1958–62, Univ. of St Andrews; Prof. of Materia Medica, Pharmacology, and Therapeutics, Univ. of Dundee, 1967–68; Hon. Lectr in Physiology, Boston Univ. Sch. of Medicine, USA, 1950; Malthe Foundn Lectr, Oslo, 1958; Sen. Commonwealth Travelling Fellowship, 1960; Vis. Prof. of Medicine, Post-Grad. Sch., Univ. of Adelaide, 1965; Vis. Prof. of Medicine, McGill Univ., 1968. Late Consultant Physician to Dundee General Hosps and Dir, Post-Grad Medical Educn. Mem., GMC; Mem., Min. of Health Cttee on Safety of Drugs, 1963-68 (Chm., Clinical Trials Sub-Cttee); Mem., UGC, 1964–68 (Chm., Medical Sub-Cttee, 1966–68); Chm., Dept of Health and Social

Security Working Party on Med. Administrators in Health Service, 1970–72. Editor, Qly Jl of Medicine, 1957–67. *Publications*: Clinical Science; *contrib*. Brit. Med. Jl, Lancet, Edinburgh Med. Jl, Qly Jl of Medicine. *Address*: Univ. of Birmingham, PO Box 363, Birmingham B15 2TT.

Hunter, Robert Leslie Cockburn; Lecturer in Jurisprudence and Comparative Law, since 1971, and Lecturer in Industrial Law since 1972, University of Aberdeen; *b* 1934; *m* 1960; two *s*. MA St Andrews 1960 (2nd cl. Medieval and Modern History), LLB Edinburgh 1963; Solicitor 1963, WS 1964; Mem., Assoc. of Inst. of Arbitrators (Arbiters) 1970, Mem., Stair Soc., Scott. Hist. Soc., Law Soc. of Scotland. Solicitor, Patrick and James, WS, Edinburgh, 1963–64; Inverness CC, 1964–66; Lectr, Univ. of Dundee, 1966–71. *Publications*: *contrib*. Jurid. Rev., Scots LT, Jl Law Soc. of Scots. *Address*: Faculty of Law, Univ. of Aberdeen, Taylor Building, King's College, Old Aberdeen AB9 2UB.

Hurford, Dr James R.; Lecturer, Linguistics Department, University of Lancaster, since 1972; *b* 1941; *m* 1964; one *d*. BA Cantab 1963, PhD London 1968; Member: Internat. Phonetic Assoc., Linguistic Soc. of Amer., Linguistics Assoc. of Gt Britain. Asst Prof., Univ. Calif. at Davis, 1968–72. *Publications*: The Linguistic Theory of Numerals, 1974; *contrib*. Foundns of Language, Jl Linguistics, Language and Speech, Lingua, Linguistic Inquiry, Linguistics, Orbis. *Address*: Dept of Linguistics, Univ. of Lancaster, Bailrigg, Lancaster LA1 4YW.

Hurst, Francis John Embleton; Librarian, New University of Ulster, since 1967; *b* 1920; *m* 1947, 1968; one *s* one *d*. BA Oxon 1946, MA Oxon 1946; MA Dublin 1959; ALA 1954; Member: Library Assoc.; Library Assoc. of Ireland (Mem. Exec. Bd, 1960– ; Pres., 1972–74). Staff-Tutor, Dept. of Extra-Mural Studies, King's Coll., Newcastle-upon-Tyne, 1947–50; Manchester Public Libraries, 1951–58; Dep. Librarian, 1958–65, Librarian 1965–67, TCD. Mem., Library Adv. Council for NI 1968– . *Publications*: *contrib*. Irish Times, Leabharlann, Libr. World. *Address*: New Univ. of Ulster Coleraine, Northern Ireland BT52 1SA

Hurst, John Stuart; Senior Staff Tutor, Extra-Mural Department, Exeter University, since 1970; *b* 1931; *m* 1957; four *s*. BA Cantab 1953, MA Cantab 1957. Lectr in English, Univ. of Bradford, 1965–70. Mem., Senate, Univ. of Bradford, 1965–70. *Publications*: *contrib*. Church Qly, Forum Mod. Lang. Studies, Theology. *Address*: Dept of Extra-Mural Studies, Cornwall Office, 5 Walsingham Place, Truro, Cornwall.

Hurstfield, Prof. Joel, DLit; Astor Professor of English History, University College, London, since 1962; *b* 1911; *m* 1938; one *s* one *d*. BA London 1934 (1st cl.), DLit London 1964. Asst Lectr, then Lectr, Univ. Coll., Southampton, 1937–40; Lectr, Queen Mary Coll., London, 1946–51; Lectr, Univ. Coll., London, 1951–53, Reader in Mod.

Hist., 1953–59, Prof. of Modern Hist., 1959–62; Fellow, UCL 1967– ; Public Orator, Univ. of London, 1967–71. Asst Comr, Nat. Savings Cttee, 1940–42; Official Historian, Offices of War Cabinet, 1942–46. *Publications*: Control of Raw Materials, 1953; The Queen's Wards, 1958; Elizabeth I and the Unity of England, 1960; The Elizabethan Nation, 1964; Freedom, Corruption and Government in Elizabethan England, 1973; ed jtly, Elizabethan Government and Society, 1961; ed, Tudor Times (English History in Pictures), 1964; ed jtly, Shakespeare's World, 1964; ed, The Reformation Crisis, 1965; ed jtly, Elizabethan People: State and Society, 1972; *contrib*. var. collective works; *contrib*. Econ. Hist. Rev., EHR, Hist., Trans Royal Hist. Soc. *Address*: Dept of History, Univ. College London, Gower Street, WC1E 6BT.

Hussey, Edward Lawrence; Lecturer in Ancient Philosophy, University of Oxford, since 1966; *b* 1940. BA Oxon 1962 (1st cl. Lit. Hum.), MA Oxon 1965. Fellow, All Souls Coll., Oxford, 1962. *Publications*: The Presocratics, 1972. *Address*: All Souls College, Oxford.

Hussey, Prof. Joan Mervyn; Pro essor of History, University of London, Royal Holloway College, since 1950. MA Oxon 1932, BLitt 1932, PhD London 1934; FRHistS 1941, FSA 1953. Res. Student, Westfield Coll., London, 1932–34; Internat. Travelling Fellow (FUW), 1934–35; Pfeiffer Res. Fellow, Girton, 1934–37; Asst Lectr in History, Univ. of Manchester, 1937–43; Lectr, 1943–47; Reader in History, Bedford Coll., Univ. of London, 1947–50; Vis. Prof., Amer. Univ. of Beirut, 1966. Governor of Girton Coll., Cambridge, 1935–37; Member of Council: St Hugh's Coll., Oxford, 1940– 46; Royal Holloway Coll., 1966– ; Pres., Brit. Nat. Cttee for Byzantine Studies, 1961–71; Vice-Pres., Internat. Cttee for Byzantine Studies, 1966– . Hon. Fellow, St Hugh's Coll., Oxford, 1968. *Publications*: Church and Learning in the Byzantine Empire 867–1185, 1937, reprinted 1961; The Byzantine World, 1957, 3rd edn 1966; ed and contrib., Cambridge Medieval History IV, Pts I and II, 1966–67; *contrib*. Byzantinische Zeitschrift, Byzantinoslavica, Jl Theol. Studies, Trans Roy. Hist. Soc., Enc. Britannica, Chambers Enc., New Catholic Enc., etc. *Address*: Royal Holloway College, Englefield Green, Egham, Surrey WT20 0EX.

Hussey, Dr Stanley Stewart, MA, PhD; Professor of Medieval English, University of Lancaster, since 1974; *b* 1925; *m* 1952; one *s*. BA London 1950 (1st cl. English), MA London 1952, PhD London 1962. Asst, Dept of English, Univ. Coll., London, 1950–52; Asst Lectr, Queen Mary Coll., London, 1952–55, Lectr, 1955–66; Sen. Lectr, Lancaster, 1966– 68, Reader in English, 1968–74; Vis. Res. Fellow, Edinburgh, 1970–71. Mem., Council, UCCA, 1971–73. *Publications*: ed, Piers Plowman: Critical Approaches, 1969; Chaucer: An Introduction, 1971; *contrib*. Sphere History of Literature I, 1970; *contrib*. Mediaev. Studies, Mod. Lang. Rev., Neup. Mitt., Neophilol., Rev. Engl. Studies. *Ad-*

dress: Dept of English, Univ. of Lancaster, Bailrigg, Lancaster LA1 4YW.

Hutchings, Donald Williams; Lecturer in Education, Department of Educational Studies, University of Oxford, since 1959; *b* 1923; *m* 1951; one *s* two *d*. BSc London 1951, DipEd London 1952, MSc London 1960; MA Oxon 1963. Brit. Steel Corp. Fellow, 1966–68; Royal Soc./IPPS Res. Offr, 1968–70; Vis. Prof., W Virginia Univ., 1969. *Publications*: Technology and the Sixth Form Boy, 1963; Discovering the Atom, 1963; Engineering Science at the University, 1963, 3rd edn 1969; The Science Undergraduate, 1967; ed, Education for Industry, 1968; *contrib*. Comp. Edn, Jl Chem. Educ., Phys. Bull., Univ. Qly. *Address*: Brasenose College, Oxford.

Hutchison, Dr Henry, MA, BD, BEd, PhD; Lecturer in Education, University of Glasgow, since 1968; *m* 1923; one *s*. MA Edinburgh 1946, BD Edinburgh 1948; PhD Glasgow 1955; BEd Toronto 1961; Teacher's Cert. 1953; Licentiate London Coll. of Music 1952. Minister, Church of Scotland, 1948–57; Headmaster, Stanstead Coll., Quebec Province, 1960–62; Lectr in Education, Brandon Univ., Canada, 1966–68. *Publications*: The Church and Spiritual Healing, 1955; This I Ask, 1958; A Faith to Live By, 1959; The Beatitudes and Modern Life, 1960; Scottish Public Educational Documents 1560–1960, 1973; *contrib*. Manit. Jl, Reformed Jl, Scott. Educnl Studies, Scott. Jl Theol., TES (Scotland). etc. *Address*: Dept of Education, Glasgow Univ., Glasgow G12 8QQ.

Hutchison, Prof. Terence Wilmot; Professor of Economics, University of Birmingham, since 1956; *b* 1912; *m* 1935; one *s* two *d*. BA Cantab 1934 (1st cl. Economics and Politics), MA 1938. Mem., Council, Royal Econ. Soc. 1967–72. Lectr, Univ. of Hull, 1946–47; Lectr, LSE, 1947–51, Reader, 1951–56; Vis. Prof., Columbia, Yale, Saarland, Dalhousie, and Keio Univs; Vis. Fellow, Univ. of Virginia, Australian Nat. Univ. *Publications*: The Significance and Basic Postulates of Economic Theory, 1938, 2nd edn 1960; Review of Economic Doctrines, 1953, Spanish and Japanese trans; Positive Economics and Policy Objectives, 1964, Italian, Spanish and Japanese trans; Economists and Economics Policy in Britain 1946–1966, 1968; *contrib*. Economica, Econ. Jl, Zeits. Nationalökon., etc. *Address*: Economics Dept, Univ. of Birmingham, PO Box 363, Birmingham B15 2TT.

Hutchison, Dr William Chalmers; Senior Lecturer, Department of Extra-Mural and Adult Education, University of Glasgow, since 1964; *b* 1922; *m* 1949; two *s* one *d*. BSc Edinburgh 1943 (1st cl. Hons Chem.), PhD Edinburgh 1946; ARIC 1947, FRIC 1957, MIBiol. Lectr in Physiol., Univ. Edinburgh, 1946–48; Lectr in Biochem., Univ. Glasgow, 1948–61; Vis. Prof. of Biochem., Univ. Western Ontario, 1958; Extra-Mural Staff Tutor in Science, Univ. Glasgow, 1961–64. Mem. Cttee, Glasgow and W of Scotland Section, Royal Inst. Chemistry, 1952–55; Sec., Glasgow and W of Scotland Cttee, Brit.

Assoc. for Advancement of Science, 1961–70. *Publications*: The Uses of the Radioisotopes of the Alkali Metals in Biology and Medicine, in, Comprehensive Treatise on Inorganic Chemistry vol. 2 suppl. 3, ed Mellor, 1963; Science, in, Approaches to Adult Teaching, ed N. Dees, 1965; *contrib*. Adult Educn, Analyst, Biochem. Jl, Biochim. Biophys. Acta, Brit. Jl Nutr., Exp. Cell Res., J. Chem. Soc., Jl Endocrin., Jl Physiol., Nature, Proc. Nutr. Soc., Scot. Adult Educn. *Address*: Univ. of Glasgow, Dept of Extra-Mural and Adult Education, 57–59 Oakfield Avenue, Glasgow G12 8LW.

Hutt, Maurice George; Reader in History, University of Sussex, since 1961; *b* 1928; *m* 1953; four *s* one *d*. BA Oxon 1951 (1st cl. History), BLitt and MA Oxon 1954. Lectr in History, Univ. of Leeds, 1952–55, 1956–61; Vis. Lectr, Cornell Univ., 1955–56. Sen. Proctor, Univ. of Sussex, 1961–64; Dep. Sen. Tutor, then Sen. Tutor of Univ., 1965–68; Chm., Hist. Subject Gp, 1970–72. *Publications*: Napoleon, 1965; Napoleon, 1972; chapter, in, The Idea of a New University, ed D. Daiches, 1964; (with C. Campos), in, French Literature and its Background, ed J. Cruickshank, vol. iv, 1969; *contrib*. Ann. Hist. Révolut. Franç., BIHR, Canad. Hist. Rev., EHR, Jl Eccles. Hist. *Address*: School of European Studies, Univ. of Sussex, Brighton BN1 9QN.

Hutton, Geoffrey John; Reader in Behavioural Sciences, School of Management, University of Bath, since 1965; *b* 1928; *m* 1949; 1961; one *s* two *d*. BSc London 1951 (Psychology). Associate, Brit. Psych. Soc.; Member: Brit. Soc. Assoc. Asst Clinical Psychologist, Tavistock Clinic, London, 1951–53; Project Officer, Tavistock Inst. of Human Relations, London, 1954–59; Dir, Social Environment Research Unit, Univ. of Edinburgh, 1959–64. Associate Consultant, Tavistock Inst. of Human Relations, London, 1969– . Mem. (Gen. Associate), European Inst. for Transnational Studies in Group and Organizational Develt (EIT); Internat. Charter Mem., Internat. Assoc. of Applied Social Scientists. *Publications*: (with Cyril Sofer) New Ways in Management Training, 1958; Thinking About Organization, 1969, 2nd edn 1972; *contrib*. Admin. Sci. Qly, Human Relations, Jl Theory Soc. Behav. *Address*: Univ. of Bath, Claverton Down, Bath BA2 7AY.

Hutton, John Philip; Senior Lecturer in Social and Economic Statistics, University of York, since 1972; *b* 1940; *m* 1964; one *s* one *d*. MA Edinburgh 1962 (1st cl. Economics); FRSS. Jun. Res. Fellow, Univ. of York, 1962–63, Asst Lectr, 1963–65, Lectr, 1965–72. Econ. Advr, HM Treasury, 1970–71 (on secondment). *Publications*: (with S. P. Gupta) Economies of Scale in Local Government Services, 1968; chapter, in, Quantitative Analysis in Public Finance, 1969; *contrib*. Brit. Jl Indus. Relat., Oxf. Econ. Papers. *Address*: Dept of Economics, Univ. of York, Heslington, York YO1 5DD.

Huxley, Prof. George Leonard, MA, FSA, MRIA; Professor of Greek, The Queen's

343

University of Belfast, since 1962; *b* 1932; *m* 1957; three *d*. BA Oxon 1955 (2nd cl. Mods, 1st cl. Greats), MA 1960; FSA, MRIA. Fellow, All Souls Coll., Oxford, 1955–61; Asst Dir, Brit. Sch. Athens, 1956–58; Vis. Lectr, Harvard Univ., 1958, 1961. Mem., Irish Nat. Cttee on Class. Studies, 1970– , on Philosophy, 1973– . Mem., Managing Cttee, Brit. Sch. Athens, 1967– , Vis. Fellow, 1973. *Publications*: Achaeans and Hittites, 1960; Early Sparta, 1962; The Early Ionians, 1966; Greek Epic Poetry from Eumelos to Panyassis, 1969; ed (with J. H. Coldstream), Kythera: Excavations and Studies, 1972; *contrib.* Ann. Brit. Sch. Athens, Greek, Roman Byzant. Studies, Jl Hellenic Studies. *Address*: Dept of Greek, The Queen's Univ., Belfast BT7 1NN.

Hyam, Dr Ronald, MA, PhD; Fellow, Librarian and Lecturer in History, Magdalene College, University of Cambridge, since 1962, and University Lecturer in History, Cambridge, since 1969; *b* 1936. BA Cambridge 1959 (1st cl. History), MA Cambridge 1963, PhD Cambridge 1963. Lecturer, Magdalene Coll., 1960–62; Asst Univ. Lectr, Cambridge, 1965–69. Treas., Cambridge Hist. Soc., 1970–72; Mngr, Smuts Mem. Fund, 1970– . *Publications*: Elgin and Churchill at the Colonial Office 1905–08: the watershed of the Empire – Commonwealth, 1968; A History of Isleworth Grammar School, 1969; The Failure of South African Expansion 1908–48, 1972; Britain's Imperial Century: a study of Empire and Expansion 1815–1914 (forthcoming); (with Ged Martin) Myths and Reappraisals in British Imperial History (forthcoming); contrib. Nineteenth Century Africa, ed P. J. M. McEwan, 1968; Churchill: a profile, ed P. Stansky, 1973; *contrib.* Hist. Jl. *Address*: Magdalene College, Cambridge.

Hyde, Prof. Francis Edwin, MA, PhD (Econ), FRHistS; Chaddock Professor of Economic History, University of Liverpool, since 1970; *b* 1908; *m* 1935; 1970; one *d*. BA Liverpool 1929 (1st cl. History), MA Liverpool 1931, PhD(Econ) London 1931; FRHistS. Pres. Liverpool Econ. Stat. Soc. Lectr, Univ. of Liverpool, 1934–48; Chaddock Prof. of Economics, 1948–70. Bd of Trade, 1941–43; Min. of Supply, 1943–45; Dean, Fac. of Arts, Univ. of Liverpool, 1949–53, Pro-Vice-Chancellor, 1961–65. *Publications*: Mr Gladstone at the Board of Trade, 1934; An Economic History of North Buckinghamshire, 1945; Blue Funnel, 1957; (jtly) A New Prospect of Economics, 1958; Shipping Enterprise and Management, 1967; (with S. Marriner) The Senior, business study of John Swire and Sons, 1968; Liverpool and the Mersey 1700–1970, 1971; Far Eastern Trade 1865–1914, 1972; *contrib.* Business Hist., Economica, Econ. Hist. Rev., Econ. Jl, Harv. Business Hist. Rev., Jap. Business Hist. *Address*: Dept of Economic History, Univ. of Liverpool, Liverpool L69 3BX.

Hyde, Dr John Kenneth, MA, DPhil; Senior Lecturer in History, Manchester University, since 1973 (Lecturer, 1964–73); *b* 1930; *m* 1959; three *d*. BA Oxon 1953, MA Oxon 1958, DipSoc Anthrop Oxon 1954, DPhil Oxon 1960; FRHistS. Asst Lectr in

History, Manchester Univ., 1961–64. *Publications*: Padua in the Age of Dante, 1966; Society and Politics in Medieval Italy, 1973. *Address*: History Dept, Manchester Univ., Manchester M13 9PL.

Hywel, John, MMus, ARCO; Lecturer, Music Department, University College of North Wales, Bangor, since 1966; *b* 1941; *m* 1970. BMus Wales 1962, MMus Wales 1964; ARCO. Dir of Music, Bangor Cathedral, 1970–71; Mem., Music Panel, N Wales Assoc. for Arts, 1969– . *Address*: Dept of Music, Univ. College of North Wales, Bangor LL57 2DG.

I

Ilersic, Prof. Alfred Roman; Professor of Social Studies, Department of Sociology, Bedford College, University of London, since 1966; *b* 1920; *m* 1944; one *s* one *d*. BCom London 1940, MSc(Econ) London 1952; FIS, FRSS; Hon. Mem., Rating and Valuation Assoc. Lectr, Univ. Coll. of the S West, 1947–53; Lectr, Bedford Coll., London, 1953–64; Reader in Econ. and Social Stats, 1964–66. Chm., Inst. of Statisticians, 1969–71; Mem., Retail Prices Adv. Cttee, 1969– . *Publications*: Statistics, 1953, 13th edn 1964; Government Finance and Fiscal Policy in Post-War Britain, 1956; Parliament of Commerce, 1960; Taxation of Capital Gains, 1963; Rate Equalisation in London, 1968; Local Government Finance in Northern Ireland, 1970; *contrib.* Canad. Tax Jl, Jl Royal Stat. Soc., Statistician. *Address*: Bedford College, Regent's Park, NW1 4NS.

Iles-Pulford, Wilfred, ARCO; Visiting Lecturer in Music, University of Bradford, since 1962; *b* 1900; *m* 1924; one *d*. ARCO. Var. Choral and Orch. Conductorships, London and provinces. *Address*: Univ. of Bradford, Bradford BD7 1DP.

Iliffe, Dr John; Assistant Director of Research, Faculty of History, University of Cambridge, since 1971; *b* 1939. BA Cantab 1961, PhD Cantab 1965. Lectr in History, Univ. of Dar es Salaam, 1965–70, Reader, 1970–71. *Publications*: Tanganyika under German Rule 1905–12, 1969; *contrib.* Jl African History. *Address*: St John's College, Cambridge.

Illsley, Prof. Raymond; Professor of Sociology, University of Aberdeen, and Director, MRC Medical Sociology Unit, since 1965; *b* 1919; *m* 1948; two *s* one *d*. PhD Aberdeen 1956. Member: Brit. Sociological Assoc.; Union Internationale pour l'étude scientifique de la population; Social Med. Soc.; Assoc. of Univ. Teachers in Sociology; Internat. Sociological Assoc.; Soc. for Study of Human Biology; Fellow of Eugenics Soc. Sociologist, MRC, Dept of Midwifery, Aberdeen Univ., 1951–64; Prof. and Head of Sociology Dept, King's Coll., Aberdeen Univ., 1964–71; Hon. Dir, Med Sociology Res. Unit (Aberdeen), MRC, 1965–71. Vis. Prof., Cornell, 1963–64; Vis. Scientist, Harvard, 1968; Vis. Prof., Boston, 1971–

72. War service, 50th (Northumbrian) Div., 1939–45, POW, Italy and Germany; Econ. Asst, Commonwealth Econ. Cttee, London, 1948; Social Res. Officer, New Town Develt Corp., Crawley, 1948–50. *Publications*: Family Growth and its Effect on the Relationship between Obstetric Factors and Child Functioning, 1967; (jtly), Mental Subnormality in the Community, 1970; Social Correlates of Perinatal Death, in Perinatal Mortality, ed Butler and Bonham, 1963; chapter in Childbearing, ed. Richardson and Guthmacher, 1967; (jtly) The Motivation and Characterisation of Internal Migrants, in, Readings in the Sociology of Migration, ed Jansen, 1970; (jtly), Social Influences on Parents and their Children, in, Child Life and Health, ed Mitchell, 1970; *contrib*. Adv. Science, Brit. Jl Educ. Psych., Brit. Jl Prev. Soc. Med., BMJ, IPPF Med. Bull., Jl Ment. Subnormality, Jl Obstet. Gynaec. Brit. Emp., Med. Officer, Milbank Mem. Fund Quat., New Society, Nursing Mirror, Proc. 52nd Annual Conf. of Nat. Assoc. for Maternal and Child Welfare, Proc. Royal Soc. Med., Soc. Rev., Soc. Sci. and Med., Trans Royal Soc. Trop. Med. Hyg. *Address*: Centre for Social Studies, Westburn Road, Aberdeen.

Ince, Prof. Walter Newcombe, MA, DUP; Professor and Head of Department of French, University of Southampton, since 1970; *b* 1926; *m* 1955; two *d*. BA Cantab 1950 (1st cl. French and Spanish), MA Cantab 1953; DU Paris 1955. Asst Lectr in French, King's Coll., London, 1953–56; Asst Lectr in French, Univ. of Leicester, 1956, Lectr, 1957, Sen. Lectr, 1966. Treas., Soc. Fr. Studies, 1957–60. *Publications*: The Poetic Theory of Paul Valéry, 1961, 2nd edn 1970; *contrib*. Forum Mod. Lang. Studies, Fr. Studies, Mod. Lang. Rev., Rev. Science Hum., Rom. Rev., etc. *Address*: Dept of French, The Univ., Southampton SO9 59H.

Ingamells, Lynn Elizabeth, MA; Lecturer in Spanish, Queen Mary College, University of London, since 1961; *b* 1935. BA London 1957 (1st cl. Spanish), MA London 1962. Asst Lecturer, Queen Mary Coll., 1958–61; Vis. Lectr, Dept of Spanish, McGill Univ., Montreal, 1967–68. Sec./Treas., Assoc. Hispanists GB and Ireland, 1970– . *Publication*: (with Peter Standish) Variedades del español actual, 1974. *Address*: Dept of Spanish, Queen Mary College, Mile End Road, E1 4NS.

Ingham, Bruce; Lecturer in Phonetics, School of Oriental and African Studies, University of London, since 1967; *b* 1942; *m* 1963; one *s* one *d*. BA Hons London 1964 (Arabic); Fellow, Brit. Soc. for Middle Eastern Studies. *Publications*: *contrib*. Audiology, Bull. SOAS. *Address*: Sch. of Oriental and African Studies, Malet Street, WC1E 7HP.

Ingham, Prof. Kenneth, OBE, MC; Professor of History, University of Bristol, since 1970; *b* 1921; *m* 1949; one *s* one *d*. BA Oxon 1941, MA Oxon 1947, DPhil Oxon 1950; FRHistS. Lectr, Makerere UC, 1950, Prof. of History, 1956–62; Dir of Studies,

RMA Sandhurst, 1962–67; Prof. of Modern History, Univ. of Bristol, 1967–70. Mem., Uganda Legislative Council, 1954–61; Chm. of Trustees, Uganda Museum, 1954–62; Mem. of Governing Council, British Inst. in E Africa, 1962– . *Publications*: Reformers in India, 1956; The Making of Modern Uganda, 1958; A History of East Africa, 3rd edn 1965. *Address*: Dept of History, Univ. of Bristol, Bristol BS8 1TH.

Inglis, Andrew Davidson, MA, PhD; Senior Lecturer in Spanish, University of Bradford, since 1969; *b* 1932; *m* 1967. MA Edinburgh 1954 (1st cl. Spanish with French), PhD Edinburgh 1956. Asst Lectr, Univ. of Birmingham, 1959–62, Lectr, 1962–69. *Address*: Modern Languages Centre, Univ. of Bradford, Bradford BD7 1DP.

Inglis, Anthony Angus Haig; Lecturer in English, University of Sussex, since 1963; *b* 1935; *m* 1958; three *d*. BA Cambridge 1958; Jnr Res. Fellow, Edinburgh, 1961–63. *Address*: Arts Building, Univ. of Sussex, Brighton BN1 9QN.

Ingram, Dr David J. E.; Principal, Chelsea College, University of London, since 1973; *b* 1927; *m* 1952; two *s* one *d*. BA Hons Oxon 1948 (Physics), DPhil, MA Oxon 1951, DSc Oxon 1959; Hon. DSc Clermont-Ferrand 1965; FInstP; FChemSoc; Fellow, Faraday Soc. University of Southampton: Res. Fellow and Lectr in Electronics, 1952–57; Reader, 1957–59; University of Keele: Prof. of Physics and Hd of Dept, 1959–73; Sen. Tutor, 1962–63. Dep. Vice Chancellor, Univ. of Keele, 1964–65, 1968–71. Mem. Physical Scis Cttee, UGC, 1970–73. *Publications*: Spectroscopy at Radio and Microwave Frequencies, 1955, 2nd edn 1967; Free Radicals as Studied by Electron Spin Resonance, 1958; Biological and Biochemical Applications of Electron Spin Resonance, 1969; Radiation and Quantum Physics, 1973; *contrib*. Jl Chem. Physics, Jl Physics, Nature, Philos. Mag., Physical Rev., Proc. Royal Soc. *Address*: Chelsea Coll., Manresa Road, SW3 5LX.

Ingram, Elisabeth; Lecturer, Department of Linguistics, University of Edinburgh, since 1969; *b* 1928; *m* 1951; one *d*. MA Edinburgh 1951 (1st cl. Psychology), Dip. Gen. Linguistics Edinburgh 1968; Mem., Lingu. Soc., Brit. Psychol. Soc. Lectr, Dept of Applied Linguistics, Univ. of Edinburgh, 1958–68. *Publications*: ed (with R. Huxley), Language Acquisition: Models and Methods, 1971; *contrib*. Brit. Jl Psychol., Internat. Rev. Appl. Lingu. *Address*: 14 Buccleuch Place, Edinburgh EH8 9LN.

Innes, Dr Doreen Cormack; Fellow and Tutor, St Hilda's College, Oxford, since 1969; University Lecturer, Oxford, since 1970; MA Aberdeen 1962, DPhil Oxon 1968, MA Oxon 1969. Randall MacIver Junior Research Fellow, St Hugh's Coll., Oxford, 1965–67; Lectr in Classical Studies, Univ. of Kent, 1967–69. *Publication*: Demetrius, On Style, in Ancient Literary Criticism, ed Russell and Winterbottom, 1972. *Address*: St Hilda's College, Oxford.

Innes, Dr Gordon; Lecturer, Department of Africa, School of Oriental and African Studies, University of London, since 1952; *b* 1924; *m* 1954; one *s* one *d*. MA Aberdeen 1950 (1st cl. Classics); PhD London 1961; Mem., Afr. Studies Assoc. UK; Mem., Folklore Soc. Bk Rev. Editor, Jl Afr. Lang., 1964– . *Publications*: A Mende Grammar, 1962; The Structure of Sentences in Mende, 1963; An Introduction to Grebo, 1966; A Grebo-English Dictionary, 1967; A Practical Introduction to Mende, 1967; A Mende-English Dictionary, 1969; *contrib*. Afr. Lang. Studies, Sierra Leone Lang. Rev. *Address*: School of Oriental and African Studies, Malet Street, WC1E 7HP.

Ionescu, George-Ghita; Professor of Government, University of Manchester, since 1969; *b* 1913; *m* 1950. Lic Droit, et Sc. Pol. Bucharest; Mem., European Research Cttee, Internat. Political Science Assoc. Nuffield Fellow, LSE, 1964–68; Reader in Government, Univ. of Manchester, 1968–69. Editor, Government and Opposition, 1965– . *Publications*: Communism in Rumania, 1965; The Politics of the European Communist States, 1966; trans. L'Avenir Politique de l'Europe Orientale, 1966; trans. Zukunftides Kommunismus, 1969; ed, Populism, 1968; (with Isabel de Madariaga) Opposition, 1969; ed, The New Politics of European Integration, 1972; Comparative Communist Politics, 1973; ed, Between Sovereignty and Integration, 1974; *contrib*. Government and Opposition, Political Qly, Political Studies, Europa-Archiv, Internat. Affairs, Annual Register, etc. *Address*: Faculty of Economic and Social Studies, Univ. of Manchester, Manchester M13 9PL.

Ireson, Prof. John Clifford, MA, DèsL; Professor of Modern French Literature, University of Hull, since 1969; *b* 1922; *m* 1949; two *s* one *d*. BA London 1942 (1st cl. French), MA London 1949; DèsL Paris 1963. Asst Lectr, Leeds Univ., 1950–53, Lectr, 1953–63, Reader, 1963–64; Prof., Sheffield Univ., 1964–69. *Publications*: A Manual of French Prose Composition for Advanced Students, 1961, 2nd edn 1966; L'Œuvre poétique de Gustave Kahn (1859–1936), 1962; ed jtly, Currents of Thought in French Literature, 1965; ed jtly, Studies in French Literature presented to H. W. Lawton, 1968; Lamartine: a revaluation, 1969; Imagination in French Romantic Poetry (inaugural lecture), 1970. *Address*: Dept of French, The Univ., Hull HU6 7RX.

Irvine, Dr Arthur Kinloch; Lecturer in Semitic Languages, Department of Near and Middle East, School of Oriental and African Studies, since 1964; *b* 1935; *m* 1970; two *s*. MA St Andrews 1957, DPhil Oxon 1964; FRAsiatS 1966 (Mem. Council 1969, Hon. Editor 1973), FRNS 1966. Asst Lectr in Semitic Langs, SOAS, 1961–64. *Publications*: *contrib*. BSOAS, JRAS, JSS, Encycl. Islam. *Address*: School of Oriental and African Studies, Univ. of London, WC1E 7HP.

Irving, Dr Henry Warwick; Lecturer in Geography, Hull University, since 1968; *b* 1942; *m* 1966; two *s*. BA Cantab 1964, MA Cantab 1966, PhD Cantab 1969. *Publications*: Elements of Social Geography, 1974; *contrib*. Environment and Behaviour, Sociol. and Social Res., Trans Bartlett Soc. *Address*: Dept of Geography, Univ. of Hull, Hull HU6 7RX.

Irving, Dr Ronald Eckford Mill; Lecturer in Politics, Centre of European Governmental Studies, University of Edinburgh, since 1969; *b* 1939; *m* 1963; four *d*. MA Oxon 1961, DPhil Oxon 1968. Lectr, Bristol Univ., 1968–69. *Publications*: Christian Democracy in France 1973; *contrib*. Parly Affairs, Pol Studies, Pol Qly, Internat. Affairs, France-Asie. *Address*: Centre of European Governmental Studies, Old College, South Bridge, Edinburgh EH8 9YL.

Irwin, Dr David George, MA, PhD, FSA, FRSA; Head of Department of History of Art, University of Aberdeen, since 1970; *b* 1933; *m* 1960; one *s* one *d*. MA Oxon 1960; PhD London 1960; FSA. Lectr in Fine Art, Glasgow Univ., 1959–70. Mem., Assoc. Internat. Crit. Art, 1968– ; Mem., Council, Walpole Soc., 1971– ; Art Panel, Scott. Arts Council, 1971– ; Neoclass., Cttee, Council of Europe, 1970–72; Vice-Pres., Brit. Soc. 18th Century Studies, 1974– . *Publications*: English Neo-classical Art, 1966; Paul Klee, 1967; Visual Arts, Taste and Criticism, 1969; Winckelmann: Writings on Art, 1972; *contrib*. Apollo, Art Bull., Burl. Mag., Connoisseur. *Address*: Dept of History of Art, King's College, Univ. of Aberdeen, Old Aberdeen AB9 2UB.

Irwin, Thomas Arthur Michael; Senior Lecturer, Department of English and American Literature, University of Kent at Canterbury, since 1971 (Lecturer, 1967–71); *b* 1934; *m* 1961; 1970; one *s* two *d*. BA Oxford 1958 (English), MA, BLitt Oxford 1961. Vis. Lectr: Catholic Univ. of Lublin, Poland, 1958–59; Univ. of Tokyo, 1961–63; Univ. of Lodz, Poland, 1963–65; Smith Coll., USA, 1965–67. *Publications*: Argument and Discussion in English, 1963; Henry Fielding: the tentative realist, 1967; Working Orders (novel), 1969; *contrib*. Essays in Criticism. *Address*: Keynes College, Univ. of Kent, Canterbury, Kent.

Ishiguro, Dr Hidé; Reader, Department of Philosophy, University College, London, since 1973; *m* 1969. BA Tokyo 1956, BPhil Oxon 1959, PhD London 1971. Mem., Aristotelian Soc. Asst Lectr in Philos., Leeds Univ., 1961–62; Lectr in Philos., Leeds Univ., 1962–64; Lectr in Philos., UCL, 1964–73. Vis. Assoc. Prof., Cornell Univ., 1969. Mem. Analysis Cttee, 1973– . *Publications*: Leibniz's Philosophy of Logic and Language, 1972; Imagination, in, British Analytical Philosophy, ed Williams and Montefiore, 1966; Use and Reference of Names, in, Studies in the Philosophy of Wittgenstein, ed Winch, 1969; A Person's Future and the Mind-Body Problem, in, Linguistic Analysis and Phenomenology, ed Mays and Brown, 1972; Theory of the Ideality of Relations, in, Leibniz, ed Frankfurt, 1972; Leibniz and the Ideas of Sensible Qualities, in,

Reason and Reality, ed Brown, 1972; *contrib.* Suppl. Proc. Aristotelian Soc., Japan Annals for Philosophy of Science. *Address*: Dept of Philosophy, Univ. Coll., Gower Street, WC1E 6BT.

Isles, Duncan; Lecturer, Department of English, University College of Wales, Aberystwyth, since 1973; *b* 1939; *m* 1962; two *d*. MA St Andrews 1962 (1st cl. English). Lectr, Dept of English, Birkbeck Coll., London Univ., 1965–73. *Publications*: Chronology and Appendix, in, Charlotte Lennox, The Female Quixote, ed M. Dalziel, 1970; Pope and Criticism, in, Alexander Pope, ed P. Dixon, 1972; Laurence Sterne, in, The English Novel: Select Bibliographical Guides, 1974; Annotd edn, The Lennox Collection (unpublished letters of Samuel Johnson and others) serialised in Harvard Library Bull., 1970–71. *contrib.* BBN, Harvard Libr. Bull., New Ramb., Notes Queries, Scriblerion, Times Lit. Supp. *Address*: Dept of English, Univ. Coll. of Wales, Aberystwyth SY23 2AX.

Isserlin, Benedikt Sigmund Johannes; Senior Lecturer and Head of Department of Semitic Studies, University of Leeds, since 1960; *b* 1916; *m* 1958; one *s*. MA Edinburgh 1939 (1st cl. History and Prehistoric Archaeol.); BA Oxon 1943 (1st cl. Orient Stud.), MA Oxon 1948, BLitt Oxon 1951, DPhil Oxon 1954; Mem., Inst. Archaeol., Soc. OT Studies. Field Dir, Leeds–London–Fairleigh Dickinson–Sydney Archaeol. Expedit. to Motya, Sicily. *Publications*: contrib. encyclopedias and report vols; *contrib.* Ann. Palest. Explor. Fund, Antiqu., Notizie Scavi, Palest. Explor. Qly, Proc. Leeds Lit. Philos. Soc., etc. *Address*: Dept of Semitic Studies, The Univ. of Leeds, Leeds LS2 9JT.

Ivamy, Prof. Edward Richard Hardy, LLB, PhD, LLD; Professor of Law, University of London, since 1960; *b* 1920; *m* 1965. LLB London 1947 (1st cl.), PhD London 1953, LLD London 1967; Barrister-at-Law; called to the Bar Middle Temple, 1949. Asst Lectr, Univ. Coll., London, 1947–50, Lectr, 1950–56, Reader, 1956–60. Hon. Sec., Soc. Public Teachers of Law, 1960–63. *Publications*: Show Business and the Law, 1955; Hire-Purchase Legislation in England and Wales, 1965; Casebook on Carriage by Sea, 1965, 2nd edn 1971; Casebook on Sale of Goods, 1966, 3rd edn 1973; General Principles of Insurance Law, 1966, 2nd edn 1970; Casebook on Mercantile Law, 1967, 2nd edn 1972; Fire and Motor Insurance, 1968, 2nd edn 1973; Marine Insurance, 1969; Casebook on Partnership, 1970; Casebook on Shipping Law, 1970; Casebook on Agency, 1971; ed, Chalmers Marine Insurance Act 1906, 6th edn 1966, 7th edn 1971; Topham and Ivamy's Company Law, 13th edn 1967, 14th edn 1970, Supp. 1973; Payne and Ivamy's Carriage of Goods by Sea, 7th edn 1963, 8th edn 1968, 9th edn 1972; Casebook on Insurance Law, 1969, 2nd edn 1972; contrib. Annual Survey of Commonwealth Law, 1967–72; *contrib.* Jl Business Law. *Address*: Faculty of Laws, Univ. College London, 4/8 Endsleigh Gardens, WC1H 0EG.

Ives, Dr Eric William; Senior Lecturer in Modern History, University of Birmingham, since 1972; *b* 1931; *m* 1961; one *s* one *d*. BA 1952 (1st cl.), PhD 1955, London; FRHistS 1964; Fellow, Selden Soc., 1970. Fellow and Lectr, Shakespeare Inst., Univ. of Birmingham, 1957–61; Asst Lectr, Mod. Hist., Univ. of Liverpool, 1961, Lectr, 1962–68; Lectr, Univ. of Birmingham, 1968–72. Mem. Council, Hist. Assoc., 1968– . *Publications*: ed, The English Revolution, 1600–1660, 1968; *contrib.* Bull. Inst. Hist. Res., Bull. John Rylands Lib., Eng. Hist. Rev., Hist., Law Qly Rev., Shakespeare Survey, Univ. Birm. Hist. Jl. *Address*: Sch. of History, Univ. of Birmingham, PO Box 363, Birmingham B15 2TT.

J

Jack, Dr Ian Robert James, MA, DPhil, LittD; Fellow and Librarian of Pembroke College, University of Cambridge, since 1961, and University Reader in English, since 1973; *b* 1923; *m* 1948; two *s* one *d*; *m* 1972. MA Edinburgh 1947 (1st cl. English), DPhil Oxon 1951; Pres., C. Lamb Soc., 1970– . Warton Lectr, Brit. Acad., 1967; Lectr in English, Brasenose Coll., Oxford, 1951–56, Sen. Res. Fellow, 1956–61; Lectr in English, Cambridge Univ., 1961–73; de Carle Lectr, Univ. of Otago, NZ, 1964; Vis. Prof., Univ. of Chicago, 1968–69, Univ. of California, Berkeley, 1969. *Publications*: Augustan Satire: Intention and Idiom in English Poetry 1660–1750, 1952, several edns, pbk edn 1966; Pope (Writers and their Work series), 1954; Sir Walter Scott (Writers and their Work series), 1958; English Literature 1815–1832 (vol. X, Oxford History of English Literature), 1963; Keats and the Mirror of Art, 1967; Browning's Major Poetry, 1973; ed, A Sentimental Journey, 1968; ed, Browning: Poetical Works 1833–1864, 1970; *contrib.* PMLA, Times Lit. Supp., etc. *Address*: Pembroke College, Cambridge.

Jack, Dr Ronald Dyce Sadler, MA, PhD; Lecturer in English Literature, University of Edinburgh, since 1968; *b* 1941; *m* 1967; two *d*. MA Glasgow 1964 (1st cl. English); PhD Edinburgh 1968. Asst Lectr, Edinburgh, 1965–68. Associate Dean, Edinburgh Univ. Fac. of Arts, 1971–73; Vis. Prof., Univ. of Virginia, 1973–74. Mem., UCCA, 1972– . Sec., Walter Scott Bicent. Conf., 1971. *Publications*: co-ed, McLellan: Jamie the Saxt, 1970; ed, Scottish Prose 1550–1700, 1971; The Italian Influence on Scottish Literature, 1972; *contrib.* Comp. Lit., Engl., Forum Mod. Lang. Studies, Mod. Lang. Rev., Rev. Engl. Studies, Studies, Scott. Lit., Scott. Church Hist. Rev. *Address*: Dept of English Literature, Univ. of Edinburgh, Edinburgh EH8 9YL.

Jackson, Dr Anthony, fil.dr; Lecturer, Department of Social Anthropology, University of Edinburgh, since 1970; *b* 1926; *m* 1960; two *d*. BA Cantab 1950, MA Cantab 1955; fil.kand Göteborg 1963; BA Hons London 1964, fil.lic Göteborg 1965, fil.dr Göteborg

1970; FRAI. Lectr, Göteborg Univ., 1962–65; Lectr, Salford Univ., 1965–70. Mem., Assoc. Social Anthropologists. *Publications*: Elementary Structures of Na-khi Ritual, 1970; *contrib*. Antropologiska studier, ASA, Bull. J. Rylands Lib., Ethnos, Folk-Lore, Hist. Science, Man, New Soc., Northern Studies, Scott. Studies, TLS, World Anthropology. *Address*: Dept of Social Anthropology, Univ. of Edinburgh, Edinburgh EH8 9LL.

Jackson, Dr Bernard Stuart; Lecturer, Department of Civil Law, University of Edinburgh, since 1969; *b* 1944; *m* 1967; one *s* one *d*. LLB Liverpool 1965, DPhil Oxon 1969; Barrister, Gray's Inn, 1966; Mem. Soc. for OT Study, 1974. Vis. Asst Prof., Univ. Georgia Sch. of Law, 1968–69; Assoc. Fellow, Oxford Centre for Postgrad. Hebrew Studies, 1973–74. *Publications*: Theft in Early Jewish Law, 1972; Essays in Jewish and Comparative Legal History, 1975; ed, Studies in Jewish Legal History in honour of David Daube, 1974; *contrib*. Amer. Jl Compar. Law, Georgia Jl Internat. and Compar. Law, Hebrew Union Coll. Annual, Irish Jurist, Jl Jewish Studies, Revue Internat. des Droits de l'Antiquité, Vetus Testamentum. *Address*: Old College, South Bridge, Edinburgh EH8 9YL.

Jackson, Dr David Edward Pritchett; Lecturer in Arabic Language and Literature, Department of Arabic Studies, University of St Andrews, since 1967; *b* 1941. MA Cantab 1964, PhD 1970; Member: Brit. Assoc. of Orientalists; Brit. Soc. for Middle Eastern Studies. Res. Fellowship, Pembroke College, Cambridge, 1967–70. *Publications*: *contrib*. Islamic Qly. *Address*: Dept of Arabic Studies, The Univ., St Andrews, Fife KY16 9AJ.

Jackson, Edward Francis, MA; Director, Oxford University Institute of Economics and Statistics, and Professorial Fellow of St Antony's College, Oxford, since 1959; *b* 1915; *m* 1942, 1954; two *s*. BCom Birmingham 1934 (1st cl. Hons), BA Oxon 1937 (Magdalen Coll., 1st cl. PPE), MA Oxon 1956; Lectr in Economics, New Coll., Oxford, 1938; Magdalen Coll., 1939; Civil Servant, 1939–51; Dep. Dir, Res. and Planning Div., UN Econ. Commn for Europe, 1951–56; University Lectr in Economic Statistics, Oxford, and Res. Fellow, St Antony's Coll., Oxford, 1956–59. Mem., Transport Adv. Council, 1965– . *Publications*: (with P. N. C. Obigbo) The Nigerian National Accounts, 1950–57; *contrib*. articles in economics jls. *Address*: Institute of Economics and Statistics, St Cross Building, Manor Road, Oxford.

Jackson, Dr Gordon; Lecturer in Economic History; University of Strathclyde, since 1965; *b* 1934; *m*; two *s* one *d*. BA London 1955 (Hons. UC Hull), CertifEd Hull 1959, PhD Hull 1960. Sen. History Master, Frederick Gough Sch., Scunthorpe, 1959–65. *Publications*: Grimsby and the Haven Company 1796–1846, 1971; Hull in the Eighteenth Century, 1972; *contrib*. Bull. Econ. Res., Durham Res. Rev., Lincs Historian, Mariner's Mirror, Transport History. *Address*: McCance Building, Richmond Street, Glasgow.

Jackson, Ian, MA; Lecturer, Department of Modern Languages, Salford University, since 1968; *b* 1932. BA Oxford 1956 (English); MA South Carolina 1959 (American Literature); MA Birmingham 1968 (English); DipEd Durham 1957; Elected Mem., Phi Beta Kappa. Mem., Brit. Assoc. Amer. Studies, Grad. Asst, Univ. of S Carolina, 1957–59. *Publications*: The Provincial Press and the Community, 1971; The Media Network, 1974. *Address*: Dept of Modern Languages, Univ. of Salford, Salford M5 4WT.

Jackson, Prof. John Archer; Professor of Social Theory and Institutions, and Head of Department of Social Studies, Queen's University, Belfast, since 1970; *b* 1929; *m* 1954; two *s* two *d*. BA Hiram College USA 1951; MA London 1956. Mem., Brit. Social Assoc. Res. Worker, Univ. of Liverpool, 1957–60; Asst Lectr, Univ. of Sheffield, 1960–62. Lectr, 1962–64; Sen. Lectr, Univ of E Anglia, 1964–69. Reader, 1969–70. Vis. Asst Prof., Hiram Coll., 1968. *Publications*: The Irish in Britain, 1963; ed, Social Stratification, 1968, Spanish edn 1970; ed, Migration, 1969; ed, Professions and Professionalization, 1970; ed, Role, 1972; *contrib*. Sociol Rev., Jl Amer. Studies. *Address*: Dept of Social Studies, Queen's Univ., Belfast BT7 1NN.

Jackson, Dr Joseph Michael; Senior Lecturer, Department of Economics, Dundee University, since 1967; *b* 1925; *m* 1953; three *s* two *d*. BA Wales 1949 (1st cl. Economics); PhD Manchester 1953. Res. Asst, Dept of Economics, Univ. Coll. of Wales, Aberystwyth, 1952–55; Asst Lectr, Dept of Sociology, Social Studies and Economics, Bedford Coll., Univ. of London, 1955–58; Lectr, Dundee Univ., 1958–67. Acting Hd, Sch. of Social Administration, 1971– . Mem., Bd of Mngmt, Dundee North. Hosps, 1971– (Convener, Fin. and Staffing Cttee). *Publications*: The Control of Monopoly in the United Kingdom, 1960; Family Income, 1963; Human Values and the Economic System, 1966; Wages and Labour Economics, 1970; ed, Little: Economics for Students, 15th edn 1971; *contrib*. Blackfr., Brit. Jl Indust. Relations, Canad. Jl Econ. Pol. Sci., Manch. Sch., Scott. Bank. Mag., Scot. Jl Pol. Econ. *Address*: Dept of Economics, The Univ., Dundee DD1 4HN.

Jackson, Prof. Kenneth Hurlstone, LittD, FBA; Professor of Celtic Languages, Literature, History, and Antiquities, Celtic Department, Edinburgh University, since 1950; *b* 1909; *m* 1936; one *s* one *d*. BA Cantab 1931 (1st cl. Classics), MA Cantab 1935, LittD Cantab 1954; Hon. AM Harvard 1940; Hon. DLitt Celt Ireland 1958; Hon. DLitt Wales 1963; Hon. MRIA 1965, Hon. DUniv. Haute-Bretagne 1971; FBA 1957, FSA Scot 1951, Corresp. Fellow, Mediaeval Acad. of America 1951, Hon. Mem., Mod. Lang. Assoc. Amer. 1958, Pres., Scott. Anthropol and Folk. Soc., 1952–60, Vice-Pres., Soc. Antiquaries Scot., 1960–63, Vice-Pres., Scott. Gaelic Texts Soc., 1951–67. Fellow, St John's Coll., Cambridge, 1934–39; Fac. Lectr in Celtic, Cambridge Univ.,

1934–39, Lectr, 1939–40; Associate Prof. of Celtic, Harvard Univ., 1940–49, Prof., 1949–50; O'Donnell Lectr, Edinburgh Univ., 1953, Oxford, 1956, Univ. of Wales, 1959; Samuel Dill Lectr, Belfast, 1954. Mem., Council: Folk. Soc., 1935–40; English Place-Names Soc., 1951– (Vice-Pres., 1973–); Mem., Comité Internat. Sci. Onomastiques, 1955– ; Royal Commn for Anc. Monum. Scotl., 1963– ; Council, Irish Texts Soc., 1967– ; Trustee, Nat. Mus. Antiqu. Scotl., 1954– ; Highlands and Islands Trust, 1952–72. *Publications*: Early Welsh Gnomic Poems, 1935; Studies in Early Celtic Nature Poetry, 1935; Cath Maighe Léna, 1938; Scéalta ón mBlascaod, 1939; A Celtic Miscellany, 1951; Language and History in Early Britain, 1953; Contributions to the Study of Manx Phonology, 1955; The International Popular Tale and Early Welsh Tradition, 1961; The Oldest Irish Tradition, a Window on the Iron Age, 1964; A Historical Phonology of Breton, 1967; The Gododdin, the Oldest Scottish Poem, 1969; The Gaelic Notes in the Book of Deer, 1972; *contrib.* Antiq. Jl, Antiq., Beal., Brit., Bull. Bd Celt. Studies, Celtica, Eigse, Eriu, Etudes Celt., Folk-Lore, Hor Yezh, Jl Celt. Studies, Jl Engl. Place-Name Soc., Jl Roman Studies, Lochlann, Man, Mod. Philol., Ogam, Proc. Brit. Acad., Proc. Scott. Anthropol Folk. Soc., Proc. Soc. Antiqu. Scotl., Scott. Gael. Studies, Scott. Hist. Rev., Scott. Studies, Speculum, Zeits. Celt. Philol. *Address*: Dept of Celtic, David Hume Tower, George Square, Edinburgh EH8 9JX.

Jackson, Margaret Cochrane; *see* Storrie, M. C.

Jackson, Dr Raymond; Lecturer in Education, School of Education, University of Reading, since 1967; *b* 1926. BSc (Econ) LSE 1957, Acad. DipEd London 1964, MA London 1968 (Educn), PhD London 1972, Teachers Dip. 1950; Licentiate, Coll. of Preceptors, 1970. Res. Officer, Schs Council, 1973–74 (on secondment from Univ. of Reading). Consultant-Expert: UNESCO, Higher Educn Div., 1971–73; OECD, 1973. *Publications*: (jtly), A Handbook of Educational Guidance, 1971; ed, Careers Guidance: practice and problems, 1973; Some Aspects of Counselling and Guidance at the Higher Educational Level, 1973; (with B. Holmes) Education in Europe (forthcoming); *contrib.* Compar. Educn, Compare, Educ. Res., Elem. Sch. Jl (Chicago), London Educ. Rev., New Univ. Paedogogik (Copenhagen), Teaching Politics. *Address*: Sch. of Education, London Road, Reading.

Jacob, Joseph Michael, LLB; Lecturer in Laws, London School of Economics, since 1970; *b* 1943; *m* 1972; one *d*. LLB Hons UCL 1966. Called to Bar, Grays Inn, 1967 (Holt Scholar, 1967, Alfsen Scholar, 1968, Lee Essay Prizeman, 1968). Coll. of Law, 1967–70. Member: Council, Soc. of Public Teachers of Law, 1973– ; Council, London Borough of Camden; Management Cttee, Camden Community Law Centre. *Address*: London School of Economics, Houghton Street, Aldwych, WC2A 2AE.

Jacob, Judith Margaret; Lecturer in Cambodian Studies, Department of South-East Asia and the Islands, School of Oriental and African Studies, since 1952; *b* 1923; *m* 1953; two *d*. BA Leeds 1944 (1st cl. Classics), DipEd Leeds 1945; BA Cantab 1948 (2nd cl. Pt 2 Classics tripos). Mem., Philol Soc., MRAS, AUT, Assoc. SE Asian Studies UK. Asst Lectr, Linguistics Dept, SOAS, London Univ., 1948–52. *Publications*: (with H. L. Shorto and E. H. S. Simmonds) Bibliographies of Mon-Khmer and Tai Linguistics, 1963; Introduction to Cambodian, 1968; Concise Cambodian-English Dictionary, 1974; *contrib.* Linguistic Comparison in South-East Asia and the Pacific, 1963; Indo-Pacific Linguistic Studies, 1965; In Memory of J. R. Firth, 1966; Current Trends in Linguistics, II, 1967; *contrib.* Bull. SOAS, 1961. *Address*: Dept of South-East Asia and the Islands, School of Oriental and African Studies, London Univ., Malet Street, WC1E 7HP.

Jacob, Roger; Lecturer, Music Department, University of Aberdeen, since 1964; *b* 1935. BMus Wales 1956, CertEd London 1957; Mem. Royal Musical Assoc., Mem. Incorp. Soc. of Musicians. Asst in Music, Aberdeen Univ., 1961–64, Asst Lectr, 1964. Mem. Academic Adv. Council, Cultural Dept of World Jewish Congress. *Publications*: Dominique Phinot, a Franco-Netherlander composer of the mid-sixteenth century, in Studies in the Italian Renaissance: A collection in honour of P. O. Kristeller, ed C. H. Clough, 1974. *Address*: Dept of Music, Powis Gate, College Bounds, Old Aberdeen AB9 2UG.

Jacobs, Denys, MA; Tutor to Bradninch Students and Lecturer in History, University of Exeter, since 1949; *b* 1914; *m* 1949; two *s* ond *d*. BA Cantab 1947, MA Cantab 1952. Asst Lectr in Adult Education, Univ. of Nottingham, 1948–49; Vis. Prof., Coll. of William and Mary, Va, 1974–75. *Publications*: ed, The Harrowby Tiverton Manuscripts: Catalogue, 1971 (private distrib.). *Address*: Univ. of Exeter, Reed Mews, Streatham Drive, Exeter.

Jacobs, Dr Eva, MA, DUP; Lecturer in French, Bedford College, University of London, since 1960; *b* 1933; *m* 1956; 1962. BA London 1954, MA London 1956, DU Paris 1959. Res. Fellow, Univ. of Nottingham, 1957–60. *Publications*: *contrib.* Mod. Lang. Rev., Nott. Fr. Studies, Rev. Sci. Hum. *Address*: Dept of French, Bedford College, Regent's Park, NW1 4NS.

Jacobs, Everett Mayer; Lecturer, Department of Economic History, Sheffield University, since 1970; *b* 1941; *m* 1967. BA Columbia, 1963, MSc (Econ) London 1966; Mem.: Nat. Assoc. of Soviet and E European Studies, Economic History Soc. Res. Fellow in Soviet Studies, UC, Swansea, 1968–70. Visiting Prof., Boston Univ., summer term, 1974; Associate, Russian and E Eur. Centre, Univ. of Illinois, summer 1974. Recorder, Sheffield Univ. Non-Professorial Staff Assoc., 1973– ; Mem.: Sheffield Univ. Faculty of Social Sciences Bd, 1971– ; Sheffield Univ.

Senate, 1973– . Treas., SCR, Swansea UC, 1969–70. *Publications*: numerous contribs in edited collections; *contrib*. Bull. Soc. for Study of Labour Hist., Government and Opposition, Jahrbuch der Wirtschaft Osteuropas, Osteuropa, Soviet and E European Abstract Series (ABSEES), Soviet Studies. *Address*: Dept of Economic History, Sheffield Univ., Sheffield S10 2TN.

Jacobs, Gabriel Cecil; Lecturer in Romance Studies, University College of Swansea, since 1966; *b* 1941; *m* 1964; two *d*. BA London (Hons French). Temp. Asst Lectr in French, UC Swansea, 1966, Asst Lectr, 1967–69. *Publications*: *contrib*. Trivium, Aumla. *Address*: Dept of Romance Studies, Univ. College of Swansea, Singleton Park, Swansea SA2 8PP.

Jacobs, John; Lecturer in Social Administration, Director of Graduate Social Work Studies, University of Sussex, since 1967; *b* 1940; *m* 1965; two *s*. BA Cantab 1962 (English), Dip. in Public and Social Admin Oxford 1964. *Address*: Univ. of Sussex, Arts Building, Falmer, Brighton BN1 9RH.

Jacobs, John Nicolas; Lecturer, Department of English, University of Bristol, since 1972; *b* 1942. BA Oxford 1964, (cl. I) MA 1967. Lectr, Balliol and St John's Colls, Oxford, 1966–72. *Publications*: *contrib*. NM, N and Q, Speculum. *Address*: Alfred Marshall Bldg, 40 Berkeley Square, Bristol.

Jacobs, Magaret; Fellow since 1955 and Tutor in German since 1957, St Hugh's College, Oxford; CUF Lecturer in German, University of Oxford, since 1952; *b* 1922. BA Oxon 1947 (1st cl. Mod. Langs), MA Oxon 1949, BLitt Oxon 1952. Asst Lectr in German, Manchester Univ., 1948–51; Cassel Lectr in German, St Hugh's Coll., Oxford, 1951–54; Asst Tutor in German, St Hugh's Coll., 1954–57. Governor: St Gabriel's Sch., Sandleford Priory, Newbury; Pusey House, Oxford. *Publications*: ed, Georg Büchner: Dantons Tod and Woyzeck, 1954, 3rd edn 1971; ed, Hugo von Hofmannsthal: Jedermann, 1957; Hugo von Hofmannsthal: Das Bergwerk zu Falun, in, Hofmannsthal, Studies in Commemoration, 1963; ed, Hofmannsthal: Four Stories, 1968; ed jtly, Hofmannsthal: Das Märchen der 672, Nacht, etc, 1973; ed, Tankred Dorst: Toller (forthcoming); *contrib*. Oxford German Stud. *Address*: St Hugh's College, Oxford.

Jacobus, Mary; Fellow and Tutor in English, Lady Margaret Hall, Oxford, since 1971; *b* 1944. BA Hons 1965 (English), DPhil 1969, MA 1969, Oxon. Joanna Randell McIver Res. Fellowship, Lady Margaret Hall, Oxford, 1968–70; Lectr, Dept of English, Manchester Univ., 1970–71. *Publications*: contrib. Bicentenary Wordsworth Studies, ed J. Wordsworth, 1971; *contrib*. E in C, N and Q, RES. *Address*: Lady Margaret Hall, Oxford.

Jaffé, Prof. Andrew Michael; Director, Fitzwilliam Museum, University of Cambridge, since 1973; *b* 1923; *m* 1964; one *s* one *d*. BA Cantab 1948 MA Cantab 1952;

FRSA. Fellow, King's Coll., Cambridge 1952– ; Commonwealth Fund Fellow, Harvard and New York Univs, 1951–53; Asst Lectr in Fine Arts, Cambridge, 1956–61; Prof. of Renaissance Art, Washington Univ., St Louis, 1960–61; Vis. Prof., Harvard Univ., 1961 and 1968–69; Lectr in Fine Arts, Cambridge, 1961–68; Reader in History of Western Art, Cambridge, 1968; Organiser (for Nat. Gall. of Canada) of Jordaens Exhibn, Ottawa, 1968–69; Head of Dept of History of Art, Cambridge, 1970–73. Member: Adv. Council, Victoria and Albert Mus.; Fine Arts Panel, Nat. Trust; Adv. Council, Paul Mellon Centre for Brit. Art and Brit. Studies; Bd of Studies (Standing Cttee), Hist. of Art, Univ. London; Working Party on Conservation of Textiles and Furniture (Standing Commn on Museums and Galls). *Publications*: Van Dyck's Antwerp Sketchbook, 1966; Rubens, 1967; Jordaens, 1968; *contrib*. Burlington Mag., Proporzioni, Master Drawings, Art Bull., Paragone, Art Qly. *Address*: Fitzwilliam Museum, Cambridge.

Jahoda, Prof. Gustav, MSc, PhD; Professor of Psychology, University of Strathclyde, since 1964; *b* 1920; *m* 1950; three *s* one *d*. BSc(Econ) London 1945 (2nd cl.), MSc London 1948, PhD London 1952; FBPS. Lectr, Manchester Univ., 1949–52; Lectr, Univ. of Ghana, 1952–56; Sen. Lectr, Glasgow Univ., 1956–63. Tutor, Oxford Extra-mural Delegacy, 1947–49; Mem., SSRC Psychol. Cttee, 1966–68; Planning Cttee, Europ. Ass. Exper. Social Psychol., 1965–69; Pres., Sect. J, Brit. Assoc., 1970; CNAA Soc. Sci. Bd. *Publications*: White Man, 1961; The Psychology of Superstition, 1969, Polish edn 1971, Italian and Swedish edns 1972; *contrib*. Brit. Jl Educnl Psychol., Brit. Jl Psychol., Brit. Jl Soc. Clin. Psychol., Child Develop., Internat. Jl Psychol., Jl Social Psychol., etc. *Address*: Dept of Psychology, Univ. of Strathclyde, Turnbull Building, 155 George Street, Glasgow G1 1RD

Jain, Dr Ravindra Kumar, MA, PhD; University Lecturer in the Social Anthropology of South Asia, and Fellow of Wolfson College, University of Oxford, since 1966; *b* 1937; *m* 1961; one *s* one *d*. MA Lucknow 1958 (1st cl. Anthropology); PhD Australian National 1965; MA Oxon 1967; FRAI, FInd Inst. Adv. Study. Asst Prof. in Anthropology, Lucknow Univ., 1958–61; Res. Schol., Australian Nat. Univ., 1961–65; Lectr in Sociol., Univ. of New England, Australia, 1965–66. Mem., Oxfam Asia Cttee, 1971–72; Mem., Cttee, Assoc. Social Anthrop., 1970–74; Consultnt., Ind. Council Social Sci. Res., 1971– . *Publications*: Ramnathpuram Experiment, 1966; South Indians on the Plantation Frontier in Malaya, American and Malaysian edns, 1970; *contrib*. East. Anthropol., Hindi Encyclop., Jl Ind. Anthropol. Soc., Man. *Address*: Institute of Social Anthropology, Univ. of Oxford, 51 Banbury Road, Oxford.

James, Prof. Alan Morien; Professor of International Relations, University of Keele, since 1974; *b* 1933; *m* 1956; four *s* two *d*. BSc(Econ) London 1954 (1st cl. International Relations). Asst Lectr, LSE, 1957–59, Lectr,

1959–66, Sen. Lectr, 1966–70; Reader in Internat. Relations, LSE, 1970–73. Rockefeller Res. Fellow in Internat. Organization, Inst. of War and Peace Studies, Columbia Univ., NY, 1968. *Publications*: The Politics of Peace-Keeping, 1969; ed, The Bases of International Order, 1973; *contrib.* Internat. Relat., Polit. Studies, Wld Today, Ybk Wld Aff. *Address*: Dept of International Relations, Univ. of Keele, Keele, Staffs ST5 5BG.

James, Carl; Lecturer, Department of Linguistics, University College of North Wales, Bangor, since 1966; *b* 1939; *m* 1968. BA Nottingham 1962 (2nd cl. German/French), DipEd Oxon 1963, DipLings Manchester 1965. Member Linguistics Assoc. GB; Brit. Assoc. App. Linguistics; Linguistics Inst. of Ireland, 1972– . Res. Fellow, Dept of Language Laboratories, Univ. of Wisconsin-Milwaukee, 1969–70. Europ. Editorial Advr, Mod. Lang. Jl, 1970. *Publications*: *contrib.* A-VLang. Jl, Internat. Rev., Appl. Lingu., Lang. Learn., Mod. Lang. Jl. *Address*: Dept of Linguistics, Univ. College of North Wales, Bangor LL57 2DG.

James, David Edward, BSc, MEd; Director of Adult Education, University of Surrey, since 1969; *b* 1937; *m* 1963; two *s* one *d*. BSc Reading 1959, BSc Reading 1960, MEd Durham 1967; DipEd Oxon 1961; DipFEd London 1968; MIBiol, ABPsS, FRSH, FRSA. Lectr, Surrey Univ., 1965–69. *Publications*: Science in Education, in, Essays in Local Government Enterprise, vol. III, ed E. Hillman, 1966; Students Guide to Efficient Study, 1967; Introduction to Psychology, 1968, 2nd edn 1971, pbk edn 1970; *contrib.* Adult Educn, Jl Medic. Educn, Nurs. Times. *Address*: Centre for Adult Education, Univ. of Surrey, Guildford, Surrey.

James, Donald William; Lecturer in Music, University of Exeter, since 1968; *b* 1935; *m* 1959; four *s*. CertifEd 1958, MA Cantab 1960; FRCO 1960, ARCM 1960, LRAM 1961. Mem. BBC Adv. Council for South West, 1972– . *Address*: Dept of Music, Univ. of Exeter, Exeter EX4 4QJ.

James, Dr Edward Donald; Lecturer in French, University of Cambridge, since 1960; *b* 1926; *m* 1955. BA Cantab 1951 (Modern and Medieval Langs), MA Cantab 1955, PhD Cantab 1958. Fellow, St John's Coll., Cambridge, 1955; Asst Lectr, Univ. of Cambridge, 1955–60. Governor, the Stamford Endowed Schs, 1970– . *Publications*: Pierre Nicole, Jansenist and Humanist, 1972; Faith, Sincerity and Morality: Bayle and Mandeville, in, Mandeville Studies (forthcoming); La Rochefoucauld et Les Moralistes, in, Histoire littéraire de la France de 1600 à 1715 (forthcoming); *contrib.* Forum for Mod. Lang. Studies, French Studies. *Address*: St John's College, Cambridge CB2 1TP.

James, Gwyn Ingli, MA; Lecturer in English, University College, Cardiff, since 1960; *b* 1928; *m* 1956; one *s* one *d*. BA Wales 1949, MA Wales 1951; Fellow, Univ. of Wales, 1951–53; Commonwealth Fund Fellow., Yale Univ., 1953–54; Asst Lectr, Univ. of London, King's Coll., 1958–59;

Asst Lectr, Cardiff, 1959–60. *Publications*: *contrib.* Apollo, Blackfr., Christ. Schol., Crit., Ess. Crit., Sewanee Rev., South. Rev. (Adelaide), TLS, Twentieth Century. *Address*: Dept of English, Univ. College, Cathays Park, Cardiff CF1 1XL.

James, Prof. John Richings, CB, OBE; Professor of Town and Regional Planning, since 1967, and Pro-Vice-Chancellor since 1970, University of Sheffield; *b* 1912; *m* 1946; five *d*. BA London; FRTPI, Hon. FRIBA. Schoolmaster, 1937–40; Res. Offr (Newcastle Regional Office), Min. of Town and Country Planning, 1946–49; Min. of Housing and Local Govt: Sen. Res. Offr (London), 1949–58; Dep. Chief Planner, 1958–61; Chief Planner, 1961–67. UK Rep. on UN Cttee for Housing, Building and Planning, 1967– ; Mem. Peterborough Develt Corp.; Governor, Centre for Environmental Studies, 1967–71. *Publications*: Greece (3 vols), 1943–45; Greece and Greek Towns and Islands, in, Chambers's Encyclopaedia; *contrib.* RSA Jl, RGS Jl, etc. *Address*: Univ. of Sheffield, Sheffield S10 2TN.

James, Dr Leslie; Staff Tutor, Board of Extra-Mural Studies, University of Cambridge, since 1949; *b* 1915; *m* 1947; one *s*. BA 1937, MA 1940, Liverpool, MA Cambridge 1954, PhD London 1967. Sen. Lectr, Univ. of Alexandria, Egypt, 1946–49. *Publication*: World Affairs since 1939: Europe, 1965. *Address*: Bd of Extra-Mural Studies, Stuart House, Cambridge.

James, Peter Anthony; Lecturer in Geography, Liverpool University, since 1971; *b* 1945; *m* 1966; one *s*. BSc Wales 1963 (Hons.) (Geog.), MSc Geography, Saskatchewan 1966 (Geog.). Teaching Asst, Saskatchewan Univ., 1966–68; Demonstrator, Nottingham Univ., 1969–71. *Publications*: *contrib.* Arctic and Alpine Res., Biul. Perygl., Geog. Mag., Brit. Geom. Res. Gp Tech. Bull. *Address*: Geography Dept, Univ. of Liverpool, PO Box 147, Liverpool L69 3BX.

James, Prof. Philip Seaforth; Professor and Head of Department of Law, Leeds University, since 1951; *b* 1914; *m* 1954; two *s*. MA Oxon 1940; Called to Bar 1939. Res. Fellow, Yale Univ., 1938–39; Fellow and Tutor, Exeter Coll., Oxford, 1946–49; Vis. Prof., Univ. of S Carolina, 1973. Chm., Yorkshire Rent Assess. Panel; Co. Ct Assessor, Race Relat. Act; Governor Swinton Conservative Coll.; Pres., Soc. Public Teachers of Law, 1971–72; Mem., Exec. Cttee, Commonwealth Legal Educn Assoc. *Publications*: An Introduction to English Law, 1951, 8th edn 1972; General Principles of the Law of Torts, 1961, 3rd edn 1969; A Shorter Introduction to English Law, 1969; *contrib.* Jl Bus. Law, Mod. Law Rev. *Address*: The Faculty of Law, Leeds Univ., Leeds LS2 9JT.

James, Prudence Anne, MA, BPhil, DottLett; Lecturer in Italian, Bedford College, University of London, since 1972; *b* 1939; *m* 1968; two *d*. BA Sydney 1961 (1st cl. Italian, 1st cl. English); BPhil Oxon 1966; DottLett Florence 1969. Teaching Fellow, Univ. of Sydney, 1962; Univ. of Cambridge:

Asst Lectr, 1966–71; College Lectr in Italian, New Hall, 1971–72; Fellow, New Hall, 1966–72. *Publications*: *contrib*. Studi danteschi. *Address*: Bedford College, Inner Circle, Regent's Park, NW1 4NS.

James, Prof. Walter; Dean and Director of Studies in Educational Studies, The Open University, since 1969; *b* 1924; *m* 1948; two *s*. BA Nottingham 1955. Resident Tutor, Univ. of Nottingham, 1958–64, Lectr in Adult Educn, 1964–69. Chm., Standing Conf. Nat. Voluntary Youth Organisations, 1971–73; Chm., Nat. Council Voluntary Youth Services, 1973– ; Trustee, Young Volunteer Force Foundn, 1971– ; Trustee, Trident Trust, 1972– ; Mem., Nat. Inst. of Adult Educn Exec. Cttee and Council, 1970– ; Mem., Nat. Council of Social Service Exec. Cttee and Policy Cttee, 1971– ; Pres., Inst. of Play Leadership, 1972– ; Mem., BBC Further Educn Adv. Council, 1971– ; Mem., Gen. Synod of C of E, 1970– ; Mem., Brit. Council of Churches, Dept of Educn, 1972–73. *Address*: The Open Univ., Walton Hall, Milton Keynes MK7 6AA.

James, Dr W. L. G., MA, DPhil; Senior Lecturer in English, University of Kent, since 1968; *b* 1932; *m* 1961; one *s* three *d*. BA Oxon 1954 (2nd English), MA Oxon 1959, DPhil Oxon 1959. Staff Tutor, Hull Univ., 1958–63; Lectr, Univ. of West Indies, 1963–66; Lectr, Kent Univ., 1966–68; Vis. Associate Prof., Univ. of S Carolina, 1969–70; Vis. Fellow, Univ. of Ibadan, 1973–74. *Publications*: Fiction for the Working Man, 1830–1850, 1962; ed, Islands that Lie Between, 1968; *contrib*. Carib. Qly, Dickens Studies Ann., Victorian Studies. *Address*: Eliot College, Univ. of Kent, Canterbury CT1 3PA.

Jameson, Andrew Leigh; Lecturer in Russian Language, Department of Russian and Soviet Studies, University of Lancaster, since 1971; *b* 1939; *m* 1964; one *s* one *d*. BA Oxon 1965 (Hons Russian); Member: Assoc. of Teachers of Russian, Brit. Univs Assoc. of Slavists, GB-USSR Assoc., Brit. Assoc. Applied Linguistics. Res. Asst in Russian, Univ. Essex, 1965–68; Portsmouth Polytechnic, 1968–71. Lectr i/c Resource Centre of ATR (information and materials service). *Publications*: trans. Ginzburg: Precipitous Journey, 1967; The Organisation of Audiovisual Materials in Education, a bibliography, 1972; *contrib*. Internat. Revue of Applied Linguistics, TES. *Address*: Dept of Russian and Soviet Studies, Univ. of Lancaster, Bailrigg, Lancaster LA1 4YN.

Jamieson, Michael Sutherland; Lecturer, School of English and American Studies, University of Sussex, since 1962; *b* 1931. MA Hons Aberdeen 1953; Member: British Assoc. for Amer. Studies; Soc. for Theatre Res. Sir John Dill Visiting Fellow, Princeton University, NJ, 1955–56; Carnegie Res. Scholar and Sen. Res. Scholar, King's Coll., Cambridge, 1956–60; Asst Lectr in English, Univ. of Keele, 1960–62; Vis. Lectr, Univ. of Rome, Summer Term, 1969. Warden of Falmer House, 1962–72. *Publications*: As You Like It: A Critical Study, 1965, 2nd edn

1971; ed, Ben Jonson: Three Comedies, 1966; *contrib*. Shakespeare Survey. *Address*: Arts Building, Univ. of Sussex, Brighton BN1 9QN.

Jaques, Prof. Elliott, MA, MD, PhD; Director, Institute of Organisation and Social Studies, Brunel University, since 1970; *b* 1917; *m* 1953; one *d*. BA Toronto 1936, MA Toronto 1937; MD Johns Hopkins Med. Sch., 1940; PhD Harvard 1950; qualified as Psycho-Analyst (British Psycho-Analytical Soc), 1951. Rantoul Fellow and Instructor in Psychology, Harvard, 1940–41; Prof. and Hd of Sch. of Social Sciences, Brunel Univ., 1965. Founder Mem. and Sen. Project Officer, Tavistock Inst. of Human Relations, 1946–51; Social consultant in industry (mainly on Glacier Project), 1952. Mem., Brit. Psycho-Analytical Soc.; Mem., Brit. Psychol Soc.; Mem., BMA; Mem., Brit. Sociol Assoc.; Fellow, Internat. Acad. of Management; Foundation Fellow, Royal Coll. of Psychiatrists. *Publications*: The Changing Culture of a Factory, 1951; Measurement of Responsibility, 1956, trans. Italian 1966, Japanese 1967; Equitable Payment, 1961, trans. French 1963, Spanish 1968, Italian 1967; (with W. Brown) Product Analysis Pricing, 1964; Time-Span Handbook, 1964, trans. French 1965, Italian 1967; (with W. Brown) Glacier Project Papers, 1965, trans. Italian 1967, Japanese 1969; Progression Handbook, 1968; Work, Creativity and Social Justice, 1970; *contrib*. California Management Rev., Harvard Bus. Rev., Hum. Rel., Int. Jl Psycho-Anal., Management, in Action, Management Today, The Manager, Mental Health, New Soc., RSH Jl, Sci. Business. *Address*: Institute of Organisation and Social Studies, School of Social Sciences, Kingston Lane, Uxbridge, Mddx UB8 3TH.

Jaques, Dr Juliette Winifred, BA, MA, PhD; Senior Lecturer, French Department, University of London, Goldsmiths' College, since 1965; *b* 1918. BA London 1946 (French), MA London 1950 (French), PhD London 1955 (French); Dip. Archive Admin. London 1953; Post-grad. Cert Ed London, 1956. Asst Lectr, Westfield Coll., Univ. of London, 1948–50. Examiner, A-level French (written), Univ. of London; Oral examiner in French, London and Oxford. *Publications*: *contrib*. Fr. Studies. *Address*: Univ. of London, Goldsmiths' College, New Cross, SE14 6NW.

Jardine, Dr Andrew Kennedy Skilling; Lecturer in Engineering Production, University of Birmingham, since 1971; *b* 1941; *m* 1964; one *s* one *d*. BSc Strathclyde 1964 (Mechanical Engineering), MSc Strathclyde 1965 (Mechanical Engineering), PhD Birmingham 1973 (Engineering Production); CEng, MIMechE, MIProdE. Lectr, Operational Research, Univ. of Strathclyde, 1966–71. *Publications*: Operational Research in Maintenance, 1970; Maintenance, Replacement and Reliability, 1973; Essentials of Statistics in Marketing, 1974; Operational Research Techniques, vol. 2, 1974; Statistical Methods in Quality Control, 1974; *contrib*. Proc. Inst. Mech. Engineers. *Address*: Dept of Engineering Production, Univ. of Birmingham, PO Box 363, Birmingham B15 2TT.

Jardine, Dr William Graham; Senior Lecturer in Geology, University of Glasgow, since 1966; *b* 1927; *m* 1955; three *s* one *d*. BSc Glasgow 1949 (1st cl. Geology), MSc McGill 1950, PhD Cantab 1957; FGS, Mem., Geol. Assoc., Mem., QRA. Lectr, Univ. of Glasgow, 1959–66. SO Soil Survey (Scotland), 1955–58; SSO, 1958–59; Mem., INQUA Sub-cttee, Brit. Nat. Cttee Geol., 1966– ; Sec., Quatern. Res. Assoc., 1970–74; Vice-Pres., Glasgow Archaeol. Soc., 1972– ; Sec.-Gen., Organising Cttee, X INQUA Congress (1977), 1973– . *Publications: contrib.* Jl Geol. Soc., Proc. Internat. Geol. Cong., Quatern., Scott. Geog. Mag., Scott. Jl Geol., Trans Geol. Soc. Glasgow. *Address:* Dept of Geology, Univ. of Glasgow, Glasgow G12 8QQ.

Jarman, Prof. Alfred Owen Hughes, MA; Professor of Welsh, University College, Cardiff, since 1957; *b* 1911; *m* 1943; two *d*. BA Wales 1932 (1st cl. Welsh), MA Wales 1936. Asst Lectr in Welsh, Cardiff, 1946–47, Lectr, 1947–55, Sen. Lectr, 1955–57. Member: Bd Celt. Studies, Univ. of Wales; Univ. of Wales Press Bd; Ct Governors, Univ. of Wales and Univ. Coll., Cardiff; Ct and Council, Nat. Libr. Wales. Editor, Llên Cymru. *Publications:* Ymiddidan Myrddin a Thaliesin, 1951, 2nd edn 1967; Chwedlau Cymraeg Canol, 1957, 2nd edn 1969; The Legend of Merlin, 1960, 2nd edn 1970; Sieffre o Fynwy/Geoffrey of Monmouth, 1966; *contrib.* Y Bywgraffiadur Cymreig, 1953; Arthurian Literature in the Middle Ages, 1959; Beiträge zur Indogermanistik und Keltologie Julius Pokorny zum 80. Geburstag gewidmet, 1967; *contrib.* Bull. Bd Celt. Studies, Llên Cymru. *Address:* Univ. College, Cardiff CF1 1XL.

Jarrett, Derek; Principal Lecturer in History, Goldsmiths' College, University of London, since 1972; *b* 1928; *m* 1965; two *d*. BA Oxon 1951 (1st cl. History), MA Oxon 1956, BLitt Oxon 1956. Lectr, Goldsmiths' Coll., 1964–65, Sen. Lectr, 1965–72. *Publications:* Britain 1688–1815, 1965; The Begetters of Revolution: England and France 1759–1789, 1973; Pitt the Younger, 1974; England in the Age of Hogarth, 1974; *contrib.* EHR. *Address:* Goldsmiths' College, SE14 6NW.

Jarrett, Dr Michael Grierson; Reader in Archaeology, University College, Cardiff, since 1970; *b* 1934. BA Dunelm 1954 (Hons Mod. History), PhD Dunelm 1958; FSA 1966. Sir James Knott Fellow, King's Coll., Newcastle upon Tyne, 1958–60; UC Cardiff: Asst Lectr, 1960–61, Lectr, 1961–68; Sen. Lectr, 1968–70. *Publications:* ed (with B. Dobson) Britain and Rome, 1966; ed, V. E. Nash-Williams: The Roman frontier in Wales, 2nd revised edn 1969; The Roman fort at Maryport, Cumberland, 1974; *contrib.* Amer. Jl Philol, Antiquity, Archaeologia Aeliana, Arch. Cambrensis, Bonner Jb., Epigraphische Studien, Historia, JRS, Trans Cumberland and Westmorland Art and Arch. Soc. *Address:* Univ. College, PO Box 78, Cardiff CF1 1XL.

Jarrett-Kerr, Rev. Fr Martin William

Robert, MA, CR; Associate Lecturer, Department of Theology, Leeds University, since 1968; *b* 1912. BA Oxford 1935 (2nd cl. Eng. Lang and Lit.), DipTheol Oxford 1935, MA 1939; Vis. Hill Prof., Gustavus Adolphus Coll., Minn., USA, 1957. *Publications:* Our Trespasses, 1948; D. H. Lawrence and Human Existence, 1951, Amer. edn 1972; The Hope of Glory, 1952; François Mauriac, in, Studies in Modern European Literature and Thought, 1954; Studies in Literature and Belief, 1954, Amer. edn 1971; African Pulse, 1960, pbk edn 1961; The Secular Promise, 1964; Christ and the New Nations, 1966; William Faulkner, in, Contemporary Writers in Christian Perspective, 1970; Patterns of Christian Acceptance, 1972; trans. W. Weidle: The Dilemma of the Arts, 1945; Pascal: Pensées (Selections, and Introduction), 1958; N. Corte: Life and Spirit of Teilhard de Chardin, 1960; *contrib.* chapters in Symposia; Doctrine of Man, in, Christian Faith and Communist Faith, ed Mackinnon, 1951; Pitfalls of the Christian Artist, in, Climate of Faith in Modern Literature, ed N. Scott, 1964; Theology and the Arts, in, A Study of Theology, ed D. T. Jenkins, 1965; Conditions of Tragedy, in, Mansions of the Spirit, ed Panichas, and in, Comparative Literature, ed A. O. Aldridge, 1969; Of Clerical Cut, in, Eliot in Perspective, ed G. Martin, 1970. *Address:* Dept of Theology, Univ. of Leeds, Leeds LS2 9JT.

Jary, David William; Senior Lecturer in Sociology, Department of Sociology, Government and Administration, University of Salford, since 1970; *b* 1938; *m* 1961; two *s* one *d*. BScEcon London 1961. Mem., Sociol Studies Bd, CNAA, 1969– . *Publications: contrib.:* Leisure and Society in Britain, ed Smith, Parker and Smith, 1973; Key Variables in Social Research, vol. II, ed, Gittus, 1974; *contrib.* Brit. Jl Soc., Univ. Qly. *Address:* Univ. of Salford, Salford M5 4NT.

Jaspan, Prof. Mervyn Aubrey, BA BSc, PhD; Director of the Centre for South-East Asian Studies and Professor of South-East Asian Sociology, University of Hull, since 1968; *b* 1926; *m* 1951; three *s*. BA Natal 1948 (Distinction Social Anthropology); BSc Oxon 1953; CertEd Exeter 1952; PhD ANU 1964; FRAI 1952, FRAS 1969. Part-time Lectr in Social Anthropology, Univ. of Manchester, 1951–52; Res. Fellow in Sociology, Univ. of Exeter, 1952–55; Prof. of Social Anthropology and Sociology, Gadjah Mada Univ., Jogjakarta, Indonesia, 1955–59; Prof., Padjadjaran State Univ., Bandung, 1959–60; Res. Fellow in Anthropology and Sociology, ANU, 1961–64; Sen. Lectr in Anthropology and Dir, Centre for Asian Studies, Univ. of W Australia, 1964–67; Vis. Prof. in Anthropology, Leiden Univ., 1967–68. Editor, Hull Monographs on SE Asia, 1968– ; Editor, Sumatra Res. Bull., 1971– . Mem., Exec. Cttee, Brit. Assoc. SE Asian Studies, 1971–73. *Publications:* The Ila Tonga Peoples of North-Eastern Rhodesia, 1952; Social Stratification and Social Mobility in Indonesia, 1959, 2nd edn 1961; Aspects of the Political Sociology of the Late Soekarno Era, 1967; Folk Literature of South

Sumatra: Redjang Ka-Ga-Nga Texts, 1964; From Patriliny to Matriliny, 1964; The Redjang Tribunal: Village Justice in South Sumatra, 1972; *contrib.* Man, Contemporary Studies of Soc. and Hist., Sosiografi Indonesia, Bijdragen tot de Taal-, Land- en Volkenkunde, Sci. and Soc. *Address:* Centre for South-East Asian Studies, The Univ. of Hull, Hull HU6 7RX.

Jay, Leslie Joseph; Senior Lecturer in Education, University of Sheffield, since 1964; *b* 1917; *m* 1943; one *s* one *d.* BA Birmingham 1938 (Hons Geography), DipEd Birmingham 1940, MA Birmingham 1949; FRGS. Mem., Inst. Brit. Geogrs, Geog. Assoc. Lectr in Educn, Sheffield, 1953–64; Vis. Lectr, Univ. of Michigan, 1961–62. Hon. Libr. and Mem., Exec. Cttee, Geog. Assoc., 1954–74. *Publications:* The Americas, 1964; *contrib.* Geog. *Address:* Dept of Education, The Univ., Sheffield S10 2TN.

Jean, Bernard; Lecturer in French, University of Manchester, since 1969; *b* 1934; *m* 1968. L-ès-L Paris 1960, Agrégé d'Anglais 1962. Special Lectr in French Thought, Univ. of Manchester, 1965–68. *Publications:* (with F. Mouret) Montaigne, Descartes et Pascal par la Dissertation, 1971; *contrib.* Etudes Angl. *Address:* Dept of French Studies, The Univ., Manchester M13 9PL.

Jeeves, Prof. Malcolm Alexander, MA, PhD, FBPsS, FAPS; Professor of Psychology, University of St Andrews, since 1969; *b* 1926; *m* 1955; two *d.* BA Cantab 1951, MA Cantab 1956, PhD Cantab 1957, PhD ad eundum gradum Adelaide 1960; FBPsS, FAPS. Member: Exper. Psychol. Soc.; Internat. Neuropsychol. Symp. Gp. Burney Studentship, Cambridge, 1952; Fellowship for Adv. Study, Harvard, 1953; Lectr, Leeds Univ., 1956–59; Prof. and Hd of Dept of Psychology, Univ. of Adelaide, 1959–69. Dean, Fac. of Arts, Univ. of Adelaide, 1962–64; Governor, Dundee Coll. Educn, 1970– ; Mem., Scott. Council, Res. Educn, 1970– . *Publications:* (with Z. P. Dienes) Thinking in Structures, 1965, French edn 1966, Italian edn, 1967, German edn 1968; (with Z. P. Dienes) The Effects of Structural Relations on Transfer, 1970, Italian edn 1972; The Scientific Enterprise and Christian Faith, 1968, American edn 1969; *contrib.* Austral. Jl Psychol., Anim. Behav., Ergonom., Jl Exper. Psychol., Jl Genet., Psychol., Neuropsychol., Psychon Sci., Qly Jl Exper. Psychol. *Address:* Psychological Laboratory, Univ. of St Andrews, Fife KY16 9AJ.

Jeffares, Prof. Alexander Norman; Professor of English, University of Stirling, since 1974; *b* 1920; *m* 1947; one *d.* BA Dublin (Classics), BA Dublin 1943 (Ancient Hist. and Polit. Science), PhD Dublin 1945 (English), MA Dublin 1946; MA Oxford 1946, DPhil Oxford 1948 (English); FRSL 1965, FRSA 1963. Fellow, Austral. Acad. Human., 1970. Lectr, Univ. of Groningen, Holland, 1946–48; Lectr, Univ. of Edinburgh, 1949–51; Jury Prof. of English Language and Literature, Univ. of Adelaide, 1951–56; Prof. of English Literature, Univ.

of Leeds, 1957–74; Founding Chm., Assoc. Commonwealth Lit. and Lang. Studies, 1966–68; Internat. Assoc. Study Anglo-Irish with Lit., 1969–70 (Co-Chm., 1971–); Sec., Austral. Human. Res. Council, 1954–57; Corresp. Mem., GB and Ireland, 1958–70; Vice-Chm., Film and TV Council S Australia, 1951–56. *Publications:* Trinity College Dublin: drawings and descriptions, 1944, 3rd edn 1945; W. B. Yeats: Man and Poet, 1949, rev. edn 1962; Seven Centuries of Poetry, 1955, rev. edn 1960; (with M. Bryn Davies) The Scientific Battleground, 1958; Oliver Goldsmith, 1959; The Poetry of W. B. Yeats, 1961; Selected Poems, 1962, Selected Prose, 1961, Selected Plays, 1964, and Selected Criticism, 1964, of W. B. Yeats; ed (with G. F. Cross), In Excited Reverie, 1965; Cowper, 1963; Selected Poetry and Prose of Whitman, 1965; ed, Fair Liberty was all his Cry: a tercentenary tribute to Swift, 1967; A Commentary on the Collected Poems of Yeats, 1968; various edns of Congreve, Goldsmith, Farquhar, Sheridan, 1963–72; *contrib.* AREL, ARIEL, Brit. Bk News, Engl. Studies, Envoy, Etudes Angl., Hermathena, Jl Commonwealth Lit., Mod. Lang. Notes, Meanjin, Neophilol., Nineteenth Cent., Rev. Engl. Studies, Shakesp. Rev., Times Litt. Supp., Wascana Rev. *Address:* Dept of English, Univ. of Stirling, Stirling FK9 4LA.

Jefferies, Alfred, MA, MLitt; Reader in Geography, University of Strathclyde, since 1964; *b* 1911; *m* 1936; three *s* one *d.* BA Dunelm 1931 (2nd cl. History), MA Dunelm 1950, Dip. Theory and Practice of Teaching Dunelm 1932, Dip. Geog. London 1935, MLitt Dunelm 1955. Hd of Geography Dept, Strathclyde, 1964–67. Editor, Scott. Geog. Mag., 1967– . *Publications: contrib.* Geog., Scott. Geog. Mag. *Address:* Dept of Geography, Univ. of Strathclyde, Glasgow G1 1XW.

Jefferson, Prof. Douglas William; Professor, School of English, University of Leeds, since 1970; *b* 1912. BA Leeds 1933 (1st cl. Hons), BLitt Oxon 1937. Univ. Leeds: Asst Lectr in Eng. Lit., 1935–38; Lectr, 1938–52; Sen. Lectr, 1952–65; Reader, 1965–70; also Lectr, Univ. of Fuad I, Cairo, 1942–46. Dean of Faculty of Arts, Leeds, 1967–69. *Publications:* ed, Pelican Book of English Prose, vol. 3, 1956; Henry James (Writers and Critics), 1960; Henry James and the Modern Reader, 1964; ed, The Morality of Art (Festschrift for G. Wilson Knight), 1969; contrib. various critical anthologies, etc; *contrib.* Cambridge Jl, Essays in Criticism, Review of Eng. Lit. *Address:* Univ. of Leeds, Leeds LS2 9JT.

Jefferys, Prof. Margot, BSc(Econ); Professor of Medical Sociology, Sociology Department, Bedford College, University of London, since 1968; *b* 1916; *m* 1940 (divorced 1958); two *s.* BSc(Econ) London 1938. Member: Brit. Sociol Assoc.; Soc. Admin. Soc.; Soc. Social. Med.; Internat. Epidemiol Assoc. Res. Fellow in Sociology, Bedford Coll., 1950–53; Lectr, then Sen. Lectr in Social Aspects of Public Health, London Sch. of Hygiene and Tropical

Medicine, 1953–65; Reader in Social Admin., Bedford Coll., 1965–68. Chm., Brit. Med. Assoc. Planning Unit, Wkng Pty on Primary Med. Care, 1967–70. *Publications*: Mobility in the Labour Market, 1954; An Anatomy of Social Welfare Services, 1965; Women in Medicine, 1966; *contrib*. Brit. Jl Soc. Prevent. Med., Brit. Med. Jl, Jl Chron. Diseases, Lancet, Med. Off., Public Hlth, Soc. Econ. Admin. *Address*: Bedford College, Regent's Park, NW1 4NS.

Jeffreys-Jones, Dr Rhodri; Lecturer in History, University of Edinburgh, since 1969; *b* 1942; *m* 1970. BA Hons UCW, Aberystwyth 1963 (Hist. 2i); PhD Cantab 1969. Asst Lectr, Univ. of Edinburgh, 1967–69; Postdoctoral Fellow, Charles Warren Center for Studies in Amer. Hist., Harvard Univ., 1971–72. *Publications*: Die Vereinigten Staaten von Amerika, ed W. Adams, 1974; The Rise of Labor, in, History of the American Peoples, vol. 10, The Rise of an Industrial Giant, ed H. S. Commager (forthcoming); *contrib*. CJAS, JAS, PAH. *Address*: Dept of History, Univ. of Edinburgh, Edinburgh EH8 9YL.

Jeffreys-Powell, Paul Roger, MA; Lecturer, Department of Humanity, University of Glasgow, since 1967; *b* 1942. BA Oxon 1963, MA Oxon 1966; Temp. Asst Lectr in Greek, Bedford Coll., London, 1966–67. *Address*: Dept of Humanity, Univ. of Glasgow, Glasgow.

Jeffs, Dr Robin Morton; Lecturer in History, Department of Mediaeval and Modern History, University of Sheffield, since 1964; *b* 1933; *m* 1966; one *s* one *step-d*. BA 1954, MA 1958, DPhil 1960, Oxon (Major Scholar in History, Trinity Coll.); FRHistS 1971, FSA 1973. Tutor, Several Oxford Colls, 1955–63; Asst Lectr, Univ. of Sheffield, 1962–64. Jun. Treas., OUDS, 1956–57. Governor, Hayfield Comprehensive Sch., Yorks, 1970– ; Dir., J. C. Clark Ltd, 1968– . Gen. Editor, The English Revolution, 1969– . *Publications*: The Works of John Day, 1963; ed, Fast Sermons to Parliament, 1640–1653, 34 vols, 1970–71; *contrib*. BIHR, P and P. *Address*: Dept of Mediaeval and Modern History, Univ. of Sheffield, Sheffield S10 2TN.

Jenkins, Dr Cecil, MA, PhD; Reader in French, University of Sussex, since 1967; *b* 1927; *m* 1952; two *s* one *d*. BA Dublin 1950 (1st cl. French and German), MA, PhD Dublin 1957. Lectr, Ecole Normale Supérieure de St Cloud, 1952–56; Asst Lectr, Univ. Coll., Londonderry, 1956–58; Lectr, Exeter Univ., 1958–63; Lectr, Sussex Univ., 1963–65, Sen. Lectr, 1965–67; Vis. Associate Prof., Univ. of British Columbia, 1972–73; *Publications*: Message from Sirius (novel), 1961; ed, Mauriac: Thérèse Desqueyroux, 1964; ed, Mauriac, 1965; ed, Malraux: La Condition Humaine, 1968; André Malraux, 1972. *Address*: Arts A, Univ. of Sussex, Falmer, Brighton.

Jenkins, Dr Dafydd; Reader in Law, University College of Wales, Aberystwyth since 1973; *b* 1911; *m* 1942; one *s*. MA 1937,

LLM 1949, LittD 1973, Cantab; FRHistS 1970. Barrister-at-Law (Gray's Inn) 1934. University College of Wales: Part-time Lectr, 1965; Lectr 1969; Sen. Lectr, 1971. Successively Organiser, Educn Officer, Sen. Exec. Officer, Welsh Agricl Organisation Soc., 1943–69. *Publications*: Tân yn Llŷn, 1937; Thomas Johnes o'r Hafod, 1948; Law for Co-operatives, 1958; Llyfr Colan, 1963; Cyfraith Hywel, 1970; Damweiniau Colan, 1973; D. J. Williams, 1973; *contrib*. Bull. Bd of Celtic Studies, Cambridge Law Jl, Trans Hon. Soc. Cymmrodorion, Welsh Hist. Rev. *Address*: Dept of Law, Univ. Coll. of Wales, Aberystwyth SY23 3DB.

Jenkins, Daniel Thomas; Visiting Professor, King's College, University of London, since 1971; *b* 1914; *m* 1942; two *s* three *d*. MA Edinburgh 1935, BD Edinburgh 1938, BA Oxon 1939; Hon DD Knox College, Toronto 1957, Hon DD Edinburgh 1963. Commonwealth Fund Fellow, USA, 1948–49; Prof. of Theology (pt-time), Univ. of Chicago, 1950–62; Chaplain and Reader, Univ. of Sussex, 1963–70, Reader (part-time), 1970–73. Sec., Christian Frontier Council, 1957–62; Member: various Wld Council of Churches Cttees; Theology Bd, CNAA. *Publications*: The Nature of Catholicity, 1942; The Gift of Ministry, 1947; Tradition and the Spirit, 1950; Congregationalism, 1953; The Strangeness of the Church, 1956; Equality and Excellence, 1961; Beyond Religion, 1962; The Christian Belief in, God, 1964; ed, The Scope of Theology; 1965; The Educated Society, 1966; etc. *contrib*. Ecumenical Rev., Jl Relig., Theol, Theol. Today, Verb. Caro, etc. *Address*: 301 Willoughby House, Barbican, EC2Y 8BL.

Jenkins, Edgar William; Lecturer, Centre for Studies in Science Education, University of Leeds, since 1966; *b* 1939; *m* 1961; two *d*. BSc Hons Leeds 1960 (1st cl. Chem.), Grad. Cert. Leeds 1961 (Distinction), ARIC 1963. Hon. Sec., Leeds AUT, 1969– ; Sec., Educn Div., Chem. Soc. *Publications*: Objective Testing: a guide, 1972; The Polymorphism of Elements and Compounds, 1973; Objective Questions in A-level Chemistry, 1973; Structured Questions in A-level Chemistry, 1973; A Safety Handbook for Science Teachers, 1974; ed, Readings in Science Education, 1974; A Bibliography of Resources for Chemistry Teachers, 1974; ed, The Teaching of Science to Pupils of Low Attainment, 1974; *contrib*. Durham Res. Rev., Educnl Res., Brit. Jl Educnl Studies, Irish Jl of Educn. *Address*: Centre for Studies in Science Education, The Univ., Leeds LS2 9JT.

Jenkins, Frank Illtyd, MA; Senior Lecturer in Architecture, University of Manchester, since 1964; *b* 1925. BArch Durham 1951, MA Durham 1953, MS (Arch.) Illinois 1955; Registered Architect 1951, ARIBA 1952–69. Lectr, Univ. of Manchester, 1956–64; Vis. Prof., Univ. of California, Berkeley, 1960–61; Vis. Prof., Univ. of Toronto, 1962. Editor, Archit. Hist., 1962–67; Chm., Soc. Archit. Hist. GB, 1967–73. *Publications*: Architect and Patron, 1961; contrib. Fletcher: History of Architecture on the Comparative Method, 17th edn, ed R. A. Cordingley, 1961, 18th edn. ed J. Palmes, 1974; Victorian Architecture, ed P. Ferriday, 1962; Concerning Architecture, ed J. Summerson, 1968; *contrib.* Archit. Hist., Archit. Rev., Country Life, Jl Soc. Archit. Hist., RIBA Jl. *Address*: School of Architecture, Univ. of Manchester, Manchester M13 9PL.

Jenkins, Dr Howell, MA, DUP; Lecturer, Department of French, University College, Cardiff, since 1960; *b* 1932. BA Wales 1953, MA Wales 1955, DUP 1957. *Address*: Univ. College, Cathays Park, Cardiff CF1 1XL.

Jenkins, Dr John Jestyn, BA, PhD; Lecturer in Philosophy, University of Edinburgh, since 1964; *b* 1937; *m* 1961; two *s* one *d*. BA Wales 1959 (1st cl. Philosophy); PhD Edinburgh 1965. Asst Lectr, Edinburgh, 1961–64. *Publications*: *contrib.* Brit. Jl Aesthet., Mind, Philos., Philos. Jl, Philos. Qly. *Address*: David Hume Tower, George Square, Edinburgh EH8 9JX.

Jenkins, Nicholas; Tutor in Graphic Design, Royal College of Art; *b* 1939; *m* 1959; two *d*. Fellow, RCA, 1972. *Publications*: Photographics, 1973; *contrib.* Penrose Ann., Design Mag. *Address*: Royal College of Art, Kensington Gore, SW7 2EU.

Jenkins, William Edward, BA; Senior Tutor in Industrial Relations, Department of Extra-Mural Studies, University College of Swansea, since 1971; *b* 1923; *m* 1950; two 2 one *d*. BA Wales 1953 (Economics and Political Science). Tutor Organiser, WEA, 1953–61; Extra-Mural Tutor in Economics and Industrial Relations, Univ. Coll. of Swansea, 1962–71; Tutor, Internat. Inst. for Labour Studies, Geneva, 1963. Pt-time Indust. Relat. Advr, Nat. Bd Prices and Incomes, 1967–70; Trade Union Educn Adv. Govt of Guyana, 1970; Mem., Council and Exec. Cttee, Coleg Harlech, 1962– . *Publications*: *contrib.* Industrial Relations in Britain, ed W. E. J. McCarthy, 1969. *Address*: Dept of Extra-Mural Studies, Univ. College of Swansea, Berwick House, 6 Uplands Terrace, Swansea.

Jenkins, Dr William Ieuan; Lecturer in Interdisciplinary Studies, University of Kent, since 1971; *b* 1941. BSc Hons London 1963, ARCS 1963, PhD London 1966, DIC 1966. Res. Associate, Dept of Social Sciences, Loughborough Univ. of Technol., 1967–71. Mem., Political Studies Assoc., UK. *Publications*: ed (with others), Social Sciences and Government, 1972; *contrib.* Public Admin. Bull., Social Science Information. *Address*: Darwin Coll., The Univ., Canterbury, Kent.

Jenkinson, Dr David Edward, BA, PhD; Senior Lecturer in German, University of London, Goldsmiths' College, since 1971; *b* 1938; *m* 1958; two *s* two *d*. BA London 1963 (1st cl. German), PhD London 1969. Lectr in German, Goldsmiths' Coll., 1966–71. *Publications*: ed, Christa Wolf: Der geteilte Himmel, 1975; *contrib.* Germ. Life Lett., Mod. Lang., New Germ. Studies. *Address*: Dept of German, Goldsmiths' College, New Cross, SE14 6NW.

356

Jenkinson, John M. M.; Lecturer (part-time), Department of Architecture, University of Sheffield, since 1960; *b* 1917; *m* 1946; one *s* one *d*. MA 1940; FRIBA 1949. *Address*: Dept of Architecture, Arts Tower, Univ. of Sheffield, Sheffield S10 2TN.

Jenkinson, John Richard; Lecturer, Classics Department, University of Hull, since 1967; *b* 1937; *m* 1963; three *d*. BA Oxford 1961 (Hon. Mods and Greats – Classics); CertEd Bristol 1962; BPhil (Classics) Oxford 1965. Asst Lectr in Classics, Hull, 1965–67. *Publications*: Interpretations of Persius Satires III and IV, in, Latomus (forthcoming); Sarcasm in Lucan I 33–66, in, Classical Review (forthcoming). *Address*: Classics Dept, The Univ., Hull HU6 7RX.

Jenner, William John Francis; Lecturer in Chinese Studies, University of Leeds, since 1966; *b* 1940; *m* 1961; 1971; two *d*. BA Oxon 1962 (1st cl. Chinese). Asst Lectr in Chinese, Univ. of Leeds, 1965–66. *Publications*: Lin Piao: a documentary study (forthcoming); trans., Aisin-Gioro P'u Yi: From Emperor to Citizen, vol. 1 1964, vol. 2 1965; ed and trans. (with G. Yang), Modern Chinese Stories, 1970; trans., Jean Esmein: The Chinese Cultural Revolution, 1973; *contrib.* Mod. Asian Studies. *Address*: Dept of Chinese Studies, Univ. of Leeds, Leeds LS2 9JT.

Jennings, Bernard, BA, MA; Senior Lecturer in History and Head of the Liberal Studies Division, Department of Adult Education and Extra-Mural Studies, University of Leeds, since 1969; *b* 1928; *m* 1950; two *s* two *d*. BA London 1948, MA Leeds 1959. Lectr, Dept of Adult Education and Extra-Mural Studies, Leeds Univ., 1961–69. Mem. Council, Yorks Archaeol. Soc., 1968– ; Co Cllr, N Riding Yorks, 1955–61. *Publications*: The Grey Friars of Richmond, 1958; (with A. Raistrick) The Lead Mining Industry of the Pennines, 1965; ed, History of Nidderdale, 1967; ed, History of Harrogate and Knaresborough, 1970; The Teaching of Local History, in, University Studies for Adults (ed A. Parker and S. G. Raybould), 1972; The Wells and Springs of Harrogate, 1974; *contrib.* Adult Educn, Victorian Studies. *Address*: Dept of Adult Education and Extra-Mural Studies, The Univ., Leeds LS2 9JT.

Jennings, Prof. Robert Yewdall, QC; Whewell Professor of International Law, University of Cambridge, since 1955; *b* 1913; *m* 1955; one *s* two *d*. BA Cantab 1935, MA Cantab 1937, LLB Cantab 1936; Whewell Schol. in Internat. Law 1936. Barrister-at-Law of Lincoln's Inn, Hon. Bencher 1970; QC 1969. Asst Lectr in Law, LSE, 1938–39; Fellow, Jesus Coll., Cambridge, 1939– ; Sen. Tutor, Jesus Coll., 1948–55; Univ. Lectr in Law, Cambridge Univ., 1946–55. Mem. Council, Brit. Inst. Internat. and Compar. Law, 1971– ; Mem., Inst. Droit Internat.; Jt Editor (with H. Waldock), Brit. Ybk Internat. Law. *Publications*: The Acquisition of Territory in International Law, 1963; General Course on the Principles of International Law, 1967;

contrib. articles in legal jls. *Address*: Jesus College, Cambridge.

Jephcott, Dr Edmund Francis Neville, PhD; Lecturer in German, School of European Studies, University of Sussex, since 1965; *b* 1938; *m* 1966; two *s* one *d*. BA Cantab 1961 (1st cl. Mod. Langs), MA Cantab 1964, PhD Cantab 1968. Lektor in English, Univ. of Münster, Germany, 1964–65; Asst Lectr in German, Univ. of Sussex, 1965–67. *Publications*: Proust and Rilke: The Literature of Expanded Consciousness, 1972; trans., Theodor W. Adorno: Minima Moralia, 1974. *Address*: Arts Building, Univ. of Sussex, Falmer, Brighton, Sussex BN1 9QN.

Jerman, James Auguste; Lecturer in Education, School of Education, University of Leicester, since 1964; *b* 1920; *m* 1946; one *s* one *d*. BA Oxon 1947 (2nd cl. French), MA Oxon 1954, DipEd Oxon 1948; Mem., Mod. Lang. Assoc., A-V Lang. Assoc. Asst Master, Royal Grammar Sch., Lancaster, 1949–55; Hd of Mod. Langs, Priory Sch., Shrewsbury, 1955–64. Teacher Fellow, Univ. of Keele, 1964. *Publications*: Essays, in, Guide to Modern Language Teaching Methods, ed Dutton, 1965; Aspects of Education No 6 (Hull Inst. of Educn), 1967; Disciplines of the Curriculum, ed Whitfield, 1971; *contrib.* Mod. Langs. *Address*: School of Education, Univ. of Leicester, Leicester LE1 7RH.

Jervis, Margaret Elliot, MA; Senior Lecturer in Education, University of Bristol, since 1969; *b* 1923. BA Cantab 1945 (Classical Tripos), DipEd Bristol 1946, MA Cantab 1949, Cert in Theology, Cambridge 1958. Lectr, Bristol Univ., 1956–69. *Publications*: (with B. R. Rees) Lampas: a new approach to Greek, 1970. *Address*: School of Education, 35 Berkeley Square, Bristol BS8 1JA.

Jessup, Frank William, CBE, MA, LLB; Director, Department for External Studies, Oxford University, since 1952; *b* 1909; *m* 1935; two *s* one *d*. BA London 1931, LLB London 1935, MA Oxford 1952; Barrister-at-Law 1935. FSA. Chm., Libr. Adv. Council (England), 1965–73; Hon. Sec., Univs Council for Adult Educn, 1969–73; Chm., Govs, Rose Bruford Coll. Speech and Drama, 1960–72. *Publications*: Local Government: current problems, 1948; (with R. F. Jessup) The Cinque Ports, 1952; Introduction to Kent Feet of Fines, 1956; A History of Kent, 1958, new edn 1974; Sir Roger Twysden, 1597–1672, 1965; Kent History Illustrated, 1966, new edn 1974; *contrib.* Archaeol. Cant. *Address*: Rewley House, Oxford.

Jevons, Prof. Frederic Raphael, MA, PhD, DSc; Professor of Liberal Studies in Science, University of Manchester, since 1966; *b* 1929; *m* 1956; two *s*. BA Cambridge 1950 (1st cl. Biochemistry), MA Cambridge 1953, PhD Cambridge 1953, DSc Manchester 1966. Fellow, King's Coll., Cambridge, 1953–59; Univ. Demonstrator, Cambridge, 1956–59; Lectr, Manchester, 1959–66. Mem., Jt Matric. Bd, 1969– ; Governor, Langley Sch., 1968–73; Mem., Adv. Bd, R and D

Mngmt, 1970– . *Publications*: The Biochemical Approach to Life, 1964, 2nd edn 1968; The Teaching of Science, 1969; Science Observed, 1973; ed jtly, University Perspectives, 1970; (jtly) Wealth from Knowledge, 1972; ed jtly, What Kinds of Graduates do we Need?, 1972. *Address*: Dept of Liberal Studies in Science, The Univ., Manchester M13 9PL.

Jewell, Charles Andrew; Senior Lecturer, Department of Agricultural Economics and Management, University of Reading, since 1964; *b* 1918; *m* 1951; two *s* one *d*. BSc (Agric.) Reading 1949. Associate Dir, Inst. of Agricl Hist. and Keeper, Mus. of English Rural Life, Univ. of Reading, 1958–64. *Address*: Museum of English Rural Life, Whiteknights, Reading RG6 2AG.

Jewell, Dr Helen Mary; Lecturer, Department of Mediæval History, University of Liverpool, since 1968; *b* 1943. BA Oxford 1965 (2nd cl. Hons Mod. Hist.), PhD Leeds 1968, MA Oxford 1969; Member: Hist. Assoc., Conservation Soc. Asst Lectr, Univ. of Liverpool, 1968–69. *Publication*: English Local Administration in the Middle Ages, 1972. *Address*: Sch. of History, Univ. of Liverpool, 8 Abercromby Square, PO Box 147, Liverpool L69 3BX.

Jillings, Lewis George; Lecturer, Department of German, University of Stirling, since 1968; *b* 1942; *m* 1966. MA Auckland, NZ 1964 (1st cl. Hons). *Address*: Dept of German, Univ. of Stirling, Stirling FK9 4LA.

Jimack, Prof. Peter David, PhD; Professor of French, University of Stirling, since 1972; *b* 1930; *m* 1953; one *s* three *d*. BA London 1951 (1st cl. French), PhD Southampton 1957. Asst Lectr, Birmingham Univ., 1959–61, Lectr, Birmingham Univ., 1961–66, Sen. Lectr, Birmingham Univ., 1966–72. *Publications*: La Genèse et la Rédaction de l'*Emile* de J.-J. Rousseau, 1960; *contrib.* French Studies, Romanic Rev., Studies on Voltaire and 18th Century. *Address*: Dept of French, Univ. of Stirling, Stirling FK9 4LA.

Jobling, Raymond George, BA, MA; University Lecturer in Sociology, and Fellow of St John's College, Cambridge, since 1968; *b* 1941; *m* 1965; one *s*. BA Liverpool 1963 (1st cl. Special Hons Social Science), MA Cantab 1965. Asst Lectr, then Lectr in Sociology, Univ. of E Anglia, 1965–68; Vis. Asst Prof. of Educnl Sociology, Univ. of British Columbia, 1967–68. *Address*: St John's College, Cambridge.

Jocelyn, Dr Henry David; Hulme Professor of Latin, University of Manchester, since 1973; *b* 1933; *m* 1958; two *s*. BA Sydney 1955, BA Cantab 1957, MA 1961, PhD 1963; Fellow, Australian Acad. of the Humanities, 1970. University of Sydney: Teaching Fellow in Latin, 1955; Lectr in Latin, 1960–64; Sen. Lectr in Latin, 1964–66; Reader in Latin, 1966–70; Prof. of Latin, 1970–73; Vis. Lectr in Classics, Yale Univ., 1967; *Publications*: The Tragedies of Ennius, 1967 (corrected repr. 1969); (with B. P. Setchell)

357

Regnier de Graaf on the Human Reproductive Organs, 1972; (with others) Entretiens sur Ennius, 1972; contrib to H. Temporini, ed, Aufstieg und Niedergang der römischen Welt, 1971– ; *contrib.* Antichthon, Class. Qly, Class. Rev., Gnomon, Harvard Studies in Class. Philol., Jl Religious Hist., L'Antiquité Classique, Latomus, Mnemosyne, Proc. Cambridge Philol Soc., Rivista di Filologia ed Istruzione Classica, Yale Class. Studies. *Address:* Dept of Latin, Univ. of Manchester, Manchester M13 9PL.

John, Dr Brian Stephen, MA, DPhil; Lecturer in Geography, University of Durham, since 1966; *b* 1940; *m* 1967; two *s.* BA Oxon 1962, MA DPhil Oxon 1966; FRGS, Mem., Inst. Brit. Geogrs, Glaciol Soc. Geomorphologist, Brit. Antarctic Survey, 1965–66. Royal Soc. European Fellowship, Stockholm Univ., 1973–74. *Publications:* The Fishguard and Pembroke Area, 1972; The Pembrokeshire Landscape, 1973; *contrib.* Antiqu., Brit. Antarctic Survey Bull., Geog. Ann., Geog. Jl, Geog. Mag., Geol. Mijnbouw, Geol. Mag., Jl Glaciol., Nature, Nature in Wales, Trans Inst. Brit. Geogrs. *Address:* Dept of Geography, Science Laboratories, South Road, Durham DH1 3LE.

John, Ieuan Gwilym; Senior Lecturer, Department of International Politics, University College of Wales, Aberystwyth, since 1964; *b* 1915; *m* 1945; three *d.* BA Wales 1937, MSc Econ London 1939; Asst Lectr in International Politics, UCW Aberystwyth, 1946–47; Lectr, 1947–64. Sub Dean, Faculty of Economic and Social Studies, 1964–67. *Publications:* Aberystwyth Papers: international politics 1939–69, ed B. Porter, 1972; *contrib.* Political Studies. *Address:* Dept of International Politics, Univ. Coll. of Wales, Llandinam Building, Penglais, Aberystwyth.

John, S. Beynon, MA; Reader in French Literature, University of Sussex, since 1967; *b* 1923; *m* 1948; two *s.* BA Wales 1948 (1st cl. French), MA Wales 1958. Mem., Soc. Fr. Studies. Organising Tutor WEA (Tyneside), 1948–51; Asst Lectr, LSE, 1951–54, Lectr, 1954–61; Lectr, Sussex Univ., 1961–63, Sen. Lectr, 1963–67; Vis. Sen. Prof. of French, Univ. of W Ontario, 1965–66. Royal Corps of Signals, 1942–45. *Publications:* contrib. Cassell's New French Dictionary, 1962; French Literature and its Background, vols iv–vi, 1969–70; Penguin Companion to Literature: Europe, 1969; Sartre: Vision and Conscience (forthcoming); *contrib.* Fr. Studies, Kontyn., Mod. Lang., Mod. Lang. Qly, Univ. Toronto Qly. *Address:* School of European Studies, Univ. of Sussex, Falmer, Brighton.

John, Stuart Griffith, MA; Senior Lecturer in French, Department of Romance Studies, University College of Wales, Aberystwyth, since 1971; *b* 1931; *m* 1959; two *s* one *d.* BA Wales 1953, DipEd Wales 1954, MA Wales 1956; Nathan Fellow, Brit. Inst. Paris, 1966. Admin. Asst, Univ. Coll. of Wales, Aberystwyth, 1958–59, Asst Lectr in French, 1959–61, Lectr in French, 1961–71; Vis. Prof., Univ. of Waikato, NZ, 1966. Chief Examiner in French, A-level, Welsh Jt Educn Cttee, 1969– . *Address:* Dept of Romance Studies,

Univ. College of Wales, Aberystywth, Cardiganshire SY23 2AX.

Johns, Ewart M.; Head of Department of Art and Environment, University of Lancaster, since 1972, *b* 1923; *m* 1949; three *s* one *d.* MA Cantab 1950; DipEd London 1948. Lectr, Univ. of Exeter, 1950–65, Sen. Lectr, 1965–72; Vis. Prof., Oklahoma State Univ., USA, 1969–70. Exhibitions of paintings: London, 1961, 1963; Exeter, 1957, 1967. *Publications:* British Townscapes, 1965; *contrib.* Area, Geog., Studio, Town and Country Planning. *Address:* Dept of Art and Environment, Univ. of Lancaster, Bailrigg, Lancaster LA1 4YW.

Johns, Dr Richard Anthony; Lecturer in International Economics, Department of Economics, Keele University, since 1966; *b* 1940. BSc(Econ) Southampton 1963 (2nd cl.), PhD Southampton 1968 (Social Science). *Address:* Dept of Economics, Keele Univ., Keele ST5 5BG.

Johnson, Alastair B.; *see* Bissett-Johnson.

Johnson, Colin Arthur, MA; Lecturer in Russian Studies, University of Leeds, since 1961; *b* 1936; *m* 1969; two *s* one *d.* BA Oxon 1959 (II Mod. Langs), MA Oxon 1960; BUAS. Asst Lectr, Leeds Univ., 1961–63. Sec., NE Region, GB-USSR Assoc. *Publications:* contrib. Yrs Wk in Mod. Lang. Studies, Yrs Wk in Engl. Lang. and Lit. *Address:* Dept of Russian Studies, The Univ., Leeds LS2 9JT.

Johnson, Prof. David Hugh Nevil, MA, LLB; Professor of International and Air Law, University of London, since 1960; *b* 1920; *m* 1952. BA Cantab 1942 (1st cl. History), MA Cantab 1947, LLB Cantab 1948 (1st cl.). Called to Bar, Lincoln's Inn 1950. Special Lectr in Internat. Law, LSE, 1949–50; University of London: Reader in Internat. Law, 1953–59; Reader in Internat. and Air Law, 1959–60; Dean of Faculty of Laws, 1968–72. Asst Legal Advr, Foreign Off., 1950–53; Sen. Legal Offr, UN Secretariat, 1956–57; Registrar, Ct of Arbitratn, Argentine–Chile Frontier Case, 1965–67. Companion, RAeS. *Publications:* Rights in Air Space, 1965; *contrib.* Aeronaut. Jl, Brit. Ybk Internat. Law, Trans Grotius Soc., Internat. Comp. Law Qly, Internat. Relat., Mod. Law Rev., Nord. Tids. Internat. Ret, Zeits. Ausländ, Öffent. Recht Völkerrecht, Netherlands Ybk Internat. Law. *Address:* London School of Economics and Political Science, Houghton Street, Aldwych, WC2A 2AE.

Johnson, David Stuart; Lecturer in History, New University of Ulster, since 1968; *b* 1943; *m* 1964; two *s.* BA Oxon 1965 (Hist.), BPhil 1968 (Econ). *Publications:* The Interwar Economy in Western Europe, 1973. *Address:* Sch. of Humanities, New Univ. of Ulster, Coleraine, Co. Londonderry BT52 1SA.

Johnson, Prof. Douglas William John; Professor of French History, University College, London, since 1968; *b* 1925; *m* 1950; one *d.* BA Oxon 1946, BLitt Oxon 1947;

FRHistS. Univ. of Birmingham: Asst Lectr, 1949; Lectr, 1952; Sen. Lectr, 1962; Prof. of Modern History, 1963; Chm. Sch. of History, 1965; Chm. Bd of Examnrs in History, London Univ., 1972. *Publications*: Guizot: Aspects of French History 1787–1874, 1963; France and the Dreyfus Affair, 1965; France, 1969; The French Revolution, 1970; A Concise History of France, 1971; ed, The Making of the Modern World, vol. I, 1971, vol. II, 1973; France: a companion to French studies, 1972; *contrib.* History, Internat. Affairs, New Society. *Address*: Univ. College, Gower Street, WC1E 6BT.

Johnson, Edwin Colin, BA, FCA; Senior Lecturer in Accounting, Department of Economics and Commerce, University of Hull, since 1970; *b* 1938; *m* 1962; two *d*. BA London 1959 (2nd cl.); ACA 1962, FCA 1973. Lectr, Univ. of Sheffield, 1964–70. *Publications*: (with G. Fridman and I. Hicks) Bankruptcy Law and Accounts, 1970; *contrib.* Acntnt. *Address*: Dept of Economics and Commerce, The Univ., Hull HU6 7RX.

Johnson, Frank; Senior Lecturer in Communication Media, Department of Education, University of Aston in Birmingham, since 1968, and Head of University's Communication Media Unit; *b* 1914; *m* 1937; three *s* one *d*. BA Oxon 1937, Certif Educn Leeds 1958 (Distinction). Audio-Visual Supervisor, Univ. of Leeds Television Service, 1965–68. Chm., Midland Univs Cttee on Audio-Visual Aids, 1973–75. *Publications*: Chapter in, University Teaching in Transition, ed David Layton, 1968; *contrib.* Brit. Jl Educnl Technology. *Address*: Communication Media, Univ. of Aston in Birmingham, Gosta Green, Birmingham B4 7ET.

Johnson, Gordon, MA, PhD; Fellow, Trinity College, since 1966, and Lecturer in the History of South Asia, Faculty of Oriental Studies, University of Cambridge, since 1974; *b* 1943. BA Cantab 1964 (1st cl. Historical Tripos), MA, PhD Cantab 1968. Res. Asst, Centre of S Asian Studies, Cambridge, 1968–69; Univ. Asst Lectr, Cambridge, 1969–74; Sec., Faculty Bd of Oriental Studies, Univ. of Cambridge, 1971– ; Editor, Modern Asian Studies, 1971– . Thirlwall Prize and Seeley Medal, 1969. *Publications*: chapter in Elites in South Asia, ed E. R. Leach and S. N. Mukherjee, 1970; chapter in Locality, Province and Nation: essays on Indian politics 1870–1940, 1973; Provincial Politics and Indian Nationalism: Bombay and the Indian National Congress 1880–1915, 1973. *Address*: Trinity College, Cambridge CB2 1TQ.

Johnson, Prof. James Henry, MA, PhD; Professor of Geography, University of Lancaster, since 1974; *b* 1930; *m* 1956; two *s* two *d*. BA Belfast 1953, MA Wisconsin 1954, PhD London 1961; FRGS. Mem., Inst. Brit. Geogrs, Econ. Hist. Soc., Reg. Studies Assoc., etc. Whitbeck Fellow, Univ. of Wisconsin, 1953–54; Asst Lectr, Univ. Coll., London, 1954–57, Lectr, 1957–65; Vis. Prof., Univ. of Minnesota, 1969. Dept Tutor, Univ. Coll., London, 1965–70; Reader in Geography, Univ. of London, at UCL, 1965–74. *Publications*: Urban Geography, 1967; ed (with R. U. Cooke), Trends in Geography, 1969; ed, Suburban Growth: geographical processes at the edge of the western city, 1974; (with J. Salt and P. Wood) Housing and the Migration of Labour in England and Wales, 1974; *contrib.* Econ. Geog., Econ. Hist. Rev., Geog. Ann., Geog. Forum, Geog. Jl, Geog. Polon., Geog. Rev., Irish Geog., Proc. Royal Irish Acad , Studia Hiber., Trans Inst. Brit. Geogrs, Ulster Folklife, Ulster Jl Archaeol., *Address*: Dept of Geography, Univ. of Lancaster. Bailrigg, Lancaster LA1 4YW.

Johnson, Dr (J.) Richard B.; Senior Lecturer in Social History, Centre for Contemporary Cultural Studies, Faculty of Arts, University of Birmingham, since 1974; *b* 1939; *m* 1963; one *d*. BA 1963 (History), PhD 1968, Cantab. Lectr, Dept of Econ. and Social Hist., Univ. of Birmingham, 1966–73, Sen. Lectr, 1973–74. Mem., Working Party on Broadening of Educn, Univ. of Birmingham, 1969–73. *Publications*: contrib. Studies in the Growth of Nineteenth Century Government, ed G. Sutherland, 1972; contrib. The Victorian Revolution, ed P. Stansky, 1973; *contrib.* Past and Present. *Address*: Centre for Contemporary Cultural Studies, Faculty of Arts, Univ. of Birmingham, Edgbaston, Birmingham B15 2TT.

Johnson, (John) Simon (Bird); Lecturer, School of Education, University of Reading, since 1964; *b* 1934; *m* 1959; two *s* one *d*. BA Dunelm 1957 (2nd cl. Music), ARCM 1956 (piano performers), ARCO 1960. Dir, Reading Bach Choir. *Address*: The School of Education, The Univ., London Road, Reading.

Johnson, Malcolm Lewis; Lecturer in Sociology, Nuffield Centre for Health Services Studies, and Associate Lecturer, Department of Social Studies, University of Leeds, since 1969; *b* 1943; *m* 1966; one *s*. BA Leicester 1964, DSAS Oxford 1966. Asst Res. Offr, Dept of Sociology, Social Res. Unit, Bedford Coll., Univ. of London, 1966–69. Convener, Brit. Sociol Assoc., Med. Sociology Gp; Mem. Nat. Exec., Age Concern. *Publications*: comp. and ed, Medical Sociology Register of Research and Teaching, 1974; *contrib.* Brit. Jl Med. Educn, Commun. Med., Brit. Jl Prev. Soc. Med., Sociol Rev., Nursing Times, Jl Soc. Policy, Soc. Sci. and Med., Brit. Jl. Sociol. *Address*: Nuffield Centre for Health Services Studies, Univ. of Leeds, Clarendon Road, Leeds LS2 9PL.

Johnson, Michael John, MA; Lecturer in German and Teutonic Philology, and Lecturer in Modern European Literature, University College of North Wales, Bangor, since 1965; *b* 1939. BA Wales 1963 (1st cl. German), MA Wales 1970. Universitätslektor, Univ. of Tübingen, 1963–65. Cttee Mem., Genootschap Nederland-Engeland, 1970– . *Address*: Dept of German and Teutonic Philology and of Russian, Univ. College, Bangor LL57 2DG.

Johnson, Nevil; Nuffield Reader in the Comparative Study of Institutions, University

359

of Oxford, since 1969; *b* 1929; *m* 1957; two *s*. BA Oxon 1952 (PPE), MA Oxon 1962. Admin. Civil Service, Min. of Supply, Min. of Housing and Local Govt, 1952–62; Lectr in Politics, Univ. of Nottingham, 1962–66; Sen. Lectr in Politics, Univ. of Warwick, 1966–69; Vis. Prof., Univ. of Bochum, 1968–69. Mem., Exec. Council, Royal Inst. Public Admin, 1964– ; Hon. Editor, Public Admin, 1967– . *Publications*: Parliament and Administration: The Estimates Committee 1945–65, 1966; Government in the Federal Republic of Germany, 1973; contrib. Specialists and Generalists, 1968; *contrib*. Döv (W Germ.), Parly Aff., Public Admin. *Address*: Nuffield College, Oxford.

Johnson, Richard; *see* Johnson, J. R. B.

Johnson, Dr Richard Hugh; Senior Lecturer, Department of Geography, University of Manchester, since 1954; *b* 1926; *m* 1958; one *s* one *d*. BA Reading 1951, MA Sheffield 1954, PhD Manchester 1966; DipEd Reading 1952. Dep. Dir of General Studies, Fac. of Arts, Manchester, 1970. Mem., Council, Manchester Geol Assoc.; Manchester Br., Geog. Assoc. *Publications*: *contrib*. Geog., New Phytol., Proc. Geol. Assoc., Proc. Yorks Geol. Soc., Trans Inst. Brit. Geogrs. *Address*: Dept of Geography, Univ. of Manchester, Manchester M13 9PL.

Johnson, Dr R(obert) Sherlaw; Lecturer in Music, University of Oxford, since 1970; Fellow, Worcester College, Oxford, since 1970; *b* 1932; *m* 1959; two *s* two *d*. BA Dunelm 1953, BMus Dunelm 1959, MA Oxon 1970, DMus Leeds 1971; ARCM 1951, LRAM 1952, ARAM 1968. Member: Composers Guild; ISM; AUT. Asst Lectr in Music, Univ. of Leeds, 1961–63; Lectr in Music, Univ. of York, 1965–70. Mem., Cttee, Central Music Libr. Ltd, London. *Publications*: Music: Sonata No 1 for Piano, 1963 (recorded), Veni sancte Spiritus for SATB and percussion, 1965; Sedit Angelus for SATB, 1965; Sonata No 2 for Piano, 1967 (recorded); Congregational Mass, 1967; Resurrection of Fêng-Huang for SATB, 1968; Seven Short Piano Pieces, 1968 (recorded); Praises of Heaven and Earth for soprano, piano and tape, 1969; Incarnatio for SATB, 1971 (recorded); Green Whispers of Gold, for sopr., piano and tape, 1971 (recorded); Carmina Vernalia, 1972; Festival Mass, 1973; Books: Olivier Messiaen (forthcoming); *other recordings*: Works by O. Messiaen: 'Harawi', Chants de terre et de ciel, Poèmes pour Mi, Catalogue d'Oiseaux, etc. *Address*: Worcester College, Oxford.

Johnson, Rosemary Anne; Lecturer, Department of Sociology, University of Edinburgh, since 1964; *b* 1928. BA Cantab 1951, MA Cantab 1953 (Classical Tripos, Natural Sciences Tripos Pt II 1960), DipSoc Studies LSE 1952. Associate Mem., Inst. Almoners, 1953. Res. Asst, Social Sciences Res. Centre, Univ. of Edinburgh, 1960–64. *Address*: Dept of Sociology, Adam Ferguson Building, George Square, Edinburgh EH8 9LL.

Johnson, Simon; *see* Johnson, J. S. B.

Johnson, Terence James, BA; Lecturer, University of Leicester, since 1972; *b* 1934; *m* 1968; one *s*. BA Leicester 1963 (1st cl. Sociology). Asst Lectr, Univ. of Ghana, 1963–64; Asst Lectr, Univ. of Leicester, 1964–65, Lectr, 1965–69; Res. Fellow, Inst. of Commonwealth Studies, Univ. of London, 1969–72. *Publications*: Professions and Power, 1972; *contrib*. Internat. Soc. Sci. Jl, Sociol. Educn, Sociol. Rev. *Address*: The Univ., Leicester SE1 7RH.

Johnson-Laird, Dr Philip Nicholas; Reader in Experimental Psychology, University of Sussex, since 1973; *b* 1936; *m* 1959; one *s* one *d*. BA Hons London 1964 (Psychol.), PhD London 1967; Member: BPsS; Linguistics Assoc.; Exptl Psychol. Soc. Department of Psychology, UCL: Asst Lectr, 1966–67; Lectr, 1967–73. *Publications*: ed (with P. C. Wason): Thinking and Reasoning, 1968; The Psychology of Reasoning, 1972; (with G. A. Miller) Perception and Language (forthcoming); *contrib*. Brit. Jl Psychol., Cognitive Psychol., Nature, Qly Jl Exptl Psychol. *Address*: Laboratory of Experimental Psychology, Univ. of Sussex, Falmer, Brighton BN1 9QY.

Johnston, Prof. Arthur, MA, DPhil; Professor of English, University College of Wales, Aberystwyth, since 1965; *b* 1924; *m* 1951; two *s* two *d*. BA Oxon 1949 (1st cl. English), MA Oxon 1949, DPhil Oxon 1956. Lectr, Bedford Coll., London, 1951–54; Lectr, Birkbeck Coll., London, 1954–65. *Publications*: Enchanted Ground, 1964; ed, Hazlitt: Lectures on the English Comic Writers, 1965; ed, Bacon: Selections, 1965; Thomas Gray and The Bard, 1966; ed, Poems of Gray and Collins, 1967; The Magus and the Monkey, 1971; ed, Bacon: Advancement of Learning, and New Atlantis, 1974; *contrib*. Mod. Lang. Rev., Rev. Engl. Studies, Shakesp. Qly. *Address*: Dept of English, Univ. College of Wales, Aberystwyth SY23 2AX.

Johnston, Dr Charlotte Stephanie, MA; Lecturer in Philosophy, University College of Wales, Aberystwyth, since 1966; *b* 1925; *m* 1951; two *s* two *d*. BA Wales 1946 (1st cl. English), BA Wales 1947 (1st cl. Philosophy), MA Wales 1949, DPhil Oxon 1956. *Publications*: *contrib*. Efryd. Athron., Jl Hist. Ideas, Mind, Rev. Internat. Philos. *Address*: Philosophy Dept, Univ. College of Wales, Aberystwyth SY23 2AX.

Johnston, David Edward, MA; Staff Tutor in Archaeology, Department of Extra-Mural Studies, Southampton University, since 1967; *b* 1934; *m* 1961; two *d*. BA Cantab 1958, MA Cantab 1961, CertEd Cantab 1959. Sec., Standing Conf. of Tutors in Arch.; Mem. Soc. for Prom. Roman Studies, Prehistoric Soc.; Mem.: Research Cttee on Ancient Agriculture; Assoc. pour l'étude de la Mosaique ancienne (Paris), etc. *Publications*: *contrib*. Antiquaries Jl, Britannia, Didaskalos, etc. *Address*: Dept of Extra-Mural Studies, The Univ., Southampton SO9 5NH.

Johnston, David J., BA, FCP; Part-time Lecturer, Bristol University School of

Education, and part-time Counsellor Open University, since 1973; *b* 1913; *m* 1940; one *s* one *d*. Teacher's Cert. London 1933, BA London 1934, AdvCertEd 1934, FCP 1963. Oxford Univ. Extra-Mural Delegacy, 1946–48; London Univ. Extra-Mural Dept, 1948–55; Adviser to Teachers, Inst. of Educn, Univ. of London, 1955–73. Mem.: Nat. Adv. Council for Training and Recruitment of Teachers, 1955–63; Governing Body, Brit. Film Inst., 1956–65; Adv. Cttee on A-V Aids in Higher Technol Educn, 1961–63; Sec./Treasr, Internat. Council on Educn for Teaching (ICET), 1954–68 (Pres., 1968–72). *Publications*: Talking Sense, Bk I 1954, Bk II 1956, Bk III 1957; School Teaching, 1960; Teachers In-Service Education, 1971; *contrib*. Brit. Jl Educnl Studies, Educn Today, Higher Educn Jl. *Address*: Bristol Univ. Sch. of Education, Berkeley Square, Bristol.

Johnston, Dr Edith Mary; Senior Lecturer in History, University of Sheffield, since 1965. MA St Andrews (ord. 1951, Hons 1953), DipEd Belfast 1952, PhD St Andrews 1956; FRHistS. Asst Lectr, Univ. of Sheffield, 1956–58, Lectr, 1958–65; Fulbright Schol. and Land-Grant Centennial Lectr, Univ. of Delaware, 1961–62; Fulbright Schol. and Vis. Lectr, Univ. of Michigan, 1962–63; Summer Sch. Lectr, McMaster Univ., 1961, 1964; Summer Sch. Lectr, Queen's Univ., Kingston, 1963; Summer Sch. Prof., Univ. of Alberta, 1968. Dep. Warden, Ranmoor Hse, Univ. of Sheffield, 1968–69; Warden, Tapton, 1969–71. *Publications*: Great Britain and Ireland, 1760–1800, 1963; A Select Bibliography of Irish History, 1968, rev. edn 1971; Ireland in the Eighteenth Century, 1974; *contrib*. Irish Hist. Studies, Proc. Royal Irish Acad. *Address*: Dept of History, The Univ., Sheffield S10 2TN.

Johnston, Prof. Ronald John; Professor of Geography, University of Sheffield, since 1974; *b* 1941; *m* 1963; one *s* one *d*. BA Manchester 1962 (Hons II i), MA 1964, PhD Monash 1967; Member: Assoc. of Amer. Geographers; Inst. of Australian Geographers; Inst. of British Geographers; NZ Geographical Soc. Teaching Fellow, Monash Univ., 1964–65; Sen. Teaching Fellow, 1965–66; Lectr, 1966–67; Lectr, Univ. of Canterbury, 1967–68; Sen. Lectr, 1969–72; Reader, 1973–74. Editor, NZ Geographer, 1969–74. *Publications*: Urban Residential Patterns, 1971; ed, Urbanisation in New Zealand: Geographical Essays, 1973; Spatial Structures, 1973; ed, Society and Environment: A Geography of New Zealand, 1974; ed, Proceedings, Sixth New Zealand Geography Conference, 1971; ed, Geography and Education, 1971; *contrib*. Ann. Assoc. Amer. Geogr., Econ. Geogr., Geogr. Ann., Geogr. Anal., NZ Geogr., Austral. Geogr., Tijds. Econ. Soc. Geogr., Envir. Plann., Trans IBG, Pac. View., Urban Studs., Austral. Geogr. Stud. *Address*: Dept of Geography, Univ. of Sheffield, Sheffield S10 2TN.

Johnston, Thomas Hamilton, MA, BMus, LRAM; Principal Lecturer in Music, College of Education, Aberdeen, and part-time Lecturer in Music, Aberdeen University,

since 1966; *b* 1928; *m* 1954; three *s*. MA Glasgow 1951, BMus Glasgow 1952, LRAM 1953. *Address*: Dept of Music, College of Education, Aberdeen.

Johnston, Prof. Thomas Lothian, MA, PhD; Professor of Economics, Heriot-Watt University, since 1966; *b* 1927; *m* 1956; two *s* three *d*. MA Edinburgh 1951, PhD Edinburgh 1955. Asst Lectr, 1953, Lectr, 1953–65, Univ. of Edinburgh; Vis. Prof., Univ. of Illinois, 1962–63. Mem.: Scottish Milk Marketing Bd, 1967–72; Nat. Industrial Relations Ct, 1971– ; Scottish Cttee on Licensing Laws, 1971–72. *Publications*: Collective Bargaining in Sweden, 1962; Economic Expansion and Structural Change, 1963; (jtly) The Structure and Growth of the Scottish Economy, 1971; *contrib*. Economica, Scottish Jl of Political Economy. *Address*: Dept of Economics, Heriot-Watt Univ., Grassmarket, Edinburgh.

Johnston, Rev. William Bryce; Associate Lecturer in Moral and Social Philosophy, Department of Business Organisation, Heriot-Watt University, since 1966; *b* 1921; *m* 1947; one *s* two *d*. MA Edinburgh 1942 (Hons), BD Edinburgh 1945 (Dist.). Cunningham Lectr, New Coll., Univ. Edinburgh, 1968–70. *Publications*: trans. Karl Barth: Church Dogmatics, vol. 2/1, 1957; trans. Calvin: Commentaries: Hebrews, Peter, 1963. *Address*: Heriot-Watt Univ., Mountbatten Building, Grassmarket, Edinburgh EH1 1HX.

Johnstone, Dr Harry Diack, MA, DPhil, MusB; Senior Lecturer in Music, University of Reading, since 1970; *b* 1935; *m* 1960; one *s* one *d*. MusB Dublin 1957, BA Oxon 1960, MA, DPhil Oxon 1968; FRCO, FTCL, ARCM. Asst Lectr, Reading Univ., 1963–65, Lectr, 1965–70. Examiner (and later Awarder) in Music, Oxf. and Camb. Schs Exam. Bd, 1961–69. *Publications*: Several edns of musical wks, mainly 18th cent. English composers; *contrib*. Musical Times, Music and Letters, Organists Rev., Proc. Royal Music. Assoc. *Address*: Dept of Music, Univ. of Reading, Reading RG6 2AH.

Johnstone, Thomas Muir; Professor of Arabic, Department of Near and Middle East, School of Oriental and African Studies, University of London, since 1970; *b* 1924; *m* 1949; two *s* three *d*. BCom London 1944, BA London 1954, PhD London 1962; FRAS. Lectr, SOAS, 1957–65, Reader, 1965–70; Chm., Bd of Studies, Orient. Langs and Lits, 1971–72. Hon. Mem., Bd of Trustees, Univ. of San'a; Jt Editor, Camb. Hist. Arab. Lit. *Publications*: Eastern Arabian Dialect Studies, 1967; *contrib*. Encyclopaedia of Islam; *contrib*. Bull. SOAS, Geog. Jl, Jl Semit. Studies, Marin. Mirr. *Address*: Dept of the Near and Middle East, School of Oriental and African Studies, Malet Street, WC1E 7HP.

Johnstone, Rev. William; Senior Lecturer, Department of Hebrew and Semitic Languages, Aberdeen University, since 1972; *b* 1936; *m* 1964; one *s* one *d*. MA Glasgow 1962 (1st cl. Hons Semitic Languages), BD 1959 (Distinction in New Testament, Distinction

361

in Old Testament); Mem. Soc. for OT Study. Lectr, Univ. of Aberdeen, 1962–72; Member: Senatus Academicus, Univ. of Aberdeen, 1967–72; Faculty of Divinity, 1962– ; Faculty of Arts, 1966– . *Publications*: trans. Fohrer: Hebrew and Aramaic Dictionary of the Old Testament, 1973; contrib. Ugaritica VI, ed J-C. Courtois, 1969; Alasia I, ed C. F. A. Schaeffer, 1972; *contrib*. ET, TGUOS, SJT, Theology. *Address*: Dept of Hebrew and Semitic Languages, King's College, Old Aberdeen AB9 2UB.

Joll, Prof. James Bysse; Stevenson Professor of International History, London School of Economics, University of London, since 1967; *b* 1918. BA Oxford 1939, MA Oxford 1945. Fellow and Tutor in Politics, New Coll., Oxford, 1948–51; Fellow and Sub-Warden, St Antony's Coll., Oxford, 1951–67; Univ. Lectr in Modern History, Oxford, 1950–67. *Publications*: The Second International (1889–1914), 1955; Three Intellectuals in Politics, 1960; The Anarchists, 1964; Europe since 1870, 1973; *contrib*. Hist. Zeits., Hist. Today, NY Rev. Bks, Past Pres., St Ant. Papers. *Address*: London School of Economics and Political Science, Houghton Street, Aldwych, WC2A 2AE.

Jolles, Charlotte, MA, Dr.phil; Reader, Department of German, Birkbeck College, University of London, since 1969; *b* 1909. Dr.phil Berlin 1937, MA London 1947. Asst Mistress, Watford Grammar Sch. for Girls, 1945–55; Lectr, Bickbeck Coll., 1955, Sen. Lectr, 1967–69. *Publications*: Theodor Fontane, 1972; ed, G. Hauptmann: Einsame Menschen, 1962; ed, T. Fontane: Sämtliche Werke vols 17 and 19, 1963–69; ed (with K. Schreinert), T. Fontane: Briefe vols 1–4, 1968–71; *contrib*. Brand. Jb., Fontane-Bl., Forsch. Brand. Pr. Gesch., Germ. Life and Lett., Jb. Schiller-Ges., Jb. Pr. Kulturbesitz. *Address*: Birkbeck College, Univ. of London, Malet Street, WC1E 7HX.

Jolles, Prof. Frank E. F., MA, Dr.phil; Professor of Modern Languages (German), New University of Ulster, since 1971; *b* 1931; *m* 1965; two *s* one *d*. BA Manchester 1952, MA Manchester 1957, Dr.phil Göttingen 1965; Mem., IVG. Temp. Asst Lectr, Southampton, 1960; Tutor, UCW Aberystwyth, 1961; Lektor, Göttingen Univ., 1962; Lectr, Magee UC, Londonderry, 1966; Sen. Lectr, New Univ. of Ulster, 1968; Vis. Associate Prof., Indiana Univ., 1967; Humboldt Fellowship, Göttingen, 1970. NI GCE German Panel. *Publications*: ed. A. W. Schlegel's Erste Übersetzung, des Sommernachtstraums, 1967; ed, A. W. Schlegel's Vorlesungen über das academische Studium, 1971; ed, Samuel Gotthold Lange, Horatzische Oden, 1977, 1971; contrib. Deutsche Literatur der Gegenwart-Aspekte und Tendenzen; *contrib*. Etudes Germ., German Life and Letters. The Year's Work in Mod. Lang. Studies. *Address*: New Univ. of Ulster, Coleraine, Co. Londonderry BT52 1SA.

Jolliffe, Flavia Rosamund, BSc, DIC; Lecturer in Department of Statistics and Operational Research, Brunel University, since 1973; *b* 1942; *m* 1970; one *s*. BSc London 1963 (Special Mathematics), DIC London 1965 (Statistics and Operational Research); FSS. Res. Asst (to Prof. C. B. Winsten), Nuffield Coll., Oxford, 1964–66; Asst Lectr, Dept of Econometrics and Social Statistics, Univ. of Southampton, 1966–68, Lectr, 1968–70; Temp. Pt-time Lectr, Dept of Econometrics and Social Statistics, Univ. of Birmingham, 1967–69; Lectr (Statistics), Dept of Economics, Queen Mary Coll., London Univ., 1970–73. *Publications*: Common-sense Statistics, 1974; *contrib*. Jl Royal Stat. Soc., Town Planning Rev. *Address*: Dept of Statistics and Operational Research, Brunel Univ., Uxbridge, Mddx UB8 3PH.

Jolowicz, John Anthony; Fellow, Trinity College, since 1952, and Reader in Common and Comparative Law, since 1972, University of Cambridge; *b* 1926; *m* 1957; one *s* two *d*. BA Cantab 1950 (1st cl. Law), MA Cantab 1955; Barrister-at-Law, 1952. Asst Lectr, 1955–59, Lectr, 1959–72, Univ. of Cambridge; Vis. Lectr, Univ. of Chicago Law Sch., 1957; British Council Lectr, Inst. of Comparative Law, Mexico, 1966; Vis. Res. Fellow, Inst. of Legal Research, Mexico, 1968. Mem.: Brighton Coll. Council, 1969– ; Adv. Cttee on Legal Educn, 1972– . Editor, Jl of Soc. of Public Teachers of Law, 1962– ; Mem., Editorial Cttee, Cambridge Law Jl, 1961– . *Publications*: ed, Lectures on Jurisprudence by the late H. F. Jolowicz; ed, Winfield on Tort, 7th edn 1963, 8th edn 1967; Winfield and Jolowicz on Tort, 9th edn 1971; ed part, Clerk and Lindsell on Torts, 12th edn 1961, 13th edn 1969; ed and contrib. The Division and Classification of the Law, 1969; *contrib*. Boletin del Instituto de Derecho Comparado de Mexico, Cambridge Law Jl, Jl of Soc. of Public Teachers of Law, Modern Law Rev., Stanford Law Rev. *Address*: Trinity College, Cambridge.

Jolowicz, Mrs P. P.; Bursar, since 1970, Secretary to the Council, since 1963, and Director of Studies in Law, Girton College, Cambridge University, since 1960; *b* 1928; *m* 1957; one *s* two *d*. BA Cantab 1950, MA Cantab 1953, LLB Cantab 1951; Barrister at Law 1952, Mem., Gray's Inn. *Address*: Girton College, Cambridge.

Jondorf, Dr Gillian; Fellow, Girton College Cambridge, and Lecturer, Department of French, Modern and Medieval Languages Faculty, University of Cambridge, since 1971; *b* 1937; *m* 1963; four *d*. BA 1959, PhD 1965 Cantab. Asst, Dept of French, Univ. of Glasgow, 1962–63; Lectr, Dept of Romance Langs, Howard Univ., Washington, DC, USA, 1966–69. *Publication*: Robert Garnier and the Themes of Political Tragedy in the Sixteenth Century, 1969. *Address*: Girton Coll., Cambridge.

Jones; *see* Duncan-Jones.

Jones, Aldwyn D.; *see* Douglas Jones.

Jones, Anthony David; Lecturer in Psychology, London School of Economics, since 1965; *b* 1934; *m* 1969. BA Oxon 1958; Mem.,

Brit. Psychol Soc. *Address*: London School of Economics, Houghton Street, WC2A 2AE.

Jones, Rev. Dr Basil Ewart, BA, BD, PhD; Lecturer in Biblical Studies, Department of Education, University College of Wales, Aberystwyth, since 1954; *b* 1914; *m* 1941; five *s* one *d*. BA Wales 1936 (Hons Hebrew), BA Wales 1937 (Hons Philosophy), BD Wales 1940 (Distinction NT Greek and Philosophy of Religion), DipEd Birmingham 1941, PhD Wales 1967. Inspector of Schools, Assam, India. 1942–54. Mem., several cttees connected with religious educn in Wales. *Publications*: A History of Assam (Indian edn), 1947; A Geography of Assam (Indian edn), 1948; (jtly) Revised Syllabus of Religious Instruction for the Schools of Wales. *Address*: Dept of Education, Univ. College of Wales, Aberystwyth SY23 2AX.

Jones, Bedwyr Lewis; Senior Lecturer, Department of Welsh Language and Literature, University College of North Wales, Bangor, since 1971 (Lecturer, 1959–71); *b* 1933; *m* 1960; two *s* one *d*. BA Wales 1953 (1st cl. Welsh), DipEd 1954 (1st cl.), MA Wales 1961. Treas., Welsh Acad. Lett., 1967–72; Mem., Trans. Adv. Panel, Welsh Off., 1966– . *Publications*: Yr Hen Bersoniaid Llengar, 1963; Blodeugerdd o'r xix Ganrif, 1965; R. Williams Parry, 1972; trans., D. Fraser: Yr Amddiffynwyr, 1967; *contrib*. Bull. Bd Celt Studies, Llên Cymru, Med. Aev. *Address*: Dept of Welsh, Univ. College of North Wales, Bangor LL57 2DG.

Jones, Benjamin Royston; Lecturer, Department of Education, University College of North Wales, Bangor, since 1964; *b* 1913; *m* 1944; two *s*. BSc Wales 1933 (1st cl. Mathematics), DipEd Aberystwyth 1934; Mem.: Math. Assoc.; Assoc. Teachers Maths. Met. Off., 1941–45. Designer of the Avon Apparatus (structural apparatus for teaching elementary mathematics), 1957. *Publications*: *contrib*. Math. Gaz., Maths Teaching, Primary Maths. *Address*: Dept of Education, Univ. College of North Wales, Bangor LL57 2DG.

Jones, C. M.; *see* Scollen, C. M.

Jones, Charles; Lecturer, Department of English Language, University of Edinburgh, since 1967; *b* 1939; *m* 1966. MA Glasgow 1962 (1st cl. Eng. Lit. and Lang.), BLitt Glasgow 1964. Lectr, Univ. of Hull, 1964–67; Vis. Prof., Univ. of Virginia, 1970–71. Treas., Linguistics Assoc. GB, 1966–69. *Publications*: Introduction to Middle English, 1972; (with J. M. Anderson) Historical English Phonology, 1974; ed (with J. M. Anderson), Proceedings of First International Conference on Historical Linguistics, 1974; *contrib*. Engl. Studies, Indogerm. Forsch., Lingua, Notes and Queries, Jl Linguistics, Edinburgh Working Papers, in Linguistics. *Address*: Dept of English Language, 15 Buccleuch Place, Edinburgh EH8 9JX.

Jones, Dr Charles L.; Lecturer in Sociology, University of Edinburgh, since 1972; *b* 1946. MA Cantab 1967, PhD Edinburgh 1973;

Mem. Brit. Sociological Assoc. **Lectr, Dept of** Educnl Sciences, Univ. of Edinburgh, 1968–72. *Publications*: *contrib*. Quality and Quantity, Jl Royal Stat. Soc. *Address*: Dept of Sociology, Univ. of Edinburgh, Edinburgh EH8 9YL.

Jones, Christopher; *see* Jones, J. C.

Jones, Dr David; Lecturer, Department of Psychology, Birkbeck College, University of London, since 1968; *b* 1938; *m* 1962; one *s* one *d*. BSc Exeter 1960 (Hons Psychology), PhD London 1965 (Psychology); Member: British Psychol. Soc., Exper. Psychol. Soc., Assoc. for Child Psychol. and Psychiatry, British Assoc. for Behavioural Psychotherapy. MRC External Scientific Staff, 1960–65 and 1966–68; Res. Assoc., State Univ. of Iowa, 1965–66. *Publications*: ed (with A. Elithorn), Artificial and Human Thinking, 1973; *contrib*. Amer. Jl Ment. Defic., Brit. Jl Psychol., Child Devel., Jl Ment. Defic. Res., Nature. *Address*: Birkbeck Coll., Malet Street, WC1E 7HX.

Jones, Dr David Cecil; Staff Tutor in Psychology, Department of Extra-Mural Studies, University College of North Wales, since 1966; *b* 1939; *m* 1965; two *d*. BA Wales, PhD Wales 1972. In Charge, Mngmt Develt Programme; Process Cnsltnt. *Publications*: Migration of Work Tradition (Leverhulme Trust Project), 1969. *Address*: Univ. College of North Wales, Bangor LL57 2DG.

Jones, David John Victor, BA, PhD; Lecturer in History, Swansea University College, since 1966; *b* 1941; *m* 1971; one *d*. BA Wales 1962, PhD Wales 1965. Secretary: Soc. Study of Welsh Labour Hist., 1970–71; Swansea Hist. Assoc. *Publications*: Before Rebecca, 1973; Chartism and the Chartists, 1974; *contrib*. Bull. Bd Celt. Studies, Bull. SS Labour Hist., Jl Mod. Hist., Welsh Hist. Rev., several co. jls. *Address*: Dept of History, Univ. College, Swansea SA2 8PP.

Jones, (David) Kenton; Senior Lecturer, Department of Architecture, University of Nottingham, since 1971; *b* 1929. BSc Hons Wales 1954 (Physics); Chartered Engineer; MIERE, MInstP. Lectr in Bldg Sci., Univ. of Sheffield, 1966–71. *Publications*: *contrib*. Acustica, Applied Acoustics, BBC Res. Reports. *Address*: Dept of Architecture, Univ. of Nottingham, University Park, Nottingham NG7 2RD.

Jones, David Maurice Clifford, BA, ACMA; Senior Lecturer in Accounting, Economics Department, University College, Cardiff, since 1971; *b* 1936; *m* 1960; one *s*. BA Wales 1960; ACMA 1964. Lectr in Accounting, Univ. Coll., Cardiff, 1964–71; Asst Dean, Fac. of Econ. and Social Studies, Univ. Coll., Cardiff, 1970–72. *Address*: Dept of Accountancy, Univ. College, Cardiff, Cathays Park, Cardiff CF1 1XL.

Jones, Prof. David Morgan, MA; Professor of Classics in the University of London, Westfield College, since 1953; *b* 1915; *m* 1965. BA Oxon 1936 (1st cl. Classical

Hon. Mods), BA Oxon 1938 (1st cl. Lit. Hum.), MA Oxon 1941. Dip. in Comparative Philology Oxon 1940. Lectr in Classics, UC of N Wales, 1940–48; Reader in Classics, Univ. of London (Birkbeck Coll.), 1949–53. *Publications*: *contrib.* classical and linguistic jls. *Address*: Westfield College, Kidderpore Avenue, Hampstead, NW3 7ST.

Jones, Rev. Prof. Douglas Rawlinson; Lightfoot Professor of Divinity, University of Durham, since 1964; *b* 1919; *m* 1946; three *s* two *d*. BA Oxon 1941, MA Oxon 1945; Deacon 1942; Priest 1943. Lectr, Wycliffe Hall, Oxford, 1945–50; Chaplain, Wadham Coll., Oxford, 1945–50, Lectr in Divinity, 1948–50; Lectr, 1951–63, Sen. Lectr, 1963–64, Univ. of Durham. Curate, St Michael and All Angels, Windmill Hill, Bristol, 1942–45; Residentiary Canon, Durham Cathedral, 1964– . *Publications*: Haggai, Zechariah and Malachi, 1962; Isaiah, 56–66 and Joel, 1964; Instrument of Peace, 1965; contrib. Peake's Commentary on the Bible, 1962; Hastings Dictionary of the Bible, 1963; The Cambridge History of the Bible, 1963; *contrib.* Jl of Theolog. Studies, Zeitschrift für die Alttestamentliche Wissenschaft, Vetus Testamentum, Theol., Scottish Jl of Theol. *Address*: Univ. of Durham, Old Shire Hall, Durham DH1 3HP.

Jones, Edgar; Lecturer, Department of Education, University College of Wales, Aberystwyth, since 1961; *b* 1921; *m* 1948; one *d*. BA Dunelm 1950 (English), DipEd Dunelm 1951, MA Dunelm 1954, MEd Dunelm 1959, PhD Wales 1974. *Publications*: *contrib.* Camb. Jl, Ess. Studies, Didask., Durham Univ. Jl. *Address*: Dept of Education, Univ. College of Wales, Aberystwyth SY23 2AX.

Jones, Prof. Emrys, MSc, PhD, FRGS; Professor of Geography, London School of Economics, University of London, since 1961; *b* 1920; *m* 1948; two *d*. BSc Wales 1941 (1st cl.), MSc Wales 1945, PhD Wales 1947; FRGS. Asst Lectr, Univ. Coll., London, 1947–50; Lectr, then Sen. Lectr, Queen's Univ., Belfast, 1950–59; Reader, LSE, 1959–61; Fellow, Rockefeller Foundn, 1948–49. Mem., Nat. Cttee of Enquiry into Allotments, 1966–69; Chm., Reg. Studies Assoc., 1968–70; Mem. Council, RGS, 1973– . *Publications*: ed, Belfast in its Regional Setting, 1951; Social Geography of Belfast, 1960; Human Geography, 1964, 2nd edn 1972, American edn 1965, Spanish edn 1966; Towns and Cities, 1966, Swedish edn 1968, French edn 1972; Atlas of London and London Region, 1960–69; ed jtly, Man and His Habitat, 1971; *contrib.* Geog., Qly Jl, Jl Assoc. Amer. Geogrs, Sociol Rev., Town Planning Rev., Trans Han. Soc. Cymmrod. *Address*: London School of Economics, Houghton Street, Aldwych, WC2A 2AE.

Jones, Mrs Emrys; *see* Everett, B.

Jones, Emrys Lloyd; Fellow of Magdalen College, University of Oxford, and University Lecturer, since 1956; *b* 1931; *m* 1965; one *d*. BA Oxford 1954 (1st cl.). *Publications*:

ed, Poems of Henry Howard, Earl of Surrey, 1964; Scenic Form in Shakespeare, 1971; *contrib.* Ess. Crit., Proc. Brit. Acad., Rev. Engl. Studies, Shakespeare Survey. *Address*: Magdalen College, Oxford.

Jones, Frank Price, BA, FSA; Senior Tutor, Extra-Mural Department, University College of North Wales, Bangor, since 1969; *b* 1920; *m* 1945; three *s*. BA Wales 1941; FSA 1961. Tutor in Welsh History, Bangor, 1947–69. Editor, Denbighs Hist. Soc., 1951– ; Clerk, Guild of Grads, Univ. of Wales, 1963– ; Member: Univ. of Wales Ct, 1963–72; Council, Nat. Eisteddfod of Wales, 1956– ; Welsh Folk Museum Cttee, 1956– (sometime chm.); Nat. Museum of Wales Ct; Welsh Off. Panel on Translations. *Publications*: The Story of Denbighshire through its Castles, 1952; Thomas Jones of Ddinbych, 1956; Crwydro Dwyrain Dinbych, 1961; Crwydro Gorllewin Dinbych, 1969; contrib. Dictionary of Welsh Biography; *contrib.* Cymmrod. Trans, Gwerin, Jl Welsh Bibliog. Soc., Lleufer, Traethodydd, Trans Anglesey, Caerns and Denbighs Hist. Soc., etc. *Address*: Extra-Mural Dept, Univ. College of North Wales, Bangor LL57 2DG.

Jones, Prof. Frederic J.; Professor of Italian, University College, Cardiff, since 1966; *b* 1925; *m* 1956. BA Oxford 1946, BLitt Oxford 1949, MA Oxford 1950, DUP 1953. Asst Lectr in French and Italian, Cardiff, 1953–55, Lectr, 1955–64, Sen. Lectr, 1964–66. Brit. Council, 1947–49. *Publications*: A Modern Italian Grammar, 1960, 2nd edn 1962, pbk 1972; ed. Gide: Les Caves du Vatican, 1961 (3rd edn); La linea esistenziale della poesia di Montale, 1963; contrib. Quasimodo e la critica, 1969; La poesia italiana contemporanea, da Gozzano a Quasimodo (forthcoming); *contrib.* Anglo-Welsh Rev., Cenobio, Ital. Studies, Mod. Lang. Rev., Nuove dimens., Poesia e crit., etc. *Address*: Dept of Italian Studies, Univ. College, Cardiff CF1 1XL.

Jones, G. E., BA, BLitt; Lecturer in Rural Sociology, Agricultural Extension and Rural Development Centre, University of Reading, since 1965; *b* 1932; *m* 1957. BA Hons Manchester 1953 (1st cl.), DipAgricEcon Oxford 1954, BLitt Oxford 1960. Lectr, Dept of Agricl Econs, Univ. of Nottingham, 1959–65. *Publications*: Rural Life: Patterns and Processes, 1973; *contrib.* Jl Agric. Econ., Sociol. Ruralis, Jl Comm. Dev., Jl Folk Life Stud., Rur. Sociol. *Address*: Agricultural Extension and Rural Development Centre, The Univ., London Road, Reading RG1 5AQ.

Jones, Dr Gareth Emlyn; Lecturer, Department of Geography, University of Strathclyde, since 1969; *b* 1944; *m* 1966; two *s* one *d*. BSc Wales (Aberystwyth) 1965, PhD Wales 1973; Mem., Inst. of British Geographers. Lectr in Geography, Queen's Univ., Belfast, 1968–69. *Address*: Livingstone Tower, Univ. of Strathclyde, Glasgow G1 1XH.

Jones, Dr Gareth H.; Fellow, and Senior Tutor of Trinity College, University of Cambridge, and University Lecturer, since

1961; b 1930; m 1959; two s one d. LLB
Cantab 1953, LLM Harvard 1954, MA
Cantab 1958, PhD London 1960, LLD
Cantab 1972; Barrister-at-Law. Lectr, King's
Coll., London, 1958–61; Vis. Professor:
Harvard Univ., 1966; Univ. of California,
Berkeley, 1967, 1971; Indiana Univ., 1971–
72. *Address*: Trinity College, Cambridge
CB2 1TQ.

Jones, George Leonard, MA, BLitt;
Lecturer in German, University College,
Cardiff, since 1963; b 1937; m 1966; two
d. BA Wales 1959 (1st cl. German), MA
Wales 1961, BLitt Oxon 1964. *Publications*:
chapter on Johann Christoph Gottsched, in,
German Men of Letters, vol. VI, 1972;
contrib. Forum Mod. Lang. Studies, Germ.
Life Lett., Oxf. Germ. Studies, Trivium.
Address: Department of German, Univ.
College, Cardiff CF1 1XL.

Jones, Dr George William, MA, DPhil;
Senior Lecturer in Political Science, London
School of Economics and Political Science,
since 1971; b 1938; m 1963; one s one d.
BA Oxon 1960, MA Oxon 1965, DPhil
Oxon 1965. Asst Lectr in Government,
Leeds Univ., 1963–65, Lectr, 1965–66;
Lectr in Political Science, LSE, 1966–71.
Sec., Pol Studies Assoc., 1965–68 (Mem.,
Exec. Cttee, 1969–); Member: Council,
Hansard Soc., 1968–70; Study of Parl. Gp,
1969– . *Publications*: Borough Politics,
1969; (with B. Donoughue) Herbert
Morrison: portrait of a politician, 1973;
contrib. Admin. Sci. Qly, Local Govt Chron.,
Local Govt Fin., Munic. Rev., Parly Aff.,
Pol Qly, Pol Studies, Public Admin., Public
Law. *Address*: Dept of Government, London
School of Economics, WC2A 2AE.

Jones, Glanville Rees Jeffreys; Reader in
Historical Geography, University of Leeds,
since 1969; b 1923; m 1959; one s one d.
BA Wales 1947 (1st cl. Geography and
Anthropology), MA Wales 1949; Mem.:
Inst. Brit. Geogrs; Econ. Hist. Soc.; Agric.
Hist. Soc. Asst Lectr, Univ. of Leeds, 1949–
52, Lectr in Geography, 1952–65, Sen.
Lectr, 1965–69. Member: Council. Inst.
Brit. Geogrs, 1968–71; Edit. Bd, 1968–70.
Publications: ed (with S. R. Eyre), Geography
as Human Ecology, 1966; ed (with M.
W. Beresford), Leeds and Its Region, 1967;
contrib. The Agrarian History of England
and Wales, vol. I: Studies of Field Systems
in the British Isles; *contrib.* Adv. Sci., Antiqu.,
Trans Inst. Brit. Geogrs, Welsh Hist. Rev.
Address: Dept of Geography, The Univ.,
Leeds LS2 9JT.

Jones, Rev. Dr Gwilym Henry, MA, PhD;
Lecturer, Department of Hebrew and Bib-
lical Studies, University College of North
Wales, Bangor, since 1966; b 1930; m 1959;
two s. BA Wales 1953 (1st cl. Hebrew), BA
Oxon 1956 (Hons Theology), MA Oxon 1960,
PhD Wales 1970. Prof. of Hebrew, Utd
Theological Coll., Aberystwyth (recognised
teacher in Theology, Univ. of Wales),
1961–66. *Publications*: Proffwydi'r Hen
Destament, 1966; Arweiniad i'r Hen Desta-
ment, 1966; *contrib.* Diwinydd., Vet. Testam.
Address: Dept of Hebrew and Biblical

Studies, Univ. College of North Wales,
Bangor LL57 2DG.

Jones, Prof. Gwyn: Professor of English,
University College, Cardiff, since 1965; b
1907; m 1928. BA Wales 1927 (1st cl. English),
MA Wales 1929. Lectr, Univ. Coll., Cardiff,
1935–40; Prof., Univ. Coll. of Wales,
Aberystwyth, 1940–64. Editor, Welsh Rev.,
1939–49; Mem., Arts Council GB; Chm.,
Welsh Arts Council, 1957–67. *Publications*: A
Prospect of Wales, 1948; Welsh Legends and
Folktales, 1955; History of the Vikings, 1968,
2nd edn 1969; Kings, Beasts and Heroes,
1972; trans. (with Thomas Jones) The
Mabinogion, 1948, 3rd edn 1972; Egil's
Saga, 1960, 2nd edn 1971; Erik the Red's
Saga, 1961, 2nd edn 1966; The Norse
Atlantic Saga, 1964, Italian edn 1966, Spanish
edn 1967; five novels, three vols short stories;
contrib. Amer.–Scand. Rev., Mod. Lang.
Rev., Med. Æv., Poetry Wales, Rev. Engl.
Studies, Times Lit. Supp. *Address*: Dept of
English, Univ. College, Cathays Park,
Cardiff CF1 1XL.

Jones, Prof. H. Gwynne, BSc. FBPsS:
Professor of Psychology, University of
Leeds, since 1969; b 1918; m 1947; one s
one d. BSc London 1940 (Hons Botany);
DipEd Wales 1946; DipPsych London 1950,
BSc London 1951 (Hons Psychology); FBPsS
1959; Corresp. Associate, Royal Coll.
Psychiatry. Lectr, Univ. London Inst.
Psychiatry, 1952–58, Sen. Lectr, 1959–63;
Sen. Lectr, St George's Hosp. Med. Sch.,
London, 1963–68. Mem. Council, Brit.
Psych. Soc., 1961–72. Hon. Gen. Sec.,
1963–67, Pres., 1970–71; Chm., Brit. Assoc.
Behavioural Psychotherapy, 1973– . Mem.
Nat. Assoc. Mental Health, Clinical Ser-
vices Commn, 1966–69. Northern Commn,
1969– ; Medical Research Council; Mem.,
Grants Commn II CRB, 1969–71; Army
Personnel Res. Commn, 1970– ; Home
Office: Mem. Consultative Cttee on Research
into the Personality of Offenders, 1972– ;
Mem., Management Cttee, Leeds (St James)
Univ. Hosp., 1970–74; Mem., Calderdale
AHA, 1973– . Mem. Court, Univ. of
Wales Inst. of Science and Technology,
1970– . *Publications*: co-author: Behaviour
Therapy and the Neuroses, ed. H. J. Eysenck,
1960; Handbook of Abnormal Psychology,
ed. H. J. Eysenck, 1960; Handbook for
Psychiatric Nurses, ed. B. Ackner, 1964;
Modern Perspectives in Child Psychiatry,
ed. J. G. Howells, 1965; Handbook of
Child Psychiatry, ed. E. Miller, 1968;
Symptoms of Psychopathology, ed. C. G.
Costello, 1970; The Psychological Assess-
ment of Mental and Physical Handicaps, ed
P. Mittler, 1970; *contrib.* various psycho-
logical and psychiatric jls. *Address*: Dept of
Psychology, Univ. of Leeds, Leeds LS2 9JT.

Jones, Prof. Henry Arthur, CBE; Vaughan
Professor of Education and Head of Depart-
ment of Adult Education, University of
Leicester, since 1968; b 1917; m 1942; two
s. BA Manchester 1937 (1st cl. English),
MA Manchester 1938, DipEd 1939 (1st cl.).
Resdt Staff Tutor, Manchester, 1947–49;
Asst Dir of Extra-Mural Studies, Liverpool,
1949–51, Dep. Dir, 1951–57; Principal,

City Lit. Inst., London, 1957–68. Mem.: Libr. Adv. Council, England, 1966–68; Cttee of Enquiry into Adult Educn (DES), 1969–73; Chm., Pubns Cttee, Nat. Inst. Adult Educn, 1967–   ; Vice-Pres., Educnl Centres Assoc., 1970–   ; Vice-Pres., Pre-Retirement Assoc., 1972–   . *Publications*: contrib. Solving the Problems of Retirement, 1968; Teaching on Equal Terms, 1969; Education without End, 1969; Teaching Techniques in Adult Education, 1971; *contrib.* *Address*: Dept of Adult Education, The Univ., Leicester LE1 7RH.

Jones, Prof. Howard; Head of Department of Social Administration, and Director of School of Social Work, University College, Cardiff, since 1969; *b* 1918; *m* 1953; one *s*. DipPA London 1942, BSc(Econ) London 1946, PhD London 1954; Mental Health Cert. LSE 1947. Lectr, Leicester Univ., 1953–61, Sen. Lectr, 1961–65; Reader, Keele Univ., 1965–69. *Publications*: Crime and the Penal System, 1956, 3rd edn 1965; Prison Reform Now, 1959; Reluctant Rebels, 1961, Dutch edn; Alcoholic Addiction, 1963, Dutch edn; Crime in a Changing Society, 1965, Czech, Dutch, Japanese, Portuguese edns; ed (with T. Grygier and J. C. Spencer), Criminology in Transition; *contrib.* App. Schs Gaz., Brit. Jl Criminol., Bull. Brit. Psych. Soc., Canad. Welf., Case Conf., How, Jl Penol., Ment. Hlth, New Soc., etc. *Address*: Univ. College, PO Box 96, Cardiff CF1 1XB.

Jones, Howard B.; *see* Bowen-Jones.

Jones, Howard Maurice; Lecturer in Philosophy, Saint David's University College, Lampeter, since 1965; *b* 1942. BA Bristol 1963. *Address*: St David's College, Lampeter, Dyfed SA48 7ED.

Jones, Huw M.; *see* Morris-Jones.

Jones, Huw Roland; Lecturer in Geography, University of Dundee, since 1961; *b* 1937; *m* 1964; two *s*. BA Aberystwyth 1958 (1st cl. Geography), MA Aberystwyth 1961. Tutorial Asst in Geography, Univ. of Leicester, 1960–61. *Publications*: contrib. Scott. Geog. Mag., Trans Inst. Brit. Geogrs, Tijdschr. Econ. Soc. Geogr., Internat. Migration, etc. *Address*: Dept of Geography, Univ. of Dundee, Dundee DD1 4HN.

Jones, Ieuan Evans, BA; Lecturer in Geography, University of Birmingham, since 1954; *b* 1924; *m* 1953; two *d*. BA Wales 1947 (1st cl. Geography), DipEd Wales 1949. Asst Lectr, Birmingham Univ., 1951–54. *Publications*: contrib. Geog., Mont. Colls, Rads Soc. Trans. *Address*: Dept of Geography, Univ. of Birmingham, PO Box 363, Birmingham B15 2TT.

Jones, Prof. Ieuan Gwynedd, MA; Sir John Williams Professor of Welsh History, University College of Wales, Aberystwyth, since 1970; *b* 1920; *m* 1946; one *s*. BA Wales 1948 (1st cl. Eng), MA Wales 1950, DipEd Wales 1951; FRHistS. Fellow, Univ. Wales at Peterhouse, Cambridge, 1951–54; Res. Fellow, Welsh Social His., Swansea, 1954–58;

Lectr in Hist., Swansea, 1958–65, Sen. Lectr, 1965; Leverhulme Fellow, 1973–74. Jt Editor, Morgannwg, 1961–71; Sec., Hist. and Law Commn of Bd of Celtic Studies. *Publications*: ed, The Religious Census of 1851 relating to Wales, vols I and II, 1974; *contrib*. Jl Merioneth Hist. S., JMH, Trans Caern. HS., TRSCymm, WHR. *Address*: Dept of Welsh History, Univ. College of Wales, Aberystwyth SY23 2AX.

Jones, Prof. J. Christopher; Professor of Design, The Open University, since 1970; *b* 1927. *Publication*: Design Methods, 1970. *Address*: The Open Univ., Milton Keynes MK7 6AA.

Jones, James Barry, BA, MA; Lecturer in Politics, University of Wales Institute of Science and Technology, since 1965; *b* 1938; *m* 1962; two *d*. BA Wales 1960 (Jt Hons Modern History and Politics), MA Alberta 1962 (Political Science). Teaching Asst, Dept of Political Economy, Univ. of Alberta, 1960–61; Govt of Alberta Res. Fellow, 1961–62. *Publications*: contrib. Pol Studies. *Address*: Dept of Applied Economics, Friary Building, Univ. of Wales Institute of Science and Technology, Cardiff.

Jones, Prof. James Rees; Professor of English History, University of East Anglia, since 1966; *b* 1925; *m* 1954; one *s* one *d*. BA Cantab 1949 (1st cl. History), MA Cantab 1951, PhD Cantab 1953. Lectr, King's Coll., Newcastle, 1952–63; Sen. Lectr, Univ. of E Anglia, 1963–66; Pro-Vice-Chancellor, 1971–74. *Publications*: The First Whigs, 1961, 2nd edn 1971; Britain and Europe in the Seventeenth Century, 1966; The Glorious Revolution of 1688, 1972; *contrib*. Bull. J. Rylands Libr., Bull. Inst. Hist. Res., Durham Univ. Jl, Hist. Jl. *Address*: School of English and American Studies, Univ. of East Anglia, University Plain, Norwich NOR 88C.

Jones, Dr John Alan; Lecturer, Department of Hispanic Studies, University of Hull, since 1967; *b* 1941; *m* 1969; one *d*. BA Leeds 1964, PhD Leeds 1971; Mem., Assoc. Hispanists of Gt Brit. and Ire.; Mem., Soc. for Renaissance Studies, Univ. of Hull, 1967–   . *Publication*: The Duality and Complexity of *Guzmán de Alfarache*: some thoughts on the structure and interpretation of Alemán's novel, in Knaves and Swindlers, ed C. J. Whitbourn, 1974. *Address*: Dept of Hispanic Studies, Univ. of Hull, Hull HU6 7RX.

Jones, John Edward; Senior Lecturer, Department of Fine Art, University of Leeds, since 1967; *b* 1926; *m* 1958; two *d*. Nat. Dip. in Design W of England Coll. of Art 1951, Art Teacher's Dip. W of England Coll. of Art 1952, Slade Dip. UCL. Lectr, Univ. of Leeds, 1961–67. *Address*: Fine Art Dept, The Univ., Leeds LS2 9JT.

Jones, John Ellis, BA; Senior Lecturer in Classics, University College of North Wales, Bangor, since 1973; *b* 1929; *m* 1958; one *s* two *d*. BA Wales 1950 (1st cl. Latin, 2nd cl. Greek 1951), DipEd 1952. Kemsley Travelling Fellow, Univ. of Wales, 1954–55; Asst Lectr in Classics, Univ. of Leicester, 1957–58; Asst Lectr in Classics, Univ. Coll. of N Wales, Bangor, 1958–60, Lectr, 1960–73. *Publications*: The Greeks, 1971; *contrib.* Brit. Sch. Athens. *Address*: Dept of Classics, Univ. College of North Wales, Bangor LL57 2DG.

Jones, (John) Stanley; Lecturer, Department of Lithography, Slade School, University College, London, since 1958; *b* 1933; *m* 1961; one *s* one *d*. Slade Dip. London 1956 (Fine Art). Studio Dir, Curwen Prints Ltd. *Publications*: Lithography for Artists, 1966; *contrib.* Studio Internat. *Address*: Slade Sch. of Fine Art, Univ. Coll., London, Gower Street, WC1E 6BT.

Jones, Prof. Kathleen, BA, PhD; Professor of Social Administration, University of York, since 1965; *b* 1922; *m* 1944; one *s*. BA London 1943 (2nd cl. History), PhD London 1953; Mem., Brit. Assoc. Social Wk, Associate Mem., Royal Coll. Psychiat. Res. Asst, Univ. of Manchester, 1951–53, Asst Lectr, 1953–57; Lectr, Univ. of Malaya, 1957–59; Lectr, Univ. of Manchester, 1959–62, Sen. Lectr, 1962–65. Mem., Cent. Council Training and Educn in Social Wk, 1971–73; Governor: St John's Coll., York, 1968– ; Wm Temple Coll., 1968–73; Mem., Archbps' Commn on Ch and State, 1966–70; Editor: Yr Bk Social Policy, 1972– ; Internat. Libr. of Social Policy, 1972– . *Publications*: Lunacy, Law and Conscience, 1955; Mental Health and Social Policy, 1960; Mental Hospitals at Work, 1962; The Teaching of Social Studies in British Universities, 1963; The Compassionate Society, 1965; contrib. Trends in the National Health Service, 1964; Trends in the Mental Health Services, 1965, etc.; *contrib.* New Soc., Sociol. *Address*: Goodricke College, Univ. of York, York.

Jones, Keith Evan; Lecturer in Philosophy, University of Kent at Canterbury, since 1968; *b* 1941. BA Keele 1964, MSc Keele 1972; Mem., Brit. Soc. Philos. of Sci. *Address*: Darwin Coll., The Univ., Canterbury, Kent CT2 7NY.

Jones, Dr Malcolm Vince, BA, PhD; Senior Lecturer in Russian, Department of Slavonic Studies, University of Nottingham, since 1973 (Lecturer, 1967–73); *b* 1940; *m* 1963; one *s* one *d*. BA Nottingham 1962 (1st cl. Russian), PhD Nottingham 1966. Asst Lectr, Univ. of Sussex, 1965–67. Member: Cttee, BUAS; Exec. Cttee, Internat. Dostoevsky Soc. *Publications*: *contrib.* Renaiss. Mod. Studies, Slav. E Europ. Rev., Jl European Studies. *Address*: Dept of Slavonic Studies, Univ. of Nottingham, University Park, Nottingham NG7 2RD.

Jones, Prof. Maldwyn Allen, MA, DPhil; Commonwealth Fund Professor of American History, University of London, since 1971; *b* 1922; *m* 1944; one *d*. BA Oxon 1949 (1st cl. Modern History), DPhil Oxon 1956. Asst Lectr in American History and Instns, Manchester Univ., 1950–54; Lectr, Manchester Univ., 1954–63; Sen. Lectr, Manchester Univ., 1963–65, Prof. of American History and Instns, 1965–71; Commonwealth Fund Fellow, Harvard Univ., 1951–52, 1959; Vis.

Prof., Univ. of Chicago, 1961–62; Vis. Prof., Univ. of Pennsylvania, 1965; Vis. Prof., Harvard Univ., 1969. Council Mem., British Assoc. for American Studies, 1958–62, Treasurer, 1962–68; Chm., 1968–71. *Publications*: American Immigration, 1960; contribs to: British Essays in American History, ed Allen and Hill, 1957; New Cambridge Modern History, vol. VII, ed Goodwin, 1965; George Washington's Opponents, ed Billias, 1969; Essays in Scotch-Irish History, ed Green, 1969; Pastmasters, ed Cunliffe and Winks, 1969; The United States: a companion to American studies, ed Welland, 1974; *contrib.* Jl Social History, Bull. John Rylands Library, Perspectives in Amer. Hist. *Address*: Dept of History, Univ. College London, Gower Street, WC1E 6BT.

Jones, Margaret Stefana Hackforth-; *see* Drower, M. S.

Jones, Martin Howard; Lecturer in German, University of London, King's College, since 1968; *b* 1944; *m* 1966; one *s* one *d*. BA Oxford 1966 (1st cl.). Lektor in English Seminar of Univ. of Erlangen-Nürnberg, W Germany, 1967–68. *Address*: Dept of German, King's Coll., Strand, WC2R 2LS.

Jones, Dr Michael Christopher Emlyn; Lecturer, Department of History, University of Nottingham, since 1969; *b* 1940; *m* 1966; one *s*. BA Oxon 1963 (2nd cl. History), MA, DPhil Oxon 1966; FRHistS 1971. Tutor, Univ. of Exeter, 1966–67; Asst Lectr, Univ. of Nottingham, 1967–69. *Publications*: Ducal Brittany 1364–1399, 1970; trans., Philippe de Commynes: Memoirs, 1972; *contrib.* Bull. Inst. Hist. Res., Camd. Misc., Jl Soc. Archivists, Mémoires de la Société d'histoire et d'archéologie de Bretagne. *Address*: Dept of History, Univ. of Nottingham, Nottingham NG7 2RD.

Jones, Myrddin; Senior Lecturer, Department of English, University of Exeter, since 1971; *b* 1927; *m* 1954; two *d*. BA Wales 1949, BLitt Oxon 1954, DipEd Oxon 1954. Univ. of Exeter, 1966– . Sub-dean, Faculty of Arts, 1973– ; Mem., Arts and Educn Faculty Bds; Governor, Rolle Coll. of Educn, 1972. *Publications*: *contrib.* Essays in Criticism, Philological Qly, Review of English Studies, Renaissance Qly. *Address*: Queen's Building, Exeter Univ., Exeter EX4 4QJ.

Jones, Norman Stewart L.; *see* Larey Jones.

Jones, Dr Owen Rogers; Senior Lecturer in Philosophy, University College of Wales, Aberystwyth, since 1964; *b* 1922; *m* 1956; two *d*. BA Wales 1949, BD Wales 1952, PhD Wales 1955, BLitt Oxon 1957. Asst Lectr, Aberystwyth, 1957–59, Lectr, 1959–64; Guest Lectr, St Olaf Coll., Minnesota, 1964–65. *Publications*: The Concept of Holiness, 1961; ed, The Private Language Argument, 1971; *contrib.* Aristot. Soc. Proc., Philos., Analysis, Amer. Philos. Qly. *Address*: Dept of Philosophy, Univ. College of Wales, Aberystwyth SY23 2AX.

Jones, Peter; Technical Officer, Department of Linguistics, University of Cambridge, since 1968; b 1927; m 1958. CEng, MIERE. *Address*: Dept of Linguistics, Sidgwick Avenue, Cambridge CB3 9DA.

Jones, Peter (Howard); Lecturer, Department of Philosophy, University of Edinburgh, since 1964; b 1935; m 1960; two d. MA Cantab (Moral Scis); Member: Aristotelian Soc., Brit. Soc. Aesthetics, Mind Assoc., Royal Inst. Philosophy. Vis. Prof. of Philosophy: Univ. Rochester, 1969–70; Dartmouth Coll., NH, 1973; Carleton Coll., Minn, 1974. Mem., British Council, 1960–61. *Publications*: Philosophy and the Novel, 1974; *contrib*. Br. Jl Aesthet., Forum Mod. Lang. Stud., Mind, Philos., Philos. Qly. *Address*: Dept of Philosophy, David Hume Tower, George Square, Edinburgh EH8 9JX.

Jones, Prof. (Peter) Hugh (Jefferd) L.; *see* Lloyd Jones.

Jones, Philip James, MA, DPhil; Fellow and Tutor in Modern History, Brasenose College, Oxford, since 1963; b 1921; m 1954; one s one d. BA Oxon 1945 (1st cl. History), MA Oxon 1946, DPhil Oxon 1950; FRHistS. Asst, Glasgow Univ., 1948–49; Lectr, Leeds Univ., 1950–59, Reader, 1959–63. *Publications*: chapters, in, Italian Renaissance Studies, ed E. F. Jacob, 1960; Cambridge Economic History, vol. I, 2nd edn 1966; Florentine Studies, ed N. Rubinstein, 1970; The Maletesta of Rimini, 1974; Studi di Storia Medievale (forthcoming); *contrib*. Econ. Hist. Rev., Jl Eccles. Hist., Riv. Storica Ital., Riv. Storia Chiesa Ital., Trans Royal Hist. Soc., etc. *Address*: Brasenose College, Oxford.

Jones, Dr Philip Nicholas; Lecturer, Department of Geography, University of Hull, since 1967; b 1940; m 1963; one s one d. BA Hons Birmingham 1961, PhD Birmingham 1965. Asst Lectr, Univ. of Hull, 1966. *Publications*: (with P. W. Lewis) Industrial Britain: the Humberside region, 1970; contrib. Occasional Papers in Geography series, Univ. of Hull; *contrib*. Trans Hon. Soc. Cymmrodorian, Trans Inst. of Brit. Geog., Transport Hist. *Address*: Dept of Geography, Univ. of Hull, Hull HU6 7RX.

Jones, Raymond Bernard W.; *see* Wood-Jones.

Jones, Prof. Reginald Victor, CB, CBE, DSc, FRS, FRSE; Professor of Natural Philosophy, University of Aberdeen, since 1946; b 1911; m 1940; one s two d. BA Oxon 1932, MA Oxon 1934, DPhil Oxon 1934, Hon. DSc Strathclyde 1969; FRS, FRSE, FRAS, FInstP. Sen. Student, Balliol Coll., 1934–36; Hon. Fellow, Wadham Coll., 1969; NZ Univs Commonwealth Prestige Fellow, 1973. Scientific Officer, 1936; Asst Dir of Intelligence, 1940–45, Dir of Intelligence (Research), 1945–46, Air Ministry; Dir of Scientific Intelligence, MoD, 1953–54. Governor, Dulwich Coll., 1966– ; Chairman: Safety in Mines Res. (Adv.) Board, 1956–60; Paul Instrument Fund Cttee, 1960– ; Electronics Res. Council, 1964–70; Inst. of Physics Cttee on Univ. Physics Depts, 1961–63; British Nat. Cttee for the History of

368

Science, Medicine and Technology, 1970– . Mem., Council of Royal Soc., 1970–72 (Vice Pres., 1971–72). *Publications*: ed, Notes and Records of Royal Soc., 1969– ; contrib. Biographical Memoirs of Fellows of the Royal Soc.; *contrib*. Chemistry and Industry, Jl of IEE, Jl RAeS, Jl of the Royal Inst, Jl of the Royal United Services Instn, Jl of Scientific Instruments, Nature, Phil. Trans Royal Soc., Proc. Physical Soc., Proc. Royal Soc. *Address*: Natural Philosophy Dept, Univ. of Aberdeen, Aberdeen AB9 2UE.

Jones, Rhodri J.; *see* Jeffreys-Jones.

Jones, Robert Maynard, MA, PhD; Senior Lecturer in Welsh Language and Literature, University of Wales, Aberystwyth, since 1969; b 1929; m 1952; one s one d. BA Wales 1949 (1st cl. Welsh), MA Wales 1951, PhD Wales 1965. Advr, Internat. Centre Bilingu. Quebec 1965; Associate Mem., Res. Lingu., Lille 1971. Lectr in Education, Wales, 1959–67, Lectr in Welsh, 1967–69. Mem.: Acad. Gymreig; Ct of Univ. of Wales; Guild of Grads Exec. (Wales); Bd of Celt. Studies; W Wales Arts Council. *Publications*: Y Gân Gyntaf, 1957; Crwydro Môn, 1957; Nid yw dŵr yn plygu, 1958; I'r Arch, 1959; Rhwng Taf a Thaf, 1960; Y Tair Rhamant, 1960; Bod yn Wraig, 1960; Llenyddiaeth Gymraeg yn Addysg Cymru, 1961; Emile, 1963; Guto'r Glyn a'i Gyfnod, 1963; Cyflwyno'r Gymraeg, 1963; Graddio Geirfa, 1963; Cymraeg i Oedolion (Llyfr yr Athro/Nodiadau'r Dysgwr) I, 1965; Tyred Allan, 1965; Man Gwyn, 1965; Cymraeg i Oedolion (Llyfr yr Athro/Nodiadau'r Dysgwr) II, 1966; Y Dyn na ddaeth adref, 1966; Yr Wyl Ifori, 1967; Ci wrth y Drws, 1968; Angau Ellis Wynne, 1968; Daw'r Pasg i Bawb, 1969; Highlights in Welsh Literature, 1969; Cyfrol Deyrnged Kate Roberts, 1969; Geiriadur Lluniau, 1969; System in Child Language, 1970; Pedwar Emynydd, 1970; Sioc o'r Gofod, 1971; Allor Wydn, 1971; Traed Prydferth, 1973; Llyfr Gwyn Rhydderch, 1973; contrib. Description and Measurement of Bilingualism, 1970; *contrib*. BBCS, Gwŷr Llên, IRAL, Llên Cym, Stud. Celt., Trans Cymmrod., Ysg. Beirn. *Address*: Adran Gymraeg, Coleg y Brifysgol, Aberystwyth, Wales.

Jones, Dr Ronald; Reader in Geography, Queen Mary College, London University, since 1971; b 1929; m 1955 (widowed). BA Wales 1949, Certif. Educn Wales 1950, MA Wales 1953, PhD Wales 1956. Mem., Inst. Brit. Geographers; Mem., Internat. Geograph. Union. Asst Lectr and Lectr, Edinburgh Univ., 1956–67; Sen. Lectr, Aberdeen Univ., 1968–71. Sec. to IGU Commn on Processes and Patterns of Urbanization; Sec., Inst. Brit. Geographers Study Gp in Urban Geography, 1964–67; Mem., Human Geography and Planning Cttee, SSRC; Academic Sec., Faculty of Social Studies, Queen Mary College. *Publications*: ed jtly and contrib., An Atlas of Edinburgh, 1965; mem. editorial bd and contrib., The Times Concise Atlas, 1973; ed and contrib., Essays in Urbanization, 1974; *contrib*. Inst. Brit. Geographers, Urban Study Group Conf. Papers, Scottish Geog. Magazine. *Address*: Dept of Geography,

Jones, Roy Elliott; Senior Lecturer in Politics, University College, Cardiff, since 1971; *b* 1933; *m* 1965; one *s* one *d*. BA Wales 1957, MA Wales 1960. Asst Lectr, subseq. Lectr, UCW, Aberystwyth, 1961–64; Lectr, Univ. York, 1964–65; Lectr, UC Cardiff, 1965–71. *Publications*: The Functional Analysis of Politics, 1967; Nuclear Deterrence, 1968; Analysing Foreign Policy, 1970; The Changing Structure of British Foreign Policy, 1974; *contrib*. Internat. Relations, Polit. Studies. *Address*: Dept of Politics, Univ. College, PO Box 96, Cardiff CF1 1XB.

Jones, Dr Russell; Lecturer in Indonesian, School of Oriental and African Studies, University of London, since 1967; *b* 1926; *m* 1966; one *d*. BA Hons 1960, PhD 1969, London. Lectr in Malay, Univ. of Sydney, 1961–65. Royal Marines, 1944–47; Colonial Service, 1948–58. *Publications*: Bustanu's-Salatin, Book IV, Part 1, 1974; *contrib*. Jl Malayan Br., RAS. *Address*: Sch. of Oriental and African Studies, Malet Street, WC1E 7HP.

Jones, Dr Schuyler; University Lecturer and Assistant Curator, Department of Ethnology and Prehistory (Pitt Rivers Museum), Oxford University, since 1970; *b* 1930; *m* 1955; one *s* one *d*. MA Edinburgh (Hons Social Anthropology), DPhil Oxon (Anthropology). Instructor, Teacher's Coll., Columbia Univ. (Afghanistan Project), 1959–61, Assoc. Profs., 1965–68. *Publications*: Under the African Sun, 1956; Annotated Bibliography of Nuristan (Kafiristan) and the Kalash Kafirs of Chitral, Pt 1, 1966; The Political Organization of the Kam Kafirs, 1967; Bibliography of Nuristan (Kafiristan) and the Kalash Kafirs of Chitral, Pt 2, 1969; Men of Influence in Nuristan, 1974; *contrib*. Acta Orientalia, Man, KUML. *Address*: Dept of Ethnology and Prehistory, Univ. of Oxford, Parks Road, OX1 3PP.

Jones, Dr Sheila; Lecturer, Department of Psychology, University College, London, since 1967; BA Oxford 1942 (Physics), BSc Oxford 1945 (Physics), Dip. Public and Social Admin, Oxford 1951, PhD London 1960, MA Oxford 1962; Member: Experimental Psychology Soc., British Psychology Soc. Res. Officer, Clarendon Laboratory, Oxford, 1942–45. Mem. MRC Industrial Psychology Research Unit, 1960–67. *Publications*: Design of Instruction, 1968; *contrib*. British Jl Educational Psychology, British Jls Psychology, Cognitive Psychology, Qly Jl Experimental Psychology, Jl of Verbal Learning and Verbal Behaviour. *Address*: Dept of Psychology, Univ. College, Gower Street, WC1E 7HP.

Jones, Stanley; *see* Jones, J. S.

Jones, Stanley, MA, PhD; Senior Lecturer, Department of French, University of Glasgow, since 1959; *b* 1916; *m* 1946; three *d*. BA Wales 1937 (1st cl. English, 1st cl. French 1938), MA Wales 1940; PhD Cambridge 1949. Vis. Prof., Univ. of Toronto, 1954. *Publications*: *contrib*. Engl. Studies, Etudes Angl., Fr. Studies, Libr., Neophilol., Notes Queries, Rev. Engl. Lit., Rev. Engl. Studies. *Address*: Dept of French Studies, The Univ., Glasgow G12 8QQ.

Jones, Prof. Stanley James, MA; Professor of Geography, University of Dundee, since 1967; *b* 1905; *m* 1944; one *s*. BA Wales 1926, MA Wales 1928; FRAI, Hon. FRSGS. Asst Lectr, Univ. of Bristol, 1928–34; Rockefeller Fellow, Chicago, 1934–35; Berkeley, 1935–36; Lectr in Geography, Univ. of Bristol, 1936–46; Vis. Lectr, Berkeley, 1939; Lectr and Hd of Dept, Univ. Coll., Dundee, 1946–53; Vis. Prof. of Geography, Berkeley, 1948; Sen. Lectr, Dundee, 1953–67; J. B. Willans Lectr, Aberystwyth, 1966. Editor, Dundee and District, 1968. *Publications*: *contrib*. Geog., Scott. Geog. Mag., Trans Inst. Brit. Geogrs. *Address*: Dept of Geography, Univ. of Dundee, Dundee DD1 4HN.

Jones, Stephen R.; *see* Rees Jones.

Jones, Trefor Thomas; Lecturer, Department of Economics, University of Dundee, since 1969; *b* 1943; *m* 1969. BA Leicester 1965, MA Leicester 1967. Asst Lectr, Queen's Coll., Univ. of St Andrews, 1966–67; Asst Lectr, Univ. of Dundee, 1967–69. *Address*: Dept of Economics, Univ. of Dundee, Dundee DD1 4HN.

Jones, Trevor Arthur; Lecturer, Department of History, University of Keele, since 1964; *b* 1936. BA Cambridge 1958 (1st cl. Geography Tripos, 1st cl. History Tripos). Univ. of Washington, Seattle, 1958–59; LSE, 1959–60; Asst Principal, CRO, London, 1960–62; Lectr, Univ. of Ghana, 1962–64. *Publication*: Ghana's First Republic (forthcoming). *Address*: Dept of History, Univ. of Keele, Keele ST5 5BG.

Jones, Trevor David, MA; Reader in German, University of Cambridge, since 1966; *b* 1908; *m* 1938; one *s* one *d*. BA Cantab 1930 (1st cl. Modern and Medieval Langs), MA Cantab 1934. Goethe Medal, Goethe Institut, Munich, 1973. Lectr, Cambridge Univ., 1937–66; Fellow, Jesus Coll., Cambridge, 1955– . *Publications*: ed, Harrap's Standard German–English Dictionary, vol. I (A–E) 1963, vol. II (F–K) 1967, vol. III (L–R) (forthcoming); trans. and ed (with J. Morris), Treptow: John Siberch – Johann Lair von Siegburg, 1970. *Address*: Jesus College, Cambridge.

Jones, Dr Trevor Owen; Lecturer in French, University of Southampton, since 1964; *b* 1937; *m* 1964; one *s* one *d*. BA Birmingham 1959 (French), PhD Birmingham 1963. Lectr, Magee Univ. Coll., 1961–64. *Address*: Dept of French, The Univ., Southampton SO9 5NH.

Jones, Dr Verina Romana, Dottore in Filosofia; Lecturer, Department of Italian Studies, University of Reading, since 1967; *b* 1939; *m* 1964. Dottore in Filosofia Turin 1962 (Philosophy), BLitt Oxon 1972. Asst Lectr, Royal Holloway Coll., London, 1965–67. *Address*: Dept of Italian Studies, Univ. of Reading, Reading RG6 2AH.

Jones, Prof. Walton Glyn, MA, PhD; Professor of Scandinavian Studies, University of Newcastle upon Tyne, since 1973; *b* 1928; *m* 1953; two *s* two *d*. BA Cantab 1952 (1st cl. Scandinavian Studies), MA, PhD Cantab 1956. Asst Lectr (Queen Alexandra Lecturer), Univ. Coll., London, 1956–58; Lectr, 1958–66; Reader, 1966–73; Vis. Prof., Univ. of Iceland, 1971. Mem., Harpur Trust, 1969–73. *Publications*: Johannes Jørgensens modne år, 1963; Johannes Jørgensen, 1969; Denmark, 1970; William Heinesen, 1974; trans., H. C. Anderson: The Fairy Tale of my Life, 1955; trans., Lund, etc: History of European Ideas, 1972; *contrib*. Fund og Forsk., Mod. Lang. Rev., Mosaic, Nord. Tids., Scand., Scand. Studies. *Address*: Dept of German and Scandinavian Studies, The Univ., Newcastle upon Tyne NE1 7RU.

Jones, Dr William Jervis; Lecturer, Department of German, Westfield College, University of London, since 1969; *b* 1941; *m* 1967; one *s* one *d*. BA Hons Oxon 1963, (1st cl.), MA Oxon 1967, DPhil Oxon 1970; Heath Harrison Travelling Scholar in German, 1962, and French, 1963. Member: Philol Soc., MHRA. Laming Travelling Fellow, Queen's Coll., Oxford, 1963–66; Asst Lectr in German, Westfield Coll., 1966–69. *Address*: Dept of German, Westfield Coll., Univ. of London, Kidderpore Avenue, Hampstead, NW3 7ST.

Jones, William Keith W.; *see* Williams-Jones.

Jones, William Richard, MA; Reader in Education, University College of North Wales, since 1968; *b* 1908; *m* 1949; one *s*. BA Wales 1930 (1st cl. Welsh/Latin), MA Wales 1933 (Education), DipEd Wales 1931. Lectr, Univ. Coll., Cardiff, 1947–49; Lectr, Univ. Coll., Bangor, 1949–60, Sen. Lectr, 1961–67. *Publications*: Bilingualism and Reading Ability in English, 1955; The Educational Attainment of Bilingual Children, 1957; Bilingualism and Intelligence, 1959; Bilingual Education in Wales (in Welsh), 1963; Bilingualism in Welsh Education, 1966; *contrib*. Brit. Jl Educnl Psychol., Brit. Jl Stat. Psychol. *Address*: Education Dept, Univ. Coll. of North Wales, Bangor LL57 2DG.

Jones, Wyndraeth Humphreys M.; *see* Morris-Jones.

Jones-Hughes, Prof. Thomas; *see* Hughes, T. J.

Jones-Lee, Dr Michael Whittaker; Senior Lecturer in Economics, University of York, since 1972; *b* 1944; *m* 1969. BEng Sheffield 1965; DPhil York 1971. University of York: Teaching Fellow, 1966–67; Jun. Lectr, 1967–68; Lectr, 1968–71; Sen. Lectr, St Andrews, 1971–72. Vice-Provost, Alcuin Coll., Univ. of York, 1973– . *Publications*: *contrib*. Applied Econs, Jl Business Finance, Econometrica, Jl Econ. Studies, Jl Finance, Jl Financial and Quantitative Analysis, Jl Pol Econ., Southern Econ. Jl, Southern Econ. Rev., Jl Transport Econs and Policy, Yorks Bull. Econ. and Soc. Res. *Address*: Dept of Economics, Univ. of York, York YO1 5DD.

370

Jope, Prof. Edward Martyn, FBA, FSA; Professor of Archaeology, The Queen's University of Belfast, since 1963; *b* 1915; *m* 1941. MA Oxon 1943; FBA, FSA. Lectr in Archaeology, 1949–54, Reader, 1954–63, QUB. Mem., Staff, Royal Commn on Ancient Monuments (Wales), 1938 (Mem., Commn, 1963–); Biochemist, Nuffield and MRC Grants, 1940. Mem., Ancient Monuments Adv. Council (NI), 1950; Pres., Section H, British Assoc., 1965. *Publications*: Early Celtic Art in the British Isles, 1972; ed, Studies in Building History, 1961; *contrib*. Biochem. Jl, Proc. RSM, Spectrochemica Acta, Trans Faraday Soc., Proc. Prehist. Soc., Antiquaries Jl, Medieval Archaeology, Oxoniensia, Ulster Jl of Archaeology, Proc. Soc. of Antiquaries of Scotland. *Address*: Queen's Univ. of Belfast, Belfast BT7 1NN.

Josipovici, Gabriel David; Lecturer in English, School of European Studies, University of Sussex, since 1966; *b* 1940. BA Oxon 1961 (1st cl. English). Asst Lectr in English, Univ. of Sussex, 1963–66. *Publications*: The Inventory (novel), 1968; Words (novel), 1971; The World and the Book, 1971; Traces (stories and plays), 1974; stories, in, Penguin Modern Stories 12, 1972; *contrib*. Adam Internat. Rev., Crit. Qly, Encoun., Europ. Juda. *Address*: Arts Building, Univ. of Sussex, Brighton BN1 9QN.

Josling, Prof. Timothy Edward; Professor of Agricultural Economics, University of Reading, since 1974; *b* 1940; *m* 1973. BSc Agric., London 1963 MSc Guelph 1965, PhD Michigan State 1967. Asst Lectr, LSE, 1968–70; Lectr, LSE, 1970–73; Reader, LSE, 1973–74. *Publications*: Interdependence among Agricultural and other Sectors of the Canadian Economy, 1966; The United Kingdom Grains Agreement (1964): An Economic Analysis, 1968; Agriculture and Britain's Trade Policy Dilemma, 1970; Burdens and Benefits of Farm Support Policies, 1972; *contrib*. Amer. Jl Agric. Econs, Can. Jl Agric. Econs, Jl Agric. Econs, Jl Farm Econs, Weltwirtschaftliches Archiv. *Address*: Univ. of Reading, Whiteknights, Reading, Berks RG6 2AH.

Joubert, John Pierre Herman, BMus, FRAM; Reader in Music, University of Birmingham, since 1968; *b* 1927; *m* 1951; one *s* one *d*. BMus Dunelm 1950; FRAM 1955. Lectr in Music, Univ. of Hull, 1950–62; Lectr in Music, Univ. of Birmingham, 1962–64, Sen. Lectr, 1964–68. Mem., Music Adv. Cttee, Brit. Council, 1971– . *Publications*: musical compositions in many forms and media; *contrib*. Composer, Musical Times. *Address*: Dept of Music, Univ. of Birmingham, PO Box 363, Birmingham B15 2TT.

Joynson, Dr Robert Billington, MA, BLitt, PhD; Senior Lecturer in Psychology, University of Nottingham, since 1958; *b* 1922; *m* 1961; one *s* one *d*. BA Oxon 1942, MA Oxon 1947, BLitt Oxon 1949, PhD Nottingham 1959; ABPsS. Asst Lectr, Nottingham, 1948–49, Lectr, 1949–58; Vis. Fulbright Lectr, Howard Univ., 1967–68. *Publications*: Psychology and Common Sense, 1974; *contrib*. Brit. Jl Psychol., Qly Jl Exper.

Psychol. *Address*: Dept of Psychology, Univ. of Nottingham, Nottingham NG7 2RD.

Jump, Prof. John Davies; John Edward Taylor Professor of English Literature, University of Manchester, since 1966; *b* 1913; *m* 1937; two *d*. BA Liverpool 1933 (1st cl. English), DipEd Liverpool 1934, MA Liverpool 1936, MA Manchester 1968. Asst Lectr, Manchester, 1937; Lectr, Manchester, 1945–50; Sen. Lectr, Manchester, 1950–59; Reader, Manchester, 1959–65; Prof., Manchester, 1965–66; Vis. Prof., Sir George Williams Univ., Montreal, 1970; Dean of Faculty of Arts, Manchester, 1970, 1971; Vis. Prof., Univ. of Victoria, BC, 1973. *Publications*: Matthew Arnold, 1955, 2nd edn 1965; Burlesque, 1972; Byron, 1972; The Ode, 1973; ed, Beaumont and Fletcher: Rollo, Duke of Normandy, 1948; ed, Marlowe: Doctor Faustus, 1962; ed, Marlowe: Tamburlaine, 1967; ed, Tennyson: The Critical Heritage, 1967; *contrib*. CQ, N and Q, RES, TLS. *Address*: English Dept, The Univ., Manchester M13 9PL.

Junankar, Pramod Nagorao; Lecturer in Economics, University of Essex, since 1969; *b* 1943. BSc(Econ) London 1964, MSc(Econ) London 1966. Tutor in Economics, LSE, 1965–66; Lectr in Economics, Univ. of Durham, 1966–69; Vis. Asst Prof., Northwestern Univ., Evanston, Ill. *Publications*: Investment: Theories and Evidence, 1972; *contrib*. Economica, Econ. Pol. Wkly. *Address*: Dept of Economics, Univ. of Essex, Wivenhoe Park, Colchester CO4 3SQ.

Juniper, Dean F.; Lecturer, School of Education, University of Reading, since 1964; *b* 1929; *m*. BA Oxford 1952, MA 1956; Member: Assoc. of Educnl Psychologists, Soc. for Study of Addiction. WEA part-time Tutor, Extra-Mural Dept, Nottingham Univ., 1959–60; Part-time tutor, Open Univ., Jan–Dec. 1972. Educational Psychologist: Huddersfield LEA, 1953–58; W Bromwich LEA, 1958–59; Holland CC LEA 1959–64. Organiser: Schs Psychol/Child Guidance Service, Boston, Lincs, 1959; Dip. in Educnl Guidance, Univ. of Reading, 1965; Dip. in Educnl Guidance, with Special Ref. to the Social Environment, Univ. of Reading, 1967; Confluent Educn Project, Marble Arch grant, 1964– . *Publications*: A Manual of Educational Guidance, 1971; Dymion, 1971; Man against Mortality, 1974; Decision-making for Secondary Schools (forthcoming); chap. in, Towards a Policy for the Education of Teachers, 1969; *contrib*. Educnl Res., Aspects of Educn, Counsellor, BPS Bull., Learning for Living, Educn and Trng. *Address*: School of Education, Univ. of Reading, 22 London Road, Reading.

K

Kaess, Dr Dale W.; Lecturer, Department of Psychology, University of Aberdeen, since 1971; *b* 1939; *m* 1968. BA Puget Sound 1964; MA Illinois 1967, PhD Illinois 1969. Instructor, Univ. of Illinois, 1968–69; Asst Prof., Washington State Univ., 1969–71. *Publications*: *contrib*. Jl Behav. Sci., Jl Com-

par. and Physiol Psychol, Develtl Psychol., Jl Exptl Child Psychol., Jl Exptl Psychol., Jl Genetic Psychol., Perception, Psychonomic Sci. *Address*: Dept of Psychology, Univ. of Aberdeen, Old Aberdeen AB9 2UB.

Kaim-Caudle, Peter Robert; Senior Lecturer in Social Administration, Department of Sociology and Social Administration, University of Durham, since 1968; *b* 1916; *m* 1945; *s* two *d*. BSc(Econ) London 1938; Barrister-at-Law, Lincoln's Inn 1956. Lectr in Economics, Sch. of Economics, Dundee, 1947–50; Extra-Mural Staff Tutor in Social Studies, Univ. of Durham, 1950–63; Lectr in Social Admin., 1963–68; Hd of Dept of Economic Studies, Univ. Coll. of Sierra Leone, 1954–55, 1961; Res. Prof., Inst. of Econ. and Soc. Res., Dublin, 1968–70 (on secondment). Mem.: Durham Co., Social Service Cttee; Ment. Hlth Rev. Trbnl (Newcastle Reg.). *Publications*: Social Security in Ireland and Western Europe, 1964; Social Policy in the Irish Republic, 1967; Dental Services in Ireland, 1969; Comparative Social Policy and Social Security, 1973; *contrib*. Admin., Local Govt, Internat. Rev. Admin. Sci., Irish Jurist, Lloyds Bank Rev. *Address*: 44/45 Old Elvet, Durham.

Kalab, Milada; Lecturer in Anthropology, University of Durham, since 1964; *b* 1924. BA Santiniketan 1952, MA Bombay 1954; MA London 1961; FRAI, FRGS. Asst Lectr, QUB, 1963–64. *Publications*: *contrib*. Geog. Jl. *Address*: Dept of Anthropology, Univ. of Durham, Durham DH1 3HP.

Kaldor, Prof. The Lord; Nicholas Kaldor, MA, FBA; Professor of Economics, University of Cambridge, since 1966; *b* 1908; *m* 1934; four *d*. BSc(Econ) London 1930 (1st cl.), MA Cantab 1950; Hon. Dr Dijon 1962; FBA 1963. Asst Lectr, Lectr, Reader in Economics, LSE, 1932–47; Fellow, King's Coll., Cambridge, 1949– ; Reader in Economics, Univ. of Cambridge, 1952–66. Res. Associate (pt-time), NIESR, 1943–45; Chief of Econ. Planning Staff, US Strategic Bombing Survey, 1945; Dir, Res. and Planning Div., ECE, Geneva, 1947–49; Mem.: UN Gp of experts on internat. measures for full employment, 1949; Royal Commn on Taxation of Profits and Income, 1951–55; Advr on tax reform. Govt of India, 1956; Econ. Advr, ECLA, Santiago, Chile, 1956; Fiscal Adv., Govt of Ceylon, 1958; Ford Vis. Res. Prof., Univ. of California, 1959–60; Fiscal Advr, Govt of Mexico, 1960; Econ. Advr, Govt of Ghana, 1961; Fiscal Advr: Govt of Brit. Guiana, 1961; Turkey, 1962; Iran, 1966; Vis. Economist, Reserve Bank of Australia, Sydney, 1963; Special Advr, Chancellor of the Exchequer, 1964–68. Cnsltnt, 1968–70. *Publications*: Quantitative Aspects of the Full Employment Problem in Britain, in, Beveridge: Full Employment in a Free Society, 1944; (jtly) Statistical Analysis of Advertising, Expenditure and Revenue of the Press, 1948; (jtly) National and International Measures for Full Employment, 1950; An Expenditure Tax, 1955, Japanese edn 1959, Italian edn 1962, Spanish edn 1963; Indian Tax Reform, 1956; Essays in Value and Distribution, 1960; Essays in Economic

Stability and Growth, 1960, Japanese edn 1962, Italian edn 1965, Spanish edn 1969, Polish edn 1970; Capital Accumulation and Economic Growth, in, The Theory of Capital, 1961; Ensayos sobre Desarrollo Economico (Mexico), 1961; Essays on Economic Policy, vols I and II, 1964, Spanish edn 1970; Causes of the Slow Rate of Growth of the United Kingdom, 1966; ed, Conflicts in Policy Objectives, 1970; *contrib*. Economet., Economica, Econ. Jl, Jl Pol. Econ., Jl Scott. Econ. Soc., Harv. Business Rev., Lloyds Bank Rev., Oxf. Econ. Papers, Oxf. Inst. Stats, Qly Jl Econ., Rev. Econ. Studies, Rev. Brasil., Sankhya. *Address*: Faculty of Economics, Sidgwick Avenue, Cambridge.

Kalton, Prof. Gordon Graham William; Leverhulme Professor of Social Statistics, Department of Econometrics and Social Statistics, University of Southampton, since 1971; *b* 1936; *m* 1962; one *s* one *d*. BSc(Econ) London 1958, MSc(Econ) London 1960; Fellow Royal Statistical Soc., FIS, Mem., American Statistical Assoc., Assoc. Mem. Market Res. Soc. Asst Lectr, 1961–64, Lectr, 1964–68, Sen. Lectr, 1968–70, Reader, 1970–71, in Social Statistics, LSE. Guest teacher and Res. Scholar, Univ. of Michigan, 1966–67. SSRC Statistics and Archives Cttees, 1972– ; Acad. Adv. Cttee, Social and Community Planning Res., 1973– . *Publications*: Introduction to Statistical Ideas for Social Scientists, 1966; The Public Schools: a Factual Survey, 1966; (with M. Shepherd, B. Cooper and A. C. Brown) Psychiatric Illness in General Practice, 1966; (with C. A. Moser) Survey Methods in Social Investigation, 2nd edn 1971. *Address*: Univ. of Southampton, Southampton SO9 5NH.

Kamat, Ramanand Padmanabh; Lecturer in Humanities and Social Sciences, Bath University, since 1962; *b* 1928; *m* 1958; two *s* three *d*. BA(Econ) Bombay 1950, MA(Econ) Bombay 1953, MSc London 1958. *Address*: Bath Univ., Claverton Down, Bath BA2 7AY.

Kamen, Dr Henry Arthur, MA, DPhil, FRHistS; Reader, Department of History, University of Warwick, since 1973; *b* 1936; *m* 1963; two *s*. BA Oxon 1960 (1st cl. History), MA Oxon 1965, DPhil Oxon 1963; FRHistS. Lectr, Edinburgh Univ., 1963–66; Lectr, Warwick Univ., 1966–71, Sen. Lectr, 1971–73. *Publications*: trans., In the Interlude: Poems 1945–1960 by B. Pasternak, 1962; The Spanish Inquisition, 1965; The Rise of Toleration, 1967; The War of Succession in Spain 1700–1715, 1969; The Iron Century: Social Change in Europe 1550–1660, 1971; A Concise History of Spain, 1974; *contrib*. Bull. Inst. Hist. Res., Econ. Hist. Rev., EHR, Past Pres. *Address*: Dept of History, Univ. of Warwick, Coventry CV4 7AL.

Kane, Prof. George, FBA; Professor of English Language and Medieval Literature, since 1965, and Head of English Department in the University of London at King's College since 1968; Dean of the Faculty of Arts, since 1973; *b* 1916; *m* 1946; one *s* one *d*. BA British Columbia 1936, MA Toronto 1937, PhD London 1946; FBA 1968, Fellow UCL 1972. Res. Fellow, Univ. of Toronto, 1936–37; Res.

372

Fellow, Northwestern Univ., 1937–38; IODE Schol. for BC, 1938–39; Asst Lectr in English, 1946–48, Lectr, 1948–53, Reader, 1953–55, UCL; Prof. of English Lang. and Lit. and Hd of English Dept, Royal Holloway Coll., Univ. of London, 1955–65; Vis. Prof., Medieval Acad. of Amer., 1970; Chambers Meml Lectr, UCL, 1965. Public Orator, Univ. of London, 1962–66. Mem., Council, Early English Text Soc., 1969; Mem., Governing Body, SOAS, 1970. Sir Israel Gollancz Meml Prize, Brit. Acad., 1963. Gen. Editor, London edn, Piers Plowman. *Publications*: Middle English Literature, 1951; Piers Plowman, the A Version, 1960; Piers Plowman: the Evidence for Authorship, 1965; (with E. Talbot Donaldson) Piers Plowman: the B Version, 1975; *contrib*. jls. *Address*: King's College, Strand, WC2R 2LS.

Kantorowich, Prof. Roy Herman; Professor of Town and Country Planning, and Director of the School of Town and Country Planning, University of Manchester, since 1961; *b* 1916; *m* 1943; one *s* two *d*. BArch Witwatersrand 1939, MA Manchester 1965; ARIBA, FRTPI, PP(SA)ITRP, MI(SA)A. Mem.: Council, S Afr. Inst. Town and Regional Planners, 1956–61 (Pres., 1960); Council, Royal Town Planning Inst. (Chm., Educn Cttee, 1965–70); NW Econ. Planning Council, 1965– ; SSRC Planning Cttee, 1968–73; CNAA Planning Panel, 1968– (Chm., 1971–). *Publ cations*: Native Housing, 1940; Cape Town Foreshore Plan, 1948; ed, Regional Shopping Centres in NW England (Haydock Report), 1964; Durban, 1985, 1968; *contrib*. S Afr. Archit. Rec., Royal Town Plan. Inst. Jl. *Address*: Dept of Town and Country Planning, Univ. of Manchester, Manchester M13 9PL.

Karn, Dr Valerie Ann; Lecturer, Centre for Urban and Regional Studies, University of Birmingham, since 1966; *b* 1939. BA Oxon 1961 (Geography); PhD Birmingham 1974. Mem., Social Admin. Assoc. Commonwealth Schol., Univ. of the Punjab, Lahore, 1961–63; Grad. Student, Dept of City and Regional Planning, GSD, Harvard, 1964; Res. Fellow, Inst. of Social and Econ. Res., Univ. of York, 1964–66. Res. Offr, Central Housing Adv. Cttee, Sub-Cttee on Housing Mngmt, 1968–69; Mem., Housing Panel, Birmingham Community Relat. Cttee, 1971– ; Rapporteur for Housing Panel, Conf. on Cities, Indianapolis, 1971. *Publications*: (with J. B. Cullingworth) The Ownership and Management of Housing in the New Towns, 1969; A Housing Survey of East Kilbride, 1970; A Housing Survey of Aycliffe, 1970; A Housing Survey of Stevenage, 1970; A Housing Survey of Crawley, 1970; Report of the Panel on Housing, in, Final Report – Conference on Cities, Indianapolis, 1971; (with H. W. Mellor and Randall Smith) Housing in Retirement, 1973; Housing Standards and Costs, 1974; Retiring to the Seaside, 1974; *contrib*. Race, Social Policy, New Community. *Address*: Centre for Urban and Regional Studies, Univ. of Birmingham, PO Box 363, Birmingham B15 2TT.

Karsten, Ian George Francis; Lecturer, Law Dept, London School of Economics and

Political Science, since 1970; *b* 1944. BA
Oxon 1965, BCL Oxon 1966, MA Oxon 1968,
Dip. Hague Acad. Internat. Law 1969;
Barrister, Gray's Inn, 1967. Asst Lectr,
Univ. of Southampton, 1966–68, Lectr,
1968–70. *Publications*: title Conflict of Laws,
in Halsbury's Laws of England, 4th edn,
1974; *contrib*. Internat Comp. Law Qly, Mod.
Law Rev. *Address*: London School of
Economics and Political Science, Houghton
Street, Aldwych, WC2A 2AE.

Kaser, Michael Charles; Professorial
Fellow of St Antony's College, and Reader in
Economics, Oxford University, since 1972;
b 1926; *m* 1954; four *s* one *d*. Economics
Tripos Cambridge (Exhibnr) 1945, MA Cam-
bridge 1950, MA Oxford 1960. Vis. Professor,
Grad. Inst. Internat. Studies, Geneva Univ.,
1959–63; Univ. of Michigan, 1966; Vis.
Lectr, Cambridge Univ., 1967–68. Foreign
Service (London and Moscow), 1947–51;
Secretariat, UN Econ. Commn for Europe,
Geneva, 1951–63; Fellow of St Antony's
Coll. and Lectr in Soviet Economics, Oxford
Univ., 1963–72; Member: Edit. Adv. Bd,
Econ. Jl; Council, Internat. Econ. Assoc.;
Cttee, Nat. Assoc. Soviet and E Europ.
Studies (Conv./Chm., 1965–73); Nat. Adv.
Bd, Soviet Studies; Edit. Bd, Abstract. Ser-
vice for Soviet and E Europ. Studies; Brit.
Cttee of Internat. Assoc. for SE Europ.
Studies; Governor, Plater Coll., Oxford.
Publications: Comecon: Integration Problems
of the Planned Economies, 1964, 2nd edn
1967, Ital. trans. 1972; ed, St Antony's
Papers 19 (Soviet Affairs 4), 1966; ed,
Economic Development for Eastern Europe,
1968; (with J. Zieliński), Planning in East
Europe, 1970, Arabic and Spanish trans 1971;
Soviet Economics, 1970, French, German,
Spanish and Swedish trans 1970, Japanese
trans. 1973; ed (with R. Portes), Planning and
Market Relations, 1971; (with A. Saint) St
Antony's College Oxford: a history of its
buildings and site, 1973; *contrib*. Ann.
URSS, Econ. Jl, Jl Develt Studies, Sov.
Studies. *Address*: St Antony's College, Ox-
ford OX2 6JF.

Katouzian, Mohammad Ali Homayoun;
Lecturer in Economics, University of Kent
at Canterbury, since 1969; *b* 1942; *m* 1964;
one *s* one *d*. BSocSc Birmingham 1967,
MScEcon London 1968; Fellow Brit. Soc.
for Middle Eastern Studies, Mem., Royal
Econ. Soc. Asst Lectr in Econs, Univ. Leeds,
1968–69; Vis. Prof., Pahlavi Univ., 1972–73;
Sen. Assoc. Mem., St Antony's Coll.,
Oxford, 1973. Casual Mem. Staff, BBC
(Persian Service), 1967–68. *Publications*: (in
Persian) International Economic Theory,
1974; trans. Persian, H. Butterfield: Univer-
sities and Higher Education Today, 1974;
contrib. Jl Peasant Studies, Kherad va
Koushesh, Mercurio, Oxford Econ. Papers,
Qly Jl Econom. Res. *Address*: Rutherford
College, Univ. of Kent at Canterbury,
Canterbury, Kent.

Katzen, Leo; Senior Lecturer, Department
of Economics, University of Leicester, since
1965; *b* 1929; *m* 1952; one *s* one *d*. BA Rand
1951 (1st cl. Economics), MSc(Econ) London
1954; Lectr, Natal Univ., Durban, 1955–58;

Sen. Lectr, Cape Town Univ., 1959–65.
Mem., Council, African Studies Assoc. of the
UK, 1969–71. *Publications*: Gold and the
South African Economy, 1964; *contrib*. South
African Jl of Econs, Optima. Internat.
Migration, Bull. of the African Studies
Assoc. of UK. *Address*: Economics Dept.,
The Univ., Leicester LE1 7RH.

Katzenellenbogen, Dr Simon E.; Lecturer
in Economic History, History Department,
University of Manchester, since 1970; *b* 1939;
two *s* two *d*. BA Michigan 1961, DPhil
Oxford 1969. Teaching Asst, Univ. of Calif.,
Los Angeles, 1961–62; Lectr, Ecole Nationale
de Droit et d'Administration, Zaïre, 1962–64;
Jun. Res. Fellow, Inst of Commonwealth
Studies, Univ. of London, 1967–68; Res.
Fellow, Dept of Econ. Hist. Leicester Univ.,
1968–70. *Publication*: Railways and the
Copper Mines of Katanga, 1973. *Address*:
Dept of History, Univ. of Manchester,
Manchester M13 9PL.

Kavanagh, Dennis Anthony; Senior Lecturer in Government, University of Manchester, since 1974 (Lecturer, 1967–74); *b*
1941; *m* 1966; one *s* two *d*. BA Manchester
1963, MA(Econ) Manchester 1966. Asst
Lectr, Hull Univ., 1965–67; Ford Foundn
Fellow, Stanford Univ., California, 1969–70.
Publications: Constituency Electioneering in
Britain, 1970; Political Culture, 1972;
Leadership and the Labour Party (forth-
coming); *contrib*. Political Participation, ed
G. B. Parry; Political Leadership in the Twen-
tieth Century, ed M. Dogan; Crisis, Choice
and Change, ed G. Almond et al.; The
Backbencher and Parliament, ed R. Leonard
and V. Herman; Between Sovereignty and
Integration, ed G. Ionescu; *contrib*. Polit.
Studies, Govt Opposit., Brit. Jl Polit. Sci.,
Comp. Polits. *Address*: Dept of Government,
Univ. of Manchester, Manchester M13 9PL.

Kazantzis, Dr George, PhD, FRCS,
MRCP, MFCM; Senior Lecturer in Com-
munity Medicine, The Middlesex Hospital
Medical School, University of London, since
1967; *b* 1924. MB BS London 1949, PhD
London 1956, FRCS 1957, MRCP 1962,
MFCM London 1972; Mem., Med. Res.
Soc., Soc. for Social Med., Soc. for Occupat.
Med., Royal Soc. of Med. Scientific Staff,
MRC, 1958–65; Lectr, Medical Professorial
Unit, Middlesex Hosp., Med. Sch., 1965–67;
Vis. Acad. Staff, London Sch. of Hygiene,
Univ. of London, 1970– . Hon. Cnsltnt in
Preventive and Social Medicine, Middlesex
Hosp., 1967– ; Mem., Bd of Studies,
Community Med., Univ. of London; Sub-
Cttee on the Toxicology of Metals, Permanent
Commn and Internat. Assoc. Occupat. Hlth,
1970; WHO Expert Adv. Panel on Food
Additives, 1972. *Publications*: chapters, in,
Reports on the Progress of Applied Chemistry
1963, 1964, 1966; in, Fundamentals of
Current Medical Treatment, 1965, 2nd edn
1970; in, The Effects of Abnormal Physical
Conditions at Work, 1967; in, Sixth Sym-
posium on Advanced Medicine, Royal
College of Physicians, 1970; in, The Medical
Annual, 1973; in, Disorders of the Respira-
tory System, 1973; *contrib*. Ann. Occupat.
Hyg., Brit. Jl Indust. Med., Brit. Med. Jl, Jl

Physiol., Internat. Jl Environm. Studies, Lancet, Nature, Qly Jl Med., Thorax. *Address*: Dept of Community Medicine, The Middlesex Hospital, W1N 8AA.

Kear, Brian Stanley, BSc, MSc; Lecturer in Geography, University of Manchester, since 1968; *b* 1936; *m* 1960; one *s* two *d*. BSc 1959 (2nd cl. Geography), MSc Manchester 1968. Asst Lectr, Manchester, 1966–68. *Publications*: Soils and Land Utilization of the Plains of Canterbury and Otago, New Zealand, 1968. *Address*: Dept of Geography, Univ. of Manchester, Manchester M13 9PL.

Kearney, Hugh Francis; Richard Pares Professor of History, University of Edinburgh, since 1970; *b* 1924; *m* 1956; two *s* one *d*. MA Cantab 1948, PhD Dublin 1955; FRHistS 1970. Lectr, UC Dublin, 1950–62; Reader, Univ. of Sussex, 1962–70. *Publications*: Strafford in Ireland, 1959; Origins of the Scientific Revolution, 1964; Scholars and Gentlemen: Universities and Society 1550–1700, 1970; Science and Change, 1971; *contrib*. Jl of Ecclesiastical History, Irish Historical Studies, Econ. Hist. Rev., Jl of History of Education. *Address*: History Dept, William Robertson Building, Univ. of Edinburgh, George Square, Edinburgh EH8 9JY.

Kearns, Edward John, PhD; Lecturer in French, University of Durham, since 1956; *b* 1930; *m*; three *d*. BA Reading 1953 (Hons in French), PhD Reading 1958 (French); Mem., Soc. French Studies. Temp. Asst Lectr, Reading, 1956. *Publications*: *contrib*. Durham Univ. Jl. *Address*: French Dept, Elvet Riverside, Durham City.

Keates, John Stanley; Senior Lecturer, Department of Geography, University of Glasgow, since 1969; *b* 1925; *m* 1950; one *s* one *d*. BA Oxon 1949 (Hons Geog.), MA Oxon 1950. Lectr, Univ. of Glasgow, 1960–69. Editor, Cartog. Jl, 1963–70; Pres., Brit. Cartog. Soc.; Member: Royal Soc. Sub-Cttee on Cartog., 1971– ; Commn VI, Cartographic Technology, Internat. Cartog Assoc.; Photogram Soc.; Technical Assessor, Cartography, SCOTECH. *Publications*: Cartographic Design and Production, 1973; *contrib*. Cartog. Jl, Internat. Ybk Cartog., Survey. Map. *Address*: Dept of Geography, Univ. of Glasgow, Glasgow G12 8QQ.

Keates, Laurence Walter; Senior Lecturer in Portuguese, Leeds University, since 1972, Lecturer in Spanish and Portuguese, 1961–72; *b* 1929; *m* 1955; one *s* three *d*. BA Birmingham 1952 (Hons Spanish), MA Birmingham 1959; Mem. Luso-Brazil. Gp, Assoc. Brit. Hispanists. Leitor em Inglês, Lisbon, 1959–61. *Publications*: The Discovery of the Atlantic (trans. of C. Brochado: O Descobrimento do Atlântico), 1960; A Treatise on Assurance (trans. of P. S. Lusitano: Tractatus de assecurationibus et sponsibus), 1961; The Court Theatre of Gil Vicente, 1962; A first course in Portuguese, 1969; A Manual of Spanish and Portuguese Prose Composition for Advanced Students, 1969; (with F. G. Tortosa) Spanish Key to above, (with F. M. Perestrelo) Portuguese Key to above, 1970; *contrib*. Rev. Fac. Let. Lisb., Rev. Litt.

Comp. *Address*: The Dept of Spanish and Portuguese, The Univ., Leeds LS2 9TJ.

Keatinge, Neil Patrick; Lecturer, Department of Political Science, Trinity College, Dublin, since 1966; *b* 1939; *m* 1964; two *s*. BA TCD 1960 (Mod.), MScEcon LSE 1963, PhD TCD 1968. Jun. Lectr, TCD, 1963–66; Tutor, 1966– . *Publications*: The Formulation of Irish Foreign Policy, 1973. *contrib*. Internat. Affairs, Internat. Relations, Osterreichische Zeitschrift für Aussenpolitik. *Address*: No 6, 22, Trinity College, Dublin 2.

Kedourie, Prof. Elie; Professor of Politics, London School of Economics, University of London, since 1965. BSc(Econ) London 1950. Asst Lectr, Lectr and Reader, LSE, 1953–65; Vis. Lectr, Univ. of California, Los Angeles, 1959; Vis. Lectr, Univ. of Paris, 1959; Vis. Prof., Princeton Univ., 1960–61; Vis. Prof., Harvard Univ., 1968–69. Editor, Middle Eastern Studies, 1964– . *Publications*: England and the Middle East: the destruction of the Ottoman Empire 1914–1921, 1956; Nationalism, 1960, 5th edn 1971, German trans. 1971; Afghani and Abduh: an essay on religious unbelief and political activism in modern Islam, 1966; The Chatham House Version, 1970; Nationalism in Asia and Africa, 1971; Arabic Political Memoirs and Other Studies, 1974; *contrib*. Cambridge Jl, Historical Jl, Jl of RAS, Orient, Middle Eastern Studies, Encounter. *Address*: London School of Economics, Houghton Street, Aldwych, WC2A 2AE.

Kedward, Harry Roderick; Lecturer in History, University of Sussex, since 1962; *b* 1937; *m* 1965; one *s* one *d*. BA Oxon 1960, BPhil Oxon 1962, MA Oxon, Leverhulme Research Fellow, 1968–69. *Publications*: The Dreyfus Affair, 1965; Fascism in Western Europe, 1968; The Anarchists, 1970. *Address*: Arts Building, Univ. of Sussex, Brighton BN1 9QN.

Kee, Dr A. Alistair; Lecturer, Department of Theology, University of Hull, since 1967; *b* 1937; *m* 1961; one *s* one *d*. MA Glasgow 1958, BD Glasgow 1961, STM Union Theol. Sem., New York, 1962, PhD UTS, New York, 1964; Licent. Ch of Scotland 1960. Lectr in Theol., Univ. Coll. of Rhodesia, 1965–67. *Publications*: The Way of Transcendence, 1971; ed, Seeds of Liberation, 1973; ed, The Development of Political Theology, 1974; *contrib*. Christ. Cent., Christ. Crisis, Expos. Times, Mod. Chman, New Christ., Nov. Testam., Record (Columbia Univ.). *Address*: Dept of Theology, The Univ., Hull HU6 7RX.

Keeble, Dr David Etherton; Lecturer, Department of Geography, Cambridge University, since 1968, and Fellow of St Catharine's College, Cambridge, since 1967; *b* 1939; *m* 1963; two *s* one *d*. BA Cambridge 1961 (1st cl. Geography), MA Cambridge 1965, PhD Cambridge 1967; Mem., Inst. Brit. Geogrs, Reg. Studies Assoc. Demonstrator, Cambridge Univ., 1963–68; Res. Fellow, St Catharine's Coll., Cambridge, 1964–67. Mem., E Anglian Econ. Planning Council, 1971– ; Mem., SSRC Geog.

Cttee, 1973– . *Publications*: (jtly) Regional Development in Britain, 1972; *contrib*. Trans Inst. Brit. Geogrs, Town Plann. Rev., Reg. Studies. *Address*: St Catharine's College, Cambridge.

Keefe, Terence, MA, BA; Lecturer in French, University of Leicester, since 1968; *b* 1940; *m* 1962; one *s* one *d*. BA Leicester 1962 (Hons French), MA Leicester 1968, BA London 1966 (Hons Philosophy); CertEd Leicester 1963. Tutorial Asst in French, Univ. of Leicester, 1965–67, Asst Lectr, 1967–68. *Publications*: *contrib*. Fr. Studies, Philos. Jl, Romanic Rev., MLR, Romance Notes. *Address*: Dept of French, Univ. of Leicester, University Road, Leicester LE1 7RH.

Keen, Maurice Hugh; Fellow and Tutor in Medieval History, Balliol College, Oxford University, since 1961; *b* 1933; *m* 1968; two *d*. BA Oxon 1957, MA Oxon 1961. Jun. Res. Fellow, Queen's Coll., Oxford, 1957–61. *Publications*: The Outlaws of Medieval Legend, 1961; The Laws of War in the late Middle Ages, 1965; A History of Medieval Europe, 1968; *contrib*. Hist., Trans Royal Hist. Soc. *Address*: Balliol College, Oxford.

Keene, Dr Geoffrey Bourton; Reader in Logic, Department of Philosophy, University of Exeter, since 1964; *b* 1923; *m* 1950; one *d*. BA Birmingham 1950 (1st cl. Philosophy), BPhil Oxon 1952, PhD Exon 1973. Asst Lectr, then Lectr, Keele Univ., 1953–60; Lectr, Exeter Univ., 1960–64. *Publications*: Abstract Sets and Finite Ordinals, 1961; Language and Reasoning, 1961, 2nd edn 1963; First-Order Functional Calculus, 1964; trans., Blanché: Axiomatics, 1962; Relational Syllogism, 1969; Formal Set Theory, 1974; *contrib*. Amer. Philos. Qly, Analysis, Mind, Philos. Qly. *Address*: Philosophy Dept, Univ. of Exeter, Exeter EX4 4QJ.

Keil, (Ellen) Teresa; Senior Lecturer in Sociology, Department of Social Sciences (formerly Department of Social Sciences and Economics), Loughborough University of Technology, since 1974 (Lecturer, 1968–74); *b* 1935; *m* 1962. BA Liverpool 1957 (Hons Social Science); Mem., Brit. Sociol Assoc. Res. Worker, Univ. of Liverpool, 1957–60; Nuffield Sociological Schol., 1960–62; Res. Worker, Univ. of Leicester, 1962–64; Lectr in Sociol., Univ. of Aston in Birmingham, 1964–68. *Publications*: *contrib*. Sociol Rev. *Address*: Dept of Social Sciences, Loughborough Univ. of Technology, Loughborough LE11 3TU.

Keil, Dr Ian John Ernest; Senior Lecturer in Economic and Social History, Department of Economics, Loughborough University, since 1971; *b* 1933; *m* 1962. BA Bristol 1955 (2nd cl. History), PhD Bristol 1964; Mem., Econ. Hist. Soc., Histl Assoc., Past Present, Brit. Agric. Hist. Tutor in Econ. Hist., Liverpool Univ., 1957–62; Asst Lectr, Loughborough, 1962–64, Lectr, 1964–71. Chm., Leics Local Hist. Council, 1971–74. *Publications*: (with D. Wix, M. Palmer and J. Roberts) Bygone Loughborough in Photographs, 1973; *contrib*. Amat. Hist., Bank.

Mag., Bristol Glos Archaeol. Soc., Dorset Archaeol. Soc., Downs. Rev., London Midx Archaeol. Soc., Notes Queries, Somerset Archaeol. Nat. Hist. Soc., Wilts Archaeol. Nat. Hist. Soc. *Address*: Dept of Economics, Univ. of Loughborough, Loughborough LE11 3TU.

Keith-Lucas, Prof. Bryan; Professor of Government, University of Kent at Canterbury, since 1965; Master of Darwin College, 1970–74; *b* 1912; *m* 1946; one *s* two *d*. MA Cambridge 1937, MA Oxford 1948; Solicitor 1937. Sen. Lectr in Local Govt, Oxford, 1948–65; Fellow, Nuffield Coll., 1950–65. Chairman: Nat. Assoc. of Parish Councils, 1964–70; Commn on Electoral System, Sierra Leone, 1954, Mauritius, 1955–56; Mem.: Roberts Cttee on Public Libraries, 1957–59; Mallaby Cttee on Staffing in Local Govt, 1964–67; Local Govt Commn for England, 1965–66. Hon. Fellow, Inst. of Local Govt Studies, Birmingham, 1973– . *Publications*: The English Local Government Franchises, 1952; ed, Redlich and Hirst: History of Local Government in England, 2nd edn 1958, 3rd edn 1970; *contrib*. Cambridge Law Jl, Econ. Hist. Rev., Law Qly Rev., Pol. Studies, Public Admin, Public Law. *Address*: Darwin College, Univ. of Kent at Canterbury, Canterbury CT2 7NY.

Keith-Smith, Brian, MLitt; Lecturer in German, Department of German, University of Bristol, since 1963; *b* 1934; *m* 1963; two *s* one *d*. BA Southampton 1958, MLitt Southampton 1968. Asst in German, Southampton, 1959; Asst Lectr, Bristol, 1960; Lektor für Anglistik und Amerikanistik, Heidelberg, 1967–68. *Publications*: Essays on Contemporary German Literature 1966, 3rd ed 1972; Johannes Bobrowski, 1970; Ermahnende Ausdeutungen, 1971; German Expressionism (forthcoming); *contrib*. Archiv; New German Studies. *Address*: Dept of German, Univ. of Bristol, Bristol BT8 1TH.

Kellas, Dr James Grant, MA, PhD; Senior Lecturer in Politics, University of Glasgow, since 1973 (Lecturer, 1964–73); *b* 1936; *m* 1962; two *s* one *d*. MA Aberdeen 1958 (1st cl. History-Politics), PhD London 1962. Tutorial Fellow in History, Bedford Coll., London Univ., 1961–62; Asst in Hist., Aberdeen Univ., 1962–64. *Publications*: Modern Scotland, 1968; chapter on Scottish Nationalism, in, D. Butler and M. Pinto-Duschinsky: The British General Election of 1970, 1971; The Scottish Political System, 1972; *contrib*. Bull. Soc. Study Labour Hist., EHR, Hist. Today, Parly Aff., Scott. Hist. Rev. *Address*: Dept of Politics, Univ. of Glasgow, Glasgow G12 8QQ.

Keller, Dr Alexander Gustave; Senior Lecturer, Department of Astronomy and the History of Science, University of Leicester, since 1974 (Lecturer, 1963–74); *b* 1932; *m* 1959; two *s* one *d*. BA Cantab 1953, MA Cantab 1960, BLitt Oxon 1956, PhD Cantab 1967; Mem.: Brit. Soc. Hist. Science Newcomen Soc. Hist. Technol.; RSA. Asst Lectr in History, Jerusalem Univ., 1956–57; Vis. Associate Prof. of Hist., Case Western

Reserve Univ., Cleveland, Ohio, 1967–68. *Publications*: A Theatre of Machines, 1964; *contrib*. Brit. Jl Hist. Sci., Endeav., Technol. Culture, Chartered Mechan. Engr, Hist. Today. *Address*: Leicester Univ., University Road, Leicester LE1 7RH.

Keller, Prof. Rudolf Ernst; Professor of German Language and Medieval Literature, University of Manchester, since 1960; *b* 1920; *m* 1947; two *d*. DrPhil Zürich 1944, MA Manchester 1949; Corresp. Mem., Inst. Deutsche Sprache, Mannheim. Asst Lectr, Manchester, 1947–49; Lectr, Royal Holloway Coll., London, 1949–52; Sen. Lectr, Manchester, 1952–59, Reader, 1959–60; Dean, Fac. of Arts, Manchester, 1968–70. *Publications*: Die Ellipse in der neuenglischen Sprache als semantisch-syntaktisches Problem, 1944; trans., Bodmer: Die Sprachen der Welt, 1955; German Dialects, 1961; Die Mundart von Jestetten, Phonai 7, 1970; *contrib*. Bull. Rylands Libr., Phonet., Trans Philol. Soc., Zeits. Mundartfors. *Address*: Dept of German, The Univ., Manchester M13 9PL.

Kellett, John Reginald, MA, PhD; Reader, Department of Economic History, University of Glasgow, since 1972; *b* 1925; *m* 1951; one *s* one *d*. MA Cantab 1950, PhD London 1951. Lectr, 1954, Sen. Lectr, 1966, Univ of Glasgow. Founder Mem., Brit. Urban Hist. Gp. *Publications*: Glasgow: a concise history, 1967; The Impact of Railways on Victorian Cities, 1969; *contrib*. British Historic Towns, ed M. D. Lobel, 1969; *contrib*. Econ. Hist. Rev., Jl Transp. Hist., Scott. Jl Pol. Econ., Vict. Studies. *Address*: Dept of Economic History, Adam Smith Building, Univ. of Glasgow, Glasgow G12 8RT.

Kells, John Henry; Reader in Greek and Latin, University College, University of London, since 1963; *b* 1910; *m* 1949; two *s* one *d*. BA Belfast 1934 (1st cl. Classics), BA Cambridge 1936 (Classics Tripos Pt II), MA Cambridge 1951–. *Publications*: ed, Sophocles: Electra, 1973; *contrib*. Bull. Inst. Class. Philol., Class. Philol, Class. Qly, Class. Rev., Philol. (Germany). *Address*: Dept of Greek, Univ. College, Gower Street, WC1E 6BT.

Kelly, Dr David Michael, BSc(Econ), PhD; Lecturer in Economics, Strathclyde University, since 1967; *b* 1940; *m* 1965; two *d*. BSc(Econ) London 1963, PhD Strathclyde 1971. Res. Asst, Strathclyde, 1963–65; Lectr, Aberdeen, 1965–67. Elected Mem., Corp. of Glasgow, 1971; Glasgow Educn Cttee; Editor, Econ. Studies, 1968– . *Publications*: Studies in the British Coal Industry, 1970; *contrib*. Econ. Studies, Internat. Rev. Social Hist. *Address*: Dept of Economics, Univ. of Strathclyde, Glasgow G1 1XW.

Kelly, Prof. John Maurice; Professor of Jurisprudence and Roman Law, Faculty of Law, University College, Dublin, since 1965; *b* 1931; *m* 1961; two *s* two *d*. BA NUI 1952, MA NUI 1953, DrJur Heidelberg 1956, BLitt Oxon 1960, MA Oxon 1961; Barrister-at-Law, King's Inns, Dublin, 1957, MRIA 1966. Pt-time Asst, Dept of Classics, UC

Dublin, 1953–54; Pt-time Asst, Faculty of Law, UC Dublin, 1957–65; Fellow and Lectr in Law, Trinity Coll., Oxford, 1961–65. Mem., Senate, Republic of Ireland (Seanad Éireann), 1969–73; Member of Dáil Éireann (TD) 1973– ; Parliamentary Secretary to the Taoiseach and the Minister of Defence, 1973– . Ed, The Irish Jurist, 1966– . *Publications*: Princeps Iudex, 1957; Fundamental Rights in the Irish Law and Constitution, 1961, 2nd edn 1967; Roman Litigation, 1966; *contrib*. Irish Jurist, Law Qly Rev., Mod. Law Rev. *Address*: Faculty of Law, Univ. College, Dublin 4.

Kelly, Rev. Canon John Norman Davidson, DD, FBA; Principal of St Edmund Hall, Oxford, since 1951; Vice-Chancellor, Oxford University, Sept.–Oct. 1966 (Pro-Vice-Chancellor, 1964–66, 1972–74); *b* 1909. 1st cl. Hon. Mods Greats and Theology Oxford; Hon. DD Glasgow 1958, Hon. DD Wales 1971; FBA 1965. Deacon, 1934, Priest, 1935; Curate, St Lawrence's, Northampton, 1934; Chaplain, St Edmund Hall, Oxford, 1935; Vice-Principal and Trustee, 1937. Select Preacher (Oxford), 1944–46, 1959, 1961, 1962; Speaker's Lectr in Biblical Studies, 1945–48; Univ. Lectr in Patristic Studies, 1948; Select Preacher (Cambridge), 1953; Paddock Lectr, Gen. Theol. Seminary, New York, 1963; Birkbeck Lectr, Cambridge, 1973. Chm., Cttee of Second Internat. Conf. on Patristic Studies, Oxford, 1955; Proctor in Convocation of Canterbury representing Oxford Univ., 1958–64; Chm., Archbishop's Commn on Roman Catholic Relations, 1964–68; accompanied Archbishop of Canterbury on his visit to Pope Paul VI, 1966; Mem. Academic Coun., Ecumenical Theological Inst., Jerusalem, 1966– ; Canon of Chichester and Prebendary of Wightring, 1948, Highleigh, 1964; Took lead in obtaining Royal Charter, new statutes and full collegiate status for St Edmund Hall, 1957. Mem.: Governing Body, Royal Holloway Coll., London, 1959–69; Governing Body, King's Sch., Canterbury: Hon. Fellow, Queen's Coll., Oxford, 1963. *Publications*: Early Christian Creeds, 1950; Rufinus, a Commentary on the Apostles' Creed, 1955; Early Christian Doctrines, 1958; The Pastoral Epistles, 1963; The Athanasian Creed, 1964; The Epistles of Peter and of Jude, 1969; Aspects of the Passion, 1970. *Address*: Principal's Lodgings, St Edmund Hall, Oxford.

Kelly, Prof. Thomas; Professor of Adult Education since 1967, and Director of Extension Studies since 1948, Liverpool University; *b* 1909; *m* 1933; two *d*. BA Hons Manchester 1929 (History), MA Manchester 1947 (History), PhD Liverpool 1957 (History); FRHistS 1957, Hon. Fellow, Birkbeck Coll., 1971. Extra-Mural Lectr, Manchester Univ., 1940–46, Deputy Dir, Extra-Mural Studies, 1946–48. Hon. Sec. Univs Council of Adult Educn, 1961–68; Chm., Nat. Inst. Adult Educn, 1968– ; Mem., Library Adv. Council for England, 1965–70; Editor, Studies in Adult Education (twice yearly), 1969–73. *Publications*: Outside the Walls, 1950; Griffith Jones Llanddowror, 1950; ed, Select Bibliography of Adult Education in Great

Britain, 1952, 3rd edn 1974; George Birkbeck, 1957; History of Adult Education in Great Britain, 1962, 2nd edn 1970; Early Public Libraries, 1966; History of Public Libraries in Great Britain, 1973; *contrib.* Adult Educn, Brit. Jl Educnl Studies, Convergence (Toronto), Educn Permanente (Paris), Soc. and Leisure (Prague), Studies in Adult Educn, etc. *Address*: Institute of Extension Studies, Liverpool Univ., Liverpool L69 3BX.

Kelsall, Malcolm Miles, MA, BLitt; Lecturer in English, University of Reading, since 1964; *b* 1938; *m* 1961. BA Oxon 1961 (1st cl. English), BLitt Oxon 1964, MA Oxon 1965. Sen. Hulme Schol., Brasenose Coll., Oxford, 1961–63; Asst Lectr, Exeter Univ., 1963–64. Mem., Reading Council for Arts. *Publications*: ed, S. Fielding: The Adventures of David Simple, 1969; T. Otway: Venice Preserved, 1969; W. Congreve: Love for Love, 1969; Joseph Trapp: Lectures on Poetry, 1973; J. M. Synge: The Playboy of the Western World, 1974; contrib. William Congreve (Mermaid Critical Commentaries), 1972; Eighteenth Century English Stage, 1972; Gulliver's Travels (Macmillan Casebooks), 1974; *contrib.* Arion, Ess. Crit., Proc. Virgil Soc., Rev. Engl. Studies, Theat. Res. *Address*: Dept of English, Faculty of Letters, Whiteknights Park, Univ. of Reading, Reading RG6 2AH.

Kelsall, Prof. Roger Keith, MA; Professor of Sociological Studies, University of Sheffield, since 1960; *b* 1910; *m* 1934. MA Glasgow 1930 (History), MA Glasgow 1932 (Political Economy). Mem., Brit. Sociol Assoc. Asst Lectr, then Lectr and Acting Hd of Dept of Economics and Commerce, Hull Univ., 1933–42; Sen. Res. Offr, LSE, 1949–54; Dir of Social Studies, Sheffield Univ., 1955–59. Chm., Brit. Sociol Assoc., 1964–66. *Publications*: Higher Civil Servants in Britain, 1955; Applications for University Admission, 1957; Women and Teaching, 1963; Population, 1967, 3rd edn 1974; (with H. M. Kelsall) The School Teacher in England and the United States, 1969; Social Disadvantage and Educational Opportunity, 1971; Stratification, 1974; (with A. Kuhn and A. Poole) Six Years After, 1970; (with A. Kuhn and A. Poole) Graduates: The Sociology of an Elite, 1972; *contrib.* Brit. Jl Sociol., Econ. Hist. Rev., Educn for Teach., EHR, Jl Bio-Social Sci., Times Educnl Supp., Times Higher Educnl Supp., Univ. Qly. *Address*: Dept of Sociological Studies, Sheffield Univ., Sheffield S10 2TN.

Kemp, Barry John; University Lecturer in Egyptology, Faculty of Oriental Studies, University of Cambridge, since 1969; *b* 1940; *m* 1964; two *d*. BA Liverpool 1962 (1st cl. Hons), MA Cantab 1965; Asst Lectr, Cambridge Univ., 1963–69. *Publications*: Egyptology Titles (a quarterly bibliog.) 1971– ; The Empire in New Kingdom Egypt (forthcoming); (jtly) Minoan Pottery in Second Millennium Egypt (forthcoming); *contrib.* Antiquity, Chronique d'Egypte, Jl Egypt Archaeol., Mitt. dt. Archaeol. Inst. Kairo, Orientalia. *Address*: Faculty of Oriental Studies, Sidgwick Avenue, Cambridge CB3 9DA.

Kemp, Betty, MA; Fellow and Tutor in Modern History, St Hugh's College, University of Oxford, since 1946; *b* 1916; BA Manchester 1940, MA Oxford 1946; FRHistS 1952, FSA 1963. Hon. Fellow, Spalding Gentlemen's Soc., 1971. Lectr, Manchester Univ., 1945–46. Mem., Council, Royal Holloway Coll., 1962–68; Governor: Burford Grammar Sch., 1957–63; Badminton Sch., 1969– . *Publications*: King and Commons 1660–1832, 1957; Sir Francis Dashwood, an 18th century Independent, 1967; Votes and Standing Orders: the Beginning, 1971; *contrib.* EHR, Hist., Vict. Studies. *Address*: St Hugh's College, Oxford.

Kemp, Dr Brian Richard, BA, PhD, FRHistS; Lecturer, Department of History, University of Reading, since 1964; *b* 1940. BA Reading 1961 (1st cl. History), PhD Reading 1966; FRHistS 1970. *Publications*: *contrib.* Berks Archaeol. Jl, Bull. Inst. Hist. Res., EHR, Trans Brist. and Glos Archaeol. Soc. *Address*: Dept of History, Univ. of Reading, Reading RG6 2AH.

Kemp, Ian, MA; Lecturer in Music, University of Cambridge, since 1972; *b* 1931; *m* 1957; one *s* four *d*. BA Cantab 1954, MA Cantab 1958. Asst Lectr, Aberdeen, 1959–61, Lectr, 1964–70, Sen. Lectr, 1970–71; Fellow, St John's Coll., Cambridge, 1972– . Gen. Sec., New Berlioz Edn, 1972– . *Publications*: ed, Michael Tippett: A Symposium, 1965; Hindemith, 1970. *Address*: St John's College, Cambridge.

Kemp, Jabez Alan, MA, MLitt; Lecturer, Department of Linguistics, Edinburgh University, since 1965; *b* 1927; *m* 1961; one *s* two *d*. BA Cantab 1948 (Classical Tripos Pt I 1st cl., Pt II 2nd cl.); MLitt Edinburgh 1967; Dip. Libr. London 1952; Mem., Internat. Phonet. Assoc. Lectr, Univ. Coll., Ibadan, Nigeria, 1955–64. *Publications*: ed, J. Wallis: Grammar of the English Language, 1972. *Address*: Dept of Linguistics, Univ. of Edinburgh, Edinburgh EH8 9YL.

Kemp, Martin John, MA; Lecturer, Department of Fine Art, University of Glasgow, since 1966; *b* 1942; *m* 1966. MA Cantab 1963 (Natural Sciences and History of Art), Acad.Dip in History of Art London 1965; Mem., Soc. Renaiss. Studies. Lectr, Dalhousie Univ., Halifax, Canada, 1965–66. *Publications*: contrib. Essays in Honour of Paul Kristeller; Sir Walter Scott Bicentenary Essays; *contrib.* Art Bull., Arte, Burl. Mag., Jl Warb. Court. Insts. *Address*: Dept of Fine Art, Univ. of Glasgow, Glasgow G12 8QQ.

Kemp, Tom, BSc(Econ); Reader in Economic History, University of Hull, since 1972; *b* 1921; *m* 1947; two *s* three *d*. BSc(Econ) London 1947. Res. Asst, Southampton, 1947–50; Asst Lectr, Hull, 1950–53, Lectr, 1950–69, Sen. Lectr, 1969–72. Royal Navy, 1941–45. *Publications*: (trans. Italian), Theories of Imperialism, 1967; Industrialization in Nineteenth Century Europe, 1969, 2nd edn 1971; Economic Forces in French History, 1971; The French Economy, 1913–1939, 1972; *contrib.* Econ. Hist. Rev., Kyklos, Sci. Soc.

Address: Dept of Economic and Social History, The Univ., Hull HU6 7RX.

Kempa, Prof. Richard Franz, PhD; Professor of Science Education, University of Keele, since 1974; *b* 1934; *m* 1958; two *s*. IngChem Essen 1956 (Chemistry), PhD London 1959; ARIC. Lectr, Coll. of St Mark and St John, London, 1959–67; Sen. Lectr in Chemical Educn, Univ. of E Anglia, 1967–74; UNESCO Science Educn Consultant, Weizmann Inst. of Science, Israel, 1971 and 1972. *Publications*: *contrib.* Jl Chem. Soc., Jl Res. Sci. Teach., Sch. Sci. Rev. *Address*: Univ. of Keele, Keele, Staffs ST5 5BG.

Kempner, Prof. Thomas; Principal, Administrative Staff College, Henley-on-Thames, and Professor and Director of Business Studies, Brunel University, since 1972; *b* 1930; *m* 1958; three *d*. BSc(Econ) London. Lectr, later Sen. Tutor, in Business Studies, Sheffield Univ., 1959–63; Prof. of Management Studies, Founder and Dir, Management Centre, Univ. of Bradford, 1963–72. Res. Officer, Admin. Staff Coll., Henley, 1954–59. Mem., Social Studies and Business Management Cttees of UGC; Mem., Management and Educn Training Cttee, NEDO, 1969– (Chm., Student Grants Sub-Cttee); Chm., Ford Industry Manpower Cttee, NEDO, 1968–71; Burnham Medal, BIM, 1970; *Publications*: (with G. Wills) Exercises in Management, 1966; (with J. Hewkin) Is Corporate Planning Necessary?, 1968; A Guide to the Study of Management, 1969; (with A. J. Tillett and G. Wills) Management Thinkers, 1970; Handbook of Management, 1971; (with Macmillan and Hawkins) Business and Society, 1974; ed and contrib. to others; *contrib.* management jls. *Address*: Administrative Staff College, Henley-on-Thames, Oxon.

Kendrick, Dr Donald Clive, PhD, FBPsS; Senior Lecturer in Psychology, University of Hull, since 1967; *b* 1934. BA Liverpool 1955 (Hons Psychology), Dip. Psychol. London 1956 (Abnormal and Educational Psychology), PhD London 1959; FBPsS. Res. Asst, Inst. of Psychiatry, London, 1956–59, Lectr, 1959–65; Lectr, Hull Univ., 1965–67. Mem., Edit. Bd, Brit. Jl Social Clin. Psychol., 1968– ; Review Ed., Brit. Jl Psychol., 1973– . *Publications*: *contrib.* Brit. Jl Psychiat., BMJ, Brit. Jl Psychol., Brit. Jl Med. Psychol., Brit. Jl Social Clin. Psychol., Devel. Psychobiol., Jl Exper. Psychol., Psychol. Rep. *Address*: Dept of Psychology, Univ. of Hull, Hull HU6 7RX.

Kennedy, Dr Barbara Anne; University Lecturer in Geography, University of Manchester, since 1973; *b* 1943. BA Cantab 1965, MA British Columbia 1967, MA Cantab 1969, PhD 1969; Member: Geologists' Assoc., Cambridge Philos Soc., Inst. Brit. Geogrs, Amer. Assoc. Advancement Science. Univ. Demonstrator, Cambridge, 1968–72; Fellow and Lectr, New Hall, Cambridge, 1968–72. *Publications*: (with R. J. Chorley) Physical Geography: a systems approach, 1971; *contrib.* Inst. of Brit. Geogrs, Special

378

Pubns. *Address*: Sch. of Geography, Univ. of Manchester, Manchester M13 9PL.

Kennedy, Dr Elspeth Mary, MA, DPhil; Tutorial Fellow of St Hilda's College, University of Oxford, since 1966, and University Lecturer in Modern Languages Faculty, since 1967; *b* 1921. BA Oxon 1947, MA, DPhil Oxon 1951. Asst Lectr, Manchester Univ., 1954–57. Lectr, 1957–66. *Publications*: contrib. articles in current edn of Encyclopaedia Britannica: King Arthur in the Prose Lancelot, in, Medieval Miscellany presented to Eugène Vinaver, 1965; The scribe as editor, in, Mélanges de langue et de littérature de Moyen Age et de la Renaissance offerts à Jean Frappier, 1970; First Part of the Old French Prose Lancelot (forthcoming); *contrib.* Med. Æv., Romania. *Address*: St Hilda's College, Oxford.

Kennedy, Dr Gavin; Senior Lecturer, Economics Department, University of Strathclyde, since 1974; *b* 1940; *m* 1973; one *d*. BA Strathclyde 1969, MSc 1971, PhD Brunel 1973. Lectr in Economics, Brunel Univ., 1971–73. *Publications*: The Military in the Third World, 1974; The Economics of War and Peace (forthcoming); The Destruction of Admiral Bligh (forthcoming). *Address*: Dept of Economics, Univ. of Strathclyde, Stenhouse Building, Cathedral Street, Glasgow.

Kennedy, Kieran A., MEconSc, BPhil, PhD, MRIA; Director, Economic and Social Research Institute, Dublin, since 1971, and Lecturer (part-time) in Political Economy, University College, Dublin, since 1965; *b* 1935; *m* 1966; two *s* two *d*. BComm Dublin 1958, MEconSc Dublin 1960, BPhil Oxon 1963, PhD Harvard 1968. Teaching Fellow, Harvard, 1964; Sen. Res. Offr, Econ. and Social Res. Inst., Dublin, 1968–71. *Publications*: Productivity and Industrial Growth, 1971; *contrib.* Econ. Soc. Rev., Admin, Proc. RIA, Jl Stat. and Social Inquiry Soc. of Ireland, Central Bank Qly Bull. *Address*: Economic and Social Research Institute, 4 Burlington Road, Dublin 4.

Kennedy, Michael Craufurd; Lecturer, Economics Department, University of Manchester, since 1965; *b* 1932; *m* 1963. BSc(Econ) London 1956. Econ. Asst, HM Treasury, 1956; Econ. Advr (First Sec.), Brit. Emb., Washington, 1960; HM Treasury, 1963. *Publications*: The Economy as a Whole, in, The UK Economy, ed A. R. Prest, 1966, 5th edn 1974; Employment Policy: What Went Wrong?, in, After Keynes, ed Joan Robinson, 1973; *contrib.* Nat. Inst. Econ. Rev. *Address*: Dept of Economics, Univ. of Manchester, Dover Street, Manchester.

Kennedy, William Gerald S.; *see* Studdert-Kennedy.

Kennelly, Prof. Brendan, MA PhD; Professor of Modern Literature, and Chairman of the English Department, Trinity College, Dublin, since 1973; *b* 1936; *m* 1969; one *d*. BA Hons TCD 1961, MA TCD 1963, PhD TCD 1967. TCD: Jun. Lectr in Eng. Lit., 1963–66; Lectr, 1966–69; Assoc. Prof., 1969–

73. Vis. Prof., Swarthmore Coll., Pennsylvania, 1971–72. A. E. Meml. Award, 1967. *Publications: verse:* Let Fall No Burning Leaf, 1963; My Dark Fathers, 1964; Up and At It, 1965; Collection One: Getting Up Early, 1966; Good Souls to Survive, 1967; Dream of a Black Fox, 1968; Selected Poems, 1969; A Drinking Cup: Poems from the Irish, 1970; Bread, 1971; Love-Cry, 1972; Salvation, the Stranger, 1972; The Voices, 1973; with R. Holzapfel: Cast a Cold Eye, 1959; The Rain, the Moon, 1961; The Dark about Our Loves, 1962; Green Townlands: Poems, 1963; *novels:* The Crooked Cross, 1963; The Florentines, 1967; ed, Penguin Book of Irish Verse, 1970. *Address:* English Dept, Trinity College, Dublin 2.

Kennerley, Prof. J. A. M.; Director, Strathclyde Business School, University of Strathclyde, since 1973; *b* 1933. BSc Manchester 1955; MSc London 1967; MIMechE 1960; AFRAeS 1960; AFIMA 1967. Asst Prof. of Mathematics, Univ. of New Brunswick, 1962–67; Lectr, Manchester Business Sch., 1967–69; Assoc. Prof., Columbia Business Sch., NY, 1969–71; Sen. Lectr, London Business Sch., 1971–73. *Publications: contrib.* Combustion and Flame, Physics of Fluids. *Address:* Univ. of Strathclyde, George Street, Glasgow G1 1XW.

Kenney, Prof. Edward John, MA, FBA; Kennedy Professor of Latin, University of Cambridge, since 1974; *b* 1924; *m* 1955. BA Cantab 1949 (1st cl. Classics), MA Cantab 1953; FBA 1968. Asst Lectr, Univ. of Leeds, 1951–52; Res. Fellow, Trinity Coll., Cambridge, 1952–53; Fellow and Libr., Peterhouse, Cambridge, 1953– ; Asst Lectr, Univ. of Cambridge, 1955–60, Lectr, 1960–70; Reader in Latin Literature and Textual Criticism, 1970–74; James C. Loeb Fellow, Harvard Univ., 1967–68; Sather Prof. of Classical Literature, Univ. of California, Berkeley, 1968. Member: Council, Almoners of Christ's Hosp., 1956– ; Stand. Cttee, Council of Univ. Class. Depts, 1968–72. Jt Editor, Class. Qly, 1959–65. *Publications:* ed, P. Ouidi Nasonis Amores, etc, 1961; ed (with P. E. Easterling), Ovidiana Graeca, 1965; ed (with F. R. D. Goodyear, etc), Appendix Vergiliana, 1966; ed, Lucretius: De Rerum Natura Book III, 1971; The Classical Text: aspects of editing in the age of the printed book, 1974; *contrib.* Arion, Class. Qly, Class. Rev., Greece and Rome, Harv. Studies Class. Philol., Hermes, Latomus, Mnemosyne, Philologus, Proc. Camb. Philol Soc., Yale Class. Studies. *Address:* Peterhouse Cambridge CB2 1RD.

Kenny, Dr Anthony John Patrick, FBA; Fellow and Tutor in Philosophy, Balliol College, since 1964 and Lecturer in Philosophy, since 1965, Oxford University; *b* 1931; *m* 1966; two *s.* PhL Gregorian Univ. Rome 1952, STL, Gregorian Univ. 1956, DPhil Oxon 1961, MA Oxon 1964; FBA 1974. Lectr in Philosophy, Exeter and Trinity Colls, Oxford, 1963–64; Wilde Lectr in Natural and Comparative Religion, Univ. of Oxford, 1969–72; Jt Gifford Lectr, Univ. of Edinburgh, 1970–73. Sen. Tutor, Balliol, 1971–72. Editor, Oxford Mag., 1972–73.

Publications: The Responsa Alumnorum of the English College, Rome, 1962–64; Action, Emotion and Will, 1963; Descartes, 1968; The Five Ways, 1969; Wittgenstein, 1972; The Anatomy of the Soul, 1973; trans., Descartes: Philosophical letters, 1970; Wittgenstein: Philosophical Grammar, 1973; contrib. vol. to Blackfriars edn of Aquinas: Summa Theologiae, 1964; *contrib.* Analysis, Mind, Phronesis, etc. *Address:* Balliol College, Oxford.

Kenny-Levick, Christopher Charles; Lecturer, Department of Marketing, University of Lancaster, since 1967; *b* 1941; *m* 1967; two *s.* BA Exeter 1966, MA Lancaster 1967; FSS 1967. *Publications: contrib.* Brit. Jl Marketing, Internat. Jl Phys. Distribution. *Address:* Furness College, Univ. of Lancaster, Bailrigg, Lancaster.

Kent, Dr Paul Welberry; Master of Van Mildert College, and Director of the Glycoprotein Research Unit, Durham University, since 1972, *b* 1923; *m* 1952; three *s* one *d.* BSc Birmingham (1st cl. Hons Chemistry), PhD Birmingham 1947 (Chemistry), MA Oxon 1951, DPhil Oxon 1953 (Biochemistry), DSc Oxon 1966, Hon. DLitt Drury USA 1973; FRIC 1951. Asst Lectr, Birmingham Univ., 1946–48; ICI Fellow, Birmingham Univ., 1948–50; Vis. Fellow, Princeton, 1948–49; Univ. Demonstrator, Biochem., Oxford, 1950–72; Student and Tutor, Christ Church, Oxford, 1956–72, Emeritus Student 1972– . Mem. Oxford City Council, 1964–72; Governor Oxford Polytechnic, 1964–72; JP 1971– . Medal of Société de Chimie Biologique, 1969; Cross of Merit, Germany, 1970. *Publications:* (with M. W. Whitehouse), Biochemistry of the Amino-Sugars, 1955; ed, Membrane-Mediated Information, vols I and II, 1973; *contrib.* Biochem. Jl, Jl Chem. Soc., European Jl Biochem. *Address:* Master's House, Van Mildert College, Durham.

Kentleton, John A.; Lecturer in Modern History, Liverpool University, since 1968; *b* 1941; *m* 1963; two *d.* BA Oxon 1963 (Hons Mod. History), MA Oxon 1968; Mem., Brit. Assoc. for Amer. Studies. Instructor in History, St Peter's Coll. NJ, 1963–64; Univ. of Liverpool: Leverhulme Res. Fellow, Dept. of Mod. History, 1964–65; Asst Lectr in Mod. History, 1965–68; Vis. Prof. in Amer. History, Univ. of Nevada, 1972–73. *Address:* Dept of Modern History, Univ. of Liverpool, PO Box 147, Liverpool L69 3BX.

Kenton Jones, David; *see* Jones, D. K.

Kenworthy, Dr Brian John; Senior Lecturer in German, University of Aberdeen, since 1968; *b* 1920; *m* 1944; two *s* one *d.* BA Bristol 1942, DipEd Bristol 1943, PhD Aberdeen 1952. Interpreter/Translator, Control Commn for Germany, 1946–47; Asst in German, Aberdeen Univ., 1947–52, Lectr in German, 1952–68. *Publications:* Georg Kaiser, 1957; (jtly) A Manual of German Prose Composition for Advanced Students, 1966; ed, G. Kaiser: Die Koralle, Gas I, Gas II, 1968; ed, H. Sudermann: Litauische Geschichten, 1971; trans., Braunbeck: The Drama of the

379

Atom, 1958; G. Kaiser: The Coral, Gas I and Gas II, in, G. Kaiser: Five Plays, 1971. *Address*: Dept of German, Univ. of Aberdeen, Taylor Building, Old Aberdeen AB9 2UB.

Kenworthy, Joan Margaret, BLitt, MA; Senior Lecturer, Department of Geography, University of Liverpool, since 1973 (Lecturer, 1960–73), and Warden of Salisbury Hall, University of Liverpool, since 1966; *b* 1933. BA Oxon 1955 (2nd cl. Geography), MA Oxon 1959, BLitt Oxon 1960; FRGS, FRMetSoc, Mem., Geog. Assoc., Inst. Brit. Geogrs, Ecol Soc., Afr. Studies Assoc. UK, Assoc. of Brit. Climatologists. Acting Tutor, St Hugh's Coll., Oxford, 1958–59; Tutorial Res. Fellow, Bedford Coll., London, 1959–60. Mem., Council, Afr. Studies Assoc., 1969–71. *Publications*: contrib. Geographers and the Tropics, ed R. W. Steel and R. M. Prothero; Liverpool Essays, 1964; Studies in East African Geography and Development, ed S. H. Ominde, 1971; Africa, ed J. I. Clarke; *contrib.* E Afr. Geog. Rev. *Address*: Dept of Geography, The Univ., PO Box 147, Liverpool L69 3BX.

Keohane, Kevin William; Professor of Science Education, Centre for Science Education, Chelsea College, University of London, and Vice-Principal, Chelsea College, since 1967; *b* 1923; *m* 1949; one *s* three *d*. BSc Hons Bristol (1st cl. Physics), PhD Bristol; FInstP. Lectr, Univ. of Bristol; Prof. of Physics, Univ. of London, 1965; Prof. of Science Educn, Univ. of London, 1967. Royal Soc. Leverhulme Prof., 1971. Ch., Sci. Div., Univ. of London Inst. of Educn; Academic Adv. Cttee, Open Univ. Member Committee: Royal Soc.; Inst. of Physics; Mem., Physics Educn. Manager, Royal Instn; Dir, Nuffield Foundn Science Teaching Projects. Chairman: Governors, Garnett Coll.; Avery Hill and Rachel Macmillan Foundn Cttee; Governor, Digby Stuart Coll. of Educn. *Publications*: *contrib.* various jls. *Address*: Chelsea Coll., Bridges Place, SW6 4HR.

Kerferd, Prof. George Briscoe; Hulme Professor of Greek, School of Classical Studies, University of Manchester, since 1973; *b* 1915; *m* 1944; one *s* one *d*. BA Melbourne 1936; BA Oxon 1939, MA Oxon 1943. Lectr in Classics, Univ. of Durham, 1939–41, 1946–51; Lectr in Greek, Univ. of Sydney, 1942–46; Sen. Lectr in Greek and Latin, Univ. of Manchester, 1951–56; Prof. of Classics, UC Swansea, 1956–67; Hulme Prof. of Latin, Manchester, 1967–73; Vis. Prof. in Classics and Philosophy, Princeton, 1971–72. Editor, Phronesis, 1973– . *Publications*: *contrib.* Bull. of The John Rylands Libr., Class. Qly, Jl of Hellenic Studies, Phronesis. *Address*: School of Classical Studies, Univ. of Manchester, Manchester M13 9PL.

Kermode, Prof. (John) Frank, MA, FBA, King Edward VII Professor of English Literature, University of Cambridge, since 1974; *b* 1919; *m* 1947, divorced 1970; one *s* one *d*. BA Liverpool 1940 (1st cl. English), MA Liverpool 1947; FRSL 1958; FBA 1973. Lectr, King's Coll., Univ. of Durham, 1947–

49; Lectr, Reading Univ., 1949–58; John Edward Taylor Prof., Manchester Univ., 1958–65; Winterstoke Prof., Bristol Univ. 1965–67; Lord Northcliffe Prof. of Modern English Literature, Univ. Coll. London, 1967–74. *Publications*: ed, English Pastoral Poetry, 1952, 2nd edn 1972; ed, Shakespeare: The Tempest, 1954, 2nd edn 1958; Romantic Image, 1957, 2nd edn 1971; John Donne, 1957, 2nd edn 1972; The Living Milton, 1960; Wallace Stevens, 1960, 2nd edn 1967; ed, Marvell: Poetry, 1967; The Sense of an Ending, 1967; Continuities, 1968; Modern Essays, 1971; Shakespeare, Spenser, Donne, 1971; *contrib.* Crit. Qly, Ess. Crit., Jl Engl. Germ. Philol., Mod. Lang. Rev., Rev. Engl. Studies. *Address*: King's College, Cambridge.

Kerr, Dr Anne Paterson; Lecturer, Department of French Studies, University of Reading, since 1971; *b* 1940. BA 1963, PhD 1971, Reading; Mem., Commn Nationale for Œuvres Complètes of Alexis de Tocqueville. Asst Lectr, Dept of French, Univ. of Aberdeen, 1967–68; Res. Fellow, Univ. of Reading, 1968–71. *Publications*: ed (with J. P. Mayer): Montesquieu: De l'Esprit des Lois, 1970; Tocqueville: Recollections, NY, London, 1970; Tocqueville: Journey to America, NY, 1972; Hobbes: Nature Humaine et Corps Politique (forthcoming). *Address*: Dept of French Studies, Fac. of Letters and Social Sciences, Univ. of Reading, Whiteknights, Reading RG6 2AH.

Kerr, Prof. John Fairhurst, BSc, PhD; Professor of Education, University of Leicester; *b* 1912; *m* 1940; two *d*. BSc Liverpool 1934; PhD Belfast 1957. Lectr, Leicester Univ., 1958–63, Sen. Lectr 1963–66, Prof., 1966; various appointments N America and several developing countries. Chm., Editorial Bd, Jl of Curriculum Studies, 1971– ; Treas., Standing Conf. on Studies in Educn, 1968– ; Inter-Univ. Council, 1968– ; Vice-Chancellors' Coordinating Cttee for Trng of Univ. Teachers; Trent RHA. *Publications*: Changing the Curriculum, 1968; Studies in Assessment, 1969; ed, Practical Work in School Science, 1963, 2nd edn 1965; *contrib.* Brit. Jl Educnl Studies, Educnl Res., Educnl Rev., Sch. Sci. Rev. *Address*: School of Education, Univ. of Leicester, 21 University Road, Leicester LE1 7RF.

Kerr, Rev. Fr Martin William Robert J.; *see* Jarrett–Kerr.

Kerrigan, Herbert Aird; Lecturer in Scots Law, within the University of Edinburgh, since 1972; *b* 1945. LLB Aberdeen 1967, (Hons 1968), MA Keele 1970; Advocate, 1970. Lectr, Criminal Law and Criminology, Univ. of Edinburgh, 1968–72. Mem., Longford Cttee on Pornography, 1971–72; Vice-Convener, Church of Scotland Moral Welfare Cttee, 1972– ; Chm., Legislation Cttee. *Publication*: An Introduction to Criminal Process in Scotland, 1972. *Address*: Dept of Scots Law, Old College, The Univ., Edinburgh EH8 9YL.

Kershaw, Dr Ian; Lecturer in History Department of History, Manchester University, since 1968; *b* 1943; *m* 1966; two *s*. BA Hons Liverpool 1965 (1st cl. Hist.), DPhil Oxford 1969; FRHistS 1972. *Publications*: Bolton Priory Rentals and Ministers Accounts, 1969; Bolton Priory, the Economy of a Northern Monastery, 1973; *contrib*. Past and Present. *Address*: Dept of History, Manchester Univ., Manchester M13 9PL.

Kershaw, Dr Roger Gordon; Lecturer in Southeast Asian Studies, Faculty of Social Sciences, University of Kent at Canterbury, since 1970; *b* 1938; *m* 1962; one *d*. BA Oxon 1961 (Mod. Hist.), DipEd Hull 1962, PhD London 1969 (Politics). Fellow in SE Asian Political Studies, Univ. Hull, 1968–70. *Address*: Keynes Coll, Univ. of Kent, Canterbury, Kent.

Kessel, Prof. William Ivor Neil; Dean of the Medical School, Professor of Psychiatry, and Director of the Department of Psychiatry, Manchester University, since 1965. BA Hons Cambridge 1945, MA Cambridge 1962, MB BChir Cambridge 1949, MD Cambridge 1963, DPM London 1958 (distinction), MSc Manchester 1968; FRCP 1967 (MRCP 1955), FRCPE 1968 (MRCPE 1965), FRCPsych 1971. Res. Asst, Inst. of Psychiatry, Univ. of London, 1959–60; Mem., Science Staff, MRC, 1960–62; Asst Dir, MRC Unit for Res. on Epidemiology of Psychiatric Illness, Edinburgh, 1964–65; Hon. Lectr, Dept of Psychiatry, Univ. of Edinburgh, 1961–63; Hon. Sen. Lectr, 1963–65. Milroy Lectr, Royal Coll. of Physicians, London, 1965; Home Off. Adv., Cttee on Misuse of Drugs, 1971; Adv. on alcoholism, Dept of Hlth and Social Security. *Publications*: (with H. J. Walton) Alcholism, 1965, 2nd edn 1972; *contrib*. Brit. Jl Prevent. Soc. Med., Brit. Jl Psychiat., Brit. Med. Jl, Jl Psychosom. Res., Jl Ment. Sci., Lancet, Proc. Royal Soc. Med. *Address*: The Medical Sch., Stopford Building, Univ. of Manchester, Manchester.

Kettle, Ann Julia; Lecturer in Mediaeval History, St Salvator's College, St Andrews University, since 1964; *b* 1939. BA Oxford 1960 (History), MA Oxford 1964; FSA. *Publications*: contrib. Victoria County History of Staffordshire, vols ii, iii, 1967, 1970; *contrib*. Staffs. Rec. Soc. *Address*: St Salvator's College, St Andrews, Fife, Scotland.

Kettle, Dr Arnold Charles; Professor of Literature, Faculty of Arts, The Open University, since 1970; Pro-Vice-Chancellor (Academic Policy), since 1973; *b* 1916; *m* 1946; two *s*. BA 1937 (1st cl. Hist. Part I, 1st cl. Eng. Part II), MA 1944, PhD 1942, Cambridge. Lectr, 1947–57, Sen. Lectr, 1957–67, Dept of English Lit., Univ. of Leeds; Prof. of Literature, Univ. of Dar es Salaam, Tanzania, 1967–70. *Publications*: An Introduction to the English Novel, vol. I, 1951, vol. II, 1953; ed, Shakespeare in a Changing World, 1964; *contrib.*: Of Books and Humankind, ed J. Butt, 1964; The Morality of Art, ed D. W. Jefferson, 1969; Critical Essays on George Eliot, ed B. Hardy, 1970; On the Novel, ed B. Bereddez, 1971; Meredith Now, ed I. Fletcher, 1971; *contrib*. Essays in Crit., Rev. Eng. Studies, Zeitschrift für

Anglistik und Amerikanistik (Berlin.) *Address*: The Open Univ., Walton Hall, Milton Keynes MK7 6AA.

Keys, Prof. Ivor Christopher Banfield, MA, DMus; Professor of Music, University of Birmingham, since 1968; *b* 1919; *m* 1944; two *s* two *d*. MA Oxon 1946, DMus Oxon 1946; FRCO 1935; Hon. RAM. Lectr in Music, 1947–50, Reader, 1950–51, Sir Hamilton Harty Prof. of Music, 1951–54, QUB; Prof. of Music, Nottingham Univ., 1954–68. Pres., RCO, 1968–70. Hon. DMus QUB, 1971. *Publications*: Sonata for Violoncello and Pianoforte; Completion of Schubert's unfinished song Gretchens Bitte; Concerto for Clarinet and Strings; Prayer for Pentecostal Fire (choir and organ); The Road to the Stable (3 Christmas songs with piano); Magnificat and Nunc Dimittis (choir and organ); (Book) The Texture of Music: Purcell to Brahms, 1961; *contrib*. Music and Letters, Musical Times. *Address*: Barber Institute of Fine Arts (Dept of Music), PO Box 363, Birmingham B15 2TS.

Khan, (Hafisullah) Akbar; Lecturer, Classics Department, Nottingham University, since 1967; *b* 1939; *m* 2nd, 1972; two *s* one *d* (of previous *m*). BA Hons Durham 1963 (1st. cl. Latin) BA Hons Newcastle upon Tyne 1964 (1st cl. Greek), MA Manchester 1968 (Latin). Asst Lectr in Classics, Univ. of WI, 1964–65. *Publications*: *contrib*. Amer. Jl Philol. Athenaeum, Class. Philol., Hermes, Latomus, Mnemosyne, Rheinisches Museum für Philologie. *Address*: Classics Dept, The Univ., Nottingham NG7 2RD.

Khan, Kabir-Rahman; Lecturer, Department of Public International Law, University of Edinburgh, since 1965; *b* 1925; *m* 1963; one *d*. BA Agra 1947, LLB Sind 1950, LLM London 1963; Barrister-at-Law (Gray's Inn) 1955. *Address*: Old College, Dept of Public International Law, Univ. of Edinburgh, Edinburgh EH9 9YL.

Kidd, Christopher John Frederick, LLB; Lecturer in Law, University of Exeter, since 1966; *b* 1941. LLB Leeds 1962; Barrister-at-Law (Gray's Inn). Lecturer in Law, Khartoum Univ., 1963–66. *Publications*: *contrib*. Mod. Law Rev., New Law Jl, Sudan Law Jl. *Address*: Faculty of Law, Univ. of Exeter, Exeter EX4 9QJ.

Kidd, Prof. Ian Gray; Professor of Ancient Philosophy, St Andrews University, since 1973; *b* 1922; *m* 1949; three *s*. MA St Andrews 1947, BA Oxon 1949. Asst Lectr, St Andrews, 1949–50, Lectr in Greek, 1950–65, Sen. Lectr, 1965–73; Vis. Prof., Univ. of Texas, 1965–66; Mem., Inst. for Advanced Study, Princeton, 1971–72. *Publications*: contrib. The Concise Encyclopaedia of Western Philosophy and Philosophers, ed J. O. Urmson, 1960; The Encyclopedia of Philosophy, ed P. Edwards, 1967; Problems in Stoicism, ed A. A. Long, 1971; Posidonius, vol. I, The Fragments, 1972; *contrib*. Class. Qly, Class. Rev., Gnomon, Philos. Qly. *Address*: Dept of Greek, Univ. of St Andrews, St Andrews, Fife KY16 9AJ.

Kidner, Richard Arundel Walton; Lecturer, Department of Law, University College of Wales, Aberystwyth, since 1970; *b* 1945; *m* 1968; two *d*. BA Oxon 1966, BCL Oxon 1968, MA Oxon 1970. Teaching Fellow, Osgoode Hall Law Sch., Toronto, 1966–67; Asst Prof., Univ. Saskatchewan, 1968–70. *Publications: contrib.* Conv. (NS), EJ, ILJ, NLJ. *Address:* Dept of Law, Llandinam Building, Penglais, Aberystwyth, Cards.

Kidson, Prof. Clarence; Professor of Physical Geography, since 1964, and Head of Department of Geography, since 1968, University College of Wales, Aberystwyth; *b* 1919; *m* 1942; two *s* one *d*. BA Hons London 1947, Associate King's Coll., London 1947, PhD London 1959; FRGS, FGS. Member: **Inst.** Geogrs; Geog. Assoc.; Geol **Assoc.**; Ussher Soc.; Quatern. Res. Assoc. Asst Lectr, Univ. of Exeter (as Univ. Coll. of S West), 1947–59, Lectr, 1949–54; Hd of Physiographic Section, Nature Conservancy, 1954–64. Mem. Commn on Mining and the Environment (Zuckerman Commn), 1972. *Publications:* chapters, in, Developments in Geomorphology, 1967; Geography at Aberystwyth, 1968; Encyclopaedia of Geomorphology, 1968; Exeter Essays in Geography, 1971; Introduction to Coastline Development, 1971; Spits and Bars, 1972; *contrib.* Chart. Surveyor, Field Studies, Geog., Geog Jl, Jl Hydraul. Div. Amer. Soc. Civ. Engrs, Nature, Proc. Brist. Nat. Soc., Proc. Geol. Assoc., Proc. Royal Geol. Soc-Cornwall, Proc. Ussher Soc., Trans Inst. Brit. Geogrs, Y Gwyddonydd (Science), Zeits. Geomorphol., Estuaries and Marine Coastal Sci. *Address:* Dept of Geography, Univ. College of Wales, Llandinam Building, Penglais, Aberystwyth, Cardiganshire.

Killham, Edgar John; Reader in English Language and Literature, University of Keele, since 1967; *b* 1922; *m* 1959; one *s* one *d*. BA London 1951 (1st cl. English), MA London 1953. Asst, Univ. Coll., London, 1951–53; Asst Lectr, Univ. Coll. of N Staffs, 1953–56, Lectr, 1956–64, Sen. Lectr, 1964–67. *Publications:* Tennyson and The Princess: Reflections of an Age, 1958; Critical Essays on the Poetry of Tennyson, 1963; *contrib.* Brit. Jl Aesth., Univ. Toronto Qly. *Address:* 5 Springpool, Univ. of Keele, Newcastle, Staffordshire.

Killick, Rachel; Lecturer in French, University of Leeds, since 1967; *b* 1943; *m* 1968; one *s*. BA Oxon 1964, MA Oxon. *Address:* French Dept, Leeds Univ., Leeds LS2 9JT.

Killingley, Dermot Hastings; Lecturer, Department of Religious Studies, University of Newcastle upon Tyne, since 1970; *b* 1935; *m* 1963; one *d*. BA Oxon 1959; FRAS, Mem., Brit. Assoc. of Orientalists. Asst Lectr, later Lectr in Sanskrit, Univ. of Malaya, 1961–68. *Address:* Dept of Religious Studies, Univ. of Newcastle upon Tyne, Newcastle upon Tyne NE1 7RU.

Kilpatrick, Rev. George Dunbar; Dean Ireland's Professor of Exegesis of Holy Scripture, Oxford; Fellow, The Queen's College, Oxford, since 1949; Fellow, University College, London, since 1967; *b* 1910; *m* 1943; one *s* three *d*. BA London 1932 (1st cl. Classics), BA Oxon 1934 (2nd cl. Lit. Hum.), (1936, 2nd cl. Theology), MA Oxon 1938, BD Oxon 1944, DD Oxon 1948; Deacon 1936, Priest 1937. Tutor, Queen's Coll., Birmingham, 1939; Lectr, Lichfield Theological Coll., 1942; Hd of Dept of Theology and Reader in Christian Theology, UC, Nottingham, 1946. Grinfield Lectr, 1945–49, Schweich Lectr, 1951, Univ. of Oxford. Asst Curate of Horsell, 1936, and of Selly Oak, 1940; Actg Warden, Coll. of the Ascension, Birmingham, 1941; Rector of Wishaw, Warks, 1942. Vice-Pres., British and Foreign Bible Soc., 1958. *Publications:* The Origins of the Gospel according to St Matthew, 1946; The Trial of Jesus, 1953; Remaking the Liturgy, 1967; ed, The New Testament in Greek, British and Foreign Bible Society's 2nd edn, 1958; *contrib.* periodicals. *Address:* The Queen's College, Oxford.

Kimbell, Dr David Rodney Bertram; Lecturer in Music, University of Edinburgh, since 1965; *b* 1939; *m* 1965; one *s* two *d*. BA Oxon 1961, MA Oxon 1965, DPhil Oxon 1968; LRAM 1957. *Publications: contrib.* Music Lett. *Address:* Dept of Music, Univ. of Edinburgh, Edinburgh EH8 9YL.

Kimber, Richard; Lecturer, Politics Department, Keele University, since 1965; *b* 1940; *m* 1969. BA Keele 1963; FSS. *Publications:* (with J. D. Lees) Political Parties in Modern Britain, 1972; (with J. J. Richardson) Campaigning for the Environment, 1974; (with J. J. Richardson) Pressure Groups in Britain, 1974; *contrib.* Pol. Studies, Parly Affairs, Man-Environment Systems, Mercurio, Public Admin, Political Qly. *Address:* Dept of Politics, Univ. of Keele, Keele, Staffordshire ST5 5BG.

Kimber, Richard Thomas, BSc, MLS; Lecturer, Department of Library and Information Studies, Queen's University, Belfast, since 1965; *b* 1940; *m* 1964; two *s* two *d*. BSc Belfast 1961 (Physics), MLS Rutgers 1963 (Librarianship). Libr. Asst, Queen's Univ., Belfast 1961–62, Sen. Libr. Asst, 1963–65. Member: Brit. Standards Inst., Data Process. Indust. User Standards Cttee, 1968–70; Aslib Council Cttee on Mechanisation, 1969–72; Aslib Computer Applications Gp Cttee, 1968–73; Ed, Program: News of Computers in Libraries, 1966–72, Chm. Edit. Bd, Program, 1972– ; Mem., Edit. Bd, Jl Document., 1968– . *Publications:* Automation in Libraries, 1968, 2nd edn 1974; *contrib.* Aslib Proc., Jl Document., Libri, Program. *Address:* Dept of Library and Information Studies, Queen's Univ., Belfast BT7 1NN.

Kindersley, Dr Richard Kerr; Faculty Lecturer in International Communism, Faculty of Social Studies, University of Oxford, and Fellow of St Antony's College, Oxford, since 1967; *b* 1922; *m* 1959. BA Cantab 1946, MA Cantab 1947, PhD Cantab 1957; Mem., Nat. Assoc. for Soviet and E European Studies. HM Foreign Service, 1957–67. *Publications:* The First Russian

Revisionists, 1962; articles and reviews. *Address*: St Antony's College, Oxford.

King, Prof. Anthony Stephen, MA, DPhil; Professor of Government, University of Essex, since 1969; *b* 1934; *m* 1965. BA Queen's (Canada) 1956 (1st cl. History), BA Oxon 1958 (1st cl. PPE), DPhil Oxon 1962. Fellow, Magdalen Coll., Oxford, 1961–65; Sen. Lectr, Essex, 1966–67, Reader, 1967–69; Vis. Prof., Univ. of Wisconsin, 1967; Ed., Brit. Jl Pol Science, 1972– . Mem., Cttee on Govtal and Legal Processes, Social Science Res. Council (USA), 1969– . *Publications*: (with D. E. Butler) The British General Election of 1964, 1965; (with D. E. Butler) The British General Election of 1966, 1966; ed, The British Prime Minister, 1969; (with Anne Sloman) Westminster and Beyond, 1973; British Members of Parliament: a self-portrait, 1974; *contrib*. Brit. Jl Pol Sci., Polity. *Address*: Dept of Government, Univ. of Essex, Wivenhoe Park, Colchester CO4 3SQ.

King, Dr Anthony Vincent; Lecturer in African Music Studies, Department of African Music Studies, School of Oriental and African Studies, University of London, since 1966; *b* 1930; *m* 1958; one *s* one *d*. BMus 1957, PhD 1968, London. Lectr in Music, Univ. of Ibadan, Nigeria, 1960–65. Editor on Music in Africa, Grove's Dictionary of Music and Musicians. *Publications*: Yoruba Sacred Music from Ekiti, 1961; A Boorii Liturgy from Katsina, 1968; Glossary of Hausa Music and its Social Contexts, 1971; Songs of Nigeria, 1973; *contrib*. African Lang. Studies, Jl of African Music Soc. *Address*: Sch. of Oriental and African Studies, Univ. of London, WC1E 7HP.

King, Prof. Cuchlaine Audrey Muriel, MA, PhD, ScD; Professor of Physical Geography, University of Nottingham, since 1969; *b* 1922. BA Cantab 1943, MA Cantab 1946, PhD Cantab 1949, ScD Cantab 1973; FRGS, FGS. Mem., Internat. Glaciol Soc., Inst. Brit. Geogrs, Geog. Assoc. Demonstrator, Durham Univ., 1949–50; Asst Lecturer, Nottingham Univ., 1951–53, Lectr, 1953–61, Reader, 1961–69; Vis. Lectr, Canterbury Univ., NZ, 1956; US Nat. Sci. Foundn Sen. Foreign Scientist Fellowship, SUNY, Binghampton, 1972–73. Member: Council, Glaciol Soc., 1970–73; Gov. Body, Kesteven Coll. of Educn, 1971– . *Publications*: Beaches and Coasts, 1959, 2nd edn 1972, Russian edn; Oceanography for Geographers, 1962, Dutch edn; Techniques in Geomorphology, 1966; (with C. Embleton) Glacial and Periglacial Geomorphology, 1968; (with J. P. Cole) Quantitative Geography, 1968; (with J. C. Doornkamp) Numerical Analysis in Geomorphology, 1971; Introduction to Marine Geology and Geomorphology, 1974; Introduction to Physical and Biological Oceanography, 1974; *contrib*. Arct. Alp. Res., E Mid. Geog., Geog., Geog. Ann. (Ser. A), Geog. Bull., Geog. Jl, Geol. Jl, Jl Glaciol., Trans Inst. Brit. Geogrs, Yorks Geol. Soc. Proc. *Address*: The Geography Dept, The Univ., Nottingham NG7 2RD.

King, Edmund James, MA, PhD, DLit; Reader in Comparative Education, King's College, University of London, since 1953; *b* 1914; *m* 1939; one *s* three *d*. BA Manchester 1935 (1st cl. Classics), MA Manchester 1937, PhD London 1955, DLit London 1966. Asst, then Sen. Asst, Dept of Extra-Mural Studies, Univ. of London, 1947–53; Vis. Lectureships, etc: Harvard, 1959, 1967; Tokyo, 1964; Tehran, 1967; Melbourne, 1970 (Fink Memorial Lectr); several USA, Canada, West Indies. Jt Ed., Comp. Educn, 1964– ; Adv., OECD, Yugoslavia, 1968; Cnsltnt, Council of Europe, 1963– ; Dir, Comp. Res. Unit, King's Coll., 1970– . *Publications*: Other Schools and Ours, 1958, 4th edn 1973; World Perspectives in Education, 1962, 2nd edn 1965; Communist Education, 1963; Society, Schools and Progress in the USA, 1965; Education and Social Change, 1966; Comparative Studies and Educational Decision, 1968; Education and Development in Western Europe, 1969; The Education of Teachers: a comparative analysis, 1970; ed, The Teacher and the Needs of Society in Evolution, 1970; (with J. A. Mundy and C. H. Moor) Post-Compulsory Education: a new analysis in Western Europe, 1974; rev. edns, W. Boyd: History of Western Education, 1964, 10th edn 1972; contrib. Encyclopaedia Britannica; *contrib*. Internat. Rev. Educn, Wld Ybk Educn, THES. *Address*: Univ. of London, King's College, WC2R 2LS.

King, Dr Edmund Joseph; Senior Lecturer in Medieval History, University of Sheffield, since 1974; *b* 1942; *m* 1967; one *s* one *d*. BA Cantab 1963 (1st cl. History), MA Cantab 1967, PhD Cantab 1968; FRHistS. Asst Lectr, Univ. of Sheffield, 1966–68, Lectr, 1968–74. Gen. Ed., Northants Rec. Soc. *Publications*: Peterborough Abbey 1086–1310: a study in the land market, 1973; *contrib*. EHR, Hist., Northants Past Pres., Past Pres. *Address*: Dept of Medieval and Modern History, The Univ., Sheffield S10 2TN.

King, Joan Faye Sendall, MBE, MA; Senior Assistant in Research, Institute of Criminology, Faculty of Law, University of Cambridge, since 1961; *b* 1917. BA London 1939 (Gen.), Dip. Social Science, Cardiff 1946. Mem., Nat. Assoc. Probation Officers. Civil Service, 1940–45; Probation Service, 1947–60. *Publications*: ed, The Probation Service, 1958, revised edn 1964; ed, The Probation and After-Care Service, 1969. *Address*: Institute of Criminology, 7 West Road, Cambridge.

King, John Ronald Beresford; Lecturer in Statistics, Department of Mathematics, The City University (also teaches econometrics), since 1967; *b* 1942. BSc(Econ) London 1964, MSc(Econ) London 1965; FSS. Mem., Amer. Stat. Assoc. Asst Lectr, City Univ., 1965–67; Seconded Civil Service Coll. (Civil Service Dept) as Lectr in Statistics, 1970–73. *Publications*: (with C. A. Moser and R. Layard) The Impact of Robbins, 1969; *contrib*. High. Educn Rev., Univ. Qly. *Address*: Dept of Mathematics, City Univ., St John Street, EC1V 4PB.

King, Peter Kenneth; University Lecturer in Dutch Language and Literature, Faculty

383

of Modern and Medieval Languages, Cambridge, since 1959; Fellow, St Edmund's House, since 1966; b 1922; m 1950; two s two d. BA London 1950, MA 1952, MA Cantab 1959. Mem., Maatschappij der Nederlandse Letterkunde. Apptd to Fac. of Mod. and Medieval Langs, Cambridge, 1952. Mem., House of Laity, Church Assembly, 1965–70. Publications: ed, European Context: studies in the literature and history of the Netherlands, presented to Theodore Weevers, 1971; Dawn Poetry in the Netherlands, 1971; Multatuli, 1972; A complete word index to J. van den Vondel's Bespiegelingen van Godt en Godtsdienst and Lucifer, 1973; ed, Dutch Studies, 1973; contrib. Leuvense Bijdragen, MLR, Nieuwe Taalgids, Spiegel der Letteren, Tijdschrift voor Nederlandse Taal-en Letterkunde, Years Work in Mod. Lang. Studies. Address: St Edmund's House, Cambridge.

King, Dr Ronald Alfred, MSc, PhD; Senior Lecturer in Sociology of Education, School of Education, University of Exeter, since 1966; b 1934; m 1956; one s two d. BSc London 1955, MSc London 1956, CertifEd 1959, DipEd 1961, PhD London 1967; Mem., Brit. Sociological Assoc., 1967. Publications: Education (Social Structure of Modern Britain Series), 1969; Values and Involvement in a Grammar School, 1969; School Organisation and Pupil Involvement, 1973; contrib. New Soc., Educnl Rev., Res. in Educn, Vocational Aspect, Social and Econ. Admin, Nature. Address: Univ. of Exeter School of Education, Gandy Street, Exeter, Devon.

King, Dr Russell Sinclair; Lecturer, Department of French, University of Nottingham, since 1964; b 1940; m 1962; three s. BA Otago 1960, MA Otago 1961 (1st cl.), DU Dijon 1964 (Mention très honorable). Temp. Asst Lectr, Univ. of Otago, 1962; Vis. Associate Prof., Univ. of Calif, Davis, 1972–74. Publications: contrib. Nott. Fr. Studies, Jl Commonwealth Lit., Rev. Litt. Comp., L'Esprit Créateur, Studies in Romanticism, Neophilologus. Address: Dept of French, Univ. of Nottingham, University Park, Nottingham NG7 2RD.

Kingman, Mrs Valerie; see Cromwell, V.

Kingsley, Dr Colin; Senior Lecturer in Music, University of Edinburgh, since 1972; b 1925; m 1955; two s two d. MusB Cantab 1946; DMus Edinburgh 1968; ARCM 1945; Mem., Incorp. Soc. of Musicians. Pianist, UCW, Aberystwyth, 1963–64; Lectr, Univ. of Edinburgh, 1964–72. Mem., Macnaghten Cttee, London, 1960–63. Pianist, specialising in contemp. music. Address: Dept of Music, Alison House, 12 Nicolson Square, Edinburgh EH8 9BH.

Kingston, Dr A. Richard; Principal Lecturer in Philosophy, School of Humanities, Ulster College, Northern Ireland Polytechnic, since 1973, and Hon. Extra-Mural Lecturer, Faculty of Theology, Queen's University of Belfast, since 1972; b 1931; m 1960; three s two d. BA Dublin 1953 (1st cl. Philosophy), MA Dublin 1960, BD Dublin 1960, PhD QUB 1970. Sen. Tutor, Edgehill Theol Coll., Belfast, and Recognised Teacher, Phil. of Religion, Christian Ethics, Faculty of Theology, QUB, 1963; Sen. Lectr. in Philosophy, Ulster Coll., NI Polytechnic, 1972. Pastoral Ministry of Methodist Church in Ireland, 1956–63. Publications: contrib. Theology, vol. LXX, No. 569 and vol. LXXI, No 576. Address: Ulster College, N Ireland Polytechnic, Jordanstown, Newtown-abbey, Co. Antrim BT37 0QB.

Kinkead-Weekes, Prof. Mark; Professor of English and American Literature, University of Kent at Canterbury, since 1974 (Senior Lecturer, 1966–74); b 1931; m 1959; two s. BA Cape Town 1951, MA Oxon 1954; Higher Cert. in Librarianship Cape Town 1951. Asst Lectr, Univ. of Edinburgh, 1956–58; Lectr, 1958–65; Lectr, Univ. of Kent, 1965–66. Publications: ed (with R. P. C. Mutter), Alexander Pope, A Selection, 1962; (with I. Gregor) William Golding, A Critical Study, 1967, 2nd edn 1968, pbk edn 1970; ed, Twentieth Century Interpretations of The Rainbow, 1971; Samuel Richardson: dramatic novelist, 1973; Samuel Richardson, the Critical Heritage (forthcoming); contrib. Kipling's Mind and Art, ed A. Rutherford, 1964; Imagined Worlds, ed M. Mack and I. Gregor, 1968; Twentieth Century Views: Richardson, 1969; Twentieth Century Interpretations of Pamela, 1969; the Brontës, 1971; Sphere History of Eng. Lit., vol. 4, 1971; contrib. Rev. Engl. Studies, Twent. Cent., Twent. Cent. Studies. Address: Rutherford College, Univ. of Kent at Canterbury.

Kinmont, David Bruce; Staff Tutor in Fine Arts, Department of Extra-Mural Studies, University of Bristol, since 1969; b 1932; m 1962; three s. ATD Manchester 1954, ATC Manchester 1954, BA Cantab 1967, MA Cantab 1972; RCA, FRSA. Sen. Lectr in Art Education, Endsleigh Coll. of Educn, Hull, 1961–65; Sen. Lectr in Art Education, Sidney Webb Coll. of Educn, London, 1968–69. Address: 32 Tyndall's Park Road, Bristol BS8 1HR.

Kinnear, Paul Roderick; Lecturer in Psychology, University of Aberdeen, since 1966; b 1938; m 1967; two s. BSc Edinburgh 1962, MSc Edinburgh 1965; Grad. Mem., BPsS; Mem., Colour Gp (GB). Asst Lectr, Univ. of Aberdeen, 1965. Publications: contrib. Die Farbe, Vision Res. Address: Dept of Psychology, King's Coll., Old Aberdeen AB9 2UB.

Kinnier Wilson, James Vincent, MA, FSA; Eric Yarrow Lecturer in Assyriology, University of Cambridge, since 1955; b 1921; m 1950. BA Oxon 1949, MA Oxon 1952, MA Cantab 1955; FSA 1970. Lectr, Durham Univ., 1950–53; Lectr, Univ. of Toronto, 1953–54, Asst Prof., 1954–55; Fellow, Univ. Coll., Cambridge, 1969. Mem., Council, Brit. Sch. Archaeol. Iraq, 1955; Chm., Fac. Bd Orient. Studies, Cambridge, 1965–67. Publications: The Nimrud Wine Lists, 1972; Indo-Sumerian, 1974; contrib. Iraq, Jl Semit. Studies. Address: Faculty of Oriental Studies, Sidgwick Avenue, Cambridge.

Kinsey, Thomas Edmund, MA; Senior Lecturer, Department of Humanity (Latin), Glasgow University, since 1972 (Lecturer, 1955–72); *b* 1930. BA Oxon 1953 (1st cl. Litterae Humaniores), MA Oxon 1956. Asst Lectr, Glasgow, 1953–55. *Publications*: ed, M. T. Ciceronis: Pro P. Quinctio Oratio, 1971; *contrib.* Latomus, Mnemosyne. *Address*: Dept of Humanity, Univ. of Glasgow, Glasgow G12 8QQ.

Kinsley, Rev. Prof. James, DLitt, FBA; Professor of English Studies, and Head of Department, University of Nottingham, since 1961; *b* 1922; *m* 1949; two *s* one *d*. MA Edinburgh 1943, BA Oxon 1947 (1st cl. English), PhD Edinburgh 1951, MA Oxon 1952, DLitt Edinburgh 1959; FBA, FRSL, FRHistS. Ordained priest 1963, public preacher, Southwell diocese 1964. Lectr, Univ. of Wales, Aberystwyth, 1947–54; Prof. of Eng. Lang. and Lit., Univ. of Wales, Swansea, 1954–61; Gregynog Lectr, Aberystwyth, 1963; Warton Lectr, Brit. Acad., 1974. Capt., RA 1943–45; Vice-Pres., Tennyson Soc., 1963; Mem., Council, Scott. Text Soc., 1958 (Vice-Pres., 1971); Dean, Fac. of Arts, Univ. of Nottingham, 1967–70; Mem., Notts Co. Rec. Cttee. Jt Editor, Renaiss. and Mod. Studies, 1961–68; Gen. Editor Oxford English Novels, 1967– ; Oxford English Memoirs and Travels, 1969– . *Publications*: ed, Lindsay: Ane Satyre of the Thrie Estaits, 1954; Scottish Poetry: A Critical Survey, 1955; Dunbar: Poems, 1958; Dryden: Poems, 1958; Lindsay: Historie of Squyer Meldrum, 1959; Burns: Poems and Songs, 1959; Dryden: Works of Virgil, 1961; (with H. Kinsley) Dryden: Absalom and Achitophel, 1961; Dryden: Poetical Works, 1962; Dryden: Selected Poems, 1963; (with J. T. Boulton) English Satiric Poetry: Dryden to Byron, 1966; Galt: Annals of the Parish, 1967; Burns: Poems and Songs, 1968; The Oxford Book of Ballads, 1969; texts of Jane Austen's Novels, 1970–71; (with G. Parfitt) Dryden's Criticism, 1970; (with H. Kinsley) Dryden: The Critical Heritage, 1971; A. Carlyle: Anecdotes and Characters, 1973; *contrib.* Med. Æv., Library Mod. Lang. Rev., Renaiss. Mod. Studies, Rev. Engl. Studies. *Address*: The Univ., University Park, Nottingham NG7 2RD.

Kiralfy, Prof. Albert Roland; Professor, Laws Faculty, King's College, London University, since 1964; *b* 1915; *m* 1960. LLB London 1935, LLM London 1936, PhD London 1949; Barrister-at-Law, Gray's Inn, 1947. Asst Lectr, King's Coll., 1937–47, Lectr, 1947–51, Reader, 1951–64. Sec., Univ. Bd of Studies in Laws, 1952–56, Chm., 1971– ; Chm., Hughes Parry Hall Council, 1970– . *Publications*: Action on the Case, 1951; The English Legal System, 1954, 5th edn 1973; Source Book of English Law, 1957; Potter's Historical Introduction to English Law, 4th edn 1958; (with G. Jones) Selden Society Guide, 1960; trans., Russian Civil Codes, 1966; Gen. Ed., Comparative Matrimonial Property Law, 1972; *contrib.* Encycl. of Soviet Law, Soviet Law since Stalin, East–West Trade Law; *contrib.* Internat. Comp. Law Qly. *Address*: Laws Faculty, King's College, Strand, WC2R 2LS.

Kirby, David Peter, MA, PhD, FRHistS; Reader, Department of History, University College of Wales, Aberystwyth, since 1973; *b* 1936; *m* 1963; one *s* one *d*. BA Dunelm 1958, MA Dunelm 1960, PhD Dunelm 1962; FRHistS. Asst Lectr, Univ. of Liverpool, 1962–64, Lectr, 1964–66; Lectr, Univ. Coll. of Wales, Aberystwyth, 1966–69, Sen. Lectr, 1969–73. *Publications*: The Making of Early England, 1967; contrib. Who Are the Scots? ed G. Menzies, 1971; ed and contrib., St Wilfrid at Hexham (Hexham Abbey Thirteen Hundredth Anniversary), 1974; *contrib.* Bull. Bd Celt. Studies, Bull. J. Rylands Libr., EHR, WHR, Studia Celt., Innes Rev. *Address*: Dept of History, Univ. College of Wales, Aberystwyth SY23 2AX.

Kirby, Prof. E. Stuart, BSc(Econ), PhD; Professor of Economics, University of Aston in Birmingham, since 1965; *b* 1909; *m* 1943; one *s* two *d*. BSc(Econ) London 1933, PhD London 1938. Mem., Reg. Studies Assoc., Royal Central Asian Soc., Royal Econ. Soc., Economics Assoc., Europ. Mvmt, Japan Soc., etc. Lectr, Fukushima Kosho, Japan, 1935–39; Lectr, SOAS, London, 1946–48; Prof. of Economics, Univ. of Hong Kong, 1948–65; Vis. Prof., Univ. of British Columbia, 1960; Simon Sen. Fellow, Manchester, 1953–54. Min. of Econ. Welfare, 1939–40; Bd of Trade, 1946–48; Cnsltncies, UN, and var business firms. Editor, Contemp. China, 1955–68. *Publications*: Economic History of England (in Japanese), 1936; Economic History of Europe (in Japanese), 1937; Japan's Economic Future (in Japanese), 1946; Essay on Japanese Culture, 1950; Introduction to the Economic History of China, 1953; Economic Development in East Asia, 1968; The Soviet Far East, 1971; *contrib.* various articles. *Address*: Univ. of Aston, Birmingham B4 7ET.

Kirby, Dr Roger Paynter; Lecturer in Geography, University of Edinburgh, since 1960; *b* 1934. BSc London 1957, Dip. Surveying London 1958, MSc McGill 1960, PhD Edinburgh 1966. Mem., Inst. Brit. Geogrs, Brit. Cartog. Soc. *Publications*: *contrib.* Geog. Jl, Scott. Jl Geol., Trans Inst. Brit. Geogrs. *Address*: Dept of Geography, Univ. of Edinburgh, Edinburgh EH8 9YL.

Kirk, Prof. Geoffrey Stephen, DSC, LittD, FBA; Regius Professor of Greek, Cambridge University, since 1974; *b* 1921; *m* 1950; one *d*. BA Cantab 1946, MA Cantab 1948, LittD Cantab 1965; MA Yale 1965; FBA 1959. Research Fellow, Trinity Hall, Cambridge, 1946–49; Commonwealth Fund Fellow, Harvard Univ., 1949–50; Fellow, Trinity Hall, 1950–70; Fellow, Trinity College, Cambridge, 1974; Asst Lectr in Classics, 1951, Lectr, 1952–61, Reader in Greek, 1961–65, Cambridge Univ.; Prof. of Classics, Yale Univ., 1965–70; Prof. of Classics, Bristol Univ., 1971–73; Vis. Lectr, Harvard Univ., 1958; Sather Prof. of Classical Literature, Univ. of California, Berkeley, 1968–69. *Publications*: Heraclitus, the Cosmic Fragments, 1954; (with J. E. Raven) The Presocratic Philosophers, 1958; The Songs of Homer, 1962 (abbrev. edn, Homer and the Epic, 1965); Euripides, Bacchae, 1970;

Myth, 1970; The Nature of Greek Myths, 1974; *contrib.* classical, archaeological and philosophical jls. *Address*: Trinity College, Cambridge.

Kirk, Maurice, JP, MA; Senior Lecturer, Department of Social Studies, University of Leeds, since 1964; *b* 1922; *m* 1948; one *s* one *d*. BA Leeds 1947 (1st cl. Geography), MA Leeds 1948. Mem., IUSSP 1961, Brit. Sociol Assoc. 1964. Lectr, Univ. of Leeds, 1948–64; Dean, Fac. Econ. Social Studies, 1963–65; Chm., Jt Fac. Bd, 1970–72. JP 1965– . *Address*: Dept of Social Studies, Univ. of Leeds, Leeds LS2 9JT.

Kirk, Prof. William; Professor of Geography and Head of Department, since 1969, and Dean of Education, 1971–74, Queen's University of Belfast; *b* 1921; *m* 1942; two *d*. BA London 1942 (1st cl. Geography), DipEd London 1947 (Distinction); FSAScot 1953. Mem., Inst. Brit. Geogrs 1950. Asst Lectr, Manchester Univ., 1947–49; Lectr, Aberdeen Univ., 1949–59; Sen. Lectr, Leicester Univ., 1959–64, Prof., of Human Geography, 1964–69. Hon. Sec. Inst. Brit. Geogrs, 1963–71; Chm., Jt Cttee (DES) for ONC, HNC awards in Surveying, Cartography, Town Planning, Estate Mngmt, 1969– ; Member: Brit. Nat. Cttee for Geography, 1969– ; Irish Nat. Cttee for Geography, 1970– ; Adv. Council to Min. of Education, N Ireland, 1971; Lelievre Cttee on Training of Teachers in N Ireland, 1972; Human Geog. Cttee, SSRC, 1973– ; Chm., N Ireland Curriculum Develt Cttee, 1973– . *Publications*: contrib. Geographical Essays on Gt Britain, ed J. Mitchell, 1965; Changing Map of Asia, ed O. H. K. Spate and G. East, 1971; Encyclopaedia Britannica; *contrib.* Geog., Ind. Geog. Jl, Geog. Rev., Proc. Royal Soc. Edin., Proc. Soc. Antiqu. Scott., Scott. Geog. Mag., Trans Inst. Brit. Geogrs, Jl Afr. Hist., Mariner's Mirror. *Address*: Dept of Geography, Queen's Univ. of Belfast, Belfast BT7 1NN.

Kirk-Greene, Anthony Hamilton Millard, MBE, MA; Senior Research Fellow in African Studies, St Antony's College, Oxford University, since 1967; *b* 1925; *m* 1967. BA Cantab 1949 (1st cl. Modern Langs), MA Cantab 1954, MA Oxon 1967. Mem., Afr. Studies Assoc. UK, Internat. Afr. Inst., Royal Afr. Soc. Sen. Lectr in Government, Inst. of Administration, Zaria, 1957–62; Reader in Public Administration, Ahmadu Bello Univ., Nigeria, 1962–66; Vis. Fellow, Clare Coll., Cambridge, 1967; Vis. Prof., Univ. of California, 1963, 1967, 1968; Associate Fellow, Inst. Commonwealth Studies, Oxford, 1970; Vis. Lectr, Univ. of Paris, 1971, 1973; Hans Wolff Vis. Prof., Indiana Univ., 1973; Commonwealth Fund (Harkness) Fellow, Northwestern Univ., 1958–59. Mem., Council, Afr. Studies Assoc., 1966–69; Advr (Staff College), E Afr. Community, 1972. Gen. Ed., Studies in African Hist. *Publications*: Adamawa Past and Present, 1958, 2nd edn 1969; Barth's Travels in Nigeria, 1962; Principles of Native Administration in Nigeria, 1965; (with S. J. Hogben) Emirates of Northern Nigeria, 1966; A Modern Hausa Reader,

1967; Hausa Proverbs, 1967; Lugard's Amalgamation of Nigeria, 1968; Crisis and Conflict in Nigeria 1966–1970, 1971; Two West African Autobiographical Narratives, 1972; Gazetteers of Northern Provinces of Nigeria, 1973; (with C. Kraft) Teach Yourself Hausa, 1973; *contrib.* Afr., Afr. Aff., Jl Afr. Admin, Jl Afr. Hist., Jl Afr. Langs, Jl Mod. Afr. Studies, Jl Nig. Hist. Soc., Times Lit. Supp. *Address*: St Antony's College, Oxford.

Kirkaldy, Prof. John Francis, DSc, FGS; Professor of Geology, Queen Mary College, University of London, since 1962; *b* 1908; *m* 1935; four *d*. BSc London 1929 (1st cl. Geology), MSc London 1932, DSc London 1946; FGS. Pres. Geol. Assoc. 1962–64, Hon. Mem., Geol. Assoc., 1971; Pres., Assoc. of Teachers of Geology, 1972–73. Demonstrator, King's Coll., London, 1929–33; Asst Lectr, Univ. Coll., London, 1933–39; Lectr, King's Coll., London, 1939–47; Reader and Head of Dept, Queen Mary Coll., London, 1947–62. Meteorol Br., RAF, 1939–45; Mem., Council, Geol Soc., 1950–55; Council, Geol Assoc., 1936–39, 1948–52, 1961–68; Senate and Acad. Council, Univ. of London, 1966– ; Fellow, King's Coll., London, 1970. *Publications*: (with A. K. Wells), Outline of Historical Geology, 2nd edn 1948, 5th edn 1966; General Principles of Geology, 1954, 5th edn 1971; The Study of Fossils, 1963; Rocks and Minerals in Colour, 1963, 2nd edn 1968; Fossils in Colour, 1967, 2nd edn 1970, French edn 1969, German and Italian edns 1971; Geological Time, 1971; *contrib.* Geol. Mag., Proc. Geol Assoc., Qly Jl Geol Soc., etc. *Address*: Geology Dept, Queen Mary College, Mile End Road, E1 4NS.

Kirkby, Prof. Michael John; Professor of Physical Geography, University of Leeds, since 1973; *b* 1937; *m* 1963; one *s* one *d*. BA Cantab 1960, PhD Cantab 1963; FRGS 1965, Member: IBG 1965, Brit. Geomorph. Res. Gp. Bristol Univ., 1966–73. *Publications*: (with M. A. Carson) Hillslope Form and Process, 1972; *contrib.* Bull. Internat. Assoc. Sci. Hydrol., Jl Geol. *Address*: Dept of Geography, Univ. of Leeds, Leeds LS2 9JT.

Kirkman, Dr John; Senior Lecturer, Department of English and Liberal Studies, University of Wales Institute of Science and Technology, since 1961; *b* 1932; *m* 1955. BA Nottingham 1953, CertEd Nottingham 1954, MA Nottingham 1957, PhD Nottingham 1967. *Address*: Univ. of Wales Institute of Science and Technology, King Edward VII Avenue, Cardiff CF1 3NU.

Kirkman, Patrick Richard Alfred; Senior Lecturer in Accountancy, Economics Department, University of Exeter, since 1973; *b* 1932; *m* 1957; four *s*. MSc Southampton 1970 (Social Science); ACIS 1957, FACCA 1958. Lectr in Accountancy, Univ. Exeter, 1970 (previously teaching in Further Educn Sector). *Publications*: Accounting under Inflationary Conditions, 1974; *contrib.* Accountant, Accountancy, Accounting and Business Research, Certified Accountants Jl,

Jl Business Finance. *Address*: Univ. of Exeter, Exeter EX4 4QJ.

Kirkpatrick, Colin Hunter; Lecturer in Economics, Department of Economics, University of Manchester, since 1968; *b* 1944; *m* 1968; one *d*. BScEcon QUB 1967 (1st cl. Hons), MSc Econ London 1968. *Publications*: *contrib*. Bull. Econ. Res., Econ. and Statistical Rev., Jl Developt Studies, Manchester Sch. of Econ. and Social Studies. *Address*: Dept of Economics, Univ. of Manchester, Oxford Road, Manchester M13 9PL.

Kirkwood, Dr Henry William, MA, PhD; Lecturer in German Language, University of Surrey, since 1964; *b* 1935. MA Edinburgh 1957 (1st cl. German Lang. and Lit.); PhD Edinburgh (Linguistics). Lektor, Univ. of Heidelberg, 1957–64. *Publications*: *contrib*. Jl Lingu., Lingu. Ber., IRAL, Philol. Prag. *Address*: Dept of Linguistic and Regional Studies, Univ. of Surrey, Guildford, Surrey GU2 5XH.

Kirkwood, Prof. Kenneth, MA; Rhodes Professor of Race Relations, University of Oxford, and Fellow of St Antony's College, since 1954; *b* 1919; *m* 1942; three *s* three *d*. BA, BSc Rand; MA. Lectr, Univ. of the Witwatersrand, 1947; Lectr, Univ. of Natal, 1948–51; Fellowship, Inst. of Commonwealth Studies, Univ. of London, 1952; Carnegie Travelling Fellowship, USA, 1953; Sen. Res. Officer, Inst. of Colonial Studies, Oxford Univ., 1953; Organiser, Inst. for Social Research, Univ. of Natal, 1954; Vis. Prof. of Race Relations (UNESCO), UC of Rhodesia and Nyasaland, 1964. Sub-Warden, St Antony's Coll., Oxford, 1968–71. Chm., Regional Cttee, S African Inst. of Race Relations in Natal, 1954, UK Rep., 1955. Investigation on behalf UNESCO into trends in race relations in British-Non-Self-Governing Territories of Africa, 1958; composed memorandum on meaning, and procedure for further study of 'racial discrimination', for UN Div. of Human Rights, 1966–67. Mem., Africa Educnl Trust, 1955–   ; Mem., Oxfam, 1955–   . Editor, St Antony's Papers: African Affairs, no 1, 1961; no 2, 1963; no 3, 1969. *Publications*: The Proposed Federation of the Central African Territories, 1952; *contrib*. Lord Hailey: An African Survey, rev. edn 1957; Cambridge History of the British Empire, 2nd edn vol. VIII, 1963; Britain and Africa, 1965; booklets and articles on race relations and international affairs. *Address*: St Antony's College, Oxford.

Kirton, Dr William J. S.; Lecturer in French, University of Aberdeen, since 1967; *b* 1939; *m* 1962; one *s* two *d*. BA Exeter 1962, PhD Exeter 1970. Tutor, Exeter Univ., 1966–67. *Address*: Dept of French, Univ. of Aberdeen, Aberdeen AB9 1AS.

Kirwan, Christopher Andrew, MA; Fellow of Exeter College, University of Oxford, since 1960, and University Lecturer in Philosophy, since 1961; *b* 1932; *m* 1959; two *s* one *d*. BA Oxon 1956 (1st cl. Hon. Mods, 1st cl. Lit. Hum.), MA Oxon 1959. Procter Vis. Fellow, Princeton Univ., 1957–58; Lectr of Merton

and Exeter Colls, Oxford, 1959–60; Vis. Associate Prof., Univ. of Michigan, 1968. Sub-Rector, Exeter Coll., 1961–63. *Publications*: Outings from Oxford, 1970; trans., Aristotle: Metaphysics, bks Gamma, Delta and Epsilon; *contrib*. Mind, Philos. Qly, Phron., Proc. Aristot. Soc. *Address*: Exeter College, Oxford.

Kistruck, Prof. John Roger Scrivener; Barclays Bank Professor of Management Information Systems, School of Industrial and Business Studies, University of Warwick, since 1971; *b* 1936. BA Cantab 1958, MA 1964. *Address*: Univ. of Warwick, Coventry CV4 7AL.

Kitch, (Joseph) Michael; Lecturer in History, School of Slavonic and East European Studies, University of London, since 1968; *b* 1941; *m* 1972; two *s* one *d*. BA Duke 1963, MA Indiana 1965; Member: Brit. Soc. for Philosophy of Sci., Brit. Soc. for Eighteenth-Century Studies. *Publication*: *contrib*. Past and Present. *Address*: Sch. of Slavonic and East European Studies, Univ. of London, WC1E 7HU.

Kitch, Malcolm James; Lecturer in History, University of Sussex, since 1967; *b* 1938; *m* 1966; two *s*. BA Oxon 1962 (1st cl. History), MA Oxon 1965. Asst Lectr in History, Univ. of Sussex, 1964–67; Vis. Associate Prof., State Univ. of NY at Stony Brook, 1973. Mem., Council, Lond. Record Soc., 1966–71; Hon. Treas., Brit. Record Soc., 1971–   . *Publications*: Capitalism and the Reformation, 1967. *Address*: School of English and American Studies, Arts Building, Univ. of Sussex, Brighton BN1 9QN.

Kitch, Michael; *see* Kitch, J. M.

Kitchen, Kenneth Anderson, BA; Lecturer in Egyptian and Coptic, School of Archaeology and Oriental Studies, University of Liverpool, since 1957; *b* 1932. BA 1956 (1st cl.Egyptology with Hebrew). Ordinary Member: Egypt Exploration Society, Palestine Exploration Fund, British Institute of Archaeology at Ankara, British School of Archaeology in Iraq, Deutsche Orient-Gesellschaft, Société Française d'Egyptologie, Fondation Egyptologique Reine Elisabeth. *Publications*: Suppiluliuma and the Amarna Pharaohs, 1962; Alter Orient u. Altes Testament, 1965, rev. English edn as Ancient Orient and Old Testament, 1966; Suppiluliuma (I Protagonisti della Storia Universale, 66), 1966; RamessideInscriptions, I/1, 1969; I/2, 1971–72; I/3, 4, 1974; II/1, 1969; II/2, 1970; II/3, 1970; III/5, 1971; II/6, 1971; IV/1, 1968; V/I, 1970; V/2, 1972; V/3, 1973; VI/1, 1969; Third Intermediate Period in Egypt, 1972; Ramesses II, 1974; *contrib*. Bull. Amer. Sch. Or. Res., Bibl. Or., Bull. Mus. Beyrouth, Chron. Egypt, Jl Amer. Res. Center Egypt, Jl Egypt. Archaeol., Orientalia NS, Or, Antiqu., Rev. Hitt. Asian., Tyn. Bull., Zeits. Äg. Spr. *Address*: School of Archaeology and Oriental Studies, The Univ., PO Box 147, Liverpool L69 3BX.

Kiteley, John Frederick; Lecturer in English, Hertford College, Oxford University, since 1965; *b* 1934; *m* 1959; one *s* one *d*. BA Oxon 1955, MA Oxon 1959, BLitt Oxon 1959. Tutor, Corpus Christi Coll., Oxford, 1959–62; Tutor, Trinity and Hertford Colls, 1962–65. *Publications*: Believe – Leave it to Wonder, 1973; contrib. Modern Critical Essays on Sir Gawain and the Green Knight, ed, Howard and Zacher, 1968; *contrib*. Anglia, Studies Lit. Imag. *Address*: Hertford College, Oxford.

Kitson, Michael William Lely; Reader in History of Art, Courtauld Institute of Art, University of London, since 1968; *b* 1926; *m* 1950; two *s*. BA Hons Cambridge 1950 (English Literature), MA 1953, Acad. Dip. London 1952 (History of Art, with distinction). Asst Lectr in History of Art, Slade Sch. of Fine Art, London, 1952–54; Lectr in History of Art, Courtauld Inst. of Art, London Univ., 1955–66, Sen. Lectr 1966–68; Vis. Lectr. Yale Univ. 1972. Mem., Adv., Council, Paul Mellon Centre for Studies in British Art, London, 1974– . *Publications*: J. M. W. Turner,1964; The Age of Baroque, 1966,1967; Claude Lorrain: Landscape with the Nymph Egeria, 1968; Rembrandt, 1969; The Complete Paintings of Caravaggio, 1969; exhibition catalogues: The Art of Claude Lorrain, 1969; ed, La Peinture romantique anglaise et les pré-raphaélites, 1972; ed, Salvator Rosa, 1973; *contrib*. Apollo, Burlington Mag., Master Drawings, Revue des Arts, Revue du Louvre, Walpole Soc., Jl Warburg and Courtauld Insts. *Address*: Courtauld Inst. of Art, 20 Portman Square, W1H 0BE.

Klappholz, Kurt; Reader in Economics, London School of Economics, since 1969; *b* 1927; *m* 1962; two *s*. BSc(Econ) London 1951 (1st cl. Hons). Instructor in Econs, Columbia Univ., NY, 1952–54; Lectr, 1954–58, Sen. Lectr, 1964–69, LSE; Warden of Hall Residence, LSE, 1967–69; Mem., Standing Cttee of Ct of Governors, LSE, 1970– . *Publications*: trans. E. Schneider: Money, Income and Employment, 1962; *contrib*. BJPS, Economica. *Address*: London School of Economics, Houghton Street, WC2A 2AE.

Klein, Dr Holger Michael; Lecturer in Comparative Literature, School of European Studies, University of East Anglia, since 1970; *b* 1938; *m* 1967; two *d*. MA Munich 1966, Drphil Munich 1970; Member: Mod. Lang. Assoc. of America, W Germany Shakespeare Assoc., British Soc. for 18th-Century Studies, Soc. for Renaissance Studies. Asst, English Dept, Univ. of Cologne, 1966–70. *Publications*: Das Portrait in der Versdichtung der englischen Renaissance, 1970; ed and trans. Wycherley: The Country Wife, 1972; Molière in English Thought on Comedy, 1660–1800, in, Molière and the Commonwealth of Letters, ed R. Golmson, 1974; Colman and Garrick: The Clandestine Marriage: An Interpretation, in, Das englische Drama im 18 und 19 Jhdt. ed H. Kosok,1974; *contrib*. Notes and Queries, Archiv. *Address*: School of European Studies, Univ. of East Anglia, Norwich NOR 88C.

Kline, Dr Paul; Reader in Psychometrics, University of Exeter, since 1973; *b* 1937; *m* 1959; one *s* three *d*. BA Hons Reading 1958

388

(classics); DipEd Wales 1959; MEd Aberdeen 1963; PhD Manchester 1968; ABPS 1968. Res. Associate, Dept of Educn, Manchester, 1963–66; Lectr in Educn, Inst of Educn, Exeter, 1966–69; Lectr in Psychol., Exeter, 1969–73. *Publications*: Fact and Fantasy in Freudian Theory, 1972; New Approaches in Psychological Measurement, 1973; *contrib*. Brit. Jl Educn Psychol., Brit. Jl Med. Psychol., Brit. Jl Psychol., Brit. Jl Soc. Clin. Psychol., Jl Personality, Jl Multiv. Exper. Personality and Clin. Psychol. *Address*: Dept of Psychology, Univ. of Exeter, EX4 4QJ.

Kloss, Günther; Senior Lecturer in European Studies and Modern Languages, Department of European Studies and Modern Languages, University of Manchester Institute of Science and Technology, since 1974; *b* 1933; *m* 1963; two *s*. Staatsexamen Tübingen 1959, Lektor, Univ. of Nottingham, 1959–61; Lectr, UMIST, 1961–74; Vis. Lectr, Univ. of Stuttgart, 1972. Warden, Hall of Res., 1963– . *Publications*: West Germany: an introduction, 1974; *contrib*. German Life Lett., Konst. Blätt. Hochschul., Minerva, THES, Wiener Libr. Bull., Wissenschaftsrecht, Wissenschaftsverwaltung, Wissenschaftsförderung. *Address*: Dept of European Studies and Modern Languages, Univ. of Manchester Institute of Science and Technology, PO Box 88, Sackville Street, Manchester M60 1QD.

Kmietowicz, Z. W.; Lecturer in Economic Statistics, University of Leeds, since 1964; *b* 1935; *m* 1960; three *d*. BA Leeds 1958, DipStats, Manchester 1960. Univ. of Nairobi, 1968–70 (secondment); UN Industrial Develt Orgn/E African Community 1970–71 (secondment). *Publications*: *contrib*. Jl Management Studies, Jl Royal Stat. Soc. *Address*: School of Economic Studies, Univ. of Leeds, Leeds LS2 9JT.

Knapp, Barbara Naomi, MCom, MA; Senior Lecturer, since 1964, and Assistant Director, Department of Physical Education, University of Birmingham, since 1965. BCom Birmingham 1941, MCom Birmingham 1948, MA Birmingham 1969; Mem., Ergonomics Research Soc. Asst Lectr, Univ. of Birmingham, 1949–51, Lectr, 1951–64. Mem., W Midlands Reg. Sports Council, 1969–72; Mem., ICCS. *Publications*: Skill in Sport: The Attainment of Proficiency, 1963; Sport et Motricité (trans. N. Ganancia and P. Dague), 1971; (with H. M. Hartley) Riding for Recreation in the West Midlands, 1971; *contrib*. Bull. Phys. Educn, Res. Phys. Educn, Res. Qly. *Address*: Dept of Physical Education, The Univ. of Birmingham, PO Box 363, Birmingham B15 2TT.

Knapp, Wilfrid Francis; Fellow and Tutor in Politics, St Catherine's College, and University Lecturer in Politics, University of Oxford, since 1950; *b* 1924; *m* 1951; two *s*. MA Oxon 1949. *Publications*: A History of War and Peace, 1939–65, 1967; Tunisia 1970. *Address*: St Catherine's College, Oxford.

Knappert, Dr Jan, MA, Dr Litt; Professor Extraordinary, University of Louvain, since 1971, and Lecturer, Department of Africa,

School of Oriental and African Studies, University of London, since 1964; *b* 1927; *m* 1955; four *s* three *d*. BA Leiden 1948 (Litt. Ind.), BA Leiden 1951 (Litt. Sem.), MA Leiden 1954 (Linguistics), Dr Litt. et Phil. Leiden 1958; FRAS, FRAI. Exch. Lectr, Univ. of Pretoria, 1958–59; Asst Lectr, Univ. of Ghent, 1960–61; Sen. Res. Fellow, Univ. Coll., Makerere, 1961–63; Sen. Res. Fellow, Univ. Coll., Dar es Salaam, 1963–64. Chm., Assoc. Brit. Orientalists, 1972– (Ed., Bull., 1969–72); Ed., Swahili, 1961–64. *Publications*: Het Epos Van Heraklios, 1958; Four Swahili Epics, 1965; Essai d'un Dictionnaire Alur-Français, 1964; Traditional Swahili Poetry, 1967; Myths and Legends of the Swahili, 1970; Myths and Legends of the Congo, 1971; Un Siècle de Classification des Langues Bantoues, 1970; Swahili Islamic Poetry, 1971; A Choice of Flowers: an anthology of Swahili love poetry, 1972; *contrib.* Afr. Lang. Studies, Afr. und Uebersee, Swahili. *Address*: Dept of Africa, School of Oriental and African Studies, Univ. of London, Malet Street, WC1E 7HP.

Kneale, (Robert) Bryan (Charles), ARA; Tutor in Sculpture School, Royal College of Art, since 1964; *b* 1930; *m* 1956; one *s* one *d*. Royal Acad. Schs Dip. 1952; Fellow, Royal Coll. of Art, 1970, ARA, Mem., Contemporary Art Soc.; Mem., Inst. Contemporary Art. Mem. Fine Art Panel, Nat. Council for Diplomas in Art and Design, 1964–70; Mem. Sculpture Panel, British Sch. at Rome 1971– ; Mem. Fine Art Panel, Arts Council of Great Britain, 1970. *Address*: Royal College of Art, Kensington Gore, SW7 2EU.

Knecht, Robert Jean, MA; Senior Lecturer in Modern History, University of Birmingham, since 1968; *b* 1926; *m* 1956. BA London 1948, DipEd 1949, MA London 1953; FRHistS. Asst Lectr, Birmingham Univ., 1956–59, Lectr, 1959–68. Mem., Hist. Subject Panel, Jt Matric. Bd, Manchester, 1969. *Publications*: The Voyage of Sir Nicholas Carewe, 1959; Francis I and Absolute Monarchy, 1969; Renaissance and Reformation, 1969; *contrib.* Hist., Univ. Birmingham Hist. Jl., Eng. Hist. Rev., TLS. *Address*: School of History, Univ. of Birmingham, PO Box 363, Birmingham B15 2TT.

Knibb, Dr Michael Anthony, BD, STM, PhD; Lecturer in Old Testament Studies, University of London, King's College, since 1964; *b* 1938; *m* 1972. BD London 1961 (1st cl.), STM Union Theol Sem. NY 1962, PhD London 1974. Hon. Sec., Palestine Explor, Fund, 1970– . *Address*: King's College, Strand, WC2R 2LS.

Knight, David Marcus, MA, DPhil; Lecturer in the History of Science, Department of Philosophy, Durham University, since 1964; *b* 1936; *m* 1962; two *s* two *d*. BA Oxon 1961 (2nd cl. Chemistry), MA, DPhil Oxon 1964, Dip. Hist. and Philos. of Science Oxford 1962; FChemSoc., Mem., Brit. Soc. Hist. Science, Royal Instn, Mem., Council, Brit. Soc. Hist. Science, 1966–70. *Publications*: Atoms and Elements, 1967, 2nd edn

1970; ed, Classical Scientific Papers, Chemistry, 1st ser. 1968, 2nd ser. 1970; Natural Science Books in English, 1972; *contrib.* Ambix, Hist. Sci., Studies Romant. *Address*: Dept of Philosophy, Univ. of Durham, Durham DH1 3HP.

Knight, John Beverley; Senior Research Officer, Institute of Economics and Statistics, Oxford University, since 1973; Fellow and Tutor in Economics, St Edmund Hall, since 1967; *b* 1939; *m* 1964; three *d*. BA Natal 1960; BA Cantab 1962. Institute of Economics and Statistics, Oxford University: Asst Res. Officer, 1963–68; Res. Officer, 1968–73. *Publications*: *contrib.* Bull. Oxford Univ. Inst. of Econs and Stats, Economic Jl, Oxford Econ. Papers. *Address*: Institute of Economics and Statistics, Manor Road, Oxford.

Knight, Prof. Kenneth Graham; Professor of German, University of Kent at Canterbury, since 1971; *b* 1921; *m* 1947; one *s* two *d*. BA Cantab 1943 (French and German), MA Cantab 1948, PhD Cantab 1951. Asst Lectr, Manchester, 1951–52; Asst Lectr, Keele, 1952–55, Lectr, 1955–60; Sec.-Libr., Inst. of Germanic Studies, Univ. of London, 1960–65; Reader in German, Univ. of Kent, 1965–71. *Publications*: trans., R. Guardini: Rilke's Duino Elegies, 1961; Deutsche Romane der Barockzeit, 1969; *contrib.* German Life Lett., Mod. Lang. Rev. *Address*: Keynes College, The Univ., Canterbury, Kent.

Knight, Michael Thomas, MA, LLB; Senior Lecturer in Law, Queen's University, Belfast, since 1971; *b* 1936. BA (Mod.) Dublin 1958 (2nd cl. (i) Legal Science), LLB Dublin 1959 (1st cl.), MA Dublin 1967. Mem., Soc. Public Teachers of Law, Brit. Sect., Internat. Commn Jurists. Asst Lectr, Univ. Coll., Cardiff, 1960–63, Lectr, 1963–64; Lectr, Queen's Univ., Belfast, 1965–71. *Publications*: Criminal Appeals, 1970; *contrib.* Crim. Law Rev., Irish Jurist, North. Ireland Legal Qly. *Address*: Faculty of Law, Queen's Univ., Belfast BT7 1NN.

Knott, Betty Irene; Senior Lecturer in Humanity and Comparative Philology, University of Glasgow, since 1968; *b* 1930. BA London 1951 (1st cl. Hons Classics), MA London 1953 (Classics, Compar. Philol., dist.); Member: Hellenic Soc., Philol Soc., Class. Assoc., Scottish Class. Assoc. Asst in Humanity, Univ. Glasgow, 1953, Lectr. 1954–68. Adviser of Studies in Arts, 1955 *Publications*: trans., Thomas a Kempis: The Imitation of Christ, 1963. *Address*: Humanity Dept, Univ. of Glasgow, Glasgow G12 8QQ.

Knowles, Anthony Vere, MA; Lecturer in Russian, University of Liverpool, since 1966; *b* 1937; *m* 1964. BA Nottingham 1962, MA Nottingham 1965. Asst Lectr, Univ. of Liverpool, 1964–66. *Publications*: (with D. Blaganje) Angleščina za vsakogar, 1962, 2nd rev. edn 1966; ed, Kak sozdavalsya Robinzon, 1968. *Address*: Dept of Russian, Modern Languages Building, PO Box 147, The Univ., Liverpool L69 3BX.

Knowles, Hubert Gordon, BSc, MSc, DipIA, AMBIM, FISM; Lecturer, Chesters Management Centre, University of Strathclyde, since 1965; b 1928; m 1957; one s one d. BSc Aston 1958, DipIA Aston 1959, MSc Strathclyde 1971; AMBIM 1960, MISM 1960, FISM 1972. Pres., BPICS (Glasgow Br.), 1970–73. Publications: Network Analysis, 1970; contrib. Superv., Superv. Mngmt. Address: Univ. of Strathclyde, Chesters Management Centre, Bearsden, Glasgow.

Knowles, Vincent; Special Lecturer in Greek and Latin, since 1948, and Registrar, University of Manchester, since 1952; b 1912; m 1940; one s one d. BA Manchester 1935 (1st cl. Classics), Teacher's Dip 1936, MA Manchester 1938. Asst in Greek and Latin, Univ. of Manchester, 1938–48. Asst Sec., Univ. of Manchester, 1945–46; Chief Asst to Registrar, 1946–50, Dep. Reg., 1950–51, Jt Reg., 1951. Publications: Studies in the late Plays of Euripides, 1938. Address: Registry, Univ. of Manchester, Manchester M13 9PL.

Knowlson, Dr Harold, BSc, PhD; Senior Lecturer in Education, and Senior Tutor for Further Professional Studies, School of Education, University of Bristol, since 1949; b 1913; m 1940; one s one d. BSc Leeds 1936 (1st cl.), PhD Leeds 1938. Lectr, Univ. of Khartoum, 1938–45. Pres., Leeds Univ. Union, 1937–38; Chm., Cttee D (inservice trng and educn), UCET. Publications: contrib. various articles on in-service training of teachers. Address: School of Education, 35 Berkeley Square, Bristol BS8 7HU.

Knowlson, Dr James Rex; Lecturer in French Studies, Reading University, since 1969; Senior Tutor, Faculty of Letters, since 1974; b 1933; m 1958; two s one d. BA Reading 1956, DipEd, PhD Reading 1964. Asst, Glasgow Univ., 1960–63, Lectr, 1963–69. Publications: Samuel Beckett: An Exhibition, 1971; Light and Darkness in Samuel Beckett's Theatre, 1972; Language and the Advancement of Learning, 1974; contrib. Hist. Today, Jl Hist. Ideas, Mod. Lang. Rev., Mod. Philol., New Theatre Mag., Studies Volt. and 18th Cent. Address: Dept of French Studies, The Univ., Whiteknights, Reading RG6 2AH.

Knox, Prof. Henry Macdonald; Professor of Education, Queen's University of Belfast, since 1951; b 1916; m 1945; one s one d. MA Edinburgh 1938, MEd Edinburgh 1940, PhD Edinburgh 1949. Lectr, Hull Univ., 1946–49; Lectr, St Andrews Univ., 1949–51. Dean of Educn, 1968–71; Governor: Stranmillis Coll., 1967– ; St Joseph's Coll. of Educn, 1968– ; Former Mem., Adv: Council on Educn, N Ireland. Publications. Scottish Education 1696–1946, 1953; ed, J. Dury: The Reformed School, 1958; Introduction to Educational Method, 1961; contrib. Brit. Jl Educnl Studies, Scott. Educnl Jl, Times Educnl Supp. Address: Dept of Education, Queen's Univ., Belfast BT7 1NN.

Koch, Hannsjoachim Wolfgang; Lecturer in History, University of York, since 1965; b 1933; m 1955; two s one d. BA Keele 1965 (1st cl. History and American Studies); Gastdozent Hochsch. Politische Wissenschaften, Muenchen, 1970– . Publications: ed, The Origins of the First World War, Great Power Rivalry and German War Aims, 1972; Hitler Youth, 1972; Der Sozialdarwinismus: Seine Genese und Einfluss auf das imperialistiche Denken, 1973; The Hitler Youth, 1974; contrib. Hist. Jl, Hist., Zeits. Pol. Wissens, Royal United Services Instn Jl. Address: Dept of History, Univ. of York, Heslington, York YO1 5DD.

Koenigsberger, Prof. Otto H.; Professor of Development Planning, School of Environmental Studies, University College London, since 1971; b 1908; m 1957. DipIng Berlin, DrIng Berlin; FIIA, FITP, FIE (India); AIV (Germany), RTPI, RIBA. Dir, Dept of Tropical Studies, Architectural Assoc., London, 1957–71 (Principal, Architectural Assoc. Sch., 1965–66); Vis. Prof., Northwestern Univ., Evanston, Illinois, 1956–57; Mellon Prof. of Planning, Columbia Univ., NY, 1968. Chief Architect and Planner, Mysore State, 1939–47; Dir of Housing, Govt of India, 1948–51; Housing Advr to UN Economic Commn for Africa, 1966–72; UN Housing and Planning Missions Ghana, Singapore, Pakistan, Nigeria, Philippines, Ceylon; Consultant to the Govts of Zambia, Costa Rica, Brazil, and Penang. Publications: Construction of Ancient Egyptian Doors, 1936; Development Plan for Jamshedpur, 1945; (with C. Abrams and V. Bodiansky) Housing in Ghana; (with R. Lynn) Roofs in the Warm Humid Tropics, 1966; Action Planning, 1964; Housing in the National Development Plan, 1970; (with C. Mahoney and M. Evans) Climate and House Design, 1970; (with T. G. Ingersoll, A. Mayhew and S. V. Szokolay), Manual of Tropical Housing and Building, 1974. Address: Development Planning Unit, School of Environmental Studies, UCL, 10/11 Percy Street, W1P 9FB.

Kogan, Prof. Maurice, MA; Professor of Government and Social Administration, since 1969, Head, School of Social Sciences, Brunel University, since 1971; b 1930; m 1961; two s. BA Cantab 1953 (1st cl. Hist. Tripos), MA Cantab 1956. Dir, Hosp. Organisation Res. Unit, Brunel Univ., 1967–70; Vis. Prof., Syracuse Univ., 1968; Harkness Fellow, Commonwealth Fund, 1960–61. Asst Sec., Dept of Educn and Science, 1966–67; Mem.: Davies Cttee on Hosp. Complaints Procedure, 1971; UGC Educn Sub-Cttee, 1970; Management Resources Cttee; Nat. Council for Educnl Technology; Public and Social Admin. Cttee, 1970. Sec. Central Adv. Council for Educn (England), 1963–66; Jt Sec. Secondary Sch. Examinations Council, 1961–63. Publications: (with S. Cang, M. Dixon and H. Tolliday) Working Relationships in the British Hospital Service, 1970; (with J. Terry) The Organisation of a Social Services Department, 1970; The Government of Education, 1970; (with E. Boyle and

A . Crosland) The Politics of Education, 1970; (with Willem van der Eyken) County Hall, 1970; Reviews of National Policies for Education: United States (OECD Rapporteur), 1970; *contrib*. Futures, New Soc., Times Educnl Supp., Times Higher Educn Supp. *Address*: School of Social Sciences, Brunel Univ., Kingston Lane, Uxbridge, Mddx UB8 3TH.

Kokosalakis, Dr Nicholas, BA, PhD; Lecturer in Sociology (Sociology of Religion, Social Theory), University of Liverpool, since 1966; *b* 1937; *m* 1970. BA Athens 1961 (Philosophy, Theology), PhD Liverpool 1969; Mem., Edit. Bd, Human Context. *Publications*: *contrib*. Hum. Cont., Sociol Ybk Relig. Engl. *Address*: Dept of Sociology, Univ. of Liverpool, Liverpool L69 3BX

Kolbert, Dr Colin Francis; University Lecturer, Department of Land Economy, University of Cambridge, since 1967, and Fellow of Magdalene College, Cambridge, since 1968; *b* 1936; *m* 1959; two *d*. BA Cantab 1959, MA Cantab 1963, PhD Cantab 1962, MA, DPhil Oxon 1964; Harold Samuel Res. Studentship, Cantab, 1959; Barrister-at-Law, Lincoln's Inn, 1960. Asst in Res., Cambridge Univ. Dept of Land Economy, 1960–63, Univ. Asst Lectr, 1963–64; Fellow and Tutor in Jurisprudence, St Peter's Coll., Oxford, 1964–67; CUF Lectr, Fac. of Law, Oxford, 1965–67; Tutor, Magdalene Coll., Cambridge, 1969– . Ed., Inc. Tax Dig. and Acntnts Rev., 1965–70; Governor: Wellingborough Sch., 1968– ; Cranleigh Sch., 1969– ; Perse Schs, Cambridge, 1970– ; Bromsgrove Sch., 1973– ; Cllr, Cambridge City Council, 1970– ; Cambridge City Educn Cttee, 1970– . *Publications*: *contrib*. Ann. Surv. Commonwealth Law, Riv. Diritto Agr. *Address*: Magdalene College, Cambridge.

Kolbuszewski, Prof. Janusz, PhD; Professor of Transportation and Environmental Planning, and Head of Department, University of Birmingham, since 1965; *b* 1915; *m* 1946; one *s* one *d*. DipIng Lwow (Poland); PhD(Eng) London 1948, DIC 1948, DSc(Eng) London 1968; Hon. Mem., Midlands Soc. for Soil Mechanics and Foundn Engrg. Prof., Dir of Studies, Polish Univ. Coll., London, 1948–50; Lectr, Sen. Lectr, Reader, in Charge of Grad. Highway and Traffic Engrg, Univ. of Birmingham, 1951–59; Prof. of Highway and Traffic Engrg, 1959–64; Prof. of Transportation, 1964–65, Univ. of Birmingham. Mem., Civil Engrg and Aero Cttee, SRC, 1967; Mem., Res. Cttee, ICE, 1966; Governor, Birmingham Coll. of Arts. Lister Prize, Midland Br. of IStructE, 1953; Nusey Prize, Soc. of Engineers, London, 1967. *Publications*: *contrib*. Geometry, Perspective, Soil Mechanics, Foundns and Highway Engrg, Transportation and Planning. *Address*: Univ. of Birmingham, PO Box 363, Birmingham B15 2TT.

Korah, Mrs Valentine Latham; Reader in English Law, Faculty of Law,s University College, London, since 1966; *b* 1928; *m* 1955; one *s* three *d*. LLB London 1949, LLM

London 1951, PhD London 1966; Barrister-at-Law 1952. Asst Lectr in Laws, Univ. Coll., London, 1951–54, Lectr in Laws, 1954–66; Vis. Prof., Univ. of Khartoum, 1966. Sen. Legal Asst, Dept of Employ. and Product., 1969–70; Sen. Legal Asst, Price Commn, 1973; Mem., Ed. Adv. Bd, and Deptl Ed., Jl Business Law. *Publications*: Monopolies, Mergers and Restrictive Practices, 1968; *contrib*. Antit. Bull., ASCL, Brit. Tax Rev., Curr. Legal Prob., Jl Assoc. Law Teachers, Jl Business Law, Mod. Law Rev., Solicitor Qly, Texas Internat. Law Forum, etc. *Address*: Faculty of Laws, Univ. College London, 4–8 Endsleigh Gardens, WC1H 0EG.

Körner, Prof. Stephan, JurDr, PhD, FBA; Professor of Philosophy, University of Bristol, since 1952, and Yale University, since 1970; *b* 1913; *m* 1944; one *s* one *d*. JurDr Prague 1935, PhD Cambridge 1944; FBA 1967. Mem., Internat. Inst. of Philosophy 1971. Lectr, Bristol Univ., 1946–52; Vis. Prof. of Philosophy: Brown Univ., 1957; Yale Univ., 1960; Texas Univ., 1964; Indiana Univ., 1967; Dawes Hicks Lectr, Brit. Acad., 1967; Eddington Lectr, Cambridge, 1971. Dean, Fac. of Arts, Bristol, 1964–66, Pro-Vice-Chancellor, 1968–71. President: Aristot. Soc., 1967; Brit. Soc. Philos. Science, 1965; Internat. Union Hist. Philos. Science, 1969; Mind Assoc., 1973. Editor, Ratio, 1961– . *Publications*: Kant, 1955; Conceptual Thinking, 1955; Philosophy of Mathematics, 1960; Experience and Theory, 1966; What is Philosophy?, 1969; Categorical Frameworks, 1970; *contrib*. philosophical jls. *Address*: Dept of Philosophy, The Univ., Wills Memorial Building, Bristol BS8 1RJ.

Kotas, Richard, BCom, MPhil, ACIS; Senior Lecturer, Department of Hotel and Catering Management, University of Surrey, since 1957; *b* 1929; *m* 1954; two *s*. BCom London 1952, MPhil Surrey 1969; ACIS 1957. FREconSoc. Mem., Brit. Acntng and Finance Assoc. Nat. Assessor in Acntng, Hotel and Cater. Inst., 1962– . *Publications*: An Approach to Food Costing, 1961; Bookkeeping in the Hotel and Catering Industry, 1964; Accounting in the Hotel and Catering Industry, 1965; Labour Costs in Restaurants, 1971; Management Accounting Problems in Hotels and Catering, 1971; (with B. E. Davis) Food Cost Control, 1973; *contrib*. Jl Hotel Cater. Inst. *Address*: Dept of Hotel and Catering Management, Univ. of Surrey, Guildford, Surrey GU2 5XH.

Koutsoyiannis, Dr Anna, BA(Econ), PhD; Senior Lecturer in Economics and Econometrics, University of Lancaster, since 1968; *b* 1932. BA(Econ) Athens 1954, PhD(Econ) Manchester 1962; Mem., Economet. Soc., Brit. Assoc. Lectr in Econs, Athens, 1962–64; Asst Prof., Univ. of Thessaloniki, 1964–65; Associate Prof., Greece, 1956–68. Hd of Stat. Sect., Nat. Tobacco Bd of Greece, 1954–59; Sen. Project Dir, Center of Planning and Econ. Res., Athens, 1962–68. *Publications*: An Econometric Study of the Leaf Tobacco

Market of Greece, 1963; Production Functions of the Greek Manufacturing Industry, 1965; Input-Output Tables of the Greek Economy, 1967; A Textbook of Microeconomics, vol. I, 1967, vol. II, 1968; Econometric Theory, 1972; *contrib.* Jl Polit. Econ. Sci. (Greece), Manch. Sch. *Address:* Dept of Economics, The Univ. of Lancaster, Lancaster LA1 4YW.

Krailsheimer, Dr Alban John; Tutor in French, since 1957, and Student (Fellow), Christ Church, Oxford University, since 1958; *b* 1921; *m* 1944; two *d.* MA Oxon 1946, PhD Glasgow 1954. Asst Lectr, Manchester, 1947–49; Lectr, Glasgow, 1949–57. *Publications:* Studies in Self-Interest, 1962; Rabelais and The Franciscans, 1963; Three Conteurs of The Sixteenth Century, 1966; trans., Pascal: Pensées, 1966; trans., Pascal: Provincial Letters, 1967; Rabelais, 1967; ed, and co-author, The Continental Renaissance, 1971; A.-J. de Rancé, Abbot of La Trappe, 1974. *Address:* Christ Church, Oxford.

Kratochvil, Dr Paul; University Lecturer in Chinese Studies, Faculty of Oriental Studies, University of Cambridge, since 1962; *b* 1932; *m* 1962; one *s.* BA Prague 1956, MA Cantab 1963, PhD Prague 1963. *Publications:* The Chinese Language Today, 1968; Lu Hsün: Three Stories, 1970; *contrib.* Archiv Orientalni, Language, Lingua, Trans Philological Society. *Address:* Faculty of Oriental Studies, Sidgwick Avenue, Cambridge.

Krausz, Dr Ernest, MSc, PhD; Senior Lecturer, Department of Social Science and Humanities, The City University, since 1970; *b* 1931; *m* 1962; two *s* two *d.* MSc London 1960, PhD London 1965; Mem., Data Comparability Wkng Party, Brit. Sociol Assoc., Brit. Assoc. Adv. Science, Steering Cttee, Stat. and Demog. Unit, Bd of Deputies of Brit. Jews; Acad. Council of Wld Jewish Cong. Sen. Res. Fellow, Nuffield Foundn, LSE, 1961–64; Principal Lectr, NE London Poly., and Mem., Ext. Bd of Examiners, Univ. of London, 1964–67; Lectr, City Univ., 1967–70; Acting Dean, Fac. of Social Sciences, 1973–74; Prof. of Sociology, Bar-Ilan Univ., 1972– . *Publications:* Leeds Jewry: Its History and Social Structure,1964; Sociology in Britain – A Survey of Research, 1969; Sociology in Britain, 1969; Ethnic Minorities in Britain, 1971; chapter, Religion, in, Data Comparability in Social Research, ed E. Gittus, 1972; (with Dr S. H. Miller) Social Research Design, 1974; *contrib.* Brit. Jl Sociol., Jewish Jl Sociol., Race, Soc. Comp. *Address:* Dept of Social Science and Humanities, The City Univ., St John Street, EC1.

Krejcl, Dr Jaroslav; Senior Lecturer in Comparative Cultural Analysis, University of Lancaster, since 1974 (Lecturer, 1970–74); *b* 1916; *m* 1940. DrJur Prague 1945; Habilitation in Economics Prague 1948. State Planning Offr, Prague, 1945–50; State Bank, Prague, 1950–53; Ext. Associate Prof., Grad. Sch. of Politics and Social Studies, 1948–50; Economics Fac. of the Technological Univ.,

Prague, 1950–52; Res. Fellow, Univ. of Lancaster, 1969–70. Political prisoner, 1954–60; CS Acad. of Science, Inst. of Econs, ext. co-worker, 1966–68; Inst. Hum. Environm., 1968. *Publications:* Income Distribution (in Czech), 1947; Economic Planning, Methodical Introduction (in Czech), 1949; Social Change and Stratification in Postwar Czechoslovakia, 1972; *contrib.* Ekonomista, Politická ekon., Rev. of Inc. and Wealth, Sociol časopis, Stat. obzor, Sov. Studies, Systemat. *Address:* Dept of Religious Studies, Univ. of Lancaster.

Kronsjö, Prof. Tom Oskar Martin, Fil.kand, Fil.lic; Professor of Economic Planning, Centre for Russian and East European Studies, and Faculty of Commerce and Social Science, University of Birmingham, since 1969; *b* 1932; *m* 1962. Fil.kand Stockholm 1956, Fil.lic Lund 1961; Mem. Economet. Soc. Vis. Asst Prof., UAR Inst. Nat. Planning, Cairo, 1964; Sen. Lectr, Birmingham, 1964–69; Vis. Prof., Purdue Univ., USA, 1972. *Publications:* *contrib.* Co-exist., Comput. Jl, Econ. Planning, Econ. Mat. Met., Ipargaz., Jbh Wirts. Osteurop., Jbh Nationalökon. Stat., Lond. Papers Reg. Sci., Math. Wirts., Papers Reg. Sci. Assoc., Rev. Franç. Inform. Rech. Operat., Zesz. Nauk. *Address:* Centre for Russian and East European Studies, Univ. of Birmingham, PO Box 363, Birmingham B15 2TT.

Kuhn, Dr Karl Heinz, BA, PhD; Senior Lecturer in Hebrew, School of Oriental Studies, University of Durham, since 1967; *b* 1919; *m* 1949; one *s* one *d.* BA Dunelm 1949 (1st cl. Theology), PhD Dunelm 1952. Res. Fellow, Durham, 1953–55; Lectr in Hebrew, Durham, 1955–67. Mem., Edit. Bd, Corpus Script. Christ. Orient., 1970– . *Publications:* Letters and Sermons of Besa (CSCO Scriptores coptici, vols 21–22), 1956; Pseudo-Shenoute: On Christian Behaviour (vols 29–30), 1960; A Panegyric on John the Baptist attributed to Theodosius Archbishop of Alexandria (vols 33–34), 1966; *contrib.* Jl Theol. Studies, Muséon. *Address:* School of Oriental Studies, Univ. of Durham, Elvet Hill, Durham.

Kumar, Jagdish Krishan; Lecturer in Sociology, Faculty of Social Sciences, University of Kent at Canterbury, since 1967; *b* 1942. BA Cantab 1964, MA Cantab 1967; MScEcon London 1965. Producer, BBC Talks and Documentaries, 1972–73. *Publications:* Revolution: the theory and practice of a European idea, 1971; *contrib.* Govt and Opposition, Sociol. *Address:* Keynes Coll., Univ. of Kent, Canterbury, Kent CT2 7ND.

Kuna, Dr Franz Matthäus, DrPhil, MA; Senior Lecturer in German, University of East Anglia, since 1964; *b* 1933; *m* 1962; three *s.* DrPhil Vienna 1958, MA East Anglia 1967. DAA Schol. Freiburg i Br., 1956–57; Brit. Council Schol., Univ. of Oxford, 1958–59; Lektor in German, Univ. of Birmingham, 1960–61; Lektor in German, Univ. of Cambridge, 1961–64; Vis. Prof., Univ. of Salzburg, 1971; Co-Editor, Jl Europ. Studies, 1971– . *Publications:* (with J. L. M. Trim)

Komm mit! (A German Course of thirty programmes, BBC 1), 1964, 2nd edn 1965; T. S. Eliot: Die Dramen, 1968, 2nd edn 1972; Kafka: Literature as Corrective Punishment, 1974; *contrib*. Engl. Studies, Ess. Crit., Lit. Krit., Publicus Engl. Goethe Soc. *Address*: School of European Studies, Univ. of East Anglia, Norwich NOR 88C.

Kuper, Dr Adam Jonathan; Lecturer in Anthropology, University College London, since 1970; *b* 1941; *m* 1966; two *s*. BA Witwatersrand 1961, PhD Cantab 1966; FRAI, Mem., Assoc. of Social Anthropologists. Lectr, Makerere Univ., Kampala, 1967–70; Vis. Lectr, Univ. of California, Santa Barbara, 1969; on attachment, Nat. Planning Agency, Jamaica, 1972–73. *Publications*: Kalahari Village Politics: an African Democracy, 1970; ed (with A. I. Richards), Councils in Action, 1971; Anthropologists and Anthropology: the British School 1922–72, 1973; *contrib*. African Affairs, African Studies, Man. *Address*: Univ. Coll. London, Gower Street, WC1E 6BT.

Kurz, Prof. Otto, FBA; Professor of the History of the Classical Tradition with special reference to the Near East, The Warburg Institute, University of London, 1965–Sept. 1975; *b* 1908; *m* 1937; one *d*. PhD Vienna 1931; FBA. Slade Professor, Oxford, 1970–71. *Publications*: *contrib*. Burl. Mag., Jl Warb. Court. Inst. *Address*: The Warburg Institute, Woburn Square, WC1H 0AB.

Kusin, Dr Vladimir V., PhD; Senior Editor, ABSEES, Institute of Soviet and East European Studies, University of Glasgow, since 1970; *b* 1929; *m* 1953; one *s* one *d*. PromHist Hons Prague 1953, PhD Prague 1968. Mem., Exec. Cttee, Nat. Assoc. for Soviet and E European Studies. Lectr, Prague Sch. of Econs, 1953–57; Res. Fellow, Comenius Centre, Univ. Lancaster, 1968–69. *Publications*: trans., Bocca: The Life and Death of Harry Oakes, 1965; trans., Bocca: Bikini Beach, 1967; trans., Stoppard: Rosencrantz and Guildenstern are Dead, 1968; The Intellectual Origins of the Prague Spring, 1971; Political Grouping in the Czechoslovak Reform Movement, 1972; ed, The Czechoslovak Reform Movement, 1968 (Proc. Reading Seminar 1971), 1973; *contrib*. Bidrag till Oststatsforskningen, Soviet Studies. *Address*: Univ. of Glasgow, Glasgow G12 8QQ.

Kuska, Dr Edward Arthur, PhD; Lecturer, Economics Department, London School of Economics, since 1961; *b* 1937. AB Idaho State 1959, PhD London 1970. Asst Lectr, LSE, 1961. *Publications*: *contrib*. Economica, Maxima, Minima, and Comparative Statics. *Address*: London School of Economics, Aldwych, WC2A 2AE.

Kyle, Peter William, BA(Econ); Lecturer in Quantitative Methods applied to Marketing, Department of Marketing, Lancaster University, since 1966; *b* 1943; *m* 1964; one *s*. BA(Econ) Manchester 1964; FRSS. Mem., Mkt Res. Soc. Vis. Lectr, Wharton Sch. of Finance and Comm., Univ. of Pennsylvania,

1969–70. *Publications*: *contrib*. Europ. Jl Mktng. *Address*: Dept of Marketing, Univ. of Lancaster, Bailrigg, Lancaster LA1 4YW.

Kynch, Prof. George James, DIC, PhD, FIMA; Professor of Mathematics, University of Manchester Institute of Science and Technology, since 1957; *b* 1915; *m* 1943; one *s* two *d*. BSc London 1935 (Physics), BSc London 1936 (Mathematics), PhD London 1939, DIC London 1939; ARCS, FIMA, FIP, MTIMS. Lectr, Birmingham Univ., 1941–50, Sen. Lectr, 1950–52; Prof. of Applied Maths, Univ. Coll. of Wales, 1952–57; Dean, Faculty of Technology (UMIST), Univ. of Manchester, 1973– . Mem., Council, Inst. Maths and Applications, 1963–66; Council Mem., Manchester Lit. Philos. Soc., 1963– (Pres., 1971–73). *Publications*: Mathematics for Chemists, 1955; *contrib*. Proc. Far. Soc., Proc. Phys. Soc., Phys. Rev., Proc. Royal Soc., A, Jl Operat. Res. *Address*: Mathematics Dept, Univ. of Manchester Institute of Science and Technology, Sackville Street, Manchester M60 1QD.

L

Lacey, Colin, BSc, PhD; Reader in Sociology of Education, University of Sussex, since 1973; *b* 1936; *m* 1960; two *s* two *d*. BSc Birmingham 1957 (2nd cl. Geology), PhD Manchester 1968. Asst Lectr, Univ. of Manchester, 1963–65; Lectr, 1965–68; Dir, Tutorial Schools Res. Project, Univ. of Sussex, 1969–73; Vis. Asst Prof., Johns Hopkins Univ., 1968–69 (jt appt). *Publications*: Hightown Grammar: The School as a Social System, 1970. 2nd pbk edn, 1971; *contrib*. Brit. Jl Sociol. *Address*: Education Development Building, Univ. of Sussex, Falmer, Brighton BN1 9RG.

Ladd, Charles Anthony; Reader in English Language, Department of English, Royal Holloway College, University of London, since 1967; *b* 1923; *m* 1961; two step-*s* one *d*. MA Oxon 1948. Lectr in English Lang., Christ Church, Oxford, 1949–52; Lecturer in English: Univ. of St Andrews, 1952–62; Royal Holloway Coll., Univ. of London, 1962–67. Warden of Deans Ct, Univ. of St Andrews, 1959–62; Mem., Royal Holloway Coll. Council, 1967–70. *Publications*: *contrib*. Bosworth-Toller, enlarged Addenda and Conigenda; *contrib*. Archivum Linguisticum, Notes and Queries, Rev. of English Studies, Proc. of IXth and Xth Internat. Congress of Linguists. *Address*: Dept of English, Royal Holloway Coll., Egham, Surrey TW20 0EX.

Lafitte, Prof. François; Professor of Social Policy and Administration, University of Birmingham, since 1959; *b* 1913; *m* 1938. Dean, Fac. of Comm. and Soc. Sci., Birmingham Univ., 1965–68. Res., Miners' Internat. Fedn, 1936–37; res. staff and subseq. Dep. Sec., PEP, 1938–43; Mem., editorial staff of The Times, 1943–59; Chm., PEP res. gps, 1943–46, and 1948–51. Mem., Home Office Adv. Council on the Treatment of

393

Offenders, 1961–64; Mem., Adv. Cttees SSRC, 1966–69; Mem., Redditch New Town Corp., 1964– ; Chm., British Pregnancy Adv. Service, 1968– . *Publications*: The Internment of Aliens, 1940; Britain's Way to Social Security, 1945; Family Planning in the Sixties, 1964; (jtly) Socially Deprived Families in Britain, 1970; PEP Planning monographs; *contrib*. Brit. Jl of Delinquency, Eugenics Rev., Chambers's Encyc., New Society, etc. *Address*: The Univ., Birmingham B15 2TT.

Laidler, Prof. David E. W., BSc, MA, PhD; Professor of Economics, University of Manchester, since 1969; *b* 1938; *m* 1965; one *d*. BSc(Econ) London 1959, MA(Econ) Syracuse 1960, PhD Chicago 1964. Temp. Asst Lectr, LSE, 1961–62; Asst Prof., Univ. of California, Berkeley, 1963–66; Actg Asst Prof., Stanford Univ., 1964; Lectr in Econs, Essex Univ., 1966–69. Mem., Econ. Bd, CNAA; Mem., Econ. Cttee, SSRC; Sec., Soc. Econ. Analysis Ltd (formerly Econ. Study Soc.). *Publications*: The Demand for Money – Theories and Evidence, 1969; Income Tax Incentives for Owner-Occupied Housing, in. The Taxation of Income from Capital, ed M. J. Bailey, 1969; The Influence of Money on Economic Activity: A Survey of Some Current Problems, in, Monetary Theory and Monetary Policy in the 1970s. ed Clayton, etc, 1971; The Phillips Curve Expectations and Incomes Policy, in, The Current Inflation, ed H. G. Johnson and A. R. Nobay, 1971; *contrib*. Banker, Bank. Mag., Canad. Jl Econ., Economica, Jl Mon. Crd. Bank., Jl Pol. Econ., Manch. Sch., Nat. Westminster Bank Rev., Oxf. Econ Papers, Swedish Jl Economics. *Address*: Faculty of Economic and Social Studies, Univ. of Manchester, Dover Street, Manchester M13 9PL.

Laing, Alexander; Senior Lecturer in Education, Department of Education, University of Leeds, since 1960; *b* 1914; *m* 1953; one *s*. MA Aberdeen 1936 (Hons English), MEd Aberdeen 1938 (1st cl.). Mem., Brit. Psychol. Soc., Mem., Soc. Res. Higher Educn. Asst. Lectr in Education, Aberdeen, 1946–48; Lectr in Educn, Aberdeen Coll. of Educn, 1948–49; Lectr in Education, Leeds, 1949–60. Advr to Overseas Students, Leeds (pt-time), 1956–72. Sec., Conf. of Univ. Advs to Overseas Students, 1960–70; Mem., Council, City of Leeds, YMCA, 1956– . *Publications*: The Art of Study, 1964, 2nd edn 1974: International Campus: an adviser to overseas students looks at his job, 1970; The Art of Lecturing, in, University Teaching in Transition, ed Layton, 1968. *Address*: Dept of Education, Univ. of Leeds, Leeds LS2 9JT.

Laing, Dr Alice F., MA, MEd; Senior Lecturer in Education, University College of Swansea, since 1973 (Lecturer, 1963–73); *b* 1928. MA St Andrews 1949 (2nd cl. History), MEd Aberdeen 1954, PhD Wales 1972; Mem., Brit. Psychol Soc. Mem., Bd of Govs, Swansea Coll. of Educn, 1970– . *Publications*: (with I. Hussell) A Biological and Psychological Background to Education, 1967; (with M. Chazan and S. Jackson) Just Before School, 1971; *contrib*. Amer. J. Ment. Def. *Address*: Dept of Education, Univ. College of Swansea, Swansea SA2 8PP.

Laird, Philip Nicholas J.; *see* Johnson-Laird.

Laithwaite, John Michael William; Senior Research Fellow, Department of English Local History, University of Leicester, since 1966; *b* 1933. BA Oxon 1958 (2nd cl. Mod. Hist.), MA Oxon 1963. Archit. historian, LCC Survey of London, 1958–66. *Publications*: An Urban House-type of the 16th and 17th Centuries (forthcoming); contrib. vols 29–34, Survey of London, 1960–66; The Buildings of Banbury pre-1700, in, VCH Oxfordshire, vol. 10, 1972; The Buildings of Burford: a Cotswold Town in the 14th to 19th Centuries, in, Perspectives in English Urban History, ed A. M. Everitt, 1973; *contrib*. Post-Mediev. Archaeol., Proc. Devon Archaeol Soc., Trans Devon Assoc., Medieval Archaeology. *Address*: Dept of English Local History, Univ. of Leicester, Leicester LE1 7RH.

Lall, Sanjaya; Research Officer, Institute of Economics and Statistics, Oxford University, since 1968; *b* 1940; *m* 1966. BA Patna Univ., India, 1960 (1st cl. Hons Economics), BA Oxford 1963 (1st cl. Hons PPE), BPhil Oxford 1965 (Economics); Mem., Royal Economic Soc. Economist, World Bank, Washington, DC, 1965–68. *Publications*: various studies for UNCTAD on effects of private foreign investment in developing countries, 1970–73; (with P. P. Streeten) Foreign Investment and Developing Countries: lessons from six country studies, 1975; bibliog. on private foreign investment and multi-nat. corps (forthcoming); *contrib*. Oxford Bull. Econs and Stats, World Develt. *Address*: Institute of Economics and Statistics, Manor Road, Oxford OX1 3UL.

Lalljee, Dr Mansur; Staff Tutor in Psychology, Department for External Studies, Oxford University, since 1968; *b* 1942; *m* 1967; two *d*. BA Hons Bombay 1963, BA Hons Oxon 1965, DPhil Oxon 1971. *Publications*: *contrib*. Brit. Jl Soc. Clinical Psychol., Language and Speech, Jl Pers. Soc. Psychol., Personnel Psychol., Semiotica. *Address*: Dept for External Studies, Wellington Square, Oxford OX1 2JA.

Lambert, Dr Audrey Munro; Lecturer in Geography, London School of Economics, since 1952. BA London 1949, PhD 1952. Univ. of Durham, 1951–52. *Publications*: The Making of the Dutch Landscape, 1971; *contrib*. Agricl Geog., Econ. Geog., Geog. *Address*: London School of Economics, Houghton Street, Aldwych, WC2 2AE.

Lambert, Dr Francis John Dalton; Lecturer in History, Latin American Institute, University of Glasgow, since 1968; *b* 1942. BA Oxon 1963 (Mod. History), MA Oxon, DPhil Oxon 1969. Mem., Soc. for Latin American Studies. Jun. Res. Fellow, Latin American Inst., Univ. London, 1966–68.

Publications: Making the Modern World: Latin America, 1973; *contrib.* Jl Latin Amer. Studies. *Address*: Latin American Institute, 5 University Gardens, Glasgow G12 8QQ.

Lambert, Malcolm David, MA; Lecturer in History, University of Bristol, since 1962; *b* 1931; *m* 1958. BA Oxon 1953 (1st cl. Hist.), MA Oxon 1957; FRHistS. Asst Lectr in History, ReadingUniv., 1959–62. *Publications*: Franciscan Poverty, 1961. *Address*: Dept of History, Univ. of Bristol, Bristol BS8 1TH.

Lambton, Prof. Ann Katharine Swynford, OBE, FBA, BA, PhD, DLit; Professor of Persian, University of London, since 1953; *b* 1912. PhD London 1939, DLit London 1953, Hon. DLitt Durham 1971, Hon. DLitt Cambridge 1973; FBA 1964. Sen. Lectr in Persian, SOAS, 1945–48; Reader in Persian, Univ. of London, 1948–53. Press Attaché, British Embassy (formerly Legn), Tehran, 1939–45. *Publications*: Three Persian Dialects, 1938; Landlord and Peasant in Persia, 1953; Persian Grammar, 1953; Persian Vocabulary, 1964; The Persian Land Reform, 1962–66, 1969; ed (with others), The Cambridge History of Islam, vols I–II, 1971. *Address*: School of Oriental and African Studies, Univ. of London, Malet Street, WC1E 7HP.

Lamont, William Montgomerie; Reader in History and Education, University of Sussex, since 1969; *b* 1934; *m* 1961; three *d*. BA London 1955, CertEd London 1956 (Distinction), PhD London 1960; FRHistS. Res. Fellow, Inst. of Historical Res., 1958–59; Lectr in History and Educn, Univ. of Sussex, 1966–69. Dir, Sussex University Post-Grad. Cert. of Educn, (1974–77). *Publications*: Marginal Prynne, 1963; Godly Rule 1603–1660, 1969; ed, The Realities of Teaching History: Beginnings, 1972; (with Sybil Oldfield) Religion, Politics and Literature in the Seventeenth Century, (forthcoming); essays in: New Movements in the Study and Teaching of History, ed M. Ballard, 1970; The Intellectual Revolution of the Seventeenth Century, ed C.Webster, (forthcoming); Educational Research in Britain, ed J. Butcher, (forthcoming); Prophecy and Millenarianism, ed A. Williams (forthcoming); *contrib.* Bull. Inst. Hist. Res., Hist. Today, Hunt. Lib. Qly, Jl Brit. Stud., Jl Eccles. Hist., Past and Pres., Teaching Hist. *Address*: Arts Building, Univ. of Sussex, Falmer, Brighton, Sussex BN1 9QN.

Lampe, Rev. Prof. Geoffrey William Hugo, MC, DD, FBA; Regius Professor of Divinity, Cambridge University, since 1971; Fellow of Gonville and Caius College, since 1960; *b* 1912; *m* 1938; one *s* one *d*. MA Oxon 1940, DD Oxon 1953; Hon. DD Edinburgh 1959; Teol. Dr (hc) Lund 1965; Ordained, 1937; FBA 1963. Fellow and Chaplain, St John's Coll., Oxford, 1943–53; Prof. of Theology, Birmingham Univ., 1953–59, Dean, Faculty of Arts, 1955–59, Vice-Principal, 1957–60; Ely Prof. of Divinity, Cambridge Univ., 1959–71. Curate of Okehampton, 1937–38; Asst Master, King's Sch., Canterbury, 1938–41; Chaplain to the Forces, 1941–45; Hon. Canon: Birmingham Cathedral, 1957–59; Ely Cathedral 1971–

(Canon, 1960–71). *Publications*: Aspects of the New Testament Ministry, 1948; The Seal of the Spirit, 1951; Reconciliation in Christ, 1956; I Believe, 1960; ed, Justification by Faith, 1954; ed, A Patristic Greek Lexicon, vol. 1, 1961, vol. 5, 1969; ed, The West from the Fathers to the Reformation (Cambridge History of the Bible), 1969; *contrib.* essays in symposia and articles in theological journals. *Address*: Gonville and Caius College, Cambridge.

Lampert, Prof. Eugene, LèsL, DPhil, FRSL; Professor and Head of Department of Russian Studies, University of Keele, since 1968; *b* 1915; *m* 1943; two *s*. LèsL Strasbourg, DPhil Oxon; FRSL. Tutor, Oxford Univ., 1949–64; Sen. Lectr, Keele Univ., 1965–68. *Publications*: N. Berdyaev and the New Middle Ages, 1948; The Apocalypse of History, 1950; Studies in Rebellion, 1958; Sons against Fathers, 1966, rev. edn 1971; contrib. Nineteenth Century Russian Literature, 1973; Encyclopaedia Britannica; *contrib.* Amer. Slav. Rev., Slav. Rev., Times Lit. Supp. *Address*: Dept of Russian Studies, Univ. of Keele, Keele ST5 5BG.

Lamport, Francis John, MA; Lecturer in German, University of Oxford, since 1961, and Fellow of Worcester College, since 1966; *b* 1935; *m* 1961; two *d*. BA Oxon 1960 (1st cl. Mod. Langs), MA Oxon 1963. *Publications*: Five German Tragedies, 1969; A Student's Guide to Goethe, 1971; *contrib.* Germ. Life Lett., Oxf. Germ. Studies. *Address*: Worcester College, Oxford.

Lancaster, Prof. Anthony, BA, PhD; Professor of Econometrics, Department of Economics and Commerce, University of Hull, since 1973; *b* 1938; *m* 1967; one *s* one *d*. BA Liverpool 1959 (1st cl. Econ.), PhD Cantab 1965; Mem., Economet. Soc., Amer. Stat. Assoc., Royal Stat. Soc. Lectr, Dept of Econometrics and Social Statistics, Birmingham Univ., 1964–69, Sen Lectr, 1969–73. *Publications*: *contrib.* Jl Royal Stat. Soc. (A), Jl Amer. Stat. Assoc., Rev. Econ. Studies. *Address*: Dept of Economics and Commerce, Univ. of Hull, Hull HU6 7RX.

Land, Prof. Frank William; Professor of Education, University of Hull, since 1961; *b* 1911; *m* 1937; two *s* one *d*. Lectr in Mathematics. Birkbeck Coll., London, 1939–40; Sen. Lectr, Univ. of Liverpool, 1950–61. Asst Master, The Grammar Sch., Hampton-on-Thames, 1933–37; Lectr in Mathematics, Coll. of St Mark and St John, Chelsea, 1937–39, Vice-Principal, 1946–49; Chm., Assoc. of Teachers in Colleges and Depts of Educn, 1956–57. *Publications*: Recruits to Teaching, 1960; The Language of Mathematics, 1961. *Address*: Univ. of Hull, Hull HU6 7RX.

Landels, Dr John G.; Lecturer, Department of Classics, University of Reading, since 1960; *b* 1926; *m* 1953. MA Aberdeen 1951 (1st cl. Classics), BA Cantab 1952 (Classics Tripos Pt I), 1953 (Pt II 1st cl.), MA Cantab 1956, PhD Hull 1961. Asst Lectr, Hull, 1953–56, Lectr, 1956–60. Jt Hon. Sec., Class. Assoc., 1969–72. *Publications*: *contrib.* Ann. Brit. Sch. Athens, Class Qly., Class.

395

Rev., Greece Rome, Jl Hellenic Studies. *Address*: Dept of Classics, Faculty of Letters, The Univ., Reading RG6 2AA.

Landon, Howard Chandler Robbins; Honorary Professorial Fellow, Department of Music, University College, Cardiff, since 1971; *b* 1926. BMus Boston 1947; Hon. DMus Boston 1969, Hon. DMus QUB 1974. Vis. Prof., Queens Coll., New York, 1969; Regents Prof., Univ. of California, Davis, 1970. *Publications*: The Symphonies of Joseph Haydn, 1955; The Mozart Companion (co-ed with Donald Mitchell), 1956; The Collected Correspondence and London Note-books of Joseph Haydn, 1959; Essays on Eighteenth-Century Music, 1969; Ludwig van Beethoven: a documentary study, 1970; critical edn of the 107 Haydn Symphonies, (completed) 1968; Haydn, vol. I, 1972; scholarly edns of eighteenth-century music; *contrib.* Music Rev., Music and Letters, Musical Times, Osterreichische Musikzeitung, etc. *Address*: Music Dept, Univ. College, Cardiff CF1 1XL.

Lane, Bernard; Staff Tutor in Geography, Extra Mural Department, University of Bristol, since 1971; *b* 1944; *m* 1973. BA Liverpool 1965 (Hons Geog.); Mem.: Inst. of British Geographers; Geographical Assoc. Tutor, Geography Dept, Univ. of Liverpool, 1967–68; Lectr, Geography Dept, University Coll., Dublin, 1968–71. *Address*: Extra Mural Dept, The Univ., Bristol BS8 1HR.

Lane, Dr David Stuart; Lecturer in Social and Political Sciences, and Fellow of Emmanuel College, Cambridge University, since 1973; *b* 1933; *m* 1962; one *s* one *d*. BSocSci Birmingham 1960 (EPS), DPhil Oxford 1966. Student, Nuffield Coll., Oxford, 1961–62; Lectr, Birmingham Univ., 1962–67, Essex Univ., 1967–71; Reader in Sociology, Essex, 1971–73. *Publications*: Roots of Russian Communism, 1969; Politics and Society in USSR, 1970; The End of Inequality?: social stratification under state socialism, 1971; (with G. Kolankiewicz) Social Groups in Polish Society, 1972; *contrib.* Sociol., Brit. Jl of Sociol., Eur. Jl of Sociol., Sov. Studies. *Address*: Emmanuel College, Cambridge.

Lane, Ronald Charles, MA, PhD; Lecturer in Russian, University of Durham, since 1964; *b* 1938; *m* 1962; two *s*. BA Cantab 1962 (2nd cl. German and Russian), MA Cantab 1964, PhD Cantab 1970. *Publications*: *contrib.* Europ. Studies. Rev., SEER, Grani, Literaturnoye Nasledstro. *Address*: Dept of Russian, Univ. of Durham, Durham DH1 3HP.

Lang, Prof. David Marshall, DLit, LittD; Professor of Caucasian Studies, School of Oriental and African Studies, University of London, since 1964, and Warden of Connaught Hall, since 1955; *b* 1924; *m* 1956; two *s* two *d*. BA Cantab 1945 (Mod. and Med. Languages), MA Cantab 1948, PhD Cantab 1949, LittD Cantab 1963; DLit London 1958; Hon. Dr Philological Sciences Tbilisi 1966; FRAS, formerly Council Mem., Royal Numism. Soc., Philol. Soc. Res.

Fellow, St John's Coll., Cambridge, 1946–52; Lectr in Georgian, SOAS, London, 1949–58; Reader in Caucasian Studies, 1958–64; Sen. Fellow, Russian Inst., Columbia Univ., 1952–53; Vis. Prof. of Caucasian Languages, UCLA, 1964–65. Former Vice-Consul, Tabriz, Iran, 1944–46; Third Sec., HM Embassy, Tehran, 1946. *Publications*: Studies in the Numismatic History of Georgia in Transcaucasia, 1955; Lives and Legends of the Georgian Saints, 1956; The Wisdom of Balahvar, 1957; The Last Years of the Georgian Monarchy, 1957; The First Russian Radical, 1959; A Modern History of Georgia, 1962; Catalogue of the Georgian Books in the British Museum, 1962; The Georgians, 1966; The Balavariani, 1966; Armenia, Cradle of Civilization, 1970 (Prix Brémond 1972); Gen. Editor, Guide to Eastern Literatures, 1971; (with C. Burney) The Peoples of the Hills, 1971; Associate Editor, Penguin Companion to Literature; contrib. Encyclopaedia Britannica; *contrib.* Bull. SOAS, Jl Royal Asiat. Soc., Numism. Chron., Times Lit. Supp. *Address*: School of Oriental and African Studies, Univ. of London, Malet Street, WC1E 7HP.

Lang, John George, MA; Special Lecturer in Education, University of Bristol, since 1973; *b* 1908; *m* 1944; two *s* four *d*. MA St Andrews 1929, DipEd St Andrews 1930, MA McGill 1931; Mem., Brit. Psychol. Soc., Brit. Sociol. Assoc., Comparative Educn Soc. Europe. Lectr in Educn, Univ. Coll., Swansea, 1939–47; Sec., Inst. Educn, Univ. of Bristol, 1947–67; Special Lectr, Univ. of Bristol, 1947–67, Sen. Lectr, 1967–73; Vis. Lectr, Univ. of British Columbia, 1964–65; Univ. of Wisconsin, 1969. Principal Offr, Bd of Trade, 1940–44; Vice-Chm., Bristol Marriage and Family Guidance Council, 1965–68. *Publications*: *contrib.* Brit. Jl Educnl Psychol., Brit. Jl Sociol. *Address*: School of Education, Univ. of Bristol, Bristol BS8 1TH.

Lang, Mervyn Francis, MA, MSc, PhD; Lecturer, Department of Modern Languages, University of Salford, since 1964; *b* 1937; *m* 1965; one *s* one *d*. MA Glasgow 1960, Teaching Dip. Jordanhill 1961, MSc Salford 1968, PhD Salford 1971, Dip. de Langue et Littérature Françaises Lyon 1958. Mem., Soc. Latin Amer. Studies, Assoc. Hispan. *Publications*: *contrib.* Hispan. Amer. Hist. Rev., Hist. Mex., Rev. Hist. Amer. *Address*: Dept of Modern Languages, Univ. of Salford, Salford M5 4WT.

Langdon, Michael David, DA, RIBA; Lecturer, Department of Architecture, University of Edinburgh, since 1966; *b* 1936; *m* 1958; one *s* one *d*. DipArch Edinburgh College of Art 1958; RIBA, ARIAS, AIArb. *Address*: Dept of Architecture, Univ. of Edinburgh, 18 George Square, Edinburgh.

Langford, Michael John; Senior Tutor, School of Photography, Royal College of Art, since 1967; *b* 1933; *m* 1954; two *d*. FRPS 1957, FIIP 1957. *Publications*: Basic Photography, 1965, 3rd edn 1973, Spanish edn 1968, Italian edn 1969; Advanced Photography, 1969, 3rd edn 1974, Italian edn 1971,

Spanish edn 1972; Visual Aids and Photography in Education, 1973; Professional Photography, 1974; (jtly), Photography Materials and Methods, 1971, 2nd edn 1974; *contrib*. Jl Royal Soc. Arts, Brit. Jl Photography, Photographic Jl. *Address*: Royal College of Art, Kensington Gore, SW7 2EU.

Langhorne, Richard Tristan Bailey; Fellow of St John's College, Cambridge, Junior Bursar, Steward and College Lecturer in History, since 1975; *b* 1940; *m* 1971; one *s*. BA Cantab 1962 (Hist. Tripos), MA Cantab 1965, Cert. in Hist. Studies Cantab 1963. Tutor, Exeter Univ., 1963–64; Lectr in History, Fac. of Humanities, Univ. of Kent, 1966–74; Master, Rutherford Coll., 1971–74. Mem., Central Council, UCCA, 1971–74. *Publications*: Historiography 1900–1918, in, The Twentieth Century Mind, ed C. B. Cox and A. E. Dyson, 1972; *contrib*. Hist. Jl. *Address*: St John's College, Cambridge.

Langley, Dr Frederick William; Lecturer, Department of French, University of Hull, since 1964; *b* 1938; *m* 1961; two *s*. BA Dunelm 1960 (Hons), DPhil Oxon 1967. Asst Lectr, Hull Univ., 1962–64. *Publications*: *contrib*. Med. Æv., Bodleian Libr. Rec. *Address*: Dept of French, Univ. of Hull, Hull HU6 7RX.

Langton, John, MA, PhD; Assistant Lecturer in Geography, University of Cambridge, since 1968, and Fellow of St John's College, Cambridge, since 1970; *b* 1942; *m* 1966; one *s* one *d*. BA Wales 1963 (1st cl. Geog.), MA Cantab 1969, PhD Wales 1970. Asst Lectr, Manchester, 1966–68. *Publications*: (with A. R. H. Baker and J. D. Hamshire) Geographical Interpretations of Historical Sources, 1970; *contrib*. Econ. Hist. Rev., Prog. Geog., Trans Lancs and Cheshire Antiquarian Soc., Area, Urban History Newsletter. *Address*: St John's College, Cambridge.

Lanham, David John, LLB, BCL, Barrister; Senior Lecturer in Law, University of Nottingham, since 1973 (Lecturer, 1965–73); *b* 1938; *m* 1962; two *s*. LLB Leeds 1962 (1st cl.), BCL Oxon 1964 (1st cl.), Barrister Lincoln's Inn 1968. Asst Lectr, Nottingham Univ., 1964–65; Vis. Lectr, Auckland Univ., 1971. Editor, Crim. Law Rev., 1973. *Publications*: Study Guide to Criminal Law, 1967; (with F. E. Camps and J. M. Cameron) Practical Forensic Medicine, 1971; *contrib*. Crim. Law Rev., Med. Science Law, Mod. Law Rev., NZ Law Jl, NZ Univ. Law Rev., Solic. Jl. *Address*: Dept of Law, Univ. of Nottingham, Nottingham NG7 2RD.

Lansberry, Dr Charles Frederick; Staff Tutor, Department for External Studies, Oxford University, since 1967; *b* 1924. MA Oxon 1959, PhD London 1964. Asst Lectr, Bedford Coll., Univ. of London, 1964–67. *Address*: Dept for External Studies, Rewley House, Wellington Square, Oxford OX1 2JA.

Lapenna, Prof. Ivo; Professor of Soviet and East European Law, University of London, since 1973; *b* 1909; *m* 1949. Dr jur

Zagreb 1933; Associate Mem., Yugoslav Acad. Sci. 1949. Docent (Asst Prof.), then Prof. of Internat. Law and Internat. Relations, Fac. of Laws, Univ. of Zagreb, 1945–49; Res. Fellow, CNRS, Paris, 1950–53; Res. Fellow, LSE, 1956–64, Lectr, 1965–66, Reader, 1966–73. Editor, Narodne Novine (Official Gazette), Zagreb, 1945–48; Mem., Editorial Bd, Arhiv, Belgrade, 1946–49; Expert-advr on Internat. Law, Peace Conf., Paris, 1946; Counsel-advocate, Internat. Ct of Justice, The Hague, 1947–48. Hon. Dr of Internat. Relations, Fort Lauderdale, USA, 1972. *Publications*: The United Nations, 1946; History of Diplomacy, Pt 1 1948, Pt 2 1949; Current Problems of International Life, 1952; Conceptions Soviétiques de Droit International Public, 1954; State and Law: Soviet and Yugoslav Theory, 1963; Soviet Penal Policy, 1968; *contrib*. Arhiv Pravne, Društ. Nauke, Internat. Comp. Law Qly, Osteuropa Recht, Politico, Ybk Wld Aff., Zborn. PF (Zagreb). *Address*: London School of Economics and Political Science, Univ. of London, WC2 2AE.

Large, David, MA, BLitt; Senior Lecturer in History, University of Bristol, since 1966; *b* 1924; *m* 1951; two *s* two *d*. BA Oxon 1948 (1st cl. Hist.), MA Oxon 1950, MA Dublin 1950, BLitt Dublin 1952. Lectr, TCD, 1949–58; Lect, Bristol Univ., 1958–66. Councillor, Bristol DC, 1974– . Sec., Bristol Record Soc., 1970; Council Mem., Brist. Glos Archaeol Soc.; Gov., Bristol Grammar Sch., Henbury Sch. *Publications*: *contrib*. Durham Univ. Jl, EHR, Irish Hist. Studies. *Address*: Dept. of History, Univ. of Bristol, Bristol BS8 1TH.

Large, David Charles, MA; Warden of St Patrick's Hall, and Lecturer in Geography, University of Reading, since 1961; *b* 1921. BA Nottingham 1950, MA Syracuse 1952; Mem., Inst. Brit. Geogrs, Assoc. Amer. Geogrs. Asst Lectr, then Lectr, Univ. of Southampton, 1952–61; Actg Warden, South Stoneham Hse, 1956–57; Vis Prof., Miami Univ., Oxford, Ohio, 1958–59. Fleet Air Arm, 1941–46; Lt (A), RNVR. *Publications*: (with W. R. Mead) How People Live in the United States of America, 1961; *contrib*. Geog. Mag., Geog. Rev., Geog. *Address*: St Patrick's Hall, Reading RG2 7HB.

Large, Prof. John Barry, BSc, MS; Professor of Applied Acoustics, Institute of Sound and Vibration Research, University of Southampton, since 1969, teaching on the sociological aspects of noise and noise control; *b* 1930; *m* 1958; two *s*. BSc(Hons) London 1953 (Aero. Eng.), MSc Purdue 1954 (Aero. Eng.). Unit Chief, Aircraft Noise Unit, Comm. Airplane Div., The Boeing Company, Seattle, Washington, 1963–69; Adjunct Prof. of Mech. Engrg, Univ. of Utah; adviser on noise matters to British Airports Authority; Consultant, Health Protection Directorate, EEC; Consultant, US Dept of Transportation; Mem., Inst. of Acoustics; Mem., Acoustical Soc. of America; Associated mem., Internat. Inst. of Social Economics; Mem., Soc. of Automotive Engineers; Mem., BSI. *Publications*: Sonic Boom: a review of current knowledge and developments, 1967;

Quieter Living: facts on noise pollution and noise reduction, 1970; contrib. Proc. of SAE/DOT Conf. on Aircraft and the Environment, 1971; Proc. 4th World Airports Conf., 1973; *contrib.* Britannica Book of the Year, Jl Inst. Physics, Physics Bull. *Address*: Institute of Sound and Vibration Research, Univ. of Southampton, Southampton SO9 5NH.

Larkin, Dr Maurice John Milner; Senior Lecturer in History, University of Kent, since 1968; *b* 1932; *m* 1958; one *s* one *d*. BA Cantab 1954 (Hist.), MA Cantab 1958, PhD Cantab 1958. Asst Lectr, Glasgow Univ., 1958–61, Lectr, 1961–65; Lectr, Univ. of Kent, 1965–68. *Publications*: Gathering Pace: Continental Europe 1870–1945, 1969; Church and State after the Dreyfus Affair: the separation issue in France, 1974; *contrib.* EHR, Hist. Jl, Jl Mod. Hist. *Address*: Rutherford College, Univ. of Kent, Canterbury, Kent.

Larkin, Steven John, MA; Lecturer, Department of French Studies, University of Newcastle upon Tyne, since 1968; *b* 1942; *m* 1965. BA 1964, MA 1968, Cantab; Member: Soc. for French Studies; Brit. Soc. for Eighteenth-Century Studies; Huguenot Soc. of London. *Address*: Dept of French Studies, Claremont Bridge, Claremont Road, Newcastle upon Tyne NE1 7RU.

Larner, John Patrick; Reader, Department of History, University of Glasgow, since 1973; *b* 1930; *m* 1960; two *s*. BA Oxon 1954 (1st cl. History), MA Oxon 1956; FRHistS 1971. Rome Mediev. Schol., Brit. Sch. Rome, 1954–57; Lectr in History, Glasgow Univ., 1957–67, Sen. Lectr, 1967–73. *Publications*: The Lords of Romagna: Romagnol society and the origins of the signorie, 1965; Culture and Society in Italy, 1290–1420, 1971. *Address*: Dept of History, The Univ., Glasgow G12 8QQ.

Lasko, Prof. Peter Erik, FSA; Director and Professor of the History of Art, Courtauld Institute, University of London, since 1974; *b* 1924; *m* 1948; three *d*. BA Hons London 1949 (Courtauld Inst.); FSA. Asst Keeper, British Museum, Dept of British and Medieval Antiquities, 1950–65; Prof. of Visual Arts, Univ. of East Anglia, 1965–73; Dean, Sch. of Fine Arts and Music, 1965–68. *Publications*: The Kingdom of the Franks, 1971; Ars Sacra, 800–1200, 1972; *contrib.* Apollo, Connoisseur, British Museum Qly. *Address*: Courtauld Inst., 20 Portman Square, W1H 0BE.

Laslett, Peter; Reader in Politics and History of Social Structure, University of Cambridge, since 1966; *b* 1915; *m* 1947; two s. MA Cantab 1946; Fellow, Trinity Coll., Cambridge, 1954– . RN, 1939–46; Chm., Viewers and Listeners Assoc. GB, 1962– ; Founder, Camb. Gp Hist. Population and Soc. Struct., 1964. *Publications*: The World We Have Lost, 1965; var. bks on J. Locke, etc. *Address*: Trinity College, Cambridge.

Lasok, Prof. Dominik, LenD, LLM, PhD, Dr jur, Barrister at Law; Professor of

European Law, Director of Centre for European Legal Studies, University of Exeter since 1968; *b* 1921; *m* 1952; two *s* three *d* LenD Fribourg 1944, LLM Durham 1948, PhD London 1954 (Laws), Dr jur Polish Univ. Abroad 1968; Barrister at Law, Middle Temple, 1954. Lectr in Internat. and Comparative Law, Exeter, 1958–64, Reader, 1964–68, Dean, 1969–72. Vis. Prof., Marshall Wythe Sch. of Law, William and Mary Univ. Williamsburg, Va, 1966–67. *Publications*: Polish Family Law, 1968; (with J. W. Bridge) Introduction to the Law and Institutions of the European Communities, 1973; Polish Civil Law, 1973; ed (and jt author), Fundamental Rights, 1973; *contrib.* Amer. Slav. E Europ. Rev., Amer. Jl Comp. Law, Assicur., Internat. Comp. Law Qly, Jl Public Law, Lucknow Law Jl, Mod. Law Rev., New Law Jl, Quis Custodiet, Rev. Gen. Droit Internat. Public, Rev. Internat. Droit Comp., R. M. Themics, Solrs Jl, Wm & Mary Law Rev. *Address*: Faculty of Law, Univ. of Exeter, Amory Building, Rennes Drive, Exeter EX4 4RJ.

Last, Rex William, MA; Lecturer, German Department, Hull University, since 1965; *m*; two *s*. BA Hull 1961, Cert Ed Hull 1962, MA Hull 1965. *Publications*: Hans Arp: the Poet of Dadaism, 1969; Erich Kästner, 1974; ed, Affinities, 1971; trans., W. Brandt: In Exile, 1971; German Dadaist Literature, 1973; trans., M. Scheele: The Essential Max Ernst, 1972; *contrib.* E. G. Germ. Life Lett., Semin., Symp., ALLC Bull. *Address*: Dept of German, The Univ., Hull HU6 7RX.

Latham, Dr Anthony John Heaton; Lecturer in International Economic History, Department of Economic History, University College of Swansea, since 1967; *b* 1940; *m* 1968. BA Birmingham 1964 (Hons Med. and Mod. Hist.), PhD Birmingham 1970 (African Studies); Mem., Econ. History Soc. Chm., Swansea Assoc. of Univ. Teachers, 1973; Mem., UC Swansea Senate, 1973. *Publications*: Old Calabar 1600–1891: The Impact of the International Economy upon a Traditional Society, 1973; *contrib.* Jl Afr. History. *Address*: Dept of Economic History, Univ. Coll. of Swansea, Singleton Park, Swansea SA2 8PP.

Latham, Dr John Derek, MA, DPhil; Reader in Arabic, University of Manchester, since 1973; *b* 1927; *m* 1955; one *s* one *d*. BA Oxon 1949 (1st cl. Oriental Studies–Arabic and Persian), Hon Mods 1947 (Classics), MA Oxon 1952, DPhil Oxon 1956; FRAS, Hon. Mem., Real Acad. Córdoba (Inst. Estud. Calif.). HM Treasury Res. Fellow, Oxford, 1950–53; Asst Libr., Near East. Books, Univ. of Manchester, 1953–57; Associate Prof. and Curator, Mid. East. Collections, Hoover Instn, Stanford Univ., 1957–58; Lectr in Arabic, Univ. of Manchester, 1958–69, Sen. Lectr, 1969–73. Cnsltnt, Special Operat. Res. Off., 1958–59; Civil Service Commn Examnr, 1968– ; Mem., Medieval Latin Dictionary Cttee (Brit. Acad.), 1971– ; Mem., Adv. Ed. Bd, Cambridge Hist. of Arabic Lit., 1971– ; Chm., Mid. East. Libr. Cttee, 1969– ;

Mem., Brit. Nat. Cttee for Mid. East. Studies, 1971– ; Fellow and Mem. Council, Brit. Soc. for Mid. East Studies, 1973– ; Mem., Asoc. Española de Orientalístas, 1969– ; Mem., Assoc. for Literary and Linguistic Computing, 1973– ; Mem., British Algerian Soc., 1973– . Editor, Islamic Quarterly; Jt Editor, Bull. Brit. Soc. for Mid. East Studies. *Publications*: (with W. F. Paterson) Saracen Archery, 1970; Arabic Literature, in, Guide to Eastern Literatures, ed D. M. Lang, 1971; contrib. L'étude des immigrations Andalouses et leur Place dans l'histoire de la Tunisie, in, Recueil d'études sur les Morisques, ed M. de Epalza and R. Petit, 1972; Encyclopaedia of Islam; var. Festschriften; Medieval Latin Dictionary; Cambridge Hist. of Arabic Lit.; Middle East and Islam, ed D. Hopwood and D. Grimwood-Jones; *contrib.* Bull. Hispan. Studies, Bull. SOAS, Cahiers de Tunisie, Iran, Islam. Qly, JAL, JESHO, Jl RAS, JSS, Rev. de l'Occident Musulman et de la Médit., Studi Medievali. *Address*: Dept of Near Eastern Studies, Univ. of Manchester, Manchester M13 9PL.

Latham, Dr Joseph Lionel; Lecturer, Department of International Economic Studies, University of Glasgow, since 1970; *b* 1928; *m* 1957; two *s* two *d*. BSc London 1949 (external degree, 1st cl. Hons Chemistry), PhD London 1952 (external degree); FRIC 1963. Lectr, Portsmouth Coll. of Technology, 1958–61; Sen. Lectr, Harris Coll., Preston, 1961–67; Sen. Lectr in Physical Chemistry, Univ. of Science and Technology, Kumasi, Ghana, 1967–69. *Publications*: Elementary Reaction Kinetics, 1962 (3rd edn forthcoming); Physics for Chemists and Biologists, 1968; Ashanti Ballads, 1969. *Address*: Adam Smith Building, Glasgow G12 8RT.

Lau, Prof. D. C.; Professor of Chinese, School of Oriental and African Studies, University of London, since 1970; *b* 1921. BA Hong Kong 1942, MA Glasgow 1949. Asst, Moral Philosophy, Univ. of Glasgow, 1949–50; Lectr, Chinese and Chinese Philosophy, SOAS, 1950–65; Reader, Chinese Philosophy, 1965–70. *Publications*: Lao Tzu: Tao te ching, 1964; Mencius, 1970; *contrib.* Asia Major, Bull. SOAS. *Address*: Sch. of Oriental and African Studies, Malet Street, WC1E 7HP.

Laughton, Prof. Eric; Firth Professor of Latin, University of Sheffield, since 1952; *b* 1911; *m* 1938; one *s* one *d*. MA Oxon 1937. Asst, Humanity Dept, Edinburgh Univ., 1934–36; Univ. of Sheffield: Asst Lectr in Classics, 1936; Lectr in Classics, 1939; Sen. Lectr, 1946; Public Orator, 1955–68; Pro-Vice Chancellor, 1968–72. *Publications*: The Participle in Cicero, 1964; verse trans. of Papyrus (17th-century Latin poem by J. Imberdis), 1952; *contrib.* various classical jls. *Address*: Univ. of Sheffield, Sheffield S10 2TN.

Launder, Victor Charles, ARIBA; Senior Lecturer, Department of Architecture, University of Bristol, since 1968; *b* 1916; *m* 1955; two *d*. ARIBA 1947. Recognised Teacher, Univ. of Bristol, 1960–63, Lectr, 1963–68;

Vice Principal, RWA Sch. of Archit., 1959–63. *Publications*: Foundations, 1972; *contrib.* Archit. Jl, Munic. Jl, RIBA Jl. *Address*: Dept of Architecture, Univ. of Bristol, 25 Great George Street, Bristol.

Laurie, Ian Charles; Senior Lecturer in Landscape Design, Department of Town and Country Planning, University of Manchester, since 1968; *b* 1925; *m* 1951; one *s* two *d*. BA Manchester 1952 (Hons TCP), DipLD Dunelm 1953; MRTPI 1955, FILA 1956. Mem., Landscape Educn Gp; Mem., Landscape Res. Gp, Manchester Univ.: Lectr in Town Planning, 1962–65; Lectr in Landscape Design, 1965–68. Hon. Editor, Landscape Research News; Mem., Min. of Housing and Local Govt Working Party, 1967–70; Mem., Inst. of Landscape Architects Educn Cttee, 1967– . *Publications*: *contrib.* Landscape Design, Landscape Architecture Qly, Planning Outlook. *Address*: Dept of Town and Country Planning, Univ. of Manchester Oxford Road, Manchester M13 9PL.

Lauterpacht, Elihu, MA, LLB, QC; Lecturer in Law, University of Cambridge, since 1955, and Fellow of Trinity College, Cambridge, since 1953; *b* 1928; *m* 1955 (wife *d* 1970), *m* 1973; one *s* two *d*. BA Cambridge 1949 (1st cl. Law), LLB Cambridge 1950 (1st cl.), Whewell Schol. in Internat. Law; Barrister 1950, QC 1970. Dir of Res. (Eng speaking sect.), Hague Acad. of Internat. Law 1959, 1960; Vis. Prof., Univ. of Delhi, 1960. Jt Sec., Interdeptal Cttee on State Immunities, 1950–51; Sec., Internat. Law Fund, 1955– ; Chm., E Afr. Common Market Tribunal, 1970– . Editor: Internat. Law Reports, 1960– ; Brit. Practice in Internat. Law, 1955– . *Publications*: Jerusalem and the Holy Places, 1968; ed, H. Lauterpacht: International Law: the collected papers, vol. I 1970; *contrib.* Brit. Ybk Internat. Law, Internat. Comp. Law Qly. *Address*: Trinity College, Cambridge.

Lavers, Robert John, BA; Fellow, Institute of Social and Economic Research, University of York, since 1968; *b* 1937; *m* 1967; four *s*. BA Oxon 1962 (PPE); FSS. Asst Lectr, in Economic and Social Statistics, Univ. of York, 1966–67, Lectr, 1967–68; Vis. Lectr, Lehigh Univ., Bethlehem, Pa, 1974. *Publications*: (with A. T. Peacock and H. Glennerster) Educational Finance, 1968; *contrib.* Jl Royal Stat. Soc., Social Trends. *Address*: Institute of Social and Economic Research, Univ. of York, Heslington, York YO1 5OD.

Lavery, (Charles Edward) Mark, MA, BLitt; Lecturer in Chinese, University of Leeds, since 1966; *b* 1936. BA Oxon 1960 (1st cl. Chinese), MA and BLitt Oxon 1964. *Address*: Dept of Chinese Studies, The Univ., Leeds LS2 9JT.

Lavin, Deborah Margaret; Lecturer, Department of Modern History, Queen's University, Belfast, since 1965; *b* 1939. BA Oxon 1961, DipEd 1962. Univ. of Witwatersrand, 1962–64. *Publications*: *contrib.* The World Today. *Address*: Dept of Modern History, Queen's Univ. of Belfast, Belfast BT7 1NN.

Law, C. M.; Senior Lecturer in Geography, Department of Economics and Geography, University of Salford, since 1973 (Lecturer, 1965–73); *b* 1938; *m* 1962; one *s* one *d*. BSc Nottingham 1959, MSc Nottingham 1961. *Publications*: *contrib*. Reg. Studies, Trans Inst. Brit. Geogrs. *Address*: Dept of Economics and Geography, Univ. of Salford, Salford M5 4WT.

Law, Michael Haldane; Lecturer, Department of Education, University of Leeds, since 1968; *b* 1925; *m* 1954; four *s*. BA Cantab 1952; Lehrbefähigungszeugnis (Vienna), 1954. *Publications*: trans., H. Kralik: The Vienna Opera House, 1955; trans., W. Hofmann: Caricature from Leonardo to Picasso, 1958; How to Read German, 1964; (co-author) Vorwärts, Stages 1 and 2, 1968–69; as Michael Kreuzenau: Pilzsuppe, 1960; Novellen I–VI, 1961–68; *contrib*. Praxis neusprach. Unterr. *Address*: Dept of Education, Univ. of Leeds, Leeds LS2 9JT.

Lawless, Dr Clive John; Lecturer in Educational Technology, Institute of Educational Technology, The Open University, since 1971; *b* 1936; *m* 1962; two *s* one *d*. BA Oxford 1959, PGCE (London) Univ. Coll. of Rhodesia 1960, MA Oxford 1966, Acad. DipEd (London) Univ. Coll. of Rhodesia 1966, PhD Reading 1973. Lectr in Educn, Univ. of Malawi, 1967–71, Sen. Lectr in Educn, 1971. *Publications*: *contrib*. Programmed Learning and Educnl Technol, Teacher Educn in New Countries. *Address*: Inst. of Educational Technology, The Open Univ., Walton Hall, Milton Keynes MK7 6AA.

Lawlor, Prof. John James; Professor and Head of Department of English, University of Keele, since 1950; *b* 1918; *m* 1941; one *s* three *d*. BA Oxford 1939 (1st cl. English), MA Oxford 1946, Sen. Mackinnon Schol., Magdalen Coll., 1946, Sen. Demy, 1947; DLitt Keele 1972; FSA 1966. Founding Mem., 1950, Internat. Assoc. Univ. Profs of Engl. (Perm. Sec.-Treas., 1971–); Contrib. Mem., Mediaev. Acad. Amer. 1962. Lectr in English, Brasenose and Trinity Colls, Oxford, 1947–50; Univ. Lectr in English Literature, Oxford, 1949–50. Ziskind Vis. Prof., Brandeis Univ., 1966; Vis. Prof., Univ. of Hawaii, 1972. Editor and publish. consltnt; Pres., N Staffs Drama Assoc., 1955– ; Brit. Drama League, County Rep., and Mem., West. Area Cttee, Brit. Drama League, 1955– . *Publications*: The Tragic Sense in Shakespeare, 1960; Piers Plowman: an Essay in Criticism, 1962; ed, Patterns of Love and Courtesy: essays in memory of C. S. Lewis, 1966; (with W. H. Auden) To Nevill Coghill, from Friends, 1966; Chaucer, 1968; ed, The New University, 1968; ed, Higher Education: Patterns of Change in the 1970s, 1972; *contrib*. Etudes Angl., Mod. Lang. Rev., Philol Qly, Rev. Engl. Lit., Rev. Engl. Studies, Sewanee Rev., Shakesp. Qly, Stratf. Studies, Va Qly Rev. *Address*: Dept of English, Univ. of Keele, Keele ST5 5BG.

Lawlor, Dr Monica Mary; Senior Lecturer, Psychology Department, Bedford College, London University, since 1966; *b* 1926. BA London 1948 (1st cl. Psychology), PhD London 1959 (Psychology). Mem., Brit. Psychol Soc., Assoc. Study Anim. Behav., Brit. Soc. Aesth. Asst, then Asst Lectr, Bedford Coll., London Univ., 1950–53; Univ. of London Fellowship, Univ. of W Ontario, 1953–55; Lectr, Bedford Coll., 1955–66; Vis. Prof., King's Coll., Univ. of W Ontario, 1969–70. *Publications*: Personal Responsibility: Growth and Limits, 1963; Out of this World: a study of Catholic Values, 1965; (with S. Clements) The McCabe Affair, 1967; *contrib*. Adv. Sci., Brit. Jl Aesth., Bull. Brit. Psychol Soc., Jl Abnorm. Soc. Psychol., Jl Soc. Psychol. *Address*: Bedford College, Regent's Park, NW1 4NS.

Lawrence, Prof. Clifford Hugh, MA, DPhil; Professor of Medieval History, University of London, since 1970; *b* 1921; *m* 1953; one *s* five *d*. BA Oxon 1948 (1st cl. History), MA Oxon 1953, DPhil Oxon 1956; FRHistS 1959. Asst Lectr, Bedford Coll., London Univ., 1951–53, Lectr, 1953–62, Reader, 1962–70. 2nd Lt, RA, 1943; Lt 1944; Capt., 1944; Major, 1945–46; Asst Archivist, Glos Co., 1949. *Publications*: St Edmund of Abingdon, 1960; ed, The English Church and the Papacy in the Middle Ages, 1965; The First Universities, 1975; *contrib*. Encyclopaedia Britannica; *contrib*. EHR, Bull. Inst. Hist. Res., Jl Eccles. Hist., History, Month. *Address*: Bedford College, Univ. of London, Regent's Park, NW1 4NS.

Lawrence, George Richard Peter; Lecturer in Geography, University of London, King's College, since 1964; *b* 1930; *m* 1958; 1968; three *s*. BSc London 1952 (Special Hons Geography), Dip. Land Surveying London 1953, MSc London 1958; FRGS, Mem., Inst. Brit. Geogrs, Geog. Assoc., Field Studies Council. Demonstrator in Geography, Univ. of Keele, 1956–58; Lectr, St Peter's Coll. of Educn, Birmingham, 1958–62; Asst Lectr in Geography, King's Coll., 1962–64. *Publications*: (jtly) Advanced Geography of Northern and Western Europe, 1967; Cartographic Methods, 1971; Randstad Holland, 1973; *contrib*. Geog., N Staffs Jl Field Studies, Proc. Geol. Assoc. *Address*: Dept of Geography, King's College, Strand, WC2R 2LS.

Lawrence, Dr Marie Collins; Recognized Lecturer in Physical Anthropology, University of Cambridge, since 1964, and Tutor, Lucy Cavendish College, Cambridge, since 1970; *b* 1927; *m* 1952; four *s* one *d*. BA Cambridge 1949, MA Cambridge 1952, PhD Cambridge 1959; Mem., Soc. Study Hum. Biol. Asst Lectr, Dept of Anatomy, Birmingham Univ., 1952–53. *Publications*: *contrib*. Man, Nature. *Address*: Lucy Cavendish College, Cambridge.

Lawrence, Prof. Raymond John, MA; Professor of Marketing, University of Lancaster, since 1965; *b* 1925; *m* 1952; one *s* one *d*. BA Cantab 1949 (1st cl. Classics), MA Cantab 1963; PhD programme, California: MBIM, Beta Gamma Sigma. Unilever Ltd, 1950–62. *Publications*: (with M. J. Thomas) Modern Marketing Management, 1971; *contrib*. Appl. Stats, Brit. Jl Mktg, Dist. Bank Rev., Jl Mngmt Studies, Jl Mktg Res.

Address: Dept of Marketing, Furness College, Univ. of Lancaster, Bailrigg, Lancaster.

Lawrenson, Prof. Thomas Edward, MA, DipEd, PhD; Professor of French Studies, University of Lancaster, since 1964; *b* 1918; *m* 1955; one *s* one *d*. MA Manchester 1939 (1st cl. French), DipEd Manchester 1940. MA Manchester 1947, PhD Manchester 1953; Mem., Soc. Fr. Studies, Internat. Fed. Theatre Res., Assoc. Internat. Etudes Franc. Asst Lectr, Manchester, 1947–50; Sen. Lectr, and Hd of Dept. Univ. Coll., Gold Coast, 1950–57; Lectr, Univ. of Glasgow, 1957–59; Warden, Crombie Hall, and Lectr in French, Univ. of Aberdeen, 1959–64. Mem., Mngmt Cttee, Theatre Res. Recherches Théâtrales, 1962– ; Cttee Soc. Fr. Studies, 1964–66; Bd of Governors, Lancaster Royal Grammar Sch., 1964– ; Lancaster CC Educn Cttee, 1964–66. Chevalier de l'Ordre National du Mérite. *Publications*: The French Stage in the Seventeenth Century, 1957; Hall of Residence Saint Anselm Hall in the University of Manchester, 1957; ed, Lesage: Crispin, rival de son maître, 1961, ed, Lesage: Turcaret, 1969; ed, Modern Miscellany: Studies in Honour of Eugène Vinaver, 1970; *contrib.* Biblio. Human. Renaiss., Centre Nat. Recherches Sci., Fr. Studies, Theatre Res./ Recherches Théâtrales. *Address*: Dept of French Studies, The Univ., Bailrigg, Lancaster LA1 4YW.

Laws, Sophie Susan Sydenham Cole, (Mrs J. G. McK. Laws), BLitt, MA; Lecturer, Theological Department, King's College, London University, since 1969; *b* 1944; *m* 1973. BA Hons 1966 (1st cl. Theol.), BLitt 1969, MA 1970, Oxford. Temp. Lectr, Dept of Theology, Leeds Univ., 1968–69. *Publications*: *contrib.* NT Studies, Theol. *Address*: Theological Dept, King's Coll., Strand, WC2R 2LS.

Lawson, Prof. Frederick Henry, DCL, FBA; Part-time Professor in Law, University of Lancaster, since 1972; *b* 1897; *m* 1933; one *s* two *d*. BA, MA Oxon 1922 (1st cl. Mod. History 1921, 1st cl. Jurisprudence 1922), DCL Oxon 1947; Hon Dr: Louvain 1958; Paris, 1964; Ghent, 1968, Hon Dr jur Frankfurt; Hon LLD Glasgow 1960; Barrister-at-Law Gray's Inn 1923, FBA 1956. Lectr in Law: Non-Collegiate Students, Oxford, 1923–26; Univ. Coll., Oxford, 1924–25; Christ Church, 1925–26; Corpus Christi Coll., 1925–26 and 1927–30; Jun. Res. Fellow, Merton Coll., Oxford, 1925–30; Official Fellow and Tutor in Law, 1930–48; Univ. Lectr in Byzantine Law, 1929–31; All Souls Reader in Roman Law, 1931–48; Prof. of Comparative Law, and Fellow of Brasenose Coll., Oxford, 1948–64; Part-time Lectr in Law, Lancaster, 1964–72; Vis. Prof., Univ. of California, 1953; Thomas M. Cooley Lectr, Univ. of Michigan Law Sch., 1953; Vis. Lectr, NY Univ. Sch. of Law, 1956, 1959, 1962, 1965; Vis. Prof., Univ. of Pennsylvania Law Sch., 1959; Univ. of Michigan Law Sch., 1959; Univ. of Houston, 1967–68. Temp. Principal, Min. of Supply, 1943–45; Mem., Internat. Social Science Council, 1952–58; Internat. Acad. Comp. Law, 1958– ; Sec. Gen., Internat. Assoc. Legal Science, 1964–69. *Publications*: (with D. L. Keir) Cases in Constitutional Law, 1928, 5th edn 1967; Negligence in the Civil Law, 1950; The Rational Strength of English Law (Hamlyn Lectures), 1951; A Common Lawyer looks at the Civil Law (Thomas M. Cooley Lectures), 1955; Introduction to the Law of Property, 1958; (with D. J. Bentley) Constitutional and Administrative Law, 1961; The Oxford Law School 1850–1965, 1968; The Roman Law Reader 1969; Remedies of English Law, 1972; ed, Stephen: Commentaries on the Laws of England, 19th edn 1928; ed, Constitutional Law, in Halsbury: Laws of England, 2nd edn 1932, 4th edn (forthcoming); ed, Buckland and McNair: Roman Law and Common Law, 2nd edn 1952; ed, Amos and Walton: Introduction to French Law, 2nd edn 1963, 3rd edn 1967; *contrib.* Jl SPTL, Law Qly Rev., NY Univ. Law Rev., Pol Studies, Rev. Internat. Droit Comp., Tulane Law Rev., Zeits. Sav. Stift. (Rom. Abt.). *Address*: 13 Eden Park, Lancaster.

Lawson, Frederick Robert; Lecturer in Environmental Studies, Department of Hotel and Catering Management, University of Surrey, since 1969; *b* 1930; *m* 1951; one *s* one *d*. MSc Salford 1968; Dips in Public Health Inspection, Environmental Health, Building, Surveying, Engineering, Fuel Technology; CEng; FIAS; FIPHE; MIHVE; MAPHI; MInstF. QUB, 1965; Research, Univ. of Salford, 1968–69. Consultant Engineer. *Publications*: (with others) Principles of Hotel Design, 1970, 2nd edn 1973; Principles of Catering Design, 1973; Restaurant Planning and Design, 1974; *contrib.* Architects Jl; Jls Assoc. Public Health Inspectors, Hotel Catering and Institutional Managers Inst., Building Services Engineer, Architect and Surveyor. *Address*: Dept of Hotel and Catering Management, Univ. of Surrey, Guildford GU2 5XH.

Lawson, Prof. Gerald Hartley; Professor of Business Finance, Manchester Business School, University of Manchester, since 1969; *b* 1933; *m* 1957; three *s*. BA(Econ) Durham 1955, MA(Econ) Durham 1959, MBA Manchester 1973; FCCA. Lectr, Univ. of Sheffield, 1959–63; Lectr, Univ. of Hull, 1963–64; Lectr, Univ. of Sheffield, 1964–66; Prof., Univ. of Liverpool, 1966–69; Vis. Prof., Univ. of Augsburg, 1971–72. Hon. Sec., Brit. Accounting and Finance Assoc. Mem., Editorial Bd, Jl Business Finance, Management Internat. Rev. *Publications*: (with D. W. Windle) Tables for DCF calculations, 1965; (with D. W. Windle) Capital Budgeting and the use of DCF Criteria in the Corporation Tax Regime, 1970; *contrib.* Acntng Rev., Acntnt, Acntnts Jl, Internat. Mngmt Rev., Jl Management Studies, etc; trans German pubns. *Address*: Manchester Business School, Booth Street West, Manchester M15 6PB.

Lawson, John; Reader in the History of Education, Department of Educational Studies, University of Hull, since 1971; *b* 1913; *m* 1939; three *s*. BA Manchester 1935 (1st cl. History), MA Manchester 1936, DipEd Manchester 1937 (1st cl.). Grad. Res.

401

Schol., Manchester, 1935; Faulkner Fellow, Manchester, 1937; Lectr, in Education, Hull Univ., 1949–63, Sen. Lectr, 1963–71. Mem., Editorial Bd, Hist. Educn. *Publications*: Primary Education in East Yorkshire 1560–1902, 1959; The Endowed Grammar Schools of East Yorkshire, 1962; A Town Grammar School Through Six Centuries, 1963; Medieval Education and the Reformation, 1967; Education, in, Victoria County History of Hull, 1969; (with H. Silver) A Social History of Education in England, 1973. *Address*: Dept of Educational Studies, Univ. of Hull, Hull HU6 7RX.

Lawson, Kenneth Steven, BA, DipPsych; Lecturer in the Psychology of Education, School of Education, University of Leeds, since 1965; *b* 1932; *m* 1954; one *s* one *d*. BA Hull 1961; DipPsych London 1962; Teachers Cert Nottingham 1956. *Publications*: Children's Reading, 1968, 2nd edn 1970; (with K. Lovell) Understanding Research in Education, 1970; *contrib.* Occupat. Psychol. *Address*: School of Education, Univ. of Leeds, Leeds LS2 9JT.

Lawton, Prof. Alan Douglas, LLB, BSc(Econ); Professor of Civil Law, Queen's University of Belfast, since 1972; *b* 1916; *m* 1942; one *s* two *d*. LLB London 1938, BSc(Econ) London 1952, Dip. en Droit Comparé Luxembourg 1965; called to the Bar, Lincoln's Inn 1957. Member: Soc. Public Teachers of Law 1964; UK Nat. Cttee for Comparative Law 1968. Vis. Lectr, Birmingham Univ., 1964–67; Vis. Lectr, King's Coll., London Univ. 1965–66; Dir of Studies, Luxembourg Univ., 1966; Lectr, Bristol Univ., 1966–72 (Sen. Lectr, 1972); Vis. Lectr, Bordeaux Univ., 1969. Mem., Univ. Appts Bd, Bristol, 1967–69; Examiner in Law, London Univ., 1969– . Pres., Commonwealth Students Bureau, 1951–52; Area Organiser, Inter Church Christian Aid, 1963–66; Member: Arnhem Link Cttee, 1966; Legal Panel, Nat. Council Social Service, 1964–66; Croydon Bor. Council, 1965–66; Croydon Educn Cttee, Libr. Cttee, and Civic Halls Cttee, 1965–66; Chm. of Governors, John Newsham Sch., Croydon, 1965–66; Governor, Croydon Tech. Coll., 1966– ; Member: Careers Adv. Bd, Bristol, 1969–72; Cttee, UK Wld Univ. Services, 1971–72; Northern Irish Bar, 1972– . UK Corresp. with European Econ. Commn, 1972– ; Common Market Cases Editor, Law Soc. Gazette, 1972– . Lectures to prof. bodies and for Home Office, 1965– . *Publications*: Estate Duty in England and Wales, 1970; contrib. Dent's Encyclopedia, 1964; Jahrbuch der Internationale Gesellschaft für Urheberrecht, 1964; Öffentlichvechtliche Grundlegung der Unternchmensverfassing, in Planung V, 1971; contribs to confs of German Comparative Law Assoc., 1969 and 1971; *contrib.* Brit. Tax Rev., Convey, Prop. Law., Jl Business Law, Jl Sar Banks Inst., Law, Guard, Legal Exec., New Law Jl, Solic. Jl, Law Soc. Gazette, Okl. Law Rev. *Address*: Queen's Univ. of Belfast, Belfast BT7 1NN.

Lawton, Richard; Professor of Geography, University of Liverpool, since 1970; *b* 1925;

m 1948; two *s* two *d*. BA Liverpool 1948 (1st cl. Geography), MA Liverpool 1950; Mem., Inst. Brit. Geogrs, Geog. Assoc., Assoc. Amer. Geogrs, Econ. Hist. Soc., Agric. Hist. Soc., Reg. Studies Assoc.; Internat. Union Sci. Study Populat. Asst Lectr, Univ. of Liverpool, 1949–52, Lectr, 1952–62, Sen. Lectr, 1962–66, Reader, 1966–70; Vis. Prof., S Illinois Univ., 1964–65; Univ. of Maryland, 1968. Mem., Council, Inst. Brit. Geogrs, 1961–62 (Hon. Sec., 1972–); Mem., Registrar General's Geog. Adv. Cttee. *Publications*: (with R. K. Gresswell) Merseyside: British Landscape through Maps, 6, 1968; ed (with R. W. Steel), Liverpool Essays in Geography, 1967; ed (with C. M. Cunningham), Merseyside: Social and Economic Studies, 1970; *contrib.* Geog. Mag., Geog., Irish Geog., Reg. Studies, Sociol Rev., Town Plan. Rev., Trans Hist. Soc. Lancs and Chesh., Trans Inst Brit. Geogrs. *Address*: Dept of Geography, Roxby Building, PO Box 147, Liverpool L69 3BX.

Layard, Peter Richard Grenville; Lecturer in Economics, London School of Economics, since 1968; *b* 1934. BA Cantab 1957 (1st cl. Hons History Pts I and II), MScEcons London 1967 (distinction). Dep. Dir, Higher Educn Research Unit, LSE, 1964– (part-time, 1968–) Sen. Res. Officer, Robbins Cttee on Higher Educn, 1961–63. *Publications*: (with T. Burgess and P. Pant) Manpower and Educational Development in India, 1961–68, 1968; (with M. Blaug and M. Woodhall) The Causes of Educated Unemployment in India, 1969; (with J. King and C. Moser) The Impact of Robbins: Expansion in Higher Education, 1969; (with J. D. Sargan, M. E. Ager and D. J. Jones) Qualified Manpower and Economic Performance: An Inter-plant Study in the Electrical Engineering Industry, 1971; ed and introd, Cost-Benefit Analysis, 1973; *contrib.* Brit. Jl Industrial Relations, Higher Educn Rev., Jl Polit. Econ., Jl Royal Stat. Soc., Minerva, Universities Qly. *Address*: London School of Economics, Houghton Street, Aldwych, WC2A 2AE.

Laycock, Blanche Eva; Lecturer (part-time), Department of French, Bedford College, University of London, since 1966; *b* 1910; *m* 1939; one *s* two *d*. Licence de lettres classiques Paris 1932 (English), Diplôme d'Etudes supérieures Paris 1935 (English). Lectrice, 1941–50, Asst Lectr, 1950–66, Bedford Coll. *Address*: Dept of French, Bedford College, Regent's Park, NW1 4NS.

Layton, Prof. David; Professor of Education, with special reference to science, since 1973, and Director of the Centre for Studies in Science Education, University of Leeds, since 1970; *b* 1925; *m* 1950; two *s* one *d*. BA Cantab 1945, MA Cantab 1955; MSc London 1955. Lectr, Univ. of Leeds, 1960–63; Dep. Head, Dept of Educn, Leeds, 1963–73. Governor, City of Leeds and Carnegie Coll. of Educn, 1969– . *Publications*: University Teaching in Transition, 1968; Science for the People, 1974; *contrib.* Brit. Jl Hist. Sci., Brit. Jl Educnl Studies, Notes Rec. Royal Soc. *Address*: Centre for Studies in

Science Education, Univ. of Leeds, Leeds LS2 9JT.

Layton-Henry, Dr Zygmunt; Lecturer, Department of Politics, University of Warwick, since 1968; *b* 1942; *m* 1968; two *d.* BSocSc Birmingham 1964, PhD 1973; Member: Political Studies Assoc.; British Sociological Assoc. Sen. Res. Asst, Brunel Univ., 1967–68. *Publications: contrib.* Jl Contemp. Hist. *Address:* Dept of Politics, Univ. of Warwick, Coventry CV4 7AL.

Lazenby, John Francis; Senior Lecturer in Ancient History, Department of Classics, University of Newcastle upon Tyne, since 1971; *b* 1934; *m* 1967; one *s* one *d.* Schol., Keble Coll., Oxford, 1952–56; Hon. Mods Oxford 1954 (1st cl. Greek and Latin Literature), BA Oxford 1956 (1st cl. Lit. Hum.); Thomas Whitcombe-Greene Schol. Oxford 1956–58, Sen. Demy, Magdalen Coll., Oxford, 1957–59; MA Oxford 1959. Lectr in Ancient History, Univ. of Newcastle upon Tyne, 1959–71. *Publications:* The Catalogue of the Ships in Homer's Iliad, 1970; (jt author) The Minnesota Messenia Expedition, 1972; (jt author) Kythera, 1972; *contrib.* Ann. Brit. Sch. Athens, Antiq., Hermes, Latomus. *Address:* Dept of Classics, The Univ., Newcastle upon Tyne NE1 7RU.

Lea, Kerrin John, MA, BLitt; Lecturer in Geography, University of Strathclyde, since 1965; *b* 1937; *m* 1964. BA Oxford 1960 (2nd Cl. Geography), BLitt Oxford 1963, MA Oxford 1965. Asst in Geog., Univ. of Glasgow, 1962–65. Mem., Geog. Assoc., Inst. Brit. Geogrs. *Publications: contrib.* Scott. Geog. Mag., Trans Inst. Brit. Geogrs. *Address:* Dept of Geography, Univ. of Strathclyde, Glasgow G1 1XW.

Leach, Edmund Ronald, MA, PhD, FBA; Provost of King's College, Cambridge, since 1966; Professor of Social Anthropology, since 1972; *b* 1910; *m* 1940; one *s* one *d.* MA Cantab; PhD London; FBA 1972; Hon. Fellow, LSE, 1973. Lectr, later Reader, in Social Anthrop., LSE, 1947–53; Lectr, Cambridge, 1953–57, Reader, 1957–72; Fellow of King's Coll., Cambridge, 1960–66; Fellow, Center for Advanced Study in Behavioral Sciences, Stanford, 1961; Sen. Fellow, Eton Coll., 1966– ; Malinowski Lectr, 1959; Reith Lectr, 1967. Anthropological Field Res. in Formosa, 1937, Kurdistan, 1938, Burma, 1939–45, Borneo, 1947, Ceylon, 1954, 1956. Mem., 1968–71, SSRC, Vice-Pres., 1964–66, 1968–70, Pres., 1971–75, Royal Anthrop. Inst. (Curl Essay Prize, 1951, 1957; Rivers Medal, 1958; Henry Myers Lectr, 1966); Chm., Assoc. of Social Anthropologists, 1966–70; Pres., British Humanist Assoc., 1970– ; Foreign Hon. Mem., Amer. Acad. of Arts and Sciences, 1968. *Publications:* Social and Economic Organization of the Rowanduz Kurds, 1940; Social Science Research in Sarawak, 1950; Political Systems of Highland Burma, 1954; Pul Eliya: a village in Ceylon, 1961; Re-thinking Anthropology, 1961; A Runaway World?, 1968; Genesis as Myth, 1970; Lévi-Strauss, 1970; Editor and contributor to various anthrop. Symposia; *contrib.* Man. Jl

Royal Anthropol Inst., American Anthropologist, South Western Jl Anthropology, Daedalus, European Archives of Sociology, New Society, Current Anthropology, etc; various articles in Encyclop. Britannica, Internat. Encyclop. of the Social Sciences. *Address:* Provost's Lodge, King's Coll., Cambridge.

Leaf, Gerald Arthur Vernon, MSc, FTI; Senior Lecturer in Textile Engineering, and Associate Lecturer, Department of Management Studies, University of Leeds, since 1970; *b* 1928; *m* 1951; two *d.* BSc London 1949, MSc London 1961; FTI, FSS. Lectr, Leeds 1965–70. Examiner, Textile Inst. *Publications: contrib.* Brit. Jl Appl. Phys., Jl Text. Inst., Text. Res. Jl. *Address:* Dept of Textile Industries, The Univ., Leeds LS2 9JT.

Leahy, Desmond Maurice; Senior Lecturer in Greek, University of Manchester, since 1963; *b* 1924; *m* 1949; one *s* three *d.* BA Oxon 1949 (1st cl. Lit. Hum.), MA Oxon 1949. Asst Lectr, Greek and Latin, Manchester Univ., 1949–52, Lectr, 1952–63, Warden, Allen Hall, Manchester, 1961–66. *Publications: contrib.* Bull. Rylands Libr., Class. Philol., Historia, Jl Hellenic Studies, Phoenix. *Address:* School of Classics, Univ. of Manchester, Manchester M13 9PL.

Leahy, James D.; Senior Lecturer and Director of Film Studies, Slade School of Fine Art, University College London, since 1971; *b* 1938; *m* 1968. BA Hons 1960 (2nd cl.), MA 1966, Cantab. Instructor in Film, Dept of Radio, TV, Film, Northwestern Univ., Evanston, Illinois, USA, 1968–71; *Publication:* The Cinema of Joseph Losey, 1967. *Address:* Unit for Study of Film, Slade Sch. of Fine Art, University Coll. London, Gower Street WC1E 6BT.

Leahy, Michael Paul Tutton; Lecturer in Philosophy, University of Kent, Canterbury, since 1967; *b* 1934; *m* 1968. BA Dublin 1961; MA Pennsylvania State 1963; Mem., Mind Assoc. Temp. Lectr, Univ. of Durham, 1966–67; Vis. Prof., Univ. of New Hampshire, 1970–71. Chm., Philos. Bd of Studies, Univ. of Kent, 1968–69, 1969–70. *Publications: contrib.* Mind, Analysis, 20th Cent. Studies, Metaphilosophy, Foundns of Language. *Address:* Rutherford College, The Univ., Canterbury, Kent.

Leakey, Prof. Felix William; Professor of French, Bedford College, University of London, since 1973; *b* 1922; *m* 1947; one *s* two *d.* BA London 1944 (1st cl. French), PhD London 1951. Asst Lectr (pt-time), Queen Mary Coll., London, 1947–48; Asst Lectr, then Lectr, Univ. of Sheffield, 1948–54; Lectr, Glasgow, 1954–64, Sen. Lectr, 1964–68, Reader, 1968–70; Prof. of French, Reading Univ., 1970–73; Carnegie Res. Fellow, 1961–62; Leverhulme Res. Fellow, 1971–72. Mem., Cttee, Soc. Fr. Studies, 1969–71, 1972–74; Jt Sec., Assoc. of Univ. Profs of French, 1972– . *Publications:* Baudelaire and Nature, 1969; ed jtly, The French Renaissance and its Heritage: Essays presented to Alan Boase, 1968; *contrib.* Fr.

Studies, Rev. Hist. Litt., Rev. Litt. Comp., Rev. Sci. Hum., Yrs Wk Mod. Lang. Studies etc. *Address*: Dept of French, Bedford College, Regent's Park, NW1 4NS.

Leaney, Rev. Prof. Alfred Robert Clare, M.A., D.D.; Professor of Christian Theology and Head of Department of Theology, University of Nottingham, since 1970; *b* 1909; *m* 1933; one *s*. BA Oxon 1932 (2nd cl. Lit. Hum.), MA Oxon 1939, BD Oxon 1952, DD Oxon 1966. Lectr, Nottingham Univ., 1956–61; Sen. Lectr, 1961–64, Reader, 1964–69; Prof. of New Testament Studies, 1969–70. Hon. Sec., Studiorum Novi Testamenti Societas, 1965–70. *Publications*: The Gospel according to St Luke, 1958, 2nd edn 1966; The Epistles to Timothy, Titus and Philemon, 1960; From Judean Caves, 1962; The Rule of Qumran and Its Meaning, 1966; The Letters of Peter and Jude, 1966; (with R. Davidson) Biblical Criticism, 1970; The New Testament, 1972; ed and contrib., A Guide to the Scrolls, 1958; contrib. Historicity and Chronology in the Gospels, 1965; Vindications, 1966; Difficulties for Christian Belief, 1966; A Dictionary of Christian Theology, 1969; *contrib.* Bull. John Rylands Library, Church Qly Rev., Colloquium, Expository Times, New Testament Studies, Scott. Jl Theol., Theol., Vigiliae Christianae. *Address*: Dept of Theology, Univ. of Nottingham, Nottingham NG7 2RD.

Leaper, Prof. R. A. B.; Professor of Social Administration, Department of Sociology, Exeter University, since 1970; *b* 1921; *m* 1950; two *s* one *d*. BA Cantab 1949, MA Cantab 1951; MA Oxon 1959, Dip. Public and Social Administration Oxon 1960. AUT; Mem. Brit. Assoc. of Social Workers; Mem. Assoc. of Community Workers. Lectr, 1960–67, Sen. Lectr, 1967–70, Acting Dir, 1969–70, UC Swansea. Chm., Standing Conf. of Councils of Social Service, 1967–69; Chm., Jt Community Work Cttee, 1969– ; Dir, Annual Summer Sch., Dept of Health and Social Security, 1969– ; Pres., Europe Region, Internat. Council on Social Welfare. *Publications*: Communities and Social Change, 1967; Administrations in Europe dealing with Social Problems, 1969; Community Work, 1969, 2nd rev. edn 1971; *contrib.* Soc. Work Today, Soc. Serv. Qly, Comm. Develt Jl. *Address*: Sociology Dept, Streatham Court, The Univ., Exeter EX4 4PU.

Learmonth, Prof. Andrew Thomas Amos; Professor of Geography, since 1970, and Dean, Faculty of Social Sciences, The Open University, since 1972; *b* 1916; *m* 1950; two *s* two *d*. MA Edinburgh 1949 (1st cl. Geography and Vans Dunlop Scholarship), PhD Edinburgh 1953; Mem., Roy. Geog. Soc., Mem., Roy. Scott. Geog. Soc., Mem., Inst. Brit. Geogrs, Mem., Inst. Austral. Geogrs, Mem., Geog. Soc. NSW, Mem., Reg. Studies Assoc. Asst Lectr, Liverpool, 1949–52, Lectr, 1952–60, Sen. Lectr, 1960–62; Prof., Australian Nat. Univ., 1962–70. Colombo Plan Assignment, Indian Stat. Inst., 1956–58; Chm., Commn on Medical Geography, IGU, 1964– . *Publications*: (with A. M. Learmonth) The Eastern Lands, 1958, 2nd

edn 1963; (with O. H. K. Spate and A. M. Learmonth) India and Pakistan, 3rd edn 1967, pbk edn 1972; (with A. M. Learmonth) Encyclopaedia of Australia, 1968; (with A. M. Learmonth) Regional Landscapes of Australia, 1971, Brit. edn 1972; contrib. Medical Geography: techniques and case studies, ed N. D. McGlashan, 1972; *contrib.* Ann. Trop. Med. Parasit., Austral. Nat. Univ. Sch. Gen. Studies Occ. Paper, Erdkunde, Geog. Jl, Ind. Geog. Jl, Scott. Geog. Mag., Trans Inst. Brit. Geogrs. *Address*: Keeley House, Tingrith, Milton Keynes MK17 9EJ.

Leary, Dr Paris, BA, DPhil; Lecturer in American Literature, Department of English and American Studies, University of Leicester, since 1963; *b* 1931. BA Louisiana 1949 (Magna cum Laude); DPhil Oxon 1958. Instructor, then Asst Prof., Univ. of Kentucky, 1958–60; Asst Prof., Bard Coll., 1960–62; Asst Prof., State Univ., NY, 1962–63; Fulbright Prof., Univ. of Leicester, 1963–64. *Publications*: Views of The Oxford Colleges and Other Poems, 1960; The Innocent Curate (novel), 1963; The Jack Sprat Cook Book, 1965; A Controversy of Poets, 1965; Poesia Americana del '900, ed and trans. by C. Izzo, 1963; The Snake at Saffron Walden (poems), 1973; *contrib.* Antioch Rev., Ch Qly Rev., Hudson Rev., Qly Rev. Lit. *Address*: English Dept, Univ. of Leicester, Leicester LE1 7RH.

Le Breton, Dr Eileen Margaret, (pen name: **Eileen Souffrin**); Reader in French Language and Literature, Bedford College, University of London, since 1964; *b* 1915; *m* 1940 (*d* 1941); *m* 1946. BA Hons London 1936 (French), LèsL Lille 1936, MA London 1938 (French), DUP 1942, Prix de l'Académie Française 1942; Member: Mod. Humanities Res. Assoc.; Soc. of French Studies, Oxford; Société française de Littérature comparée. Tutor-Librarian, Institut de Littérature Comparée, Sorbonne, 1941–44; Part-time Lectr, Brit. Inst. in Paris, 1944–45; Asst Lectr, Univ. of Glasgow, 1945–46; Lectr in French, Bedford Coll., Univ. of London, 1948–64. Gen. Editor, Athlone French Poets, series, 1973– . *Publications*: crit. edn, Banville: Les Stalactites, 1942; preface to Mallarmé: Divagations, 1942; contrib. U. Finke: French 19th century Painting and Literature, 1972; trans. (with Georges Le Breton): Les Conférences de l'Unesco, 1946; William Blake, 1947; Mark Aldanov: Le Commencement de la Fin, 1948; *contrib.* Fontaine, Fr. Studies, Revue d'Histoire littéraire de la France, Revue de Littérature comparée, Revue de Musicologie, Revue des Sciences humaines, etc, and Encyclopaedia Britannica. *Address*: French Dept, Bedford Coll., Univ. of London, Regent's Park, NW1 4NS.

Lecomber, John Richard Charles; Lecturer, Department of Economics, Bristol University, since 1969; *b* 1937; *m* 1963; one *s* one *d*. BA Oxon 1961, Cert. Stats Oxon 1962, MA Cantab 1967; Sec., Input-Output Res. Gp; Economist, Nat. Econ. Develt Off., 1963–64; Econ. Advr., DEA, 1964–66; Res. Offr, Dept of Applied Econs, Univ. of Cambridge, 1966–69; Res. Fellow, Clare Coll., Cambridge, 1966–69. *Publications*:

(with T. S. Barker) British Imports 1972, 1967; (with T. S. Barker and J. R. N. Stone) Exploring 1972, with special reference to the Balance of Payments, 1969; (with T. S. Barker) Economic Planning for 1972, 1969; Growth versus Environment: a bibliography, 1973; The Growth Objective (forthcoming); Growth Versus Environment (forthcoming); contrib. other bks; *contrib.* Econ. Plan., Jl Roy. Stat. Soc., Moorg. Wall St, Oxf. Univ. Inst. Econ. Stat. Bull., Osteuropas Jbh, Internat. Jl of Soc. Econs. *Address*: Dept of Economics, 40 Berkeley Square, Bristol.

Ledger, Philip Stevens, FRCO; Director of Music and Organist, King's College, Cambridge, since 1974; *b* 1937; *m* 1963; one *s* one *d.* BA Cantab 1960 (1st cl. Hons Music), MusB Cantab 1961, MA Cantab 1964; FRCO; LRAM; ARCM. Master of the Music, Chelmsford Cathedral, 1962–65; Director of Music, Univ. of East Anglia, 1965–73 (Dean of Sch. of Fine Arts and Music, 1968–71). An Artistic Dir, Aldeburgh Festival of Music and the arts, 1968– . Conductor Cambridge University Music Society, 1973. Limpus and Read prizes, RCO. *Publications*: (ed) Anthems for Choirs 2 and 3, 1973; other edns of Byrd, Handel and Purcell. *Address*: King's College, Cambridge CB2 1ST.

Lee, A Robert; Lecturer in American Literature, University of Kent at Canterbury, since 1967; *b* 1941. BA London 1963, MA London 1965. Eng. Speaking Union Res. Fellow, Princeton Univ., NJ, 1965–66; Vis. Lecturer: Univ. of Virginia, 1966–67; San Fernando Valley State Coll., Calif. Summer Sch., 1967; Vis. Lectr in American Studies, Bryn Mawr Coll., Pa. 1971–72; Vis. Associate Prof. of Humanities, Univ. of Louisville, Ky, Summer 1973, 1974. *Publications*: contrib. The USA and Canada: a handbook, 1972; (also ed) Studies in The Black American Novel, 1972; *contrib.* Neg. Amer. Lit. Forum, Studies, 20th Cent. Studies, Durham Univ. Qly. *Address*: Darwin College, Univ. of Kent at Canterbury, Canterbury CT2 7NY.

Lee, Clive Howard; Lecturer in Economic History, University of Aberdeen, since 1967; *b* 1942; *m* 1966. BA Cambridge 1963, MA Cambridge 1967, MLitt Cambridge 1967. Asst Lectr, Univ. of Aberdeen, 1966–67. *Publications*: Regional Economic Growth in the United Kingdom since the 1880s, 1971; A Cotton Enterprise: M'Connel and Kennedy, Fine Cotton Spinners, 1972; *contrib.* Bus. Hist., Jl Contemp. Hist. *Address*: Dept of Economic History, King's College, Univ. of Aberdeen, Aberdeen.

Lee, David Alan, MA, PhD; Lecturer in Applied Linguistics, Language Centre, University of Kent, since 1971; *b* 1939; *m* 1965; three *d.* BA Cantab 1961 (Modern and Mediaeval Langs), MA Cantab 1964; MA Essex 1970 (Theoretical Linguistics), PhD Kent 1972, Mem., Ling. Assoc. Lectr in French, Lang. Centre, Univ. of Kent, 1965–70. *Publications*: (jtly) Le Français à travers les sciences humaines, 1972; *contrib.* Lingua, Foundations of Language. *Address*:

The Language Centre, Cornwallis Building, Univ. of Kent, Canterbury, Kent.

Lee, Dr David John; Lecturer in Sociology, University of Essex, since 1969; *b* 1938; *m* 1960; two *d.* BSc(Econ) London 1959; Dip. Industrial Sociology Liverpool 1960, PhD Birmingham 1964. Mem., Brit. Sociol Assoc. Res. Associate, Education Dept, Birmingham Univ., 1960–63; Res. Fellow, Sociological Studies, Sheffield Univ., 1963–64, Asst Lectr, then Lectr, 1964–69. *Publications*: *contrib.* Sociol. Rev., Sociol. *Address*: Dept of Sociology, Univ. of Essex, Wivenhoe Park, Colchester.

Lee, Dr Geoffrey Alan, BSc(Econ), PhD, FCA; Senior Lecturer in Accountancy, Department of Industrial Economics, Nottingham University, since 1974 (Lecturer, 1966–74); *b* 1928; *m* 1951; two *s* one *d.* BSc(Econ) London 1955 (2nd cl. (i)), PhD Sheffield 1968; ACA 1951; FCA 1962; Mem., Brit. Accounting and Finance Assoc. Hon. Auditor, 1971. Res. Register Ed., Jl Business Finance, 1968–74; Mem., Jt Stand. Cttee, Degree Studies and Acctncy Profession, 1968– ; Reg. Acad. Bd, Reg. Adv. Council for Organisation of Further Educn in E Midlands, 1968– ; Council of Depts of Acctncy Studies, 1973– ; Sec., Accounting Hist. Commn in England and Wales, 1972– . *Publications*: Transport Finance and Accounting, 1965; 2nd edn 1969; Modern Financial Accounting, 1973; *contrib.* Abacus, Acctncy, The Acctnt, Chartered Acctnt in Aust., Jl Acctncy Res., Jl Business Finance, Nott. Med. Studies, Transport Hist. *Address*: Dept of Industrial Economics, The Univ., Nottingham NG7 2RD.

Lee, Hilda Iris; Lecturer in International History, London School of Economics, since 1949; *b* 1921. BA Hons London 1942 (Hist.), MA 1949. *Publications*: Malta 1813–1914: a study in constitutional and strategic development, 1973; *contrib.* Jl Malta Hist. Soc. *Address*: London Sch. of Economics, Aldwych, WC2A 2AE.

Lee, John Michael; Senior Lecturer, Department of Politics and Sociology, Birkbeck College, London, since 1972; *b* 1932; *m* 1962; one *s* one *d.* BA Oxon 1953 (Hons History), MA, BLitt Oxon 1957; FRHistS. Lectr in Govt, Manchester Univ., 1958–67; Res. Fellow, Inst. for Strategic Studies, 1967–68; Sen. Lectr, Inst. of Commonwealth Studies, 1969–72. Temp. Principal, HM Treasury and Civil Service Dept, 1968–69. *Publications*: Social Leaders and Public Persons, 1963; Colonial Development and Good Government, 1967; African Armies and Civil Order, 1969; (with Bruce Wood) The Scope of Local Initiative, 1974. *Address*: Birkbeck College, 7/15 Gresse Street, W1A 1PA.

Lee, Michael Whittaker J.; *see* Jones-Lee.

Lee, Robert; *see* Lee, A. R.

Lee, Prof. Terence Richard, MA, PhD; FBPsS; Professor of Psychology, University

405

of Surrey, since 1971; b 1924; m 1947; two d. BA Cantab 1949, MA Cantab 1954, PhD Cantab 1954; FBPsS 1971. Res. Fellow, Exeter Univ. 1953–56; Lectr, St Andrews Univ., 1956–68; Sen. Lectr, Dundee Univ., 1968–71. Member: CNAA Psychol. Bd, 1965– ; RIBA Res. Cttee, 1968– ; Scott. Council Res. Educ., 1963–71; SSRC Psychol. Cttee, 1972– . Publications: contrib. Brit. Jl Educnl Psychol., Brit. Jl Psychol., Brit. Jl Soc. Clin. Psychol., Environ. Behav., Hum. Relat., Internat. Jl Environ. Studies, Jl Royal Coll. Gen. Practit., Occup. Psychol., Psychol. Reps. Address: Dept of Psychology, Univ. of Surrey, Guildford, Surrey GU2 5XH.

Lee, Prof. Thomas Alexander, MSc, CA, ATII; Professor of Accounting, Department of Economics, University of Liverpool, since 1973; b 1941; m 1963; one s one d. MSc Strathclyde 1969 (Accounting); CA 1964, ATII 1966. Lectr in Accountancy, Univ. Strathclyde, 1966–69; Lectr in Accounting, Univ. Edinburgh, 1969–73. Sec., Scottish Accounting History Cttee, 1971– ; Editor, Auta News Review, 1971– ; Mem. Council, Brit. Accounting and Finance Assoc., 1973– . Publications: Company Auditing: Concepts and Practices, 1972; The Funds Statement, 1974; Income and Value Measurement, 1974; contrib. Accountancy, Accountant's Mag., Accounting and Business Res., Jl Accounting Res., Jl Business Finance, Singapore Accountant, S Africa Chartered Accountant. Address: Dept of Commerce, Univ. of Liverpool, PO Box 147, Liverpool L69 3BX.

Leech, Prof. Geoffrey N.; Professor of Linguistics and Modern English Language, University of Lancaster, since 1974; b 1936; m 1961; one s one d. BA London 1956, MA London 1962, PhD London 1969; Mem., Linguistic Assoc. Gt Britain; Mem., Linguistic Soc. America; Mem., Philological Soc. Asst Lectr in English, University Coll., London, 1962–65, Lectr 1965–69; Reader in English, Lancaster, 1969–74; Harkness Fellow, MIT, 1964–65; Vis. Prof. in Linguistics, Brown Univ., 1972. Publications: English in Advertising, 1966; A Linguistic Guide to English Poetry, 1969; Towards a Semantic Description of English, 1969; Meaning and the English Verb, 1971; (jtly), A Grammar of Contemporary English, 1972; Semantics, 1974; contrib. Linguistics, Lingua, Rev. Eng. Lit., Studia Neophilologica. Address: English Dept, Univ. of Lancaster, Bailrigg, Lancaster LA1 4YT.

Leedam, Stanley Dean; Academic Registrar, Chelsea College, University of London, since 1963; b 1925; m 1956; two s one d. MA Oxon 1952. Tutor, Oxford Univ. Delegacy for Extra-Mural Studies, 1949–56; Asst Registrar, Royal Coll. of Art, 1956–58; Organiser for Further Educn, Cambs, 1958–61; Asst Sec., NCDAD, 1961–63. Address: Chelsea College, Manresa Road, SW3 6LX.

Leeming, Frank Andrew; Senior Lecturer, Department of Geography, University of Leeds, since 1953; b 1926; m 1952; one s three d. BA Cantab 1949. Lectr in Geog., Univ. of

St Andrews, 1950–53; Vis. Lectr in Geog., Chinese Univ. of Hong Kong, 1969–70. Publications: contrib. Inst. Brit. Geogrs Trans and Papers, Modern Asian Studies, Scottish Geog. Mag. Address: Dept of Geography, Univ. of Leeds, Leeds LS2 9JT.

Lees, Prof. Dennis Samuel, BSc(Econ), PhD; Professor of Industrial Economics, University of Nottingham, since 1968; b 1924; m 1950; two s one d. BSc(Econ) London 1948; PhD Nottingham 1951. Lectr, then Reader, Keele Univ., 1951–65; Prof., Swansea Univ., 1965–68; Vis. Prof., Univ. of Chicago, 1963–64, Univ. of California, Berkeley, 1971. Partner, Economists Adv. Gp. 1966– ; Chm., Nat. Insurance Adv. Council, Industrial Injuries Adv. Council. Publications: Local Expenditure and Exchequer Grants, 1956; Economics of Advertising, 1967; Financial Faculties for Small Firms, 1971; contrib. Amer. Econ. Rev., Economica, Jl Indus. Econ., Jl Law Econ., Jl Pol. Econ., Lloyds Bank Rev., Public Finance. Address: Dept of Industrial Economics, Univ. of Nottingham, Nottingham NG7 2RD.

Lees, Dr John David; Senior Lecturer, University of Keele, since 1970; b 1936; m 1964; two s. BA Oxon 1960; MA Michigan 1962; PhD Manchester 1965. Asst Lectr, Keele Univ., 1964–65; Lectr, 1965–70; Vis. Prof., Arizona State Univ., 1966; State Univ of NY, Binghamton, 1970. Publications: The Committee System of the United States Congress, 1967; The Political System of the United States, 1969; ed, Political Parties in Modern Britain, 1972; ed, Committees in Legislatures: a comparative analysis, 1975; contrib. Jl Amer. Studies, Pol Studies, Parly Aff., Public Admin, Govt and Opp. Address: Dept of American Studies, Univ. of Keele, Keele ST5 5BG.

Leeson, Dr Joyce, MB ChB, DPH; Senior Lecturer in Community Medicine, Manchester University (also teaching social sciences for Medicine), since 1971; b 1930; m; one s two d. MB ChB Manchester 1954, DPH Manchester 1958; Mem., Soc. Social Med. Res. Asst, then Asst Lectr and later Lectr, Univ. of Manchester, 1958–71; Nuffield Res. Fellow, Univ. of Zambia, 1967–68. Publications: contrib. Brit. Med. Jl., Med. Care, Med Jl Zambia, Med. Off., Med. Wld. Address: Dept of Community Medicine, Stopford Building, Oxford Road, Manchester M13 9PT.

Leff, Prof Gordon, BA, PhD, LittD; Professor of History, University of York, since 1969; b 1926; m 1953; one s. BA Cantab 1950, 1951 (1st Cl. Pts I and II Hist.), PhD Cantab 1953, LittD Cantab 1968. Fellow, King's Coll., Cambridge, 1955–59; Asst Lectr, Manchester Univ., 1956–58, Lectr, 1958–64, Sen. Lectr, 1964–65; Reader, Univ. of York, 1965–69. Publications: Bradwardine and the Pelagians, 1957; Medieval Thought, 1958; Gregory of Rimini, 1961; The Tyranny of Concepts, 1961; Richard Fitzralph, 1963; Heresy in the Later Middle Ages (2 vols), 1967; Paris and Oxford Universities in the 13th and 14th Centuries,

1968; History and Social Theory, 1969; William of Ockham, 2 vols (forthcoming); *contrib*. Bull. John Rylands Library, Etudes Augustiniennes, Jl of Eccles. Hist., Past and Present, Jl of Medieval and Renaissance Studies. *Address*: Dept of History, The Univ., Heslington, York Y01 5DD.

Legeza, Ireneus Laszlo; Deputy Curator, Gulbenkian Museum, University of Durham (also teaching in the University), since 1967; *b* 1934; *m* 1957. BA London 1960. Asst Libr., Durham Univ., 1963–67. *Publications*: Guide to Transliterated Chinese, 1968–69; MacDonald Collection of Chinese Ceramics, 1972; *contrib*. var. jls. *Address*: Gulbenkian Museum, School of Oriental Studies, Elvet Hill, Durham.

Leggatt, Dr Timothy William; Senior Tutor and Fellow of King's College, Cambridge, since 1973; *b* 1933; *m* 1964; one *s* one *d*. BA Cantab 1957 (History), MA Cantab 1960; MA Chicago 1965 (Sociology), PhD Chicago 1966; Mem., Amer. Sociol Assoc., Mem., Brit. Sociol. Assoc. Lectr, Jadavpur Univ., Calcutta, 1959; Res. Offr, PEP, 1962–64; Lectr in Sociology, Sussex, 1966–73. *Publications*: New Commonwealth Students in Britain, 1965; The Training of British Managers, 1972; ed, Sociological Theory and Survey Research, 1974. *Address*: King's College, Cambridge.

Legge, Dr David, BSc, PhD; Reader in Psychology, University of London, since 1972; *b* 1936; *m* 1959; two *s*. BSc (Special) London 1959 (1st cl. Psychology), PhD London 1965; FBPsS; Mem. EPS. Lectr, UCL, 1961–70; Prin. Lectr in Psychol., City of London Poly., 1970–71. Deptal Tutor, Univ. Coll., London, 1968–70; Hon. Sec., EPS, 1968–73. *Publications*: Skills (readings), 1970; *contrib*. Brit. Jl Pharmacol., Brit. Jl Psychol., Jl Motor Behav., Percept. Motor Skills, Psychol. Rev., Qly Jl Exper. Psychol., Qly Jl Studies Att. *Address*: Dept of Psychology, Birkbeck College, Malet Street, WC1E 7HX.

Leggett, Douglas Malcolm Aufrère, MA, DSc; Vice-Chancellor, University of Surrey, 1966–Sept. 1975; *b* 1912; *m* 1943; one *s* one *d*. BA Cantab 1934, MA Cantab 1937, PhD Cantab 1939; DSc London 1960; FRAeS, FIMA. Fellow, Trinity Coll., Cambridge, 1937; Queen Mary Coll., London, 1937–39; Royal Aircraft Establishment, 1939–45; Royal Aeronautical Soc., 1945–50; King's Coll., London, 1950–60; Principal, Battersea Coll. of Technol., 1960–66. *Publications*: *contrib*. scientific and technical jls. *Address*: Univ. of Surrey, Guildford, Surrey GU2 5XH.

Lehane, John Christopher; Senior Lecturer, School of Social Sciences (Department of Economics), New University of Ulster, since 1972; *b* 1916; *m* 1956. BCom NUI 1937, Master of Economic Science, NUI, 1938; FCCA 1972, Fellow, Soc. of Commercial Accountants, 1961. Lectr, Univ. of Bath, 1967. *Address*: School of Social Sciences, New Univ. of Ulster, Coleraine BT52 1SA.

Lehmann, Prof. Andrew George; Associate Professor, School of French Studies, Warwick University, since 1968; *b* 1922; *m* 1942; two *s* one *d*. MA Oxon, DPhil Oxon; MInstM 1970. Manchester University: Asst Lectr, 1945; Lectr, 1948–51; Prof., Univ. of Reading, 1951–68; Dean, Fac. of Letters and Social Scis, Reading, 1960–66. Vis. Prof., Univ. of Mainz, 1956–57. Member: Hale Cttee, Univ. Teaching Methods, 1961–64; UGC Hong Kong, 1965–73; Academic Planning Bd, NUU, 1965–71; European Cultural Foundn, Cultural Cttee, 1970; Chm., Industrial Council for Educnl and Trng Technol., 1974. Man. Dir, Dep. Chm., Linguaphone Inst. Ltd, 1968– . *Address*: School of French Studies, Univ. of Warwick, Coventry CV4 7AL.

le Huray, Dr Peter Geoffrey; University Lecturer in Music, since 1959, and Fellow of St Catharine's College, Cambridge University, since 1958; *b* 1930; *m* 1965; one *s* one *d*. BA Cantab 1952 (1st cl. Music), MusB Cantab 1953 (University Prize), PhD Cantab 1958. Vis. Fellow, Macalester Coll., St Paul, Minn., 1969. Editor, Proc. Royal Music. Assoc., 1962–66; Mem., Council, Royal Music Assoc., 1962– ; Editorial Cttee, Early Engl. Church Music (Brit. Acad.), 1969– ; Mem., Council, Church Music Soc., 1970– ; Pres., Inc. Assoc. Organists, 1971–72; Mem., Editorial Cttee Grove's Dictionary of Music, 1970– . BBC Recitalist; soloist at BBC Promenade Concerts. *Publications*: Music and the Reformation in England, 1967; The Treasury of English Church Music, vol. II, 1966; The Collected Anthems of Thomas Weelkes, 1966; The Sources of English Church Music, 1972; *Recording*: Liszt Variations on Weinen, klagen; and Reubke's Sonata on the 94th Psalm, for organ; *contrib*. Musical Discip., Music Lett., Music. Qly. *Address*: St Catharine's College, Cambridge.

Leifer, Dr Michael; Reader in International Relations, London School of Economics and Political Science, since 1973; *b* 1933; *m* 1955; three *s*. BA Reading 1956, PhD London 1959. Mem., Royal Inst. Internat. Affairs; Mem., Internat. Inst. Strategic Studies. Lectr in Politics, Univ. of Adelaide, 1959–63; Fellow, Centre for SE Asian Studies and Lectr in Dept of Polit. Studies, 1963–69. Part-time adviser, Res. Dept, FCO, 1967–68; Hon. Sec., Assoc. of SE Asian Studies in UK, 1972– . *Publications*: Cambodia: The Search for Security, 1967; The Philippine Claim to Sabah, 1968; ed, Nationalism, Revolution and Evolution in South-East Asia, 1970; Dilemmas of Statehood in Southeast Asia, 1972; ed, Constraints and Adjustments in British Foreign Policy, 1972; The Foreign Relations of the New States, 1974; *contrib*. Asian Affairs, Internat. Affairs, Modern Asian Studies, Pacific Affairs, Parly Affairs, Round Table. *Address*: Dept of International Relations, London School of Economics, Houghton Street, Aldwych, WC2A 2AE.

Leigh, Dr Christine M.; Lecturer, Department of Geography, University of Leeds, since 1964; *b* 1941; *m* 1972. BA Leeds 1962, PhD Leeds 1970. Vis. Asst Prof., Kansas

407

State Univ., 1967–68. *Address*: Dept of Geography, Univ. of Leeds, Leeds LS2 9JT.

Leigh, Dr Leonard Herschel; Reader in Law, London School of Economics and Political Science, since 1970; *b* 1935; *m* 1960; one *s* one *d*. BA Alberta 1957, LLB Alberta 1958; PhD London 1966; admitted to Bar, Alberta 1959, North West Territories 1961. Asst Lectr, LSE, 1964–65, Lectr, 1965–70. *Publications*: The Criminal Liability of Corporations in English Law, 1969; (with J. F. Northey) Introduction to Company Law, 1971; contrib. Annual Survey of Commonwealth Law, 1968– ; Studies in Canadian Business Law, ed G. H. L. Fridman, 1970; *contrib*. Mod. Law Rev., Ottawa Law Rev., Public Law, Univ. Toronto Law Jl. *Address*: Law Dept, London School of Economics and Political Science, Aldwych, WC2A 2AE.

Leigh, Prof. Ralph Alexander, LittD, FBA; Professor of French, University of Cambridge, since 1973; *b* 1915; *m* 1945; one *s* one *d*. BA London 1936 (1st cl.), Dip Univ Paris 1938, MA Cantab 1952, LittD Cantab 1969; FBA Mem., Bibliog. Soc., etc. Lectr, Edinburgh, 1946–52; Lectr, Cambridge, 1952–69; Reader in French, Cambridge, 1969–73; Fellow, Trinity Coll., Cambridge, 1952– ; Mem., Inst. Adv. Studies, Princeton, 1967; Leverhulme Fellow, 1959, 1970; Leverhulme Prof., Sorbonne, 1973. *Publications*: (with A. J. Steele) Contemporary French, 1956; Correspondence complète de Jean-Jacques Rousseau, vols i–xxii, 1965–74; *contrib*. Fr. Studies, Hist. Jl, Libr., Mod. Lang. Rev., Rev. Litt. Comp., Volt. Studies. *Address*: Trinity College, Cambridge.

Leighton, Prof. Kenneth, MA, DMus; Reid Professor of Music, University of Edinburgh, since 1970; *b* 1929; *m* 1953; one *s* one *d*. MA Oxon 1955, DMus Oxon 1960; LRAM. Prof. of Theory, RN Sch. of Music, 1952–53; Gregory Fellow in Music, Leeds Univ., 1953–56; Lectr in Music Composition, Edinburgh Univ., 1956–58; Lectr in Music, Oxford Univ., and Fellow of Worcester Coll., 1968–70. *Compositions*: Concertos for: piano (3); violin; cello; viola and two pianos; symphonies for: strings; orchestra; two string quartets; piano quintet; sonatas for: violin and piano (2); piano (3); partita for cello and piano; orchestral works; Burlesque, Passacaglia, Chorale and Fugue; Symphony; The Birds (chorus and strings); The Light Invisible (tenor, chorus and orchestra); Fantasia Contrappuntistica (piano); incidental music for radio and television drama; church, organ, and piano music. *Address*: Faculty of Music, Univ. of Edinburgh, Alison House, Nicolson Square, Edinburgh EH8 9BH.

Leith, George Oig Manderson, MA, ABPsS; Reader in Social and Developmental Psychology, and Director of the R. M. Phillips Research Unit, University of Sussex, since 1969; *b* 1927; *m* 1954; two *s*. BA Dunelm 1952; MA London 1954; DipEd Dunelm 1955; ABPsS, Mem., IAAP, Arbeits, Emp. Päd. Forseh., Assoc. Programmed Learning

and Educnl Technol. (Vice-Pres.). Lectr in Educn (Psychol.), then Dir, Nat. Centre for Programmed Learning, Birmingham Univ., 1962–68; Vis. Prof. of Psychol., Memorial Univ., 1968, Hon. Prof. of Psychol. and Educn; Vis. Prof., Konstanz Univ., 1971. Member: UK Nat. Comm. for UNESCO; Adv. Commn on Communications; Nat. Council for Educnl Technol.; Home Off. Programmed Learning Cttee; Mem., Adv. Cttee, Memorial Univ.; Mem., Inst. Res. on Human Abilities. *Publications*: Handbook of Programmed Learning, 1964, 2nd edn 1966; What's Programmed Learning? 1965; Second Thoughts on Programmed Learning 1969; contrib. Media and Methods in Industrial Training, 1967; Methods and Media: Instructional Technology in Higher Education, 1969; Modern Trends in Education, 1971; Aspects of Educational Technology, 1967, 1968, 1971; *contrib*. Canad. Jl Behav. Sci., Educnl, Res., Educnl Rev., Impact Sci. Soc., Jl Educnl Technol., Progr. Learning Educnl Technol., Spec. Educn, Trends Educn. *Address*: R. M. Phillips Research Unit, Sussex Univ., Falmer, Brighton BN1 9RG.

Lejewski, Prof. Czeslaw; Professor of Philosophy, University of Manchester, since 1966; *b* 1913; *m* 1949 (wife *d* 1972), *m* 1973. Mag. Fil. Warsaw 1936 (Classics); PhD London 1955 (Logic and Scientific Method); MA Manchester 1970. Asst Lectr in Philos., Manchester, 1956, Lectr, 1958; Vis. Prof., Notre Dame Univ., Indiana, 1960–61; Sen. Lectr, Manchester, 1964. *Publications: contrib*. BJPS, JSL, NDJFL, Philosophy, Ratio, Studia Logica, Synthèse. *Address*: Department of Philosophy, Univ. of Manchester, Manchester M13 9PL.

Lelievre, Frank James; The Hon. the Irish Society's Professor of Greek and Latin, New University of Ulster, since 1960; *b* 1917; *m* 1940; four *s* three *d*. BA 1939, MA 1945, Cambridge (Scholar, Magdalene Coll.). Asst Lectr, Bedford Coll., London, 1947–51; Sen. Lectr, Magee University Coll., Londonderry, 1951–60, Pres., 1968. Member: Royal Irish Acad. Greek and Latin Cttee, 1967– ; Adv. Council for Educn (NI), 1965–73; NI GCE Cttee, 1961– ; Londonderry CB Educn Cttee, 1968–73; Western Educn and Library Bd, 1973– ; Exec. Cttee, Assoc. of Educn and Library Bds, (NI), 1973– ; NI Council for Educnl Res., 1973– ; Chm., Cttee of Enquiry into Teacher Training (NI), 1970–73. *Publications*: Cory's Lucretilis, 1964; Education, Initial Training and Probation of Teachers in Northern Ireland Schools, 1973; *contrib*. Class. Phil., Euphros., Greece and Rome, Phoenix, Proc. Virgil Soc. *Address*: Magee Univ. Coll., New Univ. of Ulster, Londonderry, N Ireland.

Lello, Arthur John Ernest; University Lecturer, Department of Education, University of Cambridge, since 1973; *b* 1929; *m* 1961; three *s*. BA Sheffield 1950 (2nd cl. Hist., Philos., Econs), MA 1960 (by thesis), MA Cantab 1973; Member: Hist of Educn Soc.; Headmasters' Assoc. Asst Tutor, Oxford Dept of Educn, 1959–62; Tutor (part-time), Cardiff Dept of Educn, 1962–66;

Housemaster, Atlantic Coll., 1962–66; Head-master, Tiverton Grammar Sch., Devon, 1966–73. *Publications*: Official View of Education, 1964; contrib. Techniques of Teaching, ed A. D. C. Peterson, 1965. *Address*: Cambridge Dept of Education, 17 Brookside, Cambridge.

Le May, Godfrey Hugh Lancelot; Fellow and Tutor of Worcester College, Oxford and University Lecturer in Politics, since 1968; *b* 1920; *m* 1963; one *d*. BA Rhodes 1942, BA Oxon 1950 (1st cl. Mod. Hist.), Gladstone Meml Prize, 1951, MA Oxon 1954. Lectr in History, Rhodes UC, 1947–48; Lectr in Politics, Balliol Coll., Oxford, 1951–53; Prof. of Political Studies, Witwatersrand Univ., 1953–67; Dean of Faculty of Arts and Mem. Council, Witwatersrand Univ., 1964–67; Vis. Prof., Univ. of S Carolina, 1976. *Publications*: British Government, 1914–1953: Select Documents, 1955, 2nd edn 1964; British Supremacy in South Africa, 1899–1907, 1965; Black and White in South Africa, 1971; *contrib*. SA Law Jl, SA Jl Econs, History Today, Annual Survey of SA Law. *Address*: Worcester College, Oxford.

Lemon, Dr Nigel; Lecturer in Social Psychology, University of Sussex, since 1967; *b* 1939; *m* 1965; one *s* one *d*. BSc Hull 1961, PhD Hull 1968; Member: British Psychological Soc., European Assoc. Experimental Social Psychology. Lectr, Sociology, Univ. Exeter, 1965–67. *Publications*: Attitudes and their Measurement, 1973; *contrib*. British Jl Social and Clinical Psychology, British Jl Criminol. *Address*: Arts Building, Univ. of Sussex, Falmer, Brighton BN1 9RH.

Leng, Dr Ivor John, BA, PhD; Senior Lecturer in Education, and Sub-Dean, Faculty of Arts, University College of North Wales, Bangor, since 1969; *b* 1917; *m* 1942; two *s* one *d*. BA Wales 1938 (1st cl. French), DipEd Wales 1939, PhD Wales 1965. Lectr in Educn, Univ. Coll. of N Wales, Bangor, 1955–69. *Publications*: Children in the Library, 1969. *Address*: Dept of Education, Univ. College of North Wales, Bangor LL57 2DG.

Lenman, Bruce Philip; Lecturer in Scottish History, University of St Andrews, since 1972; *b* 1938; *m* 1967; one *s* one *d*. MA Aberdeen 1960 (1st cl. History), MLitt Cantab 1964; FSA (Scot.). Asst Prof., Victoria Univ., Brit. Columbia, 1963; Lectr, Univ. of St Andrews, Queen's Coll., Dundee, 1963–67; Lectr, Univ. of Dundee, 1967–72. Mem., Council, Soc. Antiquaries Scott., 1969–71; Mem., Editorial Cttee, Proc. Soc. Antiquaries Scott., 1970–73; Mem., Council, Scott. Hist. Soc., 1969–73; Mem., Council, Scott. Soc. Indust. Archaeol., 1969–72; Mem., Council Business Archives Council Scott., 1966–72; Mem., Directorate, Nat. Registrar of Archives (Scott.), 1971–72. *Publications*: (with C. Lythe and E. Gauldie) Dundee and its Textile Industry 1850–1914, 1969; Ports of the Forth and Tay, 1974; *contrib*. Business Hist., Indust. Archaeol., Jl Soc. Army Hist. Res., Newsl. Business Archiv. Council Scotl., Scot. Hist. Rev., Town Plan. Rev. *Address*: St Salvator's College, Univ. of St Andrews, St Andrews, Fife KY16 9AJ.

Leonard, Prof. Peter; Professor of Applied Social Studies, University of Warwick, since 1973; *b* 1930; *m* 1954; one *s* two *d*. BSc(Econ) London 1952, MSc(Econ) London 1956, Dip. in Mental Health, LSE 1962. Various appointments in social work practice, 1952–62; Lectr in Social Science, Univ. Liverpool, 1963–66; Lectr, Sen. Lectr and (from 1969) Director of Social Work Education, Nat. Inst. for Social Work, London, 1966–73. Mem. Seebohn Cttee on Local Authority and Allied Personal Social Services, 1966–68. *Publications*: Sociology in Social Work, 1966; *contrib*. British Jl of Psychiatric Social Work, British Jl of Sociology, Sociological Rev. Monograph. *Address*: Dept of Applied Social Studies, Univ. of Warwick, Coventry CV4 7AL.

Le Page, Prof. Robert Brock, BA, PhD; Professor of Language, University of York, since 1964; *b* 1920; *m* 1942; one *s* two *d*. BA Oxon 1948 (2nd cl. English Lit.); PhD Birmingham 1952; Mem., Linguistic Soc. of America, Mem., Linguistics Assoc. of GB, Mem., Philological Soc. Res. Fellow, Birmingham Univ., 1948–50; Asst Lectr, Lectr, Reader, Dept of English, UC, West Indies, 1950–60; Prof. of English, Univ. of Malaya, 1960–64; Provost of Vanbrugh Coll., Univ. of York, 1967–72; Smith-Mundt and Fulbright Fellowship, Univ. of Michigan, 1953; Vis. Lectr, Univ. of Wisconsin, 1956; Vis. Prof., Univ. of Pittsburgh, 1958; Vis. Prof., Univ. of Michigan, 1967. *Publications*: Creole Language Studies, vol. I 1960, vol. II 1961; The Language Barrier, 1962; The National Language Question, 1964, repr. 1966, 1971; (with F. G. Cassidy) Dictionary of Jamaican English, 1967; contrib. to Language Problems of Developing Nations, 1968; *contrib*. Caribbean Qly, English Studies, English and Germanic Studies, Jl of English and Germanic Philol., Jl of Lings, La Linguistique, Lang. in Society, Trans Philol Soc., York Papers in Linguistics. *Address*: Dept of Language, Univ. of York, Heslington, York YO1 5DD.

Le Patourel, (Hilda E.) Jean; Lecturer, Extra-mural Department, University of Leeds, since 1967; *b* 1915; *m* 1939; three *s* one *d*. BA London 1938, DipEd London 1939; FSA 1960; Member: Soc. Medieval Archaeol.; British Archaeol Assoc.; Royal Archaeol Inst. *Publications*: The Moated Sites of Yorkshire, 1973; *contrib*. Antiquaries Jl, Château Gaillard, Medieval Archaeol., Trans. Soc. Guernesaise, Trans Thoresby Soc., Yorks Archaeol Jl. *Address*: Univ. of Leeds, Leeds LS2 9JT.

Lepper, Francis Alfred; Fellow and Tutor in Ancient History, Corpus Christi College, Oxford University, since 1939; *b* 1913; *m* 1939; one *s* one *d*. BA Oxon 1936 (1st cl. Classical Mods, 1st cl. Lit. Hum.), MA Oxon 1939. Lectr, New Coll., Oxford, 1937–39; CUF Lectr in Ancient Hist., Oxford, 1947– . Editor, JRS, 1964–68; Chairman: Editorial Cttee, Soc. Prom. Roman Studies, 1969– ; Fac. of Archaeol.,

Hist. and Lett., Brit. Sch. Rome, 1971– .
Publications: Trajan's Parthian War, 1948;
contrib. Jl Hell. Studies, Jl Rom. Studies, etc.
Address: Corpus Christi College, Oxford.

Lerner, Prof. Laurence David, MA;
Professor of English, University of Sussex,
since 1970; *b* 1925; *m* 1948; four *s*. BA Cape
Town, 1944 (distinction in English and
Latin), MA Cape Town 1945 (1st cl. Hons
Eng. Lit.); BA Cantab 1949 (1st cl. Hons).
Lectr, UC of Gold Coast, 1949–53; Lectr,
QUB, 1953–62 (Extra-Mural, 1953–57.
English, 1957–62); Lectr, 1962–64, Sen.
Lectr, 1964–66, Reader, 1966–70, Univ. of
Sussex; John Hay Whitney Vis. Fellow, USA,
1960–61; Vis. Prof., Univ. of Illinois, 1964,
Univ. of New Mexico, 1967. Univ. of
Munich, 1968–69, 1974–75. *Publications*:
English Literature: an introduction for
students abroad, 1954; The Englishmen
(novel), 1959; Domestic Interior (poems),
1959; The Truest Poetry: an essay on the
question, What is Literature?, 1960; The
Directions of Memory (poems), 1964; The
Truthtellers: Jane Austen, George Eliot,
D. H. Lawrence, 1967; A Free Man (novel),
1968; Selves (poems), 1969; The Uses of
Nostalgia: studies in pastoral poetry, 1972;
Hardy's Mayor of Casterbridge: tragedy or
social history, 1974; Arthur: The Life and
Opinions of a Digital Computer (poems),
1974; An Introduction to English Poetry,
1975; *contrib.* Critical Qly, Essays in Criti-
cism, JEGP, London Mag., Encounter.
Address: Arts Building, Univ. of Sussex,
Falmer, Brighton BN1 9QN.

Le Sage, David Ernest; Lecturer in Germanic Studies, Sheffield University, since
1968; *b* 1944; *m* 1967; one *d*. BA Hons London 1967 (German); Member: Linguistics
Assoc. of GB; Philol Soc. *Publications*: *contrib.*
Mod. Lang. Rev., Amsterdamer Beiträge
zur älteren Germanistik, German Life and
Letters. *Address*: Dept of Germanic Studies,
Univ. of Sheffield, Sheffield S10 2TN.

Leser, Prof. Conrad Emanuel Victor;
Professor of Econometrics, School of
Economic Studies, University of Leeds,
since 1967; *b* 1915; *m* 1950; two *s* two *d*. Dr
phil Zürich 1939, MSc(Econ) London 1941;
FSS, Mem., Economet. Soc. Lectr, Univ. of
Glasgow, 1947–56; Sen. Lectr, Australian
Nat. Univ., 1956–61; Res. Prof., Econ. Res.
Inst., Dublin, 1961–67. Sen. Indust. Develop.
Offr, UN, 1966–67. *Publications*: (with J. R.
Hicks and U. K. Hicks) The Problem of
Valuation for Rating, 1944; Some Aspects of
the Industrial Structure of Scotland, 1951;
contrib. The Scottish Economy, 1954;
Econometric Techniques and Problems,
1966; *contrib.* Austral. Jl Stats, Bull. Econ.
Res., Economet., Econ. Jl, Jl Amer. Stat.
Assoc., Jl Roy. Stat. Soc., Jl Stat. Soc.
Enquiry Soc. Ireland, Populat. Studies, Rev.
Econ. Studies, Scott. Jl Pol Econ. *Address*:
School of Economic Studies, Univ. of Leeds,
Leeds LS2 9JT.

Leslie, Margaret Ruth C.; Lecturer, De-
partment of Spanish, University of St
Andrews, since 1967; *b* 1938. BA Oxon 1960,
MA Oxon 1964, BLitt Oxon, 1966; Mem.,

Assoc. of British Hispanists. Asst, St
Andrews Univ., 1963–67. *Publications*: *contrib.*
Studia Neophilologica. *Address*: Dept of
Spanish, St Salvator's College, St Andrews,
Fife.

Leslie, Robert Dunbar; Lecturer, Depart-
ment of Scots Law, University of Edinburgh,
since 1969; *b* 1935; *m* 1959; two *s*. BA Cape
Town 1954, LLB Cape Town 1956, LLM
Cape Town 1963; Advocate, Rhodesia 1959,
Advocate, Lesotho 1964. Lectr, then Sen.
Lectr in Law, Univ. of Botswana, Lesotho
and Swaziland, 1964–66; Lectr, Dept of
Civil and Comparative Law, Edinburgh
Univ., 1967–69. Law Off., and other posts,
Dept of Justice, Rhodesian Govt. 1957–63.
Address: Dept of Scots Law, Edinburgh
Univ., Old College, South Bridge, Edinburgh
EH8 9YL.

Leslie, Prof. Robert Frank, BA, PhD,
FRHistS; Professor of Modern History since
1964, and Head of Department, Queen Mary
College, University of London, since 1970;
b 1918; *m* 1942; two *d*. BA London 1948 (1st
cl. History), PhD London 1951; Officer's
Cross of the Order of Polonia Restituta 1969,
FRHistS. Asst Lectr, then Lectr, and Reader,
Queen Mary Coll., 1951–64. Dean, Fac. of
Arts, Queen Mary Coll., 1967–70; Governor,
Queen Mary Coll., 1970–73. *Publications*:
Polish Politics and the Revolution of Novem-
ber 1830, 1956, 2nd edn 1969; Reform and
Insurrection in Russian Poland, 1856–1865,
1963, 2nd edn 1969; The Age of Trans-
formation, 1964, American pbk edn 1964,
rev. edn 1969; The Polish Question, 1966,
rev edn, 1971; *contrib.* Kwart. Hist., Przeg.
Hist., Slav. Rev., etc. *Address*: Dept of
History, Queen Mary College, Mile End
Road, E1 4NS.

Lesser, Anthony Harry; Lecturer, Department of Philosophy, University of Manchester, since 1970; *b* 1943; *m* 1973. BA Oxon
1965 (PPE), BPhil Oxon 1967 (Philosophy);
Mem., AUT. Lecturer in Philosophy: Univ.
of Chicago, 1967–69; Univ. of Aberdeen,
1969–70. *Publications*: *contrib.* Philosophical
Qly. *Address*: Dept of Philosophy, Univ. of
Manchester, Manchester M13 9PL.

Lessnoff, Michael Harry; Lecturer, De-
partment of Politics, University of Glasgow,
since 1966; *b* 1940. MA Glasgow 1963 (1st
cl. Politics and Political Economy); BPhil
Oxon 1965 (Politics); Mem., Pol Studies
Assoc. *Publications*: The Structure of Social
Science, 1974; *contrib.* Philos. Qly, Pol
Studies, Sociol Rev. *Address*: Dept of
Politics, Univ. of Glasgow, Glasgow G12
8QQ.

Letwin, William, PhD; Reader in Political
Science, with special reference to the government and politics of the USA, London
School of Economics, since 1966; *b* 1922;
m 1944; one *s*. BA Chicago 1943 (Econs),
PhD Chicago 1951. Teaching Asst, Economics Dept, Cornell Univ., 1946; Res.
Associate, Law Sch., Univ. of Chicago,
1952–55; Asst Prof., and Associate Prof. of
Economic Hist., MIT, 1955–66. Chm., Bd
of Studies in Economics, Univ. of London,

1972. *Publications*: Sir Josiah Child, Merchant Economist, 1959; Documentary History of American Economic Policy since 1789, 1961, 2nd edn 1972; The Origins of Scientific Economics, 1963; Law and Economic Policy in America: Evolution of the Sherman Act, 1965; *contrib*. Daed., Univ. Chic. Law Rev., Yale Law Jl. *Address*: Dept of Government, London School of Economics, Houghton Street, Aldwych, WC2A 2AE.

Lever, Jeremy Frederick, QC; Fellow, All Souls College, Oxford (Faculty of Law), since 1957; *b* 1933. MA Oxon 1956 (1st cl. Law). Barrister-at-Law, Gray's Inn, 1957. Trustee, Oxford Union Soc., 1972; Dir, (non-exec.), Dunlop Holdings Ltd. *Publications*: The Law of Restrictive Practices and Resale Price Maintenance, 1964; Asst Editor, Chitty on Contracts, 22nd edn 1961 and 23rd edn 1961 and 1968. *Address*: All Souls College, Oxford.

Lever, Dr William; Lecturer in Urban Studies, Department of Social and Economic Research, University of Glasgow, since 1968; *b* 1943; *m* 1969; one *s* one *d*. BA Oxon 1964 (1st cl. Hons), MA Oxon 1967, DPhil Oxon 1969. Asst Tutor, St Peter's Coll., Oxford, 1965–67; Asst Lectr, Glasgow Univ., 1967–68. Review Editor, Urban Studies, 1973. *Publications*: (with J. Forbes *et al.*) Studies in Social Science and Planning, 1974; *contrib*. Jl Roy. Town Plann. Inst., Land Econs, Regional Studies, Scott. Jl Polit. Econ., Trans Inst. Brit. Geogrs, Urban Studies. *Address*: Adam Smith Building, Univ. of Glasgow, Glasgow G12 8RT.

Levi, Prof. A. H. T., MA, DPhil; Buchanan Professor of French, University of St Andrews, since 1971; *b* 1929; *m* 1972. BA Oxon 1958, DPhil Oxon 1963. Tutor, Campion Hall, Oxford, 1964–71; Lectr, Christ Church Oxford, 1966–71; Reader, 1967–70, Personal chair, 1970–71, Warwick. *Publications*: French Moralists: the theory of the passions, 1585–1649, 1964; Religion in Practice, 1966 (Polish 1968, Italian 1967); ed, Humanism in France, 1970; Erasmus: The Praise of Folly (introd. and notes), 1971; numerous articles on 16th and 17th-cent. French literature. *Address*: Buchanan Building, Union Street, St Andrews, Fife.

Levick, Barbara Mary, MA, DPhil, FSA; Fellow and Tutor in Literae Humaniores, St Hilda's College, University of Oxford, since 1959, and Lecturer in St Hugh's College, Oxford, since 1966; *b* 1931. BA Oxon 1954 (1st cl. Lit. Hum.), MA Oxon 1957, DPhil Oxon 1959; Mem., Roman Soc., Mem., Class. Assoc., Mem., Brit. Inst. Archaeol., Ankara, FRNS. Libr., St Hilda's Coll., Oxford, 1956, Lectr, 1957–59. Mem., Council, Rom. Soc., 1971–73; Governor, Henley Grammar Sch., 1969– . *Publications*: Roman Colonies in Southern Asia Minor, 1967; *contrib*. Anatol. Studies, Class. Qly, Class. Rev., Historia, Jl Rom. Studies, Latomus. *Address*: St Hilda's College, Oxford OX4 1DY.

Levick, Christopher Charles K.; *see* Kenny-Levick.

Levin, Jennifer; Senior Lecturer in Laws, Queen Mary College, University of London, since 1972; *b* 1940; *m* 1960; one *s*. LLB 1961, LLM 1963, London. Barrister-at-Law, Gray's Inn. Part-time Lectr, UCL, 1962–64; Lectr, QMC, 1965–72. *Publications*: The Charter Controversy in the City of London 1660–1688, 1969; *contrib*. Mod. Law Rev., Conveyancer, Family Law. *Address*: Queen Mary Coll., Mile End Road, E1 4NS.

Levin, Dr Michael Martin John; Lecturer in Political Science, University College of Wales, Aberystwyth, since 1968; *b* 1940; *m* 1968; two *d*. BA Leicester 1964 (Soc. Scis), MScEcon London 1965 (Polit. Thought), PhD Leicester 1971; Mem., Polit. Studies Assoc. Tutorial Asst in Politics, Leicester, 1965–66; Temp. Asst Lectr in Politics, Leeds, 1966–67. Asst Lectr, UCW Aberystwyth, 1967–68. *Publications*: *contrib*. Dic. Hist. Ideas, Jl Hist. Ideas, Polit. Science Qly, Polit. Studies. *Address*: Dept of Political Science, Univ. Coll. of Wales, Aberystwyth, Aberystwyth SY23 3DB.

Levitt, John Henry, BA, JP; Senior Lecturer, Department of Adult Education, University of Keele, since 1971; *b* 1923; *m* 1950; one *s* one *d*. BA Manchester 1949 (2nd cl. English). Staff Tutor, Oxford Univ. Delegacy for Extra-Mural Studies, 1955–61; Lectr, Dept of Extra-Mural Studies, Univ. of Keele, 1961–71. JP, 1967– . *Publications*: (with J. Levitt) The Spell of Words, 1959; (with C. S. Davies) What's In a Name, 1970; *contrib*. Adult Educn. *Address*: Dept of Adult Education, Univ. of Keele, Keele ST5 5BG.

Levy, Prof. Philip Marcus, BA, PhD, FBPsS; Professor of Psychology, University of Lancaster, since 1972; *b* 1934; *m*; two *d*. BA Leeds 1955 (2nd cl. Psychology), PhD Birmingham 1960; FBPsS. Mem., Brit. Psychol Soc., Amer. Psychol Assoc., Psychomet. Soc. Res. Fellow, Birmingham, 1956–59. Sen. Res. Fellow, 1962; Lectr, 1963–69; Sen. Lectr, Birmingham, 1969–72. Mem., Council, Brit. Psychol. Soc., 1969, 1973– . Editor, Brit. Jl Math. Stat. Psychol., 1974– . *Publications*: *contrib*. Bull. Brit. Psychol Soc., Brit. Jl Educnl Psychol., Brit. Jl Stat. Psychol., Jl Clin. Psychol., Psychol. Bull. *Address*: Dept of Psychology, Univ. of Lancaster, Bailrigg, Lancaster LA1 4YW.

Lewes, Frederick Martin Meredith, BSc(Econ), MA; Senior Lecturer, Economic and Social Statistics Department, Exeter University, since 1971; *b* 1922; *m* 1945; one *s* three *d*. BSc(Econ) London External 1958, MA Exeter 1964; FRSSF. Lectr, Exeter, 1960–71. RN, 1939–59; Mem., Exeter City Council, 1966– . *Publications*: Statistics of the British Economy, 1967; (with G. A. Brady and A. Culyer) The Holiday Industry in Devon and Cornwall, 1969; (with G. A. Brady) Holidays in Britain, 1970. *Address*: Dept of Economics, Univ. of Exeter, Exeter EX4 4QJ.

Lewin, Dr John; Lecturer in Geography, University College of Wales, Aberystwyth, since 1968; *b* 1940; *m* 1966; two *d*. BA

Southampton 1962. PhD Southampton 1966; FRGS. Tutor, Univ. of Hull, 1965–66. Asst Lectr, 1966–68; Vis. Associate Prof., Univ. of Colorado, 1973. *Address*: Dept of Geography, Univ. College of Wales, Penglais, Aberystwyth.

Lewin, Moshe, BA, Doct en Hist; Reader in Soviet History and Politics, Centre for Russian and East European Studies and Department of Politics, University of Birmingham, since 1968; *b* 1921. BA Tel Aviv 1961, Doct en Hist Paris 1964. Dir d'Etudes suppléant, Ecole Pratique des Hautes Etudes, Paris, 1964; Sen. Fellow, Columbia Univ., NY, 1967–68; Mem., Inst. Adv. Study, Princeton, 1972–73. *Publications*: La Paysannerie et le Pouvoir Soviétique, 1966, English trans. Peasant and Soviet Power, 1968, American edn 1969, Italian trans. 1971, Japanese trans. 1972; Le dernier Combat de Lenine, 1967, English trans. Lenin's Last Struggle, and 6 other translations; Political Undercurrents in Soviet Economic Debates, 1974; *contrib*. Cah. Monde Russe Sov., Sov. Studies, Slavic Rev., Jl Interdisciplinary Hist. *Address*: Centre for Russian and East European Studies, Univ. of Birmingham, PO Box 363, Birmingham B15 2TT.

Lewis, Aneirin, MA; Senior Lecturer in Welsh, University College, Cardiff, since 1970; *b* 1924; *m* 1955; one *s* one *d*. BA Wales 1946 (1st cl. Welsh 1947), MA Wales 1950. Keeper of Salisbury Libr., Univ. Coll., Cardiff, 1948–57; Lectr, Dept of Welsh, 1957–70. Mem., Council, Welsh Bibliog. Soc.; Sec., Ymddiriedolaeth Bryn Taf, 1968– . *Publications*: ed, The Correspondence of Thomas Percy and Evan Evans (vol. V The Percy Letters), 1957; ed, E. Wynne: Gweledigaetheu y Bardd Cwsc (1703), 1960; ed, G. J. Williams: Agweddau ar Hanes Dysg Gymraeg, 1969; *contrib*. Efryd. Athron., Jl Welsh Bibliog. Soc., Llên Cymru. *Address*: Dept of Welsh, Univ. College, Cathays Park, Cardiff CF1 1XL.

Lewis, Prof. Bernard, BA, PhD, FBA; Professor of the History of the Near and Middle East, University of London, since 1949; *b* 1916; *m* 1947; one *s* one *d*. BA London 1936, PhD London 1939; FBA 1963; Corresp. Fellow, Inst. d'Egypte, Cairo, 1969; Hon. Fellow, Turkish Hist. Soc.; Foreign Mem., Amer. Philosophical Soc. Teacher, Univ. of London 1938– (war service 1940–45); Vis. Prof. of Hist., Univ. of California, Los Angeles, 1955–56;Columbia Univ., 1960; Indiana Univ., 1963; Class of 1932 Lectr, Princeton Univ.,1964; Vis. Mem., Inst. Adv. Study, Princeton, 1969. *Publications*: The Origins of Ismā'ilism, 1940; Turkey Today, 1940; British Contributions to Arabic Studies, 1941; Handbook of Diplomatic and Political Arabic, 1947, 2nd edn 1956; ed, Land of Enchanters, 1948; The Arabs in History, 1950, 5th rev. edn 1970; Notes and Documents from the Turkish Archives, 1952; The Emergence of Modern Turkey, 1961, rev. edn 1968; The Kingly Crown (trans. from Ibn Gabirol), 1961; ed (with P. M. Holt), Historians of the Middle East, 1962; Istanbul and the Civilization of the Ottoman Empire, 1963; The Middle East and the West, 1964; The Assassins, 1967; Race and Colour in Islam, 1971; Islam in History, 1973; ed, with others: Encyclopaedia of Islam, 1956– ; The Cambridge History of Islam, 1970; *contrib*. Bull. SOAS, Encounter, For. Aff., Internat. Aff., Mid. East. Studies, Studia Islam. *Address*: School of Oriental and African Studies, Malet Street, WC1E 7HP.

Lewis, Prof. Brian Noel; Professor of Applied Educational Sciences, Institute of Educational Technology, Open University, since 1970; *b* 1929. BSc London 1957 (Psychology). Dep. Dir, Sociological Research Unit, Univ. London Inst. Educn, 1966–68. Trustee, Community Development Trust, 1968– . *Publications*: various on research methodology, and teaching and learning and communication systems. *Address*: The Open Univ., Milton Keynes, MK7 6AA.

Lewis, Ceri Williams, BA, FSA, FRHistS; Reader in Welsh Language and Literature, University College, Cardiff, since 1973; *b* 1926; *m* 1956; one *s*. BA Wales 1952 (1st cl. Welsh), BA Wales 1953 (2nd cl. Hist.); FSA, FRHistS 1968. Asst Lectr, Univ. Coll., Cardiff, 1953–56, Lectr, 1956–65, Sen. Lectr, 1965–73; Mem., Univ. of Wales Bd of Celtic Studies, 1957– ; Atlas of Wales Cttee, 1965– ; Arthur. Soc. GB, 1972– . *Publications*: *contrib*. Archaeol. Camb., Glam. Co. Hist., Llên Cymru, Morgannwg, Studia Celt., Welsh Hist. Rev. *Address*: Dept of Welsh, Univ. College, Cathays Park, Cardiff CF1 1XL.

Lewis, Dr Colin A.; College Lecturer in Geography, University College, Dublin, since 1971; *b* 1942; *m* 1966; two *s*. BA Wales 1962; PhD NUI 1966; Mem., Geog. Soc. Ireland. Jun. Lectr, Univ. Coll., Dublin, 1964–67, Lectr, 1967–71. Hon. Sec., Geog., Soc. Ireland, 1969–72, Mem., Cttee, 1966–69; Mem. Subcttee on Teaching Geog. in Ireland, 1970– ; Subcttee for the div. of Irish Pleistocene, 1969–72; Convener, Working Gp on Field Study Centres in Ireland, 1973– ; Mem., Nat. Cttee for Geog., 1973– . *Publications*: ed, The Glaciations of Wales and adjoining regions, 1970; *contrib*. Biul. Peryglac., Brycheiniog, Geog. Jl, Geog. View., Irish Geog., Nature. *Address*: Geography Dept, Univ. College, Dublin 4.

Lewis, Colin Merritt, BA; Lecturer in Latin American Economic History, held jointly at London School of Economics and Institute of Latin American Studies, since 1970; *b* 1944; *m* 1971. BA (SS) Exeter. Res. Asst to Dir of Inst. of Latin American Studies, Univ. of London, 1968–71. *Publications*: *contrib*. Transport Hist., Inter-American Econ. Affairs. *Address*: Dept of Economic History, LSE, Houghton Street, Aldwych, WC2A 2AE.

Lewis, Dr David Malcolm, FBA; Student and Tutor in Ancient History, Christ Church, Oxford, since 1955; Faculty Lecturer in Greek Epigraphy, Oxford University, since

412

1957; b 1928; m 1958; four d. BA Oxon 1949, MA Oxon 1952, PhD Princeton 1952; FBA 1973; Mem., Hellenic and Roman Socs. Jun. Research Fellow, Corpus Christi College, Oxford, 1954–55. *Publications*: (with John Gould) A. W. Pickard-Cambridge: Dramatic Festivals of Athens, 2nd edn 1968; (with Russell Meiggs) Greek Historical Inscriptions, 1969; *contrib*. BSA, Hesperia, Historia, JHS, Num. Chron. *Address*: Christ Church, Oxford.

Lewis, Geinor (Guy) Bevan, BSc, FRGS; University Cartographer (Academic), Department of Geography, University College of Swansea, since 1965; b 1929; m 1956; one s. BSc Wales 1950, Teaching Dip Wales 1951; FRGS 1961. Mem., Geog. Assoc., Brit. Cartog. Soc., Soc. Univ. Cartog. Schoolmaster, Rhondda Educn Cttee, 1953–59; Asst Master for Geography, Mount Grace Comp. Sch., Potters Bar, 1959–65. Asst Editor, Cartog. Jl; Mem., Edit. Cttee, Brit. Cartog. Soc.; Co-opted Mem., Council, BSC, 1970– . *Publications*: *contrib*. Bull. Soc. Univ. Cartog., Canadian Cartog., Cartog. Jl, Bull. Geog. and Map Div. SLA, Amer. Geog. Soc. *Address*: Dept of Geography, Univ. College of Swansea, Swansea SA2 8PP.

Lewis, Dr Geoffrey Lewis, MA, DPhil; Senior Lecturer in Turkish, Faculty of Oriental Studies, Oxford, since 1964; Fellow, St Antony's College, since 1961; b 1920; m 1941; one s one d. BA and MA 1945, BA 1947, DPhil 1950, Oxon; FRAS, Fellow, Brit. Soc for ME Studies. Lectr in Islamic Studies, 1950–56, Sen. Lectr, 1956–64; Dir, Bilingual Humanities Project, Robert Coll., Istanbul, 1959–60; Vis. Prof., Robert Coll., 1960–68; Sen. Fellow, Council of Humanities, and Vis. Prof., Princeton, 1970–71. Trustee, Gibb Memorial Trust, 1959; Member: Council of Management, Brit. Inst. of Archaeol. in Ankara, 1962; Council, Brit. Soc. ME Studies, 1973. *Publications*: Teach Yourself Turkish, 1953; Turkey, 1955, 4th edn 1974; The Balance of Truth, 1957; Plotiniana Arabica in Plotini Opera II, 1959; Turkish Grammar, 1967, 2nd edn 1974; (with M. S. Spink) Albucasis on Surgery and Instruments, 1973; The Book of Dede Korkut, 1974. *Address*: Oriental Inst., Pusey Lane, Oxford.

Lewis, G(raham) Malcolm, MSc; Senior Lecturer, Department of Geography, University of Sheffield, since 1967; b 1930; m 1966; one d. BSc Sheffield 1952 (1st cl. Geog.), MSc Sheffield 1954. Whitbeck Fellow, Univ. of Wisconsin, 1954–55; Brit. Assoc. Amer. Studies Fellow, Univ. of Nebraska and Univ. of Denver, 1962–63; Vis. Prof., Pennsylvania State Univ., 1965 and 1967. *Publications*: *contrib*. Ann. Assoc. Amer. Geogs, E Mid. Geogr, Geog., Gt Plains Jl, Jl West, Trans Inst. Brit. Geogrs. *Address*: Dept of Geography, The Univ., Sheffield S10 2TN.

Lewis, Prof. Hywel David; Professor of the History and Philosophy of Religion, University of London, King's College, since 1955; b 1910; m 1st 1943 (widowed 1962), 2nd 1965. BA Wales 1932 (1st cl. Hons Philosophy), MA Wales 1934; BLitt Oxon 1935; Hon. DD

St Andrews; Mem., Mind Assoc. (Pres., 1948–49), Aristot. Soc. (Pres., 1962–63), Soc. Study Theol. (Pres., 1964–66), Chm., Council, Royal Inst. Philos. 1964– ; Mem., Oxf. Soc. Hist. Theol. (Pres., 1970), Lond. Soc. Study Religion (Pres., 1969–70), Inst. of Religion and Theology of GB and Ire. (Pres.1973–75), Internat. Soc. for Metaphysics (Pres., 1973–). Prof. of Philosophy, Univ. Coll., Bangor, 1947–55; Leverhulme Fellow, 1954–55; FKC; Vis. Professor: Bryn Mawr Coll., 1958–59; Harvard Divinity Sch., 1963; Yale, and Fellow, Jonathan Edwards Coll., 1964; Miami Univ. and Boston Univ., 1968–69. Gifford Lectr, Edinburgh, 1966–67, 1967–68; Wilde Lectr, Oxford, 1960–63; Edward Cadbury Lectr, Birmingham, 1962–63; Ker Lectr, Ontario, 1964; McCahan Lectr, Belfast, 1960; Owen Evans Lectr, Wales, 1964–65; Firth Lectr, Nottingham, 1966; Hobhouse Memorial Lectr, London, 1966–68; Elton Lectr, George Washington Univ., 1965; Otis Lectr, Wheaton Coll., Mass., 1969; Drew Lectr for 1973, London; Dean: Fac. of Theology, Univ. of London, 1964–68; Fac. of Arts, King's Coll., 1966–68; Fac. of Theology, King's Coll., 1970–72; Chm., Special Adv. Cttee in Religious Studies; Mem., Central Adv. Council for Educn (Wales), 1963–66; Editor: Muirhead Library of Philosophy; Religious Studies. *Publications*: Morals and the New Theology, 1947; Morals and Revelation, 1951; ed, Contemporary British Philosophy, vol. III, 1956; Our Experience of God, 1959, pbk edn 1970; Freedom and History, 1962; ed, Clarity is not Enough, 1962; Teach Yourself the Philosophy of Religion, 1965; (with R. L. Slater) World Religions, 1966; Dreaming and Experience, 1968; The Elusive Mind (Gifford Lectures), 1969; The Self and Immortality, 1973; Gwerinaeth, 1940; (with Dr. J. A. Thomas) Y Wladwriaeth a'i Hawdurdod, 1943; Ebyrth, 1943; Diogelu Dwylliant, 1945; Crist a Heddwch, 1947; Dilyn Crist, 1951; Gwybod am Dduw, 1952; Hen a Newydd, 1972; *contrib*. Analysis, Ethics, Hibbert Jl, Jl Theol Studies, Mind, Monist, Philos. Qly, Philos., Proc. Aristot. Soc., etc; *Address*: Univ. of London, King's College, Strand, WC2R 2LS.

Lewis, Prof. Ioan Myrddin; Professor of Anthropology, London School of Economics, since 1969; b 1930; m 1954; one s three d. BSc Glasgow 1951; Anthropology Dip Oxon 1952, BLitt Oxon 1953, DPhil Oxon 1957; FRAI; Mem., Internat. Afr. Inst., Assoc. Social Anthropol. Lectr, Univ. Coll. Rhodesia and Nyasaland, 1957–60; Lectr, Glasgow Univ., 1960–63; Lectr, UCL, 1963–66, Reader, 1966–69; Malinowski Meml Lectr, 1966. Council Mem., RAI, 1965–73; Hon. Sec., Assoc. Social Anthropol., 1964–67; Cnsltnt, Afr. Res. Ltd, 1964– ; Mem., Anthropol. Cttee, SSRC, 1969–73; Hon. Editor, Man, Jl Royal Anthropol Inst., 1970–73. *Publications*: Peoples of the Horn of Africa, 1955, 2nd edn 1969; A Pastoral Democracy, 1961, 4th edn 1970; (with B. W. Andrzejewski) Somali Poetry, 1964, 2nd end 1969; Modern History of Somaliland, 1965; ed, Islam in Tropical Africa, 1966, 2nd edn 1969; ed, Anthropology and History, 1968, Spanish edn 1970, pbk edn 1970; Ecstatic

413

Religion, 1971, Italian edn 1972; *contrib.* Afr., Amer. Anthropol., Man. *Address*: London School of Economics and Political Science, Houghton Street, WC2A 2AE.

Lewis, J. Windsor; Lecturer, Department of Phonetics, University of Leeds, since 1970; *b* 1926; *m* 1969. BA Wales 1951; Member: Internat. Phonetic Assoc.; Philological Soc.; Simplified Spelling Soc. (Mem. Cttee). Lecturer, Teheran, Iran, 1960–63; Oslo, Norway, 1963–70; Prof. Free Univ., Brussels, Belgium, 1968–69. *Publications*: (co-author) Pronunciation and Listening Practice, 1968; A Guide to English Pronunciation, 1969; A Concise Pronouncing Dictionary of British and American English, 1972; (co-author) Oxford Advanced Learner's Dictionary of Current English, 1974; *contrib.* Eng. Stud., Maît. Phonét., Eng. Lang. Teach., Lang. Learn., Språk. Språkund., Jl Internat. Phon. Assoc. *Address*: Dept of Phonetics, Univ. of Leeds, Leeds LS2 9JT.

Lewis, John Edward; Senior Lecturer in Financial Management, Graduate Business Centre, The City University, since 1968; *b* 1921; *m* 1949; two *s*. BA Wales 1942 (Hons Econs), MA Wales 1951; FCA (Associate 1948). Lectr in Financial Management, The City Univ., 1965. *Address*: The Graduate Business Centre, The City Univ., Lionel Denny House, 23 Goswell Road, EC1M 7BB.

Lewis, John Owen; Lecturer in Russian, University of Bath, since 1967; *b* 1925; *m* 1959; one *s* three *d*. BA London 1951 (Hons Russian Lang. and Lit.). Civil Service Interpretership (Russian) 1962. Sen. Lectr, Univ. of Strathclyde, 1963–67. *Publications*: (with N. Scorer) Russian Readers for Beginners (1–4), 1962; (with T. L. B. Wade) Russian Exercises for Language Laboratories, 1966; Collins Russian Phrasebook, 1968. *Address*: School of Modern Languages, Univ. of Bath, Claverton Down, Bath BA2 7AY.

Lewis, Dr Michael Jonathan Taunton, PhD; Senior Lecturer in Industrial Archaeology, Department of Adult Education, University of Hull, since 1971; *b* 1938. BA Cantab 1960 (1st cl. Classics), MA Cantab 1964, PhD Cantab 1963; FSA. Fellow, Corpus Christi Coll., Cambridge, 1963; Staff Tutor, Hull Univ., 1968–71. *Publications*: The Pentewan Railway, 1960; How Ffestiniog got its Railway, 1965, 2nd edn 1968; Temples in Roman Britain, 1965; Early Wooden Railways, 1970; *contrib.* Indust. Archaeol. *Address*: Dept of Adult Education, Univ. of Hull, 195 Cottingham Road, Hull.

Lewis, Peter Ronald, MA, FLA; University Librarian, University of Sussex, since 1972; *b* 1926; *m* 1952; one *s* one *d*. MA Belfast 1968; FLA 1955. Lectr, QUB, 1965–69; Librarian, The City Univ., 1969–72. BoT Libr., 1955–65; Mem., Council, Libr. Assoc., 1971– ; Chm., Edit. Bd, Jl Librship, 1972– . *Publications*: The Literature of the Social Sciences, 1960; *contrib.* Jl Document., Jl Librship. *Address*: Library, Univ. of Sussex, Falmer, Brighton BN1 9QL.

Lewis, Peter Shervey, MA; Senior Research Fellow, All Souls College, University of Oxford, since 1967; *b* 1931; *m* 1959; one *s*. BA Oxon 1953 (1st cl. Modern History), MA Oxon 1957; FRHistS. Fellow by exam., All Souls Coll., 1953, Jun. Res. Fellow, 1960; Lectr in Modern History, Wadham Coll., 1956– ; Univ. Lectr (CUF) in Modern History, 1958– . *Publications*: Later Medieval France: The Polity, 1968; ed, The Recovery of France in the Fifteenth Century, 1971; ed, Ecrits politiques de Jean Juvenal des Ursins (forthcoming); *contrib.* Europe in the Late Middle Ages, ed Hale et al., 1965; *contrib.* Ann. Midi, Bull. Inst. Hist. Res., Hist. Jl, Jl Warb. Court. Insts., Med. Æv., Past Pres., Trans Royal Hist. Soc. *Address*: All Souls College, Oxford.

Lewis, Dr Peter W.; Reader in Geography, Department of Geography, Birkbeck College, University of London, since 1971; *b* 1938; *m* 1960; one *s* one *d*. BA Manchester 1962, PhD Manchester 1968; Member: Inst. Brit. Geogrs, Assoc. Amer. Geogrs; FSS. Univ. of Manchester, 1963–64; Univ. of Hull, 1964–71; Florida State Univ. at Gainesville, 1969–70. *Publications*: A Numerical Approach to the Location of Industry, 1969; The Humberside Region (Industrial Britain Series), 1970; Maps and Statistics, 1974; *contrib.* 'Area' (Jl Inst. Brit. Geogrs), Geografiska Annaler. *Address*: Dept of Geography, Birkbeck College, London Univ. WC1E 7HX.

Lewis, Philip Simon Coleman; Senior Research Fellow, All Souls College, Oxford, since 1972; *b* 1933. BA Oxford 1955, MA 1958; Barrister-at-Law, Lincoln's Inn, 1958. Jun. Res. Fellow, All Souls Coll., Oxford, 1965. *Publications*: (with Sir Robert McEwen) ed, Gatley on Libel and Slander, 6th edn 1967, 7th edn 1974. *Address*: All Souls Coll., Oxford OX1 4AL.

Lewis, Dr Richard Albert; Senior Lecturer, Department of History, University College of North Wales, since 1963; *b* 1915. BA Birmingham 1937 (1st cl. History), PhD Birmingham 1949; FRHistS. Asst Lectr, Univ. Coll. of N Wales, 1947–51, Lectr, 1951–63. *Publications*: Edwin Chadwick and the Public Health Movement, 1832–1854, 1952; County Government since 1835, in, Victoria County History of Wiltshire, vol. V, 1957; *contrib.* Bham Hist. Jl, Econ. Hist. Rev., EHR, Hist. *Address*: Univ. College of North Wales, Bangor LL57 2DG.

Lewis, Ronald Geoffrey; Lecturer, Department of Ancient History, University of Edinburgh, since 1961; *b* 1937; *m* 1960; two *s*. BA Oxford 1959 (1st cl. Lit. Hum.), MA Oxon 1962, BLitt Oxon 1967. Asst Lectr, Univ. of Edinburgh, 1960–61. *Publications*: *contrib.* Athenaeum, Class. Rev., Hermes, Proc. Brit. Sch. Rome. *Address*: Dept of Ancient History, David Hume Tower, George Square, Edinburgh EH8 9JX.

Lewis, Roy Malcolm; Lecturer in Industrial Relations, London School of Economics, since 1968; *b* 1943. LLB London 1966, MScEcon London 1967. *Publications*: *contribs.* Brit. Jl Industrial Relations. *Address*: London

School of Economics, Houghton Street, Aldwych, WC2A 2AE.

Lewis, William Richard George; Registrar, University of Birmingham, since 1968; *b* 1923; *m* 1957; three *s*. BA Wales 1952, DipEd Wales 1953. Admin. Asst, UCW, Aberystwyth, 1954–56; Admin. Asst, Asst Registrar, Sec., Sch. of Educn and Academic Sec., Liverpool Univ., 1956–67. *Address*: Univ. of Birmingham, PO Box 363, Birmingham B15 2TT.

Lewitter, Prof. Lucjan Ryszard, PhD; Professor of Slavonic Studies, University of Cambridge, since 1968; *b* 1922. BA Cantab 1945, MA Cantab 1947, PhD Cantab 1951. Asst Lectr in Polish, Cambridge Univ., 1948–51; Christ's College: Fellow, 1951; Dir of Studies in Modern Langs, 1951–64; Tutor, 1960–68; Univ. Lectr in Slavonic Studies (Polish), Cambridge, 1953–68. *Publications: contrib.* learned jls. *Address*: Dept of Slavonic Studies, Sidgwick Avenue, Cambridge CB3 9DA.

Lewy, Dr Casimir, MA, PhD; Fellow and Lecturer in Philosophy, Trinity College, Cambridge, since 1959, and Reader in Philosophy, University of Cambridge, since 1972; *b* 1919; *m* 1945; three *s*. BA Cantab 1939 (1st cl. Moral Sciences), MA Cantab 1943, PhD Cantab 1943. Lectr in Philosophy, Liverpool Univ., 1945–52; Vis. Associate Prof., Univ. of Illinois, 1951–52; Univ. Lectr, Cambridge, 1952–72 (Sidgwick Lectr, 1955–72); Vis. Professor: Univ. of Texas, 1967; Yale Univ., 1969. Sec., Fac. Bd of Moral Science, 1953–59 (Chm., 1959–61); Mem., Gen. Bd of Facs., 1957–60. *Publications*: ed, G. E. Moore: Commonplace Book, 1963; ed, G. E. Moore: Lectures on Philosophy, 1966; *contrib.* Analysis, Mind, Proc. Aristot. Soc., Proc. Brit. Acad. *Address*: Trinity College, Cambridge.

Ley, Dr Philip, BA, DipPsych, PhD; Senior Lecturer in Clinical Psychology, Department of Psychiatry, University of Liverpool, since 1972; *b* 1933; *m* 1959; one *s* one *d*. BA Manchester 1955; DipPsych London 1956; PhD Liverpool 1969. Sen. Res. Psychol., Dept of Psychiatry, Univ. of Liverpool, 1962–65, Lectr in Clinical Psychol., 1965–72. Clin. Psychol., Nat. Hlth Service, 1957–62. *Publications*: Communicating with the Patient, 1967; Quantitative Aspects of Psychological Assessment, 1972; *contrib.* Brit. Jl Educnl Psychol., Brit. Jl Psychiat., Brit. Jl Soc. Clin. Psychol., etc. *Address*: Dept of Psychiatry, Univ. of Liverpool, PO Box 147, Liverpool L69 3BX.

Leyser, Karl Joseph, TD, MA; Official Fellow and Tutor in Modern History, Magdalen College, Oxford University, since 1948; *b* 1920; *m* 1962; two *s* one *d*. BA Oxford 1947, MA Oxford 1948; FRHistS. CUF Lectr, Oxford, 1950–65; Lectr in Medieval European History, 1965– . Sen. Dean of Arts, Magdalen Coll., 1951–55, Vice-Pres., 1971–72. *Publications*: The Polemics of the Papal Revolution, in, Trends in Medieval Political Thought, 1965; The Tenth Century in Byzantine–Western Relationships, in

East–West Relations in the Middle Ages; *contrib.* Encycl. Brit., EHR, Hist., Med. Æv., Past Pres., Trans Royal Hist. Soc. *Address*: Magdalen College, Oxford.

Lichfield, Prof. Nathaniel, PhD; Professor of the Economics of Environmental Planning, School of Environmental Studies, University College London, since 1966; *b* 1916; *m* 1942; 1970; one *s* two *d*. BSc London 1941 (Estate Management), PhD London 1956 (Economics); CEng, PPRTPI, FRICS, MIMunE. Special Lectr, Dept of Town Planning, UCL, 1950–62, Research Fellow, 1962–64; Vis. Research Economist, Univ. of California, Berkeley, 1959–60; Vis. Prof., Univ. of California, Berkeley, 1968; Vis. Prof., Hebrew Univ., Jerusalem, and Univ. of Tel Aviv and The Technion, Haifa, 1969–71. Pres., Royal Town Planning Institute, 1965; Mem., South East Economic Planning Council, 1969; Mem., SSRC 1969 (Chm., Planning Cttee, 1970); Mem. Coun. of Tavistock Inst. of Human Relations; Chm., Human Resources Centre. *Publications*: Economics of Planned Development, 1956; Cost Benefit Analysis in Urban Redevelopment, 1962; Cost Benefit Analysis in Town Planning: a case study of Cambridge, 1966; (with Peter Kettle and Michael Whitbread) Evaluation in the Planning Process, 1975; (with Alan Proudlove) Traffic and Conservation, (forthcoming); *contrib.* Estates Gazette, Jl of the Amer. Inst. of Planners, Jl RTPI, Jl of Transport Econs and Policy, Land Econs, Public Admin., Reg. Studies, The Chartered Surveyor, Town Planning Rev., Urban Studies. *Address*: School of Environmental Studies, Flaxman House, 16 Flaxman Terrace, WC1H 9AT.

Liebeschuetz, Dr John Hugo Wolfgang Gideon; Senior Lecturer in Classics, Leicester University, since 1974; *b* 1927; *m* 1955; one *s* three *d*. BA Hons UCL 1951, PhD London 1957. Schoolteaching, 1957–63. Lectr in Classics, Leicester Univ., 1963–74. *Publications*: Antioch: city and imperial administration in the later Roman Empire, 1972; *contrib.* Historia. *Address*: Dept of Classics, Leicester Univ., Leicester LE1 7RH.

Liggett, Eric; Lecturer in Politics, Department of Adult Education and Extra-mural Studies, University of Glasgow, since 1967; *b* 1926; *m* 1958; two *s* one *d*. BA Hons Manchester 1956, MLitt Glasgow 1972. *Publication*: British Political Issues, 1965. *Address*: Dept of Adult Education and Extra-mural Studies, Univ. of Glasgow, Glasgow G12 8QQ.

Limentani, Prof. Uberto; Professor of Italian, University of Cambridge, since 1962; Fellow of Magdalene College, Cambridge, since 1964; *b* 1913; *m* 1946; three *s*. Dr in Giur. Milan 1935. DottLett Milan 1939; PhD London 1946; MA Cambridge 1948; Corresp. Mem. Accad. Lett. Ital. dell'Arcadia 1964. Lector, Univ. of Cambridge, 1945–48, Asst Lectr in Italian, 1948–52. Lectr, 1952–62; Fellow Magdalene Coll., Cambridge, 1964. Co-Editor, Studi Secenteschi, 1960– ; Editor, Ital. Studies, 1962– . *Publications*: Stilistica e metrica, 1936; Poesie e lettere

415

inedite di Salvator Rosa, 1950; L'attività letteraria di Guiseppe Mazzini, 1950; trans., E. R. Vincent: Ugo Foscolo esule fra gli Inglesi, 1954; La satira nel Seicento, 1961; The Fortunes of Dante in Seventeenth Century Italy, 1964; ed, The Mind of Dante, 1965; contrib. Encyclopedia Britannica; Cassell's Encyclopedia of Literature; *contrib.* Amor Libro, Bibliofil., Gle Stor. Lett. Ital., Ital. Studies, Studi Secent. *Address*: Dept of Italian, Faculty of Modern and Medieval Languages, Raised Faculty Building, Sidgwick Avenue, Cambridge CB3 9DA.

Lindars, Rev. Dr Barnabas, SSF; Lecturer in Divinity, University of Cambridge, since 1966; *b* 1923. BA Cantab 1945 (1st cl. Or. Lang. Trip. Pt I, 1st cl. Th. Trip. Pt I 1946, 2nd cl. Th. Trip. Pt II 1947), MA Cantab 1948, BD Cantab 1961, DD Cantab 1973; Deacon 1947, Priest 1948, Mem., Soc. St Francis 1954– ; Mem., Soc. OT Studies, Soc. NT Studies. Asst Lectr, Cambridge Univ., 1961–66. Asst Sec., Soc. NT Studies, 1962– . *Publications*: New Testament Apologetic, 1961; Behind the Fourth Gospel, 1971; The Gospel of John, 1972; ed jtly, Words and Meanings, 1968; ed jtly, Christ and Spirit in the New Testament, 1973; *contrib.* Jl Theol. Studies, NT Studies, Vet. Testament. *Address*: The Divinity School, St John's Street, Cambridge CB2 1TW.

Lindley, Dr Keith John, MA; Lecturer in History, The New University of Ulster, Londonderry, since 1969; *b* 1942. BA Manchester 1964 (2nd cl. History), MA Manchester 1965, PhD Manchester 1968. Asst Lectr in History, Magee Univ. Coll., Londonderry, 1966. *Publications*: contrib. Politics, Religion and the English Civil War, ed B. S. Manning, 1973; *contrib.* Jl Eccles. Hist., Irish Hist. Stud. *Address*: History Dept, New Univ. of Ulster, Coleraine, Londonderry, N Ireland.

Lindsay, David W., MA, PhD; Lecturer in English, University College of North Wales, since 1966; *b* 1936; *m* 1959; one *s* one *d.* MA Edinburgh 1957 (1st cl. English Lang. and Lit.); PhD Aberdeen 1962. Asst in English, Aberdeen, 1959–63; Lectr in English, Belfast, 1963–66. *Publications*: *contrib.* Studies Scott. Lit., Forum Mod. Lang. Studies, Publicns Engl. Goethe Soc. *Address*: Dept of English, Univ. College of North Wales, Bangor, Caernarvonshire.

Linehan, Dr Peter Anthony, MA, PhD, FRHistS; Fellow and Lecturer in Medieval History, St John's College, Cambridge University, since 1969; *b* 1943; *m* 1971. BA Cantab 1964 (1st cl. Hist. Tripos Pt I 1963; 1st cl. Hist Tripos Pt II 1964), MA Cantab 1967, PhD Cantab 1968; Thirlwall Prizeman and Seeley Medallist, Cambridge, 1971; FRHistS. Res. Fellow, St John's Coll., Cambridge, 1966–69. *Publications*: The Spanish Church and the Papacy, 1971; *contrib.* Anu. Estudios Mediev., EHR, Hispan. Sacra, Hist. Jl, Studies Ch Hist. *Address*: St John's College, Cambridge.

Linfoot, Joyce Jones; Fellow and Bursar, Lucy Cavendish College, University of Cambridge, since 1969; *b* 1911; *m* 1935; one *s* one *d.* BA Cantab 1932 (Wrangler), MA Cantab 1937; AFIMA. Lectr, Dept of Educn, Univ. of Bristol, 1937–42; Lectr. Dept of Educn, Univ. of Cambridge, 1962–69. *Address*: Lucy Cavendish College, Lady Margaret Road, Cambridge.

Ling, Dr Roger John; Lecturer, History of Art Department, University of Manchester, since 1971; *b* 1942; *m* 1967. BA Cantab 1964 (1st cl. Classics), MA Cantab 1968, PhD Cantab 1970; Craven Student, Cambridge, 1964–65; Scholar, Brit. Sch. at Rome, 1965–67. Mem., Fac. of Archaeol., Hist. and Letters, Brit. Sch. at Rome, 1974– . Lectr in Classics, Univ. Coll. of Swansea, 1967–71. *Publications*: *contrib.* Antiqu. Jl, Archaeol. Camb., Class. Qly, Papers Brit. Sch. Rome. *Address*: History of Art Dept, The Univ., Manchester M13 9PL.

Ling, Trevor Oswald; Professor of Comparative Religion, University of Manchester, since 1973; *b* 1920; *m* 1949; three *d.* BA Oxon 1949, MA Oxon 1953, BD Oxon 1957; PhD London 1960; Mem. Royal Soc. for India, Pakistan, and Ceylon; Mem., Indian Anthropol Assoc.; Mem., Union for Scientific Study of Population. Lectr, 1963, Sen. Lectr, Univ. of Leeds, 1966; Prof. of Comparative Religion, Univ. of Leeds, 1970–73. *Publications*: Buddhism and the Mythology of Evil, 1962; Buddha, Marx and God, 1966; A History of Religion East and West, 1968; A Dictionary of Buddhism, 1972; The Buddha, 1973; *contrib.* Hibbert Jl, Population Studies, Religion, Religious Studies, South Asian Rev. *Address*: The Univ., Manchester.

Linnett, Prof. John Wilfrid, MA, DPhil, FRS; Master of Sidney Sussex College, since 1970; Professor of Physical Chemistry, University of Cambridge, since 1965; *b* 1913; *m* 1947; one *s* one *d.* MA, DPhil Oxon; FRS 1955; Mem., Faraday Soc. (Council, 1956–58, Vice-Pres., 1959–61, 1965–67, 1969–71, Pres., 1971–73); Mem., Chemical Soc. (Council, 1960–62, Hon. Sec., 1962, Vice-Pres., 1971–73); Mem., RIC (Council, 1970–73). Henry Fellow, Harvard Univ., 1937–38; Jun. Res. Fellow, Balliol Coll. Oxford, 1939–45; Lectr, Brasenose Coll., Oxford, 1944–46; Fellow of Queen's Coll., Oxford, 1945–65; Univ. Demonstrator in Chemistry, Oxford, 1944–62, Reader in Inorganic Chemistry, 1962–65; Fellow, Emmanuel Coll., Cambridge, 1965–70; Vice-Chancellor, Univ. of Cambridge, 1973–75 (Dep. Vice-Chancellor, 1971–73); Vis. Prof., Univ. of Wisconsin, 1950; Univ. of California, 1960, 1964, 1970; Victor Emmanuel Vis. Prof., Cornell Univ., 1966; Vis. Lectr, Univ. of Minnesota, 1967. Hon. Fellow, St John's Coll., Oxford, 1968; Hon. Fellow, The Queen's Coll., Oxford, 1971. JP City of Oxford, 1964–65. Coventry Award of Merit, 1966. Mem., National Register of Prominent Americans, 1969. *Publications*: Wave Mechanics and Valency, 1960; The Electronic Structure of Molecules, a New Approach, 1964; *contrib.* scientific papers in Proc. Royal Society, Trans Faraday Society, Jl Chemical Society, and other scientific jls.

Address: The Master's Lodge, Sidney Sussex College, Cambridge CB2 3HU; Dept of Physical Chemistry, Univ. of Cambridge, Lensfield Road, Cambridge CB2 1EP.

Lintott, Dr Andrew William; Lecturer in Classics (Ancient History), University of Aberdeen, since 1967; *b* 1936; *m* 1959; three *s* one *d*. BA Oxon 1958 (1st cl. Lit. Hum.), MA Oxon 1961; PhD London 1963. Asst Lectr, King's Coll., London, 1960–63, Lectr, 1963–67. *Publications*: Violence in Republican Rome, 1968; *contrib*. Class. Qly, Greece Rome, Historia, Rhein Mus. *Address*: Dept of Humanity, Univ. of Aberdeen, Aberdeen AB9 2UB.

Lipstein, Kurt; Professor of Comparative Law, Cambridge University, since 1973; *b* 1909; *m* 1944; two *d*. PhD Cantab 1936; Gerichtsreferendar 1931; Called to the Bar, Middle Temple, 1950, Hon. Bencher, 1966. Univ. Lectr, Cambridge. 1946; Reader in Conflict of Laws, Cambridge, 1962–73; Fellow, Clare Coll., 1956; Vis. Prof., Univ. of Pennsylvania, 1962; NW Univ., Chicago, 1966, 1968. Dir of Res., Internat. Assoc. Legal Science, 1954–59; Mem., UN Cttee of Experts on Enforcement of Maintenance Obligations, 1952; Cttee apptd by the Lord Chancellor to consider Hague Conventions on Private Internat Law, 1968; Internat. Academy of Comp. Law, 1962. *Publications*: The Law of the European Economic Community, 1974; ed. (with others) and contrib. Dicey's Conflict of Laws, 6th edn 1948, 8th edn 1967; Leske-Loewenfeld, Das Eherecht der Europäischen Staaten, 1963; International Encyclopaedia of Comparative Law, vol. Priv. Int. Law, 1972; *contrib*. Annales de la Faculté de droit d'Istanbul, Brit. Jl Internat. Law, Camb. Law Jl, Communicazioni e Studi, Internat. and Comp. Law Qly, Jl du Droit Internat., Modern Law Rev., Ottawa L. Rev., Rivista de l'Instituto de derecho comparado, Trans of the Grotius Soc., etc. *Address*: Clare College, Cambridge.

Lister, Dr Harold; Reader in Physical Geography, University of Newcastle upon Tyne, since 1964; *b* 1921; *m* 1954; two *s*. BSc Dunelm 1950, PhD Cantab 1956; FRSE. Vis. Prof., Dartmouth Coll., 1962. Mem., Council, Youth Exploration Trust. *Publications*: *contrib*. Encycl. Britannica, Jl Glaciol., Geogr. Jl, IASH, Geogr. Tiddscr., Med om Grøn. *Address*: Geography Dept, Univ. of Newcastle upon Tyne, Newcastle upon Tyne NE1 7RU.

Lister, Ian; Senior Lecturer in Education, York University, since 1973 (Lecturer, 1967–73); *b* 1934; *m* 1962; one *s* one *d*. BA Cantab 1956, MA Cantab 1960; CertEd Cambridge 1959; Cert. Inst. Raising of Qualifications Moscow 1960. Lectr in British Society, Univ. of Vienna, 1965–67. Chm., Educn Bd of Studies, Univ. of York, 1968–70; Governor, Read Sch., Drax, 1968– ; Editor, Gen. Educn (Longman), 1963–72. *Publications*: (with M. G. Bruce) History for Non-specialists, 1968; The Cold War, 1974; Deschooling: a reader, 1974; *contrib*. Betrifft, Camb. Rev., Comp. Educn, Internat. Jbh Braunsch. Textbk Inst., Erziehung, Bildung

und Erziehung. *Address*: Dept of Education, Univ. of York, York YO1 5DD.

Little, David George; Lecturer, Department of German, Trinity College Dublin, since 1970; *b* 1942; *m* 1967; two *d*. BA Hons Oxon 1964, BLitt Oxon 1973, MA Oxon 1973. Jun. Lectr in German, TCD, 1967–70. *Address*: Dept of German, Trinity College, Dublin 2.

Little, Prof. Ian Malcolm David, AFC, FBA; Fellow of Nuffield College, Oxford, since 1952; Professor of Economics of Underdeveloped Countries, Oxford University, since 1971; *b* 1918; *m* 1946; one *s* one *d*. MA Oxon 1945, DPhil Oxon 1950. Fellow: All Souls Coll., Oxford, 1948–50; Trinity Coll., Oxford, 1950–52. Dep. Dir, Economic Section, Treasury, 1953–55; Mem., MIT Centre for Internat. Studies, India, 1958–59 and 1965; Vice-Pres., OECD Develt Centre, Paris, 1965–67; Board Mem., British Airports Authority, 1969– ; Dir, Investing in Success Ltd, 1960–65, General Funds, 1973– ; Chm., Oxford Colls Unit Trust, 1968– . *Publications*: A Critique of Welfare Economics, 1950; The Price of Fuel, 1953; (jtly) Concentration in British Industry, 1960; Aid to Africa, 1964; (jtly) International Aid, 1965; (jtly) Higgledy-Piggledy Growth Again, 1966; (jtly) Manual of Industrial Project Analysis in Developing Countries, 1969; (jtly) Industry and Trade in Some Developing Countries, 1970; *contrib*. learned jls. *Address*: Nuffield College, Oxford.

Little, Dr John Roger Graham, BA, PhD; Lecturer in French, University of Southampton, since 1966; on secondment 1973–75 as Professor of Modern Languages, University of Sierra Leone; *b* 1938; *m* 1967. BA Dunelm 1964 (1st cl. French), PhD Dunelm 1970. Mem., Soc. Fr. Studies. Gen. Editor, Res Bibliogs and Checklists. *Publications*: Word Index of the Complete Poetry and Prose of Saint-John Perse, 1965, Supp. A, 1967; St-J. Perse: Oiseaux, trans, as Birds, 1967; St-J. Perse: Anabase (English trans.), 1970; Saint-John Perse: a bibliography for students of his poetry, 1971; trans. A. Bleikasten: William Faulkner: as I Lay Dying. 1973; ed and trans. J. de Labriolle: Claudel and the English-speaking World: a critical bibliography, 1973; ed, Saint-John Perse: Exil, 1973; Saint-John Perse, 1973; ed, J. de Baubert: The Tokoumbere Tales, 1973; *contrib*. Arlin. Qly, Forum Mod. Lang. Studies, Fr. Studies, Mod. Lang. Rev., Rev. Sci. Hum. *Address*: Dept of French, Univ. of Southampton, Southampton SO9 5NH.

Little, Prof. Kenneth Lindsay; Professor of African Urban Studies, University of Edinburgh, since 1971; *b* 1908; *m* 1955; one *s* one *d*. MA Cantab 1945; PhD London 1945. Lectr in Anthropology, LSE 1946–50; Reader in Social Anthropology, Edinburgh Univ., 1950–65, Prof. of Social Anthropology, 1965–71; Frazer Lectr, Cambridge Univ., 1963; Vis. Prof. of Anthropology. 1950–70: Fisk Univ.; California Univ.; NY Univ.; Northwestern Univ.; Khartoum Univ. Chm. Adv. Cttee to Home Off. on Race Relations Res., 1969. Pres., Sociology Section, Brit.

Assoc., 1968. *Publications*: Negroes in Britain, 1948; The Mende of Sierra Leone, 1951; Race and Society, 1952; West African Urbanization, 1965; African Women in Towns, 1973; Urbanization as a Social Process, 1974; *contrib*. Afr., Amer. Anthropol., Amer. Jl Sociol. *Address*: Adam Ferguson Building, George Square, Edinburgh EH8 9LL.

Littlechild, Prof. Stephen Charles; Professor of Applied Economics, University of Aston Management Centre, Birmingham, since 1972; *b* 1943. BCom Birmingham 1964 (1st cl.); PhD Texas 1969. Temp. Asst Lectr, Birmingham, 1964–65; Harkness Fellow, Commonwealth Fund, Stanford and Northwestern Univs., 1965–67; Murphy Res. Fellow, Northwestern, 1967–68; Foundn Mngmt Educn Fellow, Univ. of Texas, 1968–69; AT&T Postdoct. Fellow, UCLA and Northwestern, 1969; Sen. Research Lectr in Economics, Grad. Centre for Management Studies, Birmingham, 1970–72. *Publications*: *contrib*. Bell Jl, Econ. Jl, West. Econ. Jl. *Address*: Aston Management Centre, 36 Wake Green Road, Moseley, Birmingham B13 9PD.

Littlejohns, Richard; Lecturer, Department of German, University of Birmingham, since 1972; *b* 1943; *m* 1966; one *s* one *d*. BA Hons 1964 (1st cl. German), BLitt 1969, Oxon. Lektor for English, Univ. of Münster, W Germany, 1965–66; Lectr in German, Univ. of St Andrews, 1967–72. *Publication*: Types and Patterns of the Künstlerroman in the Romantic Period, 1969. *Address*: Dept of German, Univ. of Birmingham, PO Box 363, Birmingham B15 2TT.

Lively, Jack, MA; Fellow and Tutor in Politics, St Peter's College, University of Oxford, and University Lecturer in Politics, since 1965; *b* 1930; *m* 1957; one *s* one *d*. BA Cantab 1953 (1st cl. History Pt I and II), MA Cantab 1955; MA Oxon 1965. Res. Fellow, St Antony's Coll., Oxford, 1956–58; Lectr in Politics, Univ. Coll. of Swansea, 1958–61; Lectr in Politics, Univ. of Sussex, 1961–65. *Publications*: Social and Political Thought of Alexis de Tocqueville, 1962; ed, Works of Joseph de Maistre, 1965; The Enlightenment, 1966; Democracy, 1974; *contrib*. Amer. Pol Sci. Rev., EHR, Hist., Jl Politico, Mod. Lang. Rev., Philos. Studies, Pol Studies. *Address*: St Peter's College, Oxford.

Livens, Robin George; Senior Lecturer, Department of History (Sub-Department of Archaeology), University College, Bangor, since 1971; *b* 1929; *m* 1960; two *s*. BA Wales 1949, Classical Archaeology Cambridge 1953; FSAScotl. 1956, FSA 1967. Asst, Hunterian Museum, Univ. of Glasgow, 1954–60; Lectr in Archaeology, Dept of History, Univ. Coll., Bangor, 1960–71; Hon. Sec., Archaeology and Art Cttee, Bd of Celtic Studies; Jt Editor, Bull. of Bd of Celtic Studies, 1973. *Publications*: *contrib*. Antiq., Archaeol. Camb., Proc. Soc. Antiqu. Scot. *Address*: Dept of History, Univ. College, Bangor LL57 2DG.

Liversidge, Joan; Honorary Keeper, Roman Collections, Museum of Archaeology and Ethnology, Cambridge University: Dip. in Prehistoric Archaeology Cambridge 1943, MLitt Cambridge 1949; FSA. Supervisor and Lectr in Archaeology of Roman NW Provinces; Res. Fellow, Newnham Coll., Cambridge, 1955–58; Fellow and Praelector, Lucy Cavendish Coll., Cambridge, 1966. *Publications*: Furniture in Roman Britain, 1955; Roman Britain, 1958, 9th impression 1967; Britain in the Roman Empire, 1968, 2nd impression 1970, pbk edn 1973; Roman Gaul, 1974; Roman Britain, in History, ed J. Fines, 1970; Furniture and Interior Decoration, in The Roman Villa in Britain, ed A. L. F. Rivet, 1969; Greece and Rome, in, World Furniture, ed H. Hayward, 1965; *contrib*. Encyclopaedia Britannica; Encyclopedia dell'Arte Antica; *contrib*. Brit. Mus. Qly, Antiqu. Jl, Antiqu., Proc. Camb. Antiqu. Soc., Rec. Bueks., etc. *Address*: Museum of Archaeology and Ethnology, Cambridge.

Livesey, Frank; Senior Lecturer in Management Sciences, University of Manchester Institute of Science and Technology, since 1968; *b* 1933; *m* 1960; one *s* three *d*. BA(Econ) Manchester 1958. Lectr, Aberdeen Univ., 1959–60; St Andrews Univ., 1960–63; Manchester Univ., 1963–68. *Publications*: Economics, 1972; New Objective Tests in Economics, 1974; *contrib*. Scot. Jl of Pol Econ., Jl Industrial Econs, Econ. Jl, Proc. Inst. Civil Engnrs, Accountant, Urban Studies, Oxford Econ. Papers, Bull. Oxford Inst. of Econs and Stats, British Jl Industrial Relations, Town Planning Rev., European Jl of Marketing, Retail and Distribution Management, Univs Qly. *Address*: UMIST, PO Box 88, Manchester M60 1QD.

Livingstone, Prof. Arthur Stanley; Professor and Head of Department of Administrative Studies, University of Manchester, since 1958; *b* 1915; *m* 1947; one *s* one *d*. BA Melbourne 1940 (Philosophy); MSc Columbia 1950; MA Manchester 1973. Lectr, then Act. Dir, Dept of Social Studies, Univ. of Melbourne, 1944–53; Sen. Lectr, and Hd of Dept of Social Work, Panjab, W Pakistan, 1954–57; Assignment Sen. Fellow, Univ. of Manchester, 1957–58, Sen. Lectr, Dept of Administrative Studies, 1958. *Publications*: Social Work in Pakistan, 1957; The Overseas Student in Britain, 1960; Social Policy in Developing Countries, 1970; *contrib*. Public Admin. *Address*: Dept of Administrative Studies, Univ. of Manchester, Manchester M13 9QS.

Livingstone, Ian; Reader in Economics, Newcastle upon Tyne, since 1971; *b* 1933; *m* 1962; one *s* three *d*. BA Sheffield 1955, MA Yale 1957. Asst Lectr and Lectr in Econs, Makerere UC, Uganda, 1958–61; Lectr in Econ Stats, Sheffield Univ., 1961–65; Reader in Econs, Makerere Univ., 1965–68; Dir, Econ Res. Bureau and Res. Prof., Univ. of Dar es Salaam, 1968–71. *Publications*: (with H. W. Ord) An Introduction to Economics for East Africa, 1968; (with H. W. Ord) An Introduction to West African Economics, 1969; (with A. Goodall) Economics and Development: an introduction, 1970; ed, Economic Policy for Development, 1971; ed, The Teaching of Economics in Africa,

1973; *contrib.* various jls. *Address*: Economics Dept, The Univ., Newcastle upon Tyne NE1 3RU.

Livingstone, Rodney Simon; Lecturer in German, University of Southampton, since 1966; *b* 1934. BA Cantab 1956, MA Cantab 1960. Lectr, Adelaide Univ., 1960–62; Lectr, Monash Univ., 1963–66. *Publications*: trans., Th. Huber: Adventures on a Journey to New Holland, 1966; trans., G. Lukács: History and Class Consciousness, 1971; ed and trans., K. Marx: The Cologne Communist Trial, 1971; ed, G. Lukács: Political Writings 1919–1929, 1972; trans., G. Lukács: The Young Hegel, 1974; trans., K. Marx: Critique of Hegel's Philosophy of the State, 1974. *Address*: Dept of German, Univ. of Southampton, Highfield, Southampton SO9 5NH.

Llewellyn, David Thomas; Lecturer in Economics, Nottingham University, since 1967; *b* 1943; *m* 1970; one *s*. BSc (Econ) London 1964. Lectr (part-time), CS Coll., 1972–73; Economist: HM Treasury, 1964–67; Unilever, NV, Rotterdam, 1964; Examnr, Inst. of Municipal Treasurers and Accountants. *Publications*: *contrib.* Ind. Relns Jl, Nat. Westminster Bank Rev. *Address*: Univ. of Nottingham, University Park, Nottingham NG7 2RD.

Llewellyn, Mrs Frances Marion; *see* Lynch, F. M.

Llewellyn, Gwyn; Lecturer in Economic Statistics, Department of Applied Economics, University of Wales Institute of Science and Technology, since 1967; *b* 1927; *m* 1950; one *d*. BA Wales 1949 (Hons Economics, Hons Geography 1950), MA Wales 1952. Res. Asst, Univ. Coll. of Leicester, 1953–57; Brit. Nylon Spinners Ltd, 1957–61; Lectr, Univ. of Manchester Inst. Science and Technol., 1961–67. *Publications*: (with A. G. Pool) The British Hosiery Industry, 1958. *Address*: Dept of Applied Economics, Univ. of Wales Institute of Science and Technology, Cardiff CF1 3NU.

Llewellyn, Peter, MA; Lecturer, Department of History, University College of North Wales, since 1966; *b* 1937; *m* 1971. BA Oxon 1961, MA Oxon 1965. *Publications*: Rome in the Dark Ages, 1971. *Address*: Dept of History, Univ. College of North Wales, Bangor LL57 2DG.

Llewellyn, Dr Robert Terence; University Lecturer, Department of German, University of Cambridge, since 1968; *b* 1933; *m* 1962; two *s*. BA Wales 1955 (1st cl. German); PhD Cantab 1962. Asst Lectr, Hull Univ., 1962–64, Lectr, 1965; Asst Lectr, Univ. of Cambridge, 1965–68; Fellow, and Dir of Studies in German, Christ's Coll., Cambridge, 1965– . Tutor, Christ's Coll., 1970– . *Publications*: German Baroque Literature, 1973; *contrib.* Antaios, Mod. Lang. Rev. *Address*: Christ's College, Cambridge.

Llewellyn-Jones, Frank; *see* Jones, F. Ll.

Llewelyn, John Edward, BA. MA, BLitt; Senior Lecturer in Philosophy, University of Edinburgh, since 1971; *b* 1928; *m* 1959. BA Wales 1948, MA Edinburgh 1952, BLitt Oxon 1961. Lectr, Univ. of New England, Australia, 1956–64; Lectr, Univ. of Edinburgh, 1964–71. RAF Educn Br., 1948–50; French Air Force Coll., 1952–53. *Publications*: *contrib.* Amer. Philos. Qly, Austral. Jl Philos., Philos. Qly, Theoria, *Address*: Dept of Philosophy, David Hume Tower, George Square, Edinburgh EH8 9JX.

Llewelyn-Davies, Prof. The Lord; Richard Llewelyn-Davies; Professor of Urban Planning, and Head of the School of Environmental Studies, University College, London, since 1969; *b* 1912; *m* 1943; three *d*. MA Cambridge 1951, DipArch(Hons); FRIBA 1956, MRTPI 1966; Hon. Fellow, Amer. Inst. Archit. 1970. Prof. of Architecture, Univ. Coll., London, 1960–69. Dir, Investigation into function and design of hospitals, Nuffield Foundn, 1953–60; First Pres., Wld Soc. Ekistics, 1965; Chm., Centre Environm. Studies, 1967– . *Publications*: (jtly) Studies in the Function and Designs of Hospitals, 1955; (jtly) The Design of Research Laboratories, 1960; *contrib.* Archit. Jl, Archit. Rec., Archit. Rev., Jl Royal Inst. Brit. Archit., Jl Royal Inst. Chem., Jl Royal Town Plan. Inst., Nature. *Address*: Univ. College London, Flaxman House, 16 Flaxman Terrace, WC1H 9AT.

Lloyd of Hampstead, Prof. The Lord; Dennis Lloyd, LLD; Quain Professor of Jurisprudence, University College, London, since 1956; *b* 1915; *m* 1940; two *d*. LLB London 1935, BA Cantab 1937, MA Cantab 1941, LLD Cantab 1956; Called to Bar 1936. Reader in English Law, 1947–56, Dean, Fac. of Laws, 1962–64; Head of Dept of Law, UCL, Fellow of University College. Hon. Legal Adv., AUT, 1962–69; Mem., Law Reform Cttee; Consolidation Bills Cttee; Jt Cttee Theatre Censorship; Conseil Féd Brit. de l'Alliance Franç.; Chm., Nat. Film Sch. Cttee; Planning Cttee, Nat. Film Sch., Chairman of Governors, Nat. Film Sch.; Chairman of Council, University College School; Chm., Brit. Film Inst. *Publications*: Unincorporated Associations, 1938; Rent Control, 1949, 2nd edn 1955; Public Policy: A Comparative Study in English and French Law, 1953; United Kingdom: Development of its Laws and Constitution, 1955; Business Lettings, 1956; Introduction to Jurisprudence, 1959, 2nd edn 1965, 3rd edn 1972; The Idea of Law, 1964, Japanese trans. 1969, rev. edn 1973; Law (Concept Series), 1968; *contrib.* to periodicals. *Address*: Faculty of Law, Univ. College London, 4–8 Endsleigh Gardens, WC1H 0EG.

Lloyd, Prof. Antony Charles; Professor of Philosophy, University of Liverpool, since 1957; *b* 1916. BA Oxon 1938 (1st cl. Litt. Hum.). Asst, Edinburgh Univ., 1938–39; Lectr, St Andrews Univ., 1946–57; Vis. Prof., Kansas Univ., 1967. *Publications*: *contrib.* Cambridge History of Later Greek and Early Medieval Philosophy, and philos. jls. *Address*: Dept of Philosophy, Univ. of Liverpool, PO Box 147, Liverpool L69 3BX.

Lloyd, Dr Barbara Bloom (LeVine); Lecturer in Social Psychology, University of Sussex, since 1967; *b* 1933; *m* 1964; one *d*. BA Chicago 1953; MA Boston 1955 (Psychology); PhD Northwestern 1961 (Social Psychology); ABPsS. Res. Asst, Northwestern Univ., 1958–60; Lectr, 1961; Res. Fellow, Univ. of Ibadan, 1961–64; Lectr (Pt-time), Birmingham Univ., 1964–67; Fellow, Inst. of Development Studies, Univ. of Sussex, 1970–71. *Publications*: (with R. A. LeVine) Nyansongo: a Gusii Community in Kenya, in, Six Cultures: studies in child rearing, ed B. B. Whiting, 1963, pub. separately 1966; Perception and Cognition: a cross cultural perspective, 1972; *contrib.* Child Develt, Jl Cross-Cult. Psychol., Jl Social Psychol. *Address*: School of African and Asian Studies, Univ. of Sussex, Falmer, Brighton BN1 9RH.

Lloyd, Dr David Hanbury, BSc, PhD, ARAgSc; Senior Lecturer in Agricultural Management and Labour Science, University of Reading, since 1972 (Lecturer, 1955–72); *b* 1928; *m* 1950; three *s* two *d*. BSc Wales 1945; PhD Reading 1969; FOMS 1971–73; ARAgSc 1974. Mem., Brit. Soc. Agric. Lab. Science (Sec. 1970–), Organisat. and Methods Soc. Lectr, Leeds Univ., 1949–55. Convr, Jethro Tull Club, 1966–73; Dir, Brit. Poultry Science. *Publications*: Economics of Egg Production, 1955; Method Study for Advisers and Farmers, 1957, 2nd edn 1967; Business Control in Poultry Keeping, 1967; Farm Business Analysis without accounts, 1968; Development of Farm Business Analysis and Planning in Britain, 1970; Staff Management Audit, 1972; *contrib.* Farm Mngmt, Farm Econ., Jl Agric. Econ., Jl Organisat. Methods, Jl Agric. Lab. Sci. *Address*: Work Science Laboratory, Dept of Agriculture, The Univ., Whiteknights Park, Reading RG6 2AH.

Lloyd, David Tecwyn, MA; Senior Lecturer, Extra-Mural Department, University College of Wales, Aberystwyth, since 1966; *b* 1914; *m* 1955. BA Wales 1937; MA Liverpool 1961. Lectr, Aberystwyth, 1961–66. Tutor and Libr., Coleg Harlech, N Wales, 1946–55; Mem., Ct and Council, Nat. Libr. of Wales, 1948–68; Ital. For Min. Res. Fellowship, Rome, Milan, Florence, etc, 1951–52; Mem., Nat. Eisteddfod Wales, Lit. Cttee, 1948– ; Welsh Acad. Lett., 1963– ; Mem., Ct and Council, Univ. Coll. of Wales, 1969– ; Mem., Lit. Panel, Welsh Arts Council, 1972– ; Editor, Taliesin: Jl Welsh Acad. Lett., 1965. *Publications*: trans., H. I. Bell: Trwy Diroedd y Dwyrain, 1946; Erthyglau Beirniadol, 1946; Safle'r Gerbydres (Arts Council Prize), 1970; Lady Gwladys (Arts Council Prize), 1971; Y Parch John Jones MA, 1773–1853: Diaries, Text, Notes and Bibliography, 1971; *contrib.* Llên Cymru, Trivium, Barn, Planet, etc. *Address*: Extra-Mural Dept, 9 Marine Terrace, Aberystwyth, Dyfed.

Lloyd, Dr Geoffrey Ernest Richard, MA, PhD; Reader in Ancient Philosophy and Science, Cambridge University, since 1974 (University Lecturer, Classics Department, 1967–74); *b* 1933; *m* 1956; three *s*. BA Cambridge 1954 (Hons. Classics), MA Cambridge 1958, PhD Cambridge 1958; Mem., Hellenic Soc., Mem., Royal Anthropol Inst. Fellow, King's Coll., 1957– ; Asst Lectr, Cambridge Univ., 1965–67. *Publications*: Polarity and Analogy: two types of argumentation in early Greek thought, 1966; Aristotle: the growth and structure of his thought, 1968; Early Greek Science: Thales to Aristotle, 1970; Greek Science after Aristotle, 1973; *contrib.* Brit. Jl Philos. Sci., Camb. Rev., Class. Rev., Gnomon, Hist. Sci., Jl Hellenic Studies, Phronesis, Proc. Camb. Philol Soc. *Address*: King's College, Cambridge CB2 1ST.

Lloyd, Dr Howell Arnold; Senior Lecturer, Department of History, University of Hull, since 1973; *b* 1937; *m* 1962; two *s* two *d*. BA Wales 1958 (1st cl. Hons), DPhil Oxon 1964; Asst Lectr, History, Univ. of Hull, 1962–64; Lectr, 1964–73. *Publications*: The Gentry of South-West Wales, 1540–1640, 1968; (with G. Connell-Smith) The Relevance of History, 1972; The Rouen Campaign, 1590–1592: Politics, Warfare and the Early-Modern State, 1973; *contrib.* Bull. of the Institute of Historical Res., English Historical Rev., Revue Belge de Philologie et d'Histoire, Welsh History Rev. *Address*: Dept of History, Univ. of Hull, Hull HU6 7RX.

Lloyd, Michael Gordon; Lecturer in Laws, University of London, King's College, since 1968; *b* 1945. MA Oxon 1972; Barrister-at-Law (Gray's Inn), 1967. British Council Lectr in English, British Council, Oporto, Portugal, 1966–67. *Publications*: Actio Sepulchri Violati: Subsídios para o Direito Trasmontano de Túmulos, 1971; *contrib.* MLR, Recueils Jean Bodin. *Address*: King's College, Strand, WC2R 2LS.

Lloyd, Dr Peter Cutt, MA, BSc, DPhil; Reader in Social Anthropology, University of Sussex, since 1967; *b* 1927; *m* 1964; one *d*. BA Oxon 1948 (Geog.), MA Oxon 1952, BSc Oxon 1953, DPhil Oxon 1958 (Social Anthrop.). Res. Fellow, Nigerian Inst. Social and Econ. Res., 1949–56; Lands Res. Offr, Min. of Lands, Ibadan, Nigeria, 1956–59; Lectr, then Sen. Lectr in Sociology, Univ. of Ibadan, 1959–64; Sen. Lectr, then Reader in West African Sociology, Univ. of Birmingham, 1964–67. Hon. Sec., Assoc. Social Anthropol., 1967–71. *Publications*: Yoruba Land Law, 1962; ed, The New Elites of Tropical Africa, 1966; Africa in Social Change, 1967, American edn 1968, Swedish trans. 1969; ed jtly, The City of Ibadan, 1967; Classes, Crises and Coups, 1971; The Political Development of Yoruba Kingdoms, 1971; Power and Independence, 1974; *contrib.* Afr., Amer. Anthropol., Amer. Pol. Sci. Rev., Jl Afr. Law, Jl Afr. Hist., Man, Sociol. Rev. *Address*: School of Social Science, Univ. of Sussex, Brighton BN1 9QN.

Lloyd, Peter E., MA; Lecturer, Geography Department, University of Manchester, since 1964; *b* 1938; *m* 1961; one *s* one *d*. BA Birmingham 1959, MA Birmingham 1961. Lectr, Univ. of Queensland, 1961–64. *Publications*: (with M. H. Yeates) Impact of Industrial Incentives, 1971; (with P. Dicken) Location in Space: A Theoretical Approach to Economic Geography, 1972; *contrib.* Austral. Geog. Studies, Town Plan. Rev. *Address*: Dept of Geography, Univ. of Manchester, Manchester M13 9PL.

Lloyd, William Henry; Senior Lecturer in Education, Centre for Science Education, Chelsea College, University of London, since 1971; *b* 1914; *m* 1945; one *s* two *d.* BSc Leeds 1936 (Gen. Hons), DipEd Leeds 1937; Mem. ASE, Mem. AMA. Lectr, Centre for Science Educn, Chelsea Coll., 1967. Consultant on Laboratory Design; Mem., Gov. Body, Brighton College. *Publications*: contrib. The Art of the Science Teacher, 1974; *contrib.* Educn in Chemistry. *Address*: Chemical Laboratory, Science Education Centre, Chelsea College, Bridges Place, Parsons Green Lane, SW6 4HR.

Lloyd-Jones, Prof. (Peter) Hugh (Jefferd); Regius Professor of Greek in the University of Oxford, since 1960; *b* 1922; *m* 1953; two *s* one *d.* BA, MA Oxon 1947 (1st cl. Classical Mods 1941, 1st cl. Lit. Hum. 1948), MA Cantab (incorp.) 1948, Hon. DHL Chicago 1970; FBA 1966, Hon. Mem., Greek Humanistic Soc., Pres., Internat. Homeric Council, Greece. Fellow, Jesus Coll., Cambridge, 1948–54; Asst Lectr, Cambridge Univ., 1950–52, Lectr, 1952–54; Fellow, Corpus Christi Coll., Oxford, and E.P. Warren Praelector in Classics, 1954–60. *Publications*: Appendix to Aeschylus (Loeb), 1957; Menandri Dyscolus, 1960; ed, The Greeks, 1961; trans., P. Maas: Greek Metre, 1962; Tacitus, 1964; trans., Aeschylus: Agamemnon, The Libation-Bearers, The Eumenides, 1970; The Justice of Zeus, 1971; *contrib.* Antiqu. Class., Class. Qly, Class. Rev., Gnomon, Greek Roman Byzant. Studies, Harv. Studies, Jl Hellenic Studies, Maia, Rhein. Mus., Studi Ital., Yale Studies, etc. *Address*: Christ Church, Oxford.

Lloyd Thomas, David Adrian; Lecturer in Social Philosophy, Department of Philosophy, Bedford College, University of London, since 1965; *b* 1932; *m* 1958; two *d.* BA Melbourne 1956 (Hons History), MA Melbourne 1957 (Hons Philosophy); Mem.: Aristotelian Soc.; Royal Inst. of Philosophy. Tutor in Philosophy, Univ. of Melbourne, 1957; Temp. Lectr in Philosophy, Univ. of WA, 1958; Victoria Univ. of Wellington, NZ: Lectr in Philosophy, 1959–63; Sen. Lectr, 1963–65; Vis. Associate Prof. of Philosophy, Univ. of Wisconsin, Milwaukee, USA, 1972. *Publications*: *contrib.* Analysis, Canadian Jl Philos., Jl of Philos., Mind, Philos. Qly, PAS. *Address*: Bedford College, Regent's Park, NW1 4NS.

Llywelyn-Williams, Alun, MA; Director, Department of Extra-Mural Studies, University College of North Wales, Bangor, since 1948; *b* 1913; *m* 1938; two *d.* BA Wales 1934–35 (1st cl. Welsh, 2nd cl. History), MA Wales 1957. Mem., Central Adv. Council for Educn, Wales, 1961–64; Arts Council GB Welsh Cttee, 1958–67; N Wales Assoc. Arts, Exec. Cttee, 1967–   ; Dir, Welsh Theatre Co., 1967–   ; Harlech TV Ltd, 1968–   . *Publications*: Y Nos, Y Niwl, a'r Ynys (A study in Welsh romanticism), 1960; Nes Na'r

Hanesydd? (essays in literary criticism), 1969; *contrib.* Cymmrodor, Llenor, Traethodydd. *Address*: Dept of Extra-Mural Studies, Univ. College of North Wales, Bangor LL57 2DG.

Loades, Ann Lomas; Resident Tutor in Collingwood College, University of Durham, and part-time Lecturer in Theology, since 1973 (in St Mary's College, 1964–73); *b* 1938; *m* 1965. BA Durham (2nd cl. Theology), DipEd Durham 1961, MA McMaster 1965; AISTD 1968. *Address*: Collingwood College, Univ. of Durham, Durham City.

Loades, David Michael; Senior Lecturer in Modern History, University of Durham, since 1971; *b* 1934; *m* 1965. BA Cantab 1958 (1st cl. Hist. Tripos), MA Cantab 1962, PhD Cantab 1962; FRHistS 1967. Lectr in Political Science, Univ. of St Andrews, 1961–63; Lectr in Modern History, Univ. of Durham, 1963–71. Admin. Offr, RAF, 1954–55; Mem., Cttee, Eccles. Hist. Soc., 1970–73. *Publications:* Two Tudor Conspiracies, 1965; The Papers of George Wyatt, 1968; The Oxford Martyrs, 1970; *contrib.* Jl Eccles. Hist., Trans Camb. Bibliog. Soc. *Address*: Dept of Modern History, 43–46 North Bailey, Durham City.

Loasby, Prof. Brian John, BA, MLitt; Professor of Management Economics, Department of Economics, University of Stirling, since 1971; *b* 1930; *m* 1957; two *d.* BA Cantab 1952, MLitt Cantab 1957. Asst in Political Economy, Aberdeen, 1955–58; Bourneville Res. Fellow, Birmingham, 1958–61; Tutor in Mngmt Studies, Bristol, 1961–67; Arthur D. Little Mngmnt Fellow, Arthur D. Little Inc., Cambridge Mass., 1965–66; Lectr in Economics, Stirling, 1967–68, Sen. Lectr in Economics, 1968–71; Vis. Fellow, Oxford Centre for Mngmt Studies, 1974. *Publications*: The Swindon Project; *contrib.* Dist Bank Rev., Econ. Jl, Jl Mngmt Studies, Lloyds Bank Rev., R & D Mngmt. *Address*: Dept of Economics, Univ. of Stirling, Stirling FK9 4LA.

Löb, Dr Ladislaus, Dr phil; Lecturer in German, University of Sussex, since 1964; *b* 1933; *m* 1964; two *d.* Dr phil Zürich 1962. Volkshochschule, Zürich, 1961–62; Tutor in German, Sussex Univ., 1963–64; Vis. Prof., Middlebury Coll., Vermont, 1971. *Publications*: Mensch und Gesellschaft bei J. B. Priestley, 1962; (with E. R. Baer) Der arme Millionär, 1966; From Lessing to Hauptmann: studies in German drama, 1974; *contrib.* Germ. Life Lett. *Address*: School of European Studies, Univ. of Sussex, Falmer, Brighton BN1 9RH.

Lochhead, Andrew; Director, Overseas Courses, Department of Social Administration, University College of Swansea, since 1970; *b* 1911; *m* 1948; one *s* two *d.* BA Oxon 1934 (2nd cl. Mod. Greats), MA Oxon 1946. Lectr and Organizing Tutor in Social Science, Cardiff, 1952–56; Dir, Social Administration Courses, Swansea, 1961–70; Vis. Prof. in Social Administration, Khartoum, 1969; Vis. Lectr, Makerere, 1963, 1967. Gen. Sec., Bristol Council Social Service, 1948–52; Advr on Social Services, Govt of Trinidad,

1956–60; Mem., UNESCO Nat. Cttee, Social Science Panel, 1967– ; Adv. Cttee on Social Develt, Overseas Develt Admin., 1964– . *Publications*: Administration of Social Services in Trinidad, 1956; Reader in Social Administration, 1968; *contrib*. Comm. Develt Jl, Social Services Qly. *Address*: Univ. College of Swansea, Swansea SA2 8PP.

Locke, Donald Bryan, MA, BPhil; Senior Lecturer, Department of Philosophy, University of Warwick, since 1971; *b* 1938; *m* 1969; one *s* two *d*. BA New Zealand 1958, MA Canterbury NZ 1959; BPhil Oxon 1962. Asst Lectr, Univ. of Canterbury, NZ, 1960–62; Lectr, Univ. of Newcastle upon Tyne, 1962–68; Lectr, Univ. of Warwick, 1968–71. *Publications*: Perception and Our Knowledge of the External World, 1967; Myself and Others, 1968; Memory, 1970; *contrib*. Analysis, Philos. Qly, Philos. Rev., Philos. *Address*: Dept of Philosophy, Univ. of Warwick.

Lockett, Alan Geoffrey; Senior Lecturer in Management Science, Manchester Business School, since 1972 (Lecturer, 1969–72); *b* 1941; *m* 1963; two *s* one *d*. BSc Manchester 1962 (2nd cl.), MSc Manchester 1964. Lectr in Operational Res., Univ. of Hull, 1966–69. *Publications*: *contrib*. INFOR, IEEE Trans Eng. Man., Jl Finan. Quant. Analysis, Jl Mngmt Studies. Operat. Res. Qly, Operat. Res., Mngmt Sci., Internat. Jl Production Res., Personnel Rev. *Address*: Manchester Business School, Booth Street West, Manchester.

Lockett, Rev. Canon William Ernest Alfred; Senior Lecturer in Fine Art, Institute of Extension Studies, University of Liverpool, since 1966, and Canon Theologian of Liverpool Cathedral, since 1972; *b* 1916; *m* 1946; two *s* one *d*. DipTheol Lincoln 1944, ATD, DipEd; ARCA 1939, FRSA 1965. Tutor, Univ. of Liverpool, 1956–66. Hon. Art Advr, St George's Chapel, Windsor Castle; Mem., Council for Places of Worship; Chairman: Liverpool Diocesan Adv. Cttee; Nat. New Churches Cttee. *Publications*: Modern Architectural Setting of the Liturgy, 1962; Church Architecture and Social Responsibility, 1968. *Address*: Inst. of Extension Studies, Univ. of Liverpool, Abercromby Square, Liverpool.

Lockhart, Laurence; Member of the Faculty of Oriental Studies, Cambridge University, since 1957; *b* 1890; *m* 1931. (1st cl. Oriental Languages Tripos) 1915, PhD London 1936; LittD Cambridge 1959; Mem., Royal Central Asian Soc., Mem., Iran Soc. Vis. Prof., Univ. of Toronto, 1967; Vis. Lectr, McGill Univ., etc. Temp. Lectr in Persian, Univ. of Cambridge, 1957. Mem., Council Royal Central Asian Soc.; Mem., Council, Iran Soc.; sometime Vice-Pres. of both. *Publications*: Nadir Shah, a Critical Study based mainly upon Contemporary Sources, 1938; Famous Cities of Iran, 1939; The Fall of the Safavi Dynasty and the Afghan Occupation of Persia, 1958; Persian Cities, 1960; *contrib*. Jl Royal Central Asian Soc., Jl Iran Soc., etc. *Address*: Pembroke College, Cambridge.

Lockwood, Prof. David; Professor of Sociology, University of Essex, since 1968; *b* 1929;

m 1954; three *s*. BSc(Econ) London 1952, PhD London 1957. Asst Lectr/Lectr, LSE, 1953–60; Rockefeller Fellow, Univ. of California, Berkeley, 1958–59; Univ. Lectr, Faculty of Economics and Politics, and Fellow, St John's Coll., Cambridge, 1960–68; Vis. Prof., Columbia Univ., 1966–67; Dean of Social Studies, Essex, 1969–70; Chm., Dept of Sociology, Essex, 1970–72. Mem. SSRC (Chm., Sociology and Social Admin Cttee), 1973– . *Publications*: The Blackcoated Worker: a study in class consciousness, 1958; (with John H. Goldthorpe and others) The Affluent Workers, 3 vols, 1968–69; *contrib*. Brit. Jl Sociol., Sociol Rev., Sociol. *Address*: Dept of Sociology, Univ. of Essex, Colchester CO4 3SQ.

Lockwood, Geoffrey; Registrar and Secretary, University of Sussex, since 1973; *b* 1936; *m* 1962; two *d*. BSc (Econs) LSE 1959 (1st cl. Hons). Admin. Asst, Registrar's Dept, Univ. of Manchester, 1959–61; Univ. of Sussex: Asst Registrar, 1961–64; Dep. Registrar, 1964–68; Planning Officer, 1968–73. MUAAS: Founder Mem., 1961; Sec., 1964–67; Jt Sec., 1968–73; Founder Mem., SRHE (Mem. Governing Body, 1969–70); part-time Consultant: OECD, Paris, 1969–71; Internat. Inst. for Educnl Planning, UNESCO, 1969–72; Consultant on planning of higher educn, UNESCO mission to Iran, 1972; Assoc. of Univ. Teachers: Mem. Statistics Cttee, 1965–67; Mem. Admin. Staffs Panel, 1966–73; Mem. Management Cttee, Southern Univs O and M Unit, 1970–72; Univ. Rep., Univs Central Council on Admissions, 1963–66; Jt Dir, Planning and Management in Univs project, 1971–72; Mem. Cttee, Vice-Chancellors' Sub-Cttee on Trng of Admin. Staffs, 1972– . *Publications*: (jtly) Planning and Management in Universities, 1973; Institutional Planning and Management Techniques for Universities (OECD Technical Report), 1973; contrib. Teaching and Learning: an introduction to new methods and resources in higher education, 1970; Planning the development of Universities – 1, 1972; *contrib*. Higher Educn, Univs Qly. *Address*: Univ. of Sussex, Sussex House, Falmer, Brighton BN1 9RH.

Lodge, Dr David John; Reader, Department of English, University of Birmingham, since 1973; *b* 1935; *m* 1959; two *s* one *d*. BA London 1955 (1st cl. English), MA London 1959 (English); PhD Birmingham 1967. Asst Lectr in English, Univ. of Birmingham, 1960–62, Lectr, 1962–71, Sen. Lectr, 1971–73; Vis. Associate Prof., Univ. of California, Berkeley, 1969; Harkness Commonwealth Fellow in USA, 1964–65. *Publications*: The Picturegoers (novel), 1960; Ginger, You're Barmy (novel), 1962; The British Museum is Falling Down (novel), 1965; Language of Fiction, 1966; Graham Greene, 1966; ed, Emma: A Casebook, 1968; Out of the Shelter (novel), 1970; The Novelist at the Crossroads, 1971; Evelyn Waugh, 1971; ed, 20th Century Literary Criticism; *contrib*. Crit. Qly, Encounter, Ess. Crit., Mod. Lang. Rev., Nint. Cent. Fict., Novel, South Rev. *Address*: Dept of English, Univ. of Birmingham, PO Box 363, Birmingham B15 2TT.

Lodge, Kenneth Rupert; Lecturer in Linguistics and German, Language Centre, University of East Anglia, since 1969; *b* 1943; *m* 1964; one *d.* BA Manchester 1965 (Hons German); Member: Linguistic Assoc. of GB, Internat. Phonetics Assoc. Res. Fellow, Dialect Survey, Sch. of English, Leeds, 1967–68; Teaching Fellow, English and Linguistics, 1968–69. *Publications: contrib.* Archivum Linguisticum, Jl Internat. Phonetics Assocs, Maître Phonétique. *Address:* Language Centre, University Plain, Univ. of East Anglia, Norwich NOR 88C.

Lodge, Dr Raymond Anthony; Lecturer, Department of French, University of Aberdeen, since 1967; *b* 1942; *m* 1967; two *s.* BA Manchester 1965, PhD Manchester 1970; Member: Soc. for French Studies; Internat. Arthurian Soc. *Publications: contrib.* Romania, Year's Work in Mod. Lang. Studies. *Address:* Dept of French, King's College, Aberdeen.

Loewe, Dr Michael; University Lecturer in Chinese Studies, University of Cambridge, since 1963; *b* 1922. BA Hons London 1951 (Class. Chinese), PhD 1963; FSA 1972; Fellow, Clare Hall, Cambridge, 1968. Lectr in the Hist. of the Far East, Univ. of London, 1956–63. Member: Univs China Cttee, Council, RAS; Editorial Bd, Asia Major. *Publications:* Imperial China, 1966; Records of Han Administration, 1967; Everyday Life in Early Imperial China, 1968, 1973; Crisis and Conflict in Han China, 1974; *contrib.* T'oung Pao, Jl of RAS, Bull. SOAS, Asia Major. *Address:* Fac. of Oriental Studies, Sidgwick Avenue, Cambridge.

Loewe, Raphael James, MC, MA; Reader, Department of Hebrew and Jewish Studies, University College London, since 1970; *b* 1919; *m* 1952; two *d.* BA Cantab 1940 (1st cl. Part I Classics Tripos); Member: Soc. for OT Study; FRAS (formerly Mem. Council); Council Mem., Jewish Hist. Soc. of England. Lectr, Leeds Univ., 1949–54; Bye-Fellow, Caius Coll., Cambridge, 1954–57; Lectr, Leo Baeck Inst., London, 1960–63; Vis. Prof., Brown Univ., RI, 1963–64; Lectr, UCL, 1965–70. Formerly Asst Editor, Jl of Jewish Studies; Asst Editor, Bull. Inst. of Jewish Studies. *Publications:* The Position of Women in Judaism, 1966; ed, Studies in Rationalism, Judaism and Universalism in Memory of Leon Roth, 1966; *contrib.* Jl of Jewish Studies, Biblica, Trans Jewish Hist. Soc. of England, Hebrew Union Coll. Annual, etc. *Address:* Dept of Hebrew and Jewish Studies, Univ. Coll. London, Gower Street, WC1E 6BT.

Loewenthal, Dr Catherine Mary; Lecturer in Psychology, Psychology Department, Bedford College, University of London, since 1972; *b* 1941; *m* 1964; three *d.* BSc London 1963 (1st cl. Psychology), PhD London 1967 (Psychology), Mem., Brit. Psychol. Soc. Asst Lectr in Psychology, Univ. Coll. of N Wales, 1966–67; MRC Jun. Res. Fellow, 1967–68; Lectr in Psychology, City Univ., 1968–72. *Publications: contrib.* Brit. Jl Educnl Psychol., Brit. Jl Psychol., Brit. Jl Soc. Clin. Psychol., Jl Social Psychol., Psychol Rep., Psychon, Sci, Qly Jl Exper. Psychol. *Address:* Psychology Dept, Bedford College, Univ. of London, Regent's Park, NW1 4NS.

Lofmark, Prof. Carl Johan; Professor of German, St David's University College of Lampeter, since 1974; *b* 1936; *m* 1960; one *s* two *d.* BA London 1961, MA London 1964, PhD London 1973; AKC 1964; Mem., Wolfram-von-Eschenbach-Gesellschaft. Asst Lectr, KCL, 1962–64; St David's College Lampeter: Lectr i/c, German Dept, 1964; Sen. Lectr, 1969. Trivium: Germanic Editor, 1965–72; Gen. Editor, 1972– . *Publications:* trans. Pohlenz: Freedom in Greek Life and Thought, 1966; Rennewart in Wolfram's Willehalm, 1972; (jtly), A Word Index to Ulrich von Zatzikhoven's Lanzelet, 1972; *contrib.* German Life and Letters, MLN, MLR, Trivium, Zeitschrift für deutsches Altertum und deutsche Literatur. *Address:* St David's University Coll., Lampeter, Dyfed SA48 7ED.

Logan, Sir Douglas (William); DPhil; Principal of the University of London, since 1948; *b* 1910; *m* 1940; 1947; three *s* one *d.* (1st cl. Hons Mods), (1st cl. Lit. Hum.), BA Oxon 1932 (1st cl. Jurisprudence), 1933, MA Oxon 1935, BCL Oxon 1935, DPhil Oxon 1943; Hon. DCL Western Ontario; Hon. LLD: Melbourne; Madras; British Columbia; Hong Kong; Liverpool; McGill; CNAA; called to Bar, Middle Temple, 1937 (Hon. Bencher 1965); Hon. FDSRCS; Hon. FRIBA; Hon. Fellow, LSE, 1962, University Coll. Oxford, 1972; Fellow Wye Coll., 1970; Hon. Mem., Pharmaceutical Soc.; Henry Fellowship, Harvard Law Sch., 1935–36; Asst Lectr, LSE, 1936–37; Barstow Scholarship 1937; Fellow, Trinity Coll., Cambridge, 1937–43; Clerk of the Court, Univ. of London, 1944–47; Rede Lectr, 1963. Pres., British Univs Sports Fedn; Chm., British Cttee for Student Sport; Vice-Chm., Assoc. of Commonwealth Univs, 1961–67 (Chm., 1962–63), Hon. Treasurer, 1967– ; Vice-Chm., Athlone Fellowship Cttee, 1959–71; Dep. Chm., Commonwealth Scholarships Commn; Mem., Marshall Scholarships Commn. 1961–67; Mem., Nat. Theatre Bd. 1962–68; Governor, Old Vic (Vice-Chm., 1972–) and Bristol Old Vic; Trustee, City Parochial Foundn, 1953–67; Mem., Anderson Cttee on Grants to Students, 1958–60; Mem., Hale Cttee on Superannuation of Univ. Teachers, 1958–60; Mem., Northumberland Cttee on Recruitment to the Veterinary Profession, 1962–64; Mem., Maddex Working Party on the Superannuation of Univ. Teachers, 1965–68. Mem., Brit. Delegn to 1st, 2nd, 3rd and 4th Commonwealth Educn Confs, Oxford, 1959, Delhi, 1962, Ottawa, 1964, and Lagos, 1968; Mem., Commonwealth Medical Conf., Edinburgh, 1965. Chevalier de l'Ordre de la Légion d'Honneur. *Address:* The Univ. of London, Senate House, WC1E 7HU.

Lomax, Prof. Derek William; Professor of Spanish, University of Birmingham, since 1972; *b* 1933. BA Oxford 1954, MA Oxford 1958, DPhil Oxford 1961, Mem., Assoc. Hispan. Asst Lectr, Univ. of Liverpool, 1959–62, Lectr. 1962–69, Sen. Lectr, 1969–72. *Publications:* La orden de Santiago, 1170–

423

1275, 1965; *contrib.* Anu. Estudios Mediev., Archiv. Leon., Bull. Hispan. Studies, Hispan., Ibero-Rom. *Address:* Dept of Spanish, Univ. of Birmingham, PO Box 363, Birmingham B15 2TT.

Lomax, Eric Sutherland; Lecturer in Personnel Management, Chesters Management Centre, University of Strathclyde (formerly Department of Industrial Administration, Royal College of Science and Technology), since 1959; *b* 1919; *m* 1945; two *d*. Dip. Personnel Management Strathclyde 1957, Dip. Management Studies Strathclyde 1961. Mem., Newcomen Soc., FRSA. Colonial Admin. Service, Gold Coast, 1949–55; Scot. Gas Bd, Edinburgh (Ind. Rels Educn and Training), 1957–59; Trustee, Scott. Far East POW Assoc. *Publications:* A History of the Volta River Project, 1953; Report on Transport in the Northern Territories of the Gold Coast, 1953; An Introductory Guide to Systematic Personnel Selection, 1964; Human Factors in Communication, 1964, 3rd edn, 1967; The Management of Human Resources, 1971. *Address:* Chesters Management Centre, Univ. of Strathclyde, Bearsden, Glasgow G61 4AG.

Lonergan, Corinna S.; *see* Salvadori Lonergan.

Long, Prof. Anthony Arthur, BA, PhD; Gladstone Professor of Greek, Liverpool University, since 1973; *b* 1937; *m* 1960; 1970; one *s* one *d*. BA London 1960 (1st cl. Classics), PhD London 1964. Lectr, Otago Univ., NZ, 1961–64; Lectr, Nottingham Univ., 1964–66; Lectr, Univ. Coll., London, 1966–71; Reader, 1971–73; Cromer Greek Prize, British Academy (jtly) 1968; Vis. Mem., Inst. Adv. Study, Princeton, 1970; Vis. Prof. of Classical Philology, Univ. of Munich, 1973. Sec., Univ. Week Cttee, Otago Univ., 1963; Treas., Council of Univ. Classical Depts, 1970– ; Pres., London Class. Soc., 1971–72; Editor, Bull. Univ. Coll., 1971–73; Mem. Coun. Hellenic Soc., 1972– . *Publications:* Language and Thought in Sophocles, 1968; ed. Problems in Stoicism, 1971; Hellenistic Philosophy, 1974; *contrib.* Bull. Lond. Univ. Inst. Class. Studies, Class. Qly, Class. Rev., Jl Hellenic Soc., Philos. Qly, Phronesis, etc. *Address:* Sch. of Classics, Liverpool Univ., PO Box 147, Liverpool L69 3BX.

Long, Norman Ernest, BA, PhD; Reader in Anthropology, University of Durham, since 1972; *b* 1936; *m* 1960; one *s* one *d*. BA Leeds 1960 (General Studies: Anthropology, Philosophy and Biblical Studies); PhD Manchester 1967 (Social Anthropology); Mem., Assoc. Social Anthropol. GB. Res. Associate, Manchester, 1964–65, Lectr in Social Anthropology, 1965–72; Lectr (Sociology), Univ. of Zambia, 1967–68 (on secondment); Res. Fellow, Inst. Estudios Peruanos, Lima, Peru, 1970–71. Cnsltnt-Investigator, UN Res. Inst. Social Develt, Geneva, 1969. *Publications:* Social Change and the Individual: a study of the social and religious responses to innovation in a Zambian rural community, 1968, 2nd edn 1972; *contrib.* Afr. Soc. Res., Internat. Ybk Sociol. Relig. *Address:* Dept of Anthro-

pology, South End House, The Univ. of Durham, Durham.

Long, Peter; Lecturer in Philosophy, University of Leeds, since 1961; *b* 1926. BA London 1951 (1st cl.), MA Cambridge 1955. Res. Asst, Univ. Coll., London, 1951–52, Asst Lectr in Philosophy, 1954–56; Res. Fellow, Trinity Coll., Cambridge, 1955–59. *Publications:* *contrib.* Mind, Philos. Rev., Proc. Aristot. Soc. *Address:* Philosophy Dept, Univ. of Leeds, Leeds LS2 9JT.

Longbottom, David Alan; Lecturer in Quantitative Methods and Director of MSc Programme, Business School, Durham University, since 1970; *b* 1944; *m* 1971; one *s*. BSc Imperial Coll. London 1965 (Maths); ARCS; Mem., Operational Res. Soc. Operational Research Analyst, ICI Ltd, 1965–67. UK Teaching Fellow, Univ. of Durham, 1967–70. *Publications:* Management Decision Making – an approach through decision analysis (US) (forthcoming); *contrib.* Management Decision, Omega, Operational Res. Qly. *Address:* Durham Univ. Business Sch., Palmers Garth, Durham DH1 3LB.

Longrigg, Cecily V.; Lecturer in English Language and Literature, St Hilda's and St Anne's Colleges, Oxford, since 1968; *b* 1932; *m* 1959; two *s* three *d*. BA Otago, NZ, 1953, MA Hons, Otago, NZ, 1954 (1st cl. Latin), Diploma of Hons, Otago, NZ, 1955 (1st cl.), BA Hons Oxon 1959 (1st cl.). Lectr, Exeter Coll., Oxford, 1965–68. *Address:* St Hilda's Coll., Oxford.

Longrigg, James; Lecturer in Classics, University of Newcastle, since 1966; *b* 1934; *m* 1959; one *s* one *d*. BA Dunelm 1956 (1st cl. Classics). DipEd Dunelm 1957; BLitt Oxon 1961. Carl Newell Jackson Res. Fellow in Classics, Harvard Univ., 1959–60; Lecturer in Classics, Victoria Univ., Wellington, NZ, 1961–63; Nuffield Foundn Sen. Commonwealth Res. Fellow, Warburg Inst., Univ. of London, 1964–66; Vis. Prof., Inst. Res. in Humanities, Univ. of Wisconsin, 1970–71. *Publications:* contrib. Dictionary of Scientific Biography; *contrib.* Apeiron, Class. Qly, Class. Rev., Durham Univ. Jl, Harv. Studies Class. Philol., Isis, Jl Hellenic Studies, Jl Warburg and Courtauld Insts, Philologus, Phronesis, Procs Afr. Class. Assoc. *Address:* Dept of Classics, Univ. of Newcastle upon Tyne, Newcastle upon Tyne NE1 7RU.

Lonsdale, Roger Harrison; Fellow and Tutor in English, Balliol College, Oxford University, since 1963; *b* 1934; *m* 1964; one *s* one *d*. BA Oxon 1957 (1st cl. English), MA Oxon 1961, DPhil Oxon 1962. Res. Asst, Yale Univ., 1958–60; Jun. Res. Fellow, Balliol Coll., Oxford, 1960–63. *Publications:* Dr Charles Burney: a Literary Biography, 1965; The Poems of Gray, Collins, and Goldsmith, 1969; ed, W. Beckford: Vathek, 1970; ed, Dryden to Johnson (Sphere History of Literature, vol. 4), 1971; *contrib.* Papers Bibliog. Soc. Amer., Rev. Engl. Studies. *Address:* Balliol College, Oxford.

Loosemore, John Harrington, BA; Lecturer in Law; Joint Law School, University

College, Cardiff, since 1965; *b* 1937; *m* 1967; one *s* two *d*. BA Wales 1958; Solicitor 1965; Mem., Law Soc. Lectr in Economics, Welsh Coll. of Adv. Technol., 1964–65. Solicitor, private practice, 1965– . *Publications: contrib.* Law Grdn, Law Soc. Gaz., Solic. Jl. *Address:* Joint Law School, Univ. College, Cardiff CF1 1XL.

Loosmore, Robert Glyn; Lecturer, School of Education, University of Leicester, since 1964; *b* 1923; *m* 1947; one *s* one *d*. BA Wales 1951 (1st cl. English). Banking, 1939–42; Army, 1942–47; Colonial Admin. Service, 1951–63; Tutor to Commonwealth Teachers, School of Education, Leicester, 1964– . *Address:* School of Education, Leicester Univ., Leicester LE1 7RH.

Lopasic, Dr Alexander S.; Lecturer in Social Anthropology, Department of Sociology, University of Reading, since 1965; *b* 1928. DrPhil Vienna 1955; Mem., ASA, FRAI. Res. Fellow in African Anthropology (Wenner-Gren Foundn, NY), Univ. of London, 1957–59; Asst Lectr Cologne Univ., 1962–64, Lectr, 1964–65. Curator, Nigerian Museum, Lagos, 1960–61. *Publications:* Commissaire General Drag Lerman: a contribution to the history of Central Africa, 1971; *contrib.* Köln. Ethn. Mit., Man. Proc. 8th Int. Cong. Anthrop. Ethnol. Sci., Trans 6th Wld Cong. Soc. *Address:* Dept of Sociology, Univ. of Reading, Reading RG6 2AH.

Lora, Joseph G.; *see* Garcia-Lora.

Lösel, Dr Franz; Lecturer, Department of Germanic Studies, University of Sheffield, since 1972; *b* 1926; *m* 1959; two *s* two *d*. Dr phil Frankfurt/M 1955, MA TCD 1961. Lectr, Glasgow Univ., 1956–58; Lectr, Trinity College, Dublin, 1958–71, Tutor, 1961–71. Mem., Exec. Cttee, Arts Faculty, TCD, 1971; Mem. Conf. of Univ. Teachers of German. *Publications:* trans., The Book of Kells, by G. O. Simms, 1961; A Short Old High German Grammar and Reader with Glossary, 1969; *contrib.* Hermathena, Philol Qly, Wirkendes Wort. *Address:* Dept of Germanic Studies, Univ. of Sheffield, Sheffield S10 2TN.

Loudon, Dr Joseph Buist; Senior Lecturer in Social Anthropology, Department of Sociology and Anthropology, University College of Swansea, since 1966; *b* 1921; *m* 1954; one *s* two *d*. BA Oxon 1943, BM BCh Oxon 1946, MA Oxon 1947; Acad.Postgrad.Dip. Anthropol. London (Distinction) 1956; FRAI. Mem., Assoc. Social Anthropol. Asst Lectr, LSE, 1956–57; Mem., Scientific Staff, Social Psychiatry Res. Unit, MRC, 1957–64; Lectr, Univ. Coll., Swansea. 1964–66. Var. medical apptmts, 1946–56; Cnsltnt, West. Pacific Reg., WHO, 1956; Mem., Soc. Anthropol. Cttee, SSRC, 1968–72; Mem., Council, Univ. Coll., Swansea, 1970–72. *Publications:* White Farmers and Black Labour-tenants, 1970; ed. Register of Members, Association of Social Anthropologists of the Commonwealth, 1970; ed, jtly, Anthropology and Medicine, 1975; essays, in Culture and Mental Health, ed Opler, 1958; The

Social Anthropology of Complex Societies, ed Banton, 1965; Transcultural Psychiatry, ed deReuck and Porter, 1965; Socialization, the approach from Social Anthropology, ed Mayer, 1970; Studies in African Social Anthropology, ed Fortes, 1974; *contrib.* Brit. Jl Prev. Soc. Med., Brit. Jl Psychiat., Brit. Jl Sociol., Proc. Soc. Psychosomatic Res., Psychol. Med. *Address:* Dept of Sociology and Anthropology, Univ. Coll., Swansea SA2 8PP.

Lough, Prof. John, MA, PhD; Professor of French, University of Durham, since 1952; *b* 1913; *m* 1939; one *d*. BA Cantab 1934 (1st cl. Modern and Medieval Languages), PhD Cantab 1937, MA Cantab 1938; Hon. Dr Clermont 1967; Hon. DLitt Newcastle upon Tyne 1972. Asst, Aberdeen Univ., 1937–45, Lectr, 1945–46; Lectr, Cambridge Univ., 1946–52; Leverhulme Res. Fellow, 1973–74. *Publications:* Locke's Travels in France, 1953; An Introduction to Seventeenth Century France, 1954; Paris Theatre Audiences in the 17th and 18th Centuries, 1957; An Introduction to Eighteenth Century France, 1960; Essays on the Encyclopédie of Diderot and D'Alembert, 1968; The Encyclopédie in Eighteenth Century England and other Studies, 1970; The Encyclopédie, 1971; The Contributors to the Encyclopédie, 1973; ed, Diderot: Selected Philosophical Writings, 1953; Selected Articles from the Encyclopédie of Diderot and D'Alembert, 1954, 2nd edn 1969; *contrib.* Fr. Studies, Mod. Lang. Rev., Rev. Hist. Litt., Studies Volt. *Address:* Dept of French, Elvet Riverside, New Elvet, Durham.

Lovatt, Dr Roger Walford, FRHistS; Fellow, since 1962, and Senior Tutor, since 1968, Peterhouse, Cambridge; University Lecturer in History, Cambridge, since 1969; *b* 1937; *m* 1972. BA Hons Oxon 1960 (1st cl.), MA, DPhil Oxon 1966. Res. Fellow, Peterhouse, Cambridge, 1962; Official Fellow, 1964; Univ. Asst Lectr in History, Cambridge, 1965–69. *Publications: contrib.* Trans RHistS. *Address:* Peterhouse, Cambridge.

Love, Philip Noel, MA, LLB; Part-time Lecturer in Evidence and Procedure, University of Aberdeen, since 1968; *b* 1939; *m* 1963; three *s*. MA Aberdeen 1961, LLB Aberdeen 1963. Pt-time Asst in Scots Law, Aberdeen Univ., 1963–68. Mem., Council, Scott. Law Agents Soc.; Mem., Rules Council, Ct of Session; Examn for Law Soc. of Scotland in Evidence and Procedure. Mem., Rent Assessment Panel for Scotland. *Address:* Dept of Evidence and Procedure, Taylor Building, Univ. of Aberdeen, Old Aberdeen AB9 2UB.

Lovell, Dr John Christopher; Lecturer in Economic and Social History, University of Kent at Canterbury, since 1965; *b* 1940. BA Hull 1961 (1st cl. History); PhD London 1966; FRHistS. *Publications:* (with B. C. Roberts) A Short History of the TUC, 1968; Stevedores and Dockers, 1969. *Address:* Eliot College, The Univ., Canterbury, Kent CT1 3PA.

Lovell, Percy Albert; Lecturer in Music, University of Newcastle upon Tyne, since

1966; b 1919; m 1945; four s. BA Cantab 1940 (History Tripos I [2nd cl. Div. 1] MusB Pt I [1st cl.]), MA Cantab 1944, MusB Cantab 1946; LRAM 1944. Staff Tutor and Conductor, Nat. Opera and Drama Assoc. Summer Schs, 1954– , Dir, 1972– ; Dir: Camerata Singers, 1969– ; Conductor: Newcastle upon Tyne Bach Choir, 1972– ; Tyneside Chamber Orch., 1972– . *Publications:* Quaker Inheritance, 1871–1961, 1970; *contrib.* Music Lett. *Address:* Dept of Music, The Univ., Newcastle upon Tyne NE1 7RU.

Loveridge, Raymond; Professor of Manpower Management, Management Centre, University of Aston in Birmingham, since 1973; b 1932; m 1954; three d. Dip. Pol Econ. Oxon, MA Cantab, MSc London; Member: Brit. Univs Ind. Relns Assoc.; Brit. Sociol Assoc. (Co-Founder/Convenor, Ind. Sociol. Gp). Lecturer: Dept of Ind. Relns, LSE, 1967–70; Orgn Behaviour Gp, London Bus. Sch., 1970–73. Mem., Conf. Cttee on Operations Res. and Behavioural Sci., 1969– . *Publications:* Collective Bargaining by National Employees in the United Kingdom (Inst. of Labor Relations, Univ. of Michigan), 1970; (with B. C. Roberts and J. Gennard) Reluctant Militants: a study of industrial technicians, 1971; *contrib.* Brit. Jl Ind. Relns, Sociol. *Address:* The Management Centre, Univ. of Aston in Birmingham, 158 Corporation Street, Birmingham B4 6TE.

Low, Donald Alexander; Lecturer, Department of English, University of Stirling, since 1972; b 1939; m 1965; one s one d. MA St Andrews 1962, BPhil St Andrews 1965; PhD Cambridge 1968; Carnegie Scholarship 1965, Wyndham Deedes Travel Scholarship to Israel 1968. Lectr, Dept of English, Univ. of St Andrews, 1966–72. Mem., Univs Cttee on Scott. Lit., 1968– ; Treas., Assoc. Scott. Lit. Studies, 1970–71. *Publications:* Robert Burns: The Critical Heritage, 1974; ed, Critical Essays on Burns (forthcoming); contrib. New Cambridge Bibliography of English Literature, vol. 3, 1969, and vol. 2, 1971; Scott Bicentenary Essays, 1974; *contrib.* Bibliotheck, Burns Chronicle, Byron Jl, Jl Europ. Stud., Forum for Mod. Lang. Stud., N & Q, Rev. Eng. Stud., Scotsman, Scott. Lit. News, Stud. in Scott. Lit., TLS, Wordsworth Circle. *Address:* Univ. of Stirling, Stirling FK9 4LA.

Lowe, Dr Alan Darlington; Lecturer, Department of Theology, University of Leeds, since 1964; b 1932. BA Dublin 1954 (Classics), Divinity Testimonium Dublin 1956, BA supp. Dublin 1957 (Oriental Languages), PhD Cambridge 1963 (Oriental Studies). Asst Lectr, Dept of Theology, Univ. of Leeds, 1961–63. *Publications:* contrib. Hermathena. *Address:* Dept of Theology, Univ., Leeds LS2 9JT.

Lowe, Prof. Charles Ronald, Professor of Social and Occupational Medicine, Welsh National School of Medicine, University of Wales, since 1962; b 1912; m 1938; one d. MB ChB Birmingham 1936, DPh Birmingham 1948, MD Birmingham 1950, PhD Birmingham 1952; MRCP 1969, FRCGP 1972,

426

FFCM 1973; Res. Sch., Birmingham, 1948; Lectr in Public Health, Birmingham, 1949–54; Lectr in Social Med., 1954–60; Reader in Social Med., 1960–62. Med. Adv., GEC Ltd, 1954; Med. Cnslt, Dept of Employment (Wales), Mem., Indust. Injuries Adv. Council (DHSS), 1965; var. Univ. and Govt Cttees. *Publications:* (with T. McKeown) An Introduction to Social Medicine, 1966, new edn 1974; contrib. chapters in var. books; *contrib.* over 60 scientific papers, mainly in: Brit. Med. Jl, Brit. Jl Prev. Soc. Med., Brit. Jl Indust. Med., Bull. WHO, Lancet. *Address:* Welsh National School of Medicine, Heath Park, Cardiff C4X 4XN.

Lowe, David Evan; Lecturer, History Department, University of Southampton, since 1965; b 1940; m 1969. BA Wales 1963 (1st cl. History). *Address:* Dept of History, Univ. of Southampton, Southampton SO9 5NH.

Lowe, Prof. Ernest Anthony; Professor of Accounting and Financial Management, Division of Economic Studies, University of Sheffield, since 1971; b 1928; m 1956; five s one d. BScEcon London 1957; FCA 1954, ACIS 1952, Mem., TIMS. Lectr, Univ. Leeds, 1957–66; Faculty Fellow, MIT, 1961–62; Ford Foundn Fellow, Harvard Univ., 1961–62. Vis. Prof., Univ. of California, Berkeley, 1962; Sen. Lectr, Univ. of Bradford Management Centre, 1966–68; Sen. Lectr, Manchester Business Sch., 1969–71. Chm., Council of Depts of Accounting Studies (CODAS), 1974– ; Vice-Chm., British Accounting and Finance Assoc., 1971– . *Publications:* contrib. various collections; *contrib.* Accountancy, Jl Business Finance, Jl Industrial Econs, Jl Management Studies, Jl Systems Engrg. *Address:* Univ. of Sheffield, Sheffield S10 2TN.

Lowe, Geoff; Lecturer, Department of Psychology, Hull University, since 1967; b 1940; m 1960; one s two d. BA Hull 1962; PhD 1972; ABPsS. Mem., Brain Res. Assoc., Foreign Affiliate, Amer. Psychol Assoc. Asst Lectr in Psychol., Univ. of Hull, 1965–67. *Publications:* contrib. Acta Psychol, Brit. Jl Psychol, Jl Acoust. Soc. Amer., Nature, Percept. Psychophys., Psychopharm. *Address:* Dept of Psychology, Univ. of Hull, Hull HU6 7RX.

Lowe, Ian (Harlowe); Assistant Keeper, Department of Western Art, Ashmolean Museum, Oxford (also lectures), since 1962; b 1935; m 1961; one s. BA Oxon 1958 (2nd cl. English), MA Oxon 1962; Lawrence Binyon Prize 1958. Christie, Manson and Woods, 1959–61; Vis. Sch., Boston Public Libr., Boston, Mass., 1968. Sec., Friends of the Ashmolean, 1969– ; Mem., Joseph Webb Award Cttee, 1972. FRSA 1974. *Publications:* ed, Notes on Italian Monuments of the 12th to 16th Centuries, by M. H. Longhurst, 1960; contrib. Illustrations and notes, in, Oxford, by F. Markham, 1967. *Address:* Ashmolean Museum, Oxford.

Lowe, Dr Jennifer; Lecturer, Department of Hispanic Studies, University of Edinburgh, since 1966; b 1937; m 1964; two s. BA London

1959 (1st cl. Spanish), PhD London 1963. Asst Lectr, Univ. of London, 1961–64; Asst Lectr, Univ. of Edinburgh, 1964–66. *Publications*: critical study: Cervantes: Two Novelas ejemplares, 1971; *contrib.* Bull. Hispan. Studies, Forum Mod. Lang. Studies, Hispanóf., Iberorom. *Address*: Dept of Hispanic Studies, David Hume Tower, George Square, Edinburgh EH8 9JX.

Lowe, Dr John; Head of Department of Educational Studies and Director of Extra-Mural Studies, University of Edinburgh, since 1964; *b* 1922; *m* 1949; two *s* one *d*. BA Hons Liverpool 1950 (Hist.); Postgrad. CertEd London 1957, PhD London 1960. Univ. of Liverpool, 1955–63; Univ. of Singapore, 1963–64. Member: Cttee on Adult Educn (Scotland, 1970– ; Standing Consultative Council on Youth and Community Services for Scotland, 1971–73; Sec. and Treasurer, Internat. Congress of Univ. Adult Educn, 1972– ; Hd of Educnl Structures Section, OECD, 1973–74. *Publications*: Adult Education in England and Wales: a critical study, 1970; A Retrospective International Survey of Adult Education: Montreal 1960 to Tokyo 1972, 1972; ed (with M. Lowe) On Teaching Foreign Languages to Adults, 1965; ed, Adult Education and Nation-Building, 1970; *contrib.* Irish Historical Studies, Jl of Internat. Congress of Univ. Adult Educn, Studia Hibernica, Studies in Adult Educn. *Address*: Dept of Educational Studies, Univ. of Edinburgh, 11 Buccleuch Place, Edinburgh.

Lowe, John Christopher Burpee, MA, BLitt; Lecturer in Latin, Bedford College, University of London, since 1960; *b* 1930; *m* 1958; three *s*. BA Oxon 1953, MA Oxon 1956, BLitt Oxon 1961. Lectr, Queen's Coll., Oxford, 1957–60; Lectr, St Edmund Hall, Oxford, 1958–60. *Address*: Bedford College, Regent's Park, NW1 4NS.

Lowe, Julian Frank; Lecturer, Department of Industrial Economics, University of Nottingham, since 1969; *b* 1945; *m* 1968; one *s* one *d*. BA Wales 1967, MA(Econ) Manchester 1968. *Publications: contrib.* Scott. Jl Pol. Econ., Europ. Jl Marketing. *Address*: University Park, Nottingham NG7 2RD.

Lowe, Dr Peter Carlton; Lecturer in History, University of Manchester, since 1968; *b* 1941. BA Wales 1963 (1st cl. History), PhD Wales 1967; FRHistS. Asst Lectr, Manchester Univ., 1965–68. *Publications*: Great Britain and Japan 1911–15: a study of British Far Eastern policy, 1969; The Rise to the Premiership, 1914–16, in Lloyd George: Twelve Essays, ed A. J. P. Taylor, 1971; Great Britain and the Outbreak of War with Japan, 1941, in War and Society: essays in honour and memory of J. K. R. Western 1928–1971, ed M. R. D. Foot, 1973; *contrib.* Hist. Jl, Hist., TRHS. *Address*: Dept of History, Univ. of Manchester, Manchester M13 9PL.

Lowenthal, Prof. David; Professor, Department of Geography, University College London, since 1972; *b* 1923; *m* 1970. BS Harvard 1943, MA California 1950, PhD Wisconsin 1953. Asst Prof. and Chm., Dept of Geography, Vassar Coll., 1952–56. Research Assoc., Amer. Geog. Soc., 1957–72, Sec., 1967–72; Mem., Council, AAAS, 1964–72; Mem., Council, Assoc. of Amer. Geographers, 1968–71. *Publications*: George Perkins Marsh, Versatile Vermonter, 1958; The West Indies Federation: perspectives on a new nation, 1961; ed, Man and Nature, 1965, 1973; ed, Environmental Perception and Behavior, 1967; West Indian Societies, 1972; ed, West Indian Perspectives, 4 vols, 1973; *contrib.* Geog. Review, Social and Econ. Studies. *Address*: Dept of Geography, Univ. College, Gower Street, WC1E 6BT.

Lowes, Bryan; Lecturer in Economics, Management Centre, Bradford University, since 1968; *b* 1946; *m* 1969; one *d*. BSc (Hons) Bradford 1967, CertEd Leeds 1968. *Publications*: (with R. Wild) The Principles of Modern Management, 1972; (with J. Sparkes) Modern Managerial Economics, 1974; *contrib.* Econs, Jl of Bus. Policy, The Manchester Sch. *Address*: Management Centre, Emm Lane, Bradford BD9 4JL.

Lowy, (Rabbi) Simeon, MA, PhD; Lecturer in Hebrew, Department of Semitic Studies, University of Leeds, since 1960; *b* 1921; *m* 1948; two *s* two *d*. MA Jerusalem 1956 (Distinction, Hebrew and Jewish Studies), Teacher's Dip. 1967, PhD Leeds 1973; Rabbi, Fellow of Jews Coll. (London), 1960. Lectr and Res. Fellow, Inst. of Jewish Studies, Manchester, 1957–59; Fellow, Inst. of Jewish Studies, Univ. Coll., London, 1959–60; Vis. Lectr, Tel-Aviv Univ., 1968–69. *Publications: contrib.* Ann. Leeds Univ. Orient. Soc., Jl Jew. Studies, Papers Inst. Jew. Studies. *Address*: Dept of Semitic Studies, The Univ. of Leeds, Leeds LS2 9JT.

Loyn, Prof. H. R., DLitt, FSA; Professor of Medieval History, University College, Cardiff, since 1969; *b* 1922; *m* 1950; three *s*. BA Wales 1944, 1945 (2nd cl. English, 1st cl. History), MA Wales 1949, DLitt Wales 1968; FRHistS. Asst Lectr, Cardiff, 1946–49; Lectr, 1949–61; Sen. Lectr, 1961–66; Reader, 1966–69. Mem., Council, Hist. Assoc., 1964– ; Vice-Pres., and Chm., Publicns Cttee, 1970– ; Mem., Council, Soc. Mediev. Archeol., 1964–67; Vice-Pres., 1970– . *Publications*: Boroughs and Mints, in, Anglo-Saxon Coins, ed R. H. M. Dolley, 1961; Anglo-Saxon England and the Norman Conquest, 1962, pbk edn 1971; The Norman Conquest, 1965, 2nd edn 1967; ed, Annual Bulletin of Historical Literature, 1965–68; Harold Godwinson, 1966; (with Alan Sorrell) Norman Britain, 1966; Alfred the Great, 1967; contrib. Hoops: Reallexicon der Germanischen Altertumskunde, 1970– ; A Wulfstan MS: Nero Ai, 1971; *contrib.* EHR, Hist. *Address*: Dept of History, Univ. Coll., Cathays Park, Cardiff CF1 1XL.

Loynes, Prof. Robert Michael, BA, PhD; Professor of Probability and Statistics, University of Sheffield, since 1969; *b* 1935; *m* 1957; one *s* two *d*. BA Cambridge 1956, Dip. in Mathematical Statistics Cambridge 1959, PhD Cambridge 1963; FSS. Fellow, Churchill Coll., Cambridge, 1961–63; Lectr,

427

Manchester Univ., 1963–65; Lectr, Cambridge Univ., and Fellow, Trinity Hall, 1965–69; Vis. Res. Prof., Florida State Univ., 1967; Vis. Prof., Univ. of N Carolina, 1969; UNESCO expert, UNDP project, Islamabad Univ., Pakistan, 1972–73. *Publications: contrib.* Ann. Math. Stat., Jl Royal Stat. Soc., Proc. Trans Amer. Math. Soc., Zeits. Wahrschein. Anw. *Address:* Dept of Probability and Statistics, The Univ., Sheffield S3 7RH.

Lucas, Prof. Bryan K.; *see* Keith-Lucas.

Lucas, Dr John; *see* Lucas, Dr W. J.

Lucas, Dr Colin Renshaw; Fellow and Tutor in Modern History, Balliol College, Oxford, since 1973; *b* 1940; *m* 1964; one *s.* BA Oxon 1962, MA 1969, DPhil 1969. Sheffield Univ., 1965–69; Indiana Univ., 1969–70; Manchester Univ., 1970–73. *Publications:* The Structure of the Terror, 1973; *contrib.* Annales historiques de la Révolution française, Past and Present. *Address:* Balliol College, Oxford.

Lucas, John Randolph; Fellow and Tutor of Merton College, University of Oxford, since 1960; *b* 1929; *m* 1961; two *s* two *d.* BA Oxon 1951, MA Oxon 1954. Jun. Res. Fellow, Merton Coll., Oxford, 1953–56; Fellow and Asst Tutor, Corpus Christi Coll., Cambridge, 1956–59; Jane Eliza Procter Vis. Fellow, Princeton Univ., NJ, 1957–58; Leverhulme Res. Fellow in Philosophy of Science, Leeds, 1959–60. Doctrinal Commn, C of E, Mem., 1967– . *Publications:* The Principles of Politics, 1966; The Concept of Probability, 1970; The Freedom of the Will, 1970; (jtly) The Nature of Mind, 1972; A Treatise on Time and Space, 1973; (jtly) The Development of Mind, 1974; Democracy and Participation, 1975; *contrib.* Brit. Jl Philos. Sci., Monist, Philos. Qly., Philos., Philos. Science. *Address:* Merton College, Oxford.

Lucas, Dr Noah, MA, PhD; Lecturer in American Government and Politics, University of Sheffield, since 1967; *b* 1927; *m* 1965; two *d.* MA Glasgow 1951 (Hons Pol. Econ.), PhD Washington Univ., St Louis, 1961. Grad. Asst, Washington Univ., 1958–61; Asst Prof., South Illinois Univ., Edwardsville, 1961–63; Res. Assoc., Hebrew Univ., Jerusalem, 1963–66; Vis. Assoc. Prof., South Illinois Univ., 1965; Vis. Lectr, Glasgow Univ., 1966–67. Internat. Sec., Histadrut Exec. (Tel-Aviv), 1953–57. *Publications:* (as Noah Malkosh) Cooperation in Israel, 1954, 3rd edn 1962, French edn 1967; Histadrut in Israel, 1961, Spanish edn 1962; The Modern History of Israel, 1974. *Address:* Dept of Politics, Univ. of Sheffield, Sheffield S10 2TN.

Lucas, Dr Peter Jeremy, MA, PhD; Lecturer (formerly Assistant) in Old and Middle English Language and Literature, University College, Dublin, since 1965; *b* 1943; *m* 1968; one *d.* BA Oxon 1964 (English), MA Oxon 1968, PhD Leeds 1973; Gordon Duff Prize, Oxford 1968; Mem., Early English Text Soc., English Assoc., Philol Soc. Res. Asst, Leeds Univ., 1964–65. Treasurer, Dublin Medieval Soc., 1973– ; Conf. Univ. Teachers of English Cttee, 1974. *Publications: contrib.* Archiv. Lingu., Brit. Museum Qly, Engl. Studies, Leeds Studies in English, Libr., Med. Æv., Notes Queries, Scriptorium, Studia Neophilol., Studies (Dublin), Trans Camb. Bibliog. Soc. *Address:* Dept of English, Univ. College, Belfied, Dublin 4, Ireland.

Lucchesi, Dr Valerio; University Lecturer in Italian, Oxford University, since 1966; Fellow of Corpus Christi College, Oxford, since 1970; *b* 1927; *m* 1967. DottLitt Florence 1955, MA Oxon 1966. Assistente Volontario Università di Firenze, 1955–56; Asst Lectr, Univ. of Edinburgh, 1957–58; Lectr, Manchester Univ., 1959–66. *Publications: contrib.* Atti dell' Accademia Toscana di Scienze e Lettere 'La Colombaria', Mod. Lang. Review, Notes and Queries, Nuova Rivista Storica, Studi di Grammatica Italiana. *Address:* Corpus Christi College, Oxford.

Lucas, Dr (W.) John, BA, PhD; Senior Lecturer, School of English Studies, University of Nottingham, since 1971; *b* 1937; *m* 1961; one *s* one *d.* BA Reading 1959 (Hons Philosophy and English Literature), PhD Reading 1965. Lectr, Univ. of Reading, 1961–64; Lectr, Univ. of Nottingham, 1964–71; Vis. Prof., Univ. of Maryland, 1967–68. *Publications:* Tradition and Tolerance in 19th Century Fiction, 1966; George Crabbe: A Selection of his Poems, 1967; The Melancholy Man: A Study of Dickens's Novels, 1970; ed, J. Austen: Mansfield Park, 1970; ed, Literature and Politics in the 19th Century; *contrib.* Engl. Lit. Hist., Ess. Crit., Oxf. Rev., Renaissance and Modern Studies, Reviews, Mod. Studies, Vict. Studies. *Address:* School of English Studies, University Park, Nottingham NG7 2RD.

Luce, Rev. Prof. Arthur Aston, MC, DD, LittD; Berkeley Professor of Metaphysics, Trinity College, Dublin, since 1953; *b* 1882; *m* 1918; two *s.* BA Dublin 1903, BD Dublin 1907, DD Dublin 1920, LittD Dublin 1934, Hon. DLit Belfast 1953. Mem., Royal Irish Acad. Fellow, TCD, 1912; Prof. of Moral Philosophy, 1934–49. Chancellor, St Patrick's Cath., Dublin, 1936– , Precentor 1952– . *Publications:* Monophysitism Past and Present, 1920; Bergson's doctrine of intuition, 1922; Berkeley and Malebranche, 1934; Berkeley's Philosophical Commentaries. 1944; Berkeley's Immaterialism, 1945; Teach Yourself Logic, 1958; (with Jessop) The Works of George Berkeley, vols I, IV, VII, VIII, 1948–57; The Life of George Berkeley, 1949; Sense without Matter, 1954; The Dialectic of Immaterialism, 1963; *contrib.* Mind, Hermath., Proc. Royal Irish Acad. *Address:* Trinity College, Dublin 2.

Luce, John Victor, MA, FTCD; Associate Professor of Classics, Classics Department, Trinity College, University of Dublin, since 1972; *b* 1920; *m* 1948; three *d.* BA TCD 1942 (Hons), MA TCD 1945, MA Oxon 1945. Lectr in Classics, Dublin, 1942–45; Lectr in Greek, Glasgow, 1946–48; Trinity Coll., Dublin: Fellow in Classics, 1948– ; Reader in Classics, 1963–72; Sen. Tutor, 1964–67;

Public Orator, 1971– . *Publications*: The End of Atlantis, 1969, French, German and Amer. edns, 1969–71, paperback edn 1971; (with others) The Quest for America, 1971; (with W. B. Stanford) The Quest for Ulysses, 1974; Homer and the Heroic Age, 1974; *contrib*. Amer. Jl Philol., Class. Qly, Class. Rev., Greece and Rome, Hermathena, Phronesis. *Address*: Trinity College, Dublin 2, Ireland.

Lucey, Dr Denis I. F., MS, PhD; Statutory Lecturer in Economics, University College, Cork, since 1969; *b* 1942; *m* 1965; two *d*. BAgrSc National Univ. of Ireland 1963, MS Iowa State 1966, PhD Iowa State 1967. Mem., AEA, AAEA, etc. Ed., Agric. Econ. Soc. Ireland Proc. Res. Asst, Iowa State Univ., 1964–66; Res. Assoc., 1966–67; Sen. Res. Off., Econ. Dept, Agric. Res. Inst., Dublin, 1968–69. *Publications*: Rural Industrialization, 1969. *Address*: Dept of Economics, Univ. College, Cork, Ireland.

Lucy, Prof. Seán, MA; Professor of Modern English, University College, Cork (National University of Ireland), since 1967; *b* 1931; *m* 1954; three *s* two *d*. BA National Univ. of Ireland 1952, MA National Univ. of Ireland 1957. Asst Lectr, Univ. Coll., Cork, 1962–67. Mem., Cttee, Internat. Assoc. Study Anglo-Irish Lit., 1971–73; External Examnr, Univ. of Leeds, 1971– , Univ. of Dublin, 1973– , Univ. of Stirling, 1973– . *Publications*: T. S. Eliot and the Idea of Tradition, 1960; ed, Love Poems of the Irish, 1968; ed, Five Irish Poets, 1970; ed, Irish Poets in English, The Thomas Davis Lectures on Anglo-Irish Poetry, 1972; *contrib*. Irish Univ. Rev., Studies. *Address*: Dept of English, Univ. College, Cork, Ireland.

Luibhéid, Colm; Lecturer, Department of Classics, University College, Galway, since 1961; *b* 1936; *m* 1961; one *s* three *d*. BA UC Dublin 1956, MA UC Dublin 1957, PhD Princeton 1961. Fordham Univ., NY, 1959–61. *Publications*: The Essential Eusebius, 1965; Eusebius of Caesarea and the Arian Crisis, 1974; *contrib*. Class. Phil., Irish Theol. Qly., Jl Eccles. Hist. *Address*: Univ. College, Galway, Ireland.

Luke, Dr F. D.; Lecturer in German, Faculty of Modern Languages, University of Oxford, and Student of Christ Church (Tutor in German), since 1960; *b* 1921. BA Oxford 1944, MA Oxford 1947, DPhil Oxford 1948. Asst Lectr, then Lectr, Manchester Univ. 1947–60. *Publications*: Goethe: Selected Verse (Penguin Poets, bilingual series), 1964; ed and trans. (with R. Pick), Goethe: Conversations and Encounters, 1966; trans., Stifter: Limestone and other stories, 1968; trans., T. Mann: Tonio Kröger and other stories, 1970; *contrib*. Mod. Lang. Rev., Oxf. Germ. Studies, Publicns Engl. Goethe Soc. *Address*: Christ Church, Oxford.

Lukes, Steven Michael, MA, DPhil; Fellow and Tutor in Politics, Balliol College, Oxford, since 1966; *b* 1941; *m* 1964. BA Oxon 1962 (1st cl. PPE), MA Oxon 1965, DPhil Oxon 1969. Asst Lectr in Moral and Political Philosophy, Univ. of Keele, 1963; Res. Fel-

low, Nuffield Coll., Oxford, 1964–66. Mem., Editorial Bd, Archives européennes de Sociologie, 1970– . *Publications*: ed (with A. Arblaster), The Good Society, 1971; Emile Durkheim: his life and work, an historical and critical study, 1973; Individualism, 1973; Power: a Radical View, 1974; *contrib*. Archives européennes de sociologie, Brit. Jl of Sociology, Jl of the Hist. of Ideas, Political Studies, etc. *Address*: Balliol College, Oxford.

Lumsden, Dr David James, MA, DPhil, MusB; Fellow and Organist, New College, University of Oxford, and University Lecturer in Music, since 1959; *b* 1928; *m* 1951; two *s* two *d*. BA Cantab 1950 (1st cl.), MusB Cantab 1951 (Barclay Squire Prize), PhD Cantab 1957, MA DPhil Oxon 1959 (by incorporation). Dir. of Music, Keele Univ., 1957–59; Prof. of Harmony, Royal Acad. Music, 1959–61; Hugh Porter Lectr, Union Sem., NY, 1967. Pres., Inc. Assoc. Organists, 1966–68; Hon. Ed., Ch Music Soc., 1970–73. *Publications*: Anthology of English Lute Music, 1954; ed, T. Robinson: Schoole of Musicke 1603, 1971; *contrib*. Galpin Soc. Jl, Music Lett. *Address*: New College, Oxford.

Lunzer, Prof. Eric Anthony; Professor of Educational Psychology, School of Education, Nottingham University, since 1969; *b* 1923; *m* 1950; three *d*. MA Oxon, PhD Birmingham; Mem., Brit. Psych. Soc. Lectr in Child Psychology, Manchester Univ. Dept of Educn, 1957–65, Sen. Lectr, 1965–69. *Publications*: Recent Studies in Britain Based on the Work of Jean Piaget, 1960; Conservations spatiales, 1965; Manchester Scales of Social Adaptation, 1966; The Regulation of Behaviour, 1968; Development in Learning, 1968; Contexts of Education, 1969; *contrib*. Brit. Jl Educnl Psychology, Jl Child Psychology and Psychiatry, Qly Jl Exper. Psychology. *Address*: School of Education, Univ. of Nottingham, University Park, Nottingham NG7 2RD.

Lupton, Prof. Tom, MA, PhD; Professor of Organisational Behaviour, Manchester Business School, University of Manchester, since 1966; *b* 1918; *m* 1942, 1963; one *s* two *d* DipEconPolSci Oxon 1948 (Dist.), BA Oxon 1950 (PPE 2), PhD Manchester 1959. Res. Asst, Res. Fellow, Liverpool, 1951–54; Res. Fellow, Manchester, 1954, Lectr, 1958, Sen. Lectr, 1959; Head of Dept, CAT Birmingham (now Univ. of Aston), 1959–64; Prof. of Industrial Relations, Univ. of Leeds, 1964–66; Vis. Prof., Univ. of Chicago, 1971. Chm., Assoc. of Teachers of Mgmt, 1960–64; Panel Mem., Civil Service Arbitration Tribunal, 1966–72; Dept of Employment Arbitration Service, 1966– ; UGC Mgnt Educn Panel, 1964–68. Ed., Jl of Mgnt Studies, 1965– . *Publications*: On the Shop Floor, 1963; Industrial Behaviour and Personnel Management, 1965; Management and the Social Sciences, 1966, rev. edn 1970; (jtly) Neighbourhood and Community, 1954; (jtly) Technical Change and Industrial Relations, 1956; (ed) Payment Systems, 1972; (with Angela Bowey) Pay Comparisons in Collective Bargaining, 1973; (with Angela Bowey) Wages and Salaries, 1974; *contrib*. Jl of Management

429

Studies, Scott. Jl of Political Econ., Manchester Sch. *Address*: Manchester Business School, Booth Street, West, Manchester.

Luscombe, Prof. David Edward, MA, PhD, FRHistS; Head of Department and Professor of Medieval History, Department of Medieval and Modern History, Sheffield University, since 1972; *b* 1938; *m* 1960; three *s* one *d*. BA Cantab 1959 (1st cl.), MA Cantab 1963, PhD Cantab 1964; FRHistSoc 1970– . Fellow, King's Coll., Cambridge, 1962–64; Fellow, Lectr, Dir of Studies in History, Churchill Coll., Cambridge, 1964–72 and Tutor, 1969–72; Leverhulme Faculty Fellow in European Studies, 1973. Mem., Governing Body, St Edmund's House, Cambridge, 1971– . *Publications*: The School of Peter Abelard: the Influence of Abelard's Thought in the Early Scholastic Period; 1969; ed and trans., Abelard: Ethics, 1971; *contrib*. Archives d'histoire doctrinale et littéraire du moyen âge, Encyclopedia of Philosophy, Dictionnaire de spiritualité, Recherches de théologie ancienne et médiévale, Vivarium. *Address*: Dept of Medieval and Modern History, The Univ., Sheffield S10 2TN.

Lyas, Colin Anthony, BA, MA; Lecturer in Philosophy, University of Lancaster, since 1966; *b* 1938; *m* 1962. BA Keele 1961, MA McMaster 1963. Teaching Fellow, McMaster, 1962; Teaching Asst, Cornell, 1963; Susan Linn Sage Fellow in Philos., 1965. *Publications*: ed, Philosophy and Linguistics, 1971; *contrib*. Brit. Jl Aesth., Jl Philos., Philos., Philos. Bks, Proc. Aristot. Soc. *Address*: Dept of Philosophy, Bowland College, Bailrigg, Lancaster.

Lydall, Prof. Harold French; Professor of Economics, School of Social Studies, University of East Anglia, since 1970; *b* 1916; *m* 1940; one *s* two *d*. BA Univ. of S Africa 1936, MA Oxon 1950. Sen. Res. Officer, Univ. of Oxford, 1950; Reader in Economic Statistics, Univ. of WA, 1960, Prof. of Commerce, 1961; Prof. of Economics, Univ. of Adelaide, 1962. *Publications*: British Incomes and Savings, 1955; (with P. N. Dhar) The Role of Small Enterprises in Indian Economic Development, 1961; The Structure of Earnings, 1968; *contrib*. Econ. Jl, Amer. Econ. Rev., Jl Roy. Stat. Soc., Economet., Rev. Econs and Stats, Oxf. Econ. Papers, Aust. Econ. Papers, Econ. Rec., Bull. Oxf. Univ. Inst. Stats. *Address*: School of Social Studies, Univ. of East Anglia, Norwich NOR 88C.

Lydon, Prof. James F., FTCD, MRIA; Fellow, since 1965, and Associate Professor of Medieval History, Trinity College, Dublin, since 1967; *b* 1928. BA Galway (1st cl. History and English) 1950, MA Galway (1st cl. History) 1952, PhD London 1955; MRIA. Asst Lectr, Galway, 1956–59; Jun. Lectr, TCD, 1959–62; Lectr, 1962–67. *Publications*: The Lordship of Ireland in the Middle Ages, 1972; Ireland in the Later Middle Ages, 1973; *contrib*. Irish Hist. Studies, Proc. Roy. Irish Acad. *Address*: 24 Trinity College, Dublin 2.

Lynch, Frances Marion, (Mrs P. A. B.

Llewellyn), MA, FSA; Lecturer in Archaeology, Department of History, University of North Wales, since 1966; *b* 1938; *m* 1971. BA Liverpool 1960 (Hons Hist.), MA Liverpool 1962 (Archaeology); FSA, Mem., Prehist. Soc., Mem., Cambrian Archaeol. Assoc. Leverhulme Fellowship, Liverpool, 1962–64; Sen. Fellowship, Wales, 1964–66. Mem., Council, Prehist. Soc., 1970–73; Sec., CBA Gp 2 (Wales and Mon.), 1971– . *Publications*: (jtly) Megalithic Enquiries in the West of Britain, 1969; Prehistoric Anglesey, 1970; ed (with C. B. Burgess), Prehistoric Man in Wales and the West, 1972; *contrib*. Archaeol. Camb. *Address*: Dept of History, Univ. College of North Wales, Bangor LL57 2DG.

Lynch, James; Lecturer in Education, University of Southampton, since 1968; *b* 1936; *m*; one *s* two *d*. BA Hull 1958, MEd Hull 1966, PhD Durham 1974, Certif Ed 1959, Dip Ed 1962. Former Mem. Council, ATCDE, now Chm. Southern Branch. *Publications*: (with H. Dudley Plunkett) Teacher Education and Cultural Change ,1973; *contrib*. Comparative Educn, Comparative Educn Rev. *Address*: Univ. of Southampton, School of Education, Highfield, Southampton SO9 5NH.

Lynch, Prof. John, MA, PhD; Director, Institute of Latin American Studies, since 1974, Professor of Latin American History, University of London, since 1970; *b* 1927; *m* 1960; two *s* three *d*. MA Edinburgh 1952 (1st cl. history), PhD London 1955; FRHistS. Asst Lectr, then Lectr, Univ. of Liverpool, 1954–61; Lectr in Hispanic and Latin American Hist., Univ. Coll., London, 1961–64; Reader, 1964–70. *Publications*: Spanish Colonial Administration 1782–1810, 1958, Spanish edn 1963; Spain under the Habsburgs, 1964–69; (with R. A. Humphreys) The Origins of the Latin American Revolutions 1808–1826, 1965; The Spanish American Revolutions 1808–1826, 1973; *contrib*. Hispan. Amer. Hist. Rev., Jl Latin Amer. Studies. *Address*: Inst. of Latin American Studies, 31 Tavistock Square, WC1H 9HA.

Lynch, Michael Felix; Senior Lecturer, Postgraduate School of Librarianship and Information Science, Sheffield, since 1969; *b* 1932; *m* 1961; one *s* one *d*. BSc NUI 1954. PhD NUI; ARIC, MBCS. Sen. Res. Fellow, Univ. of Sheffield, 1965, Lectr, 1968. *Publications*: (with Harrison, Town and Ash), Computer Handling of Chemical Structure Information, 1971; Computer-based Information Services in Science and Technology: principles and techniques, 1974; *contrib*. Jl Chem. Soc., Inform. Stor. Retrieval, Jl Chem. Document., Computer Jl, Jl Documentation. *Address*: Western Bank, Sheffield S10 2TN.

Lynch, Prof. Patrick, MA, MRIA; Associate Professor of Political Economy, University College, Dublin, since 1966; Member, Governing Body, University College, Dublin, since 1963; *b* 1918; *m* 1965. MA National University of Ireland 1941; Elected Fellow Commoner, Peterhouse, Cambridge 1956, Elected Mem., Royal Irish Acad. 1962. Lectr in Econs, Univ. Coll., Dublin, 1952–66. Irish Civil Service, 1941–52, part as Asst Sec. to

Govt; Chm., Aer Lingus, 1954; Chm., Aerlinte Eireann, 1960; Mem. Bd, Allied Irish Banks, 1971; Nat. Indust. Econ. Council, 1963–70; Chm., Med.-Soc. Res. Bd, 1966–71; Mem., Higher Educn Authority, 1968–72; Nat. Sci. Council, 1967– ; Ed. Bds, Econ. Soc. Rev., Univ. Rev., Europ. Teacher; Econ. Consultant, OECD, Council of Europe, Dept of Finance, Dublin and Gulbenkian Inst., Lisbon; Mem., Club of Rome, 1973– . Chm., Inst. of Public Admin, 1973– . *Publications*: Planning for Economic Development in Ireland, 1959; (with J. Vaizey) Guinness's Brewery in the Irish Economy, 1960; Investment in Education, 1965; Science and Irish Economic Development, 1966 (OECD); (with J. Vaizey, *et al.*) Economics of Educational Costing, 1969; (with Brian Hillery) Ireland in the International Labour Organisation, 1969; contrib. Encyclopaedia Britannica; *contrib*. Admin., Bell, Econ. Hist. Rev., Irish Hist. Studies, Irish Jl Educn, Irish Univ. Rev. Statist. Studies. *Address*: Dept of Political Economy, Univ. College, Belfield, Dublin 4.

Lyne, Anthony Arthur, BA; Lecturer in Applied Linguistics, Language Centre, University of Sheffield, since 1966; *b* 1934; *m* 1964; two *s*. BA Leeds 1959 (1st cl. French). Mem., Lingu. Assoc. GB, Brit. Assoc. Appl. Lingu., Assoc. Lit. and Lingu. Computing. Admin. posts in 3M Co., and Dexion Ltd, 1959–64; Lectr, Manchester Coll. of Commerce, 1964–66. *Publications*: The Problem of Non-Comparability of Word-Frequency Counts, in AILA 3rd Congr. Copenhagen 1972, Procs vol. 3; *contrib*. Cah. Lexicol., IRAL, Lore and Language. *Address*: Language Centre, The Univ., Sheffield S10 2TN.

Lynn, Dr Norman, BSc, PhD; Lecturer in Mathematics and Operational Research, University of Salford, since 1964; *b* 1934; *m* 1961. BSc Belfast 1955 (1st cl. Mathematics), PhD Belfast 1959. Lectr, Liverpool Univ., 1959–62; Sen. Lectr, Welsh Coll. Adv. Technology, 1962–64. *Publications*: contrib. Proc. Phys. Soc., Proc. Royal Soc. *Address*: Dept of Mathematics, Univ. of Salford, Salford, Lancashire M5 4WT.

Lynn, Prof. Richard; Professor of Psychology, New University of Ulster, since 1972; *b* 1930; *m* 1956; one *s* two *d*. BA Cantab 1953, MA 1956; Lectr in Psychology, Univ. of Exeter, 1956–67; Prof. of Psychology, Dublin Econ. and Soc. Research Inst., 1967–71. *Publications*: Attention, Arousal and the Orientation Reaction, 1966; The Irish Braindrain, 1969; The Universities and the Business Community, 1969; Personality and National Character, 1971; An Introduction to the Study of Personality, 1972; The Entrepreneur, 1974. *Address*: New Univ. of Ulster, Coleraine, Co. Londonderry, NI BT52 1SA.

Lyon, Dr Ardon James; Lecturer in Philosophy, Department of Social Science and Humanities, The City University, since 1966; *b* 1933; *m* 1968. BA Cantab 1957 (2nd cl. Moral Sciences), PhD Cambridge 1962. Leverhulme Res. Fellow, Liverpool, 1960–61; Lectr in Philos. of Science, Durham, 1961–66. Cttee Mem., Brit. Soc. Philos. Sci., 1970– .

Publications: *contrib*. Brit. Jl Philos. Science, Mind, Studium Gen., Theoria. *Address*: Dept of Social Science and Humanities, The City Univ., St John Street, EC1 4PB.

Lyon, Michael Hazelip; Lecturer in Sociology, Aberdeen University, since 1967; *b* 1936; *m* 1963; one *s* one *d*. BA Cantab 1959. Mem., Brit. Sociol. Assoc., Mem., Inst. Race Relat. Res. Fellow, Nottingham Univ., 1966–67. *Publications*: New Community: Migration and Race Relations in an English City (forthcoming); *contrib*. Educnl Res., Jl Biosoc. Science. *Address*: Dept of Sociology, Kings College, Aberdeen.

Lyon, Peter Hazelip; Senior Lecturer in Commonwealth Studies, University of London, since 1969; *b* 1934; *m* 1957; one *s* one *d*. Bsc(Econ) London 1955, PhD London 1961. Mem., RIIA, Mem., IISS. Lectr in Politics, Univ. of Leicester, 1957–63; Lectr in Internat. Relations, LSE, 1963–69; Vis. Assoc. Prof. in Political Science, UCLA, 1967. Sec., Inst. Commonwealth Studies, 1969– ; Exec. Cttee, Pol. Studies Assoc., 1967– ; London-Cornell Cttee on SE Asia, 1966– . *Publications*: Neutralism, 1963; War and Peace in South East Asia, 1969; ed, New Orientations, 1970; *contrib*. Ann. Amer. Acad. Soc. Pol. Sci., Pol. Studies, Rev. Pol., etc. *Address*: Institute of Commonwealth Studies, 27 Russell Square, WC1B 5DS.

Lyons, Prof. Francis Stewart Leland, MA, PhD, LittD, FBA; Provost of Trinity College, Dublin, since 1974; *b* 1923; *m* 1954; two *s*. BA Dublin 1945 (1st cl. History and Political Science), PhD Dublin 1947, MA Dublin 1951; LittD Dublin 1966; FRHistS, FBA 1974. Mem., Royal Irish Acad. Lectr in Hist., Univ. Coll., Hull, 1947–51; Fellow, TCD, 1951–64; Prof. of Modern Hist., Univ. of Kent at Canterbury, 1964–74; Vis. Prof., Princeton Univ., 1960–61. Master, Eliot Coll., Univ. of Kent at Canterbury, 1969–72. *Publications*: The Irish Parliamentary Party, 1890–1910, 1951; The Fall of Parnell, 1960; Internationalism in Europe, 1815–1914, 1963; John Dillon, a biography, 1968; Ireland since the Famine, 1971; *contrib*. EHR, Hist., Irish Hist. Studies, Vict. Studies. *Address*: Provost's House, Trinity College, Dublin.

Lyons, Prof. John, MA, PhD, FBA; Professor of General Linguistics, University of Edinburgh, since 1964; *b* 1932; *m* 1959; two *d*. BA Cantab 1953 (1st cl. Classics), DipEd Cantab 1954, MA Cantab 1957, PhD Cantab 1961. Lectr, SOAS, Univ. of London, 1957–61; Lectr in Linguistics, Cambridge, and Fellow, Christ's Coll., Cambridge, 1961–64. Ed., Jl Lingu., 1964–70; Mem., Council, Philolog. Soc., 1962–66, 1969– ; Chm., Lingu. Assoc. GB. *Publications*: Structural Semantics, 1963; Introduction to Theoretical Linguistics, 1968, French edn 1970, German, Italian, Spanish edns 1971, Portuguese, Japanese, Hindi edns 1972; Chomsky, 1970, French, German, Danish edns 1971; ed, New Horizons in Linguistics, 1970; *contrib*. Internat. Jl Amer. Lingu., Jl Lingu., Lingua. *Address*: Dept of Linguistics, Univ. of Edinburgh, Edinburgh EH8 9YL.

Lyons, Dr Marianne Faith; Reader in Medieval French, Bedford College, London University, since 1956; *b* 1908. Hons Mod. Langs (French) Oxford 1931, MA Oxford 1946, D de l'U Paris 1949. Pupil, Ecole des Hautes Etudes, Paris Univ., 1931–40; Lectrice d'Anglais, Poitiers Univ., 1932–33; Asst Lectr in French, Univ. of Manchester, 1946–49; Lectr, 1949–56. Rédactrice, then Hd of Ref. Sect., Commissariat à l'Intérieur, London, 1942–44; Reg. Off. for France, Brit. Council, London, 1944–46. *Publications*: Les Eléments Descriptifs dans le Roman d'Aventure au XIII siècle, 1965; contrib. var. Miscellanies, dedicated to: M. Roques, E. Vinaver, J. Frappier and T. B. W. Reid; *contrib*. Romania. *Address*: French Dept, Bedford College, Regent's Park, NW8 4NS.

Lyons, Patrick Matthew, MA, MLitt; Lecturer in Economics, Trinity College, Dublin, since 1968; on leave of absence as full-time Member of Restrictive Practices Commission, since 1973; *b* 1941; *m* 1969; two *d*. BA Dublin 1963 (2nd cl. Economics), MA Dublin 1966. MLitt Dublin 1968. Jun. Lectr in Economics, TCD, 1965–68. Registrar, Summer Sch., TCD, 1967–71; Mem., Coll. Bd, 1971– ; Mem., Cttee on De-Pyramiding of Tariff Protection, Dept of Indust. and Comm., 1968–69; Mem., Fair Trade Commn, Dept of Indust. and Comm., 1970–72, Restrictive Practices Commn, 1972– . *Publications*: The Distribution of Personal Wealth in Ireland, in, Tait and Bristow: Ireland – Some Problems of a Developing Economy, 1972; Distribution of Personal Wealth in Ireland by County, 1966 (Stat. and Social Inquiry Soc. of Ireland), 1972–73; three reports of inquiries by Restrictive Practices Commn, 1972; Nat. Prices Commn Report no. 22, 1973; *contrib*. Econ. Soc. Rev., Rev. of Income and Wealth. *Address*: Economics Dept, 6 Trinity College, Dublin 2.

Lythe, Charlotte Margaret; Lecturer, Department of Economics, University of Dundee, since 1965; *b* 1941. MA St Andrews 1963. Mem., Royal Econ. Soc. Mem., Scott. Econ. Soc., Mem., Amer. Econ. Assoc., FSA Scot. Asst Lectr, Aberdeen Univ., 1963–65. Jt Ed., Scott. Reg. Gp, Council for Brit. Archaeol., 1969– ; Sec., Scottish Field Sch. of Archaeol., 1973– . *Publications*: contrib. Tayside: Potential for Development, 1970; *contrib*. Jl Econ. Studies. *Address*: Dept of Economics, The Univ., Dundee DD1 4HN.

Lythe, Prof. Samuel George Edgar, MA; Professor of Economic History, University of Strathclyde, since 1963; Vice-Principal, University of Strathclyde, since 1972; *b* 1910; *m* 1938; one *d*. BA Cantab 1932, MA Cantab 1935; FSAScot. Lectr, Univ. Coll., Dundee, 1954–59; Sen. Lectr, 1959–63. Chm., Co. of Scott. Hist. (Scott. Hist. Rev.), 1969– ; Mem., Anc. Monum. Bd Scotl., 1965– ; Mem., Cameron Cttee on Inshore Fisheries, 1969–71; Mem., Central Cttee on Soc. Subjects (Scottish Educn Dept), 1969– ; Gov., Hamilton Coll. of Educn, 1967– . *Publications*: British Economic History since 1760, 1950; The Economy of Scotland in its European Setting 1550–1625, 1960; *contrib*. Scott.

Hist. Rev., Scott. Jl Pol. Econ. *Address*: Dept of Economic History, Univ. of Strathclyde, Glasgow G1 1XW.

M

Maber, Richard Gervase; Lecturer, Department of French, University of Durham, since 1966; *b* 1943; *m* 1966. BA Oxon 1964 (1st cl. Mod. Lang.). *Address*: Dept of French, Univ. of Durham, Elvet Riverside, New Elvet, Durham.

Mabro, Robert Emile; Senior Research Officer in the Economics of the Middle East, Institute of Economics and Statistics, Oxford University, since 1969; Fellow of St Antony's College, Oxford, since 1971; *b* 1934; *m* 1967; two *d*. BSc (Eng) Alexandria 1956, Dip. in Philosophy, Chantilly 1964, MSc (Econ) London 1966, MA Oxon 1969; Mem.: Royal Economic Soc.; Soc. of Internat. Develt. Research Fellow, Sch of Oriental and African Studies, London Univ., 1967–69. *Publications*: The Egyptian Economy 1952–72, 1974; *contrib*. Bull. OIES, Econ. Jl, Jl Develt Studies, Oxf. Econ Papers, Projet. *Address*: St Antony's College, Oxford.

McAdams, Frank; Lecturer, Department of Librarianship, University of Strathclyde, since 1966; *b* 1932; *m* 1958; one *s* one *d*. MSc Strathclyde 1968; FLA 1962. Univ. of Strathclyde, 1964– . *Address*: Univ. of Strathclyde, Livingstone Tower, Richmond Street, Glasgow G1 1XH.

McAleese, Dermot, MA, MEconSc, PhD; Lecturer, Trinity College, Dublin, since 1972; *b* 1942; *m* 1971. BComn Dublin 1962 (1st cl.), MEconSc Dublin 1964, MA Johns Hopkins 1968; PhD Johns Hopkins 1971. Lectr, Univ. of Ghana, 1964–66; Teaching Asst, Johns Hopkins, 1968–69. Res. Off., Econ. Soc. Res. Inst., 1970–72; Lectr (part-time), Univ. Coll. Dublin, 1969–71. *Publications*: contrib. Econ. Soc. Rev., Jl Stat. Soc. Inqu. Soc. Ireland. *Address*: Dept of Economics, Trinity College, Dublin 2.

McAlindon, Dr T. E.; Senior Lecturer, Department of English, University of Hull, since 1966; *b* 1932; *m* 1962; three *s*. BA NUI 1953, MA NUI 1956, PhD Cantab 1961. Asst Lecturer: University Coll., Cork, 1960–61; Univ. of Hull, 1961. *Publications*: Shakespeare and Decorum, 1973; *contrib*. Anglia, MLR, MP, PMLA, RES, Shak. ST, SP. *Address*: Dept of English, The Univ., Cottingham Road, Hull HU6 7RX.

Mac Aodha, Breandan Seosamh; Professor of Geography, University College, Galway, since 1968; *b* 1934; *m* 1962; three *s* two *d*. BA Belfast 1955, MA Belfast 1959. Mem., Irish Geog. Soc., Amer. Geog. Soc., Econ. Social Res. Inst., Stat. Social Enqu. Soc. Irel., Irish Placenames Soc. Res. Asst, Queen's Univ., Belfast, 1955–58; Lectr, St Patrick's Teacher-Training Coll., Dublin, 1958–62; Lectr, Univ. Coll., Galway, 1962–68; Vis. Fellow, St Edmund's House, Cambridge, 1973–74; Ed., Social Sciences Res. Centre, 1966– . Principal Adv. Examiner, Dept of Education (Irish

Govt), 1959–68; Mem., Geogl Terminol. Cttee, Dept of Educn, Dublin, 1967– ; Mem., Council, Agric. Inst., Dublin, 1970–73, etc. *Publications*: (with E. A. Currie) Ireland: A Systematic and Regional Geography, 1968, 2nd edn 1971; An tSuirbhéireacht ar Ghaeltacht na Gaillimhe/ The Galway Gaeltacht Survey, vol. I (Maps), 1969, vol. II (Text), 1969; contrib., ed, L. Symons, Land Use in Northern Ireland, 1963; The Encyclopedia Americana, 1968; *contrib*. Social Sci. Res. Centre (UCG) Res. Paper Ser., Studia Hibern., Ulst. Folkl., etc. *Address*: Dept of Geography, Univ. College, Galway, Eire.

MacArthur, Dugald; University Librarian, University of St Andrews, since 1961; *b* 1910; *m* 1946; two *d*. MA Glasgow 1931, BSc Glasgow 1935; FLA 1946. Library Asst, Glasgow Univ., 1934–39; Supt of Students' Reading Room, Glasgow Univ., 1939–46; Sub-Librarian, subseq. Dep. Librarian, St Andrews Univ., 1946–61. Served RNVR, 1940–45 (Lt-Comdr). *Address*: Univ. Library, St Andrews, Fife KY16 9AJ.

McArthur, Dr Douglas George Moir, MA, DU; Senior Lecturer, Department of French Studies, University of Manchester, since 1968; *b* 1933; *m* 1955; one *s* two *d*. BA Auckland 1953, MA Auckland 1954, D de l'U Paris 1958. Mem., Lingu. Assoc. GB, Mem., Brit. Assoc. Appl. Lingu., Mem., Lingu. Soc. NZ. Lectr, Univ. of Queensland, 1959–62; Sen. Lectr, Victoria Univ., Wellington, 1962–67; Reader, 1967–68. *Publications*: Les Constructions Verbales du Français Contemporain, 1971. *Address*: Dept of French Studies, Univ. of Manchester, Manchester M13 9PL.

Macaulay, Donald; Head of Department of Celtic, Aberdeen University, since 1967; *b* 1930; *m* 1957; one *s* one *d*. MA Aberdeen 1953, BA Cambridge 1955, Dip. General Linguistics Edinburgh 1961. Lectr, English Language, Edinburgh, 1958–60; Lectr, Dept of Irish, TCD, 1960–63; Lectr, Applied Linguistics, Edinburgh, 1964–67. Dir, Scottish Internat., 1972– . *Publications*: Seóbhrach ás a'Chlaich, 1967; *contrib*. Scott. Gael. Studies. *Address*: Dept of Celtic, King's College, Aberdeen AB9 2UB.

McAuley, Alastair Nikolas Dawson; Lecturer, Department of Economics, University of Essex, since 1968; *b* 1938; *m* 1965; two *s* one *d*. BSc (Econ) 1962. Asst Lectr, Manchester Univ., 1965; Vis. Asst Prof., Princeton Univ., 1966. *Address*: Dept. of Economics, Univ. of Essex, Colchester, Essex CO4 3SQ.

McAuslan, Prof. John Patrick William Buchanan, BA, BCL; Professor, School of Law, University of Warwick, since 1972 (Reader, 1971–72); *b* 1937; *m* 1968; one *d*. BA Oxon 1960, BCL Oxon 1961; Barrister 1961. Mem., Soc. of Public Teachers of Law, Mem., Internat. Afr. Law Assoc., Mem., Town and Country Plan. Assoc., Mem., Fabian Soc. Lectr, Univ. Coll., Dar-es-Salaam, Tanzania, 1961–66; Lectr, LSE, 1966–68; Sen. Lectr, Univ. of Warwick, 1968–71; Vis. Prof., Univ. of Wisconsin, 1969; Osgoode Hall Law Sch., York Univ.,

1974. Mem., Senate, Univ. Coll., Dar-es-Salaam, 1961–64; Mem., Senate and Council, Univ. of Warwick, 1970–72. Mem. ILC Res. Adv. Cttee on Law and Development, 1972–74. *Publications*: (with Y. P. Ghai) Public Law and Political Change in Kenya, 1970; Compensation for Compulsory Acquisition, 1974; contrib. Government Enterprise, 1970; Co-operatives and Rural Development in East Africa, 1971; East African Law Today, 1966; Law and Social Change in East Africa, 1967; *contrib*. E Afr. Law Jl, E Afr. Law Rev., Internat. Comp. Law Qly, Jl Afr. Law, Jl Mod. Afr. Studies, Public Law, Mod. Law Rev. *Address*: School of Law, Univ. of Warwick, Coventry CV4 7AL.

MacBean, Prof. Alasdair Iain, PhD; Professor of Economics, University of Lancaster, since 1967; *b* 1933; *m* 1957; one *s* one *d*. MA Glasgow 1955 (1st cl. Econ.), BPhil Oxon 1959, PhD Glasgow 1965. Lectr, Glasgow, 1959–62; Res. Assoc., Harvard, 1962–64; Vis. Prof., Univ. of Michigan, 1973–74. Develop. Adv. in Pakistan, Harvard Develop. Adv. Service, 1965–66; Econ. Adv., Min. of Overseas Develop., 1966–67; Cnsltnt, UN, FAO, 1962, 1967; OECD, 1970. *Publications*: Export Instability and Economic Development, 1966; *contrib*. Amer. Econ. Rev., Bull. Oxf. Univ. Inst. Stat., Oxf. Econ. Papers, Pakistan Econ. Jl, Scott, Econ. Jl. *Address*: Dept of Economics, Univ. of Lancaster, Bailrigg, Lancaster LA1 4YW.

MacBride, Winifred Helen Baird, MA; Lecturer (in charge), Russian Department, Trinity College, Dublin, since 1962. MA Glasgow 1952 (2nd cl. French and German), MA Edinburgh 1962 (2nd cl. Russian). Asst Libr., Edinburgh Univ., 1952–62. *Address*: Russian Dept, 38 Trinity College, Dublin 2.

McBurney, Dr Charles Brian Montagu, ScD, FBA, FSA; Reader in Prehistory, University of Cambridge, since 1967; *b* 1914; *m* 1953; two *s* one *d*. BA Cantab 1937, PhD Cantab 1948, ScD Cantab 1967; FBA, FSA; Hon. corresp. mem., Istituto di Paleontologia Umana, Rome. Res. Fellow, King's Coll., Cambridge, 1940–53; Fellow, Corpus Christi Coll., Cambridge, 1962; Univ. Lectr, 1953–67. Mem. Council, Soc. Antiquaries, 1953–55; Vice-Pres., Prehist Soc., 1970–71. *Publications*: (with R. W. Hey) Prehistory and Pleistocene Geology of Cyrenaican Libya, 1955; The Stone Age of Northern Africa, 1960; The Haua Fteah (Cyrenaica) and the Stone Age of the SE Mediterranean, 1967; *contrib*. L'Anthropologie, Antiquity, JRAI, Proc. Prehist. Soc. *Address*: Corpus Christi College, Cambridge.

McCabe, John James Colin; Senior Lecturer in Education and Part-time Assistant Director, Institute and School of Education, University of Newcastle upon Tyne, since 1972; *b* 1924; *m* 1948; one *s* three *d*. BSc 1948, DipEd 1949, MEd 1955, Dunelm; MInstP, ABPsS, LRIC. *Publications: contrib*. Durham Res. Rev., etc. *Address*: Sch. of Education, Univ. of Newcastle upon Tyne, Newcastle upon Tyne NE1 7RU.

Maccabee, Geoffrey Gordon; Lecturer in Social Work, Department of Applied Social

433

Science, University of Nottingham, since 1967; *b* 1931; *m* 1958; one *s* two *d*. BA Leeds 1956 (Hons Social Studies); Mem., Brit. Assoc. of Social Workers; Mem., Nat. Assoc. of Probation Officers. *Address*: Dept of Applied Social Science, Univ. of Nottingham, University Park, Nottingham NG7 2RD.

MacCaig, Norman; Reader in Poetry, Department of English Studies, University of Stirling, since 1973; *b* 1910; *m* 1940; one *s* one *d*. MA Edinburgh 1932 (Hons Classics); FRSL. Fellowship in Creative Writing, Edinburgh Univ., 1967–69; Lectr in English Studies, Stirling Univ., 1970–73. *Publications*: *Poetry*: Far Cry, 1943; The Inward Eye, 1946; Riding Lights, 1955; The Sinai Sort, 1957; A Common Grace, 1960; A Round of Applause, 1962; Measures, 1965; Surroundings, 1966; Rings on a Tree, 1968; A Man in My Position, 1969; The White Bird, 1973; *Address*: Dept of English Studies, Univ. of Stirling, Stirling FK9 4LA.

McCail, Dr Ronald Cameron; Lecturer in Greek, Edinburgh University, since 1964; *b* 1932; *m* 1956; two *s* one *d*. MA St Andrews 1954 (1st cl. Classics), DPhil Oxon 1963. Asst Lectr in Classics, Manchester Univ., 1958–61, Lectr, 1961–64; Sec., Class. Assoc. Scotl., 1966–71. *Publications*: *contrib*. Byzantion, Jl Hellenic Studies, Rev. Etudes Byzant., etc. *Address*: Dept of Greek, David Hume Tower, George Square, Edinburgh EH8 9JX.

McCaldin, Denis James; Director of Music, Lancaster University, since 1971; *b* 1933; *m* 1958; one *s* one *d*. BSc Nottingham 1955, PhD Nottingham 1958; BMus Birmingham 1965. Lectr, Univ. of Liverpool, 1966–71. *Publications*: Beethoven's Choral Music, in, The Beethoven Companion, 1971; Stravinsky, 1972; ed, Berlioz: Te Deum, 1972; *contrib*. Music Rev., Music. Times, Music Educn, Organ Ybk, Soundings, etc. *Address*: Dept of Music, Lancaster Univ., Lancaster LA1 4YW.

Mac Cana, Prof. Proinsias, MA, PhD; Professor of Early (including Medieval) Irish, University College, Dublin, since 1971; *b* 1926; *m* 1952; one *s* one *d*. BA QUB 1948 (Celtic Languages), MA QUB 1950, PhD QUB 1953; Mem., 1971– , Council Mem., 1972– , Vice-Pres., 1974–75, RIA. Res. Assoc., Sch. of Celtic Studies, DIAS. Asst Lectr, Celtic Dept, QUB, 1951–54; Temp. Lectr, 1954–55; Asst Lectr, Old and Middle Irish, Univ. Coll., Wales, Aberystwyth, 1955–57; Lectr, 1957–61; Prof. of Welsh, UCD, 1963–71. Mem., Bd of Governors, Sch. of Celtic Studies, DIAS; Co-editor, Ériu, RIA; Gen. Editor, Med. and Mod. Welsh Series, DIAS. *Publications*: (jtly) Scéalaíocht na Ríthe; Branwen Daughter of Llyr, 1958; Celtic Mythology, 1970; *contrib*. Bull. Bd of Celtic Studies, Celtica, Ériu, Etudes celtiques, Studia Celtica, Studia Hibernica. *Address*: Dept of Early Irish, Univ. College, Belfield, Dublin 4.

McCann, William John; Lecturer in German, University of Southampton, since 1969; *b* 1943; *m* 1st 1962, 2nd 1970; one *s*. BA

434

Cantab 1965 (1st cl. Mod. and Med. Langs), MA Cantab 1969. Temp. Lectr in Celtic Studies, Dept of Anglo-Saxon, Cambridge, 1967–68. Asst Keeper, Dept of Printed Bks, Brit. Mus., 1968–69. *Address*: Dept of German, Univ. of Southampton, Southampton SO9 5NH.

McCargow, James; Secretary of the University Court and Registrar, University of Glasgow, since 1974; *b* 1920; *m* 1947; two *d*. MA Glasgow 1941. Glasgow University: Clerk of Faculty of Science, 1951–57; Asst Sec., 1957–66; Dep. Sec., 1966–74. *Address*: Univ. of Glasgow, Glasgow G12 8QQ.

McCarthy, John Lloyd; Lecturer, Department of English, University of Wales, Institute of Science and Technology, since 1960; *b* 1928; *m* 1956; four *s*. BA Oxon 1951, MA Oxon 1960; FInstArtsLett(Geneva) 1962, FInstLingu 1963. Ed., UWIST Rev., 1969–72. *Publications*: var. novels, incl. Deadfall, 1965; The Night Hawk, 1969; Take My Drums to England, 1971; *contrib*. Jl Inst. Lingu. *Address*: Dept of English, Univ. of Wales Institute of Science and Technology, Cardiff CF1 3NU.

McCarthy, Dr Michael Donald; President, University College, Cork, Ireland, since 1967; *b* 1908; *m* 1935; three *s* one *d*. BA NUI 1928, MA 1934, PhD 1939; Hon. DSc 1967, Hon. LLD TCD 1971; Mem., RIA, 1953. Lectr in Mathematics, UCC, 1931–44; Prof. of Mathematical Physics, 1944–49; Dir, Economic and Social Res. Inst., Dublin, 1966–67. Deputy Dir and Dir, Central Statistics Office, Dublin, 1949–66. Member, UN Statistical Commission, 1958–65 (Chm., 1960–65); Chm., Irish Nat. Cttee for Mathematics, and Sub-Commission for Mathematical Instruction, RIA, 1964–66; Vice-Chm., Conference of European Statisticians, 1963–66; Chm., Planning Conference, UN European Social Development Programme, 1967; Member; UN Expert Group on Nat. Accounts, 1964–66; Internat. Statistical Institute, 1951– . *Publications*: (jtly) Elements of Linear Programming, 1963; *contrib*. Annals of Mathematical Statistics, Jl Cork Historical and Archaeological Soc., PRIA, Jl Dept of Agriculture, Jl Statistical and Social Inquiry Soc. of Ireland, Proc. World Population Conference, Univ. Review, Irish Jl of Medical Science, Jl IEE, Proc. European Population Conference. *Address*: University College, Cork, Ireland.

MacCarthy, Peter A. D., MA; Senior Lecturer, and Head of Phonetics Department, Leeds University, since 1948; *b* 1912; *m* 1940; two *d*. BA Cantab 1934 (2nd cl. Mod. Languages), MA Cantab 1937. Lectr, SOAS, 1943–48. Council Mem., Internat. Phonetic Assoc., 1943– . *Publications*: English Pronunciation, 1944, 4th edn repr. 1965; English Pronouncing Vocabulary, 1945, 5th rev. edn 1967; English Conversation Reader, 1956; Practice Book of English Speech, 1965; Talking of Speaking: Papers in Applied Phonetics, 1972; The Pronunciation and Phonetics of German (forthcoming); The Pronunciation and Phonetics of French (forthcoming); *contrib*. English Lang. Teaching, Le Maître

Phonétique. *Address*: Dept of Phonetics, Univ. of Leeds, Leeds LS2 9JT.

McCarthy, William Edward John; Fellow of Nuffield College and The Oxford Centre for Management Studies, since 1965; University Lecturer in Industrial Relations, Oxford University, since 1969; *b* 1925; *m* 1956. BA Oxon 1957 PPE (1st cl. Hons), DPhil Oxon 1963; Res. Fellow, Nuffield Coll., 1960–64; Staff Tutor in Industrial Relations, Oxford Univ., 1964–65. Res. Dir, Royal Commn on Trade Unions and Employers Assocs, 1965–68; Sen. Economic Adviser, Dept of Employment, 1968–70. *Publications*: The Closed Shop in Britain, 1964; Shop Stewards in British Industry, 1966; Employers' Associations, 1967; Disputes Procedures in Britain, 1968; The Reform of Plant and Company Bargaining, 1971; Trade Unions, 1972; *contrib*. Brit. Jl of Industrial Relations; Oxford Bull. of Econs and Stats. *Address*: Nuffield College, Oxford.

McCartney, Dr Donal, MA, PhD; Statutory Lecturer in Modern Irish History, University College Dublin, since 1961; *b* 1929; *m* 1956; three *s* five *d*. BA NUI 1951, MA NUI 1954, HDip in Ed NUI 1955, PhD NUI 1971. Member: Irish Historical Soc., 1961– ; Exec. Cttee, Irish Assoc. for Amer. Studies, 1973– . Asst Lectr, UCD, 1961–73; Vis. Prof., Marquette Univ., 1969–71. Member: Governing Body, UCD, 1972– ; Exec. Cttee, Academic Staff Assoc., UCD, 1972– . *Publications*: chapters in: The Course of Irish History, ed Moody and Martin, 1967; Leaders and Men of the Easter Rising, ed Martin, 1967; Fenians and Fenianism, ed Harmon, 1968; The Easter Rising, ed Edwards and Pyle, 1968; Ireland in the War Years and After, ed Williams and Nowlan, 1969; The Making of 1916, ed Nowlan, 1969; Divided Ireland, ed O'Brien, 1971; Historical Studies VIII, ed Williams, 1971; The Scholar Revolutionary, ed Byrne and Martin, 1973; *contrib*. Irish Ecclesiastical Record, Irish Historical Studies, Jl of Contemp. Hist., Univ. Rev. *Address*: History Dept, Univ. Coll., Dublin 4.

McCaughan, Reginald Ellersley Manifold; Senior Lecturer in Civic Design, University of Liverpool, since 1949; *b* 1908; *m* 1940. BArch Hons Liverpool 1935, MA Liverpool 1938; Hon. DSc QUB 1973; FSA 1964, FRAnthI 1964. Special Lectr in Hist. of Town Plan., QUB, 1965; Univ. of Nottingham, 1972; Manchester Univ., 1972. Archaeol. Hist. Pergamon Ausgrab. Deutschen Archäol. Inst., 1958– . *Publications*: The Growth of Settlements and the Development of the Art of Civic Design in Britain to 1914, and, The Town Building of Edward I, both in, World Encyclopedia of Urban Planning, ed A. Whittick, 1974; Eine Erinnerung an Erich Boehringer, in Erich Boehringer Leben und Wirken, 1973; various reviews. *Address*: Dept of Civic Design, The Univ., Liverpool L69 3BX.

McCauley, Dr Martin; Lecturer in Russian and Soviet Institutions, School of Slavonic and East European Studies, University of London, since 1968; *b* 1934; *m* 1966; one *s*.

Diplôme d'études de Civilisation Française Sorbonne 1961, BA London 1966, PhD London 1973; ARICS 1959. Mem., Council, Sch. of Slavonic and E European Studies, Univ. of London, 1972–73. *Publications*: The Russian Revolution and the Soviet State, 1917–1921, (forthcoming); *contrib*. Mizan. *Address*: Senate House, Malet Street, WC1E 7HU.

McClean, Prof. J. David; Professor of Law, University of Sheffield, since 1973; *b* 1939; *m* 1966; one *s* one *d*. BA 1960, BCL 1961, MA 1963, Oxon; Barrister, 1963. Sheffield University: Asst Lectr in Law, 1961–63; Lectr in Law, 1963–68; Sen. Lectr in Law, 1968–73; Vis. Lectr in Law, Monash Univ., 1968. *Publications*: Criminal Justice and the Treatment of Offenders, 1969; contrib. Title: Conflict of Laws in Halsbury's Laws of England, 4th edn 1974; *contrib*. Austr. Law Jl, Crim. Law Rev., ICLQ, Sol. Qly. *Address*: Faculty of Law, The Univ., Sheffield S10 2TN

McClelland, Ivy Lilian, MA; Reader in Hispanic Studies, University of Glasgow; *b* 1908. BA Liverpool 1930 (1st cl.), MA Liverpool 1932; Assoc. Mem., Hispan. Soc. Amer. Lectr, then Sen. Lectr, Glasgow, 1930– . *Publications*: The Origins of the Romantic Movement in Spain, 1937; Tirso de Molina, 1948; Benito Jerónimo Feijoo, 1969; Spanish Drama of Pathos, 1970; Ignacio de Luzán, 1972; contrib. Encyclopaedia Britannica; Chambers' Encyclopaedia; *contrib*. Bull. Hispan. Studies, etc. *Address*: Dept of Hispanic Studies, The Univ., Glasgow G12 8QQ.

McClelland, John Scott, MA, PhD; Lecturer in Politics, University of Nottingham, since 1968; *b* 1943; *m* 1965; two *d*. BA Cantab 1964 (1st cl. Hist.), MA, PhD Cantab 1969. Asst Lectr in Politics, Nottingham, 1965–68. *Publications*: The French Right from de Maistre to Maurras, 1970. *Address*: Dept of Politics, Univ. of Nottingham, University Park, Nottingham NG7 2RD.

McClelland, Prof. Vincent Alan; Professor of Education, National University of Ireland (University College Cork), since 1969; *b* 1933; *m* 1972. BA Sheffield 1954, MA Sheffield 1955, DipEd Sheffield 1956, MA Birmingham 1958, PhD Sheffield 1968. Lectr in Educn, Liverpool Univ., 1964–69. Mem., Registration Council, Republic of Ireland, 1970– . *Publications*: Cardinal Manning: His Public Life and Influence 1865–92, 1962; English Roman Catholics and Higher Education 1830–1903, 1973; *contrib*. Catholic Hist. Rev., Victorian Studies, Innes Rev., Studies, Paedagogica Historica, Month, Tablet, Aylesford Rev., Downside Rev., Ampleforth Jl, Pax's History of Educn Soc. publns, Univs Qly, etc. *Address*: Univ. College, Cork, Eire.

McClelland, Prof. William Grigor, MA, MBA, FBIM; Director, Manchester Business School, since 1965, Professor of Business Administration since 1967; *b* 1922; *m* 1946; two *s* two *d*. BA Oxon 1948 (1st cl. PPE), MA Oxon 1957, MBA Manchester 1971; FBIM. Sen. Res. Fellow, Balliol Coll., Oxford, 1962–65; Dean, Faculty of Business Admin, Univ.

of Manchester, 1968–72. Mngng Dir, 1949–65, and Chm., 1966– , Laws Stores Ltd; Dir, Indust. Reorg. Corp., 1966–70; Mem., Nat. Econ. Develop. Council, 1969–71; Mem., Soc. Sci. Res. Council, 1971– ; Dep. Chm., Nat. Computing Centre, 1966–68; Chm., Jos. Rowntree Charitable Trust, 1965– ; Trustee, Anglo-German Foundn for Study of Industrial Soc., 1973– . *Publications*: Studies in Retailing, 1963; Costs and Competition in Retailing, 1966, pbk edn 1967; chapters, in, University Perspectives, 1970; Unorthodox Economics, 1970; Public Policy Toward Retailing: An International Study, 1972; *contrib*. Econ. Jl, Jl Indust. Econs, Jl Mngmt Studies, Sociol Rev., etc. *Address*: Manchester Business School, Booth Street West, Manchester M15 6PB.

Mac Conmara, Maitiú; Statutory Lecturer in French, University College Cork, since 1971; *b* 1940; *m* 1967; two *s*. BA NUI 1961, MA NUI 1965; Doctorat de L'Université, Aix-en-Provence, 1970. Member: Soc. for French Studies; Modern Humanities Res. Assoc.; Assoc. Internat. des Etudes Françaises. Asst, UC Cork, 1967–71. Mem. Council, Irish Fedn of Univ. Teachers, 1969–70, 1973–74. *Publications*: *contrib*. MLR, Studies. *Address*: Dept of French, Univ. Coll. Cork, Ireland.

McCord, Norman; Reader in Economic and Social History, Economics Department, University of Newcastle upon Tyne, since 1970; *b* 1930. BA Dunelm 1951 (2nd cl. Hist.), PhD Cantab 1956; FRHistS 1968. Sir James Knott Fellow, Newcastle, 1956–58; Asst Lectr in Hist., Cardiff, 1958–60; Lectr in Hist., Newcastle, 1960–69; Reader in Mod. Hist., Newcastle, 1969–70. *Publications*: The Anti-Corn Law League, 1958, 2nd edn 1968; Free Trade, 1970; (with D. J. Rowe) Northumberland and Durham: Industry in the 19th Century, 1971; Durham History from the Air, 1971; (with Allen, Clarke and Rowe) The 1871 Engineers' Strikes in North East England; Northumberland History from the Air; *contrib*. Archaeol. Ael., Econ. Hist. Rev., Hist. Jl, North. Hist., Internat. Rev. Social Hist., Trans Royal Hist. Soc. *Address*: Economics Dept., The Univ., Newcastle upon Tyne NE1 7RU.

MacCormac, Prof. Michael J.; Dean, Faculty of Commerce, University College, Dublin, since 1973; Professor of Business Administration, since 1971; *b* 1926; *m* 1950; one *d*. BA, BComm UCD 1947, MA UCD 1948, MComm UCD 1954, Post-grad. Business Admin., LSE 1948–49; FCCA. Lecturer: in Economics and Accountancy, UCD, 1949–66; in Economics and Business Admin, 1966–69; Assoc Prof., Business Admin, 1969–71. Chairman: Medico-Social Res. Bd, 1973– ; Nat. Catering Organization, 1973– ; Member: Nat. Council Educnl Awards, 1970– ; Council, IPA, 1970. *Publications*: (with J. J. Teeling) Financial Management, 1971. *contrib*. Admin., Irish Management Studies. *Address*: Faculty of Commerce, Univ. College, Belfield, Dublin 4.

MacCormack, Prof. Geoffrey Dennis; Professor of Jurisprudence, University of

Aberdeen, since 1971; *b* 1937; *m* 1965; one *d*. BA 1957, LLB 1960, Sydney; MA 1964, DPhil 1966, Oxon. Mem., NSW Bar, 1960. Lecturer: Merton Coll., Oxford, 1962–63; Magdalen and Worcester Colls, Oxford, 1963–65; Sen. Lectr in Law, Univ. of Sydney, 1966–67; Lectr in Civil Law, Univ. of Glasgow, 1967–68; Sen. Lectr in Jurisprudence, Aberdeen Univ., 1968–71. Dean, Fac. of Law, Aberdeen, 1973–74. *Address*: Dept of Jurisprudence, Univ. of Aberdeen, Aberdeen AB9 1AS.

McCormack, John Desmond; Registrar, King's College London, since 1969; *b* 1926; *m* 1955; one *s*. BA Hons London 1951 (English). Asst Sec., Inter-Univ. Council for Higher Educn Overseas, 1959–63; Registrar, Birkbeck Coll., Univ. of London, 1963–68. Member: UCCA, 1969– ; Univ. of London Careers Adv. Bd, 1969– . Governor, Bickley Park Sch., 1972– . *Address*: King's Coll., Strand, WC2R 2LS.

MacCormick, Prof. Donald Neil; Regius Professor of Public Law, University of Edinburgh, since 1972; Dean of the Faculty of Law since 1973; *b* 1941; *m* 1965; three *d*. MA Glasgow 1963 (1st cl. Philos. and Eng. Lit.), BA Oxon 1965 (1st cl. Jurisprudence), MA Oxon 1969; Barrister (Inner Temple) 1971. Lectr, St Andrew's Univ. (Queen's Coll., Dundee), 1965–67. Pro-Proctor, Oxford Univ., 1971–72; Fellow and Tutor in Jurisprudence, Balliol Coll., Oxford, 1967–72, and CUF Lectr in Law, Oxford Univ., 1968–72. *Publications*: ed, The Scottish Debate: Essays on Scottish Nationalism, 1970; contrib. Oxford Essays in Jurisprudence, 2nd series, 1973; Annual Survey of Commonwealth Law, 1970, 1971; *contrib*. Jurid. Rev., Proc. Aristot. Soc. Supp., Law Qly Rev. *Address*: Dept of Public Law, The Old College, Edinburgh EH8 9YL.

McCormick, Dr William Ormsby; Senior Lecturer in Mental Health, Queen's University of Belfast, since 1968; *b* 1929; *m* 1954; one *s* one *d*. BA Cantab 1950 (Biochemistry), MA Cantab 1971, MB, BChir Cantab 1953, DPM London 1962; MRCP London 1961, MRCPsych 1971, FRCPsych 1973. Lectr in Mental Health, Queen's Univ., Belfast, 1965–68. Mem., Council, Royal Coll. Psychiat., 1971– . *Publications*: *contrib*. Amer. Jl Orthopsychiat., Brit. Med. Jl, Psychol. Med. *Address*: Dept of Mental Health, Queen's Univ., Belfast BT7 1NN.

McCosh, Andrew McDonald; Professor of Management Accounting, Manchester Business School, since 1971; *b* 1940; *m* 1965; three *d*. BSc Edinburgh 1957, Dr Business Admin. 1963; CA, Scott. Inst. 1960. Res. Asst, Harv. Business Sch., 1964–65; Teaching Fellow in Economics, 1966; Asst and Associate Prof. of Accounting, Univ. of Michigan, 1966–71. Chm., Micah Systems Ltd, 1971– . *Publications*: Electronic Data Processing, in, The Accountants Handbook, 1970; (jtly) Practical Controllership, 1973; (jtly) Decision Support Systems, 1973; *contrib*. Accountancy, Accounting Rev., Mergers and Acquisitions, European Jl of Accountancy, Harv. Business Rev., Accountants Magazine, Hospital Financial Management, Management Accounting (US). *Address*: Manchester Business School, Booth Street West, Manchester M15 6PB

McCourt, Dr Desmond, MA, PhD; Reader in Geography, School of Environmental and Biological Studies, New University of Ulster, since 1967; *b* 1925; *m* 1960; three *d*. BA Belfast 1946 (Double Hons Econ. Hist. and Geog.), MA Belfast 1947, PhD Belfast 1950. Res. Fellow, Queen's Univ., Belfast, 1947–50; Sen. Lectr and Hd of Dept, Magee Univ. Coll., Londonderry, 1951–67; Rockefeller Foundn Fellow, and Vis. Prof., Yale Univ., 1957–58; Ed., Ulster Folklife, 1964–72; Assoc., Inst. Irish Studies, Queen's Univ., Belfast, 1972. Mem., Ulster Countryside Cttee (Min. of Develop.), 1965–71; Mem., Anc. Monum. Adv. Council (Min. of Finance), 1968–71; Mem., Hist Monum. Council (Min. of Finance); Mem., Inst. Irish Studies, Board, Queen's University, Belfast, 1972– ; Mem., Bd of Trustees, Ulster Folk Museum, 1973– ; Mem., Council, Folklife Soc., 1968–71. *Publications*: (with E. Jones and R. H. Buchanan) Man and his Habitat, 1971; *contrib*. Deuts. Jahrbuch Volksk., Econ. Hist. Rev., Folk-Liv, Ulst. Folkl., Ulst. Jl Archaeol, Irish Geog. *Address*: School of Environmental and Biological Studies, New Univ. of Ulster, Coleraine, Co. Londonderry BT52 1SA.

McCracken, Prof. John Leslie, MA, PhD; Professor of History, The New University of Ulster, since 1968; *b* 1914; *m* 1944; three *s*. BA Belfast 1936, MA Belfast 1941, PhD Belfast 1948; FRHistS. Hist. Master, Wallace High Sch., Lisburn, 1936–46; Lectr in History, Univ. of Witwatersrand, Johannesburg, 1946–50; Sir Robert Wood Res. Lectr, TCD, 1950–52; Sen. Lectr in Hist., Magee Univ. Coll., Londonderry, 1952–57; Prof. of History, 1957–68. Mem., Irish Cttee Hist. Sci., 1957– ; Mem., Cttee, Assoc. Gov. Bodies in Grammar Schs, N Ireland, 1958– ; Mem., Exec. Cttee, Brit. Council, 1970– ; Trustee, Ulster-Scot. Hist. Foundn, 1971– . *Publications*: Representative Government in Ireland, 1958; ed, Historical Studies: V, 1965; The Cape Parliament, 1854–1910, 1967; *contrib*. Irish Hist. Studies. *Address*: The New Univ. of Ulster, Coleraine, Co. Londonderry BT52 1SA.

McCulloch, Derek; Lecturer, Department of Linguistic and Regional Studies, University of Surrey, since 1965; *b* 1938; *m* 1971. BA Dunelm 1961, DipEd Dunelm 1962; Mem., Royal Music. Assoc., Mem., Conf. Univ. Teachers of German. Lektor, Tübingen Univ., W Germany, 1962–64. Founder and Dir of Baroque music ensemble: Collegium Sagittarii, 1967– ; Mem. Ed. Bd, Stuttgart Schütz Edn, 1968– . *Publications*: trans., H. J. Moser: Heinrich Schütz Life and Work, 1966; H. Stuckenschmidt: 20th Century composers, 1971. *Address*: 21 The Cloisters, Windsor Castle, Berks.

McCulloch, Ian; Lecturer, Department of Architecture and Building Science, University of Strathclyde, since 1967; *b* 1935; *m* 1959; two *s*. DA Glasgow 1957; Mem., Soc. Scottish Artists; Mem., Glasgow Group.

Has had seven one-man exhibns in Edinburgh and Glasgow, 1959–73, and taken part in numerous group exhibns; Arts Council Awards, 1967–68, 1972–73. *Address*: Univ. of Strathclyde, Dept of Architecture and Building Science, George Street, Glasgow G1 1XW.

McCulloch, James Wallace, MSc; Senior Lecturer, School of Applied Social Studies, University of Bradford, since 1969; *b* 1921; *m* 1943; two *s*. MSc Edinburgh 1965, Cert. Social Studies Edinburgh 1957, Cert. Psychiatric Social Work Edinburgh 1958; Mem., ASWT. Lectr, Univ. of Bradford, 1966–69. Vice-Chm., Postgrad. Sch. Appl. Social Studies, Univ. of Bradford, 1967– ; Vice-Chm., Undergrad. Sch. Appl. Social Studies, 1970–71; Pt-time Student Counsellor, Univ. of Bradford, 1966– . *Publications*: (with A. Munro) Psychiatry for Social Workers, 1969, German edn 1972; (with A. E. Philip) Suicidal Behaviour, 1972; contrib. Acute Barbiturate Poisoning, ed. H. Matthew, 1971; *contrib*. Acta Psychiat. Scand., Appl. Social Studies, Brit. Jl Criminol., Brit. Jl Social Clin. Psychol., Brit. Med. Jl, Brit. J. Prev. Social Med., Brit. Jl Psychiat., Brit. Jl Psychiat. Social Wk, Educnl Res., Jl Consult. Clin. Psychol., Lancet, Social Psychiat., Scot. Med. Jl. *Address*: Univ. of Bradford, Bradford BD7 1DP.

McDermott, Hubert, MA; Junior Lecturer in Modern English Literature, National University of Ireland, University College, Galway, since 1970; *b* 1943; *m* 1970; one *d*. BA NUI 1964 (1st cl. Engl., 1st cl. Latin), Higher DipEd NUI 1965, MA NUI 1968. Asst, NUI, Univ. Coll., Galway, 1965–70. Mem., Gov. Body, Univ. Coll., Galway, 1971– ; Mem., Conf. of Irish Univs, 1974– . *Publication*: The Background to Anglo-Irish Drama, in Topic: Themes in Irish Culture, 1972. *Address*: Dept of Modern English Literature, National Univ. of Ireland, Univ. College, Galway.

McDermott, Prof. Matthew; Associate Professor of Architecture, University College Dublin, since 1966; *b* 1908; *m* 1950; two *s* three *d*. BArch NUI 1930; MRIAI 1930, FRIAI 1964; ARIBA 1936. Asst, 1936; Univ. Lectr, 1943. Sometime Mem., Univ. and Professional Cttees; Hon. Sec., Irish Architectural Records Assoc., 1940– . *Publications*: various articles and contribs on aspects of architecture. *Address*: Sch. of Architecture, Univ. Coll. Dublin, Earlsfort Terrace, Dublin 2.

McDiarmid, Matthew Purdie; Reader, Department of English, University of Aberdeen, since 1966; *b* 1914; *m* 1941; two *s*. MA Glasgow 1935, BLitt Oxford 1938. Lectr, Univ. of Aberdeen, 1939–52; Sen. Lectr, Queen's Univ., Belfast, 1952–64. Council Mem., Scott. Nat. Dictionary Assoc.; Council Mem., Scott. Text Soc.; Gen. Ed., Assoc. Scott. Lit. Studies. *Publications*: The Poems of Robert Fergusson, vol. I 1954, vol. II 1956; ed, D. Lindsay: A Satire of the Three Estates, 1967; Hary: Wallace, vol. I 1968, vol. II 1969; ed, James I of Scotland: The Kingis Quair, 1972; ed, John Barbour:

437

The Bruce (forthcoming); Hugh MacDiarmid and the Colloquial Category, in, Hugh MacDiarmid: a critical survey, ed Duncan Glen, 1972; *contrib*. Etudes Angl., Forum Mod. Lang. Studies, Med. Æv., Mod. Lang. Rev., Rev. Engl. Studies, Scott. Hist. Rev., Studies in Scott. Lit. *Address*: Dept of English, Univ. of Aberdeen, Aberdeen AB9 1AS.

McDonald, Alexander Hugh, MA, PhD, DLitt, HonLLD, HonLittD, FBA; Lecturer, Faculty of History, University of Cambridge, and Fellow of Clare College, Cambridge, 1952–73, Life Fellow since 1973; *b* 1908; *m* 1941. MA New Zealand 1929, BA Cambridge 1932, MA Cambridge 1935, PhD Cambridge 1936, DLitt Cambridge 1970; HonLLD Glasgow 1948, HonLittD Auckland NZ 1968, FBA 1967. Mem., Chatham Hse, 1952. Lectr in Ancient Hist., Nottingham Univ. Coll., 1934–38; Reader in Ancient History, Univ. of Sydney, 1939–45; Prof. of Latin, Univ. of Sydney, 1945; Prof. of Ancient World History, Univ. of Sydney, 1945–51. Ed., Curr. Aff. Bull., Austral. Army, 1943–46; News Commentator, Austral. Broadcast. Commn, 1941–51; Sen. Tutor, Clare Coll., 1954–57; Chm. Archaeol. Fac., Brit. Sch., Rome, 1966–70; Pres., Roman Soc., 1971–74. *Publications*: Japanese Imperialism, 1944; ed, Trusteeship in the Pacific, 1949; Oxford Text of Livy, vol. V, 1965; Republican Rome, 1966; *contrib*. Austral. Outlk, Class. Rev., Jl Roman Studies. *Address*: Clare College, Cambridge.

McDonald, Prof. Alexander John, MA, LLB; Professor of Conveyancing, University of Dundee (formerly Queen's College), since 1955; *b* 1919; *m* 1951; two *s* two *d*. BA Cantab 1942, MA Cantab, LLB Edinburgh 1949; admitted as Solicitor and Writer to the Signet, 1950. Lectr in Conveyancing, Edinburgh Univ., 1952–55; Dean, Faculty of Law, Univ. of Dundee, 1958–62 and 1965. Mem., firm of Thorntons and Dickies, WS, Dundee. Registrar, Diocese of Brechin, 1963– . *Address*: Univ. of Dundee, Dundee DD1 4HN.

MacDonald, Eric Wray, BArch, DipCD, RIBA, MRTPI; Lecturer, Department of Architecture, Queen's University, Belfast, since 1966; *b* 1919; *m* 1943; two *s* one *d*. East Kilbride Develt Corp., 1948–53; NI Housing Trust, 1953–1966. RAF, 1940–45. *Address*: Dept of Architecture, Queen's Univ., Belfast BT7 1NN.

Macdonald, Dr Hugh John; University Lecturer in Faculty of Music, University of Oxford, since 1971; Fellow of St John's College, Oxford, since 1971; *b* 1940; *m* 1963; one *s* three *d*. BA 1961, MA 1965, PhD 1969, Cambridge. Cambridge University: Asst Lectr, 1966; Lectr, 1968; Chm., Bd of Music Studies, Cambridge Inst. of Educn, 1969–71. Gen. Editor, New Berlioz Edn, 1965– ; Mem. Exec. Cttee, Grove's Dictionary of Music, 1970– . *Publications*: ed Berlioz: Grande Symphonie Funèbre et Triomphale, 1967; ed Berlioz: Les Troyens, 1969–70; Berlioz Orchestral Works, 1969; *contrib*. Listener, Musica, Mus. Times, Music and Letters, RMA Procs, TLS. *Address*: Faculty of Music, 32 Holywell, Oxford.

Macdonald, Dr Ian Robert; Lecturer, Department of Spanish, University of Aberdeen, since 1965; *b* 1939; *m* 1962; three *s*. MA St Andrews 1961, PhD Aberdeen 1970. Adviser of Studies, Univ. of Aberdeen, 1973– . *Address*: Dept of Spanish, Univ. of Aberdeen, Aberdeen AB9 2UB.

Macdonald, J. Edwin, MA, DipPsychol, ABPsS; Lecturer, Department of Applied Psychology, University College, Cork, since 1969; *b* 1924; *m* 1957; one *s*. MA Edinburgh 1951 (Psychol.), DipPsychol London 1952 (Abnormal); Registered Psychologist, Ontario, 1966, ABPsS, ARCPsych. Lectr, Manchester Univ., 1961–65; Asst. Prof., Lakehead Univ., Ontario, 1965–67; Prof., Algoma Coll., Laurentian Univ., Ontario, 1967–68; Assoc. Prof., Univ. de Moncton, NB, 1968–69. Clinical Psychologist, 1952–55 and Sen. Psychologist, 1955–58, NHS, various hospitals; Res. Exec., Unilever Ltd, 1958–59, and Marketing Trends Ltd, 1960–61; Mem., SW Metropolitan Regional Commn Sen. Psychologists and Sub-Commn on Training, 1957–58; Chm., Dept of Psychology, Lakehead Univ., Ontario, 1966–67. *Publications*: *contrib*. Brit. Jl Psychiat. *Address*: Dept of Applied Psychology, Univ. College, Cork, Eire.

McDonald, Janet Brown Inglis; Lecturer, Department of Drama, Glasgow University, since 1968; *b* 1941; *m* 1964. MA Glasgow 1963 (2nd cl. Engl. Lang. and Lit.). Res. Fellow, Dept of Engl., Glasgow Univ., 1963–65; Asst Lectr, Dept of Engl., Glasgow Univ., 1965–66; Asst Lectr, Dept of Drama, Glasgow Univ., 1966–68. *Publications*: The Taming of the Shrew at the Haymarket Theatre, 1844 and 1847, in, Nineteenth Century Theatre, ed P. Thomson and K. Richards, 1971; *contrib*. Theat. Res./Rech. Theat. *Address*: Dept of Drama, 17 Lilybank Gardens, Univ. of Glasgow, Glasgow.

Macdonald, Prof. John, MA, BD, STM, PhD; Professor of Hebrew and Semitic Languages, University of Glasgow, since 1968; *b* 1925; *m* 1953; two *d*. BD Glasgow 1950 (1st cl.), STM(Hons) Union Theological Seminary NY 1951, MA Glasgow 1953 (1st cl. Semitic Langs), PhD Leeds 1958. Temp. Lectr, Rhodes, 1953; Lectr, Leeds, 1954–64; Sen. Lectr, Leeds, 1964–68. Permanent Examiner, London Coll. of Music, 1956– ; Ed., Leeds Univ. Orient. Soc. Annual, vols I–VI, 1959–69. *Publications*: Catalogues of Oriental MSS in The University of Leeds, 1958–62; Memar Marqah, 1963; The Theology of the Samaritans, 1964, American edn 1965; ed, A. Guillaume: Studies in the Book of Job, 1968; The Samaritan Chronicle no. II: From Joshua to Nebuchadnezzar, 1969; *contrib*. Ann. Leeds Univ. Orient. Soc., Austral. Jl of Bib. Archaeol., Encyl. Judaica, Indo-Iran., Islam. Lit., Islam. Qly, Islam. Studies, Jl Jew. Studies, Jl Semit. Studies, Musl. Wld, NT Studies, Orient. Literaturz., Scot. Jl Theol., Trans Glasgow Univ. Orient. Soc., Ugarit-Forschungen, Vet. Testam. *Address*: The Univ., Glasgow G12 8QQ.

Macdonald, John; Lecturer, Department of Theology, St David's University College, Lampeter, since 1960; *b* 1916. BA Oxford (2nd cl. Mod. Hist.) 1938, (2nd cl. Theol) 1940, MA Oxford 1942, BLitt Oxford 1958. Librarian, Pusey House, Oxford, 1954–60. Sub-Warden, Bishop Burgess Hall, 1962– . *Publications*: contrib. Oxford Dictionary of the Christian Church; *contrib.* Studia Patristica. *Address*: St David's Univ. Coll., Lampeter, Dyfed SA48 7ED.

McDonald, Rev. John Richard Burleigh; Principal Lecturer and Head of Department of Religious Studies, Stranmillis College, Queen's University, Belfast, since 1966; *b* 1917; *m* 1942; three *s* one *d*. BA TCD 1938 (1st cl. Mental and Moral Science), BD TCD 1942. Lectr, Faculty of Educn, QUB, 1967. Principal, Buwalasi Coll., Uganda, 1952–60; Sec., Assoc. of E African Theological Colls, 1958–60; Educn Officer for Church of Ireland, 1961–64. *Publications*: contrib. The Fourth R: the Durham Report on Religious Education, 1970; *contrib.* Theology. *Address*: Stranmillis College, Belfast BT9 5DY.

Macdonald, Keith Moray; Lecturer in Sociology, University of Surrey, since 1964; *b* 1930; *m* 1959; two *s*. BA(Soc) London 1962; ACA 1953, FCA 1965. Res. Asst, Univ. of Aston, 1962–64; Res. Fellow, Univ. of Edinburgh, 1969; Sen. Res. Off., Univ. of Manchester, 1969–70; Hon. Res. Fellow, Univ. of Edinburgh, 1969–70. *Publications*: *contrib.* Abitare, Admin. Science Qly, Internat. Jl Product. Res., Sociol. *Address*: Dept of Sociology, Univ. of Surrey, Guildford GU2 5XH.

McDonald, Michael Vincent; Lecturer in Arabic, University of Edinburgh, since 1968; *b* 1937; *m* 1959; three *s* one *d*. BA Cambridge 1961 (2nd cl. Arabic and Persian), MA, PhD Cambridge 1966, Dip. General Linguistics Edinburgh 1967. Asst Lectr in Arabic, Edinburgh, 1964–68. *Address*: Dept of Arabic and Islamic Studies, William Robertson Building, George Square, Edinburgh EH8 9JY.

Macdonald, Prof. Peter, MSc, PhD; Professor of Statistics, and Head of Department of Statistics and Operational Research, Brunel University, since 1970; *b* 1920; *m* 1959. BSc(Special) London 1944 (Chemistry), BSc(Special) London 1958 (Mathematics), MSc London 1961 (Statistics), PhD London 1967 (Statistics); ARIC 1949, FIMA 1967, FIS 1967. Civil Service, Fuel Res. Station, 1938–58; Building Operat. Res. Unit, 1958–60; Lectr, Brunel Coll., 1960–62, Sen. Lectr, 1962–66; Sen. Lectr, Brunel Univ., 1966–70. *Publications*: Mathematics and Statistics for Scientists and Engineers, 1966; *contrib.* Jl Appl. Chem., Jl Royal Stat. Soc., Jl Soc. Cosmet Chem. *Address*: Dept of Statistics and Operational Research, Brunel Univ., Uxbridge, Mddx UB8 3TH.

Macdonald-Ross, Michael Inman Philip; Senior Lecturer, Institute of Educational Technology, The Open University, since 1971; *b* 1939; *m* 1965. BSc London 1960 (1st cl. Hons, Zool.). Asst Lectr in Zoology,

KCL, 1962–65. Program Manager, Educnl Systems Ltd, 1965–68; Sen. Cons., Internat. Training & Education Co. Ltd, 1968–69; Partner, Instructional Systems Associates, 1969–71. Policy Editor, Instructional Sci. *Address*: The Open Univ., Walton Hall, Milton Keynes MK7 6AA.

McDonnell, Dr Kevin George Thomas; Lecturer, History Department, Queen Mary College, University of London, since 1964; *b* 1921. BSc (Econs) London 1949, PhD London 1958; Phi Kappa Theta; Member: Economic History Soc.; Newman Assoc. Res. Fellow, Queen Mary Coll., Univ. of London, 1953. Member: British Exec., World Univ. Service, 1954–66; Council, Mouvement Internat. des Intellectuals Catholiques, 1960–68 (Pres., 1968); Senior Mem., Commonwealth Hall, London Univ. 1964–66, Acting Warden, 1966–67, Vice-Warden, 1967–69; Warden, Lillian Penson Hall, Univ. of London, 1969– ; Mem., QMC Halls of Residence Cttee; Sen. Treasurer, QMC Students' Union, 1957–63; Chm., Consultative Cttee, Faculty of Arts, QMC, 1970–72. Editor, Victoria County History of Middlesex, vol. 1, 1964–66 (secondment). KSG. *Publications*: Survey of English Economic History (with D. C. Coleman and S. Pollard), 1957, 2nd edn 1966; Victoria County History of Middlesex (with J. Cockburn and P. King), vol. 1, 1969; Studies in London History (ed A. Hollaender and W. Kellaway), 1969; Medieval London Suburbs (forthcoming); *contrib.* E London Papers, Yorks Archaeol Jl. *Address*: Queen Mary College, Mile End Road, E1 4NS.

McDowall, Andrew Allen; Lecturer, School of Modern Languages, University of Bradford, since 1964; *m* 1952; one *s*. BA London (Hons), Licencié en Droit, Université l'Aurore (Shanghai). *Publication*: L'Industrie française, 1973. *Address*: University of Bradford, Bradford, Yorks BD7 1DP.

MacDowall, Dr David William, MA, DPhil, FSA; Master, University College, Durham, since 1973; *b* 1930; *m* 1962; two *d*. BA Oxon 1952 (Hons Classical Mods and Lit. Hum.), MA 1954, DPhil 1959; FRNS 1952, FRAS 1958, FSA 1960. Member: Amer. Numismatic Soc., Numismatic Soc. of India, Société Suisse de Numismatique etc. Asst Keeper, Dept of Coins and Medals, BM, 1956–65; Principal, University Grants Cttee, 1965–70; Asst Sec. 1970–73. Hon. Treasurer RNS, 1966– ; Hon. Sec, Soc. of Afghan Studies, 1972– . *Publications*: The Western Coinages of Nero, 1974; *contrib.* Jl Numismatic Soc. of India, Numismatic Chronicle, Schweizer Münzblätter, S Asian Archaeology. *Address*: Univ. College, The Castle, Durham.

McDowell, Dr C. M.; Senior Lecturer, Faculty of Law, University of Birmingham, since 1972; *b* 1940; *m* 1966; one *s*. LLB QUB 1962, PhD 1972; Member: African Studies Assoc., UK; Internat. African Law Assoc.; Royal Commonwealth Soc.; Commonwealth Legal Educn Assoc. Lecturer: Ahmadu Bello Univ., N Nigeria, 1963–66; Birmingham Univ., 1966–72. *Publications*:

contrib. Africa, Jl of African Law, Nigerian Law Jl. *Address*: Univ. of Birmingham, PO Box 363, Birmingham B15 2TT.

MacDowell, Prof. Douglas Maurice; Professor of Greek, University of Glasgow, since 1971; *b* 1931. BA Oxon 1954, MA Oxon 1958. Manchester: Asst Lectr in Greek and Latin, 1958–61; Lectr, 1961–68; Sen. Lectr, 1968–70; Reader, 1970–71. *Publications:* Andokides: On the Mysteries, 1962; Athenian Homicide Law, 1963; Aristophanes: Wasps, 1971; *contrib.* Class. Qly, Class. Rev., Jl Hellenic Studies, etc. *Address*: Univ. of Glasgow, Glasgow G12 8QQ.

McDowell, John Henry; Fellow and Praelector in Philosophy, University College, Oxford, since 1966; CUF Lecturer in Philosophy, University of Oxford, since 1967; *b* 1942. BA London 1962 (University Coll. of Rhodesia and Nyasaland), BA Oxford 1965, MA Oxford 1969. James C. Loeb Fellow in Classical Philosophy, Harvard Univ., 1969. *Publications:* trans. (with notes), Plato: Theaetetus, 1973; *contrib.* Proc. Aristot. Soc. *Address*: Univ. Coll., Oxford.

McDowell, Prof. Robert Brendan; Associate Professor of History, Trinity College, Dublin, since 1967; *b* 1913. MA, PhD TCD. Fellow, TCD, 1951– ; Jun. Dean, 1956–69. *Publications:* (with E. Curtis) Irish Historical Documents 1172–1922, 1943; Irish Public Opinion 1750–1800, 1944; Public Opinion and Government Policy in Ireland, 1801–46, 1952; British Conservatism 1832–1914, 1959; The Irish Administration 1801–1914, 1964; Alice Stopford Green: a passionate historian, 1967; The Irish Convention 1917–18, 1970; ed, Correspondence of Edmund Burke, vol. 8, (with J. A. Woods) vol. 9, 1969–70; (with W. B. Stanford) Mahaffy: a biography of an Anglo-Irishman, 1971. *Address*: School of History, Trinity College, Dublin 2.

MacEwan, James Norman Stewart; Lecturer, Law School, University of Strathclyde, since 1968; *b* 1936; *m* 1965; three *s*. MA Glasgow 1957, LLB 1960; Solicitor, Scotland, 1960. Mem., Law Sch. Bd of Study and Univ. Library Cttee, Univ. of Strathclyde, 1970–71. Mem., Stirlingshire Educn Authority, 1970– . Formerly Magistrate, Stirling Town Council. *Publications: contrib.* Scots Law Times. *Address*: Law Sch., 173 Cathedral Street, Glasgow.

McEwen, Rev. Prof. James Stevenson, DD; Professor of Church History, University of Aberdeen, since 1958; Master of Christ's College, Aberdeen, since 1971; *b* 1910; *m* 1945; two *s*. DD. Lectr in Church Hist., Univ. of Edinburgh, 1953–58. Ordained Church of Scotland, 1940; held parishes at Rathen, Hawick and Invergowrie. *Publication*: The Faith of John Knox, 1961. *Address*: Univ. of Aberdeen, Aberdeen AB9 1AS.

McEwen, Prof. Peter, BSc, PhD, FBPsS; Professor, Department of Psychology, University of Stirling, since 1966; *b* 1920; *m* 1946; three *s* one *d*. BSc Edinburgh 1945 (1st cl.), PhD QUB 1956; FBPsS 1970. Lectr, Natal UC, 1946–48; Lectr, Edinburgh Univ., 440

1948–49; Lectr, QUB, 1949–62; Sen. Lectr, QUB, 1962–66; Vis. Lectr, Oberlin Coll. Ohio, 1962–63. Mem., Council, Brit. Psychological Soc., 1969– ; Mem. Scottish Univs Council on Entrance, 1968–72. *Publications*: Figural After-Effects (Brit. Jl of Psychology Monographs), 1958; *contrib.* Brit. Jl Psychology, Amer. Jl of Psychology, Acta Psychologica. *Address*: Dept of Psychology, Univ. of Stirling, Stirling FR9 4LA.

McFadden, Rev. Prof. John Alexander, MA, BD, DD; Professor of Biblical Theology, Presbyterian College, Belfast, since 1964; *b* 1909; two *s*. MA Glasgow 1930, BD Glasgow 1934, DD Presbyterian Theological Faculty, Ireland, 1969. Pt-time Lectr, Univ. of Aberdeen, Dept of Hebrew, 1958– 64; Recognised Teacher, Queen's Univ., Belfast, 1964– . Clerk, Presbyt. of Garioch (Scotland), 1957–64; Clerk, Presbyt. of Belfast South, 1967– . *Publications: contrib.* Evang. Qly, Expos. Times. *Address*: Presbyterian College, Botanic Avenue, Belfast 7.

McFarland, Dr David John; Fellow and Tutor in Psychology, Balliol College, Oxford, since 1966, and Reader in Animal Behaviour, University of Oxford, since 1974; *b* 1938; *m* 1962; one *s* one *d*. BSc Liverpool 1961 (1st cl. Zoology), DPhil Oxon 1965 (Psychology), MA Oxon 1966. Sen. Schol., Merton Coll., Oxford, 1961–63; Lectr in Psychology, Univ. of Durham, 1964–66, Univ. of Oxford, 1966– 74; Vis. Prof., Rutgers Univ., NJ, 1971. European Ed., Anim. Behav., 1969–74. *Publications*: (with J. McFarland) An Introduction to the Study of Behaviour, 1969; Feedback Mechanisms in Animal Behaviour, 1971; ed, Motivational Control Systems Analysis, 1974; *contrib.* Anim. Behav., Physiol. Behav., Jl Comp. Physiol. Psychol., Zeits. Tierpsychol. *Address*: Balliol College, Oxford.

McFarlane, Prof. Ian Dalrymple, MBE; Professor of French Literature, Oxford, since 1971; *b* 1915; *m* 1939; one *s* one *d*. MA St Andrews 1938 (1st cl. Hons); Dr Univ. Paris 1950. Lectr in French, Cambridge Univ., 1945–61; Fellow, Gonville and Caius Coll., Cambridge, 1947, Sen. Tutor, 1956–61; Prof. of French Lang. and Lit., Univ. of St Andrews, 1961–70. Mem., Academic Planning Bd, Univ. of Stirling, 1964–67; Mem., Scott. Cert. of Educn Exam. Bd, 1964–70; Mem., Cttee on Res. and Devlop. in Mod. Langs, 1966–72. *Publications*: critical edn of M. Scève's Délie, 1966; *contrib.* learned periodicals. *Address*: Wadham College, Oxford.

McFarlane, Prof. James Walter; Professor of European Literature, School of European Studies, University of East Anglia, since 1964; *b* 1920; *m* 1944; two *s* one *d*. MA Oxon 1947, BLitt 1948; FRSA 1972. Lectr and Sen. Lectr, Dept of German and Scandinavian Studies, King's College, Univ. Durham, later Univ. Newcastle upon Tyne, 1947–63; Vis., Prof., Univ. Auckland, 1967; Leverhulme Fac. Fellow in European Studies, Univ. E Anglia, 1971–72. Univ. E Anglia: Dean of European Studies, 1964–68; Public Orator, 1964–68; Pro-Vice-Chancellor, 1968– 71. Mem., BBC Gen. Adv. Council; Chm.,

BBC E Anglian Regional Adv. Council. *Publications*: General Editor, The Oxford Ibsen, 8 vols, 1960– ; Ibsen and the Temper of Norwegian Literature, 1960; Discussions of Ibsen, 1962; Henrik Ibsen, 1970; *contrib.* Durham Univ. Jl, Mod. Lang. Rev., PMLA, Scandinavica. *Address*: School of European Studies, Univ. of East Anglia, Norwich NOR 88C.

Macfarlane, Dr Leslie John; Fellow and Tutor in Politics, St John's College, Oxford, since 1969; University Lecturer in Politics, since 1970; *b* 1924; *m* 1950; one *s* two *d*. BSc (Econ) LSE 1954 (Univ. of London evening student), PhD London 1961 (Univ. of London External), MA Oxon 1969 (by decree). Clerical and Admin. Posts, LCC, 1941–57; Lectr in Government, Birmingham Coll. of Commerce, 1957–63; Tutor in Politics, Ruskin Coll., Oxford, 1963–69. *Publications*: British Politics 1918–1964, 1965; The British Communist Party: its origin and development until 1929, 1966; Modern Political Theory, 1970, American and Japanese edns 1973; Political Disobedience, 1971; Violence and the State (forthcoming); *contrib.* Ethics, Govt and Opposition, Jl Commonwealth Polit. Stud., Polit. Qly, Polit. Studies., Past and Present, Public Law. *Address*: St John's College, Oxford.

McGann, Michael John; Senior Lecturer in Classics (Latin), Department of Latin, The Queen's University of Belfast, since 1970; *b* 1927; *m* 1954 (wife died 1969); two *s* five *d*. BA Belfast 1947, MA Belfast 1950, BLitt Oxon 1954. Hon. mem., Internat. Ovidian Soc., Bucarest. Asst Lectr in Classics, Univ. Coll., Dublin, 1948–51; Asst Lectr, Queen's Univ., Belfast, 1953–56; Lectr, Queen's Univ., Belfast, 1956–70. Asst Adv. of Studies, Fac. of Arts, Queen's Univ., Belfast, 1970– . *Publications*: Studies in Horace's First Book of Epistles, 1969; *contrib.* Archiv. Latin Med. Æv., Class. Qly, Class. Rev., Glotta, Hermes, Latomus, Rhein. Mus., Riv. Filol. *Address*: Dept of Latin, Queen's Univ., Belfast BT7 1NN.

McGeeney, Patrick; Lecturer, Department of Education, Manchester University, since 1969; *b* 1918; *m* 1947; one *s* two *d*. BA Hons 1950 (English), DipEd 1951. Res. Officer, Inst. of Community Studies, Bethnal Green, 1964–67; Sen. Res. Officer, Dept of Educn, Exeter Univ., 1967–69. *Publications*: Useful Literacy, 1960, 8th edn 1965; Progressive Literacy, 1962, 4th edn 1969; Life and Literacy, 1964, 3rd edn 1969; (with M. F. D. Young) Learning Begins at Home, 1968; Parents are Welcome, 1969, 2nd edn 1970; *contrib.* chaps in: Young Adults in School, ed Jennifer Rogers, 1972; Linking Home and School, ed M. Craft *et al*, 1972; Pastoral Care, ed M. Marland (forthcoming); *contrib.* New Statesman, Technol., Times Rev. of Ind., Use of Eng., Liberal Educn, Forum, Where, Contact, Educn, Eng. in Educn, London Educnl Rev. *Address*: Dept of Education, Univ. of Manchester, Oxford Road, Manchester.

McGhee, John Goldie; Lecturer, Department of Administration, University of

Strathclyde, since 1964; *b* 1920; *m* 1947; one *s* one *d*. DPA Glasgow 1953, BSc(Econ) London External 1956. *Address*: Dept of Administration, Univ. of Strathclyde, Glasgow G1 1XW.

MacGibbon, Prof. Iain Campbell; Professor, Public International Law, Edinburgh University, since 1966; *b* 1923; *m* 1950; two *s* one *d*. MA Edinburgh 1948, LLB Edinburgh 1950, PhD Cambridge 1957. Mem., Soc. Public Teachers of Law, Mem., Brit. Inst. of Internat. Comp. Law, Mem., Internat. Law Assoc., Mem., Americ. Soc. of Internat. Law. Sen. Lectr, Univ. of Aberdeen, 1956–67; Sen. Lectr, Univ. of Edinburgh, 1962–66. Legal Off., Secretariat Off. of Legal Aff., UN, 1959–61. *Publications*: *contrib.* Brit. Ybk Internat. Law, Internat. Comp. Law Qly. *Address*: Dept of Public International Law, Univ. of Edinburgh, Old College, South Bridge, Edinburgh EH8 9YL.

McGivney, J. V.; Lecturer in French since 1967 and Director of Language Laboratory since 1974, School of European Studies, University of Sussex; *b* 1940; *m* 1965; two *s* one *d*. BA Exeter 1962 (Hons French), LèsL Rennes 1964; Mem., Linguistics Assoc. of GB. Rennes, 1963; Paris (Sorbonne), 1964; Exeter, 1966; Nairobi (Vis. Lectr), 1970–71. *Publication*: French Pronunciation, 1973. *Address*: School of European Studies, Univ. of Sussex, Falmer, Brighton, Sussex.

McGonigle, Dr Brendan O.; University Lecturer, Department of Psychology, Edinburgh University, since 1969; *b* 1939; *m* 1965; three *d*. BA Belfast 1961, PhD Belfast 1964. Post-Doc. and Tutor, Durham Univ., 1964–65; Lectr and Tutor, Oxford Univ., 1965–67; Asst Prof. of Psychol., and Res. Assoc., Animal Behav. Labs, Inst. of Science and Engin., Pennsylvania State Univ., 1967–69. *Publications*: *contrib.* Jl Comp. Physiol. Psychol. *Address*: Dept of Psychology, Edinburgh Univ., Edinburgh EH8 9YL.

McGowan, Margaret Mary, BA, PhD; Reader in French, University of Sussex; since 1964; *b* 1931; *m* 1964. BA Reading 1954 (1st cl. French), PhD Reading 1959. Asst Lectr in French, Glasgow Univ., 1957–59, Lectr, 1959–64. *Publications*: L'Art du Ballet de Cour, Paris, 1963; ed, Racine's Bajazet, 1968; Montaigne's Deceits: The Art of Persuasion in the 'Essais', 1974; *contrib.* French Literature and its Background, 1970; Oxford History of Music; Grove's Dictionary; Gen. Editor, Renaissance Triumphs and Magnificences; *contrib.* Fr. Studies, Studi Francesi, Revue de l'Histoire du Théâtre, Baroque, The Library. *Address*: School of European Studies, Univ. of Sussex, Falmer, Brighton.

McGrath, Patrick Vincent; Reader, Department of History, Bristol University, since 1963; *b* 1914; *m* 1950; two *s* four *d*. BA London 1935 (1st cl.), MA London 1949; FRHistS. Asst Lectr, Bristol, 1946–49; Lectr, Bristol, 1949–57; Sen. Lectr, Bristol, 1957–63. Asst Dean, Fac. of Arts, 1954–57; Adv. to General Students, 1957–60; Mem., Univ. Council, 1956–58; Senate, 1961–64; Libr.

441

Cttee, 1963– ; Hon. Gen. Ed., Bristol. Res. Soc.; Rec. Sect., Bristol and Glos. Archaeol. Soc. *Publications*: Records relating to the Society of Merchant Venturers of Bristol in the Seventeenth Century, 1952; Merchants and Merchandise in Seventeenth-Century Bristol, 1955; The Merchants Avizo, 1957; Papists and Puritans under Elizabeth I, 1967, pbk edn 1969; *contrib.* EHR. *Address*: Dept of History, Univ. of Bristol., Bristol BS8 1TH.

MacGregor, Dr James; Registrar, University of Leeds, since 1971; *b* 1913; *m* 1941. BA Liverpool 1936, MEd Leeds 1949, PhD Leeds 1954; Teachers Certificate 1937. Leeds University: Lectr, Dept of Adult Educn, 1949; Asst Registrar, 1961; Dep. Registrar, 1966. Mem., Yorks Regional Health Authority, 1973– . *Address*: Univ. of Leeds, Leeds LS2 9JT.

McGregor, Prof. Oliver Ross; Professor of Social Institutions in the University of London, and Head of Department of Sociology, Bedford College, since 1964; also Director, SSRC Centre for Socio-Legal Research, Oxford, since 1972; *b* 1921; *m* 1944; three *s*. BSc(Econ) London, MA Oxon. Fellow, Wolfson Coll., Oxford, 1972. Asst Lectr and Lectr in Econ. Hist., Univ. of Hull, 1945–47; Lectr, Bedford Coll., 1947–60; Reader in Univ. of London, 1960–64; Simon Sen. Res. Fellow, Univ. of Manchester, 1959–60. Temp. Civil Servant, War Off. and Min. of Agric., 1940–44. Jt Dir, Rowntree Legal Res. Unit, 1966– ; Member: Cttee on Enforcement of Judgement Debts, 1965; Cttee on Statutory Maintenance Limits, 1966; Cttee on Land Use (Recreation and Leisure), 1967; Nat. Parks Commn, 1966–68; ITA Gen. Adv. Council, 1967–73; Countryside Commn, 1968– ; Lord Chancellor's Legal Aid Adv. Cttee, 1969– ; Cttee on One-Parent Families, 1969–73. *Publications*: Divorce in England, 1957; Bibliography of the National Association for the Promotion of Social Science, 1969; (jtly) Separated Spouses, 1970; (ed) Lord Ernle, English Farming Past and Present, 6th edn, 1960; *contrib.* Brit. Jl of Sociol., etc. *Address*: Bedford College, Inner Circle, Regent's Park, NW1 4NS; Wolfson College, Oxford.

McGregor, Ronald Stuart, MA, PhD; Lecturer in Hindi, University of Cambridge; since 1964; *b* 1929; *m* 1960; two *s* one *d*. BA New Zealand 1950, MA New Zealand 1951, Dip Hons New Zealand 1952, BA Oxon 1954, MA Oxon 1959, PhD London 1965. Mem., Royal Asiat. Soc., Philol. Soc. Asst Lectr in Linguistics, Univ. of London, 1956–57; Asst Lectr in Hindi, 1957–58, Lectr in Hindi, 1958. *Publications*: The Language of Indrajit of Orchā, 1968; ed, Exercises in Spoken Hindi, 1970; Outline of Hindi Grammar, 1972; trans., Nanddas: The Rounddance of Krishna and Uddhav's Message, 1973; *contrib.* Bull. SOAS, Ind. Lings, Jl AOS, Jl Roy. Asiat. Soc. *Address*: Faculty of Oriental Studies, Sidgwick Avenue, Cambridge.

Macgregor-Reid, George James; Lecturer, Department of Economics, Lancaster University, since 1966; *b* 1943; *m* 1968. BA 442

Leicester (Econs), MA Leicester (Public Econs). *Address*: Dept of Economics, The Univ., Bailrigg, Lancaster LA1 4YW.

McGuinness, Dr Rosamond, (Mrs George Biddlecombe); Lecturer, Music Department, Royal Holloway College, University of London, since 1969; *b* 1929; *m* 1957, 1970; one *s* four *d*. BA Vassar Coll. 1951, MA Smith Coll. 1952, DPhil 1964, MA 1969, Oxon; Mem., Royal Musical Assoc. Instructor in Music Hist.: Vassar Coll., 1955–57; Brasenose Coll. and Queen's Coll., Oxford, 1964–69; St Anne's Coll., 1965–73; St Peter's Coll. 1968–69; Randall MacIver Jun. Res. Fellow, St Anne's Coll., 1967–69; Birmingham Univ., Hilary Term, 1969; RAM, Trinity Term, 1969 and Hilary and Trinity Terms, 1970. *Publications*: English Court Odes 1660–1820, 1971; *contrib.* Die Musik in Geschichte und Gegenwart, Groves VI, Music and Letters, Proc. RMA, Soundings. *Address*: Dept of Music, Royal Holloway Coll., Univ. of London, Egham, Surrey TW20 0EX.

McGuire, Ralph Joseph, BSc, MA, MEd; Senior Lecturer in Clinical Psychology, University of Edinburgh, since 1971; *b* 1926; *m* 1951; one *s* four *d*. BSc Glasgow 1949, MA Glasgow 1949 (Maths and Physics), MEd Glasgow 1952 (Pyschology and Education); ABPsS. Sen. Lectr, Leeds Univ., 1964–71. *Publications*: chapter in, Conditioning Techniques in Clinical Practice and Research, ed C. M. Franks, 1964; in, Handbook of Abnormal Psychology, ed H. J. Eysenck, 2nd edn 1972; *contrib.* Ann. Rheum. Dis., Brit. Jl Psychiat., Brit. Med. Jl, Behav. Res. Ther., Med. Biol. Ill., Psychol. Med. *Address*: Dept of Psychiatry, Royal Edinburgh Hospital, Morningside Park, Edinburgh EH10 5HF.

McGurk, Dr Patrick Maurice; Reader in Medieval History, Birkbeck College, University of London, since 1967; *b* 1928; *m* 1961; two *d*. BA London 1949 (1st cl. History), PhD London 1954; FRHistS. Asst Lectr, Birkbeck Coll., 1953–56; Lectr, Birkbeck Coll., 1956–67; Sec., Bd of Studies in History, Univ. of London, 1967–70. *Publications*: Latin Gospel Books from AD 400–AD 800, 1961; Catalogue of Illuminated Astrological and Mythological Manuscripts of the Latin Middle Ages, vol. IV: Astrological Manuscripts in Italian Libraries (other than Rome), 1966; *contrib.* Sacris Erud., Sciptor. *Address*: Birkbeck College, Malet Street, WC1E 7HX.

McHardy, Rev. Prof. William Duff, DPhil, DD; Regius Professor of Hebrew, University of Oxford, and Student of Christ Church, Oxford, since 1960; *b* 1911; *m* 1941; one *d*. MA Aberdeen 1932, BD Aberdeen 1935, MA Edinburgh 1938; DPhil Oxon; Hon DD Aberdeen. Lectr in Aramaic and Syriac, Oxford, 1945–48; Samuel Davidson Prof. of OT Studies, London, 1948–60; Grinfield Lectr on the Septuagint, Oxford, 1959–61. Curator, Mingana Collect. of Oriental MSS, Selly Oak Colls, Birmingham; Mem., Council, Selly Oak Colls; Jt Dir, New English Bible. *Publications*: *contrib.* Jl Theol. Studies. *Address*: Christ Church, Oxford.

Machin, David John Varcoe; Research Assistant, Department of Drama, University of Bristol, since 1970; *b* 1936; *m* 1964. BA Bristol 1958; Mem. Assoc. of British Theatre Technicians. Technical Asst, Dept of Drama, Univ. of Bristol, 1964–67, Res. Asst, 1967–70. *Address:* Dept of Drama, 29 Park Row, Bristol BS1 5LT.

Machin, Dr George Ian Thom, MA, DPhil, FRHistS; Lecturer in Modern History, University of Dundee, since 1967; *b* 1937; *m* 1964; two *s* one *d*. BA Oxon 1958, MA Oxon 1961, DPhil Oxon 1961; Mem. Scottish Hist. Soc; Mem., Eccles. Hist. Soc. Asst Lectr, Singapore Univ., 1961–63, Lectr, 1963–64; Lectr, St Andrews Univ. (Queen's Coll., Dundee), 1964–67. Hon. Treas., Abertay Hist. Soc., 1966–73; Mem., Faculty Bd of Soc. Sci. and Letters, 1970–73. *Publications:* The Catholic Question in English Politics, 1820–30, 1964; *contrib.* EHR, Hist. Jl, Jl Eccles. Hist., Scott. Hist. Rev., Welsh Hist. Rev. *Address:* Dept of Modern History, Univ. of Dundee, Dundee DD1 4HN.

Machin, Robert; Resident Tutor in West Dorset, Department of Extra-Mural Studies, University of Bristol, since 1969; *b* 1942. MA Oxford 1964. Tutor Trainee, Delegacy for Extra-Mural Studies, Univ. of Oxford, 1964–65; Lectr in History, Dept of Adult Educn, Univ. of Leeds, 1965–69. *Address:* Dept of Extra-Mural Studies, Univ. of Bristol, Bristol BS8 1TH.

McHugh, Prof. Roger, MA, PhD; Professor of Anglo–Irish Literature and Drama, Department of English, University College, Dublin, since 1967; *b* 1908; *m* 1942; two *s* three *d*. BA Dublin 1928, MA Dublin 1930, PhD National University of Ireland, 1947. Mem., Royal Dublin Soc., Mem., Soc. Authors (London), Mem., American Cttee Irish Studies, Mem., Ireland–Japan Soc. Asst Lectr in Mod. Hist., Univ. Coll., Dublin, 1929; Asst Lectr in English, Univ. Coll., Dublin, 1934–46; Lectr in English, Univ. Coll., Dublin, 1947–65; Prof. of English, Univ. Coll., Dublin, 1965–67; Chm., English Dept, Univ. Coll., Dublin, 1967–69, 1971–73; Vis. Lectr, Univ. of Wisconsin, 1948; Vis. Prof., Univ. of Indiana, 1964; Vis. Prof., Univ. of Massachusetts, 1966; Univ. of San Francisco, 1967; Vis. Mellon Prof., Univ. of Pittsburgh, 1969–70; Berg Professor, New York Univ., 1972; Fellow, Sch. of Letters, Indiana Univ., 1965–71; Lecture Tours of Univs in Iceland, 1951, India, 1971, Japan 1970, Scandinavia, 1967, USA, 1962, USSR, 1967. Mem., Irish Senate, 1954–57; Trustee, Lyric Theatre, Belfast; Chm., Internat. Assoc. Study Anglo-Irish Lit., 1970–73; Pitré Internat. Folklore Award, 1957; Abbey Theatre Award, 1945. *Publications:* Henry Grattan, 1936; Letters of W. B. Yeats to K. Tynan, 1953; Dublin 1916, 1966; Ah Sweet Dancer, 1970; Jack B. Yeats, a Centenary Gathering, 1971; Plays: Trial at Green Street Courthouse, 1943; Rossa, 1948; co-ed, Jonathan Swift: a Tercentenary Tribute, 1967; *contrib.* Art in Amer., Black., Encicl. Spett., Skirnir. Studies, Texas Qly, Univ. Rev. *Address:* Room J203, Arts Block, Univ. College, Belfield, Dublin 4.

McInerney, Dr John Peter; Senior Lecturer, Department of Agricultural Economics, University of Manchester, since 1971; *b* 1939; *m* 1961; one *s* one *d*. BSc Hons London (Hons Agric. 1st cl.), Dip. Agricultural Econs Oxford, PhD Iowa State; Member: Gamma Sigma Delta, Phi Kappa Phi, 1964, Agric. Econ. Soc. (UK), Canadian Agric. Econ. Soc., American Agric. Econ. Assoc. Asst Lectr, Wye Coll., London, 1964–67; Lectr, 1967–68; Lectr, Univ. of Manchester, 1968–71. Vis. Lectr, Manitoba, 1968. Res. Consultant, Royal Canadian Commn on Farm Machinery, 1968–69; Devlt Consultant, World Bank, 1972– . *Publications: contrib.* American Jl of Agricultural Econs, Canadian Jl Agricultural Econs, Farm Economist, Jl of Agricultural Econs. *Address:* Dept of Agricultural Economics, Univ. of Manchester, Manchester M13 9PL.

McInnes, Prof. Edward O'Hara; Professor of German Studies, University of Strathclyde, since 1974; *b* 1935; *m* 1964; one *s* three *d*. BA London 1958 (1st cl. Hons), MA London 1962. Asst Lectr, King's Coll., London, 1961–62; Asst Lectr, Dept of German, Univ. of Edinburgh, 1962–64, Lectr 1964–73, Reader 1973–74. *Publications:* Hauptmann Centenary Lecture, 1964; (with A. J. Harper) German Today, 1967; *contrib.* Deuts. Vierteljahr. Lit. Gesch., Forum Mod. Lang. Study, Germ. Life Lett., Maske Koth., Zeits deutsche Philologie, Neophilologus, MLR, Orbis Litt. *Address:* Dept of German, Univ. of Strathclyde, Glasgow G1 1XW.

Macintosh, Rev. Andrew Alexander, MA; Fellow, Tutor and Assistant Dean, St John's College, Cambridge University, since 1969; *b* 1936; *m* 1962; one *s* one *d*. BA Cantab 1959, MA Cantab 1962 (Theological Tripos Pt 1 1957 (1st cl.), Theological Tripos Pt 2 1959 (2nd cl.), Theological Tripos Pt 3 1961 (2nd cl.); Deacon 1962, Priest 1963. Mem., Soc. OT Study. Curate, S Ormby, Dio. Lincoln, 1962–64; Asst Lectr, St David's Coll., Lampeter, 1964–66, Lectr, 1966–67; Chaplain, St John's Coll., Cambridge, 1967. Sec., Fac. of Divinity, Cambridge, 1970–73. *Publications: contrib.* Jl Theol. Studies, Theol., Vet. Testam. *Address:* St John's College, Cambridge.

McIntosh, Prof. Angus; Forbes Professor of English Language, University of Edinburgh, since 1964; *b* 1914; *m* 1939; two *s* one *d*. BA Oxon 1934 (1st cl. Hons English Lang. and Lit.), Dip. of Comparative Philology Oxon 1936, MA Harvard 1937 (Commonwealth Fund Fellow), MA Oxon 1938; Lectr, Dept of English, UC, Swansea, 1938–46; Univ. Lectr in Mediaeval English, Oxford, 1946–48; Lectr in English, Christ Church, Oxford, 1946–47; Student of Christ Church, 1947–48; Prof. of English Lang. and General Linguistics, Univ. of Edinburgh, 1948–64; Rockefeller Foundn Fellowship, US, June–Sept, 1949. *Publications:* books, articles and reviews on subject of English language and related topics. *Address:* David Hume Tower, George Square, Edinburgh EH8 9JX.

Macintyre, Dr Angus Donald; Official Fellow, and Tutor in Modern History,

Magdalen College, Oxford, and University Lecturer, since 1963; *b* 1935; *m* 1958; two *s* one *d*. BA Oxon 1958 (Hist.), MA Oxon 1962, DPhil Oxon 1963; FRHistS. Sen. Tutor, Magdalen Coll., 1966–68. Gov., Magdalen Coll. Sch., Brackley, 1965– ; Chm., Thomas Wall Trust, 1971– . Gen. Editor, Oxf. Hist. Monogs, 1971– . *Publications*: The Liberator, Daniel O'Connell and the Irish Parliamentary Party, 1830–47, 1965. *Address*: Magdalen College, Oxford.

McIntyre, Donald Ian; Lecturer, Department of Education, University of Stirling, since 1971; *b* 1937; *m* 1964; two *s* one *d*. MA Edinburgh 1958 (Maths and Natural Phil.), MEd Edinburgh 1960. Mem., Brit. Psychol. Soc. Res. Tutor, Univ. of Hull, 1965–67; Sen. Res. Fellow, Univ. of Stirling, 1969–71. *Publications*: (with A. T. Morrison) Teachers and Teaching, 1969; Schools and Socialization, 1971; ed (with A. T. Morrison) The Social Psychology of Teaching, 1972; *contrib.* Brit. Jl Educnl Psychol., Brit. Jl Soc. Clin. Psychol., Sociol. Rev. *Address*: Dept of Education, Univ. of Stirling, Stirling FK9 4LA.

McIntyre, Rev. James Ainslie, MA, BD; Lecturer in New Testament Language and Literature, University of Glasgow, since 1966; *b* 1936; *m* 1960; two *s*. MA Glasgow 1958 (2nd cl. Classics), BD Glasgow 1961 (distn. in New Testament). Mem., Studiorum NT Soc. Asst in NT Language and Literature, Univ. of Glasgow, 1963–66; Asst Dean, Fac. of Div., Univ. of Glasgow, 1970– . *Address*: Dept of New Testament, Univ. of Glasgow, Glasgow G12 8QQ.

McIntyre, Rev. Prof. John, MA, BD, DLitt, DD; Professor of Divinity, University of Edinburgh, since 1956; *b* 1916; *m* 1945; two *s* one *d*. MA Hons Edinburgh 1938 (1st cl. Mental Philos.), BD Edinburgh 1941 (Distinction in Systematic Theol.), DLitt Edinburgh 1953, Hon. DD Glasgow 1961. Prof. of Theol., St Andrew's Coll., Univ. of Sydney, 1946–56; Principal, St Andrew's Coll., 1950–56; Principal, New Coll., and Dean, Fac. of Divinity, Univ. of Edinburgh, 1968– . Principal Warden, Pollock Halls of Res., Univ. of Edinburgh, 1960–71; Acting Principal and Vice-Chancellor, Univ. of Edinburgh, 1973–74. *Publications*: St Anselm and His Critics, 1954; The Christian Doctrine of History, 1957; On the Love of God, 1962; The Shape of Christology, 1967; *contrib.* Scott. Jl Theol. *Address*: New College, Mound Place, Edinburgh.

McIntyre, John C., MA; Lecturer in Spanish and Latin American Studies, Department of Modern Languages, University of Strathclyde, since 1964; *b* 1941; *m* 1968; one *d*. MA Glasgow, 1962 (1st cl. Hispanic Studies and French); Mem., Assoc. of Hispanists of GB and Ireland; Mem., Assoc. of Teachers of Spanish and Portuguese, Scotland. Oral Examiner, Scot. Cert. of Ed., Exam Bd; Examiner, 'O' Level, SCE Exam Bd. *Address*: Dept of Modern Languages, Univ. of Strathclyde, Glasgow G1 1XW.

mac Íomhair, Seán; Director, Language Laboratory, University College, Galway, National University of Ireland, since 1968; *b* 1943; *m* 1967. BA Galway 1964 (1st cl. French and Irish), Basic Dip. in Sovietology, Freiburg 1965 (1st cl.), MA Galway 1965 (Hons French), Cert. Linguistique Générale Paris 1968 (Hons). Asst Lectr in French, Univ. Coll., Galway, 1965–68. Sec., Teaching Aids Cttee, UGC. Mem., Lingu. Inst. Irel., 1971– . *Publications*: trans., Pirandello: Enrico IV (Éinrí a IV), 1970; (jtly) Higher and A-Level French, 1973; *contrib.* Comhar, Louth Archaeol. Jl. *Address*: An Teanglann, Univ. College, Galway, Ireland.

Mack Smith, Denis; Senior Research Fellow, since 1962, and Dean of Visiting Fellows, since 1971, All Souls College, Oxford; *b* 1920; *m* 1963; two *d*. BA Cantab 1947, MA Cantab 1949, MA Oxon 1963. Fellow of Peterhouse, Cambridge, 1947–62; Lectr, Cambridge Univ., 1952–62. *Address*: All Souls College, Oxford.

McKane, Prof. William, MA, PhD; Professor of Hebrew and Oriental Languages, University of St Andrews, since 1968; *b* 1921; *m* 1952; three *s* two *d*. MA St Andrews 1949 (2nd cl. Philos.), MA Glasgow 1952 (1st cl. Semitic Langs), PhD Glasgow 1956; FRAS. Asst, Glasgow, 1953; Lectr, Glasgow, 1956; Sen. Lectr, Glasgow, 1965. Assessor, SCE Exam. Bd, 1968– . Mem., SOTS. Co-Dir, Church of Scotl. Selection Schs, 1967– . Editor, Trans Glasgow Univ. Oriental Soc., 1965– ; Mem., Editorial Bd, SOTS Monograph Series, 1972– . *Publications*: Al-Ghazali's Book of Fear and Hope, 1962; I and II Samuel, 1963; Prophets and Wise Men, 1965; Tracts for The Times, 1965; Proverbs, 1970; *contrib.* JSS, OTS (Leiden), VT, Trans GUOS. *Address*: Dept of Hebrew and Oriental Languages, Univ. of St Andrews, St Andrews, Fife KY16 9AJ.

Mackay, Dr Angus Iain Kenneth; Lecturer in History, University of Edinburgh, since 1969; *b* 1939; *m* 1962; one *s* one *d*. MA Edinburgh 1962 (1st cl. Hist.), PhD Edinburgh 1969. Lectr, Reading Univ., 1965–69. *Publications*: *contrib.* Past and Present. *Address*: Dept of History, Univ. of Edinburgh, George Square, Edinburgh.

MacKay, Prof. Donald Iain; Professor, Department of Political Economy, University of Aberdeen, since 1971; *b* 1937; *m* 1961; one *s* two *d*. MA Aberdeen 1959 (Econ. Science); FREconS; Fellow Scottish Econ. Soc. Lectr and Sen. Lectr in Dept of Social and Econ. Res., Univ. of Glasgow, 1965–71. Econ. Consultant to: Sec. of State for Scotland; Organisation of Econ. Co-operation and Develt; British Steel Corp.; Editor, Scottish Jl of Political Economy. *Publications*: Geographical Mobility and the Brain Drain, 1969; Local Labour Markets and Wage Structures, 1970; Labour Markets under Different Employment Conditions, 1971; *contrib.* Brit. Jl Indust. Rels, Scot. Jl Pol Econ., Jl Royal Stat. Soc., Internat. Rev. Soc. Hist., Rev. Art, Oxford Econ. Paps, Manch. Sch. of Soc. and Econ. Stud., Econ. Jl. *Address*: Dept of Political Economy, Univ. of Aberdeen, Aberdeen AB9 1AS.

MacKay, Prof. Donald MacCrimmon, BSc, PhD, FInstP; Granada Research Professor of Communication, University of Keele, since 1960; *b* 1922; *m* 1955; two *s* three *d*. BSc St Andrews 1943; PhD London 1951. KCL: Asst Lectr in Physics, 1946–48; Lectr, 1948–59; Reader, 1959–60; Rockefeller Fellow, 1951; Eddington Lectr, 1967; Vis. Prof., Univ. of California, 1969; Herter Lectr, Johns Hopkins Univ., 1971; Foerster Lectr, Univ. of Calif., Berkeley, 1973; Drummond Lectr, Univ. of Stirling, 1975. Jt Editor: Experimental Brain Research; Handbook of Sensory Physiology. *Publications*: (with M. E. Fisher) Analogue Computing at Ultra-High Speed, 1962; (ed) Christuanity in a Mechanistic Universe, 1965; Freedom of Action in a Mechanistic Universe, 1967; Information, Mechanism and Meaning, 1969; *contrib.* to books and jls on electronic computing, information theory, experimental psychology and electro-physiology. *Address*: Univ. of Keele, Keele, Staffs ST5 5BG.

McKay, Derek; Lecturer in International History, London School of Economics, since 1968; *b* 1942; *m* 1963; two *d*. BA London 1963, PhD London 1971. Lectr in Hist., York Univ., 1965–68. *Publications*: *contrib.* EHR. *Address*: London School of Economics, Aldwych, WC2A 2AE.

Mackay, Dr George Murray, BSc, SM, PhD, MICE, MIMechE; Reader in Traffic Safety, Accident Research Unit, Department of Transportation and Environmental Planning, University of Birmingham, since 1973; *b* 1937; *m* 1963; one *s* one *d*. BSc Birmingham 1958 (Mech. Eng.), SM Massachusetts Institute of Technology 1961 (Civil Eng.), PhD Birmingham 1966 (Transportation); MICE, MIMechE. Teaching Asst, MIT, 1959–61; Res. Assoc., Birmingham, 1964–66, Sen. Res. Assoc., 1966–68, Sen. Res. Fellow, 1968–73. Mem., BSI and SAE Cttees; Mem., Internat. Inst. Accid., 1968; Mem., Internat. Res. Cttee Biomech. *Publications*: contrib. Road Accidents, 1968; Technological Injury, 1970; contrib. Stapp Confs, 1967–70; FISITA meetings, 1970, 1972; *contrib.* Brit. Med. Jl, etc. *Address*: Accident Research Unit, Dept of Transportation and Environmental Planning, Univ. of Birmingham, PO Box 363, Birmingham B15 2TT.

McKay, Rev. Dr John William; Lecturer in Theology, University of Hull, since 1969; *b* 1941; *m* 1964; one *s*. MA Aberdeen 1962, BA Oxford 1964 (Theol.), PhD Cambridge 1969. Ordination training, Ridley Hall, Cambridge, 1966–69. Asst Curate, St Mary's, Cottingham, E Yorkshire, 1970– . *Publications*: Religion in Judah under the Assyrians, 1973; *contrib.* Vet. Testam., Zeits. Alttestam. Wissens. *Address*: Dept of Theology, The Univ., Hull HU6 7RX.

Mackay, Ruddock Finlay; Reader in Modern History, St Andrews University, since 1974; *b* 1922; *m* 1956; two *s* one *d*. BA New Zealand 1945, BA Oxon 1948, MA Oxon 1953, BA London 1952. Lectr in Modern History, St Andrews Univ., 1965–72, Sen. Lectr 1972–74. *Publications*: Admiral Hawke, 1965; Fisher of Kilverstone, 1973 [*i.e.* 1974];

contrib. Sources of British Military History, ed R. Higham, 1971; *contrib.* Marin. Mirr. *Address*: Dept of Modern History, Univ. of St Andrews, St Andrews, Fife KY16 9AJ.

McKeating, Dr Henry, MTh; Lecturer in Theology, University of Nottingham, since 1959; *b* 1932; *m* 1957; one *s* three *d*. BD 1955, MTh 1958, PhD 1966, London. *Publications*: Living with Guilt, 1970; God and the Future, 1974; Amos, Hosea, Micah in, New Cambridge Bible, 1971. *Address*: Dept of Theology, Univ. of Nottingham, Nottingham NG7 2RD.

McKendrick, Dr Melveena Christine, PhD; Fellow, Tutor and Lecturer in Spanish, Girton College, Cambridge, since 1970; *b* 1941; *m* 1967; two *d*. BA London 1963 (1st cl. Spanish), PhD Cantab 1967, MA Cantab 1968. Research Fellow, Girton Coll., Cambridge, 1967. *Publications*: Ferdinand and Isabella, 1968; A Concise History of Spain, 1972; The bandolera in the Spanish drama of the Golden Age, in, The Comedias of Calderón, vol. XIX, ed Cruickshank and Varey, 1973; Woman and Society in the Spanish Drama of the Golden Age, 1974; *contrib.* Bull. Hisp. Stud., Hisp. Rev. *Address*: Girton College, Cambridge.

McKendrick, Neil; University Lecturer in English Economic History, University of Cambridge, since 1964; *b* 1935; *m* 1967; two *d*. BA Cantab 1956 (Historical Tripos, 1st cl. Pt I and II with distinction), MA Cantab 1960; FRHistS. Res. Fellow, Christ's Coll., Cambridge, 1958; Official Fellow, Gonville and Caius Coll., Cambridge, 1958– ; College Lectr, Gonville and Caius Coll., Cambridge, 1958– ; Dir of Studies, Gonville and Caius Coll., Cambridge, 1959– ; Univ. Asst Lecturership, Cambridge, 1961–64; Asst Ed., Econ. Hist. Rev., 1961–63; Tutor, Gonville and Caius Coll., Cambridge, 1962–71; Sec. to History Fac., 1973–75. Consultant Editor for European Publications Ltd, 1973– . *Publications*: Josiah Wedgwood, 1730–1795, 1975; Thomas Bentley, 1730–1780, 1975; *contrib.* Essays in Economic History, vol. III, ed E. M. Carus-Wilson, 1962; Rise of Capitalism, ed Landes, 1966; Changing Perspectives in the History of Science, ed Teich and Young, 1973; ed, Historical Perspectives: Studies in English Thought and Society, 1974; *contrib.* Business Hist., Econ. Hist. Rev., Hist. Jl, Hist. Today, Horizon, Mid. Hist., Trans Royal Hist. Soc. *Address*: Gonville and Caius College, Cambridge.

McKenna, Anne; Lecturer, Department of Psychology, University College, Dublin, since 1960; *b* 1925; *m* 1949; one *s*. MA Glasgow 1945, DipPsych Dublin 1959, MPsychSci Dublin 1962; ABPsS. Mem., Irish Psychol. Soc. Founder Chm., Irish Cttee, OMEP; Mem., Panel of Experts, Grant Cttee, Internat. Fed. Univ. Women; Ed., Internat. Jl Early Childhood, 1970– . *Address*: Dept of Psychology, Univ. College, Dublin 4.

McKenna, Prof. John, PhD, FBPsS, FPSI; Associate Professor of Psychology, Royal College of Surgeons in Ireland, since 1965, and Lecturer in Psychology, University College, Dublin, since 1956; Director, Child Guidance Clinic, Dublin, since 1953; *b* 1919; *m* 1949; one *s*. MA Glasgow 1942, MEd Glasgow 1949; PhD Montreal 1955; FBPS 1965, FPSI 1971. Res. Fellow, WHO, Univ. of Montreal, 1953–55. Sec. (section J, Psychology), British Assoc. for Advancement of Science, 1956–57; Chm., Assoc. of Child Psychology and Psychiatry (Irish Br.), 1963; Cnslnt, Div. of Equality of Access to Education, UNESCO, 1968–71; Chm., Nat. Assoc. for Mentally Handicapped of Ireland, 1970–72; Mem. Council, Internat. League of Socs for Mentally Handicapped, 1973– . *Publications*: International Resources in Clinical Psychology, 1964; contrib. chapters in: International Opportunities for Advanced Training and Research in Psychology, 1966; Proceedings of III World Congress of Psychiatry, 1962; Proceedings of International Association for the Scientific Study of Mental Handicap, 1968; Proceedings of IV Congress of International League of Socieities for the Mentally Handicapped, 1969; The Present Situation and Trends of Research in the Field of Special Education, 1973; The Role of the Psychologist in Mental Health Services, 1973; *contrib.* Jl Irish Med. Assoc. *Address*: Dept of Psychology, Royal College of Surgeons, Stephens Green, Dublin.

McKennell, Dr Aubrey C., MA, PhD, FBPsS; Reader in the Methodology of Attitude Surveys, Faculty of Social Science, Southampton University, since 1971; *b* 1927; *m* 1962; one *s* one *d*. BA Hons Manchester 1951 (1st cl. Psychology), MA Manchester 1953, PhD Leeds 1956; FBPsS. Asst Lectr, then Lectr, Glasgow Univ., 1955–59; Sen. Lectr, Southampton Univ., 1967–71; Vis. Scholar, Inst. of Social Research, Univ. of Michigan, 1972–73. Ch. Psychologist, Attwood Statistics Ltd, 1959–60; Sen. and Principal Res. Off., Govt Social Survey, 1960–66; Adv. SSRC Survey Res. Unit, 1971. *Publications*: Motives in the Timing of Holidays, 1961; Noise Annoyance in Central London, 1963; Aircraft Noise Annoyance round London (Heathrow) Airport, 1963; Smoking Habits and Attitudes of Adults and Adolescents, 1967; Smoking Health and Behaviour, 1968; Surveying Attitude Structures, 1974; *contrib.* Brit. Jl Psychol., Brit. Jl Soc. Clin. Psychol., Occup. Psychol., Sociol. Rev., Sociol., Statistics, Internat. Jl of Addictions. *Address*: Faculty of Social Science, The Univ., Southampton SO9 5NH.

Mackenzie, (Alexander) Graham; University Librarian and Director of Library Research Unit, University of Lancaster, since 1963; *b* 1928; *m* 1950; one *s* one *d*. MA Glasgow 1950; ALA 1955, Mem. Library Assoc., Aslib. Keeper of Science Books, Durham Univ., 1952–60; Sub-Librarian, Nottingham Univ., 1960–61; Dep. Librarian, Brotherton Library, Leeds Univ., 1961–63. Mem., Editorial Bd, Jl of Documentation, 1965– (Chm., 1966–70). *Publications*: Bulgaria: Mechanisation of Documentation Services, 1969; Report to OECD on the Development of the University Library, Patras, 1971; jtly, and ed, Univ. of Lancaster Library, Occasional Papers, No. 1–7, 1968–72; *contrib.*

446

Aslib Proc., Brit. Libr. and Inf. Science, Jl Docum., An Leabharlann Library Trends, Program. *Address*: Library, Univ. of Lancaster, Bailrigg, Lancaster LA1 4YW.

McKenzie, Andrew Watson, BSc, DThPT, MIBiol; Senior Tutor, since 1963, Senior Lecturer, since 1953, and Head of Graduate Certificate Division, School of Education, since 1972, University of Newcastle upon Tyne; *b* 1913; *m* 1939; two *s* one *d*. BSc Dunelm 1934 (1st cl. Hons Botany with Genetics), DThPT Dunelm 1935; MIBiol. Lectr, Univ. of Durham, 1946–53; Sen. Lectr, Univ. of Durham 1953. *Address*: School of Education, Univ. of Newcastle upon Tyne, Newcastle upon Tyne NE1 7RU.

MacKenzie, Dr David Neil, MA, PhD; Reader in Iranian Languages, University of London, since 1965; *b* 1926; *m* 1951; three *s* one *d*. BA London 1951 (Persian), MA London 1953 (Old and Middle Iranian), PhD London 1957; FRAS. Mem., Philol. Soc. Lectr in Kurdish, SOAS, Univ. of London, 1955–61; Lectr in Iranian Languages, Univ. of London, 1961–65. Treas., Corpus Inscript. Iran., 1970– . *Publications*: Kurdish Dialect Studies, I, II, 1961–62; Catalogue of Pashto Manuscripts in the British Isles, 1965; Poems from the Divan of Khushâl Khân Khattak, 1965; The Dialect of Awroman, 1966; The 'Sûtra of the Causes and Effects of Actions' in Sogdian, 1970; A Concise Pahlavi Dictionary, 1971; ed, W. B. Henning: A Fragment of a Khwarezmian Dictionary, 1971; contrib. var. Festschriften; Bull. SOAS, Trans Philol. Soc. *Address*: School of Oriental and African Studies, Univ. of London, WC1E 7HP.

MacKenzie, (Donald) Kenneth (Munro); Senior Lecturer since 1973 (Staff Tutor in Literature, 1970–73), Arts Faculty, The Open University; *b* 1932; *m* 1957; two *s* one *d*. MA Hons Aberdeen 1954 (1st cl. Eng. Lang. and Lit.). Lectr in English Lit., UC of N Wales, Bangor, 1959–70. *Publications*: Open University course units: The Fox, D. H. Lawrence, 1973; The Literature of the Second World War, 1973. *Address*: The Open Univ., Walton Hall, Milton Keynes, MK7 6AA.

Mackenzie, Elizabeth Georgina Whitestone; Fellow, since 1954, and Tutor in English, since 1958, Lady Margaret Hall, Oxford, and CUF Lecturer, Oxford University, since 1954; *b* 1921. MA Oxford 1948. Libr., English Faculty Library, 1947–51; Libr., Lady Margaret Hall, 1951–68; Lectr, Lady Margaret Hall, 1951–58. Temp. Asst Principal, Min. of Agric. and Fisheries, 1943–46. *Address*: Lady Margaret Hall, Oxford.

Mackenzie, Graham; *see* Mackenzie, A. G.

McKenzie, Dr John MacDonald; Lecturer in African History, Department of History, University of Lancaster, since 1968; *b* 1943. MA Glasgow 1964 (Hons), PhD British Columbia, 1969. Sen. Tutor, County Coll., Univ. of Lancaster, 1970–73; Vis. Lecturer: Univ. of BC, 1971; Univ. of Rhodesia, 1973–74. *Publications*: contrib.

History, ed H. J. Perkin, 1970; *contrib.* Rhodes. Hist., Rhodes. Jl of Econs. *Address*: Dept of History, Furness College, Univ. of Lancaster, Lancaster LA1 4YG.

McKenzie, John Richard Philip; Lecturer in German, University of Exeter, since 1964; *b* 1940; *m* 1972. BA Manchester 1963 (Hons German Lang. and Lit.), MA Manchester 1967. *Publications*: Weimar Germany 1918–1933, 1971; *contrib.* Exeter Tapes, Thomas Mann: Tonio Kröger, 1973, and Peter Weiss: Marat/Sade, 1973; *contrib.* New German Studies. *Address*: Queen's Building, Univ. of Exeter, Exeter EX4 4QH.

MacKenzie, Kenneth; see MacKenzie, D. K. M.

MacKenzie, Norman, BSc(Econ); Director, Centre for Educational Technology, University of Sussex, since 1966, and Acting Director, School of Education, since 1973; *b* 1921; *m* 1945; two *d*. Hugh Lewis Prizewinner, 1942. BSc(Econ) London 1943 (1st cl. Hons Government). Asst Prof., Sarah Lawrence Coll., NY, 1947–48 (trans: holder Rockefeller Fellowship); Fellow, Australian Nat. Univ., Canberra, 1959–60; Res. Dir, Social Science Res. Council of Australia, 1959–60; Vis. Prof., Williams Coll., Mass., 1963–64; Lectr in Sociology, Univ. of Sussex, 1962–65; Prof. Fellow, Univ. of Sussex, 1972; Vis. Prof., Univ. of British Columbia, 1973. Asst Ed., (absences on leave) New Statesman, 1943–59; Parly Candidate, Hemel Hempstead, 1951, 1955; Cnsltncies, UNESCO, OECD, IIEP; Mem., Planning Cttee, Open Univ., 1967–69; Mem., Nat. Council Educnl Technol., 1967–73; Mem., Adv. Council, Off. Scientific Tech. Inform., 1968–73; Council Mem., Open Univ., 1969– ; Mem., Crawley, New Town Corp., 1964–65; Ed., Brit. Jl Educnl Technol. *Publications*: Socialism: a Short History, 1949; ed, Conviction, 1957; Women in Australia, 1963; Dreams and Dreaming, 1965; ed, A Guide to the Social Sciences, 1967; ed, Secret Societies, 1967; (with M. R. Eraut and H. C. Jones), Teaching and Learning: An Introduction to New Methods and Resources in Higher Education, 1970; (with S. Encel) Women in Society (forthcoming); (with Jeanne MacKenzie) The Time Traveller: a biography of H. G. Wells, 1973. *Address*: Centre for Educational Technology, Educational Development Building, Univ. of Sussex, Falmer, Brighton.

McKenzie, Dr Peter Rutherford, PhD; Senior Lecturer in Phenomenology and History of Religion, University of Leicester, since 1973 (Lecturer, 1970–73); *b* 1924; *m* 1952; one *s* two *d*. BA New Zealand 1945, MA New Zealand 1947, BD Princeton 1950, PhD Edinburgh 1953. Mem., Brit. Sect., Internat. Assoc. Hist. Relig., Mem., Soc. Afr. Ch Hist., Assoc., Mem., Afr. Stud. Assoc. UK. Lectr, Ibadan Univ., 1965–68; Sen. Lectr, 1968–70; Ed., Orita, 1967–70. Gen. Sec., NZ Student Christ. Movem., 1953–56; Presb. Parish Min., 1956–61; Stud. Chapl., Karlsruhe, 1961–65. *Publications*: Fundamentals of Christian Ethics, 1954; (jtly) Studenten und die Kirche, 1968; *contrib.* Bull.

Soc. Afr. Ch Hist., Ghana Bull. Theol., Orita, Stud. Wld. *Address*: Dept of Philosophy, Univ. of Leicester, Leicester LE1 7RH.

McKenzie, Prof. Robert Trelford, BA, PhD, Hon. LLD; Professor of Sociology with special reference to Politics, London School of Economics, since 1964; *b* 1917. BA British Columbia 1937 (1st cl. Hons), PhD London 1954; Hon. LLD, Simon Fraser 1969. Mem., Brit. Sociol. Soc., Pol. Studies Assoc. Var. appts, Royal Inst. Internat. Aff. Univ. of British Columbia, 1937–42; Asst Lectr, LSE, 1949–53; Lectr, LSE, 1953–56; Reader, LSE, 1956–64; Vis. Lectr, Harvard and Yale Univs, 1958–59. Canad. Army, 1942–46. *Publications*: British Political Parties, 1955, 2nd edn 1964, trans. German, Spanish and Japanese; (with A. Silver) Angels in Marble: Working Class Conservatives in Urban England, 1968. *Address*: London School of Economics, WC2A 2AE.

Mackerness, Eric David; Reader in English Literature, University of Sheffield, since 1968; *b* 1920. BA Cambridge 1947 (1st cl. English), MA Cambridge 1950, PhD Manchester 1952. Jane Eliza Proctor Vis. Fellow, Princeton Univ., 1948–49; Res. Fellow, Univ. of Nottingham, 1952–54; Asst Lectr, Sheffield Univ., 1954–56; Lectr, Sheffield Univ., 1956–64; Sen. Lectr, Sheffield Univ., 1964–68. *Publications*: The Heeded Voice, 1959; A Social History of English Music, 1964; ed, The Journals of George Sturt, 1967; ed, The Spirit of the Age, 1969; *contrib.* Engl., Ess. Studies, Music Lett., Queen's Qly, Rev. Engl. Lit. *Address*: Dept of English, The Univ., Sheffield S10 2TN.

Mackesy, Piers Gerald; Fellow and Tutor in Modern History, Pembroke College, Oxford University, since 1954; *b* 1924; *m* 1957; one *s* two *d*. BA Oxon 1950 (1st cl. History), DPhil Oxon 1953; FRHistS. Harkness Fellowship, Harvard, 1953–54; Vis. Fellow, Inst. Adv. Study, Princeton, 1961–62; Vis. Prof., Caltech, 1965. Mem., Council, Inst. Early Amer. Hist. and Cult., 1971–73; Mem., Council, Navy Rec. Soc. *Publications*: The War in the Mediterranean, 1803–10, 1957; The War for America, 1775–83, 1964; Statesmen at War: I, The Strategy of Overthrow, 1974; *contrib.* Great Military Battles, ed C. Falls, 1964; Essays on the American Revolution, ed D. L. Jacobson, 1971; *contrib.* Jl RUSI, etc. *Address*: Pembroke College, Oxford.

McKie, Dr Robert Lanceley Gordon; University Lecturer, Institute of Planning Studies, University of Nottingham, since 1971; *b* 1937; *m* 1962; one *s* one *d*. BA Oxon 1962 (PPE), MA Oxon 1963, MA Cantab 1964 (by Incorporation), PhD Cantab 1969. Asst. in Research, Dept of Land Economy, Cambridge 1962–68, Sen. Asst in Research, 1968–71; Vis. Lectr in Housing Studies, Dept of Land Economy, Cambridge, 1972, 1973, 1974. Sec., Bd of Land Economy, Univ. Cambridge, 1964–70; Governor, Christ's Hosp. Sch., Lincoln, 1973; Exec. Associate, The Housing Renewal Unit, 1974. *Publications*: contrib. Greater Peterborough, Draft Basic Plan, 1967; The Older Housing Areas, Greater Peterborough Supplementary Report

447

No 1, 1968; contrib. The People of Peter-borough, Greater Peterborough Supple-mentary Report No 2, 1968; Housing and the Whitehall Bulldozer, 1971; *contrib.* Town Planning Rev., Town and County Planning, Urban Studies. *Address*: Institute of Planning Studies, University Park, Nott-ingham NG7 2RD.

MacKillop, Dr Ian Duncan; Lecturer in English Literature, University of Sheffield, since 1969; *b* 1939; *m* 1972; one *d*. BA Cantab 1960, MA Cantab 1964, PhD Leicester 1972. Asst Lectr, Keele, 1968–69. Editor, Delta, 1960–73. *Publications*: *contrib.* Cambridge Qly, Delta, Essays in Criticism, Oxford Rev., Use of English. *Address*: Dept of English Lit-erature, Univ. of Sheffield, Sheffield S10 2TN.

McKinlay, H.; Professor of Management Studies, Salford University, since 1972; *b* 1928; *m* 1964; one *s* two *d*. MA Edinburgh 1951 (1st cl. Hons), BLitt Glasgow 1957. Research Fellow, Glasgow Univ., 1953–56. Strathclyde University: Lectr, 1965–67; Sen. Lectr, 1967–71; Reader, 1971–72; Chm., Bd of Social Sciences, Salford Univ., 1973. Shell Internat. Petroleum, 1956–65; Harvard Business School, 1968. *Address*: Univ. of Salford, Salford M5 4WT.

McKinnell, John Scott; Lecturer, Depart-ment of English Language and Medieval Literature, University of Durham, since 1965; *b* 1942; *m* 1965; two *s*. BA Oxon 1964 (Hons), MA Oxon 1968. Mem.: Viking Soc. for Northern Res.; Hiδ Iślenzka Bókmenntafélag. *Publications*: *contrib.* Biblio., Arnamag., Saga-Book Viking Soc. *Address*: Dept of English Language and Medieval Lit-erature, Elvet Riverside, New Elvet, Durham.

McKinney, Dr Richard William Alexander; Lecturer in Theology, Univer-sity of Nottingham, since 1968; *b* 1938; *m* 1964; one *s* two *d*. BA QUB 1962, BD Edinburgh 1965, DPhil Oxford 1970; Mem., Soc. for Study of Theol. *Address*: Dept of Theology, University Park, Nottingham NG7 2RD.

McKinnon, Prof. Donald MacKenzie, MA; Norris-Hulse Professor of Divinity, Cambridge University, and Fellow of Corpus Christi College, since 1960; *b* 1913; *m* 1939. MA Oxon 1939; Hon. DD Aberdeen 1961. Asst in Moral Philosophy, Edinburgh, 1936–37; Fellow and Tutor in Philosophy, Keble Coll., Oxford, 1937–47; Dir of Course for special courses in Philosophy for RN and RAF Cadets, Oxford, 1942–45; Lectr in Philosophy, Balliol Coll., 1945–47; Wilde Lectr in Natural and Comparative Religion, Oxford, 1945–47; Regius Prof. of Moral Philosophy, Univ. of Aberdeen, 1947–60. Lectures: Scott Holland, 1952; Hobhouse, 1953; Stanton, in the Philosophy of Religion, Cambridge, 1956–59; Gifford, Edinburgh, 1965–66; Prideaux, Exeter, 1966; Coffin, London, 1968; Riddell, Newcastle upon Tyne, 1970. *Publications*: The Notion of a Philosophy of History, 1954; A Study in Ethical Theory, 1957; (with Prof. G. W. H. Lampe), The Resurrection, 1966; Borderlands of Theology and other papers, 1968; The Stripping of the Altars, 1969; ed,

Christian Faith and Communist Faith, 1953. *Address*: Corpus Christi College, Cambridge.

Mackintosh, Prof. Athole Spalding, MA; Dean, School of Development Studies, University of East Anglia, since 1972, Pro-fessor of Economics (Development Econo-mics), since 1968, and Director, Overseas Development Group, since 1966; *b* 1926; *m* 1951; two *s* one *d*. BA Cantab 1950 (Econs), MA Cantab. Henry Fellow, Yale, 1950–51; Lectr, Univ. of Birmingham, 1951–61; Sen. Lectr, Univ. of East Anglia, 1965–69. Economic Adviser, HM Treasury, 1958–60; Dep. Dir, Overseas Develt Inst., London, 1961–64; Economic Adviser, West Pakistan, 1964–65. *Publications*: The Development of Firms, 1963; co-author, ODI series: British Aid: a survey, 1963–64. *Address*: School of Development Studies, Univ. of East Anglia, University Village, Norwich NOR 88C.

Mackrell, John Quentin Colborne; Lec-turer in History, Westfield College, Univer-sity of London, since 1970; *b* 1935; *m* 1967; BA Oxon 1958 (Mod. History), PhD London 1963. Instructor, Catholic Univ. of America, Washington, 1963–65; Lectr, Univ. of Glasgow, 1965–70. Assoc. Editor, Catholic Historical Review, 1964–65. *Publications*: The Attack on 'Feudalism' in Eighteenth-Century France, 1973; Criticism of Seig-niorial Justice in Eighteenth-Century France, in French Government and Society 1500–1850: essays in memory of Alfred Cobban, 1973; contrib. New Catholic Encycl. *Address*: History Dept, Westfield College, Kidderpore Avenue, NW3 7ST.

McLachlan, Dr Keith Stanley; Lecturer in Geography with reference to the Near and Middle East, School of Oriental and African Studies, since 1964; *b* 1937; *m* 1959; one *s* one *d*. BA Dunelm 1958, PhD Dunelm 1961. Member: Brit. Inst. Persian Studies, Soc. Libyan Studies, Assoc. Brit. Orient. Fellow-ship, SOAS, 1961–64. Sec., Assoc. Brit. Orient., 1966. *Publications*: Middle East Oil Producers, 1972; ed (with J. A. Allan and E. T. Penrose) Agriculture and the Economic Development of Libya, 1972; contrib. Revolutionizing of Iran, 1973; Cambridge History of Iran; Encyclopedia of Islam. *Address*: Dept of Geography, School of Oriental and African Studies, WC1E 7HP.

Maclagan, Michael, MA, FSA; Fellow in Medieval History, Trinity College, Oxford, since 1939, and CUF Lecturer, Oxford University, since 1948; *b* 1914; *m* 1939; 1949; two *s* two *d*. BA Oxon 1935 (1st cl. Mod. Hist.), MA Oxon 1939; FSA 1948, FRHistS. Lectr, Christ Church, Oxford, 1937–39; Sen. Proctor, Oxford, 1954–55; Vis. Prof., Univ. of S Carolina, 1974. Commnd TA, 1938; Served in 16th/5th Royal Lancers and Gen. Staff, GSO II; Mem., Oxford City Council, 1946–74; Lord Mayor of Oxford, 1970–71; Sen. Libr., Oxford Union, 1960–70; Portcullis Pursuivant, 1970. *Publications*: ed, Bede: Ecclesiastical History I and II, 1949; Trinity College, 1955; (jtly) The Colour of Heraldry, 1958; ed, R. de Bury: Philobiblon, 1960; 'Clemency' Canning, 1962 (Wheatley Gold medal); City of Constantinople, 1968;

contrib. Dictionary of National Biography; Victoria County History; *contrib.* EHR. *Address*: Trinity College, Oxford OX1 3BH.

MacLaren, Dr A. Allan, MA, PhD; Lecturer, Department of Sociology, University of Strathclyde, since 1968; *b* 1933. MA Aberdeen 1964 (History), PhD Aberdeen 1971. Lectr, Univ. of Aberdeen, 1965–68. Chm., Scott. Lab. Hist. Soc., 1970– . *Publications*: Religion and Social Class: the Disruption years in Aberdeen, 1974; Social Class in Scottish Society and History (forthcoming); *contrib.* Scott. Hist. Rev. *Address*: Dept of Sociology, Univ. of Strathclyde, Glasgow G1 1XW.

McLean, Alasdair Thomas, MBA, CA; Lecturer in Accountancy and Finance, Heriot-Watt University, since 1968; *b* 1940. MBA Strathclyde 1968; CA 1963. Asst Lectr (pt-time), Glasgow Univ., 1964–68; Stenhouse Schol., Strathclyde Univ., 1967–68. Mem., Scott. Jt Cttee for Dip. in Mngmt Studies, 1971– ; Mem. Exam. Bd, and EEC Company and Acctng Law Cttee, Inst. of CA's of Scot., 1973– . *Publications*: Accounting for Business Combinations and Goodwill, 1972; ed (and jt author), Business and Accounting in Europe; *contrib.* Accnt's Mag. *Address*: Dept of Accounting and Finance, Heriot-Watt Univ., Edinburgh EH1 2HT.

McLean, Angela Marion; Lecturer in Private Law, University of Glasgow, since 1970; *b* 1940; *m* 1964; two *s.* MA Glasgow 1961, LLB Glasgow 1963; Solicitor, Scotland, 1964. Tutor, Roman Law, 1963–64; Lectr, Scottish Private Law, 1964–67. *Publications*: *contrib.* JLS. *Address*: Faculty of Law, Univ. of Glasgow, Glasgow G12 8QQ.

Maclean, Dr Catherine Margaret Una; Lecturer, Department of Social Medicine, University of Edinburgh, since 1967; *b* 1925; *m* 1st 1951, 2nd 1963; three *s* two *d.* MB, ChB Edinburgh 1949, DPH Edinburgh 1964, MD Edinburgh 1965, PhD Edinburgh 1967. Sen. Res. Asst, Cancer Registry, Dept of Pathology, Univ. of Ibadan, Nigeria, 1960–63; Res. Fellow, Med. Res. Council Unit, Epidemiol. of Mental Illness, Dept of Psychol Med., Univ. of Edinburgh, 1964–67. *Publications*: Magical Medicine: A Nigerian Case Study, 1971; Social and Community Medicine for Students, 1971; *contrib.* Brit Jl Cancer, Brit. Jl Prev. Social Med., Brit. Med. Jl, Hum. Organisat., Jl Hlth Social Behav., Jl Trop. Med. Hyg., Scott. Med. Jl. *Address*: Dept of Social Medicine, Warrender Park Road, Edinburgh.

Maclean, Dr James Noël Mackenzie, (Maclean of Glensanda), BLitt, PhD; Lecturer in History, University of Edinburgh, since 1964; *b* 1925; *m* 1958. DipMS London 1950, BLitt Oxford 1965, PhD Edinburgh 1967; FREconS 1951, FSAScot 1953, FRHistS 1964. Mem., Convocation, Univ. of Oxford, 1969, Mem., Inst. Journalists, 1959, Assoc. Mem., BIM, 1967. AIOC Persian Lang. Schol., London, 1951. Lectr in English, Anargyrios Coll., Spetsai, Greece, 1956; Carnegie Vis. Schol., Russia and Sweden, 1968; Sir Ernest Cassel Vis. Schol., USA and

Canada, 1969; Carnegie Vis. Schol., India, 1970; Vis. Schol., Morocco, 1972. RAF, SAS Regt (Artists Rifles), Lond. Scott. Regt (Gordon Highldrs) TA; Lt-Comdr, RNR; Mngmt Trainee, Anglo-Iranian Oil Co., 1950; Exp. Mngr, Brit. & Gen. Tube Co., 1953; Dep. Ed. (Comps) Daily Mail, 1958. *Publications*: Clan Gillean (The Macleans), 1954; Memoirs of a Barra Boy, 1959; Reward is Secondary: The Life of a Political Adventurer and an Inquiry into the Mystery of Junius, 1963; The Macleans of Sweden, 1971; The Royal Visit to Edinburgh in 1822, 1972; French-Canadian Emigrants to New England, 1973; contrib. The History of Parliament: The House of Commons, 1754–1790, vol. III, ed Namier and Brooke, 1964; Studies in Diplomatic History: Essays in Memory of David Bayne Horn, ed R. Hatton and M. Anderson, 1970; Burke's Landed Gentry, 18th edn, vol. I, ed P. Townend, 1965, vol. III, ed H. Montgomery-Massingberd, 1972; *contrib.* Bull. Inst. Hist. Res., Jl Royal Soc. Arts, Scott. Geneal., S Asian Rev., Greek Gazette, New England Hist. & Gen. Register. *Address*: Dept of History, William Robertson Building, 50 George Square, Edinburgh EH8 9JY.

McLellan, Dr David, MA, DPhil; Reader in Political Theory, University of Kent, since 1972; *b* 1940; *m* 1967; two *d.* BA Oxon 1962, MA DPhil Oxon 1968. Lectr, Univ. of Kent, 1966–70; Sen. Lectr, Univ. of Kent, 1971–72. *Publications*: The Young Hegelians and Karl Marx, 1969, Japanese edn 1971, Spanish edn 1971, French edn 1972, German edn 1972; Marx before Marxism, 1970, 2nd edn 1972, Japanese edn 1972, Italian edn 1972; Karl Marx: The Early Texts, 1971; Marx's Grundrisse, 1971, 2nd edn 1972; The Thought of Karl Marx, 1971; *contrib.* Encount., Pol. Studies, Rev. Pol. *Address*: Eliot College, Univ. of Kent, Canterbury CT1 3PA.

McLennan, William Roy, MA; Lecturer in Business Studies, Division of Economic Studies, University of Sheffield, since 1969; *b* 1936; *m* 1966; one *s* two *d.* BA New Zealand 1961, MA Auckland 1963; AMBIM. Mem., BSA, ATM. Asst Lectr in Management, Otago Univ., 1964–66; Foundation for Management Education Teaching Res. Fellow, Sheffield Univ., 1967–69. Mngmt Trainee, BP (NZ) Ltd, Wellington, 1963; Dir, Postgrad. Business Programme, Sheffield Univ., 1969–71; Mem., Sheffield Br. Cttee, BIM. *Publications*: British Cases in Organizational Behaviour (forthcoming); contrib. Management Case Research Project, Cranfield Institute of Technology; *contrib.* Harv. Business Sch., Intercoll. Case Clrg Hse. *Address*: Division of Economic Studies, Univ. of Sheffield, Sheffield S10 2TN.

Macleod, Colin William; Lecturer in Classics, Oxford University, since 1969, and Tutor in Classics, Christ Church, Oxford, since 1968; *b* 1943; *m* 1969. BA Oxon 1965, MA Oxon 1968. Res. Fellow. St John's Coll., Oxford, 1966–68. *Publications*: *contrib.* Jl Theol. Studies, Class. Qly, Maia. *Address*: Christ Church, Oxford.

Macleod, Dr John Keith; Senior Lecturer, Department of Law, University of Wales

449

Institute of Science and Technology, since 1974; b 1939; m 1965; two d. LLB Nottingham 1961 (1st cl.), PhD Manchester 1966; Barrister (Gray's Inn) 1971. Asst Lectr, Manchester Univ., 1962–65; Lectr, Dept of Law, Nottingham, 1965–73. Publications: Sale and Hire Purchase, 1971; Contract title, Halsbury's Laws of England, 4th edn 1974; contrib. Crim. Law Rev., Jl Business Law. Address: UWIST, 22 The Friary, Cardiff.

Macleod, Matthew Donald; Senior Lecturer in Classics, University of Southampton, since 1971; b 1922; m 1957; one d. BA Cambridge 1947 (1st cl. Classics, pts I and II), MA Cambridge 1950. Asst Lectr in Classics, Southampton, 1948–50; Lectr, Southampton, 1950–71. Publications: Lucian vol. 7 (Loeb Classical Library), 1961; Lucian vol. 8 (Loeb Classical Library), 1967; Lucian vol. I (Oxford Classical Texts), 1972; Lucian vol. II (Oxford Classical Texts), 1974; contrib. Class. Qly, Class. Rev., Proc. Virg. Soc. Address: Dept of Classics, Univ. of Southampton, Southampton SO9 5NH.

Macleod, Prof. Robert Kenneth; Professor of Architecture, and Director, Institute of Advanced Architectural Studies, University of York, since 1969; b 1932; m 1961; one s two d. BArch UBC 1956; MRAIC 1959. Publications: Charles Rennie Mackintosh, 1968; Style and Society, 1971. Address: Univ. of York, King's Manor, Exhibition Square, York.

MacLeod, Roy Malcolm, PhD; Reader in History and Social Studies of Science, and Senior Research Fellow, Science Policy Research Unit, University of Sussex, since 1970; b 1941; m 1970. AB Harvard 1963 (summa cum laude, History and Science), PhD Cantab 1967; PBK. Fulbright Schol., Cambridge Univ., 1963–65; Res. Fellow, Univ. of Sussex, 1965–66; Res. Fellow, Churchill Coll., Cambridge, 1966–70; Vis. Prof., Univ. of Indiana, 1969; Dir d'Etudes associé, Ecole Pratique des Hautes Etudes, Paris, 1970–71;Vis. Prof., Free Univ., Amsterdam, 1973, 1974. Chm., Hist. and Social Studies of Science Div., Sch. of Math. and Physical Sciences, Univ. of Sussex, 1970– ; Mem., Cttee, Sect. X, Brit. Assoc., 1971–73; Co-Ed., Science Studies, 1971– ; Adv. Ed., Victorian Studies, 1970– ; Sec., Commn for Science Policy Studies, IUHPS, 1971– . Publications: contrib. Hist. Jl, Isis, Jl Brit. Studies, Jl Hist. Med., Med. Hist., Minerva, Nature, Notes Rec. Roy. Soc., Past Pres., Public Law, Technol. Soc., etc. Address: Physics Building, Univ. of Sussex, Brighton, Sussex.

McLintock, David Robert, MA; Reader in Department of German, Royal Holloway College, University of London, since 1967; b 1930; m 1964; one d. BA Oxon 1952 (1st cl. Mod. Langs), Dip in Comparative Philology Oxford 1954, MA Oxon 1956; Mem. Council, Philol. Soc. Lectr in Germanic Philology, Oxford, 1954–67; Tutor, Mansfield Coll., Oxford, 1961–67; Fellow, Wolfson Coll., Oxford, 1966–67. Mem., Edit. Bd, New German Studies. Publications: ed, J. K. Bostock: Handbook on Old High German

Literature, 2nd edn (forthcoming); A Historical German Reader (forthcoming); contrib. Archiv. Lingu., Beitr. z. Gesch. d. dt. Spr. u. Lit., Oxf. Germ. Studies. Address: Royal Holloway College, Egham Hill, Egham, Surrey TW20 0EX.

McLone, Dr Ronald Redman; Lecturer in Mathematics and Mathematical Education, University of Southampton, since 1967; b 1941; m 1964. BSc London 1962 (1st cl. Mathematics), PhD London 1965. Asst Lectr and Lectr, Sheffield Univ., 1965–67. Publications: The Training of Mathematicians, 1973; contrib. Bull. IMA, Int. Jl Math. Educ. Science Technol., Jl Chemical Physics, Mathematika, Proc. Royal Society, Pure and Applied Geophysics. Address: Dept of Mathematics, Univ. of Southampton, Southampton SO9 5NH.

McMahon, Dr Bryan M. E., BCL, LLB, LLM, PhD; Lecturer in Law, University College, Cork, since 1966; b 1941; m 1970. BCL National University of Ireland 1962 (1st cl.), LLB National University of Ireland 1963 (1st cl.), LLM Harvard 1965, PhD NUI 1972; Solicitor 1964. Reporter, Adv. Body, Law Reform Commn on Occupiers' Liability, 1968–71. Publications: Occupiers' Liability in Ireland: Survey and Proposals for Reform, 1972; contrib. Irish Jur. (NS), ICLQ, NILQ, Irish Law Times. Address: Law Faculty, Univ. College Cork, Cork, Ireland.

McManners, Rev. Prof. John; Regius Professor of Ecclesiastical History, Oxford, since 1972; b 1916; m 1951; two s two d. BA Oxon 1939 (1st cl. History), MA Oxon 1947, DipTh Dunelm 1947; FRHistS, FAHA. Chaplain, St Edmund Hall, Oxford, 1948, Fellow, 1949; Prof., Univs of: Tasmania, 1956–59; Sydney, 1959–67; Leicester, 1967–72; Vis. Fellow, All Souls Coll., Oxford, 1965–66. Mem., Curriculum Cttee, RMA, Duntroon, Australia, 1965–67; Trustee, Nat. Portrait Gallery, 1970; Mem., Council R. Hist. Soc., 1971. Publications: French Ecclesiastical Society under the Ancien Régime; a Study of Angers in the 18th Century, 1960; ed, France, Government and Society, 1965, 2nd edn 1971; Lectures on European History, 1789–1914; Men, Machines and Freedom, 1966; The French Revolution and the Church, 1969; Church and State in France, 1870–1914, 1972; New Cambridge Modern History, vols VI and VIII. Address: Christ Church, Oxford.

McManus, Prof. Maurice, PhD; Professor of Economics, Department of Mathematical Economics, University of Birmingham, since 1960; b 1926; m 1951 (marr. diss. 1971); one d. Hon. BCom Birmingham 1950, PhD Birmingham 1959; Mem., Royal Economic Soc., Mem., Econometric Soc. Research Asst, Leeds, 1952–55; Instructor, MIT, 1955–57; Lectr, Minnesota, 1957–58; Lectr, Aberystwyth, 1958–60. Publications: contrib. Econometrica, Amer. Econ. Rev., Economica, Internat. Econ. Rev., Metroeconomica, Rev. Econ. Studies, Southern Econ. Jl, Yorkshire Bull. Address: Faculty of Commerce, Univ. of Birmingham, PO Box 363, Birmingham B15 2TT.

McMaster, David Newcombe, MA, PhD; Reader in Geography, Department of Geography and Centre of African Studies, University of Edinburgh, since 1962; *b* 1924; *m* 1956; one *s* two *d*. BA Oxon 1951 (1st cl. Geography), MA Oxon 1955, PhD London 1960; FRGS 1952. Asst Lectr, Makerere Univ. Coll., E Africa, 1951–54; Lectr, 1954–60; Sen. Lectr, 1960–62; Lectr, Univ. of Edinburgh, 1962–67; Vis. Prof., Makerere Univ. Coll., African Studies Programme, 1966. Mem., Council, Afr. Studies Assoc. UK, 1967–69; Assoc. Dean, Fac. of Social Sciences, Univ. of Edinburgh, 1970–73. *Publications*: A Subsistence Crop Geography of Uganda, 1962; Map Reading for East Africa, 1963, 3rd edn 1970; contrib., ed, R. M. Prothero: A Geography of Africa, 1969; *contrib.* Geog. Rev., Jl Trop. Geog., Ugan. Jl, Trans Inst. Brit. Geogrs. *Address*: Centre of African Studies, Adam Ferguson Building, Univ. of Edinburgh, Edinburgh EH8 9LL.

Macmichael, Jasper Hugh Ferriby, DSO, MC; Part-time Lecturer, Business Studies, University of Edinburgh, since 1965; *b* 1918; *m* 1946; one *s* one *d*. BSc 1947 (Hons Civil Engng); CEng, MICE. Director: Wm McGeoch & Co. Ltd; Peterhead Bay (Management) Co. Ltd. *Address*: Univ. of Edinburgh, Dept of Business Studies, 50 George Square, Edinburgh.

McMillan, Prof. Duncan, BA, PhD, Dip. de l'EHE; Chevalier de la Légion d'Honneur; John Orr Professor of French Language and Romance Linguistics, Department of Romance Linguistics, University of Edinburgh, since 1955; *b* 1914; *m* 1945; one *s*. BA 1936 (1st cl. French), PhD 1938, London, Dip de l'Ecole des Hautes Etudes Paris 1950; Mem., Soc. Anc. Textes Franç., Mem., Soc. Linguist. Romane, Mem., Soc. Rencesvals. Lecteur d'anglais, Sorbonne, 1938–40; Lectr in French, Univ. of Aberdeen, 1946–50; Lectr in French and Romance Philology, Univ. of Edinburgh, 1950–55. *Publications*: La Chanson de Guillaume, 1949–50; (with G. McMillan) An Anthology of the Contemporary French Novel, 1950; Le Charroi de Nîmes, 1972; *contrib.* Cah. de Civilis. Médiév., Romania, Trav. Linguist. Litt., Zeits. Romanis. Philol. *Address*: Dept of Romance Linguistics, 8 Hope Park Square, Edinburgh EH8 9NW.

McMillan, Ian Stewart; Research Associate, Department of Social Administration and Social Work, University of Bristol, since 1973; *b* 1947. BSc (Soc) London 1968; Mem.: Social Administration Assoc.; Social Services Res. Gp. Res. Asst, Dept of Social Science and Administration, LSE, 1968–70; Res. Associate in the Residential Care of Children and Young Persons, Dept of Social Administration and Social Work, Univ. of Bristol, 1970–73. *Publications*: (with Bleddyn Davies, Andrew Barton and Valerie Williamson) Variations in Services for the Aged, 1971; (with Bleddyn Davies and Andrew Barton) Variations in Children's Services among British Urban Authorities, 1972; *contrib.* Jl Soc. Policy, Policy and Politics, Soc. and Econ. Admin. *Address*: Univ. of Bristol, 13 Woodland Road, Bristol.

Macmillan, (John) Duncan; Lecturer, Director of Studies, Department of Fine Art, Edinburgh University, since 1964; *b* 1939; *m* 1971. MA St Andrews 1961, Academic Dip. Courtauld Inst. London 1964, PhD Edinburgh 1974. *Publications*: *contrib.* Art Bull., Burl. Mag. *Address*: Dept of Fine Art, Edinburgh Univ., Edinburgh EH8 9YL.

McMillin, Dr Arnold Barratt; Lecturer in Russian Language and Literature, School of Slavonic and East European Studies, University of London, since 1965; *b* 1941; *m* 1969; one *d*. BA London 1963 (1st cl. Russian Lang. and Lit), PhD London 1971 (Slavonic Philol.). Editor, Jl of Byelorussian Studies, 1967–71. *Publications*: The Vocabulary of the Byelorussian Literary Language in the Nineteenth Century, 1973; trans. Malevich: Essays on Art, 1968; *contrib.* Jl of Byelorussian Studies, Oxford Slavonic Papers, Slav. and E European Rev. *Address* Sch. of Slavonic and East European Studies, Univ. of London, Senate House, WC1E 7HU.

McNair, John McCracken; Lecturer, Department of Education, University of Manchester, since 1966; *b* 1919; *m* 1942; one *s* one *d*. Mod. Langs Tripos Cambridge 1940, CertEd London 1947, MEd Manchester 1970. Mem., Council, Mod. Lang. Assoc., 1970– ; Dep. Chm., Assoc. Teachers of Spanish and Portuguese, 1969–70. *Address*: Dept of Education, The Univ., Manchester M13 9PL.

McNair, Prof. Philip Murray Jourdan; Serena Professor of Italian Language and Literature, University of Birmingham, since 1974; *b* 1924; *m* 1948; one *d*. BA Oxon 1948, MA Oxon 1948, DPhil Oxon 1962, PhD Cantab 1963. Univ. Lectr in Italian, Leeds Univ., 1954–61; Lectr in Italian, Bedford Coll., London Univ., 1961–63; Lectr in Italian, Cambridge Univ., 1963–74; Vis. Prof., Univ. of California, Berkeley, 1970; Fellow, Darwin Coll., Cambridge, 1965–74; Dean, Darwin Coll., Cambridge, 1965–69. *Publications*: Peter Martyr in Italy, 1967, Italian edn 1972; contrib.The Mind of Dante, 1965; Encyclopaedia Britannica; *contrib.* Ital. Studies. *Address*: Dept of Italian Language and Literature, Univ. of Birmingham, Birmingham B15 2TT.

McNicol., H., MA; Lecturer in Education, University of Nottingham, since 1947; *b* 1912; *m* 1937; two *s*. BA Hons Dublin 1934 (Mod. Hist. and Pol. Science), Higher DipEd Dublin 1935, HonsDipEd Dublin 1936, Post-Grad DipGeog Dublin 1935, MA Dublin 1944. *Publications*: History, Heritage and Environment, 1946; var. school texts and juvenile fiction; *contrib.* Jl Educn, Schoolmaster. *Address*: School of Education, The Univ., Nottingham NG7 2RD.

Macpherson, Alexander Calderwood; Lecturer (part-time), Law School, University of Strathclyde, since 1969; *b* 1939; *m* 1963; two *s*. MA Glasgow 1959, LLB Glasgow 1962; Notary Public, 1965. Asst (part-time), Dept of Scots Law, Glasgow Univ., 1962–69. *Address*: The Law School, Univ. of Strathclyde, Glasgow G1 1XW.

McPherson, Dr Frank Murdoch; Senior Lecturer, Department of Psychology, University of Dundee, since 1971; *b* 1938; *m* 1962; one *s* one *d*. MA Aberdeen, 1960; PhD Edinburgh 1969, Dip. Clin. Psychol. Edinburgh 1962; ABPsS. University of Edinburgh: Asst Lectr, 1960–63; Lectr in Psychol., 1963–71. Hon. Dir, Tayside Area Clin. Psychol. Dept, Dundee Northern Hosps, 1971– . *Publications*: Small Group Psychotherapy, 1971; contrib., Companion to Psychiatric Studies, ed A. Forrest, 1972; *contrib*. Brit. Jl Psychol., Brit. Jl Med. Psychol., Brit. Jl Soc. Clin. Psychol., Brit. Jl Psychiat. Jl Clin. Psychol., Lancet. *Address*: Dept of Psychology, The Univ., Dundee DD1 4HN.

Macpherson, Dr Ian Richard, MA, PhD; Senior Lecturer in Spanish, University of Durham, since 1972, (Lecturer, 1964–72); *b* 1934; *m* 1959; two *s*. MA Aberdeen 1951 (1st cl. French-Spanish), PhD Manchester 1956. Asst Lectr, Manchester Univ., 1959–60; Asst Lectr, Univ. of Wales, Aberystwyth, 1960–61; Lectr, Univ. of Wales, Aberystwyth, 1961–64; Vis. Prof., Univ. of Wisconsin, Madison, 1970–71. *Publications*: Spanish Philology: descriptive and historical, 1974; (with R. B. Tate) Don Juan Manuel: Libro de los estados, 1974; *contrib*. Bull. Hispan. Studies, Hispan. Rev., MLR, Rom. Philol., Studies Philol., Zeits. Romanis. Philol. *Address*: Dept of Spanish, The Univ., Durham DH1 3HP.

Macpherson, Roderick Ewen; Registrary, University of Cambridge, since 1969; Fellow of King's College, Cambridge, since 1942; *b* 1916; *m* 1941; two *s* two *d*. MA Cantab 1942. King's College, Cambridge: 3rd Bursar, 1947–50; 2nd Bursar, 1950–51; 1st Bursar, 1951–62; University Treasurer, Cambridge, 1962–69; Mem. Council of Senate, 1957–62; Mem. Financial Bd, 1955–62. *Address*: Registry, Old Schools, Cambridge CB2 1TN.

McPherson, Prof. Thomas Herdman, MA, BPhil; Professor of Philosophy, University College, Cardiff, since 1971; *b* 1925; *m* 1957; one *s* two *d*. BA New Zealand 1946, MA New Zealand 1947, BPhil Oxon 1950. Asst Lectr, Univ. Coll. of North Wales, 1951–53; Lectr, Univ. Coll. of North Wales, 1953–63; Sen. Lectr, Univ. Coll., Cardiff, 1963–68; Reader, Univ. Coll., Cardiff, 1968–71. *Publications*: The Philosophy of Religion, 1965; Political Obligation, 1967; Social Philosophy, 1970; The Argument from Design, 1972; Philosophy and Religious Belief, 1974; *contrib*. Mind, Philos., Proc. Aristot. Soc. *Address*: Dept of Philosophy, Univ. College, Cathays Park, Cardiff CF1 1XL.

Macquarrie, Rev. Prof. John, TD; Lady Margaret Professor of Divinity, and Canon of Christ Church, University of Oxford, since 1970; *b* 1919; *m* 1949; two *s* one *d*. MA Glasgow 1940, PhD Glasgow 1954, DLitt Glasgow 1964, DD Glasgow 1969, STD University of the South 1967, STD General Theological Seminary NY 1968, MA Oxon 1970. Lectr in Systematic Theology, Univ. of Glasgow, 1953–62; Prof. of Systematic Theology, Union Theol. Seminary, NY,

1962–70. Cnsltnt, Lambeth Conf., 1968; Mem., Faith and Order Commn, Wld Council Chs, 1968– ; Mem., Archbps' Commn on Doctrine, 1970– ; Dir, SCM Press, 1970– . *Publications*: An Existentialist Theology, 1955, 2nd edn 1965; The Scope of Demythologizing, 1960; Twentieth Century Religious Thought, 1963, 2nd edn 1971; Studies in Christian Existentialism, 1965; Principles of Christian Theology, 1966; God-Talk, 1967; God and Secularity, 1967; Martin Heidegger, 1968; Three Issues in Ethics, 1970; Paths in Spirituality, 1972; Existentialism, 1972; The Faith of the People of God, 1972; The Concept of Peace, 1973; *contrib*. Expos. Times, Theol., Union Sem. Qly Rev., etc. *Address*: Christ Church, Oxford OX1 1DP.

McQueen, Earl Ingram, MA, MLitt; Lecturer in Classics, University of Bristol, since 1964; *b* 1937. MA Aberdeen 1959 (1st cl. Classics), BA Cantab 1961 (1st cl. Classics), MA Cantab 1964, MLitt Cantab 1965. *Publications*: Quintus Curtius Rufus, in, Latin Biography (Studies in Latin Literature and its Influence), 1967. *Address*: Dept of Classics, Univ. of Bristol, Bristol BS8 1TH.

MacQueen, Dr Ian Alexis Gordon, OBE; Medical Officer of Health, Aberdeen, and Lecturer in Social Medicine, University of Aberdeen, since 1952; *b* 1909; *m* 1945. MA Hons Edinburgh 1932, MB, ChB Edinburgh 1937, MD (Commend.) Edinburgh 1949, DPH Edinburgh 1939, DSCHE 1968; FFCM 1972. Chm., Scott. Council for Hlth Educn, 1970– ; Pres., Scott. Br. and Co. Bor. Gp, Soc. Med. Off. of Hlth, 1960; Chm., Stand. Conf. Hlth Visitor Training Sch., 1963–65; Mem., Scott. Hlth Services Council, 1971– . *Publications*: A Study of Home Accidents in Aberdeen, 1956; (jtly) From Drains to Genetics, 1947; *contrib*. Community Med., Lancet. *Address*: St Nicholas House, Broad Street, Aberdeen.

Macqueen, James Galloway; Lecturer in Classics, University of Bristol, since 1962; *b* 1932; *m* 1959; three *s* two *d*. MA St Andrews 1954 (1st cl. Classics). Asst Lectr, Bristol Univ., 1959–62. *Publications*: Babylon, 1964, American edn 1965, Japanese edn 1972; *contrib*. Anat. Studies, Asian Aff., etc. *Address*: Dept of Classics, Univ. of Bristol, Queen's Road, Bristol BS8 1RJ.

MacQueen, Prof. John; Professor of Scottish Literature and Oral Tradition, School of Scottish Studies, University of Edinburgh, since 1972; *b* 1929; *m* 1953; three *s*. MA Glasgow 1950, BA Cambridge 1952, MA Cambridge 1955. Asst Prof. of English, Washington Univ., 1956–59; Lecturer in Medieval English and Scottish Literature, Univ. of Edinburgh, 1959–63; Masson Prof, of Medieval and Renaissance Literature, Univ. of Edinburgh, 1963–71; Dir, Sch. of Scottish Studies, Univ. of Edinburgh, 1969– . *Publications*: St Nynia, 1961; (with T. Scott), Oxford Book of Scottish Verse, 1966; Robert Henryson, 1967; Allegory, 1970, Japanese trans. 1971, Greek trans. 1972; Ballattis of Luve, 1970; (with W. W. Mac-Queen) Scottish Verse 1470–1570, 1972;

contrib. Archiv. Linguist., Dumfries Gall. Trans, Etudes Celt., Forum Mod. Lang. Studies, Folk Life, Innes Rev., Orbis, Proc. Brit. Acad., Rev. Engl. Studies, Studies Scott. Lit., Scott. Studies. *Address*: School of Scottish Studies, 27 George Square, Edinburgh.

MacRae, Dr Alexander William; Lecturer, Department of Psychology, University of Birmingham, since 1970; *b* 1939; *m* 1962; two *s* one *d*. BSc Edinburgh 1962; PhD Wales 1970; Member: BPsS; Brain Res. Assoc.; The Colour Group (GB); AISB Study Group. Univ. of Leeds, 1962–65; UCNW, 1965–70. *Publications*: contrib. Ergonomics, Psychol Bull., Qly Jl Expl Psychol. *Address*: Dept of Psychology, Univ. of Birmingham, PO Box 363, Birmingham B15 2TT.

MacRae, Dr (Charles Edward) Stuart, BCom, PhD, FCA; Senior Lecturer, Department of Administration, University of Strathclyde, since 1964; *b* 1919; *m* 1942; one *s* two *d*. BCom Edinburgh 1948, PhD Edinburgh 1960; FCA 1952. Thinking in Figures, 1964, 2nd edn 1968; The New Book-Keeping, 1965; (with S. Page) Casebook (Studies in Administration), 1966; (with S. Page) Tools for Administrators, 1967; *contrib*. Acctnts Mag. *Address*: Dept of Administration, Univ. of Strathclyde, Glasgow G1 1XW.

MacRae, Prof. Donald Gunn; Professor of Sociology, London School of Economics, University of London, since 1961; *b* 1921; *m* 1948; two *d*. MA Glasgow 1942; BA Oxon 1945, MA Oxon 1949. Asst Lectr, LSE, 1945; Univ. Lectr in Sociology, Oxford, 1949; Reader in Sociology, LSE, Univ. of London, 1954; Prof. of Sociology, Univ. of California, 1959; Fellow, Center for Advanced Studies in the Behavioral Sciences, Stanford, 1967. Editor, British Jl of Sociology, until 1965. *Publications*: Ideology and Society, 1960; *contrib*. Brit. Jl Sociol. *Address*: London School of Economics and Political Science, Houghton Street, Aldwych WC2A 2AE.

MacRae, Dr Kenneth Duncan; Lecturer in Medical Statistics, Queen's University of Belfast (also teaches Mathematical Psychology), since 1969; *b* 1942; *m* 1969. MA Aberdeen 1964 (2nd cl. Psychology), PhD Aberdeen, 1970; FSS. Asst Lectr in Psychology, Aberdeen, 1965–67; Lectr in Psychology, Belfast, 1967–69. *Publications*: contrib. Brit. Jl Cancer, Brit. Jl Psychol., Brit. Jl Surg., Brit. Med. Jl, Europ. Surg. Research, Jl Opt. Soc. Amer., Lancet, Percept. Mot. Skills, Postgrad. Med. Jl. *Address*: Dept of Medical Statistics, Queen's Univ., Belfast BT7 1NN.

McRae, Prof. Thomas W.; Professor of Finance, Bradford University Management Centre, since 1973; *b* 1932; *m* 1960; one *s* two *d*. BSc (Econ) London 1966; CA 1955. P. D. Leake Res. Fellow, LSE, 1961–63; Lecturer: in Accounting, Univ. of Hull, 1963–66; in Economics, Univ. of Manchester Bus. Sch., 1966–67; Prof. of Business Admin., Univ. of Witwatersrand, 1969–72. Mem., Post Qualifying Educn Cttee, Scottish CA, 1963–69. *Publications*: Business Computer Programming, 1963; Impact of Computers on Accounting, 1964; Analytical Management, 1969; ed, Management Information Systems, 1970; Statistical Sampling for Audit and Control, 1974; *contrib*. Abacus, Accounting Rev., Jl Accounting Res., Jl Accounting and Bus. Res. *Address*: Univ. of Bradford, Bradford BD7 1DP.

Macrae-Gibson, Dr O. Duncan; Senior Lecturer, Department of English, University of Aberdeen, since 1970; *b* 1928; *m* 1960; one *s* one *d*. BA Oxon 1955 (1st cl. English), MA Oxon 1957, DPhil Oxon 1964. Lectr, Oriel and Univ. Colls, Oxford, 1956–58; Lectr, Leicester Univ., 1958–66; Lectr, Aberdeen Univ., 1966–70. *Publications*: Learning Old English: A progressive course, 1970; ed, Of Arthour and of Merlin, vol. I, 1973 (vol. II, forthcoming); *contrib*. Engl. Studies, Med. Æv., Neophilol., Neuphilol. Mitteil., Old Engl. Newsl., System. *Address*: Dept of English, Univ. of Aberdeen, Taylor Building, King's College, Old Aberdeen AB9 2UB.

McTague, George; Senior Lecturer, Department of Adult Education and Extra-Mural Studies, University of Leeds, since 1960; *b* 1916; *m* 1948; three *s* four *d*. DA Edinburgh Coll. of Art, Cert of Fine Art Edinburgh Univ. *Publications*: Flowers and the Artist (Exhibition Cat., Harrogate Festival of Arts and Sciences), 1967; Sporting Paintings (Exhibition Cat., Harrogate Festival of Arts and Sciences), 1969. *Address*: Dept of Adult Education, The Univ., Leeds LS2 9JT.

McTavish, Ronald; Senior Lecturer, Department of Marketing, University of Strathclyde, since 1971; *b* 1933; *m* 1962; one *s* one *d*. BScEcon London 1957, MA Strathclyde 1967, ASCC 1957, Teachers' Special Certif. Jordanhill 1961; Mem. British Industrial Marketing Assoc. (Chm. Scottish Br.). Lectr in Marketing, Univ. Strathclyde, 1964–71. Formerly Editor, Marketing World. *Publications*: contrib. Jl Management Studies, Brit. Jl Marketing, Jl Scientific Business. *Address*: Dept of Marketing, Univ. of Strathclyde, Cathedral Street, Glasgow G4 0RQ.

McTurk, Roderick Walter, BA, BaccPhil Isl.; Assistant Lecturer, Department of Old and Middle English, University College, Dublin, since 1969; *b* 1942; *m* 1965; two *s*. BA Oxon 1963 (Hons Engl. Lang. and Lit.), BaccPhil Isl. Iceland 1965 (Degree in Icelandic Philology). Lectr in English, Univ. of Lund, Sweden, 1967–68; Asst, Engl. Inst., Univ. of Copenhagen, Denmark, Jan.–July 1969. Councillor and Mem., Viking Soc. for Northern Research, 1970– . *Publications*: trans. Halldor Laxness, by Peter Hallberg, 1971; *contrib*. Scandinavia. *Address*: Dept of Old and Middle English, Univ. College, Belfield Arts Block, Dublin 4, Republic of Ireland.

McVay, Dr Gordon; Lecturer in Russian, School of European Studies, University of East Anglia, since 1969; *b* 1941; *m* 1969. BA Oxon 1963 (1st cl. Hons Russian), DPhil Oxon 1969. Asst Lectr in Russian, UC

North Wales, Bangor, 1967–69. *Publications*: *contrib*. Can. Slavonic Papers, Jl Russian Studies, Mod. Lang. Rev., Novyi Zhurnal, Oxford Slavonic Papers, Russian Lit. Triquart., Slavic and E European Studies, Slavonic and E European Rev. *Address*: School of European Studies, Univ. of East Anglia, University Plain, Norwich NOR 88C.

McWatters, Prof. Keith Gordon; Professor of French (second chair), University of Liverpool, since 1974; *b* 1931; *m* 1968; two *d*. BA (Hons 1st cl.) Queensland 1952, DipEd Queensland 1954, Doctorat d'Université Grenoble 1961; Open Scholarship Queensland 1949–52, French Govt Travelling Scholar 1958–61; Carnegie Fellow 1970–71. Lectr/Sen. Lectr, Queensland 1961–64; Lectr, Leicester, 1964–65; Lectr, Glasgow, 1965–72, Sen. Lectr, 1972–74. *Publications*: Stendhal, Lecteur des Romanciers Anglais,1968; *contrib*. Austr. Jl of French Studies, Collection Stendhalienne (Aran), Essays in French Lit., Stendhal-Club. *Address*: Univ. of Liverpool, PO Box 147, Liverpool L69 3BX.

McWilliam, Colin Edgar; Senior Lecturer in Architectural History, Department of Architecture, Heriot-Watt University, since 1965; *b* 1928; one *s* two *d*. MA Cantab 1956. Officer in Charge, Scott. Nat. Bldgs Record, 1952– ; Asst Sec., Nat. Trust for Scotland, 1957– ; Vice Chm., Scott. Georgian Soc., 1966. *Address*: Edinburgh College of Art, Lauriston Place, Edinburgh EH3 9DF.

McWilliam, Prof. George Henry, MA; Professor and Head of Department of Italian, University of Leicester, since 1972; *b* 1927; *m* 1955; three *s* three *d*. BA Leeds 1953 (1st cl. Italian), MA Dublin 1961. Temp. Asst Lectr, Leeds Univ., 1954; Asst Lectr, Bedford Coll., London Univ., 1955–58; Hd of Dept of Italian, TCD, 1958–66; Reader, TCD, 1961–66; Fellow, TCD, 1964–66; Reader, Univ. of Kent, 1966–72. *Publications*: ed, U. Betti: Three Plays on Justice, 1964; ed, U. Betti: Two Plays, 1965; ed, G. Boccaccio: The Decameron, 1972; Shakespeare's Italy Revisited, 1974; *contrib*. Hermath., Ital. Studies, Tul. Drama Rev. *Address*: Dept of Italian, Univ. of Leicester, Leicester LE1 7RH.

Madariaga, Isabel de; Reader in Russian Studies, School of Slavonic and East European Studies, University of London, since 1971; *b* 1919. BA Hons London 1940 (1st cl. Russian Lang. and Lit.), PhD London 1959 (Hist.); FRHistS. Lectr in Hist., Univ. of Sussex, 1966–68; Sen. Lectr in Russian Hist., Univ. of Lancaster, 1968–71. *Publications*: Britain, Russia and the Armed Neutrality of 1780, 1962; (with G. Ionescu) Opposition, 1966, German edn 1971; *contrib*. Slav. E Europe. Rev. *Address*: School of Slavonic and East European Studies, Univ. of London, Senate House, Malet Street, WC1E 7HU.

Maddalena, Dr Caterina; Lecturer in Italian, University College of North Wales, since 1966; *b* 1939. DottLett Turin 1962. *Address*: Dept of French and Romance Studies, Univ. College, Bangor LL57 2DG.

Madden, Dr (Albert) Frederick McCulloch; Reader in Commonwealth Government, Department of Modern History and Social Studies, and Fellow of Nuffield College, Oxford University, since 1957; *b* 1917; *m* 1941; one *s* one *d*. BA Oxford 1938, BLitt Oxford 1939; DPhil Oxford 1950; FRHistS 1952. Beit Lectr in Commonwealth History, Oxford, 1947–57. Dir, Inst. Commonwealth Studies, 1960–68; Vice-Chm., Bd of Mod. Hist., 1968–73; Cnsltnt, Time-Life series on Brit. Emp., 1970–73. *Publications*: (with V. Harlow) British Colonial Developments, 1774–1834, 1953; (with K. Robinson) Essays in Imperial Government, 1963; Imperial Constitutional Documents 1765–1965, 1966; chapter, in, Cambridge History of the British Empire, 1959; chapter, in, H. Trevor-Roper: Essays in British History, 1964; *contrib*. EHR. *Address*: Nuffield College, Oxford.

Maddick, Prof. Henry, MA, AIB; Professor of Local Government Studies, since 1968, and Director of Institute of Local Government Studies, University of Birmingham, since 1964; *b* 1915; *m* 1939; three *s* one *d*. BA Oxford 1948, MA Oxford 1952; AIB 1945. Lectr, Wadham Coll., Univ. of Oxford, 1948–50; Lectr, then Sen. Lectr in Public Admin, and Reader in Local Govt, Univ. of Birmingham, 1950–68. RAF (Commnd 1941), 1940–46; Mem., Staffs Educn Cttee, 1952–56; Mem., Coventry Educn Cttee, 1964–65; Mem., Exec. Council, AUT, 1958–61. *Publications*: Democracy, Decentralisation and Development, 1963; Panchayati Raj – rural local government in India, 1970; *contrib*. Pol. Studies, Public Admin. *Address*: Institute of Local Government Studies, Univ. of Birmingham, PO Box 363, Birmingham B15 2TT.

Madgwick, Peter James, MA; Reader in Political Science, University College of Wales, Aberystwyth, since 1973 (Senior Lecturer, 1965–73); *b* 1925; *m* 1947; one *s* two *d*. BA Oxon 1950, MA Oxon 1950, DipEd Oxon 1951. Tutor, Dept of Adult Educn, Univ. of Nottingham, 1952–65. *Publications*: (with J. D. Chambers) Conflict and Community: Europe since 1750, 1968; American City Politics, 1970; Introduction to British Politics, 1970; The Politics of Rural Wales, 1973; *contrib*. Jl Amer. Studies, Parly Aff. *Address*: Dept of Political Science, Univ. College of Wales, Aberystwyth SY23 2AX.

Magee, Prof. Charles Ciaran; Professor of Accountancy and Financial Control, University College, Cardiff, since 1970; *b* 1909; *m* 1937; one *s* one *d*. BCom London 1928; Mem., Inst. Chartered Accountants (England and Wales), 1932– . *Publications*: Financial Accounting and Control, 1968; The Framework of Accountancy, 1970. *Address*: Univ. College, PO Box 78, Cardiff CF1 1XL.

Mahood, George Hamilton; Senior Lecturer since 1966, Deputy Director since 1960, Department of Extra-Mural Studies, Queen's University, Belfast; *b* 1922; *m* 1945; three *d*. BA London 1944 (Gen. Philos.), BA London 1946 (Hons Classics), MA London 1948 (Classics, Ancient Philos.). Lectr, Queen's Univ., 1956–66; Sen. Lectr (on secondment),

Univ. of Hong Kong, 1967–69. *Publications*: *contrib*. Philos. EW, Jl Chinese Philos. *Address*: Queen's Univ., Belfast BT7 1NN.

Mahood, Prof. Molly Maureen; Professor of English Literature, University of Kent, since 1967; *b* 1919. BA London 1941, MA London 1944, MA Oxford 1948. Asst Lectr, King's Coll., London, 1943–46; Tutor, St Hugh's Coll., Oxford, 1947; Fellow and Tutor, St Hugh's Coll., Oxford, 1948–54; Prof. of English, Univ. of Ibadan, 1954–63; Prof. of Lit., Univ. of Dar es Salaam, 1963–67. Mem., Inter-Univ. Council for Higher Educn Overseas, 1969– . *Publications*: Poetry and Humanism, 1950, latest edn 1970; Shakespeare's Wordplay, 1957, latest edn 1968; Joyce Cary's Africa, 1964; *contrib*. Ess. Crit., Shakesp. Surv. *Address*: Rutherford College, Univ. of Kent, Canterbury.

Maidment, Susan; Lecturer in Law, University of Keele, since 1970; *b* 1944; *m* 1969; one *s* one *d*. LLB LSE 1965, LLM LSE 1966; Barrister-at-Law (Lincoln's Inn), 1968. Univ. of Bristol, 1967–70. *Publications*: *contrib*. Brit. Yearbook Internat. Law, Internat. and Compar. Law Qly, Mod. Law Rev., New Law Jl, Public Law. *Address*: Univ. of Keele, Newcastle, Staffs ST5 5BG.

Main, Alex, MA; Lecturer in Psychology, University of Strathclyde, since 1966; seconded 1973–75 as Co-ordinating and Research Officer for the Training of University Teachers, Committee of Vice-Chancellors and Principals; *b* 1941; *m* 1966; two *s* one *d*. MA Aberdeen 1964, ABPsS. Mem., Univ. Ct, Strathclyde, 1971– ; Coordinator, In-Service Training, 1969–73; FAO, Europ. Attitudes Gp, 1970–73; Leverhulme App. Science. Res. Gp, 1971– ; Scottish Council for Research in Education, 1972– . *Publications*: Expressionism Through Illness, 1966; *contrib*. Brit. Jl Aesth. *Address*: Dept of Psychology, Univ. of Strathclyde, Glasgow G1 1XW.

Mair, Dr John Magnus; Lecturer in Social Medicine, University of Edinburgh, since 1956; *b* 1912; *m* 1940; three *s*. MB, ChB Aberdeen 1937, DPH Edinburgh 1946; MFCM 1971. Dir of Social Wk, City of Edinburgh, 1969; Mem., Council for Training in Social Wk, 1965–71; Mem., Council for Training of Hlth Visitors, 1965–71. *Address*: Dept of Social Medicine, Usher Institute, Warrender Park Road, Edinburgh.

Mair, Prof. Lucy; Honorary Professor of Anthropology, University of Kent at Canterbury, since 1972; *b* 1901. BA Cantab 1923 (Classics), MA Cantab 1925, PhD LSE 1932 (Anthropology). Hon. Sec., Royal Anthropological Inst., Dec. 1973– ; Mem., Internat. African Inst. LSE: Asst Lectr in Internat. Relations, 1927–32; Lectr in Colonial Admin, 1932–38; Reader, 1946–56; Reader in Applied Anthropol., 1956–63; Prof., 1963–66; Reader in Social Anthropol., Univ. of Durham, 1971–72. *Publications*: An African People in the 20th Century, 1934; Native Policies in Africa, 1936; Australia in New Guinea, 1948, revised edn 1970; Studies in Applied Anthropology, 1957, revised edn, Anthropology and Social Change, 1969; Primitive Government, 1962; New Nations, 1963; An Introduction to Social Anthropology, 1965, 2nd edn, 1972; African Marriage and Social Change, 1969; Witchcraft, 1969; Marriage, 1971; African Societies, 1974; *contrib*. Africa, Brit. Jl of Sociol., Cahiers d'Etudes Africaines. *Address*: 19 Hallgate, Blackheath Park, SE3 9SG.

Mair, Robert, BSc(Econ); Lecturer, Department of Politics, Glasgow University, since 1966, seconded to Civil Service College as Lecturer in Social Policy, 1973–74; *b* 1942; *m* 1965; one *s* one *d*. BSc(Econ) London 1963 (1st cl.); Mem., Pol. Studies Assoc. UK, 'Justice' (Brit. Sect. Internat. Ct Just.). Res. (Fulbright) Schol., Univ. of Chicago, 1964–65. Mem., City of Glasgow Children's Panel Adv. Cttee on Training, 1970– . *Publications*: *contrib*.: Challenges for Change, ed G. McLachlan, 1971; The Making of Social Policy (forthcoming); *contrib*. Munic. Rev., Public Admin. (Austral.), Pol Studies, Scott. Med. Jl, Social Serv. Qly. *Address*: Dept of Politics, Univ. of Glasgow, Adam Smith Building, Glasgow G12 8RT.

Major, John Samuel Harwood; Lecturer in History, University of Hull, since 1964; *b* 1936; *m* 1962; one *s* one *d*. BA Cantab 1960, MA Cantab 1964. Ed., Bull. Assoc. Contemp. Hist., 1968–72. *Publications*: (with A. M. Preston) Send a Gunboat, 1967; ed, The New Deal, 1968; The Contemporary World, 1970; The Oppenheimer Hearing, 1971. *Address*: Dept of History, Univ. of Hull, Kingston-upon-Hull HU6 7RX.

Majut, Dr Rudolf; Honorary Lecturer, German Department, University of Leicester, since 1957; *b* 1887; *m* 1939. Dr phil and MA Univ. of Greifswald, Germany 1912; Staats-Examen, Greifswald, 1913; German and English, Higher Sch. Standard Certif., French, Sch. Certif. (Standard). Prof. designatus in Pädagogische Hochschule (Training Coll.), cancelled by National Socialists; introductory (or preliminary) proceedings in Berlin Univ. as Privatdozent, 1932, prevented by National-Socialist influence. Verdienstkreuz I. Klasse. *Publications*: Farbe und Licht im Kunstgefühl Georg Büchners, Greifswald, 1912; Lebensbühne und Marionette, Berlin, 1931 (repr.); Studien um Büchner, Berlin, 1932 (repr.); German Thought, in, Germany, ed Jethro Bithell, 1st edn London 1932, 5th edn London, 1955; Der deutsche Roman vom Biedermeier bis zur Gegenwart, in, Deutsche Philologie im Aufriss, vol. II, Berlin, 1960; Über hippalogische Bezeichnungen, Berlin, 1972; *contrib*. Deutsch. für Aus., Gesells. Burschen. Geschichts., German Life and Letters, German-roman. Monats., Mod. Lang. Rev., Zeits. deutsche Phil. *Address*: Dept of German, Univ. of Leicester, Leicester LE1 7RH.

Malcolm, Dowald Alexander; Senior Lecturer, Humanity, University of Glasgow, since 1959; *b* 1919. MA Glasgow 1941, MA Oxon 1943. Lectr in Latin, Birmingham Univ., 1947–57; Lectr in Humanity, Glasgow Univ., 1957–59. Adviser on Civil Service

455

Careers. *Address*: Univ. of Glasgow, Glasgow G12 8QQ.

Maling, Dr Derek Hylton, BA, PhD; Senior Lecturer, Department of Geography, University College of Swansea, since 1964; *b* 1923; *m* 1952; one *s* one *d*. BA Dunelm 1952, PhD Dunelm 1956; FRMetSoc, FRGS, MInstNav. Asst Lectr, Univ. Coll. of Swansea, 1955–57; Lectr, Univ. Coll. of Swansea, 1957–64. RAF, 1941–46 (Commn and despatches); Falkland Is Depend. Surv., 1947–50; Mem., Royal Soc. subcttee on Cartography, 1971– ; Council Mem., Brit. Cartog. Soc., 1964–71; Mem., Jt Cttee, Nat. Certs in Survey., Cartog. and Plan., 1971– . *Publications*: (jtly) The Falkland Islands, 1960; (jtly) Plane Surveying, 1961; (jtly) The Geology of the South Orkney Islands, 1967; Coordinate Systems and Map Projections, 1973; *contrib*. Bull. Cté Franç. Cartog., Cartog. Jl, Emp. Surv. Rev., Geodez. Kartog., Internat. Ybk Cartog., Nachr. Karten. Vermess., Polar Rec. *Address*: Dept of Geography, Univ. College of Swansea, Singleton Park, Swansea SA2 8PP.

Maliphant, Dr Rodney; Lecturer in Developmental Psychology and Tutor in Educational Psychology, Department of Psychology, University College, London, since 1963; *b* 1925; *m* 1951; two *s* one *d*. BA London and Exeter 1950, BA Hons London 1953, DipEd Exeter 1951, DipPsych UCL 1954 (distinction), PhD UCL 1972; Member: Council, British Psychological Soc., 1971– , Assoc. Child Psychology and Psychiatry, 1968– . Sen. Res. Psychologist, Ford Foundn and Home Office Res. Unit, Dept of Psychology, UCL, 1959–63. Co-Editor: Bulletin, British Psychological Soc., 1967–69; Jl of Child Psychology and Psychiatry, 1968– ; Member: Home Secretary's Standing Adv. Cttee on Juvenile Delinquency, 1963–64; Publications Cttee, British Psychological Society, 1966– . Education Cttee, Inst. for the Study and Treatment of Delinquency, 1966– . *Publications*: *contrib*. Jl of Child Psychol. and Psychiatry, Jl of Criminol. *Address*: Dept of Psychology, Univ. Coll. London, Gower Street, WC1E 6BT.

Mallett, Dr Michael Edward; Reader, Department of History, University of Warwick, since 1973 (Senior Lecturer, 1967–73); *b* 1932; *m* 1961. BA Oxon 1955, MA Oxon 1959, DPhil Oxon 1959; FRSL. Lectr and Asst Prof., Univ. of Manitoba, 1960–62; Asst Dir and Libr., Brit. Sch. Rome, 1962–66. *Publications*: The Florentine Galleys in the Fifteenth Century, 1967; The Borgias: the Rise and Decline of a Renaissance Dynasty, 1969; Mercenaries and their Masters: warfare in Renaissance Italy, 1974; *contrib*. Papers Brit. Sch. Rome, Trans Amer. Philos. Soc., Econ. Hist. Rev., Florentine Studies, ed Rubinstein, Renaissance Venice, ed Hale. *Address*: Dept of History, Univ. of Warwick, Coventry CV4 7AL.

Mallinson, Prof. Vernon, MA, Officier de l'Ordre de Léopold; Professor of Comparative Education, School of Education, University of Reading, since 1967; *b* 1910. BA Leeds 1931 (Hons French), MA Leeds 1936.

Lectr in Educn, Reading, 1945–60; Reader in Educn, Reading, 1960–67; Vis. Prof., Syracuse, USA, 1958, 1959; Vis. Prof., Brit. Columbia, 1960; Vis. Prof., Missouri, 1963, 1965, 1967, 1969, 1971. Mem., Hants Educn Cttee; Chm., Mod. Lang. Assoc., 1954; Past Pres., Comp. Educn Soc. Europe (Brit. Sect.), 1968. *Publications*: Teaching a Modern Language, 1953; None Can be Called Deformed, 1956; Introduction to the Study of Comparative Education, 1957, 4th edn 1974; Power and Politics in Belgian Education, 1963; Modern Belgian Literature 1830–1960, 1966; Belgium, 1969; Man and Moralist: A Study of Montaigne (forthcoming); *contrib*. Brit. Jl Educnl Studies, Comp. Educn, Comp. Educn Rev., Internat. Rev. Educn, Times Educnl Supp. *Address*: School of Education, Univ. of Reading, London Road, Reading, Berkshire.

Malmberg, Lars Herman, CandPhil, MA; Lecturer in English Language, Department of English Language and Medieval Literature, University of Durham, since 1964; *b* 1932; *m* 1957; two *s* one *d*. CandPhil Åbo Akademi Finland 1960, BA Oxon 1963, MA Oxon 1969. Asst Lectr, Åbo Akademi, 1963–64. *Publications*: *contrib*. Neuphilol. Mitteil. *Address*: Dept of English Language and Medieval Literature, Elvet Riverside, New Elvet, Durham.

Malpas, Richard M. P.; Fellow and Tutor in Philosophy, Hertford College, Oxford, since 1959; *b* 1932. BA Oxon 1955, BPhil Oxon 1957, MA Oxon 1958. Lectr in Philosophy, Merton Coll., Oxford, 1957–58; Vis. Prof., Brown Univ., RI, USA, 1968; Bursar, Hertford Coll., Oxford, 1962–66 and 1970–72. *Publications*: *contrib*. Mind. *Address*: Hertford College, Oxford.

Maltby, Arthur; Senior Lecturer and Head of Department of Library and Information Studies, Queen's University, Belfast, since 1972; *b* 1935; *m* 1958; one *s* one *d*. BA London 1963 (Ext.), MA Liverpool 1969 (Ext.); FLA, FRSA. Lectr, QUB, 1969–72. Mem., NISE Area Educn and Lib. Bd, 1973– . *Publications*: Religion and Science (bibliog.), 1965; revd, Sayers' Manual of Classification, 4th edn 1967; Economics and Commerce: the sources of information and their organization, 1968; Classification in the 1970s, 1972; ed, The Government of Northern Ireland 1922–1972: a catalogue and breviate of Parliamentary Papers, 1974; *contrib*. Jl Librarianship, New Lib. World, Lib. Assoc. Record. *Address*: Queen's Univ., Belfast BT7 1NN.

Mann, Dr (Colin) Nicholas (Jocelyn); Official Tutorial Fellow in French, Pembroke College, Oxford, since 1973; *b* 1942; *m* 1964; one *s* one *d*. BA Cantab 1964 (1st cl. Mod. Lang.), MA Cantab 1968, PhD Cantab 1968. Res. Fellow, Clare Coll., Cambridge, 1965–67; Lectr, Dept of French Studies, Warwick, 1967–72; Vis. Fellow, All Souls Coll., Oxford, 1972. *Publications*: Petrarch Manuscripts in the British Isles, 1974; *contrib*. Ital. Medioev. Uman., Jl War. Court. Inst., Romania, Scriptor., Studi Franc. *Address*: Pembroke College, Oxford.

Mann, Dr John Cecil; Senior Lecturer in Roman-British History and Archaeology, Department of Archaeology, Durham University, since 1972 (Lecturer, 1957–72); *b* 1922; *m* 1947; one *s* four *d*. BA London 1950 (2nd cl. History), PhD London 1956; FSA. Mem., Council, Soc. Promot. Roman Studies, 1967–70, 1973– . *Publications*: The Northern Frontier in Britain from Hadrian to Honorius: Literary and Epigraphic Sources, 1969; *contrib*. Archaeol. Ael., Antiqu., Bonner Jbh, Britan., Hermes, Jl Roman Studies, Latomus. *Address*: Dept of Archaeology, The Old Fulling Mill, The Banks, Durham.

Mann, Nicholas; *see* Mann, C. N. J.

Mann, Pamela Dorothy; Lecturer in Social Administration, Department of Sociological Studies, University of Sheffield, since 1974; *b* 1925. BA New Zealand 1947 (History), Dip. Social Studies Sheffield 1963, Certif. Applied Social Studies Bristol 1964; Home Office Letter of Recognition in Child Care 1964. Mem., Brit. Assoc. Social Workers; Mem., Assoc. Teachers in Social Work Educn. Tutor in Child Care (later Tutor in Social Work), Dept of Extra-mural Studies, Sheffield Univ., 1968–74. Member: Sub-Cttee on Social Work Education, Univ. Council for Adult Educn, 1971; Sheffield Family Service Cttee, 1968; Sheffield Churches Council for Community Care, 1969; Sheffield Social Services Dept Adoption Cases Cttee, 1971; Sheffield Family Housing Assoc. Management Cttee, 1971; Adv. Council for Christian Ministry, 1972. *Address*: Dept of Sociological Studies, Univ. of Sheffield, Sheffield S10 2TN.

Mann, Dr Peter Henry; Reader, Department of Sociological Studies, University of Sheffield, since 1972; *b* 1926; *m* 1950; one *s* two *d*. BA Leeds 1950, MA Liverpool 1952, PhD Nottingham 1955. Jun. Res. Worker, Liverpool Univ., 1950–52; Univ. Res. Fellow, Nottingham Univ., 1952–54; Lectr, Sheffield Univ., 1954–64, Sen. Lectr, 1964–72. Radio Off., Merchant Navy, 1943–47. *Publications*: An Approach to Urban Sociology, 1965; Methods of Sociological Enquiry, 1968; (with J. L. Burgoyne) Books and Reading, 1969; Books, Buyers and Borrowers, 1971; Students and Books, 1974; *contrib*. Amer. Jl Sociol., Brit. Jl Sociol., Town Plan. Rev. *Address*: Dept of Sociological Studies, The Univ., Sheffield S10 2TN.

Manners, Gerald; Reader in Geography, University College, London, since 1967; *b* 1932; *m* 1959; one *s* two *d*. BA Cambridge 1954; MA Cambridge 1958; FRGS. Mem., Inst. Brit. Geogrs, Reg. Studies Assoc., Brit. Assoc. Amer. Studies. Tutor in Geography, Univ. Coll., Swansea. 1957–58; Asst Lectr in Geography, 1958–60; Lectr in Geography, 1960–67; Vis. Schol., Resources for Future Inc., Washington DC, 1964; Vis. Associate, Jt Center for Urban Studies, MIT–Harvard Univ., 1972. Mem., Location of Offices Bureau, 1970; Mem., SE Econ. Plan. Council, 1971. *Publications*: Geography of Energy, 1964, 2nd edn 1971; ed, South Wales in the Sixties, 1964; Changing World Market for Iron Ore 1950–1980, 1971; ed (jtly), Spatial Policy Problems of the British Economy, 1971; ed, Regional Development in Britain, 1972; *contrib*. Econ. Geog., Jl Indust. Econ., Town Plan. Rev., Trans Inst. Brit. Geogrs, Urban Studies. *Address*: Dept of Geography, Univ. College London, Gower Street, WC1E 6BT.

Manning, Dr David John; Lecturer in Politics, University of Durham, since 1965; *b* 1938; *m* 1967; one *s* one *d*. BSc(Econ) London 1960, PhD London 1964. Mem., Pol. Studies Assoc. Moral Tutor, St Cuthbert's Soc., 1969. Lectr in Charge, MA Course in Politics; Vis. Prof. of Politics, Univ. of Texas at Austin, 1973. *Publications*: The Mind of Jeremy Bentham, 1968. *Address*: Dept of Politics, Univ. of Durham, Durham DH1 3HP.

Manning, Maurice; Lecturer, Department of Ethics and Politics, University College, Dublin, since 1969; *b* 1943. BA National Univ. of Ireland 1964, MA National Univ. of Ireland 1966 (1st cl.). Asst, Univ. Coll., Dublin, 1966–68; Res. Fellowship, Inst. Public Admin., 1968–69; Treas., Acad. Staff Assoc., 1970. *Publications*: The Blueshirts, 1971; Irish Political Parties, 1972. *Address*: Dept of Politics, Univ. College, Dublin 4.

Manning, Dr William H., BSc, FSA; Senior Lecturer in Archaeology, University College, Cardiff, since 1973 (Lecturer, 1964–73); *b* 1936; *m* 1963; one *s*. BSc Nottingham 1958, Post-grad. Dip Arch London 1960, PhD London 1969; FSA. Asst Archaeol., Reading Mus., 1960–63; Res. Asst, Brit. Mus., 1963–64. *Publications*: (with C. Houlder) South Wales (Regional Archaeologies Series), 1966; *contrib*. Antiqu. Jl, Antiqu., Jl Roman Studies, Brit. Mus. Qly, etc. *Address*: Dept of Archaeology, Univ. College, PO Box 78, Cardiff CF1 1XL.

Mansell, Dr Antony Lowe; Lecturer in Education, Centre for Science Education, Chelsea College, University of London, since 1968; *b* 1930; *m* 1955; two *d*. BSc Manchester 1955, PhD Manchester 1959. Mem., Nuffield Advanced Science Teaching Project, 1968–70; Mem., Nuffield Gp for Res. and Innovation in Higher Educn, 1974. *Publications*: ed jtly, The Chemist in Action, 1970; contrib., Nuffield Advanced Science (Chemistry) Teachers' Guides and Students' Books, 1970; contrib., Nuffield Advanced Science (Physics) Teachers' Guides and Students' Books, 1971; *contrib*. Educn in Chemistry, Educn and Trng, Jl Chem. Soc., Nature, Jl Phys. Chem. *Address*: Centre for Science Education, Bridges Place, SW6.

Manser, Prof. Anthony Richards, MA, BPhil; Professor of Philosophy, University of Southampton, since 1970; *b* 1924; *m* 1964. BA 1948, MA 1949, BPhil 1952, Oxon. Asst Lectr, Univ. of Southampton, 1950–52, Lectr, 1952–64, Sen. Lectr, 1964–70; Vis. Lectr, Univ. of Maryland, 1964–65; Vis. Prof., Rice Univ., Houston, Texas, 1968–69. *Publications*: Sartre, a Philosophic Study, 1966, pbk (US) edn 1967; contribs. Encyclopaedia of Philosophy, 1966; Studies in the Philosophy of

457

Wittgenstein, 1969; Sartre, ed M. Warnock, 1971; Linguistic Analysis and Phenomenology, 1972; *contrib*. Philos., Proc. Aristot. Soc., Twent. Cent. Studies. *Address*: Philosophy Dept, Univ. of Southampton, Southampton SO9 5NH.

Mansergh, Prof. Philip Nicholas Seton, OBE, DLitt, LittD, FBA; Master, St John's College, Cambridge University, since 1969; *b* 1910; *m* 1939; three *s* two *d*. MA, DPhil Oxon 1936, DLitt Oxon 1960, LittD Cantab 1970; Hon. Fellow Pembroke Coll., Oxford 1954, Hon. Fellow, TCD 1971. Sec., Oxford Univ. Politics Res. Cttee, and Tutor in Politics, 1937–40; Res. Prof., British Commonwealth Relations, RIIA, 1947–53; Smuts Prof. of the History of the Brit. Commonwealth, Univ. of Cambridge, 1953–69; Fellow, St John's Coll., Cambridge, 1955–69; Vis. Prof., Australian Nat. Univ., 1951; Vis. Prof., Toronto, 1953; Vis. Prof., Duke, 1957, 1965; Vis. Prof., Indian Sch. of Internat. Studies, New Delhi, 1958, 1966. Min. of Information, 1941–46; Dominions Off., 1946–47; Ed. in Chief, India Off. Records on Transfer of Power, 1967– ; Mem., Gen. Adv. Council, BBC, 1956–62; Mem., Adv. Council on Public Records, 1966–74; Mem., Edit. Bd, Annual Register, 1947–73. *Publications*: The Irish Free State: Its Government and Politics, 1934; The Government of Northern Ireland, 1936; jt ed. Advisory Bodies, 1941; Britain and Ireland, 1942, 2nd edn 1946; The Commonwealth and the Nations, 1948; The Coming of the First World War, 1949; Survey of British Commonwealth Affairs (2 vols), 1931–39, 1952 and 1939–52, 1958; Documents and Speeches on Commonwealth Affairs, 1931–1962 (3 vols), 1953–63; South Africa: The Price of Magnaminity, 1906–1961, 1962; The Irish Question 1840–1921, 1965; The Commonwealth Experience, 1969. *Address*: Master's Lodge, St John's College, Cambridge.

Manton, John Derek, MA; Lecturer in German, Department of European Studies, Loughborough University of Technology, since 1966; *b* 1930; *m* 1958; one *s* two *d*. BA Cantab 1952 (Modern and Medieval Languages Tripos), MA Cantab 1955; AIL 1961. *Publications*: (jtly) Lustige Geschichten für die Jugend, 1966; Introduction to Theological German, 1971; (jtly) German at Work, 1972; *contrib*. Papers Purit. Conf. *Address*: Dept of European Studies, Loughborough Univ. of Technology, Loughborough LE11 3TU.

Manvell, Dr (Arnold) Roger; Visiting Fellow, Centre for Educational Technology, University of Sussex, since 1968; *b* 1909; *m* 1956. BA London 1930 (1st cl. Hons English Lang. and Lit.), PhD London 1938, DLitt Sussex 1971; Hon. DFA New England Coll., USA. Organising Tutor, Univ. of Bristol Extra-mural Dept, 1938–40; Vis. Prof. of Humanities, Univ. of Louisville, 1973. Gov., and Hd of Dept of film hist., London Film Sch.; Mem., Soc. Authors; Cttee of Mngmt, 1954–57, 1965–68. *Publications*: Film, 1944, 3rd edn 1950; On the Air, 1953; The Animated Film, 1954; The Film and the Public, 1955; The Living Screen, 1961; New Cinema in Europe, 1966; This Age of Communication, 1967; New Cinema in the USA, 1968; Ellen Terry, 1968; New Cinema in Britain, 1969; Sarah Siddons, 1970; Shakespeare and the Film, 1971; ed, International Encyclopedia of Film, 1972; contrib. var. vols on film art and history, and author with Heinrich Fraenkel of several books on history of Nazi regime; *contrib*. Annual Register. *Address*: Centre for Educational Technology, Univ. of Sussex, Falmer, Brighton, Sussex.

Mapes, Roy, DipAgricEcon, BLitt; Director, Centre for Social Science Research, University of Keele, since 1965; *b* 1923; *m* 1951; two *d*. DipAgricEcon Oxon 1959, BLitt Oxon 1963; FRSS. Sen. Res. Fellow, Univ. of Liverpool, Dept of Pharmacology, 1961–63; Univ. Lectr in Educational Statistics, Univ. of Leeds, 1963–65. Mem., Exec., Brit. Sociol Assoc., 1971– ; Rev. Ed., Sociol Rev. 1968– . *Publications*: Mathematics and Sociology, 1971; The Sociology of Planning, 1972; *contrib*. Analyst, Brit. Med. Jl, Brit. Jl Mktg, Educnl Rev., Jl Newdrugs, Jl Town Plan. Inst., Practit., Psychopharm., Sociol., Sociol Rev. *Address*: Centre for Social Science Research, Univ. of Keele, Keele ST5 5BG.

Marchant, Robert; Director of Music and Head of Department of Music, Hull University, since 1955; *b* 1916. MA Cantab 1937 (Class. Tripos 1st cl. Hons Parts I and II), MusB Cantab 1939 (1st cl.). Lectr in Music, Hull Univ., 1946. *Address*: Music Dept, Hull Univ., Hull HU6 7RX.

Marcos, Dr Manuel B.; *see* Bermejo-Marcos.

Mardia, Prof. Kantilal Vardichand, MSc, PhD, DSc, FSS; Professor of Applied Statistics, University of Leeds, since 1973; *b* 1935; *m* 1958; one *s* two *d*. BSc Bombay 1955 (1st cl. with dist.), MSc Bombay 1957, MSc Poona 1961, PhD Rajasthan 1965, PhD Newcastle 1967, DSc Newcastle 1973; FSS. Lectr, Bombay Univ., 1957–61; Lectr, Rajasthan Univ., 1961–67; Lectr, Hull Univ., 1967–69, Sen. Lectr, 1969–71, Reader in Statistics, 1971–73. *Publications*: Families of Bivariate Distributions, 1970; Statistics of Directional Data, 1972; *contrib*. Biomet., Jl Royal Stat. Soc., Ann. Math. Stat., Sankhyā. *Address*: Dept of Statistics, School of Mathematics, Univ. of Leeds, Leeds LS2 9JT.

Marett, Dr (Warwick) Paul, MA, PhD; Warden of Rutherford Hall, since 1966, and Lecturer in Asian Studies in Department of Library Studies, Loughborough University, since 1973; *b* 1926; *m* 1953. BA Bristol 1950, BSc(Econ) London 1951, BCom London 1953, BA Cambridge 1959, MA Cambridge 1963, PhD London 1970; FRHistS 1973. Lectr in Dept of Social Scis and Economics, Loughborough, 1966–72. *Publications*: A Calendar of the Register of Henry Wakefeld, Bishop of Worcester 1375–95, 1972. *Address*: Dept of Library and Information Studies, The Univ., Loughborough LE11 3TU.

Margerison, Dr Charles John; Assistant Director, Management Programmes, Management Department, University of Bradford, since 1973 (Lecturer in Organization Sociology, 1966–73); *b* 1940; *m* 1965; one *s* two *d*. BSc(Econ) London 1963, DipIndAd Liverpool 1964, PhD Bradford 1971. Mem., Brit. Sociol Assoc., 1963, Mem., Inst. Personnel Mngmt, 1964. Res. Asst, Univ. of Bradford, 1964–66. *Publications*: Four Structural Problems in Organization, 1967; Managing Effective Work Groups, 1972; Managerial Problem Solving, 1974; Planning for Human Resources, 1974; *contrib.* Brit. Jl Indust. Relat., Brit. Jl Sociol. *Address*: Univ. of Bradford Management Centre, Emm Lane, Bradford.

Margetts, Dr John, MA, DipEd, Dr phil; Lecturer, Department of German, University of Liverpool, since 1967; *b* 1937; *m* 1963; one *s* two *d*. BA Oxon 1958, MA Oxon 1962, DipEd Oxon 1959, Dr phil München 1967; FRHistS 1973. Lektor for English, München Univ., 1960–61, 1963–65; Lektor Göttingen Univ., 1965–66; Asst Lectr, Liverpool Univ., 1966–67. *Publications*: Die Satzstruktur bei Meister Eckhart, 1969; *contrib.* Germ. Life Lett., Mod. Lang. Rev., Neophilol., Neuphilol. Mitteil. *Address*: Dept of German, Univ. of Liverpool, Liverpool L69 3BX.

Markowski, Dr Stefan; Lecturer in Economics, Department of Economics, London School of Economics, since 1969; *b* 1945; *m* 1967. MSc (Econ.) Warsaw 1966, PhD LSE 1974; Mem., NIASEES. Asst Lectr in Econs, 1967–69. *Publications*: *contrib.* Mercurio, Soviet Studies, World Today, Year Book of World Affairs. *Address*: London Sch. of Economics, Houghton Street, Aldwych, WC2A 2AE.

Marks, Shula, PhD; Lecturer in the History of Southern Africa, University of London, since 1963; *b* 1936; *m* 1957; one *s* one *d*. BA Cape Town 1959 (1st cl. History and English), PhD London 1967. Lectr, jtly at Inst. of Commonwealth Studies and SOAS. Jt-Ed., Jl Afr. Hist. *Publications*: Reluctant Rebellion, 1970; *contrib.* Jl Afr. Hist. *Address*: Dept of History, School of Oriental and African Studies, Univ. of London, WC1E 7HP.

Markus, Dr Robert Austin, MA, PhD; Reader in Medieval History, University of Liverpool, since 1970; *b* 1924; *m* 1955; two *s* one *d*. BSc Manchester 1945, MA Manchester 1948, PhD Manchester 1950; FRHistS. Res. Fellow in Philosophy, Univ. of Manchester, 1948–50; Sub-Libr., Univ. of Birmingham, 1954–55; Sub-Libr., Univ. of Liverpool, 1955–59; Lectr in Medieval History, Univ. of Liverpool, 1959–69. Mem., Brit. subcommn, Commn Internat. Hist. Ecclés. Comp. *Publications*: (with A. H. Armstrong) Christian Faith and Greek Philosophy, 1960, Polish edn 1964, Spanish edn 1970; (with E. John) Papacy and Hierarchy, 1969; Saeculum: history and society in the theology of Saint Augustine, 1970; ed, Augustine: a collection of critical essays, 1972; Christianity in the Roman World, 1974; *contrib.* Jl Eccles. Hist., Jl Theol. Studies, Studies in Church Hist. *Address*: The School of History, The Univ., PO Box 147, Liverpool L69 3EX.

Markus, Prof. Thomas A., MA, MArch (MIT), RIBA; Professor of Building Science, Department of Architecture and Building Science, University of Strathclyde, since 1966; *b* 1928; *m* 1954; three *s* two *d*. BA Hon. Manchester 1949 (Architecture), MA (by Thesis) 1953, MArch (MIT) 1955; ARIBA 1950. Studio Asst, Sch. of Architecture, Univ. of Manchester, 1949–50; Asst Lectr, 1951–54; Reader in Architecture, Welsh School of Architecture, Univ. of Wales, Cardiff, 1964–66. Asst Architect, Schools Section, City Architects' Dept, Manchester, 1950–51; Architect, Engineering Services Division, ICI, London, 1954–56; Pilkington Brothers Limited, Manager, Products Application Dept, 1956–64; Member: SRC Civil and Aeronautical Engineering Cttee, and a special adviser to the Cttee, 1969–72; RIBA Bd of Educn, 1970–72; Mem., Steering Gp, Design of Learning Spaces Project, CET, 1972– ; Mem., CIE Committee, TC3.3 Principles of the Environment, 1972– ; Chm., Design Research Soc., 1973– . *Publications*: (jtly) Building Performance, 1972; *contrib.* Trans of the Royal Society, Architectural Science Rev., Architects' Jl, Light and Lighting, Building Science, Human Factors, Cahiers du Centre Scientifique et Technique du Bâtiment. *Address*: Dept of Architecture and Building Science, 131 Rottenrow, Glasgow G4 0NG.

Marlow, Arnold Norman, MA; Senior Lecturer in Latin, University of Manchester, since 1959; *b* 1914; *m* 1945; two *s*. BA London 1935 (Aegrotat), MA London 1938 (Distinction). Asst Lectr in Classics, Bangor, 1943–45; Asst Lectr in Greek and Latin, Manchester, 1945–48; Lectr, Manchester, 1948–59. Asst Tutor, Fac. of Arts, Univ. of Manchester, 1947–52; Mem., Council, Class. Assoc., 1965–68; Univ. rep., Bd of Managers, Schs in Bury, 1969. *Publications*: Radhakrishan: an Anthology, 1952; Footplate and Signal Cabin, 1956; A. E. Housman: Poet and Scholar, 1958; jt trans., Erasmus: de libero arbitrio, *and* Luther: de servo arbitrio, 1969; trans., The Latin Diary of Thomas Isham of Lamport, 1971; *contrib.* Bull. J. Rylands Libr., Jl Engl. Studies, Leeds Philos. Jl, Philos. EW. *Address*: Dept of Latin, Univ. of Manchester.

Marlow, Dr Richard Kenneth; Lecturer in Music Faculty, University of Cambridge, and Fellow, Organist, Director of Music, and Lecturer, Trinity College, Cambridge, since 1968; *b* 1939; *m* 1964; two *s*. BA Cambridge 1961 (1st cl. Music), MusB Cambridge 1962, MA Cambridge 1965, PhD Cambridge 1966; FRCO 1958. Res. Fellow, Selwyn Coll., Cambridge, 1963–65; Lectr, Southampton Univ., 1965–68. Master of Music, St Mary, Southampton, 1966–68; Gov., St Olaves Sch., 1970– ; Dir, Cambridge Univ. Chamber Choir, 1969– ; Hon. Gen. Editor, Church Music Soc., 1974. *Publications*: ed, G. and R. Farnaby: Keyboard Music (Musica Britannica XXIV), 1965; compositions: a set of responses, 1972; anthem: O Lord God, 1972; *contrib.* Music. Lett., Music. Times, Proc. Royal Music. Assoc. *Address*: Trinity College, Cambridge.

Marrian, Jacqueline; Senior Lecturer, Department of Marketing, University of Lancaster, since 1973 (Lecturer, 1966–73); *b* 1935. BCom Edinburgh 1958. Asst Lectr, Edinburgh, 1959–62; Lectr, 1962–66. Vice-Principal, Cartmel Coll., Lancaster, 1968–73. Dir, Mkting Teacher Develt Programme. Mem., Business Studies Bd, CNAA, 1973– . *Publications*: (with M. K. Adler) (also ed) Lectures in Market Research, 1965; (with A. Wilson) The Marketing of Industrial Products, 1965, 2nd edn 1972; *contrib.* Brit. Jl Mktg, Jl Sci. Business, Mktg, Mktg Forum. *Address*: Dept of Marketing, Univ. of Lancaster, Bailrigg, Lancaster LA1 4YN.

Marris, Robin; Reader in Economics, University of Cambridge, since 1972 (Lecturer, 1960–72); *b* 1924; *m* 1949; 1954; 1972; one *s* three *d*. BA Cambridge 1946, ScD Cambridge 1968. Fellow, King's Coll., Cambridge, 1950; Asst Lectr, Cambridge 1951–60; Asst Dir of Res., 1955–58; Vis. Prof., Berkeley, 1961–62; Vis. Prof., Harvard, 1967–68. Treasury, 1947–50; UN, 1950–52; Min. of Overseas Develop., 1964–66. *Publications*: Economic Arithmetic, 1958; Economic Theory of Managerial Capitalism, 1964; Economics of Capital Utilisation, 1964; ed (with H. Wood), The Corporate Economy, 1971; *contrib.* Amer. Econ. Rev., Economica, Econ. Jl, Jl Royal Stat. Soc., Proc. Manchester Stat. Soc., Qly Jl Econ., Rev. Econ. Studies. *Address*: King's College, Cambridge.

Marsden, Dr Arthur, BA, PhD, FRHistS; Senior Lecturer, Department of Modern History, University of Dundee, since 1970; *b* 1918; *m* 1949; two *s*. BA Wales 1940 (1st cl. History), PhD London 1963; FRHistS. Temp. Lectr, Univ. Coll. of Hull, 1946–47; Staff Tutor, Univ. of Hull, 1947–63; David Davies Memorial Fellow, 1958–59; Lectr, Univ. of St Andrews (Dundee from 1967) 1964–70. Staff Capt., 1940–46. *Publications*: Britain and the End of the Tunis Treaties, 1965; British Diplomacy and Tunis 1875–1902, 1971; *contrib.* EHR, Jl Mod. Hist., Att. Cong. Internaz. Studi Nord-Afr., Rev. Occid. Mussul Médit. *Address*: Dept of Modern History, Univ. of Dundee, Dundee DD1 4HN.

Marsden, Dr Eric William; Senior Lecturer in Ancient History, University of Liverpool, since 1969; *b* 1926; *m* 1954; one *s* two *d*. BA Cantab 1950 (1st cl. Classics with Distinction in Ancient History), MA Cantab 1953, PhD Cantab 1955. Asst Lectr, Liverpool Univ., 1953–56; Lectr, 1956–69; Vis. Prof., Univ. of Brit. Columbia, 1967. *Publications*: The Campaign of Gaugamela, 1964; Greek and Roman Artillery: Historical Development, 1969; Greek and Roman Artillery: Technical Treatises, 1971. *Address*: School of Classics, Liverpool Univ., PO Box 147, Liverpool L69 3BX.

Marsh, Arthur Ivor; Senior Research Fellow in Industrial Relations, St Edmund Hall, University of Oxford, since 1964; *b* 1922; *m* 1950: two *s* two *d*. MA Oxon 1948 (Modern History and PPE). Mem., Brit. Sociol Assoc., Mem., Univ. Indust. Relat. Assoc. Res. Asst, Oxford Univ. Agric.

Econ. Res. Inst., 1947–48; Staff Tutor, Delegacy for Extra-Mural Studies, 1948–64; Brit. Steel Corp. Fellow, 1971–73. Mem., Oxford City Council, 1959–62; Pay Comr, Gibraltar, 1967–72; Ind. Mem., Wages Councils, Arbitrator, Dept of Employment. *Publications*: Managers and Shop Stewards, 1963, new expanded edn 1974; Industrial Relations in Engineering, 1965; A Collection of Teaching Documents and Case Studies: Industrial Relations in Engineering, 1966; Disputes Procedures in British Industry, 1966; (with W. E. J. McCarthy) Disputes Procedures in Britain, 1968; (with J. W. Staples) Checkoff Agreements in Britain, 1968; (with E. O. Evans and P. Garcia) Workplace Industrial Relations in Engineering, 1971; (with E. O. Evans) Dictionary of Industrial Relations, 1973; *contrib.* Brit. Jl Indust. Relat., Indust. Relat. Jl, Internat. Inst. Lab. Studies Bull. *Address*: St Edmund Hall, Oxford.

Marsh, Prof. David Charles; Professor of Applied Social Science, University of Nottingham, since 1954; *b* 1917; *m* 1941; one *s*. Lectr, Univ. Coll. of Swansea, 1947–49; Prof. of Social Science, Victoria Univ. Coll., Wellington, NZ, 1949–54. Mem., Supplementary Benefits Commn, 1967– . *Publications*: National Insurance and Assistance in Great Britain, 1949; The Changing Social Structure of England and Wales, 1958; The Future of the Welfare State, 1964, new edn 1967; The Welfare State, 1970. *Address*: Univ. of Nottingham, University Park, Nottingham NG7 2RD.

Marsh, Leonard George, MEd; Principal Lecturer, and Head of Postgraduate Primary Department, University of London, Goldsmiths' College, since 1965; *b* 1930; *m* 1953; one *s* one *d*. AcadDipEd London 1955, MEd Leicester 1965. Lectr, Goldsmiths' Coll., 1961–63; Sen. Lectr, 1963–65; Vis. Lectr, Bank Street Coll., NY, and other US Univs. Cnsltnt, OECD, Portugal (Min. of Educn and Min. of Wks), 1971. *Publications*: Let's Explore Mathematics, 1964–67; Exploring Shapes and Number, 1968, 2nd edn 1970; Children Explore Mathematics, 1967, 3rd edn 1969; Exploring the Metric System, 1969, 2nd edn 1969; Exploring the Metric World, 1970; Approach to Mathematics, 1970; Alongside the Child in the Primary School, 1970; Workshop 1, 1971; Workshop 2, 1971; Workshop 3, 1970; Let's Discover Mathematics, 1971–72; Being a Teacher, 1973. *Address*: Postgraduate Primary Dept, Univ. of London, Goldsmiths' College, New Cross, SE14 6NW.

Marshak, Dr Mildred D., PhD, ABPS; Lecturer in Psychology, Institute of Education, London University, since 1961; *b* 1923; one *s*. AB California 1944 (Biology), BA San Francisco 1950 (Educnl Psychology), Teacher Credentials San Francisco 1950, PhD London 1956; ABPS. Prof. Mem., Soc. Analyt. Psychol. Lectr, Univ. Coll., London, 1955–61. Pending, Co-ord., Dip. in Remedial Educn through Art; Mem., Council, BPS Med. Sect., 1967–70; Founder Mem., Centre for Analyt. Study Student Problems; Sec., Soc. Analyt. Psychol., Child. Training

Cttee. *Publications*: contrib. New Teaching in Art Education (forthcoming); contrib. Anxiety in School Children (forthcoming); contrib. Child Development and Psychology of Teacher (forthcoming); *contrib*. Brit. Jl Med. Psychol., Didask., Jl Analyt. Psychol. *Address*: Dept of Psychology, Institute of Education, London Univ., Malet Street, WC1E 7HS.

Marshall, Geoffrey; Fellow and Praelector in Politics, The Queen's College, University of Oxford, since 1957; *b* 1929; *m* 1957; two *s*. BA Manchester 1950, MA Manchester 1952, MA Oxon 1957, PhD Glasgow 1956; FBA. Asst Lectr, Univ. of Glasgow ,1953–54; Res. Fellow, Nuffield Coll., Oxford, 1955–57. Mem., Oxford City Council, 1965– ; City Sheriff, 1970–71. *Publications*: Parliamentary Sovereignty and the Commonwealth, 1957; (with G. C. Moodie) Some Problems of the Constitution, 1959, 5th edn 1972; Police and Government, 1965; Constitutional Theory, 1971; *contrib*. Pol. Studies, Public Law. *Address*: The Queen's College, Oxford.

Marshall, Dr I. Howard; Senior Lecturer, Department of New Testament Exegesis, University of Aberdeen, since 1970; *b* 1934; *m* 1961; one *s* three *d*. MA Aberdeen 1955 (1st cl. Classics), BD Aberdeen 1959, BA Cantab 1959 (1st cl. Theology), PhD Aberdeen 1963. Asst Tutor, Didsbury Coll., Bristol, and recognised teacher in Theol Subjects, Univ. of Bristol, 1960–62; Methodist Minister, Darlington, 1962–64; Lectr, Univ. of Aberdeen, 1964–70. *Publications*: Eschatology and the Parables, 1963; Kept by the Power of God, 1969; The Work of Christ, 1969; Luke: Historian and Theologian, 1970; *contrib*. Evang. Qly, Expos. Times, Interp., Jl Theol Studies, NT Studies, Theol., Tynd. Bull. *Address*: Dept of New Testament Exegesis, King's College, Old Aberdeen AB9 2UB.

Marshall, Dr John Duncan, BSc(Econ), PhD, FRHistS; Reader in the Regional History of North-West England, Department of History, University of Lancaster, since 1969; *b* 1919; *m* 1949; one *s* two *d*. BSc(Econ) London 1949, PhD London 1956; FRHistS 1969. Sen. Lectr in Regional Hist., Univ. of Lancaster, 1965–69. *Publications*: Furness and the Industrial Revolution, 1956; ed, The Autobiography of William Stout of Lancaster, 1965; The Industrial Archaeology of the Lake Counties, 1969; The Lake District at Work Past and Present, 1971; Old Lakeland: Some Cumbrian Social History, 1971; Lancashire (City and County series), 1974; *contrib*. Econ. Hist. Rev., Jl Transp. Hist., North. Hist., Trans Cum. Westld Antiqu. Archaeol. Soc., Trans Lancs Ches. Antiqu. Soc., Trans Thorot. Soc. Notts. *Address*: Furness College, Univ. of Lancaster, Bailrigg, Lancaster.

Marshall, Prof. John Henry; Professor of Romance Philology, Westfield College, London, since 1974; *b* 1930; *m* 1960; two *s* one *d*. BA Oxon 1952 (1st cl. Mod. Lang.), MA Oxon 1956, DPhil Oxon 1963. Lectr, Durham Univ., 1955–67, Sen. Lectr, 1967–72, Reader, 1972–74. *Publications*: The Donatz Proensals of Uc Faidit, 1969; The Chansons of Adam de la Halle, 1971; The Razos de trobar of

Raimon Vidal and associated texts, 1972; *contrib*. Med. Æv., Mod. Lang. Rev., Romance Philol., Romania. *Address*: Westfield College, Kidderpore Avenue, NW3 7ST.

Marshall, Mary; University Lecturer, School of Geography, University of Oxford, since 1949; *b* 1917. BA Oxon 1939 (1st cl. Hons Geog.), MA Oxon 1943; FRGS, Mem., Geog. Assoc., IBG, Hakluyt Soc., Brit. Assoc. Dept Lectr, Sch. of Geography, Oxford, 1945–49; Lectr in Geography, Lady Margaret Hall, Oxford, 1944–61. Mem., War Agricultural Cttee, Oxon, 1939–41; Admtly NID5, 1941–46. *Address*: School of Geography, Mansfield Road, Oxford.

Marshall, Morrison Henry Bell; Lecturer in Greek, University of Glasgow, since 1968; *b* 1936. MA St Andrews 1958. Mem., Class. Assoc., Soc. Prom. Hellenic Studies. Asst, St Andrews, 1961–65; Asst, Glasgow, 1965–68. *Address*: Dept of Greek, 8 Lilybank Gardens, Univ. of Glasgow, Glasgow.

Marshall, Prof. Peter Donald; Professor of American History and Institutions, Department of American Studies, University of Manchester, since 1972; *b* 1926; *m* 1953; one *s* one *d*. BA Oxon 1950 (1st cl. Hons Mod. History), MA Yale 1952, PhD Yale 1960; Mem.: Econ. Hist. Soc.; Past and Present Soc.; Brit. Assoc. for Amer. Studies. Bristol University: Temp. Asst Lectr, 1950–51; Asst Lectr, 1953–55; Lectr, 1955–56; Vis. Asst Prof., Univ. of Calif., Berkeley, 1961–62; Prof., McGill Univ., 1966–72. *Publications*: Of Mother Country and Plantations, ed V. B. Platt and D. C. Scraggs, 1971; contrib. Perspectives of Empire, ed J. E. Flint and G. Williams, 1973; *contrib*. EHR, History, Jl Amer. Stud., Past and Present. *Address*: Dept of American Studies, Univ. of Manchester, Manchester M13 9PL.

Marshall, Sybil Mary; Reader in Primary Education, University of Sussex, since 1967; *b* 1913; *m* 1939; one *d*. MA Cambridge 1962 (Hons English); Qualified Teacher (ex cl. and head-teacher). Lectr in Primary Educn, Inst. of Educn, Univ. of Sheffield, 1962–67. Educnl Adv.,Picture Box (Granada TV). *Publications*: Experiment in Education, 1963, 2nd edn 1969; Fenland Chronicle, 1966; Adventure in Creative Education, 1968; Aspects of Art Work, 1968; Expression: (Creative Work with Lower Juniors), 1970; Creative Writing, 1974; *contrib*. Child Educn, Teach. Wld, Times Educnl Supp., Use Engl. *Address*: Education Development Building, Univ. of Sussex, Falmer, Brighton, Sussex.

Marshall, Prof. Thomas Kenneth, MD, FRCPath; Professor of Forensic Medicine, Queen's University of Belfast (teaches in Law as well as Medicine), since 1973; *b* 1924; *m* 1953; one *s* one *d*. MB, ChB Leeds 1948, MD Leeds 1959; MRCPath 1964, FRCPath 1970. Lectr in Forensic Med., Leeds, 1950–58; Pt-time Lectr in Forensic Med., Queen's Univ., Belfast, 1958–67, Pt-time Sen. Lectr, 1967–73. Past Pres., Internat. Assoc. Foren. Sciences, Mem., Brit. Acad. Foren. Sciences; Corresp. Member: Amer. Acad. Foren. Sciences; Australian Acad. Foren. Sciences;

461

Pres., Brit. Assoc. Forensic Med. *Publications*: (jtly) Disposal of the Dead, 1958, 2nd edn 1961; *contrib*. Jl Foren. Sci., Med. Sci. Law. *Address*: Institute of Pathology, Grosvenor Road, Belfast BT12 6BL.

Marsland, David; Senior Lecturer in Sociology, Brunel University, since 1972, and Director, Regional Training Consultative Unit for the Youth Services; *b* 1939; *m* 1969; two *d*. BA Cantab 1961 (Classics), MA Cantab 1965, MA Qual London 1962. Asst Lectr in Sociology, Brunel Univ., 1964–68; Lectr in Sociology, Brunel Univ., 1968–72. *Publications*: *contrib*. Sociol. Anal., Univ. Qly, Vocat. Asp. Educn, Youth and Society. *Address*: Dept of Sociology, Brunel Univ., Kingston Lane, Uxbridge, Mddx UB8 3TH.

Martin, Prof. Andrew, PhD, QC; Professor of International and Comparative Law, University of Southampton, since 1963; *b* 1906; *m* 1932; one *s*. Drjur Drpol Budapest 1927, PhD London 1942; Barrister (Middle Temple) 1940. Lectr, Ruskin Coll., Oxford, 1945–54; Sen. Lectr, Univ. of Southampton, 1954–56; Reader, Univ. of Southampton, 1956–63. Law Comr, 1965–70; Mem., Law Reform Cttee, 1970– . *Publications*: (with N. Bentwich) Commentary on the Charter of the United Nations, 1950; Collective Security, 1952; (with J. B. S. Edwards) The Changing Charter, 1955; Restrictive Trade Practices and Monopolies, 1957; (with G. Gardiner) Law Reform NOW, 1963; Legal Aspects of Disarmament, 1963; *contrib*. var articles and notes in law jls. *Address*: Faculty of Law, Univ. of Southampton, Southampton SO9 5NH.

Martin, Dr Augustine; College Lecturer in English, University College, Dublin, since 1969; *b* 1935; *m* 1960; two *s* one *d*. BA UCD 1956, MA UCD 1958, HDipEd UCD 1957, PhD UCD 1972. Asst Lectr, UCD 1965–69. Mem., Governing Body, UCD, 1969 and 1973; elected Senator of Republic of Ireland, on University panel, 1973. *Publications*: Exploring English, vol. I, 1967; Soundings, 1969; Introducing English, 1970; ed, Winter's Tales from Ireland, vol. 1, 1971; ed J. Stephens: The Charwoman's Daughter, 1972; *contrib*. Ariel, Colby Library Qly, Chicago Rev., Studies, Univ. Review (Ireland). *Address*: English Dept, Univ. College Dublin, Belfield, Dublin 4.

Martin, Bernice; Lecturer in Sociology, Bedford College, London University, since 1961; *b* 1937; *m* 1962; three *s* one *d*. BA London 1959 (1st cl. Sociol.). Res. Asst, Dept of Sociol., Univ. of Sheffield, 1960–61; Asst Lectr in Sociol., Bedford Coll., Univ. of London, 1961–64. *Publications*: *contrib*. Crit. Qly, Internat. Rev. of Social Hist., Social Compass, Sociol Yearbook of Religion in Britain. *Address*: Dept of Sociology, Bedford Coll., Regent's Park, NW1 4NS.

Martin, Charles Graham; Reader in Literature, Faculty of Arts, The Open University, since 1969; *b* 1927; *m* 1955. BSc St Andrews 1948 (Biochem.), BA Hons 1953 (1st cl. Lang. and Lit.), MA 1957 (Oxford). Assistant Lecturer: Dept of English, Univ.

of Leeds, 1955–56; Bedford Coll., Univ. of London, 1956–58, Lectr, 1958–69. *Publications*: ed, Eliot in Perspective, 1970; ed (with Harvie and Scharf), Industrialisation and Culture 1830–1914, 1970; *contrib*. Essays in Crit., Mod. Philology, Rev. of English Studies, Studies in Bibliog., Notes and Queries. *Address*: Faculty of Arts, The Open Univ., Milton Keynes MK7 6AA.

Martin, Prof. Conor J., MA, DPhil; Professor of Ethics and Politics, University College, Dublin, since 1953; *b* 1920. BA University College, Dublin 1940 (1st cl. Philosophy), MA University College, Dublin 1941 (1st cl. Philosophy), BD Maynooth 1944, DPhil Oxon 1949. Lectr, Univ. Coll., Dublin, 1949–53. *Publications*: *contrib*. Dominican Studies, Hist., Oxf. Hist. Ser. *Address*: Dept of Ethics and Politics, Univ. College, Belfield, Dublin 4.

Martin, Prof. David Alfred, BSc(Soc), PhD; Professor of Sociology, London School of Economics and Political Science, University of London, since 1971; *b* 1929; *m* 1962; three *s* one *d*. Educational Cert. Westminster College London 1952, BSc(Soc) London [External] 1959 (1st cl.), PhD London 1964. Asst Lectr, Sheffield Univ., 1961–62; Asst Lectr, LSE, 1962–64; Lectr, LSE, 1964–67; Reader, LSE, 1967–71; Edward Cadbury Lectr, Univ. of Birmingham, 1972–73. Acad. Gov., LSE, 1971– . *Publications*: Pacifism: an historical and sociological study, 1965; A Sociology of English Religion, 1967; ed, A Sociological Yearbook of Religion in Britain, 1968–70; ed, Anarchy and Culture, 1969; The Religious and the Secular, 1969; ed, 50 Key Words in Sociology, 1970; Tracts against the Times, 1973; R. D. Laing, in, The New Left, ed M. Cranston, 1970; England, in, European Social Stratification, ed M. Giner and M. S. Archer, 1971; The Behavioural Sciences and the Human Person, in, Technology and Social Justice, ed R. Preston, 1971; Religion in Europe, in, Europe, ed M. S. Archer and S. Giner, 1974; *contrib*. Brit. Jl Sociol., Europ. Jl Sociol., Internat. Jbh Relig., Rev. Mex. Sociol., Theol., Encounter, TLS, THES. *Address*: London School of Economics and Political Science, Aldwych, WC2A 2AE.

Martin, Prof. Rev. Francis Xavier, OSA; Professor of Medieval History, University College, Dublin, since 1962; *b* 1922. LPh, Augustinian College, Rome 1947, BA Univ. College Dublin 1949 (History), BD Gregorian Univ. Rome 1951, MA Univ. College Dublin 1952 (History), PhD Cambridge 1959 (History). Asst in History, Univ. Coll., Dublin, 1959–62; Vis. Prof., La Trobe Univ., Melbourne, 1972. Chm., Bd of History, Univ. Coll., Dublin, 1968–70; Mem., Irish Mss Commn, 1963– ; Mem., Royal Irish Acad., 1967– ; Trustee, Nat. Libr. Irel., 1971– ; Jt Ed, New History of Ireland, 1964– ; Mem., Council, Royal Soc. Antiqu. Irel., 1970– . *Publications*: Giles of Viterbo, 1469–1532, 1960; jt ed., Medieval Studies Presented to Aubrey Gwynn, 1961; Friar Nugent, Agent of the Counter-reformation, 1569–1635, 1962; The Irish Volunteers, 1913–

15, 1963; The Howth Gun-running, 1914, 1964; ed, 1916 and University College, Dublin, 1967; ed jtly, The Course of Irish History, 1967; ed, Leaders and Men of the Easter Rising: Dublin 1916, 1967; 1916 – Myth, Fact and Fiction (Studia Hibernica), 1968; ed jtly, The Scholar Revolutionary: Eoin MacNeill 1867–1945, 1973. *Address*: Dept of Medieval History, Univ. College, Dublin 4, Ireland.

Martin, Prof. Frederick Morris, BA, PhD; Professor of Social Administration, University of Glasgow, since 1972; *b* 1923; *m* 1947; one *s* two *d*. BA London, 1949 (1st cl. Psychology), PhD London 1953. Asst Lectr, LSE, 1949–52; Res. Fellow, London Sch. of Hygiene, and Lectr, Birkbeck Coll., 1952–55; Lectr, Univ. of Edinburgh, 1956–60; Sen. Lectr, Univ. of Edinburgh, 1960–65; Reader, Univ. of Edinburgh, 1965–67. Asst Dir of Res. and Intell., GLC, 1967–69; Head of Social Res. and Policy Div., 1969–71. Mem., Council for Educn and Trng of Health Visitors, 1971– ; Mem., Sociol. and Social Admin Cttee, SSRC, 1972– ; Chm., Wkg Party on Longitudinal Research, SSRC, 1973– ; Chm., Scott. Office Cttee on Social Work Stats, 1973– ; Mem., Central Council for Educn and Trng in Social Work, 1973– . *Publications*: (with Floud and Halsey) Social Class and Educational Opportunity, 1957; (with Rehin) Patterns of Performance in Community Care, 1968; (with Bone and Spain) Plans and Provisions for the Mentally Handicapped, 1972; *contrib*. Planning (Political and Economic Planning Series), WHO pubns. *Address*: Dept of Social Administration and Social Work, Univ. of Glasgow, Southpark Avenue, Glasgow G12 8LF.

Martin, Prof. Geoffrey Haward; Professor of History, University of Leicester, since 1973; *b* 1928; *m* 1953; three *s* one *d*. BA Oxon 1950 (2nd cl. Modern History), MA Oxon 1954, DPhil Oxon 1955; FRHistS. Asst Lectr in Economic History, Univ. Coll. of Leicester, 1952–55; Lectr in History, Univ. Coll. and Univ. of Leicester, 1955–66; Reader, 1966–73; Vis. Prof., Carleton Univ., Ottawa, 1958–59, 1967–68; Vis. Res. Fellow, Merton Coll., Oxford, 1971. Mem., Council, Brit. Records Assoc., 1966–69; Hon. Gen. Ed. (Medieval), Suffolk Records Soc., 1956– ; Public Orator, Univ. of Leicester, 1971– ; Dean of Fac. of Arts, 1972– . Besterman Medallist, Library Assoc., 1972. *Publications*: Early Court Rolls of Ipswich, 1954; The Story of Colchester, 1959; The Town, 1961; Royal Charters of Grantham, 1964; (with Sylvia McIntyre) Bibliography of British and Irish Municipal History, 1972; Ipswich Recognizance Rolls, 1294–1327: a calendar, 1973; *contrib*. Archives, Jl Transp. Hist., Trans Royal Hist. Soc. *Address*: Dept of History, The Univ., Leciester LE1 7RH.

Martin, Dr Geoffrey Thorndike, MA, PhD; Lecturer in Egyptology, University College London, since 1970; Site Director, Egypt Exploration Society, Saqqara, since 1971. BA London 1963; MA Cantab 1966, PhD Cantab 1969. Lady Wallis Budge Fellow in Egyptology, Christ's Coll., Cambridge, 1966–70. *Publications*: Egyptian Administrative and

Private-Name Seals, 1971; The Royal Tomb at El-'Amarna, vol. I, 1974. *Address*: Dept of Egyptology, Univ. College London, Gower Street, WC1E 6BT.

Martin, George McKenzie; Lecturer in German, University of Aberdeen, since 1965; *b* 1940. MA Aberdeen 1962 (1st cl. French and German). *Address*: Dept of German, Univ. of Aberdeen, Aberdeen AB9 1AS.

Martin, Graham Douglas Cameron, MA, MLitt, FIL; Lecturer in German, Department of Modern Languages, University of Strathclyde, since 1969; *b* 1937. BA Cantab 1960 (2nd cl. Mod. Langs), CertEd Cantab 1961, MA Cantab 1964, MLitt Dublin 1969 (Comp. Educn); FIL 1964, Mem. Mod. Lang. Assoc., Mem. Hist. Ver. Fürst. Liecht. Asst in English, Hochschule St Gallen für Wirtschafts- und Sozialwissenschaften, 1963–65; Asst Lectr in German, Strathclyde Univ., 1967–69. *Publications*: trans., W. Kranz: The Principality of Liechtenstein, 1967, 3rd edn 1973; *contrib*. Inc. Ling., Internat. Rev. Educn, Jahrb. Hist. Ver. Fürst. Liecht. *Address*: Dept of Modern Languages, Univ. of Strathclyde, Glasgow G1 1XH.

Martin, Graham Dunstan, MA, BLitt; Lecturer in French, University of Edinburgh, since 1967; *b* 1932; *m* 1954; 1969; three *s* one *d*. BA Oxon 1954, Cert Ed Manchester 1955; MA Oxon 1958, BLitt Oxon 1965. Asst Lectr, Edinburgh Univ., 1965–67. *Publications*: ed, and trans., P. Valéry: Cimetière marin, 1971; ed, and trans., Anthology of Contemporary French Poetry, 1972; trans. (with J. H. Scott) Love and Protest (Chinese poems), 1972; Language, Truth and Poetry, 1974; *contrib*. Mod. Lang. Rev., Forum, New Blackfriars. *Address*: Dept of French, Edinburgh Univ., Edinburgh EH8 9YL.

Martin, James Davidson; Lecturer in Hebrew and Old Testament, University of St Andrews, since 1969; *b* 1935; *m* 1961; one *s* two *d*. MA Glasgow 1957, BD Glasgow 1960, MA Glasgow 1962 (Post Grad. 1st cl. Semitic Languages), PhD Glasgow 1970. Mem., Soc. OT Study, Mem., Glasgow Univ. Oriental Soc. Minister, Parish of Dunscore, Dumfries, 1962–66; Asst in Old Testament Language and Literature, Glasgow, 1966–68; Lectr in Hebrew, Glasgow, 1968–69. *Publications*: trans. M. Noth: Numbers, 1968; trans. M. Weippert: The Settlement of the Israelite Tribes in Palestine, 1971; trans. G. von Rad: Wisdom in Israel, 1972; *contrib*. Vet. Testamen., Trans Glas. Univ. Orient. Soc. *Address*: St Mary's College, Univ. of St Andrews, Fife.

Martin, Dr John Edward; Cassel Reader in Economic Geography, University of London, since 1967; *b* 1929; *m* 1955; one *s* two *d*. BSc(Econ) London 1952 (1st cl.), PhD London 1961. Asst Lectr, LSE, 1953–57; Lectr, LSE, 1957–64; Vis. Prof., Wisconsin Univ. and Syracuse Univ., 1961–62; Sen. Lectr, LSE, 1964–67. *Publications*: Greater London: an Industrial Geography, 1966; *contrib*. Geog., Town Plan. Rev., Trans Inst. Brit. Geogrs. *Address*: Dept of Geography, London School of Economics, WC2A 2AE.

Martin, Prof. John Powell, MA, PhD; Professor of Sociology and Social Administration, University of Southampton, since 1967; *b* 1925; *m* 1951; three *s*. BA Reading 1951; Cert. in Social Science and Administration, LSE 1952; PhD London 1957, MA Cantab 1960; Mem., British Sociological Assoc., Mem., British Soc. of Criminology. Research Asst, 1952; Asst Lectr, 1953, Lectr 1957, LSE; Asst Dir of Research, Inst. Criminology, Cambridge, 1960; Fellow King's College, Cambridge, 1964–67; Hill Foundn Vis. Prof., Univ. of Minnesota, 1973; Vis. Fellow, Yale Law Sch., 1974. Mem., Exec. Cttee, Brit. Soc. Criminol., 1965–67; Mem., Sociological Studies Bd, CNAA, 1965–71; Mem., Sociology and Social Admin Cttee, SSRC, 1969–73 (Vice Chm., 1972–73); Mem., Bd of Visitors, HM Prison Albany, 1967– (Vice Chm., 1969–); Mem., Nuffield Foundn Cttee on Law and Society, 1969– . *Publications*: Social Aspects of Prescribing, 1957; Offenders as Employees, 1962; (with Gail Wilson) The Police: A Study in Manpower, 1969; (with Douglas Webster) The Social Consequences of Conviction, 1971; *contrib*. Criminology in Transition, 1964; The Future of Parole, 1972; *contrib*. Applied Stats, Brit. Jl. Criminol., Brit. Jl Sociol., New Society, Jl Royal Stat. Soc., Science Jl. *Address*: Dept of Sociology and Social Administration, The Univ., Southampton SO9 5NH.

Martin, Prof. Laurence Woodward; Professor of War Studies, University of London, King's College, since 1968; *b* 1928; *m* 1951; one *s* one *d*. BA Cambridge 1948, MA Cambridge 1952, MA Yale 1951, PhD Yale 1955. Instructor, Yale Univ., 1955–56; Asst Prof., MIT, 1956–61; Assoc. Prof., Sch. of Advanced International Studies, Johns Hopkins Univ., 1961–64; Prof. of International Politics, and Dean of the Faculty of Social Science, Univ. of Wales, 1964–68; Res. Assoc., Washington Center of Foreign Policy Res., Johns Hopkins Univ., 1966– . Mem., Soc. Science Res. Council (UK); Chm., Pol. Science Cttee; Mem., Res. Council, Georgetown Center of Internat. Strat. Studies; Acad. Adviser., Nat. Defence Coll.; Mem., Army Educn Adv. Bd; Mem., Foreign Off. Adv. Panel on Disarmament; Cnsltnt, Sandia Corp.; Stanford Res. Inst. *Publications*: (with A. Wolfers) The Anglo-American Tradition in Foreign Affairs, 1956; Peace without Victory: Woodrow Wilson and the British Liberals, 1958; Neutralism and Non-Alignment, 1963; Diplomacy in Modern European History, 1966; The Sea in Modern Strategy, 1967; Ballistic Missile Defence and the Alliance, 1969; (with R. Osgood et al.) America and the World, 1970; (with R. Osgood et al.) Retreat from Empire, 1973; Arms and Strategy, 1973; *contrib*. Amer. Pol. Science Rev., Internat. Aff., Jl Pol., Pol. Science Rev. *Address*: Univ. of London, King's College, Strand, WC2R 2LS.

Martin, Dr Roderick, MA; Official Fellow in Politics and Sociology, Trinity College, University of Oxford, and University (Faculty) Lecturer in Sociology, since 1969; *b* 1940; *m* 1963; one *s* two *d*. BA Oxon 1961 (1st cl. History), DPhil Oxon 1965, MA Oxon 464

1966. Mem., Brit. Sociol. Assoc. Asst Lectr Univ. of York, 1964–65; Lectr, 1965–66; Univ. Lectr in Sociology, Dept of Social and Administrative Studies, Oxford, and Sen. Res. Fellow, Jesus Coll., Oxford, 1966–69. *Publications*: Communism and the British Trade Unions, 1924–33; A Study of the National Minority Movement, 1969; ed (with D. E. H. Whitley), Sociology, Theology, and Conflict, 1969; (with R. H. Fryer), Redundancy and Paternalist Capitalism, 1972; *contrib*. Brit. Jl Indust. Relat., Brit. Jl Sociol., Sociol. *Address*: Trinity College, Oxford.

Martin, Ronald Haithwaite; Reader in Classics, Department of Latin, University of Leeds, since 1969; *b* 1915; *m* 1943. BA Leeds 1937, BA Cambridge 1939, MA Cambridge 1943. Asst Lectr, King's Coll., Newcastle upon Tyne, 1941–44; Asst Lectr, Univ. Coll., Southampton, 1944–46; Asst Lectr, then Lectr, and Sen. Lectr, Univ. of Leeds, 1946–69. *Publications*: ed, Terence: Phormio, 1959; *contrib*. Tacitus, ed T. A. Dorey, 1969; The Epitome Margaritae Eloquentiae of Laurentius Gulielmus de Saona, 1971; *contrib*. var. class. jls GB and overseas. *Address*: Dept of Latin, The Univ., Leeds LS2 9JT.

Martin, Tony, BA; Lecturer in Geography, University of Strathclyde, since 1966; *b* 1942; *m* 1964; one *s* one *d*. BA Liverpool 1963 (2nd cl.). *Address*: Dept of Geography, Univ. of Strathclyde, Livingstone Tower, Richmond Street, Glasgow.

Martindale, Andrew Henry Robert; Professor of Visual Arts, School of Fine Arts and Music, University of East Anglia, since 1974; *b* 1932; *m* 1959. BA Oxon 1956 (Sch. of Modern History, cl. II), Academic Diploma in History of Art (with distinction, Courtauld Inst. of Art, London Univ., 1959, MA Oxon; FSA 1968. Lectr, Courtauld Inst. of Art, London, 1959; Univ. of E Anglia: Sen. Lectr in Art History, 1965–74; Dean, Sch. of Fine Arts and Music, 1971–74. *Publications*: Man and the Renaissance, 1966; Gothic Art, 1967; The Rise of the Artist, 1972; *contrib*. Archaeol., Burlington Mag., Jl Brit. Archaeol Assoc. *Publication*: Treble Poets I, 1974. *Address*: School of Fine Arts and Music, Univ. of East Anglia, Norwich NOR 88C.

Marwick, Prof. Arthur, MA, BLitt, FRHistS; Professor of History, Open University, since 1969; *b* 1936. MA Edinburgh 1957, BLitt Oxon 1960; FRHistS. Asst Lectr, History, Aberdeen, 1959–60; Lectr, History, Edinburgh, 1960–69; Vis. Prof., SU New York, Buffalo, 1966–67. Mem., Cttee, Assoc. Contemporary Historians, 1968– ; Mem., Council, British Univ. Film Council, 1969– ; Mem., Management Cttee, Soc. of Authors, 1971– . *Publications*: The Explosion of British Society, 1963, 2nd edn 1972; Clifford Allen: the Open Conspirator, 1964; The Deluge: British Society and the First World War, 1965; Britain in the Century of Total War: war, peace and social change 1900–67, 1968; The Nature of History, 1970; War and Social Change in the Twentieth Century, 1974; *contrib*. Amer. Hist. Rev.,

Bull. of Inst. of Hist. Res., Eng. Hist. Rev., Jl Contemp. Hist., Scott. Hist. Rev. *Address*: Arts Faculty, Open Univ., Walton Hall, Milton Keynes MK7 6AA.

Marwick, Prof. Maxwell Gay, MA, BA(SS), PhD; Professor of Sociology, University of Stirling, since 1968; *b* 1916; *m* 1941; two *s*. BA South Africa 1935 (distinctions in Psychology and Geography), MA South Africa 1938 (distinction in Psychology), BA (Social Science) South Africa 1950, PhD Cape Town 1961, Univ. Educn Dip. South Africa 1939; FRAI. Mem., Assoc. Social. Anthropol. Brit. Commonwealth, Brit. Sociol. Assoc., Sociol. Assoc. Australia and NZ. Sen. Lectr, SA Native Coll., Fort Hare, 1948–49; Lectr, Univ. of Natal, 1950–53; Sen. Lectr, 1953–56; Dir, Inst. Social Res., 1955–56; Prof. of Social Anthropology, Univ. of Witwatersrand, 1957–63; Simon Sen. Fellow, Univ. of Manchester, 1962; Prof. of Anthropology and Sociology, Monash Univ., 1963–68; Disting. Vis. Prof., W Michigan Univ., 1965, 1968, 1970; Florence Purington Vis. Lectr, Mount Holyoke Coll., Mass., 1968. Fed. Govt Nominee, Council of Austral. Inst. Aborig. Studies, 1964–68. *Publications*: Sorcery in its Social Setting: a Study of the Northern Rhodesian Ceŵa, 1965; ed, Witchcraft and Sorcery: Selected Readings, 1970; *contrib*. Afr., Afr. Studies, Amer. Anthropol., Austral. Jl Science, Jl Afr. Hist. *Address*: Dept of Sociology, Univ. of Stirling, Stirling FK9 4LA.

Maslen, Elizabeth Jessie; Lecturer, Department of English, Westfield College, University of London, since 1971; *b* 1935; *m* 1960; three *s* one *d*. BA London 1957 (1st cl. Hons English), Dip. in Indo European Comparative Philology, Oxford 1959; Mem., English Assoc. Asst Lectr in English, Westfield Coll., London, 1957–59; Temp. Lectr, English Dept, Univ. of Singapore, 1967–69; Part-time Lectr, Westfield Coll., 1969–71. *Publication*: Treble Poets I, 1974. *Address*: Westfield College, Univ. of London, Kidderpore Avenue, NW3 7ST.

Mason, Dr Anthony; Lecturer, Centre for Study of Social History, University of Warwick, since 1971; *b* 1938; *m* 1962. BA Hull 1962 (Hons History), PhD Hull 1967. Dept of Adult Educn, Univ. Nottingham, 1965–66; Dept of History, Univ. Edinburgh, 1966–67; Dept of Econs, Univ. Hull, 1967–71. *Publications*: The General Strike in the North East, 1970; *contrib*. Internat. Rev. Social History. *Address*: Social History Dept, Univ. of Warwick, Coventry CV4 2AL.

Mason, Dr Christopher Michael; Lecturer, Department of Politics, University of Glasgow, since 1966; *b* 1941; *m* 1965; two *d*. BA Cantab 1963, MA Cantab 1965, PhD Cantab 1971; Member: Political Studies Assoc.; RIIA (Scottish Br.); Internat. Inst. for Strategic Studies; British Internat. Studies Assoc. First Sec. (Temporary), FCO, 1971–73. *Address*: Politics Dept, Glasgow Univ., Adam Smith Building, Glasgow G12 8RT.

Mason, Prof. Haydn Trevor; Professor of

European Literature, University of East Anglia, since 1967; *b* 1929; *m* 1955; one *s* one *d*. BA Wales 1949 (1st cl. French), MA Middlebury 1951, DPhil Oxon 1960. Instructor, Princeton Univ., 1954–57; Lectr, King's Coll., Univ. of Durham (Newcastle), 1960–63; Lectr, Univ. of Reading, 1964–65; Reader, Univ. of Reading, 1965–67. *Publications*: Pierre Bayle and Voltaire, 1963; ed, Marivaux, Les Fausses Confidences, 1964, 2nd ed 1971; ed and trans., Leibniz–Arnauld Correspondence, 1967; ed, Voltaire: Zadig and Other Stories, 1971; *contrib*. Fr. Studies, Mod. Lang. Rev., Romanic Rev., Stendahl Club, Studies on Voltaire and 18th Cent., TLS. *Address*: School of European Studies, Univ. of East Anglia, Norwich NOR 88C.

Mason, Kenneth Lewis John, BA; Senior Lecturer in Spanish, Department of Modern Languages, University of Salford, since 1971; *b* 1933; *m* 1960; one *s* one *d*. BA London 1954 (2nd cl. Spanish), DipEd Wales 1955. Lectr, Salford Univ., 1963–71. *Publications*: Advanced Spanish Course, 1967; Spanish Oral Drill Book, 1969; Key to Advanced Spanish Course, 1970; *contrib*. Bull. Hispan. Studies. *Address*: Dept of Modern Languages, Univ. of Salford, Salford M5 4WT.

Mason, Dr Sheila Mary, PhD; Lecturer in French, University of Birmingham, since 1968; *b* 1940. BA London 1962 (1st cl. French), PhD London 1971. Mem., Soc. Fr. Studies, Brit. Soc. 18th Cent. Studies. Asst Lectr, Birmingham, 1965–68. *Publications*: contrib. Livy, ed T. A. Dorey, 1971. *Address*: Dept of French, Univ. of Birmingham, PO Box 363, Birmingham B15 2TT.

Mason, Terry Robert Arthur, MA; Lecturer in Spanish, University of Newcastle upon Tyne, since 1966; *b* 1940; *m* 1965; three *d*. BA Oxon 1962 (1st cl. Spanish and French), MA Oxon 1966; CertEd (Postgrad.) Nottingham 1963. Chm., NE Assoc. Teachers of Spanish and Portuguese, 1970–72; Chm., Gov. Body: Monkseaton Middle Sch., Tyne and Wear, 1973– ; Monkseaton High Sch., Tyne and Wear, 1974– ; Vice-Chm., Gov. Body, Marden Bridge Middle Sch., 1973– . Mem., Whitley Bay Municipal Bor. Council, Northumberland, 1971–74. *Publications*: contrib. Vida Hispán., N & Q, Bull. Hisp. Stud., Hamburger Ibero-Amerikanische Studien. *Address*: Dept of Spanish and Latin American Studies, The Univ., Newcastle upon Tyne NE1 7RU.

Mason, Timothy Wright, MA, DPhil; Fellow and Tutor in Modern History, St Peter's College, University of Oxford, since 1971; *b* 1940; *m* 1970. BA Oxon 1962 (1st cl. Mod. Hist.), MA Oxon 1966, DPhil Oxon 1972. Asst Lectr, Univ. of York, 1964–65; Wiss. Asst. Free Univ., Berlin, 1965–66; Res. Fellow, St Antony's Coll., Oxford, 1966–71. Asst Ed., Past and Present, 1967–70. *Publications*: contrib. The Nature of Fascism, ed S. J. Woolf, 1968; German Democracy and the Triumph of Hitler, ed A. Nicholls and E. Matthias, 1971; *contrib*. Past Pres. *Address*: St Peter's College, Oxford.

465

Massa, Dr Ann Ruff; Lecturer in American Literature, School of English, University of Leeds, since 1971; *b* 1940. MA Edinburgh 1962, PhD Manchester 1965. Asst Lectr, Dept of English, Univ. Nottingham, 1965–67; Fellow, Dept Compar. Studies, Univ. Essex, 1967–70; ACLS Fellow, Univ. Chicago, 1970–71. *Publications*: Vachel Lindsay, 1970; *contrib.* Jl Amer. Studies. *Address*: School of English, Univ. of Leeds, Leeds LS2 9JT.

Masser, Francis Ian; Lecturer, Department of Civic Design, University of Liverpool, since 1964; *b* 1937; *m* 1962; one *d*. BA Liverpool 1958, MCD Liverpool 1960; AMTPI 1964. Mem., Reg. Science Assoc., 1969, Inst. Brit. Geogrs, 1962. Res. Fellow, Univ. of Rhodesia, 1960–61; Temp. Lectr, Univ. of Liverpool, 1961–62; Assoc. Planner, Shankland Cox Assoc., 1962–64. *Publications*: Introduction to the Use of Models in Planning, 1969; Analytical Models for Urban and Regional Planning, 1972; *contrib.* Archit. Jl, Archit. Rev., Ctt Soc., Environ. Plan., Jl TPI, Plan. Outlook, Town Plan. Rev. *Address*: Dept of Civic Design, Univ. of Liverpool, PO Box 147, Liverpool L69 3BX.

Massey, Dr David William; Lecturer in Urban Studies, Department of Civic Design, University of Liverpool, since 1970; *b* 1942. BA Leicester 1963 (Social Sciences), PhD Cantab 1970. Res. Asst, Univ. of Cambridge, 1966–67; Asst Lectr, Univ. of Glasgow, 1967–68, Lectr, 1968–70. Asst Editor, Town Planning Review, 1971– . *Address*: Dept of Civic Design, The Univ. of Liverpool, PO Box 147, Liverpool L69 3BX.

Masterman, Margaret (Mrs R. B. Braithwaite); Vice-President, Trustee and Fellow, Lucy Cavendish College, Cambridge, since 1965; Director of Research, Cambridge Language Research Unit, since 1956; *b* 1910; *m* 1932; one *s* one *d*. MA Cantab 1936 · Member: Aristotelian Soc., Linguistics Soc. Sometime Lectr, Philosophy of Language, Cambridge Univ.; Dir of Studies in Philosophy, Fitzwilliam House, Pembroke Coll., St Catharine's Coll., Cambridge. Co-Principal Investigatorship, Stanford Univ., 1969–72. Consultant: MIT 1956–57; Montreal Univ., 1968; Univ. of Victoria, 1969–72; Artificial Intelligence Unit, Stanford Univ., 1972. *Publications*: Metaphysical and Ideographic Language, in British Philosophy in the Mid-Century, ed Mace; The Potentiality of a Mechanical Thesaurus, 1956; What is a Thesaurus?, 1959; Semantic Message, Detection for Machine Translation using an Interlingua, 1961; The Nature of a Paradigm, in, Criticism and the Growth of Knowledge, ed Lakatos and Musgrave, 1972; Interlinguas (forthcoming); *contrib.* Proc. Aristotelian Soc., Proc. ASLIB Conference, TLS, Theoria and Theory, and other jls, conference procs, etc., on Information Science. *Address*: Lucy Cavendish College, Cambridge.

Masterman, Neville Charles, MA; Senior Lecturer (formerly Lecturer) in Modern History, University College, Swansea, since 1945; *b* 1912; *m* 1947; three *d*. BA Cantab 1935 (1st cl. Part I, 2nd cl. Part II), MA Cantab 1949. Lectr, Eötvös Collegium, Budapest, 1937–40. *Publications*: J. M. Ludlow, The Builder of Christian Socialism, 1963; The Forerunner: The Dilemmas of T. E. Elis, 1859–99, 1972; introd., Richard Cobden: The International Man, by J. A. Hobson, repr. 1968; *contrib.* Hist., Hist. Today, TLS, Victorian Studies, Anglo-Welsh Rev., New Hungarian Qly. *Address*: Dept of History, University College, Swansea SA2 8PP.

Masters, Lionel James; Lecturer in Archaeology, Department of Extra-Mural and Adult Education, University of Glasgow, since 1966; *b* 1942; *m* 1964; one *s* one *d*. BA Cantab 1965, MA Cantab 1969; FSAScot. Vice-Pres., Dumfries and Galloway Natural Hist. and Antiq. Soc., 1973– . *Address*: Dept of Extra-Mural and Adult Education, Univ. of Glasgow, Glasgow G12 8QQ.

Masterson, Prof. Patrick; Professor of Special Metaphysics, University College, Dublin, since 1972; *b* 1936; *m* 1964; one *s* two *d*. BA University College Dublin 1958 (1st cl. Philosophy), MA University College Dublin 1960, PhD Louvain 1962. Asst, Dept of Metaphysics, Univ. Coll., Dublin, 1963–66; Lectr, 1966–72. Chm., Irish Philos. Soc., 1971–72; Mem., Gov. Body, Univ. Coll., Dublin, 1969– ; Senate, NUI, 1972– ; Higher Educn Authority, 1972– . *Publications*: Atheism and Alienation: A Study of the Philosophical Sources of Contemporary Atheism, 1971; *contrib.* Irish Theol. Qly, Philos. Studies, Rev. Philos. Louvain, Studies. *Address*: Dept of Metaphysics, Univ. College, Belfield, Dublin 4, Ireland.

Mastin, Rev. Brian Arthur; Lecturer in Hebrew, University College of North Wales, since 1965; *b* 1938. BA Cantab 1960, MA Cantab 1963, MA Oxon (inc.) 1963. Asst Lectr in Hebrew, Univ. Coll. of North Wales, 1963–65. *Publications*: (with J. N. Sanders) A Commentary on the Gospel according to St John, 1968, pbk edn 1969; *contrib.* Ch Qly Rev., Jl Royal Anthropol. Inst., NT Studies, Palest. Explor. Qly, Scott. Jl Theol., Studia Evangelica, Zeits. für die alttestamentliche Wissenschaft. *Address*: Dept of Biblical Studies, Univ. College of North Wales, Bangor LL57 2DG.

Mather, Dr Alexander Smith; Lecturer in Geography, University of Aberdeen, since 1967; *b* 1943; *m* 1970. BSc (Hons) Aberdeen 1966, PhD 1972. Asst Lectr, Aberdeen Univ., 1967–70. *Publications*: *contrib.* Biol Conservation, Geogr. Mag., Scottish Geogr. Mag., Trans Inst. Brit. Geogrs. *Address*: Dept of Geography, Univ. of Aberdeen, St Mary's, High Street, Aberdeen AB9 2UF.

Mather, Frederick Clare, MA, FRHistS; Reader in History, University of Southampton, since 1971; *b* 1922; *m* 1965. MA Manchester 1948; Hon BA Manchester 1942; FRHistS 1963, Mem. Historical Assoc. 1949, Mem. Eccles. History Soc., 1972. Southampton University: Asst Lectr in History, 1949–51; Lectr, 1951–65; Sen. Lectr, 1965–71.

Mem. Council, Historical Assoc., 1957– , Vice-Pres., 1973– ; Mem. Senate, Univ. Southampton, 1970–72, Mem. Council, 1971–72. *Publications*: Public Order in the Age of the Chartists, 1959; contrib. Chartist Studies, ed Asa Briggs, 1959; contrib. The Layman in Christian History, ed Neill and Weber, 1963; Chartism, 1965, 2nd edn 1972; After the Canal Duke, 1970; contrib. Provincial Labour History, ed. J. H. Porter, 1972; *contrib.* Eng. Hist. Rev., History, Jl Soc. Army Hist. Res., Trans RHistS, Transport History. *Address*: Dept of History, Univ. of Southampton, Highfield, Southampton SO9 5NH.

Mathers, Dr James R., FRCPsych; Honorary Lecturer in Pastoral Studies, Department of Theology, University of Birmingham, since 1964; *b* 1916; *m* 1944; one *s* one *d*. MB ChB St Andrews 1938; DPM London 1949, FRC Psych London 1971. Med. Supt, Rubery Hill Hosp., Birmingham, 1959–71. *Address*: Dept of Theology, Univ. of Birmingham, PO Box 363, Birmingham B15 2TT.

Matheson, Prof. Arthur Alexander, QC (Scot), MA, LLB; Professor of Scots Law, University of Dundee (formerly Queen's College, University of St Andrews), since 1949; *b* 1919. MA Edinburgh (1st cl. Hons Classics), LLB Edinburgh (distinction); admitted to Faculty of Advocates, 1944; QC Scotland 1956. Queen's Coll., Dundee; Lectr in Public Internat. Law, 1950–60; Dean of Faculty of Law, 1955–58 and 1963–64; Master, 1958–66. Hon. Sheriff of Perth and Angus at Dundee, 1950. *Address*: 43 Sutherland Place, Dundee DD2 2HJ; Univ. of Dundee, Dundee DD1 4HN.

Matheson, Rev. Dr Peter Clarkson, MA, BD, PhD; Lecturer in Ecclesiastical History, University of Edinburgh, since 1966; *b* 1938; *m* 1965; one *s* one *d*. MA Otago 1960 (1st cl. History), BD Edinburgh 1963 (Dist. in Eccles. History), PhD Edinburgh 1969. Asst Lectr in Ecclesiastical History, Edinburgh, 1965–66. *Publications*: Cardinal Contarini at Regensburg, 1972; *contrib.* Juda, Scott. Ch. Hist. Soc. Rec. *Address*: Dept of Ecclesiastical History, New College, The Mound, Edinburgh.

Mathew, Dr William Mitchell; Lecturer in Economic History, University of East Anglia, since 1972; *b* 1938; *m* 1966; two *s* two *d*. MA Glasgow 1960 (1st cl. Economic History with Geography), PhD London 1964. Tutorial Asst, Dept of Economics, Leicester, 1963–64; Lectr, Dept of Economic History, Leicester, 1964–72. *Publications*: La Casa Gibbs y el Monopolío del Guano Peruano, 1974; *contrib.* Econ. Hist. Rev., Hisp. Amer. Hist. Rev., Jl Lat. Amer. Studies, Past Pres. *Address*: School of Social Studies, Univ. of East Anglia, Norwich NOR 88C.

Mathews, John Charles; Senior Lecturer, Department of Educational Research, University of Lancaster, since 1969; *b* 1923; *m* 1949; two *d*. BSc Liverpool 1943 (1st cl.), DipEd 1948; FRIC 1969. Member: Nuffield Science Teaching Projects, 1963–69; Schools Council Science Cttee, 1966–73. *Publications*:

Calculations in Chemistry, 1959, 2nd edn 1972; A Modern Chemistry Course, 1963, 2nd edn 1973; A Teacher's Guide to Assessment in Modern Chemistry, 1972; Problems in Modern Chemistry, 1971; Objective Tests in Modern Chemistry, 1972; Examinations and Assessment in Nuffield Advanced Chemistry, 1972; *contrib.* Educn in Chemistry, School Science Rev. *Address*: Dept of Educational Research, Univ. of Lancaster, Bailrigg, Lancaster.

Mathewson, Ian Robin Dighton, MA; Senior Lecturer in Classics, University of Exeter, since 1961; *b* 1916; *m* 1939; four *s*. BA Oxon 1938 (1st cl. Litt. Hum.), MA Oxon. Asst Instructor, Harvard Univ., 1938–39; Sen. Classics Master, St Paul's Sch., 1939–40, 1946–50; Lectr, Exeter Univ., 1950–60. Mem., Council, Hellenic Soc., 1955–57. *Publications*: *contrib.* Class. Qly, Greece Rome, Mnemosyne. *Address*: Dept of Classics, Queen's Building, The Univ., Exeter.

Mathias, Prof. Peter; Chichele Professor of Economic History, Oxford University, and Fellow of All Souls College, Oxford, since 1969; *b* 1928; *m* 1958; two *s* one *d*. BA Cantab 1951 (1st cl. with Dist. both pts Historical Tripos), MA Cantab 1954, MA Oxon 1969; FRHistS. Treas., Econ. Hist Soc., Asst Ed., Econ. Hist. Rev., 1955–57. Res. Fellow, Jesus Coll., Cambridge, 1953–55; Fellow, and Dir of Studies in Hist., Queens' Coll., Cambridge, 1955–68; Univ. Lectr, Hist. Faculty, Cambridge, 1955–68; Vis. Prof., Toronto, 1961; Delhi Sch. of Econ., 1967; Berkeley, 1967; Gildersleeve Prof., Barnard Coll., 1972; Penna, 1972. Chm., Business Arch. Council, 1967–72; Gov., Solihull Sch., 1966–72, Milton Abbey Sch., 1969– ; Sec., Internat. Econ. Hist. Assoc., 1960–62. *Publications*: The Brewing Industry in England, 1700–1830, 1959; English Trade Tokens, 1962; Retailing Revolution, 1967; The First Industrial Nation, 1969, American edn 1970, Japanese edn 1972; ed, Science and Society, 1972; Gen. ed., Debates in Economic History, 1967– ; *contrib.* Econ. Hist. Rev., Hist. Jl, Observer, BBC. *Address*: All Souls College, Oxford.

Mathias, William Alun, MA; Senior Lecturer in Education, University College, Cardiff, since 1972; *b* 1916; *m* 1955. BA Wales 1936 (1st cl. Welsh, 2nd cl. French 1937), DipEd Wales 1940, MA Wales 1949. Lectr, Univ. Coll., Cardiff, 1949–72. Mem., Council, Welsh Bibliog. Soc.; Ed., Educn for Develt, 1970– . *Publications*: *contrib.* Jl Welsh Bibliog. Soc., Llên Cymru. *Address*: Dept of Education, Univ. College, Cardiff CF1 1XL.

Mathur, Prof. Purushottam Narayan; Professor of Economics, University College of Wales, Aberystwyth, since 1970; *b* 1925; *m* 1951; two *s* two *d*. MA Agra 1946 (Maths), MA(Econ) Agra 1948, Dip. in Statistics Delhi 1951, Gold Medallist. Lectr, IARS, Delhi; Res. Off., Textile Enquiry Cttee; Res. Off., Planning Commission, Delhi; Sen. Lectr, Gokhale Inst., Poona Univ., 1955–59; Sen. Technical Assoc., Harvard Univ., 1959–

61; Reader, Gokhale Inst., Poona, 1961–63; Prof., 1964–70. Dir, Gokhale Inst., 1968–70; Sec., Input/Output Res. Assoc., 1965–70; Hd of Dept, Poona Univ., 1968–70. *Publications*: Studies in the Economics of Farm Management in Madhya Pradesh, 1958–62; ed, Economic Analysis and Input-Output Framework, 1967–70; *contrib*. Artha Vij., Ind. Econ. Jl, Internat. Econ. Rev., Kyklos, Rev. Econ. Studies, etc. *Address*: Economics Dept, Llandinam Building, Univ. College of Wales, Aberystwyth SY23 2AX.

Matthew, Dr Henry Colin Gray; Lecturer in Gladstone Studies, Christ Church, Oxford, since 1970; *b* 1941; *m* 1966; *s* one *d*. BA Oxon 1963, DipEd Makerere Coll., Univ. of E Africa 1964, DPhil Oxon 1970. Editor, The Gladstone Diaries, 1972– . *Publications*: The Liberal Imperialists: the ideas and politics of a post-Gladstonian élite, 1973; ed (with M. R. D. Foot) The Gladstone Diaries, vols iii and iv, 1974. *Address*: Christ Church, Oxford OX1 1DP.

Matthews, Prof. Denis; Professor of Music, University of Newcastle upon Tyne, since 1971; *b* 1919; *m* 1941, 1963; one *s* three *d*. RAM Thalberg Scholar, 1935; Blumenthal Composition Scholar, 1937. Concert pianist. Worshipful Co. of Musicians' Medal, 1938. *Publications*: In Pursuit of Music (autobiog.), 1966; Beethoven Piano Sonatas, 1967; Keyboard Music, 1972. *Address*: Dept of Music, Univ. of Newcastle upon Tyne, Newcastle upon Tyne NE1 7RU.

Matthews, Prof. Geoffrey, MA, PhD, FIMA; Shell Professor of Mathematics Education, Centre for Science Education, Chelsea College, University of London, since 1968; *b* 1917; *m* 1941; one *s* one *d*. BA Cantab 1938, MA Cantab 1942, PhD London 1959; FIMA. Mem., London Math. Soc. Chm., Teaching Cttee, Math. Assoc., 1964–68; Mem., Council, Math. Assoc., 1964– ; Jt Math. Council, UK, 1971– ; Organiser, Nuffield Math. Teaching Project, 1964–72. *Publications*: Calculus, 1964; Matrices, 1964; ed, Mathematics Through School, 1972; *contrib*. Proc. Konink. Acad. Wetens. *Address*: Centre for Science Education, Chelsea College, Bridges Place, SW6.

Matthews, Geoffrey Maurice; Reader in English Literature, University of Reading, since *s* 1966; *b* 1920; *m* 1st 1947, 2nd 1956; two *s* two *d*. BA Oxon 1948 (2nd cl. English), MA Oxon 1948, BLitt Oxon 1950. Mem. Cttee, Keats-Shelley Meml Assoc. Lectr, Turku Univ., and Åbo Akademi, Finland, 1949–55; Asst Lectr, Leeds Univ., 1956–58; Lectr, Leeds Univ., 1958–66. *Publications*: ed, Shelley: Selected Poems and Prose, 1964, 2nd edn 1966; Shelley, 1970; ed, Keats: The Critical Heritage, 1971; contrib. Shakespeare in a Changing World, 1964; The Morality of Art, 1969; contrib. New Cambridge Bibliography of English Literature; *contrib*. Ess. Crit., Engl. Lit. Hist., Jl Engl. Germ. Philol., Keats-Shelley Mem. Bull., Rev. Engl. Lit., Rev. Engl. Studies, Studia Neophilol., Times Lit. Supp. *Address*: Dept of English, Univ. of Reading, Whiteknights, Reading RG6 2AH.

Matthews, Gwynneth Margaret; Fellow and Tutor in Philosophy, St Anne's College, Oxford, since 1964; *b* 1925. BA Wales 1945, BA Oxon 1951, BPhil and MA Oxon 1953. Asst Lectr in Philosophy, Exeter, 1953–56; Lectr in Philosophy, University Coll. of N Wales, 1958–64. *Publications*: Plato's Epistemology, 1972; *contrib*. PAS, Mind. *Address*: St Anne's College, Oxford.

Matthews, Herbert Eric; Senior Lecturer, Department of Logic and Metaphysics, University of Aberdeen, since 1973 (Lecturer, 1963–73); *b* 1936; *m* 1967; two *s*. BA Oxon 1961 (1st cl. Lit. Hum.), BPhil Oxon 1964, MA Oxon 1964. *Publications*: contrib. Forum Mod. Lang. Studies, Locke Newsl., Philos. Bks, Philos. Qly, Amer. Philos. Qly, Second Order. *Address*: Dept of Logic and Metaphysics, Univ. of Aberdeen, Aberdeen AB9 1AS.

Matthews, Prof. Robert Charles Oliver, FBA; Drummond Professor of Political Economy, Oxford, and Fellow of All Souls College, since 1965; *b* 1927; *m* 1948; one *d*. BA Oxon 1947 (1st cl. Hon. Class. Mods, 1st cl. PPE), MA Oxon 1950; FBA 1968. Lectr, Merton Coll., Oxford, 1949; Asst Lectr, then Lectr, in Economics, Univ. of Cambridge, 1949–65; Fellow, St John's Coll., Cambridge, 1950–65; Vis. Prof., Univ. of California, Berkeley, 1961–62. Chm., SSRC, 1972– . *Publications*: A Study in Trade Cycle History, 1954; The Trade Cycle, 1958; (with M. Lipton and J. M. Rice) Chess Problems: introduction to an art; *contrib*. learned jls. *Address*: All Souls College, Oxford.

Matthews, Dr William Mervyn, DPhil; Lecturer, Department of Linguistic and Regional Studies, University of Surrey, since 1966; *b* 1932; *m* 1969; one *s*. BA Manchester 1955 (Hons Russian), Dip. in Economics and Politics Oxon 1956, DPhil Oxon 1961. Jun. Res. Fellow, Russian Res. Centre, Harvard, 1961–62; Jun. Res. Fellow, St Antony's Coll., Oxford, 1962–63, 1964–65; Temp. Lectr, Nottingham Univ., 1965–66; Vis. Res. Fellow, Russian Inst., Columbia Univ., NY, Spring 1969. *Publications*: Class and Society in Soviet Russia, 1972; Soviet Government, a Selection of Official Documents on Internal Policies, 1974. *Address*: Dept of Linguistic and Regional Studies, Univ. of Surrey, Guildford, Surrey GU2 5XH.

Mattingly, Prof. Harold Braithwaite; Professor of Ancient History, University of Leeds, since 1970; *b* 1923; *m* 1953; one *s* two *d*. BA Cambridge 1947 and 1948 (1st cl. Hons Classical Tripos Pts I and II), MA Cambridge 1952; FRNS 1956, FRHistS 1971, Mem., Soc. Promotion of Hellenic Studies, 1951– , Mem., Soc. Promotion of Roman Studies, 1950– . Lectr, Ancient History, Univ. of Nottingham, 1950, Reader, 1965–69. Mem. Council, RNS, 1960–64, 1968–72, Mem. Council, Soc. Promotion of Roman Studies, 1959–62, 1973–76. *Publications*: contrib. Ann. British Sch. at Athens, Athenaeum, Bull. de Corresp. Hellenique, Class. Qly, Class. Rev., Historia, Jl of Hellenic Studies, Jl of Roman Studies,

Latomus, Numismatic Chronicle, Proc. African Class. Assocs, Rivista di Cultura Classica e Medievale. *Address*: School of History, Univ. of Leeds, Leeds LS2 9JT.

Mattison, Frank Temperley; Registrar, University of Hull, since 1974; *b* 1932; *m* 1957; two *d*. BA Cantab 1954, MA Texas 1955, MA Cantab 1958, LLB London 1965. Teaching Asst, Univ. of Texas, 1954–63; Admin. Officer, Univ. of E Anglia, 1963–66; Sub-Dean, Faculty of Arts, Univ. of Liverpool, 1966–69; Dep. Sec., Univ. of Leeds, 1969–74. *Publications*: *contrib*. Jl Educn, Admin and History. *Address*: Registrar, Univ. of Hull, Hull HU6 7RX.

Mattock, Dr John Nicholas, MA, PhD; Lecturer in Arabic and Islamic Studies, University of Glasgow, since 1965; *b* 1938. BA Cantab 1961, MA Cantab 1964, PhD Cantab 1968. Res. Fellow, Pembroke Coll., Cambridge, 1963–65. Sec., Glasgow Univ. Orient. Soc., 1969–73; Co-ed, Jl Arab. Lit., 1970. *Publications*: Excerpts from Aristotle's Book of Animals, attrib. Maimonides (ATST 2), 1966; Hippocrates: On Superfoetation (ATST 3), 1968; (with M. C. Lyons) Hippocrates: On the Nature of Man (ATST 4), 1968; (with M. C. Lyons) Hippocrates: Airs, Waters and Places (ATST 5), 1969; Hippocrates: On Humours and On Nutriment (ATST 6), 1971. *Address*: Dept of Arabic and Islamic Studies, The Univ., Glasgow G12 8QQ.

Maud, *see* Redcliffe-Maud.

Maudsley, Prof. Ronald Harling; Professor of Law, King's College, London University, since 1967; *b* 1918; *m* 1949; two *s* one *d*. LLB Birmingham 1939, MA, BCL Oxford 1947, SJD Harvard 1959; Barrister-at-Law (Lincoln's Inn). Fellow, Brasenose Coll., 1947; Vis. Prof., Univ. of Miami, 1958; Univ. of Chicago, 1959; Univ. of San Diego, 1966, 1970; Cornell Univ., 1966–67; Univ. of Notre Dame, 1974. Sen. Tutor, Brasenose Coll., 1961–66; JP, Oxf., Cty, 1960–66; Governor, Millfield Sch., 1955; Council Mem., Malvern Coll., 1955; Chm., ATV Educnl Adv. Cttee, 1963; Council Mem., Bridgehead Housing Assoc., 1970; Cttee Mem., Consumer Cttee GB, 1971; Chm., Mngnt Cttee, Maudsley Hse, Oxford, 1966; Vice-Chm., Oxf. Prison Vis. Cttee; Capt., Warwicks Co. Cricket Club, 1948. *Publications*: (with Burn) Land Law: Cases and Materials, 1967, 2nd edn 1970; ed, Hanbury: Modern Equity, 9th edn 1969; (with Burn) Trusts and Trustees: Cases and Materials, 1972; *contrib*. Convey., Law Qly Rev., Mod. Law Rev., Univ. Miami Law Rev., Univ. San Diego Law Rev., Vanderbilt Law Rev. *Address*: Faculty of Laws, King's College, Strand, WC2R 2LS.

Maunder, W. Peter J.; Lecturer in Economics, Department of Economics, Loughborough University, since 1968; *b* 1943; *m* 1966; one *s* one *d*. BA Exeter 1964 (Econs), CertEd Exeter 1965, MSc Nottingham 1968 (AgricEcon). Editor of Econs, Jl of Econs Assoc. *Publications*: The Bread Industry in the United Kingdom, 1969; jtly,

Competition in British Industry, 1974; jtly, Bread: an assessment of the British bread industry, 1974. *contrib*. Jl of Agricl Econs, Bus. Economist, Economics. *Address*: Dept of Economics, Loughborough Univ., Loughborough LE11 3TU.

Maver, Prof. Thomas Watt, BSc, PhD, MIHVE; Director of the Architecture and Building Aids Computer Unit, Strathclyde (ABACUS), University of Strathclyde, since 1969; *b* 1938; *m* 1963; two *d*. BSc Glasgow 1960, PhD Glasgow 1965; MIHVE. Res. Fellow, Glasgow, 1961–67; Res. Fellow, Strathclyde, 1967–69. Vice-Chm., Design Res. Soc., 1972. *Publications*: Building Services Design, 1970; Building Performance, 1972; *contrib*. Archit. Jl, Operat. Res. Qly. *Address*: ABACUS, Dept of Architecture and Building Science, Univ. of Strathclyde, Glasgow G1 1XW.

Maw, Dr Joan Edith Mary; Lecturer in Swahili, Department of Africa, School of Oriental and African Studies, University of London, since 1966. BA Leeds 1962 (1st cl. English), Dip. General Linguistics Edinburgh 1963, PhD London 1968; London Teacher's Cert. 1949 (with distinction); ATCL 1955. Res. Fellow, SOAS, 1963–66. Mem., Steering Cttee, Centre for Lang. in Primary Educn, GLC, 1971– . *Publications*: Spoken English, 1966–68; Sentences in Swahili, 1969; Kiswahili Kusomea Certificate, 1972. *Address*: Dept of Africa, School of Oriental and African Studies, Malet Street, WC1E 7HP.

Maxcy, George Edwin; Senior Lecturer in Economics and Commerce, University of Hull, since 1964; *b* 1914; *m* 1945; one *d*. BA Cornell 1938, MA Leeds 1951. Res. Asst Hull Univ., 1951–53; Res. Asst, Dept of Applied Econs, Cambridge, 1953–56; Lectr, Hull Univ., 1957–64; Vis. Fellow, Melbourne Univ., 1960. *Publications*: The Motor Industry, in, Effects of Mergers, ed P. L. Cook, 1958; (with A. Silbertston) The Motor Industry, 1959, Japanese edn 1965; The Motor Industry, in, The Economics of Australian Industry, ed A. Hunter, 1963; *contrib*. Yorks Bull. Econ. Soc. Res. *Address*: Dept of Economics and Commerce, Hull Univ., Hull HU6 7RX.

Maxwell, Ian Stanley; Reader in Historical Geography, Department of Geography, University of Sheffield, since 1964; *b* 1917; *m* 1941; three *s* one *d*. BA Cantab 1939, MA Cantab 1948. Asst Lectr, Univ. of Sheffield, 1946–49; Lectr, Univ. of Sheffield, 1949–59; Sen. Lectr, Univ. of Sheffield, 1959–64. *Publications*: ed (with H. C. Darby) The Domesday Geography of Northern England, 1962. *Address*: Dept of Geography, Univ. of Sheffield, Sheffield S10 2TN.

Maxwell, Neville; Senior Research Officer, Institute of Commonwealth Studies, Oxford University, since 1970; *b* 1926; *m* 1958; two *s* one *d*. BA McGill 1950, MA Cantab 1958. South Asia Correspondent of The Times, 1959–67; Sen. Fellow, Sch. of Oriental and African Studies, London, 1967–69. *Publications*: India's China War, 1970; *contrib*.

469

Amer. Schol., China Qly, For. Affairs, Internat. Affairs, Pacific Commun. *Address*: Institute of Commonwealth Studies, 21 St Giles, Oxford OX1 3LA.

Maxwell, Robert Millar; Reader in Architecture, University College, London, since 1970; *b* 1922; *m* 1951 (marr. diss. 1973); one *s* two *d*. BArch Liverpool 1949 (Hons), Dip. in Civic Design Liverpool 1950; ARIBA. Sen. Lectr, UCL, 1962–70; Vis Prof., Princeton Univ., 1966– . Partner, D. Stephen and Partners (Architects), 1962– ; Mem., Council, Archit. Assoc., 1964–65; Bd of Archit. Educn, RIBA, 1967– . *Publications*: A Decade of British Architecture, 1972; *contrib*. Archit. Des., Archit. Rev., Jl Royal Inst. Brit. Archit. *Address*: School of Environmental Studies, Univ. College, Gower Street, WC1E 6BT.

May, Cedric Roger Paul, MA; Lecturer in French Language and Literature, University of Birmingham, since 1963; *b* 1934; *m* 1st 1958, 2nd 1966; two *s* three *d*. BA Leeds 1957 (1st cl. French), CertEd Leeds 1959, MA Leeds 1960. Asst Master, Qu. Eliz. Grammar Sch., Wakefield, 1959–61; Lectr in French, Macdonald Coll., McGill Univ., Montreal, 1961–63. *Publications*: contrib. Supplement to the Oxford Companion to Canadian History and Literature, ed W. Toye, 1973; *contrib*. Rev. Lett. Mod. *Address*: Dept of French, The Univ., PO Box 363, Birmingham B15 2TT.

May, Philip Radford, BA, JP; Lecturer in Education, Department of Education, University of Durham, since 1960; *b* 1928; *m* 1953; two *d*. BA Manchester 1950 (2nd cl. English Language and Lit.), Dip. and Cert. Ed Sheffield 1952 (distinction). Chm., Nat. Assoc. Christian Teachers, 1971–75. Magistrate, 1971. *Publications*: (with O. R. Johnston) Religion in Our Schools, 1968; Moral Education in School, 1971; Which Way to School?, 1972; Teenage Morality (forthcoming); *contrib*. Brit. Jl Educnl Studies, Dur. Res. Rev., Educnl Res., Learn. Liv., Spectrum. *Address*: Dept of Education, Univ. of Durham, Old Elvet, Durham City.

May, Ranald S., BCom, MA; Lecturer, Department of Economics, University of St Andrews, since 1963; *b* 1932; *m* 1968. MA St Andrews 1954 (1st cl. Econs and Hist.), BCom Queen's University Canada 1956 (1st cl.). Shell Fellow, Univ. of St Andrews, 1963–68. Treasurer, Scott. Econ. Soc., 1973– . *Publications*: *contrib*. Jl Develop. Studies, Scott. Jl Pol. Econ. *Address*: Dept of Economics, Univ. of St Andrews, St Andrews, Fife KY16 9AJ.

Mayall, James B. L.; Lecturer in International Relations, London School of Economics and Political Science, since 1966; *b* 1937; *m* 1964; one *d*. BA Cantab 1960 (1st cl. History). Sir John Dill Fellow, Princeton Univ., 1960–61. Bd of Trade, 1961–64, 1965–66; 1st Sec. (Econ.), Brit. High Commn, New Delhi, 1964–65; Mem., Civil Service Selection Bd Observer Panel, 1969– . Associate Editor, Survey and Documents on Internat. Aff., Royal Inst. Internat. Aff.,

1968–71. *Publications*: Africa: The Cold War and After, 1971; ed (with D. C. Watt) Current British Foreign Policy: Documents, Statements, Speeches 1970, 1971; 1971, 1972; ed (with D. C. Watt and C. Navari) Documents on International Affairs 1962, 1970; 1963, 1972. *Address*: Dept of International Relations, London School of Economics and Political Science, WC2A 2AE.

Mayer, Prof. Adrian Curtius; Professor of Indian Anthropology, University of London, since 1966; *b* 1922; *m* 1949; two *d*. BA St Johns College Annapolis 1943, Dip. Anthrop. London 1949, PhD London 1953; FRAnth-Inst. Res. Fellow, Australian Nat. Univ., 1953–56; Lectr, SOAS, 1956–62; Reader, SOAS, 1962–66; Vis. Prof., Col. de Mexico, 1959; Vis. Prof., Univ. of Delhi, 1970. Hon. Ed. Man. (Jl Royal Anthrop. Inst.), 1965–69. Mem. SSRC, 1973– . *Publications*: Land and Society in Malabar, 1952; Caste and Kinship in Central India, 1960; Peasants in the Pacific, 1961; Indians in Fiji, 1963. *Address*: Dept of Anthropology and Sociology, School of Oriental and African Studies, Univ. of London, Malet Street, WC1E 7HP.

Mayer, Prof. Claude Albert; Professor and Head of Department of French, University of Liverpool, since 1965; *b* 1918; *m* 1947; one *s*. BA London 1947 (1st cl. French), PhD London 1949 (French); Hon. D de l'U, Montpellier 1966. Asst, UCL 1948; Asst Lectr, UC Hull, 1949; Lectr, UC Southampton, 1950–55; Lectr, Bedford Coll., London, 1955–59; Reader, Bedford Coll., London 1959–65. *Publications*: Bibliographie des Œuvres de Clément Marot, 2 vols, vol. I Manuscrits, vol. II, Editions, Geneva, 1954; La Religion de Marot, Geneva, 1960, repr. Paris, 1973; Œuvres complètes de Clément Marot, London, vol. I, Les Epîtres, 1958, vol. II, Œuvres satiriques, 1962, vol. III, Œuvres lyriques, 1964, vol. IV, Œuvres diverses, 1966, vol. V, Les Epigrammes, 1970; Clément Marot (Anthologie), Paris, 1964, repr. 1969; Clément Marot, Paris, 1972; *contrib*. Bibliothèque d'Humanisme et Renaissance, French Studies, Studi Francesi, Rev. d'Hist. Lit. de la France, Rev. de Lit. Comp. *Address*: Dept of French, The Univ., Liverpool L69 3BX.

Mayer, Prof. Jacob Peter; Professor at the University of Reading, since 1967; *b* 1903; *m*; one *s*. Chevalier, Legion of Honour, 1959, Officier, 1974. Mem. Commn Nationale pour l'Edition des Œuvres d'Alexis de Tocqueville. LSE, 1943–45; Rockefeller Fellow, 1948–60; Nato Prof. of History, Univ. Washington, 1959–60; Prof. of History and Sociology, Univ. Colorado, 1961–62. War Service (Intelligence), 1939–43. *Publications*: Political Thought: The European Tradition, 1939, 2nd edn 1942, Amer. and Mexican edns; Alexis de Tocqueville: A Biographical Study in Political Science, 1939, 11th edn 1972, trans. French, German, Finnish, Spanish, Korean; Political Thought in France, 1943, 3rd edn 1960, trans. Japanese; Max Weber and German Politics, 1944, latest edn 1956, trans. Japanese, Spanish; Sociology of Film, 1946, augmented edn 1972; ed, Alexis de Tocqueville: Œuvres Complètes, 20 vols,

1951– ; ed, Tocqueville: Journeys to England and Ireland, 1959, revised edn 1966; ed, Tocqueville: Democracy in America, 1968, 5th edn 1973; Tocqueville: L'Ancien Régime et la Revolution, 1965, 4th augmented edn 1972; ed, Tocqueville, The Recollections, 1949, 6th edn 1966, augmented edn with A. P. Kerr 1970. *Address*: Dept of French Studies, Tocqueville Research Centre, Univ. of Reading, Whiteknights, Reading RG6 2AH.

Mayes, Dr Andrew David Hastings; Lecturer, Department of Hebrew, University of Dublin, since 1970; *b* 1943; *m* 1968; one *d*. BA TCD 1964, PhD Edinburgh 1969, MA TCD 1971; Mem., Soc. for Old Testament Study. Jun. Lectr, TCD, 1967–70. *Publications*: Israel in the Period of the Judges, 1974; *contrib*. ITQ, VT. *Address*: Trinity College, Dublin 2, Ireland.

Mayes, Anne C.; Lecturer in Economic and Social Statistics, University of Exeter, since 1968; *b* 1944; *m* 1972. BSc Wales 1967. Mem. Univ. Senate, Exeter, 1972– . *Address*: Dept of Economics, Univ. of Exeter, Exeter EX4 4QJ.

Maynard, Alan Keith; Lecturer in Economics, University of York, since 1971; *b* 1944; *m* 1968; two *s*. BA Newcastle upon Tyne 1967 (Economic Studies cl. 1); BPhil York 1968 (Econs); Member: Royal Economic Soc.; Amer. Economic Assoc. Asst Lectr and Lectr, Univ. of Exeter, 1968–71. Fellow, European Inst. for Health Care Studies, Univ. of Louvain, Belgium. *Publications*: (with M. H. Cooper) The Price of Air Travel, 1971; (with D. N. King) Rates or Prices?, 1972; *contrib*. Jl of Transport Econs and Policy, Social Sci. and Medicine, Econ. Studies, Social and Econ. Admin., Brit. Jl of Psychiatry and Medical Care. *Address*: Dept of Economics, Univ. of York, Heslington, York YO1 5DD.

Maynard, Prof. Geoffrey Walter, BSc(Econ), PhD; Professor of Economics, University of Reading, since 1965; *b* 1921; *m* 1949; two *d*. BSc(Econ) London 1950, PhD Wales 1961; FREconSoc. Asst Lectr, Univ. Coll. of Wales, Aberystwyth, 1950–51; Lectr, Univ. Coll. of S Wales, Cardiff, 1951–65; Vis. Lectr, Univ. of Birmingham, 1960–62; Fellow, Johns Hopkins Univ., Baltimore, 1957–58; Vis. Lectr, Univ. of Minnesota, 1958. Econ. Cnsltnt, HM Treasury, 1962–65; Econ. Adv., Harvard Univ. Develop. Adv. Service, 1965–67; Econ. Cnsltnt, Overseas Develop. Admin, FCO, 1967–71; IBRD, 1971–72; Under-Sec. (Econ.), Treasury, 1972–74. Ed., Bankers' Mag., 1968–72. *Publications*: Economic Development and the Price Level, 1963; Chapters, in, Economic Growth, ed E. Nelson; Development Policy: Theory and Practice, ed G. Papanek; Commonwealth Policy in a Global Context, ed Streeter and Corbet; *contrib*. Econ. Internat., Econ. Jl, Jl Develop. Studies, Ox. Econ. Papers. *Address*: Dept of Economics, Univ. of Reading, Whiteknights Park, Reading RG6 2AH.

Maynard, Winifred Annie, BA, BLitt; Senior Lecturer in English Literature, University of Edinburgh, since 1965; *b* 1924. BA Dunelm 1945 (1st cl. English), DipEd Dunelm 1946, BLitt Oxon 1950. Asst, Edinburgh Univ., 1948–51; Lectr, 1951–65. *Publications*: contrib. The Cambridge Milton; *contrib*. Rev. Engl. Studies, Music Lett. *Address*: David Hume Tower, George Square, Edinburgh EH8 9JX.

Mayo, Prof. Bernard; Professor of Moral Philosophy, University of St Andrews, since 1968; *b* 1920; *m* 1948; four *d*. BA Oxon 1947 (1st cl. Lit. Hum.), MA Oxon 1947. Lectr, Birmingham Univ., 1947–62; Reader, Birmingham Univ., 1962–68; Sub-Dean of Arts, Birmingham Univ., 1966–68; Ed., Analysis, 1956–65; Ed., Philos. Qly, 1973– ; Vis. Prof., Brown Univ., 1961. Lt and Capt., Royal Signals, 1942–45. *Publications*: The Logic of Personality, 1952; Ethics and the Moral Life, 1956; *contrib*. Analysis, Mind, Philos., Philos. Qly, Philos. Rev., Philos. Sci., Proc. Aristot. Soc. *Address*: Dept of Moral Philosophy, Univ. of St Andrews, Fife KY16 9AJ.

Mayr-Harting, Dr Henry Maria Robert Egmont, MA, DPhil; Fellow and Tutor in Modern History, St Peter's College, Oxford University, since 1968; *b* 1936; *m* 1968; one *s* one *d*. BA Oxford 1957 (1st cl. Hist.), MA, DPhil Oxford 1961; FRHistSoc. Asst Lectr, Liverpool Univ., 1960–63; Lectr, 1963–68. Treas., Canterbury and York Soc., 1966–70. *Publications*: The Acta of the Bishops of Chichester, 1075–1207 (Canterbury and York Society no. 130), 1965; The Coming of Christianity to Anglo-Saxon England, 1972; contrib. Studies in Church History, ed G. J. Cuming; *contrib*. EHR, Jl Eccles. Hist. *Address*: St Peter's College, Oxford.

Mead, Roger; Senior Lecturer in Applied Statistics since 1971, and Head of Department of Applied Statistics since 1974, University of Reading; *b* 1938; *m* 1961; two *s* one *d*. BA 1960 (2nd cl.), Dip. in Math. Stats, 1961, Cantab; Biometric Soc., RSS. Lectr, Univ. of Reading, 1966–71. *Publications*: *contrib*. Applied Stats, Biometrics, Biometrika, Computer Jl, Jl Ecol., Jl Hort. Sci., JRSS (A), Nature. *Address*: Dept of Applied Statistics, Univ. of Reading, Whiteknights, Reading RG6 2AH.

Mead, Prof. William Richard, DSc(Econ); Professor, and Head of Department of Geography, University College, London, since 1966; *b* 1915. BSc(Econ) London 1937, MSc(Econ) London 1939, PhD London 1946, DSc(Econ) London 1967; Hon. Doctorate Uppsala 1966, Helsinki 1969. Asst Lectr, Univ. of Liverpool, 1947–49; Rockefeller Fellowship, 1949–50; Lectr, then Reader, UCL, 1950–60. Hon. Sec., Royal Geog. Soc., 1967– ; Pres., Inst. Brit. Geog., 1971. *Publications*: Farming in Finland, 1953; An Economic Geography of the Scandinavian States in Finland, 1958; (with E. H. Brown) The United States and Canada, 1962, 2nd edn 1967; (with H. Smeds) Winter in Finland, 1967; Finland (Nations of the Modern World), 1968; (with W. Hall) Scandinavia, 1972; The Scandinavian Northlands, 1973. *Address*: University College London, WC1E 6BT.

Meade, James Edward, CB, MA, FBA; Nuffield Research Fellow, since 1969, and Fellow of Christ's College, Cambridge, since 1957; *b* 1907; *m* 1933; one *s* three *d*. MA Oxon 1933, MA Cantab 1957; Hon. Doc. Basel 1961, Hon. Doc. Hull 1965; Hon. Fellow, LSE; Hon. Fellow, Oriel Coll., Oxford; Hon. Fellow, Hertford Coll., Oxford; Hon. Mem., Amer. Econ. Assoc., 1962; Hon. Mem., Amer. Acad. Arts Sci., 1966. Fellow and Lectr in Economics, Hertford Coll., Oxford, 1930–37; Bursar, Hertford Coll., Oxford, 1934–37; Mem., Economic Section, League of Nations, 1938–40; Econ. Asst, Econ. Section Cabinet Offices, 1940–45; Dir, Econ. Section Cabinet Offices, 1946–47; Prof. of Commerce (Internat. Trade), LSE, 1947–57; Vis. Prof., Austral. Nat. Univ., 1956; Prof. of Political Econ., Cambridge, 1957–68. Mem., Council, Royal Econ. Soc., 1945–62 (Pres., 1964–66, Vice-Pres., 1966–); Mem., Council, Eugenics Soc., 1962–68 (Treas., 1963–67); Pres., Sect. F, Brit. Assoc. Advancement Sci., 1957: Chm., Econ. Survey Mission, Mauritius, 1960; Governor, Nat. Inst. Econ. Soc. Res., 1947– ; Governor, LSE, 1960– ; Governor, Malvern Coll., 1972– . *Publications*: Public Works in their International Aspects, 1933; The Rate of Interest in a Progressive State, 1933; Economic Analysis and Policy, 1936; Consumers' Credit and Unemployment, 1937; League of Nations World Economic Surveys, 1937–8, 1938–39; The Economic Basis of a Durable Peace, 1940; (with R. Stone) National Income and Expenditure, 1944; Planning and the Price Mechanism, 1948; The Theory of International Economic Policy, 1951–55; A Geometry of International Trade, 1952; Problems of Economic Union, 1953; The Theory of Customs Unions, 1955; The Control of Inflation, 1958; A Neo-classical Theory of Economic Growth, 1960; (jtly) Three Case Studies in European Economic Union, 1962; Efficiency, Equality and the Ownership of Property, 1964; Principles of Political Economy, 1965–71; The Theory of Indicative Planning, 1970; The Theory of Economic Externalities, 1973. *Address*: Christ's College, Cambridge.

Meadows, Prof. Arthur Jack; Professor of Astronomy, since 1971, and of the History of Science, since 1972, University of Leicester; *b* 1934; *m* 1958; one *s* two *d*. BA Oxon 1957 (1st cl. Physics), MA Oxon 1959, DPhil Oxon 1959, MSc London 1966 (Hist. of Science, with distinction); FRAS. Asst Prof., Univ. of Illinois, 1959–61; Lectr, St Andrews, 1961–64; Asst Keeper, Brit. Mus., 1964–65; Lectr, Leicester Univ., 1965–69; Sen. Lectr, Leicester Univ., 1969–71. Mem., Council, Royal Astron. Soc., 1970–73; Ed., Qly Jl RAS, 1971– . *Publications*: Stellar Evolution, 1967; The High Firmament, 1969; Early Solar Physics, 1970; Science and Controversy, 1972; Communication in Science, 1974; *contrib*. Ann. Science, Nature. *Address*: Dept of Astronomy and History of Science, Univ. of Leicester, Leicester LE1 7RH.

Meager, Ruby Lilian; Reader in Philosophy, Birkbeck College, University of London, since 1968; *b* 1916. BA 1950, BPhil, MA 1953, Oxon. Lectr, Bedford Coll., Univ. of London, 1956–68. *Publications*: *contrib*. Brit. Jl Aesthetics, Proc. Aristotelian Soc. *Address*: Dept of Philosophy, Birkbeck Coll., Malet Street, WC1E 7HX.

Meakin, David; Lecturer, Department of French, University of Bristol, since 1967; *b* 1943; *m* 1965; one *s*. BA Oxford 1965 (1st cl. Hons), BPhil Oxford 1967 (General and Comparative Literature). Lectr, Univ. of Bristol, 1967. *Publications*: *contrib*. Europ. Stud. Rev., FMLS. *Address*: Dept of French, Univ. of Bristol, Queen's Road, Bristol.

Medcalf, Stephen Ellis, BLitt, MA; Lecturer, School of European Studies, University of Sussex, since 1966; *b* 1936. BA Oxon 1959 (2nd cl. Classical Mods 1957, 1st cl. English 1959), MA Oxon 1962, BLitt Oxon 1964. Asst Master, Malvern Coll., 1962–63; Asst Lectr, Univ. of Sussex, 1963–66. *Publications*: ed, J. Glanvill: The Vanity of Dogmatizing: The Three 'Versions', 1970; 'Virgil's Aeneid', in, Literature and Western Civilisation, ed D. Daiches and A. K. Thorlby, 1972; contrib. Penguin Companion to Literature, English and Commonwealth, 1971. *Address*: Arts Building, Univ. of Sussex, Falmer, Brighton, Sussex BN1 9QN.

Meddis, Raymond, BA, PhD; Lecturer in Psychology, Bedford College, University of London, since 1965; *b* 1944; *m* 1965. BA London 1965 (1st cl. Psychology), PhD London 1969; ABPsS. *Address*: Dept of Psychology, Bedford College, Regent's Park, NW1 4NS

Medhurst, Dr Kenneth Noel; Senior Lecturer, Department of Government, University of Manchester, since 1973; *b* 1938; *m* 1968; one *s*. MA Edinburgh 1961, PhD Manchester 1969 (Polit. Science). Lectr in Govt, Univ. Manchester, 1963. *Publications*: The Basques (monograph), 1972; Allende's Chile, 1973; Government in Spain, 1973; The Changing Political Role of the Roman Catholic Church in Colombia (forthcoming); *contrib*. Govt and Opposition. *Address*: Dept of Government, Univ. of Manchester, Manchester M13 9PL.

Medley, Margaret; Curator and Honorary Lecturer in Chinese Art, Percival David Foundation of Chinese Art, and Far East Department, School of Oriental and African Studies, University of London, since 1959; *b* 1918. BA London 1950; Member: RAS; Oriental Ceramic Soc.; Internat. Inst. of Conservation; FSA. Chinese Art Librarian, Courtauld Inst. of Art and of Eastern Art Library, SOAS, 1950–59. *Publications*: Handbook of Chinese Art, 1964; Yüan Stoneware and Porcelain, 1974; *contrib*. Ars Orientalis, Oriental Art, Trans Oriental Ceramic Soc. *Address*: Percival David Foundn of Chinese Art, 53 Gordon Square, WC1.

Medlik, Prof. Slavoj, BCom, MA, FHCIMA; Professor of Hotel and Catering Administration, University of Surrey, since 1966; *b* 1928; *m* 1954; three *d*. BCom Dunelm 1954, MA Dunelm 1959; FHCIMA. Dean, Fac. of Human Studies, Univ. of Surrey, 1970–72;

Ind. Mem., Econ. Develop. Cttee, Hotel and Catering Industry, 1966– . *Publications*: The British Hotel and Catering Industry, 1961; (jtly) A Manual of Hotel Reception, 1967, 2nd edn 1969; Profile of the Hotel and Catering Industry, 1972; (jtly) Tourism: Past, Present and Future, 1974. *Address*: Dept of Hotel and Catering Management, Univ. of Surrey, Guildford, Surrey GU2 5XH.

Medwin, Prof. R. B. G.; *see* Gardner-Medwin.

Meech, Peter Hawken, BA, MA; Lecturer, Department of German, University of Stirling, since 1970; *b* 1942; *m* 1964; one *s* one *d*. BA Wales 1964; MA Manchester 1968. Lectr, Magee Univ. Coll., Londonderry, 1966–68; Lectr, New Univ. of Ulster, 1968–70. *Publications*: contrib. Forum Mod. Lang. Studies. *Address*: Dept of German, Univ. of Stirling, Stirling FK9 4LA.

Meek, Harold Alan; Senior Lecturer, Department of Architecture, Queen's University, Belfast, since 1973; *b* 1922; *m* 1943; one *d*; *m* 1973. BA Manchester 1951; FRIBA 1970. Lectr, QUB, 1967–73. Mem., Historic Bds Council, NI, 1973. *Publications*: Ancient Monuments of N Ireland in State Care, 1962, 5th edn 1966; contrib. Encyc. Mod. Arch., 1963; contrib. AR, RIBAJ, UJA. *Address*: Dept of Architecture, QUB, Belfast BT7 1NN.

Meek, Prof. Ronald Lindley, MA, LLM, PhD; Tyler Professor of Economics, University of Leicester, since 1963; *b* 1917; *m* 1951; one *s* one *d*. LLM New Zealand 1939, MA New Zealand 1946, PhD Cambridge 1949. Lectr, Glasgow Univ., 1948–59; Sen. Lectr, Glasgow Univ., 1960–63. Mem., E Midlands Econ. Plan. Council, 1967– . *Publications*: ed, Marx and Engels on Malthus, 1953; Studies in the Labour Theory of Value, 1958; The Economics of Physiocracy, 1962; Economics and Ideology, 1967; ed, Quesnay's Tableau Economique, 1971; Figuring Out Society, 1972; Turgot on Progress, Sociology and Economics, 1973; ed, Precursors of Adam Smith, 1973; contrib. Econ. Jl, Hist. Pol. Econ., Scott. Jl Pol. Econ. *Address*: Dept of Economics, Univ. of Leicester, Leicester LE1 7RH.

Meenan, Prof. James, MA; Professor of Political Economy, University College, Dublin, since 1961; *b* 1910; *m* 1945; three *d*. MA Dublin 1932; MRIA 1940. Asst Lectr in Political Economy, UC, Dublin, 1936–51, Lectr, 1951–61. Dean of Faculty of Commerce, UC, Dublin, 1961– . Pres., Statistical and Social Inquiry Soc. of Ireland, 1956–59. Mem. Council, RIA, 1960–62; Mem. Council, Econ. and Social Res. Inst., 1960– . *Publications*: The Italian Corporative System, 1944; ed (with D. A. Webb), A View of Ireland, 1956; The Irish Economy since 1922, 1970; contrib. Jl Stats and Social Inquiry Soc. of Ireland. *Address*: Univ. College, Dublin.

Meijer, Prof. Reinder Pieter, DrsLitt,

PhD; Professor of Dutch Language and Literature, University of London, Bedford College, since 1971; *b* 1926; *m* 1950; one *s* two *d*. DrsLitt Amsterdam 1950, PhD Melbourne 1958. Lectr, Univ. of Melbourne, 1951–58; Sen. Lectr, Univ. of Melbourne, 1958–66; Reader, Univ. of Melbourne, 1966–71. *Publications*: (with Jacob Smit) Dutch Grammar and Reader, 1958, 3rd edn 1969; Max Havelaar 1860–1960, 1960; Literature of the Low Countries, 1971; Dutch and Flemish: two literatures or one?, 1974; *contrib*. AUMLA, De Gids, Ons Erfdeel, Tirade. *Address*: Dept of Dutch, Bedford College, Regent's Park, NW1 4NS.

Mein, Dr Margaret; Lecturer in French, Westfield College, University of London, since 1966. BA Hons Oxon 1945 (French), Dip. in Educn Oxford 1946, BA Hons London 1950 (External) (French, cl. I), PhD London 1953 (French Lit.). Tutor and Lectr in French, St Hilda's Coll., Oxford, 1961–66. *Publications*: Proust's Challenge to Time, 1962; A Foretaste of Proust (forthcoming); *contrib*. Adam; Austr. Jl French Studies; Bull. de la Soc. des Amis de Proust; Comp. Lit; Entretiens sur Gide; Entretiens sur Valéry; L'Esprit Créateur; Europe; Forum for Mod. Lang. Studies; French Rev.; French Studies; MLR; Romanic Review. *Address*: Westfield College, Univ. of London, Kidderpore Avenue, Hampstead, NW3 7ST.

Mellaart, James, BAFSA; Lecturer in Anatolian Archaeology, Department of Western Asiatic Archaeology, Institute of Archaeology, University of London, since 1964; *b* 1925; *m* 1954; one *s*. BA London 1951 (Hons Anc. Hist. and Egyptol.); FSA. Foreign Specialist, N-East. and Anatolian Archaeol., Univ. of Istanbul, 1961–63. *Publications*: Earliest Civilisations of the Near East, 1965, French edn 1969, Dutch edn 1969, Portuguese edn 1971; The Chalcolithic and Early Bronze Ages in the Near East and Anatolia, 1966; Çatal Hüyük, a neolithic town in Anatolia, 1967, German edn 1967, French edn 1971; Excavations at Hacilar, 1970; The Neolithic of the Near East (forthcoming); *contrib*. Amer. Jl Archaeol., AJDA, Anatol. Studies, Antiqu., Belleten, Ist. Mitt. *Address*: Institute of Archaeology, Univ. of London, 31–34 Gordon Square, WC1H 0PY.

Mellers, Prof. Wilfrid Howard, MA, DMus; Professor of Music, University of York, since 1964; *b* 1914; *m* 1st 1939, 2nd 1950; two *d*. BA Cantab 1936, BMus Cantab 1938 (pt I), MA Cantab 1945, DMus Birmingham 1960; Mem., Royal Music. Assoc., 1955, Mem., Composers' Guild GB, 1958. Supervisor and Lectr in Music and English, Downing Coll., Univ. of Cambridge, 1945–48; Staff Tutor in Music, Extra-Mural Dept, Univ. of Birmingham, 1949–60; Andrew Mellon Prof. of Music, Univ. of Pittsburgh, 1960–63. Mem., Arts Council Music Panel, 1967– ; Mem., Yorks Assoc. Arts, 1970– ; Mem., several Music Festival Cttees. *Publications*: Music and Society, 1946, 2nd edn 1950; Studies in Contemporary Music, 1948; François Couperin and the French Classical Tradition, 1950; Music in the Making, 1951,

2nd edn 1952; Man and his Music, 1957, one vol. edn 1962, cheap edn 1964, pbk edn 1969, German and Italian edns 1969; Music in a New Found Land, 1964, American edn 1965; Harmonious Meeting, 1964; Caliban Reborn: renewal in 20th century music, 1966, British edn 1967, German and Swedish edns 1967; Twilight of the Gods: The Beatles in Retrospect, 1973; contrib. Grove: Dictionary of music and musicians, etc.; over 50 published compositions; contrib. Listener, Music Lett., Music. Times, New States., Music Musicians. *Address*: Dept of Music, Univ. of York, York YO1 5DD.

Melling, John; Staff Tutor, Faculty of Social Sciences, The Open University, since 1970; *b* 1910; *m* 1941; four *s* three *d*. Hon. MA Oxon 1947. Univ. of Leeds, 1947–58; McMaster Univ., 1963–70. Dir, Nat. Commn on the Indian Canadian, 1958–60; Dir., Indian–Eskimo Assoc. of Canada, 1960–63. *Publications*: Right to a Future: the native peoples of Canada, 1967; Eskimo Development: the political and administrative background, in, Canada's Aboriginal Peoples, 1974; *contrib.* Race. *Address*: The Open Univ., Walton Hall, Milton Keynes MK7 6AA.

Mellor, Enid Beatrice; Lecturer in Religious Education, University of London Institute of Education, since 1966; *b* 1926. BD London 1958 (1st cl. Hons), MTh London 1968. *Publications*: The Making of the Old Testament (Cambridge Bible Commentary), 1972. *Address*: Univ. of London Institute of Education, Malet Street, WC1E 7HS.

Mellor, Prof. Geoffrey Robertson, MA; Professor of Modern Languages, University of Salford, since 1967; *b* 1921; *m* 1945; six *d*. BA Manchester 1947 (1st cl. Mod. Lang.), MA Manchester 1950. Mem., MHRA, Mem., MLA, Mem., Fr. Studies, Mem., Ital. Studies, Mem., Hispanists, Mem., BUAS, Mem., Internat. Arthurian, Mem., Rencesvals. Asst Lectr in French, Bristol, 1948; Lectr in French, Bristol, 1951; Sen. Lectr in French and Romance Philology, 1963. *Publications*: *contrib.* Fr. Studies, Lingu. Antv., Med. Æv., Mod. Lang. Rev., Mod. Langs. *Address*: Dept of Modern Languages, Univ. of Salford, Salford M5 4WT.

Mellor, Prof. Roy Egerton Henderson; Professor of Geography (2nd Chair), University of Aberdeen, since 1967; *b* 1926; *m* 1954; one *s* one *d*. BA Manchester (Hons Geog.); FRGS, Mem., RSGS, Mem., Inst. Brit. Geogrs, Mem., Geog. Assoc. Asst Lectr, Manchester Univ., 1950–54; Cartographic Ed., Oxford Univ. Press, 1954–56; Tutor-Organiser, Extra-Mural Studies, Aberdeen Univ., 1956–57; Lectr, Aberdeen Univ., 1957–64; Sen. Lectr, Aberdeen Univ., 1964–67; Vis. Prof., Ruhr-Universität-Bochum, 1973–74. *Publications*: Geography of the USSR, 1964; Die Sowjetunion, 1966; Comecon – Challenge to the West, 1971; *contrib.* Adv. Science, Scott. Geog. Mag. *Address*: Dept of Geography, Univ. of Aberdeen, High Street, Old Aberdeen.

Mellows, Prof. Anthony Roger, TD; Director of Conveyancing Studies, King's College, University of London, since 1969; Professor of the Law of Property, King's College, London, since 1974; *b* 1936. LLB London 1957 (1st cl.), AKC London 1957; LLM London 1959 (Mark of Distinction), PhD London 1962, BD London 1968, LLD London 1973; Solicitor of the Supreme Court; FRSA. Asst Lectr, King's Coll., London, 1962–64; Lectr, 1964–69; Reader, 1971– . Mem., Ctee, City of Westminster Law Soc., 1968– . *Publications*: Local Searches and Enquiries, 1964, 2nd edn 1967; Conveyancing Searches, 1964; The Preservation and Felling of Trees, 1964; The Trustee's Handbook, 1965, 2nd edn 1971; (with D. B. Parker) The Modern Law of Trusts, 1966, 2nd edn 1970; Land Charges, 1966; Taxation for Executors and Trustees, 1967, 3rd edn 1972; The Law of Succession, 1970, 2nd edn 1973; The Taxation of Land Transactions, 1972; *contrib.* Brit. Army Rev., Conveyan., Jl Planning Law, Law Soc. Gaz., Law Times, Solic. Jl, Solic. Qly. *Address*: Faculty of Laws, King's College, Strand, WC2R 2LS.

Meltzer, Prof. Bernard, FRSE; Head of the Department of Computational Logic, School of Artificial Intelligence, University of Edinburgh, since 1965; *b* 1916; *m* 1940; one *s*. BSc Capetown 1934, PhD London 1953. Lectr, Aberdeen, 1943–46; Lectr, Reader, then Professor, Edinburgh, 1955– . Ed.-in-Chief, Artificial Intelligence, 1969– ; Mem., Internat. Jt Council of Artif. Intell., 1968; Chm., AISB Cttee (Mem., 1969). *Publications*: jt ed., Machine Intelligence Volumes, 1968–71; jt ed., Artificial Intelligence and Heuristic Programming, 1970; *contrib.* Brit. Jl Appl. Phys., Artif. Intell. *Address*: Dept of Computational Logic, Univ. of Edinburgh, Edinburgh EH8 9NW.

Mendelson, Dr Maurice Harvey, MA, DPhil; Lecturer in Laws, University of London King's College, since 1968; *b* 1943; *m* 1968; one *d*. BA Oxon 1964, MA Oxon 1968, DPhil Oxon 1971. Barrister-at-law, Lincoln's Inn, 1965. Member: RIIA; British Inst. of Internat. and Comparative Law; David Davies Meml Inst. of Internat. Studies; Internat. Law Assoc.; Soc. of Public Teachers of Law; Amer. Soc. of Internat. Law; UNA. *Publications*: *contrib.* British Yearbook of Internat. Law; Internat. and Comparative Law Qly; Jl of Soc. of Public Teachers of Law. *Address*: Faculty of Laws, Univ. of London King's College, Strand, WC2R 2LS.

Mendl, Dr Wolfgang Marco Louis; Reader in War Studies, University of London King's College, since 1971; *b* 1926; *m* 1959 (she died 1971); one *s* two *d*; *m* 1972. BA Cantab 1949, MA Cantab 1953, PhD London 1966, Postgrad. Cert. in Educn, Birmingham 1950. Member: RIIA; Conflict Res. Soc. Lectr in War Studies, KCL, 1965–71. *Publications*: Deterrence and Persuasion: French Nuclear Armament in the Context of National Policy, 1945–1969, 1970; Prophets and Reconcilers, Swarthmore Lecture, 1974; contrib. Yearbook of World Affairs, 1968, 1970; contrib. Preventing the

Spread of Nuclear Weapons, Pugwash Symposium, 1969; *contrib.* Europa Archiv; India Qly; Internat. Affairs; Survey; The World Today, etc. *Address:* Dept of War Studies, Univ. of London King's College, Strand, WC2R 2LS.

Menhennet, Prof. Alan, DPhil; Professor of German, University of Newcastle upon Tyne, since 1974; *b* 1933; *m* 1964; one *s* one *d*. BA Oxon 1956 (1st cl. German and Russian), MA Oxon 1958, DPhil Oxon 1963. Asst Lectr, Reading Univ., 1959–61, Lectr, 1961–70, Sen. Lectr in German, 1970–74. *Publications:* Order and Freedom: German Literature and Society 1720–1805, 1973; *contrib.* Forum Mod. Lang. Studies, Germ. Life Lett., Mod. Lang. Rev., Neophilol., Oxf. Germ. Studies, Stud. Neophilol., New Germ. Studies. *Address:* Dept of German, The Univ., Newcastle upon Tyne NE1 7RU.

Mennell, Stephen John; Lecturer, Department of Sociology, University of Exeter, since 1967; *b* 1944; *m* 1971. BA Cantab 1966 (Econs), MA Cantab 1970; Mem. Brit. Sociological Assoc. 1968, Mem. Amer. Sociological Assoc. 1967. Asst Lectr, Univ. Exeter, 1967–70. Councillor, City and County of City of Exeter, 1971–74. *Publications:* (with C. J. Crouch) The Universities: Pressures and Prospects, 1972; Sociological Theory: Unities and Uses, 1974; *contrib.* Jl Amer. Studies, Univs Qly. *Address:* Dept of Sociology, Univ. of Exeter, Streatham Court, Exeter, EX4 4QJ.

Mepham, Michael James; Senior Lecturer in Accountancy, Department of Accountancy and Finance, Heriot-Watt University, Edinburgh, since 1970; *b* 1932; *m* 1965; one *s* one *d*. BSc(Econ) London 1963 (Hons), Dip. in Operational Res. Strathclyde 1970; FCA 1954, ACMA 1964. Lectr, Univ. of Glasgow, 1965–69; Vis. Lectr, Univ. of Florida, 1973. *Publications:* Accounting Models: an introduction (forthcoming); *contrib.* The Acctnt, Management Acctng, The Acctnt's Mag. *Address:* Dept of Accountancy and Finance, Mountbatten Building, Heriot-Watt Univ., Grassmarket, Edinburgh.

Mercer, Prof. Alan, MA, PhD; Professor of Operational Research, University of Lancaster, since 1968; *b* 1931; *m* 1954; two *s*. BA Cantab 1952 (Maths), DipMathsStat Cantab 1953, MA Cantab 1957, PhD London 1960 (Math. Stat); FSS, Mem., Operat. Res. Soc. Sen. Lectr, Lancaster Univ., 1964–68. Mem., Central Lancs Develt Corp., 1971– ; Mem., SSRC Mngmt and Ind. Relations Cttee, 1972– . *Publications: contrib.* Biomet., Jl Ind. Econ., Jl Royal Stat. Soc., Operat. Res. Qly. *Address:* Dept of Operational Research, Univ. of Lancaster, Bailrigg, Lancaster LA1 4YW.

Merchant, Prof. William Moelwyn, MA, DLitt; Professor of English Language and Literature, and Head of Department, University of Exeter, since 1961; *b* 1913; *m* 1938; one *s* one *d*. BA Wales 1933 (1st cl. Engl., 2nd cl. Hist. 1934), DipEd Wales 1935 (1st cl.), MA Wales 1950, DLitt Wales 1960; Hon. DHL Wittenberg, Ohio, 1973. Ordained

to Anglican Orders 1940. Lectr, Univ. Coll., Cardiff, 1939–50, Sen. Lectr, 1950–61, Reader, 1961; Fulbright Fellow, 1957; Fellow, Folger Library, Wash., DC, 1957; Woodward Lectr, Yale, 1957; Dupont Lectr, Sewanee, 1963; Willett Prof., Univ. of Chicago, 1971. Mem., Welsh Cttee, Arts Council, 1960– ; Chancellor and Canon, Salisbury Cath., 1967– . *Publications:* Wordsworth's Guide to the Lakes, 1952; Reynard Library Wordsworth, 1955; Shakespeare and the Artist, 1959; Creed and Drama, 1965; ed, Shakespeare: Merchant of Venice, 1967; ed, Marlowe: Edward the Second, 1967; Comedy, 1972; contrib. Encyclopedia Britannica; *contrib.* Shakesp. Surv., Shakesp. Qly, Shakesp. Jbh, Times Lit. Supp., Warb. Jl, etc. *Address:* Dept of English, Queen's Building, The Univ., Exeter, Devon.

Mercier, Paul Jerome, MA, DipEd; Senior Lecturer, School of Education, University of Reading, since 1968; *b* 1922; *m* 1947; three *s* three *d*. BA Oxford 1949, DipEd Oxford 1950, MA Oxford 1954; Mem., Comp. Educn. Soc. Europe (Brit. Sect.), Tutor, Reading, 1961–63; Lectr, Reading, 1963–68. Chm., Univ. of Reading Sch. of Educn Training Cttee, 1969– ; Mem., Bd Sch. of Educn; Chm., Assoc. Sch. and Inst. of Educn In-Service Tutors, 1971–73. *Publications:* ed, Comparative Education and the Training of Teachers, 1966; ed, Recent Reforms in Secondary Education, 1968; ed, The Changing School Curriculum, 1969; Educational Policies since World War II (Europe 2000) – France, 1970; *contrib.* Comp. Educn, New Era. *Address:* Univ. of Reading School of Education, London Road, Reading.

Meredith, Peter, MA; Lecturer in English Language and Medieval English Literature, University of Leeds, since 1969; *b* 1933; *m* 1958; three *s* two *d*. BA Oxon 1956 (2nd cl. Engl.), MA Oxon 1960, DipEd Oxford 1957. Lectr, Univ. of Adelaide, 1961–68; Sen. Lectr, Univ. of Adelaide, 1968–69. *Publications: contrib.* Med. Æv. *Address:* School of English, Univ. of Leeds, Leeds LS2 9JT.

Merrills, John Graham; Senior Lecturer in Law, University of Sheffield, since 1974; *b* 1942; *m* 1969; one *d*. BA Oxon 1963, BCL Oxon 1964, MA Oxon 1970; Mem., Brit. Inst. Internat. and Comparative Law. Lectr in Law, Univ. of Sheffield, 1964–74; Vis. Lectr, Auckland Univ., 1971; Sub-Dean, Faculty of Law, Sheffield, 1972–74. *Publications: contrib.* Can. Bar Rev., Int. and Comp. Law Qly, Mod. Law Rev., Ottawa Law Rev., Toronto Law Jl. *Address:* Faculty of Law, Univ. of Sheffield, Sheffield S10 2TN.

Merriman, Marcus Homer; Lecturer in Modern History, University of Lancaster, since 1966; *b* 1940; *m* 1971. BA Bowdoin 1962 (with Hons in Hist.). Asst Lectr, Lancaster, 1964–65; Fellow, Inst. Hist. Res., 1965–66; Vis. Prof., Queen's Coll., NY, 1969; Syracuse Univ., NY, 1970. Mem., Senate, Lancaster Univ., 1969–72; Mem., Council, Lancaster Univ., 1971– ; Mem.,

Nat. Exec., AUT, 1972– . *Publications*: *contrib.* Scott. Hist. Rev. *Address*: Dept of History, The Univ., Lancaster LA1 4YW.

Merrington, Dr Maxine Patricia Mary; Associate Research Fellow, School of Library, Archive and Information Studies, University College, London, since 1971; *b* 1915; *m* 1939; one *s* one *d*. BSc London 1937, PhD London 1968 (Statistics); FRSS, Mem., Brit. Rec. Assoc., Mem., Biomet. Soc. Res. Asst, Univ. Coll., London, 1946–66; Lectr, Univ. Coll., London, 1966–71; Res. Assoc., Harvard Univ., 1950, 1965. Statistician, HM Prison, Wormwood Scrubs, 1938–41; Sec., Biometrika, 1941–46; Sen. Treas., Univ. Coll. Union, 1967–72. *Publications*: trans., C. Berge and A. Ghouila-Houri: Programming, games and transportation networks, 1965; da Coste: Marin Mersenne 1588–1648, 1962; (jtly) Normal centroids, medians and scores, 1968; *contrib.* Biomet., Ann. Hum. Genet., Brit. Jl Prev. Social Med., Brit. Med. Jl, Proc. 5th Berkeley Symp. Math. Stat. Prob. *Address*: School of Library, Archive and Information Studies, Univ. Coll., WC1E 6BT.

Merrison, Dr Alexander Walter, FRS; Vice-Chancellor, University of Bristol, since 1969; *b* 1924; *m* 1948, 1970; three *s* one *d*. BSc London 1944, PhD Liverpool 1957, Hon. LLD Bristol 1971; FRS 1969, FRSA 1970. Research in Radio Wave Propagation, as Experimental Officer, Signals Res. and Development Establishment, Christchurch, 1944–46; Res. in Reactor and Nuclear Physics, as Sen. Scientific Officer, AERE, Harwell, 1946–51; Res. in Elementary Particle Physics, as Leverhulme Fellow and Lectr, Liverpool Univ., 1951–57; Physicist, European Orgn for Nuclear Res. (CERN), Geneva, 1957–60; Prof. of Experimental Physics, Liverpool Univ., 1960–69 and Dir, Daresbury Nuclear Physics Lab., SRC, 1962–69. **C. V.** Boys Prizeman of Inst. of Physics and the Physical Soc., 1961, and Mem., Council, 1964–66; Mem., Council for Scientific Policy, 1967–73. Governor, Bristol Old Vic Trust, 1969– ; Chm., Cttee of Inquiry into Design and Erection of Steel Box Girder Bridges, 1970; Chm., Cttee of Inquiry into Regulation of Medical Profession, 1973– . Chm., Bristol Old Vic Trust, 1971– . *Publications*: *contrib.* scientific jls on nuclear and elementary particle physics. *Address*: The Univ., Senate House, Bristol BS8 1TH.

Merrison, Maureen Michèle; Lecturer, Department of History, University of Bristol, since 1964; *b* 1938; *m* 1970; two step-*s* one *s* one *d*. BA Hons London 1960 (2nd cl. 1st Div. History). Res. Fellow, Inst. of Historical Res., 1962–63; Jun. Res. Fellow, Bedford Coll., Univ. of London, 1963–64. *Address*: Dept of History, Univ. of Bristol, Bristol BS8 1TH.

Merritt, Prof. John E; Professor of Educational Studies, Faculty of Educational Studies, Open University, since 1971; *b* 1926; *m* 1948; two *s*. BA Dunelm 1956, DipEdPsych UCL 1957; ABPsS 1960, Member: UK Reading Assoc.; Internat. Reading Assoc.;

Assoc. of Educnl Psychologists. Lectr in Education, Univ. of Durham, 1964–71. Member: Schs Council Working Party on Special Educn, 1969; Bullock Cttee, 1972. Hon. Editor for UKRA, Monograph Series on Reading. *Publications*: A Framework for Curriculum Design, 1972; Perspectives on Reading, 1973; ed (with A. Melnik): Reading Today and Tomorrow, 1972; The Reading Curriculum, 1972; *contrib.* Reading, Reading Teacher. *Address*: The Open Univ., Walton Hall, Milton Keynes MK7 6AW.

Merry, Bruce Carmichael; College Lecturer, Department of Italian, University College, Dublin, since 1972; *b* 1944; *m* 1964; one *d*. BA Oxon 1966, MA Stanford 1968, MA Oxon 1970. Instructor, Stanford Univ., 1966–68; Lectr, Univ. of Kent, 1968–72. *Publications*: *contrib.* Forum Ital., Ital. Qly, Italica, Lond. Mag., Medit. Rev., PEN Bull., Philos. Studies, Romance Notes, Trans. Brontë Soc., Univ. Windsor Rev., Books, L'Approdo Letterario, Strumenti Critici, Ital. Studies, MLR, Mosaic, Marca Zero, Il Caffé, Jl Assoc. Teachers of Italian, Uomini e Libri, etc. *Address*: Dept of Italian, Univ. College, Dublin 4, Ireland.

Merson, Allan Leslie, MA; Senior Lecturer in History, University of Southampton, since 1964; *b* 1916; *m* 1959. BA Oxon 1937, MA Oxon 1954; FRHistS. Travelling Fellow, Queen's Coll., Oxford, 1938–39; Lectr in Hist., Univ. Coll. (later Univ.) of Southampton, 1946–64. Gen. Ed., Southampton Rec. Series, 1952– . *Publications*: ed, The Third Remembrance Book of Southampton, 1514–1602 (Southampton Records Series), 1952–65; ed, A Calendar of Southampton Apprenticeship Registers, 1609–1740 (Southampton Records Series), 1968; *contrib.* Our Hist. *Address*: Dept of History, The Univ., Southampton SO9 5NH.

Mervin, Dr David, BA, PhD; Lecturer in Politics, Department of Politics, University of Warwick, since 1966; *b* 1933; *m* 1964; one *s* one *d*. Dip. Oxford 1959 (Political Science and Econs), BA Exeter 1962, PhD Cornell 1968. Mem., Amer. Pol. Science Assoc., 1964– , Mem., Pol. Studies Assoc., 1966– . Mem., Warwick Univ. Senate, 1970– ; Mem., Warwick Univ. Council, 1971– . *Publications*: *contrib.* Jl Amer. Studies, Pol. Studies. *Address*: Dept of Politics, Univ. of Warwick, Coventry CV4 7AL.

Messenger, Thomas; Lecturer, Department of Music, University College of North Wales, since 1968; *b* 1938; *m* 1965; two *s*. BMus Glasgow 1961 (Hons), Associateship Diploma: RCM 1957; RCO 1960; Member: Royal Musical Assoc.; Assoc. of Univ. Teachers; Incorp. Soc. of Musicians. Organ Scholar, Glasgow Univ., 1957–61; Graduate Asst and Fulbright Scholar, Washington Univ., USA, 1961–62; Lectr, Royal Scottish Acad. of Music, 1962–68. Conductor: New Consort of Voices, 1966–68; Monteverdi Singers, 1970– ; Examiner, Associated Bd of Royal Schs of Music, 1969– . *Publications*: Two Part Counterpoint from the Great Masters, 1970; Editions: Three Chansons for Three Recorders, 1971, Five Imitations for

Three Recorders, 1971, Canzonets for Four Recorders, 1972; *contrib*. Jl Amer. Musicol Soc., Mus. Rev., Mus. Times, Soundings. *Address*: Dept of Music, Univ. Coll. of North Wales, Bangor LL57 2DG.

Meston, Prof. Michael Charles; Professor of Scots Law, University of Aberdeen, since 1971; *b* 1932; *m* 1958; two *s*. MA Aberdeen 1954 (1st cl. Hist.), LLB Aberdeen 1957 (Dist.), JD Chicago 1959; Solicitor 1957. Pt-time Asst, Aberdeen, 1957–58; Lectr, Glasgow Univ., 1959–64; Sen. Lectr, Aberdeen Univ., 1964–68; Prof. of Jurisprudence, Aberdeen Univ., 1968–71. Hon. Sheriff, City of Aberdeen. Mem., Valuation Appeal Cttee, City of Aberdeen. *Publications*: The Succession (Scotland) Act 1964, 1964, 2nd edn 1969; *contrib*. Scots Law Times, Jurid. Rev. *Address*: Dept of Private Law, Univ. of Aberdeen, Old Aberdeen AB9 2UB.

Metcalf, Dr David; Lecturer in Economics, London School of Economics, since 1967; *b* 1942; *m* 1968. BA(Econ) Manchester 1964 (1st cl.), MA(Econ) Manchester 1966, PhD London 1971. Asst Lectr, Manchester, 1965–67. *Publications*: Economics of Agriculture, 1969; *contrib*. Brit. Jl Indust. Relat., Econ. Hist. Rev., Economica, Fin. Times, Internat. Econ. Rev., Jl Agric. Econ., Manch. Sch., Oxf. Bull. Stat. *Address*: London School of Economics, Houghton Street, WC2A 2AE.

Metcalf, Dr David Michael; Assistant Keeper, Heberden Coin Room, Ashmolean Museum, Oxford University, since 1963; Editor, Numismatic Chronicle, since 1974; *b* 1933; *m* 1958; two *s* one *d*. BA Cambridge 1955 (Geog.), CertEd Cambridge 1956, MA Cambridge 1959, PhD Cambridge 1959, MA, DPhil Oxford 1963; FRNS, Mem., Brit. Numis. Soc., Mem., Amer. Numis. Soc., Corresp. Mem., Croatian Numis. Soc. Mem., Council, Royal Numis. Soc., 1966–69, 1973– ; Mem., Council, Brit. Numis. Soc., 1968–71. *Publications*: The Coinage of South Germany in the Thirteenth Century, 1961; Coinage in the Balkans, 820–1355, 1965, American edn 1966, rev. edn 1974; Classification of Byzantine Stamena, 1967; (with J. M. Merrick and L. K. Hamblin) Studies in the Composition of Early Medieval Coins, 1968; The Origins of the Anastasian Currency Reform, 1969, American edn 1969; Ashmolean Museum, Oxford: English Coins, 1066–1279, 1969; ed (with E. T. Hall), Methods of Chemical and Metallurgical Investigation of Ancient Coinage, 1972; Ashmolean Museum, Oxford: Coins of Henry VII 1485–1509, 1975; *contrib*. Amer. Numis. Soc. Museum Notes, Ann. Brit. Sch. Archaeol., Archaeom., Byzantion, Econ. Hist. Rev., Hamb. Beit. Numis., Hesperia, Numis. Chron., Rev. Belge Numis. *Address*: Ashmolean Museum, Oxford OX1 2PH.

Metcalfe, George Edgar; Senior Lecturer, Department of History, University of Hull, since 1966; *b* 1917; *m* 1951; one *s* two *d*. BA Oxon 1939 (1st cl. Hist), BA Oxon 1940 (1st cl. Geog.), MA Oxon 1947. Asst Lectr, Inst. Commonwealth Studies, Oxford, 1947;

Lectr, Inst. Commonwealth Studies, Oxford, 1948–51; Lectr, Univ. Coll. of the Gold Coast, 1951–57; Sen. Lectr, Univ. Coll. of the Gold Coast, 1957–61; Lectr, Hull Univ., 1961–66. *Publications*: Maclean of the Gold Coast, 1962; ed, Great Britain and Ghana 1867–1957, 1964. *Address*: Dept of History, Univ. of Hull, Hull HU6 7RX.

Metford, Prof. John Callan James; Professor of Spanish, University of Bristol, since 1960; *b* 1916; *m* 1944; one *d*. MA Liverpool 1940; Commonwealth Fund Fellow, Univ. of Yale and California, 1939–41; Brit. Council Lectr, Brazil, 1942–44; Reg. Off., Latin American Dept, British Council, 1944–46; Lectr in Latin American Studies, Univ. of Glasgow, 1946–55; Hd of Dept of Spanish and Portuguese, Univ. of Bristol, 1955–73, of Dept of Hispanic and Latin American Studies, 1973– ; Vis. Prof., Lehigh Univ., USA, 1968–69. Vice-Chm., Council, Westonbirt Sch.; Gov., St Matthias Coll., Fishponds, Bristol. *Publications*: British Contributions to Spanish and Spanish American Studies, 1950; San Martín the Liberator, 1950, 2nd edn 1970; Modern Latin America, 1964; *contrib*. Bull. Hispan. Studies, Lpool Studies Spanish, Internat. Aff., etc. *Address*: Dept of Hispanic and Latin American Studies, Univ. of Bristol, 83 Woodland Road, Bristol BS8 1US.

Mettam, Dr Roger Charles, MA, PhD; Lecturer in History, Queen Mary College, University of London, and Recognised Teacher of the University of London, since 1970; *b* 1939. BA Cantab 1961 (1st cl. Hist.), MA Cantab 1965, PhD Cantab 1967. Asst Lectr in History, York, 1964–65; Lectr in History, York, 1965–70. *Publications*: French History and Society 1589–1789, in, France: A Companion to French Studies, ed D. Charlton, 1972; (with Douglas Johnson) French History and Society: the wars of religion to the fifth republic, 1974; State and Society in the France of Louis XIV (forthcoming). *Address*: Dept of History, Queen Mary College, Mile End Road, E1 4NS.

Meudell, Peter Robert; Lecturer, Department of Psychology, University of Manchester, since 1967; *b* 1944; *m* 1967. BSc Hull 1966, MSc Manchester 1970. Res. Asst, Univ. Manchester, 1966–67. *Publications*: *contrib*. Acta Psychologica, Jl Acoustical Soc. of Amer., Jl Exper. Psychol., Perceptual and Motor Skills, Psychonomic Science. *Address*: Univ. of Manchester, Manchester M13 9PL.

Mews, Stuart Paul, MA, PhD; Lecturer in Sociology of Religion, Department of Religious Studies, University of Lancaster, since 1968; *b* 1944; *m* 1968; one *s*. BA Leeds 1964, MA Leeds 1967 (Distinction), PhD Cantab 1974, Hulsean Prize, Cantab 1968; Member: Ecclesiastical History Soc., British Sociolog. Assoc., Univ. Assoc. for the Sociol. of Religion. Asst Lectr, Lancaster, 1968–69. Pres., Cambridge Univ. Grad. Council, 1967–8; Reviews Editor, Religion, 1971– . *Publications*: *contrib*. D. Baker, Studies in Church History, vols 7, 1971, 8 1972, 9 1972; L. Bright, Search for Community, 1971; *contrib*. Miscellanea Historiae

Ecclesiasticae, Religion, Theology. *Address*: Dept of Religious Studies, Cartmel Coll., Bailrigg, Lancaster.

Meyer, Frederick Victor, PhD(Econ), BSc(Econ); Reader in International Economics, University of Exeter, since 1966; *b* 1918; *m* 1948; two *s*. BSc(Econ) London; PhD(Econ) London; Mem., Royal Inst. Internat. Aff., Mem., REconS, Mem., Europ. League Econ. Co-op. Res. Asst, Economics Res. Section, Univ. of Manchester, 1946–49; Lectr in Economics, Exeter Univ., 1949–61; Sen. Lectr in Economics, Exeter Univ., 1961–66. Council of Europe Res. Fellow, 1953–54. *Publications*: Britain's Colonies in World Trade, 1948; Britain, the Sterling Area and Europe, 1952; Inflation and Capital, 1954; United Kingdom Trade with Europe, 1957; The Seven, 1960; The Terms of Trade, 1962; (with D. C. Corner and J. E. S. Parker) Problems of a Mature Economy, 1970; The Functions of Sterling, 1973; *contrib*. Amer. Econ. Rev., Bank. Mag., Economica, Econ. Jl, Manch. Sch. Pol. Qly. *Address*: Dept of Economics, Univ. of Exeter, Streatham Court, Rennes Drive, Exeter EX4 4PU.

Meynell, Hugo Anthony; Lecturer, Department of Philosophy and Theology, Leeds University, since 1963; *b* 1936; *m* 1962; 1969; one *s* three *d*. BA Cantab 1959 (2nd cl. Music, Theology), MA Cantab 1962, PhD Cantab 1963. *Publications*: Sense, Nonsense and Christianity, 1964; Grace versus Nature (Studies in Barth's Dogmatics), 1965; The New Theology and Modern Theologians, 1967; God and the World: The Coherence of Christian Theism, 1971; *contrib*. Brit. Jl Aesth., New Blackf., Philos. Qly, Philos., Theol. *Address*: Dept of Philosophy and Theology, Leeds Univ., Leeds LS2 9JT.

Michael, Prof. Ian David Lewis, BA, PhD; Professor of Spanish, University of Southampton, since 1971; *b* 1936. BA London 1957 (1st cl. Hons. Spanish), PhD Manchester 1967. Asst Lectr, Manchester Univ., 1957–60, Lectr, Manchester Univ., 1960–68; Sen. Lectr, Manchester Univ., 1968–70. *Publications*: The Treatment of Classical Material in the 'Libro de Alexandre', 1970; Poema de Mio Cid (forthcoming); *contrib*. Anuario de Estudios Medievales, BHS, MLR. *Address*: Dept of Spanish, Univ. of Southampton, Southampton SO9 5NH.

Michie, Dr James Alexander, DLitt; Senior Lecturer in English Literature, University of Hull, since 1966; *b* 1921; *m* 1953; two *s* two *d*. MA Aberdeen 1947, BA Oxon 1950, DLitt Aberdeen 1961; Chapter V Teaching Cert. Moray House Edinburgh 1950. Asst, Aberdeen Univ., 1950–53; Lectr, Aberdeen Univ., 1953–66; Scott. Rep., Ecumen. Coll., Bossey, Geneva, 1959. *Publications*: The Loaded Spur, 1972; Sir Walter Scott, 1972; *contrib*. Aberd. Univ. Rev., Engl., Leeds Univ. Rev., Lond. Qly, Holb. Rev., Mod. Drama. *Address*: Dept of English, Univ. of Hull, Hull HU6 7RX.

Middlemas, Robert Keith, DPhil; Lecturer in Modern History, University of Sussex,

since 1966; *b* 1935; *m* 1958; one *s* three *d*. BA Cantab 1958 (1st cl. History), MA Cantab 1963, DPhil Sussex 1972. *Publications*: The Master Builders, 1963; The Clydesiders, 1965; ed, T. Jones: Whitehall Diary, 1969–71; (with A. J. L. Barnes) Baldwin, 1969; Diplomacy of Illusion (The British Government and Germany, 1937–39), 1972. *Address*: School of Social Studies, Univ. of Sussex, Falmer, Brighton BN1 9RH.

Middleton, Dr C. Richard; Lecturer, History Department, Queen's University, Belfast, since 1967; *b* 1941. BA Exeter 1963 (History), PhD Exeter 1969. Fellow, Inst. of Early American History and Culture, Williamsburg, Va, 1972–74 (on study leave from QUB). *Publications: contrib*. Bull. Inst. Hist. Res., History, Jl RUSI, Jl Amer. Studies, Parly Affairs. *Address*: Dept of History, Queen's Univ., Belfast BT7 1NN.

Middleton, Prof. John Francis Marchment; Professor of African Anthropology, Department of Anthropology, School of Oriental and African Studies, University of London, since 1972; *b* 1921. BA London 1941, BSc 1949, DPhil 1953, Oxon. Lectr, Birkbeck Coll., Univ. of London, 1953–54; Senior Lecturer: Univ. of Cape Town, 1954–55; Rhodes Univ., 1955–56; Lectr, UCL, 1956–64; Professor: Northwestern Univ., 1964–66; New York Univ., 1966–72. *Publications*: The Kikuyu and Kamba of Kenya, 1953; ed, Tribes without Rulers, 1958; Lugbara Religion, 1960; Land Tenure in Zanzibar, 1961; The Lugbara of Uganda, 1965; Zanzibar, its Society and its Politics, 1965; The Effects of Economic Development on Political Systems in Africa, 1966; The Study of the Lugbara, 1969; ed., From Tribe to Nation in Africa, 1970; *contrib*. Africa, Jl RAI, Man, Uganda Jl, etc. *Address*: Sch. of Oriental and African Studies, Malet Street, WCIE 7HP.

Middleton, Richard; *see* Middleton, C. R.

Midgley, Rev. Edward Graham; Fellow of St Edmund Hall, University of Oxford, and Tutor in English Literature, since 1951; *b* 1923. BA Oxon 1946 (1st cl. English Language and Literature), MA Oxon 1948, BLitt Oxon 1950. Lectr in English, Bedford Coll., Univ. of London, 1949–51. *Publications*: The Life of Orator Henley, 1973; *contrib*. Ess. Crit. *Address*: St Edmund Hall, Oxford.

Midgley, Ernest Brian Francis; Senior Lecturer, Department of Politics, University of Aberdeen, since 1972; *b* 1927; *m* 1951; six *s* two *d*. BA Manchester 1951 (1st cl. Hons Philosophy), MPhil London 1967; Member: Political Studies Assoc., International Assoc. for Philosophy of Law and Social Philosophy (UK Section). Asst, Univ. of Aberdeen, 1967–68; Lectr, 1968–72. Ministry of Supply (subsequently Aviation): Asst Principal, 1951–56, Principal, 1956–61; Ministry of Health: Principal, 1961–65. *Publications*: The Natural Law Tradition and the Theory of International Relations, 1974. *Address*: Dept of Politics, Univ. of Aberdeen, King's College, Old Aberdeen AB9 2UB.

Midgley, Mary Beatrice; Lecturer, Department of Philosophy, University of Newcastle upon Tyne, since 1965; *b* 1919; *m* 1950; three *s*. BA Oxon 1942 (1st cl. Lit. Hum.). Asst Lectr in Philosophy, Univ. of Reading, 1948–50. *Publications: contrib.* Mind, New States., Twent. Cent., Proc. Aristot. Soc., Philosophy. *Address:* Dept of Philosophy The Univ., Newcastle upon Tyne NE1 7RU.

Miers, David R.; Lecturer, Department of Law, University College, Cardiff, since 1973; *b* 1945. LLB Leeds 1967, LLM Leeds 1968; Mem., Soc. of Public Teachers of Law, QUB, 1968–73. Osgoode Hall Law Sch., York Univ., Toronto, 1971–72. Co-Ed., Comments Section, British Jl of Law and Soc. *Publications: contrib.* Anglo-Amer. Law Rev.; Criminal Law Rev.; NI Legal Qly; Irish Jurist; Modern Law Rev. *Address:* Dept of Law, Univ. Coll., PO Box 28, Cardiff CF1 1XL.

Miles, Dr Agnes Eva, BSc, PhD; Senior Research Fellow, Department of Sociology and Social Administration, University of Southampton, since 1969; *m*; one *s.* BSc London, PhD London 1966. Mem., Brit. Sociol. Assoc.; Mem., Royal Coll., Psychiat. Res. Fellow, Univ. of Southampton, 1966–69. *Publications:* (with N. Wansbrough) Industrial Therapy in Psychiatric Hospitals, 1968; *contrib.* Brit. Jl Criminol., Brit. Jl Med. Psychol., Brit. Jl Psychol., Jl Ment. Def. Res. *Address:* Dept of Sociology and Social Administration, Univ. of Southampton.

Miles, Prof. Charles William Noel; Professor of Estate Management, Department of Land Management and Development, University of Reading, since 1968; *b* 1915; *m* 1940; one *d.* BA Cantab 1937, MA 1947; FRICS. Univ. of Cambridge: Demonstrator, 1946–50; Lectr 1950–68. Dean, Fac. of Urban and Regional Studies, Reading, 1972. Chief Agent, Meyrick Estates, 1954–68; Pres. Chartered Land Agents' Soc. 1966–67; Mem., SE Regional Adv. Cttee, Land Commn, 1967–70; Chm., Agric. Wages Bd of England and Wales, 1972– . *Publications:* Estate Finance and Business Management, 1953, 3rd edn 1972; Estate Accounts, 1960; *contrib.* Brit. Tax Rev., Estates Gaz. *Address:* Dept of Land Management and Development, Reading Univ., Whiteknights, Reading RG6 2BU.

Miles, Prof. Hamish Alexander Drummond; Barber Professor of Fine Arts and Director of the Barber Institute, University of Birmingham, since 1970; *b* 1925; *m* 1957; two *s* two *d.* MA Edinburgh. Asst Lectr, then Lectr in the History of Art, Univ. of Glasgow, 1954–66; Prof. of History of Art, Univ. of Leicester, 1966–70; Vis. Lectr, Smith Coll., Mass, 1960–61. Asst Curator, Glasgow Art Gallery, 1953–54. Trustee, Nat. Galleries of Scotland. *Publications: contrib.* jls and catalogues. *Address:* Univ. of Birmingham, PO Box 363, Birmingham B15 2TT.

Miles, Dr Haydon Braddock, MSc, PhD, MIBiol; Senior Lecturer, Education Department, University of Hull, since 1964; *m*; two *s.* BSc Wales 1938 (1st cl. Zoolog.), MSc Wales 1956, PhD Hull 1961; MIBiol.; Vice-Pres., Eugenics Soc. Lectr, Univ. (Coll) of Hull, 1950–64. *Publications:* (all with P. M. Miles) Seashore Ecology, 1966; Freshwater Ecology, 1967; Town Ecology, 1967; Woodland Ecology, 1968; Chalkland and Moorland Ecology, 1968; *contrib.* Arch. Protistenk., Jl Protozool., Nature, Rev. Iber. Parisitol., Soil Science. *Address:* Education Dept, The Univ., Hull.

Miles, Prof. Thomas Richard, MA, PhD, FBPsS; Professor of Psychology, University College of North Wales, Bangor, since 1963; *b* 1923; *m* 1951; one *s.* Classical Hon. Mods Oxford 1942, Lit. Hum. Oxford 1947, Philos., Psychol., Physiol., Oxford 1949, PhD Wales 1963; FBPsS. Asst Lectr, Univ. Coll. of North Wales, Bangor, 1949–52; Lectr, 1952–63. Mem., Education Cttee, British Dyslexia Assoc. *Publications:* Religion and the Scientific Outlook, 1959; trans. (with Elaine Miles), A. Michotte: the Perception of Causality, 1963; Eliminating the Unconscious, 1966; On Helping the Dyslexic Child, 1970; Religious Experience, 1972; *contrib.* Brit. Jl Educn Psychol., Brit. Jl Philos. Sci., Mind, Philos., Qly Jl. Exper. Psychol. *Address:* Dept of Psychology, Univ. College of North Wales, Bangor.

Miller, Edward, MA; Master, Fitzwilliam College, Cambridge, since 1971; *b* 1915; *m* 1941; one *s.* BA Cantab 1937, MA Cantab 1945; Hon. LittD Sheffield 1972; FRHistS; MIHR. Strathcona Research Student, 1937–39, Fellow, 1939–65, St John's Coll., Cambridge; Asst Lectr in History, 1946–50, Lectr, 1950–65, Univ. of Cambridge; Prof. of Medieval History, Sheffield Univ. 1965–71. Warden, Madingley Hall, Cambridge, 1961–65; Chm., Victoria Co. Histories Cttee, IHR; Member: Councils of Selden and Lincoln Record Socs; Editorial Bd, History of Parliament Trust; Management Cttee, IHR. *Publications:* The Abbey and Bishopric of Ely, 1951; Portrait of a College, 1961; (ed jtly) Cambridge Economic History of Europe, vol. III, 1963; (ed jtly) Historical Studies of the English Parliament, 2 vols, 1970; *contrib.* Victoria Co. Histories of Cambridgeshire and York, EHR, Econ. Hist. Rev., Trans. Royal Hist. Soc., Past and Present, etc. *Address:* Fitzwilliam College, Cambridge CB3 0DG.

Miller, Gareth; *see* Miller, J. G.

Miller, Gordon Wesley; Senior Research Officer, Department of Higher Education, University of London Institute of Education, since 1965. BA Melbourne 1962, Dip. Soc. Studies Melbourne 1961, Dip. Music Melbourne 1950; PhD London 1967; ABPsS; Mem., British Sociol Assoc.; FRSA. *Publications:* Success, Failure and Wastage in Higher Education, 1970; Educational Opportunity and the Home, 1971; Higher Education Research in Australia and New Zealand, 1971; *contrib.* Austr. Jl of Social Work, Jl of Educnl Psychol., Austr. Univ., Bull. BPsS, Univs Qly. *Address:* Univ. of London Institute of Education, Malet Street, WC1E 7HS.

Miller, Henry George, MD, FRCP; Vice-Chancellor, University of Newcastle upon

479

Tyne, since 1968 (Dean of Medicine, 1966–68, and Professor of Neurology, 1964–68); *b* 1913; *m* 1942; two *s* two *d*. MB 1937, MD 1940; MRCP 1940, DPM 1943, FRCP 1953. Asst Resident Pathologist, Johns Hopkins Hosp., Baltimore, 1938; clinical appts at Hosp. for Sick Children, Gt Ormond Street, 1939; Neuropsychiatric Specialist, RAF Med. Service, 1942–46; Hammersmith Hosp. and Nat. Hosp., Queen Square, 1946–47; Asst Physician, Royal Victoria Infirmary, Newcastle upon Tyne, 1947–64. Examiner in Medicine, Univ. of Liverpool; Vis. Prof. of Medicine, Univ. of Queensland, 1963. Hon. For. Mem. Soc. Française de Neurologie; Amer. Neurological Assoc. *Publications*: Early Diagnosis, 1960; Modern Medical Treatment, 1962; (with R. Daley) Progress in Clinical Medicine, 1948–71; (with W. B. Matthews) Diseases of the Nervous System, 1972; Medicine and Society, 1973; many papers on medical and neurological subjects. *Address*: Vice-Chancellor's Lodge, Adderstone Cresent, Newcastle upon Tyne 2.

Miller, Prof. James Bennett, TD, MA, LLB; Professor of Mercantile Law, University of Glasgow, since 1963; *b* 1906; *m* 1936; one *d*. MA Glasgow 1924, LLB Glasgow 1927; Solicitor. Lectr, Administrative Law, Glasgow, 1949–63; Assessor, Univ. Court, Univ. of Glasgow, 1972– . Pres., Rent Assessment Panel for Scotland, 1965– ; Mem., Council, Scott. Univs Law Inst., 1963– ; Mem., Council, Stair Soc., 1969– ; Mem., Bd of Mngmt, Glasgow Victoria and Leverndale Hosps, 1963– ; Gov., Dollar Acad., 1966– . *Publications*: Outline of Administrative and Local Government Law in Scotland, 1961; Negotiable Instruments, 1970; Arbitration, 1970; Paisley Union Bank Robbery (Stair Society Miscellany), 1971; The Law of Partnership in Scotland, 1972; *contrib*. Jl Law Soc. Scotl., Jurid. Rev., Mod. Law Rev., Public Law, Scots Law Times. *Address*: Faculty of Law, Univ. of Glasgow, Glasgow G12 8QQ.

Miller, James Edward; Lecturer, Department of Linguistics, University of Edinburgh, since 1970; *b* 1942; *m* 1967; three *s*. MA Edinburgh 1965, Diploma in General Linguistics Edinburgh 1966, PhD Edinburgh 1970. Asst Lectr, Dept of Linguistics, Univ. of Edinburgh, 1967. *Publications*: *contrib*. Jl Linguistics, Foundations of Language. *Address*: Dept of Linguistics, 15 Buccleuch Place, Edinburgh.

Miller, John Gareth; Senior Lecturer in Law, University College, Cardiff, University of Wales, since 1972; *b* 1936; *m* 1966; one *s* one *d*. LLB Wales 1957, LLB Cantab 1959, LLM Wales 1960; Solicitor of Supreme Court 1962 (Hons). Lectr, UWIST Cardiff, 1968–72. *Publications*: Family Property and Financial Provision, 1974; *contrib*. Camb. Law Jl, Law Qly Rev., Modern Law Rev., Solicitors' Jl. *Address*: Dept of Law, Univ. Coll, PO Box 78, Cardiff CF1 1XL.

Miller, Marcus H.; Lecturer, Department of Economics, London School of Economics and Political Science, University of London, since 1967; *b* 1941; *m* 1967; one *d*. BA Oxon

1963, MA Yale 1964, PhD Yale 1971. Economist, Bank of England, 1972–73, on leave of absence. *Publications*: *contrib*. Manchester Sch.; NIER. *Address*: LSE, Houghton Street, Aldwych, WC2A 2AE.

Miller, Norma Patricia, MA; Reader in Latin, Royal Holloway College, University of London, since 1964; *b* 1925. MA Glasgow 1946 (1st cl. Classics), BA Cantab 1948 (1st cl. Classical Tripos, Pt II), MA Cantab 1952. Asst Lectr, Royal Holloway Coll., London, 1948–53; Lectr, 1953–64; Dean of Coll., 1953–55; Vice-Princ., 1964–67; Vis. Prof., Trent Univ., Ontario, 1968. Vice-Chm. Council, Church Schs Co., 1972– (Mem., 1969–). *Publications*: ed, Tacitus: Annals I, 1959, 3rd edn 1971; ed, Tacitus: Annals XV, 1972; *contrib*. Amer. Jl Philol., Bull. Inst. Class. Studies, Class. Rev., Greece Rome, Jl Roman Studies, Rhein. Mus. Philol. *Address*: Dept of Classics, Royal Holloway College, Englefield Green, Surrey.

Miller, Prof. Ronald, MA, PhD, FRSE, FRSGS; Professor of Geography, University of Glasgow, since 1953; *b* 1910; *m* 1940; one *s* one *d*. MA Edinburgh 1931 (1st cl. Geog.), PhD Edinburgh 1933; FRSE 1956, FRSGS 1958. Mem., Royal Scott. Geog. Soc., Geog. Assoc., Inst. Brit. Geogrs. Lectr, Manchester, 1933–36; Lectr, Katsina Coll., 1936–46; Lectr, Edinburgh, 1946–53. Vice-Pres., RSGS; Hon. Ed., Scott. Geog. Mag.; Mem., Livingstone Trust; Nat. Cttee for Geog.; Bd of Govs, Notre Dame Coll. of Educn. *Publications*: (with McNair) Livingstone's Travels, 1954; ed, Mungo Park, 1954; ed (and contrib. with Tivy), The Glasgow Region, 1958; ed (and contrib. with Watson), Essays in Memory of A. G. Ogilvie, 1960; Africa, 1967; (with Luther-Davies) Eday and Hoy, 1968; chapter, in, Mitchell: Great Britain: Geographical Essays, 1962; Field Studies in British Isles, 1964; New Orkney Book, ed Sherer, 1966; *contrib*. Geog., Scott. Geog. Mag., Scott. Studies. *Address*: Dept of Geography, Univ. of Glasgow, Glasgow G12 8QQ.

Miller, Dr William Lockley; Lecturer in Politics, University of Strathclyde, since 1968; *b* 1943; *m* 1967; one *s*. MA Edinburgh 1961, PhD Newcastle 1970; FSS. *Publications*: *contrib*. Jl Royal Stat. Soc., Political Studies, *Address*: Politics Dept, Univ. of Strathclyde, George Street, Glasgow G1 1XH.

Milligan, Dr David Edmond; Lecturer, Department of Philosophy, University of Bristol, since 1959; *b* 1930; *m* 1967; one *s* one *d*. MA Edinburgh 1950 (Mathematics), MA Edinburgh 1954 (Philosophy), PhD Cambridge 1963. Asst in Moral Philosophy, Edinburgh, 1956–59. Fac. Adviser, Combined Degree, 1967–70. *Publications*: *contrib*. Proc. Arist. Soc. *Address*: Dept of Philosophy, Wills Memorial Building, Queens Road, Bristol BS8 1RJ.

Milligan, Martin Orr, MA, BA; Lecturer in Philosophy, University of Leeds, since 1960; *b* 1923; *m* 1955, 1973; one *s*. MA Edinburgh 1942, BA Oxford 1945 (1st cl. PPE). Asst

Lectr in Philosophy, Leeds, 1959–60. Vice-Pres., NUS, 1944–45; Chm., Assoc. Blind and Part Sighted Teachers and Students, 1970–72; Mem., Exec. Council and Educn Cttee, Royal Nat. Inst. for the Blind, 1971– ; Mem., Radio Leeds Local Radio Council, 1972– . *Publications*: trans., K. Marx: Economic and Philosophical Manuscripts, 1959, 3rd edn 1970; *contrib.* Marxism, Today, Mod. Qly. *Address*: Dept of Philosophy, Univ. of Leeds, Leeds LS2 9JT.

Millington, Alan Fred; Lecturer in Valuation, Department of Land Management and Development, University of Reading, since 1967; *b* 1935; *m* 1963; two *s*. BSc London 1965 (Estate Management); ARICS 1967, FRVA. *Address*: Dept of Land Management and Development, The Univ., Whiteknights, Reading RG6 2AH.

Millington, Roy, MA, BA(Soc), DipFE, AMBIM, LCGI; Lecturer in Book Production and Reprography, Postgraduate School of Librarianship and Information Science, University of Sheffield, since 1963; *b* 1928; *m* 1956; two *d*. Licentiateship in Printing, CGLI, 1963, Dip. in Management Studies, AMBIM 1964. Hd of Sch. of Printing, Sheffield Poly., 1957–69. Reg. Mngr, Printing and Publishing Industry Training Bd, 1969– ; Hon. Curator, Stephenson Blake Letter-foundry Ltd, 1971– ; Co-Editor, The Crescent, 1954–59. *Publications*: History of the City of Sheffield Training College, 1956; Prelude to War, 1960; Printing as a School Craft, 1963, 2nd edn 1973. *Address*: Postgraduate School of Librarianship, Univ. of Sheffield, Sheffield S10 2TN.

Millington, Terence Alaric, BSc, FIMA; Lecturer in Mathematics Education, Centre for Science Education, Chelsea College, University of London, since 1969; *b* 1922; *m* 1946; 1964; four *s*. BSc London 1948, Teacher's Dip. London 1949; Fellow, Inst. Maths and its Applications 1966. Mem., Math. Assoc., Assoc. Teachers Maths, Univ. Depts of Educn Maths Study Gp, Soc. Authors, ATCDE. Head of Maths Dept, Haverstock Sch., 1954–57; Hd of Mathematics Dept, Furzedown Coll. of Educn, and Lectr, Univ. of London Inst. of Educn, 1957–69; Unesco Cnsltnt, Thailand, 1971–72; Unesco Expert, Thailand, 1973. Staff Off., RAF HQ, Transp. Cmnd, 1942–46; Mem., Exec. and Council, ATCDE; Chm., London Br., ATCDE, 1966–68; Coordinator, Guinness Awards Project for Encouragement of Maths, 1971– ; Mem., Ed. Bd, Educn for Teaching, 1960–66. *Publications*: Dictionary of Mathematics, 1966, 2nd edn 1972, Amer. edn 1967; Living Mathematics, 1967–72; Introduction to Sets, 1971; Sets and Numbers, 1972; Operations on Sets, 1972; History of Length, 1972; Number and Numeration, 1972; (jtly) Maths through School, 1972; History of Area, 1973; History of Mass, 1974; History of Time, 1974; *contrib.* Educn for Teaching, Teacher. *Address*: Chelsea College, Univ. of London, Bridges Place, SW6.

Mills, Anthony David, MA; Lecturer in English, Queen Mary College, London

University, since 1961; *b* 1935; *m* 1959; two *d*. BA London 1956 (Hons English), MA London 1960 (English). Res. Asst, Univ. Coll., London, 1956–58; Lektor, Uppsala Univ., 1958–61. Asst Sec., Engl. Place-Name Soc., 1962–72; Mem., Council for Name Studies GB and Irel., 1966– ; Council, Engl. Place-Name Soc., 1970– ; Jt Dir, Survey of Engl. Personal Names and Surnames, 1970– . *Publications*: The Dorset Lady Subsidy Roll of 1332, 1971; *contrib.* Engl. Place-Name Soc. Jl, Neuphilol. Mitteil., Notes Queries, Onoma, Proc. Dorset Nat. Hist. Archaeol. Soc., Studia Neophilol. *Address*: Dept of English, Queen Mary College, Mile End Road, E1 4NS.

Mills, Dr Arthur David, MA; Lecturer in English Language, University of Liverpool, since 1966; *b* 1938; *m* 1971; one *s*. BA Manchester 1959, MA Manchester 1960, PhD Manchester 1963. Leverhulme Fellow, Liverpool, 1962–63; Asst Lectr, Liverpool, 1963–66. *Publications*: (with R. M. Lumiansky) The Chester Mystery Cycle: a facsimile of MS Bodley 175, 1973; (with R. M. Lumiansky) The Chester Cycle, vol. I: Text, 1974; *contrib.* Piers Plowman: Critical Approaches, ed S. S. Hussey, 1969; *contrib.* Jl Engl. Germ. Philol., Leeds Studies Engl., Neuphilol. Mitteil., Yr's Wk Engl. Studies. *Address*: Dept of English Language, The Univ., PO Box 147, Liverpool L69 3BX.

Mills, Arthur Edward; Senior Lecturer, since 1963, and Director of Studies, School of Management, University of Bath, since 1968; *b* 1916; *m* 1942; two *s*. BA London 1938 (2nd cl. Mod. Languages) BComm London 1949 (2nd cl.), MSc(Econ) London 1958; AMBIM 1959. Asst Prof., Amer. Univ. of Beirut, 1952–59; Assoc. Prof., Amer. Univ. of Beirut, 1959–61; Sen. Lectr, Univ. of West Indies, 1961–63. *Publications*: Private Enterprise in Lebanon, 1959; Dynamics of Management Control Systems, 1967; (with J. P. Edwards) Management for Technologists, 1968; *contrib.* Jl Mngmt Studies. *Address*: School of Management, Univ. of Bath, Claverton Down, Bath BA2 7AY.

Mills, Donald; Senior Lecturer, Department of Agricultural Economics and Management, Reading University, since 1968; *b* 1921; *m* 1950; two *s* one *d*. BA Manchester 1949 (Hons Econ. and Politics), MS Cornell 1958 (Agricultural Marketing), PhD Reading 1965 (Agric. Econs); FRESoc. 1954. Mem., Agric. Econ. Soc. 1950. Asst in Agric. Economics, Manchester, 1949–50; Asst Lectr in Agric. Econs, Reading, 1950–53; Lectr, Agric. Econs, Reading, 1953–68. *Publications*: (with A. K. Giles) Farm Managers, 1970; (with A. K. Giles) More About Farm Managers, 1971; (with R. S. Cook) Competition in Milk Retailing; *contrib.* Bull. Soc. Econ., Rur., Dairy Indust., Jl Agric. Econ. Soc. *Address*: Dept of Agricultural Economics and Management, The Univ., Reading RG6 2AH.

Mills, Douglas Edgar, Lecturer in Japanese, Faculty of Oriental Studies, University of Cambridge, since 1968; Fellow of Corpus Christi College, Cambridge, since 1974; *b* 1923; *m* 1952; one *s* one *d*. BA Cantab

1944 (Mod. and Medieval Langs), MA Cantab 1947, BA (Hons) London 1945 (Japanese), PhD London 1963 (Japanese Lit.). Lectr in Classical Japanese, SOAS, 1947–63; Associate Prof., later Prof., of Oriental Languages, Univ. of California at Berkeley, 1963–68. *Publications*: A Collection of Tales from Uji: A Study and Translation of Uji Shūi Monogatari, 1970; *contrib*. Bull. of SOAS; Folklore; Jl of Amer. Oriental Soc.; Jl of RAS; Monumenta Nipponica. *Address*: Faculty of Oriental Studies, Sidgwick Avenue, Cambridge CB3 9DA.

Mills, Prof. Gordon; Professor of Economics, University of Kent at Canterbury, since 1973; *b* 1934; *m* 1960. BA Cantab 1955, MA Cantab 1958. Mem., Operat. Res. Soc. Asst Lectr, Univ. of Sheffield, 1958–61; Lectr, Univ. of Bristol, 1961–67, Reader, 1967–73; Vis. Prof., Univ. of Virginia, 1971–72. *Publications*: Introduction to Linear Algebra, 1969; *contrib*. Bull. Oxf. Univ. Inst. Stats, Econ. Jl, Jl Indust. Econ., Jl Transp. Econ. Policy, Operat. Res. Qly, Operats Res., Public Admin. *Address*: Darwin College, The Univ., Canterbury, Kent CT2 7NY.

Mills, Dr Maldwyn; Reader in English, University of Wales, since 1974; *b* 1926; *m* 1955; two *s* one *d*. BA Wales 1950 (1st cl. English), MA Wales 1952, DPhil Oxon 1960. Asst Lectr, Univ. of Wales, Aberystwyth, 1959–60, Lectr, 1960–67, Sen. Lectr, 1967–74. *Publications*: ed, Lybeaus Desconus (EETS no. 261), 1969; (ed) Six Middle English Romances, 1973; *contrib*. Med. Æv., Mod. Lang. Rev., Romania. *Address*: Dept of English, Univ. College, Aberystwyth SY23 2AX.

Mills, Roger Sydney; Lecturer in Romance Studies, University College of Wales, Aberystwyth, since 1967; *b* 1939; *m* 1966; two *d*. BA Cantab 1963. Asst Principal, Scottish Office, 1963–64. *Publications*: contrib. Studies in Modern Spanish Literature and Art presented to Helen Grant; Year's Work in Mod. Lang. Stud. *Address*: Dept of Romance Studies, Univ. Coll., Aberystwyth, Old College, Aberystwyth, SY23 2AX.

Millward, Edward Glynne; Senior Lecturer, Department of Welsh Language and Literature, University College of Wales, Aberystwyth, since 1971; *b* 1930; *m* 1965; one *s* one *d*. BA Cardiff 1950 (Welsh), DipEd Cardiff 1951, MA Wales 1954 (19th century Welsh Lit.). Dept of Educn, UC Swansea, 1960–62; Lectr, UCW Aberystwyth, 1962–71. Mem. Court, UCW Aberystwyth; Mem. Court, Univ. Wales; Mem. Standing Cttee, Univ. of Wales Guild of Graduates; Mem. Extension Bd, Univ. of Wales. *Publications*: Detholion o Ddyddiadur Eben Fardd, 1968; Pryddestau Eisteddfodol Detholedig 1911–1953, 1973; contrib. Gwŷr Llên y Bedwaredd Ganrif ar Bymtheg, 1968; Astudiaethau Amrywiol, 1968; Y Traddodiad Rhyddiaith, 1970; *contrib*. Llên Cymru, Jl Nat. Library Wales, Ysgrifau Beirniadol, etc. *Address*: Univ. Coll. of Wales, Old College, King Street, Aberystwyth SY23 2AX.

Millward, Stanley; Lecturer in Environmental Sciences, Department of Civil Engineering, University of Salford, since 1967; *b* 1920; *m*; one *s* one *d*. Fellow Assoc. Public Hlth Inspectors 1955, Fellow Royal Soc. of Hlth 1966. Lectr, Royal Coll. of Adv. Technol., Salford, 1963–67. *Publications*: Urban Renewal, annually, 1965–73; *contrib*. Environm. Hlth, Munic. Eng., Munic. Jl. *Address*: Dept of Civil Engineering, Univ. of Salford, Salford M5 4WT.

Milne, Prof. Alan J. M.; Professor of Social Philosophy, The Queen's University of Belfast, since 1973; *b* 1922; *m* 1949; two *s* one *d*. BSc(Econ) London, 1949 (1st cl.), PhD London 1952. Mem., Mind Assoc., Pol. Studies Assoc., Irish Philos. Club (North. Sec.). Commonwealth Fund (Harkness) Fellowship, Univ. of California, Berkeley, and Princeton, 1952–54; Asst Lectr, LSE, 1954–56; Lectr in Social Philos.,1956–65, Reader in Philosophy, 1965–73, Queen's Univ., Belfast. ACLS Res. Fellowship, Univ. of Calif. at Berkeley, 1963–64; Vis. Prof., San Diego State Coll., 1970. *Publications*: The Social Philosophy of English Idealism, 1962; Freedom and Rights, 1968; The Right to Dissent (inaug. lecture), 1974; Collingwood's Ethics and Political Theory, in, Critical Essays on the Philosophy of R. G. Collingwood, ed M. Krausz, 1972; Reason, Morality and Politics, in, The Morality of Politics, ed Parekh and Berki, 1972; *contrib*. Europ. Jl Sociol. Philos. Bks, Pol Studies, NI Legal Qly. *Address*: Dept of Philosophy, The Queen's Univ. of Belfast, Belfast BT7 1NN.

Milne, Dr Henry; Senior Lecturer in Zoology, University of Aberdeen (also teaches population dynamics and conservation), since 1972 (Lecturer, 1965–72); *b* 1935; *m* 1960; one *s* one *d*. BSc Aberdeen 1960, PhD Aberdeen 1963. Mem., Brit. Ecol. Soc., Brit. Ornith. Union. Asst Lecturer, Aberdeen, 1963–65. Mem., Nature Conservancy Supervisory Cttee for Loch Leven Res., 1968–72. *Publications*: contrib. Readings in Population Biology, ed Dawson and King, 1971; The Estuarine Environment, ed Barnes and Green, 1972; *contrib*. Bird Study, Ibis, Nature, Oris. Scand., Scott. Birds. *Address*: Culterty Field Station, Newburgh, Aberdeenshire.

Milne, Paul Stocks; Lecturer in Economics, Univ. of Hull, since 1968; *b* 1942; *m* 1965; one *d*. MA Aberdeen 1964 (Econ. Science). Mem., Royal Econ. Soc., Amer. Econ. Assoc. Asst Lectr, Hull Univ., 1965–68. *Address*: Dept of Economics, Univ. of Hull, Hull HU6 7RX.

Milne, Thomas Edwardson; Lecturer, Department of Management Studies, University of Glasgow, since 1969; *b* 1937; *m* 1962; two *s*. MA Glasgow 1959, MLitt Glasgow 1965; Certs ITP Harvard 1970, 1972. MInst Mktng 1967. Lectr, Dept of Business Studies, Edinburgh, 1965–69. *Publications*: Business Forecasting, A Managerial Approach (forthcoming); contrib. Studies in Scottish Business History, ed P. L. Payne, 1967; Institute of Economic Affairs, Essays in the Theory and Practice of Pricing (Institute of Economic Affairs), 1968.

Address: Dept of Management Studies, Adam Smith Building, The Univ., Glasgow G12 8RT.

Milner, Dr Alan; Fellow of Trinity College, Oxford, since 1966, and Lecturer in Law in the University of Oxford, since 1967; *b* 1936; *m* 1958; two *s* two *d*. LLB Leeds 1956 (1st cl.), LLM Yale 1958, PhD Leeds 1961, MA Oxon 1966; Barrister-at-Law, Gray's Inn, 1957. Instructor, Univ. of Pittsburgh, 1958–59; Lectr, Queen's Univ., Belfast, 1959–63; Prof. and Dean of Law, Ahmadu Bello Univ., Nigeria, 1963–65; Vis. Prof., Univ. of Pennsylvania, 1965–66; Vis. Prof., UCLA, 1970; Vis. Prof., Max Planck Inst. for Criminal Law, Freiburg, 1972, 1973. Hon. Sec., N Irel. Assoc. Study and Treatment Delinquency, 1960–63; Mem., Nigerian Council Legal Educn, 1963–65; Ed. in Chief, Afr. Law Reps, 1966– . *Publications*: African Penal Systems, 1969; Modern African Contract Cases, 1971; The Nigerian Penal System, 1972; (with S. Abrahams) Modern African Banking Cases, 1973; *contrib*. Brit. Jl Criminol., Internat. Comp. Law Qly, Jl Legal Educn, Mod. Law Rev., Nig. Law Jl. *Address*: Trinity College, Oxford.

Milner, Dr Arthur David; MA, PhD; Lecturer in Psychology, University of St Andrews, since 1970; *b* 1943; *m* 1965; two *s*. BA Oxon 1965 (2nd cl. Psychology, Philos. and Physiol.); DipPsych London 1966; MA Oxon 1970; PhD London 1971. Mem., Exper. Psychol. Soc. Res. worker, Inst. of Psychiatry, London, 1966–70. *Publications*: *contrib*. Brain, Cortex, Jl Comp. Physiol. Psychol., Neuropsychol. *Address*: Dept of Psychology, Univ. of St Andrews, St Andrews, Fife KY16 9AJ.

Milner, Charles Albert, MA; Lecturer in French, Department of European Studies, Loughborough University of Technology, since 1965; *b* 1931; *m* 1956; one *s* three *d*. BA Cantab 1954, MA Cantab 1969. *Publications*: Jean Legallois, 1971. *Address*: Dept of European Studies, Loughborough Univ. of Technology, Loughborough LE11 3TU.

Milner, Prof. George Bertram, MA, PhD; Professor of Austronesian Studies, University of London, since 1971; *b* 1918; *m* 1946; three *s*. BA Cantab 1940 (Mod. and Med. Langs), MA Cantab 1947; PhD London 1968; Academic Dip. in Anthropology London 1954; FRAS, FRAI. Lectr in Oceanic Langs, SOAS, Univ. of London, 1948, Reader (by appointment), 1964–71. *Publications*: Fijian Grammar, 1956, 3rd edn 1972; Samoan Dictionary, 1966; ed (with E. J. A. Henderson), Indo-Pacific Linguistic Studies, 1965; *contrib*. BSOAS, BSO, L'Homme, JRAI, JPS, Man, Semiotica. *Address*: Dept of South East Asia and the Islands, School of Oriental and African Studies, Malet Street, WC1E 7HP.

Milner-Gulland, Robert Rainsford; Reader in Russian, School of European Studies, University of Sussex, since 1973 (Lecturer, 1964–73); *b* 1936; *m* 1966; one *s* two *d*. BA Oxon 1959, MA Oxon 1963. Asst Lectr, Univ. of Sussex, 1962–64. Mem., Brit. Univs

Assoc. of Slavists, 1962– (Mem. Cttee, 1969– ; Treas., 1972–); Chm., Russian Studies, Univ. of Sussex, 1962–71. *Publications*: trans. and ed (with P. Levi), Yevtuskenko: Selected Poems, 1962; introd. and ed (with P. Levi), Yevtuskenko, 1963; Soviet Russian Verse, 1964; *contrib*. Oxf. Slav. Papers, Slav. E Europ. Rev., Sov. Studies. *Address*: Arts Building, Univ. of Sussex, Falmer, Sussex BN1 9QN.

Milsom, Prof. Stroud Francis Charles, FBA; Professor of Legal History, University of London, since 1964; Literary Director, Selden Society, since 1964; *b* 1923; *m* 1955. MA Cantab 1948; Hon. Bencher Lincoln's Inn; FRHistS; Corr. Fellow, Amer. Soc. Leg. Hist. Admiralty, 1944–45. Commonwealth Fund (Harkness) Fellow, Univ. of Pennsylvania, 1947–48; Yorke Prize, Cambridge, 1948; Prize Fellow, Trinity Coll., Cambridge, 1948; Fellow and Lectr, Trinity Coll., Cambridge, 1949–55; Univ. Asst Lectr and Lectr in Law, Cambridge, 1949–55; Asst Lectr, LSE, 1955–56; CUF Lectr, Oxford, 1956–64; Fellow and Tutor, New Coll., Oxford, 1956–64, Dean, 1959–64; Vis. Lectr, NY Univ. Law Sch., 1958, 1961, 1964, 1967, 1970; Vis. Prof., Yale Law Sch., 1968, 1973; Vis. Prof., Harvard Law Sch., 1973. Maitland Meml Lectures, Cambridge, 1972; Addison Harris Lectures, Indiana Univ. Law Sch., 1974. Ames Prize, Harvard, 1972; Swiney Prize for Jurisprudence, RSA, 1974. *Publications*: introd. and trans., Novae Narrationes, 1963; introd., Pollock and Maitland: History of English Law, 1968; Historical Foundations of the Common Law, 1969; *contrib*. Cambridge Law Jl, Law Qly Rev., Toronto Law Jl. *Address*: Dept of Law, London School of Economics (Univ. of London), Houghton Street, Aldwych, WC2A 2AE.

Milton, Prof. Alan, MA; Professor of Education, The New University of Ulster, since 1967; *b* 1910; *m* 1938; two *d*. BA Cambridge 1932 (1st cl. History), MA Cambridge 1937; Hon. FCP. Sec., Univ. of Exeter Inst. of Educn, 1951–53; Dir, Univ. of Exeter Inst. of Educn, 1953–61; Prof. of Educn and Dir, Inst. of Educn, Univ. Coll. of Rhodesia, 1961–67; Dean, Fac. of Educn, Univ. Coll. of Rhodesia, 1964–66; Vice-Principal, Univ. Coll. of Rhodesia, 1966, Acting Principal, 1966–67; Dir, Educn Centre, New Univ. of Ulster, 1967–72. Pro-Vice-Chancellor, New Univ. of Ulster, 1967–72, Public Orator, 1970– . *Address*: The New Univ. of Ulster, Coleraine, Co. Londonderry BT52 1SA.

Milward, Prof. Alan Steele; Professor of European Studies, University of Manchester Institute of Science and Technology, since 1971; *b* 1935. BA, PhD London. FRHistS. Member: Economic History Soc.; Economic History Assoc. Asst Lectr, Lectr in Economic History, Univ. of Edinburgh, 1960–65; Lectr, then Sen. Lectr, School of Social Studies, Univ. of East Anglia, 1965–68; Associate Prof. of Economics, Stanford Univ., 1968–71. *Publications*: The German Economy at War, 1965, German and Italian edns; The New Order and the French Economy, 1970; The

Fascist Economy in Norway, 1972; (with S. B. Saul) An Economic History of Continental Europe, 1780–1870, 1973. *Address*: Dept of European Studies, UMIST, PO Box 88, Sackville St, Manchester M60 1QD.

Minchinton, Prof. Walter Edward; Professor of Economic History, and Head of Department, University of Exeter, since 1964; *b* 1921; *m* 1945; two *s* two *d*. BSc(Econ) London 1945 (1st cl. Econ. Hist.); FRHistS. Asst Lectr, Univ. Coll., Swansea, 1948–50; Lectr, Univ. Coll., Swansea, 1950–59; Sen. Lectr, Univ. Coll., Swansea, 1959–64; Rockefeller Res. Fellow, 1959–60; Vis. Prof., Fourah Bay Coll., Sierra Leone, 1965. Mem., Council, Econ. Hist. Soc., 1954–66; Council, Brit. Agric. Hist. Soc., 1952– ; Chm., Brit. Agric. Hist. Soc., 1968–71; Mem., Brit. Nat. Cttee, Internat. Cong. Hist. Sci., 1969–73; Chm., Confed. Advance. State Educn, 1964–67; Devon Co. Educn Cttee, 1967–74; Mem., Exeter Educn Cttee, 1967–74 (Chm., 1972). *Publications*: The Trade of Bristol in the Eighteenth Century, 1957, 2nd edn 1966; The British Tinplate Industry: a history, 1957; Politics and the Port of Bristol in the Eighteenth Century, 1963; ed, Essays in Agrarian History, 1968; ed, Mercantilism: system or expediency?, 1969; ed, Industrial South Wales: essays in Welsh economic history, 1969; ed, The Growth of English Overseas Trade in the Seventeenth and Eighteenth Centuries, 1969; ed, Wage Regulation in Pre-industrial England, 1972; Devon at Work, 1974; *contrib*. Agric. Hist. Rev., Ann. Bibliog. Hist. Lit., Econ. Hist. Rev., Explor. Entrepren. Hist., Mariner's Mirror, SC Hist. Mag., Trans Brist. Glos Archaeol. Soc., Trans Royal Hist. Soc., Va Mag. *Address*: Dept of Economic History, The Univ., Exeter EX4 4PU.

Mingay, Prof. Gordon Edmund, BA, PhD, FRHistS; Professor of Agrarian History, Department of Economic and Social History, University of Kent, since 1968; *b* 1923; *m* 1945. BA Nottingham 1952 (1st cl. Econ. and Social Hist.), PhD Nottingham 1958; FRHistS. Lectr, LSE, 1956–65; Reader, Kent, 1965–68; Chm. of Subject, 1971–73; Vis. Lectr, Wisconsin, 1962–63; Brit. Columbia, 1964; Montana, 1967; Nebraska, 1969. Mem., Exec. Cttee, Brit. Agric. Hist. Soc., 1967– ; Editor, Agricultural History Rev., 1972– ; Jt Ed., Agrar. Hist. Engl. and Wales, vol. VI. *Publications*: English Landed Society in 18th Century, 1963; (with J. D. Chambers) The Agricultural Revolution 1750–1880, 1966; ed (with E. L. Jones), Land, Labour and Population in the Industrial Revolution, 1967; Enclosure and the Small Farmer in the Age of the Industrial Revolution, 1968; (with P. S. Bagwell) Britain and America, 1970; *contrib*. Agric. Hist., Agric. Hist. Rev., Econ. Hist. Rev., EHR, Ethno-psychol., Thoroton Soc. *Address*: Rutherford College, Univ. of Kent, Canterbury, Kent.

Mingay, Jean Mary, MA, BLitt; Lecturer in Education and Classics Method, Department of Education, Sheffield University, since 1966; *b* 1916; *m* 1940; three *s* one *d*. Classical Hon. Mods Oxford 1937 (1st cl.), Lit. Hum. Oxford 1939 (1st cl.), BLitt, MA Oxford 1950. Lectr in Educn, Univ. of Saskatchewan, 1970–71. Jt Assoc. Classical Teachers: Mem. Council, 1969–72; Sec. Council, 1970– ; Hon. Publications Sec., 1968– . *Publications*: contrib. Proceedings of the Symposium Aristotelicum, 1971; Islamic Philosophy and the Classical Tradition (Festschrift for Richard Walzer), 1972 *Address*: Dept of Education, The Univ., Sheffield S10 2TN.

Minio-Paluello, Dr Lorenzo; Reader in Medieval Philosophy, University of Oxford, since 1956, and Fellow of Oriel College, Oxford, since 1962; *b* 1907; *m* 1938; one *s* one *d*. Dottore in Filosofia Padua 1929, DPhil Oxon 1948, MA Oxon 1948; FBA 1957, Corresp. Fellow Mediaeval Acad. of Amer. 1970, Foreign Mem., Amer. Philos. Soc. 1971. Asst, Padua Univ., 1929–32; Fellow, Warburg Inst., Univ. London, 1947–48; Sen. Lectr, Mediev. Philos., Oxford Univ., 1948–56; Barlow Lectr, Univ. London, 1955; Prof. Straordinario de Filol. Mediev. e Uman., Padua Univ., 1956–57; Mem., Inst. for Advanced Study, Princeton, 1969–70, 1974–76. Gen. Editor, Aristoteles Latinus, 1959–72. *Publications*: trans. Italian Plato: Cratylos, 1932; Education in Fascist Italy, 1946; Critical editions: Aristotle: Categ. et De Interpr. (Greek), 1949 and 1957; Plato: Phaedo (mediaev. Latin trans.), 1950; Aristotle: Categ., De Interpr., Anal. Pr., Anal. Post., Top., Poet. (Aristot. Latinus I–V, XXXIII) 1953–69; Aristoteles Latinus: Codices, Pars Post. and Supplem. Alt. 1955, 1961; Twelfth Century Logic, vols I and II, 1956, 1958; Opuscula: The Latin Aristotle, 1972; articles in Encycl. Brit., Dizionario Biografico degli Italiani, Dict. of Scient. Biogr.; *contrib*. Class. Qly, Ital. Stud., Jl Hellenic Studies, Med. and Renaiss. Stud., Rev. Philos. de Louvain, Riv. di Filos. Neoscolastica, Studi Medievali, Traditio. *Address*: Oriel College, Oxford.

Minkes, Prof. Leonard; Professor of Business Organisation, Department of Industrial Economics and Business Studies, University of Birmingham, since 1972; Dean, Faculty of Commerce and Social Science, since 1972; *b* 1924; *m* 1948; one *s* one *d*. BA Oxon 1945 (PPE), MA Oxon 1948. Res. and lect. posts, Oxford, London, Birmingham; vis. appts and consulting work, USA, Ceylon, etc.; Dir, Grad. Centre for Management Studies, Birmingham, 1966–72. Econ. Affairs Officer, ECE Geneva, 1947–49; mem. management educn cttees, 1966–72; UNO expert, business organ. and man. develt 1973. *Publications*: contrib. Economica, Econ. Devt and Cult. Change, Jl Indust. Econs, Jl Man. Stud. *Address*: Faculty of Commerce and Social Science, Univ. of Birmingham, PO Box 363, Birmingham B15 2TT.

Minogue, Kenneth Robert; Reader in Political Science, and Dean of Undergraduate Studies, London School of Economics and Political Science, since 1971; *b* 1930; *m* 1954; one *s* one *d*. BA Sydney 1949, BSc Econ 1955 (1st cl. Govt). Asst Lectr in Public Admin, Univ. Coll., Exeter, 1955–56; Asst Lectr in Polit. Science, LSE, 1956–64; Sen. Lectr,

LSE, 1964–71. Mem., Cttee, Polit. Studies Assoc., 1965–70. *Publications*: The Liberal Mind, 1963; Nationalism, 1967; The Concept of a University, 1973; *contrib*. Amer. Schol., Europ. Jl Sociol. Pol. Studies, Encounter, etc. *Address*: Dept of Government, London School of Economics, Houghton Street, WC2A 2AE.

Minogue, Martin; Lecturer in Government and Politics, Department of Overseas Administrative Studies, Manchester University, since 1969; *b* 1937; *m* 1968. BA Cambridge 1962 (Hons Hist.), MA Cambridge 1964. Lectr in Govt and Politics, Univ. of Kent, 1966–69. 2nd Sec., HM Diplomatic Serv., 1962–66; Admissions Off., Fac. of Soc. Science, Univ. of Kent, 1968–69; Vis. Fellow in Public Administration, Univ. of Mauritius, 1971–73. *Publications*: ed (with Judith Molloy), African Aims and Attitudes, 1974; contrib. Government and Administration in Mauritius, 1973. *Address*: Dept of Overseas Administrative Studies, The Precinct Centre, Oxford Road, Manchester M13 9PL.

Minogue, Valerie P., MLitt; Lecturer in French, Queen Mary College, University of London, since 1964; *b* 1931; *m* 1954; one *s* one *d*. BA Cantab 1952, MLitt Cantab 1957; Mem., Soc. for French Studies. Assistant Lecturer: UCW, Cardiff, 1952–53; QMC, London Univ., 1962–63. *Publications*: Critical Commentary: Proust, Du Côté de Chez Swann, 1973; *contrib*. Forum for Mod. Lang. Studies; French Studies; MLR; Mod. Langs. *Address*: Queen Mary College, Mile End Road, E1 4NS.

Mirrlees, Prof. James Alexander; Professor of Economics, University of Oxford, since 1968; *b* 1936; *m* 1961; two *d*. MA Edinburgh 1957 (1st cl. Maths), BA Cantab 1959 (1st cl. Maths), PhD Cantab 1963 (Economics); Fellow Economet. Soc. Res. Assoc., MIT Center for Internat. Studies, Delhi, 1962–63; Univ. Asst Lectr, then Lectr, and Fellow, Trinity Coll., Cambridge Univ., 1963–68; Res. Assoc., Yale-Pakistan project, Karachi, 1965–66, etc; Vis. Prof., MIT, 1968, 1970; Fellow, Nuffield Coll., Oxford, 1968– ; Assoc. Ed., Rev. Econ. Studies, 1970– . Mem., Council, Economet. Soc., 1971– ; Dir, Internat. Econ. Assoc. Europ. Wkshop in Econ. Theory, 1971. *Publications*: (with I. M. D. Little) Manual of Industrial Project Analysis in Developing Countries, vol. II: Social Cost-Benefit Analysis, 1969; (with I. M. D. Little) Project Analysis and Planning, 1974; ed (with N. H. Stern), Models of Economic Growth, 1973; contrib. var. conf. proc. vols; *contrib*. Amer. Econ. Rev., Jl Econ. Theory, Jl Publ. Econ., Pak. Develop. Rev., Qly Jl Econ., Rev. Econ. Studies, Swed. Jl Econ. *Address*: Nuffield College, Oxford OX1 1NF.

Mishan, Dr Ezra Joshua, (Edward); Reader in Economics, London School of Economics, since 1963; Professor of Economics, The American University, DC; *b* 1917; *m* 1952; two *s* two *d*. BA Manchester 1946, MSc(Econ) London 1948, PhD Chicago 1951. Asst Lectr, 1956; Lectr, 1959.

Publications: Welfare Economics: 10 Introductory Essays, 1967; The Costs of Economic Growth, 1967; Welfare Economics: An Assessment, 1969; 21 Popular Economic Fallacies, 1970; Cost-Benefit Analysis, 1971; Making the World Safe for Pornography and Other Intellectual Fashions, 1973; *contrib*. Economic Jl, Economica, Oxford Economic Papers, Rev. of Economics Studies, Amer. Economic Rev., Jl of Political Economy, Canadian Jl of Econs. *Address*: London School of Economics, Houghton Street, WC2A 2AE.

Mitchell, Prof. Basil George; Nolloth Professor of the Philosophy of the Christian Religion, Oxford University, and Fellow of Oriel College, since 1968; *b* 1917; *m* 1950; one *s* three *d*. BA Oxon 1939 (1st cl. Lit. Hum.), MA Oxon 1945. Lectr, Christ Church, Oxford, 1946–47; Fellow and Tutor in Philo., Keble Coll., Oxford, 1947–67; Sen. Proctor, 1956–57; Hebdomadal Council, 1959–65; Vis. Prof., Princeton Univ., 1963; Stanton Lectr in Philos. of Religion, Cambridge Univ., 1959–62, Edward Cadbury Lectr, Univ. of Birmingham, 1966–67. Mem., Council, St David's Coll., Lampeter, 1959– . *Publications*: Law, Morality and Religion in a Secular Society, 1967; Neutrality and Commitment, 1968; (ed) Faith and Logic, 1957; (ed) The Philosophy of Religion, 1971; The Justification of Religious Belief, 1973; *contrib*. Philosoph. and theol. periodicals. *Address*: Oriel College, Oxford.

Mitchell, Dr Brian Redman, MA, PhD; University Lecturer in Economics, Cambridge University, and Fellow of Trinity College, since 1967; *b* 1929; *m* 1st 1952, 2nd 1968; two *s*. MA Aberdeen 1952 (1st cl. Econs), PhD Cantab 1955. Jun. Res. Off., Cambridge Univ. Dept of Applied Econs, 1958–60; Res. Off., Cambridge Dept of Applied Econs, 1960–66; Vis. Lectr, Univ. of Colorado, 1963; Sen. Res. Off., Cambridge Dept of Applied Econs, 1966–67. *Publications*: Abstract of British Historical Statistics, 1962; British Parliamentary Election Results 1950–64, 1966; Second Abstract of British Historical Statistics, 1971; European Historical Statistics 1750–1969, 1975; *contrib*. Jl Econ. Hist. *Address*: Trinity College, Cambridge.

Mitchell, Dr Colin Ware, FRGS; Lecturer in Geography, University of Reading, since 1967; *b* 1927; *m* 1963; three *s* two *d*. BA Oxon 1950 (2nd cl. Geography), MA Oxon 1952, MCD Liverpool 1952, Cert. Soil Science Aberdeen 1956, PhD Cantab 1971; FRGS 1949. Mem., Brit and Internat. Socs Soil Science, Mem., Brit. and Internat. Socs Photogrammetry. Min. of Defence Res. Fellow, Cambridge Univ., 1963–67. *Publications*: (with Dr T. N. Jewitt) Methods of Soil Survey in the Anglo-Egyptian Sudan, 1954; Soil Survey of a Sample Area in Equatoria: Yambio Experimental Farm, 1955; (with R. M. S. Perrin) The Subdivision of World Hot Deserts into Physiographic Units, 1966; Glossary of Local Physiographic and Hydro-geological Terms about World Hot Deserts, 1969; (with S. G. Willimott and P. M. Blaikie) Report of the Reading University Expedition to Moroccan Sahara, 1969;

(with R. M. S. Perrin) An Appraisal of Physiographic Units for Predicting Site Conditions in Arid Areas, 1970; The Interpretation of Dayas on Aerial Photographs of Arid Areas, 1970; Terrain Evaluation, 1973; Soil Classification with Particular Reference to the Seventh Approximation, 1974; *contrib.* Geoforum, Geog. Jl, Photogram. Rec., Jl Soil Science. *Address*: Dept of Geography, Univ. of Reading, Whiteknights, Reading RG6 2AF.

Mitchell, David, MA; Fellow and Tutor of Worcester College, University of Oxford, since 1946, and University Lecturer in Philosophy, Oxford; *b* 1914; *m* 1947; three *s* one *d*. BA Oxon 1937 (1st cl. Class. Hon. Mods, 1st cl. Lit. Hum. 1937). John Locke Schol., Oxford Univ., 1937; Sen. Schol., St John's Coll., Oxford, 1937–40; Vis. Prof. Brown Univ., 1965; Vis. Prof., Dartmouth Coll., 1967; Vice-Provost, Worcester Coll., 1971; Vis. Lectr, Witwatersrand Univ., 1972. Gov., Bromsgrove Sch., 1953– ; Gov., Canford Sch., 1972– ; Mem., Senate Cttee on Govt and Admin. of Univ. of Warwick, 1970; Acad. Adv. Council, RMA Sandhurst, 1969– . *Publications*: An Introduction to Logic, 1962, 2nd edn 1964, American edn 1970, Spanish edn 1968; *contrib.* Mind. *Address*: Worcester College, Oxford.

Mitchell, Prof. Geoffrey Duncan, MBE, BSc(Econ), FRAI; Professor of Sociology, since 1967, and Head of the Department of Sociology (with Social Administration), University of Exeter, since 1963; *b* 1921; *m* 1950; one *s* one *d*. BSc(Econ) London 1949; FRAI. Res. Worker, Liverpool, 1950–51; Sen. Res. Worker, Liverpool, 1951–52; Lectr, Birmingham, 1952–54; Dep. Lectr, Oxford, 1954–55; Lectr in charge, Univ. Coll. of South West, Exeter, 1954–58; Sen. Lectr, Univ. Coll. of South West, Exeter, 1958–67; Dean, Fac. Soc. Studies, 1964–67; Dep. Vice-Chancellor, Exeter, 1971–73, Acting Vice-Chancellor, 1972–73; Dir, Family Planning Res. Unit, Exeter, 1971– . *Publications*: (jtly) Neighbourhood and Community, 1954; Sociology: the Study of Social Systems, 1959, 2nd edn 1970; A Hundred Years of Sociology, 1968; ed, A Dictionary of Sociology, 1968; Sociology: An Outline for the Intending Student, 1970; *contrib.* Sociol. Rev., Hum. Rel., Public Admin. *Address*: Dept of Sociology, Univ. of Exeter, Streatham Court, Rennes Drive, Exeter EX4 4PU.

Mitchell, Prof. George Francis, FRS; Professor of Quaternary Studies, Botany, also lecturing on Art in Early Christian Ireland, Trinity College, Dublin, since 1965; *b* 1912; *m* 1940; two *d*. MA Dublin 1937, MSc Dublin 1936; MRIA 1940, FRS 1973. Lectr in Geology, 1934, Reader in Irish Archaeology, 1959–65, Univ. of Dublin; Fellow, TCD, 1944. Pres., Internat. Union for Quaternary Res., 1969. *Publications*: *contrib.* Jl Geol. Soc. London, Jl RSAI, Proc. Royal Dublin Soc., Proc. RIA, Proc. Royal Soc., Special Paper Geol. Soc. America, Proc. USSR Acad. Sci. *Address*: Trinity College, Dublin 2, Ireland.

Mitchell, Dr Joan Eileen, MA; Reader in

Economics, Nottingham University, since 1956; *b* 1920; *m* 1956; one *s* one *d*. BA Oxon 1942, PhD Nottingham 1956. Tutor, St Anne's Coll., Oxford, 1945–47; Lectr, Nottingham Univ., 1952–56. Mem., Prices and Incomes Bd, 1965–68; Mem., E Midlands Plan. Council, 1964–65. *Publications*: Crisis in Britain 1951, 1963; Groundwork to Economic Planning, 1966; The National Board for Prices and Incomes, 1972. *Address*: Dept of Economics, Univ. of Nottingham, Nottingham NG7 2RD.

Mitchell, John, BA; Lecturer, Department of French, University of Southampton, since 1965; *b* 1936; *m* 1965; one *s* one *d*. BA Birmingham 1963 (1st cl. French). Lecteur d'Anglais, Montpellier, 1963; Asst Lectr, Southampton, 1964–65. *Publications*: Stendhal: Le Rouge et le Noir (Studies in French Literature), 1973. *Address*: Dept of French, Univ. of Southampton, Highfield, Southampton SO9 5NH.

Mitchell, Prof. John David Bawden, CBE; Salvesen Professor of European Institutions, Centre of European Governmental Studies, University of Edinburgh, since 1967; *b* 1917; *m* 1945; two *d*. LLB London 1938, PhD London 1952, LLD Edinburgh 1964; Hon. Dr Lille 1965; Solicitor of the Supreme Court England 1947. Lectr, Univ. Coll. of Wales, Aberystwyth, 1947–48; Lectr, Law Soc.'s Sch., Aberystwyth, 1948–49; Lectr, LSE, Aberystwyth, 1949–52; Reader in English Law, Univ. of London, 1952–54; Prof. of Constitutional Law, Edinburgh, 1954–68. *Publications*: The Contracts of Public Authorities, 1954; Constitutional Law, 1964, 2nd edn 1968; *contrib.* Jurid. Rev., Law Qly Rev., Mod. Law Rev., CML Rev., Rev. Droit Public. *Address*: Centre of European Governmental Studies, Old College, South Bridge, Edinburgh EH8 9YL.

Mitchell, Patrick Charles; Lecturer, Department of French, University of Glasgow, since 1973; *b* 1943; *m* 1967; one *d*. BA Wales, 1966; Member: Soc. for French Studies; Brit. Soc. for Eighteenth Century Studies. Lectr, QUB, 1968–73. *Address*: The Univ., Glasgow G12 8QQ.

Mitchell, Dr Peter K.; Senior Lecturer in Geography, Centre of West African Studies, University of Birmingham, since 1974; *b* 1932; *m* 1955; two *s* one *d*. BA Durham 1954 (Hons Geog.), PhD Durham 1966; Member: Inst. of Brit. Geographers; Sierra Leone Geographical Assoc.; African Studies Assoc. of UK; Internat. Union for Scientific Study of Population. Res. Fellow in Colonial Studies, Durham, 1956–58; Lectr, later Sen. Lectr, Fourah Bay Coll., Univ. of Sierra Leone, 1959–66; Lectr, 1967–74, and Dir, Demographic Documentation Proj., Centre of West African Studies, Univ. of Birmingham, 1971–74. Pres., Sierra Leone Geographical Assoc., 1963–64; Mem. Cttee, Population Geog. Study Group, Inst. of British Geographers, 1972–74; Convener, Liaison Cttee, Drought and Famine in Africa, Internat. Congress of African Studies, 1973– . Corresp. Mem., IGU Commn on Population Geog., 1973– . Editor and publisher (for

Sierra Leone Geographical Assoc.) Sierra Leone Geographical Journal, 1962– ; Editor, Newsletter, Demographic Documentation Project. *Publications: contrib.* Qly Jl Roy. Meteor. Soc., Melita Historica, Sierra Leone Geog. Jl, Sierra Leone Stud., Pan-Afr. Jl, Afr. Lang. Rev., Agric. Meteor. *Address:* Centre of West African Studies, Univ. of Birmingham, PO Box 363, Birmingham B15 2TT.

Mitchell, Dr Sheila; Senior Lecturer, Sociology Department, University of Stirling, since 1968; *b* 1926. BSc (Econ.) Southampton 1955, PhD London 1965. Res. Asst, Univ. of Sheffield, 1955–58; Res. Associate, King's Coll., Newcastle upon Tyne, 1958–60; Res. Fellow, Inst. of Psychiatry, London, 1960–65; Lecturer in Epidemiology, Univ. of Glasgow, 1965–67; Lectr in Sociology, Univ. of Stirling, 1967–68. *Publications:* with M. Shepherd and B. Oppenheim) Childhood Behaviour and Mental Health, 1971 (trans. Spanish 1972, German 1973); *contrib.* Brit. Jl Educl Psychol., Jl Child Psychol. and Psych., Population Studies. *Address:* Sociology Dept, Univ. of Stirling, Stirling FK9 4LA.

Mitchell, Simon; Institute of Latin American Studies, University of Glasgow, since 1968; *b* 1938; *m* 1962; three *d.* MA Oxon (Hons Mod. History), MA London (Social Anthropology). *Address:* Institute of Latin American Studies, Univ. of Glasgow, Glasgow G12 8QQ.

Mitchell, Stanley; Senior Lecturer in Literature, University of Essex, since 1973; *b* 1932; *m* 1956; one *s* one *d.* BA Oxon 1956, MA Oxon; Mem., Brit. Univs Assoc. of Slavists. Asst. Lectr, Univ. Birmingham, 1960–62, Lectr, 1962–65; Lectr, Univ. Essex, 1965–73. *Publications:* trans., Georg Lukács: The Historical Novel, 1962; trans., Georg Lukács: Essays on Thomas Mann, 1965; *contrib.* Forum, Mod. Lang. Jl Univ. St Andrews, Slavonic and East European Review. *Address:* Dept of Literature, Univ. of Essex, Wivenhoe Park, Colchester CO4 3SQ.

Mitchell, Prof. Terence Frederick; Professor of Linguistics, and Head of Department of Linguistics, University of Leeds, since 1971; *b* 1919; *m* 1940; one *s* two *d.* BA London 1940 (1st cl. French with Spanish). Mem., Philol. Soc., Lingu. Assoc. GB, Lingu. Soc. Amer., Assoc. Brit. Orient. Lectr in Phonetics, SOAS, London, 1946–48; Lectr in Linguistics, SOAS, London, 1948–60; Reader, SOAS, London, 1960–64; Prof., Leeds, 1964– (Contemporary English 1964–66); English Lang. and General Lingu., Leeds, 1966–71; Chm., Sch. of English, Leeds, 1967–70; Vis. Lectr, Princeton, 1961; Vis. Lectr, Illinois, 1968; co-ed., Archiv. Lingu., 1965– ; Mem. Edit. Bd, Jl Lingu., 1968– . Sec., Assoc. Brit. Orient, 1960–64; Mem., Sub-cttee, Nat. Commn for UNESCO, 1960–64; Mem.,Nat. Cttee on Res. and Develop. in Mod. Langs, 1964–67; Mem., Council, Philol. Soc., 1965–69; Mem., Engl. Teaching Adv. Cttee, Brit. Council, 1962– ; Mem., Gov. Body, City of Leeds and Carnegie Coll. of

Educn, 1967– ; Mem., Arts Sub-Cttee, UGC, 1969– ; Mem., DES Studentship Sel. Cttee, 1970– . *Publications:* Writing Arabic, 1953, pbk edn 1971; An Introduction to Egyptian Colloquial Arabic, 1956; Teach Yourself Colloquial Arabic, 1962; Principles of Firthian Linguistics (forthcoming); contrib. on Arabic, Berber, English and general linguistics to collected and memorial vols; *contrib.* Archiv. Lingu., Bull. SOAS, Hespéris (-Tamuda), Trans Philol. Soc. *Address:* Dept of Linguistics, The Univ., Leeds LS2 9JT.

Mitchison, Rosalind Mary; Lecturer, Economic History Department, Edinburgh University, since 1967; *b* 1919; *m* 1947; one *s* three *d.* BA Oxon 1942, MA Oxon 1945; FRHistS. Asst Lectr, Manchester Univ., 1943–46; Tutor, Lady Margaret Hall, Oxford, 1946–47; Asst, Edinburgh Univ., 1954–57; Asst, Glasgow Univ., 1962–63; Pt-time Lectr, Glasgow, 1966–67. *Publications:* Agricultural Sir John, 1962; A History of Scotland, 1970; ed (with N. T. Phillipson), Scotland in the Age of Improvement, 1970; *contrib.* Econ. Hist. Rev., Listener. *Address:* Economic History Dept, Univ. of Edinburgh, Edinburgh.

Mitford, Prof. Terence Bruce; Professor of Classical Archaeology, and Research Fellow of St Leonards College, University of St Andrews; *b* 1905; *m* 1936; four *s* one *d.* MA, DLitt Oxon 1973; FSA; Corr. Member: German Archaeological Inst.; Austrian Archaeological Inst. Chm., Scottish Field Sch. of Archaeology. *Publications:* Studies in the Signaries of South Western Cyprus, 1961; The Inscriptions of Kourion; (with G. E. Bean) Journeys in Rough Cilicia, 1972; *contrib.* Amer. Jl Archaeology, Annual BS Athens, Jl Hellenic Studies, Jl Roman Studies, Opuscula Archaeologica, Opuscula Atheniensia, Wiener Deutschaiffer, etc. *Address:* Univ. of St Andrews, St Andrews, Fife KY16 9AJ.

Mittins, William Henry; Senior Lecturer in Education, University of Newcastle upon Tyne, since 1968; *b* 1914; *m* 1943; one *s.* BA London 1936 (Hons English), DipEd London 1937, Acad. DipEd London 1950, PhD Newcastle 1972. Lectr Educn, Univ. Newcastle, 1953–68; Mem., Senate, 1967–69; Mem., Acad. Cttee Inst. of Educn; Mem., Res. Cttee, Inst. of Faculty of Educn. *Publications:* Pattern in English, 1950; Grammar of Modern English, 1962; Key to Grammar of Modern English, 1966; (et al.) Attitudes to English Usage, 1970; *contrib.* Durham Univ. Jl. *Address:* Dept of Education, Univ. of Newcastle, St Thomas Street, Newcastle upon Tyne.

Mittler, Prof. Peter, MA, PhD, FBPsS; Director, Hester Adrian Research Centre, University of Manchester, since 1968; *b* 1930; *m* 1954; three *s.* BA Cambridge 1953 (2nd cl. Psychol.), MA Cambridge 1957, PhD London 1969; FBPsS 1966. Mem., Council, BPsS, Assoc. Child Psychol., and Psychiat. Clinical Psychol., Warneford and Park Hosps, Oxford, 1954–58; Principal Clin. Psychol., Fairmile, Borocourt and Smith Hosps, Reading Area Dept of Psychiatry,

1958–63. Lectr in Developmental Psychol., Birkbeck Coll., Univ. of London, 1963–68; Assoc. Ed., Brit. Jl Psychol.; Mem., Manchester RHB Mental Hlth Sub-Cttee, 1971–74. *Publications*: ed, Aspects of Autism, 1968; ed, The Psychological Assessment of Mental and Physical Handicaps, 1970; The Study of Twins, 1971; ed, Assessment for Learning in the Mentally Handicapped, 1973; *contrib*. Brit. Jl Disord. Communicat., Brit. Jl Educnl Psychol., Brit. Jl Psychol., Bull. Brit. Psychol. Soc., Develop. Med. Child Neurol., Jl Ment. Defic. Res., Jl Ment. Subnorm. *Address*: Hester Adrian Research Centre, Univ. of Manchester, Manchester M13 9PL.

Mobbs, Kenneth William, MA, MusB, FRCO, LRAM; Senior Lecturer in Music, Univ. of Bristol, since 1965; *b* 1925; *m* 1950; three *d*. BA Cantab 1946 (Nat. Sciences); MusB Cantab 1949, MA Cantab 1950; LRAM (Pianoforte Performing) 1941, ARCO 1945, FRCO (Limpus Prize) 1949. Asst Lectr in Music, Univ. of Bristol, 1950–53; Lectr, Univ. of Bristol, 1953–65. Jun. Sci. Off., Radio and Tech. Publicns, Telecommunications Res. Estab., Malvern, 1945–47; Music. Dir, Bristol Opera Sch., 1954–64; Mem., Music Bd, CNAA, 1971– ; Mem., Council, Redland High Sch., Bristol, 1968– . *Publications*: (with G. Rowell) Engaged! a comic opera in three acts adapted and arranged from Gilbert and Sullivan, 1963. *Address*: Music Dept, Royal Fort House, Univ. of Bristol, Bristol BS8 1UJ.

Moggridge, Dr Donald Edward; University Lecturer in Economics, Faculty of Economics and Politics, Cambridge University, since 1973; Fellow of Clare College Cambridge, since 1971; *b* 1943; *m* 1967. BA Toronto 1965, MA Cantab 1968, PhD Cantab 1970; Member: Royal Econ. Soc.; Canadian Econs Assoc.; Econ. Hist. Soc. Res. Fellow, Clare Coll., Cambridge, 1967–71; Jun. Res. Officer, Dept of Applied Econs, Cambridge, 1968–69; Asst Lectr in Econs, Cambridge, 1971–73. *Publications*: The Return to Gold, 1925, 1969; British Monetary Policy 1924–1931, 1972; ed, Collected Writings of John Maynard Keynes, vols 3, 4, 5, 6, 7, 8, 9, 13, 14, 1971–73; ed, Keynes: Aspects of the Man and his Work, 1974; contrib. to other vols; *contrib*. Hist. of Pol Econ., Oxford Econ. Papers. *Address*: Clare College, Cambridge CB2 1TL.

Moir, Duncan Wilson, MA; Lecturer in Spanish, University of Southampton, since 1960; *b* 1930; *m* 1963; one *s* one *d*. MA Aberdeen 1954 (1st cl. French and Spanish). Mem., Assoc. Hispan. GB and Irel., Soc. Renaiss. Studies, Assoc. Internat. Hispan. Mngmt Trainee, Yorks Copper Works, Leeds, 1954–56. Res. Student, King's Coll., Cambridge, 1956–57; Asst Lectr, Bristol Univ., 1959–60. *Publications*: ed, F. B. Candamo: Theatro de los theatros de los passados y presentes siglos, 1970; (with M. Wilson) The Golden Age: Drama 1492–1700, 1971; ed, S. de Covarrubias: Emblemas morales, 1972; ed, D. López: Declaración magistral sobre las emblemas de Alciato, 1972; *contrib*. Bull. Hispan. Studies. *Address*: Dept of Spanish, 488

Univ. of Southampton, Southampton SO9 5NH.

Moir, Rev. Dr Ian Alexander; Lecturer in Christian Origins, New Testament Department, Edinburgh University, since 1961; *b* 1914; *m* 1945; one *s* two *d*. MA Aberdeen 1936 (2nd cl. Classics), BD Aberdeen 1939 (Specialised Hebrew and New Testament), PhD Cambridge 1943; Licenced Minister, Ch of Scotl., 1939, Ordination, 1942. Mem., Internat. Crit. Greek Testam. Cttee, 1958–74; Mem., Studiorum NT Soc., 1957– ; Mem., Soc. Liturg., 1968– ; Mem., Utd Bible Soc., Europ. Trans Cttee, 1970– ; Mem., Cttee on Revision of Univ. Constitution, 1962; Warden, New Coll., Residence, 1965–68; Mem., Bd of Archaeol., 1966–74; Accomm. Cttee, 1968–70; Entrance Bursaries Cttee, 1966– ; Inform. Cttee, 1971–73; Computer Users' Cttee, 1973– ; Sec., Scott. Divinity Faculties, Inter-Fac. conf., 1964–72; Ed., Ann. of Ch Service Soc. (now Liturg. Rev.), 1968– . *Publications*: Codex Climaci Rescriptus Graecus, 1956; *contrib*. Bible Trans, Jl Theol. Studies, NT Studies, Scott. Jl Theol. *Address*: New College, Mound, Edinburgh EH1 2LX.

Molander, Christopher Frans; Lecturer in Organization Sociology, Management Centre, University of Bradford, since 1968; *b* 1938; *m* 1965; one *d*. BA Hons Liverpool 1961 (2nd cl. Sociol.), Dip. in Ind. Admin. Liverpool 1962; Member: Inst. of Personnel Admin., 1961; Brit. Sociol. Assoc. 1968. *Publications*: *contrib*. Jl of Management Studies, Management Decision, Personnel, Personnel Management. *Address*: Univ. of Bradford Management Centre, Emm Lane, Bradford, Yorks BD9 4JL.

Molland, Dr Andrew George; Lecturer in History and Philosophy of Science, University of Aberdeen, since 1967; *b* 1941; BA Cantab 1963, MA Cantab 1966, PhD Cantab 1967. Mem., Brit. Soc. Hist. Science, Mem., Brit. Soc. Philos. Science, Mem., Brit. Soc. Hist. Maths. Asst Lectr, Aberdeen Univ., 1965–67; Andrew Mellon Postdoctoral Fellow, Univ. of Pittsburgh, 1973–74. Mem., Council, Brit. Soc. Hist. Sci., 1971–73; Mem. Cttee, Brit. Soc. Hist. Maths, 1971–73. *Publications*: *contrib*. Brit. Jl Hist. Sci., Hist. Sci., Miscellanea Mediaevalia, Notes Rec. Royal Soc. Lond., Traditio. *Address*: Dept of History and Philosophy of Science, King's College, Aberdeen AB9 2UB.

Møller, Preben Christian Heigerg W.; *see* Wernberg-Møller.

Moloney, Dr Brian; Senior Lecturer in Italian, University of Leeds, since 1970; *b* 1933; *m* 1957; one *s* two *d*. MA Cantab 1957, PhD Cantab 1962. Asst Lectr, Univ. Coll., Aberystwyth, 1960–61; Lectr, Hull Univ., 1961–65; Lectr, Univ. of Leeds, 1965–70. Mem., Exec. Cttee, Soc. Ital. Studies, 1969– ; Hon. Treas., 1972– . *Publications*: ed, Novelle del Novecento, 1966, 2nd edn 1969; Florence and England, 1969; Italo Svevo: a critical introduction, 1974; contrib. var. symposia and Festschriften; *contrib*. Engl. Misc., Ital. Studies, Con., Lett. Ital., MLR,

Studies in Voltaire, Year's Work in Mod. Lang. Studies. *Address*: Dept of Italian Language and Literature, Univ. of Leeds, Leeds LS2 9JT.

Molyneux, Dr John Harold; Senior Lecturer in Classics, University of Sheffield, since 1971; *b* 1933; *m* 1958; two *s*. BA Cantab 1954 (Double 1st cl. Class.), MA Cantab 1958, PhD Sheffield 1969. Asst Lectr, Sheffield Univ., 1957–59; Lectr, Sheffield Univ., 1959–71; Vis. Assoc. Prof., Univ. of Victoria, BC, 1970–71. *Publications: contrib.* Class. Qly, Class. Rev., Didask, Hermes, Phoenix, TAPA. *Address*: Depts of Greek and Latin, The Univ., Sheffield S10 2TN

Monger, Mark, MA, JP; Senior Lecturer, School of Social Work, University of Leicester, since 1967; *b* 1919; *m* 1943; one *s* two *d*. BA Oxon 1947, MA Oxon 1947, Test. Soc. Studies Bristol 1948. Tutor, Adult Educn Dept, Leicester, 1964–67; Lecturer, Sch. of Social Work, Leicester, 1967–72. *Publications*: Casework in Probation, 1964, 2nd edn 1972; Casework in Aftercare, 1967; The English Probation Hostel, 1970; Husband Wife and Caseworker, 1971; *contrib.* Probat., Fed. Probat., etc. *Address*: School of Social Work, Univ. of Leicester, Leicester LE1 7RH.

Montague, Roger Douglas Leonard; Senior Lecturer, Department of Philosophy, University of Leicester, since 1967; *b* 1931; *m* 1957; one *s* three *d*. BA Bristol 1955, BPhil Oxon 1958. Asst, Univ. of St Andrews, 1958–61; Lectr, Hull Univ., 1961–67. *Publications: contrib.* Austral. Jl Philos., Philos. Qly, Proc. Aristot. Soc., Mind, Analysis. *Address*: Dept of Philosophy, The Univ., Leicester LE1 7RH.

Montefiore, Alan, MA; Fellow and Tutor in Philosophy, Balliol College, Oxford University, since 1961; *b* 1926; *m* 1952; one *s* two *d*. BA Oxon 1950 (1st cl. PPE), MA Oxon 1955. Asst Lectr, Keele Univ., 1951–54; Lectr, Keele Univ., 1954–60; Sen. Lectr, Keele Univ., 1960–61. Mem., Council, Keele Univ., 1962– ; Mem., Gov. Body, Froebel Educnl Inst., 1962– ; Bd of Dirs, Wiener Libr., 1962– . *Publications*: A Modern Introduction to Moral Philosophy, 1958; ed (with B. A. O. Williams), British Analytical Philosophy, 1966, Italian edn 1967; ed, Philosophy and Personal Relations, 1973; *contrib.* Geog. Studies, Harv. Educnl Rev., Mind, Philos. Qly, Philos., Rev. Internat. Philos., Proc. Aristot. Soc., Supp. Vol. Aristot. Soc. *Address*: Balliol College, Oxford.

Monypenny, Gerald Burney G.; *see* Gybbon-Monypenny.

Moodie, Prof. Graeme Cochrane, MA; Professor of Politics, University of York, since 1963; *b* 1924; *m* 1955; two *s* two *d*. MA St Andrews 1943, BA Oxon 1946 (Hons PPE), MA Oxon 1953; Member: Pol. Studies Assoc., Amer. Pol. Science Assoc., Soc. Res. into Higher Educn, Hansard Soc. Parliamentary Govt, Pol. Assoc. Lectr, Univ. of St Andrews, 1947–53; Commonwealth Fund Fellow, Princeton Univ., 1949–51; Lectr, Univ. of Glasgow, 1953–61; Sen. Lectr, 1961–63; Vis. Assoc. Prof., Princeton, 1962–63. Mem., Exec. Cttee, Pol. Studies Assoc., 1968– ; Chm., 1969–72; Mem., Gov. Council, Soc. Res. into Higher Educn, 1966– ; Chm., 1969–71. *Publications*: (with G. Marshall) Some Problems of the Constitution, 1959, 5th edn 1972; The Government of Great Britain, 1961, 3rd edn 1971; ed, Government Organisation and Economic Development, 1966; (with G. Studdert-Kennedy) Opinions, Publics, and Pressure Groups, 1970; (with R. Eustace) Power and Authority in British Universities, 1974; *contrib.* Govt Opposit., Pol Studies. *Address*: Dept of Politics, Univ. of York, Heslington, York YO1 5DD.

Moody, A. David; Senior Lecturer, Department of English and Related Literature, University of York, since 1972; *b* 1932. MA NZ 1952, BA Oxon 1955, MA Oxon 1962. University of Melbourne: Lectr, English Dept, 1958–63; Sen. Lectr, 1964–66; Lectr, Dept of English and Related Lit., Univ. of York, 1966–72. *Publications*: Virginia Woolf, 1963, 3rd edn 1970; Shakespeare: The Merchant of Venice, 1964, 2nd edn 1971; ed, The Waste Land, in, Different Voices, 1974; *contrib.* Melbourne Crit. Rev., Meanjin, Cambridge Qly, Rev. of English Studies, The Library. *Address*: Dept of English and Related Literature, Univ. of York, Heslington, York YO1 5DD.

Moody, Philippa Mairi; Lecturer, Department of English and Related Literature, York University, since 1967; *b* 1934; *m* 1956. BA Oxon 1956, MA Oxon 1964, BPhil Oxon 1966. Tutor in English, Melbourne Univ., 1959–63; Lectr in English, Melbourne Univ., 1964–67. *Publications*: Critical Commentary on Golding's Lord of the Flies, 1965; Critical Commentary on Forster's A Passage to India, 1967; *contrib.* Melbourne Crit. Rev. *Address*: Dept of English and Related Literature, Univ. of York, Heslington, York YO1 5DD.

Moody, Prof. Theodore William, MA, PhD, Hon. DLit; Professor of Modern History, University of Dublin, since 1939; *b* 1907; *m* 1935; one *s* four *d*. BA Belfast 1930 (Med. and Mod. Hist.), PhD London 1934, MA Dublin 1941, Hon. DLit Belfast 1959, FRHistS 1934, MRIA 1940. Asst in Hist., QUB, 1932–35; Lectr, QUB, 1935–39; Ed., Irish Hist. Studies, 1937– ; Fellow, TCD, 1939– ; Tutor, TCD, 1939–52; Sen. Tutor, TCD, 1952–58; Sen. Lectr, TCD, 1958–64; Dean, Fac. of Arts, 1967–69; Sen. Fellow, TCD, 1972; Ed., Studies in Irish Hist., 1944– ; Leverhulme Res. Fellow, 1964–66. Mem., Sch. of Hist. Studies, Inst. for Adv. Study, Princeton, 1965; Chm., Bd of Eds, New Hist. of Ireland (Royal Irish Acad.), 1968– ; Mem., Irish Mss Commn, 1943– ; Mem., Adv. Cttee on Cultural Relat., Ireland, 1949–63; Govt Commn on Higher Educn in Ireland, 1960–67; Irish Broadcast. Authority, 1960–72. *Publications*: The Londonderry Plantation 1609–41: the City of London and the plantation in Ulster, 1939; Thomas Davis 1814–45, 1945; (with J. C. Beckett) Queen's,

489

Belfast, 1845–1949: the history of a university, 1959; ed, Ulster Plantation Papers 1608–13 (Analecta Hibernica, no. 8), 1938; ed, and contrib. (with H. A. Cronne and D. B. Quinn) Essays on British and Irish History in honour of J. E. Todd, 1949; (with J. C. Beckett) Ulster since 1800 (1st series), 1955; (2nd series), 1957; (with F. X. Martin) The Course of Irish History, 1967; Historical Studies, vi, 1968; The Fenian Movement, 1968; ed (with J. G. Simms), The Bishopric of Derry and the Irish Society of London 1602–70, 1968; Irish Historiography 1936–70, 1971; Michael Davitt's Leaves from a Prison Diary, repr. 1972; The Ulster Question, 1603–1973, 1974; contrib. Irish Hist. Studies, Hist., Proc. Royal Irish Acad., Trans Royal Hist. Soc. Address: 40 Trinity College, Dublin 2.

Moore, Barry Charles; Research Officer, Department of Applied Economics, University of Cambridge, since 1973; b 1941; m 1966; two d. BSc (Econs) London 1965 (Hons), MSc (Econs) London 1968 (Hons); MA Cantab 1974; Mem., Royal Economic Soc. Res. Assistant: LSE, 1965–66; Queen Mary Coll., London Univ., 1966–68; Lectr, Thames Polytechnic, 1968–70. Consultant to HM Government, Min. of Housing, 1970; evidence to Trade and Industry Sub-cttee, House of Commons, 1973. Publications: Regional Economic Policy in the UK, 1973; contrib. Econ. Jl, Internat. Commerce, Scot. Jl Polit. Econ. Address: Dept of Applied Economics, Sidgwick Avenue, Cambridge.

Moore, Benjamin John Scott, BA, FRHistS; Lecturer in Economic History, Department of Economic and Social History, University of Bristol, since 1968; b 1937; m; six d. BA London 1958 (2i Hons, External); Alexander Prize, RHistS, 1963, John Nichols Local History Prize, Leicester; FRHistS 1964. Res. Fellow in Local History, Keele Univ., 1960; Lectr in Econ. History, Strathclyde Univ., 1963. Publications: Laughton: a study in the evolution of the Wealden Landscape, 1964; The Goods and Chattels of our Forefathers: Frampton Cotterell and District Probate Inventories (forthcoming); Probate and other Inventories (forthcoming); contrib. EHR, Trans RHistS. Address: Dept of Economic and Social History, Bristol Univ., Bristol BS8 1UL.

Moore, The Worshipful Chancellor the Rev. Evelyn Garth, MA; Fellow (formerly Lecturer and Director of Studies in Law), Corpus Christi College, Cambridge University, since 1947; Chancellor, Diocese of Southwark, since 1948; Chancellor, Diocese of Durham, since 1954; Chancellor, Diocese of Gloucester, since 1957; b 1906. BA Cantab 1927, MA Cantab 1931; Barrister-at-Law, Gray's Inn, 1928; Clerk in Holy Orders, 1962. Formerly: Lector, Trinity Coll., Cambridge; Tutor, Gray's Inn; Vis. Prof., Khartoum Univ., 1961; Lectr in Evidence, 1952–68, and in Criminal Procedure, Council of Legal Educn, 1957–68. Mem. Council, St David's, Lampeter, 1949–65; Mem.Governing Body, St Chad's, Durham, 1955– ; Mem. Council, Westcott House, 1961–65; formerly Mem., Gen. Council of Bar and Professional

Conduct Cttee; Dep. Chm., Hunts QS, 1948–63; Cambs QS, 1959–63; Major (RA) and local Lt-Col, Off. of JAG, 1939–45; High Bailiff, Ely Cath., 1961– ; Legal Assessor, RCVS, 1963–68; Pres. Chs Fellowship for Psychic and Spirit. Studies; Mem., Ch Assembly, 1955–62. Publications: Kenny's Criminal Cases, 8th edn (with supplement), 1935; (jtly) Ecclesiastical Law, in Halsbury's Laws of England, 3rd edn 1955; An Introduction to English Canon Law, 1966; contrib. Encyclopaedia Britannica; Chamber's Encyclopaedia; contrib. Camb. Law Jl, Law Jl, Theol., SPR Jl. Address: Corpus Christi College, Cambridge.

Moore, Dr Francis Charles Timothy; Senior Lecturer in Philosophy, University of Birmingham, since 1974; b 1940; m 1971; one d. BA 1967, MA 1967, DPhil 1967, Oxon. Lectr, Univ. of Birmingham, 1965–74; Sen. Lectr, Univ. of Khartoum, 1969–72. Publications: Claude Lévi-Strauss and the Cultural Sciences, 1969; trans. Degerando: the observation of savage peoples, 1969; The Psychology of Maine de Biran, 1970; contrib. Jl of Brit. Soc. for Phenomenology, Revue Internat. de Philosophie. Address: Dept of Philosophy, Univ. of Birmingham, Birmingham B15 2TT.

Moore, Prof. Geoffrey Herbert; Professor of American Literature and Head of Department of American Studies, University of Hull, since 1962; b 1920; m 1947 (marr. diss.); one s one d. BA Cantab 1946 (1st cl. English Tripos), MA Cantab 1951. Instr in English, Univ. of Wisconsin, 1947–49; Vis. Prof. of English, Univs of Kansas City and New Mexico, 1948, 1949; Asst Prof. of English, Tulane Univ., 1949–51; Vis. Prof. of English, Univ. of Southern California and Claremont Coll., 1950; Extra-Mural Lectr, London and Cambridge Univs, 1951–52 and 1953–54, Rose Morgan Prof., Univ. of Kansas, 1954–55; Lectr in Amer. Lit., Manchester Univ., 1955–59; Vis. Lectr, Univ. of Mainz, Göttingen and Frankfurt, 1959; Rockefeller Fellow, Harvard Univ., 1959–60; Sen. Lectr in Amer. Lit., Manchester Univ., 1960–62; Dean, Faculty of Arts, Univ. of Hull, 1967–69. Vis. Lectr, Univs of Montpellier, Aix-en-Provence and Nice, 1967, 1971; Vis. Lectr, Univs of Frankfurt, Heidelberg, Mainz, Saarbrücken, Tübingen, 1967, 1968; Vis. Lectr, Univs of Perpignan, Turin, Florence, Pisa, Rome, New Delhi, Hyderabad, Madras, Bombay, Calcutta, 1971; Vis. Prof. of English, York Univ., Toronto, 1969–70; Vis. Prof., Univ. of Tunis, Spring 1970, 1971; Vis. Prof., Harvard, Summer 1971; Vis. Lectr, Univs of Düsseldorf, Heidelberg, Freiburg, Mainz, Spring 1972; Fellow, Sch. of Letters, Indiana Univ., Summer 1970. Editor and Producer, BBC TV Talks, 1952–53; Mem. Cttee, Brit. Assoc. for Amer. Studies, 1957–60. Sen. Scholar Award, Amer. Coun. of Learned Socs, 1965. Ed, and Founder, The Bridge (Cambridge lit. mag.), 1946. Publications: Voyage to Chivalry (under pseud.), 1947; Poetry from Cambridge in Wartime, 1947; The Penguin Book of Modern American Verse, 1954; Poetry Today, 1958; American Literature and the American Imagination, 1964; American Literature,

1964; ed, 58 Short Stories by O. Henry, 1956; *contrib.* TLS, Amer. Mercury, BBC Qly, Kenyon Rev., Rev. English Lit., English Studies and other literary and scholarly jls. *Address:* Univ. of Hull, Hull HU6 7RX.

Moore, Gerald Holyoake, MA; Reader in English, School of African and Asian Studies, University of Sussex, since 1966; *b* 1924; *m* 1949 (marr. diss. 1973); one *s* two *d*; *m* 1973. BA Cantab 1950 (1st cl. Engl.), MA Cantab 1954. Regional Tutor, Extra-Mural Studies, Univ. Coll., Ibadan, 1953–56; Dir of Extra-Mural Studies, Hong Kong Univ., 1956–60; Dir of Extra-Mural Studies, Makerere Coll., 1960–66; Vis. Prof., UCLA, 1964; Vis. Prof., Univ. of Ghana, 1970; Vis. Prof., Univ. of Wisconsin, 1974. Mem., Council, Afr. Studies Assoc. UK, 1968–71. *Publications:* Seven African Writers, 1962, 2nd edn 1966; ed, Modern Poetry from Africa, 1963, 2nd edn 1968; African Literature and the Universities, 1965; The Chosen Tongue, 1969, American edn 1970; trans., T. U. Tamsi: Selected Poems, 1970; trans., Beti: The Poor Christ of Bomba, 1971; Wole Soyinka, 1972; *contrib.* Afr., Afr. Aff., Black Orph., Prés. Afr., Times Lit. Supp., Le Monde, Rev. Litt. Comp., Transit. *Address:* School of African and Asian Studies, Univ. of Sussex, Falmer, Sussex.

Moore, L. M.; *see* Briscoe, L. M.

Moore, Prof. Peter Gerald, TD, PhD, FIA; Deputy Principal since 1972 and Professor of Statistics since 1965, London Graduate School of Business Studies; *b* 1928; *m* 1958; two *s* one *d*. BSc London, 1949 (1st cl. Hons), PhD London 1956; FIA 1956 (Vice-Pres., 1973–); FRSS 1951 (Hon. Sec., 1968–). Mem., Internat. Statistical Inst. 1972. Lectr in Statistics, UCL, 1951–57; Commonwealth Fund Fellow, Princeton, 1953–54. Asst to Econ. Advisor, NCB, 1957–59; Head of Math. and Stat. Services, Reed Paper Gp, 1959–65; Dir, Shell (UK) Ltd, 1969–72. Member: UGC Management Sub-cttee, 1970– ; Prime Minister's Review Body on Doctors' and Dentists' Remuneration, 1971– ; Cttee on Security of 1971 Census, 1971–73. Rosa Morison Mem. Medal, UCL, 1949; J. D. Scaife Medal, IProdE, 1964; Guy Medal, RSS, 1970. *Publications:* Principles of Statistical Techniques, 1958, 2nd ed 1969; (with D. E. Edwards) Standard Statistical Calculations, 1964, 2nd edn 1972; Statistics and the Manager, 1966; Basic Operational Research, 1968; Risk in Business Decision, 1972; *contrib.* Applied Statistics, Biometrics, Biometrika, Jl Amer. Statistical Assoc., Jl Inst. Actuaries, Jl Man. Studies, Jl RSS, Man. Science, Operational Res. Qly. *Address:* Sussex Place, Regents Park, NW1 4SA.

Moore, Robert Ian, MA; Lecturer in Medieval and Modern History, University of Sheffield, since 1964; *b* 1941; *m* 1968. BA Oxon 1962, MA Oxon 1967. *Publications:* Popular Heresy in the Early Middle Ages, 1972; *contrib.* Bull. Inst. Hist. Res., Hist. *Address:* Dept of Medieval and Modern History, Univ. of Sheffield, Sheffield S10 2TN.

Moore, Dr Robert Samuel; Senior Lecturer in Sociology, University of Aberdeen, since 1970; *b* 1936; *m* 1969. BA Hull 1964 (Sociol. and Social Admin.); PhD Durham 1973; Mem., Brit. Sociol. Assoc., Mem., Inst. Race Relat., Mem., Brit. Assoc. Adv. Science. Res. Assoc., Univ. of Birmingham, 1964–65; Lectr, Univ. of Durham, 1965–70. Treas., Brit. Sociol. Assoc., 1970– ; Mem., Council, Brit. Assoc., 1969– ; Mem., Council, Inst. of Race Relations, 1972– ; Editor, Race Relations Abstracts, 1973– . *Publications:* Pitmen, Preachers and Politics, 1974; (with J. Rex) Race Community and Conflict, 1967, 2nd edn 1969; chapters, in Colour in Britain, 1965; chapters, in Reflections on Protest, 1967; chapters, in Inter-action, 1967; chapters, in Justice First, 1969; chapters, in Max Weber and Modern Sociology, 1971; chapter, in Working Papers in Class Imagery, 1974; *contrib.* Brit. Jl Sociol., Sociol. Anal., New Soc., Race. *Address:* Dept of Sociology, King's College, Aberdeen AB9 2UB.

Moore, Stuart Alfred, MA(Econ); Lecturer in Economic Statistics, University of Manchester, since 1966; *b* 1939; *m* 1966; two *s* one *d*. BA(Admin) Manchester 1964, MA(Econ) Manchester 1967; MBCS, Mem., Royal Econ Soc. Res. Asst in Computer Science, Univ. of Manchester, 1964–65; Res. Assoc. in Econometrics, 1965–66. *Publications:* contrib., The Demand for Food, 1972; *contrib.* Comput. Bull., Manch. Sch. *Address:* Faculty of Economic and Social Studies, The Univ., Manchester M13 9PL.

Moore, Victor William Edward; Senior Lecturer, Department of Law, University of Reading, since 1972; *b* 1929; *m* 1954; one *s* three *d*. LLB London 1959, LLM London 1967; ACCA. Lectr, Dept of Law relating to the Land, 1965–72. Mem., Justice Cttee on Admin. Law, 1966– ; Mem., Gen. Cttee, Soc. Public Teachers of Law, 1970–72. *Publications:* (with D. H. Lawrance) Compulsory Purchase and Compensation, 5th edn 1972; *contrib.* Convey. Prop. Law, Jl Prop. Law, Jl Urban Law, Legal Exec., Mod. Law Rev., New Law Jl, Public Law, Urban Law Ann. *Address:* Dept of Law, Univ. of Reading, Whiteknights, Reading, Berkshire.

Moorey, Dr Peter Roger Stuart, MA, DPhil, FSA; Senior Assistant Keeper, Ancient Egyptian and Near Eastern Collections, Ashmolean Museum, Oxford University; *b* 1937. BA Oxon 1961 (1st cl. Hist.), MA Oxon 1966, DPhil Oxon 1967; FSA. Ed., Levant, 1968– ; Sen. Treas., Oxf. Univ. Archaeol. Soc., 1971– . *Publications:* Archaeology, Artefacts and the Bible, 1969; Ancient Egypt, 1970; Catalogue of the Ancient Persian Bronzes in the Ashmolean Museum, Oxford, 1971; *contrib.* Archaeom., Iran, Iraq. *Address:* Ashmolean Museum, Oxford.

Moorhouse, Alfred Charles, MA; Reader in Classics, University College, Swansea, University of Wales, since 1962; *b* 1910; *m* 1948; one *s*. BA Cantab 1933 (1st cl. Classical Tripos), MA Cantab 1938, MA Oxon 1960. Asst Lectr, Univ. Coll., Exeter, 1938–39; Asst Lectr, Univ. Coll., Swansea, 1939–44;

Lectr, 1944–50; Sen Lectr, 1950–62. Mem., Council, Class. Assoc., 1953–56. *Publications*: Writing and the Alphabet, 1946, Japanese edn 1956; The Triumph of the Alphabet, 1953, Italian edn 1959, Mexican edn 1961; Studies in the Greek Negatives, 1959; *contrib.* Amer. Jl Philol., Class. Qly, Class. Rev. *Address*: Dept of Classics, Univ. College, Swansea SA2 8PP.

Moraes Farias, Paulo Fernando de; Lecturer, Centre of West African Studies and School of History, University of Birmingham, since 1969; *b* 1935. DMed Bahia, Brazil 1959, LicHist Bahia, Brazil 1963, MA Ghana 1966 (African Studies); Fellow, Middle East Studies Assoc. (UK), Member: African Studies Assoc. of UK; Instituto Geográfico e Histórico da Bahia. Lectr, Centro de Estudos Afro-Orientais, Fed. Univ. of Bahia, Brazil, 1963–64; Chercheur, Ecole Française d'-Afrique at the Institut Fondamental d'Afrique Noire, Univ. of Dakar, Senegal, 1966–67; Lectr, Dept of Hist., Ahmadu Bello Univ., Nigeria, 1967–69. Mem., Brit. Cttee, Fontes Historiae Africanae project (sponsored by Brit. Acad. and Internat. Union of Acads). *Publications*: *contrib.* Afro-Asia (Bahia), Bull. IFAN, JAH. *Address*: Centre of West African Studies and Sch. of History, Univ. of Birmingham, Birmingham B15 2TT.

Moran, John Michael; Lecturer, Department of Intellectual History, University of Sussex, since 1973; *b* 1935. BA Keele 1959 (1st cl. Philos. and English Lit.). Asst Lectr in Philosophy, Univ. of Keele, 1960–62; Lectr, Univ. of Sussex, 1962–73; Chm. of Intellectual History, Sussex, 1969–73; Leverhulme Faculty Fellowship in Europe (Paris and Aix-en-Provence), 1972. *Publications*: contrib. The Encyclopedia of Philosophy, 8 vols, 1967; The Dictionary of the History of Ideas, 4 vols, 1973. *Address*: Arts Building, Univ. of Sussex, Falmer, Brighton, BN1 9QN.

Morcos-Asaad, Prof. Fikry N., BArch, MArch, Sm, PhD, RIBA, FRIAS, MASCE; Professor of Architecture, University of Strathclyde, since 1970; *b* 1930; *m* 1958; three *s*. BArch(Hons) Cairo 1952, MArch Georgia Inst. of Tech. 1955, SM Mass. Inst. of Tech. 1956, PhD Illinois Inst of Tech. 1958; Mem., American Concrete Inst. 1956, MASCE 1958, Mem., RIBA, FRIAS. Asst Lectr, Faculty of Engineering, Cairo Univ., 1953–58; Lectr, Faculty of Engineering, Cairo Univ., 1958–63; Dir, Structural Studies, Liverpool Sch. of Architect., 1963–69; Vis. Prof., California Polytechnic, 1967. Architectl Cnsltnt, US Embassy, Cairo, 1960–63. Chm., various Confs; Mem., ARCUK Educn Cttee, 1973; Comr, Royal Fine Art Commn for Scotland, 1973– . *Publications*: papers, articles and various reviews. *Address*: Dept of Architecture and Building Science, Univ. of Strathclyde, Glasgow G1 1XW.

Mordey, Richard Allan; Lecturer in Town Planning, University of Wales Institute of Science and Technology, Cardiff, since 1968; *b* 1935; *m* 1958; two *s*. BA Leeds 1956 (Hons Geog.), MCD Liverpool 1959; MRTPI 1961. Various appts in local govt planning depts, 1959–68. *Publications*: contrib. Jl Planning and Environment Law, JRTPI, OAP, Town and Country Planning. *Address*: Dept of Town and Country Planning, Univ. of Wales Institute of Science and Technology, Cathays Park, Cardiff.

Moreton, Rev. Michael Joseph; Part-time Lecturer, Department of Theology, University of Exeter, since 1957; *b* 1917; *m* 1943; one *s* two *d*. BA London 1940 (History), BA Oxford 1947 (Theology), MA 1953; Wells Theological Coll., 1947; ordained deacon, Diocese of Bath and Wells, 1948, priest, 1949; Examining Chaplain to the Bishop of Exeter, 1961–73. *Publications*: Made Fully Perfect, 1974; *contrib.* Church Qly, Church Qly Rev., Studia Evangelica, Studia Patristica, Theol. *Address*: Queen's Building, The Queen's Drive, Exeter EX4 4QH.

Morgan, Dr Bernard George; Senior Lecturer, School of Architecture, University of Liverpool, since 1960; *b* 1917; *m* 1947; two *s* two *d*. BArch Liverpool 1947 (1st cl.), DipCD Liverpool 1948, PhD Liverpool 1957; ARIBA, FRHistS. Lectr, Liverpool Univ., 1948–60. *Publications*: Canonic Design in English Medieval Architecture, 1960; *contrib.* Jl Royal Inst. Brit. Archit. *Address*: School of Architecture, Univ. of Liverpool, Liverpool L69 3BX.

Morgan, David Allen Louis; Lecturer in History, University College London, since 1961; *b* 1937. MA Oxon. Jun. Lectr, Magdalen Coll., Oxford, 1961–62. *Publication*: *contrib.* Trans RHistS. *Address*: Dept of History, Univ. College, Gower Street, WC1E 6BT.

Morgan, David Eirwyn; Principal, North Wales Baptist College, Bangor, since 1970, and Lecturer in Philosophy of Religion, University College, Bangor, since 1967; *b* 1918; *m* 1953; one *s* one *d*. BA Wales 1939 (Hons Welsh), BD Wales 1943, BA Oxford 1944 (Hons Theology), MA Oxford 1947. Prof., Baptist Coll., Bangor, 1967. Sec., Welsh Hymn Soc., 1969–72, Treasurer, 1973– . *Publications*: Bedydd, Cred ac Arfer (Baptism, Belief and Practice), 1973; *contrib.* Baptist Qly, Diwinydd. *Address*: Coleg y Bedyddwyr, Bangor, Caerns.

Morgan, David George; Lecturer in Sociology, University of Kent, since 1967; *b* 1942. BA Hull 1965 (Hons Sociol. and Philos.); Mem., Brit. Sociol. Assoc. Tutorial Asst, Hull, 1965–66; Asst Lecturer, Hull, 1966–67. *Address*: Keynes College, Univ. of Kent, Canterbury, Kent.

Morgan, Dr David Hopcraft John; Lecturer in Sociology, Department of Sociology, University of Manchester, since 1967; *b* 1937; *m* 1964; one *s* one *d*. BSc (Econ.) Hull 1960, MA Hull 1964 (Soc.), PhD Manchester 1969 (Soc.); Mem., Brit. Sociol. Assoc. Asst Lectr in Sociol., Univ. of Manchester, 1964–67; Vis. Asst Prof., Univ. of Victoria, BC, 1969–70. Mem. Senate, Univ. of Manchester, 1973–76. *Publications*: ed and contrib.:

Introducing Sociology, 1970; Modern Sociology Introductory Readings, 1970; Problems of Modern Society, 1972; *contrib.* Brit. Jl Sociol., Sociol. Rev. *Address:* Dept of Sociology, Coupland Street, Univ. of Manchester.

Morgan, Dr David Rhys; Senior Lecturer in US Government, Department of Political Theory and Institutions, University of Liverpool, since 1973 (Lecturer, 1965–73); *b* 1937; *m* 1963; two *s* one *d.* BA Oxon 1960 (2nd cl. Hist.), MA Oxon 1965, PhD Cantab 1967. *Publications:* Suffragists and Democrats: the Politics of Woman Suffrage in the USA, 1972; (with Harvey Cox) City Politics and the Press, 1973; Suffragists and Liberals: the Politics of Woman Suffrage in England, 1974; *contrib.* Parl. Aff., Pol. Studies. *Address:* Dept of Politics, Roxby Building, Univ. of Liverpool, Liverpool.

Morgan, Dyfnallt, MA; Lecturer in Welsh Literature, Department of Extra-Mural Studies, University College of North Wales, Bangor, since 1964; *b* 1917; *m* 1954; one *s.* BA Wales 1938 (Hons Welsh Lang. and Lit., Hons Engl. Lang. and Lit. 1939), DipEd Wales 1940, MA Wales 1969. Res. Asst., Educn Dept, UCW, Aberystwyth, 1951–54. BBC Talks Producer, 1954–64. *Publications:* Y Llen, 1953; ed, Gwŷr Llên y Ddeunawfed Ganrif, 1966; Y Llen a Myfyrdodau Eraill, 1967; Gwŷr Llên y Bedwaredd Ganrif ar Bymtheg, 1968; Rhyw Hanner Ieuenctid, 1971; trans., Y Deyrnas (The Kingdom, Elgar), 1971; trans., Rhyw Fab o'n Hoes Ni (A Child of our Time, Tippett), 1972; Gwenallt (Writers of Wales Series), 1972; trans., mam yr Iesu (Stabat Mater, Pergolesi), 1973; trans., Ti, Dduw Dad, a tolwn (Te Deum, Dvořák), 1973; trans., Offeren yn D Leiaf (Mass in D Minor, Haydn), 1974; *contrib.* Anvil, Barn, Taliesin, Traethod, Ysgrif. Beirn. *Address:* Dept of Extra-Mural Studies, Univ. College of North Wales, Bangor LL57 2DG.

Morgan, Prof. E. Victor; Professor of Economics, University of Reading, since 1975; *b* 1915; *m* 1940; one *s* one *d.* BA Cantab 1937, MA Cantab 1940. Lectr in Econs, Univ. Coll. of Swansea, 1941–45; Prof. of Economics: Univ. Coll. of Swansea, 1945–66; Univ. of Manchester, 1966–74. *Publications:* The Theory and Practice of Central Banking, 1943; The Conquest of Unemployment, 1947; Studies in British Financial Policy, 1914–25, 1951; A First Approach to Economics, 1955, 3rd edn 1972; The Structure of Property Ownership in Great Britain, 1959; (with W. A. Thomas) The Stock Exchange, 1964, 2nd edn 1969; A History of Money, 1965; The Economics of Public Policy, 1972; *contrib.* Amer. Econ. Rev., Econ. Jl, Economica, Manch. Sch. *Address:* Dept of Economics, Univ. of Reading, Whiteknights, Reading RG6 2AH.

Morgan, Edwin George, MA; Reader in English, University of Glasgow, since 1971; *b* 1920. MA Glasgow 1947 (1st cl. Engl.). Asst Lectr, Glasgow, 1947–50; Lectr, 1950–65; Sen. Lectr, 1965–71. Mem., Lit. Cttee, Scott. Arts Council, 1966–68; Mem., Univ.

Cttee on Scott. Lit., 1968– ; Mem., Council, Assoc. Scott. Lit. Studies, 1970– ; Mem. Bd, Poetry Bk Soc., 1969– ; Co-editor: Scott. Poetry, 1966– ; Scott. Internat., 1968– . *Publications:* The Vision of Cathkin Braes, 1952; Beowulf, 1952, American pbk edn 1962; The Cape of Good Hope, 1955; Poems from Eugenio Montale, 1959; Sovpoems, 1961; ed, Collins Albatross Book of Longer Poems, 1963; Starryveldt, 1965; Emergent Poems, 1967; The Second Life, 1968; Gnomes, 1968; Proverb-folder, 1969; (with A. Bold and E. Brathwaite) Penguin Modern Poets 15, 1969; Twelve Songs, 1970; The Horseman's Word, 1970; ed, Penguin New English Dramatists 14, 1970; trans., Weöres, in S. Weöres and F. Juhász: Selected Poems, 1970; Wi the Haill Voice, 1972; Glasgow Sonnets, 1972; Instamatic Poems, 1972; From Glasgow to Saturn, 1973; *contrib.*, Encyclopedia Britannica; *contrib.* Camb. Jl, Chic. Rev., Encore, Ess. Crit., The Rev., Times Lit. Supp., Twent. Cent., Univ. Qly. *Address:* Dept of English, Univ. of Glasgow, Glasgow G12 8QQ.

Morgan, Dr Estelle, MA, PhD; Senior Lecturer, Department of German, University of Bristol, since 1955; *b* 1914; *m* 1946. MA Edinburgh 1934 (1st cl. German), PhD Edinburgh 1936; Mem., MHRA, Mem., IVG, Mem., BFUW. Lectr, Edinburgh Univ., 1937–46; Lectr, Bristol Univ., 1946–55. *Publications: contrib.* Germ. Life Lett., Mod. Lang. Rev., Mod. Langs, Neuer. Sprach. *Address:* Dept of German, Univ. of Bristol, Bristol BS8 1RJ.

Morgan, Dr Gerald Raymond; Lecturer in English, Trinity College Dublin, since 1971; *b* 1942; *m* 1967; one *s.* MA Oxon 1968, DPhil Oxon 1973. Jun. Lectr, TCD, 1968–71. *Publications: contrib.* English Studies. *Address:* Dept of English, 40 Trinity College, Dublin 2.

Morgan, Dr Kenneth Owen; Fellow and Praelector, Queen's College, Oxford, since 1966; *b* 1934; *m* 1973. BA Oxon 1955, MA 1958, DPhil 1958, Oxon; FRHistS 1964. Lectr in History, UC, Swansea, 1958–65; Sen. Lectr, 1965–66; ACLS Internat. Fellow, Columbia Univ., 1962–63; Vis. Prof., Columbia Univ., 1965. Dean of Queen's College, 1967–70. Editor, Welsh Hist. Rev., 1965– . Mem. Council, UC of Wales, Aberystwyth, 1972– . *Publications:* Wales in British Politics, 1868–1922, 1963, 2nd edn 1970; David Lloyd George: Welsh Radical as world statesman, 1963, 2nd edn 1964; Freedom or Sacrilege?, 1966; Keir Hardie, 1967; The Age of Lloyd George, 1971; ed, Lloyd George: Family Letters, 1885–1936, 1973; Lloyd George, 1974; *contrib.* English Hist. Rev., Hist. Jl, Hist., Jl of Contemporary Hist., Welsh Hist. Rev., etc. *Address:* The Queen's College, Oxford.

Morgan, Margery Mary; Reader in English, University of Lancaster, since 1973; one *d.* BA London (Hons English), MA London. Asst Lectr in English, Royal Holloway Coll., London, 1947–51, Lectr, 1951–64; Sen. Lectr, Monash Univ., 1964–67, Reader, 1967–72; Lectr, Univ. Lancaster, 1972–73.

Editor, Komos, 1967–72. *Publications*: A Drama of Political Man: A Study in the Plays of Harley Granville Barker, 1961; The Shavian Playground: An Exploration of the Art of George Bernard Shaw, 1972, 2nd edn (paperback), 1974; *contrib*. Komos, Library, Medium Ævum, Modern Drama, MLR, RES, Speculum, Theatre Notebook. *Address*: English Dept, Univ. of Lancaster, Bailrigg, Lancaster LA1 4YW.

Morgan, Sir Morien Bedford, Kt, CB, MA, FRS, CEng, FRAeS; Master of Downing College, Cambridge, since 1972; *b* 1912; *m* 1941; three *d*. BA Cantab 1934 (Seely Prize in Aeronautics 1934), MA Cantab 1939; FRS 1972. Apprenticed to Mather & Platt Ltd, 1934–35; Royal Aircraft Establishment: joined Aerodynamics Dept, 1935, engaged in flight res. and develt; Head of Aero. Flight Section, 1946–48; Head of Guided Weapons Dept, 1948–53; Dep. Dir, 1954–59; Scientific Adviser, Air Min., 1959–60; Dep. Controller of Aircraft (R&D), Min. of Aviation, 1960–63; Controller of Aircraft, 1963–66; Controller of Guided Weapons and Electronics, Min. of Technology, 1966–69; Dir, RAE, 1969–72. Pres., Royal Aeronautical Soc., 1967–68. Silver Medal, 1957, Gold Medal 1971, Royal Aeronautical Soc.; Busk Prize 1972. Hon. Fellow St Catharine's Coll., Cambridge, 1973. *Publications*: Reports and Memoranda of Aeronautical Research Council; lectures to Royal Aeronautical Soc.; *contrib*. Jl Royal Aeronautical Soc., Proc. Internat. Council Aeronautical Scis. *Address*: Downing College, Cambridge.

Morgan, Nigel John; Lecturer in Art History, School of Fine Arts and Music, University of East Anglia, since 1968; *b* 1942. BA Cantab 1964 (Trinity Coll.), MA Cantab 1968, MA East Anglia 1968. *Publications*: (ed with P. Lasko) Medieval Art in East Anglia c. 1300–1520, 1973. *Address*: School of Fine Arts and Music, Univ. of East Anglia, Norwich NOR 88C.

Morgan, Rev. Robert Chowen; Lecturer in Religious Studies, University of Lancaster, since 1967; *b* 1940; *m* 1967; two *d*. BA Cantab 1963, DipTheol Durham 1965, MA Cantab 1967; Mem., Soc. NT Studies, 1968. *Publications*: The Nature of New Testament Theology, 1973; ed (with M. Pye), The Cardinal Meaning: essays in comparative hermeneutics: Buddhism and Christianity, 1973; *contrib*. Relig. Studies, Theol. *Address*: Dept of Religious Studies, Cartmel College, Bailrigg, Lancaster.

Morgan, Prof. Thomas John; Professor of Welsh Language and Literature, University College of Swansea, since 1962, and Vice-Principal (Academic), since 1971; *b* 1907; *m* 1935; two *s*. BA Wales 1928 (1st cl. Welsh), MA Wales 1930 (with Dist.), DLitt Wales 1953; Mem., Welsh Acad. (sometime Chm.). Lectr, Univ. Coll., Cardiff, 1930–47; Sen. Lectr, Univ. Coll., Cardiff, 1947–51; Registrar, Univ. of Wales, 1951–62. Mem., Welsh Arts Council, 1963– ; Chm., Lit. Cttee 1965– ; Mem., Schs Council, Welsh Cttee; Chm. Subject-Cttees – Welsh; Chm., Welsh Studies, 1965–71; Chm., Lang. and Lit.

Cttee, Bd of Celtic Studies; Mem., Acad. Bd, Univ. of Wales, 1964– ; Mem., Univ. Council, 1967; Jt-ed., Y Llenor, 1945–48; Ed., Y Llenor, 1948–51. *Publications*: Dal Llygoden, 1937; Trwn Ac Ysgafn, 1945; Cynefin, 1948; Y Treigladau a'u Cystrawen, 1952; Ysgrifau Llenyddol, 1953; (jtly) The Saga of Llywarch the Old, 1955; Amryw Flawd, 1966; Dydd Y Farn, 1969; W. J. Gruffydd, 1970; Hirfelyn Tesog, 1971; (jtly) Y Llwybrau Gynt, 1971; Diwylliant Gwerin, 1972; *contrib*. Bull. Bd Celtic Studies, Llên Cymru, Llenor, Taliesin, Trans. Hon. Soc. Cymmrod., Ysgrif. Beirn. *Address*: Dept of Welsh, Univ. College of Swansea, Singleton Park, Swansea SA2 8PP.

Morgan, Prof. William Basil, MA, PhD; Professor of Geography, University of London, King's College, since 1971; *b* 1927; *m* 1954; one *s* one *d*. BA Oxon 1948 (1st cl. Geog.), MA Oxon 1952, PhD Glasgow 1953; FRGS. Asst, Glasgow Univ., 1948–51; Res. Asst, Glasgow Univ., 1951–53; Lectr, Univ. Coll., Ibadan, Nigeria, 1953–59; Lectr, Birmingham Univ., 1959–67; Reader, London Univ., King's Coll., 1967–71. Mem., Council, Afr. Studies Assoc. UK, 1964–66. *Publications*: (with J. C. Pugh) West Africa, 1969; (with R. J. C. Munton) Agricultural Geography, 1971; *contrib*. Afr., Ann. Assoc. Amer. Geogrs, Econ. Geog., Erdkunde, Geog. Jl, Trans Inst. Brit. Geogrs. *Address*: Dept of Geography, Univ. of London, King's College, Strand, WC2R 2LS.

Morgan, Dr William Thomas Wilson; Lecturer, Department of Geography, University of Durham, since 1968; *b* 1927. BSc (Econ.) London 1948, MSc (Econ.) London 1950; PhD Northwestern 1960. Sen. Lectr and Head of Dept of Geog., Royal Coll. Nairobi (Univ. of London), 1961–63, Prof. of Geog., 1963–64; Prof. of Geog., UC, Nairobi (Univ. of E Africa), 1964–67; Lectr in Geog., KCL, 1967–68. *Publications*: Population of Kenya: density and distribution, 1967; ed, Nairobi: city and region, 1967; ed, East Africa: its peoples and resources, 1967, 2nd edn 1972; ed, with late Sir L. Dudley Stamp, Africa: a study in tropical development, 3rd ed 1972; East Africa, 1973; *contrib*. Geogr. Jl, Trans Inst. Brit. Geogrs. *Address*: Dept of Geography, Univ. of Durham, Durham DH1 3LE.

Morgan-Wynne, Rev. John Eifion; NT Tutor, Regent's Park College, Oxford, since 1965, Lecturer (part-time) in NT Greek, University of Oxford, since 1969; *b* 1935; *m* 1962; two *s* one *d*. BA 1958 (Hist.), BA 1960 (Theol.), MA 1962, BD 1966, Oxon. *Address*: Regent's Park Coll., Oxford.

Morishima, Prof. Michio, BA, MA; Professor of Economics, London School of Economics, University of London, since 1970; *b* 1923; *m* 1935; two *s* one *d*. Keizai Gakushi (BA) Kyoto 1946; MA Oxon. Asst Prof., Univ. of Kyoto, 1950–51; Asst Prof., Univ. of Osaka, 1951–63; Fellow of Rockefeller Foundn, Oxford and Yale, 1956–58; Prof., Univ. of Osaka, 1963–69; Vis. Sen. Fellow, All Souls Coll., Oxford, 1963–64; Vis. Prof., Stanford Univ., 1964; Prof.,

Univ. of Essex, 1968–70. Mem., Econometric Soc. (Vice-Pres. 1964, Pres. 1965); Assoc. Ed., Econometrica, 1969–70; Co-ed. and Ed., Internat. Econ. Rev., 1960–70. *Publications*: Equilibrium, Stability and Growth, 1964; Theory of Economic Growth, 1969; The Working of Econometric Models, 1972; Theory of Demand: Real and Monetary, 1973; Marx's Economics, 1973; *contrib.* Econometrica, Rev. of Econ. Studies. *Address*: Dept of Economics, The London School of Economics, Houghton Street, WC2A 2AE.

Morison, John Douglas; Lecturer in Russian History, Department of Russian Studies, University of Leeds, since 1965; *b* 1937. BA Oxford 1961 (2nd cl. Hist.), MA Oxford 1966, AM Harvard 1964, Dip. in Slavonic Studies Oxford 1962, CertEd London 1963. *Publications*: *contrib.* Slav. E Europ. Rev. *Address*: Dept of Russian Studies, Univ. of Leeds, Leeds LS2 9JT.

Moritz, Prof. Ludwig Alfred, MA, DPhil; Professor of Latin, since 1960, seconded as Vice-Principal (Administration), University College, Cardiff, since 1971; *b* 1921; *m* 1949; one *s* one *d*. BA Oxon 1943, MA Oxon 1946 (1st cl. Class. hon. mods, 2nd cl. Litt. Hum.), DPhil Oxon 1954. Asst Lectr in Greek, Bedford Coll., Univ. of London, 1950–53; Coll. Lectr, Merton Coll., Oxford, 1952–53; Lectr in Latin, Univ. Coll., 1953–57; Sen. Lectr, Univ. Coll., Cardiff, 1957–60; Prof. of Classics, Univ. Coll. of Ghana, 1959–60; Dean, Fac. of Arts, Univ. Coll., Cardiff, 1967–70. Hon. Treas., Class. Assoc., 1963–72, Vice-Pres., 1972– ; Mem., Council, UCCA, 1970– ; Mem., Class. Jls Bd, 1966–72. *Publications*: Grain-Mills and Flour in Classical Antiquity, 1958; Humanitas, 1962; contrib. Pauly-Wisowa: Real-Encyclopaedie; Der Kleine Pauly; Oxford Classical Dictionary; *contrib.* Class. Philol., Class. Qly, Class. Rev., Greece Rome. *Address*: Univ. College, PO Box 78, Cardiff CF1 1XL.

Morley, Prof. Michael Francis; Professor of Accountancy, Department of Accountancy, University of Aberdeen, since 1974; *b* 1941; *m* 1961; three *s*. BA Essex 1969; ACA 1966. University of Stirling: Lectr, 1969–71; Sen. Lectr and Head of Dept. of Accountancy and Business Law, 1971–74. *Publications*: A Guide to the Taxation of Investment Institutions, 1971; *contrib.* Accountancy, Accountant, Accountant's Mag., Jl Law Soc. of Scot., Investment Analyst. *Address*: Dept of Accountancy, Univ. of Aberdeen, Aberdeen AB9 1AS.

Morley, Richard; Senior Lecturer in Economics, University of Durham, since 1972; *b* 1930; *m* 1969. BSc Econ. London 1965. Lectr in Econs, Univ. of Durham, 1965–72. *Publications*: Project to Evaluate Benefits of University Libraries, 1969; Employment in a Tourist Economy: The British Virgin Islands, 1971; Mathematics for Modern Economics, 1972. *Address*: Dept of Economics, 23–26 Old Elvet, Durham.

Morpurgo, Prof. Jack Eric; Professor of American Literature, School of English, University of Leeds, since 1969; *b* 1918; *m* 1947; three *s* one *d*. BA William and Mary 1938; Hon. DLitt Ricker 1965; Hon. LitD Elmira 1967; Hon. DHL William and Mary 1969, PhiBetaKappa, Alpha of Virginia 1938. William and Mary Res. Fellow, Durham Univ., 1938–39; Prof. of American Lit., Univ. of Geneva, 1969–70; Dir, Coll. of William and Mary History Project, 1969– . War Service, 1939–45; Ed., Penguin Bks, 1945–49; Gen. Ed., Pelican Histories, 1947–67; Educn Adv., Penguin Bks, 1963–67; Asst Dir, Nuffield Foundn, 1951–55; Dir-Gen., Nat. Bk League, 1955–69 (Vice-Pres., 1971–); Mem., var. nat. cttees. *Publications*: Charles Lamb and Elia, 1948; American Excursion, 1949; ed, I. Hunt: Autobiography, 1949; Last Days of Shelley and Byron, 1951, 2nd edn 1959; (with R. B. Nye) A History of the United States, 1955, 3rd edn 1970, also French, German, Bengali, Portuguese edns; The Road to Athens, 1963; Venice, 1964; ed, Cobbett: A Year's Residence in USA, 1965; ed, Cooper: The Spy, 1967; Barnes Wallis: A Biography, 1972; contrib. or ed, many other vols; *contrib.* Jl Documentation, Times Lit. Supp., etc. *Address*: School of English, The Univ., Leeds LS2 9JT.

Morpurgo Davies, Anna; *see* Davies, A. E.

Morrall, Dr Eric John, MA, PhD; Reader in German, University of Durham, since 1973; *b* 1920; *m* 1951; two *s* two *d*. BA London 1948 (German), MA London 1951, PhD London 1963. Lectr, Univ. of Cologne, 1949–52; Lectr and Sen. Lectr, Univ. of Durham, 1952–72. *Publications*: Heinrich von Morungen: Complete Word-index, 1957; ed, Sir J. Mandeville: Reisebeschreibung in deutscher Übersetzung von Michel Velser (forthcoming); *contrib.* Durh. Univ. Jl, Germ. Life Lett., Mod. Lang. Rev., Zeits. Deuts. Philol., etc. *Address*: Dept of German, Univ. of Durham, Elvet Riverside, Durham.

Morrall, Dr John Brimyard; Senior Lecturer in Political Science, Department of Government, London School of Economics and Political Science, University of London, since 1965; *b* 1923; *m* 1955; five *s*. BA Oxon 1944, MA Oxon 1948, BLitt Oxon 1948, PhD National University of Ireland 1954; Mem., Pol. Science Assoc. UK. Lectr in Hist., Univ. Coll. Dublin, 1950–62; Lectr in Pol. Science, LSE, 1962–65. Ed., Bull. Irish Cttee for Hist. Sci., 1958–62. *Publications*: (with S. Z. Ehler) Church and State through the Centuries, 1954, Italian edn 1958; Political Thought in Medieval Times, 1958, 3rd edn 1971, American edn 1962; Gerson and the Great Schism, 1960; The Medieval Imprint, 1967, American edn 1968, pbk edn 1970, Japanese edn 1972; ed (with J. A. Watt and F. X. Martin), Medieval Studies presented to Aubrey Gwynn, 1961; *contrib.* Camb. Jl, Francis. Studies. *Address*: London School of Economics and Political Science, Houghton Street, Aldwych, WC2A 2AE.

Morrell, David William James; Registrar, University of Strathclyde, since 1973; *b* 1933; *m* 1960; two *s* one *d*. MA Hons Edinburgh 1954, LLB 1957. Admin. Asst, King's Coll., Univ. of Durham, 1957–60; Asst Registrar and Appointments Officer, Univ. of Exeter, 1960–64; Sen. Asst Registrar, Univ. of Essex, 1964–66; Acad. Registrar, Univ. of Strathclyde, 1966–1973. Law Apprentice with Shepherd and Wedderburn WS, Edinburgh, 1954–57. Member: UCCA, 1966– ; Scottish Univs Council on Entrance, 1968– . *Address*: Royal Coll., Univ. of Strathclyde, Glasgow G1 1XW.

Morrell, Jack Bowes; Lecturer in History of Science, School of Social Sciences, University of Bradford, since 1964; *b* 1933; *m* 1962; two *d*. BSc Birmingham 1954, BA Oxon 1957, CertEd Bristol 1958. Prof., Univ. of Pennsylvania, 1970; Post-Doctoral Res. Fellow, Univ. of Edinburgh, 1973. *Publications*: *contrib*. Ambix, Brit. Jl Hist. Science, Hist. Studies, Phys. Sci., Isis, Notes Rec. Royal Soc. Lond., Sci. Studies. *Address*: School of Social Sciences, The Univ., Bradford BD7 1DP.

Morrell, Richard Charles Roy; Senior Lecturer in English Studies, New University of Ulster, since 1968; *b* 1908; *m* 1st 1935, 2nd 1947; one *s* two *d*. BA Cantab 1931, MA Cantab 1934; FZS (S). Lekt, Helsinki Univ., 1931–34; Lectr, Raffles Coll., Singapore, 1934–36, 1947–50; Johore Prof. of English, Univ. of Malaya, 1950–56; Sen. Lectr, Makerere Coll., Uganda, 1957–58; Prof. of English Literature, International Christian Univ., Japan, 1959–62; Lectr, Magee Univ. Coll., Londonderry, 1964–68. RAF (Movements), 1942–46; Mem., Council, Malay Coll., K. Kangsar, 1954–56; Mem., Art Cttee, N. Ireland Arts Council, 1971– . *Publications*: Common Malayan Butterflies, 1960, 2nd edn 1967; Thomas Hardy: the Will and the Way, 1965, 2nd edn 1968; *contrib*. Crit. Qly, Engl. Studies (Tokyo Univ.), Ess. Crit., Maker. Jl, Malay. Nature Jl, Mod. Lang. Rev., Rev. Engl. Lit., Scrut., etc. *Address*: Dept of English Studies, New Univ. of Ulster, Coleraine, Co. Londonderry BT52 1SA.

Morrice, Dr James Kenneth Watt; Clinical Senior Lecturer, Department of Mental Health, University of Aberdeen (also teaches Social Work students), since 1970; *b* 1924; *m* 1948; one *s* two *d*. MB, ChB Aberdeen 1946, MD Aberdeen 1954, DPM London 1951; FRCPsych 1972. Hon. Lectr in Forensic Psychiatry, Edinburgh Univ., 1962–68; Clinical Lectr, Aberdeen Univ., 1968–70. Hon. Chm., Sect. of Psychoth. and Social Psychiat., Royal Coll. of Psychiat., Scott. Div. *Publications*: Prototype (Verse), 1965; *contrib*. Brit. Jl Med. Psychol., Brit Jl Psychiat., Internat. Jl Soc. Psychiat. *Address*: Ross Clinic, Cornhill Road, Aberdeen.

Morrin, Francis D.; Lecturer in Political Economy, University College, Dublin, since 1962. BA University College Dublin 1958, MBA Pennsylvania 1961; Barrister-at-Law, King's Inns, Dublin, Barrister-at-Law, Inner Temple, London. *Address*: Univ. College, Dublin 4.

Morris, Arthur Stephen, MA, PhD; Lecturer in Geography, Glasgow University, since 1967; *b* 1936; *m* 1963; one *s* one *d*. BA Oxon 1960 (Geog.), MA Maryland 1962 (Geog.), PhD Wisconsin 1966 (Geog.); Mem., Inst Brit. Geogrs. Teaching Asst, Univ. of Maryland, 1960–62; Instructor, West. Michigan Univ., 1964–65; Asst Prof., West. Michigan Univ., 1965–67. Mem., Bd on Geog. Names, Washington DC, 1961. *Publications*: *contrib*. Ann. Assoc. Amer. Geogrs, Geog. Jl, Geog., Proc. Inst. Brit. Geogrs, Revista Geog. *Address*: Dept of Geography, The Univ., Glasgow G12 8QQ.

Morris, Prof. Benjamin Stephen, BSc, MEd; Professor of Education (Advanced Studies), School of Education, Bristol University, since 1956; *b* 1910; *m* 1938; two *s* one *d*. BSc Glasgow 1933, MEd Glasgow 1937; Mem., Brit. Psychol. Soc. Lectr, Univ. of Glasgow, 1940–46; Chm., Mngmt Cttee, Tavistock Inst. Hum. Relat., London, 1947–49; Dir, Nat. Foundn Educn Res. Engl. and Wales, 1950–56; Vis. Prof. of Harvard, 1969–70. *Publications*: Objectives and Perspectives in Education: Studies in Educational Theory 1955–70, 1972; Sigmund Freud, in, The Function of Teaching, ed Judges, 1959; How Does A Group Learn to Work Together?, in, How and Why Do We Learn?', ed Niblett, 1965; The Contribution of Psychology to the Study of Education, in, The Study of Education, ed Tibble, 1966; Response to Martin Trowe (Elite and Popular Functions in American Higher Education), in, Higher Education, Demand and Response, ed Niblett, 1969; Commentary: Reply to G. H. Bantock (Conflicts of Value in Teacher Education), in, Towards a Policy for the Education of Teachers, ed Taylor, 1969; *contrib*. Brit. Jl Educnl Studies, Harv. Educnl Rev., Irish Educnl Jl, Occupat. Psychol., Sociol. Rev. Monog., YBk Educn. *Address*: Univ. School of Education, 35 Berkeley Square, Bristol.

Morris, Prof. Brian Robert, MA, DPhil; Professor of English Literature, University of Sheffield, since 1971; *b* 1930; *m* 1955; one *s* one *d*. BA Oxon 1954 (2nd cl. Engl. Lang. and Lit.), MA Oxon 1957, DPhil Oxon 1963; Mem., Bibliographical Soc. Asst Lectr, Birmingham Univ., 1956–58; Lectr, Reading Univ., 1958–65; Lectr, York Univ., 1965–67; Senior Lectr, York Univ., 1967–71. Gen. Ed., New Mermaid Dramatists, 1964– ; Ed., Mermaid Critical Commentaries, 1968–72. *Publications*: The Bibliography of Cleveland's Poems, 1968; ed. Ford's: The Broken Heart, 1965; ed, Ford's: 'Tis Pity She's a Whore, 1967; ed (with Eleanor Withington), The Poems of John Cleveland, 1967; *contrib*. Shakesp. Qly, The Library. *Address*: Dept of English Literature, The Univ., Sheffield S10 2TN.

Morris, Rev. Prof. Colin, MA; Professor of Medieval History, University of Southampton, since 1969; *b* 1928; *m* 1956; two *s* one *d*. BA Oxon 1948 (1st cl. Hist. 1948, 1st cl. Theology 1951), MA Oxon 1953; FRHistS. Fellow, Pembroke Coll., Oxford, 1953–69. Supernum. Fellow, Pembroke Coll., Oxford, 1969– . *Publications*: The Discovery of the Individual 1050-1200, 1972; *contrib*. EHR, Jl Eccles. Hist., Hist. *Address*: Dept of History, Southampton Univ., Southampton SO9 5NH.

Morris, Cyril Brian; Reader in Spanish, University of Hull, since 1970; *b* 1933; *m* 1957; one *s*. BA Manchester 1955 (1st cl. Mod. Langs), MA Manchester 1956. Asst Lectr, UC, Cardiff, 1957–59, Lectr, 1959–61; Lectr, Hull Univ., 1961–64, Lectr in charge, 1964–67; Sen. Lectr in charge, Hull Univ., 1967–70. *Publications*: The Unity and Structure of Quevedo's Buscón, 1965; Rafael Alberti's Sobre los ángeles: four major themes, 1966; A Generation of Spanish Poets 1920–1936, 1969; Surrealism and Spain 1920–1936, 1972; *contrib.* Bull. of Hispanic Studies, Neophilologus, Revue de Littérature Comparée, The Romanic Rev. *Address*: Dept of Hispanic Studies, Univ. of Hull, Hull HU6 7RX.

Morris, Eleanor Kenner Smith, BArchSci, MCP, MAIP, ARTPI; Lecturer in Urban Design and Regional Planning, University of Edinburgh, since 1960; *b* 1935; *m* 1959; two *s* one *d*. AB Harvard 1956 (Architectl Science cum Laude), Dip. Town Planning London 1958, Master City Planning Pennsylvania 1959; Mem., Amer. Inst. Planners, MRTPI. Mem., Univ. of Edinburgh/Grampian TV Liaison Cttee, 1968–69; Mem., Scott. Georgian Soc., 1968–72. *Publications*: The Growing City (BBC TV for Schools), 1961; The Pedestrian in the City, ed D. Lewis, 1965; *contrib.* Archit. Des. *Address*: Dept of Urban Design and Regional Planning, Univ. of Edinburgh, Edinburgh, Scotland.

Morris, Dr Harold Stephen, BSc, Dip Anthropol, PhD; Reader, Department of Anthropology, London School of Economics, since 1973; *b* 1913; *m* 1953; two *s*. BSc Edinburgh 1934, Dip Anthropol London 1947, PhD London 1963; FRAnthropol Inst. Sen. Res. Fellow, Makerere Univ. Coll., Uganda, 1952–56; Lectr, LSE, 1956–66, Sen. Lectr, 1966–73; Vis. Prof., Col. de México, 1968; Disting. Vis. Prof., Ohio State Univ., 1970. *Publications*: A Melanau Sago Producing Community, 1952; Indians in Uganda, 1968; *contrib.* Amer. Anthropol., Jl Royal Anthropol. Inst., SW Jl Anthropol. Studies. *Address*: Dept of Anthropology, London School of Economics, Houghton Street, WC2A 2AE.

Morris, Henry Francis, PhD; Reader in African Law, School of Oriental and African Studies, University of London, since 1968; *b* 1918; *m* 1946; one *s* two *d*. BA Dublin 1940 (1st cl. Hist.), MA Dublin 1945, LLB Dublin 1946, PhD London 1957. Burma Admin. Service (cl. I), 1946–47; Colonial Admin. Service (Uganda), 1948–62; Lectr, SOAS, Univ. of London, 1963–68. *Publications*: (with B. E. R. Kirwan) A Runyankore Grammar, 1957; A History of Ankole, 1962; The Heroic Recitations of the Bahima of Ankole, 1964; (with J. S. Read) Uganda: the Development of its Laws and Constitution, 1966; Evidence in East Africa, 1968; Perspectives of East African Legal History, 1970; (with A. Phillips) Marriage Laws in Africa, 1971; (with J. S. Read) Indirect Rule and the Search for Justice, 1972; *contrib.* Jl Afr. Hist., Jl Afr. Law, Uganda Jl. *Address*: School of Oriental and African Studies, Malet Street, WC1E 7HP.

Morris, Dr J. H. C., DCL, FBA; Fellow of Magdalen College, University of Oxford, since 1936, and University Reader in Conflict of Law, since 1951; *b* 1910; *m* 1939. BA Oxon 1931 (1st cl. Jurisprudence), BCL Oxon 1932 (1st cl.), DCL Oxon 1949; Barrister-at-Law, Gray's Inn; FBA. All Souls Lectr in Private Internat. Law, 1939–51; Vis. Prof., Harvard Law Sch., 1950–51. *Publications*: ed, Theobald on Wills, 9th–11th edns, 1939–54; Cases in Private International Law, 1939, 4th edn 1968; Gen. Editor, Chitty on Contracts, 22nd edn 1961, Editor 23rd edn 1968; Gen. Editor, Dicey's Conflict of Laws, 6th–9th edns, 1949–73; (with W. B. Leach) The Rule against Perpetuities, 1956, 2nd edn 1962; The Conflict of Laws, 1971; *contrib.* Brit. Ybk Internat. Law, Camb. Law Jl, Harvard Law Rev., Law Qly Rev., Mod. Law Rev. *Address*: Magdalen College, Oxford.

Morris, James W.; *see* Walker Morris.

Morris, Dr John Anthony; Lecturer in English Literature, Division of Languages, Department of Education, Brunel University, since 1966; *b* 1937; *m* 1968; two *d*. BA Hons Nottingham 1963 (English), PhD Nottingham 1970 (English). Hugh Stewart Res. Schol., Univ. of Nottingham, 1965–66; Lectr, Dept of Extra-Mural Studies, Univ. of Nottingham, 1965–66; Vis. Lectr in English for Amer. undergrads in London, Univ. of Wisconsin, 1971–72. Examiner in Eng. Lit. for JMB, Manchester, 1968– . *Publications*: Literature and Politics (ed J. E. Flower) (forthcoming); *contrib.* Encoun., Jl Europ. Studies, Workshop New Poetry, Transcript. *Address*: Division of Languages, Dept of Education, Brunel Univ., Uxbridge, Mddx UB8 3TH.

Morris, Rev. Peter Michael Keighley; Senior Lecturer, Department of Theology, St David's University College, Lampeter, since 1969; *b* 1927; *m* 1959; two *s* two *d*. BA Oxford: 1949 (Hons Theology), 1952 (Hons Oriental Languages), MA Oxford 1955; Mem., Soc. for Old Testament Study. Lectr in Theology, St David's Coll., 1955. Asst Curate, Bedwellty, Mon, 1954–55; Exam. Chaplain to: Bishop of Monmouth (later Archbishop of Wales), 1955–67; Bishop of Monmouth, 1970– . *Publications*: (with E. B. James) A Critical Concordance of the Pentateuch (vol. of Computer Bible Project) (forthcoming); *contrib.* Exp. T., Heb. Comput., Linguist. Bull., Trivium. *Address*: Dept of Theology, St David's Univ. Coll., Lampeter, Dyfed SA48 7ED.

Morris, Prof. Terence Patrick; Professor of Sociology (with special reference to Criminology), University of London, since 1969; *b* 1931; *m* 1954, 1973; one *d*. BSc(Soc) London, PhD(Econ) London; JP Inner London 1967. Lectr in Sociol., 1955–63, Reader in Sociol. (with special ref. to Criminology), 1963–69, LSE; Vis. Prof. of Criminology, Univ. of California, 1964–65. Man. Ed., Brit. Jl of Sociol. *Publications*: The Criminal Area, 1957; (with P. Morris) Pentonville: a sociological study of an English prison, 1963; (with L. J. Blom-Cooper) A Calendar of Murder, 1964; *contrib.* Brit. Jl Criminology, Brit. Jl Sociol., Encycl. Brit.

Address: London School of Economics and Political Science, Houghton Street, Aldwych, WC2A 2AE.

Morris, Lt-Col William Edward Maxwell, BA, MSc, FIWM; Project Officer, Computer Unit, University of Durham (also teaches Operational Research), since 1965; *b* 1918; *m* 1939; three *s*. BA Cantab 1946 (Mech. Sciences), MSc Dunelm 1970 (Operational Research); Fellow, Inst. of Wks Mgrs; Passed Staff Coll., Army, 1948, Passed Tech. Staff Coll., 1950. Commnd Royal Eng., 1938; service in W Europe, 1944–45; SE Asia, 1945; Mid. East (Egypt/Palestine), 1946–47; Germany, 1950–54; Royal Mil. Coll. Sci., Shrivenham, 1954–56; Retd from Army, 1961; Gen. Wks Mgr, Heavy Eng. Indust., 1960–63; Lectr in Mathematics, Constantine Coll. of Technol., Middlesbrough, 1963–64. *Publications*: ed, Final Report on the project for evaluating the benefit from University libraries, 1969; ed, Economic Evaluation of Computer Based Systems, Bk 1: Working Party Report, 1971; (with C. W. Blaxter) Bk 2: Workshop Report, 1971. *Address*: Univ. of Durham Computer Unit, South Road, Durham City.

Morris-Jones, Prof. Huw; Professor of Social Theory and Institutions, University College, Bangor, since 1966; *b* 1912; *m* 1942; one *s* one *d*. BA Wales 1933 (1st cl. English, 1st cl. Philosophy 1934); BLitt Oxon 1937; Mem., Brit. Sociol Assoc. Lectr, Nottingham Univ., 1939–42; Lectr, Univ. Coll., Bangor, 1942–59, Sen. Lectr, 1959–66. Mem., Welsh Council, 1968–71; Mem., Nature Conserv., 1969–   ; Magistrate, 1949–   ; Mem., Welsh Reg. Cttee, BBC. *Publications*: *contrib*. Brit. Jl Aesth., Efryd Athron, Monist, Philos. *Address*: Dept of Social Theory and Institutions, Univ. College, North Wales, Bangor LL57 2DG.

Morris-Jones, Prof. Wyndraeth Humphreys; Director of the Institute of Commonwealth Studies, and Professor of Commonwealth Affairs, University of London, since 1966; *b* 1918; *m* 1953; one *s* two *d*. BScEcon London 1938 (1st cl.); Leverhulme Research Award, 1938–39; Christ's College, Cambridge, 1939–40 (Research studentship, discontinued for war service). Member: Political Studies Assoc.; International Political Science Assoc. Asst Lectr and Lectr, LSE, 1946–55; Prof. of Political Theory and Institutions, Univ. of Durham, 1955–65. Served Indian Army, 1940–46, RIASC; staff appointments in Public Relations Directorate at NW and S Commands, 1942–45; senior (Lt-Col) staff appointment at GHQ, 1945–46; Constitutional Adviser to HE the Viceroy, New Delhi, May–August 1947. *Publications*: Parliament in India, 1957; The Government and Politics of India, 1964, 3rd edn 1971; *contrib*. Asian Survey, Modern Asian Studies, Pol Studies. *Address*: Institute of Commonwealth Studies, 27 Russell Square, WC1B 5DS.

Morrison, Hon. Alasdair Andrew Orr; Lecturer in Politics, University of Bristol, since 1965; *b* 1929; *m* 1958; one *s* two *d*. BA, MA Oxon 1959, MA Chicago 1963, PhD

498

Chicago 1965. Lectr, Univ. of Chicago, 1964–65. *Publications*: *contrib*. Proc. Aristot. Soc. *Address*: 40 Berkeley Square, Bristol BS8 1HY.

Morrison, Dr Alastair; Lecturer in Geography, University of Glasgow, since 1966; *b* 1935; *m* 1963; two *s*. BA Cambridge 1958, MA Maryland 1962, PhD McGill 1966; Mem., Brit. Cartog. Soc., Inst. Brit. Geogrs, Quaternay Res. Assoc., Royal Scott. Geogl Soc. G. Philip & Sons, map publishers, 1958–59; Cartographic Asst, Univ. of Maryland, 1959–61; Asst, McGill Univ., 1961–62; St Joseph Teachers Coll., Montreal, 1961–63; Planetary Surface Interp. Project, McGill Univ. 1963–65; Asst Prof., McGill Univ., 1965–66. US Bd on Geog. Names, 1960. *Publications*: World Atlas of Photography from Tiros Satellites I to IV, 1964; Photography of the Western Sahara Desert from the Mercury MA-4 Spacecraft, 1964; Photography of Southern Africa from Tiros Satellites I to VIII, 1965; *contrib*. Arctic, Canad. Geog., Canad. Jl Bot., Cartog. Jl, Geog. Rev., Photogram. Engrg, Teach. Geog. *Address*: Dept of Geography, Univ. of Glasgow, Glasgow G12 8QQ.

Morrison, Prof. Arnold, BA MEd; Professor of Education, University of Stirling, since 1975; *b* 1928; *m* 1956; two *s* one *d*. BA Birmingham 1951, DipEd Glasgow 1956, MEd Birmingham 1963; ABPsS 1966. Lectr in Psychol., Edinburgh Univ., 1966–70; Dep. Dir, Godfrey Thomson Unit for Educnl Res., Univ. of Edinburgh, 1967–70; Sen. Lectr, Dept of Educn, Univ. of Dundee, 1970–74. Mem., Scott. Council Res. Educn, 1970–   ; Editorial Bd, Brit. Jl of Social and Clinical Psychology. *Publications*: (with D. McIntyre) Teachers and Teaching, 1969; (with D. McIntyre) Schools and Socialization, 1971; (with D. McIntyre) The Social Psychology of Teaching: Selected Readings, 1972; *contrib*. Brit. Jl Educnl Psychol., Brit. Jl Med. Educn, Brit. Jl Soc. Clin. Psychol., Educnl Res., Scott. Educnl Studies. *Address*: Dept of Education, Univ. of Stirling, Stirling FK9 4LA.

Morrison, John Sinclair; President, Wolfson (formerly University) College, Cambridge, since 1966; *b* 1913; *m* 1942; three *s* two *d*. Fellow, Trinity Coll., Cambridge, 1937–45; Asst Lectr, Manchester Univ., 1937–39; Prof. of Greek and Head of Dept of Classics and Ancient History at the Durham Colls of Univ. of Durham, 1945–50; Fellow, Tutor and Sen. Tutor of Trinity Coll., Cambridge, 1950–60; Vice-Master and Sen. Tutor of Churchill Coll., Cambridge, 1960–65, now Hon. Fellow. Leverhulme Fellow, 1965. Jt Editor, Class. Rev. Editor of Cambridge Rev., 1939–40; with Brit. Council in ME, 1941–45. Mem., Council, Hellenic Soc., 1948, 1952; Mem. Council, Class. Assoc., 1949; Mem., Sierra Leone Educn Commn, 1954, Annan Cttee on Teaching of Russian, 1961, Hale Cttee on Univ. Teaching Methods, 1961, Schools Coun., 1965–67, Jt Working Party on 6th Form Curriculum and Examinations, 1968–72, Governing Bodies Assoc., 1965; Governor, Bradfield Coll., 1963, Wellington Coll., 1963, Culford Sch., 1969,

Charterhouse Sch., 1970. *Publication*: (with R. T. Williams) Greek Oared Ships, 1968. *Address*: Wolfson College, Cambridge.

Morrison, Rhona; Senior Lecturer, School of Social Administration, University of Dundee, since 1958; *b* 1917. MA Glasgow 1938, DipSoc Studies Glasgow 1939, Cert. Int. Hosp. Almoners 1940, Cert. Psychiatric Social Wk Edinburgh 1948; Mem., Nat. Broadcast. Council Scotl., 1964–68; Exec. Cttee, Scott. Council Social Serv., 1968–71; Ind. Mem., Wages Council, Aerated Waters (Scotl.) Indust., 1968–71; Mem., Nat. Assist. Appeal Tribunal (Dundee), 1966–70. *Publications*: The Help: An Account of the Edinburgh Association for Improving the Condition of the Poor, 1968. *Address*: School of Social Administration, The Univ., Dundee DD1 4HN.

Morrison, Dr Robert Bruce, BSc, PhD, AKC; Senior Lecturer in Education, University of Reading, since 1970; *b* 1924; *m* 1954; one *s* one *d*. BSc London 1944 (1st cl. Physics), PhD London 1949, AKC London 1949. Demonstrator in Physics, King's Coll., London, 1944–46; Res. Off. in Meteorology, Imperial Coll., London, 1949–51; Lectr in Educn, Univ. of Reading, 1963–70. Dir, Educnl Measurement Res. Unit, 1969– ; Mem., Educn Cttee, Assoc. Exam. Bd, 1969– ; Council, South Reg. CSE Bd, 1971– . *Publications*: Concise Physics, 1962; (with M. J. Rolls) Science in the Garden, 1966; (with H. G. Macintosh) Objective Testing, 1969; (with D. L. Nuttall, etc) British Examinations: Techniques of Analysis, 1972; (with H. G. Macintosh, etc) Techniques and Problems of Assessment, 1974; *contrib.* Jl Sci. Inst., Maths Teach., Philos. Mag. *Address*: School of Education, Univ. of Reading, Reading, Berkshire.

Morrison, Samuel James; Director, and Senior Lecturer, Sub-Department of Operational Research, University of Hull, since 1967; *b* 1917; *m* 1944; two *d*. BSc Glasgow 1940; CEng, MIEE, MIMechE, FSS. Lectr in Operational Res., Hull, 1963–67. UK Contributing Editor, Internat. Abstracts in Operations Res. *Publications*: Appl. Stats, Eng., Glass Technol., Jl Sci. Instr., Trans Inst. Elec. Eng., Trans Soc. Glass Technol. *Address*: Sub-Department of Operational Research, Univ. of Hull, Hull HU6 7RX.

Morsbach, (Paul) Helmut, MSc, PhD; Senior Lecturer in Social Psychology, Department of Psychology, University of Glasgow, since 1974 (Lecturer, 1969–74); *b* 1937; *m* 1964; two *d*. BSc Stellenbosch 1958 (Zoology and Physiology),, BSc Stellenbosch 1959 (Hons Psychology) MSc Stellenbosch 1960 (Psychology), PhD Cape Town 1965 (Psychology); Associate Mem., Brit. Psychol Soc.; Mem., Internat. Assoc. for Cross-Cultural Psychol.; Mem., European Assoc. for Japanese Studies; Mem., Assoc. of Asian Studies. Lectr, Rhodes Univ., Grahamstown, 1964–67; Instr, Internat. Christian Univ., Tokyo, 1967–68, Asst Prof., 1968–69. *Publications*: *contrib.* Brit. Jl Criminol., Educnl Studies (Internat. Christ.

Univ.), Internat. Jl Psychol., Jap. Jl Ethnol., Jap. Jl Psychol., Jl Gen. Psychol., Jl Nervous and Mental Diseases, Jl Soc. Psychol., Personn. Guid. Jl. *Address*: Dept of Psychology, Univ. of Glasgow, Glasgow G12 8RT.

Morton, David John; Senior Lecturer, School of Education, Nottingham University, since 1970; *b* 1929; *m* 1955. BA Leeds 1953 (1st cl. Hons Classics), CertifEd, Leeds 1954; Mem. Class. Assoc. of Gt Britain, Mem. Jt Assoc. of Class. Teachers. Nottingham Univ., 1961–65 and 1969– ; Dir, Cambridge Sch. Classics Project, Cambridge Univ., 1966–69. Mem. Classics Cttee, Schools Council; Mem. Classics Cttee, Southern Univs Jt Bd. *Publications*: Classics and the Reorganisation of Secondary Schools, 1965; The Cambridge Latin Course, 1970; executive editor, The Cambridge Latin Texts, 1973; *contrib.* Cambridge Review, Didactica Classica Gandensia. *Address*: School of Education, Univ. of Nottingham, University Park, Nottingham NG7 2RD.

Morton, Richard Grenfell; Lecturer in History, Department of Extra-Mural Studies, Queen's University of Belfast, since 1967; *b* 1924; *m* 1956; two *s* one *d*. BA (Hons) 1945 (Mod. Hist.), HDipEd 1950, MA 1951, BLitt 1951, TCD, MEd Aberdeen 1951; Member: Ulster Soc. for Irish Hist. Studies; Econ. and Social Hist. Soc. of Ireland; Conf. of Local Hist. Tutors in Adult Educn. *Publications*: Standard Gauge Railways in the North of Ireland, 1962, 3rd edn 1972; Elizabethan Ireland, 1971; Victorian Bangor, 1972; introd. History of the Irish Rebellion of 1798 and Sequel by C. H. Teeling, 1972; *contrib.* Ulster Folklife, Jl of Military Hist. Soc. of Ireland, Irish Booklore, Bull. Irish Georgian Soc. *Address*: Queen's Univ. Belfast, 2 Fitzwilliam Street, Belfast BT7 1NN.

Morton, Dr Robert Steel; Lecturer in Venereal Diseases (including historical and social aspects), University of Sheffield, since 1960; *b* 1917; *m* 1945; two *s*. LRCP LRCS LRFPS 1939, MRCP 1954, FRCP 1962. Past Pres., Med. Soc. for Study of Venereal Diseases; WHO Cnsltnt, Singapore, Bangladesh and SE Asia. *Publications*: Venereal Disease, 1966; Sexual Freedom and Venereal Diseases, 1971; (jtly) Recent Advances in Sexually Transmitted Diseases, 1974; *contrib.* Brit. Jl Ven. Dis., Brit. Med. Jl. *Address*: Univ. of Sheffield, Western Bank, Sheffield.

Moseley, Laurence George; Lecturer, Department of Social Administration, University College, Swansea, since 1965; *b* 1937; *m* 1966; one *d*. BA Oxford 1961, DipSoc Admin London 1962, MA Oxford 1970. Res. Asst, Durham, 1962–65. *Publications*: *contrib.* Comm. Develt Jl, Econ. Social Admin., Social Wk, Howard Jl, Zeitschrift für Gerontologie. *Address*: Dept of Social Administration, Univ. College, Swansea SA2 8PP.

Moser, Prof. Sir Claus Adolf, KCB, CBE, FBA; Director, Central Statistical Office, and Head of UK Government Statistical Service, since 1970; Visiting Professor of Social Statistics, London School of Economics, University of London, since 1970; *b* 1922; *m* 1949; one *s* two *d*. BSc(Econ) 1943 (1st cl.); FBA, FRStatSoc., FAmerStatAssoc., Mem., Internat. Stat. Inst. Asst Lectr in Stats, LSE, 1946–49. Lectr in Stats, LSE, 1949–55; Reader in Social Stats, LSE, 1955–61; Prof. of Social Stats, LSE, 1961–70. Mem., Milner-Holland Cttee on London Housing; Mem., Perks' Cttee on Criminal Stats, etc; Stat. Adv., Robbin's Cttee on Higher Educn; Mem. Council, Brit. Acad., 1972– ; Mem., Bd of Dirs, Royal Opera Hse; Mem., Gov. Body, Royal Acad. Music; Mem., BBC Mus Adv. Cttee. *Publications*: Survey Methods in Social Investigation, 1958, 2nd edn (with G. Kalton) 1971; (with A. Carr-Saunders and D. C. Jones) Social Conditions in East and West, 1958; (with W. Scott) British Towns, 1959; *contrib.* Jl Amer. Stat. Assoc., Jl Royal Stat. Soc., etc. *Address*: London School of Economics, Aldwych, WC2A 2AE.

Moss, Dr George Dennis; Director, Centre for Educational Technology, University College, Cardiff, since 1974; *b* 1943; *m* 1968; two *d*. BSc Birmingham 1965 (1st cl. Hons Zool. and Comparative Physiol.), PhD Birmingham 1968 (Zool.), Dip. of Programmed Learning, City and Guilds, 1970; Mem., Brit. Soc. for Parasitology, 1965–72. Univ. of Glasgow, 1968–71; Lectr, Inst. of Educnl Techn., Open Univ., 1971–74. *Publication*: *contrib.* Parasitology. *Address*: Open Univ., Milton Keynes MK7 6AA.

Moss, Prof. Rowland Percy, BSc PhD; Professor of Biogeography, Department of Geography, University of Birmingham, since 1973; *b* 1928; *m* 1954; one *s* one *d*. BSc London 1951 (2nd cl. Special Geography), PhD London 1961, Soil Sci. Aberdeen 1952; FRHS 1969, Mem., Inst. Brit. Geogrs, 1960, Brit. Ecol. Soc., 1963, Brit. Soc. Soil Sci., 1962, S African Geog. Soc., 1970. Sen. Lectr, Coll. of Technol. Ibadan, 1957–62; Lectr, Univ. of Birmingham, 1962–70, Sen. Lectr, 1970–71, Reader, 1972–73. RAF, 1946–48; Soil Scientist, Colonial Agric. Service, 1952–57. *Publications*: The Classification of Soils over Sedimentary Rocks in South-western Nigeria, 1957; ed, The Soil Resources of Tropical Africa, 1968; ed (with M. R. Kettle), Southern African Studies, 1970; ed (with R. J. A. R. Rathbone), The Population Factor in Tropical African Studies, 1974; *contrib.* Ann. Assoc. Amer. Geogrs, Jl Soil Sci., Nig. Geogl Jl, Pacif. Vpnt, S Afr. Geog Jl, Trans and Papers, Inst. Brit. Geogrs. *Address*: Dept of Geography, Univ. of Birmingham, PO Box 363, Birmingham B15 2TT.

Mosse, Prof. Werner E., MA, PhD; Professor of European History, School of European Studies, University of East Anglia, since 1964; *b* 1918. BA Cantab 1939 (Double 1st cl. Hist.), MA Cantab 1943, PhD Cantab 1950; FRHistS. Res. Fellow, Corpus Christi Coll., Cambridge, 1946–48; Lectr, SSEES, London Univ., 1948–52; Sen. Lectr, Glasgow Univ., 1952–64. Mem., State Studentship Cttee, 1962–65; Dean, Sch. of Europ. Studies, Univ. of E Anglia, 1968–71. *Publications*: The European Powers and the German Question 1848–1871, 1958; Alexander II and the Modernization of Russia 1855–1881, 1959; The Rise and Fall of the Crimean System 1855–1871, 1963; ed, Entscheidungsjahr 1932, 1965, 2nd edn 1966; Deutsches Judentum in Krieg und Revolution 1916–1923, 1971; contrib. Encyclopedia Britannica; *contrib.* EHR, Jl Mod. Hist., Slav. E Europ. Rev., Sov. Studies, Ybk Leo Baeck Inst. *Address*: School of European Studies, Univ. of East Anglia, Norwich NOR 88C.

Mossop, Prof. Deryk Joseph, MA, DUP; Professor of Modern French Literature, University of Durham, since 1963; *b* 1919; *m* 1946; one *d*. BA Cape Town 1938, MA Cape Town 1939 (1st cl. French), DU Paris 1949. Temp. Lectr, Stellenbosch Univ., 1950–51; Asst, Glasgow Univ., 1951–53; Lectr, Durham Univ., 1953–63. *Publications*: Baudelaire's Tragic Hero, 1961; Pure Poetry, 1971; *contrib.* Fr. Studies, Inform. Litt., Rev. Litt. Comp. *Address*: Dept of French, Univ. of Durham, Durham DH1 3HP.

Mottram, Eric; Reader in American Literature, Department of English, King's College, University of London, since 1973 (Lecturer, 1961–73); *b* 1924. BA Cambridge 1950, MA Cambridge 1915; Mem., Brit. Assoc. Amer. Studies. Lector, Univ. of Zürich, 1952–53; Lectr, Univ. of Malaya, 1953–55; Lectr, Univ. of Gröningen, 1955–60; American Council of Learned Societies Fellow as Prof., NY Univ., 1965–66; Vis. Prof., Univ. of NY, Buffalo, 1966; Vis. Prof., Kent State Univ., Ohio, 1968, 1970–71, 1974. Mem., Poetry Soc. Gen. Council, 1970–71; Ed, Poetry Rev., 1971– . *Publications*: William Burroughs: The Algebra of Needs, 1971; Profile of William Faulkner, 1971; Inside the Whale, 1971; Shelter Island and the Remaining World, 1972; The Kenneth Rexroth Reader, 1972; Allen Ginsberg in the Sixties, 1972; The He Expression, 1972; (with M. Bradbury) The Penguin Companion to American Literature, 1973; Local Movement, 1974; *contrib.* Jl Amer. Studies, etc. *Address*: Dept of English, King's College, Univ. of London, Strand, WC2R 2LS.

Moughtin, Prof. James Clifford, PhD, MA, MCD, BArch, ARIBA, MRTPI; Professor of Town and Country Planning, Department of Town and Country Planning, Queen's University, Belfast, since 1970; *b* 1932; *m* 1957; three *s*. BArch Liverpool 1955 (2nd cl.), MCD Liverpool 1956, MA Liverpool 1964, PhD Belfast 1970; ARIBA, MRTPI. Planner, Singapore Improvement Trust, 1957–59; Architect, Kwame Nkruma Univ., Ghana, 1959–61; Lectr, Ahmadu Bello Univ., 1961–63; Planner, Univ. of Liverpool, 1963–65; Lectr, Queen's Univ., Belfast, 1965–69; Sen. Lectr, Queen's Univ., Belfast, 1969–70. *Publications*: *contrib.* Archit. Des., Archit. Jl, Archit. Rev., Jl Town Plan. Inst., Town Plan. Rev. *Address*: Dept of Town and Country Planning, The Queen's Univ. of Belfast, Belfast BT7 1NN.

Moule, Rev. Prof. Canon Charles Francis Digby, FBA; Lady Margaret's Professor of Divinity, University of Cambridge, since

1951; b 1908. BA Cambridge 1931 (1st cl. Classics), MA Cambridge 1934, Hon. DD St Andrews 1958; FBA 1966, Mem., Studiorum NT Soc., Hon. Mem., Soc. Biblical Lit. USA. Fellow, Clare Coll., Cambridge, 1944– ; Hon. Fellow, Emmanuel Coll., Cambridge, 1972– ; Univ. Lectr, Univ. of Cambridge, 1947–51. Canon Theologian, Leicester Cath., 1955– . *Publications*: An Idiom Book of New Testament Greek, 1953, 2nd edn 1959; The Sacrifice of Christ, 1956; Colossians and Philemon, 1957; Worship in the New Testament, 1961; The Birth of the New Testament, 1962; The Phenomenon of the New Testament, 1967; *contrib*. Jl Theol. Studies, NT Studies, etc. *Address*: Clare College, Cambridge.

Mounce, Howard Owen, BA; Lecturer in Philosophy, University College of Swansea, since 1968; b 1939; m 1964. BA Swansea 1961. Tutor, Univ. Coll., Swansea, 1962–63; Lecturer, Univ. Coll., Cardiff, 1963–68. *Publications*: (with D. Z. Phillips) Moral Practices, 1970; *contrib*. Analysis, Philos. *Address*: Dept of Philosophy, Univ. College, Singleton Park, Swansea SA2 8PP.

Mounfield, Peter Reginald, BA, PhD; Senior Lecturer, Department of Geography, University of Leicester, since 1973 (Lecturer, 1968–73); b 1935; m 1959; two s. BA Nottingham 1956 (1st cl. Geog.), PhD Nottingham 1962. Demonstrator, Univ. of Nottingham, 1957–58; Asst Lectr, Univ. Coll., Wales, Aberystwyth, 1958–61; Lectr, Univ. Coll., Wales, Aberystwyth, 1961–68; Vis. Assoc. Prof., Univ. of Cincinnati, 1966–67. Awarder, Oxf. Deleg. of Local Exams, 'A'- and 'S'-level Geog. *Publications*: (with M. Ortolani) Lombardy and Lancashire: a study in comparative industrial geography, 1963; *contrib*. E Midl. Geogr., Geog., N Staffs Jl Field Studies, Town Country Plan. *Address*: Dept of Geography, Univ. of Leicester, University Road, Leicester LE1 7RH.

Mount, Dr Alan John, BA, PhD; Lecturer in French, University of Hull, since 1964; b 1939; m 1971. BA Hull 1960 (1st cl. French), PhD Hull 1965, CertEd Hull 1961; Mem., Soc. Fr. Studies. Sub-Dean, Fac. of Arts, Univ. of Hull, 1968–70; Pres., Hull AUT, 1971–72. *Publications*: The Physical Setting in Balzac's Comédie Humaine, 1966. *Address*: Dept of French, Univ. of Hull, Hull HU6 7RX.

Mountjoy, Alan B., MC, MA; Reader in Geography, University of London, Bedford College, since 1964; b 1920; m 1943; three d. BA Reading 1940 (1st cl. Geog.), MA Reading 1949; FRGS, Mem., Inst. Brit. Geogrs, Mem., Geog. Assoc. Asst Lectr, Bedford Coll., Univ. of London, 1946–48; Lectr, Bedford Coll., Univ. of London, 1948–64; Vis. Examiner, Univ. of Khartoum, 1967–70. *Publications*: Industrialization and Underdeveloped Countries, 1963, 3rd edn 1971, American edn 1967; (with C. Embleton) Africa, A geographical study, 1966, 3rd edn 1970, American edn 1967; The Mezzogiorno, 1972; ed, Developing the Underdeveloped Countries, 1971; *contrib*. Econ. Geog., Geog.,

Trans Inst. Brit. Geogrs. *Address*: Bedford College, Univ. of London, Regent's Park, NW1 4NS.

Mouzelis, Dr Nicos P., PhD; Lecturer in Sociology, Department of Sociology, London School of Economics, since 1970; b 1939; m 1967; one s. Licencié ès Sciences Commerciales, Univ. of Geneva, 1960, Licencié ès Sociologie, Univ. of Geneva, 1962, PhD LSE 1966 (Sociology). Lectr in Sociology, Univ. of Leicester, 1966–69. *Publications*: Organisation and Bureaucracy; An Analysis of Modern Theories, 1967; *contrib*. BJS, Contemp. Issues, Develt and Change, Prakseol., Sociol. *Address*: London School of Economics, Houghton Street, Aldwych, WC2A 2AE.

Mowvley, Rev. Harry; Special Lecturer in Hebrew, Department of Theology, University of Bristol, since 1963; b 1919; m 1949; two d. BA Bristol 1949 (Dist. Theol.), BA Oxon 1949 (2nd cl.), MA Oxon 1951 (Theol.); Mem., Soc. OT Studies. Recog. teacher in Religious Studies, Univ. of Bristol, 1960– . *Publications*: The Testimony of Israel, 1970. *Address*: Dept of Theology, Royal Fort House, Univ. of Bristol, Bristol BS8 1TH.

Moyes, Anthony; Lecturer, Department of Geography, University College of Wales, Aberystwyth, since 1974; b 1943; m 1969. BA Manchester 1965 (Hons Geography), MA Keele 1971 (Geography); Member: Inst. of British Geographers; Geographical Assoc. Demonstrator, Univ. of Keele, 1965–68; Asst Lectr, UCW, Aberystwyth, 1968–74. *Publications*: *contrib*. Geog. N Staffs Jl Field Stud. *Address*: Dept of Geography, Univ. Coll. of Wales, Aberystwyth, Cardiganshire SY23 2AX.

Moys, Elizabeth Mary, BA, FLA; College Librarian, University of London, Goldsmiths' College, since 1968; b 1928. BA London 1949 (Engl.); ALA 1952, FLA 1965. Asst Libr., Inst. of Advanced Legal Studies, London, 1952–59; Dep. Libr., Univ. of Ghana, 1959–62; Libr., Univ. of Lagos, 1962–65; Supt, Reading Room, Univ. of Glasgow, 1965–67. Chm, Law Libr. Adv. Cttee, Accra, 1961–62; Mem., Libr. Adv. Cttee, Fed. of Nigeria, 1963–65; Mem., Bd of Dirs, Internat. Assoc. Law Libr., 1965–68; Mem., BSI Panel on Classification of Social Science, 1967– ; Mem., FID Cttee on Cataloguing and Classification of Social Science, 1968– ; Ed., Law Libr., 1969– . *Publications*: Directory of Lagos Libraries, 1965; Classification Scheme for Law Books, 1968; ed, European Law Libraries Guide, 1971; *contrib*. Internat. Pol. Sci. Abst., Law Libr. Jl, Nig. Libr., Unesco Bull. Libr. *Address*: Univ. of London, Goldsmiths' College, Lewisham Way, New Cross, SE14 6NW.

Muckle, Prof. William; Professor of Naval Architecture and Shipbuilding, University of Newcastle upon Tyne, since 1970; b 1911; m 1957. BSc Dunelm 1933, MSc Dunelm 1943, PhD Dunelm 1954, DSc Newcastle upon Tyne 1967; CEng, FRINA, FIMarE,

501

FNECInst, FIW, Mem. Soc. of Naval Archs and Marine Engrs (New York). Univ. of Durham: Lectr, 1942–51; Sen. Lectr, 1951–54; Reader, 1954– 70. Mem. Council and Vice-Pres., RINA, Mem. Council, NECInstn. *Publications*: Modern Naval Architecture, 1951; Design of Aluminium Alloy Ship Structures, 1963; Strength of Ships' Structures, 1967; *contrib.* Trans NECInstn, Trans RINA, Shipping World and Shipbuilder. *Address*: Univ. of Newcastle upon Tyne, Newcastle upon Tyne NE1 7RU.

Mudford, Peter Graham; Lecturer in English, Birkbeck College, University of London, since 1967; *b* 1936; *m* 1965. BA Oxon 1960 (1st cl. Hons Engl.), MA Oxon 1963, BLitt Oxon 1964. Asst Lectr, Manchester Univ., 1966–67. *Publications*: ed, S. Butler's Erewhon, 1971; *contrib.* Engl., Ess. Crit., Jl Hist. Ideas, Studia Neophilologica, Theatre Research, Victorian Poetry. *Address*: Dept of English, Birkbeck College, Malet Street, WC1E 7HX.

Muir, Dr Lynette Ross; Lecturer in French Language and Literature, University of Leeds, since 1961, and Deputy Director, Graduate Centre for Medieval Studies, since 1972; *b* 1930. BA London 1951 (1st cl. French), PhD London 1956. Asst, Exeter Univ., 1955–56; Lectr, Univ. Coll., Ghana, 1959–61. *Publications*: ed, P. Sala: Tristan, 1958; *trans.*, The Anglo-Norman Adam, 1970; *contrib.* Bol. Real Acad. Buenas Let. Barcelona, Fr. Studies, Med. Æv., Mod. Langs, Romania, Studia Neophilol. *Address*: Dept of French, Univ. of Leeds, Leeds LS2 9JT.

Muirhead, Rev. Ian Adair; Senior Lecturer, Department of Ecclesiastical History, University of Glasgow, since 1972; *b* 1913; *m* 1940; three *s*. MA Glasgow 1934 (1st cl. Hons Mental Philos.), BD Glasgow 1937 (Distinct. Eccles. Hist.). Mem., Soc. Study Theol., Mem., Scott. Ch Hist; Soc. Lectr in Ecclesiastical Hist., Glasgow, 1964–72. Sec., Ch of Scotl. Panel on Doctrine, 1960–68. *Publications*: Education in the New Testament, 1967; *contrib.* Innes Rev., Rec. Scott. Soc., Scott. Jl, Theol. *Address*: Univ. of Glasgow, Glasgow G12 8QQ.

Mukherjee, Dr Kartick Chandra, BT, MA, PhD; Lecturer in Comparative Education, University of London Institute of Education, since 1963; *b* 1926; *m* 1966; one *s* one *d*. BA Calcutta 1945, MA Calcutta 1947, BT Calcutta 1950, MA London 1959 (Educn) PhD London 1962 (Educn); Dip. Journalism 1952, Dip. Educn 1958; Mem., AUT, Mem., Commonwealth Corresp. Assoc. UK, Mem., Indian Journalists Assoc. London; Vis. Prof., Univ. of Illinois, 1967, 1968, 1969, 1970; Vis. Prof., Univ. of Calgary, and Kent State Univ., 1966, 1971. London Corresp., an Indian jl, 1955– . *Publications*: Under-development, Educational Policy and Planning, 1968; A Comparative Study of Some Educational Problems, 1972; contrib. Lexikon der Pädagogik; *contrib.* Brit. Jl Educnl Studies, Didask., Educnl Forum, Educnl India, Internat. Rev. Educn, New Era, Times

Educnl Supp., Wld YBk Educn. *Address*: Dept of Comparative Education, Univ. of London Institute of Education, Malet Street, WC1E 7HS.

Mulder, Prof. Johannes Wilhelmus Franciscus, SinDrs, MA, DPhil; Professor of Linguistics, since 1972, and Head of Department of Linguistics, University of St Andrews, since 1968; *b* 1919; *m* 1958; two *s*. Candidaats Exam. Leiden 1954, Doctorandus Exam. Leiden 1958 (both Chinese and Japanese Language and Literature), DPhil Oxford 1966. Librarian, Oriental Inst. Oxford, 1961–64; Sen. Librarian, 1964–68; Sen. Lectr, Linguistics, Univ. of St Andrews, 1968–72. *Publications*: Sets and Relations in Phonology, 1968; (with S.G.J.Hervey)Theory of the Linguistic Sign, 1972; *contrib.* Forum for Mod. Lang. Studies, Foundns of Lang, La Linguistique, Linguistics, Semiotica. *Address*: Dept of Linguistics, Univ. of St Andrews, St Andrews, Fife KY16 9AJ.

Mulkay, Dr Michael Joseph; Assistant Director of Research, Department of Engineering, Cambridge University, since 1970; *b* 1936; two *d*. BA London 1965 (1st cl. Sociol.), MA Simon Fraser BC 1967, PhD Aberdeen 1970; Mem., Brit. Sociol Assoc. Teaching Assoc., Simon Fraser Univ., 1965–67; Instructor, Simon Fraser Univ., 1967–68; Lectr, Univ. of Aberdeen, 1968–70. *Publications*: Functionalism, Exchange and Theoretical Strategy, 1971; The Social Process of Innovation, 1972; *contrib.* Brit. Jl Sociol., Sci. Studies, Soc. Res., Sociol. *Address*: Univ. Dept of Engineering, Trumpington Street, Cambridge.

Mulrenan, Bernard William; Director of Physical Recreation, Education Department, University College, Cardiff, since 1939; *b* 1912; *m* 1941; two *s*. BA Sheffield 1934, CertEd Sheffield 1935, DipPhysicalEd Carnegie Coll. 1939; RAF 1940–45 (Sqdn-Ldr); Mem., UK Physical Educn Assoc., Mem., Univs Physical Educn Assoc. Mem., FA Council, 1963; Vice-Pres. and Off., Univs Athletic Union, 1955; Chm., UAU Championship and Match Cttee, 1967–73; Vice-Chm., UAU, 1973– ; Mem., FA Instruction and Internat. (Amateur) Cttees, 1964; Treas., FISU, 1957–65; Chm., FISU Tech. Cttee, 1953–57. *Publications*: *contrib.* Educn, FA News, FISU, Hlth Leis. Fitness. *Address*: Univ. College, PO Box 78, Cardiff CF1 1XL.

Mulryne, Dr J. R.; Reader in English Literature, University of Edinburgh, since 1972; *b* 1937; *m* 1964; one *s* one *d*. BA Cantab 1958 (Hons), MA Cantab 1961, PhD Cantab 1962. Fellow, Shakespeare Inst., Univ. of Birmingham, 1960–62; Lectr in English Literature, Univ. of Edinburgh, 1962–72; Vis. Associate Prof., Univ. of Calif., 1970–71. *Publications*: An Honoured Guest: New Essays on W. B. Yeats (with Denis Donoghue), 1965; Much Ado About Nothing, 1965; John Webster: The White Devil, 1970; Thomas Kyd: The Spanish Tragedy, 1970; Thomas Middleton: Women Beware Women, 1974; *contrib.* Library, MLR, RES. *Address*: Dept of English Literature,

Univ. of Edinburgh, 5 Buccleuch Place, Edinburgh EH8 9LW.

Mumford, Enid; Senior Lecturer in Industrial Sociology, Manchester Business School, Manchester University, since 1969; *b* 1924; *m* 1947; one *s* one *d*. BA Liverpool 1945 (Social Science), MA Liverpool 1952 (Social Science); FInst. Person. Mngmt. Res. Worker, Univ. of Liverpool, 1949–60; Lectr, Univ. of Liverpool, 1960–66; Lectr, Manchester Univ., 1966–69. Vice-Pres., Inst. Personnel Mngmt, 1969–71. *Publications*: (with Scott, etc) Coal and Conflict, 1963; Living with a Computer, 1964; (with O. Banks) The Computer and the Clerk, 1967; (with T. B. Ward) Computers: planning for people, 1968; Computers: planning and personnel management, 1969; Systems Design for People, 1971; Job Satisfaction: a study of computer personnel, 1972; *contrib*. Mngmt Dec., Occupat. Psychol., Person. Rev., Sociol. Rev. *Address*: Manchester Business School, Booth Street West, Manchester M15 6PB.

Mumford, Michael John; Senior Lecturer, Department of Accounting and Finance, University of Lancaster, since 1972; *b* 1939; *m* 1963, two *d*. BCom Liverpool 1963 (Dunlop Scholar), MA McMaster (Canada) 1967; ACCA 1966. Lectr in Accounting, Dept of Econs, University Coll. of Wales, Aberystwyth, 1967–70; Sen. Lectr in Accounting, Univ. of Nairobi (Kenya), 1971–72. Member: Kenya Accountants and Secretaries Nat. Examinations Bd, 1971–72; Nat. Council for Business Educn, Kenya, 1971–72. *Publications*: *contrib*. Acc. and Bus. Res., Jl Ind. Econ. *Address*: Dept of Accounting and Finance, Furness College, Bailrigg, Lancaster.

Munby, Alan Noel Latimer; Librarian, King's College, Cambridge, since 1947; Fellow since 1948; *b* 1913; *m* 1945; one *s*. MA Cantab, LittD Cantab 1962; Hon Fellow, Pierpont Morgan Library, New York, Mem., Bibliographical Soc. (Vice-Pres.). J. P. R. Lyell Reader in Bibliography, Univ. of Oxford, 1962–63; Sandars Reader in Bibliography, Univ. of Cambridge, 1969–70; Vis. Fellow, All Souls Coll., Oxford, 1968. Trustee, British Museum, 1969– ; Mem., British Library Bd, 1973– . *Publications*: English Poetical Autographs (with Desmond Flower), 1938; Phillipps Studies, 5 vols, 1951–60, repr. in 2 vols, 1971; Cambridge College Libraries, 1959, 2nd edn 1962; The Cult of the Autograph Letter in England, 1962; Connoisseurs and Medieval Miniatures, 1750–1850, 1972; *contrib*. Book Collector, Library, Trans. Cambridge Bibliographical Soc., TLS. *Address*: King's College, Cambridge.

Munby, Denys Lawrence; Reader in the Economics and Organisation of Transport, Oxford University, and Fellow of Nuffield College, Oxford, since 1958; *b* 1919; *m* 1947; two *s* three *d*. BA Oxon 1946 (1st cl. Econ. 1947), MA Oxon 1946. Lectr, Christ Church, Oxford, 1948–49; Lectr, Aberdeen Univ., 1949–58; Jt Ed., Jl of Transp. Econ. and Policy, 1967– . Asst Dir, DEA, 1965–66.

Publications: Industry and Planning in Stepney, 1951; Christianity and Economic Problems, 1956; God and the Rich Society, 1961; The Idea of a Secular Society, 1963; ed, Transport, 1968; *contrib*. Jl Transp. Econ. Policy, Oxf. Econ. Papers, Scott. Jl Pol. Econ. *Address*: Nuffield College, Oxford.

Munby, Lionel Maxwell; Staff Tutor, Board of Extramural Studies, Cambridge, since 1946; *b* 1918; *m* 1947, 1972; two *s* one *d*. BA Oxon 1939 (1st cl. Hons Mod. Hist.), MA Oxon, MA Cantab, DipEd Oxon 1940; Mem., Hist. Assoc., Brit. Record Assoc. Editor (and contributor), The Local Historian (formerly The Amateur Historian). *Publications*: ed, Hatfield and its People, 1959–64; ed, History of King's Langley, 1963; Hertfordshire Population Statistics, 1964; ed, The Story of Sawbridgeworth, 1966–70; (with Ernst Wangermann) Marxism and History: a bibliography, 1967; ed, East Anglian Studies, 1967; ed, Charity School to Village College, 1968; Madingley Hall, 1970; ed, The Luddites and other Essays, 1971; ed, Short Guides to Records, 1972; ed, Wheathampstead and Harpenden, 1973, 1974– ; The Hertfordshire Landscape (forthcoming); Local History Workbook (forthcoming); *contrib*. Hist., Heimen (Norway), Századok (Hungary), Voprosyi Istorii (USSR), Zeitschrift für Anglistik und Amerikanistik (DDR). *Address*: Stuart House, Mill Lane, Cambridge CB2 1RY.

Mundle, Prof. C. W. K.; Professor of Philosophy, University College of North Wales, Bangor, since 1955; *b* 1916; *m* 1946; one *s* two *d*. MA St Andrews 1939 (1st cl. Philosophy), BA Oxon 1947 (1st cl. PPE). Hd of Philosophy Dept, Univ. Coll., Dundee, 1947–55. Pres., Soc. Psychic. Res., 1971–74. *Publications*: A Critique of Linguistic Philosophy, 1970; Perception: Facts and Theories, 1971; *contrib*. Mind, Philos. Qly, Proc. Aristot. Soc., Proc. Soc. Psychic. Res. *Address*: Dept of Philosophy, Univ. College of North Wales, Bangor LL57 2DG.

Munro, Ailie Ada; Lecturer, School of Scottish Studies, Edinburgh University, since 1968; *m*; one *s* one *d*. MA Edinburgh, LRAM, ARCM 1956, BMus Dunelm 1967; Member: ISM; WMA; EFDSS; AUT; IFMC; Saltire Soc. Member: ISM (Edinburgh) Cttee, 1969–72; Arts Faculty Council, Edinburgh Univ., 1974. *Publications*: *contrib*. Scottish Studies. *Address*: Sch. of Scottish Studies, Edinburgh Univ., Edinburgh.

Munro, Dr James Smith; Lecturer, Department of French, University of Stirling, since 1967; *b* 1940; *m* 1963; one *s* one *d*. MA Edinburgh 1961 (1st cl. French with German), PhD Edinburgh 1966. Asst Lectr, Univ. of Leeds, 1964–67. *Publications*: *contrib*. Studies Voltaire and 18th Cent. *Address*: Dept of French, The Univ., Stirling FK9 4LA.

Munton, Dr Richard John Cyril; Graduate Tutor, Department of Geography, University College London, since 1974; *b* 1943; *m* 1965; one *s* one *d*. BA 1964, PhD 1968, Birmingham; Member: Inst. Brit. Geogrs., Regnl Studies Assoc., Agricl Econs Soc. Lectr in Geog.,

UCL, 1966–74. Vis. Prof., Univ. of Waterloo, Ontario, 1973. *Publications*: (with W. B. Morgan) Agricultural Geography, 1971; *contrib*. Geographiska Annaler. *Address*: Dept of Geography, Univ. Coll., Gower Street, WC1E 6BT.

Murdoch, Dr Brian Oliver; Lecturer in German, Stirling University, since 1972; *b* 1944; *m* 1967; one *s* one *d*. BA Exeter 1965, PhD Cantab 1969; Member: MHRA; ALLC; Med. Acad. America. Lectr in German, Univ. of Glasgow, 1968–70; Asst/ Associate Prof. of German, Univ. of Illinois/ Chicago Circle, 1970–72. *Publications*: The Fall of Man in the Early Middle High German Biblical Epic, 1972; The Recapitulated Fall, 1974; Concordance to the Anegenge, 1974; contribs in collected vols, etc. *contrib*. Archiv. Comp. Lit. Studies, Doitsu Bungaku (Osaka), Etudes Germ., Euphorion, Jewish Soc. Studies, Medieval Studies, Mod. Drama, Mod. Langs, Neophilologus, Neuphil. Mitt, Rev. English Stud., Rev. Langues Vivantes, Rev. Lit. Comparée, Southern Folklore Qly, Unterrichtspraxis. *Address*: German Dept, Univ. of Stirling, Stirling FK9 4LA.

Murdoch, David Hamilton; Lecturer, School of History, Leeds University, since 1967; *b* 1937; *m* 1960; two *d*. BA Hons Cantab 1959, MA 1967, Certif. in Educn Liverpool 1960; Mem., British Assoc. for American Studies, Hist. Assoc. Asst Lectr, Leeds, 1964–67; *Address*: School of History, The Univ., Leeds LS2 9JT.

Murison, William John, OBE; Part-time Lecturer, Postgraduate School of Librarianship and Information Science, University of Sheffield, since 1966; *b* 1915; *m* 1947; three *d*. FLA 1948, FLAI 1953. Co. Libr., Berwickshire, 1947–51; Co. Libr., Antrim, 1951–58; Co. Libr., W Riding of Yorkshire, 1958–74; Mem., Libr. Adv. Council England, 1966–70; Mem., Wkng Party on Public Lending Right, 1971. *Publications*: The Public Library, 1955, 2nd edn 1971; *contrib*. An Leabhar., Libr. Assoc. Rec., Libr. Rev., Libri. *Address*: Postgraduate Sch. of Librarianship and Information Science, Univ. of Sheffield, Sheffield S10 2TN.

Murphy, Antoin E.; Lecturer in Economics, Trinity College Dublin, since 1968; *b* 1946; *m* 1973. BA UC Dublin, MA UC Dublin 1968; Barrister-at-Law, King's Inns, Dublin, 1969. *Address*: Dept. of Economics, Trinity College, Dublin 2.

Murphy, Prof. Arthur Burgess; Professor of Modern Languages (Russian), School of Humanities, New University of Ulster, since 1967; *b* 1923, *m* 1949; two *s* one *d*. BA Dublin (1st cl. French and Italian), MA London 1954 (Russian); Vice-Pres., Assoc. of Teachers of Russian. Sen. Lectr, RMA Sandhurst, 1949–63; Lectr i/c Russian, UC Swansea, 1963–67. *Publications*: (with G. M. Schatunowski) 60 Russian Proses, and, A Key to 60 Russian Proses, 1961; ed, Chekhov: The Wedding, 1963; ed. Babel: Four Stories, 1964; Aspectival Usage in Russian, 1965; ed, Zoshchenko: Stories of

the 1920's, 1969; *contrib*. Slavonic and East European Review, Jl Russian Studies, Proc. Royal Irish Acad. *Address*: New Univ. of Ulster, Coleraine, Co. Londonderry BT52 1SA.

Murphy, Dr James, MA, PhD; Reader in Education, University of Liverpool, since 1971; *b* 1910; *m* 1939; one *s*. BA Liverpool 1931, MA Liverpool 1935, PhD Liverpool 1955; FRHistS. Lectr, Liverpool Univ., 1950–60; Sen. Lectr, Liverpool Univ., 1960–71. Jt Editor, Historic Society of Lancashire and Cheshire, 1960–67. *Publications*: The Religious Problem in English Education: the Crucial Experiment, 1959; Church, State and Schools in Britain, 1971; The Education Act 1870, 1972; *contrib*. Hist. Soc. Lancs Chesh., Hist. Educn Qly. *Address*: School of Education, Univ. of Liverpool, Liverpool L69 3BX.

Murphy, Prof. John Augustin; Professor of Irish History, National University of Ireland at University College, Cork, since 1971; *b* 1927; *m* 1952; three *s* two *d*. MA (NUI) 1951. Lectr in Irish History, UC Cork, 1968–71. Vis. Prof., Loyola Univ., 1974. Member: Cork Historical and Archaeol. Soc.; United Arts Club, Dublin; Cork Art Soc. Hon. Editor, Jl of Cork Historical and Archaeol. Soc., 1964– . *Publications*: Justin McCarthy, Lord Mountcashel, 1959; Stair na hEorpa (I and II), Dublin 1954; Ireland in the Twentieth Century, 1974; (ed) Religion and Irish Society, 1974; articles in other books; *contrib*. Hist. Stud. V, Jl Cork Hist. and Archaeol. Soc., Christus Rex. *Address*: Dept of Irish History, Univ. Coll. Cork, Ireland.

Murphy, Michael Wenceslas; Junior Lecturer, Department of Education, University College, Cork, since 1968; *b* 1942; *m* 1972. BA NUI 1963, MLitt TCD 1972, HDE NUI 1966; TTG 1965. Muintir na Tire, Educn Sub-Cttee, 1968–69. *Publications*: ed, Education in Ireland 1: now and the future, 1970; ed, Educationi n Ireland 2: what should students learn?, 1971; ed, Education in Ireland 3: to unleash the potential, 1972; *contrib*. Capuchin Annual, Feasta, Furrow, Secondary Teacher. *Address*: Dept of Educn, Univ. Coll. Cork, Ireland.

Murphy, Prof. Thomas, MD, FRCPI, DPH, BSc; President, University College Dublin, since 1972; *b* 1915; *m* 1944; four *s*. MB BCh BAO National Univ. of Ireland 1940, DPH BSc (Public Health) National Univ. of Ireland 1942, MD National Univ. of Ireland 1969. Prof. of Social and Preventive Medicine, 1955–72, and Registrar, 1965–72, Univ. Coll. Dublin; Mem., Senate, Nat. Univ. Irel.; Mem., Gov. Body, Univ. Coll., Dublin; Mem., Gen. Med. Council. *Publications*: *contrib*. some 20 articles to med. jls. *Address*: Univ. College, Dublin 4.

Murray, Alexander; Lecturer in Medieval History, University of Newcastle upon Tyne, since 1963; *b* 1934. BA Oxon 1959 (2nd cl. Hist.), MA, BPhil Oxon 1965; FRHistS. Temp. Asst Lectr, Leeds, 1961–63. Royal

504

Artillery, 1954–55; Mem., Bedales Sch. Co., 1964– . Public Orator, Univ. of Newcastle upon Tyne, 1974– . *Publications*: contrib. Traditio, Studies Ch Hist. *Address*: Dept of History, Univ. of Newcastle upon Tyne, Newcastle upon Tyne NE1 7RU.

Murray, (Alice) Rosemary, MA, DPhil, JP; President, New Hall, Cambridge, since 1964 (Tutor in Charge, 1954–64); Vice-Chancellor designate, University of Cambridge (1975–77); *b* 1913. BSc Oxon 1936, DPhil Oxon 1938, MA Oxon and Cantab 1941; Hon. DSc Ulster. Lectr in Chemistry, Royal Holloway Coll., 1938–41; Lectr in Chemistry, Univ. of Sheffield, 1941–42; Lectr in Chemistry, Girton Coll., Cambridge, 1946–54; Fellow, Girton Coll., Cambridge, 1949; Tutor, Girton Coll., Cambridge, 1951; Demonstrator in Chem., Univ. of Cambridge, 1947–52. Mem., Fedn Univ. Women; Mem., Wages Councils, 1968– ; Mem., Council, GPDST, 1969– ; Mem., Lockwood Cttee 1963–65; Mem., Armed Forces Pay Rev. Body, 1971– ; Mem., C of E Higher Educn Cttee; Gov., various Schs and Colls of Educn; Chm., Cambridge Inst. of Educn. JP City of Cambridge, 1953– ; Chm. of Magistrates, 1974– . *Address*: New Hall, Cambridge.

Murray, Dr David John, MA, DPhil; Professor of Government, The Open University, since 1969; *b* 1935; *m* 1963; three *d*. BA Oxon 1959, MA Oxon 1963, DPhil Oxon 1963. Lectr, Makerere Univ. Coll., 1961–62; Lectr, Univ. Coll. Rhodesia and Nyasaland, 1963–64; Lectr, Univ. of Ibadan, 1965–67; Sen. Lectr, Univ. of Ibadan, 1967; Dir of Res., Inst. of Administration, Univ. of Ife, 1967–69; Vis. Prof., American Univ., Cairo, 1971. Mem., Exec. Council, Royal Inst. Public Admin; Jt Univ. Council for Social and Public Admin. *Publications*: The West Indies and the Development of Colonial Government, 1965; jt ed, The Progress of Nigerian Public Administration, 1968; The Work of Administration in Nigeria, 1969; The Governmental System in Southern Rhodesia, 1970; ed, Studies in Nigerian Administration, 1970; jt ed, Decisions, Organizations and Society, 1971; *contrib*. Jl Admin., Jl Admin. Overseas, Jl Commonwealth Pol. Studies. *Address*: Open Univ., Walton Hall, Milton Keynes MK7 6AA.

Murray, Dr Isobel M.; Lecturer in English, University of Aberdeen, since 1965; *b* 1939. MA Edinburgh 1960, PhD Edinburgh 1964. Asst Lectr, Univ. of Aberdeen, 1964–65; *Publications*: ed, Oscar Wilde: The Picture of Dorian Gray, 1974; *contrib*. Durham Univ. Jl, New Blackfriars. *Address*: Dept of English, King's Coll., Old Aberdeen AB9 2UB.

Murray, Prof. Peter (John), PhD, FSA; Professor of the History of Art, Birkbeck College, University of London, since 1967; *b* 1920; *m* 1947. PhD London 1956; FSA. Rhind Lectr, Edinburgh, 1967. Sen. Res. Fellow, Warburg Inst., 1961; Chm., Soc. for Renaissance Studies, 1967–70; Pres., Soc. of Architectural Historians of GB, 1969–72. *Publications*: Watteau, 1948; Index of Attributions ... before Vasari, 1959; (with L. Murray) Dictionary of Art and Artists, 1959, enlarged edn 1965; (with P. Kidson) History of English Architecture, 1962, (with P. Kidson and P. Thomson), 1965; (with L. Murray) The Art of the Renaissance, 1963; The Architecture of the Italian Renaissance, 1963; Renaissance Vol., in World Architecture, 1972; contrib. New Cambridge Modern History; Encyclopedia Britannica; *contrib*. Apollo, Burl. Mag., Warb. Court. Jl, foreign Jls. *Address*: Birkbeck College, Malet Street, WC1E 7HU.

Murray, Rosemary; *see* Murray, A. R.

Murray, Mrs Ruth Hilary; *see* Finnegan, R. H.

Murrell, Prof. Hywel; Head of Department of Applied Psychology, University of Wales Institute of Science and Technology, since 1968; *b* 1908; *m* 1938; three *d*. MA Oxon 1930; Fellow: Royal Photographic Soc., British Psychological Soc., Hon. Member: Ergonomics Res. Soc., Fedn Productivity Services Assocs, Mem. Société d'Ergonomie de Langue Française. In the printing industry, 1930–39; Royal Engineers, 1940–47; Head Naval Motion Study Unit, Admiralty, 1947–52; Dir, Dept Ergonomics, Tube Investments Ltd, 1952–54; Head, Unit for Res. on Employment of Older Workers, Dept of Psychol., Bristol, 1954–59; Res. Fellow, and Head of Unit for Res. on Human Performance in Industry, Bristol, 1959–63; Reader, Human Aspects of Management, Welsh CAT/UWIST, 1963–68. Mem. TUC Scientific Adv. Cttee, 1960–71. Distinguished Foreign Colleague Award, Human Factors Soc. of America, 1972. *Publications*: Fitting the Job to the Worker, 1958; Ergonomics, London 1965 (Ital. edn 1967, German edn 1971); *contrib*. Acta Psychologica, Applied Ergonomics, Bull. du CERP, Engineering, Ergonomics, Gerontologia Clinica, Human Factors, Internat. Jl of Production Res., Jl Applied Psychol., Jl of Gerontol., Nature, Occupational Psychol., Travail Humain. *Address*: Department of Applied Psychology, UWIST, Llwyn-y-Grant Road, Penylan, Cardiff CF3 7UX.

Murta, Kenneth Hall; Senior Lecturer in Architecture since 1972 (Lecturer, 1962–72), and Dean, Faculty of Architectural Studies since 1974, University of Sheffield; *b* 1929; *m* 1955; two *s* two *d*. BArch, Dip Arch, 1954; FRIBA. Amadhu Bello Univ. Nigeria, 1961; Sub-Dean, Fac. of Arch. Studies, Sheffield, 1970–73. Mem., New Churches Cttee, Council for Places of Worship. *Publications*: *contrib*. Arch. Rev., Jl of Arch. Teaching and Research. *Address*: Dept of Architecture, Univ. of Sheffield, Sheffield S10 2TN.

Musgrave, Stephen; Lecturer, Town and Country Planning Department, Heriot-Watt University, since 1970; *b* 1943; *m* 1971; one *s*. BA Sussex 1966 (Hons Sociology and Politics). Res. Asst, Town Planning Dept, Univ. Coll., London, 1967; Res. Associate, Urban and Regional Studies Centre, Birmingham Univ., 1969. Adviser, Craigmillar Festival Soc., 1972– . *Publication*: *contrib*. Official Arch. and Planning. *Address*: Town and Country Planning Dept, Heriot-Watt Univ',

39 Palmerston Place, Edinburgh EH12 5AU.

Musgrove, Prof. Frank; Sarah Fielden Professor of Education, University of Manchester, since 1971; *b* 1922; *m* 1944; one *d*. BA Oxon 1947, PhD Nottingham 1958; FRSA 1971. Lectureships in Univs of Leicester and Leeds, 1957–65; Vis. Prof. of Educn, Univ. of BC, 1965; Prof. of Res. in Educn, Univ. of Bradford, 1965–70; Vis. Prof. of Sociology, Univ. of California, 1969; The Chancellor's Lectr, Univ. of Wellington, NZ, 1970. Educnl Appts in England and Colonial Educn Service, E Africa, 1947–57. Editor, Research in Education. *Publications*: The Migratory Elite, 1963; Youth and the Social Order, 1964; The Family, Education and Society, 1966; (with P. H. Taylor) Society and the Teacher's Role, 1969; Patterns of Power and Authority in English Education, 1971; Ecstasy and Holiness, 1974; *contrib.* Africa, Sociological Rev., Brit. Jl of Sociology, Brit. Jl of Educnl Psychol., Econ. Hist. Rev., Brit. Jl of Sociol. and Clinical Psychol. *Address*: Victoria Univ. of Manchester, Oxford Road, Manchester M13 9PL.

Musgrove, Prof. John, BArch, ARIBA; Professor of Architecture, School of Environmental Studies, University College, London, since 1971; *b* 1920; *m* 1941; three *s*. BArch Dunelm 1952 (1st cl.); ARIBA 1953; Hon. FCIA 1973. Sen. Lectr, Univ. Coll., London, 1960–66; Reader in Architecture, Univ. Coll., London, 1966–71. Ed., Jl Archit. Res. Teaching, 1969– ; Chm., RIBA Res. Cttee, 1970– ; ARCUK Projects and Res. Awards Panel, 1970– ; Moderator, RIBA Exams Cttee. *Publications*: (jtly) The Function and Design of Hospitals, 1955; (jtly) The Design of Research Laboratories, 1960; *contrib.* Archit. Jl, Jl Archit. Res. Teaching, New Sci., RIBA Jl. *Address*: School of Environmental Studies, Univ. College London, Gower Street, WC1E 6BT.

Musson, Prof. Albert Edward; Professor of Economic History, Department of History, University of Manchester, since 1973; *b* 1920; *m* 1945; two *s*. BA Manchester 1949 (1st cl. Hons), MA Manchester 1950. Univ. of Manchester: Asst Lectr, 1951–54; Lectr, 1954–61; Sen. Lectr, 1961–73. *Publications*: The Typographical Association: Origins and History to 1949, 1954; The Congress of 1868: The Origins and Establishment of the Trades Union Congress, 1955; (with W. H. Chaloner) Industry and Technology, 1963; Enterprise in Soap and Chemicals: Joseph Crosfield & Sons Ltd, 1815–1965, 1965; (with E. H. Robinson) Science and Technology in the Industrial Revolution, 1969; (with E. H. Robinson) James Watt and the Steam Revolution, 1969; Science, Technology and Economic Growth in the Eighteenth Century, 1972; British Trade Unions 1800–1875, 1972; Trade Union and Social History, 1974; The Voice of the People: John Doherty (1798–1854), Trade Unionist, Radical, and Factory Reformer, 1974. *Address*: The Univ., Manchester M13 9PL.

Musson, Dr John Windsor; Principal Lecturer and Head of Department of English, Stranmillis College Institute of Education, Queen's University, Belfast; *b* 1914; *m* 1947; one *s* one *d*. BA Bristol 1935, DipEd Bristol 1936, MA Bristol 1940, PhD QUB 1955; Mem. Nat. Assoc. Teachers of English 1968. Mem., QUB Faculty of Educn and Bd of Studies in English, 1969– . Mem. Academic Bd, Stranmillis Coll., 1966. Mem., NI GCE English Panel, 1972. *Publications*: Reading and Reasoning, 1944; Organised Discussion, 1945; *contrib.* Jl Proc. Belfast Natural Hist. and Lit. Soc., QUB Bull. of Educn. *Address*: Stranmillis College, Belfast.

Mutch, Robert A.; Lecturer, Department of Building, Heriot-Watt University, since 1964; *b* 1933; *m* 1964; one *s* one *d*. BSc Edinburgh 1956 (Pure Science). *Address*: Dept of Building, Heriot-Watt Univ., Chambers Street, Edinburgh EH1 1HX.

Muthesius, Stefan; Lecturer, School of Fine Arts and Music, University of East Anglia, since 1968; *b* 1939; *m* 1971. Dr.phil, Philipps-Universität, Marburg an der Lahn, 1969. *Publications*: The High-Victorian Movement in Architecture 1850–1870, 1972; Das englische Vorbild: Eine Studie zu den deutschen Reformbewegungen in Architektur, Munich 1974; *contrib.* Archit. Hist. *Address*: School of Fine Arts, Univ. of East Anglia, Norwich NOR 88C.

Mutter, Prof. Reginald Patrick Charles, MA; University Professor, and Pro-Vice-Chancellor (Arts and Social Studies), University of Sussex; *b* 1924; *m* 1970; one *s* one *d*. BA Oxon 1952 (1st cl. English), MA Oxon 1952. Asst Lectr, then Lectr, King's Coll., London, 1954–62; Lectr in English and American Studies, Sussex Univ., 1962–66, Sen. Lectr, 1966–68, Reader, 1968–73, Prof., 1973; Acting Dean, Sch. of English and American Studies, Sussex Univ., 1967–68; Dean, 1968–72; Vis. Asst Prof., UCLA, 1959; Vis. Assoc. Prof., Victoria Univ., BC, 1962; Vis. Prof., UCLA, 1964; Vis. Prof., Univ. of Pittsburgh, 1966–67; Vis. Prof., Univ. of California, Berkeley, 1968. *Publications*: ed, Minor Poems of Edmund Spenser, 1957; ed (with M. Kinkead-Weekes), Selected Poems and Letters of Pope, 1962; ed, Fielding: Tom Jones, 1966; *contrib.* Times Lit. Supp. *Address*: Arts Building, Univ. of Sussex, Falmer, Brighton BN1 9QN.

Myddelton, Prof. D. R.; Professor of Finance and Accounting, Cranfield School of Management, Cranfield Institute of Technology, since 1972; *b* 1940. MBA Harvard 1964; FCA 1971 (ACA 1961); ACIS 1966. Lectr, Accounting, London Business Sch., 1969–72; Dir, MBA Programme, Cranfield, 1973– . *Publications*: The Power to Destroy: A Study of the British Tax System, 1969; (with W. Reid) The Meaning of Company Accounts, 1971, 2nd edn 1974; *contrib.* Accounting and Business Res. *Address*: Cranfield Institute of Technology, Cranfield, Bedford MK43 0AL.

Myers, Prof. Alexander Reginald; Professor of Medieval History, University of Liverpool, since 1967; *b* 1912; *m* 1940 (wife *d* 1973); three *d*. BA Manchester 1934 (1st cl. Hist.), MA Manchester 1935, PhD London 1956; FRHistS 1939, FSA 1949. Lectr, Liverpool Univ., 1938–56; Sen. Lectr, Liverpool Univ., 1956–59; Reader, Liverpool Univ., 1959–67; Dir, Combined Studies, Liverpool Univ., 1964–67. RN, 1941–45 (Lt Commdr); Pres., Liverpool Br., Hist. Assoc., 1952–55; Mem., Council Hist. Assoc., 1957–67; Vice-Pres., 1967–72; Pres., Rec. Soc. Lancs and Chesh., 1967–72; Mem., Council, Hist. Soc. Lancs, Ches., 1950–72; Council, Royal Hist. Soc., 1970–72; Pres., Historical Assoc., 1973–76. *Publications*: England in the Late Middle Ages, 1952, 8th edn 1971; The Household of Edward IV, 1959; English Historical Documents, 1327–1485, 1969; London in the Age of Chaucer, 1972; *contrib*. Bull. Inst. Hist. Res., Bull. J. Rylands Libr., EHR, Hist., Hist. Today, Hist. Jbh, Trans Hist. Soc. Lancs Chesh., Univ. Toronto Law Jl. *Address*: The School of History, The Univ., PO Box 147, Liverpool L69 3BX.

Myers, Dr Terence Frederick, BSc, PhD; Lecturer, Department of Psychology, University of Edinburgh, since 1969; *b* 1938; *m* 1968. BSc London 1964, PhD Cardiff 1973. Lectr, Reading Univ., 1966–68; Res. Staff, MRC Speech and Communication Unit, Edinburgh Univ. 1968–69. Guest of Soviet Acad. of Sciences, Pavlov Physiological Inst., 1971. *Publications*: *contrib*. Acta Psych., Psych. Rev., Jl Acou. Soc. Amer. *Address*: Psychology Dept., 7 Roxburgh Street, Edinburgh.

Myers, William Francis Teevan; Lecturer in English, Leicester University, since 1972; *b* 1939; *m* 1969; two *s*. BA Oxon 1961, MA, BLitt Oxon 1965. Asst Lectr, Nottingham, 1964, Lectr 1966; Vis. Asst Prof., Loyola, New Orleans, 1968–69. *Publications*: (jtly), Literature and Politics in the Nineteenth Century, ed John Lucas, 1971; Dryden, 1973; *contrib*. Ren. and Mod. Studies, Essays in Criticism. *Address*: Dept of English, Univ. of Leicester, Leicester LE1 7RH.

Myint, Prof. H.; Professor of Economics, London School of Economics, since 1965; *b* 1920; *m* 1944. BA Rangoon 1939, PhD London 1943, MA Oxon 1950; Hon. DLitt Rangoon 1961. Prof. of Econ., Rangoon Univ., 1945–50; Lectr in the Econs of the Underdeveloped Countries, Oxford Univ., 1950–65. Rector, Rangoon Univ., 1958–61. *Publications*: Theories of Welfare Economics, 1948; The Economics of the Developing Countries, 1964, 4th rev. edn 1973; Economic Theory and the Underdeveloped Countries, 1971; South East Asia's Economy: Development Policies in the 1970s, 1972; *contrib*. Econ. Jl, Economica, Jl Pol. Econ., Rev. Econ. Studies. *Address*: London School of Economics, Houghton Street, Aldwych, WC2A 2AE.

Mylne, Vivienne Gower; Reader in French, University of Kent at Canterbury, since 1973 (Sen. Lectr, 1966–73); *b* 1922. BA Oxford 1948 (Mod. Langs), PhD London 1952. Mem., Soc. Fr. Studies, Mem., Brit. Soc. Eighteenth-cent. Studies (Sec., 1970–71). Asst, Univ. Coll., London, 1952–55;

Asst Lectr, then Lectr, Univ. Coll. of Swansea, 1955–66. *Publications*: The Eighteenth-century French Novel, 1965, 2nd edn 1970; chapters, in, French Literature and its background, vol. 3, 1968; The Art of Criticism, 1969; Prévost: Manon Lescaut, 1972; (with A. Martin and R. L. Frautschi) Bibliographie des ouvrages romanesques en France, 1751–1800 (forthcoming); *contrib*. Brit. Jl Aesth., Fr. Studies, Mod. Lang. Rev., Rev. Hist. Litt. France. *Address*: Rutherford College, The Univ., Canterbury, Kent.

N

Nailor, Prof. Peter; Professor of Politics, University of Lancaster, since 1969; *b* 1928. BA Oxon 1952 (1st cl. Hist.), MA Oxon 1955; MBIM. Home Civil Service, 1952–69; Asst Sec., Min. of Defence, 1967. *Publications*: Problems of Security in Europe, in, International Security, 1971; The Role of Maritime Power, in, The Roles of Maritime Forces in the Security of Western Europe, 1971; Defence and Foreign Policy, in, The Management of Britain's External Relations, 1973; (with G. M. Dillon) Defence and Security, in, Britain in the EEC, 1973; The Military Bureaucracy, in, War in the Next Decade, 1974. *Address*: Dept of Politics, Univ. of Lancaster, Lancaster LA1 4YW.

Naish, Michael Charles; Lecturer in Education with special reference to the Teaching of Geography, University of London Institute of Education, since 1968; *b* 1934; *m* 1962; three *s*. BA London 1958 (1st cl. Geog.), MA 1960, PGCE London 1961, Acad. DipEd. 1970; Mem., Geog. Assoc. (Mem., Exec. Cttee, Geog. Assoc., 1973– ; Mem., Standing Cttee for Environmental Educn, 1973–). Editor: Teaching Geography Series, Geog. Assoc., 1972– ; World in Focus Series, 1974. *Publications*: contrib.: New Movements in the Study and Teaching of Geography, N. J. Graves, 1971; Handbook for Geography Teachers, ed M. Long, 1974; Geography in Education, ed W. P. Adams *et al*, 1974; *contrib*. New Era, Teaching Geog. Series, TES. *Address*: Univ. of London Inst. of Education, Malet Street, WC1E 7HS.

Nandris, Dr John G., MA, PhD, FSA, Lecturer in East European Archaeology, Institute of Archaeology, London University, since 1965; *b* 1938; *m* 1966; two *s* one *d*. BA Cantab 1962, MA Cantab 1966, PhD Cantab 1969. Mem., Prehist. Soc., Hellenic Soc., Brit. Inst. Archaeol. Ankara. Student, Brit. Sch. of Archaeol., Athens, 1963–64; Asst Dir, Knossos excavations, Crete, 1969. *Publications*: *contrib*. Alba Regia, Bull. Univ. Lond. Inst. Archaeol., Fundamenta, Man, Memoria Antique., Sci. Jl, Zbornik. *Address*: London Univ. Institute of Archaeology, 31–34 Gordon Square, WC1H 0PY.

Narain, Dr Jagat; Lecturer in the Department of Public and Comparative Law, Queen's University of Belfast, since 1968; *b* 1931. BComm Rajasthan 1950, LLB Rajasthan 1953 (1st cl.), LLM Rajasthan 1959; PhD Australian National University 1965; Mem., Soc. Public Teachers of Law, Mem., Statute Law Soc., Mem., Justice. Post-Doctoral Res. Fellow, McGill Univ., Montreal, 1964–65; Asst Lectr, QUB, 1965–68. *Publications*: Public Law in Northern Ireland: constitutional needs – working hypotheses?, 1973; Northern Ireland Public Law: a study in sphere of influence and statecraft, 1974; *contrib*. Austral. Law Jl, Jl Ind. Law Inst., Internat. Comp. Law Qly, N. Irel. Leg. Qly, Publ. Law, Kerala Law Jl, Jl Law and Econ. Develt. *Address*: Faculty of Law, Queen's Univ. of Belfast, Belfast BT7 1NN.

Narkiewicz, Olga Anna, MA, PhD; Senior Lecturer in European Studies and Modern Languages, University of Manchester Institute of Science and Technology, since 1972; *b* 1927; *m* 1946; one *d*. BA Manchester, 1962, MA Manchester 1964, PhD Manchester 1968; Mem., NASEES, Mem., PSA. Res. Asst, Dept of Government, Univ. of Manchester, 1964–66; Lectr in Mod. Langs, Univ. of Manchester Inst. of Science and Technology, 1966–72. *Publications*: The Making of the Soviet State Apparatus, 1970; History of Polish Populism, 1870–1970 (forthcoming); *contrib*. Slav. E Europ. Rev., Sov. Studies, Univ. Qly. *Address*: Dept of European Studies and Modern Languages, Univ. of Manchester Institute of Science and Technology, Sackville Street, Manchester M60 1QD.

Nath, Dr Shiv Kumar; Senior Lecturer in Economics, University of Warwick, since 1969; *b* 1936; *m* 1959; one *s* one *d*. BScEcon London 1960 (1st cl. Hons), PhD London 1964; Member: Royal Econ. Soc., American Econ. Assoc. Lectr, Univ. of Leicester, 1961–64; Reader, Univ. of Bombay, 1964–65; Lectr, Univ. of Warwick, 1965–69. *Publications*: A Reappraisal of Welfare Economics, 1969; A Perspective of Welfare Economics, 1973; *contrib*. Econ. Jl, Jl of Development Studies, Oxford Econ. Papers. *Address*: Dept of Economics, Univ. of Warwick, Coventry CV4 7AL.

Naughton, Dr James A. L.; Lecturer, Department of Psychology, University of Edinburgh, since 1949; Clinical Teacher, Department of Surgical Neurology, Edinburgh, since 1949; *b* 1917; *m* 1949; one *s* two *d*. MB and ChB Edinburgh 1939, BSc Edinburgh 1949 (1st cl. Hons Psychology); MRCP(Edin) 1972, Mem., BMA, BPS. Chm., Edinburgh Sch. of Speech Therapy, 1953–   ; Consultant Psychologist, Scottish Council for the Care of Spastics, 1949–   . *Publications*: contrib. Spinal Injury, ed P. Harris, 1965; Head Injury, ed F. J. Gillingham *et al*, 1971; *contrib*. Brit. Med. Jl, Bull. Brit. Psych. Soc., Dev. Medicine and Child Neurology, Rehabilitation. *Address*: Dept of Psychology, Univ. of Edinburgh, Edinburgh EH8 9YL.

Naumann, Dr Bernd Konrad; Statutory Lecturer, German Department, University College, Dublin, since 1972; *b* 1938; *m* 1968; one *s*. Staatsexamen Erlangen 1963, DrPhil

Erlangen 1967; Mem., GAL. Asst Lectr, Erlangen, 1964–69; Coll. Lectr, UCD, 1969–72. *Publications*: Dichter und Publikum in deutscher und lateinischer Bibelepik des frühen 12. Jahrhunderts, 1968; Wortbildung in der deutschen Gegenwartssprache, 1972. *Address*: German Dept, UCD, Belfield, Dublin 4.

Naylon, Dr John; Senior Lecturer in Geography, University of Keele, since 1970; *b* 1931; *m* 1962; one *d*. BA Birmingham 1953 (1st cl. Geog.), PhD Birmingham 1956; Mem., Inst Brit. Geogrs, Mem., Geog. Assoc., Mem., Soc. Latin Amer. Studies, Mem., Iber. Social Studies Assoc. Asst Lectr, Univ. of Keele, 1957–60; Lectr, Univ. of Keele, 1960–70. *Publications*: Andalusia, 1974; *contrib*. Ann. Assoc. Amer. Geogrs, Erdkunde, Geog. Jl, Geog. Mag., Geog. *Address*: Dept of Geography, Univ. of Keele, Newcastle, Staffordshire ST5 5BG.

Naylor, Bernard; Secretary, Interim Library Resources Co-ordinating Committee, University of London, since 1974; *b* 1938; *m* 1967; two *s* one *d*. BA Oxon 1963, MA 1965, DipLib UCL 1967; ALA 1969. Asst Grade I, For. Accessions Dept, Bodleian Library, Oxford, 1964–66; Bibliographer/Librarian, Univ. of London Inst. Latin Amer. Studies, 1966–74. Editor, New Latin American Titles, 1968–74. *Publications*: Accounts of Nineteenth Century South America: an annotated checklist of works by British and United States observers, 1969; (with Laurence Hallewell and Colin Steele) Directory of Libraries and special collections on Latin America and the West Indies, 1974. *Address*: Senate House, Univ. of London, Malet Street, WC1E 7HU.

Naylor, Eric Leslie; Lecturer in Geography, University of Aberdeen, since 1966; *b* 1942; *m* 1971. BA (Hons) Manchester 1964, MA Manchester 1968, DipAgricEcon Oxford 1966. *Address*: Dept of Geography, Univ. of Aberdeen, St Mary's, Old Aberdeen.

Naylor, Rachel, MA; Lecturer, Department of Management Sciences, University of Manchester Institute of Science and Technology, since 1961; *b* 1915. BA Oxon 1938 (2nd cl. Mod. Langs), SocSciDip Liverpool 1939; Fellow, Inst. Person. Mngmt, Mem., Nat. Inst. Indust. Psychol., Mem., Brit. Univ. Indust. Relat. Assoc., Founder Mem., Manch. Indust. Relat. Soc. Sen. Res. Asst, Dept of Mngmt Sciences, Univ. of Manchester Inst. of Science and Technology. 1960–61. Non-prof. Elected Mem., Senate, Manchester Univ.; Mem., Student Aff. Cttee, UMIST; Mem., Non-Academ. Establishment Cttee, UMIST; Mem. Bd of Governors, Hayward Schs, Bolton; Mem., Youth Employment Cttee, Bolton. *Publications*: contrib. Handbook of Industrial Relations, 1972; jt ed, A Code of Personnel Administration Practice (forthcoming); *contrib*. New Soc., Person. Rev. *Address*: Dept of Management Sciences, Univ. of Manchester Institute of Science and Technology, PO Box 88 Sackville Street, Manchester M60 1QD.

Neal, Gordon Campbell; Lecturer in

Greek and Latin, Manchester University, since 1961; b 1937; m 1970. BA Cantab 1958, MA Cantab 1962, MLitt Cantab 1964. *Address*: School of Classical Studies, The Univ., Manchester M13 9PL.

Neave, Dr Henry Robert, PhD; Lecturer (Grade A) in Statistics, University of Nottingham, since 1971; b 1942; m 1970. BSc Nottingham 1963 (1st cl.), PhD Nottingham 1967; FSS 1969, Mem. Amer. Stat. Assoc. 1973. Asst Lectr, Univ. of Nottingham, 1966; Lectr, Univ. of Nottingham, 1967; Vis. Asst. Prof., Univ. of Wisconsin, 1967–68. AFIMA, 1966–69; Mem., IMS, 1970– ; Sec. and Treas. of RSS, E. Midlands Gp, 1970–72. *Publications*: (with E. Foxley) Introduction to Programming in Algol 60 1968; *contrib.* Annals of Math. Stats, Biometrika, Jl Amer. Statistical Assoc., Jl RSS, Statistician, Rev. ISI, Technometrics. *Address*: Dept of Mathematics, Univ. of Nottingham, Nottingham NG7 2RD.

Needham, Joseph, ScD, FRS, FBA; Master of Gonville and Caius College, since 1966; b 1900; m 1924. Hon. DSc Brussels and Norwich, Hon. LLD Toronto, Hon. DLitt Hongkong. Fellow, Gonville and Caius Coll. 1924–66 (Librarian, 1959–60, Pres., 1959–66); Univ. Demonstrator in Biochem., 1928–33; Sir William Dunn Reader in Biochem., 1933–66, now Emeritus; Vis. Prof. of Biochem. at Stanford Univ., Calif., 1929; Hitchcock Prof., Univ. of California, 1950; Vis. Prof., Univ. of Lyon, 1951, Univ. of Kyoto, 1971. Hon. Counsellor, UNESCO. Hd of the Brit. Scientific Mission in China and Counsellor, Brit. Embassy, Chungking, 1942–46; Dir, Dept of Natural Sciences, UNESCO, 1946–48. Chm., Ceylon Govt Univ. Policy Commn, 1958. For. Mem. Nat. Acad. of China (Academia Sinica); Mem., Internat. Academies of Hist. of Science and of Med.; Pres., Internat. Union Hist. of Sci., 1972– ; Hon. Mem., Yale Chapter of Sigma XI. Sir William Jones Medallist, Asiatic Soc. of Bengal, 1963; George Sarton Medallist, Soc. for History of Science, 1968; Leonardo da Vinci Medallist, Soc. for History of Technology, 1968. Order of the Brilliant Star (China). *Publications*: Science, Religion and Reality (ed), 1925; Man a Machine, 1927; The Sceptical Biologist, 1929; Chemical Embryology (3 vols), 1931; The Great Amphibium, 1932; A History of Embryology, 1934; Order and Life, 1935; Christianity and the Social Revolution (ed), 1935; Adventures before Birth (tr.) 1936; Perspectives in Biochemistry (ed), 1937; Background to Modern Science (ed), 1938; Biochemistry and Morphogenesis, 1942; The Teacher of Nations (ed), 1942; Time, the Refreshing River, 1943; History is on Our Side, 1945; Chinese Science, 1946; Science Outpost, 1948; Hopkins and Biochemistry (ed), 1949; Science and Civilisation in China (7 vols), 1954– ; The Development of Iron and Steel Technology in China, 1958; Heavenly Clockwork, 1960; Within the Four Seas, 1970; The Grand Titration, 1970; Clerks and Craftsmen in China and the West, 1970; The Chemistry of Life (ed), 1970; Chart to illustrate the History of Physiology and Biochemistry, 1926; original papers in

scientific, philosophical and sinological jls. *Address*: Master's Lodge, Caius College, Cambridge.

Needleman, Prof. Lionel, MA, PhD; Professor of Economics, Department of Economics, University of Leicester, since 1970; b 1935; m 1969; one s one d. BA Oxon 1956, MA Oxon 1960, PhD Glasgow 1965. Res. Fellow, Glasgow, 1961–62; Lectr, Glasgow, 1962–63; Lectr, LSE, 1963–68; Reader, Sussex, 1968–70. *Publications*: The Economics of Housing, 1965; ed, Regional Analysis, 1968; *contrib.* Economia Internaz., Economica, Nat. Inst. Econ. Rev., Scott. Jl Pol. Econ., Urb. Studies. *Address*: Dept of Economics, Univ. of Leicester, Leicester LE1 7RH.

Neil, Michael Wells; Professor, Institute of Educational Technology, Open University, since 1971; b 1925; m 1948; two s one d. BSc London 1947, PhD London 1955; ARIC 1947 (by examination), FRIC 1956 (by election). London Hosp. Medical Coll.: Demonstrator, 1949; Lectr, 1952; Sen. Lectr, 1958; Reader, 1964; Project Manager, Science in General Management Ltd, 1965–67; International Publishing Corporation: Operations Manager, Develt Div., 1967–68; Head of Educational Div., 1968–69; Partner, Instructional Systems Associates; Chm., ISA Ltd, 1972. *Publications*: Vertebrate Biochemistry, 1961, 2nd edn 1965; *contrib.* learned jls and professional pubns. *Address*: Open Univ., Walton Hall, Milton Keynes MK7 6AA.

Neil, Rev. Dr William; Warden of Hugh Stewart Hall, since 1953, and Reader in Biblical Studies, University of Nottingham, since 1965; b 1909; m 1936; two s. MA Glasgow 1929, BD Glasgow 1932, PhD Glasgow 1936, Hon DD Glasgow 1961. Lectr, and Hd of Dept of Biblical Study, Univ. of Aberdeen, 1946–53; Croall Lectr, Univ. of Edinburgh, 1967. Minister, Bridge of Allan (Ch of Scotl.), 1937–46; Chaplain to the Forces, 1940–45; Gen. Ed., Knowing Christianity, 1964– . *Publications*: St Paul's Epistles to the Thessalonians (Moffatt Commentaries), 1950; The Rediscovery of the Bible, 1954, 5th edn 1962; The Epistle to the Hebrews (Torch Commentaries), 1955, 3rd edn 1968; The Plain Man Looks at the Bible, 1956, 8th edn 1972, Danish edn 1959; I and II Thessalonians (Torch Commentaries), 1957; One Volume Bible Commentary, 1962, 3rd edn 1973; Jeremiah and Ezekiel (Bible Guides), 1964; The Life and Teaching of Jesus, 1965; Apostle Extraordinary: The Life and Letters of St Paul, 1966; (with E. Newton) The Christian Faith in Art, 1966, German edn 1967; Galatians (Cambridge Bible Commentaries), 1967; The Truth About Jesus, 1968; The Truth About the Early Church (Croall Lectures), 1970; The Bible Story, 1971, 2nd edn 1973; The Truth about the Bible, 1972; The Acts of the Apostles (New Century Bible), 1973; Concise Dictionary of Religious Quotations, 1974; trans., Keller: The Bible as History, 1956, 11th edn 1963; trans., Bruin and Geigel: Jesus Lived Here, 1958; ed, The Bible Companion, 1959, 2nd rev. edn 1974; *contrib.*

Expos. Times, NT Studies, Scott. Jl Theol. *Address*: The Warden's House, Hugh Stewart Hall, The Univ., Nottingham NG7 2RD.

Neild, Prof. Robert Ralph; Professor of Economics, University of Cambridge, since 1971; Fellow of Trinity College, Cambridge; *b* 1924; *m* 1960; one *s* four *d*. BA Cantab 1947, MA Cantab 1952. Lectr and Fellow, Trinity Coll., Cambridge, 1956–58; Ed. Qly Econ. Rev., then Dep. Dir, Nat. Inst. of Econ. and Social Res., 1958–64; MIT Center for Internat. Studies, India Project, New Delhi, 1962–63; Econ. Adviser, HM Treasury, 1964–67; Dir, Stockholm Internat. Peace Res. Inst., 1967–71. RAF 1943–44; Operational Res., 1944–45; Secretariat of UN Econ. Commn for Europe, 1947–51; Cabinet Office and Treasury, 1951–56. *Publications*: Pricing and Employment in the Trade Cycle, 1964; *contrib*. various articles. *Address*: Trinity College, Cambridge.

Nelson, David M.; Lecturer in Psychology, University of Edinburgh, since 1968; *b* 1934; *m* 1968; two *s* one *d*. BA Oxon 1958 (2nd cl. Psychol. and Philos.), MA Oxon 1960, MA London 1960 (Dist. Occup. Psychol.); ABPsS. Lectr, Coll. of Advanced Technology, Birmingham, 1960–61; Sen. Res. Off., LSE, 1962–68. Mem., Council, Brit. Psychol. Soc., 1965–70; Rev. Sec., Psychol. Cttee, SSRC, 1966–67. *Publications*: Bibliography of British Psychological Research (SSRC), 1971; *contrib*. Occupat. Psychol. *Address*: Dept of Psychology, 60 Pleasance, Edinburgh.

Nesbitt, Prof. Joseph Edward, MA, PhD; Professor of Education, Education Centre, New University of Ulster, since 1971; *b* 1918; *m* 1944; one *s*. BA DipEd QUB 1940, Higher DipEd QUB 1941, MA QUB 1943, PhD Manchester 1962; Mem., Brit. Psy. Soc, Geog. Assoc.; Mem., Assoc. of Univ. Teachers, Mem., Internat. Assoc. of Applied Psychology. Asst to Prof. of Educn, QUB, 1943–46; Lectr in Educn, Univ. of Manchester, 1946–64; Sen. Lectr, Univ. Manchester, 1964–71. *Publications*: Chi-Square, 1966; *contrib*. Brit. Jl Educnl Psych. *Address*: Education Centre, New Univ. of Ulster, Coleraine, Co. Londonderry BT52 1SA.

Neville, Clive, BSc; Lecturer in Educational Technology, Department of Education, Brunel University, since 1965; *b* 1935. BSc London External 1959; CertEd London, 1960. Mem., AV Communication Cttee, ATCDE, 1969– . *Publications*: *contrib*. Vis. Educn. *Address*: Brunel Univ., Kingston Lane, Uxbridge, Mddx UB8 3TH.

Nevin, Prof. Edward Thomas; Professor of Economics, University College of Swansea, since 1968; *b* 1925; *m* 1947; three *s* three *d*. BA Wales 1949 (1st cl.), MA Wales 1951, PhD Cambridge 1952; Chm., Assoc. Univ. Teachers Econs. Temp. Asst Lectr, Univ. Coll. of Wales, Aberystwyth, 1949–52; Lectr, Univ. Coll. of Wales, Aberystwyth, 1952–63; Prof. of Applied Econs, Univ. Coll. of Wales, 1963–68. Mem., Welsh Econ. Council, 1965–67. *Publications*: The Problem of the National Debt, 1954; The Mechanism of Cheap Money, 1955; Textbook of Economic Analysis, 1958, 3rd edn 1967, Irish edn 1963, 2nd Irish edn 1970, Tamil edn 1965; Capital Funds in Underdeveloped Countries, 1961, Japanese edn 1962, Spanish edn 1963; (with E. W. Davis) Workbook of Economic Analysis, 1966, 2nd edn 1969; The London Clearing Banks, 1970; Introduction to Micro-Economic Theory, 1972; *contrib*. Economica, Econ. Jl. *Address*: Dept of Economics, Univ. College of Swansea, Swansea SA2 8PP.

Nevitt, Della Adam; Reader in Social Administration, Department of Social Administration, London School of Economics, since 1970; *b* 1927. BSc(Econ) London 1958. Lectr in Econs, Bedford Coll., 1958–62; Lectr in Social Admin., LSE, 1962–70. *Publications*: Housing, Taxation and Subsidies: a study of housing in the United Kingdom, 1966; The Economic Problems of Housing, 1967; (with G. Rhodes) Housing, in, The New Government of London: the first five years, 1972; *contrib*. Policy and Politics, Modern Law Rev. *Address*: London School of Economics, Houghton Street, WC2A 2AE.

New, Peter John; Lecturer in English Literature, University of Exeter, since 1967; *b* 1940; *m* 1965; two *d*. BA Cantab 1962 (1st cl. English), MA Cantab 1966. Asst Lectr, Exeter Univ., 1964–67. *Address*: Dept of English, Univ. of Exeter, Exeter EX4 4QJ.

New, Prof. Ronald William, CEng; Head of Department of Production Technology, Brunel University, since 1962; *b* 1924; one *s* one *d*. MTech, AMCT; FIMechE, FIProdE, CEng. *Address*: Dept of Production Technology, Brunel Univ., Uxbridge, Mddx UB8 3TH.

Newbery, David Michael Garrood, MA; Lecturer in Economics, University of Cambridge, since 1971; *b* 1943. BA Cantab 1965 (1st cl. Econ.), MA Cantab 1969. Fellow Churchill Coll., 1966– ; Mem., Bd of Rev. of Econ. Studies. Civil Servant, Tanzanian Treas., 1965–66; Asst Lectr in Econs, Cambridge, 1966–71; Res. Assoc., Cowles Foundn, Yale, 1969. *Publications*: (with M. F. G. Scott and J. D. MacArthur) Project Appraisal in Practice, 1974; *contrib*. Econ. Jl, Internat. Econ. Rev., Jl Econ. Theory, Oxford Econ. Papers, Jl Agric. Sci. *Address*: Churchill College, Cambridge.

Newbould, Prof. Palmer John, BA, PhD, FIBiol; Professor of Biology, New University of Ulster (also teaches Human Ecology), since 1967; *b* 1929; *m* 1954; one *s* two *d*. BA Oxon 1950 (2nd cl. Botany), PhD London 1953 (Ecology); FIBiol 1967. Mem., Brit. Ecol. Soc., Mem., Brit. Bryol. Soc., Mem., Fauna Preserv. Soc., Mem., Ecol. Soc. Amer., Mem., Conservation Soc. Asst Lectr, Univ. Coll., London, 1955–58; Lectr, Univ. Coll., London, 1958–65; Sen. Lectr, Univ. Coll., London, 1965–67. Mem., NERC Forestry and Woodlands Res. Cttee, 1966–70; Mem., Nature Conserv. Cttee for Eng., 1965–68; Mem., N Ireland Nature Reserves Cttee, 1968– ; Mem., IBP Brit. PT Cttee;

Mem., Internat. PT Cttee; Mem., N Ireland Electricity Consumers Council; Mem., Irish Nuclear Energy Bd. *Publications*: Methods for Estimating the Primary Production of Forests, 1967; *contrib*. Jl Ecol., Sci. Prog. *Address*: School of Biological and Environmental Studies, New Univ. of Ulster, Coleraine, Co. Londonderry BT52 1SA.

Newcombe, Josephine M.; Lecturer in Russian, Aberdeen University, since 1974; *b* 1935. BA Oxon 1964 (2nd cl. Modern Languages), MA Oxon 1968, Dip. in Slavonic Studies Oxon 1965. Lectr in Russian, Bristol, 1968–73. *Publications*: Leonid Andreyev, 1972; Anton Chekhov, 1975. *Address*: Dept of Russian, Taylor Building, Old Aberdeen AB9 2UB.

Newcombe, Terence Harvey; Lecturer, Department of French, University of Edinburgh, since 1967; *b* 1935; *m* 1960; three *s*. BA Nottingham 1957 (2 i), MA Nottingham 1959, Cert Educn (Div. 1) Nottingham 1959; ARCM (Clarinet) 1958. Associate Dean, Faculty of Arts, Edinburgh Univ., 1973– . *Publications*: Les poésies du trouvère Jehan Erart, 1972; The Songs of Jehan Erart: an edition of the music of a 13th century trouvère of Arras, 1974; *contrib*. Neophil., Nott. Med. Stud., Romania. *Address*: Dept of French, 4 Buccleuch Place, Edinburgh EH8 9LW.

Newcombe, Prof. Vernon Zunz; Professor of Town Planning and Director of Planning in Asian Countries Programme, University of Wales Institute of Science and Technology, since 1973; *b* 1911; *m* 1942; two *s*. Degree in architecture and town planning (with distinction) Darmstadt Technical Univ., 1934; FRIBA 1958, FRTPI 1952. Director, Centre for Planning and Housing in Developing Countries, Univ. of Edinburgh, 1965. Housing and Town Planning Adviser, OECD and UN; Mem., WHO Scientific Gp, 1971. *Publications*: professional and res. reports related to assignments in Greece, India, Jordan, Pakistan, Panama, Venezuela, 1959–72; *contrib*. RTPI Jl, Ekistics, ITCC Rev. *Address*: Dept of Town Planning, UWIST, Cardiff CF1 3NU.

Newell, Dr Martin Joseph; President, University College, Galway, since 1960; *b* 1910; *m*; four *s* one *d*. BSc NUI 1929, MSc NUI 1930, DSc NUI 1952; Hon. LLD Univ. of Dublin 1971; MRIA 1952. Lectr in Mathematics, UCG, 1935–56; Prof. of Mathematics, UCG, 1956–60. *Publications*: Algébar Iolscoile, 1947; Nua-Chúrsa Geométrachta; (with M. Power) Nótaí ar Mhion-Áireamh; *contrib*. Proc. Ed. Math. Soc., Proc. London Math. Soc., Proc. RIA, Oxford Qly Jl. *Address*: Univ. College, Galway, Ireland.

Newell, Robert Wheeler; Senior Lecturer in Philosophy, University of East Anglia, since 1968; *b* 1930; *m* 1969; two *d*. BA Virginia 1953, MA Virginia 1957, MA Cantab 1961. Fellow, St John's Coll., Cambridge, 1961–64; Lectr, Univ. of E Anglia, 1964–68; Vis. Lectr, Univ. of Virginia, 1967. *Publications*: The Concept of Philosophy, 1967;

contrib. Philos. *Address*: School of Social Studies, Univ. of East Anglia, Norwich NOR 88C.

Newey, Vincent; Lecturer, Department of English Literature, Liverpool, since 1967; *b* 1943; *m* 1970; one *s*. BA Hons Oxford 1965 (1st cl.), MA Oxford 1969, BLitt Oxford 1971. *Publications*: (with Prof. J. E. Cross) British and American Poetry, 1970; *contrib*. ELH. *Address*: Dept of English Literature, Univ. of Liverpool, PO Box 147, Liverpool L69 3BX.

Newey, Walter William; Senior Lecturer, Geography Department, University of Edinburgh, since 1970; *b* 1916; *m* 1957. MA Edinburgh 1949, BSc London 1959, PhD Edinburgh 1965; Lectr, Moray House Coll. of Educn, Edinburgh, 1961–65; Lectr, Univ. of Edinburgh, 1965–70; Dir of Studies, Univ. of Edinburgh, 1969– . *Publications*: contrib. Geography of the USSR, ed Symons, 1969; *contrib*. Bot. Soc. Edin., New Phytol., Scott. Geogl Mag., Trans Inst. Brit. Geogrs. *Address*: Geography Dept, Univ. of Edinburgh, Infirmary Street, Edinburgh.

Newick, John; Lecturer in Education (with special reference to the teaching of Art), University of London Institute of Education, since 1967; *b* 1919; *m* 1962. Art Teacher's Dip. West of England College of Art 1940. Vis. Lectr in Art Educn, Univ. of Science and Technology, Ghana, 1962–63; Reader, Univ. of Science and Technology, Ghana, 1964; Lectr in Art Educn, Makerere Univ. Coll., Uganda, 1965–66; taught courses at Univ. of California, Berkeley, 1969, Univ. of British Columbia, 1970, Stanford Univ., 1973. *Publication*: ed (with D. Field), The Study of Art and Education, 1973. *Address*: Univ. of London Institute of Education, Malet Street, WC1E 7HS.

Newitt, Malyn Dudley Dunn; Lecturer, History Department, University of Exeter, since 1965; *b* 1940. BA Oxford 1961, PhD London 1967. *Address*: History Dept., Univ. of Exeter, Exeter EX4 4QJ.

Newland, Robert Michael, MA, MSc, MInstHE; Lecturer in Transportation and Environmental Planning, University of Birmingham, since 1961; Rees Jeffreys Industrial Lectureship, since 1973; *b* 1932; *m* 1959; two *s*. BA Cantab 1956 (Hons Geography), MA Cantab 1961, MSc Birmingham 1961 (Civil Engineering); MInstHE. Cnsltnt Traffic Eng. and Transp. Planner, 1963– ; Cnsltnt Survey Dir, GEC-Elliott Traffic Automation Ltd, 1965–73; Cnsltnt, Sir A. Gibb and Partners, 1971– . *Publications*: *contrib*. Internat. Rd Saf. Traff. Rev., PTRC Sem. Proc., Rds Rd Constr., Traff. Eng. Cont. *Address*: Dept of Transportation and Environmental Planning, Univ. of Birmingham, PO Box 363, Birmingham B15 2TT.

Newland, William Rupert; Lecturer, Art Department, London University Institute of Education, since 1950; *b* 1919; *m* 1953; one *s* one *d*. NDD Painting 1949, DipCeramics Central School 1950, Art Teachers Cert. 1950; Fellow Soc. Designer Craftsmen. Mem., Nat. Council Dip. Art and Design (Summerson Cttee); Adviser, High Wycombe Coll. of Art; Assessor, Dip. Art Design, Ceramics, 1965– . *Address*: London Univ. Institute of Education, Malet Street, WC1E 7HS.

Newlyn, Prof. Walter T., BSc(Econ); Professor of Development Economics, School of Economic Studies, University of Leeds, since 1967; *b* 1915; *m* 1952; four *d*. BSc(Econ) London. Economic Adv. to the Uganda Govt, reported on Econ. Policy, 1959. *Publications*: Theory of Money, 1962; Money in an African Context; (with D. C. Rowan) Money and Banking in the British African Colonies, 1954; chapters, in, Banking in the British Commonwealth, ed R. S. Sayers, 1952; Symposium on Cost of Operating Agricultural Machinery in Tropical Africa, 1954; Federalism and Economic Growth: a symposium; *contrib*. Econ. Jl, (Yorkshire) Bull. of Econ. Res. *Address*: 61 Grove Lane, Leeds LS6 4EQ.

Newman, Aubrey Norris, MA, DPhil, FRHistS; Reader in History, University of Leicester, since 1972; *b* 1927; *m* 1954; one *s* three *d*. MA Glasgow 1949 (2nd cl. History), BA Oxon 1953 (1st cl. History), DPhil Oxon 1957, MA Oxon 1957; FRHistS 1964. Mem., Jewish Hist. Soc. Engl. Res. Fellow, Bedford Coll., London, 1954–55, 1957–58; Pt-time Temp. Lectr, Nottingham, 1958–59; Asst Lectr, Univ. of Leicester, 1959–61; Lectr, Univ. of Leicester, 1961–69; Sen. Lectr, Univ. of Leicester, 1969–72. RAF Educn Br., 1949–51; Res. Asst, History of Parliament, 1955–59. *Publications*: The Parliamentary Diary of Sir Edward Knatchbull 1722–30, 1963; The Stanhopes of Chevening, A Family Biography, 1969; Leicester House Politics 1750–60, 1969; (with H. Miller) A Bibliography of British History, 1485–1760, 1970; Migration and Settlement: Report on the First Conference of English and American Jewish Historical Societies, 1971; The Parliamentary Lists of the Early Eighteenth Century: their compilation and use, 1973; Leicester Hebrew Congregation: a centenary record, 1974; *contrib*. Bull. Inst. Hist. Res., EHR, Hist. Jl. *Address*: Dept of History, Univ. of Leicester.

Newman, Dr Colin Valpy; Lecturer, Department of Psychology, University of Birmingham, since 1969; *b* 1942; *m* 1968. BSc Hons Leicester 1965 (1st cl.), PhD Leicester 1968; ABPsS 1969; Member: Brain Res. Assoc.; Psychonomic Soc. (USA). Asst Lectr, Univ. of Leicester, 1968–69. *Publications*: *contrib*. Develtl Med. and Child Neurol., Jl of Exptl Psychol., Jl Gen. Psychol., Nature, Perception and Psychophysics, Psychonomic Sci., Qly Jl Exptl Psychol., Vision Res. *Address*: Dept of Psychol., Univ. of Birmingham, PO Box 363, Birmingham B15 2TT.

Newman, Dr Richard Kingsley; Lecturer, Department of Economic and Social History, University College of Swansea, since 1971; *b* 1939; *m* 1973. MA Auckland 1965, DPhil Sussex 1970. Jun. Lectr in History, Auckland, 1963–65; Temp. Lectr in History, Western Australia, 1971. *Address*: Dept of Economic and Social History, Univ. Coll. of Swansea, Singleton Park, Swansea, Glam. SA2 8PP.

Newson, Dr Elizabeth Ann, PhD, ABPsS; Senior Lecturer, Child Development Research Unit, University of Nottingham, since 1971 (Senior Research Fellow, 1965–71); *b* 1929; *m* 1951; one *s* two *d*. BA London 1951 (Psychology), PhD Nottingham 1955; ABPsS. Univ. Res. Fellow, Nottingham, 1959–65. Mem., Professional Adv. Cttee, Nat. Soc. Autistic Children, 1971– . *Publications*: (with J. Newson) Infant Care in an Urban Community, 1963, pbk edn 1964; Four Years Old in an Urban Community, 1968, pbk edn 1970; (with S. Hewett and J. Newson) The Family and the Handicapped Child, 1970, 2nd edn 1972. *Address*: Child Development Research Unit, The Univ., Nottingham NG7 2RD.

Newson, Dr John, PhD, ABPsS; Reader, Child Development Research Unit, University of Nottingham, since 1969; *b* 1925; *m* 1951; one *s* two *d*. BSc London 1948 (Maths and Physics), BSc London 1951 (Psychology), PhD Nottingham 1956; ABPsS. Asst Lectr, Nottingham, 1951–53; Lectr, Nottingham, 1953–65; Sen. Lectr, Nottingham, 1965–69. Mem., Professional Adv. Cttee, Nat. Soc. Autistic Children, 1971– . *Publications*: (with E. Newson) Infant Care in an Urban Community, 1963, pbk edn 1964; Four Years Old in an Urban Community, 1968, pbk edn 1970; (with S. Hewett and E. Newson) The Family and the Handicapped Child, 1970, 2nd edn 1972. *Address*: Child Development Research Unit, The Univ., Nottingham NG7 2RD.

Newton, Rev. John Anthony, MA, PhD; Recognised Teacher (Part-Time), Department of Theology, University of Bristol, since 1966; *b* 1930; *m* 1963; three *s*. BA London 1952 (History), PhD London 1956, BA Cantab 1958 (Theology), MA Cantab 1960. Mem., Eccles. Hist. Soc. *Publications*: Methodism and the Puritans, 1964; Susanna Wesley and the Puritan Tradition in Methodism, 1969; The Palestine Problem, 1972; *contrib*. Ch. Qly, Ecumen. Rev., Exp. Times, Theol. *Address*: Dept of Theology, Univ. of Bristol., Bristol BS8 1TH.

Newton, Kenneth, PhD; Research Fellow, Nuffield College, Oxford, since 1974; *b* 1940; *m* 1968; one *d*. BA Exeter 1962 (Sociology), PhD Cambridge 1966. Lectr in Political Sociology, Birmingham, 1965–73; Vis. European Schol., Univ. of Pittsburgh, 1972; ACLS Fellow, Univ. of Wisconsin, 1973–74. *Publications*: (with S. Abrams) Opportunities After O-Level, 1965; The Sociology of British Communism, 1969; *contrib*. Acta Sociol., Brit. Jl Pol. Sci., New Atlantis, Soc. Econ. Admin, Pol Studies, Jl Politics, Policy and Politics, Sociol., Trans Seventh Wld Cong. Sociol. *Address*: Nuffield College, Oxford OX1 1NF.

Newton, Dr Lucy Joy; Lecturer in French, University of Glasgow, since 1967; *b* 1939. BA Leeds 1961 (French with English Lit.), PhD London 1964 (French), Dip. de langue étrangère Rennes 1960; Fulbright Schol.,

1964–66. Instructor in French, Wellesley Coll., Mass, 1964–66; Temp. Lectr, Leicester Univ., 1966–67. Guest speaker, Council of Europe Conf. on AV media, Jan. 1972. *Publications*: Documentary film: *Emile Zola* (Glasgow Univ., TV service), 1971; Correspondance Montesquiou–Whistler: La Chauvesouris et le Papillon (forthcoming); *contrib*. Cah. Natural., Fr. Rev., Fr. Studies, Mod. Languages, Neophilol., L'Esprit Créateur. *Address*: French Dept, Univ. of Glasgow, Glasgow G12 8QQ.

Newton, Dr Peter A., PhD, FSA; Mellon Lecturer in British Medieval Art History, University of York, since 1966; *b* 1935. BA London 1956, PhD London 1961; FSA. Res. Fellow, Barber Inst., Birmingham Univ., 1962–64; Vis. Fellow, All Souls Coll., Oxford, 1972. Mem., Cttee Corpus Vitrearum Med. Aev. GB, 1966– . *Publications*: *contrib*. Antiqu. Jl. *Address*: The King's Manor, Univ. of York, York.

Niblock, Dr Timothy Colin; Lecturer in International Relations, Department of Political Science, University of Khartoum, since 1969 (on secondment from University of Reading); *b* 1942; *m* 1970; one *d*. BA Oxon 1965, Cert. of Advanced European Studies (Bruges) 1966, DPhil Sussex 1971; Mem., RIIA. Temp. res. position Univ. of Dar es Salaam, 1967–68. *Publications*: Tanzanian Foreign Policy, 1973; *contrib*. African Rev., Venture. *Address*: Dept of Political Science, Univ. of Khartoum, PO Box 321, Khartoum.

Ni Chuilleanáin, Eiléan; Lecturer in English, Trinity College, Dublin, since 1966; *b* 1942. BA National Univ. of Ireland 1962, MA National Univ. of Ireland 1964 (1st cl.), BLitt Oxon 1969. *Address*: 25 Trinity College, Dublin.

Nicholas, Prof. Barry; *see* Nicholas, J. K. B. M.

Nicholas, Brian Lewis, MA BLitt; Lecturer in French, University of Sussex, since 1964; *b* 1933; *m* 1959; one *s* one *d*. BA Oxford 1954 (1st cl. French and German), MA Oxford 1958, BLitt Oxford 1959. Asst Lectr, King's Coll., London, 1956–58; Asst Lectr, Univ. of Birmingham, 1958–60; Lectr, Univ. of Birmingham, 1960–64. *Publications*: (with I. Gregor) The Moral and the Story, 1962; chapters, in French Literature and its Background, vols 1, 2 and 5, ed J. Cruickshank, 1968–69; contrib. Penguin Companion to European Literature, ed A Thorlby, 1969; *contrib*. Mod. Lang. Rev. *Address*: Arts Building, Univ. of Sussex, Brighton BN1 9QN.

Nicholas, Edward John, MA; Senior Lecturer in Education and Senior Tutor to Postgraduate Secondary Courses, University of London, Goldsmiths' College, since 1970; *b* 1935; *m* 1959; one *s* one *d*. BA Wales 1956, Post-grad. Cert. in Educn London 1957, Acad. Dip. in Educn London 1966, MA(Educ) London 1969. *Publications*: ed, Handbook for History Teachers, Pt II, rev. edn 1971; (with others) Methods of History Teaching –

a Survey, in, Handbook for History Teachers, Pt I. *Address*: Postgraduate Education Dept, Univ. of London, Goldsmiths' College, New Cross, SE14 6NW.

Nicholas, Prof. Herbert George, MA, FBA; Rhodes Professor of American History and Institutions, University of Oxford, since 1969; *b* 1911. BA Oxon 1934 (1st cl. Lit. Hum.), MA Oxon 1938, Hon. DCL Pittsburgh 1968; FBA 1969, FRHistS 1969. Commonwealth Fund Fellow, Yale Univ., 1935–37; Lectr, Exeter Coll., Oxford, 1938–46; Fellow, Exeter Coll., Oxford, 1946–51; Fac. Fellow, Nuffield Coll., Oxford, 1948–57; Fellow, New Coll., Oxford, 1951– ; Nuffield Reader in the Comparative Study of Institutions, 1951–68; Vis. Prof., Brooking Inst, Washington, 1960; Albert Shaw Lectr in Diplomatic History, Johns Hopkins, 1961; Vis. Fellow, Inst. Adv. Studies, Princeton, 1964; Vis. Fac. Fellow, Kennedy Inst. Politics, Harvard, 1968. Amer. Div., Min. of Information and HM Embassy, Washington, 1941–46; Chm., Brit. Assoc. Amer. Studies, 1959–62; Mem., Cttee of Award, Harkness Fellowships, 1969–74. *Publications*: The American Union, 1948; The British General Election of 1950, 1951; To the Hustings, 1956; The United Nations as a Political Institution, 1959, 4th edn 1971; ed, Tocqueville: Démocratie en Amérique, 1961; Britain and the United States, 1963; *contrib*. Amer. Polit. Sci. Rev., Internat. Aff., Jl Amer. Studies, Occid., Polit. Studies, Proc. Brit. Acad., Yale Rev. *Address*: New College, Oxford.

Nicholas, Prof. (John Keiran) Barry (Moylan); Professor of Comparative Law, University of Oxford, since 1971; *b* 1919; *m* 1948; one *s* one *d*. MA Oxon 1946 (1st cl. Classical Mods 1939, 1st. cl. Law); Barrister (Inner Temple) 1950. Fellow, Brasenose Coll., Oxford, 1947– ; Vice-Principal, Brasenose Coll., Oxford, 1960–63; All Souls Reader in Roman Law, Oxford, 1949–71; Vis. Prof., Tulane Univ., 1960; Vis. Prof., Univ. of Rome, 1964; Vis. Prof., Fordham Univ., 1968. *Publications*: Introduction to Roman Law, 1962; 3rd edn of Jolowicz's Historical Introduction to Roman Law, 1972. *Address*: Brasenose College, Oxford.

Nicholl, Prof. Donald; Professor of History, University of Keele, since 1972; *b* 1923; *m* 1946; one *s* four *d*. MA Oxon 1947; FRHistS, Asst, Edinburgh Univ., 1948–52; Asst Lectr, Keele, 1953–63; Sen. Lectr, Keele, 1963–67. Reader, 1967–72; Vis. Prof., Univ. of California, 1966, 1969–70. *Publications*: Recent Thought in Focus, 1952, Italian edn 1956; trans. and ed, Dante: Monarchy, 1954; Thurstan, Archbishop of York, 1964; *contrib*. Dokumente, Downs. Rev., Dub. Rev., Vie Intell., Wort Wahr. *Address*: Dept of History, Univ. of Keele, Keele ST5 5BG.

Nicholls, Anthony James; Official Fellow, St Antony's College, and Lecturer, Oxford University, since 1968; *b* 1934; *m* 1966; one *s* one *d*. MA Oxon 1961, BPhil Oxon 1960. Lectr, Merton Coll., Oxford, 1960–61; Res. Fellow, St Antony's Coll., Oxford, 1961–68. *Publications*: Weimar and the Rise of Hitler,

513

1968; ed (with others), German Democracy and the Triumph of Hitler, 1971; (with others) The Semblance of Peace: the Political Settlement after the Second World War, 1972; contrib. European Fascism, ed S. Woolf, 1968; The History Makers, ed Wheeler-Bennett, 1973. *Address*: St Antony's College, Oxford.

Nicholls, Derek Clifford, MA, PhD; University Lecturer, Department of Land Economy, University of Cambridge, since 1974; *b* 1939; *m* 1964; one *s* one *d*. BA Cantab 1961 (Rural Est. Mngmt), MA Cantab 1965, PhD Cantab 1966. Res. Fellow, Glasgow Univ., 1964–67, Lectr, 1967–71, Sen. Lectr, 1972–73. Asst Ed., Urban Studies, 1969–71; Jt Ed., 1971– . *Publications*: (with A. Young) Recreation and Tourism in the Loch Lomond Area, 1968; Use of Land for Forestry within the Proprietary Land Unit, 1969. *Address*: Dept of Land Economy, Univ. of Cambridge, 19 Silver Street, Cambridge CB3 9EP.

Nichols, Keith Alan; Lecturer, Department of Psychology, University of Exeter, 1968; *b* 1941; *m* 1967; one *s*. BSc Leeds 1966 (Psychol.), MSc 1968 (Clinical Psychol); ABPsS. Senior Clinical Psychologist (part-time). *Publications*: *contrib.* Jl Child Psychol., Psychiatry, Expl Soc. Psychology, Perceptual and Motor Skills. *Address*: Dept of Psychology, Univ. of Exeter, Exeter EX4 4QJ.

Nicholson, Dr Arthur Richard; Senior Lecturer in Education, Department of Education, Queen's University, Belfast, since 1973; *b* 1924; *m* 1953; three *s* one *d*. BSc QUB 1949 (1st class Hons), PhD Victoria Univ. of Manchester 1953, DipEd QUB 1958. Queen's Univ., Belfast: Lectr in Educn, 1965–73; Tutor for Overseas Students, 1972– ; Sec., Youth Club Assoc., 1968– . Mem., NI VSO Cttee, 1967– . *Publications*: Cours par Correspondance à l'usage des étudiants du cycle d'orientation (Congo) (première partie) Mathématique: première année, 1967; *contrib.* Maths Teachers' Forum. *Address*: Dept of Education, Queen's Univ., Belfast BT7 1NN.

Nicholson, Peter Philip; Lecturer, Political Theory and Government, University College of Swansea, since 1963; *b* 1940; *m* 1963. BA (Social Studies) Exeter 1961 (1st cl. Government). *Publication*: *contrib.* Pol Studies. *Address*: Dept of Political Theory and Government, Univ. College, Singleton Park, Swansea SA2 8PP.

Nicholson, Prof. Roger; Professor of Textile Design, Royal College of Art, since 1958; *b* 1922. ARCA 1947, FSIA. *Address*: Royal Coll. of Art, Kensington Gore, SW7 2EU.

Nicholson, Simon; Lecturer in Design, and Chairman, Art and Environment Course Team, The Open University, since 1971; *b* 1934; *m* 1960; two *d*. ARCA 1953, BA, MA Cantab 1957 (Prehistoric Archaeology and Anthropology). Vis. Prof., Moore Coll. of Art, Pa, 1964; Associate Prof., Univ. of Califor-

514

nia: Berkeley, 1965–67; Davis, Santa Cruz, and Coll. of Creative Studies, Santa Barbara, 1967–70. Vis. Associate Prof., Carpenter Center for Visual Art, Harvard Univ., 1971; Vis. Prof.: Ontario Inst. for Studies in Educn, Toronto, 1973; Univ. of Calif., Los Angeles, 1974. Principal and Environmental Designer, Symmetry Ltd, San Francisco, 1967–70; Associate, Lawrence Halprin and Associates, San Francisco and NY, 1971–72. One-man exhibitions: London, 1964; San Francisco, 1968; Pittsburgh, 1969. Bradford Williams Medal, Amer. Soc. of Landscape Architects, 1972. *Publications*: What Do Playgrounds Teach?, 1970; The Theory of Loose Parts, 1971; Access to Communications Media as a Generator of Design, 1972; Community Participation in City Decision Making 1973; Children as Planners, 1974; *contrib.* Landscape Architecture Qly, Where, Proceedings of the California Park and Recreation Administrators Inst. *Address*: The Open Univ., Oxford Research Unit, 11–12 Berington Road, Oxford.

Nicholson, Thomas Alastair John; Professor of Production Management, London Graduate School of Business Studies, since 1972; *b* 1938; *m* 1962; one *s* two *d*. BSc Econ. London 1962, PhD London 1970 (Operational Research). London Graduate School of Business Studies: Sen. Lectr in Operations Res., 1969; Reader in Prod. Management, 1971. *Publications*: Optimisation in Industry, vols 1 and 2, 1972; Computers in Production Management, 1973; *contrib.* Internat. Jl of Production Res., Operations Res. Qly, Proc. IEE. *Address*: London Graduate Sch. of Business Studies, Sussex Place, NW1 4SA.

Nicol, Prof. Donald MacGillivray; Koraës Professor of Modern Greek and Byzantine History, Language and Literature, University of London, King's College, since 1969; *b* 1923; *m* 1950; three *s*. BA Cambridge 1948, MA Cambridge 1952, PhD Cambridge 1952; MRIA, FRHistS. Lectr in Classics, Univ. Coll., Dublin, 1952–63; Vis. Fellow, Dumbarton Oaks, Washington, DC, 1963–64; Vis. Prof. of Byzantine History, Univ. of Indiana, 1964–65; Reader in Byzantine History, Univ. of Edinburgh, 1965–69. Mem., Council, Soc. Prom. Hellenic Studies, 1966–71; Mem., Council, Eccles. Hist. Soc., 1966–72; Mem., Encyclop. Brit. Univs Adv. Cttee GB, 1967– . *Publications*: The Despotate of Epiros, 1957; Meteora: The rock monasteries of Thessaly, 1963; The Byzantine Family of Kantakouzenos (Cantacuzenus): A Genealogical and Prosopographical Study, 1968; The Last Centuries of Byzantium, 1261–1453, 1972; Byzantium: its ecclesiastical history and relations with the western world (collected studies), 1972; *contrib.* Ann. Brit. Sch. Athens, Ann. Hist. Concil., Byzantinoslavica, Byzant. Zeits., Byzant. Forsch., Byzantion, Camb. Mediev. Hist., Dumb. Oaks Papers, Greece Rome, Greek, Roman Byzant. Studies, Jl Eccles. Hist., Neo-Hellen., Proc. Royal Irish Acad., Rev. Etudes SE Europ., Studies Ch. Hist., Univ. Birmingham Hist. Jl. *Address*: Dept of Byzantine and Modern Greek Studies, Univ.

of London, King's College, Strand, WC2R 2LS.

Nicol, Rev. Dr Iain Garden; Lecturer, Department of Systematic Theology, University of Glasgow, since 1968; *b* 1934; *m* 1964; one *d*. MA Glasgow 1959, BD Glasgow 1962, PhD Glasgow 1972; Asst Lectr, Glasgow 1964–68. *Publications*: trans. (with U. Nicol) F. Hahn, etc: Anfänge der Kirche (Beginning of the Church in the New Testament), 1969. *Address*: Dept of Systematic Theology, The Univ., Glasgow G12 8QQ.

Nicoll, Prof. Ronald Ewart, MSc, FRTPI, FRICS; Professor of Urban and Regional Planning, University of Strathclyde, since 1966; *b* 1921; *m* 1943; one *s* one *d*. MSc Strathclyde 1966, DipTP 1952; FRTPI 1953, FRICS 1972. Var. appts local planning authorities, 1949– ; latterly Ch. Planning Off., Scott. Develop. Dept, 1964. Mem., Royal Commn on Environmental Pollution, 1973– . *Publications*: The Future of Development Plans, 1965; Report on Containerisation, 1970; Oceanspan, 1970; Oceanspan 2, 1971; A Future for Scotland, 1973; *contrib.* Town Country Plan. *Address*: Dept of Urban and Regional Planning, Livingstone Tower Univ. of Strathclyde, Glasgow.

Nidditch, Prof. Peter Harold; Professor and Head of Department of Philosophy, University of Sheffield, since 1969; *b* 1928; *m* 1951. BA London 1949, MA London 1951, PhD London 1953; Mem., Aristotelian Soc., Brit. Soc. Hist. Maths, Hist. Science Soc., Math. Assoc., Mind Assoc. Asst, Birkbeck Coll., London, 1953–54; Asst Lectr, QUB, 1954–56; Lectr, Liverpool Univ., 1956–59; Lectr, Bristol Univ., 1959–63; Sen. Lectr, Sussex Univ., 1963–64; Reader and Chm. of Logic, History, Policy of Science Div., Sussex Univ., 1964–70; Editor, official publications of Sussex Univ., 1965–69. *Publications*: Introductory Formal Logic of Mathematics, 1957; Elementary Logic of Science and Mathematics, 1960; Russian Reader in Pure and Applied Mathematics, 1962; Propositional Calculus, 1962; The Development of Mathematical Logic, 1962; ed, Philosophy of Science, 1968; The Intellectual Virtues, 1970; A Bibliographical and Text-historical Study of Locke's 'Some Thoughts concerning Education', 1972; Hume's Enquiries, ed Selby-Bigge, rev. edn with textual and expl notes, 1974; Locke's Essay concerning Human Understanding, with critical apparatus, introd., and glossary, 1974; Gen. Editor, Clarendon Edition of The Works of John Locke (30 vols, in progress); contrib. chapters in other books; *contrib.* The Locke Newsletter, Mind, Proc. Arist. Soc. *Address*: Dept of Philosophy, Arts Tower, Univ. of Sheffield, Sheffield S10 2TN.

Niklaus, Robert; Professor of French and Head of Department, University of Exeter, since 1952; *b* 1910; *m* 1936, 1973; two *s* one *d*. LèsL Lille 1930, BA London 1931 (1st cl. French), PhD London 1934; Hon. Ddel'U Rennes 1963; officier de l'ordre Nat. du Mérite 1972. Asst Lectr, Univ. Coll., London, 1932–38; Lectr, Univ. of Manchester, 1938–52; Prof. of French with

Spanish, Univ. of Exeter, 1958–64; with Italian, 1964– . Dean, Fac. of Arts, Univ. of Exeter, 1959–62; Dep. Vice-Chancellor, Univ. of Exeter, 1965–67; Pres., AUT, 1954–55; Pres. Internat. Assoc. Univ. Profs and Lectrs, 1960–62, 1962–64; Pres. Soc. Fr. Studies, 1968–70; Treas., Internat. Soc. 18th Cent. Studies, 1968– . Gen. Ed., Textes Français Classiques et Modernes (ULP), 1969– . *Publications*: Jean Moréas: poète lyrique, 1936; ed, D. Diderot: Pensées philosophiques, 1950, 3rd edn 1965; ed, D. Diderot: Lettre sur les avengles, 1951, 2nd edn 1963; ed (with T. Niklaus), Marivaux: Arlequin poli par l'amour, 1959; ed, J.-J. Rousseau: Confessions (Everyman series), 1960, 2nd edn 1972; ed, Sedaine: La gageure imprévue, 1970; Le Barbier de Séville by Beaumarchais (Studies in French Literature), 1968; The Eighteenth Century (Literary History of France, vol. 4), 1970; contrib. Chambers's Encyclopedia; Encyclopedia Britannica; Encyclopedia of Philosophy; textbooks for schools and universities; *contrib.* Cah. Assoc. Internat. Etudes Franç., Communicat., Diderot Studies, Europe, Filos, Geog., Romanic Rev., Studies Volt. Eighteenth Cent., Yrs Wk Mod. Lang. Studies. *Address*: Dept of French and Italian, Queen's Building, The Queen's Drive, Exeter EX4 4QH.

Nineham, Rev. Dennis Eric, DD(Hon), MA, BD; Warden of Keble College, Oxford, since 1969; *b* 1921; *m* 1946; two *s* two *d*. Asst Chaplain of Queen's Coll., Oxford, 1944; Chaplain, Queen's Coll., Oxford, 1945; Fellow and Praelector, Queen's Coll., Oxford, 1946; Tutor, Queen's Coll., Oxford, 1949; Prof. of Biblical and Historical Theology, Univ. of London (King's Coll.), 1954–58; Prof. of Divinity, Univ. of London, 1958–64; Regius Prof. of Divinity, Cambridge Univ., and Fellow, Emmanuel Coll., 1964–69. Fellow, King's Coll., London, 1963– . Select Preacher to Univ. of Oxford, 1954–56, and to Univ. of Cambridge, 1959; Proctor in Convocation of Canterbury for London Univ., 1955–64, for Cambridge Univ., 1965–69. Examining Chaplain to Archbishop of York and to Bishops of Ripon and Norwich and (1947–54) to Bishop of Sheffield. Mem., General Synod of Church of England for Oxford Univ., 1970– . Governor of Haileybury, 1966– . *Publications*: The Study of Divinity, 1960; A New Way of Looking at the Gospels, 1962; Commentary on St Mark's Gospel, 1963; ed, Studies in the Gospels, 1955; The Church's Use of the Bible, 1963; The New English Bible Reviewed, 1965; contrib. Studies in Ephesians (ed F. L. Cross), 1956; On the Authority of the Bible, 1960; Religious Education, 1944–1984, 1966; Theologians of our Time, 1966; Christian History and Interpretation, 1967; Christ for us Today, 1968, etc; *contrib.* Expository Times, Jl of Theological Studies, Theology. *Address*: Keble College, Oxford.

Nisbet, Prof. Hugh Barr, MA, PhD; Professor of German Language and Literature, University of St Andrews, since 1974; *b* 1940; *m* 1962; two *s*. MA Edinburgh 1962 (1st cl. German), PhD Edinburgh 1965. Asst Lectr in German, Bristol, 1965–67, Lectr, 1967–72,

Reader, 1972–73. *Publications*: Herder and the Philosophy and History of Science, 1970; trans., Kant: Political Writings, ed Reiss, 1970; ed (with H. S. Reiss), Goethe: Die Wahlverwandtschaften, 1971; Goethe and the Scientific Tradition, 1972; *contrib*. Deuts. Viertel. Lit. Geistes., Forum Mod. Lang. Studies, Mod. Lang. Rev., Publics Engl. Goethe Soc. *Address*: Dept of German, St Salvator's College, St Andrews KY16 9PH.

Nisbet, Prof. John Donald; Professor of Education, University of Aberdeen, since 1963; *b* 1922; *m* 1952; one *s* one *d*. MA Edinburgh 1943, BEd Edinburgh 1949; PhD Aberdeen 1952, Teacher's Cert. Edinburgh 1946, Teacher's Dip. London 1948; FBPsS 1956. Asst Lectr, Aberdeen Univ., 1949–50; Lectr, Aberdeen Univ., 1950–60; Head of Dept., Aberdeen Univ., 1960–63. Mem., Scottish Council for Res. in Educn, 1960– ; Mem., Educnl Res. Bd, 1970– ; Mem., SSRC, 1972– ; Mem., UGC Educn Sub-Cttee, 1967– ; Mem., General Teaching Council, 1966–68; Mem., Consultative Cttee on the Curriculum 1971– ; Ed., Brit. Jl Educn. Psychol., 1967– . *Publications*: Family Environment, 1953; Age of Transfer to Secondary Education, 1966; Transition to Secondary Education, 1969; Scottish Education Looks Ahead, 1969; Educational Research Methods, 1970; *contrib*. Brit. Jl Educn. Psychol. *Address*: Dept of Education, King's College, Aberdeen AB9 2UB.

Nisbet, Prof. Robin George Murdoch, FBA; Professor of Latin, Oxford, since 1970; *b* 1925; *m* 1969. MA Glasgow 1947, MA Oxford 1954; FBA 1967. Tutor in Classics, Corpus Christi Coll., Oxford, 1952–70. *Publications*: Commentary on Cicero, In Pisonem, 1961; (with M. Hubbard) on Horace, Odes I, 1970; *contrib*. CQ, CR, JRS. *Address*: Corpus Christi College, Oxford.

Nisbet, Prof. Stanley Donald, MA, MEd, FRSE; Professor of Education, University of Glasgow, since 1951; *b* 1912; *m* 1942; one *s* one *d*. MA Edinburgh 1934 (1st cl. Classics), MEd Edinburgh 1940 (with distinction); FRSE. Lectr, Manchester Univ., 1946; Prof., Queen's Univ., Belfast, 1946–51; Dean, Fac. of Arts, Glasgow Univ., 1965–67. Mem., Scott. Council Res. Educn, 1951–72; Governor, Jordanhill Coll. Educn, 1960– ; Chm., Editorial Bd, Scott. Educnl Studies, 1969– . *Publications*: Purpose in the Curriculum, 1957; (with B. L. Napier) Promise and Progress, 1970; contrib. Mental Measurements Yearbook; *contrib*. Brit. Jl Educnl Psychol. *Address*: Dept of Education, Univ. of Glasgow, Glasgow G12 8QQ.

Nish, Ian Hill, MA, PhD; Reader, Department of International History, London School of Economics, since 1973 (Senior Lecturer, 1970–73); *b* 1926; *m* 1965; two *d*. MA Edinburgh 1950 (History), PhD London 1961. Lectr, Sydney Univ., 1958–62; Lectr, LSE, 1962–70; Vis. Prof., Yale Univ., 1969–70. *Publications*: The Anglo-Japanese Alliance, 1894–1907, 1966; The Story of Japan, 1968; Alliance in Decline, 1908–23, 1972. *Address*: Dept of International History,

London School of Economics, Houghton Street, Aldwych, WC2A 2AE.

Niven, Dr Alastair Neil Robertson; Lecturer in English Studies, University of Stirling, since 1970; *b* 1944; *m* 1970. BA Cantab 1966, MA Cantab 1968, MA Ghana 1968, PhD Leeds 1972; FRCSoc 1970. Commonwealth Scholar, Univ. Ghana, 1966–68, Lectr in English, 1968–69; Temp. Lectr in Eng. Lit., Univ. Leeds, 1969–70. Chm., Public Schools Debating Assoc., 1961–62; Warden, Murray Hall, Univ. Stirling, 1973– . *Publications*: *contrib*. Commonwealth, Commonwealth Newsletter, Jl Commonwealth Lit., Literary Criterion, Planet. *Address*: Murray Hall, Univ. of Stirling, Stirling.

Nixon, Rev. Robin Ernest; Senior Tutor, St John's College, University of Durham and part-time Lecturer in Theology, since 1963; *b* 1931; *m* 1958; three *d*. BA Cambridge 1954, MA 1958; Member: Studiorum Novi, Testamenti Societas. Tutor, St John's College, Univ. of Durham, 1960–63. Editor, The Churchman, 1972– . *Publications*: The Exodus in the New Testament, 1963; Bible Study Book on John's Gospel, 1968; contrib. All in Each Place, 1965; New Bible Commentary Revised, 1970. *Address*: St John's College, Univ. of Durham, Durham DH1 3RV.

Nixon, William Lewis Benedict; Senior Lecturer in Computer Science, University of London Institute of Computer Science, since 1969; *b* 1920. *Publications*: How a Computer Works, 1968, 2nd edn 1969. *Address*: Univ. of London Institute of Computer Science, 44 Gordon Square, WC1H 0PD.

Nixson, Dr Frederick Ian; Lecturer in Economics, Manchester University, since 1971; *b* 1943; *m* 1972. BA Leeds 1964, PhD 1970. Jun. Res. Fellow in African Econ. Studies, Univ. of Leeds, 1966–67; Lectr in Economics, Makerere Univ., Kampala, Uganda, 1968–71. *Publications*: Economic Integration and Industrial Location: an East African case study, 1973. *Address*: Dept of Economics, Univ. of Manchester, Manchester M13 9PL.

Noakes, Dr Jeremy; Lecturer in Modern History, University of Exeter, since 1969; *b* 1941; *m* 1961; one *s* one *d*. BA Oxon 1963, MA Oxon 1968, DPhil Oxon 1968. Lectr, Hull Univ., 1965–68. *Publications*: The Nazi Party in Lower Saxony 1921–1933, 1971; *contrib*. Jl Contemp. Hist. *Address*: Dept of History, Univ. of Exeter, Exeter, Devon.

Noble, Grant; Lecturer in Social Psychology, Department of Psychology, Trinity College, Dublin, since 1972; *b* 1942; *m* 1971. BA Reading 1963 (Psychology and Economics), PhD London 1966. Res. Officer, Centre for Mass Communication Research, Univ. of Leicester, 1967–70. *Publications*: Growing Adult, 1967; The Facts of Sex, 1967; *contrib*. Programmed Learning, Brit. Jl Social and Clinical Psychol., Journalism Qly, J Personality and Social Psychol., Pedagogical

Europa, Sociological Rev. *Address*: Psychology Dept, Trinity College, Dublin 2.

Noble, Margaret, MA; Lecturer, Faculty of Laws, Queen Mary College, University of London, since 1967; *b* 1942; *m* 1968. MA Aberdeen 1964, BA Cantab 1966. Barrister (Lincoln's Inn), 1972. Asst Lectr, QMC, 1967–69. *Address*: Faculty of Laws, Queen Mary College, Mile End Road, E1 4NS.

Noble, Dr Peter Scott; Lecturer, Department of French Studies, University of Reading, since 1967; *b* 1941; *m* 1968. BA 1963, MA Cantab, PhD London 1973. Member: Letters Fac. Bd, 1970; Bd, 1972, Council, 1973, Sch. of Educn. *Publications*: *contrib.* Romania, Moyen Age, Studi Francesi, Mod. Lang. Rev. *Address*: Dept of French Studies, Reading Univ., Whiteknights, Reading RG6 2AH.

Noble, Thomas, MBE; Teacher of Wind Instruments, Department of Music, University College of Wales, Aberystwyth, since 1962; *b* 1909; *m* 1942; two *s* two *d*. ARCM 1940; Mem., Incorporated Soc. of Musicians. MBE 1960. *Address*: Univ. Coll. of Wales, Old College, Aberystwyth SY23 2AX.

Noble, Sir (Thomas Alexander) Fraser, MBE; Vice-Chancellor, University of Leicester, since 1962; *b* 1918; *m* 1945; one *s* one *d*. MA Aberdeen (1st cl. Hons Classics 1938, 1st cl. Hons Econ. Science 1940); Hon. LLD Aberdeen 1968. Entered Indian Civil Service, 1940; served in NW Frontier Province, 1941–47. Lectr in Pol. Economy, Univ. of Aberdeen, 1948–57; Sec. and Treas., Carnegie Trust for Univs of Scotland, 1957–62. Sec., Scottish Econ. Soc., 1954–58; Vice-Pres., Scottish Econ. Soc., 1962– . Chm., Probation Advisory and Trng Bd, 1962–65; Chm., Television Res. Cttee, 1963–69; Chm., Advisory Coun. on Probation and After-Care, 1965–70; Chm., Univs Coun. for Adult Educn, 1965–69; Chm., Min. of Defence Cttee for Univ. Assistance to Adult Educn in HM Forces, 1965–70; Chm., Advisory Bd, Overseas Students' Special Fund, 1967– , Fees Awards Scheme, 1968– ; Chm., Cttee of Vice-Chancellors and Principals of Univs of UK, 1970–71; Chm., UGC for Univ. of Botswana, Lesotho and Swaziland, 1974– . Mem., Academic Adv. Cttee, Univs of St Andrews and Dundee, 1964–66; Mem., E Midlands Econ. Planning Coun., 1965–68; Mem., Academic Adv. Coun. for Royal Defence Acad., 1969– ; Mem. Council, Assoc. of Commonwealth Univs, 1970– ; Mem. Exec. Cttee, Inter-Univ. Council for Higher Educn Overseas, 1972– ; Mem. Exec. Cttee, British Council, 1973– ; Mem., British Council Cttee for Commonwealth Univ. Exchange, 1973– ; Mem., US–UK Educnl Commn, 1973– . *Publications*: articles in economic jls. *Address*: Univ. of Leicester, University Road, Leicester LE1 7RH.

Noble, Trevor; Lecturer, Department of Sociological Studies, University of Sheffield, since 1966; *b* 1938; *m* 1965; one *d*. BA Nottingham 1959. Probationary Staff Tutor, Sheffield Univ. Dept of Extra-Mural Studies,

1963–64. Asst Lectr, Sheffield Univ., Dept of Sociol. Studies, 1964–66. *Publications*: *contrib.* Brit. Jl Sociol., Jl Th. Soc. Behav., Soc. Anal Th. *Address*: Dept of Sociological Studies, Univ. of Sheffield, Sheffield S10 2TN.

Nokes, Peter Lane, MA; Lecturer in Sociology, Division of Applied Social Studies, Department of Adult Education and Extra-Mural Studies, University of Leeds, since 1962; *b* 1932; *m* 1956; one *s* two *d*. BA Cambridge 1954 (2nd cl. History and Social Anthrop.), MA Cambridge 1956; Mem., Royal Inst. Philos. Mem., Sub-Cttee XIV (Gp and Comm. Wk with Offenders), Europ. Cttee on Crime Problems, Council of Europe, 1970–73. *Publications*: The Professional Task in Welfare Practice, 1967; *contrib.* Brit. Jl Criminol., Hum. Relat. *Address*: Division of Applied Social Studies, Univ. of Leeds, Leeds LS2 9JT.

Nolan, David, MA; College Lecturer in Italian, University College, Dublin, since 1965; *b* 1935; *m* 1964; two *s* one *d*. BA National Univ. of Ireland 1955, MA National Univ. of Ireland 1957. Asst, Univ. Coll., Dublin, 1956–57; Asst Lectr, Univ. Coll., Dublin, 1962–65. *Publications*: *contrib.* Forum Mod. Lang. Studies, Ital. Studies. *Address*: Dept of Italian, Univ. College, Dublin 4.

Nolan, Dr John R. M.; Lecturer, Department of Logic and Psychology, University College, Dublin, since 1967; *b* 1926. MA National Univ. of Ireland 1957, DD Rome 1956, MA Cantab 1964. Pres., Psychol Soc. Irel., Mem., Irish Philos. Assoc. Jun. Lectr, Univ. Coll., Dublin, 1959–67. Cnsltnt Psychol., Nat. Rehabilitation Bd. *Publications*: *contrib.* Studies (Dublin). *Address*: Univ. College, Dublin 4.

Norman, Prof. Albert Francis, MA, PhD; Professor of Classics, University of Hull, since 1968; *b* 1913; *m* 1939; two *s* one *d*. BA Oxon 1936 (1st cl. Hons Mods. 1934, Lit. Hum. 1936), MA Oxon 1939, PhD London 1955. Asst Lectr, Univ. Coll. of Hull, 1948–49; Lectr, Univ. Coll. (later Univ.) of Hull, 1949–60; Sen. Lectr, Univ. of Hull, 1960–67; Reader, Univ. of Hull, 1967–68. Mem., Council, Class. Assoc., 1971– ; Council, Jt Assoc. Class. Teachers, 1971– ; Chm., E Yorks Local Hist. Soc., 1968–69. *Publications*: Libanius' Autobiography, 1965; Libanius: Selected Works, vol. I (The Julianic Orations), Loeb Library, 1969; Themistius: Orationes, vol. II, 1971; *contrib.* Byzant. Zeits., Class. Philol., Class. Qly, Jl Hellenic Studies, Rhein. Mus. *Address*: Dept of Classics, Univ. of Hull, Hull HU6 7RX.

Norman, Rev. Edward Robert, MA, PhD, BD; Lecturer in Modern History, University of Cambridge, since 1967; *b* 1938. BA Cantab 1961, PhD Cantab 1964, MA Cantab 1965, BD Cantab 1967; FRHistS 1971. Fellow, Selwyn Coll., Cambridge, 1962–64; Fellow, Jesus Coll., Cambridge, 1964–71; Dean, Peterhouse, Cambridge, 1971– ; Asst Lectr, Cambridge Univ., 1965–67. *Publications*: The Catholic Church and Ireland in the Age of Rebellion, 1859–1873, 1964; The Catholic

Church and Irish Politics in the 1860's, 1965; The Conscience of the State in North America, 1967; Anti-Catholicism in Victorian England, 1968; The Early Development of Irish Society, 1969; A History of Modern Ireland, 1971. *Address*: Peterhouse, Cambridge.

Norman, John Malcolm; Senior Lecturer in Operational Research, University of Lancaster, since 1971; *b* 1934; *m* 1968; one *d*. BA Oxon 1955; MSc Birmingham 1961; PhD Manchester 1966. Res. Officer, Centre for Business Res., Univ. of Manchester, 1963–66. Lectr, Univ. of Lancaster, 1966–71. Vis. Prof., Indian Inst. of Technol., New Delhi, 1970. Foundn for Management Educn Fellow, Arthur D. Little Inc., 1966–67. *Publications*: Heuristic Procedures in Dynamic Programming, 1972; (with others) Planning University Development, 1973; Elementary Dynamic Programming, 1975; *contrib*. Higher Educn, Operational Res. Qly, Operations Res. *Address*: Operational Research Dept, Univ. of Lancaster, Lancaster LA1 4YW.

Norman, Kenneth Roy, MA; Lecturer in Indian Studies (Prakrit), Faculty of Oriental Studies, Cambridge University, since 1955; *b* 1925; *m* 1953; one *s* one *d*. BA Cantab 1949, MA Cantab 1954; FRAS. Fellow and Tutor, Downing Coll., Cambridge, 1952–64. Mem., Council, Philol Soc., 1970– . *Publications*: ed, Pāli Tipiṭakaṁ Concordance, vol. II, pts 4–9, 1963–73; Elders' Verses I, Theragāthā, 1969; Elders' Verses II, Therīgāthā, 1971; *contrib*. Bull. SOAS, Ind. Iran. Jl, Ind. Lingu., Jl Orient. Inst. (Baroda), Jl Royal Asiat. Soc., Trans Philol. Soc. *Address*: Faculty of Oriental Studies, Sidgwick Avenue, Cambridge.

Norris, Dr William Keith; Reader in Economics, Brunel University, since 1967; *b* 1940; *m* 1963; two *s*. BA Bristol 1961, MSc London 1967, PhD Brunel 1973. Conf. Sec., Royal Economic Soc., 1971– . *Publications*: (with J. Vaizey) Political Economy of Education, 1972; (with J. Vaizey) Economics of Research and Technology, 1973. *Address*: Brunel Univ., Uxbridge, Mddx UB8 3TH.

North, Geoffrey, MA; Senior Lecturer in Geography, University of Manchester, since 1969; *b* 1929; *m* 1964. BA Cambridge 1952, MA Cambridge 1956. Asst Lectr in Geog., Manchester, 1954–56; Lectr in Geog., Manchester, 1956–69. Sub-Warden, St Anselm Hall, Manchester Univ., 1956–63; Warden, St Anselm Hall, Manchester Univ., 1963–71; Adv., Central Acad. Adv. Service, Manchester Univ., 1972– ; Mem., Council, Inst. Brit. Geogrs, 1960–62; Sec., Inst. Brit. Geogrs, 1962–64. *Publications*: Great Britain: Geographical Essays, 1962, 2nd edn 1967; chapter on Geography, in, University Choice, ed Boehm, 1965; Face of the Earth (Adult Education TV Series), 1967–68; Law and the Common Market (Melland Schill Lectures: No. 1 Geographical Background), 1971; *contrib*. Geog., Geogl Jl, Geogl Mag. *Address*: Dept of Geography, The Univ., Manchester M13 9PL.

North, Dr John David; Assistant Curator, Museum of the History of Science, University of Oxford (also teaches History of Science), since 1969; *b* 1934; *m* 1957; one *s* two *d*. BA Oxford 1956, MA Oxon 1960, BSc London 1958, DPhil Oxford 1964; FRAS; Mem., Acad. Internat. Hist. des Sciences, Brit. Socs Hist. Science, Hist. Maths, Philos. Science. Nuffield Foundn Res. Fellow, Univ. of Oxford, 1963–68; Vis. Lectr, Univ. of Frankfurt, 1967; Vis. Prof., Univ. of Aarhus, 1974. Mem., Council of Elections, Acad. Internat. Hist. des Sciences, 1971– ; Vice. Pres., Brit. Soc. Hist. Science, 1971– ; Mem., Council, Brit. Soc. Hist. Science, 1963– ; Mem., Brit. Soc. Hist. Maths, 1972– . Editor, Archives internationales d'histoire des sciences, 1973– . *Publications*: The Measure of the Universe, 1965; Isaac Newton (Clarendon Biographies), 1967; Tolomeo, 1968; ed, Mid-nineteenth Century Scientists, 1969; Richard of Wallingford (forthcoming); *contrib*. Brit. Jl Hist. Sci., Brit. Jl Philos. Sci., Physis, Rev. Engl. Studies, Studium Gen. *Address*: Museum of the History of Science, Broad Street, Oxford.

North, Peter Machin; Fellow and Tutor in Juisprudence, Keble College, University of Oxford, since 1965; *b* 1936; *m* 1960; two *s* one *d*. BA Oxon 1959, BCL Oxon 1960, MA Oxon 1963. Teaching Asst, Northwestern Univ., Chicago, 1960–61; Asst Lectr, Univ. Coll. of Wales, Aberystwyth, 1961–62; Lectr, Univ. Coll. of Wales, Aberystwyth, 1962–63; Lectr, Univ. of Nottingham, 1964–65; Vis. Teacher, Univ. of Auckland, 1969. *Publications*: Asst Editor, Chitty on Contracts, 23rd edn 1968; Editor, Cheshire's Private International Law, 9th edn 1974; Occupiers' Liability, 1971; The Modern Law of Animals, 1972; *contrib*. Conveyan. (NS), Crim. Law Rev., Jl Business Law, Mod. Law Rev. *Address*: Keble College, Oxford.

North, Prof. Robert Joseph; Professor of French, University of Birmingham, since 1968; *b* 1913; *m* 1947; one *s* four *d*. BA London 1935 (1st cl. French), AKC London 1936 (non theological), DipEd London 1936, MA London 1947; Mem., MHRA, Soc. Fr. Studies, MLA, etc. Lectr, Sheffield, 1947–50; Lectr, Keele, 1950–62; Prof., Keele, 1962–68. Dep. Vice-Chancellor, Keele, 1965–68; Dean, Fac. of Arts, Birmingham, 1970–73; Pro-Vice-Chancellor, 1973– . *Publications*: Le Catholicisme dans l'œuvre de F. Mauriac, 1951; trans., M. M. Martin: The Making of France, 1952; trans., M. Duverger: Political Parties, 1954; trans, M. Duverger: French Political System, 1958; trans., M. Duverger: The Idea of Politics, 1966; ed, F. Mauriac: Le Feu sur la terre, 1962; ed, J. P. Sartre: Les Mouches, 1963; ed, Ionesco: Le Roi se meurt, 1966; *contrib*. Yrs Wk Mod. Langs. *Address*: Dept of French, Univ. of Birmingham, PO Box 363, Birmingham B15 2TT.

Northedge, Prof. Frederick Samuel, PhD; Professor of International Relations, The London School of Economics and Political Science (University of London), since 1968; *b* 1918; *m* 1939; two *s* one *d*. BSc(Econ)

London 1948 (1st cl.), PhD London 1953 (Economics). Mem., Royal Inst. Internat. Aff., Pol. Studies Assoc. Asst Lectr in International Relations, LSE, 1949–52; Lectr, LSE, 1952–60; Reader, LSE, 1960–68. Convener, Dept of Internat. Relat., LSE, 1969–73. *Publications*: British Foreign Policy: The Process of Readjustment, 1945–1961, 1962; The Troubled Giant: Britain among the Great Powers, 1916–1939, 1966; ed, The Foreign Policies of the Powers, 1968, rev. edn 1974; (with M. Donelan) International Disputes: The Political Aspects, 1971; (with M. J. Grieve) A Hundred Years of International Relations, 1971; Order and the System of International Politics, 1971; ed, The Use of Force in International Relations, 1974; *contrib*. Internat. Aff., Internat. Relat. *Address*: The London School of Economics and Political Science, Houghton Street, Aldwych, WC2A 2AE.

Norton, Alan Lewis; Senior Lecturer, Department of Local Government and Administration, University of Birmingham, since 1966; *b* 1926; *m* 1951; two *s*. BA Cantab 1951, MA Cantab 1958, MSocSc Birmingham 1965, CertEd London 1952. Sen. Res. Assoc., Birmingham, 1965–66; Ed., Local Govt Studies, 1971– . HM Overseas Civil Service (W Nigeria), 1952–60; Educn Dept, Barnsley, 1961–64. *Publications*: Local Government Administration in England and Wales (vol. 5, publics of Committee on Management of Local Government), 1967; Recent Reforms in the Management Arrangements of County Boroughs, 1969; Recent Reforms in the Management Arrangements of London Boroughs, 1969; Recent Reforms in the Management Arrangements of County Councils, 1970; Setting up the New Authorities, 1972; *contrib*. Public Admin, RIBA Jl, etc. *Address*: Dept of Local Government and Administration, Univ. of Birmingham, PO Box 363, Birmingham B15 2TT.

Norton-Smith, John; Reader, Department of English Language and Literature, Reading University, since 1969; *b* 1931; *m* 1956; one *d*. BA Haverford 1953, BA Oxon 1955, MA Oxon 1960, BLitt Oxon 1960. Sen. Demy, Magdalen Coll., Oxford, 1957–59; Lecturer: Univ. of St Andrews, 1960; Univ. of Hull, 1960–68; (Grade I), Univ. of Reading, 1968–69. Mem., Fac. Bd, Univ. of Reading, 1969–72; Tutor for Admissions, 1970–71. Gen. Editor, Medieval Authors Series, 1965– . *Publications*: John Lydgate: Poems, 1966, repr. 1968; James I of Scotland: The Kingis Quair, 1971; (with F. Janschka) Six Drawings and Six Poems, 1972; Geoffrey Chaucer, 1974; *contrib*. Crit. Qly, TLS, English Studies, Essays in Crit., Medium Ævum, RES. *Address*: Fac. of Letters, Whiteknights, Univ. of Reading, Reading, Berks RG6 2AH.

Nove, Prof. Alexander; Professor of Economics and Director of Institute of Soviet and East European Studies, University of Glasgow, since 1963; *b* 1915; *m* 1951; three *s*. BSc(Econ) London 1936. Reader, London Univ., 1958–63. Army, 1939–46; Civil Service (mainly BoT), 1947–58. *Publications*: The Soviet Economy, 1961, 3rd edn 1969; (with

J. A. Newth) The Soviet Middle East, 1965; Was Stalin Really Necessary?, 1965; Economic History of the USSR, 1969; ed (with D. M. Nuti), Socialist Economics, 1972; Efficiency Criteria for Nationalised Industries, 1973; Stalin and After (forthcoming). *Address*: Univ. of Glasgow, Glasgow G12 8RT.

Nowlan, Kevin Ingram, BSc, BE, Barrister-at-Law; Lecturer in Town Planning, University College, Dublin, since 1966; Head of the Department of Town Planning, since 1973; *b* 1910; *m* 1st 1939, 2nd 1970; three *s* two *d*. BSc National Univ. of Ireland 1932, BE National Univ. of Ireland 1932 (1st cl.); Pierce Malone Scholar; Barrister-at-Law, Kings Inns 1951. MIEI 1946, FRTPI 1947. Mem., Internat. Soc. City and Reg. Planners. Planning Off., Dublin CC, 1938–51; Dep. Planning Off., Dublin City, 1951–68; Special Adviser, Min. of Local Govt, 1962–64; Mem., Educn Cttee, RTPI; Mem., Planning and Develop. Cttee, Nat. Inst. Plan. Const. Res. *Publications*: *contrib*. Jl RTPI, Jl Inst. Eng. Irel. *Address*: Dept of Town Planning, Univ. College, Dublin 2.

Nunn, (Arthur) David; Lecturer in German, University College of North Wales, Bangor, since 1970; *b* 1940. BA London 1963; MA Wales 1973; FIL (German), 1965. Lectr and Hd of English Dept, Sprachen- und Dolmetscher-Institut, Frankfurt am Main, 1963–67; Volkswagen Foundn Res. Fellow, UCNW, Bangor, 1967–70. *Publications*: Advanced Interpreting, 1968, 1972; Politische Schlagwörter in Deutschland: eine publizistische Studie zum zeitgeschichtlichen Wortschatz seit 1945, 1974. *Address*: Univ. Coll. of North Wales, Bangor LL57 2DG.

Nurnberg, Monica Joan; Lecturer in French, University of Liverpool, since 1968; *b* 1942. BA Hons London 1963 (French). Temp. Asst Lectr in French, Aberystwyth, 1967–68. Member: Assoc. of Univ. Teachers; Soc. for French Studies. *Publications*: trans. Berlioz: L'Enfance du Christ, 1969. *Address*: Dept of French, The Univ., PO Box 147, Liverpool L69 3BX.

Nurse, Peter; *see* Hampshire, P.

Nursten, Jean Patricia; Senior Lecturer in Applied Social Studies, University of Bradford, since 1964; *b* 1927; *m* 1950. DipSS Leeds 1946, Cert. Psychiatric Social Wk Edinburgh 1950, MSocial Wk Smith 1962. AAPSW 1950–71; MBASW 1971– . Lectr (pt-time), Leeds Univ. Dept Social Studies, 1963; Lectr (pt-time), Dept Psychiatry, 1964–68. Chm., Undergrad. Sch. of Appl. Social Studies, 1966–70; Chm., Postgrad. Sch. of Appl. Social Studies, Bradford Univ., 1966–70; ext. examiner, Liverpool Univ., 1966–70, Newcastle Univ., 1973– ; Ed.-in-Chief, Appl. Social Studies, 1969–72. Psychiat. Soc. Worker, Leeds Co. Bor., 1950–52; Notts CC, 1952–54; W Riding CC, 1954–64; Jt Univ. Council (Social Wk Educn Cttee), 1966– ; Editor, Social Work Series: Authority in Social Casework, 1968; Social Work Supervision in Practice, 1969; Psychiatry for

Social Workers, 1969; Sociology and Social Work, 1970; Group Processes as a Helping Technique, 1970; Suicidal Behaviour, 1972; Communication in Social Work, 1972. *Publications*: Child Guidance, in, Annual Review of Residential Child Care Association, 1963; Unwillingly to School, 1964, 2nd edn 1968; School Refusal, in, International Trends in Mental Health, 1966; School Refusal – Revised concepts, in, Annual Review of Residential Child Care Association, 1971; Social Workers and their Clients, 1972; Process of Casework, 1973; *contrib.* Acta Psychopaed., Amer. Jl Orthopsychiat., Brit. Jl Criminol., Med. Off., Smith Coll. Studies Social Wk, Social Serv. Qly, Social Wk. *Address*: School of Applied Social Studies, The Univ., Bradford BD7 1DP.

Nussbaum, Gerald, MA; Senior Lecturer in Classics, University of Keele, since 1970; *b* 1931; *m* 1957; three *s* two *d*. BA Reading 1952 (1st cl. Greek), MA Birmingham 1955. Mem., Class. Assoc., Mem., Jt Assoc. Class. Teachers, Mem., Vergil Soc. Asst Lectr, Keele, 1957–61; Lectr, Keele, 1961–70. *Publications*: The Ten Thousand: A Study of Social Organization in Xenophon's Anabasis, 1967; tape, with booklet, Ore Sonandum: an aid to the reading of Vergil's hexameter poetry, 1972; *contrib.* Amer. Jl Philol., Arethusa, Class. Mediaev., Class. Qly, Didask., Latomus, Orpheus, Phoenix. *Address*: Dept of Classics, The Univ., Keele, Newcastle, Staffordshire ST5 5BG.

Nuti, Dr Domenico Mario; University Lecturer, Faculty of Economics, Cambridge University, since 1973; *b* 1937; *m* 1972; one *d*. Dottore in Giurisprudenza Rome 1961, PhD Cantab 1970. Fellow, Polish Acad. of Scis, Warsaw, 1962–63; Assistente, Univ. of Rome, 1965–66; Res. Fellow, King's Coll., Cambridge, 1966–69; Tutor, 1969–73; Univ. Asst Lectr, Fac. of Economics, Cambridge, 1971–73. *Publications*: (ed with Alec Nove) Socialist Economics, 1972, 2nd edn 1974; ed, V. K. Dmitriev: Economic Essays on Value, Competition and Utility, 1974; *contrib.* Critica Marxista, Econ. Jl, Ekonomista, Kyklos, Soviet Studies. *Address*: King's Coll., Cambridge.

Nuttall, Prof. Anthony David; Professor of English, School of English and American Studies, University of Sussex, since 1973 (Reader, 1970–73); *b* 1937; *m* 1960; one *s* one *d*. Class. Mods 1957, BA Oxon 1959, MA Oxon 1962, BLitt Oxon 1963. Asst Lectr, Sussex, 1962–64; Lectr, Sussex, 1964–70. *Publications*: ed, Shakespeare: The Winter's Tale, 1966; Two Concepts of Allegory, 1967; A Common Sky, 1974; *contrib.* Crit. Qly, Shakesp. Studies. *Address*: Arts Building, The Univ. of Sussex, Brighton, Sussex BN1 9QN.

Nuttall, Cedric Sinclair, BA; Senior Lecturer in Economics, Extramural Department, University of Birmingham, since 1971; *b* 1920; *m* 1963; two *s* two *d*. BA Wales 1949 (1st cl. Hist. and Econs). Lectr, Birmingham Univ., 1952–71. *Publications*: *contrib.* Bull. Soc. Co-op Studies, Co-op Mngmt Mktg, Midl. Industr. Comm. *Address*: Dept of

Extramural Studies, Univ. of Birmingham, PO Box 363, Birmingham B15 2TT.

Nuttall, Dr Geoffrey Fillingham; Lecturer in Church History, New College, London, since 1945, and Recognized Teacher, University of London, since 1949; *b* 1911; *m* 1944. MA Oxon 1936, DD Oxon 1945, Hon. DD Wales 1968. Pres., Eccles. Hist. Soc., 1972; Congregat. Hist. Soc., 1966–72, Friends Hist. Soc., 1953, United Reformed Church Hist. Soc., 1972– . Mem., Adv. Bd, Jl Eccles. Hist., 1950– . Chm., Bd Studies in Theology, 1957–59, Dean, Fac. of Theology, 1960–64, Univ. of London; Vis. Lectr, Marburg, 1949; Vis. Lectr, Bangor, 1957, 1964; Vis. Lectr, Harvard, 1957; Vis. Lectr, Aberystwyth, 1968. University Preacher, Cambridge, 1958, London, 1968, Oxford, 1972. *Publications*: The Holy Spirit in Puritan Faith and Experience, 1946; Visible Saints: The Congregational Way 1640–1660, 1957; The Welsh Saints 1640–1660, 1957; Christian Pacifism in History, 1958, 2nd edn 1972; ed, From Uniformity to Unity 1662–1962, 1962; Howel Harris 1714–1773: the last enthusiast, 1965; Richard Baxter, 1965; The Puritan Spirit: essays and addresses, 1967; The Faith of Dante Alighieri, 1969; *contrib.* Jl Eccles. Hist., Jl of Theol. Studies, Trans Congreg. Hist. Soc. *Address*: New College, London, 527 Finchley Road, NW3 7BE.

Nutton, Dr Vivian; Fellow, Dean and Praelector, Selwyn College, Cambridge, since 1968; *b* 1943; *m* 1973. MA Cantab 1969, PhD 1970. Res. Fellow, Selwyn Coll., 1967–68. *Publications*: *contrib.* Class. Qly, Jl of Roman Studies, Med. Hist. *Address*: Selwyn Coll., Cambridge.

O

Oakes, Dr Michael Buckley; Lecturer, Department of Mathematics, University of Salford (also teaches business studies), since 1967; *b* 1937. BSc Sheffield 1959, PhD Wales 1962; FRMetSoc., FRSS. Asst Lectr, Salford Royal Coll. of Adv. Technol., 1962–64; Lectr, Salford Royal Coll. of Adv. Technol., 1964–67. *Publications*: *contrib.* Jl Geophys. Res., Qly Jl Royal Meteorol Soc. *Address*: Dept of Mathematics, The Univ. of Salford, Salford M5 4WT.

Oakley, Robert John; Lecturer, Department of Spanish, University of Birmingham, since 1967; *b* 1938; *m* 1970; one *d*. BA 1962 (Fr. and Spanish), CertEd 1965, MA 1966 (by thesis, Compar. Lit.), BA 1967 (Spanish), Birmingham; Dip. in Teaching of English as a For. Lang., RSA, 1973; Member: Anglo-Brazilian Soc.; Assoc. of Hispanists; District Sec., Assoc. of Teachers of Spanish and Portuguese. Supervisor, Lang. Labs, Birmingham Univ., 1970– ; Mem., Cttee for Educnl Technol., Birmingham, 1972– . *Publication*: *contrib.* Vida Hispánica. *Address*: Spanish Dept, The Univ., Birmingham B15 2TT.

Oakley, Dr Stewart Philip, MA, PhD; Senior Lecturer, School of European Studies,

University of East Anglia, since 1973 (Lecturer, 1969–73); *b* 1931; *m* 1956; three *d.* BA Oxon 1952, MA Oxon 1956, PhD London 1961, DipEd Oxon 1953. Mem., Hist. Assoc. Tutor, Exeter Univ., 1959–60; Asst Lectr, Edinburgh Univ., 1960–62; Lectr, Edinburgh Univ., 1962–69; Vis. Prof., Univ. of Minnesota, 1966–67. *Publications:* The Story of Sweden, 1966, 2nd edn 1969, American edn 1966; The Story of Denmark, 1972. *Address:* School of European Studies, Univ. of East Anglia, Norwich NOR 88C.

Oates, John Claud Trewinard; Reader in Historical Bibliography, University Library, Cambridge, since 1972; Fellow of Darwin College, Cambridge, since 1964; *b* 1912; *m* 1960. BA Cantab 1935 (1st cl. Classical Tripos), MA Cantab 1938. Asst Under-Librarian, Cambridge Univ. Lib., 1936, Under-Librarian, 1950; Sandars Reader in Biobliography, Cambridge Univ., 1952 and 1964. Pres., Bibliographical Soc., 1970; Trustee, Laurence Sterne Trust. *Publications:* Catalogue of the Fifteenth-century Printed Books in the University Library, Cambridge, 1954; Shandyism and Sentiment 1760–1800, 1968; *contrib.* Book Collector, Library, Studies in Bibliography, Trans Camb. Bibliog. Soc. *Address:* Univ. Library, Cambridge.

Ó Baoill, Dr Colm Joseph Malachy; Lecturer in Celtic Studies, University of Aberdeen, since 1966; *b* 1938; *m* 1968; two *d.* BA Queen's Univ. Belfast 1960, MA 1962, PhD 1966. Departmental Asst, Queen's Univ. 1962; Asst Lectr, 1962–65; Actg Head of Dept, Spring Term, 1974. *Publications:* (with H. Wagner) Linguistic Atlas and Survey of Irish Dialects, vol. IV, 1969; Bàrdachd Shìlis na Ceapaich, 1972; *contrib.* Scottish Gaelic Studies, Trans of Gaelic Soc. of Inverness. *Address:* Dept of Celtic, King's Coll., Aberdeen AB9 2UB.

Obolensky, Prof. Dimitri, MA, PhD, FBA; Professor of Russian and Balkan History, University of Oxford, since 1961 and Student of Christ Church, since 1950; *b* 1918; *m* 1947. MA Cantab (1st cl. Mod. and Med. Langs Tripos Pts I and II); FSA, FRHistS; FBA 1974. Fellow, Trinity Coll., Cambridge, 1942–48, Faculty Asst Lectr, 1944; Lectr, 1945; Lectr, Cambridge Univ., 1946; Reader, Oxford Univ., 1949–61; Vis. Schol., Dumbarton Oaks, Harvard Univ., 1952 and 1964; Vis. Prof., Yale Univ., 1957; Birkbeck Lectr, Trinity Coll., Cambridge, 1961; Gen. Sec. 13th Internat. Congress of Byzantine Studies, Oxford, 1966; Vis. Prof., Univ. of California, Berkeley, 1973. *Publications:* The Bogomils: A Study in Balkan Neo-Manichaeism, 1948; ed, The Penguin Book of Russian Verse, 1962; (jtly) The Christian Centuries, vol. 2: The Middle Ages, 1969; Byzantium and the Slavs, 1971; The Byzantine Commonwealth, 1971; *contrib.* Oxford Slav. Papers, Dumbarton Oaks Papers, Slav. E European Rev., Ency. Brit., Chambers' Encyc., etc. *Address:* Christ Church, Oxford.

O'Brien, Prof. Denis Patrick; Professor of Economics, University of Durham, since 1972; *b* 1939; *m* 1961; one *s* two *d.* BScEcon London 1960, PhD Belfast 1969. Asst Lectr, Queen's Univ., Belfast, 1963–65; Lectr, 1965–69; Reader, 1969–72. *Publications:* (with D. Swann) Information, Agreements Competition and Efficiency, 1969; J. R. McCulloch, 1970; The Correspondence of Lord Overstowe, 3 vols, 1971; (jtly) Competition in British Industry, (forthcoming); J. R. McCulloch: Treatise on Taxation (forthcoming); *contrib.* Economica, Jl Industrial Economics, Scott. Jl Political Economy, Manchester Sch. *Address:* Dept of Economics, Univ. of Durham, 23–26 Old Elvet, Durham.

O'Brien, Donal Brian C.; *see* Cruise O'Brien.

O'Brien, Patrick Karl; University Lecturer in Economic History, Oxford University, since 1970; *b* 1935; *m* 1959; one *s* two *d.* BSc(Econ) London 1958, DPhil Oxford 1963. Mem., Econ. Hist. Assoc. Lectr, SOAS, London Univ., 1960–66; Reader in Economics, London Univ., 1966–70. *Publications:* The Revolution in Egypt's Economic System, 1966; Essays, in, Political and Social Change in Modern Egypt, ed P. M. Holt, 1968; ed M. Cook: Studies in the Economic History of the Middle East, 1970; *contrib.* Econ. Hist. Rev., Jl Developm. Studies, Mid. East Econ. Papers. *Address:* St Antony's College, Oxford.

O'Brien, Turlogh Patrick; Lecturer in Building Materials, School of Environmental Studies, University College, London, since 1964; *b* 1942; *m* 1967; one *d.* BSc Oxford 1964, MA Oxford 1967. Bldg Mats Advr, Ove Arup and Partners and Arup Associates, 1964– . *Publications: contrib.* Architects Jl, Building, Jl of Inst. of Struct. Engrs. *Address:* Sch. of Environmental Studies, Univ. Coll., Gower Street, WC1E 6BT.

Ó'Broin, Prof. Tomas P., BA, PhD; Professor of Modern Irish Literature, University College, Galway, National University of Ireland, since 1971; *b* 1909; *m* 1950; one *s* two *d.* BA NUI 1932 (1st cl. English and Irish) PhD NUI 1954. Asst in Irish, UC Galway, 1937–65; Lectr in Mod. Irish, UC Galway 1965–71; Rhys Res. Fellow, Univ. Oxford and Sen. Vis. Fellow, Jesus Coll., Oxford, 1972–73. Graduates' rep. on Gov. Body, UC Galway, 1949–70. Mem., Nat. Library of Ireland Soc.; Mem., Folklore of Ireland Soc. *Publications:* Scéalaí Tíre: study of a traditional storyteller, 1955; *contrib.* Béaloideas, Éigse, Feasta, Zeit. f. celt. Phil. *Address:* Dept of Modern Irish Literature, Univ. Coll., Galway.

Ó Carragáin, Éamonn; Statutory Lecturer, Department of English, University College, Cork, since 1972; *b* 1942; *m* 1973. BA NUI 1962, HDipEd NUI 1964, MA NUI 1965. Asst, TCD, 1964–66; Lectr, QUB, 1966–72. *Publications: contrib.* PRIA. *Address:* English Dept, Univ. Coll., Cork.

O'Connell, Prof. Charles S.; Professor of Geography, University College, Cork, since 1959; *b* 1908; *m* 1950; one *s.* BA, BComm UC Cork, 1928, HDip in Ed, UC Cork 1929; Dip. in Geog. London 1938; MA UC Cork

1942; Member: Geographical Soc. of Ireland; Inst. of British Geographers. UC Cork: Asst in Geog., 1940; Lectr, 1946. UC Cork: Dean, Faculty of Arts, 1971; Mem., Governing Body, 1971. *Address*: Univ. Coll., Cork.

O'Connell, Prof. Daniel Patrick, LLM, PhD, LLD; FRHistS; Chichele Professor of Public International Law, University of Oxford, since 1972; *b* 1924; *m* 1957; five *c*. BA Auckland, PhD Cantab 1951, LLD Cantab 1968. Reader in Law, 1953–62, Prof. of International Law, 1962–72, Univ. of Adelaide; Rockefeller Fellow, Europe and American Univs, 1957; Vis. Prof. of Internat. Law, Sch. of Foreign Service, Washington, 1960; Vis. Prof., Institut. des Hautes Etudes Internationales, Geneva, 1965. Rapporteur, Internat. Law Assoc. Cttee on State Succession to Treaties, 1961–72; Vice-Pres., Internat. Law Assoc., Australian Br., 1965– ; Dir of Studies, Internat. Law Assoc.; FASSA; Associé de L'Institut de Droit International, 1967; Mem., St John's Council, SA. Kt of Malta. *Publications*: Law of State Succession, 1956; International Law, 1965; State Succession in International Law and Municipal Law, 1967; Richelieu, 1968; *contrib.* various jls. *Address*: All Souls College, Oxford.

O'Connell, Dermot V.; University Lecturer in Architecture, University College, Dublin, since 1972; *b* 1937; *m* 1973. BArch 1961; MS Cornell 1965; MRIAI 1963 (Mem. Council, 1965, 1966); RIBA 1965. Coll. Lectr, UCD, 1965. *Address*: Sch. of Architecture, Univ. Coll., Dublin 4.

O'Connor, Dr Anthony Michael; Lecturer in Geography, University College, London, since 1967; *b* 1939; *m* 1963; one *s* one *d*. BA Cantab 1960 (1st cl. Geography), PhD Cantab 1963. Lectr, Makerere Univ., Kampala, 1963–67; Vis. Lectr, Univ. of Ibadan, 1967; Vis. Sen. Lectr, Univ. of Ibadan, 1972–73. *Publications*: Railways and Development in Uganda, 1965; An Economic Geography of East Africa, 1966, 2nd edn 1971; The Geography of Tropical African Development, 1971; *contrib.* E Afr. Geogl Rev., Jl Mod. Afr. Studies, Trans Inst. Brit. Geogrs. *Address*: Dept of Geography, Univ. College London, Gower Street, WC1E 6BT.

O'Connor, Brian J., MA, LLB; Lecturer in Commercial Law, University College, Dublin, since 1962; *b* 1932; *m* 1961; three *d*. BA University College Dublin 1952 (1st cl.), MA University College Dublin 1954, LLB University College Dublin 1955; Solicitor, admitted Dublin 1955. Examiner, Incor. Law Soc. Irel., Contract and Commercial Law, 1964– . Mem., Soc. Public Teachers of Law; Mem., Incorp. Law Soc. Irel. *Address*: Dept of Commercial Law, Faculty of Commerce, Univ. College, Belfield, Dublin 4.

O'Connor, Daniel John; Professor of Philosophy, University of Exeter, since 1957; *b* 1914. BA London 1936 (1st cl. Hons. Classics 1936, 1st cl. Philosophy 1944), PhD London 1940, MA Chicago 1947; Commonwealth Fund Fellow in Philosophy, Chicago, 1946–47. Pres., Mind Assoc., 1960, Pres., Aristot. Soc., 1968–69. Prof. of Philosophy,

Univ. of Natal, 1949–51; Prof. of Philosophy, Univ. of Witwatersrand, 1951–52; Lectr in Philosophy, Univ. Coll. of N Staffordshire, 1952–54; Prof. of Philosophy, Univ. of Liverpool, 1954–57; Dean of Soc. Studies, Exeter, 1959–61; Vis. apntmts: Brandeis Univ., 1959, Univ. of Pennsylvania, 1961–62. *Publications*: John Locke, 1952; (with A. H. Basson) Introduction to Symbolic Logic, 1953, 3rd edn 1959; Introduction to the Philosophy of Education, 1957; ed, A Critical History of Western Philosophy, 1964; Aquinas and Natural Law, 1967; Free Will, 1971; *contrib.* Mind, Philos., Philos. Qly, Proc. Aristot. Soc. *Address*: Dept of Philosophy, Univ. of Exeter, Exeter EX4 4QJ.

O'Connor, Dr Neil; Director and Honorary Lecturer, Medical Research Council Developmental Psychology Unit; *b* 1917; *m* 1949; one *s* one *d*. BA West Australia 1936, MA Oxon 1947, PhD London 1951. MRC first appointment 1948. *Publications*: (with J. Tizard) Social Problem of Mental Deficiency, 1956; ed, Recent Soviet Psychology, 1961; (with B. Hermelin) Speech and Thought in Severe Subnormality, 1963; ed, Present Day Russian Psychology, 1966; (with B. Hermelin) Psychological Experiments with Autistic Children, 1970; ed, Language and Cognition in the Handicapped, 1974; *contrib.* Brit. Jl Psychol., Jl Abn. soc. Psychol., Jl Ment. Def. Res., Neuropsychologia, Perception and Psychophysics, Qly Jl Exptl Psychol. *Address*: MRC Developmental Psychology Unit, Drayton House, Gordon Street, London WC1H 0AN.

O'Connor, Sylvester Patrick; Senior Lecturer, School of Management, Cranfield Institute of Technology, since 1971; *b* 1931; *m* 1963; two *s*. BA Wales (Econs). Lectr, Sch. of Management, Cranfield Inst. of Technol., 1966–71; Vis. Fellow, Univ. of Melbourne, Australia, 1974. *Address*: Sch. of Management, Cranfield Inst. of Technology, Cranfield, Bedford MK43 0AL.

Oddie, Prof. Guy Barrie, BArch, ARIBA; Robert Adam Professor and Head of Department of Architecture, University of Edinburgh, since 1968; *b* 1922; *m* 1952. BArch Newcastle 1944 (1st cl. Hons), DipTP Newcastle 1945; ARIBA 1946. Demonstrator, Univ. of Newcastle upon Tyne, 1944; Sen. Lectr, Birmingham Sch. of Architecture, 1950–52. Research architect, Building Research Station, 1947–50; Devel. Gp, Min. of Educn, 1952–58; Consultant to OECD, 1963– . *Publications*: School Building Resources and their Effective Use, 1966; Development and Economy in Educational Building, 1968; *contrib.* Architects Jl, Architectural Rev., RIBA Jl. *Address*: Dept of Architecture, The Univ. of Edinburgh, Edinburgh EH8 9YL.

Odgers, Prof. Frederick James, MA, LLB; Professor of Common Law, University of Liverpool, since 1971; *b* 1910; *m* 1938. MA, LLB Cantab 1950; Barrister-at-Law Lincoln's Inn 1946, Solicitor 1932. Fellow, Emmanuel Coll., Cambridge, 1950–65; Asst Dir of Res., Dept of Criminal Science, Cambridge, 1950–54; Univ. Lectr, Cambridge, 1954–65; Vis. Prof., Harvard Law Sch., 1959–60; Prof. of Law, Liverpool Univ., 1965–71. Mem., Law Reform Cttee, 1963–68; Ct of Crim. App. Cttee, 1964–65. *Publications*: var. publicns of Dept Crim. Science, Cambridge, 1950–55; jt Ed., Clerk and Lindsell: Torts, 1961–69; *contrib*. Camb. Law Jl, Law Qly Rev., Jl Soc. Public Teachers Law. *Address*: Faculty of Law, Univ. of Liverpool, PO Box 147, Liverpool L69 3BX.

Odling-Smee, Dr Francis John; Senior Lecturer, Department of Psychology, Brunel University, since 1972; *b* 1935; *m* 1971; one *d*. BA Hons UCL 1967, PhD UCL 1970. Royal Navy to 1960; Lectr, Brunel, 1970–72. *Address*: Dept of Psychology, Brunel Univ., Kingston Lane, Uxbridge, Mddx UB8 3TH.

O'Doherty, Rev. Prof. E. F., MA, PhD, FBPsS, MRIA; Professor of Logic and Psychology, University College, Dublin, since 1949; *b* 1918. MA National University of Ireland 1939, PhD Cantab 1945; FBPsS, FPsycholSoc. Irel., Mem., Royal Irish Acad., Mem., Ergonom. Res. Soc. Lectr in Logic and Psychology, Univ. Coll., Dublin, 1945–49. *Publications*: (with S. D. McGrath) The Priest and Mental Health, 1963; Religion and Personality Problems, 1964, Italian trans. 1965; Vocation and Formation, 1971; Consecration and Vows, 1971; Religious Psychology of the Junior School Child, 1972; Religious Formation of the Adolescent, 1972; *contrib*. Studies (Dublin), Irish Theol. Qly. *Address*: Univ. College, Dublin 4.

O'Donovan, Prof. John, MA, BLitt, DEconSc; Associate Professor of Economic Theory, Department of Political Economy, National University of Ireland, since 1965; *b* 1908; *m* 1936; one *s* five *d*. BA National Univ. of Ireland 1928 (1st cl. Economics and History), MA National Univ. of Ireland 1929, BLitt Oxon 1931 (Modern History), DEconSci 1941; MRIA 1957, Fellow Rockefeller Foundn, 1931–32. Univ. Lectr in Economic Theory, National Univ. of Ireland, 1951–65. Admin. Off., Dept of Finance, Dublin, 1933–41; Private Sec., Minister of Finance, 1941–43; Principal Off., 1943–51; Reg. Commnr, Cork and Kerry, 1950–51; Mem., Irish Parliament, 1954–61, 1969– ; Chm., Electricity Supply Bd Tribunal, 1963–68. *Publications*: The Economic History of Livestock in Ireland, 1940; *contrib*. Jl Stat. Soc. Inqu. Soc. Irel. *Address*: Dept of Political Economy, Univ. College, Dublin 4.

O'Donovan, Miss Katherine; Lecturer in Law, Faculty of Social Sciences, University of Kent, since 1973; *b* 1942; *m* 1971. BCL NUI 1963, LLM Harvard 1965. QUB, 1965–69; Haile Sellassie I Univ., Ethiopia, 1969–72; Univ. of Sussex, 1972–73. *Publications*: *contrib*. JEthL, JSPTL, NILQ. *Address*: Darwin College, Univ. of Kent, Canterbury, Kent.

Offler, Prof. Hilary Seton, MA, FBA; Professor of Medieval History, University of Durham, since 1956, and Chairman, Board of Studies in Modern History, 1965–68 and since 1971; *b* 1913; *m* 1951; two *s*. BA Cantab 1933 (1st cl. Hist. Tripos Pts I and II and Theol. Tripos Pt II); FBA 1974. Res. Fellow, Emmanuel Coll., Cambridge, 1936–40; served with RA, 1940–46, commnd 1942; Lectr, Bristol Univ., 1946; Reader, Durham Univ., 1947; Sec., Surtees Soc., 1950–66. *Publications*: (jtly) ed, Ockham: Opera politica, vol. I 1940, vol. II 1963; (with E. Bonjour and G. R. Potter) A Short History of Switzerland, 1952; ed, Ockham: Opera politica, vol. III 1956, vol. I ed. altera 1974; Medieval Historians of Durham, 1958; Durham Episcopal Charters 1071–1152, 1968; *contrib*. articles in English and foreign hist. jls. *Address*: Dept of History, Univ. of Durham, 43 North Bailey, Durham.

Offord, Malcolm Hugh; Lecturer, French Department, University of Nottingham, since 1969; *b* 1943; *m* 1967; two *s*. BA Leeds 1965, MPhil Leeds 1967. Magee UC, Londonderry, 1967; Magee UC/New Univ. of Ulster, 1968. *Publications*: *contrib*. Romania, Studia Neophilologica, Zeits für romanische Philologie. *Address*: French Dept, Univ. of Nottingham, University Park, Nottingham NG7 2RD.

O'Flaherty, Prof. Kathleen; Professor of French, National University of Ireland, University College, Cork, since 1969; *b* 1916. NUI: BA 1938, MA 1939, PhD 1943; Travelling Studentship, 1941. NUI, Cork: Asst Lectr in French, 1948; Lectr, 1953; Reader, 1968. Societaire, Société Chateaubriand, 1965; Chevalier de l'Ordre du Mérite, France. *Publications*: Voltaire: Myth and Reality, 1945, 2nd edn 1946; Paul Claudel and 'The Tidings Brought to Mary', 1948, Amer. edn 1949; The Novel in France 1945–65, 1973; *contrib*. Cahiers Chateaubriand, Irish Univ. Rev., Stud. *Address*: French Dept, Univ. Coll., Cork, Ireland.

O'Flaherty, Dr Wendy Doniger; Lecturer in the Ancient History of South Asia, Department of History, School of Oriental and African Studies, University of London, since 1968; *b* 1940; *m* 1964; one *s*. BA Radcliffe (Harvard) 1962 (*summa cum laude*), MA Harvard 1963, PhD Harvard 1968, DPhil Oxford 1973. Member: Phi Beta Kappa, 1961; RAS; Brit. Horse Soc. Teaching Fellow, Harvard, 1962. *Publications*: (with R. Gordon Wasson) Soma: Divine Mushroom of Immortality, NY 1968, 2nd edn 1972; Asceticism and Eroticism in the Mythology of Śiva, 1973; Hindu Myths (pbk) (forthcoming); *contrib*. Bull. SOAS, Hist. of Religions, JRAS, Purāna, S Asian Rev. *Address*: Sch. of Oriental and African Studies, Malet Street, WC1E 7HP.

Ogden, James; Lecturer in English, University College of Wales, Aberystwyth, since 1963; *b* 1936; *m* 1964; one *d*. BA Dunelm 1957 (1st cl. English), CertEd Manchester 1959, MA Dunelm 1962, BLitt Oxon 1962. Asst Lectr, St David's (Univ.) Coll., Lampeter, 1961–63. *Publications*: Isaac D'Israeli, 1969; *contrib*. Bradf. Antiqu., Heb. Union Coll. Ann., Keats-Shelley Bull., Notes Queries, Trivium. *Address*: Dept of English, Univ. College of Wales, Aberystwyth SY23 2AX.

Ogley, Roderick Clive; Reader in International Relations, University of Sussex, since 1972; *b* 1929; *m* 1960; two *s* one *d*. BA Oxon 1951 (1st cl. PPE), Cert. International Studies LSE 1959 (Distinction). Mem., Conflict Res. Soc., Mem., Pol. Studies Assoc. Res. Asst, Fac. of Economics and Social Studies, Univ. of Manchester, 1955–57; Sen. Res. Fellow, Dept of Pol. Economy, Univ. of Edinburgh, 1960–61; Lectr in Politics, Univ. of Aberdeen, 1961–65; Lectr in Internat. Relations, Univ. of Sussex, 1965–72; Nuffield Social Science Fellow, 1969–70; Hon. Res. Fellow, Harvard Center Internat. Affairs, 1970. Mem., Council, Conflict Res. Soc., 1964–65, 1967–69; Chm., Sussex Internat. Relat. Subject Gp, 1970–72. Editor, World Issues, 1972– . *Publications*: The United Nations: Its Political Role 1946–65, 1965; The Theory and Practice of Neutrality in the 20th Century, 1970; The United Nations and East–West Relations 1945–71, 1972; *contrib*. Internat. Relat., Peace Res. Soc. (Internat.) Papers, Ybk World Affairs. *Address*: Arts Building, Univ. of Sussex, Falmer, Sussex BN1 9QN.

O'Gorman, Dr Frank; Lecturer in Modern History, University of Manchester, since 1965; *b* 1940; *m* 1965; one *s* one *d*. BA Leeds 1962, PhD Cambridge 1965. *Publications*: The Whig Party and the French Revolution, 1967; Edmund Burke: his political philosophy, 1973; *contrib*. Chest. Archaeol. Jl, Govt Opposit., Studies Burke Times, Jl 18th Cent. Studies, Economist, History, EHR. *Address*: Dept of History, Univ. of Manchester, Manchester M13 9PL.

Ogston, Alexander George. FRS, MA, DSc; President of Trinity College, Oxford, since 1970; *b* 1911; *m* 1934; one *s* three *d*. DPhil Oxon 1936, MA Oxon 1937, DSc 1970; FRS 1955. Demonstrator, Balliol Coll., Oxford, 1933; Freedom Res. Fellow, London Hosp., 1935; Departmental Demonstrator (Biochem.), 1938; Univ. Demonstrator, Oxford, 1944; Reader in Biochemistry, Univ. of Oxford, 1955–59; Prof. of Physical Biochemistry, John Curtin Sch. of Medical Res., ANU, 1959–70. Marshall of ANU, 1961–66; Fellow and Dep. Master, Univ. House, ANU, 1961–65; Fellow, ANU, 1937; Bedford Lectr, 1950; Hon. Fellow, 1969, Balliol Coll.; Chm., Editorial Bd, Biochemical Jl, 1955–59 (Mem of Bd, 1951–55). Fellow, Australian Acad. of Science, 1962; Hon. Mem., American Soc. of Biological Chemists, 1965. *Publications*: scientific papers on physical chemistry and biochemistry. *Address*: The President's Lodging, Trinity College, Oxford OX1 3BH.

Ogus, Anthony Ian; Tutorial Fellow in Law, Mansfield College, Oxford, since 1969; *b* 1945. BA 1966, BCL 1967, MA 1969, Oxon. Asst Lectr, Univ. of Leicester, 1967–69. Professeur stagiaire, Council of Europe, 1973. *Publications*: Law of Damages, 1973; *contrib*. Cambridge Law Jl, MLR. *Address*: Mansfield Coll., Oxford OX1 3TF.

O'Hegarty, Sean; *see* Ó hÉigeartaigh, S.

Ó Héideáin, Prof. Eustás E., OP; Professor of Education, National University of Ireland,

University College, Galway, since 1968; *b* 1921. STL St Thomas, Rome, MA NUI, DPhil Inst. of Social Studies, St Thomas, Rome. Asst Lectr in Philosophy, Univ. Coll., Galway, 1956–58; Lectr, 1958–68. Member: Governing Body, Univ. Coll., Galway, 1971– ; Nat. Council for Educnl Awards, 1972– . *Publications*: National School Inspection in Ireland: The Beginnings, 1967. *Address*: National Univ. of Ireland, Univ. College, Galway.

Ó hÉigeartaigh, Seán; Lecturer, Education Department, University College, Dublin, since 1968; *b* 1931; *m* 1960; one *s* two *d*. MA University College Cork, HDipEd University College Cork. Lectr, Univ. Coll., Cork, 1953–54, 1956–57. Sec., AVM Cttee, Univ. Coll., Dublin, 1971; Mem., Council Nat. Film Inst., 1971; Mem., Lingu. Inst., Irel., 1971. *Publication*: Cama-Shiúlta, 1964. *Address*: Education Dept, Univ. College, Dublin 4.

O'Higgins, Dr James; Tutor for Graduates, since 1972, and Tutor in Modern History, since 1962, Campion Hall, Oxford. MA Oxford 1947 (Mod. Hist.), DPhil Oxford 1966. *Publications*: Anthony Collins: the man and his works, 1970; *contrib*. Jl of Theol Studies. *Address*: Campion Hall, Oxford.

O'Higgins, Dr Paul; University Lecturer in Law, Cambridge University, since 1965; Fellow, since 1959, and Tutor since 1970, Christ's College, Cambridge; *b* 1927; *m* 1952; one *s* three *d*. BA 1957, LLB 1957, MA 1960, TCD; MA 1959, PhD 1961, Cantab. Barrister, King's Inns, Dublin, 1957, and Lincoln's Inn, 1959. Hon Mem., Grotian Soc., Bureau Mem. for UK European Inst. of Social Security; Cttee Mem., Ind. Law Soc.; 1965– . Vis. Prof., Univ. of Kent at Canterbury, 1973–74. Mem., Council of Senate, Cambridge, 1973– ; Chm., Cambridge Br., Assoc. Univ. Teachers, 1971– ; Chm., Cambridge Br., Nat. Council of Civil Liberties, 1970– ; Mem., Staff Side Panel, CS Arbitration Tribunal, 1972– . *Publications*: Bibliography of Periodical Literature Relating to Irish Law, 1966, Supplement, 1974; (with B. A. Hepple) Public Employee Trade Unionism in the UK – Legal Framework, 1971; (with B. A. Hepple) Individual Employment Law, 1971; Jt Gen. Editor, Encyclopaedia of Labour Relations Law, 2 vols, 1972; Censorship in Britain, 1972; (with B. A. Hepple and J. Neeson) Bibliography of Labour Law, 1974; Civil Liberty in Britain, 1974; *contrib*. Amer. Jl of Legal Hist., Brit. Yearbook of Internat. Law, Cambridge Law Jl, Criminal Law Rev., Ind. Law Jl, Mod. Law Rev. *Address*: Christ's Coll., Cambridge.

O'Keeffe, Terence Míceal; Lecturer in Philosophy, School of Humanities, New University of Ulster, since 1970; *b* 1941; *m* 1973. BA QUB 1962, BD Maynooth 1965, Licence en Philosophie Paris 1967. New Univ. Ulster: Asst Lectr in Philosophy, 1968–70; Dean, Sch. of Humanities, 1971–74. *Address*: New Univ. of Ulster, Coleraine, Co. Derry, BT52 1SA.

Okell, John William Alan; Lecturer in Burmese, Department of South East Asia and the Islands, School of Oriental and African Studies, University of London, since 1962; *b* 1934. BA Oxon 1957 (Lit. Hum.), MA Oxon 1962. Asst Lectr, SOAS, Univ. of London, 1959–62. *Publications*: A Reference Grammar of Colloquial Burmese, 1969; A Guide to the Romanization of Burmese, 1972; *contrib*. Jl Royal Asiat. Soc., Jl Burm. Res. Soc., Lingua. *Address*: School of Oriental and African Studies, Malet Street, WC1E 7HP.

O'Kelly, Prof. Michael J., MA, DLitt, FSA, MRIA; Professor of Archaeology, University College, Cork, since 1947; *b* 1915; *m* 1945; three *d*. BA National University of Ireland 1939, MA National University of Ireland 1941, DLitt National University of Ireland 1963; FSA, MRIA. Mem., Nat. Monum. Adv. Council, 1945– ; Chm., 1966–70; Mem., Nat. Archaeol. Council; Council Mem., Cork Hist. Archaeol. Soc. *Publications*: *contrib*. Antiqu., Jl Cork Hist. Archaeol. Soc., Jl Royal Soc. Antiqu. Irel., Proc. Royal Irish Acad., etc. *Address*: Dept of Archaeology, Univ. College, Cork.

Okladek, Friederike W.; *see* Wilder-Okladek.

Olby, Robert; Lecturer in History and Philosophy of Science, Department of Philosophy, Leeds University, since 1969; *b* 1933; *m* 1962; two *s* three *d*. BSc London 1955, DPhil Oxford 1962, MA Oxford 1966; ARCS London 1955. Libr., Botany Sch., Oxford, 1962–69. *Publications*: Origins of Mendelism, 1966; Late 18th Century European Scientists, 1966; Charles Darwin, 1967; Early 19th Century European Scientists, 1967; The Path to the Double Helix, 1974; *contrib*. Ann. Sci., Brit. Jl Hist. Sci., Daed., Jl Chem. Educn, Jl Hist. Biol. *Address*: Dept of Philosophy, The Univ., Leeds LS2 9JT.

Oldfield, Derek Evelyn; Reader in English and Education, University of Sussex, since 1968; *b* 1924; *m* 1961; two *s* two *d*. CertifEd Oxon 1949 (Emergency Teacher Trng), BA London 1957 (Hons English), MA London 1964 (English). Lectr in Educn and English, Univ. Sussex, 1966–68. *Publications*: The Language of the Novel, in, Middlemarch: Critical Approaches to the Novel, ed B. Hardy, 1967, reprinted in, The Nineteenth Century Novel, ed. A. Kettle, 1972; (with Sybil Oldfield) Scenes of Clerical Life, in, Critical Essays on George Eliot, ed B. Hardy, 1970. *Address*: Univ. of Sussex, Falmer, Brighton BN1 9RH.

Oldfield, Dr Frank; Director, School of Independent Studies, University of Lancaster, since 1973; *b* 1936; *m* 1959; one *s* three *d*. BA Liverpool 1956 (1st cl. Geography), MA Liverpool 1960, PhD Leicester 1962. Lectr, Leicester, 1958–64; Lectr, Lancaster, 1964–67; Prof. of Geography, New Univ. of Ulster, 1967–72; Dep. Vice Chancellor, Univ. of Papua New Guinea, 1972–73. *Publications*: *contrib*. Adv. Sci., Antiqu., Bull. Cent. Etudes Rech. Sci. Biarritz, Geog. Ann., Jl Ecol., Mem. Proc. Manch. Lit. Philos. Soc., New Phytol., Rev. Palaeobotan. Palynol., Pollen Spores, Trans Inst. Brit. Geogrs, Proc. Linn. Soc. Lond. *Address*: School of

Independent Studies, Univ. of Lancaster, Lancaster LA1 4YW.

Oldfield, Sybil; (part-time) Lecturer in English, School of English and American Studies, University of Sussex, since 1965; *b* 1938; *m* 1961; two *s* two *d*. MA Canterbury 1959. Jun. Lectr in History, Univ. Canterbury, NZ, 1958–62; Asst Lectr in English, Univ. Sussex, 1962–65. *Publications*: (with D. E. Oldfield) Scenes of Clerical Life, in, Critical Essays on George Eliot, ed B. Hardy, 1970; Socio-Political Ideas of the English Romantics, in, A Social History of Western Literature, ed Daiches and Thorlby, 1973; (with William Lamont) Politics Religion and Literature in the 17th Century (forthcoming), *Address*: Arts Building, Univ. of Sussex, Falmer, Brighton BN1 9QN.

Oliver, Dr Francis Richard, MA, DPhil; Reader in Economic and Social Statistics, Department of Economics, University of Exeter, since 1970; *b* 1932. BA Cantab 1953, MA, DPhil Oxon 1959, DipStat Oxon 1957. Lectr in Economic and Social Statistics, Univ. of Exeter, 1958–69; Sen. Lectr, Univ. of Exeter, 1969–70. Mem., Exeter City Council, 1966–74; Mem., SW Econ. Plan. Council, 1968–73; Mem., (new) Devon County Council, 1973– . *Publications*: The Control of Hire-Purchase, 1961; What Do Statistics Show?, 1964; *contrib*. Appl. Econ., Appl. Stat., Economet., Jl Amer. Stat. Assoc., Jl Royal Stat. Soc. (A), Metroecon., Public Admin., Rev. Econ. Studies, Social Econ. Admin. *Address*: Dept of Economics, The Univ. Exeter EX4 4PU.

Oliver, Prof. Roland Anthony; Professor of the History of Africa, School of Oriental and African Studies, University of London, since 1963; *b* 1923; *m* 1947; one *d*. BA Cambridge, MA Cambridge, PhD Cambridge. Lectr, SOAS, 1948–58; Reader in African History, Univ. of London, 1958–63; Francqui Prof., Univ. of Brussels, 1961; Vis. Prof., Northwestern Univ., Illinois, 1962; Harvard Univ., 1967. Org. internat. Confs on Afr. Hist. and Archaeol., 1953–61 (Haile Sellassie Prize Trust Award, 1966); Mem., Council, Royal Afr. Soc.; Corresp. Mem., Acad. Royale des Sciences d'Outremer, Brussels. *Publications*: The Missionary Factor in East Africa, 1952; Sir Harry Johnston and the Scramble for Africa, 1957; ed, The Dawn of African History, 1961; (with J. D. Fage) A Short History of Africa, 1962; ed (with G. Mathew), A History of East Africa, 1963; (with A. E. Atmore) Africa since 1800, 1967; ed (with J. D. Fage), The Journal of African History, 1960–73. *Address*: School of Oriental and African Studies, Univ. of London, Malet Street, WC1E 7HP.

Olleson, Dr (Donald) Edward; University Lecturer in Music, Oxford University, since 1972, Fellow of Merton College, since 1970; *b* 1937; *m* 1965; two *s* one *d*. BA Oxon 1959, MA Oxon 1963, DPhil Oxon 1967. Asst Lectr, Univ. of Hull, 1962–63; Research Lectr, Christ Church, Oxford, 1963–66; Faculty Lectr, Oxford Univ., 1966–72. Mem., Council, Royal Musical Assoc., 1968– ; Mem., Exec. Cttee, 6th edn, Grove's

Dictionary, 1970– ; Editor, Royal Musical Assoc., 1967–74. *Publications*: Choral Music, in, The New Oxford History of Music, vol. 7, 1973; *contrib.* Haydn Yb., PRMA. *Address*: Faculty of Music, 32 Holywell, Oxford.

Olsson, Dr Yngve Bertil; Senior Lecturer, Department of English Language and General Linguistics, University of Newcastle upon Tyne, since 1968; *b* 1910; *m* 1st 1935, 2nd 1970; three *d*. fil mag Lund 1933, fil lic Göteborg 1951, fil dr Göteborg 1961. Lectr, Univ. Coll., London, 1951–54; Lectr, Univ. of Göteborg, 1956–62; Asst Prof., Göteborg, 1962–66; Lectr, Univ. of Newcastle, 1966–68; Vis. Prof., Brown Univ., Providence, RI, 1965–66; Vis. Prof., Hamburg Univ., 1972–73. Var. expert commns, Swedish Bd of Educn; Mem., Cttee, Nat. Assoc. Mod. Lang. Teachers (Sweden), 1956–65; Vice Pres., Nat. Assoc. Mod. Lang. Teachers (Sweden), 1963–65. *Publications*: On the Syntax of the English Verb, 1961; *contrib.* Årsbok Lär, Mod. Språk, Engl. Studies, Göt. Studies Engl., Notes Queries, Shakesp. Studies, Durham Univ. Jl. *Address*: School of English, Univ., Newcastle upon Tyne NE1 7RU.

O'Mahony, Sean F.; College Lecturer in Education, University College Dublin, since 1966; *b* 1930; *m* 1959; three *s* four *d*. BA Hons NUI 1955, Higher DipEd. NUI 1956, MA Hons NUI 1958, PhD NUI 1972; Post-Doctoral Fellow: RIA; British Acad. UCD: Asst, 1963–64; Asst Lectr, 1964–66. Secondary Teacher, 1956–63; Part-time Vocational Teacher, 1961–63. Mem., Convocation Cttee on Teacher Training, 1970. *Publications*: Múineadh an Dara Teanga, 1974; Marcáil Aistí, 1974; ed, Prós: díolaim, 1973; *contrib.* Comhar, *Address*: Dept of Education, Trinity Coll., Belfield, Dublin 4.

O'Malley, Dr John Brian; Lecturer in Social Theory, Department of Sociology, University of Liverpool, since 1966; *b* 1926; *m* 1956; two *s* two *d*. BA National University of Ireland 1949, LPhil Gregorian (Rome) 1952, PhD London 1962. Mem., Brit. Soc. Phenomenol. Existent. Philos., Philos. Educn Soc. GB. *Publications*: The Fellowship of Being, 1966; The Sociology of Meaning, 1972; contrib. Marcel, in, Library of Living Philosophers, 1972; contrib. Situating Marx, 1972; *contrib.* Hum. Cont., Philos. Studies, Philos. Forum. *Address*: Dept of Sociology, The Univ., PO Box 147, Liverpool L69 3BX.

O'Malley, Raymond Morgan; University Lecturer in Education, Cambridge University, since 1961; Fellow of Selwyn College, Cambridge, since 1972; *b* 1909; *m* 1949; two *s* one *d*. BA Cantab 1931 (1st cl. English), MA Cantab 1935, CertEd London 1932. Lectr in Education, Southampton Univ., 1959–61. *Publications*: One-Horse Farm, 1949; *contrib.* var. symposia. *Address*: Cambridge Univ., Dept of Education, 17 Brookside, Cambridge.

O'Meara, Prof. John Joseph, MA, DPhil; Professor of Latin, University College, Dublin, since 1948; *b* 1915; *m* 1947; one *s* two *d*. BA National University of Ireland 1938 (1st cl. Classics), MA National University of Ireland 1939 (1st cl. Classics), DPhil Oxon 1945; Mem., Royal Irish Acad., 1953. Asst, Classics Dept, Univ. Coll., Dublin, 1945–48. Vice-Pres., Royal Irish Acad., 1967; Mem., Gov. Body, Univ. Coll., Dublin, 1956–59, 1962–65; Mem., Senate, Nat. Univ. of Irel., 1964–73. *Publications*: ed, St Augustine: Against the Academics, 1950; ed, G. Cambrensis: Topography of Ireland, 1951; ed, Origen: On Prayer and Exhortation to Martyrdom, 1954; The Young Augustine: The Growth of St Augustine's Mind up to his Conversion, 1954, US edn 1964; Porphyry's Philosophy from Oracles in St Augustine, 1959; Charter of Christendom: the Significance of St Augustine's City of God, 1962; Eriugena, 1969; ed (with L. Bieler), The Wind of Eriugena, 1973; *contrib.* Arethusa, August. (Madrid), Domin. Studies, Irish Eccles. Rec., Irish Theol. Qly, Rev. Internat. Philos., Vig. Christ. *Address*: Dept of Latin, Univ. College, Dublin 4.

Ó Murchú, Prof. Máirtín; Professor of Irish, Trinity College, Dublin, since 1971; *b* 1936; *m* 1963; one *s* one *d*. BA NUI 1959, MA NUI 1961, NUI travelling studentship 1961–64. Asst Lectr, Ling. Survey of Scotland, Univ. of Edinburgh, 1964–65; Asst Lectr in Irish, Univ. Coll., Cork, 1965–67. Statutory Lectr in Irish and Linguistics, 1967–71. Mem., Council, Linguistic Inst. of Ireland, 1968–71. *Publications*: Language and Community. Urlabhra agus Pobal, 1971; *contrib.* Ériu, Lochlann, Studia Hibernica. *Address*: Trinity College, Dublin 2.

O'Neill, Prof. Patrick Geoffrey, BA, PhD; Professsor of Japanese, University of London, since 1968; *b* 1924; *m* 1951; one *d*. Lectr, Sch. of Oriental and African Studies, London Univ., 1949. *Publications*: A Guide to Nō, 1954; Early Nō Drama, 1958; (with S. Yanada) Introduction to Written Japanese, 1963; A Programmed Course on Respect Language in Modern Japanese, 1966; Japanese Kana Workbook, 1967; A Programmed Introduction to Literary-style Japanese, 1968; Japanese Names, 1972; Essential Kanji, 1973. *Address*: School of Oriental and African Studies, Malet Street, WC1E 7HP.

O'Neill, Thomas Patrick; Lecturer, Department of History, National University of Ireland at University College, Galway, since 1967; *b* 1921; *m* 1st 1948, 2nd 1965; three *s* three *d*. BA NUI 1943, MA NUI 1946; Fellow, Library Assoc. of Ireland, 1954. National Library of Ireland: Asst Librarian, 1948–52; Asst Keeper of Printed Books, 1952–67; Sec., Bibliographical Soc. of Ireland, 1949–52. *Publications*: Sources of Irish Local History, 1958; British Parliamentary Papers, 1967; James Fintan Lalor (biography, in Irish), 1962; Eamon de Valera (in Irish): vol. I, 1968, vol. II 1970; Eamon de Valera (with the Earl of Longford), 1970; ed, Private Sessions of Dáil Éireann 1921–1922, 1972; *contrib.* Irish Hist. Stud., Stud., Encyc. Amer., etc. *Address*: History Dept, Univ. Coll., Galway.

O'Neill, Tom; Lecturer, Department of Italian, Trinity College, Dublin, since 1972;

526

b 1942. MA Glasgow 1966 (French and Italian). Member: Soc. for Italian Studies; Amer. Assoc. of Teachers of Italian. Aberdeen University: Asst Lectr, 1966–68; Lectr, 1968–72; Vis. Lectr in Romance Languages, Queens Coll., City Univ. of NY, 1970–71. *Publications:* ed, Carlo Cassola: Il taglio del bosco, 1970; contrib., 2nd edn Columbia Dictionary of Modern European Literature; *contrib.* jls in Italy, USA, GB, Eire. *Address:* Dept of Italian, Trinity College, Dublin 2.

Onians, John Browning; Lecturer, School of Fine Arts and Music, University of East Anglia, since 1971; *b* 1942; *m* 1968; one *s* one *d*. BA Cambridge 1963 (Classics), Dip. History of European Art London 1965; Junior Fellow, Warburg Inst., London, 1965–67; Asst Prof., Univ. of Syracuse, NY, 1968–70; Wetenschappelijk Ambtenaar, Rijksuniversiteit Amsterdam, Holland, 1970. *Publications: contrib.* Art. Lomb., JWCI. *Address:* School of Fine Arts, Univ. of East Anglia, Earlham Hall, Norwich NOR 88C.

Opie, Roger Gilbert; Fellow and Lecturer in Economics, New College, University of Oxford, since 1961, and Special University Lecturer in Economics, since 1970; *b* 1927; *m* 1955; two *s* one *d*. MA Adelaide 1950, BA Oxon 1953 (1st cl. PPE), BPhil Oxon 1954, MA Oxon 1961. Asst Lectr, LSE, 1954–57; Lectr, LSE, 1957–61. Asst Dir, Planning Div., Dept Econ. Aff., 1964–66; Econ. Adv. to Chm. Nat. Bd Prices and Incomes, 1967–70; Mem., Monopolies Commn, 1968– . *Publications:* contrib. Causes of Crime, ed Lord Pakenham, 1968; Banking in Western Europe, ed R. S. Sayers, 1962; Sanctions against South Africa, ed R. Segal, 1964; Economic Growth in Britain, ed P. D. Henderson, 1966; Unfashionable Economics, ed P. P. Streeten, 1970; The Labour Government's Economic Record 1964–70, ed W. Beckerman, 1972. *Address:* New College, Oxford.

Oppenheim, Dr Abraham Naftali, BA, PhD; Reader in Social Psychology, University of London, since 1965; *b* 1924; *m* 1951. BA Hons Melbourne 1949 (Psychology), PhD London 1956 (Psychology); FBPsS, Mem., Inst. for Strategic Studies. Tutor, Univ. of Melbourne, 1948–49; Res. Asst, Hebrew Univ., Jerusalem, 1950; Res. Asst, Inst. of Psychiatry, Univ. of London, 1951; Res. Asst, LSE, 1952; Asst Lectr, LSE, 1952–55; Lectr, LSE, 1955–64, Sen. Lectr, LSE, 1964–65. Various internat. consultancies, incl. WHO and UNESCO. *Publications:* The Function and Training of Mental Nurses, 1955; Questionnaire Design and Attitude Measurement, 1966; (with H. T. Himmelweit and P. Vince) Television and the Child, 1958; (with M. Shepherd and S. Mitchell) Childhood Behaviour and Mental Health, 1971; (with J. V. Torney) The Measurement of Civic Attitudes in Children of Different Nations, 1974; *contrib.* Yearbook World Affs., Brit. Jl Sociology, Brit. Med. Jl. *Address:* London School of Economics, Houghton Street, WC2A 2AE.

Oppenheim, Felix W.; *see* Wedgwood-Oppenheim.

Oppenheimer, Peter Morris, MA; Student and Tutor in Economics, Christ Church, Oxford University, since 1967; *b* 1938; *m* 1964; two *s* one *d*. BA Oxon 1961 (1st cl. PPE), MA Oxon 1967. Res. Fellow, Nuffield Coll., 1964–67. *Publications: contrib.* Bull. Oxf. Univ. Inst. Econ. Stat., Jl Mon. Cred. Bank., Scott. Jl Pol. Econ., misc. Bank Revs and symposia. *Address:* Christ Church, Oxford OX1 1DP.

Ord, Henry Wilson, MA; Senior Lecturer in Economics and African Studies, University of Edinburgh, since 1971; *b* 1928; *m* 1960. BA Cantab 1952, MA Cantab 1958. Sen. Res. Fellow, E African Inst. of Soc. Res., Makerere Univ., Uganda, 1958–60; Sen. Res. Fellow, Univ. of Edinburgh, 1961–62; Lecturer in Economics, 1962–71; Vis. Prof., Makerere Univ., 1965. Chief Economist, Govt of Malawi, 1967–70. *Publications:* (with I. Livingstone) An Introduction to Economics for East Africa, 1968; (with I. Livingstone) An Introduction to West African Economics, 1969; ed (with I. G. Stewart), African Primary Products and International Trade, 1965. *Address:* Centre of African Studies, Univ. of Edinburgh, Edinburgh EH8 9YL.

O'Riordan, William Kenneth, PhD; Lecturer, Department of Political Economy, University College, Dublin, since 1969; *b* 1933. National University of Ireland: BA 1953, DipEd 1954, BComm 1957, MEconSc 1959, PhD 1964. Asst Lectr, Univ. Coll., Dublin, 1966–69. *Publications:* Economics at Work, 1970,¹2nd edn 1971; *contrib.* Econ. Soc. Rev. *Address:* Dept of Economics, Univ. College, Belfield, Dublin 4.

Orme, Dr John Edward, BA, PhD, FBPsS; Honorary Lecturer in Psychology, University of Sheffield, since 1963; *b* 1927; *m* 1952; one *s* two *d*. BA Manchester 1951 (1st cl. Psychology), PhD Sheffield 1963; FBPsS. Ch. Psychol., Sheffield Area Psychol. Service. *Publications:* Time, Experience and Behaviour, 1969; An Introduction to Abnormal Psychology, 1971; (with F. G. Spear) Psychology in Medicine, 1971; *contrib.* Brit. Jl Psychiat., Brit. Jl Psychol., Nature. *Address:* Dept of Psychology, Middlewood Hosp., Sheffield.

Orme, N. I.; Lecturer in History, Department of History, University of Exeter, since 1965; *b* 1941. MA Oxon 1966, DPhil Oxon 1969; FRHistS. *Publication:* English Schools in the Middle Ages, 1973. *Address:* Dept of History, The Queen's Building, Univ. of Exeter, Exeter EX4 4QH.

Ormerod, Milton Blackburn; Lecturer in Chemistry Method since 1967, Senior Lecturer in Education, since 1973, and Research Tutor since 1970, Department of Education, Brunel University; *b* 1922; *m* 1947; three *s*. BSc Hons Manchester 1942 (II; Chemistry), Dip. in Advanced Studies in Educn Manchester 1967 (with distinction); FRIC 1963. Lectr in Chemistry Method, Dept of Educn, Brunel Univ., 1967–73. Chm., Non-specialist Science Panel, CLEAPSE, 1973– . *Publications:* The Architecture and Properties of Matter: An Approach through Models, 1970;

PEEL Models, 1969, 1972; The Architecture and Properties of Matter: a series of filmstrips, 1st edn 1970, 2nd edn 1973; *contrib.* Chem. Brit., Educ. Chem., Sch. Sci. Rev. *Address*: Brunel Univ., Kingston Lane, Uxbridge, Mddx UB8 3PH.

Ormond, Leonée; Lecturer, Department of English, King's College, University of London, since 1968; *b* 1940; *m* 1963; one *s*. BA Oxford 1962, MA Birmingham 1965. Asst Lectr in English, KCL, 1965–68. *Publications*: George Du Maurier, 1969; (jtly) Meredith Today, 1971; (jtly) Writers and their Background: Robert Browning, 1974; *contrib.* Colby Coll. Jl. *Address*: Univ. of London King's Coll., Strand, WC2R 2LS.

Orr, Prof. Robin, (Robert Kemsley Orr), CBE; Professor of Music, University of Cambridge and Fellow of St John's College, since 1965; *b* 1909; *m* 1937; one *s* two *d*. BA MusB 1932, MA 1938 and MusD 1951, Cambridge; Hon DMus Glasgow 1972; FRCM 1965, Hon RAM 1966; Member: Royal Musical Assoc.; Incorporated Soc. of Musicians; Performing Right Soc.; Composers' Guild of GB. Asst Lectr, Univ. of Leeds, 1936–38; Organist and Dir of Studies in Music, 1938–51 and Fellow, 1948–56, St John's Coll., Cambridge; also Univ. Lectr, Cambridge, 1947–56; Prof. at RCM, 1950–56; Prof. of Music, Univ. of Glasgow, 1956–65. RAF, 1941–45. Chm., Scottish Opera, 1962– ; Trustee, Carl Rosa Opera, 1954–59; Trustee and Dir, Arts Theatre, Cambridge. *Publications*: include: Sonata for viola and piano, 1947; Oedipus at Colonus (Cambridge Univ. Greek Play), 1950; Festival Te Deum, 1950; Spring Cantata, 1955; Rhapsody for strings, 1961; Symphony in one movement, 1963; Full Circle (opera), 1967; From the Book of Philip Sparrow, 1969; Journeys and Places, 1971; Symphony No 2, 1971. *Address*: Univ. Music Sch., Downing Place, Cambridge CB2 3EL.

Orr-Ewing, John Eric Hugh, MBE, MC, MA; Registrar, Wye College, University of London, since 1966; *b* 1920; *m* 1950; two *d*. BA Cantab 1948, MA 1951. Governor, Writtle Agricultural Coll., Chelmsford, 1973– . *Address*: Wye College, Ashford, Kent TN25 2AH.

Orton, Richard Henry; Lecturer in Music, University of York, since 1967; *b* 1940; *m* 1961; two *s* one *d*. Assoc. Birmingham Sch. Music 1960, BA Cantab 1964, Mus B Cantab 1965, MA Cantab 1967. *Publications*: Four Part-Songs, 1967; Cycle for 2 or 4 Players, 1970; Kiss, 1974; For the time being, 1974; Clock Farm, 1974. *Address*: Lyons Concert Hall, Univ. of York, Heslington, York.

Osborn, Jane Mary, BPhil, MA; Fellow and Tutor in Philosophy, Lady Margaret Hall, Oxford, since 1966, and CUF Lecturer in Philosophy, Oxford University, since 1967; *b* 1940. BA Oxon 1963 (Lit. Hum.), BPhil Oxon 1965 (Philos.), MA Oxon 1966.

528

Asst Lectr, Leeds Univ., 1965–66. *Address*: Lady Margaret Hall, Oxford.

Osborn, Robert; Lecturer in English, University of Lancaster, since 1969; *b* 1944; *m* 1967; one step-*s* one step-*d*. BA Oxon 1965 (2nd cl. Hons English), MA and BLitt Oxon 1970. Associate in English, Columbia Univ. (Columbia Coll.), 1967–68, Vis. Asst Prof., 1968–69; Vis. Asst Prof., Columbia Sch. of Gen. Studies, 1971. *Publications*: Meaningful Obscurity: the Character and Antecedents of Rivers, in Bicentenary Wordsworth Studies, ed Jonathan Wordsworth, 1970; ed. Wordsworth: The Borderers (forthcoming). *Address*: English Dept, Lancaster Univ., Bailrigg, Lancaster LA1 4YW.

Osborne, Dr John; Lecturer in German, School of European Studies, University of Sussex, since 1968; *b* 1938; *m* 1962; two *d*. BA Wales 1962, PhD Cambridge 1966; Mem. Cttee, Gerhart-Hauptmann-Gesellschaft, 1973– ; Mem., Brit. Soc 18th Cent Studies. Lecturer in German, Univ. of Southampton, 1965–68; Res. Fellowship, Alexander von Humboldt-Stiftung, 1972–73. *Publications*: The Naturalist Drama in Germany, 1971; *contrib.* Germ. Life Lett., Mod. Lang. Rev., Pubns Engl. Goethe Soc., Oxford German Studies, Seminar. *Address*: School of European Studies, Univ. of Sussex, Falmer, Brighton, Sussex BN1 9QN.

Osborne, Michael John, MA; Lecturer in Classics, University of Lancaster, since 1966; *b* 1942; *m* 1962. BA Oxon 1965 (1st cl. Lit. Hum.), MA Oxon 1967. Asst Lecturer in Classics, Bristol Univ., 1965–66; Mem., Brit. Sch. Archaeol. Athens, 1966– ; Brit. Acad. Vis. Fellow, Univ. of Munich, 1973; Vis. Prof., Univ. of Oslo, 1973; Mem. Council, Hellenic Soc., 1973– . *Publications*: *contrib.* Ann. Brit. Sch. Archaeol. Athens, Historia, Hermes, Zeits. für Papyrologie und Epigraphik, Eranos, Ancient Soc., Grazer Beiträge. *Address*: Dept of Classics, Univ. of Lancaster, Bailrigg, Lancaster LA1 4YW.

Osborne, Prof. Richard Horsley, BSc(Econ), PhD; Professor of Economic Geography, University of Nottingham, since 1967; *b* 1925. BSc(Econ) London 1950 (1st cl.), PhD London 1954. Mem., Inst. British Geographers, Mem., Internat. Inst. Scientific Study of Population, Hon. Mem., Hungarian Geogr. Soc. Lectr, Univ. of Edinburgh, 1952–59; Lectr, subsequently Sen. Lectr and Reader, Univ. of Nottingham, 1959–67. Chm., East Midland Br., Regional Studies Assoc., 1966–72; Mem., Governing Body, Bishop Lonsdale Coll. of Educn, Derby; Editor, 'East Midland Geographer'. *Publications*: Eastcentral Europe, 1967; (jtly) Proc. of 3rd and 4th Anglo-Polish Geographical Seminars, 1970 and 1972; (jtly) Geographical essays in honour of K. C. Edwards, 1970; *contrib.* Advancement of Science, East Midland Geographer, Scottish Studies, Geography. *Address*: Dept of Geography, The Univ., Nottingham NG7 2RD.

Oschinsky, Dorothea, DPhil, PhD; Reader in Medieval History, University of Liverpool, since 1972; *b* 1910. DPhil Breslau 1936, PhD

London 1941; FRHistS. Asst Lectr, Liverpool, 1946–50; Lectr, Liverpool, 1950–65; Sen. Lectr, Liverpool, 1965–72. *Publications*: Walter of Henley, 1971; *contrib.* Econ. Hist. Rev. *Address*: School of History, Univ. of Liverpool, Liverpool L69 3BX.

Osmaston, Dr Henry Arthur; Lecturer in Geography, University of Bristol, since 1965; *b* 1922; *m* 1948; one *s* three *d.* BA Oxon 1945 (Forestry), MA Oxon 1947, BSc Oxon 1958, DPhil Oxon 1965; FLS, FRGS. Army (DADME), 1943–47; Uganda Forest Dept (HM Overseas Service), 1949–63. *Publications*: Working Plan for the Kibale and Itwara Forests, 1959; The Vegetation of Uganda and its bearing on land use, 1964; Guide to the Ruwenzori, 1972; *contrib.* Comm. For. Rev., Uganda Jl. *Address*: Dept of Geography, Univ. of Bristol, Bristol BS8 1TH.

Ostergaard, Geoffrey Nielsen; Senior Lecturer in Political Science, University of Birmingham, since 1965; *b* 1926; *m* 1948; one *s.* BA Oxford 1950 (1st cl. PPE), MA, DPhil Oxford 1953. Res. Fellow, Nottingham Univ., 1952–53; Asst Lectr in Government, Birmingham Univ., 1953–55; Lectr in Political Science, Birmingham Univ., 1955–65; Rockefeller Foundn Fellow, Univ. of California, Berkeley, 1958–59; Vis. Prof., Osmania Univ., Hyderabad, 1962–65. Mem., Bd of Fac. of Commerce and Social Science, Birmingham, 1955–62, 1965–68, 1971– ; Acting Hd, Dept of Pol. Science, 1965–66; Asst Examiner, London Univ. Schs Exam. Bd, 1955–62; Examiner and Awarder in Politics, Oxford and Cambridge Schs Exam. Bd, 1960–62; Mem., Adv. Bd, Internat. Arch. Sociol. Co-op., 1957–70. *Publications*: (with A. H. Halsey) Power in Co-operatives, 1965; (with M. Currell) The Gentle Anarchists: a study of the leaders of the Sarvodaya movement for non-violent revolution in India, 1971; Democracy in India, in, Dilemmas of Democratic Politics in India, ed G. S. Halappa, 1966; (with A. H. Halsey) Power in Co-operatives, in, Studies in British Society, ed J. A. Banks; Indian Anarchism, in, Anarchism Today, ed D. Apter and J. Joll, 1971; var. pamphlets; *contrib.* Agenda, Appl. Econ. Papers, Banker, Co-op. Yrbk, Ind. Jl Pol. Sci., Internat. Arch. Sociol. Co-op., Pol. Studies. *Address*: Dept of Political Science, Univ. of Birmingham, PO Box 363, Birmingham B15 2TT.

O'Sullivan, Prof. Patrick Edmund, BSc, PhD; Professor of Architectural Science, the Welsh School of Architecture, University of Wales Institute of Science and Technology, since 1970; *b* 1937; *m* 1964; three *s* one *d.* BSc Leeds 1960, PhD Dunelm 1963. Post-Doct. Res. Fellow, Newcastle, 1963–64; Warden, Gurney Hse, Newcastle, 1963–70; Res. Asst, Newcastle, 1964–66; Lectr, Newcastle, 1966–70; Vis. Lectr, Univ. Coll., Dublin, 1967–70; Sen. Lectr, Newcastle, 1970; Vis. Prof., Univ. Coll., Dublin, 1970– . Mem., Res. Cttee, RIBA, 1968– ; Mem., Editorial Bd, ART, 1970– ; Moderator and Chief Examiner in Archit. Sci., RIBA, 1969– ; Mem., Bd of Educn, RIBA, 1973– ; Mem., CNAA Architecture Panel, 1971– .

Publications: Insulation and Fenestration, 1967; Building Acoustics, 1971; *contrib.* Archit. Res. Teaching, Instn Mech. Eng. Jl, Instn Heat. Vent. Eng. Jl, RIBA Jl. *Address*: The Welsh School of Architecture, Univ. of Wales Institute of Science and Technology, King Edward VII Avenue, Cardiff CF1 3NU.

Otley, Dr Christopher Blackwood; Lecturer in Sociology, Department of Sociology, University of Lancaster, since 1970; *b* 1938; *m* 1965. BA Hull 1959 (2nd cl. Sociol./Psychol.), PhD Hull 1965 (Sociology). Asst Lectr, then Lectr in Sociol., Univ. of Sheffield, 1965–70. *Publications*: *contrib.* Armed Forces and Society, ed J. Van Doorn, 1968; *contrib.* New Soc., Sociol Rev., Soc. *Address*: Dept of Sociology, The Univ., Bailrigg, Lancaster LA1 4YW.

Otway-Ruthven, Prof. Annette Jocelyn, MA, PhD; Lecky Professor of History, Department of Medieval History, University of Dublin, since 1951; *b* 1909. BA Dublin 1931 (1st cl. History), PhD Cantab 1937, MA Dublin 1940; FRHistS, MRIA. Mem., Internat. Commn, History of Representative and Parly Instns. Lectr, TCD, 1938–51; Fellow, TCD, 1968; Dean, Fac. of Arts (Humanities), Univ. of Dublin, 1969–73; Pro-Dean, Fac. of Arts (Letters), 1969–71. Mem., Irish Hist. MSS Commn, 1943– . *Publications*: The King's Secretary and the Signet Office in the Fifteenth Century, 1939; (with C. MacNeill) The Dowdall Deeds, 1960; A History of Medieval Ireland, 1968; *contrib.* Irish Hist. Studies, Jl Royal Soc. Antiqu. Irel., Proc. Royal Irish Acad., Trans Royal Hist. Soc. *Address*: 26 Trinity College, Dublin.

Ouston, Dr Philip Anfield, MA, PhD; Senior Lecturer in French, University of St Andrews, since 1965; *b* 1923; *m* 1950; one *s* three *d.* BA London 1948 (French), MA London 1950, PhD London 1964. Lectr, Univ. Coll. Dundee, 1950–53; Lectr, Univ. of St Andrews, 1954–65; Vis. Prof., Univ. of British Columbia, 1969. *Publications*: France in the Twentieth Century, 1972; The Imagination of Maurice Barrès, 1974; *contrib.* Forum Mod. Lang. Soc. *Address*: Buchanan Building, St Andrews, Fife.

Outhwaite, Richard Brian; Senior Lecturer in Economic History, University of Leicester, since 1973 (Lecturer, 1962–73); *b* 1935; *m* 1959; two *s.* BA Nottingham 1958 (1st cl.), PhD Nottingham 1964; FRHistS 1971. Temp. Lectr, Univ. of Manchester, 1961–62. Mem., Council, Econ. Hist. Soc., 1971– ; Mem., Humanities Bd, CNAA, 1974– . *Publications*: Inflation in Tudor and Early Stuart England, 1969; *contrib.* Bull. Inst. Hist. Res., Econ. Hist. Rev., EHR, Hist. Soc., Trans RHistS. *Address*: Dept of Economic History, Univ. of Leicester, Leicester LE1 7RH.

Ovendale, Dr Ritchie; Lecturer, Department of International Politics, University College of Wales, Aberystwyth, since 1968; *b* 1944. BA Natal 1963 (1st cl.), BA Hons Natal 1964 (1st cl.), MA Natal 1966, MA McMaster 1966 (1st cl.), DPhil Oxon 1972.

Address: Dept of International Politics, Univ. Coll. of Wales, Aberystwyth SY23 3DB.

Owen, Prof. Douglas David Roy; Professor of French, University of St Andrews, since 1972; *b* 1922; *m* 1954; two *s*. BA Cantab 1948, MA Cantab 1953, PhD Cantab 1955; Mem., Soc. French Studies, MHRA, Internat. Arthurian Soc., Soc. Rencesvals. Lectr, Univ. of St Andrews, 1951–64, Sen. Lectr, 1964–71, Reader, 1971–72. Ed., Forum Mod. Lang. Studies, 1965– . *Publications*: (with R. C. Johnston) Fabliaux, 1957; The Evolution of the Grail Legend, 1968; The Vision of Hell, 1970; The Legend of Roland, 1973; ed, Arthurian Romance: Seven Essays, 1970; (with R. C. Johnston) Two Old French Gauvain Romances, 1972; trans, The Song of Roland, 1972; *contrib*. Cah. Civilis. Méd., Forum Mod. Lang. Studies, Fr. Studies, Romania, Rom. Philol., Specul., Studies Voltaire 18th Cent., StFr., Zeits. Rom. Philol. *Address*: Dept of French, Univ. of St Andrews, Fife KY16 9AJ.

Owen, Edward Roger John, BA, MA, DPhil; Lecturer in the Recent Economic History of the Middle East, Faculty of Social Studies, Oxford University, since 1964, and Fellow of St Antony's College, since 1968; *b* 1935; *m* 1960; one *d*. BA Oxon 1959 (PPE), MA, DPhil Oxon 1965. Res. Asst, PEP, London, 1960; Res. Fellow, St Antony's Coll., Oxford, 1964–68. *Publications*: Cotton and the Egyptian Economy 1820–1914: A study in trade and development, 1969; ed (with R. B. Sutcliffe), Studies in the Theory of Imperialism, 1972; *contrib*. Midd. East. Studies. *Address*: St Antony's College, Oxford.

Owen, Prof. Gwilym Ellis Lane, FBA; Laurence Professor of Ancient Philosophy, University of Cambridge, since 1973; *b* 1922; *m* 1947; two *s*. MA Oxon 1949, BPhil Oxon 1950; FBA 1969. Res. Fellow in Arts, Univ. of Durham, 1950–53; Lectr in Ancient Philos., Univ. of Oxford, 1953–57; Reader, Univ. of Oxford, 1957–63; Fellow, Corpus Christi Coll., Oxford, 1958; Prof. of Ancient Philos., Univ. of Oxford, 1963–66; Victor S. Thomas Prof. of Philos. and the Classics, Harvard Univ., 1966–73; Vis. Prof. of Philos., Pennsylvania, 1956; Vis. Prof. of Philos., Harvard, 1959; Vis. Prof. of Philos., California, 1964. *Publications*: ed (with I. Düring), Aristotle and Plato in the Mid-Fourth Century, 1960; articles in various collections; *contrib*. Classical Qly, Proc. Aristotelian Soc. *Address*: Univ. of Cambridge.

Owen, Noel Francis Calthrop; Lecturer, Department of Russian Language and Literature, Birmingham University, since 1963; *b* 1937. MA Edinburgh 1960 (Russian with German). *Publications*: trans. (with A. S. C. Ross) I. I. Revzin: Models of Language, 1966. *Address*: Dept of Russian Language and Literature, Univ. of Birmingham, PO Box 363, Birmingham B15 2TT.

Owen Smith, Eric; Senior Lecturer in Economics, Loughborough University of Technology, since 1973 (Lecturer, 1966–73); *b* 1934; *m* 1964; one *s* one *d*. BA(Econ)

Sheffield 1964, PhD Loughborough 1972. Study leave, Mannheim Univ., 1974. Mem., Ed. Bd, Indust. Relat. Jl, 1970– . *Publications*: ed (with B. J. McCormick), The Labour Market, 1969; Productivity Bargaining – a case study in the steel industry, 1971; *contrib*. Indust. Relat. Jl. *Address*: Loughborough Univ. of Technology, Loughborough LE11 3TU.

Oxley, Dr Brian Tony; Lecturer in Literature, School of Social Sciences, University of Bradford, since 1963; *b* 1929; *m* 1952; one *s* two *d*. BA Manchester 1950 (1st cl. Eng. Lang. and Lit.), MA Manchester 1951, PhD Manchester 1953, CertEd Leeds 1956. *Publications*: (with K. H. Grose) Shakespeare, 1965; George Orwell, 1967. *Address*: School of Social Sciences, Wardley House, Univ. of Bradford, Bradford.

P

Packer, Rev. James Innell, MA, DPhil; Associate Principal, Trinity College, University of Bristol, since 1972; *b* 1926; *m* 1954; one *s* two *d*. BA Oxon 1948 (1st cl. Class. Mods, 2nd cl. Lit. Hum.), 1950 (1st cl. Theology), MA, DPhil Oxon 1954. Recognized Teacher of Theology, Bristol Univ., 1955–61, 1970– ; Tutor, Tyndale Hall, Bristol, 1955–60; Warden, Latimer Hse, Oxford, 1961–69; Principal, Tyndale Hall, 1970–71. Mem., Council, Latimer Hse, 1969– ; C of E Evang. Council, 1961– ; Archbps' Commn on Christian Doctrine, 1966– . *Publications*: Fundamentalism and the Word of God, 1958, Chinese edn 1963; trans. and ed (with O. R. Johnston), Luther's Bondage of the Will, 1958; Evangelism and the Sovereignty of God, 1961, German edn 1964, Portuguese edn 1966; God has Spoken, 1965; (with A. M. Stibbs) The Spirit Within You, 1967; (with C. O. Buchanan etc.) Growing into Union, 1970; Knowing God, 1972; ed, Eucharistic Sacrifice, 1962; All in Each Place, 1965; Guidelines, 1967; Fellowship in the Gospel, 1968; Focus on Leviathan, 1973, etc; *contrib*. Chman. *Address*: Trinity College, Stoke Hill, Bristol BS9 1JP.

Paffard, Michael Kenneth; Senior Lecturer in Education, University of Keele, since 1965; *b* 1928; *m* 1953; two *s* one *d*. BA Bristol 1950 (1st cl. Hons Eng. Lang. and Lit.), DipEd Bristol 1951, MA Bristol 1964 (Educn). Lectr, UC N Staffs, 1953–65. *Publications*: Inglorious Wordsworths: A Study of Some Transcendental Experiences in Childhood and Adolescence, 1973; *contrib*. Brit. Jl Educnl Psychol., Brit. Jl Educnl Studies, Ed. Research, Researches and Studies, etc. *Address*: Education Dept, Univ. of Keele, Keele, Staffs ST5 5BG.

Page, Charles Stuart; Senior Lecturer in Public Administration, University of Strathclyde, since 1964; *b* 1918; *m* 1940; two *s*. BCom London 1954; Inst. of Public Finance accountant (Hons) 1947, ACIS, FRVA. Local Govt (varied), 1934–55; res. for Royal Commn on Local Govt in Scotland, 1967. *Publications*: Accounting for Local and

Public Authorities, 1960; Local Finance in Scotland, 1960–71; Finance for Management, 1966, rev. edn 1969; Casebook–Studies in Administration, 1966; Tools for Administrators in the Public Service, 1967; Administrative Costs of Local Authorities and Local Taxation, 1969. *Address*: Dept of Administration, Univ. of Strathclyde, Glasgow G1 1XW.

Page, Colin Michael F.; *see* Flood Page.

Page, Eric, BSc, PhD; Lecturer in Operational Research, Department of Economics and Commerce, University of Hull, since 1965; *b* 1933. BSc Birmingham 1954, PhD Birmingham 1957; FSS, Mem., Operat. Res. Soc. UK, Operat. Res. Soc. Amer., Inst. Mngmt Sci., Math. Assoc. *Publications*: Queueing Theory in Operational Research, 1972. *Address*: Sub-Dept of Operational Research, The Univ., Hull HU6 7RX.

Page, Prof. Ewan Stafford, MA, BSc, PhD, FBCS; Professor of Computing and Data Processing, and Director of Computing Laboratory, University of Newcastle upon Tyne, since 1957; Pro-Vice-Chancellor, since 1972; *b* 1928; *m* 1955; three *s* one *d*. BA Cantab 1949 (Maths), BSc London 1951 (Maths), MA Cantab 1952, PhD Cantab 1954; FBCS, FSS. Lectr in Stats, Durham Colls, 1954–57; Vis. Prof., Univ. of N Carolina, 1962, Mem., Council, Brit. Comput. Soc., 1963–66; Mem., Peterlee and Aycliffe Develop. Corp., 1969– . *Publications*: (with L. B. Wilson) Information Representation and Manipulation in a Computer, 1973; *contrib*. Biomet., Comput. Jl, Jl Royal Stat. Soc., Technomet. *Address*: Computing Laboratory, Univ. of Newcastle upon Tyne, Claremont Tower, Claremont Road, Newcastle upon Tyne NE1 7RU.

Page, John Garrard B.; *see* Burton-Page.

Page, Prof. John Kenneth; Professor of Building Science, University of Sheffield, since 1960; *b* 1924; *m* 1954; two *s* two *d*. BA Cantab 1949; Fellow Illuminating Engineering Soc. Lectr in Building Science, Liverpool Univ., 1957–60. Dean of Faculty of Architectural Studies, Sheffield, 1968–71. Mem., Econ. Planning Council Yorkshire and Humberside, 1965– ; Chm., Environmental Gp, 1971– ; Chm., UK Section, Internat. Solar Energy Soc. Mem., Yorks Water Authority. *Publications*: *contrib*. approximately 100 papers in the architectural, engineering and planning lit., and in the lit. of environmental design, and systematic design and environmental protest. *Address*: Dept of Building Science, Univ. of Sheffield, Sheffield S10 2TN.

Page, Kenneth; Resident Violinist, Archduke Trio, Music Department, Leicester University, since 1973; *b* 1927; *m* 1953; one *s* one *d*. LRAM 1948, ABSM 1951. Founder, Leader, Musical Director, Orchestra da Camera, 1957– ; Conductor, Birmingham Philharmonic Orchestra, 1959– . *Address*: Dept of Music, Leicester Univ., Leicester LE1 7RH.

Page, Dr Raymond Ian; University Lecturer, Department of Anglo-Saxon, Norse and Celtic, Cambridge, since 1961; Fellow and Librarian, Corpus Christi College, Cambridge, since 1962; *b* 1924; one *s* two *d*. BA Sheffield 1950, MA Sheffield 1951, PhD Nottingham 1959, MA Cantab 1961. Asst Lectr, English, Nottingham, 1951–54, Lectr, 1954–61. *Publications*: Gibbons Saga, 1960; Life in Anglo-Saxon England, 1970; An Introduction to English Runes, 1973; *contrib*. Anglia, Antiquaries Jl, Jl British Archaeol Assoc., JEGP, Medieval Archaeol., Medium Ævum, Nottingham Mediaeval Studies, Sagabook of the Viking Soc., Studia Neophilologica. *Address*: Corpus Christi College, Cambridge.

Paget, Ernest; Fellow of Jesus College, Oxford, since 1957, and University Lecturer in Geography, Oxford University, since 1951; *b* 1918; *m* 1950, *marr. diss.* 1963; two *d*. BA Oxon 1939 (1st cl. Geog.), MA Oxon 1946; FRGS, Mem., Inst. Brit. Geogrs. Deptal Lectr, Sch. of Geography, Oxford, 1946–51. Mem., Gen. Bd of Facs, Oxford, 1965– . *Publications*: chapter, in, Geographical Essays on British Tropical Lands, ed C. A. Fisher and R. W. Steel, 1953; *contrib*. Geog. Jl, Geog., Geog. Ann. *Address*: Jesus College, Oxford.

Pahl, Prof. Raymond Edward; Professor of Sociology, University of Kent at Canterbury, since 1972; *b* 1935; *m* 1959; two *s* one *d*. BA Cantab 1959, MA Cantab 1961, PhD London 1964. Resident Staff Tutor, Univ. of Cambridge Bd of Extra-Mural Studies, 1959–65; Lectr in Sociology, Univ. of Kent at Canterbury, 1965–68, Sen. Lectr, 1968–71. Mem., Editorial Bd, Sociology, 1969–73. Assessor, Greater London Develop. Plan Inquiry, 1970–72; Adviser, Min. of Housing and Local Govt, later Dept of Environment, 1968–72. *Publications*: Urbs in Rure, 1965; ed, Readings in Urban Sociology, 1968; Patterns of Urban Life, 1970; Whose City? and Other Essays on Sociology and Planning, 1970, 2nd rev. edn 1974; (with J. M. Pahl) Managers and their Wives, 1971. *Address*: Darwin College, The Univ., Canterbury.

Pailin, Dr David Arthur; Senior Lecturer in Philosophy of Religion, Faculty of Theology, University of Manchester, since 1973 (Lecturer, 1966–73); *b* 1936; *m* 1961; one *s* one *d*. BA Cambridge 1958, MA Cambridge 1961, MA Manchester 1965, PhD Manchester 1969. Mem., Soc. Study Theol., Mem., Christian Philosophers Gp. Mem., Methodist Connexional Faith and Order Cttee, 1968– . *Publications*: The Way to Faith, 1969; chapters, in, University Perspectives, 1971; The Living God, ed Kirkpatrick, 1971; The Twentieth Century Mind, ed Cox and Dyson, 1972; Cardinal Meaning, ed Morgan and Pye, 1974; *contrib*. Anal. Anselm., Ch Qly, Expos. Times, London Qly Hol. Rev., Faith and Thought, Process Studies, Religion, Relig. Studies. *Address*: Dept of Philosophy of Religion, Faculty of Theology, Univ. of Manchester, Manchester M13 9PL.

Pakenham-Walsh, Amory Allfrey, MA, FCCA, FCMA; Director, Graduate Course in Administration, Department of Business

Studies, University of Dublin, since 1971; b 1917; m 1941 and 1949; three d. BA Dublin 1947 (Hons Econ.), MA Dublin 1956, MA Oxon 1957; Qualified certified accountant, 1941, FCCA, FCMA, 1957, JDipMA. Dep. Chief Accountant, Arthur Guinness Son and Co., 1948–57; P. D. Leake Res. Fellow, Oxford, 1957–58; Lectr in Management, Dublin, 1959–67; Sen. Lectr, 1967– . Mem., Council, Assoc. of Certified Accountants, 1968– . *Publication*: Work Study on the Farm, 1961. *Address*: Trinity College, Dublin 2.

Palley, Prof. Claire Dorothea Taylor, BA, LLB, PhD; Professor of Law, University of Kent at Canterbury, since 1973; Master of Darwin College, since 1974; b 1931; m 1952; five s. BA Cape Town 1950 (distinction Constitutional History and Law), LLB Cape Town 1952, PhD London 1965; Barrister, Middle Temple; Advocate of the Supreme Court of S Africa, Advocate of the High Court of Rhodesia. Lectr, Univ. of Cape Town, 1953–55; Lectr, Univ. Coll. of Rhodesia and Nyasaland, 1960–65; Lectr, Queen's Univ. of Belfast, 1966–67; Reader, Queen's Univ. of Belfast, 1967–70; Prof. of Public Law, 1970–73; Dean, Fac. of Law, Queen's Univ. of Belfast, 1971–73. *Publications*: The Constitutional History and Law of Southern Rhodesia, 1966; *contrib*. Mod. Law Rev., Public Law, N Irel. Legal Qly, Race. *Address*: Darwin Coll., Univ. of Kent at Canterbury, Canterbury CT2 7NY.

Pallister, Dr Anne; Lecturer, Department of History, University of Reading, since 1967; b 1942. BA Nottingham 1963 (1st cl. History), PhD Nottingham 1966. Lectr in Hist., Univ. of Leicester, 1965–67. Warden, St David's Hall, Univ. of Reading, 1971–73. *Publications*: Magna Carta: The Heritage of Liberty, 1971. *Address*: Dept of History, Faculty of Letters and Social Sciences, Univ. of Reading, Whiteknights, Reading RG6 2AH.

Palmer, David John, MA, BLitt; Senior Lecturer, Department of English, University of Hull, since 1969; b 1935; m 1961; one s one d. BA Oxon 1958 (2nd cl. English), MA Oxon 1961, BLitt Oxon 1961. Asst Lectr, Univ. of Hull, 1960–63; Lectr, Univ. of Hull, 1963–69; Vis. Prof., Univ. of Rochester, NY, 1968–69. *Publications*: The Rise of English Studies, 1965; ed, Casebook on The Tempest, 1968; co-ed, Metaphysical Poetry, 1970; co-ed, Contemporary Criticism, 1970; ed, Shakespeare's Later Comedies: An Anthology of Criticism, 1971; co-ed, The American Novel and the Nineteen Twenties, 1972; co-ed, Shakespearian Comedy; ed, Casebook on Twelfth Night; ed, Tennyson and his Background; *contrib*. Crit. Qly, Engl. Studies, Philol. Qly, Shakesp. Qly, Stratf. Studies. *Address*: Dept of English, The Univ., Hull HU6 7RX.

Palmer, Prof. Frank Robert, MA; Professor of Linguistic Science, University of Reading, since 1965; b 1922; m 1948; three s two d. BA, MA Oxon 1947 (1st cl. Lit. Hum. 1948). Lectr, SOAS, Univ. of London, 1950–60; Prof., Univ. Coll. of N Wales, Bangor, 1960–65; Dean, Fac. of Letters and Social Sciences, 532

Univ. of Reading, 1969–72. Mem., Council, Philol Soc., 1962–67, 1969– ; Chm., Lingu. Assoc., 1965–68; Ed., Jl. Lingu., 1969– . *Publications*: The Morphology of the Tigre Noun, 1962; A Linguistic Study of the English Verb, 1965; ed, Selected Papers of J. R. Firth, 1952–59, 1968; ed, Prosodic Analysis, 1970; Grammar, 1971; *contrib*. Afr. Lang. Studies, Bull. SOAS, Jl Semit. Studies, Lingua, Mitt. Insts Orientfors., Trans Philol Soc., Word. *Address*: Dept of Linguistic Science, Univ. of Reading, Whiteknights, Reading RG6 2AA.

Palmer, John, BA; Senior Lecturer in Geography, University of Leeds, since 1973; b 1927; m; one s one d. BA Cantab 1949. Asst Lectr in Geography, Leeds, 1952–55, Lectr, 1955–73. *Publications*: *contrib*. Proc. Yorks Geol. Soc., Trans Inst. Brit. Geogrs, Zeit Geomorphol., etc. *Address*: Dept of Geography, Univ. of Leeds, Leeds LS2 9JT.

Palmer, Dr John Joseph Norman; Senior Lecturer in Medieval History, University of Hull, since 1973 (Lecturer, 1965–73); b 1939; m 1962; two s one d. BA Oxon 1960 (2nd cl. History), BLitt Oxon 1964, PhD London 1967. *Publications*: England, France and Christendom 1377–99, 1972; *contrib*. Bull. Inst. Hist. Res., EHR, Specul., Trans Royal Hist. Soc. *Address*: Dept of History, The Univ., Hull HU6 7RX.

Palmer, Nathaniel Humphrey; Senior Lecturer, Department of Philosophy, University College, Cardiff, since 1968; b 1930; m 1956; one s. BA Oxon 1953 (1st cl. Lit. Hum.), MA Oxon 1956 (2nd cl. Theology 1958), PhD Wales 1966. Lectr, Christ Church Coll., Kanpur, India, 1956–58; Asst Lectr, Univ. Coll., Cardiff, 1958–60; Lectr, Univ. Coll., Cardiff, 1960–68; Lectr, Madras Christian Coll., India, 1962–64 (on secondment). Asst Dean, Fac. of Theology, 1968–70. *Publications*: (with E. P. Palmer) Common Tamil Words, 1964; The Logic of Gospel Criticism, 1968; Analogy, 1973; trans., L. Nelson: Progress and Regress in Philosophy, vol. I, 1970, II 1971; *contrib*. Mind, NT Studies, Philos., Ratio, Theol. *Address*: Dept of Philosophy, Univ. Coll., Cardiff CF1 1XL.

Palmier, Dr Leslie Hugh, BSc(Econ), PhD; Senior Lecturer in Sociology, School of Humanities and Social Sciences, University of Bath, since 1967; b 1924; m 1956; one s two d. BSc(Econ) London 1949, PhD London 1956. Mem., Brit. Sociol Assoc., Mem., Assoc. SE Asia Studies, Mem., UK Assoc. Univ. Teachers. Res. Fellow in Southeast Asia Studies, Yale Univ., 1956–57; Assoc. Prof. of Asian Studies, Victoria Univ. of Wellington, NZ, 1957–62; Assoc. Fellow, St Antony's Coll., Oxford, 1967– . Dep. Dir, Unesco Res. Centre Social and Econ. Develop., Delhi, 1962–65; Programme Dir, UN Res. Inst. Social Develop., Geneva, 1966–67. *Publications*: Social Status and Power in Java, 1960, 2nd edn 1969; Indonesia and the Dutch, 1962; Indonesia, 1965, Spanish edn 1967; Organization of Land Redistribution Beneficiaries, 1970; Communists in

Indonesia, 1972; *contrib.* Hum. Relat., Indonesië, Internat. Aff., Mod. Asian Studies, Pacif. Aff. *Address*: The Univ., Bath BA2 7AY.

Pálsson, Stefán Hermann; Reader in Icelandic, Department of English, University of Edinburgh, since 1966; *b* 1921; *m* 1953; one *d.* Cand.mag. Iceland 1947, BA Dublin 1950 (Celtic). Lektor in Icelandic, Univ. of Edinburgh, 1950–54; Lectr, Univ. of Edinburgh, 1954–64; Sen. Lectr, Univ. of Edinburgh, 1964–66; Vis. Prof., Univ. of Toronto, 1967–68. *Publications*: Írskar fornsögur, 1953; Íslenzk mannanöfn, 1960; Sagnaskemmtun Íslendinga, 1962; Hrafnkels saga og Freysgydlingar, 1962; Eftir Thjódveldid, 1965; Sidfrædi Hrafnkels sögu, 1966; Helgafell, 1967; Art and Ethics in Hrafnkel's Saga, 1971; Hrafnkel's Saga and other Icelandic Stories, 1971; (with M. Magnusson) Njal's Saga, 1960; The Vinland Sagas, 1965; King Harald's Saga, 1966; Laxdæla Saga, 1969; (with P. Edwards) Gautrek's Saga and other Medieval Tales, 1968; Arrow-Odd, 1970; Legendary Fiction in Medieval Iceland, 1970; Hrolf Gautreksson, 1972; Eyrbyggja Saga, 1973; The Book of Settlements, 1972; (with Denton Fox) Grettir's Saga, 1973; *contrib.* Encyclopaedia Britannica, Skirnir. *Address*: Dept of English, Univ. of Edinburgh, David Hume Tower, George Square, Edinburgh EH8 9JX.

Paluello, Lorenzo M.; *see* Minio-Paluello.

Pandey, Dr Bishwa Nath, LLB, MA, PhD; Lecturer in Modern Indian History, School of Oriental and African Studies, University of London, since 1963; *b* 1929; *m* 1st 1947, 2nd 1968; two *d.* BA Banaras 1947, LLB Banaras 1949, MA Banaras 1950, PhD London 1958 (History). Lectr in Law, Banaras Univ., 1952–54; Lectr in Indian History, Bihar Univ., 1954–55. *Publications*: A Book of India, 1965; jt ed, Evolution of India and Pakistan, 1962; The Rise of Modern India, 1967; The Introduction of English Law into India, 1967; The Break-up of British India, 1969, American edn 1969. *Address*: School of Oriental and African Studies, Univ. of London, WC1E 7HP.

Panter, Prof. Kenneth Humphrey; Professor of Architecture, and Head of School of Architecture, University of Bath, since 1965; *b* 1922; *m* 1946; two *s.* MArch; ARIBA, ARWA, ASIA, FRSA. Mem., Hds of Schs Cttee, RIBA, 1960– ; Mem., Council, Brist. Som. Soc. Archit., 1962–70; Reg. Council for Further Educn in SW; Mem., Sub-cttee for Art and Design, 1965– ; Mem., Sub-cttee for Building, 1963–67; Mem., Western Centre Cttee, RSA, 1967– . *Publications*: *contrib.* Jl Royal Soc. Arts. *Address*: School of Architecture and Building Technology, Univ. of Bath, Claverton Down, Bath BA2 7AY.

Panter-Brick, Samuel Keith; Senior Lecturer in Political Science, Department of Government, London School of Economics, since 1964; *b* 1920; *m* 1949; one *s* three *d.* BA Oxon 1948 (2nd cl. PPE), BPhil Oxon 1950. Asst Lectr, LSE, 1950–54; Lectr, LSE, 1954–

64; Prof. of Public Admin, Inst. of Admin, Ahmadu Bello Univ., Nigeria, 1965–67; Vis. Prof., Univ. of Zambia, 1969. *Publications*: ed, Nigerian Politics and Military Rule, 1970, Nigerian pbk edn 1971; *contrib.* Internat. Aff., Jbh Offen. Rechts, Pol. Studies, Public Admin, Res. Pub. *Address*: Dept of Government, London School of Economics, Houghton Street, Aldwych, WC2A 2AE.

Parekh, Dr Bhikhu Chhotalal; Senior Lecturer, Department of Political Studies, University of Hull, since 1974 (Lecturer, 1964–74); *b* 1935; *m* 1959; three *s.* BA Bombay 1954, MA Bombay 1956, PhD London 1966. Lectr, Univ. of Baroda, 1957–59; Tutor, LSE, 1962–63; Asst Lectr, Univ. of Glasgow, 1963–64; Vis. Asst Prof., Univ. of British Columbia, 1968. *Publications*: ed, Politics and Experience, 1968; ed, Dissent and Disorder, 1971; ed, The Morality of Politics, 1972; ed, Bentham's Political Thought, 1973; ed, Jeremy Bentham: ten critical essays, 1973; *contrib.* Ind. Jl Pol. Sci., Cross Curr., Pol. Studies, Social Res., Jl Hist. Ideas. *Address*: Dept of Political Studies, The Univ., Hull HU6 7RX.

Parfitt, Dr George Albert Ekins; Lecturer in English Studies, University of Nottingham, since 1966; *b* 1939; *m* 1952; two *s* two *d.* BA Bristol 1962, PhD Bristol 1966. *Publications*: ed (with J. Kinsley), Dryden: Selected Criticism, 1970; The Poems of Ben Jonson (forthcoming); ed, Silver Poets of the 17th Century (forthcoming); ed, Cyril Tourneur (forthcoming); contrib. 17th Century Critical Essays, ed W. R. Keast; William Congreve, ed B. Morris; Webster's . . . Companion to . . . Literature, ed A. Pollard; *contrib.* Ess. Crit., Renaiss. Mod. Studies, Studies Engl. Lit. *Address*: School of English Studies, Univ. of Nottingham, Nottingham NG7 2RD.

Parikh, Ashok, MCom, MSc(Econ); Reader in Economics, University of East Anglia, since 1971; *b* 1936; *m* 1963; one *d.* BCom Gujarat 1957 (2nd cl.), MCom Bombay 1959, MSc(Econ) London 1962; FSS. Mem., Royal Econ. Soc. Lectr, Sardar Vallaph Vidyapith, 1959–60; Res. Assoc., Univ. of Delhi, 1963–65; Res. Assoc., Univ. of Delhi, 1963–65; Reader, Univ. of Poona, 1965–66; Lectr, Univ. of Sussex, 1966–68; Lectr, Univ. of E Anglia, 1968–71; Vis. Prof., Columbia Univ., NY, 1967, 1968. Cnsltnt, FAO, 1967; Res. Economist, IMF, Washington, DC, 1969–70; Cnsltnt, UNCTAD, 1971. *Publications*: *contrib.* Bull. Oxf. Inst. Econ. Stat., Canad. Jl Agric. Econ., Jl Develop. Studies, Ind. Econ. Jl, Ind. Jl Agric. Econ. *Address*: School of Social Studies, Univ. of East Anglia, Norwich NOR 88C.

Parish, Dr Peter Anthony; Senior Research Fellow, Medical Sociology Research Centre, University College, Swansea, since 1969; Principal in General Medical Practice, Swansea; *b* 1930; *m* 1956; two *s* one *d.* MB, ChB Sheffield 1956, MD Sheffield 1972; MRCS England, LRCP London 1956, MRCGP 1964. Hosp. and Gen. Pract. apntmts, 1956–69. *Publications*: The Prescribing of Psychotropic Drugs in General Practice (Jl RCGP Supp. 4), 1971; ed jtly,

The Medical Use of Psychotropic Drugs (Jl RCGP Supp. 2), 1973; *contrib.* BMJ, Drugs and Society, Practitioner, Nurs. Times, Gen. Practitioner, RSH Jl, Social Worker. *Address*: Medical Sociology Research Centre, Univ. College, Swansea SA2 8PP.

Parish, Peter Joseph; Senior Lecturer in American History, University of Glasgow, since 1972; *b* 1929; *m* 1957; one *d*. BA London 1950 (1st cl. History). Cataloguer, Univ. Libr., Manchester, 1955–58; ACLS Fellow, Johns Hopkins Univ., 1963–64; Lectr, Glasgow Univ., 1958–72. *Publications*: The American Civil War, 1974; *contrib.* Jl Amer. Hist. *Address*: Dept of History, Univ. of Glasgow, Glasgow G12 8QQ.

Park, Trevor; Lecturer in Industrial Relations, Department of Adult Education and Extra-mural Studies, University of Leeds, since 1972; *b* 1927; *m* 1953. BA Manchester 1948, MA Manchester 1949. Lectr, Dept of Extra-mural Studies, Univ. of Sheffield, 1960–64. MP (Lab) SE Derbyshire, 1964–70; Member of Select Committees: on Nationalised Industries, 1966–68; on Educn and Science, 1968–70. *Address*: Dept of Adult Education and Extra-mural Studies, The Univ., Leeds LS2 9JT.

Parker, Allen Mainwaring; Director of Extramural Studies, University of Birmingham, since 1955; *b* 1915; *m* 1945; one *s* two *d*. First cl. Hon Mods 1936, Second cl. Lit. Hum. 1938, MA Oxon. Sen. Classics Master, King's Coll., Auckland, NZ, 1938–39; Dept of Extramural Studies, Univ. of London, 1947–55. War service, 1940–46, KOYLI (Major). Mem., ATV Educn Adv. Cttee, 1963–72 (Chm., Adult Educn Sub-Cttee). *Publications*: University Adult Education in the Later Twentieth Century (Report of Convenor of Working Party of Universities' Council for Adult Education), 1970; (ed jtly) with Prof. S. G. Raybould) University Studies for Adults, 1972; *contrib.* Stud. Adult Educn. *Address*: Dept of Extramural Studies, Univ. of Birmingham, PO Box 363, Birmingham B15 2TT.

Parker, Anthony John; Lecturer, Department of Geography, University College Dublin, since 1969; *b* 1944; *m* 1971. BA Hons Aberystwyth 1966 (Geog. and Internat. Politics); Member: Inst. of British Geographers; Geographical Soc. of Ireland (Mem. Cttee, 1973–). Res. Asst, Dept of Geography, UCL, 1968–69. *Publications*: *contrib.* Area, Econ. and Social Rev., Geog. Mag., Geog. Viewpoint, Ir. Geog. *Address*: Dept of Geography, Univ. Coll., Dublin, Belfield, Dublin 4.

Parker, Prof. Clifford Frederick, JP, MA, LLB; Bracton Professor of Law, and Head of Department of Law, University of Exeter, since 1957; *b* 1920; *m* 1945; two *d*. Pt I Modern Languages Tripos Cambridge 1939 (1st cl.), Pt II Law Tripos Cambridge 1940 (1st cl.), LLB Cambridge 1947 (1st cl.); Admitted Solicitor of the Supreme Court 1947. Lectr, Internat. Fac. for the Teaching of Comparative Law, 1965– . Pt-time Lectr in Law, Univ. of Birmingham, 1947–48, 1949–50; Lectr in Law, 1951–57; Sen. Tutor and Asst Dir of Legal Studies, 1956–57. Dep. Vice-Chancellor, Univ. of Exeter, 1963–65; Dean, Fac. of Law, 1957–69, 1972– . JP Devon, 1969; Governor, Rolle Coll. of Educn, Exmouth. *Address*: Faculty of Law, Univ. of Exeter, Amory Building, Rennes Drive, Exeter EX4 4RJ.

Parker, Mrs Constance Mildred; *see* Howard, C. M.

Parker, Dr David; Lecturer in Modern History, University of Leeds, since 1966; *b* 1941; *m* 1965; two *d*. BA Liverpool 1963 (Hons History), PhD Liverpool 1969. *Publications*: *contrib.* Past and Present. *Address*: School of History, Univ. of Leeds, Leeds LS2 9JT.

Parker, Prof. David Berkeley; Queen Victoria Professor of Law, University of Liverpool, since 1970; *b* 1931; *m* 1970; one *s*. LLB London 1953, LLB Cantab 1955. Barrister-at-Law, Gray's Inn, 1956. Lecturer in Law: Univ. of Leeds, 1958–64; KCL, 1964–70. *Publications*: (co-author) The Modern Law of Trusts, 1st edn 1966, 3rd edn 1974; (ed jtly), Tudor on Charities, 6th edn 1967; *contrib.* Encyclopaedia of Forms and Precedents, vol. 22, 4th edn 1973. *Address*: Fac. of Law, Liverpool Univ., PO Box 147, Liverpool L69 3BX.

Parker, John Edgar Sayce; Lecturer in Economics, Exeter University, since 1963; *b* 1938; *m* 1965; one *s* one *d*. BSc(Econ) Southampton 1961, MSc(Soc. Sci.) Southampton 1963. *Publications*: (with F. V. Meyer and D. C. Corner) Problems of a Mature Economy, 1970; Economics of Innovation, 1974; *contrib.* Bank. Mag., Business Ratios, Manch. Sch., Oxf. Econ. Papers. *Address*: Dept of Economics, Univ. of Exeter, Exeter EX4 4QJ.

Parker, Dr John Morris; Senior Lecturer, Institute of Latin American Studies, University of Glasgow, since 1973 (Lecturer, 1967–73); *b* 1934; *m* 1958; three *s*. BA Cantab 1955 (1st cl. Modern Languages), MA Cantab 1959, PhD Cantab 1959; Mem., Assoc. Hispan. GB N Irel., SLAS, MHRA. Lectr, Univ. Coll. of Rhodesia and Nyasaland, 1959–63; Sen. Lectr, Univ. of Witwatersrand, 1963–66; Tutor and Adviser, Univ. of S Africa, 1965–66. *Publications*: Three Twentieth Century Portuguese Poets, 1960; Brazilian Fiction 1950–1970, 1973; *contrib.* Bull. Hispan. Studies, Rev. Lab. Fonét. Experim., Luso-Brazilian Rev., Anais do Primeiro Encontro Internacional de Estudos Brasileiros. *Address*: Institute of Latin American Studies, The Univ., Glasgow G12 8QQ.

Parker, Robert Alastair Clarke; Fellow of Queen's College, Oxford, since 1957; *b* 1927; *m* 1960; two *d*. MA Oxford 1952. Manchester University: Asst Lectr in Modern History, 1952–55; Lectr in Modern History, 1955–57; *Publications*: Das Zwanzigste Jahrhundert, Frankfurt 1967; Europe 1918–45, 1969; Coke of Norfolk: a financial and agricultural study 1707–1842 (forthcoming); *contrib.* Econ.

Hist. Rev., EHR, World Polits. *Address*: Queen's College, Oxford.

Parker, Prof. Robert Henry, BSc(Econ), FCA; Professor of Accountancy, University of Dundee, since 1970; *b* 1932; *m* 1955; one *s* one *d*. BSc(Econ) London 1954; ACA 1958, FCA 1969. Lectr, Adelaide, 1960–61; Sen. Lectr, WA, 1962–66; P. D. Leake Res. Fellow, LSE, 1966; Reader, Manchester Business Sch., 1966–69; Associate Prof., European Inst. of Business Admin, 1968–70. Mem., Council of British Accounting and Finance Assoc., 1970– ; Mem., Business Studies Bd, CNAA, 1967– . *Publications*: (jtly) Topics in Business Finance and Accounting, 1964; Management Accounting: an historical perspective, 1969; (co-ed) Readings in the Theory and Measurement of Income, 1969; Understanding Company Financial Statements, 1972; *contrib*. Abacus, Jl of Accounting Res., Jl of Business Finance. *Address*: Dept of Accountancy, Univ. of Dundee, Dundee DD1 4HN.

Parker, Prof. Roy Alfred; Professor of Social Administration, University of Bristol, since 1969; *b* 1931; *m* 1954; one *s* three *d*. BSc London 1953 (Sociology), Cert. in Applied Social Studies London 1956, PhD London 1961. Child Care Off., Berkshire CC, 1956–57; Res. Off., LSE, 1959; Lectr, LSE 1960–69. Mem., Seebohm Cttee on Local Authority and Allied Personal Social Services, 1965–68; Mem., Bd, Milton Keynes New Town Develop. Corp., 1968–71. *Publications*: Decision in Child Care – a study of prediction in fostering, 1966; The Rents of Council Houses, 1967; Planning for Deprived Children, 1971; *contrib*. Case Conf., Pol Qly, Social Wk. *Address*: Dept of Social Administration and Social Work, Univ. of Bristol, Bristol BS8 1TH.

Parker, Dr William Henry; Lecturer in the Geography of USSR, University of Oxford, since 1964; *b* 1912; *m* 1945; two *s*. BA Oxon 1934 (Hist.), 1935 (Geog.), MA Oxon 1939, BSc Oxon 1939, DPhil 1958; FRGS, Mem., Geog. Assoc., Mem., NASEES. Lectr, Royal Mil. Acad., Sandhurst, 1947–51; Sen. Lectr, Royal Mil. Acad., Sandhurst, 1951–52; Asst Prof., McMaster Univ., 1952–56; Assoc. Prof., Univ. of Manitoba, 1956–61. *Publications*: Canada, 1954; Anglo-America, 1962, 2nd edn 1971; Historical Geography of Russia, 1968; The Soviet Union, 1969; The Superpowers, 1972; The Russians, 1973; *contrib*. Canad. Hist. Rev., Geog. Jl. *Address*: Christ Church, Oxford OX1 1DP.

Parkes, Dr Edward Walter; Vice-Chancellor of The City University, since 1974; *b* 1926; *m* 1950; one *s* one *d*. MA, PhD Cantab; FIMechE, MICE. Demonstrator, subseq. Lecturer, Cambridge, and Fellow and Tutor, Gonville and Caius Coll., 1948–59; Vis. Prof., Stanford, 1959–60; Head of Dept of Engineering, Leicester, 1960–65; Professor of Mechanics, Cambridge, 1965–74. Mem., Adv. Bd for the Research Councils, 1974– . *Publications*: Braced Frameworks, 1965, 2nd edn 1974; *contrib*. Aircraft Engng, Engng, Proc. ICE, Proc. IMechE, Proc. and Phil.

Trans Roy. Soc. A, etc. *Address*: City Univ., St John Street, EC1V 4PB.

Parkes, Malcolm Beckwith; Fellow and Tutor in English Language, Keble College, Oxford, since 1965; Lecturer in Palaeography, University of Oxford, since 1971; *b* 1930; *m* 1954; two *s*. BA Hons 1953 (2nd cl. English Lang. and Lit.), MA 1957, BLitt 1959, Oxon; Gordon-Duff Prize, 1959; FSA 1971. Lectr in English Lang. and Lit., Keble Coll. and Mansfield Coll., Oxford, 1961–65; Univ. Lectr (CUF), Fac. of English Lang. and Lit., Oxford, 1964–71; Guest Lectr in Univs of Belfast, 1966–69, Cork, 1973, Durham, 1971, Konstanz, 1969, 1972, Würzburg, 1972, München, 1974; Gastprof., Universität Konstanz, 1974. Librarian, Keble Coll., Oxford, 1966–73. Mem., Internat. Editorial Adv. Cttee of Toronto Old English Series, 1973– . *Publications*: English Cursive Book Hands 1250–1500, 1969; also chapters in literary histories, and palaeographical manuals; *contrib*. Anglo-Saxon England, Medium Ævum, English Hist. Rev. *Address*: Keble Coll., Oxford OX1 3PG.

Parkin, Prof. John Michael, BA; Professor of Economics, University of Manchester, since 1970; *b* 1939; *m* 1961; one *s* two *d*. BA Leicester 1963 (1st cl.); Assoc. Inst. Cost Works Accntnts. Asst Lectr in Applied Economics, Univ. of Sheffield, 1963–64; Lectr in Economics, Univ. of Leicester, 1964–66; Lectr in Economics, Univ. of Essex, 1967–69; Sen. Lectr in Economics, Univ. of Essex, 1969–70. *Publications*: (with H. G. Johnson and others) Readings in British Monetary Economics, 1971; *contrib*. Theory of Demand, Real and Monetary, by M. Morishima, 1973; ten supp. booklets to accompany tape-recorded discussions on economic issues; *contrib*. Amer. Econ. Rev., Aust. Econ. Papers, Banker, Bull. Oxf. Univ. Inst. Econ. Stats, Economica, Economet, Economet. Mod. UK, Manch. Sch., Rev. Econ. Studies, Search. *Address*: Faculty of Economic and Social Studies, Univ. of Manchester, Manchester M13 9PL.

Parkin, Rev. Vincent; Principal, Edgehill College, Belfast, since 1973; Recognised Teacher, Department of Theology, The Queen's University, Belfast, since 1973; *b* 1915; *m* 1942; one *s*. BSc Dunelm 1936, BA Cantab 1939, MA Cantab 1942. Associate Lectr, Dept of Theology, Leeds Univ., 1954–67. Resid. Tutor, Wesley Coll., Leeds, 1953–67; Resid. Tutor, Wesley Coll., Bristol, 1967–73; Recognised Teacher, Dept of Theology, Bristol Univ., 1967–73. *Publications*: Priests in the Church of God, 1964; *contrib*. Studia Evangel. *Address*: Edgehill Coll., Lennoxvale, Belfast BT9 5BY.

Parkinson, Prof. George Henry Radcliffe; Professor of Philosophy, University of Reading, since 1974 (Reader, 1971–74); *b* 1923; *m* 1953; one *s* one *d*. BA Oxon 1949 (1st cl. Lit. Hum.), MA Oxon 1949, DPhil Oxon 1952. Asst Lectr, Reading Univ., 1950–52; Lectr, Reading Univ., 1952–64; Sen. Lectr, Reading Univ., 1964–71. Gen. Ed., Philosophical Classics series, Manch. Univ. Press, 1964– ; Mem.,

Council, Royal Inst. Philos., 1971– ; Mem., Organising Cttee, 2nd Internat. Leibniz Cong., 1972. *Publications*: Spinoza's Theory of Knowledge, 1954; Logic and Reality in Leibniz's Metaphysics, 1965; trans., Leibniz: Logical Papers, 1966; ed, The Theory of Meaning, 1968; ed, Georg Lukács: the man, his work and his ideas, 1970; Leibniz on Human Freedom, 1970; ed, Leibniz: Philosophical Writings, 1973; *contrib.* Inquiry, Mind, Monist, Philos., Philos. Qly, Studia Leibnit. *Address*: Philosophy Dept, Univ. of Reading, Whiteknights, Reading RG6 2AA.

Parkinson, Prof. John Richard; Professor of Economics, University of Nottingham, since 1969; *b* 1922; *m* 1946; two *s* two *d*. BCom Leeds 1942 (1st cl. Economics). Asst Lectr, then Lectr, Leeds Univ., 1946–48; Lectr, then Sen. Lectr, Glasgow Univ., 1954–62; Prof. of Applied Economics, Queen's Univ., Belfast, 1962–69. Asst, Prime Minister's Stat. Br., Off. of War Cabinet, 1942–45; Counsellor, OEEC, Paris, 1948–51; Adviser, Prime Minister's Stat. Br., HM Treasury, 1951–53; Adviser, Planning Commn, Pakistan, 1960. *Publications*: The Economics of Shipbuilding in the United Kingdom, 1960; (with J. Bates) Business Economics, 1963, 2nd edn 1969; *contrib.* Jl Indust. Econ., Jl Royal Stat. Soc., Oxf. Econ. Papers, Scott. Jl Pol. Econ. *Address*: Economics Dept, Nottingham Univ., Nottingham NG7 2RD.

Parkinson, Rev. Keith Edgar Hollyer, BD, MTh, AKC; Visiting Lecturer, Department of Theology and Study of Religion, University of Southampton, since 1957; *b* 1917; *m* 1943; two *s*. BD London 1941 (1st cl.), MTh London 1946, AKC London 1941. Vicar of St Augustin's, Bournemouth, 1952– ; Examining Chaplain to Bp of Winchester, 1962– . *Address*: Dept of Theology, The Univ., Southampton SO9 5NH.

Parkinson, Michael; Lecturer in Political Theory and Institutions, Liverpool University, since 1970; *b* 1944; *m* 1966. BA Liverpool 1965 (Pol Theory and Instns), MA (Econ.) Manchester 1968 (Govt). Res. Fellow, Univ. of Liverpool, 1967–70; Vis. Associate Prof., Washington Univ., St Louis, 1972–73. *Publications*: The Labour Party and the Organisation of Secondary Education, 1970; *contrib.* Pol Studies. *Address*: Dept Political Theory, Social Studies Building, Univ. of Liverpool, Liverpool L69 3BX.

Parkinson, Michael Henry; Lecturer in Comparative Literature, School of European Studies, University of East Anglia, since 1970; *b* 1945. BA Oxon 1965, MA Oxon 1969. Asst Lectr, East Anglia, 1968–70. *Address*: Univ. of East Anglia, Earlham Hall, Norwich NOR 88C.

Parkinson, Richard Nigel, MA, PhD; Lecturer in English, University of Exeter, since 1953; *b* 1919; *m* 1952; one *s* one *d*. BA Cantab 1948 (1st cl. English), MA Cantab 1951, PhD London 1964. Asst Lectr, Exeter Univ., 1950–53; Vis. Lectr, Antioch Coll., Ohio, 1961–62; Coll. of William and Mary, 1969–70. Warden, Reed Hall, 1950–52; Sen.

Warden, Duryard Halls, 1965–71. *Publications*: Edward Gibbon, 1974; *contrib.* Antioch Rev., Archiv, Crit. Surv. *Address*: Dept of English, Univ. of Exeter, Exeter EX4 4QJ.

Parmée, Douglas; University Lecturer in French, Cambridge University, since 1946, and Fellow and Director of Studies, Queens' College, Cambridge, since 1947; *b* 1914; *m* 1944; two *s* one *d*. BA Cantab 1936, MA Cantab 1940 (1st cl. MML Pts I and II with star of distinction). Steward, Queens' Coll., 1956–64; Tutor for Grad. Students, 1970– . *Publications*: Classicisme et Néoclassicisme dans l'œuvre poétique d'Henri de Régnier, 1939; Selected Critical Essays Baudelaire, 1949; Twelve French Poets, 1959, 11th edn 1971; Fifteen French Poets, 1974; trans., P. Mérimée: La Double Méprise, 1959; A. de Gobineau: Les Pléiades, 1963; T. Fontane: Unwiederbringlich, 1964; T. Fontane: Effi Briest, 1967; G. de Maupassant: Bel Ami, 1975; *contrib.* Camb. Jl, Fr. Studies, Mod. Lang. Rev., etc. *Address*: Queens' College, Cambridge.

Parr, Peter James; Senior Lecturer in Western Asiatic Archaeology, Institute of Archaeology, University of London, since 1973; *b* 1929; *m* 1959; four *d*. BA Oxon 1952, MA Oxon 1957; FSA 1959. Lectr, Inst. of Archaeology, Univ. London, 1962–73; Associate Prof., Oriental Inst., Univ. Chicago, 1971–72. Asst Dir, Brit. Sch. of Archaeology in Jerusalem, 1959–62. *Publications*: *contrib.* Bull. Inst. Archaeology, Palestine Exploration Qly, Revue Biblique, Zeitschrift des Deutschen-Palästina Vereins, Syria. *Address*: Institute of Archaeology, 31–34 Gordon Square, WC1H 0PY.

Parrinder, Rev. Prof. Edward Geoffrey Simons, MA, DD, PhD; Professor of the Comparative Study of Religions, University of London, since 1970; *b* 1910; *m* 1936; two *s* one *d*. BA London 1938 (1st cl.), BD London 1940 (1st cl.), MA London 1949, PhD London 1946, DD London 1952; FRAsiatS. Lectr, Univ. Coll., Ibadan, Nigeria, 1949–50; Sen. Lectr, Ibadan, 1950–58; Reader, Univ. of London, King's Coll., 1958–70; Fellow, King's Coll., London, 1972; Dean, Fac. of Theology, King's Coll. London, 1972–74; Charles Strong (Aust. Ch) Lectr, 1964; Wilde Lectr in Natural and Comparative Religion, Oxford, 1966–69; Teape Lectr, Delhi, Madras, 1973. Hon. Sec., Internat. Assoc. Hist. Relig., Brit. Br., 1960–72, Pres., 1972– ; Mem., Edit. Bd, Relig. Studies; Jl of Religion in Africa. *Publications*: West African Religion, 1949, 2nd edn 1961, French edn 1950; West African Psychology, 1951; Religion in an African City, 1955; Witchcraft, 1958, 2nd edn 1963, Spanish edn 1963; African Traditional Religion, 1954, 3rd edn 1974, Spanish edn 1956; Worship in the World's Religions, 1961; Comparative Religion, 1962; Upanishads Gita and Bible, 1962, Italian edn 1964, Amer. edn 1972; What World Religions Teach, 1963, 2nd edn 1968; The Christian Debate, 1964; The World's Living Religions, 1964, 2nd edn 1974, Swedish edn 1966, Norwegian edn 1967, Finnish edn 1969; Jesus in the Quran, 1965, Dutch edn 1967; African Mythology, 1968,

French edn 1969; Religion in Africa, 1969, Swedish edn 1971; A Book of World Religions, 1965, Swedish edn 1970; Avatar and Incarnation, 1970; Dictionary of Non-Christian Religions, 1971; ed, Man and his Gods, 1971; The Indestructible Soul, 1973; The Bhagavad Gita: a verse translation, 1974; contrib. Annual Register, 1958– ; *contrib.* Jl Relig. Afr., Relig. Studies, Times Educnl Supp., Times Lit. Supp. *Address:* Dept of History and Philosophy of Religion, King's College, Strand, WC2R 2LS.

Parrott, Sir Cecil, KCMG, OBE; Professor of Central and South Eastern European Studies, since 1971, and Director of the Comenius Centre, Lancaster University, since 1967; *b* 1909; *m* 1935; three *s*. BA Cambridge 1930 (Classics and English Lit.), MA Cambridge; Vice Pres. and Hon. Fellow, Inst. Linguists, 1969– . HM Minister, Moscow, 1954–57; Libr., Dir of Res. and Keeper of the Papers, Foreign Off., 1957–60; HM Ambassador, Prague, 1960–66. Prof. of Russian and Soviet Studies, Lancaster, 1966–71. *Publications:* trans., The Good Soldier Švejk (first complete English translation), 1973; various articles and broadcast talks etc on Czech music and culture. *Address:* The Univ., Bailrigg, Lancaster LA1 4YW.

Parrott, Prof. Ian, MA, DMus, FTCL, ARCO; Gregynog Professor of Music, University College of Wales, Aberystwyth, since 1916; *m* 1940; two *s*. BA, BMus Oxon 1937, DMus Oxon 1940, MA Oxon 1941; Hon. FTCL 1951; ARCO 1936. Council Mem., Incorp. Soc. Music., Mem., Soc. Prom. New Music, Mem., Peter Warlock Soc., Vice-Pres., Elgar Soc., etc. Lectr in Music, Birmingham Univ., 1947–50; Examiner, Trinity Coll. of Music, London, 1945– . Royal Signals, 1940–45; Composition, Luxor, awarded 1st prize, Royal Philharmonic Soc., 1949; Harriet Cohen Internat. Musicol. Medal, 1966. *Publications:* Pathways to Modern Music, 1947; A Guide to Musical Thought, 1955; Method in Orchestration, 1957; The Music of 'An Adventure', 1966; The Spiritual Pilgrims, 1969; Elgar (Master Musicians), 1971; var. musical compositions, commns by BBC etc; *contrib.* Musik Gesch. Gegen., Music. Times, Music Rev., etc. *Address:* Dept of Music, Univ. College of Wales, Aberystwyth SY23 2AX.

Parry, Prof. Clive, LLD; Professor of International Law, University of Cambridge, since 1969; *b* 1917; *m* 1945; one *s* one *d*. LLD Cambridge 1958; LLD Birmingham. Barrister, Gray's Inn, Associé de l'Institut de Droit Internat.; Pres., Grotian Soc., Mem., Carlyle Club. Fellow, Downing Coll., Cambridge, 1946. *Publications:* Nationality and Citizenship Laws of the Commonwealth and of the Republic of Ireland, 1957–60; The Sources and Evidences of International Law, 1965; ed, British Digest of International Law, 1965– ; ed, British International Law Cases, 1964– ; ed, Consolidated Treaty Series, 1969– . *Address:* Downing College, Cambridge.

Parry, Cyril; Senior Lecturer, Department of Social Theory and Institutions, University College of North Wales, Bangor, since 1971; *b* 1929; *m* 1954; two *s* one *d*. BSc(Econ) London 1960, PhD Wales 1968. Lectr, Univ. Coll. of N Wales, Bangor, 1965–71. Mem., Gwynedd CC. *Publications:* The Radical Tradition in Welsh Politics, 1970; *contrib.* Welsh Hist. Rev. *Address:* Dept of Social Theory and Institutions, Univ. College of North Wales, Bangor L57 2DG.

Parry, David Reginald; Lecturer in English Language and Literature, University College, Swansea, since 1968; *b* 1937. BA Sheffield 1959 (1st cl. English), MA Leeds 1965. School teacher, 1961–66; Asst Lectr, Univ. Coll., Swansea, 1966–68. *Publications:* Dialect Studies in South-East Wales, in, Patterns in Distribution, ed M. Wakelin, 1972. *Address:* Dept of English Language and Literature, Univ. College, Swansea SA2 8PP.

Parry, Prof. Geraint; Edward Caird Professor of Politics, University of Glasgow, since 1974; *b* 1936; *m* 1964; one *s* one *d*. BSc(Econ) London 1957, PhD London 1959. Temp. Asst Lectr in Politics, Univ. Coll. of Swansea, 1959–60; Asst Lectr in Philosophy, Univ. of Manchester, 1960–63, Lectr, 1963–70, Sen. Lectr in Philosophy, 1970–71, in Government, 1971–74. Vis. Lectr in Political Science, Univ. of Wisconsin, 1964–65; Vis. Prof. in Political Studies, Queen's Univ., Ontario, 1972–73. *Publications:* Political Elites, 1969, Swedish edn 1971, Italian edn 1972; ed, Participation in Politics, 1972; *contrib.* Archiv. Europ. Sociol., Gov. Opposit., Hist. Jl, Jl Commonwealth Pol. Studies, Philos. Qly, Pol. Studies. *Address:* Dept of Politics, Univ. of Glasgow, Glasgow G12 8QQ.

Parry, Dr Graham; Lecturer in English Literature, School of English, University of Leeds, since 1967; *b* 1940; *m* 1967. BA Cambridge 1961, MA Cambridge 1965, PhD Columbia 1965. Preceptor, Columbia Univ., 1962–65; Asst Prof., Univ. British Columbia, 1965–67; Maître de Conférences, Université de Toulouse, 1972–73. *Publications:* Hollar's England, 1974; introd., Inigo Jones, Stone-Heng Restored, 1972. *contrib.* Ariel, Annales de l'Université de Toulouse. *Address:* School of English, Univ. of Leeds, Leeds LS2 9JT.

Parsler, Dr Ronald; Senior Lecturer, Department of Sociology, Stirling University, since 1969; *b* 1927; *m* 1952; one *s* one *d*. BSc(Econ) London 1951, MA London 1962, PhD London 1971. Senior Lectr, Monash Univ., 1966–69. *Publications: contrib.* Sociol., Politics. *Address:* Dept of Sociology, Stirling Univ., Stirling FK9 4LA.

Parsons, David; Lecturer in Adult Education, Department of Adult Education, University of Leicester, since 1970; *b* 1936; *m* 1963; two *s* one *d*. BA Durham 1959; Member: Royal Archaeol Inst., Brit. Archaeol Assoc., Soc. for Med. Archaeol. Admin. Asst, Univ. of Glasgow, 1962–65; Organising Tutor for Leics and Rutland, Dept of Adult Education, Univ. of Leicester, 1965–70. Asst Editor (Royal Archaeol. Inst.), Archaeol Jl 1971– . *Publications:* (with N. Dees) Teachers and Taught, 1966; ed, with introd., Tenth-Century

Studies, 1973; *contrib.* Adult Educn, Archaeologia Aeliana, Archaeologia Cantiana, Archaeometry. *Address*: Dept of Adult Education, The Univ., Leicester LE1 7RH.

Parsons, Frederick William; Reader in Hausa, Department of Africa, School of Oriental and African Studies, University of London, 1968–75; *b* 1908; *m* 1954; one *d.* BA Oxon 1929 (1st cl. Hon. Mods. Classics), Hon. School of PPE Oxon 1931; Fellow, Royal Commonwealth Soc. Lectr in Hausa, SOAS, 1946–68. Admin. Service, Northern Nigeria, 1932–44. Mem., Bd of Studies in Oriental and African Languages, 1960–75. *Publications*: Hausa Translation of the Penal Code of Northern Nigeria, 1959; Hausa Translation of Criminal Procedure Code of Northern Nigeria, 1960; *contrib.* African Lang. Studies (SOAS), Jl of African Lang., Afrika und Übersee (Hamburg Univ.), Encyclopaedia of Islam. *Address*: Sch. of Oriental and African Studies, Malet Street, WC1E 7HP.

Parsons, Jack; Lecturer in Social Institutions, School of Social Sciences, Brunel University, since 1960; *b* 1920; *m* 1960; one *s* one *d.* BA Keele 1955 (Philosophy and Politics) (Mature State Scholar); Mem., Brit. Sociol. Assoc., Mem., Brit. Humanist Soc., Mem., Brit. Soc. Social Resp. in Science, Founder mem., Conservation Soc., Hon. Educn Officer, 1st three yrs, Mem., Council, 1971– , Chm., S Bucks Branch, 1970– . Mech. Eng. apprentice 1934–41; RAF pilot, 1941–46; Civil Contractors' Engr, 1946–49; NCB Cent. Sociol. Res. Unit, 1956–59. Mem., Liberal Party's Environ. Panel, 1971– ; Founder and Convenor, Brunel Environment Gp, 1972– ; Mem., Independent Commn on Transport, 1973–74. Wrote and directed documentary film, The Blackhill Campaign, 1965. *Publications*: Population versus Liberty, 1971; Population Fallacies, 1974; chapters, in, Environmental Assumptions, ed N. J. Holmes, 1975; Control of Fertility, ed Elder and Hawkins, 1975; articles, short stories, radio and TV talks. *Address*: Dept of Sociology, Brunel Univ., Kingston Lane, Uxbridge, Mddx UB8 3TH.

Parsons, Neil Simon, MA, BLitt; Lecturer in Russian, Department of Slavonic Languages, University of Glasgow, since 1966; *b* 1940; *m* 1963; one *s* one *d.* BA Oxon 1961, MA, BLitt Oxon 1965, DipEd Swansea 1962. Asst Lectr, Univ. of Glasgow, 1964–66. *Publications*: abridged trans., V. G. Kosolenko's History of my Contemporary, 1972; *contrib.* Slav. E Europ. Rev. *Address*: Dept of Slavonic Languages, Univ. of Glasgow, Glasgow G12 8QQ.

Partington, Thomas Martin; Lecturer, Department of Law, London School of Economics, since 1973; *b* 1944; *m* 1969; one *s.* BA Cantab 1965, LLB Cantab 1966; Barrister-at-Law 1970. Asst Lectr, Univ. of Bristol, 1966–69; Lectr, Univ. of Warwick, 1969–73. *Publications*: *contrib.* Crim. Law Rev., Parly Aff. *Address*: Dept of Law, London School of Economics, Houghton Street, Aldwych, WC2A 2AE.

Partridge, Prof. Monica, BA, PhD; Professor of Russian, and Head of Department of Slavonic Studies, University of Nottingham, since 1966; *b* 1915; *m* 1940. BA London 1936 (French), PhD London 1953 (Russian); Mem., Brit. Univs Assoc. Slavists. Asst, Dept of Phonetics, Univ. Coll., London, 1948–50; Asst Lectr, Nottingham Univ., 1950–52; Lectr, Nottingham Univ., 1952–63; Sen. Lectr, Nottingham Univ., 1963–66. Mem., British Council Sub-cttee for Exchanges between UK and USSR; Mem., Nat. Cttee, Assoc. Internat. Études S-E Europ.; Mem., Council and Exec. Cttee, Inter-Univ. Postgrad. Centre, Dubrovnik. *Publications*: trans. (with D. O. Jordan), Syrkin and Dyatkina: Structure of Molecules, 1950; Engl. version, S. C. Boyanus: Conversational Narratives Illustrating Spoken Russian, 1946–47; Angliskiy Jazyk iz Angilji, 1947–48, Serbo-Croatian, Yugoslav edn, 1964, British edn 1964, 2nd edn 1972; trans., Yugoslavia – A Journey Through her Art, 1972; *contrib.* Prometey. Renaiss. Mod. Studies, Rev. Slav. E Europ. Studies, Voprosy Lit. *Address*: Dept of Slavonic Studies, Univ. of Nottingham, Nottingham NG7 2RD.

Pascall, Dr Robert John; Lecturer, Department of Music, Nottingham University, since 1968; *b* 1944; *m* 1969. MA 1969, DPhil 1973, Oxford; FRCO 1963, ARCM 1960; Member: Royal Musical Assoc., RCO. *Publications*: *contrib.* Grove's Dictionary, Die Musik in Geschichte und Gegenwart, Soundings. *Address*: Music Dept, Univ. of Nottingham, Nottingham NG7 2RD.

Pasley, John Malcolm Sabine; Fellow of Magdalen College, University of Oxford, since 1958, and University Lecturer in German, since 1952; *b* 1926; *m* 1965; two *s.* BA Oxon 1949 (1st cl. Mod. Langs), MA Oxon 1953. Laming Travelling Fellow, Queen's Coll., Oxford, 1949–50; Lectr, Brasenose Coll., Oxford, 1950–65. *Publications*: ed, F. Kafka: Short Stories, 1963, 2nd edn 1968; (jtly) Kafka-Symposion, 1965; ed, F. Kafka: Der Heizer, etc, 1966; ed, Germany: Companion to German Studies, 1972; *contrib.* Deuts. Viertel. Lit. Geistes., Germ. Life Lett., Mod. Lang. Rev., Oxford Germ. Studies. *Address*: Magdalen College, Oxford.

Passey, Michael Leighton Struth; Lecturer, Faculty of Law, University of Leeds, since 1967; *b* 1937. BA Cantab 1959, MA Cantab 1964; Solicitor 1963. *Address*: Faculty of Law, Univ. of Leeds, Leeds LS2 9JT.

Paterson, Geoffrey Mitchell; Librarian, Bedford College, University of London, since 1968; *b* 1927; *m* 1953; two *s.* BA Cantab 1948; ALA 1953. Asst Libr., later Dep. Libr., Imperial Coll. of Science and Technol., 1961–68. Editor, Index to Theses, 1963– . *Address*: Bedford Coll., Regent's Park, NW1 4NS.

Paterson, Prof. John Harris; Professor of Geography, University of Leicester, since 1975; *b* 1923; *m* 1952; two *s* one *d.* BA Cambridge 1948 (1st cl. Geography), MA Wisconsin 1950; FRGS. Asst Lectr, Cambridge Univ., 1951–56; Lectr, St Andrews Univ., 1956–64, Sen. Lectr, 1964–74. *Publications*: North America, 1960, 5th edn 1974;

Land, Work and Resources, 1972. *Address*:
Dept of Geography, Univ. of Leicester,
Leicester LE1 7RH.

Paterson, Dr Ronald William Keith; Lecturer in Philosophy, Department of Adult
Education, University of Hull, since 1962;
b 1933; *m* 1964. MA St Andrews 1955, DipEd
St Andrews 1958, BPhil St Andrews 1962,
PhD Hull 1972; Member: Mind Assoc.,
Brit. Soc. for Phenomenology, Soc. Psychic.
Res. Staff Tutor, Holly Royde Coll., Dept
of Extra-Mural Studies, Univ. of Manchester, 1959–61. *Publications*: The Nihilistic
Egoist: Max Stirner, 1971; *contrib*. Adult
Educn, Philos. Qly, Ratio, Rewley House
Papers, Studies in Adult Educn. *Address*:
Dept of Adult Education, Univ. of Hull, Hull
HU6 7RX.

Paterson, Prof. Thomas Thomson; Research Professor, Chesters Management
Centre, University of Strathclyde, since
1971; *b* 1909; *m*; one *s* one *d*. BSc Edinburgh
1930 and 1933; MA Cantab 1937, PhD
Cantab 1941; FRSE. Fellow, Trinity College, Cambridge, 1936; Sen. Lectr in Industrial Relations, Univ. of Glasgow, 1951–
62; Prof., Dept of Industrial Admin., Royal
Coll. of Sci. and Technology, subseq. Univ.
of Strathclyde, 1962–71. Mem., various
Ministerial cttees; Mem., HM Commn on
Reorganization of Southern Rhodesia Public
Services, 1961–63; Adviser to various Govts;
Adviser on reorganization of Technion,
Haifa. *Publications*: Studies on the Ice Age in
the Himalaya, 1939; Eskimo String Figures,
1949; Soan, Prehistory of the Punjab, 1949;
Morale in War and Work, 1956; Glasgow
Ltd, Industrial War and Peace, 1960; Reorganization of Southern Rhodesia Public
Services, 1961; Local Government in
Southern Rhodesia, 1962; Job Evaluation in
the Public Services, 1963; Management
Theory, 1966; Job Evaluation: a new
method, 1972; Job Evaluation: a manual on
the Paterson method, 1972. *Address*: Chesters
Management Centre, Bearsden, Glasgow.

Paterson, Dr William Edgar; Volkswagen
Lecturer in German Politics, University of
Warwick, since 1970; *b* 1941; *m* 1964; two *s*.
MA St Andrews 1964, MSc London 1965,
PhD London 1973; Mem. Royal Inst. Internat. Affairs. Lectr in Internat. Relations,
Aberdeen Univ., 1967–70. *Publications*: (with
I. Campbell) Social Democracy in Post-War
Europe, 1974; The SPD and European Integration, 1974; *contrib*. Australian Outlook,
Cooperation and Conflict, Europa Archiv. Internat. Affairs, Internat. Spectator, Public
Affairs, Res Publica, etc. *Address*: Univ. of
Warwick, Coventry, Warwicks CV4 7AL.

Patmore, Prof. John Allan, BLitt, MA;
Professor of Geography, University of Hull,
since 1973; *b* 1931; *m* 1956; one *s* two *d*. BA
Oxon 1952 (1st cl. Geography), MA Oxon
1956, BLitt Oxon 1959. Tutor, then Asst
Lectr, Lectr and Sen. Lectr, Univ. of Liverpool, 1954–73; Vis. Prof., Univ. of S Illinois,
1962–63; Brit. Acad. Res. Fellowship, 1967–
69. Educn Br., RAF, 1952–54; Mem.,
Council, Inst. Brit. Geogrs, 1970–73; Mem.
Exec., Geog. Assoc., 1972– ; Mem.,

Human Geog. Cttee, SSRC, 1973– ;
Specialist Adv., House of Lords Select Cttee
on Sport and Leisure, 1971–73. *Publications*:
Atlas of Harrogate, 1962; (with J. Clarke)
Railway History in Pictures: NW England,
1968; ed (with A. G. Hodgkiss), Merseyside
in Maps, 1970; Land and Leisure, 1970, pbk
edn 1972; ed (with H. B. Rodgers), Leisure
in the North. West, 1972; *contrib*. Econ
Geog., Geog., Jl Transp. Hist., Trans Inst.
Brit. Geogrs, Geog. Jl. *Address*: Dept of
Geography, Univ. of Hull, Hull HU6 7RX.

Paton, George Edmiston Charles; Lecturer in Sociology, Department of Industrial
Administration, University of Aston in Birmingham, since 1968; *b* 1932; *m* 1962; two
s. DipPublic and Social Admin Oxon 1960,
BA Nottingham 1963, MA Nottingham
1968; Mem., Brit. Sociol. Assoc. Asst Lectr,
Strathclyde Univ., 1965–68. Res. Off. Brit.
Assoc. Colliery Mngmt, 1963–65. *Address*:
Dept of Industrial Administration, Univ. of
Aston, Birmingham B4 7ET.

Patrides, Dr C. A.; Reader in English and
Related Literature, University of York, since
1970; *b* 1930. BA Kenyon 1952, DPhil Oxon
1957; Mem., Engl. Assoc., MHRA, MLA,
Renaiss. Soc. Lectr, Univ. of California,
Berkeley, 1957–59; Asst Prof., Univ. of
California, Berkeley, 1959–63; Assoc. Prof.,
Univ. of California, Berkeley, 1964; Lectr,
Univ. of York, 1964–66; Sen. Lectr, Univ. of
York, 1966–70. *Publications*: ed, Milton's
Lycidas: The Tradition and the Poem, 1961;
Milton and the Christian Tradition, 1966;
ed, Milton's Epic Poetry, 1967; ed, Approaches to Paradise Lost, 1969; ed, The
Cambridge Platonists, 1969; ed, Ralegh's
History of the World, 1971; (jtly) Bright
Essence, 1971; The Grand Design of God,
1972; ed, Herbert's English Poems, 1974;
ed, Milton: Selected Prose, 1974; ed, Sir
Thomas Browne: Selected Prose, 1975;
contrib. Harv. Theol. Rev., Jl Hist. Ideas,
PMLA, Studies Engl. Lit., Studies Renaiss.,
etc. *Address*: Dept of English, Univ. of York,
Heslington, York YO1 5DD.

Patterson, Dr David; Cowley Lecturer in
Post-Biblical Hebrew, University of Oxford,
since 1956, Fellow St Cross Coll., Oxford,
since 1965, and Principal, Oxford Centre for
Post-Graduate Hebrew Studies, since 1972; *b*
1922; *m* 1950; two *s* two *d*. BA Manchester
1949 (1st cl. Semitic Languages), MA
Manchester 1953, MA Oxon 1956, PhD
Manchester 1962; Mem., Soc. OT Studies.
Asst Lectr, then Lectr, Manchester Univ.,
1953–56; Vis. Prof., Cornell Univ., 1966–71;
Kennicott Hebrew Fellow, Oxford, 1958–59.
Hon. Pres., IUJF, 1957; Chm., Cultural
Cttee, Wld Jewish Cong., Brit. Sect., 1962–
64; Chm., Educn Cttee, Hillel Foundn,
1960–64; Chm., Educn Cttee, B'nai Brith,
1969– ; Chm., Fac. of Oriental Studies,
Oxford, 1968–69; Chm., Grad. Studies
Cttee, Bd of Fac. of Oriental Studies, Oxford,
1969–71; Gen. Ed., Studies in Modern
Hebrew Lit., 1964– ; Series Ed., Jewish
Heritage Classics, 1967– . *Publications*:
The Foundations of Modern Hebrew Literature, 1961; Abraham Mapu, 1964; The
Hebrew Novel in Czarist Russia, 1964; trans.,

539

The King of Flesh and Blood, 1958; Children's Machzor for the New Year and Day of Atonement, 1966; contrib. Encyclopaedia Britannica; Encyclopaedia Judaica; contrib. Ann. Leeds Orient. Soc., BJRL, Jewish Jl Sociol., Jl Semit. Studies, Jl Jewish Studies, Proc. Wld Cong. Jewish Studies. *Address*: Oriental Institute, Pusey Lane, Oxford.

Pattison, Prof. Bruce, MA, PhD; Professor of Education, University of London Institute of Education, since 1948; *b* 1908; *m* 1937. BA Dunelm 1929 (English), MA Dunelm 1932, PhD Cantab 1933. Lectr in English, Univ. Coll., London, 1936–48; Reader, 1948. Bd of Trade, 1941–43; Min. of Supply, 1943–45. *Publication*: Music and Poetry of the English Renaissance, 1948, 2nd edn 1970. *Address*: Univ. of London Institute of Education, Malet Street, WC1E 7HS.

Pattison, Dr David Graham; Fellow of Magdalen College, since 1969, Lecturer in Spanish, University of Oxford, since 1966; *b* 1942; *m* 1964; two *s*. BA Oxon 1963 (2nd cl. Mod. Langs: Spanish and French), MA Oxon 1967, DPhil Oxon 1971. Asst Lectr, Queen's Univ., Belfast, 1965–66. *Publications*: contrib. Mod. Lang. Rev., Vox Romanicum, Neophilologus. *Address*: Magdalen College, Oxford OX1 4AU.

Paul, James Alexander; Senior Lecturer, Department of Education, Queen's University, Belfast, since 1973 (Lecturer, 1964–73); *b* 1929; *m* 1955; one *s* one *d*. BA Queen's Univ., Belfast 1950 (History), DipEd Queen's Univ., Belfast 1954, MEd Queen's Univ., Belfast 1962. Mem., Bd of Govs, Belfast Royal Acad., 1969– . *Address*: Dept of Education, Queen's Univ., Belfast BT7 1NN.

Paulin, Dr Roger Cole; Lecturer in German, University of Cambridge, and Fellow, Trinity College, Cambridge, since 1974; *b* 1937; *m* 1966; one *s* one *d*. MA New Zealand 1958–59, Drphil Heidelberg 1965, MA Cantab 1974. Asst Lectr, Birmingham Univ., 1963–64; Lectr in German, Bristol Univ., 1965–74; Vis. Prof., Waterloo Univ., Canada, 1971–72. *Publications*: Gryphius' 'Cardenio und Celinde' und Arnims 'Halle und Jerusalem', 1968; contrib. The Romantic Period in Germany, 1970; Zur Literatur der Restaurationsepoche, 1970; contrib. Seminar, Literaturwiss. Jbh. *Address*: Trinity College, Cambridge CB2 1TQ.

Pavlov, Alexander; Lecturer in Russian, School of Humanities, New University of Ulster, since 1968; *b* 1926; *m* 1952; two *s* one *d*. MA Glasgow 1968 (Hons), MPhil New Univ. of Ulster 1971. *Publications*: contrib. ATR, Jl Russian Stud. *Address*: School of Humanities, New Univ. of Ulster, Coleraine, Co. Londonderry BT52 1SA.

Pavlowitch, Stevan K.; Senior Lecturer in the History of the Balkans, Department of History, University of Southampton, since 1973 (Lecturer, 1965–73); *b* 1933; *m* 1967; one *s*. LèsL Paris and Lille 1956, BA London 1956, MA London 1959. *Publications*: Anglo-Russian Rivalry in Serbia 1837–1839,

1961; Yugoslavia, 1971; *contrib.* Annales, East. Chs Rev., Europ. Studies Rev., Rass. Stor. Risorg., Rev. Study Centre Yugos. Aff., Slav. Rev., Slav. E Europ. Rev., Survey. *Address*: Dept of History, The Univ., Southampton SO9 5NH.

Payne, Andrew Howard, MSc; Lecturer in Mechanics of Sport, Department of Physical Education, University of Birmingham, since 1964; *b* 1931; *m* 1960; two *s*. BSc Witwatersrand 1951, MSc Birmingham 1960, Grad. Commerce Dip. Birmingham 1961; Mem., Physical Educn Assoc., Mem., AUT. Esquire Bedell, Univ. of Birmingham, 1969. Univ. of Birmingham SCR, 1971. *Publications*: Hammer Throwing, 1969; *contrib.* ALTA, Biomech., Brit. Jl Sports Med., Bull. Physical Educn, Ergonom., Jl Physical Educn, Med. Sport. *Address*: Physical Education Dept, Univ. of Birmingham, PO Box 363, Birmingham B15 2TT.

Payne, David Frank, MA; Senior Lecturer, since 1972, and Head of Department of Semitic Studies, Queen's University of Belfast, since 1967; *b* 1931; *m* 1960; two *s* two *d*. BA Sheffield 1952 (1st cl.), MA Glasgow 1955 (1st cl.). Asst Cataloguer, Manchester Univ., 1959; Asst Lectr in Biblical History and Literature, Sheffield Univ., 1959–62; Lectr, Sheffield Univ., 1962–67. Mem., Cttee, Tyndale Fellowship for Biblical Res. *Publications*: contrib. Ann. Swedish Theol. Inst., Evang. Qly, Jl Semitic Studies. *Address*: Dept of Semitic Studies, The Queen's Univ., Belfast BT7 1NN.

Payne, Prof. Peter Lester; Professor of Economic History, University of Aberdeen, since 1969; *b* 1929; *m* 1960; one *s* one *d*. BA Nottingham 1951 (Economic and Social History), PhD Nottingham 1954. Vis. Lectr in Amer. Econ. Hist., Johns Hopkins Univ., Baltimore, 1957–58; Lectr in Econ. and Social Hist., Nottingham, 1958–59; Colquhoun Lectr in Business Hist., Glasgow, 1959–64; Sen. Lectr (Colquhoun) in Econ. Hist., Glasgow, 1964–69. Res. Off., Business Archives Council, 1959–63; Hon. Sec., Business Archives Council Scotland, 1959–69. *Publications*: (with L. E. Davis) The Savings Bank of Baltimore, 1818–1866: A Historical and Analytical Study, 1956; Rubber and Railways in the Nineteenth Century, 1961; ed, Studies in Scottish Business History, 1967; British Entrepreneurship in the Nineteenth Century, 1974; *contrib.* Aberdeen Univ. Rev., Archives, Business Hist., Business Hist. Rev., Econ. Hist. Rev., Explor. Entrepren. Hist., Jl Transp. Hist., Scott. Jl Pol. Econ. *Address*: Dept of Economic History, Univ. of Aberdeen, King's College, Old Aberdeen AB9 2UB.

Paynter, Marion Edith Stephanie; Lecturer, Department of Town and Country Planning, Heriot-Watt University, Edinburgh College of Art, since 1965; *b* 1922. Dip. Landscape Design Dunelm 1951; Dip. Civic Design Liverpool 1956; FILA 1965 (AILA 1951), MRTPI (AMPTI 1956). *Address*: Heriot-Watt Univ./Edinburgh College of Art, 39 Palmerston Place, Edinburgh EH12 5AU.

Pe, Prof. Hla, MA, PhD; Professor of Burmese, Department of SE Asia and the Islands, School of Oriental and African Studies, University of London, since 1966; *b* 1915; *m* 1970. BA Rangoon 1936 (1st cl. Burmese), MA Rangoon 1938, DipEd London 1939, PhD London 1944. Lectr, SOAS, London Univ., 1948–55; Reader, London Univ., 1955–66. *Publications*: Konmara Pya Zat (Play), vol. i, Introduction and Translation, 1952; Burmese Proverbs, 1962; Jt-Ed., A Burmese–English Dictionary pts ii, iii, iv, v, 1952– ; *contrib*. Bull. SOAS, Jl Burm. Res. Soc., Lingua. *Address*: Dept of SE Asia and the Islands, School of Oriental and African Studies, Univ. of London, WC1E 7HP.

Peace, Richard Arthur; Senior Lecturer in Charge of Russian, Sub-Department of Russian Studies, University of Bristol, since 1972; *b* 1933; *m* 1960; one *s* two *d*. BA 1957, MA 1962, BLitt 1962, Oxon. *Publications*: Dostoyevsky: an examination of the major novels, 1971; *contrib*. Jl of Assoc. of Teachers of Russian, Slav. and E European Rev. *Address*: Dept of Russian Studies, Univ. of Bristol, 81 Woodland Road, Bristol BS8 1US.

Peach, Dr Guthlac Ceri Klaus, MA, DPhil; Lecturer in Geography, Oxford University, since 1966, and Fellow of St Catherine's College, since 1969; *b* 1939; *m* 1964; two *s* one *d*. BA Oxon 1961, MA, DPhil Oxon 1964; FRGS, Mem., Inst. Brit. Geogrs. Deptal Demonstrator, Sch. of Geography, Oxford, 1964–66; Dean, St Catherine's Coll., 1971–73, Sen. Tutor, 1974. Mem., Res. Cttee, RGS, 1971. *Publications*: West Indian Migration to Britain: A Social Geography, 1968; *contrib*. Geog. Jl, Internat. Mig. Rev., Race, Soc. Econ. Studies, Sociol. Rev., Trans Inst. Brit. Geogrs. *Address*: School of Geography, Mansfield Road, Oxford.

Peacock, Prof. Alan Turner, DSC, MA; Professor of Economics, University of York, since 1962; on secondment as Chief Economic Adviser, Department of Industry, 1973–76; *b* 1922; *m* 1944; two *s* one *d*. MA St Andrews 1947 (1st cl. Econ./Polit.); Mem., Royal Econ. Soc., Mem., Internat. Inst. Public Fin. Lectr, St Andrews Univ., 1947–48; Lectr, LSE, 1948–51; Reader, LSE, 1951–56; Prof. of Econ. Science, Edinburgh Univ., 1956–62; Vis. Prof., Johns Hopkins Univ., 1958; Vis. Res. Prof., Einaudi Foundn, Turin, 1970. Lt, RNVR, 1943–45; Asst Ed., Economica, 1949–56; Mem., Council, Royal Econ. Soc., 1961–71; Mem., Allen Cttee on Impact of Rates, 1965; Pres., Internat. Inst. Public Fin., 1966–69; Mem., Commn on Constitution, 1970–73; Mem., Social Science Res. Council, 1972–73; Dep. Vice-Chancellor, Univ. of York, 1963–69. *Publications*: Economics of National Insurance, 1952; ed, Income Redistribution and Social Policy, 1954; (with D. Dosser) National Income of Tanganyika, 1958; (with H. C. Edey) National Income and Social Accounting, 1954, 3rd edn 1967; (with R. A. Musgrave) Classics in The Theory of Public Finance, 1958; (with J. Wiseman) The Growth of Public Expenditure in the UK (1890–1955), 1961, 2nd edn 1967; (with G. K, Shaw) Economic Theory of Fiscal Policy,

1971; *contrib*. Brit. Tax Rev., Econ. Jl, Economica, Finanz Archiv., Jl Polit. Econ., Jl Royal Stat. Soc., Kyklos, Nat. Tax Jl, Public Fin., Rev. Econ. Stat., Rev. Econ. Studies, Scott. Jl Pol. Econ. *Address*: Department of Industry, 1 Victoria Street, SW1H 0ET.

Peacock, Percy Gordon; Librarian, University of Stirling, since 1971; *b* 1934; *m* 1960; two *s* two *d*. BA Hons Cantab 1956 (Classics). Asst Librarian, St Andrews Univ., 1961–66; Sub Librarian, Univ. Stirling, 1966–71. *Address*: Univ. of Stirling, Stirling FK9 4LA.

Peacock, Prof. Ronald, MA, DLitt, DPhil; Professor of German, Bedford College, University of London, since 1962; *b* 1907; *m* 1933. BA Leeds 1929 (1st cl. Fr.-Ger.), MA Leeds 1930 (dist.), DPhil Marburg 1933, LittD Leeds; Mem., Mod. Hum. Res. Assoc., Mem., Engl. Goethe Soc. Asst Lectr, Leeds Univ., 1931–38; Lectr, Leeds Univ., 1938–39; Prof., Leeds Univ., 1939–45; Prof., Manchester Univ., 1945–62; Vis. Prof., Cornell Univ., 1949; Vis. Prof. of German and Comparative Literature, Heidelberg Univ., 1960–61; Prof. of Modern German Literature, Freiburg, 1965, 1967–68. Dean, Fac. of Arts, Manchester, 1954–56; Pro-Vice-Chancellor, Manchester, 1958–62. *Publications*: Hölderlin, 1938; The Poet in the Theatre, 1946, new American and pbk edn 1960; The Art of Drama, 1957, Portuguese edn 1968; Goethe's Major Plays, 1959, 2nd edn 1966; Criticism and Personal Taste, 1972; *contrib*. Deuts. Viertel. Lit. Geistes., Euphor., Ger. Life Lett., Mod. Lang. Rev., Publicns Engl. Goethe Soc., Univs Qly. *Address*: Dept of German Studies, Bedford College, Regents Park, NW1 4NS.

Pear, Prof. Richard Hatherley, BSC(Econ); Professor of Politics, University of Nottingham, since 1965; *b* 1916; *m* 1941; one *s* one *d*. BSc(Econ) London 1938 (1st cl.). Asst Lectr in Government, LSE, 1947–49; Lectr, LSE, 1949–60; Reader in Political Science (with special reference to US government and politics), LSE, 1960–65. Councillor (Labour), St Marylebone, 1955–57; Finchley, 1959–61; Chm., Europ. Assoc. Amer. Studies, 1956–60; Mem., Cttee Polit. Studies Assoc. UK, 1970– . *Publications*: American Government, 1955, 2nd edn 1963; (with Benney and Gray), How People Vote, 1956; contrib. British Essays in American History, 1957; American Civilization: an Introduction, 1968, etc; *contrib*. Mod. Law Rev., Polit. Qly. *Address*: Dept of Politics, Univ. of Nottingham, University Park, Nottingham NG7 2RD.

Pearl, Dr David Stephen, PhD; Director of Studies in Law, and Fellow, Fitzwilliam College, University of Cambridge, since 1969, and University Lecturer in Law, since 1972; *b* 1944; *m* 1967; two *s*. LLB Birmingham 1965 (1st cl.), LLB Cantab 1967 (1st cl. International Law), MA Cantab 1969, PhD Cantab 1971; Yorke Prize, 1972; Barrister, of Gray's Inn, 1968. Supervisor, Queens' Coll., Cambridge, 1966–67; Res. Fellow, Queens' Coll., Cambridge, 1967–69; Univ. Asst Lectr, Cambridge, 1967–72; Vis. Schol., Univ. of Punjab, Lahore, 1968–69. *Publications*:

541

Islamic Law on the Indian Sub-continent, 1975; *contrib.* Cambridge Law Jl, S Asian Rev., New Community, Jl Family Law. *Address*: Fitzwilliam College, Cambridge.

Pearl, Dr Valerie Louise, MA, DPhil, FRHistS; Reader in the History of London, Department of History, University College London, since 1968; *b* 1926; *m* 1949; one *d.* BA Oxon 1949 (Hons History), MA Oxon 1953, DPhil Oxon 1953; FRHistS 1968. Sen. Res. Student, St Hugh's Coll., Oxford, 1951–52; Lectr in Hist., and Rose Graham Res. Fellow, Somerville Coll., Oxford, 1965–68; Mem., Student Accomm. Cttee, UCL, 1971– ; Vis. Prof., Bryn Mawr, USA, 1974–75. Chm., London Cttee, Hist. Atlas of Town Plans of W Europe, 1968– ; Mem., Libr. Cttee, Inst. Hist Res., 1969– ; Mem., Council, London Rec. Soc., 1969– ; Editor-in-Chief, London Jl, 1974– ; Lit. Dir, RHistS, 1975– . *Publications*: London and the Outbreak of the Puritan Revolution, 1961; chapter, in, Nuove Questioni di Storia Moderna, ed L. Bulferetti, 1964; chapter, in, Studies in London History presented to P. E. Jones, ed A. E. J. Hollaender and W. Kellaway, 1969; *contrib.* London, in, Encyclopedia Americana, 1972; chapter, in, Quest for Settlement, 1646–60, ed G. E. Aylmer, 1972; *contrib.* EHR, Past and Present, TLS, Trans RHistS. *Address*: Dept of History, Univ. College London, Gower Street, WC1E 6BT.

Pears, David Francis, FBA; Student and Tutor in Philosophy, Christ Church, Oxford, since 1960, and Reader in Philosophy, University of Oxford, since 1972; *b* 1921; *m* 1963; one *s* one *d.* BA Oxon 1947 (1st cl. Lit. Hum.), MA Oxon 1947; FBA 1970. Res. Lectr, Christ Church, 1948–50; Univ. Lectr, Oxford, 1950–72; Fellow and Tutor, Corpus Christi Coll., 1950–60; Vis. Prof., Harvard, 1959; Univ. of California, Berkeley, 1964; Council of Humanities Fellow, Princeton, 1966; Vis. Prof., Rockefeller Univ., 1967; Hill Prof., Univ. of Minnesota, 1970. *Publications*: Bertrand Russell and the British Tradition in Philosophy, 1967, 2nd edn 1972; Ludwig Wittgenstein (Modern Masters series), 1971; What is Knowledge?, 1971; *contrib.* Analysis, Canad. Jl Philos., Mind, Philos. Qly, Proc. Aristot. Soc., Ratio. *Address*: Christ Church, Oxford.

Pearsall, Derek Albert, MA; Reader, Department of English and Related Literature, University of York, since 1971; *b* 1931; *m* 1952; two *s* three *d.* MA Birmingham 1952. Asst Lectr, King's Coll., London, 1959–62; Lectr, King's Coll., London, 1962–65; Vis. Prof., Univ. of Toronto, 1963–64; Lectr, Univ. of York, 1965–67; Sen. Lectr, Univ. of York, 1967–71. *Publications*: ed, The Floure and the Leafe, 1962; ed, Piers Plowman: selections from the C-text, 1967; John Lydgate, 1970; Landscapes and Seasons of the Medieval World, 1973; *contrib.* Libr., Mediaev. Studies, Mod. Lang. Rev., PMLA, Rev. Engl. Studies, Univ. Toronto Qly. *Address*: Univ. of York, King's Manor, York.

Pearson, Alan Wilfred, BSc; Senior Lecturer in Decision Analysis, Manchester Business School, University of Manchester, since 1970; *b* 1934; *m* 1959; three *s* one *d.* BSc London 1960. Lectr in Econ. Stats, Univ. of Manchester, 1964–70; Lectr in Operational Res., Manchester Business School, 1964–70. Dir, R and D Res. Unit, 1967– ; Mem., Res. Cttee, Shirley Inst., Manchester; Mem., Tech. Adv. Cttee, Internat. Inst. for Management of Technology, Milan; Mem. Edit. Bd, IEEE Trans on Engrg Management; Mem. COLRAD; Editor, R and D Management. *Publications*: *contrib.* Brit. Chem. Eng., IEEE Trans Eng. Mngmt, Indust. Mktg Mngmt, Jl Mngmt Studies, Nature, New Sci., R and D Mngmt. *Address*: Manchester Business School, Booth Street West, Manchester M15 6PB.

Pearson, Doreen, MA; Lecturer in Education, University of Newcastle upon Tyne, since 1968; *b* 1921; *m* 1945; one *d.* BA Dunelm 1941, MA Dunelm 1944, DipEd Dunelm 1942. Pt-time Lectr, King's Coll., Univ. of Durham, 1956–68. *Address*: Dept of Education, Univ. of Newcastle upon Tyne, St Thomas Street, Newcastle upon Tyne NE1 7RU.

Pearson, Mowbray Grayhurst, OBE, MA; Lecturer in Geography, University of Edinburgh, since 1966; *b* 1914. MA Edinburgh 1937; FRMetS. OC 3603 (City of Edinburgh) FCU, RAuxAF, 1948–54; Vice-Chm. (Air), Edinburgh and Lothians TAFA, 1958–69. *Publications*: *contrib.* Weather. *Address*: Dept of Geography, Univ. of Edinburgh, High School Yards, Edinburgh EH1 1NN.

Pearson, Dr Raymond; Lecturer, History Department, New University of Ulster, since 1968; *b* 1942; *m* 1968. BA Durham 1964 (Hons History), PhD Durham 1973. *Publication*: Revolution in Russia, 1973. *Address*: History Dept, New Univ. of Ulster, Coleraine, Co. Londonderry BT52 1SA.

Pearson, Dr Ronald; Senior Lecturer, Department of Zoology, Liverpool University (also teaches Historical Biogeography), since 1973 (Lecturer, 1961–73); *b* 1936; *m* 1957; two *s* one *d.* BA Cambridge 1957 (1st cl.), MA, PhD Cambridge 1960; Fellow Cambridge Philos. Soc. 1958, FZS 1959, FREntomolSoc. 1957. Asst in Res., Sub-dept of Quaternary Res., Botany Sch., Cambridge, 1957–60; Zoologist, Biophysics Unit, Kings Coll., London, 1960–61. *Publications*: Animals and Plants of the Cenozoic Era, 1964; The Avian Brain, 1972; The Vertebrate Brain (forthcoming); *contrib.* Arch. Hydrobiol., Jl Anim. Ecol., Jl Linn. Soc., Proc. Royal Entomol. Soc., Proc. Royal Soc. (B), Biol. Revs. *Address*: Univ. of Liverpool, PO Box 147, Liverpool L69 3BX.

Pedley, Prof. Robin; Head of School of Education and Dean of the Faculty of Education, University of Southampton, since 1971; *b* 1914; *m* 1951; one *s* one *d.* MA, PhD, Teaching Dip. Durham. Res. Fellow, Durham Univ., 1936–38; Schoolmaster, Friends' Sch., Great Ayton, 1938–42, and Crossley and Porter Schs, Halifax, 1943–46; Lectr, Coll. of St Mark and St John, Chelsea, 1946–47; Lectr (later Sen. Lectr), Leicester

Univ. Dept of Educn, 1947–63; Dir, Exeter Univ. Inst. of Educn, 1963–71. *Publications*: Comprehensive Schools Today, 1955; Comprehensive Education: a new approach, 1956; The Comprehensive School, 1963, rev. edn 1969; (with J. Orring) The Comprehensive School (in Hebrew, publ. Jerusalem), 1966; The Comprehensive University, 1969; *contrib.* Educn, Forum, Times Higher Educn Supp., etc. *Address*: Univ. of Southamptan, Highfield, Southampton SO9 5NH.

Peel, Prof. Edwin Arthur, PhD, DLit; Professor of Educational Psychology, University of Birmingham, since 1950; *b* 1911; *m* 1939; two *s* two *d*. BSc Leeds 1932 (Hons Chem.), MA London 1938 (Education), PhD London 1945, DLit London 1960; FBPsS. Lectr, Kings Coll., Newcastle, 1946; Reader in Psychology, Univ. of Durham, 1946–48; Prof. of Educational Psychology, Univ. of Durham,↑1948–50. Pres., Brit. Psychol. Soc., 1961; Pres., Assoc. Programmed Learning and Educnl Technol., 1967–68; Mem., Birmingham Educn Cttee, 1965–71; Chm., Midland Sect., RSA, 1968–72. *Publications*: Psychological Basis of Education, 1956, 2nd edn 1967; The Pupil's Thinking, 1960; The Nature of Adolescent Judgement, 1972; chapters, in, various bks on Educn and Educnl Psychol.; *contrib.* Brit. Jl Educnl Psychol., Brit. Jl Math. Stat. Psychol., Brit. Jl Psychol., Educnl Rev., Nature, Psychomet. *Address*: School of Education, Univ. of Birmingham, PO Box 363, Birmingham B15 2TT.

Peel, Prof. Ronald Francis Edward Waite, MBE, MA; Professor of Geography, University of Bristol, since 1957; *b* 1912; *m* 1938; one *d*. MA Cantab 1937; FRGS, FRMetSoc. Lectr, King's Coll., Durham Univ., 1935–39; Bagnold exploring expedn, Libyan Desert, 1938; served with RE, 1939–45; King's Coll., Durham Univ., 1945–46; Dept of Geog., Cambridge Univ., 1946, Lectr, Cambridge Univ., 1949, Fellow of St Catharine's Coll., 1949; Prof., Leeds Univ., 1951–57, Head of Dept, Leeds Univ., 1953–57; expedns to Ruwenzori Mountains 1952, W and C Sahara, 1961; Dean of Science, Bristol Univ., 1968–70. Pres., Inst. Brit. Geogrs, 1965; Pres., Section E, Brit. Assoc., 1967. Cuthbert Peake Award of RGS, 1950. *Publications*: Physical Geography, 1951; *contrib.* Brit. and foreign jls. *Address*: Dept of Geography, Univ. of Bristol, Bristol BS8 1TH.

Peil, Dr Margaret; Senior Lecturer, Centre of West African Studies, Birmingham University, since 1971; *b* 1929. BS Milwaukee-Downer Coll. 1951, MA Fordham 1961, PhD Chicago 1963. Mem., African Studies Assoc. of UK. Univ. of Ghana, 1963–68; Birmingham Univ., 1968– ; Univ. of Lagos, 1971–72. *Publications*: The Ghanaian Factory Worker: Industrial Man in Africa, 1972; (with D. Lucas) Survey Research Methods for West Africa, 1972; *contrib.* Africa, Br. Jl Sociol., Can. Jl Afr. Stud., Jl Mod. Afr. Stud. *Address*: Centre of West African Studies, Birmingham Univ., Birmingham B15 2TT.

Pelczynski, Dr Zbigniew Andrzej; Fellow and Lecturer in Politics, Pembroke College,

Oxford University, since 1961; *b* 1925; *m* 1961; one *s* two *d*. MA St Andrews 1949 (1st cl. Political Economy and Political Science), BPhil Oxon 1951 (Politics), DPhil Oxon 1956; Lectr in Politics, Trinity, then Balliol and Merton and later, Pembroke and Merton Colls, Oxford, 1953–61. *Publications*: (with T. M. Knox) Hegel's Political Writings, 1964; ed, Hegel's Political Philosophy, 1971; *contrib.* Internat. Aff., Parly Aff., Polit. Studies, Pol Sci. Qly, Canad. Slav. Papers, EHR, Pub. Law. *Address*: Pembroke College, Oxford OX1 1DW.

Pelling, Dr Henry Mathison; Assistant Director of Research, Faculty of History, University of Cambridge, and Fellow of St John's College, since 1966; *b* 1920. MA Cantab 1947, MA Oxon 1949, PhD Cantab 1950; Member: Brit. Assoc. for Amer. Studies; Econ. Hist. Assoc.; Pol Studies Assoc.; Assoc. of Univ. Teachers; Victorian Studies Assoc. Fellow of Queen's Coll., Oxford and Praelector in Mod. Hist., 1949–65; Tutor, 1950–65; Dean, 1962–63. *Publications*: (translations omitted) Origins of the Labour Party, 1954, 2nd edn 1965; ed, Challenge of Socialism, 1954, 2nd edn 1968; America and the British Left, 1956; (with F. W. Bealey) Labour and Politics, 1900–06, 1958; British Communist Party, 1958, 2nd edn 1974; American Labor, 1960; Modern Britain 1885–1955, 1960; Short History of the Labour Party, 1961, 5th edn 1974; History of British Trade Unionism, 1963, 2nd edn 1971; Social Geography of British Elections, 1967; Popular Politics and Society in Late Victorian Britain, 1968; Britain and the Second World War, 1970; Winston Churchill: a biography, 1974; *contrib.* Bull. of Soc. for Study of Labour Hist., Econ. Hist. Rev., Pol Studies. *Address*: St John's Coll., Cambridge.

Pembroke, Simon Geoffrey, MA; Lecturer, Department of Greek, Bedford College, University of London, since 1966; *b* 1938. BA Cantab 1961 (1st cl. Classics Pt I 1960, 1st cl. (dist.) Classics Pt II), MA Cantab 1963; Mem., Hellenic Soc., Mem., Roman Soc., Mem., Royal Anthropol. Inst. Lectr, Warburg Inst., 1963–64; Res. Fellow (Saxl Fund), 1964–65; Asst Lectr, Bedford Coll., 1965; Fellow, Kings Coll., Cambridge, 1966–70. *Publications*: contrib. Problems in Stoicism, ed A. A. Long, 1971; *contrib.* Annales (ESC), JESHO, Jl Warb. Court. Inst. *Address*: Dept of Greek, Bedford College, Regents Park, NW1 4NS.

Pender, Malcolm John, MA; Lecturer, German Section, Department of Modern Languages, University of Strathclyde, since 1964; *b* 1935; *m* 1967. BA Cantab 1957. Chm., Scott.-Germ. Soc., 1968– . *Publications*: *contrib.* Lit. Krit. *Address*: Dept of Modern Languages, Univ. of Strathclyde, Glasgow G1 1XW.

Pendry, Eric Douglas, MA, PhD; Lecturer, Department of English, University of Bristol, since 1964; *b* 1927; *m* 1954; one *s* two *d*. BA Oxon 1948 (2nd cl. English), MA Oxon 1952, PhD Birmingham 1954. Lector, Svenska Handelshögskolan, Helsinki, 1950–52; Prof., Nagoya Univ., Japan, 1954–56; Lector, Abo

543

Akademi, Finland, 1956–61; Fellow, Shakespeare Inst., Birmingham Univ., 1961–64; Vis. Prof., Hofstra Univ., NY, 1971. *Publications*: The New Feminism of English Fiction, 1956; ed, Thomas Dekker, 1967. *Address*: Dept of English, Univ. of Bristol, Bristol BS8 1TH.

Pennington, Dr Anne Elizabeth, MA, DPhil; Official Fellow and Tutor in Slavonic Languages, Lady Margaret Hall, University of Oxford, and CUF Lecturer in Russian Philology, since 1959; *b* 1934. BA Oxon 1955 (1st cl. French and Russian), Dip. Slavonic Studies Oxon 1956, MA Oxon 1959, DPhil Oxon 1964. *Publications*: trans., V. Popa: Selected Poems, 1969; trans., V. Popa: Earth Erect, 1973; *contrib.* Mod. Lang. Rev., Rev. Etudes SE Europ., Slav. E Europ. Rev., Oxf. Slav. Papers, Modern Poetry in Translation. *Address*: Lady Margaret Hall, Oxford.

Pennington, Prof. Robert R., LLD; Professor of Commercial Law, University of Birmingham, since 1968; *b* 1927; *m* 1965. LLB Birmingham 1946, LLD Birmingham 1960; Solicitor England 1951. Sen. Lectr in Commercial Law, Birmingham Univ., 1962–68. Reader, Law Soc. Sch. of Law, 1951–62; Mem., Bd of Mngmt, Coll. of Law, 1962; Govt adv. on company law reform in Trinidad, 1967; Seychelles, 1970; UN adv. on commercial legislation in developing countries, 1968– ; Adviser on Company Legislation to Commn of Europ. Communities, 1972– ; Mem., Law Soc.'s Cttee on Company Law, 1972– . *Publications*: Company Law, 1959, 3rd edn 1973; Partnership and Company Law, 1961; Companies in the Common Market, 1962, 2nd edn 1970; The Investor and the Law, 1967; Stannary Law: a history of the mining law of Cornwall and Devon, 1973; *contrib.* Acntncy Mod. Law Rev., Solic. Jl. *Address*: Faculty of Law, Univ. of Birmingham, PO Box 363, Birmingham B15 2TT.

Penny, Dr Ralph John; Lecturer in Spanish, Westfield College, University of London, since 1966; *b* 1940; *m* 1963; one *s* one *d*. MA Hons Edinburgh 1962 (1st cl.), PhD Edinburgh 1967; Member: Assoc. of Hispanists of GB and Ireland; Société de Linguistique Romane. Lectr in Spanish, Magee Univ. Coll., Londonderry, 1965–66. *Publications*: El habla pasiega: ensayo de dialectología montañesa, 1970; contrib. Medieval Hispanic studies presented to Rita Hamilton, 1974; contrib. The Year's Work in Modern Language Studies, vols 30, 31, 32, 33; *contrib.* ArchL, Orbis, RLiR, ZRP. *Address*: Westfield Coll., Hampstead, NW3 7ST.

Penrose, Prof. Edith Tilton, PhD; Professor of Economics (with reference to Asia), Department of Economic and Political Studies, School of Oriental and African Studies, University of London, since 1964; *b* 1914; *m* 1944; three *s*. AB California 1936 (Econ. Hon.), MA Johns Hopkins 1948, PhD Johns Hopkins 1951; Mem., Amer. Econ. Assoc., Royal Econ. Soc., AUT, Soc. Brit. Orient. Lectr, Johns Hopkins Univ., 1950–60; Vis. Fellow, Australian Nat. Univ.,

1955–56; Assoc. Prof., Univ. of Baghdad, 1957–59; Reader, LSE and SOAS, Univ. of London, 1960–64; Head of Dept, 1961–69; Vis. Res. Prof., Univ. of Dar Es Salaam, 1971–72. Editor, Econ. Libr. Selections, 1950–60; Mem., Sainsbury Cttee (Cttee of Enquiry into the Relationship of the Pharmaceutical Industry with the National Health Service), 1965–67; Econ. Consultant, Monopolies Commn, 1968–71; Mem., Econ. Cttee, SSRC, 1970– , Chm., 1974– ; Mem. Council SSRC, 1974– . Editor, Jl Develop. Studies, 1964–68. *Publications*: Food Control in Great Britain, 1940; The Economics of the International Patent System, 1951, Japanese edn 1957, Spanish edn 1972; The Theory of the Growth of the Firm, 1959, Japanese, French, Spanish, and Italian edns; The Large International Firm in Developing Countries: The International Petroleum Industry, 1968; (jtly) New Orientations, Essays in International Relations, 1969; The Growth of Firms, Middle East Oil and Other Essays, 1971; *contrib.* Amer. Econ. Rev., Business Hist. Rev., Econ. Jl, Economica, Jl Develop. Studies, Jl Econ Hist., Ybk Wld Aff. *Address*: Dept of Economic and Political Studies, School of Oriental and African Studies, Univ. of London, Malet Street, WC1E 7HP.

Percival, John, MA, DPhil; Senior Lecturer in Classics, University College, Cardiff, since 1972; *b* 1937; *m* 1962; two *d*. BA Oxon 1960 (Lit. Hum.), MA Oxon 1963, DPhil Oxon 1967. Asst Lectr in Ancient Hist., Univ. Coll., Cardiff, 1962–64; Lectr, 1964–72. *Publications*: *contrib.* British and foreign jls. *Address*: Dept of Classics, Univ. College, Cathays Park, Cardiff CF1 1XL.

Perkin, Rev. David Arthur, MA; Lecturer in Economic and Social History, Loughborough University of Technology, since 1966; *b* 1930. BA Oxon 1954, MA Oxon 1958. *Address*: Dept of Economics, Loughborough Univ. of Technology, Loughborough LE11 3TU.

Perkin, Prof. Harold James, MA, FRHistS; Professor of Social History, University of Lancaster, since 1967; *b* 1926; *m* 1948; one *s* one *d*. BA Cambridge 1948 (1st cl. Hist. with distinct.), MA Cambridge 1952; FRHistS, Mem., Econ. Hist. Soc., Mem., Assoc., Mem., Soc. Study Lab. Hist., Mem., Urb. Hist. Soc. Staff Tutor, Manchester Univ. Extra-Mural Dept, 1950–51; Asst Lectr, then Lectr in Social Hist., Manchester Univ., 1951–65; Sen. Lectr, Lancaster Univ., 1965–67. Pres., AUT, 1970–71; Editor, Studies in Social Hist., 1961– . *Publications*: The Origins of Modern English Society, 1780–1880, 1969, 2nd edn 1972; New Universities in the United Kingdom (OECD series Innovation in Higher Education), 1969, French edn 1969, Japanese edn 1970; Key Profession: the History of the Association of University Teachers, 1969; The Age of the Railway, 1969, 2nd edn 1970; ed, History: an Introduction for the Intending Student, 1970; *contrib.* Econ. Hist. Rev., Hist. Today, Internat. Jl Higher Educn, Soc. Hist./Hist. Soc., Trans Royal Hist. Soc., Wld Ybk Educn. *Address*: History Dept, The Univ., Lancaster.

Perkins, Dr Richard Mansfield; Lecturer, Department of Scandinavian Studies, University College London, since 1967; *b* 1939; *m* 1969. BA 1961, MA 1965, DPhil 1972 Oxon. Lectr in English, Univ. of Uppsala, Sweden, 1963–65; Asst Lectr, Dept of Scand. Studies, UCL, 1966–67. *Address:* Univ. Coll., Gower Street, WC1E 7HP.

Perman, Reginald Charles Dennis, MA; Senior Tutor, and Fellow and Tutor in French, St Peter's College, Oxford University, since 1956; *b* 1921; *m* 1941; four *d.* BA Oxon 1947 (1st cl. Mod. Langs.), MA Oxon 1948. Univ. Lectr, Oxford, and Lectr in Mod. Langs, St Peter's Coll. and Balliol Coll., 1948–56; Lectr, Corpus Christi Coll., 1959– . Sec., Mediaeval Soc., 1961– ; Gen. Ed. Blackwell's French Texts, 1968– . *Publications:* Henrì d'Arci: The Shorter Works, in, Studies in Medieval French presented to Alfred Ewert, 1961; ed, Verlaine: Selected Poems, 1965; *contrib.* Fr. Studies. *Address:* St Peter's College, Oxford.

Perrin, Prof. John Robin, BSc, MBA, PhD, MBIM; Professor and Director of the Industrial Economic and Business Research Centre, University of Warwick, since 1974; *b* 1930; *m* 1960; one *s* one *d.* BSc California 1951, MBA California 1954, PhD London 1958; MBIM, Mem., Brit. Acctng and Fin. Assoc. Asst Prof., Mount Allison, 1959–61; Lectr, Nottingham, 1962–66, Sen. Lectr, 1966–68; Prof. of Financial Control, Lancaster, 1968–74. Ed., Jl Business Fin., 1969–73; Ed., Jl Business Fin. and Acctng, 1974; Chm., Brit. Acctng and Fin. Assoc., 1971–73; Mem. Council, Inst. of Public Finance and Acctncy, 1974– ; Chm., Council of Depts of Acctng Studies, 1973–74. *Publications:* Business Success as Measured by an Accountant, in, On the Nature of Business Success, ed G. L. S. Shackle, 1968; *contrib.* Acctncy, Acctnt, Jl Business Fin., Mngmt Acctnt. *Address:* Warwick Univ., Coventry CV4 7AL.

Perrott, David Leonard; Senior Lecturer, Faculty of Law, Exeter University, since 1974 (Lecturer, 1965–74); *b* 1936; *m* 1957; two *s.* LLB Exeter 1960, BCL Oxon 1962; Mem., Soc. Public Teachers Law, Brit. Inst. Internat. Comp. Law; US Order of the Coif. Lectr, Univ. of Khartoum, 1962–65; Vis. Asst Prof., Univ. of Illinois, 1968. Acting Hd, Dept Private Law, Univ. of Khartoum, 1964–65; Mem., Sudan Council for Regulation of Legal Profession, 1963–65; Mem., Cttee, Soc. Public Teachers Law, 1966–67; Mem., Commercial Law Cttee, Assoc. of Brit. Chambers of Commerce. *Publications:* ed jtly and contrib., Fundamental Rights, 1973; contrib. Encyclopedia of European Community Law; Asst Editor, Sudan Law Rep.; *contrib.* Jl Soc. Public Teachers Law, Sudan Law Jl Rev., Sudan Law Reports. *Address:* Univ. of Exeter, Faculty of Law, Rennes Drive, Exeter, Devon.

Perrott, Prof. Elizabeth; Visiting Professor, University of Lancaster, and Director, Microteaching Research Unit, since 1972; *b* 1915; *m* 1944; one *s.* BSc Wales 1936 (1st cl. Botany), MSc Wales 1942, PhD Manchester 1957, DipEd Wales 1937; FInstBiol, FLS.

Secondary School teaching, 1937–45; Lectr Univ. Coll. of Wales, Aberystwyth, 1945–47; Sen. Lectr, Dudley Coll. of Educn, 1947–52; Lectr, then Sen. Lectr, Univ. of Keele, 1952–66; Prof. of Educn, Univ. of Stirling, 1966–73. Council Mem., Brit. Mycol. Soc., 1960–64; Mem., Royal Soc. and Inst. of Biol. Cttee on Biol. Educn, 1963–68; Sec. of State's Cttee on Educn and the Countryside, 1969–72; Schs Brdcstng Council (Scotl.) 1970–72; Gen. Teaching Council Scotl., 1971–72; Consultant to Centre for Educnl Res. and Innovation, OECD, 1972– ; Consultant on Educnl Technology to UNESCO, 1973– . *Publications:* Biology: an environmental approach (British adaptation of the American Biological Sciences Curriculum Study), 1972; *contrib.* Adv. Sci., Inst. Biol. Jl, Jl Biol. Educn, Scott. Jl Educnl Studies, Trans Brit. Mycol. Soc. *Address:* Univ. of Lancaster, Bailrigg, Lancaster LA1 4YN.

Perry, Dr Allen Howard; Lecturer, Department of Geography, University College of Swansea, since 1971; *b* 1943; *m* 1966. BSc Southampton 1965, PhD Southampton 1969; FRMetS. Lectr, Univ. Southampton, 1968–69; Lectr, UC Dublin, 1969–71. Hon. Sec., Assoc. of British Climatologists. *Publications:* Synoptic Climatology, 1973; Weather Maps, 1973; *contrib.* Weather, Meteorological Mag., Nature, Irish Geog., Scottish Geog. Mag. *Address:* Dept of Geography, Univ. Coll. of Swansea, Singleton Park, Swansea SA2 8PP.

Perry, Dr Norma; Lecturer, Department of French and Italian, University of Exeter, since 1966; *b* 1923; *m* 1958, diss. 1971; one *d.* BA London 1954 (1st cl. French), PhD London 1963. *Publications:* Cœlina ou l'enfant du mystère, 1972; Au Nom du fils, 1972; *contrib.* Fr. Studies, Proc. Huguen. Soc. Lond., Studies Voltaire Eightnth Cent. *Address:* Dept of French and Italian, Univ. of Exeter, Exeter EX4 4QJ.

Perry, Walter Laing Macdonald, OBE, FRSE; Vice-Chancellor, The Open University, since 1969; *b* 1921; *m* 1st 1946; 2nd 1971; four *s.* MB, ChB 1943, MD 1948, DSc St Andrews 1958; MRCPE 1963, FRCPE 1967. Prof. of Pharmacology, Univ. of Edinburgh, 1958–68; Vice-Principal, Univ. of Edinburgh, 1967–68. Medical Officer, Colonial Medical Service (Nigeria), 1944–46; Medical Officer, RAF, 1946–47; Mem., of Staff Medical Res. Coun., 1947–52; Dir, Dept of Biological Standards, National Inst. for Medical Res., 1952–58. Mem., Brit. Pharmacopoeia Commn, 1952–68; Sec., Brit. Pharmacological Soc., 1957–61. *Publications:* papers in Jl of Physiology, British Jl of Pharmacology and Chemotherapy, etc. *Address:* The Open Univ., Walton Hall, Milton Keynes MK7 6AA.

Petch, George Allan, BCom; Senior Lecturer in Economics, University of Newcastle upon Tyne, since 1958; *b* 1914; *m* 1945; one *s* one *d.* BCom Leeds 1939, DipEd Leeds 1940. Lectr, Leeds, 1946; Lectr, Durham, 1947–58. Mem., Inter-Univ. Council for Higher Educn Overseas, 1968– . *Publications:* Economic Development and Modern

West Africa, 1961, 2nd edn 1965. *Address*: Economics Dept, The Univ., Newcastle upon Tyne NE1 7RU.

Péter, Dr László; Lecturer in Hungarian History, History Department, School of Slavonic and East European Studies, University of London, since 1965; *b* 1929; *m* 1963; one *d*. BA Budapest 1952, DPhil Oxon 1966. *Address*: Dept of History, School of Slavonic and East European Studies, Univ. of London, WC1E 7HU.

Peterkiewicz, Prof. Jerzy; Professor of Polish Language and Literature, since 1971, Head of the Department of East European Languages and Literatures, School of Slavonic Studies, University of London, since 1964; *b* 1916; *m* 1948. MA St Andrews 1944, PhD London 1947. Lectr, Univ. of London, 1950–64, Reader, 1964–71. *Publications*: Polish Prose and Verse, 1956, 2nd edn 1970; Antologia liryki angielskiej (1300–1950), 1958; (with B. Singer) Five Centuries of Polish Poetry, 1960, 2nd rev. edn (with J. Stallworthy) 1970; The Other Side of Silence, 1970; *novels*: The Knotted Cord, 1953; Loot and Loyalty, 1955; Future to Let, 1958; Isolation, 1959; The Quick and the Dead, 1961; That Angel Burning at My Left Side, 1963; Inner Circle, 1966; Green Flows the Bile, 1969; *poetry*: Prowincja, 1936; Pogrzeb Europy, 1946; Poematy londyńskie, 1965; *contrib*. Slav. Rev., New Lit. Hist., Encounter, TLS. *Address*: School of Slavonic Studies, Univ. of London, WC1E 7HU.

Peters, Adrien John, MA, MIBiol; Senior Lecturer in Education, University of Liverpool; *b* 1915; *m* 1940; two *s* two *d*. BA Cantab 1937 (2nd cl. Natural Science and Econs Triposes), Teachers' Dip. London 1939, MA Cantab 1941; MIBiol 1953. Hd, Biol. Sect., Constantine Tech. Coll., Middlesbrough (now Teesside Poly.), 1951–59. Educn Off., Seychelles, 1947–50; Res. Off. (Tech. Educn), Nat. Foundn Educnl Res., 1955–56; Lectr in Educn, Univ. of Liverpool, 1959. Governor, F. L. Calder Coll. of Educn (Domestic Science), Liverpool, and of var. Schs. *Publications*: British Further Education, 1967; A Guide to the Study of British Further Education, 1967; Central Western Indian Ocean Bibliography, 1973; *contrib*. Atoll Res. Bull., Brit. Jl Educnl Studies, Chem. Indust., Internat. Rev. Educn, Jl Soc. Bibliog. Nat. Hist., Vocat. Asp., Jl Inst. Biol., Rep. Stud. Conf. Further Educn Staff Coll., Tech. Educn Abstr., Studies Adult Educn. *Address*: School of Education, Univ. of Liverpool, 19–23 Abercromby Square, Liverpool.

Peters, Prof. Emrys Lloyd; Professor of Social Anthropology, University of Manchester, since 1968; *b* 1916; *m* 1945; one *s*. DipEducnlPsych BA, Wales 1939, Cantab 1947, Oxon 1948, MA Cantab 1951, Manchester 1970, DPhil Oxon 1951; FRAI (Mem. Council, 1967–69, 1972–   ); Fellow, African Inst.; Mem., Hon. Soc. of Cymmrodorion. Emslie Horniman 1947, 1949, Oxford, Sen. Scarborough Student, Oxford, 1949–53; Lecturer: Cambridge, 1951–52; Manchester, 1953–58; Sen. Lectr, 1958–63, Reader, 1963–68, Univ. of Manchester. Visiting Prof.:

Pittsburgh and Chicago, 1968; Kuwait, 1970–72. Member: Cttee, SSRC, 1970–   ; Council, BritishInst. for Egyptian Studies, 1973–   ; Panel, Assoc. of Commonwealth Univs, 1973–   ; Trustee and Mem. Council, British Soc. for ME Studies, 1973–   . *Publications*: Aspects of Status and Rank in a Lebanese Village, in, Mediterranean Countryman, 1964; Some Structural Aspects of the Feud, in, Africa, 1965; Aspects of the Control of Moral Ambiguities, in, Allocation of Responsibility, 1971; Shifts in Power in a Lebanese Village, in, Rural Politics and Social Change in the Middle East, 1972; Aspects of Affinity, in, Mediterranean Kinship, 1974; Introduction to Cohesive Force, 1974; The Tied and the Free, in, Patrons and Clients (forthcoming); The Bedouin of Cyrenaica (forthcoming); *contrib*. Jl RAI, Africa, Ethnology. *Address*: Dover Street, Univ. of Manchester, Manchester M13 9PL.

Peters, Prof. George Henry, MSc; Professor of Economic Science, Department of Economics and Commerce, University of Liverpool, since 1970; *b* 1934; *m* 1959; two *d*. BSc Wales 1955, MSc Wales 1957. Mem., Royal Econ. Soc., Mem., Royal Stat. Soc., Mem., Agric. Econ. Soc. Successively Res. Asst, then demonstrator and later Univ. Lectr, Univ. of Oxford Agricultural Economics Res. Inst., 1959–67; Lectr, Liverpool Univ., 1967–69; Sen. Lectr, Liverpool Univ., 1969–70. *Publications*: Cost Benefit Analysis and Public Expenditure, 1966, 2nd edn 1968, German edn 1967; Private and Public Finance, 1970; *contrib*. Jl Agric. Econ., Farm Econ., etc. *Address*: Depts of Economics and Commerce, Univ. of Liverpool, PO Box 147, Liverpool L69 3BX.

Peters, Prof. Richard Stanley; Professor of the Philosophy of Education, University of London Institute of Education, since 1962; *b* 1919; *m* 1942; one *s* two *d*. BA Oxon 1942, BA London 1946, PhD London 1949. Mem., Amer. Nat. Acad. Educn, 1966, Mem., Aristot. Soc., Mem., Mind Assoc., Council Mem., Royal Inst. Philos., Chm., Philos. Educn Soc. GB. Pt-time Lectr, Birkbeck Coll., Univ. of London, 1946–49; Lectr, Birkbeck Coll., 1949–58; Reader in Philosophy, Birkbeck Coll., 1958–62; Vis. Prof. of Educn, Harvard Univ., 1961; Vis. Fellow, Austral. Nat. Univ., 1969. Dean, Fac. of Educn, Univ. of London, 1971; Gov., Northern Poly.; Mem., Educnl Res. Bd, SSRC, 1967–70. *Publications*: ed, Brett: History of Psychology, 1953, 2nd edn 1962; Hobbes, 1956, 2nd edn 1967; The Concept of Motivation, 1958, 2nd edn 1960; (with S. I. Benn) Social Principles and the Democratic State, 1959; Authority, Responsibility and Education, 1960; Ethics and Education, 1966; ed, The Concept of Education, 1967; ed, Perspectives on Plowden, 1969; (with P. H. Hirst) The Logic of Education, 1970; ed (with R. F. Dearden and P. H. Hirst), Education and the Development of Reason, 1972; ed (with M. Cranston), Hobbes and Rousseau, 1972; Reason, Morality and Religion (Swarthmore lecture), 1972; Reason and Compassion, 1973; ed, The Philosophy of Education, 1973; *contrib*. Analysis, Brit. Jl Educnl Psychol., Brit. Jl Educnl Studies,

Brit. Jl Philos. Sci., Mind, Philos., Philos. Educn Soc. GB Proc., Proc. Aristot. Soc. *Address*: Univ. of London Institute of Education, Malet Street, WC1E 7HS.

Pethybridge, Dr Roger William; Director, Centre of Russian and East European Studies, University College, Swansea, since 1972; *b* 1934. MA Oxon 1959, D ès sciences politiques, Geneva, 1961; Mem., Nat. Assoc. for Soviet and E European Studies. Lectr in Soviet Politics, University Coll., Swansea, 1962, Sen. Lectr, 1967, Reader, 1971; Rockefeller Foundn Fellowship, 1963. Asst to Dep. Dir-Gen. of WHO, Geneva, 1958–59. *Publications*: A Key to Soviet Politics: The Crisis of the Anti-Party Group, 1962; ed, Witnesses to the Russian Revolution, 1964 (Dutch edn 1964, Finnish and Italian edns 1967); ed, The Development of the Communist Bloc, 1965; A History of Postwar Russia, 1966 (Spanish edn 1968); The Spread of the Russian Revolution: Essays on 1917, 1972; The Social Prelude to Stalinism, 1974; *contrib.* Europ. Stud. Rev., Govt and Oppos., Osteuropa, Rev. écon. et soc., Russ. Rev., Slav. and E Europ. Rev., Sov. Stud., Pub. Opin. Qly. *Address*: Centre of Russian and East European Studies, Univ. Coll., Swansea SA2 8PP.

Petre, Prof. Edward Oswald Gabriel T.; *see* Turville-Petre.

Petre, Joan Elizabeth; *see* Turville-Petre.

Petrie, Anthony Julian; Lecturer, Department of Politics, University of Exeter, since 1969; *b* 1941; *m* 1971. BA Keele 1965; Mem., Political Studies Assoc. Asst Lectr (temp)., Univ. of Keele, 1968–69. *Publications*: *contrib.* Polit. Stud. *Address*: Dept of Politics, Univ. of Exeter, Exeter EX4 4PU.

Petrie, Gordon; Senior Lecturer, Department of Geography, University of Glasgow, since 1958; *b* 1930; *m* 1953; two *s* one *d.* MA Aberdeen 1952 (1st cl. Geog.), Dip. Surveying, London 1953, BSc Delft 1958 (Photogrammetric Engineering); Mem., Photogram. Soc., London, Mem., Brit. Cartog. Soc. Brit. Rep., Cttee VI (Educn etc), Internat. Soc. Photogram., 1965– . *Publications*: *contrib.* Cartog. Jl, ITC Publicns (Ser. A), Photogram. Rec., Photogrammetria. *Address*: Dept of Geography, Univ. of Glasgow, Glasgow G12 8QQ.

Petrucci, Dr Luciano G. D., Dr Eng, CEng, MIMechE, MIProdE; Lecturer, Department of Production Engineering, University of Aston (also teaches Italian Language), since 1964; *b* 1927; *m* 1956; one *s.* DrMechEng Pisa 1953 (1st cl.); MIMechE, MIProdE. Admissions Tutor, Dept Prod. Eng. *Publication*: Instrumentation: theory and practice, 1973. *Address*: Dept of Production Engineering, Aston Univ., Gosta Green, Birmingham B4 7ET.

Pettigrew, Dr Andrew Marshall; Lecturer in Organizational Behaviour, London Graduate School of Business Studies, since 1971; *b* 1944; *m* 1967; one *s* one *d.* BA Liverpool 1965 (Hons Social Science), Dipl.

in Industrial Admin. Liverpool 1967, PhD Manchester 1970. Res. Associate, Manchester Univ., 1966–69; Vis. Lectr, Yale Univ., 1969–71; Vis. Prof., European Institute for Advanced Studies in Management, Brussels, 1973–74. *Publications*: The Politics of Organizational Decision Making, 1973; (with Enid Mumford) Organization, Innovation and Uncertainty (forthcoming); *contrib.* Sociol., Sociol. Rev. *Address*: London Graduate School of Business Studies, Sussex Place, NW1 4SA.

Pettigrew, Dr Joyce Jane Marshall; Lecturer, Department of Social Anthropology, Queen's University, Belfast, since 1971; *b* 1940. MAEcon Manchester 1965 (Sociol. and Social Anthropol.), PhD Manchester 1969 (Social Anthropol.); Member: Royal Soc. for India, Pakistan and Ceylon, RAI, Assoc. Social Anthropologists. Res. Assoc., SOAS, 1968–71. *Publications*: Robber Noblemen, 1974; The Emigration of the Sikh Jats from the Punjab to England, ed A. C. Mayer (SSRC Report, HR 331–1); The Sikhs of Punjab: God, Land and our Past, in, Peoples of India, ed C. von Fürer-Haimendorf, 1974. *Address*: Dept of Social Anthropology, Queens Univ., Belfast BT7 1NN.

Pettit, Prof. Philip Henry; Professor of Equity, Faculty of Law, University of Bristol, since 1966; *b* 1925; *m* 1950; one *s* one *d.* BA, MA Oxon 1949; Barrister (Middle Temple) 1950. Asst Lectr, King's Coll., London, 1952–55; Lectr, Sheffield Univ., 1955–57; Sen. Lectr, Bristol Univ., 1957–66. Dean, Fac. of Law, 1968–71; Mem., Bristol Rent Assessment Panel, 1966– ; Mem., Legal Studies Bd, Council Nat. Acad. Awards, 1970– . *Publications*: Equity and the Law of Trusts, 1966, 3rd edn 1974; title Choses in Action, in Halsbury's Laws of England, 4th edn, 1974; *contrib.* Convey. Prop. Law. (NS), Law Qly Rev., Mod. Law Rev. *Address*: Faculty of Law, Univ. of Bristol, Wills Memorial Building, Queens Road, Bristol BS8 1RJ.

Pettit, Dr Philip Noel; Fellow, Trinity Hall, Cambridge University, since 1972; *b* 1945. BA NUI 1966 (Philosophy), MA NUI 1967, PhD QUB 1970, MA Cantab 1972; Mem., Irish Philosophical Soc., Mind Assoc. Teaching Asst, QUB, 1967–68; Asst Lectr, UCD, 1968–72. Editor, Cambridge Review, 1973– . *Publications*: On the Idea of Phenomenology, 1969; ed, The Gentle Revolution, 1969; contrib. W. Mays and S. C. Brown, Linguistic Analysis and Phenomenology, 1971; *contrib.* Jl Brit. Soc. Phenomenology, Philosophical Forum, Philosophical Studies (Ireland), Theory and Decision. *Address*: Trinity Hall, Cambridge.

Petyt, Keith Malcolm; Lecturer, Department of Linguistic Science, University of Reading, since 1969, and Sub-Dean of Faculty of Letters and Social Sciences since 1974; *b* 1941; *m* 1964; two *s* one *d.* BA Cantab 1962 (Classics), MA Cantab 1966, Dip. Public and Social Admin Oxon 1963, MA Reading 1968 (Linguistics). Lectr in Latin, Univ. Coll. of Cape Coast, Ghana, 1964–65; Asst Lectr in Latin, Univ. Coll.,

Cardiff, 1965–68; Lectr in Classics, Univ. Coll., Cardiff, 1968–69. *Publications*: Emily Brontë and the Haworth Dialect, 1970. *Address*: Dept of Linguistic Science, Univ. of Reading, Whiteknights, Reading RG6 2AH.

Pheifer, J. D.; Lecturer in English Language, Trinity College, Dublin, since 1964; *b* 1928; *m* 1955; two *s* two *d*. BA Notre Dame 1949 (maxima cum laude in Class.), BA Oxon 1952 (2nd cl. English), MA Oxon 1956, BLitt Oxon 1962, MA Dublin 1963 (ad eundem gradum Oxon). Asst, Univ. Coll., Dublin, 1958–60; Asst Lectr, Univ. Coll., Dublin, 1960–61; Jun. Lectr, TCD, 1961–64. Sec., Mod. Langs Sch. Cttee, 1963–73; Tutor, 1967– . *Publications*: Old English Glosses in the Epinal-Enfurt Glossary, 1974; (with M. C. Seymour et al.) On the Properties of Things, 1974. *Address*: Dept of English, 40 Trinity College, Dublin 2.

Pheysey, Diana Catherine, BA, PhD; Senior Lecturer, Management Centre, University of Aston in Birmingham, since 1973; *b* 1928. BA London 1950 (Sociol.), CertEd Leeds 1960. Affiliate Mem., Inst. Person. Mngmt 1952, Mem., Brit. Sociol Assoc. 1964. Vis. Asst Prof. of Mngmt, Kent State Univ., Ohio, 1968. Indust. posts, 1950–59; Sen. Lectr in Human Rel., High Wycombe Coll. of Techn. and Art, 1960–65; Res. Fellow, Univ. of Aston, 1965–73. *Publications*: *contrib*. Admin. Sci. Qly, Europ. Jl Soc. Psychol., Hum. Relat., Jl Mngmt Studies, Mngmt Internat. Rev., Occupat. Psychol., Org. Behav. Hum. Perf. *Address*: Univ. of Aston in Birmingham, Gosta Green, Birmingham B4 7ET.

Philips, Prof. Sir Cyril (Henry), MA, PhD, LLD, DLitt; Professor of Oriental History, University of London, since 1946, and Director, School of Oriental and African Studies, since 1957; Vice-Chancellor, University of London, since 1972; *b* 1912; *m* 1939; one *d*. MA Liverpool 1937, PhD London 1938, HonDLitt Warwick 1967, HonLLD Chinese Univ. of Hong Kong 1971. Mem., Royal Hist. Soc., Mem., Council, Royal Soc. India, Pakistan and Ceylon. Asst Lectr in Indian Hist., SOAS, 1936–39; Lectr, SOAS, 1939–45; Sen. Lectr, SOAS 1945–47. Comdnt, Army Sch. of Educn, 1943; HM Treasury, Dept of Training, 1943–46; Colonial Off. Mission on Community Develop., Africa, 1947; Mem., Soc. Develop. Cttee, Colonial Off., 1947–55; Mem., Colonial Off. Res. Council, 1955–57; Mem., UGC, 1960–69; Mem., Commonwealth Scholshp Commn, 1961–70; Mem., Postgrad. Awards Cttee, Min. of Educn, 1962–64; Mem., Mod. Langs Cttee, Min. of Educn, 1964–67; Governor, Chinese Univ. of Hong Kong, 1965– ; Mem., Inter-Univ. Council for Higher Educn Overseas, 1966– ; Dep. Vice-Chancellor, Univ. of London, 1969–70; Mem., Court, Univ. of London, 1970– . *Publications*: The East India Company, 1940, 2nd edn 1961; India, 1949; Handbook of Oriental History, 1951, 2nd edn 1962; Correspondence of David Scott, 1951; Historians of India, Pakistan and Ceylon, 1961; The Evolution of India and Pakistan, 1962; Politics and Society in India, 1963; Fort William–India

House Correspondence, 1964; History of the School of Oriental and African Studies 1917–67, 1967; The Partition of India, 1970. *Address*: School of Oriental and African Studies, Malet Street, WC1E 7HP.

Phillipps, Kenneth Charles; Senior Lecturer in English, Leicester University, since 1974 (Lecturer, 1966–74); *b* 1929; *m* 1960; one *d*. BA Liverpool 1950 (1st cl. English), MA Liverpool 1953. Lexicographer, Dictionary of the Older Scottish Tongue, Edinburgh Univ., 1964–66. *Publications*: Jane Austen's English, 1970; *contrib*. Engl. Studies, Neuphilol. Mitteil., Cornish Studies. *Address*: Dept of English, Univ. of Leicester, University Road, Leicester LE1 7RH.

Phillips, Anthony David Murray; Lecturer, Geography Department, University of Keele, since 1968; *b* 1944. BA London 1965. UCL 1962–68. *Publications*: *contrib*. Agric. Hist. Rev., Area, Etudes Rurales, Geog., Erdkunde, Trans. Inst. Brit. Geog. *Address*: Dept of Geography, Univ. of Keele, Keele, Staffs ST5 5BG.

Phillips, Charles J.; Lecturer in Educational Psychology, since 1954, and Director of the Centre for Child Study, School of Education, University of Birmingham; *b* 1914. BA London 1953 (Hons Psychol.), DipEdPsychol Birmingham 1954. *Publications*: *contrib*. Brit. Jl Disord. Commun., Brit. Jl Educnl Psychol., Brit. Jl Soc. Clin. Psychol. *Address*: Centre for Child Study, School of Education, Univ. of Birmingham, PO Box 363, Birmingham B15 2TT.

Phillips, Prof. Dewi Zephaniah, MA, BLitt; Professor of Philosophy, University College, Swansea, since 1971; *b* 1934; *m* 1959; three *s*. BA Wales 1956 (1st cl. Philos.), MA Wales 1958, BLitt Oxon 1961. Mem., Aristot. Soc., Mem., Mind Assoc., Mem., Philos. of Educn Soc. GB. Asst Lectr, Queen's Coll., Dundee, 1961–62, Lectr, 1962–63; Lectr, Univ. Coll., Bangor, 1963–65; Lectr, Univ. Coll., Swansea, 1965–67, Sen. Lectr, 1967–71. Mem., Welsh Relig. Adv. Cttee, BBC, 1971–73; Sec., Swansea Welsh Schs Assoc.; Gen. Ed., Studies in Ethics and the Philosophy of Religion, 1969– . *Publications*: The Concept of Prayer, 1965; ed, Religion and Understanding, 1967; ed, Saith Ysgrif Ar Grefydd, 1967; (with H. O. Mounce) Moral Practices, 1970; Faith and Philosophical Enquiry, 1970; Death and Immortality, 1970; (with I. Dilman) Sense and Delusion, 1971; *contrib*. Analysis, Brit. Jl Educnl Studies, Efryd. Athron., Hum Wld, Mind, Philos., Philos. Qly, Proc. Aristot. Soc., Proc. Philos. Educn Soc., Ratio, Sophia, Theol., Traethod. *Address*: Dept of Philosophy, Univ. College, Swansea SA2 8PP.

Phillips, Edward John; Lecturer in Ancient History and Classics, University of Sheffield, since 1967; *b* 1938; *m* 1968. BA Leeds 1960 (1st cl. Class.), BA Cambridge 1962 (1st cl. Class.), MA Cambridge 1968. Asst Lectr, Sheffield Univ., 1965–67. *Publications*: *contrib*. Athenaeum, Historia, Latomus, Philologus. *Address*: Dept of Ancient History, The Univ., Sheffield S10 2TN.

Phillips, Eustace Dockray, MA, FSA; Reader in Greek, The Queen's University of Belfast, since 1955; *b* 1910; *m* 1934; one *s* two *d*. BA Oxon 1933 (1st cl. Lit. Hum.), MA Oxon 1937; FSA, FAnthropolInst, FRAsiatic Soc. Temp. Asst Lectr in Class., Manchester, 1936–37; Asst Lectr, Bristol, 1937–39; Jun. Lectr, Queen's Univ., Belfast, 1939; Lectr, Queen's Univ., Belfast, 1948–55. War Service, 1940–46. *Publications*: The Royal Hordes: Nomad Peoples of the Steppes, 1965; The Mongols, 1969; History of Greek Medicine (forthcoming); *contrib.* Amer. Jl Philol. Antiqu., Archeociv., Art. Asiae, Class. Mediev., Euphros., Greek Rom. Byzant. Studies, Philos. Rev., Irish Jl Med. Sci., Jl Aesth., Jl Hellenic Studies, Philos. Rev. *Address*: Dept of Greek, The Queen's Univ., Belfast BT7 1NN.

Phillips, Dr John Patrick Norman; Senior Lecturer, Psychology Department, University of Hull, since 1969; *b* 1931; *m* 1959; one *s*. MA Oxon 1961, DipPsych London 1958, PhD 1968; Member: BPsS, Behavioural Engineering Assoc., Brit. Assoc. for Behavioural Psychotherapy, RSS, Psychometric Soc. Lectr, Univ. of Hull, 1963–69. *Publications*: *contrib.* Amer. Jl Psychology, Applied Statistics, Behaviour Res. and Therapy, Brit. Jl Mathematical and Statistical Psychology, Brit. Jl Psychiatry, Brit. Jl Social and Clinical Psychology, Computer Jl, Jl Psychosomatic Res., Mathematical Gazette, Nature, Qly Jl Experimental Psychology. *Address*: Psychology Dept, The Univ., Hull HU6 7RX.

Phillips, Dr John Roland Seymour, BA, PhD; Lecturer, Department of Medieval History, University College, Dublin, since 1968; *b* 1940. BA London 1962, PhD London 1968; FRHistS, FRSAntiquIrel, Mem., Mediev. Acad. Amer. Res., Bd of Celtic Studies, Univ. of Wales, 1966–68. *Publications*: Aymer de Valence, Earl of Pembroke, 1307–1324, 1972; Justices of the Peace in Wales and Monmouthshire, 1541–1689 (forthcoming); *contrib.* Bull. Bd Celt. Studies, Bull. Inst. Hist. Res. *Address*: Dept of Medieval History, Univ. College, Dublin 4.

Phillips, L. A. W., *see* Wolf-Phillips.

Phillips, Dr Lawrence Douglass; Senior Lecturer, Department of Psychology, Brunel University, since 1973; *b* 1934; *m* 1965. BEE Cornell 1957, PhD Michigan 1966; Member: Brit. Psychol Soc., Amer. Psychol Assoc., Amer. Inst. of Decision Sciences. Lectr, Brunel Univ., 1967–73. *Publications*: Bayesian Statistics for Social Scientists, 1973; *contrib.* IEEE Trans on Systems Science and Cybernetics, Jl Exper. Psychol. *Address*: Brunel Univ., Kingston Lane, Uxbridge, Mddx UB8 3TH.

Phillips, Nigel Godfrey; Lecturer in Austronesian Languages, Dept of SE Asia and the Islands, School of Oriental and African Studies, London University, since 1967; *b* 1934; *m* ¹1957; one *s* two *d*. BA Hons Cantab 1956 (Class.); FRAI, FRAS, Mem., Royal Inst. of Linguistics and Anthropology, Lei-

den. Res. Fellow in SE Asian Studies, SOAS, 1964–67. *Publications*: trans. and introd. (with A. Sweeney) The Voyages of Mohammed Ibrahim Munshi, 1974; *contrib.* Bull. SOAS. *Address*: Sch. of Oriental and African Studies, Univ. of London, Malet Street, WC1E 7HP.

Phillips Griffiths, Prof. Allen; *see* Griffiths, A. P.

Phillipson, Dr Nicholas Tindal, MA, BA, PhD; Lecturer in Modern History, University of Edinburgh, since 1965; *b* 1937. MA Aberdeen 1958, BA Cantab 1962 (1st cl. History), PhD Cantab 1967. Vis. Fellow, Davis Center for Historical Res., Princeton Univ., 1970–71. *Publications*: (with R. Mitchison) Scotland in the Age of Improvement, 1970. *Address*: Dept of History, Univ. of Edinburgh, Edinburgh.

Picardie, Michael; Lecturer, School of Social Work, University College, Cardiff, since 1973; *b* 1936; *m* 1960; two *d*. BA Rand 1957, BA Hons Rand 1959, MA Oxon (by decree) 1968, MA Leicester 1972, Dip. in Applied Social Studies (Psychiatric Social Work) Liverpool 1965; Mem., Brit. Assoc. of Social Workers. Lectr in Applied Social Studies, Oxford, 1968–73. Mem., DHSS Study Group on Fieldwork Trng (report, Fieldwork Training for Social Work, HMSO, 1971). *Publications*: A Metaphysical Order in Psychiatric Work, in, The Human Context, 1974; *contrib.* Social Work, Brit. Jl Psych. Social Work, Case Conference, Social Work Today. *Address*: School of Social Work, Univ. Coll., PO Box 96, Cardiff.

Picciotto, Solomon; Lecturer, School of Law, University of Warwick, since 1968; *b* 1942; *m* 1965; one *d*. BA Oxon 1963 (1st cl. Jurisprudence), JD Chicago 1964. Lectr in Law, Univ. Coll., Dar es Salaam, 1964–68. *Publications*: *contrib.* E Afr. Law Rev., Jl Mod. Afr. Studies, New Soc. *Address*: School of Law, Univ. of Warwick, Coventry CV4 7AL.

Pick, Prof. Otto; Professor in International Relations, Department of Linguistics and Regional Studies, University of Surrey, since 1973; *b* 1925; *m* 1948; one *s* two *d*. D iuris Prague 1948, BA Oxon 1950; Member: Political Studies Assoc.; Univ. Assoc. for Contemporary European Studies; Politics Assoc.; Internat. Inst. for Strategic Studies; Nat. Assoc. for Soviet and E European Studies (Mem. Exec., 1968–69); Internat. Studies Assoc., USA; Conference Gp in German Politics, USA; Nat. Council on Social Studies, USA. BBC, 1950–58; Rockefeller Res. Student, LSE, 1958–61; Lectr in History and Government, Univ. of Maryland, 1960–66; Vis. Reader, Univ. of Surrey, 1966–71, Vis. Prof., 1971–73. Dir, Atlantic Information Centre for Teachers, 1966– ; Chm., Cttee on Atlantic Studies, 1971–73, Vice-Chm., 1973– ; Chm., Standing Cttee on European Studies (Associated Examining Bd), 1973– . *Publications*: ed, Interdisciplinary Studies in Secondary Schools, 1969; ed, Learning about International Organizations, 1972; (with Julian Critchley, MP) Collective Security (forthcoming); *contrib.* Commentary (NY), Internat. Jl (Toronto), Ost-Probleme (Bonn),

Probs Communism (Wash., DC), World Today, World Survey. *Address*: Dept of Linguistics and Regional Studies, Univ. of Surrey, Guildford, Surrey GU2 5XH.

Picken, Dr Laurence Ernest Rowland, FBA; Assistant Director of Research (Oriental Music), Faculty of Oriental Studies, Cambridge, since 1966; *b* 1909. BA 1931, PhD 1935, ScD 1952, Cantab; FBA, FInstBiol. Asst Dir of Res. (Zoology), Univ. of Cambridge, 1946–66. *Publications*: The Organization of Cells and Other Organisms, 1960, 2nd edn 1962; Folk Musical Instruments of Turkey, 1974; *contrib.* Proc. Roy. Soc. A, Phil. Trans, QJMS, Jl Exp. Biol., Jl Ecol., Galpin Soc. Jl, Jl Am. Orien. S., Asia Maj., T'oung Pao, Stud. Musicol., Mus. Qly. *Address*: Faculty of Oriental Studies, Sidgwick Avenue, Cambridge.

Pickering, Sir George White, MD, FRCP, FRS; Master of Pembroke College, Oxford, since 1969; *b* 1904; *m* 1930; one *s* three *d*. 1st cl. Hons Nat. Sci. Tripos, Pts I 1925 and II 1926, MB 1930, MD 1955; Hon. DSc Durham 1957, Dartmouth (US) 1960, Hon. ScD Trinity Coll. Dublin 1962, Hon. MD Ghent 1948, Siena 1965, W Australia 1965, Hon. LLD Manchester 1964, Nottingham 1965, Hon. DUniv York 1969; FRCP 1938, FRS 1960. Formerly Asst in Dept of Clinical Res. and Lectr in Cardio-vascular Pathology, Univ. Coll. Hosp., and Mem., of Scientific Staff MRC; Herzstein Lectr, USA, 1938; Sims British Commonwealth Travelling Prof., 1949; Prof. of Medicine, Univ. of London, and Dir of Medical Clinic, St Mary's Hosp., London, 1939–56; Regius Prof. of Medicine, Oxford Univ., Student of Christ Church, and Physician to the United Oxford Hosps, 1956–68; Pro-Vice-Chancellor, Oxford Univ., 1967–69; Emeritus Student of Christ Church, 1969. Mem., UGC, 1944–54; Mem., MRC and Clinical Res. Bd, 1954–58; Mem., Lord Chancellor's Cttee on Legal Educn, 1967–71; Mem., Coun. for Scientific Policy, 1968–71. Trustee, Beit Meml Fellowship; Trustee, Ciba Foundn. Pres., BMA, 1963–64. Hon. Fellow, Pembroke Coll., Cambridge, 1959, Amer. Coll. of Physicians, Amer. Medical Assoc., RCPE, RCP Ireland, Acad. of Medicine of Mexico; Hon. FRSM. Stouffer Prize (jtly), 1970. Hon. Mem., or Corresp. Mem., numerous medical Socs and Assocs in Europe, the Commonwealth and USA; For. Hon. Mem., Amer. Acad. of Arts and Sciences; For. Associate, Amer. Nat. Acad. of Sciences, 1970. *Publications*: High Blood Pressure, 1955 (2nd edn 1968); The Nature of Essential Hypertension, 1961; The Challenge to Education, 1967; Hypertension: causes, consequences and management, 1969, 2nd edn 1974; Creative Malady, 1974; papers relating to vascular disease, high blood pressure, peptic ulcer, headache and education. *Address*: Master's Lodgings, Pembroke College, Oxford.

Pickering, Dr John Frederick; Member, Senior Directing Staff, Administrative Staff College, Henley, since 1974; Recognised Teacher, Brunel University, since 1974; *b* 1939; *m* 1967; one *d*. BSc(Econ) 1961, PhD 1965, London; Mem., Royal Econ.

Soc. Univ. of Durham, 1964–66; Univ of Sussex, 1966–73. Mem., Council of Management, Consumers' Assoc., 1969– . *Publications*: Resale Price Maintenance in Practice, 1966; The Small Firm in the Hotel and Catering Industry, 1971; Industrial Structure and Market Conduct, 1974; *contrib.* Applied Econs, Econ. Jl, European Jl Marketing, Jl Agric. Econs, Jl Ind. Econs, Jl RSS, Oxford Econ. Papers, Public Admin, Public Law, Scottish Jl Pol Econ. *Address*: Administration Staff College, Greenlands, Henley on Thames, Oxon RG9 3AU.

Pickering, Murray Ashley; Lecturer, Law Department, London School of Economics, since 1966; *b* 1934; *m* 1960; one *s* three *d*. BA NZ, 1956, MA 1958, LLB Victoria Univ. of Wellington 1961, LLM London 1963; called to Bar, Inner Temple, 1963; FREconS. *Publications*: (jtly), Company Tax from 1973, 1972; (jtly), Value Added Tax: Law and Practice, 1974; *contrib.* Brit. Tax Rev., Law Qly Rev., Mod. Law Rev. *Address*: Law Dept, London Sch. of Economics, Houghton Street, WC2A 2AE.

Pickering, Rev. Dr William Stuart Frederick; Senior Lecturer in Social Studies, Department of Social Studies, University of Newcastle upon Tyne, since 1974; *b* 1922. BD London 1949, PhD 1958; Mem., Brit. Sociol Assoc. Tutor, KCL, 1953–56; Asst Prof. in Sociol., St John's Coll., Univ. of Manitoba, 1958–62, Associate Prof., 1962–66; Lectr in Social Studies, Univ. Newcastle upon Tyne, 1966–74. *Publications*: *contrib.* Archives de Sociologie des Religions, Brit. Jl Sociol. *Address*: Dept of Social Studies, The Univ., Newcastle upon Tyne NE1 7RU.

Pickersgill, Dr Mary Joyce; Lecturer in Psychology, Bedford College, University of London, since 1962; *b* 1934. BA Oxon 1955, Dip. Psych. London 1956, MA Oxon 1958, PhD Leeds 1959; Mem., Exper. Psychol. Soc. Asst Lectr, Dept Psychiatry, Univ. Leeds, 1956–59; Res. Fellow, Radcliffe Coll., Univ. Harvard, 1959–60; Research Fellow, Bedford Coll., Univ. London, 1960–61; Lectr, Univ. Leicester, 1961–62. *Publications*: *contrib.* Nature, Qly Jl Exper. Psychol. *Address*: Bedford College, Regent's Park, NW1 4NS.

Pickett, James, BSc(Econ), MLitt; Director, David Livingstone Institute of Overseas Development Studies, since 1973 (Overseas Development Unit, 1971–73), University of Strathclyde; *b* 1929; *m* 1956; one *s* two *d*. BSc(Econ) London 1954, MLitt Glasgow 1966. Lectr, Strathclyde, 1961–69; Vis. Asst Prof., Saskatchewan, 1962–63. Statistician, Dominion Bureau Stats, Canada, 1957–59; Econ. Aff. Off., UN Ecol. Commn for Africa, 1965–67; Special Econ. Adv., 1967–68; Ed., UN Survey of Econ. Conditions in Africa, Pt II, 1969– . *Publications*: *contrib.* Canad. Jl Econ., Jl Econ. Studies, Jl Mod. African Studies. *Address*: David Livingstone Inst. of Overseas Development Studies, Univ. of Strathclyde, McCance Building, 16 Richmond Street, Glasgow G1 1XG.

Pickford, Prof. Cedric Edward, MA, DèsL; Professor of Mediaeval French Literature,

University of Hull, since 1965; *b* 1926; *m* 1956; one *s* three *d*. BA Manchester 1947, MA Manchester 1948, DèsL Paris 1958; Off. de l'Ordre des Palmes Académiques. Asst Lectr in French, Univ. Coll., Hull, 1950–52; Lectr in French, Univ. of Hull, 1952–60; Sen. Lectr in Mediaeval French Literature, 1960–64; Reader in Mediaeval French Literature, Hull, 1964–65; Dean of Faculty of Arts, 1972–74. Trésorier Internat., and Treas., Brit. Br., Soc. Internat. Arthurienne, 1966– . *Publications*: ed, Alixandre l'Orphelin, 1951; ed, Erec, roman arthurien en prose, 1959, 2nd edn 1968; L'Evolution du roman arthurien en prose, 1960; ed, La Farce de Maître Pierre Pathelin, 1967, 2nd edn 1973; ed, The Song of Songs, a twelfth century French version, 1974; *contrib*. Bull. Bibliog. Soc. Internat. Arthur., Bull. Hispan., Bull. J. Rylands Libr., etc, Yorks Archaeol. Jl. *Address*: French Dept, Univ. of Hull, Hull HU6 7RX.

Pickstock, Francis Vincent, Deputy Director, Department for External Studies, Oxford University, since 1962; Fellow of Linacre College, since 1966; *b* 1910; *m* 1933; one *s*. BA 1937 MA 1946 Oxon (PPE). Asst Sec., Univ. Tutorial Classes Cttee, 1946, Sec. 1949; Dep. Sec., Delegacy for Extra Mural Studies, 1962. Oxford City Councillor, 1952– (Lord Mayor, 1967–68); Oxfordshire County Councillor, 1974– ; Pres., Oxford AUT, 1973– . *Address*: Dept for External Studies, Rewley House, Wellington Square, Oxford.

Pickvance, C. G.; Lecturer in Sociology, Department of Sociology, University of Manchester, since 1968; *b* 1944; *m* 1969. BA (Econ.) Hons Manchester 1965, MA (Econ.) Hons Manchester 1969; Member: Brit. Sociol Assoc.; Amer. Sociol Assoc. Mem., Brit. Sociol Assoc. Working Party on Comparability, 1971– . *Publications*: ed and contrib., Problems of Modern Society, ed P. M. Worsley *et al*, 1972; contrib. Key Variables in Social Research, vol. II, Politics, Voluntary Associations and Demographic Variables, ed E. Gittus, 1974; contrib. Cities in Modern Britain, ed C. Lambert and D. T. H. Weir, 1974; trans., ed and contrib. Urban Sociology: Critical Essays (forthcoming); *contrib*. Critica Sociol., Econ. and Soc., Race, Sociol Rev., Urban Studies. *Address*: Dept of Sociology, Univ. of Manchester, Manchester M13 9PL.

Picton, J. Glyn, CBE; Senior Lecturer in Industrial Economics, Birmingham University, since 1947; *b* 1912; *m* 1939; one *s* one *d*. BCom Birmingham 1932 (1st cl.), MCom Birmingham 1933. Sub Dean, Fac. of Comm. and Social Science, 1952–58; Governor, Utd Birmingham Hosps, 1953–74; Vice-Chm., Birmingham Reg. Hosp. Bd, 1971–74; Vice-Chm., W Midlands RHA, 1973– ; Vice Chm., Nat. Health Service, Nat. Staff Cttee, 1969–73; Pres., W Midl. Rent Assessment Panel, 1966–72; Chm. of var. Wages Councils, 1960– ; Sole Comr of Inquiry, S Wales Coalfield Dispute, 1965. *Publications*: var. articles and official repts on hosps, rents and industr. relat. *Address*: Univ. of Birmingham, PO Box 363, Birmingham B15 2TT.

Pierce, Prof. Francis William, MA; Hughes Professor of Spanish, University of Sheffield, since 1953; *b* 1915; *m* 1944; three *s*. BA Queen's University Belfast 1938 (1st cl. Spanish Studies), MA Queen's University Belfast 1939; MA jure offici Dublin 1943. Asst Lectr, Liverpool Univ., 1939–40; Dep. to Prof. of Spanish, TCD, 1940–45; Hughes Lectr, Univ. of Sheffield, 1946–53; Vis. Prof., Brown and Case W. Reserve Univs, USA, 1968. Dean, Fac. of Arts, Sheffield, 1964–67; Pres., Assoc. Hispan. GB and Irel., 1971–73. *Publications:* The Heroic Poem of the Spanish Golden Age: Selections, 1947; ed, Hispanic Studies in Honour of I. González Llubera, 1959; La Poesía épica del siglo de oro, 1961, 2nd edn 1968; The Historie of Aravcana, transcribed with notes and introduction, 1964; ed (with C. A. Jones), Actas del Primer Congreso Internacional de Hispanists, 1964; ed, Two Cervantes short novels, 1970; ed, D. de Hojeda: La Cristiada, 1971; ed, Luís de Camões: Os Lusíadas, 1973; *contrib*. Bull. Hispan. Studies, Bull. Hispan., Hispan. Rev. *Address*: Dept of Hispanic Studies, The Univ., Sheffield S10 2TN.

Pierce, Gwynedd Owen, MA; Senior Lecturer in Welsh History, University College, Cardiff, since 1966, and Acting Head, Department of Welsh History; *b* 1921; *m* 1950; two *s*. BA Wales 1948 (1st cl. Welsh with Access. Welsh History), MA Wales 1953. Asst Lectr in Welsh and Welsh History, Cardiff, 1948–53; Lectr in Welsh History, Cardiff, 1953–66. Mem., Stand. Cttee, Univ. of Wales Gld of Grads, 1968– ; Univ. of Wales Court, 1969–72; Univ. of Wales Bd of Celt. Studies, 1971– ; Jt Editor, Morgannwg (Glamorgan Hist. Soc.), vols 1–17, 1957–73. *Publications*: ed, Ein Tywysogion, 1954; ed, Triwyr Penllyn, 1956; The Place-names of Dinas Powys Hundred, 1968; *contrib*. Bull. Bd Celt. Studies, etc. *Address*: Dept of Welsh History, Univ. College, Cathays Park, Cardiff CF1 1XL.

Piggott, Mary, BA, FLA; Senior Lecturer, School of Library, Archive and Information Studies, University College London, since 1960; *b* 1912. BA London 1935 (French), Dip. Librarianship 1937; FLA 1939. Lectr, Sch. of Librarianship, Univ. Coll., London, 1947–60. Mem., Libr. Assoc. Cataloguing Rules Cttee, 1951– . *Publications*: ed, Cataloguing Principles and Practice: an inquiry, 1954; ed (with R. Staveley), Government Information and the Research Worker, 2nd edn 1965. Chapters on cataloguing, in, Five Years Work in Librarianship, 1958, 1963, 1968. *Address*: School of Library, Archive and Information Studies, Univ. College London, Gower Street, WC1E 6BT.

Piggott, Prof. Stuart, CBE, FBA; Abercromby Professor of Prehistoric Archaeology, University of Edinburgh, since 1946; *b* 1910. Hon. DLittHum Columbia 1954; FBA 1953, FRSE, FSA, Mem., German Archaeolog. Inst. 1953, Hon. MRIA 1956, Foreign Hon. Mem., American Acad. of Arts and Sciences 1960. On staff, Royal Commn on Ancient Monuments (Wales), 1929–34; Asst Dir, Avebury excavations, 1934–38; Army from 1939. Research on European prehistory until

1942; in India, 1942–45, studied Oriental prehistory. Adv. Editor, Antiquity; Comr, Royal Commn on Ancient Monuments (Scot.); Trustee, British Museum, 1968– . *Publications*: Some Ancient Cities of India, 1946; Fire Among the Ruins, 1948; British Prehistory, 1949; William Stukeley: an XVIII Century Antiquary, 1950; Prehistoric India, 1950; (with G. E. Daniel) A Picture Book of Ancient British Art, 1951; Neolithic Cultures of British Isles, 1954; Scotland Before History, 1958; Approach to Archaeology, 1959; ed, The Dawn of Civilization, 1961; Ancient Europe, 1965; (with J. G. D. Clark) Prehistoric Societies, 1965; The Druids, 1968; Introduction to Camden's Britannia of 1695, 1971; (with B. W. Cunliffe and D. Bonney) Victoria History of Wiltshire, vol. I part 2, 1973; *contrib.* technical papers in archaeological jls. *Address*: Univ. of Edinburgh, Old College, South Bridge, Edinburgh EH8 9YL.

Pike, John, CBE, MA; Financial Secretary, London School of Economics, since 1967; *b* 1924; *m* 1948; two *s*. BA Oxon 1948, MA Oxon 1962. District Officer, Sarawak, 1949–55; Principal Asst Sec., 1956–61; Under-Sec., Finance and Planning, 1962–63; Financial Sec., 1964–67 (acting State Sec., 1965–66). *Address*: London School of Economics, Houghton Street, Aldwych, WC2A 2AE.

Pike, Lionel John, MA, DPhil, BMus, FRCO, ARCM; Lecturer in Music since 1968, and Organist, since 1969, Royal Holloway College, University of London; *b* 1939; *m* 1967; one *d*. BA Oxon 1962 (1st cl. Music), BMus Oxon 1964, MA Oxon 1966, DPhil Oxon 1970; ARCO, ARCM 1959, FRCO 1963. Asst Lectr in Music, Royal Holloway Coll., Univ. of London, 1965–68. Mem., Royal Musical Assoc. *Publications*: *contrib.* Consort, Music Lett., Musical Times. *Address*: Music Dept, Royal Holloway College (Univ. of London), Egham, Surrey TW20 0EX.

Pilbeam, Pamela May, BA, PhD; Lecturer, Department of History, University of London, Bedford College, since 1965; *b* 1941; *m* 1967. BA London 1962 (1st cl. History), PhD London 1966. Derby Studentship, Univ. of London, 1962–63; Res. Fellowship, Inst. of Historical Res., London, 1964–65; Vis. Lectr, Univ. of Toronto, 1971; Vis. Associate Prof., Univ. of York, Ont., 1972–73. *Publications*: *contrib.* EHR, Hist. *Address*: Bedford College, St Johns Hall, Inner Circle, Regent's Park, NW1 4NS.

Pilgrim, Jack Alfred; Lecturer, Department of Education, University of Leeds, since 1964; *b* 1929; *m* 1953; two *s* three *d*. BA Sheffield 1950, 1er Prix de Contrepoint et de Fugue, Conservatoire de Lyon 1951, CertEd Sheffield 1952, BMus Sheffield 1953. Mem., ISM. Music Adviser, Nuffield Mod. Lang. Project, 1964–70. Chm., A level Music JMB, 1973– . *Publications*: Performing Edns of Vocal Music: R. White: Lamentations, 1959; G. Carissimi: Beatus Vir, Dixit Dominus, 1969, O Anima Festina, 1970; Ah Vide Domine, Parce heu, Jonas, 1972; G. A. Homilius: Hilf Herr, Unser Vater, Siehe, das

ist Gottes Lamm, 1972; D. Cimarosa: Kyrie, 1972; Nuffield French Song Book, 1968; *contrib.* Music. Times, Music Rev., Musik Gesch. Gegen., Music and Musicians. *Address*: Dept of Education, Univ. of Leeds, Leeds LS2 9JT.

Pilgrim, John Eric, MA; Deputy Director of Extramural Studies, University of Birmingham, since 1970; *b* 1915. BA London 1936 (2nd cl. History), MA London 1939. Lectr, Birmingham Univ., 1947–59; Sen. Lectr, Birmingham Univ., 1959– . *Publications*: An approach to the Teaching of History, in, University Studies for Adults, 1972; *contrib.* Univ. Birm. Hist. Jl. *Address*: Dept of Extramural Studies, Univ. of Birmingham, PO Box 363, Birmingham B15 2TT.

Pilkington, Anthony Edward, MA, DPhil; Fellow and Tutor in Modern Languages, Jesus College, Oxford University, since 1966; *b* 1940; *m* 1966; two *s*. BA Oxon 1961 (1st cl. Mod. Lang.), MA Oxon 1966, DPhil Oxon 1971. Lectr, Lancaster Univ., 1964–66. *Publications*: ed, G. Apollinaire: Alcools, 1970; *contrib.* Fr. Studies. *Address*: Jesus College, Oxford.

Pilkington, Geoffrey Walter; Senior Lecturer in Psychology, University of Sheffield, since 1967; *b* 1928; *m* 1964; one *s* one *d*. BA London 1949 (2nd cl. History), BA London 1954 (1st cl. Psychology), Teacher's Cert. Hull 1950; ABPsS 1956. Res. Fellow in Psychology, Bedford Coll., London, 1954–55; Asst Lectr in Psychology, Univ. of Sheffield, 1955–58; Lectr in Psychology, Univ. of Sheffield, 1958–67. *Publications*: *contrib.* Brit. Jl Soc. Clin. Psychol., Brit. Jl Educnl Psychol. *Address*: Dept of Psychology, The Univ., Sheffield S10 2TN.

Pilkington, Dr Reginald, OBE, LLM, LLD; Lecturer in Law, Manchester University, since 1964; *b* 1902; *m* 1930; two *d*. LLB Leeds 1925 (1st cl.), LLM Leeds 1928, LLD Sheffield 1974; Solicitor (1st cl. Hons) 1926. Law Soc. Final Examiner, 1936–51; Mem., Council, Selden Soc., 1965– ; Mem., var. Bds of Dept of Hlth and Social Security, 1951– . *Address*: Faculty of Law, Univ. of Manchester, Manchester M13 9PL.

Pilliner, Dr Albert Edward George, PhD, BSc, ARIC; Director, The Godfrey Thomson Unit for Academic Assessment, since 1965, and Senior Lecturer, Centre for Research in Educational Sciences, University of Edinburgh, since 1965; *b* 1909; *m* 1935; one *d*. BSc Edinburgh 1931 (Chemistry), DipEd Birmingham 1932, PhD Edinburgh 1965 (Educn); ARIC 1942, Mem., Brit. Psychol. Soc. 1952. Lectr in Educn, Univ. of Edinburgh, 1949–65. Sec., Brit. Psychol. Soc. Stand. Cttee on Test Standards, 1961–73; Chm., Scott. Br., Brit. Psychol. Soc., 1962–64, Mem., Gen. Council, 1962–64. *Publications*: contrib. Mental Measurement Year Book; *contrib.* Ann. Hum. Genet., Brit. Jl Educnl Psychol., Brit. Jl Math. Stat. Psychol. *Address*: The Godfrey Thomson Unit for Academic Assessment, Univ. of Edinburgh, Edinburgh EH8 9YL.

Pincas, Anita Maria; Lecturer, Languages Division – English as a Foreign Language, University of London Institute of Education, since 1965; *m* 1969; one *s* one *d*. BA Sydney 1960 (1st cl. Hons English, 1st cl. Hons Philos.). Vis. Instructor, Columbia Univ. Teachers' Coll., 1960; Vis. Instructor, NY Univ., 1960; Tutor, Sydney Univ., 1961–64; Vis. Lectr, Tel Aviv Univ., 1964. *Publications: contrib.* Engl. Lang. Teach., Lang. Learn., Music Educn, Speech Ther. Jl Austral. *Address:* Univ. of London Inst. of Education, 36 Bedford Way, WC1.

Pinder, Dr David Antony; Lecturer, Department of Geography, Southampton University, since 1967; *b* 1944; *m* 1966; one *s* one *d*. BA Reading 1965 (1st cl. Hons), PhD Reading 1971; Mem., Inst. of Brit. Geogrs. *Publications:* with M. E. Witherick: Aspects of Change in Great Britain, 1973; Regional Contrasts in Great Britain, 1973; Population and Agriculture in the EEC, 1974; Industry and Trade in the EEC, 1974; Regional Contrasts in the USA, 1974. *Address:* Dept of Geography, Univ. of Southampton, Southampton SO9 5NH.

Pinfold, Dr Carl; Senior Lecturer, School of Architecture, Liverpool University, since 1960; *b* 1919; *m* 1952; one *s* one *d*. Cert. Arch. Cape Town 1943, PhD Liverpool 1967; RIBA. Univ. of Witwatersrand, 1948–58. *Publications: contrib.* New Scientist. *Address:* Sch. of Architecture, Liverpool Univ., Liverpool L69 3BX.

Pinion, Francis Bertram; Reader in English Studies, Division of Education, University of Sheffield, since 1973; *b* 1908; *m* 1935; one *s* one *d*. MA Hons Cantab 1930 (Eng.), DipEd Oxon 1945; Hon. Vice-Pres., Thomas Hardy Soc. Dept of Educn, Univ. of Sheffield, 1961– . Sheffield University: Sub-Dean, Fac. of Arts, 1965– ; Mem., Higher Degrees Cttee, Fac. of Arts, 1970– ; UCCA Rep. 1967– . Formerly grammar sch. appts, leading to dep. headship and headship. *Publications:* include: ed, Browning: Men and Women, 1963, 2nd edn 1967; Educational Values in an Age of Technology, 1964; A Hardy Companion, 1968, 2nd edn 1974; ed, Browning: Dramatis Personae, 1969; ed (with Evelyn Hardy) One Rare Fair Woman (Hardy's letters to Mrs Henniker, 1893–1922), 1972; A Jane Austen Companion, 1973; *contrib.* TLS, Notes and Queries, Thomas Hardy Year Book, Rev. English Studies. *Address:* Univ. of Sheffield, Western Bank, Sheffield S10 2TN.

Pinsent, Dr John; Senior Lecturer in Greek, University of Liverpool, since 1970; *b* 1922; *m*; two *s* one *d*. BA 1948, MA 1948, DPhil 1957 Oxon. Asst Lectr, Dept of Greek, Liverpool, 1950, Lectr, 1953; Actg Head of Dept, 1966, 1970–71, 1972–73; Visiting Professor: Univ. of Pennsylvania, 1958–59; Univ. of Michigan, 1969–70. *Publications:* Greek Mythology, 1969, German edn 1970; Swedish edn 1971; Myths and Legends of Ancient Greece, 1969, Swedish edn 1970, Military Tribunes and Plebeian Consuls, 1974; *contrib.* CQ, Phoenix. *Address:* Dept of Greek, The Univ., PO Box 147, Liverpool L69 3BX.

Pinto, Dr Vivian; Senior Lecturer, School of Slavonic and East European Studies, London University, since 1969; *b* 1923; *m* 1948; one *s*. MA Oxon 1947, PhD London 1952. Lecturer, SSEES, 1947–69; Mem. Bd, SEES, London Univ., 1948– . Mem., Gov. Bd, Box Hill Sch., Surrey, 1967–72. *Publications:* Bulgarian Prose and Verse, 1957; *contrib.* Bulgarian sects, in, Contrasts in Emerging Societies, 1965; *contrib.* Bulgarian sects, in, Eos, 1965; *contrib.* American Catholic Encyclopedia, 1967; *contrib.* Penguin Companion to Literature, 1969; *contrib.* Bulgarian sects, in, The Soviet Union and Eastern Europe: a Handbook, 1970; *contrib.* Cassell's Encyclopedia of Literature, 1973; Conf. on Twentieth Century Bulgarian Literature (Materials), 1972; *contrib.* Encyl. Brit., 15th edn 1974; *contrib.* Slav. E Europ. Rev. *Address:* School of Slavonic Studies, Senate House, London Univ., WC1E 7HU.

Piper, Andrew George; Senior Lecturer, Department of Accounting, University of Birmingham, since 1971; *b* 1929; *m* 1951; one *s* two *d*. BCom Birmingham 1952; FCA, FCMA, JDip, MA. Lecturer, Birmingham Univ., 1966–71. Mem., Adv. Bd for Acntncy Educn, 1970– . *Address:* Dept of Accounting, Faculty of Commerce and Social Science, Univ. of Birmingham, PO Box 363, Birmingham B15 2TT.

Piper, David W.; *see* Warren Piper.

Pirie, David B.; Lecturer, Department of English, University of Manchester, since 1967; *b* 1943; one *s* three *d*. BA Oxford 1964 (Hons Engl. Lang. and Lit.), BPhil Oxford 1967 (Mod. Engl. Studies). Asst Lectr, Univ. of Manchester, 1966–67. *Publications:* ed (with W. Empson), Coleridge's Verse: A Selection, 1972; *contrib.* Ess. Crit., Crit. Qly. *Address:* Dept of English, Univ. of Manchester, Manchester M13 9PL.

Pitt, Prof. Harry Raymond, FRS, BA, PhD; Vice-Chancellor, Reading University, since 1964; *b* 1914; *m* 1940; four *s*. HonLLD Aberdeen 1970, HonLLD Nottingham 1970; FRS 1957. Bye-Fellow, Peterhouse, Cambridge, 1936–39; Choate Memorial Fellow, Harvard Univ., 1937–38; Univ. of Aberdeen, 1939–42; Prof. of Mathematics, Queen's Univ., Belfast, 1945–50; Prof. of Pure Mathematics, Univ. of Nottingham, 1950–64; Deputy Vice-Chancellor, Univ. of Nottingham, 1959–62; Vis. Prof., Yale Univ., 1962–63. Air Ministry and Min. of Aircraft Production, 1942–45. *Publications:* Tauberian Theorems, 1957; Measure, Integration and Probability, 1963; *contrib.* mathematical papers in scientific jls. *Address:* The Univ., Reading RG6 2AH.

Pitt-Rivers, Prof. Julian; Professor of Anthropology, London School of Economics, since 1972; *b* 1919; *m* 1971. BA Oxon 1948, MA Oxon 1949, DPhil Oxon 1953. Vis. Asst Prof., Univ. of California, Berkeley, 1956–57; Vis. Prof., Univ. of Chicago, 1957–69; Dir d'études, associé à l'Ecole Pratique des Hautes Etudes, Paris, 1964–71. *Publications:* The People of the Sierra, 1954, 2nd edn 1971; *contrib.* Europ. Jl Sociol., Homme, Man.

Address: Dept of Social Anthropology, London Sch. of Economics, Houghton Street, WC2A 2AE.

Pitt-Watson, Rev. Prof. Ian; Professor of Practical Theology at Christ's College, Aberdeen, and University Lecturer and Head of Department of Practical Theology, Aberdeen, since 1972; *b* 1923; *m* 1949; one *s* two *d*. MA Edinburgh 1947 (1st cl. Hons Philosophy), BD Edinburgh 1950 (with Distinction in Systematic Theology); LRAM. Chaplain, Univ. of Aberdeen, 1952–58; Minister: St James's Parish Church, Forfar, 1958–61; New Kilpatrick Parish Church, Bearsden, Glasgow, 1961–72. *Publications*: Letters on Pacifism (with Prof. John Ferguson), 1954; Lively Oracles, 1955; Worship Now (with Prof. David Cairns and Prof. James Whyte), 1972; Theology is for Preaching (Warrack Lectures 1973) (forthcoming). *Address*: Christ's College, Aberdeen AB1 1YD.

Pittock, Dr Joan Hornby; Lecturer, English Department, University of Aberdeen, since 1966; *b* 1930; *m* 1955; one *s*. BA Manchester 1951, MA Manchester 1952, PhD Manchester 1960. Asst Lectr in Engl., Univ. of Aberdeen, 1964–66. *Publications*: The Ascendancy of Taste, 1973; *contrib*. Rev. Engl. Studies. *Address*: Dept of English, Taylor Building, King's College, Old Aberdeen AB9 2UB.

Pitty, Dr Alistair Frank, MA, DPhil; Lecturer in Geography, University of Hull, since 1965; *b* 1939; *m* 1963; one *s* one *d*. BA Oxon 1961 (1st cl. Geog.), MA, DPhil Oxon 1966. Asst Lectr, Hull, 1963; Vis. Lectr, Univ. of W Australia, 1974. *Publications*: An Approach to the Study of Karst Water, 1966; A Scheme for Hillslope Analysis, 1969–70; Introduction to Geomorphology, 1971; *contrib* Proc. Geol. Assoc. *Address*: Dept of Geography, The Univ., Hull HU6 7RX.

Pivčević, Dr Edo; Lecturer in Philosophy, University of Bristol, since 1964; *b* 1931; Equiv. BA Zagreb 1954, PhD Münster 1958, PhD London 1962. *Publications*: Ironie als Daseinsform bei Sören Kierkegaard, 1960; Husserl and Phenomenology, 1970. *Address*: Dept of Philosophy, The Univ., Bristol BS8 1TH.

Place, Ullin Thomas; Senior Lecturer, Department of Philosophy, University of Leeds, since 1974 (Lecturer, 1970–74); *b* 1924; *m* 1st 1949, 2nd 1964; one *s* one *d*. MA Oxford 1950, DipAnthropol. Oxford 1950, DLitt Adelaide 1972; ABPsS, Mem., Mind Assoc. Lectr in Psychol., Dept of Philosophy, Univ. of Adelaide, 1951–54; Clin. Psychol., Central Hosp., Warwick, 1960–64; Sen. Clin. Psychol., Hollymoor Hosp., Birmingham, 1964–66. Vis. Assoc. Prof., Dept of Philos., Univ. of Chicago, 1965; Lectr in Psychol., Dept of General Studies, Univ. of Aston in Birmingham, 1967–68; Lectr in Clin. Psychol., Dept of Psychiatry, Univ. of Leeds, 1968–69; Vis. Prof., Dept of Methodology of Psychol., Univ. of Amsterdam, 1973–74. *Publications*: *contrib*. Analysis, Austral. Jl Philos., Brit. Jl Psychol., Mind, Philos. Rev.

Address: Dept of Philosophy, Univ. of Leeds, Leeds LS2 9JT.

Plant, Dr Raymond; Lecturer in Philosophy, University of Manchester, since 1967; *b* 1945; *m* 1967; two *s*. BA London 1966 (Hons Philosophy), PhD Hull 1971. *Publications*: Social and Moral Theory in Casework, 1970; Hegel, 1973; Community and Ideology, 1974. *Address*: Dept of Philosophy, Univ. of Manchester, Manchester M13 9PL.

Plamenatz, Prof. John Petrov, FBA; Professor of Social and Political Theory, University of Oxford, since 1967; *b* 1912; *m* 1943. BA Oxon 1934 (1st cl. Hist.), MA Oxon 1937; FBA 1962. Fellow, All Souls Coll., Oxford, 1936–51; Fellow, Nuffield Coll., Oxford, 1951–67; Fellow, All Souls Coll., Oxford, 1967– . *Publications*: Consent, Freedom and Political Obligation, 1938, 2nd edn 1968; The English Utilitarians, 1949, 2nd edn 1958; The Revolutionary Movement in France, 1952; German Marxism and Russian Communism, 1954; Alien Rule and Self-Government, 1960; Man and Society, 1963; Ideology, 1970; *contrib*. Amer. Pol. Sci. Rev., Pol. Studies. *Address*: All Souls College, Oxford.

Platt, Dr Colin Peter Sherard; Lecturer, Department of History, University of Southampton, since 1964; *b* 1934; *m* 1963; two *s* two *d*. BA Oxford 1958 (1st cl.), MA Oxford 1962, PhD Leeds 1966; FSA, FRHistS. Res. Asst in Medieval Archaeology, Leeds Univ., 1960–62; Lectr in Medieval Archaeology, Leeds Univ., 1962–64. *Publications*: The Monastic Grange in Medieval England: a Reassessment, 1969; Medieval Archaeology in England: a guide to the historical sources, 1969; Medieval Southampton, 1973; Excavations in Medieval Southampton, 1953–1969, 1974; *contrib*. Archaeol. Jl, Bull. Inst. Archaeol., Hansische Geschichtsblätter. *Address*: Dept of History, The Univ., Southampton SO9 5NH.

Platt, Prof. Desmond Christopher Martin, MA, DPhil, FRHistS; Professor of Latin American History, Fellow of St Antony's Coll., and Dir, Centre of Latin American Studies, University of Oxford, since 1972; *b* 1934; *m* 1958. BA Oxon 1958 (1st cl. Hist.), MA, DPhil Oxon 1961; FRHistS. Asst Lectr, Edinburgh Univ., 1961–62; Lectr, Exeter Univ., 1962–68; Fellow, Queens' Coll., Cambridge and Univ. Lectr in Latin American History, 1969–72; Dir, Centre of Lat. Amer. Studies, Univ. of Cambridge, 1971–72. Chm., Soc. Latin American Studies, 1973–75. *Publications*: Finance, Trade and Politics in British Foreign Policy, 1815–1914, 1968; The Cinderella Service: British Consuls since 1825, 1971; Latin America and British Trade, 1806–1914, 1972; *contrib*. Bull. Inst. Hist. Res., Econ. Hist. Rev., Jl Latin Amer. Studies, Past Pres., Pol. Studies, Inter-Amer. Econ. Aff., Jl Imp. and Commonwealth Hist. *Address*: St Antony's College, Oxford.

Platt, Jennifer Ann, (Mrs C. M. Goldie); Lecturer in Sociology, University of Sussex,

554

since 1964; *b* 1937; *m* 1967; one *d*. BA Cantab 1958 (1st cl. Engl.), DPSA Oxon 1959, MA Cantab 1961, MA Chicago 1964 (Sociol.); Mem., Brit. Sociol. Assoc., For. Associate, Amer. Sociol. Assoc. Jun. Res. Off., Dept of Appl. Econs, Cambridge, 1961–64. *Publications*: (with J. H. Goldthorpe et al.) The Affluent Worker: Industrial Attitudes and Behaviour, 1968; (with J. H. Goldthorpe et al.) The Affluent Worker: Political Attitudes and Behaviour, 1968; (with J. H. Goldthorpe et al.) The Affluent Worker in the Class Structure, 1969; Social Research in Bethnal Green, 1971; *contrib.* Brit. Jl Sociol., Sociol. Rev., Sociol. *Address*: Arts Building, Univ. of Sussex, Brighton BN1 9QN.

Platts, Colin Victor, BSc, MEd, FRIC; Senior Lecturer in Education, School of Education, University of Birmingham, since 1972; *b* 1921; *m* 1948; two *s*. BSc Sheffield 1943, DipEd Sheffield 1948, MEd Birmingham 1970; FRIC, Mem., ASE. Lectr in Educn, Univ. of Birmingham, 1965–72; Admissions Tutor, Grad. Cert. Course, 1970– . Mem., Staffs CC Educn Cttee, 1968–71; W Midlands Exam. Bd, 1967–73. *Publications*: Atoms, Molecules and the Mole, 1966; Changes in School Science Teaching, 1970; *contrib.* Educnl Rev., Sch. Sci. Rev., Nuffield Sc. Proj. *Address*: School of Education, Univ. of Birmingham, PO Box 363, Birmingham B15 2TT.

Plommer, Dr William Hugh, MA; University Lecturer in Classics, Cambridge, since 1954; Fellow of Wolfson College (formerly University College), since 1965; *b* 1922. BA 1943, MA 1947, DPhil 1948, Oxon. Gustav Sachs Student at Brit. Sch. in Athens, 1947–48; Sen. Lectr, City of Leeds Sch. of Architecture, 1948–54. *Publications*: Simpson's History of Architectural Development, vol. I, 1956; (with J. M. Cook) The Sanctuary of Hemithea at Kastabos, 1966; Vitruvius and later Roman Building Manuals, 1973; *contrib.* Anatolian Studies, Annual of Brit. Sch. Athens, Antiquity, Jl of Hellenic Studies, Proc. Cambridge Philol Assoc. *Address*: Wolfson Coll., Cambridge.

Plowman, Prof. David Eric Garth; Professor of Social Administration in the University of London at London School of Economics, since 1969; *b* 1929; *m* 1954. BA Oxon 1950, MA Calif 1951; ABPsS 1955, Member; Brit. Psychol. Soc., Brit. Sociol Assoc., Social Admin Assoc. Teaching Asst in Psychol. Univ. of California, Berkeley, 1950–51; Asst Lectr in Psychol, Univ. of Manchester, 1951–55; Lectr of Psychol., UC, Swansea, 1955–63; Reader in Social Admin, LSE, 1963–69. Editor, Jl of Social Policy. *Publications*: (with A. H. Birch and others) Small Town Politics; *contrib.* Brit. Jl of Sociol., Bull. Brit. Psychol Soc., Pol Studies, Social Work, Sociol Rev. *Address*: Dept of Social Science and Admin, London School of Economics, Houghton Street, WC2A 2AE.

Plum, Dr David Robert; Lecturer, Engineering Department, University of Manchester, since 1967; *b* 1933; *m* 1959; three *d*. BSc (Eng) London 1958, PhD Manchester 1972; MIStructE 1959, MICE 1963. Vis. Lectr, Architecture, Manchester. *Publications*: *contrib.* Proc. Inst. Civ. Eng. *Address*: Engineering Dept, Univ. of Manchester, Manchester M13 9PL.

Plumb, Prof. John Harold, FBA, LittD; Professor of Modern English History, University of Cambridge, since 1966; *b* 1911. BA London 1933 (1st cl. History), PhD Cambridge 1936, LittD Cambridge 1957, Hon DLitt Leicester 1968, East Anglia 1973; FBA 1968, FRHistS, FSA, FRSL 1969, For. Hon. Mem., Amer. Acad. Arts Sci., 1970. Ehrman Res. Fellow, King's Coll., Cambridge, 1939–46; Fellow, Christ's Coll., Cambridge, 1946; Steward, 1948–50, Tutor, 1950–59; Vice-Master, 1964–68; Univ. Lectr in History, Christ's Coll., Cambridge, 1946–62; Reader in Modern English History, 1962–65; Chm., History Fac., 1966–68; Vis. Prof., Columbia Univ., NY, 1960; Ford's Lectr, Oxford, 1965–66; Saposnekow Lectr, City Coll., NY, 1968; Dist. Vis. Prof., City Univ., NY, 1971–72; Stenton Lectr, Reading Univ., 1972; Cecil and Ida Green Honors Prof., Texas Christian Univ., 1974. Trustee, Nat. Portrait Gall., 1961; Syndic., Fitzwilliam Museum, 1960; Ed., Hist. Hum. Soc., Europ. Adv. Ed., Horizon; Hist. Adv., Penguin Bks. *Publications*: England in the Eighteenth Century, 1950; (with C. Howard) West African Explorers, 1952; Chatham, 1953; ed, Studies in Social History, 1955; Sir Robert Walpole, 1956–60; The First Four Georges, 1956; The Renaissance, 1961; Men and Places, 1962; Crisis in the Humanities, 1964; Growth of Political Stability in England 1675–1725, 1967; Death of the Past, 1969; In the Light of History, 1972; contrib., Man versus Society in Eighteenth Century Britain, 1968; Churchill Revised, 1969. *Address*: Christ's College, Cambridge CB2 3BU.

Plumley, Rev. Prof. Jack Martin; Herbert Thompson Professor of Egyptology, University of Cambridge, and Fellow of Selwyn College, since 1957; *b* 1910; *m* 1938; three *s*. BA, MLitt Dunelm, MA Cantab 1950; FSA 1966. Deacon 1933, Priest 1934. Assoc. Lectr in Coptic, Cambridge Univ., 1949–57. Curacies, 1933–41; Vicar, Christ Church, Hoxton, 1942–45; Vicar, St Paul's, Tottenham, 1945–47; Rector and Vicar, All Saints', Milton, Cambridge, 1948–57. Dir, Excavations on behalf of Egypt Exploration Soc. at Qasr Ibrim, Nubia, 1963, 1964, 1966, 1969, 1972, 1974. *Address*: Selwyn College, Cambridge.

Plunkett, Dr Harold Dudley; Lecturer in Education, University of Southampton. BA Oxon, PhD Chicago. *Address*: Sch. of Education, The Univ., Southampton SO9 5NH.

Pockney, Bertram Patrick; Senior Lecturer in Russian Studies, Department of Linguistic and Regional Studies, University of Surrey, since 1970; *b* 1927; *m* 1957; two *s* one *d*. BSc(Econ) London 1947, BA London 1960. Vis. Lectr, Battersea Coll. Adv. Technol., 1964–65; Lectr, Univ. of Surrey, 1965–70. Mem., Nuffield (late Schs Council) For.

Langs Teaching Materials Project, Russian Cnsltive Cttee, 1962–72; Assoc. Exam. Bd, Mod. Langs Cttee, 1962– ; Nat. Cttee, Assoc. Teachers of Russian, 1961– . External Examnr: Essex Univ. BA, 1969–72; Lanchester Polytechnic BA, 1972– . *Publications*: (with N. A. Sollohub) Bibliography of Russian Language Teaching Materials, 1966; (with L. N. Saharova) Martian in Moscow (12 cine loops), 1968; ed, Eighty-eight Short Russian Stories, 1969; Khrushchev, Russia Today (Making of the Modern World: Russia), 1972; ed, Journey to the USSR, 1974. *Address*: Dept of Linguistic and Regional Studies, Univ. of Surrey, Guildford GU2 5XH.

Pocock, David Francis; Reader in Social Anthropology, University of Sussex, since 1966; *b* 1928. BA Cantab 1949 (1st cl. Hons Anthropology and Archaeology Tripos); FRAS, Fellow, Royal Anthropological Soc. Lectr in Indian Sociology, Oxford, 1954–66. Dean. Sch. of African and Asian Studies, Univ. of Sussex, 1970–75. Co-founder and Editor, Contributions to Indian Sociology, 1957–66. *Publications*: Social Anthropology, 1961, 2nd edn 1971; Kanbi and Patidar, 1972; Mind, Body and Wealth, 1974; trans., E. Durkheim; Sociology and Philosophy, 1951; trans., C. Bouglé: Essays on the Caste System, 1971. *Address*: School of African and Asian Studies, Univ. of Sussex, Brighton BN1 9RH.

Pocock, Dr Douglas Charles David; Lecturer, Department of Geography, University of Durham, since 1972; *b* 1935; *m* 1959; one *s* two *d*. BA Nottingham 1957 (1st cl. Geography), MA Nottingham 1960, PhD Nottingham 1967. Demonstrator, Nottingham Univ., 1959–60; Lectr, Dundee Univ., 1963–71; Vis. Asst Prof., Toronto Univ., 1970. *Publications*: *contrib.* Geog., Scott. Geog. Mag., Tijd. Econ. Soc. Geog., Trans Inst. Brit. Geogrs. *Address*: Dept of Geography, Univ. of Durham, South Road, Durham.

Podmore, David Bruce Leonard; Lecturer in Sociology, Faculty of Social Sciences, University of Aston in Birmingham, since 1971; *b* 1937; *m* 1962; two *d*. BSc(Soc) London 1964; Teachers Cert. London 1965; Mem., Brit. Sociol. Assoc. Asst Lectr, then Lectr, Univ. of Aston, 1965–68; Lectr, Univ. of Hong Kong, 1968–71. *Publications*: chapter in, Hong Kong: The Industrial Colony, ed K. Hopkins, 1971; *contrib.* Jl Comm. Pol. Studies, Internat. Jl Comp. Sociol., Jl Marriage and the Family, Jl Soc. Psychol., etc. *Address*: Faculty of Social Sciences, Univ. of Aston in Birmingham, Birmingham B4 7ET.

Podro, Prof. Michael Isaac; Professor, since 1973, and Chairman, Department of Art, since 1970, University of Essex; *b* 1931; *m* 1961; two *d*. BA Cantab 1954 (2nd cl. English), MA Cantab 1957, PhD London 1961. Hd, Dept of Art, Camberwell Sch. of Arts and Crafts, 1961–67; Lectr in Philosophy of Art, Warburg Inst., Univ. of London, 1967–69; Reader, Dept of Art, Univ. of Essex, 1969–73. *Publications*: The Manifold in Perception, 1972; *contrib.* Brit. Jl Aesth.,

Proc. Aristot. Soc. *Address*: Dept of Art, Univ. of Essex, Colchester, Essex CO4 3SQ.

Poggi, Dr Gianfranco; Reader, Department of Sociology, University of Edinburgh, since 1968; *b* 1934; *m* 1962; one *d*. Laurea Padua 1956, MA Calif (Berkeley) 1959, PhD Calif (Berkeley) 1963. Asst, Florence, 1962–64; Lectr, Edinburgh, 1964–68; Vis. Associate Prof., Victoria (BC), 1970–71; Vis. Prof., Washington (Seattle), 1971. *Publications*: Catholic Action in Italy, 1967; Images of Society, 1972; *contrib.* Br. Jl Sociol., Camb. Rev., Rass. Ital. Sociol., Quaderni Sociol. *Address*: Dept of Sociology, Univ. of Edinburgh, Edinburgh EH8 9LL.

Polack, Kenneth; Lecturer in Law, University of Cambridge, since 1966, and First Bursar, King's College, Cambridge, since 1969; *b* 1933; *m* 1961; two *d*. MA Cantab 1960, LLB Cantab 1957; Barrister (Inner Temple) 1960. Fellow, King's Coll., Cambridge, 1960– ; Asst Lectr in Law, Cambridge, 1964–66; Vis. Sen. Fellow, Univ. of Singapore, 1969–70. Tutor, King's Coll., Cambridge, 1961–69. *Address*: King's College, Cambridge.

Polding, Marjorie Eileen, MA; Lecturer in Social and Economic Statistics, Department of Sociology, Government and Administration, Salford University, since 1967; *b* 1930; *m* 1956; two *s*. BA Durham (Hons Div., General Studies), MA Liverpool 1958 (Industr. Sociol.); FSS. Res. Worker, Social Science Dept, Univ. of Liverpool, 1953–59. *Publications*: *contrib.* Person. Mngmt. *Address*: Dept of Sociology, Government and Administration, Univ. of Salford, Salford M5 4WT.

Pole, Dr David Lawrence Shmarya; Lecturer in Philosophy, King's College, University of London, since 1958; *b* 1923. BA Oxon 1949 (Mod. Hist.), BA London 1953 (Philos.), PhD London 1956; Mem., Aristot. Soc. Asst Lectr in Philos., King's Coll., London, 1955–58. *Publications*: The Later Philosophy of Wittgenstein, 1958; Conditions of Rational Inquiry, 1961; *contrib.* Analysis, Brit. Jl Aesth., Jl Brit. Soc. Phenomenol., Mind, Philos. Qly, Philos., Proc. Aristot. Soc. *Address*: King's College, Univ. of London, Strand, WC2R 2LS.

Pole, Dr Jack Richon; Reader in American History and Government, History Faculty, Cambridge University, since 1963; *b* 1922; *m* 1952; one *s* two *d*. BA Oxon 1949, PhD Princeton 1953, MA Cantab 1963; Hon. Fellow, Hist. Soc. Ghana, FRHistS, Fellow, Center Adv. Study Behav. Sci., Stanford, 1969–70. Instructor, Princeton, 1952; Asst Lectr, then Lectr, Univ. Coll., London, 1953–63; Vis. Assoc. Prof., Berkeley, 1960–61; Vis. Prof. Lectr, Chicago Univ., 1969; Vis. Prof., Univ. of Ghana, 1966; Jefferson Memorial Lectr, Berkeley, 1971; Mem., Edit. Bd, Cambridge Studies in Politics, 1965– ; Mem., Edit. Bd, Jl Amer. Studies, 1967– ; Gen. Editor, Documents of American History (series), 1974– . Mem., Council of Senate, Cambridge, 1970– . Mem. Council, Inst. of

556

Early American Hist. and Culture, Williamsburg, Va, 1973– . Co-founder, Trojan Wanderers Cricket Club. *Publications*: Abraham Lincoln, 1964; Political Representation in England and the Origins of the American Republic, 1966, pbk edn 1971; ed, the Advance of Democracy, 1967; The 17th Century: the Sources of Legislative Power, 1969; ed, The Revolution in America, 1970; jt ed, Meanings of American History, 1971; Foundations of American Independence, 1763–1815, 1972; ed, Slavery, Secession and Civil War, 1974; essays, in, British Essays in American History, 1957; essays, in, Pastmasters, 1969; *contrib*. Amer. Hist. Rev., Etudes Hist. Assembl. Etats, Hist. Jl, Hist. Today, Jl South. Hist., Maryl. Hist. Mag., Penn. Mag. Hist. Biog., Pol. Qly, Proc. NJ Hist. Soc., Times Lit. Supp., Wm Mary Qly. *Address*: Churchill College, Cambridge.

Pollard, Prof. Arthur; Professor of English, University of Hull, since 1967; *b* 1922; *m* 1948 (wife *d* 1970); *m* 1973; two *s*. BA Leeds 1948 (1st cl. Engl.), BLitt Oxford 1953. Asst Lectr, Manchester Univ., 1949–52; Lectr, Manchester Univ., 1952–64; Sen. Lectr, Manchester Univ., 1964–67; Dir of General Studies, Fac. of Arts, Manchester Univ., 1964–67. Lit. Adv., Anglican Hymn Bk, 1965. *Publications*: ed, Let Wisdom Judge (Simeon's sermons), 1959; ed (with M. M. Hennell), Charles Simeon, 1759–1836, 1959; New Poems of Crabbe, 1960; English Hymns, 1960; English Sermons, 1963; Mrs Gaskell, Novelist and Biographer, 1965; ed (with J. A. V. Chapple), Letters of Mrs Gaskell, 1966; Richard Hooker, 1966; Charlotte Brontë, 1968; Trollope's Political Novels, 1968; Satire, 1970; ed, The Victorians (Sphere History of Literature in the English Language), 1970; ed, Crabbe: The Critical Heritage, 1972; ed, Webster's New World Companion to English and American Literature, 1973. *Address*: Dept of English, Univ. of Hull, Hull HU6 7RX.

Pollard, Dr David Edward; Lecturer in Modern Chinese, School of Oriental and African Studies, University of London, since 1962; *b* 1937; *m* 1963; one *d*. BA Cantab 1961 (Oriental Stud.), PhD London 1970. Vis. Lectr, Princeton Univ., 1970–71. *Publication*: A Chinese Look at Literature, 1973. *Address*: Sch. of Oriental and African Studies, Malet Street, WC1E 7HP.

Pollard, John Graham, MA; Deputy Director, Fitzwilliam Museum, University of Cambridge, since 1970; *b* 1929; *m* 1963; one *s*. BA Cantab 1954, MA Cantab 1958; FRNS. Asst Keeper, Fitzwilliam Museum, 1954–66; Keeper, Fitzwilliam Museum, 1966–70; Fellow, Wolfson Coll., Cambridge, 1967– . Mem., Ed. Cttee, Royal Numism. Soc., 1966– . *Publications*: (with G. F. Hill) Renaissance Medals from the Kress Collection at the National Gallery of Art, 1967; Greek Coins in the Courtauld Collection, 1970; ed, G. F. Hill: The Medals of the Renaissance (forthcoming); *contrib*. Dizionario Biografico degli Italiani; *contrib*. Mitteil. Kunsthist. Insts Florenz., Numism. Chron., Studi Secent. *Address*: Fitzwilliam Museum, Cambridge.

Pollard, John Richard Thornhill, TD, MA, BLitt; Senior Lecturer in Classics, University College of North Wales, Bangor, since 1966; *b* 1914; *m* 1952; one *s* three *d*. BA London 1936 (Classics), MA London 1939 (Classics), BLitt Oxon 1947, CertEd Cambridge 1937; Student, Brit. Sch. Archaeol., Athens, 1949, FZS (Scientific). Asst in Classics, Univ. of St Andrews, 1948–49; Lectr in Classics, Univ. Coll. of N Wales, Bangor, 1949–66. Infantry Off., OTC; Army Capt., 1938–45. *Publications*: Journey to Styx, 1955; Helen of Troy, 1965; Seers, Shrines and Sirens, 1965; Appreciation to C. Day Lewis: The Aeneid of Virgil, 1969; contrib. Encyclopaedia Britannica; *contrib*. Amer. Jl Archaeol., Amer. Jl Philol., Ann. Brit. Sch. Ath., Class. Rev., Greece Rome, Ibis, Jl Hellenic Studies, Proc. Virg. Soc. *Address*: Depts of Latin and Greek, Univ. College of North Wales, Bangor LL57 2DG.

Pollard, Prof. Sidney; Professor of Economic History, University of Sheffield, since 1963; *b* 1925; *m* 1949; two *s* one *d*. BSc(Econ) London 1948 (1st cl.), PhD London 1951. Knoop Fellow in Econ. Hist., Sheffield, 1950–52; Asst Lectr in Econ. Hist., Sheffield, 1952–55; Lectr in Econ. Hist., Sheffield, 1953–60; Sen. Lectr in Econ. Hist., Sheffield, 1960–63; Vis. Prof. of History, Univ. of California, Berkeley, 1969–70; Vis. Prof., Bar-Ilan Univ., Israel, 1973. Pres., Soc. Study Lab. Hist., 1972– (Chm., 1964–66); Vice-Pres., Soc. Co-op. Studies, 1965– . *Publications*: Three Centuries of Sheffield Steel, 1954; A History of Labour in Sheffield 1850–1939, 1959; The Development of the British Economy, 1962, 2nd edn 1969; The Genesis of Modern Management, 1965, new edn 1968, Japanese edn 1972; The Idea of Progress, 1968, new edn 1971, Japanese edn 1971; (with D. W. Crossley) The Wealth of Britain, 1968; (with C. Holmes) Documents in European Economic History, 3 vols, 1968–72; The Gold Standard and Employment Policies Between the Wars, 1970; (with J. P. P. Higgins) Aspects of Capital Investment in Great Britain 1750–1850, 1971; (with J. Salt) Robert Owen, Prophet of the Poor, 1971; The Sheffield Outrages, 1971; The Economic Integration of Europe, 1815–1970, 1974; *contrib*. Econ. Hist. Rev., EHR, Jl Contemp. Hist., Jl Econ. Hist., Manch. Sch., Oxf. Econ. Papers, Past Pres., Yorks Bull. Econ. Soc. Res. *Address*: Dept of Economic History, Univ. of Sheffield, Sheffield S10 2TN.

Pollit, Kimball, DipArch, FRIBA; Lecturer (Welsh School of Architecture), and Director of Housing Studies, University of Wales Institute of Science and Technology, since 1960; *b* 1928; *m* 1952; one *s* three *d*. DipArch Leeds 1945–50; FRIBA 1968. Asst Lectr, Univ. of Wales Inst of Science and Technol., 1957–60. Chm., Ed. Bd, Architecture Wales, 1965–69; Council Mem., SWIA, 1960–67; Mem., Exec. Cttee, Central Chapter, SWIA, 1959–67. *Address*: Welsh School of Architecture, Univ. of Wales Institute of Science and Technology, Cathays Park, Cardiff CF1 3NU.

Pollock, Norman Charles, BA, BLitt, MA; Lecturer, School of Geography, University of

Oxford, since 1956; *b* 1920; *m* 1943; two *s* two *d*. BA Cape Town 1940, MA Oxford 1953, BLitt Oxon 1956; FRGS. Hd of Geography Dept, Univ. of Fort Hare, SA, 1950–56; Fellow, St Edmund Hall, Oxford, 1965; Vis. Lectr, Univ. of Brit. Columbia, 1964; Vis. Prof., Natal Univ., 1968, 1971. Mem., Council, SA Inst. Race Relat.; Chm., Senate, Univ. of Fort Hare; Mem., Anthropol. and Geog. Fac. Bd, Oxford Univ., 1962–64, 1972– . *Publications*: Historical Geography of South Africa, 1963; Maps of agriculture, minerals, power and industries, in, African Regional Economic Atlas of Africa, 1965; Africa (regional geography), 1968; Studies in Emerging Africa, 1971; Animals, Environment and Man in Africa, 1974; *contrib*. Econ. Geog., Geog., Geog. Jl. *Address*: School of Geography, Oxford.

Pollock, R. W. W.; Senior Lecturer in Russian Studies, University of Bradford, since 1971; *b* 1935. MA Cantab 1959, MA Oxon 1963, MSc Salford 1969; FIL. Lectr in Mod. Langs, Univ. Salford, 1964–71. Porson Prize for Greek, Cambridge Univ. 1955. *Publications*: *contrib*. Jl Russian Studies, Mod. Langs, Audio-Visual Lang. Jl. *Address*: Univ. of Bradford, Richmond Road, Bradford, Yorkshire BD7 1DP.

Pompa, Dr Leonardo, MA PhD; Lecturer in Philosophy, University of Edinburgh, since 1964; *b* 1933; *m* 1962; one *s* one *d*. MA Edinburgh 1956 (1st cl. Hist.), MA Edinburgh 1961 (1st cl. Philos.), PhD Edinburgh 1967; Mem., Aristot Soc. Asst Lectr, Edinburgh, 1961–64. *Publications*: *contrib*. Enqu., Hist. Theory, Philos. Qly, Systemat. *Address*: Dept of Philosophy, Univ. of Edinburgh, Edinburgh.

Pons, Prof. Valdo G. K.; Professor of Sociology, University of Hull, since 1974; *b* 1924; *m* 1949; one *s* one *d*. BSocSc Cape Town 1947, MSocSc Cape Town 1949, PhD London 1955. Lectr, Rhodes Univ., 1955–56; Lectr, Makerere Coll., 1956–60; Lectr and Sen. Lectr, Univ. Manchester, 1960–71; Sen. Lectr, Univ. Warwick, 1971–73. *Publications*: (with P. Clément and N. Xydias) Social Effects of Urbanization in Stanleyville, Belgian Congo, in, Social Implications of Industrialization and Urbanization in Africa South of the Sahara, 1956; Stanleyville, 1969; (with P. Worsley *et al*.) Introducing Sociology, 1970; ed jtly and contrib., Modern Sociology, 1970. *Address*: Dept of Sociology and Social Anthropology, Univ. of Hull, Hull HU6 7RX.

Pontiero, Dr Giovanni; Lecturer in Latin American Literature, Department of Spanish and Portuguese, University of Manchester, since 1969; *b* 1932. MA Glasgow 1960 (Hons Mod. Langs), PhD Glasgow 1962 (Latin American Lit.). Hd of English Dept., Univ. of Paraíba, Brazil, 1960–62; Dir of Studies, Cultura Inglêsa, Paraíba, 1960–61; Asst Lectr in Latin American Literature, Univ. of Manchester, 1962–65; Lectr in Latin American Literature, Univ. of Liverpool, 1966–69. *Publications*: Anthology of Brazilian Modernist Poetry, 1969; trans., C. Lispector: Laços de Familia (as Family Ties), 1972; crit. edn of

Florencio Sánchez, La Gringa and Barranca Abajo, 1972; Manuel Bandeira: poet and writer, 1974; The Prose Fiction of Dalton Trevisan, 1975; trans. Latin American prose and verse in New Directions anthology, 1968, 1972, 1975; *contrib*. Ann. Sez. Rom., Bull. Hispan. Studies, Hispania, Jl Lat. Amer. Studies, Studies Short Fict. *Address*: Dept of Spanish and Portuguese, The Univ. of Manchester, Manchester M13 9PL.

Poole, Dr Roger Carlton, MA, PhD; Lecturer in English, University of Nottingham, since 1968; *b* 1939; *m* 1969; one *s*. BA Cantab 1961 (Engl.), MA Cantab 1965, PhD Cantab 1965. Exhibnr, Trinity Coll., Cambridge, 1958, Sen. Schol., 1960, Res. Schol., 1961; Lecteur, Sorbonne, 1965–67. *Publications*: Introd. Lévi-Strauss: Totemism, 1969; contrib. Bedside Guardian No 18, 1968–69; Towards Deep Subjectivity, 1972, American edn 1972; Objective Sign and Subjective Meaning, in, The Body as a Medium of Expression, 1974; *contrib*. Blackfr. and New Blackfr., Camb. Opin., Jl Brit. Soc. Phenomenol., Renaiss. Mod. Studies, Rev. Métaphys. Morale, Scandinav., Table ronde, Twent. Cent. Studies, Books and Bookmen, TLS. *Address*: Dept of English, Univ. of Nottingham, University Park, Nottingham NG7 2RD.

Pope, Joseph Albert, DSc, PhD, WhSc; Vice-Chancellor, University of Aston in Birmingham, since 1969; *b* 1914; *m* 1940; one *s* two *d*. PhD Belfast 1944. Asst Lectr in Engineering, Queen's Univ., Belfast, 1938–44; Asst Lectr in Engineering, Univ. of Manchester, 1944–45; Lectr, then Sen. Lectr, Univ. of Sheffield, 1945–49; Prof. of Mechanical Engineering, Nottingham Univ., 1949–60; Research Dir, Mirrlees Nat. Res. Div., Stockport, 1960–69; Dir, Mirrlees National Ltd, 1960–69; Dir, Tecquipment Ltd, 1960– ; Dir, John Brown Ltd, 1970– ; Dir, Aston Technical, Management and Planning Services, 1973. *Publications*: papers on the impact of metals and metal fatigue published in Proc. of Instn of Mech. Engineers and Jl of Iron and Steel Inst. *Address*: Univ. of Aston in Birmingham, Gosta Green, Birmingham B4 7ET.

Popper, Dr Hans, BA, PhD; Senior Lecturer, Department of German, University College of Swansea, since 1973 (Lecturer, 1961–73); *b* 1924; *m* 1951; three *d*. BA Bristol 1950 (1st cl. German), PhD Bristol 1959, CertEd London 1956; Mem., Mod. Hum. Res. Assoc., Mem., Internat. Verein. Germ. Sprach. Lit. Wissen. *Publications*: contrib.: German Men of Letters, vol III, ed A. Natan, 1964; Introductions to German Literature, vol. IV, 1969; Man, Myth and Magic: Boehme, Eckhart, 1970; Affinities, ed R. W. Last, 1971; *contrib*. Antaios (Stuttgart), Germ. Studies (sections I and III), Mod. Lang. Rev., Times Lit. Supp., Triv. *Address*: Dept of German, Univ. College of Swansea, Singleton Park, Swansea SA2 8PP.

Popperwell, Dr Ronald George, MA, PhD; University Lecturer in Norwegian, Department of Scandinavian Studies, since 1953, and Fellow of Clare Hall, Cambridge

University, since 1965; b 1914; m 1940 (diss.), one d. BA Cantab 1948 (1st cl. Mod. Langs), PhD Cantab 1951, MA Cantab 1953; ARCM 1936. Deptl Lectr, Dept of Scandinavian Studies, Cambridge Univ., 1948–52; W. P. Ker Lectr in Norwegian, Univ. Coll., London, 1951–52; Vis. Prof., Univ. of Wisconsin, Madison, 1965–66. Trustee, Viking Soc. for North. Res.; Sec., IASS, 1962– ; Hon. Mem. and Mem. Cttee, MHRA; Mem., FILLM Bureau; Chm., Fac. Bd of Mod. and Med. Langs, Cambridge Univ., 1968–72, 1974; Dir, Literary and Linguistic Computing Centre, Cambridge Univ., 1971– . Mem., Mixed Commn under British–Norwegian Cultural Convention, 1974– . Ed., Year's Work in Modern Language Studies, 1970–72. Publications: (with E. Bredsdorff and B. Mortensen) An Introduction to Scandinavian Literature, 1951, repr. 1970; trans., O. Duun: Floodtide of Fate, 1960; The Pronunciation of Norwegian, 1963; trans., J. Falkberget: The Fourth Night Watch, 1968; Norway (Benn's Nations of the Modern World), 1972; ed, Expression, Communication and Experience in Literature and Language, 1973; contrib. Edda, Proc. Conf. Internat. Assoc. Scand. Studies, Scand. Studies, Scandinavica; Cassell's Encyl. of World Lit., 1953, 1973, etc. Address: Dept of Scandinavian Studies, Cambridge Univ., Sidgwick Avenue, Cambridge.

Poppleton, Pamela Kathleen, BA, PhD, ABPsS; Senior Lecturer, Department of Education, University of Sheffield, since 1970; b 1920; m 1947; one s one d. BA Sheffield 1942 (Gen. Hons), BA Sheffield 1959 (1st cl. Psychol.), PhD Sheffield 1969; ABPsS 1965. Res. Worker in Psychol., Univ. of Sheffield, 1959–61; Asst Lectr in Educn, Univ. of Sheffield, 1961–63; Lectr, Univ. of Sheffield, 1963–70; Sub-Dean, Fac. of Educnl Studies, Univ. of Sheffield, 1971. Cttee Mem., Brit. Psychol. Soc. (Educn Sect.), 1966–70; Superv. Examiner (Psychol.), Assoc. Occupat. Therap., 1971. Publications: contrib. Brit. Jl Soc. Clin. Psychol., Brit. Jl Educ. Psychol., Educ. Teach., Higher Educn Jl. Address: Dept of Education, Univ. of Sheffield, Sheffield S10 2TN.

Pörn, Dr Gustav Ingmar; Senior Lecturer in Philosophy, University of Birmingham, since 1972; b 1935. Fil kand Åbo 1960, Fil lic Åbo 1964, PhD Birmingham 1968. Asst Lectr in Philosophy, Birmingham, 1964–66, Lectr, 1966–72; Vis. Lectr, Univ. of Uppsala, 1970–71. Publications: Logic of Power, 1970; Elements of Social Analysis, 1971. Address: Dept of Philosophy, Univ. of Birmingham, PO Box 363, Birmingham B15 2TT.

Port, Michael H., MA, BLitt; Reader in Modern History, Queen Mary College, University of London, since 1974; b 1930; m 1962; two d. BA Oxon 1954, BLitt Oxon 1956, MA Oxon 1957. Asst Lectr, Lectr, and Sen. Lectr, Queen Mary Coll., London, 1961–73; Vis. Prof., Columbia Univ., 1968–69. Ed., E London Papers, 1965–70; Sec., Univ. of London Bd of Studies in Hist., 1970–72. Publications: Six Hundred New Churches, 1961; (jtly) History of the King's Works, VI (1782–1851), 1973; contrib.

Archit. Hist., Econ. Hist. Rev. Address: Dept of History, Queen Mary College, Mile End Road, E1 4NS.

Porter, Dr Bernard John, MA, PhD; Lecturer in History, University of Hull, since 1968; b 1941. BA Cantab 1963, MA Cantab 1967, PhD Cantab 1967. Fellow, Corpus Christi Coll., Cambridge, 1966. Publications: Critics of Empire, 1968. Address: Dept of History, Univ. of Hull, Hull HU6 7RX.

Porter, Dr Brian Ernest, BSc(Econ), PhD, FRHistS; Senior Lecturer in International Politics, University College of Wales, Aberystwyth, since 1971; b 1928. BSc(Econ) London 1954, PhD London 1962; FRHistS 1970. Lectr, Univ. of Khartoum (seconded from Univ. of Reading), 1963–65; Lectr, Univ. Coll. of Wales, Aberystwyth, 1965–71. Seconded Dipl. Serv., 1967; Vice-Consul, Muscat; alternate UK Deleg., World Food Program, Rome. Publications: Britain and the Rise of Communist China, 1967; ed, The Aberystwyth Papers: International Politics 1919–1969, 1972. Address: Dept of International Politics, Univ. College of Wales, Aberystwyth, Cardiganshire.

Porter, Dr Jeffrey Harvey; Lecturer, Department of Economic History, University of Exeter, since 1969; b 1943. BA Leeds 1964, PhD Leeds 1968. Tutor in Economic History, Univ. of Liverpool, 1967–69. Publications: Provincial Labour History, 1972; contrib. Bus. Hist., Econ. Hist. Rev., Manch. Sch., N. Hist., Yorks Bull. Address: Dept of Economic History, University of Exeter, Exeter EX4 4PU.

Porter, Rev. Prof. Joshua Roy, MA; Professor of Theology, University of Exeter, since 1962; b 1921. BA Oxon 1942 (1st cl. Mod. Hist.), BA Oxon 1944 (1st cl. Theology), MA Oxon 1947; Mem., Soc. OT Study, Mem., Soc. Bib. Lit., Mem., Soc. Brit. Orient., Mem., Folklore Soc. Fellow, Chaplain and Tutor, Oriel Coll., Oxford, 1949–62; University of Oxford Lectr in Theology, 1950–62; Select Preacher to Univ. of Oxford, 1953–55, and to Univ. of Cambridge, 1957; Vis. Prof., South-eastern Seminary, Wake Forest, N Carolina, 1967; Dean of Arts, Exeter Univ., 1968–71. Proctor in Convocation, 1964– ; Canon and Prebendary of Wightring, Chichester Cath., and Theological Lectr, 1965– ; Examng Chaplain to Bishops of Chichester, Peterborough and Truro. Publications: World in the Heart, 1944; Moses and Monarchy, 1963; The Extended Family in the Old Testament, 1967; Proclamation and Presence, 1970, American edn 1970; The Non-Juring Bishops, 1973; The Book of Leviticus (forthcoming); contrib. Chambers's Encycl., 1952, 1963; Promise and Fulfilment, 1963; Tradition and Interpretation (forthcoming); contrib. Ch. Qly Rev., Evang. Theol., Faith Unity, Jl Bib. Lit., Jl Theol. Studies, Svensk Exeg. Åbk, Vet. Test., Zeits. Alttest. Wissens., Expos. Times, Theology, Numen. Address: Queen's Building, Univ. of Exeter, Exeter EX4 4QH.

Porter, Air Marshal Sir Kenneth, KCB, CBE, RAF (retd); Director of Technical

559

Education Projects, Department of Education, University College, Cardiff, since 1970; *b* 1912; *m* 1940; two *s* one *d*. CEng, FIEE, FRAeS, FInstProdE, FBIM. Dir Gen. of Ground Trng, Air Min., 1961–64; Dir Gen. of Signals (Air), MoD, 1964–66; AOC in C Maintenance Comd RAF, 1966–70. *Address*: Univ. Coll., PO Box 78, Cardiff CF1 1XL.

Portes, Prof. Richard David; Professor of Economics, Birkbeck College, University of London, since 1972; *b* 1941; *m* 1963; one *s* one *d*. BA Yale 1962 (summa cum laude), MA Oxon 1965, DPhil Oxon 1969; FREconSoc., Mem., Amer. Econ. Assoc., Mem., Economet. Soc. Rhodes Schol., Oxford, 1962–65; Fellow and Tutor in Economics, Balliol Coll., Oxford, 1965–69; Asst Prof. of Economics and International Affairs, Princeton Univ., 1969–72. Mem., Gov. Bd, Econ. Study Society, 1967–69, 1972– ; For. Ed., Rev. Econ. Studies, 1969. *Publications*: ed (with M. Kaser), Planning and Market Relations, 1971; Economic Reforms in Hungarian Economy, 1974; *contrib*. Amer. Econ. Rev., Economica, Jl Pub. Econ., Oxf. Econ. Papers, Rev. Econ. Studies, Sov. Studies. *Address*: Dept of Economics, Birkbeck College, 7–15 Gresse Street, W1P 1PA.

Posner, Michael Vivian; Fellow and Director of Studies in Economics, Pembroke College, Cambridge, and University Lecturer in Economics, since 1960; *b* 1931; *m* 1953; one *s* one *d*. BA Oxford 1953, MA Oxford and Cantab 1958. Vis. Res. Prof., Brookings Instn Washington DC, 1971–72. Chairman: Fac. Bd of Econs, Cambridge, 1974; Cttee of Management, Dept of Applied Econs, 1974. Dir of Econs, Min. of Power, 1966; Econ. Advr, to HM Treasury, 1967–71; Specialist Advr to House of Commons Select Cttee on Science and Technology, 1974. *Publications*: (with S. J. Woolf) Italian Public Enterprise, 1966; Fuel Policy, 1973; *contrib*. Econ. Jl, Oxford Econ. Papers. *Address*: Pembroke Coll., Cambridge.

Posner, Rebecca; Reader, Department of Language, University of York, since 1965; *b* 1929; *m* 1953; one *s* one *d*. BA Oxon 1952 (1st cl. Mod. Langs), MA Oxon 1956, Dip. Comparative Philology Oxon 1954 (with Distinction), DPhil Oxon 1958, PhD Cantab 1960; Mem., Philol. Soc., 1953, Mem., Lingu. Soc. GB, 1963, Mem., W Afr. Lingu. Soc., 1965, Mem., Lingu. Soc. Amer., 1969. Vis. Lectr, Wesleyan Univ., Connecticut, 1957–58; Post Doct. Fellow, in Linguistics, Yale Univ., 1957–58; Bye Fellow, Girton Coll., Cambridge, 1960–63; Prof. and Hd of Mod. Langs Dept, Univ. of Ghana, 1963–65; Vis. Prof. of Romance Linguistics, Columbia Univ., 1971–72. Sen. Fellow, Ed. Bd, Romance Philol., 1964– . *Publications*: Consonantal Dissimilation in the Romance Languages, 1961; The Romance Languages: a linguistic introduction, 1966; ed, Jordan-Orr: An Introduction to Romance Linguistics, 1970; *contrib*. Archivum Linguisticum, Fr. Studies, Jl Lingu., Lang., Lingua, Romance Philol., Trans Philol. Soc. *Address*: Dept of Language, Univ. of York, Heslington, York YO1 5DD.

Post, Prof. Heinz R.; Professor of Philosophy of Science, Chelsea College, University of London, since 1972; *b* 1918; *m* 1960. BA Oxon 1941, MA Oxon 1944, PhD Chicago 1950. Reader in Hist. and Philos. of Science, Chelsea College, 1966–72. *Publications*: *contrib*. Brit. Jl Philos. Sci., Canad. Jl Res., Jl Math. Phys., Jl Phys, Mind, Phys. Rev., Phys. Educn, Phys. Lett., Proc. Phys. Soc. Lond., Studies Hist. Philos. Sci. *Address*: Chelsea College, Manresa Road, SW3 6LX.

Potter, Prof. Allen Meyers, PhD; James Bryce Professor of Politics, Department of Politics, University of Glasgow, since 1970; *b* 1924; *m* 1949; two *d*. BA Wesleyan 1947, MA Wesleyan 1948; PhD Columbia 1955; Fellow, Royal Statistical Soc. 1967. Inst., Coll. of William and Mary, 1949–51; Asst Lectr, Manchester Univ., 1951–54; Lectr, Manchester Univ., 1954–61; Sen. Lectr, Manchester Univ., 1961–62; Prof. of Politics, Univ. of Strathclyde, 1963–65; Prof. of Government, Univ. of Essex, 1965–67. Dir, SSRC Data Bank, Univ. of Essex, 1967–70. *Publications*: American Government and Politics, 1955; Organised Groups in British National Politics, 1961; chapter, in, Political Oppositions in Western Democracies (ed Dahl), 1966; *contrib*. Brit. Jl of Sociol., Manchester Sch of Econ. Social Studies, Philosophical Jl, Parly Affairs, Political Qly, Political Science Qly, Political Studies, Western Political Qly. *Address*: Dept of Politics, Univ. of Glasgow, Glasgow G12 8RT.

Potter, Dr David C.; Senior Lecturer, Social Sciences Faculty, Open University, since 1970; *b* 1931; *m* 1960; two *s* two *d*. BA California 1954, MA California, 1959, PhD London 1962. LSE, 1960–62; Oakland Univ., 1963–66; Simon Fraser Univ., 1967–70. *Publications*: Government in Rural India, 1964; (jtly), Asian Bureaucratic Systems, 1966; (ed jtly), Decisions, Organizations and Society, 1971; (ed jtly), The Practice of Comparative Politics, 1973; *contrib*. Can. Public Admin., Jl Asian Studies, Jl Commonwealth Polit. Studies, Mod. Asian Studies, Polit. Sci. Review. *Address*: PO Box 48, Milton Keynes MK7 6AA.

Potter, Jim, BA, MA(Econ); Reader in Economic History with special reference to the USA, London School of Economics, London University, since 1964; *b* 1922; *m* 1944; two *d*. BA Manchester 1947 (1st cl. Hist.), MA(Econ) Manchester 1949; Mem., Econ. Hist. Soc., Mem., Brit. Assoc. Amer. Studies, Mem., Econ. Hist. Assoc. Asst Lectr, then Lectr, LSE, 1951–64; Asst Prof., Yale Univ., 1952–53; Assoc. Prof., Univ. of N Carolina, 1958–59; Vis. Prof., Indiana Univ., 1965; Vis. Prof., Univ. of Kansas, 1968. RAF (Fl. Lt), 1942–46; Mem., Council, Econ. Hist. Soc., 1968– ; Mem., Marshall Aid Commemoration Commn, 1969– ; Mem., Econ. Soc. Hist. Cttee, SSRC, 1970– ; Adv., Gen. Course Students, LSE, 1960– ; Cnsltnt Engl. ed., Scand. Econ. Hist. Rev., 1951–61. *Publications*: Industrial America, in, British Essays in American History, ed H. C. Allen and C. P. Hill, 1957, 2nd edn 1969;

Atlantic Economy, 1815–60: the USA and the Industrial Revolution in Britain, in, Studies in the Industrial Revolution, ed L. S. Pressnell, 1960; The Study of the USA in British Education, 1963–64; The Growth of Population in America 1700–1860, in Population in History, ed D. V. Glass and D. E. C. Eversley, 1965; The American Economy, in, American Civilisation, an Introduction, ed A. N. J. den Hollander and S. Skard, 1968; Demographic History of pre-industrial societies, and American Population in the Early National Period, in Population and Economics, ed P. Deprez; *contrib.* Economica, Jl Amer. Studies, Scand., Econ. Hist. Rev. *Address*: London School of Economics, Houghton Street, Aldwych, WC2A 2AE.

Potter, Dr Lois D.; Lecturer in English, University of Leicester, since 1966; *b* 1941. BA Bryn Mawr 1961, PhD Cambridge 1965. Mem., AUT. Asst Lectr, Univ. of Aberdeen, 1964–66. *Publications*: A Preface to Milton, 1972. *Address*: Dept of English, Univ. of Leicester, Leicester LE1 7RH.

Pottinger, John; Lecturer in Applied Social Studies, Bradford University, since 1967; *b* 1931; *m* 1957; two *s*. BA Durham 1955, MA 1962; Professional Soc. Work Trng, Home Office Probation Dept, 1956. *Publications*: (with Jean Nursten and Maureen Anderson) Social Workers and their Clients, 1972; *contrib.* Applied Social Studies, Social Services Qly, Social Work Today. *Address*: Univ. of Bradford, Bradford BD7 1DP.

Potts, Dr Denys Campion; Fellow and Tutor in French, Keble College, University of Oxford, and University Lecturer in French, since 1952; *b* 1923; *m* 1957; two *s* two *d*. BA Oxon (Maths 1944, French 1949), MA Oxon 1948, DPhil Oxon 1962. Asst to Ch. Designer, Rolls-Royce (Aero Divn), 1944–47; Lecteur, Ecole Normale Supérieure, Paris, 1949–50; Vis. Prof., Univ. of Michigan, Ann Arbor, 1965. *Publications*: chapter, in, France: A Companion to French Studies, ed D. G. Charlton, 1972; contrib. Molière: Stage and Study, ed W. D. Howarth and M. Thomas, 1973; *contrib.* Fr. Studies, Mod. Lang. Rev. *Address*: Keble College, Oxford.

Potts, Dr Timothy Cyril, MA, DPhil; Lecturer in Philosophy, University of Leeds, since 1963; *b* 1929. BA Oxon 1959 (1st cl. PPE), MA Oxon 1963, DPhil Oxon 1969. Asst Lectr, Univ. of Leeds, 1962–63. *Address*: Dept of Philosophy, Univ. of Leeds, Leeds LS2 9JT.

Poulter, Dr Sebastian Murray; Lecturer in Law, University of Southampton, since 1971; *b* 1942; *m* 1972. MA Oxon 1968, DPhil 1973; Solicitor of Supreme Court, 1967. Lectr, later Sen. Lectr, Univ. of Botswana, Lesotho and Swaziland, 1967–71. *Publications*: (with V. V. Palmer) The Legal System of Lesotho, 1972; *contrib.* African Affairs, Compar. and Internat. Law Jl of Southern Africa, Jl African Law. *Address*: The Univ., Southampton SO9 5NW.

Powell, Dr Bryan Llewelyn, BSc, MA, PhD; Registrar, School of Education, Trinity College, Dublin University, since 1968; *b* 1936; *m* 1958; one *s* one *d*. BSc Wales 1958, PhD Dublin 1962, MA Dublin 1963; MIBiol, MIBiolIrel. Jun. Lectr in Zoology, TCD, 1960–63; Lectr in Zoology, TCD, 1963–67; Lectr in Educn, TCD, 1967–68; Vis. Sen. Lectr, and Science Curriculum Consultant, Univ. of the West Indies, St Augustine, Trinidad, 1969–70. Mem., Council, Irish Inst. Biol., 1967–69; Sec., Nat. Commn on Biol. in Irel., 1969; Pres., Irish Science Teach. Assoc., 1972–73. *Publications*: Intermediate Biology, 1967, 3rd edn 1971; Practical Biology for Laboratory and Field, 1970; *contrib.* Crustac. Curric. Develop., Jl Anim. Ecol., Jl Sci. Math. *Address*: School of Education, Trinity College, Dublin Univ., Dublin 2, Ireland.

Powell, Rev. Douglas Louis, MA; Lecturer, Department of Theology, University of Exeter, since 1963; *b* 1916; *m* 1951; three *s* two *d*. BA Oxon 1938 (1st cl. Hist., 2nd cl. Theology 1940), MA Oxon 1956. Pt-time Lectr in Theology, Univ. of Durham, 1954–63. Vice-Principal, St Chad's Coll., Durham, 1953–63. *Publications*: *contrib.* Anal. Bolland., Ch Qly Rev., Studia Patrist. *Address*: Queen's Building, The Univ., Exeter EX4 4QH.

Powell, Dr Henry Arthur; Senior Lecturer in Anthropology, Department of Social Studies, University of Newcastle upon Tyne, since 1971; *b* 1919; *m* 1962; two *d*. PhD London 1956; FRAI, Mem., Assoc. of Social Anthropologists. Asst Lectr, UCL, 1951–54; Lectr, Univ. of Durham (Newcastle), 1954–71. *Publications*: *contrib.* JRAI, Man (NS). *Address*: Dept of Social Studies, The Univ., Newcastle upon Tyne NE1 7RU.

Powell, Jocelyn Barcham; Lecturer, Department of Drama and Theatre Arts, University of Birmingham, since 1964; *b* 1938. BA Cantab 1959; MA; Mem., Soc. for Theatre Research. Asst Lectr, Dept of English, Birmingham, 1961; Lectr, Dept of English, Southampton, 1962. Directed operatic productions for Barber Inst. of Fine Arts, 1970– ; works directed for research include: Goethe's Faust, Part I 1968; Marlowe's Tragedy of Dido, Queen of Carthage, 1964; Gluck's Paris and Helen, 1971, and The Pilgrims of Mecca, 1973; first performances in England, John Cage's Music Circus (Birmingham and The Round House), 1972, and Reinhard Keiser's Masaniello Furioso (Birmingham and Sheffield), 1973. *Publications*: *contrib.* Alta, Procs English Goethe Soc., Stratford-upon-Avon Studies, Tulane Drama Rev. *Address*: Dept of Drama and Theatre Arts, Univ. of Birmingham, Birmingham B15 2TT.

Powell, Paul Roger J.; *see* Jeffreys-Powell.

Powell, Prof. Thomas George Eyre (Terence), MA, DLitt, FSA; Professor of Prehistoric Archaeology, University of Liverpool, since 1973 (Reader, 1966–73); *b* 1916; *m* 1944; one *s* one *d*. BA Cantab 1938, MA Cantab 1940; HonDLitt National Univ. of

Ireland 1970; FSA 1948; Corr. Mem., German Archaeol. Inst., 1955. Rankin Sen. Lectr in Prehistoric Archaeol., Univ. of Liverpool, 1948–66. Pres., Prehist. Soc., 1970–74. Mem., Lancs CC, Co. Rec. Subcttee; Mem., Brit. Cttee, Assoc. Internat. Etudes S-E Europ. *Publications*: The Celts, 1958; Prehistoric Art, 1966; (jtly) Megalithic Enquiries in the West of Britain: A Liverpool Symposium, 1969; (with G. E. Daniel) Barclodiad y Gawres, 1956; contrib. H. M. Chadwick Memorial Studies, 1950; Essays in honour of Sir Cyril Fox, 1963; Festschrift, J. Neustupny, 1966; Studies in Honour of C. F. C. Hawkes, 1971; Oxford Classical Dictionary, 2nd edn 1971; *contrib*. Antiqu. Jl, Antiqu., Archaeol., Proc. Prehist. Soc. *Address*: Dept of Prehistoric Archaeology, The Univ., PO Box 147, Liverpool L69 3BX.

Powell-Smith, Vincent; Lecturer in Law, Management Centre, University of Aston in Birmingham, since 1968; *b* 1939; *m* 1966, 1973; two *d*. LLB Birmingham 1962, DipCom Birmingham 1963, LLM Birmingham 1968, DLitt Geneva 1971; FRSA, FSAScot, APhS, Commandeur d'Education Sociale (France) 1970, Grand Prix Humanitaire de France 1971. Lectr, Leicester, 1966–68; Vis. Lectr, Univ. of Bradford Mngmt Centre, 1970– . Mem., Wages Councils under Wages Councils Act 1959, 1969– ; Cnsltnt, Cnstrctn Indust. Trng Bd, 1966–72; Jt Sec., Demolition Industry Conciliation Bd, 1972– ; Mem., Minister's Jt Adv. Cttee on Safety and Health in Construction Industry, 1973– ; Gen. Ed., The Law Students' Annual, 1969–73. *Publications*: The Law of Boundaries and Fences, 1967, 2nd edn 1974; Building Regulations Explained and Illustrated, 1967, 4th edn 1973; Blackwell's Law of Meetings, 9th edn 1967; Casebook on Contract, 1968, 2nd edn 1973; Topham's Law of Real Property, 11th edn 1969; The Law and Practice relating to Company Directors, 1969; Supplement to Emden and Gill: Building Contracts, 1972; Episcopal Heraldry in England and Wales, 1974; Kings Across the Water, 1974; *contrib*. New Law Jl, Scientia, Law Times, etc. *Address*: Management Centre, Univ. of Aston in Birmingham, Birmingham B4 6TE.

Power, Ellen, MA, FLA; Librarian, University College Dublin, since 1951; Director, School of Librarianship, University College Dublin, since 1951; *b* 1904. MA UCD, NUI, 1927 (1st cl. Hons), Dip. Librarianship 1929 (Hons), Higher DipEd 1942 (Hons), Dip. and Fellowship, Library Assoc., (London), 1938, Hon. Dip. and Fellowship, Library Assoc. (Ireland), 1970. Travelling Studentship, Univ. of Vienna, 1927; Asst Librarian, UCD, 1930–51; Lectr in Librarianship, UCD, 1935–51. Temporary Library Assistant: Univ. of Liverpool, 1947; Stadt- und Universitätsbibliothek, Bern, 1949; Counterpart Fellowship, USA, 1959; Occasional Lecturer: Univ. of Western Reserve, 1959; University Coll., Galway, 1969; St Patrick's Coll., Dublin, 1965–66; Coll. of Our Lady of Mercy, Dublin, 1965–66. Member: Exec. Bd, Library Assoc. of Ireland, 1940–51; Council, Library Council, 1952– ; Exec. Bd, Assoc. of British Library and Information Studies

Schools, 1963– ; Cttee, Nat. Science Council, 1972–73; Steering Cttee, Irish Library Co-operation, 1972– . Hon. Treas., Irish Assoc. for Documentation and Information Services; Vice-Pres. and Chm., Irish Assoc. of Sch. Librarians, 1961–71; Project Leader, Internat. Assoc. of Technological Univ. Libraries, 1965–67. National Delegate: US Atomic Energy Conference, 1963; Council of Europe Colloquy on Public Libraries, 1966; EEC Conference of Nuclear Librarians, 1971; OECD Conference on Scientific and Technical Information, 1973. *Publications*: (ed) Neylon and Henchy, Public Libraries in Ireland, 1966; (ed) Irish Publishing Record, 1967; Public Libraries and life-long integrated education, 1968; (ed) Westby, Shared Cataloguing, 1969; *contrib*. Encyclopaedia of Library and Information Science, CLS Bull., Irish Book, An Leabharlann, Libri, Oideas. *Address*: University Coll., Dublin, Belfield, Dublin 4.

Power, Dr Michael John; Lecturer in Modern History, Department of Modern History, Liverpool University, since 1969; *b* 1943; *m* 1966; one *s*. BA Southampton 1964, PhD London 1971. Asst Lectr in History, Queen Mary Coll., London, 1967–68; Asst Lectr in Mod. Hist., Univ. of Liverpool, 1968–69. *Publications*: ed, Trans Historic Soc. of Lancashire and Cheshire, 1969, 1970, 1971, 1972; contrib. to Crisis and Order in English Towns 1500–1700, ed, P. Clark and P. Slack, 1972; *contrib*. East London Papers. *Address*: Dept of History, Univ. of Liverpool. Liverpool L69 3BX.

Power, Dr Roderick Pakenham; Senior Lecturer in Psychology, The Queen's University of Belfast, since 1971; *b* 1933. BA Sydney 1961, MA Sydney 1964, PhD Sydney 1966; FBPsS, FPsSI, Mem., Exper. Psychol. Soc. Teaching Fellow, Univ. of Sydney, 1962–64; Commonwealth Schol., Univ. of Sydney, 1964–66; Lectr in Psychology, Queen's Univ. of Belfast, 1966–71. Mem., Cttee, N Ireland Br., Brit. Psychol. Soc., 1966–71, 1974– , Chm., 1970–73; Mem., Council, Psychol. Soc. Irel., 1970– , Pres., 1972–73; Co-ed., Irish Jl Psychol. *Publications*: contrib. Austral. Jl Psychol., Brit. Jl Psychiat., Brit. Jl Psychol., Irish Jl Psychol., Jl Exper. Psychol., Jl Opt. Soc. Amer., Jl Soc. Clin. Psychol., Perc. Psychophys., Psychol. Rev., Psychon. Sci., Qly Jl Exper. Psychol. *Address*: Dept of Psychology, The Queen's Univ. of Belfast, Belfast BT7 1NN.

Powesland, Peter Francis; Senior Lecturer in Psychology, University of Bristol, since 1972; *b* 1929. BA Bristol 1957 (1st cl.), MA Queen's Univ., Canada 1958; Mem., BPsS. Demonstrator in Psychol., Bristol Univ., 1958–60; Res. Asst in Psychol., Bristol Univ., 1960–62; Lectr in Psychol., Bristol Univ., 1962–72. Mem., Bristol Diocesan Educn Cttee, 1971– . *Address*: Dept of Psychology, Univ. of Bristol, 8/10 Berkeley Square, Bristol BS8 1HH.

Prais, Prof. Henry; Professor of Modern Languages since 1974, and Head of Department of Languages, since 1966, Heriot-Watt University; *b* 1918; *m* 1941; one *s* one *d*. MA

Glasgow 1957 (1st cl. French and German), PhD Edinburgh 1971. *Address*: Dept of Languages, Heriot-Watt Univ., Mountbatten Building, 31–35 Grassmarket, Edinburgh EH1 2HT.

Prandy, Dr Kenneth; Senior Research Officer, Department of Applied Economics, University of Cambridge, since 1970; *b* 1938; *m* 1961; two *d*. BSc(Econ) London 1959, PhD Liverpool 1963, MA Cantab 1968. Res. Worker, Liverpool Univ., 1963–65; Lectr, Univ. Coll. of Wales, Aberystwyth, 1965–67; Res. Off., Dept of Applied Economics, Cambridge Univ., 1967–70; Fellow, Fitzwilliam Coll., 1968. *Publications*: Professional Employees, 1965; *contrib*. Brit. Jl Sociol., Indust. Relat. *Address*: Dept of Applied Economics, Sidgwick Avenue, Cambridge.

Pratt, George; Director of Music, University of Keele, since 1964; *b* 1935; *m* 1961; two *s*. BA Oxon (1st cl.), BMus Oxon 1960; ARCO (Reed prize) 1961; Mem., RCO, ISM, RMA. *Publications*: ed, John Stanley Solos op. 1; *contrib*. Adult Educn, Comp., Music. Opin., Organ, Clergy Rev. *Address*: Univ. of Keele, Keele ST5 5BG.

Pratt, Vernon Francis John; Lecturer, Department of Philosophy, University College, Cardiff, since 1967; *b* 1943; *m*; one *s*. BA Hons Manchester 1965, BPhil Oxford 1967. Visiting Lectr, Univ. of Ife, Nigeria, 1970–71. Asst Editor, Second Order. *Publications*: Religion and Secularisation, 1970; *contrib*. Analysis, Brit. Jl Philos. Science, Jl Theoretical Biol., Philosophy, Second Order, Theoria to Theory. *Address*: Dept of Philosophy, Univ. Coll., PO Box 78, Cardiff CF1 1XL.

Prawer, Prof. Siegbert Salomon, MA, PhD, LittD, DLitt; Taylor Professor of German Language and Literature, University of Oxford, and Fellow of The Queen's College, Oxford, since 1969; *b* 1925; *m* 1949; one *s* two *d*. BA Cambridge 1947, MA Cambridge 1950, LittD Cambridge 1962, PhD Birmingham 1953, MA, DLitt Oxford 1969. Adelaide Stoll Res. Student, Christ's Coll., Cambridge, 1947–48; Asst Lectr, then Lectr and Sen. Lectr, Univ. of Birmingham, 1948–63; Prof. of German, Westfield Coll., Univ. of London, 1964–69; Vis. Prof., City Coll., NY, 1956–57; Vis. Prof., Univ. of Chicago, 1963–64; Vis. Prof., Harvard Univ., 1968; Vis. Prof., Hamburg Univ., 1969. Hon. Dir, London Univ. Inst. of Germanic Studies, 1966–68; co-ed., Oxf. Germ. Studies, 1971–74. Goethe Medal, 1973. *Publications*: German Lyric Poetry, 1952; Mörike und seine Leser, 1960; Heine's Buch der Lieder: a critical study, 1960; Heine: the tragic satirist, 1962; The Penguin Book of Lieder, 1964; The Uncanny in Literature (inaug. lect.), 1965; ed (with R. H. Thomas and L. W. Forster), Essays in German Language, Culture and Society, 1969; ed, The Romantic Period in Germany, 1970; Heine's Shakespeare, a study in contexts (inaug. lect.), 1970; ed, Seventeen Modern German Poets, 1971; Comparative Literary Studies: an introduction, 1973; *contrib*. Camb. Jl, Germ. Life Lett., Ger. Rev., Mod. Lang. Rev., Mod.

Philol., Pubns Engl. Goethe Soc. *Address*: The Taylor Institution, Oxford.

Prescott, William; Lecturer in Educational Technology, Institute of Educational Technology, The Open University, since 1970; *b* 1939; *m* 1963; two *d*. BA Hons Oxford 1962 (Mod. Hist.). Res. Fellow, Leeds Univ., 1965–67; Organizer, Res. and Evaluation Section, Mod. Langs Project, Univ. of York, 1967–70. *Publications*: various publns in field of lang. teaching and testing. *Address*: The Open Univ., Walton Hall, Milton Keynes MK7 6AA.

Presley, John Ralph; Lecturer, Department of Economics, Loughborough University, since 1968; *b* 1945; *m* 1967; two *d*. BA Lancaster 1968 (1st cl. Hons Economics); Member: Univ. Assoc. for Contemporary European Studies; Société Universitaire Européene de Recherches Financières. Course Dir, Economics (with a minor subject), Banking and Finance, Dept of Econs, Loughborough Univ.; Ext. Examnr in Econs, Wolverhampton Polytech., 1971– . *Publications*: European Monetary Integration, 1971; Europe: towards a monetary union, 1972; Monetary Union: a UK appraisal, 1970; *contrib*. Bankers' Mag., Econs, Loughborough Jl of Soc. Scis, Nat. Westminster Bank Rev., Euromoney. *Address*: Dept of Economics, Loughborough Univ., Loughborough LE11 3TU.

Press, Dr Alan Robert; Senior Lecturer in French, Queen's University, Belfast, since 1972; *b* 1932; *m* 1965; one *s* one *d*. BA Dunelm 1954 (1st cl. French), Ddel'U Bordeaux 1956. Asst Lectr, Edinburgh Univ., 1959–61; Lectr, Edinburgh Univ., 1961–66; Lectr, QUB, 1966–71. *Publications*: Anthology of Troubadour Lyric Poetry, 1971; *contrib*. Forum Mod. Lang. Studies, Romania, MLR. *Address*: Dept of French, Queen's Univ., Belfast BT7 1NN.

Prest, Prof. Alan Richmond; Professor of Economics (with special reference to the Public Sector), London School of Economics, since 1970; *b* 1919; *m* 1945; two *s* one *d*. Res. Worker, Cambridge, 1946–48; Rockefeller Fellow, USA, 1948–49; Lectr, Cambridge Univ., 1949–64; Fellow, Christ's Coll., Cambridge, 1950–64; Bursar, Christ's Coll., Cambridge, 1955–64; Prof. of Economics and Public Finance, Manchester Univ., 1964–68; Stanley Jevons Prof. of Political Economy, Manchester Univ., 1968–70; Vis. Prof., Columbia Univ., 1961–62; Vis. Prof., Pittsburgh Univ., 1969; Vis. Prof., ANU, 1971. Pres. Section F, British Assoc., 1967; Mem., Departmental Cttee on Liquor Licensing, 1971–72; Mem., Royal Commn on Civil Liability, 1973– . *Publications*: War Economics of Primary Producing Countries, 1948; (with I. G. Stewart) The National Income of Nigeria, 1950–51, 1953; Consumers' Expenditure in the UK, 1900–19, 1954; Fiscal Survey of the British Caribbean, 1957; Public Finance in Theory and Practice, 1960; Public Finance in Under-Developed Countries, 1962; ed, The UK Economy, 1966; ed Public Sector Economics, 1968; Transport Economics in Developing Countries, 1969; *contrib*.

professional jls. *Address*: London School of Economics and Political Science, Houghton Street, Aldwych, WC2A 2AE.

Prest, John Michael; Fellow and Tutor in Modern History, Balliol College, Oxford University, and CUF Lecturer, since 1954, Vice-Master, 1971–74; *b* 1928; *m* 1961; two *s* one *d*. BA Cambridge 1952, MA Cambridge 1956, MA Oxford (by incorporation). *Publications*: The Industrial Revolution in Coventry, 1959; Lord John Russell, 1972; Jowett's Correspondence with Earl Russell on Education in 1867; Robert Scott and Benjamin Jowett, in, supplements to Balliol Coll. Rec., 1965–66; *contrib.* Trans Royal Hist. Soc. *Address*: Balliol College, Oxford.

Preston, Dr David A.; Lecturer in Geography, University of Leeds, since 1962; *b* 1936; *m* 1966; one *s* one *d*. BA Sheffield 1958 (Hons Geog.), MS Illinois 1959, PhD London 1962. ESU Asst, Univ. of Illinois, 1958–59; Asst, Univ. of Brit. Columbia, 1959–60; Schol., LSE, 1960–62; Asst Lectr, Leeds, 1962. Cnsltnt, Inter-Amer. Cttee for Agric. Develop., Organization of Amer. States, 1966–67. *Publications*: (with P. R. Odell) Latin America, 1972; *contrib.* Cah. Outre-Mer, Geog. Jl, Jl Lat. Amer. Studies, Rev. Geog. (Brazil), Hum. Org., Trans Inst. Geogrs. *Address*: Dept of Geography, The Univ., Leeds LS2 9JT.

Preston, John, BLitt, MA; Senior Lecturer in English, University of Bristol, since 1968; *b* 1926; *m* three *s* one *d*. BA Oxon 1949 (2nd cl. English), MA Oxon 1953, BLitt Oxon 1954. Temp. Asst Lectr, Sheffield Univ., 1951; Asst Lectr, Bristol, 1952–55; Lectr, Bristol, 1955–68. *Publications*: The Created Self: The Reader's Role in Eighteenth-Century Fiction, 1970; *contrib.* Durh. Univ. Jl, ELH, Essays in Crit., Fr. Studies, Rev. Engl. Studies. *Address*: Dept of English, The Univ., 40 Berkeley Square, Bristol BS8 1HY.

Preston, Rev. Prof. Ronald Haydn; Professor of Social and Pastoral Theology, University of Manchester, since 1970; *b* 1913; *m* 1948; one *s* two *d*. BScEcon London 1935 (2nd cl. div. 1), BA Oxon 1940 (1st cl. Theol.), MA Oxon 1944. Industrial Sec. 1935–38, Study Sec. 1943–48, SCM; Curate, Sheffield, 1940–43; Lectr, Manchester Univ., 1948–70, Warden of St Anselm Hall, Manchester Univ., 1948–63; Examining Chaplain to Bishop of Manchester, 1948– , to Bishop of Sheffield, 1971– ; Canon Residentiary 1957–71, Sub-Dean 1970–71, Hon. Canon 1971– , Manchester Cathedral. Editor, The Student Movement, 1943–48. *Publications*: (jtly) Christians in Society, 1939; (jtly) The Revelation of St John the Divine, 1949; Technology and Social Justice, 1971; *contrib.* Theology, Guardian, etc. *Address*: Univ. of Manchester, Oxford Road, Manchester M13 9PL.

Prestwich, Menna; Fellow and Tutor in Modern History, St Hilda's College, Oxford University, since 1947; *b* 1917; *m* 1938; one *s*. BA Oxford 1938 (1st cl. Modern Hist.), MA Oxford 1943; FRHistS. *Publications*: Cranfield: Politics and Profits under the Early

Stuarts, 1966; The Making of Absolute Monarchy 1559–1683, in, France: Government and Society, ed J. M. Wallace-Hadmill and J. McManners, 1957, 2nd edn 1970; France: Monarchy and People from Henry III to Louis XIV, in, The Age of Expansion 1559–1660, ed H. R. Trevor-Roper, 1968; English Politics and Administration 1603–. 25, in, King James VI and I, ed A. G. R. Smith, 1973; *contrib.* Econ. Hist. Rev., EHR, Jl Mod. Hist., Réalités. *Address*: St Hilda's College, Oxford.

Prestwich, Michael Charles, MA, DPhil; FRHistS; Lecturer, Department of Mediaeval History, University of St Andrews, since 1969; *b* 1943. BA Oxon 1964 (1st cl. History), MA Oxon 1968, DPhil Oxon 1968. Res. Lectr, Christ Church, Oxford, 1965–68; Lectr, Christ Church, Oxford, 1968–69. *Publications*: War, Politics and Finance under Edward I, 1972; *contrib.* Bull. Inst. Hist. Res., Econ. Hist. Rev., EHR, Welsh Hist. Rev. *Address*: Dept of Mediaeval History, St Salvator's College, St Andrews, Fife KY16 9PH.

Price, Cecil John Layton; Professor of English Language and Literature, University College, Swansea (University of Wales), since 1961; *b* 1915; *m* 1940. BA Wales 1937, DipEd Wales 1938, MA Wales 1939, PhD Wales 1954, DLitt Wales 1969. Leverhulme Res. Grant 1957, Brit. Acad. Grant 1959, Fellow, Folger Shakesp. Libr. 1960, Grantee, Huntington Libr. California and Newberry Libr., Chicago 1971. Fellow, Univ. of Wales, 1947–49; Lectr in Engl., Univ. Coll. of Wales, Aberystwyth, 1949–59; Sen. Lectr in Engl., Univ. Coll. of Wales, Aberystwyth, 1959–61; Dean, Fac. of Arts, Univ. Coll., Swansea, 1971–73. *Publications*: The English Theatre in Wales in the Eighteenth and Early Nineteenth Centuries, 1948; Cold Caleb, 1956; ed, The Letters of Richard Brinsley Sheridan, 1966; ed, R. B. Sheridan: The Rivals, 1969; ed, R. B. Sheridan: The School for Scandal, 1971; ed, R. B. Sheridan: The Dramatic Works, 1973; Theatre in the Age of Garrick, 1973; *contrib.* Neuphilol. Mitteil., Rev. Engl. Studies, Times Lit. Supp. *Address*: Dept of English, Univ. College, Singleton Park, Swansea SA2 8PP.

Price, Francis Douglas; Fellow and Tutor in Modern History, Keble College, Oxford, and Lecturer in Modern History, Oxford University, since 1949; *b* 1915. BA Oxford 1936 (1st cl. Mod. Hist.), MA Oxford 1940, BLitt Oxford 1940, A. M. P. Read Schol., Oxford, 1938; FSA 1948, FRHistS. Asst Lectr, Univ. Coll. of S West, Exeter, 1938; Asst Lectr, Glasgow Univ., 1939–45; Lectr, Glasgow Univ., 1945–49; Vis. Prof., Carolina, 1964. Head of Hist. Sect., Gen. Staff, SHAEF, 1944–45. *Publications*: ed, The Wigginton Constables' Book, 1972; ed, The Commission for Ecclesiastical Causes in Bristol and Gloucester Dioceses, 1972; *contrib.* Ch. Qly Rev., EHR, Hist., Trans Brist. Glos Archaeol. Soc. *Address*: Keble College, Oxford.

Price, Prof. Glanville, MA; Professor of French, Department of Romance Studies,

University College of Wales, Aberystwyth, since 1972; b 1928; m 1954; three s one d. BA Wales 1949 (1st cl. French), MA Wales 1952, Ddel'U Paris 1956. Lectr, St Andrews Univ., 1958–64; Lectr, Leeds Univ., 1965–66; Prof. of French, Stirling Univ., 1967–72 (Prof. of French Language and Romance Linguistics, Stirling Univ., 1971–72). Mem., Scott. Central Cttee for Mod. Langs, 1971–72; Alternate Mem., Inter-Univ. Council for Higher Educn Overseas, 1969–72; Gov., Centre for Information on Lang. Teaching and Res., 1971– . Mem. Cttee, MHRA, 1972– ; Mem. Council, Philol Soc., 1973– . Editor, Year's Work in Modern Language Studies, vol. 34– , 1972– . Publications: The Present Position of Minority Languages in Western Europe: a selective bibliography, 1969; The French Language: Present and Past, 1971; trans., M. Leroy: The Main Trends in Modern Linguistics, 1967; contrib. Archiv. Lingu., Forum Mod. Lang. Studies, Mod. Lang. Rev., Orbis, Rev. Lingu. Rom., Rom. Philol., Romania, Studia Neophilol., Zeits. Rom. Philol. Address: Dept of Romance Studies, Univ. College of Wales, Aberystwyth SY23 2AX.

Price, H. S., BA, PhD; Lecturer, Department of Philosophy, University College, Swansea, since 1967; b 1929; m 1957. BA Wales 1951, PhD Wales 1961. Lectr, Univ. Coll. of Wales, Aberystwyth, 1956–57; Lectr, Univ. of Khartoum, 1958–63; Lectr, Univ. Coll. of Wales, Aberystwyth, 1964–67. Address: Univ. College, Swansea SA2 8PP.

Price, Dr John Leslie; Lecturer, Department of History, University of Hull, since 1969; b 1942. BA Hons London 1964, PhD London 1969. Asst Lectr, Univ. of Hull, 1967–69. Publications: Culture and Society in the Dutch Republic during the 17th century, 1974; contrib. Acta Historiae Neerlandicae. Address: Dept of History, The Univ., Kingston-upon-Hull HU6 7RX.

Price, Dr John Valdimir, BA, MA, PhD; Lecturer in English Literature, University of Edinburgh, since 1965; b 1937; m 1959; one s one d. BA Texas 1958, MA Texas 1960, PhD Texas 1962. Teaching Asst, Univ. of Texas, 1958–62; Instructor, San Fernando Valley State Coll., Northridge, Calif., 1962–63; Asst Prof. of English, Univ. of California, Riverside, 1963–65. Mem., Adv. Bd, Bi-Centennial Edn Wks of T. Smollett, 1968– . Publications: The Ironic Hume, 1965; David Hume, 1968; (jtly) D. Hume: A Letter from a Gentleman, 1967; ed, Smollett: The Expedition of Humphry Clinker, 1973; Hume's Dialogues concerning National Religion, 1975; contrib. JHI, Rev. Engl. Lit., Tex Studies Lit. Lang. Address: Dept of English Literature, Univ. of Edinburgh, David Hume Tower, Edinburgh EH8 9JX.

Price, Joseph Henry, MA, MBIM, MNIM; Lecturer in Politics, University of Bradford, since 1966; b 1924; m 1949; one s. BA, MA Oxon 1948; MBIM 1966, MNIM (Nigeria) 1962, FASA (USA) 1957. Lectr, Univ. Coll. of the Gold Coast (later Ghana), 1950–60; Sen. Lectr, Univ. Coll. of Ghana, 1960–61; Sen. Tutor, Commonwealth Hall, 1960–61;

Dean, Fac. of Econ. and Social Studies, Univ. of Ife, Nigeria, 1961–66; seconded as Lectr in Overseas Administrative Studies to Univ. of Manchester, 1970–73. Mem., W Riding CC, 1970– ; Gov., Askham Bryan Coll. of Agric., Ilkley Coll. of Educn, Calder High Sch., 1970– ; Mem., Nat. Adv. Cttee on Educn, 1967– ; Adv. to Govt of Bahamas on recruitment and training of sen. civil servants, 1970– . Publications: The Gold Coast General Election of 1951, 1951; contrib. Five Elections in Africa, ed Mackenzie and Robinson, 1959; Political Institutions of West Africa, 1967; Comparative Government: four modern constitutions, 1969. Address: The Univ., Bradford BD7 1DP.

Price, Dr R. J.; Senior Lecturer in Geography, Glasgow University, since 1973 (Lecturer, 1963–73); b 1936; m 1961; one s one d. BSc Wales 1957, PhD Edinburgh 1961. Mem., Royal Geog. Soc., Mem., Inst. Brit. Geogrs, Mem., |Royal Scott. Geog. Soc. Instructor, Univ. of Oklahoma, 1961–62; Asst Prof., Univ. of Oregon, 1962–63. Mem., Council, Inst. Brit. Geogrs, 1970–73; Mem., Cttee, Brit. Geomorphol. Res. Gp, 1968–70. Publications: Glacial and Fluvioglacial Landforms, 1972; contrib. Geog. Ann., Geog. Jl, Jl Art. Alp. Res., Scott. Geogr. Mag., Trans Inst. Brit. Geogrs. Address: Dept of Geography, Glasgow Univ., Glasgow G12 8QQ.

Price, Roger David; Lecturer, School of European Studies, University of East Anglia, since 1968; b 1944; m 1967; one s one d. BA Hons Wales 1965 (1st cl. Mod. Hist. and Politics). Publications: The French Second Republic: a social history, 1972; 1848 in France, 1974; contrib. European Studies Rev., Historical Jl, Jl European Studies. Address: Sch. of European Studies, Univ. of East Anglia, Norwich NOR 88C.

Price, Russell John; Senior Lecturer in Politics, Lancaster University, since 1970; b 1933; m 1965; two s. BA Wellington NZ 1958, MA Wellington NZ 1961 (1st cl. Pol Sci.); Mem., Pol Studies Assoc. UK, Soc. Ital. Studies, Soc. Renaissance Studies. Jun. Lectr in Political Science, Univ. of Wellington, 1961–62; Leverhulme Grad. Student, LSE, 1962–64; Lectr in Politics, Univ. of Lancaster, 1964–70; Mem. Senate, Lancaster Univ., 1968–71. Asst, Nat. Archives, Wellington, 1960. Mem., Edit. Panel, Europ. Studies Rev., 1970– . Publications: contrib. Europ. Studies Rev., Pol Sci., Pol Studies. Address: Dept of Politics, The Univ., Lancaster LA1 4YW.

Prichard, Prof. Alan Martin; Professor of Law, Department of Law, University of Nottingham, since 1974; b 1931; m 1957. LLB London 1951 (1st cl. Hons); Barrister-at-Law, Gray's Inn, 1952. Asst Lectr, KCL, 1952–54; Lectr, Univ. of Nottingham, 1954–62, Sen. Lectr, 1962–66, Reader, 1966–74. Publications: Leage's Roman Private Law, 3rd edn, 1961; contrib. LQR, Camb. Law Jl, Conv. (NS), Jl Bus. Law, JPL, New LJ, Sol. Jl. Address: Dept of Law, The Univ., Nottingham NG7 2RD.

Prichard, Michael John, MA, LLB; University Lecturer in Law, University of Cambridge, since 1953; *b* 1927; *m* 1953; one *s* one *d*. LLB London 1948, LLB Cantab 1950, MA Cantab 1952; Barrister-at-Law Gray's Inn. Fellow and Lectr, Gonville and Caius Coll., Cambridge, 1950–   ; Univ. Asst Lectr, Cambridge, 1952–53. *Publications: contrib.* Camb Law Jl. *Address:* Gonville and Caius College, Cambridge.

Prichard, William John, MCom; Lecturer, Department of Adult Education and Extra-Mural Studies, University of Leeds, since 1948; *b* 1915; *m* 1940; two *s*. BCom Leeds 1938 (2nd cl. Hons), Teachers' Cert. and DipEd Leeds 1939, MCom Leeds 1949. Libr., Dept of Adult Educn and Extra-Mural Studies, 1955–   . Mem., Leeds City Council, 1964–74, Leeds MDC, 1973–   ; Mem., Educn Cttee, 1965–74; Chm., Planning and Develt Cttee, 1973–   . *Address:* Albert Mansbridge College, 71/75 Clarendon Road, Leeds LS2 9PL.

Prickett, Dr (Alexander Thomas) Stephen; Lecturer in English since 1967 and Sub-Dean, School of English and American Studies, University of Sussex, since 1972; *b* 1939; *m* 1966; one *d*. BA Cantab 1961 (English, Trinity Hall), DipEd (with Distinction) Oxford 1962 (University Coll.), MA Cantab 1965, PhD Cantab 1968. Vis. Lectr in English, Smith Coll., Northampton, Mass USA 1970–71; Proctor, Univ. of Sussex, 1971–72. *Publications:* Do It Yourself Doom, 1962; Coleridge and Wordsworth: the poetry of growth, 1970; contrib. Critics on Wordsworth; *contrib.* Jl Europ. Stud., Philol. Pragensia, Theol., Twentieth Century Stud., Wordsworth Circle. *Address:* Arts Building, Univ. of Sussex, Falmer, Brighton BN1 9QN.

Pridham, Geoffrey Francis Michael, MA, PhD; Lecturer in European Politics, University of Bristol, since 1969; *b* 1942. BA Cantab 1964, MA Cantab 1968, PhD London 1969. Res. Asst, Foreign Off., 1964–67; Res. Asst, Inst. of Contemp. Hist., London, 1967–69. *Pulications:* A Dictionary of Politics, 1971; Hitler's Rise to Power, the Nazi Movement in Bavaria 1923–1933, 1973; Documents on Nazism, 1919–1945, 1974; *contrib.* Govt and Opp., Parly Aff., Jl Common Market Studies, Pol Studies. *Address:* Dept of Politics, Univ. of Bristol, 40 Berkeley Square, Bristol BS8 1HY.

Primmer, Brian Alfred Sidney, MA, MusB, ARCM, LTCL; Lecturer in Music, University of Durham, since 1965; *b* 1929; *m* 1963; one *d*. BA Cantab 1953, MA Cantab 1959, MusB Cantab 1960; ARCM 1951, LTCL 1951. Mem., RMA, 1969. *Publications:* The Berlioz Style, 1972; *contrib.* Berlioz Soc. Bull., Durh. Univ. Jl, Music Rev. *Address:* Univ. Music School, Palace Green, Durham.

Prince, Hugh, MA; Reader in Geography, University College, London, since 1965; *b* 1927; *m* 1955; two *s*. BA London 1951 (1st cl. Geog.), MA London 1953 (with dist.). Asst Lectr, then Lectr, Univ. Coll., London, 1952–65; Student, Univ. of Wisconsin,

Madison, 1954–55; Vis. Prof., Univ. of Minnesota, Minneapolis, 1966, 1968; Ed., Area, 1969–70; Vis. Prof., Clark Univ., Massachusetts, 1971. Sec., Hist. Geog. Sect., 20th Internat. Geog. Cong., 1964; Mem., Libr. and Maps Cttee, RGS; Chm., Hist. Geog. Res. Gp, IBG; Mem., Edit. Bd, Jl Hist. Geog. *Publications:* ed (with J. T. Coppock), Greater London, 1964; Parks in England, 1967. *contrib.* Agric. Hist. Rev., Amat. Hist., Archit. Assoc. Qly, Erdkunde, Geog. Jl, Geog. Mag., Geog. Rev., Geog., Jl Town Plan. Inst., Prof. Geog. *Address:* Dept of Geography, Univ. College London, Gower Street, WC1E 6BT.

Pring, Dr Julian Talbot, MA, PhD; Reader in Phonetics, University College London, since 1964; *b* 1913; *m* 1954. BA Oxon 1936 (Lit. Hum.), MA Oxon 1944, PhD London 1966. Lectr, Univ. Coll. London, 1944–64; Vis. Prof., W Washington State Coll., 1967–68. *Publications:* Grammar of Modern Greek, 1950; Colloquial English Pronunciation, 1959; Phrase Book of Modern Greek, 1960, 2nd edn 1966; New English Phonetic Reader, 1962; Modern Greek Reader, 1964; Oxford Dictionary of Modern Greek, 1965; *contrib.* Maît. Phonét., Orbis. *Address:* Dept of Phonetics, Univ. College London, WC1E 6BT.

Prins, Herschel Albert; Senior Lecturer in Social Work, University of Leicester, since 1972; *b* 1928; *m* 1958; one *s* one *d*. Dip. in Social Studies London 1951, Cert. in Mental Health London 1957 (with Distinction); AAPSW, FRSH. Lectr i/c Psychiatric Social Work Course, Dept of Psychiatry, Univ. of Leeds, 1967–72. Probation Officer, later Inspector, Probation and After-Care Dept, Home Office, 1962–67. Formerly: Mem. Exec. Cttee, Howard League for Penal Reform; Mem., Educn Cttee, ISTD (Chm., Northern Br.). *Publications:* (with M. B. H. Whyte, OBE) Social Work and Medical Practice, 1972; Criminal Behaviour, 1974; (with J. W. McCulloch) Signs of Stress (forthcoming); *contrib.* Brit. Jl of Criminology, Criminal Law Rev., Howard Jl, Jl of Criminal Law, Criminol. and Police Science (USA). *Address:* Sch. of Social Work, Univ. of Leicester, Leicester LE1 7LA.

Prior, Dr David B., BA, PhD; Lecturer, Department of Geography, The Queen's University, Belfast, since 1966; *b* 1942; *m* 1968; one *s* one *d*. BA Belfast 1964 (2nd cl. Geog.), PhD Belfast 1968. Vis. Asst Prof., Louisiana State Univ., 1968–69. Warden, Livingstone Hall, Queen's Univ., Belfast; Mem., Cttee, NI Geog. Assoc., 1971–   . *Publications: contrib.* Irish Geographical Studies, ed N. Stephens and R. G. Glasscock, 1970; *contrib.* Amer. Assoc. for Adv. Sci., Bull. Geol. Soc. Amer., Engrg Geol., Geog. Ann., Irish Geog., Inst. Brit. Geogs, Proc. Royal Irish Acad., Zeits. Geomorphol. *Address:* Geography Dept, The Queen's Univ. of Belfast, Belfast BT7 1NN.

Prior, Dr John Francis; College Lecturer, Education Department, University College, Cork, since 1968; *b* 1931; *m* 1970; two *s*. BSc 1952, MSc 1953, PhD 1956, MA 1971,

H.DipEd 1968. *Address*: Univ. Coll., Cork, Ireland.

Prior, Roger; Lecturer in English Literature, Queen's University, Belfast, since 1968; *b* 1935. MA Cantab 1959, MA Sussex 1967; Mem.: Hellenic Soc., Malone Soc. Vis. tutor in classics, Univ. of Sussex, 1966–68. *Publications*: *contrib.* Notes and Queries, Shakespeare Survey. *Address*: Dept of English, Queen's Univ. Belfast, Belfast BT7 1NN.

Pritchard, Prof. David Gwyn, BA, PhD, FRHistS; Professor of Education, University College of Swansea, since 1971; *b* 1919; *m* 1956; one *s* one *d*. BA Wales 1956 (1st cl. Hist.), PhD Liverpool 1964; FRHistS. Lectr, Liverpool Univ., 1957–63; Sen. Lectr, Liverpool Univ., 1963–71. Mem., Southport Educn Cttee, 1958–71. *Publications*: Education and the Handicapped 1760–1960, 1963, Japanese edn 1970; *contrib.* Brit. Jl Educnl Studies, Hist. Educn. Qly, Jl Spec. Educn, Slow Learn. Ch. *Address*: Dept of Education, Univ. College of Swansea, Swansea SA2 8PP.

Pritchard, Donald Frederick Laing; Lecturer in Education, School of Education, Reading University, since 1966; Educational Technology Co-ordinator for Reading University, since 1973; *b* 1922; *m* 1947; one *s*. BA London 1942 (Hons German), Teacher's Cert. London 1947, Teacher's Dip. London 1947, MA London 1951 (Education); Mem., Comp. Educn Soc. Europe, Brit. Sect. Lectr in Educn, Univ. of Ghana, 1958–61; Principal, Kawenu Teachers' Training Coll., New Hebrides, 1961–66. *Address*: School of Education, Univ. of Reading, London Road, Reading RG1 5AQ.

Pritchard, Ernest; Staff Tutor in Political Science, Department of Extra-Mural Studies, University of Birmingham, since 1971; *b* 1912; *m* 1947; one *s* two *d*. BA London 1933; FLA 1935. Extra-Mural Libr., Birmingham Univ., 1946–71. *Publications*: University Extra-Mural Libraries, 1961; *contrib.* Parly Aff., Public Admin. *Address*: Dept of Extra-Mural Studies, Univ. of Birmingham, PO Box 363, Birmingham B15 2TT.

Pritchard, Ronald Edward; Lecturer, Department of English Language and Literature, University of Keele, since 1965; *b* 1936; *m* 1963; one *s* one *d*. BA Oxon 1960 (1st cl. Hons), MA Oxon 1966. Examr, BEd degree in English, Keele Univ. 1968. *Publications*: D. H. Lawrence: Body of Darkness, 1971. *Address*: Dept of English, Univ. of Keele, Keele, Staffs ST5 5BG.

Probyn, Dr Clive Trevor; Lecturer in English Literature, University of Lancaster, since 1968; *b* 1944; *m* 1966; one *s* two *d*. BA Nottingham 1965 (1st cl. English), MA Virginia 1966, PhD Nottingham 1968; Mem., Brit. Soc. Eightnth-Cent. Studies. Tutorial Asst, Nottingham, 1966–67; English-Speaking Union Fellow, Univ. of Virginia, 1966–67. Brit. Ed., Scriblerian. *Publications*: *contrib.* Notes Queries, Scribl. *Address*: Dept of English, Bowland College, Univ. of Lancaster, Bailrigg, Lancaster.

Prochnik, Peter, MA; Lecturer in German, University of London, Royal Holloway College, since 1963; *b* 1933; *m* 1960; one *s* one *d*. BA Wales 1957; MA Wales 1959. Tutorial Asst, Cornell Univ., 1959–60; Asst Lectr, Univ. Coll. of Wales, Aberystwyth, 1960–63. *Publications*: *contrib.* Germ. Life Lett., Mod. Lang. Rev. *Address*: Dept of German, Royal Holloway College, Univ. of London, Egham, Surrey TW20 0EX.

Pronay, Nicholas; Lecturer in History, School of History, Leeds University, since 1964; *b* 1935; *m*. BA Wales 1961 (1st cl. Hons History); FRHistS. Dir Leeds Univ. History Film Project, 1969; Exec. Sec. Inter-Univ. History Film Consortium, 1970. *Publications*: *contrib.* BIHR History. *Address*: School of History, Leeds Univ. Leeds LS2 9JT.

Prosser, Dr Glyndwr Vernon; Lecturer in Psychology, University of Keele, since 1971; *b* 1923; *m* 1945; two *s* one *d*. BA Wales 1948; BD London 1955; Hons Psychol. Wales 1968 (II i); PhD Southampton 1972; ABPsS 1973; Mem., Victoria Inst. Res. Asst, Psychol. Dept, Univ. of Southampton, 1968–71 (Schools Council Project). Served War, HM Forces, 1942–45; Baptist Ministry, 1952–63. *Publications*: contrib. Schs Council Project Technical Report, 1974; *contrib.* Proc. Third Internat. Conf. on Alcoholism and Addictions; Bull. Brit. Psychol. Soc., Instruct. Sci. *Address*: Psychology Dept, Univ. of Keele, Keele, Staffs ST5 5BG.

Prothero, Iorwerth John, PhD, FRHistS; Lecturer in Modern History, Department of History, University of Manchester, since 1964; *b* 1939; *m* 1964; two *s*. BA Manchester 1961 (1st cl. Hist.), PhD Cantab 1967; FRHistS. Mem., Cttee, Soc. Study Lab. Hist., 1965–68. *Publications*: *contrib.* Bull. Soc. Study Lab. Hist., Econ. Hist. Rev., Past Pres. *Address*: Dept of History, Univ. of Manchester, Oxford Road, Manchester M13 9PL.

Prothero, Dr Ralph Mansell, MA, PhD; Reader in Geography, University of Liverpool, since 1968; *b* 1924; *m* 1951; five *s* one *d*. BA Wales 1945, MA Wales 1947, PhD Liverpool 1962; FRGS, Mem., Internat. Union Scientific Study Population. Asst, Univ. of Edinburgh, 1947–50; Lectr, Univ. College, Ibadan, 1950–54; Res. Fellow, W African Inst. Social and Econ. Res., 1954–55; Leverhulme Res. Fellow, Univ. of Liverpool, 1955–56; Lectr, Univ. of Liverpool, 1956–64; Sen. Lectr, Univ. of Liverpool, 1964–68; Vis. Prof., Hebrew Univ. of Jerusalem, 1965; Vis. Prof., Univ. of Minnesota, 1966. Cnsltnt, Wld Hlth Organisation, 1960–62, 1970; Mem., Internat. Geog. Union, Commn on Wld Population Map, 1956–64; Chm., Internat. Geog. Union, Commn on Population Geog., 1964–72. *Publications*: contrib., ed (with K. B. Barbour), Essays on African Population, 1961; ed (with R. W. Steel), Geographers and the Tropics, 1964; Migrants and Malaria, 1965; A Geography of Africa, 1969; ed (with W. Zelinsky and L. A. Kosinski), Geography and a Crowding World, 1970; *contrib.* Afr., Bull. Wld Hlth Org., Geog. Jl. *Address*: Dept of Geography, Univ.

of Liverpool, PO Box 147, Liverpool L69 3BX.

Proudfoot, Bruce; see Proudfoot, V. B.

Proudfoot, George Richard, MA, BLitt; Lecturer in English, King's College, London University, since 1966; *b* 1934; *m* 1960; two *d*. BA Oxford 1958 (Engl.), DipEd Edinburgh 1959, BLitt, MA Oxford 1961. Lectr, Univ. Coll., Univ. of Toronto, 1961–63; Lectr, Univ. of Durham, 1963–66. Mem., Council, Malone Soc., 1967; Gen. Ed., Malone Soc., 1971. *Publications*: ed, A Knack to Know a Knave, 1964; ed, Fletcher and Shakespeare: The Two Noble Kinsmen, 1970; ed, J. Heywood: Johan Johan, 1972; *contrib.* Notes Queries, Shakesp. Surv., Stratf. Studies. *Address*: Dept of English, King's College, Strand WC2R 2LS.

Proudfoot, Prof. V. Bruce, BA, PhD, FSA; Professor of Geography, Department of Geography, University of St Andrews, since 1974; *b* 1930; *m* 1961; two *s*. BA Belfast 1951 (1st cl. Hons Geog.), PhD Belfast 1957; FSA 1963, FRGS; Member: Inst. Brit. Geographers, Brit. Soc. Soil Sci., Prehistoric Soc., Ulster Archaeol. Soc., Brit. Assoc. Adv. of Science. Res. Officer, Nuffield Quaternary Res. Unit, QUB, 1954–58; Lectr in Geography: QUB, 1958–59, Durham Univ., 1959–67; Tutor and Librarian, Hatfield Coll., Durham, 1960–65; Vis. Fellow, Univ. Auckland, 1966. Univ. of Alberta: Assoc. Prof., 1967–70; Prof., 1970–74; Actg Chm., Dept of Geography, 1970–71. Co-ordinator, Socio-Economic Opportunity Studies and Staff Consultant, Alberta Human Resources Res. Council, 1971–72; Pres., Alberta Geog. Soc., 1970–71; Mem. Council, Inst. Brit. Geographers, 1967; Mem. Cttee, Jt Sec., Recorder, Section H (Anthropology), Brit. Assoc. Adv. of Science, 1957–65; Mem. Council, Prehistoric Soc., 1956–59. *Publications*: The Downpatrick Gold Find, 1955; (with Glenda Lamont) Small Town Migrants in Alberta, 1974; (jtly), Frontier Settlement Studies, 1974; *contrib.* Adv. Sci, Geog. Jl, Gwerin, Irish Geography, Jl Roy. Soc. Antiquaries, Ireland, Jl Soil Science, Medieval Archaeol., Ulster Jl Archaeol. *Address*: Dept of Geography, Univ. of St Andrews, St Andrews, Fife KY16 9AJ.

Proudlove, Prof. James Alan, MEng; Professor of Transport Studies, Department of Civic Design, University of Liverpool, since 1966; *b* 1927; *m* 1961; one *s* two *d*. BEng Liverpool 1948 (1st cl. Civil Eng.), MEng Liverpool 1950; FIMunE, FCIT, AMInstH. Lectr, Liverpool Univ., 1949–65; Vis. Prof., Univ. of Kentucky, 1960–61. Grad. Asst, Lancs Co. Surveyor and Bridgemaster, 1948–49; Cnsltnt, 1965–66. *Publications*: ed, Batson: Roads, 2nd edn 1969, Polish edn 1971. *Address*: Dept of Civic Design, Univ. of Liverpool, PO Box 147, Liverpool L69 3BX.

Prudhoe, Prof. John Edgar; Professor, Department of Drama, Manchester University, since 1973; *b* 1924. MA Cantab 1945 (II i English), DipEd Cantab 1946. Lektor in English, Zürich Univ., 1946–48; Lectr in English: Nederlandsche Opleidings-

Inst. voor het Buitenland, 1948–49; Edinburgh Univ., 1949–61; Lectr in Drama, Manchester Univ., 1961–65, Sen. Lectr, 1965–73. Mem. Bd of Dirs, Gateway Theatre, Edinburgh, 1960–62. Gen. Editor, Classics of Drama in English Translation, 1966– . *Publications*: The Reflected Star, 1962; Heart of a City, 1966, 2nd edn 1971; trans.: Goethe: Iphigenia in Tauris, 1966, 2nd edn 1971; Schiller: Wilhelm Tell, 1970, 2nd edn 1973; Goethe: Faust, 1973; The Theatre of Goethe and Schiller, 1973; *contrib.* Encyclopedia Britannica, Brit. Book News, English Studies, Mod. Lang. Rev. *Address*: The Univ., Oxford Road, Manchester M13 9PL.

Prus, Xenia G.; see Glowacki-Prus.

Pryce, Dr William Thomas Rees; Staff Tutor in Geography, Faculty of Social Sciences (with special responsibility for supervision of work of Faculty of Social Sciences in Wales), Open University, since 1971; *b* 1935; *m* 1963; two *s*. BSc Wales 1959 (Hons Geography), DipEd Wales 1960, MSc Wales 1964 (by res. thesis), PhD CNAA 1971 (by thesis); Mem., Inst. of British Geographers, 1965. Lectr in Human Geography, Lanchester Polytechnic, Coventry, 1965–70. *Publications*: *contrib.* Mont. Colls, Nat. Libr. Wales Jl, Trans Denbigh. Hist. Soc., Trans Flint. Hist. Soc., Trans Hon. Soc. Cymmrod., Trans Inst. Brit. Geog., Welsh Hist. Rev. *Address*: Open Univ. in Wales, Floor 15, Pearl Assurance House, Greyfriars Road, Cardiff, Wales.

Psacharopoulos, Dr George; Lecturer in Economics, London School of Economics, since 1971; *b* 1937; *m* 1965; one *s* one *d*. BA Athens, PhD Chicago. Asst Prof. of Econs, Univ. of Hawaii, 1968–69; Sen. Res. Officer, Higher Educn Res. Unit, LSE, 1969–71. *Publications*: Returns to Education: an international comparison, 1973; Manpower Forecasting in France, in, The Practice of Manpower Forecasting, ed B. Ahamad and M. Blaug, 1973; The Profitability of Higher Education: a review of the experience in Great Britain and the United States, in, Contemporary Problems in Higher Education, ed H. J. Butcher and E. Rudd, 1972; *contrib.* Jl of Human Resources, Jl of Pol Econ., Econ. Develt and Cult. Change, Compar. Educn Rev., Minerva, Higher Educn. *Address*: London School of Economics, Houghton Street, WC2A 2AE.

Pugh, Dr Anthony Cheal; Lecturer, Department of French, University of Durham, since 1967; *b* 1942; *m* 1973. BA Hons London 1965 (1st cl.), PhD London 1973 (ext.). Dir, Tyneside Film Theatre Ltd, Newcastle upon Tyne, 1973. *Publications*: crit. edn, Robert Pinget: Autour de Mortin, 1972; *contrib.* 20th Cent. Studies. *Address*: Elvet Riverside, New Elvet, Durham.

Pugh, Prof. Derek Salman; Professor and Chairman of Organizational Behaviour, London Graduate School of Business Studies, since 1970; *b* 1930; *m* 1954; one *s* two *d*. MA Edinburgh 1953, MSc 1956, DSc Aston 1973; FSS 1959, FBPsS 1971, Mem.

Brit. Sociol Assoc. Res. Asst, later Lectr, Edinburgh Univ., 1953–57; Lectr, later Sen. Res. Fellow and Reader, Univ. of Aston, 1957–68; Dir of Res. and Reader, London Grad. Sch. of Bus. Studies, 1968–69. Chm., Assoc. of Teachers of Management, 1970–73. *Publications*: (jtly), Writers on Organizations, 1964, 2nd edn 1971; (jtly), Exercises in Business Decisions, 1965; ed, Organization Theory: Selected Readings, 1971; *contrib.* Admin. Sci. Qly, Human Relns, Jl Management Studies, Sociol. *Address*: London Grad. Sch. of Business Studies, Sussex Place, Regent's Park, NW1 4SA.

Pugh, Prof. John Charles, MA, PhD, FRICS; Professor of Geography, and Head of Department, University of London, King's College, since 1964; *b* 1919; *m* 1944; one *s*. BA Cantab 1940, MA Cantab 1944, PhD London 1955; ARICS 1950, FRICS 1969; Mem., Geog. Assoc., Mem., Geol Soc. Lond., Mem., Inst. Brit. Geogrs, Mem., Royal Geog. Soc., Mem., RSA, etc. Lectr in Geog., Univ. Coll., Ibadan, 1949–55; Sen. Lectr in Geog., Univ. Coll., Ibadan, 1955–56; Reader in Geog., Univ. of London, King's Coll., 1956–64; Dean, Fac. of Arts, Univ. Coll., Ibadan, 1950–52; Dean, Fac. of Nat. Science, King's Coll., London, 1970–72. *Publications*: (with K. M. Buchanan) Land and People in Nigeria, 1955; (with A. E. Perry) A Short Geography of West Africa, 1960; (with W. B. Morgan) West Africa, 1969; Surveying for Field Scientists, 1974; *contrib.* Geog., Jl W Afr. Sci. Assoc., Nig. Geog. Jl, Qly Jl Geol. Soc., S Afr. Geog. Jl, Trans Inst. Brit. Geogrs. *Address*: Dept of Geography, Univ. of London, King's College, Strand, WC2R 2LS.

Pugh, Prof. Ralph Bernard, MA, DLit; Professor of English History, University of London, since 1968; *b* 1910. BA Oxon 1932 (1st cl. Mod. Hist.), MA Oxon 1937, DLit London 1972; FSA, FRHistS. Lectr in Admin. Hist., St Edmund Hall, Oxford, 1952–59; Supernum. Fellow, St Edmund Hall, Oxford, 1959– . Public Rec. Off., 1934–49 (seconded to Dominions Off., 1940–46); Hon. Ed., Wilts Rec. Soc. (until 1967 Rec. Br., Wilts Archaeol. Soc.), 1937–53; Chm., Wilts Rec. Soc., 1953–67; Pres., Wilts Rec. Soc., 1967– ; Ed., Victoria History of the Counties of England, 1949– ; Pres., Wilts Archaeol. Soc., 1950–51, 1953–55; Vice-Pres., Wilts Archaeol. Soc., 1955– ; Mem., Inst. Adv. Study, Princeton, NJ, 1963–64, 1969–70; Fellow, Folger Shakespeare Library, Washington, DC, 1973; Vice-Pres., Selden Soc., 1966–69; Mem., Nat. Trust Council, 1967– . *Publications*: Abstracts of Feet of Fines . . . Wiltshire . . . Edward I and Edward II, 1939; Calendar of Antrobus Deeds before 1625, 1947; How to Write a Parish History, 1954; The Crown Estate, an Historical Essay, 1960; The Records of the Colonial and Dominions Offices, 1964; Itinerant Justices in English History (Harte Memorial Lecture, Exeter Univ.), 1967; Imprisonment in Medieval England, 1968; Court Rolls of the Wiltshire Manors of Adam de Stratton, 1970; contrib. Victoria County History; Cambridge History of the British Empire; *contrib.* Bull. Inst.

Hist. Res., Specul., Trans Royal Hist. Soc. *Address*: Institute of Historical Research, Univ. of London, Senate House, WC1E 7HU.

Pugh Thomas, Michael; *see* Thomas, M. P.

Pulford, Wilfred I.; *see* Iles-Pulford.

Pullan, Prof. Brian Sebastian, MA, PhD; Professor of Modern History, University of Manchester, since 1973; *b* 1935; *m* 1962; two *s*. BA Cantab 1959 (1st cl. Pt I, 2nd cl. Pt II History), MA Cantab 1963, PhD Cantab 1962; FRHistS. Res. Fellow, Trinity Coll., Cambridge, 1961; Univ. Asst Lectr, Univ. of Cambridge, 1964–67, Lectr, 1967–72; Fellow, Queen's Coll., 1963–72; Sec., Fac. of History, 1971. *Publications*: ed, Sources for the History of Medieval Europe, 1966; trans., A. Tenenti: Piracy and the Decline of Venice, 1580–1615, 1967; ed, Crisis and Change in the Venetian Economy in the sixteenth and seventeenth centuries, 1968; Rich and Poor in Renaissance Venice, 1971; A History of Early Renaissance Italy, 1973; *contrib.* Renaissance Venice, ed J. R. Hale, 1973; *contrib.* Econ. Hist. Rev., Studi Venez., Studi Seicenteschi. *Address*: Dept of History, The Univ., Manchester M13 9PL.

Pullan, Dr Robert Alan; Senior Lecturer in Geography, Liverpool University, since 1972 (Lecturer, 1964–72); *b* 1932; *m* 1959; two *s* one *d*. BSc Birmingham 1953, MSc 1954; PhD Liverpool 1971. Lectr, Univ. of Edinburgh, 1958–59; Res. Fellow, Inst. of Agricl Res., Ahmadu Bello Univ., Nigeria, 1960–64; Lectr, Univ. of Zambia (on secondment), 1971–72. *Publications*: Univ. of Liverpool Dept of Geog., Res. Monograph No 6; contrib. African Ecology and Human Evolution, ed F. C. Howell and F. Bourliere, 1963; contrib. Encyclopedia of Geomorphology, ed R. W. Fairbridge, 1968; contrib. Environment and Land Use in Africa, ed M. F. Thomas and G. W. Whittington, 1969; *contrib.* Nig. Geog. Jl, Nig. Jl Sci., Soil Surv. Bull. Sam., W Afr. Sci. Assoc. Jl. *Address*: Dept of Geography, Roxby Building, PO Box 147, Liverpool L69 3BX.

Pulzer, Dr Peter George Julius, MA, DPhil, BSc(Econ); Official Student and Tutor in Politics, Christ Church, Oxford University, since 1962; *b* 1929; *m* 1962; two *s*. BA Cantab 1950 (1st cl. Hist.), MA Cantab 1954, BSc(Econ) London 1954 (1st cl.), PhD Cantab 1960. Lectr, Magdalen Coll. and Christ Church, Oxford, 1957–62. *Publications*: The Rise of Political Anti-Semitism in Germany and Austria, 1964, German edn 1966; Political Representation and Elections in Britain, 1968, 2nd edn 1972; *contrib.* Gov. Opposit., Jl Cent. Europ. Aff., Pol Qly, Pol Studies. *Address*: Christ Church, Oxford OX1 1DP.

Punnett, Robert Malcolm, BA, MA(Econ), PhD; Lecturer in Politics, Strathclyde University, since 1964; *b* 1936; *m* 1966; two *d*. BA Sheffield 1958 (2nd cl. Pol. and Hist.), MA(Econ) Sheffield 1961 (Pol.), PhD Strathclyde 1972, DipEd Sheffield 1959. Asst Lectr, Sheffield, 1963–64; Asst Prof., Carleton

Univ., Ottawa, 1967–68. *Publications*: British Government and Politics, 1968, 2nd edn 1971; Front-Bench Opposition, 1973; *contrib.* Austral. Jl Pol Hist., Parly Aff., Pol Studies, Public Admin. *Address*: Dept of Politics, Univ. of Strathclyde, McCance Building, 16 Richmond Street, Glasgow G1 1XQ.

Purdon, Noël Francis; Lecturer in Drama, Department of Drama, University of Bristol, since 1970; *b* 1941. BA Hons Sydney 1962 (1st cl.), MA Cantab 1967, Dip. di Profitto, Centro di Cultura, Florence. Teaching Fellow in English, Univ. of Sydney, Australia, 1962–63; Res. Fellow in English, Trinity Hall, Cambridge, 1967–70. *Publications*: Poliziano, selections and translations, 1974; Cambridge Rev., Cinema, Screen. *Address*: Dept of Drama, Univ. of Bristol, 29 Park Row, Bristol BS1 5LT.

Purnell, Robert S.; Lecturer, Department of International Politics, since 1966, and Sub-Dean, Faculty of Economic and Social Studies, since 1973; University College of Wales, Aberystwyth; *b* 1923; *m* 1944; 1957; one *d*. CertEd London 1957, BScEcon 1964; Member: Historical Assocn; Royal Commonwealth Soc. Asst Lectr, UCW Aberystwyth, 1964–66. *Publication*: The Society of States, 1973. *Address*: Dept of International Politics, Univ. College of Wales, Aberystwyth, Old College, Aberystwyth SY23 2AX.

Pursglove, (David) Michael; Lecturer in Russian, University of Reading, since 1974; *b* 1944; *m* 1967; one *d*. MA Cantab 1966, BPhil Oxon 1968. Lectr in Russian, New Univ. of Ulster, 1968–74. *Publications*: *contrib.* Slav. and E Europ. Jl, Slav. and E Europ. Rev., *Address*: Dept of German, Univ. of Reading, Reading, Berks, RG6 2AH.

Puttfarken, Dr Thomas; Senior Lecturer, Department of Art, University of Essex, since 1974; *b* 1943; *m* 1969; one *d*. Dr phil Hamburg 1969. Lectr, Dept of Art, Univ. of Essex, 1970–71; Wissenschaftlicher Angestellter, Kunstgeschichtliches Seminar Universität Hamburg, 1971–74. Chm., Dept of Art, Univ. of Essex, 1974– . *Publications*: Meister Francke (Katalog der Ausstellung zur Hundertjahr feier der Kunsthalle Hamburg), 1969; Masstabsfragen, 1971; *contrib.* Frühmittelalterliche Studien. *Address*: Dept. of Art, Univ. of Essex, Wivenhoe Park, Colchester CO4 3SQ.

Pyatt, Prof. Frank Graham; Professor of Mathematical Economics, Department of Economics, University of Warwick, since 1965; *b* 1936; *m* 1959; three *d*. BA (Econ.) Manchester 1957, AM Chicago 1958, Diploma in Statistics Oxford 1959, MA, PhD Cambridge 1962; Member: Royal Economic Soc.; Econometric Soc. (Jun.) Res. Officer, Department of Applied Econs, Cambridge, 1959–64; Fellow of Gonville and Caius Coll., Cambridge, 1962–64; Visitor, Univ. of Calif, Berkeley, 1964–65. Adviser, Econ. Affairs Sub-Cttee, House of Commons Select Cttee on Estimates, 1966; Jt-Dir., Centre for Industrial and Business Studies, Univ. of Warwick, 1966–69; Consultant, Coopers and Lybrand, 1969– ;

Member: SSRC Econs Cttee, 1973– ; Steering Gp, Population and Employment Project, ILO Geneva, 1973– . *Publications*: Priority Patterns and the Demand for Household Durable Goods, 1964; (with W. Galenson) Quality of Labour and Economic Development in Certain Countries, 1964; (ed, with A. S. C. Ehrenberg), Consumer Behaviour, 1971; *contrib.* Econ. Jl, Jl Roy. Statist. Soc., Rev. Econ. Stud. *Address*: Dept of Economics, Univ. of Warwick, Coventry CV4 7AL.

Pye, Edward Michael; Lecturer in Comparative Religion, Department of Theology, University of Leeds, since 1973; *b* 1939; *m* 1963; two *s* two *d*. BA Cantab 1961 (1st cl. Hons Langs and Theology). Dept of Religious Studies, Univ. Lancaster, 1969–73. Sec., Internat. Assoc. for History of Religions (British Section), 1972– . *Publications*: The Study of Kanji (Japanese Writing System), 1971; Comparative Religion, An Introduction Through Source Materials, 1972; (with R. Morgan) ed, The Cardinal Meaning, Essays in Comparative Hermeneutics: Buddhism and Christianity, 1973; Zen Buddhism and Modern Japanese Religions, 1973; *contrib.* Brit. Jl Educnl Studies, Numen, Religion, Religious Studies. *Address*: Dept of Theology, Univ. of Leeds, Leeds LS2 9JT.

Pye, Prof. Norman; Professor of Geography, University of Leicester, since 1954; *b* 1913; *m* 1940; two *s*. BA Manchester 1935 (1st cl. Geog.), DipEd Manchester 1936 (1st cl.). Lectr, Manchester Univ., 1938–53 (seconded Hydrographic Dept, Admty, 1940–46); Sen. Lectr, Manchester Univ., 1953–54. Mem., Corby Develt Corp., 1965; Mem., Schools Council, 1971; Mem., Brit. Nat. Cttee for Geog., 1971. Editor, Geography. *Publications*: ed, Leicester and its Region, 1972; *contrib.* learned jls. *Address*: Univ. of Leicester, University Road, Leicester LE1 7RH.

Pyle, Prof. William Fitzroy, PhD, FTCD, MRIA; Associate Professor of English, University of Dublin, since 1971; *b* 1907; *m* 1931; two *s* one *d*. BA Trinity College Dublin 1929 (1st cl. Mod. Lit., English and French, 1st cl. Mental and Moral Science), MA Trinity College Dublin 1933, PhD Trinity College Dublin 1933; MRIA 1955. Lectr, TCD, 1930–51; Reader, TCD, 1951–71; Fellow, TCD, 1951– ; Jun. Dean, TCD, 1951–56; Sen. Tutor, TCD, 1958–62; Sen. Proctor, TCD, 1962– . Mem., Censorship of Publicns Appeal Bd, 1946– . *Publications*: The Winter's Tale: a commentary on the structure, 1969; *contrib.* Hermath., Mod. Lang. Rev., Rev. Engl. Studies. *Address*: 27 Trinity College, Dublin 2.

Q

Quilliam, George Campbell, BArch, DipCD; Senior Lecturer, Department of Architecture, Queen's University of Belfast, since 1971; *b* 1914; *m* 1947. BArch Liverpool 1937; DipCD Liverpool 1938; RIBA 1939, MRTPI 1940. Mem., Fac. of Architecture, Univ. of Wales, 1944–47; Sch. of Architecture,

Glasgow, 1947–48. Mem., RIBA Town and Co. Plan. Cttee, 1944–45. *Address*: Dept of Architecture, The Queen's Univ. of Belfast, Belfast B17 1NN.

Quin, Prof. Ernest Gordon; Associate Professor of Celtic Languages, University of Dublin, since 1967; *b* 1910. BA Dublin 1932, MA Dublin 1935; Mem., Royal Irish Acad. Lectr, TCD, 1934–44; Fellow, TCD, 1944; Reader, TCD, 1955–67. Mem., Gov. Body, Sch. of Celtic Langs, Dublin Inst. Adv. Studies, 1943– ; Mem. Council, Royal Irish Acad., var. periods; Gen. Ed., Contributions to a dictionary of the Irish language (Royal Irish Acad.), 1953– . *Publications*: ed, Stair Ercuil ocus a bás (a 15th century Irish text), 1939; *contrib*. Celtica, Éigse, Ériu, Hermath., Irish Hist. Studies, Studia Celt. *Address*: 23 Trinity College, Dublin 2.

Quinn, Prof. David Beers, DLit, MRIA; Andrew Geddes and John Rankin Professor of Modern History, University of Liverpool, since 1957; *b* 1909; *m* 1937; two *s* one *d*. BA Queen's University Belfast 1931 (1st cl. Hist.), PhD London 1934, MA Queen's University Belfast 1956, DLit Queen's University Belfast 1958, HonDLitt Newfoundland 1964; MRIA, FRHistS. Asst Lectr, then Lectr, Univ. Coll., Southampton, 1934–39; Sen. Lectr, Queen's Univ., Belfast, 1939–44; Prof. of Hist., Univ. Coll. of Swansea, 1944–57; Vis. Harrison Prof. of Hist., Coll. of William and Mary, Williamsburg, Va., 1969–70. European Service, BBC, 1943; Mem., Council, Royal Hist. Soc., 1951–55, 1956–60; Vice-Pres., Royal Hist. Soc., 1964–68; Mem., Council, Hakluyt Soc., 1952–55, 1956–59; Vice-Pres., Hakluyt Soc., 1960– ; Corr. Mem., Colonial Soc. of Mass, 1960– ; Mem. Council Soc., Hist. Discoveries, 1972– ; Fellow, Folger Libr., 1957, 1959, 1963–64; Fellow, John Carter Brown Libr., 1963–64, 1970. *Publications*: ed, Port Books of Southampton, Edward IV, 1937–38; ed, Voyages and Colonising Expeditions of Sir Humphrey Gilbert, 1940; Raleigh and the British Empire, 1947, 4th edn 1973; ed, The Roanoke Voyages, 1955; (with P. H. Hulton), American Drawings of John White, 1964; ed (with R. A. Skelton), Hakluyt's Principal Navigations (1589), 1965; The Elizabethans and the Irish, 1966; Richard Hakluyt, editor, 1967; (with W. P. Cumming and R. A. Skelton) The Discovery of North America, 1971; American Discovery, c 1000–1612, 1971; (with N. C. Cheshire) The New Found Land of Stephen Parmenius, 1972; ed (with A. M. Quinn), Virginia Voyages from Hakluyt, 1973; England and America 1481–1620, 1974; ed, The Hakluyt Handbook, 1974; *contrib*. Actas, Cong. Internac. Hist. Descob., Geog. Jl., Hist. Studies, Irish Hist. Studies, Jl Soc. American., Proc. Amer. Philos. Soc., Proc. Royal Irish Acad., Rapp. XII Cong. Internat. Scis Hist., Shakesp. Ybk, Trans Royal Hist. Soc., Wm Mary Qly. *Address*: School of History, Univ. of Liverpool, PO Box 147, Liverpool L69 3BX.

Quinn, Hugh Michael, BA, BLitt; Senior Lecturer in English, University College, Cardiff, since 1965; *b* 1921; *m* 1951; three *s* two *d*. BA Wales 1948 (1st cl. Engl.), BLitt Oxon 1953. Lectr, Univ. Coll., Cardiff, 1952–65. *Publications*: ed, Macmillan Casebook on Henry V, 1969; *contrib*. Crit. Qly, Shakesp. Qly, Studies Philol. *Address*: Dept of English, Univ. College, Cardiff.

Quinsee, Anthony; College Librarian, Chelsea College, since 1973; *b* 1930; *m* 1959; two *s* one *d*. BA Hons London 1955; ALA 1958. Imperial College of Science and Technology: Haldane Librarian, 1958–63; Dep. Librarian, 1963–68; Actg Librarian, 1968–70; Librarian, Queen Elizabeth Coll., 1970–73. Mem., Council, Queen Elizabeth Coll., 1972–73. *Address*: Chelsea College, Manresa Road, SW3 6LX.

Quinton, Anthony Meredith, MA; Fellow of New College, Oxford University, since 1955, and University Lecturer in Philosophy, Oxford, since 1950; *b* 1925; *m* 1952; one *s* one *d*. BA Oxon 1948 (1st cl. PPE), MA Oxon 1950. Fellow, All Souls Coll., Oxford, 1949–55;! Vis. Prof., Swarthmore, 1959–60, Stanford, 1965. Chm., Govs, Stowe Sch., 1968– ; Fellow, Winchester Coll., 1969– ; Delegate, Oxf. Univ. Press, 1971– . *Publications*: ed, Political Philosophy, 1967; The Nature of Things, 1973; Utilitarian Ethics, 1973; *contrib*. Analysis, Jl Philos., Mind, Proc. Aristot. Soc. *Address*: New College, Oxford.

Quirk, Prof. (Charles) Randolph, DLit; Quain Professor of English, University of London, University College, since 1960; *b* 1920; *m* 1946; two *s*. BA London 1947 (1st cl.), MA London 1949 (with Dist.), PhD London 1951, DLit London 1965; HonFIL, Mem., Philol. Soc., Mem., Lingu. Assoc. GB, Mem., Lingu. Soc. Amer. Lectr in Engl., Univ. Coll., London, 1947–51s Vis. Faculty, Yale, 1951–52; Reader in Engl., Durham, 1953–57; Prof. of Engl. Lang., Durham, 1957–60. Mem., Lockwood Cttee, DES, 1963; Chm., DES/DHSS Cttee of Inquiry into Speech Therapy Services, 1969–72. *Publications*: Concessive Relation in Old English, 1954; (with C. L. Wrenn) An Old English Grammar, 1955; (with A. H. Smith) The Teaching of English, 1958; The Use of English, 1962; (with D. Crystal) Prosodic and Paralinguistic Features, 1964; (with J. Svartvik) Investigating Linguistic Acceptability, 1966; Essays on the English Language, 1968; (with S. Greenbaum) Elicitation Experiments in English, 1970; English Language and Images of Matter, 1972; (with S. Greenbaum, etc) Grammar of Contemporary English, 1972; (with S. Greenbaum) University Grammar of English, 1973; The Linguist and the English Language, 1974; *contrib*. Engl. Studies, Lang., Mod. Lang. Rev., Trans Philol. Soc. *Address*: Univ. College, Gower Street, WC1.

R

Rabbitt, Dr Patrick Michael; University Lecturer in Psychology, University of Oxford, since 1968; *b* 1934; *m* 1954; one *s* three *d*. BA Cantab 1957, MA Cantab 1960, PhD Cantab 1962, MA Oxon 1968; Member:

Exper. Psychol. Soc., Brit. Psychol. Soc., Inst. Applied Psychol. Soc. Scientific Staff, MRC, APRU, Cambridge, 1961–68; Fellow Queen's Coll., Oxford, 1968 . *Publications*: (ed with S. Dornich) Attention and Performance, V, 1974; *contrib.* Acta Psychologica, Brit. Jl Psychol., Amer. Jl Psychol., Jl Exper. Psychol. Nature, Qly Jl Exp. Psychol., Jl Gerontology, Psychol. Science. *Address*: Dept of Experimental Psychology, South Parks Road, Oxford.

Rachman, Dr Stanley; Reader, Department of Psychology, Institute of Psychiatry, London University, since 1973 (Senior Lecturer, 1966–73); *b* 1934; *m* 1959; one *s* two *d*. BA Hons Witwatersrand 1954 (1st cl.), MA Witwatersrand 1956, PhD London 1961. Lectr in Psychology, Witwatersrand Univ., 1956–61; Lectr in Psychology, Inst. of Psychiatry, London Univ., 1961–66. *Publications*: ed, Critical Essays on Psychoanalysis, 1961; (with H. J. Eysenck) Causes and Cures of Neurosis, 1965; Phobias: Their Nature and Control, 1968; (with J. Teasdale) Aversion Therapy and the Behaviour Disorders, 1969; The Effects of Psychotherapy, 1972; The Meanings of Fear, 1974; *contrib.* Behav. Res. Ther., Psychol. Bull. *Address*: Dept of Psychology, Institute of Psychiatry, De Crespigny Park, SE5 8AF.

Rack, Rev. Henry Denman; Lecturer in Ecclesiastical History, University of Manchester, since 1970; *b* 1931; *m* 1964; one *s* two *d*. BA Oxford 1955, BA Cantab 1957, MA Oxford 1959. Lectr in Hist. of Doctrine, Univ. of Manchester, 1965–70. *Publications*: The Future of John Wesley's Methodism, 1965; Twentieth Century Spirituality, 1969; *contrib.* Jl of Ecclesiastical Hist. *Address*: Fac. of Theology, The Univ., Manchester M13 9PL.

Rackham, James Jeffrey; Lecturer, Business School, University of Durham, since 1968; *b* 1934; *m* 1961; two *s* two *d*. MA Cantab 1957, BA Oxon 1957. Res. Asst, Imperial Coll., London, 1962–68. *Publications*: chaps in: Industrial Society, ed Pym, 1968; Industrial Organization: Behaviour and Control, ed Woodward, 1970; *contrib.* Management Educn and Develt, Personnel Management. *Address*: Durham Univ. Business Sch., Palmers Garth, Hallgarth Street, Durham.

Radcliffe, Philip Fitzhugh; Fellow of King's College, Cambridge, 1931–32 and since 1948; *b* 1905. MusB Cantab 1929, MA 1931. Univ. Lectr in Music, 1947–72. *Publications*: Mendelssohn, 1955, last edn 1967; Beethoven's String Quartets, 1965; Schubert Sonatas, 1967; *contrib.* Music Rev., Musical Times. *Address*: King's Coll., Cambridge.

Radcliffe, Dr Stanley, MA, PhD; Senior Lecturer in German, University of Bristol, since 1964; *b* 1922; *m* 1953; two *s*. BA Liverpool 1948 (1st cl. German), MA Liverpool 1955, PhD Bristol 1970. Asst Lectr, Bristol Univ., 1950–53; Lectr, Bristol Univ., 1953–64. Ch. Examiner in German, SUJB, 1958–68. *Publications*: ed, H. Löns: Naturskizzen und Erzählungen, 1959; Learn Scientific German, 1961, 2nd edn 1967; 25 Years on: Germany 1945–70, 1972; *contrib.* Germ. Life Lett., Jbh Raabe-Gesells. *Address*: Dept of German, Wills Memorial Building, The Univ., Bristol BS8 1RJ.

Radford, Dr Colin Buchan; Senior Lecturer, French Department, Queen's University of Belfast, since 1970; *b* 1931; *m* 1958; one *s* one *d*. BA Nottingham 1961 (1st cl.), MA Nottingham 1965, PhD Belfast 1970. Regular Army (RA), 1950–57; Teacher, Ashby de la Zouch Boys Grammar Sch., 1957–58; Employee Relations, Esso, 1961–62; Teacher, Up Holland Grammar Sch., 1962–66; Lectr, Queen's Univ., Belfast, 1966–70. *Publications*: ed, Seven One-act French Plays, 1974; ed, Salacrou: Boulevard Durand, 1974; *contrib.* Fr. Studies, Nott. Fr. Studies, TES, New Society, Europ. Studies Rev. *Address*: Queen's Univ., Belfast BT7 1NN.

Rado, Emil Richard; Senior Lecturer, Department of International Economic Studies, University of Glasgow, since 1967; *b* 1931; *m* 1957; one *s* two *d*. BSc(Econ) London 1952; FREconS. Univ. of Gold Coast/Ghana, 1953–60; Williams Coll., Mass, USA, 1960–61; Makerere Coll., Uganda, 1961–65; Univ. of Glasgow, 1965– ; Univ. of Nairobi (second-ment), 1967–70. *Publications*: *contrib.* E Afr. Econ. Rev., Ghana Econ. Bull., Jl Develt Stud., Jl Mod. Afr. Stud. *Address*: Dept of International Economic Studies, Univ. of Glasgow, Glasgow G12 8QQ.

Radzinowicz, Mary Ann, (Lady Radzino-wicz), PhD; University Assistant Lecturer, Faculty of English, University of Cambridge, since 1970; College Lecturer and Fellow, Girton College, since 1959; *b* 1925; *m* 1958; one *s* one *d*. BA Radcliffe Coll. 1945, MA Columbia 1947, PhD Columbia 1952, MA Cambridge 1958; Member: Renaissance Soc. of America; Mod. Lang. Assoc. Instructor and Asst Prof., Vassar Coll., 1948–51, 1952–56; Vis. Lectr, Yale Univ., 1962–63; Vis. Lectr, Univ. of Virginia, 1968. Sec., Fac. Bd of English, Cambridge, 1972–74. *Publications*: contrib. Reason and the Imagination, ed J. Mazzeo, 1962; contrib. Some Approaches to Paradise Lost, ed C. A. Patrides, 1968; ed, Paradise Lost, Bk VIII, 1974; *contrib.* Philol Qly. *Address*: Girton College, Cambridge.

Raeside, Ian Matthew Paton; Lecturer in Marathi and Gujarati, School of Oriental and African Studies, University of London, since 1958; *b* 1926; *m* 1953; three *s*. BA London 1951 (French), PhD London 1955 (French); Mem., Philol. Soc. Asst. Lectr in Linguistics, SOAS, 1954–57; Lectr in Linguistics, 1957–58. *Publications*: trans., The Rough and the Smooth, 1966; Wild Bapu of Garambi, 1969; contrib. Storia delle letterature d'Oriente, 1969; The Novel in India, 1970; *contrib.* Bull. SOAS. *Address*: School of Oriental and African Studies, Univ. of London, WC1E 7HP.

Rahtz, Philip Arthur, MA, FSA; Senior Lecturer in Medieval Archaeology, School of History, University of Birmingham, since 1970; *b* 1921; *m* 1940; three *s* two *d*. MA Bristol 1964; FSA 1963. Asst Lectr, then

Lectr in Medieval Archaeology, Univ. of Birmingham, 1963–70. Exec. of Council for Brit. Archaeol., 1966–71; Vice-Pres., Soc. Mediev. Archaeol. *Publications*: (with others) The Preparation of Archaeological Reports, 1966, rev. edn 1974; ed, Rescue Archaeology, 1974; var. monogs on archaeol., and contrib. var. Festschriften; *contrib.* Alta, Antiqu., Antiqu. Jl, Archaeol. Cant., Archaeol. Jl, Mediev. Archaeol., Jl W Afr. Studies, Proc. Dorset Nat. Hist. Archaeol. Soc., Proc. Somerset Archaeol. Nat. Hist. Soc., Proc. Univ. Brist. Spel. Soc., Trans Brist. Glos Archaeol. Soc., Trans Thor. Soc., Wilts Archaeol. Nat. Hist. Mag., Yorks Archaeol. Jl, etc. *Address*: School of History, Univ. of Birmingham, PO Box 363, Birmingham B15 2TT.

Raines, Gabrielle, BA, PhD; Lecturer in English and American Literature, Board of English and American Studies, University of Kent at Canterbury, since 1969; *b* 1940; *m* 1971; one *d*. BA Leicester 1962 (1st cl. Special Engl.), PhD Leicester 1967. Asst Lectr, Manchester Univ., 1966–69. *Address*: Darwin College, Univ. of Kent, Canterbury CT2 7NY.

Raitt, Dr Alan William; Fellow and Tutor in French, Magdalen College, Oxford University, since 1966; *b* 1930; two *d*. BA Oxon 1951 (1st cl. Mod. Langs), MA Oxon 1955, DPhil Oxon 1957; FRSL 1971. Fellow by Exam., Magdalen Coll., Oxford, 1953–55; Fellow and Lectr in French, Exeter Coll., Oxford, 1955–66. *Publications*: ed, Balzac: Short Stories, 1964; Villiers de L'Isle-Adam et le Mouvement Symboliste, 1965; ed (with P.-G. Castex), Villiers de L'Isle-Adam: Le Prétendant, 1965; French Life and Letters: The Nineteenth Century, 1965, 2nd edn 1971; Prosper Mérimée, 1970; *contrib.* Fr. Studies, Mod. Lang. Rev., Rev. Sci. Hum. *Address*: Magdalen College, Oxford.

Ralphs, Sheila; Senior Lecturer, Department of Italian Studies, University of Manchester, since 1966; *b* 1923. BA London 1946 (1st cl. Hons Italian), Dip. Theol., London 1948. *Publications*: Etterno Spiro: a study in the nature of Dante's Paradise, 1959; Dante's Journey to the Centre, 1972. *Address*: Dept of Italian Studies, Univ. of Manchester, Manchester M13 9PL.

Ramm, Agatha, MA, FRHistS; Fellow and Tutor in Modern History, Somerville College, University of Oxford, since 1952, and University Lecturer in Nineteenth Century History, Oxford, since 1965; *b* 1914. BA London 1935, MA London 1937, MA Oxon 1953; FRHistS. Asst, then Asst Lectr and later Lectr, Bedford Coll., Univ. of London, 1938–52. *Publications*: The Political Correspondence of Mr Gladstone and Lord Granville, 1868–1876, 1952; 1876–1886, 1962; The Crimean War, in, vol. X, New Cambridge Modern History, 1960; The Risorgimento (Historical Association Pamphlet), 1962, 1967; Germany, 1789–1919, 1967; trans., H. Böhme: The Foundation of the German Empire: Select Documents, 1971; Great Britain and France in Egypt, 1876–82,

in France and Britain in Africa, ed P. Gifford and R. Louis, 1971; Sir Robert Morier, Envoy and Ambassador in the Age of Imperialism, 1973; *contrib.* EHR. *Address*: Somerville College, Oxford.

Ramsay, George Daniel; Fellow and Tutor in Modern History, St Edmund Hall, Oxford University, since 1937; *b* 1909; *m* 1952; two *s* one *d*. BA Oxon 1931 (1st cl. Mod. Hist.), MA 1937, DPhil 1939; FRHistS. Lectr, Merton Coll., Oxford, 1934–36; Univ. Lectr, 1947– . Sqn Ldr, RAF (ground), 1941–45, Mem., Council, Rossall Sch., 1955– . *Publications*: The Wiltshire Woollen Industry in the 16th and 17th centuries, 1943, 2nd edn 1965; ed, Two Sixteenth-century Taxation Lists (Wilts Rec. Soc. X), 1954; English Overseas Trade during the Centuries of Emergence, 1957; ed, John Isham, Mercer and Merchant Adventurer (Northants Rec. Soc. XXI), 1962; contrib. New Cambridge Modern History, vol. III, 1968, vol. IV, 1970; *contrib.* Econ. Hist. Rev., EHR. *Address*: St Edmund Hall, Oxford.

Ramsden, Prof. Herbert; Professor of Spanish Language and Literature, University of Manchester, since 1961; *b* 1927; *m* 1953; three *s* two *d*. BA Manchester 1948 (1st cl. French), BA Manchester 1949 (1st cl. Spanish), MA Manchester 1953, Dr en Fil. y Let. Madrid 1954; Mem., Assoc. Hispan. (GB and Internat.). Asst Lectr, Manchester, 1954–57. Lectr, Manchester, 1957–61. Hispanic rep., Nat. Council for Mod. Langs, 1971–72. *Publications*: An Essential Course in Modern Spanish, 1959, 7th edn 1970; Weak-Pronoun Position in the Early Romance Languages, 1963; Azorín's La ruta de Don Quijote, 1966; Angel Ganivet's Idearium español, 1967; The Spanish 'Generation of 1898', 1974; The 1898 Movement in Spain, 1974; *contrib.* An. Gald., Bull. Hispan. Studies, Mod. Lang. Rev., etc. *Address*: Dept of Spanish and Portuguese Studies, Univ. of Manchester, Manchester M13 9PL.

Ramsey, Prof. Peter Herbert; Professor of History, University of Aberdeen, since 1966; *b* 1925; *m* 1966; three *d*. BA Oxon 1950, MA Oxon 1954, DPhil Oxon 1959; FRHistS 1970. Asst, Glasgow Univ., 1951–55; Lectr, Bristol Univ., 1955–65; Sen. Lectr, Bristol Univ., 1965–66. *Publications*: Tudor Historical Problems, 1963; ed, The Price Revolution in Sixteenth Century England, 1971; *contrib.* Econ. Hist. Rev. *Address*: Dept of History, King's College, Aberdeen AB9 2UB.

Ranawake, Dr Silvia; Lecturer, Department of German, Bedford College, University of London, since 1968; *b* 1938; *m* 1960; two *s*. Staatsexamen München 1962, DrPhil München 1970; Mem., Mod. Hum. Res. Assoc. Asst Lectr, London Univ., 1966–68. *Publication*: Höfische Strophenkunst (München), 1974. *Address*: Dept of German, Bedford Coll., Regent's Park, NW1 4NS.

Randall, John Greville; Lecturer, Department of Classics, University of Lancaster, since 1967; *b* 1939; *m* 1962; two *s*. BA Leicester 1961 (1st cl. Hons), MA 1963 (Distinction); Member: AUT, JACT. Mem.,

Cttee, ARLT, 1972– . *Address*: Dept of Classics, Univ. of Lancaster, Bailrigg, Lancaster LA1 4YW.

Randell, Dr Gerald Anthony; Senior Lecturer in Occupational Psychology, Management Centre, University of Bradford, since 1967; *b* 1930; *m* 1958; four *d*. BSc Nottingham 1956 (Hons Psychology), MSc London 1959 (Occupational Psychology), PhD London 1972 (Psychology); ABPsS, Mem., Ergonom. Res. Soc., Internat. Assoc. Appl. Psychol., Brit. Univ. Indust. Relat. Assoc., Affiliate IPM. Lectr in Occupational Psychology, Birkbeck Coll., London, 1959–67. Assessor, Civil Service Selection Bd; Chm., Occupat. Psychol. Sect., BPS, 1965–66; Council, Ind. Assessment and Res. Centre, 1969– . *Publications*: (jtly) Staff Appraisal, 1972; chapters, in, Programmierter Unterricht und Lehrmaschinen, 1963; Encyclopaedia Britannica, 1966 edn; Industrial Training Handbook, ed Barber, 1968; Studies in Organizational Behavior and Management, Porter et al., 2nd edn; International Handbook of Management Development, ed Lippitt and Taylor; *contrib*. Mngmt Decis., Occupat. Psychol., Univ. Qly. *Address*: Univ. of Bradford, Management Centre, Emm Lane, Bradford BD9 4JL.

Ranft, Dr Bryan McLean; Visiting Professor of War Studies, King's College, London, since 1970; *b* 1917; *m* 1949. BA 1939, MA 1946, DPhil 1967, Oxon; FRHistS; Member: RIIA; Internat. Inst. for Strategic Studies; Navy Records Soc., Soc. for Nautical Res. RNC Greenwich: Lectr in History, 1947–66; Prof. of History and Head of Dept of History and Internat. Affairs, 1966– . *Publications*: ed, The Hood Papers, 1952; ed, The Vernon Papers, 1958; contrib. Purnell's History of the First World War; *contrib*. Jl Mod. Hist., Mariner's Mirror, Defence, Navy Internat. *Address*: King's Coll., Strand, WC2R 2LS.

Rankin, Prof. Herbert David; Professor of Classics, University of Southampton, since 1973; *b* 1931; *m* 1957; one *s*. MA TCD 1954 (Graduated Classics). Assistant Lecturer: QMC, 1955–58; Sheffield, 1958–59; Lectr, Classics, 1959–65; Foundn Prof. and Head of Dept of Classical Studies, Monash Univ., 1965–73. *Publications*: Plato and the Individual, 1964, 1969; Petronius the Artist, 1971; *contrib*. A. Ant. Hung., A. Class., Agora, Amer. Imago, L'Ant. Class., Apeiron, Dialectica, Emerita, Eos, Eranos, Hermath, Hermes, Latomus, Philologis, Psychotherapy and Psychosomatics, Int. Logic. Rev., Rheinisches Museum, Symb. Osloensis. *Address*: Dept of Classics, Univ. of Southampton, Southampton SO9 5NH.

Ranson, Dr Edward; Lecturer in History, University of Aberdeen, since 1967; *b* 1937; *m* 1963; two *s* one *d*. BA Manchester 1959, MA Manchester 1960, PhD Manchester 1963. Asst Lectr, Univ. of Aberdeen, 1963–66; Vis. Asst Prof., Wesleyan Univ., Middleton, Conn, 1966–67. *Publications*: contrib. Historian, Jl Amer. Studies, Mil. Aff. *Address*: Dept of History, Univ. of Aberdeen, Aberdeen, Scotland.

Raphael, Prof. David Daiches, MA, DPhil; Academic Director of Associated Studies, and Professor of Philosophy, Imperial College, London, since 1973; *b* 1916; two *d*. BA Oxford 1938 (1st cl. Classical Hon. Mods, 1st cl. Lit. Hum.), DPhil Oxford 1940, MA Oxford 1940. Robinson Sen. Schol., Oriel Coll., Oxford, 1938–40; Prof. of Philosophy, Univ. of Otago, NZ, 1946–49; Lectr in Moral Philosophy, Univ. of Glasgow, 1949–51, Sen. Lectr, 1951–60; Vis. Prof., Hamilton Coll., Clinton, NY, and Univ. of S California, 1959; Mahlon Powell Lectr, Indiana Univ., 1959; Prof. of Political and Social Philosophy, Univ. of Glasgow, 1960–70; Prof. of Philosophy, Reading Univ., 1970–73. Vis. Fellow, All Souls Coll., Oxford, 1967–68. Temp. Asst Principal, Min. of Labour and Nat. Service, 1941–44; Principal, 1944–46; Ind. Mem., Cttee on Teaching Profession in Scotland (Wheatley Cttee), 1961–63; Scott. Agric. Wages Bd, 1962– ; Mem., Acad. Adv. Cttee, Heriot-Watt Univ., 1964–71; Mem., Cttee on Distribn of Teachers in Scotland (Roberts Cttee), 1965–66; Ind. Mem., Police Adv. Bd for Scotland, 1965–70; Mem., Social Sciences Adv. Cttee, UK Nat. Commn, UNESCO, 1966– ; Acad. Mem., Bd of Govs, Hebrew Univ. of Jerusalem, 1969– ; Vice-Pres., Internat. Assoc. Philos. of Law and Social Philos., 1971– ; Pres., Aristotelian Soc., 1974–75. *Publications*: The Moral Sense, 1947; ed, R. Price: Review of Morals, 1948; Moral Judgement, 1955; The Paradox of Tragedy, 1960; ed, Political Theory and the Rights of Man, 1967; ed, British Moralists 1650–1800, 1969; Problems of Political Philosophy, 1970; *contrib*. jls of philosophy and political studies. *Address*: Imperial College of Science and Technology, SW7 2AZ.

Raraty, Dr Maurice Michael, MA, PhD; Lecturer in German, Faculty of Humanities, University of Kent at Canterbury, since 1967; *b* 1938; *m* 1962; three *s*. BA Keele 1961 (1st cl. German and Economics), PhD Sheffield 1963, MA(j.o.) Dublin 1966. Jun. Lectr, TCD, 1963–66; Lectr, TCD, 1966. *Publications*: ed, E. T. A. Hoffmann: Prinzessin Brambilla, 1972; *contrib*. Hermath., Mitteil E. T. A. Hoffmann-Gesells. *Address*: Eliot College, Univ. of Kent at Canterbury, Canterbury, Kent.

Rastall, Dr (George) Richard; Lecturer in Music, University of Leeds, since 1967; *b* 1940. BA Cantab 1963, MusB Cantab 1964, MA Cantab 1967, PhD Manchester 1968; Member: Royal Mus. Assoc., Assoc. Univ. Teachers, Incorp. Soc. of Musicians. Co-director (and co-founder) and General Editor, Boethius Press. *Publications*: ed, Michel Toulouze: L'art et instruction de bien dancer, 1971; ed, Benjamin Rogers: The Complete Keyboard Works, 1972; *contrib*. Mus. and Letters, Proc. Roy. Mus. Assoc. *Address*: Dept of Music, Univ. of Leeds, 14 Cromer Terrace, Leeds LS2 9JR.

Ratcliff, Dr (Nora) Elizabeth; Lecturer in French, University of Newcastle upon Tyne, since 1966; *b* 1929. MA St Andrews 1951 (1st cl. French), PhD St Andrews 1955. *Address*:

Dept of French Studies, The Univ., Newcastle upon Tyne NE1 7RU.

Ratcliffe, Dr Barrie Michael; Lecturer, History Department, University of Manchester, since 1967; *b* 1940; *m* 1965; one *d*. BA Manchester 1963 (1st cl. Hons in Mod. Hist. with Econs and Politics), PhD Manchester 1971; Mem., Econ. Hist. Soc. Asst Lectr, Univ. of Manchester, 1964–67. *Publications*: ed, Britain and her World 1750–1914, 1974; The Free Trade Era (forthcoming); *contrib*. Cahiers de l'Institut de Science économique appliquée, Jewish Social Studies, Jl of European Econ. Hist., Jl of Transport Hist., Revue d'histoire de Banque. *Address*: History Dept, The Univ., Manchester M13 9PL.

Ratcliffe, Donald John, MA, BPhil; Lecturer in Modern History, Department of Modern History, University of Durham, since 1966; *b* 1942; *m* 1965; one *s* one *d*. BA 1963 (1st cl.), MA 1967, BPhil 1966, Oxon; CertEd Bristol 1964; Member: Brit. Assoc. for Amer. Studies; Hist. Assoc.; Organization of Amer. Historians; Inst. of Early Amer. Hist. and Culture. Ochs-Oakes Fellow, Univ. of Calif., Berkeley, 1965–66; Amer. Council of Learned Socs Res. Fellow, Ohio State Univ., 1971–72. *Publications*: *contrib*. Durham Jl, Jl Amer. Hist., Ohio Hist. *Address*: 43 North Bailey, Durham DH1 3EX.

Ratcliffe, Dr Frederick William, JP; University Librarian and Director, John Rylands University Library of Manchester, Victoria University of Manchester, since 1972; *b* 1927; *m* 1952; two *s* one *d*. BA Hons Manchester 1951, MA Manchester 1952, PhD Manchester 1956; Member: AUT; Bibliographical Soc.; Library Assoc.; Magistrates' Assoc. JP Stockport, 1971– . Manchester University Library: Asst Cataloguer, 1954–57; Cataloguer, 1957–62; Sub-Librarian, Glasgow Univ. Library, 1962–63; Dep. Librarian, Newcastle upon Tyne Univ. Library, 1963–65; Univ. Librarian, Manchester, 1965–72; Hon. Lectr in Historical Bibliography, Manchester Univ., 1969– . Member: Standing Cttee on Libraries, Vice-Chancellors and Principals Cttee, 1968– ; Exec. Bd, Friends of Nat. Libraries, 1973– . *Publications*: *contrib*. Bibliothek, Bull. John Rylands Liby, Connoisseur, Libri, Penrose Annual, Zeitschr. f. d. Philologie. *Address*: John Rylands Univ. Library of Manchester, Oxford Road, Manchester M13 9PP.

Rathfelders, Hermanis, MSc, FIL; Lecturer in Russian, Department of Modern Languages, University of Salford, since 1964; *b* 1918; *m* 1943; one *s* one *d*. MSc Salford 1967; FIL. Vis. Lectr, Univ. of Freiburg, 1970. Jt Services Sch. for Linguists, 1951–64. *Publications*: *contrib*. Acta Balt., Inst. Balt., Lett. Volkslied. *Address*: Dept of Modern Languages, Univ. of Salford, Salford, Lancashire.

Rathmell, Dr John Christopher Abbott; Lecturer in English, University of Cambridge, since 1966; *b* 1935; *m* 1963; two *d*. BA Cantab 1959 (1st cl. English), MA Cantab 1964, PhD Cantab 1964. Fellow, Christ's Coll., Cambridge, 1963; Asst Lectr, Cambridge Univ., 1963–66; Amer. Council of Learned Socs Vis. Fellow, Amherst Coll., Mass., 1971. Tutor and Dir of Studies in English, Christ's Coll., 1966; *Publications*: The Psalms of Sir Philip Sidney and the Countess of Pembroke, 1963; Literature and Politics in the Age of Jonson (forthcoming); *contrib*. Engl. Lit. Renaiss. *Address*: Christ's College, Cambridge.

Rattansi, Prof. Pyarally Mohamedally; Professor and Head of Department of the History and Philosophy of Science, University College London, since 1971; *b* 1930; *m* 1966; two *s*. BSc(Econ) London 1956, PhD London 1961, MA Cantab 1967. Leverhulme Res. Fellow in the History and Phil. of Science, Univ. of Leeds, 1962–64; Lectr in the Hist. and Phil. of Science, Leeds Univ., 1964–67; Vis. Prof., Univ. of Chicago, 1966; Sen. Res. Fellow, King's Coll., Cambridge, 1967–71; Mem., Inst. for Adv. Study, Princeton, NJ, 1969; Vis. Lectr, Princeton Univ., 1970. *Publications*: *contrib*. Ambix, Medical History, Notes and Records of the Royal Soc. *Address*: Dept of the History and Philosophy of Science, Univ. College London, Gower Street, WC1E 6BT.

Raven, Edward John Palgrave, MA; Senior Lecturer in Humanity, University of Aberdeen, since 1952; *b* 1910; *m* 1948. BA Cantab 1933 (1st cl. Classics), MA Cantab; FRNS 1937. Asst, Aberdeen Univ., 1934–40; Lectr, 1940–52. RAF Intelligence (Photog. Interpret.), 1941–45. *Publications*: *contrib*. Numism. Chron. *Address*: Dept of Humanity, King's College, Old Aberdeen.

Ravenhill, Prof. William, MA, PhD, FSA; Professor of Human Geography, since 1969, Reardon Smith Professor of Geography and Head of Department, since 1971, Exeter University; *b* 1919; *m* 1952. BA Wales 1947 (1st cl. Geography), DipEd Wales 1948, MA Wales 1951, PhD London 1957; FSA, FRGS, Mem., Inst. Brit. Geogrs. Asst Lectr, Exeter, 1948–51; Lectr, Exeter, 1951–62; Sen. Lectr, Exeter, 1962–69; Dean, Fac. of Social Studies, Exeter, 1971, 1972, 1973, 1974. Mem., Council, Inst. Brit. Geogrs, 1966–68. *Publications*: Benjamin Donn's Map of Devon, 1965; (with A. H. Shorter and K. J. Gregory) South-West England, 1967; (with K. J. Gregory) Exeter Essays in Geography, 1971; John Norden's Manuscript Maps of Cornwall; Domesday Geography of Cornwall, in, Domesday Geography of South-West England, ed H. C. Darby and Welldon-Finn, 1967; *contrib*. Antiqu., Britann., Cartog. Jl, Corn. Archaeol., Encyc. Brit., Geog. Jl, Geog. Mag., Geog., Im. Mundi, Proc. Devon Archaeol. Soc., Trans Devon. Assoc. *Address*: Dept of Geography, Queen's Building, The Queen's Drive, Exeter EX4 4QH.

Ravenscroft, Arthur; Senior Lecturer, School of English, University of Leeds, since 1966; *b* 1924; *m* 1953; one *s* two *d*. MA Cape Town 1945, BA Cambridge 1952, MA Cambridge 1961; Mem., Royal Cwealth Soc., Mem., Assoc. Cwealth Lit. and Lang. Studies, Mem., Afr. Studies Assoc. UK. Jun.

Lectr, Univ. of Cape Town, 1946; Lectr, Univ. of Stellenbosch, 1947–57; Sen. Lectr, Univ. of Stellenbosch, 1957; Lectr, Univ. Coll. of Rhodesia and Nyasaland, 1958–63; Lectr, Univ. of Leeds, 1963–66; Editor, Jl Cwealth Lit., 1965– ; Mem., Yorks Cttee for Community Relat., 1970– . *Publications*: trans., (with C. K. Johnman) Van Riebeeck: Journal, vol. III 1659–62, 1958; Chinua Achebe, 1969; Introduction, in, G. Okara: The Voice, 2nd edn 1970; Essay on The Winter's Tale, in, Seven Studies in English, ed G. Roberts, 1971; Essay on Ngugi's Novels, in, Commonwealth, ed A. Rutherford, 1972; Essay on African Novels, in, Readings in Common Wealth Literature, ed W. Walsh, 1973; *contrib*. Helikon, Jl Cwealth Lit., Lit. Criter., Rev. Engl. Lit. *Address*: School of English, Univ. of Leeds, Leeds LS2 9JT.

Ravetz, Dr Jerome R.; Reader in the History and Philosophy of Science, Department of Philosophy, University of Leeds, since 1973 (Senior Lecturer, 1963–73); *b* 1929; *m* 1953; two *s* one *d*. BA Swarthmore 1950, PhD Cambridge 1954; Mem., Acad. Internat. Hist. Sciences. Res. Fellow in Science, Durham Univ., 1954–56; Lectr in Mathematics, 1956–57; Leverhulme Res. Fellow in History and Philosophy of Science, Leeds, 1957–59; Lectr, Leeds, 1959–63; Vis. Prof., Utrecht, 1964–65. Exec. Sec. (part-time), Council for Science and Society, 1973–74. *Publications*: Astronomy and Cosmology in the Achievement of Nicolaus Copernicus, 1965; Scientific Knowledge and its Social Problems, 1971; (with I. Grattann-Guiness) Joseph Fourier 1768–1830, 1972. *Address*: Dept of Philosophy, The Univ., Leeds LS2 9JT.

Raw, Barbara, MA, FSA; Senior Lecturer in English, University of Keele, since 1967; *b* 1929. BA London 1949, MA London 1953; FSA 1973. Asst Lectr, UCL and Birkbeck Coll., Univ. of London, 1953–54; Sir James Knott Fellow, King's Coll., Univ. of Durham, 1954–56; Asst Lectr, Univ. of Birmingham, 1956–58; Asst Lectr, later Lectr, Univ. of Keele, 1959–67. *Publications*: Lives of the Saints, 1961; A Programmed Course in Old English, 1967, rev. edn 1969; *contrib*. Jl of Warburg and Courtauld Insts, Medium Ævum. *Address*: Dept of English, Univ. of Keele, Keele, Staffs ST5 5BG.

Rawson, Prof. Claude Julien, MA, BLitt; Professor of English, University of Warwick, since 1971; *b* 1935; *m* 1959; three *s* two *d*. BA Oxon 1955 (English), MA, BLitt Oxon 1959. Sir James Knott Res. Fellow, King's Coll., Newcastle upon Tyne, 1957–59; Lectr in English, Univ. of Newcastle upon Tyne, 1959–65; Lectr, then Sen. Lectr, Univ. of Warwick, 1965–71; Vis. Prof., Univ. of Pennsylvania, 1973. Vice-Pres., Brit. Soc. 18th-Cent. Studies, 1972–73, Pres., 1974; Corresp. Mem., Exec. Cttee, Austral. Soc. 18th-Cent. Studies. Adv. Ed., 18th-Cent. Studies. *Publications*: Henry Fielding (Profiles in Literature), 1968; ed, Focus: Swift, 1971; Henry Fielding and the Augustan Ideal under Stress, 1972; Gulliver and the Gentle Reader, 1973; ed, Fielding, Penguin Critical Anthology, 1973; ed, Yeats and

Anglo-Irish Literature Essays by Peter Ure, 1974; *contrib*. 18th-Cent. Studies, Ess. Crit., French Studies, Jl Engl. Germ. Philol., Mod. Lang. Rev., Mod. Philol., Rev. Engl. Studies, Shakespeare Qly, Studi Amer. *Address*: Dept of English, Univ. of Warwick, Coventry CV4 7AL.

Rawson, Elizabeth Donata, MA; College Lecturer in Classics, and Fellow, New Hall, Cambridge University, since 1967; *b* 1934. BA Oxon 1956 (1st cl. Lit. Hum.), MA Oxon 1959. Res. Fellow, New Hall, Cambridge, 1959–67; Vis. Prof., Pennsylvania State Univ., 1974. Mem., Council, Soc. Prom. Rom. Studies, 1971–74. *Publications*: The Spartan Tradition in European Thought, 1969; *contrib*. Class. Qly, Greek, Rom. Byz. Studies, Jl Rom. Studies, Proc. Brit. Sch. Rome, Proc. Camb. Philol. Soc., Arethusa, Historia, Phoenix. *Address*: New Hall, Cambridge.

Rawson, Judith Ann; Senior Lecturer since 1973 and Chairman of Department of Italian, since 1971, University of Warwick; *b* 1933; *m* 1959; three *s* two *d*. BA Oxon 1956, MA Oxon 1959. Asst Lectr, Reading Univ., 1957–59; Lectr, Leeds Univ., 1959–65; Lectr, Univ. of Warwick, 1965–73. Mem., Cttee, Soc. of Italian Studies, 1971–73. *Publications*: (ed jtly), Prose Passages for Translation into Italian, 1964; trans., Machiavelli: The History of Florence and Other Selections, ed, Myron P. Gilmore, 1970. *Address*: Dept of Italian, Univ. of Warwick, Coventry CV4 7AL.

Rawson, Philip Stanley; Curator, Gulbenkian Museum of Oriental Art, School of Oriental Studies, University of Durham, since 1960; also Tutor, Royal College of Art, since 1973; *b* 1924; *m* 1949; one *s*. BA London 1947, MA London 1952 (distinction). Demonstrator in Technology, Inst. of Archaeology, London Univ., 1950–55; Lectr in Indian Art, SOAS, London Univ., 1952–55; Asst Keeper, Museum of Eastern Art, Indian Inst., Oxford Univ., 1955–60. Chm., Visual Arts Panel, North. Arts Assoc.; Council Mem., 1968–73; Mem., Arts Council GB, Visual Arts Panel, 1969–73. *Publications*: Indian Painting, French and British edns 1961, Italian edn 1963; Japanese Paintings from Shrines and Temples, 1962; Indian Sculpture, 1966; The Indian Sword, Danish edn 1967, British edn 1968; Erotic Art of the East, American edn 1968, German edn 1969; The Arts of Southeast Asia, 1967–68; The Art of Drawing, 1969; The Appreciation of Ceramics, 1971; Tantra, 1971; Indian Art, 1972; *contrib*. Brit. Jl Aesth., Orient. Art. *Address*: Gulbenkian Museum, Elvet Hill, Durham.

Rawson, Robert R.; Senior Lecturer in Geography, London School of Economics, since 1961; *b* 1916; *m* 1945. BSc Wales 1937. RAF, 1939–45. *Publications*: The Monsoon Lands of Asia, 1963, 4th edn 1968. *Address*: London School of Economics, Houghton Street, Aldwych, WC2A 2AE.

Rawstron, Prof. Eric Mitchell, MA, FRGS; Professor of Geography and Head of

576

Department, Queen Mary College, University of London, since 1973 (Professor of Economic Geography, 1971–73); *b* 1922; *m* 1949; one *s* one *d*. BA London 1948 (1st cl. Geography), MA London 1953 (Mark of Distinction); FRGS. Asst Lectr, Nottingham Univ., 1948–51; Lectr, Nottingham Univ., 1951–59; Reader, Queen Mary Coll., 1959–71. *Publications*: (with B. E. Coates) Regional Variations in Britain, 1971; *contrib.* Adv. Sci., E Midl. Geog., Geog. Rund., Jl Geog. Assoc., Trans Inst. Brit. Geogrs. *Address*: Dept of Geography, Queen Mary College, Mile End Road, E1 4NS.

Rayfield, Donald; Lecturer, Department of Russian, Queen Mary College, University of London, since 1967; *b* 1942; *m* 1963; one *d*. BA Cambridge 1963; Mem., BUAS(Slav.). Lectr, Univ. of Queensland, 1964–67. Mem., Bd of Slav. Studies, Univ. of London, 1968– . *Publications*: introd. in, Ivanov-Razumnik: O smysle zhizni, 1971; Chekhov: Evolution of the Artist, 1974; Galaktion Tabidze – ati leksi, 1974; *contrib.* AULLA, Europ. Juda., Stand. *Address*: Dept of Russian, Queen Mary College, Mile End Road, E1 4NS.

Rayman, Robert Anthony, BCom, FCA; Lecturer in Finance, Management Centre, University of Bradford, since 1965; *b* 1939. BCom Leeds 1959; ACA 1962, FCA. Res. Asst, Univ. of Bradford Mngmnt Centre, 1964–65. *Publications*: *contrib.* Jl Acctng Res., Jl Business Fin., Acctng and Bus. Res. *Address*: The Management Centre, Univ. of Bradford, Emm Lane, Bradford BD9 4JL.

Rayner, Anthony John; Reader in Agricultural Economics, Department of Economics, University of Nottingham, since 1973; *b* 1943; *m* 1967; two *d*. BA Cantab 1965, MA(Econ) Manchester 1967. Asst Lectr, Univ. of Manchester, 1967–69, Lectr, 1969–73. Mem., Exec. Cttee, Agricl Econs Soc., 1972– (Chm., Res. Sub-Cttee, 1973–). Editorial Cons. to Jl of Agric. Econ. *Publications*: The Resource Structure of Agriculture: an economic analysis, 1970; The Demand for Food, ed W. J. Thomas, 1972; *contrib.* Amer. Jl Agricl Econs, Jl Agricl Econs, Jl Pol Econ., Manchester Sch., Rev. of Econs and Stats. *Address*: Dept of Economics, University Park, Nottingham NG7 2RD.

Raynor, John M., BScEcon, MPhil; Senior Lecturer in Educational Studies, Faculty of Education, Open University, since 1971; *b* 1929; *m* 1953; one *s* one *d*. CertifEd London 1951, BScEcon London 1961, DipEd Liverpool 1965, MPhil Sussex 1972; Mem., Brit. Sociological Assoc. Head of Sociology Dept, Brighton Coll. of Educn, 1965–71. *Publications*: Linking Home and School, 1968; The Middle Class, 1969; Cities, Communities and the Young, vol. 1, 1973; Equality and City Schools, vol. 2, 1973. *Address*: Open Univ., Milton Keynes MK7 6AA.

Raz, Dr Joseph; Fellow and Tutor, Balliol College, Oxford, since 1972; *b* 1939; *m* 1963; one *s*. MJr Hebrew Univ., Jerusalem 1964, DPhil Oxford 1967. Lectr, 1967–71, Sen. Lectr, 1971, Hebrew Univ., Jerusalem; Sen.

Res. Fellow, Nuffield Coll., Oxford, 1970–72. *Publications*: The Concept of a Legal System, 1970; *contrib.* Amer. Jl Jurisprudence, Aristotelian Soc., supp. vol., California Law Rev., Ethics, Mind, Yale Law Jl. *Address*: Balliol Coll., Oxford.

Rea, Norman, BA, DipEd; Senior Lecturer in Education, University of York, since 1973 (Lecturer, 1966–73); *b* 1935; *m* 1962; one *s* three *d*. BA Wales 1958 (Education), DipEd Wales 1959. Chm., Bd of Studies in Educn, Univ. of York, 1970–72; Dean, Langwith Coll., Univ. of York, 1970– ; Mem., Nat. Exec. Cttee, FPA, 1970– ; Mem., Nat. Council, 1971– ; UK Deleg., European Reg., IPPF, 1971– ; Vice-Chm., Educn Sect., European Reg., 1971– . *Publications*: The Race Kit, 1969; *contrib.* Jl Ment. Subnorm., Econ., Forwd Trends. *Address*: Dept of Education, Langwith College, Univ. of York, Heslington, York YO1 5DD.

Read, Prof. Donald; Professor of Modern English History, and Sub-Dean, Faculty of Humanities, University of Kent at Canterbury, since 1974; *b* 1930; *m* 1955; two *s*. BLitt, MA Oxon 1955, PhD Sheffield 1961; FRHistS. Mem., Council, Hist. Assoc. Knoop Res. Fellow in Economic Hist., Univ. of Sheffield, 1955–56; Lectr in Mod. Hist., Univ. of Leeds, 1956–65; Sen. Lectr, Univ. of Kent, 1965–69, Reader, 1969–73; Chm., Hist. Bd. Univ. of Kent, 1970–72. *Publications*: Peterloo, 1958; Press and People 1790–1850, 1961; (with E. Glasgow) Feargus O'Connor, 1961; The English Provinces 1760–1960, 1964; Cobden and Bright, 1967; Edwardian England 1901–15, 1972; ed, Documents from Edwardian England, 1973. *Address*: Darwin College, Univ. of Kent, Canterbury CT2 7NY.

Read, Edwin Charles, MA, BSc(Econ), Barrister-at-Law; Director of Extra-Mural Studies, The Queen's University of Belfast, since 1966; *b* 1915; *m* 1966; two *d*. BA Cambridge 1937 (2nd cl. Hist.), DipEd Bristol 1938, MA Cambridge 1942, BSc(Econ) London 1947 (1st cl. Economics); Barrister-at-Law, Lincoln's Inn 1956. Lectr in Educn, Univ. of Hull, 1946–49; Lectr in Adult Educn, Univ. of Southampton, 1960–64; Acad. Sec., Sch of Educn and Social Work, Univ. of Sussex, 1964–66. Sec., Central Cttee for Adult Educn in HM Forces, 1949–60. *Address*: Extra-Mural Dept, The Queen's Univ., Belfast BT7 1NN.

Read, James Stracey; Reader in African Law, School of Oriental and African Studies, University of London, since 1965; *b* 1932; *m* 1956; one *s* five *d*. LLB London 1953 (1st cl.); Barrister-at-Law, Gray's Inn 1954. Asst Lectr, Univ. Coll., London, 1956–58; Lectr in African Law, SOAS, London Univ., 1958–65; Sen. Lectr in Law, Univ. Coll., Dar es Salaam, 1963–66. Hon. Sec., SPTL, 1972– ; Mem., Editorial Cttee, Jl Afr. Law, London, 1958– ; Mem., Editorial Bd, E Afr. Law Jl, Nairobi, 1965– ; Mem., Editorial Cttee, Restatement Afr. Law, 1966– . *Publications*: (with H. F. Morris) Uganda – The Development of its Laws and Constitution, 1966; (with H. F. Morris) Indirect Rule and the Search for Justice, 1972; *contrib*. E Afr. Law Jl, E Afr. Law Rev., Jl Afr. Law. *Address*: School of Oriental and African Studies, Univ. of London, Malet Street, WC1E 7HP.

Rear, John; Senior Lecturer in Law, Faculty of Social Sciences, University of Kent at Canterbury, since 1973; *b* 1936; *m* 1960; one *s* one *d*. BA Oxford 1960 (Jurisprudence, University Coll.), MA Oxford 1965; Barrister, Inner Temple, 1961. Member: LAWASIA, Royal Asiatic Soc. Editorial Manager, Sweet and Maxwell Ltd, 1962–66; Lectr, Law, Univ. of Hong Kong, 1966–70; Sen. Lectr, 1970–73. Asst Gen. Editor, Current Law, 1961–66; Asst Editor (Law), Medicine, Science and the Law, 1963; Editor, Hong Kong Law Journal, 1970–73. *Publications*: ed, with K. Hopkins *et al.*, Hong Kong: The Industrial Colony, 1971; *contrib*. HKLJ, LAWASIA. *Address*: Rutherford Coll., The Univ., Canterbury, Kent.

Reardon, Rev. Bernard Morris Garvin; Reader and Head of Department of Religious Studies, University of Newcastle upon Tyne, since 1974 (Senior Lecturer, 1969–74); *b* 1914. BA Oxon 1935, MA Oxon 1938. Ordained priest, C of E, 1938; Chaplain to Forces, 1941–44; Vicar of Holy Cross, Hornchurch, Essex, 1946–47; Rector of Kelly, Devon, 1947–59; Hulsean Lectr, Univ. of Cambridge, 1958; Rector of Parham, Sussex, 1959–63; Hulsean Preacher, Univ. of Cambridge, 1958–59; Lectr in Divinity, Univ. of Durham, 1963; Lectr in Divinity, Univ. of Newcastle upon Tyne, 1964–69. *Publications*: trans., Man and Metaphysics, 1961; Henry Scott Holland, 1963; Religious Thought in the Nineteenth Century, 1966; Liberal Protestantism, 1968; Roman Catholic Modernism, 1970; From Coleridge to Gore, 1971; *contrib*. Amplef. Jl, Angl. Theol. Rev., Ch Qly Rev., Expos. Times, Jl Theol. Studies, Studia Patrist., Theol. *Address*: Dept of Religious Studies, Univ. of Newcastle upon Tyne, Newcastle upon Tyne NE7 7RU.

Reardon, Prof. Bryan Peter, MA, BA, DU; Professor of Classics, University College of North Wales, Bangor, since 1974; *b* 1928; *m* 1960. MA Glasgow 1951 (1st cl. Classics), BA Cantab 1953 (2nd cl. Classical Tripos Pt II), Docteur de l'Université de Nantes, 1968; Member: Council, Class. Assoc. of Canada, 1969–71; Editorial Bd, Phoenix, 1973–74; Association pour l'encouragement des Etudes Grecques. Asst Prof., Memorial Univ. of Newfoundland, 1958–64; Assoc. Prof., 1966–67; Assoc. Prof. and Chm., Dept of Classical Studies, Trent Univ., Ontario, 1967–71; Prof., 1971–74. *Publications*: trans. Lucian: Selected Works, 1965; Courants littéraires grecs des IIᵉ et IIIᵉ siècles après J.-C., 1971; *contrib*. Amer. Jl Philol., Antiq. Class., Phoenix. *Address*: Dept of Classics, Univ. College of North Wales, Bangor, Bangor LL57 2DG.

Reason, Dr James; Reader, Department of Psychology, University of Leicester, since 1972; *b* 1938; *m* 1964; two *d*. BSc Hons Manchester 1962 (Psychology (I)), PhD Leicester 1967; Member: BPsS; Aerospace Med. Assoc.; Fellow, Brit. Interplanetary

Soc. University of Leicester: Asst Lectr, 1964; Lectr, 1966. *Publications*: Man in Motion: the psychology of travel, 1974; (with others) Introducing Psychology: an experimental approach, 1970; *contrib*. Aerospace Med., Advancement of Sci., Brit. Jl Psychol., Internat. Jl Man. Machine Studies, Jl Sound and Vibration. *Address*: Dept of Psychology, Univ. of Leicester, Leicester LE1 7RH.

Reay, Pat; Lecturer in Management, Department of Sociology, Government and Administration, University of Salford, since 1963; *b* 1924; *m*; one *d*. BA (Admin) Manchester 1944; MIPM 1951, ABIM 1961. *Address*: Univ. of Salford, Salford M5 4WT.

Rebelo, Luís de Sousa, Lic.inL, PhD; Lecturer in Portuguese and Brazilian Studies, King's College, University of London, since 1956; *b* 1922. Lic. in Classical Studies Lisbon 1946 (1st cl. Greek and Latin), equiv. MA Lisbon 1947 (Portuguese Studies), Teacher's Training Dip. Lisbon 1947, PhD Lisbon 1956. Lectr in Portuguese, Univ. of Liverpool, 1947–54. Ed., Mundo Literário, Lisbon, 1946–47; Recog. Teacher, Univ. of London, 1957. *Publications*: trans., W. Faulkner: Requiem for a Nun, 1958; The Old Man, 1959, 3rd edn 1971; W. Shakespeare: Romeo and Juliet, 1961; W. Golding: Lord of the Flies, 1961; Shakespeare Para o Nosso Tempo, 1966; contrib. 45 articles, for Dicionário das Literaturas Portuguesa, Galega e Brasileira, 1960; The Penguin Companion to Literature: European, 1969; Enciclopédia Focus, 1969; Grande Dicionário da Literatura Portuguesa (forthcoming); *contrib*. Bull. Hispan. Studies, Colóquio. *Address*: Dept of Portuguese and Brazilian Studies, King's College, Univ. of London, Strand, WC2R 2LS.

Reckert, Prof. Stephen, PhD; Camoens Professor of Portuguese, and Head of Department of Portuguese and Brazilian Studies, University of London, since 1967; *b* 1923; *m* 1st 1946, 2nd 1965; two *s* one *d*. BA Yale 1945, Phi Beta Kappa, 1943, MLitt Cantab 1948, PhD Yale 1950. Instructor in Spanish, Yale, 1948–54; Fellow, Berkeley Coll., Yale, 1949–59; Curator, Spanish Collection, Yale Univ. Libr., 1952–58; Asst Prof. of Spanish, Yale, 1954–58; Prof. and Hd of Dept of Hispanic Studies, Univ. of Wales, 1958–66; Huntingdon Vis. Prof. Univ. of Madrid, 1971. Ch. Examiner in Spanish, Welsh Jt Educn Bd, 1960–64. *Publications*: (with D. Alonso) Vida y obra de Medrano, 1958; The Matter of Britain and the Praise of Spain, 1967; Lyra Minima: Structure and Symbol in Iberian Traditional Verse, 1970; (with Roman Jakobson and H. Macedo) Do Cancioneiro de Amigo, 1974; Gil Vicente: Espíritu y letra (forthcoming); *contrib*. Rev. Fac. Let. Lisb., Rev. Filol. Esp. *Address*: Dept of Portuguese and Brazilian Studies, King's College, Strand, WC2R 2LS.

Redcliffe-Maud, The Lord; John Primatt Redcliffe Redcliffe-Maud, GCB, CBE; Master of University College, Oxford, since 1963; *b* 1906; *m* 1932; one *s* two *d*. AB Harvard 1929, Hon. LLD Witwatersrand 1960, Hon. LLD Natal 1963, Hon. LLD Leeds 1967, Hon. LLD Nottingham 1968, Hon.

DSocSc Birmingham 1968. Jun. Res. Fellow, Univ. Coll., Oxford, 1929; Fellow and Dean, Univ. Coll., Oxford, 1932–39; Univ. Lectr in Politics, Univ. Coll., Oxford, 1938–39; Master of Birkbeck Coll., Univ. of London, 1939–43. Dep. Sec., later Second Sec., Min. of Food, 1941–44; Second Sec., Office of the Minister of Reconstruction, 1944–45; Sec., Office of Lord Pres. of the Council, 1945; Permanent Sec., Min. of Educn, 1945–52; Mem., Economic Planning Bd, 1952–58; Permanent Sec., Min. of Fuel and Power, 1952–59; Brit. Ambassador in S Africa, 1961–63 (High Comr, 1959–61), and High Commissioner for Basutoland, Bechuanaland Protectorate and Swaziland, 1959–63. Mem., Oxford CC, 1930–36; High Bailiff of Westminster, 1967– . Chm. Counc., Royal Coll. of Music, 1965–73; Chm., Local Govt Mngnt Cttee, 1964–67; Chm., Royal Commn on Local Govt in England, 1966–69. Pres., Royal Inst. of Public Administration, 1969– . Hon. Fellow, New Coll., Oxford, 1964; Fellow, Eton Coll., 1964; Sen. Fellow, RCA, 1961; FRCM, 1964; Associate Fellow, Jonathan Edwards Coll., Yale, 1968– . *Publications*: English Local Government, 1932; City Government: The Johannesburg Experiment, 1938; English Local Government Reformed, 1974; chapters in: Oxford and the Groups, 1934; Personal Ethics, 1935; Johannesburg and the Art of Self-Government, 1937; Education in a Changing World, 1951. *Address*: The Master's Lodgings, Univ. College, Oxford.

Reddaway, Peter Brian; Senior Lecturer in Political Science, University of London, since 1972; *b* 1939; *m* 1972. BA Cantab 1962, MA Cantab 1965; Mem., Nat. Assoc. Sov. E Europ. Studies; Mem., Amer. Assoc. Adv. Slav. Studies; Mem., Exec. Cttee, GB–USSR Assoc. Lectr in Pol Science, Univ. of London, 1965–72; Senior Fellow, Columbia Univ., 1973–74. Mem., Council, Writers and Schols Internat., 1971– ; Mem., Council, Centre for Study Relig. and Communism, 1970– . *Publications*: ed (with L. Schapiro), Lenin: the Man, the Theorist, the Leader, 1967, German trans. 1970; Soviet Short Stories, vol. 2, 1968; Uncensored Russia: The Human Rights Movement in the Soviet Union, 1972; *contrib*. Prob. Communism, Sov. Studies, Surv. *Address*: London School of Economics, Houghton Street, WC2A 2AE.

Reddaway, Prof. William Brian, CBE; Professor of Political Economy, University of Cambridge, since 1969; Fellow of Clare College, Cambridge, since 1938; *b* 1913; *m* 1938; three *s* one *d*. BA Cambridge 1934 (1st cl. Economics), MA Cambridge 1938; FBA, FREconS, FRSS. Res. Fellow, Univ. of Melbourne, 1936–38; Asst Lectr, Univ. of Cambridge, 1939–46; Lectr, Univ. of Cambridge, 1946–55; Dir, Dept of Applied Economics, Univ. of Cambridge, 1955–69. Statistician, Bd of Trade, 1940–47; Econ. Dir, OEEC, Paris, 1951–52; Ed., London and Cambridge Econ. Bull., 1949; Ed., Econ. Jl, 1971– ; Mem., Nat. Bd Prices and Incomes, 1967–71; Mem., Royal Commn on Press, 1961–62; Economic Adviser to Confederation of British Industry since 1972; *Publications*: Russian Financial System, 1935; Economics

of a Declining Population, 1939; Measurement of Production Movement, 1949; Development of the Indian Economy, 1962; Effects of UK Direct Investment Overseas – Interim Report, 1967; Effects of UK Direct Investment Overseas – Final Report, 1968; Effects of the Selective Employment Tax – First Report, 1970, Final Report, 1973; *contrib*. Econ. Jl, Econ. Rec., Ind. Econ. Rev., Lond. Camb. Econ. Bull., Rev. Econ. Studies. *Address*: Economics Building, Sidgwick Avenue, Cambridge.

Reddiford, Gordon; Senior Tutor, Division of Advanced Studies, School of Education, University of Bristol, since 1972; *b* 1930; *m* 1961; two *s*. BA Leeds 1952 (2nd cl. Philos.), DipEd Leeds 1953; Mem., Philos. Educn Soc. GB, Royal Inst. Philos., Mind Assoc. Sen. Lectr, Bristol Univ., 1965–74. *Publications*: *contrib*. Educnl Philos. Theory, Proc. Philos. Educn Soc. *Address*: Helen Wodehouse Building, 35 Berkeley Square, Bristol BS8 1JA.

Redfern, Dr Walter David; Reader, French Department, Reading University, since 1972; *b* 1936; *m* 1963; one *s* one *d*. BA Cantab 1957 (1st cl. French and Spanish), MA Cantab 1960, PhD Cantab 1960. Asst Lectr, Reading Univ., 1960–63, Lectr, 1963–72. *Publications*: The Private World of Jean Giono, 1967; Paul Nizan: Committed Literature in a Conspiratorial World, 1972; Jules Vallès: Le Bachelier, 1972; *contrib*. Fr. Rev., Jl Europ. Studies, Romanic Rev., Sympos. *Address*: French Dept, Univ. of Reading, Reading RG6 2AH.

Redgate, Geoffrey William; Senior Lecturer in Education of the Deaf, Department of Audiology and Education of the Deaf, University of Manchester, since 1973; *b* 1924; *m* 1948; one *s* two *d*. BA 1949, Teachers Dip. 1950, Cert. for Teachers of the Deaf, 1950, DipEd 1954, MEd 1964, Manchester; Mem., Nat. Coll. of Teachers of the Deaf. Lectr in Educn of the Deaf, Manchester Univ., 1954–73. Cons. and Advr on Educn of the Deaf, ODM, 1969. Mem., Bolton Area Health Authority, 1973– . *Publications*: *contrib*. various pubns of Commonwealth Soc. for Deaf. *Address*: Dept of Audiology and Education of the Deaf, The Univ., Manchester M13 9PL.

Redmond, James, MA, EdB, BA, BLitt; Lecturer, English Department, London University, Westfield College, since 1964; *b* 1937. MA Glasgow 1959, EdB Glasgow 1960, BA Cantab 1962 (1st cl. English), BLitt Oxon 1965. Editor, Year's Work in English Studies, 1972– (Asst Editor, 1968–72); Mem., Exec. Cttee, Engl. Assoc., 1971– . *Publications*: ed, W. Morris: News from Nowhere, 1970; *contrib*. Mod. Drama, Mod. Lang. Qly, Times Litt. Supp., Yrs Wk Engl. Studies. *Address*: English Dept, Westfield College, NW3 7ST.

Redpath, Dr Robert Theodore Holmes; Fellow, Lecturer, and Director of English Studies, Trinity College, Cambridge, since 1950, and University Lecturer in English, University of Cambridge, since 1954; *b* 1913;

579

m 1964; one *s* two *d*. BA Cantab 1934 (1st cl. with Special Dist. English II), MA Cantab 1937, PhD Cantab 1940 (Moral Sciences); Barrister-at-Law, Middle Temple, 1948. Univ. Asst Lectr in English, Univ. of Cambridge, 1951–54. Army Service, 1940–46; Sen. Proctor, Univ. of Cambridge, 1954–55, 1959–60; Mem., Council, Trinity Coll., Cambridge, 1961–65; Tutor, Trinity Coll., Cambridge, 1960–70; Steward, Cambridge Union Soc., 1960–70. *Publications*: ed, The Songs and Sonets of John Donne, 1956; Tolstoy, 1960, 2nd edn 1969; ed (with W. G. Ingram), Shakespeare's Sonnets, 1964, 2nd edn 1967; (with P. Hodgart) Romantic Perspectives, 1964, 2nd edn 1968; ed (with W. G. Ingram), Sixty-five Sonnets of Shakespeare, 1967; The Young Romantics and Critical Opinion, 1807–1824, 1973. *Address*: Trinity College, Cambridge.

Reed, Joselyne; Lecturer in French, University of Birmingham, since 1970; *b* 1935; *m* 1961; two *s* two *d*. BA Dunelm 1958. Lectr in French, Univ. of Keele, 1961–70. *Publications*: *contrib*. AVLang. Jl, Bull. Jeunes Rom., Mod. Langs, Prog. Cent. Philol. Rom. (Strasbourg). *Address*: Dept of French, Univ. of Birmingham, PO Box 363, Birmingham B15 2TT.

Reed, Dr Michael Arthur; Lecturer in Library and Information Studies, Loughborough University of Technology, since 1973; *b* 1930; *m* 1955; one *s*. BA Birmingham 1954 (2nd cl. Hons, Hist. and English), MA Birmingham 1958, LLB London 1966, PhD Leicester 1973. Associate Lectr, Loughborough Univ., 1967–73. *Publications*: *contrib*. Sussex Archaeol Soc. Collections, Trans Shropshire Archaeol Soc. *Address*: Dept of Library and Information Studies, Loughborough Univ. of Technology, Loughborough LE11 3TU.

Reed, Terence James; Fellow and Tutor in Modern Languages, St John's College, Oxford, and University Lecturer in German, since 1963; Senior Tutor (administrative), since 1973; *b* 1937; *m* 1960; one *s* one *d*. BA 1960, MA 1964, Oxon. Member: English Goethe Soc.; Internationale Vereinigung für Germanische Sprach- und Literaturwissenschaft. Platnauer Jun. Res. Fellow, Brasenose Coll., Oxford, 1961–63. Editor, Oxford German Studies (yearbook), 1966–74. *Publications*: ed, Thomas Mann: Der Tod in Venedig, 1971; Thomas Mann: The Uses of Tradition (monograph), 1974; *contrib*. Euphorion, German Life and Letters, Neophilologus, Oxford German Studies, TLS. *Address*: St John's Coll., Oxford.

Reed, William Paul; Lecturer in French, University of Keele, since 1966; *b* 1940; *m* 1973. BA Wales 1964 (1st cl. Hons), MA Wales 1971. *Address*: French Dept, Keele Univ., Keele, Staffs ST5 5BG.

Rees, Alwyn David; Director of Extra-Mural Studies, University College of Wales, Aberystwyth, since 1949; *b* 1911; *m* 1940; one *s*. BA Wales 1933 (1st cl. Geog. and Anthropol.), MA Wales 1947. Extra-Mural Tutor, Univ. Coll. of Wales, 1936–46; Lectr

in Geog. and Anthropol., Univ. Coll. of Wales, 1946–49; Ed., Welsh Anvil, 1949–58; Ed., Univ. Wales Rev., 1964–65; Warden, Guild of Grads, Univ. of ¡Wales, 1968–71. Mem., Court,¦ Univ. of Wales, 1955– ; Council, 1968–71; Mem., Council, Univ. Coll. of Wales, 1956–59; Mem., Council, Nat. Eisteddfod of Wales, 1966– . Ed. Barn (Welsh monthly), 1966– . *Publications*: Life in a Welsh Countryside, 1950, 2nd edn 1951; Co-Ed., Welsh Rural Communities, 1960; (with B. Rees) Celtic Heritage, 1961; var. booklets and pamphlets in Welsh and English; contrib. Proceedings of the International Congress of Celtic Studies, 1963; Saith Ysgrif ar Grefydd, ed D. Z. Phillips, 1967. *Address*: Dept of Extra-Mural Studies, Univ. College of Wales, Aberystwyth SY23 2AX.

Rees, Brinley; Senior Lecturer in Welsh, University College of North Wales, Bangor, since 1964; MA Wales 1940. Asst Lectr, Univ. Coll. of N Wales, 1947–50; Lectr, Univ. Coll. of N Wales, 1950–64. *Publications*: Dulliau'r Canu Rhydd, 1952; (with A. Rees) Celtic Heritage, 1961. *Address*: Dept of Welsh, Univ. College of North Wales, Bangor LL57 2DG.

Rees, Prof. Brinley Roderick, MA, PhD; Professor of Greek, University of Birmingham, since 1970; Dean, Faculty of Arts, since 1973; *b* 1919; *m* 1951; two *s*. BA Oxon 1944 (1st cl. Class. Mods), MA Oxon 1945, PhD Wales 1956; FRSA 1968. Asst Lectr, Univ. Coll. of Wales, Aberystwyth, 1948; Lectr, Univ. Coll. of Wales, Aberystwyth, 1949–56; Sen. Lectr, Manchester Univ., 1956–58; Prof. of Greek, Univ. Coll. of S Wales and Mon., 1958–70. Dean, Fac. of Arts, Cardiff, 1963–65; Dean of Students, 1967–68; Hon. Sec., Class. Assoc., 1963–69; Vice-Pres., and Chm., 1969– ; Sec., Council of Univ. Class. Depts. 1970–72; Chm., Bd of Mngmt, Greece and Rome, 1966–72; Mem., Gov. Body, Christ Coll., Brecon, 1961–71; Mem., Council, Hellenic Soc., 1958–61, 1965–68; Mem., Gov. Body, Cardiff Coll. of Educn, 1963–67. *Publications*: The Merton Papyri, vol. II, 1959; The Use of Greek, 1960; Papyri from Hermopolis, 1964; (with M. E. Jervis) Lampas, 1970; ed, Classics; an outline for the intending student, 1970; Aristotle's Theory and Milton's Practice, 1972; *contrib*. Amer. Jl Philol., Class. Rev., Eos., Greece Rome, Jl Egypt. Archaeol., Jl Jurist. Papyrol., Mnemosyne. *Address*: School of Hellenic and Roman Studies, Univ. of Birmingham, PO Box 363, Birmingham B15 2TT.

Rees, Dr David Arthur, MA, DPhil; Fellow and Tutor in Philosophy, Jesus College, Oxford, since 1954, and University Lecturer (CUF) in Philosophy, Oxford University, since 1954; *b* 1922; *m* 1951; one *s* one *d*. BA Oxford 1945 (1st cl. Class. Mods 1942, 1st cl. Lit. Hum.) (Merton Coll. Class. Postmaster), MA Oxford 1948, DPhil Oxford 1953; Mem., Aristot. Soc., Royal Inst. Philos., Soc. Prom. Hellenic Studies. Asst, Dept of Moral Philosophy, Aberdeen Univ., 1946–48; Asst Lectr in Philosophy, Univ. Coll. of N Wales, Bangor, 1948–51; Lectr, Univ. Coll. of N

Wales, Bangor, 1951–54; Sen. Lectr, Univ. Coll. of N Wales, Bangor, 1954; Sen. Tutor, Jesus Coll., Oxford, 1969–72, and Vice-Principal, 1971–72; Vis. Mem., Inst. Adv. Study, Princeton, 1962–63. *Publications*: ed, H. H. Joachim: Aristotle, The Nicomachean Ethics, A Commentary, 1951; contrib. var. symposia; *contrib.* Class. Rev., Jl Hellenic Studies, Philos., Proc. Aristot. Soc. *Address*: Jesus College, Oxford.

Rees, David Glyndwr; Senior Lecturer, Department of Italian, University of Birmingham, since 1973; *b* 1924; *m* 1950; two *s*. BA Oxon 1948, MA Oxon; Sec., Soc. for Italian Studies, 1962– ; Member: Soc. Nazionale Dante Alighieri; Assoc. of Teachers of Italian. University of Birmingham: Asst Lectr, 1948–51; Lectr 1951–73; Sub-Dean, Faculty of Arts, 1959–60; Mem., Court of Governors, 1967–72. *Publications*: contrib. Penguin Companion to European Literature; *contrib.* Comparative Lit., Italian Studies, N and Q. *Address*: Dept of Italian, Univ. of Birmingham, Birmingham B15 2TT.

Rees, Prof. Graham Lloyd, MA; Professor and Head of Department of Economics, University College of Wales, Aberystwyth, since 1968; *b* 1921; *m* 1949; two *d*. BA Wales 1948 (1st cl. Econ.), MA Wales 1951. Lectr, Univ. Coll., Swansea, 1948–62; Simon Fellow, Univ. of Manchester, 1958–59; Sen. Lectr, Swansea, 1962–68. Asst Comr, (Kilbrandon) Commn on Constitution of UK, 1969–73; Mem., BBC Council for Wales, 1971– . *Publications*: Britain and the European Payments Systems, 1963; Britain's Commodity Markets, 1972; (with others) Survey of the Welsh Economy, 1973; *contrib.* Economico, Lloyds Bk Rev., Manch. Sch., Nat. Prov. Bk Rev., Il Politica, Rev. Econ. Studies. *Address*: Dept of Economics, The Univ. College of Wales, Aberystwyth SY23 2AX.

Rees, Gwilym Oswald, MA; Senior Lecturer in French, University of Leeds, since 1972; *b* 1916; *m* 1961; two *s*. BA Wales 1938 (1st cl. French), MA Wales 1940; Mem., Soc. Fr. Studies, Mem., Philol. Soc., Mem., Lingu. Assoc. GB, Mem., Internat. Arthurian Soc. Asst Lectr, Univ. of Liverpool, 1946–49; Lectr, Univ. of Liverpool, 1949–69; Hon. Lectr in Comparative Philology and Lingu., Univ. of Liverpool, 1966–69; Lectr, Univ. of Leeds, 1969–72. RA and Intell. Corps, 1940–46. *Publications*: ed, Peisson: L'Anneau des Mers, 1956; ed, Escoula: Six Chevaux Bleus, 1959; ed, Muray: Une Bergère et son Chien, 1960; *contrib.* Franç. Mod., Fr. Rev., Fr. Studies, Germ.-Rom. Monats., Mod. Lang. Notes, Mod. Lang. Rev., Neuer. Spr., Neuphilol. Mitteil., Notes Queries, Yr's Wk Mod. Lang. Studies. *Address*: Dept of French, Univ. of Leeds, Leeds LS2 9JT.

Rees, John Collwyn; Reader in Political Theory, Department of Politics, University College of Swansea, since 1955; *b* 1919; *m* 1949; one *s* one *d*. MA Cantab 1945, BScEcon London 1947. Univ. Southampton, 1947–48; Univ. Birmingham, 1948–50; Univ. Leicester, 1950–55; Vis. Prof., Univ. California, Los Angeles, 1963–64. *Publications*: Mill and his

Early Critics, 1956; Lenin and Marxism, in, Lenin, ed Schapiro and Reddaway, 1967; Equality, 1971; *contrib.* Polit. Studies, Philosophy, Il Politico, Internat. Encycl. of Social Sciences. *Address*: Dept of Politics, Univ. Coll. of Swansea, Swansea SA2 8PP.

Rees, Dr (Lilian) Joan; Senior Lecturer, English Department, University of Birmingham, since 1971; *b* 1923; *m* 1950; two *s*. BA Birmingham 1943, MA London 1948, PhD Birmingham 1970. Asst Lectr, Birmingham, 1948–51; Lectr, Birmingham, 1951–71. *Publications*: Samuel Daniel, a critical and biographical study, 1964; Fulke Greville, Lord Brooke 1554–1628: a critical biography, 1971; Selected Writings of Fulke Greville, 1973; *contrib.* Mod. Lang. Rev., Notes Queries, Rev. Engl. Studies, Shakesp. Surv. *Address*: English Dept, The Univ. of Birmingham, PO Box 363, Birmingham B15 2TT.

Rees, Ray, MSc(Econ); Lecturer in Economics, Queen Mary College, University of London, since 1966; *b* 1943; *m* 1968. BSc(Econ) London 1964, MSc(Econ) London 1965. Tutor in Economics, Civil Service Coll., London, 1968–70; Pt-time Cnsltnt, HM Treasury, 1970– . *Publications*: The Penguin Dictionary of Economics, 1972; *contrib.* Econ. Jl, Economica, Reg. Studies. *Address*: Queen Mary College, Mile End Road, E1 4NS.

Rees, Roy, MA, DPE; Director of Physical Education, University College of North Wales, since 1973; *b* 1937; *m* 1959; two *s* one *d*. MA Liverpool 1968, DPE Loughborough 1961. Lectr in Phys. Educn, Univ. of Liverpool, 1964–73. *Publications*: *contrib.* Physical Educn Ybk, Sport Recreat. *Address*: Physical Education Dept, Univ. College of North Wales, Bangor LL57 2DG.

Rees Jones, Stephen; Reader, Courtauld Institute of Art, University of London, since 1965; *b* 1939; two *s*. BSc Hons 1931, DipEd 1932, MSc 1934, Wales; FInstP 1942, FSA 1958, Fellow, Internat. Inst. for Conservation of Historic and Artistic Works, 1952, MRI 1945. Courtauld Institute: Lectr, 1946–59; Sen. Lectr, 1959–65. Treas., Internat. Inst. for Conservation, 1958–61; Chm., Royal Instn. Cttee of Visitors, 1968–69. Editor, IIC Abstracts (now Art and Archaeol. Technical Abstracts), 1955–58. *Publications*: Paint and the Painter (forthcoming); *contrib.* Bull. Inst. of Physics, Studies in Conservation, Burlington Mag. *Address*: Courtauld Inst., 20 Portman Square, W1H 0BE.

Rees Pryce, William Thomas; *see* Pryce, W. T. R.

Reese, Dr Trevor Richard; Reader in History, Institute of Commonwealth Studies, University of London, since 1964; *b* 1929; *m* 1961; two *s* one *d*. BA Sheffield 1952 (1st cl. Hons), PhD London 1955; FRHistS. Lectr in History, Newcastle Univ., Australia, 1956–59; Sen. Lectr in History, Univ. Sydney, 1960–62; Leverhulme Fellow in Commonwealth Studies, Univ. Hull, 1962–64. Editor, Jl of Imperial and Commonwealth History, 1972– . *Publications*: Colonial Georgia: A

Study in British Imperial Policy in the 18th Century, 1963; Australia in the 20th Century, 1964; History of the Royal Commonwealth Society 1868–1968, 1968; Australia, New Zealand and the United States: A Survey of International Relations 1941–68, 1969; Promotional Literature of the Colony of Georgia, 1717–34, 1972; Criticisms and Defence of the Colony of Georgia, 1741–43, 1973; Earliest Journeys to the Colony of Georgia, 1974; *contrib.* Austr. Jl of Politics and History, Historical Studies, Jl Commonwealth Political Studies, William and Mary Qly. *Address:* Institute of Commonwealth Studies, 27 Russell Square, WC1B 5DS.

Reeves, Dr Nigel Barrie Reginald; Lecturer, German Department, Reading University, since 1968; *b* 1939; *m* 1965; one *s* one *d*. BA 1963 (1st cl. Hons German and Fr.), DPhil 1970, Oxon. Lektor, Univ. of Lund, Sweden, 1964–66; Alexander von Humboldt Fellow, Univ. of Tübingen, W Germany, 1974–75. *Publications:* Heinrich Heine: Poetry and Politics, 1974; *contrib.* OGS, GLL. *Address:* German Dept, Reading Univ., Whiteknights, Reading RG6 2AH.

Regan, Dr David Martin; Reader, Department of Communication, University of Keele, since 1973 (Senior Research Fellow, 1965–73); *b* 1935; *m* 1959; two *s*. BSc London 1957 (Physics), MSc London 1958 (Physics), CertEd London 1959, PhD London 1964 (Physics); ARCS, DIC. *Publications:* Evoked Potentials in Psychology, Sensory Physiology and Clinical Medicine, 1972; *contrib.* Advances Biol. Med., Brain Electroenceph. Clin. Neurophysiol., Exp. Brain Res., Jl Neurol. Neurosurg. Psychiat., Jl Opt. Soc. Amer., Jl Physiol., Med. Elect. Biol. Eng., Nature, Percept. Psychophys, Perception, Photophys., Proc. Iscerg Symp., Proc. Internat. Migraine Symp., Science, Vision Res. *Address:* Dept of Communication, Univ. of Keele, Keele ST5 5BG.

Rehfisch, F. M.; Senior Lecturer in Sociology, University of Hull, since 1969; *b* 1922; *m* 1954; one *s* one *d*. BA California 1944, MA London 1954. Mem., Assoc. Social Anthropols, Mem., Royal Anthropol. Inst. Res. Asst, Univ. Coll., London, 1952–55; Res. Fellow, Sch. of Scottish Studies, Univ. of Edinburgh, 1955–57; Asst Lectr, Univ. of Edinburgh, 1957–58; Lectr, then Sen. Lectr and later Prof., Univ. of Khartoum, 1958–69. *Publications: contrib.* Afr. Cah. Etudes Afr., Scott. Studies, Sudan Notes Rec. *Address:* Dept of Sociology, The Univ., Hull HU6 7RX.

Reibel, Dr David A., MA, PhD; Senior Lecturer in Language, University of York, since 1971; *b* 1929; *m* 1966. BA Wayne State 1953 (German Lang. and Lit.), MA Indiana 1955 (Linguistics), PhD Indiana (Linguistics); Mem., Lingu. Soc. Amer., Mem., Philol. Soc., Mem., Lingu. Assoc. GB, Mem., Brit. Assoc. Appl. Lingu., Mem., Internat. Lingu. Assoc., Mem., Internat. Phonet. Assoc., Mem., Canad. Lingu. Assoc. Lectr, English Dept, Univ. of Illinois, 1958–59; Lectr, Dept of Linguistics, Indiana Univ., 1959–62; Res. Asst, Survey of English Usage, English Dept, Univ. Coll. London,

1963–64; Asst Prof. of Linguistics, Univ. of California, San Diego, 1964–67; Lectr, Univ. of York, 1967–71; Vis. Prof., Dept of English as a Foreign Language, Univ. of Hawaii, 1972–73. *Publications:* ed (with S. A. Schane), Modern Studies in English: Readings in Transformational Grammar, 1969; *contrib.* Engl. Lang. Teach., Internat. Rev. Appl. Lingu., York Papers in Lingu. *Address:* Dept of Language, Univ. of York, Heslington, York YO1 5DD.

Reid, Alexander Livingstone; Lecturer, Department of Political Science, University of Dundee, since 1965; *b* 1936; *m* 1963. BL Edinburgh 1960, MA Edinburgh 1962, MA Yale 1963. *Address:* Dept of Political Science, The Univ., Dundee DD1 4HN.

Reid, George James M.; *see* Macgregor-Reid.

Reid, Graham Livingstone, MA; Reader in Applied Economics, Department of Social and Economic Research, University of Glasgow, since 1971; seconded as Senior Economic Adviser, Scottish Office, since 1973; *b* 1937. MA St Andrews 1959 (1st cl. Pol Econ. and Psychol.), MA Queen's (Ontario) 1960 (Economics). Asst, Dept of Social and Econ. Res., Univ. of Glasgow, 1960–63; Lectr in Applied Economics, Univ. of Glasgow, 1963–68; Sen. Lectr, Univ. of Glasgow, 1968–71; Vis. Assoc. Prof., Michigan State Univ., 1967; Vis. Res. Fellow, Indust. Relat. Centre, Queen's Univ., Ontario, 1967–69. *Publications:* ed (with D. J. Robertson), Fringe Benefits, Labour Costs and Social Security, 1965; (with G. C. Cameron) Scottish Economic Planning and the Attraction of Industry, 1966; (with L. C. Hunter) Urban Worker Mobility, 1968; (with K. J. Allen) Nationalised Industries, 1970; (with L. C. Hunter) European Economic Integration and the Movement of Labour, 1970; (with L. C. Hunter and D. Boddy) Labour Problems of Technological Change, 1970; (with K. J. Allen and D. J. Harris) Nationalised Fuel Industries, 1972; *contrib.* Brit. Jl Indust. Relat., Econ. Jl, Indust. Lab. Relat. Rev., Scott. Jl Pol. Econ. *Address:* Dept of Social and Economic Research, Adam Smith Building, Univ. of Glasgow, Glasgow G12 8RT.

Reid, Ivan; Lecturer in Educational Sociology, School of Research in Education, University of Bradford, since 1970; *b* 1940; *m* 1961; two *d*. CertEd Leeds 1961, BA Hons Leicester 1965 (Soc. Sci), MA Liverpool 1969; Member: Brit. Sociol Assoc.; ATCDE. Tutor (PT), Dept of Social Sci., Univ. of Liverpool, 1966–70. Member: UCET Cttee 'C', 1973– ; BAAS Cttee 'N', 1974; Chm.: ATCDE (Sociol. Section), 1974; Standing Cttee of Sociologists, 1974– . *Publications:* Sociology and Teacher Education, 1974; *contrib.* Brit. Jl Ed. Psych., Educ. and Psych. Measurement, Educ. Res., New Soc., Papers in Educn. *Address:* Univ. of Bradford, Bradford BD7 1DP.

Reid, Dr James Henderson: Lecturer in German, University of Nottingham, since

1967; b 1938; m 1965; two s. MA Glasgow 1960 (1st cl. French and German), PhD Glasgow 1966. Lektor, Free Univ. of W Berlin, 1963–65; Asst Lectr, Nottingham Univ., 1965–67. *Publications*: (with E. M. Boa) Critical Strategies: German Fiction in the 20th Century, 1972; Heinrich Böll, 1973; contrib. German Men of Letters, ed Natan; *contrib*. Germ. Life Lett., Mod. Lang. Rev., Britannica Book of the Year. *Address*: Dept of German, The Univ., Nottingham NG7 2RD.

Reid, Jessie Fisher, MA, MEd; Senior Lecturer, Centre for Research in Educational Sciences, University of Edinburgh, since 1972; b 1916. MA(Hons) St Andrews 1938 (English Language and Literature), MEd Edinburgh 1952; Mem., Scottish Div., Educnl and Child Psychology, 1956. Res. Fellow, Dept of Education, Univ. of Edinburgh, 1956–65, Lectr, 1965–72. *Publications*: contrib. The i.t.a. symposium, 1967; Educational Research in Britain, 1968; Reading: Problems and Practices (ed readings), 1972; Link-Up: a new reading programme, 1973; A Guide to Effective Study, 1973; Breakthrough in Action, 1974; *contrib*. Acta Psychologica, Educnl Res., Res. in Educn. *Address*: Centre for Research in Educational Sciences, 24 Buccleuch Place, Edinburgh EH8 9JT.

Reid, Prof. John Kelman Sutherland; Professor of Systematic Theology, University of Aberdeen, since 1961; b 1910; m 1950. MA Edinburgh 1933, BD Edinburgh 1938, Hon. DD Edinburgh 1966. Mem., Soc. Study Theol., Mem., Soc. NT Studiorum. Prof. of Philosophy, Scottish Church Coll., Calcutta, 1935–37; Prof. of Theology, Leeds Univ., 1952–61. Sec., Jt Cttee on New English Bible, 1947– ; Wld Council Ch. Faith Order Commn, 1961– ; Brit. Council Chs. 1961– ; Ch of Scotland Inter-Ch Relat. Cttee, 1961– ; Jt Ed., Scott. Jl Theol. *Publications*: ed and trans., Calvin: Theological Treatises, 1954; ed and trans., Calvin: Concerning the Eternal Predestination of God, 1961; The Authority of Scripture 1957, 2nd edn 1963; Our Life in Christ, 1963; Presbyterians and Unity, 1966; Christian Apologetics, 1969; *contrib*. Expos. Times, Oecumen., Scott. Jl Theol., Theol. Today. *Address*: King's College, Univ. of Aberdeen, Aberdeen AB9 2UB.

Reid, Judith; Lecturer in Law, London School of Economics, since 1967; b 1937; m 1964; one s. LLB London 1964; Barrister-at-Law, Gray's Inn, 1965. Research Officer, Law Dept, LSE, 1965–67. Mem., Editorial Cttee, Modern Law Review, 1968– ; Mem., Editorial Cttee, Industrial Law Jl, 1971– . *Publications*: (with O. Aikin) Labour Law: Employment, Welfare and Safety at Work, 1971; *contrib*. British Tax Review, Industrial Law Jl, Mod. Law Review. *Address*: London School of Economics, Houghton Street, WC2A 2AE.

Reid, Prof. Kenneth Stockdale; Professor of Spanish and Latin American Studies, University of Newcastle upon Tyne, since 1971; b 1913; m 1942. BA Dunelm 1933 (Hons French), Dip. Theory and Practice of

Teaching Dunelm 1934, BA London 1946 (Hons Spanish), PhD Dunelm 1951; Mem., Assoc. of Hispanists of Gt Britain and Ireland; Mem., Soc. for Latin Amer. Studies. Lectr in Spanish, King's Coll., Univ. Durham, 1943–54; Reader in Spanish and Latin Amer. Studies, King's Coll., Univ. Durham (from 1963, Univ. Newcastle upon Tyne), 1954–71. Univ. Durham: Dean of Faculty of Econ. Studies, 1959–61; Mem., Senate, 1959–61; Mem., Council, King's Coll., 1957–60; Mem. Council, Durham Colls, 1958–60; Vice-Chm. of Delegacy, Inst. of Educn; Chm, Shortened Courses Cttee and Bookshop Adv. Cttee; Mem. Faculties of Arts, Econ. and Social Studies, and Educn; Mem. Spending Authority, Faculty of Arts. *Publications*: (with E. Sarmiento) trans., Marías: Reason and Life: The Introduction to Philosophy, 1956; contrib. Essays presented to C. M. Girdlestone, 1960; contrib. Studies dedicated to Professor J. Manson, 1972; *contrib*. BHS, Durham Univ. Jl. *Address*: Dept of Spanish and Latin American Studies, Univ. of Newcastle upon Tyne, Newcastle upon Tyne NE1 7RU.

Reid, Prof. Robert Leslie; Professor of Psychology, University of Exeter, since 1963; b 1924; m 1949; two d. MA Hons Edinburgh 1949 (1st cl. Psychol.); FBPsS (Mem. Council, 1956–62); Mem., Exptl Psychol. Soc. Lecturer: Edinburgh Univ., 1949; Canterbury Coll., NZ, 1953; Lectr and Sen. Lectr, Aberdeen Univ., 1956. Pres., Assoc. for Programmed Learning, 1964–66. *Publications*: *contrib*. Brit. Jl of Psychol., Jl Comp. and Physiol Psychol., Occupational Psychol., Qly Jl Exptl Psychol. *Address*: Washington Singer Labs, Univ. of Exeter, Exeter EX4 4QG.

Reilly, Wyn Anthony Prowse; Senior Lecturer, Department of Overseas Administrative Studies, University of Manchester, since 1971; b 1930; m 1965; three s. BA Cantab 1953 (Geog. Tripos), MA Cantab 1957. Lectr, Dept of Overseas Administrative Studies, Manchester Univ., 1962–71; Assoc. Prof., Univ. of Mauritius (on Secondment), 1969–71. *Publications*: contrib. Practical Work in Administrative Training, 1964; *contrib*. Public Admin. *Address*: Dept of Overseas Administrative Studies, 336 Oxford Road, Manchester M13 9NG.

Reinders, Robert C.; Senior Lecturer, Department of American Studies, University of Nottingham, since 1971; b 1926; m 1955; three s. BA Notre Dame 1947, MA Notre Dame 1949, PhD Texas 1957; Mem., South. Hist. Assoc., 1960–65, Mem., Louisiana Hist. Assoc., 1958–65, Mem., Brit. Assoc. Amer. Studies, 1966– . Lectr. St Edward's Univ., USA. 1949–56; Lectr, Xavier Univ., USA, 1956–57; Lectr, Tulane Univ., USA, 1957–65; Lectr, Univ. of Nottingham, 1966–71. Sen. Fulbright Schol., Univ. of Sheffield, 1965–66. *Publications*: End of an Era: New Orleans 1850–1860, 1964; ed (with others), Dictionary of World History (forthcoming); *contrib*. Cath. Hist. Rev., Internat. Rev. Social Hist., Jl Amer. Hist., Jl South. Hist., Lab. Hist., Louis. Hist. Qly, Louis. Hist., Mid-Amer., Phylon, Wisc. Mag. Hist. *Address*: Dept of

American Studies, The Univ., Nottingham NG7 2RD.

Reiss, Prof. Hans Siegbert; Professor of German, and Head of Department, University of Bristol, since 1965; *b* 1922; *m* 1963; two *s*. BA Dublin 1943 (1st cl. Hons Mod. Lit.; Gold Medallist), Dip. in Economics and Commercial Knowledge, Dublin 1943, Dip. in History of European Art, Dublin 1945, PhD Dublin 1954, MA Dublin 1965. Asst to Prof. of German, Univ. of Dublin, 1943–46; Asst Lectr in German, LSE, 1946–49; Lectr, LSE, 1949–53; Lectr in German, Queen Mary Coll., Univ. of London, 1953–58; Vis. Prof. of German, McGill Univ., 1957–58; Prof. of German, McGill Univ., 1958–65; Chm., Dept of German and Russian, 1957–62; Chm., Dept of German, 1963–65; Vis Prof., Middlebury Coll., 1967; Vis. Prof., McGill Univ., 1968–69, 1973; Vis. Prof., Univ. of Munich, 1970–71. *Publications*: Franz Kafka, 1952, 2nd edn 1956; ed, The Political Thought of the German Romantics, 1955; ed (with H. Wegener), Emanuel Geibel, Briefe an Henriette Nölting, 1963; Goethes Romane, 1963; Das politische Denken in der Deutschen Romantik, 1966; Goethe's Novels, 1969; ed. Kant's Political Writings, 1970; ed (with H. B. Nisbet), Goethe's Die Wahlverwandtschaften, 1971; ed, Goethe und die Tradition, 1972; *contrib.* Akzente, Archiv Rechts-Socialphilos. Colloq. Germ., Deuts. Viert. Jahrs. Lit. Geistes., Germ. Life Lett., Jbh Deutsch Schiller Gesells., Jl Hist. Ideas, Mod. Lang. Qly, Mod. Lang. Rev., Pol. Viert. Jahrs., Publicns Engl. Goethe Soc., Shakesp. Jbh, Studium Gen., Trivium, Zeits. deutsch. Philologie. *Address*: Dept of German, Wills Memorial Buildings, Queen's Road, Bristol BS8 1RJ.

Rendel, Margherita Nancy; Lecturer in Educational Administration, University of London Institute of Education, since 1964; *b* 1928. BA Cantab 1951 (History Pt 1, Law Pt 2, 2nd cl.), MA Cantab 1955, PhD London 1967; Assoc. Exam. in French, Inst. of Linguists, 1953, FRSA 1971. Herts CC, Finance Dept, 1951–52; Min. of Labour, Employment Exch., 1952–54; PEP Res. Asst, 1958–59; Temp. Asst Lectr in Comparative Government, Univ. of Exeter, 1960–61; Mem., Univ. of London Careers Adv. Bd, 1967. Mem., Garner Cttee on local ombudsmen, 1969; Mem., Parly Equal Rights Gp, 1971. Mem., Wages Council on Unlicensed Places of Refreshment, 1973– ; Mem. Panel of Industrial Tribunals, 1973– . *Publications*: (with L. Tivey) Advisory Committees in British Government, 1960; Local Self-Government. The Experience of the United Kingdom, the Isle of Man and the Channel Islands, 1960; Educational Administration in England and Wales, filmstrip and teaching notes, 1967; Graduate Administrators in LEAS, 1968; (jtly) Equality for Women, 1968; The Administrative Functions of the French Conseil d'Etat, 1970; written and oral evidence to House of Lords Select Cttee on Anti-Discrimination Bill, Minutes of Evidence, session 1972–73. *Address*: Univ. of London Institute of Education, Dept of Higher Education, 55 Gordon Square, WC1H 0NT.

584

Renfrew, Dr Andrew Colin, MA, PhD, FSA; Professor of Archaeology, University of Southampton, since 1972; *b* 1937; *m* 1965; one *s* one *d*. BA Cantab 1962 (1st cl. Archaeology), MA Cantab 1964, PhD Cantab 1965; FSA. Fellow, St John's Coll., Cambridge, 1965–68; Lectr, later Sen. Lectr and Reader, Univ. of Sheffield, 1965–72; Vis. Lectr, UCLA, 1966. Mem., Council, Prehist. Soc., 1968–71; Mem., Council, Soc. Antiqu., 1971–73. *Publications*: (with J. D. Evans) Excavations at Saliagos near Antiparos, 1968; The Emergence of Civilisation: the Cyclades and the Aegean in the Third Millennium BC, 1972; Before Civilisation: the Radiocarbon Revolution and Prehistoric Europe, 1973; ed, The Exploration of Culture Change, Models in Prehistory, 1973; *contrib.* Amer. Antiqu., Amer. Jl Archaeol., Ann. Brit. Sch. Archaeol. Athens, Antiqu., Archaeom., Curr. Anthropol., Encounter, Kret. Chron., Listener, Nature, Proc. Prehist. Soc., Sci. Amer., Wld Archaeol. *Address*: Dept of Archaeology, The Univ., Southampton SO9 5NH.

Renfrew, Jane M.; Visiting Lecturer, Department of Archaeology, University of Southampton, since 1972; *b* 1942; *m* 1965; one *s* one *d*. BA Cantab 1964, MA Cantab 1968, PhD Cantab 1969; FSA Scot. 1969. Lectr in European Prehistory, Univ. Sheffield, 1967–72. *Publications*: The Life and Work of the Revd William Corus Wilson 1792–1859, 1959; Antiquary on Horseback, 1963; Palaeoethnobotany: the prehistoric food plants of the Near East and Europe, 1973. *Address*: Dept of Archaeology, Univ. of Southampton, Highfield, Southampton SO9 5NH.

Reno, Stephen Jerome; Lecturer, Department of Study of Religion, University of Leicester, since 1970; *b* 1944. BA St John's Coll. Camarillo, California 1964, MA California (Santa Barbara) 1968, PhD (Cand.) California (Santa Barbara) 1973; Member: Amer. Acad. of Religion; Brit. Inst. of Religion and Theol.; Internat. Assoc. of Hist. of Religions; Folklore Soc. Univ. of California, Santa Barbara, 1967–70. Member: Bd of Fac. of Arts, Leicester, 1973– ; Vice-Chancellor's Cttee on Teaching Methods, 1973– . *Publications: contrib.* New Scholasticism, Religious Studies, Temenos. *Address*: Dept of Study of Religion, Univ. of Leicester, Leicester LE1 7RH.

Renshaw, Patrick Richard George; Lecturer in the History of the USA, Department of Medieval and Modern History, Sheffield University, since 1968; *b* 1936; *m* 1959; three *s* one *d*. MA Oxon 1963; Mem., Brit. Assoc. for American Studies. Vis. Lectr and Fulbright Travelling Scholar, Syracuse Univ., NY, 1971–72; Sen. Res. Fellow, Maxwell Sch., Syracuse, 1972. Mem., Arts Fac. Bd, Sheffield, 1972. *Publications*: The Wobblies: the Story of Syndicalism in the United States, London and New York, 1967, Italian edn 1970, Japanese edn 1973; The General Strike, London and New York, 1975; *contrib.* Jl Contemp. Hist., Jl American Studies. *Address*: Dept of Medieval and Modern History, Sheffield Univ., Sheffield S10 2TN.

Renton, George Anthony; Senior Lecturer in Economics, London Graduate School of Business Studies, since 1974; *b* 1943; *m* 1968. BA Oxon 1964. Sen. Res. Officer, 1967–70, Lectr in Economics, 1970–74, London Grad. Sch. of Business Studies. Mem., Acad. Cttee, 1973– . *Publications:* ed, Modelling the Economy, 1974; *contrib.* Applied Econs, Bull. Oxford Univ. Inst. of Stats and Econs, Econ. Rev., Internat. Econ. Rev., Oxford Econ. Papers, Westminster Bank Rev. *Address:* London Graduate Sch. of Business Studies, Sussex Place, Regent's Park, NW1 4SA.

Revell, Prof. John Robert Stephen, BSc(Econ), MA; Professor of Economics, University College of North Wales, Bangor, since 1969; *b* 1920; *m* 1946; one *s* two *d.* BSc(Econ) London 1950, MA Cambridge 1960. Res. Off., Dept of Applied Economics, Cambridge, 1957–63; Sen. Res. Off., Dept of Applied Economics, Cambridge, 1963–68; Fellow and Tutor, Fitzwilliam Coll., Cambridge, 1965–67; Sen. Tutor, Fitzwilliam Coll., Cambridge, 1967–68. Mem., Welsh Council, 1971– . *Publications:* The Wealth of the Nation, 1967; Changes in British Banking: the Growth of a Secondary Banking System, 1968; The British Financial System, 1973. *Address:* Dept of Economics, Univ. College of North Wales, Bangor LL57 2DG.

Rex, Prof. John Arderne; Professor of Sociology, Warwick University, since 1970; *b* 1925; *m* 1st 1949, 2nd 1965; two *s* two *d.* BA South Africa 1948 (Hons 1949); PhD Leeds, 1956. Mem., Brit. Sociol. Assoc. Staff Tutor in Sociology and Philosophy, Leeds, 1949–56; Lectr in Sociology, Leeds, 1956–62; Lectr in Sociology, Birmingham, 1962–64; Prof. of Social Theory and Institutions, Durham, 1964–70; Vis. Prof., Univ. of Toronto, 1974–75. Mem., Experts Conf. on Race and Racism, 1967; Consultant, Unesco, 1973. Chm., British Soc. Assoc., 1969–71; Pres., Sect. N Brit. Assoc. Adv. Science, 1971; Ed., Internat. Library of Sociology. *Publications:* Key Problems of Sociological Theory, 1961, German, Japanese, Spanish and Portuguese edns 1970–72; (with R. Moore) Race, Community and Conflict, 1967; Race Relations in Sociological Theory, 1970; Discovering Sociology, 1972; Race, Colonialism and the City, 1972; ed, Approaches to Sociology, 1974; Sociology and the Demystification of the Modern World, 1974; *contrib.* Brit. Jl Sociol., Race. *Address:* Dept of Sociology, The Univ. of Warwick, Coventry CV4 7AL.

Reynolds, Dr Barbara; Reader in Italian Studies, University of Nottingham, since 1969, *b* 1914; *m* 1939, one *s* one *d.* BA London 1935 (Hons French) (Hons Italian 1936), MA Cantab 1940, PhD London 1948 (Italian); FRSA 1971. Hon. Mem., Lucy Cavendish Coll., Cambridge, 1969. Asst Lectr in Italian, LSE. 1937–40; Lectr in Italian, Univ. of Cambridge, 1940–63; Lectr, then Sen. Lectr, Univ. of Nottingham, 1963–69; Warden, Willoughby Hall, 1963. Mem., Council of Senate, Cambridge Univ., 1960–62. *Publications:* The Linguistic Writings of Alessandro Manzoni, 1950; The Cambridge Italian Dictionary, 1962; (with D. L. Sayers) Paradise (trans. of Dante's Paradiso), 1962; trans., Dante: Vita Nuova, 1969; trans. Ariosto: Orlando Furioso, vol. I, 1974; Concise Italian Dictionary, 1974; *contrib.* Forum Mod. Lang. Studies, Ital. Studies, Nott. Mediaev. Studies. *Address:* Dept. of Italian Studies, Univ. of Nottingham, Nottingham NG7 2RD.

Reynolds, Christopher Hanby Baillie; Lecturer in Sinhalese, School of Oriental and African Studies, London University, since 1953; *b* 1922; *m* 1952; three *s* one *d.* BA Oxford 1948 (Litt. Hum.), MA Oxford 1951, BA London 1953 (Sinhalese); FRAsiatic Soc. *Publications:* ed. and pt trans., An Anthology of Sinhalese Literature up to 1815, 1970; *contrib.* Bull. SOAS. *Address:* School of Oriental and African Studies, Univ. of London, WC1E 7HP.

Reynolds, Francis Martin Baillie, BCL, MA; Fellow of Worcester College, Oxford University, since 1960; *b* 1932; *m* 1965; two *s* one *d.* BA Oxon 1956 (1st cl. Jurisprudence), BCL Oxon 1957 (1st cl.), MA Oxon 1960; Barrister-at-Law, Inner Temple, 1961. Bigelow Teaching Fellow, Univ. of Chicago Law School, 1957; Lectr, Worcester Coll., Oxford, 1958–59; CUF Lectr, Oxford Univ., 1959– ; Vis. Lectr, Auckland Univ., 1971. *Publications:* jt ed., Bowstead on Agency, 13th edn 1968; Chitty on Contracts, 23rd edn 1968; Benjamin's Sale of Goods, 1974; *contrib.* Jl SPTL, Law Qly Rev. *Address:* Worcester College, Oxford.

Reynolds, John Frederick; Lecturer, Department of Mathematical Statistics and Operational Research, University College Cardiff, since 1966; *b* 1935; *m* 1959; two *s* one *d.* BA Cantab 1956, MA Cantab 1959; FRSS, Mem., Operat. Res. Soc. Lieut., RN. 1956–59; Scientific Off., Radar Res. Estab., Malvern, 1959–61; Lectr. RRE Coll., 1961–63; Lectr, Glamorgan Poly., 1963–66. Chm., S Wales Operat. Res. Discuss. Soc., 1969. *Publications:* *contrib.* Jl Appl. Prob., Operat. Res. *Address:* Dept of Mathematical Statistics and Operational Research, Univ. College, Cardiff CF1 1XL.

Reynolds, Josephine Preston, JP, MA, BArch, MRTPI, ARIBA; Senior Lecturer, Department of Civic Design, University of Liverpool, since 1968; *b* 1919. BArch Liverpool 1943, DipCD Liverpool 1944, MA Liverpool 1953: MRTPI, ARIBA. Asst Lectr, Liverpool, 1946–49; Lectr, Liverpool, 1949–68. JP, 1967– ; Ed., Town Planning Review. *Publications:* (jtly) Land Use in an Urban Environment, 1960; *contrib.* Jl Royal Town Plan. Inst., Town Plan. Rev. *Address:* Dept of Civic Design, Univ. of Liverpool, PO Box 147, Liverpool L69 3BX.

Reynolds, Joyce Maire, MA, FSA; University Lecturer in Classics, Cambridge, Fellow, Lecturer and Director of Studies in Classics, Newnham College, Cambridge, since 1951; *b* 1918. BA Oxon 1941 (1st cl. Lit. Hum.), MA Oxon; MA Cambridge 1957; FSA. Lectr in Ancient Hist., King's Coll., Newcastle upon Tyne, 1948–51; Asst Lectr

585

in Classics, Cambridge, 1952. Asst Principal, later Principal, BOT, 1941–46, Mem., Classical Faculty, Brit. Sch. at Rome, 1970– ; Mem., Council,Roman Soc., 1971– ; Mem., Council, Soc. for Libyan Studies, 1969– . *Publications*: (with J. B. Ward Perkins) The Inscriptions of Roman Tripolitania, 1951; *contrib*. Papers of the British Sch. at Rome, Jl Roman Studies, Libya Antiqua. *Address*: Newnham College, Cambridge.

Reynolds, Leighton Durham, MA; Fellow and Tutor in Greek and Latin Literature, Brasenose College, Oxford, since 1957, and CUF Lecturer, Oxford University, since 1958; *b* 1930; *m* 1962; one *s* two *d*. BA Wales 1950 (1st cl. Latin), BA Cambridge 1952 (1st cl. Classics), MA Cambridge 1956, MA Oxon 1956. Jun. Res. Fellow, The Queen's Coll., Oxford, 1954–57; Vis. Apntmts: Cornell Univ., 1960, 1971; Univ. of Texas, 1967; Mem., Inst. Adv. Study, Princeton, 1965. RAF, 1952–54 (Flying Off.). *Publications*: Seneca's Letters (Oxford Classical Texts), 1965; The Medieval Tradition of Seneca's Letters, 1965; (with N. G. Wilson) Scribes and Scholars, 1968, Italian edn 1969; *contrib*. Class. Rev., Class. Qly. *Address*: Brasenose College, Oxford.

Reynolds, Prof. Philip Alan; Professor of Politics and Pro-Vice-Chancellor, University of Lancaster, since 1964; *b* 1920; *m* 1946; two *s* one *d*. BA Oxon 1940 (1st cl. Mod. History), MA Oxon 1950. Asst Lectr, then Lectr in International History, LSE. 1946–50; Woodrow Wilson Prof. of Internat. Politics, Univ. Coll. of Wales, Aberystwyth, 1950–64; Vice Principal, Univ. Coll. of Wales, Aberystwyth, 1961–63; Vis. Prof. in Internat. Relations, Univ. of Toronto, 1953; Vis. Prof. in Commonwealth History and Institutions, Indian Sch. of Internat. Studies, New Delhi, 1958. Chm., Brit. Co-ord. Cttee for Internat. Studies. *Publications*: War in the Twentieth Century, 1951; British Foreign Policy in the Interwar Years, 1954; An Introduction to International Relations, 1971; chapters, in, New Cambridge Modern History, vol. XII, 1968; Studies in Politics, National and International, ed M. S. Rajan, 1970; *contrib*. Hist., Internat. Jl, Internat. Relat. Qly, Internat. Studies, Pol. Qly, Pol. Studies, Slav. Rev. *Address*: Dept of Politics, Fylde College, Univ. of Lancaster, Bailrigg, Lancaster.

Reynolds, Susan, MA; Fellow since 1964 and Dean since 1971, Lady Margaret Hall, Oxford University, and University Lecturer, Oxford, since 1965; *b* 1929. BA Oxon 1950 (2nd cl. History), Dip. Archive Admin. London 1951; FRHistS. Archive Asst, Middlesex Co. Rec. Off., 1951–52; Victoria Co. Hist., 1952–59; School-teaching Queens Coll., London, 1960–64. Mem., Culham Coll. Council, 1968– ; Mem., Wilts Rec. Cttee, 1968– . *Publications*: ed, Victoria History of Middlesex, vol. 3, 1962; Register of Roger Martival, Bishop of Salisbury, vol. 3 (Canterbury and York Soc.), 1965; *contrib*. Victoria County History; *contrib*. EHR, Wilts Archaeol. Soc. Rec. Br. Hist. *Address*: Lady Margaret Hall, Oxford.

Reynolds, Vernon; Lecturer in Physical

586

Anthropology, Department of Human Anatomy, Oxford University, since 1972; *b* 1935; *m* 1960; one *s* one *d*. BA London 1959 (Hons Anthropology), PhD London 1962 (Anthropology); FPS, Mem. RAI, ASAB. Lectr in Anthropology, Bristol Univ., 1966–72. *Publications*: Budongo, a forest and its chimpanzees, 1965, American and German edns; The Apes, 1967, American and British edns, pbk edn 1971; *contrib*. Amer–Anthropol., Folia Primatol., Man. *Address*: Anthropology Laboratory, Dept of Human Anatomy, South Parks Road, Oxford.

Rhind, Dr David; Lecturer in Geography, University of Durham, since 1973; *b* 1943; *m* 1966; one *s* one *d*. BSc Hons Bristol 1965, PhD Edinburgh 1968; Mem., Inst. Brit. Geographers, FRGS. Research Fellow: Edinburgh Univ., 1968–69; Royal Coll. of Art, 1969–73. Mem. Council, British Cartographic Soc. *Publications*: *contrib*. Bull. Geol Soc. Amer., Can. Cartographer, Cartographic Jl, Jl TPI, Math. Geology, Nachrichten aus dem Karten- und Vermessungswesen. *Address*: Dept of GEOGRAPHY, Univ. of Durham, Durham DH1 3LE.

Rhodes, Prof. Edwin, MA; Director, The New University of Ulster Institute of Continuing Education, since 1972; Director of Adult Education, The New University of Ulster, 1970–72; *b* 1920; *m* 1945; two *s* two *d*. BA London (Ext.) 1947 (1st cl. Engl.), MA London 1949. Lectr, Univ. of Toronto, 1949–55; Lectr, Magee Univ. Coll., Londonderry, 1955–68; Sen. Lectr in Adult Educn, New Univ. of Ulster, 1968–70. Mem., NI Adv. Council, BBC, 1966–70; Mem., Drama Bd, 1971– ; Mem., NI Supp. Benefits Commn, 1972– ; Mem., Western Health and Social Services Bd, 1972– . *Address*: The New Univ. of Ulster Inst. of Continuing Educn, Magee Univ. College, Londonderry, Northern Ireland.

Rhodes, John; Research Officer, Department of Applied Economics, University of Cambridge, since 1968; *b* 1941; *m* 1966; one *d*. BA Hons Liverpool 1962 (Econs), MA Cantab 1972. Lectr in Econs, Univ. of Lancaster, 1965–68. Mem., Cambridge Econ. Policy Gp. Mem., Jt Forecasting Cttee of Econ. Develt Cttee for Bldg and Civil Engrg. *Publications*: Office Dispersal and Regional Policy, 1971; Memorandum given in evidence to Trade and Industry Sub-Cttee of House of Commons Expenditure Cttee, H of C paper 42, XVI Session, 1972–73; *contrib*. Australian Econ. Papers, Econ. Jl, Jl of Management Studies, Proc. of Inst. of Fiscal Studies. *Address*: Dept of Applied Economics, Sidgwick Avenue, Cambridge.

Rhodes, Peter John, MA, DPhil; Lecturer in Classics and Ancient History, University of Durham, since 1965; *b* 1940; *m* 1971. BA Oxon 1963, MA Oxon 1966, DPhil Oxon 1969. Mem. Council, Hellenic Soc., 1972– . Craven Fellow, Univ. of Oxford, 1963–65; Harmsworth Sen. Schol., Merton Coll., Oxford, 1963–65; Libr., Univ. Coll., Durham, 1966–73. *Publications*: The Athenian Boule, 1972; Greek Historical Inscriptions, 359–323 BC, 1972; *contrib*. var. articles and reviews in class. jls. *Address*: Dept. of Classics, Univ. of Durham, 38 North Bailey, Durham.

Rhodes, Prof. Philip; Professor of Obstetrics and Gynaecology, St Thomas's Hospital Medical School, University of London, since 1964; *b* 1922; *m* 1946; three *s* two *d*. BA Cantab 1943, MBBChir 1946, FRCS(Eng) 1953, MRCOG 1956, FRCOG 1964; Mem., Brit. Med. Assoc. Dean, St Thomas's Hosp. Med. Sch., 1968– . *Publications*: Fluid Balance in Obstetrics. 1960; Introduction to Gynaecology and Obstetrics, 1967; Woman: A Biological Study, 1969; Reproductive Physiology for Medical Students, 1969; *contrib*. Brit. Med. Jl, Jl Obstet. Gynaecol. Brit. Cwealth, Lancet, Practit., etc. *Address*: St Thomas's Hospital Medical School, SE1 7EH.

Rhys, David Garel; Lecturer in Economics, University College, Cardiff, since 1971; *b* 1940; *m* 1965; one *s* two *d*. BA Wales 1963, MCom Birmingham 1967; AMInstTA. Asst Lectr in Econs, Univ. Hull, 1965–67, Lectr, 1967–71. *Publications*: The Motor Industry: An Economic Survey, 1972; *contrib*. Accounting and Business Res., Bull. Econ. Res., Jl Industrial Econs, Jl Econ. Studies, Jl Transport Econs and Policy, Scottish Jl Political Economy. *Address*: Dept of Economics, Univ. Coll. Cardiff, PO Box 96, Cardiff CF1 1XB.

Ribbans, Prof. Geoffrey Wilfrid, MA; Gilmour Professor of Spanish, University of Liverpool, since 1963; *b* 1927; *m* 1956; one *s* two *d*. BA London 1948 (1st cl. Spanish), MA London 1953; Mem., Assoc. Brit. Hispan., Mem., Internat. Assoc. Hispan., Amer., MHRA, Mem., Mod. Lang. Assoc. Amer., Mem., Soc. Lat.-Amer. Studies, Mem., Instituto de Literatura Iberoamericana. Asst Lectr, Queen's Univ., Belfast, 1951–52; Asst Lectr, St Salvator's Coll., Univ. of St Andrews, 1952–53; Asst Lectr, Univ. of Sheffield, 1953–55; Lectr, Univ. of Sheffield, 1955–61; Sen. Lectr, Univ. of Sheffield, 1961–63; Vis. Mellon Prof., Univ. of Pittsburgh, 1970–71; Threlfall Lectr and Hon. Fellow, Inst. of Linguists, 1972; Annual Lecture (on Antonio Machado), Hispan. Council, 1974. Dir, Centre for Lat.-Amer. Studies, Univ. of Liverpool, 1966–70; Ed., Bull. Hispan. Studies, Liverpool, 1964– ; Mem., Educnl Cttee, Hispan. Council, 1965– ; Mem., Lang. Bd CNAA, 1971– . *Publications*: Catalunya i València vistes pels viatgers anglesos del segle XVIIIè, 1955; Niebla y soledad: aspectos de Unamuno y Machado, 1971; ed, A. Machado: Soledades, Galerías; Otras poemas, 1974; contributions in: Hispanic Studies in Honour of I. González Llubera, 1959; Spanish Thought and Letters in the Twentieth Century, 1966; Galdós Studies, 1970; Studies in Modern Spanish Literature and Art, presented to Helen F. Grant, 1971; Studia ibérica: Festschrift für Hans Flasche, 1973; Spain: a companion to Spanish studies, ed P. E. Russell, 1973; Studies in Spanish Literature of the Golden Age, presented to Edward M. Wilson, 1973; *contrib*. Anales Galdos, Bull. Hispan. Studies, Bull. Hispan., Cuad. His-

panoamer., Cuad. Cátedra Unamuno, Filol., Hispan. Rev., Ínsula, Rev. Filol. Espan., Rev. Lit., Rev. Univ. Madrid, Rev. Valenc. Filol. *Address*: School of Hispanic Studies, The Univ., PO Box 147, Liverpool L69 3BX.

Rice, David Hugh; Official Student of Christ Church, since 1969, and CUF Lecturer in Philosophy, Oxford University, since 1970; *b* 1943; *m* 1967; one *s* one *d*. BA 1965, BPhil 1967, MA 1968, Oxford. Instructor, Univ. of Connecticut, 1967–68; Lectr, Christ Church, Oxford, 1968–69. *Address*: Christ Church, Oxford.

Rich, Prof. Edwin Ernest, MA. LittD; Master of St Catharine's College, Cambridge, since 1957 (Fellow since 1930); *b* 1904; *m* 1934; one *d*. Vere Harmsworth Prof. of Naval and Imperial History, Cambridge, 1951–70; Hon. Fellow, Trumbull Coll., Yale; Hon. Fellow, Selwyn Coll., Cambridge; Hon. Fellow, Worcester Coll., Oxford; Gen. Ed., Hudson's Bay Record Soc., 1937–60. *Publications*: Staple Courts of Bristol, 1931; Ordinances of the Merchants of the Staple, 1935; The Hudson's Bay Company, 1670–1870, 1958–59; Montreal and the Fur Trade, 1966; The Fur Trade and the Northwest, 1967. *Address*: St Catharine's College, Cambridge.

Richards, David John, MA, BLitt; Senior Lecturer in Russian, University of Exeter, since 1971; *b* 1933; *m* 1959; one *s* one *d*. BA Oxon 1957 (1st cl. Mod. Langs); BLitt Oxon 1960, MA Oxon 1961. Asst Master, Eton Coll., 1958–60; Asst Lectr, Exeter Univ., 1960–61; Lectr, Exeter Univ., 1961–71. Hon. Treas., BUAS, 1969–72. *Publications*: Zamyatin – A Soviet Heretic, 1962; ed, Lermontov: Geroi nashego vremeni, 1962, 2nd edn 1965; Soviet Chess – Chess and Communism in the USSR, 1965; Advanced Russian Unseens, 1966; Russian Critical Essays – Twentieth Century, 1971; Russian Critical Essays – Nineteenth Century, 1972; *contrib*. Forum, Mod. Lang. Studies, Slav. E Europ. Rev. *Address*: Dept of Russian, The Univ., Exeter EX4 4QJ.

Richards, Elfyn John, OBE, FRAeS, FIMechE; Vice-Chancellor of Loughborough University, 1967–Sept. 1975; *b* 1914; *m* 1941; three *d*. BSc Wales 1939; MA Cantab 1936; DSc Wales 1959; Hon. DSc Southampton 1973, Hon. LLD Wales 1973. Scientific Off., Nat. Physical Laboratory, Teddington, 1939–45; Chief Aerodynamicist and Asst Chief-Designer, Vickers Armstrong Ltd, Weybridge, 1945–50. Prof. of Aeronautical Engineering, Univ. of Southampton, 1950–64; Dir, Inst. of Sound and Vibration Research, Univ. of Southampton, 1963–67. Chm., Univs. Council for Adult Educn, 1973– ; Mem., Leics Educn Cttee, 1967– ; Mem., Science Res. Council, 1971– ; Mem., Noise Adv. Council; Mem., Gen. Adv. Council of BBC (Chm., Midlands Adv. Council, 1968–71); Mem., Cttee of Scientific Adv. Council; Mem., Wilson Cttee on Problems of Noise. Aeronautical Consultant to Vickers Armstrong Ltd, Westland Ltd, Rolls-Royce Ltd. Taylor Gold Medal of the Royal Aeronautical Soc., 1949; James Watt Medal of the Instn of Civil Engineers, 1963.

Pres., Brit. Acoustical Soc., 1968–69; Pres. Soc. of Environmental Engrs, 1971–74. *Publications*: many reports and memoranda of Aeronautical Research Council; articles and lectures in Royal Aeronautical Soc. *Address*: Vice-Chancellor's Lodge, Loughborough Univ., Loughborough, Leics LE11 3TU.

Richards, Dr Gareth; Lecturer, Hotel and Catering Management, University of Surrey, since 1964; *b* 1934; *m* 1960; two *d*. BA Hons Wales, MA Wales, PhD Surrey 1972; FSS. Consultant to OECD Tourism Cttee. *Publications*: Tourism and the Economy, 1973. *Address*: Dept of Hotel and Catering Management, Univ. of Surrey, Guildford, Surrey GU2 5XH.

Richards, Kenneth; Lecturer, Department of Economics, University College of Wales, Aberystwyth, since 1967; *b* 1943; *m* 1968; one *s* one *d*. BA Wales 1964 (1st cl. Hons), MSc (Econ.) Wales 1969. *Publications*: *contrib*. Bankers Mag., Chart. Inst. Transp. Jl, Econ. Jl, Interecon., Jl Bus. Finance, Jl Transp. Econ. Pol., New Law Jl, Town and Ctry Plan. *Address*: Dept of Economics, Univ. Coll. of Wales, Aberystwyth SY23 3DB.

Richards, Kenneth Roland; Reader in Drama, University of Manchester, since 1974; *b* 1934; *m* 1962; two *d*. Trained RADA; BA Oxon 1959, MA Oxon 1963. Lectr, Univ. of Ljubljana, 1960–63; Lectr, Univ. of Trondheim, 1963–64; Lectr, Univ. of Uppsala, 1964–66; Res. Schol., London Univ., 1966–68; Vis. Lectr, Univ. of Oslo, 1967; Lectr, Univ. of Manchester, 1968–72, Sen. Lectr, 1972–74. Ch. Ext. Examiner, Drama, Manchester Univ. Sch. of Educn, 1969–73; Chm., Drama Bd of Studies. Fellow, Folger Shakespeare Lib., Washington, 1972; Vis. Prof. in Drama, Univ. of Rome, 1974. Mem. Eng. Bd of Studies, CNAA; Mem. Mngmt Cttee, Contact Theatre Co.; Mem. Soc. Theatre Res., Internat. Fedn Theatre Res.; Editor, Theatre Research/Recherches Théâtrales, 1971– ; Gen. Ed., Drama and Theatre Studies; Gen. Ed., Plays and Playwrights. *Publications*: ed, Nineteenth Century British Theatre, 1971; The Eighteenth Century English Stage, 1972; Western Popular Theatre, 1974; contrib. Contributi Inglesi, 1974; *contrib*. Anglia, Archiv., Etudes Angl., Speech and Drama., Studia Neophilol., Theatre Notebk. *Address*: Dept of Drama, Univ. of Manchester, Manchester M13 9PL.

Richards, Dr Michael Wyndham, MA, DPhil; Lecturer in Drama, University College of North Wales, since 1970; *b* 1939; *m* 1964; one *s* two *d*. BA Oxon 1962 (2nd cl. Mediaeval and Mod. Langs), MA Oxon 1965, DPhil Oxon 1968. Lectr in German, Queen's Univ., Belfast, 1965–70. *Publications*: ed. H. Böll: Explorations, 1970; ed, H. Pinter: Englische Dichter der Moderne, 1971; *contrib*. TES. *Address*: Dept of Drama, Univ. College of North Wales, Bangor LL57 2DG.

Richards, Norman Frank, OBE; Senior Lecturer in Civil Engineering, Department of Civil Engineering, University of Bristol (also teaches History of Technology), since

1973; *b* 1914; *m* 1938. BSc Bristol 1934 (1st cl. Civil Eng.); CEng, FICE, FIStructE, MBIM. Dir of Public Wks, Somaliland and Nyasaland, 1948–61; Perm. Sec., Min. of Wks, Malawi, 1961–64. Lectr, Bristol Univ., 1964–70, Sen. Tutor, 1970–73; Mem., Gen. Purposes Cttee, Bristol Univ., 1971. *Address*: Dept of Civil Engineering, Univ. of Bristol, Bristol BS8 1TR.

Richards, Prof. Peter Godfrey, BSc(Econ), PhD; Professor of British Government, Department of Politics, University of Southampton, since 1969; *b* 1923; *m* 1954; two *d*. BSc(Econ) London 1945, PhD Southampton 1955. Tutor Organiser of Adult Educn, Univ. Coll. of Southampton, 1946; Lectr in Government, Univ. of Sotuhampton, 1947–60; Sen. Lectr, Univ. of Southampton, 1960–64; Reader in Politics, Univ. of Southampton, 1964–69. Mem., Council Hansard Soc., 1969– ; Chm., Study of Parliament Gp, 1970–73. *Publications*: Delegation in Local Government, 1956; Honourable Members, 1959, 2nd edn 1964; Patronage in British Government, 1963; Parliament and Foreign Affairs, 1967; The New Local Government System, 1968, 2nd edn 1971; Parliament and Conscience, 1971; The Backbenchers, 1972; The Reformed Local Government System, 1973; *contrib*. Parl. Aff., Polit. Qly, Polit. Studies, Public Admin, Public Law, Urban Studies. *Address*: Dept of Politics, Univ. of Southampton, Southampton SO9 5NH.

Richards, Dr Rex Edward, DSc, FRS; Warden of Merton College, Oxford, since 1969; *b* 1922; *m* 1948; two *d*. MA Oxon, DPhil Oxon, DSc Oxon 1970, Hon. DSc East Anglia 1971; FRS 1959. Fellow, Lincoln Coll., Oxford, 1947–64, Hon. Fellow, 1968; Dr Lee's Prof. of Chemistry, Oxford, 1964–70; Fellow, Exeter Coll., 1964–69; Hon. Fellow, St John's Coll., Oxford, 1968. Mem., Chemical Soc. Coun., 1957; Mem., Faraday Soc. Coun., 1963. Corday-Morgan Medal of Chemical Soc., 1954. *Publications*: *contrib*. various contribs to scientific jls. *Address*: Warden's Lodgings, Merton College, Oxford.

Richardson, Elizabeth; *see* Richardson, J. E.

Richardson, Geoffrey; Senior Lecturer, Department of Educational Studies, Hull University, since 1965; *b* 1922; *m* 1945; one *s* one *d*. BA Sheffield 1947 (Mod. Langs and Lits), DipEd Sheffield 1948, MA Sheffield 1956; Lectr in Educn, Leicester Univ., 1955–65. *Publications*: Histoires Illustrées, 1951; (jtly) Petites Histoires, 1952; (jtly) Illustrierte Geschichten, 1953; (jtly) A Book of French Verse, 1964; (jtly) Salut les Jeunes!, 1969; Histoire en Images, 1970; (jtly) Salut Correntin!, 1970; (jtly) Salut les Bouchon!, 1971; Ecris-moi bientôt!, 1972; *contrib*. Mod. Langs, Durh. Res. Rev. *Address*: Dept of Educational Studies, Univ. of Hull, Hull HU6 7RX.

Richardson, Harry Ward, MA; Director, Centre for Research in the Social Sciences, University of Kent at Canterbury, since 1969; *b* 1938; *m* 1960; two *s* one *d*. BA Manchester 1959 (1st cl. Mod. Hist., Econs and Polit.), MA Manchester 1961. Asst Lectr in Econs, Aberdeen Univ., 1960–62; Lectr, Newcastle Univ., 1962–64; Lectr, Strathclyde Univ., 1964–65; Sen. Lectr, Aberdeen, 1966–68; Vis. Prof., Univ. of Pittsburgh, 1971, 1973. *Publications*: Economic Recovery in Britain, 1932–39, 1967; (with D. H. Aldcroft) Building in the British Economy between the Wars, 1968; Regional Economics: Location Theory, Urban Structure and Regional Change, 1969; (with D. H. Aldcroft) The British Economy 1870–1939, 1969; Elements of Regional Economics, 1969; ed, Regional Economics: A Reader, 1970; Urban Economics, 1971; Input–Output and Regional Economics, 1973; Regional Growth Theory, 1973; Economics of Urban Size, 1973; *contrib.* Jl Regional Science, Business Hist., Econ. Hist. Rev., Growth Change, Lloyds Bk Rev., Oxford Econ. Papers, Scott. Jl Polit. Econ., Urb. Studies, Yorks Bull. Econ. Soc. Res., Rev. Reg. Studies, Reg. Studies. *Address*: Centre for Research in the Social Sciences, Cornwallis Building, The Univ. of Kent at Canterbury, Canterbury, Kent.

Richardson, J. Elizabeth; Head of Centre for Study of Group and Institutional Relations, School of Education, Bristol University, since 1973; Research Fellow since 1971; *b* 1915. BA 1937, DipEd 1938, MA 1948, London; MBPsS. Lecturer in Education: Univ. of Sheffield, 1949–59; Univ. of Bristol, 1959–71. *Publications*: (with others) Studies in the Social Psychology of Adolescence, 1951; The Active Teacher, 1955; Group Study for Teachers, 1967, Italian trans., 1973; The Environment of Learning, 1967, Italian trans., 1973; The Teacher, the School and the Task of Management, 1973; *contrib.* BJES, Educn for Teaching, Educ. Rev., New Era, Sociol Rev., Vocational Aspect. *Address*: Univ. of Bristol Sch. of Education, Berkeley Square, Bristol.

Richardson, Dr Jeremy John; Lecturer, Department of Politics, University of Keele, since 1969; *b* 1942; *m* 1967. BA Keele 1964 (Hons Politics and Econs), MA(Econ) Manchester 1965, PhD Manchester 1970. Asst Lectr in Politics, Keele, 1966–69. Mem., Newcastle under Lyme Bor. Council, 1970– . *Publications*: The Policy-Making Process, 1969; (with R. H. Kimber) Campaigning for the Environment, 1974; (with R. H. Kimber) British Pressure Groups, 1974; *contrib.* Local Govt Studies, Parly Aff., Polit. Studies, Public Admin, Pol Qly, Man–Environment Systems. *Address*: Dept of Politics, The Univ., Keele ST5 5BG.

Richardson, Leopold John Dixon, OBE; Hon. Professor of Classical Literature, Trinity College Dublin, since 1963; *b* 1893; *m* 1925; two *d*. BA Dublin 1916 (1st cl. Hons in Classics and Philosophy), MA Dublin 1920, MA Wales 1942; MRIA 1965. Asst Lectr in Greek, QUB, 1922–23; Dep. Prof. of Greek, QUB, 1923–24; Lectr in Latin, UC Cardiff, 1925–46; Prof. of Greek, UC Cardiff, 1946–58; Res. Associate in Greek, UCL, 1964–66. Hon. Sec., Classical Assoc. of Ireland, 1920–22; Hon. Sec., Classical Assoc. of England, 1943–63; Mem., Council,

Philological Soc., 1944–50; Mem., Council, Roman Soc., 1949–52; Mem., Council Hellenic Soc., 1955–58. Editor, Proceedings of the Classical Association, 1948–63; Editor, Studies in Mycenaean Inscriptions and Dialect, published annually by London University, 1959– ; *Publications*: Ta Indika (in Greek), 1926; *contrib.* Classical Qly, Classical Rev., Eranos, Euphrosyne, Greece and Rome, Hermathena, Phoenix, and others. *Address*: The Common Room, Trinity College, Dublin 2.

Richmond, Rev. Francis Henry Arthur; Hon. Lecturer in Biblical Studies, University of Sheffield, since 1969; *b* 1936; *m* 1966; two *s*. BA Dublin 1959, MA Dublin 1966, BTheol Strasbourg 1960, BLitt Oxon 1964. Stephenson Research Fellow, Sheffield, 1966–69. *Address*: Dept of Biblical Studies, Univ. of Sheffield, Sheffield S10 2TN.

Richmond, Rev. Dr James; Reader in Religious Studies, University of Lancaster, since 1972; *b* 1931; *m* 1962; one *s* one *d*. MA Glasgow 1952, BD Glasgow 1955 (1st cl. Systematic Theol.), PhD Glasgow 1961; Mem., Soc. for Study of Theology, Minister of Church of Scotland 1956. Lectr in Theol., Univ. Nottingham, 1961–67; Danforth Vis. Prof. in Phil. of Religion, Union Theol Seminary, 1967–68; Vis. Prof. of Religion, Barnard Coll., Columbia Univ., 1968; Sen. Lectr, Univ. Lancaster, 1968–72; Tallman Vis. Prof. of Religion, Bowdoin Coll., 1972; British Acad. Vis. European Exchange Scholar, Univ. Göttingen, 1973. *Publications*: Faith and Philosophy, 1966; (with J. S. Bowden) ed, A Reader in Contemporary Theology, 1966, 2nd enlarged edn 1971; Theology and Metaphysics, 1970; *contrib.* Can. Jl Theology, Theology, TLS. *Address*: Dept of Religious Studies, Univ. of Lancaster, Bailrigg, Lancaster LA1 4YW.

Richmond, Peter Edward, MA, BSc, MInstP; Senior Lecturer in Education, University of Southampton, since 1970; *b* 1926; *m* 1954; one *s* two *d*. BSc London 1951 (Special Physics), CertEd London 1952, DipEd London 1956, MA(Ed) London 1962; MInstP. Lectr in Educn, Southampton, 1960–70. Cnsltnt, Unesco, on Teaching Integrated Science. *Publications*: ed, New Trends in Integrated Science Teaching, vol. 1, 1971, vol. 2, 1973, vol. 3, 1974; chapter, Science Teaching, in, Education Research in Britain 3; *contrib.* Brit. Jl Educnl Psychol., Physics Educn, Sch. Sci. Rev., Sch. Sci. & Maths. *Address*: School of Education, Univ. of Southampton, Southampton SO9 5NH.

Rick, Dr John Terence, PhD; Lecturer in Psychology, University of Sheffield, since 1973; *b* 1934; *m* 1964; one *s* three *d*. BA Liverpool 1962 (1st cl. Psychol.), PhD Liverpool 1965, MSc Southampton 1967 (Biochem.); ABPsS. Mem., EPS, Mem., Biochem. Soc., Mem., EBBS, Mem., Internat. Soc. Neurochem. Demonstrator, Liverpool, 1962–65; MRC Fellow, Southampton, 1965–68; Mental Health Res. Fellow, 1968–70; Lectr in Psychology, Univ. of Birmingham, 1970–73. *Publications*: *contrib.* Comp. Biochem. Physiol., Gen. Comp. Pharmacol., Jl

Neurochem. *Address*: Dept of Psychology, Univ. of Sheffield, Sheffield S10 2TN.

Rickard, Peter, MA, DPhil, PhD; Reader in French, University of Cambridge, since 1975 (Lecturer, 1957–75); *b* 1922. BA Oxon 1948 (1st cl. Mod. Langs), MA Oxon 1948, DPhil Oxon 1952, PhD Cantab 1952 (by incorporation); Mem., Mod. Hum. Res. Assoc., Mem., Philol. Soc., Mem., Soc. Fr. Studies. Lectr in Mod. Langs, Trinity Coll., Oxford, 1949–52; CUF Lectr in French, Oxford, 1951–52; Asst Lectr, Cambridge, 1952–57; Fellow, Emmanuel Coll., Cambridge, 1953– ; Tutor, Emmanuel Coll., Cambridge, 1954–65; Dir of Studies in Mod. Langs, Emmanuel Coll., Cambridge, 1973– . *Publications*: Britain in Medieval French Literature, 1956; La langue française au XVIe siècle, Etude suivie de textes, 1968; ed, The French Language; studies presented to L. C. Harmer, 1970; ed, and trans., F. Pessoa: Selected poems, 1971; A History of the French Language, 1974; *contrib*. Archiv. Lingu., Neuphilol. Mitteil. Romania, Trans Philol. Soc. *Address*: Emmanuel College, Cambridge.

Ricketts, Dr Peter Thomas; Senior Lecturer in Romance Philology, Department of Linguistics, University of Birmingham, since 1964; *b* 1933; *m* 1960; one *s* one *d*. BA Hons Birmingham 1956 (French), PhD 1960. Lectr and Asst Prof. in French, Victoria Coll., Univ. of Toronto, 1958–59, 1961–64; Lectr in Romance Philology, Univ. of Birmingham, 1964–67; Vis. Prof. in French, Univ. of BC, Vancouver, 1967–68. *Publications*: Les poésies de Guilhem de Montanhagol, 1964; (with F. R. Hamlin and J. Hathaway) Introduction à l'étude de l'ancien provençal, 1967; Le Breviari d'Amor de Matfre Ermengaud de Béziers, vol. I (forthcoming); *contrib*. Revue des Langues Romanes, Romania. *Address*: Dept of Linguistics, The Univ., PO Box 363, Birmingham B15 2TT.

Rickman, Dr Geoffrey Edwin, MA, DPhil, FSA; Senior Lecturer and Head of Department of Ancient History, St Salvator's College, University of St Andrews, since 1968; *b* 1932; *m* 1959; one *s* one *d*. BA Oxon 1955 (1st cl. Lit. Hum.), Dip. Classical Archaeology Oxon 1958, MA Oxon 1958, DPhil Oxon 1963; FSA 1966. Jun. Res. Fellow, Queen's Coll., Oxford, 1959–62; Lectr in Ancient History, St Andrews Univ., 1962–68. *Publication*: Roman Granaries and Store Buildings, 1971. *Address*: Dept of Ancient History, Univ. of St Andrews, St Andrews, Fife KY16 9AJ.

Rickman, Hans Peter, DPhil; Reader in Philosophy, City University, London, since 1967; *b* 1918; *m* 1947. BA London 1941, DPhil Oxon 1943, MA London 1948. Staff Tutor in Philosophy and Psychology, Hull Univ., 1949–61; Sen. Lectr, City Univ., 1962–67. *Publications*: Meaning in History, 1961, American edn 1962; Preface to Philosophy, 1964, American edn 1964; Living with Technology, 1967, Japanese edn 1971; Understanding and the Human Studies, 1967; *contrib*. Encyclopedia of Philosophy, 1967; *contrib*. Symposium Volume on VICO,

1969; *contrib*. Archiv. Gesch. Philos., Brit. Jl Sociol., Germ. Life Lett., Hibb. Jl, Internat. Rev., Jl Wld Hist., Lond. Qly, Mind, Philos., Philos. Qly, Sociol. Anal. *Address*: Dept of Social Science and Humanities, The City Univ., St John Street, EC1V 4PB.

Ricks, Prof. Christopher Bruce, MA, BLitt, FRSL; Professor of English, University of Bristol, 1968–75; Professor of English, University of Cambridge, from Oct. 1975; *b* 1933; *m* 1956; two *s* two *d*. BA Oxon 1956 (1st cl. English), BLitt Oxon 1958, MA Oxon 1960. Andrew Bradley Jun. Res. Fellow, Balliol Coll., Oxford, 1957; Fellow and Tutor, Worcester Coll., Oxford, 1958–68; Vis. Prof., Berkeley and Stanford, 1965; Smith Coll., 1967; Harvard, 1971. Editor, Essays in Criticism; Vice-Pres., Tennyson Soc. *Publications*: ed (with H. Carter), A Dissertation upon English Typographical Founders, 1961; Milton's Grand Style, 1963; ed, The Poems of Tennyson, 1969; ed, Sphere History of Literature in the English Language, vols 2–3, 1969–70; Tennyson, 1972; Keats and Embarrassment, 1974; *contrib*. Ess. Crit., Rev. Engl. Studies, Vict. Studies. *Address*: Dept of English, Univ. of Bristol, Bristol BS8 1TH.

Riddall, John Gervase; Lecturer, Faculty of Law, Leeds University, since 1966; *b* 1928; *m* 1968; one *s* one *d*. MA Trinity College Dublin 1954; Barrister-at-Law. *Publications*: *contrib*. Conveyan. *Address*: Faculty of Law, The Univ., Leeds LS2 9JT.

Rideout, Prof. Roger William; Professor of Labour Law, University of London, since 1973; *b* 1935; *m* 1959; one *d*. LLB London 1956, PhD London 1958; Barrister-at-Law (Gray's Inn) 1964. Lectr, Sheffield Univ., 1960–63; Lectr, Bristol Univ., 1963–64; Sen. Lectr, Univ. Coll., London, 1964–66; Reader in English Law, Univ. Coll. London, 1966–73. Mem., Phelps Brown Cttee on Cnstrctn Indust., 1967–68. *Publications*: The Right to Membership of a Trade Union, 1963; Reforming the Redundancy Payments Act, 1969; Principles of Labour Law, 1972; The Practice and Procedure of the NIRC, 1973; Trade Unions and the Law, 1973; *contrib*. Brit. Jl, Indust. Relat., Mod. Law Rev. *Address*: Faculty of Laws, Univ. College, 4/8 Endsleigh Gardens, WC1H 0EG.

Ridgway, David W. R., BA; Lecturer in Archaeology, University of Edinburgh, since 1968; *b* 1938; *m* 1970. BA (Hons Classics) London 1960, Dip. European Archaeology Oxford 1962; For. Mem., Ist. di Studi Etruschi ed Italici, 1972 (and Mem. this inst.'s Iron Age res. cttee, 1974–). Sir James Knott Fellow, Univ. of Newcastle upon Tyne, 1965–67; Leverhulme European Schol. in Italy, 1967–68. *Publications*: ed, M. Pallottino: The Etruscans, 2nd English edn 1974; trans., R. B. Bandinelli, etc; The Buried City: Excavations at Leptis Magna, 1966; *contrib*. Greeks, Celts and Romans, ed C. and S. Hawkes, 1973; *contrib*. Archaeol. Rep. (Hellenic Soc.), Dial. Archeol., Jl Rom. Studies, Notiz. Scavi, Studi Etrus. *Address*: Dept of Archaeology, 19–20 George Square, Edinburgh EH8 9JZ.

Ridley, Prof. Frederick Fernand; Professor of Political Theory and Institutions, University of Liverpool, since 1965; *b* 1928; *m* 1967; one *s*. BSc(Econ) London 1950, PhD London 1954. Res. Fellow, CNRS, Paris, 1954; Asst Lectr, Univ. of Manchester, 1955–57; Res. Off., Cotton Bd, Manchester, 1957–58; Lectr, Univ. of Liverpool, 1958–65; Hd of Dept, 1964; Chm., Fac. of Soc. and Environmental Studies, 1971–72; Vis. Prof., Grad. Sch. of Public Affairs, Univ. of Pittsburgh, 1968; Review Editor, Parly Aff., 1968– ; Editor, Polit. Studies, 1970– ; Adv. Edit. Bd, Administration and Society, 1970– ; Mem., Jt Univ. Council Social and Public Admin, 1964– , Chm., 1972– ; Chm., Public Admin Cttee, 1971–73; Hon. Vice-Pres., Politics Assoc., 1972– ; Mem., Exec., Polit. Studies Assoc., 1969– ; Council, Hansard Soc., 1970– ; Res. Cttee, Civil Service Dept, 1970; Jt Matric. Bd of North. Univs, 1969–70; Chm., Examiners in Brit. Govt, JMB, 1965– ; Ext. Examiner, TCD, LSE and Open Univ., 1972– ; Mem., Pol Sci. Cttee, SSRC, 1972– . Mem., Jt Wking Party, Social Science Socs, 1971–73; Directing Cttee, European Gp, Internat. Inst. of Admin. Sciences, 1973– . *Publications:* (with J. Blondel) Public Administration in France, 1964, 2nd edn 1969; ed, Specialists and Generalists: A Comparative Study of the Professional Civil Service at Home and Abroad, 1968; Revolutionary Syndicalism in France: The Direct Action of its Time, 1970; The French Prefectoral System, 1973; *contrib.* Admin and Soc., Govt and Opp., PAC Bull., Parly Aff., Teaching Pol., Polit. Studies, Pub. Admin. *Address:* Dept of Political Theory and Institutions, Univ. of Liverpool, Liverpool L69 3BX.

Ridley, Tom, CEng, BSc, FRSE, FICE, MASCE; Lecturer (Part-time), Department of Architecture, University of Edinburgh, since 1960; *b* 1927; *m* 1954; three *d*. BSc 1948 (1st cl. Civil Eng.), Dip. Imperial College 1954 (Concrete Technology); Chartered Engineer, FRSE, FICE, MASCE. Leverhulme Res. Fellow, 1971; Hon. Fellow, Fac. of Social Science, 1971. Chm., CEI (Scotl.), 1970–71; Chm., ICE (Scotl.), 1967–68; Mem., Amenity Cttee, Hydro-Electric Bd. *Publications:* USA Building Package, 1971. *Address:* Dept of Architecture, Univ. of Edinburgh, Edinburgh EH8 9YL.

Rigby, Marjory Muirhead, MA, BLitt; Senior Lecturer in English, University of Birmingham, since 1973 (Lecturer, 1962–73); *b* 1927. MA Glasgow 1949 (1st cl. English), BLitt Oxon 1952; Asst Lectr, then Lectr, Univ. Coll. of N Wales, 1954–62; Ed., MHRA Annual Bibliography of Engl. Lang. and Lit., 1960–68. *Address:* Dept of English, Univ. of Birmingham, PO Box 363, Birmingham B15 2TT.

Rigelsford, Michael James Richard; Lecturer in Dutch, Department of German, University of Liverpool, since 1969; *b* 1942; *m* (separated); one *d*. BA Cantab 1964 (2nd cl. Mod. Langs), MA 1967. Member: Internat. Assoc. of Dutch Studies; Dutch Philol Conf. Assoc. Univ. Asst in Dutch, Cambridge, 1967–69. *Publications: contrib.* reviews and translations. *Address* Dept of German, Modern Languages Bldg, Univ. of Liverpool, PO Box 147, Liverpool L69 3BX.

Righter, William; Senior Lecturer in English and Comparative Literary Studies, University of Warwick, since 1969; *b* 1927; *m* 1957, 1968. AB Harvard 1949, MA Kansas 1953, BLitt Oxon 1956. Instructor in English, Cornell Univ., 1956–59; Lectr in English, Univ. Warwick, 1965–69; Prof. of Compar. Lit., Hong Kong Univ., 1970–73 (on secondment). Editor, Thames and Hudson, publishers, 1964–65. *Publications:* Logic and Criticism, 1963; The Rhetorical Hero, a study in the aesthetics of André Malraux, 1964; Myth and Literature, 1974; *contrib.* Brit. Jl Aesthetics, New Literary History. *Address:* Dept of English and Comparative Literary Studies, Univ. of Warwick, Coventry CV4 7AL.

Riley, (Conal) Stuart; Director of Tourism Research Unit, Department of Marketing, University of Lancaster, since 1970; *b* 1940; *m* 1964; one *s* one *d*. BA Keele 1962, DipPsych Liverpool 1964; ABPsS 1970; Mem., MRS 1971; Assoc. Mem., Inst. Marketing, 1973. Asst to Sen. Tutor, Univ. Keele, 1966–67; Asst Dir, Statistical Research Unit in Sociology, Univ. Keele,1967–70. Mem., Jt Industry Trng Bd Cttee on Trng in Marketing, 1971–72. *Publications: contrib.* Brit. Jl Educnl Psych., Brit. Jl Marketing, Bull. Brit. Psych. Soc., Medical Care, Traffic Engrg and Control. *Address:* Furness College, Univ. of Lancaster, Bailrigg, Lancaster LA1 4YW.

Riley, Prof. Edward Calverley, MA; Professor of Hispanic Studies, University of Edinburgh, since 1970; *b* 1923; *m* 1970. BA Oxon 1947 (French and Spanish), MA Oxon 1947, MA Dublin 1953 (ad eund.). Laming Travelling Fellowship, The Queen's Coll., Oxford, 1948–49; Asst Lectr, TCD, 1949; Lectr, TCD, 1952–57; in charge Dept of Spanish, TCD, 1953; Fellow, TCD, and Reader, 1957–65; Prof., TCD, 1965–70; Vis. Prof., Dartmouth Coll., USA, 1965–70; Mem., Nat. Cttee Mod. Lang. Studies, Ireland, 1968–69. *Publications:* Cervantes's Theory of the Novel, 1962, 2nd edn 1964, Spanish edn 1966; co-ed, Suma Cervantina, 1973; *contrib.* Anal. Cervant., Bull. Hispan. Studies, Filol., Hispan. Rev., Mod. Lang. Notes, Mod. Lang. Rev. *Address:* Dept of Hispanic Studies, David Hume Tower, George Square, Edinburgh EH8 9JX.

Riley, Patrick William Joseph, BA, PhD; Lecturer in Modern History, University of Manchester, since 1965; *b* 1926; *m* 1957; one *s* one *d*. BA Nottingham 1951 (1st cl. History), CertEd London 1952, PhD London 1957; FRHistS. Asst Teacher, Cassland Rd Sec. Sch., London, 1952–56; Sen. History Master, Bramcote Hills Grammar Sch., Nottinghamshire, 1956–62; Research Fellow, Sheffield Univ., 1963–65. Royal Signals, 1944–48. *Publications:* The English Ministers and Scotland, 1707–1727, 1964; *contrib.* Bull. Inst. Hist. Res., EHR, Scott. Hist. Rev. *Address:* Dept of History, The Univ., Manchester M13 9PL.

Riley-Smith, Dr Jonathan Simon Christopher; Assistant Lecturer in Medieval History and Fellow of Queens' College, University of Cambridge, since 1972; *b* 1938; *m* 1968; one *s* one *d*. BA Cantab 1960, MA Cantab 1964, PhD Cantab 1964; FSAScot, FRHistS. Asst Lectr, St Andrews Univ., 1964–66, Lectr, 1966–72. *Publications*: The Knights of St John in Jerusalem and Cyprus 1050–1310, 1967; Historical Introduction and Notes, in, Ayyubids, Mamlukes and Crusaders: Selections from the Tārikh al-Duwal wa'l-Muluk of Ibn-al-Furāt, ed U. and M. C. Lyons, 1971; The Feudal Nobility and the Kingdom of Jerusalem 1174–1277, 1973; contrib. Relations between East and West in the Middle Ages, ed D. Baker, 1973; *contrib.* Bull. Inst. Hist. Res., EHR, Tradit. *Address*: Queens' College, Cambridge.

Rimmer, Douglas; Senior Lecturer in Economics, Centre of West African Studies, University of Birmingham, since 1970, and Deputy Director of the Centre since 1974; *b* 1927; *m* 1st 1955, 2nd 1970; one *s* one *d*. BA Sheffield 1951 (1st cl. Mod. Hist., Econ. and Polit. Instns); Mem., Royal Econ. Soc., Mem., Afr. Studies Assoc. UK. Res. aptmts, Durham Colls, 1951–53; Univ. Coll., London, 1953–55; Lectr, Univ. Coll. of Gold Coast (Ghana), 1955–61; Lectr, Univ. of Birmingham, 1961–70; Acting Dir, Centre of West African Studies, Univ. of Birmingham, 1968, 1971. Mem., Council, Afr. Studies Assoc. UK, 1971–74. *Publications*: *contrib.* Econ. Bull. Ghana, Hobart Papers, Indust. Lab. Relat. Rev., Jl Develop. Studies, Jl Mod. Afr. Studies, Qly Jl Econ. *Address*: Centre of West African Studies, Univ. of Birmingham, PO Box 363, Birmingham B15 2TT.

Rimmer, Prof. Frederick William, MA, BMus, FRCO; Gardiner Professor of Music, University of Glasgow, since 1966, and Director of Scottish Music Archive, since 1968; *b* 1914; *m* 1941; two *s* one *d*. BMus Dunelm 1939, MA Cantab; FRCO 1934. Sen. Lectr in Music, Homerton Coll., Cambridge, 1948–51; Cramb Lectr, Glasgow Univ., 1951–56; Sen. Lectr, Glasgow Univ., 1956–66; Organist, Glasgow Univ., 1954–66. Served 11th Bn Lancs Fusiliers, Middle East, 1941–45 (Major 1944); A Dir, Scottish Opera, 1966– ; Chm., BBC's Scottish Music Adv. Cttee, 1972– ; Mem., British Council Music Cttee, 1973– . *Publications*: Five Preludes on Scottish Psalm Tunes, Pastorale and Toccata, Invenzione e Passacaglia Capricciosa (for solo organ); Sing we merrily, Christmas natus est alleluia, O Lord, we beseech thee, Five carols of the Nativity (for choir and organ); chapters 8–10, 1800–1970, in A History of Scottish Music, 1973; *contrib.* Music Rev., Org. Rev., Tempo. *Address*: Univ. of Glasgow, Glasgow G12 8QQ.

Rimmington, Donald, Lecturer, Department of Chinese Studies, University of Leeds, since 1965; *b* 1936; *m* 1962; one *s* two *d*. BA Cantab 1960, MA Cantab 1962; Asst Lectr, Leeds, 1963–65. *Address*: Dept of Chinese Studies, Univ. of Leeds, Leeds LS2 9JT.

Rinsler, Dr Norma Sybil; Lecturer, 592

Department of French, University of London, King's College, since 1962; *b* 1927; *m* 1948; one *s* two *d*. BA London 1951, PhD London 1961. *Publications:* Gérard de Nerval, 1973; ed, G. de Nerval: Les Chimères, 1973; *contrib.* Austral. Jl Fr. Studies, Ess. Fr. Lit., Fr. Studies, Mod. Lang. Rev., Philol. Qly, Rev. Hist. Litt., Rev. Hist. Théâtre, Rev. Litt. Comp., Studies Romant. *Address:* Dept of French, Univ. of London, King's College, Strand, WC2R 2LS.

Ritchie, Prof. James McPherson, MA, DPhil; Professor of German, Department of Germanic Studies, University of Sheffield, since 1970; *b* 1927; *m* 1958; two *s* one *d*. MA Aberdeen 1951 (1st cl. French–German), DPhil Tübingen 1954. Asst Lectr, Glasgow, 1954–61; Sen. Lectr, Newcastle, NSW. 1961–65; Sen. Lectr, Hull, 1965; Reader, Hull, 1967–70. Warden, MacBrayne Hall, Glasgow; Ed., Seminar; Warden of Grant Hall, Hull. *Publications:* ed, Periods in German Literature, vol. I, 1966, vol. II, 1969; ed. Seven Expressionist Plays, 1968; ed, Vision and Aftermath, 1969; ed, Carl Sternheim, 1970; ed, Georg Kaiser, 1970; ed, Th. Storm: Immensee, 1969; ed, Eichendorff: Taugenichts, 1970; Gottfried Benn, The Unreconstructed Expressionists, 1972; *contrib.* AUMLA, Euphor., Germ. Life Lett., Mod. Drama, Mod. Lang. Rev., Orb. Litt., Seminar. *Address:* Dept of Germanic Studies, Univ. of Sheffield, Sheffield S10 2TN.

Ritchie, Dr William, BSc, PhD; Lecturer, Department of Geography, Aberdeen University, since 1966; *b* 1940; *m* 1965; two *s*. BSc Glasgow 1962 (1st cl. Geog.), PhD Glasgow 1966. Res. Asst. Glasgow, 1963–64; Asst Lectr, Aberdeen, 1964–66. Sec., Sect. E, Brit. Assoc. Adv. Science. *Publications: contrib.* Scott. Geogr. Mag. *Address:* Dept of Geography, Univ. of Aberdeen, Aberdeen AB9 1AS.

Ritson, Christopher; Lecturer in Agricultural Economics and Management, University of Reading, since 1969; *b* 1945; *m* 1968; one *s*. BA Hons Nottingham 1966 (Econs), MAgrSc Reading 1968 (Agric. Econs). Res. Associate, Agricl Adjustment Unit, Univ. of Newcastle upon Tyne, 1968–69. *Publications:* (jtly) Agricultural Policy and the Common Market, 1971; (jtly) Farmers and Foreigners: the impact of the common agricultural policy on the Associates and Associables, 1973; *contrib.* Jl Agricl Econs, New Society. *Address:* Dept of Agricultural Economics, 4 Earley Gate, Whiteknights Road, Reading RG6 2AR.

Rivers, Prof. Julian P.; *see* Pitt-Rivers.

Rivet, Prof. Albert Lionel Frederick, MA, FSA; Professor of Roman Provincial Studies, Department of Classics, University of Keele, since 1974 (Reader in Romano-British Studies, 1967–74); *b* 1915; *m* 1947; one *s* one *d*. BA Oxon 1938 (Litt. Hum.), MA Oxon 1947; FSA 1953, FSAScot 1959. Corresp. Fellow, German Archaeol. Inst., 1960. Mem., Royal Archaeol. Inst., Mem., Soc. Prom. Roman Studies, Co-opted Mem., Council for Brit. Archaeol. Lectr, Dept of Classics, Univ. of

Keele, 1964–67. Asst Archaeol. Officer, Ordnance Survey, 1951–64; Mem., Council, Royal Archaeol. Inst., 1955–59, 1963–67; Mem., Exec. Cttee, 1958–59, 1965–67; Mem., Council, and Ed., Proceedings, Soc. Antiqu. Scotl., 1961–64; Mem., Council, Soc. Prom. Rom. Studies, 1967–70, 1971– ; Review Ed., Britannia, 1970– ; Mem., Fac. of Archaeol. Hist. and Lett., Brit. Sch. Rome, 1972–76; Mem., Cartog. Sub-Cttee, Brit. Nat. Cttee for Geog. (Royal Soc.), 1972–75; Mem., Edit. Bd, Hist. Rom. Provinces. *Publications*: comp., The Ordnance Survey Map of Roman Britain, 3rd edn 1956; comp., The Ordnance Survey Map of Southern Britain in the Iron Age, 1962; Town and Country in Roman Britain, 1958, 2nd edn 1964; ed, The Iron Age in Northern Britain, 1966; ed, The Roman Villa in Britain, 1969; contrib. Romano-British Villas, ed P. Corder, 1955; Problems of the Iron Age in S. Britain, ed S. S. Frere; The Civitas Capitals of Roman Britain, ed J. S. Wacher; The Oxford Classical Dictionary, ed Hammond and Scullard, 2nd edn 1970; Aufstieg und Niedergang der Römischen Welt, ed H. Temporini, 1974; *contrib*. Antiqu., Archaeol. Jl, Archaeol. Newsl., Britannia, Caesarod. *Address*: Dept of Classics, The Univ., Keele, Staffordshire ST5 5BG.

Rivière, Dr Peter Gerard; University Lecturer, Institute of Social Anthropology, Oxford University, since 1971; *b* 1934; *m* 1962; one *s* two *d*. MA Cantab 1961, BLitt Oxon 1963, DPhil Oxon 1965. Sen. Res. Fellow, Inst. of Latin American Studies, London Univ., 1966–68; Vis. Prof., Harvard, 1968–69; Univ. Lectr, Cambridge, 1970–71. Mem., Social Anthropology Cttee, SSRC, 1972– . Editor, Man, 1974– . *Publications*: Marriage Among the Trio, 1969; The Forgotten Frontier, 1972; *contrib*. Folk, Man, SW Jl of Anthropology. *Address*: Inst. of Social Anthropology, 51 Banbury Road, Oxford.

Roach, Prof. John Peter Charles, MA, PhD; Professor of Education, University of Education, University of Sheffield, since 1965; *b* 1920. BA Cantab 1946 (1st cl. Historical Tripos Pt I with Dist. 1940, 1st cl. Pt II), MA Cantab 1948, PhD Cantab 1953; FRHistS. Fellow, Corpus Christi Coll., Cambridge, 1950– ; Lectr in Education, Cambridge Univ., 1960–65. Mem., Council, Hist. Assoc., 1954–60; Gov., Harpur Trust, Bedford, 1965–71. *Publications*: ed and major contribs, Victoria History of Cambridgeshire, vol. III, 1959; ed, A Bibliography of Modern History, 1968; Public Examinations in England (1850–1900), 1971; contrib. New Cambridge Modern History, vols IX, X; *contrib*. Brit. Jl Educnl Studies, Bull. J. Rylands Libr., Camb. Hist. Jl, Jl Eccles. Hist., Paed. Europ. Vict. Studies. *Address*: Institute of Education, The Univ., Sheffield S10 2TN.

Roaf, Evelyn Christina Mervyn, MA, DPhil; Fellow and Tutor in Italian, Somerville College, Oxford University, since 1966, and University Lecturer in Italian, Oxford, since 1954; *b* 1917; *m* 1955. BA Oxon 1941 (1st cl. Mod. Langs), MA Oxon 1944, DPhil Oxon 1959; Foreign Off. Res. Dept, 1941 45;

Librarian, Information Off., Brit. Consulate, Milan, 1945; Brit. Consulate, Rome, 1946–49; Asst Lectr, Italian Dept, Univ. of Leeds, 1952–54. Governor, Bicester Sch., 1967. *Publications*: ed, B. Cavalcanti: Lettere edite e inedite, 1967; *contrib*. Ital. Studies. *Address*: Somerville College, Oxford.

Robbins, Prof. Keith Gilbert; Professor of History, University College of North Wales, Bangor, since 1971; *b* 1940; *m* 1963; three *s* one *d*. BA Oxon 1961 (1st cl. History), MA Oxon 1971, DPhil Oxon 1965; FRHistS. Asst Lectr, York Univ., 1963; Lectr, York Univ., 1964–71. *Publications*: Munich 1938, 1968, German edn 1969; Sir Edward Grey, 1971; *contrib*. Hist. Jl, Jl Eccles. Hist., Slav. E Europ. Rev., Jl Contemp. Hist, Jl Imp. Commonwealth Hist., Internat. Affairs. *Address*: Dept of History, Univ. College of North Wales, Bangor LL57 2DG.

Robbins, Dr Robin Hugh; Lecturer, Department of English Literature, University of Sheffield, since 1972; *b* 1942. BA 1964, MA 1967, DPhil 1970, Oxon. Jun. Lectr, Aligarh Muslim Univ., Uttar Pradesh, India, 1964–65; Lectr, Wadham Coll., Oxford, 1967–68; Andrew Bradley Jun. Res. Fellow, Balliol Coll., Oxford, 1969–72. *Publication*: ed, Sir Thomas Browne: Religio Medici, Hydriotaphia, and the Garden of Cyrus, 1972. *Address*: Dept of English Literature, Univ. of Sheffield, Western Bank, Sheffield S10 2TN.

Robbins Landon, Howard Chandler; *see* Landon, H. C. L.

Roberts, Dr Andrew Dunlop; Lecturer in African History, School of Oriental and African Studies, University of London, since 1971; *b* 1937. BA Cantab 1960, PhD Wisconsin 1966. Res. Fellow, UC, Dar es Salaam, 1966–68; Res. Fellow, Univ. of Zambia, 1968–71. Jt Editor, Jl of African History, 1974– . *Publications*: ed, Tanzania before 1900, 1968; A History of the Bemba, 1973; *contrib*. African Social Res., Azania, Jl of African Hist. *Address*: Sch. of Oriental and African Studies, Malet Street, WC1E 7HP.

Roberts, Prof. B. C.; Professor of Industrial Relations, London School of Economics, since 1962; *b* 1917; *m* 1945; two *s*. BA Oxford 1948, MA Oxford 1955; Pres. Internat. Indust. Relat. Assoc., 1967–73. Lectr, LSE, 1949–56; Reader, LSE, 1956–62. Ed., Brit. Jl Indust. Relat., 1963– ; Mem., Court of Govs, LSE, 1964–69. *Publications*: Trade Union Government and Administration, 1956; The Trades Union Congress, 1868–1921, 1958; National Wages Policy in War and Peace, 1958; Unions in America, 1959; Trade Unions in a Free Society, 1959, 2nd edn 1962; Industrial Relations: Contemporary Problems and Perspectives, 1962, 2nd edn 1968; Labour in the Tropical Territories of the Commonwealth, 1964; (with L. G. de Bellecombe) Collective Bargaining in African Countries, 1967; ed, Industrial Relations: Contemporary Issues, 1968; (with J. L. K. Lovell) A Short History of the TUC, 1968; (with R. O. Clarke and D. J. Fatchett)

Workers' Participation in Management in Britain, 1972; (with R. Loveridge and J. Gennard) **Reluctant Militants: a Study of Industrial Technicians**, 1972. *Address*: London School of Economics, Houghton Street, Aldwych, WC2 2AE.

Roberts, Dr Brynley Francis; Senior Lecturer, Department of Welsh, University College of Wales, Aberystwyth, since 1969; *b* 1931; *m* 1956; two *s*. BA Wales 1951, MA Wales 1954, PhD Wales 1969; Mem. Internat. Arthurian Soc., Mem. Hon. Soc. of Cymmrodorion. Asst Lectr, UCW Aberystwyth, 1957–60, Lectr, 1960–69; Sir John Rhŷs Fellow at Jesus Coll., Oxford, 1973–74. Mem. Cttee, British Br., Internat. Arthurian Soc., 1972– . *Publications*: Gwassonaeth Meir, 1961; Brut y Brenhinedd, 1971; Cyfranc Lludd a Llefelys, 1974; *contrib.* Bull. Bd Celtic Studies, Jl Welsh Bibl. Soc., Nat. Library of Wales Jl, Trans Hon. Soc. Cymmrodorion. *Address*: Dept of Welsh, Univ. Coll. of Wales, Aberystwyth 2Y23 2AX.

Roberts, Dr Christopher B., MA, PhD; Lecturer, Department of Russian, Trinity College, University of Dublin, since 1969; *b* 1941; *m* 1968; two *s*. MA Edinburgh 1964, PhD Edinburgh 1971; Member: Assoc. of Teachers of Russian, British Univs Assoc. of Slavists, Linguistics Assoc. of Gt Britain. Tutorial Assistant, Language Centre, Univ. East Anglia, 1968–69. Sec., Sch. of Mod. Langs and Lit., TCD, 1973– . *Publication*: *contrib.* Studia Slavica (Budapest) (forthcoming). *Address*: Dept of Russian, Trinity College, Dublin 2, Ireland.

Roberts, Edward Adam, BA; Lecturer in International Relations, London School of Economics, University of London, since 1968; *b* 1940; *m* 1966; one *s* one *d*. BA Oxon 1962. *Publications*: ed, The Strategy of Civilian Defence, 1967; (with Philip Windsor) Czechoslovakia 1968, 1969; trans. (with A. Lieven), Devillers and Lacouture: End of a War, 1969; Totalforsvar och Civilmotstånd, Stockholm, 1972; *contrib.* New Soc., Philosophy E and W, Survival, World Today. *Address*: London Sch. of Economics, Houghton Street, Aldwych, WC2A 2AE.

Roberts, Francis Llewellyn; Registrar, Loughborough University of Technology (formerly Loughborough College of Technology), since 1960; *b* 1921; *m* 1948; three *s* one *d*. BA Hons Wales 1949 (German); FRSA 1970. Asst Registrar, UC of the Gold Coast (later Ghana), 1955–60. Res. Asst, Air Hist. Br., Air Min., 1949–55. *Publications*: contrib. to monographs on German and Italian Air Force activities in World War II. *Address*: Loughborough Univ. of Technology, Loughborough, Leics LE11 3TU.

Roberts, Geoffrey Ransford; Senior Lecturer in Education, Department of Education, Manchester University, since 1973; *b* 1924; *m* 1954; one *s* one *d*. BA (Hons) 1951, Dip. in Teaching 1952, MA Wales 1958; Mem., UK Reading Assoc. Lectr in Educn, Manchester Univ., 1961–73. Assessor, BEd Manchester, 1969– ; Mem., Subcttee on Concurrent and

594

Combined Courses (UCET); External Examnr for Univs of Sheffield, Leicester and Lancaster. *Publications*: Reading in Primary Schools, 1969; (with Vera Southgate) Reading – which approach, 1970; English in Primary Schools, 1972; Early Reading, 1973; Student Workshop in Early Reading, 1973; contribs to several books of Readings; *contrib.* Brit. Jl of Educnl Psychol., Reading. *Address*: Educn Dept, The Univ., Manchester M13 9PL.

Roberts, Iolo Francis; Senior Lecturer in Education, University of Keele, since 1970; *b* 1925; *m* 1959; one *d*. BSc Wales 1946, MSc Wales 1962; FRIC 1962. Lectr in Educn, Univ. of Keele, 1962–70. Sen. Warden, Hawthorns Hall, Univ. of Keele, 1964–74. Member: British Cttee on Chemical Educn, 1969–72; West Midlands Reg. Adv. Council, 1965– ; Nat. Adv. Council on Educn for Industry and Commerce, 1971– . *Publications*: (with others) Further Education in England and Wales, 1969, 2nd edn 1972; Crystals and their Structures, 1974; *contrib.* Educn in Chem., New Scientist, Sch. Sci. Rev., TES. *Address*: Dept of Education, Univ. of Keele, Keele, Newcastle, Staffs ST5 5BG.

Roberts, Dr James Graeme; Lecturer in English, University of Aberdeen, since 1971; *b* 1942; *m* 1965; one *s* one *d*. MA St Andrews 1964 (1st cl. English), PhD Aberdeen 1971. Asst Lectr, Aberdeen, 1965–68; Terminable Lectr, Aberdeen, 1968–71. *Address*: Dept of English, King's College, Old Aberdeen AB9 2UB.

Roberts, Jane Annette, MA, MLitt, DPhil; Lecturer in English, King's College, University of London, since 1969; *b* 1936; *m* 1969; three *s*. BA Dublin 1956, MA Dublin 1959, Hon. DipEd Dublin 1957, MLitt Dublin 1960, MA Oxon 1960, DPhil Oxon 1966. Vice-Warden, Trinity Hall, Dublin Univ., 1956–59; Asst in English, Glasgow Univ., 1961–64; Lectr, Glasgow Univ., 1964–68; Vis. Prof., State Univ. of NY, Buffalo, summer 1968; Coll. Lectr, Univ. Coll., Dublin, 1968–69. *Publications*: *contrib.* Engl. Studies, Mediaev. Studies, Med. Ævv., Proc. Royal Irish Acad. *Address*: English Dept, King's College, Strand, WC2R 2LS.

Roberts, Dr John Cole; Lecturer in Geology, School of Biological and Environmental Studies, The New University of Ulster, since 1968; *b* 1935; *m* 1964; one *d*. BSc Wales 1957, PhD Wales 1961. Tutorial Asst, Univ. Coll., Aberystwyth, 1960–62; Asst Lectr, Magee Univ. Coll., Londonderry, 1962–65; Lectr, Magee Univ. Coll., Londonderry, 1965–68. Rep., Nat. Cttee for Adult Educn, 1972; Mem., O and A GCE Syllabus Cttee, 1970–72. *Publications*: *contrib.* Amer. Jl Sci., Geol. Jl, Geol. Mag., Proc. Royal Irish Acad. *Address*: School of Biological and Environmental Studies, The New Univ. of Ulster, Coleraine, Co Londonderry BT52 1SA

Roberts, John Metham; Lecturer, Department of German, University of Glasgow, since 1967; *b* 1939; *m* 1972. BA Oxford 1961, MA Oxford 1965. Asst, Glasgow Univ.,

1964–67. *Address*: Dept of German, The Univ., Glasgow G12 8QL.

Roberts, John Morris; Fellow and Tutor in Modern History, Merton College, Oxford University, since 1954; *b* 1928; *m* 1964; one *s* two *d*. BA Oxon 1949, MA Oxon 1953, DPhil Oxon 1954; FRHistSoc. Prize Fellow, Magdalen Coll., Oxford, 1951–53; Commonwealth Fund Fellow, Princeton and Yale, 1953–54; Vis. Prof., Univ. of S Carolina, 1961; Mem., Inst. Adv. Studies, Princeton, 1960. Sen. Proctor, Oxford Univ., 1967–68; Acting Warden, Merton Coll., 1970–71; Editor, English Historical Rev. *Publications*: ed, French Revolution Documents, vol. I, 1966; Europe 1880–1945, 1967, rev. edn 1968; Gen. Ed., History of the Twentieth Century (partwork), 1967–69; The Mythology of the Secret Societies, 1972; The Paris Commune from the Right, 1973; *contrib.* Inst. Hist. Res., EHR, Rev. d'Hist. Mod. Contemp., Trans RHistS. *Address*: Merton College, Oxford.

Roberts, Joyce Esmee; Lecturer, Social Administration Department, University of Edinburgh, since 1967; *b* 1930. Dipl. in Psychiatric Social Work, Edinburgh, 1963, MSc (Social Science) Edinburgh, 1972. Associate: Assoc. of Psychiatric Social Workers, 1963; Inst. of Organisational Analysis; Mem.: British Assoc. of Social Workers, 1968; Assoc. of Teachers in Social Work Educn, 1967; Scottish Inst. of Human Relations; Inst. for Treatment and Study of Delinquency, 1960; Race Relations Bd (Scottish Conciliation Cttee), 1971; Community Relations Commn (Edinburgh Cttee), 1971; Scottish Council on Crime, 1972. *Address*: Dept of Social Administration, Univ. of Edinburgh, Adam Ferguson Building, George Square, Edinburgh EH8 9LL.

Roberts, Kenneth, BSc(Soc), MSc(Econ); Lecturer, Department of Sociology, University of Liverpool, since 1966; *b* 1940; *m* 1964; one *s* two *d*. BSc(Soc) London 1964, MSc(Econ) London 1966; Mem., British Sociol. Assoc. *Publications*: Leisure, 1970; (with T. Lane) Strike at Pilkingtons, 1971; From School to Work, 1972; (with G. E. White and H. J. Parker) The Character-Training Industry, 1974; *contrib.* Comp. Educn, Soc. Econ. Admin., Sociol. Rev. *Address*: Dept of Sociology, Univ. of Liverpool, Liverpool L69 3BX.

Roberts, Prof. Mark, MA; Professor of English, and Head of Department of English, The Queen's University of Belfast, since 1968; *b* 1923; two *s*. BA Cantab 1949 (1st cl. English), MA Cantab 1951. Supervisor in English, Gonville and Caius Coll., Cambridge, 1949, Acting Dir of Studies, 1950; Asst Lectr, King's Coll., London, 1952–54; Asst Lectr, Sheffield Univ., 1954, Lectr, 1955–64, Sen. Lectr, 1964–68. Sub-Dean, Fac. of Arts, Sheffield, 1962–65; Rep. of Sheffield Univ. on North. Univs Jt Matric. Bd, 1967–68; Mem., Bd, Arts Council NI, 1971– . *Publications*: Browning's Men and Women, 1966; The Tradition of Romantic Morality, 1973; The Fundamentals of Literary Criticism (forthcoming); *contrib.*

Engl. Studies, Ess. Crit., Notes Queries. *Address*: Dept of English Language and Literature, The Queen's Univ. of Belfast, Belfast BT7 1NN.

Roberts, Dr Peter Raymond; Lecturer in History, Faculty of Humanities, University of Kent at Canterbury, since 1969; *b* 1939. BA Wales 1960 (1st cl. History), MA Wales 1963, MA Cantab 1965, PhD Cantab 1966; FSA, FRHistS. Fellow and Sen. Fellow, Univ. of Wales, 1962–64, 1964–65; Fellow, Corpus Christi Coll., Cambridge, 1965–68; Lectr, Westfield Coll., Univ. of London, 1968–69. *Publications*: The Tudor Union of England and Wales (forthcoming); *contrib.* Camd. Misc., Jl Nat. Libr. Wales, Trans Royal Hist. Soc. *Address*: Keynes College, Univ. of Kent, Canterbury CT2 7ND.

Roberts, Dr Philip Edward, MA; Lecturer in English Literature, University of Sheffield, since 1974; *b* 1942; *m* 1969. BA Oxon 1963, MA Oxon 1967; PhD Edinburgh 1967; Mem., Engl. Assoc. Lectr in English Literature, Univ. of Newcastle upon Tyne, 1965–73. *Publications*: Swift's Poetry, in, Swift, 1969; Mirabell and Restoration Comedy, in, Congreve, 1972; ed, Dryden: Poems, 1973; The Diary of Sir David Hamilton 1710–1714 (forthcoming); *contrib.* Jl RCP, Mod. Lang. Rev., Notes Queries, Phil. Qly. *Address*: School of English, The Univ., Sheffield S10 2TN.

Roberts, Robert Owen, MA; Senior Lecturer in Economics, University College of Swansea, since 1958; *b* 1917; *m* 1946; two *d*. BA Wales 1939 (1st cl. Econ.), CertEd 1940, MA Wales 1942; Mem., Royal Econ. Soc., Mem., Econ. Hist. Soc., Mem., Cymmrod. Soc. Asst Lectr, Univ. Coll., Swansea, 1946–48, Lectr, Univ. Coll., Swansea, 1948–58. Royal Inst. Internat. Aff., 1942–43; Res. Dept, Foreign Off., 1943–45; Ind. Mem., Min. of Employment Wages Councils (Engl. and Wales), 1962– . *Publications*: Robert Owen Y Dre Newydd, 1948; ed, Trafodion Economaidd 1953–56, 1957; ed jtly, Trafodion Economaidd a Chymdeithasol 1956–1963, 1966; Farming in Caernarvonshire around 1800, 1973; *contrib.* Bank. Mag., Business Hist., Cymmrod Trans, Economica, Manch. Sch., NLW Jl., Politico, S Wales Record Soc. Publicns, Welsh Hist. Rev., Woolwich Econ. Publicns. *Address*: Dept of Economics, Univ. College of Swansea, Singleton Park, Swansea SA2 8PP.

Roberts, Simon Arthur; Lecturer in Law, London School of Economics and Political Science, University of London, since 1968; *b* 1941; *m* 1965; one *s* one *d*. LLB London 1962, PhD London 1968. Lectr in Law, Nyasaland Inst. of Public Admin, 1963–64; Tutorial Fellow, LSE, 1964–65, Asst Lectr, 1965–68. Advr on Customary Law, Govt of Botswana, 1968–71. *Publications*: Tswana Family Law (Restatement of African Law Series), 1972; *contrib.* Jl Afr. Law. *Address*: London School of Economics and Political Science, Houghton Street, WC2A 2AE.

Roberts, Prof. Tom Aerwyn, MA, DPhil; Professor and Head of Department of

Philosophy, University College of Wales, Aberystwyth, since 1969; *b* 1924; *m* 1956; two *s* three *d*. BA Wales 1950 (1st cl. Philos.), BA Oxon 1952 (2nd cl. Theology), MA Oxon 1957, DPhil Oxon 1957. Lectr, Univ. of Keele, 1954–61; Lectr, then Sen. Lectr, Univ. Coll. of Wales, Aberystwyth, 1961–69. Editor, Efryd. Athron., 1968– . Dean, Fac. of Arts, Univ. Coll. of Wales, 1970–72. *Publications*: History and Christian Apologetic, 1960; ed, J. Butler: Fifteen Sermons, 1970; The Concept of Benevolence, 1973; *contrib.* Ch Qly Rev., Efryd. Athron., Hibb. Jl, Jl Theol. Studies, Mod. Chman, Relig. Studies. *Address*: Dept of Philosophy, Univ. College of Wales, Aberystwyth SY23 2AX.

Robertson, Alexander Gibson, MA; Director, Department of Extra-Mural Education, University of Dundee, since 1967; *b* 1918; *m* 1949; two *d*. MA St Andrews 1940 (Latin, Greek), MA St Andrews 1948 (1st cl. German Lang. and Lit.). Lectr in German, Univ. of St Andrews, 1948–63; Dir of Extra-Mural Studies, 1963–67. Governor, Newbattle Abbey Coll., 1967– . *Publications*: *contrib.* Scott. Adult Educn, Studies Adult Educn, Museums Jl. *Address*: Dept of Extra-Mural Education, The Univ., Dundee DD1 4HN.

Robertson, Alexander James; Lecturer in Economic History, Department of History, University of Manchester, since 1969; *b* 1941; *m* 1966; one *s* one *d*. MA Glasgow 1963, MA British Columbia 1965. Teaching Asst, Dept of History, Univ. of BC, Vancouver, 1963–64; Res. Asst in Bus. History, Dept of Econ. Hist., Univ. of Glasgow, 1964–66; Asst Lectr in Econ. History, Dept of Hist., Univ. of Manchester, 1966–69. *Publications*: Robert Owen, Cotton Spinner: New Lanark, 1799–1829, in, Robert Owen: Prophet of the Poor, ed S. Pollard and J. Salt, 1971; *contrib.* Bus. Hist. *Address*: Dept of History, Univ. of Manchester, Manchester M13 9PL.

Robertson, Prof. Anne Strachan; Titular Professor of Roman Archaeology since 1974, and Keeper of the Cultural Collections and of the Hunter Coin Cabinet, Hunterian Museum, University of Glasgow, since 1964. MA Glasgow (1st cl. Hons Classics), MA London (Archaeol. of Roman Empire), DLitt, Glasgow 1965; FRNS 1937, FSAScot 1941, FSA 1958, FMA 1958, Correspond. Mem. Amer. Numismatic Soc. 1950. Dalrymple Lectr in Archaeology, 1939, Reader in Roman Archaeology, 1964, Glasgow Univ.; Under-Keeper, Hunterian Museum, and Curator, Hunter Coin Cabinet, 1952. Mem., Ancient Monuments Bd for Scotland, 1962; Mem., Bd of Trustees, Nat Museum of Antiquites, Edinburgh, 1954. *Publications*: The Hunterian Museum: Handbook to the Cultural Collections, including the Roman Collections, 1954; An Antonine Fort: Golden Hill, Duntocher, 1957; The Antonine Wall, 1960, 5th edn, 1973; Sylloge of Anglo-Saxon Coins in the Hunter Coin Cabinet, 1961; Roman Imperial Coins in the Hunter Coin Cabinet: vol. 1, Augustus to Nerva, 1962, vol. 2, Trajan to Commodus, 1971, vol. 3, Pertinax to Aemilian (forthcoming); The Roman Fort at Castledykes, 1964; Excavations at Birrens, 1974; *contrib.* Britannia, Glasgow

596

Archaeol Jl, Proc. Soc. Antiquaries of Scotland, Numismatic Chronicle. *Address*: Hunterian Museum, Univ. of Glasgow, Glasgow G12 8QQ.

Robertson, Charles James Alan; Lecturer in Modern History, University of St Andrews, since 1965; *b* 1939; *m* 1970. MA St Andrews 1964 (1st cl. Mod. Hist. and Pol Econ.), AM Pennsylvania 1965 (Econ. Hist.). Thouron Schol., Univ. of Pennsylvania, 1964–65. *Address*: Dept of Modern History, St Salvator's College, St Andrews, Fife KY16 9PH.

Robertson, Prof. Charles Martin, FBA; Lincoln Professor of Classical Archaeology and Art, University of Oxford, and Fellow of Lincoln College, since 1961; *b* 1911; *m* 1942; four *s* two *d*. BA Cantab 1934, MA Cantab 1947; FBA 1967. Asst Keeper, Dept of Greek and Roman Antiquities, British Museum, 1936–48 (released for War service, 1940–46); Yates Prof. of Classical Art and Archaeology, Univ. Coll., London, 1948–61. Mem., German Archaeological Inst., 1953; Chm. Man. Cttee, British Sch. at Athens, 1958–68; Mem., Inst. for Advanced Study, Princeton, 1968–69. *Publications*: Why Study Greek Art? (inaugural lecture), 1949; Greek Painting, 1959; The Visual Arts of the Greeks, in, The Greeks, 1962; Between Archaeology and Art History (inaugural lecture), 1963; Crooked Connections (poems), 1970; indexes and editorial work, Beazley: Paralipomena, 1971; For Rachel (poems), 1972; A History of Greek Art, 1974; (with Alison Frantz) The Parthenon Frieze, 1974; *contrib.* British and foreign jls. *Address*: Lincoln College, Oxford.

Robertson, Esmonde Manning; Lecturer in International History, London School of Economics, since 1970; *b* 1923; *m* 1963; one *s*. MA Hons Edinburgh 1950 (Hist.). QUB, 1962–63; Univ. of Edinburgh, 1963–70. *Publications*: Hitler's Pre-War Policy and Military Plans, 1963; L'Europa e l'avvento di Hitler, 1933–34, in, L'Europa fra le due Guerre, Turin, 1966; Mussolini and Ethiopia: The Prehistory of the Rome Agreements, in, Studies in Diplomatic History, 1970; ed, Origins of the Second World War: Historical Interpretations, 1971; *contrib.* Vierteljahrshefte für Zeitgeschichte. *Address*: Dept of International History, London Sch. of Economics, Houghton Street, WC2A 2AE.

Robertson, Frederick; Senior Lecturer, Department of Classics, University of Reading, since 1969; *b* 1927; *m* 1953; one *s* three *d*. MA Aberdeen 1949, BA Cantab 1953; Sec. Virgil Soc. Asst Lectr, Univ. Reading, 1954; Vis. Prof., Pennsylvania State Univ., 1968–69. Warden, Windsor Hall, Univ. of Reading, 1974– . Asst Principal, Air Min., 1953. *Publications*: *contrib.* Bull. Inst. of Class. Studies, Class. Philol., Proc. Class. Assoc., Proc. Virgil Soc., Trans Amer. Philol Assoc. *Address*: Dept of Classics, Univ. of Reading, Whiteknights, Reading RG6 2AH.

Robertson, Giles Henry, MA; Watson Gordon Professor of Fine Art, University of Edinburgh, since 1972; *b* 1913; *m* 1943; four *s*

one *d*. BA Oxon 1936, MA Oxon 1947. Lectr, Univ. of Edinburgh, 1946–61, Sen. Lectr, 1961–68, Reader, 1968–72. Mem., Sch. of Hist. Studies, Inst. Adv. Study, Princeton, NJ, 1965–66. *Publications:* Vincenzo Catena, 1954; Giovanni Bellini, 1968; *contrib.* Burl. Mag., Jl Warb. Court. Insts. *Address:* Dept of Fine Art, Univ. of Edinburgh, Edinburgh EH8 9YL.

Robertson, James Joseph, MA, LLB, FSAScot; Senior Lecturer in Private Law, University of Dundee, since 1970; *b* 1932; *m* 1958; two *s* one *d*. MA St Andrews 1953 (History), LLB St Andrews 1956; Solicitor (Scotland), 1957, FSAScot. Warden, Peterson Hse, Univ. of Dundee, 1967, Sen. Advr of Studies, Fac. of Law, 1970. Mem., Cttee, Soc. Public Teachers of Law, 1967– ; Mem., Cttee, UK Nat. Cttee of Comp. Law, 1967– . *Publications: contrib.* Stair Soc. *Address:* Faculty of Law, The Univ., Dundee DD1 4HN.

Robertson, Jonathan Andrew; Lecturer in History of Art, University of Bristol, since 1966; *b* 1943; *m* 1966; two *s* one *d*. BA Manchester 1965, MA Manchester 1967. *Publications: contrib.* New Theatre Mag. *Address:* Dept of History of Art, The Univ., 93 Woodland Road, Bristol BS8 1US.

Robertson, Mary Forrest, MA, FIPM; Senior Lecturer, Department of Applied Social Science, University of Nottingham, since 1967; *b* 1914. MA Edinburgh 1935, Cert. Social Science, London 1936; FIPM 1950. Asst Lectr, Nottingham Univ., 1945–48, Lectr, 1948–67; Vis. Lectr, Duke Univ., 1960; Vis. Lectr, Univ. of Ghana, 1963; Vis. Lectr, Univ. of Zambia, 1967. Vice-Pres., IPM, 1954–56; Mem., Working Party on Mngmt Studies, 1958; Nottingham Council of Social Service Exec. Cttee, 1955– ; Mem. Bd of Visitors, Nottingham Prison, 1964– ; E Midland Race Relat. Conciliation Cttee, 1967– ; C of E Industrial Cttee, 1972. *Publications:* chapter, in, Management in the Textile Industry, 1969; *contrib.* Eng., Mngmt Dec., New Soc., Person. Mngmt. *Address:* Dept of Applied Social Science, Univ. of Nottingham, Nottingham NG7 2RD.

Robertson, Norman; Senior Tutor for the External Degree, Faculty of Urban and Regional Studies, University of Reading, since 1974; *b* 1925. BSc Aberdeen 1944, MA Aberdeen 1950, BLitt Oxford 1955. Asst Lectr, Bristol Univ., 1952–54; Lectr, 1954–66; Lectr, QUB, 1966–68, Sen. Lectr, 1968–73. *Publications:* (with J. L. Thomas) Trade Unions and Industrial Relations, 1968; (with K. I. Sams) British Trade Unionism: Select Documents, 1972. *Address:* Fac. of Urban and Regional Studies, Univ. of Reading, Whiteknights, Reading RG6 2AH.

Robertson, Seonaid Mairi; Deputy Head of Art Teacher Training Department, University of London, Goldsmiths' College, since 1960 (now part-time); *b* 1912. Dip. Design and Crafts Edinburgh 1936, ATD Edinburgh 1937; DipPsychol London 1948; Founder Mem., Brit. Soc. Aest., Founder Mem., Wld Craft Council, Mem., Soc. Educn Through Art, Mem., Internat. Soc. Educn Through Art, Mem., New Educn Fellowship, Mem., Wld Educn Fellowship, etc. Pt-time Res. Fellow, Leeds, 1953–54, Sen. Res. Fellow in Education, 1956–58; Vis. Prof., Univ. of Pennsylvania, 1965; Vis. Prof., Univ. of Washington, Seattle, 1970; Vis. Prof., Univ. of Pennsylvania, 1972. Mem., Council Soc. Educn Through Art, 1950–52; Brit. Rep. and Engl. Speaking Sec., European Cttee, INSEA; Pt-time Dir, Schs Council Res., Art and Craft for the Middle Years, 1969–71. *Publications:* Creative Crafts in Education, 1951; Craft and Contemporary Culture, 1961; Rosegarden and Labyrinth, 1963; Beginning at the Beginning with Clay; Dyes from Plants, 1972; *contrib.* var. articles, some trans. in Japanese, Portuguese, etc. *Address:* Univ. of London, Goldsmiths' College, SE14 6NW.

Robertson, Thomas; Senior Lecturer, Department of Accounting and Business Method, Edinburgh University, since 1972 (Lecturer, 1964–72); *b* 1926; *m* 1954; two *s*. FICA. Acting Hd of Dept, Edinburgh, 1966–67, 1971; Dir of Studies, 1971. Auditor, AUT (Edinburgh), 1968; Mem., Acctng Hist. Cttee for Scotland, 1971; Mem., Academic Bd, Scott. Business Sch. *Publications:* ed, A Pitman's Notebook – The Diary of Edward Smith, Houghton Colliery Viewer 1749–51, 1970; Introd., in, A Glossary of Terms Used in the Coal Trade ... 1888, 1970. *Address:* Dept of Accounting and Business Method, Univ. of Edinburgh, Edinburgh EH8 9YL.

Robertson, William, MA; Reader, Department of Economics, University of Liverpool, since 1965; *b* 1920; *m* 1951; two *d*. MA St Andrews 1947 (1st cl.). Asst Lectr, Liverpool, 1947–50, Lectr, 1950–59, Sen. Lectr, 1959–65. *Publications:* Report on World Tin Position, 1965; Welfare in Trust (A History of the Carnegie UK Trust, 1913–1963), 1965; *contrib.* Economica, Econ. Internaz., Oxf. Econ. Papers. *Address:* Dept of Economics, Univ. of Liverpool, Liverpool L69 3BX.

Robin, Gordon De Quetteville; Director, Scott Polar Research Institute, University of Cambridge, since 1958; *b* 1921; *m* 1953; two *d*. BSc Melbourne 1940 (Physics), MSc Melbourne 1942 (Physics); PhD Birmingham 1956 (Physics); MA Cambridge 1958 (Polar Studies); FInstP. Lectr, Univ. of Birmingham, 1948–49, 1952, 1956; ICI Res. Fellow, 1953–56; Sen. Fellow, Dept of Geophysics, Australian Nat. Univ., 1957–58. Naval Service, 1942–45; Lieut, RANVR; Falkland Is Dependencies Survey, 1946–48; Norwegian–Brit.–Swedish Antarctic Expedition, 1949–52 (Physicist and Sen. Brit. Mem.); Mem., Internat. Cttee for Geophysics (CIG), ICSU, 1959–63. Scientific Cttee on Antarctic Res. (SCAR), ICSU (UK Delegate), 1958– ; Sec., SCAR, 1958–70; Pres., SCAR, 1970– ; Editor, Ann. IGY, vol. 41: Glaciology. *Publications:* Scientific Reports of Norwegian–British–Swedish Antarctic Expedition, 1949–52; Glac. III Seismic Shooting and Related Investigations, 1958; *contrib.* Jl Glaciol., Nature, Phil. Trans (A) Royal Soc. *Address:* Scott Polar Research Institute, Cambridge CB2 1ER.

Robins, Dr David Lionel John; Senior Lecturer, Department of Town and Country Planning, University of Newcastle upon Tyne, since 1972 (Lecturer, 1963–72); *b* 1932; *m* 1971. BA Reading 1954 (Hons Geog.); PhD Southampton 1958; MRTPI 1960. Mem., East of Engl. Br. Cttee, Town Plan. Inst., 1959–61; Exams Bd, 1971– ; Warden, Hodgkin Hse, Newcastle Univ., 1967–72; Chm., Subfaculty of Fine Art, Architecture and Town and Country Planning, 1973– . *Publications*: Newcastle Warehouse Research Study, 1968; contrib. Rural Resource Development, 1974. *Address*: Dept of Town and Country Planning, The Univ., Newcastle upon Tyne NE1 7RU.

Robins, Ray; *see* Robins, W. R.

Robins, Prof. Robert Henry, MA, DLit; Professor of General Linguistics, University of London, since 1965; *b* 1921; *m* 1953. BA Oxon 1948 (1st cl. Lit. Hum.), MA 1948; DLit London 1968. Mem., Lingu. Soc. Amer., 1951– , Mem., Philol Soc., 1948– (Hon. Sec., 1961–). Lectr in Linguistics, SOAS, 1948–54; Reader in General Linguistics, Univ. of London, 1954–64; Res. Fellow, Univ. of California, 1951; Vis. Prof., Univ. of Washington, 1963; Vis. Prof., Univ. of Hawaii, 1968; Vis. Prof., Univ. of Minnesota, 1971. *Publications*: Ancient and Mediaeval Grammatical Theory in Europe, 1951; The Yurok Language, 1958; General Linguistics: an Introductory Survey, 1964, 2nd edn 1971; A Short History of Linguistics, 1967, 2nd edn 1970; Diversions of Bloomsbury: selected writings on Linguistics, 1971; Ideen- und Problemgeschichte der Sprachwissenschaft, 1973; *contrib.* Bull. SOAS, Canad. Jl Lingu., Found. Lang., Internat. Jl Amer. Lingu., Lang., Lingua, Trans Philol. Soc. *Address*: School of Oriental and African Studies, Univ. of London, WC1E 7HP.

Robins, William Raymond; Lecturer in Personnel Administration, Management Centre, University of Aston in Birmingham, since 1958; *b* 1925. BA Durham 1949, DipEd Durham 1950, Dip. Management Studies, Polytechnic of Central London, 1956; MIPM 1956. *Address*: Management Centre, Univ. of Aston in Birmingham, Birmingham B4 6TE.

Robinson, Adrian H. W.; Reader, Department of Geography, Leicester University, since 1969; *b* 1925; *m* 1951; one *s* one *d*. MSc London 1951, PhD London 1962; FIN 1963, FRGS. Asst Lectr, 1949–52, Lectr, 1952–69, Univ. of Leicester. *Publications*: Marine Cartography, 1962; Map Studies, 1970; The Lake District, 1970; The South West Peninsula, 1971; The West Midlands, 1971; The South East, 1971; The Welsh Marches, 1971; Cumbria, 1972; *contrib.* Geog. Jl, Inst. Navig. Jl, Proc. Geol. Assoc. *Address*: Geography Dept, Univ. of Leicester, Leicester LE1 7RH.

Robinson, Alan; Lecturer, Division of Community Studies, New University of Ulster's Institute of Continuing Education, since 1973; *b* 1940; *m* 1965; one *s*. BA Hull 1962 (special), CertEd Exeter 1963, MA

QUB 1967; Mem. Geographical Assoc. Mem. Inst. Brit. Geogrs, Mem. CAMRA. Magee University Coll., 1965–73. *Publications*: (jtly) Simulation Games for Geographers, 1972; Correlations in Geography, 1972; Networks in Geography, 1973; *contrib.* Irish Geog. Mag., Scottish Geog. Mag., New Era, Where. *Address*: Institute of Continuing Education, Magee Univ. Coll. Londonderry, N Ireland.

Robinson, Prof. Alan Ronald; Professor of German, and Head of the German, Swedish and Russian Department, University College of Wales, Aberystwyth, since 1971; *b* 1920. BA London 1944 (1st cl. German); DipEd Oxon 1945; PhD Edinburgh 1950; BA London 1966 (Swedish as Additional Subject). Asst Master, Merchant Taylors' Sch., 1945–46; Haberdashers' Aske's, 1946–47; Insp., German Sect., Foreign Off., 1947–48. Res. Award, Univ. of Edinburgh, 1948–50; Lectr in German and Swedish, Univ. Coll. of Wales, Aberystwyth, 1950–67; Vis. Prof. of German, McGill Univ., Montreal, 1963; Prof. of German, Univ. of Guelph, Ontario, 1967–71. *Publications*: ed, Fontane: Grete Minde, 1955, 2nd edn 1960; ed, A. Goes: Das Brandopfer, 1957; ed, Zuckmayer: Der Seelenbräu, 1959; *contrib.* Germ. Life Lett., Mod. Lang. Rev., Mod. Langs. *Address*: Dept of German, Swedish and Russian, Univ. College of Wales, Aberystwyth SY23 2AX.

Robinson, Christopher Frank; Official Student and Tutor in Modern Languages, Christ Church, Oxford, since 1971; *b* 1942; *m* 1970. BA Hons Oxon 1964, MA 1967. Lectr in French Studies, Univ. of Lancaster, 1966–71. Membre du Conseil International pour l'édition des Œuvres d'Erasme, 1971– . *Publication*: Luciani Dialogi, in, Erasmi Opera Omnia, vol. I. (i), 1969. *Address*: Christ Church, Oxford.

Robinson, Prof. Colin, BA(Econ), FSS; Professor of Economics, Department of Economics, University of Surrey, since 1968; *b* 1932; *m* 1957; two *s*. BA(Econ) Manchester 1957 (1st cl.); FSS; Mem., Soc. Business Econ., Manchester Stat. Soc. Economist, Procter & Gamble Ltd, 1957–60; Hd of Econ. Div., Esso Petrol. Co., 1960–66; Econ. Advr, Natural Gas, Esso Europe, 1966–68; Mem., Council, Soc. Business Econ., 1961–71; Edit. Bd, App. Econs, 1968– , Energy Policy, 1973– . *Publications*: A Policy for Fuel, 1969; Competition for Fuel, 1970; Business Forecasting: an economic approach, 1971; *contrib.* Brit. Jl Mktg, Business Econ., Jl Indust. Econ., Jl Inst. Fuel, Nat. West. Bank Rev. *Address*: Dept of Economics, Univ. of Surrey, Stag Hill, Guildford, Surrey GU2 5XH.

Robinson, David Beattie; BLitt, MA; Senior Lecturer in Greek, University of Edinburgh, since 1972; *b* 1935; *m* 1968. BA Oxon 1956, BLitt MA Oxon 1962. Lectr, St John's Coll., Oxford, 1957–58; Lectr in Greek, Univ. of Edinburgh, 1958–72; Fellow, Center for Hellenic Studies, Washington, DC, 1966–67; Vis. Lectr, Univ. of Illinois, 1969. *Publications*: *contrib.* Class. Qly.

598

Address: Dept of Greek, David Hume Tower, George Square, Edinburgh EH8 9JX.

Robinson, Prof. David Gray, MA, FRTPI; Professor of Regional Planning, Department of Town and Country Planning, University of Manchester, since 1969; *b* 1932; *m* 1958; one *s*. BA Durham 1955 (1st cl. Town and Country Planning), MA Manchester 1973; FRTPI. Lectr, Manchester Univ., 1959–66, Sen. Lectr, 1966–69. Planning Offr, Yorks W Riding and Lancs CC, 1955–59; Mem., Council, RTPI, 1965–67 (Mem., Educn Cttee, 1965–73); Mem., Construction Environ. Bd, CNAA, 1971– ; Mem., Town Plan. Subject Bd, 1966– . Mem., NERC Terrestrial Life Sciences Cttee, 1972– . *Publications*: (jtly) Regional Shopping Centres, 1964; Comprehensive Development, in, The Remoter Rural Areas of Britain, ed Ashton and Long, 1972. *Address*: Dept of Town and Country Planning, Univ. of Manchester, Manchester M13 9PL.

Robinson, Derek, MA; Senior Research Officer, Oxford University Institute of Economics and Statistics, since 1961, and Fellow, Magdalen College, Oxford, since 1969; Deputy Chairman of the Pay Board, since 1973; *b* 1932; *m* 1956; one *s* one *d*. DipEcon Pol Sci Oxon 1957, BA Oxon 1959 (1st cl. PPE), MA Oxon 1963; FREconS. Staff Tutor, Sheffield Univ., 1959–60; Lectr, Balliol Coll., Oxford, 1963–68; Vis. Prof., Univ. of California, Berkeley, 1968. Econ. Advr, NBPI, 1965–67; Sen. Econ. Advr, DEP, 1968–70. *Publications*: Non-Wage Incomes and Prices Policy, 1966; Wage Drift Fringe Benefits and Manpower Distribution, 1968; Workers' Negotiated Savings Plans for Capital Formation, 1970; ed, Local Labour Markets and Wage Structures, 1971; Incomes Policy and Capital Sharing in Europe, 1973; *contrib*. Bull. Oxf. Univ. Inst. Econ. Stats, Indust. Relat. *Address*: Institute of Economics and Statistics, St Cross Building, Manor Road, Oxford.

Robinson, Donald, DipPE; Lecturer in Physical Education, University of Leeds, since 1964; *b* 1927; *m* 1957; one *d*. Teachers Cert. Loughborough College 1946, DipPE Carnegie College 1961. Advr, Educnl Productions Ltd; Chm., Cave Leadership Training Bd. *Publications*: (with A. Greenbank) Caving and Potholing, 1964; Potholing and Caving, 1967; Cave Rescue, in, Manual of Caving Techniques, 1969; Caving, in, Hamlyn Illustrated Encyclopaedia, 1971. *Address*: Dept of Physical Education, Univ. of Leeds, Leeds LS2 9JT.

Robinson, Gordon Brian, BSc(Econ), MA; Senior Lecturer in Sociology, Department of Social Sciences, Loughborough University of Technology, since 1968; *b* 1928; *m* 1962; one *s* one *d*. BSc(Econ) London 1952, MA London 1966; CertEd London 1954, Acad. DipEd London 1956. Lectr in Sociology, Univ. of York, 1965–68; Vis. Prof. in Sociology, Dept of Pol Sci., Sociol., and Anthropol., Simon Fraser Univ., 1973–74. Mem., Senate, Loughborough, 1970–73; Mem., Council, Loughborough, 1971– . *Publications*: Private Schools and Public Policy, 1971; *contrib*. Jl

Social Econ. Admin. *Address*: Dept of Social Sciences, Loughborough Univ. of Technology, Loughborough, Leicestershire LE11 3TU.

Robinson, Guy Schuyler; Senior Lecturer, Department of Philosophy, Southampton University, since 1972 (Lecturer, 1958–72); *b* 1927; *m* 1954; one *s* two *d*. BA Bard College 1949; MA Harvard 1951. Asst Lectr, Leeds Univ., 1957–58. Hon. Sec., Mind Assoc., 1969. *Publications*: *contrib*. Analysis, Aristot. Soc. Supp. Vol., Mind, Ratio. *Address*: Dept of Philosophy, Univ. of Southampton, Southampton SO9 5NH.

Robinson, James Outram; Senior Lecturer in Psychology, University College, Cardiff, since 1970; *b* 1931; *m* 1959; two *s* one *d*. BSc Hull 1955; BSc London 1955; MSc Hull 1959; PhD London 1961; FBPsS 1970. DSIR Res. Asst, Dept of Psychology, Univ. of Hull, 1955–57; Mem., Scientific Staff, MRC, 1957–61; Lectr, UC Cardiff, 1961–70. *Publications*: The Psychology of Visual Illusions, 1972; *contrib*. Advancement of Science, Brit. Jl Psychol., Brit. Jl Soc. Clin. Psychol., Jl Preventive and Social Med., Jl Psychosom. Res. *Address*: Dept of Psychology, Univ. Coll., Cathays Park, Cardiff CF1 1XL.

Robinson, Julian; Lecturer in History, University of Nottingham, since 1968; *b* 1944. BA Oxon 1965, BPhil 1968. *Address*: Dept of History, Univ. of Nottingham, Nottingham NG7 2RD.

Robinson, Prof. Mary T. W., MA, LLB, LLM; Lecturer in European Law, Trinity College, since 1972; *b* 1944; *m* 1970; two *c*. BA Dublin 1967 (1st cl. Mod. in Legal Science), LLB Dublin 1967 (1st cl.), LLM Harvard 1968 (1st cl.), MA Dublin 1970; Barrister, King's Inns Dublin 1967 (1st cl.), and Middle Temple 1973. Mem. rep. Dublin Univ. in Irish Senate, 1969– ; Irish Legal Expert, Vedel Cttee on Instns of EEC, 1971; Mem., Jt Cttee on EEC Secondary Legislation, Irish Parlt; Mem., Select Cttee on Stat. Instruments, Irish Senate; Vice-Chm. Irish Council, European Movement; Exec. Council, Trinity Trust. *Publications*: *contrib*. Harv. Jl Internat. Law, Irish Jurist., Common Market Law Rev., Govt and Opp., Univ. W Aust. Law Rev., etc. *Address*: Dept of Law, Trinity College, Dublin 2.

Robinson, Dr Michael Finlay; Lecturer in Music, University College, Cardiff, since 1970; *b* 1933; *m* 1961; two *s*. BA Oxon 1956 (Hons Music), BMus Oxon 1957, MA Oxon 1960, DPhil Oxon 1963; Mem., Royal Musical Assoc. Lectr in Music, Durham Univ., 1961–65; Asst Prof. of Music, McGill Univ., 1965–67; Associate Prof. of Music, McGill, Univ., 1967–70. *Publications*: Opera before Mozart, 1966, 2nd edn 1972; Naples and Neapolitan Opera, 1972; *contrib*. Proc. Royal Musical Assoc., Res. Chron. of Royal Musical Assoc., Soundings. *Address*: Dept of Music, Univ. Coll. Cardiff CF1 1XL.

Robinson, Prof. Norman Hamilton Galloway, DD, DLitt; Professor of Divinity,

University of St Andrews, since 1967; *b* 1912; *m* 1936; two *s* two *d*. MA Glasgow 1935 (1st cl. Philosophy); BA Oxon 1936; BD Edinburgh 1939; DLitt. Glasgow 1948; Hon. DD Edinburgh 1964. Prof. of Divinity, Rhodes Univ., Grahamstown, SA, 1954–56; Prof. of Systematic Theology, Univ. of St Andrews, 1956–67. *Publications*: Faith and Duty, 1950; The Claim of Morality, 1952; Christ and Conscience, 1956; The Groundwork of Christian Ethics, 1971; *contrib*. Expos. Times, Hibb. Jl, Jl Theol. Studies, Philos. Qly, Philos., Relig. Studies, Scott. Jl Theol., Theol. *Address*: St Mary's College, The Univ., St Andrews, Fife.

Robinson, Dr Olivia Fiona; Lecturer in Civil Law, University of Glasgow, since 1968; *b* 1938; *m* 1960; one *s* one *d*. BA Oxon 1960, MA Oxon 1964; PhD London 1965. Asst Lectr, Univ. of Glasgow, 1966–68. *Publications*: *contrib*. RIDA. *Address*: Dept of Civil Law, Univ. of Glasgow, Glasgow G12 8QQ.

Robinson, Philip Elwyn John; Lecturer in French Literature, University of Kent at Canterbury, since 1967; *b* 1940. LLCM 1957, BA Wales 1962; Treas., Brit. Soc. for 18th Century Studies; Mem., Soc. for French Studies. *Publications*: *contrib*. Stud. on Voltaire and the 18th C, Yr's Wk in Mod. Lang. Stud. *Address*: Keynes College, Univ. of Kent at Canterbury, Canterbury, Kent.

Robinson, Dr Richard Alan Hodgson; Lecturer in Modern History, University of Birmingham, since 1968; *b* 1940. BA Oxon 1962, MA, DPhil Oxon 1968; FRHistS. Asst Lectr, Birmingham Univ., 1965–68. *Publication*: The Origins of Franco's Spain, 1970. *Address*: School of History, Univ. of Birmingham, PO Box 363, Birmingham B15 2TT.

Robinson, Prof. Ronald Edward, CBE, DFC; Beit Professor of the History of the British Commonwealth, University of Oxford, and Fellow of Balliol College, since 1971; *b* 1920; *m* 1948; two *s* two *d*. BA Cantab 1946, PhD Cantab 1949. Lectr, Cambridge Univ., 1953–66; Smuts Reader, Cambridge Univ., 1966–71; Tutor, St John's Coll., Cambridge, 1961–66, Fellow, Cambridge, 1949–71; Inst. for Advanced Studies, Princeton, 1959–60. RAF 1943–45; Res. Officer, African Studies Br., Colonial Office, 1947–49. Mem., Bridges Cttee on Trng in Public Admin, 1961–62; Chm., Cambridge Confs on Problems of Developing Countries, 1961–70. *Publications*: Africa and the Victorians, 1961; Developing the Third World, 1971; articles in Cambridge History of the British Empire, vol. III, 1959, and The New Cambridge Modern History, vol. XI, 1963; reports; *contrib*. learned jls. *Address*: Balliol College, Oxford.

Robson, Dr Brian Turnbull; Lecturer, Department of Geography, University of Cambridge, since 1967; *b* 1939. BA Cantab 1961, MA Cantab 1964, PhD Cantab 1965. Asst Lectr, Univ. Coll. of Wales, Aberystwyth, 1964–66, Lectr, 1966–67; Harkness Fellow, Commonwealth Fund, Univ. of Chicago, 1967–68; Fellow, Fitzwilliam Coll.,

Cambridge, 1968; Tutor for Admissions, 1973– . Editor, Area, 1971–74; Editor, Trans Inst. Brit. Geogrs, 1974– . Mem., Council, Inst. Brit. Geogrs, 1971– . *Publications*: Urban Analysis, 1969; Urban Growth, 1974; *contrib*. Urb. Studies. *Address*: Dept of Geography, Univ. of Cambridge, Downing Place, Cambridge.

Robson, Charles Alan; Reader in French Philology and Old French Literature, Oxford University, since 1972, and Fellow of Merton College, Oxford, since 1965; *b* 1915; *m* 1945. BA Oxon 1936, BLitt, MA Oxon 1941; Leverhulme Fellow, 1958. Lectr, Univ. Coll. of N Wales, Bangor, 1939–48; Senior Lectr in French Philology and Old French Lit., Oxford Univ., 1948–72; Sen. Tutor, Merton Coll., 1971–72. Sec., Anglo-Norman Text Soc., 1965–74. *Publications*: Maurice of Sully and the Medieval Vernacular Homily, 1952; *contrib*. Moyen Age, Rev. Lingu. Rom.; Romance Philol., Trans Philol. Soc. *Address*: Merton College, Oxford.

Robson, Prof. Sir Hugh (Norwood), Kt; MB, ChB, FRCP, FRCPE, FRACP; Principal, University of Edinburgh, since 1974; *b* 1917; *m* 1942; one *s* two *d*. Lectr, Dept of Medicine, Univ. of Edinburgh, 1947–50; Sen. Lectr, Dept of Medicine, Univ. of Aberdeen, 1950–53; Prof. of Medicine, Univ. of Adelaide, S Australia, 1953–65, Prof. Emeritus, 1965; Vice-Chancellor, Univ. of Sheffield, 1966–74. Trustee, Nuffield Provincial Hosps Trust, 1966– ; Mem., Inter-Univ. Council for Higher Educn Overseas, 1967– ; Mem., British Cttee of Award for Harkness Fellowships (Commonwealth Fund), 1968– , Chm., 1975– ; Mem., Special Steels Div. Adv. Bd, BSC, 1970– ; Chm., Central Cttee on Postgraduate Medical Educn, GB, 1968–70 (Mem., 1967); Chm., Council for Postgraduate Med. Educn in England and Wales, 1970–72; Mem., Northwick Park Adv. Cttee, 1971– ; Chm., Adv. Council on the Misuse of Drugs, 1971– ; Mem., UN University Founding Cttee, 1973; Chm., Cttee of Vice-Chancellors and Principals of Univs of UK, 1972–74 (Vice-Chm., 1970–71). *Publications*: Papers on Haematological and other subjects in Brit., Amer. and Aust. med. jls. *Address*: Principal's Office, Univ. of Edinburgh, Old College, South Bridge, Edinburgh EH8 9YL.

Robson, Robert; Fellow, Trinity College, Cambridge, since 1956; *b* 1929. MA 1957, PhD 1956, Cantab. Asst in Modern History, Univ. of Glasgow, 1956–57; Tutor for Advanced Students, Trinity Coll., Cambridge, 1960–64; Tutor, 1964–74. *Publications*: The Attorney in 18th Century England, 1959; ed, Ideas and Institutions of Victorian Britain, 1967. *Address*: Trinity Coll., Cambridge.

Robson, Prof. William Wallace, MA; Masson Professor of English Literature, University of Edinburgh, since 1972; *b* 1923; *m* 1962; two *s*. BA Oxon 1944 (1st cl. English), MA Oxon 1948. Asst Lectr, King's Coll., London, 1944–46; Lectr, Lincoln and The Queen's Colls, Oxford, 1946–48; Fellow, Lincoln Coll., 1948–70; Prof. of English,

Univ. of Sussex, 1970–72; Vis. Prof., Univ. of S California, 1953; Vis. Prof., Adelaide Univ., 1956; Vis. Prof., Univ. of Delaware, 1963–64; Elizabeth Drew Prof., Smith Coll., USA, 1968–69. *Publications*: Critical Essays, 1966; The Signs Among Us, 1968; Modern English Literature, 1970. *Address*: Dept of English Literature, Univ. of Edinburgh, Edinburgh EH8 9YL.

Roca, Ignacio Martínez; Lecturer in Spanish, Language Centre, University of Essex, since 1974 (Instructor, then Senior Instructor, 1969–74); *b* 1941. Lic en Derecho Santiago (Spain) 1963, Lic en Filología Románica Barcelona 1966, MA Essex 1972 (Linguistics); Mem., Assoc. Brit. Hispan., Mem., Ling. Assoc. of GB. Prof. Ayudante, Dept of Spanish Lit., Univ. of Barcelona, 1966; Lector, Dept of Spanish, Univ. of Durham, 1967. *Address*: Language Centre, Univ. of Essex, Colchester, Essex CO4 3SQ.

Roche, Prof. Kennedy Francis; Professor of the History of Political Theory, University College, Cork, since 1974; *b* 1911; *m* 1955; three *s*. BA NUI 1938 (1st cl. Hons), MA NUI 1943 (1st cl. Hons). Part-time Demonstrator, Dept of History, NUI, 1948–52; Full-time Asst, 1952–62; Statutory Lectr, 1962–74. *Publications*: Revolution and Counterrevolution, in Daniel O'Connell: Centenary Essays, 1949; The Relations of the Catholic Church and the State in England and Ireland, 1800–51, in, Historical Studies III, 1960; Rousseau: Stoic and Romantic, 1974. *Address*: Univ. Coll., Cork, Cork.

Rock, Dr Paul Elliot; Lecturer, Sociology Department, London School of Economics, since 1967; *b* 1943; *m* 1965; two *s*. BSc(Soc) London 1964, DPhil Oxon 1970. *Publications*: Deviant Behaviour, 1973; Making People Pay, 1973; *contrib*. Brit. Jl Sociol., Sociol., Brit. Jl Criminol. *Address*: London Sch. of Economics, Houghton Street, Aldwych, WC2A 2AE.

Rockett, Kenneth, MA; Director, Institute of Education, University of Newcastle upon Tyne, since 1972; *b* 1917; *m* 1945; one *s* one *d*. BA Manchester 1938 (1st cl. French Studies), MA Manchester 1939, DipEd Manchester 1940. Teaching Appt, Woodhouse Grove Sch., Bradford, 1940; Teaching Appt, Percy Jackson Grammar Sch., Doncaster, 1942, Hd of Mod. Langs Dept, 1944–53; Lectr in Educn, King's Coll., Newcastle, 1953–66; Asst Dir (BEd), Inst. of Educn, Newcastle Univ., 1966–72. Mem., UCET Standing Cttee A and BEd Sub-Cttee, 1967– ; Mem., var. sch. and coll. of educn gov. bodies. *Publications*: *contrib*. Educn Papers (King's Coll., Newcastle), Jl Univ. Newcastle Durh. Insts Educn, Mod. Lang. Rev., Prax. Neusprach. Unterr. *Address*: Univ. Institute of Education, St Thomas' Street, Newcastle upon Tyne NE1 7RU.

Rockwell, Joan; Lecturer, Department of Sociology, University of Reading; *b* 1919; *m* 1941 (marr. diss. 1958); two *s*. BA Chicago 1940. *Publications*: Fact in Fiction: the use of literature in the systematic study of society, 1974; *contrib*. Jl Peasant Studies.

Address: Dept of Sociology, Univ. of Reading, Whiteknights, Reading RG6 2AH.

Roderick, Dr Gordon Wynne; Senior Assistant Director, Institute of Extension Studies, University of Liverpool, since 1970; *b* 1930; *m* 1956; two *s*. BSc Hons Wales 1952 (2nd cl. Phys.), PhD London 1957, MA Liverpool 1971; MInstP 1957. Lectr in Science, Dept of Extra-Mural Studies, Univ. of Liverpool, 1962–70. *Publications*: Emergence of a Scientific Society in England, 1800–1965, 1967; Man and Heredity, 1968; (ed, with M. D. Stephens), Teaching Techniques in Adult Education 1971; (with M. D. Stephens) Scientific and Technical Education in England in the Nineteenth Century, 1973; *contrib*. Ann. Sc., BJES, Paed. Hist., Irish Jl Ed., Voc. Aspects Ed., Bull. Hist. Ed. Soc., Technik Geschichte. *Address*: Inst. of Extension Studies, Abercromby Square, Liverpool.

Rodger, Dr Gillian Burns Begg, MA, PhD; Senior Lecturer, Department of German, University of Glasgow, since 1965; *b* 1925. MA Glasgow 1947 (1st cl. French and German), PhD Glasgow 1952. Asst Lectr, Glasgow Univ., 1947–51; seconded Bedford Coll., London, 1949; Lectr, Glasgow, 1951–65. *Publications*: chapters, in German Men of Letters, vol. I, 1961; The Romantic Period in Germany, 1970; Affinities, 1971; *contrib*. Comp. Lit., Germ. Life Lett., Mod. Lang. Rev. *Address*: Dept of German, Univ. of Glasgow, Glasgow G12 8QQ.

Rodger, (Lawrence) Allan (Forbes), BSc, BArch, RIBA; Senior Lecturer, Department of Architecture, University of Edinburgh, since 1968; *b* 1935; *m* 1960; two *s* one *d*. BSc(Eng) St Andrews 1957; BArch Dunelm 1960; ARIBA 1963. Lectr, Duncan of Jordanstone Coll. of Art, Dundee, 1965–68; Sen. Lectr, Univ. of Khartoum, 1968–71. Asst Archit., 1960–64; Principal in private practice, 1964–68. *Publications*: contrib. papers to conf., The Human Environment and Development in Arab Countries, Khartoum, 1972. *Address*: Dept of Architecture, Faculty of Social Science, Univ. of Edinburgh, Edinburgh EH8 9YL.

Rodger, Prof. Leslie William; Professor and Head of Department of Business Organisation, Heriot-Watt University, since 1974; *b* 1926; *m* 1957; one *s* two *d*. BScEcon London 1947; MInstM 1957, MMS 1957 (Chm., Management Cttee, 1971–72), MBIM 1973. Marketing Manager, McCann-Erickson Ltd, 1955–60, Marketing Director, 1960–65; Management Consultant (private practice), 1965–69; General Manager, Central Marketing Services Division of Mullard Ltd, 1969–74. *Publications*: Marketing in a Competitive Economy, 1965, 4th edn 1974 (Japanese trans. 1973); Marketing Concepts and Strategies in the Next Decade, 1973. *Address*: Heriot-Watt Univ., Chambers Street, Edinburgh EH1 1HX.

Rodgers, Dr Eamonn Joseph, MA, PhD; Lecturer in Spanish, Trinity College, Dublin, since 1966; *b* 1941; *m* 1965; two *s*. BA Queen's University Belfast 1963 (1st cl. Mod.

Langs); MA Dublin 1966; PhD Queen's University Belfast 1970. Jun. Lectr, TCD, 1963–66. *Publications*: ed with introd. and notes, B. Pérez Galdós: Tormento (forthcoming); *contrib*. Anal. Galdos., Bull. Hispan. Studies, Cuad. Hispanoamer., Forum Mod. Lang. Studies. *Address*: Dept of Spanish, Trinity College, Dublin 2, Republic of Ireland.

Rodgers, Prof. Harry Brian; Professor of Geography, University of Manchester, since 1971; *b* 1924; *m* 1948; one *d*. BA Manchester 1948 (1st cl. Geography), MA Manchester 1951. Asst Lectr, Manchester, 1948–51, Lectr, 1951–63; Sen. Lectr, Keele, 1963–65, Reader, 1965–70, Prof. of Social Geog., 1970–71. Mem., Sports Council, 1972– ; Chm., Sports Council Res. Adv. Study Gp, 1968– . *Publications*: (jtly) Regions of Britain: Lancashire, Cheshire and the Isle of Man, 1966; Pilot National Recreation Survey, Report 1, 1967; Report 2 (Regional Analysis), 1969; (jtly) Atlas of American Affairs, 1969; ed jtly, Leisure in the North West, 1972; (jtly) Regional Development in Britain, 1972; *contrib*. Econ. Geog., Town Plan. Rev., Trans Inst. Brit. Geogrs, Urb. Studies, etc. *Address*: Dept of Geography, Univ. of Manchester, Manchester M13 9PL.

Rodgers, Dr Valerie Ann, MA, PhD; Lecturer in Classics, Trinity College, Dublin, since 1965; *b* 1936; *m* 1965; two *s*. BA London 1957 (1st cl. Classics), MA Dublin 1962, PhD London 1964. Jun. Lectr in Classics, TCD, 1960–65. *Publications*: *contrib*. Class. Qly, Greek, Rom. Byz. Studies. *Address*: School of Classics, Trinity College, Dublin 2, Republic of Ireland.

Rodway, Allan Edwin; Reader in English, University of Nottingham, since 1964; *b* 1919; *m* 1946; two *d*. BA Cantab 1949, MA Cantab 1952; PhD Nottingham 1951. Lectr, Nottingham Univ., 1952–63; Vis. Prof., Univ. of Oregon, 1961; Vis. Prof., Univ. of Hofstra, 1968. *Publications*: Godwin and the Age of Transition, 1952; (with V. de S. Pinto) The Common Muse, 1957, pbk edn 1965; The Romantic Conflict, 1963; Science and Modern Writing, 1964; (with M. Bradbury) Two Poets (poems), 1967; Poetry of the 1930's, 1967; The Truths of Fiction, 1971; ed, Midsummer Night's Dream, 1969; *contrib*. Pelican Guide to English Literature; *contrib*. BBC, Brit. Jl Aesth., Comp. Lit., Comp. Lit. Studies, Ess. Crit., Listener, Lond. Mag., Times Lit. Supp., Twent. Cent., Univ. Qly, etc. *Address*: English Dept, The Univ., Nottingham NG7 2RD.

Roe, Alan Raymond; Lecturer in Economics, University of Warwick, since 1971; *b* 1942; *m* 1966; one *d*. BCom Leeds 1963, MA Wales 1966, MA Cantab 1970; FREconS. Jun. Res. Officer, UCW Aberystwyth, 1964–66; Res. Fellow, UC Dar es Salaam, 1966–68; Res. Officer, Dept of Applied Econs, Cambridge, 1968–71; Vis. Prof., Washington Univ. 1970. Consultant to World Employment Programme, Research Project in Sri Lanka, 1973. *Publications*: (with J. I. Round and E. T. Nevin) The Structure of the Welsh Economy, 1966; The

Financial Interdependence of the Economy, vol. II, in, A Programme of Growth, ed R. Stone, 1971; *contrib*. E African Econs Rev., Econ. Jl, Jl Mod. African Studies, Oxford Bull. Econs and Statistics. *Address*: Dept of Economics, Univ. of Warwick, Coventry CV4 7AL.

Roe, Dr Derek Arthur, MA, PhD; University Lecturer in Prehistoric Archaeology, Department of Ethnology and Prehistory, University of Oxford, since 1965; *b* 1937; *m* 1964; one *s* one *d*. BA Cantab 1961 (1st cl. Archaeol. and Anthropol.), MA Cantab 1964; MA Oxon 1965 (by incorporation); PhD Cantab 1968. Fellow, St Cross Coll., Oxford, 1970. Sec., Palaeol. and Mesol. Res. Cttee, Council for Brit. Archaeol., 1965– ; Mem., Council, Prehist. Soc., 1966–68, 1970–72; Mem., Editorial Bd, Wld Archaeol., 1968– , Exec. Editor, 1969–71; Governor, St Edward's Sch., 1970– . *Publications*: Gazetteer of British Lower and Middle Palaeolithic Sites, 1968; Prehistory: an Introduction, 1970, pbk edn 1971; *contrib*. Proc. Prehist. Soc., etc. *Address*: Dept of Ethnology and Prehistory, Univ. of Oxford, Pitt Rivers Museum, Oxford OX1 3PP.

Roe, Harry V. S.; *see* Stopes-Roe, H. V.

Roe, Rev. Dr William Gordon; Vice-Principal, St Chad's College, University of Durham, since 1969; *b* 1932; *m* 1953; two *s* two *d*. BA Oxon 1955 (2nd cl. Mod. Lang.), MA 1957, Dip. Theol. 1957 (with Distinct.), DPhil 1962. *Publications*: Lamennais and England, 1966; *contrib*. Cahiers Mennaisiens. *Address*: St Chad's Coll., Durham.

Rogers, Dr Alan; Senior Lecturer in Medieval and Local History, Department of Adult Education, University of Nottingham, since 1973 (Lecturer, 1959–73); *b* 1933; *m* 1958; one *s* one *d*. BA Nottingham 1954, MA Nottingham 1957, PhD Nottingham 1966, CertEd Nottingham 1957; FRHistS, FSA. Lectr, King's Coll., Newcastle upon Tyne, 1957–59. Editor, Bull. Local Hist., E Midl. Reg., 1966– ; Chm., Hist. of Lincolnshire, 1966– ; Mem., Exec. Cttee, and Vice-Chm., Publicns Cttee, Standing Conf. Local Hist.; Convenor, Local Hist. Tutors Conf.; Mem., Gen. Synod, 1970– ; Mem., ACCM, 1971– ; Mem., Council, St John's Coll., Nottingham. *Publications*: The Making of Stamford, 1965; Stability and Change: some aspects of North and South Rauceby, 1968; The Medieval Buildings of Stamford, 1969; The History of Lincolnshire, 1969; Religious Institutions of Medieval Stamford, 1974; This was their World: approaches to local history, 1972; *contrib*. Amer. Jl Legal Hist., Antiqu. Jl, Bull. Inst. Hist. Res., Jl Brit. Archaeol. Assoc., Lincs Hist. Archaeol. *Address*: Dept of Adult Education, University Park, Nottingham NG7 2RD.

Rogers, Christopher David; Lecturer, Department of Economics, University of Dundee, since 1970; *b* 1944; *m* 1964; two *s*. BA Liverpool 1965, MA 1968; Mem., REconS. Asst Lectr, UC, Aberystwyth, 1967–69, Lectr, 1969–70. *Publications*: *contrib*. Interecons, Lloyds Bank Rev., Malayan

Econ. Rev. *Address*: Dept of Economics, Univ. of Dundee, Dundee DD1 4HN.

Rogers, Daniel Claude de Warrenne, MA; Senior Lecturer in Spanish, University of Durham, since 1971; *b* 1933; *m* 1961; two *s*. BA Dublin 1954 (1st cl. Moderatorship Mod. Langs), MA Dublin 1959. Jun. Lectr, TCD, 1957–63; Lectr, Durham, 1964–71. *Publications*: ed, El condenado por desconfiado, 1974; contrib. The comedias of Calderón, ed D. W. Cruickshank and J. E. Varey, vol. XIX, 1973; *contrib.* Bull. Hispan. Studies, Durh. Univ. Jl, Hispan. Rev., Rev. Lit. *Address*: Dept of Spanish, Univ. of Durham, Elvet Riverside, New Elvet, Durham.

Rogers, Dr Graham Allan John; Senior Lecturer, Department of Philosophy, University of Keele, since 1962 (Lecturer, 1962–72); *b* 1938; *m* 1969. BA Nottingham 1960, PhD Keele 1972. *Publications*: John Locke and the Scientific Revolution (forthcoming); *contrib.* Ann. Sci., Jl Hist. Ideas, Studies in the History and Philosophy of Science, John Locke Newsletter. *Address*: Dept of Philosophy, Univ. of Keele, Keele ST5 5BG.

Rogister, Dr John M. J.; Lecturer in Modern History, Department of History, University of Durham, since 1967; *b* 1941. BA Birmingham 1964; DPhil Oxon 1972. Tutor, Hatfield Coll., Univ. of Durham. *Publications*: Rexism, in, History of the 20th Century, 1969; in preparation: Biography of Louis XV; A Study of the Parlements in 18th Century France; ed, Burke's Reflections on the Revolution in France; *contrib.* Bull. Inst. Hist. Res., EHR. *Address*: Dept of History, 43–46 North Bailey, Durham.

Röhl, Dr John Charles Gerald; Reader in History, University of Sussex, since 1972; *b* 1938; *m* 1964; two *s* one *d*. BA Cantab 1961, PhD Cantab 1965. Asst Lectr, Univ. Sussex, 1964–66, Lectr 1966–72; Actg Prof. of History, Hamburg Univ., 1973. *Publications*: Germany without Bismarck: The Crisis of Government in the Second Reich, 1890–1900, 1967, German trans. 1969; From Bismarck to Hitler: The Problem of Continuity in German History, 1970; Zwei deutsche Fürsten zur Kriegsschuldfrage: Lichnowsky und Eulenburg und der Ausbruch des I. Weltkrieges, 1971 (and English edn); 1914: Delusion or Design?, 1973; *contrib.* Hist. Jl Historische Zeitschrift, Jl Contemp. History. *Address*: Arts Building, Univ. of Sussex, Brighton BN1 9QN.

Rollings, Peter James; Lecturer in Sociology, University of Reading, since 1967; *b* 1927; *m* 1953, 1965; three *s* one *d* (and one step-*s* two step-*d*). BSc London 1954 (Sociol.); Mem., Brit. Sociol Assoc. Res. Asst, LSE, 1954–56; Lectr in Sociology, UC, Gold Coast, 1956–60; Temp. Lectr in Social Psychol., UC, Swansea, 1960–62; Lectr in Sociology, Univ. of Ghana, 1962–65; Sen. Lectr in Sociology, Univ. of Ife, Nigeria, 1966–67; Chief Examnr Gen. Paper II, West African GCE A Level, 1967. Member: Standing Cttee on Univ. Studies of Africa (UK) 1972– ; Social Admin. Cttee, Jt Univ. Council for Social and Public Admin,

1973– ; Convenor, Military and Police in Soc. Seminar, 1970– . *Publications: contrib.* Ghana Jl of Sociol. *Address*: Dept of Sociology, Univ. of Reading, Whiteknights, Reading RG6 2AH.

Rolo, Prof. Paul Jacques Victor; Professor of History, University of Keele, since 1972; *b* 1917; *m* 1952; one *s* one *d*. BA Oxon 1938 (1st cl. Hist.), MA Oxon 1946; FRHistS. Lectr, Balliol Coll., Oxford, 1946–49; Lectr, Keele Univ., 1951–61, Sen. Lectr, 1961–71. *Publications*: George Canning, 1965; Entente Cordiale, 1969. *Address*: Dept of History, Univ. of Keele, Keele ST5 5BG.

Romaya, Dr Samuel Michael; Lecturer, Institute of Planning Studies, Nottingham University, since 1969; *b* 1934; *m* 1957; two *s* one *d*. BA Hons 1957, Cert TCP 1957, MA 1961, Manchester, PhD Nottingham 1972; RIBA (Professional Practice Exam.) 1958; Member: Exec. Body and Treas., Iraqi Architects' Assoc., Baghdad, 1967–68; Illuminating Eng. Soc., 1971. Baghdad Univ., 1959–61; Asst Prof. and Head of Building and Construction Dept, Coll. of Engrg Technol., Baghdad, 1961–68. Private Practice, Romaya Engineering Bureau, Baghdad, 1959–68. *Publications*: Training of Technical Personnel: paper delivered to the Eighth Iraqi Engineers' Congress, 1967; *contrib.* Lighting Res. and Technol. *Address*: Inst. of Planning Studies, University Park, Nottingham NG7 2RD.

Ronco, Daisy Dina; Senior Lecturer in Italian, University College of North Wales, since 1968; *b* 1922. DottLett Genoa 1946 (*maxima cum laude*), Dip. of piano (performer) Genoa Conservatoire 1943. Lectr, Univ. Coll. of N Wales, 1959–68. *Publications: contrib.* Boll. Soc. Studi Vald., Fr. Studies, Riv. Crit. Storia Filos. *Address*: Univ. College of North Wales, Bangor LL57 2DG.

Root, Rev. Prof. Howard Eugene; Professor of Theology, University of Southampton, since 1966; *b* 1926; *m* 1952; two *s* two *d*. BA S California 1945, BA Oxon 1951, MA Cantab 1953, MA Oxon 1970; Deacon 1953, Priest 1954. Teaching Fellow, S California, 1945–47, Instructor, 1947–49; Asst Lectr, Cambridge Univ., 1953–57, Lectr, 1957–65; Fellow, Emmanuel Coll., Cambridge, 1954–65, Chaplain, 1954–56, Dean, 1956–65. Anglican Observer, 2nd Vatican Council, 1963–65; Consultant, Lambeth Conf., 1968; Chm., Archbishops' Commn on Marriage, 1968–71; Mem., other commns; Hon. Chaplain, Winchester Cathedral, 1966–67, Canon Theologian, 1967– ; Wilde Lectr, Oxford, 1957–60; Bampton Lectr, Oxford, 1972; Jt Editor, Jl of Theological Studies, 1969– . *Address*: Univ. of Southampton, Southampton SO9 5NH.

Roots, Prof. Ivan Alan; Professor of Modern History, University of Exeter, since 1967; *b* 1921; *m* 1947; one *s* one *d*. BA Oxon 1941 (1st cl. Mod. Hist.), MA Oxon 1945; FRHistS. Asst Lectr, Univ. Coll. of S Wales and Monmouthshire, Cardiff, 1946–47, Lectr, 1947–61, Sen. Lectr, 1961–67; Vis. Prof., Lafayette Coll., Pennsylvania, 1960–61; Dean of Faculty of Arts, Exeter Univ., 1973– . Governor, Exeter Sch., 1970– ; Governor, St Luke's Coll. of Educn, Exeter, 1972– ; Mem., Post-grad. Studentship Selection Cttee, DES, 1970–73, Chm., 1974– . Mem., Editorial Bd, The English Revolution; Mem., Editorial Bd, Jl Parly Hist.; Co-founder (with Maurice Goldsmith), The Rota. *Publications*: ed (with D. H. Pennington), The Committee at Stafford 1643–45, 1957; The Great Rebellion 1642–60, 1966, 3rd edn 1972; ed, Conflicts in Tudor and Stuart England, 1967; The Late Troubles in England, 1969; Cromwell: a world profile, NY 1973, London 1974; ed, The Diary of Thomas Burton, MP (repr.), 1974; *contrib*. The English Revolution, ed E. W. Ives, 1968; *contrib*. The English Civil War and After, ed R. H. Parry, 1970; *contrib*. The Interregnum, ed G. E. Aylmer, 1972; *contrib*. Hist., Prop. Weltges., etc. *Address*: Dept of History, Univ. of Exeter, Exeter EX4 4QH.

Roper, Derek Sidney, BA, BLitt; Senior Lecturer, Department of English Literature, University of Sheffield, since 1971; *b* 1930; *m* 1956; two *d*. BA Durham 1953 (1st cl. Engl.); BLitt Oxon 1959. Temp. Lectr, Univ. of Durham, 1955–56; Instructor, Univ. of N Carolina, 1956–58; Asst Lectr, Univ. of Sheffield, 1958–61; Lectr, 1961–71. Jt Gen. Editor, Collins Annotated Student Texts, 1968– . *Publications*: ed, Wordsworth and Coleridge: Lyrical Ballads, 1968; ed, John Ford: 'Tis Pity She's a Whore, 1974; *contrib*. Bks Abroad, Delta, Mod. Lang. Rev., Notes Queries, Rev. Engl. Studies, Wisc. Studies Contemp. Lit. *Address*: Dept of English Literature, The Univ., Sheffield S10 2TN.

Roper, Hugh Redwald T.; *see* Trevor-Roper.

Rorrison, Hugh, MA; Lecturer in German, University of Leeds, since 1962; *b* 1933; *m* 1966; two *s* one *d*. MA Glasgow 1958 (1st cl. French and German). *Publications*: *contrib*. Maske und Kothurn, Theatre Qly, Theatre-facts. *Address*: Dept of German, Univ. of Leeds, Leeds LS2 9JT.

Rose, Dr Bernard William George, MA, DMus, FRCO; University Lecturer in Music, Oxford University, since 1945; *b* 1916; *m* 1939; three *s*. MusB Cantab 1938, BA Cantab 1939, MA Cantab 1944; MA Oxon 1945; DMus Oxon 1955; FRCO 1954 (ARCO 1934). Organist, The Queen's Coll., Oxford, 1939–40, 1945–57; Supernumerary Fellow, 1949, Official Fellow, 1954–57; Organist, Fellow and Informator Choristarum, Magdalen Coll., Oxford, 1957– . Mem., Council, Royal Coll. Organists, 1960– ; Gen. Editor, Novello Church Music, 1957– . Conductor, Oxford Orch. Soc., 1971– . *Publications*: Tomkins Musica Deo Sacra I, 1963; Tomkins Musica Deo Sacra II, 1964; Handel, Susanna (HHA), 1967; Tomkins Musica Deo Sacra III, 1974; *contrib*. Proc. Royal Music. Assoc. *Address*: Magdalen College, Oxford.

Rose, Prof. Edgar Alan; Professor of Town and Country Planning, University of Aston in Birmingham, since 1969; *b* 1929; *m* 1960; two *s* one *d*. DipArch Manchester 1950, DipTP Manchester 1957 (with distinction), MSc Aston 1970; ARIBA 1951, FRTPI 1965 (AMTPI 1959). Dep. City Planning Officer, Manchester City Planning Dep., 1964–68. Mem., Panel of Inquiry into Greater London Develt Plan, 1971; Mem., Town and Country Planning Assoc.; Mem., Inst. of Env. Sciences. *Publications*: Philosophy and Purpose of Planning, in, The Spirit and Purpose of Planning, ed M. J. Bruton, 1974; The Physical Environment, in, Urban Planning, ed G. Cherry, 1974; *contrib*. Internat. Jl of Environmental Studies, RTPI Jl, (T&C PA Jl, Mun. Engrg. *Address*: Dept of Architectural Planning and Urban Studies, Univ. of Aston in Birmingham, Gosta Green, Birmingham B4 7ET.

Rose, Dr Francis; Senior Lecturer in Biogeography, King's College, University of London, since 1964; *b* 1921; *m* 1943; three *s* one *d*. BSc London 1941 (Hons Botany), PhD London, 1953 (Plant Ecology); FLS 1944, Member: Brit. Bryological Soc., Brit. Lichen Soc., Botanical Soc. of Brit. Isles, Brit. Ecological Soc. Asst Lectr in Botany, Bedford Coll., London, 1949–52, Lectr, 1952–64. Chm, Kent Naturalist's Trust, 1959–65; Chm., New Forest Scientific Cttee, 1971– ; Mem. London Univ. Bds of Studies in Botany and Geography. *Publications*: contrib. Taxonomy, Phytogeography and Evolution, ed D. Valentine, 1972; contrib. Lichens and Air Pollution, 1973; *contrib*. BSBI Proc., Jl Bryology (formerly Trans Brit. Bryological Soc.), Jl Ecology, Lichenologist, Proc. Linnean Soc. *Address*: Dept of Geography, King's College, Strand, WC2R 2LS.

Rose, Prof. Harold Bertram; Esmée Fairbairn Professor of Finance, London Graduate School of Business Studies, since 1965; *b* 1923; *m* 1949; three *s* one *d*. BCom London 1947. Sen. Lectr, LSE, 1958–61, Reader 1961–65. Member: London and Cambridge Economic Service Editorial Cttee, 1958; Plowden Cttee on Primary Educn, 1963; SSRC Management Studies Cttee, 1965; UGC Business Studies Cttee, 1967; NEDO METD Working Party, 1968; Reserve Pension Bd, 1974. Director: New Throgmorton Trust, 1966; Cornhill Capital Plan Managers, 1968; Throgmorton Trust, 1973. *Publications*: Economic Background to Investment, 1960; Disclosure in Company Accounts, 1963; Management Education in the 1970's: Growth and Issues, 1969; *contrib*. Econ. Jl, Investment Analyst, Jl Accounting Research. *Address*: London Graduate School of Business Studies, Sussex Place, NW1 4SA.

Rose, Hilary; Lecturer in Social Administration, London School of Economics, since 1972; *b* 1935; *m* 1954, 1961; two *s*. BA London 1962 (Sociol.). Lectr, LSE, 1964–71; Res. Fellow, Univ. of Essex, 1971–72. *Publications*: The Housing Problem, 1968; (with S. Rose) Science and Society, 1969; (with B. Abel-Smith) Doctors, Patients and Pathology, 1972; *contrib*. var. articles. *Address*: Dept of Social Administration, London School of Economics, Houghton Street, WC2A 2AE.

604

Rose, James; Lecturer, Department of Geography, Birkbeck College, University of London, since 1968; *b* 1943; *m* 1966; two *s*. BA Leicester 1965 (1st cl. Geog.); FGS, Mem., Inst. Brit. Geogrs. *Publications: contrib.* Proc. Geologists' Assoc., Scot. Jl Geol. *Address:* Dept of Geography, Birkbeck Coll., 7/15 Gresse Street, W1P 1PA.

Rose, Dr Michael Edward, BA, DPhil; Lecturer in Economic History, Department of History, University of Manchester, since 1965; *b* 1936; *m* 1963; two *s* one *d*. BA Oxon 1960 (1st cl. Hist.), DPhil Oxon 1965. Mem., Econ. Hist. Soc., Mem., Soc. Social Hist. Med., Mem., Econ. and Social Hist. Cttee, SSRC, 1972. Asst Lectr, Univ. of Manchester, 1962–65. Chief Ext. Examiner in Hist., Teachers' Cert., Manchester ATO. *Publications:* The English Poor Law 1780–1930, 1971; The Relief of Poverty, 1834–1914, 1972; *contrib.* Brit. Jl Indust. Med, Econ. Hist. Rev., Trans Lancs Chesh. Antiqu. Soc., Northern Hist., Victorian Studies. *Address:* Dept of History, The Univ., Manchester M13 9PL.

Rose, Prof. Richard; Professor of Politics, University of Strathclyde, since 1966; *b* 1933; *m* 1956; two *s* one *d*. BA Johns Hopkins 1953 (Comparative Drama), double distinction; Phi Beta Kappa; DPhil Oxon 1960. Lectr, Manchester Univ., 1961–66. Political Public Relations, Mississippi Valley, 1954–55; Reporter, St Louis Post-Despatch, 1955–57; Election Corresp., The Times, 1964, 1966, 1970. Pres., Scottish Political Studies Assoc., 1967–68, 1972–73; Psephologist, Indep. TV News, 1970; Sec., Cttee on Political Sociology, Internat. Sociological Assoc., 1971– ; Mem. Exec. Cttee, European Consortium for Political Research, 1971– ; Mem., US–UK Fulbright Commn, 1971– ; Mem., Eisenhower Fellowship Programme, 1971– ; Dir, ISSC European Summer Sch., 1973; Guggenheim Fellowship, 1974. *Publications:* (with D. E. Butler) The British General Election of 1959; (with Mark Abrams) Must Labour Lose?, 1960; Politics in England, 1964, rev. edn 1974; ed, Studies in British Politics, 1966, rev. edn 1969; Influencing Voters, 1967; ed, Policy Making in Britain, 1969; People in Politics, 1970; ed (with M. Dogan), European Politics, 1971; Governing Without Consensus: an Irish perspective, 1971; ed, Comparative Electoral Behavior, 1974; (with T. T. Mackie) International Almanack of Electoral History, 1974; ed, Lessons from America, 1974; ed, The Management of Urban Change in Britain and Germany, 1974; *contrib.* European and American jls. *Address:* Dept of Politics, Univ. of Strathclyde, McCance Building, Richmond Street, Glasgow G1 1XQ.

Rose, Dr Saul, MA, DPhil; Lecturer in Politics, Oxford University, since 1958; *b* 1922; *m* 1946. MA Oxon 1948, DPhil Oxon 1951. Lectr, Aberdeen Univ., 1949–52; Fellow, St Antony's Coll., Oxford, 1955–63; Fellow and Bursar, New Coll., Oxford, 1963– . Mem., Pol. Science Cttee, SSRC, 1971– . *Publications:* Socialism in Southern Asia, 1959; Britain and South-East Asia, 1962; ed, Politics in Southern Asia, 1963. *Address:* New College, Oxford.

Rosen, Dr Frederick; Lecturer, Department of Government, London School of Economics, since 1971; *b* 1938; *m* 1968. BA Colgate Univ. 1960, MA Syracuse Univ. 1963, PhD London (LSE) 1965. Res. Asst, Univ. Coll., London, 1965–66; Asst Prof., Franklin and Marshall Coll., USA, 1966–68; Lectr, City Univ., 1968–71. Asst Gen. Editor, Collected Works of Jeremy Bentham, University College London, 1971– . *Publications: contrib.* Jl Hist. Ideas, Philos., Polit. Theory. *Address:* Dept of Government, London School of Economics, Houghton Street, Aldwych, WC2A 2AE.

Roskell, Prof. John Smith, MA, DPhil, FBA; Professor of Medieval History, University of Manchester, since 1962; *b* 1913; *m* 1942; one *s* one *d*. BA Manchester 1933 (1st cl. History), MA Manchester 1934; DPhil Oxon 1941; FBA, FRHistS. Asst Lectr, Manchester Univ., 1938–45, Lectr, 1945–51, Sen. Lectr, 1951–52; Prof. of Medieval History, Nottingham Univ., 1952; Pres., Lancs Parish Register Soc., 1962– ; Pres., Chetham Soc., 1972– . *Publications:* The Knights of the Shire for the County Palatine of Lancaster 1377–1460 (Chetham Soc. vol. 96 NS), 1937; The Commons in the Parliament of 1422, 1954; The Commons and their Speakers in English Parliaments, 1376–1523, 1965; *contrib.* Bull. Inst. Hist. Res., Bull. Rylands Libr., EHR. *Address:* Dept of History, Univ. of Manchester, Manchester.

Ross, Prof. Alec M.; Professor of Educational Research, and Director of School of Education, Lancaster University, since 1967; *b* 1922; *m* 1949; one *s* one *d*. BA London 1949, PhD London 1955; Teacher's Cert. 1942. Lectr, then Sen. Lectr, Univ. of Exeter, Inst. of Educn, 1959–67. Mem., Soc. Res. Higher Educn, 1968– , Chm., 1972– ; Mem., Progr. Cttee, Schs Council, 1969– ; Mem., Educn Adv. Cttee, UK Nat. Commn for UNESCO, 1971– ; Mem., CNAA, 1973– . Co-ord. Editor, Higher Educn. *Publications:* The Education of Childhood, 1960. *Address:* Dept of Educational Research, Cartmel College, The Univ., Bailrigg, Lancaster.

Ross, Rev. Dr Andrew C.; Lecturer in History of Missions, Department of Ecclesiastical History, University of Edinburgh, since 1966; *b* 1931; *m* 1953; four *s*. MA Edinburgh 1952, BD Edinburgh 1957, STM Union Theol Seminary NY 1958, PhD Edinburgh 1968. Served with Presbyterian Church in Malawi, 1958–65. Chm., Nyasaland (subseq. Malawi) Lands Tribunal, 1962–65; Vice-Chm., Nyasaland (subseq. Malawi) Nat. Tenders Bd, 1962–65. *Publications: contrib.* The Zambesian Past, 1965; *contrib.* Religion in Africa, 1965; *contrib.* Witchcraft and Healing, 1969; *contrib.* Livingstone, Man of Africa, 1973; *contrib.* Livingstone and Africa, 1974; *contrib.* New Left Rev., Union Qly Rev., Scottish Hist. Rev. *Address:* New College, The Mound, Edinburgh.

Ross, Dr Angus Macfarlane; Reader in English and Dean of the Graduate School in Arts and Social Studies, University of Sussex, since 1968; *b* 1928; *m* 1956; three *d*. MA St

Andrews 1949 (1st cl. English Lang. and Lit.); PhD Cantab 1956. Asst Lectr, St Andrews, 1955; Lectr, Univ. Coll. of West Indies, 1956–60; Lectr, Hull Univ., 1960; Lectr, Univ. of Sussex, 1961–65, Sen. Lectr, 1965–68; Vis. Prof., Columbia Univ., NY, 1958–59; Vis. Prof., Univ. of Rochester, 1961, 1965; Vis. Prof., Univ. of California, Berkeley, 1966, 1972; Univ. of New Mexico, 1969. *Publications*: ed, Defoe: Robinson Crusoe, 1966; Smollett: Humphry Clinker, 1968; Poetry of the Augustan Age, 1970; Gulliver's Travels: a study, 1968; English, 1971; ed, Gulliver's Travels, 1972. *Address*: Arts Building, Univ. of Sussex, Falmer, Brighton BN1 9QN.

Ross, Dr Charles Derek, MA, DPhil; Reader in Medieval History, University of Bristol, since 1962; *b* 1924; *m* 1946; one *s* one *d*. BA Oxon 1945 (2nd cl. History), MA Oxon 1950, DPhil Oxon 1950; FRHistS. Asst Lectr, Bristol Univ., 1947–49, Lectr, 1949–62. *Publications*: The Cartulary of St Mark's Hospital, 1959; The Cartulary of Cirencester Abbey, Gloucestershire, 1964; *contrib.* Bull. Inst. Hist. Res., Econ. Hist. Rev., EHR. *Address*: Dept of History, Univ. of Bristol, Bristol BS8 1RJ.

Ross, Prof. David John Athole; Professor of French, and Head of French Department, Birkbeck College, University of London, since 1967; *b* 1911; *m* 1938. BA Cantab 1933; MA London 1936, PhD London 1940. Lectr, King's Coll., Newcastle upon Tyne, Univ. of Durham, 1944–47; Reader in French, Birkbeck Coll., Univ. of London, 1946–67. Editor, Mod. Hum. Res. Assoc., Diss. Series. *Publications*: ed, G. Cary: The Medieval Alexander, 1956; Alexander Historiatus, 1963; Illustrated Medieval Alexander-Books in Germany and the Netherlands, 1971; *contrib.* Cah. Civilis. Mediev., Class. Mediaev., Fr. Studies, Jl Warb. Court. Insts, Med. Æv., Mod. Lang. Rev., Scriptor., Alter. *Address*: Dept of French, Birkbeck College, Malet Street, WC1E 7HX.

Ross, Graham; Lecturer, Department of Agricultural Economics, University of Newcastle upon Tyne, since 1966; *b* 1930; *m* 1956; two *s* two *d*. BA Cantab 1951, Dip. in Agriculture Cantab 1952, MA Cantab 1965; BSc(Econ) London 1965. *Address*: Dept of Agricultural Economics, The Univ., Newcastle upon Tyne NE1 7RU.

Ross, Dr Helen Elizabeth; Senior Lecturer in Psychology, University of Stirling, since 1972; *b* 1935; *m* 1971. BA Oxon 1959 (2nd cl. PPP), MA Oxon 1962; PhD Cantab 1966; Mem., EPS, BPS, Underwater Assoc., European Undersea Bio-Medical Soc. Res. Asst, Cambridge Univ., 1961–65; Asst Lectr, Hull Univ., 1965–66, Lectr, 1966–69, Lectr, Stirling Univ., 1959–72. Mem., Council, Underwater Assoc., 1969–73; Cttee, EPS, 1973– ; Cttee, Scot. BPS, 1973– . *Publications*: Behaviour and Perception in Strange Environments, 1974; *contrib.* Aerosp. Med., Brit. Jl Psychol., Brit. Jl Educnl Psychol., Ergonom., Hum. Fact., Percept. Mot. Skills, Percept. Psychophys., Psychon. So., Qly Jl

606

Exper. Psychol., Underw. Assoc. Rep. *Address*: Dept of Psychology, Univ. of Stirling, Stirling FK9 4LA.

Ross, Dr John; Senior Lecturer, Language Centre, University of Essex, since 1974; *b* 1938. MA Edinburgh 1960, PhD Edinburgh 1969. Asst Lectr, Univ. Essex, 1964–67; Lectr, Univ. Reading, 1967–69; Lectr, Language Centre, Univ. of Essex, 1969–74. *Publications*: Rendez-vous à Chaviray (Language course) for BBC; numerous translations; various papers in sociolinguistics; *contrib.* Word, TLS, etc. *Address*: Language Centre, Univ. of Essex, Colchester CO4 3SQ.

Ross, Kenneth Graham Marshall; Lecturer in International Relations, Extra-Mural Department, Leeds University, since 1966; Joint Lecturer in Extra-Mural Department and School of History since 1972; *b* 1933. MA Glasgow 1956 (1st cl. Mod. Hist.). Asst Lectr in International Relations, Extra-Mural Dept, Leeds Univ., 1964–66. *Address*: School of History, Univ. of Leeds, Leeds LS2 9JT.

Ross, Michael Inman Philip M.; *see* Macdonald-Ross.

Rosselli, Dr John; Reader in History, University of Sussex, since 1969; *b* 1927; *m* 1956; two *s*. BA Swarthmore 1946; PhD Cantab 1952. Mem., Editorial Staff, (Manchester) Guardian, 1951–64. Lectr, Sussex, 1964–66, Sen. Lectr, 1966–69. *Publications*: Lord William Bentinck and the British Occupation of Sicily, 1956; Lord William Bentinck: the Making of a Liberal Imperialist, 1974; ed, Opere Scelte di Carlo Rosselli, 1973; *contrib.* Agric. Hist. Rev., Ind. Econ. Soc. Hist. Rev., Riv. Storica Ital. *Address*: Arts Building, Univ. of Sussex, Falmer, Brighton BN1 9QN.

Roth, Sir Martin; Professor of Psychological Medicine, University of Newcastle upon Tyne, since 1956; *b* 1917; *m* 1945; three *d*. MB, BS 1943, MD 1945; FRCP 1958, London, FRC Psych 1971 (Pres., 1971–). Vis. Lectr, Swedish Univs, 1967; Mayne Guest Prof., Univ. of Queensland, 1968. Chm., Grants Cttee, Clin. Res. Bd, 1968–70; Member: WHO Expert Cttee on Mental Health Problems of Ageing and the Aged, 1958; MRC, 1964–68; Clin., Res. Bd, MRC, 1964–70; Central Health Services Council, Standing Med. Adv. Cttee, DHSS, 1968– . Hon. Mem., Soc. Royale de Médecine Mentale de Belgique, 1970; Corresp. Mem., Deutsche Gesellschaft für Psychiatrie und Nervenheilkunde, 1970; Distinguished Fellow, Med. Psychiatric Assoc., 1973; Hon. Mem., Soc. Medico-Psychologique. Co-Editor, Brit. Jl of Psychiatry, 1968– . *Publications*: (with W. Mayer-Gross and Slater) Clinical Psychiatry, 1954, 2nd edn 1961, 3rd edn 1969, trans. Italian, Spanish, Portuguese, Chinese; *contrib.* Brain, Brit. Jl Psychiatry, BMJ, Proc. RSM, WHO Bull. *Address*: Dept of Psychological Medicine, Royal Victoria Infirmary, Queen Victoria Road, Newcastle upon Tyne NE1 4LP.

Rothenberg, John; Lecturer, Department of French Language and Literature, Leeds

University, since 1963; *b* 1938; *m* 1964. BA London 1961 (1st cl. French); Mem., Soc. Fr. Studies. *Publications*: *contrib*. Forum Mod. Lang. Studies. *Address*: Dept of French, The Univ., Leeds LS2 9JT.

Rothera, Harold, MA; Lecturer in Education, University College of Swansea, since 1958; *b* 1929; *m* 1952; one *s* two *d*. BA Manchester 1950 (1st cl. Combined Subjects – French and Hist.), Cert. Ed. Nottingham 1951 (dist.); MA Manchester 1953 (French). *Publications*: *contrib*. Comp. Educn. *Address*: Dept of Education, Univ. College of Swansea, Hendrefoilan, Swansea SA2 7NB.

Rotherham, Leonard, CBE, DSc, FRS; Vice-Chancellor, Bath University, since 1969; *b* 1913; *m* 1937; one *s* two *d*. FRS 1963; CEng, FIEE, FInstF, FIM, FInstP; Hon. LLD Bristol. Physicist, Brown Firth Research Laboratories, 1935–46; Head of Metallurgy Dept, RAE, Farnborough, 1946–50; Dir, Res. and Develt, UKAEA, Industrial Gp, Risley, 1950–58. Mem. for Research, CEGB, 1958–69; Head of Research, Electricity Supply Industry and Electricity Council, 1965–69. Chm., Adv. Cttee for Scientific and Technical Information, 1970–74. Mem., Central Adv. Council for Science and Technology, 1968–70. Fellow UCL, 1959; Hon. Fellow, Inst. of Welding, 1965. Pres., Instn of Metallurgists, 1964; Pres., Inst. of Metals, 1965; Member of Council, Royal Society, 1965–66. Hon. Life Mem., Amer. Soc. of Mechanical Engineers, 1963. *Publications*: Creep of Metals, 1951; various scientific and technical papers; also lectures: Hatfield Meml, 1961; Coal Science, 1961; Calvin Rice (of Amer. Soc. of Mech. Engrs), 1963; 2nd Metallurgical Engineering, Inst. of Metals, 1963. *Address*: Bath Univ., Claverton Down, Bath BA2 7AY.

Round, Jeffery Ian; Lecturer in Economics, University of Warwick, since 1970; *b* 1943; *m* 1968; one *s*. BSc Nottingham 1964 (Maths and Econs), Dip Statistics, Wales 1965. Asst Lectr in Econs, UCW Aberystwyth, 1966–68; Harkness Fellow, Harvard Univ., 1968–70. *Publications*: (with E. T. Nevin and A. R. Roe) The Structure of the Welsh Economy, 1966; *contrib*. Regional Studies. *Address*: Univ. of Warwick, Coventry CV4 7AL.

Round, Dr Nicholas Grenville; Stevenson Professor of Hispanic Studies, University of Glasgow, since 1972; *b* 1938; *m* 1966; one *d*. BA Oxon 1959 (1st cl. Span. and Fr.), MA Oxon 1963, DPhil Oxon 1967. Lectr, Queen's Univ., Belfast, 1962–71, Reader, 1971–72. Mem., Cttee, Assoc. Hispan. GB and Ireland, 1970–72. *Publications*: *contrib*. Arch. (Oviedo), Anal. Galdos., Bull. Hispan. Studies, Forum Mod. Lang. Studies, Mod. Lang. Rev., Proc. Royal Irish Acad. *Address*: Dept of Hispanic Studies, The Univ., Glasgow G12 8QQ.

Routh, Dr Gerald Guy Cumming; Reader in Economics, School of African and Asian Studies, University of Sussex, since 1968; *b* 1916; *m* 1947; three *s* one *d*. BCom Witwatersrand 1937, PhD London 1951; FREconS, Mem. British Univs Industrial

Relations Assoc., Associate of Inst. Develt Studies. Lectr in Econs, Univ. Sussex, 1962–68. Sen. Res. Officer, Nat. Inst. of Econ. and Social Res., 1957–62. *Publications*: Occupation and Pay in Great Britain 1906 to 1960, 1965; ed jtly, The Teaching of Economics in Africa, 1973; The Origin of Economic Ideas (forthcoming); *contrib*. Economica, S Afr. Jl Econs, Polit. Qly, Monthly Labor Review, Scottish Jl Polit. Econ., Growth and Change. *Address*: Arts Building, Univ. of Sussex, Brighton BN1 9QN.

Routledge, Rev. Kenneth Graham, MA; Dean of Chapel, Fellow, since 1969, Director, Studies in Law, since 1972 (Supervisor, 1969–72), Corpus Christi College, Cambridge University; *b* 1927; *m* 1960. LLB Liverpool 1951, BA Cantab 1965, MA 1969; Barrister-at-Law, Middle Temple 1952; Ordained (C of E) deacon 1966, priest 1967. Chancellor, Diocese of Ely, 1973– . Tutor, Fac. of Law, Liverpool Univ., 1952–63; Lectr, Fac. of Law, Manchester Univ., 1966–69. *Address*: Corpus Christi College, Cambridge.

Rowan, Prof. David Culloden; Professor of Economics, University of Southampton, since 1960; *b* 1918; *m* 1949. BA (Special Econ.) Bristol 1949 (1st cl.). Asst Lectr, Birmingham, 1949–51; Res. Fellow, W African Inst. of Social and Econ. Res., 1951–52; Lectr, Bristol, 1952–54; Lectr, then Sen. Lectr, Melbourne, 1954–56; Prof. of Economics, and Dean, Univ. of NSW, 1956–60; Vis. Prof., Melbourne, 1965; Vis. Prof., Australian Nat. Univ., 1971. Vis. Res. Fellow, Fed. Res. Bank of St Louis, 1968; Cnsltnt, OECD, 1971–72; Mem., Council Royal Econ. Soc., 1969–73; Econ. Cttee, Soc. Science Res. Council, 1971– ; Econ. Cttee, CNAA, 1969–71; Dep. Vice-Chancellor, Univ. of Southampton, 1969–71. *Publications*: (with W. T. Newlyn) Money and Banking in British Colonial Africa, 1954; Output, Inflation and Growth, 1968, Spanish edn 1972; (with T. Mayer) Intermediate Macro-Economics, 1972; *contrib*. Econ. Jl, Econ. Rec., Jl Pol Econ., S Afr. Jl Econ. *Address*: Dept of Economics, The University, Southampton SO9 5NH.

Rowe, Dr Christopher James; Lecturer, Department of Classics, University of Bristol, since 1968; *b* 1944; *m* 1965; one *s* one *d*. MA, PhD, Cantab 1969. Vis. Res. Fellow, Inst. for Advanced Studies in the Humanities, Univ. of Edinburgh, 1972. *Publications*: *contrib*. Eranus Jahrbuch, Supp. Proc. Camb. Philol. Soc., also reviews. *Address*: Dept of Classics, Univ. of Bristol, Bristol BS8 1TH.

Rowe, David John, MA, BSc(Econ); Lecturer in Economics, University of Newcastle upon Tyne, since 1965; *b* 1940; *m* 1967; two *d*. BSc(Econ) Southampton 1963, MA Southampton 1965. *Publications*: ed, Records of the Company of Shipwrights of Newcastle upon Tyne 1622–1967, vol. I, 1970, vol. II, 1972; ed, London Radicalism 1830–43, 1970; (jtly) The North-east Engineers Strikes of 1871, 1971; (with N. McCord) Northumberland and Durham: Industry in the 19th Century, 1971; *contrib*.

Agric. Hist. Rev., Comm. Develop., Econ. Hist. Rev., Hist. Jl, Ind. Archaeol., Internat. Rev. Soc. Hist., North. Hist., Past Pres., Trans Hist. *Address:* Dept of Economics, The Univ., Newcastle upon Tyne NE1 7RU.

Rowe, Eric Alfred, MA, BLitt; Senior Lecturer in Politics, University of Nottingham, since 1969; *b* 1926; *m* 1955. BA Oxon 1956 (PPE), BLitt Oxon 1959, MA Oxon 1962. Asst Lectr, Liverpool Univ., 1958–59; Asst Lectr, Nottingham Univ., 1959–60, Lectr, 1960–69. Mem., Council, Elect. Ref. Soc. *Publications:* Modern Politics, 1969; Towards Fairer Voting, 1971; *contrib.* Munic. Jl, Pol Studies, Rev. Psychol. Peoples. *Address:* Dept of Politics, Univ. of Nottingham.

Rowe, Dr William John; Senior Lecturer in Modern History, Liverpool University, since 1963; *b* 1915; *m* 1956; two *s.* BA 1938, MA 1945, DPhil 1950, Oxon; FRHistS 1953; Mem., Exec. Council, Brit. Ag. Hist. Soc., 1966– . Temp. Extra Mural Lectr, Exeter, 1947; Asst Lectr, 1947–50, Lectr, 1950–63, Univ. of Liverpool; Vis. Lectr, Univ. of Calif., Berkeley, 1958. *Publications:* Cornwall in the Age of the Industrial Revolution, 1953; The Hard Rock Men, 1974; *contrib.* Agric. Hist. Rev., Folk Life. *Address:* Dept of Modern History, Liverpool Univ. 8 Abercromby Square, PO Box 147, Liverpool L69 3BX.

Rowe-Evans, Adrian; Secretary and Registrar, University of Warwick, since 1973; *b* 1923; *m* 1949; one *s.* BA London 1949. Admin. Asst, Univ. London, 1949–51; Asst/Dep. Registrar, Univ. Hong Kong, 1951–61; Sec., Makerere UC, 1961–64; Warden, International Hall, Univ. London, 1964–72. *Address:* Univ. of Warwick, Coventry CV4 7AL.

Rowell, George Rignall; Special Lecturer in Drama, University of Bristol, since 1969; *b* 1923; *m* 1959. BA Oxon 1948 (1st cl. History), MA Oxon 1948, BLitt Oxon 1950. Jun. Fellow, Bristol Univ., 1951; Asst Lectr, Bristol Univ., 1951–54, Lectr, Bristol Univ., 1954–62, Sen. Lectr, Bristol Univ., 1962–69. RA, 1942–46; aptmts incl. Adj., Field Regt RA, Staff Capt., Brit. Mil. Admin (Malaya); Gen. Editor, Theatre Res., 1961–64. *Publications:* Nineteenth Century Plays, 1953, 2nd edn 1972; The Victorian Theatre, 1956; Engaged! (play), 1963; Sixty Thousand Nights (play), 1967; Late Victorian Plays, 1968, 2nd edn 1972; The Lyons Mail (play), 1969; Victorian Dramatic Criticism, 1971; Trelawny (play), 1972. *Address:* Dept of Drama, Univ. of Bristol.

Rowland, Robert Lewis; Lecturer in Interdisciplinary Studies, School of European Studies, University of East Anglia, since 1970; *b* 1945; *m* 1970. BA Cantab 1967, MA Cantab 1971. Res. Associate, Centre for Res. in Soc. Scis, Univ. of Kent, 1967–70. Vis. Fellow, Centro Brasileiro de Análise e Planejamento, São Paulo, 1973. *Address:* Sch. of European Studies, Univ. of East Anglia, Norwich NOR 88C.

608

Rowlands, Dr John; Senior Lecturer, Department of Welsh, St David's University College, Lampeter, since 1973; *m*; two *s* one *d.* BA Wales (1st cl. Hons), MA Wales, DPhil Oxon. St David's UC, Lampeter, 1968. Sec., Yr Academi Gymreig. *Publications:* Lle Bo'r Gwenyn; Yn ôl i'w Teyrnasoedd; Ienctid yw 'Mhechod; Llawer is na'r Angylion; Bydded Tywyllwch; Arch ym Mhrâg. *Address:* Coleg Prifysgol Dewi Sant, Llanbedr Pont Steffan, Dyfed SA48 7ED.

Rowley, Prof. Brian Alan, MA, PhD; Professor of European Literature, University of East Anglia, since 1968; *b* 1923; *m* 1953; one *s* one *d.* BA Cantab 1948 (1st cl. Mod. Langs), MA Cantab 1950, PhD Cantab 1952. Asst Lectr, Univ. College, London, 1951, Lectr, 1954; Sen. Lectr, Univ. of East Anglia, 1964, Reader, 1966; Dean of the School of European Studies, 1971–74. Intelligence Corps, 1942–46. Mem., Cttee, Univ. of London Inst. of Germanic Langs and Literatures, 1962– ; Mem., Cttee, Modern Humanities Res. Assoc., 1965– ; Sec., Conf. of Univ. Teachers of German, 1959–67; Sec., English Goethe Soc., 1962– . *Publications:* ed, Novalis: Three Works, 1955; Keller: Kleider machen Leute, 1960; (with G. A. Wells) The Fundamentals of German Grammar on one card; contrib. The Thames and Hudson Encyclopaedia of the Arts, ed Sir Herbert Read, 1966; The Romantic Period in Germany, ed S. S. Prawer, 1970; *contrib.* German Life and Letters, Mod. Lang., Mod. Lang. Qly, Psychoanalysis and the Social Sciences, Publ. Engl. Goethe Soc., YWMLS. *Address:* School of European Studies, Univ. of East Anglia, Univ. Plain, Norwich NOR 88C.

Rowley, Prof. Charles Kershaw; David Dale Professor of Economics, University of Newcastle upon Tyne, since 1972, and Director of the Centre for Research in Public and Industrial Economics since 1974; *b* 1939; *m* 1961, 1971; two *s* two *d.* BA Nottingham 1960 (1st cl.), PhD Nottingham 1964. Lectr, Nottingham, 1962–65; Lectr, Kent, 1965–68; Sen. Res. Fellow, York, 1968–69; Sen. Lectr, Kent, 1969–70; Sen. Lectr in Econs, Univ. of York, 1970–72, Reader, 1972. *Publications:* The British Monopolies Commission, 1966; Steel and Public Policy, 1971; Antitrust and Economic Efficiency, 1972; (with A. T. Peacock) The Utility of Welfare Economics, 1974; *contrib.* Appl. Econ., Econ. Jl, Jl Law Econ., Jl Pol Econ., Moorg, Wall St, Scott. Jl Pol Econ., Southn. Econ. Jl, Jl Pub. Econs, Jl Long-Range Planning. *Address:* Dept of Economics, Univ. of Newcastle upon Tyne, Newcastle upon Tyne NE1 7RU.

Rowley, Dr Gwyn, PhD; Lecturer in Geography, University of Sheffield, since 1964; *b* 1938; one *s* one *d.* BA Wales 1961, PhD Wales 1967. Asst Prof., Univ. of Nebraska, 1967–68; Asst Prof., Clark Univ., 1968–69. *Publications: contrib.* Ann. Assoc. Amer. Geogrs, Area, Econ. Geog., Prof. Geog., Tijd. Econ. Soc. Geog., Trans Inst. Brit. Geogrs. *Address:* Dept of Geography, Univ. of Sheffield, Sheffield S10 2TN.

Rowlinson, William; Lecturer, Department of Education, University of Sheffield, since 1965; *b* 1931; *m* 1959; one *s* two *d*. BA Cantab 1953 (2i Mod. and Med. Lang.), CertEd Cantab 1955. Vis. Lectr, Univ. of Michigan, 1968–69. *Publications*: Sprich mal Deutsch!, 1967–69; Lies mal Deutsch!, 1973, part 2 1974; *contrib*. NALA Jl, Times Educnl Supp. *Address*: Dept of Education, Univ. of Sheffield, Sheffield.

Rowntree, Derek; Senior Lecturer in Educational Technology, Institute of Educational Technology, The Open University, since 1970; *b* 1936; *m* 1958; two *s*. BSc (Econ.) Hull 1958, CertEd Hull 1959; Member: Assoc. for Programmed Learning and Educnl Technol; Soc. of Authors. Brighton Polytechnic, 1966, Brighton Coll. of Educn, until 1969. *Publications*: Basically Branching: A Handbook for Programmers, 1966, Danish trans. 1970; Learn how to Study, 1970, Spanish trans. 1974; Educational Technology in Curriculum Development, 1974. *Address*: The Open Univ., Walton Hall, Milton Keynes MK7 6AA.

Roxbee Cox, Jeremy William, BA, BPhil; Senior Lecturer, Department of Philosophy, University of Lancaster, since 1969; *b* 1932; *m* 1962; one *s* one *d*. BA Oxon 1954 (1st cl. PPE), BPhil Oxon 1956 (Philosophy). Asst Lectr, Queen's Univ., Belfast, 1957–60, Lectr, 1960–64; Lectr, Univ. of Lancaster, 1964–69. *Publications*: contrib. Perception, a philosophical symposium, ed F. N. Sibley, 1971; *contrib*. Analysis, Mind, Philos. Qly, Philos. Rev. *Address*: Dept of Philosophy, Univ. of Lancaster, Bailrigg, Lancaster.

Roy, Donald Hubert; Senior Lecturer-in-charge, Department of Drama, University of Hull, since 1969; *b* 1930. BA (Wales) 1950 (1st cl. Hons. French), DipEd Wales 1951, MA Wales 1954; Mem. Soc. for French Studies, Mem. Assoc. of Univ. Teachers. Asst Lectr in French: Univ. St Andrews, 1958–59; Univ. Glasgow, 1959–61; Lectr in French, Univ. Glasgow, 1961–63; Lectr i/c Drama, Univ. Hull, 1963–69; Vis. Prof. in Drama, Univ. of Delaware, 1974. Mem. Bd of Management, Georgian Theatre, Richmond, and New Theatre, Hull; Mem. Cttee, Yorkshire Arts Assoc. *Publications*: (jtly), Le 'Mémoire' de Mahelot et L'Agarite de Durval: vers une reconstitution pratique, in, Le Lieu Théâtral à la Renaissance, 1963; Mahelot's 'Nights': a traditional stage effect, in, Gallica, 1968; Acteurs et spectateurs à l'hôtel de Bourgogne: vers une notation de la communication théâtrale, in, Dramaturgie et Société, 1968; Theatre Royal, Hull; or the vanishing circuit, in, Nineteenth Century British Theatre, 1971; *contrib*. Critical Survey, Drama in Educn, Jeunesse de Racine, Revue D'Histoire du Théâtre, Speech and Drama. *Address*: Dept of Drama, Univ. of Hull, Hull HU6 7RX.

Roy, Dr Ian; Lecturer in History, University of London, King's College, since 1962; *b* 1932; *m* 1957; three *d*. MA St Andrews 1954 (1st cl. Hist.), DPhil Oxon 1964. Asst Lectr, King's Coll., 1959–62. *Publications*: ed, The Royalist Ordnance Papers, 1642–1646, Pt I, 1964, Pt II, 1973; ed, Blaise de Monluc, 1971; *contrib*. Bull. Inst. Hist. Res. *Address*: Dept of History, King's College, WC2.

Roy, Dr James; Senior Lecturer, Department of Ancient History, University of Sheffield, since 1973 (Lecturer, 1963–73); *b* 1938; *m* 1965; one *s*. MA Edinburgh 1959, BA Cantab 1961, MA, PhD Cantab 1969. Humboldt-Stipendiat, Univ. of Heidelberg, 1969–70. *Publications*: *contrib*. Athenaeum, Historia, etc. *Address*: Dept of Ancient History, The Univ., Sheffield S10 2TN.

Royle, Dr Edward; Lecturer in History, University of York, since 1972; *b* 1944; *m* 1968. BA Cantab 1965, MA Cantab 1969, PhD Cantab 1969; Member: Historical Assoc., Trade Union Democratic Labour History Soc., Freethought History and Bibliography Soc. Res. Fellow, Selwyn Coll., Cambridge, 1968–69; Staff Fellow and College Lectr, Selwyn Coll., Cambridge, 1969–72. *Publications*: Descriptive Index of the Letters and Papers of G. J. Holyoake, 1968; Radical Politics, 1790–1900: religion and unbelief, 1971; Victorian Infidels: the origins of the British Secularist Movement, 1791–1866, 1974; *contrib*. Historical Jl. *Address*: Dept of History, Univ. of York, York Y01 5DD.

Rubin, Neville N.; Lecturer in African Law, Department of Law, School of Oriental and African Studies, University of London, since 1965; *b* 1935; *m* 1960; two *s*. BA 1955, LLB 1960, Cape Town; Advocate: Supreme Court of South Africa, 1962; High Court of Swaziland, 1964; Member: Royal Commonwealth Soc.; RIIA. Jun. Lectr in Comparative African Govt and Law, Univ. of Cape Town, 1961–63; Res. Officer in African Law, SOAS, Univ. of London, 1963–65; Vis. Prof. Univ. of Calif., Los Angeles, 1966; Associate Prof., Fac. of Law and Econ. Scis, Univ. of Cameroun, 1968–69. *Publications*: ed (with W. M. Warren), Dams in Africa, 1968; ed (with E. Cotran), Readings in African Law, 2 vols, 1970; ed (with E. Cotran), Annual Survey of African Law, 1967, 1968, 1969, 1970; Cameroun, an African Federation, 1971; *contrib*. Jl African Law. *Address*: Sch. of Oriental and African Studies, Univ. of London, Malet Street, WC1E 7HP.

Rudd, Ernest; Reader, Department of Sociology, University of Essex, since 1964; *b* 1924; *m* 1949; three *d*. BSc(Econ) London 1948, PhD London 1958; FSS. Founder Mem., Soc. Res. Higher Educn, 1964, Mem., Governing Council, 1964– , Treasurer, 1964–69. Dept Sci. Indust. Res., 1948–64. Mem., Cttee on Capital for Higher Educn, ODM, 1965–68; Mem., E Anglian Reg. Adv. Cttee for Further Educn, 1971– ; Mem., Transport Users' Cons. Cttee for E Anglia, 1973– . Mem. Edit. Bd, Research in Higher Educn (NY), 1973– . *Publications*: (with S. Hatch) Graduate Study and After, 1968; (with H. J. Butcher) Contemporary Problems in Higher Education, 1972; *contrib*. Higher Educn Rev., Indust. Econ., Jl Royal Stat. Soc., Minerva, Univ. Qly. *Address*: Dept of Sociology, Univ. of Essex, Colchester CO4 3SQ.

Rudd, Dr William George Allan, MA, PhD; Senior Lecturer in Curriculum Development, University of Manchester, since 1964; *b* 1916; *m* 1942; two *d.* BA London 1950 (2nd cl. Geog.), MA London 1956 (Educn), PhD London 1962 (Educn). Mem., Brit. Psychol Soc. Lectr in Education, Manchester, 1958–64; Vis. Lectr, Univ. of Chicago, 1967. Dir, NW Reg. Curriculum Develt Project, 1967–74. *Publications*: CSE: A Group Study Approach to Research and Development (Schools Council Examinations Bulletin 20), 1970; *contrib.* Educational Research in Britain, 2, 1970; *contrib.* Brit. Jl Educnl Psychol. *Address*: School of Education, The Univ., Manchester M13 9PL.

Rudden, Dr Bernard, MA; Fellow of Oriel College, Oxford University, since 1965, and University Lecturer in European Law, Oxford, since 1972; *b* 1933; *m* 1957; three *s* one *d.* BA Cantab 1956, MA Cantab 1961; PhD Wales 1965; MA Oxon 1965; Solicitor 1959. Lectr, Univ. Coll. of Wales, 1959–64; Vis. Fellow, Univ. of Leiden, Netherlands, 1964–65. *Publications*: Soviet Insurance Law, 1966; (with H. Moseley) Outline of the Law of Mortgages, 1967; (with O. Kahn-Freund and C. Lévy) Source-Book on French Law, 1972; *contrib.* Encyclopedia of Soviet Law; *contrib.* Conveyan., Internat. Comp. Law Qly Rev., Law Qly Rev., NY Law Jl. *Address*: Oriel College, Oxford.

Ruddock, Edward C.; Lecturer in Architecture, University of Edinburgh, since 1965; *b* 1930; *m* 1955; three *s.* BA Dublin 1950, MAI Dublin 1967; MSc(Eng) London 1953; MICE 1958. Mem., Brit. Geotech. Soc., Soc. Archit. Hist. Lectr, Kumasi, Ghana, 1960–65. *Publications*: Bridges of 1735–1835 (forthcoming); *contrib.* Geotech., Structural Engr, Industrial Archaeol., Trans Newcomen Soc. *Address*: Dept of Architecture, Univ. of Edinburgh, Edinburgh EH8 9YL.

Ruddock, Ralph; Senior Lecturer in Adult Education, University of Manchester, since 1971; *b* 1913; *m* 1938; one *s.* BSc(Econ) London External 1948; Mem., Nat. Inst. Adult Educn. Tutor, Holly Royde Resid. Coll., Univ. of Manchester, 1949–51; Resid. Tutor, Extra-Mural Dept, 1951–65; Sen. Staff Tutor and Dir of Courses in Social Studies, 1965–71. *Publications*: Roles and Relationships, 1969, Dutch edn 1970, Italian edn 1972; ed, Six Approaches to the Person, 1972; Sociological Perspectives on Adult Education, 1973; *contrib.* Studies Adult Educn. *Address*: Dept of Adult Education, Univ. of Manchester, Manchester M13 9PL.

Ruel, Dr Malcolm John; Lecturer in Social and Political Sciences (Social Anthropology), University of Cambridge, and Fellow of Clare College, Cambridge, since 1970; *b* 1927; *m* 1958; three *d.* BA Cantab 1951 (English and Social Anthropol.), BLitt Oxon 1952 (Social. Anthropol.), MA Cantab 1955, DPhil Oxon 1959; FRAI. Mem., Assoc. Social. Anthropol. Internat. Afr. Inst. Asst Lectr, Edinburgh Univ., 1958–62, Lectr, 1962–68; Lectr, Univ. of Ife, Nigeria, 1964–65; Sen. Lectr, Edinburgh, 1968–70. Associate Dean, Fac. of Social Science, Edinburgh

Univ., 1968–70. Hon. Treas., ASA, 1967–71; Mem., Cttee, ASA, 1966–71; Council, RAI, 1969–72. *Publications*: Leopards and Leaders: Constitutional Politics among a Cross River People, 1969; *contrib.* Afr., Jl Royal Anthropol Inst., Southw. Jl Anthropol. *Address*: Clare College, Cambridge.

Rule, Dr John Graham; Lecturer in History, University of Southampton, since 1968; *b* 1944; *m* 1967; one *s.* BA Hons Cantab 1965 (Hist.), MA 1968, PhD Warwick 1971 (Soc. Hist.). *Publications*: *contrib.* Bull. Soc. for Study of Labour Hist., Labor Hist. *Address*: Dept of History, Univ. of Southampton, Southampton S09 5NH.

Runcie, John Dick; Lecturer in American History, Department of History, University of Leicester, since 1964; *b* 1939; *m* 1968. BA Southampton 1961 (1st cl. Hons), MA Columbia 1964; Member: Brit. Assoc. for American Studies; AUT. *Publications*: *contrib.* Pennsylvania Hist., William and Mary Qly. *Address*: Dept of History, Univ. of Leicester, Leicester LE1 7RH.

Runciman, Walter Garrison, MA; Fellow of Trinity College, University of Cambridge, since 1971; *b* 1934; *m* 1963; one *s* two *d.* BA Cambridge 1958 (1st cl. Classics Pt I, 1st cl. Hist. Pt II), MA Cambridge 1963. Fellow, Trinity Coll., Cambridge, 1959–63; Pt-time Reader in Sociology, Univ. of Sussex, 1967–69; Vis. Lectr in Sociology, Harvard Univ., 1970. Mem. SSRC, 1974– . Dir, Walter Runciman & Co., Ltd, and subsid. cos, 1968– . *Publications*: Plato's Later Epistemology, 1962; Social Science and Political Theory, 1963, 2nd edn 1969, German, Spanish, Portuguese and Japanese trans; Relative Deprivation and Social Justice, 1966, pbk edn 1972, Italian trans; Sociology in its Place and Other Essays, 1970; A Critique of Max Weber's Philosophy of Social Science, 1972; *contrib.* Analysis, Brit. Jl Sociol., Mind, Philos. Qly, Philos., Sociol Rev., Sociol. *Address*: Trinity College, Cambridge CB2 1TQ.

Rundle, Bernard Bede, MA; Fellow and Lecturer in Philosophy, Trinity College, University of Oxford, since 1963; *b* 1937; *m* 1968; one *s* one *d.* MA New Zealand 1959; BPhil Oxon 1961, MA Oxon 1963. Lectr, Otago Univ., 1959; Jun. Res. Fellow, The Queen's Coll., Oxford, 1961–63; Vis. Prof., Univ. of Connecticut, 1970; Washington Univ., 1970. *Publications*: History of Logic, in, Encyclopedia of Philosophy, ed Edwards, 1967; Perception, Sensation and Verification, 1972; *contrib.* Proc. Aristot. Soc. *Address*: Trinity College, Oxford.

Runnalls, Graham Arthur, BA, MA, DipGenLing; Lecturer in French, Edinburgh University, since 1966; *b* 1937; *m* 1961; two *d.* BA Exeter 1959 (French), MA Exeter 1966, DipGenLing Edinburgh 1967. Asst Lectr, Exeter Univ., 1962–63; Lectr, N Western Poly., 1963–66. Asst Examiner in French, London Univ. GCE, 1963– ; Oxford Univ. GCE, 1963–66; Scot. Cert. of Educn, 1966– ; Sec., Ann. Conf. of Scot. Univs French Depts, 1967–71. *Publications*: Le Miracle de l'Enfant Ressuscité, 1972; Le Mystère de St Christofle, 1973; Le Mystère de la Passion, 1974; *contrib*. Med. Æv., Philol Qly, Rev. Lang. Rom., Rom. Philol., Linguistics, TES. *Address*: Dept of French, Univ. of Edinburgh, Edinburgh EH8 9YL.

Rupp, Rev. Prof. Ernest Gordon, MA, DD, FBA; Dixie Professor of Ecclesiastical History, University of Cambridge, since 1968; Principal, Wesley House, Cambridge, since 1967; *b* 1910; *m* 1938; one *s*. BA London, BA Cantab 1935, MA Cantab 1941, DD Cantab 1955; Hon. DD Aberdeen; Hon. Dr Théol. Paris; FBA 1970. Methodist Minister, Chislehurst, 1938–46; Wesley House, Cambridge, 1946–47; Richmond Coll., Surrey, 1947–52; Birkbeck Lectr, Trinity Coll., Cambridge, 1947; Lectr, Cambridge Univ., 1952–56; Prof. of Eccles. History, Manchester Univ., 1956–67. Pres., Methodist Conf., 1968–69; Mem., Central Cttee of World Council of Churches, 1969. Fellow, Emmanuel Coll., Cambridge, 1968; Hon. Fellow, Fitzwilliam Coll., Cambridge, 1969; Hon. Fellow, King's Coll., London, 1969. *Publications*: Studies in the English Protestant Tradition, 1947; Luther's Progress to the Diet of Worms, 1951; The Righteousness of God (Luther studies), 1953; Some Makers of English Religion, 1957; The Old Reformation and the New, 1967; Patterns of Reformation, 1969. *Address*: Principal's Lodge, Wesley House, Cambridge.

Rush, Dr Michael David; Lecturer in Department of Politics, University of Exeter, since 1964; *b* 1937; *m* 1964; two *s*. BA Sheffield 1962 (Mod. Hist. and Govt), PhD Sheffield 1966 (Politics); Mem., Pol Studies Assoc., Royal Inst. Public Admin, Study of Parliament Gp. Vis. Lectr, Univ. of W Ontario, 1967–68. Mem., Adv. Gp on Design of Information Systems in Social Sciences, Off. for Tech. and Sci. Information. *Publications*: The Selection of Parliamentary Candidates, 1969; (with A. Barker) The Member of Parliament and his information, 1970; (with Phillip Althoff) An Introduction to Political Sociology, 1971; ed and contrib. (with Malcolm Shaw), The House of Commons: services and facilities, 1974; chapters, in, Political Science, ed H. V. Wiseman, 1967; Political Parties in Britain, ed J. D. Lees and R. Kimber, 1972. *Address*: Dept of Politics, Univ. of Exeter, Exeter EX4 4PU.

Rushby, John George; Senior Lecturer, School of Education, University of Southampton, since 1966; *b* 1917; *m* 1946; one *s* one *d*. BSc London 1939 (1st cl.), DipEd London 1940. Lectr, Southampton Univ., 1950–66. Mem., Gov. Body, var. Colls of Educn, 1966– . *Publications*: Study Geography, 1967–71, Danish, German and American edns 1970– . *Address*: School of Education, Univ. of Southampton, Southampton SO9 5NH.

Rushton, Dr Julian Gordon; Lecturer in Music, Faculty of Music, University of Cambridge, since 1974; *b* 1941; *m* 1968; two *s*. MusB Cantab 1965, MA Cantab 1967, DPhil Oxon 1970; Mem. Royal Musical Assoc. Lectr in Music, Univ. of E Anglia,

1968–74. *Publications*: ed, Berlioz: Huit Scènes de Faust, 1970; contrib. Grove's Dictionary of Music and Musicians; *contrib*. Music and Letters, Musical Times, Music Review, Proc. RMA. *Address*: Faculty of Music, Univ. Music Sch., Downing Place, Cambridge CB2 3EL.

Russ, Charles V. J.; Lecturer in German and Linguistics, Department of Language, University of York, since 1972, *b* 1942; *m* 1969. BA Newcastle upon Tyne 1964, MLitt Newcastle upon Tyne 1967, MA Reading 1971 (Linguistics). Lectr, Dept of German, Univ. Southampton, 1967–72. *Publications*: Historical German Phonology and Morphology, 1974; *contrib*. MLR, ZDL, YPL. *Address*: Dept of Language, Univ. of York, Heslington, York YO1 5DD.

Russ, Colin Albert Harry, MA; Senior Lecturer in German, University of Kent at Canterbury, since 1971; *b* 1930; *m* 1972. BA London 1951 (1st cl. German), MA London 1954. Asst, Dept of German, Univ. of Glasgow, 1955–58, Lectr, 1958–66; Lectr, Univ. of Kent at Canterbury, 1966–71; Vis. Instructor, Columbia Univ., 1965; Vis. Associate Prof., Univ. of California, Santa Cruz, 1969; Vis. Associate Prof., Univ. of Utah, 1971; Vis. Prof., Univ. of Utah, 1972. *Publications*: ed, Goethe: Three Tales, 1964; ed, S. Lenz: Das Wrack and Other Stories, 1967, 2nd edn 1969; ed, Der Schriftsteller Siegfried Lenz: Urteile und Standpunkte, 1973; essays in var. books; *contrib*. Germ. Life Lett., PEGS. *Address*: Darwin College, Univ. of Kent at Canterbury, Canterbury CT2 7NY.

Russell, Dr Colin Archibald; Reader in the History of Science and Technology, Faculty of Arts, The Open University, since 1972; *b* 1928; *m* 1954; one *s* three *d*. BSc London 1949 (Chemistry), CertEd Hull 1950, MSc London 1958 (Hist. and Philos. Science), PhD London 1962 (Hist. and Philos. Science); FChemSoc 1952, ARIC 1953, FRIC 1962, Mem. Brit. Soc. for History of Science 1964, Mem. Royal Inst. 1972. Sen. Lectr, History of Science, Open Univ., 1970–72. Asst Lectr in Chemistry, Kingston Tech. Coll., 1950–58; Lectr, Sen. Lectr, Principal Lectr in Chemistry, Harris Coll., Preston, 1958–70; Mem. Council, British Soc. Hist. Science, 1967–71; Mem. Council, Open Univ., 1971–73. *Publications*: (jtly) Physics and Chemistry of Baking, 1963, 2nd edn 1969; Organic Chemistry Today, 2nd edn (1st edn F. W. Gibbs), 1969; The History of Valency, 1971; (jtly) Science and the Rise of Technology, 1972; ed, Science and Religious Belief, 1973; *contrib*. Annals of Science, Chem. Communications, Jl Chem. Soc. *Address*: The Open Univ., Milton Keynes, MK7 6AA.

Russell, Conrad Sebastian Robert; Reader in Modern History, Department of History, Bedford College, University of London, since 1974 (Lecturer in History, 1960–74); *b* 1937; *m* 1962; two *s*. BA Oxon 1958, MA Oxon 1962; FRHistS 1971. *Publications*: The Crisis of Parliaments: English History 1509–1660, 1971; ed, The Origins of the English Civil War, 1973; *contrib*. Bull. Inst.

Hist. Res., Econ. Hist. Rev., EHR, Jl Eccles. Hist., Jl Pol Studies, Notes and Queries. *Address*: Dept of History, Bedford College, NW1 4NS.

Russell, Donald Andrew Frank Moore, MA, FBA; Fellow and Tutor in Classics, St John's College, Oxford University, since 1948; *b* 1920; *m* 1967. BA, MA Oxon 1947 (1st cl. Lit. Hum.); FBA 1971. Res. Lectr, Christ Church, Oxford, 1947; Dean, St John's Coll., Oxford, 1957–65, Tutor for Admission, 1968–72. Mem., Council, Class. Assoc., 1967–70; Mem., Council, Hellenic Soc., 1970–73; Jt Editor, Class. Qly, 1965–70; Mem., Class. Jls Bd, 1971; Mem., Governing Body, King's Coll. Sch., Wimbledon. *Publications*: ed, Longinus: On the Sublime, 1964; (with M. Winterbottom) Ancient Literary Criticism, 1972; Plutarch, 1973; *contrib.* Class. Qly, Class. Rev., Jl Rom. Studies, Jl Hellen. Studies, Proc. Camb. Philol Soc. *Address*: St John's College, Oxford.

Russell, Joycelyne Gledhill; Fellow since 1959, Tutor in Modern History, since 1969, and Librarian, since 1953, St Hugh's College, Oxford University, and University Lecturer, since 1970; *b* 1919; *m* 1967. BA Oxford 1940 (2nd cl. Mod. Hist.), MA Oxon 1945, DPhil Oxon 1951; FRHistS. Lecturer, St Hugh's Coll., 1962–69. Aux. Territorial Service, 1940–46; UNESCO, 1946–47; Mem., Libr. Bd, Oxford Univ., 1967– ; Governor, Burford Sch. *Publications*: (as J. G. Dickinson) The Congress of Arras, 1435: A Study in medieval diplomacy, 1955; The Field of Cloth of Gold: Men and Manners in 1520, 1969; *contrib.* Bull. Inst. Hist. Res., EHR, Hist. *Address*: St Hugh's College, Oxford.

Russell, Prof. Peter Edward Lionel Russell, FRHistS; King Alfonso XIII Professor of Spanish and Director of Portuguese Studies, University of Oxford, since 1953, and Fellow of Exeter College, Oxford, since 1953; *b* 1913. BA Oxon 1935 (1st cl. Mod. Langs), MA Oxon 1939; FRHistS. Lectr, St John's Coll., 1937–53, and Queen's Coll., 1938–45, Oxford, Lectr, Oxford Univ. and Fellow of Queen's Coll., 1946–53; Norman Maccoll Lectr, Cambridge, 1969. Intelligence Corps, 1940–46. Mem., Portuguese Acad. of History, 1956; Mem., UGC Cttee on Latin-American Studies in British Univs, 1962–64. *Publications*: As Fontes de Fernão Lopes, 1941; The English Intervention in Spain and Portugal in the Time of Edward III and Richard II, 1955; Prince Henry the Navigator, 1960; (with D. M. Rogers) Hispanic Manuscripts and Books in the Bodleian and Oxford College Libraries, 1962; ed, Spain: a companion to Spanish studies, 1973; Temas de La Celestina y otras estudios (del Cid al Quijote), 1974; *contrib.* Mod. Lang. Rev., Medium Ævum, Bull. Hispanic Studies, Revista da História, Do Tempo e da História, Anuario de Estudios Medievales, etc. *Address*: Exeter College, Oxford.

Russell, Ralph; Reader in Urdu, School of Oriental and African Studies, University of London, since 1964; *b* 1918; *m* 1948; one *s* two *d*. BA Cantab 1940, BA London 1949.

Lectr in Urdu, SOAS, 1949–64. *Publications*: (with K. Islam) Three Mughal Poets, 1968, Brit. edn 1969; Ghalib, vol. I: Life and Letters, 1969, Brit. and Amer. edns; trans. A. Ahmad: The Shore and the Wave, 1971; ed, Ghalib, the Poet and his Age, 1972; *contrib.* Jl Asian Studies, Jl Royal Asiat. Soc., S Asian Rev., Modern Asian Studies. *Address*: School of Oriental and African Studies, Malet Street, WC1E 7HP.

Russell-Smith, Dame Enid Mary Russell, DBE, MA; Part-time Hon. Lecturer, Department of Politics, Durham, since 1964, and Principal, St Aidan's College, Durham University, 1949–70; *b* 1903. BA Cantab 1925 (1st cl. Mod. and Medieval Langs Tripos – French and German – Pts I and II). Civil Servant, 1925–63; ex-Dep. Sec., Min. of Health, Chm., Bp of Durham's Commn on Church in Sunderland, 1968–70; Mem., Teesside Local Educn Cttee (rep. Durham Univ.), 1969–74, Cleveland Educn Cttee, 1974– . *Address*: Dept of Politics, Durham Univ., 23–26 Old Elvet, Durham DH1 3HY.

Rutherford, Prof. Andrew; Regius (Chalmers) Professor of English Literature, University of Aberdeen, since 1968; *b* 1929; *m* 1953; two *s* one *d*. MA Edinburgh 1951 (1st cl. Eng. Lang. and Lit.); BLitt Oxon 1959. Asst Lectr, Edinburgh Univ., 1955, Lectr, 1956–64; Vis. Associate Prof., Rochester Univ., 1963; Sen. Lectr, Aberdeen Univ., 1964; 2nd Prof. of English, Aberdeen Univ., 1965–68; Byron Foundn Lectr, Nottingham Univ., 1964; Chatterton Lectr, British Acad., 1965; Stevenson Lectr, Edinburgh Univ., 1967; Byron Lectr, Byron Soc., 1973. Chm., English Bd, CNAA, 1968–73. *Publications*: Byron: A Critical Study, 1961; ed, Kipling's Mind and Art, 1964; ed, Byron: The Critical Heritage, 1970; ed, 20th Century Interpretations of A Passage to India, 1970; ed, Kipling: A Sahibs' War and Other Stories, 1971; ed, Kipling: Friendly Brook and Other Stories, 1971; *contrib.* learned jls. *Address*: Dept of English, Taylor Building, King's College, Aberdeen AB9 2UB.

Rutherford, Dr John David; Fellow and Praelector in Spanish, The Queen's College, Oxford University, since 1968; *b* 1941; *m* 1964; three *d*. BA Oxon 1963, DPhil Oxon 1970. Fac. Lectr in Spanish, Oxford, 1965– . Fellow, St Antony's College, Oxford, 1965–68. *Publications*: Mexican Society During the Revolution: a Literary Approach, 1971; An Annotated Bibliography of Novels of the Mexican Revolution, 1972; A Critical Guide to L. Alas's La Regenta, 1974. *Address*: The Queen's College, Oxford.

Ruthven, Prof. Annette Jocelyn O.; *see* Otway-Ruthven.

Rutter, John G.; *see* Gatt-Rutter.

Rutter, Prof. Michael Llewellyn, MD, DPM, FRCP; Professor of Child Psychiatry, Institute of Psychiatry, University of London, since 1973 (Reader, 1968–73); *b* 1933; *m* 1958; one *s* two *d*. MB, ChB Birmingham 1955; AcadDPM London 1961 (Distinction); MD Birmingham 1963 (Honours); MRCS, LRCP

1955, MRCP 1958, FRCP 1972, FRCPsych 1971. Nuffield Medical Travelling Fellow, Albert Einstein Coll. of Medicine, NY, 1961–62; Mem., Scientific Staff, Medical Res. Council, Social. Psychiatry Res. Unit, 1962–65; Sen. Lectr, Inst. of Psychiatry, 1965–68. Var. NHS apptmts, 1955–61; Brit. Council Lectr, Venezuela, 1965; Temp. Cnsltnt, WHO, 1967–68; Mem., Educnl Res. Bd, SSRC, 1968–73; Mem., Cttee, Assoc. Child Psychiat. Psychol., 1966–68, Chm., 1973–74; Council, Psychiat. Sect., Royal Soc. Med., 1969–72. *Publications:* Children of Sick Parents, 1966; (jtly) Education, Health and Behaviour, 1970; (jtly) A Neuropsychiatric Study in Childhood, 1970; Infantile Autism, Concepts, Characteristics and Treatment, 1971; (jtly) Children with Delayed Speech, 1972; Maternal Deprivation Reassessed, 1972; *contrib.* Jl Child Psychol. Psychiat., Brit. Jl Psychiat., Develp. Med. Child Neurol., Social Psychiat., Hum. Relat., Brit. Jl Clin. Soc. Psychol., etc. *Address:* Institute of Psychiatry, de Crespigny Park, Denmark Hill, SE5 8AF.

Ruxton, John; Lecturer, Department of Architecture and Building Science, University of Strathclyde, since 1966; *b* 1934; *m* 1956; one *s* one *d*. BSc Strathclyde 1964 (Hons Building Technology); Teacher Training Cert. Jordanhill 1964. Assessor, Scott. Assoc. Nat. Certs and Dips, 1971; Examiner, RIBA. *Address:* Univ. of Strathclyde, Dept of Architecture and Building Science, 131 Rottenrow, Glasgow G4 0NG.

Ryan, Edward Francis; Professor of Law, University College, Cork, since 1952; *b* 1914; *m* 1946, 1953; three *d*. BA Cantab 1935, MA Cantab 1952; Barrister-at-Law: Middle Temple 1939, King's Inns 1947. *Publications:* Notes of Irish Cases, 1949–1958, 1959–1968; ed, The Irish Digest, 1959–1970, 1972. *Address:* Univ. College, Cork.

Ryan, James Patrick; Lecturer in the Education of Maladjusted Children, Department of Education, University of Manchester, since 1967; *b* 1927; *m* 1958; two *d*. MA Victoria Univ. of Wellington, NZ 1957 (1st cl. Psychol.); Qualified Teacher 1952; Member: Brit. Psychol Soc., 1959– ; Cttee, Assoc. of Workers for Maladjusted Children. Sec./ Treas., Educn Section, Brit. Psychol Soc., 1971– . *Publication:* Maladjustment, in, Educational Research in Britain, vol. III, Butcher and Point, 1973. *Address:* Dept of Education, Univ. of Manchester, Manchester M13 9PL.

Ryan, Dr Terence Michael; Lecturer, Department of Social Administration, University College of Swansea, since 1963; *b* 1937; *m* 1962; one *s* two *d*. BA Oxon 1960 (2nd cl. Eng. Lang. and Lit.), Dip. Public and Social Admin Oxon 1961, PhD Wales 1967. Res. Asst, Dept of Social Admin, Manchester Univ., 1961–63. *Publications:* The Work of the Welsh Hospital Board 1948–1974, 1974; *contrib.* Brit. Jl Sociol., Comm. Med., Internat. Health Services Jl, Public Admin, Social and Econ. Admin. *Address:* Dept of Social Administration, Univ. Coll. of Swansea, Singleton Park, Swansea SA2 8PP.

Ryan, Dr William Francis; Lecturer in Russian Language and Literature, School of Slavonic and East European Studies, London University, since 1967; *b* 1937; *m* 1963; two *d*. BA Oxon 1961, DPhil Oxon 1971; Member: BUAS, BSHS, MHRA. Librarian and Asst Curator, Museum of History of Science, Oxford Univ., 1965–67. Mem. Editorial Bd, Slavonic and East European Review. *Publications:* ed jtly, M. Wheeler: Oxford Russian-English Dictionary; *contrib.* Oxford Slavonic Papers, Smithsonian Jl History. *Address:* Univ. of London, School of Slavonic and East European Studies, Malet Street, WC1E 7HU.

Rybczynski, Tadeusz Mieczrslan; Visiting Professor of Economics, University of Surrey, since 1969; *b* 1923; *m*; one *d*. BComm London 1949, MScEcon London 1952; FIB 1967; Member: Royal Econ. Soc.; Royal Stat. Soc.; Soc. of Business Economists (Chm.); Soc. of Investment Analysts; Long Range Planning Soc. Vis. Lectr, LSE, 1958–59. Dir, Lazard Securities Ltd. Vice-Chm., British Accounting and Finance Assoc.; Governor, and Mem. Exec. Cttee, Nat. Inst. for Econ. and Soc. Res.; Member Council: Trade Policy Res. Centre; Foreign Affairs Club. *Publications:* ed, The Value Added Tax, 1969; ed (jtly) The Economist in Business, 1967; ed, New Era in Competition, 1972; *contrib.* Economica. *Address:* Dept of Economics, Univ. of Surrey, Guildford, Surrey GU2 5XH.

Ryder, Dr Arthur John; Senior Lecturer, Department of History, St David's University College, Lampeter, since 1969; *b* 1913; *m* 1946. BA Oxon 1934, DPhil London 1958. Asst Lectr in History, Lampeter, 1962–64; Lectr 1964–69. *Publications:* The German Revolution, 1918–19 (Hist. Assoc. pamphlet), 1959; The German Revolution of 1918, 1967 (trans. Japanese, 1971); Twentieth Century Germany: from Bismarck to Brandt, 1973; *contrib.* European Studies Review, History, Trivium. *Address:* History Dept, St David's Univ. Coll., Lampeter, Dyfed SA48 7ED.

Ryder, Prof. Eric Charles, MA, LLB; Professor of English Law, University of London, since 1960; *b* 1915; *m* 1941. BA Cantab 1936 (1st cl. Law Tripos Pts I and II), LLB Cantab 1937 (1st cl.), MA Cantab 1940; Barrister-at-Law, Gray's Inn 1937. Lectr and Dir of Legal Studies, King's Coll., Univ. of Durham, 1944–53; Prof. of Law, Univ. of Durham, 1953–60; Dean, Fac. of Law, Durham, 1947–60. *Publications:* (with Hawkins) The Construction of Wills, 1965; *contrib.* Camb. Law Jl, Conveyan. Prop. Law., Curr. Legal Prob. *Address:* Dept of Laws, Univ. College London, 4–8 Endsleigh Gardens, WC1H 0EG.

Ryder, R. Neil; Senior Lecturer in Education, Centre for Science Education, Chelsea College, University of London, since 1968; *b* 1938; *m* 1969; one *s* one *d*. MA Cantab 1960, Postgrad. Acad. Dip. in Maths London 1964. *Television Productions and Films:* directed: 7 progs for What is Psychology? series, BBC 2, 1966; 3 progs for Engineering Research series, BBC 2, 1967; 5 progs for Engineering

Design series, BBC 1, 1967; 7 progs for
Workshop of the World series, BBC 1, 1968;
produced: 2 progs for Workshop of the
World series, BBC 1, 1968; 5 progs for In
this Case series, BBC 1, 1969; film, Equilibrium in Chemical Systems, 1972; Metallurgy: a special study, 1973; Editor: Psychology of Depth Perception, 1972; Psychology
of Motion Perception (Brain Science Information Project), 1972; Design Consultant:
Society in Britain series (forthcoming).
Address: Centre for Science Education, Chelsea Coll., Bridges Place, SW6 4HR.

Ryder, Dr Timothy Thomas Bennett;
Reader in Classics, University of Hull, since
1971; *b* 1930; *m* 1955; two *d*. BA Cantab 1952
(1st cl. Classics), MA Cantab 1956, PhD
Cantab 1956. Asst Lectr, Univ. of Hull,
1955–57, Lectr, 1957–66, Sen. Lectr, 1966–
71; Vis. Prof. in History, Michigan State
Univ., 1966–67. Sub-Dean, Fac. of Arts,
Univ. of Hull, 1963–66; Mem., Council,
Hellenic Soc., 1960–63, 1967–70; Mem.,
Council, Class. Assoc., 1967–70. *Publications*:
Koine Eirene: General Peace and Local
Independence in Ancient Greece, 1965; ed,
Dictionary of World History, 1973; *contrib.*
Class. Qly. *Address*: Dept of Classics, The
Univ., Hull HU6 7RX.

Rykwert, Prof. Joseph, Dr RCA; Professor
of Art, University of Essex, since 1967; *b*
1926; *m* 1960, 1972; one *s* one *d*. Dr RCA
1970. Lectr, Hochschule für Gestaltung,
Ulm, 1958; Lib. and Tutor, Royal Coll. of
Art, 1961–67; Vis. Fellow, Inst. Architecture
and Urban Studies, NY, 1969–71; Sen.
Fellow, Council of Humanities, Princeton
Univ., 1971; Vis. Prof., Univ. of Paris
(Vincennes), 1974. *Publications*: The Golden
House, 1947; ed, L. B. Alberti: Ten Books on
Architecture, 1955; The Idea of a Town,
1963; Church Buildings, 1966; On Adam's
House in Paradise, 1972; ed, Parole nel
Vuoti, Adolf Loos, 1972; *contrib.* Burl. Mag.,
Domus, Edl. Mod., TLS. *Address*: Dept
of Art, Univ. of Essex, Colchester CO4
3SQ.

Ryle, Stephen Francis; Lecturer, Depart-
ment of Latin, University of Liverpool, since
1969; *b* 1941. BA (Mod.) Dublin 1964, MA
Dublin 1968; BLitt Oxon 1969. Asst Lectr,
Liverpool, 1966–69. *Address*: School of
Classics, Univ. of Liverpool, PO Box 147,
Liverpool L69 3BX.

Rynne, Etienne, MA, MRIA; Lecturer in
Celtic Archaeology, Department of Celtic
Archaeology, University College, Galway,
since 1967; *b* 1932; *m* 1967; four *s*. BA
Dublin 1953, MA 1955; MRIA 1966,
Mem. Nat. Cttee for Archaeology 1971.
Editor, North Munster Antiquarian Jl,
1964– ; Asst, Irish Antiquities Division,
Nat. Museum of Ireland, 1957–66; Asst
Keeper, 1966–67; Hon. Curator, The Galway
City Museum, 1972– . *Publications*: ed and
contrib., North Munster Studies, 1967;
contrib. ACISPP, CBA Res. Reports, Jl Roy.
Soc. Antiq. Ireland, Nth Munster Antiq. Jl,
Proc. Prehist. Soc., Proc. RIA, Sborník
Národního Muzea v Praze (Czechoslovakia),
Topic: a Jl of the Liberal Arts (USA),
614

Trans Dumfriesshire and Galloway Nat.
Hist. Archaeol. Soc., Ulster Jl Archaeology.
Address: Dept of Celtic Archaeology, Univ.
College, Galway, Galway.

S

Sabine, John Arthur; Lecturer in Political
Theory and Government, University College
of Swansea, since 1961; *b* 1934; *m* 1966; one *s*
one *d*. BSc(Econ) London 1959, MA(Econ)
Manchester 1961; Mem., Internat. Inst.
Strategic Studies; Mem., Royal United
Services Inst. for Defence Studies. Res. Asst,
Univ. of Manchester, 1959–61; Vis. Asst
Prof., Queens Univ., Kingston, Ontario,
1968–69. *Address*: Dept of Political Theory
and Government, Univ. College of Swansea,
Singleton Park, Swansea SA2 8PP.

Sabri-Tabrizi, Dr Gholam-Reza, BA,
DipEd, PhD; Lecturer in Persian, the
University of Edinburgh, since 1966; *b* 1934;
m 1964; one *s* three *d*. BA Tabriz, Iran 1956,
DipEd Tabriz 1958; PhD Edinburgh 1969.
Pt-time Asst Lectr, Edinburgh, 1963–64;
Asst Lectr, 1965. Rep., Asiatic Langs,
council of Fac. of Arts. *Publications*: Devil
and Evil in Persian Mythology, in, Procs 27th
Internat. Congress of Orientalists, Ann
Arbor, Michigan, 1967; The Human Values
in Two Persian Writers, Congress of Arabic
and Islamic Studies, Brussels, 1970, in
Corresp. d'Orient; The Heaven and Hell of
William Blake, 1973; Al-Bīrūnī and Human
Values of the Eastern Renaissance, Al-Bīrūnī
Internat. Congress, Pakistan, 1973; Tolerance
in Islam, Internat. Seminar on Religion,
Morality and Law, New Delhi, 1973; The
Social Values in Sā'edi's Writings, Conf. of
British Assoc. of Orientalists, Cambridge,
1974; *contrib.* Corresp. d'Orient. *Address*:
Dept of Persian, Univ. of Edinburgh, 8
Buccleuch Place, Edinburgh EH8 9LW.

Sacker, Prof. Hugh Dyson, MA; Professor
of German, Trinity College, Dublin, since
1971; *b* 1925; *m* 1949; one *d*. BA Cantab
1950, MA Cantab 1954. Fellow, Gonville
and Caius Coll., Cambridge, 1953–55; Lectr,
UCL, 1955–65; Vis. Asst Prof., Univ. of
Chicago, 1959–60; Reader, Bedford Coll.,
London, 1965–68; Vis. Prof., Univ. of
Oregon, 1967; Vis. Prof., Univ. of Newcastle,
NSW, 1968–69. *Publications*: An Introduction
to Wolfram's Parzival, 1963; ed, Hartmann
von Aue's Der arme Heinrich, 1964; Walther
von der Vogelweide, 3rd edn 1965; (with
D. G. Mowatt) The Nibelungenlied, an
interpretative commentary, 1967; ed, Robert
Musil, Three Short Stories, 1970; *contrib.*
German Life and Letters, Germanic Rev.
Address: Dept of German, Trinity College,
Dublin 2, Eire.

Sagar, Dr Keith Milsom, MA, PhD; Senior
Staff Tutor in Literature, Extra-Mural De-
partment, University of Manchester, since
1973 (Staff Tutor, 1963–73); *b* 1934. BA Can-
tab 1955 (2nd cl. English), MA Cantab 1957;
PhD Leeds 1961. Admin. Asst, Extra-Mural
Dept, Univ. of Leeds, 1957–59; WEA Tutor-
Organizer, NE Derbys, 1959–63. *Publications*:

The Art of D. H. Lawrence, 1966; Hamlet, 1969; Ted Hughes, 1972; The Achievement of Ted Hughes, 1974; ed, D. H. Lawrence: The Mortal Coil and Other Stories, and The Princess and Other Stories, 1971; ed, D. H. Lawrence: Selected Poems, 1972; *contrib.* Camb. Qly, D. H. Lawr. Rev., Mod. Drama, Rev. Engl. Lit., Studies Short Fict. *Address:* Extra-Mural Dept, Univ. of Manchester, Oxford Road, Manchester M13 9PL.

Sagarra, Dr Eda, MA, PhD; Lecturer in German History, German Department, University of Manchester, since 1968; *b* 1933; *m* 1961; one *d.* BA National University of Ireland 1954 (1st cl. Hist.), 1st cl. Germ.), MA National University of Ireland 1955; PhD Vienna 1958. Asst Lectr, Manchester, 1958–61, Lectr, 1961–68. Tutor, Fac. of Arts, 1968– . *Publications:* Tradition and Revolution (Literature and Society series), 1971, German edn 1972; *contrib.* Germ. Life Lett., European Studies Rev., Studies Qly. *Address:* Dept of German, Univ. of Manchester, Oxford Road, Manchester M13 9PL.

Sage, Jack William; Senior Lecturer, Department of Spanish, King's College, London University, since 1956; *b* 1925; *m* 1961; one *s* one *d.* BA London 1949 (1st cl. Hons Spanish), MA London 1952 (distinction). Head of Dept of Spanish, Birkbeck Coll., London Univ., 1952–56; Lectr, Dept of Spanish, King's Coll., London Univ., 1956–72. *Publications:* (with R. O. Jones) Cassell's English–Spanish, Spanish–English Dictionary, 1959, 2nd edn 1969; Odham's Spanish Course, with records, 1961; trans., A Dictionary of Symbols, 1962, 2nd edn 1966; (with E. M. Wilson) Poesías líricas en las obras dramáticas de Calderón, 1964; La música de Juan Hidalgo para 'Los celos hacen estrellas' de Luis Vélez de Guevara, J. E. Varey and N. D. Shergold, 1965; trans. jtly, The Poetry of Luis Cernuda, ed Edkins and Harris, 1971; (with C. Swain) Music from the Middle Ages to the Renaissance: Spain *c.* 1450–1600, ed F. Sternfeld, 1973; A Critical Guide to El caballero de Olmedo, by Lope de Vega, 1974; *contrib.* Baroque, Bull. Hispanique, Early Music, Musical Times, TLS, etc. *Address:* Dept of Spanish, King's College, Strand, WC2R 2LS.

Sager, Prof. Juan Carlos, MA, FIL; Professor of Modern Languages, Department of European Studies and Modern Languages, University of Manchester Institute of Science and Technology, since 1973; *b* 1929. MA Notre Dame 1960, Dip. English Studies Edinburgh 1961. Prof. en Inglés, Tucumán, 1958; Prof. en Francés, Tucumán, 1959; Traductor Público Nacional en Alemán e Inglés, Tucumán, 1957; Notre Dame, 1959–60; Lectr, Maryland (European Di), 1961–62; Sen. Lectr, Dept of Modern Languages, Univ. of Salford, 1963–73. *Publications:* German Structure Drills, 1967; (with K. L. J. Mason) Spanish Oral Drill Book, 1969; (with P. F. McDonald) The Languages of English Journalism, 1974; *contrib.* Incorp. Lingu., Internat. Rev. Appl. Lingu. *Address:* Dept of European Studies and Modern Languages, Univ. of Manchester Inst. of

Science and Technology, Sackville Street, Manchester M60 1QD.

Saggs, Prof. Henry William Frederick, MTh, PhD, FSA; Professor of Semitic Languages, University College, Cardiff, University of Wales, since 1966; *b* 1920; *m* 1946; four *d.* AKC 1942 (1st cl.), BD London 1942 (1st cl.), MTh London 1948, MA London 1951, PhD London 1954; FSA. Lectr in Akkadian, SOAS, Univ. of London, 1953–62; Vis. Prof., Univ. of Baghdad, 1956–57; Reader in Akkadian, SOAS, 1962–66. *Publications:* The Greatness that was Babylon, 1962, German edn 1966, Polish edn 1973; Everyday Life in Babylonia and Assyria, 1965; ed, A. H. Layard: Nineveh and its Remains (abridged edn), 1970; *contrib.* Iraq, Jl Theol. Studies, RA, Sumer. *Address:* Dept of Semitic Languages and Religious Studies, Univ. College Cardiff, PO Box 78, Cardiff CF1 1XL.

Sahay, Dr Arun; Lecturer, Department of Sociological Studies, University of Sheffield, since 1969; *b* 1936; *m* 1957; one *d.* BA Patna 1955, MA Bihar 1960, PhD London 1969. Asst Lectr in Sociological Studies, Univ. Sheffield, 1968–69. *Publications:* Max Weber and Modern Sociology, 1971; Sociological Analysis, 1972; *contrib.* Sociological Analysis and Theory, Discussion Jl of Research and Ideas. *Address:* Univ. of Sheffield, Sheffield S10 2TN.

Sainsbury, Eric Edward, MA; Senior Lecturer in Social Administration, Department of Sociological Studies, University of Sheffield, since 1973 (Lecturer, 1966–73); *b* 1925; *m* 1956; one *s.* BA Oxon 1950 (Engl. Lang. and Lit.), MA Oxon 1954; Postgrad. Dip. in Social Studies Sheffield 1955 (Dist.), Cert. in Applied Social Studies London 1956; MBASW. Tutor Caseworker, Sheffield (jtly with the Sheffield Council of Social Service), 1961–66; Coal Miner, 1944–47; Schoolmaster, 1950–54; Probation Officer, 1956–61. *Publications:* Fieldwork in Social Administration Courses, 1966; Social Diagnosis in Casework, 1970; Social Work with Families, 1974; *contrib.* Indian Jl of Social Work, Internat. Social Work, Social Work To-day. *Address:* Dept of Sociological Studies, Univ. of Sheffield, Sheffield S10 2TN.

Sainsbury, Keith Arthur Frank; Senior Lecturer, Department of Politics, University of Reading, since 1964; *b* 1924; *m* 1947; one *s* one *d.* MA Hons Oxford 1948, BPhil Oxford 1950; Member: RIIA, Pol Studies Assoc. Lecturer: History and Political Science, Univ. of Adelaide, 1950–55; Political Economy, Univ. of Reading, 1955–64. Sen. Tutor, Admissions, Univ. of Reading, 1971–74; Member: Bd of Faculty of Letters and Social Sciences, 1960–63, 1966–69, 1971–74; Senate, 1969–72; Chief Examiner, Oxford and Cambridge Bd, 1964– . *Publications:* Select and Annotated Bibliography of Contemporary History, 1974; The Government of South Australia, in, The Government of the Australian States, 1959; The Second Wartime Alliance, in, Troubled Neighbours, 1972; *contrib.* Australian Outlook, Parly Affairs, Pol Studies. *Address:* Dept of Politics, Univ.

of Reading, Whiteknights Park, Reading Berks RG6 2AH.

Ste Croix, Geoffrey Ernest Maurice de; *see* de Ste Croix.

Sakwa, George, BA, MPhil; Lecturer, Politics Department, Bristol University, since 1969. Res. Asst, Politics Dept, Bristol Univ., 1966–69. *Publications: contrib.* Hist. Jl, Polish Review (NY), Preglad Historyczny (Warsaw), European Rev. *Address:* Politics Dept, Bristol Univ., Bristol BS8 1TH.

Salgādo, Dr Gāmini; Reader, School of English and American Studies, University of Sussex, since 1963; *b* 1929; *m* 1952; one *s* three *d*. BA Nottingham 1952 (1st cl. Comb. Engl. and Philos.), PhD Nottingham 1955. Lectr, Univ. of Malaya, Singapore, 1957–60; Lectr, Queen's Univ. of Belfast, 1960–63; Vis. Lectr, Earlham Coll., Indiana, 1965. *Publications:* ed, Three Jacobean Tragedies, 1965; D. H. Lawrence: Sons and Lovers, 1966; ed, Three Restoration Comedies, 1968; ed, A Casebook on Sons and Lovers, 1969; ed, Coneycatchers and Bawdybaskets, 1972; ed, Eyewitnesses of Shakespeare, 1974; ed, Four Jacobean City Comedies, 1974; *contrib.* Ess. Crit., Shakesp. Surv. *Address:* Arts Building, Univ. of Sussex, Falmer, Brighton BN1 9QN.

Salingar, Leo Gerald, MA; Lecturer in English, University of Cambridge, since 1962; *b* 1915; *m* 1944; one *d*. BA Cantab 1935 (1st cl. Engl.), MA Cantab 1939; DipEd Liverpool 1939. Staff Tutor in English, Cambridge Bd of Extra-Mural Studies, 1951–62; Fellow and Dir of Studies, Trinity Coll., Cambridge, 1962– ; Maître de Conférences associé, Faculté des Lettres, Rouen, 1968–69. *Publications:* contrib. The Pelican Guide to English Literature, vol. II, 1955, rev. edn 1969, vol. V, 1957, vol. VI, 1958, vol. VII, 1961; contrib. French edn of, Shakespeare, ed Legris and Evans, 1954–57; contrib. Dramaturgie et Société au XVI et XVII Siècles, ed Jacquot, 1968; contrib. Renaissance Drama: Shakespeare and the Tradition of Comedy, 1974; The Revenger's Tragedy, 1974; *contrib.* Ess. Studies, Forum Mod. Lang. Studies, Mod. Lang. Rev., Scrut., Shakesp. Qly. *Address:* Trinity College, Cambridge.

Salmon, Dr John Brynmor; Lecturer, Department of Ancient History, Queen's University of Belfast, since 1970; *b* 1942; *m* 1970; one *s* one *d*. MA, DPhil Oxon 1971. Asst Lectr, QUB, 1967–70. *Publications: contrib.* BSA. *Address:* Dept of Ancient History, Queen's Univ. of Belfast, Belfast BT7 1NN.

Salmon, Paul Bernard; Professor of German, Edinburgh University, since 1970; *b* 1921; *m* 1945. BA London 1947, MA London 1950, PhD London 1957. Asst Lectr, Univ. Coll., London, 1950–52; Lectr, Royal Holloway Coll., Univ. of London, 1952–62, Reader, 1962–67; Reader, Birkbeck Coll., London, 1967–70. *Publications:* Literature in Medieval Germany, 1967; *contrib.* Archiv Studium Neuer. Sprach. Lit., Beit.

Gesch. Deuts. Sprach. Lit., Euphor., Forum Mod. Lang. Studies, Germ. Life Lett., Mod. Lang. Rev., Neophilol., Trans Philol Soc. *Address:* Dept of German, Univ. of Edinburgh, David Hume Tower, George Square, Edinburgh EH8 9JX.

Salter, Charles Henry, MA; Senior Lecturer in English, University of Glasgow, since 1974; *b* 1918; *m* 1956; 1966; four *s* one *d*. BA Oxon 1941 (War Degree), MA Oxon 1947 (1st cl. Classics, 2nd cl. Lit. Hum.). Lectr in Humanity, 1949–50, in English, 1950–74, Glasgow Univ. *Publications:* Bodleiana Nova, 1939; contrib. The General Election in Glasgow, 1950, ed Chrimes, 1951; contrib. Insight III, ed Weiand, 1968; *contrib.* Camb. Rev., Poet. Rev., Rev. Engl. Studies, Victorian Poetry, Nineteenth Cent. Fict., Mod. Lang. Rev. *Address:* The Univ., Glasgow G12 8QQ.

Salter, Keith William, MA; Senior Lecturer in English, and Tutor to Overseas Students, University of Exeter, since 1949; *b* 1913; *m* 1941; two *s* two *d*. BA Bristol 1935 (1st cl. Engl.), DipEd Bristol 1936, MA Bristol 1955. Lectr, Univ. of Hong Kong, 1936–40; Lectr, Gordon Memorial Coll., Khartoum, 1946–49. Dir, Univ. of Exeter Summer Sch. for Overseas Students, 1950– ; Sub-Dean, Fac. of Arts, Exeter, 1964–68. *Publications:* Thomas Traherne, Poet and Mystic, 1964; *contrib.* Ess. Studies. *Address:* Dept of English, Queen's Building, The Queen's Drive, Exeter EX4 4QH.

Saltmarsh, John; University Lecturer, Faculty of History, University of Cambridge, since 1937, and Fellow of King's College, Cambridge, since 1931; *b* 1908. BA Cambridge 1929 (1st cl. Hist. Tripos Pts I and II), MA Cambridge 1933; FSA, FRHistS. Faculty Asst Lectr, Cambridge, 1935–37; Asst Coll. Lectr in Hist., King's Coll., 1936–37, Coll. Lectr, 1937–71; Dir of Studies in History, King's Coll., 1948–67. Librr, King's Coll., Cambridge, 1937–47; Vice-Provost, King's Coll., Cambridge, 1955–61. Foreign Off., 1940–44. *Publications:* Two Medieval Lyrics, 1933; ed, Sir J. Clapham: A Concise Economic History of Britain from the Earliest Times to 1750, 1949; King's College and its Chapel, 1957, 3rd edn 1969; King's College: a Short History, 1958 (reprint of chapter in VCH Cambridgeshire, III); Carving in King's Chapel, 1970; King Henry VI and the Royal Foundations (quincentenary memorial lecture at Eton College, 1971); *contrib.* Antiqu. Jl, Camb. Hist. Jl, Econ. Hist., Econ. Hist. Rev., Proc. Camb. Antiqu. Soc. *Address:* King's College, Cambridge CB2 1ST.

Salvadori Lonergan, Corinna; Senior Lecturer, Department of Italian, Trinity College Dublin, since 1973; *m* 1965; one *s* one *d*. BA NUI 1959 (1st cl. Hons), MA NUI 1961 (1st cl. Hons), MA TCD 1964 (*jure officii*). Lectr, Italian Dept, TCD, 1961. Mem. various mod. langs cttees, Dept of Educn; Sec., Nat. Cttee for Mod. Lang. Studies of Royal Irish Acad., 1974– . *Publications:* Yeats and Castiglione: Poet and Courtier, 1965. *Address:* Dept of Italian, Univ. of Dublin, Trinity College, Dublin 2, Ireland.

Salway, Dr Peter, MA, FSA; Regional Director, West Midlands, The Open University, since 1970; *b* 1932; *m* 1962; two *s.* BA Cantab 1954 (1st cl. Classics, Dist. in Class. Archaeol.), MA Cantab 1958, PhD Cantab 1958, MA Oxon 1965; FSA, FRGS. Sir James Knott Fellow, Newcastle, 1956–57; Fellow, Sidney Sussex Coll., Cambridge, 1957–64; Warden, Hiatt Baker Hall, Bristol, 1964–65; Fellow and Dom. Bursar, All Souls Coll., Oxford, 1965–69. Mem., Open Univ. Council, 1971–74; Former Chm., Listed Blgds Cttee, CPRE Oxon; Former Mem., Exec. Cttee, Council Brit. Archaeol.; Editor, Oxoniensia, 1967–69. *Publications:* The Frontier People of Roman Britain, 1965; ed, Sir I. Richmond: Roman Archaeology and Art, 1969; (jtly) The Fenland in Roman Times, 1970; Britain in the Early Roman Empire, 1974; *contrib.* Archaeol. Ael., Class. Rev., Proc. Camb. Antiqu. Soc. *Address:* The Open Univ., West Midlands Region, High Street, Harborne, Birmingham B17 9NB.

Sambrook, Dr Arthur James; Senior Lecturer in English, University of Southampton, since 1971; *b* 1931; *m* 1961; four *s.* BA Oxon 1955 (1st cl. Engl. Lang. and Lit.), MA Oxon 1959; PhD Nottingham 1957. Lectr, St David's Coll., Lampeter, 1957–64; Lectr, Southampton Univ., 1964–71; Sen. Res. Fellow, Dalhousie Univ., 1968–69. *Publications:* A Poet Hidden, 1962; ed, The Scribleriad, etc, 1967; ed, Thomson: The Seasons and The Castle of Indolence, 1972; William Cobbett, 1973; contrib. The Sphere History of Literature in the English Language, vol. vi, 1970; Pope and his Background, 1972. *Address:* Dept of English, Univ. of Southampton, Southampton SO9 5NH.

Samilov, Prof. Michael, BA, MA, PhD; Professor of the Comparative Philology of the Slavonic Languages, School of Slavonic and East European Studies, University of London, since 1966; *b* 1931; *m* 1958. BA City College of New York 1953 (*cum laude*); MA Columbia 1955, PhD Columbia 1960; Philol Soc. Lectr in Slavic Linguistics, Univ. of Toronto, 1956–58; Instructor, Stanford Univ., 1958–59; Asst Prof., Univ. of California, Berkeley, 1959–62; Asst Prof., Cornell Univ., 1962–63; Associate Prof. and Fellow of Silliman Coll., Yales Univ., 1963–66. *Publications:* The Phoneme Jat' in Slavic, 1964; *contrib.* Slav. E Europ. Rev., Zborn. Mat. Srp. *Address:* School of Slavonic and East European Studies, Univ. of London, WC1E 7HU.

Sampson, Geoffrey Richard; Lecturer in Linguistics, Language Studies Department, London School of Economics, since 1972; *b* 1944. BA Cantab 1965, MA 1967, MA Yale 1967, MA Oxon 1969; Member: Linguistics Assoc. of GB; Linguistic Soc. of Amer.; Philol Soc. Res. Fellow in Vietnamese, SOAS, 1967–68; Res. Fellow in Linguistics, Queen's Coll., Oxford, 1969–72. *Publications:* The Form of Language (forthcoming); *contrib.* Foundns of Lang., Lang. *Address:* Dept of Language Studies, London Sch. of Economics, Houghton Street, WC2A 2AE.

Sampson, Dr Ronald Victor; Lecturer, Department of Politics, University of Bristol,

since 1953; *b* 1918; *m* 1943; two *d.* MA Oxon 1948, DPhil Oxon 1951; John Hay Whitney Fellowship to USA, 1951–52. Lectr, Durham Univ., 1952–53. *Publications:* Progress in the Age of Reason, 1956; Equality and Power, 1965; Tolstoy: The Discovery of Peace, 1973. *Address:* Dept of Politics, Univ. of Bristol, Bristol BS8 1TH.

Samuels, Prof. John Malcolm; Professor of Business Policy, Faculty of Commerce and Social Science, University of Birmingham, since 1972; *b* 1938; *m* 1962; one *s* one *d.* BCom Birmingham 1962; FACA 1959. Asst Lectr in Industrial Economics, Univ. of Birmingham, 1962–63, Lectr, 1963–64; P. D. Leake Res. Fellowship in Accounting, Univ. of Birmingham, 1964–65, Lectr in Business Finance, 1965–66; Vis. Associate Prof. of Industrial Admin, Krannert Sch. of Business, Purdue Univ., Indiana, 1966–67; Sen. Lectr in Finance and Accounting, Graduate Centre for Management Studies, Birmingham, 1967–69; Prof. of Business Policy, Univ. of Birmingham and Univ. of Aston, 1969–72. Appl. Econ. Editor, Jl Business Policy; Sec./Treas., Brit. Acctng and Fin. Assoc.; Mem. Certified Accountants Working Party on Accounting Standards Steering Cttee. *Publications:* The Effect of Advertising on Sales and Brand Shares, 1970; (with F. M. Wilkes) The Management of Company Finance, 1971; ed, Readings in Mergers and Takeovers, 1972; Opportunity Costing: An Application of Mathematical Programming, in, Studies in Cost Analysis, ed D. Solomons, 2nd edn 1968 (also, in, Management Planning and Control, ed J. Livingstone, 1970); (with R. Manes and D. J. Smyth) Inventories and Sales: A Cross Section Study of US Companies, in, Empirical Research in Accounting, 1968; Profit Forecasts on Capital Investment Projects, in, Director's Handbook, 1969; (with K. Kristensson) Doctoral Programmes and Research in Business Policy, in, The Teaching of Business Policy, 1971; *contrib.* Acctncy, Acctnt, Austral. Econ. Papers, Bank. Mag., Economica, Jl Appl. Econ., Jl Business Fin., Jl Business Policy, Jl Fin., Jl Mngmt Studies, Rev. Econ. Studies. *Address:* Faculty of Commerce and Social Science, Univ. of Birmingham, PO Box 363, Birmingham B15 2TT.

Samuels, Prof. Michael Louis; Professor of English Language, University of Glasgow, since 1959; *b* 1920; *m* 1950; one *d.* MA Oxon 1947 (1st cl. Eng. Lang. and Lit.). Asst, Edinburgh Univ., 1948–49, Lectr, 1949–59. Mem., Council, Philol Soc., 1960–62; Mem., Scottish Dictionaries Jt Council, 1960– . *Publications:* Linguistic Evolution, 1972; *contrib.* Archiv. Lingu., Engl. Ger. Studies, Engl. Studies, Med. Æv., Trans Philol Soc. *Address:* Dept of English Language, The Univ., Glasgow G12 8QQ.

Sanders, Ivor John; Reader, Department of History, University College of Wales, Aberystwyth, since 1966; *b* 1911; *m* 1939; two *s.* BA Wales 1933 (1st cl. History), MA Wales 1935; DPhil Oxon 1938; FRHistS. Asst Lectr, 1945–47, Lectr, 1947–57, Sen. Lectr, 1957–66 UC, Aberystwyth. *Publications:* Historical Association pamphlets, 1955; Feudal

617

Military Service in England, 1956; English Baronies, a Study of their origin and descent, 1086–1327, 1960; ed, Documents of the baronial movement of reform and rebellion, 1973; contrib. in, G. E. Cokayne: Complete Peerage, 1946–50; Historical Association pamphlets, 1947; Dictionary of Welsh Biography, 1959; Handbook of British Chronology, 1961; World Book Encyclopedia, 1962; contrib. Bull. Bd Celt. Studies, Ceredig, EHR. Address: History Dept, Univ. College of Wales, Aberystwyth SY23 2AX.

Sanders, Dr John Wilbur, MA, DipEd, PhD; University Lecturer in English and Fellow, Selwyn College, University of Cambridge, since 1968; b 1936; m 1959; one s one d. BA Melbourne 1957 (1st cl. Hist. and Eng.), DipEd Melbourne 1958, MA Melbourne 1961; PhD Bristol 1965. Asst Lectr, Bristol Univ., 1965; Lectr, Sydney Univ., 1966–67. Publications: The Dramatist and the Received Idea: studies in the plays of Marlowe and Shakespeare, 1968; John Donne's Poetry, 1971; contrib. Melb. Crit. Rev. Address: Selwyn College, Cambridge.

Sanderson, Prof. George Neville; Professor of Modern History, Royal Holloway College, University of London, since 1968; b 1919; m 1960; one s two d. 1st cl. Mod. Hist. Oxon 1940, BA Oxon 1945, MA Oxon 1950, PhD London 1959; FRHistS 1972. Lectr, Gordon Memorial Coll., Univ. (Coll.) of Khartoum, 1947–53; Sen. Lectr, Khartoum, 1953–62, Prof., 1962–65, Head, Dept of History, 1958–63; Dir, Sudan Res. Unit, 1963–65; Sen. Lectr, Royal Holloway Coll., Univ. of London, 1965–66, Reader, 1966–68. Editor, Sudan Notes and Records, 1953–62; Mem., Gordon Memorial Coll. Trust Fund, Exec. Cttee, 1970– ; Mem., Cttee of Mngmt, Inst. of Cwealth Studies, Univ. of London, 1971– ; Mem. Edit. Adv. Bd, Jl Imp. and Cwealth Hist., 1972– . Publications: England, Europe and the Upper Nile, 1882–1899, 1965; contrib. France and Britain in Africa, 1972; contrib. EHR, Hist. Jl, Jl Afr. Hist., Sud. Notes Rec. Address: Dept of History, Royal Holloway College, Egham, Surrey TW20 0EX.

Sanderson, Ian McClay, MBE; Registrar, University of Bradford, since 1973; b 1932; m 1961; two s two d. BSc London 1954. Administrative Asst, Univ. of Newcastle, 1963–66; Asst Registrar, Univ. of Bradford, 1966–69; Deputy Registrar, 1969–73. Address: Univ. of Bradford, Richmond Road, Bradford, Yorks BD7 1DP.

Sanderson, John Bryan; Lecturer in Politics, Strathclyde University, since 1963; b 1937; m 1963; one s one d. BA Hull 1958 (1st cl. Government and Sociology); MA(Econ) Manchester 1960 (Government). Asst Lectr in Government, Manchester Univ., 1961–63. Publications: An Interpretation of the Political Ideas of Marx and Engels, 1969; contrib. Pol. Studies, Western Pol. Qly, Australasian Jl of Philos., Jl Eccles. Hist. Address: Dept of Politics, Strathclyde Univ., Glasgow G1 1XQ.

Sanderson, John Michael; Senior Lecturer

in Economic History, University of East Anglia, since 1973 (Lecturer, 1964–73); b 1939. BA Cantab 1960, MA Cantab 1963, PhD Cantab 1966. Asst Lectr, Univ. of Strathclyde, 1963–64. Publications: The Universities and British Industry, 1850–1970, 1972; contrib. Local Studies and the History of Education, 1972; The Universities in the Nineteenth Century, 1975; Popular Education and Socialization 1800–1900, 1975; contrib. Brit. Jl Educnl Studies, Econ. Hist. Rev., Jl Contemp. Hist., North. Hist., Sci. Studies, Yorks Bull. Econ. Soc. Res., Past and Present. Address: School of Social Studies, Univ. of East Anglia, Norwich NOR 88C.

Sanderson, Stewart Forson, MA; Director, Institute of Dialect and Folk Life Studies, School of English, University of Leeds, since 1964; b 1924; m 1953; two s one d. MA Edinburgh 1951 (1st cl. Eng. Lang. and Lit.); Korresp. LGAA 1968, Mem., Soc. Folk Life Studies, Folklore Soc. Sec.-Archivist, Sch. of Scott. Studies, Edinburgh Univ., 1952–57; Sen. Res. Fellow, 1957–60; Asst Editor, Scott. Studies, 1957–60; Lectr in Folk Life Studies, and Dir of Folk Life Survey, Leeds Univ., 1960–64, Sen. Lectr, 1965– . Mem., Cttee, Sect. H, Brit. Assoc. Adv. Sci., 1957–68 (Gen. Cttee, 1965–); Council, Folkl. Soc., 1963– (Pres., 1970–73); Cttee, Atlas of Europ. Folk Cult., 1964– ; Ed. Bd, Ethnol. Europ., 1966– ; Adv. Panel, Brit. Inst. Rec. Sound, 1970– . Publications: Hemingway, 1961, 4th edn 1970, Portuguese trans. 1963, Spanish trans. 1972; contrib. Third Statistical Account of Scotland (Edinburgh), 1966; Trans 5th Viking Congress, 1968; Studies in Folk Life, 1969; ed (with commentary) The Secret Common-Wealth, 1974; contrib. Ariel, Arts Trad. Pop., Ethnol. Europ., Folk Life, Folkl., Rev. Etnog., Scott. Studies. Address: Institute of Dialect and Folk Life Studies, Univ. of Leeds, Leeds LS2 9JT.

Sandford, Prof. Cedric Thomas, MA(Econ); Professor of Political Economy, School of Humanities and Social Sciences, University of Bath, since 1965; b 1924; m 1945; one s one d. BA(Econ) Manchester 1948, MA(Econ) Manchester 1949; BA London 1955 (Hist.); Mem., Econ. Assoc., 1950– ; Royal Econ. Soc., 1966– . Vis. Prof. of Econs and Public Finance, Univ. of Delaware, 1969. Mem., Nat. Exec. Cttee, Econ. Assoc., 1965–71; var. Sub-cttees; Governor, Bristol Poly., 1969–71; Ministerial Training Cttee, Methodist Ch, 1969–71. Publications: Taxing Inheritance and Capital Gains, 1965, 2nd edn 1967; Taxation, 1966, 2nd edn 1970; Economics of Public Finance, 1969, Spanish trans. 1971; Realistic Tax Reform, 1971; Public Expenditure and Fiscal Policy, 1971; Taxing Personal Wealth, 1971; ed (jtly) Case Studies in Economics, Economic Policy, 1970; Principles, 1971; Projects and Role Playing in Teaching Economics, 1971; Case Studies in Economics: National Economic Planning, 1972; Hidden Costs of Taxation, 1973; (with J. R. M. Willis and D. J. Ironside) An Accessions Tax; contrib. Acctng Business Res., Bank., Brit. Jl Educnl Psychol., Brit. Tax Rev., Polit. Qly, Accountancy, Nat. Westminster Bank Rev. *Address*: School of Humanities and Social Sciences, Univ. of Bath, Claverton Down, Bath BA2 7AY.

Sandford, Dr John Eric; Lecturer, German Department, Bedford College, London, since 1970; *b* 1944; *m* 1967; two *s*. BA Cantab 1966, MA 1970, PhD London 1972; Mem., MHRA. Asst Lectr in German, Bedford Coll., London, 1967–70. *Publications: contrib.* GLL. *Address*: Bedford Coll., Regent's Park, NW1 4NS.

Sandison, Dr Alan George; Lecturer, Department of English, Durham University, since 1971; *b* 1932. MA Hons Aberdeen 1958, PhD Cantab 1963. Univ. of Aberdeen, 1960–63; Univ. of Exeter, 1963–71. *Publications*: The Wheel of Empire, 1967; The Last Man in Europe: an essay on George Orwell, 1974; Rudyard Kipling: The Artist and the Empire, in, Kipling's Mind and Art, ed Rutherford, 1964; A Matter of Vision: Rudyard Kipling and Rider Haggard, in, The World of Rudyard Kipling, ed John Gross, 1972. *Address*: Dept of English, Univ. of Durham, Durham DH1 3HP.

Sansica, A.; *see* Stott, A.

Santer, Rev. Mark; Principal, Westcott House, Cambridge, since 1973; *b* 1936; *m* 1964; one *s* two *d*. BA Cantab 1960, MA 1964. Fellow and Dean of Clare Coll., Cambridge, 1967–72; Tutor of Clare Coll., 1968–72; Univ. Asst Lectr in Divinity, Cambridge, 1968–72. *Publications:* contrib. The Phenomenon of Christian Belief, ed G. W. H. Lampe, 1970; *contrib.* Jl Theol Studies, Theol. *Address*: Westcott House, Cambridge.

Sargan, Prof. John Denis; Professor of Econometrics, Department of Economics, London University, since 1964; *b* 1924; *m* 1953; two *s* one *d*. BA Cambridge 1943, MA Cambridge 1948. Asst Lectr, then Lectr, and later Reader in Economic Statistics, Leeds Univ., 1948–63. *Publications: contrib.* Economet., Jl Roy. Stat. Soc. *Address*: Dept of Economics, London School of Economics, Houghton Street, WC2A 2AE.

Sargent, John; Lecturer in Geography with Reference to the Far East, Geography Department, School of Oriental and African Studies, University of London, since 1967; *b* 1940; *m* 1970. BA Leeds 1962 (Geog.); FRGS. Res. Fellow in Geog., SOAS, 1965–67. *Publications: contrib.* CHIRI, Geog. Jl, Geog. Mag. *Address*: Sch. of Oriental and African Studies, Univ. of London, Malet Street, WC1E 7HP.

Sargent, Prof. John Richard, MA; Professor of Economics, since 1965, Pro-Vice-Chancellor, since 1970, University of Warwick; *b* 1925; *m* 1949; one *s* two *d*. BA Oxford 1948 (1st cl. PPE); FREconSoc, Mem., Council. Royal Econ. Soc. Lectr, Christ Church, Oxford, 1949–51; Fellow, Worcester Coll., Oxford, 1951–62; Res. Associate, Inst. of Econs and Statistics, Oxford, 1962–63. Pro-Vice-Chancellor, Oxford, 1970–71. Mem., Oxf. Educn Cttee, 1959–62; Econ. Cnsltnt,

HM Treasury, 1963–65; Econ. Advr, Min. of Technol., 1968–69; Governor, Nat. Inst. Econ. Res., 1969– ; Mem., Doctors and Dentists Pay Rev. Bd, 1972– ; Armed Forces Pay Rev. Bd, 1972– . *Publications*: British Transport Policy, 1958; *contrib.* Bull. Oxf. Inst. Econ. Stats, Econ. Jl, Oxf. Econ. Papers, Qly Jl Econ. *Address*: Dept of Economics, Univ. of Warwick, Coventry CV4 7AL.

Sasse, Hans Christopher; Lecturer in German, Department of German and Scandinavian Studies, University of Newcastle upon Tyne, since 1964; *b* 1936; *m* 1959; two *s*. BA Hons Adelaide 1958 (1st cl., German), MA Adelaide 1960, MLitt Cantab 1963; Mem., AUT. Tutor in German, Univ. of Adelaide, 1959–60; Donaldson Res. Scholar, Corpus Christi Coll., Cambridge, 1960–62; Asst Lectr in German, KCL, 1962–64. *Publications*: compiled (with J. Horne and C. Dixon) Cassell's New Compact German–English, English–German Dictionary, 1966, pbk 1970, 2nd edn, 6th repr., 1972; *contrib.* GLL, JES, MLR, TLS. *Address*: Dept of German and Scandinavian Studies, Univ. of Newcastle upon Tyne, Newcastle upon Tyne NE1 7RU.

Sathyamurthy, T. V.; Senior Lecturer in Politics, University of York, since 1971; *b.* 1929; *m*; one *d*. BSc Banaras 1947, MSc Banaras 1949, PhD Illinois 1962; Mem. Brit. Polit. Science Assoc. Lectr in Govt, Indiana Univ., 1961–63; Lectr in Political Science, Univ. Singapore, 1963–65; Sen. Lectr in Polit. Science and Sen. Res. Fellow, EAISR, Makerere Univ., 1965–67; Vis. Prof. of Polit. Science, Northwestern Univ., 1967; Lectr in Internat. Relations, Strathclyde Univ., 1967–68, Lectr in Politics, 1968–70; Prof. of Internat. Relations, Univ. Chile, 1970–71. Special Consultant, Dir Gen., UNESCO, 1966. *Publications*: Politics of International Cooperation: Contrasting Conceptions of UNESCO, 1964; Political History of Uganda, 1860–1971 (forthcoming); *contrib.* Polit. Studies, Current Anthrop., Acta Africana, World Politics, Internat. Organization, Internat. Rev. Educn Esprit, Analyse et Prevision, Estudios Internacionales, Estudios Orientales, Africa Today, China Now, Mawazo, Internationales Afrika Forum, etc. *Address*: Dept of Politics, Univ. of York, Heslington, York YO1 5DD.

Saul, Prof. Samuel Berrick, PhD; Professor of Economic History, Edinburgh University, since 1963; *b* 1924; *m* 1953; one *s* one *d*. BCom Birmingham 1949, PhD Birmingham 1953. Lectr, Liverpool Univ., 1951–61; Senior Lectr, 1961–63; Vis. Prof.: Berkeley, 1959; Stanford, 1969; Harvard, 1973; Dean, Faculty of Social Sciences, Edinburgh, 1970– . *Publications*: Studies in British Overseas Trade 1870–1914, 1960; The Myth of the Great Depression, 1969; Technological Change: the US and Britain in the 19th Century, 1970; (with A. S. Milward) The Economic Development of Continental Europe, vol. I, 1973. *contrib.* Econ. History Rev., Jl Econ. History, Yorkshire Bull., Business History. *Address*: Dept of Econ.

History, The Univ., George Square, Edinburgh.

Saunders, John Whiteside, MA, BLitt; Senior Lecturer in English Literature, since 1965, and Warden, Middlesbrough Adult Education Centre, University of Leeds, since 1958; *b* 1920; *m* 1944; 1971; two *s* two *d.* BA Oxon 1948, MA Oxon 1948, BLitt Oxon 1950. Asst Lectr, Leeds Univ., 1949–52, Lectr, 1952–65. Chm., Middlesbrough Civic Trust, 1962–64; Chm., Teesside Fedn of the Arts, 1968– ; Chm., Teesside Film Theatre, 1970– ; Chm., BBC Radio Teesside Council, 1970–73. *Publications*: The Profession of English Letters, 1964; P. Sheavyn: The Literary Profession in the Elizabethan Age, rev. edn 1967; contrib. var. Festschriften, 1952–70; *contrib.* Adult Educn, ELH, Ess. Crit., Shakesp. Qly, Shakesp. Surv. *Address*: Adult Education Centre, 37 Harrow Road, Middlesbrough, Cleveland TS5 5NT.

Saunders, Trevor John, BA, PhD; Senior Lecturer, Department of Classics, University of Newcastle upon Tyne, since 1972; *b* 1934; *m* 1959; two *d.* BA London 1956 (1st cl. Classics); PhD Cambridge 1962; Mem., Soc. Prom. Hellenic Studies, Mem., Class. Assoc. Asst Lectr in Latin, Bedford Coll., London, 1959–61; Asst Lectr in Classics, Univ. of Hull, 1961–62, Lectr, 1962–65; Lectr in Classics, Univ. of Newcastle upon Tyne, 1965–72. Vis. Mem., Inst. Adv. Study, Princeton, 1971–72. Mem., Council, Soc. Prom. Hellenic Studies, 1968–71, 1974–77; Mem., Council, Newman Assoc., 1967–71. *Publications*: trans. and introd., Plato: The Laws, 1970; Notes on the Laws of Plato (Supp. 28, Bull. Inst. Class. Studies), 1972; *contrib.* Class. Qly, Class. Rev., Hermes, Philologus, Philos. Qly, Eranos, Greece and Rome, Didaskalos, Jl Heil. Stud., Rev. Belge de Phil. et d'Hist. *Address*: Dept of Classics, Univ. of Newcastle upon Tyne, Newcastle upon Tyne NE1 7RU.

Saunders, Prof. Wilfred L., MA, FLA; Director, Postgraduate School of Librarianship and Information Science, University of Sheffield, since 1963; *b* 1920; *m* 1946; two *s.* BA Cambridge 1948, MA Cambridge 1953; FLA 1952. Lib., Univ. of Birmingham Inst. of Educn, 1949–56; Dep. Libr., Univ. of Sheffield, 1956–63. Seconded UNESCO (Expert in Educnl Documentation), Uganda, 1962; Mem., Libr. Adv. Council, Engl., 1970– ; Mem., ASLIB Council, 1965–71, 1972– (Chm., Educn Cttee, 1969–71); Mem., Brit. Council, 1970– ; Mem., Librarianship Board, CNAA, 1966– ; Hon. Cnsltnt, E Afr. Sch. of Librship, Makerere Univ., 1967–73; Vis. Prof., Univ. of Pittsburgh Grad. Sch. of Libr. and Info. Sciences, 1968; Cwealth Vis. Fellow, Australia, 1969; Library Science Conslt, Council of Ontario Univs, 1971–72. *Publications*: Guide to Book Lists and Bibliographies for ... School Librarians, 1956, 2nd edn 1961; Cataloguing Rules: author and title entries for the use of school librarians, 1957, 3rd edn 1966; ed, Provision and Use of Library and Documentation Services, 1966; ed, Librarianship in Britain Today, 1967; ed, University and Research Library Studies, 1968; (with H.

Schur) Education and Training for Scientific and Technological Library and Information Work, 1968; (with W. J. Hutchins and L. J. Pargeter) The Language Barrier ... in ... an Academic Community, 1971; contrib. British Library and Information Science, 1966–70, 1972; *contrib.* ASLIB Proc., Austral. Jl Librship, Educn Abstr., Educnl Rev., Inform. Sci., Jl Document., Jl Librship, Libr. Assoc. Record, Sch. Libr. *Address*: The Univ., Western Bank, Sheffield S10 2TN.

Saunderson, Barbara Maud; Lecturer in French, University College of North Wales, Bangor, since 1964; *b* 1938. BA Wales 1959 (1st cl. French), MA Wales 1962. Mem., Brit. Soc. 18th Cent. Studies. *Address*: Dept of French, Univ. College of North Wales, Bangor LL57 2DG.

Savory, Henry Jarvis, BSc, MSc; Lecturer, School of Education, University of Bristol, since 1959; *b* 1914; *m* 1949. BSc Bristol 1935 (2nd cl. Botany), DipEd Bristol 1936, MSc Bristol 1951 (Botany); Mem., BES, AETFAT. Lectr, Univ. of Ibadan, 1948, Sen. Lectr, 1949–53; Asst Dir of Educn, W Nigeria, 1953; Chief Insp. of Educn, W Nigeria, 1954–58. *Publications*: Junior Biology for Tropical Secondary Schools, 1962; Senior Biology for Tropical Secondary Schools, 1966; Caribbean Junior Biology, 1972; ed, Sciences for Tropical Schools; West African Nature Handbooks; J. A. Shaw: Biology Laboratory Management, 1965; J. A. Shaw: Chemistry Laboratory Management, 1966; E. H. Ward: Senior Physics, 1965–66; (with Wood) East African Biology, 1967; Southgate and Folivi: Junior Science, 1967–68; The use of the environment in primary science, in, Science Education in Africa, 1970; J. A. Quartey: Senior Chemistry. *Address*: School of Education, Univ. of Bristol, Bristol.

Sawyer, Rev. John Frederick Adam, MA, BD, PhD; Lecturer in Religious Studies, University of Newcastle upon Tyne, since 1965; *b* 1935; *m* 1965; one *s* two *d.* MA Edinburgh 1957 (1st cl. Classics), BD Edinburgh 1962, PhD Edinburgh 1968. Asst Lectr, Glasgow Univ., 1964–65. *Publications*: Semantics in Biblical Research, 1972; *contrib.* Ann. Swed. Theol. Inst., Biblica, Bull. SOAS, Israel Explor. Jl, Jl Semit. Studies, Jl Theol. Studies, Palest. Explor. Qly, Scott. Jl Theol., Vet. Test. *Address*: Dept of Religious Studies, Univ. of Newcastle upon Tyne, Newcastle upon Tyne NE1 7RU.

Sawyer, Prof. Peter Hayes; Professor of Medieval History, University of Leeds, since 1970; *b* 1928; *m* 1955; two *s* two *d.* BA Oxon 1951, MA Oxon 1955; FRHistS. Asst, Edinburgh Univ., 1953–56; Temp. Asst Lectr, Leeds Univ., 1956–57; Lectr, Birmingham Univ., 1957–64; Lectr, Leeds Univ., 1964–67, Reader, 1967–70; Vis. Prof., Univ. of Minnesota, 1966–67. Sec., Jt Brit. Academy – Royal Hist. Soc. Cttee on Anglo-Saxon Charters; Mem. Council, Royal Hist. Soc., 1972– . *Publications*: Textus Roffensis, 2 vols, 1957, 1962; The Age of the Vikings, 1962, 2nd edn 1971; Anglo-Saxon Charters, an annotated list and bibliography, 1968; *contrib.* Bull. John Rylands Lib., EHR,

Mediaeval Scandinavia, Past and Present, Trans Royal Hist. Soc., Univ. Birmingham Hist. Jl. *Address*: School of History, Univ. of Leeds, Leeds LS2 9JT.

Sayce, Richard Anthony, MA, DPhil; Reader in French Literature, Oxford University, since 1966, Fellow of Worcester College, Oxford, since 1950, Librarian since 1958; *b* 1917; *m* 1948; two *d*. BA Oxon 1937 (1st cl. Mod. Langs), MA Oxon 1945, DPhil Oxon 1950. Univ. Lectr in French and Lectr, Worcester and Lincoln Colls, 1947–50. Editor, The Library, 1965–70; Mem., Council, Biblio. Soc.; Sec., Mod. Hum. Res. Assoc., 1954–60. *Publications*: ed, Corneille: Polyeucte, 1949; Style in French Prose, 1953; The French Biblical Epic in the Seventeenth Century, 1955; The Essays of Montaigne, 1972; *contrib.* Biblioth. Hum. Renaiss., Comp. Lit., Fr. Studies, Libr., Mod. Lang. Rev. *Address*: Worcester College, Oxford.

Scamell, Prof. Ernest Harold; Professor of English Law, University of London, since 1966; *b* 1928; *m* 1952; two *s* two *d*. LLB London 1947, AKC London 1947, LLM London 1948; Barrister, of Lincoln's Inn. Asst Lectr, Univ. Coll., London, 1948–51, Lectr, 1951–60; Reader in English Law, Univ. of London, 1960–66. *Publications*: ed, Lindley on Partnership, 12th edn 1962, 13th edn 1971; ed (jtly), Conveyan. Prop. Law, ed (jtly), Curr. Legal Prob. *Address*: Faculty of Laws, Univ. College London, 4/8 Endsleigh Gardens, WC1E 6ST.

Scammell, Geoffrey Vaughan, MA; Lecturer in History, University of Cambridge, since 1965, and Fellow and Director of Studies in History, Pembroke College, since 1965; *b* 1925; *m* 1953; one *s*. BA Cambridge 1948 (1st cl.), MA Cambridge 1953 (Prince Consort Prizeman, Cambridge 1952); FRHistS. Res. Asst, Univ. of Durham, 1949–51, Lectr, 1951–52; Fellow, Emmanuel Coll., Cambridge, 1952–53; Lectr, Univ. of Durham, 1953–65. Mem., Council, Soc. Nautical Res., 1963–66. *Publications*: Hugh du Puiset, 1956; *contrib.* Richard Hakluyt, ed D. B. Quinn, 1974; *contrib.* Archaeol. Ael., Econ. Hist. Rev., EHR, Hist. Jl, Marin. Mirror, Trans Royal Hist. Soc. *Address*: Pembroke College, Cambridge.

Scargill, Dr David Ian, MA, DPhil; Fellow and Tutor in Geography, St Edmund Hall, Oxford, since 1962, and University Lecturer in Geography, University of Oxford, since 1964; *b* 1935; *m* 1964; one *d*. BA Oxon 1957 (1st cl. Geog.), MA Oxon 1961, DPhil Oxon 1961; FRGS. Deptl Demonstrator, Oxford Univ., 1959–64. Mem., Oxf. Co. Planning Cttee, 1971– . *Publications*: Economic Geography of France, 1968; The Dordogne Region of France, 1974; (with R. T. Jackson) The British Isles: A Systematic Regional Geography, 1975; *contrib.* Geog., Town Country Plan., Town Plan. Rev. *Address*: School of Geography, Mansfield Road, Oxford.

Scattergood, Vincent John, MA; Lecturer in English, University of Bristol, since 1964; *b* 1940; *m* 1965. BA Birmingham 1961, MA

Birmingham 1963. *Publications*: Politics and Poetry in the Fifteenth Century, 1971; *contrib.* Anglia, Archiv., Engl. Philol Studies, Libr., Med. Æv., Notes Queries. *Address*: Dept of English, Univ. of Bristol, 40 Berkeley Square, Bristol BS8 1HY.

Schaffer, Prof. Benjamin Bernard; Professorial Fellow, Institute of Development Studies, University of Sussex, since 1971; *b* 1925; *m* 1949; one *s*. BSc(Econ) London 1947 (1st cl. Government), PhD London 1956. Staff Tutor, Univ. of Southampton, 1951–56; Sen. Lectr in Public Admin, Univ. of Queensland, 1956–59, Reader, 1959–65; Sen. Lectr in Polit., Univ. of Sussex, 1965–67, Reader, 1967–71; Vis. Prof. of Government, Cornell, 1967; Fellow, Inst. of Develt Studies, Sussex, 1968–71. Associate Editor, Public Admin (Sydney), 1959–65; Mem., Editorial Bd, Jl Develt Studies, 1969– , Jl Admin and Society, 1973– ; Public Admin Cttee, Jt Univs Council on Soc. Public Admin; UK Nat. Comr for Unesco. *Publications*: (with K. W. Knight) Top Public Servants in Two States, 1963; (with D. C. Corbett) Decisions, 1966; The Administrative Factor, 1973; Administrative Training and Development, 1974; Specialists and Generalists, ed F. F. Ridley, 1968; Politics and Change in Developing Countries, ed C. T. Leys, 1969; People, Planning and Development Studies, ed R. Apthorpe, 1970; Politics in Melanesia, ed M. Ward, 1971; etc. *contrib.* Admin. Sci. Qly, Austral. Jl Polit. Hist., Jl Cwealth Polit. Studies, Polit. Sci., Polit. Studies, Public Admin, Wld Polit., etc. *Address*: Institute of Development Studies, Andrew Cohen Building, Univ. of Sussex, Falmer, Brighton BN1 9RE.

Schaffer, Prof. Heinz Rudolph, BA, PhD; Professor of Psychology, University of Strathclyde, since 1970; *b* 1926; *m* 1950; one *s* one *d*. BA London 1950 (Hons Psychol.), PhD Glasgow 1962; Mem., Brit. Psychol. Soc., Mem., Assoc. Child Psychol. Psychiat., Mem., Soc. Res. Child Develop. Lectr, Univ. of Strathclyde, 1964–65, Sen. Lectr, 1965–68, Reader, 1968–70. Co-Editor, Brit. Jl Psychol., 1968– ; Cnsltnt Editor, Child Develop., 1968–70. *Publications*: The Growth of Sociability, 1971; The Origins of Human Social Relations, 1971; *contrib.* Brit. Jl Psychol., Child Develop., Monog. Soc. Res. Child Develop. *Address*: Dept of Psychology, Univ. of Strathclyde, Glasgow G1 1XW.

Schama, Simon Michael, MA; Director of Studies in History, and Fellow of Christ's College, University of Cambridge, since 1969; *b* 1945. BA Cantab 1966 (1st cl. with dist.), MA Cantab 1970. Fellow and Asst Dir of Studies in Hist., Christ's Coll., Cambridge, 1966–69. Editor, Camb. Rev., 1969–70. *Publications*: ed, The Cambridge Mind, 1970; *contrib.* Hist. Jl, Jl Hist. Educn. *Address*: Christ's College, Cambridge CB2 3BU.

Schaper, Dr Eva; Reader in Logic, Glasgow University, since 1972; *b* 1924. Dr.Phil Münster 1950; Vice-Pres., Brit. Soc. for Phenomenology, 1970– ; Mem., Exec. Cttee, Brit. Soc. of Aesthetics, 1965– . Asst Lectr in Logic, Univ. of Glasgow, 1952–54;

Lectr, Dept of Philosophy, UC of N Wales, Bangor, 1954–58; Lectr in Logic, Univ. of Glasgow, 1958–67, Sen. Lectr, 1967–72. *Publications*: Prelude to Aesthetics, 1968; *contrib*. BJA, JBSP, Kant Studien, PAS, Phil. Forum, Phil. Qly, Rev. Met. *Address*: Dept of Logic, Univ. of Glasgow, Glasgow G12 8QQ.

Scharf, Prof. Aaron; Professor of Art History, The Open University, since 1969; *b* 1922; *m* 1966; one *s*. BA California 1951, PhD London 1962. *Publications*: Creative Photography, 1965, 2nd edn 1969, Japanese edn 1969; Art and Photography, 1968, 2nd edn 1970; *contrib*. Burl. Mag., Gaz. Beaux-Arts. *Address*: Faculty of Arts, The Open Univ., Walton, Milton Keynes MK7 6AA.

Schenk, Dr Hans Georg Artur Viktor, MA, DPhil; Senior Lecturer in European Social and Economic History, Oxford University, since 1951; *b* 1912; *m* 1944; one *s*. DLPS German Univ. Prague 1935; DPhil Oxon 1944, MA Oxon 1946; FRHistS. Asst, Inst. of Polit. Science, German Univ., Prague, 1935–38; Lectr in European Econ. and Social Hist., Oxford Univ., 1946–51; Lectr in Mod. Hist., Univ. Coll., Oxford, 1955; Fellow, Iffley Coll., Oxford, 1965; Fellow, Wolfson Coll., Oxford, 1966; Dean of Degrees, Wolfson Coll., Oxford, 1968. *Publications*: The Aftermath of the Napoleonic Wars, 1947, American edn 1967; The Mind of the European Romantics, 1966, pbk edn New York 1969, German edn 1970; contrib. The European Nobility in the Eighteenth Century, in, New Cambridge Modern History, vol. 9; *contrib*. Cam. Jl, Rev. Hist. Mod., Rev. Internat. Théorie Droit, Calif. Law Rev. *Address*: Wolfson College, Oxford.

Schlesinger, Elsa; Part-time Lecturer in Dutch, University of Salford, since 1973; free-lance translator; *b* 1909. BA Cantab Girton Coll., 1932 (Hons Mod. and Med. Langs Tripos, Germ. and Fr.), MA Cantab 1945. Lectr in Mod. Langs, Royal Coll. of Adv. Technol., Salford (now Univ. of Salford), 1963–68; Sen. Lectr, Dept of Mod. Langs, Univ. of Salford, 1968–73, retired. *Address*: Dept of Modern Languages, Univ. of Salford, Salford M5 4WT.

Schmidt, Aubrey Vincent Carlyle; Fellow and Tutor in English Language and Literature, Balliol College, Oxford, since 1973; CUF University Lecturer, since 1971; *b* 1944; *m* 1966; two *s*. BA Oxon 1965, MA 1969. Andrew Bradley Jun. Res. Fellow, Balliol Coll., Oxford, 1966–69; Lectr in Old and Middle English, UC Dublin, 1969–70; Fellow and Tutor in English, Exeter Coll., Oxford, 1970–72. *Publications*: Chaucer's General Prologue and Canon's Yeoman's Tale, 1974; *contrib*. EC, MÆ, N and Q, RES. *Address*: Balliol Coll., Oxford.

Schmitt, Charles Bernard, BChE, PhD; Lecturer in History of Science and Philosophy, Warburg Institute, University of London, since 1972; *b* 1933; *m* 1960; two *s* one *d*. BChE Louisville 1956; PhD Columbia 1963. Asst, Columbia Univ., 1957–60; Instr, Fordham Univ., 1963–64; Asst Prof., Fordham Univ., 1965–67, Associate Prof., 1967–

68; Res. Fellow, Univ. of Leeds, 1967–72; Vis. Asst Prof., UCLA, 1965–66; Fulbright Fellow, Florence, 1961–63; Res. Fellow, Harvard Univ. Centre for Ital. Renaiss. Studies, Florence, 1970–71; Amer. Philos. Soc. Res. Grant, 1965, 1973; Nat. Inst. of Hlth Res. Grant, 1966–69; Wellcome Inst. Res. Grants, 1969, 1970–72. *Publications*: Gianfrancesco Pico della Mirandola (1469–1533) and His Critique of Aristotle, 1967; A Critical Survey and Bibliography of Studies on Renaissance Aristotelianism, 1958–1969, 1971; Cicero Scepticus, 1972; *contrib*. Archiv. Reformat., Bull. Hist. Med., Cat. Trans Comment., Gesnerus, Isis, Jl Hist. Ideas, Jl Hist. Philos., Med. Hist., Mediaev. Studies, Studies Renaiss., Studies Hist. Philos. Sci., Viator, etc. *Address*: Warburg Institute, Woburn Square, WC1H 0AB.

Schmitthoff, Prof. Clive Macmillan; Visiting Professor in Law at the University of Kent at Canterbury; Visiting Professor of International Business Law at the City University; Hon. Professor of Law at the Ruhr-Universität, Bochum; *b* 1903; *m*; Dr.jur. Univ. Berlin 1927, LLM Univ. London 1936, LLD Univ. London 1953; of Gray's Inn, Barrister, 1936; Hon. Fellow of the Institute of Export, 1974. Vis. Prof. of International Business Law at the City Univ., 1972– , and Vis. Prof. at the Univ. of Kent at Canterbury, 1971– ; Hon. Prof. of Law at the Ruhr-Universität, Bochum, 1968– . Mansfield Law Club (Founder, Chm., 1948–70); Assoc. of Law Teachers (Vice-Pres. 1966–); Legal Division of the United Nations, 1966. *Publications*: The English Conflict of Laws, 1945, 3rd edn 1954; The Export Trade, 1948, 5th edn 1969; The Sale of Goods, 1951, 2nd edn 1966; Palmer's Company Law (co-ed), since 1959, 21st edn 1968; Charlesworth's Mercantile Law (co-ed), since 1960, 12th edn 1972; The Sources of the Law of International Trade (ed), 1964; Harmonisation of European Company Law (ed), 1973; *contrib*. Jl of Business Law (Founder, Editor 1957–); contributions to many legal jls. *Address*: Darwin College, Univ. of Kent, Canterbury, Kent.

Scholefield, Arthur John Buchanan; Senior Lecturer in General Management, Graduate Business Centre, The City University, since 1969; *b* 1927; *m* 1952; one *s* one *d*. BA Oxon 1948 (Chemistry), BSc Oxon 1949, MA Oxon 1964; AMBIM. Lectr, Northampton Coll. of Adv. Technol. (now The City Univ.), 1965–69. Dir, Powell and Scholefield, Ltd, 1952– ; Gen. Mngr, Viskase Ltd, 1961–64. *Publications*: *contrib*. Jl Mngmt Studies. *Address*: Graduate Business Centre, The City Univ., Lionel Denny House, 23 Goswell Road, EC1M 7BB.

Scholfield, Philip John; Lecturer, Department of Linguistics, University College of North Wales, Bangor, since 1966; *b* 1945; *m* 1970; one *d*. BA Cantab 1965 (Classics), DipEd Bangor 1966. *Address*: Dept of Linguistics, Univ. Coll. of North Wales, Bangor LL57 2DG.

Schram, Prof. Stuart Reynolds; Professor of Politics (with reference to China), University of London, School of Oriental and African Studies, since 1968; *b* 1924; *m* 1972. BA Minnesota 1944, PhD Columbia 1954. Head, Contemporary China Inst., 1968–72. Dir, Soviet and Chinese Section, Centre d'Etude des Relations Internationales, Fondation Nationale des Sciences Politiques, Paris, 1954–67. *Publications*: Protestantism and Politics in France, 1954; La théorie de la 'révolution permanente' en Chine, 1963; The Political Thought of Mao Tse-Tung, 1963, rev. edn 1969; Le marxisme et l'Asie 1853–1964, 1965, rev. and enl. English edn 1969; Mao Tse-Tung, 1966, 2nd edn 1975; trans., Mao Ze-dong, une étude de l'éducation physique, 1962; trans., Mao Tse-Tung: Basic Tactics, 1966; ed and introd.: Authority, Participation, and Cultural Change, 1973; ed and introd.: Mao Tse-Tung Unrehearsed, 1974. *Address*: School of Oriental and African Studies, Malet Street, WC1E 7HP.

Schulkind, Dr Eugene; Lecturer in European Studies, University of Sussex, since 1971; *b* 1923; *m*. BA NY 1947, DU Paris 1951 (Mention Très Honorable); Instructor and Asst Prof., Univ. of Chicago, 1958–65; Lectr in French Literature, Univ. of Sussex, 1965–71; Sen. Fulbright Fellow, UK, 1964–65. *Publications*: The Paris Commune: The View from the Left, 1972; chapters on Hugo and Stendhal, in, French Literature and its Background, vol. 4, ed, Cruickshank, 1969; *contrib*. 1848 Revues des Révs contemp., La Pensée, French Historical Studies, Liberal Educn, Int. Rev. of Social History. *Address*: Arts Building, Univ. of Sussex, Brighton BN1 9QN.

Schur, Herbert; Senior Lecturer, Postgraduate School of Librarianship and Information Science, University of Sheffield, since 1970; *b* 1925; *m* 1956; one *d*. BSc London 1951; Mem., Libr. Assoc. Industry, 1940–44; RAF, 1944–46; Amer. Foreign Service, 1946–47; Industry, 1951–53; Scientific Civil Service (DSIR, Min. of Power), 1953–64; Lectr, Univ. of Sheffield, 1964–70. Sci. Dir, First Postgrad. Course in Inform. Science, Israel, 1967–69; Mem., Inst. of Inform. Scientists Educn Cttee, 1971– . *Publications*: ed, trans. from Russian, Safety Regulations in Coal and Shale Mines, 1963; (with W. L. Saunders) Education and Training for Scientific and Technological Library and Information Work, 1968; Education and Training of Information Specialists for the 1970's, 1972; *contrib*. Aslib Proc., UNESCO Libr. Bull. *Address*: Univ. of Sheffield, Western Bank, Sheffield S10 2TN.

Schwenk, Norman Gary, MA; Lecturer in American Literature, Department of English, University College, Cardiff, since 1965; *b* 1935; *m* 1960; one *s* three *d*. BA Nebraska Wesleyan 1957; MA Pennsylvania 1960. Teaching Asst, Pennsylvania, 1959; Fulbright Lectr, Uppsala, 1960–65. Mngmt Intern., US Navy Dept, 1957–58; Mem., Court of Govs, Univ. Coll., Cardiff, 1971–72. *Publications*: ed, American Fiction and Verse, 1962, 2nd edn 1969; *contrib*. New Mex. Qly, Sewan. Rev., South. Poet. Rev. *Address*:

Arts Building, Univ. College, Cathays Park, Cardiff CF1 1XL.

Scobbie, Irene, MA; Senior Lecturer, and Head of Scandinavian Department, University of Aberdeen, since 1971; *b* 1930. BA Dunelm 1952 (Hons German), BA Dunelm 1954 (1st cl. Scand. Studies), MA Cantab 1959. Asst Lectr, Cambridge Univ., 1959–64; Lectr, Aberdeen Univ., 1964–71. English Sec., Swed. Inst. for Cult. Relat. and Off. of Swed. Cult. Attaché, Swed. Embassy, London, 1954–57. *Publications*: Pär Lagerkvist: An Introduction, 1962, 2nd edn 1963; Sweden (Nations of the Modern World Series), 1972; *contrib*. Mod. Drama, Scand., Scand. Studies. *Address*: Dept of Scandinavian Studies, Univ. of Aberdeen, Old Aberdeen AB9 2UB, Scotland.

Scobie, Rev. Geoffrey Edward Winsor; Lecturer, Department of Psychology, University of Glasgow, since 1967; *b* 1939; *m* 1961; one *s* two *d*. BSc Bristol 1962 (Psych.), GOE Tyndale Hall Theol Coll. Bristol 1963, MSc Bristol 1968 (Psych.), MA Birmingham 1970 (Theology). Asst Curate, Christchurch, Summerfield, Birmingham, 1965–66; Asst Curate, St Anne's, Mosley, Birmingham, 1966–67. Chm., Bishopbriggs Borough Labour Party; Borough Councillor, Bishopbriggs, Glasgow. *Publications*: Introduction to the Psychology of Religion (forthcoming); *contrib*. Br. Jl Psychol., Jl Religion and Religions, Jl for Co-Existence, Jl of Beh. Science. *Address*: Dept of Psychology, Adam Smith Bd, Univ. of Glasgow, Glasgow G12 8RT.

Scobie, William Everitt, LLB, Extra Master; Lecturer in Maritime Law, Department of Maritime Studies, University of Wales Institute of Science and Technology, since 1964; *b* 1914; *m* 1940; one *s* two *d*. Extra Master 1954, LLB London 1967; Mem., Inst. Navig. *Address*: Dept of Maritime Studies, Univ. of Wales Institute of Science and Technology, Cardiff.

Scofield, Martin Paul; Lecturer in English and American Literature, University of Kent at Canterbury, since 1969; *b* 1945. BA Oxon 1966 (Eng. Lang. and Lit.), BPhil Oxon 1968 (Eng. Studies). Asst Lectr, Univ. of Southampton, 1968–69. *Publications*: *contrib*. Oxford Rev., RES. *Address*: Rutherford Coll., The Univ., Canterbury, Kent.

Scola, Roger; Lecturer in Economic and Social History, University of Kent, since 1969; *b* 1943; *m* 1966. BA Manchester 1964 (Hist.), CertEd Manchester 1965; Mem., Econ. Hist. Soc. Asst Lectr, Univ. of Kent, 1966–69. *Address*: Darwin College, The Univ., Canterbury, Kent.

Scollen, Christine Mary; Lecturer, Department of French, University of Glasgow, since 1967; *b* 1940; *m* 1964 (marr. diss. 1973). BA London 1962 (1st cl. Hons), MPhil London 1967. Asst Lectr, French Dept, Univ. Glasgow, 1964–67. *Publications*: The Birth of the Elegy in France 1500–1550, 1967; Pierre de Ronsard: selected poems (chosen and ed), 1974. *Address*: French Dept, Univ. of Glasgow, Glasgow G12 8QQ.

Scorer, Rev. Peter Frank; Lecturer, Department of Russian, University of Exeter, since 1969; *b* 1942; *m* 1967; two *s* one *d.* BA Oxon 1964; Mem. Brit. Univs Assoc. of Slavists. Exeter Univ., 1968. *Address:* Queen's Building, Univ. of Exeter, Exeter EX4 4QY.

Scott, Dr Alexander Brian, BA, DPhil; Reader, Department of Latin, Queen's University, Belfast, since 1972; *b* 1933. BA Queen's University, Belfast 1955 (1st cl. Classics); DPhil Oxon 1960. Asst, Bodleian Libr., Oxford, 1958–62; Lectr, Aberdeen Univ., 1962–64; Lectr, Queen's Univ., Belfast, 1964–72. *Publications:* Hildeberti Cenomannensis Carmina Minora (Bibl. Teubneriana), 1969; *contrib.* Mediaev. Renaiss. Studies, Med. Æv., Sac. Erud. *Address:* Dept of Latin, The Queen's Univ., Belfast BT7 1NN.

Scott, Donald Wallis, MA; Director, Cecil Powell Centre for Science Education, University of Bristol, since 1966; *b* 1913; *m* 1947; one *s* one *d.* BA Cantab 1935 (2nd cl. Nat. Sci. Tripos), MA Cantab 1942. Asst Master, Rugby Sch., 1940–44; Asst Master, Shrewsbury Sch., 1946–55; Lectr, Bristol Univ., 1956–66, Sen. Lectr, 1966– ; Vis. Lectr, Harvard, 1967. Mem., Gen. Cttee, SMA. *Publications:* Light, 1960; Training of Graduate Science Teachers, 1963; Physics, 1965, 2nd edn 1971; Course of Practical Physics, 1966, 2nd edn 1972; *contrib.* Physics Educn. *Address:* Cecil Powell Centre for Science Education, Old Park Hill, Bristol BS2 8BB.

Scott, Prof. Douglas Frederick Schumacher; Professor of German, University of Durham, since 1958; *b* 1910; *m* 1942 (wife decd); two *d.* DPhil Göttingen 1934; MA London 1936. Lectr in German, King's Coll., Newcastle, 1938–40; Lectr in German, King's Coll., London, 1946–49; Reader, and Hd of Dept, Durham Coll., Univ. of Durham, 1949–58. Friends Ambulance Unit, 1940–46; Dean, Fac. of Arts, Durham Coll., Univ. of Durham, 1967–69. *Publications:* Some English Correspondents of Goethe, 1949; *contrib.* Deuts. Lit., Germ. Life Lett., Mod. Lang. Rev. *Address:* Dept of German, Univ. of Durham, Elvet Riverside, New Elvet, Durham DH1 3JD.

Scott, Dr Ian Richard; Assistant Director of Legal Studies, Senior Lecturer and Senior Tutor, Faculty of Law, University of Birmingham, since 1973; *b* 1940; *m* 1971. LLN Melbourne 1962, PhD London 1968; Barrister and Solicitor, Supreme Ct of Victoria, 1964. Asst Lectr, Univ. of Birmingham, 1967, Lectr, 1967–73; Vis. Sen. Lectr, Monash Univ., 1972. Treas., UK Nat. Cttee of Comparative Law. *Publications:* The Crown Court, 1971; *contrib.* various jls. *Address:* Fac. of Law, Univ. of Birmingham, Birmingham B15 2TT.

Scott, Malcolm, BA, DPhil; Lecturer, Department of French, University of St Andrews, since 1965; *b* 1939; *m* 1967; one *s.* BA Hull 1961 (1st cl. French); DPhil Oxon 1969; Mem., Soc. Fr. Studies. Asst Lectr,

St Andrews, 1963–65. Faculty tutor. *Publications: contrib.* Forum Mod. Lang. Studies, Fr. Studies, Nott. Fr. Studies. *Address:* Dept of French, St Salvator's College, St Andrews, Fife KY16 9PH.

Scott, Maurice FitzGerald, MA, BLitt; Official Fellow in Economics, Nuffield College, Oxford University, since 1968; *b* 1924; *m* 1953; three *d.* BA Oxon 1948 (1st cl. PPE), BLitt Oxon 1952, MA Oxon 1952; FREconS. Student of Christ Church, Oxford, 1957–68. Economist, OEEC, Paris, 1949–51; Prime Minister's Stat. Sect., London, 1951–53; Nat. Inst. Econ. Soc. Res., 1953–57; NEDO, London, 1961–63; OECD Develt Centre, Paris, 1967–68. *Publications:* A Study of United Kingdom Imports, 1963; (with Little and Scitovsky) Industry and Trade in Some Developing Countries, 1970; ed, Induction, Growth and Trade: Essays in Honour of Sir Roy Harrod, 1970; chapters, in, The British Economy in the 1950's, ed Worswick and Ady, 1962; Economic Growth in Britain, ed Henderson, 1966; Conflicts in Policy Objectives, ed Kaldor, 1971; *contrib.* Bull. Oxf. Inst. Econ. Stat., Oxf. Econ. Papers. *Address:* Nuffield College, Oxford.

Scott, Patrick Greig; Lecturer, Department of English Literature, University of Edinburgh, since 1970; *b* 1945; *m* 1973. BA Oxon 1966, MA Leicester 1969, MA Oxon 1970. Tutorial Asst in English, Leicester Univ., 1968–70; Vis. Lectr, Coll. of William and Mary, Virginia, 1974. *Publications:* Tennyson's Enoch Arden: A Victorian Best-Seller, 1970; ed, Victorian Poetry 1830–1870, 1971; ed., A. H. Clough: Amours de Voyage, 1974; *contrib.* Book Collector, Brit. Jl Educnl Studies, Harvard Library Bull., Hist. Educn Soc. Bull., Library, Notes and Queries, Studies in Church Hist., Tennyson Res. Bull., Victorian Periodicals Newsletter, Victorian Studies. *Address:* Dept of English Literature, David Hume Tower, George Square, Edinburgh EH8 9JX.

Scott, Rev. Dr Percy; Warden, Hartley Hall, Manchester, since 1973; *b* 1910; *m* 1937; one *s* two *d.* BD London 1935, D'Theol Marburg 1938. Lectr in Theology, Manchester Univ., 1952– ; Principal, Hartley Victoria Methodist Coll., Manchester, 1959–73. *Publications:* John Wesley's Lehre von der Heiligung, 1938; articles, in, Geschichte und Gegenwart, 3rd edn 1957; trans. from German, Luther Day by Day, 1946; Delling: Worship in the New Testament, 1962; Bornkamm, etc: Tradition and Interpretation in Matthew, 1963. *Address:* Hartley Hall, Alexandra Road South, Manchester.

Scott, William Cowan, MSc, FCMA, MBIM; Lecturer, Chesters Management Centre, University of Strathclyde, since 1966; *b* 1910; *m* 1941; two *s.* MSc Strathclyde 1969; FCWA 1948, MBIM 1956. *Address:* Chesters Management Centre, Univ. of Strathclyde, Bearsden, Glasgow.

Scragg, Leah, MA; Lectr in English, University of Manchester, since 1965; *b* 1939; *m* 1962. BA Liverpool 1962, MA Liverpool 1964. Leverhulme Fellow, Univ. of

Liverpool, 1964–65. *Publications*: Introduction to Facsimile Edition of Richard Wroughton's Adaptation of Shakespeare's Richard II, 1970; *contrib*. Shakesp. Surv. *Address*: Dept of English, The Univ., Oxford Road, Manchester M13 9PL.

Screech, Michael Andrew; Fielden Professor of French Language and Literature, University College, London, since 1971; *b* 1926; *m* 1956; three *s*. BA London 1950; DLitt Birmingham 1959. Asst, Univ. Coll., London, 1950–51; Lectr, then Sen. Lectr, Univ. of Birmingham, 1951–61; Reader, Univ. Coll., London, 1961–66, Prof. of French, 1966–71. Mem., Comité de publication des Textes Littéraires Français, 1967– ; Comité d'Humanisme et Renaissance, 1971– . *Publications*: The Rabelaisian Marriage, 1958; L'Evangelisme de Rabelais, 1959; Rabelais: Le Tiers Livre, 1964; Lefèvre d'Etaples: Les 52 Semaines de l'an, 1964; (with J. Jolliffe) J. du Bellay: Les Regrets et autres Œuvres poétiques, 1967; (with R. Calder) Rabelais: Gargantua, 1970; var. reprints, in, Classiques de la Renaissance en France Series; *contrib*. BHR, Etudes Rabelais., etc. *Address*: Dept of French Lang. and Lit., Univ. College London, WC1E 6BT.

Screen, John Ernest Oliver, MA, ALA; Librarian, School of Slavonic and East European Studies, University of London, since 1972; *b* 1939; *m* 1970; one *d*. BA Cantab 1960, MA 1964, Acad. Postgrad. Dip. in Librarianship London 1963; ALA 1963. Asst Librarian, Birkbeck Coll., Univ. of London, 1963–67; Dep. Librarian Birkbeck Coll., Univ. of London, 1967–72. Mem., Univ., Coll. and Res. Section Cttee, Lib. Assoc., 1972–74. *Publications*: A select bibliography of Marshal Mannerheim, 1967; Mannerheim: the years of preparation, 1970, Finnish trans. 1972; *contrib*. Historisk tidskrift för Finland, Slav. and E Eur. Rev. *Address*: Sch. of Slavonic and East European Studies, Univ. of London, Senate House, Malet Street, WC1E 7HU.

Seaborne, Dr Alexander Eric MacIntyre, MSc, PhD; Lecturer, Department of Social Psychology, London School of Economics, since 1968; *b* 1930; *m* 1954; one *s* one *d*. BSc Hons London 1957 (Psychol.), MSc Edinburgh 1961 (Psychol.), PhD London 1971 (Psychol.), HNC 1954 (Mech. Engrg). Res. Asst, Psychol. Dept, Univ. of Edinburgh, 1958–59; Res. Associate, later Lectr, Brunel Univ., 1959–67. *Publications*: (with R. Borger) The Psychology of Learning, 1966, 6th edn 1973; *contrib*. Brit. Jl Psychol., Ergonomics, Occup. Psychol., Percept. Mot. Skills. *Address*: Dept of Social Psychology, London Sch. of Economics, Houghton Street, WC2A 2AE.

Seager, Robin John; Lecturer in Ancient History, University of Liverpool, since 1966; *b* 1940. BA Oxford 1962, MA 1965 (Derby Scholarship 1962); Member: Class. Assoc., Soc. for Promotion of Roman Studies. Robinson Sen. Scholar, Oriel Coll. Oxford, 1963–66; Vis. Lectr in Hist, Univ. of Illinois at Urbana-Champaign, 1971–72. Mem.

Council, Soc. for Promotion of Roman Studies, 1973. *Publications*: ed, The Crisis of the Roman Republic, 1969; trans., M. Gelzer: The Roman Nobility, 1969; Tiberius, 1972; *contrib*. AJP, Athenaeum, CQ, CR, Historia, JHS, JRS, Latomus, SDHI. *Address*. The Univ., PO Box 147, Liverpool L69 3BX.

Sealy, Dr Kenneth Royston; Reader in Geography, London School of Economics, University of London, since 1962; *b* 1923; *m* 1950; two *s*. BSc(Econ) London 1949, MSc(Econ) London 1952, PhD London 1957; AFRAeS, FRGS, MIBG. Lectr, LSE, 1950–62. Cnsltnt, Min. of Transport, 1966; Roskill Commn, 1969, etc. *Publications*: ed, Geography of Air Transport, 1962; Air Freight and Anglo-European Trade, 1962; Regional Studies of the United States and Canada, 1968; *contrib*. Aeronaut. Jl, Geog., Geog. Jl, Transp. *Address*: Dept of Geography, London School of Economics, Aldwych, WC2A 2AE.

Sealy, Dr Leonard Sedgwick; University Lecturer in Law, since 1961, University of Cambridge, Fellow, since 1959, and Senior Tutor, since 1970, Gonville and Caius College, Cambridge. MA, LLM, PhD. *Address*: Gonville and Caius College, Cambridge.

Searby, Dr Peter; University Lecturer, Faculty of Education, University of Cambridge, since 1968; *b* 1930; *m* 1956; one *s* two *d*. BA Liverpool 1954 (Mod. Hist.), PhD Warwick, 1972 (Social Hist.). *Publications*: The Chartists, 1967; Weavers and Freemen in Coventry, 1820–1860: social and political traditionalism in an early Victorian town (forthcoming); *contrib*. Agric. Hist. Rev., Hist., Hist of Educn., Labour Hist. Bull., Trans Hist. Lancs and Ches. *Address*: 17 Brookside, Cambridge.

Searle, Dr Geoffrey Russell; Lecturer in Modern British History, School of English and American Studies, University of East Anglia, since 1967; *b* 1940. BA Cantab 1962 (1st cl. Pts I and II), MA Cantab 1966, PhD Cantab 1966; Fellow Eugenics Soc., 1971. Asst Lectr, Univ. of E Anglia, 1965–67. *Publications*: The Quest for National Efficiency: A Study in British Politics and Political Thought, 1899–1914, 1971; ed, A. White: Efficiency and Empire (1901), 1974; *contrib*. Hist., Vict. Studies. *Address*: School of English and American Studies, Univ. of East Anglia, Norwich NOR 88C.

Seaton, Robert; Secretary of the University of Dundee, since 1973; *b* 1937; *m* 1961; two *s* two *d*. MA Glasgow 1958 (1st cl. Hons Classics), LLB Edinburgh 1966. Univ. Edinburgh: Admin. Asst, 1962–66; Sen. Admin. Officer, 1966–69; Asst Sec., 1969–73. *Address*: Univ. of Dundee, Dundee DD1 4HN.

Sebald, Winfried Georg, LicèsLett, MA; Lecturer in European Studies, University of East Anglia, since 1970; *b* 1944; *m* 1967. LicèsLett Fribourg 1966; MA Manchester 1968. Lectr, Univ. of Manchester, 1966–68, 1969–70; *Publications*: Carl Sternheim, 1969;

contrib. Jl Europ. Studies, Lit. Krit., Neue Rundschau. *Address:* School of European Studies, Univ. of East Anglia, Norwich NOR 88C.

Seddon, John David; Lecturer, Overseas Development Group, University of East Anglia, since 1973; *b* 1943; *m* 1970. BA Hons Cantab 1964, MA 1968; FRAI, FRGS, Member: BSA; RIIA. Jun. Lectr, Sch. of African Studies, Univ. of Cape Town, 1964–65; Lectr, Dept of Geography and Environmental Studies, Univ. of the Witwatersrand, 1965–67; Lectr, Sch. of Oriental and African Studies, 1970–72. *Publications:* trans. Montagne: The Berbers: their social and political organisation, 1972; Relations of Production: Marxist approaches to economic anthropology, 1974; *contrib.* Current Anthropology, Man (New Series). *Address:* Overseas Development Group, Univ. of East Anglia, Earlham Hall, Norwich NOR 88C.

Seddon, Peter R., BA, PhD; Lecturer in History, University of Nottingham, since 1966; *b* 1942. BA Nottingham 1963 (1st cl.); PhD Manchester 1967. *Publications: contrib.* Renaiss. Mod. Studies. *Address:* Dept of History, Nottingham Univ., Nottingham NG7 2RD.

Sedge, Dr Douglas; Lecturer in English, University of Exeter, since 1965; *b* 1940. BA Birmingham 1962, MA Birmingham 1963, PhD Birmingham 1966. *Publications: contrib.* Yrs Wk Engl. Studies. *Address:* Dept of English, Univ. of Exeter, Exeter EX4 4QJ.

Sedgwick, Peter; Lecturer, Department of Politics, University of York, since 1968; *b* 1934. BA Oxon 1956 (PPP), MA Oxon 1959. Demonstrator in Psychology, Univ. of Liverpool, 1957–59; Educnl Psychol., Liverpool Child Guidance Centre, 1960–63; Tutor-Organiser, HM Psychiat. Prison, Grendon, 1963–65; Res. Psychol., Rivermead Hosp., Oxford, 1965–67; Vis. Tutor, Ruskin Coll., Oxford, 1965–67. Vis. Prof. in Sociology, Queen's Coll., NY, 1970–71. *Publications:* ed, V. Serge: Memoirs of a Revolutionary, 1963, 2nd edn 1967; ed, V. Serge: Year One of the Russian Revolution, 1972; *contrib.* numerous articles on Marxist ideology, political analysis, and problems of method in psychology and psychiatry. *Address:* Dept of Politics, Univ. of York, Heslington, York YO1 5DD.

Sedgwick, Robert; Lecturer in Economics, Division of Economic Studies, University of Sheffield, since 1969; *b* 1945; *m* 1971. BSc Econ Hull 1967. Temp. Lectr in Econs, Univ. Sheffield, 1968. *Publications:* ed (jtly), Monetary Theory and Policy in the 1970's, 1971; (jtly) Introducing Economics, 1974. *Address:* Division of Economic Studies, Univ. Sheffield, Sheffield S10 2TN.

Seed, Dr Geoffrey; Senior Lecturer, Department of Modern History, University of St Andrews, since 1954; *b* 1917; *m* 1942; one *s* two *d.* BA Dunelm 1938 (1st cl. History), MA Dunelm 1946; PhD St Andrews 1949. Lectr, Univ. Coll., Dundee, 1946–54; Vis. Prof., Queen's Univ., Kingston, Ontario, 1952–53; Vis. Prof., Union Coll.,

Schenectady, NY, 1958–59; Vis. Prof., Dalhousie Univ., Halifax, NS, 1966; Wisconsin State Univ., 1966–67; Vis. Prof. Queen's Univ., Kingston, 1968. Warden, J. Burnet Hall, St Andrews, 1971– . *Publications: contrib.* Hist., Jl Amer. Studies, Jl Royal Asiat. Soc., Penn. Mag. Hist. Biog., Pol Sci. Qly. *Address:* Dept of Modern History, Univ. of St Andrews, St Andrews, Fife KY16 9AJ.

Seed, Philip; Senior Lecturer in Social Work, Social Work Department, University of Aberdeen, since 1973; *b* 1930; *m* 1956; three *s.* MA Hons Cantab 1956, Cert. in Social Sci. and Admin LSE 1954; Mem., Brit. Assoc. of Social Workers. Sen. Lectr in Sociol. Univ. of Aberdeen, 1969–73. Convener, Jt Univ. Council for Social and Public Admin Cons. Gp on Community Work, 1971– . *Publications:* The Psychological Problem of Disarmament, 1966; The Expansion of Social Work in Britain, 1973; *contrib.* Brit. Jl of Social Work. *Address:* Univ. of Aberdeen, King's Coll., High Street, Old Aberdeen.

Seers, Dudley; Fellow, Institute of Development Studies and Professor of Development Studies at the University of Sussex, since 1972 (Director, 1967–72); *b* 1920; *m* 1943; one *s* three *d.* BA Cambridge 1943; MA Oxford 1946. Sen. Lectr in Economic Stats, Oxford Univ., 1946–53; Vis. Prof., Yale Univ., 1961–63; Dir.-Gen., Econ. Planning Staff, Min. of Overseas Development, 1964–67. Leader, ILO missions to Colombia, 1970, Ceylon, 1971; Vice-Pres., Soc. Internat. Develop., UK Chapter, Hon. Vice-Pres., Intermed. Technol. Develop. Gp Ltd. *Publications:* ed, Cuba: The Economic and Social Revolution, 1964; ed (with L. Joy), Development in a Divided World, 1971; ed (with M. Faber), Crisis in Planning, 1972; *contrib.* Bull. Inst. Develop. Studies, Econ. Jl, Internat. Develop. Rev., Internat. Lab. Rev., Jl Develop. Studies, Jl Wld Trade Law, Soc. Econ. Studies. *Address:* Institute of Development Studies, Univ. of Sussex, Brighton BN1 9RE.

Segal, Prof. Judah Benzion, MC, MA, DPhil, FBA; Professor of Semitic Languages, School of Oriental and African Studies, University of London, since 1961; *b* 1912; *m* 1946; two *d.* BA Cantab 1935, MA Cantab 1939, DPhil Oxon 1939; FBA. Lectr in Mod. Hebrew, SOAS, 1946–55; Reader in Aramaic and Syriac, 1955–61. DADPS, Sudan Govt, 1939–41; GHQ, MEF, 1942–44; Brit. Mil. Admin., Tripolitania, 1945–46. *Publications:* The Diacritical Point and the Accents in Syriac, 1953; The Hebrew Passover, 1962; Edessa: The Blessed City, 1970; *contrib.* Bull. SOAS, Iraq, Jl Semit. Studies. *Address:* School of Oriental and African Studies, Malet Street, WC1E 7HP.

Seglow, Peter; Lecturer in Industrial Sociology, Department of Sociology, Brunel University, since 1967; *b* 1934; *m* 1965; one *s.* Dip. in Ind. Admin, Liverpool 1962, MA Leicester 1967 (Sociol.); Member: Brit. Sociol Assoc.; Brit. Univs Indus. Relns Assoc. Research Officer PEP, 1962–64; Cons. OECD,

1964; Management Cons., 1964–67; Part-time Ind. Relns Advr: NBPI, 1969–71; Office of Manpower Econs, 1971; Pay Bd, 1972–73. *Publications*: Attitudes in British Management, 1966; Business Education and the EEC; ed, The Future of Productivity Bargaining; *contrib*. Ind. Relns Jl. *Address*: Brunel Univ., Uxbridge, Mddx UB8 3TH.

Seiffert, Dr Leslie, Drphil; Reader in German, University of Oxford, Fellow of Hertford College, and Lecturer in German, Jesus College, since 1973; *b* 1934; *m* 1968; one *s* one *d*. BA Sydney 1955 (1st cl. and Medal, German), DipEd Sydney 1956, Drphil Munich 1965, MA Oxon 1973. Asst Lectr in German, Birmingham Univ., 1959–62; Lectr, 1962–69, Sen. Lectr, 1969–73, Birmingham Univ. *Publications*: Wortfeld-theorie und Strukturalismus, 1968, English edn forthcoming; contrib. German Linguistics, ed Hartmann, 1973; contrib. Hartmann von Aue, ed Kuhn/Cormeau, 1973; *contrib*. Deut. Viertel. Lit. Geistes., Jl Ling., Med. Æv., Oxf. Germ. Studies. *Address*: Hertford College, Oxford OX1 3BW.

Self, Prof. Peter John Otter; Professor of Public Administration, University of London, since 1963; *b* 1919; *m* 1959; two *s*. MA Oxon 1960. Extra-Mural Lectr, London Univ., 1944–49; Lectr, 1948–61, Reader, 1961–63, LSE. Editorial staff, The Economist, 1944–62; Dir of Studies (Admin), Civil Service Dept, 1969–70. Mem. Exec. and Council, 1954, Vice-Chm. Exec., 1955–61, 1969– , Chm. Exec., 1961–69, Town and Country Planning Assoc.; Mem. SE Regional Economic Planning Council, 1966– . *Publications*: Regionalism, 1949; Cities in Flood: The Problems of Urban Growth, 1957; (with H. Storing) The State and the Farmer, 1962; Metropolitan Planning, 1972; Administrative Theories and Politics, 1972; *contrib*. numerous articles. *Address*: London School of Economics and Political Science, Houghton Street, Aldwych, WC2A 2AE.

Sellar, William David Hamilton; Lecturer, Department of Scots Law, University of Edinburgh, since 1969; *b* 1941. BA Oxon, LLB Edin; Solicitor. Secretary, Co. of Scottish History, Ltd, 1972– ; Legal Assessor, Scottish Land Court, 1967–68. *Publications: contrib*. Scottish Historical Rev., Scottish Studies, Scots Law Times. *Address*: Dept of Scots Law, Univ. of Edinburgh, Old College, South Bridge, Edinburgh EH8 9YL.

Selmes, Dr Cyril; Senior Lecturer in Education, since 1974, and Director of Studies, since 1969, School of Education, University of Bath; *b* 1930; *m* 1951; two *s* two *d*. BA Hons 1951, CertEd 1952, MA 1955, Cantab, PhD Bath 1971; MIBiol 1955. Sen. Biologist, The Crypt Sch., Gloucester, 1952–56; Head of Biology Dept, 1956–59, Head of Science Dept, 1959–66, Corby Grammar Sch.; Lectr in Educn, Sch. of Educn, Univ. of Bath,1966–74. *Publications*: ed, New Movements in the Study and Teaching of Biology, 1974; *contrib*. Jl Biol Educn, Sch. Sci. Rev. *Address*: Sch. of Education, Northgate House, Upper Borough Walls, Bath, Somerset.

Selwyn, Rev. David Gordon; Lecturer in Theology, St David's University College, Lampeter, since 1968; *b* 1938. BA Cantab 1962, BA Oxon 1965 (by incorp.), MA Cantab 1966, MA Oxon 1966. Mem. Eccles. History Soc., Mem. Bibliog. Soc. Sir Henry Stephenson Fellow, Univ. Sheffield, 1964–65; Hastings Rashdall Student, New Coll., Oxford, 1965–68; Sub-Editor Trivium. *Publications*: *contrib*. Jl Theol Studies, Library. *Address*: St David's Univ. Coll., Lampeter, Dyfed SA48 7ED.

Selwyn, Norman, LLM, JP; Lecturer in Law, Management Centre, University of Aston in Birmingham, since 1965; *b* 1927; *m* 1962; two *s* one *d*. LLB Manchester 1957, LLM Manchester 1967, DipEcon Oxon 1951; ACCS 1962, ACIS 1969, Barrister-at-Law (Gray's Inn) 1962, JP, 1971– . *Publications*: Industrial Law Notebook, 1969; Guide to the Industrial Relations Act, 1971; Selected Questions and Answers on the Industrial Relations Act, 1972; *contrib*. Mod. Law Rev. *Address*: Management Centre, Univ. of Aston, Gosta Green, Birmingham B4 7ET.

Semeonoff, Dr Boris; Reader in Psychology, University of Edinburgh, since 1964; *b* 1910; *m* 1939; two *s* two *d*. MA Edinburgh 1931, MEd Edinburgh 1933, PhD Edinburgh 1936; FBPsS 1941, Mem., Exper. Psychol. Soc., Hon. Fellow, Brit. Soc. Projective Psychol. and Personality Study 1963. Univ. Asst, Univ. of Edinburgh, 1933–38, Lectr, 1938–56, Sen. Lectr, 1956–64. Pres., Brit. Psychol. Soc., 1968–69; Pres., Sect. J, Brit. Assoc. Adv. Sci., 1969; Ed., Brit. Jl Psychol., 1958–64; Mem., Psychol. Cttee, SSRC, 1971–73. *Publications*: (with E. L. Trist) Diagnostic Performance Tests, 1958; Personality Assessment: Selected Readings, 1966, 2nd edn 1970; *contrib*. Brit. Jl Med. Psychol., Brit. Jl Psychol., Hum. Relat. *Address*: Dept of Psychology, Univ. of Edinburgh, Edinburgh EH8 9TJ.

Sen, Prof. Amartya Kumar; Professor of Economics, University of London, since 1971; *b* 1933; *m* 1960; two *d*. MA, PhD Cantab. Prof. of Econs, Jadavpur Univ., Calcutta, 1956–58; Prize Fellow, 1957–61, Staff Fellow, 1961–63, Trinity Coll., Cambridge; Prof. of Econs 1963–71, Chm., Dept of Econs, 1966–68, Hon. Prof., 1971– , Delhi Univ.; Vis. Prof., MIT, 1960–61; Vis. Prof., Univ. of Calif. at Berkeley, 1964–65; Vis. Prof., Harvard Univ., 1968–69. Hon. Dir, Agric. Econs Res. Centre, Delhi, 1966–68 and 1969–71. Chm., UN Expert Gp Meeting on Role of Advanced Skill and Technology, NY, 1967. *Publications*: Choice of Techniques: an aspect of planned economic development, 1960, 3rd edn 1968; Growth Economics, 1970; Collective Choice and Social Welfare, 1971; On Economic Inequality, 1973; *contrib*. various jls. *Address*: London School of Economics and Political Science, Houghton Street, Aldwych, WC2A 2AE.

Serjeant, Prof. Robert Bertram; Sir Thomas Adams's Professor of Arabic since 1970, and Director of Middle East Centre since 1965, University of Cambridge; *b* 1915;

m 1941; one *s* one *d*. MA Edinburgh 1936 (1st cl. Semitic Langs), PhD Cantab 1939. Tweedie Fellow, Edinburgh Univ., 1939; Post-graduate student, SOAS, London Univ., 1940; Lectr, SOAS, London Univ., 1941; Colonial Res. Fellow, Hadramawt, 1947–48; Reader in Arabic, 1948; Prof. of Arabic, SOAS, London Univ., 1955–64; Lectr, Islamic Hist., Cambridge Univ., 1964–66 Reader, 1966–70. Ed., Arabic Listener, 1943–45. Mem., Minister of Educn's mission to examine instruction in Arabic, Nigeria, 1956; Mem., Sec. of State for Colonies' mission to examine Muslim educn in E Africa, 1957; Mem., Inter-Univ. Council's Adv. Delegn on Univ. of N Nigeria, 1961; Mem., ME Comd Expedn to Socotra, 1967. Co-editor, Arabian Studies, 1973– . *Publications*: Catalogue of Arabic, Persian and Hindustani MSS in New College, Edinburgh, 1942; Materials for a History of Islamic Textiles, 1942–51, repr. 1973; Prose and Poetry from Hadramawt, I, 1950; Saiyids of Hadramawt, 1957; Portuguese off the South Arabian Coast, 1961; The South Arabian Hunt, 1974; *contrib*. BSOAS, JRAS, Le Muséon, Rivista d. Studi Orientali, Islamic Culture, etc. *Address*: Faculty of Oriental Studies, Sidgwick Avenue, Cambridge.

Seton, Francis, MA, DPhil; Official Fellow, Nuffield College, Oxford University, since 1953; *b* 1920; *m* 1950; two *s* one *d*. BA Oxford 1946 (1st cl. Russ. Lang. and Lit.), BA Oxford 1948 (1st cl. Econs); Mem., Royal Econ. Soc., Economet. Soc., Amer. Assoc. Study Soviet-Type Econ. Res. Fellow, Nuffield Coll., Oxford, 1950–52; Res. Associate, Harvard Univ., 1952–53; Vis. Prof., Osaka Univ., Japan, 1958; Vis. Prof., Columbia Univ., 1959; Vis. Prof., Pennsylvania Univ., 1963; Vis. Prof., Univ. of Waterloo, Canada, 1970. Cnsltnt, ECE (UNO), Dept of Econ. Aff., Bd of Trade; Govt Adv., Iran, Chile, Indonesia. *Publications*: Shadow Wages in the Chilean Economy, 1972; *contrib*. Economet., Econ. Jl, Oxf. Econ. Papers, Sov. Studies. *Address*: Nuffield College, Oxford.

Seton-Watson, Christopher Ivan William, MC, MA; Fellow of Oriel College, Oxford, since 1946, and Lecturer in Politics, University of Oxford, since 1951; *b* 1918. BA Oxon 1945, MA Oxon 1946; FRHistS. Chm., UK Council of World Univ. Service, 1964–69; Chm., Czechoslovak Student Scholarship Fund, 1969–73. *Publications*: Italy from Liberalism to Fascism, 1967. *Address*: Oriel College, Oxford.

Seton-Watson, George Hugh Nicholas; Professor of Russian History and Head of History Department, School of Slavonic and East European Studies, University of London, since 1951; *b* 1916; *m* 1947; three *d*. BA Oxon 1938 (1st cl. PPE), MA Oxon 1946; FBA, FRHistS. Fellow and Praelector in Politics, Univ. Coll., Oxford, 1946–51; Vis. Prof., Columbia Univ., NY, 1957; Fellow, Center for Advanced Studies in Behavioural Sciences, Stanford, California, 1963–64; Vis. Fellow, Australian Nat. Univ., 1964; Vis. Prof., Indiana Univ., 1973; Walker-Ames Vis. Prof., Washington Univ., 1973. Mem., Council, Royal Inst. Internat. Aff., 1951– ;

Mem., ed. bd, var. learned jls. *Publications*: Eastern Europe between the Wars, 1945; The East European Revolution, 1950; The Decline of Imperial Russia, 1952; The Pattern of Communist Revolution, 1953; Neither War nor Peace, 1960; The New Imperialism, 1961; Communism and Nationalism: essays, 1964; The Russian Empire 1801–1917, 1967; *contrib*. var. articles on hist. and pol. sci. to jls in Britain, US, Germany, Yugoslavia, Roumania, Hungary. *Address*: School of Slavonic and East European Studies, Univ. of London, WC1E 7HU.

Severin, Dr Dorothy Sherman; Lecturer, Department of Spanish, Westfield College, University of London, since 1969; *b* 1942; *m* 1966; one *d*. AB, AM, PhD, Harvard; Mem., Assoc. of Hispanists. Teaching Fellow and tutor, Harvard Univ., 1964–66; Vis. Lectr, Univ. of West Indies, Jamaica, 1967–68; Asst Prof., Vassar Coll., NY, 1968–69. *Publications*: ed, F. de Rojas: La Celestina (Madrid), 1969, 2nd edn 1971; Memory in La Celestina, 1970; ed, D. de San Pedro: La pasión trobada (Naples), 1973; ed, D. de San Pedro: Obras completas III, Poesía (Madrid), 1975; *contrib*. Medieval Hispanic Studies, presented to Rita Hamilton; *contrib*. Anuario de Estudios Medievales, Romanische Forschungen. *Address*: Westfield Coll., Kidderpore Avenue, Hampstead, NW3 7ST.

Seymour, Dr Philip Herschel Kean; Lecturer, Department of Psychology, Dundee University, since 1966; *b* 1938; *m* 1962; one *s* one *d*. BA Oxon 1962; DipEd St Andrews 1965, MEd St Andrews 1966; PhD Dundee 1971; Secondary Sch. Teaching Cert., 1965; Member: BPsS; Exptl Psychol. Soc. *Publications*: *contrib*. Brit. Jl Psychol., Acta Psychologica, Qly Jl Exptl Psychol., Perception and Psychophysics, Memory and Cognition, Jl Exptl Psychol. *Address*: Dept of Psychology, The Univ., Dundee DDI 4HN.

Seymour-Ure, Dr Colin, DPhil; Senior Lecturer in Politics, University of Kent at Canterbury, since 1965; *b* 1938; *m* 1963; one *s* one *d*. BA Oxon 1961 (2nd cl. PPE), MA Carleton 1962, DPhil Oxon 1968. Jun. Lectr, Magdalen Coll., Oxford, 1962–65; Vis. Prof., Univ. of N Carolina, 1970. *Publications*: The Press, Politics and the Public, 1968; The Political Impact of Mass Media, 1974; *contrib*. Parly Aff., Govt Opposit., Pol Qly. *Address*: The Univ., Canterbury, Kent CT2 7NZ.

Shackle, Dr Christopher; Lecturer in Urdu and Panjabi, Department of India, Pakistan and Ceylon, School of Oriental and African Studies, University of London, since 1969; *b* 1942; *m* 1964; one *s* one *d*. BA 1963, Dip. Soc. Anthrop. 1965, BLitt 1966, Oxon, PhD London 1972. Fellow in Indian Studies, SOAS, 1966–69. *Publications*: Punjabi (Teach Yourself Books), 1972; (with D. J. Matthews) An Anthology of Classical Urdu Love Lyrics, 1972. *Address*: School of Oriental and African Studies, Univ. of London, Malet Street, WC1E 7HP.

Shackleton, Dr N. J.; Assistant Director of Research, Sub-dept of Quaternary Research, Cambridge University, since 1972, also lecturing on acoustics in the Faculty of Music; *b* 1937; *m* 1967. BA Cantab 1961, MA Cantab 1965, PhD Cantab 1967; FGS; Mem., Glaciological Soc.; Mem., Galpin Soc. Asst in Res., 1961, Sen. Asst in Res., 1966, Sub-dept of Quaternary Res., Cambridge Univ. *Publications*: *contrib.* Brit. Sch. Archaeol. Athens Pub., Geol. Soc. Lond. Special Pub., Nature, Jl Sci. Instrum., Proc. Royal Soc. *Address*: Sub-Department of Quaternary Research, 5 Salisbury Villas, Station Road, Cambridge.

Shackleton, Dr Robert, DLitt, FBA, FSA, FRSL, FRHistS; Bodley's Librarian, Oxford University, since 1966; *b* 1919. BA Oxon 1940 (1st cl. Mod. Langs), MA Oxon 1945, DLitt Oxon 1966; Hon. Dr Bordeaux 1966, Hon LittD Dublin 1967; FBA 1966, FSA, FRSL. Corresp. Mem., Acad. de Bordeaux 1954, Acad. Montesquieu (Bordeaux) 1956, Hon. Mem., Assoc. Internat. de Bibliophilie, Hon. For. Corresp. Mem., Grolier Club NY, For. Hon. Mem., Amer. Acad. Arts Sci., 1971, Pres., Soc. Fr. Studies, 1959–60, Pres., Internat. Comp. Lit. Assoc., 1964–67, Vice-Pres., Internat. Soc. Eightnth-Cent. Studies, 1971– . Lectr, Trinity Coll., Oxford, 1946–49; Fellow, Brasenose Coll., Oxford, 1946– ; Libr., Brasenose Coll., Oxford, 1948–66; Sen. Dean, Brasenose Coll., Oxford, 1954–61; Vice-Princ., Brasenose Coll., Oxford, 1963–66; Lectr in French, Oxford Univ., 1949–65; Reader in French Literature, 1965–66; Vis. Prof., Univ. of Wisconsin, 1968; Zaharoff Lectr, Oxford Univ., 1970; Hon. Fellow, Oriel Coll., Oxford, 1971; Hon. Prof. Fellow, Univ. Coll. of Wales, 1972; Associate Fellow, Silliman Coll., Yale, 1972. Mem., Ed. Bd, Fr. Studies; Gen. Ed., 1965–67; Mem., Ed. Bd, Archives Internat. d'hist. des idées, 1962– ; Mem., Internat. Adv. Bd, Comp. Lit. Studies, 1974– ; Chm., Cttee on Oxf. Univ. Librs, 1965–66; Deleg., Clarendon Press, 1971– ; Mem., Council, Brit. Acad., 1971– . *Publications*: Ed, Fontenelle: Entretiens sur la pluralité des mondes, 1955; Montesquieu, a critical biography, 1961; The Encyclopédie and the Clerks, 1970; contrib. Encyclopaedia Britannica; *contrib.* Act. Acad. Bord., Fr. Studies, Mod. Lang. Rev., Rev. Internat. Philos., Rev. Litt. Comp., Rev. Hist. Litt. Fran., Studies Volt. 18th Cent., Trans Amer. Philos. Soc. *Address*: Bodleian Library, Oxford.

Shaefer, Ivor Thomas; Director, Management Development, School of Management, Cranfield Institute of Technology, since 1968; *b* 1918; *m* 1941; two *d*. FCIS 1957. Advr, NEDO. *Address:* Sch. of Management, Cranfield Inst. of Technology, Cranfield, Bedford MK43 0AL.

Shaffer, Leonard Henry, PhD; Senior Lecturer, Department of Psychology, Exeter University, since 1971; *b* 1929; *m* 1964; one *s* one *d*. BSc London 1955 (1st cl. Psychology), PhD London 1959 (Psychology); Mem., Exper. Psychol. Soc. Res. Sci., MRC Appl. Psychol. Res. Unit, Cambridge, 1959–65; Lectr, Exeter, 1965–71. Treas., Exper. Psychol. Soc., 1972. *Publications*: *contrib.* Brit. Jl Psychol., Jl Exper. Psychol., Percept. Psychophys., Qly Jl Exper. Psychol. *Address*: Dept of Psychology, Univ. of Exeter, Exeter EX4 4QJ.

Shanbhag, Dr Damodar Nagesh; Lecturer, Department of Probability and Statistics, University of Sheffield, since 1971; *b* 1937; *m*; one *s* one *d*. MSc Karnatak 1960, PhD Karnatak 1967. Research Fellow: CSIR, New Delhi, 1963–65; UGC, New Delhi, 1965–66; Lectr, Univ. Poona, 1966–68; Sen. Lectr, Univ. Western Australia, 1969–70. *Publications:* numerous in applied probability theory; *contrib.* Austr. Jl Statistics, Annals Math. Statist., Annals Stat. Maths, Biometrika, Biometrics, Calcutta Stat. Bull., Jl Appl. Prob., Jl Royal Stat. Soc., Jl Amer. Stat. Assoc., Proc. Camb. Phil. Soc., Ops Res., etc. *Address*: Dept of Probability and Statistics, Univ. of Sheffield, Sheffield S3 7RH.

Shanin, Prof. Teodor, PhD; Professor of Sociology, University of Manchester, since 1974; *b* 1930; *m* 1970. BA Jerusalem 1963 (SocEcon); PhD Birmingham 1968; Cert. Qualified Social Worker Jerusalem 1951. Professional Social Worker, 1951–56; Med. Social Worker, 1956–58; District Rehabil. Offr, 1958–60; Study Leave Abroad (rehabil. handicapped), 1960–61; Dir, Rehabil. Unit for Handicapped, 1961–63; Lectr, Sheffield Univ., 1965–70; Vis. Lectr, CREES, Univ. of Birmingham, 1968–69; Sen. Lectr in Sociology, 1970–72, Assoc. Prof., 1972–73, Univ. of Haifa; Vis. Fellow, St Antony's Coll., Oxford, 1973–74. *Publications*: Peasants and Peasant Societies, 1971; ed, The Awkward Class: Political Sociology of Peasantry in a Developing Society: Russia 1910–1925, 1972; ed, The Rules of the Game: Models in Scholarly Thought, 1972; *contrib.* Europ. Jl Sociol., Sociol. Rev., Sociol., Sov. Studies, Jl Contemp. Asia (co-editor), Jl Peasant Studies (co-editor). *Address*: Dept of Sociology, Univ. of Manchester, Manchester M13 9PL.

Shannon, Dr Richard Thomas; Reader in English History, School of English and American Studies, University of East Anglia, since 1971; *b* 1931. MA New Zealand 1953 (1st cl. Hist.), PhD Cantab 1960; FRHistS. Asst Lectr, Univ. Coll., Auckland, 1955–57; Lectr, 1960–61; Sen. Lectr, 1962–63; Lectr, Sch. of English and American Studies, Univ. of E Anglia, 1963–65; Sen. Lectr, 1965–71. *Publications*: Gladstone and the Bulgarian Agitation, 1876, 1963, repr. 1974; The Crisis of Imperialism: a history of Britain 1865–1915, 1974; contrib. Festschriften for W. Airey and G. K. Clark; contrib. Pressures from Without, ed P. M. Hollis, 1974; *contrib.* Hist. Studies (Austral. NZ). *Address*: School of English and American Studies, Univ. of East Anglia, Norwich NOR 88C.

Shapira, Morris; Lecturer in English, Faculty of Humanities, University of Kent at Canterbury, since 1967; *b* 1929. BA Cantab 1953, MA Cantab 1958. Graham Robertson Res. Fellow, Downing Coll., Cambridge, 1957–60; Dir of Studies in English, Downing Coll., Cambridge, 1962–65; Vis. Lectr, La Trobe Univ., Melbourne. *Publications*: ed., Henry James: Selected Literary Criticism, with introd. by F. R.

Leavis. *Address*: Rutherford College, Univ. of Kent at Canterbury, Canterbury, Kent.

Shapiro, Esmée Esther; Lecturer in Private Law, University of Glasgow, since 1967; *b* 1933; *m* 1952; two *s* one *d*. BL Glasgow 1965. Asst in Private Law, Univ. Glasgow, 1965–67. Adviser of Studies, Univ. Glasgow. *Publications*: *contrib*. Jl Law Soc. Scotland. *Address*: Dept of Private Law, 63 Hillhead Street, Glasgow G12 8QQ.

Sharp, Dr Clifford Henry; Reader in Transport Economics, Department of Economics, Leicester University, since 1973; *b* 1922; *m* 1959; two *s* one *d*. BA London 1944, BSc Econ London 1946, PhD Birmingham 1954; Dip. Public Admin London 1943. Res. Asst, Exeter, 1947–50; Asst Lectr, Birmingham, 1952–53; Res. Assoc., 1953–58; Lectr, Leicester, 1965–68, Sen. Lectr, 1968–73. Consltnt, Econ. Commn Asia and Far East, 1959–60; Specialist Adv., House of Commons Estimates Sub-Cttee, 1969–70, Sel. Cttee on Nationalised Industries, 1973. *Publications*: The Problem of Transport, 1965; Problems of Urban Passenger Transport, 1967; Living with the Lorries, 1973; Transport Economics, 1974; *contrib*. Econ. Jl, Jl Indust. Econ., Jl Transp. Econ. Policy. *Address*: Dept of Economics, Univ. of Leicester, Leicester LE1 7RH.

Sharp, Derrick William Hackett; Lecturer in Education, with special reference to English Studies, University College of Swansea, since 1962; *b* 1922; *m* 1947; two *s* two *d*. BA London 1947 (1st cl. English), Teachers' Dip. London 1948 (practical distinction), MA London 1952 (Education); Mem., Exec. Cttee, Nat. Assoc. the Teaching Engl.; Mem., Brit. Assoc. for Applied Linguistics. Dir, Schs Council Projects on Attitudes, and English in Wales, 8–13, 1967–71, 1973–76; Ed., Univ. Coll. of Swansea Collegiate Fac. of Educn Jl, 1963– . *Publications*: (with G. W. Dennis) The Art of Summary, 1966; Language in Bilingual Communities, 1973; (jtly) Attitudes to Welsh and English in the Schools of Wales, 1973. *Address*: Dept of Education, Univ. College of Swansea, Hendrefoilan, Swansea SA2 7NB.

Sharp, Stanley, MA, DipEd; Senior Lecturer in Adult Education and Staff Tutor in Literature, Department of Extra-Mural Studies, University of Bristol, since 1973 (Resident Tutor, 1954–73); *b* 1921; *m* 1945; three *s* one *d*. BA Leeds 1942, DipEd Leeds 1946, MA Leeds 1952. Resid. Tutor, Univ. Coll. of W Indies, 1949–54. *Address*: Extra-Mural Dept, 30/32 Tyndall's Park Road, Bristol BS8 1HR.

Sharpe, Eric John, MA, TeolD; Senior Lecturer in Religious Studies, University of Lancaster, since 1970; *b* 1933; *m* 1962. BA Manchester 1957, MA Manchester 1964, Teol. Lic Uppsala 1961, TeolD Uppsala 1965; Mem., Viking Soc., North. Res., Folklore Soc. Res. Fellow, Uppsala, 1961–65; Docent in History of Mission, Uppsala, 1965; Vis. Prof., Manchester Coll., Indiana, 1965–66; Lectr in Comparative Religion, Univ. of Manchester, 1966–70. Vis. Prof., Northwestern Univ., Evanston, Ill, 1973. Dep. Sec. Gen., Internat.

Assoc. Hist. of Religions, 1970–71, Act. Sec. Gen., 1971– ; Mem., Shap Working Party on Wld Religions in Educn, 1969– ; Ed. Bd, Religion, 1970– . *Publications*: J. N. Farquhar: A Memoir, 1963; Not to Destroy but to Fulfil, 1965; The Theology of A. G. Hogg, 1971; Fifty Key Words: Comparative Religion, 1971; Thinking about Hinduism, 1971; (ed jtly) Hinduism, 1972; (ed jtly) Man and his Salvation, 1973; Trans.: B. Gärtner: John 6 and the Jewish Passover, 1960; The Theology of the Gospel of Thomas, 1962; B. Gerhardsson: Memory and Manuscript, 1961; R. Sjölinder: Presbyterian Reunion in Scotland, 1962; P. Beskow: Rex Gloriae, 1963; R. A. Carlson: David, the Chosen King, 1964; O. Hartman: Earthly Things, 1968; etc; *contrib*. Relig., Relig. Studies, Svensk Missionstidskr, Evang. Qly. *Address*: Dept of Religious Studies, Cartmel College, Bailrigg, Lancaster.

Sharpe, Laurence James; University Lecturer in Public Administration, and Fellow of Nuffield College, Oxford, since 1965; *b* 1930 *m* 1959; two *s* two *d*. BSc (Econ.) LSE 1957, MA Oxon 1965 (by decree). Lectr in Govt, LSE, 1962–65; Vis. Prof., Queens Univ., Canada, 1970–71. Dir of Intelligence, Royal Commn on Local Govt in England, 1966–69. *Publications*: A Metropolis Votes, 1963; Why Local Democracy?, 1965; ed, Voting in Cities, 1967; *contrib*. Brit. Jl Pol. Sci., Brit. Jl Sociol., Pol Qly, Pol. Studies, Public Admin. *Address*: Nuffield Coll., Oxford.

Sharpe, Dr Robert A.; Senior Lecturer, Department of Philosophy, St David's University College, Lampeter, since 1972; *b* 1935; *m* 1959; one *s* one *d*. BA Bristol 1956, MA Bristol 1959, PhD London 1962; Member: Mind Assoc., Aristotelian Soc. Res. Fellow, Univ. Reading, 1962–64; Asst Lectr, St David's Coll., 1964–65; Lectr in Philosophy, St David's Coll., 1965–72; Amer. Council of Learned Societies Internat. Fellow, Univ. Michigan, Ann Arbor, 1967–68; *Publications*: *contrib*. Mind, Brit. Jl Aesthetics, Ratio, Trans Peirce Soc., Music Review, Inquiry, etc. *Address*: St David's Univ. Coll., Lampeter, Dyfed SA48 7ED.

Sharples, Hedley, BA; Lecturer, Department of Education, University of Sheffield, since 1963; *b* 1932. BA Durham 1956 (1st cl. Span. and Lat. Amer. Studies): Dip. Ed. Durham 1960 (distinctions in Theory and Practice). Mem., Mod. Lang. Assoc., Assoc. Teachers of Span. and Portug., Anglo-Span. Soc. Asst Lectr in Education, Sheffield, 1960–62; Vis. Lectr in Educn and Spanish, Univ. of Michigan, 1962–63. Mem., Span. Cnsltive Cttee, Sch. Council, 1968–72; Chm., Assoc. Teachers of Span. and Portug., 1970–73; Mem., Educn Cttee, Hispanic Council, 1973– . *Publications*: Bibiography of Spanish Teaching Materials, 1968; *contrib*. Teach. Coll. Rec., Teach. Wld, Vida Hispán. *Address*: Dept of Education, The Univ., Sheffield S10 2TN.

Sharrock, Prof. Roger Ian, MA, BLitt; Professor of English Language and Literature, King's College, London, since 1968; *b* 1919; *m* 1940; one *s* two *d*. BA Oxon 1943 (1st cl. English), MA, BLitt Oxon 1947. Asst Master, Rugby Sch., 1944–46; Lectr, Southampton Univ., 1946–62, Reader, 1962–63; Prof., Durham Univ., 1963–68; Vis. Prof., Notre Dame Univ., 1958–59; Vis. Prof., ANU, 1970; Vis. Prof., Virginia Univ., 1972. Trustee, Dove Cottage, 1968– ; Trustee, Rydal Mount Trust, 1970– ; Chm., English Assoc., 1972– ; Ed., Durham Univ. Jl, 1964–68. *Publications*: Songs and Comments, 1946; John Bunyan, 1954, 2nd edn 1968; Selected Poems of Wordsworth, 1958, 4th edn 1966; ed, Bunyan, The Pilgrim's Progress, 1960, 2nd edn 1968; ed, Bunyan, Grace Abounding, 1962; Selected Poems of Dryden, 1963, 5th edn 1968; Keats: Selected Poems and Letters, 1964; ed, The Pilgrim's Progress, 1965; The Pilgrim's Progress (monograph), 1966; ed, Grace Abounding and The Pilgrim's Progress, 1966; Solitude and Community in Wordsworth's Poetry, 1969; Pelican English Prose, 1970; *contrib.* DUJ, EC, ESEA, MLR, NQ, RES. *Address*: Dept of English, King's College, Strand, WC2R 2LS.

Sharwood Smith, John Edward, DFC, MA; Senior Lecturer in Education, with special reference to the teaching of Classics, Institute of Education, London University, since 1959; *b* 1919; *m* 1949; two *s* one *d*. BA Cantab 1947 (1st cl. Classics, 2nd cl. Mod. Hist.), MA Cantab 1949. Mem., Council, Class. Assoc., 1960–63; Mem., Council, Soc. Prom. Hellenic Studies, 1968–71; Mem., Council, Hamilton Lodge Sch. Deaf Children, 1963– ; Mem., Council, Channing Sch., 1968–72; Editor, Didaskalos, 1963– . *Publications*: ed, Modern Stories of Ancient Greece, 1969; The Bride from the Sea: an introduction to the study of Greek Mythology, 1973. *Address*: Univ. of London Inst. of Education, Malet Street, WC1E 7HS.

Shaw, Dr David Henry, MA, PhD, AKC, MRIPHH; Senior Lecturer in English, University of London, Goldsmiths' College, since 1967; *b* 1928. BA London 1953, MA London 1958, PhD London 1968, AKC 1953; Teacher's Cert., Borough Road College, Isleworth 1948; MRIPHH 1948. Lectr in English, Goldsmiths' Coll., 1966–67. *Address*: English Dept, Univ. of London, Goldsmiths' College, New Cross, SE14 6NW.

Shaw, Dr Dennis Frederick, CBE; Fellow and Tutor in Physics, Keble College, University of Oxford, since 1957, and Chairman of Education Department; *b* 1924; *m* 1949; one *s* three *d*. BA Oxon 1943, MA Oxon 1950, DPhil Oxon 1950; Ord. FZS 1962, FInstP 1971, Mem., Amer. Physics Soc., 1957. Res. Off., Oxford Univ., 1950–57; Sen. Res. Off., 1957–64; Vis. Sci., CERN, 1961–62; Univ. Lectr, Oxford, 1964– ; Chm., Oxford Univ. Delegacy for Educnl Studies, 1968– . Mem., Oxf. City Council, 1963–67; Mem., Home Off. Sci. Adv. Council, 1965– . *Publications*: An Introduction to Electronics, 1962, 2nd edn 1970; contrib. Essays to a Young Teacher, 1966; *contrib.* Cryog., Educn Sci., Jl Sci. Inst., New Sci., Nucl. Phys., Nucl. Inst.,

Phys. Lett., Proc. Phys. Soc. *Address*: Keble College, Oxford.

Shaw, Dr Donald Leslie, MA, PhD; Reader in Hispanic Studies, University of Edinburgh, since 1968; *b* 1930; *m* 1958; one *s* one *d*. BA Manchester 1952 (1st cl. Mod. Langs), MA Manchester 1954, PhD Dublin 1961. Asst Lectr, TCD, 1955–57; Lectr, Glasgow, 1957–64; Lectr, Edinburgh, 1964–68, Sen. Lectr, 1968–72; Vis. Prof., Brown Univ., 1968. *Publications*: ed, V. Malvezzi: Historia de los primeros años del reinado de Felipe IV, 1968; ed, E. Mallea: Todo verdor perecerá, 1968; ed, P. Baroja: El mundo es ansi, 1970; A Literary History of Spain: The Nineteenth Century, 1972; *contrib.* Bull. Hispan. Studies, Hispan. Rev., Mod. Lang. Rev., Rev. Ibero-amer. *Address*: Dept of Hispanic Studies, Univ. of Edinburgh, Edinburgh EH8 9YL.

Shaw, Rev. Douglas William David; Senior Lecturer in Divinity, University of Edinburgh; Dean, Faculty of Divinity, since 1974 (Acting Dean, 1973–74); *b* 1928. BA Cantab 1948, LLB Edinburgh 1951, BD Edinburgh 1960; WS 1951. Lectr in Divinity, Univ. Edinburgh, 1963– . *Publications*: Who is God?, 1968, 2nd edn 1970; trans., F. Heyer: The Catholic Church 1648–1870, 1969. *Address*: New College, Mound Place, Edinburgh EH1 2LX.

Shaw, Dr Frank; Lecturer, Department of German, University of Bristol, since 1967; *b* 1928; *m* 1965; two *s* one *d*. BA Manchester 1950 MA 1951, Drphil Bonn 1966. English Lektor, Univ. of Bonn, 1956–67. *Publications*: *contrib.* ZfdPh, GLL. *Address*: Dept of German, Univ. of Bristol, Wills Memorial Bldg, Bristol BS8 1RJ.

Shaw, John Calman; Lecturer (part-time) in Accounting and Business Method, University of Edinburgh, and in Accountancy and Finance, Heriot-Watt University; *b* 1932; *m* 1960; three *d*. BL Edinburgh 1953; CA 1955, FCMA 1960, JDipMA 1965, MBCS 1970. *Publications*: ed, Bogie on Group Accounts, 3rd edn, 1973; *contrib.* Accountants' Magazine. *Address*: 31 Queen Street, Edinburgh EH2 1LB.

Shaw, John James B.; *see* Byam Shaw.

Shaw, Dr Marjorie; Senior Lecturer in French, University of Sheffield, since 1963; *b* 1914. BA London 1937 (Hons French), DipEd Cantab 1940, DUP 1946. Asst Lectr, Univ. of Sheffield, 1947–49, Lectr, 1949–63. *Publications*: ed, Musset: Lorenzaccio and Un Caprice, 1963; ed, Current Research in French Studies at Universities and University Colleges in the United Kingdom, 1972– ; *contrib.* MLR, Revue d'Histoire littéraire de France, RSHum, Year's Work in Modern Language Studies. *Address*: The Dept of French, The Univ., Sheffield S10 2TN.

Shaw, Martin; Lecturer, School of Social Work, University of Leicester, since 1968; *b* 1935; *m* 1959; one *s* one *d*. MA Glasgow 1957, Cert. of Social Study Glasgow 1958,

Dipl. in Social Admin Liverpool 1959; Home Office Cert. in Child Care, 1959. Mem., BASW. *Publication*: (with D. Jehu, P. Hardiker and M. Yelloly) Behaviour Modification in Social Work, 1972. *Address*: Sch. of Social Work, Univ. of Leicester, Leicester LE1 7RU.

Shaw, Richard Wright; Lecturer in Economics, University of Stirling, since 1969; *b* 1941; *m* 1965; one *s*. MA Cantab 1966. Univ. of Leeds: Asst Lectr, Management Div. of Dept of Econs, 1964–66; Lectr, Sch. of Econ. Studies, 1966–69. *Publications: contrib.* Jl Ind. Econs, Jl Management Studies. *Address*: Dept of Economics, Univ. of Stirling, Stirling FK9 4LA.

Shaw, Prof. Roy; Professor and Director, Department of Adult Education, University of Keele, 1962–75; Secretary-General, Arts Council, from July 1975; *b* 1918; *m* 1946; five *s* two *d*. BA Manchester 1945. Lectr in Philos. and Adult Educn, Univ. Leeds, 1947–59; Warden, Leeds Univ. Centre, Bradford ,1959–62. Member: Planning Cttee, Open Univ.; BBC Gen. Adv. Council, 1957–72; Arts Council, 1971– ; Chm., Arts Council Regional Develt Cttee, 1972– ; Chm., Standing Conf. on Broadcasting, 1973–. *Publications: contrib.* Adult Educn, Jl World History, Studies in Adult Educn. *Address*: Dept of Adult Education, Univ. of Keele, Staffs ST5 5BG.

Shaw, Dr Valerie Anne; Lecturer, Department of English Literature, University of Edinburgh, since 1967; *b* 1941. Dip. Edinburgh Coll. of Domestic Science 1963, MA Edinburgh 1966 (1st cl. Hons English), PhD Yale, 1971. Dir of Studies, Edinburgh, 1972. *Address*: Dept of English Literature, Univ. of Edinburgh, David Hume Tower, George Square, Edinburgh EH8 9JX.

Shearer, John Gilmour Spence; Lecturer, Department of Extra-Mural and Adult Education, University of Glasgow, since 1950; *b* 1920; *m* 1947; one *d*. MA Glasgow 1948 and 1950; FSAScot. Co-editor, Scottish Jl of Adult Educn. *Publications: contrib.* Parly Affairs, Studies in Adult Educn., *Address*: Dept of Extra-Mural and Adult Educn., Univ. of Glasgow, Glasgow G12 8QQ.

Shearman, Prof. John K. G.; Professor of the History of Art, Courtauld Institute of Art, University of London, since 1974; *b* 1931; *m* 1957; one *s* three *d*. BA London 1955 (1st cl. Hist. of Art), PhD London 1957. Asst Lectr, Courtauld Inst., 1957–61, Lectr, 1961–66, Sen. Lectr, 1966–67, Reader, 1967–74; Fellow, Inst. Adv. Studies, Princeton, 1964. *Publications*: Andrea del Sarto, 1965; Mannerism, 1967, 2nd edn 1970, Polish edn 1970; Raphael's Cartoons, 1972; *contrib.* Art Bull., Burl. Mag., var. Fr., Ital., Germ. jls. *Address*: Courtauld Institute of Art, 20 Portman Square, W1H 0BE.

Sheddick, Prof. V. G., BA, PhD; Professor of Sociology, New University of Ulster, since 1967; *b* 1915; *m* 1940; one *s*. BA Wales 1937 (Geog.), PhD London 1951 (Soc. Anthropol.); FRAI, FRGS, FEugenics Soc. Lectr, King's Coll., Univ. of Durham; Lectr, Univ. of Newcastle upon Tyne, 1950–67. *Publications*:

The Southern Sotho, 1953; Land Tenure in Basutoland, 1954; contrib. New Towns as Socio-scientific experiments, in, Planning Outlook IV, 1958; contrib. The contribution of anthropology to the study of human ecology, in, The Education of Human Ecologists, ed P. Rogers, 1972. *Address*: New Univ. of Ulster, Coleraine, Co. Londonderry BT52 1SA.

Sheehy, Dr Maurice P., DLitt; Lecturer in Palaeography, Diplomatic and Late Latin, University College, Dublin, since 1967; *b* 1928; *m* 1969. BA Dublin 1949 (1st cl. Philos.), BD Gregoriana 1951, Lic Hist Gregoriana 1955, Dr Hist Gregoriana 1957, PhD Dublin 1960, DLitt Dublin 1966. Dip. Sch. of Palaeography, Diplomatic and Archive Sci., Vatican Libr., 1954–57. Lectr in Medieval Lit. and Philos., Univ. Coll., Dublin, 1963–67. Gov., Michael Collins Educnl Foundn, 1966– . *Publications*: Pontificia Hibernica: the Medieval Papal Chancery Documents concerning Ireland, 640–1261, 1962–64; La France et l'Irlande, 1970; The Celtic Legacy: church, state and Christianity in medieval Ireland, 1974; *contrib.* Archiv. Hibern., Bull. Inst. Mediev. Canon Law, Collect. Hibern., Ir. Eccles. Rec., Ir. Theol. Qly. *Address*: Dept of Palaeography and Late Latin, Univ. College, Dublin 4.

Sheehy, Dr Seamus J., BAgrSc, PhD; Lecturer in Agricultural Economics, and Head of Department of Applied Agricultural Economics, University College, Dublin, since 1969; *b* 1935; *m* 1968; one *d*. BAgrSc National Univ. of Ireland 1957, PhD Pennsylvania State 1964. Coll. Lectr, UC, Dublin, 1964–69. *Publications*: Irish Agriculture in a Changing World, 1971; *contrib.* Amer. Jl Agric. Econ. *Address*: Dept of Applied Agricultural Economics, Univ. College, Glasnevin, Dublin 9.

Sheerman, Barry John, BSc(Econ), MSc; Lecturer, Department of Political Theory and Government, since 1969, and Secretary of American Studies Board, University College, Swansea, University of Wales, since 1967; *b* 1940. BSc(Econ) London 1965, MSc London 1966. Mem., Brit. Assoc., Amer. Studies Assoc. Asst Lectr, UC, Swansea, 1966–69. *Publications*: in preparation: Harold Laski and American Democratic Theory; *contrib.* Jl Amer. Studies. *Address*: Dept of Political Theory and Government, Univ. College, Swansea SA2 8PP.

Shefton, Brian Benjamin; Senior Lecturer in Greek Archaeology and Ancient History, Department of Classics, University of Newcastle upon Tyne, since 1960; *b* 1919; *m* 1960; one *d*. MA Oxon 1947 (1st cl. Lit. Hum.). Corresp. Mem., Germ. Archaeol. Inst. British Sch., Athens, 1948–50; Lectr in Classics, Exeter, 1950–55; Lectr in Greek Archaeol. and Ancient Hist., Newcastle, 1955–60; Vis. Res. Fellow, Merton Coll., Oxford, 1969. Mem., Council, Soc. Prom. Hellenic Studies. *Publications*: (with P. E. Arias and M. Hirmer) A History of Greek Vase Painting, 1962; *contrib.* Perachora II, ed T. J. Dunbabin, 1962; *contrib.* Amer. Jl

Archaeol., Ann. Brit. Sch. Ath., Bull. Corresp. Hellen., Hamb. Beitr. Archäol., Hesper., Jl Hell. St., Rev. Arch., Wiss. Zeits. Univ. Rost. *Address*: Dept of Classics, The Univ., Newcastle upon Tyne NE1 7RU.

Sheldon, Charles D., PhD; University Lecturer in Japanese History, University of Cambridge, since 1963; *b* 1918; *m* 1950; one *s* one *d*. BA California 1950 (with highest hons Far Eastern Studies), MA California 1951 (Hist.), PhD California 1955 (Hist.); Phi Beta Kappa, 1950– ; Fulbright Schol. and Ford Foundn Fellow, Kyoto Univ. Japan, 1953–54. Asia Foundn, Kyoto, 1955–57; US Dept of State, 1957–60; Asst Univ. Lectr, Cambridge, 1960–63; Vis. Prof., Univ. of Washington, 1965–66, Univ. of Colorado, 1966. Sec., Fac. Bd of Oriental Studies, Cambridge, 1969; Dir of Studies in Oriental Studies, Christ's Coll., Cambridge, 1969– . *Publications*: The Rise of the Merchant Class in Tokugawa Japan, 1600–1868, 1958, expanded edn 1973; Feudal Japan, in, Half the World, The History and Culture of China and Japan, ed A. Toynbee, 1973; Japan in Civilization (CRM Books), 2 vols, 1973; The Politics of the Civil War of 1868, in, Aspects of Modern Japan, ed W. G. Beasley (forthcoming); *contrib*. Camb. Opin., Kyoto Univ. Econ. Rev., Mod. Asian Studies, Pacif. Aff. *Address*: Faculty of Oriental Studies, Sidgwick Avenue, Cambridge.

Shelston, Alan John; Lecturer in English Literature, University of Manchester, since 1968; *b* 1937; *m* 1963; two *s*. BA Hons London 1964 (1st cl. Eng.), MA 1968 (Eng.). Asst Lectr in English, Univ. of Manchester, 1966–68. *Publications*: ed. with Introd. and Notes, Thomas Carlyle: Selected Writings, 1971; ed, with Introd. and Notes, Mrs Gaskell: The Life of Charlotte Brontë, 1974; *contrib*. Crit. Qly, Crit. Survey. *Address*: Dept of English, Univ. of Manchester, Manchester M13 9PL.

Shennan, Prof. Joseph Hugh, BA, PhD; Professor of European Studies, University of Lancaster, since 1974; *b* 1933; *m* 1958; three *s*. BA Liverpool 1955 (1st cl. Mod. and Med. Hist.), PhD Cantab 1963; FRHistS. Asst Lectr, Liverpool Univ., 1960–63; Lectr, Liverpool Univ., 1963–65; Lectr, Lancaster Univ., 1965–68, Sen. Lectr, 1968–71, Reader, 1971–74. Editor, Europ. Studies Rev., 1970– . *Publications*: The Parlement of Paris, 1968, American edn 1968; Government and Society in France, 1461–1661, 1969, repr. 1972; The Origins of the State in Early Modern Europe, 1974; *contrib*. EHR, Hist. Jl. *Address*: Dept of History, Univ. of Lancaster, Bailrigg, Lancaster LA1 4YW.

Shepherd, Frank Cavendish, LLB; Part-time Lecturer, Faculty of Law, University of Manchester, since 1946; *b* 1918; *m* 1946; two *d*. LLB Manchester 1940; Solicitor 1944, Comr for Oaths, Notary Public 1950, FIA 1970. Temp. part-time Asst, Manchester, 1941–46. Sen. partner, firm of solicitors; Mem., Cttee on Commercial Banks, IBA, 1971; Mem., Panel of part-time Chairmen of VAT Tribunals. *Address*: Faculty of Law, Univ. of Manchester, Manchester M13 9PL.

Sheppard, David Kent, AB, MA, PhD; Senior Lecturer, Graduate Centre for Management Studies, University of Birmingham, since 1969; *b* 1933; *m* (marr. diss.); two *s* one *d*. AB 1958, MA 1962, PhD 1970, Harvard; Mem., Amer. Econ. Assoc. Lectr, Univ. of Birmingham, 1963–69; Hon. Sen. Lectr, Mathematical Economics Dept, Univ. of Birmingham, 1971– . Res. Econ., Internat. Monetary Fund, 1965–67 (on leave of absence); Econ. Cltnt, OECD, 1971; Mem., Exec. Cttee, GMC, 1970. *Publications*: Growth and Role of UK Financial Institutions 1880–1962, 1971; *contrib*. Economica. *Address*: Mathematical Economics Dept, Faculty of Commerce, Univ. of Birmingham, Birmingham B15 2TT.

Sheppard, Dr June A.; Reader, Department of Geography, Queen Mary College, University of London, since 1973; *b* 1928. BA London External 1949, MA London External 1951, DipEd 1951, PhD London 1956. Asst Lectr, Queen Mary Coll., 1953–57, Lectr, 1957–73; Vis. Lectr, Univ. of New England, NSW, 1962. *Publications: contrib*. Agric. Hist. Rev., Geog. Ann., Trans Inst. Brit. Geogrs. *Address*: Dept of Geography, Queen Mary College, Mile End Road, E1 4NS.

Sheppard, Richard William; Lecturer, School of European Studies, University of East Anglia, since 1970; *b* 1944; *m* 1966; one *s* one *d*. BA Cantab 1965, DipEd Oxon 1967, MA Cantab 1969. Asst Lectr, Univ. East Anglia, 1967–70. *Publications*: On Kafka's Castle, 1973; *contrib*. Colloquia Germanica, German Life and Letters, German Qly, Jahrbuch der Schiller-Gesellschaft, Jl of European Studies, Mod. Langs Review, St Andrews Forum for Mod. Langs Theology. *Address*: School of European Studies, Univ. of East Anglia, Norwich NOR 88C.

Shepperdson, Michael John; Lecturer in Social Administration, University College Swansea, since 1967; *b* 1939; *m* 1965; one *d*. BA Hons Cantab (Hist. and Soc. Anthrop.); MA London. *Publications*: Tradition and Change in a Punjabi Village in West Pakistan, 1962 (Budhopur Report); Social Problems and Welfare Services in Swansea, 1974. *Address*: Dept of Social Administration, Univ. Coll. of Swansea, Swansea SA2 8PP.

Shepperson, Prof. George Albert, MA; William Robertson Professor of Commonwealth and American History, Department of History, Edinburgh University, since 1963; *b* 1922; *m* 1953; one *d*. BA Cantab 1943 (1st cl. English, 1st cl. Hist. 1947), MA Cantab 1948; CertEd Cambridge 1948 (1st cl.). Lectr, Edinburgh Univ., 1948–59, Sen. Lectr, 1960–61, Reader, 1961–62; Vis. Prof., Roosevelt Univ., 1959; Vis. Prof., Chicago Univ., 1959; Vis. Prof., Makerere Univ., 1962; Convenor, Centre of African Studies, Edinburgh Univ., 1962–65; Canada Council Vis. Prof., Dalhousie Univ., 1968–69. Editor, Bull. Brit. Assoc. Amer. Studies, 1957–62; Mem., cttees, BAAS, Royal Afr. Soc., Chm., Brit. Assoc. Amer. Studies, 1971; Pres., St Andrew Soc., Edinburgh, 1971; Chm., Mungo Park Bicent. Cttee, 1970–72. *Publications*: Independent African, 1958, 3rd edn

633

1968; David Livingstone and the Rovuma, 1965; *contrib*. Afr., Jl Afr. Hist., Jl South. Hist., Phylon, Rev. Belge Philol. Hist., Rhodes-Livingst. Jl, Scott. Hist. Rev., Wm Mary Qly, etc. *Address*: Dept of History, William Robertson Building, Edinburgh Univ., George Square, Edinburgh EH8 9JY.

Sherborne, James Wilson, MA; Senior Lecturer in History, University of Bristol, since 1964; *b* 1924; *m* 1954; two *s* one *d*. BA Oxon 1947, MA Oxon 1952; FRHistS. Asst Lectr, Univ. of Bristol, 1948–51; Lectr, 1951–64. *Publications*: *contrib*. Bull. Inst. Hist. Res., EHR, Past Pres. *Address*: Dept of History, Wills Memorial Building, Univ. of Bristol, Bristol BS8 1RJ.

Shergold, Prof. Norman David; Professor of Hispanic Studies, University College, Cardiff, University of Wales, since 1967; *b* 1925. BA Cantab 1950 (1st cl. Hons), MA Cantab 1952, PhD Cantab 1954; Member: MHRA, Assoc. of Hispanists. Lectr, Dept of Spanish and Latin American Studies, King's Coll., Newcastle upon Tyne, later Univ. of Newcastle upon Tyne, 1954–64, Sen. Lectr, 1964–67. *Publications*: A History of the Spanish Stage from Medieval Times until the end of the Seventeenth Century, 1967; (with J. E. Varey): ed, Tirso de Molina, El Burlador de Sevilla, 1954; Los autos sacramentales en Madrid en la época de Calderon, 1637–1681: Estudio y documentos, 1961; ed, Juan Vélez de Guevara, Los celos hacen estrellas, 1970; Teatros y comedias en Madrid: 1600–1650; Estudio y documentos, 1971; Teatros y comedias en Madrid: 1651–1665; Estudio y documentos 1973; *contrib*. Boletin de la Biblioteca de Menéndez Pelayo, Bull. Hispanic Studies, Bull. Hispanique, Clavileño, Estudios Escénicos, Hispanic Rev., Hispanófila, Mod. Lang. Rev., Revista de la Biblioteca, Archivo y Museo de Madrid, Year's Work in Mod. Lang. Studies. *Address*: Dept of Hispanic Studies, Univ. College, Cathays Park, Cardiff CF1 1XL.

Sheridan, Prof. Lionel Astor, LLD, PhD, Hon LLD; Professor of Law, University College, Cardiff, since 1971; *b* 1927; *m* 1948; one *s* one *d*. LLB London 1947, PhD Belfast 1953, LLD London 1969; Hon. LLD Singapore 1963; Barrister-at-Law, Lincoln's Inn, 1948. Pt time lectr, Nottingham Univ., 1949; Lectr, Belfast Univ., 1949–56; Prof. of Law, Univ. of Malaya (Singapore), 1956–63; Prof. of Comparative Law, Belfast Univ., 1963–71. Chm., N Ireland Land Law Working Party, 1967–71. *Publications*: Fraud in Equity, 1957; (with B. T. Tan) Elementary Law, 1957; (with V. T. H. Delany) The Cy-Près Doctrine, 1959; The Federation of Malaya Constitution, 1961, 2nd edn (The Constitution of Malaysia, with H. E. Groves), 1967; (jtly) Malaya, Singapore, The Borneo Territories, 1961; Constitutional Protection, 1963; (with G. W. Keeton) Equity, 1969; (jtly) Survey of the Land Law of Northern Ireland, 1971; (with G. W. Keeton) The Modern Law of Charities, 2nd edn 1971; *contrib*. Alb. Law Rev., Anglo-Amer. Law Rev., Cambrian Law Rev., Cah. Droit, Canad. Bar Rev., Conveyan. Prop. Law., Curr. Legal Prob., De Paul Law Rev.,

Internat. Comp. Law Qtly, Irish Jur., Jbh Öffent. Rechts Gegen., Jl Inst. Bank. Ireland, Jl Soc. Public Teachers Law, Jl Stat. Soc. Enqu. Soc. Ireland, Law Qly Rev., Mal. Law Rev., Mal. Law Jl, Mod. Law Rev., N Ireland Legal Qly, Public Law, Solic. Qly, Univ. W. Austral. Ann. Law Rev., YB Wld Aff. *Address*: Dept of Law, Univ. College, Cardiff CF1 1XL.

Sherrard, Dr Philip; Lecturer in History of Orthodox Church, King's College, School of Slavonic and East European Studies, University of London, since 1970; *b* 1922; *m* 1948; two *d*. MA Cantab 1942, PhD London 1952, MA Oxford 1956. St Antony's Coll., Oxford, 1957. *Publications*: The Marble Threshing Floor, 1956; The Greek East and Latin West, 1959; Athos: The Mountain of Silence, 1961; (with E. L. Keeley) Six Poets of Modern Greece, 1963; The Pursuit of Greece, 1964; Constantinople: Iconography of a Sacred City, 1965; Byzantium, 1966; (with E. L. Keeley) George Seferis: Collected Poems 1924–1955, 1967; (with John Campbell), Modern Greece, 1968; Essays in Neo-Hellenism, 1971; (with E. L. Keeley) C. P. Cavafy: Selected Poems, 1972; (with E. L. Keeley) C. P. Cavafy: Collected Poems, 1974; *contrib*. Studies in Compar. Religion, Sobornost, etc. *Address*: King's Coll., Strand, WC2R 2LS.

Sherrin, Dr C. H.; Lecturer, Faculty of Law, University of Bristol, since 1967; *b* 1944; *m* 1967; one *s* one *d*. LLB London 1965, LLM London 1966, PhD London 1972; Barrister, Gray's Inn, London. Univ. of Bristol, 1967– . *Publications*: ed, Williams on Wills, 4th edn (forthcoming); *contrib*. Chitty's Law Jl, New Law Jl, Solic. Jl, Times. *Address*: Faculty of Law, Univ. of Bristol, Bristol.

Sherry, Prof. Norman, BA, PhD; Professor of English, University of Lancaster, since 1970; *b* 1925; *m* 1955. BA Dunelm 1955 (Hons Engl.), PhD Singapore 1964. Lectr, Univ. of Singapore, 1960–66; Lectr, Univ. of Liverpool, 1966–68, Sen. Lectr, 1968–70. *Publications*: Conrad's Eastern World, 1966; Jane Austen, 1966; Charlotte and Emily Brontë, 1968; Conrad's Western World, 1971; Conrad, the Critical Heritage, 1973; Conrad and his World, 1973; Nostromo (Everyman edn), 1972; ed and introd.: Nostromo, The Secret Agent, The Nigger and the Narcissus, Lord Jim, new collected edns, 1974; *contrib*. Mod. Lang. Rev., Mod. Philos. 19th Cent. Fict., Notes Queries, PMLA, Rev. Engl. Studies, Philos. Qly, Times Lit. Supp. *Address*: Dept of English, Univ. of Lancaster, Lancaster LA1 4YW.

Sherwin-White, Adrian Nicholas, MA, FBA; Reader in Ancient History, University of Oxford, since 1966; Fellow and Tutor of St John's College, Oxford, since 1936; Keeper of the Groves, 1970; *b* 1911. MA Oxon 1937; FBA 1956. Sarum Lectr, Oxford Univ., 1960–61; Gray Lectr, Cambridge Univ., 1965–66. Editor, Geographical Handbook Series, Admiralty. *Publications*: Roman Citizenship, 1939, 2nd edn 1972–73; Ancient Rome (Then and There Series), 1959;

Roman Law and Roman Society in the New Testament, 1963; Historical Commentary on the Letters of Pliny the Younger, 1966; Racial Prejudice in Imperial Rome, 1967; *contrib.* Jl Roman Studies. *Address*: St John's College, Oxford.

Sherwood, Henry Chetwynd, MA; Senior Staff Tutor, and Staff Tutor in Literature, Extra-Mural Department, University of Manchester, since 1946; *b* 1906; *m* 1939; one *s* one *d*. BA Birmingham 1928, DipEd Birmingham 1929, MA Birmingham 1934. Staff Tutor, Dept of Extra-Mural Studies, Liverpool, 1937–46. *Publications*: The Poetry of Gerard Manley Hopkins, 1969; *contrib.* Times Lit. Supp. *Address*: Extra-Mural Dept, The Univ., Manchester M13 9PL.

Shewell, Michael Edward Joseph, BSc, MA, FRIC; Senior Lecturer in Education, University of Manchester, since 1966; *b* 1917; *m* 1941; two *d*. BSc Manchester 1938 (1st cl. Chemistry), DipBiol London 1939, DipEd London 1940, MA London 1952 (Education); FRIC. Lectr, Manchester Univ., 1954–66. Ch. Examiner, NUJMB (Gen. Studies, A Level), 1959– . *Publications*: ed, The Story of the Scriptures, 1960–68; (with R. W. Crossland) Science Work Books, 1962–64; How Your Body Works, 1967. *Address*: Dept of Education, The Univ., Manchester M13 9PL.

Shibata, Dr Hirofumi, BA, MA, PhD; Reader in Economics, Department of Economics, University of York, since 1971; *b* 1929; *m* 1966; one *s*. BA Kobe 1953, MA McGill 1962, PhD Columbia 1965. Mem., Amer. Econ. Assoc., Canad. Econ. Assoc., Internat. Inst. Public Fin., Soc. Public Choice. Asst Prof., Queen's Univ., Canada, 1965–67; Assoc. Prof., Queen's Univ., 1967–68; Lectr, Univ. of York, 1968–69, Sen. Lectr, 1969–71; Vis. Assoc. Prof., Univ. of Maryland, 1970– 71. Asst Min. of Finance, Japan, 1953–59. *Publications*: (with H. G. Johnson and P. Wonnacott) Harmonization of National Economic Policies under Free Trade, 1968; Fiscal Harmonization under Free Trade, 1969; (with R. A. Musgrave, etc) Taxation and Public Finance, 1971; *contrib.* Amer. Econ. Rev., Canad. Jl Econ., Economica, Jl Pol. Econ. *Address*: Dept of Economics and Related Studies, Univ. of York, Heslington, York YO1 5DD.

Shields, Maureen Margaret; Lecturer in Child Development, University of London Institute of Education, since 1972; *b* 1918; *m* 1941; three *s* two *d*. BA Oxford 1939 (PPE), Teacher's Cert. and Froebel Cert. 1954, Dip. Child Development 1966. Res. Asst, Nuffield Coll., and Extra-Mural Tutor, Oxford Univ., 1944–47; Teacher, LCC, 1948–64; Lectr in Education, Goldsmiths' Coll., 1965–67, Sen. Lectr, 1967–71. Mem., SSRC Pre School Language Project, 1971–72; Asst, Min. of Supply, 1940–42; Foreign Off., Foreign Press and Res. Dept, 1942–43. *Publications*: contrib. Essays in Local Government, ed Wilson, 1947; *contrib.* Educnl Res. *Address*: Dept of Child Development, Univ. of London Inst. of Education, Malet Street, WC1E 7HS.

Shields, Dr Robert Wylie; Lecturer, Department of Child Development and Educational Psychology, London University Institute of Education, since 1962; *b* 1919; *m* 1943; two *d*. BA Leeds 1941, BD 1943, PhD London 1950; Psycho-analyst; Mem., Brit. Psychoanalytical Soc., 1962, FBPsS. *Publications*: The Child's First Five Years, 1950; A Cure of Delinquents, 1960, 2nd edn 1971; *contrib.* Internat. Jl Psycho-analysts, New Era, Psychoanalytic Forum. *Address*: London Univ. Inst. of Education, Malet Street, WC1E 7HS.

Shimmin, Prof. Sylvia, BSc, FBPsS; Professor of Behaviour in Organizations, University of Lancaster, since 1969; *b* 1925. BSc London 1945, BSc Special London 1946 (Psychology); FBPsS. Asst Lectr, Univ. of London, 1947–52; Lectr, Extra-mural Studies, Univ. of Sheffield, 1963–68, Sen. Lectr, 1968–69. MRC Appl. Psychol. Res. Unit, 1946–47; Res. staff OCSR, 1952–53; MRC Indust. Psychol. Res. Unit, 1953–63; Mem., Council, Brit. Psychol. Soc., 1968–71; Chm., BPS Occupat. Psychol. Div., 1971– . *Publications*: Payment by Results, 1959; Supplement to NBPI Report no 65, 1968; *contrib.* Brit. Jl Psychol., Occupat. Psychol. *Address*: Dept of Behaviour in Organizations, Univ. of Lancaster, Bailrigg, Lancaster LA1 4YW.

Shipley, Patricia; Lecturer, Department of Occupational Psychology, Birkbeck College, London University, since 1967; *b* 1937. BA Southampton 1959; BA Hons London 1964; ABPsS; Mem., Ergonomics Res. Soc.; Grad. Mem., Inst. Work Study Practitioners, 1961– 63. *Publications*: *contrib.* Ergonomics. *Address*: Dept of Occupational Psychology, Birkbeck Coll., Malet Street, WC1E 7HX.

Shipman, Dr Marten Dorrington; Visiting Professor, Department of Sociology, University of Surrey; Director of Research and Statistics for Inner London Education Authority, since 1973; *b* 1926; *m* 1958; two *s*. BSc London 1956 (1st cl. Sociology), CertifEd 1957, DipEd 1960, PhD London 1965. Sen. Lectr in Educn, Univ. of Keele, 1968–72 (Lectr, 1968–71). Chm., ATCDE Sociology Section, 1969–70. *Publications*: Sociology of the School, 1968; Participation and Staff–Student Relations, 1969; Education and Modernisation, 1971; The Limitations of Social Research, 1972; Childhood: a sociological perspective, 1972; *contrib.* Brit. Jl Ed. Psych., Brit. Jl Soc., Ed. Res., Moral Ed. *Address*: Dept of Sociology, Univ. of Surrey, Guildford GU2 5XH.

Shippey, Thomas Alan, MA; Fellow, St John's College, Oxford, since 1972; *b* 1943; *m* 1966; one *s* two *d*. BA Cantab 1964 (1st cl.), MA Cantab 1967. Asst Lectr, Birmingham, 1965–68, Lectr, 1968–72. *Publications*: Old English Verse, 1972; *contrib.* Comp. Lit., Mod. Lang. Rev., Notes Queries. *Address*: St John's College, Oxford.

Shirley, Dr Arthur Wilfred, BA, MEd, PhD; Lecturer, Department of Psychology, Glasgow University, since 1960; *b* 1920; *m* 1949; four *s* four *d*. BA Lampeter 1949, MEd

Glasgow 1952, PhD Glasgow 1964; ABPsS. *Publications*: *contrib*. Brit. Jl Med. Psychol., Brit. Jl Physiol. Opt. *Address*: Dept of Psychology, Adam Smith Building, Univ. of Glasgow, Glasgow G12 8RT.

Shirt, Dr David John, BA, PhD; Lecturer in French, University of Newcastle upon Tyne, since 1962; *b* 1938; *m* 1965; one *s* one *d*. BA Manchester 1959 (French), PhD Manchester 1970. *Publications*: ed, H. Queffélec: Un Recteur de l'Ile de Sein, 1972; Henri Queffélec et les traditions sénanes, in Annales de Bretagne, 1973. *Address*: Dept of French, Univ. of Newcastle upon Tyne, Newcastle upon Tyne NE1 7RU.

Shirt, Marion Audrey, MA; Lecturer, Department of Phonetics, Leeds University, since 1956; *b* 1934. MA Edinburgh 1955. *Address*: Dept of Phonetics, The Univ., Leeds LS2 9JT.

Shone, Sir Robert (Minshull), CBE; Visiting Professor of Applied Economics, Graduate Business Centre, The City University, since 1966; *b* 1906. BEng Liverpool 1927 (1st cl.), MEng Liverpool 1930, MA (Econ) Chicago 1934; FREconSoc, FSS, Hon. Fellow, LSE, Hon. Vice-Pres., Iron and Steel Inst. Lectr, LSE, 1935–36; Res. Fellow, Nuffield Coll., Oxford, 1966–67; Special Prof., Dept of Economics, Nottingham Univ., 1971–73. Exec. Mem., Iron and Steel Bd, 1953–62; Dir Gen., Nat. Econ. Develop. Off., 1962–66; Dir, M. and G. Securities Ltd, 1966– ; Dir, Rank Organisation Ltd; Dir, APV Holidays, 1970– . *Publications*: Problems of Investment, 1971; *contrib*. Econ. Jl, Jl Inst. Actuar., Jl Royal Stat. Soc., etc. *Address*: City Univ., Gresham College, Basinghall Street, EC2.

Short, Dr Ian; Lecturer in French, Westfield College, University of London, since 1970; *b* 1939; *m* 1963; one *s* one *d*. BA London 1962, PhD 1966. Univ. of Hull, 1966–68; Univ. of California, Berkeley, 1968–70. *Publications*: The Anglo-Norman Pseudo-Turpin Chronicle of William de Briane, 1973; *contrib*. CCM, CN, MÆ, Mittellateinisches Jahrbuch, Rom., RPh. *Address*: Westfield Coll., Hampstead, NW3 7ST.

Short, Robert Stuart, DPhil; Senior Lecturer, School of European Studies, University of East Anglia, since 1974 (Lecturer, 1967–74); *b* 1938; *m* 1965; one *d*. BA Cambridge 1959 (2nd cl. Hist.), MA Cambridge 1964, DPhil Sussex 1965, DipEd Cambridge 1961. Asst Lectr in Political Studies, Univ. of Hull, 1965–67. Europ. Acad. Adv., American Peoples Encyclopedia. *Publications*: Contre-Attaque, in, Surréalisme, ed F. Alquié, 1968; (with Roger Cardinal) Surrealism: Permanent Revelation, 1970; Surrealism, in, French Literature and its Background, vol. 6, ed J. Cruickshank, 1970; *contrib*. Jl Contemp. Hist. *Address*: School of European Studies, Univ. of East Anglia, Norwich NOR 88C.

Shorto, Prof. Harry Leonard; Professor of Mon-Khmer Studies, University of London, since 1971; *b* 1919; *m* 1953; one *s* one *d*. BA Cantab 1940 (2nd cl. Mod. Lang. Tripos, Pts

I and II), MA Cantab 1947; FRAsiatS, FRAnthropInst; Mem. Philol Soc., Folk Soc., Galpin Soc. Lectr, Univ. of London, 1948–64, Reader, 1964–71. Hon. Sec., Royal Asiat. Soc., 1966–70; Hon. Editor, Jl Royal Asiat. Soc., 1970–73; Mem., Council, Philol. Soc., 1969– . *Publications*: A Dictionary of Modern Spoken Mon, 1962; (with J. M. Jacob and E. H. S. Simmonds) Bibliographies of Mon-Khmer and Tai Linguistics, 1963; ed, Linguistic Comparison in South East Asia and the Pacific, 1963; A Dictionary of the Mon Inscriptions from the Sixth to the Sixteenth Centuries, 1971; contrib. var. symposia; *contrib*. Bull. SOAS, Lingua, Wiss. Zeits. K.-Marx-Univ. *Address*: School of Oriental and African Studies, Univ. of London, Malet Street, WC1E 7HP.

Shotter, Dr David Colin Arthur, BA, PhD; Senior Lecturer in Classics, University of Lancaster, since 1973 (Lectr, 1966–73); *b* 1939; *m* 1962; one *s* one *d*. BA Southampton 1961 (1st cl. Classics), PhD Southampton 1964. Asst Lectr in Greek and Latin, Magee Univ. Coll., Londonderry, N Ireland, 1964–66. *Publications*: Romans in Lancashire, 1973; *contrib*. Class. Qly, Historia, Latomus, Britannia. *Address*: Dept of Classics, Univ. of Lancaster, Bailrigg, Lancaster LA1 4YW.

Showler, Brian; Lecturer in Social Administration, University of Hull, since 1968; *b* 1943; *m* 1964; one *s* one *d*. BScEcon Hull 1966, MScEcon Hull 1969; FIScB 1971, MRES 1972. Asst Editor, Internat. Jl of Social Econs. *Publications*: The Employment Service and Management, 1972; Onto a Comprehensive Employment Service, 1973; *contrib*. IJSE, YBESR. *Address*: Dept of Social Administration, Univ. of Hull, Cottingham Road, Hull HU6 7RX.

Shukman, Dr Harold, BA, MA, DPhil; Lecturer in Modern Russian History, University of Oxford, since 1969; *b* 1931; *m* 1st, 1956, diss. 1971; two *s* one *d*; *m* 2nd, 1973. BA Nottingham 1956, DPhil Oxon 1961, MA Oxon 1965. Vis. Fellow, Russian Res. Center, Harvard, 1960; Fellow, St Antony's Coll., Oxford, 1961– . *Publications*: Lenin and the Russian Revolution, 1966; (with G. Katkov) Lenin's Path to Power, 1971; trans., Penguin Soviet Plays, 1965; The Holy Well, Kataev; Short Stories, Daniel; *contrib*. articles and revs. *Address*: St Antony's College, Oxford.

Sibbons, John Louis Harry; Lecturer, Department of Geography, Sheffield University, since 1957; *b* 1928. BA Oxford 1950, BSc Oxford 1952, MA Oxford 1955. Mem., Geog. Assoc., Mem., Royal Meteorol Soc. Res. Demonstrator, Sheffield, 1952–54; Asst Lectr, Sheffield, 1954–57. Councillor, Royal Meteorol Soc., 1963–66. *Publications*: *contrib*. Adv. Sci., Geog. Ann., Geog. Jl, Jl Appl. Physiol. *Address*: Dept of Geography, The Univ., Sheffield S10 2TN.

Sibley, Prof. Frank Noel; Professor of Philosophy, University of Lancaster, since 1964; *b* 1923; *m* 1943; two *d*. BA Oxon 1947 (1st cl. PPE), MA Oxon 1948. Asst Prof., Yale Univ., 1949–53; Asst Prof., State Univ. of Iowa, 1953–55; Lectr, Univ. of Michigan,

1955–56; Asst and Assoc. Prof., Cornell Univ., 1956–64. *Publications*: ed, Perception, 1971; *contrib*. Jl Philos., Mind, Philos. Rev., Proc. Aristot. Soc., Rev. Metaphysics. *Address*: Dept of Philosophy, Univ. of Lancaster, Bowland College, Bailrigg, Lancaster LA1 4YW.

Siefken, Dr Hinrich Gerhard; Senior Lecturer, Department of German, Saint David's University College, Lampeter, since 1973; *b* 1939; *m* 1968; one *s* one *d*. DrPhil Tübingen 1964, Staatsexamen (German/ English) 1964. Tutor, German Dept, Tübingen, 1962–65; Lektor, German Dept, Bangor, 1965–66; Wiss. Ass., German Dept, Tübingen, 1966–67; Asst Lectr, German Dept, SDUC Lampeter, 1967–68, Lectr, 1968–73. *Publications*: Überindividuelle Formen und der Aufbau des Kudrun-Epos (Medium Ævum vol. 11), 1967; (with Alan Robinson) ed, Erfahrung und Überlieferung: Festschrift for C. P. Magill, 1974; *contrib*. Euphorion, Germanistik, GLL, Trivium (Lampeter), ZfdPh. *Address*: Dept of German, Saint David's Univ. Coll., Lampeter, Dyfed SA48 7ED.

Sigsworth, Prof. Eric Milton; Professor of Economic and Social History, Department of Economics and Related Studies, University of York, since 1970; *b* 1923; *m* 1951; one *s* two *d*. BA Leeds 1948 (1st cl. Econ. and Hist.), PhD Leeds 1954. Res. Student, Leeds, 1948–51, Res. Asst, 1951–54, Lectr in Econ. Hist., 1954–63; Lectr in Econ. Hist., York, 1963–64, Reader in Econ. Hist., 1964–70. Editor, Yorks Bull. Econ. Social Res., 1967–71; Mem., Edit. Adv. Bd, North. Hist.; Mem., Jl Textile Hist.; Chm., Yorks Indust. Hist. Gp. *Publications*: Black Dyke Mills: A History, 1958; Bradford 1830–60, in, Round About Industrial Britain 1830–60, ed C. R. Fay, 1952; York Since 1800, in, Victoria County History of York, 1961; contrib. Encyclopaedia Britannica; *contrib*. Amer. Bened. Rev., Archit. Jl, Borthw. Papers, Econ. Hist. Rev., Jl Bradf. Textile Soc., Jl Nat. Hous. Town Plan. Council, Jl Textile Inst., Jl Urb. Studies, Sci. Soc. 1600–1900, Vict. Studies, Yorks Bull. Econ. Social Res. *Address*: Dept of Economics and Related Studies, Univ. of York, Heslington, York YO1 5DD.

Silberston, (Zangwill) Aubrey; Official Fellow in Economics, Nuffield College, Oxford, since 1971; *b* 1922; *m* 1945; one *s* one *d*. BA Cantab 1943, MA 1950, MA Oxon 1971. Res. Fellow, St Catharine's Coll., Cambridge, 1950–53; Asst Lectr and Lectr in Econs, Univ. of Cambridge, 1951–71; Fellow, St John's Coll., Cambridge, 1958–71. Chm., Fac. Bd of Econs, Cambridge, 1966–70. Mem., Monopolies Commn, 1965–68; Non-Exec. Bd Mem., BSC, 1967– ; Mem., Econs Cttee, SSRC, 1969–73; Econ. Advr, CBI, 1972–74. *Publications*: Education and Training for Industrial Management, 1955; (with George Maxcy) The Motor Industry, 1959; (in collab.) Economies of Large-scale Production in British Industry, 1965; (in collab.) The Patent System-Administration, 1967; (with C. T. Taylor) The Economic Impact of the Patent System, 1973; *contrib*.

Bull. Oxford Inst. of Stats, Econ. Jl, Jl RSS, Oxford Econ. Papers. *Address*: Nuffield Coll., Oxford.

Silburn, Richard Lionel; Lecturer in Applied Social Science, University of Nottingham, since 1964; *b* 1938; *m* 1964; three *s*. BA Nottingham 1961 (2nd cl. Social Admin). Mem., Brit. Sociol. Assoc., Mem., Soc. Admin Assoc. Res. Asst, Nottingham Univ., 1962, Asst Lectr, 1962–64. *Publications*: (with K. S. Coates) Poverty, Deprivation and Morale, 1967, 2nd edn 1968; Poverty: the Forgotten Englishmen, 1970, rev. edn (pbk), 1973; contrib. An Introduction to the Study of Social Administration, ed D. C. Marsh, 1965. *Address*: The Univ., Nottingham NG7 2RD.

Silk, Robert K.; *see* Kilroy-Silk.

Silva, M. W. Sugathapala de; *see* de Silva.

Silver, Harold; Reader in Educational History, Centre for Science Education, Chelsea College, University of London, since 1971; *b* 1928; *m* 1950; two *d*. MA Cantab 1952, MEd Hull 1963. Chelsea Coll., Univ. London: Sen. Lectr, Humanities, 1961–68; Sen. Lectr, Social History, 1968–71. *Publications*: trans. V. I. Chuikov: The Beginning of the Road, 1963; The Concept of Popular Education, 1965; Robert Owen on Education, 1969, Italian edn 1972; (with J. Ryder) Modern English Society, 1970; (with S. J. Teague) History of British Universities, 1970; (with J. Lawson) A Social History of Education in England, 1973; Equal Opportunity in Education, 1973; (with P. Silver) The Education of the Poor, 1974; *contrib*. History of Educn. *Address*: Centre for Science Education, Chelsea College, Univ. of London Bridges Place, SW6.

Silvey, Jonathan, MA, DipPsych; Lecturer in Social Science, Department of Applied Social Science, University of Nottingham, since 1964; *b* 1934; *m* 1966; two *s*. BA Cantab 1957 (Hist. Trip.), MA Cantab 1960, DipPsych London 1959; Member: Brit. Sociol Assoc.; African Studies Assoc. Sen. Res. Fellow, Univ. of E Africa, 1962–64. Res. Officer, Home Office Res. Unit, 1959–61. *Publications*: Deciphering Data, 1974; *contrib*. Criminal Law Rev., Race, Rhodes-Livingstone Jl, Occup. Psychol., Transition. *Address*: The Univ., Nottingham NG7 2RD.

Simmonds, Prof. Edward Harold Stuart; Professor of Languages and Literatures of South East Asia, University of London, since 1970; *b* 1919; *m* 1953. BA Oxon 1948 (English Lang. and Lit.), MA Oxon 1952; FRAsiatS 1954, Dir, 1965–68; Vice-Pres., 1968–72; Pres., 1973– . Lectr in Linguistics, SOAS, Univ. of London, 1948–51; Lectr in Tai, SOAS, Univ. of London, 1951–66; Reader in Tai Lang. and Lit., SOAS, Univ. of London, 1966–70. Act. Hd of Dept of SE Asia and Islands, SOAS, Univ. of London, 1966–69; Hd of Dept, 1969– . *Publications*: (with H. L. Shorto and J. M. Jacob) Bibliographies of Mon-Khmer and Tai Linguistics, 1963; *contrib*. Asia Maj.,

Bull. SOAS, Jl Royal Asiat. Soc. (Malysn Br.), Jl Siam Soc., Lingua, Mod. Asian Studies, etc. *Address*: School of Oriental and African Studies, Univ. of London, Malet Street, WC1E 7HP.

Simmonds, Prof. Kenneth; Professor of Marketing and International Business, London Graduate School of Business Studies, since 1969; *b* 1935; *m* 1960; two *s* one *d*. BCom New Zealand 1956, MCom New Zealand 1960 (1st cl. Econ.), DBA Harvard 1963, PhD London 1965; Hon. MGCE EUTG 1974; CA (NZ) 1956, CMA (NZ) 1956, FCIS 1956, FCMA 1960, FInstM 1973. Pt-time Lectr, Univ. of Wellington, 1957–59; Res. Asst, Harvard Univ., 1960–61; Ford Foundn Fellow, 1961–62; Vis. Sen. Lectr, Cranfield Inst. Technol., 1963–64; Asst Prof., Indiana Univ., 1964–66; Prof., Univ. of Manchester, 1966–69. Clerk, Guardian Trust Co., 1950–53; Asst Co. Sec., Gordon and Gotch (NZ) Ltd, 1953–55; Asst Acntnt, then Acntnt and later Cost Acntnt, Wm Cable Ltd, 1955–59; Cnsltnt, A. D. Little, Inc., 1959–60; Cnsltnt, Harbridge House, Inc., 1962–64; Mktg Adv., Internat. Publish. Corp., 1967– ; Dir, BSC Construct. Eng., 1970–72; Dir, Redpath Dorman Long Ltd, 1972– ; Dir, Bracken Kelner & Assoc. Ltd, 1973– ; Mem., Textile Council, 1968–70; Mem., Intern. Mngmt Adv. Council, Brit. Inst. Mngmt, 1970– ; Mem., Mktg Cttee, Confed. Brit. Indust., 1971– ; Mem., SSRC Mgt and Ind. Rel. Cttee, 1971–72. *Publications*: (with S. Robock) International Business and Multilingual Enterprises, 1973; (with D. Leighton) Case Problems in Marketing, 1973; *contrib*. Acntncy Business Res., Col. Jl Wld Business, Jl Indust. Econ., Jl Mngmt Studies, Operat. Res. Qly. *Address*: London Graduate School of Business Studies, Sussex Place, Regents Park, NW1 4SA.

Simmonds, Prof. Kenneth Royston; Visiting Professor of Law, Queen Mary College, London, since 1972; *b* 1927; *m* 1958; one *s* one *d*. BA Oxon 1951, MA Oxon 1955, DPhil Oxon 1955; Assoc. de l'Acad. Internat. de droit Comp., 1970. Mem., UK Nat. Council of Comp. Law, 1959– , Chm., 1974– (Sec., 1960–66), Mem., SPTL, and Convener, Europ. Law Cttee, Mem., Amer. Soc. Internat. Law. Lectr, UCW, 1953–61; Sen. Lectr, QUB, 1961–63; Vis. Prof., McGill Univ., Montreal, 1963; Dir, Brit. Inst. Internat. Comp. Law, 1965– ; Vis. Prof., Wyoming and California, 1969; Prof. of Law, Univ. of Kent at Canterbury, 1970–72; Vis. Prof., Brussels, 1972– . Gen. Editor, Internat. Comp. Law Qly, 1966– ; Editor, Comm. Mkt Law Rev., 1967– ; Mem., Brit. Council Legal Adv. Cttee, 1966– ; Mem., Edit. Cttee, Brit. YB Internat. Law, 1967– . Vice-Pres., Internat. Assoc. of Legal Science, 1973– . *Publications*: Resources of the Ocean Bed, 1970; ed, Legal Problems of an Enlarged European Community, 1972; Gen. Editor, Encyclopaedia of European Community Law, 1973– ; ed, New Directions in the Law of the Sea, vol. III, 1974; *contrib*. Comm. Mkt Law Rev., Internat. Comp. Law Qly, Jbh Internat. Recht, Köln. Schrif. Europ., McGill Law Jl,

Savigny-Zeitsch. *Address*: Queen Mary College, E1 4NS.

Simmonds, Paula, MA; Lecturer in English Language, University of Dublin, since 1971; *b* 1934. BA Dublin 1957 (Moderatorship), MA Dublin 1962. Career mainly in journalism, 1957–66; Asst, Dublin Univ., 1966–68, Jun. Lectr, 1968–71. *Address*: Dept of English, Trinity College, Dublin 2.

Simmons, Dr Ian Gordon, BSc, PhD; Senior Lecturer in Geography, University of Durham, since 1970; *b* 1937; *m* 1962; one *s* one *d*. BSc(Special) London 1959 (1st cl. Geog.), PhD London 1962. Mem., Inst. Brit. Geogrs, Mem., Brit. Ecol. Soc., Mem., Quatern. Res. Assoc., Mem., Conservation Soc. Lectr, Univ. of Durham, 1962–70; ACLS Fellow, Univ. of California, Berkeley, 1964–65; NATO Travelling Fellow (Cultural Programme), 1968; Vis. Assoc. Prof., Univ. of California, Berkeley, 1969; Churchill Memorial Travelling Fellow, 1971–72; Vis. Prof., York Univ., Toronto, 1972–73. Rep., Min. of Environment, Yorks Dales (NR), Nat. Park Planning Cttee, 1963–72; Chm., Durham Council Social Service; Chm., Rural Cttee, 1968–72. *Publications*: Dartmoor Essays, 1964; The Yorkshire Dales, 1971; Ecology of Natural Resources, 1974; *contrib*. Canad. Geogr., New Phytol., Tidj. Econ. Soc. Geogr., Trans Inst. Brit. Geogrs, Yorks Archaeol. Jl, Proc. Prehist. Soc., Biol Cons. *Address*: Dept of Geography, Science Laboratories, South Road, Durham City.

Simmons, Prof. Jack; Professor of History, University of Leicester, since 1947; *b* 1915. MA Oxon; FRSL, FRHistS. Beit Lectr, Oxford Univ., 1943–47. Mem., Adv. Council, Science Museum, 1970– ; Pres., Leicester Soc. of Artists, 1969–71; Hon. Ed., 1948–61, Pres., 1966– , Leicestershire Archaeological and Historical Soc.; Chm., Leicester Local Broadcasting Council, 1967–70. Jt Ed., Jl Transport History, 1953–73; Ed., a Visual History of Modern Britain. *Publications*: ed (with Margery Perham), African Discovery: An Anthology of Exploration, 1942; Southey, 1945; Edition of Southey's Letters from England, 1951; Journeys in England: an Anthology, 1951; Parish and Empire, 1952; Livingstone and Africa, 1955; New University, 1958; The Railways of Britain: an Historical Introduction, 1961; Transport, 1962; Britain and the World, 1965; St Pancras Station, 1968; Transport Museums, 1970; A Devon Anthology, 1971; Life in Victorian Leicester, 1971; ed, The Railway Traveller's Handy Book, 1971; Leicester Past and Present, 2 vols, 1974. *Address*: Dept of History, Univ. of Leicester, University Road, Leicester LE1 7RH.

Simmons, James Stewart Alexander; Lecturer in English Studies, New University of Ulster, since 1968; *b* 1933; *m* 1955; one *s* four *d*. BA Leeds 1958 (Hons English). Lectr, Ahmadu Bello Univ., Nigeria, 1963–68. Treas., N Irel. Soc. Teachers of English, 1962; Ed., Poetry and Audience, Leeds, 1958; Ed., Out on the Edge, Leeds, 1958. *Publications*: Poetry: Ballad of a Marriage, 1966; Late but in Earnest, 1967; Ten

Poems, 1968; In the Wilderness, 1969; No Ties, 1970; Energy to Burn, 1971; No Land is Waste, Dr Eliot, 1972; ed, New Poems from Ulster, 1972; The Long Summer Still to Come, 1973; ed, Ten Irish Poets, 1974; Play: Aikin Mata, 1967; Songs: Songs for Derry, 1969; Record: City and Eastern, 1971; Essays: Joyce Cary in Ireland, in, On the Novel, 1971; The Diction of Yeats, in, Confrontation; var., in, The Honest Ulsterman, 1968– . *Address*: English Studies, New Univ. of Ulster, Coleraine, Co. Londonderry BT52 1SA.

Simmons, Dr Richard Clive; Senior Lecturer in American History, University of Birmingham, since 1973; *b* 1937; *m* 1965; one *d*. BA Cantab 1958 (Hons History), PhD Univ. of Calif. 1965. Univ. of Birmingham: Asst Lectr in Mod. Hist., 1964–65; Lectr, 1965–73. Editor: University of Birmingham Historical Journal, 1965–71; Midland History, 1971– . *Publications*: ed, William Ames: A Fresh Suit against Human Ceremonies, 1972; ed, William Bradshaw: English Puritanism and other Works, 1972; ed, William Ames: Church Controversies, 1973; North America and the West Indies, in, The Making of Empires, 1973; The Middle Colonies, in, America, ed H. S. Commager, 1974; *contrib*. Delaware Hist., Hist. Today, Jl Amer. Hist., Jl Amer. Stud., New Eng. Qly, Wm and Mary Qly. *Address*: School of History, The Univ., Birmingham B15 2TT.

Simms, Dr John Gerald; Fellow, Trinity College, Dublin, since 1966, and Lecturer in Modern History, University of Dublin, since 1964; *b* 1904; *m* 1930; one *s* three *d*. BA Oxon 1927 (1st cl. Lit. Hum.), MA Oxon 1933, PhD Dublin 1952; MRIA, Mem., Irish Hist. Soc., Mem., Mil. Hist. Soc. Irel. Indian Civil Service, 1929–49; Asst to Prof. of Modern Hist., Univ. of Dublin, 1957–64. Mem., Cult. Relat. Cttee, Dept of Foreign Aff., Irel., 1964– . *Publications*: The Williamite Confiscation in Ireland, 1690–1703, 1956; Jacobite Ireland, 1685–91, 1969; *contrib*. Irish Hist. Studies, Irish Sword. *Address*: Trinity College, Dublin 2.

Simon, Prof. Brian, MA; Professor of Education, University of Leicester, since 1966; *b* 1915; *m* 1941; two *s*. BA Cantab 1937, MA Cantab 1952. Lectr, Leicester Univ., 1950–64, Reader, 1964–66. Gov., Countesthorpe Coll.; Gov., City of Leicester Coll. of Educn; Gov., Wreake Valley Coll. *Publications*: A Student's View of the Universities, 1943; Intelligence Testing and the Comprehensive School, 1953; The Common Secondary School, 1955; ed, Psychology in the Soviet Union, 1957; ed, New Trends in English Education, 1957; Studies in the History of Education 1780–1870, 1960; ed (with J. Simon), Educational Psychology in the USSR, 1963; ed, The Challenge of Marxism, 1963; ed, Non-Streaming in the Junior School, 1964; Education and the Labour Movement 1870–1920, 1965; Education, the new perspective: an inaugural lecture, 1967; ed, Education in Leicestershire 1540–1940, 1968; (with D. Rubinstein) Evolution of the Comprehensive School

1926–1966, 1969, 2nd edn 1926–72, 1973; (with C. Benn) Half-Way There, 1970, 2nd edn 1972; Intelligence, Psychology and Education, 1971; ed, The Radical Tradition in Education in Britain, 1972. *Address*: School of Education, 21 University Road, Leicester LE1 7RF.

Simon, John Hedley, MA; Senior Lecturer, Department of Humanity (Latin), University of St Andrews, since 1959; *b* 1920; *m* 1948; one *s* one *d*. MA Oxon 1948. Lectr, Univ. Coll., Cardiff, 1948–51; Lectr, Univ. of St Andrews, 1951–59. *Publications*: *contrib*. Class. Rev. *Address*: Dept of Humanity, Univ. of St Andrews, St Andrews, Fife KY16 9AJ.

Simon, Rev. Prof. Ulrich Ernst, DD; Professor of Christian Literature, King's College, University of London, since 1971; *b* 1913; *m* 1949; two *s* one *d*. BD London 1938, MTH London 1943, DD London 1960; Priest, C of E, 1939. Lectr, London Univ., 1954–59, Reader, 1959–71; Fellow, King's Coll., London, 1957; Vis. Prof., St Mary's, Baltimore, 1969. *Publications*: Theology of Crisis, 1948; Theology of Salvation, 1953; Heaven in the Christian Tradition, 1958; The Ascent to Heaven, 1961; The End is not yet, 1964; Theology Observed, 1966; A Theology of Auschwitz, 1967; The Trial of Man, 1973; Story and Faith, 1974; *contrib*. Ch Qly Rev., Theol. *Address*: King's College, Strand, WC2R 2LS.

Simpson, Prof. (Alfred William) Brian, MA, JP; Professor of Law, University of Kent, since 1973; *b* 1931; *m* 1969; one *s* one *d*. BA Oxon 1954, MA Oxon 1958. Jun. Res. Fellow, St Edmund Hall, Oxford, 1954–55; CUF Lectr, Oxford, 1956–73; Fellow of Lincoln Coll., Oxford, 1955–73; Vis. Prof., Dalhousie Univ., 1964– ; Dean, Fac. of Law, Univ. of Ghana, 1968–69. JP, Oxford Co. *Publications*: Introduction to the History of the Land Law, 1961; contrib. Oxford Essays in Jurisprudence, 1st series, 1969, ed 2nd ser., 1973; contrib. Annual Survey of Commonwealth Law, 1965, 1966, 1968, 1970; *contrib*. Law Qly Rev. *Address*: Keynes College, Canterbury, Kent CT2 7ND.

Simpson, Dr David Rae Fisher; Reader in Economics, University of Stirling, since 1973 (Senior Lecturer, 1969–73); *b* 1936. MA Edinburgh 1959 (1st cl. Econ.), PhD Harvard 1963. Instructor, Harvard Univ., 1963–64; Lectr, Univ. Coll., London, 1967–69. Harvard Econ. Res. Project, 1962–64; Stat. Off., UN, NY, 1964–65; Res. Off., Econ. Res. Inst., Dublin, 1965–67. *Publications*: Problems of Input–Output Tables and Analysis, 1966, French edn 1966, Spanish edn 1969; *contrib*. Ectrica, Rev. Econ. Stat. *Address*: Dept of Economics, Univ. of Stirling, Stirling FK9 4LA.

Simpson, Derek Douglas Alexander, MA, FSA; Lecturer in Archaeology, University of Leicester, since 1960; *b* 1938; *m* 1960; one *s* one *d*. MA Edinburgh 1958; FSA 1966. Mem., Prehist. Soc. 1956, Soc. Antiqu. Scotl. 1957. Mem., Council, Prehist. Soc., 1966–69; Mem., Exec. Council for Brit.

Archaeol., 1961–65. *Publications*: Guide Catalogue of the Neolithic and Bronze Age Collections, Devizes Museum, 1964; ed, Studies in Ancient Europe, 1968; ed, Economy and Settlement in Neolithic and Bronze Age Britain and Europe, 1971; *contrib*. Antiqu., Jl Glasgow Archaeol. Soc., Proc. Prehist. Soc., Proc. Soc. Antiqu. Scott., Trans Dumfries Gall. Archaeol. Soc., Wilts Archaeol. Mag. *Address*: Dept of Archaeology, Univ. of Leicester, Leicester LE1 7RH.

Simpson, Derek John; University Librarian and Director of Media Resources, Open University, since 1969; *b* 1929; *m* 1960; one *s* one *d*. BScEcon London 1957; FLA 1954. Dep. Librarian, UMIST, 1965–67; Sub-Librarian, Manchester Univ., 1967; Dep. Librarian, Glasgow Univ., 1967–69. Asst Librarian in public libraries, 1945–60; Librarian, IBM UK Ltd, 1960–65. *Publications*: *contrib*. Aslib Proc., Library Assoc. Record. *Address*: Open Univ. Library, Walton Hall, Milton Keynes MK7 6AA.

Simpson, Ian Gordon; Lecturer in Agricultural Economics, University of Leeds, since 1956; *b* 1926; *m* 1952; two *s* one *d*. BSc Reading 1947 (Agric.), MSc Reading 1955 (Agric. Economics). Mem., Agric. Econ. Soc. Agric. Econ., Univ. of Leeds, 1948–56; Sudan Gov., on secondment, 1963–66. Mem., Exec., Agric. Econ. Soc., 1970–73. *Publications*: *contrib*. Farm Econ., Jl Agric. Econ., Land Econ. *Address*: School of Economic Studies, Univ. of Leeds, Leeds LS2 9JT.

Simpson, John; Lecturer in Politics, University of Southampton, since 1967; *b* 1943; *m* 1966; two *s*. BSc(Econ) London 1964, MSc(Econ) London 1965. Asst Lectr, Southampton, 1965–67. *Publications*: (with F. Gregory and G. Williams) Crisis in Procurement: A Case Study of the TSR-2, 1969; *contrib*. ORBIS, Public Admin., RUSI Jl. *Address*: Dept of Politics, Univ. of Southampton, Highfield, Southampton SO9 5NH.

Simpson, John Montgomery; Lecturer, Department of Scottish History, University of Edinburgh, since 1964; *b* 1938; *m* 1960; one *s* two *d*. MA St Andrews 1960 (1st cl. Mod. and Med. Hist.). Mem., Scott. Hist. Soc. (Council Mem., 1968–72), Mem., Scott. Mediaev. Conf. (Sec.), 1971–74, Mem., Soc. Study Lab. Hist. Asst Lectr, Dept of Hist., Univ. of Sheffield, 1962–64; Dir of Studies, Fac. of Arts, Univ. of Edinburgh, 1968– . *Publications*: Who Steered the Gravy Train, 1707–1766?, in, Scotland in the Age of Improvement, ed N. T. Phillipson and R. Mitchison, 1970; contrib. The History of Parliament: The House of Commons, 1715–1754, ed R. Sedgwick, 1970. *Address*: Dept of Scottish History, Univ. of Edinburgh, 50 George Square, Edinburgh.

Simpson, J. M. Y.; Head of Department of Linguistics and Phonetics, University of Glasgow. *Address*: Dept of Linguistics and Phonetics, Univ. of Glasgow, Glasgow G12 8QQ.

Simpson, John Vivian, BSc(Econ); Senior Lecturer in Economics, Queen's University,

Belfast, since 1969; *b* 1932; *m* 1961; two *d*. BSc(Econ) Queen's Univ., Belfast, 1954. Lectr, Queen's Univ., Belfast, 1964–69. Asst Dean, Fac. of Econ. and Social Science, 1969–72; NI Youth Employment Service Bd, 1968– ; Pres., AUT, 1969–71; Econ. Advr, NI Min. of Commerce, 1972–73. *Publications*: *contrib*. Econ. Soc. Rev. (Irel.), Jl Develop. Studies, Stat. Social Inqu. Soc. (Irel.). *Address*: Dept of Economics, Queen's Univ., Belfast BT7 1NN.

Simpson, Prof. Michael George; Professor of Operational Research, and Head of Department, University of Lancaster, since 1967; *b* 1929; *m* 1954; one *s* one *d*. BSc London 1949, PhD London 1955. Mem., Operat. Res. Soc., Operat. Res. Soc. Amer., Brit. Inst. Mngmt, Inst. Mngmt Science. Vis. Prof., Univ. of Belgrade, 1961; Reader in Operational Res., Lancaster, 1964–67. Council Mem., Operat. Res. Soc., 1960–63; Mem., Cent. Adv. Water Cttee, 1970–71; Mem.; Air Traffic Control and Navig. Cttee, 1970–71. *Publications*: (jtly) Operational Research in Management, 1957; Some Techniques of Operational Research, 1962; (jtly) Planning University Development, 1972; *contrib*. Operat. Res. Soc. *Address*: Operational Research Dept, Cartmel College, Univ. of Lancaster, Bailrigg, Lancaster LA1 4YW.

Simpson, Robert William; Lecturer, Department of Moral Philosophy, University of Aberdeen, since 1966; *b* 1941; *m* 1963. MA Aberdeen 1963 (1st cl. Mental Philosophy), BPhil Oxon 1965. Asst Lectr in Moral Philosophy, Univ. of Aberdeen, 1965–66. *Address*: Dept of Moral Philosophy, Univ. of Aberdeen, Aberdeen AB9 1AS.

Sims, Bernard James; Lecturer in Classics, University of Newcastle upon Tyne, since 1963; *b* 1918; *m* 1944; one *s* one *d*. MA Cantab 1946. *Publications*: *contrib*. Class. Qly, Durham Univ. Jl, Jl Hellen. Studies. *Address*: Dept of Classics, Univ. of Newcastle upon Tyne, Newcastle upon Tyne NE1 7RU.

Sims, Nicholas (Roger) Alan; Lecturer in International Relations, Department of International Relations, London School of Economics, since 1969; *b* 1945; *m* 1969; one *d*. BSc (Econ.) London 1967 (Internat. Relns). Asst Lectr in Internat. Relns, LSE, 1968–69. Conflict Res. Society: Council Mem., 1966–73, Hon. Sec., 1970–73; Rapporteur, Defence and Disarmament Working Party, Brit. Council of Chs, 1969–72. *Publications*: Opting for Development, 1968; (rapporteur) The Search for Security: a Christian appraisal, 1973; Approaches to Disarmament: an introductory analysis, 1974; *contrib*. Internat. Relns, Nature, Politique Etrangère, Survival. *Address*: London Sch. of Economics, Houghton Street, WC2A 2AE.

Sims, Dr Richard Leslie; Lecturer in History of Far East, Department of History, School of Oriental and African Studies, University of London, since 1966; *b* 1940; *m* 1964; two *s*. BA London 1962 (1st cl. Hons History), PhD London 1968 (History). *Publications*: Modern Japan, 1973; *contrib*. Trans

Asiatic Soc. Japan. *Address*: Dept of History, School of Oriental and African Studies, Univ. of London, Malet Street, WC1E 7HP.

Sinclair, Crawford Donald; Lecturer in Statistics, University of St Andrews, since 1963; *b* 1940; *m* 1963; three *s* one *d*. BSc St Andrews 1961. *Address*: Dept of Statistics, Univ. of St Andrews, St Andrews, Fife KY16 9AJ.

Sinclair, Prof. John McHardy; Professor of Modern English Language, Department of English Language and Literature, University of Birmingham, since 1965; *b* 1933; *m* 1956; two *s* one *d*. MA Edinburgh 1955. *Address*: Dept of English Language and Literature, Univ. of Birmingham, PO Box 363, Birmingham B15 2TT.

Sinclair, Robert Finlayson, MA; Senior Lecturer in German and Swedish, Department of German and Scandinavian Studies, University of Newcastle upon Tyne, since 1973 (Lecturer, 1942–73); *b* 1918. MA Edinburgh 1941 (1st cl. German). *Address*: Dept of German and Scandinavian Studies, Univ. of Newcastle upon Tyne, Newcastle upon Tyne NE1 7RU.

Sinfield, Alan; Lecturer in English, School of English and American Studies, University of Sussex, since 1965; *b* 1941. BA London 1964, MA London 1967. Res. Asst, Univ. Coll., London, 1964. *Publication*: The Language of Tennyson's In Memoriam, 1971. *Address*: Arts Building, Univ. of Sussex, Brighton BN1 9QN.

Sinfield, Robert Adrian, BA, DipSocAdmin; Senior Lecturer in Sociology, University of Essex, since 1971; *b* 1964; two *d*. BA Oxon 1961 (2nd cl. Lit. Hum.), DipSocAdmin London 1963 (with distinction); Mem., Brit. Sociol. Assoc., CPAG. Res. Asst, LSE, 1963–64; Asst Lectr in Sociology, Univ. of Essex, 1965–67, Lectr, 1967–71; Vis. Lectr in Social Policy, Bryn Mawr Coll. and Columbia Univ., 1969–70. Soc. Welf. Admin., Lutheran Wld Service, Hong Kong, 1961–62; Res. Assoc., NY State Mental Hlth Res. Unit, Syracuse, 1964–65; Cnsltnt on Long-Term Unemployed, OECD, Paris, 1965–68; Assessor, Council of Social Wk Training, 1966–69; Cnsltnt on Indust. Social Welf., UN, 1970–71. *Publications*: The Long-Term Unemployed, 1968; Which Way for Social Work?, 1969. *Address*: Dept of Sociology, Univ. of Essex, Wivenhoe Park, Colchester, Essex CO4 3SQ.

Singer, Bernard Roy, BSc; Senior Lecturer in Psychology, University of Reading, since 1971; *b* 1929; *m* 1965. BSc London 1955; ABPsS. Mem., Soc. Authors. Lectr, St Andrews Univ., 1956–60; Lectr, Queen's Coll., Dundee, 1960–61; Lectr, Reading Univ., 1961–71. *Publications*: Penguin Dictionary of Psychology, 1952, 3rd edn 1967; *contrib*. Brit. Jl Psychol,, Jl Hist. Behav. Sci. *Address*: Building No 3, Earley Gate, Whiteknights Park, Reading.

Singh, Prof. Ghan Shyam; Professor of Italian and Head of Italian Department, Queen's University, Belfast, since 1971; *b* 1926. MA Rajasthan 1950 (1st cl.), PhD Rajasthan 1954, DipEd Perugia 1957, Dott-Lett Milan 1959, DottLett Bologna 1960; PhD London 1961. Lectr, Agra Univ., 1950– ; Lectr, Muslim Univ., Aligarh, 1954; Reader, Bocconi Univ., Milan, 1961; Lectr, Queen's Univ., Belfast, 1965; Reader, Queen's Univ., Belfast, 1968. *Publications*: Swinburne's Early Poetry, 1956; Leopardi and the Theory of Poetry, 1964; Le poesie di Kabir (by Ezra Pound and Singh), 1966; ed, Le opere di Tagore, 1966; ed, Essäyer av F. R. Leavis, 1966; Leopardi e l'Inghilterra, 1968; ed, Contemporary Italian Verse, 1968; ed, Poesie di Thomas Hardy (with Preface by Eugenio Montale), 1968; ed, Sotto che Re, briccone?, 1969; ed, Xenia by Montale, 1970; ed, The Butterfly of Dinard, 1970; ed, Selected Poems by Montale, 1974; A Critical Study of Montale's Poetry, Prose and Criticism, 1973; ed, Da Swift a Pound: Saggi Critici di F. R. Leavis, 1973; *contrib*. Books Abroad, Forum Italicum, Horisont, Il Mondo, Italica, Italian Studies, Le Parole e le Idee, London Magazine, TLS, Il Verri. *Address*: Italian Dept, Queen's Univ., Belfast BT7 1NN.

Singleton, Frederick Bernard, MA; Senior Lecturer, School of Contemporary European Studies, University of Bradford, since 1969; *b* 1926; *m* 1957; two *s* two *d*. BA Leeds 1950 (Hons Geog.), DipEd Leeds 1951, MA Leeds 1952; FRGS. Lectr in Geog., Bradford, 1963–69. Chm., Post-Grad. Sch. of Yugoslav Studies, Bradford Univ.; Exec. Sec., Nat. Assoc. Sov. and E Europ. Studies; Mem., Edit. Bd, Sov. Studies; ABSEES and Sov. and E Europ. Studies Monog. Series, Camb. Univ. Press; Chm., Brit. Yugoslav Soc., North. Br. *Publications*: (with W. E. Tate) A History of Yorkshire, 1960, 3rd edn 1967; (with M. Heppell) Yugoslavia (Nations of the Modern World), 1961; (with A. J. Topham) Workers Control in Yugoslavia, 1963; Background to Eastern Europe, 1965, 2nd edn 1969; Yugoslavia: Country and People, 1970; Industrial Revolution in Yorkshire, 1970; *contrib*. Geog. Mag., Jbh Wirts. Osteurop., Jl Soc. Study Lab. Hist., World Today. *Address*: School of Contemporary European Studies, Univ. of Bradford, Bradford BD7 1DP.

Singleton, Howard Raymond, BSc, FGS, FZS, FMA; Director, Department of Museum Studies, University of Leicester, since 1966; *b* 1915; *m* 1940; one *s* one *d*. BSc Reading 1937 (Gen. Hons); FGS, FZS, FMA. Science Tutor, Millfield Sch., 1938–40. Military Service, 1940–46. Keeper of Geology, Nottingham Nat. Hist. Museum, 1947–49; Liverpool Museum, 1949–51; Dir, Sheffield City Museum, 1951–65. Mem., Council Museums Assoc., 1961–71 (Chm., Educn Cttee, 1969–71); Mem., Internat. Council of Museums (ICOM), 1959– ; Chm., ICOM Internat. Cttee for Training Museum Personnel, 1967–73. *Publications*: Chronology of Cutlery, 1965; Guide to Old Sheffield Plate, 1966; Primer Seminairo de Perfecionamiento Museologico, 1971; *contrib*. ICOM News, Museums, Museums Jl. *Address*: Dept. of Museum Studies, 152 Upper New Walk, Leicester LE1 7QA.

Singleton, Prof. William Thomas, MA, DSc; Professor of Applied Psychology, and Head of Department, University of Aston in Birmingham, since 1965, Dean of Social Sciences, since 1972; *b* 1924; *m* 1950; one *s* four *d*. BA Cantab 1947 (Nat. Sciences), MA Cantab 1950 (Moral Sciences, Psychol.), DSc Aston 1970. Mem., Ergonom. Res. Soc., Foreign Affil., Amer. Psychol. Assoc., Distinguished Foreign Colleague, Hum. Factors Soc. Sen. Lectr in Ergonomics and Systems Design, Coll. of Aeronautics, Cranfield, 1960–65. Chm., Ergonom. Res. Soc.; Mem., Council, Nat. Inst. Indust. Psychol.; Exec. and Res. Cttee. *Publications*: (with R. S. Easterby and D. Whitfield) The Human Operator in Complex Systems, 1967; (with J. G. Fox and D. Whitfield) Measurement of Man at Work, 1970; Introduction to Ergonomics, 1972; Man Machine Systems, 1973; (with P. Spurgeon) Measurement of Human Resources, 1973; *contrib.* Appl. Ergonom., Brit. Jl Psychol., Ergonom., Hum. Factors, Occupat. Hlth. *Address*: Applied Psychology Dept, Aston Univ., Birmingham B4 7ET.

Sinnhuber, Karl Aemilian, Mag.phil, Dr.phil; Reader in Geography, and Head of Geography Section, Department of Linguistic and Regional Studies, University of Surrey, since 1967; *b* 1919; *m* 1952; two *s* one *d*. Dr.phil Innsbruck 1947 (Prehist. Archaeol., with distinction), Mag.phil, Innsbruck 1948 (with distinction); DipSoc Geog. Glasgow 1951; FRGS. Mem., Geog. Assoc. (Pres., Guildford Br., 1971–73), Inst. Brit. Geogr., Österr. Geog. Ges.; Verb deutscher Hochschullehrer der Geographie. Temp. Asst Lectr, Southampton Univ. Coll., 1950–51; Asst Lectr, then Lectr, Univ. Coll. London, 1951–66; Recognized Teacher, Univ. of London, 1961; Vis. Prof., Free Univ., Berlin, 1971. Mem., Conf. of Hds of Dept of Geog. of the Brit. Isles. Leverhulme Foundn Fac. Fellowship in European Studies, 1972. *Publications*: Die Glan bei Salzburg, 1949; Die Altertümer vom 'Himmelreich' bei Wattens, 1949; Germany: its geography and growth, 1961, 2nd edn 1970; ed, The Eisenstadt Area, Burgenland, 1962; *contrib.* Encyclopaedia Britannica; *contrib.* Cartog. Jl, Erdkunde, Geog. Runds., Scott. Geog. Mag., Trans Inst. Brit. Geog., Westerm. Lexikon der Geog., Wien. Geog. Schr. *Address*: Dept of Linguistic and Regional Studies, Univ. of Surrey, Guildford GU2 5XH.

Sirc, Ljubo, DrRerPol; Senior Lecturer in Political Economy, Univ. of Glasgow, since 1968; *b* 1920; *m* 1960 divorced. DipIur Ljubljana 1943, DrRerPol Fribourg 1961. Vis. Lectr, Univ. of Dacca, 1960–61; Lectr, Univ. of St Andrews (Queen's Coll., Dundee), 1962–65; Lectr, Univ. of Glasgow, 1965–68. *Publications*: Economic Devolution in Eastern Europe, 1969; Nesmisel in Smisel, 1969; Outline of International Trade, 1973; Outline of International Finance, 1974; Economic Reform in Jugoslav Industry (forthcoming); *contrib.* Econ. Internaz., Ordo-Jbh. *Address*: Dept of Political Economy, The Univ., Glasgow G12 8QQ.

Sisam, Celia; Fellow, and Tutor in English, St Hilda's College, Oxford University, since 1957; *b* 1926. BA Oxon 1947, MA Oxon 1951. Lectr in English, Queen Mary Coll., Univ. of London, 1948–52; Res. Fellow, Lady Margaret Hall, Oxford, 1952–57. *Publications*: (jtly) The Paris Psalter, 1958; (with K. Sisam) The Salisbury Psalter, 1959; (with K. Sisam) The Oxford Book of Medieval English Verse, 1970; *contrib.* Rev. Engl. Studies. *Address*: St Hilda's College, Oxford OX4 1DY.

Sissons, Dr John Brian; Reader in Geography, University of Edinburgh, since 1966; *b* 1926; *m* 1950; one *s* one *d*. BA Cantab 1950 (1st cl. Hons), MA Cantab 1954, PhD Cantab 1954, DSc Edinburgh 1972; Mem. Inst. Brit. Geogrs. Asst Lectr, Univ. Edinburgh, 1953–54, Lectr, 1954–66; Vis. Prof., McGill Univ., 1957–58. *Publications*: The Evolution of Scotland's Scenery, 1967; *contrib.* Geogr. Annaler, Geol Mag., Geol Soc. Amer. Bull., Nature Phys. Sci., Proc. Yorks Geol Soc., Qly Jl Engrg Geol., Scott. Geogr. Mag., Scott. Jl Geol., Trans Edinb. Geol Soc., Trans Inst. Brit. Geogr., Trans Roy. Soc. Edinb. *Address*: Dept of Geography, High School Yards, Edinburgh EH1 1NR.

Sizer, Prof. John; Professor of Financial Management, and Head of Department of Management Studies, University of Technology, Loughborough, since 1970; Dean of School of Human and Environmental Studies; *b* 1938; *m* 1965; three *s*. BA Nottingham 1964 (Upper 2nd cl. Indust. Econ.); ACMA 1961, AMBIM 1965, FCMA 1973, FRSA 1973; Mem., Amer. Acctng Assoc. Teaching Fellow, Edinburgh, 1965–67; Lectr, Edinburgh, 1967–68; Sen. Lectr, London Grad. Sch. of Business Studies, 1968–70. Mem., Res. and Tech. Cttee and Posts Qualifying Educn Cttee, Inst. Cost and Management Acctnts, 1968– . *Publications*: An Insight into Management Accounting, 1970; Case Studies in Management Accounting, 1974; *contrib.* Acctncy, Acctncy Mngmt, Acctng Business Res., Jl Bus. Finance, Jl Indust. Econ., Jl Mngmt Studies, Omega, Aust. Ch. Acctnts. *Address*: Dept of Management Studies, Univ. of Technology, Loughborough LE11 3TU.

Skegg, Peter Donald Graham; Fellow of New College, Oxford, since 1971, and Lecturer (CUF) in Law in the University of Oxford, since 1972; *b* 1944; *m* 1968; one *s* one *d*. LLB Auckland 1969, MA Oxford 1971. Barrister, Supreme Ct of NZ, 1968. Jun. Lectr, Univ. of Auckland, 1968–69. *Publications*: *contrib.* CLJ, MLR, Med. Sci. L. *Address*: New Coll., Oxford.

Skemp, Prof. Richard Rowland, MA, PhD, FBPsS; Professor of Education, University of Warwick, since 1973; *b* 1919; *m* 1961; one *s*. MA Oxon 1948 (Maths), MA Oxon 1955 (Psychol. and Physiol.), PhD Manchester 1958; FBPsS. Hon. Mem., Soc. Medical Hypnosis, Hon. Mem., Assoc. Professional Psychotherapists. Asst Lectr, 1955–58, Lectr, 1958–66, Sen. Lectr, 1966–73, Univ. of Manchester. *Publications*: Understanding Mathematics, 1964–70; The Psychology of Learning Mathematics, 1971; *contrib.*

642

Brit. Jl Educnl Psychol., Maths Teaching. *Address*: Dept of Education, Univ. of Manchester, Oxford Road, Manchester M13 9PL.

Skerratt, L. C. L; Lecturer, Department of Economics, Lancaster University, since 1966; *b* 1942; *m* 1966; one *s* one *d*. BSc(Econ) London 1964. Ordination training, Chichester Theol. Coll., and Trinity Coll., Oxford, 1964–66. *Publications: contrib.* Jl Business Fin. *Address*: Lonsdale College, Bailrigg, Lancaster.

Skillend, Dr William Edward, MA, PhD; Lecturer in Korean, School of Oriental and African Studies, University of London, since 1953; *b* 1926; *m* 1953; two *s*. BA 1950, MA 1952, PhD 1956, Cantab. Chm., Centre for Far Eastern Studies, 1971– . *Publications*: Kodae Sosol, A Survey of Korean Traditional Style Popular Novels, 1968; *contrib.* Asia Major, Chosen Gakuho, Jl Asiatic Studies of Korea Univ., Jl Inst. Asiatic Studies of Seoul Univ. *Address*: Sch. of Oriental and African Studies, Univ. of London, WC1E 7HP.

Skilliter, Dr Susan Anne, MA, PhD; Lecturer in Turkish, Faculty of Oriental Studies, University of Cambridge, since 1965; *b* 1930. BA Cantab 1954 (2nd cl. Orient. Studies), MA Cantab 1958, PhD Manchester 1965; FRAsiat Soc. Asst Under-Libr., Oriental Dept, Cambridge Univ. Libr., 1954–62; Lectr, Manchester Univ., 1962–64; Vis. Prof., Wisconsin Univ., 1972. Hon Sec., Camb. Bibliog. Soc., 1957–59; Organising Sec., 3rd Internat. Cong. Turkish Art, Cambridge, 1967; Mem., Council Royal Asiat. Soc., 1968– , Hon. Sec., 1970– ; Mem., Council Hakluyt Soc., 1969–73; Fac. Bd Orient. Studies, Cambridge, 1966– . *Publications*: contrib. Documents from Islamic Chanceries, 1965; Iran and Islam, 1971; *contrib.* Bull. SOAS, Jl Royal Asiat. Soc. *Address*: Faculty of Oriental Studies, Sidgwick Avenue, Cambridge CB3 9DA.

Skinner, Basil Chisholm, MA; Senior Lecturer, Department of Educational Studies, University of Edinburgh, since 1966; *b* 1923; *m* 1951; two *s*. MA Edinburgh 1951; FSA Scotl. Hon. Sec., Soc. Antiqu. Scotl., 1965– . *Publications*: Scots in Italy in the 18th Century, 1966; *contrib.* Burl. Mag., Scott. Art Rev., Scott. Hist. Rev., Scott. Studies. *Address*: Dept of Educational Studies, Univ. of Edinburgh, Edinburgh EH8 9YL.

Skinner, David N.; Senior Lecturer, Department of Architecture, Heriot-Watt University, since 1967, and Professor of Landscape Architecture, Delhi School of Planning and Architecture, India, since 1971; *b* 1928; *m* 1954; two *s*. BArch Liverpool 1954, MLArch Penna 1957; ARIBA 1955, AILA 1960. *Publications*: *contrib.* Plan. Outlk, Landsc. Des. *Address*: Dept of Architecture, Heriot-Watt Univ., Edinburgh EH1 1HX.

Skinner, Quentin Robert Duthie; Fellow of Christ's College, Cambridge, since 1962, and Lecturer in History, Cambridge University, since 1967; *b* 1940. BA Cambridge 1962 (1st cl. with distinction, Hist. Tripos

Pts I and II), MA Cambridge 1965; FRHistS 1971. Asst Lectr in Hist., Cambridge Univ., 1965–67; Vis. Fellow, Res. Sch. of Social Science, Austral. Nat. Univ., 1970; Vis. Fellow, Inst. for Advanced Study, Princeton, 1974–75. *Publications: contrib.* Comp. Studies, Hist. Jl, Hist. Theory, Past Pres., Philos. Qly, Philos., Pol. Studies, New Lit. Hist., Pol. Theory, Rev. Philosophique. *Address*: Christ's College, Cambridge.

Skinner, Thomas Beveridge; Secretary, University of Aberdeen, since 1968; *b* 1921; *m* 1943; two *s*. MA Hons Edinburgh 1942 (English Lit. and Lang.). Scottish Office, 1945–68; Principal, Dept of Health for Scotland, 1949–59; Sec., Gen. Bd of Control for Scotland, 1957–59; Asst Sec., Scottish Home and Health Dept, 1959–68; Dir, Scottish Prison Service, 1963–68. *Address*: Univ. of Aberdeen, Marischal Coll., Aberdeen AB9 1AS.

Skone, Dr John Francis; Lecturer in Public Health, University of Bristol, since 1959; *b* 1924; *m* 1951; one *s* one *d*. MD London 1952, MRCS Eng., LRCP London 1948, DCH (RCP and S) 1950, DIH (RCP and S) 1952, DPH London 1952 (distinction). Foundn Fellow, Fac. of Community Medicine, Fellow Soc. Med. Off. of Hlth, Mem. Soc. Social Med. Jun. Paediatric Registrar, Dept of Child Hlth, Welsh Nat. Sch. of Medicine, 1950–51; Clinical Asst, Utd Oxford Hospitals, 1952–55. Mem., Glenside-Barrow Gp Hosp. Mngnt Cttee, 1971– ; Dep. Med. Off. of Hlth, Dep. Principal Sch. Med. Off., and Dep. Port-Med. Off., City and County of Bristol; Dep. Med. ref., Bristol Corp. Crematoria, 1959– ; Med. Insp. of Aliens, 1959– , and under Commonwealth Immigrants Act, 1962– . *Publications*: Public Health Aspects of Immigration, 1968, 2nd edn 1970; *contrib.* Encyclopaedia Britannica: *contrib.* Brit. Med. Bull., Brit. Med. Jl, Lancet, Med. Off., Postgrad. Med. Jl, Public Hlth, Royal Soc. Hlth Jl. *Address*: Dept of Public Health, Canynge Hall, Whiteladies Road, Bristol BS8 2PR.

Slack, Paul Alexander, MA, DPhil; Fellow and Tutor in Modern History, Exeter College, Oxford, since 1973; *b* 1943; *m* 1965; two *d*. BA Oxon 1964 (1st cl. Hist.), MA Oxon 1969, DPhil Oxon 1972. Jun. Res. Fellow in Hist., Balliol Coll., Oxford, 1966–69; Lectr in History, Univ. of York, 1969–72. *Publications*: ed (with P. A. Clark), Crisis and Order in English Towns 1500–1700, 1972. *Address*: Exeter College, Oxford.

Slade, Dr Cecil Frederick; Reader in Charge of Archaeology, Department of History, University of Reading, since 1969; *b* 1921; *m* 1942; one *s* one *d*. BA Reading 1946, PhD 1957; FRHistS, FSA. Reading University: Asst Lectr, 1946–49; Lectr, 1949–60; Sen. Lectr, 1960–69. Pres., Berkshire Archaeol Soc., 1966– ; Chm., Berkshire Archaeol Cttee, 1972– ; Hon. Editor, Berkshire Archaeol Jl, 1968– . *Publications*: Pipe Roll – 12 John, 1951; Leicestershire Survey, 1956; ed (jtly), Early Medieval Miscellany for D. M. Stenton, 1960; Historic Towns: Reading, 1968; *contrib.* VCH Staffordshire

643

(Domesday), 1958; Steinberg's Dictionary of British History, 1964; *contrib.* Berkshire Archaeol Jl. *Address*: Dept of History (Archaeology), Univ. of Reading, White-knights, Reading RG6 2AH.

Slater, Dr Lucy Joan; Head of Computing, Department of Applied Economics, University of Cambridge, since 1961; Fellow, Lucy Cavendish College, Cambridge; *b* 1923. PhD 1953, ScD 1968, Cantab, BA 1944, BA Hons 1947, MA 1949, PhD 1951, DLitt 1956, London. Asst Tutor, UC, Southampton, 1945–47; Research Fellow: Bedford Coll., London 1947–53; Newnham Coll., Cambridge, 1953–58; Res. Officer, Dept of Applied Econs, Cambridge, 1958–61. *Publications*: chap. in Handbook of Mathematical Tables, 1958; Confluent Hypergeometric Functions, 1960; Generalized Hypergeometric Functions, 1965; Fortran Programs for Economists, 1967; (with Prof. Stone *et al*) A Program for Growth, vols 1–12, 1960–73; First Steps in Basic Fortran, 1970; More Fortran Programs for Economists, 1972; *contrib.* London Math. Jl, and Proc., Oxford Qly Jl, Cambridge Philos. Soc. Proc., Computer Jl. *Address*: Dept. of Applied Economics, Sidgwick Avenue, Cambridge.

Slater, Dr Maya; Lecturer, French Department, Westfield College, London University, since 1969; *b* 1941; *m* 1966; two *d.* BA 1964 (1st cl.), MA 1968, DPhil 1970, Oxon; Mem., Conservation Soc. Asst Lectr, French Dept, Westfield Coll., London, 1966–69. *Publications*: Proust and his Times (forthcoming); *contrib.* MLR. *Address*: Westfield Coll., Kidderpore Avenue, Hampstead NW3 7ST.

Slater, Dr Michael Derek, MA, DPhil; Lecturer, Department of English, Birkbeck College, University of London, since 1967; *b* 1936. BA Oxon 1960 (2nd cl. English), MA Oxon 1965, DPhil Oxon 1965. Res. Asst, Birkbeck Coll., 1962–65; Asst Lectr, Birkbeck Coll., 1965–67. Hon. Ed., Dickensian, 1968– ; Mem., Bd of Trustees, Dickens House, London, 1970– . *Publications*: ed, Dickens 1970, 1970; ed. Dickens's Christmas Books, 1971; Dickens's Nicholas Nickleby, 1973; *contrib.* Dickens Studies, Ninetnth Cent. Fict., Etudes Anglaises. *Address*: Birkbeck College, Malet Street, WC1E 7HX.

Slater, Dr Peter James Bramwell, BSc, PhD; Lecturer in Animal Behaviour, University of Sussex, since 1968; *b* 1942; *m* 1968; one *s.* BSc Edinburgh 1964 (1st cl. Zool.), PhD Edinburgh 1968. Mem., Brit. Ornithol. Union. Shaw Macfie Lang Fellow, Edinburgh, 1964–66; Univ. Demonstrator, 1966–68. Trustee, Fair Isle Bird Observatory, 1963– ; Dir, Hampton Properties Ltd, 1966–72. *Publications*: *contrib.* Anim. Behav., Behav., Jl Zool. *Address*: School of Biology, Univ. of Sussex, Brighton BN1 9RH.

Slatter, John Douglas; Lecturer, Department of Russian, University of Durham, since 1968; *b* 1945; *m* 1966. BA Hons Cantab 1966; Member: BUAS; AUT. Temp. Lectr in Russian, Univ. of Durham, 1968. *Address*: Dept of Russian, Univ. of Durham, Elvet Riverside, Durham.

Slattery, Daniel Gabriel; Senior Lecturer in Economics, Queen's University of Belfast, since 1974; *b* 1937; *m* 1972; one *s* one *d.* BSc (Econ.) QUB 1965. Queen's Univ. of Belfast: Clement Wilson Res. Fellow, 1965–66; Lectr, 1966–74. Econ. Advr, HM Treasury, 1969–71. *Publications*: *contrib.* NI Legal Qly, Jl Stat. and Social Inquiry Soc. of Ireland, Econ. and Social Res. Inst. (Dublin) Papers. *Address*: Dept of Economics, Queen's Univ. of Belfast, Belfast BT7 1NN.

Slay, Dr Desmond, MA, PhD; Reader, Department of English Language and Literature, University College of Wales, Aberystwyth, since 1972; *b* 1927; *m* 1958; four *s* one *d.* BA Oxon 1948 (1st cl. English), MA Oxon 1952, PhD Wales 1959. Pres., Viking Soc. North. Res., 1970–72; Mem., Philol. Soc., 1951– . Asst Lectr, 1948–50, Lectr, 1950–62, Sen. Lectr, 1962–72, Univ. Coll. of Wales, Aberystwyth; Life Gov., Univ. Coll. of Wales, 1969– . *Publications*: Codex Scardensis, 1960; Hrólfs Saga Kraka, 1960; The Manuscripts of Hrólfs Saga Kraka, 1960; Romanes, 1972; ed jtly, Proc. First Internat. Saga Conf., Edin. 1971, 1973; *contrib.* Afmælisrit Jóns Helgasonar (Festschrift), Bibliotheca Arnamagnæan, Trans Philol. Soc. *Address*: Dept of English Language and Literature, Univ. College of Wales, Aberystwyth SY23 2AX.

Sleeman, Allan Godfrey; Lecturer, Department of Political Economy, University of Glasgow, since 1967; *b* 1938; *m* 1966. BSc(Econ) London 1960. *Publications*: *contrib.* Oxf. Econ. Papers. *Address*: Dept of Political Economy, Univ. of Glasgow, Glasgow G12 8QQ.

Sloane, Dr Peter James, BA(Econ), PhD; Lecturer, Department of Industrial Economics, University of Nottingham, since 1969; *b* 1942; *m* 1969; one *s.* BA(Econ) Sheffield 1964, PhD Strathclyde 1968. Asst Lectr in Political Econ., Aberdeen Univ., 1966–67; Lectr, Aberdeen Univ., 1967–69. Seconded as Econ. Adviser, Dept of Employment, 1973–74. Mem., Nottingham and Dist. Local Employment Cttee, 1969– ; Bd of Edit. Adv., Indust. Relat. Jl. *Publications*: *contrib.* Jl Econ. Studies, Brit. Jl Indust. Relat., Scott. Jl Pol. Econ., Applied Econ. *Address*: Dept of Industrial Economics, Univ. of Nottingham, Univ. Park, Nottingham NG7 2RD.

Sloman, Aaron; Lecturer in Philosophy, School of Social Sciences, University of Sussex, since 1964; *b* 1936; *m* 1965; two *s.* BSc Cape Town 1956, DPhil Oxon 1962. Rhodes Schol. 1957. Temp. Lectr in Maths, Univ. Cape Town, 1957; Sen. Schol., St Antony's Coll., Oxford, 1960–62; Lectr in Philos., Hull Univ., 1962–64; Sen. Vis. Fellow, Dept Computational Logic, Sch. of Artificial Intelligence, Edinburgh Univ., 1972–73. *Publications*: *contrib.* Amer. Philos. Qly, Analysis, Aristotelian Soc. Proc., Artificial Intelligence, Inquiry, Mind, Philosophy. *Address*: Arts Building, School of Social Sciences, Univ. of Sussex, Brighton BN1 9QN.

Sloman, Albert Edward, DPhil; Vice-Chancellor, University of Essex, since 1962;

b 1921; *m* 1948; three *d*. Mediaeval and Mod. Langs, 1941, MA Oxon, MA Dublin, DPhil Oxon. Lectr in Spanish, Univ. of California, Berkeley, USA, 1946–47; Reader in Spanish, in charge of Spanish Studies, Univ. of Dublin, 1947–53; Fellow, TCD, 1950–53; Gilmour Prof. of Spanish, Univ. of Liverpool, 1953–62; Dean, Faculty of Arts, 1961–62. Reith Lectr, 1963; Granada Guildhall Lectr, 1970. Chm., Dept of Educn State Studentship Cttee (Humanities), 1965– ; Mem. Council of Europe Cttee for Higher Educn and Research, 1963–73; Mem., Conf. of European Rectors and Vice-Chancellors, 1965– (Pres. 1969–); Mem., Adm. Bd, Internat. Assoc. of Univs, 1965– ; Mem., Bd of Governors, Univ. of Guyana, 1966– . Ed. of Bull. of Hispanic Studies, 1953–62. *Publications*: The Sources of Calderón's El Principe constante, 1950; The Dramatic Craftsmanship of Calderón, 1958; A University in the Making, 1964; *contrib*. Mod. Lang. Rev., Bull. Hispanic Studies, Hispanic Rev., Romance Philol. and other jls. *Address*: The Univ. of Essex, Colchester, Essex CO4 3SQ.

Sluckin, Prof. Wladyslaw, BSc(Eng), BSc, PhD, FBPsS; Professor of Psychology, University of Leicester, since 1965; *b* 1919; *m* 1942; two *s*. BSc London 1942 (Engineering), BSc London 1950 (Psychol.), PhD London 1955. Mem., Exper. Psychol. Soc., Mem., Assoc. Anim. Behav. Res. Asst, Univ. of Durham, 1951–53; Lectr in Psychol., Univ. of Durham, 1953–60; Lectr in Psychol., Univ. of Leicester, 1960–62; Reader, Univ. of Leicester, 1962–65. Ed., Brit. Jl Psychol., 1967–73. *Publications*: Principles of Alternating Currents, 1951, 2nd edn 1959, Swedish edn 1965; (with T. G. Connolly) Statistics for the Social Sciences, 1953, 3rd edn 1971, Spanish edn 1956, Swedish edn 1958; Minds and Machines, 1954, 2nd edn 1960, Spanish edn 1956, Polish edn 1957, Italian edn 1964, Portuguese edn 1965; Imprinting and Early Learning, 1964, American edn 1965, Spanish edn 1969; Early Learning in Man and Animal, 1970, American edn 1972; Early Learning and Early Experience (Readings), 1971. *Address*: Dept of Psychology, The Univ., Leicester LE1 7RH.

Small, Alan, MA, FSA, FSAScot; Senior Lectr in Geography, University of Dundee, since 1969; *b* 1937; *m* 1968; one *d*. MA Aberdeen 1959; FSA, FSAScot. Asst Lectr, Aberdeen Univ., 1961–62; Lectr, 1962–69. *Publications*: ed, The Fourth Viking Congress, 1965; ed, St Ninian's Isle and its Treasure, 1972; *contrib*. Norsk. Geog. Tids., Scott. Geog. Mag., Proc. Soc. Antiqu. Scotl., Saga-Book, Folk Life, etc. *Address*: Dept of Geography, Univ. of Dundee, Dundee DD1 4HN.

Small, Ian, OBE, BSc, CEng, FICE; Lecturer, Department of Building Engineering, University of Liverpool, since 1963; *b* 1918; *m* 1940; one *s* one *d*. BSc Belfast 1938 (1st cl. Civil Eng.); MICE 1943, FICE 1961. Civil Eng. in-Chief's Dept, Admiralty, 1939–52; Dir, W Afr. Build. Res. Inst., 1952–63; Chm., Ghana Jt Gp of Engineers, 1957; UN Cnsltnt, Mauritius, 1967; Indonesia, 1968;

Zambia, 1970; Nigeria, 1971. *Publications*: *contrib*. Pubns W Afr. Build. Res. Inst. *Address*: The Univ., PO Box 147, Liverpool L69 3BX.

Small, Prof. John Rankin; Professor and Head of Department of Accountancy and Finance, Heriot-Watt University, since 1967; Dean of Faculty of Economic and Social Studies; *b* 1933; *m* 1957; one *s* two *d*. BSc(Econ) London 1956; FCCA 1958, FCMA 1961, JDipMA 1964. Mem., Council, Assoc. Cert Acctnts; Mem., Council, Scott. Bus. Educ. Council; Business Studies Bd, CNAA; Educn Cttee, UEC. *Publications*: Introduction to Managerial Economics, 1966, Italian edn 1970, Swedish edn 1971, Finnish edn 1971; *contrib*. Acctnts Mag., Cert. Acctnts Jl, Mngmt Acctnt. *Address*: Mountbatten Building, Heriot-Watt Univ., Edinburgh.

Small, Dr Ronald John, MA, PhD; Reader in Geography, University of Southampton, since 1971; *b* 1930; *m* 1954; one *s* four *d*. BA Cantab 1953 (1st cl. Geog.), MA Cantab 1956, PhD Southampton 1958. Asst Lectr, Southampton Univ., 1954–57; Lectr, Southampton Univ., 1957–68; Sen. Lectr, Southampton Univ., 1968–71. Ed., Southampton Res. Series in Geog. *Publications*: The Study of Landforms, 1969; *contrib*. Geog., Proc. Geol. Assoc. Lond., Trans Inst. Brit. Geogrs. *Address*: Dept of Geography, Univ. of Southampton, Southampton SO9 5NH.

Smalley, Rev. Stephen Stewart, MA, BD; Lecturer in New Testament Studies, Department of Biblical Criticism and Exegesis, University of Manchester, since 1970; *b* 1931. BA Cantab 1955 (English and Theol.), MA Cantab 1958, BD Eden Theol Seminary 1957. Mem., Studiorum NT Soc., 1966– . Chaplain, Peterhouse, Cambridge, 1960–63; Acting Dean, Peterhouse, Cambridge, 1962–63; Lectr, Ibadan Univ., 1963–67; Sen. Lectr, Ibadan Univ., 1967–69. Warden, St Anselm Hall, Manchester Univ., 1972– . *Publications*: Building for Worship, 1967; Heaven and Hell, 1968; The Spirit's Power, 1972; ed. and contrib., Christ and Spirit in the New Testament, 1973; contrib: New Bible Dictionary, 1962; Work, 1968; Encounter with Books, 1970; Baker's Dictionary of Christian Ethics, 1973; *contrib*. Expos. Times, Jl Bib. Lit., NT Studies, Nov. Test., Scott. Jl Theol., Tynd. Bull. *Address*: Faculty of Theology, The Univ., Manchester M13 9PL.

Smallman, Prof. Frederic Basil Rowley, MA, BMus, ARCO; Alsop Professor of Music, University of Liverpool, since 1965; Pro-Vice-Chancellor, since 1973; *b* 1921; *m* 1949; two *s* one *d*. BA, BMus Oxon 1946, MA Oxon 1948, DipEd Oxon 1947; ARCO 1939. Mem., Royal Music. Assoc., Incorp. Soc. of Music. Lectr, Nottingham Univ., 1950–61; Sen. Lectr, 1961–64. Liverpool University: Dean, Fac. of Arts, 1968–71; Public Orator, 1972–73. Chm., Cwealth Music Conf., Liverpool, 1965. *Publications*: The Background of Passion Music, 1957, 2nd edn 1971; *contrib*. Music Lett., Musical Times. *Address*: Dept. of Music, Univ. of Liverpool, 80 Bedford Street South, Liverpool.

Smallwood, Dr Edith Mary, MA, PhD, FSA; Reader in Classics, Department of Latin, Queen's University, Belfast, since 1967; *b* 1919. BA Cantab 1942 (1st cl. Classics), MA Cantab 1946, PhD Cantab 1951; FSA 1972. Temp. Asst Lectr, Univ. of Liverpool, 1945–46; Res. student, Cambridge, 1946–48 (holding Craven Studentship, 1946–47); Jex-Blake Res. Fellow, Girton Coll., Cambridge, 1948–51; Lectr in Classics, Dept of Latin, Queen's Univ., Belfast, 1951–63; Sen. Lectr, Queen's Univ., Belfast, 1963–67; Exch. Lectr, Univ. of Ibadan, Nigeria, 1963–64; Vis. Lectr, Univ. of Cape Town, 1967; Mem., Inst. Adv. Study, Princeton, NJ, 1971–72. *Publications*: Philonis Alexandrini *Legatio Ad Gaium*, 1961, 2nd edn 1970; Documents illustrating the Principates of Nerva, Trajan and Hadrian, 1966; Documents illustrating the Principates of Gaius, Claudius and Nero, 1967; *contrib.* Class. Philol., Greece Rome, Historia, Jl Jew. Studies, Jl Rom. Studies, Jl Theol. Studies, Latomus. *Address*: Dept of Latin, Queen's Univ., Belfast BT7 1NN.

Smart, Alastair; *see* Smart, P. A. M.

Smart, Dr Brian Joseph; Lecturer in Philosophy, University of Keele, since 1968; *b* 1941; *m* 1969. BA Bristol 1962 (Philos. and Classics), PhD London 1967. Asst Lectr in Philosophy, UCNW Bangor, 1965–68. *Publications*: *contrib.* Analysis, Philosophical Studies. *Address*: Dept of Philosophy, Univ. of Keele, Keele, Staffs ST5 5BG.

Smart, John David; Lecturer in Classics, University of Leeds, since 1961; *b* 1937; *m* 1960; one *s* one *d*. BA Oxon 1960 (1st cl. Lit. Hum.), MA Oxon 1965. Vis. Asst Prof., Trinity Coll., Toronto, 1966–67; Vis. Fellow, Pennsylvania State Univ., 1969; Vis. Asst Prof., Univ. of Brit. Columbia, 1970. Mem., Council, Hellen. Soc., 1971–74. *Publications*: contrib. Dictionary of World History, 1973; *contrib.* Jl Hellen. Studies, Phoenix. *Address*: Dept of Greek, The Univ., Leeds LS2 9JT.

Smart, Kenneth Frank; Lecturer, School of Education, University of Reading, since 1956; *b* 1924; *m* 1948; four *s*. BA Oxon 1948, MA Oxon 1949, DipEd Oxon 1949. Mem., Comp. Educn Soc. Europe. UNESCO Cnsltnt, Mauritius, 1962–64; Mem., UNESCO Reg. Gp for Educnl Planning in Africa, 1966–68. *Address*: School of Education, The Univ., Reading RG1 5AQ.

Smart, Patricia; Lecturer in Philosophy, University of Surrey, since 1965; *b* 1931. Teaching Certif. Bishop Otter Coll. 1951, BA Exeter 1961 (Philos.), MPhil London 1968, MSc London 1970 (Philos. of Science). *Publications*: Thinking and Reasoning, 1972; Indoctrination, in, New Essays in the Philosophy of Education, 1973; *contrib.* Proc. Philos. Educn Soc. *Address*: Univ. of Surrey, Stag Hill, Guildford, Surrey GU2 5XH.

Smart, Prof. (Peter) Alastair (Marshall), MA, DA, FRSA; Professor, since 1963, and Head of the Department of Fine Art, University of Nottingham, since 1956; *b* 1922; *m* 1960; one *s* one *d*. MA Glasgow 1942

(English), Gen. Ord. Exam. Edinburgh Theological College 1946, DipArt Edinburgh College of Art 1949; FRSA 1966. Staff Tutor in Art Hist., Adult Educn Dept, and Lectr (pt-time), Hist. Dept., Univ. of Hull, 1949–56; Hd of Dept of Fine Art, Univ. of Nottingham, 1956–63; Commonwealth Fund Fellow, NY Univ. and Columbia Univ., 1954–55; Mem., Inst. Adv. Study, Princeton, NJ, 1966–67. Army, 1942–43, Mem., Council, Walpole Soc.; Former Mem., Art Panel, Arts Council GB. *Publications*: The Life and Art of Allan Ramsay, 1952; Paintings and Drawings by Allan Ramsay (Exhibit. Cat., Royal Acad.), 1964; Allan Ramsay, 1966; Fra Angelico, 1967; The Assisi Problem and the Art of Giotto: A Study of the Legend of St Francis . . . at Assisi, 1971; The Renaissance and Mannerism in Italy, 1972; The Renaissance and Mannerism outside Italy, 1972; var. exhibition catalogues, etc; Catalogue raisonné of the Portraits of Allan Ramsay (forthcoming); *contrib.* Apollo, Burl. Mag., Renaiss. Mod. Studies, Rev. Engl. Studies. *Address*: Dept of Fine Art, The Univ. of Nottingham, University Park, Nottingham NG7 2RD.

Smart, Robert George, MArch, ARIBA, MRTPI; Lecturer in Urban Design, Heriot-Watt University, since 1964; *b* 1932; *m* 1969. DipArch Edinburgh College of Art 1959, DipTP Edinburgh College of Art 1963, MArch Cornell 1962; ARIBA 1960, MRTPI 1968, Registered Architect 1959. *Address*: Dept of Architecture, Edinburgh College of Art, Lauriston Place, Edinburgh.

Smart, Prof. (Roderick) Ninian, MA, BPhil, HLD; Professor of Religious Studies, University of Lancaster, since 1967; *b* 1927; *m* 1954; one *s* two *d*. BA Oxon 1951 (1st cl. Greats), MA Oxon 1953, BPhil Oxon 1954; Hon. HLD Loyola (Chicago) 1970. Asst Lectr in Philos., Univ. Coll. of Wales, Aberystwyth, 1952–55; Lectr, Univ. Coll. of Wales, Aberystwyth, 1955; Vis. Lectr in Philos., Yale, 1955–56; Lectr in Hist. and Philos. of Religion, Univ. of London, 1956–61; H. G. Wood Prof. of Theology, Univ. of Birmingham, 1961–67; Vis. Prof. of Philos. and Hist., Univ. of Wisconsin, 1965; Vis. Prof. of Religion and Sen. Fellow of Council of the Humanities, Princeton Univ., 1971; Vis. Prof., Otago Univ., Dunedin, 1972. *Publications*: Reasons and Faiths, 1958; A Dialogue of Religions, 1950, reissued as World Religions: A Dialogue, 1966; Historical Selections in the Philosophy of Religion, 1962; Philosophers and Religious Truth, 1964, rev. edn 1969; Doctrine and Argument in Indian Philosophy, 1964; The Yogi and the Devotee, 1968; Secular Education and the Logic of Religion, 1968; The Religious Experience of Mankind, 1969, British edn 1971; The Concept of Worship, 1972; The Phenomenon of Religion, 1972; The Science of Religion and the Sociology of Knowledge, 1973; *contrib.* Monist, Philos. Qly, Relig., Relig. Studies, Scott. Jl Theol., Theol. *Address*: Dept of Religious Studies, Cartmel College, Univ. of Lancaster, Bailrigg, Lancaster LA1 4YW.

Smee, Francis John O.; *see* Odling-Smee.

Smeed, Dr John William, MA. PhD; Senior Lecturer in German, Durham University, since 1967; *b* 1926; *m* 1952. BA Wales 1951 (1st cl. German), MA Wales 1953, PhD Wales 1956. Asst Lectr in German, King's Coll., London, 1956–58. Lectr in German, Durham, 1958–67. *Publications:* Jean Paul: Dreams, 1966; ed, J. Paul: Schmelzle, 1966; ed, Goethe: Faust, Parts i and ii, 1969; *contrib.* Comp. Lit., Deuts. Vjs., Germ. Life Lett., J-Paul-Jbh. *Address:* Dept of German, The Univ., Durham DH1 3HP.

Smeed, Prof. Reuben Jacob, CBE, PhD; Professor of Traffic Studies, Department of Civil and Municipal Engineering, University College, London, since 1966; *b* 1909; *m* 1938; one *s* one *d.* BSc London 1931 (1st cl. Maths), PhD London 1933 (Eng.). MICE, MInstHE, Mem., Inst. Maths and Application, FSS. Demonstrator, Maths Dept, Imperial Coll., London, 1933–35; Asst Lectr, Maths Dept, Imperial Coll., London, 1935–39; Royal Aircraft Estab., Farnborough, 1939–40; Telecommunications Res. Estab., 1940–41; RAF Bomber Command, 1941–47; Dep. Dir, Road Res. Lab., 1947–65; Ch. Scientist, Min. of Land and Natural Resources, 1965–66. Chairman: Cttee on Road Pricing, 1962–64; OTA/PIARC Sub-cttee of Experts, 1950– ; Chm., Univs Transp. Study Gp, 1967– ; *Publications:* contrib. Accident Analysis and Prevention; *contrib.* Bull. Inst. Internat. Stats, Highway Res. Rec., Jl Inst. Civil Eng., Jl Internat. Inst. Stats, Jl Royal Stat. Soc., Nature, Philos. Mag., Royal Soc. Lond. Proc., Transp. Sci., Jl Transp. Econs and Policy. *Address:* Univ. College London, Research Group in Traffic Studies, Department of Civil and Municipal Engineering, Gower Street, WC1E 6BT.

Smiley, Dr Timothy John; Lecturer in Philosophy, Cambridge University, since 1962; *b* 1930; *m* 1954; four *d.* BA Cantab 1952, MA, PhD Cantab 1956; Barrister, Gray's Inn, 1956. Fellow, Clare Coll., Cambridge, 1955– ; Asst Tutor, 1959–65; Sen. Tutor, 1966–69; Asst Lectr, Cambridge Univ., 1957–62; Vis. Prof., Cornell Univ., 1964; Vis. Prof., Univ. of Virginia, 1972. Scientific Off., Air Min., 1955–57. *Publications: contrib.* Analysis, Jl Symb. Logic, Mind, Proc. Aristot. Soc. *Address:* Clare College, Cambridge.

Smith, Dr A. Hassell, BA, PhD; Senior Lecturer in History, School of English and American Studies, University of East Anglia, since 1969; *b* 1926; *m* 1961; one *d.* BA London 1952, PhD London 1959. Jt Ed., Norfolk Rec. Soc., 1969– . *Publications:* The County and The Court: Administration and Politics in Norfolk 1558–1603; *contrib.* Bull. Inst. Hist. Res., Hunt. Lib. Qly. *Address:* School of English and American Studies, Univ. of East Anglia, Norwich NOR 88C.

Smith, Alan; Senior Lecturer, Postgraduate Diploma Course in Art Gallery and Museum Studies, Department of Art History, University of Manchester, since 1970; *b* 1925; *m* 1947; two *s* two *d.* DA Manchester 1945, ATD 1946; FMA 1972. Keeper of Ceramics and Applied Art, City of Liverpool Museums, 1964–70. Professional Councillor, Museums Assoc. *Publications:* Liverpool Pottery, 1968; Liverpool Herculaneum Pottery, 1970; The Lancashire Watch Co., Prescot, England, 1973 (USA); *contrib.* English Ceramic Circle Trans, Proc. Antiquarian Horological Soc. *Address:* Gallery and Museum Studies, Dept of Art History, Univ. of Manchester, Manchester M13 9PL.

Smith, Dr Alan Gordon Rae, MA, PhD; Lecturer in History, University of Glasgow, since 1964; *b* 1936; *m* 1972. MA Glasgow 1959 (1st cl. Hist.), PhD London 1962; FRHistS 1968. Asst in History, Univ. of Glasgow, 1962–64. *Publications:* The Government of Elizabethan England, 1967; The New Europe, 1969; Science and Society in the Sixteenth and Seventeenth Centuries, 1972; (with J. Hurstfield) Elizabethan People: State and Society, 1972; ed, The Reign of James VI and I, 1973; *contrib.* EHR, Hist., Hist. Today. *Address:* Dept of History, Univ. of Glasgow, Glasgow G12 8QQ.

Smith, Prof. Albert James; Professor of English, University of Southampton, since 1974; *b* 1924; *m* 1950; one *s.* BA Wales 1951 (1st cl. English), MA Wales 1954. Lectr, Univ. of Florence, 1955–56; Lectr, Univ. Coll. of Swansea, 1959–67, Sen. Lectr, 1967–71, Actg Head of Dept, 1970–71; Prof. of English, Keele, 1971–74. Leverhulme European Schol., Florence, 1955–56; Leverhulme Fellow, 1967–68. *Publications:* (with W. H. Mason) Short Story Study, 1961; Shakespeare Stories, 1962; John Donne: The Songs and Sonets, 1964; John Donne: The Complete English Poems, 1971; ed, Donne: Quatercentenary Studies, 1972; *contrib.* AW Rev., Bull. J. Rylands Libr., Mod. Lang. Qly, Mod. Lang. Rev., Rev. Engl. Studies, English, Crit. Qly, Essays in Crit., Times Lit. Supp. *Address:* Dept of English, Univ. of Southampton, Southampton SO9 5NH.

Smith, Alexander Louis MacGregor, MA; Reader in Politics, University of Strathclyde, since 1966; *b* 1921; *m* 1941; one *s* one *d.* MA Glasgow 1950 (2nd cl. Economics and Politics). Sen. Lectr, Strathclyde, 1964–66. Chairman: Bridgeton Employment Cttee, 1965– ; Glasgow Fabian Soc., 1969– . *Publications:* jtly, Political Stratification and Democracy, 1972; jtly, Class, Religion and Politics in Glasgow (forthcoming). *Address:* Dept of Politics, Univ. of Strathclyde, Glasgow G1 1XW.

Smith, Ann Dorothea; Lecturer, Department of Criminology, Edinburgh University, since 1967; *b* 1918; *m* 1940; two *d.* BA Oxon 1939, PhD Edinburgh 1960. Mem., Soc. Public Teachers of Law, Harvard League, ISTD. Asst Lectr, Edinburgh, 1965–67. JP; Mem., Scott. Central Adv. Cttee for JPs; Parole Bd for Scotl., 1967–70; Ellis Cttee on Remand Homes; Russell Cttee on Succession of Illegit. Children. *Publications:* Women in Prison, 1962; A Home for Young Offenders, 1972; *contrib.* Brit. Jl of Criminology, Sociol. Rev., Scots Law Times. *Address:* Dept of Criminology, Univ. of Edinburgh, Edinburgh EH8 9YL.

Smith, Arthur Edward, OBE, MA; Senior Tutor, Department of Adult Education, University of Nottingham, since 1966; *b* 1920; *m* 1948; two *d*. BA Leeds 1942 (1st cl. English), MA Leeds 1943. Tutor, Dept of Adult Educn, Nottingham Univ., 1947–66. Chm., Cttee for Engl., Nature Conservancy Council, 1973– (Mem., Nature Conservancy, 1956–67; Chm., 1971–73); Mem., Nature Conservancy Council, 1973– (Nature Conservancy, 1967–73); Hon. Sec., Soc. Prom. Nature Reserves, 1963– ; Lincs Trust for Nature Conservation, 1948–68, Chm., 1968– . *Publications*: The Birds of Lincolnshire, 1955; The Conservation of Nature in Lincolnshire, in, Nottingham and its Region (BA Handbook), 1966. *Address*: Dept of Adult Education, 14 Shakespeare Street, Nottingham NG1 4FJ.

Smith, Barbara Mary Dimond; Lecturer, Centre for Urban and Regional Studies, University of Birmingham, Faculty of Commerce, since 1967; *b* 1929; *m* 1951. BCom Birmingham 1950 (2nd cl.). Res. Asst, Fac. of Commerce, Univ. of Birmingham, 1950–58, Res. Assoc., 1958–62, Res. Fellow, 1962–66; Res. Off., Bd of Trade Reg. Off. in Birmingham, 1966–67. Univ. rep., Greater Birmingham Employment Cttee; Mem., Hat, Cap and Millinery (GB) Wages Council; Mem., Licensed Resid. Establishment and Licensed Restaurant Wages Council; Mem. Hollow-ware Wages Council; Mem., Retail Food Trade Wages Council; Mem., Industrial Tribunals. *Publications*: Industry and Trade, 1880–1960, in, Victoria History of the County of Warwick, vol. VII, 1964; (with S. A. Ruddy and G. E. Cherry) Employment Problems in a County Town: a study of Bridgnorth, Shropshire, 1971; (with H. Parsons) The Rugeley Study, 1971; The Administration of Industrial Overspill, 1972; Black Country Employment 1959–1970, 1973; *contrib*. Business Hist., Econ. Hist. Rev., Hans. Soc. Parly Govt, Jl Town Plan. Inst., Urb. Studies. *Address*: Centre for Urban and Regional Studies, Univ. of Birmingham, Selly Wick House, Selly Wick Road, Birmingham.

Smith, Bernard B.,; *see* Babington Smith.

Smith, Prof. Brian A.; *see* Abel-Smith.

Smith, Dr Brian Clive, BA, MA, PhD; Senior Lecturer in Public Administration, University of Bath, since 1972; *b* 1938; *m* 1960; one *s* one *d*. BA Exeter 1959 (Government), MA McMaster 1963 (Polit. Econ.), PhD Exeter 1970. Asst Lectr, Exeter Univ., 1963–65; Lectr, Inst. of Administration, Zaria, N Nigeria, 1965–66; Lectr, Exeter Univ., 1966–70; Lectr, Civil Service Coll., 1970–72. *Publications:* Regionalism in England (three monogs), 1964–65; Field Administration, 1967; Advising Ministers, 1969; *contrib*. Admin. Sci. Qly, Pol. Studies, Public Admin. *Address*: School of Humanities and Social Sciences, Univ. of Bath, Claverton Down, Bath BA2 7AY.

Smith, Brian K.; *see* Keith-Smith.

Smith, Catherine D.; *see* Delano Smith.

Smith, Charles Gordon, MA; University Lecturer in Geography, University of Oxford, since 1950, and Fellow of Keble College, Oxford, since 1957; *b* 1921; *m* 1954; three *s*. BA Oxon 1948 (1st cl. Geog.), MA Oxon 1952; FRGS. Mem., Geog. Assoc., Mem., Inst. Brit. Geogrs. Asst Lectr, Leeds Univ., 1949–50; Vis. Prof., Osmania Univ., India, 1959–60. Brit. Army, 1939–46 (Capt. RASC); Mem., Council, Inst. Brit. Geogrs, 1958–60; Ext. Examiner, Birmingham Univ., 1963–65; Sen. Proctor, Oxford Univ., 1968–69. *Publications*: contrib. Oxford Economic Atlas of the Middle East and North Africa, 1960; contrib. Illustrated World Geography, 1960; contrib. Oxford Bible Atlas, 1962; contrib. Encyclopaedia Britannica; contrib. The World and Man (Elsevier's Encyclopaedia of Geography) (forthcoming); *contrib*. Geog., Geog. Mag., Jl Contemp. Hist., Met. Mag., Trans Inst. Brit. Geogrs, Weather, Wld Today. *Address*: Keble College, Oxford.

Smith, Dr Christopher Colin; University Lecturer in Spanish, Cambridge, and Fellow and Tutor of St Catharine's College, since 1968; *b* 1927; *m* 1954; three *d*. BA Hons Cantab 1950 (1st cl. Fr. and Spanish), MA, PhD Cantab 1954; Member: Assoc. of Hispanists; Modern Humanities Res. Assoc. (Mem. Cttee). Univ. of Leeds: Asst Lectr, Dept of Spanish, 1953–56, Lectr, 1956–64; Sub-dean of Arts, Social Studies and Law, 1963–67. Chm., Bd of Fac. of Mod. and Medieval Langs, Cambridge, 1973. Treas., 12th FILLM Congress, Cambridge, 1972. Editor, Hispanic section, MLR, 1974– . *Publications*: ed, Spanish Ballads, 1964, repr. 1970; (with G. A. Davies and H. B. Hall) Langenscheidt's Standard Dictionary of the English and Spanish Languages, 1966; (with M. Bermejo Marcos and E. Chang-Rodríguez) Collins Spanish–English, English–Spanish Dictionary, 1971, repr. 1972 and 1974, Spanish edn 1972; ed, Poema de mio Cid, 1972; *contrib*. BH, BHS, MÆ, MLR, R, RFE. *Address*: St Catharine's Coll., Cambridge.

Smith, Dr Christopher Norman; Lecturer in School of European Studies, University of East Anglia, since 1968; *b* 1936; *m* 1961; one *d*. BA Cantab 1960 (Mod. and Med. Langs), DipEd Oxon 1962, MA Cantab 1964, PhD Cantab 1969. Asst Lectr, Aberdeen Univ., 1966. *Publications*: ed (with K. M. Hall), J. de La Taille: The Dramatic Works, 1972; ed, A. de Montchrestien: Two Tragedies, 1972; contrib. Introds, French emblem bks, Scolar Press reprint series; *contrib*. Forum Mod. Lang. Studies, Jl Europ. Studies, Jl Amer. Studies, Kentucky Romance Qly. *Address*: School of European Studies, Univ. of East Anglia, Norwich NOR 88C.

Smith, Prof. Clifford Thorpe; Professor of Latin American Geography, and Director of the Centre for Latin American Studies, Liverpool University, since 1970; *b* 1924; *m* 1949; two *s* one *d*. MA Cambridge 1949. Mem., Econ. Hist. Soc., Mem., Royal Geogl Soc., Mem., Soc. Lat. Amer. Studies, Mem., Inst. Brit. Geogrs. Asst Lectr, Univ. Coll. of Leicester, 1948–51; Asst Lectr, Dept of

Geography, Cambridge Univ., 1951–55; Lectr, Dept of Geog., Cambridge Univ., 1955–70; Fellow, St John's Coll., Cambridge, 1960–70; Tutor, St John's Coll., Cambridge, 1963–70. Co-Ed., Jl Lat. Amer. Studies, 1970– . *Publications*: (jtly) The Making of the Broads, 1960; Historical Geography of Western Europe before 1800, 1968; co-ed, Latin America: Geographical Perspectives, 1971; *contrib*. Geogl Jl, Geog., Curr. Anthrop., Geography. *Address*: Centre for Latin American Studies, Univ. of Liverpool, Liverpool L69 3BX.

Smith, Prof. Colin, MA, PhD; Professor of French, University of Reading, since 1967; *b* 1914; *m* 1943; two *d*. BA Manchester 1935 (1st cl. French), MA Manchester 1937, PhD London 1950, Teacher's Dip. Manchester 1936. Asst, Univ. of Manchester, 1937; Asst Lectr, 1938–46, Lectr, 1946–57; Sen. Lectr, Univ. Coll., London, 1957–62; Reader, Univ. of London, 1962–67; Sen. Vis. Prof., Univ. of W Ontario, 1965–66. Army, 1939–45; Mem., Council, Royal Inst. of Philos., 1956– . *Publications*: ed, E. Renan: Caliban: drame philosophique, 1954; Contemporary French Philosophy, 1964; trans., M. Merleau-Ponty: Phenomenology of Perception, 1962; trans. (with A. Lavers), R. Barthes: Writing, degree zero and Elements of Semiology, 1967; contrib. Encyclopaedia of Philosophy, 1967; ed, Stuart Mill, Philosophes de tous les temps, 1973; *contrib*. Brit. Jl Phenom., Fr. Studies, Mod. Lang. Rev., Philos., Rev. Métaphys. Morale, Rev. Internat. Philos. *Address*: Dept of French Studies, Faculty of Letters and Social Sciences, Univ. of Reading, Whiteknights, Reading RG6 2AA.

Smith, Colin; Lecturer, Department of Librarianship, Strathclyde University, since 1964; *b* 1919; *m* 1946; one *s*. MA Strathclyde 1971; FLA. Dep. Libr., Univ. Coll., Nairobi, 1960–63; *Publications*: Library Resources in Scotland, 1968, rev. edn 1972. *Address*: Dept of Librarianship, Univ. of Strathclyde, Glasgow G1 1XH.

Smith, David Ingle; Lecturer, Department of Geography, University of Bristol, since 1959; *b* 1935; *m* 1958; one *s* one *d*. BSc London: 1956 (Geog.), 1957 (Geol.), MSc McGill 1959 (Geog.); FRGS, AKC. *Publications*: ed, Limestone and Caves of the Mendip Hills, 1974; *contrib*. Geograph. Jl, Jl of Hydrol., Qly Jl of Geol. Soc., etc. *Address*: Dept of Geography, The Univ., Bristol BS8 1SS.

Smith, Denis M.; *see* Mack Smith.

Smith, Dame Enid Mary R. R.; *see* Russell-Smith.

Smith, Eric O.; *see* Owen Smith.

Smith, Ernest Anthony, MA, FRHistS; Senior Lecturer in History, University of Reading, since 1964; *b* 1924; *m* 1948; one *s* one *d*. BA Cantab 1949, MA Cantab 1955, DipEd Reading 1950; FRHistS 1957. Asst Lectr in Hist., Reading Univ., 1951–54, Lectr, Reading Univ., 1954–64. Mem., South. Univ. Jt Bd Sch. Exams, 1962– ; Mem.,

FSSU Central Council, 1968– . *Publications*: ed, Letters of Princess Lieven to Lady Holland, 1847–57, 1955; ed (with A. Aspinall), English Historical Documents, vol. XI 1783–1832, 1959, 2nd edn 1969; History of the Press, 1968; Whig Principles and Party Politics: Earl Fitzwilliam and the Whig Party 1748–1833 (forthcoming); contrib. The House of Commons 1754–90, ed L. B. Namier and J. Brooke, 1964; contrib. The Prime Ministers, ed H. van Thal, 1974; *contrib*. EHR, Hist. Jl, Hist. Today, North. Hist., Parly Aff. *Address*: Dept of History, Univ. of Reading, Whiteknights, Reading RG6 2AH.

Smith, F. S., BA, MSc; Lecturer in Education, Brunel University, since 1966; *b* 1927; *m* 1947; two *d*. BA Wales 1953 (Hons Econs), MSc Surrey 1972. Ch. Examiner, Assoc. Exam. Bd; Ch. Examiner, South. Univs Bd; Ch. Examiner, Middlesex Reg. Exam. Bd; Mem., Econ. Assoc. Teacher-Training Cttee; Chm. Res. Cttee, Assoc. for Liberal Educn; Mem., Educn Adv. Bd, Encyclopaedia Britannica. *Publications*: Earning and Spending, 1969; Jt Ed., The New Transport Revolution, 1972; contrib. Curriculum Development in Economics, 1974. *Address*: Dept of Education, Brunel Univ., Uxbridge, Middlesex UB8 3TH.

Smith, Dr Francis John; Director, Computer Centre, The Queen's University of Belfast, since 1970; *b* 1935; *m* 1965; four *s*. BSc Belfast 1956, MA Catholic University of America 1959, PhD Belfast 1962; FIMA 1969, FBCS 1970. Asst Lectr, Queen's Univ., Belfast, 1960–62; Lectr, Queen's Univ., Belfast, 1962–66; Res. Assoc., Univ. of Maryland, 1963–64; Reader, Queen's Univ., Belfast, 1966–70. *Publications*: *contrib*. Computer Jl, Jl Chem. Phys., Mol. Phys., Proc. Phys. Soc. *Address*: Computer Centre, The Queen's Univ. of Belfast, Belfast BT7 1NN.

Smith, Prof. Frederick Viggers; Professor of Psychology, University of Durham, since 1950; *b* 1912. BA Sydney 1938 (1st cl. Psychol.), MA Sydney 1941 (1st cl. Psychol.), PhD London 1948; FBPsS. Pres., Brit. Psychol. Soc., 1958–59. Lectr, 'Teachers' Coll., Sydney, 1938–46; Lectr, Birkbeck Coll., London, 1946–48; Lectr, Univ. of Aberdeen, 1948–50; Vis. Prof., Cornell Univ., 1957; Vis. Prof., Univ. of New Zealand, 1960. UNESCO Consultant: Univ. of Riyadh, 1973; Peoples' Democratic Republic of Yemen, 1974. Mem., Council, Brit. Psychol. Soc., 1946–61; Council, Internat. Ethnol. Soc., 1969. *Publications*: Explanation of Human Behaviour, 1951, 2nd edn 1960; Attachment of the Young, 1969; Purpose in Animal Behaviour, 1971; *contrib*. Anim. Behav., Austral. Jl Philos. Psychol., Brit. Jl Psychol. *Address*: Dept of Psychology, Science Laboratories, South Road, Durham DH1 3LE.

Smith, Geoffrey Simon N.; *see* Nowell-Smith.

Smith, Gerald Rex; Assistant Lecturer in Arabic Studies, University of Cambridge, since 1970; *b* 1938; *m* 1961; three *s*. BA Hons

London 1961 (Arabic (class.)), MA Cantab 1970; FRAS 1969. Lectr in Arabic, UC, Durban, S Africa, 1966–69. Student Liaison Officer, Govt of Aden, London, 1961–62; Asst Advr, W Aden Protectorate, 1962–65. Editorial Sec., Bd of Editors of Cambridge History of Arabic Literature, 1971– . *Publications*: The Ayyūbids and early Rasūlids in the Yemen, 2 vols, 1973–74; *contrib*. African Studies, Arabian Studies, Islamic Culture, Semitics. *Address*: Fac. of Oriental Studies, Univ. of Cambridge, Cambridge CB3 9DA.

Smith, Dr Grahame Francis; Senior Lecturer in English Studies, University of Stirling, since 1970; *b* 1933; *m* 1964; two *s* one *d*. MA Aberdeen 1960 (1st cl. Eng. Lang. and Lit.), PhD Cantab 1963. Asst Prof., Univ. Calif, Los Angeles, 1963–65; Lectr, UC Swansea, 1965–70. *Publications*: Dickens, Money and Society, 1968; Bleak House, 1974; *contrib*. Dickensian, Human World, Mod. Lang. Rev., Victorian Studies. *Address*: Dept of English Studies, Univ. of Stirling, Stirling FK9 4LA.

Smith, Henry Sidney; Edwards Professor, and Head of Department of Egyptology, University College, London, since 1970; *b* 1928; *m* 1961. MA Cambridge 1956. Lectr, Fac. of Oriental Studies, Cambridge, 1954–63; Tutor, Christ's Coll., Cambridge, 1961–63; Reader, Dept of Egyptology, Univ. Coll., London, 1963–70. Field Dir, Egypt Explor. Soc. Nubian Survey, 1960–62; Field Dir, Egypt Explor. Soc., Sakkara, 1971–73; Hon. Sec., Brit. Inst. Hist. and Archaeol. in E Afr., 1966–71. *Publications*: Preliminary Reports of the Egypt Exploration Society's Nubian Survey, 1962; *contrib*. ACTA Orient., Jl Egypt. Archaeol., Kush. *Address*: Dept of Egyptology, Univ. College London, Gower Street, WC1E 6BT.

Smith, Herbert William; Lecturer and Course Tutor in Italian, School of Modern Languages, Bath University, since 1965; *b* 1919; *m* 1957; one *s* one *d*. BA General London 1952, PGCE 1953, BA Hons 1955; FIL 1957. External Examiner in Italian for the BA degree, Univ. of Strathclyde, 1971– ; Sec., International Assoc. of Teachers of Italian, 1972– ; Chm., Assoc. of Teachers of Italian, 1970–71; Vice Pres., Bath Anglo-Italian Soc., 1972– ; Editor, Jl of the Assoc. of Teachers of Italian, 1969– . *Publications*: Antologia della Stampa Italiana, 1970; A First Itlain Reader for Adults, 1971; Using Italian, 1972; The Greatness of Dante Alighieri, 1974; *contrib*. Jl Assoc. of Teachers of Italian, Technology and Society, TES. *Address*: School of Modern Languages, Bath Univ., Claverton Down, Bath BA2 7AY.

Smith, James Leslie Clarke, MA, BLitt; Lecturer, English Department, University of Southampton, since 1965; *b* 1936. BA Oxon 1960 (1st cl. English), MA, BLitt Oxon 1966. Henry Fellow, Yale Univ., 1962–63; Lectr, Univ. of Brit. Columbia, 1963–64. *Publications*: ed, The Great McGonagall, 1968; ed, W. McGonagall: Last poetic gems, 1968; The Jew of Malta in the Theatre, in, Christopher Marlowe, ed B. Morris, 1968; Melodrama, 1973; ed, Vanbrugh, The provoked wife,

650

1974; *contrib*. Studies Scott. Lit. *Address*: Dept of English, Univ. of Southampton, Highfield, Southampton SO9 5NH.

Smith, Prof. John Cyril, FBA; Professor of Law, University of Nottingham, since 1958; Pro-Vice-Chancellor, since 1973; *b* 1922; *m* 1957; two *s* one *d*. BA Cantab 1949, LLB Cantab 1950, MA Cantab 1954. Called to Bar, Lincoln's Inn, 1950. Asst Lectr, Nottingham Univ., 1950–52; Lectr, Nottingham Univ., 1952–56; Reader, Nottingham Univ., 1956–57; Commonwealth Fund Fellow, Harvard Law Sch., 1952–53. *Publications*: (with J. A. C. Thomas) A Casebook on Contract, 1957, 5th edn 1973; (with Brian Hogan) Criminal Law, 1965, 3rd edn 1973; Law of Theft, 1968, 2nd edn 1972; *contrib*. legal jls. *Address*: Univ. of Nottingham, University Park, Nottingham NG7 2RD.

Smith, John Edward S.; *see* Sharwood Smith.

Smith, Prof. John Harold; Professor of Sociology, University of Southampton, since 1964; Deputy Vice-Chancellor, since 1974; *b* 1927; *m* 1951; two *s* one *d*. BA London 1950 (2nd cl.). Mem., Brit. Sociol. Assoc. Asst Lectr, LSE, 1952–55; Lectr, LSE, 1955–64; Sen. Lectr, LSE, 1964; Rockefeller Fellow, 1962; Fellow, Center for Adv. Study in Behavioral Science, Stanford, 1962–63; Vis. Prof., Univ. of Texas, 1967. RN, 1944–48; Mem., Acton Soc. Trust, 1950–52; Dean, Fac. of Social Science, Univ. of Southampton, 1967–70; Chm., Combined Studies (Soc. Scis) Bd, CNAA, 1971– (Mem., CNAA, 1967–74); Mem., Central Council for Educn and Training in Social Wk, 1971– ; Mem., Social Science Adv. Cttee, UK Nat. Commn for UNESCO, 1965– . *Publications*: The Teaching of Industrial Sociology, 1960; (jtly) Married Women Working, 1963; co-ed, Manpower Policy and Employment Trends, 1966; (jtly) The Social Sciences in Higher Technical Education, 1969; *contrib*. Brit. Jl Indust. Relat., Brit. Jl Sociol., Occupat. Psychol., Sociol. Rev. *Address*: Dept of Sociology and Social Administration, Univ. of Southampton, Highfield, Southampton SO9 5NH.

Smith, John N.; *see* Norton-Smith.

Smith, Jonathan Simon Christopher R.; *see* Riley-Smith.

Smith, Joseph Edward; Senior Lecturer in Management Accounting, Management Centre, University of Aston in Birmingham, since 1962; *b* 1924; *m* 1950; one *s*. BSc Aston 1968, JDipMA 1970; FCMA 1968. Chm., Educn and Trng Cttee, ICMA. *Publications*: Financial Aspects of Supervisory Management, 1966; Hardy Heating Co. Ltd – Text and Cases in Management Accounting, 1969; *contrib*. Management Accounting. *Address*: Management Centre, Univ. of Aston in Birmingham, Birmingham B4 7ET.

Smith, Dr Keith; Senior Lecturer, Department of Geography, University of Strathclyde, since 1971; *b* 1938; *m* 1961; one *s* one *d*. BA Hull 1960, PhD Hull 1964. Tutor in

Geogr., Univ. Liverpool, 1963–65; Lectr in Geogr., Univ. Durham, 1965–70. *Publications*: Water in Britain, 1972; Principles of Applied Climatology, 1974; *contrib*. Jl Hydrology, Meteorological Mag., Water and Water Engrg, Weather. *Address*: Dept of Geography, Livingstone Tower, Richmond Street, Glasgow G1 1XH.

Smith, Kenneth Edward; Lecturer in Literature, School of Human Purposes and Communication, University of Bradford, since 1973; *b* 1944; *m* 1968; one *s*. BA Oxon 1966 (1st cl. Hons), BPhil Oxon 1968. Lectr in English, UCW Aberystwyth, 1968–73. *Address*: School of Human Purposes and Communication, Univ. of Bradford, Bradford BD7 1DP.

Smith, Lawrence D.; Senior Lecturer in Agricultural Economics, Department of Political Economy, University of Glasgow, since 1972; *b* 1939; *m* 1963; one *s* two *d*. BScAgric London 1961; Associate, Inst. for Develt Studies, Sussex, 1973– . Dept Lectr, Agric. Econs Res. Inst., Univ. Oxford, 1963–66; Lectr in Agric. Econs, Dept Polit. Economy, Glasgow, 1966–72, on secondment, 1968–71; Res. Fellow, Inst. Develt Studies, Univ. Nairobi, 1968–70, Sen. Res. Fellow, 1970–71. Mem., ILO Employment Mission to Kenya, 1972. *Publications*: (with M. E. Kempe) ed, Strategies for Improving Rural Welfare (Inst. Develt Studies, Nairobi, Occ. Paper No. 4), 1971; *contrib*. E Afr. Jl, E Afr. Jl Rural Develt, Farm Economist, Westminster Bank Review. *Address*: Dept of Political Economy, Adam Smith Building, Univ. of Glasgow, Glasgow G12 8RT.

Smith, Leslie Allan, BSc(Econ), FCI, FRSA; Head of the Curriculum Laboratory, Department of Arts, Science and Education, University of London, Goldsmiths' College, since 1970; *b* 1922; *m* 1943; one *s*. BSc(Econ) London 1952; Fellowship Institute of Commerce 1971, Certificated Teacher 1949, Nat. Cert. in Commerce 1947. Mem., Brit. Pol. Assoc., Mem., Hist. Assoc., Mem., Internat. Evaluation of Achievement Assoc., Mem., Brit. Soc. Authors; Hon. Life Mem., Irish Assoc. Curriculum Develt. Hdmaster, Mark Hse Sec. Sch., Essex, 1957–66; Dir of Consultative Services, Curriculum Lab., Univ. of London, Goldsmiths' Coll., 1966– ; Ed. of Publications, Univ. of London, Goldsmiths' Coll., 1967– ; Recognised Teacher, Inst. of Educn, Univ. of London, 1968– . Chm., Nat. Cttee, Engl. and Wales, Civic Educn, IEA, 1967– ; Rep. for Engl. and Wales, Internat. Cttee Civic Educn, IEA, 1967– ; Mem., Working Party on Hist. Assoc. Exam Bd, 1968– ; Mem., Schs Council Working Party on Hlth Educn, 1969– ; Mem., Stand. Cttee on Sec. Educn, Inst. of Educn, Univ. of London, 1968– ; Co-Dir (Engl) Harvard Univ. W Europ. Yth Survey, 1970–72; Dir, Totem Community Educn Services Ltd, 1971– ; Co-Dir, Amer. Pol. Science Assoc. Class Room Poll, 1970–73; Co-founder and Hon. Cnsltnt, Teachers' Center, Greenwich, Conn, 1972– . Mem., Edit Bd, Pol. Assoc., 1970– ; Mem., Adv. Cttee, BBC, on Further Educn, 1971– . *Publications*: ed, Ideas, series one (Library edn), 1970;

(jtly) The British People 1902–1968, 1970, 2nd edn 1972; British Government and International Affairs, 1973; (jtly) Towards a Freer Curriculum, 1974; Tradition and Change in Contemporary Education, 1975; contrib. published papers; *contrib*. Amer. Pol. Sci. Assoc., Harv. Univ., Hist. Assoc., Internat. Evaluation of Achievement Assoc. (IEA), Goldsmiths' Coll., Jl Curric. Studies. *Address*: Curriculum Laboratory, Univ. of London, Goldsmiths' College, New Cross, SE14 6NW.

Smith, Prof. Louis P. F.; Associate-Professor of Political Economy (International Trade), University College, Dublin, since 1954; *b* 1923; *m* 1950; three *s* three *d*. BA Univ. Coll. Dublin 1947, MA Univ. Coll. Dublin 1948, PhD Univ. Coll. Dublin 1956, DEconSc Univ. Coll. Dublin 1961; Bar Final, King's Inns Dublin. Res. Asst, Manchester, 1949–54. Econ. Adv., Nat. Farmers Assoc., 1954–64; Chm., Irish Council of European Gov., 1966–68; Econ. Cnsltnt, Allied Irish Banks, 1971. *Publications*: Evolution of Agricultural Cooperation, 1961; Elements of Economics, 1971; Finance Costs in Agriculture, 1967; *contrib*. Jl Stat. Social Inqu. Soc. Irel., Manch. Sch. *Address*: Dept of Political Economy, Univ. College, Belfield, Dublin 4.

Smith, Dr Malcolm Crawford; Lecturer in French, University of Leeds, since 1967; *b* 1941. BA London 1962 (1st cl. French), PhD London 1967. Asst Lectr, Leeds Univ., 1964–67; Vis. Prof., Univ. of W Ontario, 1970–71; Postdoctoral Fellow, Soc. for Humanities, Cornell Univ., 1973–74. *Publications*: ed, P. de Ronsard: Sonnets pour Hélène, 1970; Joachim Du Bellay's veiled victim, 1974; *contrib*. Biblioth. Hum. Renaiss., Cah. Assoc. Internat. Etudes Franç., etc. *Address*: Dept. of French, The Univ., Leeds LS2 9JT.

Smith, Malcolm Philip Dominic B.; *see* Baker-Smith.

Smith, Martin Ferguson, MA, MLitt; Senior Lecturer in Classics, University College of North Wales, since 1973; *b* 1940; *m* 1964; one *d*. BA Dublin 1962 (1st cl. Classics), MA Dublin 1965, MLitt Dublin 1965. Foundn Schol. and Tyrrell Gold Medalist, TCD, 1960. Asst Lectr, 1963–66, Lectr, 1966–73, UCNW. Mem. Council, Soc. Promotion Hellenic Studies. *Publications*: trans., Lucretius: On The Nature of Things, 1969; ed, Lucretius, De Rerum Natura, 1974; Thirteen New Fragments of Diogenes of Oenanda, 1974; *contrib*. Amer. Jl Archaeol., Anatolian Studies, Class. Qly, Class. Rev., Greece and Rome, Hermath., Jl Hellen. Studies. *Address*: Dept of Classics, Univ. College of North Wales, Bangor, Gwynedd LL57 2DG.

Smith, Prof. Michael G.; Professor of Anthropology, University College, London, since 1969; *b* 1921; three *s*. BA London 1948, PhD London 1951. Res. Fellow, Inst. of Social and Econ. Res., UC of the West Indies, 1952–56; Sen. Res. Fellow, UC of the West Indies, 1956–58; Sen. Res. Fellow,

651

Nigerian Inst. of Social and Econ. Res., Ibadan, 1958–60; Sen. Lectr in Sociology, UC of West Indies, 1960–61; Prof. of Anthropology, Univ. of California, Los Angeles, 1961–69. *Publications*: The Economy of Hausa Communities of Zaria, 1955; Government in Zazzau, 1800–1950, 1960; Kinship and Community in Carriacou, 1962; West Indian Family Structure, 1962; Dark Puritan, 1963; The Plural Society in the British West Indies, 1965; Stratification in Grenada, 1965; ed (with L. Kuper), Pluralism in Africa, 1969. *Address*: Univ. College, Gower Street, WC1E 6BT.

Smith, Michael Peter H.; *see* Hornsby-Smith.

Smith, Dr Michael Quinton; Lecturer-in-charge, Sub-Department of History of Art, Bristol University, since 1964; *b* 1933; *m* 1969. BA Cantab 1957, MA Cantab 1960, PhD Glasgow 1965. Res. Asst, Edinburgh Univ., 1958–59; Rivoira Schol., 1960; Rome Schol., 1961; Asst Lectr, Glasgow Univ., 1962–64. *Publications*: The Medieval Churches of Bristol, 1970; *contrib.* Explor. Entrepen. Hist., Papers Brit. Sch. Rome. *Address*: Sub-Dept of History of Art, The Univ., Bristol BS8 1TH.

Smith, Dr Neilson Voyne; Reader in Linguistics, University College, London, since 1972; *b* 1939; *m* 1966; two *s*. BA Cantab 1961, MA Cantab 1964, PhD London 1964. Lectr in West African Langs, 1964–70, Lectr in Linguistics and W African Langs, 1970–72; Harkness Fellow, Commonwealth Fund, 1966–68; Post-Doctoral Fellow, MIT, 1966–67; Vis. Fellow, UCLA, 1968. *Publications*: Outline Grammar of Nupe, 1967; The Acquisition of Phonology, 1973; *contrib.* Afr. Lang. Studies, Jl Afr. Langs. *Address:* Univ. College, Gower Street, WC1E 6BT.

Smith, Dr Paul; Lecturer in History, University of London, King's College, since 1965; *b* 1937; *m* 1969. BA Oxon 1958 (1st cl. Mod. Hist.), MA Oxon 1964, DPhil Oxon 1965; FRHistS. Asst Lectr, Queen's Univ. of Belfast, 1963–64; Asst Lectr, King's Coll., London, 1964–65. Mem., Exec., Brit. Univs Film Council, 1969–74; Mem., Hist. Selection Cttee, Nat. Film Archive, 1969– . *Publications*: Disraelian Conservatism and Social Reform, 1967; ed, Lord Salisbury on Politics: a Selection from His Articles in the Quarterly Review, 1860–1883, 1972. *Address*: Dept of History, King's College, Strand, WC2R 2LS.

Smith, Dr Pauline Mary; Senior Lecturer in French, University of Hull, since 1971; *b* 1940. BA London 1961 (Hons French), PhD London 1964 (French Lit.); Member: AUT, Soc. of Authors. Lectrice d' Anglais, Faculté des Lettres, Université de Lyon, 1963–64; Asst Lectr in French, Univ. Birmingham, 1964–67, Lectr, 1967–71. *Publications*: The Anti-Courtier Trend in C16th French Literature, 1966; Clément Marot, Poet of the French Renaissance, 1970; *contrib.* Bibliothèque d'humanique et Renaissance. *Address*: Dept of French, Univ. of Hull, Cottingham Road, Hull HU6 7RX.

Smith, Peter Beaumont; Senior Lecturer, Department of Music, University of Manchester, since 1972; *b* 1928. MSc Juilliard Sch. of Music, NY 1951, BA, MusB 1955, MA Cantab. Asst Lectr, Dept of Music, Univ. of Manchester, 1957–60, Lectr, 1960–72. Sen. Tutor, 1958, Sub-Warden, 1965–67, St Anselm Hall, Univ. of Manchester. *Publications*: Church Music in Italy, c. 1660–1750, in, New Oxford History of Music (forthcoming); articles in Grove's Dictionary of Music and Musicians, 6th edn (forthcoming). *Address*: Dept of Music, Denmark Road, The Univ., Manchester M13 9PL.

Smith, Dr Peter Bevington; Lecturer in Social Psychology, School of Social Sciences, University of Sussex, since 1966; *b* 1937; *m* 1961; two *d*. BA Cambridge 1959, PhD Cambridge 1962; ABPsS. Res. Fellow in Industrial Mngmt, Univ. of Leeds, 1962–64; Lectr in Mngmt Studies, Univ. of Leeds, 1964–66; Dir of Studies, Graduate Programme in Social Psychology, Sussex, 1970–73. Res. Associate, Univ. of Calif, Santa Cruz, 1973. *Publications*: Improving Skills in Working with People: the T-group, 1969; ed, Group Processes, 1970; Groups within Organisations, 1973; *contrib.* Admin. Sci. Qly, Brit. Jl So. Clin. Psychol., Hum. Relat., Jl Applied Behavioural Sci., Jl Mngmt Studies. *Address*: School of Social Sciences, Univ. of Sussex, Brighton BN1 9QN.

Smith, Dr Peter Frederick, MA, PhD, FRIBA; Senior Lecturer, Department of Architecture, University of Sheffield, since 1973 (Lecturer, 1965–73); *b* 1930; *m* 1957; one *s* two *d*. BA Cantab 1955, MA Cantab 1957, PhD Manchester 1962; ARIBA 1964, FRIBA 1970. Prin., Ferguson Smith and Assoc., Chartered Architects, 1968– . *Publications*: Third Millennium Churches, 1973; Dynamics of Urbanism, 1974; Environment and Human Need, in, Between Religion and Art (forthcoming); *contrib.* Ch Building, Built Environment, Archit. Psychol. Newsletter, Architectl Design, Leonardo, Jl RIBA, Jl RTPI. *Address*: Dept of Architecture, Arts Tower, Univ. of Sheffield, Sheffield SI0 2TN.

Smith, Dr Ralph Bernard; Reader in the History of South East Asia, School of Oriental and African Studies, University of London, since 1971; *b* 1939. BA Leeds 1959 (Hist.), PhD Leeds 1963. Lectr in the Hist. of S East Asia, SOAS, 1962–71. *Publications*: Viet-Nam and the West, 1968; Land and Politics in the England of Henry VIII, 1970; *contrib.* Bull. SOAS, Mod. Asian Studies, Past Pres. *Address*: School of Oriental and African Studies, Malet Street, WC1E 7HP.

Smith, Randall Clive; Senior Lecturer, School for Advanced Urban Studies, Bristol University, since 1974; *b* 1936; *m* 1964. BA Oxon 1960 (2nd cl. PPP). Mem., Brit. Sociol. Assoc., Mem., Soc. Admin. Assoc., Mem., Educn for Planning Assoc. Res. Off., Acton Soc. Trust, 1960–64; Temp. Lectr in Applied Sociology, Dept of Social and Economic Res., Univ. of Glasgow, 1964–67; Lectr in Urban and Reg. Studies, Birmingham Univ., 1967–72; Lectr in Soc. Policy, CS Coll., 1972–74.

Publications: (with D. Brooks) Mergers I: Past and Present, 1963; (with R. Stewart and P. Wingate) Mergers II: The Impact on Managers, 1963; (with D. Brooks) Mergers III: The Impact on the Shopfloor, 1966; (with G. Sumner) Planning Local Authority Services for the Elderly, 1969. *Address*: Sch. for Advanced Urban Studies, The Univ., Bristol BS8 1TH.

Smith, Prof. Reginald Donald; Professor and Head of Liberal and Contemporary Studies, Institute of Continuing Education, New University of Ulster, Coleraine; *b* 1914; *m* 1939. BA Birmingham 1936 (Hons Eng.), MA Examination (thesis not submitted) 1937, Secondary Sch. Teaching Dip. 1938. Actg Dep. Postmaster General, Govt of Palestine, 1944–45; BBC Writer/Producer, 1945–73. Mem. Drama Panel, North Ireland Arts Council, 1973, Governor, NI Arts Council, 1974. Premio d'Italia, 1973. *Address*: Institute of Continuing Education, New Univ. of Ulster, Londonderry BT52 1SA.

Smith, Richard Norville Watson; Senior Lecturer, Department of Logic and Metaphysics, University of St Andrews, since 1965; *b* 1916; *m* 1964. MA Glasgow 1937 (1st cl. Classics), MA Oxford 1947 (2nd cl. Lit. Hum.). Asst, Univ. of St Andrews, 1947–49; Lectr, Univ. of St Andrews, 1949–65; Vis. Asst Prof., Union Coll., Schenectady, NY, 1959–60. RNVR, 1939–46; Adv. of Studies, Fac. of Arts, Univ. of St Andrews, 1966–69. *Publications*: *contrib.* Philos. Qly. *Address*: Dept of Logic and Metaphysics, Univ. of St Andrews, NE Fife KY16 9AJ.

Smith, Dr Robert, DMus, FTCL, LGSM; Senior Lecturer in Music, University College of North Wales, Bangor, since 1969; *b* 1922; *m* 1945; one *s* two *d.* BMus Wales 1946, MMus Wales 1948, DMus Wales 1959; FTCL 1948, LGSM 1942. Lectr, Univ. Coll. of N Wales, Bangor, 1947–69. Lieut, R. Signals, 1942–45; Mem., Exec. Cttee, Guild for Prom. of Welsh Music, 1958–66; Vice-Chm., Exec. Cttee, Guild for Prom. of Welsh Music, 1964–66; Mem., Music Cttee, Schs Council, 1965–72; Ch. Examiner, A level Music, WJEC, 1962–71, 1974– . *Publications*: Catalogues of Contemporary Welsh Music, 1960–68; A Complete Catalogue of Contemporary Welsh Music, 1972; *contrib.* Anglo-Welsh Rev., Music Rev., Musik. Anal, Welsh Music. *Address*: Depot of Music, Univ. College of North Wales, Bangor LL57 2DG.

Smith, Prof. Roland; Carrington Viyella Professor of Marketing, University of Manchester Institute of Science and Technology, since 1965; *b* 1928; *m* 1954. BA Birmingham 1950, PhD 1954 (Econ.), MSc Manchester 1970; FBIM. Member: Manchester Industrial Soc., REconS. Lectr in Economics, Univ. of Liverpool, 1960–64; Dir, Liverpool Business School, 1964–65. Chm., Management Sciences Dept, UMIST, 1970– . *Publications*: numerous. *Address*: UMIST Sackville Street, Manchester M60 1QD.

Smith, Roland Cecil Yates; Lecturer in German, Modern Languages Centre, Uni-

versity of Bradford, since 1966; *b* 1926; *m* 1963; two *s* one *d.* BA London 1951 (2nd German), CertEd 1954, Cert. Proficiency in Russian Leeds 1966, MA Bradford 1971. Asst Master, Bemrose Sch., Derby, 1954–57; Asst Master, Wath-on-Dearne Grammar Sch., 1957–63; Lectr in German, Huddersfield Coll. of Technol., 1964–66. *Address*: Modern Languages Centre, Univ. of Bradford, Bradford BD7 1DP.

Smith, Sheila Mary, MA; Senior Lecturer, Department of English, University of Nottingham, since 1974; *b* 1930. BA London 1951 (1st cl. English), CertEd 1952, MA London 1956. Asst Lectr in English, 1952–55; Lectr, 1955–74, Nottingham Univ. *Publications*: ed, Mr. Disraeli's Readers, 1966; *contrib.* Renaiss. Mod. Studies, Rev. Engl. Studies. *Address*: Dept. of English, The Univ., Nottingham NG7 2RD.

Smith, Sydney Herbert C.; *see* Clague-Smith.

Smith, Trevor A., BSc(Econ); Senior Lecturer in Political Science and Government, Department of Economics, Queen Mary College, University of London, since 1972; *b* 1937; *m* 1960; two *s*. BSc(Econ) London 1958. Mem., Pol. Studies Assoc. Temp. Asst Lectr in Public Administration, Univ. of Exeter, 1959–60; Lectr in Political Studies, Univ. of Hull, 1962–67; Lectr in Political Science and Govt, Queen Mary Coll., London, 1967–72; Vis. Assoc. Prof., Los Angeles State Univ., 1969. Res. Adv., Acton Soc. Trust, 1968– ; Res. Adv., Joseph Rowntree Social Service Trust, 1969– . *Publications*: (jtly) Training Managers, 1962; (jtly) Town Councillors, 1964; Town and County Hall, 1966; Anti-Politics: consensus, reform and protest in Britain, 1972; jt ed, Direct Action and Democratic Politics, 1972; *contrib.* Govt and Opposition, Parl. Aff. *Address*: Queen Mary College, Mile End Road, E1 4NS.

Smith, Dr Verity Anne; Lecturer, Department of Spanish, University of London, since 1966; *b* 1939; *m* 1961; two *d.* BA London 1960 (Hons Spanish), PhD London 1965. Asst Lectr, Univ. of London, 1963–66. *Publications*: Valle-Inclán: Tirano Banderas, 1971; Ramon del Valle-Inclán, 1972. *Address*: Dept of Spanish, Westfield College, Univ. of London, NW3 7ST.

Smith, Vincent P.; *see* Powell-Smith.

Smith Brindle, Reginald; *see* Brindle, R. S.

Smithers, Dr Alan George, BSc, PhD, MSc; Senior Lecturer in Education, University of Bradford, since 1969; *b* 1938; *m* 1962; two *d.* BSc London 1959 (1st cl. Botany), PhD London 1966; MSc(Educn) Bradford, 1972; MIBiol. 1966. Mem., Soc. Res. Higher Educn, 1966, Mem. Council, 1972– . Asst Lectr, then Lectr in Botany, Birkbeck Coll., Univ. of London, 1964–67; Res. Fellow in Educn, Univ. of Bradford, 1967–69. *Publications*: *contrib.* Ann. Bot., Brit. Jl Educnl Psychol., Brit. Jl Indust. Relat., Brit. Jl Soc. Clin. Psychol., Educn

Res., Educnl Rev., Jl Exper. Bot., Nature, Res. Educn. *Address*: School of Research in Education, Univ. of Bradford, Bradford BD7 1DP.

Smyth, Robert Leslie, B(Com)Sc; Senior Lecturer in Economics, University of Keele, since 1965; *b* 1922; *m* 1951; one *s* one *d*. B(Com)Sc Belfast 1948, B(Com)Sc Belfast 1950 (2nd cl.). Asst Lectr in Econs, Queen's Univ., Belfast, 1950–51; Lectr in Econs, Univ. of Hull, 1951–59; Lectr in Econs, Univ. of Keele, 1959–63; Sen. Lectr in Commerce, Univ. of W Australia, 1963–65. *Publications*: The Distribution of Fruit and Vegetables, 1959; ed, Essays in Economic Method, 1962; ed, Essays in the Economics of Socialism and Capitalism, 1964; (with D. H. Briggs) Distribution of Groceries, 1967; ed, Essays in Modern Economic Development, 1969; The History of Section F of the British Association 1835–1970, in, Conflicts in Policy Objectives, ed N. Kaldor, 1971; *contrib*. Adv. Sci., Scott. Jl Pol. Econ., Austral. Qly, Econ. Rec., Yorks Bull. *Address*: Dept of Economics, Univ. of Keele, Staffordshire ST5 5BG.

Snaith, John Graham; University Lecturer in Hebrew and Aramaic, Faculty of Oriental Studies, Cambridge University, since 1971; *b* 1934; *m* 1960; one *s* one *d*. BA 1957, MA 1960, Oxon, BD London 1959, MA Cantab 1971; Mem., Soc. for OT Study. Lectr, Univ. of Ibadan, Nigeria, 1961–63; Asst Lectr, 1966–67, Lectr, 1967–71, Univ. of Nottingham. *Publications*: Ecclesiasticus, Cambridge Bible Commentary, 1974; *contrib*. Jl Semitic Studies, Jl of Theol Studies, Vetus Testamentum. *Address*: Fac. of Oriental Studies, Sidgwick Avenue, Cambridge CB3 9DA.

Snellgrove, David Llewellyn, MA, PhD, LittD, FBA; Professor of Tibetan, Departments of India and the Far East, School of Oriental and African Studies, University of London, since 1974; *b* 1920. BA Cantab 1948, MA Cantab 1951, PhD London 1953, LittD Cantab 1969; FBA 1969. Lectr, 1949–59, Reader, 1960–74, SOAS. Accred. Cnsltnt, Secretariat for non-Christian religions, Vatican, 1967– . *Publications*: Buddhist Himālaya, 1957; Hevajra Tantra, 1959; Himalayan Pilgrimage, 1961; Four Lamas of Dolpo, 1967; Nine Ways of Bon, 1967; (with H. E. Richardson) A Cultural History of Tibet, 1968; *contrib*. Arts Asiat., Bull. Secret. Non-Christ. Relig., Cent. Asian Jl, etc. *Address*: School of Oriental and African Studies, Univ. of London, WC1E 7HP.

Snodgrass, Dr Anthony McElrea; Reader in Classical Archaeology, University of Edinburgh, since 1969; *b* 1934; *m* 1959; four *d*. BA Oxon 1959 (1st cl. Mods/Greats), MA Oxon 1963, DPhil Oxon 1963. Lectr in Classical Archaeology, Univ. of Edinburgh, 1961–69. Mem., Council, Hellen. Soc., 1964–67, 1973– ; Mngng Cttee, Brit. Sch. Athens, 1969–73. *Publications*: Early Greek Armour and Weapons, 1964; Arms and Armour of the Greeks, 1967; The Dark Age of Greece, 1971; *contrib*. Jl Hellen. Studies, Proc. Pre-

hist. Soc. *Address*: Dept of Classical Archaeology, 18–20 George Square, Edinburgh EH8 9JZ.

Snodgrass, Giulia Louise Margaret, MA, FLA; Lecturer, Department of Librarianship, University of Strathclyde, since 1964; *b* 1915. MA St Andrews 1936 (2nd cl. English Lang. and Lit.); FLA 1955. Organiser of Sch. Librs, Stirlingshire, 1957–63. *Address*: Dept of Librarianship, Univ. of Strathclyde, Livingstone Tower, Richmond Street, Glasgow G1 1XH.

Soddy, Dr Kenneth, MD, BS, FRCPsych; Lecturer in Child Psychiatry, University College Hospital Medical School, since 1948, and Honorary Lecturer in Psychology, University College, London, since 1952; *b* 1911; *m* 1936; 1972; one *s* two *d*. MB, BS London 1934, MD London 1938, DPM (RCP and S) 1937; FRCPsych, FRSocMed. Mem., Brit. Psychol. Assoc., Mem., Assoc. Child Psychol. Psychiat. Chm., Inst. Relig. Med., 1964–71; Pro-Chm., Inst. Relig. Med., 1971–74; Mem., HMC, St Lawrence's Hosp., Caterham, 1961–74; Gov., Cranborne Chase Sch.; Mem., Expert Panel, Wld Hlth Organisation. *Publications*: Clinical Child Psychiatry, 1960; (with R. F. Tredgold) Tredgold's Textbook of Mental Deficiency, 9th, 10th and 11th edns, 1956, 1963, 1970; (with R. H. Ahrenfeldt) Mental Health in a Changing World, 1965; Mental Health and Contemporary Thought, 1967; Mental Health in the Service of the Community, 1967; (with M. C. Kidson) Men in Middle Life, 1967; Ed., Mental Health and Infant Development, 1955; Cross Cultural Studies in Mental Health: Identity; Mental Health and Value Systems, 1961; *contrib*. numerous articles. *Address*: Univ. College Hospital, Gower Street, WC1E 6AU.

Sorabji, Richard Rustom Kharsedji; Lecturer, Department of Philosophy, King's College, University of London, since 1970; *b* 1934; *m* 1958; one *s* two *d*. BA 1959, BPhil 1962, Oxon. Asst Prof., 1962–67, Associate Prof., 1967–70, Cornell Univ. *Publications*: Aristotle on Memory, 1972; ed (jtly), Aristotle, 4 vols (forthcoming); *contrib*. Amer. Philos. Qly, Class. Qly, Philos. Qly, Philos. Rev., Philos., Proc. Aristotelian Soc. *Address*: Dept of Philosophy, King's College, Strand, WC2R 2LS.

Soskice, David William; Official Fellow and Tutor in Economics, University College, Oxford, and University Lecturer in Economics, Oxford, since 1967; *b* 1942; *m* 1965; one *s* one *d*. BA 1961, MA 1969, Oxon. *Address*: Univ. Coll., Oxford.

Souffrin, E.; *see* Le Breton, E. M.

Southern, Richard William, FBA; President of St John's College, Oxford, since 1969; *b* 1912; *m* 1944; two *s*. BA Oxon 1932 (1st cl. Hons Mod. Hist); Hon. DLitt Glasgow 1964, Hon. DLitt Durham 1969, Hon. DLitt Cantab 1971, Hon. DLitt Bristol 1974; FBA 1960, FRHistS (Pres., 1968–). Junior Res. Fellow, Exeter Coll., Oxford, 1933–37; Fellow and Tutor, Balliol Coll., Oxford, 1937–61 (Hon. Fellow, 1966); Jun. Proctor, Oxford

Univ., 1948–49; Birkbeck Lectr in Ecclesiastical Hist., Trinity Coll., Cambridge, 1959–60; Chichele Prof. of Mod. Hist., Oxford, 1961–69. Lectures, at Brit. Acad., 1962, and at Glasgow Univ., 1963 and 1970–72. Pres., Selden Soc., 1973– . Corr. Fellow, Medieval Acad. of America, 1965; For. Hon. Mem., Amer. Acad. Arts and Sciences, 1972; Hon. Fellow, Sidney Sussex Coll., Cambridge, 1971. *Publications*: The Making of the Middle Ages, 1953 (numerous for. translations); Western Views of Islam in the Middle Ages, 1962; ed, Eadmer's Vita Anselmi, 1963; St Anselm and his Biographer, 1963; ed (with F. S. Schmitt), Memorials of St Anselm, 1969; Medieval Humanism and other studies, 1970 (RSL award 1970); Western Society and the Church in the Middle Ages, 1970; *contrib*. English Historical Review, Medieval and Renaissance Studies, Trans RHistS, etc. *Address*: President's Lodgings, St John's College, Oxford.

Southgate, Donald George, BA, DPhil; Reader in Political and Constitutional History, University of Dundee, since 1969; *b* 1924; *m* 1950; two *s* one *d*. BA London 1944 (1st cl. Hist.), DPhil Oxon 1949; FRHistS. Asst Lectr, Exeter, 1947–50; Lectr, Exeter, 1950–51; Sen. Lectr, Rhodes Univ., S Africa, 1951–53; Temp. Aptmt (Politics), Glasgow Univ., 1955–56; Lectr, Univ. of St Andrews (Queen's Coll., Dundee), 1956–65; Sen. Lectr, Univ. of St Andrews (Queen's Coll., Dundee), 1965–67; Sen. Lectr, Univ. of Dundee, 1967–69. Mem., Univ. Court, 1971. *Publications*: The Passing of the Whigs 1832–85, 1962; The Most English Minister, The Policies and Politics of Palmerston, 1966; ed, The Conservative Leadership 1830–1937, 1974; contrib. Britain Pre-Eminent, ed C. J. Bartlett, 1971; Victorian Liberalism, ed F. S. L. Lyons (forthcoming); Annual Register (British section), 1947–51; *contrib*. Third Stat. Acc. of Scot. (Glasgow, Dundee, Angus Volumes), Abertay Histl Soc. pubs. *Address*: Dept of Modern History, Univ. of Dundee, Dundee DD1 4HN.

Southgate, Vera; *see* Booth, V. S.

Sowden, Dr John Kenneth; Lecturer in German, University of Bradford, since 1966; *b* 1920; *m* 1948; one *s*. BA London External 1951 (2nd cl.), PhD Leicester 1962. Lektor, Univ. des Saarlandes, 1952–61; Akademischer Rat (Anglistik) und Lehrbeauftragter (Dolmetscherinst), 1961–66. Mem., Bd, Wissenschaft, Prüfung. Lehramt Höheren Schulen; Regierungsrat Hochschuldienst. *Publications*: contrib. Germ. Life Lett., Mod. Lang. Rev. *Address*: School of Modern Languages, Univ. of Bradford, Bradford BD7 1DP.

Sowter, Dr Anthony Peter; Lecturer, Economics Department, University of Nottingham, since 1968; *b* 1946; *m* 1967, 1973. BSc Nottingham 1966 (2nd cl., jt Hons, Maths/Econs), PhD Nottingham 1969; FSS 1968. Asst Lectr, Univ. of Nottingham, 1968–70. Various consultancies. *Publications*: contrib. Applied Econs, Brit. Jl Marketing, Jl of Marketing Res. *Address*: Economics Dept, University Park, Nottingham NG7 2RD.

Spalding, Prof. Keith, MA, PhD; Professor of German, University College of North Wales, Bangor, since 1953; *b* 1913; *m* 1946. BA Birmingham 1937, MA Birmingham 1938, PhD Birmingham 1940; Hon. Dr phil Tübingen 1972. Asst Lectr, Univ. Coll. of Swansea, 1946–48; Lectr, Univ. Coll., Swansea, 1948–50; Hd of Dept of German and Teutonic Philology, Bangor, 1950–53. Mem., Council and Bd of Govs, Bangor, 1955–58, 1968–71; Dean, Fac. of Arts, Bangor, 1956–58; Mem., Univ. of Wales Acad. Bd, 1958–62. *Publications*: Kultur oder Vernichtung, 1933, 2nd edn 1947; An Introduction to the German Language, 1939; ed, Der Ackermann aus Böhmen, 1950; ed, Selections from Adalbert Stifter, 1952; An Historical Dictionary of German Figurative Usage, 1952– ; ed, German Advanced Unseens, 1958, 3rd edn 1964; German Word Patterns, 1962; ed, German Simple Unseens, 1963; ed, Grillparzer's Sappho, 1965; ed, Stifter's Abdias. 1966; ed, Goethe's Hermann und Dorothea, 1968; Assoc. Ed., Langenscheidts Enzyklopädisches Wörterbuch, English–German, Deutsch–Englisch, 1951– ; *contrib*. Archiv. Lingu., Germ. Life Lett., Gwerin, Mod. Lang. Rev., Mod. Langs, Muttersprache, Zeits. Deuts. Wortfors. *Address*: Dept. of German and Teutonic Philology and of Russian, Univ. College of North Wales, Bangor, Gwynedd LL57 2DG.

Spark, Barbara Mary; Lecturer in Physical Education and Outdoor Activities, University College of North Wales, Bangor, since 1965; *b* 1936. Dip. in Physical Education I. M. Marsh College 1957; Mountain Instructors Adv. Cert., Brit. Assoc. Ski Instructors Grade III. *Address*: Physical Education Dept, Univ. College of North Wales, Bangor LL57 2DG.

Sparkes, Dr Brian A., BA, AKC, PhD; Senior Lecturer, Department of Classics, Southampton University, since 1971; *b* 1933; *m* 1959; one *s* one *d*. BA London 1955 (1st cl. Classics), AKC London 1955, PhD London 1957. Asst Lectr, Southampton, 1958–60; Lectr, Southampton, 1960–71; Ed., Jl Hellen. Studies, 1964–72; Vis. Fellow, Inst. Adv. Studies, Princeton, 1962–63. Mem., Council, Soc. Prom. Hellen. Studies, 1964–72; Mngr's Cttee, Inst. Classical Studies, London, 1964–72; Brit. Sch. Athens. *Publications*: (with L. Talcott) Pots and Pans of Classical Athens, 1959; (with L. Talcott) The Athenian Agora, vol. XII: Black and Plain Pottery of the 6th, 5th and 4th centuries BC, 1970; *contrib*. Antike Kunst, Jl Hellen. Studies. *Address*: Dept of Classics, Univ. of Southampton, Southampton SO9 5NH.

Sparkes, John R.; Lecturer in Economics, School of Studies in Management, University of Bradford, since 1965; *b* 1942; *m* 1966; one *s* one *d*. BA Wales 1963, MScEcon 1965. Asst Lectr in Economics, Univ. of Bradford, 19 65 67. Warden of Halls of Residence, 1968– . *Publications*: (with C. L. Pass) Industry and Trade: A Study of the UK in the World Economy, in, Bradford Exercises in Management, 1966; The Structure of Industry, in, Principles of Modern Management, 1972; (with B. Lowes) Modern Managerial nomics, 1974; (with B. Taylor) Corporate and Strategic Planning (forthcoming); *contrib.* Bus. Economist, Bus. Horizons, Jl Bus. Policy, Econs, Management Accounting, Management Decision, Michigan Bus. Rev. *Address*: Univ. of Bradford, Management Centre, Emm Lane, Bradford BD9 4JL.

Sparks, Bruce Wilfred, MA; University Lecturer in Geography, University of Cambridge, since 1954; *b* 1923; *m* 1946; three *s* one *d*. BA London 1947 (1st cl. Geog.), MA London 1949 (with distinction), MA Cambridge 1949; FGS, FLS, FRGS. Lectr, Queen Mary Coll., London, 1947–49; Univ. Demonstrator, Cambridge, 1949–54; Fellow, Jesus Coll., Cambridge, 1962; Steward, Jesus Coll., Cambridge, 1964–69; Sen. Tutor, Jesus Coll., Cambridge, 1970– . *Publications*: Geomorphology, 1960, 2nd edn 1972; Rocks and Relief, 1971; (with R. G. West) The Ice Age in Britain,1972; trans., Guilcher: Coastal and Submarine Morphology, 1958; *contrib.* Eiszeit. Gegen., Geog. Jl, Geol. Mag., Jl Conch., Jl Ecol., Phil. Trans Royal Soc. B, Proc. Geol. Assoc., Proc. Jl Linn. Soc., Proc. Malac. Soc., Trans Inst. Brit. Geogrs. *Address*: Jesus College, Cambridge.

Sparks, Dr Richard Franklin, BSc, PhD; Assistant Director of Research, Institute of Criminology, University of Cambridge, since 1967; *b* 1933; *m* 1961; one *s* two *d*. BSc Northwestern 1954, PhD Cantab 1966. Lectr in Criminal Law and Criminology, Univ. of Birmingham, 1964–67. *Publications*: (with R. G. Hood) Key Issues in Criminology, 1970; Local Prisons: the Crisis in the English Penal System, 1971; *contrib.* Brit. Jl Criminol., Crim. Law Rev., Mod. Law Rev., Sociol. Rev. Monogs. *Address*: Institute of Criminology, 7 West Road, Cambridge.

Sparrow, John Hanbury Angus, OBE; Warden of All Souls College, Oxford, since 1952; *b* 1906. Hon. Mods Oxford 1927 (1st cl.), Lit. Hum. Oxford 1929 (1st cl.), Hon. DLitt Warwick 1967. Fellow of All Souls Coll., 1929, re-elected 1937, 1946. Called to Bar, Middle Temple, 1931; practised in Chancery Division, 1931–39. DAAG and AAG, War Office, 1942–45; resumed practice at Bar 1946–52; Hon. Bencher, Middle Temple, 1952. Fellow of Winchester Coll., 1951; Hon. Fellow, New Coll., 1956. *Publications*: various; mostly reviews and essays in periodicals, some of which were collected in Independent Essays, 1963, and Controversial Essays, 1966; Mark Pattison and the Idea of a University (Clark Lectures), 1967; After the Assassination, 1968; Visible Words (Sandars Lectures), 1969. *Address*: All Souls College, Oxford.

Spear, Hilda D.; Lecturer, English Department, University of Dundee, since 1969; *b* 1926; *m* 1952; two *d*. BA London 1951, MA London 1953, PhD Leicester, 1972; Teacher's Cert. 1946. Mem., Engl. Assoc. Lectr, Dept of English, Purdue Univ., USA, 1957–58; Lectr, Sch. of Educn, Leicester, 1965–67; Tutor, Dept of English, Leicester, 1967–68. *Publications*: ed, The English Poems of C. S. Calverley, 1974; contrib. Pelican Guide to English Literature; *contrib.* Notes Queries, Univ. Kansas City Rev., Use Engl. *Address*: Dept of English, Dundee Univ., Dundee DD1 4HN.

Spear, Ruskin, RA; Tutor, Painting School, Royal College of Art; *b* 1911; *m* 1935; one *s* one *d*. RA 1954 (ARA 1944), RCA 1950; Pres., London Gp, 1950. Mem., many selection cttees in London and provinces. Exhibitions, London, Moscow, and most provincial galleries. *Publication*: contrib. William Gaunt, Concise History of English Painting, 1964. *Address*: Royal Coll. of Art, Kensington Gore, SW7 2EU.

Spearing, Anthony Colin; University Lecturer, Faculty of English, Cambridge University, since 1964; *b* 1936; *m* 1961; one *s* one *d*. BA Cantab 1957, MA Cantab 1960. Res. Fellow, Gonville and Caius Coll., Cambridge, 1959–60; Asst Lectr in English, Cambridge, 1959–64; Off. Fellow, Queens' Coll., Cambridge, 1960– ; Dir of Studies in English, Queens' Coll., 1967– ; Libr., Queens' Coll., 1964–69. Sec., Fac. Bd of Engl., Cambridge, 1969–70. *Publications*: Criticism and Medieval Poetry, 1964, 2nd edn 1972; (with M. Hussey and J. Winny) An Introduction to Chaucer, 1965, 3rd edn 1972; ed, Chaucer: Pardoner's Tale, 1965, 2nd edn 1971; ed, Chaucer: Franklin's Tale, 1966, 2nd edn 1971; ed, Chaucer: Knight's Tale, 1966; The Gawain-Poet, 1970; ed (with J. E. Spearing), Shakespeare: The Tempest, 1972; ed (with J. E. Spearing), Poetry of the Age of Chaucer, 1974; *contrib.* Anglia, Jl Engl. Germ. Philol., Mod. Philol., Rev. Engl. Studies, Specul. *Address*: Queens' College, Cambridge.

Spears, David Alan, BSc, PhD; Lecturer in Geology, University of Sheffield, since 1965; *b* 1938; *m* 1962; two *s* two *d*. BSc Sheffield 1959, PhD Sheffield 1963. Mem., Yorks Geol. Soc., SEPM. Res. Asst, Univ. of Sheffield, 1963–65. Mem., Council, Yorks Geol. Soc., 1970– . *Publications*: Compte Rendu, Carboniferous Congress, 1967; *contrib.* Clays Clay Min., Econ. Geol., Geochim. Cosmo., Jl Sed. Petrol., Oil Jl, Proc. Yorks Geol. Soc., Qly Jl Eng. Geol., Sediment. *Address*: Dept of Geology, Univ. of Sheffield, Sheffield S1 3JD.

Speight, Harold; Senior Lecturer, School of Economic Studies, University of Leeds, since 1966; *b* 1916. BA London 1938, DipEd London 1939. Asst Lectr, Leeds, 1947–50; Lectr, Leeds, 1950–66. Mem., Gov. Body of Sec. Schs, Rothwell Div. W Riding CC, 1955–64; Mem. Bd of Governors, Park Lane Coll. Further Educn, Leeds, 1962–67. *Publications*: Economics: The Science of Prices and Incomes, 1960, 3rd edn 1968; Economics and Industrial Efficiency, 1962, 3rd edn 1970; *contrib.* Bank. Mag., Jl Indust. Econ. *Address*: School of Economic Studies, The Univ., Leeds LS2 9JT.

Speitel, Dr Hans-Henning; Lecturer, Linguistic Survey of Scotland, University of Edinburgh, since 1964; *b* 1937; *m* 1963; two *d*. PhD Edinburgh 1969 (Linguistics). Mem., Philological Soc. Part-time Asst Lectr, Univ. Edinburgh, 1961–64. *Publications*: *contrib.* ZMF, Phon., A Ling. *Address*: Linguistic

Survey of Scotland, Univ. of Edinburgh, 24 Buccleuch Place, Edinburgh EH8 9LN.

Spence, Prof. John Edward; Professor of Politics, University of Leicester, since 1973; *b* 1931; *m* 1959; one *d*. BA Hons Rand 1952, BScEcon London 1957; Member: Inst. of Strategic Studies; RIIA; African Studies Assoc. of UK. Lectr in Politics, Univ. of Natal, 1958–60; Rockefeller Jl Res. Fellow, LSE, 1961–62; Univ. Coll., Swansea: Lectr in Politics, 1962–68; Sen. Lectr in Politics, 1968–72; Reader in Politics, 1972–73; Vis. Prof., Univ. of Calif., LA, 1965–66 and 1970–71. Member: Adv. Panel on Arms Control and Disarmament, FCO, 1968– ; Pol Sci. Cttee, SSRC, 1969–74; Council, African Studies Assoc. of UK, 1970–74; Exec. Cttee, Brit. Internat. Studies Assoc., 1974– ; Combined Studies Panel, Council for Nat. Academic Awards, 1974. Jt Editor, Jl of Southern African Studies, 1974– . *Publications*: Republic under Pressure, 1965; Lesotho: the politics of dependence, 1967; The Strategic Significance of Southern Africa, 1970; contrib. Oxford History of South Africa, vol. 2; *contrib*. African Affairs, Europa Archiv, Govt and Opposition, Jl Commonwealth Pol Studies, World Today, Theoria, Round Table, Survival. *Address*: Dept of Politics, Univ. of Leicester, Leicester LE1 7RH.

Spence, Dr Nicol Christopher William; Reader in French, Bedford College, London University, since 1966; *b* 1924; *m* 1959; one *s* one *d*. BA Leeds 1948 (1st cl. Mod. Langs), PhD London 1955. Asst Lectr, Queen's Univ., Belfast, 1951–54; Asst Lectr, Univ. Coll. N Staffs, 1954–55; Temp. Lectr, Queen's Univ., Belfast, 1955; Lectr, Queen's Univ., Belfast, 1956–60; Reader, Queen's Univ., Belfast, 1961–66. *Publications*: A Glossary of Jersey-French, 1960; (with M. M. Pelan) Narcisus (poème du XII siècle), 1964; contrib. Encyclopaedia of Linguistics, Information and Control, 1969; *contrib*. Archiv. Lingu., Lingua, Linguist., Neophilol., Rev. Lingu. Rom., Rev. Rom., Rom. Jbh., Trans Philol. Soc., Vox Rom., Word. *Address*: Dept of French, Bedford College, Regent's Park, NW1 4NS.

Spence, Dr Nigel; Lecturer, Department of Geography, London School of Economics, since 1968; *b* 1944; *m* 1969; one *d*. BSc Wales 1966; PhD London1974. *Publications*: contrib. Prog. in Geog., Regnl Studies. *Address*: London Sch. of Economics, Houghton Street, Aldwych, WC2A 2AE.

Spencer, Dr Herbert; Senior Research Fellow, Readability of Print Research Unit, Royal College of Art, since 1966; *b* 1924; *m* 1954; one *d*. Dr RCA 1970; RDI 1965, FSIA 1948. Internat. Pres., Alliance Graphique Internationale (AGI), 1971–74. Editor: Typographica Magazine, 1949–67; The Penrose Annual, 1964–73. *Publications*: Design in Business Printing, 1952; The Visible Word, 1969; Pioneers of Modern Typography, 1969, German edn 1970; (with Colin Forbes) New Alphabets A to Z, 1973. *Address*: Royal Coll. of Art, Kensington Gore, SW7 2EU.

Spencer, Prof. John C., MA, PhD; Professor of Social Administration, University of Edinburgh, since 1967; *b* 1915; *m* 1950; one *s* one *d*. BA Oxon 1938 (2nd cl. PPE), MA Oxon 1947, Cert. Social Science LSE 1939 (dist.), PhD London 1951; FRSA. Mem., Brit. Sociol. Assoc., Brit. Assoc. Social Workers. Lectr, LSE, 1946–53; Res. Fellow, Bristol Univ., 1953–58; Sen. Simon Res. Fellow, Manchester Univ., 1958–59; Prof., Toronto Univ., 1959–67. Chm., Scott. Adv. Cttee, Council for Educn and Training in Social Work; Mem. Council. Chm., Children's Panel Adv. Cttee, Edinburgh; Vice-Chm., Scott. Council Social Serv.; Mem., Adv. Council Social Wk in Scott.; Cttee on Criminal Procedure Scot.; Ed. Bd: Brit. Jl Criminol.; Brit. Jl Social Policy. *Publications*: Crime and the Services, 1954; ed (with T. Grygier and H. Jones), Criminology in Transition, 1965; (with N. Dennis and J. Tuxford) Stress and Release in an Urban Estate, 1964; contrib. Encyclopaedia Britannica; *contrib*. Brit. Jl Delinq., Canad. Jl Correct., Criminol. Police Sci., Jl Crim. Law, Soc. Serv. Rev., Sociol. Rev. *Address*: Dept of Social Administration, Univ. of Edinburgh, Edinburgh EH8 9LL.

Spencer, Prof. John Ervine; Professor of Economics, New University of Ulster, since 1971; *b* 1942. BScEcon QUB 1964 (1st cl. Hons); Member: Royal Econ. Soc., Amer. Econ. Assoc., Econometric Soc., Statistical and Social Inquiry Soc. of Ireland. Lectr in Econs, QUB, 1964–69; Henry Fellow at Yale Univ., 1965–66; Lectr in Econs, LSE, 1969–71; Sen. Lectr, NUU, 1971. *Publications*: (with R. C. Geary) Elements of Linear Programming with Economic Applications (No 15 of Griffin's Statistical Monographs and Courses), 2nd edn 1973 (1st edn by Geary and McCarthy); (with R. C. Geary) Exercises in Mathematical Economics and Econometrics, 1974; *contrib*. Nat. Inst. Econ. Review. *Address*: School of Social Sciences, New Univ. of Ulster, Coleraine BT52 1SA.

Spencer, John Walter; Director, Institute of Modern English Language Studies, and Senior Lecturer, School of English, University of Leeds, since 1965; *b* 1922; *m* 1944. BA Oxford 1949 (Engl. Lang. and Lit.), MA Oxford 1956. Mem., Philol. Soc., Mem., Internat. Phonet. Assoc., Mem., Brit. Assoc. Appl. Lingu., Afr. Studies Assoc. UK. Lectr, Univ. of Lund, Sweden, 1949–52; Asst Lectr, Phonetics Dept, Univ. of Edinburgh, 1955–56; Assoc. Prof., English Lang. Inst., Allahabad, India, 1956–58; Vis. Reader, Linguistics Inst., Univ. of the Panjab, Pakistan, 1958–59; Hd of Dept of Phonetics, Univ. of Ibadan, Nigeria, 1959–62; Lectr, Sch. of English, Univ. of Leeds, 1962–65. Ed., Jl W Afr. Langs, 1963–71; Ed., W Afr. Lang. Monogs, 1963– . *Publications*: Workers for Humanity, 1963; ed, Language in Africa, 1963; (with Enkvist and Gregory) Linguistics and Style, 1964; (with Wollman) Modern Poems for the Commonwealth, 1966; ed, The English Language in West Africa, 1971; *contrib*. Curr. Trends Lingu., Lingua, Phonet., Sierra Leone Lang. Rev., etc. *Address*: Institute of Modern English

Language Studies, School of English, Univ. of Leeds, Leeds LS2 9JT.

Spencer, Robin; Lecturer in the History of Art, Department of Fine Arts, St Salvator's College, University of St Andrews, since 1969 (on leave of absence as Director, Krazy Kat Arkive, since 1974); *b* 1944; *m* 1970. BA Manchester 1966, MA London 1968. Res. Asst, Whistler Collections etc, Univ. of Glasgow, 1968–69; Leverhulme Fellow in the History of Western Art, Jesus Coll., Cambridge, 1972–73. *Publications*: Whistler, 1969 (exhibition catalogue); The Aesthetic Movement; Theory and Practice, 1972. *Address*: Dept of Fine Arts, St Salvator's Coll., Univ. of St Andrews, St Andrews, Fife KY16 9AJ.

Spencer, Prof. Terence John Bew; Professor of English Language and Literature, University of Birmingham, since 1958; Director, Shakespeare Institute, since 1961; *b* 1915; *m* 1948; three *d*. BA London, PhD London. Asst, King's Coll., London, 1938–40; Brit. Council Lectr, Rome and Athens, 1939–41; Asst Lectr, subseq. Lectr, UCL, 1946–55; Prof. of English, Queen's Univ., Belfast, 1955–58; Turnbull Prof. of Poetry, Johns Hopkins Univ., 1968; Berg Prof. of English, NY Univ., 1974. Hon. Sec., Shakespeare Assoc., 1950– ; Mem., Bd, Nat. Theatre, 1968– ; Gov., Royal Shakespeare Theatre, 1968– . Gen. Ed., New Penguin Shakespeare; Gen. Ed., Penguin Shakespeare Libr.; English Ed., 1956– , Gen. Ed., 1960– , Mod. Lang. Rev.; Ed., Year Bk of English Studies, 1971– . *Publications*: Fair Greece, Sad Relic: Literary Philhellenism from Shakespeare to Byron, 1954; ed (with James Sutherland), W. P. Ker: On Modern Literature, 1955; From Gibbon to Darwin, 1959; The Tyranny of Shakespeare, 1959; Byron and the Greek Tradition, 1960; Shakespeare: The Roman Plays, 1963; ed, Shakespeare's Plutarch, 1964; ed, Shakespeare: A Celebration, 1964; ed, Romeo and Juliet, 1967; ed, A Book of Masques, 1967; Elizabethan Love Stories, 1968; *contrib*. books and jls. *Address*: The Shakespeare Institute, Univ. of Birmingham, Birmingham B15 2TT.

Spiller, Michael Ryder Gordon; Lecturer, Department of English, University of Aberdeen, since 1966; *b* 1941; *m* 1962; two *d*. MA Hons Edinburgh 1963 (1st cl. Eng. Lang. and Lit.), BLitt Oxford 1968. Teaching Fellow, Univ. of Michigan, Ann Arbor, USA, 1963–64. *Publication*: *contrib*. Rev. English Studies. *Address*: Dept of English, Taylor Bldg, Univ. of Aberdeen, Aberdeen AB9 2UB.

Spink, Ian; Reader and Head of Music Department, since 1971, and Dean, Faculty of Arts, since 1973, Royal Holloway College, University of London; *b* 1932; *m* 1960; two *s* three *d*. BMus London 1952, MA Birmingham 1958; FTCL, ARCM. Lectr in Music, Univ. of Sydney, 1962–65, Sen. Lectr, 1966–69; Sen. Lectr in Music, Royal Holloway Coll., Univ. of London, 1969–71. *Publications*: incl. An Historical Approach to Musical Form, 1967; English Song, 1625–1660, in, Musica Britannica,

xxxiii, 1971; English Song: Dowland to Purcell, 1974; *contrib*. Acta Musicologica, Music and Letters, Proc. Royal Musical Assoc., etc. *Address*: Royal Holloway Coll., Egham, Surrey TW20 0EX.

Spolton, Lewis; Senior Lecturer in Education, University College of Swansea, since 1967; *b* 1916; *m* 1940; one *s* one *d*. BSc London (1st cl. Geog.), DipEd, MEd Nottingham 1951; FRMetS 1942. Lectr in Educn, Univ. Coll., Swansea, 1961–67; Warden, Neuadd Sibly, 1969–73. RAF Meteorol. Br., 1943–46; Chm., Comp. Soc. Europe, Brit. Sect., 1971–73. *Publications*: The Upper Secondary School: a comparative survey, 1967; (with D. Riley) World Weather and Climate, 1974; *contrib*. Brit. Jl Educnl Studies, Comp. Educn. *Address*: Univ. College, Singleton Park, Swansea SA2 8PP.

Spooner, Dr Derek John; Lecturer in Geography, University of Hull, since 1970; *b* 1943; *m* 1969. BA Cantab 1965, MA Cantab 1969, PhD Cantab 1972; Member: Inst. Brit. Geogrs, Regional Studies Assoc. Asst Lectr, Univ. Hull, 1968–70. Hall Tutor, Univ. Hull, 1968–69; Tutor-in-charge, Godolphin House, Univ. Hull, 1969–70. *Publications*: *contrib*. Regional Studies, Town Planning Review. *Address*: Dept of Geography, Univ. of Hull, Hull HU6 7RX.

Spooner, Prof. Frank Clyffurde, MA, PhD; Professor of Economic History, University of Durham, since 1966; *b* 1924. BA Cantab 1948 (1st cl. Hist. Tripos, Pts I and II), MA Cantab 1949, PhD Cantab 1953; FRHS, Lauréat de l'Acad. des Sciences Morales et Pol. 1957; Member: Amer. Econ. Assoc., Camb. Hist. Soc., Econ. Hist. Assoc., Econ Hist. Soc., Hakluyt Soc., Royal Econ. Soc., Soc. Franç. Numismat., Veren. Neder. Econ.-Hist. Archief. Chargé de Recherches, CNRS Paris, 1949; Fellow, Christ's Coll., Cambridge, 1951–57; Commonwealth Fund Fellow, 1955–57; Ecole Pratique des Hautes Etudes, Sorbonne, 1957–61; Lectr, Oxford, 1958–59; Vis. Lectr in Econs, Harvard, 1961–62; Irving Fisher Res. Prof. of Econs, Yale, 1962–63; Lectr, Durham, 1963; Reader, Durham, 1964–66. Hd of Dept of Econ. Hist., Durham, since 1965; Senate since 1965; Curator of the Library, 1967–70; Council, 1968–71; Director of the Inst. of European Studies since 1969. *Publications*: L'economie mondiale et les frappes monétaires en France, 1493–1680, 1956; The International Economy and Monetary Movements in France 1493–1725, 1972; chapters, essays, etc.: (with F. Braudel) Les métaux monétaires et l'economie du XVIe siècle, 1955; A la côte de Guinée sous pavillon français, in, Studi in onore di Armando Sapori, 1957; La Normandie à l'époque des guerres civiles: un problème de l'économie internationale, in, Annales de Normandie, VIII, 1958; The Reformation in France, 1519 to 1559 and The Hapsburg–Valois Rivalry, 1519 to 1559, in, The Revised Cambridge Modern History, vol. II, 1958; Venice and the Levant: an aspect of monetary history (1610–1614), in Studi in onore di Amintore Fanfani, 1962; Secular price movements and problems in capital accumulation, 1965; (with

F. Braudel) The History of Prices in Europe (1450–1760), in, The Cambridge Economic History of Europe, vol. IV, 1965; The Economy of Europe, 1559 to 1609, in, The Revised Cambridge Modern History, vol. III, 1969; The Economy of Europe, 1609 to 1650, in, The Revised Cambridge Modern History, vol. IV, 1970; The Suez Canal and the growth of the international economy, 1869–1914, in, Mediterraneo e Oceano Indiano, ed, M. Cortelazzo, 1970; Monetary Disturbance and Inflation, 1590–1593: the case of Aix-en-Provence, 1972; *contrib.* Cah. Ann., Camb. Hist. Jl. *Address*: Dept of Economic History, Univ. of Durham, Durham DH1 3HY.

Spraos, Prof. John; Professor of Political Economy, University College, University of London, since 1965; *b* 1926; *m* 1956; one *s* one *d*. MA Edinburgh 1950 (1st cl. Econs). Res. Fellow, Univ. of Sheffield, 1953–57; Lectr, Univ. Coll., London, 1957–64; Reader, Univ. Coll., London, 1964–65. Mem., Ed. Bd, Rev. Econ. Studies, 1955–65; Exec. Cttee, Assoc. Univ. Teachers of Econ., 1966– ; Econ. Adv. Bd, Penguin Educn, 1966– ; Chm., Greek Cttee Against Dictatorship, 1967– . *Publications*: The Decline of the Cinema: an Economist's Report, 1962; *contrib.* Econ. Jl, Economica, Manch. Sch., Qly Jl Econ. *Address*: Univ. College, Gower Street, WC1E 6BT.

Sprigg, Richard Keith, MA, PhD; Reader in Phonetics, University of London, since 1968; *b* 1922; *m* 1952; one *s* one *d*. BA Cantab 1944 (1st cl. Classics), MA Cantab 1947, PhD London 1969. Lectr, London Univ., 1948–67. *Publications*: contrib. Studies in Linguistic Analysis, 1957, 2nd edn 1962; Linguistic Comparison in South East Asia and the Pacific, 1963; In memory of J. R. Firth, 1966; Prosodic Analysis, 1970; *contrib.* AM (NS), Anthropol. Lingu., AOH, Bull. SOAS, Bull. Tibetol., JBRS. Magy. Tud. Akad. I. *Address*: Dept of Phonetics and Linguistics, School of Oriental and African Studies, Univ. of London, Bloomsbury, WCIE 7HP.

Sprigge, Dr Timothy Lauro Squire; Reader in Philosophy, School of English and American Studies, University of Sussex, since 1970; *b* 1932; *m* 1959; one *s* two *d*. BA Cantab 1955, PhD Cantab 1961, MA Cantab 1961; Member: Mind Assoc.; Aristotelian Soc. Lecturer: UCL, 1961–63; Univ. of Sussex, 1963–70. *Publications*: ed, The Correspondence of Jeremy Bentham, vols 1 and 2, 1968; Facts, Words and Beliefs, 1970; Santayana: an examination of his philosophy, 1974; *contrib.* Inquiry, Mind, Philos. *Address*: Arts Building, Univ. of Sussex, Falmer, Brighton BN1 9QN.

Spring, Dr Derek William; Hayter Lecturer in Russian and East European History, Department of History, University of Nottingham, since 1967; *b* 1939; *m* 1965; one *s* one *d*. BA London 1961 (Hons Hist.), CertEd London 1962, PhD London 1968. Mem., Nat. Assoc. Sov. E Europ. Studies, Mem., Brit. Univ. Assoc. Slavists. Asst Lectr in Russian and E Europ. Hist., Univ. of Nottingham, 1965–67. *Address*: Dept of

History, Univ. of Nottingham, University Park, Nottingham NG7 2RD.

Spruce, Dorothy Jill, LLB; Lecturer in Law, Bristol University, since 1967; *b* 1939; *m* 1959; one *s* one *d*. LLB London 1964; Barrister-at-Law, Gray's Inn, 1966. *Address*: Faculty of Law, Bristol Univ., Queen's Road, Bristol.

Spufford, Dr Peter, MA, PhD; Reader in History, University of Keele, since 1973; *b* 1934; *m* 1962; one *s* one *d*. BA Cantab 1956 (1st cl. History), MA Cantab 1959, PhD Cantab 1963; FRHistS. Fellow Jesus Coll., Cambridge, 1958–60; Lectr, 1960–68, Sen. Lectr, 1968–73, Univ. of Keele; Vis. Fellow, Clare Hall, Cambridge, 1969–70. Hon. Sec., British Numismatic Soc., 1960–63; Hon. Sec., British Record Soc., 1960– . *Publications*: Origins of the English Parliament, 1967; Monetary Problems and Policies in the Burgundian Netherlands, 1970. *Address*: Dept of History, Univ. of Keele, Keele, Staffs ST5 5BG.

Squire, Dr Peter Stansfeld; Lecturer in Russian, University of Cambridge, since 1953; *b* 1920; *m* 1954. BA Cantab 1948 (1st cl. Russian), MA Cantab 1950, PhD Cantab 1958. Fellow, Churchill Coll., Cambridge, 1960– ; Dir of Studies in Modern Languages, Churchill Coll., Cambridge, 1961– ; Vis. Prof., Columbia Univ., 1965. Tutor, Adv. Students, Churchill Coll., 1963– . *Publications*: ed, Fourman: Science Russian Course, 1961; The Third Department, 1968; trans., The Memoirs of Ivanov–Razumnik, 1965; *contrib.* Slav. E Europ. Rev. *Address*: Dept of Slavonic Studies, Faculty of Modern and Medieval Languages, Univ. of Cambridge.

Squires, Finlay; *see* Squires, J. F. R.

Squires, J. E. R.; Lecturer in Logic and Metaphysics, University of St Andrews, since 1964; *b* 1940; *m* 1962; one *s* one *d*. BA Oxon 1961 (1st cl. PPE), MA Oxon 1966, BPhil Oxon 1964. *Publications*: *contrib.* Analysis, Mind, Philos. Qly, Philos. Rev., Philos. *Address*: Dept of Logic and Metaphysics, Univ. of St Andrews, Fife KY16 9AJ.

Squires, (James) Finlay (Robertson); Principal Lecturer, Department of Religious Education, Aberdeen College of Education, also Recognised Teacher, University of Aberdeen, since 1966; *b* 1932; *m* 1960; two *s* one *d*. MA Aberdeen 1957, BD Glasgow 1960 (with distinction); Post-grad. research, Princeton 1961, Marburg 1962. Asst Lectr, Glasgow Univ., 1962–65. *Address*: Dept of Religious Education, Aberdeen Coll. of Education, Hilton Place, Aberdeen AB9 1FA.

Stacey, Prof. Frank Arthur, MA, BPhil; Francis Hill Professor of Local Government, Department of Politics, University of Nottingham, since 1974; *b* 1923; *m* 1945; three *s* two *d*. BA Cambridge 1948 (1st cl. Hist. Tripos Pt II), BPhil Oxford 1950 (Politics). Asst Lectr in Politics, Swansea Univ. Coll., 1951–53; Lectr in Politics, Swansea Univ. Coll., 1953–67, Sen. Lectr, Dept of Political Theory and Govt, 1967–74. Hon. Sec., Public

Admin. Cttee, Jt Univ. Council for Social and Public Admin., 1968–71. *Publications*: The Government of Modern Britain, 1968; The British Ombudsman, 1971; A New Bill of Rights for Britain, 1973; *contrib*. Public Admin. *Address*: Dept of Politics, Univ. of Nottingham, Nottingham NG7 2RD.

Stacey, Prof. Margaret; Professor of Sociology, University of Warwick, since 1974; *b* 1922; *m* 1945; three *s* two *d*. BSc(Econ) London 1943 (1st cl. Sociol.). Foundn Mem., Brit. Sociol. Assoc., Hon. Gen. Sec., 1968–70. Extra-mural tutor, Oxford Univ., 1944–48; Jt extra-mural and social training tutor, Oxford Univ., 1948–51; Res. Off., Sociol., Lower Swansea Valley Project, Univ. Coll. of Swansea, 1961–62; Res. Fellow in Social Studies, Univ. Coll., Swansea, 1962–63; Lectr in Sociol., 1963–70, Sen. Lectr, 1970–74, Univ. Coll., Swansea. Mem., Welsh Hosp. Bd, 1970–74; Mem., Michael Davies Cttee on Hosp. Complaints Procedure, 1971–73. *Publications*: Tradition and Change: A Study of Banbury, 1960, pbk edn 1970; Methods of Social Research, 1969; ed, Comparability in Social Research, 1969; ed, Hospitals, Children and their Families, 1970; *contrib*. Brit. Jl Sociol., Sociol. Rev., Urb. Studies. *Address*: Dept of Sociology, Univ. of Warwick, Coventry CV4 7AL.

Stalker, Rev. David Muir Gibson; Senior Lecturer, and Head of Department of Biblical Studies, University of Edinburgh, since 1948; *b* 1909; *m* 1938; one *d*. MA Edinburgh 1932 (1st cl. Classics), BD Edinburgh 1935 (distinction, Hebrew and OT). Mem., Old Testament Soc., 1945, Mem., Soc. Study NT, 1945. Lectr in Biblical Studies, Univ. of Edinburgh, 1948–72; Kerr Lectr, Univ. of Glasgow, 1953–57. *Publications*: Old Testament parts in Syllabus of Religious Education for Secondary Schools in Scotland, 1945–53; Genesis, 1949; Genesis, 1956; trans., Von Rad: Studies in Deuteronomy, 1953; trans, Von Rad: Old Testament Theology, I, 1962, II, 1965; Ezekiel, 1968; trans, Westermann: Isaiah 40–66, 1970; trans, Bornkamen, Paul, 1971; *contrib*. Internat. Bible Read. Assoc., Jl Theol. Studies, Rec. Scott. Ch. Hist. Soc. *Address*: Dept of Biblical Studies, Univ. of Edinburgh, Edinburgh EH8 9YL.

Stammers, Robert Brian; Lecturer in Applied Psychology, University of Aston, since 1972; *b* 1947; *m* 1968; two *d*. BSc Hull 1968 (Psychol.); ABPsS 1972. Res. Asst, Hull, 1968–71; Res. Fellow, Aston, 1971–72. Sec. Trng Cttee, Ergonomics Res. Soc., 1973–74. *Publication*: (with others) Task Analysis. *Address*: Dept of Applied Psychology, Univ. of Aston, Birmingham B4 7ET.

Stamp, Prof. Edward, MA, CA; Professor of Accounting Theory, and Director of the International Centre for Research in Accounting, since 1971, Head of Department of Accounting and Finance, since 1973, University of Lancaster; *b* 1928; *m* 1953; one *s* three *d*. BA Cantab (1st cl. Hons, Nat. Scis), MA Cantab; CA. Sen. Lectr in Accountancy, Victoria Univ. of Wellington, NZ, 1962–65, Prof., 1965–67; Prof. and Hd of Dept of

Accounting and Finance, Univ. of Edinburgh, 1967–71; Vis. Professor: Univ. of Sydney, 1966; Univ. of NSW, 1967; European Inst. of Business Admin (INSEAD), Fontainebleau, 1967, 1970; Univ. of Nairobi, 1969, 1972. With Arthur Young, Clarkson, Gordon & Co., Chartered Accountants and Management Conslts, Toronto and Montreal, 1951–62 (Manager, 1957; Partner, 1961); Advr, HM Treasury, 1971– . Mem., Jt Standing Cttee on Degree Studies and Accounting Profession (UK), 1967–72 (Mem., Exec. Cttee, 1969–72); Mem., UK Adv. Bd of Accountancy Educn, 1969–72; Chm., Brit. Accounting and Finance Assoc., 1968–71 (Life Vice-Pres., 1971); Mem., Steering Cttee, Long-Range Enquiry into Accounting Educn, 1971– ; Mem., Editorial Board: Abacus (Australia), 1969– ; Jl of Business Finance, 1969– ; Internat. Register of Res. in Accounting and Finance, 1971– ; Accounting Rev., USA, 1972– . *Publications*: The Elements of Consolidation Accounting, 1965; Looking at Balance Sheets, 1967; Accounting Principles and the City Code: the case for reform, 1970; Corporate Financial Reporting, 1972; *contrib*. jls in England, Scotland, Canada, USA, Australia, NZ and South Africa, incl. Abacus, Accountancy, Accountants Jl (NZ), Accountants Mag., CA in Australia, Jl Accountancy (US), Jl Accountancy Res. (US), Jl Business Finance, Management Accounting. *Address*: Univ. of Lancaster, University House, Bailrigg, Lancaster LA1 4YW.

Standring, Dr Bernard, BA, PhD; Lecturer, Department of German, University of Birmingham, since 1964; *b* 1931; *m* 1966; one *s* one *d*. BA Birmingham 1960 (1st cl. German), PhD Birmingham 1969. Asst Lectr, Birmingham Univ., 1962–64. *Publication*: Die Gedichte des Wilden Mannes, 1963. *Address*: Dept of German, Univ. of Birmingham, PO Box 363, Birmingham B15 2TT.

Standring, John, MA; Senior Lecturer, Department of European Studies and Modern Languages, University of Manchester Institute of Science and Technology, since 1965; *b* 1915; *m* 1947. BA Cantab 1937, MA Cantab 1941, MA Manchester 1957. Lectr, Univ. of Manchester Inst. of Science and Technol., 1957–65. Mem., Oldham Educn Cttee. *Publications*: (with H. S. Jackson) French Course for Technologists and Scientists, 1960, American edn 1964; Bossuet: A Prose Anthology, 1962; Amusez-vous bien, 1965. *Address*: Dept of European Studies and Modern Languages, Univ. of Manchester, Institute of Science and Technology, Manchester M60 1QD.

Standwell, Graham John Burgoyne; Lecturer, Department of Linguistic Science, Reading University, since 1968; *b* 1938; *m* 1966; two *d*. BA Hons Durham 1959, MLitt 1963, FilKand Stockholm 1968; PGCE 1963 (Eng. as For. Lang.). *Publications*: *contrib*. AVLJ, Norw. Jl Linguistics, ZDL. *Address*: Dept of Linguistic Science, Univ. of Reading, Whiteknights Park, Reading RG6 2AH.

Stanford, Dr Stanley Charles; Senior Lecturer in Prehistory, Department of

Extramural Studies, University of Birmingham, since 1960; b 1927; m 1952; one s two d. BA London 1952, PGCE London 1953, PhD Birmingham 1972; FSA 1961, Member: Royal Archaeol Inst., 1958; Soc. for Med. Archaeol., 1957; Prehist. Soc., 1957; Soc. for Promotion of Roman Studies. *Publications*: Croft Ambrey, 1974; Invention, adoption and imposition: the evidence of the hill-forts, in, The Iron Age and its Hill-forts, ed M. Jesson and D. Hill, 1971; Welsh Border hill-forts, in, The Iron Age in the Irish Sea Province, ed C. Thomas, 1972; The function and population of hill-forts in the Central Marches, in, Prehistoric Man in Wales and the West, 1972; *contrib*. Archaeol Jl, Birmingham Archaeol Soc., Woolhope Naturalists' Field Club. *Address*: Dept of Extramural Studies, Univ. of Birmingham, Birmingham B15 2TT.

Stanford, Prof. William Bedell; Regius Professor of Greek, Trinity College, Dublin University, since 1940; b 1910; m 1935; two s two d. BA Dublin 1932 (1st cl. Classics and Anc. Hist., gold medals), MA Dublin 1935, LittD Dublin 1940; Mem., Royal Irish Acad. Fellow TCD, 1934, Sen. Fellow, 1962; Public Orator 1970–71. Sec., Aptmts Assoc., 1936–37; Mem., Bd of TCD, 1962– ; Univ. Council, 1967– ; Chm., Disciplinary Cttee, 1968–69; Chm., Amenities Cttee, 1969– ; Chm., Coun. of Dublin Inst. for Advanced Studies, 1972– . *Publications*: Greek Metaphor, 1936; Ambiguity in Greek Literature, 1939; Aeschylus in his Style, 1942; ed, Homer: Odyssey, 1947–48, 2nd edn 1961–62; The Ulysses Theme, 1954, 2nd edn 1963; ed, Aristophanes: Frogs, 1957, 2nd edn 1963; ed, Sophocles: Ajax, 1963; The Sound of Greek, 1967; (with R. B. McDowell) Mahaffy, 1971; *contrib*. Class. Phil., Class. Rev., Hermath., Phoenix, Jl Hellenic Studies, Proc. Royal Irish Acad. *Address*: 40 Trinity College, Dublin 2.

Stanforth, Dr Anthony William, MA, DrPhil; Lecturer in German, Department of German and Scandinavian Studies, University of Newcastle upon Tyne, since 1965; b 1938; m 1971. BA Dunelm 1960, MA Dunelm 1962, DrPhil Marburg 1964. Earl Grey Memorial Fellow, King's Coll., Newcastle, 1962–64; Lectr in German, Univ. of Manchester, 1964–65; Vis. Asst Prof., Univ. of Wisconsin, 1970–71. *Publication*: Die Bezeichnungen für 'gross', 'klein', 'viel' und 'wenig' im Bereich der Germania, 1967. *Address*: Dept of German and Scandinavian Studies, The Univ., Newcastle upon Tyne NE1 7RU.

Staniland, Martin; Lecturer, Department of Politics, University of Glasgow, since 1969; b 1941. BA Cantab 1963, MA Ghana 1965 (African Studies); Mem. African Studies Assoc. of UK. Fellow, Inst. Develt Studies, Univ. Sussex, 1967–69. Dep. Chm., Sub-Faculty of Social Sciences, Glasgow Univ. *Publications*: contrib. Politics and Change in Developing Countries, ed C. Leys, 1969; contrib. African Perspectives: Essays Presented to Thomas Hodgkin, ed Allen and Johnson, 1970; *contrib*. Afr. Affairs, Etudes Congolaises, Jl Admin Overseas, Jl

Afr. History, Jl Develt Studies, Jl Mod. Afr· Studies. *Address*: Dept of Politics, Univ. of Glasgow, Glasgow G12 8RT.

Stanley, Michael James; Lecturer in Geography, University of Edinburgh, since 1961; b 1937; m 1960. BA Birmingham; Mem. IBG, Mem., Econ. Hist. Soc., Mem., Agricultural History Soc. *Address*: Dept of Geography, High School Yards, Edinburgh.

Stansfield, David Eric; Lecturer in Politics, Institute of Latin American Studies, University of Glasgow, since 1969; b 1942; m 1966; one d. BA Wales 1964, MScEcon London 1966; Mem.: Soc. for Latin American Studies (Mem. Exec. Cttee 1971–75); Conseijo Europeano de Investigaciones Sociales sobre América Latina (CEISAL), 1974–75. Formerly: Lectr in Politics, Univ. Lancaster; Ford Foundn Fellow, Univ. New Mexico; Lecturer in Latin Amer. Politics, Univ. Glasgow; Vis. Lectr, Inter-Univ. Center for Latin Amer. Res. and Documentation, Amsterdam. Sec.-Gen., European Group on Latin American Politics, 1973– . *Publications*: Cuban Foreign Policy, in, The Other Powers, ed R. P. Barston, 1972; The Mexican Cabinet: An indicator of political change, 1973; 'Political Oppositions' in Mexico: the political climate, ed Focus Research, 1973; *contrib*. Political Studies, Amer. Pol. Science Rev., Internat. Affairs, Latin Amer. Res. Rev., Bull. Soc. for Latin Amer. Studies. *Address*: Institute of Latin American Studies, Univ. of Glasgow, Glasgow G12 8QQ.

Stansfield, Ronald Grubb, MA, BSc, Reader in Industrial Sociology, Department of Social Science & Humanities, The City University, London, since 1962; b 1915; m 1947; one s one d. BA Cantab 1936 (Nat. Sciences, Physics), MA Cantab 1940, BSc London 1936; FRAI, FPhysLond, MBPsS, Mem., Brit. Sociol. Assoc., Founder-mem., Ergonom. Res. Soc., Mem., Operat. Res. Soc. Scientific Civil Service, 1939–62; Air Min., MAP, 1941; Min. of Wks, 1945; Bd of Trade, 1948; Treas., 1950; Dept of Science and Indust. Res., 1951. Sec., DSIR Hum. Scis Cttee, 1957–59. *Publications*: contrib. Ergonom., Jl Cloth. Inst., Jl Inst. Elec. Eng., Jl Inst. Navig., Occupat. Psychol., Proc. Camb. Philos. Soc. *Address*: Dept of Social Science & Humanities, The City Univ., St John Street, EC1V 4PB.

Stanton, Glyn Rhys Thomas, MSc, DipArch, RIBA; Director of Studies for BArch (formerly Lecturer), School of Architecture and Building Technology, University of Bath, since 1962; b 1932; m 1957; two s one d. DipArch Wales 1957 (with distinction), MSc Loughborough 1963; Registered Archit. 1959, RIBA 1960. Mem., Ergonom. Res. Soc., 1963. Res. Fellow, Univ. of Technology, Kumasi, Ghana, 1960–61; Nuffield Schol., Loughborough, 1961–62. Articles, Montgomery CC, 1948–52; Pres., Students Union, Welsh CAT, 1955–56; Welsh Vice-Pres., NUS, 1956–57; Archit. Asst, MOPBW, 1957–58; Asst Reg. Archit., Ashanti, Ghana, 1959–60; Ergonom. Cnsltnt, DHSS, 1969– ; Mem., BSI Cttee OC27/4,

1971– . *Publication*: A Guide to User Activity Measurement in Health Buildings, 1969. *Address*: Acacia Lodge, Kensington Place, Bath, Avon.

Stanyer, Jeffrey; Lecturer, Department of Politics, The University of Exeter, since 1964; *b* 1936; *m* 1962; one *s* one *d*. BA Oxon 1958 (1st cl. PPE), BPhil Oxon 1960 (Politics). Mem., Pol Studies Assoc., Royal Inst. Public Admin. Res. Fellow in Local Government, Univ. of Exeter, 1960–62; Asst Lectr, Dept of Politics, 1962–64. *Publications*: County Government in England and Wales, 1967; *contrib*. Pol Studies, Public Admin. *Address*: Dept of Politics, The Univ., Streatham Court, Exeter EX4 4PU.

Stark, Dr Thomas; Lecturer, School of Social Sciences, New University of Ulster, since 1968; *b* 1941; *m* 1967; one *d*. BAEcon Manchester 1962, MAEcon Manchester 1963, PhD Manchester 1967; Member: Royal Econ. Soc., Scottish Econ. Soc. Res. Asst, Univ. Manchester, 1964–66; Res. Associate, Univ. Manchester, 1966–67; Asst Prof., Univ. Alberta, 1967–68. Mem. Council, Football Assoc. of Ireland, 1973–74; Mem. British Univ. Sports Fedn Football Cttee, 1972– . *Publications*: (with J. L. Ford) Long and Short Term Interest Rates: An Econometric Analysis, 1967; Distribution of Income in the United Kingdom 1949–63, 1972; *contrib*. Manchester School, Bull. Oxford Univ. Inst. Econs and Statistics. *Address*: New Univ. of Ulster, Coleraine, N Ireland BT52 1SA.

Starkie, David Nicholas Martin; Lecturer, Department of Geography, Reading University, since 1968; *b* 1942; *m* 1966; BSc(Econ) London 1963, MSc(Econ) London 1966. Assoc. Lectr, Centre for Transport Studies, Leeds Univ., 1966–68. Sen. Econ., R. Travers Morgan and Partners, 1966; Mem., Freight Gp, Trans. Co-ord. Council for London, 1969; Mem., Ashford-Hasting Jt Local Authority Steering Cttee; Special Adv., Hse of Commons Select Cttee on Expenditure, 1972, 1974; Asst Ed., Jl Reg. Studies, 1971– . *Publications*: Traffic and Industry, 1967; Transportation Planning and Public Policy, 1973; Economic Value of Peace and Quiet (forthcoming); *contrib*. Reg. Studies, Jl Transp. Econ. Policy. *Address*: Dept of Geography, Univ. of Reading, Whiteknights, Reading RG6 2AH.

Starr, James Moore Wesley; Senior Lecturer in Education, Queen's University of Belfast, since 1971; *b* 1932; two *s* one *d*. BSc Belfast 1952 (2nd cl. Physics), MEd Belfast 1959. Mem., Assoc. Science Educn. Lectr in Educn, QUB, 1963–71. Mem., NI Schs Curriculum Cttee, 1968–72; Mem., NI Council for Nurses and Midwives, 1973– . *Publications*: *contrib*. Durh. Res. Rev., Educnl Res., Educnl Rev. *Address*: Dept of Education, Queen's Univ., Belfast BT7 1NN.

Startup, Richard; Lecturer in Sociology, Department of Sociology and Anthropology, University College of Swansea, since 1966; *b* 1942. BA Oxon 1963, MA Oxon, Dipl.

Mathl Stats Cantab 1964. Mem., Brit. Sociol. Assoc. Fellow in Social Stats, Swansea, 1964–66. *Publications*: *contrib*. Educnl Res., Sociol. Qly, Sociol., Univ. Qly, Res. in Educn, Higher Educn Rev. *Address*: School of Social Studies, Univ. College, Singleton Park, Swansea SA2 8PP.

Staveley, Dr Eastland Stuart; Reader in Ancient History, Bedford College, University of London, since 1957; *b* 1926; *m* 1952; one *s*. BA Oxon (1st cl. Class. Mods, 1st cl. Lit. Hum.), MA Oxon 1948, DPhil Oxon 1952. Sen. Lectr in Ancient History, Univ. St Andrews, 1951–57. *Publications*: Greek and Roman Voting and Elections, 1972; *contrib*. Amer. Jl Philology, Athenaeum, Historia, Jl Roman Studies, Rhenisches Museum für Philologie. *Address*: Bedford College, Regent's Park, NW1 4NS.

Stchedroff, Marcel; Lecturer in Philosophy, Queen's University of Belfast, since 1967; *b* 1937; *m* 1963; one *s*. BA City Univ., New York 1958, MA New York 1960. Temp. Asst Lectr, Southampton Univ., 1964–65; Asst Lectr, Queen's Univ., Belfast, 1965–67. *Address*: Dept of Philosophy, Queen's Univ., Belfast BT7 1NN.

Stead, Rev. Prof. George Christopher, MA; Ely Professor of Divinity, Cambridge University, since 1971; *b* 1913; *m* 1958; two *s* one *d*. BA Cambridge 1935 (1st cl. Classics Pt I, 1st cl. Mor. Science Pt II), MA Cambridge 1938, BA Oxford 1935, MA Oxford 1949. Fellow, and Lectr in Divinity, King's Coll., Cambridge, 1938–48; Fellow, and Chaplain, Keble Coll., Oxford, 1949–71; Prof. Fellow, King's Coll., Cambridge, 1971– . Asst Master, Eton Coll., 1940–44; Exam. Chaplain, Bp of Hereford, 1951– ; Bp of Winchester, 1958– ; Sec., Oxf. Soc. Hist. Theol., 1953–71; Canon, Ely Cath., 1971– . *Publications*: Divine Substance (forthcoming); *contrib*. Faith and Logic, ed B. G. Mitchell, 1957; New Testament Apocrypha II, ed R. McL. Wilson, 1965; *contrib*. Jl Theol. Studies, Texte Untersuch. *Address*: The Divinity School, St John's Street, Cambridge.

Stead, Peter Price; Lecturer in History, University College of Swansea, since 1966; *b* 1943; *m* 1971. BA Wales 1964 (1st cl. Hist.). Vis. Lectr, Wellesley Coll., Mass, 1973–74. Sec., Glamorgan Hist. Soc., Treas., 'Llafur' – Soc. Study Welsh Lab. Hist. *Publications*: contrib. The British General Election of 1966, 1966; *contrib*. Glam. Hist., Welsh Hist. Rev., Llafur, Hist. Jl. *Address*: History Dept, Univ. College of Swansea, Swansea, West Glamorgan SA2 8PP.

Stedman, Maurice Bernard; Lecturer, Department of Geography, Birmingham University, since 1952; *b* 1924; *m* 1951; two *s*. Pt I Mod. and Med. Lang. Tripos, Cambridge 1943, Latin cl. I, French cl. II, BA Cantab 1948 (1st cl. Geog.), MA Cantab 1951. Asst Lectr, Birmingham, 1949–52. *Publications*: *contrib*. Geog. Mag., Geog., Trans. Inst. Brit. Geogrs. *Address*: Dept of Geography, Univ. of Birmingham, PO Box 363, Birmingham B15 2TT.

Steed, Michael; Lecturer, Department of Government, University of Manchester, since 1967; *b* 1940; *m* 1969. BA Cantab 1962; Member: Pol Studies Assoc.; Univ. Assoc. for Contemp. European Studies. Asst Lectr, Dept of Govt, Univ. of Manchester, 1965–67. Tutor, MA in European Community Studies, Univ. of Manchester, 1972. *Publications*: An Analysis of the Results, in, The British General Election of 1964, D. E. Butler and Anthony King, 1965; An Analysis of the Results, in, The British General Election of 1966, D. E. Butler and Anthony King, 1966; France, in, European Political Parties, ed S. Henig and J. Pinder, 1969; An Analysis of the Results, in, The British General Election of 1970, D. E. Butler and M. Pinto-Duschinsky, 1971; The European Parliament: the significance of direct election, in The New Politics of European Integration, ed G. Ionescu, 1972; Participation through Western Democratic Institutions, in, Participation in Politics, ed G. Parry, 1972; (with S. E. Finer) Great Britain, in, Modern Political Systems, R. Macridis and R. E. Ward, 3rd edn 1972; *contrib*. Govt and Opp. *Address*: Dept of Government, Univ. of Manchester, Manchester M13 9PL.

Steeds, David; Senior Lecturer in Far Eastern Studies, Department of International Politics, University College of Wales, Aberystwyth, since 1973 (Lecturer, 1963–73); *b* 1935; *m* 1966. BA Bristol 1956 (1st cl. Hist.). Asst Lectr, Glasgow Univ., 1961–63. *Address*: Dept of International Politics, Univ. College of Wales, Aberystwyth SY23 9DB.

Steel, Eileen Margaret; Lecturer (Supervisor of School Practice), School of Education, University of Liverpool, since 1958; *b* 1915; *m* 1940; one *s* two *d*. BA Oxon 1937 (2nd cl. Geog.), DipEd Oxford 1938, MA Oxon 1941. Mem., Geog. Assoc. Lectr in Geog., School of Educn, Univ. of Liverpool, 1958–70. *Publications*: (with R. W. Steel) Africa: a certificate geography, 1974; *contrib*. Bibliog. Internat. Géog., Geog. *Address*: School of Education, Univ. of Liverpool, PO Box 147, Liverpool L69 3BX.

Steel, Prof. Robert Walter; John Rankin Professor of Geography, University of Liverpool, since 1957; *b* 1915; *m* 1940; one *s* two *d*. BA Oxon 1937 (1st cl. Geog.), MA Oxon 1941, BSc Oxon 1950; FRGS. Mem., Inst. Brit. Geogrs (Pres., 1968), Geog. Assoc. (Pres., 1973), Afr. Studies Assoc. (Pres., 1971), Internat. Afr. Inst., Internat. Population Union. Lectr in Geog., Univ. of Oxford, 1939–47; Sen. Lectr in Commonwealth Geog., Univ. of Oxford, 1947–56; Fellow, Jesus Coll., Oxford, 1954; Univ. of Liverpool: Dean, Fac. of Arts, 1965–68; Pro-Vice Chancellor, 1971–73; Vis. Prof., Univ. of Ghana, 1964; Vis. Prof. (Australian Vice-Chancellor's Cttee), 1965; Vis. Prof., Carleton Univ., Ottawa, 1970. Dir, Commonwealth Geographical Bureau, 1972– . Ed, Trans Inst. Brit. Geogrs, 1950–60. *Publications*: ed (with A. F. Martin), The Oxford Region: an historical and scientific survey, 1953; (with C. A. Fisher) Geographical Essays on British Tropical Lands, 1956; (with R. M. Prothero) Geographers and the Tropics: Liverpool Essays, 1964; (with R. Lawton) Liverpool Essays in Geography: a jubilee collection, 1967; (with E. M. Steel) Africa: a certificate geography, 1974;) *contrib*. Bibliog. Internat. Géog., Geog. Jl, Geog., Trans Inst. Brit. Geogrs, etc. *Address*: Dept of Geography, Univ. of Liverpool, PO Box 147, Liverpool L69 3BX.

Steel, William Lindsay; Senior Lecturer, Department of Physical Education, Manchester University, since 1948; *b* 1917; *m* 1942; one *s*. MA Glasgow 1939 (maths and science), EdB Glasgow 1948; Grad. Teacher's Cert. 1940, Dip. Physical Educn and Hygiene (Scotland) 1940. Mem., Brit. Psychol. Soc., Brit. Soc. Sports Psychol., Brit. Assoc. Sport Med. Mem., N West Sports Council, 1966–68. *Publications*: Fitness for Rugby, 1963; *contrib*. Jl Brit. Assoc. Sport Med., Jl Physical Educn, Res. Physical Educn. *Address*: Dept of Physical Education, Manchester Univ., Manchester M13 9PL.

Steele, Prof. Alan John; Professor of French, University of Edinburgh, since 1961; *b* 1916; *m* 1947; one *s* one *d*. MA Edinburgh 1938 (1st cl. French Lang. and Lit.). Lectr, Edinburgh, 1946–59; Sen. Lectr, Edinburgh, 1959–61. Dean, Fac. of Arts, 1968–71; Ed. for French, Mod. Lang. Rev., 1971; Chm., Scott. Nat. Cttee Mod. Langs, 1972; Chevalier, Légion d'Honneur, 1973. *Publications*: (with R. A. Leigh) Contemporary French Translation Passages, 1956; Three Centuries of French Verse, 1511–1819, 1956, 2nd edn 1961; *contrib*. Cah. Assoc. Internat. Etudes, Franç., Forum Mod. Lang. Studies. *Address*: Dept of French, Univ. of Edinburgh, 4 Buccleuch Place, Edinburgh EH8 9LW.

Steele, David Brian, BA, MA; Fellow, Institute of Development Studies, University of Sussex, since 1969; *b* 1934; *m* 1960; one *s* one *d*. BA Dunelm 1959, MA Dunelm 1962. Mem., Reg. Studies Assoc. Asst Lectr, Nottingham Univ., 1960–62; Lectr, Nottingham Univ., 1962–63; NEDO, 1963–64; DEA, 1964–67; OECD Cnsltnt, Middle East Tech. Univ., 1967–69; NIESR, 1968–69; Kenya Govt TA Adviser, 1969–71; UN Sen. Econ. Planning Adviser, 1972–74. *Publications*: *contrib*. Jl Develt Stud., Oxf. Econ. Papers, Reg. Studies, Town Plan. Rev., Urb. Studies. *Address*: Inst. of Development Studies, Sussex Univ., Brighton BN1 9RE.

Steele, Dr Edward David; Lecturer in Modern History, School of History, Leeds University, since 1965; *b* 1934; *m* 1961. MA Cantab 1962, PhD Cantab 1964; FRHistS 1969. Asst in Modern Hist., Univ. Coll., Dublin, 1962, Asst Lectr 1963–64; Temp. Lectr in Govt, Univ. Coll. of Rhodesia and Nyasaland, 1956. *Publications*: Irish Land and British Politics, 1974; *contrib*. Hist. Jl, Irish Hist. Studies. *Address*: School of History, The Univ., Leeds LS2 9JT.

Steer, Prof. John Richardson, MA, BA; Professor of Fine Arts, University of St Andrews, since 1967; *b* 1928. BA Oxon 1951 (Mod. Hist.), MA Oxon 1956, BA London 1953 (Hist. of Art). Gen. Asst, Dept of Art, City Museum and Art Gall., Birmingham,

663

1953–56; Asst Lectr, Dept of Fine Art, Univ. of Glasgow, 1956–59; Lectr, Hist. of European Art, Univ. of Bristol, 1959–67. Vice Chm., Scott. Theatre Ballet, 1970–71. *Publications*: A Concise History of Venetian Painting, 1970; *contrib*. Burl. Mag., Art Quarterly. *Address*: Dept of Fine Arts, St Salvator's College, St Andrews, Fife KY16 9PH.

Steer, Mireille, Agrégée de l'Université; College Lecturer in French, Somerville College, Oxford University, since 1965; *b* 1937; *m* 1964; one *d*. BLitt Oxon. *Address*: Somerville College, Oxford.

Stein, Prof. Peter Gonville, FBA; Regius Professor of Civil Law, University of Cambridge, and Fellow of Queens' College, Cambridge, since 1968; *b* 1926; *m* 1953; three *d*. BA Cantab 1949, LLB Cantab 1950, MA Cantab 1951, PhD Aberdeen 1955; FBA 1974. Solicitor of the Supreme Court, 1951. Italian Govt Schol., Univ. of Pavia, 1951–52; Asst Lectr, Nottingham Univ., 1952–53; Lectr, Aberdeen Univ., 1953–56; Prof. of Jurisprudence, Aberdeen Univ., 1946–68; Dean, Fac. of Law, Aberdeen Univ., 1961–64; Vis. Prof., Univ. of Virginia Law Sch., 1965–66; Vis. Prof., Univ. of Colorado, 1966; Vis. Prof., Witwatersrand Univ., 1970. Mem., Bd of Mngmt, Royal Cornhill and Assoc. Hosps, Aberdeen (Chm., 1967–68); Sec. of State for Scotland's Working Party on Hosp. Endowments, 1966–69; Council, Max Planck Inst. Europ. Legal Hist., Frankfurt, 1966– ; Council, Selden Soc., 1969– ; Council, Internat. Assoc. Soc. Legal Hist., 1970– ; JP, Cambridge City, 1970; Mem., UGC, 1971– . *Publications*: Fault in the Formation of Contract in Roman Law and Scots Law, 1958; ed, Buckland's Textbook of Roman Law, 3rd edn 1963; Regulae iuris, from juristic rules to legal maxims, 1966; Roman Law and English Jurisprudence (inaugural lecture), 1969; (with J. Shand) Legal Values in Western Society, 1974; *contrib*.: Dictionary of History of Ideas; Encyclopaedia Britannica; *contrib*. Camb. Law Jl, Jurid. Rev., Jus Rom., Med. Ævv., Law Qly Rev., Rev. Internat. Droits Antiqu., Scott. Hist. Rev., S African Law Jl, Tulane Law Rev., Va Law Rev. *Address*: Queens' College, Cambridge CB3 9ET.

Stein, Walter, BA; Senior Lecturer, Department of Adult Education and Extramural Studies, University of Leeds, since 1969; *b* 1924; *m* 1954; two *s* two *d*. BA Manchester 1947 (Hons English and Philos.). Asst Lectr, Univ. of Leeds, 1949–52, Lectr, 1952–69; William Noble Fellow, Univ. of Liverpool, 1965–67; Vis. Lectr, Manhattanville Coll., NY, 1968. Mem., Peace Cttee, Commn Internat. Justice and Peace of Episcopal Conf. of Engl and Wales (RC), 1971. *Publications*: ed, Nuclear Weapons and Christian Conscience, 1961; ed, Peace on Earth: The Way Ahead, 1966; Criticism as Dialogue, 1969; contrib. The Twentieth Century Mind (ed Cox and Dyson), 1972; co-ed (with I. Gregor) The Prose for God: religious and anti-religious aspects of imaginative literature, 1973; *contrib*. Continuum, Crit. Qly, Cross Curr., Dub. Rev., Ess. Crit., Humanitas, New Blackf., Wldview. *Address*: Dept of Adult

Education and Extramural Studies, Univ. of Leeds, Leeds LS2 9JT.

Steinberg, Prof. Hannah, BA, PhD; Professor of Psychopharmacology, Department of Pharmacology, University College, University of London, since 1970. BA London 1948 (1st cl. Psychol.), PhD London 1953. Hon. Res. Asst, Dept of Pharmacol., Univ. Coll., London, 1950–54; Asst Lectr, Univ. Coll., London, 1954; Lectr, Univ. Coll., London, 1955–62; Reader, Univ. Coll., London, 1962–70; Hon. Cnsltng Clin. Psychologist, Dept of Psychol. Med., Royal Free Hosp., London, 1970– . Pres., Univ. of London Union, 1947–48; FBPsS, Sci.FZS. Mem., Brit. Pharmacol. Soc.; Mem., Coll. Internat. Neuro-Psychopharmacol.; Vice-Pres., Coll. Internat. Neuro-Psychopharmacol., 1968– ; Mem.: Exper. Psychol. Soc. UK; Med. Res. Council Working Parties, 1968–69, 1971– ; ed, Bull. Brit. Psychol. Soc., 1956–62; Mem., Ed. Bd, Psychopharmacologia, 1965– ; Brit. Jl Pharmacol., 1965–72; Mem., Assoc. Study Anim. Behav.; Mem., Brain Res. Assoc. GB, 1969– . *Publications*: Animal Behaviour and Drug Action (with A. V. S. de Reuck and J. Knight eds), Biol. Council Symposium jointly with CIBA Foundation, 1964; Scientific Basis of Drug Dependence, Biological Council Symposium, 1969; *contrib*. Brit. Jl Pharmacol., Brit. Jl Psychol., Brit. Med. Bull., Brit. Med. Jl, Jl Psychosom. Res., Nature (London), Psychopharmacologia; Percep. and Mot. Skills; Qly Jl Exp. Psychol., Rev. Psychol. Appl., Thérapie. *Address*: Dept of Pharmacology, Univ. College London, Gower Street, WC1E 6BT.

Steinberg, Dr Jonathan; Fellow since 1966, and Tutor, since 1967, Trinity Hall, Cambridge; University Lecturer in History, since 1968; *b* 1934; *m* 1960; three *s*. BA Harvard 1955 (*magna cum laude*), MA 1963, PhD 1965, Cantab; FRHistS 1970. Res. Fellow, Christ's Coll., Cambridge, 1963–66; Univ. Asst Lectr, 1966–68; Dir of Studies, Trinity Hall, Cambridge, 1966–74; Vis. Lectr, Harvard, 1968–69. Sec., Cambridge Hist. Soc., 1971–74; Member: Faculty Bd of Hist., 1969–73; Degree Cttee (Hist.), 1969–73. *Publications*: Yesterday's Deterrent: Tirpitz and the birth of the German Battle Fleet, 1965, NY, 1966; Inside Switzerland(forthcoming);Diplomatic als Wille und Vorstellung: Die Berliner Mission Lord Haldanes im Februar 1912, in, Marine und Marinepolitik 1871–1914, H. Schottelius and W. Deist, 1972; *contrib*. Hist. Jl, Past and Present, Jl of Contemp. Hist., Proc. Royal Hist. Soc. Amer. Hist. Rev. *Address*: Trinity Hall, Cambridge CB2 1TJ.

Steiner, Prof. George, MA, DPhil, FRSL; Extraordinary Fellow, Churchill College, Cambridge University, since 1969; Professor of English and Comparative Literature, University of Geneva, since 1974; *b* 1929; *m* 1955; one *s* one *d*. BèsL et Phil Paris 1947, BA Chicago 1948, MA Harvard 1950, DPhil Oxon 1955; FRSocLit 1964– . Mem., Inst. Adv. Study, Princeton, 1956–58; Fellow, and Dir of English Studies, Churchill Coll., 1961–69; Vis. Prof., Yale, Vis. Prof., NY Univ., Harvard, Univ. of Zürich, etc.

Publications: Tolstoy or Dostoevsky, 1958, 2nd edn 1971; The Death of Tragedy, 1960, 2nd edn 1962; Anno Domini, 1964; Language and Silence, 1967, 2nd edn 1970; Extraterritorial, 1971; In Bluebeard's Castle, 1971; After Babel: aspects of language and translation, 1975. *Address*: Churchill College, Cambridge; Faculty of Letters, Univ. of Geneva.

Steiner, Hillel Isaac; Lecturer in Political Philosophy, Department of Government, University of Manchester, since 1971; *b* 1942; *m* 1966. BA Hons Toronto 1964 (Pol Sci. and Econs), MA Carleton 1965 (Pol and Pub. Admin). Lectr in Politics and Public Admin, Univ. of Saskatchewan, 1966–67; Res. Associate, Dept of Govt, Univ. of Manchester, 1967–71. Res. Asst, Canadian Royal Commn on Bilingualism and Biculturalism, 1965–66. *Publications*: *contrib.* Mind, Proc. Aristotelian Soc., Ratio. *Address*: Dept of Government, Univ. of Manchester, Manchester M13 9PL.

Steiner, William Anthony Frederick Paul; Librarian, Institute of Advanced Legal Studies, University of London, since 1971; *b* 1918; *m* 1950; one *s* three *d*. Dip. Consular Acad., Vienna 1938, LLB London 1945, LLM 1948, MA Cantab 1962; Barrister-at-law, Gray's Inn, 1942; ALA 1953, Cert. of competence, Amer. Assoc. of Law Libraries, 1967; Member: Brit. and Irish Assoc. of Law Librarians; Internat. Assoc. of Law Libraries; Amer. Soc. of Internat. Law; SPTL. Asst Librarian: Brit. Lib. of Pol and Econ. Sci., LSE, 1946–58; Squire Law Lib., Univ. of Cambridge, 1959–68; Sec. and Librarian, Inst. Advanced Legal Studies, Univ. of London, 1968–71. Pres., Special Section A, 8th Internat. Congress of Compar. Law, 1970; Gen. Reporter, Special Section A2, 9th Internat. Congress of Compar. Law, 1974. Asst Editor, Index to Foreign Legal Periodicals, 1959–68, Gen. Editor, 1968– . *Publications*: Modern Law Rev.: index to vols 1–21, 1959; ed, Cambridge Law Jl: index 1921–70, 1972; ed, Univ. of Cambridge, Squire Law Library: Catalogue of international law, 1972; ed, Univ. of Cambridge, Squire Law Library: Catalogue, 1973– ; Classification scheme and lists of subject headings for the Squire Law Library of the Univ. of Cambridge, 1973; *contrib.* Annuaire européen, European Yearbook, Bull. Internat. Assoc. of Law Libraries, Internat. Jl of Law Libraries. *Address*: Univ. of London, Inst. of Advanced Legal Studies, 25 Russell Square, WC1B 5DR.

Steiner, Dr Zara; Fellow in Modern History, New Hall, Cambridge University, since 1961; *b* 1928; *m* 1958; one *s* one *d*. BA Swarthmore College 1948, BA St Anne's College 1950, PhD Harvard 1955. Lectr, Harvard Univ., 1954–55; Lectr, Vassar Coll., 1955–56; Res. Assoc., Princeton Univ., Center of Internat. Studies, 1957–58, 1960–61. *Publications*: The Wriston Report . . . Four Years Later, 1958; Problems of the Foreign Service, 1961; The Foreign Office and Foreign Policy, 1898–1914, 1969; *contrib.* Canad. Hist. Rev., Hist. Jl, Hist., Jl Mod. Hist. *Address*: New Hall, Cambridge.

Stenhouse, Lawrence Alexander, MA, MEd; Director, Centre for Applied Research in Education, University of East Anglia, since 1970; *b* 1926; *m* 1949; one *s* two *d*. MA St Andrews 1951 (2nd cl. English), MEd Glasgow 1956 (1st cl); William Boyd Prize in Education Glasgow 1956. Staff Tutor, Univ. of Durham Inst. of Educn, 1957–61; Principal Lectr in Educn, Jordanhill Coll. of Educn, Glasgow, 1961–67; Dir, Nuffield Foundn and Schs Council Humanities Curriculum Project, 1967–72; Council of Europe Vis. Prof., Univ. of Uppsala, 1964. *Publications*: Culture and Education, 1967, 2nd edn 1970; ed, Discipline in Schools, 1967; *contrib.* Brit. Jl Educnl Studies, Internat. Rev. Educn, Jl Curric. Studies, Paedagog. Europ., Paedagogik, Scand. Jl Educnl Res., Theory Pract., Times Educnl Supp. *Address*: Centre for Applied Research in Education, Univ. of East Anglia, Univ. Village, Norwich NOR 88C.

Stephen, Dr Kenneth David, BSc, PhD, CEng, FIEE, MIEEE, MRTS; Director of Television, Television Centre, Heriot-Watt University (also teaches education and social studies), since 1971; *b* 1928; *m* 1954. BSc Edinburgh 1953, PhD Heriot-Watt 1971; CEng, FIEE, MIEEE, MRTS. Design Eng., BTH Co. Ltd, 1953–59; Sen. Design Eng., AEI Ltd, 1959–64; Lectr, Heriot-Watt Univ., 1964–67; Sen. Lectr, Heriot-Watt, 1967–71; Hon. Dir of Television, Heriot-Watt, 1965–71. Chm., IEE, Scott. Centre Educn and Training Circle Cttee, 1968–69; Chm., Scott. Reg., NECCTA, 1969–71; Vice-Chm., NECCTA, 1972–73; Chm., NECCTA Editorial Bd, 1972–73. *Publications*: *contrib.* British Compressed Air Society publicns; IEE Conference publicns; Inter-University Power Engineers Conference Proc.; *contrib.* NECCTA Bull. *Address*: Television Centre, Heriot-Watt Univ., Grassmarket, Edinburgh EH1 2HT.

Stephens, David James; Lecturer and Assistant Tutor to the Faculty of Laws, University College London, since 1972; *b* 1943. LLB Wales 1965, LLB Cantab 1967, LLM Wales 1969; Barrister, Lincoln's Inn, 1971. Lectr: Univ. of Newcastle upon Tyne, 1967–70; Univ. of Bristol, 1970–72. *Publications*: *contrib.* Crim. Law Rev., New Law Jl. *Address*: Fac. of Laws, Univ. Coll. London, 4–8 Endsleigh Gardens, WC1H 0EG.

Stephens, James Edwin; Lecturer, Department of Educational Studies, University of Hull, since 1965; *b* 1929; *m* 1953; three *s* one *d*. BA Nottingham 1952, MEd Leeds 1963. Ch. Examiner, N Ireland GCE, 1963–68; South. Univs Jt Bd GCE, 1972; Mem., Scunthorpe Educn Cttee, 1967–70. *Publications*: Aubrey on Education, 1972; *contrib.* Brit. Jl Educnl Studies, Country Life, Educn, Hist., Jl Educnl Admin, Yorks Archaeol. *Address*: Dept of Educational Studies, Univ. of Hull, 173 Cottingham Road, Hull.

Stephens, Prof. Michael Dawson; Robert Peers Professor of Adult Education, University of Nottingham, since 1974; *b* 1936; *m* 1961; one *s* two *d*. BA Hull 1960, MA

665

Johns Hopkins 1962, PhD Edinburgh 1965, MEd Leicester 1970; FRGS 1961. Res. Fellow, Johns Hopkins Univ., 1960–62; Demonstrator, Univ. of Edinburgh, 1962–64; Lectr, 1964–69, Asst Dir and Head of Adult Educn Div., Inst. of Extension Studies, Univ. of Liverpool, 1969–74. General Editor, World Education Series. *Publications*: ed (jtly), Teaching Techniques in Adult Education, 1971; (jtly) Scientific and Technical Education in 19th Century England, 1972; *contrib*. Annals Sci., Paedagogica Historica, Brit. Jl of Ed. Studies, Vocational Aspect of Ed., Hist. of Ed. Soc. Bull., Jl of Admin and Hist. of Ed, etc. *Address*: 1 Abercromby Square, Liverpool L69 3BX.

Stephens, Prof. Nicholas; Professor of Geography, University of Aberdeen, since 1974; *b* 1926; *m* 1952; one *s* one *d*. BSc Bristol 1949 (2nd cl.), DipEd Bristol 1950, MSc Bristol 1952, PhD Belfast 1966. Demonstrator in Geography, Bristol, 1950–51; QUB: Asst Lectr, 1951–54; Lectr, 1954–66; Sen. Lectr, 1966–68; Reader, 1968–73. Vis. Sen. Res. Fellow, Univ. of Tasmania, 1964–65. Recorder, Sect. E Brit. Assoc. Adv. Science, 1961–64; Mem., Council, Inst. Brit. Geogrs, 1972–74; *Publications*: Jt Ed., Irish Geographical Studies, 1970; *contrib*. Eng. Geol., Geog. Ann., Irish Geog., Proc. Royal Irish Acad., Proc. Royal Soc. Lond., Trans Inst. Brit. Geogrs. *Address*: Dept of Geography, Univ. of Aberdeen, St Mary's, High Street, Aberdeen AB9 2UF.

Stephens, Dr William Brewer; Senior Lecturer, Education Department, University of Leeds, since 1970; *b* 1925; *m* 1955; one *s* one *d*. BA London 1951 (Hons Hist.), PhD London 1954 (Hist.), MA Exeter 1959 (Education); FSA, FRHistS, Teacher's Certificate 1952. Dep. Gen. Ed., Victoria County Histories, Inst. of Hist. Res., London Univ., 1961–67; Lectr, Leeds Univ., 1967–70. Jt Ed., Jl Educnl Admin. Hist., 1968– . *Publications*: Seventeenth Century Exeter: A Study of Industry and Trade 1625–1688, 1958; (jtly) Teaching of History in Secondary Schools, 1959; ed, History of Birmingham (VCH Warwickshire vol. VII), 1964; ed, History of Coventry and Warwick (VCH Warwickshire vol. VIII), 1969; ed, History of Congleton, 1970; ed, Sources for the History of Population and their Uses, 1971; Sources for English Local History, 1973; Regional Variations in Education during the Industrial Revolution 1780–1870, 1973; *contrib*. Agric. Hist., Comp. Educn Rev., Econ. Hist. Rev., Jl Educnl Admin. Hist., Jl Textile Hist., Jl Transp. Hist., Trans Devon. Assoc., Trans Hist. Soc. Lancs Chesh. *Address*: Dept of Education, The Univ., Leeds LS2 9JT.

Stephenson, Dr Geoffrey Michael, BA, PhD; Senior Lecturer in Psychology, Department of Psychology, University of Nottingham, since 1973 (Lecturer, 1966–73); *b* 1939; *m* 1962; one *s* one *d*. BA Nottingham 1960 (1st cl. Psychol.), PhD Nottingham 1963; ABPsS. Lectr in Psychol., Univ. of Keele, 1962–66. Hon. Sec. and Treasurer, Soc. Psychol. Sect., BPsS, 1972– (Mem., 1970–72); Mem. Psychol. Cttee, SSRC, 1972– .

Publications: The Development of Conscience, 1966; The Social Psychology of Bargaining (forthcoming); Intergroup Relations and Negotiating Behaviour, in, Psychology at Work, 1971; *contrib*. Amer. Jl Orthopsychiat., Brit. Jl Psychiat., Brit. Jl Psychol., Brit. Jl Social Clin. Psychol., Indust. Relat. Jl, Jl Exper. Social Psychol., Jl. Ment. Sci., Jl Social Psychol. *Address*: Dept of Psychology, The Univ., Nottingham NG7 2RD.

Stern, Axel; Senior Lecturer in Philosophy, University of Hull, since 1967; *b* 1912; *m* 1969. LèsSc Geneva 1939, Teaching Dip. Geneva 1939, DPhil Geneva 1944. Asst in Moral Philos., Edinburgh, 1950–54; Lectr in Philos., Hull, 1954–67. Vis. Prof. in Philos., Tübingen, 1974–75. Founder and Sec., Brit. Soc. French Speaking Philosophers, 1954– ; Mem., Cttee and Ed. Bd, Brit. Soc. Phenomenol. and its Jl. *Publications*: Poème métaphysique en prose, 1940; Morale de la liberté, 1944; L'existentialisme contre l'existence, 1945; Le vrai en art et en science, 1945; ed, I. Benrubi: Morale et connaissance, 1946; Metaphysical Reverie, 1956; The Science of Freedom, 1969; Creative Ethics (forthcoming); *contrib*. Archiv Philos., Jl Brit. Soc. Phenomenol., Proc. Aristot. Soc., Rev. Univ. Sci. Mor. *Address*: Dept of Philosophy, The Univ., Hull HU6 7RX.

Stern, Prof. Joseph Peter; Head of Department of German and Professor in the University of London, Department of German, University College, since 1972; *b* 1920; *m* 1944; two *s* two *d*. BA Hons 1945 (Mod. and Med. Langs), CertEd 1946, MA 1947, PhD 1950, Cantab; Fellow, Center for Humanities, Wesleyan Univ., 1972. Supervisor in German, St John's Coll., Cambridge, 1946–72; Assistant Lecturer in German: Bedford Coll., London, 1950–52; Univ. of Cambridge, 1952–54; Lectr in German, Univ. of Cambridge, 1954–72; Lewis Fry Meml Lectr, Univ. of Bristol, 1973. (Moral) Tutor, St John's Coll., Cambridge, 1963–70, 1972; Mem. Coll. Council, St John's Coll., Cambridge at various periods. Visiting posts: City Coll. NY, w/s, 1958–59; Univ. of Calif., Berkeley, w/s, 1964–65 and Summer and Fall Quarters, 1967; Merton Prof., Univ. of Göttingen, s/s, 1965; State Univ. of NY, Buffalo, w/s, 1969–70; Univ. of Virginia, Charlottesville, w/s, 1971–72. *Publications*: Ernst Jünger: a writer of our time, 1952; G. C. Lichtenberg: a doctrine of scattered occasions, US, 1959; Re-Interpretations: seven studies in nineteenth-century German literature, 1964; Thomas Mann (Columbia Series on Modern Writers), 1967; Idylls and Realities: studies in nineteenth-century German literature, 1971; On Realism (Concepts of Literature series), 1973; ed with Introd. and notes, Arthur Schnitzler: Liebelei, Leutnant Gustl, Die letzten Masken, 1966; trans. R. W. Meyer: Leibnitz and the seventeenth-century revolution, 1952; trans. H.-E. Holthusen: R. M. Rilke: a study of his later poetry, 1952; *contrib*. Cambridge Jl, Cambridge Rev., Cent. European Observer (London), Daily Telegraph, Economist, Erasmus, Forum (St Andrews), Germanic Qly, German Life and Letters, Göttinger, Deutsche Universitätszeitung, Jl European Studies, Listener, Mod. Lang. Rev., Spectator, TLS. *Address*: Dept. of German, Univ. Coll., Gower Street, WC1E 6BT.

Stern, Karen Margaret; Lecturer in Medieval Studies, English Department, University of York, since 1968; *b* 1941; *m* 1970. BA Cantab 1963 (Hons English), MPhil London 1972 (English). Asst Lectr, Univ. York, 1965–68. *Publications*: *contrib*. Archiv für das Neueren Sprachen und Literaturen, Scriptorium. *Address*: Centre for Medieval Studies, King's Manor, York.

Stern, Walter Marcel; Senior Lecturer in Economic History, London School of Economics and Political Science, University of London, since 1963; *b* 1912; *m* 1940; one *s* one *d*. BSc (Econ.) London 1949. Asst Lectr in Econ. Hist., 1949–52, Lectr, 1952–63, LSE. *Publications*: The Porters of London, 1960; Britain Yesterday and Today, 1962, 2nd edn 1969, pbk 1971; *contrib*. Econ. Hist. Rev., Economica, Guildhall Miscellany. *Address*: London Sch. of Economics, Houghton Street, Aldwych, WC2A 2AE.

Sternfeld, Dr Frederick William, PhD; Reader in the History of Music, University of Oxford, since 1972; *b* 1914; *m* 1943. PhD Yale 1943, MA Oxon 1956. Mem., Royal Music. Assoc., Vice-Pres., 1971– . Instructor, Wesleyan Univ., USA, 1940–44; Asst Prof., Wesleyan Univ., USA, 1944–46; Asst Prof., Dartmouth Coll., USA, 1946–54; Prof., Dartmouth Coll., USA, 1954–56; Mem., Inst. Adv. Study, Princeton, 1954–55; Fellow, Exeter Coll., Oxford, 1965; Act. Prof. of Music, Oxford, 1971–72, Lectr in Music, 1956–72. *Publications*: Goethe and Music, 1954; Music in Shakespearean Tragedy, 1963, 2nd edn 1967; Songs from Shakespeare's Tragedies, 1964; ed (with Fellowes and Greer), English Madrigal Verse, 1967; ed, New Oxford History of Music, vol. VII, 1973; ed, History of Western Music, vol. I, 1973; contrib. New Cambridge Modern History, vols VI, VIII, IX, 1965–70; *contrib*. Music Lett., Music. Qly, Shakesp. Qly, Shakesp. Surv. *Address*: Faculty of Music, Univ. of Oxford, 32 Holywell, Oxford OX1 3SL.

Stevens, Dr John Edgar; Reader in English and Musical History, University of Cambridge; *b* 1921; *m* 1946; two *s* two *d*. MA Cantab, PhD Cantab. Bye Fellow, subseq., Res. Fellow, and Fellow and Tutor of Magdalene Coll., Cambridge. *Publications*: ed, Medieval Carols, 1952, 2nd edn 1958; Music and Poetry in the Early Tudor Court, 1961; ed, Music at the Court of Henry VIII, 1962; (with Cudworth, Winton Dean and Fiske) Shakespeare in Music, 1966; (with R. Axton) trans., Medieval French Plays, 1971; Medieval Romance, 1973; ed, Early Tudor Songs and Carols (forthcoming). *Address*: Magdalene College, Cambridge.

Stevens, Dr John Harold, BSc, PhD; Lecturer in Geography (Soil Science), University of Durham, since 1966; *b* 1940; *m* 1966; one *s* one *d*. BSc Durham 1961 (2nd cl. Geog.), PhD Durham 1973; FRGS, Mem., Inst.

Brit. Geogrs, Mem., Geog. Assoc., Mem., Brit. Soc. Soil Science, Mem., Internat. Soc. Soil Science, Mem., Amer. Geog. Soc. Sci. Off., Macaulay Inst. Soil Res., Aberdeen, 1961–66; Coll. Tutor, Univ. College, Durham Univ., 1969– . Mem. Senate, Durham Univ., 1972– . Rapporteur-General, Internat. Subcommn on Salt Affected Soils, 1973. Mem., Council, Brit. Assoc. Adv. Science, 1971; Sec., Sect. E, Brit. Assoc. Advancement of Science, 1972– . *Publications*: contrib.: Africa, ed J. I. Clarke, 1974; African Studies, ed R. B. Sergeant and G. R. Bidwell, 1974; *contrib*. Geog. Jl, Jl Soil Water Cons., Jl Soil Science, Quatern, Geography, Jl Roy. Central Asian Soc., Met. Mag. *Address*: Dept of Geography, Science Laboratories, South Road, Durham City, DH1 3LE.

Stevens, Mildred, MEd; formerly Head of Course for Teachers of the Severely Subnormal, National Association for Mental Health, 1961–71; *b* 1923; *m* 1953. Teaching Cert., Crewe College of Educn 1943, MEd Manchester 1953. Mem., Brit. Psychol. Soc., Mem., Nat. Assoc. Ment. Hlth, Mem., Froebel Soc., Mem., Assoc. Special Educn ATCDE, Mem., Guild Teachers of Backward Children, Mem., Educl Develop. Assoc., Mem., Assoc. All Speech Impaired Children. Pt-time Special Lectr, Univ. of Manchester, 1964– . *Publications*: Observing Children who are Severely Subnormal, 1968; The Educational Needs of Severely Subnormal Children, 1971; contrib. Proceedings of Conference in Copenhagen, Warsaw, International Association for the Scientific Study of Mental Deficiency 1964: 1970; *contrib*. Jl Ment. Defic. *Address*: Dept of Education, Univ., Manchester M13 9PL.

Stevens, Richard John; Lecturer in Psychology, Faculty of Social Science, Open University, since 1972; *b* 1939; *m* 1958; three *s*. MA Edinburgh 1962 (1st cl.), MA Dublin 1970 (de jure officii); Mem., Brit. Psychol. Soc. Jun. Lectr in Psychol., TCD, 1964–67; Lectr in Psychol., TCD, 1967–72; Coll. Tutor, TCD, 1969–72; Act. Hd, Dept of Psychol., TCD, 1968–69. Dir of Drama, BBC-TV, London, 1962–64; Clin. Psychologist (pt-time), St Patrick's Hosp., Dublin, 1965–68; Clin. Psychologist (pt-time), Dublin Hlth Authority, 1966–72; Mem., Selection Cttee, Irish Civil Service, 1967–72. *Address*: Walton Hall, Walton, Milton Keynes MK7 6AA.

Stevenson, Leslie F.; Lecturer, Department of Logic and Metaphysics, University of St Andrews, since 1968; *b* 1943; *m* 1972. BA 1965, MA 1969, BPhil 1968, Oxon; Mem., Mind Assoc. Res. Lectr, Merton Coll., Oxford, 1967–68. *Publications*: Seven Theories of Human Nature, 1974; *contrib*. Analysis, Metaphilosophy, Religious Studies, Notre Dame Jl Formal Logic, Philos. Qly. *Address*: Dept of Logic and Metaphysics, Univ. of St Andrews, Fife KY16 9AJ.

Stevenson, Olive; Reader in Applied Social Studies, Department of Social and Administrative Studies, University of Oxford, and Professorial Fellow, St Anne's College,

Oxford, since 1969; *b* 1930. BA Oxon 1951 (2nd cl. Eng. Lang. and Lit.), MA Oxon 1956, Cert. Social Studies London 1952, Cert. Child Care London 1953; Tavistock Clinic Adv. Social Casework Course 1958, Mem., Brit. Assoc. Social Workers 1970 (and equivalents previously). Child Care Officer, Devon CC, 1954–58. Pt-time Lectr, and Susan Isaacs Res. Fellow, Bristol Univ., 1959–60; Lectr in Applied Social Studies, Oxford Univ., 1960–68. Social Wk Adviser, Supplementary Benefits Commn, DHSS, 1968–70; Mem., Royal Commn on Civil Liability, 1973. *Publications*: Someone Else's Child, 1952; Client or Claimant: a social worker's view of the Supplementary Benefits Commission, 1972; *contrib*. Brit. Jl Child Psychol. Psychiat., Brit. Jl Psychiat., Social Wk, Case Conf., Psychoanalytic Study Child. *Address*: St Anne's College, Oxford.

Stevenson, Richard Charles; Lecturer, Department of Economics, University of Liverpool, since 1967; *b* 1941; *m* 1970; two *s* two *d*. BSc (Econ.) London 1962, MA Stanford 1964. Univ. of Reading, 1966–67. *Address*: Dept of Economics, Univ. of Liverpool, PO Box 147, Liverpool L69 3BX.

Stewart, Alasdair McIntosh, MA, PhD; Lecturer, Department of German, University of Aberdeen, since 1967; *b* 1934; *m* 1964; one *s*. MA Hons 1956 (French), 1958 (German), DipEd 1959, PhD 1973 (Eng. Lit.) Edinburgh, GTC Registered Teacher of French and German, Moray House Coll. of Educn, Edinburgh, 1959. Lecteur d'Anglais, Caen, 1954–55; Englischer Lektor,Giessen, 1962–67; Lehrbeauftragter, TU Darmstadt, 1965; Mem., English Fac., European Div., Univ. of Maryland, 1963–67. Flying Officer, Educn Branch, RAF, 1959–62. *Address*: Dept of German, Taylor Bldg, King's Coll., Old Aberdeen AB9 2UB.

Stewart, Dr Anthony Terence Quincey; Lecturer in Irish History, Department of Modern History, The Queen's University, Belfast, since 1968; *b* 1929; *m* 1963; two *s*. BA Hons 1952 (1st cl.), MA 1956 (by thesis), PhD 1967 (by thesis), QUB; Mem., Hist. Assoc. Fellow-Commoner, Peterhouse, Cambridge, 1965–66. *Publications*: The Ulster Crisis, 1967, pbk 1969; The Pagoda War, 1972. *Address*: 10 University Square, Belfast BT7 1NN.

Stewart, David Hamilton, DA, MSc, MRTPI; Lecturer in Urban Planning, University of Edinburgh, since 1965; *b* 1933; *m* 1957; one *s* two *d*. Dip. Arch. Edinburgh 1960, Dip. Urban Design Edinburgh 1962, MSc Edinburgh 1969; Mem., Royal Town Plan. Inst., Registd Archit. Res. Unit, Univ. of Edinburgh, 1962–65. Planning Res. Adv., Nat. Inst. Physical Planning and Cnstctn Res., Dublin, 1970– . *Publications*: ed (with Wright), The Exploding City, 1972; *Address*: Dept of Urban and Regional Planning, Univ. of Edinburgh, Edinburgh EH8 9YL.

Stewart, Prof. Ian George, MA; Professor of Economics, University of Edinburgh, since 1967; *b* 1923; *m* 1949; one *s* two *d*. MA St Andrews 1948 (1st cl. Econ. and Pol.

668

Science), MA Cantab 1954; Mem., Royal Econ. Soc., Mem., Scott. Econ. Soc., Commonwealth Fund Fellow, Harvard and Chicago, 1948–50; Res. Off., Dept of Applied Econ., Cambridge, 1950–57; Lectr, Edinburgh Univ., 1957–58, Sen. Lectr 1958–61, Reader 1961–67; Vis. Assoc. Prof., Univ. of Michigan, 1962; Assoc. Dean, Fac. of Social Science, Edinburgh, 1964–66. Mem., Council, Royal Econ. Soc., 1970–75. *Publications*: (with A. R. Prest) The National Income of Nigeria 1950/51, 1953; ed (with H. W. Ord), African Primary Products and International Trade, 1965; ed, Economic Development and Structural Change, 1969; *contrib*. Econ. Jl, Scott. Jl Pol. Econ. *Address*: Dept of Economics, Univ. of Edinburgh, George Square, Edinburgh EH8 9JY.

Stewart, James Blythe; Lecturer in Law, Department of Business Organisation, Heriot-Watt University, since 1969; *b* 1943. MA Edinburgh 1963 (Ordinary), LLB Edinburgh 1966 (2nd cl.), LLB London 1972. Advocate 1969. Res. Asst in Law, Univ. of St Andrews, 1966; Tutorial Asst, Univ. of St Andrews, 1967; Asst Lectr, Heriot-Watt Univ., 1967–69. *Publications*: (jtly) Sale of Goods, Trade Descriptions and Hire Purchase, 1970; *contrib*. Jurid. Rev., Scots Law Times. *Address*: Mountbatten Building, 31–5 Grassmarket, Edinburgh EH1 2HT.

Stewart, Prof. John David; Associate Director, since 1970, and Professor of Local Government and Administration, since 1971, Institute of Local Government Studies, University of Birmingham; *b* 1929; *m* 1953; two *s* two *d*. BA Oxon 1952 (PPE), DPhil Oxon 1954. Sen. Lectr, Univ. of Birmingham, Inst. of Local Govt Studies, 1966–71. Member: Library Adv. Council; Police Trng Council. *Publications*: British Pressure Groups, 1958; Management in Local Government: a view point 1971; (with R. Greenwood) Corporate Management in English Local Government: an analysis of readings, 1974; The Responsive Local Authority, 1974. *Address*: Inst. of Local Government Studies, Univ. of Birmingham, PO Box 363, Birmingham B15 2TT.

Stewart, Jonathan; Lecturer in Econometrics, University of Manchester, since 1969; *b* 1944; *m* 1965; four *s*. BA(Econ) Manchester 1966 (1st cl. Economet.), MA(Econ) Manchester 1968 (Dist. Economet.). Res. Asst, Manchester, 1966–68; Lectr, New Univ. of Ulster, 1968–69. *Address*: Dept of Econometrics, Univ. of Manchester, Manchester M13 9PL.

Stewart, Dr Michael Alexander; Lecturer in Philosophy, University of Lancaster, since 1965; *b* 1937. MA St Andrews 1960 (2nd cl. Greek and Logic and Metaphysics), PhD Pennsylvania 1965. Teaching Fellow, Univ. of Pennsylvania, 1961–63; Lectr, Brooklyn Coll., NY, 1963–64; Lectr, Univ. of W Ontario, 1964–65. Dean, Lonsdale Coll., Lancaster Univ., 1970–72. Editor, Philosophical Books, 1975– . *Publications*: *contrib*. Dur. Univ. Jl, Philos. Qly., Arch. Gesch. Phil. *Address*: Dept of Philosophy, Bowland College, Bailrigg, Lancaster LA1 4YT.

Stewart, Michael James; Reader, Department of Political Economy, University College London, since 1969; Special Adviser (part-time) to Secretary of State for Trade, 1974; *b* 1933; *m* 1962; three *d*. BA Oxon 1955, MA 1958. Economic Adviser: Treasury, 1961–62; Cabinet Office, 1964–67 (Sen. Econ. Advr, 1967); Kenya Treasury, 1967–69. *Publications*: Keynes and After, 1967, 2nd edn 1972. *Address*: Dept of Political Economy, Univ. Coll. London, Gower Street, WC1E 6BT.

Stewart, Dr Robert Howard Mackenzie; Lecturer in Medical Services Administration, Department of Family and Community Medicine, University of Newcastle upon Tyne, since 1956; *b* 1914; *m* 1942; two *s* three *d*. MB, ChB Liverpool 1940, MD Liverpool 1948, FFCM 1972. Sen. Admin. Med. Off., Newcastle Reg. Hosp. Bd, 1956–74; Cnsltnt, WHO, 1966; Mem., Bd, Fac. of Community Medicine, Royal Colls of Physicians UK, 1972–73. *Publications*: contrib. Brit. Med. Jl, Lancet, Newc. Med. Jl. *Address*: Dept Family and Community Medicine, Medical School, The Univ., Newcastle upon Tyne NE1 7RU.

Stewart, Stanley Oliphant; University Librarian, University of Keele, since 1962; *b* 1913; *m* 1941; one *d*. MA Glasgow 1936; ALA 1939. Asst, Glasgow Univ. Library, 1936–39; Asst and Dep. Librarian, Liverpool Univ. Library, 1946–49; Librarian, UC North Staffs, 1949–62. War Service, 1939–45. *Address*: Univ. of Keele, Keele, Staffs ST5 5BG.

Stewart, Vivien Frances; University Lecturer, Department of Land Economy, Cambridge University, and Fellow of New Hall, Cambridge, since 1964; *b* 1933. MA St Andrews 1955; Mem., Reg. Studies Assoc., Urb. Studies Conf. Asst in Res., Cambridge, 1957–59; Univ. Asst Lectr, Cambridge, 1959–64. Dir of Studies in Economics, New Hall, Cambridge, 1965; Mem., Bd of Land Econ., Cambridge Univ., 1965; Bursar, New Hall, 1965–70; Treas., Reg. Studies Assoc., E Anglia Gp, 1971. *Publications*: (with R. Denman) Farm Rents, 1956; *contrib.* Farm Econ. *Address*: New Hall, Cambridge.

Stewart, Prof. William Alexander Campbell, MA, PhD, DL; Vice-Chancellor, University of Keele, since 1967; *b* 1915; *m* 1947; one *s* one *d*. BA London 1937, MA London 1941, PhD 1947, Dip. in Educn 1938; Hon. DLitt Ulster 1973. Asst Lectr and Lectr in Education, Univ. Coll., Nottingham, 1944–47; Lectr in Educn, Univ. of Wales (Cardiff), 1947–50; Prof. of Education, Univ. of Keele, 1950–67; Vis. Prof., McGill Univ., 1957; Vis. Prof., Univ. of California, Los Angeles, 1959; Simon Vis. Prof., Manchester Univ., 1962–63; Prestige Fellow, NZ Univs, 1969. Chm., YMCA Educn Cttee, 1962–67; Chm., Nat. Adv. Council for Child Care, 1968–71; Chm., Univs Council for Adult Educn, 1969–73; Mem., Inter-Univ. Council for Higher Educn Overseas; Mem., Commonwealth Univ. Interchange Council; Mem., British Council, 1968– ; Mem., Adv. Council on Trng and Supply of Teachers, 1973– ; Mem., Council, Fourah Bay Coll., Sierra Leone, 1968–72; Mem., Governing Body, Abbotsholme Sch., Derbyshire, 1960– ; Fellow, Internat. Inst. of Art and Letters. *Publications*: Quakers and Education, 1953; ed (with J. Eros), Systematic Sociology of Karl Mannheim, 1957; (with K. Mannheim) An Introduction to the Sociology of Education, 1962; contrib. The American College (ed Sanford), 1962; The Educational Innovators (vol. 1, with W. P. McCann), 1967; The Educational Innovators (vol. 2), 1968; Progressives and Radicals in English Education, 1750–1970, 1972; *contrib.* Brit. Jl Educnl Sociol., Sociol. Rev., Year Bk of Educn, Brit. Jl Educnl Sociol. Psychol. *Address*: The Clock House, The Univ., Keele, Staffs ST5 5BG.

Still, Dr Arthur William; Lecturer in Psychology, Durham University, since 1965; *b* 1935; *m* 1955; three *d*. BA Cambridge 1959, PhD Cambridge 1965; Mem., Exper. Psychol. Soc. Asst in Res., Cambridge, 1963–65. *Publications*: contrib. Qly Jl Exper. Psychol. *Address*: Dept of Psychology, Science Laboratories, Durham DH1 3LE.

Stillmark, Alexander; Lecturer, German Department, University College London, since 1964; *b* 1937; *m* 1964; one *s* one *d*. BA Cantab 1961 (Mod. and Med. Langs Trip. (German and Russian)), MA 1965, JSSL (Cert. in Russian) 1957. *Publications*: contrib. FMLS, GLL, OGS. *Address*: Univ. Coll. London, Gower Street, WC1E 6BT.

Stirling, Prof. Arthur Paul, MA, DPhil; Professor of Sociology, University of Kent at Canterbury, since 1965; *b* 1920; *m* 1948; two *s* two *d*. MA Oxon 1947 (1st cl. Lit. Hum.), DPhil Oxon 1951 (Social Anthrop.); Mem., Assoc. Soc. Anthrop., Mem., Royal Anthrop. Inst., Mem., Brit. Sociol. Assoc., Mem., Assoc. Brit. Orient., Mem., Brit. Soc. for ME Studies. Asst Lectr in Anthrop., LSE, 1952–54; Lectr in Anthrop., LSE, 1954–65. Mem., Council, Royal Anthrop. Inst., 1967–69. *Publications*: Turkish Village, 1965; contrib. Tensions in the Middle East, ed P. W. Thayer, 1958; Mediterranean Countrymen, ed J. Pitt-Rivers, 1964; contrib. Mediterranean Sociology, ed J. Peristiany, 1968; contrib. Choice and Change, ed J. Davis; *contrib.* Anthrop. Qly, Brit. Jl Sociol., Internat. Social Science Bull., Mid. East Jl, New Atlan. *Address*: Eliot College, The Univ., Canterbury, Kent CT1 3PA.

Stirling, John Fullarton; Librarian, University of Exeter, since 1972; *b* 1931; *m* 1960; two *d*. BA Liverpool 1953, MA Liverpool 1961; Mem. Library Assoc. 1953. Asst Librarian, UCL, 1956–62; Sub-Librarian/Dep., Univ. York, 1962–66; Librarian, Univ. Stirling, 1966–71. *Publications*: contrib. Jl Documentation, Liverpool Public Libraries Bull., SLA News. *Address*: Univ. Library, Prince of Wales Road, Exeter EX4 4PT.

Stockman, Norman; Lecturer in Sociology, Department of Sociology, Aberdeen University, since 1968; *b* 1944; *m* 1968. BA Oxford 1966, MA Essex 1967. Mem., British Sociolog. Assoc. Temp. Asst Lectr in Sociology,

Univ. of Essex, 1967–68. *Publications: contrib.* Sociolog. Rev. *Address:* Dept of Sociology, King's College, Aberdeen AB9 2UB.

Stoddart, Dr David Ross; University Lecturer, Department of Geography, Cambridge University, since 1967; *b* 1937; *m* 1961; one *s* one *d*. BA Cantab 1959, MA Cantab 1963, PhD Cantab 1964; Mem., Royal Geog. Soc., Mem., Inst. Brit. Geogrs, Mem., Brit. Ecol. Soc., Mem., Geog. Assoc. Univ. Demonstrator, Cambridge, 1962–67; Fellow, Churchill Coll., Cambridge, 1966– ; Scientific Co-ordinator, Royal Soc. Aldabra Res. Programme, 1968– . Ed., Atoll Res. Bull.; Ed. Progress in Geog. Adv.; Ed., Jl Hum. Ecol. *Publications:* (with C. M. Yonge) Regional Variation in Indian Ocean coral reefs, 1971; *contrib.* Atoll Res. Bull., Geog. Jl, Phil. Trans Royal Soc. Lond., Trans Inst. Brit. Geogrs. *Address:* Dept of Geography, Downing Place, Cambridge CB2 3EN.

Stokes, Dr Antony Derek, MA, PhD; Fellow and Praelector in Russian, University College, Oxford, since 1967; Faculty Lecturer in Russian, University of Oxford, since 1967; *b* 1927; *m* 1973; three *d*. BA Cambridge 1951 (Mod. and Med. Langs, Pembroke), MA 1955, PhD Cambridge 1959; Mem., British Universities Assoc. of Slavists. Asst Lectr, Russian, Univ. of Liverpool, 1955–57; SSEES, Univ. of London, 1957–67. *Publications:* (with J. L. I. Fennell) Early Russian Literature, 1974; *contrib.* Penguin Companion to Literature, SEER, YWML. *Address:* Univ. College, Oxford.

Stokes, Prof. Eric Thomas, MA, PhD; Smuts Professor of the History of the British Commonwealth, University of Cambridge, since 1970; *b* 1924; *m* 1949; four *d*. MA Cantab 1949, PhD Cantab 1953. Lectr, Malaya Univ., 1950–55; Lectr, Bristol Univ., 1955–56; Prof. of History, UC Rhodesia and Nyasaland, 1956–63; Lectr, Cambridge Univ. and Fellow and Tutor, St Catharine's Coll., 1963–70; Reader, Cambridge Univ., 1970. *Publications:* The English Utilitarians and India, 1959; The Political Ideas of English Imperialism: an inaugural lecture, 1960; ed (with Richard Brown), The Zambesian Past, 1966; contrib. Historians of India, Pakistan and Ceylon, ed Philips, 1961; contrib. Elites in South Asia, ed Leach and Mukherjee, 1970; *contrib.* Historical Jl, Past and Present, etc. *Address:* St Catharine's College, Cambridge.

Stone, Brian Ernest, MC, MA; Reader in Literature, Arts Faculty, Open University, since 1969; *b* 1919; *m* 1945; four *s* one *d*. BA Hons London 1951 (English), MA Hons 1954. LRAM Speech and Drama (Teacher) 1949. Founder Council Mem., NATE. *Publications:* Prisoner from Alamein, 1944; verse trans with introds: Sir Gawain and The Green Knight, 1959, 2nd edn 1974; Medieval English Verse, 1963; The Owl and The Nightingale, Cleannes, St Eikenwald, 1971. *Address:* Arts Fac., Open Univ., Walton Hall, Milton Keynes MK7 6AA.

Stone, David Clifford; Visiting Lecturer in Violin, Music Department, Reading University, since 1964; *b* 1936; *m* 1958; one *s*. Polack Exhibitioner, Music and Classics, King's Coll., Cambridge; BA Cantab 1957, MA Cantab; Member: ISM, ESTA. Univ. of Canterbury, NZ, 1958–61; Univ. of Sheffield, 1962–63. Principal, Menuhin Festival Orchestra; conductor and coach, various youth orchestras, etc.; Examiner, Associated Bd, Royal Schs of Music. *Publications:* ed, Joseph Gibbs: Sonatas for Violin and Continuo, 1974; *contrib.* Stud. Mus.; recordings: Teilhard de Chardin, Interludes to Mass on the World, 1972; Delius Sonatas 2 and 3, Legend, 1973; Beethoven/Mozart Sonatas, 1974. *Address:* The Old Post Office, Leighterton, Tetbury, Glos.

Stone, Eric, MA, DPhil; Fellow, and Tutor in Medieval History, Keble College, Oxford University, since 1955, and Senior Tutor, since 1965; *b* 1924; *m* 1950; two *s* two *d*. BA Oxon 1947 (1st cl. Hist.), MA Oxon 1948, DPhil Oxon 1956; FRHistS, FSA. Asst Lectr, Manchester Univ., 1948–51; Lectr, Manchester Univ., 1951–54. *Publications:* Oxfordshire Hundred Rolls of 1279: the Hundred of Bampton (Oxfordshire Record Society, vol. xlvi), 1968; *contrib.* Trans Royal Hist. Soc. *Address:* Keble College, Oxford OX1 3PG.

Stone, Dr Gerald Charles; University Lecturer in Slavonic Languages and Fellow of Hertford College, Oxford, since 1972; *b* 1932; *m* 1953; 1974; two *s* one *d*. BA Hons London 1964 (1st cl. Russian Lang. and Lit.), PhD 1968; MA Cantab 1971, MA (Oxford) 1972; Member: Linguistics Assoc. of GB; Assoc. of Teachers of Russian; Philol Soc.; Brit. Univs Assoc. of Slavists. Lectr, Nottingham Univ., 1966–71; Asst Dir of Res., Cambridge Univ., 1971–72. *Publications:* Lexical Changes in the Upper Sorbian Literary Language during and following the National Awakening, 1971; The Smallest Slavonic Nation, 1972; *contrib.* Oxford Slav. Papers, Trans Philol Soc., Pamiętnik Słowiański, Slavonic and E European Rev., Studia z filologii polskiej i słowiańskiej. *Address:* Hertford Coll., Oxford OX1 3BW.

Stone, Dr Jeffrey Charles; Senior Lecturer, Department of Geography, Aberdeen University, since 1973 (Lecturer, 1965–73); *b* 1936; *m* 1967; one *d*. MA Edinburgh, 1958 (1st cl. Geog.); PhD Aberdeen 1972. Overseas Service Course Cambridge 1959. Admin. Off., Govt of N Rhodesia and Zambia, 1959–65. *Publications: contrib.* O'Dell Mem. Monog. Series, Scott. Geog. Mag., Trans Dumf. Gall. Nat. Hist. Antiqu. Soc., Imago Mundi, Geog. Mag., Jl Trop. Geog., Northern Scotland. *Address:* Dept of Geography, St Mary's, High Street, Aberdeen AB9 2UF.

Stone, Prof. (John) Richard (Nicholas), CBE, FBA; P. D. Leake Professor of Finance and Accounting, University of Cambridge, since 1955, Fellow of King's College, Cambridge, since 1945; *b* 1913; *m* 1941; 1960; one *d*. MA, ScD Cantab 1957, HonDr Oslo 1965, HonDr Brussels 1965, HonDr Geneva 1971; FBA 1956, Mem., Internat. Statistical

Inst., Pres., Econometric Soc. 1955, Hon. Mem., Soc. of Incorp. Accountants 1954, For. Hon. Mem., Amer. Acad. of Arts and Sciences 1968. Dir, Dept of Applied Econs, Cambridge Univ., 1945–55. With C. E. Heath and Co., Lloyd's Brokers, 1936–39; Min. of Econ. Warfare, 1939–40; Central Statistical Office, 1940–45. *Publications*: The Role of Measurement in Economics, 1951; (jtly) The Measurement of Consumers' Expenditure and Behaviour in the United Kingdom 1920–1938, vol. 1 1954, vol. 2 1966; Quantity and Price Indexes in National Accounts, 1956; Input–Output and National Accounts, 1961; (with G. Stone, 9th edn) National Income and Expenditure, 1966; Mathematics in the Social Sciences, and other Essays, 1966; Mathematical Models of the Economy, and other Essays, 1970; Demographic Accounting and Model Building, 1971; gen. ed. and pt author series, A Programme for Growth, 1962– ; numerous articles. *Address*: King's College, Cambridge.

Stone, Olive Marjorie; Reader in Law, London University, since 1964; *b* 1910. BSc(Econ) London 1947, LLB London 1949, PhD London 1964; Called to the Bar (Gray's Inn) 1951. Asst Lectr, London Univ., 1950–52; Lectr, London Univ., 1952–64. *Publications*: Jt ed., Commonwealth and Dependencies, in, Halsbury: Laws of England, 3rd edn 1953; (jtly) Family Law, in, Reform the Law Now, 1963; The World of Wedlock, in, In Her Own Right, 1968; *contrib*. Amer. Jl Fam. Law, Archiv. Civilist. Praxis, Fam. Law Qly, Internat. Corp. Law Qly, Jl Soc. Public Teachers Law, Mod. Law Rev. *Address*: London School of Economics and Political Science, Houghton Street, Aldwych, WC2A 2AE.

Stoneman, Colin Frank; Lecturer, Department of Education, University of York, since 1967; *b* 1930; *m* 1956; two *s*. BSc Gen Hons London 1951 (Botany, Chemistry Zoology), BSc Spec. Hons London 1952 (Botany); Postgrad. Certificate in Educn, London 1953. FIBiol, Mem., Associates for Science Educn. *Publications*: Maintenance of the Organism (Nuffield Advanced Biological Science), 1970; Metabolism, 1970; Biological Barriers, 1971; Space Biology, 1972; Enzymes and Equilibria, 1974; *contrib*. Jl of Biol. Educn, Sch. Science Rev. *Address*: Dept of Educn, Univ. of York, Heslington YO1 5DD.

Stoneman, Patricia Mary, MA; Part-time Lecturer in English Literature, Hull University, since 1969; *b* 1940; *m* 1962; two *d*. BA London 1962 (1st cl. Engl. Lang. and Lit.), MA London 1964. Asst Lectr, Hull Coll. of Educn, 1964–66; Asst Lectr, Hull Univ., 1966–67; Lectr, Hull Univ., 1967–69. *Address*: Dept of English, Hull Univ., Cottingham Road, Hull HU6 7RX.

Stones, Prof. Edgar; Professor of Education, University of Liverpool, since 1972; *b* 1922; *m* 1948; one *s* one *d*. BA Sheffield 1951, MA Sheffield 1957 (Educn), DipEd Sheffield 1952, DipEdPsychol Manchester 1958, PhD Birmingham 1970. Lectr Educn (Psychol.), Univ. of Birmingham, 1964–72. *Publications*: An Introduction to Educational Psychology,

1966, Spanish edn 1969, French edn 1972, Russian edn (forthcoming); Learning and Teaching: a programmed introduction, 1968, Italian edn 1970, Spanish, Danish, German edns 1972; Readings in Educational Psychology, 1970, Spanish edn 1972; Educational Objectives and the Teaching of Educational Psychology, 1972; (with S. Morris) Teaching Practice: Problems and Perspectives, 1972; *contrib*. Brit. Jl Educnl Psychol., Programmed Learning, Educn Res., Educn Rev. *Address*: School and Institute of Education, Univ. of Liverpool, 19–23 Abercromby Square, Liverpool L69 3BX.

Stones, Prof. Edward Lionel Gregory, MA, PhD, FSA; Professor of Medieval History, University of Glasgow, since 1956; *b* 1914; *m* 1947; one *s* one *d*. MA Glasgow 1936 (1st cl. Engl. Lang. and Lit.), BA Oxford 1939 (1st cl. Mod. Hist.), MA Oxford 1943, PhD Glasgow 1950; FSA 1962, FRHistS 1950. Asst Lectr, Glasgow, 1939–45; Lectr, Glasgow, 1945–51; Sen. Lectr, Glasgow, 1951–56. GSO2, Signals Directorate, GHQ, India, 1943–45; Mem., Anc. Monum. Bd for Scotl., 1964; Chm., Anc. Monum. Bd for Scotl., 1968–73; Mem., Council, Royal Hist. Soc., 1968–72; Pres., Glasgow Archaeol. Soc., 1969–72, Mem., Council Soc. Antiq., London, 1972–74. *Publications*: Anglo-Scottish Relations, 1174–1328, 1965, rev. edn 1971; *contrib*. Antiqu. Jl, Archives, Bull. Inst. Hist. Res., EHR, Hist., Innes Rev., Scott. Hist. Rev., Trans Royal Hist. Soc. *Address*: Dept of History, The Univ., Glasgow G12 8QQ.

Stoney, Peter John Milton; Lecturer, School of Business Studies, University of Liverpool, since 1970; *b* 1940; *m* 1965; one *s* two *d*. BA Liverpool 1966, MA(Econ) Manchester 1967; Mem., Manch. Stat. Soc.; Mem., Assoc. Teachers of Management. Student Demonstrator, Univ. of Manchester, 1966–67; Asst Lectr, Univ. of Manchester, 1967–68; Lectr, Univ. of Salford, 1968–70. Pt-time cnsltnt, NBPI, 1970, Office of Manpower Econs, 1972. *Publications*: *contrib*. Manch. Sch., Rev. Econ. Studies, Management, Educn and Develt. *Address*: 11 Abercromby Square, Liverpool L69 3BX.

Stopes-Roe, Dr Harry V., MSc, PhD; Senior Lecturer in Science Studies (formerly Physics), Department of Extramural Studies, University of Birmingham, since 1972; *b* 1924; *m* 1948; two *s* two *d*. BSc, ARCS London 1944, MSc Cantab 1949 (Nat. Sciences), PhD Cantab 1957 (Moral Sciences); FRAS 1946. Demonstrator in Physics, Imperial Coll., London, 1944–45; Lectr in Physics, incl. Philos. and Sociol. of Sci., Birmingham, 1958–72. Vis. Lectr, Univ. of Washington, Seattle, 1965. *Publications*: *contrib*. Philos. of Sci., Jl Symbolic Logic, Nature, etc. *Address*: Dept of Extramural Studies, Univ. of Birmingham, PO Box 363, Birmingham B15 2TT.

Stopford, Prof. John Morton; Professor of International Business, London Business School, since 1974; *b* 1939; *m* 1966; two *s*. BA Oxon 1961, SM MIT 1962, DBA Harvard 1968. Vis. Sen. Lectr, Manchester Bus. Sch.,

1968–70; Vis. Asst Prof., Harvard Bus. Sch., 1970–71; Reader in Business Policy, London Business Sch., 1971–74. Chm., Bus. Policy Area, LBS. Director: Shell (UK) Ltd; Bracken, Kelner and Associates; Orbit Business Soc., Geneva. *Publications*: (with L. T. Wells) Managing the Multinational Enterprise, US and UK, 1972, Fr. and Japanese edns 1974; (with D. F. Channon and D. Norburn) British Business Policy: a casebook, 1975; *contrib.* Admin. Scene Qly. *Address*: London Business Sch., Sussex Place, Regent's Park, NW1 4SA.

Stopp, Elisabeth Charlotte; Lecturer in German, University of Cambridge, since 1966; *b* 1911; *m* 1937. BA Cantab 1932, MA Cantab 1935, PhD Cantab 1937; FRSL 1963. Ottilie Hancock Res. Fellow, Girton Coll., Cambridge, 1935–37; Lectr, Royal Holloway Coll., Univ. of London, 1956–57. *Publications*: De adhaerendo Deo, St Albert the Great, 1948, 2nd edn 1956; St Francis de Sales: Selected Letters, 1960; Madame de Chantal, 1962, Spanish trans. 1964; St Francis de Sales: A Testimony by St Chantal, 1967; C. Brentano: Chronika des fahrenden Schülers, 1971; *contrib.* Deutsche Vjschr., Fr. Studies, Litwiss. Jb., Mod. Lang. Rev., Month, Oxf. Germ. Studies, Salesian Studies. *Address*: Faculty of Modern and Medieval Languages, Sidgwick Avenue, Cambridge.

Stopp, Frederick John, MBE; MA, PhD; Reader in Renaissance German Studies, University of Cambridge, since 1971; *b* 1911; *m* 1937. BA Cantab 1932, MA Cantab 1947, PhD London 1948; FRNumS. Lectr, Univ. of Cambridge, 1947–71; Sandars Lectr, Cambridge, 1972; Fellow, Gonville and Caius Coll., Cambridge, 1958– ; Sen. Tutor, Gonville and Caius Coll., Cambridge, 1961–65. Germanic Ed., Mod. Lang. Rev., 1960–72. *Publications*: Manual of Modern German, 1957; Evelyn Waugh, Portrait of an Artist, 1958; Emblems of the Altdorf Academy: medals and medal orations 1577–1626, 1974; *contrib.* Deutsche Vierteljahrsschrift, Jl Warb. Court. Inst., Literaturwiss. Jb. d. Görresg., Mod. Lang. Rev. *Address*: Gonville and Caius College, Cambridge.

Storey, Prof. Robin Lindsay; Professor of English History, University of Nottingham, since 1973; *b* 1927; *m* 1956; one *s* one *d*. BA Oxon 1951, PhD Dunelm 1954, MA Oxon 1955; FRHistS. Asst Keeper, Public Rec. Off. 1953–62. Lectr in History, 1962–64, Sen. Lectr in History, 1964–66, Reader, 1966–73, Univ. of Nottingham. Hon. Gen. Ed., Canterbury and York Soc., 1968– ; Thoroton Soc. Rec. Series, 1966– . *Publications*: ed, The Register of Thomas Langley (Surtees Soc.), 1956–70; Diocesan Administration in the Fifteenth Century, 1959; Thomas Langley and the Bishopric of Durham, 1961; Index of Warrants for Issues and Indentures of War, 1963; The End of the House of Lancaster, 1966; The Reign of Henry VII, 1968; ed (with D. A. Bullough), The Study of Medieval Records, 1971; Diocesan Administration in Fifteenth-Century England, 1972; Chronology of the Medieval World, 1973; contrib. The Reign of Richard II, ed F. R. H.

Du Boulay and C. M. Barron, 1971; contrib. Fifteenth-century England, ed S. B. Chrimes, C. D. Ross and R. A. Griffiths, 1972; *contrib.* EHR. *Address*: Dept of History, The Univ., Nottingham NG7 2RD.

Stork, Francis Colin, MA, PhD; Head of Language Centre, University of Sheffield, since 1971; *b* 1936; *m* 1958; one *s* two *d*. BA Birmingham 1957 (German), CertEd Birmingham 1958, MA Birmingham 1961, PhD Manchester 1971. Asst Lectr, then Lectr in Mod. Langs, Univ. of Manchester Inst. of Science and Technol., 1962–66; Lectr in Applied Linguistics, Univ. of Sheffield, 1966–70. *Publications*: (with R. Hartmann) Dictionary of Language and Linguistics, 1972; (with J. D. A. Widdowson) Learning About Linguistics: an introductory workbook, 1974; *contrib.* AV Lang. Jl, Brit. Jl Disord. Comm., Leb. Sprach., Mod. Langs, Nordfries. Jb. *Address*: The Language Centre, Univ. of Sheffield, Sheffield S10 2TN.

Storm-Clark, Christopher Connington; Lecturer in Economic and Social History, Department of Economics and Related Studies, University of York, since 1967; *b* 1942. BA Cantab 1963 (1st cl. Hons, History); Mem., Econ. History Soc., 1960– , Hon. Sec., Oral History Soc., 1973– . Asst Lectr, Econ. and Social History, Univ. of York, 1965–67. Hon. Sec., AUT, York Local Assoc., 1968–73. *Publications*: contrib. Victorian Studies. *Address*: Dept of Economics and Related Studies, Univ. of York, Heslington, York YO1 5DD.

Storrie, Dr Margaret Cochrane, (Mrs C. I. Jackson); Lecturer, Geography Department, Queen Mary College, University of London, since 1962; *b* 1935; *m* 1963. BSc Glasgow 1957 (Hons Geog.), PhD Glasgow 1962; Mem., Inst. Brit. Geogrs, Mem., Royal Scott. Geog. Soc. Lectr, Glasgow Univ., 1957–60; Lectr, Bedford Coll., Univ. of London, 1960–62; Lectr, Queen Mary Coll., Univ. of London, 1962– ; Sen. Leverhulme Fellow, 1969–70. *Publications*: (trans. with C. I. Jackson) L. E. Hamelin: Canada: a geographical perspective, 1973; Isle of Islay (forthcoming); *contrib.* Cartog. Jl, Folk Life, Geog. Mag., Geog. Rev., Geog. Ann., Scott. Geog. Mag., Scott. Studies, Trans Inst. Brit. Geogrs. *Address*: Queen Mary College, Mile End Road, E1 4NS.

Stott, Dr Antonia; Lecturer in Italian, University of Edinburgh, since 1968; *b* 1923; *m* 1949; two *s*. Laurea in Lettere e Filosofia, Milan 1945. Lectr, Glasgow Univ., 1964–68. *Publications*: contrib. Agenda, Scottish Internat. *Address*: Italian Dept, David Hume Tower, George Square, Edinburgh EH8 9JX.

Strachan, Dr Alan James; Lecturer in Geography, University of Leicester, since 1969; *b* 1940; *m* 1970. MA Hons Edinburgh 1963, MS Wisconsin 1964, PhD Edinburgh 1969; Mem., Inst. Brit. Geogrs. Univ. of Leeds, 1968–69. *Publications*: contrib. Town and Country Planning, Geographia Polonica. *Address*: Dept of Geography, Univ. of Leicester, Leicester LE1 7RH.

Strachan, John Christopher Gibson; Lecturer in Classics, University of Hull, since 1965; *b* 1938; *m* 1962; three *d*. MA Edinburgh 1960. Asst Lectr in Classics, Hull, 1963–65. *Publications*: trans. (with R. Strachan), A. Stern: The Science of Freedom, 1969; *contrib.* Class. Qly, Class. Philol. *Address*: Dept of Classics, Univ. of Hull, Hull HU6 7RX.

Straker, Dermot, MA, FBPsS; Senior Lecturer, Department of Psychology, University of Liverpool, since 1970; *b* 1912; *m* 1938; two *s* two *d*. BA Cantab 1935 (2nd cl. Nat. Sciences, Tripos Pt I, 1st cl. Moral Sci., Tripos Pt II [Psychol.]), MA Cantab 1949; FBPsS. Pt-time Lectr, Univ. Coll., Wellington, NZ, 1951–54; Lectr, Univ. of Liverpool, 1954–70; Sub-Dean, Univ. of Liverpool, 1963–66. Mem., Council, Brit. Psychol. Soc., 1955–68; Chm., NZ Br., BPS, 1952–54; Gov., Bedales Sch., 1946–49; Mem., Sci. Staff, Nat. Inst. of Indust. Psychol., 1935–48; Temp. Psychologist, Admiralty, 1948–49. *Publications*: (jtly) Training Operatives for Machine Shops, 1944; (jtly) The Academic Record of Science Students in the University of New Zealand, 1955; *contrib.* Bull. Brit. Psychol. Soc., Occupat. Psychol. *Address*: Dept of Psychology, Univ. of Liverpool, PO Box 147, Liverpool L69 3BX.

Strang, Prof. Barbara Mary Hope; Professor of English Language and General Linguistics, since 1964, and Head of School of English, University of Newcastle upon Tyne, since 1970; *b* 1925; *m* 1955; one *d*. BA London 1945 (Hons English Lang. and Lit.), MA London 1947. Mem., Philol. Soc., Foundn Mem. and former Sec., Lingu. Assoc. Asst Lectr, Westfield Coll., London, 1947–50; Lectr, King's Coll., Newcastle, 1950–63. Chm., Univ. Libr. Cttee, 1969– . *Publications*: Modern English Structure, 1962, 2nd edn 1968; A History of English, 1970; contrib. var. wks jt authorship; *contrib.* Durh. Univ. Jl, Trans Philol. Soc., Zeits. Mundart., etc. *Address*: School of English, The Univ., Newcastle upon Tyne NE1 7RU.

Straw, Prof. Allan, BA, PhD; Professor of Geography, University of Exeter, since 1971; *b* 1931; *m* 1955; two *s* one *d*. BA Nottingham 1954 (1st cl. Geog.), PhD Sheffield 1964. Mem., Inst. Brit. Geogrs, Mem., Geog. Assoc., Mem., Geol. Assoc., Mem., Yorks Geol. Soc., Mem., Quatern Res. Assoc. Jun. Res. Fellow, Sheffield Univ., 1954–57; Lectr, Sheffield Univ., 1957–65, 1967–68; Asst Prof., McMaster Univ., 1965–67; Sen. Lectr, Sheffield Univ., 1968–71. Pres., Lincoln Br., Geog. Assoc., 1970– . *Publications*: *contrib.* Bull. Geol. Soc. Amer., Canad. Geog., Proc. Geol. Assoc., Proc. Yorks Geol. Soc., Trans Papers Inst. Brit. Geogrs. *Address*: Dept of Geography, Univ. of Exeter, Exeter EX4 4QJ.

Strawson, Prof. Peter Frederick, FBA; Waynflete Professor of Metaphysical Philosophy, University of Oxford, and Fellow of Magdalen College, Oxford, since 1968; *b* 1919; *m* 1945; two *s* two *d*. BA Oxon 1940 (2nd cl. PPE), MA Oxon 1946; FBA 1960. Foreign Hon. Mem., Amer. Acad. Arts Sci.,

1971. Asst Lectr in Philosophy, Univ. Coll. of N Wales, Bangor, 1946–47; Lectr in Philosophy, 1947–48, and Fellow and Praelector in Philosophy, Univ. Coll., Oxford, 1948–68; Reader, Univ. of Oxford, 1966–68. Pres., Aristot. Soc., 1969–70. *Publications*: Introduction to Logical Theory, 1952; Individuals, 1959; The Bounds of Sense, 1966; ed, Philosophical Logic, 1967; ed, Studies in the Philosophy of Thought and Action, 1968; Logico-Linguistic Papers, 1971; Freedom and Resentment, 1974; *contrib.* Analysis, Jl Philos., Mind, Philos. Qly, Philos. Rev., Philos., Proc. Aristot. Soc. *Address*: Magdalen College, Oxford.

Street, Prof. Harry, LLM, PhD, FBA; Professor of English Law, University of Manchester, since 1956; *b* 1919; *m* 1947; two *s* one *d*. LLB Manchester 1938, LLM Manchester 1947, PhD Manchester 1951; FBA 1968. Lectr, Manchester, 1946–51; Prof. of Law, Nottingham, 1952–56; Vis. Prof., Harvard Law Sch., 1957–58. Chm., Street Report on Race Relat.; Mem., Royal Commn on the Constitution, 1969–73; Mem., Monopolies and Mergers Commn, 1973– . *Publications*: (with J. A. G. Griffith) Principles of Administrative Law, 5th edn 1973; A Comparative Study of Governmental Liability, 1953; Torts, 5th edn 1972; Damages, 1962; Freedom, the Individual and the Law, 3rd edn 1972; *contrib.* Law Qly Rev., Mod. Law Rev., New Soc. *Address*: Law Faculty, Univ. of Manchester, Manchester M13 9PL.

Street, Dr John, MA, PhD; Lecturer in Latin American Studies, Department of Spanish and Faculty of History, Cambridge University, since 1951; *b* 1922; *m* 1st 1947, 2nd 1971; one *s* one *d*. BA Cantab 1946 (1st cl.), MA Cantab 1947, CertEd Cambridge 1947, PhD Cantab 1950; FRHistS. War Service, 1942–45; Tutor, then Fellow, Fitzwilliam Coll., Cambridge, 1958– ; Chm., Faculty Bd of Modern and Medieval Langs, Cambridge Univ., 1964–67; Dir of Studies in Modern and Medieval Langs, Fitzwilliam Coll., 1968– ; Dir, Cambridge Centre for Latin American Studies, 1966–70. Ed., CUP Latin American Series, 1967– ; Mem., ed. Bd, Jl Lat. Amer. Studies, 1967– ; Mem., Cttee of Mngmt, Camb Centre Lat. Amer. Studies, 1966– ; Past Chm., Soc. Lat. Amer. Studies; Mem., UGC Cttee on Lat. Amer. Studies (Parry Cttee), 1962–64. *Publications*: Artigas and the Emancipation of Uruguay, 1959, Spanish edn 1967; La Gran Bretaña y la emancipación del Virreinato del Río de la Plata, 1968; trans., G. Morón: A History of Venezuela, 1964; ed (with F. Street), F. García Lorca: La zapatera prodigiosa, 1962; *contrib.* Hispan. Amer. Hist. Rev., Rev. Hist. (Montevideo). *Address*: Fitzwilliam College, Cambridge.

Streeten, Paul Patrick, MA; Director, Institute of Commonwealth Studies, Warden of Queen Elizabeth House, and Fellow of Balliol College, Oxford University, since 1968; *b* 1917; *m* 1951; one step *s* two *d*. MA Aberdeen 1944, BA Oxon 1947 (PPE), Hon. Schol., Balliol Coll., Oxford, MA Oxon 1952; FREconS. Mem., Amer. Econ. Assoc. Fellow, Balliol Coll., Oxford, 1948–64, 1968– ;

Prof., Univ. of Sussex; Fellow, and Act. Dir, Inst. of Development Studies, Univ. of Sussex, 1966–68. Dep. Dir Gen., Econ. Planning, Min. of Overseas Develop., 1964–66; Mem., Cwealth Develop. Corp., 1967–72; Mem., UNESCO UK Nat. Commn; Mem., Prov. Council, Univ. of Mauritius; Mem., Gov. Body: Inst. of Develt Studies; Queen Elizabeth Hse; Dominion Students' Hall Trust, London Hse; Mem. Council, Overseas Develt Inst. *Publications*: ed, Value in Social Theory, 1958; Economic Integration, 1961, 2nd edn 1964; ed (with Lipton), The Crisis of Indian Planning, 1968; ed, Unfashionable Economics, 1970; (with D. Elson) Diversification and Development: the Case of Coffee, 1971; ed (with H. Corbet), Commonwealth Policy in a Global Context, 1971; The Frontiers of Development Studies, 1972; Trade Strategies for Development, 1974; *contrib*. Amer. Econ. Rev., Bull. Oxf. Inst. Econ., Econ Jl, Oxf. Econ. Papers, Qly Jl Econ., Rev. Econ. Studies. *Address*: Queen Elizabeth House, 21 St Giles, Oxford OX1 3LA.

Streeter, David Thomas, BSc, MIBiol, FLS; Lecturer in Ecology, School of Biological Sciences, University of Sussex, since 1965; *b* 1937; *m* 1967; one *s*. BSc London 1959; MIBiol 1962, FLS. Asst Lectr in Botany, Kings Coll., London, 1962–65. Mem., Exec. Cttee, Council for Nature; Mem., Exec. Cttee, SPNR; Chm., Conservation Liaison Cttee; Mem., Council, Brit. Ecol Soc.; Mem., Exec. Cttee, Field Studies Council. Working Party on Nat. Resource Mngmt, UN Conf. in Hum. Environ., 1971–72. *Publications*: *contrib*. Sci. Prog., Symp. Brit. Ecol. Soc., Trans Brit. Bryol. Soc. *Address*: School of Biological Sciences, Univ. of Sussex, Falmer, Brighton BN1 9QG.

Strelcyn, Stefan; Reader in Semitic Languages, University of Manchester, since 1973 (Lecturer, 1970–72); *b* 1918; *m* 1940; two *s*. L ès L Sorbonne 1948, Dip ENLOV Paris 1948, Dip ILOA Inst. Cath Paris 1949, Dip EPHE 4 Section Paris 1950; Haile Selassie I Award for Ethiopian Studies 1967. Attaché de Recherches, CNRS, Paris, 1949; Asst Prof., Univ. of Warsaw, 1950; Prof., Univ. of Warsaw, 1954–69; Hd of Dept of Semitic Studies, Univ. of Warsaw, 1950–69; Vis. Lectr, SOAS, Univ. of London, 1969–70; Dep.-Dir, Inst. Orient. Studies, Polish Acad., 1953–62; Vice-Pres., Cttee of Orient. Studies, Polish Acad., 1954–66; Dir, Inst. Orient. Studies, Univ. of Warsaw, 1961–65; Dir., Centre of Afr. Studies, Univ. of Warsaw, 1962–69; Ed., Catalogue des MSS orientaux des Collections Polonaises, 1959–67; Africana Bull., 1964–69; Co-ed., Rocznik orientalistyczny, 1954–68; Prace orientalistyczne PAN, 1954–68. Mem., Pol. Tow. Orient., Pol. Tow Językoz., Soc. Asiat., Soc. Lingu., GLECS, Soc. Africanistes, ASAUK, SOTS. *Publications*: Catalogue des manuscrits éthiopiens de la Collection Griaule, vol. IV, 1954; Prières magiques éthiopiennes pour délier les charmes, 1955; Kebra Nagast, 1956, Mission scientifique en Ethiopie, 1960. Médecine et plantes d'Ethiopie, vol. I, 1968, vol. II, 1973; *contrib*. Bull. SOAS, Euhemer, CR GLECS, Jl Asiat., Przegląd Orient., Jl Ethiop. Studies, Jl Sem.

Studies, Rass. Studi Etiop., Rocznik Orient. *Address*: Dept of Near Eastern Studies, Univ. of Manchester, Manchester M13 9PL.

Stringer, Dr Edward Trevor; Senior Lecturer, Geography Department, University of Birmingham, since 1967; *b* 1928; *m* 1957; two *s*. BSc Birmingham 1949 (1st cl.), PhD Birmingham 1951; FRMetS, FRGS. Professional Mem., Amer. Meteorol. Soc., Mem., Inst. Brit. Geogrs, Mem., Geog. Assoc., Brit. Assoc. Lectr in Meteorology and Climatology, Univ. of Birmingham, 1955–66; Sen. Lectr in Charge, Postgrad. Sch. of Climatology and Applied Meteorology, 1967–   ; Vis. Prof. of Climatology, McGill Univ., 1964–65; Sci. Dir, Edgbaston Meteorol. Observatory (Univ. of Birmingham), 1967–   . *Publications*: Foundations of Climatology, 1971; Techniques of Climatology, 1971; Climate in the Service of Man, 1972. *Address*: Dept of Geography, Univ. of Birmingham, PO Box 363, Birmingham B15 2TT.

Strong, Kenneth; Lecturer in Japanese, Department of Far East, School of Oriental and African Studies, University of London, since 1965; *b* 1925; *m* 1953; one *s* one *d*. BA Oxon 1947 (Classics), MA Oxon 1957, BA London 1951 (Japanese), BA London 1957 (English). Lectr, Univ. of Sydney, 1963–64. *Publications*: trans., The Buddha Tree, 1966; Footprints in the Snow, 1970; Pillar of Fire, 1972; The Broken Commandment (forthcoming); Biography of Tanaka Shōzō (forthcoming); *contrib*. Bull. Orient. Soc. Austral., Monum. Nippon. *Address*: School of Oriental and African Studies, Univ. of London, WC1E 7HP.

Strongman, Dr Kenneth Thomas, BSc, PhD; Lecturer in Psychology, University of Exeter, since 1964; *b* 1940; *m* 1964; one *s* one *d*. BSc London 1962 (Psychol.), PhD London 1964. MBPsS. *Publications*: Psychology of Emotion, 1973; *contrib*. Brit. Jl Psychol., Canad. Jl Psychol., Jl Exper. Psychol., Psychol. Rec., Qly Jl Exper. Psychol. *Address*: Psychology Dept, Washington Singer Laboratories, Univ. of Exeter, Exeter.

Stuart, Charles Harborne, MA, FRHistS; Student and Tutor of Christ Church, Oxford, since 1948, and University Lecturer in Modern History, Oxford University, since 1950; *b* 1920; *m* 1951; one *s* one *d*. BA Oxon 1941 (1st cl. Hist.), MA Oxon 1945; FRHistS 1971. Lectr in Mod. Hist., Queen's Coll., Oxford, 1946–47; Lectr in Mod. Hist., Christ Church, Oxford, 1947–48, Censor, 1953–58; Examiner in Final Hons School Mod. Hist., 1953–55, 1963–64 (Chm., 1964); Ext. Examiner in Mod. Hist., Univ. of St Andrews, 1962–65; Vis. Prof., Simpson Coll., Iowa, 1964; Sec., Gov. Body, Christ Church, 1966–70. Special Dept, Foreign Off., 1941–45; Foreign Off., 1945. *Publications*: ed, B. Williams: The Whig Supremacy, rev. edn 1962; contrib. Essays in British History, ed H. Trevor-Roper, 1964; *contrib*. Trans Royal Hist. Soc. *Address*: Christ Church, Oxford.

Stuart, Denis Gwynne; Senior Lecturer in History, Department of Adult Education, University of Keele, since 1971; *b* 1919; *m*

1947; one *d*. BA London 1950 (1st cl. Hist.), MA London 1958. Staff Tutor, Oxford Univ. Delegacy for Extra-Mural Studies, 1951–61. *Publications*: (with M. W. Greenslade) History of Staffordshire, 1965; *contrib*. Lichf. S Staffs. Archaeol. Hist. Soc. Trans. *Address*: Dept of Adult Education, Univ. of Keele, Keele, Staffordshire ST5 5BG.

Stubbings, Frank Henry, MA, PhD, FSA; Lecturer in Classics, Cambridge University, since 1949; *b* 1915; *m* 1945; two *d*. BA Cambridge 1937, MA Cambridge 1944, PhD Cambridge 1948; FSA, Corresp. Mem., Deuts. Archäol. Inst. Res. Fellow, Emmanuel Coll., Cambridge, 1945–49; Official Fellow, 1949; Coll. Libr., 1959– ; Vice-Master, Emmanuel Coll., Cambridge, 1965–69. *Publications*: Mycenaean Pottery from the Levant, 1951; ed (with A. J. B. Wace), A Companion to Homer, 1962; Prehistoric Greece (World of Archaeology series), 1972; *contrib*. Ann. Brit. Sch. Athens, Antiqu., Class. Rev., Jl Hellen. Studies. *Address*: Emmanuel College, Cambridge.

Stubbs, Hugh William; Senior Lecturer, Department of Classics, Exeter University, since 1969; *b* 1917; *m* 1954; two *s* one *d*. BA Oxon 1940, MA Oxon 1943. Mem., Class. Assoc. 1936. Asst Lectr, Univ. Coll. of the S West, 1942–47; Lectr, Univ. Coll. of the S West, 1947–69. Chm., Exeter Folkl. Soc., 1967–72. *Publications*: *contrib*. Class. Rev., Erasmus, Folkl., Orpheus, Proc. Class. Assoc., Proc. Virg. Soc. *Address*: Dept of Classics, Queen's Building, The Univ., Exeter, Devon EX4 4QH.

Stubbs, Dr Peter Charles, MA, PhD; Senior Lecturer, Department of Economics, University of Manchester, since 1972; *b* 1937; *m* 1962; four *s*. BA Cantab 1960, MA Cantab 1964, PhD Melbourne 1967. Res. Fellow, Inst. of Applied Econ. and Soc. Res., Univ. of Melbourne, 1963–69; Lectr, Univ. of Manchester, 1969–72. RAF 1955–57; The Economist, 1960–62. *Publications*: Innovation and Research, 1968; The Australian Motor Industry, 1972; (with N. Lee) A History of Dorman Smith 1878–1972, 1972; *contrib*. Austral. Econ. Rev., Econ. Rec. *Address*: Dept of Economics, Univ. of Manchester, Manchester M13 9PL.

Studd, Dr John Robert; Lecturer in History, University of Keele, since 1969; *b* 1941; *m* 1968; three *d*. BA Leeds 1963, PhD Leeds 1971. Temp. Asst Lectr, School of History, Univ. of Leeds, 1966–67; Asst Lectr in History, Keele, 1967–69. *Address*: Dept of History, Univ. of Keele, Keele, Staffordshire ST5 5BG.

Studdert-Kennedy, William Gerald; Lecturer, Faculty of Commerce and Social Science, University of Birmingham, since 1973; *b* 1933; *m* 1971; one *s* one *d*. BA Cambridge 1957 (English), MA California 1964 (Berkeley, Pol Science). Production Asst, BBC TV (Talks), 1959–62; Teaching Asst, Univ. of California, Berkeley, 1964–66; Lectr, Dept of Politics, Univ. of York, 1967–73. *Publications*: (with G. C. Moodie) Opinions, Publics and Pressure Groups, 1970;

Evidence and Explanation in Social Science, 1974; *contrib*. Jl Aesthetics and Art Crit., Burlington, Govt and Opposition, Jl Royal Statistical Soc., Pol Studies. *Address*: Faculty of Commerce and Social Science, Univ. of Birmingham, PO Box 363, Birmingham B15 2TT.

Sturdy, David; Lecturer in the Early Medieval Archaeology of Russia and Eastern Europe, jointly in the Institute of Archaeology and the School of Slavonic and East European Studies, University of London, since 1969; *b* 1935; *m* 1967; two *s*. BA Oxon 1958, MA Oxon 1961, BLitt Oxon 1963. Asst Keeper, Dept of Antiquities, Ashmolean Museum, Oxford, 1958–66; Lectr in Medieval Archaeology, Univ. of Liverpool, 1967–69. *Address*: Institute of Archaeology, 31–34 Gordon Square, WC1H 0PY.

Sturdy, Dr David John; Lecturer in History, New University of Ulster, since 1970; *b* 1940; *m* 1969; one *d*. BA Hull 1962, PhD Dublin 1970. Jun. Lectr in History, TCD, 1965–70. *Publications*: Europe and the World, 1763–1960, 1971; The Lost Peace, 1971; Royal Authority in France, 1589–1643, 1973. *Address*: New Univ. of Ulster, Coleraine, N Ireland BT52 1SA.

Sturdy, Rev. John Vivian Mortland; Dean of Gonville and Caius College, Cambridge University, since 1965; *b* 1933; *m* 1962; three *s* two *d*. Oxford, 1st cl. Classical Mods 1952, 2nd cl. Lit. Hum. 1954, 1st cl. Theology 1956, Cambridge, 2nd cl. Oriental Studies (Hebrew and Aramaic) 1958. Mem., Soc. OT Study. Mem., and Libr., Fac. of Divinity, Univ. of Cambridge. Sec., Degree Cttee, Fac. of Divinity, 1968– ; GOE examiner, 1965–72. *Publications*: trans: E. Linnemann: Parables of Jesus, 1966; E. Hammershaimb: The Book of Amos, 1972; H. Ringgren: Religions of the Ancient Near East, 1973; J. Moltmann: Man, 1974; O. Kaiser: Introduction to the Old Testament, 1974; *contrib*. Ch. Qly, Vet. Testam. *Address*: Gonville and Caius College, Cambridge.

Sturgess, Keith Malcolm, MA, BLitt; Lecturer, Department of English, University of Lancaster, since 1966; *b* 1940; *m* 1962; two *s* one *d*. BA Oxon 1963, BLitt Oxon 1966. Univ. of Khartoum (on secondment), 1969–71. *Publications*: Three Elizabethan Domestic Tragedies, 1969; John Ford, Three Plays, 1970; *contrib*. Libr. *Address*: Dept of English, Univ. of Lancaster, Bailrigg, Lancaster LA1 4YW.

Stuvel, Dr Gerhard; University Lecturer in Economic Statistics, University of Oxford, since 1960; *b* 1917; *m* 1949. DrEcon Rotterdam 1950, MA Oxon 1961. Mem., Royal Econ Soc., Mem., Royal Stat. Soc. Res. Fellow, Dept of Applied Econ., Cambridge, 1946–47; Faculty Mem., Inst. of Soc. Studies, The Hague, 1957–62, 1968–71; Vis. Prof., Yale Univ., 1959; Guest Fellow, Branford Coll., 1959; Philips Vis., Haverford Coll., 1960; Vis. Prof., Pennsylvania Univ., 1965; ed, Bull. Oxf. Inst. Stat., 1969– . Neth. Works Admin., 1941; Neth. Min. of Transport, 1941–42; Neth. Cent. Bur. of Stat.,

1942–45; Chief, Macro-Econ. Plan Div., Neth. Cent. Plan. Bureau, 1945–51; Chief, Nat. Acc. Div., OEEC, Paris, 1951–60. *Publications*: The Exchange Stability Problem, 1950; ed, Income Redistribution and the Statistical Foundations of Economic Policy, 1964; Systems of Social Accounts, 1965, Japanese edn 1969, Portuguese edn 1970; *contrib.* Econometrica, Econ. Jl, Econ. (London), Econ (Amsterdam), Inc. Wlth, Jl Royal Stat. Soc., Rev. Econ. Stat., Rev. Econ. Studies. *Address*: Institute of Economics and Statistics, Univ. of Oxford, Oxford.

Stych, Franklin Samuel, MA, FLA; Senior Lecturer, Postgraduate School of Librarianship and Information Science, University of Sheffield, since 1973 (Lecturer, 1964–73); *b* 1916. BA London 1951 (Hons Ital.), MA London 1956; FLA. Birmingham Public Libr., 1933–63. *Publications*: Chapter, in, A Guide to Foreign Language Grammars and Dictionaries, 1964, 2nd edn 1967; How to Find Out about Italy, 1970; Pinocchio in Gran Bretagna e Irlanda, 1971; *contrib.* Libr., Rass. Lucch., R. Q. *Address*: Postgraduate School of Librarianship and Information Science, The Univ., Western Bank, Sheffield S10 2TN.

Styler, Rev. Leslie Moreton; Chaplain and Fellow, Brasenose College, since 1947, and CUF Lecturer in Theology and Classics, Oxford University, since 1965; *b* 1908. BA Oxford 1930 (1st cl. Hon. Mods Classics 1928, 1st cl. Lit. Hum.), MA Oxford 1933. Sixth form master, St Edward's Sch., Oxford, 1931–47. Sen. Tutor, Brasenose Coll., 1965– ; Vice-Principal, Brasenose Coll., 1966–69; Sec., Oxford Colls Admissions Off., 1962–65. *Publications*: Foundation of Greek Prose Composition, 1934, 2nd edn 1954; Euchologium Anglicanum, 1963. *Address*: Brasenose College, Oxford.

Styler, Prof. William Edward; Director and Professor, Department of Adult Education, Hull University, since 1960; *b* 1907; *m* 1933; one *s* one *d*. MA Birmingham 1937. Staff Tutor and Sen. Staff Tutor, Manchester Univ., 1939–48; Adviser, Tutorial Classes, and Dept. Dir of Extra-Mural Studies, 1949–59; Assoc. Dir, 1959–60. Mem., Exec. Cttee, Univs Council Adult Educn, 1965–70; Mem., Council and Exec. Cttee, Nat. Inst. Adult Educn, 1966– ; Vice-Pres., Educnl Centres Assoc., 1969– . *Publications*: Adult Education in India, 1967; ed, F. D. Maurice: Learning and Working, 1968; A Bibliographical Guide to Adult Education in Rural Areas, 1973; contrib. Aspects of the History of Adult Education, 1974; numerous reports and pamphlets; *contrib.* Adult Educn, Aspects Educn, Comm. Develop., Internat. Rev. Educn, Jl Internat. Cong. Univ. Adult Educn. *Address*: Dept of Adult Education, Univ. of Hull, Hull HU6 7RX.

Subiotto, Prof. Arrigo Victor, BA, MA, PhD; Professor of German, University of Birmingham, since 1971; *b* 1928; *m* 1966; two *s*. BA London 1950 (1st cl. German), MA London 1952, DipEd London 1955; PhD Aberdeen 1969. Lectr, Keele Univ., 1956–64; Lectr, Aberdeen Univ., 1965–69; Sen.

Lectr, Stirling Univ., 1969–70. CNAA, 1971– . *Publications*: Bertolt Brecht's Adaptations for the Berliner Ensemble; various articles, essays and chapters in books; *contrib.* Essays in Contemp. German Lit., FMLS, German Life and Letters, Studia Neophilologica, YWMLS, Modern Langs. *Address*: German Dept, Univ. of Birmingham, Birmingham B15 2TT.

Sugden, Dr D. E., BA, DPhil; Senior Lecturer in Geography, University of Aberdeen, since 1973 (Lecturer, 1966–73); *b* 1941; *m* 1966; one *s* one *d*. BA Oxon 1962 (1st cl. Geog.), DPhil Oxon 1965. Mem., Brit. Antarctic Survey, 1965–66. *Publications*: *contrib.* Brit. Art. Surv. Bull., Geog. Jl, Inst. Arctic Alp. Res., Scott. Geog. Mag., Trans Inst. Brit. Geogrs, etc. *Address*: Dept of Geography, Univ. of Aberdeen, Aberdeen AB9 2UF.

Sullivan, John, MA; Lecturer in Russian, University of St Andrews, since 1964; *b* 1937; *m* 1961; two *s* one *d*. BA Manchester 1959 (Russian Studies), MA Manchester 1961. Res. Asst, Clarendon Press, 1961–64; Admissions Off., Fac. of Arts, St Andrews Univ., 1970–73. *Publications*: *contrib.* Bibliothek, Forum Mod. Lang. Studies, Oxf. Slav. Papers. *Address*: Dept of Russian, Univ. of St Andrews, St Andrews, Fife KY16 9AJ.

Sultana, Dr Donald Edward; Senior Lecturer in English Literature, University of Edinburgh, since 1973 (Lecturer, 1965–72); *b* 1924; *m* 1964. BSc Malta 1942, MD Malta 1946, BA Oxon 1951, MA Oxon 1953, DPhil Oxon 1964; Rhodes Schol. for Malta, 1946–50. Carnegie Vis. Fellow, 1959; Lectr in English Lit., Royal Univ. of Malta, 1951–64. *Publications*: Samuel Taylor Coleridge in Malta and Italy, 1969; *contrib.* Times Lit. Supp., European univ. jls. *Address*: David Hume Tower, George Square, Edinburgh EH8 9JX.

Summerfield, Prof. Arthur; Professor of Psychology, University of London, and Head of the Department of Psychology, Birkbeck College, since 1961; *b* 1923; *m* 1946; one *s* one *d*. BScTech Manchester 1947 (Elec. Eng.), BSc London 1949 (1st cl. Psychol.); FBPsS, Sci.FZS. Mem., Amer. Psychol. Assoc., Brit. Pharmacol. Soc., Coll. Internat. Neuropsychopharm., Exper. Psychol. Soc. Asst Lectr in Psychol., Univ. Coll., London, 1949–51; Lectr, Univ. Coll., London, 1951–61; Hon. Res. Assoc., Univ. Coll., London, 1961–71, Hon. Res. Fellow, 1971– ; Vis. Prof., Univ. of California, 1968. Mem., Council, Brit. Psychol. Soc., 1953–65, 1967– ; Hon. Gen. Sec., Brit. Psychol. Soc., 1954–59; Dep. Pres., Brit. Psychol. Soc., 1959–62; Pres.-elect, Brit. Psychol. Soc., 1962–63; Pres., Brit. Psychol. Soc., 1963–64; Vice-Pres., Brit. Psychol. Soc., 1964–65; Mem., Gen. Assembly, Internat. Union of Psychol. Sci., 1957– ; Exec. Cttee, 1963– ; Ed., Brit. Jl Psychol., 1964–67; Asst Ed., Brit. Jl Stat. Psychol., 1950–54; Dep. Chm., Organizing Cttee, XIX Internat. Cong. Psychol., 1966–69. Chm., Dept of Educn and Sci. Working Party on Psychologists in Educn Services, 1965–68; Gov., Enfield Coll.

of Technol., 1968– ; Dean (first), Fac. of Econ., Birkbeck Coll., 1971– . *Publications*: trans. and ed (with H. Steinberg), D. Katz: Animals and Men, 1953; Sci. Ed., British Medical Bulletin issues on: Experimental Psychology, 1964; Cognitive Psychology, 1971; *contrib.* Brit. Jl Psychol., Brit. Jl Sociol., Nature, Psychomet., Qly Jl Exper. Psychol. *Address*: Birkbeck College (Univ. of London), Malet Street, London WC1E 7HX.

Summerfield, Geoffrey; Senior Lecturer in English and Education, University of York, since 1965; *b* 1931. BA London. Lectr in English and Educn, Univ. York, 1965–68; Vis. Prof., Univ. Nebraska, 1968–69; Sen. Lectr, Univ. York, 1969–71; Vis. Prof., English, Univ. Calif. at Berkeley, 1971–72. *Publications*: John Clare: The Shepherd's Calendar, 1964; The Later Poems of John Clare, 1964; Topics in English, 1965, 3rd edn 1971; Voices, 1968; English in Practice, 1969; John Clare: Selected Poetry and Prose, 1969; Junior Voices, 1970; The Creative Word, 1972; Worlds, 1974. *Address*: Univ. of York, Heslington, York YO1 5DD.

Summers, Mrs Janet Margaret; *see* Bateley, J. M.

Summers, Dr Norman; Senior Lecturer, Department of Architecture, University of Nottingham, since 1965; *b* 1916; *m* 1939; one *d*. Dip Archit. Assoc. London, PhD Nottingham 1967. Lectr, Nottingham, 1964–65. *Publications*: A Prospect of Southwell, 1974; *contrib.* Trans Thorot. Soc. Notts. *Address*: Dept of Architecture, Univ. of Nottingham, Nottingham NG7 2RD.

Sumner, Michael Thomas; Lecturer in Economics, University of Manchester, since 1970; *b* 1943; *m* 1967; one *s* one *d*. BA(Econ) Manchester 1965 (1st cl.). Douglas Knoop Res. Fellow in Econs, Sheffield, 1965; Asst Lectr, Sheffield, 1966–69; Lectr, Essex, 1969–70. *Publications*: ed (with others) and contrib., Incomes Policy and Inflation, 1972; *contrib.* Bull. Oxf. Univ. Inst. Stat., Manch. Sch., Scott. Jl Pol Econ., Jl Pol Econ., Proc. AUT Econs. *Address*: Dept of Economics, Univ. of Manchester, Manchester M13 9PL.

Sunderland, Prof. Eric, MA, PhD; Professor of Anthropology, University of Durham, since 1971; *b* 1930; *m* 1957; two *d*. BA Wales 1950 (1st cl. Geog. with Anthrop.), MA Wales 1951, PhD London 1954; FRAI, Eugenics Soc. Lectr, Univ. of Durham, 1958–66; Sen. Lectr, 1966–71. Mem., Council, Royal Anthrop. Inst., 1966–69, 1970–73; Recorder, Anthrop. Sect., Brit. Assoc., 1973– ; Mem., Cttee and Programme Sec., Soc. Study Hum. Biol., 1968– ; Mem., Council, Eugenics Soc., 1973– . Book Reviews Ed., Annals of Human Biology. *Publications*: Elementary Human and Social Geography: some anthropological perspectives, 1973; ed (with D. F. Roberts), Genetic Variation in Britain, 1973; contrib. Cambridge History of Iran, vol. 1, 1968; *contrib.* Acta Genet., Amer. Jl Phys. Anthrop., Ann. Hum. Genet., Eugen. Rev., Geog., Gwyddn., Hum. Biol., Jl Royal Anthrop. Inst., Man, Nature, Jl Biosoc. Sci., Phil. Trans Roy. Soc.

of London. *Address*: Dept of Anthropology, Univ. of Durham, Durham DH1 3TG.

Sutcliffe, Dr Anthony Richard; Lecturer, Department of Economic History, Sheffield University, since 1970; *b* 1942; *m* 1972. MA Oxon 1963, DUP 1966. Res. Fellow, Sch. of Hist., Birmingham Univ., 1966–70. *Publications*: The Autumn of Central Paris: the defeat of town planning 1850–1970, 1970; (with R. J. Smith) History of Birmingham, vol. III, 1974; Multi-Storey Living, 1974. *Address*: Dept of Economic History, Sheffield Univ., Sheffield S10 2TN.

Sutcliffe, Prof. Frank Edmund; Professor of Classical French Literature, University of Manchester, since 1966; *b* 1918; *m* 1966. BA Manchester 1940 (1st cl. French), MA Manchester 1948, PhD Manchester 1958. Asst Lectr, Manchester, 1946–49; Lectr, 1949–55; Sen. Lectr, 1955–61; Prof. Modern French Lit., 1961–66. Dean, Fac. of Arts, 1972–74. *Publications*: La pensée de Paul Valéry, 1955; Guez de Balzac et son temps: littérature et politique, 1960; Le réalisme de Charles Sorel: problèmes humains du XVIIᵉ siécle, 1965; ed, F. de la Noue: Discours politiques et militaires, 1967; trans., Descartes: Discours de la Méthode and other writings, 1968; Politique et Culture 1560–1660, 1973; *contrib.* Bull. J. Rylands Libr. *Address*: Dept of French Studies, The Univ., Manchester M13 9PL.

Sutherland, Alister, MA; University Lecturer in Economics and Fellow of Trinity College, University of Cambridge, since 1966; *b* 1934; *m* 1967. BA Oxon 1956 (1st cl. PPE), MA Yale 1960, MA Oxon 1961, MA Cantab 1966. Mem., Royal Econ. Soc., Amer. Econ. Assoc. Lectr, Wesleyan Univ., Conn. Asst, Yale, 1960; Lectr, Univ. Coll., London Univ., 1961–64. Econ. Adv. Registrar of Restrictive Trading Agreements, 1962–64, 1966–67; Econ. Cnsltnt, HM Treasury, 1964–66; Cnsltnt, Bd of Trade, Min. of Housing, Civil Service Select. Bd; Econ. Assessor, Greater London Develpt Plan Inquiry, 1970–72. *Publications*: The Monopolies Commission in Action, 1969; contrib. The Managed Economy, ed A. K. Cairncross, 1970; *contrib.* Econ. Jl, Jl Indust. Econ., Oxf. Econ. Papers. *Address*: Faculty of Economics, Univ. of Cambridge, Sidgwick Avenue, Cambridge.

Sutherland, Gillian, MA, DPhil; Official Fellow, and Lecturer in History, Newnham College, Cambridge University, since 1966; *b* 1942; *m* 1967. BA Oxon 1963 (1st cl. Hist.), BA Cantab 1965, MA Cantab 1967, MA Oxon 1970, DPhil Oxon 1970. Asst Lectr, Newnham Coll., Cambridge, 1965; Dir of Studies in Soc. and Pol Sci., History Pt II, 1970– . *Publications*: Elementary Education in the Nineteenth Century, 1971; ed, Studies in the Growth of Nineteenth Century Government, 1972; Policy Making in Elementary Education 1870–1895, 1973; ed, Matthew Arnold on Education, 1973; *contrib.* Hist., Victorian Studies. *Address*: Newnham College, Cambridge.

Sutherland, Sir Gordon (Brims Black McIvor), FRS; Master of Emmanuel College,

Cambridge, since 1964; *b* 1907; *m* 1936; three *d*. MA St Andrews 1928, BSc St Andrews 1929; PhD Cantab 1933; ScD Cantab 1948; Hon. LLD St Andrews 1958, Hon. DSc Strathclyde 1966; FRS 1949. Fellow and Lectr, Pembroke Coll., Cambridge, 1935–49; Head of group carrying out extra-mural research in Cambridge Univ. for Min. of Aircraft Prodn, Min. of Supply and Admiralty, 1941–45; Asst Dir of Res. in Dept of Colloid Science, Cambridge, 1944–47; Reader in Spectroscopy, Cambridge, 1947–49; Univ. Proctor, Cambridge, 1943–44; Mem., Council of Senate, Cambridge; Prof. of Physics, Univ. of Michigan, 1949–56; Guggenheim Fellow, Univ. of Michigan, 1956. Dir, Nat. Physical Laboratory, 1956–64; Vice-Pres., Royal Society, 1961–63; Vice-Pres., Internat. Cttee on Data for Science and Technol., 1968–72; Vice-Pres., Internat. Union of Pure and Applied Physics, 1963–69; Pres., Inst. of Physics and the Physical Soc., 1964–66 (Glazebrook Medal, 1972); Pres., Sect. X, British Assoc., 1968; A Trustee of the National Gallery, 1971– ; Hon. Fellow, Pembroke Coll., Cambridge, 1959; For. Hon. Mem., Amer. Acad. of Arts and Sciences, 1968. *Publications*: Infra-Red and Raman Spectra, 1935; Scientific papers and articles on Infra-red Spectroscopy, Molecular Structure and Science Policy. *Address*: The Master's Lodge, Emmanuel College, Cambridge CB2 3AP.

Sutherland, Dr John A.; Lecturer, English Department, University College London, since 1971; *b* 1938; *m* 1967. BA Leicester 1964, MA 1966, PhD Edinburgh 1973. Lectr, Edinburgh Univ., 1965–71. *Publications*: Thackeray at Work, 1974; *contrib*. MP, MLR, VP, MLQ, EIC, NQ, Ang., ES, PULC. *Address*: Dept of English, Univ. Coll. London, Gower Street, WC1E 6BT.

Sutherland, Prof. Margaret Brownlie; Professor and Head of Department of Education, University of Leeds, since 1973; *b* 1920. MA Glasgow 1942 (1st cl. Fr., Germ.), MEd Glasgow 1945 (1st cl. Educ. and Psychol.), PhD Belfast 1955; ABPsS. Lectr, 1947–60, Sen. Lectr; 1960–72, Reader, QUB, 1972–73; Vis. Lectr, Rhodes Univ., Grahamstown, S Africa, 1962–63. Mem., BBC Adv. Council, NI, 1964–68; Chm., Brit. Sect., Comp. Educn Soc. in Europe, 1968–71; Dep. Chm., NI Adv. Council Educn, 1969–72; Mem., NI Council Nurses and Midwives, 1970–72; Pres., S Yorks Soc. for Autistic Children, 1973– . *Publications*: Everyday Imagining and Education, 1971; *contrib*. Brit. Jl. Educnl Psychol., Brit. Jl Educnl Studies. *Address*: Univ. of Leeds, Leeds LS2 9JT.

Sutherland, Dr Nicola Mary, MA, PhD; Lecturer in History, Bedford College, London University, since 1964; *b* 1925. BA Cantab 1947, MA Cantab 1954, PhD London 1958; FRHistS. Asst Lectr, Bedford Coll., Univ. of London, 1962–64. *Publications*: The French Secretaries of State in the Age of Catherine de Medici, 1962; Catherine de Medici and the Ancien Régime, 1966; The Massacre of St Bartholomew and the European Conflict 1559–1572, 1973; Antoine de

Bourbon, King of Navarre, and the French Crisis of Authority 1559–1562, in, French Government and Society 1500–1850, ed J. F. Bosher, 1973; *contrib*. Annali, EHR, Hist., History Today, Jl Eccles. Hist., Proc. Huguenot Soc. Lond. *Address*: Bedford College, Regent's Park, NW1 4NS.

Sutherland, Prof. Norman Stuart, MA, DPhil; Professor of Experimental Psychology, University of Sussex, since 1964; *b* 1927; *m* 1957; two *d*. BA Oxon 1949 (1st cl. Lit. Hum., 1st cl. PPP 1953), MA Oxon 1952, DPhil Oxon 1957; Mem., AISB, Mem., Soc. Anim. Behav., Mem., Soc. Exper. Psychol. Fellow, Magdalen Coll., Oxford, 1954–58; Lectr, Magdalen Coll., Oxford, 1958–64; Univ. Lectr in Exper. Psychol., Oxford, 1958–64; Lectr, Oriel Coll., 1959–64; Lectr, Corpus Christi Coll., 1959–64; Lectr, Merton Coll., 1960–64; Fellow, Merton Coll., Oxford, 1963–64; Vis. Prof. of Exper. Psychol., MIT, 1964–65; Ed., Qly Jl Exper. Psychol., 1970–72; Mem., SRC Comput. Science Cttee, 1966–69; Mem., SRC Biol. Cttee, 1969– ; Mem., Steering Cttee, Europ. Brain Behav. Org., 1970– . *Publications*: Shape Discrimination in Animals, 1961; (with W. R. Gilbert) | Animal Discrimination Learning, 1969; (with N. J. Mackintosh) Mechanisms of Animal Discrimination Learning, 1971; *contrib*. Brit. Jl Psychol., Jl Comp. Phys. Psychol., Jl Exper. Psychol., Nature, Proc. Royal Soc., Qly Jl Exper. Psychol. *Address*: Laboratory of Experimental Psychology, Univ. of Sussex, Falmer, Brighton.

Sutherland, Stewart Ross; Senior Lecturer, Department of Philosophy, University of Stirling, since 1972 (Lecturer, 1968–72); *b* 1941; *m* 1964; one *s* two *d*. MA Aberdeen 1963 (1st cl.), BA Cambridge 1965 (1st cl.), MA Cantab 1969; Mem., Aristot. Soc., Mem., Brit. Soc. Aesth. Lectr, Univ. Coll. of N Wales, Bangor, 1965–68. Vis. Fellow, ANU, 1974; Gillespie Vis. Prof., Wooster Coll., Ohio, 1975. *Publications*: *contrib*. Brit. Jl Aesth., Hum. Wld, Jl Theol Studies, Relig. Studies, Scott. Jl Theol., Theol. *Address*: Dept of Philosophy, Univ. of Stirling, Stirling, Scotland FK9 4LA.

Sutton, Dr Clive Remer, Lecturer in Education, School of Education, University of Leicester, since 1967; *b* 1936; *m* 1960; two *s* two *d*. BSc Liverpool 1956, PhD Liverpool 1959, PGCE London; Associate, Royal Inst. of Chemistry. Coordinator, Science Teacher Educn Project, 1970–73. *Publications*: (with J. T. Haysom) Innovation in Teacher Education, 1974; ed (with J. T. Haysom), and contrib. to: The Art of the Science Teacher, Theory into Practice, and Activities and Experiences, 1974; *contrib*. Arch. Biochem. Biophys., Educn for Teaching. *Address*: 21 University Road, Leicester LE1 7RF.

Sutton, Laurence Paul E.; *see* Elwell-Sutton.

Sutton, Philip; Lecturer, Slade School of Art, University College London; *b* 1928; *m* 1954; one *s* three *d*. Slade Dip. of Fine Art. *Address*: Slade Sch. of Art, Univ. Coll., Gower Street, WC1E 6BT.

Swaisland, Dr Henry Charles, BCom, DPhil; Senior Lecturer, Institute of Local Government Studies, University of Birmingham, since 1968; b 1919; m 1949; two d. BCom (Social Study), Birmingham 1949, DPhil Oxon 1968; Mem., Royal Afr. Soc., Mem., Afr. Studies Assoc. UK, Mem., Royal Inst. Public Admin. Provincial Admin., Nigeria, 1949–63. Recognized Lectr, Centre for W Afr. Studies, Univ. of Birmingham, 1967; Prof.: Local Govt Admin, Univ. of Mauritius (on secondment), 1969–70, Public Admin. and Local Govt, 1973– . *Publications*: Report on local government in Eastern Ngwa, Nigeria, 1955; Chapter on Birmingham, in, Great Cities of the World and their Administration, ed Robson and Regan, 3rd edn 1972. *Address*: Inst. of Local Government Studies, Univ. of Birmingham, PO Box 363, Birmingham B15 2TT.

Swales, Dr Martin William; Reader in German, King's College, University of London, since 1972; b 1940; m 1966; one s one d. BA Cantab 1961, PhD Birmingham 1963. Lectr in German, Univ. Birmingham, 1964–70; Prof. of German, Univ. Toronto, 1970–72. *Publications*: Arthur Schnitzler: A Critical Study, 1971; *contrib*. Deutsche Vierteljahrsschrift, German Life and Letters, Mod. Lang. Rev., Pubns of English Goethe Soc., Wirkendes Wort. *Address*: Dept of German, King's College, Univ. of London, Strand, WC2R 2LS.

Swann, Prof. Dennis; Professor of Economics, Loughborough University of Technology, since 1968; b 1932; m 1957; two d. BA(Econ) Leeds 1955, PhD Leeds 1960. Asst Lectr in Econ., Leeds Univ., 1957–59; Asst Lectr in Econ., Queen's Univ., Belfast, 1959–60; Reader in Econ., Queen's Univ., Belfast, 1967–68. Mem., Exec., AUT, 1968– ; Chm., AUT Salaries and Grading Cttee, 1968–70; Ch. Examiner, N Irel. GCE A Level Econ. and Pol., 1970– . *Publications*: Competition Policy in the Economic Community, 1967; Concentration or Competition: A European Dilemma?, 1967; Information Agreements, Competition and Efficiency, 1968; The Economics of the Common Market, 1970, 2nd edn 1972; (with others) Competition in British Industry: restrictive practices legislation in theory and practice, 1974; (with others) Competition in British Industry: case studies of the effects of restrictive practices legislation, 1974; *contrib*. Econ. Jl, Manch. Sch., Scott. Jl. Pol Econ. *Address*: Univ. of Technology, Dept of Economics, Ashby Road, Loughborough, Leicestershire.

Swanston, Rev. Dr Hamish F. G.; Lecturer in Theology, University of Kent at Canterbury, since 1972; b 1933. BA Dunelm 1954 (Hons Eng. Lang. and Lit.), MA Dunelm 1957, MLitt Dunelm, 1966, PhD Canterbury 1970; Mem. Egyptian Exploration Soc. 1964. Vis. Prof. of Theology, Manhattanville Coll., NY, 1966; Prof. of Theology, Manhattanville, 1967; Prof. of Theology, Boston Theol Inst., 1971. *Publications*: Community Witness, 1966 (Italian trans. 1968); Kings and the Covenant, 1968; Studies in the Sacraments, 2 vols, 1969;

Early Histories of Israel, 1971; Later Histories of Israel, 1972; Minor Prophets, 1972; Ideas of Order, 1974; contrib. Theology and University, Religious Education, Church Membership and Inter-Communion, Prose for God. *Address*: Eliot College, Univ. of Kent at Canterbury, Canterbury, Kent.

Swanwick, Keith, MEd, PhD, GRSM; Lecturer in Education, with special reference to Music, London University Institute of Education, since 1966; b 1937; m 1959; one s two d. LRAM 1958, GRSM 1959, ARCO 1960, MEd Leicester 1965, PhD Leicester 1972; MTC London 1960. Hd of Music Dept., Rutherford Sch., 1960–62; Hd of Music Dept, Wyggeston Boys' Sch., 1962–66. *Publications*: Popular Music and the Teacher, 1968; *contrib*. Music, Music Educn, Music Teach. *Address*: Music Dept, Institute of Education, Malet Street, WC1E 7HS.

Swart, Prof. Dr Koenraad Wolter; Professor of Dutch History and Institutions, University of London, since 1966; b 1916; m 1951; two s two d. JurCand Leiden 1935, DLitt Leiden 1949; FRHistS, Mem., Dutch Royal Acad. of Sciences. Vis. Lectr, Univ. of Illinois, 1950–52; Asst Prof., Georgetown Univ., 1952–53; Prof., Brenau Coll., 1954–56; Assoc. Prof., Agnes Scott Coll., 1956–66; Vis. Prof., Temple Univ., 1969–70. Res. Assoc., Netherlands State Inst. for War Documentation, 1947–49. *Publications*: Sale of Offices in the Seventeenth Century, 1949; The Sense of Decadence in Nineteenth-Century France, 1964; The Miracle of the Dutch Republic as seen in the Seventeenth Century, 1969; *contrib*. Jl Hist. Ideas, Rev. Pol. *Address*: Dept of History, Univ. College London, Gower Street, WC1E 6BT.

Sweeney, Very Rev. Canon Garrett Daniel; Master, St Edmund's House, Cambridge, since 1964; b 1912. BA London 1940, MA Cantab 1952. Priest (RC), 1937; Asst Priest, Leicester, 1937–41; Parish Priest, Shirebrook, Derbyshire, 1941–46. Asst Master, St Hugh's Coll., Tollerton, Nottingham, 1948–56; Headmaster, St Hugh's Coll., Tollerton, Nottingham, 1956–64. *Address*: St Edmund's House, Cambridge CB3 0BN.

Sweet, Dr David Whinfield, MA, PhD; Lecturer, Department of Modern History, University of Durham, since 1965; b 1938; m 1969. BA Cantab 1962 (1st cl. Hist.), MA Cantab 1966, PhD Cantab 1972. 2nd Lieut., Royal Corps of Signals, 1958–59. *Publications*: *contrib*. Hist. Jl. *Address*: Dept of History, 43 North Bailey, Durham.

Sweet, Rev. J. P. M.; Lecturer in Divinity, University of Cambridge, since 1964; b 1927; m 1961; one s two d. BA Oxon 1949 (2nd cl. Lit. Hum., 1st cl. Theol. 1953), MA Oxon 1952, MA Cantab 1958; Mem., Studiorum NT Soc. Fellow, Selwyn Coll., Cambridge, 1958; Asst Lectr, Cambridge Univ., 1960–63. *Publications*: *contrib*. NT Studies. *Address*: Selwyn College, Cambridge CB3 9DQ.

Sweeting, Elizabeth Jane, MBE, MA; Administrator, University Theatre, University of Oxford, since 1961, and Tutor in English

Studies, St Catherine's College, University of Oxford, since 1967; *b* 1914. BA London 1936 (1st cl. Engl.), MA London 1938, MA Oxford 1960. Lectr, Univ. Coll., London, 1940–46; Ext. Examiner in Drama, Colls of Educn, Birmingham area, 1965–68; Sec., Curators of the Univ. Theatre, 1961– . Mngr, Aldeburgh Festival, 1948–55; Gen. Mngr, Oxford Playhouse, 1956–61; Mem., Arts Council Drama Panel, 1965–68; Chm., Arts Council Drama Panel Cttee on Training for Theatre Admin., 1971– ; Ext. Examiner, Poly. of Central London course in Training for Arts Admin, 1970– ; Gov., Wyvern Theatre and Arts Centre, Swindon; Dir, Watermill Theatre, Bagnor, Newbury, Berkshire; Adv., Theatre Royal, Bury St Edmunds; Gov., Brit. Inst. Recorded Sound; Mem., Exec. Cttee, Assoc. Brit. Theatre Technicians; Mem., Exec. Cttee, Southern Arts Assoc. *Publications*: Studies in Early Tudor Criticism, Literary and Linguistic, 1940; Theatre Administration, 1970; Beginners Please: Working in the Theatre, 1971; *contrib*. Mod. Lang. Rev., Rev. Engl. Studies. *Address*: Oxford Univ. Theatre, Oxford Playhouse, Beaumont Street, Oxford OX1 2LW.

Sweeting, Dr Marjorie Mary; Fellow of St Hugh's College, and University Lecturer in Geography, Oxford University, since 1954; *b* 1920. BA Cantab 1941, MA Cantab 1945, PhD Cantab 1948, MA Oxon 1951; FRGS. Res. Fellow, Newnham Coll., Cambridge, 1948–51; Lectr, St Hugh's Coll., Oxford, 1951–54. Mem., Council, Royal Geog. Soc. 1969– ; Mem., Field Studies Council Cttee, Royal Geog. Soc., 1970– ; Dean, St Hugh's Coll., 1960–66; Mem., Sch. Council, Abbot's Bromley Sch.; Sen. Tutor, St Hugh's, 1966– . *Publications*: Kanst Landfoms, 1972; (with J. N. Jennings) The Limestone Ranges, Fitzroy Area, 1963; *contrib*. Inst. Brit. Geogrs, Geog. Jl, Trans Cave Res. Gp, Zeits. Geomorphol., etc. *Address*: St Hugh's College, Oxford.

Sweetman, Dr John Edward; Lecturer in Fine Art and History of Art, University of Southampton, since 1967; *b* 1929; *m* 1963; one *s* one *d*. NDD, Birmingham Coll. of Art 1950, BA London (Hons Hist. of Art), PhD London 1955; AMA 1963, Mem. Royal Archaeological Inst. 1957; Mem. Oriental Ceramic Soc. 1966, Mem. Council, 1974. Curator, Barlow Collection of Chinese Ceramics, Bronzes and Jades, Univ. Sussex, 1973– . Keeper, Temple Newsam House, Leeds, 1965–67. *Publications*: *contrib*. Apollo, Burlington Mag., Jl Courtauld and Warburg Insts, Museums Jl, etc. *Address*: Univ. of Southampton, Highfield, Southampton SO9 5NH.

Swift, Dr Bernard Christopher, MA, PhD; Senior Lecturer in French, University of Stirling, since 1973 (Lecturer, 1972–73); *b* 1937; *m* 1962; two *s*. BA Manchester 1959, MA Manchester 1961, PhD Aberdeen 1971. Mem., Soc. Fr. Studies. Asst, Univ. of Geneva, 1961–63; Asst Lectr, Univ. of Aberdeen, 1963–66, Lectr, 1966–72; Vis. Asst Prof., Univ. of Saskatchewan, 1969. Adv. of Studies, Fac. of Arts, Univ. of Aberdeen, 1971–72; Principal Examiner in French, Cert.

of Sixth Yr Studies, Scott. Cert. of Educn Exam. Bd, 1972– . *Publications*: trans., B. Gagnebin: Encounter with Henry Dunant, 1963; J. Starobinski: A History of Medicine, 1963; J. Starobinski: The Invention of Liberty, 1964; *contrib*. Wasc. Rev., West. Canad. Studies Mod. Langs Lit., MLR, Yrs Wk in Mod. Lang. Studies. *Address*: Dept of French, The Univ., Stirling FK9 4LA.

Swift, Prof. Donald Francis; Professor of Sociology of Education, The Open University, since 1970; *b* 1932; *m* 1957; one *s* two *d*. Teacher's Certif. 1954, BScEcon Hull 1959, PhD Liverpool 1963, MA Oxon 1968; Mem. Brit. Sociological Assoc., Mem. Amer. Sociological Assoc. Calgary Univ., 1962–64; Liverpool Univ., 1964–66; Oxford Univ., 1966–70. *Publications*: Foundation Disciplines and the Study of Education, 1968; The Sociology of Education, 1969; Basic Readings in the Sociology of Education, 1970; School and Society: A Sociological Reader, 1971. *contrib*. Brit. Jl Sociology, Brit. Jl Educnl Psych., Educnl Res. *Address*: The Open Univ., Walton Hall, Milton Keynes MK7 6AA.

Swigg, Dr Richard; Lecturer, Department of English Language and Literature, University of Keele, since 1966; *b* 1938; *m* 1964; one *s* one *d*. BA Liverpool 1963, PhD Bristol 1967. *Publications*: Lawrence, Hardy and American Literature, 1972; *contrib*. Agenda, MLR. *Address*: Dept of English Language and Literature, Univ. of Keele, Keele, Staffs ST5 5BG.

Swinbank, Dr Peter; Senior Lecturer, Department of History of Science, University of Glasgow, since 1967; *b* 1928. BSc Birmingham 1949 (2nd cl. Physics), PhD Birmingham 1953; MInstP, Mem., Brit. Soc. Hist. Science. Res. Fellow, Natural Philosophy Dept, Glasgow, 1955–58; Lectr in Natural Philosophy, Glasgow, 1958–60; Lectr in Physics, Birmingham, 1960–67; Lectr in Hist. of Science, Glasgow, 1967. *Publications*: Exhibition catalogues: James Watt Bicentenary, 1969; Treasures of the University of Glasgow, 1970; *contrib*. var. articles and reviews, sci. and hist. jls. *Address*: Dept of History of Science, The Univ., Glasgow G12 8QQ.

Swinburne, Prof. Richard Granville; Professor of Philosophy, and Head of the Department of Philosophy, University of Keele, since 1972; *b* 1934; *m* 1960; two *d*. BA Oxon 1957 (1st cl. PPE), BPhil Oxon 1959 (Philos.), DipTheol Oxon 1960 (with distinction), MA Oxon 1961. Fereday Fellow, St John's Coll., Oxford, 1958–61; Leverhulme Res. Fellow in Hist. and Philos. of Sci., Univ. of Leeds, 1961–63; Lectr, Univ. of Hull, 1963–69, Sen. Lectr, 1969–72; Vis. Assoc. Prof., Univ. of Maryland, 1969–70. Mem., Analysis Cttee, 1968– ; Sec., 1971– . *Publications*: Space and Time, 1968; The Concept of Miracle, 1971; An Introduction to Confirmation Theory, 1973; ed, The Justification of Induction, 1974; *contrib*. Amer. Philos. Qly, Analysis, Ann. Science, Austral. Jl Philos., Brit. Jl Philos. Science, Ch Qly Rev., Mind, Philos. Qly Philos., Philos. Science, Proc.

Aristol. Soc., Relig. Studies. *Address*: Dept of Philosophy, Univ. of Keele, Keele, Staffordshire ST5 5BG.

Swinden, Dr Patrick; Lecturer, Department of English Language and Literature, University of Manchester, since 1967; *b* 1941; *m* 1966; one *s*. BA Hull 1963 (1st cl. Hons English), PhD Cantab 1968 (English). *Publications*: ed, George Eliot: Middlemarch, A Casebook, 1972; Unofficial Selves: Character in Fiction from Dickens to the Present Day, 1973; An Introduction to Shakespeare's Comedies, 1973; *contrib*. Critical Qly, Critical Survey, Twentieth Century Mind. *Address*: Dept of English, Univ. of Manchester, Manchester M13 9PL.

Swinfen, Dr David Berridge; Lecturer, Department of Modern History, University of Dundee (formerly Queen's College, University of St Andrews), since 1964; *b* 1936; *m* 1960; two *s* three *d*. BA Oxford 1960, DPhil Oxford 1965. Asst Lectr, Queen's Coll., Univ. of St Andrews, 1963–64. *Publications*: Imperial Control of Colonial Legislation, 1813–65, 1970; *contrib*. Jurid. Rev. *Address*: Dept of Modern History, Univ. of Dundee, Dundee DD1 4HN.

Swingewood, Dr Alan W.; Lecturer in Sociology, London School of Economics, since 1967; *b* 1938; *m* 1962; two *s*. BSc (Sociol.), PhD, London. *Publications*: (jtly) The Sociology of Literature, 1972; Marx and Modern Social Theory, 1974; The Novel and Revolution (forthcoming); *contrib*. Brit. Jl Sociol., Sociol Rev., New Literary Hist. *Address*: Room 233, Dept of Sociology, London Sch. of Economics, Houghton Street, Aldwych, WC2A 2AE.

Swoboda, Victor, MA; Senior Lecturer in Russian and Ukrainian, School of Slavonic and East European Studies, University of London, since 1973; *b* 1925; *m* 1958; one *s* one *d*. BA London 1953 (1st cl. Russian), MA London 1958 (Russian Lang. and Lit., with distinction). Asst Lectr, 1955–59, Lectr, 1959–73, Sch. of Slav. and E Europ. Studies, London. *Publications*: The 'Slavonice' Part of the Oxford Heptaglot Lexicon, 1956; ed, T. Shevchenko: Song out of Darkness, 1961; *contrib*. Ann. Ukr. Acad. Arts Sci. US, Conflict Studies, Index, Slav. E Europ. Rev., Welt Slaven, Yrs Wk Mod. Lang. Studies. *Address*: School of Slavonic and East European Studies, Univ. of London, WC1E 7HU.

Sykes, Alan; Lecturer in Modern History, University of St Andrews, since 1970; *b* 1942; *m* 1964; one *s* two *d*. BA Oxon 1964. Univ. Adelaide, 1964–70. *Address*: Dept of Modern History, Univ. of St Andrews, St Andrews, Fife KY16 9AJ.

Sykes, Prof. Andrew James Macintyre, MA, PhD; Professor of Sociology, University of Strathclyde, since 1966; *b* 1924. MA Glasgow 1950, PhD Glasgow 1960; FRAI. Reader, and Hd of Dept of Sociology, Strathclyde, 1964–66. *Publications*: *contrib*. Hum. Relat., Sociol. Rev., Sociol. *Address*: Dept of Sociology, Univ. of Strathclyde, Richmond Street, Glasgow.

Sykes, Dr Donald Armstrong; Senior Tutor, since 1970, and Fellow in Theology, Mansfield College, Oxford, since 1959; *b* 1930; *m* 1962; two *s*. MA St Andrews 1952 (2nd cl. classics), BA Oxon 1957 (1st cl. Theol.), DipEd Glasgow 1958, MA Oxon 1961, DPhil Oxon 1967. Vis. Prof. in Religion, Saint Olaf Coll., Northfield, Minn., 1969–70. *Publications*: *contrib*. Jl Theol. Studies. *Address*: Mansfield College, Oxford OX1 3TF.

Sykes, Dr Elizabeth Ann Bowen, MSc, PhD, ABPsS; Lecturer in the Department of Psychology, University College of North Wales, since 1965; *b* 1936. BSc(Spec.) London 1959, MSc London 1962; PhD Edinburgh 1970; ABPsS 1964, Mem., Brit. Psychol. Soc., Assoc. Study Anim. Behav. Visiting Asst Prof. of Psychol., Wilson Coll., Chambersburg, Pa, 1972–73; Res. Asst, Univ. of Edinburgh, 1962–65. Res. Staff. Nat. Inst. Indust. Psychol., 1959–61. *Publications*: *contrib*. Biochem. Pharmacol., Fed-PMC, Neuropsychopharm., Psychopharm, Psychonom. Sci., Brit. Jl Psychol. *Address*: Dept of Psychology, Univ. College of North Wales, Bangor LL57 2DG.

Sykes, Joseph Donald, BSc, NDA, DipAgricEcon; Senior Lecturer in Agricultural Economics, School of Rural Economics and Related Studies, Wye College, University of London, since 1965; *b* 1925; *m* 1948; one *s* one *d*. BSc Leeds 1951, DipAgricEcon Oxford 1952, Nat. Dip. Agric. Asst Agric. Economist, Leeds Univ., 1948–52; Lectr, Wye Coll., 1952–65. Chm., Canterbury Farmers Club. *Publications*: (with G. P. Wibberley) Problems and Prospects of Farming in South East England, 1956; (with J. B. Hardakers) The Potato Crop: Policy and Practices, 1961; The Economics of Grain Maize Prodn, 1971. *Address*: School of Rural Economics and Related Studies, Wye College, Univ. of London, Ashford, Kent TN25 5AH.

Sykes, Dr Peter, MSc, PhD, FRIC; Lecturer in Organic Chemistry, University of Cambridge, since 1955, Fellow and Director of Studies, Christ's College, Cambridge, since 1956; *b* 1923; *m* 1946; two *s* one *d*. BSc Manchester 1943, MSc Manchester 1944, PhD Cantab 1946; FRIC. Univ. Demonstrator, Cambridge, 1947–55; Res. Fellow, St John's Coll., Cambridge, 1948–51; Vis. Res. Prof., Coll. of Wm and Mary, Virginia, 1970–71. Gov., Rydal Sch., 1958– ; Pres., Sci. Masters Assoc. (East Reg.), 1960–62; Mem., IUPAC Commn on Teaching Chemistry, 1963– ; Sec., IUPAC Commn on Teaching Chemistry, 1963–66; Mem., Brit. Cttee on Chem. Educn, 1965–67, 1972– ; Mem., Nuffield Jt Cttee A Level Physical Scis, 1964–71; Mem., UK Commn, Anglo-Span. Mixed Commn, 1967–73. *Publications*: The Silicones, 1957; Guidebook to Mechanism in Organic Chemistry, 1961, 3rd edn 1970, German, Japanese and Spanish edns 1964, French edn 1966, Italian edn 1967, Portuguese edn 1969; The Search for Organic Reaction Pathways, 1972, German edn 1973, Japanese, Spanish, Portuguese, Italian, Polish edns (forthcoming); *contrib*. Chem. Indust., Chem. Commun., Jl Chem. Soc.

Address: Univ. Chemical Laboratory, Lensfield Road, Cambridge CB2 1EW.

Sykes, Robert Neil; Lecturer, Department of Psychology, University College, Swansea, since 1969; *b* 1944; *m* 1965; two *s* one *d*. BSc London 1965; Grad. Mem., British Psychological Soc. Asst Lectr, Univ. Coll., Swansea, 1966–69. *Publications*: *contrib*. Acta Psychol., Am. Jl Psychol. *Address*: Dept of Psychology, Univ. College, Singleton Park, Swansea SA2 8PP.

Sykes, Rev. Prof. Stephen Whitefield, MA; Van Mildert Canon Professor of Divinity, University of Durham, since 1974; *b* 1939; *m* 1962; one *s* two *d*. BA Cantab 1961 (1st cl. Theol.), Pt III Theol. Tripos 1962 (1st cl. with dist.), MA Cantab 1964. Fellow and Dean, St John's College, Cambridge, 1964–74; Univ. Asst Lectr, in Divinity, Cambridge Univ., 1964–68; Univ. Lectr, 1968–74. Mem., Westcott Hse Council, 1967–71; Mem., Archbps' Cttee on Relig. Educn, 1967; Sec., Camb. AUT, 1968–71, Vice-Pres., 1973–74; Exam. Chaplain, Bp of Chelmsford, 1970– . *Publications*: Friedrich Schleiermacher, 1971; Christian Theology Today, 1971; ed, Christ, Faith and History, 1972; *contrib*. Relig. Studies. *Address*: 14 The College, Durham Cathedral, Durham.

Sylvester, David William, MA; Lecturer, Department of Education, University of Leeds, since 1966; Director Schools Council Project: History 13–16, 1972–75; *b* 1934; *m* 1957; two *s* one *d*. BA Oxon 1955, MA Oxon 1959, DipEd Oxon 1959. *Publications*: Clive in India, 1968; (with P. J. Gosden) History for the Average Child, 1968; Educational Documents 800–1816, 1970; Captain Cook and the Pacific, 1971; Robert Lowe and Education, 1974. *Address*: Dept of Education, Univ. of Leeds, Leeds LS2 9JT.

Symmons, Sarah; Lecturer, Department of Art, University of Essex, since 1971; *b* 1942. BA London 1967, MA London 1968. Vis. Lectr, Univ. Essex, 1968–69; Part-time Lectr, Univ. Essex, 1969–71. *Publications*: *contrib*. Burlington Mag., Listener. *Address*: Dept of Art, Univ. of Essex, Wivenhoe Park, Colchester, Essex CO4 3SQ.

Symon, Iain Walker, MA, CA; Lecturer in Accountancy, Faculty of Law, University of Dundee, since 1972; *b* 1937; *m* 1964; three *d*. MA St Andrews 1959. Mem., Inst. Chartered Accountants Scotl., 1964. Asst Lectr, 1963–65; Lectr, Univ. of St Andrews, 1965–67; Lectr, Dept of Econs, Dundee, 1967–72. Mem., Res. and Publicns Cttee, ICAS, 1970– . *Publications*: The Balance Sheet: what is its function?, 1972; *contrib*. Acctnt's Mag. *Address*: The Univ. of Dundee, Dundee DD1 4HN.

Symons, Dr Leslie John, BSc(Econ), PhD; Reader in the Geography of Russia, Department of Geography and Centre of Russian and East European Studies, University College of Swansea, since 1973; *b* 1926; *m* 1954; two *d*. BSc(Econ) London 1953 (1st cl. Geog.), PhD Belfast 1958. Member: Inst. Brit. Geogrs; Geog. Soc. NZ; Nat. Assoc.

for Soviet and E European Studies. Asst Lectr in Geography, 1953–55; Temp. Lectr in Geography, 1955–56; Lectr in Geography, 1956–63; Vis. Lectr, Univ. of Canterbury, NZ, 1960; Lectr, Univ. of Canterbury, NZ, 1963; Sen. Lectr, Univ. of Canterbury, NZ, 1964–70; Sen. Lectr, Univ. Coll. of Swansea, 1970–73; Simon Sen. Res. Fellow, Univ. of Manchester, 1967–68. Embarkation Staff Off., RE (MCS), Bristol Channel Ports, 1947–48. *Publications*: ed, Land Use in Northern Ireland, 1963; Agricultural Geography, 1967; (with L. Hanna) Northern Ireland: a Geographical Introduction, 1967; Russian Agriculture: a Geographical Survey, 1972; (with C. White et al.) Russian Transport (forthcoming); *contrib*. Geog., Irish Geog., Jl Stat. Social Inqu. Soc. Irel., NZ Geog., NZ Jl Geog., Pacif. Viewpt, Scott. Geog. Mag., Soviet Studies. *Address*: Dept of Geography, Univ. College of Swansea, Singleton Park, Swansea SA2 8PP.

Szreter, Richard; Senior Lecturer, School of Education, University of Birmingham, since 1970; *b* 1927; *m* 1950; two *s* one *d*. BSc(Econ) London 1950, BA London 1955, CertEd Leicester 1952. School teacher, 1952–60; Lectr, School of Educn, Univ. of Birmingham, 1960–70. *Publications*: *contrib*. Teaching Economics, ed N. Lee, 1967; ed and trans., W. Kula: Problems and Methods of Economic History (forthcoming); *contrib*. Brit. Jl Educnl Studies, Jl Royal Stat. Soc., Univ. Qly, Univ. Birm. Hist. Jl, etc. *Address*: School of Education, Univ. of Birmingham, PO Box 363, Birmingham B15 2TT.

T

Tabrizi, Gholam-Reza S.; *see* Sabri-Tabrizi.

Tagg, Dr Eric Donovan; Senior Lecturer, since 1971, and Chairman since 1972, Department of Mathematics, University of Lancaster; *b* 1913; *m* 1939; three *s*. BA Cantab 1933 (B* Wrangler), MA Cantab 1937, PhD Cantab 1938; FIMA 1966, MBCS 1970, Fellow, Camb. Philos. Soc., 1934– . Commonwealth Fund Fellow, Princeton Univ., 1935–37; Housemaster and Sen. Maths Master, Oundle Sch., 1937–67; Vis. Prof., Wesleyan Univ., Conn., 1962; Dir, Res. Project in the Accelerated Teaching of Higher Level Maths, Univ. of Lancaster, 1968–70. Chm., BCS Schs Cttee, 1966–70 (Mem., 1964–); Mem., IMA Council, 1969–71; Gov., Baines Grammar Sch., 1968– ; Mem., IFIP Working Group on Computer Educn in Schs, 1967– . *Publications*: *contrib*. IAG Jl, Internat. Jl Math. Educn Sci. Technol., Jl Lond. Math. Soc. *Address*: Dept of Mathematics, Cartmel College, Univ. of Lancaster, Bailrigg, Lancaster.

Tailby, John Edward; Lecturer, Department of German, University of Leeds, since 1963; *b* 1938; *m* 1963; one *s* one *d*. MA St Andrews 1961, BPhil St Andrews 1966. Lektor, Univ. of Erlangen, 1962–63. *Address*: Dept of German, The Univ., Leeds LS2 9JT.

Tait, Prof. Alan A., MA, PhD; Professor of Monetary and Financial Economics, University of Strathclyde, since 1971; *b* 1934; *m* 1963; one *s*. MA Edinburgh 1957; PhD Trinity College, Dublin 1966. Lectr, TCD, 1959–68; Vis. Prof., Univ. of Illinois, 1965; Fellow, TCD, 1968, Sen. Tutor, 1970–71; Vis. Prof., IMF, 1972; IMF adviser to Pakistan Tax Commn, 1973–74. *Publications:* The Taxation of Personal Wealth, 1967; Spanish edn 1972; Economic Policy in Ireland, 1968; The Value Added Tax, 1972; Some Problems of a Developing Economy: Ireland, 1972; *contrib.* Finanz., Nat. Tax Jl, Public Fin., Rev. Econ. Stat., Scott. Jl Pol Econ. *Address:* Dept of Economics, Univ. of Strathclyde, Glasgow.

Tait, David A.: Lecturer, Department of Geography, University of Glasgow, since 1968; *b* 1943. BSc Glasgow 1965 (Hons Geography), BSc ITC (Delft, Netherlands) 1967 (Photogrammetric Engineering); FSA Scot; Member: British Cartographic Soc.; British Photogrammetric Soc.; Amer. Soc. of Photogrammetry. ITC, Delft, Netherlands, 1967–68. *Publications: contrib.* Archs Jl, Photogram. Rec. *Address:* Dept of Geography, Univ. Glasgow, Glasgow G12 8QQ.

Tait, James Adie, MA, MSc, FLA; Senior Lecturer, Department of Librarianship, University of Strathclyde, since 1970; *b* 1922; *m* 1955. MA Edinburgh 1943; MSc Strathclyde 1968. FLA 1951. Lectr, Scott. Coll. of Commerce, 1962–64; Lectr, Univ. of Strathclyde, 1964–70. Hon. Treasurer, Scott. Libr. Assoc., 1974– . *Publications:* Descriptive Cataloguing, 1968, 2nd edn 1971; Authors and Titles, 1969; *contrib.* Libr. Rev. *Address:* Dept of Librarianship, Univ. of Strathclyde, Richmond Street, Glasgow.

Tait, Thomas, MBE, MA; Administrative Head of Postgraduate Department, University of London, Goldsmiths' College, since 1965; *b* 1917; *m* 1948; three *d.* BA Oxon 1939, CertEd 1939, MA Oxon 1945. Admin. Asst, Educn Dept, Berkshire CC, 1946; Asst Master, St John's Sch., Leatherhead (Head of English Dept), 1947–61; Lectr, Goldsmiths' Coll., 1961; Sen. Lectr, 1962–64; Princip. Lectr, Goldsmiths' Coll., 1964– . Major, Indian Army (MBE), 1939–45. *Address:* Univ. of London, Goldsmiths' College, New Cross, SE14.

Tajfel, Prof. Henri, MA, PhD; Professor of Social Psychology, University of Bristol, since 1967; *b* 1919; *m* 1948; two *s*. BA London 1954 (1st cl. Psychol.), MA Oxon 1956, PhD London 1961; FBPsS. Res. Asst, Univ. of Durham, 1954–56; Tutor, then Fellow, Linacre Coll., and Univ. Lectr, in Social Psychol., Oxford Univ., 1956–66; Vis. Lectr in Social Psychol., Harvard Univ., 1958–59; Vis. Prof., Univ. of W Ontario, 1964; Fellow, Center for Adv. Studies Behav. Science, Stanford, Calif., 1966–67; SSRC Prof. Fellow, Ecole Pratique des Hautes Etudes, Univ. of Paris, 1970; Vis. Prof., Univ. of Leiden, 1971–73; Katz-Newcomb Lectr, Univ. of Michigan, 1974. Member: SSRC Cttee on Psychol., 1964–68; Cttee on Social Psychol., Amer. Soc. Science Res. Council, 1966– ; Nuffield Foundn

Social Science Adv. Council, 1968– ; Nuffield Foundn Fellowships Council, 1969– ; OECD panel nat. soc. sci. policies in France, 1973–74; Pres., Europ. Assoc. Exper. Social Psychol., 1969–72; Chm., Social Psychol. Sect., Brit. Psychol. Soc., 1970–72. *Publications:* ed, Disappointed Guests, 1965; ed, The Context of Social Psychology, 1972; contrib. Social Psychology through Experiment, ed Humphrey and Argyle, 1962; Politische Psychologie, 1964; International Encyclopedia of the Social Sciences, 1968; The Handbook of Social Psychology, ed Lindzay and Aronson, 1969; Inter-disciplinary Relationships in the Social Sciences, ed Sherif, 1969; Introduction à la psychologie sociale, ed Moscovici, 1972; *contrib.* Acta Psychol., Brit. Jl Psychol., Brit. Jl Social Clin. Psychol., Europ. Jl Social Psychol., Internat. Jl Psychol., Jl Abnorm. Social Psychol., Jl Pers., Jl Pers. Social Psychol., Psychol. Rev., Sci. Amer. *Address:* Dept of Psychology, Univ. of Bristol, Bristol BS8 1HH.

Talbot, Dr Michael Owen; Lecturer, Department of Music, University of Liverpool, since 1968; *b* 1943; *m* 1970. ARCM 1961, BA Cantab 1964, MusB 1965, PhD 1969; Mem., Royal Musical Assoc. Asst Lectr, Dept of Music, Univ. of Liverpool, 1968–69. Vice-Chm., Internat. Antonio Vivaldi Soc., 1971– . *Publications: contrib.* Music and Letters, Music Rev., Vivaldi-Informations. *Address:* Dept of Music, The Univ., Liverpool L69 3BX.

Talbot, Reginald John, MSc, BSc(Eng), ACGI; Lecturer in Ergonomics, Building Department, University of Manchester Institute of Science and Technology, since 1967; *b* 1941; *m* 1967; one *s* one *d.* BSc(Eng), ACGI London 1963 (Aero. Eng.), MSc Cranfield 1965 (Ergonomics and Systems Design); Mem., Ergonom. Res. Soc., Design Res. Soc. Asst Lectr, Univ. of Manchester Inst. of Science and Technol., 1965–67. Member: UMIST Bd of Fac., 1971; Council Design Res. Soc., and Conf. Sec., 1971; Soc. for Gen. Systems Res., 1972; Soc. for Academic Gaming and Simulation in Educn and Training, 1971– . *Publications:* Educational Gaming and Simulation; Everyday Ergonomics; Functions and Futures of Technical Conferences; *contrib.* Ergonom., Applied Ergonomics, Programmed Learning. *Address:* Design Research Laboratory, Pariser Building, Univ. of Manchester Institute of Science and Technology, Manchester M60 1QD.

Tall, Dr David Orme, MA, DPhil; Lecturer in Mathematics, with special reference to Education and Mathematics Education (joint appointment), University of Warwick, since 1969; *b* 1941; *m* 1963; two *s* one *d.* BA Oxon 1963 (1st cl. Maths) MA Oxon 1967, DPhil Oxon 1967. Lectr, Sussex Univ., 1966–69. *Publications:* Functions of a Complex Variable, 1970; *contrib.* Jl Lond. Math. Soc. Topol. *Address:* Mathematics Institute, Univ. of Warwick, Coventry CV4 7AL.

Tanner, Michael Francis, MSc(Econ); Lecturer in Geography, University of Birmingham, since 1963; *b* 1936; *m* 1960; three *d.* BSc(Econ) London 1960, MSc(Econ)

683

London 1963. Tutor and Res. Asst, LSE, 1960–62; Tutor in Geography, Univ. of Liverpool, 1962–63. *Publication*: Water Resources and Recreation, 1973. *Address*: Dept of Geography, The Univ. of Birmingham, PO Box 363, Birmingham B15 2TT.

Tann, Dr Jennifer; Reader in Economic History, Management Centre, University of Aston, since 1973; *b* 1939; *m* 1963; one *s*. BA Manchester 1960, PhD Leicester 1964; Member: Economic History Soc.; Business Archives Council. Asst Lectr, Univ. of Aston, 1967, Lectr, 1968. Mem. Exec. Council, Business Archives Council. *Publications*: Gloucestershire Woollen Mills, 1966; The Development of the Factory, 1970; contrib. Textile History and Economic History, essays in Honour of Miss J. de Lacy Mann; *contrib*. Bus. Arch., Bus. Hist., Hist., Text. Hist. *Address*: Management Centre, Univ. of Aston, Birmingham B4 7ET.

Tanner, Paul Antony, MA, PhD; University Lecturer, English Faculty, Cambridge, since 1966, and Director of English Studies, Kings College, Cambridge University, since 1961; *b* 1935; *m* 1965. BA Cambridge 1958 (English), PhD Cambridge 1964. Mem., BAAS. Harkness Fellow, 1958–60; ACLS Fellow, 1962–63; Fellow, Kings Coll., Cambridge, 1960– ; Univ. Asst Lectr, Kings Coll., Cambridge, 1964–66. *Publications*: Lord Jim, 1963; The Reign of Wonder, 1965; Saul Bellow, 1965; ed, A Hazard of New Fortunes, 1965; ed, Mansfield Park, 1966; ed, James: Hawthorne, 1968; Three Novels by James, 1968; ed, James: Modern Judgments, 1968; City of Words, 1971; ed, Pride and Prejudice, 1972; *contrib*. Crit. Qly, Encount., Jl BAAS, Lond. Mag., Part. Rev., TriQly, etc. *Address*: King's College, Cambridge.

Taplin, Oliver Paul; Lecturer in Greek and Latin (Lit. Hum.), University of Oxford, since 1973; *b* 1943; *m* 1964; one *s* one *d*. BA Oxon 1966, MA Oxon 1969, DPhil Oxon 1974; Cromer Greek Prize, British Academy, 1971; Conington Prize, 1974; Fellow by Examination, Magdalen Coll., Oxford, 1968–72; Fellow, Center for Hellenic Studies, Washington, DC, 1970–71; Lectr in Classics, Univ. of Bristol, 1972–73. *Publications*: *contrib*. CR, G and R, GRBS, HSCP. *Address*: Magdalen College, Oxford.

Tappe, Prof. Eric Ditmar; Professor of Rumanian Studies, School of Slavonic and East European Studies, University of London, since 1974 (Reader, 1964–74); *b* 1910. BA Oxon 1932 (1st cl. Hon. Mods, 2nd cl. Lit. Hum.), MA Oxon 1935; FSA. Lectr in Rumanian Language and Lit., SSEES, Univ. of London, 1948–64. Hon. Sec., Brit. Cttee, Internat. Assoc. SE Europ. Studies, 1970– . *Publications*: Rumanian Prose and Verse, 1956; Documents concerning Rumanian History (1427–1601) collected from British archives, 1964; trans., M. Eliade and M. Niculescu: Fantastic Tales, 1969; *contrib*. Rev. Etudes Roum., Rev. Etudes SE Europ., Slav. E Europ. Rev. *Address*: Univ. of London, School of Slavonic and East European Studies, Malet Street, WC1E 7HU.

Tapper, Colin Frederick Herbert, MA, BCL; Fellow and Tutor in Law, Magdalen College, Oxford University, since 1965; *b* 1934; *m* 1961. BA Oxon 1958 (1st cl. Jurisprudence), BCL Oxon 1959 (1st cl.), MA Oxon 1965; Barrister-at-Law, Gray's Inn 1961. Asst Lectr in Law, LSE, 1959–62; Lectr in Law, LSE, 1962–65; CUF Lectr in Law, Oxford, 1966– ; Vis. Prof., Univ. of Alabama Law Sch., 1970; Vis. Prof., NY Univ. Law Sch., 1970. Statutes and Reports Ed., Mod. Law Rev., 1964– ; Exp. Cnsltnt, Council of Europe Computers and Law Cttee, 1968– ; Mem. Council, Soc. for Computers and Law, 1973– . *Publications*: Computers and Law, 1973; contrib. Annual Survey of Commonwealth Law, 1966–69, 1973– ; Oxford Essays in Jurisprudence, 2nd edn 1972; *contrib*. Alab. Law Rev., Camb. Law Jl, Jl Soc. Public Teachers Law, Mod. Law Rev. *Address*: Magdalen College, Oxford OX1 4AU.

Tapper, Dr Edward Robert; Lecturer, Department of Politics, University of Sussex, since 1968; *b* 1940; *m* 1972; one *s*. BA Exeter 1962, MA Oregon 1964, PhD Manchester 1968. *Publication*: Young People and Society, 1971. *Address*: Dept of Politics, Univ. of Sussex, Falmer, Brighton BN1 9RH.

Tapper, Dr Richard Lionel; Lecturer in Anthropology with special reference to the Middle East, Department of Anthropology and Sociology, School of Oriental and African Studies, University of London, since 1967; *b* 1942; *m* 1965. BA Cantab 1964, PhD London 1972; FRAI, Fellow, Soc. for Afghan Studies. *Address*: Dept of Anthropology and Sociology, School of Oriental and African Studies, Univ. of London, Malet Street, WC1E 7HP.

Tarn, Prof. John Nelson, BArch, PhD, FRIBA; Roscoe Professor of Architecture, University of Liverpool, since 1973; *b* 1934. BArch Dunelm 1957 (1st cl.), PhD Cantab 1961; FRIBA. Lectr, Dept of Architecture, Sheffield Univ., 1963–70; Prof. and Head of Dept of Architecture, Nottingham Univ., 1970–73. *Publications*: Working Class Housing Policies in Nineteenth Century Britain, 1971; The Peak District National Park: Its Architecture, 1971; *contrib*. Archit. Rev., Town Plann. Rev., Urb. Studies, Vict. Studies. *Address*: School of Architecture, Univ. of Liverpool, Liverpool L69 3BX.

Tarr, Roger Paul; Lecturer in Art History, Fine Art Department, Edinburgh University, since 1966; *b* 1940. BA Oxon 1963, Postgraduate Diploma in History of Art, Courtauld Inst., London, 1966. *Address*: Fine Art Dept, Edinburgh Univ., 19 George Square, Edinburgh.

Tarrant, Dr John Rex; Senior Lecturer since 1974, and Dean, 1974–77, School of Environmental Sciences, University of East Anglia; *b* 1941; *m* 1966. BSc Hull 1963 (spec. Hons Geog.), PhD Hull 1966; Mem. Inst. Brit. Geogrs. Asst Lectr, UC Dublin, 1966–68; Lectr, Sch. of Environmental Scis, Univ. of E Anglia, 1968–74. *Publications*: Agricultural Geography, 1974; *contrib*. Econ.

Geography, Geog. Analysis, Geog. Mag., Geography, Irish Geography, Jl Brit. Interplanetary Soc., Professional Geographer, Trans Inst. Brit. Geogrs, Tijdschrift voor Econishe en Sociale Geografie. *Address*: School of Environmental Sciences, Univ. of East Anglia, Norwich NOR 88C.

Tate, Elizabeth Priscilla; Lecturer, Department of Social Administration, London School of Economics, University of London, since 1966; *b* 1912; *m* 1941; three *d*. BA Oxford 1934 (Hons Modern and Mediaeval History), Certificate in Applied Social Studies LSE, 1961. Sen. Sch. Care Organiser, LCC, 1936–41 and 1956–65; Princ. Social Worker, London Borough of Hackney, 1965–66. *Publication*: Health and Welfare, in, The Government of London: the first five years, ed G. Rhodes, 1970. *Address*: Dept of Social Administration, London School of Economics, Houghton Street, Aldwych, WC2A 2AE.

Tate, Prof. Robert Brian, MA, PhD; Professor of Spanish, University of Nottingham, since 1958; *b* 1921; *m* 1951; one *s* one *d*. BA Belfast 1948 (1st cl. French and Spanish), MA Belfast 1950, PhD Belfast 1955. Lectr, Manchester Univ., 1949–51; Lectr, Queen's Univ., Belfast, 1951–56; Reader, Nottingham Univ., 1956–58. *Publications*: Joan Margarit, Bishop of Gerona, 1955; ed, F. P. de Guzmán: Generaciones y Semblanzas, 1965; Ensayos sobre la historiografía peninsular del siglo XV, 1970; ed, F. de Pulgar: Claros varones de Castilla, 1971; ed (with I. R. Macpherson), J. Manuel: Libro de los estados, 1974; trans. P. Vilar: Spain: a Brief History, 1967; *contrib*. Bull. Hispan. Studies, Hispan. Rev., Rom. Ph., Sp., Mod. Lang. Rev. *Address*: Spanish Dept, Univ. of Nottingham, Nottingham NG7 2RD.

Tattersall, Arthur; Secretary, University College London, since 1964; *b* 1912; *m* 1937; one *s* one *d*. BA Cantab 1934 (Open Scholar, Christ's Coll.; Class. Tripos Pt I, cl. I, 1933, Pt II, cl. I, 1934), MA 1946. Classics Master, King Henry VIII Sch., Coventry, 1934–40; Army (Royal Tank Regt), 1940–45; Asst Dir of Educn, Hunts, 1945–50; Dep. Academic Registrar, Univ. of London, 1950–55; Sec., Makerere Coll., Uganda (now Makerere Univ.), 1955–61; Warden, Internat. Hall, Univ. of London, and Sec., Hale Cttee on Univ. Teaching Methods, 1961–64. *Address*: Univ. College London, Gower Street, WC1E 6BT.

Tawney, David A.; Senior Research Associate, Centre for Applied Research in Education, University of East Anglia, since 1974; *b* 1931; *m* 1955; two *s* one *d*. BA Cantab 1953, MA Cantab 1957, Certif. of Educn Cantab 1954; MInstP 1964, Mem., Assoc. for Science Educn. Various secondary schs, 1955–67; Lectr in Educn, Univ. of Keele, 1967. Dir, Evaluation Study of Schs Council Project on Technology, 1969–72. *Publications*: contrib. Evaluation in Curriculum Development: twelve case studies, 1973; contrib. Science Teacher Educn Project Pubns: The Art of the Science Teacher, 1974; Activities and Experiences,

1974; Meadowbank School: case studies in education, 1974; *contrib*. Jl Curric. Stud., Paed. Eur., Phys Educn, Sch. Sci. Rev. *Address*: Centre for Applied Research in Education, Univ. of East Anglia, Norwich NOR 88C.

Taylor, Alan John Percivale, FBA; Fellow of Magdalen College, Oxford University, since 1938; Hon. Director, The Beaverbrook Library; *b* 1906; *m* 1st 1931, 2nd 1951; four *s* two *d*. BA Oxon 1927 (1st cl. Hist.), MA Oxon 1932, Hon. DCL New Brunswick 1961, Hon. D Univ. York 1970; FBA. Lectr, Manchester Univ., 1930–38; Tutor, Magdalen Coll., Oxford, 1938–63; Ford Lectr, Oxford, 1956; Leslie Stephen Lectr, Cambridge, 1961; Lectr, Oxford Univ., 1953–63. *Publications*: The Course of German History, 1945, Italian edn 1965; The Habsburg Monarchy, 1948, Slovene edn 1951; Bismarck, 1955, German edn 1956, Italian edn 1963; The Struggle for Mastery in Europe, 1954, Russian, Hebrew, Serbo-Croat and Italian edns; The Troublemakers, 1957; The Origins of the Second World War, 1961, 11 foreign edns; The First World War, 1963, 3 foreign edns; English History 1914–45, 1965, Italian and Japanese edns; From Sarajevo to Potsdam, 1966, French and Swedish edns; War by Time-Table, 1969, French, Spanish, Swedish and Dutch edns; The Second World War, 1974; ed, Lloyd George: Twelve Essays, 1971; ed, Lloyd George: a Diary by Frances Stevenson, 1971; Beaverbrook, 1972; ed, Off The Record by W. P. Crozier, 1973. *contrib*. EHR. *Address*: Magdalen College, Oxford.

Taylor, Prof. Andrew, MA; Professor of Education, University College, Cardiff, University of Wales, since 1967; *b* 1920; *m* 1945; one *s* one *d*. BA New Zealand 1946, MA New Zealand 1948 (1st cl.), DipEd New Zealand 1949. Lectr, Univ. Coll. of the Gold Coast, 1950–55, Sen. Lectr, 1955–58, Dir, Inst. of Educn, 1958–60; Prof., and Dir, Inst. of Educn, Univ. of Ibadan, 1960–67. Chm., Nigerian Council for Educnl Res., 1965–67; Gov., Centre for Educnl Development Overseas, 1971– . *Publications*: Equipping the Classroom, 1953; Educational and Occupational Selection in British West Africa, 1960; *contrib*. Educn Develop., Teach. Educn, W Afr. Jl Educn, YBk Educn. *Address*: Faculty of Education, Univ. College, Cardiff CF1 1XL.

Taylor, Arnold Rodgers, MA; Senior Lecturer in English, and Supervisor of Icelandic Studies, University of Leeds, since 1956; *b* 1913; *m* 1942; one *s* one *d*. BA Manchester 1934 (English Lang. and Lit.), DipEd Manchester 1936, MA Manchester 1935. Pres., Viking Soc. North. Res., 1952–54; Vice-Pres. in Council, VSNR. Lector in English, Univ. of Jena, 1937; Asst Lectr, Univ. of Leeds, 1946; Lectr, Univ. of Leeds, 1947–56. *Publications*: ed, E. V. Gordon: Introduction to Old Norse, rev. edn 1957; Icelandic-English Pocket Dictionary, 1955; English-Icelandic Pocket Dictionary, 1955; *contrib*. Leeds Studies Engl., Saga Bk Vik. Soc. *Address*: School of English, The Univ., Leeds LS2 9JT.

685

Taylor, Prof. Arthur John, Professor of Modern History, Leeds University, since 1961; *b* 1919; *m* 1955; one *s* two *d.* BA Manchester 1946, MA Manchester 1947; FRHistS 1955. Mem., Econ. Hist. Soc., Mem., Hist. Assoc. Asst Lectr, Univ. Coll., London, 1948–50, Lectr, 1950–61; Chm., Sch. of History, Leeds, 1962–71; Pro-Vice-Chancellor, Leeds, 1971– . Chm., Jt Matric. Bd, 1970– ; Mem., Council, Royal Hist. Soc., 1964–67. *Publications*: ed and trans., E. Halévy: Thomas Hodgskin, 1956; contrib. Studies in the Industrial Revolution, ed L. S. Pressnell, 1960; Edwardian England, ed S. Nowell-Smith, 1964; Victoria County History of Staffordshire, vol. II, 1967; *contrib.* Econ. Hist. Rev., Economica, Hist. *Address*: Univ. of Leeds, Leeds LS2 9JT.

Taylor, Basil Frederick; Reader in Portfolio Investment, Graduate Business Centre, The City University, since 1969; *b* 1926; *m* 1958; one *s* one *d.* BSc(Econ) UCL 1951 (1st cl. Hons); Mem., Soc. of Investment Analysts. Res. Studentship, Balliol Coll., Oxon, and Nuffield Coll., Oxon, 1951–53; City employment, portfolio investment, 1954–67; Esmée Fairbairn Sen. Res. Fellow in Finance, City Univ., 1967–69. Dir, Giles Taylor Ltd, 1963– . *Publications*: ed and contrib. Investment Analysis and Portfolio Management: Readings from British Publications, 1970 (also Amer. and Spanish edns); *contrib.* Invest. Anal., Investor's Chronicle, Lloyds Bank Rev., Stock Exch. Jl, Westminster Bank Rev. *Address*: Gresham College, Basinghall Street, EC2.

Taylor, Brian K.; Lecturer in Social Administration, University College of Swansea, since 1965; *b* 1924; *m* 1953; three *s* one *d.* BA Rhodes 1948, MA London 1957. Mem., Internat. Soc. Community Develop., Mem., Assoc. Community Workers. Lectr, Swansea Univ. Coll., 1961; Lectr, Univ. of Adelaide, 1962–64. Colonial Social Science. Res. Fellow, 1949–52; Community Develop. Off., Uganda, 1953–60; Social Welf. Adv., W Cameroon, 1967; Community Develop. Adv., Uganda, 1968; Community Develop. and Yth Wk Adv., Cyprus, 1968–71; Ed., Community Develop. Jl, 1971– . *Publications*: The Western Lacustrine Bantu, 1962, 2nd edn 1969. *Address*: Social Administration Dept, Univ. College of Swansea, Swansea SA2 8PP.

Taylor, Christopher Charles Whiston; Fellow and Tutor in Philosophy, Corpus Christi College, Oxford University, since 1963; *b* 1936; *m* 1965; one *s* one *d.* MA Edinburgh 1958 (1st cl. Classics), BA Oxon 1960 (1st cl. Lit. Hum.), BPhil Oxon 1962 (Philos.), MA Oxon 1964. Fellow, Magdalen Coll., Oxford, 1962; CUF Lectr, Oxford Univ., 1964– ; Loeb Fellow in Classical Philos., Harvard Univ., 1970. Sec., Sub-fac. of Philos., Oxford Univ., 1967–72; Tutor for Graduates, Corpus Christi Coll., 1971– . *Publications*: *contrib.* Analysis, Mind, Phron., Philos. Qly, Proc. Aristot. Soc. *Address*: Corpus Christi College, Oxford.

Taylor, Daniel Malcolm; Senior Lecturer in Philosophy, University of Kent at Canter-
686

bury, since 1966; *b* 1934. BA Oxford 1956 (PPE), BA Oxford 1958 (PPP). Lectr in Psychol., Australian Nat. Univ., 1959–62; Lectr in Philos., Liverpool Univ., 1962–66. Mem., Senate and Senate Exec., 1970–71; Mem., Humanities Fac., 1968–70; Eliot Coll. Cttee. *Publications*: Explanation and Meaning: An Introduction to Philosophy, 1970; *contrib.* Mind, Philos. Qly. *Address*: Eliot College, Univ. of Kent, Canterbury CT1 3PA.

Taylor, David Stewart; Lecturer in Applied Experimental Psychology, Management Centre, University of Bradford, since 1964; *b* 1940; *m* 1968. BSc Leeds 1964 (Hons Psychology); ABPsS 1971; Member: British Psychological Soc.; Ergonomics Res. Soc.; Internat. Assoc. of Applied Psychology. Co-editor, Jl of European Training, 1972– . *Publications*: *contrib.* Brit. J. Mkt, Ergon. *Address*: Managemen. Centre, Univ. of Bradford, Emm Lane, Bradford BD9 4JL.

Taylor, Eric; Lecturer, Faculty of Law, University of Manchester, since 1965; *b* 1931; *m* 1958. LLB Manchester 1952, LLM Manchester 1954; Solicitor (II Hons) 1955; SPTL; Mem. Council, Law Soc. Asst Lectr, Faculty of Law, Univ. of Manchester, 1958. *Publications*: contrib. Modern Conveyancing Precedents, 1964; ed jtly, Modern Wills Precedents, 1969; *contrib.* Crim. Law Rev., Law Soc. Gaz. *Address*: Faculty of Law, The Univ., Manchester M13 9PL.

Taylor, Prof. Eric Robert, MA, DMus, ARCO, Hon. ARAM; Professor of Music, University of Durham, since 1968; *b* 1928; *m* 1950; two *s.* BA Oxon 1949, MA, BMus Oxon 1954, DMus Oxon 1961; ARCO; Hon. ARAM. Lectr, Reading Univ., 1959–66 (also Prof. of composition, harmony, etc, Royal Acad. of Music); Sen. Lectr, Reading Univ., 1966–68. Dir of Music, Stonyhurst Coll., 1955–59. *Publications*: A Method of Aural Training, 1955; Playing from an Orchestral Score, 1967; An Introduction to Score Playing, 1970; *contrib.* Music & Lett., Music Rev. *Address*: The Music School, Palace Green, Durham.

Taylor, Dr Frank, MA PhD, FSA; Deputy Director and Principal Keeper, The John Rylands University Library of Manchester, since 1972; Hon. Lecturer in Manuscript Studies, University of Manchester, since 1967. BA Manchester 1930 (History), MA Manchester 1931, PhD Manchester 1938; FSA 1955. Res. for Cttee on History of Parliament, 1934–35; John Rylands Library: Keeper of Western Manuscripts, 1935–49; Keeper of Manuscripts, 1949–72; Librarian, 1970–72. RN 1942–46 (Lieut). Hon. Sec., Lancs Parish Register Soc., 1937– ; Editor, Bulletin of John Rylands (University) Library, 1948– ; Mem. Cttee, Medieval Latin Dictionary, 1973– . *Publications*: various calendars of manuscripts and charter room collections in John Rylands Library, 1937– ; The Chronicle of John Strecche for the Reign of Henry V, 1932; An Early 17th Century Calendar of Records preserved in Westminster Palace Treasury, 1939; The Parish Registers of Aughton, Lancs (1541–

1764), 1942; (contrib.) Some 20th Century Interpretations of Boswell's Life of Johnson (ed J. L. Clifford), 1970; The Oriental Manuscript Collections in the John Rylands Library, 1972; (with J. S. Roskell) The Gesta Henrici Quinti (forthcoming); *contrib.* Bull. John Rylands Lib., Ind. Arch. *Address*: The John Rylands University Library of Manchester, Manchester.

Taylor, George; Part-time Teaching Fellow, Education Department, University of Leeds, since 1965; *b* 1900; *m* 1937; three *d.* BA Manchester 1921 (2nd cl. Hist.), MA Manchester 1923 (Hist.); Barrister-at-Law 1933. Chief Educn Off., City of Leeds, 1950–65. Chm., Consult. Cttee on Mod. Langs Teaching Materials Project, Nuffield Foundn, 1962–70; Chm., Schs Council Consult. Cttee on Mod. Langs, 1970–73. *Publications*: (with G. Unwin) Oldknow and the Arkwrights, 1925; Sketch Map History of Britain and Europe, 1937; ed, New Law of Education, 6th edn 1965, 7th edn 1971; ed, Teacher as Manager, 1970; Born and Bred Unequal, 1970. *Address*: Dept of Education, Univ. of Leeds, Leeds LS2 9JT.

Taylor, George William; Lecturer, Drama Department, University of Manchester, since 1967; *b* 1940. Manchester University: BA 1964 (Hons History), Diploma in Drama 1965, MA 1973 (Drama). Artistic Dir, Chester Playhouse, 1965–66; Graduate Asst, Drama Dept, Manchester Univ., 1966–67. *Publications*: The Just Deliniation of the Passions: Theories of Acting in the Age of Garrick, in, The Eighteenth-Century English Stage, ed K. Richards and P. Thomson, 1972; *contrib.* Theatre Res. *Address*: Drama Dept, Univ. of Manchester, Oxford Road, Manchester M13 9PL.

Taylor, Dr (Gloria) Clare; Lecturer, Department of History, University College of Wales, Aberystwyth, since 1967; *b* 1934. MA Edinburgh 1957, PhD Edinburgh 1960. Mem., Brit. Assoc. Amer. Studies, Mem., Victorian Soc., Mem., Cardigan. Antiqu. Soc. Asst Lectr, Univ. Coll. of Wales, Aberystwyth, 1963–67. *Publications*: ed (with G. A. Shepperson), The Estlin Papers, 1962; Wales and America – A Documentary Survey, 1972; British and American Abolitionists: An Episode in Transatlantic Understanding (forthcoming); *contrib.* Bull. Brit. Assoc. Amer. Studies, Bull. Jam. Hist. Soc., Ceredig. *Address*: Dept of History, Univ. College of Wales, Aberystwyth SY23 2AX.

Taylor, Harold James Strickland; Lecturer, Institute of Education, University of Leeds, since 1963; *b* 1922; *m* 1954; one *s* one *d.* BA Cambridge 1948 (Hist.), DipEd Cambridge 1949, MA Cambridge 1953. Mem., AUT 1963– , Mem., Internat. Assoc. Teachers of English as a Foreign Lang. Lectr in the Teaching of English as a Second Language, Leeds, 1966– . Ext. Examiner, Overseas Teachers Courses, Inst. of Educn, Univ. of Exeter, 1968–73. *Publications*: reviser, Guided Composition, new edn; *contrib.* Eng. Lang. Teach., Mod. Eng. Teacher, Levende Talen. *Address*: Institute of Education, Univ. of Leeds, Leeds LS2 9JT.

Taylor, Prof. Ian Galbraith; Ellis Llwyd Jones Professor of Audiology and Education of the Deaf, University of Manchester, since 1964; *b* 1924; *m* 1954; two *d.* MB, ChB Manchester 1949, DPH Manchester 1954, MD Manchester 1962 (Gold Medal); MRCP 1973; Member: British Soc. of Audiology; Manchester Paediatric Club; Hon. FCST. Dept of Audiology and Educn of Deaf, Univ. of Manchester: Hon. Special Lectr and Ewing Foundn Fellow, 1956–60; Lectr in Clinical Audiology, 1960–63; Sen. Lectr in Clinical Audiology, 1963–64. *Publications*: Neurological Mechanisms of Hearing and Speech, 1964; Audiometry, in, Biomedical Technology in Hospital Diagnosis, ed Elder and Neill, 1972; (with others) Linguistic Development, in, Scientific Foundations of Paediatrics, ed J. Dobbing and J. Davis, 1974; The Future of Audiology in the Hospital Service (Paper read to Sect. of Otology, RSM, Feb. 1972). *Address*: Dept of Audiology and Education of the Deaf, Univ. of Manchester, Manchester M13 9PL.

Taylor, Ian Roger; Lecturer in Criminology, Criminology Unit, Faculty of Law, University of Sheffield, since 1971; *b* 1944. BA Durham 1965 (Modern History), Diploma in Criminology, Cantab, 1966; Member: British Sociological Assoc.; Soc. for Study of Social Problems, USA. Res. Asst, Dept of Social Studies, Univ. of Durham, 1966–68; Asst Lectr in Sociology, Univ. of Glasgow, 1968–69; Sessional Lectr in Sociology, Queen's Univ., Kingston, Ont, Canada, 1969–70; SSRC Project Officer, Dept of Sociology, Univ. of Bradford, 1970–71. Mem. Cttee, Nat. Deviancy Conf. (UK). *Publications*: (with P. Walton and J. Young) The New Criminology, 1973; (co-ed. with Laurie Taylor) Politics and Deviance, 1973; (co-ed with P. Walton and J. Young) Critical Criminology (forthcoming); *contrib.* Brit. Jl Sociol., Brit. Jl Criminol., Hum. Cont., Prob. Polit. et Soc., New Soc., Times High. Ed. *Address*: Criminology Unit, Faculty of Law, Univ. of Sheffield, Sheffield S10 2TN.

Taylor, James Allan, MA; Reader in Geography, University College of Wales, Aberystwyth, since 1972 (Senior Lecturer, 1967–72); *b* 1925; *m* 1962; one *s* one *d.* BA Liverpool 1945 (1st cl.), DipEd Liverpool 1946, MA Liverpool 1949; FRGS, FRMetSoc. Asst Lectr, Aberystwyth, 1950–52. Council Mem., Inst. Brit. Geogrs, Mem., Edit. Bd, Inst. Brit. Geogrs, 1966–68; Founder and Co-organizer mem., Internat. Geog. Union Commn on Agric. Typology, 1964– ; Ch. Examiner, 'A' level Geog., WJEC, 1971–75; Conv. of ann. symp. in agric. and applied meteorol., Aberystwyth, 1958–72; Organizer of land use and vegetation surveys of Wales, 1960–66. *Publications*: British Weather in Maps, 1958, 2nd edn 1967; Weather and Agriculture, 1967; Geography at Aberystwyth, 1968; Weather Economics, 1970; The Role of Water in Agriculture, 1970; Research Papers in Forest Meteorology: An Aberystwyth Symposium, 1972; Weather Forecasting for Agriculture and Industry, 1972; Climatic Resources and Economic Activity, 1974; *contrib.* Geog.,

Nature., Trans Brit. Geog., Trans Inter. Peat Symposia (1952, 1963, 1968 and 1972). *Address*: Dept of Geography, Univ. College of Wales, Llandinam Building, Penglais, Aberystwyth.

Taylor, Jane Hilary Margaret, MA, DPhil; Lecturer in Medieval French, University of Manchester, since 1966; *b* 1941; *m* 1964. BA Oxon 1963, MA Oxon 1970, DPhil Oxon 1970. *Address*: Dept of French, Univ. of Manchester, Manchester M13 9PL.

Taylor, John, MA; Reader in Medieval History, University of Leeds, since 1970; *b* 1925; *m* 1955; two *s*. BA Oxon 1950 (2nd cl. Hist.), MA Oxon 1950; FRHistS. Asst Lectr, Univ. of Leeds, 1950–53; Lectr, Univ. of Leeds, 1953–65; Sen. Lectr, Univ. of Leeds, 1965–70; Vis. Assoc. Prof., Princeton Univ., 1961–62. Ed., Leeds Philos. Lit. Soc., Lit. and Hist. Sect., 1959– . *Publications*: Kirkstall Abbey Chronicles, 1952; Medieval Historical Writing in Yorkshire, 1961; The Use of Medieval Chronicles, 1965; The Universal Chronicle of Ranulf Higden, 1966; *contrib*. EHR, Med. et Humanistica. *Address*: School of History, Univ. of Leeds, Leeds LS2 9JT.

Taylor, John Bernard; Recognized Lecturer in Theology, University of Birmingham and Reader in Islamics, Selly Oak Colleges, Birmingham, since 1965; on leave of absence as Assistant Director, Dialogue with People of Living Faiths and Ideologies, World Council of Churches, Geneva, 1973–76; *b* 1937; *m* 1962; two *s* one *d*. BA Cantab 1961 (1st cl. Classics and Oriental Langs), MA Cantab 1964, PhD McGill 1972. Mem., Internat. Assoc. Hist. of Religions. Sen. Rouse Ball Studentship, Trinity Coll., Cambridge, 1965; Assoc. Teacher, Centre for W African Studies, Univ. of Birmingham, 1970; Vis. Schol., Center for Study of Wld Religions, Harvard Univ., 1971–72. Mem., Consult. Cttee, Schs Council Project on Religious Educn in Sec. Schs, Lancaster Univ., 1970–73. *Publications*: Thinking about Islam, 1971; *contrib*. Islam Cult., Jl Relig. Studies. *Address*: Selly Oak Colleges, Birmingham B29 6LE; WCC, 150 Rte de Ferney, 1211 Geneva 20.

Taylor, Dr John Laverack, PhD, MSc, DipArch, RIBA, MRTPI; Senior Lecturer in Town and Regional Planning, and Director, Sheffield Centre for Environmental Research, University of Sheffield, since 1971; *b* 1937; *m* 1960; one *s* two *d*. DipArch Leeds 1960, MSc Columbia 1963, PhD Sheffield 1969; Registd Architect RIBA, Chartd Town Planner, MRTPI. ESU Univ. Fellow, Columbia Univ., 1962–63; Vis. Lectr, Univ. of Kentucky, 1963–64; Lectr, Univ. of Sheffield, 1966–71; Vis. Nuffield Social Science Fellow, Univ. of Michigan, and Univ. of S California, 1971–72. Cnsltnt, OECD; Amer. Inst Archit.; Fed. Housing and Urb. Renewal Agency; Min. of Overseas

Develop.; Ed., SCUPAD Bull.; Mem. Edit. Bd, Simulation Games. *Publications*: ed, Instructional Simulation Systems, 1970–71; Instructional Planning Systems, 1971; Simulation in the Classroom, 1972; Planning for Urban Development, 1972; *contrib*. Archit. Jl, Archit. Des., Build., Etristics, Jl Royal Town Plan. Inst., Plan. Outlk, Technol. Soc., Urb. Studies, Werk. *Address*: Dept of Town and Regional Planning, Univ. of Sheffield, Sheffield S10 2TN.

Taylor, John Percy W.; *see* West-Taylor.

Taylor, Dr Maxwell; Lecturer, Department of Psychology, University College of North Wales, since 1970; *b* 1945; *m* 1967; one *s* one *d*. BA Hons Wales 1967, PhD Liverpool 1971. Demonstr, Liverpool, 1967–70. *Publications*: *contrib*. Psychopharmacologia. *Address*: Dept of Psychology, Univ. College of North Wales, Bangor LL57 2DG.

Taylor, Michael John; Senior Lecturer, Department of Government, University of Essex, since 1971; *b* 1942. BSc Hons London 1964; MSc Essex 1965; Member: Amer. Pol. Sci. Assoc.; Conflict Res. Soc.; Public Choice Soc. (US); Conservation Soc. Lectr, Essex, 1968–71. Vis. Lectr, Yale Univ., 1970–71. Fellow, Netherlands Inst. for Advanced Study, 1973–74. *Publications*: The Analysis of Political Cleavages, 1970; Anarchy and Cooperation, 1975; *contrib*. Amer. Pol Sci. Rev., Behav. Sci., Brit. Jl Pol Sci., Comp. Pol., Europ. Jl Pol Res., Hum. Relat., Polity, Public Choice. *Address*: Dept of Government, Univ. of Essex, Colchester CO4 3SQ.

Taylor, Michael John, MA; Lecturer in French, School of Modern Languages, University of Bath, since 1966; *b* 1936; *m* 1959; one *d*. BA Dunelm 1958 (2nd cl. French), DipEd Dunelm 1959, MA Dunelm 1963. *Publication*: Martin du Gard: Jean Barois, 1974. *Address*: School of Modern Languages, Univ. of Bath, Claverton Down, Bath BA2 7AY.

Taylor, Dr Philip Arthur Michael, MA, PhD; Reader in American Studies, University of Hull, since 1972; *b* 1920; *m* 1949; one *d*. BA Cantab 1946 (1st cl. Pts I and II Hist.), MA Cantab 1948, PhD Cantab 1952. Asst Lectr, Aberdeen Univ., 1949; Instructor, Univ. of Iowa, 1950; Asst Prof., Univ. of Iowa, 1951–53; Tutor, Extra-mural Dept, Birmingham Univ., 1953–62; Lectr, Hull Univ., 1962–66, Sen. Lectr, 1966–72. *Publications*: ed, The Industrial Revolution in Britain, 1958, 2nd edn 1970; ed, The English Civil War, 1960; Expectations Westward: Mormons and Emigration of British Converts, 1965; The Distant Magnet: European Emigration to United States, 1971; *contrib*. Econ. Hist. Rev., Jl Amer. Studies, Univ. Birm. Hist. Jl, Utah Hist. Qly. *Address*: Dept of American Studies, Univ. of Hull, Hull HU6 7RX.

Taylor, Philip Hampson; Professor of Education, University of Birmingham, since 1966; *b* 1923; *m* 1952; two *s*. BA Leeds 1950, MEd Manchester 1956; Teachers' Dip. 1951, DipEd 1953. Lectr, Univ. of Leicester, 1960–66. Adv., Min. of Educn, 1963–64; Dir. of Res., Schs Council, 1964–66. *Publications*: Society and the Teacher's Role, 1969; How Teachers Plan their Courses, 1970; *contrib.* Brit. Jl Educn Psychol., Educnl Rev., High. Educn Rev., Internat. Jl Educnl Sci., Paedagog. Europ. *Address*: School of Education, The Univ., PO Box 363, Birmingham B15 2TT.

Taylor, Richard K. S.; Lecturer, Department of Adult Education and Extra-mural Studies, University of Leeds, since 1973; *b* 1945; *m* 1967; one *s* two *d*. BA Oxford 1967 (Hons PPE; Exeter Coll., 1964–67). Univ. of Lancaster, 1967–70; Univ. of Leeds, 1970. *Address*: Adult Education Dept, Univ. of Leeds, Leeds LS2 9JT.

Taylor, Prof. Ronald J.; Professor of German, University of Sussex, since 1965; *b* 1928; *m* 1950; one *s* one *d*. MA London 1952, PhD London 1956; LRAM. Lectr in German, Univ. Coll. of Swansea, 1951–57; Sen. Lectr, Univ. Coll. of Swansea, 1957–65; Prof. of German, Univ. of Chicago, 1960; Prof. of German, Northwestern Univ., 1963–64. *Publications*: (with A. T. Hatto) The Songs of Neidhart von Reuental, 1959; Die Melodien der weltlichen Lieder des Mittelalters, 1963; E. T. A. Hoffmann, 1964; The Art of the Minnesinger, 1968; The Romantic Tradition in Germany, 1970; The Intellectual Tradition of Modern Germany, 1973; Literature and Society in Germany, 1918–1945, 1974; var. trans from German; *contrib.* Encyclopedia Britannica; *contrib.* Germ. Life and Lett., Mod. Lang. Rev., Times Lit. Suppl. etc. *Address*: Univ. of Sussex, Falmer, Brighton BN1 9RH.

Taylor, Ronald Yearsley; Lecturer in Economics and Accountancy, Department of Accounting, Manchester University, since 1950; *b* 1913; *m* 1951. BA Admin; FICA. Chartered Accountant in public practice. *Address*: Dept of Accounting, The Univ., Oxford Road, Manchester M13 9PL.

Taylor, Samuel Sorby Brittain, BA, PhD; Reader in French, University of St Andrews, since 1972; *b* 1930; *m* 1956; two *d*. BA Birmingham 1952 (French), PhD Birmingham 1957 (French). Dunlop Rubber Co. Ltd, 1958–60; Inst. et Musée Voltaire, Geneva, as Asst to T. Besterman (Voltaire's correspondence), 1960–63; Asst Lectr, Univ. of St Andrews, 1963, Lectr, 1964–72; Canada Council Vis. Prof. in Romance Langs, 1967–68. RN, 1956–58; Sec., 2nd Internat. Cong. on Enlightenment, St Andrews, 1967; Sec.-Gen., Internat. Soc. Eightnth Cent. Studies, 1967–70; Mem., edit. cttee, Complete Works of Voltaire, 1968– . *Publications*: Gen. Ed., The Age of the Enlightenment: Studies presented to Theodore Besterman, 1967; contrib. New Cambridge Bibliography of English Literature, vol. 2, 1971; *contrib.* Forum Mod. Lang. Studies, Studies Volt. Eightnth Cent. *Address*: Dept of French,

Univ. of St Andrews, St Andrews, Fife KY1 9AJ.

Taylor, Dr Stanley William; Senior Lecturer, French Department, University of Bristol, since 1964; *b* 1921; *m* 1947; three *s* two *d*. BA Bristol 1949, PhD Bristol 1958. Asst Lectr, Bristol Univ., 1950, Lectr, 1953. *Address*: Dept of French, The Univ., Queens Road, Bristol BS8 1RJ.

Taylor, Sydney; Lecturer, School of Education, University of Reading, since 1963; *b* 1909; *m* 1963. BA Reading 1932 (2nd cl. French), DipEd Reading 1933, L-ès-L Lille 1935. Mem., AUT, MLA, IAAM, AVLA, CESE. Sen. Steward, Sen. Common Room, 1970–71. *Address*: Reading Univ. School of Education, London Road, Reading RG1 5AQ.

Taylor, Dr William, BScEcon, PhD; Director, University of London Institute of Education, since 1973; *b* 1930; *m* 1954; one *s* two *d*. BSc(Econ) London 1952 (Sociology), CertEd London 1953, DipEd London 1954 (with distinction), PhD London 1961 (Sociol. of Educn). Teacher, primary and sec. schs, 1953–59; Colls of Educn, 1959–64; Lectr and Tutor, Oxford Univ. Dept of Educn, 1964–66; Prof. of Educn, Univ. of Bristol, 1966–73; Dir, Univ. of Bristol Area Training Organisation, 1967–73. Res. Adv., Dept of Educn and Science, 1968–73; Chm., Europ. Cttee on Educnl Res., 1969–71. *Publications*: The Secondary Modern School, 1963; Society and the Education of Teachers, 1969; Heading for Change, 1969; ed, Towards a Policy for the Education of Teachers, 1969; ed (with G. Baron), Educational Administration and the Social Sciences, 1969; (with S. Moore) '. . . and Gladly Teach', 1970; Policy and Planning in Post-Secondary Education, 1971; Theory into Practice, 1972; ed, Research Perspectives in Education, 1973; *contrib.* Educn Teach., Jl Educnl Technol., Sociol. Rev. *Address*: Institute of Education, Malet Street, WC1E 7HS.

Teasdale, Dr James Arthur; Senior Lecturer, Department of Naval Architecture and Shipbuilding, University of Newcastle upon Tyne, since 1972; *b* 1931; *m* 1954; two *s* three *d*. BSc Durham 1954, MSc Newcastle 1966, PhD Newcastle 1970; FRINA 1972. Lectr, Dept of Naval Arch. and Shipbldg, Univ. of Newcastle upon Tyne, 1965. Dir, A. & P. Appledore (London) Ltd. Mem. Council, NE Coast Instn of Engrs and Shipbuilders. *Publications*: *contrib.* Procs Inst. Marine Engrs, Korean Soc. of Naval Architects, NE Coast Instn, RINA. *Address*: Dept of Naval Architecture and Shipbuilding, Univ. of Newcastle upon Tyne, Newcastle upon Tyne.

Telfer, Elizabeth Ann, MA, BPhil; Senior Lecturer, Department of Moral Philosophy, University of Glasgow, since 1971; *b* 1936. BA Oxon 1959 (1st cl. Lit. Hum.), MA Oxon 1962, BPhil Oxon 1963. Asst Lectr, Glasgow Univ., 1963; Lectr, Glasgow Univ., 1964–71. *Publications*: (with R. S. Downie) Respect for Persons, 1969; (with R. S. Downie and E. M. Loudfoot) Education and Personal Relationships, 1974; *contrib.* Philos. Qly, Philos.,

Proc. Aristot. Soc., Proc. Phil. Educn Soc. GB. *Address*: Dept of Moral Philosophy, Univ. of Glasgow, Glasgow G12 8QQ.

Temperley, Dr Howard Reed; Senior Lecturer in American History, University of East Anglia, since 1967; *b* 1932; *m* 1966; one *s* two *d*. BA Oxon 1956 (2nd cl. Hist.), MA Yale 1957, PhD Yale 1961. Asst Lectr, Univ. Coll. of Wales, Aberystwyth, 1960–61; Asst Lectr, Univ. of Manchester, 1961–63; Lectr, Univ. of Manchester, 1963–67; Amer. Council of Learned Societies Fellow, Brown Univ., 1965–66. Gen. Ed., Brit. Assoc. Studies, Books on America Series, 1963– . *Publications*: contrib. Anti-slavery Vanguard, ed M. Duberman, 1965; British Anti-slavery, 1833–70, 1972; contrib. Pressure from Without, ed P. Hollis, 1974; *contrib*. Amer. Qly, Jl Negro Hist. *Address*: School of English and American Studies, Univ. of East Anglia, Norwich NOR 88C.

Templeman, Geoffrey, MA, PhD, FSA; Vice-Chancellor, University of Kent at Canterbury, since 1963; *b* 1914; *m* 1939; two *s* one *d*. MA London, PhD Birmingham; FSA. Univ. of Birmingham: Teaching History from 1938, Registrar, 1955–62. Chairman: Northern Univs Jt Matric. Bd, 1961–64; Univs Central Council on Admissions, 1964– ; Schs Commn Bd of Educn, General Synod of C of E, 1971– ; Member: Review Body on Doctors' and Dentists' Remuneration, 1965–70. SE Metropolitan Reg. Hosp. Bd, 1972–74; SE Thames Reg. Hosp. Authority, 1974– . *Publications*: Dugdale Society Publications, vol. XI; *contrib*. Cambridge Hist. Jl, Trans Royal Hist. Soc., etc. *Address*: The Univ., Canterbury, Kent CT2 7NZ.

Templeton, Janet Macduff, MA; Lecturer in Scottish Language, University of Glasgow, since 1966; *b* 1929. MA St Andrews 1953. Res. Fellow, Edinburgh Univ., 1958–65; Hon. Lectr, Edinburgh Univ., 1965–66; Asst Ed., Dictionary of Older Scottish Tongue, 1958–66, Hon. Assoc. Ed., 1970– . *Publications*: *contrib*. Studies Scott. Lang. *Address*: Dept of English Language, Univ. of Glasgow, Glasgow G12 8QQ.

Terry, Prof. Arthur Hubert; Professor of Literature, Department of Literature, University of Essex, since 1973; *b* 1927; *m* 1955; two *s* one *d*. BA Cantab 1947, MA Cantab 1950; Member: Assoc. of British Hispanists; Anglo-Catalan Soc. Queen's Univ. of Belfast: Asst Lectr in Spanish, 1950–54; Lectr, 1954–60; Sen. Lectr, 1960–62; Prof. of Spanish, 1962–72. Mem. Editorial Bd, Bulletin of Hispanic Studies, 1968– . *Publications*: La Poesía de Joan Maragall, 1963; An Anthology of Spanish Poetry, 1500–1700: Part One (1500–1580), 1965; Part Two (1580–1700), 1968; Catalan Literature, 1972; Antonio Machado: Campos de Castilla, 1973; *contrib*. BHS, ER. *Address*: Dept of Literature, Univ. of Essex, Wivenhoe Park, Colchester CO4 3SQ.

Tester, Stanley Jim, BA; Senior Lecturer in Classics, University of Bristol, since 1962; *b* 1924; *m* 1950; three *d*. BA London 1950 (1st cl. Classics). Asst Lectr, Bristol, 1950–53,

Lectr, 1953–62. *Publications*: trans., Boethius: De Consolatione Philosophiae (Loeb Classical Library), 1972; A Short History of Western Astrology (forthcoming); *contrib*. Downs. Rev., Educnl Rev., Hibb. Jl. *Address*: Dept of Classics, Wills Memorial Building, Queens Road, Bristol BS8 1RJ.

Tew, Prof. John Hedley Brian, PhD; Midland Bank Professor of Money and Banking, University of Nottingham, since 1967; *b* 1917; *m* 1944; one *s* one *d*. BSc(Econ) London, PhD Cantab. Prof. of Econs, Adelaide Univ., 1947–49; Prof. of Econs, Nottingham Univ., 1950–67. Iron and Steel Control, 1940–42; Min. of Aircraft Prodn, 1942–45; Industrial and Commercial Finance Corp., 1946. Pt-time Mem., Iron and Steel Bd, 1964–67; Pt-time Mem., E Mids Electricity Bd, 1965– ; Pt-time Mem., Tubes Div., BSC, 1969–73; Mem., Cttee of Enquiry on Small Firms, Dept Trade and Industry, 1969–71. *Publications*: Wealth and Income, 1950; International Monetary Co-operation, 1952; ed (jtly), Studies in Company Finance, 1959; Monetary Theory, 1969. *Address*: Univ. of Nottingham, University Park, Nottingham NG7 2RD.

Thacker, Dr Christopher; Senior Lecturer in French, University of Reading, since 1973; *b* 1931; *m* 1954; four *s* one *d*. BA Oxon 1954 (2nd cl. Mod. Langs), MA Oxon 1958, DipEd Oxon 1959, PhD Indiana 1963, MA Trinity College Dublin 1967; FRSA. Jun. Lectr, TCD, 1963–66; Lecturer: TCD, 1966–67; Reading, 1967–73. Ed., Garden Hist. Soc., 1971– . *Publications*: ed, Voltaire: Candide, 1968; Voltaire, 1971; ed, Garden History, vol. I 1972, vol. II 1973; *contrib*. Garden Hist. Soc., Occ. Papers, Studies Volt. Eightnth Cent. *Address*: Dept of French Studies, The Univ., Reading RG6 2AH.

Thacker, Prof. Thomas William, MA; Director of School of Oriental Studies and Professor of Semitic Philology, University of Durham, since 1951; *b* 1911; *m* 1939; one *s*. BA Oxon 1933, MA Oxon. Asst Lectr, UC North Wales, Bangor, 1937; Reader, Durham Univ., 1938–45; Foreign Office, 1940–45; Prof. of Hebrew and Oriental Langs, Durham Univ., 1945–51. Mem., Egypt Exploration Soc.'s Expedn to Tell-el-Amarna, 1935. Foreign Mem., Royal Flemish Acad.; Examiner, Univs of Wales (Hebrew, Old Testament), Manchester, Liverpool and Leeds (Semitic Langs), Oxford (Egyptology, Hebrew). *Publications*: The Relationship of the Semitic and Egyptian Verbal Systems, 1954; *contrib*. various jls. *Address*: School of Oriental Studies, Elvet Hill, Durham.

Thakur, Prof. Shivesh Chandra; Professor of Philosophy, University of Surrey, since 1973; *b* 1936; *m* 1st, 1956 (widowed 1968), 2nd, 1969; two *s* one *d*. BA Patna 1954 (1st cl. Hons Philosophy), MA Patna 1956 (1st cl. Philosophy), PhD Durham 1966, Dip. in History and Philosophy of Science, Oxon, 1966; Member: Aristotelian Soc., Mind Assoc.; Royal Inst. of Philosophy; Amer. Acad. of Religion. Commonwealth Scholar, 1963–66; Lectr in Philosophy: Patna Univ., 1956–58; Ranchi Univ., 1959–63 and 1966–

67; Victoria Univ., Wellington, NZ, 1967–69; Sen. Lectr in Philosophy, Univ. of Auckland, NZ, 1969–72; Vis. Prof. and Larwill Lectr, Kenyon Coll., Ohio, 1972. *Publications*: Christian and Hindu Ethics, 1969; *contrib.* Aust. Jl Philos., Internat. Philos. Qly, Philos. Stud., Philos. Qly. *Address*: Dept of Philosophy, Univ of Surrey, Guildford, Surrey GU2 5XH.

Thanh, Dr Pham Chi; Lecturer in Political Economy, University College London, since 1968; Professor of Economics, Queen's University, Ontario, Canada, since 1971; *b* 1939; *m* 1970. Lic. en Droit Saigon 1958; BCom (Econs) New South Wales 1962, PhD New South Wales 1966; Member: Econometric Soc.; Bd, Economic Study Soc. Univ. of NSW, 1963–65; Univ. of Sydney, 1964–65; Univ. of Oslo, 1966; Univ. of Southampton, 1966–68; Univ. of Wisconsin, 1969; Univ. of Western Ontario, 1970–71. Dir, Economic Study Soc. Ltd, 1968–73. *Publications*: *contrib.* Econometrica, Economica, Internat. Econ. Rev., Econ. Record. *Address*: Dept of Political Economy, Univ. Coll. London, WC1E 6BT.

Thirlwall, Dr Anthony Philip; Reader in Economics, University of Kent, since 1971; *b* 1941; *m* 1966; one *s*. BA Leeds; MA Clark; PhD Leeds. Teaching Fellow, Clark Univ., 1963; Asst Lectr, Univ. of Leeds, 1964–66; Lectr, then Sen. Lectr, Univ. of Kent, 1966–71; Vis. Prof., W Virginia Univ., 1967; Vis. Res. Econ., Princeton Univ., 1971–72. Econ. Adv., Dept of Employment, 1968–70. *Publications*: Growth and Development: with Special Reference to Less Developed Countries, 1972; Inflation, Saving and Growth in Developing Economies, 1974; *contrib.* Brit. Jl Indust. Relat., BNQR, Bull. Oxf. Univ. Inst. Stats, Econ. Jl, Manch. Sch., Oxf. Econ. Papers, PDR, Scott. Econ Jl, Scott. Jl Pol Econ., YB. *Address*: Keynes College, Univ. of Kent, Canterbury, Kent CT2 7ND.

Thirsk, Dr Joan, MA, PhD, FBA, FRHistS; Reader in Economic History, University of Oxford, since 1965; *b* 1922; *m* 1945; one *s* one *d*. BA London 1947 (1st cl. History); MA Oxon 1965; PhD London 1950; FBA 1974, FRHistS 1955. Asst Lectr in Sociology, LSE, 1950–51; Sen. Res. Fellow in English Agrarian History, Leicester Univ., 1951–65. Mem., Editorial Bd, Past and Present, 1956– ; Mem., Council, Econ. Hist. Soc., 1955– ; Mem., Exec. Cttee, British Agricultural Hist. Soc., 1953– ; Vice-Chm., Exec. Cttee, Standing Conf. Local History, 1965– . Gen. Editor, History of Lincs, 1967– ; Editor, Agric. Hist. Rev., 1964–72; Dep. Gen. Editor, Agrarian History of England and Wales, 1966– . *Publications*: Fenland Farming in the Sixteenth Century, 1953; English Peasant Farming, 1957; Suffolk Farming in the Nineteenth Century (Suffolk Records Soc.), 1958; Tudor Enclosures, 1959; ed and part author, Agrarian History of England and Wales, IV, 1500–1640, 1967; (with J. P. Cooper) Seventeenth-Century Economic Documents, 1972; *contrib.* Agricultural Hist. Rev., Econ. Hist. Rev., History, Jl Modern History, Past and Present. *Address*: St Hilda's College, Oxford.

A W W—AA

Thoburn, Dr John Thomas; Lecturer in Economics, University of East Anglia, since 1967; *b* 1941; *m* 1965; two *s*. BA Leicester 1962 (Social Science), MA Leicester 1964 (Internat. Econs), PhD Alberta 1971 (Econs). Tutorial Asst, Leicester Univ., 1963; Grad. Teaching Asst, Univ. of Alberta, 1964–66; Res. Student, LSE, 1966–67. *Publications*: *contrib.* Canad. Jl Econ. Pol Sci., Oxford Econ. Papers, Oxford Bull. of Econs and Stats. *Address*: School of Social Studies, Univ. of East Anglia, Norwich NOR 88C.

Thody, Prof. Philip Malcolm Waller; Professor of French Literature, University of Leeds, since 1965; *b* 1928; *m* 1954; two *s* two *d*. MA London 1953. Temp. Asst Lectr, Univ. of Birmingham, 1954–55; Asst Lectr, then Lectr, Queen's Univ. of Belfast, 1956–65; Chm., Dept of French, Univ. of Leeds, 1968–72; Chm., Bd, Faculties of Arts, Econs, Social Studies and Law, 1972–74; Vis. Prof., Univ. of W Ontario, 1963–64; Berkeley Summer Sch., 1964; Harvard Summer Sch., 1968. *Publications*: Albert Camus: a study of his work, 1957; Jean-Paul Sartre: a literary and political study, 1960; Albert Camus, 1913–1960, 1961; Jean Genet: a study of his novels and plays, 1968; Jean Anouilh, 1968; Choderlos de Laclos, 1970; Jean-Paul Sartre: a Biographical Introduction, 1971; Aldous Huxley: a biographical introduction, 1973; *contrib.* Encount., Fr. Studies, Lond. Mag., Mod. Lang. Rev., Times Lit. Supp., Twent. Cent. *Address*: Dept of French, The Univ., Leeds LS2 9TJ.

Thomaneck, Dr Jürgen Karl Albert, MEd, Dr phil; Lecturer, German Department, King's College, University of Aberdeen, since 1969; *b* 1941; *m* 1964; one *d*. Staatsexamen, Kiel, Germany, 1966; Teacher's Certificate (Secondary), Aberdeen Coll. of Educn, 1968; MEd Aberdeen 1969, Dr phil Kiel 1969. Part-time Asst, Aberdeen Univ., 1968–69. *Publications*: (co-author) Deutsches Abiturienten Lexikon, Munich 1968, 3rd edn 1971; Ernest Hemingway: Adjektiv und Adverb als Stil- und Deutungsmittel, 1974; *contrib.* Eng. and Amer. Stud. Germ., Germ. Life and Lett., Lang. and Speech, New Germ. Stud., Stud. Short Fict. *Address*: Taylor Building, King's College, Aberdeen.

Thomas, Alan Keith; Senior Lecturer in Science Education, Education Centre, New University of Ulster, since 1968; *b* 1928; *m* 1957; one *s* four *d*. BSc Manchester 1949, Teacher's Dip., Manchester 1952; MIBiol 1953; Member: Assoc. for Sci. Educn; Brit. Ecol Soc.; Royal Microscopical Soc. Schoolmaster: Victoria Coll., Alexandria, 1955–56; Dauntsey's Sch., Wilts 1957–68; seconded to Nuffield Foundn Sci. Teaching Project (O-level Biol. Project), 1963–65. Member: Schs Council Sci. Cttee, 1965–67; NI GCE Board (formerly Cttee), 1968–73. *Publications*: (with others) Nuffield O-level Biology Project's *Text* and *Teacher's Guide*, 1966; *contrib.* Nature, Jl Biol Educn, Sch. Sci. Rev. *Address*: Education Centre, New Univ. of Ulster, Coleraine, BT52 1SA.

Thomas, Prof. Antony Charles, MA, FSA; Professor of Cornish Studies, and Director,

691

Institute of Cornish Studies, University of Exeter, since 1972; *b* 1928; *m* 1959; two *s* two *d*. BA Oxon 1951 (Hons Jurispr.), DipPrehistEuropArchaeol London 1953, MA Oxon 1955; FSA, FSAScot; Hon. Mem., RIA, 1973. Lectr in Archaeology, Univ. of Edinburgh, 1958–67; Prof. of Archaeology, Univ. of Leicester, 1967–72; Leverhulme Fellow, 1966–68; Hunter Marshall Lectr, Univ. of Glasgow, 1968; O'Donnell Lectr, Univ. of Edinburgh, 1970. Pres., Council Brit. Archaeol., 1970–73; Pres., Royal Instn of Cornwall, 1970–72; BBC Archaeol Adv., 1962–63; Hon. Adviser Archaeol., Nat. Trust, 1966– ; Mem., Councils, var. nat. socs; Ed., Cornish Archaeol., 1961– ; Cornish Studies, 1973. *Publications*: The Christian Antiquities of Camborne, 1967; The Early Christian Archaeology of North Britain, 1971; Britain and Ireland, AD 400 to 800, 1971; (jtly) St Ninian's Isle and its Treasure, 1973; contrib. chapters, in var. bks, 1963– ; *contrib.* Antiqu., Mediev. Archaeol. *Address*: Institute of Cornish Studies, Trevenson House, Pool, Redruth, Cornwall TR15 3RE.

Thomas, Beryl Dorothy; Lecturer in Education, University College of Wales, Swansea, since 1966; *b* 1937; *m* 1963; one *d*. BA Wales 1958 (1st cl. Welsh), DipEd Wales 1959 (Cert. Biblical Studies), MA Wales 1961 (Welsh). Teacher and Coll. of Educn Lectr, to 1966. *Address*: Education Dept, Univ. College, Hendrefoilan, Swansea SA2 7NB.

Thomas, Prof. Brinley, CBE, PhD, FBA; Director, Manpower Research Unit, University College, Cardiff, since 1973; *b* 1906; *m* 1943; one *d*. BA Wales 1926 (1st cl. Economics); PhD London 1931; FRStatS. Lectr, LSE, 1933–39; Prof. of Econs, Univ. Coll., Cardiff, 1946–73. Vis. Prof., Duke Univ., 1957; Vis. Prof., Univ. of Illinois, 1960; Vis. Prof., ANU, 1965; Vis. Prof., Johns Hopkins Univ., 1968; Vis. Prof., Brown Univ., 1971; Vis. Prof., Stanford Univ., 1974. Dir Northern Section, Political Intelligence Dept, FO, 1942–45; Mem., Nat Assistance Bd, 1948–53; Mem., Anderson Cttee on Grants to Students, 1958–60; Chm., Assoc. Univ. Teachers of Economics, 1965–68; Chm., Welsh Council, 1968–71; Mem., Min. of Employment Cost of Living Adv. Cttee, Mem., Exec. Cttee of British Council; Mem., Gov. Body Centre for Environmental Studies. *Publications*: Monetary Policy and Crises: a study of Swedish experience, 1937; Migration and Economic Growth, 1954, 2nd edn 1972; ed, The Economics of International Migration, 1958; International Migration and Economic Development: a trend report and bibliography, 1961; ed, The Welsh Economy: studies in expansion, 1962. Migration and Urban Development, 1972; *contrib.* Jl Royal Statist. Soc., Econ. Jl, Economica. *Address*: Manpower Research Unit, Univ. College, Cardiff CF1 1XL.

Thomas, Dr Colin; Lecturer in Geography, School of Biological and Environmental Studies, New University of Ulster, Coleraine, since 1970; *b* 1939; *m* 1969; two *s*. BA Wales 1961 (Geog. and Anthrop.), PhD Wales 1965. Res. Asst, Centre for Russian and E Europ. Studies, Univ. of Birmingham, 1964–

692

65; Asst Lectr, Univ. of Leicester, 1965–67; Lectr, Univ. Coll. of Wales, Aberystwyth, 1967–70. *Publications*: contrib. Agric. Hist. Rev., Geog., Rev. Géog. Est, Trans Inst. Brit. Geogrs. *Address*: New Univ. of Ulster, Coleraine, Co. Londonderry BT52 1SA.

Thomas, Dafydd Rhys; *see* Ap-Thomas.

Thomas, Rev. Daniel Rowland; Lecturer, Department of Education, University College of Wales, Aberystwyth, since 1963; *b* 1912; *m* 1940; two *s* one *d*. BA Wales 1938 (Hons Semitics and Hons Philosophy), BA Cantab 1938 (Theology Tripos Part II), MA Cantab 1943. Lecturer: Biblical Studies; Philosophy of Educn. *Publications*: Proffwydir Wythfed Ganrif, 1948; Actau'r Apostolion, 1948; Beth yw Dyn?, 1949, Athronwyr ac Addysg, 1969. *Address*: Dept of Education, Univ. of Wales, Aberystwyth SY23 2AX.

Thomas, Prof. David; Professor of Geography, St David's University College, Lampeter, University of Wales, since 1970; *b* 1931; *m* 1955; one *s* one *d*. BA Wales 1954, MA Wales 1957, PhD London 1967. Asst Lectr, 1957; Lectr, 1960; Reader, 1968. *Publications*: Agriculture in Wales during the Napoleonic Wars, 1963; London's Green Belt, 1970; *contrib.* numerous jls. *Address*: Saint David's Univ. College, Lampeter, Dyfed SA48 7ED.

Thomas, David Adrian L.; *see* Lloyd Thomas.

Thomas, Rev. (David Albert) Terence; Staff Tutor in Religion, Faculty of Arts, Open University in Wales, since 1971; *b* 1931; *m* 1956; three *s*. BA St David's University Coll., Lampeter 1956 (Hons Welsh), BA Oxon 1958 (Hons Theology), MA Oxon 1962, MTh Serampore, India, 1973; Mem.: Nat. Inst. of Adult Educn; Soc. for Study of Theology. Lectr in New Testament Studies, United Theological Coll., Poona, India (affil. Serampore Univ.), 1962–69; Lectr, New Testament and Christian Doctrine, United Theological Coll., Bangalore (affil. Serampore Univ.), 1969–71. *Publications*: contrib. Ind. Jl Theol., Rel. and Soc. *Address*: Open Univ. in Wales, Pearl Assurance House, Greyfriars Road, Cardiff.

Thomas, David Arthur; Fellow of Trinity Hall, Cambridge, and Assistant Director of Research in Criminology, University of Cambridge, since 1971; *b* 1938; *m* 1961; two *d*. BA Cantab 1960; LLB Cantab 1961; MA Cantab 1970. Asst Lectr in Law, LSE, 1961–64, Lectr in Law, 1964–70; Vis. Prof., Univ. of Alabama Sch. of Law, 1968. *Publications*: Principles of Sentencing, 1970; *contrib.* Crim. Law Rev., Mod. Law Rev. *Address*: Trinity Hall, Cambridge.

Thomas, Dr David Oswald; Senior Lecturer, Philosophy Department, University College, Aberystwyth, University of Wales, since 1965; *b* 1924; *m* 1965; one *d*. BA Wales 1950, MA Wales 1952, PhD London 1956; Mem., Royal Inst. Philos., Mem., Mind Assoc., Mem., Aristot. Soc., Mem., Pol. Studies Assoc. Lectr, Univ. Coll., Aberystwyth, 1960–65. *Publications: contrib.* Efryd. Athron., Philos., Proc. Aristot. Soc. *Address:* Dept of Philosophy, Univ. College, Aberystwyth SY23 2AX.

Thomas, David Roy; Senior Lecturer, Department of Economics, University College, Cardiff, since 1973; *b* 1937; *m* 1968. BA Oxford 1959 (1st cl. PPE), BPhil(Econ) Oxford 1961. Asst Lectr, Univ. of Reading, 1962–65; Lectr, Univ. Coll., Cardiff, 1965–73. *Publications:* Industry in Rural Wales, 1966; *contrib.* Bull. Oxf. Univ. Inst. Stats, Scott. Jl Pol., Jl Bus. Finance, Jl Inst. Transport. Econ. *Address:* Dept of Economics, Univ. College, Cardiff CF1 1XL.

Thomas, Dr Gwyn, MA, DPhil; Senior Lecturer, Welsh Department, University College of North Wales, Bangor, since 1973; *b* 1936; *m* 1964; two *s*. BA Wales 1957 (1st cl. Welsh), MA Wales 1961, DPhil Oxon 1966. Fellow, Univ. of Wales, 1959–63; Lectr, 1963–73. Mem., Yr Acad. Gymreig, 1965– ; Sec., Yr Acad. Gymreig, 1967–72; Mem., Lit. Panel, N Wales Assoc. Arts, 1968– ; Mem., Welsh Arts Council's Lit. Cttee, 1971– . *Publications:* Chwerwder yn y Ffynhonnau, 1963; Y Weledigaeth Haearn, 1965; Ysgyrion Gwaed, 1967; The Caerwys Eisteddfodau, 1968; Diweddgan (trans. and ed, S. Beckett: Fin de Partie), 1969; ed, Yr Aelwyd Hon, 1970; Y Bardd Cwsg, 1971; Amser Dyn, 1972; Enw'r Gair, 1972; (ed jtly) Presenting Saunders Lewis, 1973; *contrib.* Bull. Bd Celt. Studies, Llên Cymru, Poetry Wales, Ysgrif. Beirn. *Address:* Dept of Welsh, Univ. College of North Wales, Bangor LL57 2DG.

Thomas, Dr Howard; Director of the Decision Analysis Unit, since 1971, Senior Lecturer in Quantitative Methods, since 1972, and Director of Doctoral Programme, since 1972, London Graduate School of Business Studies; *b* 1943; *m* 1968; two *s*. BSc London 1964, MSc London 1965, MBA Chicago 1966, PhD Edinburgh 1970. Lectr, Dept of Business Studies, Univ. of Edinburgh, 1966–69; Vis. Asst Prof., Graduate Sch. of Business Administration, Harvard Univ., 1969–70; Lectr, London Graduate Sch. of Business Studies, 1969–72; Vis. Prof. of Management, European Inst. for Advanced Studies in Management, Brussels, 1972– . *Publications:* (with Dr H. Behrend, J. Davies and H. Lynch) Incomes Policy and the Individual, 1967; Decision Theory and the Manager, 1972; *contrib.* Jl Roy. Stat. Soc., Jl Man. Stud., Op. Res. Qly, Jl Bus. Fin., Man. Today, Harvard Bus. Rev. *Address:* London Graduate School of Business Studies, Sussex Place, NW1 4SA.

Thomas, Prof. Hugh Swynnerton; Professor of History, University of Reading, since 1966; *b* 1931; *m* 1962; two *s* one *d*. BA Cantab 1953 (1st cl. Hist. Tripos pt I, 2nd cl. pt II), MA Cantab 1957. Foreign Off., 1954–57. *Publications:* The World's Game, 1957; The Oxygen Age, 1958; ed, The Establishment, 1959; The Spanish Civil War, 1961; The Story of Sandhurst, 1961; The Suez Affair, 1967; ed, Crisis in the Civil Service, 1969; Cuba or the Pursuit of Freedom, 1971; ed,

Selected Writings and Speeches of José Antonio Primo de Rivera, 1972; Goya's The Third of May 1808, 1973; Europe, the Radical Challenge, 1973; John Strachey, 1973. *Address:* Dept of History, Univ. of Reading, Whiteknights, Reading RG6 2AH.

Thomas, Dr J. David; Senior Lecturer, Department of Palaeography and Diplomatic, University of Durham, since 1973; *b* 1931; *m* 1956; two *s*. BA Oxon 1955, MA Oxon 1958, PhD Wales 1965; Mem., Assoc. Internat. Papyrol. Lectr, Univ. Coll. of Wales, Aberystwyth, 1955–66; Lectr, Univ. of Durham, 1966–73; Mem., Inst. Adv. Study, Princeton, 1972. *Publications:* The Merton Papyri III (BICS, Suppl. xvii), 1967; chap. XI, Egypt, in, A. H. M. Jones: Cities of the Eastern Roman Provinces, 2nd rev. edn 1971; (jtly) The Oxyrhynchus Papyri XXXVIII, 1971; XLIII, 1974; *contrib.* Chron. d'Egypte, Jl Egypt. Archael., Zeits. Papyrol. Epigraph., Bull. Inst. Class. Stud. *Address:* Dept of Palaeography, Univ. of Durham, South Road, Durham.

Thomas, Dr James Edward; Senior Lecturer in Social Studies, Department of Adult Education, University of Hull, since 1974; *b* 1933; *m* 1957; two *s*. BA Oxon 1957, MA Oxon 1963, BSc London 1966, DPhil York 1970. Lectr in Social Studies, Dept of Adult Educn, Univ. of Hull, 1967–74. *Publications:* The English Prison Officer since 1850, 1972; *contrib.* Adult Educn (UK), Australian Jl Adult Educn, Australian and NZ Jl Criminol., Continuing Educn in NZ, Geographical Jl, Studies in Adult Educn. *Address:* Dept of Adult Educn, Univ. of Hull, HU6 7RX.

Thomas, Rev. John H.; *see* Heywood Thomas.

Thomas, John Hugh; Senior Tutor in Music, Department of Extra-Mural Studies, University College of Wales, Swansea, since 1973; *b* 1935; *m* 1957; three *d*. University Coll. of Wales, Cardiff: BA 1956 (Hons), DipEd 1957, MA Wales 1972. Tutor in Music, Univ. Coll. of Wales, Swansea, 1960–73. Founder-conductor of Swansea Bach Soc. and Dir of Swansea Bach Week. *Publications: contrib.* Mus. Rev. *Address:* Dept of Extra-Mural Studies, Berwick House, 6 Uplands Terrace, Swansea.

Thomas, Rev. Canon John Roland Lloyd; Principal of St David's University College, Lampeter, since 1953; *b* 1908; *m* 1949; three *d*. BA Lampeter 1930 (1st cl. Hons Hist.), BA Oxon 1932 (2nd cl. Th. Hons), MA Oxon 1936; Deacon 1932, Priest 1933; Curate of St John Baptist, Cardiff, 1932–40, CF(EC) 1940–44, Rector of Canton, Cardiff 1944–49, Vicar of St Mark's, Newport 1949–52, Dean of Monmouth and Vicar of St Woolos Parish, Newport 1952–53, Canon of St David's Cathedral 1956, Chancellor of St David's Cathedral 1963, CF(TA) 1949–52, SCF(TA) 1950–52, Hon. CF 1952. Supernumerary Fellow, Jesus College, Oxford, 1953 (in turn every fourth year); Mem., Commonwealth Univs Council, 1955; Mem., Court, UC, Cardiff, 1957; Mem., UCCA Council,

693

1966; Mem., UCCA Exec., 1971; Mem., Univ. of Wales Court and Council, 1971; Mem., Court, Univ. Coll., Swansea; Mem., Council, Trinity Coll., Carmarthen. Mem., Governing and Rep. Bodies, Church in Wales, 1945; Governor, Christ Coll., Brecon, 1953; Governor, National Library of Wales, 1965; Mem., Council, National Library of Wales, 1971. *Address*: St David's Univ. College, Lampeter, Dyfed SA48 7ED.

Thomas, Prof. Joseph Anthony Charles, MA, LLB; Professor of Roman Law in the University of London, Faculty of Laws, University College, since 1965; *b* 1923; *m* 1949 (diss. 1970); three *s* one *d*. BA Cambridge 1948 (1st cl. Law), MA Cambridge 1949, LLB Cambridge 1949 (1st cl.); of Gray's Inn, Barrister-at-Law 1950. Lectr, Nottingham Univ., 1949–54; Sen. Lectr, Glasgow Univ., 1954–57; Douglas Prof. of Civil Law, Glasgow Univ., 1957–65. Mem., UK Nat. Cttee Comp. Law, 1952– ; Treas., UK Nat. Cttee Comp. Law, 1955–65; Mem., Comitato Internaz. Scientifico, IURA, 1969– ; Mem., Council, Soc. Rom. Studies, 1968–71. *Publications*: Private International Law, 1955; (with J. C. Smith) Casebook on Contract, 1957, 5th edn 1973; *contrib.* Ann. Fac. Giurisprud. Macerata, Anu. Hist. Derecho Españ., IURA, Jurid. Rev., Law Qly Rev., Rev. Internat. Droits Antiqu., Temis, Tijds. Rechtsgesch., Zeits. Sav.-Stift. *Address*: Faculty of Laws, Univ. College London, 4–8 Endsleigh Gardens, WC1H 0EG.

Thomas, Keith Vivian; Fellow and Tutor in Modern History, St John's College, Oxford University, since 1957; *b* 1933; *m* 1961; one *s* one *d*. BA Oxon 1955 (1st cl. Mod. Hist.), MA Oxon 1959; FRHistS. Fellow, All Souls Coll., Oxford, 1955–57; Vis. Prof., Louisiana State Univ., 1970. Mem., Edit. Bd, Past and Pres., 1968– ; Jt Lit. Dir, Royal Hist. Soc., 1970– . *Publications*: Religion and the Decline of Magic, 1971 (Wolfson Literary Award for History, 1972); *contrib.* Ideas in Cultural Perspective, ed A. Noland and P. P. Wiener, 1962; *contrib.* Crisis in Europe, ed T. Aston, 1965; *contrib.* Hobbes Studies, ed K. C. Brown, 1965; *contrib.* Writing in England Today, ed K. Miller, 1968; *contrib.* Witchcraft Confessions and Accusations, ed M. Douglas, 1970; *contrib.* The Interregnum, ed G. E. Aylmer, 1972; *contrib.* Jl Hist. Ideas, Past and Pres. *Address*: St John's College, Oxford OX1 3JP.

Thomas, Prof. Lionel Hugh Christopher, MA, PhD; Professor of German, University of Hull, since 1970; *b* 1922; *m* 1947; two *s*. Heath Harrison Travelling Schol., 1948, BA Oxon 1948 (1st cl. Mod. Langs, German and Russian), MA Oxon 1949, PhD Leeds 1952, MA Dublin 1960 (ad eundem); Cross of Merit (1st cl.), German Federal Republic 1971 (for services to study of German Lit.). Asst Lectr in German, Leeds Univ., 1948–50; Lectr, Leeds Univ., 1950–58; Reader, and Hd of German Dept, TCD, 1958–65; Prof. of German, TCD, 1965–70; Prof. Fellow, TCD, 1967. Ext. Examiner, Nat. Univ. Irel., 1967; Univ. of Wales, 1967–70; Univ. of Wales

(Higher Degrees), 1970; Univ. of Exeter (Higher Degrees), 1971; New Univ. of Ulster, 1972; Univs of Keele and Southampton, 1973. *Publications*: ed, Grillparzer: König Ottokars Glück und Ende, 1953, 3rd edn 1963; ed, Halm: Die Marzipan-Lise, 1957; trans., Droste-Hülshoff: The Jew's Beech, 1957; ed, Mörike: Selected Poems, 1960, 2nd edn 1964; trans., Gaiser: Aniela, and Lampe: Spanish Suite, in, Modern German Stories, ed H. M. Waidson, 1961; Willibald Alexis (biography), 1964; ed, Keller: Two Stories, 1966; *contrib.* Encyclopedia Britannica; The Comic Spirit in Nineteenth Century German Literature (Inaugural Lecture, Univ. of Hull), 1972; *contrib.* Bär Berl., Forum Mod. Lang. Studies, Germ. Life Lett., Hermath., Mod. Lang. Rev., Proc. Leeds Philos. Soc., Zeits. Deut. Philol., Fontane–Blätter. *Address*: Dept of German, Univ. of Hull, Hull HU6 7RX.

Thomas, Dr Michael Frederic; Lecturer in Geography, University of St Andrews, since 1964; *b* 1933; *m* 1956; one *s* one *d*. BA Reading 1955 (1st cl. Geog.), MA Reading 1957, PhD London 1967. Mem., Inst. Brit. Geogrs, Mem., Brit. Geomorphol. Res. Gp, Mem., Afr. Studies Assoc., UK. Asst Lectr in Geography, Magee Univ. Coll., Londonderry, 1957–60; Lectr in Geography, Univ. of Ibadan, Nigeria, 1960–64; Vis. Lectr, Univ. of Canterbury, NZ, 1969–70. Mem., Council, Afr. Studies Assoc., UK, 1972– ; Mem., Cttee, Brit. Geomorphol. Res. Gp, 1970–73. *Publications*: co-ed, Environment and Land Use in Africa, 1969; Tropical Geomorphology, 1974; *contrib.* Trans Inst. Brit. Geogrs, Zeits. Geomorphol. *Address*: Dept of Geography, Univ. of St Andrews, St Andrews, Fife KY16 9AL.

Thomas, Michael James; Head of Department and Senior Lecturer, Department of Marketing, University of Lancaster, since 1971; *b* 1933; *m* 1958; one *s* one *d*. BSc (Econ) 1956 (Hons; University Coll. London and LSE), MBA (Ind.) 1957; FInstM 1973; Associate Member: Market Res. Soc.; Amer. Marketing Assoc. E-SU Fellow, Indiana Univ., 1956–57; Sch. of Management, Syracuse University: Res. Associate, 1960–62; Instructor, 1962–67; Asst Prof., 1967–71; Ford Foundn Res. Fellow, Univ. of Chicago, 1964; Vis. Sen. Lectr, Univ. of Lancaster, 1969–70. Treas., Central NY Chapter, Amer. Marketing Assoc., 1963–64; Vice-Pres. and Conservation Chm., Onondaga Audubon Soc., 1968–69 and 1970–71; Member: Nat. Audubon Soc., 1960– ; British Trust for Ornithology, 1968– ; Lancashire Naturalists Trust,1969– ; British Ornithologists' Union, 1974– ; Council Mem., Inst. of Marketing, 1974– (Mem. Pubns Bd, 1972–). *Publications*: International Marketing Management, 1969; International Marketing Management, 1970; Modern Marketing Management (with Prof. R. J. Lawrence), 1971; The Theory of Trade and Development Revisited, in, New Essays in Marketing Theory, ed G. F. Fisk, 1971; *contrib.* Amer. Bus. Law Jl, Amer. Econ., Cong. Rec., Chem. and Ind., Internat. Develt Rev., Jl Bus. *Address*: Dept of Marketing, Univ. of Lancaster, Bailrigg, Lancaster LA1 4YW.

Thomas, Dr Michael Pugh; Senior Lecturer, Department of Biology, University of Salford (also teaches Environment); *b* 1932; *m* 1960. BSc 1955 (Hons Zool.), PhD 1958; MIBiol 1956. Mem., Brit. Ecol. Soc., Mem., Freshwater Biol. Assoc., Mem., Internat. Limnological Assoc. Mem., Council, Inst. Biol., 1967–72. *Publications: contrib.* Archiv. Hydrobiol., Entomol., Proc. Internat. Limnol Assoc. *Address:* Dept of Biology, The Univ., Salford M5 4WT.

Thomas, Neil Martin; Lecturer, Institute of Local Government Studies, University of Birmingham, since 1971; *b* 1942; *m* 1966; one *s*. BSc(Econ) Wales 1965. Res. Asst, Dept of Social Admin, Univ. of Birmingham, 1965–66; Asst Lectr, Dept of Social Admin, Univ. of Birmingham, 1966–68; Lectr, Dept of Social Admin, Univ. of Birmingham, 1968–70. *Publications:* Business Studies: A Guide to First Degree Courses in UK Universities and Colleges, 1967, 2nd edn 1969; The Seebohm Committee, in, Government by Commission, ed R. A. Chapman, 1972; *contrib.* Local Govt Chron., Munic. Public Serv. Jl. *Address:* Institute of Local Government Studies, Univ. of Birmingham, PO Box 363, Birmingham B15 2TT.

Thomas, Noel L'Estrange, PhD; Senior Lecturer in German, Department of Modern Languages, University of Salford, since 1973; *b* 1929; *m* 1954; two *d*. BA Manchester 1950 (German), CertEd London 1951, MA Liverpool 1958, PhD Salford 1973. Lectr, Univ. of Salford, 1964–73. *Publications:* (with G. Weischedel) Modern Prose Passages for Translation into German, 1968; (with G. Weischedel) Modern German Prose Passages, 1972. *Address:* Dept of Modern Languages, Univ. of Salford, Salford M5 4WT.

Thomas, Dr Peter David Garner; Reader in History, University College of Wales, Aberystwyth, since 1971; *b* 1930; *m* 1963; two *s* one *d*. BA Wales 1951 (1st cl. Hist.), MA Wales 1953, PhD London 1958; FRHistS. Asst, Glasgow Univ., 1956–59; Lectr, Glasgow Univ., 1959–65; Lectr, Univ. Coll. of Wales, 1965–68; Sen. Lectr, Univ. Coll. of Wales, 1968–71. *Publications:* The House of Commons in the Eighteenth Century, 1971; *contrib.* Bull. Inst. Hist. Res., EHR, Welsh Hist. Rev. *Address:* Dept of History, Univ. Coll. of Wales, Aberystwyth SY 23 2AX.

Thomas, Philip Aneurin; Lecturer, Department of Law, University College, Cardiff, since 1970; *b* 1940; *m* 1966; one *s* one *d*. LLB Wales 1962, LLM 1965. Lectr in Law, Univ. Coll., Dar es Salaam, Tanzania, 1966–68; Res. Fellow, School of Law, Univ. of Zambia, 1968–69; W. Cook Res. Fellow, The Law School, Univ. of Michigan, 1969–70. *Publications:* ed, Private Enterprise in East Africa, 1969; (jtly) Cases and Materials on Business Associations in Eastern Africa, 1974. *Address:* Univ. College, Cardiff, PO Box 78, Cardiff CF1 1XL.

Thomas, Prof. Raymond Elliott, MCom; Professor of Business Administration, and Head of School of Management, Bath University, since 1966; *b* 1923; *m* 1971. BCom London 1943 (2nd cl. Trades and Transp.), MCom Birmingham 1949; MBIM. Lectr, Scott. Coll. of Commerce (now Univ. of Strathclyde), 1948–52; Sen. Lectr, Univ. of Strathclyde, 1952–62; Hd of Dept, Univ. of Strathclyde, 1956–62; Sen. Lectr, Bristol Coll. of Science and Technol. (now Univ. of Bath), 1962–66. *Publications:* (with Jenkinson and Hunnaford) Commercial Apprenticeship, 1962; Responsibilities of Management Decisions, 1968; (with E. Cleary) Economic Consequences of the Severn Bridge, 1973. *Address:* Univ. of Bath, Claverton Down, Bath BA2 7AY.

Thomas, Prof. Richard George; Professor of English, University College, Cardiff, since 1968; *b* 1914; *m* 1943; two *s*. BA Wales 1936, MA Wales 1939, PhD Wales 1943. Lectr, Cardiff Univ. Coll., 1945–50; Sen. Lectr, Cardiff Univ. Coll., 1950–68. Army in Iceland, India, Burma, Ceylon, SE Asia, 1940–46; Mem., Council, Viking Soc., 1952–64, 1966–68; Trustee, Viking Soc., 1967– ; Mem., Bd of Eds, Yrs Wk Eng. Studies, 1955–59; Mem., Philol. Soc., 1962– ; Mod. Hum. Res. Assoc., 1954– . *Publications:* trans., Hrafnkels saga Freysgoða: A Study by S. Nordal, 1958; Myles Davies: Athenae Britannicae (ARS), 1962; R. S. Thomas (Writers and their Works), 1964; Charles Dickens: Great Expectations (Studies in Lit.), 1964; Ten Miracle Plays (York Medieval Texts), 1966; Letters from Edward Thomas to Gordon Bottomley, 1968; (with J. H. McGrew) Sturlunga Saga, 1970– ; Edward Thomas (Writers of Wales), 1972; *contrib.* Engl., Germ. Rev., Mod. Lang. Qly, Mod. Lang. Rev., Nuove Dimens, Saga Bk, Trans Hon. Soc. Cymmrod., Yrs Wk Engl. Studies. *Address:* English Dept, Univ. College, Cathays Park, Cardiff CF1 1XL.

Thomas, Prof. Richard Hinton, MA, PhD; Professor of German Studies, and Chairman of Department of German Studies, University of Warwick, since 1969; *b* 1912; *m* 1940; two *d*. BA Cantab 1934 (2nd cl. Mod. Langs Tripos), MA Cantab 1938, PhD Birmingham 1952. Lectr, Birmingham Univ., 1946–56; Sen. Lectr, Birmingham Univ., 1956–64; Prof., Birmingham Univ., 1964–69. War service, 1940–45 (Maj., Intell. Corps and Control Commn for Germany). *Publications:* (with R. H. Samuel) Expressionism in German Life, Literature and the Theatre 1910–1924, 1939, American edn 1971; (with R. H. Samuel) Education and Society in Modern Germany, 1949, American edn 1971; Liberalism, Nationalism and the German Intellectuals, 1952; Thomas Mann: The Mediation of Art, 1958; Poetry and Song in the German Baroque, 1963; ed, Seventeen Modern German Stories, 1965; The Commitment of German Studies (Inaugural Lecture), 1965; (with W. van der Will) The German Novel and the Affluent Society, 1968, German trans. 1969; jt-Ed., Studies in German Language, Literature and Society, 1969; *contrib.* Germ. Life Lett., Mod. Lang. Rev., Publ. Eng. Goethe Soc., Times Lit. Supp. *Address:* Dept of German Studies, Univ. of Warwick, Coventry CV4 7AL.

Thomas, Roy, MA; Lecturer in Education, University College of Swansea, since 1966; *b* 1919; *m* 1942; two *d*. BA Wales 1940 (1st cl. English), DipEd Wales 1946 (1st cl.), MA Wales 1949. *Publications*: How to Read a Poem, 1962. *Address*: Dept of Education, Univ. College of Swansea, Singleton Park, Swansea SA2 8PP.

Thomas, Dr Stuart Denis; Senior Lecturer in Business Policy, London Graduate School of Business Studies, since 1969; *b* 1938; *m* 1965; one *s*. BSc Bristol 1963 (Hons), MBA Harvard Business Sch. 1965 (with Distinction), DBA Harvard Business Sch. 1969. Instructor in Business Admin., Harvard Business Sch., Harvard Univ., 1966–69; Lectr in Business Policy, London Business Sch., London Univ., 1969–72; Dir, London–Sloan Fellowship Programme, London Business Sch., 1971– . *Publications*: *contrib*. Jl Bus. Pol. *Address*: London Graduate School of Business Studies, Sussex Place, Regent's Park, NW1 4SA.

Thomas, Rev. Terence; *see* Thomas, Rev. D. A. T.

Thomas, Trevor Cawdor, MA, LLB; Vice-Chancellor, University of Liverpool, since 1970; *b* 1914; *m* 1943. LLB Wales 1936, BA, LLB Cantab 1938, MA Cantab 1945; Hon. LLD Liverpool 1972; Barrister-at-Law of Gray's Inn (1st cl. with Cert. of Hon., 1941). Lectr, Univ. of Leeds, 1939–41; Fellow, Trinity Hall, Cambridge, 1945–60; Lectr in Law, Univ. of Cambridge, 1945–60; Fellow, and Sen. Bursar, St John's Coll., Cambridge, 1960–70; Hon. Fellow, Trinity Hall and Darwin Coll., Cambridge, 1973. Mem., Stat. Commn Royal Univ. of Malta, 1960–70; JP, 1966–70. *Publications*: co-Ed., Jenks: Digest of English Civil Law, 4th edn 1947; *contrib*. Camb. Law Jl. *Address*: Senate House, Univ. of Liverpool, Liverpool L69 3BX.

Thomas, Prof. Watkin James; Professor of Agricultural Economics, University of Manchester, since 1953; *b* 1919; *m* 1943; 1973; two *s*. BSc Wales 1939, MSc 1946, MAEcon Manchester 1967; Member: Agric. Econ. Soc. (Pres., 1973–74); Manchester Stat. Soc.; Internat. Soc. of Agric. Economics. Lectr, Univ. Coll. Aberystwyth, 1940–46; Univ. of Leeds, 1949–53. Min. of Agriculture, 1946–49; Member: Forestry Commn Res. Cttee, 1960– ; National Food Survey Cttee, 1960– ; Sometime Mem., Agric. Econ. Exec. Cttee. *Publications*: The Demand for Food, 1972; *contrib*. Agric. Economics, Agric. Rev., Brit. Assoc., International Jl Agric. Econ., etc. *Address*: Univ. of Manchester, Oxford Road, Manchester M13 9PL.

Thomas, William Eden Sherwood, MA, FRHistS; Student and Tutor in Modern History, Christ Church, Oxford, and University Lecturer, Oxford University, since 1968; *b* 1936; *m* 1959; two *s* one *d*. BA Oxon 1959 (1st cl. Hist.), MA Oxon 1967. Jun. Res. Fellow, Merton Coll., Oxford, 1960–63; Lectr, Univ. of York, 1963–67; Lectr in Modern Hist., Christ Church, 1967–68. *Publications*: *contrib*. EHR, Guildh. Misc.,

Hist. Jl, Hist. *Address*: Christ Church, Oxford OX1 1DP.

Thomas, Wyndham Harwood, MA, ARCO; Lecturer, Department of Music, University of Bristol, since 1966; *b* 1938; *m* 1962; two *s*. BA Durham 1960 (2nd cl. Div. 1. Music), DipEd Durham 1961 (1st cl.), MA Durham 1968; ARCO 1968. *Publications*: *contrib*. ISCM Jl, Music. Times. *Address*: Dept of Music, Royal Fort House, Bristol BS8 1UJ.

Thomason, Prof. George Frederick, MA, PhD, MBIM, MIPM; Montague Burton Professor of Industrial Relations, Department of Industrial Relations and Management Studies, University College, Cardiff, since 1969; *b* 1927; *m* 1953; one *s* one *d*. BA Sheffield 1952 (Hons Econ.), MA Toronto 1953 (Pol. Econ.), PhD Wales 1963 (Sociol.). Member: Brit. Inst. Mngmt, 1969, Inst. Person. Mngmt, 1954, RSA. Res. Asst, Univ. Coll., Cardiff, 1953–54, Asst Lectr, 1954–56, Res. Assoc., 1956–59, Lectr, 1959–60, 1962–63, Sen. Lectr, 1963–69, Reader, 1969. Asst to Mng Dir, Flexfasteners Ltd, 1960–62; Member: SSRC Management Cttee; Exec. Cttee, Council Social Serv. Wales, 1963– ; Four Wages Councils, 1966– . *Publications*: Welsh Society in Transition, 1963; Personnel Manager's Guide to Job Evaluation, 1968; The Professional Approach to Community Work, 1969; The Management of Research and Development, 1970; Experiments in Participation, 1971; The Management of Industrial Relations, 1971; Improving the Quality of Organisation, 1973; *contrib*. Brit. Jl of Management Studies, European Business. *Address*: Dept of Industrial Relations, Univ. College, Newport Road, Cardiff CF2 1TA.

Thompson, Prof. Alan Eric, MA, PhD; Professor of the Economics of Government, Heriot-Watt University, since 1972; *b* 1924; *m* 1960; three *s* one *d*. MA Edinburgh 1951 (1st cl. Economic Science), PhD Edinburgh 1953. Asst Lectr, Edinburgh, 1952, Lectr, Edinburgh, 1953–59, 1964–72; Vis. Prof., Stanford Univ., USA, 1966 and 1968. MP (Lab.) Dunfermline Burghs, 1959–64; Parly Adviser, Scott. Television Ltd, 1964– ; Economic Cnslnt, Scotch Whisky Assoc., 1965–70; Mem., Public Schools Commn (Scott. Cttee), 1968–70; Mem., Donaldson Cttee, MoD, 1970–71; Jt Chm., Northern (Maritime) Offshore Resources Study, 1974– ; Chm., Adv. Bd on Economics Educn (Esmée Fairbairn Econ. Res. Cert.), 1969– . *Publications*: The Economics of Government, in, New Developments in the Teaching of Economics, ed K. Lumsden, 1967; Economics in the UK, in, Recent Research in Economics Education, ed K. Lumsden, 1970; *contrib*. Polit. Qly, Scott. Jl of Polit. Econ., etc. *Address*: Dept of Economics, Heriot-Watt Univ., Edinburgh EH1 1HX.

Thompson, Arthur Frederick; Fellow and Tutor in Modern History, Wadham College, Oxford, since 1947, and University Lecturer in Modern History, Oxford University, since 1950; *b* 1920; *m* 1942; two *s* one *d*. BA Oxon

1941 (1st cl. Mod. Hist.), MA Oxon 1946; FRHistS. Sen. Demy and Lectr, Magdalen Coll., Oxford, 1946–47; Vis. Prof., Stanford Univ., 1967–68, Kratter Vis. Prof., 1973–74. Mem., Edit. Cttee, Gladstone Diaries, 1962– ; Ed., Oxf. Hist. Monogs, 1970– . *Publications*: (with H. A. Clegg and A. Fox) A History of British Trade Unions since 1889, vol. 1, 1964; *contrib*. EHR, etc. *Address*: Wadham College, Oxford.

Thompson, Dr Barbara; Sociologist, Medical Research Council, Medical Sociology Unit, University of Aberdeen, since 1953; *b* 1921. BA Manchester 1946; Dip. Social Studies Manchester 1947, PhD Aberdeen 1965; AIMSW 1948. Mem., Council, Eugenic Soc., 1969– . WHO Consultant. *Publications*: contrib. Population Growth and Socio-Economic Change in West Africa (ed. J. C. Caldwell) (forthcoming); *contrib*. Brit. Jl Prev. Soc. Med., Brit. Jl Sociol., Jl Biosoc. Sci., Jl Obstet. Gynaec. Brit. Cwealth, Jl Trop. Paediat., Lancet, Milb. Mem. Fund Qly, Sociol. Rev., Trans Royal Soc., Trop. Med. Hyg., New Soc., Bull. Jl Ven. Diseases, Human Biology IBP Handbk No. 9. *Address*: Medical Research Council, Medical Sociology Unit, Centre for Social Studies, Westburn Road, Aberdeen AB9 2ZE.

Thompson, Dr Bruce; Lecturer, Department of German, University of Stirling, since 1972; *b* 1941; *m* 1971; one *d*. BA London 1963, MA McMaster 1964, PhD London 1971; Member: English Goethe Soc., Internationale Vereinigung für Germanische Sprach- und Literaturwissenschaft. Lectr in German, Univ. Liverpool, 1964–72. *Publications*: *contrib*. German Life and Letters. *Address*: Dept of German, Univ. of Stirling, Stirling FK9 4LA.

Thompson, Dr Christopher Warwick; Lecturer, School of French Studies, University of Warwick, since 1971; *b* 1938. BA Cantab 1961, PhD Cantab 1969. Lectr, Univ. Edinburgh, 1966–67; Research Fellow, Clare Coll., Cambridge, 1967–71. *Publications*: Victor Hugo and the Graphic Arts, 1970; *contrib*. Gazette des Beaux-Arts, Revue de Littérature Comparée, Mod. Lang. Review. *Address*: School of French Studies, Univ. of Warwick, Coventry, Warwicks CV4 7AL.

Thompson, Dr David Michael; Assistant Lecturer, Faculty of Divinity, University of Cambridge, since 1970; *b* 1942; *m* 1969. BA Cantab 1964 (1st cl. Hist.), MA Cantab 1968, PhD Cantab 1969. Fellow, Fitzwilliam Coll., Cambridge, 1965– ; Libr., Fitzwilliam Coll., Cambridge, 1967–73; Praelector, 1969– . *Publications*: Nonconformity in the Nineteenth Century, 1972; *contrib*. Studies Ch Hist., Vict. Studies. *Address*: Fitzwilliam College, Cambridge CB3 0DG.

Thompson, Prof. Donald, LLB, PhD, Barrister-at-Law; Professor of Law, University of Keele, since 1964; *b* 1928; *m* 1953; two *s* one *d*. LLB Nottingham 1953, PhD Nottingham 1957; Barrister-at-Law Gray's Inn 1958. Asst Lectr, then Lectr, Univ. of Manchester, 1955–63; Dir of Res., and Ed.,

Internat. Commn Jurists, Geneva, 1963–64; Mem., Legal Studies Bd, CNAA, 1965– ; Public Admin. Bd, 1967– ; Town Plan. Studies Bd, 1966–71. *Publications*: Il precedente giudizario nel diritto costituzionale inglese, in, La Dottrina del Precedente nella Giurisprudenza della Corte Costituzionale, ed G. Treves, 1971; *contrib*. Canad. Bar Rev., Mod. Law Rev., Public Law. *Address*: Univ. of Keele, Staffordshire ST5 5BG.

Thompson, Dorothy Katharine Gane; Lecturer in Modern History, School of History, University of Birmingham, since 1970; *b* 1923; *m* 1948; two *s* one *d*. MA Cantab 1946; FRHS. Fellowship in History, Univ. Birmingham, 1968–70. *Publications*: La presse de la classe ouvrière anglaise, in La Presse Ouvrière, ed Jacques Godediot, 1966; The British People 1760–1902, 1969; The Early Chartists, 1972; Antologia di Scritti Cartisti (forthcoming); Bull. Soc. for Study of Labour History, TLS. *Address*: School of History, Univ. of Birmingham, Birmingham B15 2TT.

Thompson, Prof. Edward Arthur, FBA; Professor of Classics, University of Nottingham, since 1948; *b* 1914. Lectr, Dublin, 1939–41; Lectr, Swansea, 1942–45; Lectr, King's Coll., London, 1945–48; Vis. Bentley Prof. of Hist., Michigan Univ., 1969–71. *Publications*: The Historical Work of Ammianus Marcellinus, 1947; A History of Attila and The Huns, 1948; A Roman Reformer and Inventor, 1952; The Early Germans, 1965; The Visigoths in the Time of Ulfila, 1966; The Goths in Spain, 1969. *Address*: Univ. of Nottingham, University Park, Nottingham NG7 2RD.

Thompson, Prof. Francis Michael Longstreth; Professor of Modern History, Bedford College, University of London, since 1968; *b* 1925; *m* 1951; two *s* one *d*. BA Oxon 1949 (1st cl. Hist.), MA Oxon 1949, DPhil Oxon 1956; FRHistS. Asst Lectr, Univ. Coll., London, 1951–53, Lectr, 1953–63, Reader in Economic Hist., 1963–68; Editor, Econ. Hist. Rev., 1968– . Staff Captain RA (E Bengal), 1946–47. Member Council: Agric. Hist. Soc., 1966– ; Econ. Hist. Soc., 1966– ; Royal Hist. Soc., 1971– ; elected Mem., Senate and Acad. Council, London Univ., 1970– ; Mem., Council, Bedford Coll., 1971–74; Gov., Brentwood Coll. of Educn, 1970– . *Publications*: English Landed Society in the Nineteenth Century, 1963, 2nd edn 1971; Chartered Surveyors: the Growth of a Profession, 1968; Hampstead: Building a Borough, 1650–1964, 1974; contrib. var. bks of jt authorship; *contrib*. Econ. Hist. Rev., EHR, Hist., Oxf. Econ. Papers. *Address*: History Dept, Bedford College, Regent's Park, NW1 4NS.

Thompson, Harry Llewellyn Bacon, BA; Lecturer in Drama, University of Hull, since 1964; *b* 1919. BA Bristol 1961 (Hons French and Drama). *Address*: Dept of Drama, Univ. of Hull, Hull HU6 7RX.

Thompson, Dr Ian Bentley; Senior Lecturer, Department of Geography, University of Southampton, since 1972 (Lecturer, 1962–72); *b* 1936; *m* 1961; four *d*. BA Durham 1957, MA Indiana 1958, PhD Durham 1960. Instr, Indiana Univ., 1957–58; Tutor, Durham Univ., 1958–59; Asst Lectr, Leeds Univ., 1959–62; Vis. Asst Prof., Miami Univ., Ohio, 1967. *Publications*: The St Malo Region, Brittany, 1968; Modern France: A Social and Economic Geography, 1970; Corsica, 1971; The Paris Basin, 1972; La France, Population, Economie et Régions, 1973; trans. and ed, France: a Geographical Study; *contrib*. Geog., Scott. Geogl Mag., Soton Res. Series Geog., Tijd. Econ. Sociale, Geog. Jl. *Address*: Dept of Geography, The Univ., Southampton SO9 5NH.

Thompson, Dr Irving Alexander Anthony; Lecturer, Department of History, University of Keele, since 1969; *b* 1938. BA Hons Cantab · 1959, MA Cantab, PhD Cantab 1965, PhD Adelaide 1966. Asst Lectr, Dept of History, Univ. of Reading, 1963–65; Lectr, Sch. of Social Sciences, Flinders Univ., South Australia, 1966–68. *Publications*: War and Government in Habsburg Spain 1560–1620, 1975; *contrib*. Econ. Hist. Rev., EHR, Historical Jl. *Address*: Dept of History, Univ. of Keele, Keele, Staffs ST5 5BG.

Thompson, Dr John Alexander; Lecturer, Faculty of History, University of Cambridge, since 1973; *b* 1938. BA Cantab 1962, PhD Cantab 1969. Asst Lectr in Amer. History, UCL, 1966–68, Lectr 1968–71; Asst Lectr in History, Univ. Cambridge, 1971–73. *Publications*: *contrib*. Jl Amer. History, Jl Amer. Studies. *Address*: St Catharine's College, Cambridge.

Thompson, Malcolm Wilfred; Lecturer in Classics, Queen Mary College, University of London, since 1967; *b* 1939. BA Exeter 1961 (1st cl. Hons Classics); Member: Virgil Soc.; Soc. for Promotion of Roman Studies. Asst Lectr, Queen Mary Coll., Univ. London, 1964–67. *Publications*: *contrib*. Class. Qly, Proc. Virgil Soc. *Address*: Queen Mary College, Mile End Road, E1 4NS.

Thompson, William David James C.; *see* Cargill Thompson.

Thomson, Prof. Derick Smith, MA, BA; Professor of Celtic, University of Glasgow, since 1964; *b* 1921; *m* 1952; four *s* one *d*. MA Aberdeen 1947 (1st cl. Celtic and English), BA Cantab 1948 (1st cl. Archaeol. and Anthropol. Sect. B). Asst, Edinburgh Univ., 1948–49; Lectr, Glasgow Univ., 1949–56; Reader, Aberdeen Univ., 1956–63; Ed., Scott. Gael. Studies, 1961– ; O'Donnell Lectr, Univ. of Wales, 1968; Osborn Bergin Memorial Lecture, 1974. Pres., Scott. Gael. Texts Soc., 1964– ; Ch., Gael. Soc. Inverness, 1969; Chm., Gael. Bks Council, 1968– ; Ed., Gairm, 1952– . *Publications*: The Gaelic Sources of MacPherson's 'Ossian', 1952; Branwen Verch Lyr, 1961, 2nd edn 1968; (with J. L. Campbell) Edward Lhuyd in the Scottish Highlands, 1699–1700, 1963; (with I. Grimble) The Future of the Highlands, 1968; three collections of Gaelic verse: 1951, 1967, 1970; An Introduction to Gaelic Poetry, 1974; *contrib*. Scott. Gael.

Studies, Scott. Studies, Trans Gael. Soc. Inverness. *Address*: Dept of Celtic, Univ. of Glasgow, Glasgow G12 8QQ.

Thomson, Hector; Senior Lecturer in Modern Greek, University of Aberdeen, since 1967; *b* 1917; *m* 1941. BA Oxon 1938 (2nd cl. Hon. Mods, 2nd cl. Lit. Hum.), MA Oxon 1943; Gaisford Greek Verse Prize 1937. Asst in Greek, Aberdeen, 1946–48; Lectr in Modern Greek, Aberdeen, 1948–67. Temp. Sec., Brit. Embassy, Bagdad, 1941–46; Mem., Macdonald Art Cttee, Aberdeen Art Gall., 1950– ; Adv. of Studies, Fac. of Arts, 1966– . *Publications*: *contrib*. Class. Qly, Class. Rev., Cyp. Studies, Greek Gaz. *Address*: Dept of Greek, King's College, Aberdeen AB9 2UB.

Thomson, Dr John Aidan Francis; Senior Lecturer in Mediaeval History, University of Glasgow, since 1974; *b* 1934; *m* 1970. MA Edinburgh 1955 (1st cl. Hist.), DPhil Oxon 1960; FRHistS. Asst, Glasgow Univ., 1960–61; Lectr, 1961–74; *Publications*: The Later Lollards 1414–1520, 1965, 2nd edn 1968; *contrib*. EHR, Innes Rev., Jl Eccles. Hist., Specul., Bull. IHR. *Address*: Dept of Mediaeval History, Univ. of Glasgow, Glasgow G12 8QQ.

Thomson, Patricia, MA; Reader in English, Queen Mary College, University of London, since 1965; *b* 1921; *m* 1970. BA Oxon 1943 (1st cl. English Lang. and Lit.), MA Oxon 1947. Asst Lectr, Univ. of Sheffield, 1946–49, Lectr, 1949–54; Lectr, Queen Mary Coll., London Univ., 1954–65. Mil. Service, 1943–46. *Publications*: Sir Thomas Wyatt and his Background, 1964; Elizabethan English Lyrical Poets, 1967; ed (with K. Muir), Collected Poems of Sir Thomas Wyatt, 1969; The Early Tudor Period Excluding Drama, in, Year's Work in English Studies, annually 1959–68; *contrib*. Comparative Lit., HLQ, Mod. Lang. Rev., Notes Queries, Rev. Engl. Studies. *Address*: Queen Mary College, Mile End Road, E1 4NS.

Thomson, Dr Patricia, (Mrs Maurice Evans); Reader, School of English and American Studies, Sussex University, since 1967; *b* 1920; *m* 1st 1946, 2nd 1966; one *s*. MA Aberdeen 1942 (1st cl. English), PhD Cantab 1946. Lectr, Aberdeen, 1946, 1954–64; Lectr, Sussex, 1964–66; Vis. Prof., State Univ. of NY, Buffalo, 1966–67. *Publications*: The Victorian Heroine, 1956; ed, The Changeling, 1964, 2nd edn 1971; *contrib*. Ess. Crit., Mod. Lang. Rev., Ninetnth Cen. Fict., Studia Neophilol., RES. *Address*: School of English and American Studies, Arts Building, Univ. of Sussex, Brighton BN1 9QN.

Thomson, Peter William; Lecturer in English and Drama, University College, Swansea, since 1971; *b* 1938; *m* 1963; two *s* two *d*. BA Cantab 1961 (English); Mem. Soc. for Theatre Research. Lectr in Drama, Univ. Manchester, 1964–71. *Publications*: ed, Julius Caesar, 1971; ed, Nineteenth Century British Theatre, 1971; ed, The Eighteenth Century English Stage, 1972; *contrib*. Shakespeare Survey. *Address*: English

Dept, Univ. College, Swansea, Singleton Park, Swansea SA2 8PP.

Thomson, Robert, MA; Senior Lecturer in Psychology, University of Leicester, since 1964; *b* 1921; *m* 1962; one *s* two *d*. BA Oxon 1948, MA Oxon 1949. Censor and Tutor, Univ. Coll., Durham, 1949–55; Lectr in Philosophy, Durham Univ., 1949–55; Sen. Tutor, Univ. Coll., Durham, 1955–64; Lectr in Psychology, Durham Univ., 1955–64; Vis. Lectr in Psychology, King's Coll., Newcastle upon Tyne, 1956–61. Psychologist, Civil Service Select. Bd (Method II). *Publications*: The Psychology of Thinking, 1959; Tänkandet: Psykologi, 1963; The Pelican History of Psychology, 1968 (Danish, Japanese, Swedish, Italian and Spanish trans); contrib. Key Papers in Cybernetics, ed C. R. Evans and A. D. J. Robertson; *contrib*. Brit. Jl Philos. Sci. *Address*: Dept of Psychology, Astley Clarke Building, The Univ., Leicester LE1 7RH.

Thomson, Robert Leith; Reader in Celtic, School of English, University of Leeds, since 1971; *b* 1924. BA Leeds 1949 (1st cl. Latin and English), Dip. Comp. Philol. Oxford 1951, BLitt Glasgow 1953, MA Leeds 1958. O'Donnell Lectr, Edinburgh, 1961 and Oxford, 1974; Rhŷs Memorial Lectr, Brit. Academy, 1969. Asst Lectr, Leeds, 1953–55, Lectr, 1955–64, Sen. Lectr, 1964–71. Dep. Dir, Grad. Centre for Medieval Studies, Leeds, 1967–72, Dir, 1972–77. *Publications*: Pwyll Pendeuic Dyuet, 1957, 2nd edn 1972; A dtimchiol an Chreidimh, 1962; Owein, 1968; Foirm na n-Urrnuidheadh, 1970; *contrib*. Celt., Etudes Celt., Jl Manx Mus., Scott. Gael. Studies, Studia Celt., Zeits. Celt. Philol. *Address*: School of English, The Univ., Leeds LS2 9JT.

Thomson Vessey, David William; *see* Vessey, D.W.T.

Thorlby, Prof. Anthony Kent; Professor of Comparative Literature, School of European Studies, University of Sussex, since 1967; *b* 1928; *m* 1962; three *d*. BA Cantab 1949 (Mod. Langs), MA Cantab 1955, PhD Yale 1952 (Compar. Lit.). Instructor in English, Yale, 1952–53; Lektor in English, Zürich, 1955–56; Lectr in German, UC Swansea, 1956–61; Lectr in German, Sussex, 1961–67; Vis. Prof., Northwestern Univ., 1968–69; Vis. Prof., Univ. Nice, 1974–75. *Publications*: Flaubert, 1959; The Romantic Movement, 1966; ed and contrib., The Penguin Companion to Literature vol. 2: European, 1969; (with D. Daiches) ed and contrib., Literature and Western Civilization, 6 vols, 1972– ; Kafka, 1972. *Address*: Univ. of Sussex, Falmer, Brighton BN1 9RH.

Thornberry, Cedric Henry Reid; Lecturer in Law, London School of Economics and Political Science, since 1963; *b* 1936; *m* 1st 1959, 2nd 1970; three *s* one *d*. BA Cantab 1957, LLB Cantab 1958, MA Cantab 1960; Barrister-at-Law, Gray's Inn, 1961. Res. Fellow, Brit. Inst. Internat. Comp. Law, 1960–61; Asst Lectr, LSE, 1961–63. Mem., Nat. Cttee for Cwealth Immigrants, 1966–68; (Special) Foreign Corresp., The Guardian,

1967–70. *Publications*: (with C. Parry) British Digest of International Law, vol. 6: Aliens, 1965; *contrib*. Internat. Comp. Law Qly, Mod. Law Rev. *Address*: London School of Economics, Houghton Street, Aldwych, WC2A 2AE.

Thorne, Christopher Guy; Reader in International Relations, University of Sussex, since 1972; *b* 1934; *m* 1958; two *d*. BA Oxon 1958 (Hons Mod. Hist.), MA Oxon. Lectr in Internat. Relations, Univ. Sussex, 1968–72. Head of Further Educn, BBC Radio, 1966–68. *Publications*: Ideology and Power, 1965; Chartism, 1966; The Approach of War, 1938–39, 1967; The Limits of Foreign Policy, 1972; *contrib*. Amer. Hist. Rev., Hist. Jl, Jl Contemp. History, Orbis, etc. *Address*: Arts Building, Univ. of Sussex, Falmer, Brighton BN1 9QN.

Thorne, James Peter, MA, BLitt; Reader in English Language, University of Edinburgh, since 1971; *b* 1933; *m* 1960; two *s*. BA Oxon 1954, MA, BLitt Oxon 1959, Dip. Gen. Linguistics Edinburgh 1961. Res. Fellow, Bedford Coll., London, 1957–58; Asst Lectr, Edinburgh, 1959–62; Lectr, Edinburgh, 1962–71; Vis. Assoc. Prof., Univ. of California, Berkeley, 1967; Vis. Assoc. Prof., Univ. of California, San Diego, 1969. Asst Dir., USAF Mechanical Analysis of Lang. Project, 1961–62. *Publications*: contrib. Commun. ACM, Jl Lingu., Mod. Philol., Nature. *Address*: Dept of English, Univ. of Edinburgh, Edinburgh EH8 9YL.

Thornely, John Wilfrid Athlone, MA; University Lecturer in Law, University of Cambridge, since 1949, Fellow, and Director of Studies in Law, Sidney Sussex College, Cambridge, since 1948; *b* 1917; *m* 1942; one *s* two *d*. BA Cantab 1940, MA Cantab 1943; Barrister, Inner Temple, 1947 (Hon. Bencher 1972). Faculty Asst Lectr in Law, Cambridge Univ., 1948. Tutor, Sidney Sussex Coll., 1962–65, Sen. Tutor, 1965–75. Book Review Editor, Cambridge Law Jl, 1960– . *Publications*: contrib. Cambridge Law Jl. *Address*: Sidney Sussex College, Cambridge CB2 3HU.

Thornes, Dr John Barrie, MSc, PhD; Lecturer, Department of Geography, London School of Economics, since 1969; *b* 1940; *m* 1962; one *s* one *d*. BSc London 1962, MSc McGill 1964, PhD London 1967. Asst Lectr, LSE, 1966–69; Vis. Asst Prof., Univ. of Toronto, 1970–71. *Publications*: contrib. Geog. Anal., Trans Inst. Brit. Geogrs. *Address*: Dept of Geography, London School of Economics, Houghton Street, WC2A 2AE.

Thornhill, William; Senior Lecturer in Political Theory and Institutions, University of Sheffield, since 1959; *b* 1920; *m* 1942; two *s*. BSc(Econ) London 1944, MSc(Econ) London 1948. Civics Res. Fellow, Natal Univ. Coll., Durban, 1946–48; Asst Lectr in Public Economics and Public Administration, Univ. of Sheffield, 1948–50; Lectr, Univ. of Sheffield, 1950–59. *Publications*: The Nationalized Industries: An Introduction, 1968; The Growth and Reform of English Local Government, 1971; The Case for Regional

Reform, 1972; ed and contrib., The Modernization of British Government, 1975; *contrib.* Internat. Rev. Admin. Sci., Local Govt Chron., Parly Aff., Yorks Bull. Econ. Social Res. *Address*: Dept of Political Theory and Institutions, The Univ., Sheffield S10 2TN.

Thornley, Denis Glyn, BA, FRIBA; Reader in Architecture, University of Manchester, since 1964; *b* 1916; *m* 1945; two *s*. BA Manchester 1939 (1st cl. Archit.), CertTP Manchester 1939; ARIBA 1940, FRIBA 1970. Studio Asst, Manchester Univ., 1939–40; Sen. Lectr and Acting Hd, Nottingham Sch. of Architecture, 1946–49; Lectr in Architecture, Manchester Univ., 1950–56; Sen. Lectr in Architecture, Manchester Univ., 1958–64; Vis. Lectr, Toronto Univ., 1962; Vis. Lectr, Hochschule für Gestatung, Ulm, 1961. *Publications*: Jt ed., Conference of Design Method, 1963; *contrib.* Jl Manch. Univ. Eng. Soc., RIBA Jl, York Studies Archit. Hist. *Address*: School of Architecture, Univ. of Manchester, Oxford Road, Manchester M13 9PL.

Thornton, Alan Henry; Deputy Director, Department of Adult Education, University of Nottingham, since 1954; *b* 1912; *m* 1966; one *s* two *d*. BA Dunelm 1935 (Hons History), DipEd Dunelm 1936, MA Dunelm 1947, BCL Dunelm 1950. Resident Tutor, Dept of Adult Educn, Univ. of Nottingham, 1947–54; Actg Dir, Dept Adult Educn, 1960–62 and 1968–70; Vice-Dean, Faculty of Educn, 1962–65. Mem. Lincs Educn Cttee; Chm. Jt Industrial Council, Hosiery Dyers and Bleachers. *Publications*: (with F. J. Bayliss) Adult Education and the Industrial Community, 1966; The Industrial Relations Bill: For and Against, 1971; *contrib.* Adult Educn, Jl Industrial Relations. *Address*: Dept of Adult Education, 14–22 Shakespeare Street, Nottingham.

Thornton, Dr Douglas Stanley, BSc(Agric), PhD, BA; Reader in Agricultural Economics, University of Reading, since 1966; *b* 1924; *m* 1949; two *s* one *d*. BSc(Agric) Reading 1949, BA London 1952 (1st cl. Geog.), PhD Reading 1961; Mem., Agric. Econ. Soc., Mem., Agric. Hist. Soc. Lectr, Reading, 1953–62; Sen. Lectr, then Prof., Univ. of Khartoum, 1962–66. Mem., ESCOR (Overseas Develop. Admin). *Publications*: *contrib.* Jl Agric. Econ. Soc., Trop. Agric. *Address*: Dept of Agricultural Economics, Univ. of Reading, Reading RG6 2AH.

Thornton, Dr Robert Kelsey Rought; Lecturer, Department of English, University of Newcastle upon Tyne, since 1967; *b* 1938; *m* 1961; two *s*. BA Manchester 1960, MA Manchester 1961, PhD Manchester 1972; FRSA. Mem., North. Arts Lit. Panel. *Publications*: ed, Poetry of the 'Nineties, 1970; Gerard Manley Hopkins: The Poems, 1973. *Address*: Dept of English, Univ. of Newcastle upon Tyne, Newcastle upon Tyne NE1 7RU.

Thorp, Martin Barrymore, MA; Statutory Lecturer, Geography Department, University College, Dublin, since 1969; *b* 1939; *m* 1965; two *d*. BA Liverpool 1960, MA Liverpool 1962. Lectr, Ahmadu Bello Univ., Nigeria, 1962–68; Assoc. Prof., UCLA, 1968. Mem., Cttee Nig. Geog. Assoc., 1966–68; Hon. Sec., Irish Geog. Soc. *Publications*: *contrib.* Nig. Geog. Jl, Trans Inst. Brit. Geogrs, Zeits. Geomorphol., Geog. Viewpoint. *Address*: Dept of Geography, Univ. College, Belfield, Dublin 4, Ireland.

Thorp, Rosemary; Research Officer, Latin American Economics, University of Oxford, since 1970; *b* 1940; *m* 1964; one *s* one *d*. BA Oxon 1962 (PPE), MA Oxon 1965; Mem. Soc. for Latin Amer. Studies. Jun. Res. Officer, Oxford Univ., 1962–67; Lectr (part-time), St Anne's Coll., Oxford, 1965–67; Lectr, Univ. Calif, Berkeley, 1967–70. *Publications*: (with Urquidi) ed, Latin America in the International Economy, 1973; *contrib.* Bull. Oxford Univ. Inst. Econs and Statistics. *Address*: Univ. of Oxford, Institute of Economics and Statistics, Manor Road, Oxford OX1 3UL.

Thorpe, Ellis; Lecturer in Sociology, University of Aberdeen, since 1970; *b* 1938; *m* 1960; two *d*. BA Leicester 1967, MSc Salford 1969; Mem. Brit. Sociological Assoc. Tutorial Asst, Univ. Salford, 1967–68; Res. Fellow, Univ. Durham, 1968–70. *Publications*: *contrib.* Health Visitor, Lancet, Occupational Mental Health, Social Work Today, Sociology. *Address*: Dept of Sociology, King's College, Aberdeen AB9 2UB.

Thorpe, Prof. Harry, MA, MLitt, PhD, FRGS, FSA; Professor of Geography, since 1964, and Head of the Department of Geography, University of Birmingham, since 1971; *b* 1913; *m* 1940; two *s* two *d*. BA Dunelm 1934 (1st cl. Geog.), MLitt Dunelm 1936, MA Dunelm 1937, PhD Birmingham 1954; Maltby Prizeman, Durham Univ. 1933; Teachers' Cert., Durham 1934; FRGS 1946, FSA 1957, Mem., Inst. Brit. Geogrs, 1946, Mem., Geog. Assoc. Demonstrator, Durham Univ., 1934–36; Lectr, Birmingham Univ., 1946–54; Reader, Birmingham Univ., 1955–63. Mil. service, RE, Europe, SE Asia, 1939–46; Pres., Geog. Assoc., 1974– ; Mem., Council, Inst. Brit. Geogrs; Mem., Res. Cttee, Royal Geog. Soc.; Chm., Birm. Br., Geog. Assoc., 1954–71, Pres., 1971; Pres., Worcs. Br., Geog. Assoc., 1964– ; Pres., Birm. and Warwicks Archaeol Soc., 1970– ; Chm., Govt Cttee of Inquiry into Allotments, 1965–69; Pres., Nat. Allts and Gdns Soc., 1973– . *Publications*: The City of Lichfield: A Study of its Growth and Function, 1950; Lancaster and Adjacent Areas, 1958; (with P. D. A. Harvey) The Printed Maps of Warwickshire, 1959; Report of the Departmental Committee of Inquiry into Allotments, 1969; *contrib.* Birmingham and its Regional Setting, 1950; *contrib.* The British Isles: A Systematic Survey, 1964; *contrib.* A Computer Mapped Flora for Warwickshire, 1971; *contrib.* Geog., Geog. Jl, Trans Birm. Archaeol Soc., Trans Inst. Brit. Geogrs. *Address*: Dept of Geography, Univ. of Birmingham, PO Box 363, Birmingham B15 2TT.

Thorpe, Prof. Lewis (Guy Melville), PhD, D de l'U; Professor of French Language and Literature, University of Nottingham, since

1958; b 1913; m 1939; one s one d. BA London 1935 (1st cl. French), LèsL Lille 1939, PhD London 1948, D de l'U Paris 1957; FIAL, FRHistS, FRSA, Fellow Assoc. Scrittori Veneti., Mem., MCC. Lectr, Nottingham Univ., 1946–54; Reader, Nottingham Univ., 1954–58; Vis. Prof., Univ. of Munich, 1966. Treas., Assoc. Univ. Teachers of French, 1951–52; Sec., Assoc. Univ. Teachers of French, 1953–55; Pres., Assoc. Univ. Teachers of French, 1956; Sec., Brit. Br., Internat. Arthur. Soc., 1951–66; Pres., Brit. Br. Internat. Arthur. Soc., 1966– ; Internat. Sec., Internat. Arthur. Soc., 1966– ; Ed., Nottingham Mediaeval Studies, 1957– ; Ed., Nottingham French Studies, 1962– ; Mem., Calvin Ed. Cttee, Wld Alliance Reformed and Protestant Chs, 1964– ; Ed., Bibliographical Bull. of the Internat. Arthur. Soc., 1967– . Publications: La France Guerrière, 1945; Le Roman de Laurin, fils de Marques le Sénéchal, 1950; Le Roman de Laurin, text of MS BN f fr. 22548, 1960; The History of the Kings of Britain, 1966, 3rd edn 1973; (with B. Reynolds) Guido Farina, Pittore di Verona, 1896–1957, 1967, English edn 1967; Two Lives of Charlemagne, 1969, 4th edn 1974; The History of the Kings of Britain, Folio Soc., 1969; Einhard the Frank: The Life of Charlemagne, 1970; Le roman de Silence, 1972; The Bayeux Tapestry and the Norman Invasion, 1973; The History of the Franks, by Gregory of Tours, 1974; contrib. Eras., Fr. Studies, Mod. Lang. Notes, Mod. Lang. Rev., Riv. Lett. Mod., Romania, Scriptor., etc. Address: Dept of French, The Univ., Nottingham NG7 2RD.

Thring, Meredith Wooldridge; Professor, and Head of Department of Mechanical Engineering, Queen Mary College, London University (also teaches Social Consequences of Engineering), since 1964; b 1915; m 1940; two s one d. BA Cantab 1937 (1st cl. Maths Pt I, Physics Pt II), ScD Cantab 1964 (Eng.); FIMechE 1964, FIEE 1964, FInstP 1943, FInstF 1951, FRAeS 1969, FIChemE 1956. Prof., and Hd of Dept of Fuel Technol. and Chem. Eng, Sheffield Univ., 1953–64. Gen. Supt of Res., Internat. Flame Res. Foundn, 1949–70; Hon. Gen. Supt of Res., Internat. Flame Res. Foundn, 1970– ; Mem., Clean Air Council, 1957–62; Pres., Inst. of Fuel, 1962–63. Publications: The Science of Flames and Furnaces, 1952, 2nd edn 1962; (with R. E. Johnstone) Pilot Plants: Models and Scale-up Methods in Chemical Engineering, 1957; Air Pollution, 1957; Nuclear Propulsion, 1961; The Principles of Applied Science, 1964; Man, Machines and Tomorrow, 1973; Machines – Masters or Slaves of Man?, 1973; contrib. Bull. Inst. Physics, Electron. Power, Internat. Symp. Combust., Jl ISI, Jl Inst. Fuel, CME. Address: Dept of Mechanical Engineering, Queen Mary College, Mile End Road, E1 4NS.

Thrower, James Arthur, MA, BLitt; Lecturer in Religious Studies, University of Aberdeen, since 1970; b 1936; m 1960; three d. BA Dunelm 1958, MA Dunelm 1960; BLitt Oxon 1963; Mem. Internat. Assoc. Hist. Relig. Lectr, Univ. of Ghana, 1964–68; Lectr, Bede Coll., Univ. of Durham, 1968–70. Mem., Council, Legon Hall, Univ. of Ghana, 1967–68; Sen. Resid., Balgownie Lodge, Univ. of Aberdeen, 1971– ; Vis. Res. Fellow, Inst. for Comparative Study for Religion, Helsinki, 1974. Publications: A Short History of Western Atheism, 1971; Letters of Heloise and Abelard, 1974; Phenomenon of Irreligion: East and West, 1975; contrib. •New Humanist, Question, Scot. Jl Theology, Religion in Africa, Scot. Bull. Missionary Studies. Address: Dept of Religious Studies, Univ. of Aberdeen, Aberdeen AB9 1AS.

Thurley, Keith Ernest; Senior Lecturer in Industrial Sociology, Department of Industrial Relations, London School of Economics and Political Science, since 1966; b 1931; m 1957; two s one d. BScEcon London 1952, IPM Diploma 1953; Member: Brit. Sociological Assoc., Inst. Personnel Management, Brit. Univs Industrial Relations Assoc., European Assoc. for Japanese Studies. Research Officer, 1959, Lectr in Social Admin, LSE, 1960–66. Vis. Asst Prof., Internat. Christian Univ., Tokyo, 1965, 1966, 1970. Mem. Council, Tavistock Inst. of Human Relations, 1969– ; Chief Exam. (Educn and Trng), IPM 1971– ; Mem. Business Studies Bd, CNAA, 1973– . Publications: (with A. C. Hamblin) The Supervisor and his Job, 1963; (with H. Wirdenius) Supervision: a reappraisal, 1973; (with H. Wirdenius) Approaches to Supervisory Development, 1973; contrib. Brit. Jl Industrial Relations, Japan Inst. Lab. Jl. Address: London School of Economics, Houghton Street, Aldwych WC2A 2AE.

Thurlow, Peter Arthur; Lecturer, German Department, Reading University, since 1962; b 1938. BA Reading 1961 (1st cl. German). Address: The German Dept, Univ. of Reading, Reading RG6 2AH.

Thurmer, Rev. John Alfred, MA; Part-time Lecturer in History, Exeter University, since 1973; b 1925. BA Oxon 1950 (2nd cl. Hist.), MA Oxon 1955; Deacon 1952, Priest 1953 (C of E). Chaplain, Salisbury Theol. Coll., 1955–63; Lazenby Chaplain, and Part-time Lecturer in History and Theology, 1963–73. Publications: contrib. Ch Qly Rev. Address: Queen's Building, The Queen's Drive, Exeter EX4 4QH.

Thwaites, Dr Bryan, MA, PhD; Principal of Westfield College, since 1966; b 1923; m 1948; four s two d. MA Cantab 1950, PhD London; FIMA (Pres., 1966–67). Scientific Off., Nat. Phys. Lab., 1944–47; Lectr, Imperial Coll., London, 1947–51; Special Lectr, Imperial Coll., London, 1951–58; Asst Master, Winchester Coll., 1951–59; Prof. of Theoretical Mechanics, Southampton Univ., 1959–66; Gresham Prof. in Geometry, City Univ., 1969–72. Shadow Vice-Chancellor, Independent Univ., July–Nov., 1971; Mem., Acad. Adv. Cttees, Univ. of Bath, 1963–71; Mem., Open Univ., 1969– ; Dir, School Mathematics Project, 1961– ; Mem., US Educnl Commn, 1966– ; Chm., and Mem. of various cttees, Aeronautical Res. Council, 1948–69; Chairman: Council of C of E Colls of Educn, 1969–71; Northwick Park Hosp. Management Cttee, 1970–74; Collegiate Council, London

Univ., 1973– ; Brent and Harrow AHA, 1973; Governor various schs. *Publications*: ed, Incompressible Aerodynamics, 1960; ed, on Teaching Mathematics, 1961; *contrib*. Proc. Royal Soc., Reports and Memoranda of Aeronautical Res. Council, Qly Jl Applied Mech., Jl Royal Aeronautical Soc. *Address*: The Old House, Westfield College, NW3 7ST.

Tibawi, Dr Abdul Latif; Lecturer in Education in Developing Countries, University of London, since 1963; *b* 1910; *m*; two *d*. BA Beirut 1929, Teachers Certif. Palestine 1931, DipEd London 1951, PhD London 1952 (Educn), DLit London 1962 (Middle East history and educn). Res. Fellow, Harvard Univ. 1960–63. Sen. Educn Officer, Palestine, until 1948; Asst Editor, Arabic Listener (BBC), 1948–49. *Publications*: Arab Education in Mandatory Palestine 1918–48, 1956; British Interests in Palestine 1800–1901: A Study of Religions and Educational Work, 1961; Lectures on the History of the Arabs and Islam, vol. 1 1963, vol. 2 1966 (in Arabic); American Interests in Syria 1800–1901: A Study of Religious and Educational Work, 1966; A Modern History of Syria including Lebanon and Palestine, 1969; Islamic Education: Its Traditions and Modernization into the Arab National Systems, 1972; Arabic and Islamic Themes: Historical, Educational and Literary Studies, 1974; various works in Arabic: monographs, articles, reviews; *contrib*. Islamic Qly, Internat. Rev. Educn, Middle East Forum, Middle East Jl, Revue de l'academie arabe de Damas, Royal Central Asian Jl, Die Welt des Islams, etc. *Address*: Institute of Education, Univ. of London, Malet Street, WC1E 7HS.

Tierney, Prof. James Joseph; Professor of Greek, University College, Dublin, since 1948; *b* 1910; *m* 1942; two *d*. BA NUI 1931, MA NUI 1932, Higher DipEd 1932; Member: Hellenic Soc., 1936– , Royal Soc. Antiquaries of Ireland, 1937– , Royal Irish Acad., 1945– . Assistant Lecturer: Latin, QUB, 1932–36; Ancient Classics, UCD, 1936–48. Hon. Gen. Sec., Royal Soc. Antiq. Ireland, 1939–45; Dean, Faculty of Arts, UCD, 1957–69; Mem., Senate, NUI, 1959–72. *Publications*: ed, Dicuili Liber de Mensura Orbis Terrae (Scriptores Latini Hiberniae vol VI), 1967; *contrib*. Hellenica (Athens), Jl Hellenic Studies, Proc. Royal Irish Acad., Rheinisches Museum für Philologie. *Address*: Univ. College, Dublin, Arts Building, Belfield, Dublin 4.

Tiley, John; University Lecturer in Law, University of Cambridge, since 1972; *b* 1941; *m* 1964; two *s* one *d*. BA Oxford 1962, BCL Oxford 1963; MA Oxford 1967; MA Cantab 1967; Barrister-at-Law Inner Temple 1964. Lectr, Lincoln Coll., Oxford, 1963–64; Lectr, Univ. of Birmingham, 1964–67; Asst Lectr, Univ. of Cambridge, 1967–72; Fellow, Queens' Coll., Cambridge, 1967– ; Vis. Prof., Dalhousie Law School, 1972–73. *Publications*: A Casebook on Equity and Succession, 1968; ed, Beattie: Elements of Estate Duty, 7th edn 1970; *contrib*. Camb. Law Jl, Law Qly Rev., Mod. Law Rev. *Address*: Queens' College, Cambridge.

Till, John Roger, MA; Senior Staff Tutor in Extra-Mural Studies, University of Durham, since 1970; *b* 1911; *m* 1951; one *s* two *d*. Journalism Dip. London 1932 (dist. Engl. Lit. and Crit.), BA Oxon 1949 (2nd cl. Shortened Hons Engl.), after war service in Navy; MA Oxon 1952; Mem., Nat. Bk League, Mem., Crit. Qly Soc. Staff Tutor in Extra-Mural Studies, Durham Coll., Durham Univ., 1950–70; Vis. Lectr and Examiner, Toronto Univ. Extension Div. Summer Session, 1965. Coll. Tutor, Van Mildert Coll., Durham Univ., 1965–73; Pres., Durham English Soc., 1964–66; Dir of Studies, Brit. Council Summer Sch., Durham, 1966, 1968, 1970, 1973; former Journalist (Hornsey Jl, Birm. Post, BBC), and Schoolmaster (Blundell's, King Edward VI Sch., Five Ways, Birmingham). *Publications*: Wills of Bristol, 1954; contrib. verse, in, In Praise of Cricket, ed J. Aye, 1946; verse, in, The Sleep Book, ed A. M. Laing, 1948; New Statesman Competitions, ed A. Marshall, 1955; Durham County and City with Teesside, ed J. C. Dewdney, 1970; *contrib*. Durh. Univ. Jl, Highway, New States., Time & Tide. *Address*: Dept of Extra-Mural Studies, Univ. of Durham, 32 Old Elvet, Durham DH1 3JB.

Till, Rev. Michael Stanley; Dean of King's College, Cambridge, since 1970; College Lecturer in Divinity and Director of Studies since 1970; *b* 1935; *m* 1965; one *s* one *d*. BA Oxon: 1960 (Hons History), 1962 (Hons Theology); Deacon 1964, priest 1965. Chaplain, King's Coll., Cambridge, 1967–70. *Address*: King's College, Cambridge.

Tillotson, Howard Thomas; Lecturer, Department of Transportation and Environmental Planning, University of Birmingham, since 1968; *b* 1940; *m* 1964; one *d*. BA Oxon 1962 (Natural Philos.), MA Oxon 1969 (Natural Philos.); Fellow of Visible Record and Minicomputer Soc., 1972, MInstP 1974. Res. Assoc., Univ. Birmingham, 1966, Sen. Res. Assoc. 1967. *Publications*: *contrib*. Surveyor, Local Govt Technology, Traffic Engrg and Control. *Address*: Univ. of Birmingham, Birmingham B15 2TT.

Tilmouth, Prof. Michael, MA, PhD; Tovey Professor of Music, University of Edinburgh, since 1971; *b* 1930; *m* 1966; one *s* one *d*. BA Cantab 1954 (1st cl. Music), MA Cantab 1958, PhD Cantab 1960; Scholar, Christ's Coll., Cambridge, 1953, Wm Barclay Squire Prizeman, Cambridge, 1955. Lectr, Glasgow Univ., 1959–71. Ed., Royal Music. Assoc. Res. Chron., 1968– ; Mem., Proc. Cttee, Royal Music. Assoc., 1968–72; Mem., Council, Royal Music. Assoc., 1970– ; Mem., Ed. Cttee, Musica Britannica, 1972– ; *Publications*: A Calendar of References to Music 1660–1719, 1961, 2nd edn 1968; Matthew Locke: Chamber Music I (Musica Britannica vol. XXXI), 1971; Matthew Locke: Chamber Music II (Musica Britannica vol. XXXII), 1972; *contrib*. Music Qly, Music. Times, Music Lett., Proc. Roy. Mus. Assoc. *Address*: Dept of Music, Univ. of Edinburgh, Alison House, 12 Nicolson Square, Edinburgh EH8 9BH.

702

Timings, Edward Kenneth; Lecturer, School of Archive and Information Studies, University College, London; *b* 1918. BA Cantab (1st cl. Hons History), MA Cantab 1940. Principal Asst Keeper Public Record Office, London, Head of Search Dept, 1967– . *Publications:* Navy Record Society vol. CV, 1963 and vol. CXII, 1969; *contrib.* English Hist. Review, Jl Brontë Soc. Trans, Modern Lang. Notes, Mariners' Mirror. *Address:* Univ. College, Gower Street, WC1E 6BT.

Timms, Prof. Duncan William Graham; Professor of Sociology, University of Stirling, since 1972; *b* 1938; *m* 1960; one *s* one *d*. BA Cantab 1959 (1st cl. Geog.), PhD Cantab 1963; Mem., Sociol. Assoc. Austral. NZ (Vice-Pres., 1970–71), Mem., Amer. Sociol. Assoc., Mem., Pacif. Sociol. Assoc., Mem., Soc. Study Social Problems (US). Lectr, Univ. of Queensland, Australia, 1962–64; Sen. Lectr, Univ. of Queensland, Australia, 1965–67; Prof. of Sociol., Univ. of Auckland, NZ, 1968–71. Hon. Cnsltnt, Dept of Psychol. Med., Auckland Hosp., 1968–71; Mem., Urb. Develop. Working Party, Nat. Develop. Conf. (NZ), 1970–71. *Publications:* The Urban Mosaic, 1971; Stirling and its Region, 1974; *contrib.* Austral. NZ Jl Sociol., Pacif. Sociol. Rev., Sociol. Soc. Res., Envt and Planning. *Address:* Dept of Sociology, Univ. of Stirling, Stirling FK9 4LA.

Timms, Prof. Noel, MA; Professor of Social Work, University of Newcastle upon Tyne, since 1975; *b* 1927; *m* 1956; three *s* three *d*. BA London 1949 (Hons Hist.), MA London 1960 (Sociol.), Dip. Public Social Admin Oxford 1950, Dip. Mental Hlth London 1955. Lectr, Cardiff Univ. Coll., 1957–61; Lectr, Birmingham Univ., 1961–63; Lectr, LSE, 1963–70; Prof. of Applied Social Studies, Univ. of Bradford, 1970–75. *Publications:* Psychiatric Social Work in Great Britain (1939–1962), 1964; Social Casework, Principles and Practice, 1964, 2nd edn 1966; A Sociological Approach to Social Problems, 1967; Language of Social Casework, 1968; Social Work: An Outline for the Intending Student, 1970. *Address:* Univ. of Newcastle upon Tyne, Newcastle upon Tyne NE1 7RU.

Tinker, David; Director of Visual Art Studies, University College of Wales, Aberystwyth, University of Wales, since 1962; *b* 1924; *m* 1948; two *s* one *d*. Dip. Fine Art London 1949. Mem., Art Cttee, Welsh Arts Council; Mem., Exec. and Art Cttees, N Wales Assoc. for Arts. Commissions in Sculpture and Painting; exhibitions of both. *Address:* Art Dept, Univ. College of Wales, Visual Art Building, Llanbadarn Road, Aberystwyth, Dyfed.

Tinnion, John Wesley; Lecturer in Law, University of Leeds, since 1973; *b* 1941; *m* 1963; two *s*. LLB Sheffield 1962. Admitted Law Soc. 1965. Part-time Tutor, Univ. Leeds, 1968–73. *Address:* Univ. of Leeds, Leeds LS2 9JT.

Tinsley, Rev. Prof. Ernest John, MA, BD; Professor of Theology, University of Leeds, since 1962; *b* 1919; *m* 1947; two *d*. BA Durham 1940 (1st cl. Engl. Lang. and Lit., 1st cl. Theol. 1942), MA Durham 1943, BD Durham 1945. Lectr in Theology, Univ. Coll., Hull, 1946–54; Lectr in Charge, Dept of Theology, Hull Univ., 1954–61; Sen. Lectr and Hd of Dept, Hull Univ., 1961–62. Mem., Durham Commn on Religious Educn, 1967–69; Mem., Archbps' Commn on Doctrine, 1967–69; Hon. Canon, Ripon Cath., 1966– . *Publications:* The Imitation of God in Christ, 1960; The Gospel according to Luke, 1964; ed, Modern Theology, 1973; *contrib.* Ch Qly, Ch Qly Rev., Concil., Hibb. Jl, Scott. Jl Theol. *Address:* Dept of Theology, The Univ., Leeds LS2 9JT.

Tipton, Ian Charles, MA, BLitt; Lecturer in Philosophy, University College of Wales, Aberystwyth, since 1967; *b* 1937; *m* 1963; two *s*. BA Wales 1959 (1st cl. Philos.), MA Wales 1962, BLitt Oxon 1965. Asst Lectr, Keele, 1964–66; Lectr, Keele, 1966–67. *Publications:* Berkeley: The Philosophy of Immaterialism, 1974; *contrib.* Hermath., Jl Hist. Ideas. *Address:* Dept of Philosophy, Univ. Coll. of Wales, Aberystwyth SY23 2AX.

Tisdall, Caroline; Lecturer, Department of Fine Art, University of Reading, since 1968; *b* 1945; *m* 1969. BA London 1968 (Hons History of Art). Art Critic, Guardian, 1970– . *Publications:* Metaphysical Art, 1971; Futurism, 1972; Joseph Beuys: The Secret Block for a Secret Person in Ireland, 1974; A Dutch Dozen, 1974; Art into Society: German Political Art, 1974; The Energy Plan for the Western Man, 1974. *Address:* Dept of Fine Art, Univ. of Reading, Whiteknights, Reading RG6 2AH.

Titmus, Colin John, BA, PhD; Senior Lecturer, Extra-Mural and Adult Education, University of Glasgow, since 1969; *b* 1927; *m* 1950; one *s* two *d*. BA London 1947 (Hons French), Teacher's Dip. London 1950, PhD London 1955 (French). Staff Tutor, Glasgow Univ., 1961–67; Sen. Tutor, Glasgow Univ., 1967–69. *Publications:* Adult Education in France, 1967; *contrib.* Adult Educn, Fr. Studies, Mod. Lang. Rev., Studies in Adult Educn. *Address:* Dept of Extra-Mural and Adult Education, 57–59 Oakfield Avenue, Glasgow.

Tivey, Leonard James; Senior Lecturer in Public Administration, University of Birmingham, since 1969; *b* 1926; *m* 1954; one *s*. BSc(Econ) London 1953 (1st cl.). Res. Off., Pol. Econ. Planning (PEP), 1953–60, Sen. Inform. Off., Treasury, 1960–61. Lectr in Public Admin, Univ. of Birmingham, 1961–69. *Publications:* Nationalisation in British Industry, 1966, rev. edn 1973; (jtly) PEP reports on Industrial Trade Associations, 1957; Advisory Committees in British Government, 1960; The Nationalized Industries since 1960, 1973; *contrib.* var. PEP broadsheets; *contrib.* Parl. Aff., Pol. Qly. *Address:* Dept of Political Science, Univ. of Birmingham, PO Box 363, Birmingham B15 2TT.

Tivy, Dr Joy, BA, BSc, PhD, FRSGS; Reader, Department of Geography, University of Glasgow, since 1972; *b* 1924. BA

703

Trinity College Dublin (1st cl. Nat. Science), BSc Trinity College Dublin 1946, PhD Edinburgh 1955; FRSGS 1965. Asst, Edinburgh, 1950–53; Lectr, Edinburgh, 1953–56; Lectr, Glasgow, 1956–65, Sen. Lectr, 1965–72. Ed., Scott. Geog. Mag., 1955–65; Hon. Sec./Ed., Scott. Fld Studies Assoc., 1965– . *Publications*: ed, The Glasgow Region, 1958; Biogeography, 1971; Organic Resources of Scotland, 1973; *contrib*. Scott. Geog. Mag., Trans Inst. Brit. Geogrs. *Address*: Dept of Geography, The Univ. of Glasgow, Glasgow G12 8QQ.

Tizard, Dr Barbara; Senior Research Fellow (Dr Barnardo's), Thomas Coram Research Unit, Department of Child Development, Institute of Education, London, since 1967; *b* 1926; *m* 1947; three *s* two *d*. BA Oxon 1948, PhD London 1957; Associate Mem. British Psychological Soc., Mem. Experimental Psychology Soc. Lectr, Dept Exper. Neurology, Inst. of Psychiatry, London, 1963–67. *Publications*: *contrib*. Acta Psychiat. et Neurol., Amer. Jl Ment. Defic., Brit. Jl Soc. and Clin. Electroenceph., Clin. Neurophysiol., Child Development, Jl Ment. Sci., Jl Neurol. Neurosurg. Psychiat., Jl Child Psychol., Psychiat., Medical History, Nature, New Society, Psychol. Bull. *Address*: Thomas Coram Res. Centre, A1 Brunswick Square, WC1N 1AZ.

Tizard, Prof. Jack; Professor of Child Development, University of London Institute of Education, since 1964, Research Professor, since 1971; *b* 1919; *m* 1947; three *s* two *d*. MA New Zealand 1940 (1st cl. Psychol.), BLitt Oxford 1948 (Social Studies), PhD London 1951 (Psychol.); FBPsS, FAmer Assoc. Ment. Defic., FRSoc Med. Lectr in Psychology, St Andrews Univ., 1947–48. Scientific Staff, MRC, Soc. Psychiatry Res. Unit, Inst. of Psychiatry, 1948–64; Cnsltnt in Ment. Hlth, WHO, 1954– ; Cnsltnt Adv. in Ment. Hndcp, Dept of Hlth, 1964– ; Chm., Sec. of State's Adv. Cttee on Hndcpd Children, 1968–72; Council Mem., SSRC, and Chm., Educnl Res. Bd, 1968–71. *Publications*: (with N. O'Connor) The Social Problem of Mental Deficiency, 1956; (with J. C. Grad) The Mentally Handicapped and their Families, 1961; Community Services for the Mentally Handicapped, 1964; (with M. Rutter and K. Whitmore) Education, Health and Behaviour, 1971; (with R. D. King and N. U. Raynes) Patterns of Residential Care, 1972. *Address*: Thomas Coram Research Unit, 41 Brunswick Square, WC1.

Tobias, Ruth Kathleen; Lecturer in Mathematics, Department of Educational Studies, University of Hull, since 1971; *b* 1925. BA Reading 1946, DipEd Reading 1947, MA Reading 1949; Founder Fellow, Inst. Mathematics and Applications, Vice-Pres., Mathematical Assoc. Lectr, Univ. of Nottingham, 1968–71. *Publications*: contrib. Teaching of Analysis in Sixth Forms, 1963; Mathematics Laboratories in Schools, 1968; Count Me In: Numeracy in Education, 1968; *contrib*. Int. Jl Math. Educ. Sci. Technol. *Address*: The Univ., Cottingham Road, Hull HU6 7RX.

Todd, The Lord; Alexander Robertus Todd, DSc, DPhil, MA, FRS, FRIC; Master of Christ's College, Cambridge, since 1963 (Fellow 1944), (first) Chancellor, University of Strathclyde, Glasgow; *b* 1907; *m* 1937; one *s* two *d*. DSc Glasgow, Dr Phil nat Frankfurt, DPhil Oxon, MA Cantab, Hon. LLD Glasgow, Melbourne, Edinburgh, California, Manchester, Hon. Dr rer nat Kiel, Hon. DSc London, Madrid, Exeter, Leicester, Aligarh, Sheffield, Wales, Yale, Strasbourg, Harvard, Liverpool, Adelaide, Strathclyde, Oxford, ANU, Paris, Warwick, Durham, Michigan, Hon. DLitt Sydney; FRS 1942. Asst in Medical Chemistry, Univ. of Edinburgh, 1934–35; Beit Meml Research Fellow, Univ. of Edinburgh, 1935–36; Mem., Staff, Lister Inst. of Preventive Medicine, London, 1936–38; Reader in Biochemistry, Univ. of London, 1937–38; Sir Samuel Hall Prof. of Chemistry and Dir of Chemical Laboratories, Univ. of Manchester, 1938–44; Prof. of Organic Chemistry, Univ. of Cambridge, 1944–71. Chm., Adv. Council on Scientific Policy, 1952–64; Pres., Chemical Soc., 1960–62; Pres., Internat. Union of Pure and Applied Chemistry, 1963–65; Pres., Brit. Assoc. Advancement of Science, 1969–70; Mem., Council, Royal Society, 1967–70; Mem., NRDC, 1968– ; Chm., Bd of Governors, United Cambridge Hosps, 1969–74; Dir, Fisons Ltd; Hon. Mem., French, German, Spanish, Belgian, Swiss, Chemical Socs; Foreign Mem., Amer. and other Acads of Science or Arts and Sciences; Hon. Fellow, Oriel Coll., Oxford, Churchill Coll., Cambridge, RSE, Manchester Coll. of Technology, Australian Chem. Inst.; Chm., Nuffield Foundn; Meldola Medal, 1936; Lavoisier Medallist, French Chem. Soc., 1948; Davy Medal of Royal Society, 1949; Royal Medal of Royal Society, 1955; Nobel Prize for Chemistry, 1957; Cannizzaro Medal, Italian Chem. Soc., 1958; Paul Karrer Medal, Univ. Zürich, 1962; Stas Medal, Belgian Chem. Soc., 1962; Longstaff Medal, Chemical Soc., 1963; Copley Medal, Royal Society, 1970; Pour le Mérite, German Federal Republic, 1966. *Publications*: numerous scientific papers in chemical and biochemical jls. *Address*: Master's Lodge, Christ's College, Cambridge.

Todd, Christopher; *see* Todd, F. C. C.

Todd, Dr (Francis) Christopher (Crew); Lecturer in French, University of Leeds, since 1967; *b* 1939; *m* 1964; one *s* one *d*. BA London 1964, PhD London 1969. Vis. Assoc. Prof., Queen's Univ., Kingston, Ontario, 1972–3. *Publications*: Voltaire's Disciple: Jean-François de La Harpe, 1972; *contrib*. MLR, Studies on Voltaire and the Eighteenth Century. *Address*: Dept of French, Univ. of Leeds, Leeds LS2 9JT.

Todd, Malcolm; Senior Lecturer, Department of Classical and Archaeological Studies, University of Nottingham, since 1974; *b* 1939; *m* 1964; one *s* one *d*. BA St David's UC 1961, Dip. Class. Archaeology, Oxon 1963 (distinction); FSA 1970. Lectr, Dept of Class. and Arch. Stud., Univ. of Nottingham, 1965–74. *Publications*: The Roman Fort at Great Casterton, 1968; Everyday Life of the Barbarians, 1972; The Coritani, 1973; The Northern Barbarians: 100 BC–AD 300, 1975; *contrib.* Antiquaries Jl, Britannia, Bonner Jahrbücher, Amer. Jl Archaeology. *Address*: Univ. of Nottingham, University Park, Nottingham NG7 2RD.

Tomiak, Janusz Jozef; Hayter Lecturer in Russian and Soviet Education, University of London Institute of Education, and School of Slavonic and East European Studies, since 1967; *b* 1924; *m* 1949; two *s.* BSc London 1953 (Econ.), MA London 1965 (Educn), Acad.Dip. London 1958 (Educn); Mem., Comp. Educn Soc. Europe (Brit. Sect.). Lectr in Comparative Educn, Univ. of London Inst. of Educn, 1966–67; Vis. Prof., Kent State Univ., Ohio, 1967. Mem., Gov. Body, Kennington Coll., London, 1970– . *Publications*: The Soviet Union (World Education Series), 1972; *contrib.* Comp. Educn Rev., Polish Rev., Kwart. Pedagog. *Address*: Dept of Comparative Education, Univ. of London Institute of Education, Malet Street, WC1E 7HS.

Tomkins, Cyril Robert; Senior Lecturer, Department of Accountancy and Finance, University of Strathclyde, since 1972; *b* 1939; *m* 1963; two *s.* BA Bristol 1962, MSc London 1967; Member: Inst. Public Finance Accountants 1965 (prize for 2nd place) (formerly IMTA), Amer. Accounting Assoc., Amer. Finance Assoc., British Accounting and Finance Assoc. Lectr, Univ. Hull, 1967–70; Lectr and Sen. Res. Officer, UCNW, 1970–72. *Publications*: Income and Expenditure Accounts for Wales, 1965–1968, 1971; Financial Planning in Divisionalised Companies, 1973; *contrib.* Accounting and Business Research, Accountancy, Econ. Jl, Jl Business Finance, Jl Financial and Quantitative Analysis. *Address*: 173 Cathedral Street, Glasgow.

Tomlin, Dr Roger Simon Ouin; Lecturer in Classics, University of Durham, since 1973. BA Oxon 1965 (1st cl. Hons Class. Mods and Greats), DPhil Oxon 1974; Mem. Soc. for Promotion of Roman Studies, etc. Craven Fellow, Oxford, 1965. Vis. Asst Prof., Cornell Univ., 1968–70; Lectr in Class. Studies, Univ. Kent at Canterbury, 1970–73. *Publications*: *contrib.* Amer. Jl Philology, Britannia, Jl Roman Studies, Yorks Archaeological Jl. *Address*: Dept of Classics, 38 North Bailey, Durham.

Tomlinson, (Alfred) Charles; Reader in English Poetry, Department of English, University of Bristol, since 1968; *b* 1927; *m* 1948; two *d.* BA Cantab, MA London. Lectr, Univ. Bristol, 1956–68; Vis. Prof., Univ. New Mexico, 1962–63; O'Connor Prof. of English, Colgate Univ., 1967. Mem., Arts Council Poetry Panel, 1964–66. *Publications*: The Necklace, 1955; Seeing Is Believing, 1958; (with H. Gifford) trans., Versions from Tyutchev, 1960; A Peopled Landscape, 1963; (with H. Gifford) trans., Castilian Ilexes: Versions from Machado, 1963; American Scenes, 1966; The Way of a World, 1969; (with H. Gifford) trans, Ten Versions from Trilce by Cesár Vallejo, 1970; (with Roubaud, Sanguineti and Paz)

Renga, 1971; Written on Water, 1972; Words and Images 1972; *contrib.* Agenda, Essays in Criticism, Hudson Review, Poetry (Chicago), Sewanee Review. *Address*: Dept. of English, Univ. of Bristol, Bristol BS8 1TH.

Tomlinson, Charles; *see* Tomlinson, A. C.

Tomlinson, Clive; Lecturer in Surveying, Department of Geography, University College of Swansea, since 1963; *b* 1932; *m* 1954; four *s.* BA Reading 1953; FRGS; Mem., Assoc. Brit. Geodesists, Mem., Fld Surv. Assoc., Mem., Photogram. Soc., Mem., Brit. Cartog. Soc. Land Surveyor, Directorate of Overseas Surveys, 1953–58; Soil Surv. and Res., BWI Soils Res., Imperial Coll. Trop. Agric., Trinidad, 1958–60; Lectr in Surveying, Dept of Surveying and Engineering, Coll. of Estate Management, Univ. of London, 1960–63; Assoc. Prof. of Cartography, Dept of Geog., Univ. of Victoria, BC, 1970–71. *Publications*: Survey Instruments and Techniques, 1962; *contrib.* Estates Gaz. *Address*: Dept of Geography, Univ. College, Swansea SA2 8PP.

Tomlinson, Prof. Richard Allan, MA, FSA; Professor of Ancient History and Archaeology, University of Birmingham, since 1971; *b* 1932; *m* 1957; three *s* one *d.* BA Cantab 1954 (1st cl. Classics), MA Cantab 1958; FSA. Temp. Asst, Edinburgh, 1957; Asst Lectr, Birmingham, 1958–61; Lectr, Birmingham, 1961–70; Sen. Lectr, Birmingham, 1970–71. Mem., Mngng Cttee, Brit. Sch. Athens, 1972– . *Publications*: Argos and The Argolid, 1972; *contrib.* Ann. Brit. Sch. Athens, Jl Hellen. Studies, Amer. Jl Archaeology. *Address*: Dept of Ancient History and Archaeology, The Univ., PO Box 363, Birmingham B15 2TT.

Tong, Robert Percy, OBE, ERD; Registrar and Secretary, Queen Mary College, University of London, since 1946; *b* 1911; *m* 1941. CertifEd Cantab 1936, MA Cantab 1938; psc 1940. Dep. Chm., UCCA, 1972–75; Mem., Essex Educn Cttee, 1951–64; Vice-Chm., Barking/Havering Area Health Authority, 1973; Chm., Brentwood Group Hosp. Management Cttee, 1958–74. JP NE London 1960. *Address*: Queen Mary College, Mile End Road E1 4NS.

Tonkin, Dr Jessica Elizabeth Ann, MA, DPhil; Lecturer in Social Anthropology, Centre of West African Studies, University of Birmingham, since 1970; *b* 1934. BA Oxford 1955, MA Oxford 1961, DipSocAnthrop Oxford 1967, DPhil Oxford 1971, CertEd London 1963. Educn Off., HMOCS, Kenya (at Kenya High Sch.), 1958–63; Lectr, Dept of Engl., Ahmadu Bello Univ., Nigeria, 1963–66. *Publications*: Some coastal pidgins of West Africa, in, Social Anthropology and Language, ed E. Ardener. *Address*: Centre of West African Studies, Univ. of Birmingham, PO Box 363, Birmingham B15 2TT.

Topham, Anthony John; Lecturer in Industrial Studies, Department of Adult Education, University of Hull, since 1973; *b* 1929; *m* 1957; two *s.* BA Leeds 1950 (Econs and Polit. Sci.), MA Leeds 1952. Mem. Soc.

705

Industrial Tutors, Mem. WEA. Tutor in Social Studies, Univ. Hull, 1962–65, Tutor in Industrial Studies, 1965–73. *Publications*: (with F. Singleton) Workers' Control in Yugoslavia, 1962, 2nd edn 1970; (with K. Coates) Industrial Democracy in Great Britain, 1968, 2nd edn revised as Workers Control, 1970; ed and contrib., Trade Union Register 1969, 1969; ed and contrib., Trade Union Register 1970, 1970; (with K. Coates) The New Unionism, 1972, 2nd revised edn 1974; The Organised Worker, Book IV, Industrial Studies for Trade Unions series, 1975; *contrib.* Jl Soc. Industrial Tutors. *Address*: Dept of Adult Education, Univ. of Hull, Cottingham Road, Hull HU6 7RX.

Topham, Neville; Senior Lecturer in Economics, University of Salford, since 1972; *m* 1967; two *s* one *d*. BSc(Econ) Hull 1963. Economist Brit. Nylon Spinners Ltd (ICI) 1963–64; Asst Lectr in Econ., Univ. of Hull, 1964–65, Lectr, 1965–72. *Publications*: *contrib.* Jl Royal Stat. Soc., Manch. Sch. *Address*: Univ. of Salford, Salford M5 4WT.

Topsfield, Dr Leslie Thomas; Lecturer in Provençal and French, University of Cambridge, since 1958; *b* 1920; *m* 1943; two *s*. MA Cantab 1948, PhD Cantab 1951; Member: MHRA, Internat. Arthurian Soc., Soc. for French Studies, Soc. for Study of Med. Langs and Lit., Anglo-Norman Text Soc. Asst Lectr in Provençal and French, Cambridge, 1950–58. St Catharine's Coll., Cambridge: Fellow, 1953; Dir of Studies in Germanic Langs, 1953; Praelector, 1955; Domestic Bursar, 1960; Tutor, 1966. *Publications*: ed, The Year's Work in Modern Language Studies, vols XVII, XVIII, XIX, 1955–57; contrib. The Penguin Companion to Literature: European, 1969; Les Poésies du troubadour Raimon de Miraval, 1971; Troubadours and Love, 1975; *contrib.* FS, MAe, MLR, NMi. *Address*: St Catharine's College, Cambridge.

Tordoff, Prof. William; Professor of Government, Department of Government, University of Manchester, since 1971; *b* 1925; *m* 1951; two *d*. BA Cantab 1950, MA Cantab 1955; PhD London 1961; Mem., Political Studies Assoc., Mem., African Studies Assoc. Univ. of Ghana: Resident Tutor, Inst. of Extra-Mural Studies, 1950–58; Lectr and Sen. Lectr in Political Science, Dept of Econs, and Tutor and Actg Sen. Tutor, Commonwealth Hall, Legon, 1958–62; Univ. of Manchester: Ford Foundn Sen. Fellow in Govt, 1962–65, seconded as Sen. Lectr in Govt to Inst. of Public Admin., UC, Dar-es-Salaam, 1963–64; Lectr, Sen. Lectr and Reader in Govt, 1965–71, seconded as Prof. of Political Science, to Univ. of Zambia, 1966–68; Dir of Studies, Graduate Sch., Dept of Govt, 1970– . *Publications*: Ashanti under the Prempehs, 1965; Government and Politics in Tanzania, 1967; ed, Government and Politics in Zambia, 1974; *contrib.* Jl Admin. Overs., Jl Brit. Studies, Jl of Comm. Pol. Studies, Jl Develt Studies, Jl Mod. Afric. Studies, Pol. Studies. *Address*: Dept of Government, Univ. of Manchester, Dover Street, Manchester 13.

Torrance, Rev. James Bruce, MA, BD; Senior Lecturer in Christian Dogmatics, University of Edinburgh, since 1971; *b* 1923; *m* 1955; one *s* two *d*. MA Edinburgh 1947 (1st cl. Hons Philosophy), BS Edinburgh 1950 (Distinction). Lectr in Divinity and Dogmatics, in History of Christian Thought, Edinburgh Univ., 1961–71; Dir, Adult Christian Educn, Edinburgh Univ., 1964–71. Tutor, St Colm's Missionary Coll., Edinburgh, 1962–70. *Publications*: trans. Cullman, Early Christian Worship, 1953; contrib. to Essays in Christology for Karl Barth, 1955; *contrib.* Church Service Annual, Interpretation, Luth. W., Ref. W., Scot. Jl Theol. *Address*: New College, The Mound, Edinburgh EH1 2LX.

Torrance, Rev. Prof. Thomas Forsyth; Professor of Christian Dogmatics, University of Edinburgh, since 1952; *b* 1913; *m* 1947; two *s* one *d*. MA Edinburgh 1934, BD Edinburgh 1937, DrTheol Basel 1946, DLitt Edinburgh 1970; Pres., Academie Internat. Sci. Relig., 1965 (Mem., 1965–), Mem., Soc. Internat. Etude Philos. Mediév., 1970, Mem., Soc. Internat. Scot., Founder Mem., Soc. Study Theol., 1952, Mem., Scott. Ch Theol. Soc., 1946. Protopresbyter of Gk Orthodox Church (Patriarchate of Alexandria), 1973. Prof. of Systematic Theology, Auburn, NY, 1938–39; Prof. of Church History, Edinburgh Univ., 1950–52. Mem., Ch of Scot. Delegation for reunion discussions with C of E, 1952–59; Mem., Faith Order Commn, Wld Council of Chs, 1952–62; Founder, and Ed., with J. K. S. Reid, Scott. Jl Theol., 1948– . *Publications*: Doctrine of Grace in the Apostolic Fathers, 1949, 2nd edn 1958; Calvin's Doctrine of Man, 1949, 2nd edn 1957; Royal Priesthood, 1955, 2nd edn 1963; Kingdom and Church, 1956; The School of Faith, 1959; Conflict and Agreement in the Church, 1959–60; Karl Barth: An Introduction to His Early Theology, 1910–1930, 1962; Theology in Reconstruction, 1965; Theological Science, 1969, 2nd edn 1971; Space, Time and Incarnation, 1969; God and Rationality, 1971; Newton, Einstein and Scientific Theology, 1972; (with G. W. Bromiley) Barth: Church Dogmatics, vols I–IV, 1956–69; (with D. W. Torrance) Calvin's New Testament Commentaries, vols 1–12, 1959–72; Calvin's Tracts and Treatises, 1958; (with R. S. Wright) A Manual of Church Doctrine, 1960, 2nd edn 1965; *contrib.* Bijdragen, Evang. Theol., Evang. Qly, Jl Eccles. Hist., Jl Theol. Studies, Keryg. Dogma, Proc. Internat. Acad. Relig. Sci., Relig. Studies, Renov., Rev. Théol. Philos., Rev. Hist. Philos. Relig., Scott. Jl Theol., Theol. Today, Theol. Zeits., Verb. Caro. *Address*: New College, Mound Place, Edinburgh EH1 2LX.

Tosh, Michael G.; *see* Gearin-Tosh.

Towers, Brian, BA(Com), BSc(Econ); Lecturer in Economics, Department of Adult Education, University of Nottingham, since 1966; *b* 1936; *m* 1957; one *s* two *d*. BA (Com) Manchester 1957, Hon. BSc(Econ) London 1965. Mem., Royal Econ. Soc. Ed., Indust. Relat. Jl, 1970– . *Publications*: Markets and Prices, 1970; The New Bargainers, 1970; Bargaining for Change, 1972; *contrib.* Jl Indust. Relat., Relat. Indust. *Address*: Industrial Relations Unit, The Univ., University Park, Nottingham NG7 2RD.

Towler, Dr Robert Charles; Lecturer in Sociology, University of Leeds, since 1969; *b* 1942. BA Leeds 1964 (Psychol. and Sociol.), PhD Leeds 1970 (Sociol.). *Publication*: Homo Religiosus, 1974. *Address*: Univ. of Leeds, Leeds LS2 9JT.

Townend, Prof. Gavin Bernard, MA; Professor of Latin, University of Durham, since 1966; *b* 1919; *m* 1955; one *d*. BA Oxon 1942 (1st cl. Hon. Mods, 1st cl. Greats), MA Oxon 1945. Asst Lectr, then Lectr, and later Sen. Lectr in Classics, Univ. of Liverpool, 1946–66; Dean, Arts Fac., Durham, 1969–71. Mem., Council, Rom. Soc., 1962–65, 1969– ; Mem., Council Classical Assoc., 1972–75; Chm., Greece and Rome; Rev. Ed., Jl Rom. Studies. *Publications*: contrib. Cicero, ed Dorey, 1965; Lucretius, ed Dudley, 1965; Latin Biography, ed Dorey, 1967; *contrib.* Amer. Jl Philol., Class. Jl, Class. Qly, Hermes, Historia, Latomus, Greece Rome, Jl Rom. Studies. *Address*: Dept of Classics, Univ. of Durham, 38 North Bailey, Durham.

Townsend, Alan Robson; Reader and Director of North-East Area Study, Faculty of Social Sciences, University of Durham, since 1972; *b* 1939; *m* 1971. MA Cantab 1961 (Geography). Passed all examns, Town Plan. Inst., 1969. Mem., Reg. Studies Assoc., Sec. North. Br., 1971– ; Mem., Inst. Brit. Geogrs, 1969– . Asst Res. Off., Bd of Trade, Manchester, 1961–63; Res. Off., Glasgow, 1963–65; Town Planner, H. Wilson and L. Womersley, 1965–67; Lectr, Durham Univ., 1967–72. *Publications*: *contrib.* Town Plan. Rev. *Address*: 49 North Bailey, Univ. of Durham, Durham City.

Townsend, Prof. Peter Brereton; Professor of Sociology, University of Essex, since 1963; *b* 1928; *m* 1949; four *s*. BA Cantab 1950. Res. Fellow, LSE, 1957–60; Lectr in Social Admin, LSE, 1960–63. Pres. Psychiatric Rehabilitation Assoc., 1967– ; Chairman: Fabian Soc., 1965–66; Child Poverty Action Gp, 1969– ; Mem., UGC Social Studies Sub-Cttee, 1969–74. *Publications*: The Family Life of Old People, 1957; (with B. Abel-Smith and R. M. Titmuss) National Superannuation, 1957; (with C. Woodroffe) Nursing Homes in England and Wales, 1961; The Last Refuge, 1962; (with B. Abel-Smith) The Poor and the Poorest, 1965; (with D. Wedderburn) The Aged in the Welfare State, 1965; (with E. Shanas *et al*) Old People in Three Industrial Societies, 1968; (ed) The Concept of Poverty, 1970; (ed) Labour and Inequality, 1972; The Social Minority, 1973; Sociology and Social Policy, 1974. *Address*: Univ. of Essex, Wivenhoe Park, Colchester CO4 3SQ.

Townsin, Dr Robert Lewis; Senior Lecturer, Department of Naval Architecture and Shipbuilding, University of Newcastle upon Tyne, since 1969; *b* 1926; *m* 1950; two *s* two *d*. BSc (Hons) Dunelm 1949, PhD Dunelm 1958; CEng, FRINA, FIMarE. Mem. Coun-

cil, RINA. *Publications*: The Ship and Her Environment, 1973; *contrib.* Royal Photographic Soc., Trans NEC Inst., Trans RINA. *Address*: Dept. of Naval Architecture and Shipbuilding, Univ. of Newcastle upon Tyne, Newcastle upon Tyne NE1 7RU.

Toyne, Peter, BA; Lecturer in Geography, University of Exeter, since 1965; *b* 1939; *m* 1969; one *s*. BA Bristol 1962 (1st cl. Geog.). *Publications*: World Problems, 1970; Techniques in Human Geography, 1971; Recreation and Environment, 1974; Organisation, Location and Behaviour, 1974; *contrib.* Hormes Terres Nord. *Address*: Dept of Geography, Queen's Buildings, Univ. of Exeter, Exeter EX4 4QH.

Trainer, Prof. James, MA, PhD; Professor of German, University of Stirling, since 1969; *b* 1932; *m* 1958; two *s* one *d*. MA St Andrews 1955, PhD St Andrews 1958. Lectr, St Andrews Univ., 1958–67; Vis. Prof., Yale Univ., 1964–65; Lectr, Stirling Univ., 1967–68; Sen. Lectr, Stirling Univ., 1968–69. *Publications*: Ludwig Tieck: from Gothic to Romantic, 1964; ed, C. Reeve: Old English Baron, 1967; contrib. Cambridge Bibliography of English Literature; *contrib.* EG, Forum Mod. Lang. Studies, Germ. Life Lett., Mod. Lang. Notes, Mod. Lang. Qly, Mod. Lang. Rev., Mod. Langs, Yrs Wk Mod. Lang. Studies. *Address*: Dept of German, Univ. of Stirling, Stirling FK9 4LA.

Tranchell, Peter Andrew; University Lecturer in Music, Cambridge University, since 1952; *b* 1922. BA Cantab 1948 (1st cl. Music), MusB Cantab 1949 (with distinction), MA Cantab 1950. Mem., Composers Guild GB, Mem., ISM, Mem., PRS. Univ. Asst Lectr, Cambridge, 1950–52; Fellow, Gonville and Caius Coll., Cambridge, 1960. Sec., Univ. Fac. Bd of Music; Dir of Music Studies, sometime, totalling 8 years, for: Caius, Clare, Fitzwilliam, New Hall Colls; Dir of Music, since 1960, and Precentor, since 1962, Caius Coll.; Dom. Bursar, Caius Coll., 1963–67; Dir, Arts Theatre, Cambridge, for about 10 years; *Publications*: var. compositions (some listed in Grove: Dictionary of Music and Musicians); *contrib.* Bks Today, Camb. Rev., Music Lett. *Address*: Caius College, Cambridge.

Trapp, Joseph Burney; Librarian, Warburg Institute, University of London, since 1966; *b* 1925; *m* 1953; two *s*. MA New Zealand 1947. Jun. Lectr, Victoria Univ. Wellington, 1950–51; Asst Lectr, Univ. Reading, 1951–53; Asst Librarian, Warburg Inst., 1953–66; Vis. Reader, Univ. Reading, 1965; Vis. Prof., Univ. Toronto, 1969. *Publications*: ed, Oxford Anthology of English Literature, Medieval vol., 1973; ed jtly, Oxford–Warburg Studies, etc; *contrib.* Jl Warburg and Courtauld Insts. *Address*: Univ. of London, Warburg Institute, Woburn Square, WC1H 0AB.

Trasler, Prof. Gordon Blair; Professor of Psychology, University of Southampton, since 1964; Dean of Social Sciences since 1970; *b* 1929; *m* 1953. BSc London 1952, PhD London 1955, MA Exeter 1960; FBPsS 1963. Tutorial Asst, Univ. Coll., Exeter,

1952–53; Res. Schol., Univ. Coll., Exeter, 1953–55; Lectr in Social Psychology, Univ. of Southampton, 1957–64. Psychologist, Prison Commn, 1955–57; Mem., Adv. Council on the Penal System, 1968– ; Mem., Psychol. Cttee, SSRC, 1969– ; Mem., Council, Brit. Psychol. Soc., 1965–67. *Publications*: In Place of Parents, 1960; The Explanation of Criminality, 1962; The Shaping of Social Behaviour (inaug. lectr), 1967; contrib. The Formative Years, 1968; contrib. Handbook of Abnormal Psychology, 2nd edn 1972; *contrib*. Adv. Sci., Brit. Jl Criminol, Educnl Res., Ment. Hlth, Int. Jl Offender Therapy and Comp. Criminol. *Address*: Dept of Psychology, The Univ., Southampton SO9 5NH.

Travers, David Thomas; Lecturer in Politics, University of Lancaster, since 1968; *b* 1942; *m* 1972. BA Wales 1963 (Internat. Pol.). Asst Lectr, Lancaster, 1965–68; Vis. Asst Prof., Univ. of Waterloo, Canada, 1969; Vis. Schol., Inst. War and Peace Studies, Columbia Univ., 1971. *Address*: Dept of Politics, Univ. of Lancaster, Bailrigg, Lancaster LA1 4YW.

Trebilcock, Ronald Clive, MA; University Lecturer in Modern Economic History, University of Cambridge, since 1969; *b* 1942; *m* 1964; two *d*. BA Cantab 1964 (1st cl. Hist.), MA Cantab 1967; FRHistS. Staff Fellow, Pembroke Coll., Cambridge, 1965–67; Univ. Asst Lectr, Pembroke Coll., Cambridge, 1967–69. *Publications*: *contrib*. Econ. Hist. Rev., Jl Contemp. Hist. *Address*: Pembroke College, Cambridge.

Treble, Dr James Henry, PhD; Lecturer in Economic History, University of Strathclyde, since 1966. BA Leeds 1959 (1st cl. Hist.), PhD Leeds 1969. Res. Asst Dept of Economic Hist., Univ. of Birmingham, 1962–64; Asst Lectr, Dept of Economic Hist., Univ. of Strathclyde, 1964–66. *Publications*: contrib. Popular Movements 1830–50, ed J. T. Ward, 1970; Robert Owen: Prince of Cotton Spinners, ed J. Butt, 1971; Studies in Working Class Housing, ed S. D. Chapman, 1971; The Victorians and Social Protest, ed I. F. Clarke and J. Butt, 1973; *contrib*. Internat. Rev. Soc. Hist., Jl Eccles. Hist., North. Hist., Scott. Jl Lab. Hist., Trans Hist., Jl Educn Admin and Hist. *Address*: Dept of Economic History, Univ. of Strathclyde, Glasgow G1 1XW.

Tregenza, Peter Roy, BArch, MBdgSc, PhD, RIBA; Lecturer in Architecture, University of Nottingham, since 1966; *b* 1939; *m* 1961; three *s*. BArch Dunelm 1963, MBdgSc Sydney 1966, PhD Nottingham, 1972; Architect. Mem., Royal Inst. Brit. Archit. Lectr, Sydney Univ., 1965–66. Mem., Council, Illum. Eng. Soc., 1969–71. *Publications*: *contrib*. Archit. Sci. Rev., Bldg Sci. *Address*: Dept of Architecture, Nottingham Univ., University Park, Nottingham NG7 2RD.

Treherne, Arthur Alan; Lecturer in Philosophy, University of Keele, since 1967; *b* 1938; *m* 1962; two *d*. BA Keele 1961 (1st cl. Maths and Philos.). Lectr in Mathematics,

708

Univ. of Glasgow, 1962–67. *Address*: Dept of Philosophy, Univ. of Keele, Keele, Staffordshire ST5 5BG.

Treisman, Dr Anne Marie, MA, DPhil; University Lecturer, Department of Psychology, Oxford, since 1968; Fellow, St Anne's College, Oxford, since 1967; *b* 1935; *m* 1960; two *s* two *d*. BA Cantab: Mod. and Med. Langs 1956, Natural Sciences (Psychology Part II) 1957, DPhil Oxon 1961 (Psychology). Scientific Staff, MRC Psycholinguistics Res. Unit, Oxford, 1962–66; Vis. Scientist, Bell Telephone Laboratories, New Jersey, 1966–67. *Publications*: *contrib*. Psychol. Rev., Attention and Performance, Qly Jl Exper. Psychol., Jl verb. Learn. verb. Behav., Perception and Psychophysics. *Address*: Dept of Experimental Psychology, South Parks Road, Oxford OX1 3PS.

Treisman, Dr Michel; Lecturer in Psychology, Department of Experimental Psychology, University of Oxford, and Fellow of New College, since 1972; *b* 1929; *m* 1960; two *s* two *d*. MB, BCh Witwatersrand 1952, BA Oxon 1956 (1st cl. Hons), MA Oxon 1960, DPhil Oxon 1962; Member: BMA, BPS, EPS. Jun. Lectr in Exper. Psychol., Oxford, 1959–63; Lectr in Psychol., Oxford, 1963–67; Mem. Techn. Staff, Bell Labs, Murray Hill, NJ 1966–67; Prof. of Psychol., Univ. Reading, 1967–72. *Publications*: *contrib*. Acta Psychologica, Brit. Jl Psychol., B. Jl Math. and Stat. Psychol., Brit. Jl Phil. Sci, Jl Acoust. Soc. Amer., Nature, Perception and Psychophysics, Psychol. Bull., Psychol. Rev., Psychol. Monog., Qly Jl Exp. Psychol., Psychometrika. *Address*: Dept of Experimental Psychology, South Parks Road, Oxford OX1 3PS.

Treitel, Guenter Heinz, BCL, MA; All Souls Reader in English Law, Oxford University, since 1964; Fellow of Magdalen College, since 1954; *b* 1928; *m* 1957; two *s*. BA Oxon 1949 (1st cl. Jurisprudence), BCL Oxon 1951 (1st cl.). Barrister-at-Law, Gray's Inn, 1952. Asst Lectr, LSE, 1951; Lectr, Univ. Coll., Oxford, 1953–54; Vis. Lectr, Univ. of Chicago Law Sch., 1963–64; Vis. Prof., Univ. of Chicago Law Sch., 1968–69, 1971–72. *Publications*: The Law of Contract, 3rd edn 1970; ed (with others), Dicey and Morris, Conflict of Laws, 8th edn 1967; ed (with others), Chitty on Contracts, 23rd edn 1968; *contrib*. Law Qly Rev., Modern Law Rev. *Address*: Magdalen College, Oxford.

Trejo, Enrique E. C.; *see* Caracciolo-Trejo.

Trenaman, Nancy Kathleen, (Mrs M. S. Trenaman); Principal, St Anne's College, Oxford, since 1966; *b* 1919; *m* 1967. BA Oxon 1938 (1st cl. Hons English Lang. and Lit.), MA Oxon 1945. Bd of Trade, 1941–51; Asst Sec., Ministry of Materials, 1951–54; Counsellor, Brit. Embassy, Washington, 1951–53; Bd of Trade, 1954–66; Under-Sec., 1962–66. Mem., Commn on the Constitution, 1969–73. *Address*: St Anne's College, Oxford.

Trend, The Rt Hon. Lord; Burke St John Trend, PC, GCB, CVO; Rector of Lincoln

College, Oxford, since 1973; *b* 1914; *m* 1949; two *s* one *d*. BA Oxon 1936 (1st cl. Hon. Mods 1934, 1st cl. Lit. Hum. 1936), MA Oxon 1956; Hon. DCL Oxon 1969; Hon. LLD St Andrews 1974; Hon. Fellow, Merton Coll., Oxford, 1964. Home Civil Service Admin. Class, 1936; Min. of Educn, 1936; transferred to HM Treasury, 1937; Asst Private Sec. to Chancellor of Exchequer, 1939–41, Principal Private Sec., 1945–49; Under Sec., HM Treasury, 1949–55; Office of the Lord Privy Seal, 1955–56; Dep. Sec. of the Cabinet, 1956–59; Third Sec., HM Treasury, 1959–60, Second Sec., 1960–62; Sec. of the Cabinet, 1963–73. *Address*: Lincoln College, Oxford.

Tress, Ronald Charles, CBE, DSc; Master of Birkbeck College, University of London, since 1968; *b* 1915; *m* 1942; one *s* two *d*. BScEcon London, DSc Bristol. Res. Fellow, Manchester Univ., 1937–38; Asst Lectr, UC Exeter, 1938–41; Econ. Asst, War Cabinet Offices, 1941–45; Econ. Adviser, Cabinet Secretariat, 1945–47; Reader, London Univ., 1947–51; Prof. of Polit. Economy, Bristol Univ., 1951–68. Man. Ed., London and Cambridge Econ. Service, 1949–51; Develt Comr, 1959– ; Chm., SW Econ. Planning Council, 1965–68; Mem., Council, Royal Econ. Soc., 1960–70. Mem., Reorganisation Commn for Pigs and Bacon, 1955–56; Mem., Fiscal Commns, Nigeria, 1957–58; Mem., Economic and Fiscal Commn, E Africa, 1960; Mem., Fiscal Commn, Uganda, 1962; Chm., Fiscal Commn, Kenya, 1962–63; Mem., Deptl Cttee on Rating of Charities, 1958; Mem., Financial Enquiry, Aden Colony, 1959; Mem., Nat. Incomes Commn, 1963–65. *Publications*: *contrib*. Econ. Jl, Economica, LCES Bull., etc. *Address*: Birkbeck College, Malet Street, WC1E 7HX.

Trethowan, Prof. William Henry; Professor of Psychiatry, University of Birmingham, since 1962; *b* 1917; *m* 1941; one *s* two *d*. MA, MB, BChir Cambridge 1942; MRCS, LRCP 1943, MRCP 1948, DPM 1951, FRACP 1961, FRCP 1963, FRCPsych 1971, FANZCP (Hon.) 1965. Hon. Teaching Fellow, Harvard Univ., 1951; Lectr in Psychiatry, Univ. of Manchester, 1951–53; Sen. Lectr, Univ. of Manchester, 1953–56; Prof. of Psychiatry, Univ. of Sydney, 1956–62. Dean, Fac. of Medicine, Univ. of Birmingham, 1968–74; Mem., Birm. Reg. Hosp. Bd, 1964– ; Chm., Standing Ment. Hlth Adv. Cttee, Dept of Hlth and Soc. Security; Mem., Standing Ment. Hlth Adv. Cttee, Central Hlth Services Council; Hon. Cnsltnt Psychiatrist, Utd Birm. Hosps. *Publications*: (with Anderson) Psychiatry, 1967; (with Enoch and Barker) Uncommon Psychiatric Syndromes, 1967; *contrib*. Acta Psychiat. Scand., Austral. Med. Jl, Brit. Jl Psychiat., Brit. Med. Jl, Jl Nerv. Ment. Dis., Jl Psycho-som. Res., Lancet. *Address*: Dept of Psychiatry, Queen Elizabeth Hospital, Birmingham B15 2TH.

Trevor-Roper, Prof. Hugh Redwald; Regius Professor of Modern History, Oxford University, since 1957; *b* 1914; *m* 1954. BA Oxon 1936, MA Oxon 1939. Res. Fellow, Merton Coll., Oxford, 1937–39; Student of Christ Church, Oxford, 1946–57; Censor,

1947–52. *Publications*: Archbishop Laud, 1940; The Last Days of Hitler, 1947; The Gentry, 1540–1640, 1953; ed, Hitler's Table Talk, 1953; ed (with J. A. W. Bennett), The Poems of Richard Corbett, 1955; Historical Essays, 1957; ed, Hitler's War Directives 1939–45, 1964; ed, Essays in British History Presented to Sir Keith Feiling, 1964; The Rise of Christian Europe, 1965; Religion, the Reformation and Social Change, 1967; ed, The Age of Expansion, 1968; The Philby Affair, 1968. *Address*: Oriel College, Oxford.

Trice, John Edward; Lecturer in Law, University College of Wales, Aberystwyth, since 1968; *b* 1941. BA Cantab 1963, LLB Cantab 1964, MA Cantab 1966; Mem. Soc. of Public Teachers of Law, 1967. Asst Lectr in Law, UCW Aberystwyth, 1966–68. Chm. of Law Dept Bd, UCW Abersytwyth, 1970–72; Staff Examr, London Univ. External LLB Exam., 1972. *Publications*: *contrib*. Cambrian Law Rev., Conveyancer and Property Lawyer, Criminal Law Rev., Jl Planning and Environment Law, Law Qly Rev., Mod. Law Rev., Public Law, New Law Jl, Jl Soc. Public Teachers of Law. *Address*: Law Dept, Univ. College of Wales, Aberystwyth, Penglais, Llandinam Building, Aberystwyth.

Trickett, Mabel Rachel; Principal, St Hugh's College, Oxford, since 1973; *b* 1923. BA Oxon (1st cl. Hons English), MA Oxon. Lectr in English, Univ. Hull, 1946–54; Fellow and Tutor in English, and Univ. Lectr, St Hugh's Coll. Oxford, 1954–73. *Publications*: The Honest Muse, 1967; *Novels*: The Return Home; The Course of Love; Point of Honour; A Changing Place; The Elders; A Visit to Timon; *contrib*. Rev. of English Studies, Yale Rev. TLS, Essays and Studies. *Address*: St Hugh's College, Oxford.

Trigg, Dr Roger Hugh, MA, DPhil; Lecturer in Philosophy, University of Warwick, since 1966; *b* 1941; *m* 1972. BA Oxon 1964, MA Oxon 1967, DPhil Oxon 1968. *Publications*: Pain and Emotion, 1970; Reason and Commitment, 1973; *contrib*. Mind. *Address*: Dept of Philosophy, Univ. of Warwick, Coventry, CV4 7AL.

Trim, John Leslie Melville, MA; Director of the Department of Linguistics, University of Cambridge, since 1970; *b* 1924; *m* 1948; four *d*. BA London 1949 (1st cl. German), MA Cantab 1959; Mem., Nat. Council for Mod. Langs. Asst Lectr, Univ. Coll., London, 1949–52; Lectr, Univ. Coll., London, 1952–58; Univ. Lectr in Phonetics, Cambridge, 1958–64, in Linguistics, 1964–70; Hd of Dept of Linguistics, 1966–70; Fellow, Selwyn Coll., 1963; Hon. Organiser, 2nd Internat. Cong. Appl. Ling., 1969; Dir, Council of Europe Project for European unit/credit scheme in mod. langs for adult learners. *Publications*: English Pronunciation Illustrated, 1965; co-ed, In Honour of Daniel Jones, 1964; co-ed, Applications of Linguistics, 1971; *contrib*. ELT, Lang. Speech, MPhon, Speech, Word. *Address*: Dept of Linguistics, Univ. of Cambridge, Sidgwick Avenue, Cambridge.

Triseliotis, Dr John Paul; Senior Lecturer, Department of Social Administration, University of Edinburgh, since 1965; *b* 1929; *m*; one *s* one *d*. DipSoc London 1959, Certif. Mental Health Edinburgh 1960, PhD Edinburgh 1969; Mem., Brit. Assoc. of Social Workers. Mem. Central Council for Educn and Trng in Social Work, 1971. *Publications*: Evaluation of Adoption Policy and Practice, 1970; Social Work with Coloured Immigrants and their Families, 1972; In Search of Origins, 1973; *contrib*. Case Conference, Brit. Jl Psychiatric Social Work, Child Adoption, Brit. Jl Social Work, Social Work Today. *Address*: Adam Fergusson Building, Univ. of Edinburgh, George Square, Edinburgh EH8 9LL.

Tristram, P. M.; *see* Moody, P. M.

Troeller, Ruth Reta, BA, MSc(Econ); Senior Lecturer in International Economics, University of Surrey, since 1969; *b* 1928; *m* 1946; one *s* one *d*. BA London 1956 (Philos.), MSc(Econ) London 1962. Lectr, Univ. of Surrey, 1963–69; Vis. Prof. Santiago de Compostela, 1972; N Illinois Univ., 1972–73; Hd of Sub-dept of Internat. Econ., Univ. of Surrey, 1966–70. *Publications*: *contrib*. Jl Wld Trade Law, Irish Banking Rev., Rev. du Marché Commun. *Address*: Dept of Economics, Univ. of Surrey, Guildford, Surrey GU2 5XH.

Tropp, Prof. Asher, BSc(Econ), PhD; Professor of Sociology, University of Surrey, since 1967; *b* 1925; *m* 1947; one *s*. BSc(Econ) London 1951, PhD London 1954. Mem., Brit. Sociol. Assoc., Mem., Amer. Sociol. Assoc. Jun. Res. Off., LSE, 1953–54; Asst Lectr, then Lectr, and later Reader, LSE, 1954–67; Vis. Prof., Univ. of Puerto Rico, 1961–62; Vis. Prof., Univ. of Texas, 1966–67; Vis. Prof., UCLA, 1971. *Publications*: The Schoolteachers, 1957; *contrib*. Ybk Educn, Rev. Mex. Sociol., Hum. Relat., Soc. Econ. Studies. *Address*: Univ. of Surrey, Guildford, Surrey GU2 5XH.

Trotman-Dickenson, Dr Aubrey Fiennes; Principal, University of Wales Institute of Science and Technology, Cardiff, since 1968; *b* 1926; *m* 1953; two *s* one *d*. MA Oxon 1951, BSc Oxon 1948, PhD Manchester 1952, DSc Edinburgh 1958. Fellow, National Res. Council, Ottawa, 1948–50; Asst Lectr, ICI Fellow, Manchester Univ., 1950–53; E. I. du Pont de Nemours, Wilmington, USA, 1953–54; Lectr, Edinburgh Univ., 1954–60; Professor, Univ. Coll. of Wales, Aberystwyth, 1960–68. Mem., Welsh Council, 1971– . *Publications*: Gas Kinetics, 1955; Free Radicals, 1959; Tables of Bimolecular Gas Reactions, 1967; contribs to learned jls. *Address*: UWIST, Cardiff CF1 3NU.

Truman, Dr Ronald William, MA, DPhil; University Lecturer in Spanish, University of Oxford, since 1963, and Student and Tutor of Christ Church, Oxford, since 1964; *b* 1934. BA Oxon 1957 (1st cl. Spanish and French), MA Oxon 1961, DPhil Oxon 1964. Asst Lectr, then Lectr, Birkbeck Coll., London, 1959–63; Lectr, Christ Church and Brasenose Coll., 1963; Jun. Censor,

Christ Church, 1967; Sen. Censor, Christ Church, 1969–72. Lt Cdr, RNR, 1966– ; Gov., Dean Close Sch., Cheltenham, 1970– ; Registrar, Pusey Hse, Oxford, 1970– . *Publications*: contrib. The Continental Renaissance, ed, A. J. Krailsheimer, 1971; *contrib*. Bull. Hispan. Studies, Mod. Lang. Rev., Times Lit. Supp., Jl Theol. Studies. *Address*: Christ Church, Oxford.

Trump, Dr David Hilary, MA, PhD, FSA; Staff Tutor in Archaeology, Board of Extra-Mural Studies, University of Cambridge, since 1964; *b* 1931; *m* 1961; three *s*. BA Cantab 1954 (1st cl. Archaeol. and Anthropol.), MA Cantab 1956, PhD Cantab 1957; FSA. Res. Fellow, Pembroke Coll., Cambridge, 1956–58; Curator of Archaeol., Nat. Museum, Malta, 1958–63. Mem., Council, Prehist. Soc., 1970–73. *Publications*: Central and Southern Italy before Rome, 1966; Skorba and the Prehistory of Malta, 1966; (with W. Bray) A Dictionary of Archaeology, 1970, pbk edn 1972; Malta: An Archaeological Guide, 1972; *contrib*. Antiqu., Bull. Paletnol. Ital., Papers Brit. Sch. Rome, Proc. Prehist. Soc., Rept Mus. Dept Malta. *Address*: Board of Extra-Mural Studies, Univ. of Cambridge, Mill Lane, Cambridge CB2 1RY.

Tuck, Prof. John Philip, MA; Professor of Education, University of Newcastle upon Tyne, since 1963; *b* 1911; *m* 1936; two *s*. BA Cantab 1933, CertEd 1934, MA Cantab 1937; FRSA; Hon. FCST. Lectr in Educn, King's Coll., Newcastle upon Tyne, Univ. of Durham, 1946–48; Prof., Univ. of Durham, 1948–63. Sch. teacher, 1935–40, 1946; Infantry Off., and AEC Off., 1940–46. *Publications*: *contrib*. Brit. Jl Educnl Studies, Durh. Res. Rev. *Address*: School of Education, Univ. of Newcastle upon Tyne, Newcastle upon Tyne NE1 7RU.

Tuck, Dr Patrick James Noel, MA, DPhil; Lecturer, School of History, University of Liverpool, since 1966; *b* 1942. BA Oxon 1964, MA Oxon 1970, DPhil Oxon 1971. *Address*: School of History, Univ. of Liverpool, 8 Abercromby Square, Liverpool.

Tuck, Prof. Ronald Humphrey; Head of Department of Agricultural Economics, University of Reading, and Provincial Agricultural Economist (Reading Province), since 1965, now Department of Agricultural Economics and Management; Dean, Faculty of Agriculture and Food, University of Reading, since 1971; *b* 1921; *m* 1942; one *s* two *d*. MA Oxon 1947. Res. Economist, Reading Univ., 1947–49, Lectr, 1949–62, Reader, 1962–65. *Publications*: An Essay on the Economic Theory of Rank, 1954; An Introduction to the Principles of Agricultural Economics, 1961 (trans. Italian 1970); *contrib*. Jl Agric. Econs, Econ. Jl. *Address*: Univ. of Reading, Whiteknights, Reading, Berks RG6 2AH.

Tucker, Henry Frank Greenslade, MA; Senior Lecturer in Adult Education, since 1968, and Senior Resident Tutor in Gloucestershire, Department of Extra-Mural Studies, University of Bristol, since 1970;

710

b 1912; *m* 1943; two *d*. BA Bristol 1933 (1st cl. Mod. Hist.), MA Bristol 1936 (Colonial Hist.), DipEd Bristol 1934. Res. Tutor in Gloucestershire, Bristol Univ., 1938–70. Mem., Council, Europ. Atlantic Mvmnt, Vice-Chm., Europ. Assoc. Teachers (UK Sect.), 1971– ; Gov., N Glos. Coll. Technol., 1968– ; Chosen Hill Sch., Gloucester, 1968– ; Gov., Cirencester Sch., 1972– . *Address*: Dept of Extra-Mural Studies, Univ. of Bristol, Bristol.

Tucker, Peter Edwin, BLitt, MA, ALA; University Librarian, University of Warwick, since 1963; *b* 1926; *m* 1957; one *s* one *d*. BA Oxon 1951, BLitt Oxon 1954, MA Oxon 1955; ALA 1956. Assistant Librarian: Liverpool, 1953; Leeds, 1954; Sub-Librarian, Inst. of Educn, Leeds, 1958. University of Warwick: Member: Senate, 1965– ; Council, 1969–71. *Publications*: contrib. Essays on Malory, ed, J. A. W. Bennett, 1963; *contrib.* Jl Doc., Mod. Lang. Studies. *Address*: Univ. Library, Univ of Warwick, Coventry CV4 7AL.

Tudor, Andrew Frank; Lecturer, Department of Sociology, University of York, since 1970; *b* 1942; *m* 1967; one *s*. BA (Hons) Leeds 1965. Lectr: Univ. of Essex, 1966–70. Associate Editor, Screen. *Publications*: Theories of Film, 1974; Image and Influence: Studies in the Sociology of Film, 1974; *contrib.* Internat. Jl of Comparative Sociology, Screen, Sociology. *Address*: Dept of Sociology, University of York, Heslington, York YO1 5DD.

Tudor, Henry, BA; Senior Lecturer in Politics, Durham University, since 1973; *b* 1937. BA Harvard 1959 (Hist. and Lit., magna cum laude). Res. Asst, LSE, 1962–63; Lectr, Politics, Univ. of Durham, 1963–73. Assoc. Ed., Transatl. Rev., 1961–63. Resid. Tutor, St Cuthbert's Soc., Univ. of Durham, 1966–72. *Publications*: Political Myth, 1973. *Address*: Dept of Politics, 23–26 Old Elvet, Durham City.

Tunkel, Victor; Senior Lecturer, Faculty of Laws, Queen Mary College, University of London, since 1973; *b* 1933; *m* 1959; one *s* one *d*. LLB Nottingham 1954; Barrister, Gray's Inn 1956. Asst Lectr, Univ. Bristol, 1960–62, Lectr, 1962–67; Lectr, Queen Mary Coll., 1967–73. Sec., Selden Soc., 1968– . *Address*: Faculty of Laws, Queen Mary College, Mile End Road, E1 4NS.

Tunstall, Prof. C. Jeremy; Professor of Sociology, Department of Social Science, City University, since 1974; *b* 1934; *m* 1967; two *d*. BA Cantab 1958, MA Cantab. Research Fellow, Manchester Univ., 1961; Research Officer, LSE, 1962–65; Fellow, Univ. Essex, 1965–69; Sen. Lectr in Sociology, Open Univ., 1969–74. *Publications*: The Fishermen, 1962; The Advertising Man, 1964; Old and Alone, 1966; The Westminster Lobby Correspondents, 1970; ed, Media Sociology, 1970; Journalists at Work, 1971; (with K. Thompson) ed, Sociological Perspectives 1971; ed, The Open University Opens, 1974. *Address*: Dept of Social Science and Humanities, The City Univ. St John Street, EC1V 4PB.

Turk, Dr Christopher Cyril Ross, MA, DPhil; Lecturer in English, University of Wales Institute of Science and Technology, since 1966; *b* 1942; *m* 1968; one *s* one *d*. BA Cantab 1964 (English Lit.), DPhil Sussex 1970 (English Lit.). *Address*: Dept of English, Univ. of Wales Institute of Science and Technology, Cathays Park, Cardiff CF1 3NU.

Turk, Dr Frank Archibald; Reader in Natural History and Oriental Art, Department of Extra-Mural Studies, University of Exeter, since 1972; *b* 1911; *m* 1932 and 1947; one *s* one *d*. Dott. di. Filosofia Turin 1936; FRAS, Mem. Assoc. British Orientalists, Mem. Japan Soc. Part-time Tutor, Univ. Exeter, 1936; Tutor Corn. Adult Ed. Jt Comm., 1960; Lectr, Univ. Exeter, 1968–72. *Publications*: Japanese Objets d'Art, 1962; The Prints of Japan, 1966; *contrib.* Apollo, Coin and Medal Bull., Connoisseur, Netsuke, Numismatic Notes, Oriental Art. *Address*: Dept of Extra-Mural Studies, Univ. of Exeter, Gandy Street, Exeter.

Turner, Arthur Sydney; Lecturer in Modern History, University of Dundee, since 1968; *b* 1941; *m* 1965; one *s* one *d*. BA Oxon 1962 (1st cl. Mod. History), MA Oxon 1969, Dip. Business Management, Manchester Business Sch. 1965. *Address*: Dept of Modern History, Univ. of Dundee, Dundee DD1 4HN.

Turner, Barry Arthur; Lecturer, Department of Sociology, Exeter University, since 1970; *b* 1937; *m* 1961; two *d*. BSocSc Birmingham 1966; Mem., Brit. Sociol. Assoc. Res. Officer, then Sen. Res. Officer, Industrial Sociology Unit, Imperial Coll., 1966–69; Sen. Res. Fellow, Centre for Utilisation of Social Science Res., Loughborough Univ. of Technol., 1969–70. *Publications*: Exploring the Industrial Subculture, 1971; Industrialism, 1974; *contrib.* Admin. Sci. Qly. *Address*: Dept of Sociology, Exeter Univ., Exeter EX4 4QJ.

Turner, David, MA; Lecturer in German, University of Hull, since 1963; *b* 1937; *m* 1960; two *s* one *d*. BA London 1959, MA London 1966. Lektor, Freie Univ., Berlin, 1961–63. *Publications*: *contrib.* Font. Blätt., Forum Mod. Lang. Studies, Germ. Life Lett. *Address*: Dept of German, The Univ., Hull HU6 7RX.

Turner, Prof. Eric Gardner, FBA; Professor of Papyrology, University College, London, since 1950; *b* 1911; *m* 1940; one *s* one *d*. BA Oxon 1934 (1st cl. Class. Mods and Lit. Hum.), Hon. DPhil et Lettres Brussels 1965; FBA. Asst, Aberdeen Univ., 1936; Lectr, Aberdeen Univ., 1938–48; Reader, London Univ., 1948–50; first Dir, Inst. of Classical Studies, London Univ., 1953–63; Vis. Mem., Inst. for Advanced Study, Princeton, 1961, 1964, 1968. Pres., Internat. Assoc. of Papyrologists; Vice-Pres., Hellenic Soc. (Pres., 1968–71); Vice-Pres., Roman Soc., Vice-Pres., Union Académique Internationale, 1971–74; Chm., Organising Cttee, 3rd Internat. Congress of Classical Studies, London, 1959; Chm., Cttee, Egypt Exploration Soc.; Jt Editor, Graeco-Roman pubns.

Publications: Catalogue of Greek Papyri in University of Aberdeen, 1939; (with C. H. Roberts) Catalogue of Greek Papyri in John Rylands Library, vol. IV, 1951; The Hibeh Papyri, Part II, 1955; (jtly) The Oxyrhynchus Papyri Part XXIV, 1957, Part XXV, 1959, Part XXVII, 1962, Part XXXI, 1966, Part XXXIII, 1968, Part XXXVIII, 1971, Part XLI, 1973; (jtly) The Abbinæus Papyri, 1962; New Fragments of the Misoumenos of Menander, 1965; Greek Papyri, an Introduction, 1968; Greek Manuscripts of the Ancient World, 1970; trans. Menander: The Girl from Samos, 1972; *contrib.* learned jls. *Address*: Univ. College, Gower Street, WC1E 6BT.

Turner, Gerard L'Estrange, MA, MSc, FInstP; Senior Assistant Curator, Museum of the History of Science, University of Oxford, since 1964; *b* 1926; *m* 1956; one *s* one *d*. BSc London 1949, MSc London 1959, MA Oxon 1965; FInstP 1968, FRMS 1964. Lectr, London Univ., 1959–61; Vis. Fellow, Clare Hall, Cambridge, 1974; Royal Microscop. Soc.: Quekett Lectr, 1971; Council Mem., 1965– ; Hon. Sec., 1969–73; Pres.-Elect, 1973; Mem., Council, Brit. Soc. Hist. Science, 1967– ; Hon. Treas., Brit. Soc. Hist. Science, 1969– ; Project Hd, Information Retrieval Gp, Museums Assoc., 1970–73. *Publications*: ed, Historical Aspects of Microscopy, 1967; (with T. H. Levere) Martinus van Marum: Life and Work, vol. IV, 1973; Descriptive Catalogue of Van Marum's Scientific Instruments in Teyler's Museum, 1973; *contrib.* Ann. Sci., Hist. Sci., Jl Royal Microscop. Soc., N. R. Royal Soc., Orient. Art, Physis. *Address*: Linacre College, Oxford.

Turner, Dr Harold Walter; Lecturer in Religious Studies, Department of Religious Studies, University of Aberdeen, since 1973; *b* 1911; *m* 1939; one *s* three *d*. BA NZ 1933, MA NZ 1935, BD Melb. Coll. Div. 1943, DD Melb. Coll. Div. 1963; Member: African Studies Assoc. UK, Internat. Assoc. Hist. of Religions, Internat. Assoc. for Mission Studies, Deutsche Gesellschaft für Missionswissenschaft. UC Sierra Leone, 1955–62; Univ. Nigeria, 1963–66; Univ. Leicester, 1966–70; Emory Univ. 1970–72. Chaplain to Students, Dunedin, 1941–47; Warden, Arana Hall, Univ. Otago, 1943–51; Minister, Parish of Opoho, Dunedin, 1951–54. *Publications*: Halls of Residence, 1953; Profile through Preaching, 1965; (with R. C. Mitchell) Bibliography of Modern African Religious Movements, 1966, 2nd edn 1971; African Independent Church, 2 vols, 1967; Living Tribal Religions, 1971, 2nd edn 1973; *contrib.* Cahiers des Religions Africaines, Compar. Studies in Society and History, Hibbert Jl, Internat. Review of Mission, Jl African History, Jl Religion in Africa, Numen, Religion, Scottish Jl Theology, Zeitschrift für Religion- und Geistesgeschichte. *Address*: Dept of Religious Studies, Univ. of Aberdeen, Aberdeen AB9 2UB.

Turner, Prof. Herbert Arthur (Frederick), BScEcon, PhD; Montague Burton Professor of Industrial Relations, University of Cambridge, since 1963; Fellow of Churchill College; *b* 1919. BScEcon London 1939, PhD

Manchester 1960, MA Cantab 1963. Lectr, Manchester Univ., 1950; Sen. Lectr, Manchester Univ., 1959; Montague Burton Prof. of Industrial Relations, Leeds Univ., 1961–63. Mem., TUC Res. and Econ. Dept, 1944; Asst Educn Sec., TUC, 1947; Mem., NBPI, 1967–71; Sometime Adv. to Govts of Congo, UAR, Tanzania, Fiji, Papua-New Guinea, Iran, Zambia and other African states; Chm., Commn on Pay and Incomes Policies, E African Community, 1973–74. *Publications*: Trade Union Growth, Structure and Policy, 1962; Wages: the Problems for Underdeveloped Countries, 1965; Prices, Wages and Incomes Policies, 1966; Labour Relations in the Motor Industry, 1967; Is Britain Really Strike-Prone?, 1969; Do Trade Unions Cause Inflation?, 1972; *contrib.* various reports of ILO, monographs, papers etc. *Address*: Churchill College, Cambridge.

Turner, Paul Digby Lowry; University Lecturer in English Literature, Oxford University, since 1964; *b* 1917; *m* 1940; two *d*. Classical Tripos Pt I Cambridge 1937, English Tripos Pt I Cambridge 1939, MA Cantab 1944, MA Oxford 1964. Asst Lectr in English, King's Coll., London, 1946–48; Univ. Asst Lectr in English, Cambridge, 1948–53; Lectr in English, Univ. Coll., London, 1955–61, 1962–63; Prof. of English, Ankara Univ., 1961–62, 1963–64; Fellow, Linacre Coll., Oxford, 1964– . *Publications*: trans., J. Barclay: Euphormio: Satyricon, 1954; Longus: Daphnis and Chloe, 1956, 2nd edn 1968; Apollonius of Tyre, 1956; The Ephesian Story, 1957; Lucian: True history and Lucius or the Ass, 1958; E. T. A. Hoffmann: The King's Bride, 1959; Fouqué: Undine, 1960; Lucian: Satirical Sketches, 1961, 2nd edn 1968; ed, P. Holland: Pliny's Natural History, 1962; ed, T. North: Plutarch's Lives, 1963; trans., More: Utopia, 1965, 6th edn 1971; Ovid: Technique of Love and Remedies for Love, 1968; ed, Swift: Gulliver's Travels, 1970; ed, Browning: Men and Women, 1972; *contrib.* Camb. Jl, Class. Qly, Engl. Studies, Greece Rome, Engl. Germ. Philol., Notes Queries, Novel, Rev. Engl. Studies, Vict. Studies. *Address*: Linacre College, Oxford.

Turner, William Henry Keith; Senior Lecturer in Geography, University of Dundee, since 1968; *b* 1920; *m* 1949; one *d*. BA Wales 1947 (1st cl. Geog.), DipEd and Practical Teaching Wales 1948 (1st cl.), MA Wales 1953. Lectr, Univ. Coll., Dundee, Univ. of St Andrews, 1948–68. *Publications*: *contrib.* Scott. Geog. Mag., Trans Inst. Brit. Geogrs. *Address*: Dept of Geography, The Univ., Dundee DD1 4HN.

Turnock, Dr David; Lecturer in Geography, University of Leicester, since 1969; *b* 1938; *m* 1965; two *s*. BA Cantab 1961 (1st cl. Geog.), MA Cantab 1964, PhD Cantab 1964. Mem., Inst. Brit. Geogrs. Asst Lectr, Univ. of Aberdeen, 1964–66; Lectr, Univ. of Aberdeen, 1966–69. *Publications*: Patterns of Highland development, 1970; contrib. North East Scotland: a survey of its development potential, ed M. Gaskin, 1969; Handbook of the Soviet Union and Eastern Europe, ed G. Schopflin, 1970; Scotland's Highlands and

Islands, 1974; An Economic Geography of Romania, 1974; *contrib.* Area, Ann. Assoc. Amer. Geogrs, Geog. Ann., Geog., Scott. Geogl Mag., Scott. Studies, Tijds. Econ. Soc. Geog., Trans Inst. Brit. Geogrs. *Address*: Dept of Geography, The Univ., Leicester LE1 7RH.

Turpin, Kenneth Charlton; Provost, Oriel College, Oxford, since 1957; Pro-Vice-Chancellor, Oxford University, 1964–66, and since 1969 (Vice-Chancellor, 1966–69); Member, Hebdomadal Council, since 1959; *b* 1915. HM Treasury, 1940–43; Asst Private Sec. to C. R. Attlee, Lord Pres., and Dep. Prime Minister, 1943–45; 2nd Asst Registrar, Univ. Registry, Oxford, 1945–47; Sec. of Faculties, Univ. of Oxford, 1947–57; Professorial Fellow, Oriel Coll., 1948. Hon. Fellow, Trinity Coll., Dublin, 1968. *Address*: Provost's Lodgings, Oriel College, Oxford.

Turton, Brian John; Lecturer, Department of Geography, Keele University, since 1961; *b* 1934; *m* 1964; one *s* one *d*. BSc Nottingham 1956 (1st cl.), PhD Nottingham 1961. Mem., Inst. Brit. Geogrs. Demonstrator, Univ. of Keele, 1960–61. *Publications*: *contrib.* Town Plan. Rev., Trans Inst. Brit. Geogrs, Transp. Hist. *Address*: Dept of Geography, Keele Univ., Newcastle, Staffordshire ST5 5BG.

Turull, Dr Antoni; Lecturer, Department of Spanish and Portuguese, Bristol University, since 1964; *b* 1933; *m* 1959; two *s* one *d*. DPhil Athenaeum Angelicum Rome 1955, Lic Fil Let Barcelona 1958. Asst Lectr, Univ. of Glasgow, 1959–61. *Publications*: A l'oreig del capvespre, 1971; *contrib.* Gran Enciclopèdia Catalana. *Address*: Dept of Spanish and Portuguese, 87 Woodland Road, Bristol BS8 1US.

Turville-Petre, Prof. Edward Oswald Gabriel, FBA; Vigfússon Reader in Ancient Icelandic Literature and Antiquities, Oxford University, since 1941, with title of Professor since 1953; *b* 1908; *m* 1943; three *s*. MA Oxford 1937, BLitt Oxford 1937; FBA 1973; Corresp. Mem., Icelandic Acad. Science, 1959, Hon. DPh Iceland 1961, Kt of Falcon (Ice.) 1956, Comdr 1963. Lectr, Univ. of Iceland, 1936–38; Hon. Lectr in Modern Icelandic, Univ. of Leeds, 1935–50; Vis. Prof., Univ. of Melbourne, 1965. *Publications*: Viga-Glúms Saga, 1940, 2nd edn 1960; The Heroic Age of Scandinavia, 1951; Origins of Icelandic Literature, 1953, 2nd edn 1967; Hervarar Saga, 1956; Myth and Religion of the North, 1964; Nine Norse Studies, 1972; *contrib.* Mediev. Studies, Med. Æv., Saga-Bk Vik. Soc., Skírnir, Studia ISL, etc. *Address*: Christ Church, Oxford.

Turville-Petre, Joan Elizabeth; Lecturer in English Language, Somerville College, Oxford University, since 1946; *b* 1911; *m* 1943; three *s*. BA Oxon 1933 (2nd cl. English), DipCompPhilol Oxon 1935, BLitt Oxon 1935, MA Oxon 1938. Asst Lectr in English Lang., Somerville Coll., 1936–41; Fellow and Tutor, Somerville Coll., 1941–46; Res. Fellow, Somerville Coll., 1966–73 (Hon. Fellow, 1973–). *Publications*: contrib. The Beowulf Poet, ed D. K. Fry, 1968; *contrib.* Arkiv

Nord. Filol., Jl Engl. Germ. Philol., Saga Bk Vik. Soc., Tradit. *Address*: Somerville College, Oxford.

Twine, Sydney Walter; Senior Lecturer, Department of Mathematics, City University, London, since 1969; *b* 1911; *m* 1944. BSc Bristol 1933, DipEd Bristol 1934, MSc Bristol 1935, BScEcon London 1944, MScEcon London 1947; FSS, Mem., London Math. Soc., Mem., Math. Assoc. Lectr in Mathematics, City Univ., 1966–69. *Publications*: *contrib.* Jl of the London Math. Soc. *Address*: Dept of Mathematics, City Univ., St John Street, EC1V 4PB.

Twining, Prof. William Lawrence; Professor of Law, University of Warwick, since 1972; *b* 1934; *m* 1957; one *s* one *d*. BA Oxon 1955 (1st cl. Jurisprudence), MA Oxon 1960, JD Chicago 1958 (cum laude). Lectr, Univ. of Khartoum, 1958–61; Sen. Lectr, Univ. Coll., Dar es Salaam, 1961–65; Prof. of Jurisprudence, Belfast, 1965–72; Vis. Lectr, Chicago, 1964; Sen. Fellow, Yale Law Sch., 1965; Vis. Prof., Univ. of Pennsylvania, 1971. Ed., Sudan Law Jl Reps, 1959–61; Mem., Kaya Council Legal Educn, 1962–65; IUC Cnsltnt on Legal Educn, Botswana, Lesotho and Swaziland, 1971; Mem., Bentham Cttee, 1972– ; Cttee on Legal Educn in N Ireland, 1972–73. *Publications*: The Place of Customary Law in the National Legal Systems of E Africa, 1964; The Karl Llewellyn Papers, 1968; Karl Llewellyn and the Realist Movement, 1973; *contrib.* Law Qly Rev., Mod. Law Rev., Jl Afr. Law, Jl Soc. Public Teachers Law, etc. *Address*: School of Law, Univ. of Warwick, Coventry CV4 7AL.

Twiss, Brian Charles; Senior Lecturer and Assistant Director of Post Experience Programmes, Management Centre, University of Bradford, since 1968; *b* 1926; *m* 1958; one *s* one *d*. MA Cantab 1947, MSc Cranfield Inst. Tech.; CEng, AFRAeS. Cranfield Inst. of Technology: Sen. Res. Fellow, 1965–66; Mutual Security Fund Lectr in Management, 1966–68. Dir of Sen. Exec. and Bradford Exec. Programmes, 1968–73. *Publications*: Organisational Problems in European Manufacture, vols 1 and 2, 1973; Managing Technological Innovation, 1974; *contrib.* Long Range Planning Jl, Production Engineer. *Address*: Univ. of Bradford, Management Centre, Heaton Mount, Keighley Road, Bradford BD9 4JU.

Twitchett, Prof. Denis Crispin, FBA; Professor of Chinese, University of Cambridge, since 1968; *b* 1925; *m* 1956; two *s*. MA Cantab 1954, PhD Cantab 1955; FBA 1967. Lectr, London Univ., 1954–56; Lectr, Cambridge Univ., 1956–60; Prof. of Chinese, SOAS, London Univ., 1960–68. *Publications*: The Financial Administration under the T'ang Dynasty, 1963, 2nd edn 1971. *Address*: St Catharine's College, Cambridge.

Twyman, Dr Michael Loton, BA, PhD, MSIA; Senior Lecturer in Typography, University of Reading, since 1971; *b* 1934; *m* 1958; two *s* one *d*. BA Reading 1957 (1st cl. Fine Art), PhD Reading 1966; MSTD, MIOP and Graphic Communication. Asst

Lectr, Univ. of Reading, 1959–62; Lectr, Univ. of Reading, 1962–71. Chm., Working Party on Typographic Teaching, 1967– ; Mem., Cttee, Print. Hist. Soc., 1966– ; Assoc. ed., Jl Print. Hist. Soc., 1971– ; Graphic Des. Panel, Nat. Council Dips Art Des., 1971– . *Publications*: (with W. Rollinson) John Soulby, Printer, Ulverston, 1966; Lithography 1800–1850: the techniques of drawing on stone in England and France and their application in works of topography, 1970; Printing 1770–1970: an illustrated history of its development and uses in England, 1970; *contrib*. Jl Print. Hist. Soc., Penrose Ann. *Address*: Dept of Typography and Graphic Communication, Univ. of Reading, 2 Earley Gate, Whiteknights, Reading.

Tyacke, Nicholas Robert Noel; Lecturer in History, University College London, since 1968; *b* 1941; *m* 1971. BA Oxon 1962, MA Oxon 1970, DPhil Oxon 1970. Tutor, Dept of History, 1970– . Sen. Mem., Commonwealth Hall, 1965–68. *Address*: Dept of History, Univ. College London, Gower Street, WC1E 6BT.

Tydeman, William Marcus; Senior Lecturer, Department of English, University College of North Wales, since 1970; *b* 1935; *m* 1961; two *d*. BA Oxon 1959 (1st cl. English), MA Oxon 1969, BLitt Oxon 1969. Asst Lectr, Univ. Coll. of N Wales, 1961–64; Lectr, Univ. Coll. of N Wales, 1964–70. *Publications*: ed, English Poetry, 1400–1580, 1970; jt editor: Six Christmas Plays, 1971; Casebook: Wordsworth, Lyrical Ballads, 1972; Casebook: Coleridge, The Ancient Mariner and other Poems, 1973. *Address*: Dept of English, Univ. College of North Wales, Bangor LL57 2DG.

Tyler, Edward Lawson Griffin; Lecturer, Faculty of Law, University of Liverpool, since 1971; *b* 1937; *m* 1961; three *s* one *d*. BA Oxon 1961, MA Oxon 1966; Barrister, Lincoln's Inn and Northern Circuit. Tutor (pt-time), Liverpool Univ., 1965–66; Lectr and Tutor (pt-time), Liverpool Univ., 1966–71. *Publications*: ed, Fisher and Lightwood: Law of Mortgage, 8th edn 1969; Family Provision, 1971; (with E. G. Bowman) The Elements of Conveyancing, 1972; co-ed., Crossley Vaines: Personal Property, 5th edn 1973; Cases and Statutes on Land Law, 1974; *contrib*. Conv. (NS), New Law Jl. *Address*: Faculty of Law, Univ. of Liverpool, Liverpool L69 3BX.

Tyler, Godfrey John, MA, MSc(Agric); University Lecturer in Agricultural Economics, Oxford University, since 1968; *b* 1929; *m* 1961; three *d*. BSc(Agric) London 1954, MSc(Agric) London 1959, MA Oxon 1969. Mem., Agric. Econ. Soc., Internat. Assoc. Agric. Econ. Res. Asst, Wye Coll., London Univ., 1954–56; Asst Lectr, London Univ., 1957–60; Lectr, London Univ., 1960–61; Econ. Res. Off., NSW Govt, 1961–63; Lectr, Bristol Univ., 1963–68; Fellow, St Cross Coll., Oxford, 1970. *Publications*: *contrib*. Farm Econ., Jl Agric. Econ., Rev. Mktg Agric. Econ., Oxford Agrarian Studies. *Address*: St Cross College, Oxford.

714

Tyler, John William; Lecturer in Education and Tutor for Overseas Students, University of Bristol, since 1963; *b* 1924; *m* 1966; one *s* one *d*. BSc London 1950 (Hons Anthrop.); FRAI, Mem. Assoc. Social Anthropologists, Mem. African Studies Assoc. of UK. Research Fellow, Makerere Coll. Uganda, 1950–53; Research Fellow, Univ. Bristol, 1963–68. Educn Officer, Uganda, 1956–63. *Publications*: (with J. La Fontaine) The Zinza, in, East African Chiefs, ed, A. I. Richards, 1960; Education and National Identity, in, Tradition and Transition in East Africa, ed, P. M. Gulliver, 1969. *Address*: Univ. of Bristol School of Education, Bristol BS8 1JA.

Tyler, Prof. William Edwin, MA, FLA; Professor, and Head of Department of Librarianship, University of Strathclyde, since 1964 and Dean of School of Arts and Social Studies, since 1972; *b* 1920; *m* 1944; two *s* one *d*. MA Strathclyde 1967 (Econ. Hist.); FLA 1950. Dep. City Libr., Salford, 1949–50; Mem., Council, Libr. Assoc., 1962–67; Council, Scott. Libr. Assoc., 1951– ; Pres., 1970; Mem., Scott. Educn Dept Working Party on Standards for Public Librs Scotl., 1968–69. *Publications*: *contrib*. Libr. Assoc., Rec., Libr. Wld, Scott. Libr. Assoc. News. *Address*: Dept of Librarianship, Univ. of Strathclyde, Livingstone Tower, Richmond Street, Glasgow G1 1XH.

Tymms, Prof. Ralph Vincent, MA; Professor of German, Royal Holloway College, University of London, since 1956, Vice-Principal, since 1969; *b* 1913. BA Oxon 1934 (1st cl. German), MA Oxon 1941. Asst Lectr, Manchester Univ., 1936–45; Lectr, Manchester Univ., 1945–48; Reader, London Univ., 1948–56; Hd of Dept of German, Royal Holloway Coll., 1948. Intell. Corps, 1941–45 (Major 1945). *Publications*: Doubles in Literary Psychology, 1949; German Romantic Literature, 1955; *contrib*. Germ. Life Lett., Mod. Lang. Rev. *Address*: Royal Holloway College, Egham, Surrey TW20 0EX.

Tyson, John Colin, MA; Lecturer in Education, University of Newcastle upon Tyne, since 1963; *b* 1923; *m* 1949; one *d*. BA Sheffield 1948 (Hons Hist.), DipEd Sheffield 1949, MA Birmingham 1960. Gen. Ed., Univ. of Newcastle upon Tyne School of Educn Archive Teaching Units, 1968– ; Pres., NE Counties Br., Hist. Assoc., 1973– . *Publications*: King Edward VI Elementary Schools (Victoria County History of Warwickshire, vol. VII), 1964; (with L. Turnbull) Coals from Newcastle, 1968; (with G. W. Hogg) Popular Education 1700–1870, 1969; (with J. P. Tuck) The Origins and Development of the Training of Teachers in the University of Newcastle upon Tyne, 1971. *Address*: School of Education, Univ. of Newcastle upon Tyne, Newcastle upon Tyne NE1 7RU.

Tyson, Robert Edward; Lecturer in Economic History, University of Aberdeen, since 1964; *b* 1937; *m* 1963; one *s* one *d*. BA Manchester 1961, MA Manchester 1962; Mem. Econ. History Soc. Res. Asst, Dept of Econ. History, Univ. Glasgow, 1962–63.

Adviser of Studies, Univ. Aberdeen, 1970. *Publications*: Scottish Investment in American Railways, in, Studies in Scottish Business History, ed, P. L. Payne, 1967; The Cotton Industry, in, The Development of British Industry and Foreign Competition 1875–1914, ed, D. H. Aldcroft, 1968; contrib. Dictionary of Labour Biography, ed, Joyce M. Bellamy and J. Saville, vol. 1, 1972, vol. 2, 1974. *Address*: Dept of Economic History, King's College, Univ. of Aberdeen, Aberdeen.

Tyzack, Charles Richard Peregrine; Lecturer in English, University College, Cardiff, since 1966; *b* 1937. BA Oxon 1961, BLitt Oxon 1963, MA Oxon 1965. Asst Lectr, St David's Coll., Lampeter, 1964–66. *Address*: Dept of English, Univ. College, Cardiff CF1 1XL.

Tzoannos, John; Lecturer in Econometrics, University of Aston Management Centre, since 1972; *b* 1944. BA Hons Manchester 1966 (Econ.), MSc Southampton 1968 (Soc. Sci.), PhD Birmingham 1974; FSS. Lectr, Grad. Centre for Management Studies, Birmingham, 1968–72. *Publications*: contrib. Applied Econs, Jl Business Finance. *Address*: Univ. of Aston Management Centre, 36 Wake Green Road, Birmingham B13 9PD.

U

Uche, Dr U. U.; Lecturer, Department of Law, School of Oriental and African Studies, University of London, since 1967; *b* 1934; *m* 1964; two *s* two *d*. LLB London 1962, LLM London 1964, PhD London 1967; Grade I Teacher 1957, Barrister-at-Law Gray's Inn 1965. Prof. and Head of Dept of Public Law, Univ. of Nairobi, 1972–74. Chm., Res. and Curriculum Cttee, Univ. of Nairobi, 1972–74. *Publications*: Contractual Obligations in Ghana and Nigeria, 1971; contrib. Annual Survey of African Law, 1967–72; *contrib*. African Studies Bull. (UK), Jl of African Law, Univ. of Ghana Law Jl. *Address*: Dept of Law, School of Oriental and African Studies, Malet Street, WC1E 7HX.

Uglow, Euan; Lecturer, Slade School of Fine Art, University College, London, since 1961; *b* 1932. Slade Dip. 1953; Mem. London Group. Mem. Fine Art Adv. Panel, Nat. Council for Diplomas in Art and Design. *Address*: Slade School of Fine Art, Univ. College, Gower Street, WC1E 6BT.

Uldall, Elizabeth T.; Senior Lecturer in Phonetics, Linguistics Department, Edinburgh University, since 1965; *b* 1913; *m* 1939; one *d*. BA Columbia 1935 (Engl. Lit.), MA London 1939 (Comp. Philol. [Phonetics]); Mem., Philol. Soc., Internat. Phonet. Assoc. Asst, English Dept, Barnard Coll., Columbia Univ., 1936–37; Asst, Phonetics Dept, Univ. Coll., London, 1938–39; Lectr, American Univ., Cairo, 1941–43; Lectr, Univ. of Tucumán, Argentina, 1948; Lectr, Edinburgh Univ., 1949–65. *Publications*: Amerika-Eigo Na Oncho (The Intonation of American English), 1958; contrib. In Honour of Daniel

Jones, 1964; Form and Substance, 1971; Proc., 8th Int. Cong. Ling., 1958; Proc., 4th Int. Cong. Phon. Sci., 1962; Proc., 5th Int. Cong. Phon. Sci., 1965; Proc. Stockholm Speech Communication Seminar, 1962; *contrib*. Arch. Ling., IJAL, L and S, MF, Rev. Lab. Fonét. Exper. *Address*: Linguistics Dept, Adam Ferguson Building, Edinburgh Univ., Edinburgh EH8 9LL.

Ullendorff, Prof. Edward, FBA; Professor of Ethiopian Studies, School of Oriental and African Studies, University of London, since 1964; *b* 1920; *m* 1943. MA Jerusalem and Manchester, DPhil Oxon, Hon. DLitt St Andrews; FBA, FRAS. Res. Off. and Libr., Oxford Univ. Inst. of Col. Studies, 1948–49; Lectr, later Reader, in Semitic Languages, St Andrews Univ., 1950–59; Prof. of Semitic Languages, Manchester Univ., 1959–64; Jt Ed., Jl Semitic Studies, 1961–64; Chm., Ed. Bd, Bull. SOAS, 1968– ; Schweich Lecturer, Brit. Acad., 1967. War service, Ethiopia, 1941–46; Pres., Soc. OT Studies, 1971; Vice-Pres., Anglo-Ethiop. Soc., Chm., Assoc. Brit. Orient., 1963–64. Haile Selassie Internat. Prize for Ethiopian Studies, 1972. *Publications*: The Definite Article in the Semitic Languages, 1942; Exploration and Study of Ethiopia, 1945; Catalogue of Ethiopic MSS in the Bodleian Library, 1951; The Semitic Languages of Ethiopia, 1955; The Ethiopians, 1960, 3rd edn 1973; Catalogue of Ethiopic MSS in Cambridge University Library, 1961; (jtly) Introduction to Comparative Grammar of Semitic Languages, 1964; The Challenge of Amharic, 1965; An Amharic Chrestomathy, 1965; Ethiopia and the Bible, 1968; Comparative Semitics (Current Trends in Linguistics), 1970; etc; *contrib*. Bull. SOAS, Jl Royal Asiat. Soc., Jl Semitic Studies, Orientalia, etc. *Address*: School of Oriental and African Studies, London Univ., WC1E 7HP.

Ullmann, Prof. Stephen, MA, PhD, DLitt; Professor of the Romance Languages, University of Oxford, and Fellow of Trinity College, Oxford, since 1968; *b* 1914; *m* 1939; one *s* two *d*. PhD Budapest 1936, DLitt Glasgow 1949, MA Oxon 1968. Pres., Philol. Soc., 1970– ; Pres., Mod. Lang. Assoc., 1973; Hon. Fellow, Inst. Lingu., 1968– (Diamond Jubilee Medal, 1972); Mem., Soc. Fr. Studies, MHRA. Lectr, then Sen. Lectr, Glasgow Univ., 1946–53; Prof., Leeds Univ., 1953–68; Vis. Prof., Toronto Univ., 1964, 1966; Vis. Prof., Univ. of Michigan, 1965; Vis. Prof., ANU, 1974. Jt Ed., Archiv. Lingu., 1949–64; Mem., Arts Sub-Cttee, UGC, 1969– ; Mem., Advisory Bd, Archiv. Lingu., Mem., Advisory Council, Fr. Studies, Mem., Advisory Bd, Lang. Style, Mem., Ed. Bd, Romance Philol., Mem., Ed. Bd, Style; Mem., Council, Soc. Lingu. Romane; Gen. Ed., Lang. Style series. *Publications*: Words and their Use, 1951 (Japanese trans.); The Principles of Semantics, 1951, 2nd edn 1963 (German and Japanese trans.); Style in the French Novel, 1957; The Image in the Modern French Novel, 1960; Semantics, 1962 (Japanese, Italian, Portuguese, German and Spanish trans.); Language and Style, 1964 (Italian, German and Spanish trans.); Précis de sémantique française, 1952, 2nd edn 1959 (Spanish trans.); Meaning and Style, 1973; *contrib.* Archiv. Lingu., Fr. Studies, Mod. Lang. Rev., Mod. Langs, var. foreign jls. *Address*: Trinity College, Oxford.

Ullmann, Prof. Walter, JUD, LittD, FBA; Professor of Medieval History, University of Cambridge, since 1972; *b* 1910; *m* 1940; two *s*. JUD Innsbruck 1933, MA Cantab 1949, LittD Cantab 1956; FRHistS, FBA; Hon. Dr rer. pol. Innsbruck 1972. Lectr in Medieval Hist., Univ. of Leeds, 1947–49; Univ. Lectr in Medieval Hist., Cambridge, 1949–57; Reader in Medieval Ecclesiastical Institutions, Cambridge, 1957–65; Prof. of Humanities, Johns Hopkins Univ., 1964–65; Prof. Medieval Ecclesiastical History, Cambridge, 1965–72; Maitland Memorial Lectr, Cambridge, 1948–49; Birkbeck Lectr, Cambridge, 1968–69; Vis. Prof., Tübingen, Munich, 1973. Ed., Camb. Studies in Medieval Life and Thought, 1969– . Pres., Eccles. Hist. Soc., 1969–70; Co-ed., Päpste und Papsttum, 1970– . *Publications*: The Medieval Idea of Law, 1946; The Origins of the Great Schism, 1948; Medieval Papalism, 1949; The Growth of Papal Government in the Middle Ages, 1955, 4th edn 1970, German edn 1960; Principles of Government and Politics in the Middle Ages, 1961, 3rd edn 1974, Spanish edn 1971, Italian edn 1972; A History of Political Ideas in the Middle Ages, 1965, rev. edn 1970; Individual and Society in the Middle Ages, 1966, Japanese edn 1972, German edn 1973, Italian edn 1974; The Carolingian Renaissance, 1969; A Short History of the Papacy in the Middle Ages, 1972, 2nd edn 1974; ed, Liber regie capelle (Henry Bradshaw Soc.), 1961; Papst und König im Mittelalter, 1967; The Future of Medieval History, 1973; *contrib.* Ann. Storia Ammin., Ann Storia d.dir., Atti Accurs., Camb. Hist. Jl, Cath. Hist. Rev., Citeaux, EHR, Ephemerides iur. can., Europa Dir. Rom., Hist. Jb, Hist. Zeits, Jl Eccles. Hist., Jl Theol. Studies, Juridical Rev., Law Quart. Rev., Misc. Hist. Pontif., Rec. Soc. J. Bodin, Rev. Bénédict., Sav. Zeits, Sett. Spol., Rev. Hist. Droit, S Afric. Law Jl, Specul. Hist., Studi Bart., Studi Greg., Studia Grat., Studia Patrist., Studies Ch Hist., Trans R. Hist. Soc., Virginia Jl of Internat. Law, Yorks Arch. Jl, etc. *Address*: Trinity College, Cambridge CB2 1TQ.

Unwin, David John; Lecturer, Department of Geography, University of Leicester, since 1973; *b* 1943; *m* 1968. BSc London 1965 (Special), MPhil London 1970; FRMetS, Mem. Inst. Brit. Geogrs. Lectr, UCW, Aberystwyth, 1967–73. *Publications*: *contrib.* Area, Jl Hydrology, Jl Glaciology, Trans Inst. Brit. Geogrs. *Address*: Dept of Geography, University Road, Leicester LE1 7RH.

Unwin, Derick James, BSc, MA; Senior Lecturer in Education, New University of Ulster, since 1968; *b* 1931; *m* 1st 1958, 2nd 1970; one *s* four *d*. BSc Leeds 1956, MA Loughborough 1966; FRSS. Res. Asst, Loughborough Univ., 1963–65. Ed., Progr. Learn. Educnl Technol., 1971– ; Vice-Pres., Assoc. Prog. Learn. Educnl Technol., 1965– . *Publications*: Programmed Learning

716

in the Schools, 1965, 2nd edn 1971, Danish edn 1969; The Computer in Education, 1968; Media and Methods, 1969; *contrib.* Brit. Jl Educnl Studies, Educnl Rev., Educnl Technol. *Address*: The Education Centre, New Univ. of Ulster, Coleraine, Co. Londonderry BT52 1SA.

Upton, Anthony Frederick; Senior Lecturer, Department of Modern History, St Andrews University, since 1966; *b* 1929; *m* 1951; three *s*. BA Oxon 1951 (1st cl. Hist.), AM Duke 1953 (Hist.); FRHistS. Asst Lectr, Leeds Univ., 1953–56; Lectr, St Andrews Univ., 1956–66. *Publications*: Sir Arthur Ingram, 1961; Finland in Crisis, 1964, Finnish trans., Välirauha, 1966; Kommunismi Suomessa, 1970, British edn (The Communist parties of Scandinavia and Finland), 1973. *Address*: Dept of Modern History, St Salvator's College, St Andrews, Fife KY16 9PH.

Upton, Martin; Lecturer in Agricultural Economics, University of Reading, since 1966; *b* 1933; *m* 1964; three *s* one *d*. BSc Reading 1957 (Agric.), PGDip. Farm Management Leeds 1958, MSc Reading 1963; Mem. Agric. Econs Soc. Research Agriculturalist, Reading, 1957–59; Lectr, Univ. Ibadan, 1959–65; Lectr, QUB, 1965–66. *Publications*: (with Q. B. O. Anthonio) Farming as a Business, 1965, 2nd edn 1970; Farm Management in Africa, 1973; *contrib.* Jl Agric. Econs. *Address*: Dept of Agricultural Economics, TOB 4, Earley Gate, Whiteknights Road, Reading RG6 2AH.

Ure, Colin S.; *see* Seymour-Ure.

Urmson, James Opie, MC, MA; Fellow of Corpus Christi College, Oxford University, and Tutor in Philosophy, since 1959; *b* 1915; *m* 1940; one *d*. BA Oxon 1938 (1st cl. Lit. Hum.), MA Oxon 1944. Fellow by Examination, Magdalen Coll., Oxford, 1939; Student of Christ Church, Oxford, 1945–55; Prof. of Philosophy, Univ. of St Andrews, 1955–59; Vis. Prof., Univ. of Michigan, 1960, 1965–66, 1969. *Publications*: Philosophical Analysis, 1956; ed, Encyclopaedia of Western Philosophy, 1960; Emotive Theory of Ethics, 1968; *contrib.* Mind, Proc. Aristot. Soc. *Address*: Corpus Christi College, Oxford.

Urquhart, Prof. Donald John, CBE; External Professor, Department of Library and Information Studies, University of Loughborough, and Hon. Lecturer, Postgraduate School of Librarianship and Information Science, University of Sheffield, since 1973; *b* 1909; *m* 1939; two *s*. BSc Sheffield 1931, PhD Sheffield 1937; Hon. DSc Heriot-Watt, Salford, Sheffield, 1973; FLA. Dir, Nat. Lending Library, until 1973; Dir-Gen., British Library Lending Div., 1973–74. Pres. Library Assoc., 1972; Chm. Standing Conf. of Nat. and University Libraries, 1968–70. *Address*: Dept of Librarianship, Univ. of Loughborough, Loughborough LE11 3TU.

Urquhart, Roderick Mackenzie, OBE, MA; Secretary and Registrar, University of Southampton, since 1966; *b* 1917; *m* 1942;

three *d.* MA St Andrews 1939; FSAScot 1965. Univ. Sheffield: Asst Bursar, 1950–52; Dep. Bursar, 1952; Bursar, 1952–66. Colonial Audit Service, 1940–50. Mem. Area Health Authority (T) for Hampshire, 1973; FSSU Exec., 1953– ; USS Adv. Cttee, 1974– ; Mem. numerous inter-University Cttees incl. those connected with Non-Teaching Staffs, 1953– . *Publication*: Scottish Burgh and County Heraldry, 1973. *Address*: Univ. of Southampton, Highfield, Southampton SO9 5NH.

Urry, Prof. Sydney Allandale, BSc(Eng), CEng, AFRAeS; Professor, Division of Building Technology, Brunel University (also teaches Operational Research), since 1971; *b* 1925; *m* 1947; two *s* one *d.* BSc(Eng) London 1945; CEng, AFRAeS. Dir. of Industrial Training, Brunel Univ., 1964–71; Goldsmith's Travelling Fellow, 1965. *Publications*: Solution of Problems in Strength of Materials, 1953, 2nd edn 1957, rev. edn 1960, Asia edn 1962, French edn 1966, SI metric edn 1974; Solution of Problems in Aerodynamics, 1956; Solution of Problems in Applied Heat and Thermodynamics, 1962; *contrib.* Jl Royal Aero. Soc., Jl Inst. Aero. Sci. *Address*: Division of Building Technology, Brunel Univ., Uxbridge, Middlesex UB8 3TH.

Urry, Dr William George; Reader in Medieval Western Palaeography, History Department, Oxford University, since 1969; Fellow of St Edmund Hall, Oxford University; *b* 1913; *m* 1947; one *s* one *d.* BA London 1935 (Gen., Engl., Fr., Latin), BA London 1939 (Hons Hist.), PhD London 1956, MA Oxon (by decree) 1969; FSA 1955, FRHistS 1958. Pt-time Lectr in History, Univ. of Kent at Canterbury, 1966–69; Vis. Fellow, All Souls Coll., Oxford, 1968. War service, 1940–46 (Lieut. RA, later Royal E Kent Regt); Asst Libr.-Archivist, Canterbury Cath., 1946–48; Keeper, Cath. and Corpn Archives, Canterbury, 1948–69. *Publications*: Canterbury under the Angevin Kings, 1967; *contrib.* Ann. Normandie, Archaeol. Cant., Spicil. Becc., Times Lit. Supp. *Address*: St Edmund Hall, Oxford OX1 4AR.

Urwin, Derek William; Lecturer in Politics, Strathclyde University, since 1965; *b* 1939; *m* 1965; two *s.* BA Keele 1962 (1st cl. English and Politics), MA(Econ) Manchester 1963. Mem., Pol. Studies Assoc. Asst Lectr, Strathclyde Univ., 1963–65; Vis. Res. Fellow, Yale Univ., 1969–70; Docent in Comparative Politics, Univ. of Bergen, 1972. *Publications*: (jtly) Scottish Political Behaviour, 1966; Western Europe since 1945, 1968, 2nd edn 1972; *contrib.* Comp. Pol. Studies, Pol. Studies, Scott. Hist. Rev. *Address*: Dept of Politics, Univ. of Strathclyde, George Street, Glasgow G1 1XW.

Usher, Gwilym Arthur; Senior Lecturer in History, University College of North Wales, since 1966; *b* 1923; *m* 1947; two *s* one *d.* BA Wales 1947 (1st cl. Hist.), MA Wales 1954. Res. Fellow, Inst. of Historical Res., 1948–49; Lectr in Medieval Hist., Univ. of St Andrews, 1949–52; Lectr, Univ. Coll. of N Wales, 1952–66; Sen. Lectr-in-Charge, Dip. Course

in Archive Admin., 1965; Vis. Prof., Wilmington Coll., Ohio, Vis. Prof., UCLA, 1963–64. RN, 1942–45. *Publications*: Gwysaney and Owston: a History of the Family of Davies-Cooke, 1964; *contrib.* Bull. Bd Celt. Studies, Nat. Libr. Wales Jl, Trans Anglesey Antiqu. Soc., Trans Denbighs. Hist. Soc., Trans Royal Hist. Soc. *Address*: Dept of History, Univ. College of North Wales, Bangor LL57 2DG.

Usher, Dr Stephen, MA, PhD; Senior Lecturer in Classics, Royal Holloway College; London University, since 1974 (Lecturer, 1960–74); *b* 1931; *m* 1959; two *s.* BA Wales 1951, MA Wales 1953, PhD London 1955. Mem., Class. Assoc., Mem., Hellen. Soc. Lectr in Classics, Victoria Univ., Wellington, NZ, 1957–60. Sec., Bd of Studies in Classics, London Univ., 1967–70. *Publications*: The Historians of Greece and Rome, 1969, pbk edn 1970, American edn 1970; ed, Dionysius: Critical Essays (Loeb Classical Library) (forthcoming); *contrib.* Amer. Jl Philol., Class. Rev., Eranos, Jl Hellen. Studies. *Address*: Royal Holloway College, Egham Hill, Egham, Surrey TW20 0EX.

Ussher, Dr Robert Glenn; Reader in Greek and Latin, New University of Ulster, since 1973 (Senior Lecturer, 1968–73); *b* 1927; *m* 1954. BA Dublin 1949, MA Dublin 1959, PhD Belfast 1967. Asst Lectr in Greek and Latin, Magee Univ. Coll., Londonderry, 1949–53; Lectr in Greek and Latin, Magee Univ. Coll., Londonderry, 1953–68. Mem., Council, Hellen. Soc., 1970–73. *Publications*: The Characters of Theophrastus, 1960; Aristophanes Ecclesiazusae, 1972; *contrib.* Class. Philol., Eranos, Greece Rome, Hermes, etc. *Address*: New Univ. of Ulster, Coleraine, Co. Londonderry BT52 1SA.

Uzzell, Peter Stanley; Lecturer in Education, School of Education, University of Exeter, since 1964; *b* 1931; *m* 1962; one *s* one *d.* BSc Bristol 1955, Certif. Ed., Bristol 1956; ARIC 1955. *Publications*: Aspects of Isomerism, 1971. *Address*: School of Education, Univ. of Exeter, Exeter EX4 4JZ.

V

Vaines, (James) Crossley; Senior Lecturer in Law, University of Liverpool, since 1958; *b* 1916; *m* 1951. LLB Liverpool 1939 (1st cl.), LLM Liverpool 1941; Barrister, Gray's Inn and Northern Circuit 1942. Lecturer in Law, Liverpool, 1942–58. Temp. Asst Clerk, War Off., 1940–43; Chm., Nat. Insurance Local Appeals Tribunals, 1951–70; Dep. Chm. or Chm., Wages Councils, 1962– ; Pt-time Chm., Indust. Tribunals, 1968– . *Publications*: ed, Batt: Law of Master and Servant, 4th edn 1950; Crossley Vaines on Personal Property, 1954, 4th edn 1967, 5th edn, ed E. L. G. Tyler and N. E. Palmer, 1973. *Address*: Faculty of Law, The Univ., PO Box 147, Liverpool L69 3BX.

Vaizey, Prof. John, MA, DTech; Professor of Economics, Brunel University, since 1966; *b* 1929; *m* 1961; two *s* one *d.* BA Cantab 1951

717

(1st cl. Econ.), Gladstone Prizeman 1952, MA Cantab 1954, MA Oxon 1956, DTech Brunel 1971; Mem., Order of El Sabio, 1969; FREconS. Fellow, St Catharine's Coll., Cambridge, 1952–57; Lectr, Oxford Univ., 1956–60; Dir, Res. Unit, London Univ., 1960–62; Fellow and Tutor, Worcester Coll., Oxford, 1962–66; Rathbone Lectr, Durham, 1966; O'Brien Lectr, Dublin, 1968. UN Geneva, 1951–52; Cnsltnt, UN, OECD, ILO, UNESCO; Mem., Nat. Adv. Council on Supply and Training for Teachers, 1962–72; Mem., Public Schools Commn, 1966–68; Mem., Nat. Council Educnl Technol., 1967–73; Mem., Oxf. City Educn Cttee, 1958–60; Mem., Inner Lond. Educn Auth., 1970–72; Mem., Governing Bd, Internat. Inst. for Educnl Planning, 1971– ; Mem., Arts Cttee, Gulbenkian Foundn, 1972– ; Hon. Treas., Brit.-Irish Assoc., 1972– ; Trustee, Acton Soc. Trust, 1962– ; Trustee, King George VI and Queen Elizabeth Foundn, 1973– ; Governor, Ditchley Foundn, 1973– . *Publications*: The Costs of Education, 1958; Scenes from Institutional Life, 1959; (with P. Lynch) Guinness's Brewery in the Irish Economy, 1960; The Brewing Industry, 1886–1951, 1961; The Economics of Education, 1962, 2nd edn 1963; Education for Tomorrow, 1962, 5th edn 1971; The Control of Education, 1963; Barometer Man, 1966; ed (with E. A. G. Robinson), The Economics of Education, 1966; Education in the Modern World, 1966, 2nd edn 1969; The Sleepless Lunch, 1967; (with J. Sheehan) Resources for Education, 1968; (with J. Sheehan, etc) The Economics of Educational Costing, 1969–71; The Type to Succeed, 1970; Capitalism, 1971; Social Democracy, 1971; Education in Europe since 1945, 1971; (with K. Norris and J. Sheehan) The Political Economy of Education, 1972; The Economics of Education, 1973; (with K. Norris) The Economics of Research and Technology: The History of British Steel, 1974; *contrib.* Arquivo, Econ. Jl. *Address*: Dept of Economics, Brunel Univ., Uxbridge, Mddx UB8 3TH.

Vale, Vivian, MA; Lecturer in Politics, University of Southampton, since 1957; *b* 1920; *m* 1953; three *d*. BA Cantab 1947 (1st cl. Hist.), MA Cantab 1948. Res. Student, Jesus Coll., Cambridge, 1947; Lectr in Political Theory and Institutions, Univ. of Durham, 1948–57; Tutor, Univ. Coll., Durham, 1950–57; Harkness Fellow, Harvard Univ. and Univ. of Wisconsin, 1952–53; Vis. Lectr, Portsmouth Coll. of Educn, 1960–68; Vis. Prof. of Pol. Sci., Univs of S Carolina and California, 1967; Vis. Prof. of Govt, Cornell Univ., 1974. Warden, South Stoneham Hse, Univ. of Southampton, 1957– . *Publications*: Labour in American Politics, 1971; American Political Institutions in the 1970's, 1974; *contrib.* Bull. Brit. Assoc. Amer. Studies, Camb. Hist. Rev., Durh. Univ. Jl, Govt Opposit., Jl Amer. Studies, Parl. Aff., Pol. Studies, Public Admin, West. Pol. Qly, etc. *Address*: South Stoneham House, Swaythling, Southampton SO9 4WL.

Valentine, Dr Donald Graham, MA, LLB, DrJur; Reader in Law, London School of Economics, University of London, since

1967; *b* 1929. BA Cantab 1952, LLB Cantab 1953, DrJur, Utrecht 1954, MA Cantab 1956; Barrister-at-Law 1956. Asst Lectr, LSE, 1954–57; Lectr, LSE, 1957–64; Sen. Lectr, LSE, 1964–67. Prof., and Dean of Law Fac., Univ. of Nigeria, 1966–67; Dir, Professional Law Sch., E Nigeria, 1966–67; Jt Ed., Com. Mkt Law Rep., 1962– . *Publications*: The Court of Justice of the European Coal and Steel Community, 1955; The Court of Justice of the European Communities, 1965; *contrib.* Brit. Ybk Internat. Law, Mod. Law Rev. *Address*: London School of Economics, Houghton Street, Aldwych, WC2A 2AE.

Vallance, Elizabeth Mary; Lecturer in Government and Political Science, Department of Economics, Queen Mary College, University of London, since 1968; *b* 1945; *m* 1967; one *d*. MA St Andrews 1967 (Philosophy), MSc London 1968 (Politics). *Publications*: The State, Society and Self-Destruction, 1974; Three Languages of Change: Democracy, Technocracy and Direct Action, in, Direct Action and Democratic Politics, ed, Benewick and Smith. *Address*: Dept of Economics, Queen Mary College, Mile End Road, E1 4NS.

Vallance, Peter James; Lecturer in Management, and Head of Industrial Training, National College of Food Technology, University of Reading, since 1964; *b* 1934; *m* 1964; two *s* one *d*. LLB Bristol 1956; AMBIM 1964, MOMS 1969. Mem., Bd, NCFT. *Address*: National College of Food Technology, Univ. of Reading, St George's Avenue, Weybridge.

Vallat, Prof. Sir Francis Aimé, KCMG, QC; Professor of International Law since 1970 and Director of International Law Studies since 1968, King's College, University of London; *b* 1912; *m* 1939; one *s* one *d*. BA Toronto, LLB Cantab; QC 1961. Called to Bar, Gray's Inn, 1935, Bencher 1971. Asst Lectr, Bristol Univ., 1935–36; practised at Bar, London, 1936–39; RAFVR, 1941–45; Asst Legal Adviser, Foreign Office, 1945–50; Legal Adviser, UK Perm. Delegn to UN, 1950–54; Dep. Legal Adviser 1954–60, Legal Adviser 1960–68, FO; (on leave of absence) Actg Dir, Inst. of Air and Space Law, and Vis. Prof. of Law, McGill Univ., 1965–66; Dir of Studies, Internat. Law Assoc., 1969–72; Reader, King's Coll., London, 1969–70. Mem., Senate, Univ. of London, 1972–73; Assoc. Mem., Institut de Droit international, 1965– ; Mem., Internat. Law Commn, 1973– . *Publications*: International Law and the Practitioner, 1965; *contrib.* Brit. Ybk of Internat. Law, etc. *Address*: King's College, Strand, WC2R 2LS.

van der Loon, Prof. Piet; Professor of Chinese, University of Oxford, since 1972; *b* 1920; *m* 1947; two *d*. LittCand Utrecht 1942, LittDrs Leiden 1946, MA Cantab 1949. Asst Lectr, Cambridge, 1948–49; Lectr, Cambridge, 1949–72. *Publications*: *contrib.* Asia Maj., T'oung Pao. *Address*: Oriental Institute, Pusey Lane, Oxford.

van der Will, Wilfried, DPhil; Lecturer in German, University of Birmingham, since

718

1963; b 1935; m 1962. DPhil Cologne 1962; Deutscher Germanistenverband. Colloquiel Asst 1962–63. *Publications*: Voraussetzungen und Möglichkeiten einer Symbolsprache im Werk Gerhart Hauptmanns, 1962; Pikaro heute, 1967; (with R. H. Thomas) The German Novel and the Affluent Society, 1968 (trans. and enlarged German edn 1969); essays in: Modern Languages, 1966; Mitteilungen der Vereinigung ehemaliger Abiturienten des Gymnasiums Geldern, 1967; Innovations and Experiments in University Teaching Methods, 1969; Essay in German Language, Culture and Society, 1969. *Address*: Dept of German, The Univ., Birmingham B15 2TT.

Vandome, Prof. Peter, MA; Professor of Econometrics, University of Edinburgh, since 1967; b 1930; m 1958; two s. BA Cantab 1954 (Maths), DipStat Manchester 1955, MA Cantab 1958, MA Oxon 1960. Asst Res. Off., Inst. of Economics and Statistics, Oxford, 1955–63; Res. Off., Inst. of Economics and Statistics, Oxford, 1963–65; Sen. Res. Off., Inst. of Economics and Statistics, Oxford, 1965–66; Sen. Lectr, Edinburgh Univ., 1966–67; Vis. Lectr, Univ. of Kentucky, 1958–59; Univ. of Pennsylvania, 1962–63. Mem., Econ. Bd, Council Nat. Acad. Awards, 1968– . *Publications*: (jtly) An Econometric Model of the United Kingdom, 1961; *contrib*. Bull. Oxf. Univ. Inst. Econ. Stats. *Address*: Dept of Economics, Univ. of Edinburgh, Edinburgh EH8 9YL.

van Emden, Prof. Wolfgang Georg; Professor of French, University of Reading, since 1974; b 1931; m 1960; one s one d. BA London 1952 (1st cl. French), PhD London (External) 1963. Temp. Lectr, Edinburgh Univ., 1957–58; Asst Lectr, Nottingham Univ., 1958–60, Lectr, 1960–69; Sen. Lectr, Lancaster Univ., 1969–74. *Publications*: ed, Girart de Vienne (forthcoming); *contrib*. Cah. Civilis. Médiév., Festschriften, Nott. Mediaev. Studies, Romania, French Studies, Actes of Congress of Soc. Rencesvals. *Address*: Dept of French Studies, Univ. of Reading, Whiteknights, Reading, Berks RG6 2AH.

van Heyningen, William Edward, MA, ScD; Master of St Cross College, Oxford, since 1965 (also Reader in Bacterial Chemistry, University of Oxford, since 1966); b 1911; m 1940; one s one d. MSc Stellenbosch 1932, PhD Cantab 1936, MA Oxon 1949, ScD Cantab 1952, DSc Oxon 1954. Commonwealth Fund Fellow, USA, 1936–38; Sen. Student of Royal Commn for Exhibn of 1851, 1938–40. Staff Mem., Wellcome Physiological Res. Laboratories, 1943–46; Sen. Res. Off., Sir William Dunn Sch. of Pathology, Oxford Univ., 1947–66. Sec., Soc. for Gen. Microbiology, 1946–52; Curator of the Bodleian Library, 1961– ; Mem., Hebdomadal Council, Oxford Univ., 1963–69. Vis. of the Ashmolean Museum, 1969– . Expert Consultant, Pakistan-SEATO Cholera Res. Lab., 1968–69. *Publications*: Bacterial Toxins, 1950; articles in various books and jls. *Address*: St Cross College, Oxford.

Van Noorden, Roger John; Lecturer in Economics, Oxford University, and Fellow in

Economics, Hertford College, Oxford, since 1963; b 1939. BA Oxon 1962, MA Oxon 1966. *Address*: Hertford College, Oxford.

Varcoe, Dr Ian; Lecturer in Sociology, University of Leeds, since 1970; b 1944; m 1972. BA Leicester 1965 (Soc.), DPhil Oxon 1971; Mem. Brit. Sociological Assoc. Asst Lectr in Sociology, Univ. Leeds, 1968–70. *Publications*: Organizing for Science in Britain, 1974; *contrib*. Minerva. *Address*: Dept of Sociology, Univ. of Leeds, Leeds LS2 9JT.

Varey, Prof. John Earl; Professor of Spanish, Westfield College, University of London, since 1963; b 1922; m 1948; two s one d. BA Cantab 1946 (emergency regs: 1st cl. Pt II, Mod. and Mod. Langs Tripos, 1947), MA Cantab 1948, PhD Cantab 1951. Lectr, Westfield Coll., 1952–57; Reader, Westfield Coll., 1957–63; Gen. Ed., Colección Támesis, 1963– ; Mem. Ed. Bd, Segismundo, 1965– ; Vice-Principal, Westfield Coll., 1969–70; Jt Ed., Critical Guides to Spanish Texts, 1969– ; Vis. Prof., Univ. of Indiana, 1970, 1971; Jt Ed., Research Bibliographies and Check-Lists, 1970– ; Leverhulme Fellowship, 1970–71. Dean, Fac. of Arts, 1966–68; Mem., Frances Mary Buss Foundn, 1964– ; Chm., Bd of Studies in Rom. Langs and Lits, Univ. of London, 1972– . *Publications*: ed (with N. D. Shergold), T. de Molina: El burlador de Sevilla, 1954, 2nd edn 1967; Historia de los títeres en España, 1957; Títeres, marionetas y otras diversiones populares, 1959; (with N. D. Shergold) Los autos sacramentales en Madrid en la época de Calderón, 1961; ed, Galdós Studies, 1970; ed (with N. D. Shergold), J. Vélez de Guevara: Los celos hacen estrellas, 1970; Pérez Galdós: Doña Perfecta, 1971; (with N. D. Shergold) Fuentes para la historia del teatro en España, vol. III, 1972, vol. IV, 1973, vol. VII, 1972; *contrib*. Barague, Bol. Real Ac. de la Hist., Bull. Hispan. Studies, Bull. Hispan., Bol. Biblio. M. Pelayo, Clavil., Estudios Escén., Hispan. Rev., Hispanóf., Inst. Estudios Madril., Mod. Lang. Rev., Renaiss. Drama, Rev. Filo. Españ., Rev. Filol. Valenc., Rev. Bibliot. Archivo Mus., Madrid, Segism., Symp. *Address*: Westfield College, Kidderpore Avenue, Hampstead, NW3 7ST.

Varley, Donald E.; Senior Lecturer, Department of Industrial Economics, University of Nottingham, since 1963; b 1924; m 1949; one s three d. BA Cantab (Econ. Tripos), MA Cantab. Asst Lectr, Univ. of Nottingham, 1949–52, Lectr, 1952–63. Warden, Rutland Hall, 1967; Pres. (UK), AUT, 1968–69; Hon. Treas., Internat. Assoc. Univ. Profs and Lecturers, 1968–71; Pres., Internat. Assoc. Univ. Profs and Lecturers, 1971– . *Publications*: A History of the Midland Counties Lace Manufacturers Association (incorporating a History of the 19th Century Lace Trade), 1959; John Heathcoat: a short biography, 1970; *contrib*. Brit. Univ. Ann., Jl Textile Hist. *Address*: Dept of Industrial Economics, Univ. of Nottingham, Nottingham NG7 2RD.

Varley, Douglas Harold; University Librarian, University of Liverpool, since 1966;

b 1911; *m* 1936; three *d*. BA Oxon 1932, MA Oxon 1938, Dip. Librarianship and Archives London 1933; FLA 1937. Lectr in Bibliography, Univ. Cape Town Sch. of Librarianship, 1940–61; Sec. and Chief Librarian, South African (National) Library, Cape Town, 1938–61; Librarian, UC Rhodesia and Nyasaland (later UCR), 1961–66. Mem. Council, S African Library Assoc., 1938–61 (Pres., 1946–48); Chm., Central African Library Assoc., 1962–66; Hon. Sec. for Southern Africa, Hakluyt Soc., 1946–61; Chm., Standing Conf. on Library Materials on Africa, 1971–73; Chm., Liverpool Bibliographical Soc., 1970–72; Pres., N W Br. Library Assoc., 1974. *Publications*: African Native Music, 1936, repr. 1970; The School Library: Handbook for teacher-librarians, 1942; ed, Aspects of Library Work in South Africa, 1948; Adventures in Africana, 1949; South Africa in Print, 1952; ed, Cape Journals of Archdeacon Merriman, 1957; South African Reading in Earlier Days, 1959; Rôle of the Librarian in the New Africa, 1963; Intellectual Freedom: Trends Abroad, South Africa, 1970; Mr Chronometer: Sir John Barrow, In, Libraries and People, 1970; *contrib*. Africana Notes and News, Library, Library Assoc. Record, Library Trends, Qly Bull. of SA Library (ed), South African Libraries (ed). *Address*: PO Box 123, Liverpool L69 3DA.

Varty, Prof. E. Kenneth C., BA, PhD, FSA; Stevenson Professor of French, University of Glasgow, since 1968; *b* 1927; *m* 1958; two *d*. BA Nottingham 1951 (1st cl. French), PhD Nottingham 1954; FSA 1969. Asst Lectr, Keele Univ., 1953–56; Lectr, Keele Univ., 1956–61; Lectr, Leicester Univ., 1961–65; Sen. Lectr, Leicester Univ., 1965–68; Pt-time Vis. Lectr, Univ. of Warwick, 1967. Mem., Exec. Cttee, Soc. Fr. Studies, 1967–69; Treas., Soc. Fr. Studies, 1971–72; Mem., Cttee, Assoc. Univ. Profs, Fr., 1970–72; Sec., Brit. Br., Internat. Arthurian Soc., 1971– ; Asst Ed., Bibliog. Bull. Internat. Arthurian Soc., 1968– . *Publications*: The Jeu de Robin et de Marion, 1960; Christine de Pisan's Rondeaux, Ballades and Virelais, 1965; Reynard the Fox: a study of the Fox in medieval English art and literature, 1967; *contrib*. Archiv. Lingu., Fr. Studies, Jl Court. Warb. Inst., Mod. Lang. Notes, Mod. Langs Nott. Fr. Studies, Trans Leics. Hist. Archaeol. Assoc. *Address*: Dept of French, Univ. of Glasgow, Glasgow G12 8QL.

Vatikiotis, Prof. P. J., BA, PhD; Professor of Politics, with special reference to the Near and Middle East, University of London, since 1965; *b* 1928; *m* 1956; one *s* two *d*. BA American (Cairo) 1948, PhD Johns Hopkins 1954. Instructor, American Univ. Cairo, 1948; Instructor, Johns Hopkins Univ., 1952–53; Instructor in Government, Indiana Univ., 1953–57; Asst Prof. of Government, 1957–60; Assoc. Prof. of Government, 1960–63; Prof. of Government, 1963–65; Vis. Prof., Johns Hopkins Sch. of Adv. Internat. Studies, 1967; Vis. Prof., Univ. of Michigan, 1960; Vis. Prof., UCLA, 1969; Vis. Prof. and Vis. Sen. Fellow on Council of the Humanities, Princeton Univ., 1973–74. Chm., Centre Mid. East. Studies, SOAS, Univ. of London,

1966–69; Mem., Adv. Ed. Bd, Mid. East. Studies, 1964– . *Publications*: The Fatimid Theory of the State, 1957; The Egyptian Army in Politics, 1961; Politics and the Military in Jordan, 1967, pbk edn 1972; ed, Egypt since the Revolution, 1968; The Modern History of Egypt, 1969; Conflict in the Middle East, 1971; ed, Revolution in the Middle East and other case studies, 1972; contrib. Tensions in the Middle East, ed P. W. Thayer, 1967; Foreign Policy in World Politics, 2nd rev. edn, ed R. C. Macridis, 1962; Islam and International Relations, ed J. P. Harris, 1965; Political and Social Change in Modern Egypt, ed P. M. Holt, 1968; Political Dynamics of the Middle East, ed Hammond and Alexander, 1971; Encyclopaedia of Islam, 2nd edn; *contrib*. Amer. Pol. Sci. Rev., APSR, Mid. East. Studies, New Soc., Pol Qly. *Address*: Dept of Economic and Political Studies, School of Oriental and African Studies, Univ. of London, WC1E 7HP.

Vaughan, Dr David Hughes, MB, ChB, MFCM, DPH; Senior Lecturer in Community Medicine, University of Manchester, since 1967; *b* 1927; *m* 1951; two *s* two *d*. MB, ChB Edinburgh 1950, MFCM 1972, DPH Manchester 1958. Mem., BMA, Mem., Soc. Social Med., FSocMOH. Lectr, Manchester Univ., 1963–67. *Publications*: *contrib*. Brit. Jl Prev. Soc. Med., Jl Royal Coll. Gen. Pract., Social Sci. Med. *Address*: Stopford Building, The Univ., Manchester M13 9PT.

Vaughan, George Douglas; Senior Tutor, since 1969, and Senior Lecturer in Managerial Economics, Graduate Business Centre, The City University, London, since 1966; *b* 1921; *m* 1946; one *s* one *d*. BSc(Econ) London 1952 (1st cl.). Lectr, City Univ., 1963–66. Min. Housing and Loc. Govt, 1947–57; 1959–62; HM Treasury, 1957–59. *Publications*: Applied Economics, 1972; *contrib*. Jl Public Admin, Pol. Econ. Plan. *Address*: Graduate Business Centre, The City Univ., Lionel Denny House, 23 Goswell Road, EC1M 7BB.

Vaughan, John Edmund; Tutor/Librarian, School and Institute of Education, University of Liverpool, since 1966; *b* 1935. BA Bristol 1956, CertifEd Exeter 1957, MA Bristol 1960; Member: Library Assoc., Bibliograph. Soc., etc. *Publications*: The Parish Church and Institute of Education, University Norton, 7th edn 1973; (with O. M. V. Argles) British Government Publications concerning Education, 3rd edn 1969; The English Guide Book c. 1780–1870, 1974; *contrib*. Library Assoc. Record, Local Historian, Paedagogica Historica. *Address*: 22 Abercromby Square, PO Box 147, Liverpool L69 3BX.

Vaughan, Prof. Michalina Ewa Francisca, L en Droit, DipEtPol, D en Droit d'Etat, DES (Sociol.); Professor of Sociology, University of Lancaster, since 1972; *b* 1932. L en Droit Paris 1951, D en Droit d'Etat Paris 1954, DipEtPol Paris Institute of Political Studies 1951, DES (Sociol.) Sorbonne 1954, DipIHEI Sorbonne 1954, DipEBAP (UN sponsored) Brazilian Sch. of Public Admin

Rio de Janeiro 1952; FIL. Lectr, LSE, 1959–70; Sen. Lectr, 1970–72. Progr. Asst, Div. Internat. Co-op., Dept Social. Sci., UNESCO, 1955–57. *Publications*: (with G. Langrod) L'Irlande 1968; (with M. S. Archer) Social Conflict and Educational Change in England and France, 1789–1848, 1971; trans., R. Boudon: A quoi sert la notion de structure? (The Uses of Structuralism), 1971; *contrib*. Archiv. Europ. Sociol., Brit. Jl Sociol., Czasop. Prawnohist., Rev. Mex. Sociol., Stato Soc. *Address*: Univ. of Lancaster, Bailrigg, Lancaster LA1 4YW.

Vaughan, Trefor Doloughan; Lecturer in Adolescent Development, University of London Institute of Education, since 1968; *b* 1932; *m* 1960; one *s* two *d*. BA Hons QUB 1956, DipEd QUB 1957, MA QUB 1960, MEd QUB 1965; Mem. British Psychological Soc. *Publications*: Education and Vocational Guidance Today, 1970; Education and the Aims of Counselling: a European perspective, 1975; *contrib*. Econ. Geography, Geography, Irish Geography, New Era, Revue Française de Pedagogie, Vocational Aspect of Educn. *Address*: Institute of Education, Malet Street, WC1E 7HS.

Veasey, Richard George; Lecturer in French, School of European Studies, University of Sussex, since 1968; *b* 1939; *m* 1965; one *s* one *d*. BA Southampton 1961 (2nd cl.), MPhil Sussex 1963. Asst Lectr, Sussex, 1965–68. *Publications*: Libertinism and the novel, in, French Literature and its Background, vol. 2, ed J. Cruickshank, 1968; Notes on various modern French novelists, in, Penguin Companion to European Literature, ed A. Thorlby, 1969; The novel of action, in, French Literature and its Background, vol. 6, ed J. Cruickshank, 1970. *Address*: Arts Building, Univ. of Sussex, Falmer, Brighton, Sussex BN1 9QN.

Vermes, Dr Geza, MA, DTheol; Reader in Jewish Studies, University of Oxford, since 1965; *b* 1924; *m* 1958. Lic en Hist Philol Orient Louvain 1952, DTheol 1953, MA Oxon 1965. Mem., Soc. OT Study. Lectr, Newcastle Univ., 1957–64; Sen. Lectr, 1964–65; Ed., Jl Jew. Studies, 1971– ; Vis. Prof., Brown Univ., 1971; Prof. Fellow, Wolfson Coll., Oxford, 1971. Chm., Curators, Orient. Inst., Oxford, 1971–73; Gov., Oxford Centre for Postgraduate Hebrew Studies, 1972– . *Publications*: Les Manuscrits du désert de Juda, 1953, 2nd edn 1954; Discovery in the Judean Desert, 1956; Scripture and Tradition in Judaism, 1961, 2nd edn 1973; The Dead Sea Scrolls in English, 1962, 3rd edn 1968; Jesus the Jew, 1973; editor and reviser: E. Schürer, The History of the Jewish People in the Age of Jesus Christ, vol. I, 1973; P. Winter, On the Trial of Jesus, 2nd edn 1974; trans., A. Dupont-Sommer: The Essene Writings from Qumran, 1961; *contrib*. Ann. Leeds Univ. Orient Soc., Jl Jew. Studies, Jl Semit. Studies, Rev. Qumran. *Address*: Oriental Institute, Pusey Lane, Oxford OX1 2LE.

Versey, Dr John; Senior Lecturer in Child Development, Department of Child Development and Educational Psychology, University of London Institute of Education, since 1974; *b* 1932; *m* 1965. LTCL 1956, BSc London 1961, PhD London 1974; ABPsS. Lectr in Psychol. of Educn, Univ. of London Inst. of Educn, 1968–74. Jt Editor, Bulletin of British Psychological Soc. *Address*: Univ. of London Institute of Education, Malet Street, WC1E 7HS.

Vesey, Prof. Godfrey Norman Agmondisham, MA, MLitt; Professor of Philosophy, The Open University, since 1969; *b* 1923; *m* 1949; two *d*. BA Cantab 1950 (1st cl. Pts I and II, Moral Sci. Tripos). Lectr, King's Coll., London, 1952–65; Reader, King's Coll., London, 1965–69; Vis. Prof., Carlton Coll., Minn., 1966; Vis. Prof., Univ. of Oregon, 1966. Asst Ed., Philos., 1964–69; Hon. Dir, Royal Inst. Philos., 1965– . *Publications*: ed, Body and Mind, 1964; The Embodied Mind, 1965; Perception, 1971; Personal Identity, 1974; *contrib*., 8 collected wks; forewords to Royal Institute of Philosophy Lectures; *contrib*. Analysis, Austral. Jl Philos., Mind, Philos., Philos. Rev., Philos. Qly. *Address*: The Open Univ., Walton Hall, Milton Keynes MK7 6AA.

Vessey, Dr David William Thomson; Lecturer, Department of Classics, Queen Mary College, University of London, since 1969; *b* 1944. BA Cantab 1965 (1st cl. Hons), MA Cantab 1969, PhD Cantab 1969; FRHistS, FRSA, FSAScot, Member: Roman Soc., Hellenic Soc., Virgil Soc. Asst Lectr, Queen Mary Coll., Univ. London, 1967–69. *Publications*: Statius and the Thebaid, 1973; The Ice Age and Other Poems 1973; *contrib*. Amer. Jl Philology, L'Antiquité Classique, Bull. Inst. Class. Studies, Class. Bull., Class. Jl, Class. Philology, Class. Qly, Class. World, Contemp. Review, Hermes, Latomus, Mediaeval Studies, Mnemosyne, Philologus, Proc. Virgil Soc., Royal Stuart Papers. *Address*: Dept of Classics, Queen Mary College, Mile End Road, E1 4NS.

Vick, Sir (Francis) Arthur, OBE, DSc, PhD; President and Vice-Chancellor, Queen's University of Belfast, since 1966; *b* 1911; *m* 1943; one *d*. Hon. DSc Keele 1972, Hon. LLD Dublin 1973; FIEE, FInstP, MRIA. Asst Lectr in Physics, Univ. Coll. London, 1936–39; Lectr, Univ. Coll. London, 1939–44; Asst Dir of Scientific Res., Min. of Supply, 1939–44; Lectr in Physics, Manchester Univ., 1944–47; Sen. Lectr, Manchester Univ., 1947–50; Prof. of Physics, Univ. Coll. of N Staffs, 1950–59 (Vice-Principal, 1950–54, Actg Principal, 1952–53); Dep. Dir, AERE, Harwell, 1959–60; Dir, AERE, Harwell, 1960–64; Dir of Research Gp, UKAEA, 1961–64; Mem. for Research, 1964–66. Mem. Bd, Inst. of Physics, 1946–51, Vice-Pres., Inst. of Physics, 1953–56; Hon. Sec., Inst. of Physics, 1956–60. Chm., Naval Educn Adv. Cttee, 1964–70; Chm., RDA Academic Adv. Council, MoD, 1969– ; Hon. Mem., Assoc. for Sci. Educn, 1969; Hon. Mem., Assoc. of Teachers in Colls and Depts of Educn, 1972 (Pres., 1964–72). Vice-Pres., Arts Council of NI, 1966– . Mem., UGC, 1959–66; Mem., Colonial Univ. Grants Adv. Cttee, 1960–65; Mem., Nuclear Safety Adv. Cttee, Min. of Power, 1960–66;

Mem., Governing Body, Nat. Inst. for Res. in Nuclear Science, 1964–65. Kt Comdr, Liberian Humane Order of African Redemption, 1962. *Publications*: various scientific and educnl papers and contribs to books; *contrib*. Adv. of Sci., Brit. Jl Appl. Phys., Contemp. Phys., Jl Sci. Instr., Nature, Proc. Phys. Soc., Proc. Roy. Soc., Sch. Sci. Rev., Sci. Progress, Univ. Qly. *Address*: Vice-Chancellor's Lodge, 16 Lennoxvale, Belfast BT9 5BY.

Vile, Prof. Maurice J. C.; Professor of Political Science, University of Kent, since 1968; *b* 1927. BSc(Econ) London 1951, PhD London 1954, MA Oxon 1962. Lectr, Univ. of Exeter, 1954–62; Fellow, Nuffield Coll., Oxford, 1965–68; Reader, Univ. of Kent, 1965–68; Dean, Fac. of Social Sci., 1969– ; Vis. Prof., Univ. of Massachusetts, 1960. *Publications*: The Structure of American Federalism, 1961; Constitutionalism and the Separation of Powers, 1967; Politics in the USA, 1970, French edn 1972; Federalism in the United States, Canada and Australia, Res. Paper No. 2, Commn on the Constitution, 1973; *contrib*. Amer. Pol. Sci. Rev., Brit. Jl Pol Sci., Pol Qly, Pol Sci. Qly. *Address*: Keynes College, The Univ., Canterbury, Kent CT2 7ND.

Vincent, Prof. John Russell; Professor of Modern History, University of Bristol, since 1970; *b* 1937. BA Cantab 1959, MA, PhD Cantab 1963. Lectr in History, Cambridge Univ., 1967–70. *Publications*: The Formation of the Liberal Party, 1966; Pollbooks: How Victorians Voted, 1967; ed (with A. B. Cooke), Lord Catlingford's Journal, 1971; ed (with M. Stenton), McCalmont's Parliamentary Pollbook 1832–1918, 1971; *contrib*. Econ. Hist. Rev., Hist. Jl, Irish Hist. Studies. *Address*: Univ. of Bristol, Queen's Road, Bristol BS8 1RJ.

Vincent, Paul, BSc(Econ); Senior Lecturer, Department of Sociology, University of Strathclyde, since 1963; *b* 1929; *m* 1960; one *s* one *d*. BSc(Econ) London 1955 (2nd cl.). *Publications*: *contrib*. Jew. Jl Sociol. *Address*: Dept of Sociology, Univ. of Strathclyde, Glasgow G1 1XW.

Vincent, Paul Frank, MA; Lecturer in Dutch, Bedford College, University of London, since 1967; *b* 1942; *m* 1964; two *s*. BA Cantab 1964 (Mod. and Med. Langs), MA Cantab 1968. Asst in Dutch, Univ. Cambridge, 1966–67. *Publications*: ed, European Context: Studies in the history and literature of the Netherlands presented to Theodoor Weevers, 1972; *contrib*. Mod. Lang. Review. *Address*: Bedford College, Regent's Park, NW1 4NS.

Virgoe, Dr Roger; Senior Lecturer in History, School of English and American Studies, University of East Anglia, since 1971; *b* 1932; *m* 1963; one *s* two *d*. BA London 1954, PhD London 1964; FRHistS. Temp. Lectr, Queen Mary Coll., Univ. of London, 1959–61; Lectr in History, Univ. of Khartoum, 1961–64; Lectr in History, Univ. of E Anglia, 1964–71. *Publications*: contrib. var. articles in essay collections; *contrib*. Bull.

Inst. Hist. Res., Bull. J. Rylands Libr., Jl Soc. Archiv., Norfolk Archaeol. *Address*: School of English and American Studies, Univ. of East Anglia, Norwich NOR 88C.

Vittorini, Edwina E., BA; Lecturer in French, Department of Romance Studies, University College of Swansea, since 1962; *b* 1935; one *s* one *d*. BA Dunelm 1958 (1st cl. Hons French). Temp. Lectr in French, Durham Colls, 1962. *Publications*: trans., The Mother, and Wartime Autobiography: On Being a Writer, in Italian Short Stories 2 (Penguin Parallel Text series), 1971; *contrib*. Durham Univ. Jl. *Address*: Dept of Romance Studies, Univ. College of Swansea, Singleton Park, Swansea SA2 8PP.

Vlasto, Dr Alexis Peter; Lecturer, Department of Slavonic Studies, University of Cambridge, since 1960; *b* 1915; *m* 1945; one *s* one *d*. BA Cantab 1937, MA Cantab 1945, PhD Cantab 1953. Res. Fellow, King's Coll., Cambridge, 1945–51; Asst Lectr, Cambridge, 1954–60; Fellow, Selwyn Coll., Cambridge, 1969. *Publications*: The Entry of the Slavs into Christendom, 1970. *Address*: Selwyn College, Cambridge.

Vokes, Rev. Prof. Frederick Ercolo; Archbishop King's Professor of Divinity, Trinity College, Dublin University, since 1957; *b* 1910; *m* 1937; one *s* two *d*. BA Cantab 1933 (1st cl. Classics, 1st cl. Theol.), MA Cantab 1947, BD Cantab 1953, MA Dublin 1967. Prof. of Hebrew and Theology, St David's Coll., Lampeter, 1955–57. *Publications*: The Riddle of the Didache, 1938; *contrib*. Ch Qly, Hermath., Studia Evangel., Studia Patrist. Theol., Irish Theol. Qly, Doctrine and Life, Hermathena. *Address*: 25 Trinity College, Dublin 2.

von Fürer-Haimendorf, Christoph; *see* Fürer-Haimendorf.

von Leyden, Dr Wolfgang Marius; Reader in Philosophy, University of Durham, since 1962; *b* 1911; *m* 1953; one *s* one *d*. PhD Florence 1936, DPhil Oxon 1944. Lectr, Durham Univ., 1946–56; Sen. Lectr, Durham Univ., 1956–62; Vis. Prof., State Univ. of NY, Binghamton, 1966–67. *Publications*: ed, J. Locke: Essays on the Law of Nature, 1954, 2nd edn 1958; Remembering, 1961, pbk edn 1970; Seventeenth-Century Metaphysics, 1968, pbk edn 1971; Three Political Philosophers: Aristotle, Hobbes, Locke (forthcoming); *contrib*. Archiv. Philos., Jl Hist. Ideas, Hist. Theor., Mind, Philos., Philos. Qly, Pol. Studies, Proc. Aristot. Soc., Rev. Metaphys., Sophia. *Address*: Dept of Philosophy, Univ. of Durham, Durham DH1 3HP.

von Tunzelmann, George Nicholas; University Assistant Lecturer, Department of Economics, University of Cambridge, since 1970; *b* 1943. MA Canterbury 1966, MA Cantab 1970. Asst Lectr, Univ. Canterbury, 1966, Lectr 1967; Student, Nuffield Coll., Oxford, 1967–70; Fellow, St John's Coll., Cambridge, 1970; Dir of Studies in Econs, St John's Coll., 1971. *Publications*: contrib. The Industrial Revolution, ed, Hartwell, 1970; contrib. The New Economic History, ed Andreano, 1970; contrib. The Use of Economics Literature, ed, Fletcher, 1971; *contrib*. Econ. History Review, Explorations in Econ. History, Austr. Econ. Papers. *Address*: St John's College, Cambridge.

W

Wacher, John Stewart, BSc, FSA; Reader in Archaeology, University of Leicester, since 1970; *b* 1927; *m* 1957, 1972; one *s*. BSc London 1951; FSA, FSAScot. Mem., Royal Archaeol. Inst., Soc. Prom. Rom. Studies. Asst Lectr, Leicester Univ., 1960–62; Lectr, Leicester Univ., 1962–70. Mem., Council, Soc. Prom. Rom. Studies, 1962–65; Council, Royal Archaeol. Inst.; Mem., Council, Soc. Antiqu., 1963–64; Mem., Res. Cttee, Soc. Antiqu., 1963–65; Mem., Res. Cttee, Royal Archaeol. Inst., 1964–65; Mem., Res. Cttee, Iron Age and Roman Periods, CBA, 1963–65; Council Brit. Archaeol., 1963– . *Publications*: ed, The Civitas Capitals of Roman Britain, 1966; Excavations at Brough-on-Humber, 1958–61 (Reports of the Research Committee, Society of Antiquaries, no 25), 1969; contrib. Soldier and Civilian in Roman Yorkshire, 1971; Corinium, 1971; The Towns of Roman Britain, 1974; *contrib*. Antiqu. Jl, Antiqu., Archaeol. Jl, Britann., var. jls of C. Archaeol. Soc. *Address*: Dept of Archaeology, The Univ., Leicester LE1 7RH.

Waddell, Prof. David Alan Gilmour, MA, DPhil; Professor of Modern History, University of Stirling, since 1968; *b* 1927; *m* 1951; two *s* one *d*. MA St Andrews 1949 (1st cl. Hist.), DPhil Oxon 1954; FRHistS 1965. Lectr, Univ. Coll. of W Indies, 1954–59; Lectr, Edinburgh Univ., 1959–63, Sen. Lectr, 1963–68; Vis. Prof., Univ. del Valle, Colombia, 1967; Univ. of California, Irvine, 1971. Mem., DES Studentship Select. Cttee, 1970– . *Publications*: British Honduras, 1961; The West Indies and the Guianas, 1967; *contrib*. Amer. Jl Internat. Law, Carib. Qly, Econ. Hist. Rev., Hispan. Amer. Hist. Rev., Hist. Jl, Libr. *Address*: Dept of History, Univ. of Stirling, Stirling FK9 4LA.

Waddicor, Dr Mark Hurlstone, BA, PhD; Lecturer in French, University of Exeter, since 1966; *b* 1939. BA Bristol 1960 (1st cl. French); PhD Bristol 1965. Mem., Soc. Fr. Studies, Mem., Brit. Soc. Eightnth Cent. Studies. Asst Lectr, Univ. of Exeter, 1963–66. *Publications*: Montesquieu and the Philosophy of Natural Law, 1970. *Address*: Dept of French, Univ. of Exeter, Queen's Building, The Queen's Drive, Exeter EX4 4QH.

Wade, Prof. Henry William Rawson, QC, FBA, MA, LLD, DCL; Professor of English Law, University of Oxford, and Fellow of St John's College, since 1961; *b* 1918; *m* 1943; two *s*. MA Cantab 1946, LLD Cantab 1959; DCL Oxon 1961; QC 1968; FBA 1969. Called to Bar, Lincoln's Inn, 1946, Hon. Bencher, 1964. Henry Fellow, Harvard Univ., 1939; Treasury, 1940–46; Fellow, Trinity Coll.,

Cambridge, 1946–61; Reader, Univ. of Cambridge, 1959; Lectr, Council of Legal Educn, 1957; Brit. Council Lectr in Scandinavia, 1958, and Turkey, 1959; Cooley Lectr, Michigan Univ., 1961; Vithalbai Patel Lectr, New Delhi, 1971; Chettyar Lectr, Madras, 1974. Mem., Council on Tribunals, 1958–71; Mem., Relationships Commn, Uganda, 1961; Mem., Royal Commn on Tribunals of Inquiry, 1966. Ed., Annual Survey of Commonwealth Law. *Publications*: (with R. E. Megarry) The Law of Real Property, 1957, 3rd edn 1966; Administrative Law, 1961, 3rd edn 1971; Towards Administrative Justice, 1963; (with B. Schwarz) Legal Control of Government, 1972; *contrib*. Cambridge Law Jl, Law Qly Rev. *Address*: St John's College, Oxford.

Wager, Dr Jonathan Field; University Lecturer, Department of Town and Country Planning, University of Manchester, since 1967; *b* 1937; *m* 1963; two *s* one *d*. BA Cantab 1961 (Est. Man.), Certif. Proficiency in Est. Man. Cantab 1961, MA Cantab 1966, PhD Cantab 1966; MRTPI 1974, Mem. Regional Studies Assoc., Mem. Town and Country Planning Assoc. Harold Samuel Research Student, Dept of Land Economy, Univ. Cambridge, 1961–64; Vis. Sen. Lectr in Regional Planning, Univ. of Umeå, Sweden, 1970–71. Sen. Planning Asst, Durham County Council, 1964–67. *Publications*: contrib. Jl RTPI. *Address*: Univ. of Manchester, Manchester M13 9PL.

Wagner, Prof. H. H.; Professor of Celtic and Comparative Philology, since 1969 (Professor of Celtic, 1958–69), The Queen's University, Belfast; *b* 1923; *m* 1951; one *d*. Dr phil Zürich 1950; MRIA. Prof. of Germanic Philology, Univ. of Utrecht, 1951; Prof. of German Philology, Univ. of Basel, 1953. Editor, Zeitschrift für celtische Philologie (Niemeyer, Tubingen). Hon. Consul of Switzerland for N Ireland, 1971– . *Publications*: Linguistic Atlas and Survey of Irish Dialects, 4 vols, 1958–69; Das Verbum in den Sprachen der Britischen Inseln, 1959; The Origins of the Celts and of Early Celtic Civilisation, 1971; *contrib*. numerous jls. *Address*: Department of Celtic, Queen's Univ., Belfast BT7 1NN.

Wagstaff, John Malcolm; Lecturer in Geography, University of Southampton, since 1966; *b* 1940; *m* 1962; two *s*. BA Liverpool 1962 (Special Studies, Geog.). Res. Asst in Geography, Centre of Middle Eastern and Islamic Studies, Durham, 1963–66; NATO Fellow, 1966–68. *Publications*: contrib. Balk. Studies, Erdkunde, Geog., Trans Inst. Brit. Geogrs. *Address*: Dept of Geography, The Univ., Southampton SO9 5NA.

Waidson, Prof. Herbert Morgan, MA, DrPhil; Professor of German, University College of Swansea, since 1960; *b* 1916; *m* 1941; three *d*. BA Birmingham 1936 (1st cl. German), DipEd Birmingham 1937, MA Birmingham 1938, DrPhil Leipzig 1939. Mem., Mod. Hum. Res. Assoc., Mod. Lang. Assoc., Internat. Assoc. Germanic Studies. Asst Lectr, then Lectr, and later Sen. Lectr, Hull Univ., 1946–60. Pres., Assoc. Teachers

German, 1966–68. *Publications*: F. M. Klingers Stellung zur Geistesgeschichte seiner Zeit, 1939; Jeremias Gotthelf: An Introduction to the Swiss Novelist, 1953; Ed, Gotthelf: Die schwarze Spinne, 1956, 3rd edn 1972; trans., Gotthelf: The Black Spider, 1956; ed, German Short Stories 1945–1955, 1957, 5th edn 1967; The Modern German Novel, 1959, 2nd edn (as The Modern German Novel 1945–1965), 1971; ed, German Short Stories 1900–1945, 1959, 2nd edn 1966; ed, Goethe: Egmont, 1960, 2nd edn 1967; trans., Goethe: Kindred by Choice, 1960, Indian edn 1962; ed, E. K. Bennett: A History of the German Novelle, 2nd edn 1961, 4th edn 1970; ed, Modern German Stories, 1961; ed (with G. Seidmann), Böll: Doktor Murkes gesammeltes Schweigen, 1963, 3rd edn 1974; ed, German Short Stories 1955–1965, 1969, 2nd edn 1971; contrib. on Prose Fiction, in, Twentieth Century German Literature, ed A. Closs, 1969, 2nd edn 1971; contrib. on Robert Walser and Dürrenmatt, in, Swiss Men of Letters, ed A. Natan, 1970; contrib. on F. M. Klinger, in, German Men of Letters, vol. vi, ed A. Natau and B. Keith-Smith; contrib. on Vernon Watkins, in, Affinities, Essays in German and English Literature, ed R. W. Last; contrib. (with T. M. Holmes) on the Shakespearean Strain, in, The German Theatre and R. Hayman; *contrib.* Germ. Life Lett., Mod. Lang. Rev., Forum for Mod. Lang. Studies, Anglo-Welsh Rev., Books Abroad, Times Lit. Supp., etc. *Address*: Dept of German, Univ. College of Swansea, Singleton Park, Swansea SA2 8PP.

Wain, Prof. John Barrington; Professor of Poetry, University of Oxford, since 1973; *b* 1925; *m* 1960; three *s*. BA 1946 (1st cl. Eng. Lang. and Lit.), MA 1950, Oxon. FRSL, 1960–61. Fereday Fellow, St John's Coll., Oxford, 1946–49; Lectr, Eng. Lit., Univ. of Reading, 1947–55; Churchill Vis. Prof., Univ. of Bristol, 1967; Vis. Prof., Centre Universitaire Expérimentale de Vincennes, 1969; Fellow in creative arts, Brasenose Coll., Oxford, 1971–72. *Publications*: *poetry*: A Word Carved on a Sill, 1956; Weep Before God, 1961; Wildtrack, 1965; Letters to Five Artists, 1969; The Shape of Feng, 1972; *criticism*: Preliminary Essays, 1957; Essays on Literature and Ideas, 1963; The LivingWorld of Shakespeare, 1964; A House for the Truth, 1972; *autobiography*: Sprightly Running, 1962; *fiction*: Hurry on Down, 1953; Living in the Present, 1955; The Contenders, 1958; A Travelling Woman, 1959; Nuncle and other stories, 1960; Strike the Father Dead, 1962; The Young Visitors, 1965; Death of the Hind Legs and other stories, 1966; The Smaller Sky, 1967; A Winter in the Hills, 1970; The Life Guard and Other Stories, 1971. *Address*: Brasenose Coll., Oxford.

Wake, Dr Clive Harold; Senior Lecturer in French, University of Kent at Canterbury, since 1969; *b* 1933; *m* 1965; one *s*. BA Cape Town 1953, MA Cape Town 1954, D de l'U Paris 1958. Lectr in French, Univ. Coll. of Rhodesia, 1958–66; Lectr, Univ. of Kent at Canterbury, 1966–69. Trustee, Treas., 1969–72, Budiriro Trust, 1969– . *Publications*: (with J. Reed) A Book of African Verse, 1964; ed (with J. Reed), L. S. Senghor: Selected Poems, 1964; Anthology of African and Malagasy Poetry in French, 1965; ed (with J. Reed), L. S. Senghor: Prose and Poetry, 1965; ed (with J. Reed), L. S. Senghor: Nocturnes, 1969; (with J. Reed) French African Poetry, with English translations, 1972; The Novels of Pierre Loti, 1973; *contrib.* Bks Abroad, Comp. Lit. Studies, Forum Mod. Lang. Studies, Fr. Rev., Rev. Nat. Lit. *Address*: Darwin College, The Univ., Canterbury, Kent CT2 7NY.

Wakeford, Dr John; Senior Lecturer in Sociology, University of Lancaster, since 1969; *b* 1936; *m* 1965; one *s* one *d*. BA Nottingham 1959 (Sociol.), PhD Brunel 1968. Mem., Brit. Sociol. Assoc., Mem., Amer. Sociol. Assoc., Mem., Soc. Res. Higher Educn. Asst Lectr, then Lectr, Univ. Coll., Cardiff, 1960–64; Asst Producer TV, BBC, 1964–65; Lectr, Univ. of Exeter, 1965–67; Lectr, Brunel Univ., 1967–69; Vis. Asst Prof., Univ. of New Brunswick, 1966–67. Ed. New Perspect. in Sociol., 1969– . *Publications*: The Strategy of Social Enquiry, 1968; The Cloistered Elite, 1969; ed, Power in Britain, 1973; contrib. Elites and Power in British Society, ed A. Giddens; Yearbook of Political Sociology, ed I. Crewe; *contrib.* Brit. Jl Sociol., Hosp., New Soc., Sociol. Rev. *Address*: Dept of Sociology, The Univ., Lancaster LA1 4YW.

Wakelin, Dr Martyn F., MA, PhD; Lecturer in English, Royal Holloway College, University of London, since 1967; *b* 1935; *m* 1966; one *s* two *d*. BA Leeds 1959, MA Leeds 1960 (with distinction), PhD Leeds 1970. Ed. Asst, Leeds Survey of English Dialects, 1961; later Asst Ed., and then Co-Ed. *Publications*: ed, W. Renwick and H. Orton: The Beginnings of English Literature, 3rd edn 1966; (with H. Orton) Survey of English Dialects, vol. IV, 1967–68; ed, Patterns in the Folk Speech of the British Isles, 1972; English Dialects: An Introduction, 1972; Language and History in Cornwall, 1974; *contrib.* Anglia, Folk Life, Leeds Studies Engl. (NS), Studia Neophilol. *Address*: Dept of English, Royal Holloway College, Egham Hill, Egham, Surrey TW20 0EX.

Walbank, Prof. Frank William, FBA; Professor of Ancient History and Classical Archaeology, University of Liverpool, since 1951; *b* 1909; *m* 1935; one *s* two *d*. BA Cantab 1931 (1st cl. Classics), MA Cantab 1935; FBA. Asst Lectr, Liverpool Univ., 1934–36; Lectr, Liverpool Univ., 1936–46; Prof. of Latin, Liverpool Univ., 1946–51; Gray Meml Lectr, Cambridge, 1957; Vis. Prof., Pittsburgh Univ., 1964; Myres Meml Lectr, Oxford, 1965; Mem., Inst. Adv. Studies, Princeton, 1970; Sather Prof., Univ. of California, Berkeley, 1971. Mem., Council, Class. Assoc., 1944–48, 1958–61; Mem., Council, Rom. Soc., 1948–51; Mem., Ed. Bd, Class. Jl, 1949–66; Mem., Council, Hellen. Soc., 1951–64; Mem., Ed. Cttee, Rom. Soc., 1958– ; Review ed., Jl Rom. Studies, 1959–68; Pres., Rom. Soc., 1961–65; Vice-Pres., Rom. Soc., 1953–61, 1965– ; Pres., Class. Assoc., 1969–70; Vice-Pres., 1970– ; Mem., Birkenhead Educn Cttee,

1949–57; Mem., Liverpool City Council, Mem., Arts and Culture Sub-Cttee. *Publications*: Aratos of Sicyon, 1933; Philip V of Macedon, 1940, 2nd edn 1967; The Decline of the Roman Empire in the West, 1946, American edn 1953, Japanese edn 1963; A Historical Commentary on Polybius, vol. I, 1957, 2nd edn 1970, vol. 2, 1967; Speeches in Greek Historians, 1965; The Awful Revolution, 1969; Polybius, 1972; *contrib*. Bull. Inst. Class. Studies, Class. Med., Class. Philol., Class. Qly, Class. Rev., Gk, Rom. Byz. Studies, Historia, Jl Egypt. Archaeol., Jl Hellen. Studies, Jl Rom. Studies, Mus. Helv., Kokalos, Pheonix, Pros. Camb. Philol. Soc. *Address*: School of Classics, The Univ., PO Box 147, Liverpool L69 3BX.

Walcot, Prof. Peter; Professor, Department of Classics, University College, Cardiff, since 1973; *b* 1931; *m* 1956; two *s* one *d*. BA London 1952, MA Yale 1954, PhD London 1955. Jt Ed., Greece and Rome, 1969– . Asst Lectr, Univ. Coll., Cardiff, 1957–59; Lectr, 1959–66, Sen. Lectr, 1966–73, Univ. Coll., Cardiff. *Publications*: Hesiod and the Near East, 1966; Greek Peasants, Ancient and Modern, 1970; *contrib*. Class. Qly, Greece Rome, Rev. Etudes Grec., Symb. Oslo., Ugarit Forsch. *Address*: Univ. College, Cardiff CF1 1XL.

Waley, Dr Pamela Joan; Lecturer in Spanish and Italian, Westfield College, University of London, since 1960; *b* 1921; *m* 1945; one *s* two *d*. BA London 1942 (1st cl. Italian), BA London 1957 (1st cl. Spanish), PhD London 1967. Pt-time Lecturer in Italian, Westfield Coll., 1956–60, Foreign Off., 1942–45. *Publications*: trans., Botero: The Reason of State, 1956; Verzone: From Theodoric to Charlemagne, 1968; Pignatti: Pietro Longhi, 1969; Briganti: View Painters of Europe, 1970; ed, J. de Flores: Grimalte y Gradissa, 1971; *contrib*. Bull. Hispan. Studies, Hispanóf., Ital. Studies, Neophilol., Rev. Filos. Españ. *Address*: Dept of Spanish, Westfield College, Kidderpore Avenue, Hampstead, NW3 7ST.

Wales, Kathleen Margaret; Lecturer in English, Royal Holloway College, University of London, since 1968; *b* 1946; *m* 1971; one *s*. BA London 1967 (1st cl. Hons English); Mem.: Philological Soc. of Gt Britain, Linguistics Assoc. of Gt Britain, Soc. for Study of Med. Langs and Lit., Assoc. for Literary and Linguistic Computing. Tutorial Research Student, Royal Holloway Coll., 1967–68. Asst Warden, Royal Holloway Coll., 1968–71; Treas., Coll. Br. of Assoc. of Univ. Teachers. 1970–73. *Publications*: *contrib*. Times Educnl Supplement. *Address*: Dept of English, Royal Holloway College, Egham, Surrey TW20 OEX.

Walford, Rex Ashley; University Lecturer in Education, University of Cambridge, since 1973; *b* 1935; *m* 1969. BScEcon London 1955, CertifEd London 1956, BD London 1958, MA Northwestern 1961, MA Cantab 1973; FRGS 1955, Mem. Geograph. Assoc. 1957. Sen. Tutor, Maria Grey Coll. of Educn, Univ. London, 1968–73. *Publications*: ed jtly, On the Spot Geographies (9 books), 1966–69; Games in Geography, 1969 (trans. German

1972); (with J. L. Taylor) Simulation in the Classroom, 1972 (trans. German, Dutch, French); ed, New Directions in Geography Teaching, 1973; (with J. L. Bale and N. J. Graves) ed, Perspectives in Geographical Education, 1973; (with G. W. Dinkele and S. Cotterell) Geographical Games, 1974; *contrib*. Geography. *Address*: Dept of Education, Univ. of Cambridge, Brookside, Cambridge.

Walker, Arthur David McKinnon; Lecturer, Department of Philosophy, University of Hull, since 1970; *b* 1943. BA Oxon 1964 (1st cl. Hons Lit. Hum.). Asst Lectr in Philos., Univ. Hull, 1967–70. *Publications*: (with G. Wallace) ed, The Definition of Morality, 1970; *contrib*. Analysis, Mind. *Address*: Dept of Philosophy, Univ. of Hull, Hull HU6 7RX.

Walker, Dr Colin Alexander Stewart; Lecturer in German and Germanic Studies, Queen's University, Belfast, since 1970; *b* 1938; *m* 1963; one *s* one *d*. BA QUB 1959, PhD Bristol 1973. Asst Lectr, Bristol Univ., 1961–64, Lectr, 1964–70; Lectr, QUB, 1970–73. *Publications*: *contrib*. GLL. *Address*: Dept of German, Queen's Univ., Belfast BT7 1NN.

Walker, Rev. Canon David Grant; Senior Lecturer, Department of History, University College of Swansea, University of Wales, since 1973; *b* 1923; *m* 1951; one *s* one *d*. BA Bristol 1949 (1st cl.), DPhil Oxon 1954; FSA 1960, FRHistS 1962. Asst Lectr, Swansea, 1951–53; Lectr, Swansea, 1953–63. Subdean, Fac. of Arts, 1962–66; Dean, Fac. of Arts, 1969–71; Mem., Senate and Sub-Cttees; Exam. Chaplain, Bp of Swansea and Brecon; OCF, RAF; Canon of Brecon, 1972. Hon. Editor, Hist. Soc. of the Church in Wales, 1973. *Publications*: A Short History of St Mary's, Swansea, 1959, 3rd edn 1967; The Big Ten, 1960; Nerth yr Eglwys, 1964; William the Conqueror, 1968; ed. and contrib., Swansea and Brecon, 1923–73; jt ed. and contrib., Swansea and Brecon Historical Essays, 1974; Charters of the Earldom of Hereford, 1095–1201, in, Camden Miscellany XXII, 1964; Some Charters relating to St Peter's, Gloucester, in, Pipe Roll Society (NS) 36, 1967; The Organisation of Material in Medieval Cartularies, in, The Study of Medieval Records, 1971; *contrib*. Brist. Gloucs Archaeol. Soc., Bull. Inst. Hist. Res., Ch Qly Rev., Durh. Univ. Jl, EHR, Mod. Chman, Morgannwg, Trans Woolhope Soc., Welsh Hist. Rev. *Address*: Univ. College, Singleton Park, Swansea SA2 4PP.

Walker, Prof. David Maxwell, QC, MA, PhD, LLD; Regius Professor of Law, Department of Private Law, University of Glasgow, since 1958; *b* 1920; *m* 1954. MA Glasgow 1946, LLB Glasgow 1948, PhD Edinburgh 1952, LLB London 1957, LLD Edinburgh 1960, LLD London 1968, Hon. LLD Edinburgh 1974; Advocate of the Scottish Bar 1948, Barrister-at-Law, Middle Temple, 1957, Queen's Counsel (Scotland) 1958, FSAScot. Dir, Scottish Univs Law Inst., 1974– . Prof. of Jurisprudence, Glasgow, 1954–58; Dean, Fac. of Law, 1956–59. Indian Army, 1939–45; Hon.

Sheriff, Lanarkshire, 1966– . *Publications*: Faculty Digest of Decisions, 1940–50, 1953; Law of Damages in Scotland, 1955; The Scottish Legal System, 1959, 3rd edn 1969; Law of Delict in Scotland, 1966; Principles of Scottish Private Law, 1970; Law of Prescription in Scotland, 1973; Law of Civil Remedies in Scotland, 1974; ed, Scottish part of Topham and Ivamy: Company Law, 12th, 13th, 14th edns, 15th edn 1974; chapters in collaborative vols; *contrib*. Jl Soc. Public Teachers Law, Jurid. Rev., Mod. Law Rev., Scotts Law Times. *Address*: Dept of Private Law, Univ. of Glasgow, Glasgow G12 8QQ.

Walker, (George) Marshall, MA; Lecturer in English Literature, University of Glasgow, since 1965; *b* 1937; *m* 2nd 1970; one *s* four *d*. MA Glasgow 1960; CertEd Jordanhill 1961. Mem., Brit. Assoc. Amer. Studies. Lectr, Rhodes Univ., S Africa, 1962–65; Vis. Prof., George Peabody Coll., Nashville, Tennessee, 1968–69; Vis. Prof., Memphis State Univ., and Idaho State Univ., 1970–71. *Publications*: *contrib*. Dubliner, Engl. Studies Afr., Scott. Internat., Standpunkte, Studies Lit. Imag. *Address*: Dept of English Literature, Univ. of Glasgow, Glasgow G12 8QQ.

Walker, Prof. Kenneth Richard; Professor of Economics with special reference to China, Head of Department of Economic and Political Studies, School of Oriental and African Studies, University of London, since 1972; *b* 1931; *m* 1959; one *s* one *d*. BA Leeds 1953 (Econs), DipAgricEcons Oxon 1954, DPhil Oxon 1959. Asst Lectr in Polit. Econ., Univ. Aberdeen, 1956–59; School of Oriental and African Studies: Research Fellow, 1959–61; Lectr in Econs, 1961–66; Reader in Econs, 1966–72. Mem. Liaison Cttee on Contemp. Chinese Studies, SSRC of USA, 1965–71; Mem. Exec. Editorial Cttee, China Quarterly, 1968– . *Publications*: Planning in Chinese Agriculture: Socialisation and the Private Sector, 1956–62, 1965; *contrib*. China Quarterly, Econ. Develt and Cultural Change, Scottish Jl Polit. Economy. *Address*: School of Oriental and African Studies, Univ. of London, Malet Street, WC1E 7HP.

Walker, Prof. Nigel David; Wolfson Professor of Criminology and Director of Institute of Criminology, University of Cambridge, since 1973; *b* 1917; *m* 1939; one *d*. MA Oxon, PhD Edinburgh, DLitt Oxon; Vice-Pres. Howard League, Mem. British Soc. of Criminology. Reader in Criminology, Univ. Oxford, 1961–73. Chm. Home Secretary's Adv. Council on Probation and After-Care, 1970– ; Mem. Inter-departmental Cttee on Mentally Abnormal Offenders, 1973– ; Mem. Scottish Council on Crime, 1972– ; Mem. Editorial Boards of British Jl of Criminology, Criminal Law Review, etc. *Publications*: Delphi: a Latin poem, 1937; A Short History of Psychotherapy 1957 (various translations); Morale in the Civil Service, 1961; Crime and Punishment in Britain, 1965, 2nd edn 1968; Crime and Insanity in England, vol. 1 1968, vol. 2 1973; Sentencing in a Rational Society, 1969, 2nd edn 1971; Crimes, Courts and Figures, 1971; *contrib*. Brit. Jl Criminology,

Brit. Jl Philos. of Science, Brit. Jl Psychiatry, Criminal Law Review. *Address*: King's College, Cambridge.

Walker, Lt-Comdr Peter H., MSc, FRMetS, MRTS, ASIA, RNR; Lecturer in Television and Communication, Television Centre, Heriot-Watt University, since 1968; *b* 1934; *m* 1961; one *d*. BSc Manchester 1955, MSc Manchester 1966; FRMetS 1956; Mem., Royal Television Soc., 1969; Associate Mem., Soc. Industrial Artists and Designers, 1973. *Address*: Heriot-Watt Univ., 31–35 Grassmarket, Edinburgh EH1 2HT.

Walker, Dr Ralph Charles Sutherland; Fellow and Tutor in Philosophy, Magdalen College, Oxford, since 1972; *b* 1944. BA McGill 1964, BPhil Oxon 1966, DPhil Oxon 1970, MA Oxon 1971. Fellow of Merton Coll., Oxford, 1968–72; Vis. Lectr, Makerere Univ., 1972. *Address*: Magdalen College, Oxford OX1 4AU.

Walker, Robert Scott, MA, FLA; Lecturer in Bibliographical Studies, Department of Librarianship, University of Strathclyde, since 1964; *b* 1921; *m* 1956; two *s*. MA Strathclyde 1970; FLA 1960. Hon. Sec., Scott. Libr. Assoc., 1967– ; Mem., Working Party on Standards for Public Libr. Service Scotl., 1967–69. *Publications*: Library Resources in Scotland, 1968, 2nd edn 1972; *contrib*. Ann. Libr. Science, Libr., Libr. Assoc. Rec., Libr. Rev., Scott. Libr. Assoc. News. *Address*: Dept of Librarianship, Univ. of Strathclyde, Glasgow G1 1XW.

Walker, Dr Roger Michael, BA, PhD; Reader in Spanish, Birkbeck College, University of London, since 1972; *b* 1938; *m* 1960; one *s* one *d*. BA Manchester 1960 (1st cl. Mod. Langs), PhD London 1970. Asst Lectr, Bristol Univ., 1961–63; Asst Lectr, 1963–64, Lectr, 1964–72, Birkbeck Coll., London; Vis. Prof., Univ. of Georgia, 1970. *Publications*: (with B. Dutton and L. P. Harvey) Cassell's Compact Spanish Dictionary, 1969, American edns 1969, 1970; Estoria de Santa María Egiçiaca, 1972; Tradition and Technique in El Libro del Cavallero Zifar, 1974; *contrib*. Bull. Hispan. Studies, Filol., Forum Mod. Lang. Studies, Med. Æv., Mod. Lang. Notes, Mod. Lang. Rev., Rev. Camon. *Address*: Dept of Spanish, Birkbeck College, Malet Street, WC1E 7HX.

Walker, Dr William Michael; Lecturer in Sociology, University College, Cardiff, since 1965; *b* 1935; *m* 1960; one *d*. BCom Birmingham 1958 (1st cl.), PhD Birmingham 1965. Res. Assoc., Manchester Univ., 1962–65. Vis. Associate Prof. of Sociology, Univ. of New Hampshire, 1973. *Publications*: *contrib*. Brit. Jl Sociol. *Address*: Dept of Sociology, Univ. College, Cardiff CF1 1XL.

Walkland, Stuart Alan; Senior Lecturer, Department of Political Theory and Institutions, University of Sheffield, since 1965; *b* 1925; *m* 1965. MA St Andrews 1951 (1st cl.). Mem., AUT, Study Parlt Gp. Asst Lectr in Politics, Univ. of Aberdeen, 1956–57; Asst Lectr in Politics, Univ. of Sheffield, 1957–59; Lectr, Univ. of Sheffield, 1959–65. Mem.,

Jt Matric. Bd, for Univ. of Sheffield, 1968– .
Publications: The Legislative Process in Great
Britain, 1968; *contrib.* Parl. Aff., Pol Qly, Pol
Studies, Public Admin. *Address*: Univ. of
Sheffield, Sheffield S10 2TN.

Wall, David, BSc(Econ); Lecturer in
Economics, School of Social Sciences, Uni-
versity of Sussex, since 1965; *b* 1940; *m* 1963;
two *s* one *d*. BSc(Econ) 1962 (2nd cl.). Vis.
Prof., Univ. of Wisconsin, Milwaukee, 1969;
Vis. Fellow, Univ. of Chicago, 1969–70.
Cnsltnt, UN Corp. on Trade and Develop-
ment, 1965, 1966, 1968; FAO IBRD/ICO
Coffee Study, 1967; Min. of Overseas
Develop., 1968; UN Develop. Programme,
1969; Cwealth Secretariat, 1972; IBRD
(World Bank), 1972–74. *Publications*: Rondoy,
1964; The Third World Challenge, 1968; ed,
Chicago Essays in Economic Development,
1972; The Charity of Nations, 1973; contrib.
Trade Strategy for Rich and Poor Nations,
ed H. G. Johnson, 1971; Destiny or Delusion,
ed D. Evans, 1971; The UK, EEC and the
Third World, 1971; *contrib.* Economica, Jl
Econ. Studies, Jl Develop. Studies. *Address*:
School of Social Sciences, Univ. of Sussex,
Brighton BN1 9QN.

Wall, John Leonard, BA, PhD; Senior
Lecturer in Education, Goldsmiths' College,
London University, since 1968; *b* 1919; *m*
1957; one *s* one *d*. BA London (External)
1950 (Hons English), BA (Hons Classics)
qualifying for MA London (Internal) 1955,
PhD London 1968 (Classics), Acad. DipEd
London 1971; Teachers' Cert. 1948, Cert. in
Education of Junior School Children, London
Inst. of Educn, 1956. Mem., Soc. Prom. Rom.
Studies; Life Mem., Birkbeck Coll., 1969.
Teacher, Primary and Secondary Schs, 1948–
59; Dep. Hd, Tanys Dell Jun. Sch., Harlow,
1959–62; Hd, Latton Green Jun. Sch.,
Harlow, 1962–66; Lectr, London Inst. of
Educn, 1967– ; Lectr in Educn, Gold-
smiths' Coll., Univ. of London, 1966–68.
Address: Goldsmiths' College, London Univ.,
New Cross, SE14 6NW.

Wall, Rachel Frances, MA; Lecturer in
International Politics, Department of Social
Studies, Oxford University, since 1964;
b 1933. BA Manchester 1955 (2nd cl. Politics
and Mod. Hist.), MA Cantab 1961, MA Oxon
1964. Scholar, Inst. ital. di studi storici,
1955–56. Royal Inst. of Internat. Affairs,
1956–61. Eugene Strong Res. Fellow, Girton Coll., Cambridge, 1961–64; Lectr in
Politics, St Hugh's Coll., 1964– , and Lady
Margaret Hall, 1964–72; Fellow, St Hugh's
Coll., 1965– . *Publications*: (with G. Barraclough) Survey of International Affairs 1955–
56, 1960; (with G. Barraclough) Survey of
International Affairs 1956–58, 1962; (with G.
Barraclough) Survey of International Affairs
1958–60, 1964; Japan's Century, 1964; Die
Washington Konferenz aus Die Folgen von
Versailles 1919–1924, 1968; Japans Politik in
den Vorkriegsjahren aus Weltpolitik 1933–
1939, 1973; *contrib.* Times Lit. Supp., etc.
Address: St Hugh's College, Oxford.

Wall, Dr William Douglas; Professor of
Educational Psychology, University of London, since 1972; *b* 1913; *m* 1936, 1960; three *s*

one *d*. BA London 1934 (1st cl. English),
PhD Birmingham 1947 (Psychol.); Mem.
BPsS (Cttee of Prof. Psychologists: Social
Psych. Sect.: Child and Ed. Psych. Sect.).
Univ. of Birmingham, Educn Dept, 1945–
51, Reader, 1948–53; Head Educn and Child
Develop. Unit, UNESCO Paris, 1951–56;
Dir, Nat. Foundn for Educn Res. in England
and Wales, 1956–68; Dean, Univ. of London
Inst. of Educn, 1968–72; Vis. Prof.: Univ. of
Michigan, 1957; Univ. of Jerusalem, 1962;
Univ. of Tel Aviv, 1967. Chm., Internat.
Project Evaluation of Educn Attainment,
1958–62; Mem., Police Trng Council,
1970– ; Mem., BBC TV Cttee on Social
Effects of TV; Co-dir and Chm., Nat. Child
Develop. Study, 1958; Mem., Council Internat. Children's Centre, Paris, 1970– . *Publications*: Adolescent Child, 1948, 2nd edn
1952 (trans. Portuguese, Italian, 1970, 1971);
Education and Mental Health, 1955 (trans.
German, French, Spanish, Arabic, Polish,
etc.); Psychological Services for Schools,
1956 (Fr. trans. 1958, German trans. 1956);
Child of Our Times, 1959; Failure in School,
1962; Adolescents in School and Society,
1968 (Italian, French trans); Longitudinal
Studies and the Social Sciences, 1970; Con-
structive Education – the first decade, vol. i,
1974; *contrib.* Brit. Jl Educnl Psych., Brit. Jl
Psych., Ed. Res., Ed. Rev., Enfance, Human
Develop., Internat. Rev. Ed., Ed. and Mental
Health Bull. *Address*: Univ. of London,
Institute of Education, Malet Street, WC1E
7HS.

Wallace, Richard; Lecturer in Classics,
University of Keele, since 1965; *b* 1941; *m*
1968; one *d*. BA Leicester 1963, MA Mc-
Master 1964. *Address*: Dept of Classics,
Univ. of Keele, Keele, Staffordshire.

Wallace, Dr William John Lawrence;
Lecturer, Department of Government, University of Manchester, since 1967; *b* 1941;
m 1968. BA Cantab 1962 (Hist.), MA Cantab
1966, BA Oxon 1965 (incorporated), PhD
Cornell 1968. Teaching Asst, Cornell Univ.,
1962–65; Carpenter Fellow, Cornell Univ.,
1965–67; Studentship, Nuffield Coll., Oxford,
1965–67. *Publications*: Foreign Policy and the
Political Process, 1972; *contrib.* Govt Opposit.,
Pol Studies, Jl Common Market Studies,
Internat. Affairs. *Address*: Dept of Government, Univ. of Manchester, Manchester M13
9PL.

Wallace, Prof. William Villiers, MA;
Professor of History, New University of
Ulster, since 1967; *b* 1926; *m* 1953; two *s* one
d. MA Glasgow 1950 (Hist.), MA London
1953 (Czechoslovak Reg. Studies); FRHistS.
Lectr, Pittsburgh Univ., 1953–54; Lectr,
Aberdeen Univ., 1957–59; Lectr, Durham
Univ., 1959–67. Sub-Lt, RNVR, 1944–47;
Mem., Exec., AUT, 1969– , Vice-Pres.,
1973–74; Pro-Vice-Chancellor, New Univ.
of Ulster, 1971– . *Publications*: Czechoslo-
vakia, 1974; *contrib.* EHR, Internat. Aff., Jl
Amer. Studies, Slav. E Europ. Rev. *Address*:
School of Humanities, New Univ. of Ulster,
Coleraine, Co. Londonderry BT52 1SA.

Wallace-Hadrill, Prof. John Michael;
Chichele Professor of Modern History and

727

Fellow of All Souls College, Oxford, since 1974; *b* 1916; *m* 1950; two *s*. MA Oxon, DLitt Oxon; FBA 1969. Fellow, Corpus Christi Coll., Oxford, 1946–47; Fellow and Tutor, Merton Coll., Oxford, 1947–55; Prof. of Med. History, Manchester, 1955–61; Sen. Res. Fellow, Merton Coll., Oxford, 1961–74; Ford's Lectr, Oxford, 1969–70; Birkbeck Lectr, Cambridge, 1973–74. Editor, English Historical Review, 1965–74. *Publications*: The Barbarian West, 1952, 3rd edn 1967 (trans. Italian and Spanish); (with J. McManners) France, Government and Society, 1957; The Chronicle of Fredegar, 1960; The Long-Haired Kings, 1962; Early Germanic Kingship, 1971. *Address*: All Souls College, Oxford.

Waller, Dr Bruce; Lecturer, Department of History, University College of Swansea, since 1965; *b* 1932; *m* 1959; two *d*. BA Florida 1954, PhD London 1963. Asst Lectr, UC Swansea, 1963–65. *Publications*: Bismarck at the Crossroads: The Reorientation of German Foreign Policy after the Congress of Berlin, 1974. *Address*: History Dept, Univ. College of Swansea, Singleton Park, Swansea SA2 8PP.

Waller, (David) Michael, MA, BA; Lecturer in Government, University of Manchester, since 1971; *b* 1934; *m* 1970; one *d*. BA Oxon 1958 (Lit. Hum.), PGCE London 1959, BA Manchester 1963 (Hons Russian), MA Oxon. Lectr in Russian and Soviet Studies, Lancaster Univ., 1964–71. *Publications*: The Language of Communism, 1972; *contrib*. Cambridge Opinion, Govt and Opposition, Incorporated Linguist, Soviet Studies. *Address*: Dept of Government, Faculty of Economic and Social Studies, Dover Street, Manchester M13 9PL.

Waller, Michael; *see* Waller, D. M.

Waller, Philip John; Fellow and Tutor in Modern History, Merton College, Oxford, since 1971; *b* 1946; *m* 1971. BA Oxon 1967 (1st cl. Hons), MA Oxon. Fellow, Magdalen Coll., Oxford, 1968–71; CUF Lectr, Oxford Univ., 1972. *Publications*: Racial Phobia: The Chinese Scare 1906–1914, in, Essays Presented to C. M. Bowra, 1970. *Address*: Merton College, Oxford.

Waller, Dr Richard Edmund Ashton, MA, DPhil; Lecturer in French, University of Liverpool, since 1970; *b* 1941; *m* 1962; one *s* one *d*. BA Oxon 1963, MA Oxon 1967, DPhil Oxon 1972. Asst Lectr, Queen's Univ., Belfast, 1963–64; Instructor, Univ. of Victoria, BC, 1964–66. *Address*: Dept of French, Modern Languages Building, PO Box 147, Univ. of Liverpool, Liverpool L69 3BX.

Wallis, Dr Kenneth Frank; Reader in Statistics, with Special Reference to Econometrics, London School of Economics, since 1972; *b* 1938; *m* 1963. BSc Manchester 1959, MScTech Manchester 1961, PhD Stanford 1966. Mem., Council, Royal Stat. Soc., Mem., Royal Econ. Soc., Mem., Economet. Soc. Res. Staff Economist and Lectr, Yale Univ., 1965–66; Lectr in Stats,

with special reference to Econometrics, LSE, 1966–72. *Publications*: Introductory Econometrics, 1972; Topics in Applied Econometrics, 1973; *contrib*. Economet., Jl Econ. Lit., Jl Royal Stat. Soc., Rev. Econ. Stats, Economica (Jt Editor), Jl Amer. Stat. Assoc. *Address*: London School of Economics, Houghton Street, WC2A 2AE.

Wallis, Peter John; Reader in Historical Bibliography of Education, School of Education, University of Newcastle upon Tyne, since 1970; *b* 1918; *m* 1939; three *s* two *d*. BA Cantab 1939, DPA London 1940, MA Cantab 1943, Teacher's Diploma 1947; FIMA 1964, FRHistSoc 1964. Lectr in Educn, Univ. Newcastle upon Tyne, 1963–70. Res. Mathematician on radar, 1941–45; Sen. Maths, Sixth Form and House Master in schools, 1945–53; Head Master, 1953–62. Mem. Nat. Council, Math. Assoc. (Local Pres.); Dir, Biobibliography of British Maths, 1966– ; Dir, Book Subscription Lists Project, 1972– . *Publications*: Sheffield Church Burgesses, 1957; ed, Guide to Digital Computers, 1962; William Crashawe: The Sheffield Puritan, 1963; Histories of Old Schools, 1965, 2nd edn 1966; Book Subscriptions Lists: a Preliminary (revised) Guide 1972, 1974; contrib. The Art of the Librarian, 1973; *contrib*. Accountants' Mag., Bibliotheck, Bod. Lib. Record, Br. Jl Ed. Studies, Br. Jl Hist. Sc., Centaurus, Cumb. and Westmorland Soc. Trans, Derb. Arch. Jl, Dict. Sc. Biog., Durham Res. Rev., Hist. Math., Jl IEE, Jl Inst. Nav., Leeds Univ. Res. and Studies, Library, Math. Gaz., Maths in School, North Notes, Phil Mag., Trans Camb. Bib. Soc., Trans Lancs and Cheshire Hist. Soc., Yorks Arch. Soc. Jl. *Address*: School of Education, The University, Newcastle upon Tyne NE1 7RU.

Wallis, Roy William, BCom, AIMTA; Lecturer in Accounting and Business Finance, since 1964, and sometime Tutor to the Faculty of Economics and Social Studies, University of Manchester; *b* 1932; *m* 1958; two *s*. BCom London 1954 (External); AIMTA 1956 (Chartd Municipal Treas.). HM Comr of Public Wks Loans Bd, 1968–72. Vis. Fellow in Public Finance, Mauritius, 1972–74. *Publications*: Accounting: a modern approach, 1970; Financial Management in the Health Services, in, Health Services: Administration, Research and Management, ed P. Ferrer, 1972; *contrib*. Loc. Govt Fin. *Address*: Dept of Accounting and Business Finance, Univ. of Manchester, Manchester M13 9PL.

Walls, Andrew Finlay; Senior Lecturer, Head of the Department of Religious Studies, and Riddoch Lecturer in Comparative Religion, University of Aberdeen, since 1970; *b* 1928; *m* 1953; one *s* one *d*. BA Oxon 1948 (1st cl. Theol.), MA Oxon 1952, BLitt Oxon 1954. Recog. Teacher in Theological Subjects, Bristol Univ., 1951–52; Lectr in Theology, Univ. Coll. of Sierra Leone, 1957–62; Hd of Dept of Religion (Sen. Lectr, 1962–65, Assoc. Prof., 1965), Univ. of Nigeria, Nsukka, 1962–65; Lectr in Church History, Aberdeen Univ., 1966–69; Sen. Lectr in Church History, Aberdeen Univ.,

1969–70; Vis. Prof., Univ. of Botswana, Lesotha and Swaziland, 1972. Libr., Tyndale Hse, Cambridge, 1952–57; Sec., Scott. Inst. Missionary Studies, 1969– ; Hon. Ed., Soc. Afr. Ch Hist., 1963– ; Mem., Cttee, Internat. Assoc. Mission Studies, 1970– ; Mem. Council, Afr. Stud. Assoc. UK, 1973– ; Aberdeen City Educn Cttee; Ed., Jl Relig. Afr. *Publications*: (with A. M. Stibbs) I Peter, an introduction and commentary, 1959; Guide to Christian Reading, 1962; Bibliography of the Society for African Church History, 1967; contrib. New Bible Commentary, 1953, rev. edn 1970; New Bible Dictionary, 1962; Apostolic History and the Gospel, ed Martin and Gasque, 1970; The Mission of the Church and the Propagation of the Faith, ed Cuming, 1970; Melvill Horne's Letters on Missions (forthcoming); (with G. H. Anderson) 500 Basic Books for Missionary Studies, (forthcoming); *contrib*. Internat. Rev. Miss., Jl Relig. Afr., NT Studies, S Leone Bull. Relig., Studia Patrist., Vigil. Christ. *Address*: Dept of Religious Studies, Univ. of Aberdeen, Aberdeen AB9 2UB.

Wallwork, Dr Kenneth Lee; Senior Lecturer in Geography, School of Biological and Environmental Studies, New University of Ulster, since 1968; *b* 1933; *m* 1958 (decd 1972); two *s* one *d*. BA Manchester 1954 (Geog.), MA Manchester 1955, PhD Leicester 1966; Member: Geog. Assoc., Inst. Brit. Geogrs, Reg. Studies Assoc. Asst Lectr, Univ. Manchester, 1956–57; Lectr, Univ. Leicester, 1957–67. *Publications*: (with A. H. W. Robinson) Map Studies with Related Field Excursions, 1970; Derelict Land: the Origins and Prospects of a Land Use Problem, 1974; *contrib*. E Midland Geogr, Geography, Geograph. Jl, Internat. Salt Symposium Proc., Irish Geography, Trans and Papers Inst. Brit. Geogrs. *Address*: School of Biological and Environmental Studies, New Univ. of Ulster, Coleraine BT52 1SA.

Walsh, Amory Allfrey P.; *see* Pakenham-Walsh.

Walsh, Prof. Patrick Gerard, MA, PhD; Professor of Humanity, University of Glasgow, since 1972; *b* 1923; *m* 1953; four *s* one *d*. BA Liverpool 1949 (1st cl. Classics), MA Liverpool 1951, PhD National Univ. of Ireland 1957. Lectr, Univ. Coll., Dublin, 1952–59; Lectr, Edinburgh Univ., 1959–66; Vis. Prof., Toronto, 1966–67; Reader, Edinburgh Univ., 1967–70; Vis. Prof., Yale, 1970–71; Prof. of Medieval Latin, Edinburgh, 1970–72. *Publications*: Livy, his historical aims and methods, 1961; ed (with A. Ross), Aquinas: Courage, 1965; Letters of St Paulinus of Nola, 1966–67; The Roman Novel, 1970; Courtly Love in the Carmina Burana, 1972; ed Livy XXI, 1973; Poems of Paulinus of Nola, 1974; *contrib*. Amer. Jl Philol., Class. Philol., Class. Rev. Gnomon, Greece Rome, Jl Rom. Studies. *Address*: Dept of Humanity, Univ. of Glasgow, Glasgow G12 8QQ.

Walsh, Prof. William, FRSA; Professor of Commonwealth Literature, School of English, University of Leeds, since 1972; *b* 1916; *m* 1945; one *s* one *d*. MA Cantab 1945, MA London 1951; FRSA 1970. Lectr in Educn, UC N Staffs, 1951–53; Lectr, Edinburgh Univ., 1953–57; Prof. of Educn and Head of Dept of Educn Leeds Univ., 1957–72. Chm., Sch. of Educn, and Douglas Grant Fellow in Commonwealth Lit., Univ. of Leeds, 1969– ; Chm., Bd of combined Faculties of Arts, Econs, Social Studies and Law, Leeds Univ., 1964–66; Pro-Vice-Chancellor, Leeds Univ., 1965–67; Vis. Prof., ANU, 1968; Australian Commonwealth Vis. Fellow, 1970. Schoolmaster, 1943–51. Chm., Bd of Adult Educn, 1969– . Dir, Yorkshire Television, 1967– . *Publications*: Use of Imagination, 1959; A Human Idiom, 1964; Coleridge: the work and the relevance, 1967; A Manifold Voice, 1970; R. K. Narayan, 1972; V. S. Naipaul, 1972; Commonwealth Literature, 1972; (ed) Readings in Commonwealth Literature, 1973; D. J. Enright, 1974; contribs to, From Blake to Byron, 1957; Young Writers, Young Readers, 1960; Speaking of the Famous, 1962; F. R. Leavis, Some Aspects of his Work, 1963; The Teaching of English Literature Overseas, 1963; Contemporary Poets, 1970; Contemporary Novelists, 1972; Higher Education: patterns of change in the 1970s, 1972; The Literature of England, 1974; *contrib*. Brit. and Amer. Jls. *Address*: Univ. of Leeds, Leeds LS2 9JT.

Walsh, Prof. William Henry; Professor of Logic and Metaphysics, Philosophy Department, University of Edinburgh, since 1960; *b* 1913; *m* 1938; one *s* two *d*. BA Oxford 1936 (1st cl. Lit. Hum.), MA Oxford 1939; FBA 1969. Lectr in Philos., Univ. Coll., Dundee, 1946–47; Fellow and Tutor, Merton Coll., Oxford, 1947–60; Lectr in Philos., Univ. of Oxford, 1947–60; Vis. Prof., Ohio State Univ., 1957–58; Vis. Prof., Dartmouth Coll., 1965; Vis. Prof., Univ. of Maryland, 1969–70. Pres., Aristot. Soc., 1964–65; Sen. Tutor, Merton Coll., Oxford, 1954–60; Dean, Fac. of Arts, Edinburgh Univ., 1966–68. *Publications*: Reason and Experience, 1947; An Introduction to Philosophy of History, 1951; Metaphysics, 1963; Hegelian Ethics, 1969; *contrib*. Hist. Theory, Kant-Studien, Mind, Philos. Qly, Philos., Proc. Aristot. Soc. *Address*: Philosophy Dept, Univ. of Edinburgh, Edinburgh EH8 9YL.

Walters, Prof. Alan Arthur; Cassel Professor of Economics, with special reference to money and banking, London School of Economics, since 1968; *b* 1926; *m* 1950; one *d*. BSc(Econ) London (1st cl.), Gerstenberg Prize, Nuffield Studentship; FEconometSoc. Lectr, then Sen. Lectr, Univ. of Birmingham, 1952–61; Prof., and Hd of Dept of Econometrics and Social Statistics, Univ. of Birmingham, 1961–68. Econ. Adv., Sec. of State for Hlth and Soc. Security, 1970– ; Mem., Roskill Commn on Third London Airport, cost-benefit study, 1967–70; Cnsltnt to Govts of Israel, Singapore, Malaysia and ECAFE; Jt Mngng Ed., Rev. Econ. Studies, 1971; Governor, Centre for Environm. Studies, 1971– ; Mem. Editl Bd, Jl Money Credit and Banking, Urban Economics; Dir, Economists Bookshop; Principal, Inter Counsel. *Publications*: Report on Cost, Price and Competition in Transport in UK, 1958; (with M. Harwitz, et al) Growth without

Development, 1966; Integration in Freight Transport, 1968; The Economics of Road User Charges, 1968; An Introduction to Econometrics, 1968; (with E. Bennathan) Economics of Ocean Freight Rates, 1969; Money in Boom and Slump, 3 edns; An Introduction to Econometrics, 2nd edn 1970; *contrib.* Amer. Econ. Rev., Economet., Econ. Jl, Economica, Jl Pol Econ., Jl Royal Stat. Soc., Oxf. Econ. Papers. *Address*: London School of Economics, Houghton Street, WC2A 2AE.

Walters, David Beverley, Lecturer in Foreign and Comparative Law, Department of Civil Law, University of Edinburgh, since 1967; *b* 1935; *m* 1961. LLB London 1963, LLM London 1966; Member: Selden Soc., Class. Assoc., Soc. Public Teachers of Law, etc. Mem., Senatus Academicus, 1970– ; Course Dir for British Council European Lawyers' Visits, 1970– ; Dir of Studies, Edinburgh, 1972– . *Publications: contrib.* Jl Law Soc. of Scotland, Juridical Review, Zeitschrift der Savigny-Stiftung (RA), etc. *Address*: Dept of Civil Law, Univ. of Edinburgh, Old College, South Bridge, Edinburgh EH8 9YL.

Walters, Patricia Ann; Lecturer, Department of Sociology, Government and Administration, University of Salford, since 1968; *b* 1942; *m* 1962; one *d*. BA(Econ) Manchester 1962 (1st cl. Soc. Anthropol.). Mem., BSA, BSSRS. Teaching Fellow, Univ. of Michigan, 1963–64; Asst Lectr, Univ. of Manchester, 1966–68. Res. Staff, Royal Commn on Hlth Services, Ottawa, 1962–63. *Publications*: Jt Author, Women and Top Jobs, 1971. *Address*: Dept of Sociology, Government and Administration, Univ. of Salford, Salford M5 4WT.

Walton, Alan Dickinson; Lecturer, Department of Geography, University of Keele, since 1958; *b* 1925; *m* 1955; one *s*. BA London 1951, MA Wisconsin 1952; CertEd Manchester 1954; Mem., Inst. Brit. Geogrs; Mem., Assoc. Amer. Geogrs; Mem., Geog. Assoc.; Mem., Brit. Photogram. Soc.; Mem., Amer. Soc. Photogram; Mem., Remote Sensing Soc. Asst Lectr in Geography, Keele, 1954–58. Vis. Prof., Univ. of Brit. Columbia, 1961–62; responsible for Air-photo Libr., 1962– , (6,500,000 prints. Univ. of Keele is Custodian for Min. of Defence and Public Rec. Off. of part of Nat. archives). *Publications*: Air Photo Pack No 1: Casella and the Geographical Association, 1968; Air-photo Pack No 2: Casella and the Geographical Association, 1970; *contrib.* Adv. Sci., Jl Textile Inst., Jl Inst. Bank., Vis. Educn. *Address*: Dept of Geography, Univ. of Keele, Keele, Staffordshire ST5 5BG.

Walton, Prof. Henry John, MD, PhD, FRCP, FRCPsych, DPM; Professor of Psychiatry, University of Edinburgh, since 1970; *b* 1924; *m* 1959. MB, ChB Cape Town 1946, MD Cape Town 1954, DPM Royal Coll. Physicians 1956, DPM London 1956, PhD Edinburgh 1966, FRCP 1968, FRCPsych 1971. Res. Fellow, Coll. of Physicians and Surgeons, Columbia Univ., NY, 1960–61. Pres., Assoc. Med. Educn

Europe, 1970– ; Mem., Council, Royal Coll. Physicians, Edinburgh, 1969–70; Chm., Assoc. Study Med. Educn, 1968– ; Past Chm., Soc. Res. Higher Educn. *Publications*: (with N. Kessel) Alcoholism, 1965, Polish edn 1967, Danish edn 1968, Norwegian edn 1969, Finnish edn 1969; ed, Small Group Psycho-Therapy, 1971, Ital. edn, 1972; *contrib.* Amer Jl Psychiat., Brit. Jl Med. Educn, Brit. Jl Med. Psychol., Brit. Jl Psychiat., Brit. Med. Jl, Jl Med. Educn, Lancet, etc. *Address*: Univ. Dept of Psychiatry, Univ. of Edinburgh, Morningside Park, Edinburgh EH10 5HF.

Walton, J. Michael; Lecturer, Drama Department, University of Hull, since 1965; *b* 1939; *m* 1967; one *s* one *d*. MA St Andrews 1962, DipDrama Bristol 1963. Vis. Asst Prof., Univ. of Denver, 1972–73. *Publications: contrib.* New Theat., Theat. Res. (Rech. Théat.). *Address*: Drama Dept, Univ. of Hull, Hull HU6 7RX.

Walton, Prof. James Kirkwood; Professor of English Literature, University of Dublin, since 1969; *b* 1918; *m* 1948; two *s* two *d*. BA Trinity Coll. Dublin 1941, BLitt Trinity Coll. Dublin 1944, MA Trinity Coll. Dublin 1947, Barrister-at-Law 1946; Fellow, TCD, 1964, DLitt TCD 1973; Mem., Royal Irish Acad., 1972. Prof. of English, Univ. of Mysore, 1947–49; Lectr in English, Auckland Univ. Coll., 1951–55; Foyle Fellow, Shakespeare Inst., Univ. of Birmingham, 1956–57; Lectr in English, TCD, 1957–69. *Publications*: The Copy for the Folio Text of Richard III, 1955; The Quarto Copy for The First Folio of Shakespeare, 1971; *contrib.* Hermath., Rev. Engl. Studies, Shakesp. Surv. *Address*: 40 Trinity College, Dublin 2.

Walton, John, MA; Senior Lecturer, Institute of Education, University of Exeter, since 1966; *b* 1924; *m* 1950; one *s* one *d*. BA Sheffield 1949 (Hist.), MA Sheffield 1952 (Econ. Hist.), DipEd, CertEd Sheffield 1950. Gov., Plymouth Coll. of Further Educn, 1968– ; Gov., Weymouth Coll. of Educn, 1970– . *Publications*: The Integrated Day: Theory and Practice, 1970; Curriculum Organisation and Design, 1971; The Secondary School Timetable, 1972; (co-ed with P. Taylor) The Curriculum: research innovation and change, 1973; *contrib.* Forum. *Address*: The Institute of Education, The Univ., Gandy Street, Exeter.

Walton, Prof. Kenneth; Professor of Geography, University of Aberdeen, since 1965; *b* 1923; *m* 1949; two *s*. MA Edinburgh 1948 (1st cl. Geog.), PhD Aberdeen 1951; FRSE, FRSGS. Mem., Inst. Brit. Geogrs, Inst. Naut. Res., etc. Res. Fellow, Aberdeen, 1948–49; Lectr, Aberdeen, 1949–60; Sen. Lectr, Aberdeen, 1960–65; Reader, Aberdeen, 1965. Mem., SCEEB Exam. Panel, 1964–70; Countryside Commn (NE Scot.), 1972; Sec., Sect. E, Brit. Assoc., 1964–68. *Publications*: (with A. C. O'Dell) The Highlands and Islands of Scotland, 1961; The Arid Zones, 1969; ed, General and Regional Geography, 1965; *contrib.* Royal Scotl. Geog. Soc., Trans Inst. Brit. Geogrs, etc. *Address*: Dept of Geography, St Mary's High Street, Old Aberdeen AB9 2UF.

Walton, Dr Ronald Gordon; Lecturer in Social Work, School of Social Work, University College, Cardiff, since 1973; *b* 1936; *m* 1961; three *d*. BA Admin Manchester 1960, MA Econ 1967, PhD 1972; Tutor in Social Work, Manchester, 1965–72. *Publication*: Women in Social Work (forthcoming). *Address*: School of Social Work, Univ. Coll. Cardiff, PO Box 78, Cardiff CF1 1XL.

Walz, Prof. H. P. H.; Research Professor in German, University of Surrey, since 1972; *b* 1907; *m* 1957; two *s* two *d*. PhD Freiburg 1930. Mem., Germanist Soc., Mem., Comput. Science, NPL (Brain Res. Assoc.), Mem., RIIA, Mem., Assoc. Univ. Profs of French. Lectr, Univ. of Heidelberg, 1931–36; Political Refugee in England, 1936–48; Lectr, Heidelberg, 1948–67; Lectr, Univ. of Surrey, 1967–68, Prof. of Lingu. and Reg. Studies, 1968–72; Hd of English Dept, Dolmetscher Inst., Heidelberg, 1931–36, 1948–67; Founder and Dir, Sprachkybernetisches Forschungszentrum, Heidelberg, 1963–68. *Publications*: Die Jugendwerke George Merediths und ihre Bedeutung für die spätere Entwicklung des Dichters, 1931; Against the Tide, 1943; Das Britische Kolonialreich, 1955; Britain Past and Present, 1957; England, 1958; Contemporary Britain, 1965; Audio-oraler Französischkurs im Fernunterrichtsverfahren, 1966; Language Mystery and the Human Brain, 1973; *contrib*. Europa-Archiv., IRAL, Leben Fremds., Neu. Sprach., Praxis Neusprach. Unter., Rup. Carola. *Address*: Dept of Linguistic and Regional Studies, Univ. of Surrey, Guildford, Surrey GU2 5XH.

Wang, Alfredo; Lecturer, and Leader of University Ensemble, University College, Cardiff, since 1952; *b* 1918; *m* 1st 1941, 2nd 1966; two *s* one *d*. Lauréat SAM Vienna 1938. Lectr, Univ. of Sucre, Bolivia, 1940–41; Lectr, Univ. of Santiago, 1941–51; Vis. Lectr, Univ. of Oslo, 1966–67; Vis. Lectr, Univ. of Lund, 1969– . *Address*: Dept of Music, Univ. College, Cardiff CF1 1XL.

Wangermann, Ernst, MA, DPhil; Senior Lecturer in Modern History, University of Leeds, since 1969; *b* 1925; *m* 1966; two *s*. BA Oxon 1949 (2nd cl. Hist.), MA Oxon 1953, DPhil Oxon 1953; FRHistS. Lectr. Univ. of Leeds, 1962–69. *Publications*: From Joseph II to the Jacobin Trials, 1959, 2nd edn 1969, German edn 1966; The Austrian Achievement, 1700–1800, 1973; contrib. New Cambridge Mod. Hist., vol. VIII, 1965. *Address*: School of History, The Univ., Leeds LS2 9JT.

Wankowski, Dr Janislaw Adam; Lecturer, University of Birmingham School of Education and Researcher and Student Counsellor, University of Birmingham Educational Survey and Counselling Unit, since 1964; *b* 1919; *m* 1943; three *s* two *d*. BA Wales 1950, MA Wales 1958, PhD Birmingham 1972; Mem. Soc. for Research into Higher Educn. *Publications*: Temperament, Motivation and Academic Achievement (Univ. of Birmingham Survey and Counselling Unit); contrib. Student Wastage: the Birmingham Experience, in, Contemporary Problems in Higher Education, ed, Butcher and Rudd, 1972; contribs to Conferences on Research into Higher Educn; *contrib*. British Student Health Assoc., Bull. British Psychological Soc., Jl Curriculum Stud., Soc. for Research into Higher Educn. *Address*: Univ. of Birmingham, PO Box 363, Aston Webb Building, Birmingham B15 2TT.

Warburton, Dr Irene P., PhD; Lecturer in Linguistic Science, University of Reading, since 1970; *b* 1938; *m* 1965; one *s* one *d*. BA Athens 1962, PhD Indiana 1966. Indiana Univ. 1965–67; Univ. California, Irvine, 1967–69. *Publications*: On the Verb in Modern Greek, 1970; *contrib*. Glotta, JL, Lingua. *Address*: Dept of Linguistic Science, Univ. of Reading, Whiteknights, Reading, Berks RG6 2AH.

Ward, Alan; Lecturer in English Language, Wadham College, Oxford, since 1950, and Official Fellow of St Cross College, Oxford, since 1965; *b* 1923; *m* 1955; one *s*. MA Oxon 1949, BLitt Oxon 1973; Associate of Drama Board 1966. *Publications*: ed and trans., Eilert Ekwall: Historische neuenglische Laut- und Formenlehre, 1974. *Address*: St Cross College, Oxford; Wadham College, Oxford.

Ward, Rev. Dr Arthur Marcus; Lecturer in New Testament, University of London, Heythrop College, since 1972; *b* 1906; *m* 1932; three *d*. BA London 1926 (1st cl.), DipEd Cantab 1927, BA Cantab 1930 (1st cl. Theol.), MA Cantab 1933; Hon. DD Serampore 1955. Asst Tutor, Richmond Coll., 1930–32; Wesley Coll., Madras, 1932–36; Prof. of Theology, Utd Theological Coll. of India and Ceylon, Bangalore, 1936–55; Tutor, Richmond Coll., 1955–72. Mem., Negotiating Cttee for Ch Union in S India, 1937–47; Cnsltnt of Theol. Educn and Christian Lit. Funds, Wld Council of Chs. *Publications*: Our Theological Task, 1946; The Byzantine Church, 1953; Outlines of Christian Doctrine, 1954, 4th edn 1966; The Pilgrim Church, 1954; Commentary on St Matthew, 1961; The Churches Move Together, 1968; *contrib*. Expos. Times, Internat. Rev. Missions, Lond. Qly, Sobornost. *Address*: Heythrop College, Cavendish Square, W1M 0AN.

Ward, Rev. Prof. Conor Kieran; Professor of Social Science, University College, Dublin, since 1973; *b* 1930. BA National Univ. of Ireland 1950, STL Rome 1954, PhD Liverpool 1959. Asst, 1959–66, Lectr, 1966–73, Univ. Coll., Dublin. Mem., Cttee for Admin. Ford Foundn Grant for Soc. Sci. in Irel.; Chm., Dublin Inst. of Adult Educn; Mem., Irish Council of Churches; Mem., RC Church Jt Study Gp on Soc. Problems; Mem., Med.-Soc. Res. Bd; Mem., Nat. Soc. Service Council (Chm. Develt Cttee). *Publications*: Priests and People, 1961, 2nd edn 1965; Manpower in a Developing Community, 1967; New Homes for Old, 1969. *Address*: Dept of Social Science, Univ. College, Belfield, Dublin 4, Ireland.

Ward, Prof. Dennis; Professor of Russian, University of Edinburgh, since 1963; *b* 1924; *m* 1946; two *s* one *d*. BA Cantab 1948, MA Cantab 1951; Mem. BUAS, IPA. Univ.

of Edinburgh: Lectr, 1949–59; Sen. Lectr, 1959–61; Reader, 1961–63; Convener, Bd of Studies in Mod. Langs, 1969–72. *Publications*: Russian Pronunciation, 1958; Russian for Scientists, 1960; Keep up Your Russian, 1960, 2nd edn 1963; Starting Russian, 1962; Lermontov: Demon, 1961, 2nd edn 1963; Introduction to Russian, 1964; The Russian Language Today, 1965; Russian Pronunciation Illustrated, 1966; (with M. Greene) Graded Russian Reader, Bk 1 1961, Bk 2 1961, Bk 3 1962; (with D. Jones) The Phonetics of Russian, 1969; *contrib*. Archivum Linguisticum, Forum for Mod. Lang. Studies, IJSLP, Le maître phonétique, MLR, SEER. *Address*: Dept of Russian, David Hume Tower, George Square, Edinburgh EH8 9JX.

Ward, Ian, MA, MEd; Director of Physical Education, University of Liverpool, since 1971; *b* 1929; *m* 1958; two *d*. DipPE Loughborough 1952, DipPE Leeds 1957, MA N Carolina 1961, MEd Birmingham 1969. Asst Lectr, Univ. of Birmingham, 1958–60. Governor, I. M. Marsh Coll., 1970– . *Publications*: (with D. C. V. Watts) Athletics for Student and Coach, 1967; *contrib*. Physical Educn. *Address*: Sub-Dept of Physical Education, Univ of Liverpool, Liverpool L69 3BX.

Ward, Jennifer Clare, MA, PhD; Senior Lecturer in History, University of London, Goldsmiths' College, since 1972; *b* 1938. BA Oxford 1959 (2nd cl. Hist.), MA Oxford 1963, PhD London 1962. Lectr in History, Goldsmiths' Coll., 1965–72. *Publications*: (with K. Marshall and I. G. Robertson) Old Thorndon Hall, 1972; *contrib*. Proc. Suffolk Inst. Archaeol., Trans Monum. Brass Soc. *Address*: Dept of History, Univ. of London, Goldsmiths' College, SE14 6NW.

Ward, John Powell; Lecturer, Department of Education, University College, Swansea, since 1963; *b* 1937; *m* 1965; two *s*. BA Toronto 1959 (Latin and English), BA Cantab 1961 (English), MA Cantab 1970, MSc(Econ) Wales 1970 (Sociology). Mem., Brit. Sociol. Assoc., Mem., Welsh Acad. *Publications*: The Other Man (poems), 1969; The Line of Knowledge (poems), 1972. *Address*: Dept of Education, Univ. College, Singleton Park, Swansea SA2 8PP.

Ward, Rev. (John Stephen) Keith; Lecturer in Philosophy of Religion, King's College, University of London, since 1971; *b* 1938; *m* 1963; one *s* one *d*. BA Wales 1962, BLitt Oxon 1968. Lectr in Logic, Glasgow Univ., 1964–66; Lecturer in Moral Philosophy: Glasgow Univ., 1966–69; St Andrews Univ., 1969–71. *Publications*: 50 Key Words in Philosophy, 1968 (trans. Swedish 1970); Ethics and Christianity, 1970; The Development of Kant's View of Ethics, 1972; The Concept of God, 1974; *contrib*. Analysis, Jl Theol Studies, Mind, Philosophy, Philos. Quarterly, Religious Studies, Scottish Jl Theology, Theology. *Address*: Dept of Philosophy of Religion, King's College, Strand, WC2R 2LS.

Ward, Dr John Towers, MA, PhD; Senior Lecturer in Economic History, University of Strathclyde, since 1963; *b* 1930; *m* 1958; one *s*. BA Cantab 1953 (1st cl. Hist. Tripos, pts 1 and 2), MA Cantab 1957, PhD Cantab 1957. Bye-Fellow, Magdalene Coll., Cambridge, 1955; Lectr in Mod. Hist., Queen's Coll., Dundee (Univ. of St Andrews), 1956–63. Sec., Scott. Constitut. Cttee, 1968–70. *Publications*: The Factory Movement, c. 1830–1855, 1962; Sir James Graham, 1967; introd., J. Fielden: Curse of the Factory System, 1969; ed, Popular Movements, 1830–1850, 1970; The Factory System, 1970; co-ed, Land and Industry, 1971; *contrib*. Encyclopaedia Britannica; *contrib*. Bull. Inst. Hist. Res., EHR, Scott. Hist. Rev., Transp. Hist., Yorks Bull., etc. *Address*: Dept of Economic History, Univ. of Strathclyde, Glasgow G1 1XW.

Ward, Rev. Keith; see Ward, Rev. J. S. K.

Ward, Robin Harwood; Deputy Director, SSRC Research Unit on Ethnic Relations, University of Bristol, since 1972; *b* 1937; *m* 1964; one *s* one *d*. BA Cantab 1961, MA Cantab 1963, Dip. Adv. Studies Indust. Sociol. Manchester 1965. O&M Off., Cadbury Bros, Ltd, 1961–63; Lectr in Sociology, Univ. of Manchester, 1965–72. Mem., panel for Indust. Tribunals, 1971– . *Publications*: (with P. Worsley, et al.) Introducing Sociology, 1970; *contrib*., ed (with P. Worsley, et al.), Modern Sociology: Introductory Readings, 1970; ed (with P. Worsley, et al.), Problems of Modern Society, 1972; *contrib*. Race. *Address*: SSRC Research Unit on Ethnic Relations, Univ. of Bristol, 8 Priory Road, Bristol BS8 1SZ.

Ward, Dr Roy Charles; Senior Lecturer in Geography, University of Hull, since 1972; *b* 1937; *m* 1966; two *d*. BA Reading 1958 (1st cl. Geog.), PhD Reading 1962. Asst Lectr, Hull Univ., 1960–63, Lectr, 1963–72. *Publications*: Principles of Hydrology, 1967, 2nd edn 1974; Small Watershed Experiments, 1971; *contrib*. Geogl Jl, Geog., Jl Hydrol., Nature, Weather. *Address*: Dept of Geography, The Univ., Hull HU6 7RX.

Ward, Prof. William Reginald; Professor of Modern History, University of Durham, since 1965; *b* 1925; *m* 1949; two *s* one *d*. BA Oxford 1946 (1st cl. Mod. Hist.), MA, DPhil Oxford 1951; FRHistS 1954. Mem., Eccles. Hist. Soc., Pres., 1970–71. Res. Tutor, Ruskin Coll., Oxford, 1946–49; Asst Lectr, then Lectr, and later Sen. Lectr in Mod. Hist., Univ. of Manchester, 1949–65; Warden, Needham Hall, 1959–65. *Publications*: English Land Tax in the 18th Century, 1953; Georgian Oxford, 1958; Victorian Oxford, 1965; Religion and Society in England 1790–1850, 1972; The Early Correspondence of Jabez Bunting, 1972; contrib. Cambridge Mod. Hist.; Victoria County Hist. of Wiltshire; Statesmen, Scholars and Merchants (essays presented to Lucy Stuart Sutherland, ed Whetman, Dickson and Bromley), 1973; *contrib*. Bull. Inst. Hist. Res., Bull. J. Rylands Libr., EHR, Jl Eccles. Hist., Scott. Hist. Rev., Studies Ch Hist., Baptist Qly, Durham Univ. Jl. *Address*: Dept of History, Univ. of Durham, 43–6 North Bailey, Durham DH1 3EX.

Wardman, Prof. Harold William, BA, PhD; Professor of French Studies, University of Lancaster, since 1972; *b* 1919; *m* 1946; one *s* one *d.* BA London 1947 (1st cl. French), PhD London 1949. Lectr, Magee Univ. Coll., 1951–53; Lectr, then Sen. Lectr, Univ. of Ghana, 1953–61; Sen. Lectr, Univ. of W Australia, 1961–65; Sen. Lectr, Univ. of Lancaster, 1965–69; Reader, Univ. of Lancaster, 1969–72. *Publications:* Ernest Renan: A Critical Biography, 1964; *contrib.* Ess. Fr. Lit., Fr. Studies, Mod. Lang. Rev. *Address:* Dept of French Studies, Univ. of Lancaster, Bailrigg, Lancaster LA1 4YW.

Ware, Rev. Dr Kallistos Timothy; Spalding Lecturer in Eastern Orthodox Studies, University of Oxford, since 1966; *b* 1934. BA Oxon 1956 (1st cl. Lit. Hum.), MA Oxon 1959, DPhil Oxon 1965. Jane Eliza Proctor Vis. Fellow, Princeton Univ., 1959–60; Fellow, Pembroke Coll., Oxford, 1970– . Ed., East. Chs Rev., 1967– ; Archimandrite, Gk Orth. Ch, 1967– ; Mem., Brthd of Monastery of St John Theologian, Patmos, Greece, 1966– . *Publications:* The Orthodox Church, 1963, 6th edn 1973, French trans. 1968; Eustratios Argenti: A Study of the Greek Church under Turkish Rule, 1964; ed, The Art of Prayer: an Orthodox Anthology, 1966; ed and trans., The Festal Menaion, 1969. *Address:* Pembroke College, Oxford.

Ware, Prof. Niall John, MA, PhD; Professor of Spanish, University College, Cork, since 1964; *b* 1937; *m* 1964; one *s* two *d.* BA National Univ. of Ireland 1957, MA National Univ. of Ireland 1958, PhD National Univ. of Ireland 1964. Mem., Assoc. Hispan. GB Irel., Mem., Mod. Hum. Res. Assoc. Asst Lectr, Univ. Coll., Cork, 1960–64. *Publications: contrib.* Bull. Hisp. Studies, Hispan. Rev. *Address:* Dept of Spanish, Univ. College, Cork, Ireland.

Waring, Edward, MA, MLitt; Senior Lecturer in Adult Education (in Philosophy), Department of Extra-Mural Studies, University of Bristol, since 1971; *b* 1925; *m* 1950; one *s* one *d.* BA Cantab 1950 (1st cl. English), MA Cantab 1954, MLitt Cantab 1955 (Moral Science). Res. Tutor in W Dorset, Bristol Univ. Dept of Extra-Mural Studies, 1955–67; Staff Tutor in Philosophy, Bristol Univ. Dept of Extra-Mural Studies, 1967–71. *Address:* Dept of Extra-Mural Studies, Univ. of Bristol, 32 Tyndalls Park Road, Bristol.

Warman, Stephen Aidan; Lecturer in French, University of Bristol, since 1967; *b* 1939; *m* 1961; one *s* one *d.* BA Oxon 1962, MA Oxon 1965, BLitt Oxon 1968. Asst Lectr in French, Univ. Bristol, 1964–67. *Publications: contrib.* Studi Secenteschi. *Address:* Dept of French, Univ. of Bristol, Bristol BS8 1TH.

Warmington, Brian Herbert, MA; Reader in Ancient History, University of Bristol, since 1961; *b* 1924; *m* 1945; two *d.* BA Cantab 1948 (1st cl. Classics and Hist.), MA Cantab 1950. Asst Lectr in Classics, Bristol, 1951–54; Lectr in Ancient Hist., Bristol, 1954–61; Dep. Dean, Fac. of Arts, Bristol, 1970–72. Mem.,

Council, Soc. Prom. Rom. Studies, 1961–63, 1967–70; Pres., Bristol Br., AUT, 1965–67. *Publications:* The North African Provinces from Diocletian to the Vandal Conquest, 1954, 2nd edn 1972; Carthage, 1960, 2nd edn 1970, French edn 1961, German edn 1963, Hungarian edn 1967, Italian edn 1968; Nero, 1970; *contrib.* Papers Brit. Sch. Rome, Byz. Zeits. *Address:* Dept of Classics, The Univ., Bristol BS8 1TH.

Warner, Prof. Alan John; Professor of English, New University of Ulster, since 1967; *b* 1912; *m* 1937, 1968; one *s* one *d.* BA Cantab 1935 (1st cl. Pts I and II English Tripos), MA Cantab 1938, PhD Witwatersrand 1950. Lectr, Rhodes Univ. Coll., 1939–45; Lectr, Univ. of Witwatersrand, 1946–50; Prof., Makerere Univ. Coll., 1951–60; Prof., Magee Univ. Coll., 1961–67. *Publications:* A Short Guide to English Style, 1961; William Allingham: An Introduction, 1971; Clay is the Word (Patrick Kavanagh, 1904–1967), 1974; William Allingham, 1974; *contrib.* Dubl. Mag., Engl., Rev. Engl. Lit. *Address:* The New Univ. of Ulster, Coleraine, Co. Londonderry BT52 1SA.

Warner, Dr Elizabeth Ann, MA, PhD; Lecturer in Russian Studies, University of Hull, since 1967; *b* 1940; *m* 1966. MA Edinburgh 1962 (1st cl. Russian), PhD Edinburgh 1970 (Russian). Lectr in Russian, Univ. of St Andrews, 1964–67. *Publications: contrib.* Folkl., Sovetskaya etnografiya, Forum. *Address:* Dept of Russian Studies, Univ. of Hull, Hull HU6 7RX.

Warner, Francis; Fellow and Tutor in English Literature, St Peter's College, since 1965, and University Lecturer in English, University of Oxford: *b* 1937; *m* 1958; two *d.* BA Cantab 1959, MA Cantab. St Catharine's Coll., Cambridge, 1960–65. Messing Internat. Award for Distinguished Contribs to World of Literature, 1972. *Publications:* Perennia, 1962; Early Poems, 1964; Experimental Sonnets, 1965; Madrigals, 1967; Poetry of Francis Warner, 1970; Maquettes, 1972; Lying Figures, 1972; Meeting Ends, 1974; *contrib.* various jls. *Address:* St Peter's College, Oxford.

Warner, Ian Robin; Lecturer, Department of Hispanic Studies, University of Sheffield, since 1965; *b* 1940; *m* 1964; one *s.* BA Leeds 1963, PhD Leeds 1970. *Address:* Dept of Hispanic Studies, The Univ., Sheffield S10 2TN.

Warnock, Geoffrey James; Principal, Hertford College, Oxford, since 1971; *b* 1923; *m* 1949; two *s* three *d.* BA Oxon 1948, MA Oxon 1952. Fellow, Magdalen Coll., Oxford, 1949–50; Fellow and Tutor: Brasenose Coll., Oxford, 1950–53; Magdalen Coll., Oxford, 1953–71. *Publications:* Berkeley, 1953, 2nd edn 1969; English Philosophy since 1900, 1958, 2nd edn 1969; Contemporary Moral Philosophy, 1967; The Object of Morality, 1971; *contrib.* Mind, Proc. Aristotelian Soc. *Address:* Hertford College, Oxford.

Warren, Dr Andrew; Lecturer, Department of Geography, University College, London, since 1964; *b* 1937; *m* 1967; one *s* one *d*. BSc Aberdeen 1959, PhD Cantab 1967. *Publications*: (with R. U. Cooke) Geomorphology in Deserts, 1973; (with F. B. Goldsmith) ed, Conservation in Practice, 1974; *contrib*. Geograph. Jl, Sedimentology, Zeitschrift für Geomorphology. *Address*: Dept of Geography Univ. College, Gower Street, WC1E 6BT.

Warren, Donald Anson, BA; Lecturer in French, University of Kent, since 1967; *b* 1937. BA London 1960 (Hist.), CertEd London 1961. Lecteur, Sorbonne, 1963–64; Asst, then Lectr, Glasgow Univ., 1964–67. British Acad. Trav. Fellow, 1973. *Publications*: ed (with G. Almansi), l'Esploratore Turco di G. P. Marana, 1968; ed, La lettre d'un Sicilien à un de ses amis (forthcoming); *contrib*. Studi Secent. *Address*: Keynes College, Univ. of Kent, Canterbury, Kent CT2 7ND.

Warren, Dr Kenneth; University Lecturer in Geography, University of Oxford, and Fellow and Tutor in Geography, Jesus College, Oxford, since 1970; *b* 1931; *m* 1957; three *s*. BA Cantab 1954, PhD Cantab 1960; Mem. Inst. Brit. Geogrs. Asst Lectr, Univ. Leicester, 1956–59, Lectr, 1959–66; Lectr, Univ. Newcastle upon Tyne, 1966–70. *Publications*: The British Iron and Steel Sheet Industry since 1840: an Economic Geography, 1970; jtly, Regional Development in Britain, 1972; North East England (Problem Regions of Europe Series), 1973; Mineral Resources, 1973; The American Steel Industry 1850–1970, a Geographical Interpretation, 1973; *contrib*. Econ. Geog., Geog. Jl Regional Studies, Scottish Geog. Mag., Trans and Papers of Inst. Brit. Geogrs, Urban Studies. *Address*: School of Geography, Mansfield Road, Oxford.

Warren, Neil; Lecturer in Social Psychology, School of African and Asian Studies, University of Sussex, since 1966; *b* 1936; *m* 1967; one *s* one *d*. BA Cantab 1960, MA London 1963. Asst Lectr in Psychol., Brunel Univ., 1964–66; Lectr in Social Psychol., Makerere UC, 1968–70. *Publications*: (with Marie Jahoda) ed, Attidudes, 1966, 2nd revised edn 1973; *contrib*. Amer. Psychologist, Brit. Jl Social and Clin. Psychol., Child Develt, Psychological Bull., Science Studies. *Address*: School of African and Asian Studies, Univ. of Sussex, Brighton BN1 9RH.

Warren, Prof. Raymond H. C., MA, MusD; Stanley Hugh Badock Professor of Music, University of Bristol, since 1972; *b* 1928; *m* 1953; three *s* one *d*. BA Cantab 1952 (1st cl. Music), MusB Cantab 1952, MA Cantab 1956, MusD Cantab 1967; Mem., Composers' Guild, Mem., Inc. Soc. Music. Lectr, Queen's Univ. of Belfast, 1955–64; Reader in Music, Queen's Univ. of Belfast, 1964–66; Prof. of Composition, Prof. of Music, 1966–70, 1970–72. Mem., Arts Council N Irel., 1970; Mem., Council, Inc. Soc. Music., 1970. *Publications*: The Passion, 1964; String Quartet No 1, 1967; Violin Concerto, 1967; Songs of Old Age, 1971. *Address*: Music Dept, Univ. of Bristol, Bristol BS8 1TH.

Warren, Roger; Lecturer, Department of English, University of Leicester, since 1970; *b* 1943. BA Oxon 1964 and 1968, MA Oxon 1968. Leverhulme Fellow in Drama, Univ. Southampton, 1967–70. *Publications*: John Webster (Mermaid Critical Commentaries), 1970; *contrib*. Notes and Queries, Shakespeare Survey. *Address*: English Dept, Univ. of Leicester, University Road, Leicester LE1 3BX.

Warren, Prof. Wilfred Lewis; Professor and Head of Department of Modern History, The Queen's University of Belfast, since 1973 (Reader in History, 1969–73); *b* 1929; *m* 1960; one *s* two *d*. BA Oxon 1952, MA, DPhil Oxon 1956; FRHistS. Asst Lectr, Queen's Univ., Belfast, 1955–58; Lectr, Queen's Univ., Belfast, 1958–69. Warden, Alanbrooke Hall, Queen's Elms Halls of Resid., 1963–70; Chm., Bd of Wardens, 1967–68. *Publications*: King John, 1961, rev. edn 1966; 1066: The Year of the Three Kings, 1966; Henry II, 1973; *contrib*. Hist., Hist. Today, Jl Eccles. Hist. *Address*: Dept of Modern History, The Queen's Univ., Belfast BT7 1NN.

Warren Piper, David, MSc, ABPsS; Senior Lecturer in Higher Education, University of London Institute of Education, since 1970; Acting Head of University Teaching Methods Unit, since 1973; *b* 1937; *m* 1961; three *s*. BSc London 1961 (2nd cl. Special Psychol.), MSc London 1964 (Occupat. Psychol.); ABPsS, Mem., Soc. Res. Higher Educn, Mem., RSA. Res. Fellow, Res. Unit for Student Problems, Univ. of London, 1961–65; Lectr in Psychol. and Management, Hornsey Coll. of Art, 1966–68; Lectr in Occupational Psychology, Bradford Univ. Management Centre, 1968–70; seconded to Architectural Assoc., three days a week; First Year Master AA Sch. of Architecture, 1970–72. Mem., Nat. Council Dips Art Des., 1968–71; Mem., Nat. Adv. Cttee on Art Educn, Jt Working Party (3rd Coldstream Rep.), 1968–70. *Publications*: Readings in Art and Design Education, 1972; *contrib*. Des. Educn, Occupat. Psychol., Studio Internat., Univ. Qly. *Address*: Univ. Teaching Methods Unit, 55 Gordon Square, WC1H 0NT.

Warrender, Prof. James Howard; Professor of Political Theory and Institutions, University of Sheffield, since 1972; *b* 1922; *m* 1947. BA Oxon 1943 (1st cl. PPE), MA Oxon 1948. Hd of Pol. Science Dept (Lectr, then Sen. Lectr, and later Reader), Univ. of Glasgow, 1946–59; Prof. of Pol. Science, The Queen's Univ. of Belfast, 1959–72. *Publications*: The Political Philosophy of Hobbes, 1957; The Study of Politics, 1963; contrib. The General Election in Glasgow, 1950; Hobbes-Forschungen, 1969; *contrib*. Philos. Qly, Philos., Pol. Studies, Riv. Crit. Storia Filos. *Address*: Dept of Political Theory and Institutions, The Univ., Sheffield S10 2TN.

Warwick, Dr Gordon Thomas, MBE; Reader in Geomorphology, Department of Geography, University of Birmingham, since 1969; *b* 1918; *m* 1950; one *d*. BSc

Bristol 1939 (1st cl.), PhD Birmingham 1953 (Official Degree); FRGS, FGS, Mem., British Cave Res. Assoc., Mem., Engl. Ceram. Circle, Mem., Geol. Assoc., Mem., Glaciol. Soc. Asst Lectr in Geog., Univ. of Birmingham, 1946–48; Lectr in Geog., Univ. of Birmingham, 1948–63; Sen. Lectr in Geog., Univ. of Birmingham, 1963–69. Pt-time Reg. Off., Min. of Land and Nat. Resources, 1965–67; Admin Off., Min. Hsng and Loc. Govt, 1967–70; Admin Off., Dept of Environm., 1970– ; Comm. Mem., Inst. Brit. Geogrs, 1953–55; Hon. Treas., Brit. Geomorphol. Res. Gp, 1959–69; Vice-Pres., Internat. Speleol. Union, 1965–73; Mem., W Midl. Sports Council, 1965– ; Mem., Cttee, Nat. Caving Assoc., 1969–72; Mem., Senate, Univ. of Birmingham, 1969–75, Mem. Acad. Exec., 1973–75. Gold Medal, Internat. Spel. Congr., Czechoslovakia, 1973. *Publications*: Birmingham in its Regional Setting, ed M. J. Wise, 1950; contrib. British Caving, ed C. H. D. Cullingford, 1953, 2nd edn 1963; A Computer-Mapped Flora of Warwickshire, ed D. A. Cadbury, etc, 1971; *contrib*. Erdkunde, Geog. Jl, Proc. Internat. Speleol. Congs, Trans Cave Res. Gp, Zeits. Geomorphol. *Address*: Dept of Geography, The Univ., PO Box 363, Birmingham B15 2TT.

Wason, Dr Peter Cathcart; Reader in Psycholinguistics, Department of Phonetics and Linguistics, University College, London, since 1970; *b* 1924; *m* 1951; two *d*. BA Oxon 1948 (Eng. Lit.), MA Oxon 1953, BA London 1953 (Psychol.), PhD London1957 (Psychol.); FBPsS 1964, Mem. Exper. Psychol Soc., 1960. Asst Lectr, Eng. Lit., Aberdeen Univ., 1949–50; Hon. Res. Asst, Psychol. Dept., UCL, 1956–67; Sen. Vis. Res. Fellow, Center for Cognitive Studies, Harvard Univ., 1962–63. *Publications*: (with P. N. Johnson-Laird) ed, Thinking and Reasoning, 1968; (with P. N. Johnson-Laird) Psychology of Reasoning, 1972; *contrib*. Brit. Jl Psychol., Brit. Med. Bull., Cognitive Psychol., Jl Verbal Learning and Verbal Behavior, Qly Jl Exper. Psychol. *Address*: Psycholinguistics Research Unit, Univ. College, Wolfson House, 4 Stephenson Way, NW1 2HE.

Wassell, Richard Peter; Lecturer, Department of Educational Studies, Edinburgh University, since 1966; *b* 1922; *m* 2nd 1967; one *s* one *d*. MA Oxon 1948; Mem., Pol Studies Assoc. Lectr, Nottingham Univ. Extra-Mural Dept., 1957–62. *Address*: Dept of Educational Studies, 11 Buccleuch Place, Edinburgh.

Wasserman, Sidney; Lecturer, School of Applied Social Studies, University of Bradford, since 1967; *b* 1924. BA Ohio State Univ. 1946, MSSA Case-Western Reserve Univ. 1954, DSW Case-Western Reserve 1964. Lectr, Case-Western Reserve, Cleveland, Ohio, 1961–64; Asst Prof., Smith Coll., Northampton, Mass, 1964–66, Associate Prof., 1966–67. *Publications*: contrib. Children, Clin. Jl Soc. Work, Ment. Hygiene, Soc. Casework, Soc. Work (USA). *Address*: Univ. of Bradford, School of Applied Social Studies, Bradford BD7 1DP.

Waterhouse, Dr John Charles Graeme; Staff Tutor in Music, Extramural Department, University of Birmingham, since 1973; *b* 1939. BA Oxford 1960 (Music), MA Oxford 1964, DPhil Oxford 1969; Life Mem., Royal Music. Assoc., Mem., Inc. Soc. Music. Asst Lectr in Music, 1966–67, Lectr, 1967–72, Extra-Mural Dept, Queen's Univ., Belfast. *Publications*: contrib. encyclopedias of music; *contrib*. Listener, Music Lett., Music. Times, Music Musicians, Opera, Current Musicology, Proc. Royal Music. Assoc., Rass. Music. Curci, Ricord., Tempo, Times Lit. Supp. *Address*: Extramural Dept, Univ. of Birmingham, Birmingham B15 2TT.

Waters, Donald; Lecturer in German, University of Strathclyde, since 1965; *b* 1931; *m* 1958; one *s* two *d*. MA Glasgow 1952 (2nd cl.), Akad. Geprüfter Übersetzer Heidelberg 1955. *Address*: Dept of Modern Languages, Univ. of Strathclyde, Glasgow G1 1XW.

Waters, Prof. Ronald Sidney; Professor of Geography, University of Sheffield, since 1965; *b* 1922; *m* 1944; three *s* one *d*. BA Reading 1948 (1st cl.), MA Reading 1951; FRGS, Mem., Inst. Brit. Geogrs, Mem., Geog. Assoc., Mem., NZ Geog. Soc. Lectr, Sheffield Univ., 1949–54; Lectr, Exeter Univ., 1954–61; Prof., Canterbury, Christchurch, NZ, 1962–65. Sec., NZ Geog. Soc., 1962–65. *Publications*: contrib. Biul. Peryglac., Geog. Jl, Geog., Trans Inst. Brit. Geogrs. *Address*: Dept of Geography, The Univ., Sheffield S10 2TN.

Waterson, Natalie; Lecturer in Phonetics, Department of Phonetics and Linguistics, School of Oriental and African Studies, University of London, since 1950; *m* 1949; one *s* one *d*. BA London 1948 (Hons Russian). Recog. Teacher, Univ. of London, 1964. *Publications*: contrib. In Memory of J. R. Firth, ed C. E. Bazell, et al., 1966; Prosodic Analysis, ed F. R. Palmer, 1970; *contrib*. Bull. SOAS, Jl Internat. Phonet. Assoc., Jl Lingu., Trans Philol Soc. *Address*: Dept of Phonetics and Linguistics, School of Oriental and African Studies, Univ. of London, Malet Street, WC1E 7HP.

Watkin, Margaret Auriol, JP, BA; Lecturer, Department of Education, University College of Wales, Aberystwyth, since 1952; *m* 1951. BA Wales 1939 (1st cl. Econ. and Pol Science; Geog. and Anthropol. 1940), DipEd Wales 1941 (1st cl. both pts). Lectr, Univ. Coll., Swansea, 1947–55. Mem., Home Off. Res. Adv. Cttee on Probation and After Care; Mem., Central Council, Probation and After-Care; Mem., Exec. and Prison Welf. and After-Care and Adult Probation Hostels Sub-Cttees; Mem., Council, Magistrates' Assoc.; Mem., Juvenile Courts Cttee; Mem., Reg. Council, NACRO; Chm., Cards. Probation and After-Care Cttee; Chm., Talybont Petty Sessional Div.; Mem., S Wales Severn Reg. Consultative Cttee on After-Care Hostels; Mem., Bd of Visitors, HM Prison, Swansea; Chm., Supp. Benefits Tribunal; Mem., Schs' Council Working Party on Hlth Educn. *Publications*: contrib. Ysgrifau ar Addysg

(Essays on Education), 1962; *contrib.* Anthro, Hered., Magist. Man, Proc. Internat. Soc. Criminol. *Address*: Dept of Education, Univ. College of Wales, Aberystwyth SY23 2AX.

Watkins, John Howard, MA, DipEd; Senior Lecturer in French and Romance Studies, University College of North Wales, Bangor, since 1953; *b* 1915; *m* 1960. BA Wales 1937 (1st cl. French and German), DipEd Wales 1938 (1st cl.), MA Wales 1948. Asst Lectr, Univ. Coll., Bangor, 1946–49; Lectr, Univ. Coll., Bangor, 1949–53; Act. Hd of Dept, Univ. Coll., Bangor, 1951. Mem., Lit. Panel, N Wales Assoc. for Arts, 1968– . *Publications*: contrib. Dictionnaire des Lettres Françaises; contrib. Encyclopaedia Britannica; *contrib.* Fr. Studies, Mod. Langs, Mod. Lang. Rev., Moy. Age, Studia Celt., Trans Hon. Soc. Cymmrod, Ysgrif. Beirn. *Address*: Dept of French and Romance Studies, Univ. College of North Wales, Bangor LL57 2DG.

Watkins, Prof. John William Nevill, DSC, BSc(Econ), MA; Professor of Philosophy, University of London, since 1967; *b* 1924; *m* 1952; one *s* three *d.* BSc(Econ) London 1949 (1st cl.), MA Yale 1950. Asst Lectr, LSE, 1950–53; Lectr, LSE, 1953–57; Reader, LSE, 1957–67. Dist. Vis. Prof., Grinnell Coll., 1961. *Publications*: Hobbes's System of Ideas, 1965, American pbk edn 1969, rev. edn 1973; contrib. Readings in the Philosophy of Science, ed Feigl and Brodbeck, 1953; Theories of History, ed Gardiner, 1959; The Critical Approach to Science and Philosophy, ed Bunge, 1964; Problems in the Philosophy of Science, ed Lakatos and Musgrave, 1968; Readings in the Philosophy of Social Sciences, ed Brodbeck, 1968; The Problem of Inductive Logic, ed Lakatos, 1968; The Nature and Scope of Social Science: A Critical Anthology, ed Krimerman, 1969; Explanation in the Behavioural Sciences, ed Borger and Cioffi, 1970; *contrib.* Analysis, Brit. Jl Philos. Science, Mind, Philos., Philos. Qly, Proc. Aristot. Soc., Ratio. *Address*: Dept of Philosophy, London School of Economics, Houghton Street, WC2A 2AE.

Watkins, Owen Clifford, MA; Lecturer, School of Education, University of Leicester, since 1966; *b* 1922; *m* 1950; two *d.* BA London 1950 (1st cl. Engl.), MA London 1952. Lectr in charge Gen. Studies, AEI (Manchester) Wks Sch., 1953–60; Sen. Lectr, Nat. Coll. for Training Youth Leaders, Leicester, 1961–66. Mem., Min. of Educn Cttee on Gen. Studies, 1962. *Publications*: The Puritan Experience, 1972; Professional Training for Youth Work, 1972; *contrib.* Lib. Educn. *Address*: Univ. of Leicester School of Education, 21 University Road, Leicester LE1 7RF.

Watkins, Thomas Arwyn, MA; Senior Lecturer in Welsh Language and Literature, University College of Wales, since 1962; *b* 1924; *m* 1955; two *s* one *d.* BA Wales 1949 (1st cl. Welsh), MA Wales 1951, Teaching Dip. Wales 1948; Fellow Univ. of Wales 1951–52. Asst Lectr, Univ. Coll. of Wales, 1952–54; Lectr, Univ. Coll. of Wales, 1954–62; Vis.

Prof., Dublin Inst. Adv. Studies, 1971. *Publications*: Ieithyddiaeth, 1961; (with A. Conway) Hanes yr Unol Daleithiau, 1965; *contrib.* Bull. Bd Celt. Studies, Lochlann. *Address*: Univ. College of Wales, Aberystwyth SY23 2AX.

Watkins, Dr Trevor Francis, BA, PhD; Lecturer, Department of Archaeology, University of Edinburgh, since 1966; *b* 1938; *m* 1964; one *s* two *d.* BA Birmingham 1960 (Anc. Hist. and Archaeol.), PhD Birmingham 1964; FSAScot. Res. Fellow, Birmingham, 1963–66. *Publications*: *contrib.* Report of the Department of Antiquities, Cyprus, 1970. *Address*: Dept of Archaeology, Univ. of Edinburgh, 19/20 George Square, Edinburgh EH8 9JZ.

Watson; see Seton-Watson.

Watson, Alan; see Watson, W. A. J.

Watson, Andrew John, BA; Lecturer, Department of International Economic Studies, University of Glasgow, since 1968; *b* 1942; *m* 1965; two *s.* BA Hons London 1964 (Modern Chinese). *Publications*: Transport in Transition: The Evolution of Traditional Shipping in China (Michigan Abstracts No. 3), 1972; A Revolution to touch men's souls: The Family, Interpersonal Relations and Daily Life, in, Authority Participation and Cultural Change in China, ed, S. R. Schram, 1973; Life in People's China (forthcoming). *Address*: Dept of International Economic Studies, Univ. of Glasgow, Glasgow G12 8QQ.

Watson, Dr Anthony Irvine, BA, PhD; Professor since 1972 and Head of Spanish Department since 1957, Birkbeck College, University of London; *b* 1926. BA London 1952 (1st cl. Spanish), PhD London 1956. Asst Lectr, TCD, 1953–55; Lectr, Univ. Coll., Cardiff, 1955–57; Lectr and Hd of Spanish Dept, Birkbeck Coll., 1957–64; Sen. Lectr, 1964–72; Act. Hd of Spanish Dept, TCD, 1966. Moderator in Spanish, London, O and A Levels, 1963–68; Ch. Examiner in Spanish, Welsh Jt Educn Cttee, 1967–72; Moderator in Spanish, Lanchester Poly., 1967–72. *Publications*: Juan de la Cueva and the Portuguese Succession, 1971; Spanish for Beginners, 1963; Oigan Señores, 1965; Mosairco Español, 1969; contrib. Critical Essays on the Theatre of Calderón, ed B. W. Wardropper, 1965; Homage Volume for William L. Fichter, 1971; *contrib.* Bull. Hispan. Studies, Clavil., RJ. *Address*: Dept of Spanish, Birkbeck College, Malet Street, WC1E 7HX.

Watson, Bruce Anderson; Lecturer, Department of German, Bedford College, University of London, since 1967; *b* 1941; *m* 1966; two *d.* BA Oxon 1963 (1st cl. Mod. Langs), MA; Mem., Engl. Goethe Soc. Pt-time Teaching, Engl. Dept, Univ. of Freiburg, 1963–64; Asst Lectr, Dept of German, Univ. of Reading, 1964–67. Mem., Acad. Bd, Bedford Coll., 1970–73; Mem., Univ. Bd of Studies in Germ. Lang. and Lit., 1968– . *Publications*: (with Watson-Kröger) Leben um Leben, 1969 (trans. of novel by A. A. T.

736

Davies published 1967 as The Horses of Winter); editor, The Classical Era (German), The Year's Work in Modern Language Studies, 1973– ; *contrib.* Germ. Life Lett. *Address:* Dept of German, Bedford College, Regent's Park, NW1 4NS.

Watson, David Robin; Senior Lecturer in Modern History, University of Dundee (formerly Queen's College, Dundee University of St Andrews), since 1972; *b* 1935; *m* 1959; one *s* two *d.* BA Oxford 1956 (1st cl. Mod. Hist.), MA Oxford 1960, BPhil Oxford 1960 (European Hist.); Mem., Soc. Hist. Mod. Contemp. (Paris). Lectr in Mod. Hist., Dundee, 1961–72; Vis. Assoc. Prof. of French Hist., Queen's Univ., Kingston, Ontario, 1971–72. *Publications:* Clemenceau: a political biography, 1974; The Life of Charles I, 1972; contrib. The Nationalist Movement in Paris 1900–1906, in, The Right in France, ed D. Shapiro, 1962; The British constitution and the development of Parliamentary government in western Europe, in, Britain Pre-eminent, ed C. J. Bartlett, 1968; The making of the treaty of Versailles, in, Troubled Neighbours, ed N. Waites, 1971; *contrib.* EHR, Hist. Jl, Mod. Lang. Rev., Past Pres. *Address:* Dept of History, Univ. of Dundee, Dundee DD1 4HN.

Watson, Donald Henry; Special Lecturer in French Drama (pt-time), Department of French, University of Bristol, since 1969; *b* 1920. BA London 1950 (1st cl. French); Chevalier des Palmes Académiques 1967. Jun. Fellow, Dept of French, Univ. Coll., Swansea, 1955–57; Jun. Fellow, Dept of French, Univ. of Bristol, 1957; Asst Lectr, Dept of French, Bristol Univ., 1959; Lectr, Dept of French, Bristol Univ., 1960–69. *Publications:* trans of plays of Ionesco: The Lesson, The Chairs, The Bald Prima Donna, Jacques, 1958; Amédée, The New Tenant, Victims of Duty, 1958; The Killer, Improvisation, Maid to Marry, 1960; Exit the King, The Motor Show, Foursome, 1963; A Stroll in the Air, Frenzy for Two, 1965; Hunger and Thirst, The Picture, Salutations, 1968; Here Comes a Chopper, The Oversight, At the Foot of the Wall, 1971; Ionesco's Essays: Notes and Counternotes, 1964, American edn 1964; trans of plays of De Obaldia: Jenusia and Seven Impromptus for Leisure, 1965; The Satyr of La Villette, Wide Open Spaces and The Unknown General, 1970; trans., Pinget: L'Inquisitoire: The Inquisitory, 1966, American edn 1967; ed, Ionesco: Bald Prima Donna, including a trans. of a previously unpublished scene, 1966. *Address:* Dept of French, Univ. of Bristol, Bristol BS8 1TH.

Watson, Elizabeth Porges; Lecturer, English Department, University of Nottingham, since 1964; *b* 1935; *m* 2nd 1971. BA Oxford 1958 (1st cl.), BLitt Oxford 1963. Mem., Nat. Arts Colls Fund, Folklore Soc. Asst Lectr, Nottingham, 1962–64. *Publications:* Spenser, 1968; ed Gaskell: Cranford, 1972; *contrib.* Renaiss. Mod. Studies, Studia Patrist. *Address:* Dept of English, Univ. of Nottingham, Nottingham NG7 2RD.

Watson, Frank Richard; Lecturer in

Education, Institute of Education, University of Keele, since 1965; *b* 1930; *m* 1955; one *s* two *d.* BA Cantab 1953, CertEd Oxford 1954, MA Cantab 1957; AFIMA. *Publications:* An Introduction to Algol Bell, 1974; contrib. Grade 11 and 12 texts, UNESCO Mathematics Project for the Arab States; contrib. The Art of the Science Teacher, 1974; *contrib.* Educnl Res., Int. Jl Math. Educn Sci. Technol., Math. Gaz., Math. Spectrum, Maths Teaching, Math. in Sch., Computer Educ. *Address:* Institute of Education, Univ. of Keele, Keele, Staffs ST5 5BG.

Watson, George Grimes; University Lecturer in English, University of Cambridge, since 1959, and Fellow of St John's College; *b* 1927. BA Oxon 1950, MA Oxon 1954, MA Cantab 1959; Mem. Bibliographical Soc. London. Vis. Lectr, Univ. Minnesota and New York Univ., 1957–58; Lectr, UC Swansea, 1958–59. *Publications:* Cambridge Bibliography of English Literature vol. 5, 1957; Concise Cambridge Bibliography of English Literature, 1958; The Literary Critics 1962; Coleridge the Poet, 1966; The English Petrarchans, 1967; The Study of Literature, 1969; New Cambridge Bibliography of English Literature, 1969–74; The Literary Thesis: a guide to research, 1970; The English Ideology: Studies in the Language of Victorian Politics, 1973; also edns of Coleridge, Dryden, Maria Edgeworth; *contrib.* Critical Qly, Encounter, Essays in Criticism, Jl European Studies, Listener, Review of English Studies, TLS. *Address:* St John's College, Cambridge.

Watson, George J. B., BA, BLitt; Lecturer, Department of English, University of Aberdeen, since 1966; *b* 1942; *m* 1968; one *d.* BA Belfast 1964 (1st cl. Engl.), BLitt Oxon 1968. *Publications:* ed, T. Middleton: A Trick to Catch the Old One, 1968; Shakespeare's Hamlet: an introduction, 1971; Shakespeare's Julius Caesar: an introduction, 1971. *Address:* Dept of English, Univ. of Aberdeen, Aberdeen AB9 2UB.

Watson, George Ronald, MA, MLitt; Senior Lecturer in Classics, University of Nottingham, since 1968; *b* 1917; *m* 1945; one *d.* BA Dunelm 1939, MA Dunelm 1945, MLitt Dunelm 1953; Asst Lectr, Nottingham Univ., 1949–52; Lectr, Nottingham Univ., 1952–68. Loc. Sec., AUT, 1964–73; Vice-Chm., 1973–74; Hon. Treas., Classical Assoc., 1972– . *Publications:* The Roman Soldier, 1969; contrib. Britain and Rome, 1965; Christianity in Britain 300–700, 1968; Parker: Roman Legions, 1958; Oxford Classical Dictionary, 2nd edn 1970; *contrib.* Historia, Jl Rom. Studies. *Address:* Dept of Classics and Archaeological Studies, The Univ., Nottingham.

Watson, Ian P.; *see* Pitt-Watson.

Watson, Prof. James Wreford; Professor of Geography and Head of Department of Geography, University of Edinburgh, since 1954; *b* 1915; *m* 1939; one *s* one *d.* MA Edinburgh 1936, PhD Toronto 1945; FRCS, FRSE. Lectr, Sheffield Univ., 1937–39; Prof. of Geog., McMaster Univ., 1945–49.

737

Chief Geographer, Canada, and Dir of Geographical Br., Dept of Mines and Technical Surveys, 1949–54; Ed., Scottish Studies, 1957–64; Chm., Centre of Canadian Studies, Edinburgh Univ., 1974– . Award of Merit, Amer. Assoc. of Geogrs, 1949; Gov. General's Medal, Canada (Literary), 1953; Murchison Award, RGS, 1956; Res. Medal, RSGS, 1965. *Publications*: Of Time and the Lover, 1953; Unit of Five, 1957; General Geography, 1957; North America: Its Countries and Regions, 1963; A Geography of Bermuda, 1965; Canada: Problems and Prospects, 1968; ed (with R. Miller), Geographical Essays; ed, The British Isles: A Systematic Geography, 1964; ed, Collins-Longmans Advanced Atlas, 1968; ed (with T. O'Riordan), The American Environment, its Perception and Use, 1974; *contrib*. Geog., Scott. Geog. Magazine, Geog. Rev., Jl Geog., Canadian Jl Econs and Pol Sci., etc., also Canadian and British literary jls. *Address*: Dept of Geography, Univ. of Edinburgh, Edinburgh.

Watson, Joanna I. R.; Lecturer in English, University of Aberdeen, since 1968; *b* 1942; *m* 1968; one *d*. BA Oxon 1964 (2nd cl. Engl.), BLitt Oxon 1970. Asst Lectr in Engl., Queen Mary Coll., Univ. of London, 1966–68. *Publications*: contrib. to New CBEL, vol. I. *Address*: Dept of English, The Univ., Aberdeen, Scotland.

Watson, Dr John Richard, MA, PhD; Senior Lecturer in English, University of Leicester, since 1974 (Lecturer, 1966–74); *b* 1934; *m* 1962; one *s* two *d*. BA Oxon 1958 (1st cl. Engl.), MA Oxon 1964, PhD Glasgow 1966; Matthew Arnold Memorial Prize, Oxford 1961, Ewing Prize, Glasgow 1962. Asst, Glasgow Univ., 1962–64; Lectr, 1964–66; Vis. Lectr, Univ. of British Columbia, 1963; Vis. Lectr, Netherlands-England Soc., 1970. *Publications*: Picturesque Landscape and English Romantic Poetry, 1970; Turner and the Romantic Poets, in, Encounters, ed J. D. Hunt, 1971; ed, Browning, Men and Women, 1974; *contrib*. Crit. Qly, Crit. Survey, Ess. Crit., Philos. Jl, Rev. Engl. Studies, Yrs Wk Engl. Studies. *Address*: Dept of English, Univ. of Leicester, University Road, Leicester.

Watson, (John) Steven, MA, FRSE, FRHistS, JP; Principal, University of St Andrews, since 1966; *b* 1916; *m* 1942; two *s*. BA Oxon 1939 (1st cl. Hons Mod. Hist.); Hon. DLitt DePauw. Admin Asst to Controller-General, Min. of Power and Fuel, 1942; Private Sec. to Ministers of Fuel and Power, 1942–45. Lectr, Student and Tutor, Christ Church, Oxford, 1945–66; Censor, Christ Church, Oxford, 1955–61; Chm., Bd of Modern History, Oxford, 1956–58; Ed., Oxford Historical series, 1950–66; Chm., Scott. Academic Press. Wiles Lectr, 1968. Mem., Franks Commn of Univ. Inquiry, 1964–66; Mem., Cttee to examine operation of Sect. 2 of Official Secrets Act, 1971. TV scripts and performances. *Publications*: (with Dr W. C. Costin) The Law and Working of the Constitution 1660–1914, 2 vols, 1952; The Reign of George III 1760–1815 (vol. XII, Oxf. Hist. of England), 1960; A History

of the Salters' Company, 1963; essays in various collections and jls. *Address*: Univ. House, The Scores, St Andrews, Fife.

Watson, Prof. Newton, BArch, ARIBA; Bartlett Professor of Architecture, University College London, since 1969; *b* 1923; *m* 1944; two *d*. BArch Dunelm 1951 (1st cl.); ARIBA 1953. Lectr, UCL, 1960–63; Sen. Lectr, UCL, 1963–69; Vis. Prof., Univ. of California at Berkeley, 1965–66. Architectural Practice, 1951–55; Nuffield Research Fellow, 1955–57; Mem., Bd of Educn, ARCUK, 1968– ; Mem., Schs Cttee, RIBA, 1969– . *Publications*: contrib. RIBA Jl. *Address*: School of Environmental Studies, Univ. College, Gower Street, WC1E 6BT.

Watson, Thomas Edward; Senior Lecturer in Organisation, School of Industrial and Business Studies, University of Warwick, since 1970; *b* 1926; *m* 1953; three *d*. MA Edinburgh 1949, MA Edinburgh 1951 (Hons Psychol.); ABPsS 1955, MIPM 1963, Mem. Div. of Occupational Psychol. of Brit. Psychological Soc. 1971. Management trainee, Supervisor Organisation Planning, Ford Motor Co., 1951–57; Consultant, Management Selection Ltd, and Dir, MSL Trustees Ltd, 1957–63; Organisation and Personnel Adviser, Dir, Unbrako Ltd, and Group Dir, Unbrako Ltd, Unbrako Steel Co. Ltd and Unbrako Schrauben. GmbH, 1963–66. Mem. Directing Staff, Ashborne Hill Coll., 1966–70. *Publications*: (with H. E. Roff) Job Analysis, 1961; Job Evaluation, in, Director's Handbook of Management Techniques; *contrib*. Acct's Mag. *Address*: Univ. of Warwick, Coventry CV4 7AL.

Watson, Dr Thomas John, MC, MA, PhD; Reader in Audiology and Education of the Deaf, University of Manchester, since 1964; *b* 1912; *m* 1952; one *s*. MA Edinburgh 1934 (Hons Hist.), DipEd Manchester 1937, PhD Edinburgh 1949; Mem., Nat. Coll. Teachers of the Deaf, Mem., Brit. Soc. Audiol., Mem., Internat. Soc. Audiol. Lectr in Educn of the Deaf, Manchester, 1947–49; Sen. Lectr in Education of the Deaf, Manchester, 1949–64; Vis. Prof., Univ. of Minnesota, 1960–61. Chm., Nat. Coll. of Teachers of the Deaf, 1956–68. *Publications*: Education of Hearing Handicapped Children, 1967; *contrib*. Internat. Audio., Teach. Deaf, Volta Rev. *Address*: Dept of Audiology and Education of the Deaf, Manchester Univ.

Watson, Prof. William, FBA; FSA; Professor of Chinese Art and Archaeology of the University of London, at the School in Oriental and African Studies, and Head of the Percival David Foundation of Chinese Art, since 1966; *b* 1917; *m* 1940; four *s*. MA Cantab 1943 (Modern and Medieval Langs); Asst Keeper, British Museum, first in Dept of British and Medieval Antiquities, then in Dept of Oriental Antiquities, 1947–66; Slade Prof. of Fine Art, Cambridge Univ., 1975–76. *Publications*: The Sculpture of Japan, 1959; Archaeology in China, 1960; China before the Han Dynasty, 1961; Jade Books in the Chester Beatty Library, 1963; Cultural Frontiers in Ancient East Asia, 1971; *contrib*. Jl RAS, Oriental Art, Burlington Mag., BM Qly, etc. *Address*: Sch. of Oriental and African Studies, Malet Street, WC1E 7HP.

Watson, Prof. William Alexander Jardine, (Alan Watson), DPhil, DCL; Professor of Civil Law, Edinburgh University, since 1968; *b* 1933; *m* 1958; one *s* one *d*. MA Glasgow 1954, LLB Glasgow 1957, BA Oxon 1957 (by Decree), MA Oxon 1958, DPhil Oxon 1960, DCL Oxon 1973; FSAScot. Lectr, Wadham Coll., Oxford, 1957–59; Lectr, 1959–60; Fellow, Oriel Coll., Oxford, 1960–65; CUF Lectr, Oxford, 1959–65; Douglas Prof. of Civil Law, Univ. of Glasgow, 1965–68; Vis. Prof., Tulane Univ. Law Sch., 1967; Vis. Prof., Univ. of Virginia Law Sch., 1970, 1974; Vis. Prof., Univ. of Cape Town, 1974; Mem., Council, Stair Soc., 1970– . *Publications*: (as Alan Watson) Contract of Mandate in Roman Law, 1961; Law of Obligations in Later Roman Republic, 1965; Law of Persons in Later Roman Republic, 1967; Law of Property in Later Roman Republic, 1968; Law of the Ancient Romans, 1970; Roman Private Law Around 200 BC, 1971; Law of Succession in Later Roman Republic, 1971; Law Making in Later Roman Republic, 1974; Legal Transplants, an approach to comparative law, 1974; ed, Daube Noster, 1974; *contrib*. Class. Rev., Glotta, Index, Irish Jurist, Israel Law Rev., IURA, Jl Rom. Studies, Klio, Labeo, Law Qly Rev., Rev. Internat. Droits Antiqu., Studi Urbinati, Studia Doc. Hist. Iuris, Tijds. Rechtsgesch., Tulane Law Rev., Zeits. Sav.-Stift. *Address*: Dept of Civil Law, Univ. of Edinburgh, Old College, Edinburgh EH8 9YL.

Watson, Rev. William Lysander Rowan; Fellow, Chaplain and Tutor of St Peter's College, Oxford, and Lecturer in Ecclesiastical History, Faculty of Theology, Oxford University, since 1957; *b* 1926; *m* 1968; one *s* one *d*. BA Dublin 1947 (1st cl. Mod. Hist. and Pol Science), Divinity Testimonium Dublin 1949, Higher DipEd Dublin 1950, MA Dublin 1950, MA Cantab 1952, MA Oxford 1957; Ordained Deacon 1950, Ordained Priest 1951. Tutor, Ridley Hall, Cambridge, 1951–53; Chaplain, Ridley Hall, Cambridge, 1953–57. *Address*: St Peter's College, Oxford.

Watt, Donald Cameron, MA, FRHistS; Professor of International History, London School of Economics and Political Science, University of London, since 1972; *b* 1928; *m* 1st 1951, 2nd 1962; one *s* one *d*. BA Oxon 1951 (1st cl. PPE), MA Oxon 1954; FRHistS. Asst Lectr, LSE, 1954–56; Lectr, LSE, 1956–62; Sen. Lectr, LSE, 1962–65; Reader in Internat. History, LSE, 1965–72; Rockefeller Fellow in Social Sciences, 1960–61; Ed., Survey of Internat. Affairs, Documents on Internat. Affairs, and Hd of Survey Dept, Royal Inst. Internat. Affairs, 1962–71 (pt-time); Asst Ed., Documents on German Foreign Policy, 1918–1945, For. Off., 1951–54, 1957–59 (pt-time); Ed., Bull. European Assoc. American Studies, 1962–66; Chm., Cttee EAAS, 1963–66; Sec., Assoc. Contemp. Hist., 1967– ; Chm., LSE Local Assoc., AUT, 1970– ; Lees-Knowles Lectr, Cambridge, 1973–74; Mem., Editorial Bd, Political Quarterly. *Publications*: Britain Looks to Germany, 1965, German edn 1965; Personalities and Policies, 1965, American edn 1965; Survey of International Affairs 1961, 1966; ed (with K. Bourne), Studies in International History, 1967, American edn 1967; (with F. Spencer and N. Brown) A History of the World in the Twentieth Century, 1967, American edn 1968; ed, Contemporary History in Europe, 1969; ed, Hitler's Mein Kampf, 1970; ed, Survey of International Affairs 1962, 1970; ed (with J. Mayall), Current British Foreign Policy, 1970, 1971; Current British Foreign Policy, 1971, 1972; *contrib*. Camb. Jl, Internat. Aff., Jl Cont. Hist., Jl Mod. Hist., Jl Royal Cent. Asian Soc., Jl Royal Utd Serv. Instn, Jl Soc. Archiv., Pol Qly, Rev. Hist. Gu. Mo., Rev. Mil. Gen., Rev. Pol., Slav. E Europ. Rev., US Nav. Inst. Proc., Vjh. Zg., Wehrwiss. Rundsch. *Address*: London School of Economics and Political Science, Aldwych, WC2A 2AE.

Watt, Dr Donald Elmslie Robertson; Senior Lecturer in Mediaeval History, University of St Andrews, since 1965; *b* 1926; *m* 1959; two *d*. MA Aberdeen 1950 (1st cl. Hist.), DPhil Oxon 1957; FRHistS, FSAScot. Lectr in Mediaeval Hist., Univ. of St Andrews, 1953–65; Vis. Prof., Columbia Univ., NY, 1966–67. Gov., Morrison's Acad., Crieff, 1971– ; Jt Ed., Scott. Hist. Rev., 1963–71. *Publications*: Fasti Ecclesiae Scoticanae Medii Aevi, 1959, 2nd edn 1969; *contrib*. Aberd. Univ. Rev., Scott. Hist. Rev., Specul., Trans Royal Hist. Soc. *Address*: Dept of Mediaeval History, St Salvator's College, St Andrews, Fife KY16 9PH.

Watt, Dr John Anthony; Reader in Medieval History, University of Hull, since 1970; *b* 1927; *m* 1954; two *s* three *d*. BA Leeds 1950 (1st cl. Hist.), PhD Cantab 1954; FRHistS. Asst Lectr, then Lectr, Univ. Coll., Dublin, 1953–63; Lectr, Hull Univ., 1963–65; Sen. Lectr, Hull Univ., 1965–70. *Publications*: The Theory of Papal Monarchy, 1965; The Church and the Two Nations in Medieval Ireland, 1970; John of Paris: On royal and papal power, 1971; The Church in Medieval Ireland, 1972; *contrib*. Irish Hist. Studies, Mediaev. Studies, Studia Grat., Tradit. *Address*: Dept of History, The Univ., Hull HU6 7RX.

Watt, Prof. W. Montgomery, PhD, DD; Professor of Arabic and Islamic Studies, University of Edinburgh, since 1964; *b* 1909; *m* 1943; one *s* four *d*. MA Edinburgh 1930 (1st cl. Classics), BA Oxon 1932 (2nd cl. Lit. Hum.), BLitt Oxon 1933, MA Oxon 1936, PhD Edinburgh 1944, Hon. DD Aberdeen 1966. Asst Lectr in Moral Philos., Univ. of Edinburgh, 1934–38; Arabic Specialist, Anglican Bishopric, Jerusalem, 1943–46; Lectr in Ancient Philos., Edinburgh Univ., 1946–47; Lectr in Arabic, Edinburgh Univ., 1947–52; Sen. Lectr, Edinburgh Univ., 1952–55; Reader, Edinburgh Univ., 1955–64; Vis. Prof., Toronto Univ., 1963; Vis. Prof., Collège de France, Paris, 1970. Chm., Assoc. Brit. Orient., 1964–65. *Publications*: Free Will and Predestination in Early Islam, 1949; The Faith and Practice of al-Ghazali, 1953;

Muhammad at Mecca, 1953; Muhammad at Medina, 1956; The Reality of God, 1958; The Cure for Human Troubles, 1959; Islam and the Integration of Society, 1961; Muhammad: Prophet and Statesman, 1961; Islamic Philosophy and Theology, 1962; Muslim Intellectual, 1963; Truth in the Religions, 1963; Islamic Spain, 1965; A Companion to the Qur'an, 1967; What is Islam?, 1968; Islamic Political Thought, 1968; Islamic Revelation and the Modern World, 1970; Bell's Introduction to the Qur'an, 1970; The Influence of Islam on Mediaeval Europe, 1972; The Formative Period of Islamic Thought, 1973; The Majesty that was Islam, 1974; var. edns in French, Spanish, Turkish, Persian, Japanese; *contrib.* Islam, Jl Royal Asiat. Soc., Oriens. *Address:* Dept of Arabic and Islamic Studies, Univ. of Edinburgh, Edinburgh EH8 9YL.

Watt, Prof. William Smith; Professor of Humanity, University of Aberdeen, since 1952; *b* 1913; *m* 1944; one *s.* MA Glasgow 1934 (1st cl. Classics), BA Oxon 1937 (1st cl. Classical Hon. Mods,   ' it. Hum.), MA Oxon 1940. Lectr in Greek and Greek History, Glasgow Univ., 1937–38; Fellow and Tutor in Classics, Balliol Coll., Oxford, 1938–52; Univ. Lectr in Latin Literature, Oxford Univ., 1946–52. Civilian Off., Admiralty (Naval Intell. Div.), 1941–45; Hon. Sec., Classical Jls Bd, 1950–64; Curator of Libr., Aberdeen Univ., 1955–59, Dean, Fac. of Arts, 1963–66, Senatus Assessor, Univ. Court, 1966– , Vice-Principal, 1969–72; Chm. of Governing Body, Aberdeen Coll. of Educn, 1971– ; Convenor, Scottish Univ. Council on Entrance, 1973– . *Publications:* ed, Ciceronis Epistulae ad Quintum fratrem, etc, 1958; ed., Ciceronis Epistularum ad Atticum Libri I–VIII, 1965; *contrib.* Class. Qly, Eranos, Hermath., Rhein. Mus. Philol., Mnemos. *Address:* King's College, Aberdeen AB9 2UB.

Watts, Dr Cedric Thomas, MA, PhD; Lecturer, School of English and American Studies, University of Sussex, since 1965; *b* 1937; *m* 1963; one *s* two *d.* BA Cantab 1961 (1st cl. Engl.), MA Cantab 1965, PhD Cantab 1965. *Publications:* Joseph Conrad's Letters to R. B. Cunninghame Graham, 1969. *Address:* Arts Building, Univ. of Sussex, Falmer, Brighton, Sussex BN1 9QN.

Watts, Dr David, PhD; Lecturer, Department of Geography, University of Hull, since 1963; *b* 1935. BA London 1956, MA California 1959, PhD McGill 1963; Mem., Assoc. Amer. Geogrs 1961. Temp. Lectr, Univ. Coll. Swansea, 1962–63; Vis. Prof., McGill Univ., Montreal, 1969–70. *Publications:* Man's Influence on the Vegetation of Barbados, 1966; Principles of Biogeography, 1971, North American edn 1971; *contrib.* Canad. Geog. *Address:* Dept of Geography, The Univ., Hull HU6 7RX.

Watts, Dr Derek Arthur, MA, DU; Reader in Classical French Literature, University of Exeter, since 1970; *b* 1929; *m* 1958; three *s* three *d.* BA Cantab 1949, MA Cantab 1953, D de l'U Paris 1954. Lectr, Univ. Coll., Bangor, 1955–63; Lectr, Exeter Univ., 1964–

66; Sen. Lectr, Exeter Univ., 1966–70. *Publications:* ed, Corneille: Cinna, 1964; Cardinal de Retz: La Conjuration de Fiesque, 1967; Rotrou: Hercule Mourant, 1971; *contrib.* Fr. Studies, Rev. Sci. Hum. *Address:* Dept of French, Queen's Building, The Queen's Drive, Exeter EX4 4QH.

Watts, Hugh Douglas; Lecturer, Department of Geography, University of Sheffield, since 1969; *b* 1941. BA Leicester 1962, MA Hull 1964. Asst Lectr, Hull, 1964–65; Asst Lectr, Aberystwyth, 1965–67; Lectr, Aberystwyth, 1967–69. *Publications: contrib.* Business Hist., Econ. Geog., Jl Town Plan. Inst., Tijds. Econ. Soc. Geog., Geography, Geoforum, Trans Inst. Brit. Geogrs. *Address:* Dept of Geography, The Univ., Sheffield S10 2TN.

Watts, Dr Michael Robert; Lecturer in History, University of Nottingham, since 1964; *b* 1936; *m* 1962; one *s* one *d.* BA Oxon 1959 (1st cl. Hist.), DPhil Oxon 1966. Asst, Glasgow Univ., 1961–64. *Address:* Dept of History, Univ. of Nottingham, Nottingham NG7 2RD.

Watts, Nita Grace Mary, OBE; Vice-Principal, Fellow and Tutor in Economics, St Hilda's College, and Senior Research Officer, Institute of Economics and Statistics, Oxford University, since 1965; *b* 1920. BSc(Econ) London 1940, MA Oxford 1965. Mem., Royal Econ. Soc., Mem., Royal Stat. Soc., Mem., Nat. Assoc. SE Europ. Studies. Mem., Econ. Sect., War Cabinet Off., and later HM Treasury, 1941–55; Res. Div., UN Econ. Commn for Europe, 1955–64; Nat. Econ. Develop. Off., 1964–65. *Publications: contrib.* Bull. Oxf. Univ. Inst. Econ. Stats. *Address:* St Hilda's College, Oxford.

Watts, Victor Ernest; Lecturer in English Language and Medieval Literature, University of Durham, since 1962; *b* 1938; *m* 1962; one *s* two *d.* BA Oxon 1961, MA Oxon 1964. *Publications:* trans., Boethius: the Consolation of Philosophy, 1969; Place Names, in, Durham City and County with Teesside, 1970; ed, De Proprietatibus Rerum, Book XVII, trans. John Trevisa, 1974; *contrib.* Durham Univ. Jl, Med. Æv. *Address:* Dept of English Language and Medieval Literature, Elvet Riverside, New Elvet, Durham.

Webb, Julian Barry, MA, MusB; Senior Lecturer in Music, School of Fine Arts and Music, University of East Anglia, since 1970; *b* 1936; *m* 1961; three *s.* BA Cantab 1957, MusB Cantab 1958, MA Cantab 1960. Lectr in Music, Univ. of Manchester, 1961–66; Lectr in Music, Univ. of E Anglia, 1966–70. Mem., Ad Solem Ensemble, Univ. of Manchester, 1961–66; Music. Dir, Norwich Sinfonia, 1967– ; Examiner, Assoc. Bd, Royal Schs Music, 1969– ; Orch. Cndctr, Norwich Philharm. Soc., 1971– . *Address:* School of Fine Arts and Music, Music Centre, Univ. Plain, Norwich NOR 88C.

Webb, Michael Gordon, MA; Lecturer in Economics, University of Leicester, since 1964; Visiting Lecturer, UN Asian, Institute for Economic Development and Planning,

1972–74; *b* 1940; *m* 1961; two *s* one *d*. BA Leicester 1962 (2/II Social Science, Econ.), MA Leicester 1966 (Econ., with distinct.). *Publications*: Economics of Nationalised Industries: A Theoretical Approach, (forthcoming); *contrib*. Manch. Sch., Oxf. Bull., Oxf. Econ. Papers, Scott. Jl Pol Econ. *Address*: Dept of Economics, Univ. of Leicester, Leicester LE1 7RH.

Webster, Alexander Bruce; Senior Lecturer in History, University of Kent at Canterbury, since 1967; *b* 1929; *m* 1958; three *s* one *d*. MA Glasgow 1950 (1st cl. Hist.), BA Oxon 1954 (1st cl. Hist.), MA Oxon 1957; FRHistS 1965, FSA 1966. Asst in Hist., Glasgow Univ., 1954–56; Lectr, Glasgow Univ., 1956–66; Lectr in Medieval History, Univ. of Kent at Canterbury, 1966–67. *Publications*: *contrib*. Trans Royal Hist. Soc. *Address*: Keynes College, The Univ., Canterbury, Kent CT2 7ND.

Webster, Graham Alexander, MA, PhD, FSA, AMA; Reader in Romano-British Archaeology, Extra-Mural Department, Birmingham University, since 1971; *b* 1915; *m* 1938; two *s*. MA Manchester 1950, PhD Birmingham 1957; FSA 1947; Associate, Museums Assoc.; Corresp. Mem., German Archaeol. Inst. Curator, Grosvenor Museum, Chester, 1948–54; Edward Cabdury Sen. Res. Fellow, Birmingham, 1954–57; Staff Tutor in Archaeology, Extra-Mural Dept, Birmingham, 1957–71. Vive-Pres., Royal Archaeol. Inst., 1965–68; Vice-Pres., Council Brit. Archaeol., 1967–70; Chm. W Midlands Rescue Archaeol. Cttee. *Publications*: (with D. R. Dudley) The Rebellion of Boudicca, 1962; Practical Archaeology, 1963, 2nd edn 1974; CBA Romano-British Coarse Pottery Student Guide, 1964, 2nd edn 1969; (with D. R. Dudley) The Roman Conquest of Britain, 1965, 2nd edn 1973; The Roman Imperial Army, 1969; The Cornovii (forthcoming); *contrib*. Antiqu. Jl, Archaeol Jl, Birm. Archaeol Soc. Trans, Britann., Chester Archaeol Soc. Jl, Derbys. Archaeol Jl, Dorset Archaeol Soc. Trans, Jl Rom. Studies, Shrops. Archaeol Trans, etc. *Address*: Dept of Extra-Mural Studies, The Univ., PO Box 363, Birmingham B15 2TT.

Webster, Prof. John Roger, MA, PhD; Professor of Education, and Dean of the Faculty of Education, University College of North Wales, Bangor, since 1966; *b* 1926; *m* 1963; one *s* one *d*. BA Wales 1947, DipEd 1948, MA Wales 1952, PhD Wales 1959. Lectr in Educn, Univ. Coll., Swansea, 1952–61. Dir for Wales, Arts Council GB, 1961–66; Mem., Lloyd Cttee on Nat. Film Sch., 1966; James Cttee on Teacher Educn and Training, 1971; Council, Open Univ., Chm., Adv. Cttee on Educnl Studies, 1969– ; Mem., Exec. Cttee, N Wales Arts Assoc., 1966– ; Anglesey, Caernarvon. and Flints Co. Educn Cttees, 1969–74; Mem., Clwyd Co. Educn Cttee, 1974– ; Chm., Standing Conf. on Educnl Studies, 1973– ; Chm., Educn Cttee of Prince of Wales Cttee, 1973– . *Publications*: Ceri Richards, 1961; Joseph Herman, 1962; Dyheadau's Bedwaredd Ganrif ar Bymtheg, in, Addysg i Gymru, ed J. L. Williams, 1966; *contrib*. Welsh Hist.

Rev. *Address*: Dept of Education, Univ. College of North Wales, Bangor LL57 2DG.

Webster, Robert Lovett, BSc, DLC; Lecturer, Education Department, University College, Cardiff, since 1965; *b* 1936; *m* 1965; two *d*. BSc Bristol 1958, DipPhysEd Loughborough 1959, DipEd 1959. *Address*: The Gymnasium, 49 Park Place, Cardiff.

Wedderburn, Dorothy Enid Cole; Reader in Industrial Sociology, since 1970, and Director, Industrial Sociology Unit, since 1973, Imperial College, University of London; *b* 1925. BA Cantab 1946, MA Cantab 1950. Jun. Res. Off., Dept of App. Econs, Univ. of Cambridge, 1950; Res. Off., Univ. of Cambridge, 1951; Sen. Res. Off., Univ. of Cambridge, 1952–65; Lectr in Industrial Sociol., Imperial Coll., 1965–70. Mem., Exec. Cttee, PEP, 1970– ; Mem., Nat. Adv. Council, Nat. Corp. Care of Old People, 1969– . *Publications*: (jtly) The Aged in the Welfare State, 1962; (jtly) The Economic Circumstances of Old People, 1962; White Collar Redundancy, 1964; Redundancy and the Railwaymen, 1964; (jtly) Old People in Three Industrial Societies, 1968; (jtly) Workers' Attitudes and Technology, 1972; ed, Poverty, Inequality and Class Structure, 1974; *contrib*. Amer. Behav. Sci., Jl Royal Stat. Soc., Sociol Rev. *Address*: Industrial Sociology Unit, Imperial College, 11 Princes Gardens, SW7.

Wedderburn, Prof. Kenneth William, MA, LLB; Cassel Professor of Commercial Law, University of London, (London School of Economics), since 1964; *b* 1927; *m* 3rd, 1969; two *s* two *d*. BA Cantab 1948 (1st cl., Star, Law, and George Long Prize for Jurisprudence), LLB Cantab 1949 (1st cl., Star, and Vice-Chancellor's Medal for English Law), MA Cantab 1953; Barrister-at-Law Middle Temple 1953 (Cert. of Hon.). Fellow, Clare Coll., Cambridge, 1952–64; Lectr in Law, Cambridge Univ., 1953–64; Vis. Prof., Harvard Law Sch., 1969–70; UCLA Law Sch., 1967. Gen. Ed., Mod. Law Rev., 1971; Chm., London and Provincial Theatre Councils, 1971; Dep. Chm., 1969–71; Staff Panel Mem., Civil Service Arbit. Trbnl, 1968; Mem., Post Off. Arbit. Trbnl, 1971. *Publications*: The Worker and the Law, 1965, 2nd edn 1971; asst ed, Clerk and Lindsell: Torts, 12th edn 1966, 13th edn 1969; Cases and Materials on Labour Law, 1967; (with P. L. Davies) Employment Grievances and Disputes Procedures in Britain, 1969; asst ed, Gower: Modern Company Law, 3rd edn 1969; ed (with B. Aaron), Industrial Conflict: a comparative survey, 1972; *contrib*. Camb. Law Jl, Mod. Law Rev., Internat. Comp. Law Qly. *Address*: London School of Economics, Houghton Street, Aldwych, WC2A 2AE.

Wedell, Prof. Eberhard (Arthur Otto) George; Professor of Adult Education and Director of Extra-Mural Studies, University of Manchester, since 1964; *b* 1927; *m* 1948; three *s* one *d*. BSc(Econ) London 1947, HonMEd Manchester 1968. Mem., Royal TV Soc. Staff, Min. of Educn, 1950–58; Sec., Bd Soc. Responsibility, Ch Assembly,

1958–60; ITA, 1960–64; Gov., Centre Educnl Develop. Overseas, 1970– ; Chm., IURU, 1969–71; SCUTREA, 1971–72; Manchester Univ. Centre for Overseas Educnl Develop., 1972– . *Publications*: ed, Together in Britain: a Christian Handbook on Race Relations, 1960; The Use of Television in Education, 1963; The Reform of Church Government, 1965; Broadcasting and Public Policy, 1968; (with H. D. Perraton) Teaching at a Distance, 1968; ed, Structures of Broadcasting, 1969; (with R. Glatter) Study by Correspondence, 1970; The Place of Education by Correspondence in Permanent Education, 1971; *contrib.* Adult Educn, Carn. Enf., Govt Opposit., Jl Overseas Public Admin. *Address*: Dept of Adult Education, Univ. of Manchester, Manchester M13 9PL.

Wedgwood-Oppenheim, Felix; Lecturer, Institute of Local Government Studies, University of Birmingham, since 1968; *b* 1938; *m* 1961; two *s*. BA Keele 1964, MSc Birmingham 1968 (Operational Research); Mem., Operational Res. Soc. *Address*: Univ. of Birmingham, Institute of Local Government Studies, PO Box 363, Edgbaston, Birmingham B15 2TT.

Weekes, Mark K.; *see* Kinkead-Weekes.

Weidmann, Dr Ulrich; Senior Lecturer, Department of Psychology, University of Leicester, since 1970; *b* 1925; *m* 1952; two *s* one *d*. DrPhil Zürich 1955 (Zoology). Mem., Amer. Assoc. Adv. Science, Assoc. Study Anim. Behav., Soc. Exper. Biol., Brit. Ornithol. Union. Res. Asst to Dr N. Tinbergen, Oxford Univ., 1953–56; Lectr, Birkbeck Coll., London Univ., 1956–66; Vis. Prof., Dept of Zoology, Univ. of Freiburg, 1963; Inst. Animal Behaviour, Pennsylvania State Univ., 1963; Dept of Psychology, Columbia Univ., NY, 1965; NSF Sen. Scientific Fellow, and Vis. Prof., Dept of Psychology, Univ. of Tennessee, Knoxville, 1966–67; Lectr, Univ. of Leicester, 1967–70. *Publications*: *contrib.* Anim. Behav., Rev. Comp. Anim., Rev. Suisse Zool., Zeits. Tierpsychol. *Address*: Dept of Psychology, The Univ., Leicester LE1 7RH.

Weightman, Prof. John George, BA, LèsL, PhD; Professor of French, Westfield College, University of London, since 1968; *b* 1915; *m* 1940; one *s* one *d*. BA Dunelm 1938 (1st cl. French), LèsL Poitiers 1938, PhD London 1955. Lectr in French, King's Coll., London, 1950–63; Reader, Westfield Coll., 1963–68. Mem. Cttee, London Libr.; Mem. Cttee, Translators Assoc., 1969–71. *Publications*: On Language and Writing, 1947; trans., J. Guéhenno: Jean-Jacques Rousseau, 1966; (with J. D. Weightman) C. Lévi-Strauss: The Raw and the Cooked, 1969; trans., C. Lévi-Strauss: Tristes Tropiques, 1973; The Concept of the Avant-Garde, 1973; *contrib.* Encounter, Europ. Studies, Times Litt. Supp., NY Rev. Books. *Address*: Westfield College, Kidderpore Avenue, NW3 7ST.

Weiner, Prof. Joseph Sidney, DSc, MRCP, MRCS, FIBiol; Professor of Environmental Physiology, London School of Hygiene and Tropical Medicine, University of London,

742

since 1965; *b* 1915; *m* 1943; one *s* one *d*. BSc Witwatersrand 1934, MSc Witwatersrand 1937, MA Oxon 1945, PhD London 1946, MRCS, LRCP 1947, DSc Oxon 1971, MRCP 1973; FIBiol 1963, FSA 1968. Reader in Physical Anthropology, Oxford, 1945–62; Dir, MRC Environmental Physiology Unit, 1962– . Pres., Royal Anthropol. Inst., 1963–64; Convenor, Hum. Adaptability Sect., Internat. Berlyne Programme, 1962– ; Ed., Ergonom., 1964–68; Mem., Royal Soc. Cttee for IBP. *Publications*: The Piltdown Forgery, 1955; (jtly) Human Biology, 1964; Human Biology; A Guide to Field Methods, 1969; Man's Natural History, 1971; *contrib.* Jl Physiol., Jl Appl. Physiol., Trans Royal Soc. B, Brit. Jl Indust. Med. *Address*: London School of Hygiene and Tropical Medicine, Gower Street, WC1E 7HT.

Weingreen, Prof. Jacob, MA, PhD, FTCD; Professor of Hebrew, University of Dublin, since 1937; *b* 1908; *m* 1934. BA Dublin 1929 (1st cl. Moderatorship), PhD Dublin 1931; FTCD 1956. Mem., Royal Irish Acad. Life Trustee, Chester Beatty Libr., Mem., Acad. Council Irish Coll. of Ecumenics. Lectr in Hebrew, Dublin, 1931–37; Lectr in Arabic, 1941– . Mem., Council, Wld Union Jew. Studies, 1969. *Publications*: A Practical Grammar for Classical Hebrew, 1939, 2nd edn 1957; Classical Hebrew Composition, 1957; *contrib.* Bull. J. Rylands Libr., Hermath., Jl Semit. Studies, Trans Wld Union Jew. Studies, Vet. Test. *Address*: East Chapel, Trinity College, Dublin 2.

Weinstein, William Leon; Fellow and Tutor in Politics, Balliol College, Oxford University, since 1962; *b* 1934; *m* 1959; one *s* one *d*. BA Columbia 1955, BPhil Oxon 1958, MA Oxon 1962. Res. Fellow, Nuffield Coll., Oxford, 1961–62; Vis. Fellow in Philosophy, Australian Nat. Univ., 1966, 1973; Vis. Lectr, Makerere Univ., 1968. Tutor for Admissions, Balliol Coll., Oxford, 1967–71. *Publications*: *contrib.* Mind, Pol Studies. *Address*: Balliol College, Oxford.

Weir, Dr Alan John; Reader in Mathematics and Education, Mathematics Division, University of Sussex, since 1966; *b* 1927; *m* 1956; four *s*. MA Cantab 1949, PhD Cantab 1953. Commonwealth Fellow, Princeton, USA, 1952–54; Lectr in Mathematics, Queen Mary Coll., Univ. of London, 1954–62 and 1963–66; Vis. Lectr, MIT, 1962–63. *Publications*: Notes on Algebraic Geometry, 1963; Linear Geometry (with K. W. Gruenberg), 1967; Lebesgue Integration and Measure, 1973; General Integration and Measure, 1974; *contrib.* Proc. AMS, Mathemat., Math. Gaz. *Address*: Mathematics Division, Univ. of Sussex, Falmer, Brighton, Sussex BN1 9QH.

Weir, Dr Alastair James, MA, DPhil; Senior Lecturer in Psychology, University of Glasgow, since 1968; *b* 1927; *m* 1958; one *s* one *d*. MA Glasgow 1948 (1st cl. Econ. with Psychol.), DPhil Oxon 1951. Asst Lectr in Psychology, Glasgow Univ., 1951–54; Commonwealth Fund Fellow, Clark Univ., 1954–56; Lectr in Psychology, Glasgow Univ., 1956–68; Vis. Lectr, Univ. of Kansas, 1963–

64. Vice-Chm., Exec., Scott. Assoc. Ment. Hlth, 1962– ; Chm., UK and Eire Cttee, Wld Fedn Ment. Hlth, 1965– ; Ed., Qly Bull. Wld Fedn Ment. Hlth, 1969–71; Mem., and Lectr, Glasgow Retirement Council, 1958– . *Publications*: Social Attitudes towards the Retired in the Community, in, Solving the Problems of Retirement, ed H. B. Wright, 1968; *contrib.* Internat. Rec. Med. Gen. Pract. Clinics, Jl Ment. Sci., Vita Hum. *Address*: Dept of Psychology, Adam Smith Building, Univ. of Glasgow, Glasgow G12 8RT.

Weir, Catherine G.; Lecturer, Department of Psychology, University College, London, since 1970; *b* 1943; *m* 1967; one *s*. BA Colorado College 1965, BSc (Qual) London 1966, PhD 1970. Lectr, Reading Univ., 1968–70. *Address*: Psychology Dept, Univ. College, Gower Street, WC1E 6BT.

Weir, David Thomas Henderson; Senior Lecturer in Sociology, Manchester Business School, since 1971; *b* 1939; *m* 1967; one *s* one *d*. BA Oxon 1960 (2nd cl. Hons PPE); Dip. in Public and Social Administration, Oxford Univ., 1961; Member: British Sociological Assoc. (Mem. Exec. Cttee, 1968–72 and 1973–75); Assoc. of Teachers of Management; Amer. Sociological Assoc.; Internat. Assoc. of Survey Statisticians. Sociologist, Obstetric Medicine Res. Unit, Univ. of Aberdeen, 1961–62; Lectr in Sociology and Criminology, Dept of Extra-Mural Studies, Leeds Univ., 1962–63; Res. Asst, Asst Lectr, Lectr, Dept of Sociology, Hull Univ., 1963–66; Lectr in Sociology, Manchester Univ., 1966–71; Vis. Prof. in Sociology, Western Mich. Univ., USA, Summer Session 1968 and 1969. Member: Senate, Manchester Univ., 1970–73 and 1973–75; Editorial Bd, Sociology, 1973–75; External Examiner, Manchester Polytechnic. *Publications*: The Sociology of Modern Britain (with Eric Butterworth) 1970; Social Problems of Modern Britain (with Eric Butterworth), 1972; Locality (with Camilla Filkin), in, Key Variables in Social Research, 1972 (for British Sociological Association); Computerguide 3: Programs for Social Scientists (with J. C. Mitchell and G. C. Thorn), 1972; Men and Work in Modern Britain, 1973; Cities in Modern Britain (with Camilla Lambert), 1974. *Address*: Manchester Business School, Booth Street West, Manchester M15 6PB.

Weir, Dr Ian Brash Louden, OBE; BSc. MBChB, DPH, DPA, FFCM; Part-Time Lecturer in Community and Occupational Medicine, University of Dundee, since 1953; *b* 1911; *m* 1939; two *s*. BSc Glasgow 1932 (Pure Science), MBChB Glasgow 1935, DPH Glasgow 1937, DPA Glasgow 1947; FFCM 1972. Asst Lectr to DPH Classes, Glasgow Univ., 1947–53; Pt-time Lectr to Health Visitor Training Courses, Duncan of Jordanstone Coll., Dundee. MOH, Dundee, 1953–74; District Med. Officer, Dundee Dist, Tayside Hlth Bd, 1974– ; Mem., Scott. Hlth Services Council, 1954–67; Mem., Scott. Adv. Council on Food Hygiene, 1963– ; Mem., Sub-Cttee on Epidemiol., 1965– ; Pres., Royal Sanitary Assoc. Scotl.,

1972–73. *Publications*: Annual Report of MOH, Dundee, 1953–1970; *contrib.* BMJ, Glasg. Med. Jl, Jl Hyg. *Address*: Dept of Community and Occupational Medicine, Univ. of Dundee, 9 Dudhope Terrace, Dundee.

Weir, John Antony, MA, MCL; Lecturer in Law, University of Cambridge, since 1966, and Fellow of Trinity College, Cambridge, since 1962; *b* 1936. BA Cantab 1960 (1st cl. Classics and Law), MCL Tulane 1962. Asst Prof., Tulane Univ., 1962–63; Asst Lectr in Law, Cambridge Univ., 1963–66; Vis. Prof., Cornell Univ., 1967; Univ. of Pennsylvania, 1970. *Publications*: Casebook on Tort, 1967, 3rd edn 1974; *contrib.* Camb. Law Jl, Tul. Law Rev. *Address*: Trinity College, Cambridge.

Weischedel, Gisela; Lecturer, Department of Modern Languages, University of Salford, since 1964; *b* 1937; *m* 1964 (marr. diss.); one *s* one *d*. Diplom-Dolmetscher Mainz 1963, Auslandskorrespondent 1957. Teaching posts in Germany, 1962–64. Interpreter for various internat. confs; free-lance technical translator. *Publications*: (co-author) Modern Prose Passages for Translation into German, 1967; (co-author) Twentieth Century Literary Guide), 1969; (co-author) Modern German Prose Passages, 1972. *Address*: Dept of Modern Languages, Univ. of Salford, Salford M5 4WT.

Welbourn, Rev. Frederick Burkewood; Senior Lecturer in Religious Studies, Department of Theology and Religious Studies, Bristol University, since 1966; *b* 1912; *m* 1946; one *s* one *d*. BA Cambridge 1934, MA Cambridge 1938; Member: Internat. African Inst.; Royal African Soc.; African Studies Assoc. of UK; Internat. Assoc. for History of Religion. Chaplain variously of Caius Coll., Trinity Hall and Trinity Coll., Cambridge, 1938–43; variously Chaplain, Tutor in Physics, Warden of Mitchell Hall, and Sen. Lectr in Religious Studies, Makerere Coll., Uganda, 1946–64. *Publications*: Science and Humanity, 1948; East African Rebels, 1961; East African Christian, 1965; Religion and Politics in Uganda, 1952–1962, 1965; (with B. A. Ogot) A place to feel at home, 1966; Atoms and Ancestors, 1968; *contrib.* Jl Rel. in Afr. *Address*: Dept of Theology and Religious Studies, Bristol University, Royal Fort, Bristol BS8 1UJ.

Welbourne, Michael, BPhil, MA; Lecturer in Philosophy, University of Bristol, since 1963; *b* 1933; *m* 1962; one *s* one *d*. BA Oxon 1958 (Lit. Hum.), BPhil Oxon 1960, MA Oxon 1961. Asst, Edinburgh Univ., 1960–61; Lectr, Magdalen Coll. and Christ Church, Oxford, 1961–63. *Address*: Dept of Philosophy, Univ. of Bristol, Bristol BS8 1TH.

Welham, Dr Philip John; Senior Lecturer, Department of Economics, Heriot-Watt University, since 1971; *b* 1936; *m* 1962; one *s* one *d*. BA (Econ) Leeds 1958, PhD (Econ.) Leeds 1967. Aberdeen Univ., 1960–62; Keele Univ., 1962–67; Leeds Univ., 1967–68; Heriot-Watt Univ., 1968– . *Publications*:

Monetary Circulation in the UK, 1969; (with others) Demand for Housing in Scotland, HMSO, 1972. *Address*: Dept of Economics, Heriot-Watt Univ., Edinburgh EH1 1HX.

Welland, Prof. Dennis Sydney Reginald; Professor of American Literature, Department of American Studies, University of Manchester, since 1965; *b* 1919; *m* 1942; one *s*. BA London 1940 (1st cl. English), PhD Nottingham 1951, Hon. MA Manchester 1969. Tutorial Asst and Asst Lectr, Univ. Coll., Nottingham, 1947–49; Lectr, Univ. of Nottingham, 1949–59; Sen. Lectr, Univ. of Nottingham, 1959–62; Reader, Univ. of Manchester, 1962–65; Vis. Prof., Indiana Univ. and Amherst Coll., 1968. Editor, Jl Amer. Studies, 1967– ; Treas., Brit. Assoc. Amer. Studies, 1956–63. *Publications*: The Pre-Raphaelites in Literature and Art, 1953; Wilfred Owen: a Critical Study, 1960; Arthur Miller, 1961, 3rd edn 1970; Selections from Shelley's Poetry and Prose, 1961; ed, Benjamin Franklin's Autobiography and other pieces, 1971; ed, The United States: a Companion to American Studies, 1974; *contrib*. Bull. NY Public Libr., Rev. Engl. Studies. *Address*: Dept of American Studies, Univ. of Manchester, Manchester M13 9PL.

Wellesley, Kenneth; Reader, Department of Humanity (Latin), University of Edinburgh, since 1967; *b* 1911; *m* 1940; one *s* one *d*. BA Cantab 1934 (1st cl. Classics Pts I and II), MA Cantab 1937. Schoolmaster, 1934–48; Lectr, Edinburgh Univ., 1949–62; Sen. Lectr, Edinburgh Univ., 1962–67. Mem., Council Rom. Soc., 1964–67. *Publications*: trans., Tacitus: Histories, 1964; ed, Tacitus: Histories III, 1972; contrib. Tacitus, ed Dorey, 1969; *contrib*. Acta Class. Univ. Debrec., Amer. Jl Philol., Class. Philol., Class. Qly, Class. Rev., Jl Rom. Studies, Wienstudien. *Address*: Dept of Humanity, David Hume Tower, George Square, Edinburgh EH8 9LJ.

Wells, Dr Brian Walter Pierrepont, MA, PhD; Lecturer in Psychology, University of Strathclyde, since 1965; *b* 1933; *m* 1957; one *d*. BA Bristol 1959, MA Bristol 1962, PhD Liverpool 1964. Lectr, Univ. of Liverpool, 1962–65; Vis. Prof., Univ. of Wisconsin, 1968. RAF, 1951–53; W. H. Smith (Alacra) Ltd, 1953–57; Psychologist, Cheadle Royal Hosp., 1960–62. *Publications*: Psychedelic Drugs: psychological, medical and social issues, 1973; contrib. var. vols of collected works; *contrib*. Archit. Jl, Archit. Assoc. Qly, Brit. Jl Vener. Dis., Brit. Jl Soc. Clin. Psychol., Biol. Hum. Aff., Design, Hlth Bull., Jl Ment. Sci., Lancet, Psychiat. Qly Supp. *Address*: Dept of Psychology, Univ. of Strathclyde, Glasgow G1 1RD.

Wells, Prof. David Arthur, PhD; Professor of German, Queen's University of Belfast, since 1974; *b* 1941. BA Cantab 1963, MA, PhD Cantab 1967. Lectr in German: Univ. of Southampton, 1966–69; Bedford Coll., Univ. of London, 1969–74. Hon. Sec., Mod. Hum. Res. Assoc., 1969–. *Publications*: The Vorau Moses and Balaam, 1970; A complete Concordance to the Vorauer Bücher Moses, 1974; *contrib*. Mod. Lang. Rev.,

Studia Neerland., Times Lit. Supp., Yrs Wk Mod. Lang. Studies, Zeits. Deuts. Altert. *Address*: Dept of German, Queen's Univ. of Belfast, Belfast BT7 1NN.

Wells, Prof. George Albert, BSc, MA, PhD; Professor of German, University of London, Birkbeck College, since 1968; *b* 1926; *m* 1957. BA London 1947 (1st cl. German), MA London 1950 (German), PhD London 1954 (Philosophy), BSc London 1963 (2nd cl. Geology). Asst Lectr in German, Univ. Coll., London, 1949–52; Lectr in German, Univ. Coll., London, 1952–64; Reader in German, Univ. Coll., London, 1964–68. Sec., London Univ. Bd of Studies in Germanic Langs and Lits, 1965–68; Dean, Fac. of Arts, Birkbeck Coll., 1971–73. *Publications*: Herder and After, 1959; The Plays of Grillparzer, 1969; The Jesus of the Early Christians, 1971; *contrib*. Brit. Jl Hist. Sci., Germ. Life Lett., Jl Engl. Germ. Philol., Jl Hist. Ideas, Mod. Lang. Rev., Publicns Engl. Goethe Soc. *Address*: Birkbeck College, Malet Street, WC1E 7HX.

Wells, Dr John Christopher, PhD; Lecturer in Phonetics, University College, London, since 1965; *b* 1939. BA Cantab 1960 (1st cl. Classical Tripos Pt I, 2nd cl. Pt II), MA Cantab 1964, MA London 1962 (Gen. Linguistics and Phonetics), PhD London 1971. Asst Lectr, Univ. Coll., London, 1962–65. Dep. Sec., Internat. Phonet. Assoc., 1969– . Jt Ed., Jl Internat. Phonet. Assoc. *Publications*: The EUP Concise Esperanto and English Dictionary, 1969; (with G. Colson) Practical Phonetics, 1971; Jamaican Pronunciation in London, 1973; *contrib*. Jl Internat. Phonet. Assoc., Jl Lingu. *Address*: Dept of Phonetics and Linguistics, Univ. College London, Gower Street, WC1E 6BT.

Wells, Dr Stanley William, BA, PhD; Reader in English, since 1972 (Senior Lecturer, 1971–72), and Fellow of the Shakespeare Institute, University of Birmingham, since 1962; *b* 1930. BA London 1951, PhD Birmingham 1961. Mem., Council, Malone Soc., 1968– ; Pres., Shakesp. Club, Stratford upon Avon, 1971–72. Res. Assoc., Shakespeare Inst., 1961–62, Fellow, 1962–64, Lectr, 1964–71; Dir, Royal Shakesp. Theatre Summer Sch., 1971– . *Publications*: ed, Selected Works of Thomas Nashe, 1964; ed, A Midsummer Night's Dream, 1967; ed, Richard II, 1969; Shakespeare: A Reading Guide, 1969, 2nd edn 1970; Literature and Drama, 1970; Assoc. Ed., New Penguin Shakespeare, 1972; ed, The Comedy of Errors, 1972; ed, C. J. Sisson, The Boar's Head, 1972; ed, Shakepeare: select bibliographical guides, 1973; *contrib*. Shakesp. Survey, Strat. Studies, Shakesp. Jhb, Shakesp. Qly. *Address*: The Shakespeare Institute, Stratford upon Avon.

Werbner, Dr Richard P; Senior Lecturer, Department of Social Anthropology, University of Manchester, since 1974; *b* 1937; *m* 1971. BA Brandeis Univ. 1959, PhD Manchester 1968; FRAI; Mem., Assoc. of Social Anthropologists; Fellow, Amer. Anthropological Assoc. Res. Asst, Univ. of Manchester, 1961–62, Asst Lectr, 1962–66, Lectr, 1966–73. Member: Post-graduate Bd, Manchester Univ.; PhD Bd, Manchester Univ. *Publications*: Constitutional Ambiguities and the British Administration of Royal Careers, in, Law in Culture and Society, ed L. Nader, 1969; Sin, Blame, and Ritual Mediation, in, The Allocation of Responsibility, ed M. Gluckman, 1972; *contrib*. Africa, Amer. Anth., Botswana Notes and Recs, Man, Myth and Magic. *Address*: Dept of Social Anthropology, Univ. of Manchester, Manchester M13 9PL.

Wernberg-Møller Preben Christian Heiberg, MA, DPhil; Reader in Semitic Philology, University of Oxford, since 1968; *b* 1923; *m* 1955; one *s* four *d*. Cand Theol Copenhagen 1948, DPhil Oxford 1956, MA Oxford 1968; Mem., Cttee, Soc. OT Study, 1971– . Asst Lectr, Manchester Univ., 1954–57; Lectr, Manchester Univ., 1957–63; Sen. Lectr, Manchester Univ., 1963–68; Prof. Fellow, St Peter's Coll., Oxford, 1968– . Mem., Bd, Fac. of Oriental Studies, Oxford, 1969– . *Publications*: The Manual of Discipline, 1957; Codex Babylonicus Petropolitanus, 1971; contrib. Encyclopedia Judaica; *contrib*. Booklist of Soc. OT, Studies, Leeds Univ. Oriental Soc. Ann., Jl Bib. Lit., Jl Jew. Studies, Jl Semit. Studies, Jl Theol. Studies, Rev. Qum., Studia Theol., Textus, Vet. Test., Zeits. Altest. Wissens. *Address*: Oriental Institute, Pusey Lane, Oxford.

Werner, Dr Karel; Spalding Lecturer in Indian Philosophy and Religion, School of Oriental Studies, University of Durham, since 1969; *b* 1925; *m* 1st 1948, 2nd 1970; two *s*. PhD Olomouc 1949. Lectr, Palacky Univ. of Olomouc, Czechoslovakia, 1948–51. Var. forced manual occupations (incl. mines and gas works) after dismissal from Univ. by Communist authorities. *Publications*: Hatha Yoga, 1968, 2nd edn 1971; *contrib*. Bharat. Vid., Hum. Context, Wld Buddh., Yoga Qly Rev. *Address*: School of Oriental Studies, Univ. of Durham, Elvet Hill, Durham.

Wernham, Prof. Archibald Garden; Regius Professor of Moral Philosophy, University of Aberdeen, since 1960; *b* 1916; *m* 1942; two *s*. MA Aberdeen 1938 (1st cl. Classics), BA Oxon 1943 (1st cl. Lit. Hum.); Lectr, St Andrews Univ., 1945–53; Sen. Lectr, St Andrews Univ., 1953–59; Reader, St Andrews Univ., 1959–60. Gov., Robert Gordon's Colls, Aberdeen, 1967– ; Dean, Fac. of Arts, Aberdeen Univ., 1970– . *Publications*: Spinoza: The Political Works, 1958; Liberty and Obligation in Hobbes, in, Hobbes Studies, 1965; *contrib*. Philos. Qly. *Address*: Dept of Moral Philosophy, King's College, Aberdeen AB9 2UB.

Werth, Paul Nicholas; Lecturer, Department of Linguistics, University of Hull, since 1974; *b* 1942; *m* 1966; two *d*. BA (Hons) Leeds, 1965; Mem., Linguistics Assoc. of GB. Lectr, Dept of English, Univ. of Hull, 1967–74; Dir of Studies, British Council summer courses, 1968–74; Mem., Cttee, Yorks. Dialect Soc., 1970–74. *Publications*: Relativization and Semantic Theory (forth-

coming); (jtly) Style and Usage (forthcoming); *contrib*. Linguistics. *Address*: Dept of English, Univ. of Hull, Cottingham Road, Hull HU6 7RX.

West, Dr D. J., MD, PhD, MRCPsych; Reader in Clinical Criminology, Cambridge University, since 1973 (Lecturer in Criminology, 1968–73); *b* 1924. MB, ChB Liverpool 1947, DipPsycholMed London 1952, MD Liverpool 1958, PhD Cantab 1967, McDougall Award (jtly) for distinguished work in Parapsychology, 1958; Mem., Royal Coll. Psychiatrists, 1971; Mem., Acad. Forensic Sciences, Mem., Brit. Soc. Criminol., Vice-Pres., former Pres., Soc. Psychic. Res.; Asst Dir of Res. in Criminology, Univ. of Cambridge, 1960–68; Fellow, Darwin Coll., Cambridge, 1966– ; Vis. Prof. of Psychiatry, Univ. of Missouri, 1970. Hon. Cnsltnt Psychiatrist, Cambridge, 1961– ; Assessor, Brit. Jl Psychiat.; Mem., Parole Bd of Engl., 1967–69; Mem., and Chm., of Res. and Develop. Cttee, Home Off. Adv. Council on Child Care, 1969–71; Gen. Rapporteur, 10th Council of Europe Conf. of Dirs of Criminol Res. Insts, 1972. *Publications*: Psychical Research Today, 1954, rev. edn 1962; Homosexuality, 1955, rev. edn 1968; Eleven Lourdes Miracles, 1959; The Habitual Prisoner, 1963; Murder followed by Suicide, 1965; The Young Offender, 1967; Present Conduct and Future Delinquency, 1969; The Future of Parole, 1972; Who Becomes Delinquent, 1973; *contrib*. Brit. Jl Criminol., Internat. Jl Soc. Psychiat., Jl Parapsychol., Jl Proc. Soc. Psychic. Res. *Address*: Institute of Criminology, 7 West Road, Cambridge CB3 9DT.

West, Prof. David Alexander, MA, BA; Professor of Latin, University of Newcastle, since 1969; *b* 1926; *m* 1953; three *s* two *d*. MA Aberdeen 1949, BA Cantab 1952; Mem., Class. Assoc., Mem., Rom. Soc. Asst Lectr, Sheffield, 1952–55; Lectr, Edinburgh, 1955–69. *Publications*: Reading Horace, 1967; The Imagery and Poetry of Lucretius, 1969; *contrib*. Class. Qly, Hermes, Jl Rom. Studies, Philol. *Address*: The Univ., Newcastle upon Tyne NE1 7RU.

West, George; *see* West, S. G.

West, Prof. Martin Litchfield, MA, DPhil, FBA; Professor of Greek, Bedford College, University of London, since 1974; *b* 1937; *m* 1960; one *s* one *d*. BA Oxon 1959, MA Oxon 1962, DPhil Oxon 1963. Woodhouse Jun. Res. Fellow, St John's Coll., Oxford, 1960–63, CUF Lectr, Oxford, 1964; Fellow and Praelector, UC Oxford, 1963–74. Vis. Lectr, Harvard, 1967. Editor, Liddell and Scott: Greek Lexicon, 1965. *Publications*: ed, Hesiod: Theogony, 1966; (with R. Merkelbach) Fragmenta Hesiodea, 1967; (with F. Solmsen and R. Merkelbach) Hesiodi Opera, 1970; Early Greek Philosophy and the Orient, 1971; Sing Me, Goddess, 1971; Iambi et Elegi Graeci, 1971–72; Textual Criticism and Editorial Technique, 1973; Studies in Greek Elegy and Iambus, 1974; *contrib*. Class. Qly, Class. Rev., Glotta, Maia, Philol., etc. *Address*: St John's Hall, Inner Circle, Regent's Park, NW1 4NS.

West, Prof. (Sidney) George, OBE, MA; Visiting Professor in Portuguese, Department of Portuguese and Brazilian Studies, King's College, University of London, since 1971; *b* 1909; *m* 1939; one *s* two *d.* BA London 1929 (1st cl. Hons English), MA (with Distinction) London 1932; AKC 1929, FKC 1953. Corresp. Mem., Lisbon Acad. of Sciences, 1959; Mem., Assoc. of Hispanists of GB and Ireland. Student-Lectr in English, King's Coll., London, 1929–30; Post-graduate Student-Librarian, King's Coll., London, 1931–32; Lectr, Univ. of Coimbra, Portugal, 1934–36; Lectr and Head of Dept of Portuguese, King's College, London, 1936–37; Lectr, Univ. of Lisbon, 1938–40, Dir, British Inst. in Portugal, and British Council Rep., 1938–48; British Council: Representative, Brazil, 1948–51; Head Office, London, 1951–70; Controller, European Div., 1962–70. Mem., British-Portuguese Mixed Commn, 1954– ; Vice-Pres., Anglo-Portuguese Soc.; Officer, Portuguese Order of Public Instruction, 1940. *Publications:* The New Corporative State of Portugal, 1937, 2nd edn 1939; ed, English edn, Eduardo Brazão: The Anglo-Portuguese Alliance, 1957; Anglo-Portuguese Bibliography (forthcoming); *contrib.* Garc. Orta, Int. Affrs, Mod. Lang. Rev., Rev. Eng. Stud., Rev. Litt. Comp., Rev. Port. *Address:* Univ. of London King's College, Strand, WC2R 2LS.

West, Dr Stephanie Roberta; College Lecturer in Classics, Hertford College, Oxford, since 1967; *b* 1937; *m* 1960; one *s* one *d.* BA Oxford 1960, DPhil Oxford 1964. *Publications:* The Ptolemaic Papyri of Homer, 1967; *contrib.* Class. Qly, Jl Egypt. Arch., Zeits. f. Papyr. u. Epig. *Address:* Hertford College, Oxford.

West, Prof. William Alexander, LLM; Head of Department of Law, and Professor of Law relating to the Land, University of Reading, since 1967; *b* 1916; *m* 1st 1947, 2nd 1963; one *s* four *d.* LLB London 1951, LLM London 1960; Barrister-at-Law of Gray's Inn, 1947. Lectr, Coll. of Estate Management, 1951–55; Hd of Dept of Law, Coll. of Estate Management, 1955–72. Mem., CNAA; Mem., Adv. Panel, Inst. Econ. Aff., Chm., SPACE. *Publications:* Law of Housing, 1955, 2nd edn 1965; Law of Dilapidations, 1954, 5th edn 1964; (with F. G. Pennance) Housing Market Analysis and Policy (Hobart Paper 48), 1969; The Law and the Land: the need for a policy, 1966; contrib. Development of Settlement Patterns (Inst. of Archaeology), 1972; *contrib.* Conveyan. Prop. Law, Est. Gaz., Law Qly Rev., Mod. Law Rev. *Address:* Faculty of Urban and Regional Studies, Univ. of Reading, Reading RG6 2AH.

West-Taylor, John Percy; Registrar, University of York, since 1961; *b* 1924; *m* 1960; two *s* one *d.* BA Cantab 1948 (Trinity Hall), MA Cantab 1951. *Address:* Univ. of York, Heslington, York YO1 5DD.

Westergaard, John Harald; Reader in Sociology, University of London, since 1970; *b* 1927; *m* 1950; one *s* one *d.* BSc(Econ) London 1951. Res. Asst, Univ. Coll.,

746

London, 1951–55; Res. Fellow, Nottingham Univ., 1955–56; Asst Lectr, LSE, 1956–59, Lectr, 1959–66, Sen. Lectr, 1966–70; Vis. Lectr, Brown Univ., USA, 1963–64; Res. Assoc., Centre for Urban Studies, Univ. Coll., London, 1958– . Mem., SSRC Sociol. Cttee, 1970– ; Mem., SSRC Survey Archive Cttee, 1972– ; Mem., CNAA Town Planning Panel, 1972– ; Mem., Exec. Cttee, Council Acad. Freedom, 1971– . *Publications:* Scandinavian Urbanism, 1968; jtly, or contrib., London – Aspects of Change, 1964; Towards Socialism, ed Anderson and Blackburn, 1965; (with R. Glass) London's Housing Needs, 1965; Housing in Camden, 1969; *contrib.* Brit. Jl Sociol., Social. Reg., Town Plan. Rev. *Address:* London School of Economics, Houghton Street, WC2A 2AE.

Westland, Gordon Lindsay; Lecturer, Department of Humanities and Social Sciences, University of Surrey, since 1966; *b* 1925; *m* 1950. BSc Glasgow 1945, MA Glasgow 1947, MEd Glasgow 1949. Mem., Brit. Psychol. Soc. *Publications: contrib.* Brit. Jl Aesth., Univ. Qly. *Address:* Dept of Humanities and Social Sciences, Univ. of Surrey, Guildford, Surrey GU2 5XH.

Wetherick, Dr Norman Edward, BA, PhD; Senior Lecturer in Psychology, University of Aberdeen, since 1972; *b* 1929; *m* 1961; one *s.* BA Bristol 1953, BA London 1960, PhD Liverpool 1965; ABPsS. Staff Tutor, Liverpool Univ., 1964–66; Lectr, Bradford Univ., 1966–68; Sen. Lectr, Bradford Univ., 1968–71. Treasurer, Brit. Soc. for the Philos. of Science, 1969–72. *Publications: contrib.* Brit. Jl Psychol., Internat. Jl Psychol., Jl Brit. Soc. Phenom., Lang. Speech. *Address:* Dept of Psychology, The Univ., Old Aberdeen.

Wetherill, Dr Peter Michael, MA, Ddel'U; Senior Lecturer, Department of French, University of Manchester, since 1968; *b* 1932; *m* 1958; two *d.* BA Birmingham 1954 (1st cl. French), MA Birmingham 1956, Ddel'U Strasbourg 1962. Mem., Soc. Fr. Studies. Lectr, Univ. of New England, Australia, 1958–60; Asst Lectr, then Lectr, Leeds, 1961–68. *Publications:* Charles Baudelaire et la Poésie d'Edgar Allan Poe, 1962; Flaubert et la Creation littéraire, 1966; The Literary Text: an examination of critical methods, (forthcoming); *contrib.* Mod. Lang. Qly, Rom. Rev., Symp., Zeits. Franz. Spr. Lit. *Address:* Dept of French, The Univ., Manchester M13 9PL.

Wharfe, Harold; Senior Lecturer, School of Architecture, University of Newcastle upon Tyne, since 1974; *b* 1916; *m* 1951; three *s.* MA Dunelm 1956, Dipl. in Architecture, Leeds Sch. of Architecture, 1938, Dipl. in Town and Country Planning, Leeds Sch. of Architecture, 1939; ARIBA 1940, FRIBA 1960; Associate, Royal Town Planning Inst., 1946–70. Lectr, Sch. of Architecture, Univ. of Newcastle upon Tyne, 1948–74. Military Service, RE, 1940–46; architectural practice (partnership), 1948–72. *Address:* School of Architecture, Univ. of Newcastle upon Tyne, Newcastle upon Tyne NE1 7RU.

Whatley, Herbert Allan, MA, FLA; Senior Lecturer, Department of Librarianship, University of Strathclyde, since 1964; *b* 1913; *m* 1940; one *s* one *d.* MA Strathclyde 1968; FLA 1937. Life Mem., Libr. Assoc., 1931– . Lectr, Scottish Coll. of Commerce, 1953–63; Sen. Lectr, Scottish Coll. of Commerce, 1963–64 (from 1964 as Univ. of Strathclyde); Vis. Lectr, Kent State Univ., Ohio, 1970. Birmingham Public Librs, 1930–53; Exch. visit, Montclair, NJ, Public Libr., 1938–39; Study tours: Germany, Czechoslovakia, USSR, Hungary, Bulgaria, Italy; Ed., Libr. Science Abstr., 1951–68. *Publications*: A Survey of the Major Indexing and Abstracting Services for Library Science and Documentation, 1966; A British View of Libraries in ... the USSR, 1966; Ed., British Librarianship and Information Science, 1966–70, 1971; *contrib.* Konyv. Figy., Libr., Libr. Assoc. Rec., Libr. Jl, Libr. Rev., Libr. Wld, Scott. Libr. Assoc. News, Stech.-Haf. Bk News, Unesco Bull. Librs. *Address*: Dept of Librarianship, Univ. of Strathclyde, Livingstone Tower, Richmond Street, Glasgow G1 1XH.

Wheare, Sir Kenneth Clinton, CMG, FBA, DLitt; Chancellor of Liverpool University, since 1972; Fellow of All Souls College, Oxford; *b* 1907; *m* 1934; 1943; three *s* two *d.* BA Melbourne 1929, MA 1949, BA Oxon 1932 (1st cl. Hons Sch. of Philosophy, Politics and Economics), MA 1935, DLitt 1957; Hon. LHD Columbia 1954, Hon. LittD Cambridge 1969, Hon. LLD Exeter 1970, Hon. LLD Liverpool 1972; FBA 1952. Lectr, Christ Church, Oxford, 1934–39; Beit Lectr in Colonial History, Oxford, 1935–44; Fellow of Univ. Coll., Oxford, 1939–44, and Dean, 1942–45; Gladstone Prof. of Government and Public Administration, Univ. of Oxford, and Fellow of All Souls Coll., Oxford, 1944–57; Fellow of Nuffield Coll., 1944–58; Rector, Exeter Coll., Oxford, 1956–72. Mem., Hebdomadal Council, 1947–67; Vice-Chancellor, Oxford Univ., 1964–66, Pro-Vice-Chancellor, 1958–64, 1966–72. A Rhodes Trustee, 1948– ; Nuffield Trustee, 1966– ; Mem., UGC, 1959–63; Mem., Governing Body, Sch. of Oriental and African Studies, 1970– . Mem., Oxford CC, 1940–57. Pres., British Academy, 1967–71. Hon. Fellow, Nuffield, Exeter, Oriel, University and Wolfson Colls. *Publications*: The Statute of Westminster, 1931, 1933; The Statute of Westminster and Dominion Status, 1938, (5th edn 1953); Federal Government, 1946, (4th edn 1963); Abraham Lincoln and the United States, 1948; Modern Constitutions, 1951; Government by Committee, 1955; The Constitutional Structure of the Commonwealth, 1960; Legislatures, 1963; Maladministration and its Remedies, 1973. *Address*: All Souls College, Oxford.

Wheatcroft, Prof. George Shorrock Ashcombe; Professor Emeritus of English Law, University of London, 1959–68, and now occasional lecturer, London School of Economics; *b* 1905; *m* 1930; two *s* one *d.* BA Oxon 1926, MA Oxon 1952; Solicitor 1929, FBIM. Master of Supreme Ct, 1951–59; Vice-Chm., Hambro Life Ass. Co., 1971– ;

Cnsltng Ed., Brit. Tax Rev.; Ed., Brit. Tax Rev., 1956–69; Cnsltng Ed., Brit. Tax Encyclop.; Ed., Brit. Tax Encyclop., 1962–70; Cnsltng Ed., VAT Encyclopedia, 1973– ; Cnsltng Ed., Hambro Tax Guide, 1972, 1973. *Publications*: The Taxation of Gifts and Settlements, 1953, 3rd edn 1958; The Law of Income Tax, Surtax and Profits Tax, 1962; Estate and Gift Taxation, 1965; (with P. Whiteman) Whiteman and Wheatcroft on Income Tax and Surtax, 2nd edn, 1970; (with P. Whiteman) Wheatcroft and Whiteman on Capital Gains Tax, 2nd edn 1971; Guide to the Estate Duty Statutes, 2nd edn 1972; contrib. Halsbury: Laws of England, 3rd edn 1962–68; *contrib.* Brit. Tax Rev. *Address*: 80 Campden Hill Court, W8.

Wheeler, Prof. Marcus Christopher Corbet; Professor of Slavonic Studies, The Queen's University of Belfast, since 1967; *b* 1927; *m* 1960; one *s* two *d.* BA Oxon (Lit. Hum. 1949, Russian 1955), BLitt Oxon, 1952, MA Oxon 1953; Civil Service Commn Interpretership in Russian, 1953. HM Foreign Service, 1959–65; Res. Specialist, Royal Inst. Internat. Aff., 1966–68. Mem., Cttee Nat. Assoc. Sov. E Europ. Studies, 1966–68. *Publications*: Oxford Russian-English Dictionary, 1972; *contrib.* Amer. Jl Philol., Ann. Ist. Orient. (Naples), Govt Opposit., Greece Rome, Jl Hist. Ideas, Studia Lingu. *Address*: Dept of Slavonic Studies, The Queen's Univ., Belfast BT7 1NN.

Whincup, Michael Hynes; Senior Lecturer in Law, University of Keele, since 1969; *b* 1929; *m* 1957; one *s* one *d.* LLB Liverpool 1950, LLM Liverpool 1952; Barrister-at-Law 1953. Mem., Indust. Law Soc. Lectr, Coll. of Adv. Technol., Birmingham, 1957–65; Lectr, Univ. of Keele, 1965–69; Vis. Lectr, Univ. of Auckland, NZ, 1969, 1974. Mem., ed. adv. bd, Occupat. Hlth. *Publications*: Safety and the Law, 1963, 2nd edn 1964, Argentinian edn 1964; Redundancy and the Law, 1967; Industrial Law, 1968; Consumer Protection Law in America, Canada and Europe, 1973; *contrib.* Modern Law Rev., Jl Business Law, NI Legal Qly, Jl Soc. Public Teachers Law, New Law Jl. *Address*: Dept of Law, Univ. of Keele, Keele, Staffs ST5 5BG.

Whinnom, Prof. Keith; Professor of Spanish, University of Exeter, since 1967; *b* 1927; *m* 1955; two *d.* BA Oxon 1948 (1st cl. Mod. Langs), MA Oxon 1953. Laming Travelling Fellow, The Queen's Coll., Oxford, 1950–51; Lectr, Univ. of Hong Kong, 1952–55; Lectr, TCD, 1956–61; Prof., Univ. of W Indies, 1962–67; Vis. Prof., Emory Univ., 1965. *Publications*: Spanish Contract Vernaculars in the Philippine Islands, 1956; A Glossary of Spanish Bird-Names, 1966; Spanish Literary Historiography, 1967; ed (with G. D. Trotter), La Comedia Thebaida, 1969; ed, D. de San Pedro: Obras, 3 vols, 1972– ; D. de San Pedro, TWAS, 1973; *contrib.* AION (Sez. Rom.), Amer. Anthropol., Bull. Hispan. Studies, Ekon. Keuan. Indon., Filol., Hispan. Rev., Jl Orient. Studies, Mod. Lang. Rev., Orbis, Rev. Filol. Espñ., Rev. Litt. Comp.,

747

Symp., Theol., Zeits. Rom. Philol. *Address*: Dept of Spanish, Univ. of Exeter, Exeter, Devon EX4 4QJ.

Whiston, Thomas George; Lecturer in Psychology, University of Manchester, since 1967; *b* 1938; *m* 1966. BSc Aston 1959, MSc Loughborough 1961, MSc Toronto 1965; ARIC, 1962; AMInst CS, 1970; ERS, 1970. Teaching Fellowship, Univ. of Toronto, 1964–66; Staff Scientist, Ontario Centennial Centre of Sci. and Technol., 1966–67. Res. Scientist, Central Elec. Gen. Bd, 1962–64; Cnsltnt, Ontario Centennial Centre, 1967– ; Cnsltnt Which?, 1971– . *Publications*: *contrib*. Analyst, Educn Chem., Percept. Phychol., Bull. Psychol., Ergonom. Abstr., Readings Int. Cybern. Symp. *Address*: Dept of Psychology, Univ. of Manchester, Manchester M13 9PL.

Whitaker, Prof. Dorothy Stock; Professor, Department of Social Administration and Social Work, University of York, since 1973; *b* 1925; *m* 1963; one *s*. PhB Chicago, 1944, MA Chicago 1947, PhD Chicago 1951; Dip. Clin. Psychol., American Bd of Examiners in Professional Psychol., Member: American Psychol Assoc., Amer. Gp Psychotherapy Assoc., Gp-Analytic Society. Asst Prof., Univ. of Chicago, 1957–63; Assoc. Prof., 1963–64; Lectr, Univ. of Leeds, 1964–73. *Publications*: (with M. A. Lieberman) Psychotherapy through the Group Process, 1964; (jtly) Small Group Therapy, 1971; as D. Stock: (with H. A. Thelen) Emotional Dynamics and Group Culture, 1958. *Address*: Dept of Social Administration and Social Work, Univ. of York, Heslington, York YO1 5DD.

Whitaker, Dr Katherine Po Kan; Reader in Classical Chinese, Far East Department, School of Oriental and African Studies, University of London, since 1956; *b* 1912; *m* 1941; one *d*. BA Univ. of Hong Kong 1934, BA Oxford 1938 (Hons), MA Oxford 1942, PhD London 1952; Member: Royal Central Asian Soc.; China Soc.; Soc. for Afghan Studies. Temp. Lectr, University of Hong Kong, 1939; Special Lectr, Sch. of Oriental and African Studies, Univ. of London, 1944. *Publications*: 1200 Chinese Basic Characters for Students of Cantonese, 1953, 2nd edn 1958; Structure Drill in Cantonese, 1954, 2nd edn 1959; Cantonese Sentence Series, 1955; *contrib*. Asia Major (NS), BSOAS. *Address*: Far East Dept, School of Oriental and African Studies, Univ. of London, Malet Street, WC1E 7HP.

Whitaker, Dr Philip, MA, PhD; Lecturer in Political Science, University of Dundee, since 1964; *b* 1927; *m* 1959; one *d*. BA Dublin 1951, MA Dublin 1954, PhD Manchester 1956. Mem., Afr. Studies Assoc. UK, Mem., Afr. Studies Assoc. USA, Mem., Pol Studies Assoc. UK. Res. Asst, Univ. of Manchester, 1956; Lectr, Makerere Coll., Uganda, 1957–63; Vis. Fellow, Univ. of Chicago, 1963. Mem., Forfar Dist Council, 1971– ; Mem., Represent. Ch Council, Episcopal Ch of Scotl., 1972. *Publications*: The General Election in the Western Region of Nigeria, 1956, in, Five Elections in Africa,

ed Mackenzie and Robinson, 1960; Political Theory and East African Problems, 1964; *contrib*. Jl Afr. Admin, Mak. Jl, Pol Studies. *Address*: Dept of Political Science, Univ. of Dundee, Dundee DD1 4HN.

Whitaker, Shelagh M., BA; Lecturer (part-time), Department of Psychology, University of Keele, since 1968; *b* 1924; *m* 1955; two *s*. BA London 1946. Mem., Brit. Psychol. Soc. Jun. Lectr, Inst. of Psychiatry, Univ. of London, 1948–51. *Address*: Dept of Psychology, Univ. of Keele, Keele, Staffs ST5 5BG.

Whitaker, Sidney Francis; Senior Lecturer (Language Teaching Group), Department of Education, University College of North Wales, Bangor, since 1964; *b* 1924; *m* 1951; two *s* one *d*. BA Oxon 1948, MA Oxon 1952. Mem., IATEFL, Mem., BAAL, Mem., NATE. Lectr, French Dept, Glasgow Univ., 1949–59; Colombo Plan Adviser, Min. of Educn, Vietnam, 1957–58; Dir of Studies, Brit. Inst., Caracas, 1959–64. *Publications*: *contrib*. Engl. Lang. Teach., Rev. Litt. Comp. *Address*: Dept of Education, Univ. College of North Wales, Bangor LL57 2DG.

Whitbourn, Christine Janet; Lecturer in Spanish, University of Nottingham, since 1973; *b* 1934. BA Nottingham 1956 (Hons Spanish), MA Hull 1968. Asst Lectr, Hull Univ., 1965–67. Admin. Staff, Univ. of London, 1957–61; Univ. of Sussex, 1961–63; Dep. Warden, Thwaite Hall, Univ. of Hull, 1963–65; Lectr in Spanish, Univ. of Hull, 1967–72. *Publications*: The Arcipreste de Talavera and the Literature of Love, 1970; ed, Knaves and Swindlers: essays on the picaresque novel in Europe, 1974. *Address*: Dept of Spanish, The Univ., Nottingham NG7 2RD.

White, Adrian Nicholas S.; *see* Sherwin-White.

White, Prof. Alan Richard; Ferens Professor of Philosophy, University of Hull, since 1961; *b* 1922; *m* 1948; one *s* two *d*. BA Dublin 1945 (1st cl. Classics and Mental and Moral Science). Univ. Student in Classics, Dep. Lectr in Logic, TCD, 1945; Asst Lectr, then Lectr, and later Sen. Lectr, Univ. of Hull, 1946–61; Vis. Prof., Univ. of Maryland, 1967–68. Hon. Sec., Mind Assoc., 1960–69; Pres., Mind Assoc., 1972. *Publications*: G. E. Moore, 1958; Attention, 1964; The Philosophy of Mind, 1967; ed, The Philosophy of Action, 1968; Truth, 1970; *contrib*. Amer. Philos. Qly, Analysis, Mind, Philos. Qly, Philos. Rev., Proc. Aristot. Soc., etc. *Address*: Dept of Philosophy, The Univ., Hull HU6 7RX.

White, Dr Alfred Douglas; Lecturer, Department of German, University College, Cardiff, since 1966; *b* 1941. BA Oxon 1963, MA Oxon 1968, DPhil Oxon 1968. *Publications*: *contrib*. Germ. Life Lett., Mod. Lang. Rev., Theat. Qly, New German Studies. *Address*: Dept of German, Univ. College, PO Box 95, Cardiff CF1 1XA.

White, Rev. Principal Barrington Raymond, MA, DPhil; Principal of Regent's

Park College, Oxford, since 1972; *b* 1934; *m* 1957; two *d*. BA Cantab 1956 (Theol.), MA Cantab 1960, DPhil Oxon 1961. Lectr in Ecclesiastical Hist., Regent's Park Coll., Oxford, 1963–72. *Publications*: The English Separatist Tradition, 1971; ed, Association Records of the Particular Baptists, Pts I–III, 1971–74; *contrib*. Jl Eccles. Hist., Jl Theol Studies. *Address*: The Principal's Lodging, Regent's Park College, Oxford.

White, Prof. Donald Maxwell, MA, PhD; Professor of Italian Language and Literature, University of Leeds, since 1968; *b* 1920; *m* 1950; one *s* one *d*. BA Cantab 1950 (1st cl. Italian), MA Cantab 1954, PhD Manchester 1958. Asst Lectr, Manchester Univ., 1950–53; Lectr, Manchester Univ., 1953–64; Sen. Lectr and Hd of Dept, Leeds Univ., 1964–68. Sec., Manch. Philol. Club, 1953–61; Mem., Exec. Cttee, Soc. Ital. Studies, 1965– ; Treas., Soc. Ital. Studies, 1967–72. *Publications*: Zaccaria Seriman (1709–1784) and the 'Viaggi di Enrico Wanton': A Contribution to the Study of the Enlightenment in Italy, 1961; ed, G. Verga: Pane Nero and other Stories, 1962, 2nd edn 1965; (with A. C. Sewter) Disegni di G. B. Piazzetta nella Biblioteca Reale di Torino, 1969; contrib. The Music Masters, vol. IV, ed Bacharach, 1954; *contrib*. Apollo, Art Qly, Boll. Musei Venez., Connoiss., Rass. Storica Tosc., Yrs Wk Mod. Lang. Studies. *Address*: Dept of Italian Language and Literature, Univ. of Leeds, Leeds LS2 9JT.

White, Dr Douglas John; Professor, Department of Decision Theory, Manchester University, since 1971; *b* 1933; *m* 1958; one *s* one *d*. MA Oxford 1956 (Maths), MSc Birmingham 1959 (Operational Res.), PhD Birmingham 1962 (Operational Res.); Member: British Operational Res. Soc.; Amer. Operations Res. Soc.; Inst. of Management Sciences; Math. Programming Soc. Res. Fellow, Birmingham Univ., 1960–62; Sen. Res. Fellow, Manchester Univ., 1962–65; Reader in Operational Res., Strathclyde Univ., 1965–68, Prof. of Operational Res., 1968–71. *Publications*: Dynamic Programming, 1969; Decision Theory, 1969; (with N. L. Lawrie and W. A. Donaldson), Introduction to Operational Research, 1969; *contrib*. Jl Math. Anal. and Applic., Man. Sci., Ops Res., OR Qly. *Address*: Dept of Decision Theory, Manchester Univ., Dover Street, Manchester.

White, Graham Edmund; Lecturer, Department of Sociology, University of Liverpool, since 1969; *b* 1943; *m* 1968; one *s* one *d*. Cert in Education Liverpool 1965, BA Liverpool 1967 (Hons Sociology), MA Liverpool 1973 (Sociology). Asst Lectr, Dept of Sociology, Univ. of Liverpool, 1968. Vice-Chm., Granby Sch. Managers, 1971–74. *Publications*: (with Roberts and Parker) The Character Training Industry, 1973; contrib. Penelope Hall's Social Services of England and Wales; *contrib*. New Era (in Home and School), Brit. Jl Soc. Work, Pers. Man. *Address*: Dept of Sociology, Univ. of Liverpool, Liverpool L69 3BX.

White, Prof. Henry Patrick; Professor of Geography and Chairman of Department, Department of Economics and Geography, University of Salford, since 1973; *b* 1920; *m* 1948; one *s* two *d*. BA London 1948, MA London 1950. Asst Lectr, Univ. of Edinburgh, 1949–52; Lectr, Univ. of Ghana, 1952–56; Sen. Lecturer: Fourah Bay Coll., 1956–58; Univ. of Ibadan, 1958–62; Royal Coll. of Advanced Technology, later Univ. of Salford: Lectr, 1962; Sen. Lectr, 1966; Reader, 1967. *Publications*: (with W. J. Varley) The Geography of Ghana, 1958; A Regional History of the Railways of Great Britain: vol. 2, Southern England, 1961, 3rd edn 1969; vol. 3, Greater London, 1963, 2nd edn 1970, paperback edn 1973; (with M. B. Gleave) An Economic Geography of West Africa, 1971; *contrib*. Econ. Geog., Geog. Jl, Geogr. Rev., Geog., Geog. Polon., Scott. Geog. Mag., Tijd. Econ. Soc. Geog., Urban Stud. *Address*: Dept of Economics and Geography, Univ. of Salford, Salford M5 4WT.

White, James Dunlop; Lecturer in Soviet and East European History, Institute of Soviet and East European Studies, University of Glasgow, since 1964; *b* 1941; *m* 1969. MA Glasgow 1963, Cert. Proficiency in Russian Lang. and Lit., Glasgow 1964; PhD Glasgow 1972. *Publications*: *contrib*. Sov. Studies. *Address*: Institute of Soviet and East European Studies, Univ. of Glasgow, Glasgow G12 8QQ.

White, Prof. John Edward Clement Twarowski; Durning-Lawrence Professor of History of Art, University College, London, since 1971; *b* 1924; *m* 1950. BA London 1950, PhD London 1962, MA Manchester 1963. Jun. Res. Fellow, Warburg Inst., 1950–52; Lectr, Courtauld Inst., 1952–58; Alexander White Vis. Prof., Chicago Univ., 1958; Reader, Courtauld Inst., 1958–59; Pilkington Prof. of History of Art and Dir of Whitworth Art Gall., Manchester Univ., 1959–66; Vis. Ferens Prof. of Fine Art, Hull Univ., 1961–62; Prof. of History of Art and Chm., Dept of History of Art, Johns Hopkins Univ., 1966–71. *Publications*: Perspective in Ancient Drawing and Painting, 1956; The Birth and Rebirth of Pictorial Space, 1957; Art and Architecture in Italy, 1250–1400, 1966; *contrib*. Burlington Mag., Jl Warburg and Courtauld Insts, Art Bull. *Address*: Dept of History of Art, Univ. College, Gower Street, WC1E 6BT.

White, Prof. Kenneth Douglas; Professor of Classics, University of Reading, since 1971; *b* 1908; *m* 1936; one *s* two *d*. BA Liverpool 1929, BA Cantab 1931, MA Cantab 1936. Mem., Council, Roman Soc., 1969–72. Asst in Greek, Univ. of Edinburgh, 1931–33; Asst Lectr in Classics, Univ. of Leeds, 1933–38; Prof. and Hd of Dept of Classics, Rhodes Univ., Grahamstown, 1938–58; Prof. and Hd of Dept of Classics, Univ. of Natal, 1958–62; Prof. of Ancient History, Univ. of Ibadan, 1962–65; Reader in Classics, Univ. of Reading, 1967–71; Commonwealth Fellow, St John's Coll., Cambridge, 1960–61; Res. Fellow, Merton Coll., Oxford, 1972; Vis. Prof., Univ. of Toronto, 1971–72. Chm., S Afr. Assoc. Univ. Teachers, 1956–59; Dep. Mayor,

Grahamstown, 1957–58; Mem., Gov. Council, Univ. of S Africa, 1961–62. *Publications*: Agricultural Implements of the Roman World, 1967; Roman Farming, 1970; A Bibliography of Roman Agriculture, 1970; Roman Farm Equipment, 1974; Aspects of Greek and Roman Technology, 1974; *contrib.* Agric. Hist., Antiqu., Greece Rome. *Address*: Dept of Classics, Univ. of Reading, Whiteknights, Reading RG6 2AH.

White, Patricia Ann, MA; Senior Lecturer in Philosophy of Education, Philosophy of Education Department, University of London Institute of Education, since 1974 (Lecturer, 1965–74); *b* 1937; *m* 1962; one *d*. BA Bristol 1958, Acad. Dip. London 1964, MA London 1966. Mem., Philos. of Educn Soc. GB. *Publications*: contrib. Education and the Development of Reason; contrib. The Philosophy of Education; *contrib.* Proc. Philos. Educn Soc. GB. *Address*: Univ. of London Institute of Education, Malet Street, WC1E 7HS.

Whitehead, Francis Stafford, MA; Reader in English and Education, Division of Education, University of Sheffield, since 1973 (Senior Lecturer, 1962–73); *b* 1916; *m* 1st 1939, 2nd 1951; two *s* three *d*. BA Cantab 1938, Teaching Dip. London 1939, MA Cantab 1945, MA London 1953. Lectr, Univ. of London Inst. of Educn, 1948–62. Hon. Chm., Nat. Assoc. Teaching Engl., 1965–67; Assoc. Dir, Dartmouth Seminar (Anglo-Amer. Seminar on Teaching Engl.), 1966. *Publications*: The Disappearing Dais, 1966, 2nd edn 1971; Creative Experiment: Writing and the Teacher, 1970; *contrib.* Brit. Jl Educnl Psychol., Use Engl. *Address*: Institute of Education, Univ. of Sheffield, Sheffield S10 2TN.

Whitehead, Laurence Andrew, MA; Official Fellow since 1969 and Senior Tutor since 1970, Nuffield College, Oxford; *b* 1944. BA Oxon 1966 (PPE), MA Oxon 1970. Faculty Fellow, St Antony's Coll., Oxford, 1968–69. *Publications*: The United States and Bolivia, 1969; chapters in: Financing Development in Latin America, ed, K. Griffin, 1971; The Widening Gap, ed B. Ward and others, 1971; Latin American Urban Research, vol. III, 1974; *contrib.* Annali Fond. Luig. Ein., Bull. Oxf. Univ. Inst. Econs and Stats, Curr. Hist, Desarr. Econ., Estud. And., Jl Politico, Jl Internat. Affs, Parly Affs, Polit. Stud., Pop. Stud., Stud. Stor., World Today. *Address*: Nuffield College, Oxford OX1 1NF.

Whitehouse, John Colin, MA; Lecturer in French, School of Modern Languages, University of Bradford, since 1965; *b* 1932; *m* 1957; four *s* two *d*. BA Sheffield 1953 (Hons French), MA Sheffield 1965; FIL 1957. *Publications*: trans., Mouchette, 1966; Advanced Conversational French, 1968; Le Realisme dans les Romans de Bernanos, 1969. *Address*: School of Modern Languages, The Univ., Bradford BD7 1DP.

Whitehouse, Prof. Walter Alexander; Professor of Theology, University of Kent, since 1965, and Master, Eliot College, University of Kent, 1965–69, 1973– ; *b* 1915; *m* 1946. Hon. DD Edinburgh 1960. Minister, Elland Cong. Ch, 1940–44; Chaplain, Mansfield Coll., Oxford, 1944–47; Reader in Divinity, Univ. of Durham, 1947–65. Principal, St Cuthbert's Soc., Univ. of Durham, 1955–60; Pro-Vice-Chancellor, and Sub-Warden, 1961–64. *Publications*: Christian Faith and the Scientific Attitude, 1952; Order, Goodness, Glory (Riddell Memorial lectures), 1959. *Address*: The Univ., Canterbury, Kent CT2 7NZ.

Whiteley, Prof. Charles Henry, PhD, MA; Professor of Philosophy, University of Birmingham, since 1969; *b* 1911; *m* 1944. BA Oxon 1933 (1st cl. Lit. Hum.), MA Oxon 1938, PhD Birmingham 1951. Asst Lectr, Birmingham Univ., 1935–38; Lectr, Birmingham Univ., 1938–52; Reader, Birmingham Univ., 1952–69; Pres., Aristotelian Soc., 1973–74. *Publications*: Introduction to Metaphysics, 1950, rev. edn 1955; (with W. M. Whiteley) The Permissive Morality, 1964; (with W. M. Whiteley) Sex and Morals, 1967; Mind in Action, 1973; *contrib.* Analysis, Mind, Philos. Qly, Philos. *Address*: Dept of Philosophy, Univ. of Birmingham, PO Box 363, Birmingham B15 2TT.

Whiteley, Rev. Denys Edward Hugh; Lecturer, Department of Theology, and Chaplain, University of Oxford, since 1947; *b* 1914; *m* 1943 (wife died) and 1968; two *s* one *d*. BA Oxon: Classical Hon. Mods 1935, Lit. Hum. 1937, Theology 1938; Holy Orders 1939; Mem., Soc. of NT Studies, 1950. Secretary of Faculty of Theology, Oxford Univ., 1953, Chm. of Bd and Faculty, 1967; Vice-Principal and Actg Principal of Jesus Coll., 1967. Moderator, Gen. Ordination Exam., 1960. *Publications*: The Theology of St Paul, 1964 (2nd edn forthcoming); Thessalonians, 1969; *contrib.*, Anal. Bib. (Rome), JTS, Texte und Unt. (Berlin). *Address*: Jesus College, Oxford.

Whiteman, Elizabeth Anne Osborn; Vice-Principal, since 1971, Tutor in Modern History, since 1946, Lady Margaret Hall, Oxford, and CUF Lecturer in Modern History, Oxford University, since 1950; *b* 1918. BA Oxford 1940, MA Oxford 1945, DPhil Oxford 1951; FRHistS 1951, FSA 1958. Fellow, Lady Margaret Hall, 1948– . Chm. Bd, Fac. of Modern History, Oxford Univ., 1969–71; Mem., Bd, Fac. of Modern Hist., 1963–72; Hebdomadal Council, Oxford Univ., 1968– ; Acad. Planning Bd, Warwick Univ., 1962–70. *Publications*: contrib. Victoria Country History: Wiltshire, vol. III, 1956; New Cambridge Modern History, vol. V, 1961; From Uniformity to Unity, ed G. F. Nuttall and O. Chadwick, 1962; ed, Compton Census of 1676 (forthcoming); *contrib.* Bodl. Libr. Rec., Trans Royal Hist. Soc. *Address*: Lady Margaret Hall, Oxford.

Whiteman, Philip Morgan, MA, FLA; Head of Department of Social and Management Studies, College of Librarianship Wales, since 1972; *b* 1926; *m* 1953; two *d*. MA Belfast 1969; FLA 1951. Hd of Dept of Librarianship, Manchester Coll. of Commerce, 1961–64; Sch. of Library and Information Studies,

QUB: Lectr, 1965–68; Sen. Lectr, 1968–72 Dep. Dir, 1965–70, Dir, 1970–72. *Publications: contrib.* Aslib Proc., Jl Librship, Lib. Assoc. Rec., Libr. Rev. *Address:* College of Librarianship Wales, Llanbadarn Fawr, Aberystwyth SY23 3AS.

Whiteside, Michael Thomas, BA, MEd; Lecturer in Sociology of Education, School of Education, Leicester University, since 1967; *b* 1943; *m* 1967; one *d.* BA Leicester 1964 (Social Science), CertEd Leicester 1965, MEd Leicester 1971. *Publications: contrib.* Brit. Jl Educnl Studies, Paedagog. Europ., Sociol. Rev., Vocat. Asp., Erzieher ohne Status? *Address:* School of Education, Leicester Univ., Leicester LE1 7RH.

Whitfield, David John Christopher, MA MSc; Senior Lecturer, Applied Psychology Department, University of Aston in Birmingham, since 1972 (Lecturer, 1965–72); *b* 1938; *m* 1960; one *s* one *d.* BA Cantab, 1959 (Nat. Sciences, Exper. Psychol.), MSc London 1962 (Occupat. Psychol.), MA Cantab 1964. Mem., Ergonom. Res. Soc., Mem., Hum. Factors Soc. USA. Psychologist, Ergonom. Lab., EMI Electronics Ltd, 1961–63; Res. Fellow, Coll. of Aeronautics, 1963–65. *Publications:* ed (with W. T. Singleton and R. S. Easterby), The Human Operator in Complex Systems, 1967; ed (with W. T. Singleton and J. G. Fox), Measurement of Man at Work, 1971; *contrib.* Ergonom., Hum. Factors. *Address:* Applied Psychology Dept, Univ. of Aston, Birmingham B4 7ET.

Whitfield, Dr Richard Charles; University Lecturer, Department of Education, University of Cambridge, since 1969; *b* 1938; *m* 1961; three *s.* BSc Leeds 1960 (1st cl. Chem.), PhD Leeds 1963 (Organic Chem.), MA Cantab 1966, MEd Leicester 1968 (with distinction); ARIC 1961. Demonstrator in Organic Chemistry, Leeds, 1961–63; Deptl Lectr in Educn, Cambridge, 1966–69; Dir of Studies in Educn, Christ's and Pembroke Colls, Cambridge, 1969– . Mem., IEA Internat. Science Cttee; Topic Gp Leader, Science Teacher Educn Project. *Publications:* A Guide to Understanding Basic Organic Reactions, 1966, trans into Japanese, Italian, German, Portuguese, Korean; Spectroscopy in Chemistry, 1969, German and Italian trans 1971; Multiple Choice Tests for Advanced Level Chemistry, 1971, German trans 1971; Disciplines of the Curriculum, 1971; Situations in Teaching, 1972; *contrib.* Chem. Soc. Rev., Educnl Res., Teach. Coll. Rec., Sch. Sci. Rev., etc. *Address:* Univ. Dept of Education, 17 Brookside, Cambridge CB2 1JG.

Whiting, Dr (Harold Thomas Anthony) John, MA, PhD, DLC, ABPsS; Senior Lecturer, Department of Physical Education, University of Leeds, since 1969; *b* 1929; *m* 1953; three *s.* Dip Loughborough College 1953 (2nd cl.), Teacher's Cert. Nottingham 1952 (distinctions in Maths and Physical Educn), MA Leeds 1964 (Psychol.), PhD Leeds 1967 (Exper. Psychol.); ABPsS 1967. Chm., Brit. Soc. Sports Psychol., 1972– . Lectr in Physical Educn, Univ. of Leeds, 1960–69. Ed., Human Movement Series

(Henry Kimpton), 1971– ; Gen. Ed., Jl Human Movement Studies, 1975– . *Publications:* Acquiring Ball Skill: a psychological interpretation, 1969; Teaching the Persistent Non-swimmer: a scientific approach, 1970; (with P. R. Morris) Motor Impairment and Compensatory Education, 1971; ed, Readings in Sports Psychology, 1971; ed, Reading in Aesthetics of Sport, 1972; (with K. Hardman, etc.) Personality and Performance in Physical Education and Sport, 1974; ed (with J. D. Brooke) Human Movement: a field of study, 1972; *contrib.* Brit. Jl Soc. Clin. Psychol., Educnl Res., Ergonom., Jl Motor Behav., Jl Sports Med. Physical Fit., Res. Qly, Internat. Jl Sports Psychol., Sportswissenschaft. *Address:* Dept of Physical Education, Univ. of Leeds, Leeds LS2 9JT.

Whitley, Eileen Marjorie; Reader in Phonetics, Department of Phonetics and Linguistics, School of Oriental and African Studies, University of London, since 1972; *b* 1910; *m* 1951; one *d.* BA London 1932 (Hons French), DipEd London 1934; Member: Philological Soc.; Linguistics Assoc. of GB; RAS. Asst Lectr, UCL, 1933–37, Lectr, 1937–39; Asst Prof., Sch. of Celtic Studies, Dublin Inst. for Advanced Studies, 1940–41; Lectr, Sch. of Oriental and African Studies, 1941, Sen. Lectr, 1946; Leverhulme Res. Fellow, 1946; Vis. Professor: Deccan Coll., Poona, 1966; Sch. of Celtic Studies, Dublin Inst. for Advanced Studies, 1972. *Address:* Dept of Phonetics and Linguistics, School of Oriental and African Studies, Univ. of London, WC1E 7HP.

Whitley, John Stuart, MA; Lecturer, School of English and American Studies, University of Sussex, since 1966; *b* 1940; *m* 1968; one *d.* BA Sheffield 1961 (1st cl. Hons English), MA Sheffield 1962 (English); Mem., British Assoc. of Amer. Studies. Instructor in English, Univ. of Mich., 1963–64; Asst Lectr, Sch. of English and Amer. Studies, Sussex Univ., 1964–66; Vis. Asst Prof. of English, Univ. of Mich., 1967–68. *Publications:* (ed with David Galloway) Ten Modern American Short Stories, 1969; William Golding: Lord of the Flies, 1970; (ed, with Arnold Goldman) American Notes, 1972; *contrib.* PMAAS, LR. *Address:* School of English and American Studies, Arts Building, Univ. of Sussex, Falmer, Brighton BN1 9QN.

Whittall, Dr Arnold, MA, PhD, ARCO; Senior Lecturer in Music, University College, Cardiff, since 1971; *b* 1935; *m* 1964. BA Cantab 1959, MA Cantab 1961, PhD Cantab 1963; ARCO 1954. Lectr in Music, Nottingham, 1964–69; Lectr in Music, Cardiff, 1969–71. *Publications:* Schoenberg Chamber Music, 1972; *contrib.* Music Lett., Music Rev., Proc. Royal Music. Assoc., Tempo. *Address:* Dept of Music, Univ. College, Cardiff CF1 1XL.

Whittam, Dr John Richard; Lecturer in History, University of Bristol, since 1964; *b* 1935; *m* 1959; one *s* two *d.* BA Oxon 1957 (2nd cl. Hist.), BPhil Oxon 1959, MA Oxon 1963, PhD London 1968. Instructor, Univ. of

Pennsylvania, 1960–61; Temp. Lectr, Royal Holloway Coll., 1961–62; Asst Lectr, Westfield Coll., 1962–64. *Publications*: Ricasoli as Prime Minister, 1971; *contrib*. EHR, Hist. *Address*: Dept of History, Univ. of Bristol, Bristol BS8 1TH.

Whittington, Dr Geoffrey, BSc(Econ), MA, PhD, FCA; Professor of Accountancy and Finance, University of Edinburgh, 1972–75; Professor of Accounting and Finance, University of Bristol, from Aug. 1975; BSc(Econ) London 1959, MA Cantab 1966, PhD Cantab 1971; ACA 1963. Jun. Res. Off., Dept of Applied Economics, Cambridge, 1962–64; Res. Off., Dept of Applied Economics, Cambridge, 1964–71, Sen. Res. Off., 1971–72; Res. Fellow, Fitzwilliam Coll., Cambridge, 1966–68, Fellow, 1968–72; Dir, Studies in Econs, Fitzwilliam Coll., 1967–72. *Publications*: (with A. Singh) Growth, Profitability and Valuation, 1968; The Prediction of Profitability, and other studies of company behaviour, 1971; *contrib*. Econ. Jl, Rev. Econ. Stats, Acctg and Bus. Res., Jl Indust. Econ. *Address*: Univ. of Edinburgh, William Robertson Building, 50 George Square, Edinburgh EH8 9JY; Univ. of Bristol, Bristol BS8 1TH.

Whittington, Dr Graeme Walter; Senior Lecturer, Department of Geography, University of St Andrews, since 1972; *b* 1931. BA Reading 1956, PhD Reading 1959. Asst, St Andrews, 1959, Lectr, 1962; Vis. Lectr, Natal, 1971. Mem., British Assoc. Cttee on Ancient Fields, 1958– . *Publications*: Environment and Land Use in Africa (with M. F. Thomas), 1969; *contrib*. Erdk., Scot. Geog. Mag., Tijd. Econ. Soc. Geog., Trans Inst. Brit. Geog., Wilts Archaeol. Mag. *Address*: Dept of Geography, St Salvator's College, The Univ., St Andrews, Fife KY16 9AL.

Whittle, Edward Watney; Lecturer in Greek, University of Birmingham, since 1960; *b* 1931; *m* 1958. BA Cantab 1953, MA Cantab 1957, MA Birmingham 1957. Asst Lectr in Classics, Univ. Coll. of N Staffs, 1954–57; Res. Fellow in Greek, Birmingham, 1957–59; Asst Lectr in Greek, Birmingham, 1959–60. *Publications*: *contrib*. Class. Mediaev., Class. Qly. *Address*: School of Hellenic and Roman Studies, Univ. of Birmingham, PO Box 363, Birmingham B15 2TT.

Whittle, Dr Paul, PhD; University Lecturer in Experimental Psychology, University of Cambridge, since 1967; Fellow of Darwin College, since 1969; *b* 1938; two *s* one *d*. BA Cantab 1959, PhD Cantab 1963. Res. Associate, Brown Univ., 1963–65; Univ. Demonstrator in Experimental Psychology, 1965–67. *Publications*: *contrib*. Jl Gen. Phys., Percept. and Psych., Vis. Res. *Address*: Psychological Laboratory, Downing Street, Cambridge.

Whitton, Dr Kenneth Stuart, MA, DipEd, PhD; Lecturer in German Studies, since 1966, Deputy Chairman, School of European Studies, since 1973, University of Bradford; *b* 1925; *m* 1954; one *s* one *d*. MA Edinburgh 1951 (Hons German with French), DipEd Edinburgh 1952, PhD Bradford 1971; FIL,

752

1959. Teacher of German: grammar schs, Bradford, Rotherham, 1952–60; Leeds Grammar Sch., 1960–66. Chief Examnr in German: Yorks Reg. Exams Bd, 1963– ; A-level, London Univ., 1974– (Examnr, 1964–74). Chm., Mod. Lang. Assoc., 1963–64; Hon. Treas. and Sec. for German Affairs, Yorks Br., Mod. Lang. Assoc., 1965– ; Founder Mem., AUT German. *Publications*: trans., Lohse: Australia and the South Seas, 1959; Hundert Nacherzählungen, 1965; Wir waren vier, vol. I, 1966, vol. II, 1967; Advanced Nacherzählungen, 1969; The Spectrum of the Comic in the Komödien of Friedrich Dürrenmatt (forthcoming); trans. and ed, Fischer-Dieskau: The Lieder of Franz Schubert (forthcoming); trans. Hügin and Gerschwiler: A Manual of Ice Skating (forthcoming); *contrib*. German Life and Letters, New German Studies, Adnv Jl, Mod. Langs. *Address*: Univ. of Bradford, Bradford BD7 1DP.

Whittow, Dr John Byron; Senior Lecturer in Geography, since 1973 (Lecturer, 1961–73), and Warden of St David's Hall, University of Reading, since 1968; *b* 1929; *m* 1957; one *d*. BA Reading 1952 (Geog.), DipEd Reading 1953; PhD Reading 1957; FRGS; FGS. Asst Lectr, Magee Univ. Coll., Londonderry, 1954–57; Lectr, Makerere Univ. Coll., Uganda, 1957–60; Res. Assoc., UCLA, 1960–61; Vis. Lectr, Univ. of New England, NSW, 1966–67; Vis. Lectr, Univ. of Oxford, 1968. Chm., Landscape Res. Gp, London, 1973– . *Publications*: ed (with P. D. Wood), Essays in Geography for Austin Miller, 1965; ed (with J. R. Hardy), A. E. Trueman: Geology and Scenery in England and Wales, 2nd edn 1972; Geology and Scenery in Ireland, 1974; *contrib*. Geog. Jl, Jl Glaciol., Proc. Geol Assoc. *Address*: Dept of Geography, Univ. of Reading, Reading, Berkshire RG6 2AH.

Whitworth, Thomas, MA, DPhil, FGS; Master of Hatfield College, University of Durham, since 1956; *b* 1917; *m* 1941; one *s* two *d*. BA Oxon 1947 (1st cl. Geol.), MA Oxon 1947, DPhil Oxon 1950; FGS. Deptl Demonstrator, Oxford, 1947; Univ. Demonstrator, Oxford, 1949; Lectr, Oriel Coll., Oxford, 1949–56. Governor, Schs Multilateral Unit, Hartlepool, 1957–65; Ed., Yorks Geol Soc., 1958–61; Mem., Cttee, Durham County RFU, 1963– ; Pres., Durham Univ. RFC, 1963– ; Treas. and Sen. Trustee, Durham Union Soc., 1963– ; Dep. Chm., Durham County Referees' Soc., 1971– . *Publications*: The Miocene Hyracoidea of East Africa, 1954; Miocene Ruminants of East Africa, 1958; Yellow Sandstone and Mellow Brick (an account of Hatfield College, Durham, 1846–1971), 1971; *contrib*. Bull. Overseas Geol. and Min. Resources, Jl South Afr. Arch. Soc., Qly Jl Geol. Soc. *Address*: Hatfield College, Durham City DH1 3RQ.

Whybray, Rev. Roger Norman, MA, DPhil; Reader in Theology, University of Hull, since 1969; *b* 1923; *m* 1948; one *s*. BA Oxon 1944 (Theol.), MA Oxon 1947, DPhil Oxon 1962; Mem., Soc. OT Study, Mem., Soc. Bib. Lit. Exegesis USA. Fellow, Tutor and Instructor, General Theol. Seminary, NY, 1948–50; Lectr and Tutor (pt-time), Queen's Coll., Birmingham, 1951–52; Prof. of Old Testament and Hebrew, Central Theol. Coll., Tokyo, 1952–65; Kennicott Hebrew Fellow, Oxford, 1960–62; Lectr, Hull Univ., 1965–69. Mem., Council, USPG, 1965– ; Mem., Overseas Cttee, 1969– ; Mem., Cttee, SOTS, 1970– . Ed., SOTS Book List, 1973– . *Publications*: A Survey of Modern Study of the Old Testament (in Japanese), 1961; Wisdom in Proverbs, 1965; The Succession Narrative, 1968; The Heavenly Counsellor in Isiaiah xl 13–14, 1971; Cambridge Bible Commentary on Proverbs, 1972; The Intellectual Tradition in the Old Testament, 1974; *contrib*. Ch Qly Rev., Vet. Test., Zeits. Alttest. Wissens. *Address*: Dept of Theology, Univ. of Hull, Hull HU6 7RX.

Whyman, John; Lecturer in Economic and Social History, University of Kent at Canterbury, since 1968; *b* 1939. BSc Econ London 1961, Dip Personnel Management; MIPM; Member: Econ History Soc., Agric. History Soc., Oral History Soc. Editor, Cantium; Mem.: County Local History Cttee, Kent Council of Social Service; Kent Archaeological Soc. Records Publication Cttee. *Publications*: (with W. Johnson and G. Wykes) A Short Economic and Social History of Twentieth Century Britain, 1967; (with Margaret Roake) ed, Essays in Kentish History, 1973; *contrib*. Perspectives in English Urban History, ed A. Everitt, 1973; *contrib*. Archaeologia Cantiana, Cantium, Local Population Studies. *Address*: Rutherford College, Univ. of Kent at Canterbury, Canterbury, Kent CT2 7NX.

Whyman, Peter; Reader, Department of Architecture and Building Science, University of Strathclyde, since 1972; *b* 1920; *m* 1951; one *s* two *d*. Dipl. in Architecture, Manchester 1949; ARIBA 1950, ARIAS 1966. Res. Fellow, Univ. of Strathclyde, 1966, Sen. Lectr, 1970; Vice-Dean, Sch. of Architecture, Building Science and Planning, Univ. of Strathclyde. District Councillor, Old Kilpatrick DC. *Publications*: (joint authorship under name of Building Performance Research Unit) Building Performance 1972; *contrib*. Bg, Mod. Qly. *Address*: Dept of Architecture and Building Science, Univ. of Strathclyde, Glasgow G4 0NG.

Whyte, Rev. Prof. James Aitken; Professor of Practical Theology and Christian Ethics, St Mary's College, University of St Andrews, since 1958, and Dean of Faculty of Divinity, 1968–72; *b* 1920; *m* 1942; two *s* one *d*. MA Edinburgh 1942 (1st cl. Phil.); Ordained 1945. Guest Lectr, Inst. for Study of Worship and Religious Architecture, Birmingham, 1965–66; Kerr Lectr, Glasgow Univ., 1969–72; Croall Lectr, Edinburgh Univ., 1972–73. Chaplain to the Forces, 1945–48; Minister of Dunollie Road, Oban, 1948–54; Minister of Mayfield and Fountainhall, Edinburgh, 1954–58. *Publications*: contrib. Towards a Church Architecture, 1962; Preparing for the Ministry of the 1970's, 1965; A Dictionary of Christian Ethics, 1967; *contrib*. jls, etc. *Address*: St

Mary's College, Univ. of St Andrews, St Andrews, Fife.

Whyte, Dr John Henry, MA, BLitt, PhD; Reader in Political Science, Queen's University of Belfast, since 1971; *b* 1928; *m* 1966; two *s* one *d*. BA Oxon 1949 (Mod. Hist.), BLitt Oxon 1951, MA Oxon 1953, PhD Belfast 1970. Lectr in History, Makerere Univ. Coll., Uganda, 1958–61; Coll. Lectr in Politics, Univ. Coll., Dublin, 1961–66; Lectr in Pol Science, Queen's Univ. of Belfast, 1966–71. Res. Fellow, Center for Internat. Affairs, Harvard Univ., 1973–74. *Publications*: The Independent Irish Party, 1850–59, 1958; Church and State in Modern Ireland, 1923–70, 1971; *contrib*. EHR, Irish Hist. Studies. *Address*: Dept of Political Science, Queen's Univ., Belfast BT7 1NN.

Wibberley, Prof. Gerald Percy, CBE, PhD; Professor of Countryside Planning, University of London, since 1968; *b* 1915; *m* 1944; one *d*. BSc Wales 1939 (1st cl. Agric. Econ.); MSc Illinois 1938; PhD Wales 1942; FRTPI (MTPI 1949). Reader, London Univ., 1958–62, Prof. of Rural Economy, 1962–68. Mem., Adv. Council, Min. of Lands and Natural Resources, 1968–69; Mem., Council, Small Industries in Rural Areas, 1964– ; Mem., Nature Conservancy Council, 1973– . *Publications*: Agriculture and Urban Growth, 1958; Studies in Rural Land Use, 1955– ; *contrib*. Jl Agric. Econ. Soc., Jl RTPI. *Address*: School of Rural Economics, Wye College, Ashford, Kent TN25 5AH; Sch. of Environmental Studies, UCL, 16 Flaxman Terrace, WC1H 9AT.

Wickens, Michael Roden; Reader in Econometrics, Economics Department, University of Essex, since 1974; *b* 1940; *m* 1964; two *s* one *d*. MSc(Econ) London 1965; Mem., Economet. Soc., Mem., Amer. Stat. Assoc., Mem., Amer. Econ. Assoc. Lectr, Univ. of Exeter, 1965–68; Lectr, Univ. of Bristol, 1968–74; Vis. Assoc. Prof., Rutgers Univ., 1973–74. Econ. Cnsltnt, UN Food and Agric. Org., 1970– . *Publications*: *contrib*. Economet., Econ. Jl, Economica, Rev. Econ. Stat. *Address*: Economics Dept, Univ. of Essex, Wivenhoe Park, Colchester CO4 3SQ.

Wicker, Brian John, MA; Senior Lecturer in English Literature, Department of Extra-Mural Studies, University of Birmingham, since 1968; *b* 1929; *m* 1953; one *s* two *d*. BA Oxon 1952 (1st cl. Engl. Lang. and Lit.), MA Oxon 1956, MA Birmingham 1960 (Philos.). Asst Sec., Appointments Bd, Birmingham Univ., 1956–60; Lectr in Engl. Lit., Dept of Extra-Mural Studies, 1960–68; Vis. Prof. of Engl., E Michigan Univ., 1968–69; Resid. Staff Tutor, Birmingham, 1960– . 1st Clarinet, Univ. Orchestra, 1956– ; Chm., Univ. Music. Soc., 1971; Chm., Pax Christi in UK. *Publications*: Culture and Liturgy, 1963; Culture and Theology, 1966 (American title: Towards a Contemporary Christianity); First the Political Kingdom, 1967; ed (with T. Eagleton), From Culture to Revolution, 1968; *contrib*. Blackfr., Commonweal, Critic, Ess. Crit., Guardian, Life Spirit, Slant. *Address*: Dept of Extra-Mural Studies, PO Box 363,

Univ. of Birmingham, Birmingham B15 2TT.

Wickham, Prof. Glynne William Gladstone; Professor of Drama, University of Bristol, since 1960, Dean of Faculty of Arts, 1970–72; *b* 1922; *m* 1954; two *s* one *d*. BA Oxon 1947, DPhil Oxon 1951. Asst Lectr, Bristol Univ., 1948; Sen. Lectr and Hd of Drama Dept, Bristol Univ., 1955; Rockefeller Trav. Award, 1953; Vis. Prof., Iowa Univ., 1960; G. F. Reynolds Meml Lectr, Colorado Univ., 1960; Judith E. Wilson Lectr, Cambridge Univ., 1960–61; Brit. Council Lectr, Europe, 1969– ; Ferens Vis. Prof., Hull Univ., 1969; Vis. Prof., Yale Univ., 1970. Consultant to Finnish Nat. Theatre and Theatre Sch., 1963 and to E Africa Univ., 1965 on estab. of drama depts in Helsinki Univ. and UC, Dar-es-Salaam; Festvortrag für Deutsche Shakespeare Gesellschaft, Bochum, 1973; Governor, Bristol Old Vic Trust., 1963– ; Governor, Dartington Arts Coll., 1964– ; Dir, Theatre Seminar, Vaasa, 1965; External Examiner, Ibadan Univ., 1965–68; Mem., Engl. Panel, CNAA, 1968– ; Mem., Coun. Clifton High Sch. for Girls, 1968– ; Chm., Nat. Drama Conf., Nat. Council of Social Service, 1970– ; Mem., Internat. Adv. Cttee, World Shakespeare Congress, Vancouver, 1971 (Chm., Elizabethan Theatre Panel). *Publications*: Early English Stages, 1300–1660: vol. I (1300–1576) 1959, vol. II (1576–1660), Pt I 1962, Pt 2 1971; Drama in a World of Science, 1962; Shakespeare's Dramatic Heritage, 1968; The Medieval Theatre, 1974; ed, The Relationship between Universities and Radio, Film and Television, 1954; Gen. Introd., Munro: London Shakespeare (6 vols), 1958. *Address*: Dept of Drama, Univ. of Bristol, 29 Park Row, Bristol BS1 5LT.

Wickham, Rev. Lionel Ralph; Lecturer, Department of Theology and the Study of Religion, University of Southampton, since 1967; *b* 1932; *m* 1963; three *s* one *d*. BA Cantab 1957, MA Cantab 1961. *Publications*: *contrib*. Jl Theol. Stud. *Address*: Dept of Theology and the Study of Religion, The Univ., Southampton SO9 5NH.

Wicks, Russell P.; Senior Lecturer in Psychology, University of Surrey; *b* 1925; *m* 1948. BSc Special London 1955, MSc London 1956 (Occupat. Psychol.); ABPsS, Mem., ERS. Lectr, Univ. of Surrey, 1961. *Address*: Dept of Humanities and Social Sciences, Univ. of Surrey, Guildford, Surrey GU2 5XH.

Widdowson, Dr John David Allison, MA; Senior Lecturer in English Language, University of Sheffield, since 1973 (Lecturer, 1965–73); *b* 1935; *m* 1960; two *s* one *d*. BA Oxon 1959, MA Oxon 1963; MA Leeds 1966; PhD Newfoundland 1973. Lectr, Memorial Univ. of Newfoundland, 1962–64; Asst Lectr, Sheffield Univ., 1964–65; Hon. Res. Fellow, Inst. of Dialect and Folk Life Studies, Leeds Univ., 1971– ; Hon. Res. Assoc., Memorial Univ. of Newfoundland Folklore and Language Archive, 1971– . Director: Survey of Language and Folklore, Sheffield Univ., 1964– ; Archives of Cultural Tradi-

tion, Sheffield Univ., 1964– . Editor, Lore and Language. *Publications*: (with F. C. Stork) Learning About Linguistics, 1974; ed (with others), Linguistic Atlas of England (forthcoming); ed (with others), Dictionary of Newfoundland English (forthcoming); *contrib*. Folia Lingu., Canad. Jl Lingu., Folkl. *Address*: Dept of English Language, The Univ., Sheffield S10 2TN.

Wiener, Philip Bernard; Lecturer in German, University of Birmingham, since 1961; *b* 1933. BA Birmingham 1954, MA Birmingham 1955; Constance Naden Medal 1956. Asst Lectr, Birmingham Univ., 1958–61. Res. Dept, Foreign Off. Libr., Whaddon, 1958–59. *Publications*: Heinrich Simon in German Politics, 1960; 'Die Parteien der Mitte', in, Entscheidungsjahr 1932, ed W. E. Mosse, 1965, 2nd edn 1966; 'Bertha von Suttner and the Political Novel', in, Essays in German Language, Culture and Society, ed Prawer, etc, 1969; *contrib*. Univ. Birm. Hist. Jl. *Address*: Dept of German, Univ. of Birmingham, PO Box 363, Birmingham B15 2TT.

Wiggins, Prof. David, MA; Professor of Philosophy, University of London, since 1967; *b* 1933. BA Oxon 1955 (1st cl. Classical Hon. Mods, 1st cl. Lit. Hum.), MA Oxon 1957; Mem., Aristot. Soc., Mem., Mind Assoc. Lectr and Fellow, New Coll., Oxford, 1959–67; Vis. Assoc. Prof., Stanford Univ., 1965, 1966; Vis. Prof. of Philosophy, Harvard Univ., 1968; James Loeb Fellow, Harvard, 1972; Vis. Fellow, All Souls Coll., Oxford, 1973. *Publications*: Identity and Spatiotemporal Continuity, 1967; *contrib*. Analysis, Philos. Rev., Proc. Aristotl Soc. *Address*: Dept of Philosophy, Bedford College, Regent's Park, NW1 4NS.

Wight, Robert Muir; Senior Lecturer in Education, since 1961, and Director of Physical Education, University of Leicester, since 1964; *b* 1915; *m* 1941. BL Aberdeen 1937, Dip Loughborough College 1940. Lectr in Educn, 1948–61. Pres., Commn pour L'Etude du Sport Universitaire, 1960. *Publications*: *contrib*. Jl Physical Educn, Traguardi. *Address*: Univ. of Leicester, University Road, Leicester LE1 7RH.

Wightman, Prof. David Randal, BSc(Econ), PhD; Professor of International Economic Organisation, University of Birmingham, since 1971; *b* 1925; *m* 1953; one *s* one *d*. BSc(Econ) London 1946 (1st cl.), PhD Birmingham 1957; Mem., Royal Inst. Internat. Aff. Asst Lectr in Econ. Hist., Birmingham Univ., 1947–50; Lectr in Econ. Hist., Birmingham Univ., 1950–59; Rockefeller Foundn Fellow, 1955; Sen. Lectr in Internat. Econ. Hist., Birmingham Univ., 1959–64; Reader in Internat. Econ. Hist., Birmingham Univ., 1964–71; Vis. Fellow, Inst. Internat. Econ. Studies, Univ. of Stockholm, 1966. Cnsltnt, UN/FAO Wld Food Programme, 1966; Cnsltnt UN Dept Econ. Social Aff., 1967–68, 1971; Assoc., Inst. Develop. Studies, Univ. of Sussex, 1968– . *Publications*: Economics Cooperation in Europe, 1956; Towards Economic Cooperation in Asia, 1963; (with G. Mydral, etc.) Asian

Drama: An Inquiry into the Poverty of Nations, 1968; *contrib*. Internat. Concil., Internat. Org., Wld Today. *Address*: Faculty of Commerce and Social Science, Univ. of Birmingham, PO Box 363, Birmingham B15 2TT.

Wilbie-Chalk, Derrick; Lecturer, Faculty of Arts (Architecture), Newcastle upon Tyne, since 1949; *b* 1922; *m* 1951; one *s* three *d*. Dip-Arch., Cert. in Town Planning, Manchester 1944; ARIBA. Demonstrator in Architecture, Univ. of Manchester, 1944–46; Asst Lectr in Architecture, Univ. of Manchester, 1946–49; Asst, Univ. of Manchester Inst. Science and Technol., 1947–49; Lectr in Architecture, Newcastle, 1949. Dep. Tech. Dir, Manchester Univ. Theatre, 1947–49; Senate Rep. in drama, Newcastle Univ. Inst. of Educn, 1969– ; Mem. Curricula Studies Gp, Schs of Architecture Council, 1973– . *Publications*: contrib. var. tech. jls. *Address*: School of Architecture, Univ. of Newcastle upon Tyne, Newcastle upon Tyne NE1 7RU.

Wilcox, Prof. Max, MA, BD, PhD; Professor and Head of Department of Biblical Studies, University College of North Wales, Bangor, since 1973; *b* 1927; *m* 1951; one *s* three *d*. BA Melbourne 1947 (2nd cl. Philos.), MA Melbourne 1948 (Philos.), BD Melbourne Coll. of Divinity 1950; BD Hons 1951 (2nd cl. New Testament with Palestinian Aramaic), PhD Edinburgh 1955; Mem., Studiorum NT Soc., 1957, FR Asiat. Soc., 1958; Mem., Soc. OT Study, 1965. Lectr in Semitic Studies (Pt-time), Univ. of Melbourne, 1958–62; Alexander von Humboldt-Stiftung Forschungs-stipendiat, Heidelberg Univ., 1963–64; Lectr in Divinity, 1964–67, Reader and Hd of Dept of Religious Studies, 1967–73, Univ. of Newcastle upon Tyne; Vis. Prof., Brown Univ., 1971. Licenciate, Presbyt. Ch of Australia, 1951; ordained, 1955. *Publications*: The Semitisms of Acts, 1965; ed (with E. E. Ellis), Neotestamentica et Semitica, 1969; *contrib*. Abr-Nahrain, Austral. Bibl. Rev., NT Studies. *Address*: Dept of Biblical Studies, Univ. College of North Wales, Bangor LL57 2DG.

Wild, Barbara; Lecturer, School of Humanities and Social Sciences, University of Bath, since 1965; *b* 1923; *m* 1st 1946, 2nd 1970. BA London 1944 (Engl. Lang. and Lit.), DipEd London 1945, Dip. in Public and Social Admin Oxford 1949, Mental Health Cert. London 1952. *Address*: Univ. of Bath, Claverton Down, Bath BA2 7AY.

Wild, Dr John Peter, MA, FSA; Lecturer in Archaeology, Department of Archaeology, Manchester University, since 1968; *b* 1940; *m* 1968; one *s* one *d*. BA Cantab 1961 (Classics), MA Cantab 1964, PhD Cantab 1967; FSA. Asst Lectr in Classics, Manchester Univ., 1965–68. *Publications*: Textile Manufacture in the Northern Roman Provinces, 1970; *contrib*. Antiqu., Bonner Jbh., Britann., Class. Qly, Derbys Archaeol. Jl, Germ., Latomus. *Address*: Dept of Archaeology, Univ. of Manchester, Manchester M13 9PL.

Wild, Martin Trevor; Lecturer in Geography, Hull University, since 1967; *b* 1940; *m* 1969. BA Birmingham 1961, PhD Birm-

ingham 1972; Mem., Inst. Brit. Geogrs. Asst Lectr in Geog., Aberdeen, 1964–66; Asst Lectr in Geog., Hull, 1966–67. Mem., Vacation Grants Cttee, Univ. of Hull, 1971– . *Publications*: contrib. The Yorkshire Textile Industry, in, The Wool Textiles of Great Britain, ed G. Jenkins, 1972; *contrib*. Textile Hist. *Address*: Dept of Geography, Univ. of Hull, Hull HU6 7RX.

Wilder, William D., MA; Lecturer in Anthropology, University of Durham, since 1966; *b* 1939; *m* 1963; one *s* one *d*. AB Harvard 1961, MA London 1963. Assoc., London Cttee, London–Cornell project for E and SE Asian Studies, 1967– . *Publications*: contrib. Amer. Anthropol., Assoc. Social Anthrop. Monogs., Bijdragen tot de taal-, land- en volkenkunde, Man, Mod. Asian Studies. *Address*: Dept of Anthropology, Univ. of Durham, South End House, South Road, Durham City DH1 3TG.

Wilders, Dr John Simpson, MA, PhD, DPhil; Tutorial Fellow in English, Worcester College, Oxford University, since 1968; *b* 1927; *m* 1953; two *s* one *d*. BA Cantab 1950 (1st cl. Engl.), PhD Cantab 1954, MA Cantab 1955, DPhil Oxon 1968. Instructor in English, Princeton Univ., 1953; Jun. Fellow, Bristol Univ., 1954; Asst Lectr, Bristol Univ., 1955–57; Lectr, Bristol Univ., 1957–67; Sen. Lectr, Bristol Univ., 1967. Gov., Royal Shakesp. Theatre, 1965; Mem., Exec. Council, Royal Shakesp. Theatre, 1968; Dir, Royal Shakesp. Theatre Summer Sch., 1959–70. *Publications*: ed, S. Butler: Hudibras, 1967; ed, The Merchant of Venice: A Casebook, 1969; ed (with A. H. de Quehen), S. Butler: Hudibras and selected other writings, 1973; *contrib*. Camb. Rev., Ess. Crit., Notes Queries, Rev. Engl. Studies. *Address*: Worcester College, Oxford.

Wilding, Dr John Martin, MA, PhD; Lecturer in Psychology, Bedford College, University of London, since 1966; *b* 1936; *m* 1963; three *s*. BA Oxon 1962 (1st cl. Lit. Hum.), BA Oxon 1964 (2nd cl. PPP), MA Oxon 1965, PhD London 1970. Asst Lectr, Bedford Coll., Univ. of London, 1964–66. *Publications*: *contrib*. Acta Psychol., Brit. Jl Psychol., Nature, Psychonom. Sci. *Address*: Dept of Psychology, Bedford College, Regent's Park, NW1 4NS.

Wilding, Dr Paul Roger; Senior Lecturer, Department of Applied Social Science, University of Nottingham, since 1974; *b* 1938; *m* 1969. BA Oxon 1961, DipEd Oxon 1962, MA Oxon 1965, Dipl. in Social Administration, Manchester 1965, PhD Manchester 1970. Asst Lectr, 1967, Lectr, 1968–74, Univ. of Nottingham. *Publications*: (with V. George) Motherless Families, 1972; *contrib*. Jl of Soc. Pol., Pub. Admin., Soc. and Econ. Admin., Sociol. Rev. *Address*: Dept of Applied Social Science, Univ. Park, Nottingham NG7 2RD.

Wiles, Rev. Canon Prof. Maurice Frank, DD; Regius Professor of Divinity, Oxford University, since 1970; *b* 1923; *m* 1950; two *s* one *d*. BA Cantab 1947, MA Cantab 1950, BD Cantab 1963, DD Cantab 1970. Lectr, Univ. Coll. of Ibadan, Nigeria, 1955–59;

Lectr, Univ. of Cambridge, and Dean of Clare College, 1959–67; Prof. of Christian Doctrine, Univ. of London, King's Coll., 1967–70. Canon of Christ Church, Oxford. *Publications*: The Spiritual Gospel, 1960; The Christian Fathers, 1966; The Divine Apostle, 1967; The Making of Christian Doctrine, 1967; *contrib.* Jl Theol. Studies, Relig. Studies, Theol. *Address*: Christ Church, Oxford.

Wiles, Prof. Peter John de la Fosse; Professor of Russian Social and Economic Studies, University of London, since 1965; *b* 1919; *m* 1946 (marr. diss.); one *s* two *d*; *m* 1960. BA Oxford 1939 (shortened war course) (Dist. in Class. Hon. Mod.), MA Oxford 1941. Fellow, All Souls Coll., 1946; Fellow, New Coll., 1947–60; Prof., Brandeis Univ., 1960–63; Res. Associate, Inst. för Internationell Ekonomi, 1963; Vis. Prof., City Coll., NY, 1964 and 1967. *Publications*: Price, Cost and Output, 1956, 2nd edn 1961; The Political Economy of Communism, 1962; Communist International Economics, 1969; ed, The Prediction of Communist Economic Performance, 1971; *contrib.* Analyse et Prévis., Econ. Jl, Economica, Mysl Gospod., Ost-Europa, Oxf. Econ. Papers, Oxf. Inst. Stats Bull., Survey. *Address*: London School of Economics, Houghton Street, WC2A 2AE.

Wilkerson, Terence Edward; Lecturer in Philosophy, University of Nottingham, since 1972; BA Oxon 1966 (PPE), BPhil Oxon 1968 (Philosophy), MA Oxon 1971. Lectr in Philosophy, Univ. of Keele, 1968–72. *Publications*: Minds, Brains and People, 1974; *contrib.* Kant-Stud., Mind, Philos. Qly, Philos. Rev., Philos. *Address*: Dept of Philosophy, Univ. of Nottingham, Nottingham NG7 2RD.

Wilkes, Alan Lawson; Senior Lecturer, Department of Psychology, University of Dundee, since 1973; *b* 1937; *m* 1960; two *d*. BSc Manchester 1959, BSc Oxon 1964. Lectr, Psychology, Dundee Univ., 1964–73. *Publications*: *contrib.* Br. Jl Psychol., Jl Exper. Psychol., Jl Verbal Learning and Verbal Behaviour, Qly Jl Exper. Psychol. *Address*: Dept of Psychology, Univ. of Dundee DD1 4HN.

Wilkie, Prof. John Ritchie, MA; Professor of German, University of Leeds, since 1972; *b* 1921; *m* 1951; one *d*. MA Aberdeen 1943, BA Cantab 1945, MA 1972. Temp. Asst in German, Aberdeen Univ., 1945–46; Asst, Aberdeen Univ., 1947–50; Lectr in German, Leeds Univ., 1950–61; Sen. Lectr, Leeds Univ., 1961–72. Elder, United Ref. Ch. *Publications*: (with W. W. Chambers) A Short History of the German Language, 1970; *contrib.* Encyclopaedia Britannica; *contrib.* Germ. Life Lett., Mod. Lang. Rev. *Address*: Dept of German, The Univ., Leeds LS2 9JT.

Wilkin, Andrew; Lecturer in Italian, Department of Modern Languages, University of Strathclyde, since 1967; *b* 1944; *m* 1965; one *s* one *d*. BA Manchester 1967 (Hons Italian Studies). Treasurer, Assoc. of Teachers of Italian (Scotland), 1971– ;

756

Vis. Examr in Italian, Scottish Certif. of Educn Examination Bd, 1973– . *Publications*: introduction and glossary, Giovanni Verga: Little Novels of Sicily (trans. D. H. Lawrence) 1973; *contrib.* Assoc. Teach. Ital. Jl, Mod. Langs, Mod. Lang. Rev., Year's Work Mod. Langs. *Address*: Dept of Modern Languages, Univ. of Strathclyde, Glasgow G1 1XH.

Wilkins, David Arthur; Lecturer, Department of Linguistic Science, University of Reading, since 1966; *b* 1936; *m* 1959; one *s* two *d*. BA Manchester 1960 (Hons French), Post-graduate Certif. in Educn London 1961, Dipl. in Applied Linguistics Edinburgh 1966; Member: Linguistics Assoc. of GB; Linguistics Soc. of America; British Assoc. for Applied Linguistics. *Publications*: Linguistics in Language Teaching, 1972; Second Language Learning and Teaching (forthcoming). *Address*: Dept of Linguistic Science, Univ. of Reading, Whiteknights, Reading RG6 2AH.

Wilkins, Dr John Barrington; Lecturer in Classics, Queen Mary College, University of London, since 1965; *b* 1935; *m* 1958; one *s* two *d*. Univ. of Cambridge: BA 1957, MA 1961, PhD 1961. Scholar, King's Coll., Cambridge, 1954–58; Sandys Student, Univ. of Cambridge, 1958; Rome Scholar, British Sch. at Rome, 1958–61. Lectr, Dept of Latin, Univ. of Wales, Cardiff, 1961–65; Consultant Linguist, Cambridge Sch. Classics Project, Univ. of Cambridge, 1965–68. *Publications*: *contrib.* Trans Philol Soc., Didask., Jl Lings. *Address*: Dept of Classics, Queen Mary College, Univ. of London, E1 4NS.

Wilkins, Dr Nigel Edward, BA, PhD, LTCL; Lecturer in French, University of St Andrews, since 1964; *b* 1936; *m* 1962; two *d*. BA Nottingham 1960 (1st cl. French), PhD Nottingham 1964, CertEd Nottingham 1961, LTCL London 1960. Asst Prof. of French, Memorial Univ. of Newfoundland, 1962–64. *Publications*: The Works of Jehan de Lescurel, 1966; A Fourteenth-century Repertory from the Codex Reina, 1966; A Fifteenth-century Repertory from the Codex Reina, 1966; The Lyric Works of Adam de la Halle, 1967; One Hundred Ballades, Rondeaux and Virelais, 1969; Guillaume de Machaut: La Louange des Dames, 1972; Two Miracles, 1972; Three Madrigals by Jacopo da Bologna, 1973; The Writings of Erik Satie, 1974; *contrib.* Grove's Dictionary; *contrib.* Musica Discip., Nott. Mediaev. Studies, Rev. Belge Musicol., Zeits. Philol. *Address*: Dept of French, The Univ., St Andrews, Fife KY16 9AJ.

Wilkinson, Prof. Alexander Birrell; Professor of Private Law, since 1972, and Dean of Faculty of Law, since 1974, Dundee University; *b* 1932; *m* 1965; one *s* one *d*. MA St Andrews 1954 (Hons Classics), LLB Edinburgh 1959 (with Distinction); Admitted to Faculty of Advocates, 1959. Lectr in Scots Law, Univ. of Edinburgh, 1965–69. Practice at Scottish Bar, 1959–69; Sheriff of Stirling, Dunbarton and Clackmannan at Stirling and Alloa, 1969–72; Vice-Chm., Scottish Marriage Guidance Council. *Publications*: *contrib.* legal periodicals. *Address*: Univ. of Dundee, Dundee DD1 4HN.

Wilkinson, Prof. Elizabeth M., PhD, LLD, DLit; FBA; Professor of German, University of London, since 1960; b 1909. BA London 1932, DipEd Oxford 1933, PhD London 1943; Hon. LLD Smith College, Northampton, Mass. 1966, Hon. DLit Kent 1971. Temp. Asst Lectr, Univ. Coll., London, 1940–43; Temp. Lectr, Univ. Coll., London, 1943–46; Lectr, Univ. Coll., London, 1946–47; Reader, Univ. Coll., London, 1947–60; Elected to Chair of German, Univ. Coll. of London, 1961. Sec., Bd of Studies, Germanic Langs and Lits, 1946–52; Sec., Engl. Goethe Soc., 1953–   ; Pres., Mod. Lang. Assoc. GB, 1964. *Publications*: J. E. Schlegel: A German Pioneer in Aesthetics, 1945; (with L. A. Willoughby) Goethe: Poet and Thinker, 1962; ed, and trans. (with L. A. Willoughby), F. Schiller: On the Aesthetic Education of Man, 1967; *contrib*. Germ. Life Lett., Mod. Lang. Rev., Proc. Engl. Goethe Soc. *Address*: Dept of German, Univ. College London, Gower Street, WC1E 6BT.

Wilkinson, Harold William; Senior Lecturer, Faculty of Law, Bristol University, since 1969; b 1931; m 1962; two d. LLB Manchester 1949, LLM Manchester 1963; Solicitor, 1955; Mem. Law Soc. Lectr in Law, Bristol Univ., 1966. *Publications*: Pipes, Mains, Cables and Sewers, 1967, 2nd edn 1970; Personal Property, 1971; The Standard Conditions of Sale of Land, 1972, 2nd edn 1974; *contrib*. Conveyancer, Modern Law Review. *Address*: Faculty of Law, The Univ., Bristol BS8 1TH.

Wilkinson, Joan Hazel; *see* Carter, J. H.

Wilkinson, Lancelot Patrick, FRSL; Brereton Reader in Classics, Cambridge University, 1969–74, and Orator of Cambridge University, 1958–74; b 1907; m 1944; two s. BA Cantab 1930, MA Cantab 1933; a Vice-Pres., Class. Assoc. (Pres., 1972). Lectr in Classics, Cambridge, 1936–67; Reader in Latin Literature, Cambridge, 1967–69; Fellow, King's Coll., 1932–   ; Dean, King's Coll., 1932–45; Sen. Tutor, King's Coll., 1946–56; Vice-Provost, King's Coll., 1961–65. Mem., Council, New Hall, 1954–65; Mem., Council of Senate, Cambridge Univ., 1952–56; Gov., Queen Mary Coll., London, 1954–57; Gov., Charterhouse Sch., 1954–69; Mem., Conseil Consultatif, Fondation Hardt (Geneva), 1959–63. *Publications*: Horace and his Lyric Poetry, 1945; Letters of Cicero, 1949; Ovid Recalled, 1955; abr. edn as Ovid Surveyed, 1962; Golden Latin Artistry, 1963; ed (with R. H. Bulmer), King's College Register, 1919–1958, 1963, 1945–1970, 1974; The Georgics of Virgil, 1969; *contrib*. Class. Rev., Greece Rome, Hermes, Jl Rom. Studies. *Address*: King's College, Cambridge.

Wilkinson, Paul; Lecturer in Politics, Department of Economics, University of Wales (University College, Cardiff), since 1968; b 1937; m 1960; two s one d. BA Swansea 1959 (Jt Hons Mod. Hist. and Pol.), MA Wales 1968; Mem., ACH, Mem., I Iss, Mem., PSA. Asst Lectr, Cardiff, 1966–68. RAF, 1960–65. *Publications*: Social Movement, 1971; Political Terrorism, 1974; *contrib*. Jl Contemp. Hist., Govt and Opposition, Pol Studies. *Address*: Dept of Politics, Univ. College, PO Box 78, Cardiff CF1 1XL.

Wilkinson, William John, MSc, MInstP; Lecturer, Department of Educational Studies, University of Hull, since 1964; b 1933; m 1962; three s one d. BSc Belfast 1957 (1st cl. Physics), MSc Belfast 1959, BSc London 1970 (2nd cl. Psychol.), Dip. Adv. Study in Education Manchester 1965; MInstP; ABPsS. Mem., Educn Sect. Mem., Yorks Br., Assoc. Science Educn Cttee, 1967–70; Mem., Hull-York Cttee, ASE, 1968–71; Mem., Conceptual Thinking in Science Gp, Science Teacher Educn Project, 1969–74. *Publications*: *contrib*. Asp. Educn, Contemp. Phys., Durh. Educnl Rev., Educn Teaching, Educn Science, Educnl Rev., Sch. Science Rev. *Address*: Dept of Educational Studies, Applied Science Building, The Univ., Hull HU6 7RX.

Wilks, Brian John; Lecturer in Education, Department of Education, University of Leeds, since 1968; b 1933; m 1959; one s one d. BA UC of N Wales, Bangor, 1959 (1st cl. Hons), MA Bangor 1963. *Publications*: ed and introd. (with R. Chapman), Snap Out Of It, 1973 (Playscript); chapters in: Drama in Education: The Annual Survey, vol. 1 1972, vol. 2 1973. *Address*: Dept of Education, The Univ., Leeds LS2 9JT.

Wilks, Prof. Michael John, MA, PhD; Professor of Medieval History, Birkbeck College, University of London, since 1974 (Reader in History of Political Ideas, 1967–74); b 1930; m 1954; two s. BA Cantab 1954 (1st cl. Hist.), MA Cantab 1957, PhD Cantab 1958. Fellow, Trinity Coll., Cambridge, 1957–62; Asst Lectr, Birkbeck Coll., London, 1957–59; Lectr, Birkbeck Coll., London, 1959–67. *Publications*: The Problem of Sovereignty in the Later Middle Ages, 1963; *contrib*. August., Bull. J. Rylands Libr., Jl Theol. Studies, SCH, Studia Patrist., etc. *Address*: Dept of History, Birkbeck College, Malet Street, WC1E 7HX.

Willcock, Prof. Malcolm Maurice, MA; Professor of Classics, University of Lancaster, since 1965; b 1925; m 1957; four d. BA Cantab 1950 (1st cl. Classics), MA Cantab 1951. Res. Fellow, Pembroke Coll., Cambridge, 1951; Fellow, Sidney Sussex Coll., 1952; Asst Lectr, Cambridge, 1961–65; Principal, Bowland Coll., Lancaster, 1966; Vis. Prof., Univ. of Minnesota, 1971. *Publications*: A Commentary on Homer's Iliad Books I–VI, 1970; *contrib*. Bull. Inst. Class. Stud., Class. Qly. *Address*: Dept of Classics, Univ. of Lancaster, Bailrigg, Lancaster LA1 4YW.

Willcocks, Dr Arthur John; Professor of Social Administration, Nottingham University, since 1972; b 1924; m 1951; two s two d. BCom Birmingham 1951 (1st cl. Soc. Studies), PhD Birmingham 1953; Mem., Royal Inst. Public Admin, Mem., Soc. Admin Assoc., Mem., Brit. Sociol Assoc. Lectr, Nottingham Univ., 1956–66, Sen. Lectr, 1966–72. Mem., Exec. Council, Nottm and Notts., Nat. Hlth Serv., 1960–68; Nottm and Dist Hosp. Mngmt Cttee, 1968–   ; Adv. Council, Nat.

Corp. for Care of Old People, 1969– ;
Univ. Senate, Council and var. cttees.
Publications: Creation of the National Health
Service, 1967; Demand and Need for Dental
Care, 1968; contrib. Problems and Progress
in Medical Care (Annual Vol. of Essays,
Nuffield Provincial Hospitals Trust); *contrib.*
Soc. Econ. Admin., Sociol. Rev. *Address:*
Dept of Applied Social Science, Univ. of
Nottingham, Nottingham NG7 2RD.

Willett, Ralph, MA; Lecturer, Department
of American Studies, Hull University, since
1966; *b* 1935; *m* 1963. BA Nottingham 1956,
DipEd Nottingham 1957, MA London
1964. Teaching Fellow, Western Reserve
Univ., Cleveland, 1964–65; Lectr, King's
Coll., London, 1965–66. Mem., Cttee, Brit.
Assoc. Amer. Studies, 1971– . *Publications:*
(with J. White) Slavery in the American
South, 1970; ed, Studies in Pierre, 1971; jt
ed., Webster's New World Biographical and
Critical Guide to English and American
Literature, 1973; *contrib.* Jl Amer. Studies,
PMLA, S Atl. Qly, Yrs Wk Engl. Studies.
Address: Dept of American Studies, Univ. of
Hull, Hull HU6 7RX.

Willetts, Prof. Ronald Frederick, MA;
Professor of Greek, University of Birming-
ham, since 1970; *b* 1915; *m* 1945; one *d.* BA
Birmingham 1937 (1st cl. Classics), MA
Birmingham 1938, DipEd Birmingham 1939;
Leverhulme Res. Award 1971; Mem.,
Hellen. Soc., Mem., Internat. PEN, Mem.,
Soc. Authors. Lectr in Greek, Univ. of
Birmingham, 1946–57; Sen. Lectr, Univ. of
Birmingham, 1957–63; Reader, Univ. of
Birmingham, 1963–69. Mem., Council,
Hellen. Soc., 1967–70. *Publications:* Aristo-
cratic Society in Ancient Crete, 1955; The
Ion of Euripides, 1958; Cretan Cults and
Festivals, 1962; Ancient Crete: A Social
History, 1965; The Plutus of Aristophanes,
1965; The Law Code of Gortyn, 1967; Every-
day Life in Ancient Crete, 1969; Blind Wealth
and Aristophanes, 1970; gen. ed., States and
Cities of Ancient Greece, 1970– ; *contrib.*
numerous articles in learned jls, procs and
bks. *Address:* The Dept of Greek, Univ. of
Birmingham, PO Box 363, Birmingham B15
2TT.

Williams, Alan Francis; Lecturer in De-
partment of Geography, University of Birm-
ingham, since 1965; *b* 1933; *m* 1958; two *s*
one *d.* BA Bristol 1955 (Hons Geog.), PhD
Bristol 1960. Mem., Inst. Brit. Geogrs, Mem.,
Canad. Assoc. Geogrs, Mem., Geog. Assoc.
Demonstrator, Univ. of Bristol, 1957–58;
Asst Lectr, Univ. of Birmingham, 1958–59;
Asst Lectr, Univ. of Glasgow, 1959–62; Asst
Prof., Memorial Univ. of Newfoundland,
1962–65; Prof. and Act. Hd of Dept of
Geography, Memorial Univ., 1971–72 (on
leave of absence). *Publications:* (with B.
Fullerton) Scandinavia, 1972. *Address:* Dept
of Geography, Univ. of Birmingham, PO
Box 363, Birmingham B15 2TT.

Williams, Prof. Alan Harold; Professor,
Department of Economics, University of
York, since 1968; *b* 1927; *m* 1953; two *s*
one *d.* BCom Birmingham 1951. Asst Lectr,
Univ. of Exeter, 1954–56; Lectr, Univ. of

Exeter, 1956–61; Vis. Lectr, MIT, 1957–58;
Vis. Lectr, Princeton, 1961–62; Sen. Lectr,
York, 1962–66; Dir of Econ. Studies, Centre
for Admin. Studies, and Econ. Cnsltnt, HM
Treasury, 1966–68. *Publications:* Public
Finance and Budgetary Policy, 1963; *contrib.*
Economica, Jl Pol Econ., Jl Pub. Econ., Nat.
Tax Jl, Public Fin. *Address:* Dept of Econ-
omics, Univ. of York, York YO1 5DD.

Williams, Dr Allan Peter Owen; Senior
Lecturer in Occupational and Organizational
Psychology, Graduate Business Centre, City
University, since 1974; *b* 1935; *m* 1959; one *s*
two *d.* BA Manchester 1957 (Psychology),
MA Birkbeck Coll., London Univ. 1959
(Occupational Psychology), PhD Birkbeck
Coll. 1963 (Psychology); ABPsS 1963;
Member: Nat. Inst. of Industrial Psychology;
Internat. Assoc. of Applied Psychology;
Group Relations Trng Assoc. Lectr, Grad.
Bus. Centre, City Univ., 1963–74. Mem.,
Psychologists' Panel, CS Selection Bd, CS
Commn, 1966– ; Hon. Treasurer, British
Psychological Soc., 1970– . *Publications:*
contrib. Jl Man. Stud., Occup. Psych. *Ad-
dress:* Graduate Business Centre, City Univ.,
23 Goswell Road, EC1M 7BB.

Williams, Alun L.; *see* Llewelyn-Williams.

Williams, Arthur, BA, MA; Lecturer in
German, Modern Languages Centre, Uni-
versity of Bradford, since 1970; *b* 1940; *m*
1967. BA Keele 1963 (French/German),
MA Keele 1967. Lektor, English, Univ. of
Saarbrücken, 1963–64; Res. Asst in German,
Modern Languages Centre, Univ. of Brad-
ford, 1967–70. *Publications:* *contrib.* Germ.
Life Lett. *Address:* Modern Languages
Centre, Univ. of Bradford, Bradford BD7
1DP.

Williams, Prof. Bernard Arthur Owen,
FBA; Knightbridge Professor of Philosophy,
University of Cambridge, and Fellow of
King's College, since 1967; *b* 1929; *m*
1955 (marr. diss. 1974); one *d.* BA Oxon
1951, MA Oxon 1954. Fellow, All Souls
Coll., Oxford, 1951–54; Fellow, New Coll.,
Oxford, 1954–59; Vis. Lectr, UC Ghana,
1958–59; Lectr, Univ. Coll., London, 1959–
64; Prof. of Philosophy, Bedford Coll., London, 1964–67; Vis. Prof., Princeton Univ.,
1963; Vis. Fellow, Austr. Nat. Univ., 1969;
Vis. Prof., Harvard, 1973. Trustee, Sadler's
Wells; Mem., Public Schools Commn, 1965–
70. Mem., Institut Internat. de Philosophie.
Publications: ed (with A. C. Montefiore),
British Analytical Philosophy, 1966; Morality, 1971; Problems of the Self, 1973; (with
J. J. C. Smart) Utilitarianism, 1973; *contrib.*
jls, etc. *Address:* King's College, Cambridge.

Williams, Dr Christopher John Fardo;
Reader in Philosophy, University of Bristol,
since 1972; *b* 1930. BA Oxon 1954 (1st cl.
Class. Hon. Mods, 1st cl. Lit. Hum.), MA
Oxon 1956, DPhil Oxon 1965. Asst Lectr,
Hull Univ., 1962–64; Lectr, 1964–66; Lectr,
Bristol Univ., 1966–72; Vis. Prof., Univ. of
Notre Dame, 1970; Ed., Analysis, 1971.
Mem., Downside Symp. Gp, 1960–72; Chm.,
1966–68; Mem., Council, Downside Centre

for Relig. Studies, 1967– . *Publications*: *contrib*. Analysis, Downs. Rev., Mind, Philos. Qly, Philos., Proc. Aristot. Soc., Relig. Studies, Sophia. *Address*: Dept of Philosophy, Univ. of Bristol, Bristol BS8 1RJ.

Williams, David Anthony; Lecturer, French Department, University of Hull, since 1968; *b* 1942; *m* 1964; two *s* one *d*. BA Oxford 1963, BPhil Oxford 1966 (Gen. and Comparative Literature). Lecteur d'Anglais, Aix-en-Provence, 1966–68. *Publications*: Psychological Determinism in Madame Bovary, 1973; *contrib*. For. Mod. Lang. Stud. *Address*: French Dept, Univ. of Hull, Cottingham Road, Hull HU6 7RX.

Williams, Dr David Gareth; University Lecturer in Psychology, School of Cultural and Community Studies (Psychology), University of Sussex, since 1968; *b* 1943. BSc Bristol 1964 (Special Hons Psychology), PhD Bristol 1969; Associate Mem., British Psychological Soc. Temp. Asst Lectr in Psychology, Univ. of Bristol, 1965–66. *Publication*: *contrib*. J. Psych. *Address*: School of Cultural and Community Studies, Univ. of Sussex, Arts Building, Falmer, Brighton BN1 9QN.

Williams, David Malcolm, MA; Lecturer in Economic History, University of Leicester, since 1964; *b* 1940; *m* 1963; one *s* one *d*. BA Liverpool 1961, MA Liverpool 1963. Tutor, Univ. of Liverpool, 1962–63. *Publications*: *contrib*. Business Hist. *Address*: Dept of Economic History, The Univ., Leicester LE1 7RH.

Williams, Dr David Sydney Mabe; Lecturer in History of Asiatic Russia, Department of History, School of Slavonic and East European Studies, University of London, since 1964; *b* 1928; *m* 1965; two *d*. BA London 1963 (Hons), PhD London 1969. *Publications*: *contrib*. Asian Affs, Cent. Asian Rev., Slav. and E Eur. Rev. *Address*: School of Slavonic and East European Studies, Univ. of London, Senate House, WC1E 7HU.

Williams, Elizabeth Glenys, MA; Lecturer in English Language and Medieval English Literature, School of English, University of Leeds, since 1968; *b* 1938. BA London 1961 (1st cl. English), MA London 1964. Asst Lectr in English Language and Medieval English Literature, School of English, Univ. of Leeds, 1965–68. *Publications*: *contrib*. Leeds Studies Engl. *Address*: School of English, The Univ., Leeds LS2 9JT.

Williams, Gareth, MA, BLitt; Lecturer in Russian, University College of Swansea, since 1967; *b* 1936; *m* 1961; two *s* one *d*. BA Oxon 1959 (1st cl. Russian and French), MA Oxon 1965, BLitt Oxon 1966. Instructor, Univ. of British Columbia, 1963–65. Asst Prof., 1965–67. *Publications*: *contrib*. Canad. Slav. Papers, Welt der Slaven. *Address*: Dept of German, Univ. College of Swansea, Singleton Park, Swansea SA2 8PP.

Williams, Geraint Lynn, MA; Lecturer in Political Theory and Institutions, Sheffield University, since 1968; *b* 1942; *m* 1970. BA Wales 1963, MA Wales 1968. Lectr, Univ. Coll., Swansea, 1966–68; Vis. Prof., Univ. of Calgary, 1971–72. *Address*: Dept of Political Theory and Institutions, The Univ., Sheffield S10 2TN.

Williams, Prof. Glanmor, MA, DLitt, FRHistS; Professor of History, University College of Swansea, since 1957; *b* 1920; *m* 1946; one *s* one *d*. BA Wales 1941 (1st cl. Hist.), MA Wales 1947, DLitt Wales 1963; FRHistS. Asst Lectr, Swansea, 1945; Lectr, Swansea, 1946–52; Sen. Lectr, Swansea, 1952–57. Mem., Council, Royal Hist. Soc., 1958–62, 1966–70; Mem., RCAM, Wales, 1963– ; Mem., Hist. Bdngs, Council, Wales, 1963– ; Gov., BBC, 1965–71; Chm., Bd of Celtic Studies, 1969– ; Mem., British Library Bd, 1973– . *Publications*: Bywyd Ac Amserau Yr Esgob Richard Davies, 1953; The Welsh Church from Conquest to Reformation, 1962; Owen Glendower, 1966; (with G. M. Richards) Llyfr Gweddi Gyffredin, 1567, 1966; Welsh Reformation Essays, 1967; Reformation Views of Church History, 1970; ed, Glamorgan County History, vol. III, 1971; *contrib*. Camb. Jl, Hist., Welsh Hist. Rev. *Address*: Univ. College, Singleton Park, Swansea SA2 8PP.

Williams, Prof. Glanville Llewelyn, QC, LLD, FBA; Rouse Ball Professor of English Law, University of Cambridge, since 1968; *b* 1911; *m* 1939; one *s*. LLB Wales 1931, PhD Cantab 1936, MA Cantab 1938, LLD Cantab 1946, Hon LLD Nottingham 1963; Barrister of the Middle Temple, 1935; Hon. Bencher, 1967; QC 1968; FBA. Pres., Abortion Law Reform Assoc., Fellow, Eugenics Soc., Mem., Selden Soc., Howard League. Res. Fellow, St John's Coll., Cambridge, 1936–42; Reader in English Law, and successively Prof. of Public Law and Quain Prof. of Jurisprudence, Univ. of London, 1945–55; Carpentier Lectr, Columbia Univ., 1956; Cohen Lectr, Hebrew Univ. of Jerusalem, 1957; first Walter E. Meyer Vis. Res. Prof., NY Univ., 1959–60; Charles Inglis Thompson Guest Prof., Univ. of Colorado, 1965. Special Cnsltnt for Amer. Law Inst. Model Penal Code, 1956–58; Mem., Criminal Law Revision Cttee, 1959– ; Mem., Law Commn's Working Party on Codification of Criminal Law, 1967– ; Mem., Cttee on Mentally Abnormal Offenders, 1972– . *Publications*: Liability for Animals, 1939; The Law Reform (Frustrated Contracts) Act, 1944; Learning the Law, 1945, 8th edn 1973; Crown Proceedings, 1948; Joint Obligations, 1949; Joint Torts and Contributory Negligence, 1950; Criminal Law, The General Part, 1953, 2nd edn 1961; The Proof of Guilt, 1955, 3rd edn 1963; The Sanctity of Life and the Criminal Law, 1956, British edn 1958; The Mental Element in Crime, 1965; *contrib*. Camb. Law Jl, Crim. Law Rev., Law Qly Rev., Mod. Law Rev. *Address*: Jesus College, Cambridge.

Williams, Prof. Gordon W.; Professor of Humanity, University of St Andrews, since 1963; *b* 1926; *m* 2nd 1970; one *s* one *d*. BA Trinity College Dublin 1947, MA Trinity

College Dublin 1951, MA Oxon 1953. Asst Lectr, King's Coll., London, 1948–51; Lectr, Univ. Coll., Cardiff, 1951–53; Fellow and Tutor, Balliol Coll., Oxford, 1953–62; Vis. Prof., Univ. of Indiana, 1969; Sather Prof., Univ. of California, Berkeley, 1973. *Publications*: Tradition and Originality in Roman Poetry, 1968; The Third Book of Horace's Odes, 1969; Nature of Roman Poetry, 1970; Horace, 1972; *contrib*. Class. Qly, Class. Rev., Gnomon, Hermes, Jl Rom. Studies. *Address*: Dept of Humanity, St Salvator's College, St Andrews, Fife KY16 9PH.

Williams, Prof. Gwyn A.; Professor of History, University College, Cardiff, since 1974; *b* 1925; *m* 1950; one *s*. BA Wales 1950 (1st cl. Hons), MA Wales 1952, PhD London 1960. Fellow, Univ. of Wales, 1952–54; Res. Student, Goldsmiths' Company, 1952–54; Lectr, Univ. Coll. Wales, Aberystwyth, 1954–63; Sen. Lectr, later Reader, Univ. of York, 1963–65, Professor, 1965–74; Alexander Prize, Royal Historical Soc., 1960. *Publications*: Medieval London: from commune to capital, 1963, pbk 1973; Artisans and Sans-culottes, 1968; Banner Bright, 1973; Antonio Gramsci, the Turin movement of factory councils and the origins of Italian communism, 1974; Goya and the impossible Revolution (forthcoming); *contrib*. Welsh History Rev., Bull. Bd of Celtic Studies, Trans Royal Historical Soc., Hon. Soc. Cymmrodorion, Jl History of Ideas. *Address*: Dept of History, Univ. College, Cardiff, PO Box 78, Cardiff CF1 1XL.

Williams, Prof. Harri Llwyd H.; *see* Hudson-Williams.

Williams, Harry; Deputy Head of Department of Architecture, Heriot-Watt University, since 1973; *b* 1919; *m* 1945; one *s*. BArch Liverpool 1947 (Hons 1), DipCD Liverpool 1948; ARIBA 1948, MRTPI 1949, ARIAS 1955. Sen. Lectr, Dept of Architecture, Heriot-Watt Univ., 1955. *Address*: Dept of Architecture, Heriot-Watt Univ., Edinburgh EH1 1HX.

Williams, Prof. Hugh Trefor, CBE, BA; Professor of Agricultural Economics, University College of Wales, Aberystwyth, since 1964; *b* 1912; *m* 1942; one *s* one *d*. BA Wales 1934; FRAgS, Mem., Agric. Econ. Soc. Economist, and Hd of Econ. Br., Min. of Agriculture, 1940–54; Dep. Principal, Seale-Hayne Agricultural Coll., 1954–64. Mem., Cttee of Inquiry into Statutory Smallholdings, 1963–66; Mem., Adv. Cttee to Min. of Agriculture on Working Capital Grants to Agric. Cooperatives, 1965–67; Mem., Meat and Livestock Commn, 1967–73; Mem., Merseyside and N Wales Electric. Bd, 1967; Chm., Council, Welsh Agric. Organisation Soc., 1971– . *Publications*: Principles for British Agricultural Policy, 1961; *contrib*. Jl Agric. Econ. Soc. *Address*: Dept of Agricultural Economics, Univ. College of Wales, Aberystwyth SY23 2AX.

Williams, Ioan Miles; Senior Lecturer in English, Department of English and Comparative Literary Studies, University of Warwick, since 1973; *b* 1941; *m* 1964; three *d*.

BA Oxford 1963 (1st cl. Hons English Language and Literature, St Catherine's Coll.), MA, BLitt Oxford 1965 (St Catherine's Coll.). Asst Lectr in English, Exeter Univ., 1964–66; Lectr in English, Dept of English, Warwick Univ., 1966–73. *Publications*: Robert Browning, 1968; Sir Walter Scott on Novels and Novelists, 1968; W. M. Thackeray, 1969; Novel and Romance, 1700–1800, 1970; The Criticism of Henry Fielding, 1970; George Meredith, the Critical Heritage, 1971; Sandra Belloni and Vittoria, in Meredith Now, ed I. Fletcher, 1971; The Realist Novel in England, 1974; *contrib*. RES, Vict. Stud., Planet, TES. *Address*: Dept of English, Univ. of Warwick, Coventry, CV4 7AL.

Williams, Dr Iolo Wyn; Lecturer in Education, University College of Swansea, since 1961; *b* 1934; *m* 1962; one *s*. BSc Wales 1955 (1st cl. Chem.), PhD Wales 1958; FRIC 1970. Sen. Lectr, Univ. of W Indies, 1968–69. Dep. Ed., Y Gwyddonydd. *Publications*: *contrib*. Educn Chem., Sch. Science Rev. *Address*: Education Dept, Univ. College of Swansea, Hendrefoilan, Swansea SA2 7NB.

Williams, Prof. Jac L., BA, BSc(Econ), PhD; Professor of Education, and Dean of Faculty, University College of Wales, Aberystwyth, since 1961; *b* 1918; *m* 1946; two *d*. BA Wales 1939 (1st cl. Welsh), BSc(Econ) London 1944, DipEd Wales 1940, DPA London 1943, PhD London 1954. Adv. Off., Fac. of Educn, 1956–60. Mem., Welsh Jt Educn Cttee; Schs Council Cttee for Wales; Gov. Body, and Liturgical Commn, Ch in Wales. *Publications*: Bibliography of Bilingualism, 1971; Editor: Welsh Studies in Education, 1967– ; Ysgrifau ar Addysg, 1965– ; Cyfres y Dysgwyr, 1961– ; Dictionary of Welsh Technical Terms, 1973. *Address*: Dept of Education, Univ. College of Wales, Aberystwyth, Dyfed SY23 1NU.

Williams, Prof. John Ellis Caerwyn; Professor of Irish, University College of Wales, Aberystwyth, since 1965; *b* 1912; *m* 1945. BA Wales 1934 (Hons Latin; Welsh), MA Wales 1936, BD Wales (Church Hist., Greek, Distinctions); Hon. DLitt Celt. Ireland 1967. Res. Lectr, Univ. Coll. of North Wales, Bangor, 1937–39; Fellow, Univ. of Wales, 1939–41; Lectr, Bangor, 1939–51; Sen. Lectr, Bangor, 1951–53; Prof. of Welsh, Bangor, 1953–65; Leverhulme Fellow, 1963–64; Vis. Prof. of Celtic, UCLA, 1968; Summer Sch., Harvard, 1968. Chm., Welsh Acad., 1965– ; ed., Y Traethodydd, 1965– ; ed., Ysgrifau Beirniadol, I–VII; ed., Studia Celtica, I–VI. *Publications*: Ystoriau ac Ysgrifau Pádraic ó Conaire, 1947; Yr Ebol Glas, 1954; Traddodiad, Llenyddol Iwerddon, 1958; Edward Jones, Maes-Y-Plwm, 1963; trans., I. Williams: Canu Taliesin (Poems of Taliesin), 1968; The Court Poet in Medieval Ireland, 1972; Y Storïwr Gwyddeleg a'i Chwedlau, 1972; *contrib*. Bull. Bd Celt. Studies, Celtica, Etudes Celt., Taliesin, Trans Caerns. Hist. Soc., Trans Royal Soc. Cymmrod. *Address*: Univ. College of Wales, Aberystwyth SY23 2AX.

Williams, Prof. John Gwynn; Professor of Welsh History, University College of North

760

Wales, Bangor, since 1963; *b* 1924; *m* 1954; three *s*. BA Wales 1948 (Hist.), MA Wales 1952; Gladstone Memorial Essay Prize 1948, Prince Llywelyn ap Gruffydd Medal 1952. Sec., History and Law Cttee, Bd of Celtic Studies, 1963–72; Dean, Fac. of Arts, Univ. Coll. of N Wales, 1972–73, Vice-Principal, 1974– . Mem., Royal Commn on Anc. Monum., Wales and Monmouth., 1967– ; ed., Jl Flints Hist. Soc., 1969– . *Publications:* *contrib.* Nat. Libr. Wales Jl, Rev. Hist. *Address:* Dept of Welsh History, Univ. College of North Wales, Bangor LL57 2DG.

Williams, Kathleen W.; Lecturer, Department of Modern Languages, University of Aston in Birmingham, since 1967; *b* 1911; widow; one *s*. BA London 1933 (French, German, Spanish), Dip. Internat. Affairs 1951; BA London 1963 (Hons Russian Lang. and Lit.), MA London 1968 (Russian Lang. and Lit.); Psychology Cert. London 1928, Social Sci. Cert. London 1940. Pilgrim Trust Schol., LSE, 1939–40. Brit. Embassy, Moscow, 1945–46; Mem., Unesco Secretariat, Paris, 1946–48; Council Mem., Soc. Cult. Relat. with USSR; Mem., delegation to USSR, Jan. 1971. *Publications: contrib.* Anglo-Sov. Jl, THES. *Address:* Univ. of Aston in Birmingham, Gosta Green, Birmingham B4 7ET.

Williams, John Valentine; Senior Lecturer, Centre for Journalism Studies, University College, Cardiff, since 1974; *b* 1936; *m* 1959; one *s* two *d*. BA Hull 1958; Proficiency Certif. Nat. Council for Training of Journalists, 1960. Cumberland Evening News, Carlisle, 1958; Reuters, 1960; Sheffield Morning Telegraph, 1964. Univ. of Canterbury, Christchurch, NZ, 1967; Lectr, Centre for Journalism Studies, University Coll., Cardiff, 1970–74. *Address:* Centre for Journalism Studies, 34 Cathedral Road, Cardiff CF1 9YG.

Williams, Penry Herbert; Fellow and Tutor in History, New College, Oxford University, since 1964; *b* 1925; *m* 1952; one *s* one *d*. BA Oxon 1949 (Hons Mod. Hist.), MA Oxon 1957, DPhil Oxon 1955; FRHistS. Asst Lectr, Manchester Univ., 1951–54; Lectr, Manchester Univ., 1954–63; Sen. Lectr, Manchester Univ., 1963–64. *Publications:* The Council in the Marches of Wales under Elizabeth I, 1958; Life in Tudor England, 1964; *contrib.* Past Pres., Welsh Hist. Rev. *Address:* New College, Oxford.

Williams, Peter H.; *see* Havard-Williams.

Williams, Philip Maynard; Official Fellow of Nuffield College, Oxford University, since 1958; *b* 1920. BA Oxon 1940 (1st cl. Hist.), MA Oxon 1944. Lectr, Trinity Coll., Oxford, 1946–53; Fellow, Nuffield Coll., Oxford, 1950–53; Fellow, Jesus Coll., Oxford, 1953–58; Vis. Prof., Columbia Univ., 1956–57; Princeton Univ., 1968. *Publications:* Politics in Post-war France, 1954, 3rd edn (as Crisis and Compromise) 1964, French edn 1971; (with M. Harrison) De Gaulle's Republic, 1960; The French Parliament 1958–67, 1968; Wars Plots and Scandals in Post-war France, 1970; (with M. Harrison

and D. B. Goldey) French Politicians and Elections, 1970; (with M. Harrison) Politics and Society in De Gaulle's Republic, 1971; *contrib.* Amer. Schol., EHR, Par. Aff., Pol Qly, Pol Sci. Qly, Pol Studies, Rev. Franç. Sci. Pol. *Address:* Nuffield College, Oxford.

Williams, Prof. Raymond Henry; Fellow of Jesus College, Cambridge, since 1961; Professor of Drama, University of Cambridge, since 1974 (Reader, 1967–74); *b* 1921; *m* 1942; two *s* one *d*. MA Cantab 1946, LittD Cantab 1969. Staff Tutor in Literature, Oxford Univ. Extra-Mural Delegacy, 1946–61. Gen. Editor, New Thinkers' Library, 1962; Editor: Politics and Letters, 1946–47; May Day Manifesto, 1968. *Publications:* Reading and Criticism, 1950; Drama from Ibsen to Eliot, 1952; Drama in Performance, 1954, rev. edn 1968; Culture and Society, 1958; Border Country, 1960; The Long Revolution, 1961; Communications, 1962, rev. edn 1966; Second Generation, 1964; Modern Tragedy, 1966; Public Inquiry, 1967; Drama from Ibsen to Brecht, 1968; The English Novel from Dickens to Lawrence, 1970; A Letter from the Country, 1971; Orwell, 1971; The Country and the City, 1973. *Address:* Jesus College, Cambridge.

Williams, Richard H.; *see* Hodder-Williams.

Williams, Prof. Robert Deryck, MA; Professor of Classics, University of Reading, since 1971; *b* 1917; *m* 1945; three *d*. BA Cantab 1939 (1st cl. Classics), MA Cantab 1945. Lectr, Reading Univ., 1945–57; Sen. Lectr, Reading Univ., 1957–62; Reader, Reading Univ., 1962–71; Vis. Prof., Chicago Univ., 1964; Vis. Prof., Australian Nat. Univ., 1966; Pennsylvania State Univ., 1968. Sec., Res. Bd, Univ. of Reading, 1950–56; Mem., Reading Educnl Adv. Cttee on Adult Educn, 1953–62; Council, Abbey Sch., Reading, 1961– ; Council, Rom. Soc., 1970–73; Pres., Virgil Soc., 1972–75. *Publications:* ed, Virgil: Aeneid V, 1960; ed, Virgil: Aeneid III, 1962; Virgil (New Surveys in the Classics, Greece and Rome), 1967; ed, Virgil: Aeneid I–XII, 1972–73; ed, Statius: Thebaid 10 (Mnemosyne, Supp. XXII), 1972; Aeneas and the Roman Hero, 1973; *contrib.* Class. Qly, Class. Rev., Proc. Virg. Soc. *Address:* Dept of Classics, Univ. of Reading, Reading RG6 2AH.

Williams, Roderick Trevor, MC, MA; Reader in Greek Art and Archaeology, Department of Classics, University of Durham, since 1969; *b* 1916; *m* 1941; one *s* one *d*. BA Wales 1938 (1st cl. Latin, Greek), MA Wales 1958; FRNS. Lectr, Durham Univ., 1946–61; Sen. Lectr, 1961–69. Royal Welch Fusiliers; 53rd Reconn. Regt (RAC), 1939–45; Mem., Council, Soc. Prom. Hellen. Studies, 1963. *Publications:* Confederate Coinage of the Arcadians, 1965; (with J. S. Morrison) Greek Oared Ships, 1968; Silver Coinage of the Phokians, 1972; *contrib.* Antike Kunst, Durh. Univ. Jl, Greece Rome, Jl Hellen. Studies, Museum Notes (ANS), Numism. *Address:* Dept of Classics, 38 North Bailey, Durham.

Williams, Prof. William David, MA, DPhil; Professor of German, University of Liverpool, since 1954; *b* 1917; *m* 1946; one *s* one *d*. BA Oxon 1939 (1st cl. Mod. Langs), MA Oxon 1943, DPhil Oxon 1952. Asst Lectr, Leeds Univ., 1946–48; Lectr, Oxford Univ., 1948–53; Sen. Lectr, Oxford Univ., 1953–54. *Publications*: Nietzsche and the French, 1952; ed, C. F. Meyer: Die Versuchung des Pescara, 1958; The Stories of C. F. Meyer, 1962; *contrib.* Erasm., Germ. Life Lett., Mod. Lang. Rev. *Address*: German Dept, Modern Language Building, PO Box 147, Liverpool L69 3BX.

Williams, Prof. William Morgan, MA; Professor of Sociology and Anthropology, University of Wales, Swansea, since 1963; *b* 1926; *m* 1948; one *s* one *d*. BA Wales 1950 (Geog. and Anthrop.), MA Wales 1952. Asst Lectr in Geography, Univ. of Keele, 1952–55; Lectr in Social Geography, Univ. of Keele, 1955–60; Sen. Lectr, Univ. of Keele, 1960–63; Reader, Univ. of Keele, 1963. Mem., Welsh Econ. Council, and Welsh Council, 1964– ; Chm., Hlth and Soc. Serv. Panel, Welsh Council, 1969– ; Mem., Welsh Management Steering Cttee, NHS Re-Organization in Wales, 1971–73; Chm., W Glamorgan AHA, 1973– ; Mngng Ed., Sociol. Rev., Ed., Studies in Sociol.; Gen. Ed., Medicine, Illness and Society. *Publications*: The Sociology of an English Village: Gosforth, 1956; The Country Craftsman, 1958; A West Country Village: Ashworthy, 1963; ed jtly, The Medical Use of Psychotropic Drugs, 1973; Occupational Choice, 1974; *contrib.* Geog. Polon., Geog. Jl, Geog. Studies, Man, N Staffs Jl Field Studies, Sociol. Rur., Sociol. Rev., Trans Cumb. Westm. Antiqu and Archaeol. Soc. *Address*: Dept of Sociology and Anthropology, Univ. College, Swansea SA2 8PP.

Williams, Dr Wynne; Lecturer, Department of Classics, Keele University, since 1968; *b* 1941. BA Oxon 1963, MA Oxon 1966, DPhil Oxon 1971; Member: Classical Assoc.; Soc. for Promotion of Roman Studies. Asst Lectr in Classics, Keele Univ., 1965–68. *Publications*: *contrib.* Historia. *Address*: Dept of Classics, The Univ., Keele, Staffs ST5 5BG.

Williams-Jones, William Keith, MA; Lecturer in Welsh History, University College of North Wales, Bangor, since 1963; *b* 1925; *m* 1959. BA Wales 1950, MA Wales 1967, DipArchive Admin. Liverpool 1951. *Publications*: ed, The Calendar of the Merioneth Quarter Sessions Rolls, vol. I, 1965; *contrib.* Bull. Bd Celt. Studies, Welsh Hist. Rev. *Address*: Dept of Welsh History, Univ. College of North Wales, Bangor LL57 2DG.

Williamson, John; Lecturer, Philosophy Department, University of Liverpool, since 1966; *b* 1933; *m* 1961; two *s* one *d*. BSc Manchester 1954, CertEd London 1957, MA London 1961; Mem., Aristot. Soc., Mem., BSPS, Mem., Mind Assoc. Lectr, Monash Univ., Melbourne, 1961–66. *Publications*: *contrib.* Jl Philos. Phenomenol. Res., Mind, Philos. Qly. *Address*: Dept of Philosophy, Univ. of Liverpool, Liverpool L69 3BX.

Williamson, Prof. John (Harold); Professor of Economics, University of Warwick, since 1970, on leave of absence as Adviser to Research Department, IMF, 1972–74; *b* 1937. BSc(Econ) London 1958, PhD Princeton 1963; Mem., Royal Econ. Soc., Mem., Amer. Econ. Assoc. Lectr, Univ. of York, 1963–67; Vis. Asst Prof., MIT, 1967; Reader, Univ. of York, 1967–68. Scientific Adv., Air Min., 1959–60; Cnsltnt, HM Treasury, 1968–70; Chm., Econ. Study Soc., 1969–72. *Publications*: The Crawling Peg, 1965; The Choice of a Pivot for Parities, 1971; On Estimating the Income Effects of British Entry to the EEC, 1971; *contrib.* Econ. Jl, Economica, Oxford Econ. Papers, Rev. Econ. Studies, Jl of Internat. Econ., IMF Staff Papers. *Address*: Dept of Economics, Univ. of Warwick, Coventry CV4 7AL.

Willis, Dr Peter, FRIBA; Lecturer in Architecture, University of Newcastle upon Tyne, since 1965; *b* 1933; *m* 1968; one *s*. BArch Dunelm 1956 (1st cl.), PhD Cantab 1962; FRIBA 1970. Fellow, Dumbarton Oaks Res. Libr. and Coll., Harvard Univ., 1964–65; Vis. Prof., Univ. of Minnesota, 1968–69. Architect, Sir Robert Matthew, Johnson-Marshall and Ptnrs, Edinburgh, 1961–64; Hon. Treas., Soc. Archit. Hist. GB, 1967– . *Publications*: Charles Bridgeman, 1974; ed, Furor Hortensis, 1974; *contrib.* Apollo, Burl. Mag., Eightnth-cent. Studies, Studies Volt. 18th Cent. *Address*: School of Architecture, The Univ., Newcastle upon Tyne NE1 7RU.

Willis, Dr Robert Clive, MA, PhD; Senior Lecturer in Portuguese, University of Manchester, since 1969; *b* 1934; *m* 1961; two *s* two *d*. BA Cantab 1956 (2nd cl. Mod. Langs Tripos), MA Cantab 1960, PhD Manchester 1968; Mem., Assoc. Brit. Hispan., Mem., Soc. Lat. Amer. Studies, Mem., Canning Hse Centre. Asst Lectr in Portuguese, Manchester Univ., 1956–60; Lectr, Manchester Univ., 1960–69. *Publications*: Langenscheidt/ Methuen Universal Dictionary, English– Portuguese, Portuguese–English, 1960; Essential Course in Modern Portuguese, 1965; rev. edn 1971; assoc. ed., Twentieth Century Writing, 1969; *contrib.* Bull. Hispan. Studies, Ocid. *Address*: Dept of Spanish and Portuguese Studies, The Univ., Manchester M13 9PL.

Willis, Dr Roy Geffrey; Lecturer, Department of Social Anthropology, University of Edinburgh, since 1967; *b* 1927; *m* 1968; one *s* one *d*. Diploma in Social Anthropology Oxford 1961, BLitt Oxford 1962, DPhil Oxford 1966; Member: Assoc. of Social Anthropologists, 1966 (Mem. Cttee, 1971–); African Studies Assoc. of UK, 1970 (Mem. Council, 1972–). Res. Asst, UCL, 1965–67. *Publications*: Fipa and Related Peoples of S-W Tanzania and N-W Zambia, 1966; Man and Beast, 1974; *contrib.* Afr., Ethnol., Man, New Soc. *Address*: Dept of Social Anthropology, Univ. of Edinburgh, Edinburgh EII8 9YL.

Willmer, M. A. P., MA; Reader in Operational Research, Manchester Business School, Manchester University, since 1971; *b* 1932;

m 1959; one *s* one *d*. BSc London 1954, DCAe Cranfield 1956, MA Oxon 1967. Mem., Operat. Res. Soc. Res. Fellow, Nuffield Coll., Oxford, 1967–70. *Publications*: Crime and Information Theory, 1970; contrib. Aero. Res. Council R + M Series; Proc. NATO Conference on Operational Res., 1968; *contrib.* Brit. Jl Criminol., Gen. Syst., Jl Res. Crime Delinqu., Operat. Res. Qly. *Address*: Manchester Business School, Univ. of Manchester, Booth Street West, Manchester M15 6PB.

Wills, Prof. Gordon Stanley Clifford, BA, DMS, FInstM, MBIM, FIScB; Professor of Marketing and Logistics, School of Management, Cranfield Institute of Technology, since 1972; *b* 1937; *m* 1967; two *s*. BA Reading 1961 (Hons Pol Econ.), Dip. Mngmt Studies (with distinction) Dept of Education of Science 1964; FInstMktng 1972, Mem., Brit. Inst. Mngmt 1970, FInst Sci. Business 1964. Lectr in Marketing, Univ. of Bradford, 1965–67; Sen. Lectr, Univ. of Bradford, 1967–68; Prof., Univ. of Bradford, 1968–72; Vis. Prof., Univ. of Alberta, 1970. Mem., Bd, Centre for Physical Distrib. Mngmt, 1969– ; Dir, Roles and Parker Ltd; Yorks Fin. and Mngmt Co. Ltd; MCB Ltd; Ed., Europ. Jl Mktng; Ed., Internat. Jl Physical Distrib. *Publications*: (with T. Kempner) Bradford Exercises in Management, 1966; (with R. Yearsley) Handbook of Management Technology, 1967; Marketing Through Research (now in seven languages), 1967; Sources of UK Marketing Information, 1969; jt ed., Pricing Strategy, 1969; ed, Technological Forecasting and Corporate Strategy, 1969; New Ideas in Retail Management, 1970; jt ed., Management Thinkers, 1970; ed, Marketing Research, 1970; Exploration in Marketing Thought, 1971; jt ed., Long Range Planning for Marketing and Diversification, 1971; Technological Forecasting, 1971; Contemporary Marketing, 1971; Organisational Design for Marketing Futures, 1972; jt ed., Marketing Logistics and Distribution Planning, 1972; jt ed., Fashion Marketing, 1972; jt ed., Creating and Marketing New Products, 1972; *contrib.* Comment., Mktng Wld, Mngmt Decis., Jl Mngmt Studies, Indust. Mktng Jl, Advert. Qly, Brit. Jl Mktng. *Address*: School of Management, Cranfield Inst. of Technology, Cranfield, Bedford MK43 0AL.

Willson, Dr Francis Michael Glenn; Warden of Goldsmiths' College, University of London, since 1974; *b* 1924; *m* 1945; two *d*. BA (Administration), Manchester 1950 DPhil Oxon 1953, MA 1956; Res. Officer, Royal Institute of Public Administration, 1953–60; Res., Fellow, Nuffield Coll., 1955–60; Lectr in politics, St Edmund Hall, Oxford, 1958–60; Prof., Univ. Coll., Rhodesia and Nyasaland, 1961–64, and Dean, Faculty of Social Studies, 1962–64; Prof., Univ. California, Santa Cruz, 1965–74; Provost, Adlai E. Stevenson Coll., 1967–74; Vice-Chancellor Coll. and Student Affairs, 1973–74. *Publications*: Administrators in Action, 1961; (with D. N. Chester) The Organisation of British Central Government, 2nd edn 1968; *contrib.* Public Admin, Pol Studies, Parly Affairs, etc.

Address: Goldsmiths' College, New Cross, SE14 6NW.

Willson, Prof. Harold Bernard, MA; Professor of German and Head of Department, University of Leicester, since 1970; *b* 1919; *m* 1948; three *s* one *d*. BA Cantab 1940 (1st cl. Mod. Langs), MA Cantab 1944; Mem., Mod. Hum. Res. Internat. Arthurian Soc. Asst Lectr in German, Univ. of Leicester, 1947–48; Lectr, Univ. of Leicester, 1948–65; Sen. Lectr, Univ. of Leicester, 1965–70; Vis. Prof., Univ. of Illinois, 1968–69. Foreign Off., 1940–45. *Publications*: *contrib.* Beit. Gesch. Deuts. Sprache Lit., Deuts. Viertel-Euph., Germ. Life Lett., Germ. Rev., Germ. Rom., Monats., Germ. Qly, Jl Engl. Germ. Philol., Med. Æv., Mod. Lang. Notes, Mod. Lang. Rev., Mod. Philol., Nott. Mediev. Studies, Specul., Wolf-Jb, Zeits. Deuts. Altert., Zeits. Deuts. Philol. *Address*: Dept of German, Univ. of Leicester, University Road, Leicester LE1 7RH.

Willson, Nora Kathleen, MA, PhD; Principal Lecturer, Homerton College, Cambridge, Head of French Department, since 1955, and Fellow of Lucy Cavendish College, Cambridge, since 1966; *b* 1919. BA Cantab 1941 (2nd cl. Mod. Langs), MA Cantab 1945, PhD Cantab 1952. Trustee, Lucy Cavendish Coll., Cambridge; Trustee Homerton Coll., Cambridge. *Publications*: Cassell's Encyclopedia of Literature, 1953. *Address*: Homerton College, Cambridge.

Wilson, Prof. Alan Geoffrey, MA; Professor of Urban and Regional Geography, University of Leeds, since 1970; *b* 1939; *m* 1965. BA Cantab 1960 (Maths), Mathematical Tripos, Pt III (Distinction), Cantab 1961; MA Cantab 1964; FRGS. Mem., Inst. Brit. Geogrs, Operat. Res. Soc., Reg. Science Assoc. Res. Off., Univ. of Oxford, 1964; Assoc. Ed., Transp. Res., 1967– ; Ed., Environm. Planning, 1969– . Scientific Off., Rutherford Lab., 1961; Math. Adv., Min. of Transp., 1966; Asst Dir, Centre Environm. Studies, 1968. *Publications*: Entropy in Urban and Regional Modelling, 1970; Papers in Urban and Regional Analysis, 1972; Urban and Regional Models in Geography and Planning, 1974; *contrib.* Geog. Analysis, Jl Reg. Science, Res., Jl Transp. Econ. Policy, Papers Reg. Science Assoc., Reg. Studies, Transp. Rds., Urb. Studies. *Address*: Dept of Geography, Univ. of Leeds, Leeds LS2 9JT.

Wilson, Alan Greenwood G.; *see* Greenwood-Wilson.

Wilson, Alan John Nisbet, MA, DPhil; Senior Lecturer in Greek and Latin, University of Manchester, since 1971; *b* 1915; *m* 1957, diss. 1962; one *s*. BA Oxon 1938 (1st cl. Hon. Mods, 1st cl. Lit. Hum.), DPhil Oxon 1949; Mem., Hellen. Soc., Mem., Rom. Soc., Mem., Class. Assoc. Asst Lectr, Univ. Coll., Leicester, 1947–50; Lectr, Univ. of Manchester, 1950–71. Bd of Trade, 1940–45. *Publications*: Emigration from Italy in the Republican Age of Rome, 1965; *contrib.* Bull. J. Rylands Libr., Crit. Qly. *Address*: Dept of Classics, The Univ., Manchester M13 9NR.

Wilson, Prof. Alexander Thomson Macbeth; Professor of Organisational Behaviour, London Graduate School of Business Studies, University of London, since 1970; *b* 1905; *m*; one *d*. BSc, MB, ChB (Hons) Glasgow; W of Scotland Prize 1929; MD 1940 (1st cl. Hons and Gold Medal); Associate Mem., British Psycho-Analytical Soc., 1950; FBPsS 1934, FRC Psych 1972; Fellow, London Business Sch, 1968; Burnham Medal, BIM, 1968. Lectr in Physiology, Middlesex Hosp. Med. Sch., 1931–34; Rockefeller Res. Fellow and Physician, Tavistock Clinic, 1934–39; T. Lt-Col, RAMC, WO, 1941–46; Founder Mem. and later Chm., Management Cttee, Tavistock Inst. of Human Relations, 1946–58; Adviser, Use of Social Sciences, Unilever Ltd, 1958–70. Vis. Professor of Social Science: N Western Univ., 1949; Univ. of Mich, 1951 and 1954; Harvard Med. Sch., 1957; Regents Lectr, Univ. of Calif., Berkeley, 1964. Hon. Officer and Sec., RSM, 1949–54; Chairman: WHO Cttee on Automation and Mental Health, 1949; Cttee on Management Educn in Social Science, DES, 1957; Council-Staff Cttee, Tavistock Inst., London, 1973– ; Member: Bd, also Treas., Internat. Univ. Contact for Management Educn, 1962–68; Management Studies Cttee, SSRC, 1965–68; Cttee on Recruitment and Selection of Administrative Cl., CS, 1968–69; Council, Brunel Univ., 1963– ; Cons., FAO, 1962; Trustee, Columbus Trust, 1967– ; Adviser, Inst. of Manpower Studies, Univ. of Sussex and LSE, 1972– ; External Doctorate and Masters Examiner, LSE, 1971– ; Adv. Editor, Human Relations, and, Management Today. *Publications*: Social Science Research in Industry (with A. B. Cherns and Jeremy Mitchell), 1971; chapters in, Aspects of Manpower Planning, ed Smith and Morris, 1971; Manpower and Management Sciences, ed Bartholomew and Smith, 1973; Management Research, ed Farrow, 1969; Manpower Studies, ed Leicester, 1974; *contrib.* Br. Med. Jl, Lancet, Jl Physiol., Br. Jl Med. Psych. (London), Hum. Relat., Ind. Mgmt Rev., Information (Unesco), Jl Mgmt Stud., Sociol Rev., Inst. Stud. of Mgmt Organ. *Address*: London Graduate School of Business Studies, Sussex Place, Regent's Park, NW1 4SA.

Wilson, Prof. Angus Frank Johnstone, CBE, CLit; Professor of English Literature, Department of English and American Studies, University of East Anglia, since 1966; *b* 1913. BA Oxon 1936; FRSL. Ewing Lectr, UCLA, 1960; Northcliffe Lectr, London Univ., 1961; Leslie Stephen Lectr, Cambridge Univ., 1963; Beckman Prof., Univ. of California Berkeley, 1967; John Hinkley Prof., Johns Hopkins Univ., 1974. Mem., Arts Council, 1966–70; Chm. NBL, 1971–74; President: Powys Soc., 1971– ; Dickens Fellowship, 1973–75. *Publications*: The Wrong Set, 1949; Such Darling Dodos, 1950; Emile Zola, 1952; Hemlock and After, 1952; For Whom the Cloche Tolls, 1953; Mulberry Bush, 1956; Anglo Saxon Attitudes, 1956; A Bit off The Map, 1957; Old Men at the Zoo, 1961; The Wild Garden, 1963; Late Call, 1964; No Laughing Matter, 1967; The World of Charles Dickens, 1970; As If By Magic,

1973. *Address*: Felsham Woodside, Bradfield St George, Bury St Edmunds, Suffolk IP30 0AQ.

Wilson, Sir (Archibald) Duncan, GCMG; Master of Corpus Christi College, Cambridge, since 1971; HM Diplomatic Service, retired; *b* 1911; *m* 1937; one *s* two *d*. 1st cl. Hon. Mods, Lit. Hum., Oxford. Taught at Westminster Sch., 1936–37; Asst Keeper, Brit. Museum, 1937–39; Min. of Economic Warfare, 1939–41; empl. FO, 1941–45; CCG, 1945–46; entered Foreign Service, 1947; served Berlin, 1947–49; Yugoslavia, 1951–53; Dir of Res. and Acting Librarian, 1955–57; Chargé d'Affaires, Peking, 1957–59; Asst Under-Sec., FO, 1960–64; Ambassador, to Yugoslavia, 1964–68, to USSR, 1968–71. Fellow, Center of Internat. Affairs, Harvard Univ. (on secondment, 1959–60). *Publications*: Life and Times of Vuk Stefanović Karadžić, 1970. *Address*: The Master's Lodge, Corpus Christi College, Cambridge.

Wilson, Dr Brian James; Lecturer, Department of Mathematics, Chelsea College, London (also teaches history of mathematics), since 1962; *b* 1934; *m* 1963; one *s* one *d*. BSc London 1958, MSc London 1961, PhD London 1970. *Address*: Dept of Mathematics, Chelsea College, Manresa Road, SW3 6LX.

Wilson, Bryan R.; Reader in Sociology, University of Oxford, since 1962, and Fellow of All Souls, Oxford, since 1963. BSc(Econ) London 1952 (1st cl.), PhD London 1955, MA Oxon 1962; Commonwealth Fund Fellow, Harkness Foundn, 1957–58; Fellow, Amer. Council Learned Socs, 1966–67. Asst Lectr, Leeds Univ., 1955–57; Lectr, Leeds Univ., 1957–62. Pres., Conf. Internat. Sociol. Relig., 1971– . *Publications*: Sects and Society, 1961, American edn 1961; Religion in Secular Society, 1966, pbk edn 1969, Spanish edn 1969; ed, Patterns of Sectarianism, 1967; The Youth Culture and the Universities, 1970; ed, Rationality, 1970, American edn 1970; Religious Sects, 1971, French edn 1971, German edn 1971, Spanish edn 1971, Swedish edn 1971, Japanese edn 1973; Magic and the Millennium, 1973; Equality Education and Society (forthcoming); The Noble Savages (forthcoming); *contrib.* Amer. Jl Sociol., Amer. Sociol. Rev., Archiv. Sociol. Relig., Brit. Jl Sociol, Crim. Law Rev., Sociol Rev., Theol., Jl Relig. in Africa. *Address*: All Souls College, Oxford.

Wilson, Prof. Charles Henry, FBA; Professor of Modern History, University of Cambridge, since 1965; *b* 1914; *m* 1939 (marr. diss.); one *d*; *m* 1972. BA Cantab 1936 (1st cl. Hist. and English), MA Cantab 1938, HonLittD Groningen 1965; FBA, FRHistS (Vice-Pres., 1971). Overseas Fellow, Royal Danish Acad., 1969; Royal Belgian Acad., 1971. Commander, Order of Oranje-Nassau, 1973. Fellow, Jesus Coll., Cambridge, 1938–39; Univ. Lectr in Hist., Cambridge Univ., 1945–64; Reader, Cambridge Univ., 1964–65; Ford Lectr, Oxford, 1968; Vis. Prof., Harvard, 1954; Vis. Prof., Leiden, 1970; Vis. Prof., Louvain, 1970; Jt Ed., Econ. Hist. Rev., 1957–67. Hd of Cabinet Div., Admiralty, 1939–45; (special

Reserve RNVR); Bursar, Jesus Coll., 1945–54; Mem., Anglo-Netherl. Mixed Culture Commn, 1949– ; Mem., Lord Chancellor's Cttee on Public Records, 1971; Mem., Gov. Cttee, Datini Inst. Econ. Hist., Prato, Italy, 1971. *Publications*: Anglo-Dutch Commerce and Finance, 1940, 2nd edn 1966; History of Unilever, 1954–68, 2nd edn 1971; Mercantilism, 1958; Profit and Power, 1957; England's Apprenticeship, 1967; The Dutch Republic and The Civilisation of the Seventeenth Century, 1968, French, German, Italian, Spanish, United States, Dutch edns 1968, Japanese edn 1971; Economic History and the Historian, 1969; Queen Elizabeth and the Revolt of the Netherlands (Ford Lectures), 1970; *contrib.* Econ. Hist. Rev., EHR, Camb. Hist. Jl, Harv. Business Hist. Rev., Hist., Trans Royal Hist. Soc., Trans Royal Hist. Soc. Utrecht. *Address*: Jesus College, Cambridge.

Wilson, Prof. David Mackenzie, MA, FSA; Professor of Medieval Archaeology, University of London, since 1971; Joint Head, Department of Scandinavian Studies, University College, London, since 1973; *b* 1931; *m* 1955; one *s* one *d*. BA Cantab 1953, MA Cantab 1958; FSA. Res. Asst, Cambridge, 1954; Asst Keeper, BM, 1954–64; Reader in Archaeology of the Anglo-Saxon Period, 1964–70; Jarrow Lectr, 1969, Dalrymple Lectr, Glasgow Univ., 1971. Corresp. Mem., German Archaeological Inst. Royal Gustav Adolfs Acad. of Sweden; Sec. Soc. Medieval Archaeology, 1957– ; Pres., Brit. Archaeological Assoc., 1962–69; Pres., Viking Soc. Northern Res., 1968–70; Sec., King's Lynn Archaeological Res. Commn, 1963– ; Mem., Archaeological Cttees. *Publications*: The Anglo-Saxons, 1960, 2nd edn 1970; Anglo-Saxon Metalwork 700–1100 in British Museum, 1964; (with O. Klindt Jensen) Viking Art, 1966; (with G. Bersu) Three Viking Graves in the Isle of Man, 1969; The Vikings and their Origins, 1970; (with P. G. Foote) The Viking Achievement, 1970; Reflections on the St Ninians Isle Treasure (Jarrow Lecture), 1970; *contrib.* Archaeologia, Antiquaries Jl, Acta Archaeologica, Medieval Archaeology, etc. *Address*: Univ. College, Gower Street, WC1E 6BT.

Wilson, David Raoul, MA, BLitt, FSA; Senior Assistant in Research, Department of Geography, University of Cambridge, since 1965; *b* 1932; *m* 1965. BA Oxon 1955, MA Oxon 1960, BLitt Oxon 1961; FSA 1967, Member: British Inst. of Archaeol., Ankara, Soc. Promotion of Roman Studies. Res. Asst, Archaeol. of Roman Empire, Oxford, 1960–65. *Publications*: (jtly) rev. edn, A. H. M. Jones, Cities of the Eastern Roman Provinces, 1937, 1971; The Roman Frontiers of Britain, 1967; ed R. G. Collingwood and I. A. Richmond, The Archaeology of Roman Britain, 1969; *contrib.* Anatolian Stud., Britannia, Jl Roman Stud. *Address*: c/o Cttee for Aerial Photography, Univ. of Cambridge, Cambridge.

Wilson, Dr Deirdre Susan Moir; Lecturer in Linguistics, Department of Linguistics, University College, London, since 1970; *b* 1941. BA Oxford 1964 (1st cl. Hons PPE), BPhil Oxford 1967 (Philosophy), PhD MIT 1973 (Linguistics). Lectr in Philosophy, Somerville Coll., Oxford, 1967–68; Harkness Fellowship in Philosophy and Linguistics, MIT, 1968–70. *Publications*: *contrib.* Ling Inq. *Address*: Dept of Linguistics, Univ. College London, Gower Street, WC1E 6BT.

Wilson, Dr Dudley Butler; Reader in French, University of Durham, since 1969; *b* 1923; *m* 1958; one *s* two *d*. BA Cantab 1947 (Mod. and Med. Langs), MA Cantab 1949, Ddel'U Paris 1952; Mem., Bibliog. Soc. Asst, Univ. of Aberdeen, 1950–53, Lectr, Univ. of Durham, 1953–64; Sen. Lectr, Univ. of Durham, 1964–69; Vis. Prof., Univ. of Saskatchewan, 1969. Gen. Ed., French Renaissance Facsimiles (Scolar Press), 1971. *Publications*: Ronsard Poet of Nature, 1961; Descriptive Poetry in France from Blason to Baroque, 1967; ed, French Renaissance Scientific Poetry, 1974; *contrib.* Bibl. Hum. Renaiss., Cah. Assoc. Internat. Etudes Franç., Durh. Univ. Jl, Etudes Rabelais, Fr. Studies, Libr., Studi Franc., Yrs Wk Mod. Lang. Studies. *Address*: Dept of French, Elvet Riverside, Durham.

Wilson, Edward Peter, BA, BLitt, MA; Lecturer, Department of English Literature, University of Edinburgh, since 1969; *b* 1940; *m* 1972; one *d*. BA Hull 1962, MA Oxon 1966, BLitt Oxon 1968. Lectr, St Edmund Hall and Univ. Coll., Oxford, 1965–69. *Publications*: A Descriptive Index of the English Lyrics in John of Grimestone's Preaching Book, 1973; *contrib.* Bk Coll., Engl. Philol Studies, Med. Ævv., Neuphilol. Mitteil., Notes Queries, Rev. Engl. Studies. *Address*: Dept of English Literature, Univ. of Edinburgh, David Hume Tower, Edinburgh EH8 9JX.

Wilson, Frank Arnal; Lecturer, Project Planning Centre for Developing Countries, University of Bradford, since 1969; *b* 1942; *m* 1964; one *s* two *d*. BSc Leeds 1964 (Agricultural Economics), MPhil Leeds 1972 (Research); Member: Agricultural Econs Soc.; African Studies Assoc.; UK Chapter, Soc. for Internat. Develt. Lectr, Univ. of Glasgow (on secondment to University Coll., Nairobi, Univ. of E Africa, 1967–69; on secondment to Barclays International, 1972–74 (Agricultural Develt Adviser in Zambia)). *Publications*: (with T. J. Aldington) Beef Marketing in Kenya, 1968; ed, Financing Rural Development (forthcoming). *Address*: Project Planning Centre for Developing Countries, Univ. of Bradford, Bradford BD7 1DP.

Wilson, Prof. Geoffrey Philip; Chairman of Law School, University of Warwick, since 1967; *b* 1930. LLB, MA Cantab; Barrister-at-Law, Gray's Inn 1953. Fellow, Queen's Coll., Cambridge, 1953–67; Praelector and tutor, 1959–67; Lectr in Law, Univ. of Cambridge, 1955–67; Harkness Fellow, Yale and Berkeley, 1960–61. *Publications*: Cases and Materials in Constitutional and Administrative Law, 1966; Cases and Materials on the English Legal System, 1973. *Address*: School of Law, Univ. of Warwick, Coventry CV4 7AL.

Wilson, Henry Summerville; Senior Lecturer, History Department, York University, since 1968; *b* 1928; *m* 1962. BA Durham 1949, BLitt Oxford 1955; FRHistS. Mem., Brit. Assoc. Afr. Studies. Lectr, Fourah Bay Coll., Univ. of Sierra Leone, 1956–59; Lectr, Univ. Coll. of Wales Aberystwyth, 1959–68. *Publications*: Origins of West African Nationalisation, 1969; *contrib*. Afr. Aff., Amer. Jl Sociol., Muslim Wld, Sierra Leone Bull. Relig., Sierra Leone Studies. *Address*: History Dept, Vanbrugh College, York.

Wilson, James Vincent K.; *see* Kinnier Wilson.

Wilson, J. D. R.; Lecturer in Sociology, University of Stirling, since 1968; *b* 1943; *m* 1973. BA, Dip. Social Studies Keele 1966, MA Essex 1967. Jun. Res. Fellow, Univ. of York, 1967–8. *Publications*: *contrib*. Soc. Work Today. *Address*: Dept of Sociology, The Univ., Stirling FK9 4LA.

Wilson, John; Senior Lecturer, Department of Architecture, Sheffield University, since 1961; *b* 1915; *m* 1940; one *s* two *d*. ARCA 1947. Lectr, Univ. of Sheffield, 1951–61. *Publications*: Decoration and Furnishing, 1960; *contrib*. Arch. Jl, Die Mappe. *Address*: Dept of Architecture, Arts Tower, Sheffield S10 2TN.

Wilson, Dr John Cameron; Official Fellow and Lecturer in French, Jesus College, Cambridge, since 1966; *b* 1942 *m* 1966; one *s* one *d*. BA Cantab 1963 (Modern and Medieval Languages Tripos: Pt I, cl. I; Pt II, cl. I), MA Cantab 1967, PhD Cantab 1968; Mem. Soc. for French Studies. Res. Fellow, Jesus Coll., Cambridge, 1965–66; Tutor, Jesus Coll., Cambridge, 1967– . *Publication*: The Style of Molière (forthcoming). *Address*: Jesus College, Cambridge CB5 8BL.

Wilson, Prof. John F.; Professor of Law, Faculty of Law, University of Southampton, since 1966; *b* 1924; *m* 1950; one *s* one *d*. BA Oxford 1949, MA Oxford 1950. Asst Lectr, UCW, Aberystwyth, 1949, Lectr, 1952; Univ. of Southampton: Sen. Lectr, 1959; Reader, 1964; Dean, Faculty of Law, 1962–68; Dep. Vice-Chancellor, 1970–74; Vis. Professor: Tulane Univ., USA, 1957, Univ. of Auckland, NZ, 1970. Hon. Sec., Soc. of Public Teachers of Law, 1963–72; Chm., Police Council Arbitration Tribunal, 1973– ; Independent Mem., Wages Councils, 1969–; Mem., Lord Chancellor's Legal Educn Cttee, 1968–71. *Publications*: Principles of the Law of Contract, 1957; Survey of Legal Education in the United Kingdom, 1966; *contrib*. CLJ, LQR, MLR, Tulane LR. *Address*: Faculty of Law, The Univ., Southampton SO9 5NH.

Wilson, Rev. Dr (John) Michael; Lecturer in Pastoral Studies, Department of Theology, University of Birmingham, since 1971; *b* 1916; *m* 1941 and 1962; five s. two *d*. MB, BS London 1942, MD London 1948, DTM&H London 1948; MRCS, LRCP 1942, MRCP 1948; Mem, Inst. of Religion and Medicine. Sen. Med. Officer, University

Coll. of Gold Coast, 1950–55; Lectr, St Martin-in-the-Fields, London, 1963–67; Res. Fellow, Dept of Theology, Birmingham Univ., 1967. Mem., S Birmingham HMC Nurse and Midwifery Educn Cttee. *Publications*: The Christian Nurse, 1960 (trans. Danish); The Church is Healing, 1966; The Hospital, a place of Truth, 1971. *Address*: Theology Dept, Univ. of Birmingham, Birmingham B15 2TT.

Wilson, Prof. John Stuart Gladstone, MA, DipCom; Professor of Economics and Commerce, University of Hull, since 1959; *b* 1916; *m* 1943. DipCom. MA W Austr. Lectr, Tasmania Univ., 1941–43; Lectr, Sydney Univ., 1944–45; Lectr, Canberra Univ., 1946–47; Hackett Res. Student, 1947; Lectr, LSE, 1948–49; Reader, LSE, 1950–59; Leverhulme Res. Award, 1955; Dean, Fac. of Social Sciences and Law, Hull Univ., 1962–65; Head, Dept of Econs, Hull Univ., 1959–71, 1974– . Cnsltnt, OECD, 1965–66; Cnsltnt, Harvard Adv. Develt Service, Liberia, 1967; headed Enquiry into Sources of Capital and Credit to UK Agriculture, 1970–73; Cnsltnt, Dir.-Gen. Agric., EEC, 1974; Mem., Man. Cttee, Inst. Commonwealth Studies, London, 1960– ; Gov., SOAS, London, 1963– ; Mem., Yorks Council for Further Educn, 1963–67; Mem., Nat. Adv. Council on Educn for Industry and Commerce, 1964–66; Sec.-Gen., Société Universitaire Européene de Recherches Financières, 1968–72, Pres., 1973– . Ed., Yorks Bull. of Econ. and Social Res., 1964–67; Mem., Ed. Adv. Bd, Mod. Asian Studies, 1966– . *Publications*: French Banking Structure and Credit Policy, 1957; Economic Environment and Development Programmes, 1960; Monetary Policy and the Development of Money Markets, 1966; Economic Survey of the New Hebrides, 1966; Availability of Capital and Credit to UK Agriculture, 1973; ed (with C. R. Whittlesey), Essays in Money and Banking in Honour of R. S. Sayers, 1968; contrib. Sayers: Banking in the British Commonwealth, 1952; contrib. Sayers: Banking in Western Europe, 1962; contrib. Hamilton and others: A Decade of the Commonwealth, 1955–64, 1966; *contrib*. Economica, Econ. Jl, Jl Pol Econ., Econ. Record. *Address*: Dept of Economics and Commerce, Univ. of Hull, Hull HU6 7RX.

Wilson, Mrs Katherine; *see* Duncan-Jones, K.

Wilson, Kathleen Jean Wallace, BSc, PhD, RGN, SCM, RNT; Senior Research Fellow, Health Services Research Centre, University of Birmingham, since 1973; seconded to West Midlands Regional Health Authority as Nursing Research Liaison Officer; *b* 1922. BSc Edinburgh 1960 (Pure Science), PhD Edinburgh 1971; RGN 1945, SCM 1946, RNT 1952. Lectr, Dept of Nursing Studies, Univ. of Edinburgh, 1961–71, Sen. Lectr, 1971–73. Editor, Internat. Jl Nursing Studies; Member: Chief Scientist's Cttee, DHSS; Standing Nursing and Midwifery Adv. Cttee, DHSS. *Publications*: Foundations of Nursing, 1956, 5th edn 1970; Foundations of Anatomy and Physiology, 1963, 4th edn 1973. *Address*: Health Services

Research Centre, Social Medicine Dept, Univ. of Birmingham, Birmingham B15 2TT.

Wilson, Laurence; Registrar, University College at Buckingham, since 1973; *b* 1920; *m* 1959; three *s* one *d*. BA Oxon 1941 (1st cl. Hons Maths), MA Oxon 1945; Barrister, Gray's Inn, 1951. Asst Registrar, Univ. Manchester, 1962–66; Registrar, Coll. of Aeronautics, Cranfield, 1967–69; Registrar, Cranfield Inst. Technology, 1969–73. Legal posts, Shell Petroleum Gp, 1948–56; Principal Scientific Officer (Safety Assessment), UKAEA, 1956–62. *Address:* Univ. College, Buckingham MK18 1EG.

Wilson, Margaret; *see* Borland, W. M. D.

Wilson, Michael; *see* Wilson, J. M.

Wilson, Nigel Guy, MA; Fellow and Tutor in Classics, Lincoln College, Oxford University, since 1962; *b* 1935. BA Oxon 1957, MA Oxon 1960. Res. Lectr, Merton Coll., Oxford, 1957–62. *Publications:* (with L. D. Reynolds) Scribes and Scholars, 1968, rev. edn 1974, Italian trans. 1969, French trans. forthcoming; (with D. M. Jones) Scholia graeca in Aristophanis Equites, 1969; An Anthology of Byzantine Prose, 1971; Mediaeval Greek Booklands, 1973; *contrib.* Class. Qly, Class. Rev., Gnomon, GGA, Gk Rom. Byz. Studies, etc. *Address:* Lincoln College, Oxford.

Wilson, Prof. Raymond, BA; Professor of Education, University of Reading, since 1968; *b* 1925; *m* 1950; two *s* one *d*. BA London 1954 (1st cl. English), Hd of English, Dulwich Coll., 1957–65; Lectr, Southampton Univ., 1965–68. Univ. and Exec. Mem., South. Reg. Council for Further Educn; Univ. Mem., Nat. Adv. Council Educn in Indust. Comm.; Gov., Berks. Coll. of Educn; Mem., Reading Educn Cttee; UCET. *Publications:* ed, Reading Aloud, 1960; A Coleridge Selection, 1963; Solo and Chorus, 1964; Rhyme and Rhythm, 1965; Poems to Compare, 1966; Untravelled Worlds, 1966; Language in New Directions in the Teaching of English, 1969; *contrib.* Crit. Qly, Crit. Qly Survey, Listener, Use Engl., THES. *Address:* School of Education, Univ. of Reading, Reading RG6 2AH.

Wilson, Dr Richard George; Senior Lecturer in Economic History, School of Social Studies, University of East Anglia, since 1970; *b* 1938; *m* 1962; two *s* one *d*. Leeds Univ., 1957–63, BA, PhD. Asst Lectr, Univ. of Strathclyde, 1963–65, Lectr, 1965–66; Lectr, Univ. of E Anglia, 1966–70. *Publications:* Gentlemen Merchants, 1971; (ed, with J. T. Ward) Land and Industry, 1971; *contrib.* Bus. Hist., Econ. Hist. Rev. *Address:* School of Social Studies, Univ. of East Anglia, Norwich NOR 88C.

Wilson, Rev. Prof. Robert McLachlan, MA, BD, PhD; Professor of New Testament, University of St Andrews, since 1969; *b* 1916; *m* 1945; two *s*. MA Edinburgh 1939 (1st cl. Classics), BD Edinburgh 1942 (Dist. NT),

PhD Cantab 1945. Lectr, St Andrews, 1954–64; Sen. Lectr, St Andrews, 1964–69; Vis. Prof., Vanderbilt Divinity Sch., 1964. Assoc. Ed., NT Studies, 1967– ; Mem., Cttee, Studiorum NT Soc.; Mem., Edit. Bd, Nag Hammadi Studies; Hon. Mem., Soc. of Biblical Literature. *Publications:* The Gnostic Problem, 1958; Studies in the Gospel of Thomas, 1960; ed and trans., The Gospel of Philip, 1962; Gnosis and the New Testament, 1968, French edn 1969, German edn 1971; ed, Eng. trans., Hennecke-Schneemelcher, New Testament Apocrypha, 1963–65; ed, Eng. trans., Haenchen: The Acts of the Apostles, 1971; ed, Eng. trans., Foerster, Gnosis vol. i, 1972, vol. ii, 1974; *contrib.* Jl Theol. Studies, NT Studies, Scott. Jl Theol., Vig. Christ. *Address:* St Mary's College, St Andrews, Fife KY16 9JU.

Wilson, Stuart Swinford, MA; University Lecturer, Department of Engineering Science, Oxford University, since 1955 (including energy economics, development studies, design and educational reform); *b* 1923; *m* 1953; one *s* two *d*. BA Oxon 1944 (1st cl. Eng. Science), MA Oxon 1948. Deptl Demonstrator, Oxford Univ., 1946; Lectr, Brasenose Coll., 1947–55; Lectr, Corpus Christi Coll., 1964; Fellow, St Cross Coll., Oxford, 1965; Vis. Fellow, Univ. of New South Wales, 1968. *Address:* Dept of Engineering Science, Parks Road, Oxford.

Wilson, Prof. Thomas, OBE, MA, PhD; Adam Smith Professor of Political Economy, University of Glasgow, since 1958; *b* 1916; *m* 1943; one *s* two *d*. BA Queen's Univ., Belfast 1938, PhD London 1940, MA Oxford 1946 (by decree); Mem., Royal Econ. Soc., Mem., Amer. Econ. Soc. Fellow, Univ. Coll., and Lectr, Univ. of Oxford, 1946–58. Civil Servant: Min. of Econ. Warfare, Min. of Aircraft Production, Prime Minister's Stat. Br., 1940–46; Official Cnsltncy wk in Nigeria, Canada, N Ireland; Gen. Ed., Oxf. Econ. Papers, 1948–58. *Publications:* Fluctuations in Income and Employment, 1942; Oxford Studies in the Price Mechanism, 1951; Inflation, 1961; Planning and Growth, 1964; Pensions, Inflation and Growth, 1974; var. Monogs on reg. develop.; *contrib.* Econ. Jl, Economica, Oxf. Econ. Papers, Rev. Econ. Studies, Rev. Econ. and Stats, Manch. Sch., Rd Table, etc. *Address:* Dept of Political Economy, Adam Smith Building, The Univ., Glasgow G12 8RT.

Wilson, Thomas Brendan; Reader in Music, Extra-Mural Department, Glasgow University, since 1972; *b* 1927; *m* 1952; three *s*. MA Glasgow 1951, BMus Glasgow 1954; ARCM 1954; Vice-Chm., Composers Guild (Scotland); Mem., Soc. for Promotion of New Music. Tutor in Music, Extra-Mural Dept, Glasgow Univ., 1957. Mem., Scottish Arts Council, 1968–74. *Publications:* Variations for orch. Toccata for orch.; Piano Sonata; Soliloquy for guitar; Clarinet Sonatina; 3 Pieces for guitar; Coplas del ruiseñor; Piano Sonatina; Piano Trio; Concerto da Camera; Touchstone: portrait for orch.; Symphony No 2; Concerto for orch.; Threnody for orch.; Te Deum, Missa pro mundo conturbato; String quartet No. 3;

Ritornelli per archi, Complementi; Pas de Quoi for strings; Canti Notturni; Carmina Sacra for high voice and strings; 3 Pieces for piano; Sinfonia for 7 instruments; Fantasia for solo cello; Violin Sonata; Cello Sonata; Carol: A Babe is Born; Night Songs (SATB). *Other works*: opera: The Charcoal Burner; Sequentiae Passionis; ballet: Embers of Glencoe. *contrib.* musical magazines (e.g. Musical Times); also newspaper articles, reviews, broadcast talks, performances, etc. *Address*: Extra-Mural Dept, Univ. of Glasgow, Glasgow G12 8QQ.

Wilson, Dr Thomas Roger, MA, PhD; Senior Lecturer in Psychopharmacology, Medical School, University of Manchester (also teaches Social Psychology), since 1973 (Lecturer, 1965–73); *b* 1938. BA Liverpool 1960 (Spec. Hons Psychol.), MA Liverpool 1962, PhD Liverpool 1964; MIBiol 1971, FRSM 1968. Mem., Brit. Psychol. Soc., 1957, Mem., Royal Coll. Psychiat., 1961; Mem., Assoc. Study Animal Behav., 1967; Mem., Brit. Soc. Gastroenterol., 1967; Mem., Brit. Pharmacol. Soc., 1968. Tutor in Psychology, Liverpool Univ., 1960–65; Demonstrator in Pharmacology, Liverpool Univ., 1962–65. *Publications*: contrib. Age and Function, ed Heron and Chown, 1964; Peptic Ulcer, ed Pfeiffer, 1971; *contrib.* Acta Genet. Med., Brit. Jl Pharmacol., Gerontol., Scand. Jl Gastroenterol. *Address*: Dept of Pharmacology, Univ. Medical School, Manchester M13 9PT.

Wilson, Prof. William Adam; Professor of Law, Department of Scots Law, University of Edinburgh, since 1972; *b* 1928. MA Glasgow 1948, LLB 1951; Admitted solicitor, 1951. Lectr in Scots Law, Univ. of Edinburgh, 1960–65; Sen. Lectr, 1965–72. *Address*: Old College, South Bridge, Edinburgh EH8 9YL.

Wilton-Ely, John; Lecturer in Fine Art, Nottingham University, since 1963; *b* 1937; *m* 1971; two *s*. BA Cantab 1961, MA 1966, Acad. Dip. in Art History, London 1963; Mem., Exec. Cttee, Soc. Archit. Hist. GB, 1969– ; Mem., Exec. Cttee, British Soc. for 18th Cent. studies, 1974– ; Mem., Walpole Soc., Mem., Soc. Furniture Hist. Mem., Archit. Sub-Cttee, Council of Europe exhib.: Age of Neo-classicism, 1971–72. *Publications*: Giovanni Battista Piranesi: The Polemical Works, 1972; *contrib.* Apollo, Archit. Hist., Archit. Rev., Country Life. *Address*: The Univ., Nottingham NG7 2RD.

Winch, Prof. Donald; Professor of History of Economics, University of Sussex, since 1969; *b* 1935. BSc(Econ) 1956, PhD Princeton 1960; FREconSoc. Vis. Lectr, Univ. of California, Berkeley, 1959–60; Lectr, Edinburgh Univ., 1960–63; Lectr, Univ. of Sussex, 1963–66; Reader, Univ. of Sussex, 1966–69. Dean, Sch. of Soc. Sciences, Univ. of Sussex, 1968– ; Publicns Sec., Royal Econ. Soc., 1971– . *Publications*: Classical Political Economy and Colonies, 1965; James Mill, Selected Economic Writings, 1966; Economics and Policy, A Historical Study, 1969; The Emergence of Economics as a Science, 1750–1900, 1971; *contrib.* Econ. Jl, Economica, Jl Pol Econ. *Address*: Arts Building, Univ. of Sussex, Falmer, Brighton BN1 9QN.

Winch, Prof. Peter Guy, BA, BPhil; Professor of Philosophy, University of London, King's College, since 1967; *b* 1926; *m* 1947; two *s*. BA Oxon 1949 (PPE), BPhil Oxon 1951; Mem., Aristot. Soc., Mem., Mind Assoc., Mem., Royal Inst. Philos. Asst Lectr, 1951–54, Lectr, 1954–59, Sen. Lectr, Univ. Coll., Swansea, 1959–64; Reader, Univ. of London (Birkbeck Coll.), 1964–67; Vis. Prof., Univ. of Rochester, 1961–62; Vis. Prof., Univ. of Arizona, 1970; Ed., Analysis, 1965–71. Mem., Council Royal Inst. Philos., 1969; Mem., Exec. Royal Inst. Philos., 1971; Editor, Analysis, 1965–71; Edl Bd, Library of Philosophy and Logic, 1971– . *Publications*: The Idea of a Social Science, 1958, trans. into German, Portuguese, Italian; ed, Studies in the Philosophy of Wittgenstein, 1969, Argentinian edn 1971; Moral Integrity, 1968; Ethics and Action, 1972; *contrib.* Amer. Philos. Qly, Analysis, Brit. Jl Sociol., Hum. Wld, Inquiry, Monist, Proc. Aristot. Soc., Univ. Qly, Ratio. *Address*: King's College, Strand, WC2R 2LS.

Windsor Lewis, J.; *see* Lewis, J. W.

Winearls, Jane; Dance Lecturer, Birmingham University, since 1965; *b* 1908; *m* 1945 (widowed 1966); one step *s*. Certs and Dips in all brs Dance; freelance teacher, dancer, choreographer, producer; wkd in var. instns in Educn and Theatre in England and Europe; Sigurd Leeder Sch., London, and Folkwangschule, Essen (K. Jooss . . . training sch. and Ballets Jooss), 1947–52; opened 1st training course for Theatre Dance (Alexander Technique of psycho-physical re-educn) as The Jane Winearls Studio, Morley Coll.; currently the only professional dance lecturer in full-time Univ. lectureship. *Publications*: Modern Dance, 1958, 2nd edn 1968, Japanese trans. 1971; contrib. 1st Symposium, International Society of Posturography and Instituto N. do Psicologia Aplicada Psicotecnia, Juan Huarte do San Juan I, Madrid, 1971; Dance Studies, vols 1–10: Modern Dance in Notation Form (forthcoming); *contrib.* Dancing Times, Dance and Dancers. *Address*: Dept of Physical Education, Univ. of Birmingham, PO Box 363, Birmingham B15 2TT.

Wing, Prof. John Kenneth, MD, PhD; Director, MRC Social Psychiatry Unit, since 1965; Professor of Social Psychiatry, Institute of Psychiatry and London School of Hygiene, since 1970. DPM London 1956, PhD London 1959, MD London 1960; FRCPsych. Hon. Cnsltnt, Maudsley and Bethlem Royal Hosps, 1961– ; Mem., Epidemiol. Cttee, Med. Res. Council, 1967; Mem., Council, Royal Coll. Psychiat., 1971. *Publications*: Early Childhood Autism, 1966, Italian edn 1970, German edn 1973; Schizophrenia and Social Care, 1966; Institutionalism and Schizophrenia, 1970; Psychiatric Epidemiology, 1970; Roots of Evaluation, 1973; Measurement and Classification of Psychiatric Symptoms, 1974; *contrib.* Brit. Jl Prev. Soc. Med., Brit. Jl Psychiat., Brit.

Med. Jl, Psychol. Med., Soc. Psychiat. *Address*: Social Psychiatry Unit, Institute of Psychiatry, de Crespigny Park, SE5 8AF.

Wingard, Peter Graham; Senior Lecturer in the Teaching of English Overseas, Department of Education, Manchester University, since 1962; *b* 1924; *m* 1951; two *s* one *d*. BA Oxon 1949, MA Oxon 1949, Teacher's Dip. London 1949; Mem., Brit. Assoc. App. Lingu., Lingu. Assoc., Nat. Assoc. Teaching Engl., Internat. Assoc. Teaching Engl. as a Foreign Lang., Teaching Engl., UK Reading Assoc. Res. Fellow in Educn, Univ. Coll. of E Africa, 1957–59; Lectr in Educn, 1959–62. Mem., Brit. Council Engl.-Teaching Adv. Cttee, 1967–69. *Publications*: Gen. ed. (with S. H. Olu Tomori), Progressive English, course for Nigerian schools, 1965–72; contrib. Language in Africa, ed J. Spencer, 1963; other symposia; *contrib*. Engl. Lang. Teach., Rev. Educnl Res. *Address*: Dept of Education, The Univ., Manchester M13 9PL.

Winston, Frederick Denis Dyson; Lecturer in West African Languages, School of Oriental and African Studies, University of London, since 1952; *b* 1925; *m* 1954; one *s* one *d*. BA Cantab 1948 (Classics). Mem., Afr. Studies Assoc. UK. *Publications*: *contrib*. Afr. Lang. Studies. *Address*: School of Oriental and African Studies, Malet Street, WC1E 7HP.

Winter, Henry James Jacques, DSc, PhD; Senior Lecturer, Science Education Centre, University of Exeter, since 1957; *b* 1912; *m* 1940; one *s*. BSc London 1934 (Hons. Physics), CertEd Nottingham 1935 (dist. Adv. Art), MSc London 1939 (Hist. and Philos. of Sci.), PhD London 1945 (Hist. and Philos. of Sci.), DSc London 1954; FRAsiatSoc. Lectr in Educn, Univ. Coll. of the S West, Exeter, 1947–57. Tech. Off., Royal Aircraft Establishment, 1940–44. *Publications*: Eastern Science, 1952; *contrib*. Ann. Science, Archeion, Archiv. Internat. Hist. Sci., Brit. Jl Hist. Science, Centaur., Isis, Jl Royal Asiat. Soc., Philos. Mag., Physis, Sch. Science Rev. *Address*: Science Education Centre, Univ. of Exeter, Exeter.

Winterbottom, Herbert Wager; Director of Music and University Organist, University of Salford, since 1967; *b* 1921; *m* 1955; two *d*. MSc Salford 1973; LTCL 1942, LRAM 1945, ARCM 1960, FNSM 1963. Dir of Music and College Organist, Royal Technical Coll., Salford, 1956– (later Royal Coll. Advanced Technology, subsequently Univ. of Salford). *Address*: Music Dept, Peel Building, Univ. of Salford, Salford M5 4WT.

Winterbottom, Michael, MA, DPhil; Fellow and Tutor in Classics, Worcester College, Oxford University, since 1967; *b* 1934; *m* 1963; one *s*. BA Oxon 1956 (1st cl. Lit. Hum), MA Oxon 1959, DPhil Oxon 1964. Lectr in Latin and Greek, Univ. Coll., London, 1962–67; Ed., Class. Qly, 1970– . *Publications*: M. F. Quintiliani: Institutio Oratoria, 1970; Problems in Quintilian, 1970; (with D. A. Russell) Ancient Literary Criticism, 1972; The Elder Seneca, 1974; *contrib*. Celtica, Class. Qly, Class. Rev., Jl

Rom Studies, Med. Æv., Philol. *Address*: Worcester College, Oxford.

Winton, Malcolm George Hardy; Tutor, Department of Graphic Design, School of Graphic Design, Royal College of Art, since 1966; *b* 1936. *Publications*: *contrib*. Arts Mag. NY. *Address*: Graphic Design Dept, Royal College of Art, Exhibition Road, SW7 2EU.

Wirtz, Erika Anna; Lecturer in German, University of Liverpool, since 1951; *b* 1913. BA Reading 1946 (1st cl. Hons), MA Liverpool 1954. Univ. of Liverpool: Temp. Lectr, 1947–48; Asst Lectr, 1948–51. *Publications*: Stilprobleme bei Thomas Mann, in, Stil- und Formprobleme in der Literatur, ed P. Boeckmann, 1957; Der Zauber des Zauberbergs, in, Tradition und Ursprünglichkeit, ed W. Kohlschmidt and H. Meyer, 1966; *contrib*. MLR, GLL, Modern Languages, Wirkendes Wort, Jl Gypsy Lore Soc. *Address*: Modern Languages Building, PO Box 147, Liverpool L69 3BX.

Wisbey, Prof. Roy Albert, MA, DrPhil; Professor of German, University of London, King's College, since 1971; *b* 1929; *m* 1951; one *s*. BA Cantab 1952 (1st cl. Mod. and Med. Langs Tripos), MA Cantab 1956, DPhil Frankfurt am Main 1956. Hon. Sec., Mod. Hum. Res. Assoc., 1960–63, Hon. Treas., 1963– . Res. Fellow, Bedford Coll., Univ. of London, 1955–56; Lectr in German, Univ. of Durham, 1956–58; Asst Lectr, then Lectr, Univ. of Cambridge, 1958–71; Dir of Lit. and Lingu. Computing Centre, Univ. of Cambridge, 1964–71; Fellow (later Dir of Studies, Libr., Actg Bursar), Downing Coll., Cambridge, 1959–71; Vis. Prof., Univ. of Colorado, 1967, 1969. Founder Chm., Assoc. for Lit. and Lingu. Computing, 1973. Ed., Publics of the Lit. and Lingu. Computing Centre, 1969– ; Gen. Ed., COMPENDIA (Computer Generated Aids to Lit. and Lingu. Res.), 1968– ; Germ. Ed., MHRA Diss. Series, 1970– . *Publications*: Das Alexanderbild Rudolfs von Ems, 1966; Vollständige Verskonkordanz zur Wiener Genesis, 1967; Concordance to the Vorau and Strassburg Alexander, 1968; Word-index to the Speculum Ecclesiae, 1968; Concordance to the Rolandslied, 1969; ed, The Computer in Literary and Linguistic Research, 1971; ed (with others), Studien zur frühmittelhochdeutschen Literatur, 1974; contrib. var. coll. wks; *contrib*. Jb. Internat. Germ., Mod. Lang. Rev., Trans Philol. Soc., Yrs Wk Mod. Lang. Studies, Zeits. f. Deut. Altert. *Address*: Dept of German, King's College, Strand, WC2R 2LS.

Wise, Prof. Douglass; Professor of Architecture, since 1965, and Head of the School of Architecture, University of Newcastle upon Tyne, since 1970; *b* 1927; *m* 1958; one *s* one *d*. BArch Dunelm 1951 (1st cl.), DipTP Dunelm 1952; ARIBA 1953, FRIBA 1968. Lectr in Architecture, Newcastle, 1959–65. Mem., RIBA Bd of Educn, 1971; Chm., RIBA Moderators, 1970; Chm., RIBA Exams Cttee, 1970; Chm., RIBA Schs Cttee, 1971; RIBA Special Entry Cttee, 1971; Dir, N East. Housing Assoc., 1967. *Publications*: *contrib*. Archit. Jl, Builder, North. Archit.,

RIBA Jl. *Address*: School of Architecture, The Univ., Newcastle upon Tyne NE1 7RU.

Wise, Prof. Michael John, MC, BA, PhD; Professor of Geography, London School of Economics and Political Science (University of London), since 1958; *b* 1918; *m* 1942; one *s* one *d*. BA Birmingham 1939 (Geog.), Birmingham 1951; FRGS. Mem., Inst. Brit. Geogrs, Mem., Geog. Assoc., Mem., Econ. Hist. Soc. Asst Lectr, Birmingham Univ., 1946–48; Lectr, Birmingham Univ., 1948–51; Lectr in Geography, LSE, 1951–54; Sir Ernest Cassel Reader in Economic Geography, 1954–58; Erskine Fellow, Univ. of Canterbury, NZ, 1970. Chm., Deptl Cttee of Inquiry into Statutory Smallholdings, 1963–67; Mem., UGC, Hong Kong, 1967–73; Hon. Sec., RGS, 1963–73; Hon. Treas., Geog. Assoc.; Vice-Pres., Internat. Geog. Union, 1968– ; Pres., Sect. E, Brit. Assoc., 1965; Pres., Inst. Brit. Geogrs, 1974; Mem., DoE Landscape Adv. Cttee on Trunk Roads, 1971– . A Governor, Birkbeck Coll., 1968– . *Publications*: Hon. Ed., Birmingham and Its Regional Setting, 1951; *contrib*. Agric. Hist., Econ. Geog., Geog. Jl, Geog., Jl Town Plan. Inst., Town Country Plan., Univ. Birm. Hist. Jl. *Address*: London School of Economics and Political Science, Houghton Street, Aldwych, WC2A 2AE.

Wiseman, Prof. Donald John, OBE, DLit, FBA; Professor of Assyriology, University of London, since 1961; *b* 1918; *m* 1948; three *d*. BA London 1939, BA Oxon 1948, MA Oxon 1951, DLit London 1969; FBA, FSA. Mem., Soc. OT Studies. RAFVR, 1939–45; Asst Keeper, Brit. Museum, 1948–61; Jt-Dir, Brit. Sch. Archaeol. Iraq, 1962–65; Chm. Council, 1971– ; Council, Brit. Inst. Archaeol. Ankara; Brit. Sch. Archaeol. Jerusalem; Jt Editor, Iraq, 1953– . *Publications*: The Alalakh Tablets, 1953; Chronicles of Chaldean Kings, 1956; Vassal-Treaties of Esarhaddon, 1958; Cylinder Seals of Western Asia, 1959; Illustrations from Biblical Archaeology, 1959, rev. edn 1963, German edn 1965; catalogue of Western Asiatic Seals – I, 1960; The Expansion of Assyrian Studies, 1962; Assyriology in Europe, 1968; ed, Peoples of Old Testament Times, 1973; etc; *contrib*. Bull. SOAS, Iraq, Jl Cunéif. Studies, Semit. Studies, Syria, etc. *Address*: School of Oriental and African Studies, Univ. of London, WC1E 7HP.

Wiseman, Prof. Jack, BSc(Econ); Prof. of Applied Economics, and Director of the Institute of Social and Economic Research, University of York, since 1964; *b* 1919; *m* 1949; one *d*. BSc(Econ) London 1949. Mem., Royal Econ. Soc., Vice-Pres., Internat. Inst. Public Fin. Asst Lectr, then Lectr, and later Reader, LSE, 1949–63; Vis. Prof., Univ. of California, at Berkeley, 1963. Mem., Adv. Cttee, Inst. Econ. Aff.; Hon. Adv., Indust., Educnl and Res. Foundn; Jt Ed., Univ. of York Studies in Econ., Mem., Ed. Bd, Jl Public Fin.; Partner, Econ. Adv. Gp; Consultant, OECD. *Publications*: (with A. T. Peacock) The Growth of Public Expenditure in the United Kingdom, 1961, 2nd edn 1967; (with E. H. Phelps Brown) A Course in Applied Economics, 1964, 2nd edn 1966; *contrib*. Economica, Econ. Jl, Kyklos, Oxf. Econ. Papers, Public Fin., Scott. Jl Polit. Econ., South. Econ. Jl. *Address*: Institute of Social and Economic Research, Univ. of York, Heslington, York YO1 5DD.

Wiseman, Dr Timothy Peter; Reader in Roman History, University of Leicester, since 1973 (Lecturer in Classics, 1965–73); *b* 1940; *m* 1962. BA Oxon 1961 (1st cl. Lit. Hum.), MA Oxon 1964, DPhil Oxon 1967. Asst Lectr, Leicester Univ., 1963–65; Vis. Assoc. Prof., Univ. Coll., Toronto, 1970–71. Mem., Council, Soc. Prom. Rom. Studies, 1970–73; Fac. of Archaeol., Hist. and Letters, Brit. Sch. Rome, 1970–74. *Publications*: Catullan Questions, 1969; New Men in the Roman Senate 139 BC–AD 14, 1971; Cinna the Poet and other Roman Essays, 1974; *contrib*. Class. Qly, Class. Rev., Historia, Jl Rom. Studies, Paper Brit. Sch. Rome, etc. *Address*: Dept of Classics, The Univ., Leicester LE1 7RH.

Witherick, Dr Michael Edward, BA; Lecturer in Urban Geography, University of Southampton, since 1966; *b* 1936; *m* 1965; one *s* one *d*. BA Birmingham 1958 (1st cl. Geog.), PhD Birmingham 1963. Asst Lectr, Queen Mary Coll., London Univ., 1960–63; Lectr, Queen Mary Coll., London Univ., 1963–66. Mem., Geog. Panel, South. Univs Jt Bd for Sch. Exams, 1971– ; Chief Examnr, Geog. A level, Univ. of London, 1974– . *Publications*: *contrib*. Area, Geog., Housing Plan. Rev., Town Country Plan. *Address*: Dept of Geography, Univ. of Southampton, Southampton SO9 5NH.

Withrington, Donald John; Senior Lecturer in Scottish History, University of Aberdeen, since 1969; Director, Centre for Scottish Studies, University of Aberdeen, since 1970; *b* 1931; *m* 1957; three *d*. MA Edinburgh 1953, DipEd Edinburgh 1954, MEd Edinburgh 1955; FRHistS. Godfrey Thomson Res. Fellow and Hon. Lectr in Educn, Univ. Edinburgh, 1958–61; Lectr in Educn, Univ. Edinburgh, 1961–69; Lectr in History, Univ. Aberdeen, 1964–69. Jt Editor, Scottish Historical Review, 1971– ; Jt Editor, Northern Scotland, 1971– ; Chm., Scottish History of Educn Soc., 1967– . *Publications*: (with Margaret Donaldson) A Study of Children's Thinking, 1963; *contrib*. Scotland in the Age of Improvement, ed N. T. Phillipson and R. Mitchison 1970; *contrib*. Essays on Class and Society, ed A. A. Maclaren, 1974; *contrib*. Aberdeen Univ. Rev., Educn in the North, Local Historian, Northern Scotland, Recs Scot. Church Hist. Soc., Scot. Educn. Stud., Scot. Hist. Rev. *Address*: King's College, Old Aberdeen AB9 2UB.

Witte, Prof. William; Professor of German, University of Aberdeen, since 1951; *b* 1907; *m* 1937; one *s* one *d*. BA London 1940 (1st cl. German), MA London 1943, Dr rer pol Breslau 1930, PhD Aberdeen 1935, DLit London 1966. Asst in German, Aberdeen, 1931–36; Asst in German, Edinburgh, 1936–37; Lectr, Aberdeen, 1937–45; Sen. Lectr, and Hd of Dept, Aberdeen, 1945–47; Reader,

Aberdeen, 1947–51; Dean, Fac. of Arts, Aberdeen, 1960–63. Mem., Scott. Univs Entrance Bd, 1949–58; Adv. Council on Educn in Scotl., Special Cttee, 1959–61; Selection Cttee, Scott. Postgrad. Studentship, 1962– . *Publications*: Modern German Prose Usage, 1937; Schiller, 1949; ed, Schiller: Wallenstein, 1952; ed, T. Mann: Two Stories, 1957; Schiller and Burns, and Other Essays, 1959; ed, Schiller: Wallensteins Tod, 1962; ed, Schiller: Maria Stuart, 1965; ed, Goethe: Clavigo, 1973; *contrib.* Aberd. Univ. Rev., Forum Mod. Lang. Studies, Germ. Life Lett., Hermath., Mod. Lang. Rev., Oxf. Germ. Studies, Publicns Engl. Goethe Soc., Edin. Carlyle Soc. *Address*: Dept of German, King's College, Univ. of Aberdeen, Aberdeen AB9 2UB.

Witton-Davies, Ven. Carlyle; Archdeacon of Oxford, and Canon of Christ Church, University of Oxford, since 1956; *b* 1913; *m* 1941; three *s* four *d*. BA Wales 1934 (1st cl. Hebrew), BA Oxon 1937 (2nd cl. Theol.), MA Oxon 1940; Junior Hall Houghton LXX Prize, Oxford 1938, Senior Prize 1939. Mem., Soc. OT Studies. Subwarden, St Michael's Coll., Llandaff, 1940–44; Examng Chaplain: Bp of Monmouth, 1940–44; Anglican Bp in Jerusalem, 1945–49; Bp of St Davids, 1950–57; Bp of Oxford, 1965– ; Chm., Gov., Culham Coll. of Educn, 1965– . *Publications*: Journey of a Lifetime, 1962; trans., M. Buber: Hasidism, 1948; M. Buber: The Prophetic Faith, 1949, pbk edn 1960; contrib. Oxford Dictionary of the Christian Church, 1957, 2nd edn 1972; Mission of Israel, 1963; *contrib.* Jl Theol. Studies, Theol. *Address*: Christ Church, Oxford.

Witts, Allan Gavin; Lecturer in Accounting, School of Economic Studies, Leeds University, since 1963; *b* 1937; *m* 1966; two *s*. BCom Leeds 1958; ACA 1961, FCA 1972. Asst Lectr in Accounting, Leeds, 1961–63. *Address*: School of Economic Studies, The Univ., Leeds LS2 9JT.

Wohlgemuth, Dr Ernest; Senior Lecturer in Politics, Dept of Politics, University of Leicester, since 1974 (Lecturer, 1964–74); *b* 1924; *m* 1954; one *s*. BSc Econ London 1948, MA Chicago 1953 (Social Science), PhD Chicago 1956. Asst Prof., Kansas State Univ., USA, 1950; Research Fellow, Univ. of Chicago, 1951–54; Vis. Prof., State Univ. of New York, 1971. Chm., Univ. Assoc. for Contemp. Europ. Studies, 1973– . Senior Research Officer, PEP, London, 1954–59; HM Treasury, 1959–61; Mem. Staff, EFTA Secretariat, Geneva, 1961–64. *Publications*: Industrial Trade Associations, 1957; European Organisations, 1959; European Unity, 2nd edn 1968; *contrib.* PEP broadsheets, Political Qly, Treasury Bull. for Industry, EFTA Bull. *Address*: Dept of Politics, Univ. of Leicester, Leicestershire LE1 7RH.

Woledge, Prof. Brian, MA, Ddel'U; Honorary Research Fellow in French, University College, London, since 1971; *b* 1904; *m* 1933; one *s* one *d*. BA Leeds 1926, MA Leeds 1928, Ddel'U Paris 1930; Hon. Ddel'U Aix-Marseille, 1969. Asst Lectr, Univ. Coll., Hull, 1930–32; Lectr, Univ. of Aberdeen,

1932–39; Fielden Prof. of French, Univ. Coll., London, 1939–67; Vis. Prof., Pittsburg, 1967; Emeritus Prof. of French, Univ. of London, 1971– . *Publications*: L'Atre périlleux, Études, 1930; L'Atre périlleux, Roman de la Table ronde, 1936; Bibliographie des roman en prose antérieurs à 1500, 1954; The Penguin Book of French Verse, I, To the Fifteenth Century, 1961: (with H. P. Clive) Répertoire des premiers textes en prose française, 1964; *contrib.* Med. Æv., Mod. Lang. Rev., Romania. *Address*: Univ. College, WC1E 6BT.

Wolf-Phillips, Leslie A.; Lecturer in Political Science, London School of Economics and Political Science, since 1960; *b* 1929; *m* 1960; one *s* one *d*. BSc(Econ) London 1958 (1st cl. Govt), LLM London 1970; CertEd Bristol 1953, Cert. Relig. Educn London 1954. Grad. Tutor, LSE, 1958–60; Vis. Lecturer in Politics, Univ. of Southampton, 1969. *Publications*: ed, Constitutions of Modern States, 1968; Comparative Constitutions, 1972; *contrib.* Pol. Studies, Parly Affairs, ME Studies. *Address*: London School of Economics and Political Science, WC2A 2AE.

Wolfe, Prof. James Nathan; Professor of Economics, University of Edinburgh, since 1964; *b* 1927; *m* 1954; two *d*. BA McGill 1948, MA McGill 1949, BLitt Oxford 1953. Mem., Amer. Econ. Assoc., Royal Econ. Soc., Economet. Soc., Scott. Econ. Soc. Lectr in Political Economy, Univ. of Toronto, 1952–60; Vis. Prof., Purdue Univ., 1959–60; Vis. Prof., Univ. of California, Berkeley, 1960–61; Prof. of Economics, Univ. of California, Santa Barbara, 1961–64. Econ. Cnsltnt, Dept Econ. Aff., and Sec. of State for Scotl., 1965– ; Mem., Cttee Long Term Population Distrib., 1967–70; Cttee on Tourism in Scotl., 1967–69. *Publications*: Taxation and Development in the Maritimes, 1959; ed, Value Capital and Growth: Papers in Honour of Sir John Hicks, 1968; Res. Dir and co-ed., An Economic and Geographical Study of the Central Borders, 1968; ed, Government and Nationalism in Scotland, 1970; ed (with J. Erickson), The Armed Services and Society, 1970; ed (with M. F. G. Scott and W. Eltis), Induction Growth and Trade: Essays in Honour of Sir Roy Harrod, 1970; *contrib.* Canad. Jl Econ. Pol. Science, Econ. Jl, Jl Pol Econ., Qly Jl Econ., Rev. Econ. Studies. *Address*: Dept of Economics, William Robertson Building, George Square, Edinburgh EH8 9JY.

Wolfram, Sybil, MA, DPhil; Fellow and Tutor in Philosophy, Lady Margaret Hall, University of Oxford, since 1964; *b* 1931; *m* 1952; two *s*. BA Oxon 1952 (1st cl. PPE), MA Oxon 1957, DPhil Oxon 1957 (Soc. Anthropol.). Lectr in Philos., St Hilda's Coll., Oxford, 1958–64. *Publications*: contrib. Modes of Thought, ed R. Horton and R. Finnegan, 1973; *contrib.* Analysis, l'Homme, Mind, Philos. Qly. *Address*: Lady Margaret Hall, Oxford.

Wolkowinski, Roscislaw; Chief Instructor, Language Centre (Russian Department), University of Essex, since 1971; *b* 1914; *m*

1946; three *s*. LLM Warsaw 1939, BA London 1960 (Russian Lang. and Lit). Mem., Sch. Assoc. Teachers Russ. Instructor, Jt Services Sch. for Linguists, 1951–61; Asst Master, Bognor Regis Grammar Sch., 1961–66; Sen. Instructor, Univ. of Essex, 1966–71. *Address*: Language Centre, Univ. of Essex, Wyvenhoe Park, Colchester .Essex CO4 3SQ.

Wollheim, Prof. Richard Arthur, FBA; Grote Professor of Philosophy of Mind and Logic, University of London, since 1963; *b* 1923; *m* 1950, 1969; two *s*. MA Oxon 1949. University College, London: Asst Lectr, 1949; Lectr, 1951; Reader, 1960; Vis. Prof., Columbia Univ., 1959–60, 1970; Vis. Prof., Visva-Bharati Univ., 1968; Hill Vis. Prof., Minnesota Univ., 1972. Army, 1942–45 (POW 1944). Pres., Aristot. Soc., 1967–68; Vice-Pres., Brit. Soc. of Aesthetics, 1969– . *Publications*: F. H. Bradley, 1959, rev. edn 1969; Socialism and Culture, 1961; ed, F. H. Bradley: Ethical Studies, 1961; ed, Hume on Religion, 1963; On Drawing an Object (Inaugural Lecture), 1965; Art and its Objects, 1968; ed, F. H. Bradley: Appearance and Reality, 1968; A Family Romance (fiction), 1969; Freud, 1971; ed, Adrian Stokes: Selected Writings, 1972; On Art and the Mind, 1973; *contrib*. Anthologies, philos. and lit. jls. *Address*: Univ. College, Gower Street, WC1E 6BT.

Wood, Bruce; Lecturer, Department of Government, University of Manchester, since 1970; *b* 1943; *m* 1967; one *s* one *d*. BScEcon London 1964. Res. Asst, Greater London Gp, LSE, 1964–66; Res. Associate, subseq. Asst Lectr, Lectr, Univ. Manchester, 1968–70. Asst Res. Officer, Royal Commn on Local Govt in England, 1966–68. *Publications*: contrib. Trends in British Society since 1900, ed A. H. Halsey, 1972; (with J. M. Lee) The Scope of Local Initiative: A Study of Cheshire County Council, 1961–74, 1974; (with Lord Redcliffe-Maud) English Local Government Reformed, 1974; *contrib*. Political Qly, Public Administration. *Address*: Dept of Government, Univ. of Manchester, Manchester M13 9PL.

Wood, Dr Douglas; Senior Lecturer in Economics, Faculty of Business Administration, University of Manchester, since 1973 (Lecturer, 1966–73); *b* 1942; *m* 1967; two *d*. BComm Birmingham 1963, MComm Birmingham 1965; PhD Manchester 1970. Dptl Demonstrator, Dept of Agricl Econs, Univ. of Oxford, 1963–66. Dir, Doctoral Prog.; Co-ordinator, Graduate Course. *Publications*: *contrib*. European Jl of Marketing, Jl of Business Finance, Jl of Industrial Econs, Jl of Management Studies. *Address*: Manchester Business School, Booth Street West, Manchester M15 6PB.

Wood, Geoffrey Edward; Lecturer in Economics, University of Warwick, since 1968; *b* 1945; *m* 1968. MA Aberdeen 1967, MA Essex 1968. *contrib*. Jl Internat. Econs, Southern Econ. Jl, Surrey Econ. Paper, Scottish Jl Polit. Economy. *Address*: School of Economics, Univ. of Warwick, Coventry CV4 7AL.

Wood, George Alexander McDougall; Lecturer in English Studies, University of Stirling, since 1968; *b* 1938. BA London 1962; Member: Bibliographical Soc., Oxford Bibliographical Soc., Malone Soc. Res. Asst UCL, 1962; Librarian, Osborn Collection, Yale Univ., 1962–66; Asst Prof., Univ. California Santa Barbara, 1966–68. *Publications*: (with D. Simpson) Change of Currency, 1972; contrib. Scott Centenary Essays, 1973; *contrib*. Bibliotheck, Library, Notes and Queries, Philological Qly, Studies in Scottish Literature. *Address*: Univ. of Stirling, Stirling FK9 4LA.

Wood, George Cecil, OBE, MA; Registrar, University of London Goldsmiths' College, since 1958; *b* 1913; *m* 1948. BA Oxon 1935 (Physics) (Open Exhibnr, New Coll., Oxford, 1932–35), MA Oxon 1939. Gordon Memorial College (subseq. Univ. Khartoum): Lectr in Physics, 1939–45; Sen. Lectr and Head of Physics Dept, 1945; Dean of Science, 1946; Vice-Principal (Admin), 1950; Registrar, UC Khartoum, 1951–56; Registrar (subseq. Academic Sec.), Univ. Khartoum, 1956–58. Asst Master, Edinburgh Academy, 1935–39. *Publications*: section on University of Khartoum, Sudan, in, Relations between Governments and Universities (collected Seminar papers, Inst. Commonwealth Studies), 1967. *Address*: Univ. of London Goldsmiths' College, New Cross, SE14 6NW.

Wood, Prof. John Harold, MA, PhD; Esmée Fairbairn Professor of Investment, Economics Department, University of Birmingham, since 1971; *b* 1933; *m* 1958; one *s* two *d*. BSc Ohio 1955, MA Michigan St., 1959, PhD Purdue 1964. Mem., Amer. Econ. Assoc., Mem., Royal Econ. Soc., Mem., Amer. Fin. Assoc., Mem., Economet. Soc. Lectr in Economics, Univ. of Birmingham, 1965–67; Assoc. Prof. of Finance, Univ. of Pennsylvania, 1967–71. Economist, Bd of Govs, Federal Reserve System, 1962–65. *Publications*: contrib. Amer. Econ. Rev., Jl Fin., Jl Pol. Econ., Qly Jl Econ. *Address*: Economics Dept, Univ. of Birmingham, PO Box 363, Birmingham B15 2TT.

Wood, Michael, BSc; Lecturer in Geography (Cartography), University of Aberdeen, since 1969; *b* 1941; *m* 1966; two *d*. BSc Aberdeen 1963 (Hons Geog.), Dip. Cartography Glasgow 1964. Res. Asst, Dept of Geography, Univ. of Glasgow, 1964–66; Asst Lectr in Geography, Univ. of Glasgow, 1966–69. Mem., Council, Brit. Cartog. Soc., 1970–71. *Publications*: contrib. Cartog. Jl, Scottish Geog. Mag., Brit. Antarctic Survey Report. *Address*: Dept of Geography, Univ. of Aberdeen, Old Aberdeen AB9 2UF.

Wood, Oscar Patrick; Student and Tutor in Philosophy, Christ Church, University of Oxford, since 1956; *b* 1924; *m* 1950; two *s* one *d*. BA, MA Oxon 1948. Mem., Aristot. Soc., 1948. Fellow by Exam., Magdalen Coll., Oxford, 1948; Vis. Prof., Brown Univ., 1968. *Publications*: *contrib*. Proc. Aristot. Soc. *Address*: Christ Church, Oxford.

Wood, Dr Peter Anthony; Lecturer in Geography, University College, London, since 1968; *b* 1940. BSC Birmingham 1961, PhD Birmingham 1966; CertEd London 1962. Asst Lectr, Univ. Coll., London, 1965–68; Vis. Lectr, Queens Univ., Kingston, Ontario, 1967. Mem., Exec. Cttee, Reg. Studies Assoc., 1970–71; Vice-Chm., Reg. Studies Assoc., 1971–73. *Publications*: (with G. M. Lomas) Employment Location in Regional Economic Planning, 1970; (with K. E. Rosing) Character of a Conurbation: a Computer Atlas of the West Midlands Conurbation, 1971; *contrib.* Area, Geog., Jl Town Plan. Inst., Trans Inst. Brit. Geogrs. *Address*: Dept of Geography, Univ. College, Gower Street, WC1E 6BT.

Wood, Susan Meriel; Fellow and Tutor in Medieval History, St Hugh's College, Oxford, since 1952; *b* 1925; *m* 1950; two *s* one *d*. BA Oxon 1945 (1st cl. Hist.), MA Oxon 1949, BLitt Oxon 1950; FRHistS. Asst Lectr, Nottingham Univ., 1948–49; Lectr, St Hugh's Coll., Oxford, 1949–52. *Publications*: English Monasteries and their Patrons in the Thirteenth Century, 1955; contrib. Victoria Country History of Oxfordshire, vol. V, 1957. *Address*: St Hugh's College, Oxford.

Wood, Rev. Prof. Thomas, MA, BD; D. J. James Professor of Pastoral Theology, St David's University College Lampeter, since 1957; *b* 1919; *m* 1945; three *s*. BA Leeds 1941 (1st cl. Eng. Lang. and Lit.), BD Leeds 1945, MA Leeds 1947 (distinction). Dep. Principal, St David's UC Lampeter, 1971– . Member: Standing Doctrinal Commn, Church in Wales, 1969– ; Commn on Church and Society of Church in Wales, 1973– ; Churches' Council on Gambling, 1965– ; Select Preacher, Univ. Cambridge, 1961. *Publications*: English Casuistical Divinity during the Seventeenth Century, 1952; The Pastoral Responsibility of the Church Today, 1958; Five Pastorals, 1961; Some Moral Problems, 1961; Chastity Not Outmoded, 1965; contrib. A Dictionary of Christian Ethics, 1967; *contrib.* Church Qly Rev., Theology, Trivium. *Address*: Dept of Pastoral Theology, St David's Univ. College, Lampeter, Dyfed SA48 7ED.

Wood-Jones, Dr Raymond Bernard, MA, PhD, BArch, ARIBA, FSA; Senior Lecturer in Architecture, University of Manchester, since 1960; *b* 1920; *m* 1955; one *s* one *d*. BArch Liverpool 1949 (1st cl.), MA Liverpool 1953, PhD Manchester 1958; FSA, ARIBA, RIBA Neale Bursary 1959. Lectr, Manchester Univ., 1952–60. RAFVR, 1940–46; Archit. in private practice, 1952– ; Cathedral Archit., Manchester, 1963–69; Hon. Archit. Hist. to Cathedral, 1969– ; Mem., Royal Commn on Ancient Monuments in Wales and Mon., 1963– ; Mem., Council, 1953– , Hon. Ed., 1964–68, Chm., 1969–71, Vice-Pres., 1971– , Ancient Monuments Soc.; Mem., Council, RSA, 1967– ; Blackburn Dioc. Adv. Cttee, 1965– . *Publications*: Traditional Domestic Architecture in the Banbury Region, 1963; Gothic Architecture, 1972; contrib. Encyclopaedia Britannica; New World Encyclopaedia; *contrib.* Oxon., Trans Anc. Monums Soc., Trans Lancs Chesh. Antiqu. Soc. *Address*:

School of Architecture, Univ. of Manchester, Manchester M13 9PL.

Woodham, Ronald; Professor of Music, University of Reading, since 1951; *b* 1912; *m* 1949; three *s*. BA Oxford 1935, DMus Oxford 1939; FRCO, ARCM. Cramb Lectr in Music, Glasgow Univ., 1947–51. Mem., Exec. Cttee, South. Arts Assoc. *Publications*: *contrib.* Music Lett., Music Rev., Music. Times. *Address*: Dept of Music, Univ. of Reading, 35 Upper Redlands Road, Reading.

Woodhead, Arthur Geoffrey, MA, FSA; Lecturer in Classics, University of Cambridge, since 1951, and Fellow of Corpus Christi College, Cambridge, since 1948; *b* 1922; *m* 1949. BA Cantab 1946 (1st cl. with dist., Classics), MA Cantab 1949, Dip. Class. Archaeol., with dist., Cantab 1947; BSA. Asst Lectr in Classics, Cambridge, 1949–51; Mem., Inst. Adv. Study, Princeton, NJ, 1947–48, 1956–57, 1961–62, 1968–72; Martin Lectr, Oberlin Coll., 1968; Distinguished Vis. Prof., Ohio State Univ., 1974. Mem., Council, Hellen. Soc., 1953–59; Mem., Class. Jls Bd, 1955–74; Chm., 1967–74; Gov., St Paul's Schs, London, 1970– . *Publications*: Supplementum Epigraphicum Graecum, vols XI–XXV, 1954–71; The Study of Greek Inscriptions, 1959; Documents of the Flavian Emperors, 1961; (with M. McCrum) The Greeks in the West, 1962; Thucydides on the Nature of Power, 1970; *contrib.* Amer. Jl Archaeol., Amer. Jl Philol., Ann. Brit. Sch. Athens, Hesp., Historia, Jl Hellen. Studies, Mnemos., Phoenix. *Address*: Corpus Christi College, Cambridge CB2 1RH.

Woodhead, John Laughton; Lecturer in Phonetics, University of Leeds, since 1952; *b* 1925. BA Cantab 1948 (2nd cl. Mod. and Med. Langs, Pt II, 1949), MA Cantab 1950. Mem., Philol. Soc., Lingu. Assoc. GB and N Irel. Asst Lectr, Leeds, 1949–52; Sen. Lectr in Language and Linguistics, Univ. Coll., Dar-es-Salaam, Tanzania, (on secondment) 1966–69; Hd of Dept of Language and Linguistics, 1967–69. *Address*: Phonetics Dept, The Univ., Leeds LS2 9JT.

Woodhouse, Rev. Prof. Hugh Frederic; Regius Professor of Divinity, and Head of Department, University of Dublin, since 1963; *b* 1912; *m* 1944; two *s* one *d*. BA Dublin 1934 (Gold Medallist), BD Dublin 1937, DD Dublin 1951, MA Dublin 1968, HDipEd; Mem., Irish Theol. Assoc., Mem., Soc. Study Theol. Prof. of Church Hist., Wycliffe Coll., Toronto, 1951–54; Principal and Prof., Anglican Theol. Coll., Vancouver, 1954–59; Prof. of Dogmatic Theology, Univ. of King's Coll., Halifax, NS, 1959–63; Mem., Summer Sch. Staff, Univ. of S Sewanee, Tenn., 1969. *Publications*: ed, G. D. Salmon: Infallibility of the Church, 1952; The Doctrine of the Church in Anglican Theology (1547–1603), 1954; The Life Giver at Work, 1955; *contrib.* Angl. Jl Theol., Ch Qly Rev., Scott. Jl Theol., Theol., Biblical Theol. *Address*: East Chapel, Trinity College, Dublin 2, Eire.

Woodhouse, Dr John Robert; University Lecturer, and Lecturer in Italian, Jesus College, Oxford, since 1973; Fellow, St Cross College, Oxford, since 1973; *b* 1937; *m* 1967. BA Oxford 1961, (Hons. Sch. Mod. Langs) (Hertford Coll.), MA Oxford 1964, PhD Wales 1969. Member: Soc. for Italian Studies, Soc. for Renaissance Studies, Assoc. of Teachers of Italian. Asst in Italian, King's Coll., Aberdeen, 1961–62; British Council Res. Scholar, Scuola Normale Superiore, Pisa, 1962–63; Lecturer: Italian, Univ. Coll. North Wales, Bangor, 1963–66; Univ. of Hull, 1966–72, Sen. Lectr, 1972–73; Old Dominion Foundn Fellow, Harvard Univ., 1969–70. *Publications:* Italo Calvino: a Reappraisal and Appreciation of the Trilogy, 1968; ed, Calvino: Il Barone Rampante, 1970; ed, Borghini: Scritti Inediti o Rari Sulla Lingua, 1971; ed, Borghini: Storia della Nobiltà Fiorentina, 1973; *contrib.* Barn, Forum for Mod. Lang. Studies, Ital. Qly, Ital. Studies, Lingua Nostra, Studi Secenteschi, Studi sul Boccaccio. *Address:* Taylor Institute, St Giles', Oxford.

Woodland, David J. A.; Lecturer in Sociology, School of Social Studies, University of East Anglia, since 1966; *b* 1935; *m* 1967; one *s.* BA Exeter 1960 (1st cl. Sociology); Mem. Brit. Sociological Assoc., Foreign Associate, Amer. Sociological Assoc. Fellow, Brown Univ., 1960–61; research, St John's Coll., Cambridge, 1961–63; Asst Lectr in Sociology, Univ. Exeter, 1963–66. *Publications:* contrib. A Dictionary of Sociology, ed G. D. Mitchell, 1968. *Address:* School of Social Studies, Univ. of East Anglia, University Plain, Norwich NOR 88C.

Woodman, Dr Anthony John; Lecturer, Department of Classics, University of Newcastle upon Tyne, since 1968; *b* 1945. BA Dunelm 1965, PhD Cantab 1970; Member: Cambridge Philological Soc., Class. Assoc., Soc. for Promotion of Roman Studies. *Publications:* contrib. Hommages Renard, 1968; ed jtly and contrib., Quality and Pleasure in Latin Poetry, 1974; *contrib.* Amer. Jl Philology, Class. Qly, Greece and Rome, Jl Roman Stud., Latomus. *Address:* Dept of Classics, Univ. of Newcastle upon Tyne, Newcastle upon Tyne NE1 7RU.

Woodruff, Graham James Michael, BA, MA; Director of Drama and Head of Department of Drama and Theatre Arts, University of Birmingham, since 1972; *b* 1935. BA Bristol 1959 (1st cl. Drama, Latin, Philos.), MA Georgia 1961. Asst Lectr, Manchester, 1961–64; Lectr, Manchester, 1964–66; Lectr, Birmingham, 1968–72, Sen. Lectr 1972; Dir and Co. Mngr, Library Theatre-in-the-round Scarborough, 1965; Mngr and Licensee, Univ. Theatre, Manchester, 1965–66; Assoc. Dir, Liverpool Playhouse, 1966–68; Guest Dir, Birmingham's Rep. Theatre, 1969. *Publications:* contrib. Theat. Res. *Address:* Dept of Drama and Theatre Arts, Univ. of Birmingham, PO Box 363, Birmingham B15 2TT.

Woods, Dr John Aubin; Reader in Modern History, University of Leeds, since 1971; *b* 1927. BA Cantab 1948, MA Cantab 1952, PhD Rochester 1952; FRHistS. Temp. Asst Lectr, Univ. of Manchester, 1954–55; Lectr, Univ. of Leeds, 1961–66; Sen. Lectr, Univ. of Leeds, 1966–71. Assoc. Ed., Correspondence of Edmund Burke. *Publications:* Roosevelt and Modern America, 1959; ed, Correspondence of Edmund Burke, vols IV, 1963, VII, 1968, IX, 1970; ed, H. B. Stowe: Uncle Tom's Cabin, 1965. *Address:* The School of History, The Univ., Leeds LS2 9JT.

Woods, Michael John, BPhil, MA; Fellow and Tutor in Philosophy, Brasenose College, Oxford University, since 1961; *b* 1934. BA Oxon 1956 (Lit. Hum.), BPhil Oxon 1958, MA Oxon 1959. Lectr, Christ Church and Magdalen Coll., Oxford, 1959–61; Univ. Lectr in Philosophy, Oxford, 1961– ; Vis. Lectr, Univ. of Minnesota, 1963; Vis. Prof., Cornell Univ., 1968; Radcliffe Res. Fellow, 1973–75. *Publications:* contrib. Jl Philos., Mind, Proc. Aristot. Soc. *Address:* Brasenose College, Oxford.

Woodward, Donald Malcolm, MA; Lecturer, Department of Economic and Social History, University of Hull, since 1968; *b* 1942; *m* 1965; two *s.* BA Manchester 1963 (Mod. Hist. with Econ. and Pol.), MA Manchester 1965. Asst Lectr, Hull Univ., 1965–68. *Publications:* The Trade of Elizabethan Chester, 1970; *contrib.* Hist., Loc. Hist., Trans Hist. Soc. Lancs Chesh. *Address:* Dept of Economic and Social History, Univ. of Hull, Hull HU6 7RX.

Woodward, Dr James Brian, MA, DPhil; Senior Lecturer in Russian, Department of German, University College of Swansea, since 1970; *b* 1935; *m* 1959; two *d.* BA Oxon 1959 (1st cl. Russian and Italian), MA Oxon 1963, DPhil Oxon 1965. Instructor, Univ. of British Columbia, 1962–65; Lectr, Univ. Coll. of Swansea, 1965–70. *Publications:* Selected Poems of Aleksandr Blok, 1968; Leonid Andreyev: a Study, 1969; *contrib.* Canad. Slav. Papers, Canad. Slav. Studies, Etudes Slav. E-Europ., Mod. Drama, Mod. Lang. Rev., Oxf. Slav. Papers, Russ. Lit., Scando-Slav., Slav. E.-Europ. Jl, Slav. E.-Europ. Rev., Welt Slav. *Address:* Dept of German, Univ. College of Swansea, Singleton Park, Swansea SA2 8PP.

Woodward, Prof. Leslie James, MA; Professor of Spanish, University of St Andrews, since 1964; *b* 1916; *m* 1941; four *d.* BA Cantab 1939, MA Cantab 1944. Lectr, St Andrews, 1948–64; Mellon Prof., Pittsburgh, 1965; Vis. Prof., Montana, 1969. Pres., Brit. Assoc. Hispan., 1964–66. *Publications:* contrib. Bull, Hispan., Bull. Hispan. Studies, Forum Mod. Lang. Studies, Jl Europ. Studies, Mod. Lang. Notes, Mod. Lang. Rev. *Address:* Dept of Spanish, St Salvator's College, Univ. of St Andrews, St Andrews KY16 9PH.

Woodward, Dr W. Mary, BA, PhD; Senior Lecturer in Psychology, University College of Swansea, since 1966; *b* 1921. BA London 1950 (Psychol.), PhD London 1956; FBPsS. Lectr in Psychol., Univ. Coll. of Swansea, 1961–66. *Publications:* The Development of

Behaviour, 1971; *contrib.* Brit. Jl Educnl Psychol., Brit. Jl Soc. Clin., Jl Child Psychol., Psychiat. *Address*: Dept of Psychology, Univ. College of Swansea, Singleton Park, Swansea SA2 8PP.

Woolf, Rosemary, BLitt, MA; Fellow and Tutor in English Language and Medieval Literature, Somerville College, Oxford University, since 1961; *b* 1925. BA Oxon 1946 (English), BLitt Oxon 1949, MA Oxon 1950. Asst Lectr, Hull Univ., 1948–50; Lectr, Hull Univ., 1950–61. *Publications*: The English Religious Lyric in the Middle Ages, 1968; The English Mystery Plays, 1972; *contrib.* Med. Æv., Rev. Engl. Studies, Specul. *Address*: Somerville College, Oxford.

Woolf, Prof. Stuart Joseph; Professor of History, History Department, University of Essex, since 1975; *b* 1936; *m* 1959; one *d*. BA Oxon 1956, MA Oxon 1960, DPhil Oxon 1960, PhD Cantab 1961 (by incorp.). Fellow and Asst Dir of Studies in History, Pembroke Coll., Cambridge, 1961–65; Reader, Dept of Italian Studies, and Dir, Centre for Advanced Study of Italian Soc., Univ. of Reading, 1965–74; Asst Dir, Inst. Contemp. History, London, 1967–70; Chm., Grad. Sch. Contemp. European Studies, Univ. Reading, 1968–71. *Publications*: (trans, Levi: If this is a Man, 1961; Studi sulla nobiltà piemontese nell'epoca dell'assolutismo, 1963; trans., Levi: The Truce, 1965; (with M. V. Posner) Italian Public Enterprise, 1967; ed and contrib., European Fascism, 1968; trans. and adapted, Marongiu: Medieval Parliaments, 1968; ed and contrib., The Nature of Fascism, 1968; The Italian Risorgimento, 1969; (with E. L. Jones) ed and contrib., Agrarian Change and Economic Development: the Historical Problems, 1969; ed and contrib., The Rebirth of Italy, 1943–50, 1972; ed and introd., Venturi: Italy and the Enlightenment, 1972; Storia d'Italia: Dal primo Settecento all' Unità: La storia Politica e sociale, 1973; *contrib.* Econ. History Rev., English Miscellany, History of the 20th Century, Jl Contemp. History, New Camb. Mod. History, New Society, various Italian jls, etc. *Address*: Dept of History, Univ. of Essex, Wivenhoe, Colchester CO4 3SQ.

Woolford, Alfred John; Staff Tutor, Department of External Studies, University of Oxford, since 1946; *b* 1917; *m* 1945; one *s* two *d*. BA Cantab 1938 (Hons History), MA Cantab 1942, MA Oxon 1949. Hon. Captain RA, 1945. Sec. Assoc. of Tutors in Adult Educn, 1966–67; Sec., New Dover Gp 1971–73. *Publications*: *contrib.* Scrutiny. *Address*: External Studies, Rutherford College, Univ. of Kent at Canterbury, Canterbury, Kent.

Woolhouse, Dr Roger Stuart; Senior Lecturer, Department of Philosophy, University of York, since 1973 (Lecturer, 1968–73); *b* 1940; *m* 1970. BA London 1961 (1st cl. Philos.), PhD Cantab 1968. Lectr, Univ. Coll., Cardiff, 1964–68. *Publications*: Locke's Philosophy of Science and Knowledge, 1971; *contrib.* Jl Hist. Philos., Jl Phil. Logic, Mind, Phil. Phen. Res., Phil. Stud., Philos., Ratio.

Address: Dept of Philosophy, Univ. of York, Heslington, York YO1 5DD.

Woolrych, Prof. Austin Herbert, MA, BLitt, FRHistS; Professor of History, University of Lancaster, since 1964; *b* 1918; *m* 1941; one *s* one *d*. BA Oxon 1948 (1st cl. Hist.), MA, BLitt Oxon 1952; FRHistS. Asst Lectr, Leeds Univ., 1949–52; Lectr, Leeds Univ., 1952–58; Sen. Lectr, Leeds Univ., 1958–64. Mem., DES State Studentship Selection Cttee, 1969–73; Brit. Nat. Cttee, Internat. Cong. Hist. Sci., 1970– . *Publications*: Battles of the English Civil War, 1961, pbk edn 1964; Oliver Cromwell, 1964; etc.; contrib. The English Revolution 1600–60, ed E. W. Ives, 1968; contrib. The Interregnum, ed G. E. Aylmer; contrib. vol. VII, Yale edn Complete Prose Works of John Milton, 1974; *contrib.* Camb. Hist. Jl, EHR. *Address*: Furness College, Bailrigg, Lancaster.

Wooster, Arthur Dennis; Lecturer, School of Education, University of Nottingham, since 1965; *b* 1931; *m* 1963; one *s*. BA Bristol 1962; ABPsS. *Publications*: Parents' Problems with Children, 1968; *contrib.* Brit. Jl Disorders Communication, Brit. Jl Mental Subnormality, Jl Moral Educn, Educnl Res. *Address*: School of Education, Univ. of Nottingham, Nottingham NG7 2RD.

Wordie, Dr James Ross; Lecturer, Department of History, University of Reading, since 1970; *b* 1941; *m* 1964; two *s*. BA Cantab 1963, CertifEd Cantab 1964, MA Cantab 1967, PhD Reading 1967. Mem. Brit. Agric. History Soc., Mem. Econ. History Soc. St David's UC 1967–70. *Publications*: chapter in, Agrarian History of England and Wales, vol. V (1640–1750), ed H. P. R. Finberg (forthcoming); *contrib.* Econ. History Rev. *Address*: Dept of History, Univ. of Reading, Whiteknights, Reading RG6 2AH.

Wordsworth, Jonathan Fletcher; Fellow in English Literature, Exeter College, Oxford University, since 1957; *b* 1932; *m* 1958; four *s*. BA Oxon 1955 (1st cl. English), MA Oxon 1958. Mem., MLA. Vis. Assoc. Prof., Cornell, 1966–67, 1970; Chatterton Lectr, Brit. Acad., 1969. Hon Sec., Trustees, Dove Cottage, Grasmere (Wordsworth Archive). *Publications*: The Music of Humanity, 1969; William Wordsworth 1770–1969 (Chatterton Lectr 1969), in, Proceedings of the British Academy, 1970; ed, Bicentenary Wordsworth Studies, 1970; *contrib.* Ariel, Coll. Engl., Cornell Libr. Bull., JEGP, Times Lit. Supp. *Address*: Exeter College, Oxford.

Wormell, Prof. Donald Ernest Wilson, PhD, SFTCD; Professor of Latin, University of Dublin, since 1942; *b* 1908; *m* 1941; three *s* one *d*. BA Cantab 1930 (1st cl. Classics), MA Cantab 1933, PhD Yale 1933, BA, MA Dublin 1939; Mem., Royal Irish Acad. Fellow, St John's Coll., Cambridge, 1933–36; Asst Lectr, Univ. Coll. of Swansea, 1936–39; Fellow, TCD, 1939–68; Sen. Fellow, 1968– ; Public Orator, 1952–69. Air Min. and Foreign Off., 1942–44. *Publications*: (with H. W. Parke) The Delphic Oracle, 1956; contrib. Encyclopaedia Britannica; *contrib.* Class. Qly, Class. Rev., Hermat. *Address*: 40 Trinity College, Dublin 2.

Worsley, Geoffrey Leonard, MA, ARIBA, FRSA, AIArb; Lecturer, School of Architecture, University of Manchester, since 1966; *b* 1931; *m* 1956; one *d.* BA(Arch) 1954 (1st cl. Hons), MA 1956; FRSA. Asst Lectr, Univ. of Manchester, 1955–66. RAF Flying Officer, 1955–58; Mem., Lancashire CC, 1958–60; Mem., NW Met. Reg. Hosp. Bd, 1960–66. Sen. Partner, G. L. Worsley and Assocs. *Publications*: *contrib.* Architects Jl. *Address*: School of Architecture, Univ. of Manchester, Manchester M13 9PL.

Worsley, Prof. Peter Maurice; Professor of Sociology, University of Manchester, since 1964; *b* 1924; *m* 1950; two *d.* BA Cantab 1947 (Social Anthropology); MA(Econ) Manchester 1951 (Social Anthropology); PhD ANU 1954 (Social Anthropology); Pres., British Sociol Assoc., 1971– . Vis. Prof., Sir George Williams Univ., Montreal, 1966 and 1968; Vis. Prof., Michigan State Univ., 1969; Vis. Prof., Brandeis Univ., 1970; Public Lecture, Heriot-Watt Univ., 1971; Colloquium, Memorial Univ., Newfoundland, 1971. Mass Education Officer, Overseas Food Corp., Tanganyika, 1948–49. Dir. Northern Research, Center for Community Studies, Saskatchewan, 1960–61; Cnsltnt, Council of Ont. Univs on postgrad. studies, 1973–74. Mem., British Econ. Mission to Tanzania, 1965. Mem., Penguin Educn Sociology Series Adv. Bd, 1968– ; Mem., Develt Panel, SSRC, UK, 1970. *Publications*: The Trumpet Shall Sound, 1957, Italian edn 1961, Russian edn 1963, 2nd edn NY 1967, London 1968; The Third World, 1964, 2nd edn 1967, Mexican edn 1966; ed and contrib., Introducing Sociology, 1970; ed, Modern Sociology: Introductory Readings, 1970; ed, Two Blades of Grass: Rural Cooperatives and Agricultural Development, 1971; ed jtly, Basic Concepts of Rural Sociology, 1971; ed and contrib., Problems of Modern Society: Introductory Readings in Sociology, 1972; Inside China, 1974; Problems of the Have-Not World, in, The Times History of Our Times 1945–1970, 1971; *contrib.* Sociol. Rev., American Anthropologist, Jl Anthropol Inst., Science and Society, New Society, Past and Present, The Listener, New Reasoner, La Cultura Poplare (Milan), Acta Ethnographica Academiae Scientiarium Hungaricae (Budapest), Studie Socjologiczne (Warsaw). *Address*: Dept of Sociology, Univ. of Manchester, Dover Street, Manchester M13 9PL.

Worthen, Dr John; Lecturer, Department of English, University College of Swansea, since 1970; *b* 1943. BA Cantab 1965, MA Kent 1967, PhD Kent 1970. Univ. Virginia, 1968–69; Jun. Res. Fellow, Univ. Edinburgh, 1969–70. *Publications*: *contrib.* D. H. Lawrence Review. *Address*: Dept of English, Univ. College of Swansea, Singleton Park, Swansea SA2 8PP.

Wortley, Prof. Ben Atkinson; Professor of Jurisprudence and International Law, Manchester University, since 1946; *b* 1907; *m* 1935; two *s* one *d.* LLB Leeds 1928 (1st cl.), LLM Leeds 1934, LLD Manchester 1940; OBE (Mil) 1946; Hon. Dr Rennes 1955, Strasbourg 1965, Commendatore Italy 1960, Mem., Royal Netherlands Acad. 1960; Solicitor 1929 (1st cl.), Barrister (Grays Inn) 1947, QC 1969. Pres., Soc. Public Teachers Law, 1964–65: Assoc. 1956, Mem. 1967, Inst. Droit Internat. Asst, LSE, 1931–33; Lectr, Manchester Univ., 1933–34; Reader, Birmingham Univ., 1934–36; Reader, Manchester, 1936–46; Vis. Prof., Tulane Univ., New Orleans, 1959. Min. Home Security, 1939–43; Instructor Cdr, RN, 1943–46; Mem., Lord Chancellor's Cttee on Private Internat. Law, 1952–63; Mem., Gov. Council, Internat. Inst. for Unification of Private Law, Rome, 1948– ; Inst. Adv. Legal Studies, 1947– . *Publications*: jt ed., Dicey: Conflict of Laws, 1949; ed, UN: The first 10 years, 1957; Expropriation in Public International Law, 1959; ed, Schill Lectures on International Law, Jurisprudence, 1967; ed, Introduction to Common Market Law, 1972; contrib. publicns UNIDROIT; *contrib.* Brit. YBk Internat. Law, Rec. Acad. Internat. Haye. *Address*: Law Faculty, Univ. of Manchester, Manchester M13 9PL.

Wragg, Prof. Edward Conrad, BA, MEd, PhD; Professor of Education, University of Nottingham, since 1973; *b* 1938; *m* 1960; two *d.* BA Dunelm 1959 (1st cl. German), DipEd Dunelm 1960 (1st cl.), MEd Leicester 1967, PhD Exon 1972. Lectr, Exeter Univ., 1966–73. Teacher at schs in Wakefield and Leicester, 1960–66. *Publications*: Krimis, 1968; Life in Germany, 1968; Teaching Teaching, 1974; Teaching Mixed Ability Groups, 1974; *contrib.* Educn, Educn Teach., Educnl Res., Jl Mental Subnormality, Mod. Lang. Jl, Times Educnl Supp. *Address*: Univ. Sch. of Education, University Park, Nottingham NG7 2RD.

Wright, Prof. Barbara, PhD, FTCD; Associate Professor of French, Trinity College, Dublin, since 1970; *b* 1935; *m* 1961; one *s.* BA Trinity College Dublin 1956 (1st cl. Mod. Langs), MA Trinity College Dublin 1960, LLB Trinity College Dublin 1956, PhD Cantab 1962. Asst Lectr, Manchester Univ., 1960–61; Temp. Lectr, TCD, 1961–63; Asst Lectr, Exeter Univ., 1963–64; Lectr, Exeter Univ., 1964–65; Lectr, TCD, 1965–70; Tutor, TCD 1965–72; Fellow TCD, 1968– . Sec., Irish Nat. Cttee Mod. Lang. Studies, Royal Irish Acad., 1969–74. *Publications*: ed, E. Fromentin: Dominique, 1965, French edn 1966; ed, E. Fromentin and E. Beltrémieux: Gustave Drouineau, 1969; (with P. Moisy) Moreau et Eugène Fromentin, 1972; E. Fromentin: a bibliography, 1973; *contrib.* Bull. du Biblioph., Fr. Rev., Fr. Studies, Mod. Lang. Rev., Studi Franc. *Address*: Dept of French, 38, Trinity College, Dublin 2.

Wright, Barry Forsyth, MA, BSc, FCS, JP; Lecturer in Psychology, Department of Social Science and Humanities, The City University, since 1968; Deputy Warden, Finsbury Hall; *b* 1934; *m* 1968; one *d.* HNC Heriot-Watt 1958 (Chemistry), BSc Edinburgh 1963, MA Edinburgh 1964; Fellow Royal Soc. St George. Univ. Edinburgh, 1956–58; Dept Chemistry Univ. St Andrews, 1958–59. Psychologist: Home Office (Prison Dept), 1964–65; Horton Hosp., Epsom, 1965–66; Research Officer, Nat. Children's

Bureau, London, 1967–68. JP Inner London, 1972– . *Publications: contrib.* Biological Jl, Quest. *Address:* Psychology Unit, City Univ., St John Street, EC1V 4PB.

Wright, Colin Bernard, MA; Lecturer in the History and Philosophy of Science, Department of Philosophy, University of Exeter, since 1966; *b* 1927; *m* 1958. BA Cantab 1948, MA Cantab 1952, Cambridge Cert. in Hist. and Philos. of Science, 1962. Mem., Brit. Soc. Philos. Science, Aristot. Soc. Lectr in Physical Metallurgy, Univ. of Birmingham, 1954–56; Asst Prof. in Philosophy, Univ. of Kansas, 1964; Asst Prof., Carleton Coll., Minnesota, 1964–65; Asst Prof. in Philosophy, S Illinois Univ., 1965. *Address:* Univ. of Exeter, Queen's Building, The Queen's Drive, Exeter EX4 4QJ.

Wright, David Frederick, MA; Senior Lecturer, Department of Ecclesiastical History, since 1973 (Lecturer, 1964–73), and Associate Dean, Faculty of Divinity, since 1973, Edinburgh University; *b* 1937; *m* 1967; one *s* one *d.* BA Cantab 1961, MA Cantab 1964. *Publications:* Common Places of Martin Bucer, 1972; *contrib.* Jl Theol. Studies, Rech. August. *Address:* New College, Mound Place, Edinburgh EH1 2LX.

Wright, Edward Maitland, MA, DPhil, LLD, FRSE; Principal and Vice-Chancellor, University of Aberdeen, since 1962; *b* 1906; *m* 1934; one *s.* Lectr, King's Coll., London, 1932–33; Lectr, Christ Church, Oxford, 1933–35; Prof. of Mathematics, Univ. of Aberdeen, 1935–62; Vice-Principal, Univ. of Aberdeen, 1961–62. Principal Scientific Officer, Air Ministry, 1943–45; Mem., Anderson Cttee on Grants to Students, 1958–60; Mem., Hale Cttee on Univ. Teaching Methods, 1961–64; Mem., Scottish Univs Entrance Bd, 1955–62 (Chm.); Mem., Royal Commn on Medical Educn, 1965–67. Vice-Pres., RUSI, 1969–72. Hon. Fellow, Jesus Coll., Oxford, 1963. *Publications:* (with Prof. G. H. Hardy) Introduction to the Theory of Numbers, 1938, 2nd edn 1945, 3rd edn 1954, 4th edn 1960; mathematical papers in scientific jls. *Address:* Univ. of Aberdeen, Aberdeen AB9 1AS.

Wright, Prof. Esmond; Director, Institute of United States Studies, and Professor of American History, University of London, since 1971; *b* 1915; *m* 1945. BA Dunelm (1st cl. Mod. History), MA Virginia, Glasgow Univ., 1946–67, Prof. of Modern History, Glasgow Univ., 1957–67; MP (C) Glasgow, Pollok, March 1967–70; Vis. Prof., various Amer. univs; Vis. Prof., Strathclyde Univ., 1970– . Founder Mem., British Assoc. for Amer. Studies (Chm., 1965–68); Mem., Brit. Nat. Commn for Unesco; Mem., Marshall Aid Commemoration Commn; Chm., Brit. Cttee for Loyalist Studies and Publications. *Publications:* A Short History of our own Times, 1951; George Washington and the American Revolution, 1957; Fabric of Freedom, 1961; The World Today, 1961, 3rd edn 1971; ed, Illustrated World History, 1964; Benjamin Franklin and American Independence, 1966; ed, Causes and Consequences of the American Revolution, 1966;

ed, American Themes, 1967; American Profiles, 1967; ed, Benjamin Franklin: a profile, 1970; A Time for Courage, 1971; *contrib.* various jls. *Address:* Institute of United States Studies, 31 Tavistock Square, WC1H 9EZ.

Wright, Evan Cyril; Registrar, University of Bristol, since 1973; *b* 1924; *m* 1951; two *d.* BA Oxon 1948, MA 1952; Graduate Asst, Oxford, 1949–50; Asst Registrar and Secretary, Bristol, 1950–62; Deputy Registrar and Secretary, Bristol, 1962–73. *Address:* Senate House, Tyndall Avenue, Bristol BS8 1TH.

Wright, Rev. Canon. Frank Sidney; Staff Tutor in Religious Studies, Extra-Mural Department, University of Manchester, since 1967; *b* 1922; *m* 1949; two *s* one *d.* MA Oxon 1947; ordained 1949. *Address:* Extra-Mural Dept, Univ. of Manchester, Manchester M13 9PL.

Wright, Prof. Henry Myles; Lever Professor of Civic Design, University of Liverpool, since 1954; *b* 1908; *m* 1939; two *d.* MA Cantab 1936; FRIBA, MRTPI. Mem., Federal Capital Commn, W Indies, 1956; Chm., UN Mission to Zambia, 1964. *Publications:* Plan for Cambridge, 1950; Plan for Corby New Town, 1957; A Planner's Notebook, 1948; ed, Land Use in an Urban Environment, 1961; Advisory Plan for the Dublin Region, 1967. *Address:* Univ of Liverpool, PO Box 147, Liverpool L69 3BX.

Wright, Prof. Jack Clifford, MA, BA; Professor of Sanskrit, School of Oriental and African Studies, University of London, since 1964; *b* 1933; *m* 1958; one *s.* MA Aberdeen 1955 (1st cl. French and German), BA London 1959 (1st cl. Sanskrit); FRAS, MPhilSoc. Lectr, SOAS, Univ. of London, 1959–64. *Publications:* Non-classical Sanskrit Literature, 1966; *contrib.* Bull. SOAS, Jl Royal Asiat. Soc. *Address:* Dept of India, Pakistan and Ceylon, School of Oriental and African Studies, Univ. of London, Malet Street, WC1E 7HP.

Wright, James Robertson Graeme; Lecturer in Humanity (Latin), University of Edinburgh, since 1966; *b* 1939; *m* 1966; two *d.* MA Edinburgh 1961, BA Cantab 1963, MA Cantab 1968. Asst Lectr, Humanity (Latin), Univ. Edinburgh, 1965–66. Sen. Warden, Pollock Halls of Residence, 1973– . *Publications:* Form and Content in the Moral Essays, in, Seneca, ed C. D. N. Costa, 1974; *contrib.* Class. Qly, Mnemosyne. *Address:* David Hume Tower, George Square, Edinburgh EH8 9JX.

Wright, John Farnsworth; Special Lecturer in Economics, Oxford University, since 1970, and Fellow of Trinity College, Oxford, since 1955; *b* 1929; *m* 1954; two *s.* BA Oxon 1952 (1st cl. PPE), MA Oxon 1956. Lectr in Economics, Trinity Coll., 1953– ; Res. Fellow, Nuffield Coll., 1954–55; Univ. Lectr (CUF), Oxford Univ., 1955–70; Gen. Ed., Oxf. Econ. Papers, 1965– . Estates Bursar, Trin. Coll., 1958–68, 1970– ; Special Adv., Bd of Trade, 1968–69; Econ. Adv., 1969–70.

777

Publications: contrib. Econ. Hist. Rev, Econ. Jl, Jl Econ. Hist., Oxf. Econ. Papers. *Address:* Trinity College, Oxford.

Wright, Laurence Marshall; Lecturer in French, University College of North Wales, Bangor, since 1967; *b* 1941; *m* 1966; one *s* one *d.* BA Bristol 1963. Asst Lectr, Magee UC, 1966–67. *Publications: contrib.* Medium Ævum, Music and Letters. *Address:* Dept of French, Univ. College of North Wales, Bangor LL57 2DG.

Wright, Dr Lawrie W.; Lecturer in Geography, Queen Mary College, University of London, since 1967; *b* 1940. BA London 1962, PhD London 1971. Lectr, Univ. of Auckland, NZ, 1965–67. *Address:* Queen Mary College, Mile End Road, E1 4NS.

Wright, Maureen Rosemary; Lecturer, Department of Classics, University College of Wales, Aberystwyth, since 1964; *b* 1933; *m* 1968; two *s* two *d.* BA London 1954 (Latin), MA London 1956 (Classics), BLitt Oxon 1963 (Lit. Hum.). Lectr, Dept of Classics, Univ. of Queensland, 1957–59; Fellow, Center for Hellenic Studies, Washington, DC, 1967–68. *Publications: contrib.* Class. Rev., Pegasus, Proc. Vergil Soc. *Address:* Dept of Classics, Univ. College of Wales, Aberystwyth SY23 2AX.

Wright, Moorhead, BA, MA, PhD; Lecturer in International Politics, University College of Wales, since 1965; *b* 1934; *m* 1968; two *s* two *d.* BA cum laude Princeton 1956; MA Johns Hopkins 1963 (with distinction), PhD Johns Hopkins 1971. Foreign Affairs Analyst, Library of Congress, 1963. *Publications:* ed, Theory and Practice of the Balance of Power, 1974; contrib. The Aberystwyth Papers, 1972; *contrib.* Internat. Aff., Internat. Relat., Polit. Stud. *Address:* Dept of International Politics, Univ. College of Wales, Aberystwyth SY23 2AX.

Wright, Dr Peter; Senior Lecturer, Modern Languages Department, Salford University, since 1971; *b* 1923; *m* 1956; two *s* three *d.* BA Leeds 1949 (English), PhD Leeds 1954, AdvDipEd London 1960. Res. Asst, Leeds Univ., 1949–52; Sen. Lectr, Sheffield City Coll. of Educn, 1960–65; Lectr in Modern Languages, Salford Univ., 1965–71. *Publications:* Dialect of the Fleetwood Fishing Community, 1960; Language at Work, 1968; Success in Spelling, 1968; O-Level English Language, 1968; The Lanky Twang, 1971; The Yorkshire Yammer, 1972; The Language of British Industry, 1974; The Cheshire Croak, 1974; *contrib.* Leeds Studies Engl., Publicns Yorks Lancs Lakeland Dialect Soc. *Address:* Modern Language Dept, Salford Univ., Salford M5 4WT.

Wright, Robert; Lecturer in Geography, University of Aberdeen, since 1970; *b* 1943; *m* 1968; one *s* one *d.* BSc Glasgow 1966 (Hons Geog.), BSc ITC (Netherlands) 1968 (Photogrammetric Engrg); Member: Inst. Brit. Geogrs, Brit. Soc. Photogrammetry. Asst Lectr, Univ. Aberdeen, 1968–70. *Address:* Dept of Geography, St Mary's, High Street, Old Aberdeen AB9 2UF.

Wright, Dr Vincent; Reader in Political Science, London School of Economics, since 1974; *b* 1937. BScEcon London 1960, PhD London 1965. Lecteur, Univ. Bordeaux, 1963–65; Lectr, Univ. Newcastle upon Tyne, 1965–69; Sen. Res. Associate, St Antony's Coll., Oxford, 1969–70; Lectr, 1970–72, Sen. Lectr 1972–74, Dept of Government, LSE. *Publications:* Le Conseil d'Etat sous le Second Empire, 1972; (with B. Le Clère) Les Préfets du Second Empire, 1973; (with F. Marx) Les universités britanniques, 1973; *contrib.* Annales du Midi, Etudes et Documents du Conseil e'Etat, Govt and Opposition, Internat. Rev. Social History, Parly Affairs, Polit. Studies, Revue Administrative, Revue d'Histoire Moderne et Contemporaine, Revue d'Histoire de l'Eglise de France, Revue Historique. *Address:* London School of Economics, Houghton Street, Aldwych, WC2A 2AE.

Wright, William David Chapel, MA; Lecturer in Economics, University of Edinburgh, since 1961; *b* 1935; *m* 1959; one *s.* MA Edinburgh 1957 (Econ). Computer exec., A. C. Nielsen Co., Oxford, 1957–59; Res. Fellow, Univ. of Edinburgh, 1959–61. Vis. Prof., Univ. of Buffalo and Washington Univ., St Louis, 1970–71; Lectr (pt-time), Univ. of Glasgow, 1965–70. *Publications: contrib.* Jl Pol Econ. *Address:* Dept of Economics, Univ. of Edinburgh, Edinburgh EH8 9JY.

Wrigley, Dr Edward Anthony; Lecturer in Geography, University of Cambridge, and Fellow of Peterhouse, since 1958; *b* 1931; *m* 1960; one *s* three *d.* BA Cantab 1952, MA Cantab 1956, PhD Cantab 1957; Co-founder, Cambridge Gp for History of Population and Social Structure, 1964. William Volker Res. Fellow, Univ. Chicago, 1953–54; Bye-Fellow, Peterhouse, Cambridge, 1955–56; Univ. Demonstrator in Geog., Cambridge, 1956–58; Mem., Princeton Inst. for Advanced Study, 1970–71. Senior Bursar, Peterhouse, 1964– . *Publications:* Industrial Growth and Population Change, 1960; ed, Introduction to English Historical Demography, 1966; Population and History, 1969; ed, Nineteenth Century Society, 1972; ed, Identifying People in the Past, 1973; *contrib.* Econ. History Rev., Jl Interdisciplinary History, Past and Present. *Address:* Peterhouse, Cambridge CB2 1RD.

Wrigley, Prof. Jack, BSc, MEd, PhD, FBPsS; Professor of Curriculum Research and Development, University of Reading, and Director of Studies and Head of Research Group, Schools Council, since 1967; *b* 1923; *m* 1946; two *s.* BSc Manchester 1943 (2nd cl. Maths), DipEd Manchester 1945 (1st cl.), MEd Manchester 1951, PhD Queens University of Belfast 1956; FBPsS; Mem., Maths Assoc., Mem., Assoc. Teachers Maths. Res. Asst, Manchester Univ., 1950–51; Lectr in Educn, Queen's Univ., Belfast, 1951–57; Lectr, Univ. of London Inst. of Educn, 1958–63; Prof. of Educn, Univ. of Southampton, 1963–67. *Publications: contrib.* Brit. Jl Educnl Psychol., Brit. Jl Psychol., Educnl Psychol Meas., Educnl Rev., Maths Teaching. *Address:* School of Education, Univ. of

Reading, London Road, Reading, Berkshire RG1 5AQ.

Wulstan, David; Lecturer in the History of Music, Magdalen College, Oxford University, since 1968; *b* 1937; *m* 1965; one *s*. BA Oxon 1964 (1st cl. Music), MA Oxon 1967. Fellow by Exam., Magdalen Coll., Oxford, 1964–68. Dir Clerkes of Oxenford, 1961– ; Publicns Sec., Plainsong and Mediaev. Music Soc., 1968– . *Publications*: Orlando Gibbons: Verse Anthems, 1965; An Anthology of Carols, 1968; An Anthology of English Church Music, 1971; A Handbook of Early Music (forthcoming); Aspects of the Mediaeval Lyric (forthcoming); ed, Essays on Plainsong and Mediaeval Music (forthcoming); *contrib.* Jl Theol. Studies, Music and Lett., Studies East. Chant. *Address*: Magdalen College, Oxford.

Wylie, John Cleland Watson; Senior Lecturer, Department of Law, University College, Cardiff, since 1972; *b* 1943; *m* 1973. LLB QUB 1965, LLM Harvard 1967. Asst Lectr, QUB, 1965–66 and 1967–68; Lectr, QUB, 1968–71; Lectr, UC Cardiff, 1971–72. Editor, Northern Ireland Legal Quarterly, 1970– . *Publications*: jtly, Survey of the Land Law of Northern Ireland, 1971; *contrib.* Northern Ireland Legal Qly. *Address*: Dept of Law, Univ. College Cardiff, PO Box 78, Cardiff CF1 1XL.

Wynn, Dr John Barrie; Senior Lecturer in English and Liberal Studies, University of Wales Institute of Science and Technology, since 1960; *b* 1924; *m* 1951; one *s*. BA Wales 1949 (1st cl.), MA Wales 1951, PhD Manchester 1956, DPhil Oxford 1962. Mem., Engl. Assoc., Philol Soc., Lingu. Assoc. GB; Mem., Internat. Phonetic Assoc. Asst Lectr in English Language, Univ. of Manchester, 1952–55; Fellow, Univ. of Wales, 1955–57; Asst Lectr in English Lang., Univ. Coll. of N Wales, Bangor, 1958–59; Lectr in Linguistics, Univ. of Wales Inst. Sci. and Technol., 1960– ; Chm., Bd of Studies in English, 1968–73; Chm., Bd of Examiners in English, 1968–73. *Publications*: contrib. Anglo-Saxon Dictionary, ed Bosworth and Toller, 1972; *contrib.* Med. Æv. *Address*: Univ. of Wales Institute of Science and Technology, Dept of English and Liberal Studies, 57 Park Place, Cardiff.

Wynne, John Eifion M.; *see* Morgan-Wynne.

Y

Yale, David Eryl Corbet; Reader in English Legal History, Cambridge University, since 1969; *b* 1928; *m* 1959; two *s*. BA Cantab 1949, LLB Cantab 1950, MA Cantab 1953; Barrister-at-Law Inner Temple 1951. Asst Lectr, then Lectr, Cambridge, 1952–69; Fellow, Christ's Coll., Cambridge, 1950– . *Address*: Christ's College, Cambridge.

Yamey, Prof. Basil Selig, CBE, BCom; Professor of Economics, University of London, London School of Economics, since

1960; *b* 1919; *m* 1948; one *s* one *d*. BCom Cape Town 1938. Lectr, Rhodes Univ., 1941, 1945–46; Sen. Lectr, Cape Town Univ., 1946–47; Lectr, LSE, 1947–49; Associate Prof., McGill Univ., 1949–50; Reader, Univ. of London, 1950–60. Pt-time Mem., Monopol. and Mergers Commn, 1966– . *Publications*: The Economics of Resale Price Maintenance, 1954; (with P. T. Bauer) The Economics of Under-developed Countries, 1957; (with H. C. Edey and H. W. Thomson) Accounting in England and Scotland, 1543–1800, 1963; (with R. B. Stevens) The Restrictive Practices Court, 1965; (with P. T. Bauer) Markets, Market Control and Marketing Reform, 1968; *contrib.* Economica, Econ. Hist. Rev., Econ. Jl, Jl Acnting Res., Jl Law Econ., Jl Pol. Econ., Oxf. Econ. Papers, Public Law. *Address*: London School of Economics, Houghton Street, WC2A 2AE.

Yannopoulos, George N.; Lecturer, Department of Economics and Deputy-Chairman, Graduate School of Contemporary European Studies, University of Reading, since 1965; *b* 1938. MScEcon London 1963. *Publications*: (with R. Clogg) ed, Greece under Military Rule, 1972; The Local Impact of Decentralised Offices, 1973; *contrib.* Economic Integration in Europe, ed G. R. Denton; *contrib.* Regional Studies, Built Environment, Bankers' Magazine. *Address*: Dept of Economics, Univ. of Reading, Whiteknights, Reading, Berks RG6 2AH.

Yardley, Prof. David Charles Miller, LLB, MA, DPhil; Barber Professor of Law, University of Birmingham, since 1974; *b* 1929; *m* 1954; two *s* two *d*. LLB Birmingham 1949, MA Oxon 1954, DPhil Oxon 1953; of Gray's Inn Barrister 1952. Fellow and Tutor in Jurisprudence, St Edmund Hall, Oxford, 1953–74; Bigelow Teaching Fellow, Univ. of Chicago, 1953–54; Lectr in Law, St Peter's Hall, Oxford, 1956–63; Univ. Sen. Proctor, 1965–66; Vis. Prof. of Law, Univ. of Sydney, 1971. Chm., Thames Valley Rent Trib., 1963– ; Chm., Oxf. Area Local Appeal Trib., Nat. Insurance, 1969– ; Oxf. City Councillor, 1966–74; Mem., Isis Gp Hosp. Mngmt Cttee, 1966–70; Curator, Oxf. Playhouse Theatre, 1965– ; Chm., Govs, St Helen's Sch., Abingdon, 1968– ; Gov., Oxf. Poly., 1970– . *Publications*: Introduction to British Constitutional Law, 1960, 4th edn 1974; A Source Book of English Administrative Law, 1963, 2nd edn 1970; The Future of the Law, 1964; ed, Geldart: Elements of English Law, 8th edn 1975; ed Hanbury: English Courts of Law, 4th edn 1967; jt ed., Manual of Military Law; jt ed., Halsbury: Laws of England; *contrib.* ASCL, Irish Jurist, Jurid. Rev., Law Qly Rev., Mod. Law Rev., New Law Jl, N Irel. Law Qly, Parl. Aff., Public Law, Solic. Jl. *Address*: Faculty of Law, The Univ., Birmingham B15 2TT.

Yarker, Patrick Maurice, MA; Senior Lecturer, Department of English, King's College, University of London, since 1969; *b* 1915; *m* 1959; two *s* one *d*. BA London 1949 (1st cl. English), MA London 1954 (distinction). Asst Lectr, King's Coll., London, 1951–55; Lectr, King's Coll., London, 1955–59. Hon. Treas., Engl. Assoc., 1963–72.

Publications: ed, W. Wordsworth: The Prelude, Books I–IV, 1968; ed, Ruskin: Unto This Last, 1970; *contrib.* Ess. Studies, Ninetnth Cent. Fict., Yrs Wk Eng. Studies. *Address*: Univ. of London, King's College, Strand, WC2R 2LS.

Yarlott, Dr Geoffrey, MA, PhD; Lecturer in Education, Nottingham University, since 1963; *b* 1927; *m* 1955; two *s*. BA Nottingham 1950 (English, Philos., Hist.), CertEd Nottingham 1951, MA Nottingham 1953, PhD Nottingham 1957. *Publications*: Coleridge and the Abyssinian Maid, 1967; Education and Children's Emotions, 1972; *contrib.* Educnl Res., Educnl Rev. *Address*: Dept of Education, Univ. of Nottingham, Nottingham NG7 2RD.

Yarnold, Rev. Edward John, SJ, MA; Senior Tutor, Campion Hall, Oxford University, since 1972; *b* 1926. BA Oxon 1954 (Litt. Hum.), MA Oxon 1957, STL Heythrop Coll. 1961. Chaplain, Campion Hall, 1964, Master, 1965–72, Tutor, 1964–72; Select Preacher, 1970–71, Sarum Lectr, 1972–73 Oxford. Mem., Council of Mngmt, Oxfam, 1966– ; Anglican–RC Internat. Commn, 1970– ; Gov., Heythrop Coll., 1971– ; Gen. Ed., Theology Today series. *Publications*: The Awe-Inspiring Rites of Initiation, 1972; The Theology of Original Sin, 1971; *contrib.* Amer. Jl Philol., Heyth. Jl, Jl Theol Studies, Texte Untersuch. Geschicht. altchrist Lit. *Address*: Campion Hall, Oxford.

Yarrow, Prof. Philip John, MA, Ddel'U; Professor of French, University of Newcastle upon Tyne, since 1963; *b* 1917; *m* 1939; one *s* one *d*. BA Cantab 1938 (Mod. and Med. Lang. Tripos: Pt I, 1936, 1st cl. French and German; Pt II, 1st cl.), MA Cantab 1942, Ddel'U Paris 1960. Mem., MHRA, Soc. Fr. Studies. Sen. Mod. Lang. Master, Royal Masonic Sch., Bushey, 1938–39; Sen. Fr. Master, Sedbergh Sch., 1939–40, 1946–47; Lectr, Univ. Coll. of the S West, Exeter (later Univ. of Exeter), 1948–60; Sen. Lectr, Univ. of Exeter, 1960–63; Mil. Service, 1940–46. *Publications*: (with J. Petit) Barbey d'Aurevilly: Journaliste et Critique, 1959; La Pensée politique et religieuse de Barbey d'Aurevilly, 1961; Corneille, 1963; The Seventeenth Century (vol. II of Benn's Literary History of France), 1967; (with E. Suddaby) Lady Morgan in France, 1971; ed, Molière: l'Avare, 1959; Corneille: Horace, 1967; T. Corneille and D. de Visé: La Devineresse, 1971; Hugo: Châtiments, 1974; trans., A. Bassi: Del Mal del Segno, 1958; *contrib.* Fr. Studies, Mod. Lang. Rev., etc. *Address*: Dept of French Studies, Univ. of Newcastle upon Tyne, Newcastle upon Tyne NE1 7RU.

Yates, Prof. William Edgar; Professor of German, University of Exeter, since 1972; *b* 1938; *m* 1963; one *s*. BA Cantab 1961, MA Cantab 1965, PhD Cantab 1965. Lectr, Durham Univ., 1963–72. *Publications*: ed, H. von Hofmannsthal: Der Schwierige, 1966; ed, F. Grillparzer: Der Traum ein Leben, 1968; Grillparzer: A Critical Introduction, 1972; Nestroy: Satire and Parody in Vien-

nese Popular Comedy, 1972; Humanity in Weimar and Vienna: the continuity of an ideal, 1973; *contrib.* Forum Mod. Lang. Studies, Maske Koth., MLR, Germanic Rev. *Address*: Dept of German, Univ. of Exeter, Exeter EX4 4QH.

Yeats, Ian Martin; Lecturer in Law, Queen Mary College, University of London, since 1967; *b* 1941. MA Aberdeen 1963, BCL Oxon 1966, MA Oxon 1970; Barrister, Inner Temple, 1972. Asst Lectr, Queen Mary Coll., 1966–67; Vis. Lectr, Univ. Adelaide, 1974. *Address*: Faculty of Laws, Queen Mary College, Mile End Road, E1 4NS.

Yehia, Mohamed Bakri Ahmed; Tutor, School of Siversmithing and Jewellery, Royal College of Art, since 1970; *b* 1925; *m* 1955; one *s* one *d*. BSc Cairo, Des RCA. Tutor and Asst Prof., Applied Art Coll., Cairo, 1955–68, Prof. 1970. *Publications*: The Art of Enameling, 1969 (in Arabic); *contrib.* Art and Architecture (Cairo). *Address*: Royal College of Art, Kensington Gore, SW7 2EU.

Yeoman, Dr Glyndwr David, BSc, PhD, ARIC; Senior Lecturer in Education, University of Nottingham, since 1973 (Lecturer, 1964–73); *b* 1928; *m* 1963; one *s* one *d*. BSc Wales 1949 (1st cl. Chem.), PhD Wales 1952; ARIC. Mem., Gov. Body, Bp Grosseteste Coll., Lincoln; Heanor Grammar Sch. *Publications*: Calculations and Problems in Organic Chemistry, 1964; An Experiment in the Oral Examining of Chemistry, 1971; *contrib.* Educnl Rev., Educn in Chem., Educn in Sci. *Address*: School of Education, The Univ., Nottingham NG7 2RD.

Yeomans, George John; Lecturer, Department of Town Planning, University of Wales Institute of Science and Technology, since 1967; *b* 1937; *m* 1960; one *s* two *d*. BA Cantab 1960 (St John's Coll.), MA Cantab 1964, Diploma in Town Planning, Birmingham Sch. of Planning 1967; Mem., Royal Town Planning Inst., 1967– . Dir, Civic Trust for Wales, 1970–73; Assoc. Dir, CTW, 1973– ; Member: Prince of Wales' Cttee, Welsh Environment, 1972– ; Wales Cttee, European Architectural Heritage Year 1975, 1973– ; Council of Town and Country Planning Sch., 1969–72. *Publications*: *contrib.* Built Environment, Jl of Royal Town Planning Inst. *Address*: Dept of Town Planning, UWIST, Cathays Park, Cardiff.

Yeomans, Keith Antony; Senior Lecturer in Economic and Social Statistics, University of Aston Management Centre, since 1974; *b* 1939; *m* 1962; two *s* one *d*. BA Keele 1962, DipEd Keele 1962, MSc Keele 1970; FSS 1965, MIS 1972. Lectr, Econ. and Social Stats, Univ. of Aston Management Centre, 1967–74. *Publications*: Statistics for the Social Scientist, vol. I Introducing Statistics, vol. II Applied Statistics, 1968; *contrib.* Jl Royal Statistical Soc., Series C. *Address*: Univ. of Aston Management Centre, Maple House, 158 Corporation Street, Birmingham B4 6TE.

Yorke, David Arthur; Lecturer in Management Sciences, University of Manchester Institute of Science and Technology, since 1970; *b* 1938; *m* 1961; three *s* one *d.* BCom Liverpool 1960 (Hons); Mem., Industrial Marketing Res. Assoc. Lectr in Industrial Management, Univ. of Liverpool, 1964–67; Senior Res. Fellow in Marketing, UMIST, 1967–68. *Address*: UMIST, PO Box 88, Sackville Street, Manchester M60 1QD.

Youings, Prof. Joyce A., BA, PhD, FRHistS; Professor of English Social History, Department of History, University of Exeter, since 1973; *b* 1922. BA London 1944 (1st cl. History), PhD London 1950; FRHistS. Lectr in History, UC of South West, Exeter, 1950, Univ. of Exeter, 1955, Sen. Lectr, 1965, Reader in Tudor Hist., 1968–73. Mem., Council, Historical Assoc., 1960–63; Mem., Council, Brit. Records Assoc., 1962–73; Mem., Editorial Bd, Archives, 1964–73; Mem., Devon County Records Cttee, 1965–74, Vice-Chm., 1970–74; Chm., Exeter Centre, National Trust, 1968–72; Governor, the Maynard Sch., Exeter, 1971– . *Publications*: Devon Monastic Lands: A Calendar of Particulars for Grants, 1536–58; Tuckers Hall Exeter, 1968; The Dissolution of the Monasteries, 1972; *contrib.* Archives, Trans Devonshire Assoc., EHR, Trans Royal Hist. Soc. *Address*: Dept of History, Queen's Building, The Univ., Exeter EX4 4QJ.

Young, Prof. Andrew McLaren; Professor, Department of Fine Art, University of Glasgow, since 1965; *b* 1913; *m* 1941; one *s* one *d.* Hon. MA Glasgow 1954; FMA, FRSA. Edinburgh Univ., 1936–39; Asst, Barber Inst. Fine Arts, Birmingham, 1946–49; Lectr, Univ. Glasgow, 1949–65. Mem. Scottish Arts Council 1965–68. *Publications*: James McNeill Whistler: Catalogue of Exhibition in London and New York, 1960; ed and contrib., Glasgow at a Glance: an Architectural Handbook, 1965, 2nd edn 1971; Charles Rennie Mackintosh: Catalogue of Exhibition in Edinburgh and London, 1968; *contrib.* Apollo, Connoisseur, Times Lit. Suppl. *Address*: Dept of Fine Art, Univ. of Glasgow, Glasgow G12 8QQ.

Young, Dr Anthony, MA, PhD; Reader, School of Environmental Sciences, University of East Anglia, since 1969; *b* 1932; *m* 1957; one *s* one *d.* BA Cantab 1954 (Geog.), PhD Sheffield 1958; FRGS, Mem., Inst. Brit. Geogrs, Mem., Brit. Soc. Soil Sci. Jun. Res. Fellow, Sheffield, 1954–58; Lectr, Sheffield, 1962–63; Lectr, Sussex, 1963–68; Lectr, East Anglia, 1968–69; Vis. Prof., Nanyang Univ., Singapore, 1970–71. Soil Surveyor, Nyasaland, 1958–62; Hunting Tech. Serv. (Malaya), 1965–66; Cnsltnt soil survey, Pakistan, Niger; Geomorphol., Royal Soc./Royal Geog. Soc. Xavantina-Cachimbo Expedit., Brazil, 1968. *Publications*: World Vegetation, 1966; Slopes, 1972; *contrib.* Geog. Jl, Geog., Jl Soil Sci., Nature, Trans Inst. Brit. Geogrs, Zeits. Geomorphol. *Address*: School of Environmental Sciences, Univ. of East Anglia, Norwich NOR 88C.

Young, David; Lecturer in Economics,

Dundee University, since 1971; *b* 1941; *m* 1964; one *s* one *d.* MA St Andrews 1964 (1st cl. Econ.). Asst Lectr, Univ. of St Andrews, 1964–67; Lectr, Univ. of St Andrews, 1967–69; Lectr, Univ. of Natal S Africa, 1969–71. *Publications*: International Economics, 1969. *Address*: Dept of Economics, The Univ., Dundee DD1 4HN.

Young, David J.; Lecturer in English, University of Wales Institute of Science and Technology, since 1962; *b* 1931. BA Birmingham 1953 (1st cl. Hons), BLitt Oxon 1956, Dip. Linguistics Edinburgh 1971. Foreign Lectr, Dept English, Uppsala, 1958–62; Asst Lectr, Dept English, Welsh CAT, 1962–63, Lectr 1963–68. *Address*: Dept of English, Univ. of Wales Institute of Science and Technology, 57 Park Place, Cardiff CF1 3AT.

Young, Sir Frank (George), FRS, DSc, PhD, MA; (First) Master of Darwin College, Cambridge, since 1964; Professor of Biochemistry, University of Cambridge, since 1949; Hon. Consultant Biochemist to United Cambridge Hospitals; *b* 1908; *m* 1933; three *s* one *d.* DSc, PhD London, MA Cantab; Hon. LLD Aberdeen, Dr *hc* Catholic Univ. of Chile, Dr *hc* Univ. Montpellier; FRS 1949, FRSM, FRIC. Beit Memorial Fellow at UCL, Univ. of Aberdeen, and Univ. of Toronto, 1932–36; Mem. of Scientific Staff, Medical Res. Council, 1936–42; Prof. of Biochemistry, Univ. of London, 1942–49. Croonian Lectr, Royal Soc., 1962; numerous lectureships abroad. Mem., Medical Res. Council, 1950–54; Mem., Commn on Higher Educn for Africans in Central Africa, 1952; Mem., Inter-Univ. Council for Higher Educn Overseas, 1961–72; Mem., Medical Sub-Cttee, UGC, 1964–73; Mem., Royal Commn on Medical Educn, 1965–68; Mem., Council of Nestlé Foundn, Lausanne, 1970– . Trustee, Kennedy Meml Trust, 1964– . Pres., Brit. Nutrition Foundn, 1970– ; Pres., Internat. Diabetes Fedn, 1970–73 (Hon. Pres., 1973); Vice-Pres., Internat. Council of Scientific Unions, 1970–72. Chm., Smith Kline and French Trustees (UK), 1963– ; Chm., Clinical Endocrinology Cttee (MRC), 1965–72; Chm., Adv. Cttee on Irradiation of Food (UK), 1967– ; Chm., Exec. Coun., and Trustee, Ciba Foundn, 1967– . Hon. or corresp. member of many foreign medical and scientific bodies. *Publications*: Scientific papers in Biochemical Journal and other scientific and medical jls on hormonal control of metabolism, diabetes mellitus, and related topics. *Address*: Darwin College, Cambridge.

Young, Dr James Alexander Taylor; Lecturer, since 1966, and Director of Studies, Department of Geography, University of Edinburgh, since 1970; *b* 1940; *m* 1966. BSc Aberdeen 1962 (1st cl.), PhD Edinburgh 1966. Univ. Demonstrator, Edinburgh, 1962–66. *Publications*: *contrib.* Geol. Soc. Amer. Bull., Artic Alp. Res., Scott, Jl Geol. *Address*: Dept of Geography, Univ. of Edinburgh, Edinburgh EH1 1NR.

Young, Dr Johnathan Cameron; Lecturer in Geography, University of Durham, since 1971; *b* 1945; *m* 1973. BSc Dunelm 1966, PhD Dunelm 1973; Mem. Inst. Brit. Geogrs.

(Librarian and Map Curator, 1968–71.) Hatfield College: Tutor, 1969– ; Tutor for Admissions in Arts, 1970–71; Bursar, 1971– . *Publications: contrib.* Annals Assoc. Amer. Geogrs, Professional Geographer, Community Medicine, Occasional Paper Series of Dept of Geography, Univ. Durham. *Address:* Hatfield College, Durham.

Young, Dr Michael John Lewis, MA, PhD, FRAS; Lecturer in Arabic, Department of Semitic Studies, University of Leeds, since 1963; *b* 1935; *m* 1968; two *s.* BA Cantab 1958, MA Cantab 1962, PhD Melbourne 1963; FRAS 1963, Mem. Soc. Genealogists. Lectr in Arabic, Univ. Melbourne, 1960–63. Sec. and Treas., Leeds Univ. Oriental Soc., 1968– . *Publications:* (with R. Y. Ebied) The Story of Joseph in Arabic Verse; *contrib.* Abr Nahrain, Islamic Studies, Jl Semitic Studies, Le Muséon, Parole de L'Orient. *Address:* Dept of Semitic Studies, Univ. of Leeds, Leeds LS2 9JT.

Young, Nigel James; Lecturer in Peace Studies, University of Bradford, since 1974; *b* 1938; *m* 1964; three *d.* BA Oxon 1961, MA Oxon 1963, PhD California Berkeley 1968 (distinction). Member: Peace Research Assoc., Commonweal Collection, Peace Research in History Assoc. Asst, Northwestern Univ., 1963–64; Univ. California at Berkeley: Asst/Associate, 1964–66; Research Fellow, Inst. of Internat. Studies, 1966–68; Instructor summer course/experimental courses, 1966–68; Lectr in Polit. Sociol., Depts of Polit. Sci. and Sociol., Univ. of Birmingham, 1968–74. *Publications:* Nationalism and Corporativism, 1969; Culture of the English Working Class, in, Problems of Modern Society, ed Worsley, 1972; On War, National Liberation and the State, 1972 (trans. German, French, Norwegian); Crisis of the New Left (forthcoming); *contrib.* Dialectics of Incorporation, Jl of Sociology, Peace Research and Peace Movement, Agora. *Address:* School of Peace Studies, Univ. of Bradford, Bradford BD7 1DP.

Young, Ralph Aubrey; Lecturer, Department of Government, University of Manchester, since 1969; *b* 1939; *m* 1965; one *d.* BA Amherst 1961, MA California (Los Angeles) 1963; Phi Beta Kappa 1961; Mem., Polit. Studies Assoc.; Mem., Amer. Polit. Science Assoc. Dept of Govt, Univ. Manchester: Res. Associate, 1966–67; Asst Lectr (backdated), 1966–69. Lectr, Dept of Polit. Science, Univ. Zambia, 1968–70 (on secondment). *Publications:* The 1968 General Elections, in, Zambia in Maps, ed D. Hywel Davies, 1971. *Address:* Dept of Government, Univ. of Manchester, Manchester M13 9PL.

Yudkin, Leon Israel; Lecturer in Modern Hebrew, Department of Near-Eastern Studies, University of Manchester, since 1966; *b* 1939; *m* 1967. BA London 1960, MA London 1963 (with distinct.). Lectr in Hebrew and Judaica, Univ. of S Africa, 1965–66. *Publications:* Isaac Lamdan: A Study in 20th Century Hebrew Poetry, 1971; ed (with B. Tammuz), Meetings with the Angel, 1973; Escape into Siege: Israeli literature today, 1974; *contrib.* Europ. Jud., Jew. Qly, Jew.

Spect., Jl Semit. Studies, Tarbut. *Address:* Dept of Near-Eastern Studies, Univ. of Manchester, Manchester M13 9PL.

Yuill, Prof. William Edward, MA; Professor of German, University of Nottingham, 1965–75; Professor of German, Bedford College, University of London, from Oct. 1975; *b* 1921; *m* 1947; four *d.* MA Aberdeen 1947 (1st cl. French and German), MA London 1951. Tutorial Student, King's Coll., London, 1947–49; Lectr, then Sen. Lectr, Sheffield Univ., 1949–65; Vis. Prof., Univ. of Chicago, 1965–66. *Publications:* ed, Grillparzer: Der Traum Ein Leben, 1955; (with G. Kolisko) Practice in German Prose, 1957, 7th edn 1972; (with H. H. Neville) Translation from German for Chemists, 1959, 2nd edn 1964; Key to Practice in German Prose, 1961, 2nd edn 1965; ed, C. F. Meyer: Two Stories, 1963; ed, C. M. Wieland: Der Prozess um des Esels Schatten, 1964; German Narrative Prose, 1966; (with E. L. Stahl) German Literature of 18th and 19th Centuries, 1970; *contrib.* Deuts. Beit. Geist. Überl., Forum Mod. Langs, Germ. Life Lett., Mod. Lang. Rev., Yrs Wk Mod. Lang. Studies. *Address:* Dept of German, Univ. of Nottingham, Nottingham NG7 2RD; (from Oct. 1975) Dept of German, Bedford College, Regent's Park, NW1 4NS.

Z

Zaina, Lucrezia Alexandra; Senior Lecturer and Head of Department of Italian, University of Liverpool, since 1964; *b* 1921. Certif. Italian Liverpool 1942, BA Liverpool 1943 (1st cl. Hons French), CertifEd Cantab 1944, MA Liverpool 1947 (French). Lectr in French, Univ. Liverpool, 1948–64. Rankin Hall of Residence: Sen. Tutor, 1956–72; Warden, 1972–73; Sen. Tutor to Women Students, Faculty of Arts, Univ. Liverpool, 1973– . *Publications:* Don Renato, in, Corvo 1860–1960: Centenary Essays, ed Woolf and Sewell, 1961; The Prose of John Gray, in, Two Friends, John Gray and André Raffalovich, ed Sewell, 1963; *contrib.* MLR, TLS. *Address:* Dept of Italian, Univ. of Liverpool, PO Box 147, Liverpool L69 3BX.

Zangwill, Prof. Oliver Louis; Professor of Experimental Psychology, University of Cambridge, since 1952; *b* 1913; *m* 1947. MA Cantab 1939; FBPsS, Mem., Assoc. Brit. Neurologists, Mem., Exper. Psychology Soc. Asst Dir., Inst. Exper. Psychology, Univ. Oxford, 1945–51; Sen. Lectr in Gen. Psychology, Univ. Oxford, 1947–52. Vis. Psychologist, Nat. Hosp. for Nervous Diseases, Queen Square, London, 1946– ; Mem., Biological Research Bd MRC, 1962–66; Consultant in Psychology to United Cambridge Hosps, 1969– . Pres., Brit. Psychological Soc., 1974–75. *Publications:* An Introduction to Modern Psychology, 1950, reprinted with new Appendix 1963; ed jtly and contrib., Modern Problems in Animal Behaviour, 1961; Cerebral Dominance and its Relation to Psychological Function, 1960; ed jtly and contrib., Amnesia, 1966;

contrib. Brain, Brit. Jl Psychol., Brit. Jl Psychiat., Jl Neurol. Neurosurg. Psychiat, Qly Jl Exp. Psychol. *Address*: Psychological Laboratory, Downing Street, Cambridge CB2 3EB.

Zanker, Francis William Alan; Lecturer in Accounting, School of Economic Studies, University of Leeds, since 1964; *b* 1938; *m* 1961; one *s* one *d*. BCom Leeds 1959; Chartered Accountant. Mem. Academic Planning Cttee, 1971. *Address*: School of Economic Studies, Univ. of Leeds, Leeds LS2 9JT.

Zarnecki, Prof. George, CBE, FBA, FSA; Professor of History of Art, and Deputy Director of Courtauld Institute, University of London, since 1963; *b* 1915; *m* 1945; one *s* one *d*. MA Cracow 1938; PhD London 1950; FBA, FSA. Asst Inst. of Hist. of Art, Cracow Univ., 1936–39; on Staff of Courtauld Inst. of Art, Univ. of London, 1945– ; Slade Prof. of Fine Art, Univ. of Oxford, 1960–61; Reader of Hist. of Art, Univ. of London, 1959–63; Mem., Inst. for Advanced Study, Princeton, 1966. Mem., Corpus Vitrearum Cttee, Brit. Acad., 1956– ; Mem. Council, Soc. Antiquaries, 1969–72 (Vice-Pres., 1969–72); Mem., Postgrad. Studentship Selection Cttee, Dept Educ. and Science, 1970–72; Mem., Arts Sub-Cttee Univ. Grants Cttee, 1972– ; Mem., Royal Commn on Hist. Monuments, 1972– ; Mem., Canterbury Cathedral Stained Glass Cttee, 1972– ; Trustee, York Glaziers Trust, 1972– ; Mem., Ed. Staff, Jl of the Warburg and Courtauld Inst., 1960– . *Publications*: English Romanesque Sculpture, 1951; Later English Romanesque Sculpture, 1953; English Romanesque Lead Sculpture, 1957; Early Sculpture of Ely Cathedral, 1958; Gislebertus, sculpteur d'Autun, 1960, 2nd edn 1969, English edn 1961, German edn 1962; Romanesque Sculpture at Lincoln Cathedral, 1964, 2nd edn 1971; La sculpture à Payerne, 1966; Romanik, 1970, Eng. and Amer. edn, Romanasque Art, 1970; (with others) Westminster Abbey, 1972; The Monastic Achievement, 1972; *contrib.* Archaeol. Jl, Jl of the Brit. Archaeol. Assoc. *Address*: Courtauld Institute of Art, 20 Portman Square, W1H 0BE.

Zauberman, Dr Alfred; Part-time Lecturer in Economics, London School of Economics, since 1970; *b* 1903; *m* 1948. LLM Cracow 1924, LLD Cracow 1927 (Econ.). Res. student, LSE, 1945–47; Hon. Tutor, Univ. of Oxford, 1946–47; Lectr, LSE, 1960–67; Reader in Economics, LSE, 1967–70; Res. Assoc., Harvard Univ., 1967; Vis. Prof., Univ. of California, 1970–71; Vis. Prof., Univ. of Toronto, 1971–72; Sen. Fellow, Columbia Univ., NY, 1972–73; Vis. Prof., Konstanz Univ., 1973–74. Cnsltnt, FAO (UN), 1967. *Publications*: Industrial Progress in Poland, Czechoslovakia and East Germany, 1937–1962, 1964; Aspects of Planometrics, 1967; Mathematical Revolution in Soviet Economics Thinking (forthcoming); Mathematization of Soviet Planning Thought (forthcoming); *contrib.* Amer. Econ. Rev., Bull. Oxf. Inst. Econ. Stat., Economet., Econ. Internaz., Economica, Kyklos, Manch.

Sch., Qly Jl Econ. *Address*: London School of Economics, Houghton Street, WC2A 2AE.

Zawadzki, Krzysztof Konrad Feliks, MA, MSc(Econ); Senior Lecturer in Economics, Department of Economics, University of Newcastle upon Tyne, since 1969; *b* 1919; *m* 1945. MA St Andrews 1945, MSc(Econ) London 1950; FREconSoc. Asst Lectr in Economics, Polish Univ. Coll., London, 1946–49; Lectr in Economics, Polish Univ. Coll., London, 1950–53; Holder of res. grant from Leon Bequest, Univ. of London, 1953–54; Lectr in Economics, Univ. of Newcastle (until 1963 Newcastle Div. of Univ. of Durham), 1954–69. *Publications*: The Economics of Inflationary Processes, 1965; *contrib.* Kyklos, Oxf. Econ. Papers, Rev. Econ. Studies. *Address*: Dept of Economics, Univ. of Newcastle upon Tyne, Newcastle NE1 7RU.

Zeldin, Dr Theodore; Senior Tutor, and Dean, St Antony's College, University, Oxford, since 1963; *b* 1933. BA Oxford 1954 (1st cl. Mod. Hist.), MA, DPhil Oxford 1957; FRHistS. Res. Fellow, Centre Nat. de la Rech. Sci., Paris, 1955–56; Res. Fellow, St Antony's Coll., 1937–63; Official Fellow, St Antony's Coll., 1963– ; Lectr, Christ Church, Oxford, and Univ. Lectr, Oxford Univ., 1959– ; Vis. Prof. of History, Harvard Univ., 1969–70. *Publications*: The Political System of Napoleon III, 1958, pbk edn 1970; ed, Journal d'Emile Ollivier, 1961; Emile Ollivier and the Liberal Empire of Napoleon III, 1963; ed, Conflicts in French Society: Anticlericalism, Education and Morals in the 19th Century, 1970; France 1848–1945, (Oxford History of Modern Europe) vol. 1, 1973; *contrib.* EHR, Jl Contemp. Hist., Hist. Jl, Hist. Today, Times Lit. Supp. *Address*: St Antony's College, Oxford.

Ziderman, Dr Adrian; Senior Lecturer in Economics, Queen Mary College, University of London, since 1971; *b* 1937; *m* 1972; one *s*. BA Cantab 1959, AM Stanford 1961, PhD London. Instr. in Economics, Stanford Univ., 1960–61; Res. Off., Higher Educn Res. Unit, LSE, 1963–65; Lectr in Economics, Queen Mary Coll., London Univ., 1965–71. Econ. Cnsltnt, Dept Educn and Science, 1967–71. *Publications*: (with M. Blaug and M. H. Peston) The Utilization of Educated Manpower in Industry, 1967; *contrib.* Brit. Jl Ind. Rel., Economica, Econ. Trends, Jl Hum. Resources, Manch. Sch., Oxford Econ. Papers, Public Fin. Jl. *Address*: Dept of Economics, Queen Mary College, London Univ., Mile End Road, E1 4NS.

Zielinski, Dr Janusz G.; Reader in International Economic Studies, University of Glasgow, since 1971; *b* 1931; *m* 1st 1953, 2nd 1968; one *s*. BA Central School of Planning and Statistics, Warsaw 1952, MA Central School of Planning and Statistics, Warsaw 1953, PhD Central School of Planning and Statistics, Warsaw 1960, DSc Central School of Planning and Statistics, Warsaw 1961. Lectr, Central Sch. of Planning and Statistics, Warsaw, 1953–56; Sen. Lectr, Central Sch. of Planning and Statistics, Warsaw, 1956–61; Reader, Central Sch. of Planning and Statistics, Warsaw, 1961–68; Assoc. Sen. Mem., St Antony's Coll., Oxford, 1968; Glasgow Univ.: Res. Fellow, 1969; Sen. Lectr, 1970. Hd, Res. Unit for Price and Incentive Theory, 1965–68; Vis. Lectr, Yale Univ., 1962; Vis. Sen. Lectr, Ibadan Univ., 1964; Vis. Prof., UN Inst of Econ. Develop. and Planning, Dakar, 1965; Vis. Prof., Tufts Univ., Fletcher Sch. of Law and Diplomacy, 1970; Res. Fellow, Harvard Univ. Russian Res. Center, 1974. Ed., Econ. Life, Warsaw, 1958–68; Ed., Soviet Studies, 1970. Mem., Sci. Council, Inst. for Training Managerial Personnel, Warsaw, 1967–68; Co-ed., Comparative Study of Economic Reforms in Eastern Europe series, 1969. *Publications*: In Polish: Labour Accounting Day in Soviet Collective Farms, 1955; Economic Calculation in a Socialist Economy, 1961, 3rd edn 1967; Big Business: The New Management Techniques and Their Relevance for Socialist Economy, 1962; contrib. Outline of the Theory of Socialist Economy, ed A. Wakar, 1965; The Theory of Socialist Trade, ed. A. Wakar, 1966; Political Economy of Socialism, ed M. Pohorille, 1968; Public Economics, ed J. Margolis and H. Guitan, 1969; In English: Lectures on the Theory of Socialist Planning, 1968, Spanish edn 1972, Italian edn 1973; (with M. Kaser) Planning in East Europe: Industrial Management by the State, 1970, Arabic edn 1971, Spanish edn 1971; Economic Reforms in Polish industry, 1973; *contrib.* Amer. Econ. Rev., Cah. ISEA, Co-exist., Econ. Internat., Econ. Plan., Ekon., Gospod. Planowa, Nig. Jl Econ. Soc. Studies, Quad. Rev. Politico, Rev. Est, Social Science Inform., Sov. Studies, Zycie Gospod,

Jrb. der Wirtschaft Osteuropas. *Address*: The Univ., 9 Southpark Terrace, Glasgow.

Ziff, Dr Larzer; University Lecturer in English, University of Oxford, and Fellow of Exeter College, since 1973; *b* 1927; *m* 1952; three *s* one *d.* MA Chicago 1952, PhD Chicago 1955. Asst Prof., subseq. Prof., Univ. California, 1956–73. *Publications*: The Career of John Cotton, 1962; The American 1890's, 1966; The Literature of America: Colonial Period, 1970; Puritanism in America, 1973. *Address*: Exeter College, Oxford OX1 3DP.

Zubaida, Sami Daoud, BA, MA; Lecturer in Sociology, Birkbeck College, London, since 1969; *b* 1937. BA Hull 1961 (Sociol. and Psychol.), MA Leicester 1964 (Sociol.). Asst Lectr, Leicester Univ., 1963–65; Lectr, Leicester Univ., 1965–69. Mem., Exec. Ctte, Brit. Sociol. Assoc., 1967–71; Mem., Council, Internat. Sociol. Assoc., 1970–74. Mem., Edit. Bd, Economy and Society. *Publications*: ed, Race and Racialism, 1970. *Address*: Dept of Politics and Sociology, Birkbeck College, Malet Street, WC1E 7HX.

Zuckerman, Azriel Adrian Sorin; Official Fellow and Praelector in Jurisprudence, University College, Oxford, since 1973; *b* 1943. LLB Jerusalem 1967, LLM Jerusalem 1969, MA Oxon 1972; Mem. Israeli Bar, 1968. Teaching Asst, Hebrew Univ., Jerusalem, 1967; Jun. Res. Fellow, Balliol Coll., Oxford, 1971. *Publications*: *contrib.* Law Qly Rev., Modern Law Rev. *Address*: Univ. College, Oxford OX1 4BH.